The Irwin Business and Investment Almanac 1996

The IRWIN
Business and Investment Almanac 1996

Edited by

Sumner N. Levine
Professor Emeritus
State University of New York
at Stony Brook
and Editor
Financial Analyst's Handbook
and
The Investment Manager's Handbook

and

Caroline Levine

IRWIN
Professional Publishing®
Chicago • London • Singapore

ISSN 1072-6136
ISBN 0-7863-0453-7

Printed in the United States of America
 2 3 4 5 6 7 8 9 0 BP 2 1 0 9 8 7 6

Preface

This 20th edition of the annual *Irwin Business and Investment Almanac* contains a number of new features in response to the rapidly changing business and investment scene as well as updates on our standard features.

The editors and publisher are, of course, pleased with the acceptance of the *Irwin Business and Investment Almanac* as a standard and unique reference for the business and investment community. As always, we continue to invite suggestions from our readers. All suggestions should be sent to: *Irwin Business and Investment Almanac,* P.O. Box 2118, Setauket, New York, 11733.

TO ORDER COPIES

If copies are not available at your local bookstore call 1-800-634-3966 or write: Order Department, 1333 Burr Ridge Parkway, Burr Ridge, IL 60521.

We appreciate your suggestions.

The Editors

Foreword

The *Irwin Business and Investment Almanac* is one book I would take to a desert island if I had to start a new economy. Why? A virtual library in one book, this almanac is a very effective business tool kit, providing summaries, graphs, and statistics from a variety of respected business sources. You didn't save the Fortune 500? No problem. You don't know where to find the Lipper Gauge in *Barron's*? Don't worry. You don't understand a mutual fund statement? No sweat. It's all here in this attractive, extensively indexed annual compendium.

The Editors, Sumner and Caroline Levine, have created a text that should delight the student, the investor, business people, and the information professional. The book is easy to use, with a detailed table of contents, bibliography, and index.

How does one use the *Irwin Business and Investment Almanac*? There are so many uses for the data that it really depends on you, your project, and where you've already looked. This book is a great place to start, and often you will find that it has sufficiently answered your question. If you need to go into more detail, the authors have clearly sourced and footnoted each chart and provided a bibliography for more searching.

Here are a few more examples and the chapters where you can find information. Starting your own business?
- Small Business Investment Companies

Getting up to speed?
- How to Read Mutual Fund Quotations
- How to Understand Options and Futures

Investing in the stock market?
- Quarterly Dow Jones Averages
- Industry Surveys
- General Business & Economic Indicators

Doing business in another state?
- State Information Guide
- State Business Assistance Publications
- State Information Offices

Creating a new woman-owned business?
- Women in Business

Where else can I look?
- Business Information Directory
- General Reference Sources
- Selected Bibliography

Whether you are a professional researcher or a consumer, it's a value-added asset to have all the work done for you and to know that the Editors have used the most reliable publications found in business libraries.

Colin McQuillan, Manager
Business Information Center
General Mills, Inc.

Contents

Business in Review

October 1994–September 1995°

°All dates refer to the day on which the report appeared in *The Wall Street Journal,* usually the day after the event.

Source: Reprinted by permission of THE WALL STREET JOURNAL, © 1994/1995 Dow Jones & Company, Inc. All Rights Reserved Worldwide.

October 1994

3 The U.S. and Japan reached a trade pact, as Japan made concessions to deflect U.S. pressure on its auto industry. The countries resolved disputes on government purchasing practices, insurance, window glass and formulas to measure progress.

A GATT panel upheld U.S. fuel-efficiency laws for cars, turning back a challenge by the European Union. Separately, the House approved a bill designed to give the U.S. leverage to open foreign banking markets.

Disposable income rose 0.4% in August, the seventh straight gain, while consumer spending jumped 0.9%.

4 The manufacturing sector showed strong growth in September, a survey of purchasing managers indicated, further evidence that the economic expansion still has plenty of steam. The National Association of Purchasing Management's index rose to 58.2%, its highest point since September 1988.

5 Stock prices sank on fears of higher interest rates. The Dow Jones industrials fell 45.76 to 3801.13. The 30-year Treasury bond dropped nearly three-eighths of a point to yield 7.88%, its highest yield in over two years.

Economic expansion is likely to continue through 1994, the government's chief gauge of future economic activity suggests. The index of leading indicators rose 0.6% in August.

U.S. vehicle sales remained strong in September as inventory shortages began to ease, leaving auto executives bullish about the rest of 1994.

Sematech will give up its $90 million annual federal appropriation. Member companies will continue supplying $90 million each year to the semiconductor-research consortium.

Merger-and-acquisition activity surged 51% to $173.5 billion for the first nine months of the year. Salomon Brothers led investment banks in the rankings, serving as an adviser in transactions valued at $45.63 billion.

6 Factory orders surged 4.4% in August, the latest in a series of upbeat reports that have led economists to forecast growth into next year, but that also have fanned fears about inflation. The increase was the largest gain in orders in nearly two years.

The report pushed stock and bond prices lower, as investors worried that another interest-rate increase is on the way. The Dow Jones industrials fell 13.79 to 3787.34. The Treasury's 30-year bond dropped more than five-eighths of a point to yield 7.94%.

Companies must disclose more about their derivatives holdings under a new rule issued by the Financial Accounting Standards Board. But critics say the rule fails to adequately warn investors about the risks that derivatives trading poses to the companies.

7 Retailers reported disappointing sales for September and blamed lingering warm weather, especially in the Midwest. Sales at stores open at least a year rose 3.9%, Salomon Brothers said. Apparel sales were particularly weak, while consumer electronics and hard goods sold well.

The economy shows no signs of slowing, according to a Business Council survey of economists.

The nation's poverty rolls grew by 1.3 million last year to 39.3 million, the Census Bureau reported, despite an improving economy. The slight rise kept the poverty rate at 15.1%. The rate for children was 22.7% in 1993, the highest of any age group.

10 The unemployment rate fell 0.2 percentage point to 5.9% in September, the lowest in four years. The report reflects the growing contrast between the service sector, where employment and wages are rising briskly, and manufacturing, where payrolls declined last month.

Federal Reserve Chairman Greenspan warned bankers that, after several months of sharply increased bank lending, they may have become too accommodating to their borrowers.

12 Prudential Securities has reached a preliminary accord with prosecutors that will head off criminal charges involving the sale of limited partnerships, according to people close to the situation. Under the pact, the securities firm would be indicted only if it commits future wrongdoing. The investigation of the tactics Prudential used to sell $8 billion of the risky partnerships is set to end soon.

13 Steven Spielberg, Jeffrey Katzenberg and David Geffen said they will form a new movie studio and entertainment company and, according to people familiar with the situation, may try to buy a large stake in MCA from Matsushita Electric Industrial.

14 Producer prices fell sharply in September, signaling that inflation remains under control despite the economy's strength. The 0.5% decline was the largest in more than a year.

Stock and bond prices gained on the strength of the soothing inflation report. The Dow Jones Industrial Average rose 14.80 to 3889.95, giving up most of an early jump of 50 points.

17 PaineWebber has worked out the final details of an agreement to buy General Electric's Kidder Peabody unit for common and preferred stock valued at about $670 million. The acquisition would give PaineWebber, long viewed as a second-tier brokerage firm, a crack at major-league standing in the securities business. GE would get an initial stake of 22% in PaineWebber, which could rise to 25%.

Microsoft's agreement to buy Intuit, giving it popular software for personal finances and an electronic system for bill payment and other transactions, could be a threat to banks. But it may raise antitrust concerns.

Consumer prices rose 0.2% and retail sales moved up 0.6% in September. Industrial production showed no change. The signs of a gently expanding economy eased inflation fears.

18 The U.S. found that GM pickup trucks with side-mounted gasoline tanks were defective, a decision that could lead to a recall of up to 6 million trucks. The Transportation Department said that the design of trucks sold by GM between 1973 and 1987 made the fuel tanks vulnerable to rupture in collisions and that GM knew of the problem for years. The cost of a recall could reach $1.2 billion.

Ford is halting production of its new compact sedans for a week because of a fuel-leakage problem.

The dollar sank to a two-year low against the mark after German Chancellor Kohl's election victory on Sunday. The dollar was quoted at 1.4990 marks in late New York trading.

21 Bond prices sank and yields soared to nearly 8% as an unexpectedly strong housing-market report rattled investors. Housing starts increased 4.4% in September, heightening expectation of an interest-rate increase. The Treasury's 30-year bond tumbled more than 1⅛ points.

IBM reported stronger-than-expected third-quarter earnings and said it may use part of its $10.8 billion cash hoard to make at least one "multibillion-dollar" acquisition.

24 The SEC is examining whether insider trading may have worsened shareholder losses at Community Bankers U.S. Government Money Market Fund, the first money fund ever to "break the buck." The agency is interested in the large outflows from the fund shortly before its net asset value dropped below $1 a share.

Financial regulators are moving to strengthen their formal examinations of banks' dealings in derivatives. The Office of the Comptroller of the Currency is announcing detailed procedures for its examiners to follow in monitoring activity in derivatives.

25 Long-term yields topped 8%, the first time they have passed that level in 2½ years. The rise pushed stocks lower, as the Dow Jones industrials fell 36.00 points to 3855.30. The Treasury's 30-year issue fell nearly three-quarters of a point to yield 8.04%. Bond dealers say yields could rise further in the days ahead, causing more havoc in the jittery markets.

26 Workers' wages and benefits continued to grow slowly, another sign that inflation is under control. The Labor Department's employment-cost index rose 0.7% in the third quarter.

Sales of existing homes remained strong in September, nearly matching year-earlier sales despite interest-rate increases of more than two points.

27 Durable-goods orders edged up 0.1% in September, a sign that the manufacturing sector is growing but not in danger of overheating.

The number of mortgage loans to blacks and Hispanics last year grew more than for whites, but the denial rate for minorities remained higher.

The U.S. issued a rule to protect consumers from being overcharged for mortgage escrow accounts.

28 British companies have surpassed Japanese firms as the leading foreign investors in the U.S., according to a study to be released next week.

The Ziff family agreed to sell its Ziff-Davis media company for $1.4 billion to surprise bidder Forstmann Little. The buyout firm said Ziff-Davis would be run by its current management team, headed by Eric Hippeau.

31 RJR Nabisco plans to sell 19% of its Nabisco food company to the public in a stock offering and use the proceeds, expected to top $1 billion, to repay bank debt. The move is seen as the first step in dividing RJR into food and tobacco companies. Separately, the company is dropping its plan to acquire 20% of Borden. It also plans a 30-cent-a-year cash dividend.

Strong economic growth raised expectations that the Federal Reserve will increase interest rates in November. Gross domestic product grew at a 3.4% annual rate in the third quarter.

Stock and bond prices rallied. The Dow Jones industrials jumped 55.51, or 1.43%, to 3930.66, and long-term bond yields fell back below the 8% level.

November 1994

1 The SEC and the Commodity Futures Trading Commission are investigating whether Bankers Trust violated federal laws in selling risky derivatives to Procter & Gamble and Gibson Greetings. The inquiries could lead to tougher regulation of the market for privately traded derivatives.

Disposable personal income rose 0.4% in September, its third straight gain, while consumer spending was unchanged after August's 0.7% rise.

2 The manufacturing sector opened the fourth quarter strongly, as the National Association of Purchasing Management's index climbed to 59.7% in October, its highest level in nearly seven years. At the same time, the index showed sharp inflation pressure.

Stock prices skidded as the report sent bond yields higher. The Dow Jones Industrial Average tumbled 44.75 to 3863.37. The 30-year Treasury

bond dropped seven-eighths of a point as its yield rose to nearly 8.06%.

3 Economic expansion is accelerating in several parts of the country, the Federal Reserve reported. But wage pressures have remained sluggish in most districts, it said. Separately, the index of leading economic indicators for September remained unchanged.

The Federal Reserve intervened to boost the sagging dollar, but traders said the effort won't help the currency unless the Fed raises interest rates. The dollar was trading at 97.50 yen and 1.5143 marks late in New York.

Stock and bond prices slumped as investors worried about interest rates and the dollar. The Dow Jones industrials fell 26.24 to 3837.13. The Treasury's 30-year bond fell nearly three-eighths of a point to yield 8.09%.

4 Sales at big retailers remained lackluster in October, disappointing analysts but not dashing hopes for a strong Christmas season. Stores open at least a year registered a 3.8% increase, Salomon Brothers said.

U.S. vehicle sales increased 9% in October despite shortages of some important new American models related to slow production startups.

The Federal Reserve moved again to bolster the dollar. The U.S. currency rose a bit, and traders predicted the Fed would continue to intervene. The dollar was trading at 97.75 yen and 1.5185 marks late in New York.

7 An interest-rate boost by the Federal Reserve appears all but certain following the release of October jobs data. Unemployment dropped 0.1 percentage point, to 5.8% of the work force. The economy's surprising show of strength put more pressure to fight inflation on the central bank, as it approaches a key policy meeting next week.

Bond prices declined on the jobs report, pushing yields to their highest level in more than three years. The Treasury's 30-year bond lost more than ¾ point, lifting its yield to 8.15%. Stock prices dropped as well.

Corporate profits continued to surge in the third quarter. Companies chalked up the strong performance to a healthy U.S. economy, which lifted earnings in virtually every industry, and to manufacturing price gains and improved overseas sales.

Stock investors are ignoring the solid quarterly earnings and have begun shifting more assets into cash and bonds. The profit gains have been overshadowed by worries about rising interest rates and inflation.

The IBM-Apple agreement to forge a common computer design may be insufficient to challenge the industry dominance of Microsoft and Intel, critics say, because it doesn't include a common software system. Motorola will join the IBM-Apple effort.

8 OPEC's crude-oil output rose in October even as world petroleum demand seemed weaker than previously forecast for this quarter. The report, from the International Energy Agency, had a bearish effect on world oil markets.

Americans' credit usage rose at a 14.6% annual rate in September. While analysts are uncertain about the reasons for the continued borrowing, it is clear that consumer spending has picked up for durable goods.

9 China will enter talks to buy two Canadian-designed nuclear reactors valued at a total of $2.58 billion. The decision gives Canadian nuclear-equipment manufacturers a key foothold in what is expected to be the largest new market for nuclear power.

Business-related litigation will be significantly affected by a high court ruling that a party to a lawsuit can't get a lower-court defeat erased from the law books merely by settling the dispute while the case is on appeal.

10 Financial markets reacted cautiously to the GOP's victory. Stocks were little changed, with the Dow Jones industrials gaining 1.01 to 3831.75. Bond prices climbed, and the dollar rose. Meanwhile, many business executives across the country found much to applaud in the Republicans' success.

The world trade pact still has a good chance of clearing Congress, but administration officials acknowledge that the accord's chances may have been hurt by the election results. Also, organized labor emerged as one of the biggest losers in the midterm voting.

Soros Fund Management lost $400 million to $600 million on a dollar-yen wager, traders say. In February, the hedge-fund firm admitted to losing more than $600 million on such a bet.

11 Sears Roebuck plans to spin off its $9 billion controlling stake in its huge Allstate insurance subsidiary, a move that will complete the firm's return to its retailing roots. The company also announced that its chairman and CEO, Edward Brennan, will retire when the Allstate transaction is completed next year.

Producer prices posted larger-than-expected declines for the second consecutive month, falling 0.5% in October to match September's drop. But economists say the report doesn't indicate that overall inflation is abating.

The FCC loosened its reins on cable-TV rates, giving cable operators greater flexibility to raise rates when they add new channels. The decision will let operators offer packages of new program channels that essentially would be unregulated.

15 Indonesia plans to unveil transportation, construction and energy projects that will generate billions of dollars in business for U.S. corporations. Exxon is expected to win the biggest plum, developing a natural gas field.

16 The Fed raised short-term interest rates by three-quarters of a percentage point. It said the increase, which was sharper than expected, was necessary to keep inflation at bay. In contrast with previous rate moves, the Fed didn't indicate that it expects this increase to be the last for a while, an omission prompting speculation that further increases are likely before the end of 1995.

Stock and bond prices gyrated in the wake of the Fed's move, jumping after the rise was announced, then falling sharply, ending the day little changed. The dollar strengthened.

The economy continued to show strength at the start of the fourth quarter as production at the nation's factories, mills and mines grew 0.7% in October and retail sales gained 1.1%.

17 Nasdaq Stock Market traders narrowed the "spreads" on many well-known stocks after the disclosure of a Justice Department antitrust investigation. But spreads haven't changed much for smaller, less-active issues.

Consumer prices rose just 0.1% in October after a 0.2% rise the month before, showing inflation under control despite concern it could heat up.

18 Sony took a $2.7 billion charge to clean up the books of its Columbia Pictures unit, a stunning acknowledgment of its disastrous foray into Hollywood. The charge, to write off goodwill from the 1989 purchase of the movie studio, led to speculation that Sony plans to sell Columbia, which Sony denied. The charge contributed to a $3.2 billion second-quarter loss.

Matsushita Electric Industrial has hired an investment bank to value its MCA unit, a sign that it is serious about tackling its dispute with the U.S. entertainment company, whose managers are seeking more control.

Housing starts fell 5.2% in September after increasing for three straight months, as rising interest rates began to slow the pace of home building.

Big aluminum makers are pushing through price rises of roughly 50% on an industry mainstay, can sheet.

The latest rise in interest rates has sparked worries that the auto industry's sales boom may stall next year if too many consumers, worried about further rate increases, rush to buy cars over the next several weeks.

GM investors, after a series of meetings with the company, scaled back hopes about how soon GM's North American auto business will reach competitive profitability levels.

23 Stocks plunged as worries intensified over a slowing economy and rising interest rates. The Dow Jones Industrial Average fell 91.52, or 2.4%, to 3677.99, bringing its two-day loss to 137.27 points. Among broader averages, Standard & Poor's 500-stock index skidded 8.21, or 1.79%, to 450.09. The Nasdaq Composite Index tumbled 16.53, or 2.2%, to 741.21. Bonds rose.

Tokyo stocks retreated, with the key Nikkei index closing below the 19000 level for the first time since February. Hong Kong shares fell 3.8%.

25 Factory orders declined 1.5% in October, a sign that the Federal Reserve's attempts to slow the economy may be beginning to take effect.

28 Retailers opened the Christmas season with strong sales as many posted better-than-expected gains over the long holiday weekend. In an encouraging sign for retailers, sales of clothing and electronic toys were brisk, and many shoppers indicated optimism about the economy.

Saudi Arabia's continuing cash shortage has begun to influence its petroleum policy. It is seeking to boost oil prices by holding output steady as rising consumption tightens supplies.

29 The sales pace of previously owned homes held steady in October despite a sharp increase in interest rates.

Ford agreed to acquire a 45% stake in an assembler of Ford automobiles in South Africa, moving toward becoming the first U.S. auto maker to make a major investment in that country since apartheid was dismantled.

30 The House approved the General Agreement on Tariffs and Trade, setting the stage for a showdown in the Senate tomorrow. The trade pack is expected to pass there as well, but its outcome remains in doubt because it must win three-fifths of the vote, not just a simple majority.

The consumer confidence index surged to its highest level in four years, rebounding from four months of declines. The index jumped 12 points in November to 101.3, but some analysts suggested that the rise was an aberration triggered by the election.

December 1994

1 Gross domestic product grew at a 3.9% annual rate in the third quarter, a half percentage point faster than estimated a month ago, heightening economists' concerns about inflation.

President Clinton plans to call for the creation of an Americas Free Trade Agreement, which would meld five trade agreements involving countries of North and South America.

The chief opponent of the world-trade accord, Senator Ernest Hollings, acknowledged the pact has enough support to win today's Senate vote.

2 The World-Trade pact was approved by the Senate in a 76–24 vote. The GATT accord cuts tariffs globally by roughly 40%, extends intellectual-property rights and tightens rules on investment and trade in services. The accord still needs to be ratified by a number of countries, many of which were waiting for the Congress to act before voting on the accord.

The economic expansion shows no signs of slowing down. Manufacturing surged in November to its strongest level in 10 years, according to the National Association of Purchasing Managers' index. And personal income and consumer spending gained in October, as did construction spending.

Retailers rang up modest sales gains in November, with healthy increases over the Thanksgiving weekend helping to offset a slow start. Analysts continued to project gains of 6% to 8.5% for the holiday season.

5 The unemployment rate fell to 5.6% in November from 5.8% in October. The

October index of leading economic indicators slipped 0.1%, but economists continued to see strong growth.

6 The Manager of the Orange County, Calif., investment fund resigned after the $20 billion portfolio plunged at least $1.5 billion in value. Robert Citron made his name using leverage arrangements and large purchases of derivatives, but was caught short by rising interest rates.

U.S. vehicle sales rose 4.3% in November as buoyant consumer confidence and a rush to buy four-wheel-drive vehicles before winter strengthened results in a normally slow month.

7 California's Orange County defaulted on about $2 billion of reverse repurchase agreements with CS First Boston. Earlier in the day, speculation that the county could file for bankruptcy protection to prevent a run on its battered investment fund sent tremors through stock and bond markets. The scandal threatens to embroil Merrill Lynch and other firms that bankrolled the fund. Meanwhile, the SEC has mounted a two-pronged investigation of the fund's losses.

8 Orange County said it would be able to maintain public services for the immediate future. But the California county's bankruptcy filing throws many long-term projects into doubt, including a multibillion-dollar expansion of Disneyland. On Wall Street, brokerage firms are scrambling to sell about $10 billion of securities held as collateral for loans to the county and its investment fund.

Federal Reserve Chairman Alan Greenspan said there is little evidence of an economic slowdown. His remarks were in step with the Fed's latest survey of its 12 district banks.

HMOs will cut prices for the first time in at least seven years, according to a survey by an industry group, which found HMOs plan to reduce premiums 1.2% on average next year.

Britain increased its base lending rate to 6.25% from 5.75%, the second half-point rise in three months.

9 Concerns about interest rates and the Orange County financial crisis sent stocks skidding in heavy trading. The Dow Jones Industrial Average dropped 49.79, or 1.33%, to 3685.73.

12 Orange County's financial crisis deepened as legal action threatened to disrupt its restructuring under the federal bankruptcy code. Meanwhile, falling bond prices and Wall Street's

rush to sell bonds repossessed from the county's troubled investment fund may have deepened the fund's losses to $2.5 billion.

More mutual-fund companies are bailing out their money-market funds because of the Orange County fiasco.

13 IBM halted shipments of its high-power PCs that use Intel's Pentium chip, saying that Intel has underestimated the potential for error arising from a bug in the chip. Intel disputed IBM's test results. The move may have little impact on IBM, which uses the Pentium chip in only about 5% of its machines. But the dispute could hurt rival computer makers such as Gateway, Dell and Packard Bell, which rely on Pentium for more of their sales.

The U.S. and Japan reached an accord aimed at opening the Japanese sheet-glass market to imports, an agreement that may serve as a model for other industries. The pact doesn't set any specific import targets.

15 Amtrak plans a sweeping cutback that will reduce its passenger-train service by 21% and cut at least 5,500 jobs from its work force of 25,000. The plan, a bid to close a $200 million budget gap and block efforts to end Amtrak's federal subsidy, eliminates service entirely on some routes and drops parts of other routes.

The economy continues to show strength with little sign of inflation. Industrial output rose 0.5% in November, while consumer prices moved up 0.3%. The reports reinforce expectations that the Fed won't raise interest rates when it meets next week.

Stock prices rallied on the economic reports, as the Dow Jones industrials surged 30.95 to 3746.29.

16 Foreign investment in emerging economies is beginning to slow after a four-year surge. Investments and loans will total about $177.6 billion this year, according to the Institute of International Finance, down from a peak of $205.1 billion in 1993.

19 Housing starts rose 6.9% in November as warm weather helped push the measure to an eight-month high.

Retailers reported brisk sales during the last shopping weekend before Christmas and many continue to expect to meet or beat projections of a 5% to 6% increase in holiday sales.

21 Intel offered to replace all of its flawed Pentium chips, bowing to mounting pressure from customers. The recall, forced on Intel by PC makers who were pledging replacement chips, will cost Intel an estimated $200 million or more in an after-tax charge. Intel shares rose 5.9%.

Microsoft postponed the release of Windows 95 until August, the second big delay for the operating system.

The Mexican peso plunged 12.7% after the country's new administration effectively devalued the currency by lowering its trading floor.

The U.S. trade deficit jumped to $10.14 billion in October, the second-highest monthly gap on record, and the gap with Japan hit a new high.

Exports of cars and light trucks built in the U.S. and Canada have surged at least 25% this year.

The Federal Reserve left short-term interest rates unchanged. But it is widely expected to boost rates early next year unless the economy falters.

22 Mexican stocks plunged and interest rates soared after the government said it will focus on its ballooning trade deficit at the expense of strong economic growth. Stocks fell 11% during the session before closing with a loss of 3.1%. The sell-off follows a 12.7% devaluation of the peso Tuesday.

U.S. stock prices climbed, led by rebounding technology and cyclical issues. The Dow Jones Industrial Average jumped 34.65 to 3801.80.

23 Mexico abandoned efforts to support its currency, sending the peso down nearly 15% in foreign exchange markets, while Mexico's interest rates soared and stock prices gyrated wildly. The government's decision to float the peso caught many investors off guard, damaging Mexico's credibility in financial markets.

Japan plans to propose relaxing rules that now bar most foreign investment advisers from managing part of the country's $200 billion public pension fund. The move could hasten a U.S.–Japan accord on financial trade.

27 Many retailers met their sales goals during the Christmas season, helped by last-minute shoppers. But results were uneven, as brisk sales of electronics, toys, jewelry and home-related items were partially offset by tepid apparel sales at many retailers.

Mexican government officials acknowledge that they have lost so much control over the economy following last week's devaluation of the peso that they will have to wait for the markets to quiet before proposing new economic steps. The peso fell a fur-

ther 6% against the dollar yesterday.

28 Sales of existing homes declined 2.6% in November to the lowest level in 17 months as rising interest rates finally began to discourage potential buyers. Sales of previously owned single-family homes fell to a seasonally adjusted rate of 3.81 million last month from October's pace of 3.91 million.

Consumer confidence jumped to a four-and-a-half-year high, suggesting the economy still has considerable momentum as the year draws to an end. The Conference Board's consumer confidence index rose to 102.2 this month from 100.4 in November.

29 The peso rebounded against the dollar as word spread that Mexico's government was close to completing a plan to bolster the economy. According to people familiar with the plan, the government is considering letting U.S. and other foreign financial institutions expand more broadly in Mexico in an effort to draw funds into the beleaguered economy.

The Japanese government ordered communications giant NTT to open key private telephone lines to competitors, effectively loosening NTT's grip on Japan's local phone systems.

New construction contracts rebounded 3% in November, led by a surge in nonresidential building.

Precious metals prices surged as investors and speculators fleeing the dollar sought a safe haven.

30 Investors pulled money out of bond mutual funds at a record pace in November, the ninth month in a row of bond-fund withdrawals. Stock-fund inflows slowed to a trickle. December results are running only slightly better.

Some junk-bond funds, like emerging-market mutual funds, have been hurt by Mexico's economic crisis.

The economy showed further signs of future strength, as the index of leading economic indicators rose 0.3% in November, its largest gain in four months. Plant and equipment orders posted sharp gains, pointing to continued strength in manufacturing.

January 1995

3 The economy will slow to nearly half its current rate of growth by the second half of 1995 as the Federal Reserve continues to raise interest rates and successfully engineers a "soft landing," economists predict in *The Wall Street Journal*'s semiannual survey. While they expect slower growth, most don't believe the economy is heading for a recession or that inflation will pick up substantially.

The U.S. and China moved closer to a trade war. The U.S. threatened to place 100% tariffs on more than $1 billion of Chinese goods unless Beijing moves to halt piracy of videotapes, compact disks and computer software. China responded quickly with a retaliatory list of trade penalties.

Mexico put together a broad rescue plan that includes some $18 billion in emergency credit lines. The credit lines, principally from foreign governments, also include a vote of confidence from U.S. commercial banks, which are contributing $3 billion.

4 Manufacturers continued to show strength through the end of the year. The National Association of Purchasing Management's index registered 57.8% in December, down from 61.2% in November but still well above the 50% level that signals growth.

Venture-capital funds raised some $4.2 billion in 1994, nearly 45% more than the $2.9 billion raised in 1993, according to an industry newsletter.

5 Companies in the U.S. are feeling the pinch of Mexico's currency crisis as the devalued peso hobbles exports and forces writedowns of assets. Mattel will take a charge of 8 cents a share to reflect the lower value of its Mexican inventory and receivables. Although some firms are shrugging off the peso's slide, others are postponing expansion in Mexico and many see Mexican sales falling.

Mexico's new finance minister faces the urgent task of persuading mutual funds and other investors to roll over billions of dollars of government debt that will mature soon.

Auto-sales reports for December indicate the industry sold about 15.1 million vehicles in 1994, the best year since 1988. Auto executives are predicting an even better year in 1995.

The Big Three auto makers, flush with cash thanks to booming vehicle sales, are preparing to make record profit-sharing and bonus payouts.

Construction spending rose 0.7% in November, as rising interest rates had little effect on building activity.

A Chinese factory accused of being a major producer of pirated compact and laser video disks was established and half-owned by European electronics giant Philips Electronics.

6 Factory orders jumped 2.6% in November, sparking predictions of prosperity in the manufacturing sector over the next several months.

December retail sales fell short of gains projected by retailers and analysts, rising 4.9% according to one index and 4.5% according to another.

9 The economy showed little sign of being hampered by higher interest rates as the unemployment rate fell to 5.4% in December from 5.6% in November, with 256,000 new jobs created.

The peso plunged a further 6.3% against the dollar. The effects of the currency crisis are beginning to spread through the Mexican economy, with lending nearly halted, construction slowing and layoffs expected.

10 The Federal Reserve intervened in foreign exchange markets to prop up the peso. The intervention, believed to total $559 million, strengthened the peso, but Mexican stocks plummeted.

Consumer debt surged in November, the 24th increase in a row, further evidence that the economy didn't slow much at the end of the year.

North Korea announced it will lift import restrictions on many U.S. products, the State Department said. The U.S., meanwhile, will lift some financial and economic restrictions on trade with North Korea later this month.

11 Mexico's economic crisis deepened as the country's stock market and currency both fell more than 6%, showing that investors aren't convinced that the country can return to stability soon. The crisis helped send emerging-market debt securities plunging for the second straight day, as traders reacted to a poor response to a debt offering by Mexico.

The Canadian dollar continued its long slide, falling to an eight-and-a-half-year low against the U.S. dollar.

Producer prices rose just 0.2% in December and only 1.7% for the year, despite the economy's vigorous growth. But many economists doubt such modest inflation can last.

IBM offered to buy back $1.1 billion in preferred stock it sold during the depths of its financial crisis, partially answering questions about what it will do with its growing cash hoard.

Johnson & Johnson plans to plead guilty to shredding documents related to a federal probe into whether the company illegally promoted its Retin-A acne drug as a wrinkle remover.

Japan agreed to open up parts of its financial-services sector to foreign companies, giving financial institutions and investment advisers a crack at the country's huge pension funds.

12 Mexican markets recovered, bolstered by comments by Clinton that greater U.S. financial support would be available if necessary. Meanwhile, hedge funds and others purchased emerging-market debt, and some bonds reversed course after a plunge that sent them close to record lows.

The consumer price index rose just 0.2% in December, holding its gain for the year to 2.7%. The so-called core rate of inflation, which excludes food and energy costs, rose only 2.6%, the smallest annual increase in 30 years.

13 A new academic study suggests that dealers on the Nasdaq Stock Market frequently violate market rules on speedy reporting of transactions, to the detriment of individual investors.

16 The economy showed signs of cooling off as consumer spending slipped in December. Retail sales fell 0.1% last month, and November sales, originally reported as showing a healthy 1.2% gain, were restated to show a rise of just 0.2%. The report raised questions about the strength of the economy and whether the Fed will see the need to raise interest rates further when it meets later this month.

Investors sent stock prices sharply higher on hopes for lower interest rates. The Dow Jones Industrial Average surged 49.46 to 3908.46.

France signed a $2.83 billion agreement to supply two nuclear reactors to China, which aims to sharply boost its electricity-generating capacity.

17 China has moved closer to American demands to improve enforcement of copyright, trademark and patent laws, U.S. trade officials said. China said yesterday it will crack down on compact-disk piracy. Tensions between the two countries are easing on the eve of resumed trade talks, which broke down last month.

A strong quake hit western Japan, trapping hundreds in collapsed buildings. The predawn earthquake reportedly killed at least 10 people, but the death toll was expected to climb. Hundreds of people were reported trapped in rubble, and fires broke out in Kobe, one of Japan's largest ports. The quake, measuring 7.2 on the Richter scale, was described as the most powerful to have struck a densely populated urban area in Japan in two decades. Television showed footage of a collapsed section of the elevated Kobe-Osaka highway.

Stock prices climbed, buoyed by a growing conviction that the Federal Reserve may not lift interest rates later this month. The Dow Jones Industrial Average rose 23.88 to 3932.34.

18 Kmart ousted its chairman, Joseph Antonini, naming Donald Perkins as his successor. Antonini remains president and chief executive, but the struggling discount retailer plans to name a new president from outside the company soon, people familiar with the situation said.

Mexico sold $400 million of government bonds, its first successful debt auction since the peso was devalued in December, a sign that foreign investors are regaining confidence.

Industrial production rose 1.0% in December, raising doubts about earlier signs of a slowing economy.

19 The Federal Reserve is likely to raise short-term interest rates again later this month, probably by another one-half percentage point. Despite hints of weakness in retail sales and home buying, Fed officials see few convincing signs that the economy has slowed significantly. The latest Fed review of regional economic conditions found "economic expansion remained vibrant" in most areas.

Orange County reduced its estimate of portfolio losses to $1.69 billion from $2.02 billion after receiving higher-than-expected prices for some securities and finding cash that hadn't been factored into earlier estimates.

20 Stocks slumped as investors resigned themselves to the probability of another interest-rate increase. The Dow Jones Industrial Average sank 46.77 to 3882.21. Worries about interest rates and inflation also drove bond prices lower. Helping to depress markets was concern that political opposition in Congress could stall a planned rescue package for Mexico.

Mexican stock prices sank 4.8% and the peso fell 2.7% against the dollar on nervousness about U.S. approval of the rescue package.

Japan's quake deaths topped 4,000 and new fires erupted in Kobe. Survivors struggled with freezing temperatures and food shortages as rescue teams found more bodies in the wreckage. Nearly 100 new fires broke out in the port city, but fire-fighters were stymied by crushed water mains. Some 800 aftershocks have riddled the Kobe-Osaka region. After a period of indecision, the government agreed yesterday to accept international aid. Six U.S. Air Force planes brought in supplies, and Switzerland dispatched a search team.

Ford is cutting output of three new vehicles, including the Windstar minivan, a sign of softening demand.

GM shut down two assembly plants because of a strike at a parts-making site. More plants are expected to close today if the strike continues.

23 Housing starts fell just 1% in December from November's strong pace, helped by warm weather. For the year, housing starts rose 12.9%.

24 World stock markets tumbled, rattled by rising damage estimates from the Kobe earthquake and growing fear about higher U.S. interest rates.

IBM posted sharply improved fourth-quarter earnings, but revenue growth of just 2% and a poor showing by the company's personal-computer division disappointed Wall Street.

IBM tapped the head of its Asian operations, Robert Stephenson, to fill its top U.S. sales position.

26 Fed Chairman Alan Greenspan predicted economic growth will slow, but he signaled that another interest-rate increase may be on the way.

The proposed U.S. rescue package for Mexico is being assailed as a bail-out mainly benefiting Wall Street.

The Mexican auto industry is girding for a 30% to 40% sales drop in the wake of the peso's devaluation.

27 The auto industry showed signs of slower growth as Ford set plans to idle two more factories and Chrysler offered hefty rebates on minivans.

Chrysler is being urged by safety officials to voluntarily recall minivans and replace the rear-door latch.

Durable-goods orders rose 1.4% last month, but the report suggested the economy may be cooling down.

30 U.S. gross domestic product grew at an annual rate of 4.5% in the fourth quarter while an inflation measure, the fixed-weighted price index, rose just 2.5%. Despite the low inflation, the Fed is expected to raise interest rates again when it meets this week.

31 The peso plunged to new lows as President Clinton scrambled to shore up flagging support for the proposed Mexican rescue package. The peso lost nearly 10% of its value against the dollar, and Mexican stocks and other Latin American securities sank in its wake. The turmoil may help convince U.S. lawmakers they risk starting a grave financial downturn if they don't back the rescue plan.

Personal income jumped 0.7% in December while spending edged up 0.2%, another sign that consumer buying patterns may be slowing.

February 1995

1 Clinton abandoned the proposed $40 billion rescue plan for Mexico, offering instead a package of loans and financial aid that expands an existing safety net and doesn't require congressional approval. The new plan buoyed Mexico's markets, and the peso bounced back from the new lows it hit Monday, when it appeared that balky U.S. lawmakers would fail to ratify the original rescue plan.

U.S. stock and bond prices gained and the dollar rallied on the surprise rescue package. But worries about the U.S. economy have intensified. The Federal Reserve is widely expected to raise interest rates by 0.5% today.

Employment costs, a measure of workers' wages, salaries and benefits, rose just 3% in 1994, despite rising employment and a booming economy.

2 The Federal Reserve pushed up short-term interest rates another half percentage point to their highest levels in four years, giving no indication that it will stop tightening. Most analysts expect the Fed to continue increasing rates this year, perhaps by another percentage point.

The economy continues to expand, three new reports indicated. The purchasing-management index edged up in January. The index of leading economic indicators showed a 0.1% gain for December, while construction spending rose 1.1% in the month.

Ford reported that its earnings for the fourth quarter more than doubled to $1.57 billion, helped by a turnaround in international operations. The results met most analysts' forecasts, but included some disappointments.

GM, Chrysler and most of the leading foreign auto makers reported disappointing U.S. sales for January.

The peso continued to recover, rising another 6.9% against the dollar. But Mexican stocks declined 4.6%.

3 Big retailers reported stronger-than-expected January sales as shoppers jumped for post-Christmas discounts. But analysts warned that aggressive markdowns will eat into profits and that rising interest rates may make consumers more cautious.

6 Trade relations between the U.S. and China deteriorated further as the two countries battled over intellectual-property rights. The U.S. imposed tough sanctions on a number of Chinese exports, including cellular telephones, sporting goods and plastic articles, and China responded with its own sanctions. But the tariffs won't go into effect until February 26, and many analysts expect a pact before then.

The unemployment rate jumped 0.3 percentage point to 5.7% in January, its first increase in more than a year and a sign that the economy is cooling. Employers created 134,000 jobs, about half the pace of previous months.

Stocks posted strong gains after the jobless report raised investors' hopes that interest rates have peaked. The Dow Jones Industrial Average rose 57.87, or 1.50%, to 3928.64.

8 Some short-term interest rates fell sharply in Mexico's latest debt auction, but the rate for one-year notes remained above 20%, indicating investor concern about long-term stability.

Productivity jumped 2.2% in 1994, the Labor Department reported, up from a 1.5% rise the previous year.

13 A $3 billion bank loan to Mexico has run into difficulty as possible participants criticized terms set by lead banks Citicorp and J.P. Morgan.

Producer prices rose 0.3% in January, showing inflation at the wholesale level remains mild, but there were hints of higher prices coming.

14 A Japanese firm agreed to buy the huge Comdex computer trade show and related properties for $800 million from Sheldon Adelson's Interface Group. The price surprised some analysts, but those based in Tokyo praised the move. The sale would be one of the biggest recent acquisitions in the U.S. by a Japanese company.

Corporate health-care costs fell 1.1% last year, after outpacing inflation for decades, as employees shifted to managed care and employers offered fewer traditional plans.

Clinton's economic advisers say the trend in U.S. productivity growth may be improving, boosting the prospects for growth in living standards.

Manufacturers are optimistic for the short term, a Dun & Bradstreet survey found, but are concerned about interest rates and the potential for slowed orders later in the year.

15 Microsoft's antitrust settlement . was struck down. A federal judge, portraying the accord as too lenient, said the pact doesn't deal with many practices that the company has been accused of, including charges that it announces products far in advance of their being ready for market in order to discourage customers from buying rivals' software.

January retail sales rose a tiny 0.2% before inflation, another sign that the economy may be slowing.

The report pushed stocks up, with the S&P 500 edging up to a record high, the first major index to break into new territory in more than a year.

16 The Dow Jones industrials closed at a record 3986.17 on growing confidence that the economy is slowing down, easing interest-rate fears. The average at one point was within 2.05 points of 4000, and the S&P 500 set a second consecutive record, edging up to 484.54. Stocks were helped by a report that industrial output rose in January at about half the pace of the prior two months. But there were signs that inflation may be picking up.

Mexico's markets were thrown into turmoil as interest rates on Mexican treasury bills soared to 40% and a major conglomerate defaulted on some short-term debt. The stock market's IPC index fell 6.41%. The peso lost 2.7% of its value against the dollar.

17 The U.S. economy appears to be slowing, and the slowdown could help keep inflation in check. In the latest report reflecting the shift, the Commerce Department said housing starts dropped 9.8% in January, with single-family home starts tumbling 12.4%.

Mexico's stocks were volatile, with the main IPC index tumbling to a loss of more than 3% at times before recovering to close 1.9% higher. Mexico's currency weakened further, breaking again the psychologically important level of six pesos to the dollar.

Concerns about the U.S. aid package for Mexico and a potential wave of Mexican corporate-bond defaults depressed bond prices in emerging markets, particularly Latin America.

A hacker's theft of 20,000 credit-card numbers raises concerns about the security of data on the Internet.

21 Quarterly profits were surprisingly strong for 1994's fourth period, lifted by improved efficiency and the ability to raise prices for the first time in years. According to a *Wall Street Journal* survey, 668 major companies posted a cumulative 61% increase in earnings compared with the year-earlier period. Meanwhile, some analysts say the fierce tug of war between earnings growth and interest rates is entering a crucial stage.

The trade deficit narrowed in December, to $7.34 billion from a November $10.04 billion, but widened for 1994.

The Fed is "close" to success in its preemptive inflation strike and must be ready to cut rates to pre-empt recession when circumstances warrant, Vice Chairman Alan Blinder said.

22 The U.S. reached agreement with Mexico on a $20 billion rescue plan. The long-awaited pact contains such tough conditions that Mexican markets initially fell on the news.

Tobacco companies were dealt two more setbacks in the escalating legal battle over cigarettes as Florida and Mississippi moved ahead with separate attempts to recoup welfare funds spent on smoking-related illnesses.

A global labor study predicts rising unemployment in industrialized nations for the rest of the century.

23 Greenspan said the Fed might refrain from further interest-rate increases even if inflation measures move up a bit. Bonds rallied sharply on the news, and stocks followed the bond market higher. The yield on the benchmark 30-year Treasury fell to nearly 7.54%, its lowest since September. Though Greenspan didn't rule out further increases, the comments were his first public hint that he thinks the current rate cycle may be near its end.

Mexico's stock market showed a loss for much of the day, and the peso fell a further 4%, as investors responded to worries that terms of a U.S. loan package may push interest rates high enough to cause a recession.

Auto sales in Mexico fell 22.2% in January, and the industry is bracing for a bigger decline this month.

24 The Dow Jones Industrial Average closed above 4000 for the first time, driven by growing optimism that the Federal Reserve can engineer an economic "soft landing" that will produce slower but sustained growth. This and a growing disenchantment with volatile foreign markets suggests to some analysts that stock prices will see gains the rest of the year.

Mexico's weakened economy and devalued peso will reverberate strongly in the U.S., shaving up to 0.4% off growth this year, according to Fed economists. Up to 380,000 jobs may be lost over four years, an analyst said.

U.S. businesses plan to boost spending on buildings and equipment 6.6% this year, the Commerce Department said, sharply less than in 1994.

27 British investment bank Barings PLC collapsed after a huge loss from derivatives trading wiped out its capital. The losses were attributed to a single Barings employee trading Japanese stock-index futures contracts. The Bank of England, which failed in an attempt to fashion a rescue package, put the loss at more than $800 million and said the figure could grow.

China and the U.S. signed an accord averting a major trade war.

In a comprehensive pact hailed as a triumph for Clinton's carrot-and-stick strategy, China agreed to crack down on piracy of computer software, compact disks, videotapes and other intellectual property. The Chinese also pledged to open their market to U.S. movies, music and software. "This agreement will go a long way to improving the balance of our economic relationship with China," U.S. Trade Representative Kantor said.

Clinton said the pact will "mean thousands of jobs for Americans in key industries," including software, publishing, pharmaceuticals, chemicals and audio-visual products.

Durable-goods orders increased 0.6% in January, helped by a jump in orders for industrial equipment.

28 Barings PLC's estimated loss jumped to $1.2 billion and world stock markets were rocked by the news of the collapse of the British investment bank, with Japanese stocks tumbling 3.8%. Meanwhile, authorities continued to search for the young trader being blamed for the debacle. In the U.S., Dillon Read, 40%-owned by Barings, plans to buy back the stake.

Investors pulled out of international stock funds in January, putting their money back into U.S. funds. For stock funds investing abroad, outflows totaled $37.8 million. Overall, stock funds had inflows of $6.2 billion.

March 1995

1 Rising Japanese stocks narrowed Barings PLC's estimated loss on futures contracts and options by about $100 million, although the loss still amounts to about $1.1 billion. Talks with potential buyers continued.

Sales of existing homes fell 4.5% in January, hitting their lowest level in nearly two years, a sign that higher interest rates are having an effect.

Mexico arrested the brother of ex-President Salinas in an assassination case.

The attorney general's office said Raul Salinas, the former president's older brother, is suspected of orchestrating the September slaying of Jose Francisco Ruiz Massieu, who was the No. 2 official in the ruling party when he was killed. Raul Salinas, a powerful businessman, has been dogged by press allegations of close links to some hard-liners in the ruling PRI who oppose democracy.

The arrest came on the heels of a statement by Salinas denying charges of a cover-up in last year's slaying of PRI presidential candidate Colosio.

2 Manufacturing activity continued to slow in February and price pressures for materials eased a bit, a purchasing-managers survey suggests. Separately, the Commerce Department said the economy grew at a 4.6% rate in the fourth quarter, a slight upward revision of an earlier report.

U.S. vehicle sales softened in February. GM, Chrysler and other auto makers, whose combined sales account for about two-thirds of the U.S. vehicle market, said sales fell 7%.

Canada's gross domestic product rose at a 5.9% rate in the fourth quarter, led by surging exports to the U.S.

3 The Senate narrowly rejected the balanced-budget amendment.

As expected, the GOP proposal fell a single vote short of the 67 needed for two-thirds approval, blocked by a band of Democrats citing concerns for Social Security. The outcome was 66–34, until Majority Leader Dole switched to the opposition to give him the right, under Senate rules, to demand another vote at any time. That put the official tally at 65–35. "This is not going to go away," the Kansas Republican warned.

Defeat of the proposed amendment, the centerpiece of the GOP's ambitious legislative agenda, raises questions about their resolve for erasing the federal budget deficit without it.

The U.S. bought dollars on foreign-exchange markets to bolster the currency after it fell to new lows against the yen. The dollar slipped to 94.95 yen before the action, then edged up to 95.25 yen in late New York trading.

Consumer spending was flat in January. Separately, new-home sales increased 3.8% in the month.

Retailers posted mildly disappointing February results as a slowing economy helped restrain sales growth.

6 Dutch financial giant Internationale Nederlanden Groep agreed to acquire collapsed investment bank Barings PLC, beating out a joint bid from ABN-Amro Holdings and Smith Barney. ING said it would immediately inject $1.06 billion to enable Barings to resume operations. Meanwhile, senior Barings executives face questions from investigators about whether they may have known enough to prevent the collapse.

Central banks intervened to support the dollar, following the Federal Reserve's effort to shore up the currency. But the dollar fell to new lows against the yen and continued sliding against major European currencies, and further declines are expected.

Factory orders jumped 0.6% in January, a strong pace but still the slowest in three months. Citing signs of a slowdown, analysts expect the Fed to hold interest rates steady this month.

7 The dollar continued to fall against the yen and the mark, but the U.S. remained on the sidelines, declining to intervene, unlike last week. Currency worries battered European markets, helping to send U.S. stocks sharply lower in early trading. But stocks recovered to end the day mixed. U.S. companies, meanwhile, see the falling dollar as an opportunity to increase sales at home and abroad.

The peso tumbled nearly 10% against the dollar but rebounded after Mexico's central bank intervened forcefully, spending an estimated $350 million to bolster the currency. Still, the peso lost 4.1% for the day.

Brazil moved to devalue its currency, the real, by as much as 12%, in a bid to avoid the kind of financial upheaval that is gripping Mexico.

8 The dollar went into a free fall against the mark and yen, hitting new lows

and jolting the U.S. stock market. Other currencies, including the British pound and the French franc, also fell to record lows against the mark, and some executives and traders worried that the declines could become a global crisis, dragging down markets around the world. Others were less concerned, noting that U.S. stocks remain close to historic highs.

Prices for gold and other precious metals rocketed higher in a sudden response to world currency turmoil.

9 The dollar regained some ground after its recent losses, helped by the jawboning of central bankers in Europe and the U.S., but traders said the move didn't signal a real turnaround. Federal Reserve Chairman Alan Greenspan blamed the dollar's weakness on the U.S. budget deficit and on Congress's failure to pass a balanced-budget amendment.

10 The Mexican peso sank to another record low as investors worried about the government's repeated delays in releasing a new economic-recovery plan. A government official said the plan will include tax increases, sharp rises in electricity and gas prices and tighter monetary policy. He acknowledged that interest rates would soar and that some companies would fail as a result.

Argentina sought additional financing from the International Monetary Fund to help its banking sector.

13 China and the U.S. reached agreements that should further open Chinese markets to U.S. agricultural products and facilitate Beijing's entry into the World Trade Organization. China also agreed to lift suspension of a 1992 market-access accord with the U.S. and open discussions on allowing U.S. telecommunications and insurance services into the country.

Job growth showed surprising strength in February, raising questions about whether the economy is slowing enough to keep the Fed from raising interest rates. Unemployment fell to 5.4% from January's 5.7%.

The jobs report and a stabilizing dollar helped send stock prices to record highs. The Dow Jones Industrial Average gained 52.22 to 4035.61.

14 Argentina has asked central banks from several leading industrial countries to help arrange a $3 billion credit line to shore up the country's banking system. Argentina not only is seeking the central banks' help but also is asking them to persuade commercial banks to participate.

Pentagon spending cuts and defense industry consolidation, which have eliminated more than 1.1 million jobs since 1987, will erase nearly 700,000 more during the next three years, according to the latest Labor Department and defense industry estimates.

15 Clinton blocked Conoco's plans to help Iran develop two oil fields, saying he will issue an order barring U.S. companies from such ventures with Tehran. Conoco, a unit of DuPont, immediately said it would terminate the contract. Some industry analysts said the U.S. stance will cede business to European firms, hurting U.S. oil companies more than Iran.

Retail sales slid 0.5% in February to $192.85 billion, the first decline since April, another sign that the economy is slowing under higher interest rates.

The sales report helped push stock and bond prices higher. The Dow Jones industrials climbed 23.52 to 4048.75. The price of the 30-year Treasury bond rose more than 1⅛ points.

The U.S. trade deficit surged to $155.7 billion last year from $103.9 billion in 1993, the 13th straight year that exports have fallen short of imports.

Japan's global trade surplus expanded 5.3% in February despite the strong yen. Its surplus with the U.S. jumped 13%, to $4.89 billion.

16 Kohlberg Kravis unloaded its remaining stake in RJR Nabisco, six years after buying the food and tobacco giant for $25 billion. The leveraged buyout firm transferred its 8% stake, valued at roughly $640 million, to its recently purchased Borden unit. Borden is expected to sell the shares on the open market. KKR probably will see a single-digit annual return on its RJR investment, far lower than any broader stock market index.

New reports suggested the economy is slowing but is far from weak. Industrial production rose 0.5% in February and businesses operated at close to capacity, but inventories piled up. Producer prices rose 0.3%. The reports bolster expectations that the Fed won't lift interest rates this month.

Mexican interest rates soared and the peso sank 4.5%, a sign that investors remain leery about the country's recently unveiled economic plan.

The dollar fell sharply against the mark and yen, stung by hints of U.S. inflation and worries about Mexico.

17 Consumer prices rose slightly last month, while housing starts declined sharply, two more signs that the economy is slowing down while inflation remains modest. Stocks moved higher on the news, with the Dow Jones industrials gaining 30.78 to 4069.15. Bond prices initially surged, too, but ended the day a bit lower.

Derivatives regulators, exchanges and dealers around the world are seeking a variety of reforms in the wake of the collapse of Barings PLC. But a consensus will be difficult to reach.

Germany's central bank declined to cut interest rates. A reduction could bolster the sinking dollar and strengthen weak European currencies. Nevertheless, the dollar moved higher against the mark and the yen.

The number of auto recalls in the U.S. declined 45% last year after rising for four straight years. A total of 6.1 million vehicles were recalled in 1994.

20 Credit Lyonnais posted a 1994 loss of $2.4 billion, far more than expected. The loss, the biggest in French banking history, forced Credit Lyonnais to seek another state bailout, its second in a year. Under the plan, the bank will spin off about $27 billion of assets into a new company backed by the state. Potential losses on those assets could total another $10 billion.

21 Nasdaq proposed a new system for handling small-investor orders, an attempt to dispel criticism of the market's trading practices. Nasdaq President Joseph Hardiman and other Nasdaq officials said the new system isn't a response to an antitrust probe of the market. The plan is subject to approval by the SEC, which blocked an earlier Nasdaq proposal.

Police began a massive probe of a nerve-gas attack on Tokyo subway trains.

The attack killed seven people and sickened nearly 4,700, but no clear suspects or motive have emerged. Tokyo police mobilized 300 detectives to investigate the case. Authorities said at least five unidentified suspects left various containers filled with sarin on trains. Sarin is a gas developed by German scientists between the two world wars, which cripples the nervous system and can kill in minutes. The Japanese army's anti-chemical warfare units decontaminated five trains and 16 stations on three of the city's subway lines. The U.S. said it was prepared to offer technical assistance to help Japan.

22 Genetic Therapy received rights to a patent covering experimental "gene therapy" techniques being tested against cancer and other illnesses.

Base-metals prices were boosted by reports showing that consumers continue to draw down inventories of aluminum, copper and other metals at London Metal Exchange warehouses.

23 The U.S. trade gap ballooned to a record $12.2 billion in January as the effects of Mexico's financial crises spread across the border. With big declines in autos and grain sales, U.S. exports to Mexico fell 10%. Exports to South and Central America also dropped precipitously. Overall, merchandise exports declined nearly 6% and merchandise imports grew 3%, while the service surplus shrank 12%.

The dollar fell, stung by the deficit report and worries about Mexico. In late New York trading, the dollar was at 89.00 yen and 1.4025 marks.

24 The dollar continued to fall against the yen, touching another record low despite intervention by the Bank of Japan during Asian trading. Traders and analysts are betting the drop is far from over. Meanwhile, economists said that although the lower dollar hasn't narrowed the U.S. trade gap, ultimately the deficit will shrink if the currency remains weak.

Mexico may be forced to raise interest rates well beyond their current levels of nearly 100% to stabilize the country's weakened currency, a central-bank official said. He said the stance is necessary to prove Mexico's commitment to stabilizing the peso.

Citicorp has suspended plans to expand its retail banking business in Mexico, citing the economic turmoil there following the peso's decline.

An investment fund managed by the state of Wisconsin lost $95 million because of derivative investments, the latest in a series of derivative losses suffered by public investment funds.

27 The airline industry is showing signs of a long-awaited recovery. Traffic figures are up this year, advance bookings are strong and stock analysts are raising their earnings estimates.

Leaders of USAir's pilots' union agreed to a 20% pay cut and other concessions under a tentative accord that could save the troubled airline $190 million annually for five years.

28 Stock and bond prices surged on new signs that the economy is slowing. The Dow Jones Industrial Average rose

18.67 to 4157.34, its seventh record in the past 11 sessions. Airline stocks jumped higher, reflecting signs that the battered industry may finally be finding some economic success.

Existing-home sales fell in February to their lowest level in two years, further evidence that higher interest rates have hurt the market.

29 Mitsubishi Bank and Bank of Tokyo plan to merge, forming the largest private bank in the world. The merger could revitalize Japan's ailing bank industry, a root of the country's economic problems. But terms of the combination haven't been worked out, and the heads of the two banks gave no word on the value and financing of the deal, who will run the new bank, or how the merger will affect their big California units.

30 New home sales sank 14% in February to the slowest annual rate in nearly three years, with activity off in every region of the country.

31 Germany's Central Bank unexpectedly cut interest rates, boosting the sagging dollar. The moves pushed German rates to their lowest level in five years and caught currency markets by surprise. Central banks in Switzerland, Austria, the Netherlands and Belgium quickly followed the Bundesbank's decision with interest-rate cuts of their own.

The dollar rallied against the mark and yen after the Bundesbank's move. In late New York trading, the dollar was at 1.4095 marks and 89.60 yen.

April 1995

3 The U.S. economy closed out 1994 with a stronger-than-expected quarter, but the growth may have contributed to the first quarter's signs of slowing. Fourth-quarter GDP was revised to 5.1% from 4.6%, while reports on more recent data show weakness.

4 The U.S. moved to bolster its currency, buying dollars on world markets. Despite the intervention, the dollar slipped to new lows against the yen. Traders increasingly believe that only higher interest rates can help the dollar, but the Fed opted not to lift rates at its meeting last week and isn't expected to raise them anytime soon.

Japanese stocks sank 4.7% on mounting concern about the economy and the dollar's persistent weakness.

The rapid expansion in manufacturing showed signs of tailing off in March, more evidence of an economic slowdown. Separately, consumer spending inched up 0.1% in February, the smallest rise in nearly a year.

Auto sales in March, traditionally the industry's second-busiest month, were disappointing. Chrysler Chairman Robert Eaton said the continued slowdown will hurt earnings.

5 Merrill Lynch risk managers repeatedly sought to rein in the firm's business with Orange County long before the county's financial collapse. Merrill's top risk manager even took the unusual step of visiting the county's treasurer to express concern about his highly leveraged portfolio.

U.S. stock funds surged 7.16% in the first three months of 1995, their strongest gain in two years. But stock funds that invest abroad lost 1.85%. Bond funds, meanwhile, gained 3.85%.

Construction spending fell 0.5% in February, its second straight decline, suggesting that higher interest rates are prompting builders to cut back.

Stock and bond prices rose as investors cheered signs of a slowing economy. The Dow Jones industrials gained 33.20 to a record 4201.61.

6 The U.S., Germany and Japan made a coordinated effort to bolster the dollar, but the intervention failed to push the sagging currency higher. Concern about the dollar's slide has begun to make Wall Street uneasy.

Seagram is close to completing a sale of its 24.2% stake in DuPont back to the chemical giant for close to $10 billion and is in exclusive negotiations with Matsushita Electric Industrial for the purchase of its MCA unit.

The index of leading economic indicators fell 0.2% in February, only the second time in 19 months that the economic barometer has declined. Separately, wholesalers' inventories rose 1.2%, suggesting that weakening consumer demand could lead to production cutbacks in coming months.

7 Daimler-Benz swung to a profit in 1994 after its first postwar loss in 1993. The rebound followed a cost-cutting drive that included a 20% work-force reduction and big concessions from unions. Other German firms have taken similar actions, fueling the nation's recovery and boosting the mark.

March sales were even slower than big retailers expected, with a number of companies showing declines, including

Gap, Limited and J.C. Penney. Dayton Hudson said sales fell 4.7% and warned that first-quarter net didn't match year-earlier profit.

The dollar slipped to yet another new low against the yen. But concern about further intervention steadied the dollar against other currencies. Late in New York, the dollar was trading at 1.3735 marks and at 85.34 yen.

U.S. stock and bond investors remained ambivalent about the dollar's woes. Stock prices finished mostly higher and bond prices rose a bit. The Dow Jones industrials edged up 4.84 to 4205.41, another record high.

10 Seagram agreed to acquire 80% of MCA from Matsushita Electric Industrial for $5.7 billion. Seagram won't assume any MCA debt. Many on Wall Street and in Hollywood speculate that Seagram's next move will be an investment in a network. People close to Seagram say there are no such plans at the moment, but they don't rule out a possible investment that would give MCA a distribution link.

The comptroller of the currency warned bankers that credit standards are slipping and announced the formation of a panel to monitor loan standards at federally chartered banks.

Manufacturing employment declined in March, and the drop, the first in 15 months, suggests that the economy could be headed for a "soft landing." Overall, the unemployment rate rose to 5.5% in March from 5.4%.

11 Kemper has agreed to be acquired by an investor group led by Zurich Insurance Group of Switzerland for $49.50 a share, or $2 billion, according to people familiar with the transaction. Kemper would receive $47.50 a share in cash and $2 a share in securities. The deal would cap Kemper's long search for a buyer, a hunt sparked by a hostile takeover bid made by a GE subsidiary last March.

The dollar recovered from an overnight pounding in Asian trading to finish New York trading modestly higher against the yen. Stock prices, initially hurt by the dollar's drop, rebounded as well, ending with small gains.

12 The chairman of the American Stock Exchange will ask its board to overhaul its controversial section for tiny, unproven stocks, the Emerging Company Marketplace, and toughen listing standards for companies on the Amex's main exchange. The intended revamping of the small-company section, a

move that critics say is long overdue, is part of an attempt to boost the exchange's image.

The dollar faces a new challenge in Asia, where central bankers are under pressure to keep selling dollars and buying yen because of debt owed—in yen—to Japan. Currency trading cooled after Monday's sharp swings, with the dollar slipping slightly.

The producer price index was unchanged last month, the latest sign that the economic expansion isn't producing higher levels of inflation. Stagnant prices, economists said, are due in part to a backlog of inventories.

13 Chrysler received a massive takeover proposal from its biggest shareholder, Kirk Kerkorian, and its former chairman, Lee Iacocca. At $55 a share, the $20 billion proposal topped Chrysler's Tuesday closing price by more than 40%. Chrysler shares rose 24% to $48.75, reflecting the proposal's sketchy financing plans. Iacocca said he isn't seeking to return to the auto maker's helm. Chrysler said it isn't for sale.

Consumer prices edged up 0.2% in March, the smallest increase this year, but underlying numbers raised questions about whether inflation is under control or beginning to pick up.

14 Chrysler faces pressure from large investors to respond to Kirk Kerkorian's $20 billion takeover bid with a major share repurchase or other steps, although questions remain about Mr. Kerkorian's ability to finance the deal. The auto maker reported a 37% drop in first-quarter earnings and predicted that second-quarter results will be off as well.

Retail sales edged up 0.2% in March after February's 1.0% decline, another sign the economy is cooling.

17 Industrial production fell in March, another sign that manufacturing is slowing and the economy is approaching a "soft landing." Also, business inventories rose in February.

Japan's merchandise trade surplus shrank only slightly in March overall, and rose against the U.S., helped by auto, chip and machinery exports.

Japan's four largest brokerage companies expect losses on their securities holdings for the year ended March 31, the latest sign of trouble in the country's financial sector. The four—Nomura, Daiwa, Nikko and Yamaichi—are to report combined losses of nearly $1 billion on investments.

Some large U.S. companies have profited from the dollar's decline in recent months as corporate treasurers have taken best against it in the futures market, observers say.

Importers and others too small to invest in hedge positions are shifting production back to the U.S. and using other strategies, such as price increases and tougher negotiations, to offset the effects of a weaker dollar.

18 Conrail is considering selling or abandoning up to 4,000 miles, or one-third, of its rail routes in the Northeast and Midwest to boost profit margins and to concentrate spending on more successful lines. The contemplated streamlining would eliminate its least productive routes without reducing revenue sharply.

The dollar fell sharply as traders signaled their dissatisfaction with a Japanese plan to lower the value of the yen. The Bank of Japan intervened to stem the U.S. currency's slide.

19 The dollar sank again as trade tensions thickened between the U.S. and Japan, which ended their latest round of talks without a breakthrough. The dollar, sinking toward record lows, dragged stock prices down. The head of IMF blasted the Fed for failing to raise interest rates to boost the dollar, saying that the U.S. and world economies are threatened by the currency's weakness.

Housing starts tumbled 7.9% in March, falling to their lowest annual rate in two years, another sign that the economy has lost momentum.

20 Bear Stearns, under pressure from Chrysler, has decided not to serve as financial adviser to Kirk Kerkorian in his bid for the auto maker. Chrysler also is pressing its top banks to refrain from financing the hostile offer, according to people on Wall Street, who see Kerkorian faltering in his efforts to line up financing.

Ford's earnings jumped 71% in the first quarter, but profit from U.S. auto operations edged up only 1.1%.

21 IBM's first-quarter net more than tripled, with sales increasing for all its product lines for an overall sales rise of 18%. The stronger-than-expected showing sent IBM shares up 2.2% and prompted analysts to boost earnings projections for the rest of the year.

24 Stocks rallied, lifting the Dow Jones Industrial Average to its second straight record. The industrial average gained 39.43, or 0.93%, to 4270.09. The dollar slipped a bit from earlier gains. Analysts worry that the dollar could be pushed even lower by increasingly strained relations between the U.S. and Japan, set to resume auto trade talks this week.

The U.S. trade gap will balloon to $200 billion this year, an economic think tank predicted. The Institute for International Economics forecasts that the trade gap will remain at the $200 billion level for several years.

25 Chrysler's board spurned Kerkorian's $20 billion takeover proposal, but didn't offer a plan to prop up the auto maker's sagging stock. Charging that the takeover bid would cripple the company, Chrysler reiterated its need to maintain a big cash hoard to weather a recession. Chrysler shares slipped 62.5 cents to $44.50.

Mexican stocks jumped 5.1% on the peso's increasing strength and better-than-expected results at the country's largest banking company. The peso has increased 15.6% this month.

Treasury Secretary Rubin described the U.S. agenda for remaking international financial institutions in the wake of Mexico's financial crisis.

26 Employment costs rose 0.6% in the first quarter, the smallest increase since the measure was begun in 1982. Benefits costs inched up only 0.2%.

Existing-home sales rose 5.8% in March from February, helped in part by lower mortgage rates, but sales were 12% off the year-ago level.

Finance ministers from the Group of Seven nations said they would like to see a stronger dollar but didn't offer any plan to boost the currency.

27 The Supreme Court opened the way for health-care reform efforts at the state level, clearing New York regulations that impose surcharges on insurers and HMOs to help pay for care for the poor. At least 21 states have similar regulations, and many others now are likely to follow suit. Employers warned that the ruling will increase their insurance premiums and force them to consider limiting health coverage for workers.

Chrysler shares slid 5.7% after Kerkorian acknowledged late Tuesday that he has failed to line up financing for a proposed $20 billion takeover.

Some U.S. manufacturers are starting to pass along rising raw-material costs, leading some economists to forecast modestly higher inflation.

28 The U.S. filed suit to block Microsoft's $2 billion acquisition of Intuit, arguing that the deal would hinder competition in the market for personal-finance software, one of the last PC-related areas where Microsoft remains a minor player. The Justice Department also cited concern about the deal's effect on new markets, such as on-line data services and banking. Competitors cheered the suit, which Microsoft and Intuit vowed to fight.

May 1995

1 Profits surged at big U.S. companies in the first quarter despite signs of a slowing economy. According to a *Wall Street Journal* survey, 674 major companies reported net income rose a cumulative 48%, with all industry groups posting gains for the period. The performance surprised analysts, who doubted companies could keep up the pace of earlier quarters.

The economy expanded at a 2.8% annual rate in the first quarter, the slowest growth since the summer of 1993, and economists expect the rate to remain in that range with only modest inflation for the rest of the year.

2 Car sales sank in April despite aggressive spending by auto makers on consumer incentives, a sign that the first-quarter slump may be turning into a rout. General Motors' car and light-truck sales were off 7% while Chrysler's slid 18%. The results were particularly disappointing for Chrysler, which saw falling sales for minivans and sport-utility vehicles.

GM raised its common stock dividend by 50%, an effort to catch up with increases by Ford and Chrysler.

Northern States Power and Wisconsin Energy agreed to merge. The $3 billion combination, the biggest ever for U.S. electric utilities, could accelerate an industry consolidation that has been fueled by deregulation.

3 The surging yen is hurting Japanese car companies in the U.S. Nearly all big Japanese auto makers reported substantial sales declines for April.

New home sales rose 3% in March from February but remained 20% below the March 1994 level, a further sign that the economy is slowing down.

4 Stocks soared to new highs, sparked by a rally in the bond market. The Dow Jones industrials rose 44.27 to 4373.15, as investors were cheered by new signs of a slowing economy. Factory orders fell in March, and the index of leading indicators declined. The reports fueled optimism that the Federal Reserve won't increase interest rates again.

Ford bucked the trend of slower vehicle sales, reporting a 3.6% increase for April. But auto-industry sales overall were down 6.1% for the month, leading auto makers and industry watchers to cut 1995 sales predictions for the second time in two months.

5 Hoechst agreed to acquire Marion Merrell Dow for $25.75 a share, or $7.1 billion, making the German company the world's third-largest drug concern. Hoechst will purchase Dow Chemical's 71% stake in Marion Merrell and make a tender offer for the remaining shares.

U.S. retailers posted disappointing sales for April, failing to rebound from a flat March, and are expected to report weak first-quarter earnings.

Japan said it would take its trade dispute with the U.S. to the World Trade Organization if current auto trade talks fail and the U.S. imposes threatened economic sanctions.

The Commerce Department is overhauling its economic-statistics operation, changing the inflation measure it uses to calculate economic growth. The department is scuttling its index of leading indicators.

8 Unemployment jumped 0.3 percentage point to 5.8% in April, raising concern that the economy may be slowing too much. But economists doubt the slowdown will deteriorate into recession. The jobs report, the latest sign that growth has cooled, led many investors to believe the Federal Reserve's next move could be to lower interest rates rather than raise them.

Paris Mayor Chirac won France's presidential election.

Gaullist Jacques Chirac, regarded only three months ago as a has-been, staged a comeback by defeating Socialist Lionel Jospin by roughly 52% to 48%, according to incomplete returns. Chirac's election brings to a close Mitterrand's 14-year reign and ends a period of unwieldy power-sharing between a Socialist president and conservative parliament. Chirac's ambiguous stance on European relations and conflicting signals on monetary policy may signal a rocky phase in the drive toward European unity.

In his victory statement last night, Chirac said, "Our principal battle has a name: the fight against unemployment. The classic remedies have failed. We need a new approach."

The U.S. is expected to announce this week tariffs totaling $2 billion to $4 billion on Japanese goods, including electronic products, luxury cars and minivans, after failing to make headway in its trade talks with Japan.

9 The U.S. plans to target Japanese luxury cars and minivans with hefty tariffs to price them out of the market, a sharp escalation in the countries' long-running trade dispute. Japan has said that it will appeal any sanctions to the World Trade Organization.

10 Bond prices surged, sending long-term interest rates below 7% for the first time in more than a year. But the gains unsettled the stock market, where prices finished mixed as investors worried about the effect of an economic slowdown on corporate profits. Still, the Dow Jones Industrial Average edged up to yet another record, rising 6.91 to 4390.78.

Productivity inched up in the first quarter, growing at a 0.7% annual rate for the period. Labor costs, meanwhile, rose at a 3.4% annual rate.

11 Swiss Bank agreed to acquire the investment-banking operations of S. G. Warburg, Britain's largest investment bank, for $1.36 billion. The deal doesn't include Warburg's 75% interest in Mercury Asset Management.

Economic activity is proceeding "at a somewhat slower pace" than earlier this year, the Fed's latest survey of its 12 district banks suggests.

Slumping car sales have dashed hopes for another year of record earnings for the Big Three auto makers.

12 The dollar surged, driven by near panic buying as surprised traders rushed to cover big bets that the currency would decline. The dollar was buoyed by optimism about the U.S.'s budget deficit and trade gap.

The majority owner of New York's Rockefeller Center sought bankruptcy protection for the midtown Manhattan office towers after losses of more than $600 million on the property.

The American Stock Exchange will close its controversial section for tiny, unproven stocks, the Emerging Company Marketplace, which opened three years ago with 23 companies.

Producer prices rose 0.5% in April, the largest increase in five months. But a separate report showed that consumer spending continues to slow, helping to allay inflation concerns.

15 The dollar continued to rebound on signs that the U.S. may be moving to reduce its trade and budget deficits. For the week, the dollar gained more than 5% against the mark and 3.3% against the yen. Many traders and money managers—but not all—are now convinced that the dollar has seen its lows for the year, but few believe the currency's recent gains are the start of a lasting rally.

Consumer prices rose 0.4% in April, the largest gain since August, but many economists say inflation is likely to remain in check over the next few months. Separately, business inventories increased 0.7% in March.

16 Dow Corning filed for protection under bankruptcy laws, in a move to limit its escalating legal exposure to breast-implant lawsuits. The move disrupts a global settlement fund that now totals $4.23 billion.

Manufacturers expect fewer new orders this summer, a trend that will further slow factory production and prompt some firms to lower prices.

17 The U.S. took even harsher steps than expected in its trade dispute with Japan, threatening sanctions that could virtually halt sales of 13 Japanese luxury cars. U.S. officials said that 100% tariffs would go into effect retroactively in three days, meaning that cars arriving at U.S. ports after Friday would be subject to any tariffs imposed next month. The stance won bipartisan support in Washington but was criticized by the European Union.

Industrial production fell 0.4% in April after a 0.3% drop in March, the first back-to-back declines in more than three years. Separately, housing starts increased 0.4% last month.

18 Japanese luxury-car dealers worried that threatened U.S. sanctions could lead to massive employee layoffs, and at least one Japanese auto maker rushed a load of cars to port in the U.S. to beat a Saturday deadline. Meanwhile, industry experts said that while some U.S. parts makers would benefit from greater access to the Japanese market—a key goal for the U.S. in the trade battle—not many American jobs would be gained.

19 The U.S. trade gap narrowed a bit in March, with the overall deficit in goods and services shrinking to $9.12 billion from February's $9.15 billion.

But the trade gap with Japan jumped to $6.14 billion from $4.71 billion.

Eastman Kodak accused Japan and rival Fuji Photo Film of choking Kodak's access to the Japanese photographic film and paper market, stepping up its long-running battle with Fuji in the wake of threatened U.S. trade sanctions on Japanese cars.

22 Microsoft abandoned its plan to acquire Intuit three weeks after the Justice Department sued to block the purchase, alleging it would give Microsoft total dominance over the burgeoning market for personal-finance software. Microsoft could face similar pressure with its planned on-line service, which is being examined by a U.S. antitrust team.

Customers flocked to Japanese luxury-car showrooms, rushing to make purchases before possible U.S. sanctions on the models take effect.

23 The United Rubber Workers abandoned a 10-month strike at Bridgestone/Firestone, ending a walkout that cost it thousands of jobs and prompted its decision to merge with the United Steelworkers union.

24 Stock and bond prices rallied after the Federal Reserve left interest rates unchanged. Many economists, though not all, expect the Fed's next move will be to cut rates, but predict that the central bank will take a wait-and-see stance through the summer. Buoyed by the hope of lower rates later this year, the Dow Jones Industrial Average gained 40.81 to 4436.44 and the 30-year Treasury bond rose nearly three-quarters of a point.

U.K. regulators set new media-ownership rules that effectively halt Rupert Murdoch's British expansion.

25 Durable-goods orders fell 4% in April, the biggest drop in more than three years, suggesting the economic slowdown has spread beyond weakening car and home sales. Bond prices surged on the news, with the 30-year Treasury bond gaining nearly $1^3/4$ points. Stocks gyrated but ended the day little changed.

Vanguard Group's president, John Brennan, will succeed John Bogle as chief executive of the fund company.

30 The U.S. and Japan wrangled over when to resume trade talks on auto parts. The U.S., trying to force Tokyo to agree to demands that it open its auto-parts market, wants to delay negotiations until June 20, just one week before punitive sanctions on Japanese luxury cars would go into effect. Japan is seeking an earlier date but may not be able to force the issue.

Nissan plans to ship about 4,000 luxury cars to the U.S. in coming weeks, becoming the second Japanese auto maker to gamble that the U.S. won't carry out threatened sanctions.

31 Toyota and Nissan scaled back efforts to protect their U.S. luxury-car dealers from threatened trade sanctions. The Japanese auto makers are reducing the number of high-priced vehicles to be shipped to the U.S., and Toyota is cutting its luxury-car production in Japan. Meanwhile, Mitsubishi said it won't produce Diamante luxury cars scheduled to be built in June for the U.S. market.

The Clinton administration is stepping up pressure on Tokyo to resume talks over U.S. airlines' rights to serve Japan and other Asian markets.

Japan's jobless rate rose to 3.2% in April, the highest level since the nation began keeping records in 1953.

June 1995

1 Stocks soared to record highs on signs that the economy isn't slowing too quickly. The Dow Jones Industrial Average surged 86.46 to 4465.14. The U.S. nudged down its estimate of economic growth for the first quarter, but details in the report suggested that the economy, while slowing, isn't sliding into a recession. Separately, new-home sales fell 2.7% in April. Falling mortgage rates are expected to bolster sales later this year.

Kirk Kerkorian abandoned his $20 billion bid for Chrysler. But his holding company, Tracinda, said that it won't sell its 10% stake in the auto maker and that it hired Wasserstein Perella to evaluate its options.

2 Federal Reserve officials don't anticipate a recession and therefore are unlikely to cut interest rates in the near future. The Fed is braced for a wave of reports showing that the economy has slowed, such as yesterday's data indicating that manufacturing growth and new factory orders declined this spring. But officials expect growth to pick up by year end.

Major retailers reported sales gains for May, but stores often had to offer discounts to attract shoppers. Apparel sales showed some improvement for the first time this year.

Sales of new cars and trucks remained sluggish in May, though partial results indicate that they improved from April's anemic levels.

5 Recession concerns were bolstered by grim May employment data, including the largest drop in nonfarm payrolls in four years. The price of the 30-year Treasury rallied sharply, for a short time equaling its largest one-day gain of the decade, before ending 1¼ points higher. Its yield plunged to 6.52% on the prospect that, absent a soft landing for the economy, the Fed might reduce interest rates.

The U.S. backs trade liberalization with Europe that would reduce barriers and seek common agreement on standards and technical issues but falls short of a full free-trade pact.

Japan and the U.S. agreed to one round of talks aimed at resolving an auto-trade dispute but disagreed over the terms for subsequent meetings.

6 Job stability fell in the 1980s, a federal study said, contradicting other recent indications of little change in the rate at which employees switch jobs.

8 Japan's Finance Ministry is said to be considering measures to handle insolvent banks, a sign it may be preparing for its first bank failures in more than 50 years as a loan crisis widens.

9 Economists have cut their estimates for second-quarter economic growth to the lowest levels in nearly four years amid further signs of a slowdown, though they expect lower interest rates to ward off recession.

12 Lotus agreed to be acquired by IBM for $3.52 billion, or $64 a share, capitulating less than a week after the hostile bid was announced. In a surprise move, Lotus Chairman Jim Manzi is to join IBM as Lotus's CEO. He was widely expected to depart, and the appointment may pose strategic and managerial problems as the software maker is integrated into IBM.

Producer prices were unchanged in May, indicating inflation pressure may be falling as the economy slows.

Bond prices tumbled despite the positive inflation news. The benchmark 30-year bond slid 1⅝ points on Friday, lifting its yield to 6.72% and pulling stocks lower. The Dow Jones industrials fell more than 50 points before recovering to close 34.58 lower.

13 Canada's economic growth slowed sharply in the first quarter, partly due to the softening U.S. economy.

The justices dealt a severe blow to federal affirmative-action programs.

In a 5–4 decision, the Supreme Court ruled that Congress must meet an extremely tough legal standard to justify any contracting or hiring practice based on race. Though the court stopped short of striking down any particular program, the decision is certain to provoke court challenges against minority-preference programs.

The high court stepped up pressure on federal courts to wind down their supervision of school desegregation, throwing out a desegregation plan ordered by a district judge in Kansas City, Mo.

14 Retail sales grew 0.2% in May, less than expected, heightening concerns about the economy's health. Separately, consumer prices rose 0.3%.

Bonds and stocks rallied on hopes the Fed may soon consider interest-rate cuts to spur the economy. The price of the benchmark 30-year Treasury jumped nearly 2¼ points, pushing its yield sharply lower, to 6.54%. The Dow Jones industrials rose 38.05.

15 Inventories grew in April and sales declined, the government said, further signs that economic growth is slowing.

21 Greenspan said the economy will grow "very little" in the current quarter, or perhaps even shrink slightly. Meanwhile, housing starts slid 1.3% in May, the fourth decline in five months, further evidence of a slowdown. Stocks closed mixed and bond prices fell slightly as investors awaited an evening speech by Greenspan, hoping to gain insight into the Fed's intentions on interest rates ahead of a July policy meeting.

Japan is considering placing tariffs on certain U.S. exports if Washington's sanctions on Japanese luxury cars take effect next week as planned.

Japan's economy fared poorly in the latest period, and by one measure slid into recession. Gross domestic product grew at a 0.3% annual rate, and gross national product fell 0.2%.

22 The trade deficit widened unexpectedly in April, to $11.37 billion from March's $9.79 billion, and economists again lowered second-quarter economic expectations. Though trade figures with Japan improved a bit, imports of Japanese cars grew, boosting pressure on the U.S. in the current trade dispute over autos.

The Fed found "indications of some softening" of the economy, particularly on the coasts, in its region-by-region survey. But it also said economic activity "remains at a high level" in most parts of the U.S.

26 Mickey Kantor, the U.S. trade representative, plans to meet with his Japanese counterpart, Ryutaro Hashimoto, to discuss the trade dispute over autos as tariffs loom. The challenge for the U.S. is to obtain specific commitments from auto makers that they will buy more U.S.-made parts; the auto makers are leery of being locked into purchase targets. Sanctions totaling $5.9 billion on Japanese luxury cars are to begin this week.

Honda is increasing its imports to Japan of foreign-made parts, partly to cut costs by taking advantage of the yen's strength against the dollar.

Factory orders rose 2.5% in May, their largest increase since November. The figures suggest the slowing economy may stabilize by year's end, analysts said. Separately, machine-tool orders jumped in May, and are up 20% so far this year, on rising exports.

27 Kerkorian offered $700 million for 14 million Chrysler shares, just weeks after dropping his attempt to purchase the auto maker outright. The $50-a-share tender offer would boost the stake held by Kerkorian, who is already Chrysler's biggest holder, to 13.6% from nearly 10%. The offer, set to begin today, faces a hurdle in Michigan related to insurance regulations; two Chrysler insurance units are based there.

Germany's Dresdner Bank agreed to acquire British investment bank Kleinwort Benson for $1.59 billion.

28 Japan released another plan to help its economy, this one hastening deregulation and accelerating public-works spending. The Nikkei fell 2.6%, even though the package also aims to nurture the weakened stock market.

Tokyo's privatization plans are suffering as the market tumbles. Officials said a sale of state-owned railroads is now "unlikely" this year.

29 The U.S. and Japan compromised, avoiding a trade war over access to Japan's auto market. Japan agreed to deregulate the sale of replacement parts, and its auto makers pledged to buy more U.S.-made goods. However, no spe-

cific purchase targets were set, as the U.S. had sought. One clear winner is the U.S. parts industry; Clinton said the pact should eventually lift annual sales to Japan by $9 billion, or about 45% from 1994 levels.

Orange County voters rejected a sales-tax increase that would have helped to avert a possible default on the county's debt, and officials met to ponder a new approach. One consequence of the vote may be to aid Merrill in its legal fight with the county.

30 Kodak's claims of unfair trade practices by Fuji Photo in the Japanese market will be investigated soon by the U.S. Kodak alleges Fuji controls Japan's largest distributors of photo supplies. Fuji has denied the charges, but U.S. officials have long considered the case a strong one. The probe comes on the heels of the climactic end to the lengthy auto dispute.

The U.S. will decide next month whether to set sanctions in a conflict involving Federal Express, the next in a string of trade confrontations with Japan that have marked recent years.

New-home sales jumped 19.9% in May, the Commerce Department said, a sharp change from a lackluster performance earlier this year. Separately, unemployment claims fell. The data suggest the worst may be over for the housing market and the broader economy, analysts and others said.

Bonds plummeted on signs that the economy is too strong to warrant a Fed interest-rate cut. The 30-year Treasury's price ended nearly two points lower; stock prices closed mixed.

The Commodity Futures Trading Commission approved a sweeping overhaul of rules governing disclosures by commodity pools and trading advisers, a move meant to simplify how they report investment performance and to cut management fees.

July 1995

3 Merger activity set a record in the first half of the year. Announced deals in which the target was a U.S. company totaled $164.4 billion, a 20% jump from 1994's first half, as companies sought to grow through acquisitions to offset the effects of an economic slowdown. The pace is likely to continue, though not at record levels due to last year's strong finish.

Factory orders rose 1.4% in May, their first increase since January. These and other figures hint that the economy may see a slight rebound.

5 Economists are upbeat that the economy will pick up by late summer, a survey found. They foresee a burst of spending driven by recent interest-rate declines. Meanwhile, personal income and construction spending fell, and growth in manufacturing slowed, but analysts said the data are consistent with slow growth and harbor little recession threat.

Fed policy makers meet today and tomorrow, and they appear divided on whether to cut short-term rates to nudge the economy. The markets are looking for guidance on rates following weeks of shifting expectations.

6 The Dow Jones Industrial Average jumped more than 30 points, closing above 4600 for the first time, as investors indicated they believe the Federal Reserve will cut short-term rates soon. Bonds traded narrowly, as did the dollar, as markets awaited a move by Fed policy makers, whose two-day meeting concludes today. Any change in rates would likely be announced early this afternoon.

Ford and Chrysler broke sales records in June, leading an auto-industry rebound from lackluster sales earlier this year. However, the gains were driven largely by discounting, which indicates a weakness in the market.

Bond prices rallied in Japan to an eight-year high amid uncharacteristically gloomy assessments of the economy by policy makers. The shift in rhetoric was taken as a sign the central bank may cut interest rates to aid the economy, which would lift bonds.

Mexican stocks saw one of their strongest rallies of the year, with the IPC index closing up 121.84 points, or 5.6%, at 2306.30. It was its highest close since January 2 and a sign that foreign investors are returning to the market.

7 The Fed trimmed a pivotal short-term rate by 0.25%, its first loosening of rates in nearly three years, and markets welcomed the news. The benchmark 30-year Treasury bond's yield tumbled to 6.49%, its lowest in 17 months, and the Dow Jones industrials soared more than 48 points to 4664, another record close.

Consumers spent cautiously last month amid concerns over the economy, producing lackluster sales growth at major retailers. Sales at stores open at least a year rose about 3.4%, below analyst expectations.

The index of leading indicators fell 0.2% in May, its fourth straight decline. Analysts said the data hint at slowing growth but not a downturn.

Chinese officials said they favor Mercedes over Ford and Chrysler for a $1 billion minivan venture; separately, Shanghai's mayor canceled a U.S. business meeting. The developments feed fears that U.S.–China political tension may take a business toll.

10 A high-ranking executive at Archer-Daniels-Midland has been an informant for federal investigators for three years, and the efforts of the 38-year-old biochemist, Mark Whitacre, led to a current probe of ADM and other grain processors on allegations they colluded to fix prices.

Tokyo and Washington teamed up to prop the dollar on Friday, following last week's global round of rate cuts by central banks. These and other developments accompany a striking drop in inflation pressures world-wide.

Most major banks pared their prime rates to 8.75% from 9%. Meanwhile, some analysts expect the Fed to continue trimming rates this year.

Unemployment slid to 5.6% in June, its second straight drop. Though the figures were unexpectedly strong, analysts were wary of considering them a vigorous sign of economic rebound.

11 France will end most remaining restrictions on investors from outside the EU, in a bid to attract more foreign investment and enhance Paris's standing as a financial center.

12 Consumer debt grew at a 14.6% annual rate in May. The figures suggest that, although Americans are buying considerably less than they did late last year, they are still relying heavily on credit for what they do purchase.

13 Germany's Mercedes-Benz won "basic agreement" for a $1 billion joint venture to build minivans and engines in China, beating out U.S. rivals Ford and Chrysler. Chinese officials denied a link between the Mercedes deal and deteriorating relations between the U.S. and China.

17 Consumer prices edged up only 0.1%, their best showing this year, and retail sales rose a healthy 0.7%. The June figures, which include the first increase in industrial production since

January, are new indications that the economy is seeing a soft landing.

Bond prices slid amid signs of a firming economy, which decreases the likelihood that the Fed will further cut short-term rates any time soon.

18 Business inventories grew only 0.4% in May, the slowest pace in five months, and sales rose 0.5%. The healthy economic signs suggest manufacturers won't have to cut production.

Japan's trade surplus with the U.S. fell 12% last month in dollar terms, a sharp decline. Economists cited a waning demand for imports amid slower U.S. economic growth, but the auto-trade dispute also played a role.

19 The U.S. trade deficit grew in May to a record, an unexpected development given the weaker dollar, which makes U.S. goods cheaper abroad.

20 Stock prices sank in a sell-off led by plummeting technology issues as well as eroding bond prices, which were driven down by Fed Chairman Greenspan's upbeat assessment of the economy. The Nasdaq Composite Index tumbled 35.66 to 952.87, its second-largest point drop ever. The Dow Jones Industrial Average fell more than 132 points before recovering to close 57.41 lower at 4628.87.

Greenspan told Congress that a revival in economic growth is likely, and that inflation risk is slim, suggesting that further cuts in the short-term rates set by the Fed are unlikely.

Housing starts fell 0.1% last month, but single-family home starts rose 3.9% to the highest level in four months, suggesting a rebound in that segment due to mortgage-rate cuts.

25 Middle-aged and elderly families are in significantly worse financial condition than previously projected, according to a comprehensive Rand Corp. survey. An analysis of the data paints a stark picture of wealth inequalities in the U.S., with minority couples especially vulnerable as they near retirement.

26 Labor costs rose only 2.9% in the year ended in June, less than the 3% inflation rate. The data indicate a lack of upward pressure on wages more than four years into the economic expansion. Separately, housing starts rose 6.5% in June from the previous month, and consumer confidence grew in July after a decline in June.

Markets surged on signs of stability in the economy. The Dow Jones industrials jumped 45.78 to 4714.45 and the 30-year bond rose nearly ⅝ point.

27 Three major unions agreed to merge by the turn of the century, creating by far the largest U.S. industrial union with nearly two million members. The three—United Auto Workers, United Steelworkers of America and International Association of Machinists—also agreed to link their organizing and lobbying efforts ahead of the merger's completion.

28 The U.S. has videotape evidence that senior Archer-Daniels-Midland executives met with global competitors, perhaps in an effort to lift prices for a popular livestock-feed additive. The federal probe of possible criminal price collusion by grain processors is now focusing on two top executives: Michael Andreas, long considered the eventual heir to Archer Daniels' top positions, which are now held by his father, and Terrance Wilson.

Durable-goods orders slid 0.1% in June, but new construction contracts rose 4% to the highest dollar volume this year. The divergent data paint a mixed picture of the U.S. economy.

A sweeping overhaul of securities law was introduced by House GOP leaders. Its critics, including state regulators and consumer groups, say the plan would shift the balance of power on Wall Street away from investors.

31 The economy was listless in the second quarter, as GDP grew at only a 0.5% rate, the slowest rise in almost four years. But the composition of growth suggests that the economy is about to perk up.

Exports showed strength, growing at an annual rate of 7.2% in the quarter. Helping the growth were pulp, industrial machines, telecommunications equipment and chemicals.

Fuji Photo charged that Kodak acts monopolistically in the U.S., which Kodak emphatically denies. Fuji's assertion comes in a response to Kodak's claim that Fuji unfairly dominates the Japanese photography market.

Simpler mutual-fund disclosures are to be unveiled by regulators and eight fund companies. The easily read forms are intended to supplement the standard lengthy prospectuses.

August 1995

1 Disney agreed to purchase Capital Cities/ABC for $19 billion in stock and cash, the second-largest acquisition in

U.S. history, creating a global entertainment powerhouse. The surprise pact will force fundamental change on the media and entertainment landscape as competitors scramble to respond. The stocks of both firms—and those of a host of others—surged as Wall Street tried to anticipate other acquisition candidates.

2 Westinghouse will buy CBS for $81 a share, or $5.4 billion, transforming the industrial company into a broadcast powerhouse that reaches more than one-third of all U.S. households, but leaving it debt-laden. The purchase will be financed by bank loans and through asset sales; Westinghouse is expected to put its lucrative Thermo-King refrigeration-equipment business on the market, which could bring as much as $1 billion.

Disney's growth will be driven increasingly by overseas development. About 23% of revenue last year came from abroad, a percentage that will rise as the ABC purchase permits cross-promotions and other efficiencies, particularly in TV programming.

The manufacturing sector grew in July, according to a survey of purchasing managers, reversing two months of declines and suggesting that the U.S. economy is bouncing back.

Bond prices were driven lower by indications of economic strength. The price of the benchmark 30-year Treasury fell as much as 1¼ points over the course of the day, though it recovered to end more than ¾ point lower.

U.S. auto sales stumbled in July, according to initial reports, reversing signs in June that sales had recovered from a lackluster spring. The figures may mean that auto makers will need incentives to lure buyers as they start rolling out 1996 models next month.

3 The White House will push for federal regulation of cigarette sales to minors, a move likely to draw strong industry protest. The initiative, which is still in formative stages, may seek to ban vending machines in certain places, limit advertising and require buyers to provide proof of age.

The dollar soared 3% against the yen after Tokyo unveiled surprise regulatory changes designed to trim the yen. Japanese and U.S. central banks bought dollars in support of the new policy, and Tokyo stocks rallied 2.2%.

Stocks fell in the U.S., reversing an early surge, as enthusiasm about the dollar and Japan's moves faded. The

Dow Jones industrials slid 10.22, led by technology issues and fears that a stronger dollar may hurt exports.

New-home sales rose 6.1% in June, the Commerce Department said, and the index of leading economic indicators rose 0.2%, its first gain this year. The data are further indication that the economy is gaining strength.

4 Union Pacific agreed to acquire Southern Pacific in a cash-and-stock pact valued at $3.9 billion, or $25 a share. The combination produces the largest U.S. railroad, with $9.5 billion in annual revenue, and may raise antitrust questions. The company's strength would be focused in the western two-thirds of the country, though analysts say Southern Pacific's operations require significant upgrading.

Major U.S. retailers reported uneven July sales. Consumers responded strongly to apparel clearance sales, which helped results at department stores and chains. However, specialty stores and others were down sharply.

Factory orders slipped in June, as did orders for durable goods. Separately, new claims for initial unemployment benefits fell 51,000 last week, the largest decline in a year.

7 Corporate profit grew a surprisingly strong 15% on average in the second quarter, according to a *Wall Street Journal* survey of major U.S. companies. Though earnings have remained healthy despite a lack of vigor in the economy, the gain in the most recent period was the smallest since 1993's second quarter. Analysts expect a further slowdown ahead.

Oil reserves in the Alaska wildlife refuge may be only half the size once thought, new U.S. estimates show. The figures come as oil firms appear on the verge of winning drilling rights from Congress and may aid critics of development. The field is thought to be the largest U.S. find in 20 years.

Unemployment changed little in July, rising to 5.7% from June's 5.6%. However, factories cut 85,000 jobs last month, their largest reduction in 3½ years and an indication of economic uncertainty among manufacturers.

Auto makers are revising their models of the economy to reflect the expectations of a smaller auto industry, a shift with broad ramifications.

8 General Motors plans to spin off Electronic Data Systems, which would make EDS the world's largest independent computer-services company and free it to expand. Under the plan, only holders of GM's Class E shares would receive EDS equity; those shares, which have a market value of $22.31 billion, currently are tied to EDS earnings. GM said the transaction won't proceed unless the IRS rules it to be tax-free.

NBC agreed to pay a record $1.27 billion to air the Summer and Winter Olympic Games in 2000 and 2002. The network made its offer with the proviso that it would be withdrawn if the Olympic committee sought other bids.

10 Clinton will declare nicotine in cigarettes to be a drug that can be regulated by the FDA and will ask the agency to draft a federal rule to curtail smoking by minors. The main thrust of his proposal, to be unveiled today, is a landmark extension of FDA jurisdiction to nicotine. However, the president is expected to say he may back away from federal regulations if Congress passes a law to restrict youths' access to cigarettes.

Netscape's shares opened at $71 apiece—more than double Tuesday's IPO price—kicking off frantic trading in the 16-month-old company, which makes software for browsing the Internet. The closing price of $58.25 puts a value of $2.2 billion on Netscape, which has yet to show a profit.

Most regional economies are growing, though their strength varies, according to the latest survey of the 12 Fed district banks. The job market is mixed as well, but inflation pressure is moderating. Overall, the report rebuts the few economists who may feel the economy is headed for a downturn.

11 The FDA outlined stricter-than-expected regulations to curtail minors' access to cigarettes. Tobacco and advertising interests responded with court action that aims to halt the initiative. The FDA's report about addictiveness may give ammunition to plaintiffs' lawyers in class-action lawsuits against tobacco companies, but in the short term, the proposed rules aren't likely to seriously harm the $45 billion industry.

Toyota selected the charismatic Hiroshi Okuda to be its next president, ending the reign of the Toyoda family as the world's third-largest auto maker and marking a sharp cultural shift. Mr. Okuda said a priority will be to shift production abroad, a strategy with major ramifications for Detroit.

Producer prices were unchanged in July, aided by a steep 2.5% decline in energy prices. The data indicate inflation pressures continue to fade.

14 Tobacco allies are attacking on several fronts in response to proposed federal regulations. Lawmakers plan legislation to supersede the FDA rules, and cigarette makers and others are casting the FDA plan as bureaucracy reminiscent of Prohibition. However, there are signs of rifts in the ranks.

The consumer price index rose a mild 0.2% in July, and retail sales fell 0.1%, led by a sharp drop in car sales. The data show a slowly growing economy that faces little inflation threat.

Recent jumps in housing activity stand to benefit a range of industries, in part by cutting inventories at makers of furniture, appliances and other household goods. In the process, the broader economy also should gain.

15 Disney hired Michael Ovitz, co-founder and chairman of Creative Artists, to be Michael Eisner's second-in-command, filling a long-standing gap. Mr. Ovitz, who built CAA into the world's largest talent agency, will be Disney's president and have responsibility for its three operating divisions as well as Capital Cities/ABC, once the planned acquisition of the network is complete.

Business inventories grew a modest 0.2% in June, the Commerce Department reported, but a separate survey indicates that manufacturing executives remain wary of the prospect of an increase in their stockpiles.

16 The central banks of the U.S., Japan and Germany teamed up to buy dollars, sharply lifting the currency against the yen and mark. Those gains helped to boost bond prices late in the day, which tempered earlier sharp declines in stocks. The Dow Jones industrials ended 19.02 lower at 4640.84.

Japan's merchandise trade surplus plunged 23% in July, in dollar terms, largely on the effects of a strong yen.

Industrial production rose 0.1% in July, its first gain in five months, though largely on a jump in electricity production prompted by hot weather. Overall, activity remained sluggish.

17 Housing starts rose 6.7% in July, their fourth straight advance and the biggest in 16 months, as buyers took advantage of lower mortgage rates.

Mexico's economic output tumbled 10.5% in the second quarter. The decline is the worst on record and exceeded expectations, raising concerns about the country's ability to end its deep recession in coming months.

The dollar continued to strengthen against the yen, and Japanese stocks rose 4% on Wednesday in response.

21 The dollar is expected to rally further in the weeks ahead, analysts said, possibly testing the 1.50-mark and 100-yen levels. The dollar's recent surge against the yen could help lure Japanese investors back to U.S. markets.

22 Congressional leaders overseeing an overhaul of federal securities laws and regulations have received heavy campaign contributions by the nation's financial-services firms.

Eurotunnel shares plunged 17% to an all-time low amid growing fears that disappointing summer traffic could force the European rail-tunnel operator into a new cash crisis.

23 Fed officials left short-term rates unchanged, a decision that was widely anticipated in the financial markets. Separately, an unexpected contraction in the German money supply increased speculation that the Bundesbank will cut rates soon.

Bond prices eased after the Fed decision and the dollar strengthened. Stocks edged higher. The Dow Jones industrials gained 5.64 to 4620.42.

24 Two utilities, Public Service Co. of Colorado and Southwestern Public Service, agreed to merge in a transaction valued at $1.26 billion. The agreement continues an industry trend of consolidation, but observers warn that the number of "healthy" merger partners is limited.

Tire makers are the focus of a price-fixing probe by the Justice Department. Goodyear and Bridgestone/Firestone are among those that have responded to the agency.

25 Germany's Central Bank lowered two key interest rates, amid signs of a slowing economic recovery and complaints from German companies that the nation's strong currency is hurting business. The rate cuts spurred big swings in the value of the dollar. The German action was quickly followed by Austria, Belgium, Denmark and the Netherlands.

Durable-goods orders fell 1.7% in July, the fifth decline in six months. The drop sparked concern that economic growth for the rest of the year may be slower than expected.

Bond prices surged on the report, with the Treasury's long bond rising more than 1¼ points. Stocks were mixed. The Dow Jones industrials declined 4.23 points to 4580.62.

Russian banks were thrown into a crisis when they stopped lending to one another. The turmoil followed speculation in the press that some fairly large banks may be unsound.

U.S. researchers said the number of patients infected with an antibiotic-resistant strain of a potentially deadly bacterium is rising at an alarming rate. The rapid spread of drug-resistance threatens to complicate treatment of diseases ranging from pneumonia to a common type of childhood ear infection.

28 Fed policy makers were deeply divided about their decision to cut short-term interest rates last month, according to a summary of their meeting.

Existing-home sales jumped 5% in July from June to their highest level in more than a year. The increase, prompted by lower mortgage rates, is the third consecutive monthly gain.

29 Mutual-fund investors poured cash into stock funds in July, but bond funds didn't fare as well. Stock-fund net inflows surged to $13.9 billion, up nearly 70% from June's $8.2 billion.

New-home sales rose 0.4% in July to an annual rate of 715,000, the government said, their highest level in more than a year. Separately, new contracts for residential construction slid 5% last month, F. W. Dodge said; overall, building contracts fell 3%.

Job growth in construction and services will be relatively strong in the next decade, government projections indicate, but declines are seen in mining, military and farm employment.

U.S. airport delays are expected to worsen in coming weeks because of a confluence of security threats, radar-equipment failures and strained labor relations. Bomb scares at airports in Philadelphia and Houston inconvenienced passengers a day after a bomb threat briefly closed all three New York airports.

30 The merger of Chase and Chemical in a $10 billion stock swap marks a fundamental change in the banking industry, which faces stiffening competition from an array of financial-service providers. More alliances are likely as banks move to cut costs and consolidate strengths, though the trend raises concerns about job losses and declining competition. In New York, about 4,000 jobs will be cut in the Chemical merger, and many branches will be closed.

The International Monetary Fund is scaling back its forecast for short-term economic growth in the industrialized world, in part because of the weakness of the Japanese economy. In a draft report, the IMF also cautions the Fed against further U.S. rate cuts.

Japanese investors bought a net $18.4 billion in dollar-denominated U.S. securities in the first half, resuming a pace not seen since the late 1980s. The surprising data suggest investors in Japan believe the yen has peaked.

Russia's banking system began to revive, with some banks starting to lend among themselves again for the first time since Thursday, when rumors of weakness prompted banks to stop doing business with one another.

Foreign-born residents made up 8.7% of the U.S. population last year, the highest proportion of immigrants since World War II, a Census Bureau study says. The study says the proportion has nearly doubled since 1970, and that one-fifth of the immigrants arrived in the past five years. One-third of the immigrants live in California.

31 Japanese regulators took over two major lenders in the wake of unreported runs on both institutions, taking a major step to address the nation's $400 billion bad-loan crisis. The move wiped out Japan's deposit-insurance fund, though officials said the two closures would be the biggest of their kind. However, there is some risk of a domino effect, and Tokyo faces resistance to any plans for a taxpayer-backed bailout of lenders.

Japan's vehicle exports to the U.S. plummeted 45.6% in July, their largest drop in postwar history, the Japan Automobile Manufacturers Association said. World-wide vehicle exports fell for the seventh straight month.

Gross domestic product grew at a 1.1% annual rate in the second quarter. The figure, revised from 0.5%, is further evidence of moderate growth.

September 1995

1 Time Warner reached a tentative agreement to purchase Turner for $8 billion. The broad pact won key support from TCI Chairman Malone, whose company owns 21% of Turner. The combination would create the world's largest media company, but the deal could still collapse due to its unusually complex nature and the diverse interests of the three parties.

Factory orders fell again in July, while disposable income rose slightly and consumer spending stalled. Economists were hesitant to interpret the mixed bag of statistics ahead of today's release of other key indicators.

Retail sales grew only 1.5% in August, less than expected. Heat was blamed for apparel's poor showing, but electronics sales revived.

Japan's markets reacted calmly to the takeover of two major lenders, but new data suggest the country's weak economy still faces high hurdles. Industrial output, housing starts and steel exports fell in recent periods.

The dollar tumbled against the Japanese currency, closing in New York at 97.34 yen, down from 99.00.

5 August's strong employment figures indicate a strengthening economy, but manufacturing is still weak, according to job-growth statistics and data from purchasing managers.

The Dow Jones industrials gained 36.98 to 4647.54 on Friday, their biggest advance in more than two weeks.

A jury awarded $2 million to a former smoker, handing the tobacco industry a major defeat. The San Francisco state-court jury said Lorillard and former filter maker Hollingsworth & Vose should be liable for a rare disease that the plaintiff claims he contracted from a type of cigarette filter.

Most auto makers reported strong U.S. sales for August, as car makers used generous leases and cash rebates to reduce their summer inventories.

7 Western Europe's two largest economies slumped in the second quarter. Germany's gross domestic product declined to 2.2% from 2.9% in the first period, while France's output dropped to 2.8% from 3.8%.

8 Chrysler's board doubled to $2 billion its stock-buyback program, in a bid to placate Kirk Kerkorian and others who may consider joining him in forcing changes at the auto maker. Directors also decided not to allow retired Chairman Iacocca to cash in stock options in exchange for severing ties with Kerkorian. Separately, Kerkorian's Tracinda agreed to pay Jerome York $25 million as part of a pact to leave IBM for Tracinda.

Second-quarter productivity hit a nine-year high, revised government figures show, but analysts were divided over the change's implications.

Hardware and software accessory sales are booming as a result of big Windows 95 sales, retailers and wholesalers say, and Microsoft's other products are benefiting as well.

12 Mitsubishi Estate abruptly abandoned its four-month effort to retain its ownership stake in Rockefeller Center. It sets the stage for the property's largest creditor and a group led by investor Sam Zell, which includes Walt Disney Co., to take control of the office complex. It effectively ends the involvement of the Rockefeller family with the site since the Rockefeller Group, in which the family owns a 20% stake, will give up title.

The yen's recent retreat against the dollar is raising corporate Japan's expectations of improved earnings for this fiscal year, and may also lower costs for U.S. technology companies.

13 The Dow soared more than 42 points to its first record in nearly two months, driven by more signs that inflationary threats are receding. Bonds rallied and the dollar pushed past 100 yen, its highest level against the Japanese currency since January. Government data showed producer prices slipped 0.1% in August, the third straight month without an increase. But the trade deficit widened to record $43.62 billion in the second quarter.

The Fed isn't likely to trim short-term interest rates when it meets this month, central bank officials indicate, because the economy seems healthier than in July, when rates were last cut.

Goldman Sachs launched a bid to derail investor Sam Zell's effort to gain control of Rockefeller Center. Zell's group was joined by General Electric and agreed to invest $250 million in the site's mortgage holder.

14 Consumer prices rose a minuscule 0.1% in August and just 2.6% from August 1994, amid an absence of inflation signals. Meanwhile, the Fed's latest survey of regional economic conditions hailed signs of "further expansion," with few inflationary signals. The benign inflation news lifted stocks, sending major averages to another batch of records. The Dow Jones industrials rose 18.31 points to 4765.52, the blue-chip indicator's second consecutive record.

The dollar continued to rise, and traders and economists say it could still climb another 4% to 7%. However, they warn that the currency still faces a number of important obstacles.

Clinton said he is "sick and tired" of rising juvenile crime, and he swore to stop Republicans from dismantling legislation he signed into law a year ago. The president told an audience of middle-school children in Maryland that youth violence is the No. 1 problem in the country.

15 Retail sales rose only 0.6% in August, on weaker-than-expected spending in most areas except cars and home furnishings. Meanwhile, initial claims for state unemployment benefits rose more than was expected.

Stocks and bonds rallied on the economic reports, which were viewed as confirming moderate growth with no signs of inflation. The Dow Jones industrials jumped 36.28 points to 4801.80, their third consecutive record. The Treasury's 30-year bond climbed ⅞ point. The dollar weakened.

Eurotunnel suspended interest payments on $12.4 billion of debt while it seeks to work out a restructuring plan with its creditor banks. The move won't affect the day-to-day business of the Channel Tunnel, which is run by the Franco-British firm.

18 Industrial output rose 1.1% in August, and the Fed revised July's figure upward to 0.3%. Two straight months of surprising production gains may signal inventory overages are easing.

Australia is the world's richest nation and the U.S. is in 12th place in a new World Bank ranking of per-capita wealth based on countries' man-made, natural and human resources.

19 Japan's domestic output grew faster than expected in the second quarter, but the 0.8% rate belies weaknesses that the government hopes to address in a huge economic-stimulus package to be released tomorrow.

Inventories grew 0.3% in July, the smallest rise in seven months, and retailers trimmed stocks 0.7%. That reflects sluggish sales and conservative ordering, meaning retailers may be able to avoid heavy discounting.

20 A detailed report on the Nasdaq Stock Market recommends it be split off from its parent, the National Association of Securities Dealers. Under the new structure, the NASD would be a holding company with two subsidiaries: one to police Nasdaq dealers and other brokerage firms, and one to operate the market itself. The independent Rudman panel, which prepared the report, also found lapses in Nasdaq's mission to protect investors.

Housing starts rose 0.6% in August, continuing their four-month revival, driven by low mortgage rates and an uptick in new-home sales. The government also revised July's big increase in housing starts upward to 7.1%.

21 AT&T will break up into three independent companies, jettisoning an ailing computer unit and a potent equipment business to refocus on its communications mainstay, marking the second split of the industry's biggest empire. The plan could free AT&T of distractions as it tries to grow and protect operations that provide 80% of annual profit and 60% of sales. AT&T shares jumped 11% on the announcement and led a blue-chip rally.

The U.S. trade deficit inched up to a record $11.5 billion in July, as a drop in exports more than offset a decline in imports. Significant improvement isn't expected because of the economic weakness of key trading partners.

Tokyo stocks sank 1.3% as investors gave a thumbs-down to Japan's $136 billion economic-stimulus package. Although bigger than expected, the plan mirrored previous efforts that had failed to spark robust growth.

22 U.S. companies doing business in Mexico are feeling surprisingly little pain from its economic crisis, an informal survey found. Many firms have turned to other markets, and some have benefitted from the weaker peso.

Canada's Supreme Court struck down that country's tough law on tobacco advertising and health warnings. The law was challenged by the Canadian tobacco industry, which claimed the advertising ban violated its constitutional right to free expression.

25 Time Warner's unveiling of its agreement to buy Turner for $7.5 billion in stock was met by a U.S. West lawsuit to block it. The Baby Bell, which has an ownership stake in a Time Warner unit, is said to be weighing how to sever the arrangement. Comcast and Continental Cablevision, Turner board members, protested Time Warner's concessions to TCI's chairman in return for his blessing as Turner's biggest outside shareholder.

Germans, wary of a single European currency, are investing heavily in Swiss-franc asset funds. Upheavals among Europe's currencies and the dollar's sudden plunge have unhinged Japanese and European markets.

26 Baltimore Gas & Electric and Potomac Electric Power agreed to one of the largest domestic utility combination ever, a $3.1 billion stock deal that would create the nation's ninth-largest utility. The friendly merger, the fourth since May, would cost 1,200 jobs. The combined utility's service area would stretch from Baltimore and surrounding counties to Washington.

Low mortgage rates and high consumer confidence drove sales of existing homes up 3% in August from July, to the highest sales rate in 15 months. Prices were higher and supply dwindled to its lowest level since January.

27 Daiwa Bank said a rogue trader in its New York office secretly racked up $1.1 billion in losses over 11 years by trading U.S. Treasury securities. Toshihide Iguchi confessed to Daiwa that he covered his losses by selling other Daiwa securities and forging documents to hide their sale. The Japanese bank fired the trader and will take a $1.1 billion write-off.

Federal Reserve policy makers left interest rates unchanged amid indications of a reviving economy. It looks more likely that the Fed will wait to see if Congress and the president agree on a deficit-reduction plan.

Stocks finished mostly lower as an early technology-led rally fizzled when the Fed held short-term rates steady.

Consumers' faith in the economy flagged in September, indicating growth was mostly from businesses' capital outlays. The consumer confidence index fell to 97.4 from a revised 102.4 in August and 101.4 in July.

Former Prime Minister Andreotti went on trial in Italy on charges that he protected, helped and consorted with Mafia figures who, in turn, delivered Sicilian votes for Andreotti's Christian Democrats. The 76-year-old seven-time premier has denied the charges, saying they are part of a Mafia plot to punish him for his crackdowns on crime.

28 The SEC put forward new trading rules designed to put individual investors on more-equal footing with big investors on the Nasdaq Stock Market and elsewhere. Big firms are worried the rules may reduce their profit.

Durable-goods orders jumped 4.9% in August, the biggest increase in a year, sparking speculation that manufacturing is picking up. Also, total construction starts in August rose 6%.

29 Regulators are stepping up efforts to punish brokerage firms for misstating broker employment records. Some firms have been faulted for letting rogue brokers roam from firm to firm without detailing their abuses.

Industry Surveys

Annual Report on American Industry[1]

The following provides data on the profitability, growth rates, earnings, sales, net income, and profit margin of leading companies in major industries. Also shown are the industry median values. Editor

For return on capital, we divide a firm's total capitalization into the sum of three items—aftertax profits, the amount remaining if the interest paid on long-term debt was taxed, and minority interest. Most companies (except for electric utilities) don't report interest expense on long-term debt. In such cases we estimate this expense for the latest 12 months. We assume a 34% corporate tax

How we calculate the results	Profitability				Growth				Sales	Net income	Profit margin
	Return on equity		Return on capital		Sales		Earnings per share				
	5-year average %	latest 12 mos %	latest 12 mos %	Debt/ capital %	5-year average %	latest 12 mos %	5-year average %	latest 12 mos %	latest 12 mos $mil	latest 12 mos $mil	latest 12 mos %

Profitability

We calculate return on equity by taking primary earnings per share and dividing them by common shareholders' equity per share at the start of the fiscal year. In calculating common equity, we assume that all convertible preferred stock is converted into common. The liquidation value of nonconvertible preferred shares is subtracted from total stockholders' equity. Net income and earnings per share include gains or losses from discontinued operations but exclude extraordinary items like tax-loss carryforwards.

Five-year average return on equity is calculated with a modified version of the sum-of-the-years digits method. This emphasizes recent results. If a firm lost money during any fiscal year but started that year with positive equity, we calculated the percentage lost on equity and factored this result into our equation for that year. Companies were penalized for the years in which they had negative equity. If a company shows a return on equity exceeding 100% in a given year, this value is automatically scaled back to 100%, in order to knock out outrageous and unreasonable returns.

rate to compute the tax break derived from interest expense. We define total capitalization as long-term debt, common and preferred equity, deferred taxes, investment tax credits and minority interest in consolidated subsidiaries.

Growth Rates

We use a modified version of the least-squares method to calculate sales and earnings growth rates. This equation adjusts for sharp fluctuations and yields a result that closely reflects the average rate of growth. Example: During a four-year period a corporation's earnings go from 50 cents to 75 cents, then to $1 and finally to $1.15 in the last year. That's a 50% jump from the first year to the second, a 33% increase in the third and a 15% increase between the third and fourth year. Least-squares says that on average, earnings grew at a compound annual rate of 32.1%. The regression formula calculates the slope of a line that best fits the data points for four years. If you do the math yourself—starting with 50 cents—you'll get $1.15 in the fourth year.

There's one limitation to the least-squares method. It can't handle negative values. If earnings are negative at the beginning of the period, we calculate the growth rate for a shorter period, starting with the first positive year. If a company lost money during the middle of a measuring period, FORBES dropped the year from the calculation and

[1] Excerpted from the **FORBES** *Annual Report on American Industry*. Page 125 in the footnotes to the Exhibits in this section refers to the page in *Forbes,* January 2, 1995. The corresponding page in the *Almanac* is 1.

measured the growth rate over the remaining positive periods. Our assumption: A single loss is not representative of long-term performance. If a company lost money in more than one year, however, the five-year earnings growth rate is not calculated and the result is listed as not meaningful (NM).

Our computer checked all least-squares growth rates with a comparison method to see if the earnings pattern made sense. Here's an extreme case showing why we check: If a company's per-share earnings plunge from $1 in the first year to 15 cents in the second, then jump to $4 in the third and dive again to 15 cents in the fourth year, the formula says the annual growth rate is -21.4%. This does a terrible job of describing year-to-year changes, so we marked such wildly fluctuating patterns also as not meaningful (NM).

Time Periods

The five-year growth rates we use require six years' worth of data. These rates are based on latest fiscal year-end results. All growth rates covering a period of less than five years are footnoted. When the range of available data is less than four years, we marked it as not available (NA).

Latest-12-month comparisons are between the most recent four quarters for which financial results have been announced and the comparable quarters in the previous period. Sales, net income figures and profit margins are measured over the latest 12 months. Debt as a percentage of total capital is based on the most recent balance sheet.

Definitions

FORBES defines sales as net sales plus other operating revenue. For banks, sales are total interest income plus other operating income. Sales for insurance companies include premium income plus net investment and other income. Debt as a percentage of capital is long-term debt, including capitalized leases, divided by total capitalization as defined above.

Medians are calculated by listing the companies in rank order and selecting the value of the middle company. If there is an even number of firms, we average the data on the two middle companies. All companies, including those with negative values, are ranked in calculating the industry median, except for those marked NA. The all-industry median is the median for all ranked firms in this survey other than biotechnology companies, which are not counted because they are much smaller than the other survey companies and most are not yet profitable.

Aerospace & defense	Profitability				Growth				Sales	Net income	Profit margin
	Return on equity		Return on capital	Debt/capital %	Sales		Earnings per share				
Company	5-year average %	latest 12 mos %	latest 12 mos %		5-year average %	latest 12 mos %	5-year average %	latest 12 mos %	latest 12 mos $mil	latest 12 mos $mil	latest 12 mos %
General Dynamics	31.6	20.4	18.5	13.3	-22.3	-6.3	NM	-75.6	3,113	244	7.8
Litton Industries	28.3*	8.8	7.4	7.9	-0.7	-0.8	-12.6	-47.6	3,446	51	1.5
General Electric	21.5	21.1	12.7	55.3	3.2	10.1	9.4	8.1	64,618	5,435	8.4
Martin Marietta	21.1	23.7	15.7	29.2	7.6	33.5	6.9	46.0	10,275	615	6.0
Sundstrand	20.3	27.6	22.5	32.3	NM	-6.5	NM	50.5	1,371	145	10.6
Raytheon	19.9	13.5	13.4	0.5	1.9	7.9	6.5	-14.2	9,800	577	5.9
Boeing	18.5	10.9	9.1	21.0	9.8	-17.7	19.6	-23.0	22,460	1,003	4.5
GenCorp	18.1	12.1	6.5	94.0	NM	-6.7	-24.0	-14.3	1,773	29	1.6
Rockwell Intl	18.0	21.6	17.2	19.8	-3.0	2.6	NM	12.5	11,123	634	5.7
Thiokol	16.4	14.6	12.3	18.0	-1.3	-12.5	22.8	-1.3	1,024	61	5.9
E-Systems	16.2	12.5	12.6	1.0	8.1	-6.1	8.5	-19.3	1,999	98	4.9
Loral	16.0	18.8	10.2	53.7	30.3	39.2	9.5	36.7	5,013	262	5.2
AlliedSignal	15.8	30.5	18.7	33.7	NM	4.4	6.9	17.9	12,342	732	5.9
Teleflex	15.2	13.9	9.8	39.4	15.7	21.1	5.3	14.6	771	38	5.0
McDonnell Douglas	13.2	8.8	7.1	37.3	NM	-14.3	31.6	-77.0	13,278	301	2.3
Northrop Grumman	13.1	9.0	10.2	52.2	-1.3	14.4	-27.6†	-38.1	6,087	121	2.0
Alliant Techsystems	13.0*	8.8	7.2	9.6	-10.3	-7.9	NM	D-P	775	9	1.1
Lockheed	12.7	15.4	10.6	38.9	3.2	6.3	-8.4	6.9	13,025	443	3.4
Teledyne	12.5	def	2.7	58.2	-6.7	-7.6	-20.8	P-D	2,380	-9	def
Textron	12.1	15.0	7.4	75.5	4.2	10.5	6.4	14.4	9,733	424	4.4

(continued)

Aerospace & defense (concluded)

Company	Profitability — Return on equity 5-year average %	latest 12 mos %	Return on capital latest 12 mos %	Debt/ capital %	Growth — Sales 5-year average %	latest 12 mos %	Earnings per share 5-year average %	latest 12 mos %	Sales latest 12 mos $mil	Net income latest 12 mos $mil	Profit margin latest 12 mos %
Precision Castparts	10.7	12.2	11.4	2.8	NM	−1.0	4.3	500.0+	424	27	6.4
Oshkosh Truck	6.6	11.6	8.8	8.2	11.6	8.9	120.4†	154.2	692	13	1.9
UNC	6.4	def	def	60.2	NM	43.8	30.8†	P-D	546	−49	def
Fairchild	4.4	49.3	10.9	75.8	−3.3	−0.2	NM	D-P	455	32	7.0
United Technologies	2.8	13.8	11.9	22.0	2.9	−0.8	NM	D-P	20,754	608	2.9
GM Hughes Electronics	1.8	3.4	14.4	4.4	3.6	7.3	NM	25.0	14,111	1,100	7.8
Kaman	1.1	6.6	8.4	14.1	NM	1.0	NM	D-P	803	19	2.3
Rohr	0.5	3.8	5.5	79.6	NM	−21.9	NM	D-P	918	7	0.8
ESCO Electronics	def	4.5	5.0	12.3	−5.1	3.1	NM	53.2	474	8	1.8
Sequa	def	def	1.5	49.8	NM	−12.8	NM	D-D	1,493	−22	def
SPS Technologies	def	def	def	42.8	−6.8	2.5	NM	D-D	330	−26	def
Avondale Industries	def	def	12.2	28.1	−4.1	−7.8	NM	D-D	452	−4	def
Hexcel	def	def	def	102.5	−2.8	−8.5	NM	D-D	317	−57	def
Talley Industries	def	def	4.4	84.5	−3.8	−1.4	NM	D-D	316	−2	def
Coltec Industries	NE	NE	36.2	223.1	−2.9	0.0	−14.6	36.1	1,331	91	6.9
Abex	NA	NE	21.8	147.5	−13.0	−31.1	NA	D-P	361	15	4.1
Aviall	NA	NA	3.5	47.7	−2.0	−12.8	NA	NA	850	10	1.1
Industry medians	12.7	11.3	10.2	37.3	−3.0	−0.8	−20.8	10.3	1,493	51	3.4
All-industry medians	11.4	12.6	9.4	32.8	5.5	6.3	−18.8	11.8	1,449	60	4.3

D-D: Deficit to deficit.   D-P: Deficit to profit.   F-D: Profit to deficit.   def: Deficit.   NM: Not meaningful.
†Four-year average.   †Three-year average.   For further explanation, see page 125.   NA: Not available.   NE: Negative equity.

Sources: Forbes; Value Line Data Base Service via OneSource Information Services.
Source: Reprinted By Permission of FORBES Magazine © Forbes Inc., 1995.

Capital goods	Profitability				Growth				Sales	Net income	Profit margin
	Return on equity		Return on capital		Sales		Earnings per share				
Company	5-year average %	latest 12 mos %	latest 12 mos %	Debt/capital %	5-year average %	latest 12 mos %	5-year average %	latest 12 mos %	latest 12 mos $mil	latest 12 mos $mil	latest 12 mos %
Electrical equipment											
Premier Industrial	26.5	23.8	22.6	1.4	4.0	8.3	7.2	9.6	760	98	12.8
General Electric	21.5	21.1	12.7	55.3	3.2	10.1	9.4	8.1	64,618	5,435	8.4
Honeywell	21.4	16.2	13.8	22.3	NM	−1.8	−4.2*	23.0	5,939	287	4.8
Emerson Electric	20.0	20.2	17.8	7.1	3.6	5.3	5.6	11.7	8,607	789	9.2
Mark IV Industries	17.2	16.8	9.6	59.0	11.9	12.2	NM	18.8	1,361	58	4.3
Hubbell	16.6	12.7	12.8	0.5	6.0	15.4	NM	−25.1	948	72	7.6
Andrew	14.6	19.5	17.6	16.6	10.9	29.6	24.4	56.4	558	44	8.0
Thomas & Betts	13.1	13.2	8.8	36.2	17.4	7.1	−3.7	10.1	1,136	65	5.7
National Service	10.8	11.8	10.2	3.2	3.8	4.3	NM	9.9	1,882	83	4.4
Valmont Industries	8.6	6.3	6.6	22.0	NM	4.1	−10.5	−61.3	452	7	1.6
Genlyte Group	5.8	8.8	7.2	62.8	−3.9	−1.4	−27.6	D-P	426	5	1.3
MagneTek	3.5	def	def	77.8	5.8	−22.6	NM	P-D	1,128	−41	def
Westinghouse	def	def	def	53.2	−7.4	−0.8	NM	D-D	8,721	−294	def
Imo Industries	def	NE	def	103.3	NM	−32.3	NM	D-D	500	−240	def
Willcox & Gibbs	NA	9.0	7.0	47.9	7.8	85.9	NM	D-P	929	9	1.0
Medians	**13.9**	**12.7**	**9.6**	**36.2**	**3.8**	**5.3**	**−27.6**	**9.9**	**1,128**	**58**	**4.4**
Heavy equipment											
Federal Signal	21.5	22.2	19.6	8.7	8.3	15.4	15.4	17.3	632	44	7.0
Stewart & Stevenson	18.6	17.4	14.9	14.8	14.0	15.6	16.5	23.4	1,050	62	5.9
Caterpillar	12.6	37.5	17.5	58.2	NM	21.3	NM	54.1	13,568	824	6.1
Trinity Industries	11.1	12.7	11.0	29.7	9.9	22.6	NM	13.4	2,019	74	3.7
Ingersoll-Rand	10.8	14.9	11.6	16.5	4.9	8.3	−4.5	56.6	4,356	201	4.6
McDermott Int'l	9.5	3.7	5.0	41.5	5.4	−0.9	NM	−82.7	3,063	27	0.9
Tenneco	8.5	25.8	10.2	48.6	−0.7	1.9	NM	D-P	13,447	570	4.2
Nacco Industries	7.4	13.9	7.9	63.7	16.6	15.6	−24.1	134.8	1,746	33	1.9
Deere & Co	5.5	26.4	14.2	44.6	2.5	16.2	−26.0	500.0+	8,689	544	6.3
Harnischfeger Inds	4.7	3.5	3.6	29.5	−6.8	−7.7	−16.5	D-P	1,140	18	1.6

(continued)

Capital goods (concluded)

Company	Profitability — Return on equity 5-year average %	Return on equity latest 12 mos %	Return on capital latest 12 mos %	Debt/ capital %	Growth — Sales 5-year average %	Sales latest 12 mos %	Earnings per share 5-year average %	Earnings per share latest 12 mos %	Sales latest 12 mos $mil	Net income latest 12 mos $mil	Profit margin latest 12 mos %
Clark Equipment	1.5	46.8	29.5	29.8	-10.1	8.4	NM	500.0+	917	140	15.3
Indresco	0.8	11.1	10.9	0.0	-10.7	-11.7	-18.8	D-P	469	31	6.7
Terex	def	NE	0.2	125.1	11.5	-12.7	NM	D-D	724	-16	def
AGCO	NA	42.9	23.5	61.9	18.0	107.5	NA	203.2	1,058	76	7.2
Case	NA	NA	NA	50.3	-9.0*	19.9	NA	NA	4,143	86	2.1
Medians	**8.5**	**16.2**	**11.3**	**41.5**	**4.9**	**15.4**	**-26.0**	**95.6**	**1,746**	**74**	**4.6**
Other industrial equipment											
BWIP Holding	27.5*	def	1.2	35.4	9.3	2.7	NM	P-D	432	-1	def
Nordson	25.0	22.1	20.7	7.8	13.8	7.7	6.3	15.2	488	45	9.2
Briggs & Stratton	21.8	28.2	23.0	15.2	7.1	12.7	32.1*	36.8	1,315	107	8.2
EG&G	20.0	1.3	1.4	0.3	15.1	-40.5	5.6	-92.4	1,633	7	0.4
Dover	18.2	21.7	17.3	20.5	4.1	22.7	2.5	25.9	2,927	189	6.5
Illinois Tool Works	16.8	20.0	15.4	15.2	9.8	8.4	5.6	25.4	3,333	252	7.6
Donaldson	16.8	17.6	17.1	4.0	8.2	11.8	15.3	17.9	615	34	5.5
Keystone Intl	16.1	12.3	11.0	18.7	9.5	1.3	NM	-15.2	522	33	6.4
Crane	15.2	16.6	15.1	53.1	-1.2	17.6	-5.9	-8.5	1,534	49	3.2
Danaher	13.4	19.7	16.1	23.6	8.0	16.3	NM	58.5	1,212	73	6.1
Watts Industries	13.3	12.0	10.1	20.5	18.0	11.1	5.6	35.7	541	42	7.7
Giddings & Lewis	13.2*	8.0	8.0	0.0	28.7	-3.6	25.1	-22.7	553	35	6.3
York International	13.1*	-8.9	15.0	39.8	10.8	18.1	125.8†	17.3	2,332	86	3.7
Tyco International	12.6	13.0	10.4	27.4	11.1	6.6	NM	70.3	3,300	130	3.9
Ametek	12.2	6.9	4.7	73.2	7.7	6.8	NM	-54.4	791	7	0.9

Goulds Pumps	11.9	10.8	9.9	15.2	3.8	3.1	-11.6†	2.1	573	20	3.5
Pentair	11.9	12.7	9.9	48.4	7.6	18.3	NM	3.8	1,548	51	3.3
Cooper Industries	11.7	def	1.2	32.9	7.3	-21.6	4.1	P-D	4,947	-3	def
Stanley Works	11.2	11.5	9.7	23.1	3.5	5.7	-4.3	8.0	2,425	110	4.5
Commercial Intertech	8.7	17.3	13.0	23.1	1.9	4.6	NM	78.1	483	25	5.2
Tecumseh Products	8.6	16.4	16.3	1.3	NM	14.3	NM	66.1	1,468	113	7.7
General Signal	8.5	15.4	13.0	29.9	-3.5	8.7	NM	297.7	1,645	82	5.0
Kennametal	6.7	14.0	11.9	21.1	7.9	35.2	-20.2	D-P	846	40	4.7
Parker Hannifin	6.5	8.1	7.8	18.8	NM	7.7	-13.4	21.6	2,681	80	3.0
Bearings	5.6	9.2	7.7	33.8	8.1	13.1	NM	31.3	961	13	1.4
Applied Power	5.2	18.3	11.0	35.4	5.9	20.3	-16.0	396.0	434	17	3.8
Blount	4.6	16.9	12.2	32.6	-11.4	-9.0	NM	205.4	536	29	5.4
Amphenol	0.3	19.0	9.8	47.1	5.8	16.6	NM	128.6	659	37	5.6
Timken	def	1.8	2.3	20.4	1.9	11.9	NM	0.0	1,866	13	0.7
Great American Mgmt	def	def	def	65.6	-3.9	NA	NM	NA	955	-78	def
Trinova	def	20.2	12.8	43.8	-3.7	4.0	-29.4	328.6	1,740	52	3.0
SKF Group	def	def	1.5	48.7	5.0	9.6	NM	D-D	3,971	-23	def
Lincoln Electric	def	def	def	50.7	7.8	1.9	NM	D-D	864	-24	def
Cincinnati Milacron	NE	def	def	51.4	NM	17.9	NM	P-D	1,149	-23	def
Eagle-Picher Inds	NE	NE	def	NE	-4.1	13.9	NM	P-D	737	-1,133	def
Interlake	NE	NE	5.9	206.1	-6.1	3.5	NM	D-D	716	-21	def
Medians	**11.4**	**12.5**	**10.0**	**25.5**	**6.5**	**8.7**	**NM**	**17.3**	**1,055**	**35**	**3.8**
Industry medians	**10.8**	**13.0**	**10.2**	**29.8**	**5.2**	**8.4**	**NM**	**17.6**	**1,138**	**43**	**4.3**
All-industry medians	**11.4**	**12.6**	**9.4**	**32.8**	**5.5**	**6.3**	**-18.8**	**11.8**	**1,449**	**60**	**4.3**

D-D: Deficit to deficit.   D-P: Deficit to profit.   def: Deficit.   NA: Not available.   NE: Negative equity.   NM: Not meaningful.

*Four-year average.   †Three-year average.   P-D: Profit to deficit.   For further explanation, see page 125.

Sources: Forbes; Value Line Data Base Service via OneSource Information Services.

Source: **Reprinted By Permission of FORBES Magazine © Forbes Inc., 1995.**

Chemicals

| Company | Profitability | | | | Growth | | | | Sales | Net income | Profit margin |
| | Return on equity | | Return on capital | Debt/ capital | Sales | | Earnings per share | | | | |
	5-year average %	latest 12 mos %	latest 12 mos %	%	5-year average %	latest 12 mos %	5-year average %	latest 12 mos %	latest 12 mos $mil	latest 12 mos $mil	latest 12 mos %
Diversified											
FMC	35.9	20.4	12.7	65.9	3.4	2.8	-17.3	-54.8	3,918	46	1.2
A Schulman	16.2	15.2	14.7	6.2	2.7	9.3	6.4	14.4	749	45	6.0
Monsanto	12.7	20.0	15.3	27.2	-1.7	2.3	-4.4	11.6	8,064	626	7.8
PPG Industries	11.7	15.8	13.2	13.8	NM	4.5	-10.7	35.1	6,050	418	6.9
Rohm & Haas	10.9	15.1	10.9	29.5	4.9	5.2	-10.3	182.1	3,434	243	7.1
Dow Chemical	9.7	8.1	7.5	32.9	1.6	4.1	-32.1	50.3	19,026	668	3.5
El du Pont de Nemours	8.0	21.0	13.2	32.0	1.4	4.5	-24.2	500.0+	33,970	2,318	6.8
Hercules	7.8	17.7	14.2	19.0	-1.0	0.9	37.9†	33.9	2,782	241	8.7
Rhone-Poulenc	5.7	3.9	6.3	35.9	4.2	-1.4	-24.4	-38.4	15,131	346	2.3
Union Carbide	5.6*	18.0	12.4	36.0	-3.8	-2.7	-29.5	97.7	4,628	276	6.0
Univar	4.4	def	def	38.6	7.5	0.5	-29.8	P-D	1,841	-17	def
First Mississippi	1.3	18.7	13.2	31.2	NM	25.2	NM	D-P	552	32	5.8
Olin	def	def	def	34.6	NM	8.5	NM	P-D	2,579	-58	def
Imperial Chemical Inds	NA	def	2.4	28.4	-3.7†	0.6	NM	D-D	13,248	-19	def
Medians	8.0	15.5	12.6	31.6	0.2	3.5	-24.3	24.1	4,273	242	5.9
Specialized											
Lyondell Petrochem	45.6	NE	22.1	80.2	-4.0	-15.7	NM	500.0+	3,584	134	3.7
Vigoro	37.7	26.5	15.2	28.2	3.4	30.1	NM	18.6	756	50	6.6
Crompton & Knowles	28.6	21.4	20.1	12.1	13.9	3.7	23.8	3.1	574	52	9.0
Nalco Chemical	26.5	19.7	14.1	8.0	7.2	-1.3	8.3	-25.2	1,381	115	8.3
Great Lakes Chemical	24.6	22.3	22.3	15.1	25.5	9.3	21.1	6.5	1,930	277	14.4
Valspar	22.9	22.8	22.0	20.2	7.9	13.4	15.1	12.4	787¹	45¹	5.8
Sigma-Aldrich	22.0	13.6	18.3	2.4	14.3	15.5	13.5	6.3	823	110	13.4
Betz Laboratories	21.3	16.8	15.5	0.0	9.5	1.8	8.2	-13.7	701	65	9.2
Loctite	21.1	21.2	21.1	0.7	7.2	10.8	7.5	5.4	673	76	11.3
Intl Flavors & Frags	19.7	24.7	24.2	1.6	7.6	7.3	9.0	19.2	1,270	218	17.2
RPM	17.8	18.5	12.8	57.1	15.3	28.6	9.5	15.7	860	56	6.5
Sherwin-Williams	17.3	17.9	17.1	2.3	8.8	6.1	9.5	14.8	3,064	182	6.0
Sterling Chemicals	16.2	26.8	8.3	68.3	NM	35.1	-34.7	D-P	701	19	2.7
Lubrizol	16.0	23.9	22.1	6.2	6.6	4.5	NM	163.0	1,577	174	11.1
NCH	14.6	10.9	10.7	2.2	3.3	2.2	NM	-7.1	689	31	4.6

Morton International	14.2	18.5	16.5	12.0	14.1	24.4	11.4	80.1	2,976	246	8.3
Airgas	13.1	15.5	8.2	48.7	16.3	32.6	NM	57.0	601	26	4.3
Wellman	13.1	8.4	6.0	29.7	21.5	7.2	-3.1	-21.7	895	44	4.9
Stepan	13.0	9.1	6.5	38.0	6.3	-1.8	NM	-6.4	433	10	2.3
Cabot	12.8	15.6	9.9	24.9	NM	4.1	NM	117.8	1,680	79	4.7
Air Prods & Chems	12.3	11.2	7.9	26.6	5.6	4.7	NM	17.0	3,485	234	6.7
HB Fuller	11.9	9.5	9.1	30.6	7.4	8.1	9.2	-19.0	1,049	24	2.3
Ferro	11.0	12.6	11.2	15.9	0.7	7.9	NM	-13.4	1,146	51	4.4
Scotts	10.5*	16.6	14.7	55.2	12.1	30.1	94.5†	18.7	606	24	3.9
Grow Group	10.3	10.4	9.5	0.6	-1.4	13.8	NM	-5.4	424	14	3.3
Dexter	9.1	11.8	9.4	36.4	2.1	6.1	NM	7.0	945	37	3.9
Georgia Gulf	7.9	NE	34.3	97.7	-7.6	8.8	-36.0	82.5	842	75	8.9
Witco	7.7	7.0	5.4	26.1	5.2	3.9	-12.6	5.9	2,183	54	2.5
Akzo Nobel	6.5	4.4	4.3	18.4	-1.0	-2.0	-18.9	-31.2	9,498	199	2.1
BF Goodrich	5.8	13.4	10.4	31.7	-3.6	7.6	NM	209.3	2,093	119	5.7
MA Hanna	5.7	3.7	4.5	44.2	7.6	16.7	-33.0	-65.6	1,732	12	0.7
WR Grace	4.1	18.1	11.3	48.8	-5.0	0.6	-35.5	D-P	4,812	265	5.5
NL Industries	2.8	NE	1.2	114.0	-4.3	3.2	NM	D-D	848	-50	def
IMC Global	def	7.8	8.2	30.0	NM	69.3	NM	D-P	1,596	41	2.6
Terra Industries	def	14.9	11.5	13.3	-4.5	30.1	NM	62.5	1,507	37	2.4
Albemarle	NA	11.1	6.5	29.3	2.9	16.8	NA	NA	1,029	47	4.5
Cytec Industries	NA	31.2	18.7	0.0	-2.9	4.8	NA	D-P	1,060	45	4.2
Eastman Chemical	NA	25.3	10.0	48.5	6.4	6.6	NA	NA	4,140	270	6.5
Ethyl	NA	22.6	13.4	44.7	NA	NA	NA	NA	1,007	78	7.7
Geon	NA	14.9	10.9	21.8	-6.4	17.6	NA	D-P	1,106	35	3.2
Intl Specialty Prods	NA	6.7	5.1	6.6	6.2	3.4	NM	0.0	577	36	6.2
Praxair	NA	28.8	13.8	44.8	6.3	5.7	NA	103.0	2,602	188	7.2
Rexene	NA	NE	6.5	86.9	-10.4	15.0	NA	NA	489	1	0.1
Medians	**13.1**	**15.5**	**11.2**	**26.6**	**5.9**	**7.5**	**-35.1**	**14.8**	**1,049**	**52**	**4.9**
Industry medians	**12.1**	**15.5**	**11.3**	**29.3**	**3.4**	**6.1**	**-29.6**	**14.8**	**1,381**	**54**	**5.5**
All-industry medians	**11.4**	**12.6**	**9.4**	**32.8**	**5.5**	**6.3**	**-18.8**	**11.8**	**1,449**	**60**	**4.3**

D-D: Deficit to deficit.   D-P: Deficit to profit.   P-D: Profit to profit.   def. Deficit.   NA: Not available.   NE: Negative equity.   NM: Not meaningful.
*Four-year average.   †Three-year average.   ‡Does not reflect spinoff of McWhorter Technologies.   For further explanation, see page 125.

Sources: *Forbes; Value Line Data Base Service via OneSource Information Services.*

Source: **Reprinted By Permission of FORBES Magazine © Forbes Inc., 1995.**

Computers & communications

Company	Profitability				Growth				Sales	Net income	Profit margin
	Return on equity		Return on capital	Debt/ capital	Sales		Earnings per share				
	5-year average %	latest 12 mos %	latest 12 mos %	%	5-year average %	latest 12 mos %	5-year average %	latest 12 mos %	latest 12 mos $mil	latest 12 mos $mil	latest 12 mos %
Major systems											
Compaq Computer	18.7	27.7	27.5	7.8	22.9	53.1	NM	81.9	9,816	775	7.9
Dell Computer	17.5	22.3	19.9	16.0	64.8	15.8	NM	D-P	3,186	107	3.4
Apple Computer	16.7	15.0	11.9	9.5	12.0	15.2	-15.6	257.5	9,189	310	3.4
Hewlett-Packard	15.1	18.2	17.6	5.7	15.8	23.0	12.7	32.0	24,991	1,599	6.4
Stratus Computer	14.1	6.7	6.9	1.6	13.6	14.6	NM	-43.7	574	30	5.3
Sun Microsystems	13.1	13.5	12.7	4.7	21.0	13.4	16.8	41.3	5,003	218	4.4
AST Research	12.7	1.4	1.9	35.5	38.8	43.2	NM	D-P	2,348	5	0.2
Silicon Graphics	9.7	18.5	18.1	19.2	40.7	38.4	32.5	49.6	1,607	157	9.8
Cray Research	9.1	9.0	8.5	10.6	2.8	20.4	-10.5	500.0+	987	71	7.2
Harris	9.0	10.8	8.8	35.3	6.1	7.4	31.2	9.3	3,374	126	3.7
SCI Systems	6.4	7.8	5.7	47.7	12.6	15.9	NM	-28.2	2,050	23	1.1
Teradyne	5.6	14.1	14.3	2.0	3.7	18.2	NM	107.5	635	61	9.7
NEC	0.8	1.0	2.8	55.0	2.4	1.8	-36.3	D-P	36,380	83	0.2
Intergraph	def	def	def	3.3	7.2	-7.0	NM	D-D	1,013	-122	def
Raychem	def	def	def	24.2	6.5	7.5	NM	P-D	1,497	-53	def
Tandem Computers	def	21.9	20.3	8.5	4.6	3.8	NM	D-P	2,108	170	8.1
Itel	def	54.2	11.9	31.1	NM	-3.3	NM	D-P	1,751	216	12.4
Unisys	def	8.1	8.5	41.0	-5.4	-6.6	NM	-31.6	7,378	278	3.8
Amdahl	def	def	def	10.3	NM	-20.2	NM	D-D	1,583	-7	def
IBM	def	11.4	7.9	36.7	NM	1.1	NM	D-P	63,552	2,172	3.4
Data General	def	def	def	34.0	-3.5	4.0	NM	D-D	1,121	-88	def
Control Data Systems	def	def	def	0.0	-15.0	13.1	NM	P-D	528	0	def
Digital Equipment	def	def	def	23.5	1.7	-3.7	NM	D-D	13,558	-2,197	def
Gateway 2000	NA	29.7	28.8	7.7	118.0	57.4	NM	-10.9	2,423	88	3.6
Wang Laboratories	NA	NA	NA	0.6	-21.0	-23.1	NA	NA	837	7	0.8
Medians	**5.6**	**9.9**	**8.5**	**10.6**	**6.1**	**13.1**	**NM**	**36.6**	**2,108**	**83**	**3.4**

Peripherals & equipment											
Cisco Systems	63.4	50.7	52.9	0.0	**101.9**	79.9	**106.3**	70.3	1,387	350	25.2
Cabletron Systems	46.6	32.9	32.5	0.0	**60.6**	38.0	**53.3**	36.6	699	139	19.9
Intl Game Technology	41.3	35.3	31.9	17.6	**34.8**	41.1	**63.8**	11.5	674	140	20.8
EMC	29.0	47.3	33.0	31.9	**42.7**	85.8	**120.0†**	108.9	1,195	220	18.4
Future Now	27.7*	def	def	68.1	**96.4**	35.1	**34.4***	P-D	817	-41	def
Intel	27.0	29.1	28.3	3.1	**24.5**	29.5	**32.8**	17.6	10,682	2,510	23.5
Cirrus Logic	26.4	18.2	17.8	5.8	**66.9**	65.2	**19.6**	352.1	707	62	8.8
Micron Technology	25.7	60.0	54.7	10.2	**30.7**	96.6	**NM**	268.3	1,629	401	24.6
Solectron	23.3	20.6	15.6	29.8	**61.3**	74.2	**39.7**	65.0	1,457	56	3.8
Tech Data	19.7	16.3	16.3	3.7	**43.4**	57.9	**32.2**	30.1	1,948	36	1.8
Quantum	19.4	35.5	25.7	31.1	**57.5**	34.6	**45.7**	500.0+	2,609	151	5.8
Pioneer-Standard Elec	18.4	20.9	18.6	28.9	**12.8**	37.6	**18.4**	34.2	687	22	3.2
Advanced Micro	18.3	22.4	20.8	4.6	**8.9**	22.5	**NM**	16.4	2,003	306	15.3
Seagate Technology	16.8	17.1	12.9	26.2	**16.9**	19.0	**22.5**	17.1	3,659	212	5.8
Anthem Electronics	16.5	7.9	8.0	0.0	**19.4**	10.1	**10.8**	-35.0	692	17	2.4
AMP	15.7	16.5	15.3	8.2	**5.4**	11.1	**NM**	14.9	3,803	340	8.9
Applied Materials	14.6	29.5	26.4	11.4	**21.4**	57.8	**NM**	126.3	1,519	185	12.2
Motorola	14.4	20.6	18.2	13.1	**14.1**	32.5	**11.8**	51.6	20,785	1,385	6.7
Marshall Industries	13.9	15.4	13.2	9.1	**8.0**	20.7	**9.7**	35.2	846	34	4.1
Vishay Intertech	13.7	13.1	9.4	40.7	**24.5**	13.3	**10.4**	18.3	918	50	5.5
Arrow Electronics	13.6	18.8	14.5	31.2	**20.0**	56.9	**105.8†**	11.8	3,589	95	2.6
Varian Associates	12.6	18.2	16.2	11.7	**2.2**	18.4	**15.5†**	76.2	1,552	79	5.1
Molex	12.4	12.3	12.2	0.8	**11.5**	14.0	**9.2**	28.8	1,000	101	10.1
Merisel	12.1	11.2	7.5	44.1	**47.3**	61.0	**NM**	-1.2	4,544	26	0.6
Wyle Laboratories	10.1	def	0.0	13.3	**8.1**	22.9	**9.8**	P-D	726	-1	def
Texas Instruments	9.5	26.3	22.1	22.1	**5.7**	21.8	**NM**	50.1	9,907	636	6.4
Natl Semiconductor	8.5	27.7	26.4	1.0	**6.5**	9.1	**NM**	69.2	2,290	266	11.6
Avnet	8.0	10.1	9.6	21.5	**11.5**	40.3	**6.4**	53.8	3,623	107	3.0
Analog Devices	5.4	14.9	13.0	13.7	**8.5**	17.8	**NM**	74.7	749	67	8.9
Bell Industries	2.9	10.9	9.6	27.4	**NM**	24.2	**NM**	D-P	472	10	2.2
Tektronix	2.5	14.8	13.5	17.4	**-1.9**	4.1	**NM**	D-P	1,341	67	5.0
Storage Technology	1.6	0.9	3.1	25.6	**12.2**	6.4	**NM**	D-P	1,509	20	1.3
Dynatech	1.0	def	def	18.2	**3.8**	-6.8	**NM**	P-D	468	-28	def
3Com	0.3	def	def	0.3	**15.3**	42.0	**NM**	P-D	914	-26	def
M/A-Com	def	3.0	4.2	33.3	**-4.3**	0.5	**NM**	D-P	342	3	1.0

(continued)

Computers & communications (concluded)

Company	Profitability				Growth				Sales	Net income	Profit margin
	Return on equity		Return on capital	Debt/capital	Sales		Earnings per share				
	5-year average %	latest 12 mos %	latest 12 mos %	%	5-year average %	latest 12 mos %	5-year average %	latest 12 mos %	latest 12 mos $mil	latest 12 mos $mil	latest 12 mos %
VLSI Tech	def	13.3	11.3	28.3	17.6	14.8	NM	D-P	571	30	5.2
Western Digital	def	52.1	34.1	14.6	7.6	38.7	NM	D-P	1,719	113	6.6
LSI Logic	def	28.2	15.5	29.7	10.9	20.9	NM	78.5	835	88	10.5
Conner Peripherals	def	35.6	10.9	61.8	50.4	6.8	NM	D-P	2,348	74	3.2
Maxtor	def	def	def	66.0	30.6	-26.6	NM	D-D	971	-193	def
General Instrument	NA	50.0	19.1	62.8	NM	48.5	NA	205.7	1,904	201	10.6
Medians	**13.7**	**18.2**	**15.3**	**17.6**	**15.3**	**24.2**	**7.8**	**51.6**	**1,387**	**79**	**5.5**
Software											
Microsoft	39.7	29.8	31.8	0.0	43.5	25.4	42.1	23.1	4,913	1,223	24.9
Oracle Systems	30.7	45.6	40.9	8.8	25.3	35.5	NM	81.7	2,160	308	14.2
Computer Associates	27.5	25.2	20.4	3.3	13.4	16.5	34.7	9.7	2,308	328	14.2
Novell	24.3	20.4	22.8	0.0	31.4	69.6	NM	D-P	1,821	255	14.0
Lotus Development	16.2	def	def	7.2	16.5	3.8	NM	P-D	985	-6	def
Legent	16.1	13.6	14.0	0.0	35.3	13.5	NM	-16.3	502	51	10.2
Cadence Design	9.8	6.6	7.0	1.2	42.4	7.9	NM	94.1	413	15	3.6
Policy Management Sys	5.5	6.1	5.0	0.9	17.7	1.0	NM	D-P	476	28	5.9
Mentor Graphics	def	cef	def	19.6	NM	-2.2	NM	D-D	332	-17	def
Borland Intl	def	def	def	5.7	1.8	-30.8	NM	D-D	313	-17	def
Computervision	NA	NE	def	NE	-4.5	-27.8	NM	D-D	641	-4	def
Medians	**16.2**	**6.6**	**7.0**	**1.2**	**17.7**	**7.9**	**NM**	**9.7**	**641**	**28**	**5.9**
Telecommunications											
MCI Communications	23.5	15.7	10.5	33.4	16.2	13.1	10.2	5.7	13,065	751	5.8
Alltel	18.7	19.0	10.7	46.6	17.5	28.1	5.7	14.7	2,844	297	10.4

AT&T	17.8	32.4	16.2	33.6	1.8	9.4	NM	-3.0	72,443	4,354	6.0
LDDS Communications	16.7†	8.9	8.1	22.0	27.4	72.7	19.3	464.7	1,668	156	9.4
Ameritech	16.7	13.7	9.3	27.9	3.2	6.4	3.5	-22.2	12,275	1,140	9.3
Citizens Utilities	16.0	13.6	9.2	35.3	16.3	33.1	6.3	9.5	817	137	16.8
Bell Atlantic	15.2	16.1	9.4	38.2	3.4	4.4	1.8	-3.8	13,500	1,425	10.6
Southwestern Bell	13.7	20.1	11.8	31.8	4.7	7.6	6.2	14.3	11,309	1,610	14.2
GTE	13.1	12.4	7.5	43.7	4.0	-0.3	-9.0	-34.5	19,759	1,292	6.5
Rochester Telephone	13.0	15.8	10.8	34.2	13.5	11.9	2.9	33.5	979	109	11.2
BellSouth	10.3	9.5	7.0	31.8	3.0	5.8	-7.8	-18.1	16,575	1,348	8.1
Corning	9.6	6.3	6.5	31.6	13.8	21.9	NM	-39.3	4,580	125	2.7
Pacific Telesis	9.4*	8.5	6.1	47.2	0.4*	-0.5	-29.8*	-50.5	9,176	469	5.1
Comsat	8.6	10.5	7.4	31.9	12.0	23.4	NM	-1.4	777	81	10.5
US West	8.6	20.8	11.1	42.5	2.3	4.9	-17.9	176.9	10,780	1,281	11.9
Scientific-Atlanta	7.6	10.5	10.6	0.3	7.9	19.7	-8.4	58.3	874	40	4.6
DSC Communications	7.0	21.2	19.9	1.5	13.3	34.6	16.6	78.9	909	138	15.2
So New Eng Telecom	6.6	def	0.0	39.0	0.4	4.5	NM	P-D	1,707	-44	def
Nynex	5.9	def	def	35.1	0.7	-0.1	NM	P-D	13,309	-648	def
Tele & Data Systems	4.4	3.5	32.8	23.4	24.3	23.3	14.4	6.2	686	48	7.1
AirTouch Commun	3.2†	3.2	3.8	1.8	15.4*	8.2	NA	340.0	1,062	110	10.3
Cincinnati Bell	2.9	def	def	49.5	8.1	3.8	NM	P-D	1,161	-52	def
Northern Telecom	2.5	7.2	6.2	29.8	9.6	4.3	NM	D-P	8,583	221	2.6
Sprint	NA	21.9	12.0	45.5	8.3	11.6	-7.9	118.4	12,398	867	7.0
Medians	**9.6**	**11.5**	**8.6**	**33.5**	**8.2**	**8.8**	**-7.9**	**5.9**	**6,582**	**189**	**7.6**
Industry medians	**10.2**	**13.7**	**10.7**	**19.6**	**12.0**	**15.2**	**NM**	**31.1**	**1,629**	**101**	**5.5**
All-industry medians	**11.4**	**12.6**	**9.4**	**32.8**	**5.5**	**6.3**	**-18.8**	**11.8**	**1,449**	**60**	**4.3**

NA: Not available.   NE: Negative equity.   NM: Not meaningful.

D-D: Deficit to deficit.   D-P: Deficit to profit.   P-D: Profit to deficit.   def: Deficit.
*Four-year average.   †Three-year average.   For further explanation, see page 125.
Sources: Forbes; Value Line Data Base Service via OneSource Information Services.
Source: Reprinted By Permission of FORBES Magazine © Forbes Inc., 1995.

Construction	Profitability				Growth				Sales	Net income	Profit margin
	Return on equity		Return on capital	Debt/capital	Sales		Earnings per share				
Company	5-year average %	latest 12 mos %	latest 12 mos %	%	5-year average %	latest 12 mos %	5-year average %	latest 12 mos %	latest 12 mos $mil	latest 12 mos $mil	latest 12 mos %
Commercial builders											
Jacobs Engineering	18.2	10.7	10.8	0.0	8.2	2.0	13.1	-34.8	1,166	19	1.6
Fluor	14.8	17.9	16.8	4.6	6.4	10.7	NM	221.1	8,293	188	2.3
Butler Manufacturing	13.1	36.9	25.5	35.0	-3.4	15.2	-15.6	223.5	639	23	3.6
Foster Wheeler	10.5	16.2	10.7	46.6	21.3	-11.8	13.7	22.1	2,308	65	2.8
Morrison Knudsen	8.9	def	def	4.8	6.2	1.0	-14.7*	P-D	2,641	-24	def
Apogee Enterprises	7.1	6.0	5.9	29.5	6.5	17.5	-26.9	21.4	729	7	0.9
Granite Construction	7.0	11.3	9.6	9.9	4.2	27.8	-29.9	500.0+	687	19	2.8
CBI Industries	4.3	def	0.4	38.9	3.9	7.9	NM	P-D	1,799	-26	def
Forest City Enterprises	2.8	def	3.4	90.5	11.7	2.7	NM	P-D	503	-2	def
Turner	def	def	def	49.5	-5.0	-3.8	NM	P-D	2,643	-6	def
Perini	def	def	1.1	30.2	5.3	-20.1	NM	D-D	942	0	def
Guy F Atkinson	def	def	def	14.4	-13.1	0.4	NM	P-D	482	-12	def
Medians	**7.0**	**2.3**	**4.7**	**29.9**	**5.8**	**2.3**	**NM**	**-34.8**	**1,054**	**4**	**0.5**
Residential builders											
Clayton Homes	19.4	17.6	15.3	13.1	21.1	31.5	23.0	22.2	661	73	11.0
Pulte	15.4	26.0	19.8	19.1	6.6	7.0	15.5	88.5	1,699	146	8.6
Oakwood Homes	14.1	13.6	9.7	43.4	38.5	79.7	37.2	22.2	579	34	5.9
Kaufman & Broad Home	12.1	11.7	6.1	60.0	NM	4.4	-17.9	9.8	1,305	46	3.5
Centex	11.3	17.1	13.9	23.4	9.9	20.6	8.9	61.6	3,391	116	3.4
Lennar	10.5	15.3	9.4	33.8	6.0	52.5	8.7	59.2	841	72	8.6
Del Webb	8.3	10.3	4.1	63.3	20.5	41.7	NM	500.0+	585	20	3.5
Skyline	6.5	9.6	9.6	0.0	8.9	17.0	NM	52.1	599	16	2.7
Hovnanian Enterprises	6.2	6.1	2.7	57.0	7.7	31.1	NM	-25.8	638	11	1.7
Ryland Group	5.2	8.6	6.1	56.0	2.2	13.0	NM	D-P	1,627	28	1.7

MDC Holdings	def	8.9	7.3	60.2	-7.2	26.4	NM	145.7	766	18	2.3
Beazer Homes USA	NA	NA	NA	43.3	38.4	95.1	NA	21.4	537	16	3.0
US Home	NA	11.7	5.6	52.5	NM	21.2	NM	14.2	944	31	3.3
Medians	**10.5**	**11.7**	**8.3**	**43.4**	**7.7**	**26.4**	**NM**	**52.1**	**766**	**31**	**3.4**
Cement & gypsum											
Vulcan Materials	13.2	12.3	10.4	11.6	0.8	5.7	-8.9	0.0	1,186	87	7.3
Hanson	12.7	8.3	5.5	47.6	6.1	12.0	-9.7	-31.9	11,422	963	8.4
Florida Rock Inds	4.9	8.1	6.3	8.8	-8.8	12.0	-32.7	145.2	320	14	4.5
CalMat	4.3	4.1	3.5	19.1	-13.6	7.9	-31.8	D-P	365	15	4.0
Lafarge	def	6.3	6.2	35.3	1.9	5.4	NM	D-P	1,557	51	3.3
Southdown	def	3.1	5.8	30.8	-2.9	9.7	NM	D-P	582	16	2.7
USG	NA	NA	NA	85.3	-4.3	17.7	NA	NA	2,185	NA	NA
Medians	**4.6**	**7.2**	**6.0**	**30.8**	**-2.9**	**9.7**	**-32.3**	**D-P**	**1,186**	**34**	**4.2**
Other materials											
Carlisle Cos	9.6	15.1	13.1	22.1	NM	16.4	7.8	24.1	674	34	5.1
Masco	9.0	12.9	9.4	39.3	7.9	14.4	NM	24.3	4,330	265	6.1
Manville	6.5	4.0	5.4	56.5	1.2	7.0	-26.8	-60.8	2,432	49	2.0
TJ International	5.9	6.2	10.8	18.2	9.1	21.3	-14.1	34.9	615	15	2.5
Ply Gem Industries	5.5	def	0.0	42.6	11.5	13.5	-11.5	P-D	785	-6	def
Mueller Industries	4.4†	10.4	10.3	26.1	NM	3.1	NA	28.2	517	24	4.7
Noland	2.9	5.8	5.1	24.5	-3.0	6.9	-8.1	120.5	430	6	1.4
Hughes Supply	2.9	8.6	6.5	42.0	3.6	23.2	-10.8	50.0	767	9	1.2
Ameron	def	def	def	43.2	3.7	-10.1	NM	P-D	414	-25	def
Morgan Products	def	def	def	48.4	-2.9	-4.0	NM	D-D	368	-10	def
Eljer Industries	def*	NE	21.4	132.8	-2.4	4.5	NM	500.0+	407	8	2.1
Nortek	def	12.2	9.9	63.5	-9.6	-4.0	NM	D-P	728	13	1.8
Robertson-Ceco	def	NE	def	187.8	NM	-3.4	NM	D-P	379	-22	def
Owens-Corning	NE	NE	409.6	311.6	NM	10.1	-15.1	-25.1	3,219	64	2.0
Medians	**2.9**	**4.9**	**7.9**	**42.9**	**-2.7**	**7.0**	**-26.8**	**26.2**	**645**	**11**	**1.9**
Industry medians	**5.9**	**8.4**	**6.2**	**39.1**	**3.7**	**10.4**	**-31.8**	**24.1**	**748**	**18**	**2.5**
All-industry medians	**11.4**	**12.6**	**9.4**	**32.8**	**5.5**	**6.3**	**-18.8**	**11.8**	**1,449**	**60**	**4.3**

D-D: Deficit to deficit. D-P: Deficit to profit. P-D: Profit to deficit. def: Deficit. NA: Not available. NE: Negative equity. NM: Not meaningful.
*Four-year average. †Three-year average. For further explanation, see page 125.
Sources: Forbes; Value Line Data Base Service via OneSource Information Services.
Source: Reprinted By Permission of FORBES Magazine © Forbes Inc., 1995.

Consumer durables

	Profitability				Growth				Sales	Net income	Profit margin
	Return on equity		Return on capital	Debt/ capital	Sales		Earnings per share				
Company	5-year average %	latest 12 mos %	latest 12 mos %	%	5-year average %	latest 12 mos %	5-year average %	latest 12 mos %	latest 12 mos $mil	latest 12 mos $mil	latest 12 mos %
Automobiles & Trucks											
Chrysler	11.2	53.3	26.5	44.2	3.4	19.3	NM	58.2	49,916	3,322	6.7
General Motors	9.8	163.5	20.8	77.0	1.9	9.5	NM	D-P	149,666	5,263	3.5
Paccar	9.7	20.0	12.7	44.5	NM	26.2	-13.4	58.6	4,258	193	4.5
Ford Motor	5.1	33.1	9.8	70.7	2.4	15.6	NM	500.0+	122,637	4,458	3.6
Toyota Motor‡	4.9	2.6	2.2	25.6	3.2	-8.3	-21.3	-28.4	95,150	1,279	1.3
Honda Motor	4.4	2.3	2.3	38.8	2.1	-6.5	-23.6	-37.9	39,255	241	0.6
Nissan Motor‡	def	def	def	60.0	3.7	-6.4	NM	D-D	58,952	-883	def
Volvo	def	def	NA	26.2	NM	80.5	NM	D-P	20,368	NA	NA
Navistar Intl	def	30.3	6.7	54.5	NM	12.0	NM	D-P	5,076	81	1.6
Daimler-Benz	NA	def	def	27.5	6.8	14.1	NM	D-D	67,749	-451	def
Medians	**4.9**	**11.3**	**6.7**	**44.4**	**2.3**	**13.1**	**NM**	**58.4**	**54,434**	**241**	**1.6**
Automotive parts											
Bandag	30.2	21.8	20.5	0.0	3.7	6.2	4.3	16.1	627	89	14.3
TBC	23.1	16.5	16.5	0.0	3.7	-4.3	12.7	-12.5	554	19	3.5
Cooper Tire & Rubber	22.4	21.3	19.5	4.9	10.1	12.1	20.2	7.7	1,337	117	8.8
Genuine Parts	20.0	19.4	18.7	0.8	7.3	13.1	5.2	11.3	4,746	280	5.9
Modine Manufacturing	16.1	20.5	16.9	21.2	9.5	33.4	9.6	37.0	796	53	6.7
AlliedSignal	15.8	30.5	18.7	33.7	NM	4.4	6.9	17.9	12,342	732	5.9
Snap-on	13.0	13.7	12.3	10.4	4.8	7.2	-9.0	29.9	1,193	96	8.1
Goodyear	12.9	23.6	18.8	29.4	1.7	2.9	NM	9.9	11,994	544	4.5
Eaton	12.9	21.7	17.5	40.9	2.9	24.1	-8.0	33.2	5,562	274	4.9
Echlin	12.4	17.0	14.6	25.8	8.2	14.7	22.3	28.8	2,229	121	5.4
Allen Group	11.0	14.9	12.5	18.0	-5.1	12.1	NM	41.8	322	29	8.9
Standard Products	10.9	13.3	9.7	38.7	8.3	11.3	NM	-14.6	892	31	3.5
Johnson Controls	10.8	13.5	11.6	24.3	12.7	11.1	10.3	20.3	6,871	165	2.4
AO Smith	9.9	19.5	12.2	33.3	2.8	15.8	NM	31.3	1,332	53	4.0
Excel Inds	9.7	15.0	13.0	21.8	15.2	19.9	NM	93.6	592	16	2.8

TRW	9.4	19.2	12.4	30.5	2.9	7.4	-5.9	35.9	8,646	296	3.4
Dana	9.3	25.6	15.2	43.6	NM	17.3	-18.4	66.1	6,373	204	3.2
Cummins Engine	7.2	27.5	24.1	9.6	4.2	10.4	NM	34.6	4,577	235	5.1
Arvin Industries	7.2	9.2	6.9	44.5	7.6	3.5	25.8	-1.1	1,993	39	2.0
Standard Motor Prods	7.1	11.9	9.4	37.9	7.8	11.9	NM	20.1	636	22	3.5
Barnes Group	6.8	13.3	9.4	38.2	NM	9.4	-24.0	168.7	550	14	2.6
Douglas & Lomason	6.3	def	def	29.3	2.8	17.5	NM	P-D	497	-2	def
MascoTech	6.2	10.9	7.0	54.9	-0.9	-15.5	NM	-6.9	1,500	68	4.5
Hayes Wheels Intl	5.2*	16.6	12.0	34.4	-5.2	23.0	NM	68.3	509	31	6.0
SPX	5.2	25.8	12.6	64.6	NM	30.5	-22.6	D-P	989	43	4.3
Federal-Mogul	4.1	12.3	9.1	18.3	5.5	15.1	NM	101.4	1,774	59	3.3
Varity	1.7	20.7	16.1	17.2	4.8	-17.6	-18.1	189.1	2,443	125	5.1
Borg-Warner Auto	NA	12.5	10.8	21.9	-1.4	20.1	NA	NA	1,161	59	5.1
Collins & Aikman	NA	NA	NA	409.1	0.8*	16.3	NA	NA	1,496	NA	NA
Detroit Diesel	NA	16.2	13.8	13.5	12.5	6.1	NA	58.9	1,631	33	2.1
Harvard Industries	NA	NE	16.3	17.0	NM	-0.3	NA	D-D	615	7	1.1
Lear Seating	NA	29.9	NA	66.0	18.4*	56.6	NM	62.1	2,814	22	0.8
Medians	**9.9**	**16.6**	**12.8**	**27.6**	**3.7**	**12.0**	**-20.5**	**30.6**	**1,417**	**59**	**4.3**
Appliances											
Sunbeam-Oster	15.3†	21.2	17.8	12.5	4.0	11.3	NA	30.9	1,163	102	8.7
Whirlpool	12.2	18.8	14.7	31.3	9.8	6.0	16.5	35.9	7,909	318	4.0
Harman International	8.5	16.9	12.3	38.6	9.1	35.6	NM	70.1	927	30	3.2
Maytag	6.4	23.2	14.2	43.1	6.6	7.7	-24.5	227.9	3,257	151	4.6
Toro	6.0	14.0	11.1	32.1	1.9	16.1	NM	62.9	794	22	2.8
Pioneer Electronic	5.3	0.5	0.9	8.9	4.1	-13.5	-15.2	-81.0	5,181	17	0.3
Electrolux Group	4.1	3.7	5.4	57.2	3.8	24.5	-35.0	176.9	13,614	71	0.5
Sony	4.0	1.1	2.6	42.5	10.7	-6.9	-28.1	-54.3	36,686	155	0.4
Black & Decker	3.1	10.0	6.6	62.4	15.3	4.7	NM	D-P	5,066	109	2.2
Matsushita Electric	2.8	0.7	1.5	27.7	4.5	-6.1	-37.6	-35.8	67,313	249	0.4
Sanyo Electric	0.8	def	0.9	33.0	4.4	-0.6	NM	D-D	15,822	-16	def
Philips Electronics	def	15.6	11.5	38.1	0.9	0.5	NM	D-P	33,844	957	2.8
Zenith Electronics	def	def	def	47.8	-12.4	10.0	NM	D-D	1,377	-47	def
Medians	**4.1**	**10.0**	**6.6**	**38.1**	**4.4**	**6.0**	**NM**	**35.9**	**5,181**	**102**	**2.2**
Home furnishings											
Mohawk Industries	34.8†	15.8	9.8	58.5	23.8*	31.6	40.8*	-2.0	1,426	38	2.6
Newell Co	20.9	19.3	16.7	22.4	10.1	24.4	13.9	12.1	1,972	189	9.6
Rubbermaid	20.9	19.9	19.6	1.7	10.4	8.0	13.1	9.4	2,076	224	10.8
Leggett & Platt	16.0	20.3	15.7	25.6	11.0	23.5	12.5	34.0	1,763	107	6.1
Premark International	12.1	24.7	22.3	16.2	5.0	10.0	12.2	40.9	3,340	210	6.3

(continued)

Consumer durables (concluded)	Profitability				Growth				Sales	Net income	Profit margin
	Return on equity		Return on capital latest 12 mos %	Debt/ capital %	Sales		Earnings per share				
Company	5-year average %	latest 12 mos %			5-year average %	latest 12 mos %	5-year average %	latest 12 mos %	latest 12 mos $mil	latest 12 mos $mil	latest 12 mos %
La-Z-Boy Chair	11.9	12.6	10.9	16.2	6.9	13.4	2.8	12.9	839	37	4.4
Kimball International	11.4	10.1	9.5	0.2	6.5	11.3	NM	2.5	834	34	4.1
Oneida	8.9	12.1	8.6	45.9	4.4	-1.8	-15.9	113.0	461	10	2.3
Bassett Furniture Inds	8.4	8.7	8.6	0.0	NM	2.4	14.7	-6.4	515	25	4.9
Springs Industries	6.3	9.8	7.9	32.9	1.8	1.3	NM	16.5	2,058	54	2.6
Fieldcrest Cannon	4.4	15.7	8.8	57.0	-5.1	0.2	NM	23.0	1,049	29	2.8
Armstrong World Inds	3.6	17.6	14.4	20.6	-0.8	6.8	-23.9	125.7	2,672	141	5.3
Thomas Industries	3.4	7.4	6.7	36.7	3.1	1.5	-30.6	124.4	455	9	2.0
LADD Furniture	1.0	4.0	3.5	42.8	4.9	8.2	NM	0.0	569	6	1.0
Foamex International	NA	13.1	8.3	88.8	18.4	51.8	NA	NA	959	8	0.8
Interco	NA	14.9	9.6	59.8	-3.3	8.5	NA	NA	1,783	52	2.9
Medians	**10.1**	**14.0**	**9.6**	**29.2**	**4.9**	**8.3**	**-6.6**	**14.7**	**1,238**	**38**	**3.5**
Recreation equipment											
Harley-Davidson	16.7	13.0	12.9	0.9	10.4	21.5	NM	-40.3	1,458	42	2.9
Fleetwood Enterprises	11.3	15.4	12.8	24.0	8.0	29.2	NM	41.4	2,596	82	3.1
Anthony Industries	10.4	13.6	8.7	46.6	5.3	12.6	NM	13.1	476	12	2.6
Huffy	8.7	def	0.7	30.4	17.6	-9.6	NM	P-D	713	-3	def
Coachmen Industries	6.6	20.9	20.3	4.4	-4.1	17.2	NM	3.0	377	13	3.4
Winnebago Industries	5.4	21.2	20.1	4.7	NM	17.7	NM	86.5	452	17	3.9
Brunswick	2.0	11.9	9.6	20.5	-8.5	20.8	NM	450.0	2,581	106	4.1
Outboard Marine	def	29.8	17.1	47.4	-4.9	4.2	NM	D-P	1,078	49	4.5
Coleman	NA	15.2	10.3	41.9	19.3	24.8	NA	3.2	696	34	4.9
Medians	**7.7**	**15.2**	**12.8**	**24.0**	**5.3**	**17.7**	**NM**	**13.1**	**713**	**34**	**3.4**
Industry medians	**8.4**	**15.2**	**11.6**	**31.7**	**3.9**	**11.3**	**NM**	**30.4**	**1,769**	**54**	**3.4**
All-industry medians	**11.4**	**12.6**	**9.4**	**32.8**	**5.5**	**6.3**	**-18.8**	**11.8**	**1,449**	**60**	**4.3**

D-D: Deficit to deficit.   D-P: Deficit to profit.   P-D: Profit to deficit.   def: Deficit.   NA: Not available.   NE: Negative equity.   NM: Not meaningful.
†Four-year average.   ‡Three-year average.   ‡Results not based on US GAAP accounting.   For further explanation, see page 125.

Sources: Forbes; Value Line Data Base Service via OneSource Information Services.

Source: Reprinted By Permission of FORBES Magazine © Forbes Inc., 1995.

Consumer nondurables	Profitability				Growth				Sales	Net income	Profit margin
	Return on equity		Return on capital		Sales		Earnings per share				
Company	5-year average %	latest 12 mos %	latest 12 mos %	Debt/capital %	5-year average %	latest 12 mos %	5-year average %	latest 12 mos %	latest 12 mos $mil	latest 12 mos $mil	latest 12 mos %
Personal products											
Avon Products	60.2	75.7	48.6	35.9	5.3	6.1	55.5*	0.3	4,162	236	5.7
Tambrands	41.1	78.7	55.2	42.7	2.7	-0.5	NM	9.3	627	88	14.1
Gillette	36.2	33.0	21.1	26.4	9.1	11.1	12.3	-10.0	5,888	503	8.6
Johnson & Johnson	30.6	34.7	27.8	18.1	10.2	7.5	14.5	13.4	15,175	1,963	12.9
Kimberly-Clark	20.2	23.2	15.8	21.6	5.8	2.7	3.1	82.1	7,207	571	7.9
First Brands	19.9	17.4	12.8	27.5	-2.1	-1.3	NM	7.7	1,039	59	5.7
Church & Dwight	19.8	9.4	7.9	4.5	8.6	-4.6	22.9	-47.7	499	16	3.2
Stanhome	19.2	19.0	19.3	0.0	9.2	3.7	NM	53.7	770	49	6.4
Clorox	18.8	21.2	16.0	16.8	5.4	10.3	11.7	-4.6	1,864	187	10.0
BIC	17.8	21.9	21.9	0.0	8.4	3.4	14.2	12.8	460	50	10.8
Colgate-Palmolive	16.9	26.5	16.4	36.3	9.3	5.1	NM	13.2	7,432	565	7.6
Procter & Gamble	16.8	24.2	18.7	22.6	7.5	2.6	NM	417.5	30,893	2,333	7.6
Duracell Intl	15.8	19.1	13.6	20.6	8.6	10.1	NM	63.6	1,926	209	10.8
Alberto-Culver	15.0	14.9	12.4	19.1	12.0	5.9	6.6	9.0	1,216	44	3.6
Block Drug	12.9	8.8	8.6	2.5	9.6	3.1	4.5	-19.2	635	46	7.2
Service Corp Intl	12.8	14.1	7.9	50.2	7.8	22.8	12.9†	21.5	1,048	126	12.0
Carter-Wallace	10.6	def	def	2.3	5.5	7.9	-8.2	P-D	706	-27	def
Helene Curtis Inds	10.0	9.1	5.9	41.1	14.4	3.5	NM	5.8	1,224	17	1.4
Gibson Greetings	9.8	def	def	18.4	4.9	9.5	-20.5	P-D	573	-17	def
James River Corp Va	def	def	2.1	46.4	-5.6	5.8	NM	D-D	4,904	1	0.0
Scott Paper	def	def	def	59.5	NM	-2.4	NM	P-D	4,654	-235	def
Dial	NA	27.0	14.2	57.2	NM	13.0	NM	101.9	3,447	135	3.9
Paragon Trade Brands	NA	18.0	18.1	0.0	15.6	5.1	NA	-30.5	576	30	5.3
Medians	**16.9**	**19.0**	**14.2**	**21.6**	**7.8**	**5.1**	**-14.3**	**7.7**	**1,224**	**59**	**6.4**

(continued)

Consumer nondurables (concluded)

Company	Profitability				Growth				Sales	Net income	Profit margin
	Return on equity		Return on capital	Debt/capital	Sales		Earnings per share				
	5-year average %	latest 12 mos %	latest 12 mos %	%	5-year average %	latest 12 mos %	5-year average %	latest 12 mos %	latest 12 mos $mil	latest 12 mos $mil	latest 12 mos %
Apparel & shoes											
Jones Apparel Group	55.0	26.6	26.5	3.9	26.1	14.3	38.1	8.2	600	52	8.7
Stride Rite	28.2	9.5	9.2	0.8	9.0	-5.1	15.7	-47.2	550	28	5.2
NIKE	27.2	17.2	16.9	0.7	18.0	-2.2	12.7	-15.8	3,852	291	7.6
Fruit of the Loom	25.2	15.8	9.4	54.4	13.1	14.8	21.4	-17.1	2,162	166	7.7
Liz Claiborne	23.9	10.4	10.3	0.1	14.0	-0.6	6.2	-34.8	2,192	101	4.6
Reebok International	22.5	29.3	27.6	12.7	12.6	7.5	10.6	143.4	3,174	252	7.9
Phillips-Van Heusen	21.9	13.2	10.6	40.8	12.4	8.5	19.1	-16.3	1,211	33	2.7
VF	18.7	16.4	13.4	22.7	12.3	12.4	11.6	-1.2	4,780	261	5.5
Instrument Systems	18.2	18.3	16.5	10.6	2.3	11.9	19.4*	66.7	489	30	6.1
Justin Industries	17.4	19.9	14.0	26.5	14.8	-1.7	41.1	12.2	475	38	8.1
Oxford Industries	13.0	16.6	14.9	8.3	1.9	9.2	22.4	29.4	641	20	3.1
Russell	13.0	12.7	10.5	20.6	11.2	11.3	NM	37.3	1,043	74	7.1
Kellwood	10.7	12.0	9.3	32.1	10.3	4.6	NM	8.9	1,240	37	3.0
Tultex	7.3	0.2	2.4	61.0	10.1	1.9	-14.9	-98.0	552	2	0.3
LA Gear	def	def	def	26.5	NM	11.1	NM	D-D	426	-22	def
Hartmarx	def	7.4	6.5	64.5	-8.3	-4.9	NM	75.0	722	9	1.2
Salant	def	36.9	14.0	58.2	NM	5.3	NM	D-P	421	19	4.5
Warnaco Group	NE	37.1	19.6	55.0	6.1	11.2	NM	11.4	761	60	7.8
Interco	NA	14.9	9.6	59.8	-3.3	8.5	NA	NA	1,783	52	2.9
Nine West Group	NA	36.4	28.8	18.1	8.2	20.7	NA	22.4	631	60	9.6
Medians	**17.8**	**16.1**	**12.0**	**24.6**	**10.2**	**8.5**	**11.1**	**8.9**	**742**	**45**	**5.3**

Textiles										
Cone Mills	26.7	21.6	13.0	21.9	5.4	1.5	NM	−17.8	780	38	4.9
Unifi	21.6	13.8	10.8	26.3	12.5	5.7	14.4	−36.0	1,419	79	5.6
Shaw Industries	21.1	18.8	14.4	33.4	16.9	12.0	17.3	15.8	2,715	132	4.9
Guilford Mills	11.1	11.5	8.4	38.0	3.9	7.5	20.5†	−13.7	704	25	3.6
Delta Woodside Inds	7.3	def	def	34.8	4.4	−10.5	NM	P-D	609	−15	def
Dixie Yarns	def	def	1.1	45.9	−2.3	23.5	−22.8	P-D	677	−3	def
Triarc Cos	def	NE	5.6	87.3	−2.8	2.8	NM	D-D	1,060	−7	def
Burlington Industries	def	20.6	8.6	55.9	NM	3.4	NM	46.0	2,127	99	4.7
WestPoint Stevens	NA	NE	def	114.9	−3.5	4.0	NA	NA	1,564	−210	def
Medians	9.2	11.5	8.4	38.0	3.9	4.0	NM	−26.9	1,060	25	3.6
Photography & toys										
Polaroid	25.9	10.7	8.2	33.6	3.9	3.5	NM	69.4	2,299	99	4.3
Mattel	23.8†	20.8	17.2	18.6	23.0*	9.4	7.1*	−18.8	2,929	185	6.3
Hasbro	14.8	13.3	12.3	13.4	17.5	0.6	21.5	−11.0	2,662	174	6.6
Tyco Toys	0.5	def	def	31.7	23.3	3.1	NM	D-D	754	−78	def
Actava Group	def	def	def	51.8	5.9	−39.6	NM	D-D	723	−95	def
Eastman Kodak	NA	16.5	8.6	52.8	2.9	1.4	NM	9.9	14,050	562	4.0
Medians	14.8	12.0	8.4	32.7	11.7	2.3	NM	−14.9	2,481	137	4.2
Industry medians	16.9	16.1	11.5	26.5	8.0	5.2	−11.5	3.0	1,136	51	5.0
All-industry medians	11.4	12.6	9.4	32.8	5.5	6.3	−18.8	11.8	1,449	60	4.3

D-D: Deficit to deficit.   P-D: Profit to profit.   def: Deficit.   NA: Not available.   NE: Negative equity.   NM: Not meaningful.
*Four-year average.   †Three-year average.   For further explanation, see page 125.
Sources: Forbes; Value Line Data Base Service via OneSource Information Services.
Source: **Reprinted By Permission of FORBES Magazine © Forbes Inc., 1995.**

Energy	Profitability				Growth				Sales	Net income	Profit margin
	Return on equity		Return on capital		Sales		Earnings per share				
Company	5-year average %	latest 12 mos %	latest 12 mos %	Debt/capital %	5-year average %	latest 12 mos %	5-year average %	latest 12 mos %	latest 12 mos $mil	latest 12 mos $mil	latest 12 mos %
International oils											
Exxon	14.7	13.2	9.0	18.3	4.5	-2.5	5.7	-9.4	97,705	4,700	4.8
Texaco	12.8	8.1	6.3	32.4	NM	-6.4	-12.7	-20.3	32,139	850	2.6
Royal Dutch Petroleum	10.8	9.4	8.0	9.1	5.8	12.4	-2.8	4.4	97,154	3,148	3.2
Amoco	10.6	13.4	9.9	20.5	2.8	0.7	-7.5	2.8	25,633	1,837	7.2
Chevron	10.4	9.1	7.0	15.0	4.5	-1.9	NM	-32.6	30,305	1,364	4.5
Mobil	10.3	8.8	7.3	17.4	3.3	0.0	NM	-29.9	57,115	1,585	2.8
British Petroleum	7.0	8.6	5.4	44.8	5.4	5.1	-16.6	D-P	54,924	1,113	2.0
Medians	**10.6**	**9.1**	**7.3**	**18.3**	**4.5**	**0.0**	**-12.7**	**-9.4**	**54,924**	**1,585**	**3.2**
Other energy											
Holly	46.5	43.4	19.8	46.3	8.9	-12.5	NM	3.7	551	21	3.8
Adams Res & Energy	26.7	26.7	20.4	27.2	63.1	-11.7	-13.4	371.4	636	3	0.4
Union Texas Petrol	26.6	19.6	5.9	34.6	-10.0	8.7	-11.2	28.6	723	55	7.6
Mapco	24.6	11.9	7.2	41.6	8.1	6.4	6.4	-26.2	2,782	76	2.8
Tosco	15.1	15.2	9.8	52.1	19.9	93.5	NM	D-P	5,710	79	1.4
Atlantic Richfield	13.6	4.5	4.2	43.8	NM	-11.5	-25.8	-71.6	15,495	278	1.8
Valero Energy	10.1	0.1	2.6	43.0	8.9	25.2	12.5	-98.5	1,557	8	0.5
Ashland Oil	9.4	13.7	9.3	45.3	2.4	-1.0	6.1	30.1	9,457	197	2.1
Burlington Resources	9.2†	5.9	5.2	26.4	10.6	-2.3	36.4	-48.5	1,246	153	12.3
Diamond Shamrock	9.2	11.1	7.7	38.6	6.9	-1.4	-18.1	125.0	2,558	62	2.4
Apache	9.1	5.6	4.3	35.9	25.7	12.4	14.8	1.4	519	43	8.4
Unocal	9.1	5.9	5.2	46.4	-4.1	-10.6	31.5	-53.3	6,872	208	3.0
Phillips Petroleum	8.9	10.7	7.2	36.9	NM	-3.5	-17.2	-8.5	12,074	342	2.8
El du Pont de Nemours	8.0	21.0	13.2	32.0	1.4	4.5	-24.2	500.0+	33,970	2,318	6.8
Witco	7.7	7.0	5.4	26.1	5.2	3.9	-12.6	5.9	2,183	54	2.5
Pennzoil	7.5	def	def	54.8	1.7	-3.5	NM	P-D	2,391	-180	def
Murphy Oil	6.3	8.9	7.6	9.0	NM	2.6	9.6	17.5	1,713	109	6.3
Fina	5.7	4.8	4.4	39.9	4.3	-6.1	-23.4	-44.3	3,319	53	1.6
Kerr-McGee	4.6	4.3	3.9	26.2	3.3	1.3	-10.0	D-P	3,356	70	2.1
Louisiana Land	4.1	0.4	1.2	49.4	1.9	4.4	NM	-88.9	791	2	0.2

USX-Marathon	2.9	6.3	3.7	45.6	NM	-2.6	NM	D-P	10,344	196	1.9
Quaker State	1.8	9.4	8.7	16.8	-3.1	-2.9	NM	D-P	720	18	2.5
Amerada Hess	1.6	def	0.3	51.2	5.0	13.6	NM	D-D	6,534	-69	def
Howell	1.6	0.5	3.0	26.3	12.8	-10.4	NM	-88.9	408	3	0.7
Oryx Energy	1.3	def	def	58.9	NM	-11.3	NM	D-D	1,040	-270	def
Sun Co	0.7	8.0	6.4	27.1	-3.8	-7.4	NM	-38.3	7,153	158	2.2
Crown Central Pet	def	def	def	13.3	4.1	-8.7	NM	D-D	1,450	-18	def
Occidental Petroleum	def	def	2.4	45.5	-19.8	3.3	NM	D-D	8,692	21	0.2
Santa Fe Energy Res	def	def	def	38.8	8.6	-13.4	NM	D-D	396	-71	def
Tesoro Petroleum	def	15.5	9.8	54.6	NM	-0.3	NM	D-P	858	22	2.5
Hadson	def	NE	def	57.4	-8.3	40.1	NM	D-D	706	-11	def
Maxus Energy	def	def	2.1	66.5	6.6	-8.3	NM	P-D	722	-24	def
Castle Energy	def	NE	30.0	84.9	NM	42.0	NM	-47.6	826	30	3.6
Westmoreland Coal	def	def	def	21.2	-4.2	-8.9	NM	D-D	430	-100	def
Pittston Minerals	def	NE	def	124.8	8.0	13.9	NM	NA	765	-106	def
Petroleum Heat & Pwr	NE	NE	10.7	144.9	1.5	-0.5	NM	D-D	546	3	0.5
Ultramar	NA	14.4	11.0	46.0	6.8	-5.1	NA	NA	2,376	80	3.4
Medians	**5.1**	**5.6**	**5.2**	**43.0**	**2.4**	**-1.4**	**NM**	**-44.3**	**1,557**	**30**	**1.9**
Oilfield services											
Schlumberger	17.8	11.5	11.0	7.7	7.7	1.1	10.0	-17.8	6,662	505	7.6
Dresser Industries	9.9	31.4	22.1	23.6	7.2	21.5	NM	283.6	4,942	351	7.1
Tidewater	6.0†	7.9	7.8	0.3	6.7	3.0	NM	50.9	523	45	8.5
Baker Hughes	5.9	7.7	6.5	33.9	NM	-7.3	NM	150.0	2,505	131	5.2
Halliburton	def	0.4	1.4	26.1	5.1	-8.9	NM	D-P	5,784	8	0.1
Camco International	NA	8.0	6.6	18.2	10.9	5.9	NA	NA	606	29	4.7
Western Atlas	NA	def	def	29.8	9.8*	NA	NA	NA	2,210	-127	def
Medians	**6.0**	**7.9**	**6.6**	**23.6**	**7.2**	**2.0**	**NM**	**150.0**	**2,505**	**45**	**5.2**
Gas producers & pipeliners											
Sonat	15.8	12.4	9.8	36.1	NM	13.5	21.6	-34.1	1,869	169	9.1
Western Gas Resources	15.4*	1.3	3.1	47.0	46.7	27.4	38.4	-90.7	1,072	14	1.3
Enron	13.9	18.4	6.5	38.9	NM	-20.2	18.9	36.1	8,619	449	5.2
Tejas Gas	10.7	10.3	7.1	54.7	29.4	69.2	10.5	39.6	1,111	30	2.7
Williams Cos	10.6	13.7	8.2	36.9	9.2	-27.7	13.7	-9.3	1,878	235	12.5
Panhandle Eastern	6.9	10.5	6.6	37.8	5.9	-1.7	NM	-5.2	2,292	176	7.7
Mitchell Energy	5.6	2.0	1.9	55.3	10.7	-3.6	8.0	-76.3	941	16	1.7
Coastal	3.0	10.1	6.0	50.8	4.3	2.9	NM	D-P	10,412	227	2.2
Transco Energy	def	def	5.2	65.0	NM	-0.3	NA	P-D	2,922	15	0.5
El Paso Natural Gas	NA	12.5	7.4	43.1	-4.0	-2.8	NA	3.0	875	88	10.1
USX-Delhi	NA	def	def	22.4	NM	7.5	NA	NA	568	-30	def
Medians	**10.6**	**10.3**	**6.5**	**43.1**	**4.3**	**-0.3**	**10.5**	**-7.2**	**1,869**	**88**	**2.7**

(continued)

Energy (concluded)

Company	Profitability				Growth				Sales	Net income	Profit margin
	Return on equity		Return on capital	Debt/ capital	Sales		Earnings per share				
	5-year average %	latest 12 mos %	latest 12 mos %	%	5-year average %	latest 12 mos %	5-year average %	latest 12 mos %	latest 12 mos $mil	latest 12 mos $mil	latest 12 mos %
Gas distributors											
Nicor	16.2	16.0	9.7	40.0	1.4	2.9	1.6	2.5	1,752	112	6.4
MCN	14.6	18.0	9.0	49.4	3.0	7.2	NM	42.8	1,581	85	5.4
Piedmont Natural Gas	13.3	12.8	7.6	46.8	5.6	4.7	3.2	-7.9	579	37	6.3
Washington Gas Light	12.3	12.8	8.4	35.9	4.7	2.3	2.9	8.0	915	60	6.6
Peoples Energy	12.0	11.8	7.4	40.5	1.7	1.6	-1.5	0.9	1,279	74	5.8
Laclede Gas	11.6	11.6	7.6	35.5	NM	4.0	2.9	-11.8	524	22	4.2
Brooklyn Union Gas	11.1	11.9	7.5	39.9	6.7	11.0	2.9	6.9	1,339	87	6.5
Atlanta Gas Light	10.6	10.8	7.7	41.0	4.7	6.2	3.9	8.3	1,200	63	5.3
UtiliCorp United	10.3	10.2	6.9	45.1	19.2	0.7	-3.7	13.1	1,555	94	6.1
Assoc Natural Gas	9.7	8.7	7.4	45.8	50.0	52.8	58.2*	-11.6	2,017	19	0.9
Wicor	9.2	12.4	8.8	30.9	1.7	7.4	NM	13.5	892	34	3.9
UGI	8.9	9.2	6.8	45.0	16.9	3.5	-8.2	6.2	757	38	5.0
Southwest Gas	3.9	5.8	4.3	56.5	-3.7	2.3	-25.1	11.8	709	20	2.9
Eastern Enterprises	3.6	def	1.9	42.3	9.9	3.8	NM	P-D	1,147	-6	def
Medians	**10.9**	**11.7**	**7.5**	**41.6**	**4.7**	**3.9**	**0.1**	**6.6**	**1,174**	**49**	**5.3**

Integrated gas

Questar	13.0	18.7	11.9	30.4	6.5	-0.4	21.8	37.7	654	118	18.0
Equitable Resources	11.7	9.6	6.2	27.1	20.0	38.2	7.8	-10.2	1,398	70	5.0
National Fuel Gas	11.0	11.1	7.5	29.9	5.6	11.9	4.0	3.7	1,141	82	7.2
Oneok	10.1	9.8	6.1	38.6	5.0	0.4	1.7	-6.3	792	36	4.6
KN Energy	9.8†	3.0	3.9	34.5	17.4	10.2	NA	-62.6	1,106	13	1.2
Consol Natural Gas	9.4	9.0	5.9	27.6	2.7	11.3	-2.0	-3.2	3,278	196	6.0
Enserch	4.0	5.8	4.6	39.6	-4.8	-15.1	NM	D-P	1,898	49	2.6
NorAm Energy	1.8	2.3	5.3	61.7	8.0	-1.8	NM	116.7	2,956	23	0.8
Columbia Gas System	def	18.7	8.3	47.9	NM	-7.3	NM	42.1	3,074	242	7.9
Pacific Enterprises	def	13.7	7.7	39.9	-16.2	-6.0	NA	24.3	2,772	169	6.1
Trident NGL Holding	NA	def	3.3	63.6	3.8	NA	NA	NA	533	-4	def
Medians	**9.6**	**9.6**	**6.1**	**38.6**	**5.0**	**0.0**	**-2.0**	**14.0**	**1,398**	**70**	**5.0**
Industry medians	**9.1**	**8.9**	**6.6**	**39.6**	**4.5**	**1.1**	**-23.4**	**0.9**	**1,581**	**55**	**2.8**
All-industry medians	**11.4**	**12.6**	**9.4**	**32.8**	**5.5**	**6.3**	**-18.8**	**11.8**	**1,449**	**60**	**4.3**

D-D: Deficit to deficit. D-P: Deficit to profit. def: Deficit. NA: Not available. NE: Negative equity. NM: Not meaningful.
*Four-year average. †Three-year average. For further explanation, see page 125.

Sources: Forbes; Value Line Data Base Service via OneSource Information Services.

Source: **Reprinted By Permission of FORBES Magazine © Forbes Inc., 1995.**

Food, drink & tobacco

Company	Profitability				Growth				Sales	Net income	Profit margin
	Return on equity		Return on capital	Debt/ capital	Sales		Earnings per share				
	5-year average %	latest 12 mos %	latest 12 mos %	%	5-year average %	latest 12 mos %	5-year average %	latest 12 mos %	latest 12 mos $mil	latest 12 mos $mil	latest 12 mos %
Food processors											
General Mills	37.7	32.4	16.5	39.1	8.5	2.5	2.6	-9.8	8,408	455	5.4
Wm Wrigley Jr	33.6	39.3	37.8	0.0	9.5	12.6	14.5	32.9	1,555	226	14.5
Kellogg	32.9	41.4	29.4	23.2	8.4	6.3	11.3	10.3	6,536	702	10.7
Thorn Apple Valley	29.3	14.1	12.6	21.5	4.0	4.9	-9.0†	3.3	777	13	1.6
Ralston-Purina	26.7†	26.1	12.2	53.8	4.3	-2.6	NA	-17.2	5,759	231	4.0
Quaker Oats	26.6	27.6	17.5	41.3	4.1	5.0	11.6	-33.4	6,057	201	3.3
HJ Heinz	25.2	25.4	17.0	39.7	4.2	1.1	6.0	14.4	7,200	605	8.4
Lancaster Colony	24.8	28.4	24.9	11.9	8.0	13.3	29.4	28.5	738	62	8.4
Campbell Soup	24.5	35.7	26.6	19.4	2.9	2.1	NM	149.1	6,791	661	9.7
CPC International	23.9	17.4	13.9	27.6	7.8	5.5	8.4	-16.2	7,155	335	4.7
McCormick & Co	23.9	22.4	14.0	40.3	5.7	6.4	15.4	12.2	1,647	104	6.3
Pioneer Hi-Bred Intl	20.7	26.0	22.7	6.4	11.4	10.1	20.9	56.9	1,479	213	14.4
Universal Foods	18.7	19.2	12.1	35.8	2.2	4.3	4.8	4.2	930	51	5.5
Hershey Foods	18.5	17.3	14.7	8.9	9.9	4.1	8.1	-9.7	3,563	252	7.1
Smithfield Foods	18.2	17.3	12.5	48.1	12.0	16.8	NM	500.0+	1,521	29	1.9
ConAgra	18.0	17.9	12.3	43.0	14.4	11.0	9.9	17.1	24,071	446	1.9
Hormel Foods	17.7	20.7	20.5	0.9	4.5	7.4	10.4	17.6	3,065	118	3.9
Dreyer's Grand	17.3	2.9	3.1	38.8	20.3	16.4	14.5	-79.8	533	4	0.7
Dean Foods	16.2	15.4	12.3	25.7	6.8	8.5	2.9	20.5	2,486	77	3.1
JM Smucker	16.0	13.0	11.8	16.2	6.4	10.9	3.7	-15.9	538	31	5.7
Lance	16.0	11.9	11.0	0.0	2.7	3.0	-4.5	-6.9	480	29	6.1
Sara Lee	15.9	6.1	5.0	19.7	6.4	8.4	NM	-67.8	16,030	244	1.5
Savannah Foods	14.9	2.1	2.9	37.7	3.2	-3.8	-7.9	-82.2	1,092	4	0.4
Unilever NV	14.8	13.1	10.4	12.0	4.7	1.4	3.3	-13.1	44,661	1,813	4.1
Flowers Industries	13.7	11.4	8.9	22.9	4.9	3.8	NM	-17.6	1,006	31	3.1

Tyson Foods	13.0	def	1.7	44.2	12.7	8.6	NM	P-D	5,110	-2	def
Archer Daniels	12.0	10.6	8.9	25.7	7.7	17.3	3.6	11.0	11,776	570	4.8
Pet	11.7*	25.3	12.3	57.2	-3.6	2.7	NM	D-P	1,574	84	5.4
WLR Foods	11.3	12.7	10.6	26.3	9.1	15.8	NM	29.1	759	19	2.5
Pilgrim's Pride	11.0	23.5	12.5	41.9	6.9	3.9	6.0	39.5	923	31	3.4
Grand Metropolitan	10.4	5.2	4.8	41.8	5.3	1.3	-27.7*	-53.2	10,759	357	3.3
Seaboard	10.2	8.4	6.2	36.0	23.0	-8.8	-4.7	-6.5	1,038	26	2.5
IBP	10.1	20.5	13.4	38.1	5.5	0.4	8.9	71.4	11,671	127	1.1
Dole	9.9	4.4	3.6	52.4	7.0	8.3	-9.1	-37.6	3,682	47	1.3
Hudson Foods	9.5	15.1	9.9	25.2	10.9	13.1	NM	60.4	1,041	27	2.6
Interstate Bakeries	8.0*	7.8	5.7	48.5	1.6	-1.2	NM	-44.4	1,147	15	1.3
Intl Multifoods	6.6	16.7	10.0	40.5	3.2	0.6	NM	500.0+	2,225	42	1.9
American Maize	4.3	9.2	6.7	33.9	NM	13.6	NM	D-P	598	20	3.3
Michael Foods	4.3	def	def	34.3	19.5	9.4	NM	P-D	505	-10	def
Imperial Holly	1.1	def	1.3	46.7	-1.1	-3.6	NM	D-D	634	-2	def
Valhi	def	4.4	5.4	59.7	0.9	7.5	NM	D-P	835	9	1.1
Chiquita Brands Intl	def	def	1.0	64.1	-7.1	-5.4	NM	D-D	2,447	-75	def
Borden	def	def	def	60.1	-4.5	-5.3	NM	P-D	5,552	-763	def
ERLY Industries	43.5	43.5	10.6	66.8	NM	65.3	NA	D-P	432	5	1.2
Doskocil Cos	NA	def	4.1	83.0	NM	2.3	NA	D-D	705	-1	def
Ralcorp Holdings	NA	42.1	13.3	69.5	11.8	9.3	NA	32.5	987	54	5.4
Ralston-Continental	NA	def	def	75.1	0.3	-2.4	NA	P-D	1,949	-26	def
Medians	**15.4**	**15.1**	**11.0**	**38.1**	**5.5**	**5.0**	**-4.7**	**3.3**	**1,574**	**47**	**3.1**
Beverages											
Coca-Cola	48.4	53.8	41.0	21.6	11.6	12.3	15.1	17.3	15,528	2,453	15.8
PepsiCo	25.7	26.8	12.9	43.5	13.6	13.6	14.0	24.6	27,072	1,713	6.3
Brown-Forman	21.5	31.3	18.1	34.6	8.2	0.2	8.6	5.1	1,417	146	10.3
Coca-Cola Bottling	18.8	49.8	6.2	79.7	16.6	2.3	NM	12.8	709	15	2.1
Anheuser-Busch Cos	18.5	22.1	13.4	32.0	5.4	5.0	NM	80.8	11,949	1,023	8.6
Whitman	15.7*	20.1	11.8	48.4	4.1	6.1	NM	0.0	2,631	104	3.9
Canandaigua Wine	13.4	7.5	6.8	42.8	28.0	105.5	30.0	-43.1	630	12	1.9
Seagram	9.9	9.5	7.8	37.0	5.6	0.5	-8.4	-14.8	5,260	471	9.0
Coca-Cola Enterprises	def	-4.8	3.6	54.5	7.6	7.8	NM	D-P	5,846	61	1.0
Dr Pepper/Seven-Up	NE	NE	28.8	183.2	7.4	8.3	NM	-29.2	752	85	11.3
Adolph Coors	NA	def	def	21.1	5.2	3.8	NM	P-D	1,644	-27	def
Snapple Beverage	NA	38.1	32.8	-5.9	118.8	51.4	NA	NA	686	61	8.9
Medians	**17.1**	**21.1**	**12.4**	**39.9**	**7.9**	**7.0**	**NM**	**12.8**	**2,138**	**95**	**7.4**

(continued)

Food, drink & tobacco (concluded)

Company	Profitability				Growth				Sales	Net income	Profit margin
	Return on equity		Return on capital	Debt/ capital	Sales		Earnings per share				
	5-year average %	latest 12 mos %	latest 12 mos %	%	5-year average %	latest 12 mos %	5-year average %	latest 12 mos %	latest 12 mos $mil	latest 12 mos $mil	latest 12 mos %
Tobacco											
UST Inc	58.8	79.2	73.6	9.5	13.0	8.7	19.6	7.8	1,158	375	32.4
Philip Morris Cos	34.4	34.3	17.9	53.7	12.7	2.5	14.5	-9.4	52,248	3,972	7.6
Monk-Austin	20.4	def	def	19.3	18.8	-23.3	NM	P-D	463	-8	def
American Brands	19.5	15.3	11.3	33.8	3.7	2.1	5.0	-9.3	8,555	650	7.6
Universal	19.5*	6.6	5.8	43.0	5.0	1.0	NM	-66.2	2,940	26	0.9
Dibrell Brothers	17.2	def	def	60.3	7.5	-5.9	NM	P-D	925	-15	def
Loews	11.0	5.3	4.7	24.9	4.4	-3.7	-4.2	D-P	12,339	327	2.7
Std Commercial	0.6	def	def	40.7	4.5	-5.0	NM	D-D	1,055	-21	def
RJR Nabisco	0.6*	def	3.5	41.1	4.7	1.5	NM	P-D	15,373	173	1.1
Brooke Group	NE	NE	def	NE	8.4	-26.8	NM	D-P	418	28	6.8
Medians	18.4	2.6	4.1	37.3	6.3	-1.3	NM	-37.8	2,049	101	1.9
Industry medians	15.9	14.1	10.6	38.1	6.4	4.3	-8.7	1.7	1,644	61	3.3
All-industry medians	11.4	12.6	9.4	32.8	5.5	6.3	-18.8	11.8	1,449	60	4.3

D-D: Deficit to deficit. D-P: Profit to deficit. def: Deficit. NA: Not available. NE: Negative equity. NM: Not meaningful.
*Four-year average. †Three-year average. For further explanation, see page 125.

Sources: Forbes; Value Line Data Base Service via OneSource Information Services.

Source: **Reprinted By Permission of FORBES Magazine** © Forbes Inc., 1995.

| Forest products & packaging | Profitability | | | Debt/capital % | Growth | | | | Sales | Net income | Profit margin |
| | Return on equity | | Return on capital | | Sales | | Earnings per share | | | | |
Company	5-year average %	latest 12 mos %	latest 12 mos %	latest %	5-year average %	latest 12 mos %	5-year average %	latest 12 mos %	latest 12 mos $mil	latest 12 mos $mil	latest 12 mos %
Paper & lumber											
Universal Forest Prod	16.6*	15.9	14.4	46.8	13.0	33.2	21.6	-1.7	843	10	1.2
PH Glatfelter	13.4	2.4	1.8	20.9	-3.7	-6.4	-20.2	-60.0	459	11	2.4
Louisiana-Pacific	12.3	18.9	15.3	7.4	5.5	21.8	NM	25.1	2,927	322	11.0
Willamette Inds	9.8	10.6	7.1	42.2	8.5	11.2	-15.8	44.9	2,847	132	4.7
Consolidated Papers	9.5	7.6	6.1	8.3	NM	-0.7	-21.2	19.0	956	72	7.5
Weyerhaeuser	9.0	12.7	6.8	48.3	-1.6	10.4	NM	-2.0	10,256	502	4.9
Federal Paper Board	8.7	3.3	3.9	44.4	4.2	1.8	NM	481.8	1,454	34	2.3
Potlatch	7.7	4.1	3.8	37.7	4.0	5.6	-20.2	13.2	1,426	38	2.6
Westvaco	7.7	2.5	2.8	35.2	1.4	5.2	-21.2	-52.1	2,463	46	1.9
Pope & Talbot	6.5	8.5	6.2	38.3	NM	7.1	NM	-21.6	657	17	2.6
International Paper	6.3	5.9	4.2	33.3	6.9	3.6	-27.4	500.0+	14,185	368	2.6
Albany International	5.8	9.0	6.8	48.3	3.4	-0.6	-30.2	85.0	550	22	4.0
Union Camp	5.8	4.2	3.8	34.8	3.3	6.4	-35.6	60.3	3,267	76	2.3
Mead	5.4	9.6	6.5	45.6	1.1	-5.9	-22.6	28.0	4,511	155	3.4
Chesapeake	4.8	8.3	6.5	42.9	4.0	2.2	-30.4	500.0+	917	31	3.4
Georgia-Pacific	2.5	5.1	4.7	53.5	4.9	5.0	NM	-9.9	12,639	121	1.0
Rayonier	2.0*	9.1	9.5	39.2	-2.3	9.8	NM	D-P	1,031	55	5.4
Champion Intl	def	def	0.7	43.2	-0.7	2.9	NM	D-D	5,153	-69	def
Bowater	def	def	2.1	45.2	NM	-20.5	NM	D-D	1,209	-21	def
Boise Cascade	def	def	def	49.0	-2.0	4.2	NM	D-D	4,029	-112	def
Medians	**6.4**	**6.8**	**5.4**	**42.6**	**2.4**	**4.6**	**-33.0**	**16.1**	**1,959**	**42**	**2.6**
Packaging											
Sonoco Products	17.3	16.3	11.2	36.7	3.8	18.0	NM	31.4	2,233	125	5.6
Bemis	16.1	18.4	14.0	27.1	2.6	10.7	4.7	56.5	1,325	69	5.2
Crown Cork & Seal	14.5	10.1	7.9	38.2	19.9	4.0	13.6	-30.0	4,296	126	2.9
Continental Can	12.0	6.2	5.8	58.4	46.2	4.9	-15.5	500.0+	515	4	0.8
Owens-Illinois	10.6†	def	0.7	82.1	1.9	-1.1	NM	P-D	3,585	-188	def

(continued)

Forest products & packaging (concluded)

Company	Profitability				Growth				Sales	Net income	Profit margin
	Return on equity		Return on capital	Debt/capital	Sales		Earnings per share				
	5-year average %	latest 12 mos %	latest 12 mos %	%	5-year average %	latest 12 mos %	5-year average %	latest 12 mos %	latest 12 mos $mil	latest 12 mos $mil	latest 12 mos %
Longview Fibre	10.0	7.7	5.1	41.3	NM	6.2	−18.8	−28.9	741	30	4.1
Temple-Inland	9.5	5.2	4.5	41.6	6.2	3.3	−18.1	3.2	2,856	90	3.1
Greif Brothers	8.8	9.1	8.8	8.5	5.0	6.0	NM	14.0	553	29	5.3
Ball	3.4†	def	1.9	39.1	26.2	5.4	NM	P-D	2,539	−8	def
St Joe Paper	3.0	3.5	3.6	2.7	−2.1	10.5	−33.9	452.6	653	32	4.9
Riverwood Intl	2.7†	def	3.7	59.4	11.7	4.8	NA	12.5	1,194	18	1.5
Stone Container	def	def	0.6	75.3	4.5	4.3	NM	D-D	5,370	−244	def
Gaylord Container	def	def	def	100.9	0.9	6.9	NM	D-D	784	−84	def
Sealed Air	NE	NE	28.1	92.3	5.4	10.6	NM	34.4	494	34	6.8
ACX Technologies	NA	4.1	4.0	0.0	7.4	14.9	NA	NA	696	17	2.5
Jefferson Smurfit	NA	NA	4.2	129.3	0.4*	4.5	NA	NA	3,083	−42	def
Rock-Tenn	NA	14.9	13.1	15.0	6.7	8.5	NM	44.0	706	38	5.3
Medians	**9.2**	**4.6**	**4.5**	**41.3**	**5.0**	**6.0**	**NM**	**12.5**	**1,194**	**29**	**2.9**
Industry medians	**7.1**	**5.6**	**4.7**	**41.6**	**3.8**	**5.2**	**NM**	**13.2**	**1,426**	**32**	**2.6**
All-industry medians	**11.4**	**12.6**	**9.4**	**32.8**	**5.5**	**6.3**	**−18.8**	**11.8**	**1,449**	**60**	**4.3**

D-D: Deficit to deficit.   D-P: Deficit to profit.   def: Deficit.   NA: Not available.   NE: Negative equity.   NM: Not meaningful.

*Four-year average.   †Three-year average.   P-D: Profit to deficit.   For further explanation, see page 125.

Sources: Forbes; Value Line Data Base Service via OneSource Information Services.

Source: **Reprinted By Permission of FORBES Magazine © Forbes Inc., 1995.**

Company	Profitability Return on equity 5-year average %	Profitability Return on equity latest 12 mos %	Return on capital latest 12 mos %	Debt/ capital %	Growth Sales 5-year average %	Growth Sales latest 12 mos %	Earnings per share 5-year average %	Earnings per share latest 12 mos %	Sales latest 12 mos $mil	Net income latest 12 mos $mil	Profit margin latest 12 mos %
Drugs											
Merck	49.0	29.2	24.0	7.7	12.5	39.6	14.7	26.6	14,099	2,898	20.6
American Home Prods	47.3	39.3	30.5	17.2	5.3	3.7	6.3	5.2	8,496	1,511	17.8
Schering-Plough	44.2	57.6	46.8	9.1	8.1	6.4	19.6	15.2	4,544	907	20.0
Abbott Laboratories	39.4	40.6	37.1	7.4	11.8	7.6	15.2	11.7	8,902	1,485	16.7
Perrigo	34.7*	20.2	15.9	18.7	27.7	13.0	67.8	11.8	679	55	8.1
Bristol-Myers Squibb	34.3	33.9	30.9	9.6	6.2	4.3	17.9	−11.1	11,729	2,000	17.1
Rhone-Poulenc Rorer	32.4	20.7	15.1	24.0	36.0	−1.1	26.7	−34.3	4,019	311	7.7
Marion Merrell Dow	32.3	21.2	19.6	0.7	29.6	4.3	19.0	14.3	2,997	446	14.9
Warner-Lambert	31.4	26.0	22.7	25.1	8.7	8.6	NM	−41.4	6,230	359	5.8
Glaxo Holdings	29.2	26.5	23.1	4.4	18.0	14.7	14.4	9.2	8,888	1,972	22.2
ICN Pharmaceuticals	24.1	19.8	16.5	7.2	37.8	7.1	19.0	32.9	392	31	8.0
Upjohn	21.5	23.7	18.9	15.7	6.6	−2.3	14.1	39.5	3,625	553	15.3
Eli Lilly	19.6	10.0	8.9	15.4	10.7	9.9	−7.1	−63.5	6,934	472	6.8
IVAX	19.1*	18.6	14.2	31.7	56.1*	8.2	152.3†	9.6	1,016	90	8.9
Pfizer	16.5	28.2	23.8	11.3	7.3	7.2	NM	102.5	7,970	1,253	15.7
McKesson	13.7	15.9	13.2	24.6	12.9	8.0	NM	−11.0	12,922	134	1.0
Bergen Brunswig	12.2	13.3	9.8	42.3	13.9	9.7	−4.5	92.4	7,484	56	0.8
Cardinal Health	12.2†	10.5	8.8	36.3	28.6*	27.6	29.9*	NA	6,318	39	0.6
SmithKline Beecham	11.8	11.9	9.0	15.7	9.3	15.7	NM	34.7	9,492	814	8.6
Bindley Western Inds	10.0	6.4	5.7	28.0	22.0	17.9	13.3	17.9	3,890	11	0.3
Mallinckrodt Group	5.3	10.7	8.2	33.2	12.5	8.7	NM	D-P	1,983	103	5.2
FoxMeyer Health	def	4.3	7.1	37.7	14.0	−0.6	NM	D-P	5,259	36	0.7
Medians	22.8	20.5	16.2	16.5	12.7	8.1	14.3	14.3	6,274	403	8.3

(continued)

Health (continued)

Company	Profitability				Growth				Sales	Net income	Profit margin
	Return on equity		Return on capital	Debt/ capital	Sales		Earnings per share				
	5-year average %	latest 12 mos %	latest 12 mos %	%	5-year average %	latest 12 mos %	5-year average %	latest 12 mos %	latest 12 mos $mil	latest 12 mos $mil	latest 12 mos %
Health care services											
Mid Atlantic Medical	66.8	65.1	63.4	4.7	54.8	12.9	62.2	144.9	714	50	7.0
WellPoint Health	63.9	17.2	17.2	0.0	11.3	13.0	58.7*	26.0	2,703	212	7.8
US Healthcare	54.6	48.5	47.9	1.7	29.1	13.8	75.4	40.3	2,816	375	13.3
Maxicare Health	43.0†	14.3	19.0	0.0	-18.4	1.0	NM	D-P	434	10	2.3
Health Systems Intl	40.9	29.0	14.0	44.6	144.3	16.9	11.1*	-9.8	2,221	46	2.1
United HealthCare	39.0	24.4	26.9	0.0	44.1	54.0	65.6*	35.3	3,373	259	7.7
National Health Labs	34.1	21.7	10.9	75.6	19.9	4.5	10.9	-42.9	807	30	3.7
PacifiCare Health	31.3	25.8	25.4	19.6	34.0	30.3	45.0	34.2	2,893	85	2.9
Foundation Health	24.8	24.5	19.5	25.6	17.9	-1.8	30.8*	28.8	1,607	83	5.2
HealthTrust	23.2†	24.5	14.0	60.9	10.4	24.0	38.2†	22.2	2,970	173	5.8
Manor Care	20.5	18.0	11.0	32.9	13.2	14.4	30.0	16.5	1,200	83	6.9
Quorum Health Group	19.0*	22.9	15.9	42.2	86.1†	111.0	NM	103.8	744	43	5.8
Value Health	19.0*	4.5	5.2	1.2	64.0	69.1	30.3†	-54.8	879	17	1.9
NovaCare	18.3	14.6	10.6	40.2	53.2	41.1	37.8	-4.4	844	56	6.6
FHP International	16.3	13.5	7.8	23.8	28.1	33.3	10.8	19.9	2,851	69	2.4
Hillhaven	13.0*	25.2	9.8	60.9	7.1	4.0	NM	31.3	1,470	62	4.2
Columbia/HCA	12.3†	19.6	11.6	42.3	7.3*	6.0	NM	12.8	10,766	694	6.5
American Medical	10.7	19.7	9.9	52.5	-3.4	6.4	NM	106.9	2,382	139	5.8
Universal Health	10.4	11.9	10.8	17.1	5.0	2.7	32.9	19.3	771	28	3.6
HealthSouth Rehab	9.0	4.5	3.5	69.8	46.4	85.8	NM	-60.8	865	19	2.2
Humana	8.6	17.7	16.7	7.5	35.6	12.0	NM	133.3	3,447	157	4.6
Continental Medical	4.0	def	def	57.1	50.3	6.1	NM	P-D	998	-36	def
Coventry	2.5*	28.0	23.0	21.0	39.2	22.2	6.3	64.7	664	25	3.8
Beverly Enterprises	2.0	9.6	7.5	45.0	7.3	3.9	NM	D-P	2,937	74	2.5
National Medical	def	def	def	13.4	-3.3	-20.5	NM	P-D	2,858	-320	def

OrNda HealthCorp	def†	def	0.8	73.5	8.9	32.5	NM	P-D	1,274	-47	def
Caremark Intl	NA	17.5	17.4	31.4	27.3	31.7	NA	NA	2,250	76	3.4
Charter Medical	NA	def	def	72.3	-7.1	0.8	NA	D-D	905	-47	def
GranCare	NA	12.8	8.7	66.4	140.0	10.9	NA	-44.9	526	10	2.0
Health Care & Retire	NA	12.2	8.7	28.2	10.8	10.6	NA	22.4	602	40	6.7
Kinder-Care Learning	NA	10.4	8.1	43.9	9.6	11.8	NA	NA	498	20	4.1
Physician Corp Amer	NA	26.9	27.5	6.5	74.9	50.8	NM	24.8	741	52	7.1
Medians	**18.6**	**17.6**	**11.0**	**32.1**	**23.6**	**13.0**	**10.8**	**22.3**	**1,237**	**51**	**4.0**
Medical supplies											
Johnson & Johnson	30.6	34.7	27.8	18.1	10.2	7.5	14.5	13.4	15,175	1,963	12.9
Dentsply Intl	29.9†	22.0	16.4	15.6	18.4*	-3.3	NA	85.2	533	54	10.1
Medtronic	24.5	24.1	23.1	1.3	14.3	15.8	18.3	22.6	1,540	258	16.8
Stryker	24.4	24.0	22.2	18.4	26.4	14.8	31.3	20.2	622	69	11.1
Hillenbrand Inds	22.7	14.7	13.5	24.0	10.8	6.4	16.6	-24.6	1,531	94	6.1
VWR	17.4	2.3	3.6	60.1	8.8	1.7	-7.6	-87.5	519	1	0.2
Pall	17.3	18.4	16.9	8.0	6.9	2.0	9.9	26.5	701	99	14.1
CR Bard	17.2	28.6	25.4	14.0	6.1	2.4	NM	156.1	1,003	109	10.9
Bausch & Lomb	16.9	10.4	7.8	18.6	13.3	2.4	9.3	-47.6	1,858	97	5.2
Owens & Minor	15.4	3.9	5.6	49.6	11.1	54.0	34.2	-67.5	2,042	6	0.3
Becton Dickinson	14.4	15.5	11.8	30.4	7.2	3.8	3.2	12.5	2,559	227	8.9
Amsco International	13.9*	def	def	48.6	15.7	-7.7	9.7	P-D	480	-51	def
Allergan	13.8	19.7	17.4	15.0	2.6	4.9	NM	-0.6	908	106	11.7
US Surgical	13.7	def	def	27.9	35.3	-16.0	NM	P-D	937	-125	def
Millipore	9.7	14.8	13.2	24.4	NM	-8.4	-5.4	119.8	481	69	14.3
Corning	9.6	6.3	6.5	31.6	13.8	21.9	NM	-39.3	4,580	125	2.7
Perkin-Elmer	9.5*	21.4	20.6	10.6	5.2	2.5	NM	390.0	1,028	65	6.3
Angelica	9.2	6.7	6.6	26.8	5.4	10.1	-7.7	29.1	464	13	2.8
Beckman Instruments	5.6	def	def	26.7	3.3	-1.6	NM	P-D	875	-33	def
Baxter International	4.7	def	def	40.7	7.2	4.9	NM	P-D	9,219	-168	def
Medians	**14.9**	**14.8**	**12.5**	**24.2**	**9.5**	**3.1**	**-5.4**	**6.0**	**970**	**69**	**6.2**
Biotechnology											
Amgen	35.0	33.1	30.0	12.9	81.9	19.3	NM	0.3	1,571	406	25.9
Diagnostic Products	16.4	11.6	11.9	0.0	18.3	8.7	NM	-6.8	115	15	12.8
Life Technologies	14.9	15.9	15.8	0.0	10.8	11.9	2.9	5.4	228	18	7.7
Biogen	8.1	def	def	0.0	49.4	-10.4	NM	P-D	137	-10	def
Collagen	7.5	10.3	9.1	0.0	6.1	25.7	NM	-52.5	68	5	8.1

(continued)

Health (concluded)

Company	Profitability — Return on equity, 5-year average %	Profitability — Return on equity, latest 12 mos %	Return on capital, latest 12 mos %	Debt/capital %	Growth — Sales, 5-year average %	Growth — Sales, latest 12 mos %	Earnings per share, 5-year average %	Earnings per share, latest 12 mos %	Sales, latest 12 mos $mil	Net income, latest 12 mos $mil	Profit margin, latest 12 mos %
Immucor	7.0	2.7	3.2	0.0	27.6	-2.4	-10.4	-42.1	29	1	2.8
Genentech	1.6	10.8	10.2	10.5	12.1	20.2	NM	169.2	708	124	17.6
Applied BioScience	1.1	def	def	31.6	31.9	-1.7	NM	D-D	167	-13	def
Genzyme	def	def	def	26.6	69.5	12.0	NM	P-D	295	-16	def
Genetics Institute	def	def	def	0.0	29.3	37.7	NM	D-D	132	-7	def
Molecular Biosystems	def	def	def	16.2	-12.3	271.3	NM	D-D	15	-14	def
Synergen	def	def	def	0.0	29.8	-21.5	NM	D-D	14	-110	def
Vertex Pharmaceutical	def†	def	def	4.5	121.1†	197.8	NM	D-D	32	-4	def
MedImmune	def†	def	def	5.2	22.1*	99.1	NM	D-D	19	-15	def
Gilead Sciences	def*	def	def	6.0	45.8†	19.7	NM	D-D	5	-29	def
Repligen	def	def	def	0.0	29.4	-14.6	NM	D-D	19	-23	def
T Cell Sciences	def	def	def	0.0	NM	-11.2	NM	D-D	8	-9	def
Scios Nova	def	def	def	1.5	25.3	9.6	NM	D-D	53	-34	def
US Bioscience	def	def	def	0.0	NM	20.6	NM	D-D	6	-38	def
Alliance Pharmaceut	def	def	def	0.0	-19.5	208.2	NM	D-D	5	-37	def
Sepracor	def†	def	def	10.1	72.1	-24.9	NM	D-D	12	-27	def
Chiron	def	5.1	3.9	38.6	63.4	44.7	NM	D-P	413	28	6.8
Gensia	def*	NE	def	1.5	NM	85.5	NM	D-D	55	-66	def
Centocor	def	def	def	103.2	9.2	-4.8	NM	D-D	75	-91	def
Cell Genesys	NA	def	def	4.4	NA	43.2	NM	D-D	9	-14	def
Cephalon	NA	def	def	11.9	NM	18.2	NM	D-D	19	-32	def
Medians	def	def	def	3.0	25.3	18.8	NM	D-D	43	-14	def
Industry medians	17.3	17.9	13.4	24.2	12.7	8.1	9.5	16.5	1,921	72	5.8
All-industry medians	11.4	12.6	9.4	32.8	5.5	6.3	-18.8	11.8	1,449	60	4.3

D-D: Deficit to deficit.   D-P: Profit to deficit.   def: Deficit.   NA: Not available.   NE: Negative equity.   NM: Not meaningful.
*Four-year average.   †Three-year average.   For further explanation, see page 125.

Metals	Profitability				Growth				Sales	Net income	Profit margin
	Return on equity		Return on capital	Debt/capital	Sales		Earnings per share				
Company	5-year average %	latest 12 mos %	latest 12 mos %	%	5-year average %	latest 12 mos %	5-year average %	latest 12 mos %	latest 12 mos $mil	latest 12 mos $mil	latest 12 mos %
Steel											
Allegheny Ludlum	21.6	4.2	4.1	26.4	-2.6	-6.6	-14.9	-75.5	1,017	17	1.6
Worthington Inds	17.0	19.3	16.0	8.4	5.6	16.1	7.0	23.0	1,341	90	6.7
J&L Specialty Steel	13.7†	19.5	11.7	35.2	-4.9	1.4	NA	27.4	674	51	7.5
Oregon Steel Mills	13.4	1.9	3.0	27.8	27.0	37.2	-10.4	-51.8	799	5	0.7
Nucor	12.6	20.6	15.0	15.2	13.7	35.3	NM	65.1	2,788	186	6.7
Carpenter Technology	10.6	16.0	9.8	31.7	NM	15.7	NM	53.4	655	40	6.2
Lukens	10.5	0.7	2.6	37.1	7.8	-0.8	-17.4	-93.7	897	4	0.4
Commercial Metals	9.2	11.0	9.2	23.6	6.5	6.9	NM	19.7	1,666	26	1.6
Birmingham Steel	7.9	8.7	7.4	22.9	6.9	73.8	NM	143.0	796	30	3.7
AM Castle & Co	6.5	18.4	11.4	34.9	-2.4	10.8	-15.0	151.5	514	13	2.5
Quanex	6.2	4.6	5.8	34.2	5.0	8.1	-40.9	D-P	663	15	2.2
Central Steel & Wire	4.7	10.7	10.7	0.0	-5.8	16.6	-36.5	228.2	572	14	2.5
Lone Star Tech	4.6	def	def	46.9	-13.5	-1.4	-58.0†	P-D	346	-8	def
Texas Industries	4.1	11.2	8.1	29.3	NM	17.8	NM	500.0+	739	35	4.8
Acme Metals	2.8	15.7	15.9	56.0	NM	14.9	NM	414.9	500	15	3.0
WHX	0.1†	20.9	12.2	29.8	-2.9	14.7	NA	D-P	1,137	82	7.2
Geneva Steel	def	def	def	66.6	-2.1	4.5	NM	D-D	486	-17	def
Intermet	def	4.6	3.8	50.8	2.7	6.3	NM	D-P	471	3	0.7
Weirton Steel	def	68.6	10.2	87.6	-4.1	6.8	NM	D-P	1,258	21	1.7
Inland Steel Inds	def	3.0	6.8	42.3	-2.4	15.5	NM	D-P	4,319	51	1.2
USX-US Steel	def	42.2	13.7	60.0	-6.0	12.5	NM	D-P	5,971	235	3.9
National Steel	def	def	4.0	68.2	-1.9	5.7	NM	D-D	2,542	2	0.1
Bethlehem Steel	def	def	def	38.4	-5.9	13.0	NM	D-D	4,725	-193	def
Armco	def	NE	def	277.7	-10.4	-21.7	NM	D-D	1,466	-23	def
AK Steel Holding	NA	NA	34.0	95.5	NM	NA	NA	NA	1,883	95	5.1
LTV	NA	NA	47.3	17.8	-4.4	11.2	NA	NA	4,441	334	7.5
Northwestern Steel	NA	17.9	9.9	74.2	3.5	11.9	NM	D-P	604	10	1.7
Medians	**4.6**	**10.7**	**9.2**	**35.2**	**-2.6**	**11.6**	**NM**	**65.1**	**897**	**17**	**2.2**

(continued)

Metals (concluded)

Company	Profitability			Debt/ capital %	Growth				Sales latest 12 mos $mil	Net income latest 12 mos $mil	Profit margin latest 12 mos %
	Return on equity		Return on capital		Sales		Earnings per share				
	5-year average %	latest 12 mos %	latest 12 mos %		5-year average %	latest 12 mos %	5-year average %	latest 12 mos %			
Nonferrous metals											
Newmont Mining	34.2	10.7	10.0	29.9	3.6	-2.4	-16.9	-11.5	600	76	12.7
Freeport-McMoRan	20.6	0.0	7.1	48.1	-4.1	24.0	NM	D-P	1,907	34	1.8
Broken Hill	18.9	15.4	9.2	28.8	8.1	3.8	NM	-21.2	12,433	935	7.5
Phelps Dodge	16.2	12.2	9.2	19.1	1.0	13.3	-12.5	17.0	2,941	249	8.5
Inco	11.4	def	def	34.7	-9.4	0.3	-49.5	P-D	2,232	-128	def
Engelhard	7.7	4.5	4.6	15.7	-1.8	7.0	-33.6†	-77.0	2,309	23	1.0
Maxxam	7.4	NE	def	95.9	20.4	-1.1	NM	D-D	2,081	-156	def
Tredegar Industries	5.0*	22.1	13.8	14.3	-7.3	9.3	NM	178.9	492	37	7.5
Magma Copper	3.6	8.8	6.7	32.0	5.8	3.0	-19.7	112.8	818	60	7.3
Handy & Harman	3.3	16.7	8.8	61.8	NM	21.3	NM	58.0	760	15	2.0
Alcoa	2.5	def	3.0	17.2	-2.5	4.1	NM	P-D	9,573	-12	def
Alcan Aluminum	1.4	def	1.5	27.7	-3.9	7.8	NM	D-D	7,814	-14	def
Asarco	0.9	0.2	1.5	32.4	-3.5	6.0	NM	D-P	1,879	3	0.2
Cyprus Amax Minerals	0.3	2.6	4.2	33.8	3.0	59.5	-23.5	-80.1	2,599	100	3.9
Reynolds Metals	def	def	def	45.8	-1.7	6.0	NM	D-D	5,587	-186	def
Homestake Mining	def*	15.7	10.3	18.3	2.5	-2.2	NM	500.0+	673	81	12.0
Alumax	NA	def	def	44.1	-1.9	7.4	NA	NA	2,575	-75	def
Medians	4.3	2.6	4.6	32.0	-1.8	6.0	NM	-16.3	2,232	23	1.8
Industry medians	4.6	6.7	7.3	34.0	-2.4	7.8	NM	27.4	1,300	19	1.9
All-industry medians	11.4	12.6	9.4	32.8	5.5	6.3	-18.8	11.8	1,449	60	4.3

D-D: Deficit to deficit.   D-P: Deficit to profit.   def: Deficit.   NA: Not available.   NM: Not meaningful.
*Four-year average.   †Three-year average.   For further explanation, see page 125.   NE: Negative equity.

Sources: Forbes; Value Line Data Base Service via OneSource Information Services.

Source: **Reprinted By Permission of FORBES Magazine © Forbes Inc., 1995.**

Retailing	Profitability				Growth				Sales	Net income	Profit margin
	Return on equity		Return on capital		Sales		Earnings per share				
Company	5-year average %	latest 12 mos %	latest 12 mos %	Debt/ capital %	5-year average %	latest 12 mos %	5-year average %	latest 12 mos %	latest 12 mos $mil	latest 12 mos $mil	latest 12 mos %
Department stores											
May Dept Stores	20.1	19.1	13.0	33.7	5.3	4.8	11.2	12.1	11,980	746	6.2
Younkers	17.8*	7.1	6.5	28.2	13.6	-6.0	16.1	-57.0	583	12	2.0
Dillard Dept Stores	14.8	11.8	8.9	35.9	15.0	8.0	12.8	1.4	5,437	244	4.5
JC Penney	14.8	18.8	12.9	31.1	4.0	4.2	NM	18.2	20,657	1,068	5.2
Mercantile Stores	8.5	7.6	7.5	16.7	4.3	1.6	-10.4	18.1	2,779	101	3.6
Sears, Roebuck	7.9	10.9	8.5	42.7	2.4	3.8	15.1	D-P	53,144	1,314	2.5
Strawbridge	7.3	9.0	7.6	44.9	1.3	2.4	-11.7	46.3	994	23	2.3
Neiman Marcus Group	0.1	def	4.8	45.3	6.9	2.9	NM	P-D	2,105	21	1.0
Broadway Stores	NA	def	def	73.5	-5.8	-2.4	NA	NA	2,069	-67	def
Carson Pirie Scott	NA	NA	9.3	49.6	2.2*	1.5	NA	NA	1,156	38	3.2
Federated Dept Stores	NA	9.9	6.2	46.5	-1.0*	5.3	NA	34.6	7,524	226	3.0
Medians	11.6	9.5	7.6	42.7	4.0	2.9	0.4	18.1	2,779	101	3.0
Apparel											
Gap	35.7	27.4	26.1	0.0	22.1	12.9	29.1	43.0	3,573	311	8.7
TJX Cos	28.6*	16.9	13.7	24.6	13.9	5.2	NM	-20.5	3,771	102	2.7
Goody's Family	24.5†	10.2	9.5	1.5	20.2	18.4	NA	-32.3	578	9	1.6
Filene's Basement	24.1*	def	def	25.4	13.9	8.6	NM	P-D	608	-3	def
Limited	24.0	15.8	12.7	19.1	12.9	-0.7	9.3	-10.0	7,203	388	5.4
Talbots	18.8*	15.2	12.5	8.9	13.6*	17.2	NM	31.3	802	45	5.7
Ross Stores	18.1	16.0	13.9	26.4	12.2	10.3	4.1	17.5	1,216	37	3.1
Charming Shoppes	17.7	11.6	11.4	3.7	12.1	4.1	17.3	-18.1	1,284	63	4.9
Edison Bros Stores	15.2	3.7	4.1	27.9	10.4	-1.8	-7.4	-74.1	1,473	15	1.0
Nordstrom	14.9	16.6	14.0	19.3	9.0	7.3	3.7	49.4	3,811	194	5.1
Dress Barn	14.5	11.4	11.3	0.0	13.1	9.0	NM	-15.1	457	16	3.5
Burlington Coat	13.7	11.9	10.6	19.8	16.6	22.4	15.6	-5.6	1,526	41	2.7
Melville	13.6	13.0	13.9	1.0	9.7	6.9	-9.4	172.7	11,134	332	3.0
J Baker	12.8	12.3	8.5	51.0	24.0	25.6	6.7	12.6	1,008	25	2.5
Merry-Go-Round	8.4	def	def	44.0	25.1	-2.2	NM	P-D	905	-107	def

(continued)

Retailing (continued)

Company	Profitability				Growth				Sales	Net income	Profit margin
	Return on equity		Return on capital	Debt/capital	Sales		Earnings per share				
	5-year average %	latest 12 mos %	latest 12 mos %	%	5-year average %	latest 12 mos %	5-year average %	latest 12 mos %	latest 12 mos $mill	latest 12 mos $mill	latest 12 mos %
Jacobson Stores	4.7	1.0	2.8	54.5	2.2	−3.3	−23.2	−72.2	403	1	0.2
AnnTaylor Stores	3.6†	8.6	7.3	34.3	11.9	15.6	123.7†	121.3	562	23	4.2
US Shoe	0.7	7.1	6.1	15.8	2.0	−2.3	NM	D-P	2,583	33	1.3
Brown Group	def	def	def	36.1	−1.1	−9.3	NM	P-D	1,511	−22	def
Petrie Stores	def	def	def	6.4	4.2	2.0	NM	D-D	1,484	−24	def
Genesco	def	def	def	56.7	3.9	−16.8	NM	P-D	482	−145	def
Medians	**14.5**	**11.4**	**9.5**	**19.8**	**12.2**	**6.9**	**−16.3**	**−15.1**	**1,284**	**25**	**2.7**
Consumer electronics											
Circuit City Stores	22.1	19.9	19.5	14.4	18.3	30.0	12.5	15.7	4,692	143	3.1
Sun TV & Appliances	17.3	13.5	13.1	6.7	30.1	39.2	37.1	17.2	652	18	2.8
Intelligent Electron	16.8	16.4	16.7	0.0	34.3	30.1	31.1	75.9	2,971	37	1.3
MicroAge	14.9	16.8	14.8	0.7	38.7	33.0	15.8	35.3	2,009	16	0.8
Best Buy	14.0	14.1	10.6	39.2	42.9	80.8	58.2	52.2	3,784	44	1.2
Good Guys	12.0	13.5	13.5	0.0	27.9	31.2	NM	76.7	725	14	1.9
Inacom	11.6	def	0.1	18.7	45.0	23.6	NM	P-D	1,708	−2	def
Tandy	7.9	11.5	10.5	3.9	NM	15.3	−27.8	D-P	4,576	219	4.8
Fretter	2.0	def	def	56.2	18.8	107.7	NM	P-D	766	−9	def
CompUSA	def	def	def	51.2	70.4	51.4	NM	P-D	2,295	−19	def
Medians	**13.0**	**13.5**	**11.8**	**10.6**	**32.2**	**32.1**	**−7.7**	**26.3**	**2,152**	**17**	**1.2**
Drug & discount											
Wal-Mart Stores	29.2	23.5	15.2	42.0	27.4	22.3	22.5	13.4	78,454	2,520	3.2
Venture Stores	28.3	13.1	10.9	27.2	7.7	10.0	16.3	−25.2	1,967	35	1.8
Value City Dept Stores	24.3†	21.8	18.6	12.6	15.2	2.7	23.6*	−3.2	865	39	4.5
Family Dollar Stores	21.4	19.2	18.3	0.0	13.8	10.1	25.3	−4.3	1,428	62	4.3
Walgreen	20.3	20.4	18.0	0.9	11.3	11.3	12.5	15.2	9,235	282	3.1
Dollar General	19.6	25.4	25.3	1.5	13.5	29.3	35.7	43.5	1,347	63	4.7
Caldor	17.0†	14.7	10.9	47.4	8.8	15.7	102.5*	−3.3	2,669	43	1.6
Genovese Drug Stores	15.5	15.0	9.8	34.1	5.5	11.7	15.2	6.0	538	9	1.6
Consolidated Stores	15.0	17.1	15.4	28.7	12.1	16.2	104.7†	18.8	1,175	46	3.9
ShopKo Stores	15.0	8.6	6.2	44.1	6.6	6.9	NM	−24.2	1,819	32	1.8

Dayton Hudson	14.7	14.1	9.1	55.6	9.5	9.2	3.8	26.5	20,594	433	2.1
Fred Meyer	13.0	13.2	9.6	41.1	7.6	7.1	22.3†	12.9	3,122	75	2.4
Longs Drug Stores	12.8	9.4	8.8	0.0	5.3	2.7	-3.4	-2.5	2,548	48	1.9
Arbor Drugs	12.8	11.8	10.4	14.7	15.8	15.8	NM	104.5	642	15	2.3
Fay's	12.8	13.0	10.8	48.1	13.3	9.2	NM	31.9	1,007	13	1.3
Mac Frugal's Bargains	11.9	13.3	12.8	1.6	7.8	16.7	NM	0.0	678	34	5.0
F&M Distributors	10.7†	def	0.6	73.2	13.2	0.2	NA	P-D	733	-9	def
Rite Aid	10.2	1.5	2.2	39.9	7.6	2.0	7.2	-88.5	4,172	13	0.3
Big B	10.1	14.6	9.8	41.1	13.8	16.5	NM	28.5	655	14	2.1
Kmart	5.0	def	def	38.9	5.6	0.9	NM	P-D	35,990	-1,021	def
Pamida Holdings	4.8	def	6.6	96.9	2.1	5.4	NM	Z-D	667	-1	def
Drug Emporium	0.7	2.8	4.1	55.9	13.9	-0.1	NM	D-P	755	1	0.2
Woolworth	def	def	def	20.4	3.6	-14.0	NM	D-D	8,549	-154	def
Perry Drug Stores	def	def	def	63.2	0.6	5.7	NM	P-D	729	-18	def
Jamesway	def	def	def	84.5	NM	-8.3	NM	D-D	724	-31	def
Rose's Stores	def	def	def	164.3	-2.8	-27.3	NM	D-D	1,006	-108	def
Ames Dept Stores	NA	46.3	27.4	61.2	-11.3	-4.8	NA	NA	2,208	28	1.3
Bradlees	NA	12.3	7.3	53.9	-1.2	1.6	NA	11.9	1,886	20	1.1
Eckerd	NA	NE	14.1	117.7	7.6	7.5	NM	104.3	4,339	60	1.4
Hills Stores	NA	NA	NA	47.0	NM	5.9	NA	NA	1,825	NA	NA
Revco DS	NA	8.6	7.8	45.8	NM	16.9	NA	86.4	2,677	42	1.6
Medians	**12.8**	**12.6**	**9.7**	**42.0**	**7.6**	**7.1**	**NM**	**0.0**	**1,819**	**30**	**1.6**
Home improvement											
Home Depot	23.4	19.7	15.7	21.2	36.2	33.3	35.8	27.9	11,687	571	4.9
Lowe's Cos	11.8	22.6	14.7	31.7	12.6	34.1	12.2	65.8	5,769	203	3.5
Waban	8.6	def	1.2	36.5	17.0	-1.9	NM	P-D	3,569	-1	def
Hechinger	2.9	6.1	5.1	43.5	15.4	18.3	-13.5	14.3	2,399	31	1.3
Grossman's	def	def	2.2	47.5	-6.2	-5.5	NM	D-D	781	-1	def
Payless Cashways	NA	13.9	8.5	55.0	6.7	6.1	NA	500.0+	2,713	50	1.9
Wickes Lumber	NA	500.0+	15.7	94.2	-4.5*	13.8	NA	NA	918	13	1.5
Medians	**8.6**	**13.9**	**8.5**	**43.5**	**12.6**	**13.8**	**-13.5**	**21.1**	**2,713**	**31**	**1.5**
Home shopping											
Service Merchandise	55.7	22.4	10.7	70.4	4.0	5.7	NM	-22.2	3,962	65	1.6
Lands' End	26.2	21.9	21.2	0.0	12.9	19.8	10.1	5.4	961	39	4.0
Blair	23.6	20.9	20.7	0.0	4.5	3.8	NM	25.5	527	38	7.2
Viking Office Prods	21.4	25.6	27.1	0.0	36.0	31.3	31.1	70.0	618	36	5.8
CUC International	19.7	35.0	33.9	3.9	20.2	18.1	49.5*	34.2	956	103	10.7

(continued)

Retailing (concluded)

| Company | Profitability | | | | Growth | | | | Sales | Net income | Profit margin |
| | Return on equity | | Return on capital | Debt/ capital | Sales | | Earnings per share | | | | |
	5-year average %	latest 12 mos %	latest 12 mos %	%	5-year average %	latest 12 mos %	5-year average %	latest 12 mos %	latest 12 mos $mil	latest 12 mos $mil	latest 12 mos %
Fingerhut Cos	16.1†	14.4	12.3	32.6	11.2	6.7	14.8†	7.3	1,874	74	4.0
Spiegel	9.8	13.1	7.5	65.0	11.7	22.2	-11.6	150.9	2,976	72	2.4
QVC	8.8	7.9	8.6	1.1	25.9	11.7	NM	-32.2	1,286	48	3.7
Home Shopping	3.8	7.1	5.5	1.2	8.7	6.4	NM	500.0+	1,121	14	1.3
Hanover Direct	def	28.3	16.7	21.9	5.1	32.7	NM	-37.5	771	15	1.9
Medians	**17.9**	**21.4**	**14.5**	**2.6**	**11.5**	**14.9**	**NM**	**16.4**	**1,041**	**44**	**3.8**
Specialty retailers											
CML Group	36.4	21.9	18.1	21.1	28.8	17.6	39.7†	-25.4	794	45	5.7
AutoZone	31.6	28.4	28.7	0.8	22.7	23.9	55.8	32.2	1,508	116	7.7
Toys 'R' Us	17.4	15.3	12.8	18.5	14.5	12.3	11.6	10.7	8,257	488	5.9
Musicland Stores	15.6	10.0	9.3	46.4	14.1	18.9	42.8*	2.2	1,329	28	2.1
Michaels Stores	14.9	13.6	10.8	22.8	19.6	50.6	38.6†	9.4	853	27	3.2
CPI	14.4	6.2	5.6	27.3	8.0	10.7	-13.4	-33.3	496	11	2.2
Trans World Entertain	14.2	5.0	4.7	33.5	13.1	8.4	-6.5	-39.3	521	6	1.2
Heilig-Meyers	14.1	14.1	10.8	33.1	19.3	35.5	18.0	32.5	1,010	63	6.3
Jenny Craig	13.8*	def	def	0.0	16.0	-22.2	NM	P-D	383	-4	def
Pep Boys	12.4	13.9	10.6	34.1	13.5	12.5	9.9	25.7	1,368	77	5.7

Office Depot	12.4	15.9	11.3	37.1	80.7	70.0	45.1	61.2	3,820	94	2.5
Smart & Final	11.8	14.4	14.4	1.3	14.5	9.3	NM	6.7	906	16	1.8
Tiffany	9.6	14.7	10.9	34.0	12.5	27.5	NM	D-P	652	28	4.3
General Nutrition Cos	9.6*	23.9	15.0	55.1	8.7	20.5	NM	92.4	624	41	6.5
Pier 1 Imports	9.5	4.1	5.1	39.8	9.4	6.4	-15.7	-57.7	692	8	1.2
Price/Costco	9.0	def	def	29.9	16.1	6.3	NM	P-D	16,481	-112	def
Staples	9.0	13.1	9.1	29.8	60.4	57.6	44.0*	61.0	1,664	32	1.9
Fabri-Centers of Amer	7.5	1.9	2.7	43.1	16.3	3.0	-26.6	-20.5	603	3	0.5
Jostens	6.9	def	def	17.1	3.9	-10.9	NM	D-D	810	-17	def
Amerco	6.3*	8.2	7.7	48.7	7.0*	11.6	NM	58.6	1,203	65	5.4
Egghead	5.5	def	def	0.1	17.8	4.3	NM	P-D	792	-1	def
House of Fabrics	1.0	def	def	0.3	12.0	-8.5	NM	D-D	514	-38	def
Getty Petroleum	0.6	5.9	7.3	38.6	-6.0	-12.6	NM	19.4	721	5	0.7
Dart Group	0.6	def	2.0	22.4	14.6	0.7	NM	P-D	1,310	-4	def
General Host	def	def	def	66.8	3.9	1.8	NM	D-D	572	-48	def
Levitz Furniture	NE	NE	10.7	95.0	0.8	5.3	NM	D-P	1,019	20	2.0
Barnes & Noble	NA	5.7	5.5	37.2	14.1	20.0	NA	46.5	1,514	13	0.9
Kohl's	NA	23.9	20.0	23.5	16.1*	17.5	49.2†	18.8	1,447	63	4.3
OfficeMax	NA	NA	NA	0.3	106.6*	NA	NA	NA	1,701	27	1.6
Medians	**9.6**	**7.2**	**8.4**	**29.9**	**14.5**	**11.1**	**-26.6**	**8.0**	**906**	**20**	**1.9**
Industry medians	**12.8**	**11.8**	**9.3**	**32.6**	**12.1**	**8.5**	**-13.5**	**9.4**	**1,347**	**28**	**1.9**
All-industry medians	**11.4**	**12.6**	**9.4**	**32.8**	**5.5**	**6.3**	**-18.8**	**11.8**	**1,449**	**60**	**4.3**

D-D: Deficit to deficit. D-P: Deficit to profit. P-D: Profit to deficit. Z-D: Zero to deficit. def: Deficit. NE: Negative equity. NM: Not meaningful.

*Four-year average. †Three-year average. For further explanation, see page 125. NA: Not available.

Sources: Forbes; Value Line Data Base Service via OneSource Information Services.

Source: Reprinted By Permission of FORBES Magazine © Forbes Inc., 1995.

Travel

Company	Profitability — Return on equity (5-year average %)	Return on equity (latest 12 mos %)	Return on capital (latest 12 mos %)	Debt/ capital %	Growth — Sales (5-year average %)	Sales (latest 12 mos %)	Earnings per share (5-year average %)	Earnings per share (latest 12 mos %)	Sales (latest 12 mos $mil)	Net income (latest 12 mos $mil)	Profit margin (latest 12 mos %)
Airlines											
British Airways	13.6	12.0	5.2	70.4	7.2	13.2	-9.2	D-P	9,905	228	2.3
Southwest Airlines	12.0	18.2	11.7	30.1	20.5	20.6	14.6	37.2	2,574	197	7.7
Amtran	5.0	8.2	5.5	31.8	13.4	20.3	NM	96.2	548	6	1.1
AMR	def	1.0	4.0	59.3	12.0	-0.4	NM	D-P	15,733	105	0.7
Alaska Air Group	def	4.2	4.1	72.3	6.7	14.8	NM	D-P	1,275	7	0.6
UAL	def	def	3.8	103.1	9.8	0.6	NM	D-D	14,152	1	0.0
Delta Air Lines	def	def	def	58.8	9.9	1.2	NM	D-D	12,296	-397	def
USAir Group	def	def	def	92.2	3.7	2.9	NM	D-D	7,118	-479	def
America West Airlines	NA	NA	NA	45.5	10.7	10.7	NA	NA	1,415	NA	NA
Continental Airlines	NA	NA	NA	70.6	-7.3	-0.8	NA	NA	5,630	NA	NA
Northwest Airlines	NA	NE	12.7	106.7	6.6*	7.9	NA	NA	9,101	341	3.7
Medians	def	1.0	4.1	70.4	9.8	7.9	NM	66.7	7,118	7	0.7
Hotels & gaming											
Circus Circus	38.9	23.5	11.8	46.5	14.4	33.1	13.9	20.2	1,164	131	11.3
Carnival	20.4	22.2	14.7	35.9	17.1	11.6	NM	16.4	1,721	362	21.0
Caesars World	19.5	16.6	12.1	26.9	2.8	3.3	10.8	-6.2	1,016	78	7.7
Walt Disney	19.2	21.7	16.2	19.6	16.2	17.9	5.9	65.9	10,055	1,110	11.0
Promus Cos	17.3†	24.4	13.4	54.5	7.0	26.0	44.6†	74.6	1,500	132	8.8
Mirage	13.4	9.9	8.1	27.6	38.7	36.3	-5.5†	38.5	1,223	95	7.8
Club Med	11.1	8.5	7.2	16.2	5.2	1.6	18.8	-15.3	561	27	4.8
Hilton Hotels	10.7	10.9	7.3	53.2	7.9	7.7	-4.5	18.8	1,435	116	8.1
Aztar	3.9	5.4	5.9	50.5	0.9	3.1	NM	53.1	535	19	3.6
Bally Entertainment	def	def	1.2	72.6	-9.7	-15.6	NM	D-D	1,037	-60	def
Resorts Intl	def†	NE	def	83.5	-0.8	-13.6	NM	D-D	384	-148	def
Host Marriott	NA	def	2.4	65.6	NA	9.5	NA	D-D	1,446	-42	def
Marriott Intl	NA	25.0	15.9	38.1	NA	-4.0	NA	11.3	7,656	184	2.4
Medians	13.4	10.9	8.1	46.5	7.0	7.7	-4.5	16.4	1,223	95	7.7
Industry medians	10.7	8.3	6.5	53.8	7.6	7.8	NM	18.8	1,473	87	3.0
All-industry medians	11.4	12.6	9.4	32.8	5.5	6.3	-18.8	11.8	1,449	60	4.3

D-D: Deficit to deficit.   D-P: Deficit to profit.   P-D: Profit to deficit.   def: Deficit.   NE: Negative equity.   NM: Not meaningful.   NA: Not available.
*Four-year average.   †Three-year average.   For further explanation, see page 125.

Sources: Forbes; Value Line Data Base Service via OneSource Information Services.

Source: **Reprinted By Permission of FORBES Magazine © Forbes Inc., 1995.**

BUSINESS INVESTMENT AND PLANS
(all dollar figures in text are in current dollars)

Percentage of Planned Business Investment by Sector: 1995

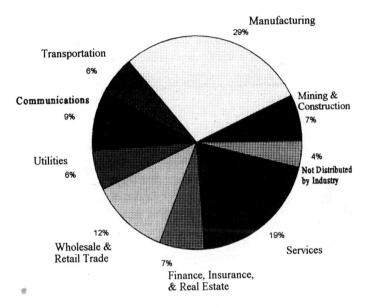

Note: Data presented in this graph are subject to sampling variability and nonsampling error.

U.S. businesses plan to invest nearly $593 billion for capital goods in 1995, according to estimates reported today by the Commerce Department's Bureau of the Census. This is an increase of 7 (± 4)[1] percent from 1994 and over 21 percent from 1993 levels. The spending data for 1994 and 1995 are based on information collected in the new semiannual Investment Plans Survey (IPS). The 1993 data are based on the Annual Capital Expenditures Survey (ACES). Business investment represents domestic expenditures for depreciable capital assets such as buildings and other structures, and machinery and other equipment. Spending in 1994 was estimated at $556 billion and $489 billion in 1993.

[1]The statement "7 (± 4) percent increase," appearing in the text, indicates the range (+3 to +11 percent) in which the actual percent change is likely to have occurred. The range given for the percent change is a 90 percent confidence interval that accounts only for sampling variability. If the range had contained zero, it would have been uncertain whether there was an increase or decrease; that is, the change would not have been statistically significant. For any comparison cited without a confidence interval, the change is statistically significant.

Source: U.S. Department of Commerce, Bureau of the Census.

VALUE OF MANUFACTURERS' SHIPMENTS FOR INDUSTRY GROUPS
(Millions of dollars)

Industry	Seasonally adjusted						Not seasonally adjusted[1]						
	Monthly			Percent Change			Monthly				Percent change	Year to date	
	Apr. 1995p	Mar. 1995r	Feb. 1995	Mar.-Apr.	Feb.-Mar.	Jan.-Feb.	Apr. 1995p	Mar. 1995r	Feb. 1995	Apr. 1994	Apr. 95/94	1995p	1994
All manufacturing industries	295,637	298,437	298,556	-0.9	0.0	+0.3	292,695	313,519	295,576	272,953	+7.2	1,170,147	1,070,651
Manufacturing Industries													
with unfilled orders	161,589	163,087	162,069	-0.9	+0.6	+0.2	157,785	173,633	159,547	144,619	+9.1	634,969	571,342
without defense capital goods	289,070	291,794	291,914	-0.9	0.0	+0.3	286,610	306,509	289,218	266,482	+7.6	1,145,152	1,044,320
Durable goods industries	158,259	161,571	161,206	-2.0	+0.2	+0.1	157,102	174,202	160,976	147,235	+6.7	634,967	578,785
With unfilled orders	126,794	128,552	127,849	-1.4	+0.5	+0.2	123,509	138,707	125,667	114,154	+8.2	500,293	452,237
Stone, clay, and glass products	6,634	7,045	7,212	-5.8	-2.3	0.0	6,868	6,951	6,656	6,868	0.0	26,543	24,511
Primary metals	15,016	15,305	15,152	-1.9	+1.0	-0.7	15,317	16,123	15,456	12,594	+21.6	61,399	48,938
Blast furnaces, steel mills	6,336	6,538	6,467	-3.1	+1.1	+2.3	6,450	6,918	6,571	5,682	+13.5	26,052	22,384
Iron and steel foundries	1,298	1,329	1,335	-2.3	-0.4	-2.8	1,360	1,419	1,384	1,225	+11.0	5,451	4,723
Nonferrous and other primary metals	7,382	7,438	7,350	-0.8	+1.2	-2.8	7,507	7,786	7,501	5,687	+32.0	29,896	21,831
Fabricated metal products	15,693	15,695	15,858	0.0	-1.0	-2.2	15,638	16,547	15,882	14,938	+4.7	62,782	59,117
Industrial machinery and equipment	30,200	30,351	30,131	-0.5	+0.7	+3.4	29,167	35,220	29,401	25,836	+12.9	118,416	103,481
Engines and turbines	1,997	1,799	2,023	+11.0	-11.1	+3.0	1,865	1,999	1,887	1,629	+14.5	7,314	6,558
Farm and garden machinery	1,855	1,890	1,904	-1.9	-0.7	+3.7	2,469	2,524	2,256	2,314	+6.7	8,905	8,096
Construction, mining and material handling equipment	3,059	3,112	3,170	-1.7	-1.8	+1.3	3,163	3,435	3,349	2,721	+16.2	12,763	10,672
Metalworking machinery	3,404	3,297	3,332	+3.2	-1.1	+1.0	3,176	3,539	3,223	2,642	+20.2	12,674	10,424
Computer and office equipment	8,229	8,494	7,990	-3.1	+6.3	+5.2	6,641	10,641	6,995	5,827	+14.0	29,971	26,280
Electronic and other electrical equipment	24,794	25,138	24,491	-1.4	+2.6	-0.5	23,590	26,568	23,889	21,225	+11.1	95,651	83,422
Electrical transmission and distribution equipment and industrial apparatus	2,743	2,900	2,821	-5.4	+2.8	+1.6	2,734	3,202	2,922	2,574	+6.2	11,302	10,264
Household appliances	1,826	1,864	1,883	-2.0	-1.0	-3.2	1,837	2,009	1,800	1,932	-4.9	7,278	7,097
Electric lighting and wiring equipment	1,928	1,954	1,948	-1.3	+0.3	+0.2	1,837	2,076	2,013	1,710	+7.4	7,648	6,851
Household audio and video equipment	1,121	1,119	1,130	+0.2	-1.0	+1.7	898	1,057	1,035	818	+9.8	3,904	3,437
Communications equipment	5,893	5,853	5,700	+0.7	+2.7	-1.5	5,472	6,328	5,255	4,607	+18.8	21,785	17,565
Electronic components	9,070	9,319	8,886	-2.7	+4.9	+0.4	8,816	9,798	8,886	7,514	+17.3	35,741	29,828

Industry Group												
Transportation equipment	38,291	39,926	40,171	-4.1	-0.6	-0.1	39,759	43,438	42,205	39,739	+0.1	161,246	156,135
Motor vehicles and parts	26,603	28,445	28,686	-6.5	-0.8	-0.3	28,227	30,988	31,065	28,940	-2.5	116,769	112,277
Aircraft, missiles, space vehicles, and parts.	8,779	8,455	8,688	+3.8	-2.7	+2.2	8,438	9,183	8,357	7,880	+7.1	32,731	33,404
Shipbuilding and tanks	857	898	820	-4.6	+9.5	-14.0	826	942	804	972	-15.0	3,352	3,683
Instruments and related products	11,330	11,600	11,624	-2.3	-0.2	+1.4	10,706	12,341	11,192	10,360	+3.3	44,379	41,735
Search and navigation equipment	2,658	2,655	2,614	+0.1	+1.6	-1.1	2,407	2,841	2,524	2,284	+5.4	9,978	9,342
Measuring and controlling devices	3,395	3,690	3,575	-8.0	+3.2	+4.3	3,266	4,074	3,487	3,032	+7.7	13,994	12,389
Medical instruments and supplies	3,010	3,095	3,120	-2.7	-0.8	+0.5	2,869	3,293	3,055	2,841	+1.0	12,095	11,554
Photographic goods	1,859	1,767	1,925	+5.2	-8.2	+2.0	1,753	1,728	1,751	1,834	-4.4	6,767	7,062
All other durable goods	16,301	16,511	16,567	-1.3	-0.3	-2.3	16,057	17,014	16,295	15,675	+2.4	64,551	61,446
Nondurable goods industries	137,378	136,866	137,350	+0.4	-0.4	+0.5	135,593	139,317	134,600	125,718	+7.9	535,180	491,866
With unfilled orders	34,795	34,535	34,220	+0.8	+0.9	+0.5	34,276	34,926	33,880	30,465	+12.5	134,676	119,105
Food and kindred products	36,172	36,010	36,167	+0.4	-0.4	-1.0	35,077	36,681	35,374	33,898	+3.5	140,425	137,598
Meat products	8,356	8,045	8,150	+3.9	-1.3	+0.6	8,172	7,983	7,957	7,749	+5.5	31,676	31,224
Dairy products	4,713	4,733	4,792	-0.4	-1.2	-1.6	4,633	4,803	4,679	4,532	+2.2	18,614	18,141
Beverages	5,333	5,339	5,279	-0.1	+1.1	-0.5	5,264	5,311	4,751	5,134	+2.5	19,800	19,218
All other foods, except fats and oils	15,873	15,793	15,970	+0.5	-1.1	-2.0	15,111	16,484	16,011	14,758	+2.4	62,408	61,673
Tobacco products	2,992	2,843	3,044	+5.2	-6.6	+0.2	2,866	2,936	2,761	2,703	+6.0	11,038	10,633
Textile mill products	6,290	6,424	6,380	-2.1	+0.7	-0.2	6,057	6,740	6,194	5,869	+3.2	24,516	23,145
Broadwoven fabrics and other textiles	3,913	4,011	3,995	-2.4	+0.4	-0.1	3,792	4,289	3,951	3,635	+4.3	15,558	14,512
Paper and allied products	13,706	13,469	13,372	+1.8	+0.7	+2.5	13,327	13,719	13,490	10,667	+24.9	53,159	42,879
Pulp, paper, and paperboard mill products	6,077	5,858	5,697	+3.7	+2.8	+3.6	5,889	5,968	5,788	4,149	+41.9	22,986	16,902
Paperboard containers and boxes	3,580	3,629	3,609	-1.4	+0.6	+2.9	3,612	3,698	3,580	2,922	+23.6	14,284	11,016
Miscellaneous converted paper products	4,049	3,982	4,066	+1.7	-2.1	+0.7	3,826	4,053	4,122	3,596	+6.4	15,889	14,961
Chemicals and allied products	30,111	30,488	30,695	-1.2	-0.7	+0.6	31,069	32,372	30,456	28,983	+7.2	122,828	110,080
Industrial chemicals	16,519	16,819	16,832	-1.8	-0.1	-0.1	16,948	17,607	17,046	14,721	+15.1	67,636	56,440
Drugs, soaps, and toiletries	10,314	10,281	10,334	+0.3	-0.5	+1.0	9,829	10,690	9,978	9,763	+0.7	40,419	39,534
Petroleum and coal products	13,583	13,082	13,400	+3.8	-2.4	+5.2	13,295	11,847	12,100	11,586	+14.8	48,569	42,511
Rubber and plastics products	10,037	10,111	10,100	-0.7	+0.1	-0.1	10,245	10,680	10,137	9,514	+7.7	40,538	36,607
All other nondurable goods	24,487	24,439	24,192	+0.2	+1.0	-0.7	23,657	24,342	24,088	22,498	+5.2	94,107	88,413

P Preliminary.   r Revised.

¹ Shipments and new orders are the totals for the period and are adjusted for trading-day and calendar-month variations.
Note: Estimates of manufacturers' shipments, inventories and orders are subject to survey error and revision. One major component of survey error is nonsampling error, which includes errors of coverage, response, and nonreporting. Since the survey panel is not a probability sample, estimates of sampling error cannot be calculated. Further details on survey design, methodology, and data limitations are contained in our most recent annual benchmark publication, Current Industrial Reports: M3-1(92), "Manufacturers' Shipments, Inventories, and Orders: 1982-1992."

Source: Manufacturers' Shipments, Inventories, and Orders, Bureau of the Census, U.S. Department of Commerce.

MEDIA GENERAL INDUSTRY INDEXES (for week ended 06/30/95)

Jan. 2, 1970 = 100

M/G Composite Index 200 days Ago: 524.36

Industry	Week's Close	Previous Week's Close	30 Days Ago	90 Days Ago	52-Wk Moving Average	For Week	30 Days	90 Days	Year To Date	P/E Ratio Now	5-Year Average P/E	12 Mos. Earnings Change (%)	5-Year Earnings Growth (%)	Dividend Yield (%)	Return On Equity (%)	Profit Margin (%)
			Index				Percent Change					Fundamental				
Composite	566.13	570.35	541.20	504.68	515.31	-.7	4.6	12.1	16.8	18.3	22.7	45	0	2.4	12.5	5.1
01. Aerospace	1104.19	1122.10	1031.32	891.73	903.60	-1.6	7.0	23.8	29.2	19.2	13.2	11	6	1.6	13.2	4.2
02. Airlines	365.32	363.11	318.24	269.17	298.71	.6	14.7	35.7	48.6	NC	NC	NE	NC	.9	NE	-.8
03. Automotive	307.90	309.63	293.74	273.37	292.97	-.5	4.8	12.6	7.0	7.2	NC	177	NC	3.0	15.9	3.5
04. Banking	450.90	456.69	430.31	395.69	409.78	-1.2	4.7	13.9	23.5	10.7	17.8	37	23	3.5	14.3	11.0
05. Building	415.70	410.37	400.58	375.55	376.05	1.3	3.7	10.6	16.6	15.1	NM	100	-4	2.3	13.1	4.4
06. Building-Heavy	622.66	605.61	616.66	581.41	702.60	2.8	.9	7.0	3.3	NM	NM	-57	-52	1.4	7.7	.2
07. Business Data Proc	343.35	348.84	318.31	273.12	270.99	-1.5	7.8	25.7	29.9	32.4	NC	NE	NC	.4	9.6	3.8
08. Business Equipment	269.52	270.39	265.75	246.18	248.39	-.3	1.4	9.4	15.2	17.2	72.2	206	-5	2.4	18.6	5.1
09. Business Services	345.03	345.80	335.84	323.15	325.98	-.2	2.7	6.7	11.0	23.0	26.2	100	-12	1.8	12.0	4.8
10. Chemicals	887.23	883.08	865.74	806.90	828.08	.4	2.4	9.9	13.6	15.4	22.5	147	-10	2.6	15.9	6.0
11. Communications	654.81	656.80	619.18	598.53	640.74	-.3	5.7	9.4	10.0	18.4	NM	57	9	3.0	16.4	9.4
12. Cosmetic-Personal	570.29	570.06	534.29	503.28	497.19	.0	6.7	13.3	16.4	24.7	26.2	36	16	1.6	33.4	7.3
13. Credit	440.01	447.38	427.39	383.27	400.08	-1.6	2.9	14.8	35.2	12.6	15.9	4	-6	1.7	8.0	3.0
14. Distillers-Brewers	684.48	671.88	668.58	589.43	635.76	1.8	2.3	16.1	10.9	16.7	33.9	129	-4	2.2	16.4	8.0
15. Drug Manufacturers	1079.11	1094.05	974.88	939.11	910.81	-1.3	10.6	14.9	21.6	22.8	22.8	37	5	2.4	23.0	13.2
16. Electrical Equip	824.02	832.38	808.31	756.21	744.87	-1.0	1.9	8.9	14.6	18.2	25.1	7	1	2.5	10.9	4.7
17. Electronics	985.05	1007.32	872.80	706.36	731.84	-2.2	12.8	39.4	52.7	25.4	28.4	27	9	.4	8.2	3.9
18. Food Production	850.90	849.92	811.69	802.90	841.49	.1	4.8	5.9	14.8	25.9	21.2	-17	3	2.4	15.6	3.5
19. Food-Packed Goods	1510.35	1516.32	1443.66	1384.48	1361.75	-.3	4.6	9.0	11.3	18.1	18.1	35	6	2.2	27.1	5.3
20. Food-Meats-Dairy	1082.53	1070.27	1059.34	1054.52	1013.51	1.1	2.1	2.6	8.8	21.0	NM	1	6	1.0	10.2	1.7
21. Food-Confections	1816.49	1855.94	1688.99	1569.91	1560.30	-2.1	7.5	15.7	20.0	25.1	23.9	28	21	1.5	21.2	7.5
22. Freight-Shipping	432.70	435.62	451.99	449.09	449.15	-.6	-4.2	-3.6	-2.2	23.8	27.1	12	-1	1.2	9.8	2.3
23. Health	651.10	671.25	637.75	626.02	612.25	-3.0	2.0	4.0	8.6	30.2	32.0	77	11	.5	8.8	3.8
24. Hotels-Motels-Res	822.73	816.70	787.68	714.14	749.13	.7	4.4	15.2	25.2	24.9	32.9	431	-7	.5	13.5	6.1
25. Housewares-Furn.	519.78	514.21	519.96	531.42	530.30	1.0	-.0	-2.1	1.9	18.0	22.2	9	2	1.7	11.2	3.5

Industry																
26. Insurance	569.19	577.54	555.39	519.32	514.41	-1.4	2.4	9.6	17.1	13.8	14.1	23	-1	1.9	9.3	5.4
27. Investments	163.42	165.49	159.14	150.73	152.58	-1.2	2.6	8.4	15.0	18.0	11.4	-49	18	5.7	14.0	6.0
28. Machinery-Heavy	651.47	643.96	633.37	565.81	575.56	1.1	2.8	15.1	20.2	17.1	NM	81	-1	1.7	13.8	4.5
29. Machine-Lt-Equip	525.98	515.71	519.26	473.03	474.51	1.9	1.2	11.1	21.3	16.7	61.7	134	-9	1.7	10.5	3.9
30. Metals Fabrication	640.87	627.91	640.67	578.12	587.99	2.0	.0	10.8	16.7	16.4	NM	90	2	1.4	11.7	3.9
31. Metals-Iron-Steel	219.95	213.63	215.03	209.24	226.27	2.9	2.2	5.1	-1.9	11.4	NC	NE	NC	1.3	9.7	3.7
32. Metals-Nonf-Coal	243.69	237.74	225.39	215.28	229.03	2.5	8.1	13.2	9.1	15.9	NM	NC	NC	1.7	7.3	3.9
33. Metals, Rare	507.97	529.38	496.43	433.85	483.37	-4.0	2.3	17.0	12.8	67.0	92.5	-14	NC	1.0	8.0	10.2
34. Multi-Industry	323.66	324.05	314.14	293.49	289.85	-.1	3.0	10.2	18.1	17.2	28.5	35	-4	2.3	15.3	4.5
35. Oil, Nat Gas Svcs	496.55	496.63	503.79	438.80	467.90	-.0	-1.4	13.1	15.4	56.4	29.5	-26	NC	1.7	5.5	2.7
36. Oil, Nat Gas Prod	282.51	281.74	286.36	261.06	273.50	.2	-1.3	8.2	13.1	20.2	NM	-79	NC	2.3	6.6	4.0
37. Oil Refin, Mkting	743.17	746.75	755.85	697.23	696.60	-.4	-1.6	6.5	11.3	19.5	19.4	11	-7	4.1	10.3	3.9
38. Paper, Packaging	787.37	780.89	732.10	707.44	704.26	.8	7.5	11.3	19.2	28.4	38.8	419	-29	1.8	9.3	3.3
39. Personal Services	384.61	383.26	355.07	328.83	337.17	.3	8.3	16.9	21.0	29.0	28.3	14	2	1.3	9.3	5.0
40. Precision Instruments	277.98	280.66	258.69	228.39	235.55	-.9	7.4	21.7	31.2	18.6	30.8	14	-11	1.4	8.3	3.5
41. Publishing	974.13	987.61	941.11	897.24	878.13	-1.3	3.5	8.5	10.9	15.6	37.4	95	11	1.3	12.7	8.5
42. Railroads	839.19	835.56	817.06	784.65	762.67	.4	2.7	6.9	18.9	16.5	64.4	31	NC	2.2	12.8	8.4
43. Real Estate Inves	185.46	188.77	180.63	166.08	170.78	-1.7	2.6	11.6	16.5	36.1	41.5	-5	8	5.2	11.9	13.5
44. Real Estate	81.17	80.53	79.13	77.49	78.49	.7	2.5	4.7	6.8	19.5	NC	NE	NC	2.7	1.2	1.1
45. Recreation-Luxury	311.23	314.93	304.08	302.75	304.29	-1.1	2.3	2.8	.9	66.0	39.6	58	-14	1.3	11.3	3.7
46. Recreation-Bdcstg	2915.05	2888.91	2623.27	2607.43	2800.43	.9	11.1	11.8	16.8	31.5	NM	96	NC	.2	8.4	4.8
47. Recreation-Mov-Sp	2217.76	2329.81	2160.38	2060.85	1966.74	-4.8	2.6	7.6	18.3	23.3	68.6	17	-7	.7	12.3	6.5
48. Retail-Apparel	1437.49	1430.37	1403.50	1341.12	1428.29	-.5	2.4	7.1	6.6	14.8	26.1	-23	-1	1.6	9.8	3.0
49. Retail-Dept Strs	399.91	398.43	370.05	338.72	371.51	.3	8.0	18.0	18.7	22.1	48.5	9	-4	2.2	13.3	3.3
50. Retail-Disc, Drug	1199.35	1198.50	1092.51	1102.65	1121.92	.0	9.7	8.7	15.7	22.1	27.1	62	3	1.0	14.3	2.3
51. Retail-Food Strs	922.79	933.70	897.39	847.46	886.01	-1.1	2.8	8.8	10.1	18.1	39.0	13	NC	1.2	19.9	1.5
52. Retail-Misc	1073.25	1079.37	1030.93	1061.44	1052.70	-.5	4.1	1.1	3.1	26.5	24.9	-1	0	.9	9.4	1.8
53. Rubber-Plastic	586.30	583.89	594.50	560.88	556.06	.4	-1.3	4.5	8.7	14.2	20.2	25	3	2.3	13.2	4.8
54. Savings and Loan	511.24	511.42	491.67	444.09	453.06	-.0	3.9	15.1	26.5	12.9	NC	151	27	2.2	7.4	7.8
55. Shoes-Leather	1001.74	1007.30	967.37	943.48	940.76	-.5	3.5	6.1	2.4	16.3	16.8	21	3	1.1	16.6	5.8
56. Textile Mfg	469.11	469.85	492.79	476.98	491.44	-.1	-4.8	-1.6	-5.1	42.5	24.8	-11	-7	1.1	5.8	1.8
57. Textiles-Apparel	511.16	499.10	482.82	484.16	509.05	2.4	5.8	5.5	5.5	18.1	NM	-15	5	1.4	11.0	3.4
58. Tobacco	1770.50	1797.04	1664.20	1467.99	1591.55	-1.4	6.3	20.6	24.3	12.9	13.3	112	9	4.5	30.9	6.6
59. Utilities-Electric	175.55	176.56	168.31	170.41	164.19	-.5	4.3	3.0	9.7	12.9	14.5	10	2	6.2	11.5	9.7
60. Utilities-Gas-Oth	321.52	324.96	326.62	309.11	310.55	-1.0	-1.5	4.0	7.2	15.0	25.3	70	-3	4.4	7.7	5.6

Source: Media General Financial Services, Inc., Richmond, VA.

MEDIA GENERAL P/E DISTRIBUTIONS BY MARKET (for week ended 06/30/95)

P/E Ratios Now
Rankings as of June 30, 1995

Stocks by P/E Ranking*	Composite		NYSE		ASE		OTC	
	Now	52 Weeks Ago	Now	52 Weeks Ago	Now	52 Weeks Ago	Now	52 Weeks Ago
Top 5%	50.5	51.4	40.5	49.3	60.7	48.4	53.6	52.4
10%	37.5	38.0	30.5	35.7	43.8	41.3	40.3	39.3
15%	30.4	30.8	26.3	29.3	35.5	33.6	33.0	31.6
20%	26.4	26.4	23.5	25.8	28.4	29.0	28.2	26.6
25%	23.4	23.7	21.0	23.0	23.5	24.6	25.0	23.8
30%	20.8	21.4	19.5	21.1	20.8	22.2	22.3	21.6
35%	19.2	19.4	18.4	19.2	19.4	19.0	19.9	19.7
40%	17.7	18.0	17.3	17.8	17.7	17.6	18.1	18.2
45%	16.6	16.7	16.4	16.8	16.8	16.0	16.7	16.8
50%	15.5	15.7	15.5	15.9	15.3	14.8	15.5	15.7
55%	14.5	14.7	14.8	14.9	13.7	14.0	14.4	14.7
60%	13.6	13.9	14.0	14.1	13.1	13.1	13.4	13.7
65%	12.9	13.0	13.3	13.5	12.1	12.6	12.6	12.9
70%	12.1	12.2	12.7	12.6	11.4	11.8	11.8	12.1
75%	11.3	11.4	11.8	11.7	10.4	10.8	11.1	11.3
80%	10.6	10.5	11.1	10.9	9.7	9.8	10.3	10.4
85%	9.7	9.6	10.4	10.1	8.8	9.1	9.4	9.4
90%	8.6	8.5	9.4	9.0	7.5	8.3	8.2	8.3
95%	6.8	7.1	7.6	7.4	5.8	6.8	6.6	6.9
No. of Companies	4,865	4,377	1,657	1,484	442	391	2,766	2,502

P/E Ratio Ranges	Composite		NYSE		ASE		OTC	
	Now	52 Weeks Ago	Now	52 Weeks Ago	Now	52 Weeks Ago	Now	52 Weeks Ago
0.1 to 1.9	.2%	.1%	.2%	.0%	.6%	.2%	.1%	.1%
2.0 to 2.9	.2	.1	.1	.1	.4	.1	.3	.1
3.0 to 3.9	.3	.2	.1	.1	.5	.4	.4	.2
4.0 to 4.9	.6	.6	.5	.5	.5	.7	.7	.6
5.0 to 5.9	.6	.7	.6	.8	.9	.6	.6	.6
6.0 to 6.9	1.1	.9	1.1	.9	1.6	.6	1.0	1.0
7.0 to 7.9	1.7	1.8	1.2	1.6	2.0	1.5	1.8	1.9
8.0 to 8.9	2.2	2.2	1.7	1.9	2.0	3.0	2.6	2.2
9.0 to 9.9	2.7	2.5	3.0	2.8	3.0	3.0	2.5	2.3
10.0 to 11.9	7.8	6.3	8.5	7.3	7.0	4.9	7.6	6.1
12.0 to 13.9	7.6	6.4	9.1	6.7	7.0	6.4	7.0	6.2
14.0 to 15.9	6.0	5.8	8.4	7.2	3.3	5.1	5.3	5.1
16.0 to 17.9	5.0	4.6	6.9	5.8	4.6	3.2	4.1	4.1
18.0 to 19.9	4.0	3.6	5.7	3.9	2.8	2.5	3.4	3.7
20.0 to 24.9	6.0	6.0	7.2	6.5	5.9	4.1	5.3	6.0
25.0 to 29.9	4.2	3.4	4.3	4.4	3.0	3.1	4.3	3.0
30.0 to 39.9	4.1	3.8	3.7	3.6	2.7	3.8	4.5	3.8
40.0 to 49.9	2.0	1.9	1.3	1.8	2.6	2.7	2.3	1.7
50.0 And Over	3.1	3.0	2.0	2.9	4.2	2.3	3.5	3.2
Cannot Calculate	40.3	46.3	34.3	41.2	45.4	51.7	42.6	48.1
No. of Companies	8,151		2,522		810		4,819	

*Excludes negative and zero earnings companies.

Source: Media General Financial Services, Inc., Richmond, VA.

U.S. Trade and Key Export Industries

U.S. Trade

U.S. TRADE IN GOODS AND SERVICES ($ Billion)

Year	EXPORTS			IMPORTS			TRADE BALANCE		
	Total	Goods	Services	Total	Goods	Services	Total	Goods	Services
1960	25.9	19.7	6.3	22.4	14.8	7.7	3.5	4.9	−1.4
1961	26.4	20.1	6.3	22.2	14.5	7.7	4.2	5.6	−1.4
1962	27.7	20.8	6.9	24.4	16.3	8.1	3.4	4.5	−1.2
1963	29.6	22.3	7.3	25.4	17.0	8.4	4.2	5.2	−1.0
1964	33.3	25.5	7.8	27.3	18.7	8.6	6.0	6.8	−0.8
1965	35.3	26.5	8.8	30.6	21.5	9.1	4.7	5.0	−0.3
1966	38.9	29.3	9.6	36.0	25.5	10.5	2.9	3.8	−0.9
1967	41.3	30.7	10.7	38.7	26.9	11.9	2.6	3.8	−1.2
1968	45.5	33.6	11.9	45.3	33.0	12.3	0.3	0.6	−0.4
1969	49.2	36.4	12.8	49.1	35.8	13.3	0.1	0.6	−0.5
1970	56.6	42.5	14.2	54.4	39.9	14.5	2.3	2.6	−0.3
1971	59.7	43.3	16.4	61.0	45.6	15.4	−1.3	−2.3	1.0
1972	67.2	49.4	17.8	72.7	55.8	16.9	−5.4	−6.4	1.0
1973	91.2	71.4	19.8	89.3	70.5	18.8	1.9	0.9	1.0
1974	120.9	98.3	22.6	125.2	103.8	21.4	−4.3	−5.5	1.2
1975	132.6	107.1	25.5	120.2	98.2	22.0	12.4	8.9	3.5
1976	142.7	114.7	28.0	148.8	124.2	24.6	−6.1	−9.5	3.4
1977	152.3	120.8	31.5	179.5	151.9	27.6	−27.2	−31.1	3.8
1978	178.4	142.1	36.4	208.2	176.0	32.2	−29.8	−33.9	4.2
1979	224.1	184.4	39.7	248.7	212.0	36.7	−24.6	−27.6	3.0
1980	271.8	224.3	47.6	291.2	249.8	41.5	−19.4	−25.5	6.1
1981	294.4	237.0	57.4	310.6	265.1	45.5	−16.2	−28.0	11.9
1982	275.2	211.2	64.1	299.4	247.6	51.7	−24.2	−36.5	12.3
1983	266.0	201.8	64.2	323.8	268.9	54.9	−57.8	−67.1	9.3
1984	290.9	219.9	71.0	400.1	332.4	67.7	−109.2	−112.5	3.3
1985	288.8	215.9	72.9	410.9	338.1	72.8	−122.1	−122.2	0.1
1986	309.5	223.3	86.1	448.3	368.4	79.8	−138.8	−145.1	6.3
1987	348.0	250.2	97.8	500.0	409.8	90.2	−152.0	−159.6	7.6
1988	430.2	320.2	110.0	545.0	447.2	97.9	−114.8	−127.0	12.1
1989	489.0	362.1	126.8	579.3	477.4	101.9	−90.3	−115.2	24.9
1990	537.6	389.3	148.3	616.0	498.3	117.7	−78.4	−109.0	30.7
1991	581.2	416.9	164.3	609.1	490.7	118.4	−27.9	−73.8	45.9
1992	616.9	440.4	176.6	657.3	536.5	120.9	−40.4	−96.1	55.7
1993	641.7	456.9	184.8	717.4	589.4	128.0	−75.7	−132.6	56.9
1994	696.4	502.8	193.6	804.5	669.1	135.4	−108.1	−166.3	58.2

Note: Balance of payments basis for goods reflects adjustments for timing, coverage, and valuation to the data compiled by the Census Bureau. The major adjustments concern military trade of U.S. defense agencies, additional nonmonetary gold transactions, and inland freight in Canada and Mexico. Goods valuation: f.a.s. for exports and customs value for imports. Data reflect all revisions through June 1994.

Source: Department of Commerce: Bureau of Economic Analysis, Bureau of the Census

Source: *U.S. Global Trade Outlook 1995–2000.* U.S. Department of Commerce.

TOP 50 PARTNERS IN TOTAL U.S. TRADE IN GOODS, 1988–94 ($ Million)

Country	1988	1989	1990	1991	1992	1993	1994
Canada	153,020	166,762	175,054	176,214	189,224	211,661	243,389
Japan	127,244	138,046	138,264	139,636	145,227	155,138	172,630
Mexico	43,888	52,144	58,436	64,407	75,803	81,499	100,303
United Kingdom	36,341	39,156	43,679	40,459	42,893	48,168	51,896
Germany	40,929	41,927	46,922	47,439	50,069	47,494	50,986
China	13,532	17,745	20,044	25,247	33,146	40,303	48,068
Taiwan	36,843	35,647	34,157	36,205	39,846	41,269	43,789
South Korea	31,337	33,195	32,889	32,523	31,321	31,900	37,686
France	22,478	24,593	26,818	28,679	29,390	28,546	30,397
Singapore	13,741	16,347	17,823	18,760	20,938	24,476	28,382
Italy	18,351	19,148	20,743	20,334	21,036	19,679	21,904
Hong Kong	15,925	16,014	16,438	17,416	18,870	19,428	21,143
Malaysia	5,833	7,614	8,697	10,001	12,657	16,627	20,942
Netherlands	14,675	16,174	17,974	18,322	19,052	18,282	19,606
Belgium/Luxembourg	11,904	13,077	15,036	14,906	14,749	14,841	17,286
Brazil	13,561	13,214	12,946	12,865	13,360	13,537	16,826
Thailand	5,172	6,668	8,284	9,875	11,518	12,308	15,168
Saudi Arabia	9,396	10,731	14,070	17,457	17,538	14,369	13,697
Australia	10,514	12,204	12,984	12,392	12,563	11,574	12,901
Venezuela	9,769	9,796	12,588	12,835	13,625	12,730	12,420
Switzerland	8,808	9,626	10,530	11,133	10,185	12,779	11,990
Israel (including Gaza)	6,216	6,067	6,517	7,395	7,893	8,849	10,229
Philippines	4,545	5,270	5,855	5,736	7,113	8,423	9,608
Indonesia	4,209	4,775	5,238	5,132	7,309	8,206	9,334
Spain	7,419	8,113	8,524	8,322	8,539	7,160	8,179
India	5,440	5,772	5,683	5,192	5,697	7,332	7,598
Sweden	7,684	8,030	8,342	7,811	7,561	6,887	7,564
Colombia	3,915	4,479	5,197	4,688	6,123	6,266	7,242
Ireland	3,558	4,048	4,295	4,628	5,124	5,248	6,306
Argentina	2,490	2,430	2,690	3,332	4,479	4,981	6,191
Dominican Republic	2,769	3,291	3,407	3,750	4,472	5,021	5,894
Russia	(NA)	(NA)	(NA)	(NA)	2,594	4,714	5,814
Nigeria	3,635	5,774	6,535	6,000	6,104	6,196	4,939
Chile	2,247	2,707	2,977	3,141	3,854	4,061	4,598
Turkey	2,829	3,375	3,426	3,473	3,845	4,626	4,329
South Africa	3,200	3,190	3,429	3,841	4,161	4,033	4,203
Norway	2,375	3,028	3,111	3,112	3,248	3,170	3,641
Costa Rica	1,470	1,844	1,991	2,187	2,768	3,084	3,513
Egypt	2,553	2,838	2,647	2,926	3,523	3,381	3,392
Denmark	2,633	2,586	2,989	3,235	3,140	2,756	3,337
Austria	1,821	2,008	2,193	2,319	2,563	2,736	3,122
New Zealand	2,101	2,326	2,332	2,216	2,525	2,456	2,929
Ecuador	1,909	2,117	2,054	2,275	2,343	2,499	2,923
Finland	1,964	2,339	2,388	2,037	1,970	2,456	2,872
Algeria	2,544	2,585	3,577	2,829	2,274	2,521	2,716
Guatemala	1,023	1,270	1,558	1,844	2,286	2,507	2,638
Kuwait	1,147	1,826	972	1,264	1,618	2,818	2,620
Angola	1,317	2,025	2,056	1,961	2,460	2,266	2,258
Peru	1,453	1,509	1,574	1,616	1,743	1,826	2,248
Honduras	917	976	1,055	1,182	1,593	1,813	2,109

NA Not available

Note: Census basis; f.a.s. for exports and customs value for imports

Source: Department of Commerce, Bureau of the Census

Source: *U.S. Global Trade Outlook 1995–2000*. U.S. Department of Commerce.

TOP 50 PURCHASERS OF U.S. GOODS EXPORTS, 1988–94 ($ Million)

Country	1988	1989	1990	1991	1992	1993	1994
Canada	71,622	78,809	83,674	85,150	90,594	100,444	114,441
Japan	37,725	44,494	48,580	48,125	47,813	47,891	53,481
Mexico	20,628	24,982	28,279	33,277	40,592	41,581	50,840
United Kingdom	18,364	20,837	23,490	22,046	22,800	26,438	26,833
Germany	14,457	16,956	18,760	21,302	21,249	18,932	19,237
South Korea	11,232	13,459	14,404	15,505	14,639	14,782	18,028
Taiwan	12,129	11,335	11,491	13,182	15,250	16,168	17,078
France	9,970	11,579	13,664	15,345	14,593	13,267	13,622
Netherlands	10,117	11,364	13,022	13,511	13,752	12,839	13,591
Singapore	5,768	7,344	8,023	8,804	9,626	11,678	13,022
Hong Kong	5,687	6,291	6,817	8,137	9,077	9,874	11,445
Belgium/Luxembourg	7,410	8,522	10,451	10,789	10,047	9,439	10,944
Australia	6,973	8,331	8,538	8,404	8,876	8,276	9,781
China	5,021	5,755	4,806	6,278	7,418	8,763	9,287
Brazil	4,266	4,804	5,048	6,148	5,751	6,058	8,118
Italy	6,775	7,215	7,992	8,570	8,721	6,464	7,193
Malaysia	2,141	2,870	3,425	3,900	4,363	6,064	6,965
Saudi Arabia	3,776	3,574	4,049	6,557	7,167	6,661	6,010
Switzerland	4,196	4,911	4,943	5,557	4,540	6,806	5,614
Israel (including Gaza)	3,244	2,828	3,203	3,911	4,077	4,429	5,006
Thailand	1,962	2,288	2,995	3,753	3,989	3,766	4,861
Spain	4,215	4,796	5,213	5,474	5,537	4,168	4,625
Argentina	1,054	1,039	1,179	2,045	3,223	3,776	4,466
Colombia	1,754	1,924	2,029	1,952	3,286	3,235	4,070
Venezuela	4,612	3,025	3,108	4,656	5,444	4,590	4,042
Philippines	1,878	2,202	2,471	2,265	2,759	3,529	3,888
Ireland	2,183	2,483	2,540	2,681	2,862	2,728	3,416
Egypt	2,332	2,612	2,249	2,720	3,088	2,768	2,844
Indonesia	1,059	1,247	1,897	1,891	2,779	2,770	2,811
Dominican Republic	1,359	1,645	1,656	1,743	2,100	2,350	2,800
Chile	1,066	1,414	1,664	1,839	2,466	2,599	2,776
Turkey	1,850	2,003	2,243	2,467	2,735	3,429	2,754
Russia	(NA)	(NA)	(NA)	(NA)	2,112	2,970	2,579
Sweden	2,700	3,138	3,405	3,287	2,845	2,354	2,520
India	2,500	2,458	2,486	1,999	1,917	2,778	2,296
South Africa	1,688	1,659	1,732	2,113	2,434	2,188	2,173
Costa Rica	696	882	986	1,034	1,357	1,542	1,867
United Arab Emirates	705	1,238	1,004	1,455	1,553	1,811	1,593
New Zealand	940	1,117	1,135	1,007	1,307	1,249	1,508
Peru	795	695	772	840	1,005	1,072	1,408
Austria	746	873	875	1,056	1,256	1,326	1,373
Guatemala	590	662	763	945	1,205	1,312	1,355
Panama	637	723	869	978	1,103	1,187	1,276
Norway	929	1,037	1,281	1,489	1,279	1,212	1,268
Denmark	969	1,051	1,311	1,574	1,473	1,092	1,215
Ecuador	681	643	678	948	999	1,100	1,196
Algeria	730	756	951	727	688	938	1,191
Kuwait	683	853	403	1,228	1,337	999	1,175
Finland	761	969	1,126	952	785	848	1,069
Jamaica	762	1,006	943	961	938	1,116	1,066

NA Not available

Note: Census basis; f.a.s. for exports and customs value for imports

Source: Department of Commerce, Bureau of the Census

Source: *U.S. Global Trade Outlook 1995–2000.* U.S. Department of Commerce.

U.S. Trade and Key Export Industries

TOP 50 SUPPLIERS OF U.S. GOODS IMPORTS, 1988–94 ($ Million)

Country	1988	1989	1990	1991	1992	1993	1994
Canada	81,398	87,953	91,380	91,064	98,630	111,216	128,948
Japan	89,519	93,553	89,684	91,511	97,414	107,246	119,149
Mexico	23,260	27,162	30,157	31,130	35,211	39,917	49,493
China	8,511	11,990	15,237	18,969	25,728	31,540	38,781
Germany	26,472	24,971	28,162	26,137	28,820	28,562	31,749
Taiwan	24,714	24,313	22,666	23,023	24,596	25,101	26,711
United Kingdom	17,976	18,319	20,188	18,413	20,093	21,730	25,063
South Korea	20,105	19,737	18,485	17,018	16,682	17,118	19,658
France	12,508	13,014	13,153	13,333	14,797	15,279	16,775
Singapore	7,973	9,003	9,800	9,957	11,313	12,798	15,360
Italy	11,576	11,933	12,751	11,764	12,314	13,216	14,711
Malaysia	3,692	4,744	5,272	6,101	8,294	10,563	13,977
Thailand	3,210	4,379	5,289	6,122	7,529	8,542	10,307
Hong Kong	10,238	9,722	9,622	9,279	9,793	9,554	9,698
Brazil	9,294	8,410	7,898	6,717	7,609	7,479	8,708
Venezuela	5,157	6,771	9,480	8,179	8,181	8,140	8,378
Saudi Arabia	5,620	7,157	10,021	10,900	10,371	7,708	7,687
Indonesia	3,150	3,529	3,341	3,241	4,529	5,435	6,523
Switzerland	4,611	4,714	5,587	5,576	5,645	5,973	6,376
Belgium/Luxembourg	4,493	4,555	4,585	4,117	4,703	5,402	6,342
Netherlands	4,559	4,810	4,952	4,811	5,300	5,443	6,015
Philippines	2,666	3,068	3,384	3,471	4,355	4,894	5,720
India	2,940	3,314	3,197	3,192	3,780	4,554	5,302
Israel (including Gaza)	2,972	3,239	3,313	3,484	3,815	4,420	5,223
Sweden	4,985	4,892	4,937	4,524	4,716	4,534	5,044
Nigeria	3,278	5,284	5,982	5,168	5,103	5,301	4,430
Spain	3,204	3,317	3,311	2,848	3,002	2,992	3,554
Russia	(NA)	(NA)	(NA)	(NA)	481	1,743	3,235
Colombia	2,161	2,555	3,168	2,736	2,837	3,032	3,172
Australia	3,541	3,873	4,447	3,988	3,688	3,297	3,120
Dominican Republic	1,410	1,646	1,752	2,008	2,373	2,672	3,094
Ireland	1,375	1,566	1,755	1,948	2,262	2,519	2,890
Norway	1,446	1,991	1,830	1,624	1,969	1,958	2,373
Denmark	1,664	1,535	1,678	1,661	1,667	1,664	2,122
Angola	1,216	1,928	1,904	1,775	2,303	2,092	2,061
South Africa	1,513	1,531	1,697	1,728	1,727	1,845	2,030
Chile	1,181	1,292	1,313	1,302	1,388	1,462	1,822
Finland	1,203	1,370	1,262	1,085	1,185	1,608	1,803
Austria	1,074	1,135	1,318	1,264	1,307	1,411	1,749
Ecuador	1,228	1,474	1,376	1,327	1,344	1,399	1,727
Argentina	1,436	1,391	1,511	1,287	1,256	1,206	1,725
Costa Rica	774	962	1,005	1,154	1,412	1,541	1,646
Turkey	979	1,371	1,182	1,006	1,110	1,198	1,575
Algeria	1,814	1,829	2,626	2,103	1,586	1,583	1,525
Kuwait	464	973	569	36	281	1,818	1,445
New Zealand	1,161	1,209	1,197	1,209	1,218	1,208	1,421
Guatemala	433	609	794	899	1,081	1,194	1,283
Gabon	173	437	701	712	921	961	1,155
Trinidad and Tobago	719	768	1,020	866	848	803	1,109
Honduras	441	461	491	557	782	914	1,097

NA Not available

Note: Census basis; f.a.s. for exports and customs value for imports

Source: Department of Commerce, Bureau of the Census

Source: *U.S. Global Trade Outlook 1995–2000.* U.S. Department of Commerce.

Key Export Industries

Automotive Parts

SUMMARY

The U.S. automotive parts industry is emerging from a massive restructuring that has enabled it to greatly strengthen its competitive position in relation to Japan, its major rival. Since 1987, productivity has increased about 3 percent annually, helping the industry narrow the cost gap with the Japanese, and quality has improved greatly. This enhanced competitive stance will be tested as U.S. automotive parts suppliers attempt to position themselves globally to meet the changing international sourcing strategies of automakers. The U.S. parts industry will be further challenged by its customers' demands for continued cost cuts and quality improvements, and by foreign—mainly Japanese—competition.

U.S. automotive parts exports have grown 16 percent annually from 1989 to 1994, to $37.1 billion. However, the trade deficit ($7 billion in 1994) remains a major problem, primarily because of the large and growing value of imports from Japan and lack of access to the Japanese market for foreign producers. The global automotive parts market will total about $460 billion in 1995 and an estimated $519 billion in 2000. Growth in mature major markets is expected to average less than 2 percent annually, so the biggest opportunities for U.S. exporters will be in the fast-growing markets in Asia and Latin America.

The U.S. automotive parts industry, as defined here, comprises manufacturers of automotive stampings; carburetors, pistons, piston rings, and valves; vehicular lighting equipment; storage batteries; engine electrical equipment; and other motor vehicle parts and accessories.[1]

Critical Issues

During the late 1980s, the U.S. industry underwent a massive restructuring, greatly narrowing cost, quality, and productivity gaps with Japan, its major competitor in

Source: *U.S. Global Trade Outlook 1995–2000*, U.S. Department of Commerce.

The *U.S. Global Trade Outlook 1995–2000* contains more complete discussions of the industries excerpted for the *Almanac*.

[1] Based on Standard Industrial Classification (SIC) codes 3465, 3592, 3647, 3691, 3694, and 3714.

U.S. FOREIGN TRADE

The U.S. is top exporter and importer

Value ($ Billion)

		1989	1993	1994
World	Exports	17.5	33.5	37.1
	Imports	32.0	38.3	44.9
Canada	Exports	9.8	18.3	20.1
	Imports	9.4	10.3	11.3
Mexico	Exports	3.3	7.3	7.7
	Imports	4.5	7.4	9.7
Japan	Exports	0.6	1.1	1.5
	Imports	10.6	12.3	14.3
Germany	Exports	0.4	0.8	0.8
	Imports	1.9	2.0	2.2
UK	Exports	0.4	0.6	0.7
	Imports	0.6	0.5	0.6
BEMs	Exports	0.6	1.4	2.0
(less Mexico)	Imports	2.4	2.7	3.2
Rest of	Exports	2.3	3.9	4.4
World	Imports	2.6	3.1	3.6

Average Annual Percent Change

		1989–93	1993–94
World	Exports	17.7	11.0
	Imports	4.6	17.1
Canada	Exports	16.8	9.9
	Imports	2.4	9.5
Mexico	Exports	21.9	4.7
	Imports	13.3	31.9
Japan	Exports	16.2	31.4
	Imports	3.9	16.2
Germany	Exports	17.7	6.2
	Imports	1.4	10.4
UK	Exports	7.3	10.1
	Imports	−5.2	11.0
BEMs	Exports	25.5	39.8
(less Mexico)	Imports	3.0	18.1
Rest of	Exports	14.7	12.5
World	Imports	4.1	15.3

Sources: U.S. Department of Commerce: Bureau of the Census; International Trade Administration (ITA). United Nations.
Note: Exports are total f.a.s. Imports are customs value.

world markets. In 1994 the industry's remaining 4,500 firms produced a record $113 billion worth of automotive parts while having only about 565,000 employees; further downsizing is expected. The industry will be challenged to continue cost and quality improvements, withstand foreign—mainly Japanese—competition, and go global with its customers.

Going Global Without Going Bust

More competition at home and the increasing globalization of the U.S. motor vehicle industry are driving competitive U.S. automotive parts suppliers toward the world market to gain more business. To comply with the global sourcing strategies of automakers, U.S. suppliers must not only continually adjust their manufacturing capabilities and product lines to increase export sales, but they must also increase their manufacturing presence in foreign markets. Although the major U.S. automotive parts manufacturers have long had a substantial presence in the European, Canadian, and Mexican markets, many U.S. suppliers are increasing their role in these and other markets through acquisitions and mergers to capitalize on opportunities there.

An effective global strategy must take into account the increasingly stringent requirements of U.S. automakers, who began demanding significant annual cost cuts and quality improvements from their suppliers in the early 1990s. U.S. suppliers have to continually refine their operations to meet these requirements. Many suppliers are finding that they are hitting a wall of diminishing returns: Each additional improvement is becoming increasingly more difficult to attain, so profit levels are growing more slowly. Suppliers must juggle the costs of staying competitive with the costs and risks of going global, picking the right mix of products and customers in both the U.S. and foreign markets.

Japanese Competition Will Continue

Competition from the Japanese automotive industry and its parts suppliers was the primary impetus behind the restructuring of the U.S. industry. Their practices forced the Big Three U.S. manufacturers (General Motors, Ford, and Chrysler) to put pressure on the U.S. parts industry to improve quality and productivity. This will continue to be a key challenge in the coming years. Until recently, almost all U.S.-based Japanese automotive parts firms supplied U.S.-based Japanese automakers, with only a few shipping to the Big Three. However, as financial pressures have loosened the ties between Japanese automakers and their U.S.-based affili-ated suppliers, many of these parts producers have begun to solicit more business from the Big Three. These financial pressures also are forcing parts manufacturers in Japan to achieve dramatic cost reductions. This process may chisel away at the cost advantage U.S. manufacturers now have over imported Japanese parts due to the strong yen.

Competitiveness in World Markets

Leading U.S. automotive parts firms now have adopted manufacturing processes and products—such as agile production and parts commonization—that make them better able to compete in the global marketplace. In addition, many manufacturers are now able to finance and perform functions, including product design, prototyping, and testing, previously performed by automakers, allowing the latter to focus more of their resources on global design and product management.

U.S. Advantages

In recent years competition in the major automotive markets has become increasingly technology-based, aimed at meeting higher environmental, fuel efficiency, and safety standards. The U.S. industry is a world leader in high-tech systems—such as antilock brakes, air bags, emissions control, and engine management—giving it an important advantage as foreign governments adopt more stringent standards. The Clinton Administration's Partnership for a New Generation of Vehicles (the "clean car") is designed to spur technological breakthroughs in components and systems that could possess outstanding export potential.

Competitive Challenges and Obstacles

The U.S. industry is likely to continue to face global competitive challenges from recently restructured, leaner firms in Japan and Western Europe. Japan, which already has significant investment in the U.S. industry, has important investments and influence in the Asia-Pacific region. The European automotive parts industry has plans to expand its international presence in Eastern Europe and the Asia-Pacific region.

U.S. competitiveness in foreign markets has been adversely affected by tariff and nontariff barriers. U.S. access to Japan's automotive parts market, the world's second-largest, is restricted by various regulations and business practices. The majority of emerging markets levy high, often prohibitive, tariffs (20 to 100 percent) on imported automotive parts, as well as other taxes. The GATT Uruguay Round did not significantly lower tariffs in these markets, although many countries agreed on tariff ceilings. Many developing countries also have systems of nontariff barriers, including local content and investment requirements, discriminatory tax treatment, and preferential treatment of locally based foreign firms. These measures impede U.S. trade and investment in these markets.—*Mary Ann Slater, Office of Automotive Affairs, 202-482-1420, March 1995.*

REFERENCES

U.S. Automotive Parts Trade Statistics (quarterly), U.S. Department of Commerce, Office of Automotive Affairs, Washington, DC 20230, 202-482-1418.

Automotive News, Crain Communications Inc., 965 E. Jefferson, Detroit, MI 48207-3185, 800-678-9595.

Automotive Parts and Accessories Association, 4600 East-West Highway, Third Floor, Bethesda, MD 20814, 301-654-6664.

The Autoparts Report, International Trade Services, P.O. Box 5950, Bethesda, MD 20824-5950, 301-857-8454.

Global Automotive Review and Outlook (monthly), Global Automotive Information Services, 4813 Pelican Way, West Bloomfield, MI 48323, 810-683-2686.

Motor and Equipment Manufacturers Association, P.O. Box 13966, Research Triangle Park, NC 27709-3966, 919-549-4800.

Ward's Automotive Reports (weekly); *Ward's Automotive International* (bimonthly); and *Ward's Automotive Yearbook,* Ward's Communications, Suite 2750, 3000 Town Center, Southfield, MI 48075, 313-962-4433.

World Automotive Outlook, 1994–2000, 1994, AutoFacts International, 1595 Paoli Pike, West Chester, PA 19380, 215-429-9900.

World Motor Vehicle Data 1994 (annual), American Automobile Manufacturers Association, Suite 900, 1401 H St., NW, Washington, DC 20005, 202-326-5500.

Computer Equipment

SUMMARY

The U.S. computer equipment industry (producing computer systems, peripherals, and parts) controls more than 75 percent of the world computer market through its global operations. Continuously declining computer prices, steadily rising performance, and increasingly sophisticated uses have all stimulated domestic sales and exports. Yet the ever-accelerating tempo of technical change and product introductions has raised the costs and complexity of research and product development. The industry's operations have become more global, and companies have formed domestic and foreign alliances to ensure that the lowest-cost components and latest technology are available.

The computer equipment industry suffered a slight erosion in its world export market share during the early 1990s, and a traditionally strong U.S. trade surplus turned into a deficit. Imports rose almost three times faster than exports, which grew at a moderate rate of 5.8 percent annually from 1989 to 1993. U.S. exports were $34.6 billion—about 13 percent higher—in 1994, and should increase 8 percent in 1995 and then nearly 7 percent a year through 2000, to $52 billion. Recovery in Western Europe and Japan and robust growth in the rapidly expanding markets of Asia and Latin America will boost U.S. exports. Some of the fastest U.S export growth will be in the Big Emerging Markets (BEMs), particularly India and China.

The $60 billion U.S.-based industry encompasses electronic computer systems, peripherals, and parts. Electronic computer systems include digital computers of all sizes, from supercomputers to handheld portables, as well as computer kits assembled by the purchaser. Peripherals are storage devices, terminals, printers, plotters, graphics displays, and other input/output equipment.

Critical Issues

Expansion of U.S. Operations Overseas

The U.S computer industry continues to become increasingly global in nature, entering and expanding in fast-growing markets around the world. Annual investment of U.S. firms in overseas operations has averaged more than $21 billion since 1990. A significant portion of this investment went to the European Union (EU) because of that market's progress toward unification and its growing importance. Spending in Asia also

U.S. FOREIGN TRADE

Canada and Japan remain our largest markets

Value ($ Billion)

		1989	1993	1994
World	Exports	24.5	30.7	34.6
	Imports	21.7	38.7	46.9
Canada	Exports	2.8	4.9	5.6
	Imports	1.5	2.3	3.2
Japan	Exports	3.2	3.3	3.8
	Imports	8.6	13.0	15.0
UK	Exports	3.1	3.0	3.6
	Imports	0.6	1.0	1.2
Germany	Exports	2.5	2.7	2.6
	Imports	0.4	0.6	0.7
Netherlands	Exports	1.6	2.3	2.1
	Imports	0.1	0.1	0.1
BEMs	Exports	3.1	4.9	6.0
	Imports	5.4	10.3	12.3
Rest of World	Exports	8.2	9.6	10.9
	Imports	5.1	11.4	14.4

Average Annual Percent Change

		1989–93	1993–94
World	Exports	5.8	12.7
	Imports	15.6	21.2
Canada	Exports	15.0	14.3
	Imports	11.3	39.1
Japan	Exports	0.8	15.2
	Imports	10.9	15.4
UK	Exports	−0.8	20.0
	Imports	13.6	20.0
Germany	Exports	1.9	−3.7
	Imports	10.7	16.7
Netherlands	Exports	9.5	−8.7
	Imports	—	—
BEMs	Exports	12.1	22.4
	Imports	17.2	19.4
Rest of World	Exports	4.0	13.5
	Imports	22.3	26.3

Sources: U.S. Department of Commerce: Bureau of the Census; International Trade Administration (ITA). United Nations.
Note: Exports are total f.a.s. Imports are customs value.

has risen, as suppliers establish manufacturing operations to serve burgeoning markets in China and South Korea, and to benefit from lower labor rates. Another major factor in the industry's globalization has been the attempt to circumvent tariff and nontariff barriers in many countries.

In response to mounting costs of performing R&D in several component and systems-level technologies and of establishing new manufacturing plants, U.S. computer firms and foreign partners will continue current practices and seek to form strategic alliances during the 1990s. The purpose of these alliances ranges from cooperating on and sharing advanced technologies to jointly developing, manufacturing, and marketing products (Table 1).

Competitiveness in World Markets

U.S. computer firms are price and performance leaders and occupy the foremost position in the relentless drive for higher performance at lower cost. Small computer systems, such as personal computers and workstations, have become extremely sensitive to price and technological factors. In addition, suppliers have shortened product life cycles from several years to as little as nine months. During 1994, the pace continued unabated. The average retail price of personal computers dropped below $2,000, but these computer systems are now equipped with processing and storage capabilities that surpass those of more expensive systems five years ago.

U.S. suppliers producing all types of computer systems draw on strengths in research, design, software development, marketing, and customer support to maintain their lead in the world marketplace. Other factors that contribute to U.S. competitiveness include favorable exchange rates (vis-a-vis the Japanese yen, for instance) and improved protection of intellectual property rights in key foreign markets. The U.S. industry has a

trade deficit despite these favorable competitive factors because of its global sourcing strategies, including the production of peripherals and parts in Asia.

Japan Remains Competitive

Japanese firms pose the strongest challenge to the U.S. computer equipment industry. Building upon a solid base in semiconductors and other enabling technologies, they have succeeded in reaching parity with U.S. firms across a wide range of products, especially computer peripherals. However, this strength has been largely confined to the Japanese market and has not resulted in many exports of computer systems, an area in which Japan is not competitive internationally.

Japanese companies' profit margins have rapidly diminished as equipment has become more commodity-like. They were late to recognize the shifts in the international marketplace from proprietary mainframes to smaller, more open systems. Most of the leading Japanese suppliers reported declines in their 1993 domestic and export sales.

The Western European computer industry has lagged far behind its U.S. and Japanese competitors in technological capability and market share. It has lost money and has been forced to undergo painful restructuring accompanied by major layoffs. The major European firms have increasingly come to rely on technology linkages with U.S. and Japanese companies.

Many foreign governments continue to pursue restrictive trade and investment policies that adversely affect U.S. exports by limiting imports. Many governments nurture domestic computer industries through such measures as support for R&D, "buy national" procurement policies, low-interest financing, export subsidies, and tied aid. They also erect tariff and nontariff barriers to protect local suppliers and force the transfer of technology. Such policies often distort trade by

TABLE 1   MAJOR COMPUTER ALLIANCES BETWEEN U.S. AND FOREIGN FIRMS

	U.S. Firm	Foreign Partner	Product Area
Joint Developments	Apple	Sharp (Japan)	Palmtop PC
	EO	Olivetti (Italy)	Handheld PC
	Hewlett-Packard	Hitachi (Japan)	Workstation Microprocessor
	IBM	NEC (Japan)	Operating System
Distribution Agreements	Convex	NK EXA (Japan)	Minisupercomputer
	Hewlett-Packard	Oki (Japan)	Workstation
	IBM	Canon (Japan)	Notebook PC
	IBM	Mitsubishi (Japan)	Mainframe

Sources: Department of Commerce; Dataquest

limiting competition and slowing innovation. Over time, users in these countries end up with products with higher prices and outdated technologies. Brazil is a typical example of this—it built a domestic computer industry starting in the early 1980s through its Informatics Policy.—*Tim Miles, Office of Computers and Business Equipment, 202-482-2990, March 1995.*

REFERENCES

Best Market Reports, 1994, Computers and Peripherals, U.S. Department of Commerce, National Trade Data Bank, Office of Business Analysis, Washington, DC 20230, 202-482-1405.

Tariffs and Other Taxes on Computer Hardware and Software, U.S. Department of Commerce, Office of Computers and Business Equipment, Washington, DC 20230, 202-482-0571.

Computer and Business Equipment Manufacturers Association, 311 First St., NW, Suite 500, Washington, DC 20001, 202-626-5730.

"Computer and Office Equipment," *Panorama of EC Industry 94,* European Commission, Luxembourg, 1994.

Datamation, 275 Washington St., Newton, MA 02158, 617-964-3030.

Dataquest, Inc., 1290 Ridder Park Dr., San Jose, CA 95131, 408-437-8000.

Electronic Business, 275 Washington St., Newton, MA 02158-1630, 617-964-3030.

Electronic Engineering Times, 600 Community Dr., Manhasset, NY 11030, 516-562-5000.

Gartner Group, Inc., 56 Top Gallant Rd., Stamford, CT 06904, 203-967-6752.

"The Information Revolution 1994," *Business Week,* McGraw-Hill, Inc., 1221 Avenue of the Americas, New York, NY 10020, 212-512-2000.

International Data Corporation, 5 Speen St., Framingham, MA 01701, 800-343-4952.

"Unleashing the Power," *The Wall Street Journal,* June 27, 1994, 200 Liberty St., New York, NY 10281, 212-416-2000.

"Wired for What?," *Wilson Quarterly,* Summer 1994, 901 D St., SW, Suite 704, Washington, DC 20024, 202-287-3000.

Computer Software

SUMMARY

U.S. software vendors were the leading suppliers of the $77 billion packaged software market in 1994. U.S. vendors' future competitiveness depends on several critical policy and technical issues, the most significant of which is the level of protection of intellectual property rights worldwide. U.S. software suppliers will also face challenges stemming from the emergence of multimedia technologies, the growing importance of services and electronic commerce, lingering export restrictions, and more suppliers around the world. Up-to-date market information and export assistance will be essential for the industry's many small- and medium-sized firms to take full advantage of export opportunities.

The near-term outlook for the packaged software market remains bright. According to International Data Corporation, the world market for packaged software will increase from $86 billion in 1995 to $153 billion in 2000. Asia (including Japan) and Latin America will be the fastest-growing markets for packaged software during this period, reaching $19 billion and $4 billion, respectively, in 2000. The markets in Western Europe will expand more slowly, but will still reach $45 billion in 2000.

The $77 billion world market for packaged software comprises application tools, application solutions, and systems software and utilities. U.S. vendors have the largest share in systems and utilities software, which includes operating systems, operating system enhancements, and data center management software (automated operations programs, for instance). U.S. firms also supply the lion's share of the world markets for application tools and application solutions. Application tools include data management/design software; application solutions encompass software specific to industries (such as banking) or functions (such as payroll and accounting). The United States and Europe are the largest markets.

Critical Issues

Intellectual Property Rights

Vigorous protection of intellectual property rights (IPR—which include patents, copyrights, trademarks, trade secrets, and semiconductor mask works) is critical to trade in software. Although many countries have improved their IPR practices in recent years, the Business Software Alliance, an industry trade association, estimates that piracy deprived software developers of about $13 billion in worldwide revenues in 1993 (Figure 1).

The level of IPR protection varies by country. In its annual Special 301 review of the IPR policies and IPR-related market-access practices of U.S. trading partners, the U.S. Trade Representative (USTR) identified 27 countries that deny adequate and effective IPR protection. In June 1994, USTR designated China a "priority foreign country"; seven countries and one regional grouping were put on the "priority watch list"; and

FIGURE 1 LOSSES DUE TO SOFTWARE PIRACY, 1993

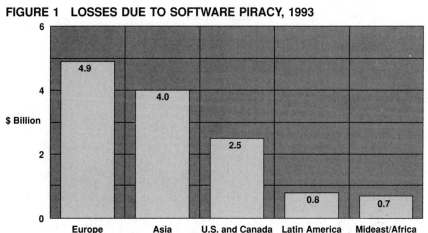

Source: Business Software Alliance

18 countries were placed on the "watch list" (Figure 2). The U.S. government has been working with these countries to improve their IPR policies and practices. In February 1995, USTR revoked China's designation as a priority foreign country after reaching agreement on IPR enforcement. Implementation of the Uruguay Round's Agreement on the Trade-Related Aspects of Intellectual Property, or TRIPs, will help reduce the incidence of piracy. TRIPs will protect software as a literary work for a minimum of 50 years and provide an exclusive rental right for the owners of computer programs.

FIGURE 2   RESULTS OF U.S. REVIEW OF IPR PRACTICES

Priority Watch List	Watch List
Argentina	Australia
European Union	Chile
Greece	Colombia
India	Cyprus
Japan	Egypt
Saudi Arabia	El Salvador
South Korea	Guatemala
Turkey	Indonesia
	Italy
	Pakistan
	Peru
	Philippines
	Poland
	Spain
	Taiwan
	Thailand
	United Arab Emirates
	Venezuela

Source: U.S. Trade Representative, as of February 1995

Rapidly Changing Market Challenges U.S. Firms

Several trends will substantially alter the nature of the packaged software industry in the years ahead. The emergence of multimedia products, which combine video, animation, pictures, voice, music, graphics, and text, will blur the lines between formerly distinct products and industries. The international alliances that dominate this nascent field are an indication that multimedia products will be developed globally. Electronic commerce and online distribution will expand product areas, speed product dissemination and updates, and change distribution methods. U.S. companies will need to adapt to these developments to remain competitive.

Offshore programming and the development of strong software industries elsewhere will continue. While the United States will remain a principal site for software development, some U.S. firms are taking advantage of lower labor costs by using programmers in India, Russia, and other countries. This practice is encouraged by governments seeking to develop strong indigenous software industries. The growing importance of software support services, such as training and network implementation, also favors local vendors.

U.S. firms will need up-to-date information on exporting, readily available export financing, and fewer export restrictions (particularly on security features for data transmission) to capitalize on their technological strengths in the international market. If these measures are available, many small- and medium-sized U.S. packaged software firms may overcome their reluctance to export.

Competitiveness in World Markets

United States Is Leader

U.S. vendors lead the world in packaged software development (Table 1). According to IDC, U.S. vendors supplied 75 percent of the $70 billion world packaged software market in 1993—91 percent of the $21 billion systems software market, 77 percent of the $20 billion application tools market, and 63 percent of the $29 billion application solutions market. Of the world's top 10 software suppliers, six were American.

TABLE 1   PACKAGED SOFTWARE MARKETS, 1993–2000 ($ Million)

Item	1993	1994	1995	2000
World	69,918	77,416	86,060	152,816
United States	31,400	35,600	40,000	74,263
Western Europe[1]	24,703	26,563	28,970	45,243
Japan	7,008	7,499	8,365	14,562
Canada	1,276	1,457	1,613	2,694
Australia	1,044	1,183	1,345	2,551
Latin America[2]	1,640	1,770	1,840	4,250
Asia[3]	1,079	1,334	1,647	4,786
Other	1,768	2,010	2,279	4,466

[1] Austria, Belgium, Denmark, Finland, France, Germany, Italy, Greece, Ireland, Netherlands, Norway, Portugal, Spain, Sweden, Switzerland, and United Kingdom; [2] Argentina, Brazil, Chile, Mexico, and Venezuela; [3] China, Hong Kong, India, Malaysia, Singapore, South Korea, Taiwan, and Thailand
Source: International Data Corporation

U.S. packaged software vendors dominate in each region. They supplied 63 percent of the Western European market and 54 percent of the Japanese market, regions where domestic suppliers traditionally hold stronger positions. They hold the largest market share in countries outside Western Europe and Japan, supplying 73 percent of these markets. The strong U.S. position in these countries (generally in Asia and Latin America) reflects the high quality of and receptivity to U.S. software, and the relatively small international presence of European and Japanese software vendors.

U.S. Technological Advantages

Several factors contribute to the competitive strength of the U.S. industry. Foremost is the leading role U.S. vendors played in developing the software industry. This has given U.S. firms a technological edge and made the United States the locus of high-quality, innovative software development. The size and sophistication of the U.S. market also contributed to the competitiveness of U.S. vendors, resulting in a variety of niche products, a great number of firms, and intense competition.

Competition from Europe and Japan

The principal competition to U.S. vendors comes from companies in Japan and Western Europe. Three Japanese firms and one European firm are among the world's top 10 software suppliers. Competition is strongest within Japan and Europe. For different reasons, Japanese and European software suppliers have little international presence. European software suppliers generally specialize in custom software and services. Japanese suppliers are typically aligned with major Japanese hardware vendors and concentrate on the domestic market. Software suppliers from other countries, such as China, India, and Brazil, will likely grow in influence in the coming years. However, they now trail U.S., Japanese, and European vendors in technological innovation.—*Mary Smolenski, Office of Computers and Business Equipment, 202-482-0551, March 1995.*

REFERENCES

Copyright Protection for Computer Software, U.S. Department of Commerce, Office of Computers and Business Equipment, Washington, DC 20230, 202-482-0571.

Software/Systems International, U.S. Department of Commerce, Office of Computers and Business Equipment, Washington, DC 20230, 202-482-0571.

Tariffs and Other Taxes on Computer Hardware and Software, U.S. Department of Commerce, Office of Computers and Business Equipment, Washington, DC 20230, 202-482-0571.

Business Software Alliance, 2001 L St., NW, Suite 400, Washington, DC 20036, 800-688-2721.

Datamation, 275 Washington St., Newton, MA 02158, 617-964-3030.

Information Technology Association of America, 1616 N. Fort Myer Dr., Suite 1300, Arlington, VA 22209, 703-522-5055.

Interactive Multimedia Association, 3 Church Circle, Suite 800, Annapolis, MD 21401, 410-626-1380.

International Data Corporation, 5 Speen St., Framingham, MA 01701, 800-343-4952.

Software Publishers Association, 1730 M St., NW, Suite 700, Washington, DC 20036, 202-452-1600.

Information Services

SUMMARY

The phenomenal growth of the information services industry is fueled by worldwide demand for rapid access to information; the restructuring and downsizing of industry; and efforts to keep pace with complex and constantly changing information technologies. Electronic commerce—the use of computer networks to transact business—also contributes to the strength of the industry. The most common types of electronic commerce include electronic data interchange, electronic mail, and electronic funds transfer. World expenditures for information services are expected to amount to $324.7 billion in 1995 and grow by 13 percent annually over the next five years.

The United States is the world's leader in the provision, use, and export of information services. In 1994, the United States captured 46 percent of world information services revenues. Critical issues include the industry's ability to respond to rapidly changing information needs and to develop appropriate technology and applications to deliver services quickly and efficiently. The industry is especially sensitive to international policies governing market access, intellectual property protection, and delivery of telecommunications services.

New opportunities to provide information services are cropping up all over the world. In many countries, information services providers face few barriers. Because of their technological capability and broad experience, U.S. information services firms are in an excellent position to take advantage of these export opportunities. Over the next five years, the United Kingdom, Japan, Canada, Germany, France, and Italy will constitute the best markets in developed countries. China, Taiwan, Hong Kong, South Korea, and Mexico (once it recovers from the 1994–95 crisis) are expected to offer the best opportunities among the Big Emerging Markets (BEMs).

Critical Issues

The speed and agility with which information services firms can adapt to rapidly changing needs and growing world demand are critical for the industry. Demand is created by evolving business needs, including the shift from paper to electronic transactions, the proliferation of credit and debit cards, and the demand for rapid access to financial and other business information. The

U.S. FOREIGN TRADE

Europe and Japan are the largest markets

Value ($ Million)
Sales/payments to unaffiliated companies

		1989	1993	1994*
World	Exports	1,183	2,877	3,222
	Imports	77	377	424
EU	Exports	325	1,265	1,300
	Imports	26	280	310
Japan	Exports	145	331	371
	Imports	20	10	12
Canada	Exports	90	232	259
	Imports	12	22	25
Australia	Exports	36	162	185
	Imports	1	21	25
Taiwan	Exports	9	113	120
	Imports	—	1	2
BEMs	Exports	104	346	398
	Imports	2	7	10
Rest of World	Exports	474	541	589
	Imports	16	35	40

Average Annual Percent Change

		1989–93	1993–94*
World	Exports	24.8	11.9
	Imports	48.7	12.5
EU	Exports	40.4	2.7
	Imports	81.1	10.7
Japan	Exports	22.9	12.1
	Imports	−15.9	20.0
Canada	Exports	26.7	11.6
	Imports	16.3	14.2
Australia	Exports	45.6	14.2
	Imports	114.0	19.1
Taiwan	Exports	88.2	6.2
	Imports	100.0	100.0
BEMs	Exports	35.1	15.0
	Imports	36.8	42.8
Rest of World	Exports	3.4	8.9
	Imports	21.6	14.3

Sources: U.S. Department of Commerce: Bureau of the Census; International Trade Administration (ITA). United Nations.
Note: Exports are total f.a.s. Imports are customs value.
*ITA forecasts.

resulting complexity of computer tasks often requires businesses to subcontract for data management and other information services—an important and growing sector of the industry.

The industry includes companies that electronically process financial accounts such as payrolls, credit cards, and utility bills and companies that provide professional services including consulting, custom software development, systems integration, and training. Outsourcing, the process of contracting with a third party to perform a company's computer system or data management tasks, is a large and growing business area for information services companies. Firms that provide electronic information services such as bulletin boards, online databases, and CD-ROM databases to both home and business consumers, are also included in the information services industry. The commercialization of Internet, a global computer network with 23 million users, has also helped the industry. Established online services are adding gateways to the Internet and others have started new services that are available through the Internet.

Government Policies Key to Industry Growth

The information services industry is especially sensitive to government policies regarding market access, intellectual property protection, privacy protection, security of data, and telecommunications services. Implementation of the Uruguay Round agreements will alleviate some concerns about market access and intellectual property protection, although enforcement in some countries remains a major problem.

Telecommunications policy in the United States, Europe, Asia, and elsewhere is an area of concern for the industry, as are issues related to privacy protection and security. Information services companies need efficient, reliable, telecommunications services at reasonable, nondiscriminatory, cost-based rates in order to operate successfully. These terms are still not available in many countries. The industry is constantly fighting proposals that would create excessive privacy protection regulations that could severely cripple its growth. Security of information remains an unresolved issue.

Eliminating the financial, regulatory, legal, and technical barriers to establishing information superhighways in the United States and elsewhere is another critical issue for the industry. The creation of these superhighways will stimulate the information services industry and will benefit all of its sectors. It will require professional services to plan, design, and build the infrastructure;

it will also generate opportunities for database producers and others to customize services for individuals, the health care sector, education community, and others who are linked to the networks.

Competitiveness in World Markets

The United States is expected to maintain its leadership position in the use, provision, and export of information services, but Europe and Japan are beginning to pose a challenge. U.S. companies are competitive in the global marketplace because of their reputation and broad experience. Using the most advanced software and equipment, U.S. firms are able to produce innovative solutions to complex information technology problems and are expert in developing new services. Because English is so widely spoken throughout the world, U.S. producers of electronic databases have an added advantage over databases in other languages.

In 1994, the world market for information services was $282 billion. The market shares by region were as follows: the United States controlled 46 percent of the world market followed by Europe, 32.5 percent; Asia/Pacific, 18.1 percent; Canada, 1.5 percent; Latin America, 1.5 percent; and Africa/Middle East, 0.4 percent.

The major U.S. competitors are located in Europe and Japan. In Europe, the major providers of information services are Group Bull, ICL, Cap Gemini, Siemens Nixdorf, Olivetti, and Sema Group. Major Japanese information services providers are NEC, Toshiba, NTT, Mitsubishi, and Nomura. Reuters of the United Kingdom is the world's largest electronic information services company. Canada also has a large information services company, Systemshouse, that is competitive with U.S. companies in providing professional services in the United States and abroad.

While these companies dominate their own markets, their exports to the United States are small. The United States has always maintained a large trade surplus in this field, and this trend is expected to continue over the next five years. Japanese computer manufacturers are becoming more aggressive in the professional services sector. However, U.S. firms still have about 50 percent of the global market for professional services.

EU Takes Steps to Unify European Information Services

The European Commission has reactivated its EU Action Plan for Information Technology. Its goals include decreasing European dependency on U.S. databases and becoming more competitive with U.S. suppliers of professional services by eliminating regulatory barriers that have prevented a Europeanwide information services industry from coming into being. The EU Action Plan will also help U.S. firms by harmonizing intra-EU policies and regulations on standards, intellectual property protection, privacy, security, and telecommunications.

France's Minitel, a national information network, has been successful in bringing online information to home users. Over 6.5 million users can access Minitel's 23,000 services. In 1993, Minitel had revenues of $1.1 billion. However, attempts to market Minitel in the United States have not been successful. Similar U.S. services such as Prodigy, CompuServe, Delphi, and America Online have grown tremendously over the past two years, reaching a customer base of nearly 5 million. These companies, especially CompuServe, are believed to have a number of foreign subscribers.

U.S. Dominates in Databases

According to Gale Research's *Directory of Databases,* the United States produced 4,956 or 66 percent of the 7,538 electronic databases around the world in 1993. The next largest producers were the United Kingdom, 641; Canada, 480; Germany, 342; and France, 288.—*Mary Inoussa, Office of Service Industries, 202-482-5820, March 1995.*

REFERENCES

Industry Sector Reports, *National Trade Data Bank,* U.S. Department of Commerce, Washington, DC 20230, 202-482-2164.

Survey of Current Business, The Economic Bulletin Board, U.S. Department of Commerce, Bureau of Economic Analysis, Washington, DC 20230, 202-482-1986.

Datamation, 275 Washington St., Newton, MA 02158, 617-558-4281.

Dataquest, Inc., 1290 Ridder Park Dr., San Jose, CA 95131, 202-437-8000.

Gale Research, Inc., *Directory of Databases,* P.O. Box 33477, Detroit, MI 48226, 313-961-2243.

Input, 1881 Landings Dr., Mountain View, CA 94043, 415-961-3300.

Information Industry Association, Suite 800, 555 New Jersey Ave. NW, Washington, DC 20001, 202-639-8262.

Information Technology Association of America, 1616 North Fort Myer Dr., Suite 1300, Arlington, VA 22209, 703-522-5055.

Interactive Services Association, Suite 865, 8403 Colesville Rd., Silver Spring, MD 20910, 301-495-4955.

Medical Equipment and Supplies

SUMMARY

The U.S. medical equipment and supplies industry is respected worldwide for its quality, cutting-edge technology, and services. The industry has consistently produced trade surpluses for the United States, rising from $1.6 billion in 1989 to $3.4 billion in 1993. International demand for U.S. medical equipment and supplies is expected to grow significantly over the next five years from $9.2 billion in 1994 to $10 billion in 1995, reaching about $18 billion by 2000.

The Food and Drug Administration's (FDA) product approval process and export regulatory requirements are critical issues affecting the competitiveness of U.S. exports of medical equipment and supplies. According to the industry, regulatory delays are one of the key reasons that U.S. manufacturers have relocated some of their production and R&D facilities overseas. Reduction or removal of trade barriers achieved through international agreements, as well as the inability of developing countries to manufacture high-technology medical equipment, will also bolster the future export performance of the U.S. medical equipment and supplies industry.

While strong growth in medical goods consumption and trade is likely to continue, existing patterns in demand have already begun a major shift away from the traditional markets in industrialized countries and toward rapidly developing economies in Latin America and Asia. U.S. medical equipment suppliers have begun to alter their global export strategies to establish a presence in these major markets of the future.

Western Europe remains the industry's largest market; like most developed economies, it has an aging population with sufficient income to afford health care. But the bulk of future growth should come in developing countries, which have rising income levels and recognize the need to upgrade their health care delivery systems. As a result, exports to the Big Emerging Markets (BEMs) should grow by 20 percent a year over each of the next five years compared to 12 percent for Western Europe.

Critical Issues

Globally competitive and technologically diverse, the U.S. medical equipment and supplies industry has managed to capture dominant shares in most major international markets. The industry is divided into five sectors: surgical and medical instruments,

U.S. FOREIGN TRADE

World export growth rates climb steadily

Value ($ Billion)		1989	1993	1994
World	Exports	4.6	8.3	9.2
	Imports	3.0	4.9	4.9
Japan	Exports	0.8	1.2	1.4
	Imports	0.7	1.1	1.1
Canada	Exports	0.5	1.0	1.0
	Imports	0.1	0.2	0.2
Germany	Exports	0.6	0.9	1.0
	Imports	0.8	1.1	1.0
France	Exports	0.3	0.5	0.6
	Imports	0.1	0.3	0.2
UK	Exports	0.3	0.5	0.5
	Imports	0.2	0.3	0.3
BEMs	Exports	0.7	1.3	1.4
	Imports	0.3	0.7	0.8
Rest of World	Exports	1.4	2.9	3.1
	Imports	0.8	1.2	1.2

Average Annual Percent Change		1989–93	1993–94
World	Exports	15.9	10.8
	Imports	13.0	—
Japan	Exports	10.7	16.7
	Imports	12.0	—
Canada	Exports	18.9	—
	Imports	18.9	—
Germany	Exports	10.7	11.1
	Imports	8.3	−9.1
France	Exports	13.6	20.0
	Imports	31.6	−33.3
UK	Exports	13.6	—
	Imports	10.7	—
BEMs	Exports	16.7	7.7
	Imports	23.6	14.3
Rest of World	Exports	20.0	6.9
	Imports	10.7	—

Sources: U.S. Department of Commerce: Bureau of the Census; International Trade Administration (ITA). United Nations.
Note: Exports are total f.a.s. Imports are customs value.

surgical appliances and supplies, dental equipment and supplies, X-ray apparatus and tubes, and electromedical equipment.

Despite its leadership in advanced technologies, the industry faces major critical issues such as U.S. government regulatory requirements; disparities among U.S. and foreign regulations; escalating costs and supply disruptions arising from liability suits; and government pressure to curtail rising health care costs.

Effects of Regulation

The industry has voiced concerns that requirements and separate regulations governing exports have hampered trade in medical equipment. The Safe Medical Devices Act of 1990 established new requirements for U.S. manufacturers to ensure that products entering both the domestic and international market are safe and effective, often resulting in shipping delays of two months or more. In response to industry complaints, however, the FDA has made great progress in streamlining its procedures, cutting the export processing time from an average of 65 days in 1993 to about 20 days in 1994.

In addition to the pre-export inspections, U.S. medical products often encounter lengthy approval processes once they reach their destination in key overseas markets, such as the EU and Japan. This lack of global harmonization of standards and regulations has resulted in duplicative testing and approvals for U.S. medical equipment. Globalization of standards has become an increasingly important issue in developing countries that are establishing their own medical equipment industries and regulatory controls.

Although other countries may approve American medical devices for sale in their markets, U.S. export requirements sometime delay exports. Consequently, some U.S. firms have resorted to doing R&D and production in other developed countries such as Japan and Germany where products can be developed and shipped in a more timely fashion. By relocating their production and R&D facilities, U.S. manufacturers have benefited from lower production costs and proximity to foreign markets. Recent data shows a significant increase in overseas investment by medical device firms. Foreign direct investment capital outflows from the United States grew significantly during the 1989–92 period, from an annual flow of $333 million in 1989 to more than $1 billion in 1992.

Lawsuits Hamper Production

Risks of being associated with manufacturers of medical technologies in costly product liability suits have induced many suppliers of materials and components to restrict the use of their products, particularly in implants and invasive technologies, such as teflon used in making pacemakers. Such actions are threatening the supply of crucial materials for current and future medical innovations.

A growing awareness of rising health care costs has increased buyers' resistance, both here and abroad, to purchasing expensive medical equipment. Hospitals and other medical facilities in search of equipment that can provide higher performance at a lower cost have increased their demand for used or reconditioned medical equipment. Although a major portion of used medical equipment is sold in the United States, export markets are emerging in Latin America, China, Canada, Eastern Europe, Russia, and other former Soviet republics.

Technology Is the Key to U.S. Leadership

Despite domestic and foreign challenges, U.S. companies are the world's leading sources for discoveries in medical technologies. U.S. leadership in advanced medical research and practice and the industry's reputation for high-quality medical products have benefited other critical industries, such as computerized imaging and virtual reality. The U.S. medical equipment industry, capable of fulfilling the broad spectrum of medical technology needs in the world's rapidly developing nations, supplies about 52 percent of the $88 billion global market.

The industry's commitment to R&D has enabled it to maintain its leadership in the manufacturing of technologically advanced and high-quality medical products. The result has been shorter hospital stays and quicker recovery for patients. These advanced medical technologies are highly sought after by physicians and scientists from around the world who become familiar with these products while training at U.S. institutions.

This competitive position has allowed the American medical device industry to take advantage of the growing economic opportunities in the emerging markets in Asia and Latin America. To remain competitive in these markets, the U.S. government and industry are working to reduce export practices that impede business and to help implement procedures in major developing countries that would enhance sales of U.S. medical goods.

Competitiveness in World Markets

Over the past 10 years, the U.S. medical equipment industry underwent major changes that altered its competitiveness and price sensitivity. In developed countries, sharply rising health care expenditures, combined with fiscal budgetary constraints, have led to increasing cost-containment pressures, inducing private sector and government health care purchasers to seek value as well as technological sophistication.

For example, U.S. buyers have resisted making major investments in capital-intensive electromedical equipment such as magnetic resonance imaging (MRI), pressuring suppliers to provide high-performance medical equipment at lower cost. Over the past five years, the cost of medical equipment in the United States increased an average of 2.9 percent a year, slower than the overall inflation rate of 3.8 percent.

Favorable Financing, a Key to BEMs Trade

In major developing countries, sustained economic growth rates have expanded market opportunities for U.S. medical equipment, but access to adequate currency to pay for imports remains a problem. Although they account for an increasing share of global demand for medical equipment, most developing countries are not wealthy by world standards. Medical equipment suppliers, eager to establish an early market presence in countries such as India and Russia, have found that they often need to reduce their prices or offer favorable financing to match the purchasing capacity of their potential customers.

Major developing countries in Asia are improving their capacity to produce high-technology medical equipment, meaning it will become increasingly difficult for U.S. medical equipment manufacturers to increase their share of markets in these countries. The United States also faces strong competition in East Asian countries such as China and Korea, where Japanese companies have moved out ahead of U.S. firms.

Foreign Governments Assist Competitors

Foreign government assistance programs also affect the U.S. medical equipment industry's competitiveness. Programs ranging from research subsidies to preferential export credits for developing new products and entering new markets are common among European and Asian companies. Clearly, government assistance has helped competitor nations such as Germany and Japan to move rapidly into East Asian BEMs where their market shares now rival those of U.S. medical equipment companies.

The United States is the leader in most major markets worldwide, and remains technologically superior in most medical equip-

ment categories. Of the 20 largest medical equipment and supplies businesses in the world, 13 are U.S.-based companies, six are European, and one is Japanese (Table 1). These 20 companies accounted for nearly $50 billion in sales in 1992, or well over half of the global medical equipment and supplies sales that year. U.S. manufacturers are most competitive in areas of medical implants, diagnostic imaging, patient monitoring, and other high-technology devices.— *Victoria Kader and Matthew Edwards, Office of Microelectronics, Medical Equipment, and Instrumentation, 202-482-4073, March 1995.*

TABLE 1 WORLD'S LEADING MEDICAL TECHNOLOGY FIRMS

Company	Country
3M	United States
Abbot	United States
Bard	United States
Baxter	United States
Becton Dickinson	United States
Boehringer Mannheim	Germany
Bristol-Myers Squib	United States
Eli Lilly	United States
General Electric	United States
Hewlett-Packard	United States
Johnson & Johnson	United States
Medtronic	United States
Miles	Germany
Ohmeda	United Kingdom
Pfizer	United States
Philips	Netherlands
Siemens	Germany
Smith and Nephew	United Kingdom
Toshiba	Japan
U.S. Surgical	United States

Source: Health Industry Manufacturers Association

REFERENCES

Annual Survey of Manufacturers, Statistics for Industry Groups and Industries, 1991, M90(AS)-1, M90(AS)-2, U.S. Department of Commerce, Bureau of the Census, Washington, DC 20233.

Industry and Trade Summary: Medical Goods, pub. 2674, September 1993, U.S. International Trade Commission, Office of the Secretary, 500 E St., SW, Washington, DC 20436, 202-205-1809.

Dental Manufacturers of America, 123 South Broad St., Fidelity Bldg., Suite 2531, Philadelphia, PA 19109, 215-731-9975.

Diagnostic Imaging, 600 Harrison St., San Francisco, CA 94107, 415-905-2550.

Europe Drugs and Device Report, Washington Business Information, Inc., 1117 19th St., Arlington, VA 22203 and Thompson-Lesser Publishing, Inc., 1725 K St., NW,

Washington, DC 20006, 703-247-3400 and 202-785-8851.

The Global Medical Device Market Update, 1994 ed., Health Industry Manufacturers Association, January 1994, Washington, DC 20005-3814, 202-783-8700.

Health Care Reform, Regulation, and Innovation in the Medical Devices Industry, Hudson Institute Competitiveness Center, Indianapolis, IN.

Health Care Technology Institute, Alexandria, VA 22314, 703-739-9437.

Medical Device and Diagnostic Industry. Canon Communications, Inc., Santa Monica, CA 90403, 310-392-5509.

The Value Line Investment Survey, June 18, 1993 (vol. 48, no. 40), pp. 193–238, Value Line Publishing, Inc., New York, NY 10017-4064, 212-687-3965.

Motor Vehicles

SUMMARY

Worldwide sales volume of cars, trucks, and buses have grown by just 1.2 percent annually during the past 10 years because markets in developed countries are nearly saturated. In many developing countries, however, unit sales and production are growing rapidly—some at double-digit rates. The motor vehicle industry is undergoing global reorganization to adjust to long-term changes in demand. Perhaps as few as 10 mega-manufacturing alliances will dominate developed markets within the next 10 years as companies consolidate and restructure. U.S. firms have become increasingly competitive; the quality of their products and the productivity of their workforces have improved significantly. Nevertheless, varying safety and environmental standards (requiring vehicle model changes) and other foreign market barriers still impede U.S. export performance.

U.S. exports of new cars and commercial vehicles increased more than 13 percent to $22 billion in 1994, but the trade deficit grew to $51 billion. The vehicle trade deficit with Japan alone—the object of ongoing market-opening trade negotiations—was $24 billion. Significant U.S. export opportunities are likely to arise in the developing markets, which are expected to account for nearly one-third of the total U.S. export growth in the world motor vehicle market during the next five years.

This section covers new, on-road, volume-produced completed vehicles for carrying passengers or cargo. Commercial vehicles include medium and heavy trucks and buses. Sales of new motor vehicles and car bodies in the United States will increase an estimated 3 percent in 1995, to 15.9 million units or an ex-factory reference value of about $214 billion.[1] Sales in developing countries could total $181 billion, up 6½ percent over 1994, and could reach $221 billion five years later. U.S. firms are beginning to focus more intently on these emerging markets to gain new customers, help sustain U.S. production, and maintain cost and price competitiveness.

[1] Reference value is a measure of the value of motor vehicle production, expressed in terms of the average value of 1992–93 U.S. production multiplied by estimates for local unit sales. U.S. export estimates are based on U.S.-declared customs values to each country in 1992–93. Therefore, all estimates and forecasts are in real terms, or constant dollars.

U.S. FOREIGN TRADE

Trade deficits with Japan and Canada remain high

		Value ($ Billion)		
		1989	1993	1994
World	Exports	13.3	19.4	22.0
	Imports	54.5	63.1	72.6
Canada	Exports	8.6	9.3	11.4
	Imports	19.6	26.8	31.0
Japan	Exports	0.5	1.2	2.0
	Imports	22.9	23.3	26.0
Taiwan	Exports	0.8	1.2	1.2
	Imports	—	—	—
Saudi Arabia	Exports	0.4	1.5	0.9
	Imports	—	—	—
Germany	Exports	0.4	0.9	0.8
	Imports	5.1	5.4	5.8
BEMs (less Taiwan)	Exports	0.2	1.9	1.8
	Imports	3.3	4.5	6.3
Rest of World	Exports	2.4	3.4	3.9
	Imports	3.6	3.0	3.5

		Average Annual Percent Change	
		1989–93	1993–94
World	Exports	9.8	13.8
	Imports	3.7	15.1
Canada	Exports	1.8	22.6
	Imports	8.1	15.7
Japan	Exports	23.1	66.7
	Imports	0.4	11.6
Taiwan	Exports	13.4	—
	Imports	—	—
Saudi Arabia	Exports	37.7	-40.0
	Imports	—	—
Germany	Exports	20.3	-11.0
	Imports	1.7	7.4
BEMs (less Taiwan)	Exports	83.5	-5.3
	Imports	8.3	40.0
Rest of World	Exports	8.6	23.5
	Imports	-4.0	16.7

Sources: U.S. Department of Commerce: Bureau of the Census; International Trade Administration (ITA). United Nations.
Note: Exports are total f.a.s. Imports are customs value.

Critical Issues

Future Restructuring

The long-term market stagnation now evident in the developed countries suggests that a shakeout among the major international producers is inevitable. Today, 26 firms serve the major developed markets. Unrelenting competition is forcing them to drive down manufacturing costs, while markets, fractured into ever smaller niche segments, demand an increasing number of products. Firms that successfully make maximum use of their enormous investments in assembly plants can generate billions of dollars in profits in a single year. Therefore, all the large firms in the major markets seek ways to generate high-volume production runs of several vehicle models and types from a single vehicle platform. Some are doing so by sharing manufacturing resources and coordinating marketing plans with their competitors. These mostly temporary arrangements could lead the principal companies to combine many of their operations into new, permanent entities. Within 10 years as few as 10 mega-manufacturing alliances may serve all the developed countries.

Growing Role of Developing Countries

Emerging markets are increasingly important for U.S. automakers. These markets accounted for almost 21 percent of worldwide motor vehicle output and sales in 1993 (Figure 1), and this share will grow rapidly. Many new local and regional producers are attempting to serve their home countries and are struggling to enter the seemingly attractive, high-volume motor vehicle markets of the developed nations. Developed country suppliers generally serve newly emerging markets first with direct exports, then with limited local "screwdriver" assembly facilities (with no actual manufacturing capability) as local governments seek domestic employment opportunities. Although sometimes inefficient, these operations often blossom into full-scale local factories.

Governments in the developing world now play a major role in shaping the global motor vehicle industry through their efforts to develop local manufacturing capabilities. Despite efforts in the GATT Uruguay Round to liberalize investment requirements, governments increasingly require foreign motor vehicle investors to undertake joint-venture local production as the price of admission. Several developing countries now are unwilling to accept tooling and technology for discontinued products because they want to develop an internationally competitive industry. Some major foreign manufacturers will agree to these terms with the understanding that in return they will be protected from competitive imports. At the same time, they often win the exclusive right to import for locally emerging low-volume, high-profit niche market segments. The social and environmental policies of developed-country governments that impose substantial costs on motor vehicle production at home have encouraged some manufacturers to relocate production to emerging markets.

Competitiveness in World Markets

Around the globe, the primary determinant of motor vehicle sales is price; indeed, price overshadows all other factors. Greatly

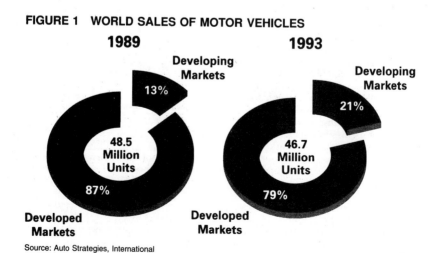

FIGURE 1   WORLD SALES OF MOTOR VEHICLES

1989

Developing Markets
13%

48.5 Million Units

87%

Developed Markets

1993

Developing Markets
21%

46.7 Million Units

79%

Developed Markets

Source: Auto Strategies, International

improved productivity coupled with recent currency trends have made the United States the lowest-cost motor vehicle production site in the developed world. U.S. competitiveness in world markets has risen proportionately, but it has not been immediate because of locked-in contract prices for inputs purchased from outside firms. Japanese automotive manufacturers are responding to this situation by shifting more of their production to the United States; they are developing a rapidly growing export capability in those plants. According to industry estimates, Japanese producers can manufacture some models in the United States for export at $1,000 less per unit than in Japan.

Importance of Quality and Productivity

Responding to the intense pressure of Japanese-affiliated manufacturers, U.S.-owned motor vehicle producers have made enormous improvements in the quality of their products and in the productivity of their workforces. Part of this success derives from reducing the number of parts used per vehicle and sharing more components across model lines, a strategy now being adopted by the Japanese producers. In the process, several U.S. plant closings and worker layoffs unfortunately have occurred. However, a leaner industry is now much better positioned for the challenges posed by the continuing globalization of the industry, Japanese cost reductions achieved in order to compete at disadvantageous currency values, and European industry's determination to catch up with Japan and the United States. The quality of U.S.-produced passenger vehicles is now virtually on par with that of the Japanese firms. In fact, when pricing and service are competitive, the decisive factor in consumer purchases in many markets apparently is moving toward exterior styling and interior features, traditional strengths of U.S. producers.

Local Competition from Japan and Europe

Japanese manufacturers continue to lead in the search for new foreign markets and in efforts to build new facilities, particularly in the United States, Western Europe, and Asia. The Big Three also are producing more overseas, but smaller U.S.-owned producers of trucks and buses will depend primarily upon their U.S. factories to fill their international order books. The three major German producers are expanding and establishing limited production facilities in both the Western Hemisphere and China, and the two big French producers are pursuing actively opportunities in Asia and South America. The remaining European firms are likely to remain focused predominantly on their own region.

U.S. and Foreign Regulations Mean Higher Costs

There are no directly imposed U.S. government barriers to exports of nonmilitary motor vehicles from the United States. However, U.S. measures to strengthen regulations concerning motor vehicle safety, fuel economy, and emissions could inadvertently hamper U.S. producers' international competitiveness by adding significant overhead costs to each vehicle produced in the United States. For example, some industry sources claim that U.S. environmental regulations are responsible for substantial costs associated with building a new U.S. auto assembly plant. To upgrade existing factories to meet environmental standards already announced or planned for the year 2000, the Big Three reportedly may have to spend up to $3 billion, plus an additional $600 million in higher operating costs.

U.S. firms are on the leading edge of motor vehicle product content and manufacturing technology. However, they face an inherent disadvantage in exporting because of the disparate certification procedures in the United States and abroad. The U.S. government requires that manufacturers assume the burden of certifying compliance with federal safety and emission regulations; there are no government testing centers. On the other hand, most other countries use a government-conducted type-designation system that relieves manufacturers from proving that their vehicles meet specified standards. Because of these differing approaches, U.S. exporters often are required to deliver their vehicles to foreign government facilities for testing, a costly and time-consuming procedure. Country-specific or European-oriented technical standards being adopted by many emerging markets further complicate matters. Therefore, the United States supports UN efforts that eventually could produce greater openness and universality in motor vehicle safety and environmental standards.

If their upward spiral continues, health care and product liability costs could undermine the competitiveness of U.S. products. According to the Big Three, health care now adds nearly $1,000 per unit to their production costs. Producers in Japan are believed to incur costs of just half that amount. The National Center for Manufacturing Sciences reports that product liability defense claims add about $500 each to the costs of a U.S.-made automobile as opposed to $50 for most imports.—*Randall Miller, Office of Automotive Affairs, 202-482-0669, March 1995.*

TABLE 1   MARKETS FOR U.S. MOTOR VEHICLES, 1995 AND 2000*

	1995				2000			
	Total Market		U.S. Exports		Total Market		U.S. Exports	
	Units	Value	Units	Value	Units	Value	Units	Value
Country	(thousands)	($ million)	(thousands)	($ million)	(thousands)	($ million)	(thousands)	($ million)
Big Emerging Markets	**8,100**	**109,350**	**165.0**	**2,714**	**10,040**	**135,540**	**226.4**	**3,713**
Argentina	480	6,480	12.0	194	540	7,290	13.5	218
Brazil	1,200	16,200	7.6	183	1,260	17,010	8.0	192
China and Hong Kong	1,200	16,200	57.4	917	1,720	23,220	82.3	1,314
India	370	4,995	0.4	5	420	5,670	1.3	17
Indonesia	290	3,915	0.3	33	360	4,860	0.4	43
Mexico	370	4,995	20.0	350	700	9,450	24.3	662
Poland	570	7,695	1.0	6	600	8,100	1.1	7
South Africa	300	4,050	0.7	13	320	4,320	0.8	15
South Korea	2,060	27,810	3.8	62	2,600	35,100	4.8	78
Taiwan	620	8,370	60.9	925	760	10,260	74.7	1,135
Turkey	640	8,640	0.9	26	760	10,260	1.1	32
Other Developing Markets	**1,820**	**24,570**	**169.8**	**2,643**	**2,160**	**29,160**	**179.1**	**2,780**
Chile	170	2,295	22.5	249	200	2,700	26.5	293
Colombia	190	2,565	9.1	231	210	2,835	10.1	257
Israel	140	1,890	21.4	295	160	2,160	24.5	338
Kuwait	40	540	21.0	310	40	540	22.2	328
Malaysia	210	2,835	0.9	22	280	3,780	1.5	36
Saudi Arabia	220	2,970	72.7	1,216	220	2,970	72.7	1,216
Thailand	640	8,640	0.7	12	850	11,475	0.9	15
United Arab Emirates	80	1,080	11.3	165	80	1,080	11.3	165
Venezuela	130	1,755	10.2	143	120	1,620	9.4	132
Developed Markets	**22,230**	**300,105**	**1,289.8**	**18,565**	**24,550**	**331,425**	**1,613.6**	**23,309**
Australia	610	8,235	9.2	68	730	9,855	11.8	87
Canada	1,310	17,685	987.9	13,965	1,590	21,465	1,231.5	17,409
Japan	6,920	93,420	143.4	2,447	7,600	102,600	207.2	3,535
European Union	12,430	167,805	132.6	1,830	13,590	183,465	145.0	2,001
Other West Europe	960	12,960	16.7	255	1,040	14,040	18.1	277
Rest of World	**3,490**	**47,115**	**118.7**	**1,299**	**4,180**	**56,430**	**209.0**	**2,288**
Total Foreign Markets	**35,640**	**481,140**	**1,743.3**	**25,221**	**40,930**	**552,555**	**2,227.7**	**32,090**
less Canada	34,630	467,505	8,558	12,368	39,650	535,275	1,287.6	18,018
United States	**15,850**	**213,975**			**14,800**	**199,800**		
Total World Market	**51,490**	**695,115**			**55,730**	**752,335**		

*Reference value

Source: Department of Commerce

REFERENCES

Compilation of Foreign Motor Vehicle Import Regulations (issued periodically), U.S. Department of Commerce, Office of Automotive Affairs, Washington, DC 20230, 202-482-0669.

U.S. Motor Vehicle Trade Statistics (quarterly), U.S. Department of Commerce, Office of Automotive Affairs, Washington, DC 20230, 202-482-0669.

Automotive News, Crain Communications Inc., 965 E. Jefferson, Detroit, MI 48207-3185, 800-678-9595.

Global Automotive Review and Outlook (monthly), Global Automotive Information Services, 4813 Pelican Way, West Bloomfield, MI 48323, 810-683-2686.

International Automobile Industry in the United States, 1993, Association of International Automobile Manufacturers, Suite 1200, 1001 19th St. North, Arlington, VA 22209, 703-525-8817.

Ward's Automotive Reports (weekly); *Ward's Automotive International* (bimonthly); and *Ward's Automotive Yearbook,* Ward's Communications, Suite 2750, 3000 Town Center, Southfield, MI 48075, 313-962-4433.

World Automotive Outlook, 1994–2000, 1994, AutoFacts International, 1595 Paoli Pike, West Chester, PA 19380, 215-429-9900.

World Motor Vehicle Data 1994 (annual), American Automobile Manufacturers Association, Suite 900, 1401 H St. NW, Washington, DC 20005, 202-326-5500.

World Motor Vehicle Markets 1984–93 (annual), Auto Strategies International, 12305 Oak Park Blvd., Garfield Heights, OH 44125, 216-581-6323.

Paper Products

SUMMARY

The U.S. paper industry is mature yet dynamic. Faced with stagnating domestic shipments, it refocused on export sales and continues to gain global market share. The industry is the most modern in the world because of continued large capital expenditures. This spending, largely driven by production improvements, environmental concerns, and the goal of increased recycling, totaled nearly $11 billion in 1994.

The most important issue for the U.S. industry is the need to meet increasingly stringent air and water anti-pollution regulations. It is making progress in meeting these requirements. The industry is recycling more paper products; the United States is the leading exporter of recovered paper. Industry leaders are working to accelerate tariff reductions under the NAFTA and WTO agreements and to reduce barriers to the $60 billion Japanese market.

Relatively low-cost raw materials and energy, combined with modern facilities, make U.S. paper producers competitive worldwide. They accounted for 18 percent of world paper exports in 1992. It is more economical for the industry to produce finished products domestically rather than invest in facilities outside of North America. Canada has the world's most competitive paper products industry, followed by the United States and the Scandinavian countries.

U.S. exports of all paper products were valued at $11.3 billion in 1994, up nearly 18 percent from 1993. By 2000, U.S. exports will be nearly $15.2 billion and imports $14.5 billion, yielding a trade surplus of $700 million. Major export markets are Canada—by far the largest, Mexico, the European Union (EU), and Japan, although many other countries offer good export growth potential for U.S. firms.

Critical Issues

Industry Strives to Exceed Clean Air and Water Standards

The U.S. industry has met or exceeded mandatory environmental targets. New standards proposed by the Environmental Protection Agency (EPA) are currently under review by government and industry officials. Since 1988, the industry has spent more than $1 billion in response to the environmental and health concerns surrounding dioxin. As a result, dioxin generation has been reduced by more than 90 percent.

U.S. FOREIGN TRADE

Canada is the largest U.S. trading partner

Value ($ Billion)

		1989	1993	1994
World	Exports	8.6	9.6	11.3
	Imports	11.5	10.6	11.3
Canada	Exports	1.0	2.1	2.3
	Imports	8.9	7.8	8.3
Mexico	Exports	1.0	1.4	1.7
	Imports	0.4	0.1	0.2
Japan	Exports	1.5	1.2	1.2
	Imports	0.2	0.2	0.3
South Korea	Exports	0.6	0.4	0.6
	Imports	0.1	0.1	0.1
Germany	Exports	0.5	0.4	0.4
	Imports	0.3	0.3	0.3
BEMs (less Mexico, S. Korea)	Exports	0.9	1.1	1.4
	Imports	0.4	0.4	0.4
Rest of World	Exports	3.1	3.0	3.7
	Imports	1.2	1.7	1.7

Average Annual Percent Change

		1989–93	1993–94
World	Exports	2.8	17.7
	Imports	−2.0	6.6
Canada	Exports	20.4	9.5
	Imports	−3.2	6.4
Mexico	Exports	8.8	21.4
	Imports	−29.3	100.0
Japan	Exports	−5.4	—
	Imports	—	50.0
South Korea	Exports	−9.6	50.0
	Imports	—	—
Germany	Exports	−5.2	—
	Imports	—	—
BEMs (less Mexico, S. Korea)	Exports	5.2	27.3
	Imports	—	—
Rest of World	Exports	−1.0	23.3
	Imports	9.1	—

Sources: U.S. Department of Commerce: Bureau of the Census; International Trade Administration (ITA). United Nations.
Note: Exports are total f.a.s. Imports are customs value.

Pulp and paper producers in Europe (especially Germany and Scandinavia) have similar environmental goals and face costs comparable to those of U.S. producers. Other regions, including Asia and Latin America, have yet to reach this high level of environmental capital outlays for improvement of the environment. Therefore, the lack of environmental regulations in these countries gives them a distinct cost competitive advantage.

In 1993, the industry attained a wastepaper recovery rate of 42 percent, and recovered paper accounted for over 30 percent of fiber used in paper and paperboard mills. During the balance of this decade, the industry will spend more than $10 billion in retrofitted or new manufacturing capacity, which will enable the production of more recycled products. The only other markets having similar recycling standards are some European countries and Japan. An important benefit of environmental regulations for U.S. producers is the large quantity of paper and paperboard that does not end up in domestic landfills. According to industry reports, for the first time more paper and paperboard were recycled in 1993 than were put in landfills. This trend is expected to continue.

International environmental concerns have had a noticeable effect on international trade patterns and have strongly boosted U.S. exports of wastepaper. The United States is the world's leading exporter of recovered paper, especially to Mexico and Asia. In 1994, the U.S. exported nearly 7 million metric tons of recovered paper (valued at more than $845 million). This has helped to improve the U.S. trade balance in paper products. Taiwan, South Korea, Mexico, and Japan, countries which lack large local raw materials bases, have a strong economic impetus to import wastepaper. These countries

have been unable to develop adequate domestic pulping industries, but still require large quantities of papermaking fiber that can be supplied by the United States. Imports of newsprint from Canada have declined since 1989, primarily because of increased U.S. production of newsprint recycled from old newspapers.

Competitiveness in World Markets

The world's largest paper exporters are the EU, Canada, the United States, and the Scandinavian countries in that order of importance (Figure 1). More than 70 percent of EU exports represent intra-EU trade; the EU is a large net importer of paper products. Most Canadian exports are destined for the United States. A number of U.S. paper companies have subsidiaries and operating facilities in Canada, and also harvest some Canadian timber. The United States is a major supplier of wood pulp and kraft linerboard to Europe, with total sales to the EU exceeding $1.8 billion, or 9 percent of the total. Although substantial, Canadian exports to the EU are less than half the value of U.S. exports there. The Scandinavian countries are the largest exporters to the EU market. Japan and Brazil are smaller exporters but are important players in regional markets.

U.S. Competitive Advantages

U.S. companies accounted for more than 18 percent of world paper exports in 1992. The United States has advantages in raw materials, energy, technology, a skilled workforce, and investment in capital equipment. Thus, the position of U.S. exporters has improved in most of the world, with the notable exceptions of Japan and the EU, where market access barriers and currency devaluations in Scandinavian countries have limited U.S. market shares. Fairly high U.S. wage

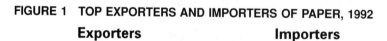

FIGURE 1   TOP EXPORTERS AND IMPORTERS OF PAPER, 1992

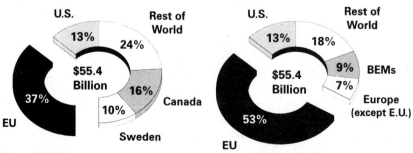

Exporters

U.S.
13%

Rest of World
24%

$55.4 Billion

37%
EU

16%
Canada

10%
Sweden

Importers

U.S.
13%

Rest of World
18%

$55.4 Billion

9% BEMs

7%

53%
EU

Europe (except E.U.)

Source: United Nations

TABLE 1   U.S. EXPORTS OF PAPER PRODUCTS, 1993–2000 ($ Million)

Country	1993	1995*	2000*
Canada	1,936	2,618	3,344
European Union	1,864	2,225	2,812
Mexico	1,376	1,904	2,052
Japan	1,151	1,404	1,829
Other BEMs	1,452	1,964	2,736
Rest of World	1,754	1,785	2,427
TOTAL	9,533	11,900	15,200

* Estimate

Source: Department of Commerce

rates are roughly similar to those in Canada, Japan, the Scandinavian countries, and most other industrialized nations. Wage rates are therefore not a competitive factor with these countries, but they are with such developing nations as Brazil and Malaysia.

Since the U.S. dollar has been relatively strong compared with the Canadian and Scandinavian currencies, U.S. producers have had to reduce prices to maintain international competitiveness. Economic slowdowns in the major markets of Japan and the EU, combined with industry overcapacity, have resulted in a global paper and paperboard surplus, leading to lower prices in the early 1990s. However, paper product prices have increased substantially in 1994 because of increased global demand and improved economic performance in major markets.

Canadian competitors have invested in more advanced technology and have improved their forest management techniques to remain competitive. Competitors in Europe and Japan have focused much of their investment on consolidations to gain market share. For example, several Scandinavian producers have heavily invested in the EU paper sector to obtain captive markets where products are only for local consumers. There has been a steady consolidation of the Japanese paper industry, which has made it harder for outside suppliers to sell products in the already complicated and concentrated Japanese distribution system.— *Gary Stanley, Office of Metals, Materials, and Chemicals, 202-482-0375, March 1995.*

REFERENCES

1994 Statistics of Paper, Paperboard, and Wood Pulp, American Forest and Paper Association, 1111 19th St. NW, Suite 800, Washington, DC 20036, 202-463-2700.

Board Converting News and Recycling Markets, NV Business Publishers Corp., 43 Main St., Avon-By-The-Sea, NJ 07717, 908-502-0500.

Boxboard Containers, Maclean Hunter Publishing Co., 29 N. Wacker Dr., Chicago, IL 60606, 312-726-2802.

Exports of Pulp, Paper, Paperboard, and Converted Products to World Markets, American Forest and Paper Association, 1111 19th St. NW, Suite 800, Washington, DC 20036, 202-463-2700.

Monthly Statistical Summary, American Forest and Paper Association, 1111 19th St. NW, Suite 800, Washington, DC 20036, 202-463-2700.

Official Board Markets, Magazines for Industry, Inc., 233 N. Michigan Ave., Chicago, IL 60601, 312-938-2300.

Paper Age, Global Publications, Inc., 420 Washington St., Braintree, MA 02184, 617-849-0226.

Papermaker Magazine, ASM Communications, Inc., 57 Executive Park South, Suite 310, Atlanta, GA 30329, 404-325-9153.

Pulp and Paper, Pulp and Paper International, Miller Freeman Publications, 600 Harrison St., San Francisco, CA 94107, 415-905-2200.

Recycled Paper News, 6732 Huntsman Blvd., Springfield, VA 22152, 703-569-8670.

TAPPI Journal, Technology Park/ Atlanta, P.O. Box 105113, Atlanta, GA 30348, 404-446-1400.

Walden's Fiber and Board Report, Walden-Mott Corporation, 225 N. Franklin Turnpike, Ramsey, NJ 07446, 201-818-8630.

General Business and Economic Indicators

SELECTED BUSINESS STATISTICS

SEASONALLY ADJUSTED WHERE APPLICABLE

EXPANSION PEAKS (P), RECESSION TROUGHS (T)

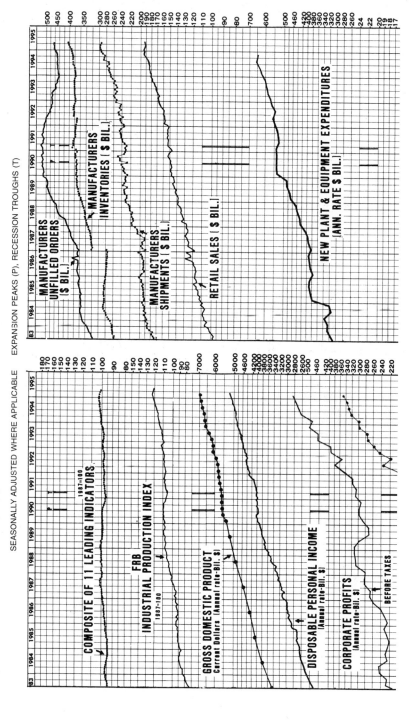

COMPOSITE OF 11 LEADING INDICATORS

FRB
INDUSTRIAL PRODUCTION INDEX
1987=100

GROSS DOMESTIC PRODUCT
Current Dollars (Annual rate–Bil. $)

DISPOSABLE PERSONAL INCOME
(Annual rate–Bil. $)

CORPORATE PROFITS
(Annual rate–Bil. $)

BEFORE TAXES

MANUFACTURERS
UNFILLED ORDERS
($ BIL.)

MANUFACTURERS
INVENTORIES ($ BIL.)

MANUFACTURERS
SHIPMENTS ($ BIL.)

RETAIL SALES ($ BIL.)

NEW PLANT & EQUIPMENT EXPENDITURES
(ANN. RATE $ BIL.)

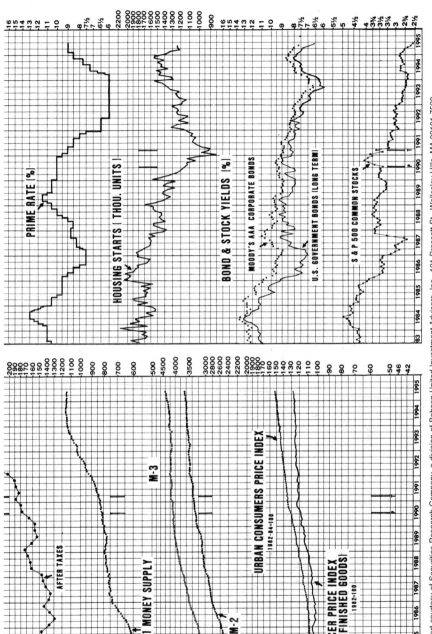

Source: Chart courtesy of Securities Research Company, a division of Babson-United-Investment Advisors, Inc., 101 Prescott St., Wellesley Hills, MA 02181-7528.

COMPOSITE INDEXES*

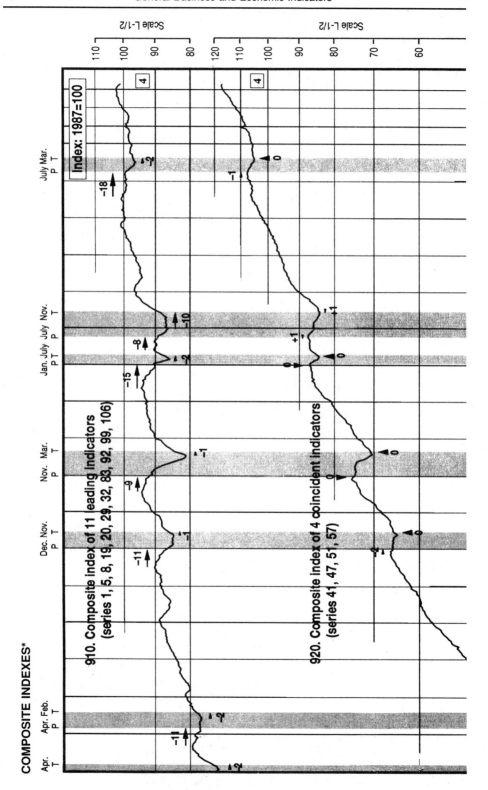

910. Composite index of 11 leading indicators
(series 1, 5, 8, 19, 20, 29, 32, 83, 92, 99, 106)

920. Composite index of 4 coincident indicators
(series 41, 47, 51, 57)

Index: 1987=100

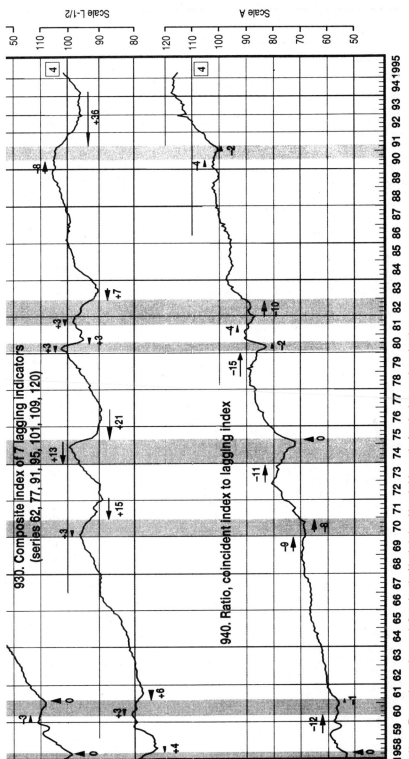

930. Composite index of 7 lagging indicators
(series 62, 77, 91, 95, 101, 109, 120)

940. Ratio, coincident index to lagging index

Scale L-1/2

Scale A

NOTE.—The numbers and arrows indicate length of leads (−) and lags (+) in months from business cycle turning dates.

* For notes and definitions see page 80.

Source: *Survey of Current Business*, U.S. Department of Commerce, Bureau of Economic Analysis.

Composition of Leading, Coincident, and Lagging Indicators

I. THE ELEVEN LEADING INDICATORS

1. Average weekly hours of production or non-supervisory workers, manufacturing.
5. Average weekly claims for unemployment insurance, State programs.
8. Manufacturers' new orders in 1987 dollars, consumer goods and materials industries.
19. Index of stock prices, 500 common stock prices.
20. Contracts and orders for plant and equipment in 1987 dollars.
29. Index of new private housing units authorized by local building permits.
32. Vendor performance, slower deliveries diffusion Index.
83. Index of consumer expectations.
92. Change in manufacturer's unfilled orders for the durable goods industry.
99. Change in sensitive materials prices, smoothed.
106. Money supply (M2 in 1987 dollars).

II. THE FOUR COINCIDENT INDICATORS

41. Employees on non-agricultural payrolls.
47. Index of industrial production.
51. Personal income less transfer payments in 1987 dollars.
57. Manufacturing and trade sales in 1987 dollars.

III. THE SEVEN LAGGING INDICATORS

62. Change in index of labor costs per unit of output, manufacturing, smoothed.
77. Ratio, manufacturing, and trade inventories to sales in 1987 dollars.
91. Average duration of unemployment in weeks.
95. Ratio, consumer installment credit outstanding to personal income.
101. Commercial and industrial loans outstanding in 1987 dollars.
109. Average prime rate charged by banks.
120. Change in Consumer Price Index for services, smoothed.

Source: *Survey of Current Business.*

Notes

The following notes explain general features of the charts.

- Business cycle peaks (P) and troughs (T), as designated by the National Bureau of Economic Research, Inc., are indicated at the top of each chart. The shaded areas represent recessions.

- For each series classified as a cyclical indicator, the timing classifications at peaks, at troughs, and overall are shown in a box adjacent to the title. (L = leading, C = coincident, Lg = lagging, U = unclassified.) A complete list of series titles and sources is shown on pages C-30 through C-32 in the April 1995 SURVEY OF CURRENT BUSINESS.

- *Arithmetic scales* are designated "Scale A." On the same arithmetic scale, equal vertical distances represent equal differences in data. (For example, the vertical distance from 10 to 15 is the same as the distance from 100 to 105.)

- *Logarithmic (log) scales* are designated L-1, L-2, or L-3 to indicate their relative size. On log scales of the same size, equal vertical distances represent equal percentage changes. (For example, the vertical distance from 10 to 15 is the same as the distance from 100 to 150.) Compared with an L-1 scale, the same percentage change covers half the distance on an L-2 scale and one-third the distance on an L-3 scale.

- Data are monthly unless otherwise indicated. Quarterly data are indicated by a "Q" following the series title.

- Some series include a centered moving average, which is shown as a heavy line superimposed on the actual monthly data.

- Parallel lines across a plotted series indicate a missing data value, change in definition, or other significant break in continuity.

- The box near the end of each plotted series indicates the latest data month (Arabic numeral) or quarter (Roman numeral) shown or, for series computed over a span of time (diffusion indexes and rates of change), the latest data period used in computing the series.

NATIONAL INCOME (Billions of dollars; quarterly data at seasonally adjusted annual rates)

Period	National income	Compensation of employees[1]	Proprietors' income with inventory valuation and capital consumption adjustments — Farm	Proprietors' income — Nonfarm	Rental income of persons with capital consumption adjustment	Corporate profits with inventory valuation and capital consumption adjustments — Total	Profits with inventory valuation adjustment and without capital consumption adjustment — Total	Profits before tax	Inventory valuation adjustment	Capital consumption adjustment	Net interest
1989	4,249.5	3,100.2	40.2	307.0	-13.5	362.8	325.4	342.9	-17.5	37.4	452.7
1990	4,491.0	3,297.6	41.9	321.4	-14.2	380.6	354.7	365.7	-11.0	25.9	463.7
1991	4,608.2	3,404.8	36.7	339.5	-10.5	390.3	370.9	365.2	5.8	19.4	447.4
1992	4,829.5	3,591.2	44.4	374.4	-5.5	405.1	389.4	395.9	-6.4	15.7	420.0
1993	5,131.4	3,780.4	37.3	404.3	24.1	485.8	456.2	462.4	-6.2	29.5	399.5
1994	5,458.4	4,004.6	39.5	434.2	27.7	542.7	505.0	524.5	-19.5	37.7	409.7
1982: IV	2,551.5	1,940.4	10.2	169.6	24.1	150.3	160.0	168.6	-8.6	-9.6	256.8
1983: IV	2,884.3	2,101.2	6.3	193.8	22.2	229.1	216.2	223.8	-7.6	12.9	281.8
1984: IV	3,134.4	2,288.1	21.9	217.7	24.3	261.3	223.6	220.1	-3.5	37.7	321.1
1985: IV	3,341.9	2,442.5	17.8	250.9	14.0	284.9	228.0	231.8	-3.8	56.9	331.9
1986: IV	3,486.0	2,582.5	23.6	260.9	4.7	264.6	225.0	235.7	-10.7	39.6	349.7
1987: IV	3,828.8	2,785.1	42.4	282.6	6.8	343.3	293.4	311.2	-17.8	49.9	368.6
1988: IV	4,127.6	3,004.9	30.9	302.5	2.8	378.3	340.5	372.2	-31.7	37.9	408.1
1989: IV	4,305.2	3,162.8	38.4	311.4	-21.6	354.5	320.6	334.1	-13.5	33.9	459.8
1990: IV	4,539.2	3,344.2	43.8	325.1	-11.1	362.8	349.3	368.9	-19.5	13.5	474.4
1991: IV	4,663.9	3,459.1	36.6	349.8	-8.1	394.7	372.3	373.1	-.8	22.4	431.8
1992: IV	4,964.9	3,671.0	46.0	392.4	5.1	432.5	415.6	413.5	2.1	16.9	418.0
1993: I	5,031.1	3,713.1	49.6	394.8	16.5	442.5	421.5	432.7	-11.2	21.0	414.6
II	5,094.0	3,761.1	39.4	399.4	23.4	473.1	446.6	456.6	-10.0	26.5	397.6
III	5,138.5	3,801.7	15.8	404.5	26.3	493.5	461.7	458.7	3.0	31.7	396.7
IV	5,262.0	3,845.8	44.4	418.5	30.3	533.9	495.1	501.7	-6.5	38.8	389.1
1994: I	5,308.7	3,920.0	47.2	423.8	15.3	508.2	471.2	483.5	-12.3	37.0	394.2
II	5,430.7	3,979.3	39.3	431.9	34.1	546.4	509.0	523.1	-14.1	37.4	399.7
III	5,494.9	4,023.7	29.8	437.1	32.6	556.0	518.5	538.1	-19.6	37.5	415.7
IV	5,599.4	4,095.3	41.7	444.0	29.0	560.3	521.4	553.5	-32.1	38.8	429.2
1995: I ʳ	5,687.8	4,158.2	43.5	449.2	25.1	568.8	530.8	569.5	-38.7	38.0	443.1

Source: Department of Commerce, Bureau of Economic Analysis.

[1] Includes employer contributions for social insurance.

Source: *Economic Indicators*, Council of Economic Advisers.

Gross Domestic Product as a Measure of U.S. Production

As of late 1991, the Bureau of Economic Analysis (BEA) features gross domestic product (GDP), rather than gross national product (GNP), as the primary measure of U.S. production. This change in emphasis recognizes that GDP is more appropriate for many purposes for which an aggregate measure of the Nation's production is used. GNP will remain a key aggregate in the national income and product accounts (NIPA's) and will continue to be published regularly.

How Do the GDP and GNP Concepts Differ?

Both GDP and GNP are defined in terms of goods and services produced, but they use different criteria for coverage. GDP covers the goods and services *produced by labor and property located in the United States.* As long as the labor and property are located in the United States, the suppliers (that is, the workers and, for property, the owners) may be either U.S. residents or residents of the rest of the world. GNP covers the goods and services *produced by labor and property supplied by U.S. residents.* As long as the labor and property are supplied by U.S. residents, they may be located either in the United States or abroad.

As shown in table 1, to move from GNP to GDP one must subtract factor income receipts from foreigners, which represent the goods and services produced abroad using the labor and property supplied by U.S. residents, and add factor income payments to foreigners, which represent the goods and services produced in the United States using the labor and property supplied by foreigners. Factor incomes are measured as compensation of employees, corporate profits (dividends, earnings of unincorporated affiliates, and reinvested earnings of incorporated affiliates), and net interest.

Why Feature GDP?

GDP refers to production taking place in the United States. It is, therefore, the appropriate measure for much of the short-term monitoring and analysis of the U.S. economy. In particular, GDP is consistent in coverage with indicators such as employment, productivity, industry output, and investment in equipment and structures.

In addition, the use of GDP facilitates comparisons of economic activity in the

Source: *Survey of Current Business,* Bureau of Economic Analysis, U.S. Department of Commerce.

United States with that in other countries. GDP is the primary measure of production in the System of National Accounts, the set of international guidelines for economic accounting that the U.S. economic accounts will be moving toward in the mid-1990's, and virtually all other countries have already adopted GDP as their primary measure of production. Canada, for example, began featuring GDP in 1986.

The emphasis on GDP is consistent with measurement considerations. Data from BEA's direct investment survey, which is one of the primary sources for estimating factor income payments and receipts, are not available for the first two of the three quarterly estimates of GNP. For these two estimates, factor income payments and receipts are based on judgments about trends in the pace of economic activity in the United States and abroad and about the value of the dollar in foreign countries, on announced profits of individual companies, and on other information. Even when all of the source data become available, BEA does not have the information needed to make a full set of adjustments to reflect the concepts underlying the NIPA's. For example, the profits of foreign affiliates do not include inventory valuation and capital consumption adjustments, and they are affected by intracompany transfer prices and exchange rates. In addition, the deflation of current-dollar factor incomes is problematic because incomes such as interest and dividends cannot be separated into price and quantity components. Lacking a component-specific deflator, BEA uses the implicit price deflator for net domestic product to derive constant-dollar estimates.

GNP, however, continues to be a useful concept. Because it refers to the income available to U.S. residents as the result of their contribution to production, it is appropriate for analyses related to sources and uses of income. For example, saving rates are normally expressed as a percentage of income, and GNP is the more appropriate measure for this purpose. In addition, GNP is better than GDP for analyses that focus on the availability of resources, such as the Nation's ability to finance expenditures on education.

How Much Do the Estimates of GDP and GNP Differ?

For the United States, the dollar levels of GDP and GNP differ little—that is, the net receipts (receipts from foreigners less payments to foreigners) of factor income have been small (tables 1 and 2). The main reason is that the value of the property owned abroad by U.S. residents (U.S. investment abroad) less the value of the property owned

TABLE 1. RELATION OF GNP AND GDP

	1990	
	Billions of dollars	Billions of 1982 dollars
GNP	5,465.1	4,157.3
Less: Factor income receipts from foreigners	137.4	102.2
Plus: Factor income payments to foreigners	95.7	70.3
GDP	5,423.4	4,125.4

TABLE 2. DIFFERENCES BETWEEN GNP AND GDP

Year or quarter	GNP less GDP (Billions of dollars)	GNP less GDP, as a percent of GDP	Growth rate of GNP less growth rate of GDP, based on 1982 dollars (Percentage points)
1980	47.6	1.8	0
1981	52.1	1.7	−.1
1982	51.2	1.6	0
1983	49.9	1.5	−.1
1984	47.4	1.3	−.2
1985	40.7	1.0	−.2
1986	34.4	.8	−.2
1987	29.0	.6	−.2
1988	33.5	.7	.1
1989	37.6	.7	0
1990	41.7	.8	.1
1990: I	41.6	.8	−.1
II	31.6	.6	−.8
III...............	42.9	.8	.7
IV...............	50.8	.9	.5
1991: I	54.8	1.0	.2
II	42.4	.8	−.9

NOTE.—The quarterly estimates are based on seasonally adjusted annual rates.

by foreigners in the United States (foreign investment in the United States) has been small relative to the size of the U.S. economy. (The value of labor supplied to, and by, foreigners is even smaller.) Since 1929, the receipts by U.S. residents from their investments abroad have exceeded payments to foreigners for their investments here, so GNP has been larger than GDP. The largest percentage difference, 1.8 percent, was in 1980. In 1990, GNP was 0.8 percent larger than GDP.

In some countries, the difference between GDP and GNP is much larger. For example, there is much more foreign investment in Canada than Canadian investment abroad; consequently, its GNP was 3.6 percent smaller than its GDP in 1990. However, the difference in France, Japan, the United Kingdom, and several other industrialized countries is now similar, at 1 percent or less, to that in the United States.

Although the differences between the dollar levels of U.S. GNP and GDP are small, their growth rates sometimes differ. Table 2 shows that the annual growth rate of real GNP was slightly less than that of real GDP in most years of the 1980's. Differences between growth rates tend to be larger and to fluctuate more.

GROSS DOMESTIC PRODUCT

BILLIONS OF DOLLARS (RATIO SCALE)

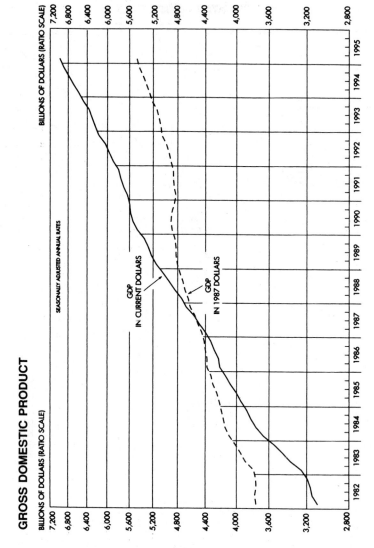

SEASONALLY ADJUSTED ANNUAL RATES

GDP IN CURRENT DOLLARS

GDP IN 1987 DOLLARS

BILLIONS OF DOLLARS (RATIO SCALE)

SOURCE: DEPARTMENT OF COMMERCE

COUNCIL OF ECONOMIC ADVISERS

[Billions of current dollars; quarterly data at seasonally adjusted annual rates]

Period	Gross domestic product	Personal consumption expenditures	Gross private domestic investment	Net exports	Exports	Imports	Government purchases Total	Federal Total	Federal National defense	Federal Non-defense	State and local	Final sales of domestic product	Gross domestic purchases	Addendum: Gross national product
1986	4,268.6	2,850.6	717.6	−132.5	319.2	451.7	833.0	367.8	276.7	91.1	465.3	4,260.0	4,401.2	4,277.7
1987	4,539.9	3,052.2	749.3	−143.1	364.0	507.1	881.5	384.9	292.1	92.9	496.6	4,513.7	4,683.0	4,544.5
1988	4,900.4	3,296.1	793.6	−108.0	444.2	552.2	918.7	387.0	295.6	91.4	531.7	4,884.2	5,008.4	4,908.2
1989	5,250.8	3,523.1	832.3	−79.7	508.0	587.7	975.2	401.6	299.9	101.7	573.6	5,217.5	5,330.5	5,266.8
1990	5,546.1	3,761.2	808.9	−71.4	557.1	628.5	1,047.4	426.5	314.0	112.5	620.9	5,539.3	5,617.5	5,567.8
1991	5,724.8	3,902.4	744.8	−19.9	601.1	620.9	1,097.4	445.8	322.8	123.1	651.6	5,726.6	5,744.7	5,740.8
1992	6,020.2	4,136.9	788.3	−30.3	638.1	668.4	1,125.3	449.0	314.2	134.8	676.3	6,017.2	6,050.5	6,025.8
1993	6,343.3	4,378.2	882.0	−65.3	659.1	724.3	1,148.4	443.6	302.7	140.9	704.7	6,327.9	6,408.6	6,347.8
1994	6,738.4	4,628.4	1,032.9	−98.2	718.7	816.9	1,175.3	437.3	292.3	145.0	738.0	6,686.2	6,836.6	6,726.9
1982: IV	3,195.1	2,128.7	464.2	−29.5	265.6	295.1	631.6	281.4	205.5	75.9	350.3	3,241.4	3,224.6	3,222.6
1983: IV	3,547.3	2,346.8	614.8	−71.8	286.2	358.0	657.6	289.7	222.8	66.9	367.9	3,527.1	3,619.1	3,578.4
1984: IV	3,869.1	2,526.4	722.8	−107.1	308.7	415.7	727.0	324.7	242.9	81.9	402.2	3,818.1	3,976.2	3,890.2
1985: IV	4,140.5	2,739.8	737.0	−135.5	304.7	440.2	799.2	356.9	268.6	88.3	442.4	4,107.9	4,276.0	4,156.2
1986: IV	4,336.6	2,923.1	697.1	−133.2	333.9	467.1	849.7	373.1	278.6	94.5	476.6	4,355.4	4,469.8	4,340.5
1987: IV	4,683.0	3,124.6	800.2	−143.2	392.4	535.6	901.4	392.5	295.8	96.7	509.0	4,623.7	4,826.2	4,690.5
1988: IV	5,044.6	3,398.2	814.8	−106.0	467.0	573.1	937.6	392.0	296.8	95.2	545.7	5,027.3	5,150.7	5,054.3
1989: IV	5,344.6	3,599.1	825.2	−73.9	523.8	597.7	994.5	405.1	302.5	102.6	589.3	5,314.6	5,418.7	5,365.0
1990: IV	5,597.9	3,836.6	756.4	−71.6	577.6	649.2	1,076.5	436.5	322.5	114.0	640.0	5,621.8	5,669.5	5,630.0
1991: IV	5,796.6	3,955.7	756.8	−13.7	623.7	637.5	1,097.9	438.3	311.6	126.6	659.7	5,782.3	5,810.4	5,810.7
1992: IV	6,169.3	4,251.3	822.0	−42.2	649.2	691.4	1,138.1	454.8	316.0	138.7	683.3	6,160.0	6,211.4	6,167.0
1993: I	6,235.9	4,294.6	853.8	−49.6	646.8	696.4	1,137.1	446.9	307.0	139.9	690.2	6,215.8	6,285.5	6,243.9
II	6,299.9	4,347.3	869.7	−63.3	660.1	723.5	1,146.3	445.2	305.8	139.4	701.2	6,281.4	6,363.3	6,303.3
III	6,359.2	4,401.2	882.2	−77.0	649.0	726.0	1,152.9	442.7	299.0	143.6	710.2	6,345.4	6,436.3	6,367.8
IV	6,478.1	4,469.6	922.5	−71.2	680.3	751.4	1,157.2	439.8	299.1	140.7	717.4	6,469.2	6,549.3	6,476.2
1994: I	6,574.7	4,535.0	966.6	−86.7	674.2	760.9	1,159.8	437.8	291.7	146.1	722.0	6,550.6	6,661.4	6,574.0
II	6,689.9	4,586.4	1,034.4	−97.6	704.5	802.1	1,166.7	435.1	291.7	143.5	731.5	6,622.5	6,787.5	6,682.5
III	6,791.7	4,657.5	1,055.1	−109.6	730.5	840.1	1,188.8	444.3	300.5	143.8	744.5	6,729.1	6,901.3	6,779.6
IV	6,897.2	4,734.8	1,075.6	−98.9	765.5	864.4	1,185.8	431.9	285.3	146.6	753.8	6,842.4	6,996.1	6,871.3
1995: I ʳ	6,979.7	4,785.8	1,110.1	−113.1	775.8	888.9	1,196.9	433.6	283.8	149.8	763.3	6,924.4	7,092.8	6,957.9

Source: Department of Commerce, Bureau of Economic Analysis.

[1] GDP less exports of goods and services plus imports of goods and services.

Source: Economic Indicators, Council of Economic Advisers.

GROSS DOMESTIC PRODUCT IN 1987 DOLLARS (Billions of 1987 dollars; quarterly data at seasonally adjusted annual rates)

Period	Gross domestic product	Personal consumption expenditures	Gross private domestic investment — Nonresidential fixed investment	Gross private domestic investment — Residential fixed investment	Gross private domestic investment — Change in business inventories	Exports and imports of goods and services — Net exports	Exports	Imports	Government purchases — Total	Government purchases — Federal Total	Government purchases — Federal National defense	Government purchases — Federal Non-defense	Government purchases — State and local	Final sales of domestic product	Gross domestic purchases	Addendum: Gross national product
1986	4,404.5	2,969.1	500.3	226.2	8.5	-155.1	329.6	484.7	855.1	373.0	280.6	92.4	482.4	4,395.9	4,559.6	4,413.5
1987	4,539.9	3,052.2	497.8	225.2	26.3	-143.1	364.0	507.1	881.5	384.9	292.1	92.9	496.6	4,513.7	4,683.0	4,544.5
1988	4,718.6	3,162.4	530.8	222.7	19.9	-104.0	421.6	525.7	886.8	377.3	287.0	90.2	509.6	4,698.6	4,822.6	4,726.3
1989	4,838.0	3,223.3	540.0	214.2	29.8	-73.7	471.8	545.4	904.4	376.1	281.4	94.8	528.3	4,808.3	4,911.7	4,852.7
1990	4,897.3	3,272.6	546.5	194.5	5.7	-54.7	510.5	565.1	932.6	384.1	283.6	100.4	548.5	4,891.6	4,951.9	4,916.5
1991	4,867.6	3,259.4	515.4	169.5	-1.1	-19.5	542.6	562.1	944.0	386.7	281.4	105.3	557.2	4,868.7	4,887.2	4,882.3
1992	4,979.3	3,349.5	525.9	196.9	2.5	-32.3	578.8	611.2	936.9	373.5	261.4	112.2	563.3	4,976.9	5,011.6	4,985.7
1993	5,134.5	3,458.7	591.6	213.0	15.3	-73.9	602.5	676.3	929.8	356.6	243.7	113.0	573.1	5,119.3	5,208.4	5,140.3
1994	5,344.0	3,579.6	672.4	231.3	47.8	-110.0	657.0	766.9	922.8	337.6	226.7	110.9	585.2	5,296.2	5,454.0	5,337.3
1982: IV	3,759.6	2,539.3	417.2	131.2	-44.9	-19.0	280.4	299.4	735.9	316.0	229.4	86.6	419.9	3,804.5	3,778.6	3,791.7
1983: IV	4,012.1	2,678.2	449.6	190.6	29.3	-83.7	291.5	375.1	748.1	322.2	242.9	79.3	425.9	3,982.8	4,095.8	4,046.6
1984: IV	4,194.2	2,784.8	509.6	198.8	47.9	-131.4	312.8	444.2	784.3	341.7	254.3	87.4	442.6	4,146.2	4,325.5	4,216.4
1985: IV	4,333.5	2,895.3	525.5	207.4	30.2	-155.4	312.0	467.4	830.5	363.7	272.1	91.6	466.7	4,303.3	4,488.9	4,349.5
1986: IV	4,427.1	3,012.5	495.5	230.5	-20.1	-156.0	342.9	498.9	864.8	377.5	282.2	95.3	487.3	4,447.2	4,583.1	4,430.8
1987: IV	4,625.5	3,074.7	510.6	223.3	59.9	-136.0	386.1	522.1	893.0	391.6	295.0	96.6	501.4	4,565.6	4,761.5	4,633.0
1988: IV	4,779.7	3,202.9	538.8	225.3	20.9	-102.7	438.2	540.9	894.5	378.4	285.7	92.7	516.1	4,758.7	4,882.4	4,789.0
1989: IV	4,856.7	3,242.0	536.7	208.0	24.9	-67.4	487.7	555.0	912.6	376.1	281.5	94.7	536.5	4,831.8	4,924.1	4,875.1
1990: IV	4,867.2	3,265.9	540.2	176.3	-20.9	-36.8	520.4	557.2	942.4	386.5	285.7	100.8	555.8	4,888.0	4,904.0	4,895.4
1991: IV	4,880.8	3,265.3	506.9	177.5	13.5	-16.9	562.6	579.4	934.4	374.1	265.8	108.2	560.4	4,867.3	4,897.6	4,893.9
1992: IV	5,060.7	3,403.4	540.9	207.7	6.6	-38.5	590.7	629.3	940.6	377.0	262.4	114.6	563.6	5,054.1	5,099.2	5,061.0
1993: I	5,075.3	3,417.2	560.3	210.4	18.5	-57.6	589.2	646.8	926.5	361.6	248.2	113.3	564.9	5,056.8	5,132.9	5,083.9
II	5,105.4	3,439.2	581.0	206.3	18.9	-69.3	600.2	669.6	929.3	358.3	246.8	111.5	571.0	5,086.5	5,174.7	5,110.1
III	5,139.4	3,472.2	597.9	211.0	13.0	-86.3	595.3	681.6	931.8	355.6	240.9	114.7	576.2	5,126.5	5,225.8	5,148.4
IV	5,218.0	3,506.2	627.2	224.5	10.8	-82.2	625.2	707.4	931.5	351.1	238.7	112.4	580.4	5,207.2	5,300.2	5,218.7
1994: I	5,261.1	3,546.3	643.6	229.9	25.4	-104.0	619.6	723.6	919.9	341.7	228.5	113.2	578.3	5,235.7	5,365.1	5,262.7
II	5,314.1	3,557.8	657.0	233.8	59.2	-111.8	643.9	755.6	917.1	334.7	226.1	108.7	582.4	5,254.9	5,425.8	5,310.5
III	5,367.0	3,584.7	680.0	230.2	57.1	-117.0	666.5	783.5	932.0	343.5	233.0	110.5	588.5	5,310.0	5,484.0	5,359.9
IV	5,433.8	3,629.6	708.2	231.5	49.4	-107.1	697.9	805.0	922.2	330.4	219.1	111.3	591.8	5,384.4	5,540.9	5,416.0
1995: I [r]	5,470.0	3,646.1	742.3	230.0	52.3	-120.0	702.2	822.2	919.4	326.9	215.0	111.8	592.5	5,417.7	5,590.0	5,455.3

Source: Department of Commerce, Bureau of Economic Analysis.

[1] GDP less exports of goods and services plus imports of goods and services.

Source: *Economic Indicators*, Council of Economic Advisers.

PERSONAL CONSUMPTION EXPENDITURES IN 1987 DOLLARS (Billions of 1987 dollars, except as noted; quarterly data at seasonally adjusted annual rates)

Period	Total personal consumption expenditures	Durable goods				Nondurable goods						Services			Retail sales of new passenger cars (millions of units)	
		Total durable goods	Motor vehicles and parts	Furniture and household equipment	Other	Total nondurable goods	Food	Clothing and shoes	Gasoline and oil	Fuel oil and coal	Other	Total services[1]	Housing	Medical care	Domestics	Imports
1989	3,223.3	440.7	196.4	165.8	78.5	1,051.6	515.0	187.8	87.3	11.4	250.2	1,731.0	469.2	408.6	7.1	2.8
1990	3,272.6	443.1	192.7	171.6	78.7	1,060.7	523.9	186.2	86.4	10.5	253.8	1,768.8	474.6	424.6	6.9	2.6
1991	3,259.4	425.3	170.0	179.2	76.1	1,047.7	518.8	184.7	83.1	10.7	250.5	1,786.3	479.0	437.7	6.1	2.3
1992	3,349.5	452.6	181.8	193.3	77.5	1,057.7	514.7	193.2	85.6	11.2	253.0	1,839.1	485.2	454.3	6.3	2.1
1993	3,458.7	489.9	196.1	214.1	79.7	1,078.5	524.0	197.8	86.5	12.1	258.2	1,890.3	492.6	466.4	6.7	2.0
1994	3,579.6	532.1	208.2	238.7	85.2	1,109.5	535.6	208.8	87.2	11.9	265.9	1,938.1	501.3	479.0	7.3	2.0
1982: IV	2,539.3	272.3	123.7	96.4	52.3	880.7	458.3	135.7	73.4	10.5	202.8	1,386.2	411.0	327.8	6.0	2.5
1983: IV	2,678.2	319.1	151.6	109.3	58.1	915.2	467.1	147.7	76.9	11.4	212.2	1,443.9	419.7	334.8	7.4	2.6
1984: IV	2,784.8	347.7	164.3	118.7	64.8	942.9	475.1	154.7	79.0	11.1	222.0	1,494.2	431.3	344.9	7.7	2.6
1985: IV	2,895.3	369.6	173.9	128.6	67.1	968.7	488.2	161.7	79.5	11.4	228.0	1,557.1	438.1	359.1	7.0	3.1
1986: IV	3,012.5	415.7	193.6	141.4	80.7	1,000.9	496.9	171.9	84.6	12.4	235.2	1,595.8	444.8	372.0	7.7	3.4
1987: IV	3,074.7	404.7	183.6	145.9	75.2	1,014.6	502.4	174.5	85.4	11.9	240.4	1,655.5	457.0	390.7	6.6	3.3
1988: IV	3,202.9	439.2	197.7	160.3	81.2	1,046.8	518.0	182.8	87.5	12.0	246.4	1,716.9	465.6	403.0	7.5	3.0
1989: IV	3,242.0	436.8	188.3	167.9	80.5	1,058.9	515.6	190.9	88.6	12.0	251.8	1,746.3	471.3	411.8	6.2	2.6
1990: IV	3,265.9	433.2	182.1	172.3	78.8	1,057.5	525.8	184.5	84.6	9.5	253.1	1,775.2	475.9	429.4	6.6	2.4
1991: IV	3,265.3	427.7	171.6	181.2	74.9	1,040.4	514.9	182.8	82.4	10.7	249.7	1,797.3	481.4	444.7	6.1	2.2
1992: IV	3,403.4	468.8	188.2	202.0	78.6	1,074.2	522.0	198.1	86.0	11.3	256.3	1,860.4	487.8	459.0	6.4	2.0
1993: I	3,417.2	472.5	189.7	205.2	77.6	1,070.0	520.7	194.0	86.1	12.0	257.2	1,874.8	489.8	463.1	6.4	2.0
II	3,439.2	483.7	195.1	209.9	78.7	1,074.3	522.3	196.1	85.7	11.8	258.3	1,881.2	491.5	464.3	6.9	2.1
III	3,472.2	492.7	195.0	216.6	81.1	1,081.7	525.1	198.6	87.5	12.2	258.4	1,897.8	493.7	467.6	6.7	2.0
IV	3,506.2	510.8	204.7	224.6	81.5	1,088.0	528.1	202.4	86.6	12.2	258.8	1,907.4	495.4	470.4	7.1	1.9
1994: I	3,546.3	521.7	213.7	225.9	82.0	1,098.3	531.9	203.8	86.1	13.4	263.1	1,926.3	497.7	473.2	7.4	2.0
II	3,557.8	522.2	205.3	232.5	84.4	1,104.3	536.1	204.9	86.7	11.4	265.1	1,931.4	500.0	477.4	7.2	2.0
III	3,584.7	529.6	202.0	241.7	86.0	1,113.4	535.7	210.2	88.0	11.7	267.6	1,941.8	502.6	481.0	7.1	2.0
IV	3,629.6	554.8	211.9	254.5	88.4	1,121.9	538.5	216.4	88.2	11.1	267.6	1,952.9	505.0	484.4	7.4	1.8
1995: I[p]	3,646.1	549.1	202.7	256.2	90.1	1,129.0	541.2	216.9	90.3	11.6	269.1	1,968.0	507.4	486.8	7.0	1.8

1 Includes other items, not shown separately.

Source: Economic Indicators, Council of Economic Advisers.

Source: Department of Commerce, Bureau of Economic Analysis.

CORPORATE PROFITS

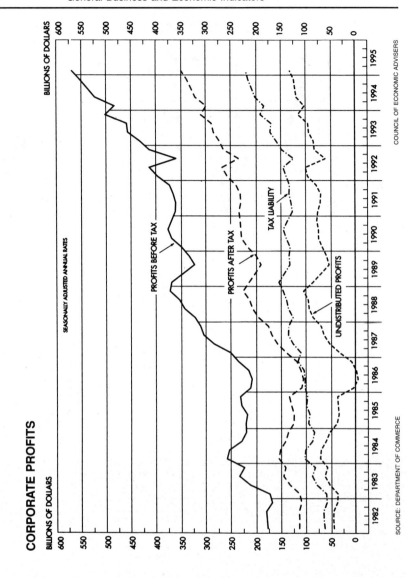

BILLIONS OF DOLLARS

SOURCE: DEPARTMENT OF COMMERCE

COUNCIL OF ECONOMIC ADVISERS

[Billions of dollars; quarterly data at seasonally adjusted annual rates]

Period	Profits (before tax) with inventory valuation adjustment[1]						Profits before tax	Tax liability	Profits after tax			Inventory valuation adjustment
	Total[2]	Domestic industries										
		Total	Financial	Nonfinancial					Total	Dividends	Undistributed profits	
				Total[3]	Manufacturing	Wholesale and retail trade						
1986	227.6	194.6	35.8	158.9	59.0	46.3	217.8	106.5	111.3	109.8	1.6	9.7
1987	273.4	233.9	36.4	197.5	87.0	39.9	287.9	127.1	160.8	106.2	54.6	-14.5
1988	320.3	271.2	41.8	229.4	117.5	37.1	347.5	137.0	210.6	115.3	95.2	-27.3
1989	325.4	266.0	50.6	215.3	108.0	39.7	342.9	141.3	201.6	134.6	67.1	-17.5
1990	354.7	286.7	65.7	221.1	109.1	37.2	365.7	138.7	227.1	153.5	73.6	-11.0
1991	370.9	302.4	84.3	218.1	90.1	46.7	365.2	131.1	234.1	160.0	74.1	5.8
1992	389.4	328.8	81.9	246.9	94.5	54.8	395.9	139.7	256.2	171.1	85.1	-6.4
1993	456.2	391.0	103.7	287.3	114.2	61.2	462.4	173.2	289.2	191.7	97.5	-6.2
1994	505.0	444.6	104.0	340.6	145.6	67.6	524.5	202.5	322.0	205.2	116.9	-19.5
1982: IV	160.0	130.8	23.0	107.8	50.1	33.8	168.6	58.7	109.9	72.5	37.5	-8.6
1983: IV	216.2	182.6	22.1	160.5	90.5	40.7	223.8	82.2	141.6	84.2	57.4	-7.6
1984: IV	223.6	192.9	20.3	172.6	79.2	50.8	220.1	83.8	136.3	83.4	52.9	3.5
1985: IV	228.0	193.5	29.0	164.5	83.3	39.0	231.8	97.6	134.2	97.4	36.9	-3.8
1986: IV	225.0	192.5	34.7	157.8	63.9	43.1	235.7	116.6	119.2	111.0	8.2	-10.7
1987: IV	293.4	246.3	39.4	207.0	98.7	39.3	311.2	135.2	176.0	106.3	69.7	-17.8
1988: IV	340.5	285.9	46.1	239.7	129.3	39.3	372.2	146.2	226.0	121.0	105.0	-31.7
1989: IV	320.6	254.8	52.5	202.3	94.5	39.2	334.1	134.2	200.0	141.3	58.7	-13.5
1990: IV	349.3	273.8	66.6	207.2	98.5	36.2	368.9	137.0	231.8	153.7	78.1	-19.5
1991: IV	372.3	301.4	84.6	216.8	85.3	47.4	373.1	133.1	240.0	160.9	79.1	-.8
1992: IV	415.6	361.0	86.7	274.3	101.3	64.6	413.5	148.6	264.8	182.1	82.7	2.1
1993: I	421.5	354.0	95.9	258.0	96.2	56.0	432.7	159.8	273.0	188.2	84.7	-11.2
II	446.6	383.8	100.1	283.7	114.2	63.3	456.6	171.8	284.8	190.7	94.1	-10.0
III	461.7	392.6	103.9	288.7	112.4	62.0	458.7	169.9	288.9	193.2	95.6	3.0
IV	495.1	433.4	114.6	318.8	134.2	63.7	501.7	191.5	310.2	194.6	115.6	-6.5
1994: I	471.2	410.1	89.6	320.5	145.1	59.0	483.5	184.1	299.4	196.3	103.0	-12.3
II	509.0	448.2	106.4	341.8	143.0	72.0	523.1	201.7	321.4	202.5	118.9	-14.1
III	518.5	458.1	112.6	345.5	143.3	70.1	538.1	208.6	329.5	207.9	121.6	-19.6
IV	521.4	461.7	107.2	354.5	150.9	69.2	553.5	215.6	337.9	213.9	124.0	-32.1
1995: I p	530.8	463.6	114.2	349.4	....	....	569.5	220.2	349.4	217.1	132.2	-38.7

[1] See p. 81 for profits with inventory valuation and capital consumption adjustments.
[2] Includes rest of the world, not shown separately.
[3] Includes industries not shown separately.

Source: Department of Commerce, Bureau of Economic Analysis.

Source: Economic Indicators, Council of Economic Advisers.

Price Data

Definitions are applicable to the exhibit on pages 91–92.

Price data are gathered by the Bureau of Labor Statistics from retail and primary markets in the United States. Price indexes are given in relation to a base period (1982 = 100 for many Producer Price Indexes or 1982–84 = 100 for many Consumer Price Indexes, unless otherwise noted).

DEFINITIONS

The **Consumer Price Index** (CPI) is a measure of the average change in the prices paid by urban consumers for a fixed market basket of goods and services. The CPI is calculated monthly for two population groups, one consisting only of urban households whose primary source of income is derived from the employment of wage earners and clerical workers, and the other consisting of all urban households. The wage earner index (CPI–W) is a continuation of the historic index that was introduced well over a half-century ago for use in wage negotiations. As new uses were developed for the CPI in recent years, the need for a broader and more representative index became apparent. The all urban consumer index (CPI–U) introduced in 1978 is representative of the 1982–84 buying habits of about 80 percent of the noninstitutional population of the United States at that time, compared with 32 percent represented in the CPI–W. In addition to wage earners and clerical workers, the CPI–U covers professional, managerial, and technical workers, the self-employed, short-term workers, the unemployed, retirees, and others not in the labor force.

The CPI is based on prices of food, clothing, shelter, fuel, drugs, transportation fares, doctor's and dentist's fees, and other goods and services that people buy for day-to-day living. The quantity and quality of these items are kept essentially unchanged between major revisions so that only price changes will be measured. All taxes directly associated with the purchase and use of items are included in the index.

Data collected from more than 19,000 retail establishments and 57,000 tenants in 85 urban areas across the country are used to develop the "U.S. city average." Separate estimates for 15 major urban centers are presented in the table on page 92. The areas listed are as indicated in footnote 1 to the table. The area indexes measure only the average change in prices for each area since the base period, and do not indicate differences in the level of prices among cities.

NOTES ON THE DATA

In January 1983, the Bureau changed the way in which homeownership costs are measured for the CPI–U. A rental equivalence method replaced the asset-price approach to homeownership costs for that series. In January 1985, the same change was made in the CPI–W. The central purpose of the change was to separate shelter costs from the investment component of homeownership so that the index would reflect only the cost of shelter services provided by owner-occupied homes. An updated CPI–U and CPI–W were introduced with release of the January 1987 data.

For additional information on consumer prices, contact the Division of Consumer Prices and Price Indexes: 202-606-7000.

Source: *Monthly Labor Review*, U.S. Department of Labor Statistics, Bureau of Labor Statistics.

CONSUMER PRICE INDEX—U.S. CITY AVERAGE AND AVAILABLE LOCAL AREA DATA: ALL ITEMS

(1982–84=100, unless otherwise indicated)

Area[1]	Pricing schedule[2]	All Urban Consumers							Urban Wage Earners						
		1994				1995			1994				1995		
		Feb.	Mar.	Nov.	Dec.	Jan.	Feb.	Mar.	Feb.	Mar.	Nov.	Dec.	Jan.	Feb.	Mar.
U.S. city average	M	146.7	147.2	149.7	149.7	150.3	150.9	151.4	144.0	144.4	147.3	147.2	147.8	148.3	148.7
Region and area size[3]															
Northeast urban	M	154.0	154.3	156.7	156.3	157.1	157.6	158.0	151.4	151.7	154.3	154.0	154.8	155.2	155.5
Size A—More than 1,200,000	M	154.6	155.1	157.2	156.6	157.7	158.3	158.7	150.9	151.4	153.8	153.3	154.3	154.8	155.1
Size B—500,000 to 1,200,000	M	153.0	152.7	154.8	155.3	155.4	155.7	155.9	150.7	150.6	152.6	153.1	153.3	153.7	153.9
Size C—50,000 to 500,000	M	151.9	152.2	155.4	155.0	155.7	156.0	156.6	153.2	153.4	157.1	156.7	157.4	157.6	158.1
North Central urban	M	142.1	142.6	145.8	145.7	146.1	146.7	147.3	139.0	139.4	142.8	142.7	143.0	143.6	144.2
Size A—More than 1,200,000	M	143.2	143.9	146.8	146.8	147.3	148.0	148.5	139.4	140.0	143.1	143.1	143.5	144.2	144.7
Size B—360,000 to 1,200,000	M	141.3	141.8	144.5	144.1	144.4	145.2	146.1	137.6	137.9	141.0	140.6	140.9	141.8	142.6
Size C—50,000 to 360,000	M	143.0	143.1	147.4	147.1	147.4	147.7	148.3	140.6	140.6	144.8	144.6	144.9	145.2	145.6
Size D—Nonmetropolitan (less than 50,000)	M	137.2	137.8	141.3	141.2	141.5	142.3	142.7	135.8	136.3	139.9	139.7	139.8	140.4	141.0
South urban	M	142.9	143.6	146.0	146.1	146.7	147.4	148.0	141.2	141.9	144.8	144.9	145.3	145.9	146.5
Size A—More than 1,200,000	M	143.4	144.4	145.9	146.0	146.6	147.3	148.0	141.3	142.3	144.3	144.3	144.8	145.4	146.1
Size B—450,000 to 1,200,000	M	144.6	145.4	148.4	148.4	148.9	149.6	150.4	141.2	141.8	145.2	145.3	145.6	146.3	146.9
Size C—50,000 to 450,000	M	141.6	142.0	145.0	145.3	145.7	146.2	146.6	141.3	141.6	145.1	145.3	145.7	146.1	146.5
Size D—Nonmetropolitan (less than 50,000)	M	140.7	141.3	144.3	144.3	145.2	146.1	146.6	141.0	141.4	144.7	144.7	145.6	146.4	146.7
West urban	M	148.3	149.0	151.1	151.2	152.0	152.4	152.8	145.4	145.9	148.2	148.5	149.2	149.4	149.8
Size A—More than 1,250,000	M	149.9	150.5	151.9	152.2	152.9	153.1	153.6	145.4	145.9	147.6	147.9	148.5	148.7	149.1
Size C—50,000 to 330,000	M	148.3	148.7	153.8	153.3	154.1	155.1	155.2	146.0	146.3	151.1	150.7	151.4	152.2	152.2
Size classes:															
A (12/86 = 100)	M	133.3	133.9	135.6	135.6	136.2	136.7	137.2	132.1	132.7	134.8	134.7	135.3	135.7	136.2
B	M	146.1	146.5	149.4	149.4	149.9	150.5	151.1	143.4	143.8	146.8	146.9	147.3	147.9	148.5
C	M	144.9	145.2	148.9	148.8	149.3	149.8	150.2	144.1	144.3	148.2	148.1	148.6	149.0	149.3
D	M	141.5	142.0	145.3	145.3	145.9	146.6	147.1	140.8	141.2	144.8	144.8	145.2	145.8	146.3

(continued)

CONSUMER PRICE INDEX—U.S. CITY AVERAGE AND AVAILABLE LOCAL AREA DATA: ALL ITEMS (concluded)

(1982–84 = 100, unless otherwise indicated)

Area[1]	Pricing schedule[2]	All Urban Consumers							Urban Wage Earners						
		1994				1995			1994				1995		
		Feb.	Mar.	Nov.	Dec.	Jan.	Feb.	Mar.	Feb.	Mar.	Nov.	Dec.	Jan.	Feb.	Mar.
Selected local areas															
Chicago, IL-Northwestern IN	M	146.8	147.6	150.4	150.5	151.8	152.3	152.6	142.3	143.0	145.7	145.8	147.1	147.5	147.8
Los Angeles-Long Beach, Anaheim, CA	M	152.2	152.5	152.9	153.4	154.3	154.5	154.6	146.9	147.0	147.7	148.1	149.0	149.2	149.3
New York, NY-Northeastern NJ	M	157.4	157.9	159.4	158.9	159.9	160.3	160.9	153.5	154.0	155.9	155.4	156.3	156.6	157.1
Philadelphia, PA-NJ	M	152.9	153.5	156.7	155.4	156.6	157.8	158.0	152.2	152.8	156.1	155.1	156.4	157.5	157.5
San Francisco-Oakland, CA	M	147.4	148.2	149.8	149.4	150.3	150.5	151.1	145.0	145.6	147.6	147.4	148.2	148.3	148.9
Baltimore, MD	1	—	145.0	148.6	—	148.7	—	150.3	—	144.2	147.6	—	147.7	—	149.1
Boston, MA	1	—	155.0	156.7	—	158.0	—	158.4	—	153.5	155.8	—	157.0	—	156.9
Cleveland, OH	1	—	143.3	146.0	—	146.6	—	147.3	—	135.7	138.8	—	139.0	—	139.7
Miami, FL	1	—	143.5	144.5	—	147.3	—	148.7	—	141.1	142.7	—	145.3	—	146.6
St. Louis, MO-IL	1	—	139.7	143.3	—	142.9	—	144.5	—	138.7	142.9	—	142.3	—	143.9
Washington, DC-MD-VA	1	—	151.5	153.0	—	153.8	—	155.1	—	148.9	150.6	—	151.2	—	152.4
Dallas-Ft. Worth, TX	2	139.2	—	—	141.9	—	143.3	—	138.1	—	—	141.7	—	142.7	—
Detroit, MI	2	141.7	—	—	145.5	—	147.3	—	137.0	—	—	141.0	—	142.7	—
Houston, TX	2	137.0	—	—	137.8	—	139.3	—	136.3	—	—	137.8	—	138.9	—
Pittsburgh, PA	2	142.6	—	—	146.5	—	147.3	—	136.3	—	—	140.3	—	141.1	—

[1] Area definitions are those established by the Office of Management and Budget in 1983, except for Boston-Lawrence-Salem, MA-NH, Area (excludes Monroe County); and Milwaukee, WI, Area (includes only the Milwaukee MSA). Definitions do not include revisions made since 1983. Excludes farms and the military.

[2] Foods, fuels, and several other items priced every month in all areas; most other goods and services priced as indicated:
M—Every month.
1 —January, March, May, July, September, and November.
2 —February, April, June, August, October, and December.

[3] Regions are defined as the four Census regions.
—Data not available.

NOTE: Local area CPI indexes are byproducts of the national CPI program. Because each local index is a small subset of the national index, it has a smaller sample size and is, therefore, subject to substantially more sampling and other measurement error than the national index. As a result, local area indexes show greater volatility than the national index, although their long-term trends are quite similar. Therefore, the Bureau of Labor Statistics strongly urges users to consider adopting the national average CPI for use in escalator clauses.

Source: Monthly Labor Review, U.S. Department of Labor, Bureau of Labor Statistics.

Purchasing Power of the Dollar:
1950–1994

1950 to 1992

[Indexes: PPI, 1982 = $1.00; CPI, 1982–84 = $1.00. Producer prices prior to 1961, and consumer prices prior to 1964, exclude Alaska and Hawaii. Producer prices based on finished goods index. Obtained by dividing the average price index for the 1982 = 100, PPI; 1982–84 = 100, CPI base periods (100.0) by the price index for a given period and expressing the result in dollars and cents. Annual figures are based on average of monthly data]

YEAR	ANNUAL AVERAGE AS MEASURED BY—		YEAR	ANNUAL AVERAGE AS MEASURED BY—		YEAR	ANNUAL AVERAGE AS MEASURED BY—	
	Producer prices	Consumer prices		Producer prices	Consumer prices		Producer prices	Consumer prices
1950.....	$3.546	$4.151	1965....	2.933	3.166	1979....	1.289	1.380
1951.....	3.247	3.846	1966....	2.841	3.080	1980....	1.136	1.215
1952.....	3.268	3.765	1967....	2.809	2.993	1981....	1.041	1.098
1953.....	3.300	3.735	1968....	2.732	2.873	1982....	1.000	1.035
1954.....	3.289	3.717	1969....	2.632	2.726	1983....	0.984	1.003
1955.....	3.279	3.732	1970....	2.545	2.574	1984....	0.964	0.961
1956.....	3.195	3.678	1971....	2.469	2.466	1985....	0.955	0.928
1957.....	3.077	3.549	1972....	2.392	2.391	1986....	0.969	0.913
1958.....	3.012	3.457	1973....	2.193	2.251	1987....	0.949	0.880
1959.....	3.021	3.427	1974....	1.901	2.029	1988....	0.926	0.846
1960.....	2.994	3.373	1975....	1.718	1.859	1989....	0.880	0.807
1961.....	2.994	3.340	1976....	1.645	1.757	1990....	0.839	0.766
1962.....	2.985	3.304	1977....	1.546	1.649	1991....	0.822	0.734
1963.....	2.994	3.265	1978....	1.433	1.532	1992....	0.812	0.713
1964.....	2.985	3.220						

Source: U.S. Bureau of Labor Statistics. Monthly data in U.S. Bureau of Economic Analysis, Survey of Current Business.

Source: Statistical Abstract of the United States, U.S. Department of Commerce.

1993–1994

YEAR	ANNUAL AVERAGE AS MEASURED BY—	
	Producer prices	Consumer prices
1993.................	0.802	0.692
1994.................	0.797	0.675

Source: U.S. Department of Commerce, U.S. Bureau of Economic Analysis.

CONSUMER PRICES—ALL URBAN CONSUMERS

INDEX, 1982-84 = 100 (RATIO SCALE)

INDEX, 1982-84 = 100 (RATIO SCALE)

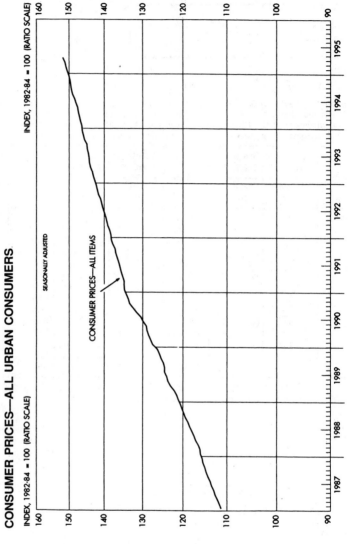

SEASONALLY ADJUSTED

CONSUMER PRICES—ALL ITEMS

SEE NOTE ON TABLE BELOW
SOURCE: DEPARTMENT OF LABOR

COUNCIL OF ECONOMIC ADVISERS

[1982-84=100, except as noted; monthly data seasonally adjusted, except as noted]

Period	All items¹ Not seasonally adjusted (NSA)	All items¹ Seasonally adjusted	Food	Total¹	Housing Total	Shelter Total	Shelter Rent ers' costs (Dec. 1982=100)	Shelter Home own ers' costs (Dec. 1982=100)	Shelter Mainte nance and repairs (NSA)	Fuel and other utili ties	Ap parel and up keep	Transportation Total¹	Transportation New cars	Transportation Motor fuel	Medi cal care	En ergy²	All items less food and energy
Rel. imp.³	*100.0*		*15.8*	*41.2*	*28.0*	*8.0*	*19.9*	*0.2*		*7.1*	*5.7*	*17.1*	*4.1*	*3.1*	*7.3*	*7.0*	*77.2*
1985	107.6	....	105.6	107.7	109.8	115.4	113.1	106.5	106.5	105.0	106.4	106.1	98.7	113.5	101.6	109.1
1986	109.6	....	109.0	110.9	115.8	121.9	119.4	107.9	104.1	105.9	102.3	110.6	77.1	122.0	88.2	113.5
1987	113.6	....	113.5	114.2	121.3	128.1	124.8	111.8	103.0	110.6	105.4	114.6	80.2	130.1	88.6	118.2
1988	118.3	....	118.2	118.5	127.1	133.6	131.1	114.7	104.4	115.4	108.7	116.9	80.9	138.6	89.3	123.4
1989	124.0	....	125.1	123.0	132.8	138.9	137.3	118.0	107.8	118.6	114.1	119.2	88.5	149.3	94.3	129.0
1990	130.7	....	132.4	128.5	140.0	146.7	144.6	122.2	111.6	124.1	120.5	121.0	101.2	162.8	102.1	135.5
1991	136.2	....	136.3	133.6	146.3	155.6	150.2	126.3	115.3	128.7	123.8	125.3	99.4	177.0	102.5	142.1
1992	140.3	....	137.9	137.5	151.2	160.9	155.3	128.6	117.8	131.9	126.5	128.4	99.0	190.1	103.0	147.3
1993	144.5	....	140.9	141.2	155.7	165.0	160.2	130.6	121.3	133.7	130.4	131.5	98.0	201.4	104.2	152.2
1994	148.2	....	144.3	144.8	160.5	169.4	165.5	130.8	122.8	133.4	134.3	136.0	98.5	211.0	104.6	156.5
1994:																
Apr	147.4	147.4	143.2	144.0	159.3	167.6	164.4	130.2	122.9	133.6	133.2	135.0	96.7	209.2	103.6	155.8
May	147.5	147.6	143.5	144.4	159.7	168.1	164.8	131.0	122.6	133.9	132.8	135.4	95.4	209.9	102.7	156.2
June	148.0	148.1	143.9	144.4	159.8	168.5	164.9	131.5	122.6	134.7	133.7	135.9	96.1	210.7	103.0	156.7
July	148.4	148.5	144.7	144.7	160.2	168.5	165.3	131.3	122.8	134.2	134.7	136.5	98.8	211.5	104.4	157.0
Aug	149.0	149.1	145.4	145.1	160.9	169.2	166.1	131.2	123.0	133.0	136.0	136.9	101.8	212.4	105.9	157.4
Sept	149.4	149.4	145.7	145.4	161.3	169.1	166.8	131.6	122.6	132.8	136.2	137.5	101.1	213.3	105.3	157.7
Oct	149.5	149.6	145.8	145.7	161.8	169.7	167.3	130.8	122.6	132.8	136.1	137.6	100.4	214.3	105.0	158.0
Nov	149.7	149.8	146.0	145.9	162.2	170.2	167.7	131.2	122.9	132.4	136.3	137.4	101.1	215.2	105.5	158.3
Dec	149.7	150.1	147.1	145.9	162.3	170.1	167.8	132.7	122.7	132.1	136.6	137.6	101.3	216.2	105.4	158.5
1995:																
Jan	150.3	150.6	146.7	146.5	162.8	170.5	168.4	133.1	123.3	133.0	137.4	137.7	101.7	216.9	105.7	159.2
Feb	150.9	151.0	147.1	146.9	163.3	171.0	168.9	133.8	123.3	132.2	137.9	138.1	101.3	217.6	105.6	159.6
Mar	151.4	151.3	147.1	147.2	163.8	172.0	169.2	134.2	123.1	132.2	138.7	138.1	100.9	218.2	105.1	160.1
Apr	151.9	151.9	148.2	147.6	164.4	172.7	169.8	134.2	123.4	132.1	139.7	138.9	101.5	218.8	105.5	160.7

¹ Includes items not shown separately.
² Household fuels—gas (piped), electricity, fuel oil, etc.—and motor fuel. Motor oil, coolant, etc. excluded beginning 1983.
³ Relative importance, December 1994.

NOTE.—Data incorporate a rental equivalence measure for homeownership costs (beginning 1983).

Source: Department of Labor, Bureau of Labor Statistics.

Source: *Economic Indicators*, Council of Economic Advisers.

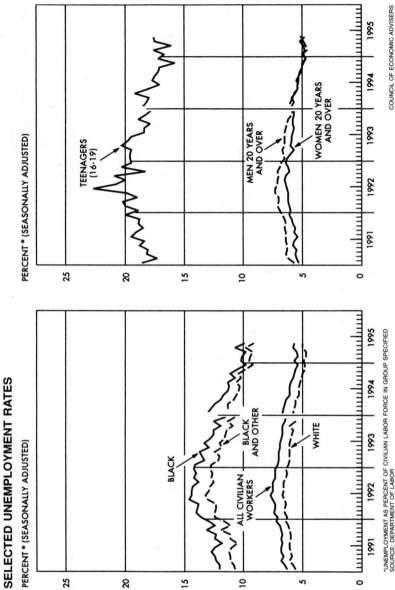

SELECTED UNEMPLOYMENT RATES
PERCENT * (SEASONALLY ADJUSTED)

PERCENT * (SEASONALLY ADJUSTED)

TEENAGERS
(16-19)

MEN 20 YEARS
AND OVER

WOMEN 20 YEARS
AND OVER

BLACK

BLACK
AND OTHER

ALL CIVILIAN
WORKERS

WHITE

COUNCIL OF ECONOMIC ADVISERS

*UNEMPLOYMENT AS PERCENT OF CIVILIAN LABOR FORCE IN GROUP SPECIFIED
SOURCE: DEPARTMENT OF LABOR

[Monthly data seasonally adjusted]

Period	By sex and age				By race			By selected groups				
	All civilian workers	Men 20 years and over	Women 20 years and over	Both sexes 16–19 years	White	Black and other	Black	Experienced wage and salary workers	Married men, spouse present	Women who maintain families	Full-time workers [1]	Part-time workers [1]
1985	7.2	6.2	6.6	18.6	6.2	13.7	15.1	6.8	4.3	10.4	7.1	7.5
1986	7.0	6.1	6.2	18.3	6.0	13.1	14.5	6.6	4.4	9.8	6.9	7.4
1987	6.2	5.4	5.4	16.9	5.3	11.6	13.0	5.8	3.9	9.2	6.0	6.9
1988	5.5	4.8	4.9	15.3	4.7	10.4	11.7	5.2	3.3	8.1	5.3	6.4
1989	5.3	4.5	4.7	15.0	4.5	10.0	11.4	5.0	3.0	8.1	5.1	6.2
1990	5.5	4.9	4.8	15.5	4.7	10.1	11.3	5.3	3.4	8.2	5.4	6.3
1991	6.7	6.3	5.7	18.6	6.0	11.1	12.4	6.5	4.4	9.1	6.7	6.9
1992	7.4	7.0	6.3	20.0	6.5	12.7	14.1	7.1	5.0	9.9	7.4	7.4
1993	6.8	6.4	5.9	19.0	6.0	11.7	12.9	6.5	4.4	9.5	6.8	7.1
1994 [2]	6.1	5.4	5.4	17.6	5.3	10.5	11.5	5.9	3.7	8.9	6.1	6.0
1994: May	6.1	5.4	5.4	18.1	5.3	10.6	11.7	5.9	3.7	8.9	6.1	6.2
June	6.1	5.3	5.4	17.1	5.3	10.4	11.3	5.9	3.6	8.8	6.1	5.9
July	6.1	5.5	5.3	17.7	5.3	10.3	11.2	6.0	3.6	7.9	6.1	6.0
Aug	6.0	5.3	5.3	17.5	5.2	10.6	11.3	5.8	3.5	8.8	6.0	6.2
Sept	5.8	5.1	5.2	17.2	5.1	10.2	10.7	5.7	3.4	8.9	5.8	5.8
Oct	5.7	5.0	5.0	17.1	5.0	10.4	11.1	5.5	3.3	8.9	5.8	5.6
Nov	5.6	4.9	5.0	15.8	4.8	9.8	10.5	5.4	3.2	8.7	5.6	5.4
Dec	5.4	4.7	4.7	17.2	4.8	9.2	9.8	5.3	3.2	8.8	5.3	5.9
1995: Jan	5.7	5.0	4.9	16.7	4.9	9.5	10.2	5.4	3.4	8.9	5.5	6.2
Feb	5.4	4.6	4.8	17.6	4.7	9.4	10.1	5.1	3.0	8.1	5.3	6.0
Mar	5.5	4.7	4.9	16.1	4.7	9.2	9.8	5.2	3.2	7.6	5.4	5.8
Apr	5.8	4.9	5.2	17.5	5.0	9.8	10.7	5.6	3.4	9.0	5.6	6.3
May	5.7	5.1	4.8	17.6	5.0	9.1	9.9	5.6	3.4	8.0	5.6	6.1

[1] Revised definition; for details, see *Employment and Earnings*, February 1994.
[2] Data beginning January 1994 are not directly comparable with data for earlier periods. See *Employment and Earnings*, February 1994.

Note.—Data relate to persons age 16 years and over.
Source: Department of Labor, Bureau of Labor Statistics.

Source: *Economic Indicators*, Council of Economic Advisers.

MONEY STOCK, LIQUID ASSETS, AND DEBT MEASURES

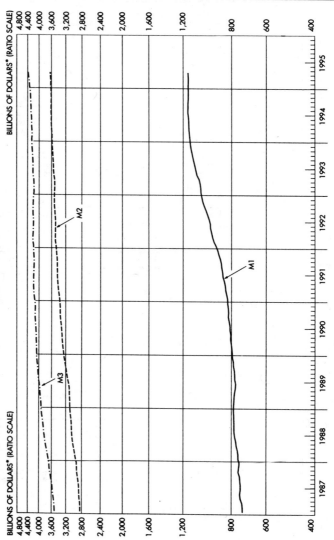

BILLIONS OF DOLLARS* (RATIO SCALE)

M3

M2

M1

*AVERAGES OF DAILY FIGURES; SEASONALLY ADJUSTED
SOURCE: BOARD OF GOVERNORS OF THE FEDERAL RESERVE SYSTEM

COUNCIL OF ECONOMIC ADVISERS

[Averages of daily figures, except as noted; billions of dollars, seasonally adjusted]

Period	M1 — Sum of currency, demand deposits, travelers' checks, and other checkable deposits (OCDs)	M2 — M1 plus overnight RPs and Eurodollars, MMMF balances (general purpose and broker/dealer), MMDAs, and savings and small time deposits	M3 — M2 plus large time deposits, term RPs, term Eurodollars, and institution-only MMMF balances	L — M3 plus other liquid assets	Debt — Debt of domestic nonfinancial sectors (monthly average)[1]	Percent change from year or 6 months earlier[2] M1	M2	M3	Debt
1985: Dec	619.9	2,576.1	3,200.2	3,827.5	6,902.1	12.3	8.3	7.3	14.8
1986: Dec	724.4	2,820.3	3,488.7	4,129.1	7,785.2	16.9	9.5	9.0	12.8
1987: Dec	749.8	2,922.3	3,675.8	4,334.8	8,544.6	3.5	3.6	5.4	9.8
1988: Dec	786.9	3,083.6	3,915.7	4,670.1	9,315.0	4.9	5.5	6.5	9.0
1989: Dec	794.2	3,243.1	4,066.1	4,896.5	10,045.1	.9	5.2	3.8	7.8
1990: Dec	825.9	3,355.9	4,123.0	4,973.5	10,690.2	4.0	3.5	1.4	6.4
1991: Dec	897.3	3,457.9	4,176.0	4,990.9	11,171.1	8.6	3.0	1.3	4.5
1992: Dec	1,024.4	3,515.3	4,182.9	5,061.1	11,706.1	14.2	1.7	.2	4.8
1993: Dec	1,128.6	3,583.6	4,242.5	5,150.3	12,335.3	10.2	1.9	1.4	5.4
1994: Dec	1,147.8	3,615.1	4,304.5	5,294.0	12,965.0	1.7	.9	1.5	5.1
1994: Mar	1,141.1	3,597.4	4,240.6	5,165.5	12,498.1	6.6	2.2	1.3	5.3
Apr	1,142.8	3,605.4	4,250.8	5,181.2	12,546.3	5.3	2.3	1.3	5.5
May	1,143.5	3,608.5	4,251.4	5,188.4	12,591.6	3.8	1.8	.8	5.3
June	1,147.0	3,605.3	4,256.6	5,185.1	12,641.4	3.3	1.2	.7	5.0
July	1,152.2	3,616.2	4,273.8	5,208.4	12,681.1	3.5	1.5	1.3	4.7
Aug	1,150.8	3,614.2	4,272.7	5,208.1	12,738.5	2.4	1.6	1.9	4.7
Sept	1,151.0	3,613.3	4,278.4	5,211.9	12,800.0	1.7	.9	1.8	4.8
Oct	1,148.1	3,609.0	4,284.9	5,231.6	12,856.5	.9	.2	1.6	4.9
Nov	1,147.5	3,610.3	4,291.4	5,244.9	12,919.2	.7	.1	1.9	5.2
Dec	1,147.8	3,615.1	4,304.5	5,294.0	12,965.0	.1	.5	2.3	5.1
1995: Jan	1,148.8	3,626.9	4,327.7	5,327.0	13,021.9	-.6	.6	2.5	5.4
Feb	1,147.1	3,622.7	4,335.8	5,375.8	13,096.8	-.6	.5	3.0	5.6
Mar	1,147.9	3,630.3	4,356.8	P 5,426.0	P 13,154.9	-.5	.9	3.7	5.5
Apr	1,149.7	3,642.9	4,377.9	....	....	.3	1.9	4.3	

[1] Consists of outstanding credit market debt of the U.S. Government, State and local governments, and private nonfinancial sectors; data from flow of funds accounts.

[2] Annual changes are from December to December and monthly changes are from 6 months earlier at a simple annual rate.

Source: Board of Governors of the Federal Reserve System.

Source: Economic Indicators, Council of Economic Advisers.

OUTPUT, CAPACITY, AND CAPACITY UTILIZATION[1] (Seasonally adjusted)

Series	1994 Q2	Q3	Q4	1995 Q1	1994 Q2	Q3	Q4	1995 Q1	1994 Q2	Q3	Q4	1995 Q1
	Output (1987=100)				Capacity (percent of 1987 output)				Capacity utilization rate (percent)[2]			
1 Total industry...................	117.4	118.8	120.5	122.1	140.0	140.9	141.9	143.1	83.8	84.3	84.9	85.3
2 Manufacturing...................	118.9	120.5	122.7	124.5	143.1	144.2	145.3	146.6	83.1	83.6	84.5	84.9
3 Primary processing[3].........	114.7	115.9	118.4	119.7	131.0	131.6	132.3	133.2	87.6	88.1	89.5	89.9
4 Advanced processing[4].......	120.9	122.7	124.8	126.8	148.7	150.0	151.3	152.9	81.3	81.8	82.5	83.0
5 Durable goods................	124.1	126.5	129.4	131.7	150.2	151.6	153.1	154.9	82.6	83.4	84.6	85.0
6 Lumber and products.........	105.4	106.6	107.9	109.4	115.5	116.0	116.5	117.1	91.2	91.9	92.7	93.4
7 Primary metals..............	114.4	114.1	119.4	120.2	125.0	125.2	125.4	126.7	91.6	91.1	95.2	94.9
8 Iron and steel..............	120.2	115.8	123.3	125.0	127.9	128.4	128.8	130.9	93.9	90.2	95.8	95.5
9 Nonferrous..................	106.9	111.4	113.9	113.8	120.5	120.5	120.5	120.9	88.7	92.4	94.5	94.2
10 Industrial machinery and equipment	157.6	162.6	167.5	171.6	179.0	181.6	184.1	187.8	88.0	89.6	91.0	91.4
11 Electrical machinery	156.8	163.5	169.4	173.7	179.9	184.1	188.5	193.8	87.1	88.8	89.9	89.6
12 Motor vehicles and parts...............	133.3	135.0	141.5	146.3	158.5	160.3	162.2	164.2	84.1	84.2	87.2	89.1
13 Aerospace and miscellaneous transportation equipment..........	84.2	82.1	80.8	80.4	129.8	129.4	129.1	128.8	64.9	63.5	62.6	62.5
14 Nondurable goods.............	113.1	113.8	115.3	116.6	134.8	135.5	136.3	137.1	83.9	84.0	84.6	85.0
15 Textile mill products..................	108.7	108.9	111.6	112.2	120.8	121.4	122.0	122.7	90.1	89.7	91.4	91.4
16 Paper and products...................	115.9	118.5	120.0	120.0	126.6	127.1	127.7	128.4	91.6	93.2	94.4	93.4
17 Chemicals and products	123.6	124.4	126.0	129.4	151.9	153.3	154.7	156.2	81.4	81.1	81.4	82.9
18 Plastics materials.................	124.3	126.9	130.2	...	130.0	130.8	131.6	...	95.6	97.0	98.9	...
19 Petroleum products	106.3	104.9	106.5	108.3	115.3	115.2	115.1	115.1	92.2	91.1	92.5	94.1
20 Mining................................	100.7	100.1	99.2	100.0	111.5	111.5	111.4	111.4	90.3	89.8	89.0	89.7
21 Utilities............................	117.2	118.1	116.3	117.0	135.0	135.4	135.8	136.3	86.8	87.2	85.6	85.8
22 Electric.............................	118.0	118.2	117.3	118.2	132.6	133.1	133.6	134.1	89.0	88.8	87.8	88.1

Series	1973 High	1975 Low	Previous cycle[5] High	Low	Latest cycle[6] High	Low	1994 Mar.	1994 Oct.	Nov.	Dec.[r]	1995 Jan.[r]	Feb.[r]	Mar.[p]
	Capacity utilization rate (percent)[2]												
1 Total industry...................	89.2	72.6	87.3	71.8	84.9	78.0	83.7	84.4	84.8	85.5	85.6	85.4	84.9
2 Manufacturing	88.9	70.8	87.3	70.0	85.2	76.6	82.9	83.8	84.4	85.2	85.3	84.9	84.5
3 Primary processing[3].........	92.2	68.9	89.7	66.8	89.0	77.9	86.8	88.3	89.5	90.8	90.3	89.7	89.5
4 Advanced processing[4]........	87.5	72.0	86.3	71.4	83.5	76.2	81.3	82.1	82.4	83.0	83.3	83.0	82.6
5 Durable goods................	88.8	68.5	86.9	65.0	84.0	73.7	82.3	83.9	84.3	85.4	85.4	85.0	84.5
6 Lumber and products.........	90.1	62.2	87.6	60.9	93.3	76.3	90.3	91.7	91.6	94.7	94.3	93.2	92.8
7 Primary metals..............	100.6	66.2	102.4	46.8	92.8	74.0	89.8	92.5	95.0	96.0	96.0	94.5	94.1
8 Iron and steel..............	105.8	66.6	110.4	38.3	95.7	72.1	91.4	92.4	94.6	100.3	96.5	94.9	95.1
9 Nonferrous..................	92.9	61.3	90.5	62.2	88.7	75.0	87.9	92.7	95.6	95.2	95.5	94.1	92.9
10 Industrial machinery and equipment.....	96.4	74.5	92.1	64.9	84.0	72.5	86.9	90.9	91.0	91.1	92.0	91.3	90.9
11 Electrical machinery...........	87.8	63.8	89.4	71.1	84.9	76.6	86.1	89.3	89.6	90.8	90.3	89.7	89.0
12 Motor vehicles and parts.........	93.4	51.1	93.0	44.5	85.1	57.6	88.2	85.7	87.2	88.8	89.4	89.8	88.1
13 Aerospace and miscellaneous transportation equipment.....	77.0	66.6	81.1	66.9	88.4	79.4	64.4	62.6	62.6	62.5	62.3	62.5	62.6
14 Nondurable goods..............	87.9	71.8	87.0	76.9	86.7	80.4	83.8	83.9	84.6	85.2	85.4	85.0	84.7
15 Textile mill products...........	92.0	60.4	91.7	73.8	92.1	78.9	89.7	90.8	91.7	91.8	92.7	90.8	90.8
16 Paper and products...........	96.9	69.0	94.2	82.0	94.8	86.5	91.7	93.2	95.0	95.2	93.5	93.5	93.3
17 Chemicals and products...........	87.9	69.9	85.1	70.1	85.9	78.9	81.6	80.2	81.6	82.5	83.4	82.7	82.5
18 Plastics materials.............	102.0	50.6	90.9	63.4	97.0	74.8	94.3	93.3	98.5	105.0	105.6	...	...
19 Petroleum products.............	96.7	81.1	89.5	68.2	88.5	83.7	89.6	90.4	93.5	93.7	93.4	93.4	95.6
20 Mining...........................	94.4	88.4	96.6	80.6	86.5	86.0	90.2	89.0	88.2	89.8	89.6	90.0	89.5
21 Utilities........................	95.6	82.5	88.3	76.2	92.6	83.2	87.5	86.4	85.8	84.7	85.3	87.3	85.0
22 Electric.........................	99.0	82.7	88.3	78.7	94.8	86.5	88.6	88.3	88.0	87.1	87.5	89.7	87.1

1. Data in this table also appear in the Board's G.17 (419) monthly statistical release. For the ordering address, see the inside front cover. The latest historical revision of the industrial production index and the capacity utilization rates was released in November 1994. See "Industrial Production and Capacity Utilization: A Revision," *Federal Reserve Bulletin*, vol. 81 (January 1995), pp. 16–26. For a detailed description of the industrial production index, see "Industrial Production: 1989 Developments and Historical Revision," *Federal Reserve Bulletin*, vol. 76 (April 1990), pp. 187–204.
2. Capacity utilization is calculated as the ratio of the Federal Reserve's seasonally adjusted index of industrial production to the corresponding index of capacity.

3. Primary processing includes textiles; lumber; paper; industrial chemicals; synthetic materials; fertilizer materials; petroleum products; rubber and plastics; stone, clay, and glass; primary metals; and fabricated metals.
4. Advanced processing includes foods; tobacco; apparel; furniture and fixtures; printing and publishing; chemical products such as drugs and toiletries; agricultural chemicals; leather and products; machinery; transportation equipment; instruments; and miscellaneous manufactures.
5. Monthly highs, 1978–80; monthly lows, 1982.
6. Monthly highs, 1988–89; monthly lows, 1990–91.

Source: *Federal Reserve Bulletin*, Board of Governors of the Federal Reserve System.

INDUSTRIAL PRODUCTION Indexes and Gross Value[1]

Group	1992 proportion	1994 avg.	Mar.	Apr.	May	June	July	Aug.	Sept.	Oct.	Nov.[r]	Dec.[r]	Jan.[r]	Feb.[r]	Mar.[p]
							Index (1987 = 100)								
MAJOR MARKETS															
1 Total index	100.0	118.1	116.6	116.7	117.4	118.0	118.2	119.1	119.0	119.5	120.3	121.7	122.2	122.3	121.9
2 Products	60.9	115.9	114.7	114.7	115.3	115.9	116.2	116.7	116.4	116.9	117.5	118.7	119.3	119.3	118.8
3 Final products	46.6	118.4	117.4	117.3	117.8	118.4	118.5	119.2	118.9	119.2	119.8	121.2	121.9	122.0	121.4
4 Consumer goods, total	28.5	113.2	112.9	112.9	112.8	113.5	113.3	113.8	113.0	113.0	113.9	115.5	116.1	116.1	115.2
5 Durable consumer goods	5.5	119.4	119.0	117.8	116.4	118.0	118.0	119.5	124.9	123.8	124.5	127.1	131.1	131.6	133.2
6 Automotive products	2.5	125.5	126.4	124.1	120.1	121.0	119.5	115.0	126.0	122.5	122.3	126.5	131.4	132.7	134.8
7 Autos and trucks	1.6	125.4	127.7	125.0	118.1	118.5	115.0	86.5	91.7	90.2	92.9	94.0	100.5	103.6	103.6
8 Autos, consumer	.9	94.9	98.8	96.0	90.4	89.6	86.5	91.7	90.2	92.9	94.0	100.5	103.6	103.6	103.1
9 Trucks, consumer	.7	180.7	179.6	177.2	168.0	170.7	166.6	189.0	181.5	175.5	185.8	187.3	184.6	191.0	181.7
10 Auto parts and allied goods	.9	123.2	121.1	119.8	121.9	123.8	126.6	120.0	123.9	126.6	125.7	127.8	126.5	127.1	126.7
11 Other	3.0	114.1	112.7	112.5	113.2	115.4	116.7	117.1	115.2	115.2	115.0	116.8	117.9	115.6	113.3
12 Appliances televisions and air conditioners	.7	126.0	124.3	120.7	125.6	132.8	129.7	135.1	130.2	124.9	126.9	131.5	130.4	124.7	120.1
13 Carpeting and furniture	.8	105.0	103.1	104.5	103.3	103.6	108.4	106.9	104.1	107.4	105.9	108.0	110.2	107.9	106.3
14 Miscellaneous home goods	1.5	113.8	112.8	113.2	113.1	114.2	115.3	114.6	114.6	114.9	114.5	114.9	116.4	115.6	113.9
15 Nondurable consumer goods	23.0	111.8	111.5	111.0	112.0	112.5	112.5	110.6	111.2	111.9	112.2	112.4	114.3	114.8	115.1
16 Foods and tobacco	10.3	110.5	109.8	110.2	110.9	110.5	110.6	111.2	111.9	112.2	112.4	112.4	114.3	114.8	114.7
17 Clothing	2.4	95.9	95.7	96.4	97.2	96.3	96.5	95.9	95.5	96.2	96.2	96.8	96.2	94.8	94.1
18 Chemical products	4.5	129.7	130.3	128.4	129.5	131.4	131.1	129.8	127.5	127.2	130.5	134.0	136.5	135.0	135.2
19 Paper products	2.9	104.7	103.9	105.1	105.6	105.8	105.2	105.9	105.2	103.6	104.6	104.3	103.4	103.8	103.4
20 Energy	2.9	113.9	114.5	110.0	112.4	115.5	114.3	113.1	110.5	109.8	110.6	109.6	109.7	112.6	110.2
21 Fuels	.9	106.7	105.8	108.3	107.4	106.5	105.8	105.8	107.4	103.9	109.8	107.4	107.4	108.8	113.8
22 Residential utilities	2.1	116.8	118.1	110.5	114.4	119.3	117.8	116.1	111.8	112.2	110.7	110.3	110.5	114.1	108.5
23 Equipment	18.1	126.5	124.3	124.9	125.4	125.8	126.4	127.5	128.0	128.8	128.9	130.1	130.8	131.0	131.1
24 Business equipment	14.0	146.7	142.6	143.5	144.5	145.5	146.9	148.9	149.5	150.9	151.0	152.6	153.7	154.1	154.6
25 Information processing and related	5.7	176.4	170.0	170.2	171.8	173.7	177.1	179.7	181.1	183.2	184.2	188.3	188.6	189.1	191.6
26 Computer and office equipment	1.5	284.2	270.9	270.8	271.6	276.5	282.6	288.9	295.8	300.5	305.7	311.9	317.5	324.8	331.3
27 Industrial	4.0	120.9	117.8	119.2	120.7	120.6	120.6	122.1	122.3	123.0	124.4	124.1	124.1	125.8	126.5
28 Transit	2.6	137.9	139.3	138.0	135.3	136.1	132.6	137.9	136.8	137.1	137.5	137.8	139.7	140.8	138.8
29 Autos and trucks	1.2	148.0	148.1	145.9	140.0	141.7	138.2	149.4	147.7	149.2	151.6	152.6	157.2	158.5	155.4
30 Other	1.7	129.4	123.3	127.1	129.4	130.5	132.6	133.5	133.3	134.3	133.1	133.1	133.9	132.8	132.0
31 Defense and space equipment	3.4	71.0	73.7	73.6	72.4	71.3	69.9	69.2	68.8	68.7	69.0	68.7	68.6	67.9	67.8
32 Oil and gas well drilling	.5	90.8	92.1	93.2	94.6	94.2	93.7	89.6	93.9	88.3	86.0	86.0	86.7	89.1	85.7
33 Manufactured homes	.2	137.3	135.6	132.4	135.2	137.8	133.3	134.5	138.4	142.0	143.1	153.6	153.6	147.4	...
34 Intermediate products, total	14.3	108.1	106.3	106.9	107.7	108.5	109.1	109.3	108.2	108.6	109.9	110.6	110.9	111.1	110.9
35 Construction supplies	5.3	108.8	103.2	104.7	106.1	106.4	107.9	108.2	108.6	109.7	109.8	111.6	112.1	111.4	111.5
36 Business supplies	9.0	109.1	108.4	108.5	108.8	110.1	110.0	109.9	108.7	110.1	111.3	110.7	110.8	111.1	110.7
37 Materials	39.1	121.5	119.5	119.7	120.5	121.2	121.4	122.8	122.9	123.4	124.6	126.3	126.9	126.9	127.7
38 Durable goods materials	20.6	131.2	128.3	129.2	129.8	130.0	130.9	132.6	133.3	134.2	136.0	138.6	139.3	139.1	139.1
39 Durable consumer parts	3.9	132.2	131.5	130.1	129.7	129.2	130.4	133.3	133.1	133.8	135.8	139.7	139.6	139.7	138.3
40 Equipment parts	7.5	143.1	137.9	139.6	140.5	142.1	143.8	145.2	146.7	149.0	150.7	152.3	153.7	155.0	156.0
41 Other	9.1	121.3	119.3	120.4	121.2	120.8	121.1	122.3	122.8	122.7	124.6	127.3	127.8	126.5	126.3
42 Basic metal materials	3.0	119.7	116.7	115.9	118.2	118.1	118.6	120.3	119.8	120.3	121.5	122.8	122.6	122.9	123.2
43 Nondurable goods materials	8.9	118.4	116.7	115.9	118.2	118.4	118.4	117.5	117.5	118.0	118.7	118.7	120.3	121.5	123.2
44 Textile materials	1.1	105.3	104.0	104.4	104.2	104.8	104.8	104.8	104.7	104.5	105.6	105.4	105.3	105.4	105.3
45 Paper materials	1.8	118.7	117.8	116.1	118.9	118.4	122.9	123.4	124.8	124.0	124.6	125.9	127.5	128.2	129.4
46 Chemical materials	4.0	123.2	120.6	120.6	121.5	124.8	124.0	124.6	124.8	124.0	124.6	119.5	119.3	123.4	120.2
47 Other	2.0	116.9	115.6	113.3	114.8	116.5	116.6	116.1	116.1	115.6	105.2	104.9	105.3	106.5	105.3
48 Energy materials	9.6	105.2	105.0	104.8	104.6	106.7	105.2	106.1	105.6	105.2	104.9	105.3	105.4	102.5	101.5
49 Primary energy	6.3	100.3	100.5	100.9	100.4	100.2	100.3	100.9	101.1	101.1	100.8	100.3	100.7	101.7	101.7
50 Converted fuel materials	3.3	114.9	114.0	112.5	112.8	119.9	114.9	116.3	115.1	115.1	113.4	112.3	112.9	114.5	113.0
SPECIAL AGGREGATES															
51 Total excluding autos and trucks	97.2	117.6	116.1	116.2	117.1	117.7	118.1	118.7	118.6	119.1	119.8	121.1	121.6	121.6	121.3
52 Total excluding motor vehicles and parts	95.2	117.1	115.5	115.7	116.6	117.3	117.7	118.2	118.0	118.5	119.2	120.5	120.9	121.0	120.7
53 Total excluding computer and office equipment	98.3	115.4	114.0	114.1	114.8	115.4	115.5	116.4	116.1	116.6	117.4	118.7	119.1	119.1	118.7
54 Consumer goods excluding autos and trucks	26.9	112.4	111.9	111.5	112.4	113.2	113.2	113.2	113.0	112.4	113.1	114.5	115.0	114.9	114.1
55 Consumer goods excluding energy	25.6	113.1	112.7	112.5	112.8	113.2	113.2	113.8	113.3	113.3	114.2	116.2	116.8	116.5	115.7
56 Business equipment excluding autos and trucks	12.8	146.5	142.0	143.2	144.8	145.7	147.7	148.8	149.5	151.0	150.9	152.5	153.3	153.6	154.4
57 Business equipment excluding computer and office equipment	12.5	130.7	127.6	128.5	129.4	130.0	131.1	132.7	132.7	133.8	133.6	134.7	135.5	135.3	135.3
58 Materials excluding energy	29.5	127.3	124.8	125.1	126.2	126.4	127.2	128.8	129.2	129.9	131.6	133.8	134.2	134.2	134.3

(continued)

INDUSTRIAL PRODUCTION Indexes and Gross Value[1] *(concluded)*

Group	SIC code	1992 pro-por-tion	1994 avg.	1994 Mar.	Apr.	May	June	July	Aug.	Sept.	Oct.	Nov.	Dec.r	1995 Jan.r	Feb.r	Mar.p
								Index (1987 = 100)								
MAJOR INDUSTRIES																
59 Total index.................	...	100.0	118.1	116.6	116.7	117.4	118.0	118.2	119.1	119.0	119.5	120.3	121.7	122.2	122.3	121.9
60 Manufacturing..............	...	85.5	119.7	118.0	118.4	119.0	119.3	119.8	120.9	120.9	121.5	122.6	124.2	124.7	124.5	124.4
61 Primary processing........	...	26.5	115.3	113.3	114.0	115.2	114.7	115.3	116.3	116.2	116.6	118.4	120.3	120.0	119.5	119.5
62 Advanced processing.......	...	59.0	121.8	120.2	120.5	120.8	121.5	121.9	123.1	123.1	123.8	124.6	126.0	126.9	126.9	126.7
63 Durable goods.............	...	45.1	125.5	122.9	123.7	124.0	124.6	125.2	127.0	127.2	128.0	129.1	131.2	131.8	131.7	131.6
64 Lumber and products......	24	2.0	106.0	104.0	103.9	106.0	106.2	106.8	105.5	107.6	106.7	106.7	110.4	110.1	109.1	108.9
65 Furniture and fixtures.....	25	1.4	111.4	107.7	110.2	110.1	111.8	114.0	115.5	112.4	114.8	113.0	114.7	116.0	115.3	114.3
66 Stone, clay, and glass products..............	32	2.1	104.9	103.7	105.0	105.5	104.4	104.3	105.8	105.8	105.4	106.9	110.1	108.2	106.8	107.4
67 Primary metals............	33	3.1	114.5	112.1	114.8	114.8	113.7	112.7	113.5	116.0	115.9	119.1	123.0	121.4	119.7	119.5
68 Iron and steel...........	331,2	1.7	118.3	116.7	121.5	120.9	118.2	116.1	113.0	118.2	118.8	121.9	129.3	125.9	124.2	124.7
69 Raw steel.............		.1	107.9	106.0	105.3	105.7	106.3	104.7	107.0	109.9	109.0	114.2	121.9	114.6	117.2	...
70 Nonferrous.............	333–6,9	1.4	109.3	106.0	106.2	106.9	107.6	108.0	113.6	112.7	111.8	115.2	114.8	115.3	113.7	112.5
71 Fabricated metal products...	34	5.0	110.8	108.5	109.6	110.0	110.2	111.7	112.4	111.6	112.2	113.3	115.3	116.3	115.9	115.4
72 Industrial machinery and equipment..........	35	7.9	159.9	154.0	156.1	157.7	158.9	160.6	162.6	164.6	166.5	167.5	168.5	171.3	171.4	172.1
73 Computer and office equipment..........	357	1.7	284.2	270.9	270.8	271.6	276.5	282.6	288.9	295.8	300.5	305.7	311.9	317.5	324.8	331.3
74 Electrical machinery......	36	7.3	160.0	152.6	154.3	156.5	159.5	161.5	164.1	165.0	166.9	168.8	172.5	173.2	173.8	174.2
75 Transportation equipment .	37	9.6	120.9	110.7	109.5	107.6	107.5	105.7	109.5	108.8	109.0	110.5	111.9	112.5	113.3	112.2
76 Motor vehicles and parts .	371	4.8	137.9	138.8	136.2	131.6	132.2	129.6	138.1	137.4	138.4	141.4	144.6	146.1	147.5	145.4
77 Autos and light trucks .	371	2.5	131.9	134.7	131.7	124.4	124.6	120.8	131.9	128.4	128.6	132.7	138.4	140.0	142.0	138.8
78 Aerospace and miscellaneous transportation equipment	372–6,9	4.8	82.6	83.8	84.1	84.6	83.8	82.8	82.3	81.4	80.8	80.9	80.6	80.3	80.5	80.5
79 Instruments	38	5.4	107.4	106.9	106.6	106.4	106.8	108.5	108.7	108.0	108.2	107.7	108.9	108.5	107.8	108.5
80 Miscellaneous	39	1.3	116.2	114.1	115.2	115.4	115.8	118.6	117.1	117.0	118.4	118.6	117.6	119.1	120.2	118.7
81 Nondurable goods	...	40.5	113.3	112.5	112.4	113.4	113.4	113.6	114.0	113.7	114.2	115.4	116.4	116.8	116.6	116.4
82 Foods	20	9.4	112.8	112.9	111.9	112.8	112.8	113.4	113.7	114.6	113.4	113.9	114.7	115.6	115.7	115.6
83 Tobacco products........	21	1.6	96.5	93.0	98.1	98.5	95.9	93.7	96.2	96.1	104.5	101.5	108.0	107.8	109.3	108.1
84 Textile mill products......	22	1.8	109.0	107.9	108.6	108.9	108.7	109.4	109.0	108.3	110.6	112.0	112.2	112.5	111.5	111.7
85 Apparel products........	23	2.2	96.3	95.7	96.2	97.1	97.0	97.0	96.8	96.8	96.9	96.8	97.0	96.6	95.7	94.5
86 Paper and products.......	26	3.6	117.4	115.7	114.4	116.7	116.6	116.6	120.2	118.7	118.9	121.3	121.7	119.8	120.1	120.0
87 Printing and publishing....	27	6.8	101.1	101.3	101.7	101.6	102.4	102.1	101.5	100.9	101.4	102.0	101.6	101.3	101.2	100.9
88 Chemicals and products ...	28	9.9	124.1	123.1	122.4	124.0	124.4	124.7	124.7	123.7	123.8	126.2	128.0	129.9	129.1	129.3
89 Petroleum products.......	29	1.4	105.3	103.4	107.5	107.0	104.5	104.3	105.2	105.3	104.0	107.6	107.7	107.4	107.5	110.1
90 Rubber and plastic products .	30	3.5	133.5	130.9	130.8	132.4	132.8	134.5	134.5	134.7	136.7	138.3	140.0	140.6	140.7	139.3
91 Leather and products	31	.3	85.8	87.0	87.6	85.9	85.5	86.3	85.5	85.4	85.6	84.5	84.4	82.9	82.7	82.6
92 Mining..................	...	6.8	99.8	100.5	100.7	100.7	100.6	100.1	100.0	100.1	99.2	98.3	100.1	99.8	100.3	99.8
93 Metal.................	10	.4	159.4	165.2	157.0	156.4	162.8	159.5	156.6	160.0	158.9	154.3	156.2	158.4	158.3	158.2
94 Coal.................	12	1.0	112.0	117.7	118.3	111.5	113.4	108.6	111.4	110.7	110.2	110.1	117.8	117.9	118.6	116.9
95 Oil and gas extraction	13	4.7	93.0	92.9	93.2	93.8	94.3	93.5	93.7	92.2		91.2	91.9	91.2		
96 Stone and earth minerals ...	14	.6	107.0	104.7	105.9	108.1	105.6	107.9	106.6	106.7	109.3	109.9	109.9	113.6	112.2	114.8
97 Utilities	...	7.7	118.1	117.9	114.7	115.8	121.1	119.0	118.8	116.5	117.2	116.5	115.2	116.0	118.9	115.9
98 Electric	491,3PT	6.1	117.8	117.2	116.4	116.2	121.4	119.0	118.4	117.1	117.9	117.5	116.5	117.2	120.3	116.9
99 Gas..................	492,3PT	1.6	119.2	120.5	107.9	114.1	120.0	118.9	120.4	114.2	114.4	112.3	109.8	111.3	113.3	111.7
SPECIAL AGGREGATES																
100 Manufacturing excluding motor vehicles and parts	...	80.7	118.6	116.7	117.3	118.2	118.6	119.2	119.8	119.9	120.5	121.5	122.9	123.4	123.2	123.1
101 Manufacturing excluding office and computing machines ...	...	83.8	116.5	114.9	115.3	115.9	116.2	116.6	117.6	117.5	118.1	119.1	120.6	121.1	120.8	120.6
	...	**1,707.0**	**2,006.2**	**1,985.6**	**1,985.8**	**1,990.7**	**2,002.5**	**2,002.1**	**2,020.2**	**2,015.6**	**2,020.4**	**2,037.2**	**2,056.5**	**2,062.6**	**2,065.9**	**2,060.8**
						Gross value (billions of 1987 dollars, annual rates)										
MAJOR MARKETS																
102 Products, total	...	1,314.6	1,576.3	1,563.6	1,559.9	1,561.7	1,571.1	1,569.3	1,586.6	1,584.2	1,584.4	1,598.4	1,615.1	1,621.0	1,625.7	1,621.2
103 Final	...	866.6	982.5	981.3	976.0	977.1	983.0	979.0	987.3	981.5	977.0	988.5	999.6	1,000.2	1,002.3	997.1
104 Consumer goods	...	448.0	593.8	582.3	583.9	584.5	588.1	590.3	599.3	602.7	607.3	609.9	615.5	620.8	623.3	624.1
105 Equipment..............	...	392.5	429.8	422.0	425.9	429.0	431.4	432.9	433.5	431.4	436.0	438.8	441.4	441.5	440.3	439.6
106 Intermediate.............																

1. Data in this table also appear in the Board's G.17 (419) monthly statistical release. For the ordering address, see the inside front cover. The latest historical revision of the industrial production index and the capacity utilization rates was released in November 1994. See "Industrial Production and Capacity Utilization: A Revision," *Federal Reserve Bulletin*, vol. 81 (January 1995), pp. 16–26. For a detailed description of the industrial production index, see "Industrial Production: 1989 Developments and Historical Revision," *Federal Reserve Bulletin*, vol. 76, (April 1990), pp. 187–204.
2. Standard industrial classification.

Source: *Federal Reserve Bulletin*, Board of Governors of the Federal Reserve System.

PERSONAL INCOME AND SAVING

Billions of current dollars except as noted; quarterly data at seasonally adjusted annual rates

Account	1992	1993	1994	1994 Q1	Q2	Q3	Q4	1995 Q1
PERSONAL INCOME AND SAVING								
1 Total personal income	5,154.3	5,375.1	5,701.7	5,555.8	5,659.9	5,734.5	5,856.6	5,963.1
2 Wage and salary disbursements	2,974.8	3,080.8	3,279.0	3,208.3	3,257.2	3,293.9	3,356.4	3,403.2
3 Commodity-producing industries	757.6	773.8	818.2	801.9	811.6	821.8	837.3	848.8
4 Manufacturing	578.3	588.4	617.5	609.4	612.8	618.3	629.5	638.8
5 Distributive industries	682.3	701.9	748.5	728.6	742.5	753.5	769.6	778.8
6 Service industries	967.6	1,021.4	1,109.5	1,082.0	1,101.2	1,114.3	1,140.5	1,160.0
7 Government and government enterprises	567.3	583.8	602.8	595.7	601.9	604.4	609.0	615.6
8 Other labor income	328.7	355.3	381.0	373.2	378.4	383.7	388.7	399.6
9 Proprietors' income[1]	418.7	441.6	473.7	471.0	471.3	467.0	485.7	493.8
10 Business and professional[1]	374.4	404.3	434.2	423.8	431.9	437.1	444.0	448.7
11 Farm[1]	44.4	37.3	39.5	47.2	39.3	29.8	41.7	45.1
12 Rental income of persons[2]	−5.5	24.1	27.7	15.3	34.1	32.6	29.0	25.6
13 Dividends	161.0	181.3	194.3	185.7	191.7	196.9	202.7	205.5
14 Personal interest income	665.2	637.9	664.0	631.1	649.4	674.2	701.1	724.5
15 Transfer payments	860.2	915.4	963.4	947.4	957.6	969.0	979.7	1,004.6
16 Old–age survivors, disability, and health insurance benefits	414.0	444.4	473.5	463.8	470.7	476.5	483.1	496.2
17 LESS: Personal contributions for social insurance	248.7	261.3	281.4	276.3	279.9	282.9	286.6	293.7
18 EQUALS: Personal income	5,154.3	5,375.1	5,701.7	5,555.8	5,659.9	5,734.5	5,856.6	5,963.1
19 LESS: Personal tax and nontax payments	648.6	686.4	742.1	723.0	746.4	744.1	754.7	774.3
20 EQUALS: Disposable personal income	4,505.8	4,688.7	4,959.6	4,832.8	4,913.5	4,990.3	5,101.9	5,188.8
21 LESS: Personal outlays	4,257.8	4,496.2	4,756.5	4,657.3	4,712.4	4,787.0	4,869.3	4,918.8
22 EQUALS: Personal saving	247.9	192.6	203.1	175.5	201.1	203.3	232.6	270.0
MEMO								
Per capita (1987 dollars)								
23 Gross domestic product	19,489.7	19,878.8	20,475.8	20,235.2	20,389.7	20,536.5	20,739.8	20,842.5
24 Personal consumption expenditures	13,110.4	13,390.8	13,715.4	13,639.8	13,650.9	13,716.6	13,853.5	13,872.9
25 Disposable personal income	14,279.0	14,341.0	14,696.0	14,535.0	14,625.0	14,697.0	14,927.0	15,057.0
26 Saving rate (percent)	5.5	4.1	4.1	3.6	4.1	4.1	4.6	5.2
GROSS SAVING								
27 Gross saving	722.9	787.5	920.6	886.2	923.3	922.6	950.3	n.a.
28 Gross private saving	980.8	1,002.5	1,053.5	1,037.3	1,041.4	1,052.7	1,082.7	n.a.
29 Personal saving	247.9	192.6	203.1	175.5	201.1	203.3	232.6	270.0
30 Undistributed corporate profits[1]	94.3	120.9	135.1	127.7	142.3	139.5	130.7	n.a.
31 Corporate inventory valuation adjustment	−6.4	−6.2	−19.5	−12.3	−14.1	−19.6	−32.1	−36.5
Capital consumption allowances								
32 Corporate	396.8	407.8	432.2	432.2	425.9	432.6	438.0	445.3
33 Noncorporate	261.8	261.2	283.1	301.8	272.1	277.3	281.3	284.8
34 Government surplus, or deficit (−), national income and product accounts	−257.8	−215.0	−132.9	−151.1	−118.1	−130.1	−132.3	n.a.
35 Federal	−282.7	−241.4	−159.1	−176.2	−145.1	−154.0	−161.1	n.a.
36 State and local	24.8	26.3	26.2	25.2	27.0	23.9	28.8	n.a.
37 Gross investment	731.7	789.8	889.7	850.2	899.3	901.5	907.9	n.a.
38 Gross private domestic investment	788.3	882.0	1,032.9	966.6	1,034.4	1,055.1	1,075.6	1,119.3
39 Net foreign investment	−56.6	−92.3	−143.2	−116.4	−135.1	−153.6	−167.7	n.a.
40 Statistical discrepancy	8.8	2.3	−30.9	−36.1	−24.0	−21.1	−42.4	n.a.

1. With inventory valuation and capital consumption adjustments.
2. With capital consumption adjustment.

SOURCE. U.S. Department of Commerce, *Survey of Current Business.*

Source: *Federal Reserve Bulletin,* Board of Governors of the Federal Reserve System.

HOURLY COMPENSATION COSTS

Indexes of hourly compensation costs for production workers in manufacturing, 29 countries or areas and selected economic groups, selected years, 1975–93

[Index, United States = 100]

Country or area	1975	1980	1985	1988	1989	1990	1991	1992	1993
United States	100	100	100	100	100	100	100	100	100
Canada	94	88	84	97	104	107	110	106	97
Mexico.	23	22	12	9	10	11	12	14	16
Australia.	88	86	63	82	87	88	87	81	73
Hong Kong.	12	15	13	17	19	21	23	24	26
Israel.	35	38	31	55	54	57	56	56	—
Japan	47	56	49	91	88	86	94	101	114
Korea.	5	10	9	16	22	25	29	30	32
New Zealand	50	54	34	59	54	56	54	49	48
Singapore.	13	15	19	19	22	25	28	31	32
Sri Lanka	4	2	2	2	2	2	3	—	—
Taiwan	6	10	12	20	25	26	28	32	31
Austria	71	90	58	104	99	119	116	126	120
Belgium	101	133	69	114	108	129	127	137	127
Denmark	99	110	62	109	101	120	117	124	114
Finland.	72	83	63	113	118	141	136	123	99
France	71	91	58	93	88	102	98	104	97
Germany[1].	100	125	74	131	124	149	147	157	152
Greece.	27	38	28	38	38	45	44	46	—
Ireland	48	60	46	72	67	79	78	83	—
Italy.	73	83	59	101	101	119	119	121	95
Luxembourg	100	121	59	99	95	110	107	—	—
Netherlands	103	122	67	114	105	123	118	127	120
Norway	106	117	80	133	128	144	139	142	120
Portugal	25	21	12	20	21	25	27	32	27
Spain.	40	60	36	61	62	76	78	83	69
Sweden	113	127	74	121	122	140	142	152	107
Switzerland.	96	112	74	129	117	140	139	144	135
United Kingdom	53	77	48	76	74	85	88	89	76
Trade-weighted measures[2]									
23 foreign economies[3]. . . .	61	67	52	77	77	83	86	89	86
OECD[4]	76	84	66	98	97	105	108	110	106
Europe.	81	102	62	105	100	118	117	123	111
European Union . .	79	100	61	102	98	115	114	121	110
Asian NIE's	8	12	13	18	23	25	27	30	31

[1] Former West Germany.
[2] For description of trade-weighted measures and economic groups, see text.
[3] 29 countries or areas less the United States and 5 countries for which 1993 data are not available.
[4] Organization for Economic Cooperation and Development less Mexico, which became a member in 1994.
Dash indicates data are not available.

Source: *Monthly Labor Review,* Department of Labor, Bureau of Labor Statistics.

OUTPUT IN MANUFACTURING, 12 COUNTRIES[1]

(Indexes: 1982=100)

Year	United States	Canada	Japan	Belgium	Denmark	France	Germany	Italy	Nether-lands	Norway	Sweden	United Kingdom
1950	NA	29.1	3.1	NA	29.8	20.9	17.8	12.3	22.6	37.9	34.8	61.0
1955	NA	37.7	6.9	NA	32.8	26.0	33.8	19.0	30.9	46.4	40.3	71.7
1960	NA	44.1	15.1	37.6	45.4	35.1	51.0	28.0	42.7	56.0	51.8	82.9
1961	NA	45.9	18.1	39.2	47.9	37.7	54.0	30.8	44.2	58.3	55.3	83.0
1962	NA	51.1	19.7	42.3	52.0	40.5	56.7	34.1	46.3	58.8	59.5	83.2
1963	NA	54.5	21.9	44.3	52.7	43.6	57.8	36.3	48.3	62.3	62.5	86.1
1964	NA	60.0	25.5	48.3	58.9	47.6	62.8	36.8	52.9	66.8	68.0	94.0
1965	NA	66.0	26.5	49.9	62.7	50.0	67.5	38.7	56.6	70.3	72.8	96.7
1966	NA	70.3	30.0	52.8	64.0	54.6	68.7	42.3	59.6	74.5	74.9	98.4
1967	NA	71.8	36.0	53.4	64.7	57.2	67.1	46.5	62.0	76.9	77.3	99.1
1968	NA	76.6	41.6	57.1	69.7	60.4	74.1	50.8	67.8	78.8	81.3	106.0
1969	NA	82.0	48.4	63.9	73.5	67.6	82.8	54.1	74.4	84.5	87.7	110.1
1970	NA	78.5	55.1	70.4	75.7	72.7	87.0	58.4	80.3	88.4	91.1	110.5
1971	NA	83.5	57.8	73.5	77.2	77.2	87.9	59.3	82.3	91.5	91.7	109.3
1972	NA	90.3	63.8	79.1	83.9	80.8	90.6	62.7	85.3	95.9	92.2	111.6
1973	NA	100.0	71.8	86.3	88.5	87.0	96.4	70.7	91.2	101.3	98.7	121.9
1974	NA	103.0	69.7	89.7	89.9	88.7	95.4	75.6	95.2	106.4	104.1	120.4
1975	NA	96.1	67.1	83.0	87.7	86.9	91.0	71.1	88.3	104.1	104.4	112.1
1976	NA	103.1	73.6	89.3	91.9	92.0	98.0	81.6	94.2	104.3	104.4	114.2
1977	104.3	106.9	76.4	89.6	92.3	96.2	99.8	84.6	95.2	102.2	98.5	116.4
1978	108.7	111.7	79.8	90.8	92.0	98.4	101.7	88.8	97.9	99.8	95.8	117.0
1979	109.3	115.9	86.5	93.2	97.3	101.3	106.9	97.9	101.0	102.7	102.0	116.8
1980	102.0	110.7	91.5	95.7	101.7	100.6	104.7	103.1	101.5	101.7	102.4	106.7
1981	105.0	114.8	95.7	95.6	98.4	99.0	103.6	101.1	101.5	100.7	99.7	100.1
1982	100.0	100.0	100.0	100.0	100.0	100.0	100.0	100.0	100.0	100.0	100.0	100.0
1983	103.2	106.5	104.3	106.3	106.7	99.9	101.5	100.8	101.9	99.3	105.8	102.1
1984	111.3	120.2	113.2	109.9	111.7	98.7	104.6	105.4	107.9	105.0	113.6	105.9
1985	114.0	127.0	121.2	111.8	115.3	99.1	108.4	108.9	111.1	108.8	115.7	108.9
1986	115.2	127.9	117.9	111.9	115.3	99.1	110.1	111.5	113.8	108.8	117.1	110.3
1987	123.5	134.1	126.5	112.3	110.6	98.9	108.1	116.3	115.4	110.8	120.0	115.5
1988	130.0	140.9	138.2	118.0	112.3	104.6	111.5	125.0	119.7	105.5	123.7	123.6
1989	131.2	142.1	149.3	125.0	113.6	110.3	115.4	129.7	125.2	103.8	125.1	129.1
1990	130.6	136.8	160.6	126.5	112.4	112.4	121.7	132.3	129.3	104.5	124.3	128.9
1991	128.2	127.5	170.8	125.9	111.1	110.6	126.2	132.1	129.9	102.3	117.4	121.9
1992	130.1	128.3	167.7	125.8	112.5	109.8	123.3	132.4	129.0	104.2	113.3	121.1
1993	135.4	134.7	160.7	120.5	113.2	106.3	113.8	129.6	125.8	105.9	115.1	122.8

NA: Not Available.

Source: U.S. Department of Labor, Bureau of Labor Statistics, February 1995.

[1] See notes on page 107.

UNIT LABOR COSTS IN MANUFACTURING, NATIONAL CURRENCY BASIS, 12 COUNTRIES[1]

(Indexes: 1982=100)

Year	United States	Canada	Japan	Belgium	Denmark	France	Germany	Italy	Nether-lands	Norway	Sweden	United Kingdom
1950	NA	25.3	NA	NA	17.0	16.0	33.3	12.6	25.8	14.8	16.4	9.1
1955	NA	29.2	41.4	NA	21.3	22.3	33.2	12.9	30.1	19.4	23.8	12.1
1960	NA	31.9	35.5	38.0	23.8	25.7	36.4	13.5	33.4	21.3	25.8	14.2
1961	NA	31.0	36.4	39.7	25.3	26.6	38.8	13.9	36.2	22.5	26.9	15.2
1962	NA	29.9	39.7	40.5	26.3	27.7	41.1	14.7	37.5	24.7	27.9	15.6
1963	NA	30.0	41.0	43.1	27.7	28.6	42.0	17.0	39.9	25.0	29.1	15.5
1964	NA	29.9	40.6	45.8	27.7	28.8	42.0	18.0	42.5	25.3	29.2	15.5
1965	NA	30.1	43.9	48.4	29.3	29.2	43.4	17.3	44.8	26.4	30.0	16.5
1966	NA	31.8	44.1	50.0	31.7	28.6	45.3	16.9	47.2	27.7	31.5	17.2
1967	NA	33.1	43.7	51.7	33.2	28.9	45.0	17.8	48.9	29.8	32.2	17.0
1968	NA	33.3	45.4	50.8	33.5	29.7	44.7	17.6	48.7	31.0	32.0	17.0
1969	NA	34.1	47.0	51.0	36.2	29.7	45.6	18.6	50.5	31.2	32.3	18.1
1970	NA	37.3	49.7	52.6	39.0	31.5	51.9	21.3	52.7	33.7	35.4	20.4
1971	NA	37.5	54.2	56.8	42.0	33.4	56.0	24.1	57.1	37.1	38.0	22.6
1972	NA	38.4	56.2	58.9	43.0	35.2	58.3	24.9	60.0	39.0	40.5	24.7
1973	NA	39.1	63.2	61.8	47.4	37.7	61.9	27.1	64.5	41.4	42.2	26.3
1974	NA	44.3	80.9	71.3	55.5	43.8	68.1	33.1	70.8	46.4	47.6	31.0
1975	NA	52.4	90.4	83.0	60.2	51.7	71.9	43.3	82.8	56.3	57.5	42.1
1976	NA	56.1	90.8	85.5	64.8	55.8	72.3	47.3	83.3	63.0	66.3	46.8
1977	65.3	58.8	95.7	91.0	70.3	59.9	76.7	54.8	86.8	71.1	73.5	52.4
1978	70.5	62.6	96.7	92.5	76.4	64.6	79.8	59.3	88.4	77.1	79.8	60.3
1979	78.4	68.4	95.4	95.5	81.4	69.9	82.1	65.6	90.4	76.6	79.8	71.1
1980	89.7	78.7	97.8	99.4	85.1	80.1	90.6	73.5	94.2	84.3	87.4	86.7
1981	95.1	86.3	100.4	102.0	92.2	90.1	94.4	86.8	95.9	93.5	96.6	95.8
1982	100.0	100.0	100.0	100.0	100.0	100.0	100.0	100.0	100.0	100.0	100.0	100.0
1983	100.5	98.9	100.2	95.0	101.9	107.9	99.7	111.2	98.1	105.2	103.2	99.5
1984	102.4	95.5	98.1	97.7	108.3	115.2	101.0	116.1	92.7	107.8	106.9	101.9
1985	104.2	97.6	95.8	102.0	114.9	120.2	102.6	123.4	93.9	114.2	116.1	107.5
1986	105.8	102.9	102.4	104.7	124.5	123.2	106.2	127.1	96.1	126.4	123.4	112.3
1987	101.6	105.0	96.8	105.0	136.8	125.5	112.6	130.5	98.4	137.5	129.1	118.0
1988	103.2	109.2	93.1	103.0	136.5	121.8	113.0	132.6	96.0	147.1	135.6	119.4
1989	106.7	112.8	92.4	103.8	139.5	122.2	114.6	141.4	93.5	146.3	145.4	126.2
1990	110.4	117.2	92.7	110.0	148.3	126.4	117.8	151.3	94.7	149.8	158.0	128.9
1991	113.7	123.4	93.2	114.4	153.8	131.5	121.3	162.1	98.3	155.6	170.6	137.2
1992	116.0	123.5	97.5	115.9	155.1	133.0	129.4	165.6	103.3	157.3	169.5	144.2
1993	116.1	121.4	99.9	117.0	150.5	135.9	136.8	167.2	105.1	155.5	156.6	147.8

NA: Not Available

Note: The data relate to employees (wage and salary earners) in Belgium, Denmark, Italy, the Netherlands, and the United Kingdom, and to all employed persons (employees and self-employed workers) in the other countries.

Source: U.S. Department of Labor, Bureau of Labor Statistics, February 1995.

[1] See notes on page 107.

General Notes

BLS has changed the labor input measures for Japan, France, Germany, Norway, and Sweden from an employees (wage and salary worker) basis to an all-employed-persons basis. Employed persons include the self-employed and unpaid family workers in addition to employees. This change puts the measures for these countries on the same employment basis as the comparative measures for the United States and Canada, which have always been reported on an employed-persons basis. The labor input measures for Belgium, Denmark, Italy, the Netherlands, and the United Kingdom continue to refer to employees only.

The change to an employed-persons basis has no effect on hourly compensation costs because, as with the United States and Canada, hourly compensation costs of employed persons are assumed to be the same as for employees.

BLS does not have consistent total labor input series back to 1950 for any of the five countries converted to an employed-persons basis. The employment series for France, Germany, and Norway are consistent back to 1950, but average hours of the self-employed and family workers are estimated for 1950 to 1969 for France, for 1950 to 1959 for Germany, and for 1950 to 1961 for Norway based on the trend in the previous series on average hours of employees. The Swedish indexes for both employment and hours for 1950 to 1959 are based on the trend in the previous employee series. The Japanese indexes have only been carried back to 1955. Japanese household labor force survey data on the self-employed were linked at 1970 to national accounts-based estimates, which are derived largely from the household survey. Average hours of the self-employed for 1955 to 1967 are held constant at the 1968 level since the data available to BLS do not indicate any trend over the period; for 1971 and 1972, they are prorated between figures that are available for 1970 and 1973.

Source: U.S. Department of Labor, Bureau of Labor Statistics, February 1995.

U.S. EXPORTS AND IMPORTS

(Billions of dollars, annual rates)

Goods and Services

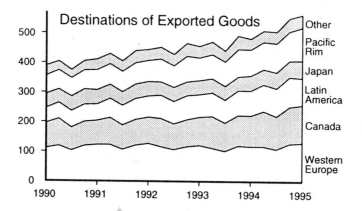

Destinations of Exported Goods

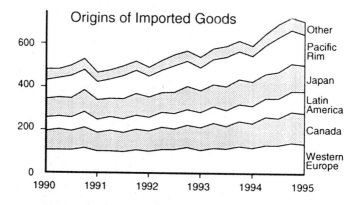

Origins of Imported Goods

Notes: Figures reflect general imports, customs value, and total exports (including re-exports), FAS value. Except where noted, they are not adjusted to the balance-of-payments basis, and thus include military goods and non-monetary gold. The totals, goods and services subtotals, and end-use breakouts are seasonally adjusted; all other series are unadjusted.

Economic and Financial Trends for the Major Developed Countries

Introduction

Main Economic Indicators is mainly designed to provide statistics on recent economic developments in OECD Member countries. It has been divided into two main parts: Indicators by subject and Indicators by country.

The following points should be noted:

1. Index numbers are shown with 1990 = 100, in conformity with international recommendations for a standard reference year.
2. Many series are shown in both seasonally adjusted and unadjusted form. Where seasonally adjusted data are not available from national sources, the series have been adjusted by the Secretariat according to the U.S. *Bureau of the Census* Method II, X-11 version.
3. The 12-month rate of change shown in the tables is calculated as the percentage variation between the latest period shown for each series and the corresponding period of the previous year.

Data for Mexico have been included in some area totals
The statistics for Germany in this publication refer to *western Germany* (Federal Republic of Germany before the unification of Germany)
As data become available for unified Germany, they will be incorporated, duly indicated, in the relevant tables and graphs of this publication.
Monetary, economic and social union between the Federal Republic and the German Democratic Republic took place on 1st July 1990. The series affected are: interest rates, foreign finance.

The data in the following series refer to unified Germany starting from the given time period:

National product: gross domestic product at current and constant prices, third quarter 1990

Domestic finance: original series for money supply data and other domestic finance series, June 1990
Foreign trade, balance of payments: all series, July 1990. Ships completed, October 1990
Seasonally adjusted money supply series, industrial production: crude steel, January 1991
New passenger car registrations, January 1992
Commercial vehicles, production of passenger cars, share prices, January 1993
Labour: employment in manufacturing and monthly hours worked, January 1991; unemployment and unfilled vacancies, September 1990
Construction: work put in place, residential and private non-residential, 1992; cost of construction, first quarter 1991
Wholesale sales (value) and retail sales (value), January 1991
Indices of industrial production, July 1990

COUNTRY GRAPHS

Country graphs give a view of the developments over the last five years of a selection of important short-term economic indicators: Output, Demand, Labour, Prices, Finance and Balance of payments. Data underlying the indicators which are presented in the graphs may be found in the country tables, with the exception of leading indicators for which data may be found in Part I of this publication. Scales have been harmonised for indicators presented on the same graph and across countries according to the method described below in the section on scaling and cross-country comparisons.

On each graph, the most prominent indicator is represented by a solid black line referring to the left scale when two scales are present on the graph. The second indicator represented by a solid grey line, refers to the right scale. When a third indicator is present it is shown as a dotted line and the associated scale is indicated below the curve. A break on the vertical axis indicates that the scale does not start at zero. Grids are shown on each graph for easy reading.

Output

The key indicator in this category is *Gross domestic product* (GDP) at constant market prices, generally presented on a quarterly basis. Two other indicators are presented where available: the index of *Industrial production* and the *OECD composite leading indicator*. The latter is a composite indicator, based on indicators of economic activity, which signals cyclical movements in industrial production six to nine months in advance. The OECD system of leading indicators is described in *OECD leading indicators and business cycles in Member countries, 1960–1985, Sources and Methods*, No. 39, (January 1987).

Demand

This graph shows some of the most closely monitored demand indicators in a given country. For many countries these are monthly data on construction and new passenger car registrations.

Labour Market

The key indicator for the Labour market is the *Unemployment rate*, shown with an indicator on job vacancies. For most countries the latter is *Unfilled vacancies*, though in some cases *New vacancies* or *Help wanted advertising* has been used. The *Unemployment rate* is shown with a constant scale range of 8 percent for all countries.

Prices

This graph shows the two most important price indices, the *Consumer price index* and the *Producer price index*. For more information on these indicators see *Sources and Methods: Consumer Price Indices*, April 1994 and *Sources and Methods: Producer price Indices*, April 1994.

Financial Markets

This graph shows the movements of the typical long and short-term *interest rates* for each country together with a leading *share price index*.

Balance of Payments

The *trade* and the *current balance* aggregates of the balance of payments are presented in this graph.

Harmonising variations in the graphs

The scales of the graphs have been adjusted with the following main objectives:

- to make the representation of the relative variation of different indicators in the same graph less arbitrary;
- to harmonise scale ranges across countries in order to facilitate cross-country comparisons.

Intra-subject scaling

When several indicators expressed in different units are presented on the same graph, the variations of the indicators are not necessarily comparable. If scales were not adjusted, movements in the *Industrial production index*, for example, shown against the right scale, would not be comparable with movements in *GDP* expressed in currency units on the left scale. Not adjusting scales for differences in units could give an arbitrary picture of the variations of the one indicator compared to those of the other indicator.

The following method has been adopted in calculating left and right-hand scales: a given length on the two scales represents the same percentage change in the corresponding indicators.

This method has been applied to the Output and Demand graphs. Since indicators on Prices and Balance of payments are expressed in the same units, harmonisation was not necessary. The method has not been applied to financial indicators because movements in *Share prices* do not easily relate to movements in *Interest rates*.

For most countries the Labour market indicators presented are the *Unemployment rate* and *Job vacancies*. Over the past five years the number of unemployed persons has varied considerably in most OECD countries whereas the change in the number of new job vacancies has been very small in comparison. Because it is not possible to harmonise variations without flattening the *Job vacancies* curve, some distortion remains between the movements of the two indicators on the Labour market graphs. However, it is kept constant across countries.

Another constraint to this graph is cross country comparability, for which the scale range of the *Unemployment rate* has been fixed at 8 percent. The common distortion factor then gives the range for the *Job vacancies* indicator.

Harmonising scale ranges across countries

The scale range has been calculated by category for all countries. Ideally, the largest range would then be used for all countries. However, this is not always possible without flattening some of the graphs. Therefore for each category three different scale ranges were used, which correspond to three groups of countries. The first group covers the majority of "standard" variation countries; the two other groups cover countries with high variation indicators. For instance, for price indicators high inflation countries are in the second group and very high inflation countries in the third group.

The following table lists by subject the countries which are included in the two high variation groups:

	Group II	Group III
Output	Turkey	Iceland
	Mexico	
Demand	Austria	Netherlands
	Denmark	
	Greece	
	Luxembourg	
	Norway	
	Turkey	
Labour Market	Spain	Finland
	Sweden	
Prices	Greece	Turkey
	Portugal	
	Mexico	
Interest Rates	Australia	Iceland
	Canada	Ireland
	Denmark	Mexico
	Finland	
	Italy	
	New Zealand	
	Norway	
	Sweden	
	United Kingdom	
Share Prices	Finland	Turkey
	Switzerland	

DEFINITIONS

Unless otherwise specified, the following definitions apply:

Subject definitions

Construction: Excludes civil engineering.
Domestic trade: Wholesale sales exclude indirect taxes; retail sales include them.
Jobs vacant: Includes part-time jobs.
Time lost through labour disputes: Excludes time lost due to shortages or strikes in related industries.
Official reserves: Gross holdings of special drawing rights and foreign exchange plus reserve position in IMF.
Foreign trade: Special trade, excluding non-monetary gold.

Geographic coverage

Belgium-Luxembourg: Foreign finance, foreign trade and balance of payments statistics refer to the Belgo-Luxembourg Economic Union.
United Kingdom: Great Britain and Northern Ireland.
Germany: Western Germany (Federal Republic of Germany before the unification of Germany).

SHARE PRICES

COURS DES ACTIONS

January 1986 = 100 — Janvier 1986 = 100

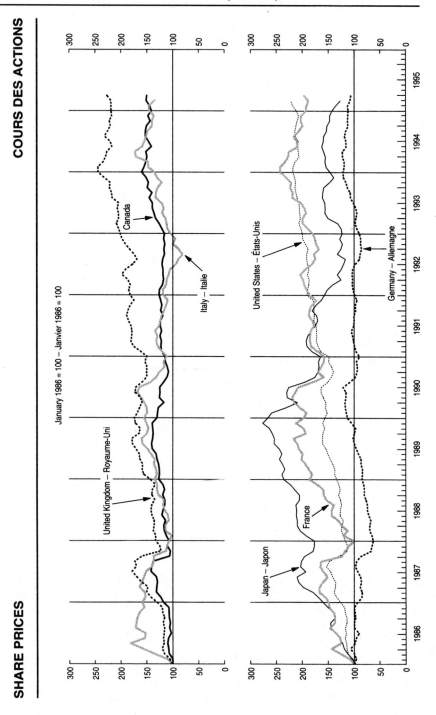

1990 = 100

	1992	1993	1994	1994 Q2	1994 Q3	1994 Q4	1995 Q1	1994 Sep	1994 Oct	1994 Nov	1994 Dec	1995 Jan	1995 Feb	1995 Mar	1995 Apr	12-month rate of change / Variation sur 12 mois
Canada[1]	99	114	125	123	126	123	121	127	125	120	123	117	121	126	125	0.3
Mexico - Mexique[1]	289	326	442	412	463	440	320	482	448	455	417	367	272	321	344	-14.5
United States - États-Unis[2]	125	136	139	136	139	137	142	140	139	138	136	138	143	145		3.7
Japan - Japon[1]	63	70	73	75	75	71	64	73	73	70	70	68	65	60		-18.9
Australia - Australie	106	122	133	134	130	122	121	128	124	121	120	119	121	124		-13.3
New Zealand - Nouvelle-Zélande	91	114	134	133	132	128	125	132	134	127	122	123	126	127	141	5.1
Austria - Autriche[3]	66	65	74	75	73	69	66	73	70	68	68	68	64	65	62	-18.0
Belgium - Belgique[4]	96	101	114	117	115	109	104	114	108	111	107	106	105	100	103	-12.0
Denmark - Danemark[1]	85	88	103	104	101	96	96	97	96	96	97	98	98	93		-14.4
Finland - Finlande[1]	69	116	179	172	182	188	180	189	190	191	184	190	183	167		-5.4
France	97	108	115	116	111	106	101	109	105	107	107	102	101	99	104	-13.2
Germany - Allemagne[5]	88	95	108	111	108	103	102	107	103	104	103	103	104	99	98	-13.1
Greece - Grèce	77	80	91	91	84	83	81	84	84	81	86	83	81	80	80	-17.3
Ireland - Irlande[6]	84	101	119	116	116	117	119	122	117	117	117	118	119	121		-1.4
Italy - Italie	70	83	104	116	105	96	98	103	97	97	95	100	101	93		-8.0
Netherlands - Pays-Bas	108	125	148	147	146	146	147	147	144	146	147	148	149	144	146	-3.1
Norway - Norvège[3]	84	107	138	137	137	134	138	135	133	132	138	140	141	133	139	-1.0
Portugal	74	85	114	113	111	115		114	114	115	115					12.4
Spain - Espagne	88	101	120	122	116	113	106	114	112	114	112	107	108	103		-19.1
Sweden - Suède[1]	80	106	133	131	131	134	135	128	131	136	133	137	137	132		3.9
Switzerland - Suisse[7]	108	137	159	159	154	152		151	149	153	155	149	153			-9.1
Turkey - Turquie[1]	100	279	527	409	614	666	781	667	619	701	678	628	724	991	1160	208.8
United Kingdom - Royaume-Uni[1]	115	132	142	139	140	137	136	140	137	138	135	136	136	136	141	-1.1

Note: Industrial share prices for Australia, Belgium, Finland, Norway and United Kingdom ("500" share index), for all other countries data refer to all shares. Unless otherwise specified monthly data are averages of daily quotations. Quarterly and annual data are monthly averages.

(1) Monthly data refer to end of period.
(2) Composite index.
(3) Monthly data refer to the 15th of month.
(4) Monthly data refer to the 25th of month.
(5) Data refer to Germany after unification.
(6) Monthly data refer to beginning of period.
(7) Monthly data refer to last workday of month.

Note: Actions industrielles pour l'Australie, la Belgique, la Finlande, la Norvège et le Royaume-Uni (indice de "500" actions). Pour tous les autres pays les données se réfèrent à l'ensemble des actions. Sauf indication contraire, les données mensuelles sont les moyennes des quotations journalières. Les données trimestrielles et annuelles sont les moyennes des mois.

(1) Les données mensuelles se réfèrent à la fin de la période.
(2) Indice composite.
(3) Les données mensuelles se réfèrent au 15 du mois.
(4) Les données mensuelles se réfèrent au 25 du mois.
(5) Les données se réfèrent à l'Allemagne après l'unification.
(6) Situation en début de mois.
(7) Les données mensuelles se réfèrent au dernier jour ouvrable du mois.

AUSTRALIA   AUSTRALIE

OUTPUT   PRODUCTION

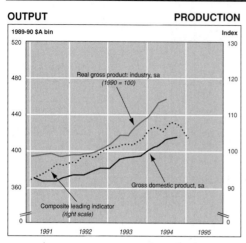

DEMAND   DEMANDE

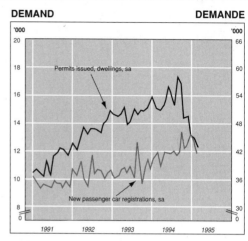

LABOUR MARKET   MARCHÉ DU TRAVAIL

PRICES   PRIX

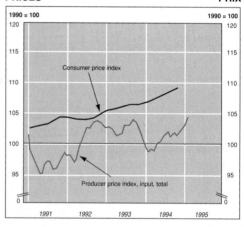

FINANCIAL MARKETS   MARCHÉS FINANCIERS

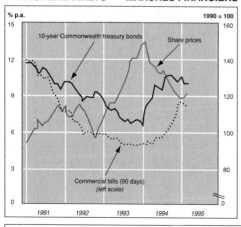

BALANCE of PAYMENTS   BALANCE des PAIEMENTS

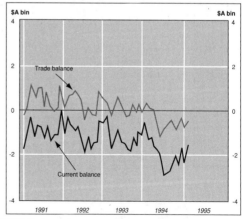

| left scale | ———— | échelle de gauche | | right scale | ———— | échelle de droite |

CANADA   CANADA

OUTPUT   PRODUCTION

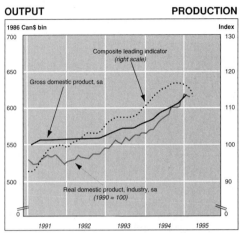

1986 Can$ bin | Index

- Composite leading indicator *(right scale)*
- Gross domestic product, sa
- Real domestic product, industry, sa *(1990 = 100)*

DEMAND   DEMANDE

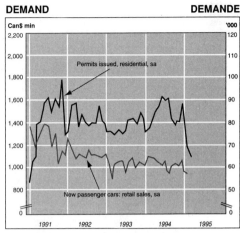

Can$ min | '000

- Permits issued, residential, sa
- New passenger cars: retail sales, sa

LABOUR MARKET   MARCHÉ DU TRAVAIL

% | 1990 = 100

- Unemployment rate, sa
- Help wanted advertising, sa

PRICES   PRIX

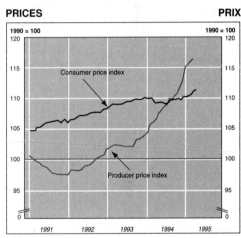

1990 = 100 | 1990 = 100

- Consumer price index
- Producer price index

FINANCIAL MARKETS   MARCHÉS FINANCIERS

% p.a. | 1990 = 100

- Federal government bonds
- Share prices
- 90-day deposit receipts *(left scale)*

BALANCE of PAYMENTS   BALANCE des PAIEMENTS

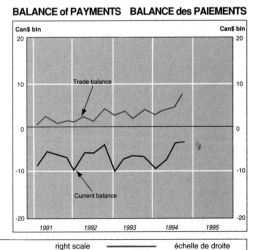

Can$ bin | Can$ bin

- Trade balance
- Current balance

---

left scale ▬▬▬ échelle de gauche   right scale ▬▬▬ échelle de droite

FRANCE   FRANCE

OUTPUT   PRODUCTION

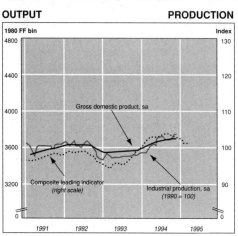

DEMAND   DEMANDE

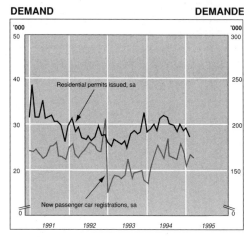

LABOUR MARKET   MARCHÉ DU TRAVAIL

PRICES   PRIX

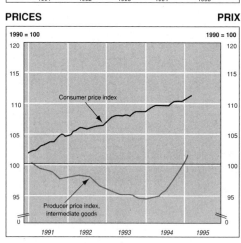

FINANCIAL MARKETS   MARCHÉS FINANCIERS

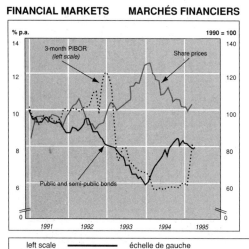

BALANCE of PAYMENTS   BALANCE des PAIEMENTS

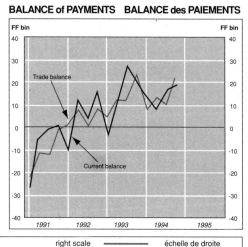

| left scale | ——— | échelle de gauche | right scale | ——— | échelle de droite |

GERMANY   ALLEMAGNE

OUTPUT   PRODUCTION

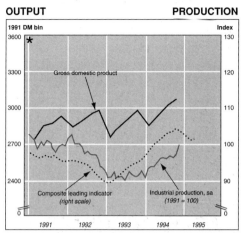

1991 DM bin / Index

Gross domestic product

Composite leading indicator
(right scale)

Industrial production, sa
(1991 = 100)

DEMAND   DEMANDE

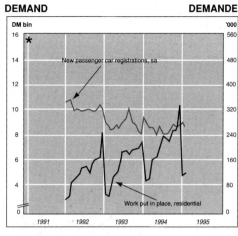

DM bin / '000

New passenger car registrations, sa

Work put in place, residential

LABOUR MARKET   MARCHÉ DU TRAVAIL

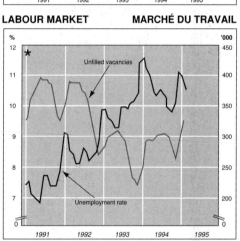

% / '000

Unfilled vacancies

Unemployment rate

PRICES   PRIX

1990 = 100 / 1990 = 100

Consumer price index

Producer price index

FINANCIAL MARKETS   MARCHÉS FINANCIERS

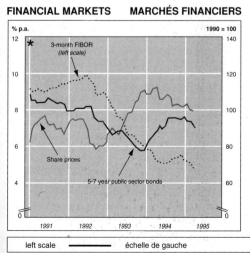

% p.a. / 1990 = 100

3-month FIBOR
(left scale)

Share prices

5-7 year public sector bonds

BALANCE of PAYMENTS   BALANCE des PAIEMENTS

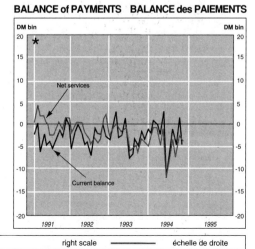

DM bin / DM bin

Net services

Current balance

| left scale | ——— | échelle de gauche | | right scale | ——— | échelle de droite |

★ Germany after unification. See introduction for details.   ★ Allemagne après l'unification. Voir l'introduction pour les détails.

ITALY

ITALIE

OUTPUT

PRODUCTION

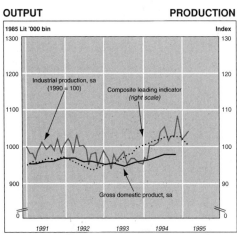

1985 Lit '000 bin — Index

Industrial production, sa (1990 = 100)

Composite leading indicator *(right scale)*

Gross domestic product, sa

DEMAND

DEMANDE

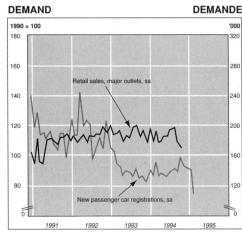

1990 = 100 — '000

Retail sales, major outlets, sa

New passenger car registrations, sa

LABOUR MARKET

MARCHÉ DU TRAVAIL

Unemployment rate, sa

B

PRICES

PRIX

1990 = 100 — 1990 = 100

Consumer price index

Producer price index

FINANCIAL MARKETS

MARCHÉS FINANCIERS

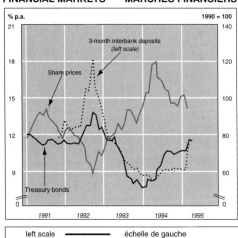

% p.a. — 1990 = 100

3-month interbank deposits *(left scale)*

Share prices

Treasury bonds

BALANCE of PAYMENTS

BALANCE des PAIEMENTS

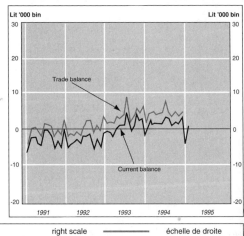

Lit '000 bin — Lit '000 bin

Trade balance

Current balance

---

left scale ——— échelle de gauche   right scale ——— échelle de droite

B Break in continuity of series   **B** Rupture d'homogénéité dans la série

JAPAN   JAPON

OUTPUT   PRODUCTION

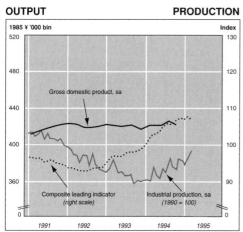

DEMAND   DEMANDE

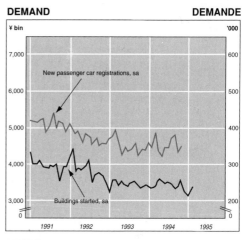

LABOUR MARKET   MARCHÉ DU TRAVAIL

PRICES   PRIX

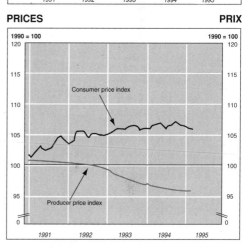

FINANCIAL MARKETS   MARCHÉS FINANCIERS

BALANCE of PAYMENTS   BALANCE des PAIEMENTS

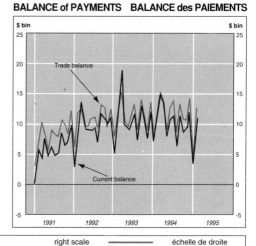

| left scale | ——— | échelle de gauche | right scale | ——— | échelle de droite |

MEXICO   MEXIQUE

OUTPUT   PRODUCTION

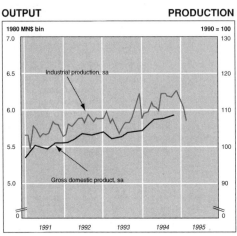

DEMAND   DEMANDE

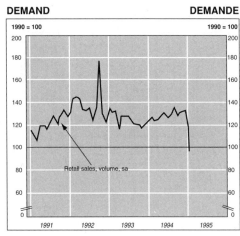

LABOUR MARKET   MARCHÉ DU TRAVAIL

PRICES   PRIX

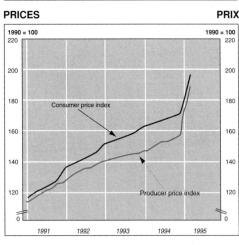

FINANCIAL MARKETS   MARCHÉS FINANCIERS

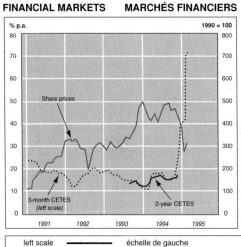

BALANCE of PAYMENTS   BALANCE des PAIEMENTS

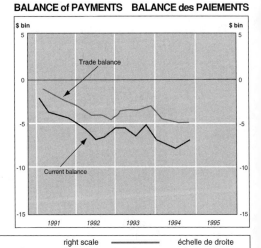

| left scale ———— échelle de gauche | right scale ———— échelle de droite |

SPAIN   ESPAGNE

OUTPUT   PRODUCTION   ## DEMAND   DEMANDE

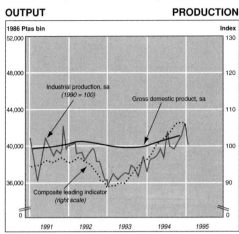

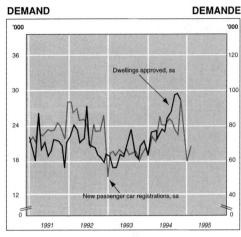

LABOUR MARKET   MARCHÉ DU TRAVAIL   ## PRICES   PRIX

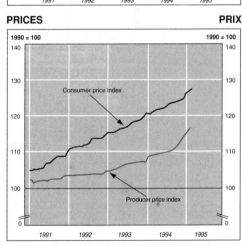

FINANCIAL MARKETS   MARCHÉS FINANCIERS   ## BALANCE of PAYMENTS   BALANCE des PAIEMENTS

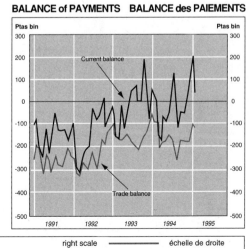

| left scale ——— | échelle de gauche | right scale ——— | échelle de droite |

SWITZERLAND SUISSE

OUTPUT PRODUCTION

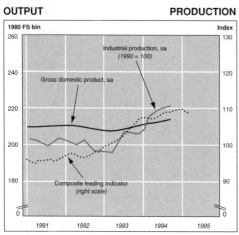

DEMAND DEMANDE

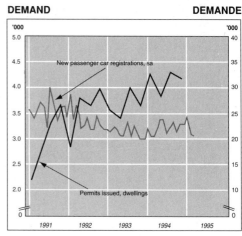

LABOUR MARKET MARCHÉ DU TRAVAIL

PRICES PRIX

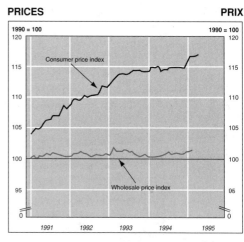

FINANCIAL MARKETS MARCHÉS FINANCIERS

EXTERNAL POSITION POSITION EXTÉRIEURE

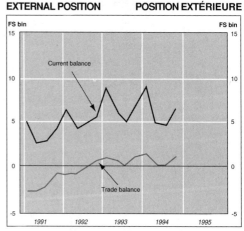

| left scale | ———— | échelle de gauche | right scale | ———— | échelle de droite |

UNITED KINGDOM   ROYAUME UNI

OUTPUT   PRODUCTION

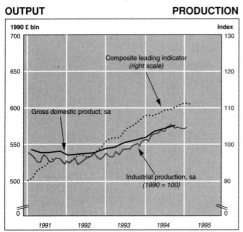

DEMAND   DEMANDE

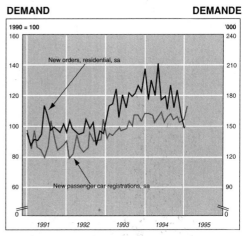

LABOUR MARKET   MARCHÉ DU TRAVAIL

PRICES   PRIX

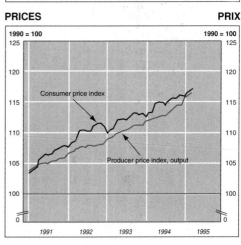

FINANCIAL MARKETS   MARCHÉS FINANCIERS

BALANCE of PAYMENTS   BALANCE des PAIEMENTS

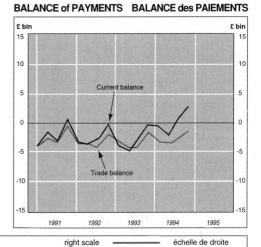

| left scale | ——————— | échelle de gauche | right scale | ——————— | échelle de droite |

UNITED STATES   ÉTATS-UNIS

OUTPUT   PRODUCTION

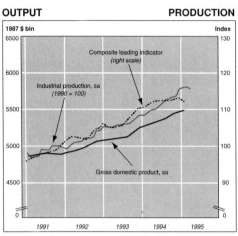

DEMAND   DEMANDE

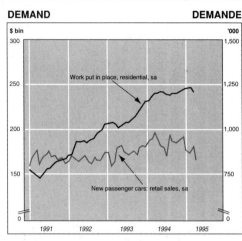

LABOUR MARKET   MARCHÉ DU TRAVAIL

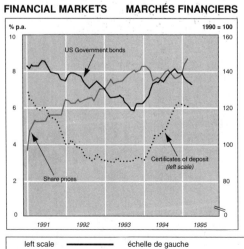

PRICES   PRIX

FINANCIAL MARKETS   MARCHÉS FINANCIERS

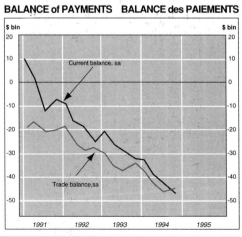

BALANCE of PAYMENTS   BALANCE des PAIEMENTS

| left scale | ——— | échelle de gauche | right scale | ——— | échelle de droite |

Selected Regional Trade Arrangements in the Western Hemisphere

Arrangement	Countries	Type	Status	Economic Indicators	Highlights	Comments
Andean Pact	Bolivia, Colombia, Ecuador, Peru, Venezuela	Customs Union	Founded with Cartagena Agreement, 1969 Act of Barahona 12/4–5/91	Population: 96.33 million Total GDP: $480.6 billion U.S. exports: $10.2 billion U.S. imports: $13.5 billion	The Andean countries have significantly liberalized their trade and investment regimes through coordinated efforts under the auspices of the Andean Pact. Free trade between Ecuador, Bolivia, Colombia and Ecuador in October 1992. The Andean Pact is finalizing negotiations on a common external tariff (CET) with a structure of 5, 10, 15, and 20 percent.	Peru suspended its participation in 1992 but its reintegration is scheduled to be complete by June 1995.
Caribbean Common Market (CARICOM)	Antigua and Barbuda, Barbados, Belize, Dominica, Grenada, Guyana, Jamaica, Montserrat, St. Kitts and Nevis, St. Lucia, St. Vincent and Grenadines, Trinidad and Tobago	Customs Union; eventual Common Market	Founded 1973 Grand Anse Declaration 7/89	Population: 5.79 million Total GDP: $28.6 million U.S. exports: $3.0 billion U.S. imports: $2.1 billion	Despite its name, the CARICOM currently operates as a customs union and not a common market. The CARICOM common external tariff (CET), first proposed in 1973, has never been implemented by all member countries.	In May 1992, four of CARICOM's smallest members agreed to pursue political union. In July 1991, Cuba expressed an interest in joining the group.
Central American Common Market (CACM)	Costa Rica, El Salvador, Guatemala, Honduras, Nicaragua	Common Market	Founded 1960 Puntarenas Declaration 1973	Population: 28.5 million Total GDP: $81.2 billion U.S. exports: $4.8 billion U.S. imports: $4.3 billion	El Salvador, Guatemala, Honduras and Nicaragua have recently moved to lower mutual trade and investment barriers. CACM countries have established a common external tariff with a ceiling of 20 percent and have dropped tariffs on intra-regional trade in agricultural products, but this is not effective for all countries.	Panama is slowly increasing its participation in CACM.

(continued)

125

SELECTED REGIONAL TRADE ARRANGEMENTS IN THE WESTERN HEMISPHERE *(concluded)*

Arrangement	Countries	Type	Status	Economic Indicators	Highlights	Comments
G-3	Colombia, Venezuela, Mexico	Free Trade Area	Signed 6/13/94 Subject to ratification by all three countries	Population: 145.5 million Total GDP: $1.1 billion U.S. exports: $49.4 billion U.S. imports: $51.1 billion	The G-3 Agreement is not as comprehensive as the NAFTA, but includes all the same chapters, except the energy chapter. Tariffs will be phased out over ten years, with a number of important exceptions will apply.	Bolivia, Ecuador, Peru and Chile have stated an interest in joining.
Southern Common Market (Mercosur)	Argentina, Brazil, Paraguay, Uruguay	Common Market	Agreement on Argentine-Brazilian Integration 7/29/86 Treaty of Asuncion 3/26/91	Population: 198 million Total GDP: $1 trillion U.S. exports: $10.6 billion U.S. imports: $8.9 billion	Phased reduction of tariffs with zero tariff on intragroup trade to be implemented January 1995. A common external tariff between 0 and 20 percent will be applied to most imported goods beginning in 1995. Little progress in harmonization of fiscal and monetary policy.	
North American Free Trade Agreement (NAFTA)	Canada, Mexico and the United States	Free Trade Area	Signed 12/1992 Effective 1/1/1994	Population: 376.3 million Total GDP: $7.736 trillion U.S. exports: $142 billion U.S. imports: $151 billion	Eliminates tariffs and non-tariff barriers and includes disciplines on government procurement, product standards, investment, services, and intellectual property rights.	

Source: *Business America*, U.S. Department of Commerce.

Government Budget, Receipts, and Deficits: Historical Data[1]

Overview of the Budget Process

Executive Budget Formulation Process

During budget formulation, the President establishes general budget and fiscal policy guidelines. Under a multi-year planning system, policy guidance is given to agencies for both the upcoming budget year and for the four following years and provides the initial guidelines for preparation of agency budget requests.

The budget formulation process begins not later than the spring of each year, at least nine months before the budget is transmitted. Executive branch agencies prepare their budget requests based on the guidelines provided by the President through the Office of Management and Budget (OMB) and the detailed instructions on preparation of budget estimates provided in this Circular.

Last year, the Executive branch budget review process was expanded to provide for greater participation of agency heads and their staff. Building on that process, OMB is working with agency staff to identify major issues for the upcoming budget; undertake the analysis necessary to provide the context for decision-making; identify major options for the fall budget review process; and develop and implement multi-year plans for analysis of issues that will need decisions in future years.

Through the spring and summer, the process focuses on review of program performance, as well as on ways to ensure efficient use of government resources and successful implementation of programs and policies. Ideas are exchanged on potential reorganization of functions, consolidation of activities, and proposals to restructure programs. In addition, a wide range of management practices are explored to ensure high-quality program performance, evaluation of near- and longer-term program results, and timely assessment of the need for policy redirection through administrative action or legislative changes.

Executive branch departments and agencies are required to submit initial budget materials to OMB beginning early in the fall, in accordance with the schedule in section 10.3. Other materials are submitted later in the fall and winter on a schedule supplied by OMB. Budget data are required for the past, current, and upcoming budget year, as well as for the four years following the budget year.

In the fall, major issues and options will be prepared for consideration by the President, organized around major Administration themes and cross-cutting issues. OMB will then review agency budget requests, based on Presidential priorities, program performance, and budget constraints. A complete set of budget proposals will be presented to the President by early December for his approval.

After the review process is completed, decisions on budget requests are passed back to the agencies. Upon receipt of final decisions for the current and budget year, agencies revise their budget requests to bring them into accord with these decisions. These final estimates are transmitted to Congress in the President's budget. In accordance with current law, the budget must be transmitted to Congress not later than the first Monday in February.

The multi-year planning estimates included in the President's budget then become the starting point in planning for the budget to be transmitted to Congress the following year.

Executive and Congressional Budget Processes

The executive budget formulation process described above is prescribed by OMB, in accordance with the Budget and Accounting Act of 1921, as amended. The following timetable highlights significant dates culminating in transmittal of the President's budget and subsequent updates of the budget. It also reflects the congressional budget procedures established by the Congressional Budget Act of 1974 and certain requirements of the Balanced Budget and Emergency Deficit Control Act of 1985, as they both were amended by the Budget Enforcement Act of 1990 (BEA).

Source: Office of Management and Budget, Circular No. A-11 Revised.

[1] See page 146 for notes to Exhibits on pages 134–145.

THE BUDGET PROCESS

	ACTION TO BE COMPLETED	
The Executive Budget Process	Timing	The Congressional Budget Process
Agencies subject to executive branch review submit initial budget request materials.	September 9	
Fiscal year begins.	October 1	Fiscal year begins.
Agencies not subject to executive branch review submit budget request materials.	October 15	
	10 days after end of session	CBO issues its final sequester report.
OMB issues its final sequestration report;[1] President issues sequestration order, if necessary.	15 days after end of session	
	30 days later	Comptroller General issues compliance report.
Legislative branch and the judiciary submit budget request materials.	November–December	
	5 days before President's budget transmittal	CBO issues its sequestration preview report
President transmits the budget to Congress, including OMB sequestration preview report.	Not later than the first Monday in February	
	February 15	Congressional Budget Office reports to the Budget Committees on the President's budget.
	Within 6 weeks of President's budget transmittal	Committees submit views and estimates to Budget Committees.

Executive action	Date	Congressional action
OMB issues budget planning guidance.	April	
	April 1	Senate Budget Committee reports concurrent resolution on the budget.
	April 15	Congress completes action on concurrent resolution.
	May 15	House may consider appropriations bills in the absence of a concurrent resolution on the budget.
	June 10	House Appropriations Committee reports last appropriations bill.
	June 15	Congress completes action on reconciliation legislation.
	June 30	House completes action on annual appropriations bills.
	After completion of action on discretionary, direct spending, or receipts legislation.	CBO provides estimate of the impact of legislation as soon as practicable.
President transmits the Mid-Session Review, updating the budget estimates.	July 15	
OMB and agencies discuss budget issues and options in preparation for fall budget review and decision making.	Late June—early August	
OMB issues its sequestration update report.	August 15	
	August 20	CBO issues its sequestration update report.

1 A "within session" sequestration is triggered within 15 days after enactment of appropriations that are enacted after the end of a session for the budget year and before July 1, if they breach the category spending limit for that fiscal year. A "lookback" reduction to a category limit is applied for appropriations enacted after June 30th for the fiscal year in progress that breach a category limit for that fiscal year and is applied to the next fiscal year.

Note.—OMB also reports to Congress on the impact of enacted legislation and provides an explanation of any differences between OMB and CBO estimates, within 5 calendar days of enactment of legislation.

Glossary of Budget Terms[1]

BALANCES OF BUDGET AUTHORITY—These are amounts of budget authority provided in previous years that have not been outlayed. Obligated balances are amounts that have been obligated but not yet outlayed. Unobligated balances are amounts that have not been obligated and that remain available for obligation under law.

BREACH—A breach is the amount by which new budget authority or outlays within a category of discretionary appropriations for a fiscal year is above the cap on new budget authority or outlays for that category for that year.

BUDGET—The *Budget of the United States Government* (this document) sets forth the President's comprehensive financial plan and indicates the President's priorities for the Federal Government.

BUDGET AUTHORITY (BA)—Budget authority is the authority provided by Federal law to incur financial obligations that will result in outlays. Specific forms of budget authority include:

- provisions of law that make funds available for obligation and expenditure (other than borrowing authority), including the authority to obligate and expend offsetting receipts and collections;

- borrowing authority, which is authority granted to a Federal entity to borrow (e.g., through the issuance of promissory notes or monetary credits) and to obligate and expend the borrowed funds;

- contract authority, which is the making of funds available for obligation but not for expenditure; and

- offsetting receipts and collections as negative budget authority.

BUDGETARY RESOURCES—Budgetary resources comprise new budget authority, unobligated balances of budget authority, direct spending authority, and obligation limitations.

BUDGET TOTALS—The budget includes totals for budget authority, outlays, and receipts. Some presentations in the budget distinguish on-budget totals from off-budget totals. On-budget totals reflect the transactions of all Federal Government entities except those excluded from the budget totals by law. Off-budget totals reflect the transactions of Government entities that are excluded from the on-budget totals by law. Currently excluded are the social security trust funds (Federal Old-Age and Survivors Insurance and Federal Disability Insurance Trust Funds) and the Postal Service. The on- and off-budget totals are combined to derive a total for Federal activity.

CAP—This is the term commonly used to refer to legal limits on the budget authority and outlays for each fiscal year for each of the discretionary appropriations categories. A sequester is required if an appropriation for a category causes a breach in the cap.

CATEGORIES OF DISCRETIONARY APPROPRIATIONS—Through 1993, discretionary appropriations are categorized as defense, international, or domestic. Separate spending limits (caps) are applied to each category. The appropriations in each of the categories are determined by lists of existing appropriations in a 1990 congressional report[2] or, in the case of new appropriations, in consultation among the Office of Management and Budget and the congressional Committees on Appropriations and the Budget. For 1994 and 1995, all discretionary appropriations constitute a single category.

COST—The term cost, when used in connection with Federal credit programs, means the estimated long-term cost to the Government of a direct loan or loan guarantee, calculated on a net present value basis. The term excludes administrative costs and any incidental effects on governmental receipts or outlays. Present value is a standard financial concept

---

[1] These basic terms and other budget terms, concepts, and procedures are described more fully in *The Budget System and Concepts of the United States Government*, a pamphlet available from the Government Printing Office. References to requirements in law generally refer to the Balanced Budget and Emergency Deficit Control Act of 1985 (also known as the Gramm-Rudman-Hollings Act), as amended. The Act was most recently amended by the Budget Enforcement Act of 1990 (Title XIII of Public Law 101–508). These requirements are discussed in various parts of the *Budget*.

[2] The joint statement of the managers accompanying the conference report on the Omnibus Budget Reconciliation Act of 1990 (Public Law 101–508).

that allows for the time value of money, that is, for the fact that a given sum of money is worth more at present than in the future because interest can be earned on it. The cost of direct loans and loan guarantees is a net present value because collections are offset against disbursements.

CREDIT PROGRAM ACCOUNT—A credit program account receives an appropriation for the cost of a direct loan or loan guarantee program, from which such cost is disbursed to a financing account for the program.

DEFICIT—A deficit is the amount by which outlays exceed Governmental receipts.

DIRECT LOAN—A direct loan is a disbursement of funds by the Government to a non-Federal borrower under a contract that requires the repayment of such funds with or without interest. The term includes the purchase of, or participation in, a loan made by another lender. The term does not include the acquisition of a federally guaranteed loan in satisfaction of default claims or the price support loans of the Commodity Credit Corporation. (*Cf.* LOAN GUARANTEE.)

DIRECT SPENDING—Direct spending, which sometimes is called mandatory spending, is a category of outlays from budget authority provided in law other than appropriations acts, entitlement authority, and the budget authority for the food stamp program. (*Cf.* DISCRETIONARY APPROPRIATIONS.)

DISCRETIONARY APPROPRIATIONS—Discretionary appropriations is a category of budget authority that comprises budgetary resources (except those provided to fund direct-spending programs) provided in appropriations acts. (*Cf.* DIRECT SPENDING.)

EMERGENCY APPROPRIATION—An emergency appropriation is an appropriation in a discretionary category that the President and the Congress have designated as an emergency requirement. Such appropriations result in an adjustment to the cap for the category.

FEDERAL FUNDS—Federal funds are the moneys collected and spent by the Government other than those designated as trust funds. Federal funds include general, special, public enterprise, and intragovernmental funds. (*Cf.* TRUST FUNDS.)

FINANCING ACCOUNT—A financing account receives the cost payments from a credit program account and includes other cash flows to and from the Government resulting from direct loan obligations or loan guarantee commitments made on or after October 1, 1991. At least one financing account is associated with each credit program account. For programs with direct and guaranteed loans, there are separate financing accounts for direct loans and guaranteed loans. The transactions of the financing accounts are not included in the budget totals. (*Cf.* LIQUIDATING ACCOUNT.)

FISCAL YEAR—The fiscal year is the Government's accounting period. It begins on October 1st and ends on September 30th, and is designated by the calendar year in which it ends.

GENERAL FUND—The general fund consists of accounts for receipts not earmarked by law for a specific purpose, the proceeds of general borrowing, and the expenditure of these moneys.

LIQUIDATING ACCOUNT—A liquidating account includes all cash flows to and from the Government resulting from direct loan obligations and loan guarantee commitments prior to October 1, 1991. (*Cf.* FINANCING ACCOUNT.)

LOAN GUARANTEE—A loan guarantee is any guarantee, insurance, or other pledge with respect to the payment of all or a part of the principal or interest on any debt obligation of a non-Federal borrower to a non-Federal lender. The term does not include the insurance of deposits, shares, or other withdrawable accounts in financial institutions. (*Cf.* DIRECT LOAN.)

MANDATORY SPENDING—See DIRECT SPENDING.

MAXIMUM DEFICIT AMOUNTS—These are amounts specified in and subject to certain adjustments under law. If the deficit for the year in question is estimated to exceed the adjusted maximum deficit amount for that year by more than a specified margin, a sequester of the excess deficit is required.

INTRAGOVERNMENTAL FUNDS—Intragovernmental funds are accounts for business-type or market-oriented activities conducted primarily within and between Government agencies and financed by offsetting collections that are credited directly to the fund.

OBLIGATIONS—Obligations are binding agreements that will result in outlays, immediately or in the future. Budgetary resources must be available before obligations can be incurred legally.

OFF-BUDGET—See BUDGET TOTALS.

OFFSETTING COLLECTIONS—Offsetting collections are collections from the public that result from business-type or market-oriented activities and collections from other

Government accounts. These collections are deducted from gross disbursements in calculating outlays, rather than counted in Governmental receipt totals. Some are credited directly to appropriation or fund accounts; others, called offsetting receipts, are credited to receipt accounts. The authority to spend offsetting collections is a form of budget authority. (*Cf.* RECEIPTS, GOVERNMENTAL.)

ON-BUDGET—See BUDGET TOTALS.

OUTLAYS—Outlays are the measure of Government spending. They are payments to liquidate obligations (other than the repayment of debt), net of refunds and offsetting collections. Outlays generally are recorded on a cash basis, but also include many cash-equivalent transactions, the subsidy cost of direct loans and loan guarantees, and interest accrued on public issues of the public debt.

PAY-AS-YOU-GO—This term refers to requirements in law that result in a sequester if the estimated combined result of legislation affecting direct spending or receipts is an increase in the deficit for a fiscal year.

PUBLIC ENTERPRISE FUNDS—Public enterprise funds are accounts for business or market-oriented activities conducted primarily with the public and financed by offsetting collections that are credited directly to the fund.

RECEIPTS, GOVERNMENTAL—Governmental receipts are collections that result primarily from the Government's exercise of its sovereign power to tax or otherwise compel payment. They are compared to outlays in calculating a surplus or deficit. (*Cf.* OFFSETTING COLLECTIONS.)

SEQUESTER—A sequester is the cancellation of budgetary resources provided by discretionary appropriations or direct spending legislation, following various procedures prescribed in law. A sequester may occur in response to a discretionary appropriation that causes a breach, in response to increases in the deficit resulting from the combined result of legislation affecting direct spending or receipts (referred to as a "pay-as-you-go" sequester), or in response to a deficit estimated to be in excess of the maximum deficit amounts.

SPECIAL FUNDS—Special funds are Federal fund accounts for receipts earmarked for specific purposes and the associated expenditure of those receipts. (*Cf.* TRUST FUNDS.)

SUBSIDY—This term means the same as cost when it is used in connection with Federal credit programs.

SURPLUS—A surplus is the amount by which receipts exceed outlays.

SUPPLEMENTAL APPROPRIATION—A supplemental appropriation is one enacted subsequent to a regular annual appropriations act when the need for funds is too urgent to be postponed until the next regular annual appropriations act.

TRUST FUNDS—Trust funds are accounts, designated by law as trust funds, for receipts earmarked for specific purposes and the associated expenditure of those receipts. (*Cf.* SPECIAL FUNDS.)

Source: *Budget of the United States Government, Fiscal 1994,* Executive Office of the President, Office of Management and Budget.

THE FEDERAL GOVERNMENT DOLLAR FISCAL YEAR 1996 ESTIMATES

WHERE IT COMES FROM...

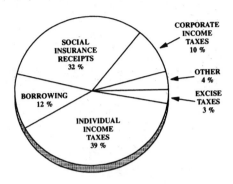

WHERE IT GOES...

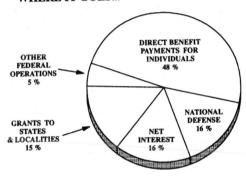

RECEIPTS, OUTLAYS, AND DEFICITS
(In billions of dollars)

	1994	1995	1996	1997	1998	1999	2000
Receipts	1,257.7	1,346.4	1,415.5	1,471.6	1,548.8	1,624.7	1,710.9
Outlays	1,460.9	1,538.9	1,612.1	1,684.7	1,745.2	1,822.2	1,905.3
Deficit (−)	−203.2	−192.5	−196.7	−213.1	−196.4	−197.4	−194.4
On-budget deficit (−)	(−258.8)	(−251.8)	(−262.0)	(−284.5)	(−274.8)	(−283.3)	(−288.6)
Off-budget surplus	(55.7)	(59.3)	(65.3)	(71.4)	(78.4)	(85.9)	(94.2)

Source: *Budget of the United States Government*, Fiscal year 1996. Executive Office of the President, Office of Management and Budget.

RECEIPTS BY SOURCE AS PERCENTAGES OF GDP: 1934–2000

Fiscal Year	Individual Income Taxes	Corporation Income Taxes	Social Insurance Taxes and Contributions			Excise Taxes	Other	Total Receipts		
			Total	(On-Budget)	(Off-Budget)			Total	(On-Budget)	(Off-Budget)
1934	0.7	0.6	*	(*)	......	2.2	1.3	4.9	(4.9)	......
1935	0.8	0.8	*	(*)	......	2.1	1.6	5.3	(5.3)	......
1936	0.9	0.9	0.1	(0.1)	......	2.1	1.1	5.1	(5.1)	......
1937	1.3	1.2	0.7	(0.4)	(0.3)	2.2	0.9	6.2	(5.9)	(0.3)
1938	1.5	1.5	1.8	(1.3)	(0.4)	2.1	0.9	7.7	(7.2)	(0.4)
1939	1.2	1.3	1.8	(1.2)	(0.6)	2.1	0.8	7.2	(6.6)	(0.6)
1940	0.9	1.3	1.9	(1.3)	(0.6)	2.1	0.7	6.9	(6.3)	(0.6)
1941	1.2	1.9	1.7	(1.1)	(0.6)	2.3	0.7	7.7	(7.1)	(0.6)
1942	2.3	3.3	1.7	(1.1)	(0.6)	2.4	0.6	10.3	(9.7)	(0.6)
1943	3.7	5.4	1.7	(1.1)	(0.6)	2.3	0.5	13.7	(13.0)	(0.6)
1944	9.8	7.4	1.7	(1.1)	(0.6)	2.4	0.5	21.7	(21.0)	(0.6)
1945	8.7	7.5	1.6	(1.0)	(0.6)	3.0	0.5	21.3	(20.7)	(0.6)
1946	7.6	5.6	1.5	(0.9)	(0.6)	3.3	0.6	18.5	(17.9)	(0.6)
1947	8.0	3.9	1.5	(0.9)	(0.7)	3.2	0.6	17.3	(16.6)	(0.7)
1948	7.8	3.9	1.5	(0.9)	(0.7)	3.0	0.6	16.8	(16.2)	(0.7)
1949	5.9	4.3	1.4	(0.8)	(0.6)	2.9	0.5	15.0	(14.4)	(0.6)
1950	5.9	3.9	1.6	(0.8)	(0.8)	2.8	0.5	14.8	(14.0)	(0.8)
1951	6.9	4.5	1.8	(0.8)	(1.0)	2.8	0.5	16.5	(15.5)	(1.0)
1952	8.2	6.2	1.9	(0.8)	(1.1)	2.6	0.5	19.4	(18.4)	(1.1)
1953	8.2	5.8	1.9	(0.7)	(1.1)	2.7	0.5	19.1	(18.0)	(1.1)
1954	8.0	5.7	2.0	(0.7)	(1.2)	2.7	0.5	18.9	(17.7)	(1.2)
1955	7.5	4.6	2.0	(0.7)	(1.3)	2.4	0.5	17.0	(15.7)	(1.3)
1956	7.7	5.0	2.2	(0.7)	(1.5)	2.4	0.5	17.9	(16.4)	(1.5)
1957	8.1	4.8	2.3	(0.7)	(1.5)	2.4	0.6	18.3	(16.7)	(1.5)
1958	7.7	4.5	2.5	(0.7)	(1.8)	2.4	0.7	17.8	(16.0)	(1.8)
1959	7.6	3.6	2.4	(0.7)	(1.7)	2.2	0.6	16.5	(14.8)	(1.7)
1960	8.1	4.3	2.9	(0.8)	(2.1)	2.3	0.8	18.3	(16.2)	(2.1)
1961	8.0	4.1	3.2	(0.8)	(2.3)	2.3	0.7	18.3	(15.9)	(2.3)
1962	8.2	3.7	3.1	(0.9)	(2.2)	2.3	0.7	18.0	(15.7)	(2.2)
1963	8.1	3.7	3.4	(1.0)	(2.4)	2.3	0.8	18.2	(15.8)	(2.4)
1964	7.8	3.8	3.5	(0.9)	(2.6)	2.2	0.8	18.0	(15.4)	(2.6)

Fiscal Year	Individual income taxes	Corporation income taxes	(On-budget)	Social insurance total	(Off-budget)	Excise taxes	Other	Total	(On-budget)	(Off-budget)
1965	7.3	3.8	(0.8)	3.3	(2.5)	2.2	0.9	17.4	(14.9)	(2.5)
1966	7.5	4.1	(0.9)	3.5	(2.6)	1.8	0.9	17.8	(15.2)	(2.6)
1967	7.8	4.3	(1.0)	4.1	(3.1)	1.7	0.9	18.8	(15.7)	(3.1)
1968	8.1	3.4	(1.1)	4.0	(2.9)	1.7	0.9	18.1	(15.1)	(2.9)
1969	9.4	4.0	(1.1)	4.2	(3.1)	1.6	0.9	20.2	(17.1)	(3.1)
1970	9.2	3.3	(1.1)	4.5	(3.4)	1.6	1.0	19.6	(16.2)	(3.4)
1971	8.2	2.5	(1.1)	4.5	(3.4)	1.6	1.0	17.8	(14.4)	(3.4)
1972	8.3	2.8	(1.1)	4.6	(3.5)	1.3	1.1	18.1	(14.6)	(3.5)
1973	8.1	2.8	(1.3)	5.0	(3.6)	1.3	0.9	18.1	(14.5)	(3.6)
1974	8.5	2.8	(1.5)	5.3	(3.8)	1.2	1.0	18.8	(14.9)	(3.8)
1975	8.1	2.7	(1.5)	5.6	(4.1)	1.1	1.0	18.5	(14.3)	(4.1)
1976	7.8	2.5	(1.4)	5.4	(3.9)	1.0	1.0	17.7	(13.8)	(3.9)
TQ	8.7	1.9	(1.6)	5.7	(4.0)	1.0	1.0	18.3	(14.2)	(4.0)
1977	8.2	2.9	(1.5)	5.6	(4.0)	1.0	1.0	18.5	(14.5)	(4.0)
1978	8.4	2.8	(1.7)	5.6	(4.0)	0.9	0.9	18.5	(14.6)	(4.0)
1979	9.0	2.7	(1.7)	5.7	(4.0)	0.8	0.9	19.1	(15.0)	(4.0)
1980	9.2	2.4	(1.7)	6.0	(4.3)	0.9	1.0	19.6	(15.3)	(4.3)
1981	9.6	2.1	(1.8)	6.2	(4.4)	1.4	1.0	20.2	(15.8)	(4.4)
1982	9.5	1.6	(1.9)	6.5	(4.6)	1.2	1.1	19.8	(15.2)	(4.6)
1983	8.7	1.1	(1.9)	6.3	(4.4)	1.1	0.9	18.1	(13.7)	(4.4)
1984	8.1	1.5	(2.0)	6.5	(4.5)	1.0	0.9	18.0	(13.5)	(4.5)
1985	8.4	1.5	(2.0)	6.7	(4.7)	0.9	0.9	18.5	(13.8)	(4.7)
1986	8.3	1.5	(2.0)	6.7	(4.7)	0.8	1.0	18.2	(13.5)	(4.7)
1987	8.8	1.9	(2.0)	6.8	(4.8)	0.7	0.9	19.2	(14.4)	(4.8)
1988	8.3	2.0	(1.9)	7.0	(5.0)	0.7	0.9	18.9	(13.9)	(5.0)
1989	8.6	2.0	(1.9)	6.9	(5.1)	0.7	0.9	19.2	(14.1)	(5.1)
1990	8.5	1.7	(1.8)	6.9	(5.1)	0.6	1.0	18.8	(13.7)	(5.1)
1991	8.2	1.7	(1.8)	7.0	(5.2)	0.7	0.9	18.6	(13.4)	(5.2)
1992	8.0	1.7	(1.9)	7.0	(5.1)	0.8	0.9	18.4	(13.3)	(5.1)
1993	8.1	1.9	(1.9)	6.8	(5.0)	0.8	0.8	18.4	(13.4)	(5.0)
1994	8.2	2.1	(1.9)	7.0	(5.1)	0.8	0.9	19.0	(13.9)	(5.1)
1995 estimate	8.4	2.1	(1.9)	6.9	(5.0)	0.8	0.9	19.2	(14.2)	(5.0)
1996 estimate	8.4	2.1	(1.9)	6.9	(5.0)	0.8	0.9	19.1	(14.1)	(5.0)
1997 estimate	8.2	2.1	(1.9)	6.8	(5.0)	0.7	0.9	18.8	(13.9)	(5.0)
1998 estimate	8.3	2.1	(1.8)	6.8	(4.9)	0.7	0.9	18.8	(13.8)	(4.9)
1999 estimate	8.2	2.1	(1.8)	6.7	(4.9)	0.7	0.9	18.7	(13.7)	(4.9)
2000 estimate	8.2	2.1	(1.8)	6.7	(4.9)	0.7	1.0	18.6	(13.7)	(4.9)

* 0.05 percent or less.

Source: Budget of the United States Government, Historical Tables, Fiscal Year 1996, Executive Office of the President, Office of Management and Budget.

PERCENTAGE COMPOSITION OF RECEIPTS BY SOURCE: 1934–2000

Fiscal Year	Individual Income Taxes	Corporation Income Taxes	Social Insurance Taxes and Contributions Total	(On-Budget)	(Off-Budget)	Excise Taxes	Other	Total Receipts Total	(On-Budget)	(Off-Budget)
1934	14.2	12.3	1.0	(1.0)	.....	45.8	26.7	100.0	(100.0)	.....
1935	14.6	14.7	0.9	(0.9)	.....	39.9	30.0	100.0	(100.0)	.....
1936	17.2	18.3	1.3	(1.3)	.....	41.6	21.6	100.0	(100.0)	.....
1937	20.3	19.3	10.8	(5.9)	(4.9)	34.8	14.9	100.0	(95.1)	(4.9)
1938	19.1	19.1	22.8	(17.1)	(5.7)	27.6	11.5	100.0	(94.3)	(5.7)
1939	16.3	17.9	25.3	(17.3)	(8.0)	29.7	10.7	100.0	(92.0)	(8.0)
1940	13.6	18.3	27.3	(18.9)	(8.4)	30.2	10.7	100.0	(91.6)	(8.4)
1941	15.1	24.4	22.3	(14.4)	(7.9)	29.3	9.0	100.0	(92.1)	(7.9)
1942	22.3	32.2	16.8	(10.6)	(6.1)	23.2	5.5	100.0	(93.9)	(6.1)
1943	27.1	39.8	12.7	(8.0)	(4.7)	17.1	3.3	100.0	(95.3)	(4.7)
1944	45.0	33.9	7.9	(5.0)	(3.0)	10.9	2.2	100.0	(97.0)	(3.0)
1945	40.7	35.4	7.6	(4.7)	(2.9)	13.9	2.4	100.0	(97.1)	(2.9)
1946	41.0	30.2	7.9	(4.8)	(3.2)	17.8	3.1	100.0	(96.8)	(3.2)
1947	46.6	22.4	8.9	(5.1)	(3.8)	18.7	3.5	100.0	(96.2)	(3.8)
1948	46.5	23.3	9.0	(5.1)	(3.9)	17.7	3.5	100.0	(96.1)	(3.9)
1949	39.5	28.4	9.6	(5.3)	(4.3)	19.0	3.5	100.0	(95.7)	(4.3)
1950	39.9	26.5	11.0	(5.7)	(5.3)	19.1	3.4	100.0	(94.7)	(5.3)
1951	41.9	27.3	11.0	(4.9)	(6.0)	16.8	3.1	100.0	(94.0)	(6.0)
1952	42.2	32.1	9.7	(4.3)	(5.4)	13.4	2.6	100.0	(94.6)	(5.4)
1953	42.8	30.5	9.8	(3.9)	(5.9)	14.2	2.7	100.0	(94.1)	(5.9)
1954	42.4	30.3	10.3	(3.8)	(6.6)	14.3	2.7	100.0	(93.4)	(6.6)
1955	43.9	27.3	12.0	(4.2)	(7.8)	14.0	2.8	100.0	(92.2)	(7.8)
1956	43.2	28.0	12.5	(3.9)	(8.6)	13.3	3.0	100.0	(91.4)	(8.6)
1957	44.5	26.5	12.5	(4.0)	(8.5)	13.2	3.3	100.0	(91.5)	(8.5)
1958	43.6	25.2	14.1	(4.0)	(10.1)	13.4	3.7	100.0	(89.9)	(10.1)
1959	46.3	21.8	14.8	(4.3)	(10.5)	13.3	3.7	100.0	(89.5)	(10.5)
1960	44.0	23.2	15.9	(4.4)	(11.5)	12.6	4.2	100.0	(88.5)	(11.5)
1961	43.8	22.2	17.4	(4.6)	(12.8)	12.6	4.0	100.0	(87.2)	(12.8)
1962	45.7	20.6	17.1	(4.8)	(12.3)	12.6	4.0	100.0	(87.7)	(12.3)
1963	44.7	20.3	18.6	(5.3)	(13.3)	12.4	4.1	100.0	(86.7)	(13.3)
1964	43.2	20.9	19.5	(5.0)	(14.5)	12.2	4.2	100.0	(85.5)	(14.5)

1965	41.8	21.8	19.0	(4.7)	(14.3)	12.5	4.9	100.0	(85.7)	(14.3)
1966	42.4	23.0	19.5	(4.9)	(14.6)	10.0	5.1	100.0	(85.4)	(14.6)
1967	41.3	22.8	21.9	(5.5)	(16.4)	9.2	4.7	100.0	(83.6)	(16.4)
1968	44.9	18.7	22.2	(5.9)	(16.3)	9.2	5.0	100.0	(83.7)	(16.3)
1969	46.7	19.6	20.9	(5.4)	(15.5)	8.1	4.7	100.0	(84.5)	(15.5)
1970	46.9	17.0	23.0	(5.7)	(17.4)	8.1	4.9	100.0	(82.6)	(17.4)
1971	46.1	14.3	25.3	(6.1)	(19.2)	8.9	5.4	100.0	(80.8)	(19.2)
1972	45.7	15.5	25.4	(6.1)	(19.2)	7.5	6.0	100.0	(80.7)	(19.2)
1973	44.7	15.7	27.3	(7.4)	(20.0)	7.0	5.2	100.0	(80.0)	(20.0)
1974	45.2	14.7	28.5	(8.0)	(20.5)	6.4	5.2	100.0	(79.5)	(20.5)
1975	43.9	14.6	30.3	(7.9)	(22.4)	5.9	5.4	100.0	(77.6)	(22.4)
1976	44.2	13.9	30.5	(8.2)	(22.3)	5.7	5.8	100.0	(77.7)	(22.3)
TQ	47.8	10.4	31.0	(8.9)	(22.2)	5.5	5.3	100.0	(77.8)	(22.2)
1977	44.3	15.4	29.9	(8.3)	(21.6)	4.9	5.3	100.0	(78.4)	(21.6)
1978	45.3	15.0	30.3	(8.9)	(21.4)	4.6	4.8	100.0	(78.6)	(21.4)
1979	47.0	14.2	30.0	(8.8)	(21.2)	4.0	4.8	100.0	(78.8)	(21.2)
1980	47.2	12.5	30.5	(8.6)	(21.9)	4.7	5.1	100.0	(78.1)	(21.9)
1981	47.7	10.2	30.5	(8.8)	(21.7)	6.8	4.8	100.0	(78.3)	(21.7)
1982	48.2	8.0	32.6	(9.4)	(23.2)	5.9	5.3	100.0	(76.8)	(23.2)
1983	48.1	6.2	34.8	(10.3)	(24.5)	5.9	5.0	100.0	(75.5)	(24.5)
1984	44.8	8.5	35.9	(11.0)	(24.9)	5.6	5.2	100.0	(75.1)	(24.9)
1985	45.6	8.4	36.1	(10.8)	(25.4)	4.9	5.0	100.0	(74.6)	(25.4)
1986	45.4	8.2	36.9	(10.9)	(26.0)	4.3	5.2	100.0	(74.0)	(26.0)
1987	46.0	9.8	35.5	(10.5)	(25.0)	3.8	4.9	100.0	(75.0)	(25.0)
1988	44.1	10.4	36.8	(10.2)	(26.6)	3.9	4.8	100.0	(73.4)	(26.6)
1989	45.0	10.4	36.3	(9.7)	(26.6)	3.5	4.8	100.0	(73.4)	(26.6)
1990	45.3	9.1	36.9	(9.5)	(27.3)	3.4	5.4	100.0	(72.7)	(27.3)
1991	44.4	9.3	37.6	(9.7)	(27.9)	4.0	4.7	100.0	(72.1)	(27.9)
1992	43.6	9.2	37.9	(10.2)	(27.7)	4.2	5.0	100.0	(72.3)	(27.7)
1993	44.2	10.2	37.1	(10.1)	(27.0)	4.2	4.3	100.0	(73.0)	(27.0)
1994	43.2	11.2	36.7	(10.1)	(26.6)	4.4	4.6	100.0	(73.4)	(26.6)
1995 estimate	43.7	11.2	36.0	(9.9)	(26.1)	4.3	4.8	100.0	(73.9)	(26.1)
1996 estimate	44.0	11.1	36.0	(9.8)	(26.2)	4.0	4.8	100.0	(73.8)	(26.2)
1997 estimate	43.7	11.3	36.2	(9.8)	(26.4)	4.0	4.9	100.0	(73.6)	(26.4)
1998 estimate	43.9	11.2	36.1	(9.8)	(26.3)	3.8	5.0	100.0	(73.7)	(26.3)
1999 estimate	44.1	11.0	36.1	(9.7)	(26.4)	3.7	5.0	100.0	(73.6)	(26.4)
2000 estimate	44.2	11.1	35.9	(9.6)	(26.4)	3.6	5.1	100.0	(73.6)	(26.4)

Source: Budget of the United States Government, Historical Tables, Fiscal Year 1996, Executive Office of the President, Office of Management and Budget.

TOTAL GOVERNMENT EXPENDITURES AS PERCENTAGES OF GDP: 1947–1994

Fiscal Year	Total Government Expenditures	Federal Government Outlays			Addendum: Federal Grants	State and Local Government Expenditures From Own Sources (NIPA Basis)
		Total	On-Budget	Off-Budget		
1947	20.4	15.5	15.3	0.1	(0.7)	4.9
1948	17.7	12.1	11.9	0.1	(0.7)	5.6
1949	21.0	14.8	14.6	0.2	(0.8)	6.2
1950	23.1	16.0	15.8	0.2	(0.9)	7.1
1951	21.0	14.5	14.1	0.4	(0.8)	6.4
1952	26.3	19.9	19.4	0.5	(0.8)	6.4
1953	27.2	20.9	20.3	0.6	(0.7)	6.3
1954	26.0	19.3	18.5	0.8	(0.8)	6.8
1955	25.1	17.8	16.8	1.0	(0.8)	7.3
1956	24.2	17.0	15.8	1.2	(0.8)	7.2
1957	25.0	17.5	16.1	1.4	(0.8)	7.5
1958	26.4	18.4	16.7	1.7	(1.0)	8.0
1959	27.2	19.2	17.3	1.9	(1.3)	8.0
1960	26.1	18.3	16.1	2.2	(1.4)	7.8
1961	27.3	18.9	16.6	2.3	(1.3)	8.4
1962	27.7	19.2	16.8	2.4	(1.4)	8.4
1963	27.6	19.0	16.5	2.6	(1.4)	8.5
1964	27.5	19.0	16.4	2.5	(1.6)	8.6
1965	26.2	17.6	15.2	2.5	(1.6)	8.6
1966	27.0	18.3	15.6	2.7	(1.7)	8.7
1967	28.8	19.8	17.3	2.6	(1.9)	9.0
1968	30.3	21.0	18.4	2.6	(2.1)	9.3
1969	29.5	19.8	17.1	2.7	(2.1)	9.6

1970	29.7	19.9	17.1	2.8	(2.3)	9.8
1971	30.4	20.0	16.9	3.1	(2.5)	10.4
1972	30.3	20.1	16.9	3.2	(2.8)	10.2
1973	29.0	19.3	15.7	3.6	(3.2)	9.7
1974	29.1	19.2	15.5	3.7	(3.0)	10.0
1975	32.4	22.0	18.0	4.0	(3.2)	10.4
1976	32.4	22.1	17.9	4.1	(3.4)	10.4
TQ	32.1	21.6	17.2	4.4	(3.5)	10.5
1977	31.0	21.3	17.1	4.2	(3.5)	9.7
1978	30.4	21.3	17.1	4.2	(3.5)	9.1
1979	29.7	20.7	16.6	4.1	(3.3)	9.0
1980	31.5	22.3	18.0	4.3	(3.3)	9.2
1981	31.9	22.9	18.3	4.6	(3.0)	9.0
1982	33.3	23.9	19.0	4.8	(2.7)	9.4
1983	33.8	24.4	19.9	4.4	(2.6)	9.4
1984	32.1	23.1	18.6	4.5	(2.5)	9.0
1985	33.0	23.9	19.4	4.5	(2.5)	9.2
1986	32.9	23.5	19.1	4.3	(2.6)	9.4
1987	32.5	22.5	18.2	4.4	(2.3)	9.9
1988	32.0	22.1	17.9	4.2	(2.3)	9.9
1989	31.9	22.1	18.0	4.1	(2.2)	9.8
1990	33.0	22.9	18.7	4.1	(2.3)	10.2
1991	34.0	23.3	19.1	4.3	(2.6)	10.7
1992	34.1	23.3	19.1	4.3	(2.8)	10.8
1993	33.3	22.5	18.2	4.3	(2.9)	10.7
1994	32.7	22.0	17.8	4.2	(2.9)	10.7

Source: *Budget of the United States Government, Historical Tables, Fiscal Year 1996*, Executive Office of the President, Office of Management and Budget.

TOTAL GOVERNMENT EXPENDITURES BY MAJOR CATEGORY OF EXPENDITURE AS PERCENTAGES OF GDP: 1947–1994

Fiscal Year	Total Government	Defense and International	Net Interest	Federal Payments For Individuals		Other Federal	State and Local From Own Sources (Except Net Interest)
				Social Security and Medicare	Other		
1947	20.4	8.3	1.9	0.2	3.9	1.2	4.8
1948	17.7	5.5	1.8	0.2	3.5	1.1	5.6
1949	21.0	7.3	1.8	0.2	3.6	1.9	6.1
1950	23.1	6.9	1.8	0.3	4.9	2.1	7.0
1951	21.0	8.7	1.5	0.5	2.8	1.1	6.4
1952	26.3	14.3	1.4	0.6	2.6	1.0	6.4
1953	27.2	15.1	1.4	0.7	2.3	1.4	6.3
1954	26.0	13.8	1.3	0.9	2.5	0.7	6.8
1955	25.1	11.7	1.3	1.1	2.6	1.1	7.3
1956	24.2	10.8	1.2	1.3	2.4	1.3	7.2
1957	25.0	11.1	1.2	1.5	2.4	1.3	7.5
1958	26.4	11.2	1.3	1.8	2.9	1.3	8.0
1959	27.2	10.9	1.2	2.0	2.8	2.4	8.0
1960	26.1	10.1	1.4	2.3	2.5	2.0	7.8
1961	27.3	10.2	1.3	2.4	3.0	2.1	8.4
1962	27.7	10.4	1.3	2.5	2.7	2.3	8.4
1963	27.6	10.0	1.3	2.6	2.7	2.4	8.5
1964	27.5	9.5	1.3	2.6	2.6	2.9	8.6
1965	26.2	8.3	1.2	2.5	2.4	3.1	8.6
1966	27.0	8.7	1.2	2.8	2.3	3.3	8.7
1967	28.8	9.7	1.2	3.1	2.4	3.4	9.1
1968	30.3	10.3	1.2	3.4	2.5	3.5	9.4
1969	29.5	9.4	1.3	3.6	2.6	2.9	9.7

1970	29.7	8.7	1.3	3.7	2.9	3.1	10.0
1971	30.4	7.9	1.3	4.1	3.6	3.0	10.5
1972	30.3	7.3	1.2	4.2	3.9	3.3	10.3
1973	29.0	6.3	1.2	4.5	3.7	3.4	9.9
1974	29.1	6.1	1.3	4.7	3.9	3.0	10.2
1975	32.4	6.2	1.2	5.1	5.0	4.1	10.7
1976	32.4	5.7	1.3	5.3	5.4	4.1	10.6
TQ	32.1	5.6	1.3	5.4	4.8	4.2	10.7
1977	31.0	5.4	1.3	5.4	4.8	4.1	9.9
1978	30.4	5.2	1.3	5.4	4.4	4.6	9.5
1979	29.7	5.1	1.3	5.4	4.2	4.3	9.5
1980	31.5	5.5	1.3	5.7	4.8	4.3	9.9
1981	31.9	5.8	1.6	6.0	4.9	3.9	9.8
1982	33.3	6.3	1.8	6.5	5.0	3.4	10.3
1983	33.8	6.7	1.8	6.8	5.2	3.0	10.3
1984	32.1	6.6	2.1	6.4	4.4	2.6	9.9
1985	33.0	6.8	2.3	6.5	4.3	3.0	10.1
1986	32.9	6.8	2.3	6.4	4.3	2.7	10.4
1987	32.5	6.6	2.2	6.4	4.2	2.3	10.8
1988	32.0	6.3	2.3	6.3	4.1	2.3	10.8
1989	31.9	6.1	2.3	6.3	4.1	2.4	10.8
1990	33.0	5.7	2.4	6.5	4.2	3.1	11.1
1991	34.0	5.1	2.5	6.7	4.7	3.3	11.6
1992	34.1	5.3	2.5	7.0	5.3	2.4	11.7
1993	33.3	4.9	2.3	7.1	5.4	1.9	11.6
1994	32.7	4.5	2.2	7.2	5.2	2.1	11.5

Source: *Budget of the United States Government, Historical Tables, Fiscal Year 1996*, Executive Office of the President, Office of Management and Budget.

TOTAL GOVERNMENT EXPENDITURES BY MAJOR CATEGORY OF EXPENDITURE: 1947–1994

(in billions of dollars)

Fiscal Year	Total Government	Defense and International	Net Interest	Federal Payments For Individuals		Other Federal	State and Local From Own Sources (Except Net Interest)
				Social Security and Medicare	Other		
1947	45.4	18.6	4.3	0.4	8.6	2.6	10.8
1948	43.6	13.7	4.4	0.5	8.5	2.7	13.8
1949	55.0	19.2	4.6	0.6	9.5	5.0	16.1
1950	61.3	18.4	4.9	0.7	12.9	5.7	18.7
1951	65.7	27.2	4.7	1.5	8.8	3.4	20.1
1952	89.4	48.8	4.7	2.0	8.9	3.4	21.7
1953	98.9	54.9	5.2	2.6	8.3	5.1	22.8
1954	95.9	50.9	4.8	3.3	9.3	2.6	25.0
1955	96.5	45.0	4.9	4.3	10.0	4.3	27.9
1956	100.8	44.9	5.2	5.4	9.8	5.4	30.0
1957	109.6	48.6	5.4	6.5	10.5	5.6	32.9
1958	118.4	50.2	5.7	8.0	12.9	5.7	35.9
1959	130.6	52.2	5.9	9.5	13.2	11.4	38.4
1960	131.8	51.1	7.1	11.4	12.8	10.0	39.5
1961	141.3	52.8	6.8	12.2	15.3	10.7	43.5
1962	153.7	58.0	7.0	14.0	14.9	13.0	46.7
1963	161.1	58.7	7.9	15.5	15.5	13.9	49.6
1964	172.2	59.7	8.2	16.2	16.0	18.4	53.7
1965	176.0	55.9	8.4	17.1	16.0	20.6	58.0
1966	198.4	63.7	9.0	20.3	16.8	24.4	64.3
1967	228.7	77.0	9.5	24.5	18.7	27.0	72.0
1968	256.9	87.2	10.1	28.4	21.4	30.0	79.7
1969	272.7	87.1	11.7	33.0	24.2	26.6	90.1

1970	292.2	86.0	12.8	36.4	28.4	30.4	98.1
1971	319.2	83.0	13.2	42.6	38.0	31.7	110.6
1972	347.4	84.0	14.2	47.7	45.3	38.2	118.1
1973	369.1	80.8	15.3	57.2	47.5	42.8	125.5
1974	409.1	85.1	17.8	65.7	54.7	42.4	143.5
1975	489.6	93.6	18.7	77.7	76.2	61.6	161.9
1976	546.4	96.1	22.5	89.6	91.0	68.4	178.9
TQ	142.7	24.7	6.0	24.0	21.5	18.8	47.7
1977	594.7	103.6	25.6	104.5	92.5	78.7	189.8
1978	655.6	112.0	28.4	116.7	95.0	99.5	203.9
1979	722.3	123.8	30.8	130.8	103.1	103.8	230.1
1980	834.2	146.7	34.6	151.0	127.5	113.2	261.1
1981	945.1	170.6	46.3	179.1	145.5	114.2	289.4
1982	1,038.9	197.6	57.3	203.1	154.8	105.2	320.9
1983	1,120.2	221.8	59.3	224.0	172.5	100.3	342.4
1984	1,185.6	243.3	78.1	237.0	164.2	96.2	366.8
1985	1,311.0	268.9	91.9	256.1	171.2	120.7	402.2
1986	1,387.3	287.5	95.7	270.7	180.5	115.5	437.2
1987	1,445.6	293.6	97.8	285.0	186.3	100.3	482.6
1988	1,538.5	300.8	108.7	302.5	198.1	110.8	517.5
1989	1,651.5	313.1	118.9	324.4	211.6	124.7	558.7
1990	1,809.8	313.1	131.7	353.8	230.3	171.3	609.6
1991	1,928.5	289.1	143.3	380.7	269.6	189.5	656.3
1992	2,020.7	314.5	146.2	414.3	313.4	139.3	693.0
1993	2,081.1	308.3	145.6	444.7	338.0	118.9	725.6
1994	2,168.8	298.6	148.6	476.2	346.0	137.1	762.2

Source: *Budget of the United States Government, Historical Tables, Fiscal Year 1996*, Executive Office of the President, Office of Management and Budget.

SUMMARY OF RECEIPTS, OUTLAYS, AND SURPLUSES OR DEFICITS (−) IN CURRENT DOLLARS, CONSTANT (FY 1987) DOLLARS, AND AS PERCENTAGES OF GDP: 1940–2000

(dollar amounts in billions)

Fiscal Year	In Current Dollars			In Constant (FY 1987 Dollars)			Addendum: Composite Deflator	As Percentages of GDP		
	Receipts	Outlays	Surplus or Deficit (−)	Receipts	Outlays	Surplus or Deficit (−)		Receipts	Outlays	Surplus or Deficit (−)
1940	6.5	9.5	−2.9	67.0	96.3	−29.9	0.0978	6.9	9.9	−3.1
1941	8.7	13.7	−4.9	86.3	135.3	−49.0	0.1009	7.7	12.1	−4.4
1942	14.6	35.1	−20.5	131.2	315.1	−183.9	0.1115	10.3	24.8	−14.5
1943	24.0	78.6	−54.6	200.2	655.2	−455.0	0.1199	13.7	44.8	−31.1
1944	43.7	91.3	−47.6	377.1	787.1	−410.0	0.1160	21.7	45.3	−23.6
1945	45.2	92.7	−47.6	395.8	812.6	−416.8	0.1141	21.3	43.7	−22.4
1946	39.3	55.2	−15.9	329.4	463.0	−133.6	0.1193	18.5	26.0	−7.5
1947	38.5	34.5	4.0	257.4	230.6	26.9	0.1496	17.3	15.5	1.8
1948	41.6	29.8	11.8	269.3	192.9	76.4	0.1543	16.8	12.1	4.8
1949	39.4	38.8	0.6	249.1	245.5	3.7	0.1582	15.0	14.8	0.2
1950	39.4	42.6	−3.1	241.4	260.5	−19.1	0.1634	14.8	16.0	−1.2
1951	51.6	45.5	6.1	324.2	285.9	38.3	0.1592	16.5	14.5	1.9
1952	66.2	67.7	−1.5	406.7	416.0	−9.3	0.1627	19.4	19.9	−0.4
1953	69.6	76.1	−6.5	406.6	444.5	−37.9	0.1712	19.1	20.9	−1.8
1954	69.7	70.9	−1.2	394.9	401.4	−6.5	0.1765	18.9	19.3	−0.3
1955	65.5	68.4	−3.0	363.4	380.0	−16.6	0.1801	17.0	17.8	−0.8
1956	74.6	70.6	3.9	391.1	370.4	20.7	0.1907	17.9	17.0	0.9
1957	80.0	76.6	3.4	396.6	379.7	16.9	0.2017	18.3	17.5	0.8
1958	79.6	82.4	−2.8	374.9	388.0	−13.0	0.2124	17.8	18.4	−0.6
1959	79.2	92.1	−12.8	352.4	409.5	−57.1	0.2249	16.5	19.2	−2.7
1960	92.5	92.2	0.3	393.4	392.1	1.3	0.2351	18.3	18.3	0.1
1961	94.4	97.7	−3.3	392.1	406.0	−13.9	0.2407	18.3	18.9	−0.6
1962	99.7	106.8	−7.1	406.8	436.0	−29.2	0.2450	18.0	19.2	−1.3
1963	106.6	111.3	−4.8	418.9	437.6	−18.7	0.2544	18.2	19.0	−0.8
1964	112.6	118.5	−5.9	433.8	456.6	−22.8	0.2596	18.0	19.0	−0.9
1965	116.8	118.2	−1.4	440.8	446.1	−5.3	0.2650	17.4	17.6	−0.2
1966	130.8	134.5	−3.7	478.9	492.4	−13.5	0.2732	17.8	18.3	−0.5
1967	148.8	157.5	−8.6	529.0	559.8	−30.7	0.2813	18.8	19.8	−1.1
1968	153.0	178.1	−25.2	522.6	608.6	−86.0	0.2927	18.1	21.0	−3.0
1969	186.9	183.6	3.2	604.4	593.9	10.5	0.3092	20.2	19.8	0.4

Year	Receipts	Outlays	Surplus or Deficit	Receipts (constant)	Outlays (constant)	Surplus or Deficit (constant)	Composite deflator	Receipts (% GDP)	Outlays (% GDP)	Surplus or Deficit (% GDP)
1970	192.8	195.6	−2.8	587.5	596.1	−8.7	0.3282	19.6	19.9	−0.3
1971	187.1	210.2	−23.0	533.5	599.1	−65.7	0.3508	17.8	20.0	−2.2
1972	207.3	230.7	−23.4	554.9	617.5	−62.6	0.3736	18.1	20.1	−2.0
1973	230.8	245.7	−14.9	582.7	620.3	−37.6	0.3961	18.1	19.3	−1.2
1974	263.2	269.4	−6.1	611.2	625.4	−14.2	0.4307	18.8	19.2	−0.4
1975	279.1	332.3	−53.2	586.6	698.5	−111.9	0.4758	18.5	22.0	−3.5
1976	298.1	371.8	−73.7	584.7	729.3	−144.6	0.5098	17.7	22.1	−4.4
TQ	81.2	96.0	−14.7	153.6	181.5	−27.9	0.5287	18.3	21.6	−3.3
1977	355.6	409.2	−53.7	643.8	740.9	−97.2	0.5523	18.5	21.3	−2.8
1978	399.6	458.7	−59.2	674.0	773.9	−99.8	0.5928	18.5	21.3	−2.7
1979	463.3	504.0	−40.7	719.2	782.4	−63.2	0.6442	19.1	20.7	−1.7
1980	517.1	590.9	−73.8	728.1	832.1	−104.0	0.7102	19.6	22.3	−2.8
1981	599.3	678.2	−79.0	766.6	867.7	−101.0	0.7817	20.2	22.9	−2.7
1982	617.8	745.8	−128.0	738.2	891.1	−152.9	0.8369	19.8	23.9	−4.1
1983	600.6	808.4	−207.8	684.3	921.1	−236.8	0.8776	18.1	24.4	−6.3
1984	666.5	851.8	−185.4	730.4	933.5	−203.2	0.9125	18.0	23.1	−5.0
1985	734.1	946.4	−212.3	776.6	1,001.3	−224.6	0.9452	18.5	23.9	−5.4
1986	769.1	990.3	−221.2	790.0	1,017.3	−227.3	0.9735	18.2	23.5	−5.2
1987	854.1	1,003.9	−149.8	854.1	1,003.9	−149.8	1.0000	19.2	22.5	−3.4
1988	909.0	1,064.1	−155.2	877.3	1,027.1	−149.8	1.0361	18.9	22.1	−3.2
1989	990.7	1,143.2	−152.5	916.2	1,057.2	−141.0	1.0813	19.2	22.1	−2.9
1990	1,031.3	1,252.7	−221.4	914.1	1,110.4	−196.2	1.1282	18.8	22.9	−4.0
1991	1,054.3	1,323.4	−269.2	894.7	1,123.2	−228.4	1.1783	18.6	23.3	−4.7
1992	1,090.5	1,380.9	−290.4	895.1	1,133.4	−238.4	1.2183	18.4	23.3	−4.9
1993	1,153.5	1,408.7	−255.1	921.9	1,125.8	−203.9	1.2513	18.4	22.5	−4.1
1994	1,257.7	1,460.9	−203.2	981.7	1,140.3	−158.6	1.2812	19.0	22.0	−3.1
1995 estimate	1,346.4	1,538.9	−192.5	1,022.0	1,168.1	−146.1	1.3174	19.2	21.9	−2.7
1996 estimate	1,415.5	1,612.1	−196.7	1,041.3	1,186.0	−144.7	1.3593	19.1	21.8	−2.7
1997 estimate	1,471.6	1,684.7	−213.1	1,048.8	1,200.6	−151.9	1.4032	18.8	21.6	−2.7
1998 estimate	1,548.8	1,745.2	−196.4	1,070.5	1,206.2	−135.7	1.4468	18.8	21.2	−2.4
1999 estimate	1,624.7	1,822.2	−197.4	1,089.4	1,221.8	−132.4	1.4914	18.7	20.9	−2.3
2000 estimate	1,710.9	1,905.3	−194.4	1,112.8	1,239.2	−126.5	1.5375	18.6	20.7	−2.1

Source: Budget of the United States Government, Historical Tables, Fiscal Year 1996, Executive Office of the President, Office of Management and Budget.

NOTES TO HISTORICAL TABLES

Because of the numerous changes in the way budget data have been presented over time, there are inevitable difficulties in trying to produce comparable data to cover so many years. The general rule underlying all of these tables is to provide data in as meaningful and comparable a fashion as possible. To the extent feasible, the data are presented on a basis consistent with current budget concepts. When a structural change is made, insofar as possible the data are adjusted for all years.

In November 1990, the Omnibus Budget Reconciliation Act of 1990 was enacted. Part of this legislation was the Budget Enforcement Act, which not only provided new enforcement mechanisms, but also included significant changes in budget concepts. The major conceptual change concerns the measurement of Federal credit activity in the budget. Under current law, only the subsidy cost (the cost to the Government, including the cost associated with loan defaults) of direct loans or loan guarantees be recorded as budget authority and outlays. The remaining financial transactions are recorded as means of financing the deficit. This concept applies only to direct loan obligations and loan guarantee commitments made in 1992 and later years. Unfortunately, the historical data prior to 1992 could not be converted to this new measurement basis. Thus, data prior to 1992 are on a cash flow or pre-credit reform basis. Data for 1992 and beyond are on a cash flow basis for direct loans and loan guarantees obligated or committed in earlier years, but the budget program accounts providing direct loans or loan guarantees reflect the subsidy cost for subsequent obligations and commitments.

Coverage

The Federal Government has used the unified or consolidated budget concept as the foundation for its budgetary analysis and presentation since the 1969 budget. The basic guidelines for the unified budget were presented in the *Report of the President's Commission on Budget Concepts* (October 1967). The Commission recommended the budget include all Federal fiscal activities unless there were exceptionally persuasive reasons for exclusion. Nevertheless, from the very beginning some programs were perceived as warranting special treatment. Indeed, the Commission itself recommended a bifurcated presentation: a "unified budget" composed of an "expenditure account" and a "loan account." The distinction between the expenditure account and the loan account proved to be confusing and caused considerable complication in the budget for little

benefit. As a result, this distinction was eliminated starting with the 1974 budget. However, even prior to the 1974 budget, the Export-Import Bank had been excluded by law from the budget totals, and other exclusions followed. The structure of the budget was gradually revised to show the off-budget transactions in many locations along with the on-budget transactions, and the off-budget amounts were added to the on-budget amounts in order to show total Federal spending.

The Balanced Budget and Emergency Deficit Control Act of 1985 (Public Law 99–177) repealed the off-budget status of all then existing off-budget entities, but it included a provision immediately moving the Federal old-age, survivors, and disability insurance funds (collectively known as social security) off-budget. To provide a consistent time series, the budget historical data show social security off-budget for all years since its inception, and show all formerly off-budget entities on-budget for all years. Subsequent law (OBRA 1989) moved the Postal Service fund off-budget, starting in fiscal year 1989. Prior to that year, the Postal Service fund is shown on-budget.

Though social security and the Postal Service are now off-budget, they continue to be Federal programs. Indeed, social security currently accounts for around one-third of all Federal receipts and one-quarter of all Federal spending. Hence, the budget documents include these funds and focus on the Federal totals that combine the on-budget and off-budget amounts. Various budget tables and charts show total Federal receipts, outlays, and surpluses and deficits, and divide these totals between the portions that are off-budget and the remainder of Federal transactions, all of which are on-budget.

Changes in Historical Outlays and Deficit

The outlay and deficit totals for 1979, 1991 and 1993 have changed from those published in the 1995 Budget. In 1979, the Department of Transportation assumed responsibility for paying interest and principal on $547 million of bonds issued by the Washington Metropolitan Area Transit Authority (WMATA). This was effectively a grant to WMATA financed by borrowing, i.e., the Federal assumption of WMATA debt. This transaction was not recorded as a budget outlay at the time. Correction of this scoring error increases outlays, debt and the deficit for 1979 by $547 million.

NOTE ON THE FISCAL YEAR

The Federal fiscal year begins on October 1 and ends on the subsequent September

30. It is designated by the year in which it ends; for example, fiscal year 1993 began October 1, 1992 and ended on September 30, 1993. Prior to fiscal year 1977 the Federal fiscal years began on July 1 and ended on June 30. In calendar year 1976 the July–September period was a separate accounting period (known as the transition quarter or TQ) to bridge the period required to shift to the new fiscal years.

Concepts Relevant to the Historical Tables

Budget (or "on-budget") receipts constitute the income side of the budget; they are composed almost entirely of taxes or other compulsory payments to the Government. Any income from business-type activities (e.g., interest income or sale of electric power), and any income by Government accounts arising from payments by other Government accounts is offset in computing *budget outlays* (spending). This method of accounting permits users to easily identify the size and trends in Federal taxes and other compulsory income, and in Federal spending financed from taxes, other compulsory income, or borrowing. *Budget surplus* refers to any excess of budget receipts over budget outlays, while *budget deficit* refers to any excess of budget outlays over budget receipts.

The terms *off-budget receipts, off-budget outlays, off-budget surpluses,* and *off-budget deficits* refer to similar categories for off-budget activities. The sum of the on-budget and off-budget transactions constitute the consolidated or total Federal Government transactions.

The budget is divided between two fund groups, federal funds and trust funds. The Federal funds grouping includes all receipts and outlays not specified by law as being trust funds. All Federal funds are on-budget except for the Postal Service fund starting with fiscal year 1989. All trust funds are on-budget, except that, as explained in the general notes above, the two social security retirement trust funds are shown off-budget for all years.

The term *trust fund* as used in Federal budget accounting is frequently misunderstood. In the private sector, "trust" refers to funds of one party held by a second party (the trustee) in a fiduciary capacity. In the Federal budget, the term "trust fund" means only the law requires that the funds must be accounted for separately and used only for specified purposes and that the account in which the funds are deposited is designated as being a "trust fund." A change in law may change the future receipts and the terms under which the fund's resources are spent. The determining factor as to whether a particular fund is designated as a "Federal" fund or "trust" fund is the law governing the fund.

The largest trust funds are for retirement and social insurance (e.g., civil service and military retirement, social security, medicare, and unemployment benefits). They are financed largely by social insurance taxes and contributions and payments from the general fund (the main component of Federal funds). However, there are also major trust funds for transportation (highway and airport and airways) and for other programs that are financed in whole or in part by *user charges*.

The budget documents do not separately show user charges. Frequently there is confusion between the concept of user charges and the concept of offsetting collections. User charges are charges for services rendered. Such charges may take the form of taxes (budget receipts), such as highway excise taxes used to finance the highway trust fund. They may also take the form of business-type charges, in which case they are off-setting collections—offset against budget outlays rather than being recorded as budget receipts. Examples of such charges are the proceeds from the sale of electric power by the Tennessee Valley Authority and medical insurance premiums paid to the supplementary medical insurance trust fund. User charges may go to the general fund of the Treasury or they may be "earmarked." If the funds are earmarked, it means the collections are separately identified and used for a specified purpose—they are not commingled (in an accounting sense) with any other money. This does not mean the money is actually kept in a separate bank account. All money in the Treasury is merged for efficient cash management. However, any earmarked funds are accounted for in such a way that the balances are always identifiable and available for the stipulated purposes.

U.S. BUDGET RECEIPTS AND OUTLAYS[1] (millions of dollars)

Source or type	Fiscal year 1993	Fiscal year 1994	1993 H1	1993 H2	1994 H1	1994 H2	1995 Jan.	1995 Feb.	1995 Mar.
RECEIPTS									
1 All sources	1,153,226	1,257,453	593,212	582,038	652,236	625,557	131,801	82,544	92,532
2 Individual income taxes, net	509,680	543,055	255,556	262,073	275,053	273,474	79,162	33,863	26,846
3 Withheld	430,211	459,699	209,517	228,423	225,387	240,062	49,432	40,643	44,561
4 Presidential Election Campaign Fund	28	70	25	2	63	10	0	4	18
5 Nonwithheld	154,989	160,364	113,510	41,768	118,245	42,031	29,980	1,061	4,284
6 Refunds	75,546	77,077	67,468	8,115	68,642	9,207	245	7,845	22,016
Corporation income taxes									
7 Gross receipts	131,548	154,205	69,044	68,266	80,536	78,392	5,415	3,483	17,238
8 Refunds	14,027	13,820	7,198	6,514	6,933	7,331	2,157	1,423	2,375
9 Social insurance taxes and contributions, net	428,300	461,475	227,177	206,176	248,301	220,141	40,442	38,653	39,379
10 Employment taxes and contributions[2]	396,939	428,810	208,776	192,749	228,714	206,613	26,096	35,667	38,646
11 Self-employment taxes and contributions[3]	20,604	24,433	16,270	4,335	20,762	4,135	1,279	1,718	1,862
12 Unemployment insurance	26,556	28,004	16,074	11,010	17,301	11,177	1,069	2,630	320
13 Other net receipts[4]	4,805	4,661	2,326	2,417	2,284	2,349	372	357	413
14 Excise taxes	48,057	55,225	23,398	25,994	26,444	30,062	4,555	3,485	5,143
15 Customs deposits	18,802	20,099	8,860	10,215	9,500	11,042	1,539	1,435	1,470
16 Estate and gift taxes	12,577	15,225	6,494	6,617	8,197	7,071	1,005	916	1,218
17 Miscellaneous receipts[5]	18,273	22,041	9,879	9,227	11,170	13,305	1,839	2,131	3,612
OUTLAYS									
18 All types	1,408,532	1,461,067	673,915	727,685	710,620	751,642	115,172	120,536	142,168
19 National defense	291,086	281,451	140,535	146,672	133,841	141,092	18,499	21,461	26,533
20 International affairs	16,826	17,249	6,565	10,186	5,800	12,056	999	1,108	425
21 General science, space, and technology	17,030	17,602	7,996	8,880	8,502	8,979	1,194	1,374	1,628
22 Energy	4,319	5,398	2,462	1,663	2,036	2,949	488	260	569
23 Natural resources and environment	20,239	20,902	8,592	11,221	9,829r	12,373	1,571	1,374	1,951
24 Agriculture	20,443	15,131	11,872	7,516	7,451	7,697	1,049	1,264	1,195
25 Commerce and housing credit	−22,725	−4,851	−14,537	−1,490	−5,114	−2,678	−1,469	−2,978	−1,853
26 Transportation	35,004	36,835	16,076	19,570	16,754r	20,489	3,080	2,799	3,167
27 Community and regional development	9,051	11,877	4,929	4,288	4,855r	7,070	1,140	228	971
28 Education, training, employment, and social services	50,012	44,730	24,080	26,753	19,258r	25,887	4,650	4,078	4,678
29 Health	99,415	106,495	49,882	52,958	53,195r	54,128	9,440	8,918	10,625
30 Social security and Medicare	435,137	464,314	195,933	223,735	232,777	236,819	39,734	39,461	43,209
31 Income security	207,257	213,972	107,870	102,380	109,080	101,743	16,326	20,583	24,708
32 Veterans benefits and services	35,720	37,637	16,385	19,852	16,686	19,757	1,996	3,023	4,642
33 Administration of justice	14,955	15,283	7,482	7,400	7,718	7,800	1,568	1,099	1,488
34 General government	13,009	11,348	5,205	6,531	5,084r	7,393	−233	1,170	1,680
35 Net interest[6]	198,811	202,957	99,635	99,914	99,844	109,435	19,568	18,002	19,671
36 Undistributed offsetting receipts[7]	−37,386	−37,772	−17,035	−20,344	−17,308	−20,065	−2,911	−2,688	−2,829

1. Functional details do not sum to total outlays for calendar year data because revisions to monthly totals have not been distributed among functions. Fiscal year total for outlays does not correspond to calendar year data because revisions from the *Budget* have not been fully distributed across months.
2. Old-age, disability, and hospital insurance, and railroad retirement accounts.
3. Old-age, disability, and hospital insurance.
4. Federal employee retirement contributions and civil service retirement and disability fund.

5. Deposits of earnings by Federal Reserve Banks and other miscellaneous receipts.
6. Includes interest received by trust funds.
7. Rents and royalties for the outer continental shelf, U.S. government contributions for employee retirement, and certain asset sales.

SOURCES. U.S. Department of the Treasury, *Monthly Treasury Statement of Receipts and Outlays of the U.S. Government;* and U.S. Office of Management and Budget, *Budget of the U.S. Government, Fiscal Year 1996.*

Source: *Federal Reserve Bulletin,* Board of Governors of the Federal Reserve System.

FEDERAL DEBT SUBJECT TO STATUTORY LIMITATION
Billions of dollars, end of month

	Item	1993				1994				1995
		Mar. 31	June 30	Sept. 30	Dec. 31	Mar. 31	June 30	Sept. 30	Dec. 31	Mar. 31
1	**Federal debt outstanding**	**4,250**	**4,373**	**4,436**	**4,562**	**4,602**	**4,673**	**4,721**	**4,800**	**4,864**
2	Public debt securities.	4,231	4,352	4,412	4,536	4,576	4,646	4,693	n.a.	↑
3	Held by public.	3,188	3,252	3,295	3,382	3,434	3,443	3,480	3,543	
4	Held by agencies	1,043	1,100	1,117	1,154	1,142	1,203	1,213	1,257	
5	Agency securities.	20	21	25	27	26	28	29	27	n.a.
6	Held by public.	20	21	25	27	26	27	29	27	
7	Held by agencies	0	0	0	0	0	0	0	0	↓
8	**Debt subject to statutory limit**	**4,140**	**4,256**	**4,316**	**4,446**	**4,491**	**4,559**	**4,605**	**4,711**	**4,775**
9	Public debt securities	4,139	4,256	4,315	4,445	4,491	4,559	4,605	4,711	4,774
10	Other debt[1].	0	0	0	0	0	0	0	0	0
	Memo									
11	Statutory debt limit.	4,145	4,370	4,900	4,900	4,900	4,900	4,900	4,900	4,900

1. Consists of guaranteed debt of U.S. Treasury and other federal agencies, specified participation certificates, notes to international lending organizations, and District of Columbia stadium bonds.

SOURCES. U.S. Department of the Treasury, *Monthly Statement of the Public Debt of the United States* and *Treasury Bulletin.*

Source: *Federal Reserve Bulletin,* Board of Governors of the Federal Reserve System.

Largest Companies

The 200 Largest U.S. Corporations

RANK 1994	1993*	COMPANY	REVENUES $ millions	% change from 1993	PROFITS $ millions	Rank	% change from 1993	ASSETS $ millions	Rank	STOCK-HOLDERS' EQUITY $ millions	Rank
1	1	GENERAL MOTORS Detroit	154,951.2	12.1	4,900.6†	3	98.7	198,598.7	6	12,823.8	14
2	2	FORD MOTOR Dearborn, Mich.	128,439.0	18.4	5,308.0	1	109.9	219,354.0	3	21,659.0	4
3	3	EXXON Irving, Texas	101,459.0E	2.0	5,100.0	2	(3.4)	87,862.0	27	37,415.0	1
4	S	WAL-MART STORES Bentonville, Ark.[1]	83,412.4	22.7	2,681.0	12	14.9	32,819.0	76	12,726.0	17
5	S	AT&T New York[2,3]	75,094.0	11.8	4,676.0	6	—	79,262.0	30	17,921.0	7
6	5	GENERAL ELECTRIC Fairfield, Conn.	64,687.0¶	5.1	4,726.0	4	9.5	194,484.0	7	26,387.0	2
7	4	INTL. BUSINESS MACHINES Armonk, N.Y.	64,052.0	2.1	3,021.0	9	—	81,091.0	29	23,413.0	3
8	6	MOBIL Fairfax, Va.	59,621.0E	4.5	1,079.0	47	(48.2)	41,542.0	60	17,146.0	9
9	S	SEARS ROEBUCK Chicago	54,559.0	(0.6)	1,454.0**	33	(38.8)	91,896.0	25	10,801.0	23
10	7	PHILIP MORRIS New York	53,776.0E	6.2	4,725.0	5	52.9	52,649.0	44	12,786.0	16
11	8	CHRYSLER Highland Park, Mich.	52,224.0	19.8	3,713.0	7	—	49,539.0	47	10,694.0	25
12	S	STATE FARM GROUP Bloomington, Ill.[4]	38,850.1	4.8	(244.3)	480	(111.8)	76,670.0	32	21,164.9	5
13	S	PRUDENTIAL INS. CO. OF AMERICA Newark, N.J.[4]	36,945.7	(5.1)	(1,175.0)	493	(233.7)	211,902.0	5	9,484.0	32
14	10	E.I. DU PONT DE NEMOURS Wilmington, Del.	34,968.0E	4.8	2,727.0	11	391.4	36,892.0	67	12,822.0	15
15	S	KMART Troy, Mich.[1]	34,313.0	(7.2)	296.0	203	—	17,029.0	124	6,032.0	59
16	9	TEXACO White Plains, N.Y.	33,768.0E	(4.0)	910.0	62	(14.8)	25,505.0	93	9,749.0	28
17	S	CITICORP New York	31,650.0	(1.7)	3,366.0	8	51.7	250,489.0	2	17,769.0	8
18	11	CHEVRON San Francisco	31,064.0E	(5.9)	1,693.0	25	33.8	34,407.0	71	14,596.0	11
19	12	PROCTER & GAMBLE Cincinnati[5]	30,296.0	(0.5)	2,211.0	16	—	25,535.0	92	8,832.0	37
20	15	PEPSICO Purchase, N.Y.	28,472.4	13.8	1,752.0	24	10.3	24,792.0	94	6,856.1	48
21	13	AMOCO Chicago	26,953.0E	4.5	1,789.0	23	(1.7)	29,316.0	84	14,382.0	12
22	19	HEWLETT-PACKARD Palo Alto[6]	24,991.0	23.0	1,599.0	29	35.9	19,567.0	112	9,926.0	27
23	S	ITT New York	23,767.0	0.2	1,022.0	50	11.9	100,854.0	20	5,459.0	67
24	16	CONAGRA Omaha[7]	23,512.2	9.3	413.1	156	67.7	10,721.8	183	2,226.9	211
25	S	KROGER Cincinnati	22,959.1	2.6	242.2*	237	—	4,707.7	286	(2,153.7)	500
26	S	AMERICAN INTERNATIONAL GROUP New York	22,385.7	11.4	2,175.5	18	12.2	114,346.1	16	16,421.7	10
27	S	METROPOLITAN LIFE INSURANCE New York[4]	22,257.9	6.5	80.4	376	(44.7)	136,125.3	13	6,309.0	54
28	23	MOTOROLA Schaumburg, Ill.	22,245.0	31.1	1,560.0	30	52.6	17,536.0	120	9,096.0	35
29	14	BOEING Seattle	21,924.0	(13.8)	856.0	65	(31.2)	21,463.0	104	9,700.0	29
30	S	DAYTON HUDSON Minneapolis[1]	21,311.0	10.8	434.0	148	15.7	11,697.0	172	3,043.0	149
31	18	UNITED TECHNOLOGIES Hartford	21,197.0	0.6	585.0	110	20.1	15,624.0	136	3,752.0	120
32	S	J.C. PENNEY Plano, Texas[1]	21,082.0	7.7	1,057.0	48	12.4	16,202.0	130	5,615.0	64
33	21	DOW CHEMICAL Midland, Mich.	20,015.0	10.8	931.0	58	44.6	26,545.0	89	8,212.0	42
34	S	GTE Stamford, Conn.	19,944.3	1.0	2,444.6	14	173.8	42,499.8	58	10,483.3	26
35	S	UNITED PARCEL SERVICE Atlanta	19,575.7	10.1	943.3	57	16.5	11,182.4	177	4,647.2	86
36	S	FED. NATL. MORTGAGE ASSN. Washington, D.C.	18,572.4	15.7	2,131.6	20	13.8	272,508.3	1	9,540.7	31
37	S	TRAVELERS INC. New York	18,465.0	171.7	1,326.0	36	44.8	115,297.0	15	8,640.0	39
38	S	CIGNA Philadelphia	18,392.0	(0.1)	554.0	115	136.8	86,102.0	28	5,811.0	62
39	S	AMERICAN STORES Salt Lake City[1]	18,355.1	(2.2)	345.2	183	39.7	7,031.6	225	2,050.9	224
40	S	MERRILL LYNCH New York	18,233.1	9.9	1,016.8	51	(25.2)	163,749.3	11	5,817.5	61
41	26	XEROX Stamford, Conn.	17,837.0	(0.7)	794.0	70	—	38,585.0	66	4,177.0	107
42	S	AETNA LIFE & CASUALTY Hartford	17,524.7	2.4	467.5	137	—	94,172.5	24	5,503.0	66
43	20	EASTMAN KODAK Rochester, N.Y.	16,862.0¶	(16.8)	557.0*	114	—	14,968.0	138	4,017.0	112
44	S	BELLSOUTH Atlanta	16,844.5	6.1	2,159.8	19	145.4	34,397.0	72	14,367.3	13
45	24	USX Pittsburgh	16,799.0E	4.1	501.0	128	—	17,517.0	121	4,302.0	100
46	S	BANKAMERICA CORP. San Francisco[8]	16,531.0	4.0	2,176.0	17	11.4	215,475.0	4	18,891.0	6
47	S	PRICE/COSTCO Kirkland, Wash.[9,10]	16,480.6	109.8	(112.4)	473	(198.7)	4,235.7	303	1,685.0	259
48	32	COCA-COLA Atlanta	16,172.0	15.9	2,554.0	13	17.4	13,873.0	143	5,235.0	74
49	S	AMR Fort Worth	16,137.0	2.0	228.0	250	—	19,486.0	115	3,380.0	135
50	S	SUPERVALU Eden Prairie, Minn.[11]	15,936.9	26.8	185.3	290	12.6	4,042.4	309	1,275.5	314

*An "S" indicates an appearance on last year's Service 500. Definitions, explanations, and footnotes are on pages 158–159.

MARKET VALUE 3/31/95 $ millions	Rank	PROFITS AS % OF... REVENUES %	Rank	ASSETS %	Rank	STOCK-HOLDERS' EQUITY %	Rank	EARNINGS PER SHARE 1994 $	% change from 1993	1984–94 annual growth rate %	Rank	TOTAL RETURN TO INVESTORS 1994 %	Rank	1984–94 annual rate %	Rank	Industry table number	RANK 1994
33,188.5	15	3.2	311	2.5	304	38.2	18	5.15	141.8	(3.2)	300	(22.0)	394	6.1	335	31	1
27,529.1	27	4.1	274	2.4	308	24.5	55	4.97	118.5	6.6	172	(10.8)	315	19.6	62	31	2
82,734.6	2	5.0	227	5.8	154	13.6	242	4.07	(3.3)	1.9	248	0.8	209	16.1	126	33	3
58,892.0	5	3.2	309	8.2	84	21.1	86	1.17	14.7	25.6	15	(14.4)	352	25.1	24	22	4
81,196.1	3	6.2	186	5.9	146	26.1	40	3.01	—	9.2	120	(1.9)	236	14.5	158	44	5
92,321.6	1	7.3	153	2.4	307	17.9	136	2.77	9.7	8.2	140	0.1	217	17.2	101	14	6
48,265.7	8	4.7	241	3.7	241	12.9	262	5.02	—	(7.3)	325	32.1	22	(1.4)	377	11	7
36,638.8	13	1.8	379	2.6	299	6.3	393	2.55	(49.4)	(2.0)	289	11.0	111	18.0	87	33	8
20,674.4	38	2.7	335	1.6	341	13.5	249	3.66	(40.3)	(0.9)	278	(10.0)	310	11.1	256	22	9
55,699.2	6	8.8	110	9.0	68	37.0	22	5.45	54.8	19.7	29	8.8	130	23.7	34	17	10
14,823.7	55	7.1	160	7.5	98	34.7	24	10.11	—	1.9	246	(6.3)	281	17.5	93	31	11
N.A.		(0.6)	467	(0.3)	462	(1.2)	454	N.A.	—	—		—		—		26	12
N.A.		(3.2)	475	(0.6)	464	(12.4)	468	N.A.	—	—		—		—		26	13
41,215.4	11	7.8	135	7.4	102	21.3	83	4.00	393.8	7.3	152	20.1	55	17.5	91	8	14
6,282.9	143	0.9	420	1.7	333	4.9	417	0.63	—	(6.8)	323	(35.9)	434	5.2	338	22	15
17,288.1	48	2.7	331	3.6	252	9.3	352	3.17	(15.2)	11.9	86	(2.8)	248	13.6	189	33	16
16,840.3	49	10.6	78	1.3	360	18.9	110	7.03	56.2	8.1	141	13.4	96	12.3	228	9	17
31,280.2	21	5.5	219	4.9	183	11.6	306	2.60	33.7	1.5	252	6.8	148	16.6	111	33	18
45,478.2	9	7.3	154	8.7	73	25.0	53	3.09	—	8.7	127	11.3	108	19.3	69	42	19
30,988.1	22	6.2	187	7.1	110	25.6	46	2.18	11.2	24.2	20	(9.6)	307	24.8	27	19	20
31,583.0	20	6.6	171	6.1	138	12.4	277	3.60	(1.6)	(0.7)	275	16.2	79	13.5	196	33	21
30,706.1	23	6.4	181	8.2	83	16.1	182	6.14	32.0	9.0	123	28.1	28	12.4	223	11	22
10,844.6	76	4.3	265	1.0	390	18.7	117	8.57	17.1	11.2	95	(0.6)	222	14.6	155	12	23
8,214.2	106	1.8	382	3.9	232	18.6	121	1.81	70.8	15.3	55	21.5	52	20.3	56	17	24
3,080.1	277	1.1	416	5.1	177	—		2.13	—	2.0	241	19.9	60	24.0	33	18	25
32,910.2	16	9.7	89	1.9	329	13.2	256	6.87	12.4	20.3	26	12.2	102	18.9	75	26	26
N.A.		0.4	443	0.1	453	1.3	442	N.A.	—	—		—		—		26	27
32,024.9	19	7.0	163	8.9	70	17.2	154	2.65	48.9	12.5	80	26.4	35	22.8	39	14	28
18,327.4	43	3.9	280	4.0	228	8.8	365	2.51	(31.4)	0.5	266	11.0	110	13.5	195	2	29
5,122.7	174	2.0	364	3.7	243	14.3	222	5.77	15.6	8.0	142	8.5	135	10.8	268	22	30
8,511.8	99	2.8	327	3.7	238	15.6	195	4.40	24.6	(1.1)	281	4.5	170	9.3	288	2	31
10,430.4	81	5.0	228	6.5	124	18.8	115	4.29	13.8	11.4	93	(12.5)	330	19.0	73	22	32
20,297.8	39	4.7	243	3.5	255	11.3	316	3.37	44.6	5.3	189	23.2	45	18.6	79	8	33
32,154.9	17	12.3	52	5.8	158	23.3	68	2.55	174.2	3.3	218	(8.0)	296	14.9	149	44	34
N.A.		4.8	236	8.4	77	20.3	93	1.63	16.4	(5.3)	315	—		—		32	35
22,238.8	35	11.5	61	0.8	411	22.3	74	7.77	13.9	—		(4.4)	262	32.6	7	12	36
12,375.9	68	7.2	157	1.2	378	15.3	202	3.86	3.2	—		(15.3)	362	—		26	37
5,399.7	168	3.0	316	0.6	418	9.5	348	7.66	135.7	22.7	22	6.3	155	9.3	286	26	38
3,796.3	239	1.9	377	4.9	185	16.8	161	2.42	178.2	13.0	72	27.3	32	20.2	57	18	39
7,986.0	112	5.6	213	0.6	421	17.5	146	4.75	(20.6)	24.9	17	(12.9)	335	13.4	198	6	40
12,424.5	67	4.5	259	2.1	320	19.0	109	6.73	—	10.3	107	14.2	90	15.6	135	40	41
6,423.8	139	2.7	334	0.5	433	8.5	368	4.14	—	14.8	60	(17.8)	369	8.4	300	26	42
18,092.0	44	3.3	306	3.7	242	13.9	232	1.66	—	(4.2)	307	(12.2)	328	8.7	298	40	43
29,531.3	24	12.8	47	6.3	133	15.0	209	4.35	145.8	4.3	202	(2.2)	241	15.1	145	44	44
N.A.		3.0	319	2.9	286	11.6	304	N.A.	—	—		—		—		33	45
18,059.4	46	13.2	40	1.0	391	11.5	309	5.36	11.9	11.7	90	(11.8)	324	10.8	266	9	46
2,873.6	292	(0.7)	468	(2.7)	474	(6.7)	463	(0.51)	(121.2)	—		(33.1)	428	(4.4)	379	43	47
71,930.7	4	15.8	18	18.4	6	48.8	8	1.98	18.6	17.4	37	17.4	72	28.9	13	5	48
4,912.9	181	1.4	399	1.2	376	6.7	387	4.51	—	0.3	268	(20.5)	386	4.0	348	3	49
1,901.1	349	1.2	410	4.6	201	14.5	218	2.58	11.7	9.5	115	(30.6)	422	6.8	326	53	50

(continued)

The 200 Largest U.S. Corporations *(continued)*

RANK 1994	1993*	COMPANY	REVENUES $ millions	% change from 1993	PROFITS $ millions	Rank	% change from 1993	ASSETS $ millions	Rank	STOCK-HOLDERS' EQUITY $ millions	Rank
51	S	FLEMING Oklahoma City	15,753.5	20.3	56.2	403	59.7	4,608.3	290	1,078.6	341
52	30	JOHNSON & JOHNSON New Brunswick, N.J.	15,734.0	11.3	2,006.0	21	12.3	15,668.0	135	7,122.0	46
53	22	ATLANTIC RICHFIELD Los Angeles	15,682.0E	(11.8)	919.0	61	241.6	24,563.0	95	6,278.0	55
54	S	SAFEWAY Oakland	15,626.6	2.7	239.7	240	94.4	5,022.1	275	643.8	399
55	S	AMERICAN EXPRESS New York	15,593.0	(20.5)	1,413.0	35	(4.4)	97,006.0	22	6,433.0	52
56	27	SARA LEE Chicago5	15,536.0	6.6	199.0†	279	(71.7)	11,665.0	173	3,357.0	139
57	25	RJR NABISCO HOLDINGS New York	15,366.0	1.7	519.0*	124	—	31,408.0	80	10,908.0	22
58	31	MINNESOTA MINING & MFG. St. Paul	15,079.0	7.6	1,322.0	37	4.7	13,496.0	151	6,734.0	49
59	46	MERCK Whitehouse Station, N.J.	14,969.8	42.6	2,997.0	10	38.4	21,856.6	102	11,139.0	20
60	33	INTERNATIONAL PAPER Purchase, N.Y.	14,966.0	9.4	357.0	178	23.5	17,836.0	118	6,514.0	50
61	41	CATERPILLAR Peoria, Ill.	14,328.0	23.4	955.0	56	46.5	16,250.0	129	2,911.0	163
62	S	UAL Elk Grove Township, Ill.	13,950.0	(3.9)	51.0†	409	—	11,764.0	171	(316.0)	491
63	S	BELL ATLANTIC Philadelphia	13,791.4	6.2	(754.8)*	491	(153.8)	24,271.8	96	6,081.3	57
64	S	LOEWS New York	13,515.2	(1.3)	267.8	220	(54.9)	50,336.0	45	5,405.3	69
65	29	DIGITAL EQUIPMENT Maynard, Mass.5	13,450.8	(6.4)	(2,156.1)	494	—	10,579.8	188	3,279.8	144
66	S	MCI COMMUNICATIONS Washington, D.C.	13,338.0	11.9	795.0	69	36.6	16,366.0	128	9,004.0	36
67	S	NYNEX New York	13,306.6	(0.8)	792.6	71	—	30,068.0	81	8,581.4	40
68	34	TENNECO Houston	13,222.0	(0.2)	396.0	165	(3.9)	12,542.0	160	2,900.0	164
69	28	MCDONNELL DOUGLAS Berkeley, Mo.	13,176.0	(9.0)	598.0	106	51.0	12,216.0	166	3,872.0	116
70	35	LOCKHEED Calabasas, Calif.12	13,130.0	0.5	445.0	145	5.5	9,113.0	201	2,807.0	170
71	S	NATIONSBANK CORP. Charlotte, N.C.	13,126.0	27.3	1,690.0	26	12.6	169,604.0	10	11,011.0	21
72	38	ALLIEDSIGNAL Morris Township, N.J.	12,817.0	8.4	759.0	75	84.7	11,321.0	175	2,982.0	154
73	36	GEORGIA-PACIFIC Atlanta	12,738.0	3.3	310.0	197	—	10,728.0	182	2,620.0	179
74	S	CHEMICAL BANKING CORP. New York	12,685.0	2.1	1,294.0	39	(19.3)	171,423.0	9	10,712.0	24
75	S	SPRINT Westwood, Kans.	12,661.8	11.4	888.2	63	1,598.3	14,936.3	139	4,524.8	93
76	S	AMERITECH Chicago	12,569.5	7.3	(1,063.0)*	492	(170.3)	19,946.8	111	6,055.1	58
77	S	HOME DEPOT Atlanta1	12,476.7	35.0	604.5	103	32.2	5,778.0	248	3,442.2	130
78	S	MCKESSON San Francisco14	12,428.2	6.5	136.2†	323	18.7	3,192.7	342	678.6	391
79	37	PHILLIPS PETROLEUM Bartlesville, Okla.	12,367.0E	(1.4)	484.0	134	99.2	11,436.0	174	2,953.0	158
80	S	DELTA AIR LINES Atlanta5	12,359.0	3.0	(409.0)	484	—	11,896.0	169	1,467.0	285
81	40	GOODYEAR TIRE & RUBBER Akron	12,288.2	5.5	567.0	112	46.2	9,123.3	200	2,803.2	171
82	S	MAY DEPARTMENT STORES St. Louis1	12,223.0	10.9	782.0	74	10.0	9,472.0	195	4,135.0	108
83	39	IBP Dakota City, Nebr.	12,075.4	3.5	182.3	294	102.4	1,865.0	420	780.5	379
84	S	NEW YORK LIFE INSURANCE New York4	12,066.6	0.7	404.3	159	9.9	68,925.7	34	3,723.2	122
85	43	ANHEUSER-BUSCH St. Louis	12,053.8E	4.8	1,032.1	49	73.6	11,045.4	179	4,415.5	96
86	44	BRISTOL-MYERS SQUIBB New York	11,983.6	5.0	1,842.0	22	(6.0)	12,910.0	155	5,704.0	63
87	S	J.P. MORGAN & CO. New York	11,915.0	(0.2)	1,215.0	42	(23.4)	154,917.0	12	9,568.0	30
88	S	ALBERTSON'S Boise1	11,894.6	5.4	400.4	162	17.9	3,621.7	327	1,687.9	258
89	S	SBC COMMUNICATIONS San Antonio15	11,618.5	8.7	1,648.7	28	—	26,005.3	91	8,355.6	41
90	56	INTEL Santa Clara, Calif.	11,521.0	31.2	2,288.0	15	(0.3)	13,816.0	144	9,267.0	34
91	S	US WEST Englewood, Colo.	11,506.0	4.6	1,426.0	34	—	23,204.0	98	7,382.0	45
92	48	ARCHER DANIELS MIDLAND Decatur, Ill.5	11,374.4	15.9	484.1	133	(14.7)	8,746.9	205	5,045.4	78
93	S	MELVILLE Rye, N.Y.	11,285.6	8.1	307.5	198	(7.3)	4,735.5	283	2,381.6	196
94	45	ROCKWELL INTERNATIONAL Seal Beach, Calif.16	11,204.7	2.6	634.1	95	12.8	9,860.8	192	3,355.6	140
95	S	CHASE MANHATTAN CORP. New York	11,187.0	(2.0)	1,205.0	43	24.7	114,038.0	17	8,665.0	38
96	S	NATIONWIDE INS. ENTERPRISE Columbus, Ohio4	11,183.1	2.0	445.3	144	(11.1)	47,696.0	52	4,819.6	81
97	S	COLUMBIA/HCA HEALTHCARE Nashville17	11,132.0	96.9	630.0*	97	353.2	12,339.0	163	5,022.0	79
98	S	WINN-DIXIE STORES Jacksonville5	11,082.2	2.3	216.1	262	(8.6)	2,146.6	394	1,057.5	346
99	S	SYSCO Houston5	10,942.5	9.2	216.8	261	7.4	2,811.7	364	1,240.9	316
100	76	COMPAQ COMPUTER Houston	10,866.0	51.1	867.0	64	87.7	6,166.0	238	3,674.0	125

MARKET VALUE 3/31/95 $ millions	Rank	PROFITS AS % OF... REVENUES %	Rank	ASSETS %	Rank	STOCK-HOLDERS' EQUITY %	Rank	EARNINGS PER SHARE 1994 $	% change from 1993	1984–94 annual growth rate %	Rank	TOTAL RETURN TO INVESTORS 1994 %	Rank	1984–94 annual rate %	Rank	Industry table number	RANK 1994
846.3	420	0.4	444	1.2	370	5.2	410	1.51	57.3	(5.6)	316	(1.6)	235	(0.6)	374	53	51
38,236.1	12	12.7	49	12.8	20	28.2	36	3.12	13.9	16.3	45	25.0	38	22.4	41	34	52
18,486.7	42	5.9	198	3.7	239	14.6	215	5.63	239.2	9.8	111	2.0	195	14.5	157	33	53
3,591.8	247	1.5	394	4.8	192	37.2	21	1.96	92.2	—		50.0	13	2.3	364	18	54
17,293.3	47	9.1	104	1.5	350	22.0	78	2.75	(5.8)	7.0	163	11.0	112	9.3	287	12	55
12,510.9	66	1.3	406	1.7	334	5.9	400	0.37	(73.6)	(0.9)	279	3.9	177	23.6	35	17	56
9,911.7	82	3.4	299	1.7	336	4.8	422	0.25	—	—		(13.7)	344	—		47	57
24,400.6	31	8.8	112	9.8	46	19.6	103	3.13	7.6	7.2	156	1.5	202	14.3	164	40	58
53,187.5	7	20.0	3	13.7	17	26.9	39	2.38	27.3	20.4	25	14.9	85	25.1	26	34	59
9,379.5	87	2.4	354	2.0	323	5.5	405	2.86	22.2	11.8	89	13.8	91	14.2	171	20	60
11,124.5	73	6.7	170	5.9	148	32.8	26	4.70	46.2	—		24.9	41	15.2	143	25	61
1,306.1	391	0.4	441	0.4	438	—		(0.61)	—	—		(40.2)	439	7.6	311	3	62
23,064.7	33	(5.5)	482	(3.1)	477	(12.4)	469	(1.73)	(153.7)	—		(11.7)	323	15.7	133	44	63
5,824.8	153	2.0	368	0.5	430	5.0	414	4.45	(52.0)	1.0	254	(5.6)	275	11.3	251	12	64
5,555.3	160	(16.0)	494	(20.4)	492	(65.7)	476	(15.80)	—	—		(2.9)	250	(5.0)	380	11	65
14,015.7	58	6.0	193	4.9	188	8.8	364	1.32	153.8	26.6	12	(34.8)	430	17.4	94	44	66
16,671.8	50	6.0	194	2.6	294	9.2	355	1.89	—	(2.9)	299	(2.7)	246	13.8	183	44	67
8,893.3	98	3.0	317	3.2	274	13.7	241	2.20	(9.8)	(5.8)	317	(16.5)	367	7.0	322	25	68
6,506.0	138	4.5	251	4.9	186	15.4	200	5.05	50.0	6.5	174	34.4	20	10.4	273	2	69
4,592.2[13]	191	3.4	297	4.9	187	15.9	185	7.00	4.5	2.9	227	9.9	120	8.9	295	2	70
14,034.6	57	12.9	44	1.0	393	15.3	201	6.12	5.9	11.6	92	(4.2)	258	13.7	184	9	71
11,112.9	74	5.9	196	6.7	122	25.5	49	2.68	84.8	0.6	259	(12.6)	331	12.2	229	2	72
7,214.0	122	2.4	346	2.9	284	11.8	298	3.48	—	13.6	70	6.4	151	14.4	161	20	73
9,227.3	91	10.2	83	0.8	413	12.1	289	4.64	(19.6)	(3.3)	301	(6.8)	284	7.2	318	9	74
10,536.9	79	7.0	162	5.9	143	19.6	104	2.55	1,600.0	7.1	157	(18.1)	371	14.7	151	44	75
22,747.8	34	(8.5)	485	(5.3)	483	(17.6)	470	(1.94)	(169.8)	—		11.6	106	18.8	77	44	76
20,044.5	40	4.8	235	10.5	35	17.6	145	1.32	30.7	37.3	8	16.9	74	39.0	4	43	77
1,773.6	359	1.1	415	4.3	212	20.1	99	3.17	17.8	5.3	188	—		—		53	78
9,581.0	84	3.9	278	4.2	213	16.4	170	1.85	98.9	0.5	265	15.8	80	14.2	172	33	79
3,175.8	272	(3.3)	476	(3.4)	478	(27.9)	473	(10.32)	—	—		(7.2)	286	3.3	356	3	80
5,564.2	158	4.6	246	6.2	135	20.2	94	3.75	42.0	6.8	167	(25.0)	404	13.6	191	38	81
9,185.7	92	6.4	182	8.3	80	18.9	111	3.06	10.5	9.5	116	(12.1)	327	17.2	97	22	82
1,553.7	379	1.5	395	9.8	47	23.4	67	3.79	101.6	—		17.8	70	—		17	83
N.A.		3.4	303	0.6	424	10.9	328	N.A.	—	—		—		—		26	84
15,216.4	53	8.6	118	9.3	62	23.4	66	3.91	80.2	12.2	83	6.6	149	18.0	86	5	85
32,108.9	18	15.4	22	14.3	14	32.3	28	3.62	(4.7)	7.7	147	4.7	169	12.4	222	34	86
11,522.9	70	10.2	84	0.8	410	12.7	271	6.02	(22.8)	7.1	158	(15.6)	363	15.5	136	9	87
8,184.5	108	3.4	301	11.1	33	23.7	61	1.58	17.9	18.0	35	10.0	118	25.1	25	18	88
25,185.5	30	14.2	31	6.3	130	19.7	102	2.74	—	6.2	179	1.0	206	19.3	68	44	89
35,172.2	14	19.9	4	16.6	8	24.7	54	5.24	0.8	24.9	16	3.3	180	21.3	47	14	90
18,796.0	41	12.4	51	6.1	137	19.3	106	3.14	—	3.1	219	(18.1)	372	13.7	186	44	91
9,611.0	83	4.3	269	5.5	162	9.6	346	1.40	(11.4)	14.6	61	43.3	14	20.0	59	17	92
3,935.2	229	2.7	329	6.5	125	12.9	261	2.75	(8.3)	4.3	201	(20.8)	388	8.5	299	43	93
8,470.3	100	5.7	209	6.4	127	18.9	113	2.87	12.5	5.9	181	(1.0)	225	12.3	227	14	94
6,316.4	141	10.8	72	1.1	388	13.9	230	5.87	22.5	2.7	229	5.7	158	10.6	272	9	95
N.A.		4.0	275	0.9	400	9.2	354	N.A.	—	—		—		—		26	96
15,615.2	52	5.7	208	5.1	179	12.5	272	1.80	95.7	—		10.5	113	—		23	97
4,167.3	213	2.0	371	10.1	38	20.4	91	2.90	(6.8)	7.4	150	(1.3)	231	16.4	119	18	98
4,839.4	184	2.0	369	7.7	93	17.5	148	1.18	9.3	16.0	49	(10.7)	314	20.9	52	53	99
8,982.4	96	8.0	131	14.1	16	23.6	62	3.23	77.8	45.1	5	60.4	8	43.0	2	11	100

(continued)

The 200 Largest U.S. Corporations *(continued)*

RANK 1994	1993*	COMPANY	REVENUES $ millions	% change from 1993	PROFITS $ millions	Rank	% change from 1993	ASSETS $ millions	Rank	STOCK-HOLDERS' EQUITY $ millions	Rank
101	S	TEACHERS INS. & ANNUITY ASSN. New York[4]	10,550.8	4.7	463.3	139	57.8	73,347.8	33	3,437.8	131
102	S	PACIFIC GAS & ELECTRIC San Francisco	10,447.4	(1.3)	1,000.2	53	(5.7)	27,809.1	87	9,368.0	33
103	50	WEYERHAEUSER Federal Way, Wash.	10,398.0	8.9	589.0	109	1.7	13,007.0	154	4,290.0	102
104	54	ALCOA Pittsburgh	10.391.5	13.6	375.2*	171	7,716.7	12,353.2	162	3,999.2	113
105	S	GREAT ATLANTIC & PACIFIC TEA Montvale, N.J.[11]	10,384.1	(1.1)	4.0	452	—	3,098.7	349	994.4	355
106	58	TEXAS INSTRUMENTS Dallas	10,315.0	21.0	691.0	86	46.4	6,989.0	227	3,039.0	151
107	S	WMX TECHNOLOGIES Oak Brook, Ill.	10,097.3	10.5	784.4	73	73.2	17,538.9	119	4,541.0	91
108	S	WALT DISNEY Burbank, Calif.[16]	10,055.1	17.9	1,110.4	46	270.4	12,826.3	157	5,508.3	65
109	52	RAYTHEON Lexington, Mass.	10,012.9	8.8	596.9	107	(13.9)	7,395.4	221	3,928.2	114
110	47	COASTAL Houston	10,012.7[E]	(1.2)	232.6	246	102.1	10,534.6	189	2,457.2	190
111	51	MARTIN MARIETTA Bethesda, Md.[12]	9,873.7	4.6	635.6	94	2,947.4	8,538.0	207	3,371.0	137
112	57	TEXTRON Providence	9,683.0	6.7	433.0	149	14.2	20,925.0	106	2,882.0	165
113	S	CSX Richmond	9,608.0	7.5	652.0	92	81.6	13,724.0	147	3,731.0	121
114	S	NORTHWESTERN MUTUAL LIFE INS. Milwaukee[4]	9,581.4	7.2	398.4	164	(21.9)	48,110.6	51	2,225.3	212
115	49	ASHLAND Russell, Ky.[16]	9,505.3[E]	(1.1)	197.0	280	38.5	5,815.0	245	1,594.6	269
116	S	PACIFIC TELESIS GROUP San Francisco	9,494.0	(7.9)	1,159.0	44	—	20,139.0	110	5,233.0	75
117	64	OCCIDENTAL PETROLEUM Los Angeles	9,416.0[E]	10.2	(36.0)	465	(112.7)	17,989.0	116	4,457.0	94
118	S	MORGAN STANLEY GROUP New York[18]	9,376.0	2.2	395.0	166	(49.7)	117,400.0[19]	14	4,555.0[19]	90
119	55	BAXTER INTERNATIONAL Deerfield, Ill.	9,324.0	5.0	596.0	108	—	10,002.0	191	3,270.0	145
120	S	WALGREEN Deerfield, Ill.[9]	9,235.0	11.3	281.9	207	27.2	2,908.7	357	1,573.6	271
121	42	WESTINGHOUSE ELECTRIC Pittsburgh	9,208.0	(20.4)	77.0	379	—	10,624.0	185	1,792.0	247
122	—	LEHMAN BROTHERS New York[20]	9,190.0	—	75.0†	381	—	109,947.0	18	3,395.0	134
123	67	APPLE COMPUTER Cupertino, Calif.[16]	9,188.7	15.2	310.2	196	258.2	5,302.7	264	2,383.3	194
124	59	ABBOTT LABORATORIES Abbott Park, Ill.	9,156.0	8.9	1,516.7	32	8.4	8,523.7	208	4,049.4	111
125	S	NORTHWEST AIRLINES St. Paul	9,142.9	5.7	236.2	245	—	8,070.1	215	(1,370.7)	499
126	68	TRW Cleveland	9,087.0	14.3	333.0	188	70.4	5,636.0	251	1,822.0	244
127	72	DEERE Moline, Ill.[6]	9,029.8	16.5	603.6	104	—	12,781.2	158	2,557.9	185
128	S	LIBERTY MUTUAL INS. GROUP Boston[4]	8,985.5	(5.1)	407.0	158	36.1	33,427.0	75	3,539.0	127
129	S	ENRON Houston	8,983.7	12.7	453.4	140	36.4	11,966.0	168	2,880.3	166
130	60	AMERICAN HOME PRODUCTS Madison, N.J.	8,966.2	8.0	1,528.3	31	4.0	21,674.8	103	4,254.1	104
131	S	TOYS "R" US Paramus, N.J.[1]	8,745.6	10.1	531.8	120	10.1	6,571.2	232	3,428.9	133
132	S	PUBLIX SUPER MARKETS Lakeland, Fla.	8,742.5	15.7	238.6	241	32.3	2,302.3	387	1,473.2	281
133	62	EMERSON ELECTRIC St. Louis[16]	8,607.2	5.3	788.5†	72	11.4	8,215.0	211	4,341.8	98
134	S	FLUOR Irvine, Calif.[6]	8,556.3	7.3	192.4	284	15.3	2,824.8	362	1,220.5	319
135	63	GENERAL MILLS Minneapolis[7]	8,516.9	4.7	469.9	136	(7.2)	5,198.3	267	1,151.2	329
136	S	FEDERAL EXPRESS Memphis[7]	8,479.5	8.6	204.4	270	279.4	5,992.5	242	1,924.7	234
137	61	AMERICAN BRANDS Old Greenwich, Conn.	8,441.5¶[E]	1.9	734.1	78	56.3	9,794.4	193	4,621.8	87
138	S	MARRIOTT INTERNATIONAL Washington, D.C.	8,415.0	13.3	200.0	277	58.7	3,207.0	341	767.0	380
139	S	SCECORP Rosemead, Calif.	8,345.0	6.7	722.0	81	13.0	22,390.0	101	6,144.0	56
140	S	MCDONALD'S Oak Brook, Ill.	8,320.8	12.3	1,224.4	41	13.1	13,591.9	148	6,885.4	47
141	S	FEDERATED DEPARTMENT STORES Cincinnati[1,21]	8,315.9	15.0	187.6	287	(2.9)	12,379.7	161	3,639.6	126
142	S	SOUTHERN Atlanta	8,297.0	(2.3)	989.0	54	(1.3)	27,042.0	88	8,186.0	43
143	S	WOOLWORTH New York[1]	8,293.0	(13.8)	47.0	415	—	4,173.0	304	1,358.0	302
144	74	PFIZER New York	8,281.3	10.7	1,298.4**	38	97.5	11,098.5	178	4,323.9	99
145	70	MONSANTO St. Louis	8,272.0	4.7	622.0	99	25.9	8,891.0	204	2,948.0	159
146	S	UNION PACIFIC Bethlehem, Pa.	8,140.0	7.7	546.0	116	3.0	15,942.0	132	5,131.0	77
147	73	WHIRLPOOL Benton Harbor, Mich.	8,104.0	7.6	158.0	312	209.8	6,655.0	231	1,723.0	256
148	S	PRINCIPAL MUTUAL LIFE INSURANCE Des Moines[4]	8,006.7	11.6	152.1	315	(28.2)	44,116.6	56	1,927.3	233
149	S	ALCO STANDARD Wayne, Pa.[16]	7,996.1	21.2	70.6	387	70,509.0	3,502.3	331	1,367.1	299
150	S	BANC ONE CORP. Columbus, Ohio[22]	7,857.1	8.7	1,005.1	52	(11.8)	88,922.6	26	7,564.9	44

MARKET VALUE 3/31/95 $ millions	Rank	PROFITS AS % OF... REVENUES %	Rank	ASSETS %	Rank	STOCK-HOLDERS' EQUITY %	Rank	EARNINGS PER SHARE 1994 $	% change from 1993	1984–94 annual growth rate %	Rank	TOTAL RETURN TO INVESTORS 1994 %	Rank	1984–94 annual rate %	Rank	Industry table number	RANK 1994
N.A.		4.4	262	0.6	420	13.5	247	N.A.	—	—		—		—		26	101
10,752.8	78	9.6	92	3.6	251	10.7	332	2.21	(5.2)	(1.7)	286	(25.4)	406	12.2	230	13	102
7,994.2	111	5.7	207	4.5	202	13.7	238	2.86	1.1	10.9	98	(13.5)	341	11.0	263	20	103
7,424.1	121	3.6	294	3.0	276	9.4	351	2.10	13,900.0	3.0	223	27.5	29	12.2	231	29	104
864.7	419	0.0	453	0.1	450	0.4	447	0.10	—	(22.4)	344	(30.6)	421	3.1	358	18	105
8,202.4	107	6.7	168	9.9	41	22.7	73	7.27	44.5	5.3	190	19.3	63	8.4	301	14	106
13,306.5	62	7.8	137	4.5	204	17.3	151	1.62	74.2	16.0	48	1.3	204	18.4	80	52	107
27,798.8	26	11.0	67	8.7	74	20.2	97	2.04	270.9	28.2	11	8.6	133	29.4	11	16	108
8,985.5	95	6.0	192	8.1	88	15.2	205	4.51	(11.7)	12.1	84	(1.1)	227	15.5	137	14	109
3,011.3	283	2.3	357	2.2	318	9.5	349	2.05	105.0	4.4	199	(7.6)	292	13.4	199	33	110
4,262.6[13]	206	6.4	178	7.4	101	18.9	114	6.00	—	—		1.8	196	14.4	160	2	111
4,986.2	180	4.5	257	2.1	319	15.0	210	4.80	14.0	11.9	85	(11.3)	318	15.3	141	2	112
8,246.9	103	6.8	166	4.8	194	17.5	147	6.23	80.1	7.1	162	(13.0)	336	15.1	146	37	113
N.A.		4.2	273	0.8	405	17.9	137	N.A.	—	—		—		—		26	114
2,164.8	326	2.1	363	3.4	260	12.4	282	2.94	30.1	—		3.9	176	14.7	150	33	115
12,828.0	65	12.2	53	5.8	157	22.1	77	2.73	—	2.6	231	(21.2)	391	15.4	139	44	116
6,941.8	130	(0.4)	463	(0.2)	458	(0.8)	452	(0.36)	(145.0)	—		19.4	62	3.9	349	8	117
5,117.2	175	4.2	271	0.3	443	8.7	367	4.18	(56.4)	—		(15.0)	359	—		12	118
9,245.7	90	6.4	183	6.0	142	18.2	126	2.13	—	26.1	14	20.6	54	11.9	239	40	119
5,922.8	151	3.1	315	9.7	50	17.9	135	2.28	27.4	12.6	77	8.6	134	16.4	118	18	120
5,044.7	177	0.8	421	0.7	416	4.3	424	0.07	—	(26.5)	346	(12.0)	326	2.9	360	14	121
1,881.7	351	0.8	423	0.1	452	2.2	437	N.A.	—	—		—		—		6	122
4,256.9	207	3.4	300	5.8	152	13.0	260	2.61	257.5	17.4	38	35.3	17	11.3	252	11	123
28,667.2	25	16.6	15	17.8	7	37.5	20	1.87	10.7	16.2	47	12.9	98	22.7	40	34	124
2,287.5	319	2.6	341	2.9	280	—		N.A.	—	—		—		—		3	125
4,470.0	198	3.7	292	5.9	144	18.3	125	5.05	67.8	3.5	213	(2.0)	237	10.0	280	31	126
7,028.0	126	6.7	169	4.7	195	23.6	63	7.01	—	16.3	46	(8.0)	297	11.5	245	25	127
N.A.		4.5	253	1.2	371	11.5	311	N.A.	—	—		—		—		26	128
8,347.7	102	5.0	226	3.8	236	15.7	191	1.80	36.4	2.5	233	7.7	143	16.3	120	35	129
21,792.6	36	17.0	13	7.1	111	35.9	23	4.97	5.1	8.4	135	1.7	200	14.2	170	34	130
7,112.3	124	6.1	189	8.1	87	15.5	198	1.85	13.5	17.0	43	(25.1)	405	14.9	148	43	131
N.A.		2.7	328	10.4	37	16.2	176	1.03	35.5	(4.1)	306	—		—		18	132
14,864.5	54	9.2	101	9.6	52	18.2	129	3.52	11.7	7.5	148	6.3	153	13.9	181	14	133
3,992.1	224	2.2	360	6.8	118	15.8	189	2.32	14.3	72.4	1	7.6	144	12.5	215	15	134
9,409.3	86	5.5	216	9.0	65	40.8	14	2.95	(4.8)	9.0	124	(2.7)	245	21.3	48	17	135
3,783.3	240	2.4	349	3.4	259	10.6	334	3.65	272.4	3.8	209	(15.0)	357	5.7	336	32	136
7,904.6	114	8.7	113	7.5	98	15.9	184	3.63	56.5	7.3	153	19.5	61	14.1	176	47	137
4,311.8	204	2.4	355	6.2	134	26.1	41	1.51	—	—		(2.0)	238	—		24	138
6,996.9	128	8.7	116	3.2	268	11.8	301	1.52	6.3	(0.4)	274	(21.1)	389	10.0	279	13	139
23,836.8	32	14.7	27	9.0	66	17.8	141	1.68	15.5	13.2	71	3.5	179	18.9	76	19	140
4,033.4	220	2.3	359	1.5	347	5.2	412	1.41	(7.8)	—		(7.2)	288	—		22	141
13,376.8	61	11.9	56	3.7	247	12.1	288	1.52	(3.2)	0.1	272	(2.4)	242	16.7	108	13	142
2,450.9	314	0.6	434	1.1	381	3.5	430	0.36	—	(10.7)	334	(37.8)	437	8.8	296	43	143
26,944.9	28	15.7	20	11.7	30	30.0	33	4.19	104.4	10.5	103	15.2	82	17.2	98	34	144
9,330.3	89	7.5	148	7.0	113	21.1	85	5.32	29.8	7.0	165	(0.8)	223	16.6	115	8	145
11,300.8	72	6.7	167	3.4	258	10.6	333	2.66	3.1	2.9	226	(25.4)	407	11.7	241	37	146
4,133.6	215	1.9	372	2.4	310	9.2	358	2.10	213.4	(2.1)	290	(22.8)	397	11.6	242	14	147
N.A.		1.9	376	0.3	442	7.9	378	N.A.	—	—		—		—		26	148
3,951.3	228	0.9	419	2.0	321	5.2	411	1.10	—	(2.6)	297	16.6	76	18.3	84	53	149
11,314.1	71	12.8	48	1.1	379	13.3	254	2.42	(18.8)	9.8	113	(26.0)	409	15.3	142	9	150

(continued)

The 200 Largest U.S. Corporations *(concluded)*

RANK 1994	1993*	COMPANY	REVENUES $ millions	% change from 1993	PROFITS $ millions	Rank	% change from 1993	ASSETS $ millions	Rank	STOCK-HOLDERS' EQUITY $ millions	Rank
151	75	SUN Philadelphia	7,792.0E	3.4	90.0	359	(68.8)	6,465.0	233	1,863.0	236
152	69	RALSTON PURINA St. Louis[16]	7,705.3	(2.5)	188.7	286	85.7	4,622.3	289	355.6	451
153	S	VIACOM New York[23]	7,636.6	280.9	89.6*	363	(47.6)	28,273.7	86	11,791.6	19
154	77	COLGATE-PALMOLIVE New York	7,587.9	6.3	580.2	111	205.5	6,142.4	239	1,822.9	242
155	S	BANKERS TRUST NEW YORK CORP. New York	7,503.0	(3.8)	615.0	100	(38.2)	97,016.0	21	4,704.0	83
156	S	BERGEN BRUNSWIG Orange, Calif.[16]	7,483.8	9.7	56.1	405	115.5	1,995.1	408	461.9	431
157	81	CPC INTERNATIONAL Englewood Cliffs, N.J.	7,425.4	10.2	345.1	184	(24.1)	5,668.0	250	1,748.8	251
158	71	UNISYS Blue Bell, Pa.	7,399.7	(4.4)	100.5	352	(82.2)	7,323.9	223	2,604.5	180
159	S	TIME WARNER New York	7,396.0	12.4	(91.0)	471	—	16,716.0	126	1,148.0	330
160	79	KIMBERLY-CLARK Irving, Texas	7,364.2	5.6	535.1	119	4.7	6,715.7	230	2,595.8	182
161	S	LIMITED Columbus, Ohio[1]	7,320.8	1.0	448.3	143	14.7	4,570.1	293	2,761.0	173
162	—	SUPERMARKETS GENL. HLDGS. Woodbridge, N.J.[24]	7,226.5	57.0	(41.8)	466	—	1,133.8	472	(1,300.6)	498
163	66	UNOCAL Los Angeles	7,072.0E	(6.1)	(153.0)	477	(171.8)	9,337.0	198	2,815.0	169
164	78	H.J. HEINZ Pittsburgh[25]	7,046.7	(0.8)	602.9	105	52.1	6,381.1	234	2,338.6	199
165	85	ELI LILLY Indianapolis	7,000.8¶	8.5	1,286.1	40	167.8	14,507.4	140	5,355.6	71
166	S	USAIR GROUP Arlington, Va.	6,997.2	(1.2)	(684.9)	490	—	6,808.0	228	(896.9)	496
167	S	LINCOLN NATIONAL Fort Wayne	6,984.4	(15.7)	349.9	181	9.7	49,330.1	48	3,042.1	150
168	S	FEDERAL HOME LOAN MORTGAGE McLean, Va.	6,923.0	26.9	983.0	55	25.1	106,199.0	19	5,162.0	76
169	88	JOHNSON CONTROLS Milwaukee[16]	6,870.5	11.1	165.2	307	939.0	3,806.9	318	1,202.8	321
170	98	DANA Toledo	6,740.5	21.2	228.2	249	186.7	5,110.8	270	939.8	361
171	104	NORTHROP GRUMMAN Los Angeles	6,711.0	32.5	35.0	428	(63.5)	6,047.0	240	1,290.0	311
172	91	AMERADA HESS New York	6,698.8E	14.1	73.7	383	—	8,337.9	209	3,099.6	148
173	83	CAMPBELL SOUP Camden, N.J.[26]	6,690.5	1.6	630.3	96	7,586.6	4,992.0	278	1,989.0	227
174	109	FARMLAND INDUSTRIES Kansas City[27]	6,677.9	41.4	N.A.		—	1,926.6	416	585.0	410
175	S	DEAN WITTER DISCOVER New York	6,602.6	13.4	740.9	77	22.7	31,859.4	79	4,108.0	109
176	86	KELLOGG Battle Creek, Mich.	6,562.0	4.2	705.4	82	3.6	4,467.3	295	1,807.5	246
177	82	BORDEN Columbus, Ohio	6,494.8¶	(3.1)	(597.7)	487	—	3,822.3	317	(92.1)	487
178	S	EQUITABLE New York	6,447.3	(0.5)	252.0	227	16.2	94,640.0	23	3,013.8	152
179	92	WARNER-LAMBERT Morris Plains, N.J.	6,416.8	10.8	694.0	85	109.7	5,532.8	255	1,816.4	245
180	94	W.R. GRACE Boca Raton, Fla.	6,381.0¶	10.0	83.3*	370	220.4	6,230.6	237	1,504.5	279
181	S	CAPITAL CITIES/ABC New York	6,379.2	12.4	679.8	88	49.3	6,768.2	229	4,288.6	103
182	140	TOSCO Stamford, Conn.	6,365.8	78.9	83.8	369	4.1	1,797.2	424	575.5	412
183	93	PPG INDUSTRIES Pittsburgh	6,331.2	10.0	514.6	126	2,218.0	5,893.9	244	2,557.0	186
184	S	SALOMON New York	6,278.0	(28.7)	(399.0)	483	(148.2)	172,732.0	8	3,792.0	119
185	S	UNICOM Chicago[28]	6,277.5	19.3	354.9	180	215.7	23,121.0	99	5,448.0	68
186	87	COOPER INDUSTRIES Houston	6,258.0¶	(0.3)	(19.9)	464	(105.4)	6,361.7	236	3,009.6	153
187	S	FIRST UNION CORP. Charlotte, N.C.	6,253.6	8.7	925.4	59	13.2	77,313.5	31	5,397.5	70
188	S	CONSOLIDATED EDISON OF NEW YORK New York	6,239.6E	(0.4)	727.6	80	11.6	13,728.4	146	5,853.3	60
189	S	UNITED SERVICES AUTOMOBILE ASSN. San Antonio	6,181.4	3.2	564.4	113	(15.9)	19,548.3	113	4,073.7	110
190	S	GUARDIAN LIFE INS. CO. OF AMERICA New York[4]	6,133.8	(13.8)	143.7	320	(42.2)	13,566.9	149	1,012.3	353
191	—	AFLAC Columbus, Ga.	6,110.8	22.2	292.8	204	14.7	20,287.1	109	1,751.8	250
192	S	LOWE'S North Wilkesboro, N.C.[1]	6,110.5	34.7	223.6	258	69.6	3,106.0	348	1,419.9	292
193	90	LEVI STRAUSS ASSOCIATES San Francisco[29]	6,074.3	3.1	321.0†	192	(34.8)	3,925.3	313	1,471.6	282
194	99	GILLETTE Boston	6,070.2	12.2	698.3	83	142.2	5,494.0	257	2,017.3	226
195	89	HONEYWELL Minneapolis	6,057.0	1.6	278.9	210	(13.4)	4,885.9	279	1,854.7	238
196	115	EATON Cleveland	6,052.0	37.5	333.0	188	92.5	4,682.0	287	1,680.0	260
197	S	NORWEST CORP. Minneapolis	6,032.0	14.3	800.4	68	22.5	59,315.9	39	3,846.4	117
198	101	REYNOLDS METALS Richmond	6,013.2	13.6	121.7	337	—	7,461.3	219	2,271.7	207
199	97	COCA-COLA ENTERPRISES Atlanta	6,011.0	10.0	69.0	389	—	8,738.0	206	1,339.0	304
200	S	ENTERGY New Orleans	5,963.3	33.0	341.8	185	(38.1)	22,613.5	100	6,350.8	53

MARKET VALUE 3/31/95 $ millions	Rank	PROFITS AS % OF... REVENUES %	Rank	ASSETS %	Rank	STOCK-HOLDERS' EQUITY %	Rank	EARNINGS PER SHARE 1994 $	% change from 1993	1984-94 annual growth rate %	Rank	TOTAL RETURN TO INVESTORS 1994 %	Rank	1984-94 annual rate %	Rank	Industry table number	RANK 1994
3,047.8	281	1.2	411	1.4	354	4.8	419	0.84	(68.9)	(15.8)	341	4.1	175	7.2	316	33	151
4,796.5	186	2.4	345	4.1	221	53.1	6	2.04	—	—		—	—	—		17	152
15,990.6	51	1.2	408	0.3	444	0.8	446	0.07	(94.7)	(24.3)	345	(9.2)	303	—		16	153
9,568.8	85	7.6	143	9.4	58	31.8	30	3.82	253.7	24.4	19	4.3	172	21.4	46	42	154
4,079.1	218	8.2	126	0.6	419	13.1	259	7.17	(37.7)	4.2	204	(26.3)	410	12.4	220	9	155
1,062.6	409	0.7	427	2.8	287	12.2	286	1.52	111.1	8.9	125	20.0	57	9.4	284	53	156
7,943.4	113	4.6	244	6.1	139	19.7	101	2.25	(23.7)	8.5	133	14.9	84	21.9	44	17	157
1,610.9	375	1.4	402	1.4	356	3.9	427	(0.11)	(104.1)	—		(31.7)	424	(5.3)	381	11	158
14,271.2	56	(1.2)	469	(0.5)	463	(7.9)	465	(0.27)	—	—		(19.9)	382	14.3	166	16	159
8,419.2	101	7.3	155	8.0	89	20.6	89	3.33	4.7	10.4	104	0.3	215	19.4	67	20	160
8,226.7	104	6.1	188	9.8	44	16.2	174	1.25	15.7	17.2	41	8.6	132	16.2	122	43	161
N.A.		(0.6)	465	(3.7)	480	—		N.A.	—	—		—		—		18	162
6,997.5	127	(2.2)	474	(1.6)	471	(5.4)	462	(0.78)	(206.8)	—		0.6	211	7.2	317	33	163
9,374.5	88	8.6	119	9.4	57	25.8	43	2.35	53.6	10.7	100	6.5	150	16.4	117	17	164
21,367.5	37	18.4	6	8.9	71	24.0	58	4.45	173.0	10.2	108	15.5	81	18.4	82	34	165
370.9	445	(9.8)	487	(10.1)	487	—		(12.73)	—	—		(67.0)	451	(18.4)	387	3	166
3,822.6	238	5.0	229	0.7	417	11.5	310	3.37	8.0	7.1	160	(16.1)	366	11.1	258	26	167
10,907.6	75	14.2	30	0.9	401	19.0	108	5.08	24.8	—		3.2	181	—		12	168
2,073.4	334	2.4	351	4.3	210	13.7	237	3.80	2,135.3	4.9	194	(5.2)	269	12.9	208	31	169
2,518.8	310	3.4	298	4.5	205	24.3	56	2.31	168.6	3.1	220	(19.0)	377	10.3	274	31	170
2,410.3	315	0.5	438	0.6	426	2.7	432	0.72	(63.8)	(14.9)	340	16.8	75	6.2	334	2	171
4,591.8	192	1.1	414	0.9	403	2.4	436	0.79	—	(8.9)	330	2.4	189	8.3	302	33	172
12,052.4	69	9.4	95	12.6	23	31.7	31	2.51	8,266.7	13.0	74	10.4	115	20.5	54	17	173
N.A.		—		—		—		N.A.	—	—		—		—		17	174
6,950.9	129	11.2	66	2.3	313	18.0	132	4.35	—	—		(0.9)	224	—		12	175
12,978.2	64	10.7	73	15.8	10	39.0	17	3.15	7.1	14.2	63	5.1	161	22.2	43	17	176
N.A.		(9.2)	486	(15.6)	491	—		(4.16)	—	—		(26.6)	411	4.4	345	17	177
3,132.7	273	3.9	279	0.3	447	8.4	372	1.51	26.9	—		(32.2)	426	—		26	178
10,535.7	80	10.8	70	12.5	26	38.2	19	5.17	111.0	13.9	67	18.0	68	19.5	65	34	179
5,007.1	178	1.3	405	1.3	362	5.5	404	0.88	214.3	(7.9)	328	(1.6)	233	11.9	240	8	180
13,632.3	60	10.7	76	10.0	39	15.9	186	4.42	59.1	14.9	58	37.8	15	18.0	88	16	181
1,153.2	402	1.3	403	4.7	198	14.6	217	2.27	(4.6)	—		2.1	193	21.0	50	33	182
7,785.3	117	8.1	127	8.7	72	20.1	98	2.43	2,214.3	8.4	134	0.8	210	20.1	58	8	183
3,585.6	248	(6.4)	484	(0.2)	459	(10.5)	466	(4.31)	(161.5)	—		(20.1)	384	3.6	353	6	184
5,087.0	176	5.7	210	1.5	344	6.5	390	1.66	654.5	(9.3)	332	(9.0)	301	7.3	315	13	185
4,530.8	195	(0.3)	461	(0.3)	461	(0.7)	451	(0.64)	(123.3)	—		(28.0)	415	12.7	213	14	186
7,633.6	118	14.8	25	1.2	373	17.1	155	4.98	5.3	8.7	129	4.3	171	13.3	202	9	187
6,401.0	140	11.7	57	5.3	170	12.4	278	2.98	12.0	2.9	225	(13.8)	346	12.7	214	13	188
N.A.		9.1	102	2.9	285	13.9	233	N.A.	—	—		—		—		26	189
N.A.		2.3	356	1.1	387	14.2	224	N.A.	—	—		—		—		26	190
4,085.9	217	4.8	238	1.4	351	16.7	163	2.84	16.9	17.7	36	13.8	92	23.2	37	26	191
5,499.5	162	3.7	293	7.2	105	15.7	190	1.44	60.9	13.0	73	17.4	73	20.6	53	43	192
N.A.		5.3	222	8.2	82	21.8	80	N.A.	—	—		—		—		4	193
18,075.8	45	11.5	58	12.7	22	34.6	25	3.14	143.4	17.1	42	27.3	31	30.0	10	28	194
4,826.5	185	4.6	247	5.7	159	15.0	208	2.15	(10.4)	5.4	185	(5.2)	270	10.6	271	40	195
4,229.7	209	5.5	217	7.1	107	19.8	100	4.40	78.1	5.3	187	0.3	214	14.1	175	31	196
7,844.6	115	13.3	38	1.3	359	20.8	88	2.45	15.0	22.7	23	(1.0)	226	24.7	28	9	197
3,062.7	279	2.0	366	1.6	337	5.4	407	1.42	—	(7.7)	327	9.6	121	14.1	173	29	198
2,691.5	303	1.1	412	0.8	408	5.2	413	0.52	—	—		18.4	66	—		5	199
4,746.5	187	5.7	205	1.5	348	5.4	406	1.49	(52.8)	(6.3)	321	(35.1)	432	9.2	291	13	200

Source: FORTUNE 500, "© 1995 Time Inc. All rights reserved."

NOTES: DEFINITIONS AND EXPLANATIONS

Revenues All companies on the list must publish financial data—and must report part or all of their figures to a government agency. Private companies and cooperatives that produce a 10-K are included; subsidiaries of foreign companies incorporated in the U.S. are excluded. Revenues are as reported, including revenues from discontinued operations when they are published. The revenues for commercial banks and savings institutions are the sum of interest and noninterest revenues. Such figures for insurance companies include premium and annuity income, investment income, and capital gains or losses, but exclude deposits. Revenue figures for all companies include consolidated subsidiaries and exclude excise taxes. Data shown are for the fiscal year ended on or before January 31, 1995. All figures are for the year ended December 31, 1994, unless otherwise noted.

Profits Profits are shown after taxes, after extraordinary credits or charges if any appear on the income statement, and after cumulative effects of accounting changes. Figures in parentheses indicate a loss. Profit declines over 100% reflect swings from 1993 profits to 1994 losses. Cooperatives provide only net margin figures, which are not comparable with the profit figures in these listings, and therefore N.A. is shown in that column. Profits for insurance companies are based on statutory accounting and footnoted as such.

Assets Assets shown are the company's year-end total.

Stockholders' Equity Stockholders' equity is the sum of all capital stock, paid-in capital, and retained earnings at the company's year-end. Preferred stock that is technically construed to be debt has been excluded. Redeemable preferred stock whose redemption is either mandatory or outside the control of the company is therefore excluded. Dividends paid on such stock have been subtracted from the profit figures.

Market Value The figure shown was arrived at by multiplying the number of common shares outstanding by the price per common share as of March 31, 1995. Shares traded on a when-issued basis are excluded.

Earnings per Share The figures shown for each company are the primary earnings per share that appear on the income statement. Per share earnings for 1993 and 1984 are adjusted for stock splits and stock dividends. They are not restated for mergers, acquisitions, or accounting changes. Though earnings per share numbers are not marked by any footnotes, if a company's profits are footnoted to indicate an extraordinary charge or credit, it can be assumed that earnings per share are affected as well. Results are listed as not available (N.A.) if the companies are cooperatives or joint ventures, if the figures were not published, or if the stock traded on a limited basis or was not widely held. The 1984–94 growth rate is the annual rate, compounded.

Total Return to Investors Total return to investors includes both price appreciation and dividend yield to an investor in the company's stock. The figures shown assume sales at the end of 1994 of stock owned at the end of 1984 and 1993. It has been assumed that any proceeds from cash dividends, the sale of rights and warrant offerings, and stock received in spinoffs were reinvested when they were paid. Returns are adjusted for stock splits, stock dividends, recapitalizations, and corporate reorganizations as they occur; however, no effort has been made to reflect the cost of brokerage commissions or of taxes. Results are listed as not available (N.A.) if shares are not publicly traded or are traded on a limited basis. If companies have more than one class of shares outstanding, only the more widely held and actively traded has been considered. Total return percentages shown are the returns received by the hypothetical investor described above. The 1984–94 return is the annual rate, compounded.

Medians The median figures in the tables refer only to results of companies in the 500 (or 1,000 for industry categories), and no attempt has been made to calculate them in groups of fewer than four companies. The medians for profit changes from 1993 do not include companies that lost money in both 1993 and 1994, because no meaningful percentage changes can be calculated in such cases.

Credits Most of the figures in this FORTUNE 500 Directory were prepared by Henry Goldblatt and Richard Tucksmith, who are responsible for the columns reporting on companies' revenues, profits, assets, and stockholders' equity as well as for the industry table numbers. They were assisted by Richard Odson and Kimberly Seals McDonald. Earnings per share and total return to investors were compiled by Angela Such and Cathi Haight from information found in company annual reports and data supplied by Deloitte & Touche's PeerScape. Market value data are also attributable to the latter source.

Footnotes

E Excise taxes have been deducted.

N.A. Not available.

° Reflects an extraordinary charge of at least 10%.

°° Reflects an extraordinary credit of at least 10%.

†Reflects a net SFAS 106, 109, and/or 112 charge of at least 10%.

‡Reflects a net SFAS 106, 109, and/or 112 credit of at least 10%.

¶Includes sales of discontinued operations of at least 10%.

[1] Figures are for fiscal year ended January 31, 1995.

[2] Acquired McCaw Cellular Communications (1993 Service 500 rank: S-70), September 19, 1994.

[3] Name changed from American Telephone & Telegraph, April 20, 1994.

[4] Financial data for company are based on statutory accounting.

[5] Figures are for fiscal year ended June 30, 1994.

[6] Figures are for fiscal year ended October 31, 1994.

[7] Figures are for fiscal year ended May 31, 1994.

[8] Acquired Continental Bank Corp. (1993 Service 500 rank: B-34), September 1, 1994.

[9] Figures are for fiscal year ended August 31, 1994.

[10] Figures reflect merger with Costco Wholesale (1993 Service 500 rank: R-19), October 21, 1993.

[11] Figures are for fiscal year ended February 28, 1994.

[12] Figures do not reflect merger between Lockheed and Martin Marietta, March 15, 1995.

[13] Figure as of December 31, 1994.

[14] Figures are for fiscal year ended March 31, 1994.

[15] Name changed from Southwestern Bell, October 3, 1994.

[16] Figures are for fiscal year ended September 30, 1994.

[17] Figures reflect merger with Hospital Corp. of America (1993 Service 500 rank: S-20), February 10, 1994.

[18] Fiscal year-end changed from November 30. Figures are for fiscal year ended January 31, 1995.

[19] Figure as of October 31, 1994.

[20] Fiscal year-end changed from December 31. Figures are for fiscal year ended November 30, 1994.

[21] Acquired R. H. Macy (1993 Service 500 rank: R-26), December 19, 1994.

[22] Acquired Liberty National Bancorp (1993 Service 500 rank: B-91), August 15, 1994.

[23] Acquired Paramount Communications (1993 Service 500 rank: S-25), March 11, 1994.

[24] Figures are for four quarters ended October 31, 1994.

[25] Figures are for fiscal year ended April 30, 1994.

[26] Figures are for fiscal year ended July 31, 1994.

[27] Cooperatives provide only net margin figures, which are not comparable with the profit figures on the list.

[28] Name changed from Commonwealth Edison, September 1, 1994.

[29] Figures are for fiscal year ended November 30, 1994.

The World's 100 Largest Corporations

RANK 1994	1993		Company		REVENUES $ millions	% change from 1993	PROFITS $ millions	Rank	% change from 1993	ASSETS $ millions	Rank	STOCK-HOLDERS' EQUITY $ millions	Rank	EMPLOYEES Number	Rank	Industry table number
1	S		MITSUBISHI[1]	JAPAN	175,835.6	9.8	218.7	311	28.4	109,256.0	83	11,764.8	69	36,000	294	37
2	S		MITSUI[1]	JAPAN	171,490.5	4.9	263.8	283	85.8	82,461.8	107	6,592.4	172	80,000	137	37
3	S		ITOCHU[1]	JAPAN	167,824.7	8.2	81.6	400	—	74,062.9	117	5,138.5	228	7,345	468	37
4	S		SUMITOMO[1]	JAPAN	162,475.9	3.1	73.2	408	8.2	58,973.6	133	8,074.8	127	22,000	372	37
5	1		GENERAL MOTORS	U.S.	154,951.2	12.1	4,900.6	4	98.7	198,598.7	40	12,823.8	53	692,800	2	24
6	S		MARUBENI[1]	JAPAN	150,187.4	3.9	104.4	373	105.0	78,802.8	113	5,532.0	207	9,911	453	37
7	2		FORD MOTOR	U.S.	128,439.0	18.4	5,308.0	2	109.9	219,354.0	33	21,659.0	20	337,778	9	24
8	3		EXXON	U.S.	101,459.0[E]	2.0	5,100.0	3	(3.4)	87,862.0	102	37,415.0	6	86,000	124	25
9	S		NISSHO IWAI[1]	JAPAN	100,875.5	5.7	52.7	419	(47.0)	56,412.6	137	2,804.2	353	17,008	403	37
10	4		ROYAL DUTCH/SHELL GROUP	BRIT./NETH.	94,881.3[E]	(0.3)	6,235.6	1	38.4	108,300.0	84	56,375.2	1	106,000	92	25
11	5		TOYOTA MOTOR[2]	JAPAN	88,158.6	3.4	1,184.6	75	(19.6)	98,037.1	93	49,028.1	3	110,534	82	24
12	6		WAL-MART STORES[3]	U.S.	83,412.4	22.7	2,681.0	17	14.9	32,819.0	197	12,726.0	58	600,000	3	17
13	S		HITACHI[1]	JAPAN	76,430.9	11.4	1,146.7	80	89.6	105,257.5	87	34,926.6	7	331,673	11	11
14	S		NIPPON LIFE INSURANCE[1]	JAPAN	75,350.4	6.2	2,682.1	16	(4.5)	422,350.8	9	3,129.5	331	90,132	110	19
15	S		AT&T[4,5]	U.S.	75,094.0	11.8	4,676.0	7	—	79,262.0	111	17,921.0	27	304,500	14	35
16	S		NIPPON TELEGRAPH & TELEPHONE[1]	JAPAN	70,843.6	14.9	767.9	129	66.1	146,776.9	62	49,759.9	2	194,700	32	35
17	8		MATSUSHITA ELECTRIC INDUSTRIAL[1]	JAPAN	69,946.7	13.9	911.0	106	301.3	94,440.7	95	37,481.0	5	265,397	17	11
18	S		TOMEN[1]	JAPAN	69,901.5	8.2	10.2	451	(29.7)	27,014.1	222	1,317.0	426	3,192[6]	490	37
19	9		GENERAL ELECTRIC	U.S.	64,687.0	5.1	4,726.0	5	9.5	194,484.0	41	26,387.0	10	221,000	23	11
20	10		DAIMLER-BENZ	GERMANY	64,168.6	8.6	649.9	149	78.5	60,365.3	131	12,971.9	50	330,551	12	24
21	7		INTL. BUSINESS MACHINES	U.S.	64,052.0	2.1	3,021.0	12	—	81,091.0	108	23,413.0	13	243,039	20	8
22	11		MOBIL	U.S.	59,621.0[E]	4.5	1,079.0	84	(48.2)	41,542.0	173	17,146.0	33	58,500	200	25
23	12		NISSAN MOTOR[1]	JAPAN	58,731.8	9.2	(1,671.7)	496	—	82,820.0	106	16,454.4	35	145,582	50	24
24	S		NICHIMEN[1]	JAPAN	56,202.6	5.1	39.7	430	12.7	24,635.4	239	1,695.1	406	2,591[6]	492	37
25	S		KANEMATSU[1]	JAPAN	55,856.1	5.9	(153.0)	469	—	19,430.5	268	943.1	454	8,431	463	37
26	S		DAI-ICHI MUTUAL LIFE INSURANCE[1]	JAPAN	54,900.4	9.2	1,823.1	39	(9.6)	299,470.4	18	2,101.5	385	71,797	154	19
27	S		SEARS ROEBUCK	U.S.	54,825.0	(0.1)	1,454.0	55	(38.8)	91,896.0	99	10,801.0	78	360,000	6	17
28	15		PHILIP MORRIS	U.S.	53,776.0[E]	6.2	4,725.0	6	52.9	52,649.0	143	12,786.0	56	165,000	41	13
29	19		CHRYSLER	U.S.	52,224.0	19.8	3,713.0	9	—	49,539.0	153	10,694.0	81	121,000	66	24
30	17		SIEMENS[7]	GERMANY	51,054.9	1.3	1,067.6	85	(4.0)	50,579.1	147	13,123.5	49	382,000	5	11
31	13		BRITISH PETROLEUM	BRITAIN	50,736.9	(3.3)	2,416.1	20	161.6	48,699.4	155	17,320.8	31	60,000	196	25
32	S		TOKYO ELECTRIC POWER[1]	JAPAN	50,359.4	15.1	870.8	111	51.6	157,097.4	56	17,232.3	32	43,115	263	10
33	•		U.S. POSTAL SERVICE[G,7]	U.S.	49,383.4	3.8	(913.6)	486	—	46,415.6	161	(5,961.5)	497	728,944	1	20
34	18		VOLKSWAGEN	GERMANY	49,350.1	6.6	91.9	385	—	52,329.1	145	7,090.7	156	242,318	21	24
35	S		SUMITOMO LIFE INSURANCE[1]	JAPAN	49,063.1	9.8	2,061.2	31	1.4	259,372.3	23	2,416.2	368	70,911	157	19
36	20		TOSHIBA[1]	JAPAN	48,228.4	12.4	449.9	216	299.9	62,904.9	128	12,882.1	52	190,000	35	11
37	21		UNILEVER	BRITAIN/NETHERLANDS	45,451.2	8.6	2,388.5	21	22.7	28,438.2	211	8,354.1	124	304,000	15	13
38	16		IRI[G]	ITALY	45,388.5	(10.1)	(1,085.9)	491	—	116,625.5	73	4,572.8	250	292,695	16	22
39	22		NESTLÉ	SWITZERLAND	41,625.7	7.0	2,377.8	22	21.7	34,562.6	191	12,934.4	51	212,687	27	13
40	S		DEUTSCHE TELEKOM[8]	GERMANY	41,071.2	10.6	794.2	121	—	107,485.8	86	23,143.3	15	223,000	22	35
41	26		FIAT	ITALY	40,851.4	17.7	627.3	160	—	59,127.6	132	12,218.2	64	248,810	19	24
42	S		ALLIANZ HOLDING	GERMANY	40,415.2	10.0	593.8	176	82.9	152,722.5	60	7,720.3	136	69,859	162	19
43	27		SONY[1]	JAPAN	40,101.1	15.9	(2,953.2)	500	(2,183.0)	48,634.7	156	11,604.0	71	138,000	55	11
44	S		VEBA GROUP	GERMANY	40,071.9	8.1	823.9	118	65.2	38,628.5	181	10,052.7	90	126,875	62	37
45	24		HONDA MOTOR[1]	JAPAN	39,927.2	11.5	619.4	165	182.0	34,708.2	190	11,715.2	70	92,800	104	24
46	23		ELF AQUITAINE	FRANCE	39,459.1	1.5	(980.6)	489	(619.1)	48,915.7	154	14,308.5	42	89,500	117	25
47	•		STATE FARM GROUP	U.S.	38,850.1	4.8	(244.3)	472	(111.8)	76,670.0	114	21,164.9	21	68,353	165	19
48	29		NEC[1]	JAPAN	37,945.9	14.4	355.5	251	480.7	47,798.7	158	9,104.8	108	151,069	47	11
49	S		PRUDENTIAL INS. CO. OF AMERICA	U.S.	36,945.7	(5.1)	(1,175.0)	492	(233.7)	211,902.0	35	9,484.0	104	99,000	96	19
50	•		OESTERREICHISCHE POST	AUSTRIA	36,766.0	—	1,858.6	36	—	178,322.8	47	26,299.9	11	56,983	208	35

*An "S" indicates an appearance on last year's Global Service 500. Definitions, explanations, and footnotes are on pages 161–162.

RANK 1994	1993	Company		REVENUES $ millions	% change from 1993	PROFITS $ millions	Rank	% change from 1993	ASSETS $ millions	Rank	STOCK-HOLDERS' EQUITY $ millions	Rank	EMPLOYEES Number	Rank	Industry table number
51	S	MEIJI MUTUAL LIFE INSURANCE[1]	JAPAN	36,343.7	13.8	1,455.2	54	(0.4)	180,333.7	45	1,727.7	404	49,050	236	19
52	33	DAEWOO	SOUTH KOREA	35,706.6	15.6	761.1	131	57.7	50,029.2	150	8,034.7	128	80,600	136	11
53	30	E.I. DU PONT DE NEMOURS	U.S.	34,968.0E	4.8	2,727.0	14	391.4	36,892.0	184	12,822.0	54	107,000	90	6
54	S	UNION DES ASSUR. DE PARIS	FRANCE	34,597.0	(14.1)	282.7	276	12.5	160,212.0	53	7,556.6	142	50,448	230	19
55	41	MITSUBISHI MOTORS[1]	JAPAN	34,369.9	25.8	127.0	360	145.4	32,544.0	198	5,517.3	208	28,742[6]	325	24
56	S	KMART[3]	U.S.	34,313.0	(7.2)	296.0	271	—	17,029.0	285	6,032.0	188	335,000	10	17
57	28	TEXACO	U.S.	33,768.0E	(4.0)	910.0	107	(14.8)	25,505.0	231	9,749.0	96	30,042	320	25
58	32	PHILIPS ELECTRONICS	NETHERLANDS	33,516.7	5.8	1,168.0	77	10.4	27,719.5	215	7,305.9	147	253,032	18	11
59	S	ÉLECTRICITÉ DE FRANCE[G]	FRANCE	33,466.6	3.3	227.0	304	(39.5)	125,867.0	71	28,174.5	9	117,575	74	10
60	S	DEUTSCHE BANK	GERMANY	33,069.2	(1.0)	823.7	119	(37.2)	369,810.9	12	13,359.8	46	73,450	149	7
61	36	FUJITSU[1]	JAPAN	32,795.1	12.7	453.2	214	—	42,761.3	168	12,669.1	59	164,364	42	8
62	37	MITSUBISHI ELECTRIC[1]	JAPAN	32,726.4	13.7	423.8	227	120.9	39,594.1	179	9,591.3	100	110,573	81	11
63	25	ENI[G]	ITALY	32,565.9E	(6.4)	1,993.5	34	647.9	54,569.1	140	12,058.0	65	91,544	108	25
64	35	RENAULT[G,9]	FRANCE	32,188.0	7.4	655.5	145	246.7	42,357.4	170	8,005.2	129	138,279	54	24
65	S	DAIEI[10]	JAPAN	32,062.3	31.6	(503.8)	479	(1,106.8)	22,964.3	247	1,521.5	415	49,682	233	14
66	S	CITICORP	U.S.	31,650.0	(1.7)	3,366.0	10	51.7	250,489.0	26	17,769.0	28	82,600	129	7
67	S	INDUSTRIAL BANK OF JAPAN[1]	JAPAN	31,072.3	9.5	298.8	268	47.3	470,446.1	8	16,221.8	37	5,433[6]	478	7
68	31	CHEVRON	U.S.	31,064.0E	(5.9)	1,693.0	45	33.8	34,407.0	192	14,596.0	39	45,758	251	25
69	39	HOECHST	GERMANY	30,604.2	9.9	545.7	189	93.6	26,187.2	227	7,241.7	152	165,671	40	6
70	34	PROCTER & GAMBLE[2]	U.S.	30,296.0	(0.5)	2,211.0	25	—	25,535.0	230	8,832.0	113	96,500	100	33
71	40	ALCATEL ALSTHOM	FRANCE	30,223.9	9.5	652.6	147	(47.7)	51,256.8	146	11,597.3	72	196,900	31	11
72	44	PEUGEOT	FRANCE	30,112.3	17.3	559.3	183	—	26,266.9	226	10,014.8	91	139,800	53	24
73	S	FUJI BANK[1]	JAPAN	30,103.3	19.7	46.8	424	(84.7)	615,189.4	3	22,854.3	17	16,252[6]	408	7
74	S	MITSUBISHI BANK[1]	JAPAN	29,990.9	10.0	254.0	285	(42.3)	592,446.6	6	21,046.4	22	15,701[6]	411	7
75	38	ABB ASEA BROWN BOVERI	SWITZERLAND	29,718.0	5.0	760.0	132	1,017.6	29,055.0	209	4,017.0	281	207,557	28	11
76	S	SUMITOMO BANK[1]	JAPAN	29,620.6	14.4	(2,857.3)	499	(966.7)	613,855.7	4	22,217.7	18	17,247[6]	400	7
77	45	NIPPON STEEL[1]	JAPAN	29,003.8	13.8	(40.0)	461	—	52,360.0	144	9,996.4	92	96,800	99	22
78	S	SANWA BANK[1]	JAPAN	28,799.0	13.7	224.9	307	(46.9)	624,393.5	1	23,406.2	14	14,909[6]	418	7
79	43	MITSUBISHI HEAVY INDUSTRIES[1]	JAPAN	28,676.0	11.1	784.3	127	6.0	46,222.2	162	13,565.5	45	53,048	222	18
80	S	ITO-YOKADO[10]	JAPAN	28,631.5	8.1	709.0	139	31.5	17,131.2	282	7,818.7	132	66,710	171	14
81	S	RWE GROUP[2]	GERMANY	28,628.3E	(4.8)	546.8	187	(2.7)	39,744.5	176	4,925.6	237	117,958	72	25
82	48	PEPSICO	U.S.	28,472.4	13.8	1,752.0	43	10.3	24,792.0	238	6,856.1	163	471,000	4	15
83	42	PEMEX (PETRÓLEOS MEXICANOS)[G]	MEXICO	28,194.7	6.1	985.5	96	1.5	37,843.8	183	22,203.1	19	119,928	67	25
84	S	CIE GÉNÉRALE DES EAUX	FRANCE	28,153.1	10.1	603.2	171	6.6	41,805.0	172	6,445.1	177	215,281	26	12
85	S	CRÉDIT AGRICOLE	FRANCE	27,753.1	(5.3)	1,044.8	88	7.4	328,243.8	13	17,680.6	29	72,500	150	7
86	46	AMOCO	U.S.	26,953.0E	4.5	1,789.0	41	(1.7)	29,316.0	207	14,382.0	40	43,205	262	25
87	50	BASF	GERMANY	26,927.7	9.8	791.7	124	52.6	25,078.3	233	10,158.4	88	106,266	91	6
88	S	ING GROUP	NETHERLANDS	26,926.3	0.8	1,265.3	67	15.8	206,607.1	37	12,533.4	61	46,975	247	9
89	49	BAYER	GERMANY	26,771.1	8.0	1,214.6	73	51.4	27,339.8	218	10,714.4	79	146,700	48	6
90	S	ASAHI MUTUAL LIFE INSURANCE[1]	JAPAN	26,505.5	13.9	716.9	138	(19.5)	135,306.2	66	861.9	458	39,499	283	19
91	S	DAI-ICHI KANGYO BANK[1]	JAPAN	26,500.2	3.4	282.1	277	161.5	622,927.0	2	22,868.3	16	19,061[6]	391	7
92	S	CRÉDIT LYONNAIS	FRANCE	26,388.1	(23.5)	(2,181.8)	498	—	327,995.3	14	5,949.3	191	68,291	166	7
93	S	SAKURA BANK[1]	JAPAN	26,069.0	7.1	225.7	305	6.6	600,513.9	5	21,030.1	23	21,600	376	7
94	64	BMW (BAYERISCHE MOTEREN WERKE)	GER.	25,972.6	48.0	427.3	226	34.8	24,971.3	234	5,033.9	233	109,362	87	24
95	S	FRANCE TÉLÉCOM	FRANCE	25,706.3	14.6	1,787.0	42	110.7	53,918.8	141	25,494.4	12	152,886	46	35
96	S	KANSAI ELECTRIC POWER[1]	JAPAN	25,585.3[11]	—	443.9[11]	221	—	75,868.6	115	13,856.6	44	26,707	338	10
97	56	HEWLETT-PACKARD[12]	U.S.	24,991.0	23.0	1,599.0	50	35.9	19,567.0	266	9,926.0	93	98,400	98	8
98	51	TOTAL	FRANCE	24,653.0	3.1	610.3	168	16.6	25,225.0	232	9,607.6	99	51,803	225	25
99	S	EAST JAPAN RAILWAY[1]	JAPAN	24,643.4	13.5	659.8	143	25.6	83,951.1	105	7,153.6	154	79,709[6]	138	28
100	S	LONG-TERM CREDIT BANK OF JAPAN[1]	JAPAN	24,605.1	12.3	71.3	410	(77.4)	392,681.4	10	12,777.0	57	3,877[6]	483	7

E Excise taxes have been deducted.
G Government owned.
N.A. Not available.
¶ Includes sales of discontinued operations of at least 10%.
[1] Figures are for fiscal year ended March 31, 1995.
[2] Figures are for fiscal year ended June 30, 1994.
[3] Figures are for fiscal year ended January 31, 1995.
[4] Acquired McCaw Cellular Communications (1993 U.S. Service 500 rank: S-70), September 19, 1994.
[5] Name changed from American Telephone & Telegraph, April 20, 1994.

[6] Parent company figure only.
[7] Figures are for fiscal year ended September 30, 1994.
[8] Name changed from Deutsche Bundespost Telekom (DBT) in connection with company privatization, January 1, 1995.
[9] Figures prepared in accordance with International Accounting Standards.
[10] Figures are for fiscal year ended February 28, 1995.
[11] No percent change calculated because consolidated figures this year are not comparable with prior-year parent-only figures.
[12] Figures are for fiscal year ended October 31, 1994.

DEFINITIONS AND EXPLANATIONS

Revenues & Profits   All companies on the list must publish financial data and report part or all of their figures to a government agency. In the U.S., private companies and cooperatives that produce a 10-K are included. Revenues are as reported, including revenues from discontinued operations when they are published. The revenues for commercial banks and savings institutions are the sum of interest and noninterest revenues. Such figures for insurance companies include premium and annuity income, investment income, and capital gains or losses, but exclude deposits. Revenue figures include consolidated subsidiaries unless footnoted and exclude excise taxes. Profits are shown after taxes, after extraordinary credits or charges if any appear on the income statement, and after cumulative effects of accounting changes. Figures in parentheses indicate a loss. Profit declines over 100% reflect swings from 1993 profits to 1994 losses. Data shown are for the fiscal year ended on or before March 31, 1995. Revenue and profit figures for non-U.S. companies have been converted to dollars at the average official exchange rate during each company's fiscal year (ended December 31, 1994, unless otherwise noted).

Assets & Stockholders' Equity   Assets shown are those at the company's fiscal year-end. Stockholders' equity is the sum of capital stock, paid-in capital, and retained earnings on the same date. Minority interest is not included. Figures for non-U.S. companies have been converted to dollars at the official exchange rate at each company's fiscal year-end.

Employees   The figure shown is either a fiscal year-end or yearly average number, as published by the corporation.

Industry Tables   Companies are included in the industry that represents the greatest volume of their revenues. Industry groups are based on categories established by the U.S. Office of Management and Budget.

Credits   Figures for this Global 500 Directory were prepared by reporters Cindy Kano (Tokyo) and Richard Tucksmith.

Corporate Contact Directory

BUSINESS WEEK 1000
Alphabetical List of Companies

The number to the left of the company's name identifies its rank in market value among the Business Week 1000. The numbers immediately to the right identify the company's rank in sales, profits, and assets, respectively, among all Business Week 1000 companies.

MKT. RANK	COMPANY	OTHER RANKINGS		
		SALES	PROFITS	ASSETS

A

MKT. RANK	COMPANY	SALES	PROFITS	ASSETS
25	**ABBOTT LABORATORIES**	118	32	232
	One Abbott Park Rd, Abbott Park, IL 60064/708-937-6100			
537	**ADAPTEC**	882	602	925
	691 South Milpitas Blvd, Milpitas, CA 95035/408-945-8600			
570	**ADC TELECOMMS.**	865	820	946
	4900 West 78th St, Minneapolis, MN 55435/612-938-8080			
425	**ADOBE SYSTEMS**	815	943	857
	1585 Charleston Rd, Mountain View, CA 94043/415-961-4400			
340	**ADVANCED MICRO DEVICES**	447	208	511
	One AMD Place, Sunnyvale, CA 94088/408-732-2400			
622	**ADVANTA**	879	499	448
	300 Welsh Rd, Horsham, PA 19044/215-657-4000			
613	**AES**	840	522	584
	1001 North 19th St, Arlington, VA 22209/703-522-1315			
158	**AETNA LIFE & CASUALTY**	38	139	22
	151 Farmington Ave, Hartford, CT 06156/203-273-0123			
275	**AFLAC**	175	213	103
	1932 Wynnton Rd, Columbus, GA 31999/706-323-3431			
434	**AHMANSON (H.F.)**	319	269	37
	4900 Rivergrade Rd, Irwindale, CA 91706/818-960-6311			
172	**AIR PRODUCTS & CHEMICALS**	292	260	331
	7201 Hamilton Blvd, Allentown, PA 18195/610-481-4911			
920	**AIRGAS**	798	881	852
	100 Matsonford Rd, Radnor, PA 19087/610-687-5253			
64	**AIRTOUCH COMMUNS.**	639	525	375
	1 California St, San Francisco, CA 94111/415-658-2000			
831	**ALBEMARLE**	652	792	722
	451 Florida Blvd, Baton Rouge, LA 70801/504-388-8011			
949	**ALBERTO-CULVER**	606	810	859
	2525 Armitage Ave, Melrose Park, IL 60160/708-450-3000			
118	**ALBERTSON'S**	85	166	415
	250 Parkcenter Blvd, Boise, ID 83706/208-385-6200			
804	**ALC COMMUNICATIONS**	826	700	963
	30300 Telegraph Rd, Bingham Farms, MI 48025/810-647-4060			
276	**ALCO STANDARD**	138	584	401
	825 Duportail Rd, Wayne, PA 19087/610-296-8000			
823	**ALEXANDER & ALEXANDER**	593	983	471
	1185 Ave of the Americas, New York, NY 10036/212-840-8500			
800	**ALEXANDER & BALDWIN**	620	647	573
	822 Bishop St, Honolulu, HI 96801/808-525-6611			
744	**ALLEGHANY**	489	684	414
	Park Ave Plaza, New York, NY 10055/212-752-1356			
584	**ALLEGHENY LUDLUM**	653	913	735
	1000 Six PPG Place, Pittsburgh, PA 15222/412-394-2800			
350	**ALLEGHENY POWER SYSTEM**	411	267	276
	12 East 49th St, New York, NY 10017/212-752-2121			
508	**ALLERGAN**	690	477	738
	2525 Dupont Dr, Irvine, CA 92715/714-752-4500			

MKT. RANK	COMPANY	SALES	PROFITS	ASSETS
996	**ALLIANCE SEMICONDUCTOR**	989	920	996
	3099 North First St, San Jose, CA 95134/408-383-4900			
77	**ALLIEDSIGNAL**	69	79	187
	101 Columbia Rd, Morristown, NJ 07962/201-455-2000			
694	**ALLMERICA PROPERTY**	465	515	316
	440 Lincoln St, Worcester, MA 01653/508-855-1000			
69	**ALLSTATE**	27	136	34
	2775 Sanders Rd, Northbrook, IL 60062/708-402-5000			
179	**ALLTEL**	357	229	350
	One Allied Dr, Little Rock, AR 72202/501-661-8000			
706	**ALTERA**	957	927	987
	2610 Orchard Pkwy, San Jose, CA 95134/408-894-7000			
656	**ALUMAX**	379	812	468
	5655 Peachtree Pkwy, Norcross, GA 30092/404-246-6600			
133	**ALUMINUM CO. OF AMERICA**	106	148	165
	425 6th Ave, Pittsburgh, PA 15219/412-553-4545			
499	**ALZA**	938	742	801
	950 Page Mill Rd, Palo Alto, CA 94303/415-494-5000			
599	**AMBAC**	949	405	374
	One State St Plaza, New York, NY 10004/212-668-0340			
644	**AMDAHL**	524	646	625
	1250 East Arques Ave, Sunnyvale, CA 94088/408-746-6000			
218	**AMERADA HESS**	161	653	230
	1185 Ave of the Americas, New York, NY 10036/212-997-8500			
975	**AMERCO**	609	706	494
	1325 Airmotive Way, Reno, NV 89502/702-688-6300			
741	**AMERICA ONLINE**	958	971	992
	8619 Westwood Center Dr, Vienna, VA 22182/703-448-8700			
125	**AMERICAN BRANDS**	65	63	207
	1700 East Putnam Ave, Old Greenwich, CT 06870/203-698-5000			
153	**AMERICAN ELECTRIC POWER**	194	119	131
	One Riverside Plaza, Columbus, OH 43215/614-223-1000			
47	**AMERICAN EXPRESS**	56	35	21
	World Finl Center, New York, NY 10285/212-640-2000			
987	**AMERICAN FREIGHTWAYS**	870	891	940
	2200 Forward Dr, Harrison, AR 72601/501-741-9000			
147	**AMERICAN GENERAL**	216	203	47
	2929 Allen Pkwy, Houston, TX 77019/713-522-1111			
428	**AMERICAN GREETINGS**	487	413	622
	One American Rd, Cleveland, OH 44144/216-252-7300			
35	**AMERICAN HOME PRODUCTS**	121	31	241
	Five Giralda Farms, Madison, NJ 07940/201-660-5000			
16	**AMERICAN INTL. GROUP**	24	18	16
	70 Pine St, New York, NY 10270/212-770-7000			
633	**AMERICAN NATIONAL**	572	299	291
	One Moody Plaza, Galveston, TX 77550/409-763-4661			
547	**AMERICAN POWER**	906	667	965
	132 Fairgrounds Rd, West Kingston, RI 02892/401-789-5735			
720	**AMERICAN PREMIER**	486	950	379
	One East Fourth St, Cincinnati, OH 45202/513-579-6600			

(continued)

BUSINESS WEEK 1000 (continued)

The number to the left of the company's name identifies its rank in market value among the Business Week 1000. For explanation of other rankings, see page 163.

MKT. RANK	COMPANY	SALES	PROFITS	ASSETS
560	AMERICAN RE 555 College Rd East, Princeton, NJ 08543/609-243-4200	512	528	271
287	AMERICAN STORES 709 East South Temple, Salt Lake City, UT 84102/801-539-0112	36	184	260
817	AMERICAN WATER WORKS 1025 Laurel Oak Rd, Voorhees, NJ 08043/609-346-8200	749	618	440
31	AMERITECH 30 South Wacker Dr, Chicago, IL 60606/312-750-5000	74	47	108
93	AMGEN 1840 Dehavilland Dr, Thousand Oaks, CA 91320/805-447-1000	522	200	588
22	AMOCO 200 East Randolph Dr, Chicago, IL 60601/312-856-6111	19	24	75
116	AMP 470 Friendship Rd, Harrisburg, PA 17111/717-564-0100	265	175	402
712	AMPHENOL 358 Hall Ave, Wallingford, CT 06492/203-265-8900	773	828	837
213	AMR 4333 Amon Carter Blvd, Fort Worth, TX 76155/817-963-1234	44	280	104
535	AMSOUTH BANCORP. 1900 Fifth Ave North, Birmingham, AL 35203/205-320-7151	611	438	121
376	ANADARKO PETROLEUM 17001 Northchase Dr., Houston, TX 77060/713-875-1101	862	836	545
496	ANALOG DEVICES Three Technology Way, Norwood, MA 02062/617-329-4700	739	594	798
422	ANDREW 10500 West 153rd St, Orland Park, IL 60462/708-349-3300	824	799	919
56	ANHEUSER-BUSCH One Busch Place, St. Louis, MO 63118/314-577-2000	83	51	189
964	ANNTAYLOR STORES 142 West 57th St, New York, NY 10019/212-541-3300	812	890	872
284	AON 123 North Wacker Dr, Chicago, IL 60606/312-701-3000	257	177	113
576	APACHE 2000 Post Oak Blvd, Houston, TX 77056/713-296-6000	835	824	627
208	APPLE COMPUTER One Infinite Loop, Cupertino, CA 95014/408-996-1010	111	143	307
258	APPLIED MATERIALS 3050 Bowers Ave, Santa Clara, CA 95054/408-727-5555	491	265	602
86	ARCHER DANIELS MIDLAND 4666 Faries Pkwy, Decatur, IL 62526/217-424-5200	80	100	210
243	ARCO CHEMICAL 3801 West Chester Pike, Newtown Square, PA 19073/610-359-2000	305	232	405
960	ARGONAUT GROUP 1800 Ave of the Stars, Los Angeles, CA 90067/310-553-0561	899	635	552
530	ARMSTRONG WORLD 313 West Liberty St, Lancaster, PA 17604/717-397-0611	380	304	522
488	ARROW ELECTRONICS 25 Hub Dr, Melville, NY 11747/516-391-1300	231	475	563
906	ARROW INTERNATIONAL 3000 Bernville Rd, Reading, PA 19605/610-378-0131	963	878	980
716	ASARCO 180 Maiden Lane, New York, NY 10038/212-510-2000	459	701	431
476	ASHLAND 1000 Ashland Dr, Russell, KY 41169/606-329-3333	109	356	294
2	AT&T 32 Ave of the Americas, New York, NY 10013/212-387-5400	5	6	28
689	AT&T CAPITAL 44 Whippany Rd, Morristown, NJ 07962/201-397-3000	574	518	243
883	ATLANTA GAS LIGHT 303 Peachtree St NE, Atlanta, GA 30308/404-584-4000	635	845	628
779	ATLANTIC ENERGY 6801 Black Horse Pike, Pleasantville, NJ 08232/609-645-4100	699	548	491
41	ATLANTIC RICHFIELD 515 South Flower St, Los Angeles, CA 90071/213-486-3511	52	62	87
573	ATMEL 2125 O'Nel Dr, San Jose, CA 95131/408-441-0311	908	735	901
503	AUTODESK 111 McInnis Pkwy, San Raphael, CA 94903/415-507-5000	873	751	904
103	AUTOMATIC DATA One ADP Blvd, Roseland, NJ 07068/201-994-5000	395	178	476
260	AUTOZONE 3030 Poplar Ave, Memphis, TN 38111/901-325-4600	538	451	772
457	AVERY DENNISON 150 North Orange Grove Blvd, Pasadena, CA 91103/818-304-2000	363	483	612
566	AVNET 80 Cutter Mill Rd, Great Neck, NY 11021/516-466-7000	277	467	574
255	AVON PRODUCTS Nine West 57th St, New York, NY 10019/212-546-6015	252	237	570

B

MKT. RANK	COMPANY	SALES	PROFITS	ASSETS
959	BABY SUPERSTORE 605 Haywood Rd, Greenville, SC 29607/803-675-0299	970	940	997
361	BAKER HUGHES 3900 Essex Lane, Houston, TX 77027/713-439-8600	407	412	454
811	BALL 345 South High St, Muncie, IN 47305/317-747-6100	398	657	617
280	BALTIMORE G&E 39 West Lexington St, Baltimore, MD 21203/410-234-5000	374	196	240
74	BANC ONE 100 East Broad St, Columbus, OH 43271/614-248-5800	142	55	24
709	BANCORP HAWAII 130 Merchant St, Honolulu, HI 96813/808-537-8111	693	459	169
567	BANDAG 2905 North Hwy 61, Muscatine, IA 52761/319-262-1400	796	546	873
312	BANK OF BOSTON 100 Federal St, Boston, MA 02110/617-434-2200	249	150	48
152	BANK OF NEW YORK 48 Wall St, New York, NY 10286/212-495-1784	263	80	44
784	BANK SOUTH 55 Marietta St NW, Atlanta, GA 30303/404-529-4111	860	564	267
42	BANKAMERICA 555 California St, San Francisco, CA 94104/415-622-3456	49	17	4
734	BANKERS LIFE HOLDING 222 Merchandise Mart Plaza, Chicago, IL 60654/312-396-6000	565	411	389
200	BANKERS TRUST N.Y. 280 Park Ave, New York, NY 10017/212-250-2500	164	106	20
805	BANPONCE 209 Munoz Rivera Ave, Hato Rey, PR 00918/809-765-9800	673	445	171
607	BARD (C. R.) 730 Central Ave, Murray Hill, NJ 07974/908-277-8000	670	645	768
871	BARNES & NOBLE 122 Fifth Ave, New York, NY 10011/212-633-3300	552	932	763

MKT. RANK	COMPANY	OTHER RANKINGS		
		SALES	PROFITS	ASSETS
226	**BARNETT BANKS**	337	134	54
	50 North Laura St, Jacksonville, FL 32202/904-791-7720			
958	**BATTLE MOUNTAIN GOLD**	947	938	835
	333 Clay St, Houston, TX 77002/713-650-6400			
480	**BAUSCH & LOMB**	484	931	488
	One Chase Square, Rochester, NY 14604/716-338-6000			
100	**BAXTER INTERNATIONAL**	115	112	206
	One Baxter Pkwy, Deerfield, IL 60015/708-948-2000			
482	**BAY NETWORKS**	724	670	784
	4401 Great America Pkwy, Santa Clara, CA 95052/408-988-2400			
700	**BAYBANKS**	715	485	197
	175 Federal St, Boston, MA 02110/617-482-1040			
448	**BEAR STEARNS**	317	297	30
	245 Park Ave, New York, NY 10167/212-272-2000			
867	**BECKMAN INSTRUMENTS**	707	808	794
	2500 Harbor Blvd, Fullerton, CA 92634/714-871-4848			
285	**BECTON, DICKINSON**	397	271	455
	One Becton Dr, Franklin Lakes, NJ 07417/201-847-6800			
916	**BED BATH & BEYOND**	893	889	990
	715 Morris Ave, Springfield, NJ 07081/201-379-1520			
32	**BELL ATLANTIC**	58	34	88
	1717 Arch St, Philadelphia, PA 19103/215-963-6000			
24	**BELLSOUTH**	39	19	66
	1155 Peachtree St NE, Atlanta, GA 30309/404-249-2000			
728	**BELO (A. H.)**	806	680	778
	400 South Record St, Dallas, TX 75202/214-977-6606			
610	**BEMIS**	573	658	774
	222 South Ninth St, Minneapolis, MN 55402/612-376-3000			
481	**BENEFICIAL**	446	298	143
	301 North Walnut St, Wilmington, DE 19801/302-425-2500			
750	**BERGEN BRUNSWIG**	144	736	558
	4000 Metropolitan Dr, Orange, CA 92668/714-385-4000			
28	**BERKSHIRE HATHAWAY**	260	69	98
	1440 Kiewit Plaza, Omaha, NE 68131/402-346-1400			
851	**BEST BUY**	248	788	567
	7075 Flying Cloud Dr, Eden Prairie, MN 55344/612-947-2000			
526	**BETHLEHEM STEEL**	221	604	296
	1170 Eighth Ave, Bethlehem, PA 18016/610-694-2424			
675	**BETZ LABORATORIES**	768	656	881
	4636 Somerton Rd, Trevose, PA 19053/215-355-3300			
729	**BEVERLY ENTERPRISES**	355	633	557
	1200 South Waldron Rd, Fort Smith, AR 72903/501-452-6712			
491	**BHC COMMUNICATIONS**	883	550	536
	767 Fifth Ave, New York, NY 10153/212-421-0200			
967	**BIC**	867	783	934
	500 BIC Dr, Milford, CT 06460/203-783-2000			
618	**BIOGEN**	975	952	931
	14 Cambridge Center, Cambridge, MA 02142/617-679-2000			
498	**BIOMET**	895	650	900
	Airport Industrial Park, Warsaw, IN 46580/219-267-6639			
415	**BLACK & DECKER**	206	437	313
	701 East Joppa Rd, Towson, MD 21286/410-716-3900			
251	**BLOCK (H & R)**	598	361	783
	4410 Main St, Kansas City, MO 64111/816-753-6900			
555	**BMC SOFTWARE**	919	677	908
	2101 City West Blvd, Houston, TX 77042/713-918-8800			
252	**BOATMEN'S BANCSHARES**	452	179	74
	800 Market St, St. Louis, MO 63101/314-466-6000			
860	**BOB EVANS FARMS**	759	786	912
	3776 South High St, Columbus, OH 43207/614-491-2225			

MKT. RANK	COMPANY	OTHER RANKINGS		
		SALES	PROFITS	ASSETS
51	**BOEING**	26	66	97
	7755 East Marginal Way South, Seattle, WA 98108/206-655-2121			
676	**BOISE CASCADE**	259	978	364
	1111 Jefferson St, Boise, ID 83702/208-384-6161			
516	**BORDEN**	193	998	387
	180 East Broad St, Columbus, OH 43215/614-225-4000			
932	**BOSTON CHICKEN**	988	925	917
	14103 Denver West Pkwy, Golden, CO 80401/303-278-9500			
726	**BOSTON EDISON**	544	443	413
	800 Boylston St, Boston, MA 02199/617-424-2000			
451	**BOSTON SCIENTIFIC**	877	612	914
	One Boston Scientific Place, Natick, MA 01760/508-650-8000			
682	**BOWATER**	582	951	466
	55 East Camperdown Way, Greenville, SC 29601/803-271-7733			
933	**BOYD GAMING**	828	924	795
	2950 South Industrial Rd, Las Vegas, NV 89109/702-792-7200			
973	**BREED TECHNOLOGIES**	922	714	973
	5300 Old Tampa Hwy, Lakeland, FL 33811/813-284-6000			
794	**BRIGGS & STRATTON**	584	472	818
	12301 West Wirth St, Wauwatosa, WI 53222/414-259-5333			
602	**BRINKER INTERNATIONAL**	689	682	866
	6820 LBJ Fwy, Dallas, TX 75240/214-980-9917			
19	**BRISTOL-MYERS SQUIBB**	84	22	161
	345 Park Ave, New York, NY 10154/212-546-4000			
788	**BRODERBUND SOFTWARE**	979	922	995
	500 Redwood Blvd, Novato, CA 94948/415-382-4400			
710	**BROOKLYN UNION GAS**	590	570	546
	One Metrotech Center, Brooklyn, NY 11201/718-403-2000			
419	**BROWN-FORMAN**	566	401	685
	850 Dixie Hwy, Louisville, KY 40210/502-585-1100			
156	**BROWNING-FERRIS**	228	201	268
	757 North Eldridge, Houston, TX 77079/713-870-8100			
942	**BRUNO'S**	362	804	781
	800 Lakeshore Pkwy, Birmingham, AL 35211/205-940-9400			
493	**BRUNSWICK**	388	433	550
	One North Field Court, Lake Forest, IL 60045/708-735-4700			
985	**BURLINGTON INDUSTRIES**	440	549	594
	3330 West Friendly Ave, Greensboro, NC 27410/910-379-2000			
196	**BURLINGTON NORTHERN**	212	160	249
	777 Main St, Fort Worth, TX 76102/817-333-2000			
205	**BURLINGTON RESOURCES**	662	383	342
	5051 Westheimer, Houston, TX 77056/713-624-9000			

C

MKT. RANK	COMPANY	OTHER RANKINGS		
		SALES	PROFITS	ASSETS
347	**CABLETRON SYSTEMS**	754	391	856
	35 Industrial Way, Rochester, NH 03866/603-332-9400			
637	**CABLEVISION SYSTEMS**	725	996	538
	One Media Crossways, Woodbury, NY 11797/516-364-8450			
646	**CABOT**	507	534	650
	75 State St, Boston, MA 02109/617-345-0100			
810	**CADENCE DESIGN**	887	858	936
	555 River Oaks Pkwy, San Jose, CA 95134/408-943-1234			
715	**CALLAWAY GOLF**	878	623	969
	2285 Rutherford Rd, Carlsbad, CA 92008/619-931-1771			
75	**CAMPBELL SOUP**	154	92	314
	Campbell Place, Camden, NJ 08103/609-342-4800			
994	**CANANDAIGUA WINE**	764	921	776
	116 Buffalo St, Canandaigua, NY 14424/716-394-7900			
61	**CAPITAL CITIES/ABC**	167	93	279
	77 West 66th St, New York, NY 10023/212-456-7777			

(continued)

BUSINESS WEEK 1000 (continued)

The number to the left of the company's name identifies its rank in market value among the Business Week 1000. For explanation of other rankings, see page 163.

MKT. RANK	COMPANY	SALES	PROFITS	ASSETS
692	**CAPITAL ONE FINANCIAL** 2980 Fairview Park, Falls Church, VA 22042/804-967-1000	792	542	449
458	**CARDINAL HEALTH** 655 Metro Place South, Dublin, OH 43017/614-761-8700	157	819	585
667	**CAREMARK INTERNATIONAL** 2215 Sanders Rd, Northbrook, IL 60062/708-559-4700	412	608	694
141	**CARNIVAL** 3655 NW 87th Ave, Miami, FL 33178/305-599-2600	493	173	410
245	**CAROLINA POWER & LIGHT** 411 Fayetteville St, Raleigh, NC 27601/919-546-6111	361	204	237
874	**CASCADE COMMUNS.** Five Carlisle Rd, Westford, MA 01886/508-692-2600	998	939	1000
81	**CATERPILLAR** 100 NE Adams St, Peoria, IL 61629/309-675-1000	55	58	126
849	**CBI INDUSTRIES** 800 Jorie Blvd, Oak Brook, IL 60521/708-572-7000	478	785	566
250	**CBS** 51 West 52nd St, New York, NY 10019/212-975-4321	283	217	525
596	**CENTERIOR ENERGY** 6200 Oak Tree Blvd, Independence, OH 44131/216-447-3100	414	231	202
989	**CENTEX** 3333 Lee Pkwy, Dallas, TX 75219/214-559-6500	314	500	569
748	**CENTOCOR** 200 Great Valley Pkwy, Malvern, PA 19355/610-651-6000	995	986	955
211	**CENTRAL & SOUTH WEST** 1616 Woodall Rodgers Fwy, Dallas, TX 75202/214-777-1000	287	165	191
762	**CENTRAL FIDELITY BANKS** 1021 East Cary St, Richmond, VA 23219/804-782-4000	775	474	205
999	**CENTRAL NEWSPAPERS** 135 North Pennsylvania St, Indianapolis, IN 46204/317-231-9200	849	825	905
955	**CENTURY COMMUNS.** 50 Locust Ave, New Canaan, CT 06840/203-972-2000	902	977	635
546	**CENTURY TELEPHONE** 100 Century Park Dr, Monroe, LA 71203/318-388-9000	838	519	646
597	**CERIDIAN** 8100 34th Ave South, Bloomington, MN 55425/612-853-8100	698	619	832
263	**CHAMPION INTERNATIONAL** One Champion Plaza, Stamford, CT 06921/203-358-7000	200	704	222
146	**CHASE MANHATTAN** One Chase Manhattan Plaza, New York, NY 10081/212-552-2222	91	45	13
85	**CHEMICAL BANKING** 270 Park Ave, New York, NY 10017/212-270-6000	72	40	9
948	**CHESAPEAKE** 1021 East Cary St, Richmond, VA 23219/804-697-1000	680	854	759
20	**CHEVRON** 225 Bush St, San Francisco, CA 94104/415-894-7700	13	29	63
740	**CHICAGO & NORTH WESTERN** 165 North Canal St, Chicago, IL 60606/312-559-7000	641	585	532
982	**CHIPCOM** 118 Turnpike Rd, Southborough, MA 01772/508-460-8900	935	912	976
399	**CHIRON** 4560 Horton St, Emeryville, CA 94608/510-655-8730	891	885	755
789	**CHRIS-CRAFT INDUSTRIES** 767 Fifth Ave, New York, NY 10153/212-421-0200	863	699	528
52	**CHRYSLER** 12000 Chrysler Dr, Highland Park, MI 48288/313-956-5741	11	7	42
139	**CHUBB** 15 Mountain View Rd, Warren, NJ 07059/908-903-2000	191	127	102
175	**CIGNA** 1601 Chestnut St, Philadelphia, PA 19192/215-761-1000	35	121	26
612	**CINCINNATI BELL** 201 East Fourth St, Cincinnati, OH 45202/513-397-9900	610	640	624
348	**CINCINNATI FINANCIAL** 6200 South Gilmore Rd, Fairfield, OH 45014/513-870-2000	555	319	348
264	**CINERGY** 139 East Fourth St, Cincinnati, OH 45202/513-381-2000	360	284	239
518	**CINTAS** 6800 Cintas Blvd, Mason, OH 45040/513-459-1200	827	745	892
793	**CIPSCO** 607 East Adams St, Springfield, IL 62739/217-523-3600	721	573	615
455	**CIRCUIT CITY STORES** 9950 Mayland Dr, Richmond, VA 23233/804-527-4000	209	387	512
417	**CIRCUS CIRCUS** 2880 Las Vegas Blvd South, Las Vegas, NV 89109/702-734-0410	634	416	664
798	**CIRRUS LOGIC** 3100 West Warren Ave, Fremont, CA 94538/510-623-8300	744	748	860
98	**CISCO SYSTEMS** 170 West Tasman Dr, San Jose, CA 95134/408-526-4000	547	192	683
43	**CITICORP** 399 Park Ave, New York, NY 10043/800-285-3000	17	8	2
379	**CITIZENS UTILITIES** High Ridge Park, Stamford, CT 06905/203-329-8800	734	415	428
840	**CLARK EQUIPMENT** 100 North Michigan St, South Bend, IN 46601/219-239-0100	691	708	718
623	**CLAYTON HOMES** 623 Market St, Knoxville, TN 37902/615-970-7200	774	638	830
803	**CLEAR CHANNEL** 200 Concord Plaza, San Antonio, TX 78216/210-822-2828	956	904	923
317	**CLOROX** 1221 Broadway, Oakland, CA 94612/510-271-7000	475	330	633
450	**CMS ENERGY** 330 Town Center Dr, Dearborn, MI 48126/313-436-9200	289	317	255
217	**CNA FINANCIAL** CNA Plaza, Chicago, IL 60685/312-822-5000	94	859	49
330	**COASTAL** Nine Greenway Plaza, Houston, TX 77046/713-877-1400	102	272	198
4	**COCA-COLA** One Coca-Cola Plaza NW, Atlanta, GA 30313/404-676-2121	43	13	147
363	**COCA-COLA ENTERPRISES** One Coca-Cola Plaza NW, Atlanta, GA 30313/404-676-2100	184	678	226
832	**COLEMAN** 250 North St. Francis St, Wichita, KS 67202/316-832-2653	755	865	855
91	**COLGATE-PALMOLIVE** 300 Park Ave, New York, NY 10022/212-310-2000	145	115	285
698	**COLTEC INDUSTRIES** 430 Park Ave, New York, NY 10022/212-940-0400	591	547	791
638	**COLUMBIA GAS SYSTEM** 20 Montchanin Rd, Wilmington, DE 19807/302-429-5000	364	259	266
53	**COLUMBIA/HCA HEALTHCARE** One Park Plaza, Nashville, TN 37203/615-327-9551	93	81	183
273	**COMCAST** 1500 Market St, Philadelphia, PA 19102/215-665-1700	576	080	335

MKT. RANK	COMPANY	SALES	PROFITS	ASSETS
		OTHER RANKINGS		
835	COMDISCO	453	762	343
	6111 North River Rd, Rosemont, IL 60018/708-698-3000			
307	COMERICA	415	171	67
	500 Woodward Ave, Detroit, MI 48226/313-222-4000			
780	COMMERCE BANCSHARES	821	537	242
	1000 Walnut, Kansas City, MO 64106/816-234-2000			
96	COMPAQ COMPUTER	96	65	284
	20555 State Highway 249, Houston, TX 77070/713-370-0670			
791	COMPASS BANCSHARES	801	520	218
	15 South 20th St, Birmingham, AL 35233/205-933-3000			
94	COMPUTER ASSOCIATES	410	174	459
	One Computer Associates Plaza, Islandia, NY 11788/ 516-342-5224			
360	COMPUTER SCIENCES	335	506	598
	2100 East Grand Ave, El Segundo, CA 90245/310-615-0311			
548	COMPUWARE	864	750	907
	31440 Northwestern Hwy, Farmington Hills, MI 48334/ 810-737-7300			
894	COMSAT	731	626	571
	6560 Rock Springs Dr, Bethesda, MD 20817/301-214-3000			
111	CONAGRA	21	142	170
	One Conagra Dr, Omaha, NE 68102/402-595-4000			
222	CONRAIL	281	194	235
	2001 Market St, Philadelphia, PA 19101/215-209-2000			
878	CONSECO	490	382	192
	11825 North Pennsylvania St, Carmel, IN 46032/317-817-6100			
148	CONSOLIDATED EDISON	168	83	144
	Four Irving Place, New York, NY 10003/212-460-4600			
885	CONS. FREIGHTWAYS	227	730	502
	3240 Hillview Ave, Palo Alto, CA 94304/415-494-2900			
294	CONS. NATURAL GAS	345	338	309
	625 Liberty Ave, Pittsburgh, PA 15222/412-227-1000			
439	CONSOLIDATED PAPERS	667	575	665
	231 First Ave North, Wisconsin Rapids, WI 54495/715-422-3111			
864	CONSOLIDATED STORES	601	760	862
	300 Phillipi Rd, Columbus, OH 43228/614-278-6800			
381	CONTEL CELLULAR	831	949	540
	245 Perimeter Center Pkwy, Atlanta, GA 30346/404-804-3400			
757	CONTINENTAL CORP.	207	999	130
	180 Maiden Lane, New York, NY 10038/212-440-3000			
215	COOPER INDUSTRIES	233	212	275
	First City Tower, Houston, TX 77002/713-739-5400			
404	COOPER TIRE & RUBBER	570	435	743
	701 Lima Ave, Findlay, OH 45840/419-423-1321			
853	CORAM HEALTHCARE	876	987	879
	1121 Alderman Dr, Alpharetta, GA 30202/404-442-2160			
773	CORDIS	904	821	954
	14201 NW 60th Ave, Miami Lakes, FL 33014/305-824-2000			
221	CORESTATES FINANCIAL	405	254	73
	1345 Chestnut St, Philadelphia, PA 19101/215-973-3100			
129	CORNING	222	218	290
	One Riverfront Plaza, Corning, NY 14831/607-974-9000			
588	COUNTRYWIDE CREDIT	694	464	278
	155 North Lake Ave, Pasadena, CA 91109/818-304-8400			
115	CPC INTERNATIONAL	146	185	299
	700 Sylvan Ave, Englewood Cliffs, NJ 07632/201-894-4000			
620	CRACKER BARREL	767	718	886
	305 Hartmann Dr, Lebanon, TN 37088/615-444-5533			
855	CRANE	518	755	740
	100 First Stamford Place, Stamford, CT 06902/203-363-7300			
939	CREDIT ACCEPTANCE	997	905	918
	25505 West 12 Mile Rd, Southfield, MI 48034/810-353-2700			
558	CRESTAR FINANCIAL	659	366	145
	919 East Main St, Richmond, VA 23219/804-782-5000			
857	CROMPTON & KNOWLES	819	789	916
	One Station Place, Stamford, CT 06902/203-353-5400			
266	CROWN CORK & SEAL	245	427	345
	9300 Ashton Rd, Philadelphia, PA 19136/215-698-5100			
110	CSX	110	97	150
	901 East Cary St, Richmond, VA 23219/804-782-1400			
246	CUC INTERNATIONAL	679	479	823
	707 Summer St, Stamford, CT 06901/203-324-9261			
495	CUMMINS ENGINE	223	249	480
	500 Jackson St, Columbus, IN 47202/812-377-5000			
735	CYPRESS SEMICONDUCTOR	892	791	880
	3901 North First St, San Jose, CA 95134/408-943-2600			
392	CYPRUS AMAX MINERALS	372	369	315
	9100 East Mineral Circle, Englewood, CO 80112/303-643-5000			

D

MKT. RANK	COMPANY	SALES	PROFITS	ASSETS
397	DANA	158	278	326
	4500 Dorr St, Toledo, OH 43615/419-535-4500			
529	DANAHER	599	599	726
	1250 24th St NW, Washington, DC 20037/202-828-0850			
931	DAUPHIN DEPOSIT	900	673	328
	213 Market St, Harrisburg, PA 17101/717-255-2121			
194	DAYTON HUDSON	29	155	176
	777 Nicollet Mall, Minneapolis, MN 55402/612-370-6948			
673	DEAN FOODS	401	613	704
	3600 North River Rd, Franklin Park, IL 60131/708-678-1680			
138	DEAN WITTER, DISCOVER	210	82	76
	Two World Trade Center, New York, NY 10048/212-392-2222			
143	DEERE	113	96	154
	John Deere Rd, Moline, IL 61265/309-765-8000			
552	DELL COMPUTER	300	394	654
	9505 Arboretum Blvd, Austin, TX 78759/512-338-4400			
703	DELMARVA POWER	678	486	484
	800 King St, Wilmington, DE 19899/302-429-3011			
337	DELTA AIR LINES	79	994	181
	1050 Delta Blvd, Atlanta, GA 30320/404-715-2600			
409	DELUXE	502	406	703
	1080 West County Rd F, St. Paul, MN 55126/612-483-7111			
845	DENTSPLY INTERNATIONAL	843	768	906
	570 West College Ave, York, PA 17405/717-845-7511			
911	DEPARTMENT 56	952	860	970
	6436 City West Pkwy, Eden Prairie, MN 55344/612-944-5600			
237	DETROIT EDISON	298	161	188
	2000 Second Ave, Detroit, MI 48226/313-237-8000			
408	DIAL	296	407	400
	1850 North Central Ave, Phoenix, AZ 85077/602-207-4000			
993	DIAMOND SHAMROCK	396	639	649
	9830 Colonnade Blvd, San Antonio, TX 78230/210-641-6800			
760	DIEBOLD	753	703	842
	5995 Mayfair Rd, North Canton, OH 44720/216-489-4000			
199	DIGITAL EQUIPMENT	59	1000	211
	111 Powdermill Rd, Maynard, MA 01754/508-493-5111			
322	DILLARD DEPT. STORES	189	250	358
	1600 Cantrell Rd, Little Rock, AR 72202/501-376-5200			
26	DISNEY (WALT)	97	43	164
	500 South Buena Vista St, Burbank, CA 91521/818-560-1000			

(continued)

BUSINESS WEEK 1000 *(continued)*

The number to the left of the company's name identifies its rank in market value among the Business Week 1000. For explanation of other rankings, see page 163.

MKT. RANK	COMPANY	SALES	PROFITS	ASSETS
574	**DOLE FOOD**	273	685	409
	31355 Oak Crest Dr, Westlake Village, CA 91361/818-879-6600			
505	**DOLLAR GENERAL**	587	709	882
	104 Woodmont Blvd, Nashville, TN 37205/615-783-2000			
144	**DOMINION RESOURCES**	241	129	151
	901 East Byrd St, Richmond, VA 23219/804-775-5700			
185	**DONNELLEY (R. R.)**	218	235	365
	77 West Wacker Dr, Chicago, IL 60601/312-326-8000			
299	**DOVER**	336	318	556
	280 Park Ave, New York, NY 10017/212-922-1640			
39	**DOW CHEMICAL**	31	59	80
	2030 Dow Center, Midland, MI 48674/517-636-1000			
290	**DOW JONES**	451	344	514
	200 Liberty St, New York, NY 10281/212-416-2000			
420	**DPL**	624	376	437
	1065 Woodman Dr, Dayton, OH 45432/513-224-6000			
524	**DQE**	608	371	366
	301 Grant St, Pittsburgh, PA 15279/412-393-6000			
267	**DRESSER INDUSTRIES**	205	312	373
	2001 Ross Ave, Dallas, TX 75201/214-740-6000			
242	**DSC COMMUNICATIONS**	675	372	702
	1000 Coit Rd, Plano, TX 75075/214-519-3000			
113	**DUKE POWER**	242	102	162
	422 South Church St, Charlotte, NC 28242/704-594-0887			
101	**DUN & BRADSTREET**	217	104	317
	187 Danbury Rd, Wilton, CT 06897/203-834-4200			
10	**DUPONT**	12	11	60
	1007 Market St, Wilmington, DE 19898/302-774-1000			
204	**DURACELL INTERNATIONAL**	464	294	509
	Berkshire Corporate Park, Bethel, CT 06801/203-796-4000			

E

MKT. RANK	COMPANY	SALES	PROFITS	ASSETS
585	**E-SYSTEMS**	460	539	684
	6250 LBJ Fwy, Dallas, TX 75240/214-661-1000			
219	**EASTMAN CHEMICAL**	247	188	370
	100 North Eastman Rd, Kingsport, TN 37660/615-229-2000			
45	**EASTMAN KODAK**	60	120	136
	343 State St, Rochester, NY 14650/716-724-4000			
254	**EATON**	181	190	352
	1111 Superior Ave NNE, Cleveland, OH 44114/216-523-5000			
460	**ECHLIN**	425	434	643
	100 Double Beach Rd, Branford, CT 06405/203-481-5751			
899	**ECKERD**	246	676	667
	8333 Bryan Dairy Rd, Largo, FL 34647/813-399-6000			
568	**ECOLAB**	621	583	749
	370 North Wabasha St, St. Paul, MN 55102/612-293-2233			
611	**EDWARDS (A. G.)**	619	423	541
	One North Jefferson Ave, St. Louis, MO 63103/314-289-3000			
940	**EG&G**	589	970	810
	45 William St, Wellesley, MA 02181/617-237-5100			
743	**EL PASO NATURAL GAS**	713	562	518
	100 North Stanton St, El Paso, TX 79901/915-541-2600			
778	**ELECTRONIC ARTS**	861	770	943
	1450 Fashion Island Blvd, San Mateo, CA 94404/415-571-7171			
NR	**ELECTRONIC DATA**	NR	NR	NR
	3044 West Grand Blvd, Detroit, MI 48202/313-556-5000			

MKT. RANK	COMPANY	SALES	PROFITS	ASSETS
302	**EMC**	575	252	691
	171 South St, Hopkinton, MA 01748/508-435-1000			
54	**EMERSON ELECTRIC**	124	71	227
	8000 West Florissant Ave, St. Louis, MO 63136/314-553-2000			
997	**ENERGY SERVICE**	937	856	811
	1445 Ross Ave, Dallas, TX 75202/214-922-1500			
388	**ENGELHARD**	418	458	677
	101 Wood Ave, Iselin, NJ 08830/908-205-5000			
112	**ENRON**	123	137	179
	1400 Smith St, Houston, TX 77002/713-853-6161			
304	**ENRON OIL & GAS**	825	397	597
	1400 Smith St, Houston, TX 77002/713-853-6161			
834	**ENSERCH**	483	598	467
	300 South St. Paul St, Dallas, TX 75201/214-651-8700			
783	**ENSERCH EXPLORATION**	969	894	724
	1817 Wood St, Dallas, TX 75201/214-748-1110			
193	**ENTERGY**	182	144	92
	639 Loyola Ave, New Orleans, LA 70113/504-529-5262			
403	**EQUIFAX**	568	454	748
	1600 Peachtree St NW, Atlanta, GA 30309/404-885-8000			
313	**EQUITABLE**	165	195	18
	787 Seventh Ave, New York, NY 10019/212-554-1234			
769	**EQUITABLE OF IOWA**	795	524	244
	604 Locust St, Des Moines, IA 50309/515-245-6911			
818	**EQUITABLE RESOURCES**	571	726	565
	420 Blvd of the Allies, Pittsburgh, PA 15219/412-261-3000			
895	**EQUITY RESIDENTIAL**	964	887	695
	Two North Riverside Plaza, Chicago, IL 60606/312-474-1300			
688	**ETHYL**	632	527	745
	330 South Fourth St, Richmond, VA 23219/804-788-5000			
962	**EXIDE**	669	903	804
	1400 North Woodward Ave, Bloomfield Hills, MI 48304/ 810-258-0080			
3	**EXXON**	3	4	25
	225 East John W. Carpenter Fwy, Irving, TX 75062/ 214-444-1000			

F

MKT. RANK	COMPANY	SALES	PROFITS	ASSETS
980	**FAMILY DOLLAR STORES**	563	712	864
	10401 Old Monroe Rd, Matthews, NC 28105/704-847-6961			
36	**FANNIE MAE**	33	20	1
	3900 Wisconsin Ave NW, Washington, DC 20016/202-752-7000			
870	**FASTENAL**	974	911	998
	2001 Theurer Blvd, Winona, MN 55987/507-454-5374			
279	**FEDERAL EXPRESS**	122	244	288
	2005 Corporate Ave, Memphis, TN 38132/901-369-3600			
80	**FEDERAL HOME LOAN**	156	52	17
	8200 Jones Branch Dr, Mclean, VA 22102/800-424-5401			
666	**FEDERAL PAPER BOARD**	540	665	490
	75 Chestnut Ridge Rd, Montvale, NJ 07645/201-391-1776			
841	**FEDERAL SIGNAL**	784	809	894
	1415 West 22nd St, Oak Brook, IL 60521/708-954-2000			
352	**FEDERATED DEPT. STORES**	134	332	238
	Seven West Seventh St, Cincinnati, OH 45202/513-579-7000			
998	**FERRO**	627	807	803
	1000 Lakeside Ave, Cleveland, OH 44114/216-641-8580			

MKT. RANK	COMPANY	OTHER RANKINGS		
		SALES	PROFITS	ASSETS
759	**FHP INTERNATIONAL**	325	610	517
	9900 Talbert Ave, Fountain Valley, CA 92708/714-963-7233			
305	**FIFTH THIRD BANCORP**	631	261	138
	38 Fountain Square Plaza, Cincinnati, OH 45263/513-579-5300			
702	**FINA**	306	512	503
	8350 North Central Expwy, Dallas, TX 75206/214-750-2400			
965	**FINGERHUT**	471	815	753
	4400 Baker Rd, Minnetonka, MN 55343/612-932-3100			
843	**FINOVA GROUP**	889	705	295
	1850 North Central Ave, Phoenix, AZ 85004/602-207-6900			
859	**FIRST AMERICAN**	833	554	247
	300 Union St, Nashville, TN 37237/615-748-2000			
184	**FIRST BANK SYSTEM**	461	163	83
	601 Second Ave South, Minneapolis, MN 55402/612-973-1111			
929	**FIRST BRANDS**	665	767	805
	83 Wooster Heights Rd, Danbury, CT 06813/203-731-2300			
220	**FIRST CHICAGO**	229	91	32
	One First National Plaza, Chicago, IL 60670/312-732-4000			
737	**FIRST COLONY**	560	386	219
	901 E Byrd St, Richmond, VA 23219/804-775-0300			
165	**FIRST DATA**	519	308	363
	11718 Nicholas St, Omaha, NE 68154/402-222-2000			
739	**FIRST EMPIRE STATE**	743	473	200
	One M&T Plaza, Buffalo, NY 14203/716-842-4200			
241	**FIRST FIDELITY BANCORP.**	406	145	62
	550 Broad St, Newark, NJ 07102/201-565-3200			
228	**FIRST FINANCIAL MGMT.**	438	375	443
	Three Corporate Square, Atlanta, GA 30329/404-321-0120			
884	**FIRST HAWAIIAN**	837	634	251
	1132 Bishop St, Honolulu, HI 96813/808-525-7000			
160	**FIRST INTERSTATE**	261	84	36
	633 West Fifth St, Los Angeles, CA 90071/213-614-3001			
443	**FIRST OF AMERICA BANK**	480	295	86
	211 South Rose St, Kalamazoo, MI 49007/616-376-9000			
669	**FIRST SECURITY**	487	408	178
	79 South Main St, Salt Lake City, UT 84111/801-246-6000			
629	**FIRST TENNESSEE NATL.**	661	399	201
	165 Madison Ave, Memphis, TN 38103/901-523-4444			
117	**FIRST UNION**	173	60	29
	One First Union Center, Charlotte, NC 28288/704-374-6161			
454	**FIRST USA**	701	410	282
	2001 Bryan Tower, Dallas, TX 75201/214-746-8400			
696	**FIRST VIRGINIA BANKS**	820	470	246
	6400 Arlington Blvd, Falls Church, VA 22042/703-241-4000			
486	**FIRSTAR**	616	310	134
	777 East Wisconsin Ave, Milwaukee, WI 53202/414-765-4316			
782	**FISERV**	829	853	676
	255 Fiserv Dr, Brookfield, WI 53045/414-879-5000			
232	**FLEET FINANCIAL GROUP**	256	107	46
	50 Kennedy Plaza, Providence, RI 02903/401-278-5800			
802	**FLEET MORTGAGE GROUP**	851	761	535
	1333 Main St, Columbia, SC 29201/803-929-7900			
792	**FLEETWOOD ENTERPRISES**	381	580	697
	3125 Myers St, Riverside, CA 92503/909-351-3500			
986	**FLEMING**	45	754	357
	6301 Waterford Blvd, Oklahoma City, OK 73118/405-840-7200			
609	**FLIGHTSAFETY INTL.**	927	648	806
	Marine Air Terminal, La Guardia Airport, Flushing, NY 11371/718-565-4100			
332	**FLORIDA PROGRESS**	376	293	298
	One Progress Plaza, St. Petersburg, FL 33701/813-824-6400			
247	**FLUOR**	127	323	469
	3333 Michelson Dr, Irvine, CA 92730/714-975-2000			
433	**FMC**	266	358	425
	200 East Randolph Dr, Chicago, IL 60601/312-861-6000			
358	**FOOD LION**	141	385	499
	2110 Executive Dr, Salisbury, NC 28144/704-633-8250			
27	**FORD MOTOR**	2	3	3
	The American Rd, Dearborn, MI 48121/313-322-3000			
830	**FORE SYSTEMS**	996	941	999
	174 Thorn Hill Rd, Warrendale, PA 15086/412-772-6600			
416	**FOREST LABORATORIES**	896	543	834
	909 Third Ave, New York, NY 10022/212-421-7850			
708	**FOSTER WHEELER**	436	696	559
	Perryville Corporate Park, Clinton, NJ 08809/908-730-4000			
534	**FOUNDATION HEALTH**	470	933	603
	3400 Data Dr, Rancho Cordova, CA 95670/916-631-5000			
865	**FOURTH FINANCIAL**	823	592	248
	100 North Broadway, Wichita, KS 67202/316-261-4444			
151	**FPL GROUP**	196	118	167
	700 Universe Blvd, Juno Beach, FL 33408/305-552-3552			
956	**FRANCHISE FINANCE**	990	896	867
	17207 North Perimeter Dr, Scottsdale, AZ 85255/602-585-4500			
957	**FRANKLIN QUEST**	946	866	982
	2200 West Pkwy Blvd, Salt Lake City, UT 84119/801-975-1776			
316	**FRANKLIN RESOURCES**	722	246	613
	777 Mariners Island Blvd, San Mateo, CA 94404/415-312-3000			
395	**FREEPORT-McMORAN**	467	659	371
	1615 Poydras St, New Orleans, LA 70112/504-582-4000			
224	**FREEPORT-McMORAN C&G**	617	431	451
	1615 Poydras St, New Orleans, LA 70112/504-582-4000			
545	**FRONTIER**	682	480	618
	180 South Clinton Ave, Rochester, NY 14646/716-777-1000			
520	**FRUIT OF THE LOOM**	429	729	442
	233 South Wacker Dr, Chicago, IL 60606/312-876-1724			

G

MKT. RANK	COMPANY	OTHER RANKINGS		
		SALES	PROFITS	ASSETS
121	**GANNETT**	275	140	406
	1100 Wilson Blvd, Arlington, VA 22234/703-284-6000			
209	**GAP (THE)**	294	205	578
	One Harrison St, San Francisco, CA 94105/415-952-4400			
872	**GARTNER GROUP**	968	914	978
	56 Top Gallant Rd, Stamford, CT 06904/203-964-0096			
630	**GATEWAY 2000**	387	538	814
	610 Gateway Dr, North Sioux City, SD 57049/605-232-2000			
868	**GATX**	636	552	411
	500 West Monroe St, Chicago, IL 60661/312-621-6200			
412	**GAYLORD ENTERTAINMENT**	776	707	751
	1 Gaylord Dr, Nashville, TN 37214/615-316-6000			
303	**GEICO**	385	305	333
	5260 Western Ave, Chevy Chase, MD 20815/301-986-3000			
166	**GENENTECH**	741	446	620
	450 Point San Bruno Blvd, South San Francisco, CA 94080/415-225-1000			
333	**GENERAL DYNAMICS**	342	291	483
	3190 Fairview Park Dr, Falls Church, VA 22042/703-876-3000			
1	**GENERAL ELECTRIC**	8	1	5
	3135 Easton Turnpike, Fairfield, CT 06431/203-373-2211			
257	**GENERAL INSTRUMENT**	457	255	551
	181 West Madison St, Chicago, IL 60602/312-541-5000			

(continued)

BUSINESS WEEK 1000 *(continued)*

The number to the left of the company's name identifies its rank in market value among the Business Week 1000. For explanation of other rankings, see page 163.

MKT. RANK	COMPANY	OTHER RANKINGS SALES	PROFITS	ASSETS
89	**GENERAL MILLS** One General Mills Blvd, Minneapolis, MN 55426/612-540-2311	129	141	301
18	**GENERAL MOTORS** 3044 West Grand Blvd, Detroit, MI 48202/313-556-5000	1	2	6
850	**GENERAL NUTRITION** 921 Penn Ave, Pittsburgh, PA 15222/412-288-4600	808	837	871
288	**GENERAL PUBLIC UTILITIES** 100 Interpace Pkwy, Parsippany, NJ 07054/201-263-6500	285	329	217
79	**GENERAL RE** 695 East Main St, Stamford, CT 06901/203-328-5000	274	95	100
536	**GENERAL SIGNAL** One High Ridge Park, Stamford, CT 06904/203-329-4100	549	508	686
821	**GENETICS INSTITUTE** 87 Cambridgepark Dr, Cambridge, MA 02140/617-876-1170	980	963	921
207	**GENUINE PARTS** 2999 Circle 75 Pkwy, Atlanta, GA 30339/404-953-1700	220	215	576
824	**GENZYME** One Kendall Square, Cambridge, MA 02139/617-252-7500	929	960	865
961	**GEON** 6100 Oak Tree Blvd, Independence, OH 44131/216-447-6000	618	744	807
664	**GEORGIA GULF** 400 Perimeter Center Terrace, Atlanta, GA 30346/404-395-4500	688	450	896
140	**GEORGIA-PACIFIC** 133 Peachtree St NE, Atlanta, GA 30303/404-652-4000	70	193	194
605	**GIANT FOOD** 6300 Sheriff Rd, Landover, MD 20785/301-341-6100	284	557	682
44	**GILLETTE** Prudential Tower Bldg, Boston, MA 02199/617-421-7000	177	88	310
928	**GLATFELTER (P. H.)** 228 South Main St, Spring Grove, PA 17362/717-225-4711	866	985	846
799	**GLENAYRE TECHNOLOGIES** 4201 Congress St, Charlotte, NC 28209/704-553-0038	972	870	960
NR	**GM HUGHES ELECTRONICS** 7200 Hughes Terrace, Los Angeles, CA 90045/310-568-7868	NR	NR	NR
418	**GOLDEN WEST FINANCIAL** 1901 Harrison St, Oakland, CA 94612/510-446-6000	474	276	70
714	**GOODRICH (B. F.)** 3925 Embassy Pkwy, Akron, OH 44333/216-374-2000	439	694	504
173	**GOODYEAR TIRE & RUBBER** 1144 East Market St, Akron, OH 44316/216-796-2121	76	116	216
233	**GRACE (W. R.)** One Town Center Rd, Boca Raton, FL 33486/407-362-2000	208	590	281
323	**GRAINGER (W. W.)** 5500 West Howard St, Skokie, IL 60077/708-982-9000	346	436	663
981	**GREAT A&P TEA** Two Paragon Dr, Montvale, NJ 07645/201-573-9700	100	991	457
238	**GREAT LAKES CHEMICAL** One Great Lakes Blvd, West Lafayette, IN 47906/317-497-6100	449	221	539
386	**GREAT WESTERN** 9200 Oakdale Ave, Chatsworth, CA 91311/818-775-3411	350	251	51
374	**GREEN TREE FINANCIAL** 345 St. Peter St, St. Paul, MN 55102/612-293-3400	852	343	614
17	**GTE** One Stamford Forum, Stamford, CT 06904/203-965-2000	32	14	50
886	**GTECH HOLDINGS** 55 Technology Way, West Greenwich, RI 02817/401-392-1000	770	775	812

H

MKT. RANK	COMPANY	OTHER RANKINGS SALES	PROFITS	ASSETS
230	**HALLIBURTON** 500 North Akard St, Dallas, TX 75201/214-978-2600	188	348	318
879	**HANNA (M. A.)** 200 Public Square, Cleveland, OH 44114/216-589-4000	504	857	711
756	**HANNAFORD BROTHERS** 145 Pleasant Hill Rd, Scarborough, ME 04074/207-883-2911	431	713	788
341	**HARCOURT GENERAL** 27 Boylston St, Chestnut Hill, MA 02167/617-232-8200	327	510	436
459	**HARLEY-DAVIDSON** 3700 West Juneau Ave, Milwaukee, WI 53208/414-342-4680	546	507	831
631	**HARNISCHFEGER** 13400 Bishops Lane, Brookfield, WI 53005/414-671-4400	637	910	587
521	**HARRIS** 1025 West Nasa Blvd, Melbourne, FL 32919/407-727-9100	301	428	489
745	**HARSCO** 350 Poplar Church Rd, Camp Hill, PA 17011/717-763-7064	561	576	692
881	**HARTFORD STEAM BOILER** One State St, Hartford, CT 06102/203-722-1866	813	781	780
353	**HASBRO** 1027 Newport Ave, Pawtucket, RI 02861/401-431-8697	390	347	516
828	**HAWAIIAN ELECTRIC** 900 Richards St, Honolulu, HI 96813/808-543-5662	629	609	322
679	**HBO** 301 Perimeter Center North, Atlanta, GA 30346/404-393-6000	920	883	972
910	**HEALTH & RETIREMENT** 400 Centre St, Newton, MA 02158/617-332-3990	992	782	793
806	**HEALTH CARE & RETIREMENT** One Seagate, Toledo, OH 43604/419-252-5500	809	830	836
934	**HEALTH CARE PROPERTY** 10990 Wilshire Blvd, Los Angeles, CA 90024/310-473-1990	986	795	884
680	**HEALTH MANAGEMENT** 5811 Pelican Bay Blvd, Naples, FL 33963/813-598-3131	874	780	924
639	**HEALTH SYSTEMS INTL.** 21600 Oxnard St, Woodland Hills, CA 91367/818-719-6775	427	571	786
753	**HEALTHCARE COMPARE** 3200 Highland Ave, Downers Grove, IL 60515/708-241-7900	966	790	981
619	**HEALTHSOURCE** Two College Park Dr, Hooksett, NH 03106/603-268-7000	822	842	920
695	**HEALTHSOUTH** Two Perimeter Park South, Birmingham, AL 35243/205-967-7116	642	774	687
308	**HEALTHTRUST** 4525 Harding Rd, Nashville, TN 37205/615-383-4444	316	336	388
717	**HEILIG-MEYERS** 2235 Staples Mill Rd, Richmond, VA 23230/804-359-9171	650	691	721
88	**HEINZ (H. J.)** 600 Grant St, Pittsburgh, PA 15219/412-456-5700	149	122	259
189	**HERCULES** 1313 North Market St, Wilmington, DE 19894/302-594-5000	368	226	462
231	**HERSHEY FOODS** 100 Crystal A Dr, Hershey, PA 17033/717-534-6799	290	337	465
23	**HEWLETT-PACKARD** 3000 Hanover St, Palo Alto, CA 94304/415-857-1501	20	23	106
971	**HIBERNIA** 313 Carondelet St, New Orleans, LA 70130/504-533-3333	888	643	277

MKT. RANK	COMPANY	SALES	PROFITS	ASSETS
471	HILLENBRAND INDUSTRIES	536	565	481
	700 State Route 46 East, Batesville, IN 47006/812-934-7000			
297	HILTON HOTELS	553	452	463
	9336 Civic Center Dr, Beverly Hills, CA 90210/310-278-4321			
37	HOME DEPOT	75	109	297
	2727 Paces Ferry Rd, Atlanta, GA 30339/404-433-8211			
904	HOME SHOPPING NETWORK	643	917	909
	2501 118th Ave North, St. Petersburg, FL 33716/813-572-8585			
441	HOMESTAKE MINING	769	624	710
	650 California St, San Francisco, CA 94108/415-981-8150			
839	HON INDUSTRIES	720	766	938
	414 East Third St, Muscatine, IA 52761/319-264-7400			
214	HONEYWELL	180	220	338
	Honeywell Plaza, Minneapolis, MN 55408/612-951-1000			
461	HORMEL FOODS	338	422	717
	One Hormel Place, Austin, MN 55912/507-437-5611			
648	HOSPITALITY FRANCHISE	926	773	802
	339 Jefferson Rd, Parsippany, NJ 07054/201-428-9700			
540	HOST MARRIOTT	550	969	397
	10400 Fernwood Rd, Bethesda, MD 20058/301-380-9000			
234	HOUSEHOLD INTL.	232	176	65
	2700 Sanders Rd, Prospect Heights, IL 60070/708-564-5000			
210	HOUSTON INDUSTRIES	267	151	173
	4400 Post Oak Pkwy, Houston, TX 77027/713-629-3000			
519	HUBBELL	672	497	742
	584 Derby-Milford Rd, Orange, CT 06477/203-799-4100			
270	HUMANA	293	353	575
	500 West Main St, Louisville, KY 40202/502-580-1000			
969	HUNT (J. B.)	622	838	758
	615 J. B. Hunt Corporate Dr, Lowell, AR 72745/501-820-0000			
400	HUNTINGTON BANCSHARES	615	264	112
	Huntington Center, Columbus, OH 43287/614-480-8300			

I

MKT. RANK	COMPANY	SALES	PROFITS	ASSETS
9	IBM	7	9	27
	Old Orchard Rd, Armonk, NY 10504/914-765-1900			
581	IBP	82	340	593
	IBP Ave, Dakota City, NE 68731/402-494-2061			
829	IDAHO POWER	836	644	543
	1221 West Idaho St, Boise, ID 83702/208-388-2200			
944	IES INDUSTRIES	745	687	599
	200 First St SE, Cedar Rapids, IA 52401/319-398-4411			
595	ILLINOIS CENTRAL	818	468	693
	455 North Cityfront Plaza Dr, Chicago, IL 60611/312-755-7500			
192	ILLINOIS TOOL WORKS	302	222	506
	3600 West Lake Ave, Glenview, IL 60025/708-724-7500			
523	ILLINOVA	534	352	305
	500 South 27th St, Decatur, IL 62525/217-424-6600			
614	IMC GLOBAL	505	663	482
	2100 Sanders Rd, Northbrook, IL 60062/708-272-9200			
723	INFINITY BROADCASTING	925	867	876
	600 Madison Ave, New York, NY 10022/212-750-6400			
380	INFORMIX	869	690	910
	4100 Bohannon Dr, Menlo Park, CA 94025/415-926-6300			
300	INGERSOLL-RAND	239	303	412
	200 Chestnut Ridge Rd, Woodcliff Lake, NJ 07675/201-573-0123			
653	INLAND STEEL INDUSTRIES	240	491	427
	30 West Monroe St, Chicago, IL 60603/312-346-0300			
606	INTEGRA FINANCIAL	660	367	149
	Four PPG Place, Pittsburgh, PA 15222/412-644-7669			

MKT. RANK	COMPANY	SALES	PROFITS	ASSETS
650	INTEGRATED DEVICE	903	675	895
	2975 Stender Way, Santa Clara, CA 95054/408-727-6116			
15	INTEL	88	16	156
	2200 Mission College Blvd, Santa Clara, CA 95052/408-765-8080			
992	INTERNATIONAL CABLETEL	1000	968	853
	150 East 58th St, New York, NY 10155/212-371-3714			
181	INTERNATIONAL FLAVORS	602	296	678
	521 West 57th St, New York, NY 10019/212-765-5500			
504	INTL. GAME TECHNOLOGY	779	418	779
	520 South Rock Blvd, Reno, NV 89502/702-688-0100			
90	INTERNATIONAL PAPER	54	157	114
	Two Manhattanville Rd, Purchase, NY 10577/914-397-1500			
369	INTERPUBLIC GROUP	466	466	453
	1271 Ave of the Americas, New York, NY 10020/212-399-8000			
625	INTUIT	945	974	947
	155 Linfield Dr, Menlo Park, CA 94025/415-322-0573			
672	IPALCO ENTERPRISES	777	536	553
	25 Monument Circle, Indianapolis, IN 46204/317-261-8261			
758	ITEL	501	934	690
	Two North Riverside Plaza, Chicago, IL 60606/312-902-1515			
82	ITT	22	68	19
	1330 Ave of the Americas, New York, NY 10019/212-258-1000			
500	IVAX	640	559	746
	8800 NW 36th St, Miami, FL 33178/305-590-2200			

J

MKT. RANK	COMPANY	SALES	PROFITS	ASSETS
974	J&L SPECIALTY STEEL	766	772	843
	One PPG Place, Pittsburgh, PA 15222/412-338-1600			
468	JAMES RIVER	197	957	245
	120 Tredegar St, Richmond, VA 23219/804-644-5411			
429	JEFFERSON SMURFIT	323	935	478
	8182 Maryland Ave, St. Louis, MO 63105/314-746-1100			
355	JEFFERSON-PILOT	603	277	286
	100 North Greene St, Greensboro, NC 27401/910-691-3000			
882	JOHN NUVEEN	951	741	944
	333 West Wacker Dr, Chicago, IL 60606/312-917-7700			
12	JOHNSON & JOHNSON	46	21	139
	One Johnson & Johnson Plaza, New Brunswick, NJ 08933/908-524-0400			
463	JOHNSON CONTROLS	153	368	392
	5757 North Green Bay Ave, Glendale, WI 53209/414-228-1200			
827	JOSTENS	737	964	889
	5501 Norman Center Dr, Minneapolis, MN 55437/612-830-3300			

K

MKT. RANK	COMPANY	SALES	PROFITS	ASSETS
589	KANSAS CITY POWER	714	504	477
	1201 Walnut St, Kansas City, MO 64106/816-556-2200			
561	KANSAS CITY SOUTHERN	648	503	549
	114 West 11th St, Kansas City, MO 64105/816-556-0303			
72	KELLOGG	163	87	355
	One Kellogg Square, Battle Creek, MI 49016/616-961-2000			
693	KELLY SERVICES	421	723	858
	999 West Big Beaver Rd, Troy, MI 48084/810-362-4444			
615	KEMPER	531	579	146
	One Kemper Dr, Long Grove, IL 60049/708-320-4700			
1000	KENNAMETAL	709	805	827
	Route 981 South, Latrobe, PA 15650/412-539-5000			
371	KERR-McGEE	312	555	407
	Kerr-McGee Center, Oklahoma City, OK 73125/405-270-1313			
132	KEYCORP	204	67	31
	127 Public Square, Cleveland, OH 44114/216-689-3000			

(continued)

BUSINESS WEEK 1000 *(continued)*

The number to the left of the company's name identifies its rank in market value among the Business Week 1000. For explanation of other rankings, see page 163.

MKT. RANK COMPANY	SALES	OTHER RANKINGS PROFITS	ASSETS
108 KIMBERLY-CLARK	150	126	269
545 East John Carpenter Fwy, Irving, TX 75062/214-830-1200			
963 KIMCO REALTY	981	840	825
3333 New Hyde Park Rd, New Hyde Park, NY 11042/ 516-869-9000			
641 KING WORLD PRODUCTIONS	886	627	863
1700 Broadway, New York, NY 10019/212-315-4000			
627 KLA INSTRUMENTS	921	864	945
160 Rio Robles, San Jose, CA 95134/408-434-4200			
168 KMART		14	243	105
3100 West Big Beaver Rd, Troy, MI 48084/810-643-1000			
339 KNIGHT-RIDDER	394	362	510
One Herald Plaza, Miami, FL 33132/305-376-3800			
583 KOHL'S	564	710	822
N54 W13600 Woodale Dr, Menomonee Falls, WI 53051/ 414-783-5800			
333 KROGER	23	234	361
1014 Vine St, Cincinnati, OH 45202/513-762-4000			
767 KU ENERGY	803	622	638
One Quality St, Lexington, KY 40507/606-255-2100			

L

MKT. RANK COMPANY	SALES	PROFITS	ASSETS
718 LA QUINTA INNS	911	851	797
112 East Pecan St, San Antonio, TX 78205/210-302-6000			
683 LAFARGE	541	603	644
11130 Sunrise Valley Dr, Reston, VA 22091/703-264-3600			
761 LAM RESEARCH	810	759	885
4650 Cushing Pkwy, Fremont, CA 94538/510-659-0200			
787 LANCASTER COLONY	748	689	933
37 West Broad St, Columbus, OH 43215/614-224-7141			
342 LDDS COMMUNICATIONS	515	380	475
515 East Amite, Jackson, MS 39201/601-360-8600			
820 LEAR SEATING	329	732	708
21557 Telegraph Rd, Southfield, MI 48034/810-746-1500			
924 LEE ENTERPRISES	890	765	902
215 North Main St, Davenport, IA 52801/319-383-2100			
776 LEGENT	847	763	824
575 Herndon Pkwy, Herndon, VA 22070/703-708-3000			
543 LEGGETT & PLATT	482	465	736
One Leggett Rd, Carthage, MO 64836/417-358-8131			
489 LEHMAN BROTHERS	382	441	12
Three World Financial Center, New York, NY 10285/ 212-526-7000			
642 LEUCADIA NATIONAL	586	660	353
315 Park Ave South, New York, NY 10010/212-460-1900			
649 LG&E ENERGY	729	711	519
220 West Main St, Louisville, KY 40202/502-627-2000			
38 LILLY (ELI)	190	46	141
Lilly Corporate Center, Indianapolis, IN 46285/317-276-2000			
154 LIMITED (THE)	152	146	360
Three Limited Pkwy, Columbus, OH 43230/614-479-7000			
142 LIN BROADCASTING	710	117	445
5400 Carillon Point, Kirkland, WA 98033/206-828-1902			
970 LINCARE HOLDINGS	955	849	986
19337 U.S. 19 North, Clearwater, FL 34624/813-530-7700			
235 LINCOLN NATIONAL	155	181	43
1300 South Clinton St, Fort Wayne, IN 46802/219-455-2000			

MKT. RANK COMPANY	SALES	OTHER RANKINGS PROFITS	ASSETS
472 LINEAR TECHNOLOGY	948	679	957
1630 McCarthy Blvd, Milpitas, CA 95035/408-432-1900			
544 LITTON INDUSTRIES	309	746	521
21240 Burbank Blvd, Woodland Hills, CA 91367/818-598-5000			
663 LIZ CLAIBORNE	444	595	706
1441 Broadway, New York, NY 10018/212-354-4900			
202 LOCKHEED	66	147	220
4500 Park Granada Blvd, Calabasas, CA 91399/818-876-2000			
551 LOCTITE	772	596	840
Ten Columbus Blvd, Hartford, CT 06106/203-520-5000			
170 LOEWS	61	236	41
667 Madison Ave, New York, NY 10021/212-545-2000			
907 LONE STAR STEAKHOUSE	959	888	989
224 East Douglas, Wichita, KS 67202/316-264-8899			
494 LONG ISLAND LIGHTING	339	209	157
175 East Old Country Rd, Hicksville, NY 11801/516-755-6650			
846 LONGVIEW FIBRE	718	801	747
End of Fibre Way, Longview, WA 98632/206-425-1550			
293 LORAL	195	223	337
600 Third Ave, New York, NY 10016/212-697-1105			
470 LOTUS DEVELOPMENT	685	965	782
55 Cambridge Pkwy, Cambridge, MA 02142/617-577-8500			
713 LOUISIANA LAND	738	993	668
909 Poydras St, New Orleans, LA 70112/504-566-6500			
315 LOUISIANA-PACIFIC	344	183	479
111 SW Fifth Ave, Portland, OR 97204/503-221-0800			
182 LOWE'S	176	290	446
Hwy 268 East, North Wilkesboro, NC 28659/910-651-4000			
319 LSI LOGIC	705	484	700
1551 McCarthy Blvd, Milpitas, CA 95035/408-433-8000			
550 LTV	238	439	304
25 West Prospect Ave, Cleveland, OH 44115/216-622-5000			
430 LUBRIZOL	532	354	679
29400 Lakeland Blvd, Wickliffe, OH 44092/216-943-4200			
487 LYONDELL PETROCHEMICAL	272	292	639
1221 McKinney St, Houston, TX 77010/713-652-7200			

M

MKT. RANK COMPANY	SALES	PROFITS	ASSETS
991 MAGMA COPPER	706	574	675
7400 North Oracle Rd, Tucson, AZ 85704/602-575-5600			
389 MALLINCKRODT GROUP	458	476	496
7733 Forsyth Blvd, St. Louis, MO 63105/314-854-5200			
506 MANOR CARE	607	572	707
10750 Columbia Pike, Silver Spring, MD 20901/301-681-9400			
432 MANPOWER	250	586	715
5301 North Ironwood Rd, Milwaukee, WI 53217/414-961-1000			
732 MANVILLE	403	695	398
717 17th St, Denver, CO 80202/303-978-2000			
549 MAPCO	341	615	542
1800 South Baltimore Ave, Tulsa, OK 74119/918-581-1800			
134 MARION MERRELL DOW	340	152	385
9300 Ward Pkwy, Kansas City, MO 64114/816-966-4000			
749 MARK IV INDUSTRIES	567	715	607
501 John James Audubon Pkwy, Amherst, NY 14228/ 716-689-4972			
269 MARRIOTT INTERNATIONAL	130	321	438
10400 Fernwood Rd, Bethesda, MD 20058/301-380-3000			

MKT. RANK	COMPANY	OTHER RANKINGS SALES	PROFITS	ASSETS
159	**MARSH & McLENNAN** 1166 Ave of the Americas, New York, NY 10036/212-345-5000	304	172	394
474	**MARSHALL & ILSLEY** 770 North Water St, Milwaukee, WI 53202/414-765-7700	630	544	168
216	**MARTIN MARIETTA** 6801 Rockledge Dr, Bethesda, MD 20817/301-897-6000	107	103	224
889	**MARTIN MARIETTA MATERIALS** 2710 Wycliff Rd, Raleigh, NC 27607/919-781-4550	850	740	870
569	**MARVEL ENTERTAINMENT** 387 Park Ave South, New York, NY 10016/212-696-0808	846	717	813
248	**MASCO** 21001 Van Born Rd, Taylor, MI 48180/313-274-7400	244	327	372
198	**MATTEL** 333 Continental Blvd, El Segundo, CA 90245/310-252-2000	326	245	507
816	**MAXIM INTEGRATED** 120 San Gabriel Dr, Sunnyvale, CA 94086/408-737-7600	960	876	984
95	**MAY DEPARTMENT STORES** 611 Olive St, St. Louis, MO 63101/314-342-6300	77	77	212
517	**MAYTAG** 403 West Fourth St North, Newton, IA 50208/515-792-8000	310	389	498
375	**MBIA** 113 King St, Armonk, NY 10504/914-273-4545	881	241	319
253	**MBNA** 400 Christiana Rd, Newark, DE 19713/800-441-7048	514	258	208
514	**McCORMICK** 18 Loveton Circle, Sparks, MD 21152/410-771-7301	508	721	657
582	**McDERMOTT INTL.** 1450 Poydras St, New Orleans, LA 70112/504-587-5400	352	833	383
33	**McDONALD'S** One McDonald's Plaza, Oak Brook, IL 60521/708-575-3000	133	42	152
145	**McDONNELL DOUGLAS** J. S. McDonnell Blvd & Airport Rd, Berkeley, MO 63134/ 314-232-0232	64	110	175
286	**McGRAW-HILL** 1221 Ave of the Americas, New York, NY 10020/212-512-2000	378	314	458
60	**MCI COMMUNICATIONS** 1801 Pennsylvania Ave NW, Washington, DC 20006/ 202-872-1600	62	73	125
553	**McKESSON** One Post St, San Francisco, CA 94104/415-983-8300	67	992	419
738	**MCN** 500 Griswold St, Detroit, MI 48226/313-256-5500	545	606	527
310	**MEAD** Courthouse Plaza NE, Dayton, OH 45463/513-495-6323	237	563	339
935	**MEDAPHIS** 2700 Cumberland Pkwy, Atlanta, GA 30339/404-319-3300	939	918	939
913	**MEDIA GENERAL** 333 East Grace St, Richmond, VA 23219/804-649-6000	807	462	808
660	**MEDITRUST** 197 First Ave, Needham Heights, MA 02194/617-433-6000	971	607	653
136	**MEDTRONIC** 7000 Central Ave NE, Minneapolis, MN 55432/612-574-4000	527	227	626
171	**MELLON BANK** One Mellon Bank Center, Pittsburgh, PA 15258/412-234-5000	270	154	59
296	**MELVILLE** One Theall Rd, Rye, NY 10580/914-925-4000	90	207	347
562	**MERCANTILE BANCORP.** 721 Locust St, St. Louis, MO 63101/314-425-2525	668	374	174
819	**MERCANTILE BANKSHARES** Two Hopkins Plaza, Baltimore, MD 21201/410-237-5900	871	577	303

MKT. RANK	COMPANY	OTHER RANKINGS SALES	PROFITS	ASSETS
577	**MERCANTILE STORES** 9450 Seward Rd, Fairfield, OH 45014/513-881-8000	366	505	560
6	**MERCK** One Merck Dr, White House Station, NJ 08889/908-423-1000	53	10	94
502	**MERCURY FINANCE** 40 South Skokie Blvd, Northbrook, IL 60062/708-564-3720	944	600	733
892	**MERCURY GENERAL** 4484 Wilshire Blvd, Los Angeles, CA 90010/213-937-1060	832	641	787
527	**MERIDIAN BANCORP** 35 North Sixth St, Reading, PA 19601/610-655-2000	612	373	137
126	**MERRILL LYNCH** 250 Vesey St, New York, NY 10281/212-449-1000	37	53	10
896	**MEYER (FRED)** 3800 SE 22nd Ave, Portland, OR 97202/503-232-8844	332	880	651
421	**MFS COMMUNICATIONS** 3555 Farnam St, Omaha, NE 68131/402-271-2890	934	989	666
423	**MGIC INVESTMENT** 250 East Kilbourn Ave, Milwaukee, WI 53202/414-347-6480	859	392	670
632	**MGM GRAND** 3799 Las Vegas Blvd South, Las Vegas, NV 89109/ 702-891-3333	758	654	725
624	**MICHIGAN NATIONAL** 27777 Inkster Rd, Farmington Hills, MI 48334/810-473-3000	703	288	229
945	**MICRO WAREHOUSE** 535 Connecticut Ave, Norwalk, CT 06854/203-899-4000	747	884	979
938	**MICROCHIP TECHNOLOGY** 2355 West Chandler Blvd, Chandler, AZ 85224/602-786-7200	961	872	974
150	**MICRON TECHNOLOGY** 2805 East Columbia Rd, Boise, ID 83706/208-368-4000	485	132	605
11	**MICROSOFT** One Microsoft Way, Redmond, WA 98052/206-882-8080	203	38	292
837	**MID ATLANTIC MEDICAL** Four Taft Court, Rockville, MD 20850/301-294-5140	756	764	968
557	**MIDLANTIC** 499 Thornall St, Edison, NJ 08837/908-321-8000	663	219	155
930	**MIDWEST RESOURCES** 666 Grand Ave, Des Moines, IA 50306/515-242-4300	657	628	493
677	**MILLIPORE** 80 Ashby Rd, Bedford, MA 01730/617-275-9200	853	733	891
34	**MINNESOTA MINING & MFG.** 3M Center, St. Paul, MN 55144/612-733-1110	51	37	153
925	**MINNESOTA POWER** 30 West Superior St, Duluth, MN 55802/218-722-2641	802	719	604
431	**MIRAGE RESORTS** 3400 Las Vegas Blvd South, Las Vegas, NV 89109/ 702-791-7111	604	444	647
908	**MITCHELL ENERGY** 2001 Timberloch Place, The Woodlands, TX 77380/ 713-377-5500	717	895	520
13	**MOBIL** 3225 Gallows Rd, Fairfax, VA 22037/703-846-3000	6	26	52
937	**MOBILE TELECOMMS.** 200 South Lamar St, Jackson, MS 39201/601-944-1300	977	962	828
814	**MODINE MFG.** 1500 De Koven Ave, Racine, WI 53403/414-636-1200	716	731	883
362	**MOLEX** 2222 Wellington Court, Lisle, IL 60532/708-969-4550	664	492	714
97	**MONSANTO** 800 North Lindbergh Blvd, St. Louis, MO 63167/314-694-1000	137	105	223
658	**MONTANA POWER** 40 East Broadway, Butte, MT 59701/406-723-5421	674	469	497

(continued)

BUSINESS WEEK 1000 *(continued)*

The number to the left of the company's name identifies its rank in market value among the Business Week 1000. For explanation of other rankings, see page 163.

MKT. RANK COMPANY	OTHER RANKINGS SALES PROFITS ASSETS		
71 **MORGAN (J. P.)** 60 Wall St, New York, NY 10260/212-483-2323	131	44	11
190 **MORGAN STANLEY GROUP** 1251 Ave of the Americas, New York, NY 10020/212-703-4000	114	167	14
854 **MORRISON RESTAURANTS** 4721 Morrison Dr, Mobile, AL 36609/205-344-3000	645	720	913
225 **MORTON INTERNATIONAL** 100 North Riverside Plaza, Chicago, IL 60606/312-807-2000	331	238	486
14 **MOTOROLA** 1303 East Algonquin Rd, Schaumburg, IL 60196/708-576-5000	25	30	116
600 **MULTIMEDIA** 305 South Main St, Greenville, SC 29601/803-298-4100	805	556	833
479 **MURPHY OIL** 200 Peach St, El Dorado, AR 71730/501-862-6411	496	496	523
393 **MYLAN LABORATORIES** 130 17th St, Pittsburgh, PA 15222/412-232-0100	915	501	897

N

MKT. RANK COMPANY	OTHER RANKINGS SALES PROFITS ASSETS		
405 **NALCO CHEMICAL** One Nalco Center, Naperville, IL 60563/708-305-1000	588	532	701
239 **NATIONAL CITY** 1900 East Ninth St, Cleveland, OH 44114/216-575-2000	373	158	69
790 **NATIONAL FUEL GAS** Ten Lafayette Square, Buffalo, NY 14203/716-857-7000	646	605	562
796 **NATIONAL GYPSUM** 2001 Rexford Rd, Charlotte, NC 28211/704-365-7300	804	593	869
707 **NATIONAL HEALTH LABS.** 4225 Executive Square, La Jolla, CA 92037/619-550-0600	712	877	750
452 **NATIONAL SEMICONDUCTOR** 2900 Semiconductor Dr, Santa Clara, CA 95052/408-721-5000	430	228	608
634 **NATIONAL SERVICE INDS.** 1420 Peachtree St NE, Atlanta, GA 30309/404-853-1000	476	582	729
58 **NATIONSBANK** 100 North Tryon St, Charlotte, NC 28255/704-386-5000	68	27	8
754 **NAVISTAR INTERNATIONAL** 455 North Cityfront Plaza Dr, Chicago, IL 60611/312-836-2000	201	513	344
195 **NBD BANCORP** 611 Woodward Ave, Detroit, MI 48226/313-225-1000	307	123	45
863 **NEVADA POWER** 6226 West Sahara Ave, Las Vegas, NV 89102/702-367-5000	751	597	586
435 **NEW ENGLAND ELECTRIC** 25 Research Dr, Westborough, MA 01582/508-366-9011	435	309	334
733 **NEW PLAN REALTY TRUST** 1120 Ave of the Americas, New York, NY 10036/212-869-3000	985	757	845
755 **NEW WORLD COMMUNS.** 3200 Windy Hill Rd, Atlanta, GA 30339/404-955-0045	909	975	637
575 **NEW YORK STATE E&G** 4500 Vestal Pkwy East, Binghamton, NY 13902/607-729-2551	477	331	323
436 **NEW YORK TIMES** 229 West 43rd St, New York, NY 10036/212-556-1234	422	300	439
272 **NEWELL** 29 East Stephenson St, Freeport, IL 61032/815-235-4171	454	325	501
298 **NEWMONT GOLD** 1700 Lincoln St, Denver, CO 80203/303-863-7414	817	589	640
321 **NEWMONT MINING** 1700 Lincoln St, Denver, CO 80203/303-863-7414	816	637	641

MKT. RANK COMPANY	OTHER RANKINGS SALES PROFITS ASSETS		
670 **NEXTEL COMMUNICATIONS** 201 Route 17 North, Rutherford, NJ 07070/201-438-1400	991	984	472
444 **NIAGARA MOHAWK POWER** 300 Erie Blvd West, Syracuse, NY 13202/315-474-1511	258	351	209
654 **NICOR** 1844 Ferry Rd, Naperville, IL 60563/708-305-9500	530	482	534
188 **NIKE** One Bowerman Dr, Beaverton, OR 97005/503-671-6453	262	197	495
813 **NINE WEST GROUP** Nine West Broad St, Stamford, CT 06902/203-324-7567	793	702	958
465 **NIPSCO INDUSTRIES** 5265 Hohman Ave, Hammond, IN 46320/219-853-5200	513	357	390
657 **NOBLE AFFILIATES** 110 West Broadway, Ardmore, OK 73401/405-223-4110	914	946	766
786 **NORDSON** 28601 Clemens Rd, Westlake, OH 44145/216-892-1580	842	803	930
289 **NORDSTROM** 1501 Fifth Ave, Seattle, WA 98101/206-628-2111	271	315	500
99 **NORFOLK SOUTHERN** Three Commercial Place, Norfolk, VA 23510/804-629-2600	235	94	195
346 **NORTHEAST UTILITIES** 107 Selden St, Berlin, CT 06037/203-665-5000	286	191	196
328 **NORTHERN STATES POWER** 414 Nicollet Mall, Minneapolis, MN 55401/612-330-5500	408	263	293
507 **NORTHERN TRUST** 50 South La Salle St, Chicago, IL 60675/312-630-6000	558	342	110
427 **NORTHROP GRUMMAN** 1840 Century Park East, Los Angeles, CA 90067/310-553-6262	160	862	289
456 **NORTHWEST AIRLINES** 2700 Lone Oak Pkwy, Eagan, MN 55121/612-726-2111	119	211	236
114 **NORWEST** Sixth St & Marquette Ave, Minneapolis, MN 55479/ 612-667-1234	179	72	35
122 **NOVELL** 122 East 1700 South, Provo, UT 84606/801-429-7000	462	326	572
891 **NOVELLUS SYSTEMS** 81 Vista Montana, San Jose, CA 95134/408-943-9700	950	817	966
203 **NUCOR** 2100 Rexford Rd, Charlotte, NC 28211/704-366-7000	353	283	568
48 **NYNEX** 1113 Westchester Ave, White Plains, NY 10604/914-644-6000	63	75	72

O

MKT. RANK COMPANY	OTHER RANKINGS SALES PROFITS ASSETS		
155 **OCCIDENTAL PETROLEUM** 10889 Wilshire Blvd, Los Angeles, CA 90024/310-208-8800	116	973	119
283 **OFFICE DEPOT** 2200 Old Germantown Rd, Delray Beach, FL 33445/ 407-278-4800	253	502	583
838 **OGDEN** Two Pennsylvania Plaza, New York, NY 10121/212-868-6000	450	686	424
687 **OHIO CASUALTY** 136 North Third St, Hamilton, OH 45025/513-867-3000	542	567	404
314 **OHIO EDISON** 76 South Main St, Akron, OH 44308/216-384-5151	420	206	221
603 **OKLAHOMA G&E** 101 North Robinson, Oklahoma City, OK 73102/405-272-3000	583	448	474

MKT. RANK	COMPANY	SALES	PROFITS	ASSETS
652	**OLD KENT FINANCIAL** One Vandenberg Center, Grand Rapids, MI 49503/616-771-5000	711	417	199
984	**OLD NATIONAL BANCORP** 420 Main St, Evansville, IN 47708/812-464-1434	933	816	380
655	**OLD REPUBLIC INTL.** 307 North Michigan Ave, Chicago, IL 60601/312-346-8100	511	390	280
742	**OLIN** 120 Long Ridge Rd, Stamford, CT 06904/203-356-2000	393	553	564
604	**OLSTEN** 175 Broad Hollow Rd, Melville, NY 11747/516-844-7800	433	672	821
484	**OMNICOM GROUP** 437 Madison Ave, New York, NY 10022/212-415-3600	499	488	508
62	**ORACLE SYSTEMS** 500 Oracle Pkwy, Redwood Shores, CA 94065/415-506-7000	419	187	621
722	**ORYX ENERGY** 13155 Noel Rd, Dallas, TX 75240/214-715-4000	655	979	426
724	**OUTBACK STEAKHOUSE** 550 North Reo St, Tampa, FL 33609/813-282-1225	875	846	975
905	**OVERSEAS SHIPHOLDING** 1114 Ave of the Americas, New York, NY 10036/212-869-1222	913	953	591
586	**OWENS-CORNING** Fiberglas Tower, Toledo, OH 43659/419-248-8000	313	651	434
671	**OWENS-ILLINOIS** One Seagate, Toledo, OH 43666/419-247-5000	295	621	311
593	**OXFORD HEALTH PLANS** 800 Connecticut Ave, Norwalk, CT 06854/203-852-1442	763	886	952

P

MKT. RANK	COMPANY	SALES	PROFITS	ASSETS
532	**PACCAR** 777 106th Ave NE, Bellevue, WA 98004/206-455-7400	251	313	391
469	**PACIFIC ENTERPRISES** 633 West Fifth St, Los Angeles, CA 90071/213-895-5000	391	339	312
76	**PACIFIC GAS & ELECTRIC** 77 Beale St, San Francisco, CA 94106/415-973-7000	98	54	78
668	**PACIFIC TELECOM** 805 Broadway, Vancouver, WA 98660/206-905-5800	771	601	673
67	**PACIFIC TELESIS GROUP** 130 Kearny St, San Francisco, CA 94108/415-394-3000	117	48	107
483	**PACIFICARE HEALTH** 5995 Plaza Dr, Cypress, CA 90630/714-952-1121	334	558	723
178	**PACIFICORP** 700 NE Multnomah, Portland, OR 97232/503-731-2000	299	138	182
538	**PAGING NETWORK** 4965 Preston Park Blvd, Plano, TX 75093/214-985-4100	858	961	826
528	**PAINEWEBBER GROUP** 1285 Ave of the Americas, New York, NY 10019/212-713-2000	269	873	61
407	**PALL** 2200 Northern Blvd, East Hills, NY 11548/516-484-5400	765	516	767
301	**PANHANDLE EASTERN** 5400 Westheimer Ct, Houston, TX 77056/713-627-5400	234	286	252
424	**PARAMETRIC TECHNOLOGY** 128 Technology Dr, Waltham, MA 02154/617-398-5000	936	666	953
411	**PARKER HANNIFIN** 17325 Euclid Ave, Cleveland, OH 44112/216-531-3000	365	495	561
678	**PAYCHEX** 911 Panorama Trail South, Rochester, NY 14625/716-385-6666	942	869	994
164	**PECO ENERGY** 2301 Market St, Philadelphia, PA 19101/215-841-4000	264	153	135
87	**PENNEY (J. C.)** 6501 Legacy Dr, Plano, TX 75024/214-431-1000	30	50	127
311	**PENNSYLVANIA POWER** Two North Ninth St, Allentown, PA 18101/610-774-5151	383	262	213
426	**PENNZOIL** 700 Milam St, Houston, TX 77002/713-546-4000	402	995	349
947	**PENTAIR** 1500 County Rd B2 West, St. Paul, MN 55113/612-636-7920	521	771	699
852	**PEOPLES ENERGY** 130 East Randolph Dr, Chicago, IL 60601/312-240-4000	623	728	595
909	**PEOPLESOFT** 4440 Rosewood Dr, Pleasanton, CA 94588/510-225-3000	983	928	991
467	**PEP BOYS** 3111 West Allegheny Ave, Philadelphia, PA 19132/215-229-9000	580	629	705
21	**PEPSICO** 700 Anderson Hill Rd, Purchase, NY 10577/914-253-2000	18	25	85
684	**PERKIN-ELMER** 761 Main Ave, Norwalk, CT 06859/203-762-1000	666	671	796
770	**PERRIGO** 515 Eastern Ave, Allegan, MI 49010/616-673-8451	782	779	898
373	**PET** 400 South Fourth St, St. Louis, MO 63102/314-622-7700	537	471	720
815	**PETRIE STORES** 70 Enterprise Ave, Secaucus, NJ 07094/201-866-3600	885	956	631
797	**PETSMART** 10000 North 31st Ave, Phoenix, AZ 85051/602-944-7070	844	947	941
29	**PFIZER** 235 East 42nd St, New York, NY 10017/212-573-2323	136	39	203
261	**PHELPS DODGE** 2600 North Central Ave, Phoenix, AZ 85004/602-234-8100	318	230	382
7	**PHILIP MORRIS** 120 Park Ave, New York, NY 10017/212-880-5000	10	5	39
102	**PHILLIPS PETROLEUM** Fourth & Keeler Sts, Bartlesville, OK 74004/918-661-6600	78	135	186
880	**PHYSICIAN CORP.** 5835 Blue Lagoon Dr, Miami, FL 33126/305-267-6633	736	778	848
497	**PINNACLE WEST CAPITAL** 400 East Van Buren St, Phoenix, AZ 85004/602-379-2500	509	282	261
345	**PIONEER HI-BRED INTL.** 400 Locust St, Des Moines, IA 50309/515-248-4800	557	306	662
180	**PITNEY BOWES** One Elm Croft Rd, Stamford, CT 06926/203-356-5000	321	182	254
777	**PITTSTON SERVICES GROUP** 100 First Stamford Place, Stamford, CT 06902/203-978-5200	481	611	771
162	**PNC BANK** 5th Ave & Wood St, Pittsburgh, PA 15265/412-762-2000	224	108	33
903	**POLARIS INDUSTRIES** 1225 Hwy 169 North, Minneapolis, MN 55441/612-542-0500	761	697	964
608	**POLAROID** 549 Technology Square, Cambridge, MA 02139/617-386-2000	426	461	533
877	**POLICY MGMT. SYSTEMS** I-77 & U.S. 21 North, Blythewood, SC 29016/803-735-4000	855	955	893
781	**PORTLAND GENERAL** 121 SW Salmon St, Portland, OR 97204/503-464-8820	686	509	416
665	**POTLATCH** One Maritime Plaza, San Francisco, CA 94111/415-576-8800	559	800	555
413	**POTOMAC ELECTRIC POWER** 1900 Pennsylvania Ave NW, Washington, DC 20068/202-872-2000	492	281	265
123	**PPG INDUSTRIES** One PPG Place, Pittsburgh, PA 15272/412-434-3131	171	130	327

(continued)

BUSINESS WEEK 1000 *(continued)*

The number to the left of the company's name identifies its rank in market value among the Business Week 1000. For explanation of other rankings, see page 163.

MKT. RANK	COMPANY	OTHER RANKINGS SALES	PROFITS	ASSETS
318	**PRAXAIR**	386	316	418
	39 Old Ridgebury Rd, Danbury, CT 06810/203-837-2000			
356	**PREMARK INTERNATIONAL**	303	285	530
	1717 Deerfield Rd, Deerfield, IL 60015/708-405-6000			
464	**PREMIER INDUSTRIAL**	746	517	890
	4500 Euclid Ave, Cleveland, OH 44103/216-391-8300			
847	**PRICE (T. ROWE)**	905	722	956
	100 East Pratt St, Baltimore, MD 21202/410-547-2000			
334	**PRICE/COSTCO**	40	324	341
	10809 120th Ave NE, Kirkland, WA 98033/206-803-8100			
8	**PROCTER & GAMBLE**	16	15	79
	One Procter & Gamble Plaza, Cincinnati, OH 45202/513-983-1100			
354	**PROGRESSIVE**	416	225	354
	6300 Wilson Mills Rd, Mayfield Village, OH 44143/216-461-5000			
278	**PROMUS**	535	419	582
	1023 Cherry Rd, Memphis, TN 38117/901-762-8600			
897	**PROPERTY TRUST**	967	811	696
	7777 Market Center Ave, El Paso, TX 79912/915-877-3900			
766	**PROVIDENT LIFE**	377	421	120
	One Fountain Square, Chattanooga, TN 37402/615-755-1011			
292	**PROVIDIAN**	348	210	89
	400 West Market St, Louisville, KY 40202/502-560-2000			
492	**PS OF COLORADO**	455	364	378
	1225 17th St, Denver, CO 80202/303-571-7511			
131	**PUBLIC SERVICE ENT.**	185	86	124
	80 Park Plaza, Newark, NJ 07101/201-430-7000			
617	**PUGET SOUND POWER**	628	456	422
	411 108th Ave NE, Bellevue, WA 98004/206-454-6363			
918	**PYXIS**	978	863	983
	9380 Carroll Park Dr, San Diego, CA 92121/619-625-3300			

Q

MKT. RANK	COMPANY	SALES	PROFITS	ASSETS
223	**QUAKER OATS**	174	328	329
	321 North Clark St, Chicago, IL 60610/312-222-7111			
579	**QUALCOMM**	930	926	942
	6455 Lusk Blvd, San Diego, CA 92121/619-587-1121			
711	**QUESTAR**	789	798	658
	180 East First South St, Salt Lake City, UT 84111/801-534-5000			
862	**QUORUM HEALTH GROUP**	750	806	844
	155 Franklin Rd, Brentwood, TN 37027/615-371-7979			

R

MKT. RANK	COMPANY	SALES	PROFITS	ASSETS
890	**RALCORP**	677	769	829
	901 Chouteau Ave, St. Louis, MO 63102/314-982-5900			
197	**RALSTON PURINA GROUP**	186	274	399
	Checkerboard Square, St. Louis, MO 63164/314-982-1000			
525	**RAYCHEM**	554	972	680
	300 Constitution Dr, Menlo Park, CA 94025/415-361-3333			
869	**RAYONIER**	656	674	661
	1177 Summer St, Stamford, CT 06905/203-348-7000			
92	**RAYTHEON**	104	111	257
	141 Spring St, Lexington, MA 02173/617-862-6600			
983	**READ-RITE**	762	832	839
	345 Los Coches St, Milpitas, CA 95035/408-262-6700			
186	**READER'S DIGEST**	359	307	537
	Reader's Digest Rd, Pleasantville, NY 10570/914-238-1000			

MKT. RANK	COMPANY	OTHER RANKINGS SALES	PROFITS	ASSETS
335	**REEBOK INTERNATIONAL**	320	248	645
	100 Technology Center Dr, Stoughton, MA 02072/617-341-5000			
587	**REGIONS FINANCIAL**	702	400	163
	417 North 20th St, Birmingham, AL 35202/205-326-7100			
662	**RELIASTAR FINANCIAL**	539	489	204
	20 Washington Ave South, Minneapolis, MN 55401/612-372-5432			
367	**REPUBLIC NEW YORK**	424	186	55
	452 Fifth Ave, New York, NY 10018/212-525-5000			
681	**REVCO D.S.**	328	822	529
	1925 Enterprise Pkwy, Twinsburg, OH 44087/216-425-9811			
719	**REYNOLDS & REYNOLDS**	733	669	850
	115 South Ludlow St, Dayton, OH 45402/513-443-2000			
324	**REYNOLDS METALS**	183	453	258
	6601 West Broad St, Richmond, VA 23230/804-281-2000			
176	**RHONE-POULENC RORER**	255	180	376
	500 Arcola Rd, Collegeville, PA 19426/610-454-8000			
453	**RITE AID**	254	839	548
	30 Hunter Lane, Camp Hill, PA 17011/717-761-2633			
746	**RIVERWOOD INTL.**	600	937	544
	3350 Cumberland Circle, Atlanta, GA 30339/404-644-3000			
120	**RJR NABISCO HOLDINGS**	48	78	71
	1301 Ave of the Americas, New York, NY 10019/212-258-5600			
438	**ROADWAY SERVICES**	236	908	577
	1077 Gorge Blvd, Akron, OH 44309/216-384-8184			
972	**ROBERTS PHARMACEUTICAL**	984	915	950
	Four Industrial Way West, Eatontown, NJ 07724/908-389-1182			
914	**ROCHESTER G&E**	676	649	505
	89 East Ave, Rochester, NY 14649/716-546-2700			
107	**ROCKWELL INTERNATIONAL**	92	98	177
	2201 Seal Beach Blvd, Seal Beach, CA 90740/310-797-3311			
268	**ROHM & HAAS**	297	240	393
	100 Independence Mall West, Philadelphia, PA 19106/215-592-3000			
856	**ROLLINS**	811	797	959
	2170 Piedmont Rd NE, Atlanta, GA 30324/404-888-2000			
833	**ROUSE**	787	942	464
	10275 Little Patuxent Pkwy, Columbia, MD 21044/410-992-6000			
556	**ROYAL CARIBBEAN CRUISES**	633	403	592
	1050 Caribbean Way, Miami, FL 33132/305-539-6000			
774	**RPM**	700	747	765
	2628 Pearl Rd, Medina, OH 44258/216-273-5090			
191	**RUBBERMAID**	441	279	630
	1147 Akron Rd, Wooster, OH 44691/216-264-6464			
691	**RUSSELL**	647	617	728
	755 Lee St, Alexander City, AL 35010/205-329-4000			
661	**RUST INTERNATIONAL**	510	756	609
	100 Corporate Pkwy, Birmingham, AL 35242/205-995-7878			
509	**RYDER SYSTEM**	226	384	340
	3600 NW 82nd Ave, Miami, FL 33166/305-593-3726			

S

MKT. RANK	COMPANY	SALES	PROFITS	ASSETS
291	**SAFECO**	282	202	128
	4333 Brooklyn Ave NE, Seattle, WA 98185/206-545-5000			
825	**SAFETY-KLEEN**	742	794	752
	1000 North Randall Rd, Elgin, IL 60123/708-697-8460			

MKT. RANK	COMPANY	OTHER RANKINGS SALES	PROFITS	ASSETS
274	**SAFEWAY** 201 Fourth St, Oakland, CA 94660/510-891-3000	47	253	330
359	**SALLIE MAE** 1050 Thomas Jefferson St NW, Washington, DC 20007/ 202-333-8000	343	164	38
265	**SALOMON** Seven World Trade Center, New York, NY 10048/212-783-7000	170	997	7
385	**SAN DIEGO GAS & ELECTRIC** 101 Ash St, San Diego, CA 92101/619-696-2000	468	402	356
923	**SANTA FE ENERGY** 1616 South Voss, Houston, TX 77057/713-507-5000	901	919	737
249	**SANTA FE PACIFIC** 1700 East Golf Rd, Schaumburg, IL 60173/708-995-6000	389	322	306
601	**SANTA FE PACIFIC GOLD** 6200 Uptown Blvd NE, Albuquerque, NM 87110/505-880-5300	907	749	799
68	**SARA LEE** Three First National Plaza, Chicago, IL 60602/312-726-2600	41	242	180
30	**SBC COMMUNICATIONS** 175 East Houston, San Antonio, TX 78205/210-821-4105	86	28	82
445	**SCANA** 1426 Main St, Columbia, SC 29201/803-748-3000	594	378	369
128	**SCECORP** 2244 Walnut Grove Ave, Rosemead, CA 91770/818-302-1212	132	85	93
765	**SCHERER (R. P.)** 2075 West Big Beaver Rd, Troy, MI 48084/810-649-0900	848	843	851
57	**SCHERING-PLOUGH** One Giralda Farms, Madison, NJ 07940/201-822-7000	230	61	367
59	**SCHLUMBERGER** 277 Park Ave, New York, NY 10172/212-350-9400	162	125	233
946	**SCHOLASTIC** 555 Broadway, New York, NY 10012/212-343-6100	780	868	899
764	**SCHULMAN (A.)** 3550 West Market St, Akron, OH 44333/216-666-3751	723	802	878
383	**SCHWAB (CHARLES)** 101 Montgomery St, San Francisco, CA 94104/415-627-7000	658	420	250
522	**SCIENTIFIC-ATLANTA** One Technology Pkwy South, Norcross, GA 30092/404-903-5000	684	734	849
161	**SCOTT PAPER** Scott Plaza, Philadelphia, PA 19113/610-522-5000	291	239	302
406	**SCRIPPS (E. W.)** 1105 North Market St, Wilmington, DE 19899/302-478-4141	614	449	623
531	**SEAGATE TECHNOLOGY** 920 Disc Dr, Scotts Valley, CA 95066/408-438-6550	268	256	450
876	**SEALED AIR** Park 80 East, Saddle Brook, NJ 07662/201-791-7600	845	855	951
46	**SEARS, ROEBUCK** Sears Tower, Chicago, IL 60684/312-875-2500	9	41	23
752	**SECURITY CAPITAL** 14100 East 35th Place, Aurora, CO 80011/303-375-9292	994	898	716
462	**SENSORMATIC** 500 NW 12th Ave, Deerfield Beach, FL 33442/305-420-2000	752	588	671
364	**SERVICE CORP. INTL.** 1929 Allen Pkwy, Houston, TX 77019/713-522-5141	644	426	325
501	**SERVICEMASTER** One Servicemaster Way, Downers Grove, IL 60515/708-964-1300	351	409	709
943	**SHARED MEDICAL SYSTEMS** 51 Valley Stream Pkwy, Malvern, PA 19355/610-219-6300	834	861	932
437	**SHAW INDUSTRIES** 616 East Walnut Ave, Dalton, GA 30720/706-278-3812	371	430	636
325	**SHAWMUT NATIONAL** 777 Main St, Hartford, CT 06115/203-728-2000	434	268	68
343	**SHERWIN-WILLIAMS** 101 Prospect Ave NW, Cleveland, OH 44115/216-566-2000	333	334	580
511	**SIGMA-ALDRICH** 3050 Spruce St, St. Louis, MO 63103/314-771-5765	719	478	792
442	**SIGNET BANKING** Seven North Eighth St, Richmond, VA 23219/804-747-2000	596	393	160
201	**SILICON GRAPHICS** 2011 North Shoreline Blvd, Mountain View, CA 94043/ 415-960-1980	498	355	652
704	**SIMON PROPERTY GROUP** 115 West Washington St, Indianapolis, IN 46204/317-636-1600	868	835	554
592	**SNAP-ON** 2801 80th St, Kenosha, WI 53141/414-656-5200	626	523	712
801	**SOLECTRON** 847 Gibraltar Dr, Milpitas, CA 95035/408-957-8500	523	716	800
390	**SONAT** 1900 Fifth Ave North, Birmingham, AL 35203/205-325-3800	495	404	417
447	**SONOCO PRODUCTS** North Second St, Hartsville, SC 29550/803-383-7000	428	432	601
63	**SOUTHERN** 64 Perimeter Center East, Atlanta, GA 30346/404-393-0650	135	49	81
808	**SOUTHERN NATIONAL** 500 North Chestnut St, Lumberton, NC 28358/910-671-2000	797	481	228
440	**SO. NEW ENGLAND TEL.** 227 Church St, New Haven, CT 06510/203-771-5200	506	350	420
351	**SOUTHERN PACIFIC RAIL** One Market Plaza, San Francisco, CA 94105/415-541-1000	330	257	381
533	**SOUTHLAND** 2711 North Haskell Ave, Dallas, TX 75204/214-828-7011	159	551	579
542	**SOUTHTRUST** 420 North 20th St, Birmingham, AL 35203/205-254-5000	597	359	115
384	**SOUTHWEST AIRLINES** 2702 Love Field Dr, Dallas, TX 75235/214-904-4000	399	346	470
701	**SOUTHWESTERN PS** 600 South Tyler St, Amarillo, TX 79101/806-378-2121	730	529	611
842	**SPELLING ENTERTAINMENT** 5700 Wilshire Blvd, Los Angeles, CA 90036/213-965-5700	897	901	770
731	**SPIEGEL** 3500 Lacey Rd, Downers Grove, IL 60515/708-986-8800	347	899	492
84	**SPRINT** 2330 Shawnee Mission Pkwy, Westwood, KS 66205/ 913-624-3000	73	64	142
887	**SPS TRANSACTION** 2500 Lake Cook Rd, Riverwoods, IL 60015/708-405-0200	941	852	816
512	**ST. JOE PAPER** 1650 Prudential Dr, Jacksonville, FL 32207/904-396-6600	778	829	660
541	**ST. JUDE MEDICAL** One Lillehei Plaza, St. Paul, MN 55117/612-483-2000	912	614	775
240	**ST. PAUL** 385 Washington St, St. Paul, MN 55102/612-221-7911	225	149	117
836	**STANDARD FEDERAL BANK** 2600 West Big Beaver Rd, Troy, MI 48084/810-643-9600	728	457	184
515	**STANLEY WORKS** 1000 Stanley Dr, New Britain, CT 06053/203-225-5111	404	442	632
578	**STAPLES** 100 Pennsylvania Ave, Framingham, MA 01701/508-370-8500	463	841	769
659	**STAR BANC** 425 Walnut St, Cincinnati, OH 45202/513-632-4000	785	463	214
902	**STARBUCKS** 2401 Utah Ave South, Seattle, WA 98124/206-447-1575	918	929	922

(continued)

BUSINESS WEEK 1000 *(continued)*

The number to the left of the company's name identifies its rank in market value among the Business Week 1000. For explanation of other rankings, see page 163.

MKT. RANK	COMPANY	SALES	PROFITS	ASSETS
366	STATE STREET BOSTON	479	311	96
	225 Franklin St, Boston, MA 02110/617-786-3000			
901	STERLING SOFTWARE	857	959	875
	8080 North Central Expwy, Dallas, TX 75206/214-891-8600			
747	STEWART & STEVENSON	649	692	789
	2707 North Loop West, Houston, TX 77008/713-868-7700			
446	STONE CONTAINER	187	988	262
	150 North Michigan Ave, Chicago, IL 60601/312-346-6600			
690	STOP & SHOP	280	616	619
	1385 Hancock St, Quincy, MA 02169/617-380-8000			
826	STORAGE TECHNOLOGY	526	834	600
	2270 South 88th St, Louisville, CO 80028/303-673-5151			
640	STRATACOM	976	906	988
	1400 Parkmoor Ave, San Jose, CA 95126/408-294-7600			
449	STRYKER	781	661	817
	2725 Fairfield Rd, Kalamazoo, MI 49002/616-385-2600			
320	SUN	105	533	273
	1801 Market St, Philadelphia, PA 19103/215-977-3000			
809	SUN HEALTHCARE GROUP	814	882	734
	5131 Masthead St NE, Albuquerque, NM 87109/505-821-3355			
327	SUN MICROSYSTEMS	199	247	460
	2550 Garcia Ave, Mountain View, CA 94043/415-960-1300			
591	SUNAMERICA	697	363	140
	1999 Ave of the Stars, Los Angeles, CA 90067/310-772-6000			
475	SUNBEAM-OSTER	625	494	730
	200 East Las Olas Blvd, Fort Lauderdale, FL 33301/ 305-767-2100			
590	SUNDSTRAND	577	540	656
	4949 Harrison Ave, Rockford, IL 61125/815-226-6000			
953	SUNGARD DATA SYSTEMS	884	823	903
	1285 Drummers Lane, Wayne, PA 19087/610-341-8700			
149	SUNTRUST BANKS	322	128	53
	25 Park Place NE, Atlanta, GA 30303/404-588-7711			
926	SUPERIOR INDUSTRIES	872	752	937
	7800 Woodley Ave, Van Nuys, CA 91406/818-781-4973			
513	SUPERVALU	42	777	362
	11840 Valley View Rd, Eden Prairie, MN 55344/612-828-4000			
922	SURGICAL CARE AFFILIATES	943	875	949
	102 Woodmont Blvd, Nashville, TN 37205/615-385-3541			
349	SYBASE	732	568	838
	6475 Christie Ave, Emeryville, CA 94608/510-922-3500			
912	SYBRON	880	818	877
	411 East Wisconsin Ave, Milwaukee, WI 53202/414-274-6600			
995	SYMANTEC	924	897	985
	10201 Torre Ave, Cupertino, CA 95014/408-253-9600			
898	SYNOPSYS	954	916	977
	700 East Middlefield Rd, Mountain View, CA 94043/ 415-962-5000			
626	SYNOVUS FINANCIAL	794	578	287
	901 Front Ave, Columbus, GA 31901/706-649-2311			
187	SYSCO	87	270	461
	1390 Enclave Pkwy, Houston, TX 77077/713-584-1390			

T

MKT. RANK	COMPANY	SALES	PROFITS	ASSETS
736	TALBOTS	726	787	887
	175 Beal St, Hingham, MA 02043/617-749-7600			
564	TAMBRANDS	799	561	926
	777 Westchester Ave, White Plains, NY 10604/914-696-6000			

MKT. RANK	COMPANY	SALES	PROFITS	ASSETS
477	TANDEM COMPUTERS	442	345	616
	19333 Vallco Pkwy, Cupertino, CA 95014/408-285-6000			
370	TANDY	215	287	435
	1800 One Tandy Center, Fort Worth, TX 76102/817-390-3700			
391	TECO ENERGY	585	379	430
	702 North Franklin St, Tampa, FL 33602/813-228-4111			
785	TECUMSEH PRODUCTS	548	455	698
	100 East Patterson St, Tecumseh, MI 49286/517-423-8411			
771	TEKTRONIX	578	652	744
	26600 SW Pkwy, Wilsonville, OR 97070/503-627-7111			
66	TELE-COMMUNICATIONS	243	831	109
	5619 DTC Pkwy, Englewood, CO 80111/303-267-5500			
651	TELEDYNE	417	954	669
	1901 Ave of the Stars, Los Angeles, CA 90067/310-277-3311			
394	TELEPHONE & DATA	760	727	487
	30 North Lasalle St, Chicago, IL 60602/312-630-1900			
414	TELLABS	854	662	929
	4951 Indiana Ave, Lisle, IL 60532/708-969-8800			
357	TEMPLE-INLAND	358	425	172
	303 South Temple Dr, Diboll, TX 75941/409-829-5511			
377	TENET HEALTHCARE	384	302	432
	2700 Colorado Ave, Santa Monica, CA 90404/310-998-8000			
104	TENNECO	81	101	166
	1010 Milam St, Houston, TX 77002/713-757-2131			
635	TERADYNE	783	668	847
	321 Harrison Ave, Boston, MA 02118/617-482-2700			
950	TERRA INDUSTRIES	516	753	815
	600 Fourth St, Sioux City, IA 51101/712-277-1340			
49	TEXACO	15	56	84
	2000 Westchester Ave, White Plains, NY 10650/914-253-4000			
130	TEXAS INSTRUMENTS	101	90	263
	13500 North Central Expwy, Dallas, TX 75265/214-995-2011			
127	TEXAS UTILITIES	192	99	99
	1601 Bryan St, Dallas, TX 75201/214-812-4600			
206	TEXTRON	108	156	101
	40 Westminster St, Providence, RI 02903/401-421-2800			
398	THERMO ELECTRON	556	531	456
	81 Wyman St, Waltham, MA 02254/617-622-1000			
598	THERMO INSTRUMENT	800	758	754
	504 Airport Rd, Santa Fe, NM 87504/505-438-3171			
643	THOMAS & BETTS	654	948	713
	1555 Lynnfield Rd, Memphis, TN 38119/901-682-7766			
295	3COM	671	976	854
	5400 Bayfront Plaza, Santa Clara, CA 95052/408-764-5000			
775	TIDEWATER	841	826	773
	1440 Canal St, New Orleans, LA 70112/504-568-1010			
647	TIG HOLDINGS	497	776	283
	65 East 55th St, New York, NY 10022/212-446-2700			
55	TIME WARNER	148	981	122
	75 Rockefeller Plaza, New York, NY 10019/212-484-8000			
402	TIMES MIRROR	311	440	377
	Times Mirror Square, Los Angeles, CA 90053/213-237-5000			
727	TIMKEN	472	683	596
	1835 Dueber Ave SW, Canton, OH 44706/216-438-3000			
812	TJX	278	514	648
	770 Cochituate Rd, Framingham, MA 01701/508-390-1000			

MKT. RANK	COMPANY	OTHER RANKINGS SALES	PROFITS	ASSETS
988	TOOTSIE ROLL INDUSTRIES	928	850	948
	7401 South Cicero Ave, Chicago, IL 60629/312-838-3400			
331	TORCHMARK	473	233	231
	2001 Third Ave South, Birmingham, AL 35233/205-325-4200			
763	TOSCO	169	587	610
	72 Cummings Point Rd, Stamford, CT 06902/203-977-1000			
721	TOTAL SYSTEM SERVICES	965	902	993
	1200 Sixth Ave, Columbus, GA 31901/706-649-2310			
119	TOYS 'R' US	128	131	253
	461 From Rd, Paramus, NJ 07652/201-262-7800			
271	TRANSAMERICA	198	159	56
	600 Montgomery St, San Francisco, CA 94111/415-983-4000			
636	TRANSATLANTIC HOLDINGS	696	541	423
	80 Pine St, New York, NY 10005/212-770-2000			
990	TRANSCO ENERGY	367	936	396
	2800 Post Oak Blvd, Houston, TX 77056/713-439-2000			
900	TRANSTEXAS GAS	916	930	874
	363 North Sam Houston Pkwy East, Houston, TX 77060/ 713-447-3111			
70	TRAVELERS	34	36	15
	65 East 55th St, New York, NY 10022/212-891-8900			
277	TRIBUNE	445	266	473
	435 North Michigan Ave, Chicago, IL 60611/312-222-9100			
915	TRIMAS	839	793	868
	315 East Eisenhower Pkwy, Ann Arbor, MI 48108/313-747-7025			
628	TRINITY INDUSTRIES	448	620	681
	2525 Stemmons Fwy, Dallas, TX 75207/214-631-4420			
951	TRINOVA	494	693	756
	3000 Strayer, Maumee, OH 43537/419-867-2200			
730	TRITON ENERGY	999	967	861
	6688 North Central Expwy, Dallas, TX 75206/214-691-5200			
227	TRW	120	189	300
	1900 Richmond Rd, Cleveland, OH 44124/216-291-7000			
256	TURNER BROADCASTING	369	814	395
	100 International Blvd, Atlanta, GA 30303/404-827-1700			
262	TYCO INTERNATIONAL	276	398	441
	One Tyco Park, Exeter, NH 03833/603-778-9700			
282	TYSON FOODS	202	944	408
	2210 West Oaklawn Dr, Springdale, AR 72762/501-290-4000			

U

MKT. RANK	COMPANY	OTHER RANKINGS SALES	PROFITS	ASSETS
396	U.S. BANCORP	469	388	95
	111 SW 5th Ave, Portland, OR 97204/503-275-6111			
368	U.S. CELLULAR	917	923	659
	8410 West Bryn Mawr, Chicago, IL 60631/312-399-8900			
137	U.S. HEALTHCARE	354	168	672
	980 Jolly Rd, Blue Bell, PA 19422/215-628-4800			
873	U.S. SHOE	400	871	727
	One Eastwood Dr, Cincinnati, OH 45227/513-527-7000			
699	U.S. SURGICAL	695	909	732
	150 Glover Ave, Norwalk, CT 06856/203-845-1000			
705	UAL	57	632	185
	1200 East Algonquin Rd, Elk Grove Village, IL 60007/ 708-952-4000			
572	UJB FINANCIAL	651	424	133
	301 Carnegie Center, Princeton, NJ 08543/609-987-3200			
807	ULTRAMAR	409	724	629
	Two Pickwick Plaza, Greenwich, CT 06830/203-622-7000			
177	UNICOM	172	162	91
	10 South Dearborn St, Chicago, IL 60690/312-394-4321			
485	UNIFI	562	591	760
	7201 West Friendly Rd, Greensboro, NC 27410/910-294-4410			

MKT. RANK	COMPANY	OTHER RANKINGS SALES	PROFITS	ASSETS
697	UNION BANK	638	642	123
	350 California St, San Francisco, CA 94104/415-445-0200			
281	UNION CAMP	308	460	351
	1600 Valley Rd, Wayne, NJ 07470/201-628-2000			
229	UNION CARBIDE	219	169	332
	39 Old Ridgebury Rd, Danbury, CT 06817/203-794-2000			
259	UNION ELECTRIC	456	199	272
	1901 Chouteau Ave, St. Louis, MO 63103/314-621-3222			
78	UNION PACIFIC	143	57	129
	Eighth & Eaton Ave, Bethlehem, PA 18018/610-861-3200			
539	UNION TEXAS PETROLEUM	757	688	688
	1330 Post Oak Blvd, Houston, TX 77056/713-623-6544			
554	UNISYS	147	487	256
	Township Line & Union Meeting Rds, Blue Bell, PA 19424/215-986-4011			
772	UNITED ASSET MGMT.	856	738	777
	One International Place, Boston, MA 02110/617-330-8900			
124	UNITED HEALTHCARE	279	216	421
	9900 Bren Rd East, Minnetonka, MN 55343/612-936-1300			
109	UNITED TECHNOLOGIES	28	114	132
	One Financial Plaza, Hartford, CT 06103/203-728-7000			
410	UNITRIN	581	396	359
	One East Wacker Dr, Chicago, IL 60601/312-661-4600			
917	UNIVERSAL FOODS	704	664	819
	433 East Michigan St, Milwaukee, WI 53202/414-271-6755			
135	UNOCAL	140	447	215
	1201 West Fifth St, Los Angeles, CA 90017/213-977-7600			
326	UNUM	288	381	158
	2211 Congress St, Portland, ME 04122/207-770-2211			
157	UPJOHN	315	139	324
	7000 Portage Rd, Kalamazoo, MI 49001/616-323-4000			
40	US WEST	95	33	90
	7800 East Orchard Rd, Englewood, CO 80111/303-793-6500			
616	USF&G	324	273	148
	100 Light St, Baltimore, MD 21202/410-547-3000			
751	USG	432	982	524
	125 South Franklin St, Chicago, IL 60606/312-606-4000			
875	USLIFE	520	535	264
	125 Maiden Lane, New York, NY 10038/212-709-6000			
167	UST	613	170	820
	100 West Putnam Ave, Greenwich, CT 06830/203-661-1100			
212	USX-MARATHON GROUP	71	198	190
	600 Grant St, Pittsburgh, PA 15219/412-433-1121			
382	USX-U.S. STEEL GROUP	178	320	274
	600 Grant St, Pittsburgh, PA 15219/412-433-1121			
645	UTILICORP UNITED	551	545	444
	911 Main St, Kansas City, MO 64105/816-421-6600			

V

MKT. RANK	COMPANY	OTHER RANKINGS SALES	PROFITS	ASSETS
978	VALASSIS COMMUNS.	830	945	971
	36111 Schoolcraft Rd, Livonia, MI 48150/313-591-3000			
952	VALERO ENERGY	488	892	485
	530 McCullough Ave, San Antonio, TX 78215/512-246-2000			
848	VALHI	727	907	809
	5430 LBJ Fwy, Dallas, TX 75240/214-233-1700			
968	VALLEY NATIONAL	940	737	403
	1445 Valley Rd, Wayne, NJ 07470/201-305-8800			
954	VALSPAR	740	813	935
	1101 Third St South, Minneapolis, MN 55415/612-332-7371			
580	VALUE HEALTH	683	796	888
	22 Waterville Rd, Avon, CT 06001/203-678-3400			

(continued)

BUSINESS WEEK 1000 *(continued)*

The number to the left of the company's name identifies its rank in market value among the Business Week 1000. For explanation of other rankings, see page 163.

MKT. RANK	COMPANY	SALES	PROFITS	ASSETS
768	**VANGUARD CELLULAR**	973	958	915
	2002 Pisgah Church Rd, Greensboro, NC 27455/910-282-3690			
674	**VARIAN ASSOCIATES**	525	569	757
	3050 Hansen Way, Palo Alto, CA 94304/415-493-4000			
565	**VARITY**	423	490	589
	672 Delaware Ave, Buffalo, NY 14209/716-888-8000			
387	**VASTAR RESOURCES**	517	395	642
	15375 Memorial Dr, Houston, TX 77079/713-584-6000			
919	**VENCOR**	894	874	928
	400 West Market St, Louisville, KY 40202/502-569-7300			
306	**VF**	213	224	429
	1047 North Park Rd, Wyomissing, PA 19610/610-378-1151			
50	**VIACOM**	151	429	77
	1515 Broadway, New York, NY 10036/212-258-6000			
685	**VIKING OFFICE PRODUCTS**	786	847	967
	13809 South Figueroa St, Los Angeles, CA 90061/213-321-4493			
621	**VISHAY INTERTECHNOLOGY**	681	739	689
	63 Lincoln Hwy, Malvern, PA 19355/610-644-1300			
976	**VIVRA**	932	879	962
	400 Primrose, Burlingame, CA 94010/415-348-8200			
888	**VONS**	211	893	531
	618 Michillinda Ave, Arcadia, CA 91007/818-821-7000			
977	**VORNADO REALTY TRUST**	993	844	927
	Park 80 West, Saddle Brook, NJ 07663/201-587-1000			
490	**VULCAN MATERIALS**	605	526	719
	One Metroplex Dr, Birmingham, AL 35209/205-877-3000			

W

MKT. RANK	COMPANY	SALES	PROFITS	ASSETS
163	**WACHOVIA**	356	124	57
	301 North Main St, Winston-Salem, NC 27102/910-770-5000			
5	**WAL-MART STORES**	4	12	64
	702 SW Eighth St, Bentonville, AR 72716/501-273-4000			
169	**WALGREEN**	112	214	447
	200 Wilmot Rd, Deerfield, IL 60015/708-940-2500			
83	**WARNER-LAMBERT**	166	89	308
	201 Tabor Rd, Morris Plains, NJ 07950/201-540-2000			
936	**WASHINGTON FEDERAL**	931	566	384
	425 Pike St, Seattle, WA 98101/206-624-7930			
927	**WASHINGTON GAS LIGHT**	708	743	674
	1100 H St NW, Washington, DC 20080/703-750-4440			
686	**WASHINGTON MUTUAL**	595	360	111
	1201 Third Ave, Seattle, WA 98101/206-461-2000			
344	**WASHINGTON POST**	529	365	634
	1150 15th St NW, Washington, DC 20071/202-334-6000			
921	**WASHINGTON WATER**	788	630	590
	1411 East Mission Ave, Spokane, WA 99202/509-489-0500			
822	**WEINGARTEN REALTY**	982	827	841
	2600 Citadel Plaza Dr, Houston, TX 77008/713-866-6000			
725	**WEIS MARKETS**	543	636	785
	1000 South Second St, Sunbury, PA 17801/717-286-4571			
861	**WELLMAN**	692	698	741
	1040 Broad St, Shrewsbury, NJ 07702/908-542-7300			
309	**WELLPOINT HEALTH**	370	301	515
	21555 Oxnard St, Woodland Hills, CA 91367/818-703-4000			
105	**WELLS FARGO**	214	70	40
	420 Montgomery St, San Francisco, CA 94104/415-477-1000			

MKT. RANK	COMPANY	SALES	PROFITS	ASSETS
563	**WENDY'S INTERNATIONAL**	579	530	739
	4288 West Dublin-Granville Rd, Dublin, OH 43017/614-764-3100			
858	**WESCO FINANCIAL**	987	900	764
	301 East Colorado Blvd, Pasadena, CA 91101/818-585-6700			
795	**WEST ONE BANCORP**	790	511	225
	101 South Capitol Blvd, Boise, ID 83702/208-383-7000			
401	**WESTERN ATLAS**	443	625	513
	360 North Crescent Dr, Beverly Hills, CA 90210/310-888-2500			
979	**WESTERN NATIONAL**	791	655	234
	5555 San Felipe Rd, Houston, TX 77056/713-888-7800			
478	**WESTERN RESOURCES**	528	333	321
	818 Kansas Ave, Topeka, KS 66612/913-575-6300			
174	**WESTINGHOUSE ELECTRIC**	125	631	193
	11 Stanwix St, Pittsburgh, PA 15222/412-244-2000			
365	**WESTVACO**	375	414	386
	299 Park Ave, New York, NY 10171/212-688-5000			
106	**WEYERHAEUSER**	99	113	159
	33663 Weyerhaeuser Way South, Federal Way, WA 98003/206-924-4560			
378	**WHEELABRATOR**	592	335	433
	Liberty Lane, Hampton, NH 03842/603-929-3000			
244	**WHIRLPOOL**	139	377	270
	2000 M-63 North, Benton Harbor, MI 49022/616-923-5000			
473	**WHITMAN**	392	498	547
	3501 Algonquin Rd, Rolling Meadows, IL 60008/708-818-5000			
336	**WILLAMETTE INDUSTRIES**	349	349	452
	3800 First Interstate Tower, Portland, OR 97201/503-227-5581			
372	**WILLIAMS**	500	370	320
	One Williams Center, Tulsa, OK 74172/918-588-2000			
866	**WILMINGTON TRUST**	898	581	346
	1100 North Market St, Wilmington, DE 19890/302-651-1000			
236	**WINN-DIXIE STORES**	89	289	526
	5050 Edgewood Court, Jacksonville, FL 32254/904-783-5000			
966	**WISCONSIN CENTRAL**	953	848	911
	6250 North River Rd, Rosemont, IL 60018/708-318-4600			
329	**WISCONSIN ENERGY**	503	341	368
	333 West Everett St, Milwaukee, WI 53203/414-221-2345			
559	**WITCO**	437	493	581
	One American Lane, Greenwich, CT 06831/203-552-2000			
65	**WMX TECHNOLOGIES**	103	76	118
	3003 Butterfield Rd, Oak Brook, IL 60521/708-572-8800			
466	**WOOLWORTH**	126	990	336
	233 Broadway, New York, NY 10279/212-553-2000			
510	**WORTHINGTON INDUSTRIES**	569	521	790
	1205 Dearborn Dr, Columbus, OH 43085/614-438-3210			
844	**WPL HOLDINGS**	735	681	606
	222 West Washington Ave, Madison, WI 53703/608-252-3311			
183	**WRIGLEY (WM.) JR.**	533	275	761
	410 North Michigan Ave, Chicago, IL 60611/312-644-2121			

XYZ

MKT. RANK	COMPANY	SALES	PROFITS	ASSETS
73	**XEROX**	50	74	58
	800 Long Ridge Rd, Stamford, CT 06904/203-968-3000			
571	**XILINX**	923	784	961
	2100 Logic Dr, San Jose, CA 95124/408-559-7778			

MKT. RANK	COMPANY	SALES	PROFITS	ASSETS
893	**XTRA**	910	725	762
	60 State St, Boston, MA 02109/617-367-5000			
594	**YORK INTERNATIONAL**	413	560	655
	631 South Richland Ave, York, PA 17403/717-771-7890			

MKT. RANK	COMPANY	SALES	PROFITS	ASSETS
941	**ZURICH REINSURANCE**	962	966	731
	One Chase Manhattan Plaza, New York, NY 10005/ 212-898-5000			

Source: Reprinted from March 27, 1995 issue of *Business Week* by special permission, copyright © 1995 by McGraw-Hill, Inc.

(continued)

Companies That Rate Insurance Companies

Company	Telephone	Address
A.M. Best & Co.	908-439-2200	A.M. Best Road Oldwich, NJ 08858-9999
Duff & Phelps/ Credit Rating Co.	312-368-3157	55 East Monroe Street Chicago, IL 60603
Moody's Investor's Service, Inc.	212-553-0377	99 Church Street New York, NY 10007
Standard & Poor's Corp.	212-208-1527	25 Broadway New York, NY 10004
Weiss Research, Inc.	800-289-9222	P.O. 2923 West Palm Beach, FL 33402

America's Biggest Brokers

Rank 1993	1994	Firm	Total consolidated capital ($ millions)	Equity capital ($ millions)	Long-term debt ($ millions)	"Excess" net capital ($ millions)	Total assets ($ millions)
1	1	Merrill Lynch & Co.	$20,681.0	$5,818.0	$14,863.0	$2,198.0	$163,749.0
2	2	Salomon Inc.	19,694.0	4,492.0	15,202.0	888.0	172,732.0
3	3	Goldman, Sachs & Co.[1]	19,189.0	4,771.0	14,418.0	1,418.0	95,296.0
4	4	Lehman Brothers[2]	14,716.0	3,395.0	11,321.0	1,281.0	109,947.0
5	5	Morgan Stanley & Co.[3]	13,582.0	4,471.0	9,111.0	572.0	115,988.0
6	6	Bear, Stearns & Co.	5,810.0	2,307.0	3,503.0	991.0	66,842.0
7	7	CS First Boston	5,557.0	1,784.0	3,773.0	686.0	109,838.0
8	8	PaineWebber	4,130.0	1,631.0	2,499.0	646.0	35,856.0
9	9	Smith Barney	3,158.0	2,181.0	977.0	1,119.0	44,425.0
11	10	Donaldson, Lufkin & Jenrette	1,777.0	1,045.0	732.0	467.0	33,116.0
10	11	Prudential Securities	1,760.0	1,325.0	435.0	572.0	18,912.0
12	12	Dean Witter Reynolds	1,751.0	1,376.0	375.0	608.0	13,578.0
14	13	J.P. Morgan Securities	1,036.0	486.0	550.0	401.0	35,526.0
15	14	Nomura Holdings America	1,031.7	404.1	627.6	356.1	33,761.4
19	15	A.G. Edwards & Sons	892.0	892.0	0.0	541.0	2,300.0
17	16	BT Securities Corp.	883.0	426.0	457.0	497.0	20,188.0
18	17	UBS Securities	876.0	326.0	550.0	143.0	28,957.0
16	18	Shelby Cullom Davis & Co.	742.9	742.9	0.0	559.1	4,658.3
35	19	Chase Securities	542.0	307.0	235.0	344.0	9,730.0
—	20	Internationale Nederlanden (U.S.) Capital Holdings Corp.	537.0	337.0	200.0	249.0	8,458.0
21	21	Citicorp Securities	530.0	385.0	145.0	316.0	8,672.0
24	22	Chemical Securities	492.0	392.0	100.0	267.6	11,359.0
20		Charles Schwab & Co.	492.0	367.0	125.0	254.0	7,735.0
—	24	NationsBanc Capital Markets	476.0	326.0	150.0	291.0	13,279.0
22	25	Greenwich Capital Markets	437.6	217.6	220.0	297.0	21,797.6
31	26	Spear, Leeds & Kellogg	375.0	268.0	107.0	103.0	7,871.0
23	27	D.E. Shaw & Co.	370.0	370.0	0.0	46.3	2,716.0
26	28	Alex. Brown & Sons	359.0	339.0	20.0	224.0	1,237.0
29	29	Fidelity Brokerage Services	353.7	353.7	0.0	218.8	4,660.0
25	30	Daiwa Securities America	346.1	196.1	150.0	154.9	31,290.3
32	31	Yamaichi International (America)[4]	336.0	136.0	200.0	165.0	16,172.0
28	32	Oppenheimer & Co.	335.8	257.1	78.7	112.6	2,957.2
30	33	Legg Mason	325.7	223.2	102.5	89.6	901.3
27	34	Deutsche Bank Securities Corp.	321.0	125.0	196.0	140.0	12,971.0
39	35	Edward D. Jones & Co.	307.0	171.0	136.0	144.0	891.0
33	36	Kemper Securities	296.2	252.7	43.5	59.8	705.0
36	37	John Nuveen & Co.	286.0	286.0	0.0	213.0	349.0
34	38	Aubrey G. Lanston & Co.	268.0	268.0	0.0	154.0	2,091.0
56	39	First Chicago Capital Markets	256.0	196.0	60.0	174.0	9,342.0
38	40	Dillon, Read & Co.	247.0	182.0	65.0	132.0	2,657.0
—	41	Crédit Lyonnais Securities (USA)	244.0	124.0	120.0	222.0	680.0
45	42	S.G. Warburg & Co.	235.0	160.0	75.0	97.0	NA
37	43	Nikko Securities Co. International	233.1	133.1	100.0	185.6	9,536.5
44	44	Instinet Corp.	232.0	232.0	0.0	55.0	279.0
41	45	Raymond James Financial	231.0	231.0	0.0	139.0	1,658.0
43	46	Quick & Reilly Group[1]	229.0	229.0	0.0	157.0	2,854.0
46	47	Sanwa Securities (USA) Co.	228.0	128.0	100.0	112.8[5]	17,104.0
53	48	Jefferies & Co.	222.8	163.2	59.6	71.1	1,557.3
42	49	Gruntal Financial Corp.	217.3	189.0	28.3	16.1	2,278.2
40	50	Allen & Co.	216.0	216.0	0.0	76.0	417.0
52	51	Fuji Securities	214.8	114.8	100.0	184.3	13,108.8
51	52	Piper, Jaffray	213.0	171.0	42.0	66.0	699.0
47	53	Wertheim Schroder & Co.	180.8	165.7	15.1	44.9	5,583.0

(continued)

America's Biggest Brokers *(concluded)*

Rank 1993	1994	Firm	Total consolidated capital ($ millions)	Equity capital ($ millions)	Long-term debt ($ millions)	"Excess" net capital ($ millions)	Total assets ($ millions)
48	54	Barclays de Zoete Wedd Securities	$ 180.0	$ 130.0	$ 50.0	$ 131.0	$ 14,628.0
50	55	M.A. Schapiro & Co.	179.4	179.4	0.0	137.6	1,019.1
—	56	Cantor Fitzgerald Securities Corp.	156.0	156.0	0.0	48.0	8,592.0
55	57	Brown Brothers Harriman & Co.	155.0	155.0	0.0	0.0	1,549.9
54	58	Neuberger & Berman	152.0	57.0	95.0	102.0	1,530.0
—	59	NYLIFE Distributors	147.0	147.0	0.0	41.0	207.0
68	60	Dain Bosworth	141.0	116.0	25.0	27.0	486.0
57	61	Arnhold & S. Bleichroeder	139.0	139.0	0.0	84.0	3,523.0
73	62	Wheat First Butcher Singer	138.8	113.8	25.0	54.1	749.2
61	63	McDonald & Co. Securities	133.7	108.7	25.0	71.5	471.8
67	64	Herzog, Heine, Geduld	132.0	101.0	31.0	95.0	660.0
62	65	Morgan Keegan & Co.	131.0	131.0	0.0	75.0	836.0
59	66	Lazard Frères & Co.	125.0	125.0	0.0	69.0	978.0
66	67	J.C. Bradford & Co.	122.7	98.6	24.1	59.1	695.8
49	68	D.H. Blair Investment Banking Corp.	122.0	122.0	0.0	20.0	207.0
71	69	Bernard L. Madoff Investment Securities	121.8	121.8	0.0	75.8	373.2
64	70	Stephens Inc.	119.0	119.0	0.0	56.0	406.0
63	71	Van Kampen American Capital Distributors	117.0	117.0	0.0	38.0	186.0
—	72	HSBC Securities	114.0	114.0	0.0	6.0	4,714.0
69	73	Janney Montgomery Scott	113.9	89.9	24.0	69.1	438.9
—	74	Furman Selz	112.7	62.7	50.0	40.3	230.0
58	75	Cowen & Co.	110.9	89.4	21.5	35.0	1,893.8
75	76	SBCI-Swiss Bank Corp. Investment Banking	110.0	45.0	65.0	63.0	1,520.0
59	77	Glickenhaus & Co.	108.0	108.0	0.0	28.0	610.0
70	78	Toronto Dominion Securities (USA)	107.0	22.0	85.0	41.0	211.0
74	79	Interstate/Johnson Lane Corp.	102.5	81.5	21.0	34.9	843.0
72	80	Paribas Corp.	101.6	79.6	22.0	66.1	13,675.0
—	81	ABN Amro Securities (USA)	97.8	47.8	50.0	80.7	1,965.3
79	82	Robert W. Baird & Co.	97.4	89.0	8.4	33.1	384.7
78	83	S.D. Securities	93.0	93.0	0.0	71.0	544.2
82	84	Fahnestock & Co.	89.0	76.0	13.0	71.0	510.0
76		Republic New York Securities Corp.	89.0	89.0	0.0	67.0	1,200.0
83	86	Chicago Corp.	85.8	64.8	21.0	32.7	562.2
77	87	Mabon Securities Corp.	85.1	13.1	72.0	36.3	1,424.8
81	88	Tucker Anthony	80.0	80.0	0.0	25.0	480.0
84	89	Smith New Court	79.4	49.4	30.0	31.8	298.9
—	90	Serfin Securities	78.8	18.8	60.0	28.9	85.8
80	91	Montgomery Securities	77.5	47.5	30.0	36.4	382.5
87	92	J.J.B. Hilliard, W.L. Lyons	72.6	69.4	3.2	39.0	173.0
88	93	BHC Securities	72.0	6.0	66.0	49.3	546.8
—	94	Keefe, Bruyette & Woods	71.1	70.4	0.7	47.9	100.3
90	95	Advest	68.0	68.0	0.0	23.0	536.0
93	96	Hambrecht & Quist	66.7	66.7	0.0	7.0	181.4
86	97	Harris Nesbitt Thomson Securities	65.6	20.6	45.0	42.1	6,116.9
91	98	William Blair & Co.	65.0	65.0	0.0	18.0	258.0
		Brown & Co. Securities Corp.	65.0	50.0	15.0	49.0	632.0
96		Principal Financial Securities	65.0	65.0	0.0	19.0	338.0

[1] As of 11/25/94.   [2] As of 11/30/94.   [3] As of 10/31/94.   [4] As of 9/30/94.   [5] Liquid capital.

50 Leading Retained Executive Search Firms in North America[*]

Allerton Heneghan & O'Neill
70 W. Madison St., Ste. 2015
Three First National Plaza
Chicago, IL 60602
Tel: 312-263-1075
Donald Allerton

Martin H. Bauman Assoc., Inc.
375 Park Ave., Ste. 2002
New York, NY 10022
Tel: 212-752-6580
Martin H. Bauman

Bishop Partners, Ltd.
708 Third Ave., Ste. 2200
New York, NY 10017
Tel: 212-986-3419
Susan K. Bishop

Boyden
364 Elwood Ave.
Hawthorne, NY 10532-1239
Tel: 914-747-0093
Richard Foy

The Caldwell Partners Amrop Int'l.
64 Prince Arthur Ave.
Toronto, ON M5R 1B4 Canada
Tel: 416-920-7702
C. Douglas Caldwell

Callan Assoc., Ltd.
1550 Spring Rd.
Oak Brook, IL 60521
Tel: 708-832-7080
Robert M. Callan

Cejka & Co.
222 S. Central, Ste. 400
St. Louis, MO 63105
Tel: 314-726-1603
Susan Cejka

Clarey & Andrews, Inc.
1200 Shermer Rd., Ste. 108
Northbrook, IL 60062
Tel: 708-498-2870
John R. "Jack" Clarey

Coleman Lew & Assoc., Inc.
326 W. Tenth St.
Charlotte, NC 28202
Tel: 704-377-0362
Charles E. Lew

**Conrey Paul Ray Berndtson
 International**
Palo Santo #6
Col. Lomas Altas
Mexico City, MX CP 11950 Mexico
Tel: 52 5 5 70 74 62
Craig J. Dudley

Thorndike Deland Assoc.
275 Madison Ave., 13th Floor
New York, NY 10016
Tel: 212-661-6200
Howard Bratches

Dieckmann & Assoc., Ltd.
180 N. Stetson Ave., Ste. 5555
Two Prudential Plaza
Chicago, IL 60601
Tel: 312-819-5900
Ralph E. Dieckmann

Robert W. Dingman Co., Inc.
32129 W. Lindero Canyon Rd., Ste. 206
Westlake Village, CA 91361
Tel: 818-991-5950
Robert W. Dingman

Diversified Search, Inc.
One Commerce Sq.
2005 Market St., Ste. 3300
Philadelphia, PA 19103
Tel: 215-732-6666
Judith M. von Seldeneck

Bert H. Early Assoc., Inc.
55 E. Monroe St., Ste. 4530
Chicago, IL 60603-5805
Tel: 312-236-6868
Bert H. Early

---

[*]Retained executive search firms primarily require an advance fee and progress payments versus payments contingent on hiring.

Source: Reprinted with permission of *Executive Recruiter News®*, published monthly since 1980 by Kennedy Publications, Templeton Rd., Fitzwilliam, NH 03447, 603-585-6544, publishers also of *The Directory of Executive Recruiters*.

Fenwick Partners
57 Bedford St., Ste. 101
Lexington, MA 02173
Tel: 617-862-3370
Charles A. Polachi, Jr.

Ferneborg & Assoc., Inc.
555 Twin Dolphin Drive, Ste. 190
Redwood City, CA 94066
Tel: 415-637-8100
John R. Ferneborg

Francis & Assoc.
6923 Vista Drive
West Des Moines, IA 50266
Tel: 515-221-9800
N. Kay Francis

Jay Gaines & Company, Inc.
450 Park Ave.
New York, NY 10022
Tel: 212-308-9222
Jay Gaines

Gould, McCoy, & Chadick, Inc.
300 Park Ave.
New York, NY 10022
Tel: 212-688-8671
William E. Gould

Hayden Group, Inc.
One Post Office Sq., Ste. 3830
Boston, MA 02109
Tel: 617-482-2445
James A. Hayden

Heidrick & Struggles, Inc.
125 S. Wacker Drive, Ste. 2800
Chicago, IL 60606-4590
Tel: 312-372-8811
Robert E. Hallagan

The Heidrick Partners, Inc.
20 N. Wacker Drive, Ste. 2850
Chicago, IL 60606
Tel: 312-845-9700
Robert L. Heidrick

The Hetzel Group
Williamsburg Village
1601 Colonial Pkwy.
Inverness, IL 60067
Tel: 708-776-7000
William G. Hetzel

Hockett Associates
One First St., Ste. 14
P.O. Box 1765
Los Altos, CA 94023
Tel: 415-941-8815
Bill Hockett

William C. Houze & Co.
48249 Vista De Nopal
La Quinta, CA 92253
Tel: 619-564-6400
William C. Houze

Houze, Shourds & Montgomery, Inc.
Greater LA World Trade Ctr.
One World Trade
Long Beach, CA 90831-1840
Tel: 310-495-6495
James Montgomery

Isaacson, Miller
334 Boylston St., Ste. 500
Boston, MA 02116-3805
Tel: 617-262-6500
John Isaacson

Pendleton James & Assoc., Inc.
200 Park Ave., Ste. 3706
New York, NY 10166
Tel: 212-557-1599
E. Pendleton James

A. T. Kearney Executive Search
222 W. Adams St.
Chicago, IL 60606
Tel: 312-648-0111
Charles W. Sweet

Kenny, Kindler, Hunt & Howe
1 Dag Hammarskjold Plaza, 34th Floor
New York, NY 10017
Tel: 212-355-5560
Roger M. Kenny

Korn/Ferry Int'l.
237 Park Ave.
New York, NY 10017
Tel: 212-687-1834
Richard Ferry

Lamalie Amrop Int'l.
489 Fifth Ave.
New York, NY 10017-6105
Tel: 212-953-7900
John F. Johnson

Herbert Mines Assoc., Inc.
399 Park Ave., 27th Floor
New York, NY 10022
Tel: 212-355-0909
Herbert Mines

Mirtz Morice, Inc.
One Dock St., 3rd Floor
Stamford, CT 06902
Tel: 203-964-9266
P. John Mirtz

Nadzam, Lusk & Assoc., Inc.
3211 Scott Blvd., Ste. 205
Santa Clara, CA 95054-3091
Tel: 408-727-6601
Richard J. Nadzam

Norman Broadbent Int'l., Inc.
200 Park Ave.
New York, NY 10166
Tel: 212-953-6990
William B. Clemens, Jr.

Preng & Assoc., Inc.
2925 Briarpark, Ste. 1111
Houston, TX 77042
Tel: 713-266-2600
David E. Preng

Paul Ray Berndtson
301 Commerce St., Ste. 2300
Ft. Worth, TX 76102
Tel: 817-334-0500
Paul R. Ray, Jr.

Russell Reynolds Assoc., Inc.
200 Park Ave.
New York, NY 10166
Tel: 212-351-2000
Hobson Brown, Jr.

Norman Roberts & Assoc., Inc.
1800 Century Park E., Ste. 430
Los Angeles, CA 90067-1507
Tel: 310-552-1112
Norman C. Roberts

Seitchik, Corwin & Seitchik, Inc.
1830 Jackson St., Ste. C
San Francisco, CA 94109
Tel: 415-928-5717
Jack Seitchik

SpencerStuart
277 Park Ave., 29th Floor
New York, NY 10172
Tel: 212-366-0200
Dayton Ogden

Tanton Mitchell/Paul Ray Berndtson
710-1050 W. Pender St.
Vancouver, BC V6E 3S7 Canada
Tel: 604-685-0261
Kyle Mitchell

Travis & Co., Inc.
325 Boston Post Rd.
Sudbury, MA 01776
Tel: 508-443-4000
John A. Travis

Ward Howell International, Inc.
99 Park Ave., Ste. 2000
New York, NY 10016-1699
Tel: 212-697-3730
John F. Raynolds, III

Daniel Wier & Assoc.
333 S. Grand Ave., Ste. 2980
Los Angeles, CA 90071
Tel: 213-628-2580
Daniel C. Wier

Wilkinson & Ives
One Bush St., Ste. 550
San Francisco, CA 94104
Tel: 415-834-3100
William R. Wilkinson

**Witt/Kieffer, Ford, Hadelman
& Lloyd**
2015 Spring Rd., Ste. 510
Oak Brook, IL 60521
Tel: 708-990-1370
John Lloyd

Egon Zehnder Int'l., Inc.
55 E. 59th St., 14th Floor
New York, NY 10022
Tel: 212-838-9199
A. Daniel Meiland

America's Most Admired Corporations*

America's Most Admired Companies

RANK	LAST YEAR	Company	SCORE	Quality of management	Quality of product or services	Financial soundness
1	1	**Rubbermaid** Rubber	8.65	8.99	9.13	8.72
2	3	**Microsoft** Computer & data services	8.42	8.90	8.31	9.15
3	3	**Coca-Cola** Beverages	8.39	8.82	8.49	9.08
4	6	**Motorola** Electronics, electrical equipment	8.38	8.73	9.01	8.31
5	2	**Home Depot** Specialist retailers	8.24	8.97	8.40	8.38
6	*	**Intel** Electronics, electrical equipment	8.17	8.50	8.74	8.37
7	8	**Procter & Gamble** Soaps, cosmetics	8.13	8.69	8.76	8.67
8	5	**3M** Sci., photo & control equipment	8.09	8.40	8.50	8.23
9	10	**United Parcel Service** Trucking	8.05	8.69	8.46	8.63
10	19	**Hewlett-Packard** Computers, office equipment	8.04	8.50	8.50	8.40

°HOW IT WAS DONE. The 13th annual Corporate Reputations survey includes 395 companies in 41 industry groups that appeared in the 1994 FORTUNE 500 Industrial and FORTUNE 500 Service directories. More than 10,000 senior executives, outside directors, and financial analysts were asked to rate the ten largest companies (or sometimes fewer) in their own industry. They measured the contenders by eight attributes: quality of management; quality of products or services; innovativeness; long-term investment value; financial soundness; ability to attract, develop, and keep talented people; responsibility to the community and the environment; and wise use of corporate assets.

Companies are assigned to a group according to the activity or business that contributed most to their revenues. Philip Morris, for example, is listed under food because brands like Kraft and General Foods contributed $31 billion in revenues vs. the $28 billion pulled in by its cigarettes.

... and how they scored

Value as a long-term investment	Use of corporate assets	Innovativeness	Community or environmental responsibility	Ability to attract, develop, and keep talented people
8.44	8.39	9.03	8.22	8.27
8.46	8.05	8.49	6.99	9.02
8.78	8.30	7.44	7.77	8.49
8.59	8.09	8.77	7.19	8.38
8.02	8.07	8.53	7.35	8.19
7.92	7.78	8.82	6.93	8.27
8.21	7.68	8.00	7.03	7.99
7.87	7.59	8.52	7.63	7.95
8.25	7.80	7.47	7.36	7.75
7.99	7.79	7.83	7.27	8.08

Deals of the Year

BIGGEST U.S. DEALS[1]

Target (Advisers)	Acquirer (Advisers)	Type of deal	Price ($ millions)	Effective date
1 **McCaw Cellular Communications** (Salomon Brothers, Lazard Frères, NM Rothschild, Donaldson, Lufkin & Jenrette)	**AT&T Corp.** (Morgan Stanley)	acquisition of remaining 89.45 percent via stock swap and assumption of liabilities	$18,923.4	9/19/94
2 **Paramount Communications** (Lazard Frères)	**Viacom, a unit of National Amusements** (Bear Stearns, Smith Barney, Goldman Sachs)	merger via tender offer	9,600.0	7/7/94
3 **American Cyanamid Co.** (Morgan Stanley, CS First Boston)	**American Home Products Corp.** (Gleacher & Co.)	merger via tender offer	9,267.2	12/21/94
4 **Blockbuster Entertainment** (Merrill Lynch, Kidder Peabody)	**Viacom, a unit of National Amusements** (Smith Barney)	acquisition via stock swap	7,971.1	9/29/94
5 **HCA-Hospital Corp. of America** (Goldman Sachs)	**Columbia Healthcare Corp.** (Merrill Lynch)	acquisition via reverse stock swap	5,605.0	2/10/94
6 **Syntex Corp.** (Goldman Sachs, Allen & Co.)	**Roche Holdings** (J. P. Morgan)	merger via tender offer	5,307.2	11/3/94
7 **PCS Health Systems, a unit of McKesson Corp.** (Morgan Stanley)	**Eli Lilly & Co.** (Lehman Brothers)	acquisition	4,000.0	11/21/94
8 **KeyCorp** (Salomon Brothers)	**Society Corp.** (CS First Boston)	acquisition via stock swap	3,923.9	3/1/94
9 **Gerber Products Co.** (Wasserstein Perella, Goldman Sachs)	**Sandoz** (Morgan Stanley)	merger via tender offer	3,689.9	12/19/94
10 **UAL Corp.** (CS First Boston, Lazard Frères)	**United Airlines Union Coalition** (Houlihan Lokey)	employees' acquisition of 55 percent stake in UAL	3,467.5*	7/12/94
11 **R.H. Macy & Co.** (Blackstone Group, Merrill Lynch, Wasserstein Perella, Houlihan Lokey)	**Federated Department Stores** (Smith Barney, Citicorp)	acquisition	3,449.2	12/19/94
12 **Liberty Media** (Merrill Lynch)	**Tele-Communications Inc.** (CS First Boston)	acquisition of remaining 95 percent interest	3,411.0	8/4/94
13 **Sterling Winthrop, a unit of Eastman Kodak Co.** (Goldman Sachs)	**SmithKline Beecham** (Wasserstein Perella, Kleinwort Benson)	acquisition	2,925.0	11/2/94
14 **Diversified Pharmaceutical Services, a unit of United Healthcare Corp.** (Goldman Sachs)	**SmithKline Beecham Corp., a unit of SmithKline Beecham** (Wasserstein Perella, Kleinwort Benson)	acquisition	2,300.0	5/27/94

Target (Advisers)	Acquirer (Advisers)	Type of deal	Price ($ millions)	Effective date
15 **Continental Bank** (Goldman Sachs)	**BankAmerica Corp.** (Lazard Frères, Montgomery Securities)	acquisition via stock swap	2,162.0	9/1/94

* *Estimated value.*   Source: Securities Data Co.

[1] RANKING THE BIGGEST DEALS
The table "Biggest U.S. Deals" shows the 15 largest deals involving a U.S. target company that were completed between January 1 and December 31, 1994. The table "Biggest Canadian and Latin American Deals" shows the ten largest deals involving a Canadian or Latin American target company that were completed in the same period.

Advisers received credit only for those deals on which they served as financial advisers; firms that acted only as providers of fairness opinions were not credited.

These figures do not include buybacks or repurchases, spin-offs, split-offs, self-tenders or minority stake purchases, unless the stake purchase was for the remaining interest of a company that the acquirer already partially owned.

Source: Securities Data Co. for *Institutional Investor.* Securities Data Company, Newark, New Jersey.

Editor's Addenda:

The Disney acquisition of Capital Cities/ABC Company in August 1995 for $19 billion was the second highest ever reported. (The largest was the Kohlberg Kravis acquisition of RJR Nabisco for $25 billion.)

The merger of Chase and Chemical banks in a $10 billion stock swap was announced in late August 1995.

BIGGEST CANADIAN AND LATIN AMERICAN DEALS[1]

Target (Advisers)	Acquirer (Advisers)	Type of deal	Price ($ millions)	Effective date
1 **Lac Minerals** (Canada) (Goldman Sachs, RBC Dominion Securities, Wood Gundy, Rothschild Canada)	**American Barrick Resources Corp.** (Canada) (Bunting Warburg, Kidder Peabody)	merger via tender offer	$1,604.3	10/17/94
2 **Bow Valley Energy, a unit of British Gas** (Canada) (Morgan Stanley, Goldman Sachs)	**Talisman Energy** (Canada)	acquisition	1,042.8	8/11/94
3 **Trizec Corp., a unit of Carena Bancorp's Carena Properties** (Canada) (Donaldson, Lufkin & Jenrette)	**Investor group of Horsham Corp. and Argo Partnership** (Canada) (Merrill Lynch, J.P. Morgan)	acquisition of 68.5 percent stake	740.0	7/25/94
4 **Hidroeléctrica Piedro de Aquila** (Argentina)	**Investor group of TransAlta Energy and Duke Energy Corp.** (U.S.) (Merrill Lynch)	acquisition of 57 percent interest in state-owned utility	520.0	1/17/94
5 **Laurentian Group** (Canada) (Wood Gundy)	**Société Financière des Caisses Desjardins, a unit of Confédération des Caisses** (Canada)	acquisition via tender offer	481.4	1/3/94
6 **Banco de Colombia, a unit of Financial Institutions Guarantees Fund** (Colombia) (CS First Boston)	**Bancol, a unit of Gilinski Group** (Colombia) (Morgan Grenfell)	acquisition of 75 percent from state-owned fund	432.6	1/20/94
7 **Lawson Mardon Group** (Canada) (CS First Boston, Swiss Bank)	**Alusuisse-Lonza Holding** (Switzerland) (Baring Brothers, Dillon Read, Burns Fry)	acquisition via tender offer	424.7	2/2/94
8 **Sociedad Minera Cerro Verde** (Peru) (Morgan Grenfell)	**Cyprus Climax Metals, a unit of Cyprus Amax Minerals Co.** (U.S.)	acquisition from state-owned mining company	409.0*	3/21/94
9 **Empresa Minera Especial Tintaya** (Peru)	**Magma Copper Co.** (U.S.) (CS First Boston)	acquisition of 96.43 percent interest from state-owned mining company	358.0	11/30/94
10 **El Abra copper deposit, a unit of Codelco** (Chile)	**Cyprus Minerals** (U.S.) (NM Rothschild)	acquisition of 51 percent interest from state-owned company	346.5	6/28/94

Estimated value.   Source: Securities Data Co.

[1] See footnote with table "Biggest U.S. Deals" on page 190.

Source: Securities Data Co. for *Institutional Investor.* Securities Data Company, Newark, New Jersey.

INTERNATIONAL

The scoreboard

Deal	Bankers	Deal	Bankers
Akzo Skr 16.6 billion Acquisition of Nobel Industrier from Securum	S.G. Warburg (adviser to Akzo), Goldman Sachs Int'l (adviser to Securum)	**Istituto Nazionale delle Assicurazioni** L4.5 trillion 1.89 billion shares	Goldman Sachs Int'l, Istituto Mobiliare Italiano (global coordinators)
Banca Commerciale Italiana L2.7 trillion 50 million shares	Lehman Bros., Banca Commerciale Italiana (global coordinators)	**P.T. Indonesian Satellite Corp.** $1.051 billion 362.4 million shares	Merrill Lynch & Co., P.T. (Persero) Danareksa (global coordinators)
British Gas £200 million 7.125% 50-year bonds	CS First Boston (book runner); Baring Bros., Goldman Sachs Int'l, Kleinwort Benson, Salomon Bros., UBS Int'l, S.G. Warburg Securities (co-lead managers)	**Republic of Italy** ¥300 billion 3.5% notes due 2001	Daiwa Europe, J.P. Morgan Securities (book runners)
People's Republic of China $1 billion 6.5% ten-year global notes	Merrill Lynch International (lead manager)	$4 billion Three-tranche multicurrency floating-rate note	Merrill Lynch (global coordinator), UBS, IMI Luxembourg, Nomura, Banca di Roma, Deutsche Bank, Banca Naz. del Lavoro
Elf Aquitaine Ffr23.6 billion 60.3 million shares	Banque Paribas, Crédit Lyonnais (global coordinators); Merrill Lynch; Daiwa Securities Co.	**Koninklijke PTT Nederland** Dfl 6.9 billion Sale of 30% stake by Dutch gov't	ABN Amro Bank (global coordinator), S.G. Warburg Securities, Morgan Stanley & Co., CS FirstBoston
Eurotunnel $1.39 billion Rights issue, 324 million shares	Indosuez Capital, Morgan Grenfell & Co., S.G. Warburg Securities	**Republic of Lebanon** $400 million Three-year Eurobond	Merrill Lynch Int'l (lead manager)
Hub River Power Co. Debt: $686 million Offshore senior debt facility	Citibank (global syndication coordinator)	**Nacional Financiera** $250 million Dragon bonds	Lehman Bros. Asia, Wardley Group (lead managers)
Debt: 3,012 billion rupees Senior facility	National Development Finance Corp. and others	**Pakistan Telecommunications** $900 million 5 million vouchers	Jardine Fleming & Co., Muslim Commercial Bank (global coordinators)
Official debt: $641 million	British Commonwealth Development Corp., Coface, Japanese Export-Import Bank, MITI, SACE, World Bank	**Republic of Portugal** $2 billion Medium-term-note program	Lehman Bros. (global arranger), Paribas Capital Markets
International equity: $145 million 13.4 million GDRs	Morgan Grenfell Emerging Markets (global coordinator)	**Tele Danmark** Dkr19.6 billion 63.2 million shares	Den Danske Bank, Goldman, Sachs & Co. (global coordinators); Barclays de Zoete Wedd, UBS
Domestic equity: $30 million 69.28 million shares	Bear Stearns Jahangir Siddiqui (lead manager)	**Viag** Dm5.5 billion Acquisition of Bayernwerk	Lehman Bros. (adviser to State of Bavaria)

Source: *Institutional Investor*, January 1995.

Noteworthy Deals

DERIVATIVES

The scoreboard

Institutional Investor has selected the following derivatives deals as
the most noteworthy of the year.

Deal	Bankers
Eastman Kodak Co. Unwound $7.3 billion in derivatives in conjunction with $4.8 billion debt tender offer	CS First Boston, Lehman Brothers
Elf Aquitaine Leveraged participation plan, enabling Elf employees to purchase 10 percent of shares offered in $6 billion privatization	Bankers Trust International
Modesto Irrigation District Financing Authority Sold option for $7.5 million to advance-refund $119.7 million of bonds	Lehman Brothers

REAL ESTATE

The scoreboard

Institutional Investor has selected the following real estate deals as the most noteworthy of the year.

Deal	Participants
Comptoir des Entrepreneurs French mortgage bank securitizes $1.69 billion of commercial real estate assets in the largest-ever commercial-mortgage-backed security	Comptoir des Entrepreneurs; Bankers Trust International adviser and underwriter
IBM Company sells 590 Madison Avenue office building to speculative investor group for approximately $205 million	IBM; Edward S. Gordon Co., adviser to IBM; Odyssey Partners L.P. and Edward Minskoff, buyers
Trizec Corp. Simultaneous $760 million equity infusion and $1.4 billion debt restructuring results in largest recap ever of a real estate company	Trizec Corp.; Goldman, Sachs & Co., Dominion Securities, advisers to Trizec; Horsham Corp., Argo Partnership, investors; Merrill Lynch, adviser to Horsham; Donaldson, Lufkin & Jenrette, adviser to senior creditors

Source: *Institutional Investor,* January 1995.

PROJECT FINANCE

The scoreboard

Institutional Investor has selected the following project finance deals as the most noteworthy of the year.

Deal	Bankers*
Deer Park Refining L.P. $400 million, 14-year, 6.47% notes issued under Rule 144A	**Goldman, Sachs & Co.,** Lehman Brothers, co-agent
Energy Investors Fund $125 million, 9.45%, 17-year secured bonds issued under Rule 144A	**Lehman Brothers,** CS First Boston
Indiantown Cogeneration L.P. $505 million taxable project finance debt securities $125 million tax-exempt project finance debt securities (November pricing)	**Morgan Stanley & Co.,** Goldman, Sachs & Co., Kidder, Peabody & Co., Lehman Brothers
Selkirk Cogen Funding Corp. $392 million first-mortgage bonds issued under Rule 144A: $165 million, 8.65%, 13-year; $227 million, 8.98%, 18-year $65 million equity restructuring	**CS First Boston,** Chase Securities, Morgan Stanley & Co.

Lead managers are indicated in bold.

Source: *Institutional Investor,* January 1995.

Capital Sources for Startup Companies and Small Businesses

Sources of Venture Capital

Small Business Investment Companies (SBICs)

Small Business Administration (SBA)
409 Third Street, S.W.—6th Floor
Washington, D.C. 20416
Telephone: 202-205-7586

The Small Business Investment Companies (SBIC) are licensed by the SBA. They are privately organized and privately managed investment firms, yet they are participants in a vital partnership between government and the private sector economy. With their own capital and with funds borrowed at favorable rates from the Federal government, SBICs provide venture capital to small independent businesses, both new and already established. Today there are two types of SBICs—the original, or regular SBICs and SSBICs (Specialized Small Business Investment Companies). SSBICs are specifically targeted toward the needs of entrepreneurs who have been denied the opportunity to own and operate a business because of social or economic disadvantage.

For further information call your regional SBA office listed below or the Answer Desk at 800-827-5722. See also page 209.

Regular Small Business Investment Companies

Alabama

First SBIC of Alabama
David C. DeLaney, President
16 Midtown Park East
Mobile, AL 36606
Tel: 205-476-0700

Source: *Directory of Operating Small Business Investment Companies*, U.S. Small Business Administration, Investment Division.

Note: In addition to the companies listed in this section of the *Almanac*, the *Directory of Small Business Investment Companies* includes SBICs designed to assist small businesses owned by socially or economically disadvantaged persons. The *Directory* also includes some specifics about each entry.

Hickory Venture Capital Corporation
J. Thomas Noojin, President
200 W. Court Square
Huntsville, AL 35801
Tel: 205-539-1931

Arizona

First Commerce & Loan LP
Ross M. Horowitz, GP & Manager
5620 N. Kolb
Tucson, AZ 85715
Tel: 520-298-2500

First Interstate Equity Corp.
Edmund G. Zito, President
100 West Washington Street
Phoenix, AZ 85003
Tel: 602-528-6647

Sundance Venture Partners, L.P.
(Main Office: Cupertino, CA)
Gregory S. Anderson, Vice-President
2828 N. Central Avenue
Phoenix, AZ 85004
Tel: 602-279-1101

Arkansas

Small Business Inv. Capital, Inc.
Charles E. Toland, President
10003 New Benton Hwy.
Mail: P.O. Box 3627
Little Rock, AR 72203
Tel: 501-455-6599

California

Aspen Ventures West II, L.P.
Alexander Cilento & David Crocket, Mgrs.
1000 Fremont Avenue
Los Altos, CA 94024
Tel: 415-917-5670

AVI Capital, L.P.
P. Wolken, B. Weinman & B. Grossi, Mgrs.
One First Street
Los Altos, CA 94022
Tel: 415-949-9862

BT Capital Corp.
(Main Office: New York, NY)
300 South Grand Avenue
Los Angeles, CA 90071
Tel: NONE

Citicorp Venture Capital, Ltd.
(Main Office: New York, NY)
2 Embarcadero Place
2200 Geny Road
Palo Alto, CA 94303
Tel: 415-424-8000

Developers Equity Capital Corporation
Larry Sade, Chairman of the Board
1880 Century Park East
Los Angeles, CA 90067
Tel: 310-277-0330

Draper Associates, a California LP
Timothy C. Draper, President
400 Seaport Court
Redwood City, CA 94063
Tel: 415-599-9000

First SBIC of California
Robert L. Boswell, Senior Vice President
650 Town Center Drive
Costa Mesa, CA 92626
Tel: 714-556-1964

First SBIC of California
(Main Office: Costa Mesa, CA)
5 Palo Alto Square
Palo Alto, CA 94306
Tel: 415-424-8011

First SBIC of California
(Main Office: Costa Mesa, CA)
155 North Lake Avenue
Pasadena, CA 91109
Tel: 818-304-3451

G C & H Partners
Edwin Huddleson, General Partner
One Maritime Plaza
San Francisco, CA 94110
Tel: 415-981-5252

Hall, Morris & Drufva II, L.P.
Ronald J. Hall, Managing Director
25401 Cabbot Road
Laguna Hills, CA 92653
Tel: 714-707-5096

Imperial Ventures, Inc.
Ray Vadalma, Manager
9920 South La Cienega Blvd.
Mail: P.O. Box 92991; L.A. 90009
Inglewood, CA 90301
Tel: 310-417-5710

Jupiter Partners
John M. Bryan, President
600 Montgomery Street
San Francisco, CA 94111
Tel: 415-421-9990

Marwit Capital Corp.
Martin W. Witte, President
180 Newport Center Drive
Newport Beach, CA 92660
Tel: 714-640-6234

Merrill Pickard Anderson & Eyre I
Steven L. Merrill, President
2480 Sand Hill Road
Menlo Park, CA 94025
Tel: 415-854-8600

New West Partners II
Timothy P. Haidinger, Manager
4350 Executive Drive
San Diego, CA 92121
Tel: 619-457-0723

Northwest Venture Partners
(Main Office: Minneapolis, MN)
3000 Sand Hill Road
Menlo Park, CA 94025
Tel: 503-223-6622

Norwest Equity Partners IV
(Main Office: Minneapolis, MN)
3000 Sand Hill Road
Menlo Park, CA 94025
Tel: 503-223-6622

Norwest Growth Fund, Inc.
(Main Office: Minneapolis, MN)
3000 Sand Hill Road
Menlo Park, CA 94025
Tel: 503-223-6622

Novus Ventures, L.P.
Daniel D. Tompkins, Manager
20111 Stevens Creek Boulevard
Cupertino, CA 95014
Tel: 408-252-3900

Pacific Mezzanine Fund, L.P.
David C. Woodward, General Partner
88 Kearny Street, Suite 1850
San Francisco, CA 94108
Tel: 415-362-6776

Ritter Partners
William C. Edwards, President
150 Isabella Avenue
Atherton, CA 94025
Tel: 415-854-1555

Sorrento Growth Partners I, L.P.
Robert Jaffe, Manager
4225 Executive Square, Suite 1450
San Diego, CA 92037
Tel: 619-452-6400

Sundance Venture Partners, L.P.
Larry J. Wells, General Manager
10600 N. DeAnza Blvd.
Cupertino, CA 95014
Tel: 408-257-8100

Union Venture Corp.
Kathleen Burns, Vice President
445 South Figueroa Street
Los Angeles, CA 90071
Tel: 213-236-5658

VK Capital Company
Franklin Van Kasper, General Partner
600 California Street
San Francisco, CA 94108
Tel: 415-391-5600

Walden-SBIC, L.P.
Arthur S. Berliner, Manager
750 Battery Street
San Francisco, CA 94111
Tel: 415-391-7225

Colorado
Hanifen Imhoff Mezzanine Fund, L.P.
Edward C. Brown, Manager
1125 17th Street
Denver, CO 80202
Tel: 303-291-5209

Connecticut
AB SBIC, Inc.
Adam J. Bozzuto, President
275 School House Road
Cheshire, CT 06410
Tel: 203-272-0203

All State Venture Capital Corporation
Ceasar N. Anquillare, President
The Bishop House
32 Elm Street, P.O. Box 1629
New Haven, CT 06506
Tel: 203-787-5029

Canaan SBIC, L.P.
Gregory Kopchinsky, Manager
105 Rowayton Avenue
Rowayton, CT 06853
Tel: 203-855-0400

Capital Resource Co. of Connecticut
Morris Morgenstein, General Partner
2558 Albany Avenue
West Hartford, CT 06117
Tel: 203-236-4336

Financial Opportunities, Inc.
Ms. Robin Munson, Manager
One Vision Drive
Enfield, CT 06082
Tel: 203-741-4444

First New England Capital, LP
Richard C. Klaffky, President
100 Pearl Street
Hartford, CT 06103
Tel: 203-293-3333

Marcon Capital Corp.
Martin A. Cohen, President
10 John Street
Southport, CT 06490
Tel: 203-259-7233

RFE Capital Partners, L.P.
Robert M. Williams, Managing Partner
36 Grove Street
New Canaan, CT 06840
Tel: 203-966-2800

RFE Investment Partners V, L.P.
James A. Parsons, General Partner
36 Grove Street
New Canaan, CT 06840
Tel: 203-966-2800

District of Columbia
Allied Investment Corporation
Cabell Williams, President
1666 K Street, N.W.
Washington, DC 20006
Tel: 202-331-1112

Allied Investment Corporation II
William F. Dunbar, President
1666 K Street, N.W.
Washington, DC 20006
Tel: 202-331-1112

Legacy Fund Limited Partnership
John Ledecky, Manager & General Partner
1400 34th Street
Washington, DC 20007
Tel: 202-965-2020

Florida
Allied Investment Corporation
(Main Office: Washington, DC)
Executive Office Center
2770 N. Indian River Blvd.
Vero Beach, FL 32960
Tel: 407-778-5556

Florida Capital Ventures, Ltd.
Warren E. Miller, President
880 Riverside Plaza
100 W. Kennedy Blvd.
Tampa, FL 33602
Tel: 813-229-2294

J & D Capital Corp.
Jack Carmel, President
12747 Biscayne Blvd.
North Miami, FL 33181
Tel: 305-893-0303

Market Capital Corp.
Donald Kolvenbach, President
1102 North 28th Street
Mail: P.O. Box 31667
Tampa, FL 33631
Tel: 813-247-1357

Quantum Capital Partners, Ltd.
Michael E. Chaney, President
4400 NE 25th Avenue
Fort Lauderdale, FL 33308
Tel: 305-776-1133

Western Financial Capital Corporation
(Main Office: Dallas, TX)
AmeriFirst Bank Building
18301 Biscayne Boulevard
N. Miami Beach, FL 33160
Tel: 305-933-5858

Georgia

Cordova Capital Partners, L.P.
Paul DiBella & Ralph Wright, Managers
3350 Cumberland Circle
Atlanta, GA 30339
Tel: 404-951-1542

Investor's Equity, Inc.
I. Walter Fisher, President
945 E. Paces Ferry Road
Atlanta, GA 30326
Tel: 404-266-8300

North Riverside Capital Corporation
Tom Barry, President
50 Technology Park/Atlanta
Norcross, GA 30092
Tel: 404-446-5556

Hawaii

Bancorp Hawaii SBIC
Robert Paris, President
111 South King Street
Honolulu, HI 96813
Tel: 808-521-6411

Illinois

Continental Illinois Venture Corp.
John Willis, President
209 South LaSalle Street
Mail: 231 South LaSalle Street
Chicago, IL 60693
Tel: 312-828-8023

First Capital Corp. of Chicago
J. Mikesell Thomas, President
Three First National Plaza
Chicago, IL 60670
Tel: 312-732-5400

Heller Equity Capital Corporation
John M. Goense, President
500 West Monroe Street
Chicago, IL 60661
Tel: 312-441-7200

Walnut Capital Corp.
Burton W. Kanter, Chairman of the Board
Two North LaSalle Street
Chicago, IL 60602
Tel: 312-346-2033

Indiana

1st Source Capital Corporation
Eugene L. Cavanaugh, Jr., Vice President
100 North Michigan Street
Mail: P.O. Box 1602; South Bend 46634
South Bend, IN 46601
Tel: 219-235-2180

Cambridge Ventures, LP
Ms. Jean Wojtowicz, President
8440 Woodfield Crossing
Indianapolis, IN 46240
Tel: 317-469-9704

Circle Ventures, Inc.
Carrie Walkup, Manager
26 N. Arsenal Avenue
Indianapolis, IN 46201
Tel: 317-636-7242

Iowa

MorAmerica Capital Corporation
David R. Schroder, President
101 2nd Street, SE
Cedar Rapids, IA 52401
Tel: 319-363-8249

Kansas

Kansas Venture Capital, Inc.
Rex E. Wiggins, President
6700 Antioch Plaza
Overland Park, KS 66204
Tel: 913-262-7117

Kansas Venture Capital, Inc.
(Main Office: Overland Park, KS)
Thomas C. Blackburn, Vice President
One Main Place
Wichita, KS 67202
Tel: 316-262-1221

KCEP I, L.P.
Paul H. Hanson, Manager
4200 Somerset Drive
Prairie Village, KS 66208
Tel: 913-649-1771

Kentucky

Mountain Ventures, Inc.
L. Ray Moncrief, President
P.O. Box 1738, 362 Old Whitley Road
London, KY 40743
Tel: 606-864-5175

Louisiana

First Commerce Capital, Inc.
William Harper, Manager
821 Gravier Street
New Orleans, LA 70119
Tel: 504-561-1491

Premier Venture Capital Corporation
G. Lee Griffin, President
451 Florida Street
Baton Rouge, LA 70821
Tel: 504-332-4421

Maine

North Atlantic Venture Fund II, L.P.
David M. Coit, Manager
70 Center Street
Portland, ME 04101
Tel: 207-772-1001

Maine Capital Corp.
David M. Coit, President
Seventy Center Street
Portland, ME 04101
Tel: 207-772-1101

Maryland

Anthem Capital, L.P.
William M. Gust, II, Manager
16 S. Calvert Street
Baltimore, MD 21202
Tel: 410-625-1510

Greater Washington Investments, Inc.
Haywood Miller, Manager
5454 Wisconsin Avenue
Chevy Chase, MD 20815
Tel: 301-656-0626

Massachusetts

Advent Atlantic Capital Company, LP
David D. Croll, Managing Partner
75 State Street
Boston, MA 02109
Tel: 617-345-7200

Advent Industrial Capital Company, LP
David D. Croll, Managing Partner
75 State Street
Boston, MA 02109
Tel: 617-345-7200

Advent V Capital Company LP
David D. Croll, Managing Partner
75 State Street
Boston, MA 02109
Tel: 617-345-7200

BancBoston Ventures, Incorporated
Frederick M. Fritz, President
100 Federal Street
Mail: P.O. Box 2016 Stop 01-31-08
Boston, MA 02110
Tel: 617-434-2442

Business Achievement Corporation
Michael L. Katzeff, President
1172 Beacon Street
Newton, MA 02161
Tel: 617 965-0550

Chestnut Capital International II LP
David D. Croll, Managing Partner
75 State Street
Boston, MA 02109
Tel: 617-345-7200

Chestnut Street Partners, Inc.
David D. Croll, President
75 State Street
Boston, MA 02109
Tel: 617-345-7220

First Capital Corp. of Chicago
(Main Office: Chicago, IL)
One Financial Center
Boston, MA 02111
Tel: 617-457-2500

LRF Capital, Limited Partnership
Joseph J. Freeman, Manager
189 Wells Avenue
Newton, MA 02159
Tel: 617-964-0049

Mezzanine Capital Corporation
David D. Croll, President
75 State Street
Boston, MA 02109
Tel: 617-345-7200

Northeast SBI Corp.
Joseph Mindick, Treasurer
16 Cumberland Street
Boston, MA 02115
Tel: 617-267-3983

Pioneer Ventures Limited Partnership
Frank M. Polestra, Managing Partner
60 State Street
Boston, MA 02109
Tel: 617-742-7825

Pioneer Ventures Limited Partnership II
Leigh Michl, Managing Partner
60 State Street
Boston, MA 02109
Tel: 617-742-7825

Seacoast Capital Partners, L.P.
Mr. Eben Moulton, Manager
55 Ferncroft Road
Danvers, MA 01923
Tel: 508-777-3866

UST Capital Corp.
Arthur F. Snyder, President
40 Court Street
Boston, MA 02108
Tel: 617-726-7000

Zero Stage Capital V, L.P.
Paul Kelley, Manager
Kendall Square
1010 Main Street
Cambridge, MA 02142
Tel: 617-876-5355

Michigan

Capital Fund, The
Barry Wilson, President
6412 Centurion Drive
Lansing, MI 48917
Tel: 517-323-7772

White Pines Capital Corporation
Mr. Ian Bund, President & Manager
2929 Plymouth Road
Ann Arbor, MI 48105
Tel: 313-747-9401

Minnesota

FBS SBIC, Limited Partnership
John M. Murphy, Jr., Managing Agent
601 Second Avenue South
Minneapolis, MN 55402
Tel: 612-973-0988

Northland Capital Venture Partnership
George G. Barnum, Jr., President
613 Missabe Building
Duluth, MN 55802
Tel: 218-722-0545

Norwest Equity Partners V, L.P.
John F. Whaley, Manager
2800 Piper Jaffray Tower
222 South 9th Street
Minneapolis, MN 55402
Tel: 612-667-1667

Northwest Venture Partners
Robert F. Zicarelli, Managing G.P.
2800 Piper Jaffray Tower
222 South 9th Street
Minneapolis, MN 55402
Tel: 612-667-1650

Norwest Equity Partners IV
Robert F. Zicarelli, General Partner
2800 Piper Jaffray Tower
222 South 9th Street
Minneapolis, MN 55402
Tel: 612-667-1650

Norwest Growth Fund, Inc.
Daniel J. Haggerty, President
2800 Piper Jaffray Tower
222 South 9th Street
Minneapolis, MN 55402
Tel: 612-667-1650

Piper Jaffray Healthcare Capital L.P.
Lloyd (Buzz) Benson, Manager
222 South 9th Street
Minneapolis, MN 55402
Tel: 612-342-6335

Missouri

Bankers Capital Corp.
Raymond E. Glasnapp, President
3100 Gillham Road
Kansas City, MO 64109
Tel: 816-531-1600

CFB Venture Fund I, Inc.
James F. O'Donnell, Chairman
11 South Meramec
St. Louis, MO 63105
Tel: 314-746-7427

CFB Venture Fund II, LP
Bart S. Bergman, President
1000 Walnut Street
Kansas City, MO 64106
Tel: 816-234-2357

Gateway Partners, L.P.
8000 Maryland Avenue
St. Louis, MO 63105
Tel: 314-721-5707

MorAmerica Capital Corporation
(Main Office: Cedar Rapids, IA)
911 Main Street
Commerce Tower Building
Kansas City, MO 64105
Tel: 816-842-0114

United Missouri Capital Corporation
Noel Shull, Manager
1010 Grand Avenue
Mail: P.O. Box 419226; K.C., MO 64141
Kansas City, MO 64106
Tel: 816-556-7333

Nebraska

United Financial Resources Corp.
Joan Boulay, Manager
7401 "F" Street
Mail: P.O. Box 1131; Omaha, NE 68101
Omaha, NE 68127
Tel: 402-339-7300

New Jersey

Bishop Capital, L.P.
Charles J. Irish, General Partner
500 Morris Avenue
Springfield, NJ 07081
Tel: 201-376-0495

CIT Group/Venture Capital, Inc.
Colby W. Collier, Manager
650 CIT Drive
Livingston, NJ 07932
Tel: 201-740-5429

ESLO Capital Corp.
Leo Katz, President
212 Wright Street
Newark, NJ 07114
Tel: 201-242-4488

DFW Capital Partners, L.P.
Donald F. DeMuth, Manager
Glenpointe Center East
300 Frank W. Burr Blvd.
Teaneck, NJ 07666
Tel: 201-836-2233

Fortis Capital Corporation
Martin Orland, President
333 Thornall Street
Edison, NJ 08837
Tel: 908-603-8500

MidMark Capital, L.P.
Denis Newman, Manager
466 Southern Boulevard
Chatham, NJ 07928
Tel: 201-822-2999

Tappan Zee Capital Corporation
Jack Birnberg, President
201 Lower Notch Road
Little Falls, NJ 07424
Tel: 201-256-8280

New York

399 Venture Partners
William Comfort, Chairman
399 Park Avenue
New York, NY 10043
Tel: 212-559-1127

ASEA-Harvest Partners II
Harvey Wertheim, General Partner
767 Third Avenue
New York, NY 10017
Tel: 212-838-7776

Argentum Capital Partners, LP
Daniel Raynor, Chairman
405 Lexington Avenue
New York, NY 10174
Tel: 212-949-8272

Atalanta Investment Company, Inc.
L. Mark Newman, Chairman of the Board
650 5th Avenue
New York, NY 10019
Tel: 212-956-9100

BT Capital Corp.
Noel E. Urben, President
280 Park Avenue
New York, NY 10017
Tel: 212-454-1903

Barclays Capital Investors Corp.
Graham McGahen, President
222 Broadway
New York, NY 10038
Tel: 212-412-3937

CB Investors, Inc.
Edward L. Kock III, President
270 Park Avenue
New York, NY 10017
Tel: 212-286-3222

CIBC Wood Gundy Ventures, Inc.
Gordon Muessel, Vice President
425 Lexington Avenue
New York, NY 10017
Tel: 212-856-3713

CMNY Capital II, L.P.
Robert G. Davidoff, General Partner
135 East 57th Street
New York, NY 10022
Tel: 212-909-8432

Chase Manhattan Capital Corporation
Gustav H. Koven, President
1 Chase Plaza
New York, NY 10081
Tel: 212-552-6275

Chemical Venture Capital Associates
Jeffrey C. Walker, Managing General Partner
New York, NY 10017
Tel: 212-270-3220

Citicorp Venture Capital, Ltd.
William Comfort, Chairman of the Board
399 Park Avenue
New York, NY 10043
Tel: 212-559-1127

Edwards Capital Company
Edward H. Teitlebaum, President
Two Park Avenue
New York, NY 10016
Tel: 212-686-5449

Eos Partners SBIC, L.P.
Marc H. Michel, Manager
520 Madison Avenue
New York, NY 10022
Tel: 212-832-5814

Exeter Equity Partners, L.P.
Keith Fox, Timothy Bradley, Jeff Weber
10 East 53rd Street
New York, NY 10022
Tel: 212-872-1170

Exeter Venture Lenders, L.P.
Keith Fox, Manager
10 East 53rd Street
New York, NY 10022
Tel: 212-872-1170

Fifty-Third Street Ventures, L.P.
Patricia Cloherty & Dan Tessler, G.P.
155 Main Street
Cold Spring, NY 10516
Tel: 914-265-4244

First Wall Street SBIC, LP
Alan Farkas, G.P.
26 Broadway
New York, NY 10004
Tel: 212-742-3770

Fundex Capital Corp.
Howard Sommer, President
525 Northern Blvd.
Great Neck, NY 11021
Tel: 516-466-8551

Furman Selz SBIC, L.P.
Brian Friedman, Manager
230 Park Avenue
New York, NY 10169
Tel: 212-309-8200

Genesee Funding, Inc.
Stuart Marsh, President & CEO
100 Corporate Woods
Rochester, NY 14623
Tel: 716-272-2332

IBJS Capital Corp.
Peter D. Matthy, President
One State Street
New York, NY 10004
Tel: 212-858-2000

InterEquity Capital Partners, LP
Irwin Schlass, President
220 Fifth Avenue
New York, NY 10001
Tel: 212-779-2022

J.P. Morgan Investment Corporation
David M. Cromwell, Managing Director
60 Wall Street
New York, NY 10260
Tel: 212-483-2323

KOCO Capital Company, L.P.
Walter Farley, CFO
111 Radio Circle
Mount Kisco, NY 10549
Tel: 212-397-1800

Kwiat Capital Corp.
Sheldon F. Kwiat, President
579 Fifth Avenue
New York, NY 10017
Tel: 212-223-1111

LEG Partners SBIC, L.P.
Lawrence E. Golub, Manager
230 Park Avenue
New York, NY 10169
Tel: 212-207-1585

Mercury Capital, L.P.
David W. Elenowitz, Manager
650 Madison Avenue
New York, NY 10022
Tel: 212-838-0888

M & T Capital Corp.
Phillip A. McNeill, Vice President
One Fountain Plaza
Buffalo, NY 14203
Tel: 716-848-3800

NYBDC Capital Corp.
Robert W. Lazar, President
41 State Street
P.O. Box 738
Albany, NY 12201
Tel: 518-463-2268

NatWest USA Capital Corporation
Phillip Krall, General Manager
175 Water Street
New York, NY 10038
Tel: 212-602-1200

Needham Capital SBIC, L.P.
John Michaelson, Manager
400 Park Avenue
New York, NY 10022
Tel: 212-705-0291

Norwood Venture Corp.
Mark R. Littell, President
1430 Broadway
New York, NY 10018
Tel: 212-869-5075

Odyssey Partners SBIC, L.P.
Alain Oberrotman, Manager
31 West 52nd Street
New York, NY 10019
Tel: 212-708-0641

Paribas Principal Incorporated
Steven Alexander, President
787 Seventh Avenue
New York, NY 10019
Tel: 212-841-2000

Prospect Street NYC Discovery Fund, L.P.
Richard E. Omohundro, CEO
250 Park Avenue
New York, NY 10177
Tel: 212-490-0480

Pyramid Ventures, Inc.
Brian Talbot, Vice President
130 Liberty Street
New York, NY 10006
Tel: 212-250-9571

R & R Financial Corp.
Imre Rosenthal, President
1370 Broadway
New York, NY 10036
Tel: 212-356-1400

Rand SBIC, Inc.
Donald Ross, President
1300 Rand Building
Buffalo, NY 14203
Tel: 716-853-0802

Sterling Commercial Capital, Inc.
Harvey L. Granat, President
175 Great Neck Road
Great Neck, NY 11021
Tel: 516-482-7374

TLC Funding Corp.
Phillip G. Kass, President
660 White Plains Road
Tarrytown, NY 10591
Tel: 914-332-5200

Tappan Zee Capital Corporation
(Main Office: Little Falls, NJ)
120 North Main Street
New City, NY 10956
Tel: 914-634-8890

UBS Partners, Inc.
Justin S. Maccarone, President
299 Park Avenue
New York, NY 10171
Tel: 212-821-6490

Vega Capital Corp.
Victor Harz, President
80 Business Park Drive
Armonk, NY 10504
Tel: 914-273-1025

Winfield Capital Corp.
Stanley M. Pechman, President
237 Mamaroneck Avenue
White Plains, NY 10605
Tel: 914-949-2600

North Carolina

First Union Capital Partners, Inc.
Kevin J. Roche, Senior Vice President
One First Union Center
301 South College Street
Charlotte, NC 28288
Tel: 704-374-6487

NationsBanc Capital Corporation
(Main Office: Dallas, TX)
100 N. Tryon
Charlotte, NC 28255
Tel: 704-386-8063

NationsBanc SBIC Corp.
George W. Campbell, Jr., President
901 West Trade Street
Charlotte, NC 28202
Tel: 704-386-7720

Springdale Venture Partners, LP
S. Epes Robinson, General Partner
2039 Queens Road, East
Charlotte, NC 28207
Tel: 704-344-8290

North Dakota

North Dakota SBIC, L.P.
David R. Schroder, Manager
417 Main Avenue
Fargo, ND 58103
Tel: 701-237-6132

Ohio

Banc One Capital Partners Corporation
(Main Office: Dallas, TX)
10 West Broad Street
Columbus, OH 43215
Tel: NONE

Clarion Capital Corp.
Morton A. Cohen, President
Ohio Savings Plaza
1801 East 9th Street
Cleveland, OH 44114
Tel: 216-687-1096

Key Equity Capital Corporation
Raymond Lancaster, President
127 Public Square
Cleveland, OH 44114
Tel: 216-689-5776

National City Capital Corporation
William H. Schecter, President & G.M.
1965 East Sixth Street
Cleveland, OH 44114
Tel: 216-575-2491

River Cities Capital Fund L.P.
R. Glen Mayfield, Manager
221 East Fourth Street
Cincinnati, OH 45202
Tel: 513-621-9700

Oklahoma

Alliance Business Investment Company
Barry Davis, President
17 East Second Street
One Williams Center
Tulsa, OK 74172
Tel: 918-584-3581

BancFirst Investment Corp.
T. Kent Faison, Manager
101 North Broadway
Mail: P.O. Box 26788
Oklahoma City, OK 73126
Tel: 405-270-1000

Oregon

Northern Pacific Capital Corporation
Joseph P. Tennant, President
937 S.W. 14th Street
Mail: P.O. Box 1658
Portland, OR 97207
Tel: 503-241-1255

Shaw Venture Partners III, L.P.
Ralph R. Shaw, Manager
400 Southwest Sixth Avenue
Portland, OR 97204
Tel: 503-228-4884

U.S. Bancorp Capital Corporation
Gary Patterson, President
111 S.W. Fifth Avenue
Portland, OR 97204
Tel: 503-275-5860

Pennsylvania

CIP Capital L.P.
Winston Churchill, Jr., Manager
20 Valley Stream Parkway
Malvern, PA 19355
Tel: 215-695-2066

Enterprise Venture Cap Corp of Pennsylvania
Don Cowie, CEO
111 Market Street
Johnstown, PA 15901
Tel: 814-535-7597

Fidelcor Capital Corp.
Elizabeth T. Crawford, President
Fidelity Building
123 South Broad Street
Philadelphia, PA 19109
Tel: 215-985-3722

First SBIC of California
(Main Office: Costa Mesa, CA)
Daniel A. Dye, Contact
P.O. Box 512
Washington, PA 15301
Tel: 412-223-0707

Meridian Capital Corp.
Pamela E. Davis, President
601 Penn Street
Reading, PA 19603
Tel: 215-655-2924

Meridian Venture Partners
Raymond R. Rafferty, General Partner
The Fidelity Court Building
259 Radnor-Chester Road
Radnor, PA 19087
Tel: 215-254-2999

PNC Capital Corp.
Gary J. Zentner, President
Pittsburgh National Building
Fifth Avenue and Wood Street
Pittsburgh, PA 15265
Tel: 412-762-2248

Rhode Island

Domestic Capital Corp.
Nathaniel B. Baker, President
815 Reservoir Avenue
Cranston, RI 02910
Tel: 401-946-3310

Fleet Equity Partners VI, L.P.
Robert Van Degna & Habib Y. Gorgi, Mgrs.
111 Westminster Street
Providence, RI 02903
Tel: 401-278-6770

Fleet Venture Resources, Inc.
Robert M. Van Degna, President
111 Westminster Street
Providence, RI 02903
Tel: 401-278-6770

Moneta Capital Corp.
Arnold Kilberg, President
99 Wayland Avenue
Mail: 285 Governor Street
Providence, RI 02906
Tel: 401-454-7500

NYSTRS/NV Capital, Limited Partnership
Robert M. Van Degna, Managing Partner
111 Westminster Street
Providence, RI 02903
Tel: 401-278-5597

Richmond Square Capital Corporation
Harold I. Schein, President
1 Richmond Square
Providence, RI 02906
Tel: 401-521-3000

Wallace Capital Corp.
Lloyd W. Granoff, President
170 Westminster Street
Providence, RI 02903
Tel: 401-273-9191

South Carolina

Charleston Capital Corporation
Henry Yaschik, President
111 Church Street
P.O. Box 328
Charleston, SC 29402
Tel: 803-723-6464

Floco Investment Company, Inc. (The)
William H. Johnson, Sr., President
Highway 52 North
Mail: P.O. Box 919; Lake City, SC 29560
Scranton, SC 29561
Tel: 803-389-2731

Lowcountry Investment Corporation
Joseph T. Newton, Jr., President
4444 Daley Street
P.O. Box 10447
Charleston, SC 29411
Tel: 803-554-9880

Tennessee

Byrd Business Investment, L.P.
Damon W. Byrd, General Partner
2000 Glen Echo Road
Nashville, TN 37215
Tel: 615-383-8673

Pacific Capital, L.P.
Stephen F. Wood, President
109 Westpart Drive
Brentwood, TN 37027
Tel: 615-371-9600

Sirrom Capital, LP
George M. Miller, II, Manager
511 Union Street
Nashville, TN 37219
Tel: 615-256-0701

Texas

AMT Capital, Ltd.
Tom H. Delimitros, CGP
8204 Elmbrook Drive
Dallas, TX 75247
Tel: 214-905-9760

Alliance Business Investment Company
(Main Office: Tulsa, OK)
911 Louisiana
One Shell Plaza
Houston, TX 77002
Tel: 713-224-8224

Banc One Capital Partners Corporation
Michael J. Endres, President
300 Crescent Court
Dallas, TX 75201
Tel: 214-979-4360

Capital Southwest Venture Corp.
William R. Thomas, President
12900 Preston Road
Dallas, TX 75230
Tel: 214-233-8242

Catalyst Fund, Ltd. (The)
Richard L. Herrman, Manager
Three Riverway
Houston, TX 77056
Tel: 713-623-8133

Central Texas SBI Corporation
Robert H. Korman II, Director
1401 Elm Street
Dallas, TX 75202
Tel: 214-508-0900

Charter Venture Group, Incorporated
Winston C. Davis, President
2600 Citadel Plaza Drive
P.O. Box 4525
Houston, TX 77008
Tel: 713-622-7500

Citicorp Venture Capital, Ltd.
(Main Office: New York, NY)
717 North Harwood
Dallas, TX 75201
Tel: 214-880-9670

Ford Capital, Ltd.
C. Jeff Pan, President
200 Crescent Court
Mail: P.O. Box 2140; Dallas, TX 75221
Dallas, TX 75201
Tel: 214-871-5177

HCT Capital Corp.
Vichy Woodward Young, Jr., President
4916 Camp Bowie Boulevard
Fort Worth, TX 76107
Tel: 817-763-8706

Houston Partners, SBIP
Harvard Hill, President, CGP
Capital Center Penthouse
401 Louisiana
Houston, TX 77002
Tel: 713-222-8600

Jiffy Lube Capital Corporation
Mark Youngs, Manager
700 Milam Street
Mail: P.O. Box 2967
Houston, TX 77252
Tel: 713-546-8910

Mapleleaf Capital Ltd.
Patrick A. Rivelli, Manager
Three Forest Plaza
12221 Merit Drive
Dallas, TX 75251
Tel: 214-239-5650

NationsBanc Capital Corporation
David Franklin, President
901 Main Street
Dallas, TX 75202
Tel: 214-508-0900

SBI Capital Corp.
William E. Wright, President
6305 Beverly Hill Lane
Mail: P.O. Box 570368; Houston, TX 77257
Houston, TX 77057
Tel: 713-975-1188

SBIC Partners, L.P.
Gregory Forrest & Jeffrey Brown, Manager
201 Main Street
Fort Worth, TX 76102
Tel: 714-729-3222

Stratford Capital Group, Inc.
Michael D. Brown, President
200 Crescent Court
Dallas, TX 75201
Tel: 214-740-7377

UNCO Ventures, Ltd.
Walter Cunningham, Managing Partner
520 Post Oak Blvd.
Houston, TX 77027
Tel: 713-622-9595

Ventex Partners, Ltd.
Richard S. Smith, President
1000 Louisiana
Houston, TX 77002
Tel: 713-659-7860

Victoria Capital Corp.
David Jones, President
One O'Connor Plaza
Victoria, TX 77902
Tel: 512-573-5151

Victoria Capital Corp.
(Main Office: Victoria, TX)
Jeffrey P. Blanchard, Vice President
750 E. Mulberry #305   Mail: Box 1561
San Antonio, TX 78212
Tel: 210-736-4233

Western Financial Capital Corporation
Andrew S. Rosemore, President
17290 Preston Road
Dallas, TX 75252
Tel: 214-380-0044

Utah

First Security Bus. Investment Corp.
Louis D. Alder, Manager
79 South Main Street
Salt Lake City, UT 84111
Tel: 801-246-5737

Wasatch Venture Corporation
W. David Hemingway, Manager
1 South Main Street
Salt Lake City, UT 84133
Tel: 801-524-8939

Vermont

Green Mountain Capital, L.P.
Michael Sweatman, General Manager
RD 1, Box 1503
Waterbury, VT 05676
Tel: 802-244-8981

Queneska Capital Corporation
Albert W. Coffrin, III, President
123 Church Street
Burlington, VT 05401
Tel: 802-865-1806

Virginia

Rural America Fund, Inc.
Fred Russell, Chief Executive Officer
2201 Cooperative Way
Herndon, VA 22071
Tel: 703-709-6750

Walnut Capital Corp.
(Main Office: Chicago, IL)
8000 Tower Crescent Drive
Vienna, VA 22182
Tel: 703-448-3771

Washington

Pacific Northwest Partners SBIC, L.P.
Theodore M. Wight, Manager
Suite 800, Koll Center Bellevue
500 108th Avenue, N.E.
Bellevue, WA 98004
Tel: 206-646-7357

West Virginia

Anker Capital Corporation
Thomas Loehr, Manager
208 Capitol Street
Charleston, WV 25301
Tel: 304-344-1794

WestVen Limited Partnership
Thomas E. Loehr, President
208 Capitol Street
Charleston, WV 25301
Tel: 304-344-1794

Wisconsin

Banc One Venture Corp.
H. Wayne Foreman, President
111 East Wisconsin Avenue
Milwaukee, WI 53202
Tel: 414-765-2274

Bando-McGlocklin SBIC
George Schonath, Chief Executive Officer
13555 Bishops Court
Brookfield, WI 53005
Tel: 414-784-9010

Capital Investments, Inc.
James R. Sanger, President
Commerce Building
744 North Fourth Street
Milwaukee, WI 53203
Tel: 414-273-6560

M & I Ventures Corp.
John T. Byrnes, President
770 North Water Street
Milwaukee, WI 53202
Tel: 414-765-7910

MorAmerica Capital Corporation
(Main Office: Cedar Rapids, IA)
600 East Mason Street
Milwaukee, WI 53202
Tel: 414-276-3839

Polaris Capital Corp.
Richard Laabs, President
One Park Plaza
11270 W. Park Place
Milwaukee, WI 53224
Tel: 414-359-3040

Washington, D.C.

First Legacy Fund, Inc.
Jonathan Ledecky, Manager
1400 34th Street, N.W.
Washington, DC 20007
Tel: 202-659-1100

Directories

Directory of Small Business Investment Companies. Contains a listing of SBICs by state including branch offices, contact persons, and types of businesses funded. Free of charge, the *Directory* is available by calling the Small Business Administration at 202-205-6666.

Pratt's Guide to Venture Capital Sources. Provides extensive information on all leading venture capital firms in the U.S.A. and around the world. Available from:

Venture Economics
40 West 57th Street
New York, NY 10102-0968

Corporate Finance Source Book. This volume provides a listing of thousands of US and world financial sources. Published by:

National Register Publishing Co.
121 Chanlon Road
New Providence, NJ 07974

National Venture Capital Association (NVCA) *Membership Directory* lists members of the association and information about it.

National Venture Capital Association
1655 North Fort Meyer Drive
Arlington, VA 22209
Tel: 703-528-4370

Small Business Administration (SBA) Field Offices

REGIONAL OFFICES

REGION I
155 Federal St.
Ninth Floor
Boston, MA 02110
Tel: (617) 451-2023
TDD: (617) 451-0491

REGION II
26 Federal Plaza
Room 31-08
New York, NY 10278
Tel: (212) 264-1450
TDD: (212) 264-5669

REGION III
475 Allendale Road
Suite 201
King Of Prussia, PA 19406
Tel: (215) 962-3700
TDD: (215) 962-3739

REGION IV
1375 Peachtree St. N.E.
Fifth Floor
Atlanta, GA 30367-8102
Tel: (404) 347-2797
TDD: (404) 347-5051

REGION V
300 S. Riverside Plaza
Suite 1975 S
Chicago, IL 60606-6617
Tel: (312) 353-5000
TDD: (312) 353-8060

REGION VI
8625 King George Drive
Building C
Dallas, TX 75235-3391
Tel: (214) 767-7633
TDD: (214) 767-1339

REGION VII
911 Walnut St.
13th Floor
Kansas City, MO 64106
Tel: (816) 426-3608
TDD: (816) 426-2990

REGION VIII
999 18th St.
Suite 701
Denver, CO 80202
Tel: (303) 294-7186
TDD: (303) 294-7096

REGION IX
71 Stevenson St.
20th Floor
San Francisco, CA 94105-2939
Tel: (415) 744-6402
TDD: (415) 744-6401

REGION X
2615 Fourth Ave.
Room 440
Seattle, WA 98121
Tel: (206) 553-5676
TDD: (206) 553-2872

DISTRICT, BRANCH AND POST-OF-DUTY OFFICES

ALABAMA
2121 8th Ave., N.
Suite 200
Birmingham, AL 35203-2398
Tel: (205) 731-1344
TDD: (205) 731-2265

ALASKA
222 W. 8th Ave.
Room 67
Anchorage, AK 99513-7559
Tel: (907) 271-4022
TDD: (907) 271-4005

ARIZONA
2828 N. Central Ave.
Suite 800
Phoenix, AZ 85004-1025
Tel: (602) 640-2316
TDD: (602) 640-2357

300 W. Congress St.
Room 7-H
Tucson, AZ 85701-1319
Tel: (602) 670-4759
TDD: None Listed

ARKANSAS
2120 Riverfront Drive
Suite 100
Little Rock, AR 72202
Tel: (501) 324-5278
TDD: (501) 324-7849

CALIFORNIA
2719 N. Air Fresno Drive
Fresno, CA 93727-1547
Tel: (209) 487-5189
TDD: (209) 487-5917

330 N. Brand Blvd.
Suite 1200
Glendale, CA 91203-2304
Tel: (818) 552-3210

880 Front St.
Suite 4-S-29
San Diego, CA 92188-0270
Tel: (619) 557-7252
TDD: (619) 557-6998

211 Main St.
Fourth Floor
San Francisco, CA 94105-1988
Tel: (415) 744-6820
TDD: (415) 744-6778

901 W. Civic Center Drive
Suite 160
Santa Ana, CA 92703-2352
Tel: (714) 836-2494
TDD: (714) 836-2200

660 J St.
Room 215
Sacramento, CA 95814-2413
Tel: (916) 551-1426
TDD: None Listed

6477 Telephone Road
Suite 10
Ventura, CA 93003-4459
Tel: (805) 642-1866
TDD: None Listed

COLORADO
721 19th St.
Suite 426
Denver, CO 80202-2259
Tel: (303) 844-3984
TDD: (303) 844-5638

CONNECTICUT
330 Main St.
Second Floor
Hartford, CT 06106
Tel: (203) 240-4700
TDD: (203) 524-1611

DISTRICT OF COLUMBIA
1110 Vermont Ave., N.W.
Suite 900
Washington, DC 20041
Tel: (202) 606-4000

DELAWARE
920 N. King St.
Suite 412
Wilmington, DE 19801
Tel: (302) 573-6295
TDD: (302) 573-6644

FLORIDA
1320 S. Dixie Highway
Suite 501
Coral Gables, FL 33146-2911
Tel: (305) 536-5521
TDD: (305) 530-7110

7825 Baymeadows Way
Suite 100-B
Jacksonville, FL 32256-7504
Tel: (904) 443-1900
TDD: (904) 443-1909

501 E. Polk St.
Suite 104
Tampa, FL 33602-3945
Tel: (813) 228-2594
TDD: None Listed

5601 Corporate Way
Suite 402
West Palm Beach, FL 33407
Tel: (407) 689-3922
TDD: None Listed

GEORGIA
1720 Peachtree Road, NW
Sixth Floor
Atlanta, GA 30309
Tel: (404) 347-4749
TDD: (404) 347-0107

52 N. Main St.
Room 225
Statesboro, GA 30458
Tel: (912) 489-8719
TDD: None Listed

GUAM
238 Archbishop F.C. Flores St.
Room 508
Agana, GU 96910
Tel: (671) 472-7277
TDD: None Listed

HAWAII
300 Ala Moana Blvd.
Room 2213
Honolulu, HI 96850-4981
Tel: (808) 541-2990
TDD: (808) 541-3650

IDAHO
1020 Main St.
Suite 290
Boise, ID 83702-5745
Tel: (208) 334-1696
TDD: (208) 334-9637

ILLINOIS
500 W. Madison St.
Room 1250
Chicago, IL 60661-2511
Tel: (312) 353-4528
TDD: (312) 886-5108

511 W. Capitol St.
Suite 302
Springfield, IL 62704
Tel: (217) 492-4416
TDD: (217) 492-4418

INDIANA
429 N. Pennsylvania
Suite 100
Indianapolis, IN 46204-1873
Tel: (317) 226-7272
TDD: (317) 226-5338

IOWA
215 4th Ave., SE
Suite 200
Cedar Rapids, IA 52401
Tel: (319) 262-6405

210 Walnut St.
Room 749
Des Moines, IA 50309
Tel: (515) 284-4422
TDD: (515) 284-4233

KANSAS
100 E. English St.
Suite 510
Wichita, KS 67202
Tel: (316) 269-6273
TDD: (316) 269-6205

KENTUCKY
600 Dr. M.L. King Jr. Place
Room 188
Louisville, KY 40202
Tel: (502) 582-5971
TDD: (502) 582-6715

LOUISIANA
1661 Canal St.
Suite 2000
New Orleans, LA 70112
Tel: (504) 589-6685
TDD: (504) 589-2053

500 Fannin St.
Room 8A-08
Shreveport, LA 71101
Tel: (318) 676-3196
TDD: None Listed

MAINE
40 Western Ave.
Room 512
Augusta, ME 04330
Tel: (207) 622-8378
TDD: (207) 626-9147

MARYLAND
10 N. Calvert St.
Third Floor
Baltimore, MD 21202
Tel: (410) 962-4392
TDD: (410) 962-7458

MASSACHUSETTS
10 Causeway St.
Room 265
Boston, MA 02222-1093
Tel: (617) 565-5590
TDD: (617) 565-5797

1550 Main St.
Room 212
Springfield, MA 01103
Tel: (413) 785-0268
TDD: None Listed

MICHIGAN
477 Michigan Ave.
Room 515
Detroit, MI 48226
Tel: (313) 226-6075
TDD: (313) 226-2958

228 West Washington St.
Room 11
Marquette, MI 49885
Tel: (906) 225-1108
TDD: (906) 228-4126

MINNESOTA
100 N. Sixth St.
Suite 610
Minneapolis, MN 55403-1563
Tel: (612) 370-2324
TDD: (612) 777-2332

MISSISSIPPI
101 W. Capitol St.
Suite 400
Jackson, MS 39201
Tel: (601) 965-4378
TDD: (601) 965-5328

1 Hancock Plaza
Suite 1001
Gulfport, MS 39501-7758
Tel: (601) 863-4449
TDD: (601) 865-9926

MISSOURI
323 W. Eighth St.
Suite 501
Kansas City, MO 64105
Tel: (816) 374-6708
TDD: (816) 374-6764

815 Olive St.
Room 242
St. Louis, MO 63101
Tel: (314) 539-6600
TDD: (314) 539-6654

620 S. Glenstone St.
Suite 110
Springfield, MO 65802-3200
Tel: (417) 864-7670
TDD: (417) 864-8855

MONTANA
301 S. Park
Room 528
Helena, MT 59626
Tel: (406) 449-5381
TDD: (406) 449-5053

NEBRASKA
11145 Mill Valley Road
Omaha, NE 68154
Tel: (402) 221-4691
TDD: (402) 498-3611

NEVADA
301 E. Stewart St.
Room 301
Las Vegas, NV 89125-2527
Tel: (702) 388-6611
TDD: None Listed

50 S. Virginia St.
Room 238
Reno, NV 89505-3216
Tel: (702) 784-5268
TDD: None Listed

NEW HAMPSHIRE
143 N. Main St.
Suite 202
Concord, NH 03302-1257
Tel: (603) 225-1400
TDD: (603) 225-1462

NEW JERSEY
60 Park Place
Fourth Floor
Newark, NJ 07102
Tel: (201) 645-2434
TDD: (201) 645-4653

2600 Mt. Ephraim Ave.
Camden, NJ 08104
Tel: (609) 757-5183
TDD: None Listed

NEW MEXICO
625 Silver Ave., S.W.
Suite 320
Albuquerque, NM 87102
Tel: (505) 766-1870
TDD: (505) 766-1883

NEW YORK
26 Federal Plaza
Room 3100
New York, NY 10278
Tel: (212) 264-2454
TDD: (212) 264-9147

100 S. Clinton St.
Room 1071
Syracuse, NY 13260
Tel: (315) 423-5383
TDD: (315) 423-5723

111 W. Huron St.
Room 1311
Buffalo, NY 14202
Tel: (716) 846-4301
TDD: (716) 846-3248

333 E. Water St.
4th Floor
Elmira, NY 14901
Tel: (607) 734-8130
TDD: (607) 734-0557

35 Pinelawn Road
Room 102E
Melville, NY 11747
Tel: (516) 454-0750
TDD: None Listed

100 State St.
Room 410
Rochester, NY 14614
Tel: (716) 263-6700
TDD: None Listed

Leo O'Brian Building
Room 815
Albany, NY 12207
Tel: (518) 472-6300
TDD: None Listed

NORTH CAROLINA
200 N. College St.
Charlotte, NC 28202
Tel: (704) 344-6563
TDD: (704) 344-6640

NORTH DAKOTA
657 Second Ave., N.
Room 218
Fargo, ND 58108-3086
Tel: (701) 239-5131
TDD: (701) 239-5657

OHIO
1240 E. Ninth St.
Room 317
Cleveland, OH 44199
Tel: (216) 522-4180
TDD: (216) 522-8350

2 Nationwide Plaza
Suite 1400
Columbus, OH 43215-2592
Tel: (614) 469-6860
TDD: (614) 469-6684

525 Vine St.
Suite 870
Cincinnati, OH 45202
Tel: (513) 684-2814
TDD: (513) 684-6920

OKLAHOMA
200 N.W. Fifth St.
Suite 670
Oklahoma City, OK 73102
Tel: (405) 231-4301
TDD: None Listed

OREGON
222 S.W. Columbia
Suite 500
Portland, OR 97201-6605
Tel: (503) 326-2682
TDD: (503) 326-2591

PENNSYLVANIA
475 Allendale Road
Suite 201
King Of Prussia, PA 19406
Tel: (215) 962-3804
TDD: (215) 962-3806

960 Penn Ave.
Fifth Floor
Pittsburgh, PA 15222
Tel: (412) 644-2780
TDD: (412) 644-5143

100 Chestnut St.
Room 309
Harrisburg, PA 17101
Tel: (717) 782-3840
TDD: (717) 782-3477

20 N. Pennsylvania Ave.
Room 2327
Wilkes-Barre, PA 18702
Tel: (717) 826-6497
TDD: (717) 821-4174

PUERTO RICO
Carlos Chardon Ave.
Room 691
Hato Rey, PR 00918
Tel: (809) 766-5572
TDD: (809) 766-5174

RHODE ISLAND
380 Westminster Mall
Fifth Floor
Providence, RI 02903
Tel: (401) 528-4561
TDD: (401) 528-4690

SOUTH CAROLINA
1835 Assembly St.
Room 358
Columbia, SC 29201
Tel: (803) 765-5376
TDD: (803) 253-3364

SOUTH DAKOTA
101 W. Main Ave.
Suite 101
Sioux Falls, SD 57102-0527
Tel: (605) 330-4231
TDD: (605) 331-3527

TENNESSEE
50 Vantage Way
Suite 201
Nashville, TN 37228-1500
Tel: (615) 736-5881
TDD: (615) 736-2499

TEXAS
4300 Amon Carter Blvd.
Suite 114
Fort Worth, TX 76155
Tel: (817) 885-6500
TDD: (817) 885-6552

10737 Gateway West
Suite 320
El Paso, TX 79935
Tel: (915) 540-5676
TDD: (915) 540-5196

222 E. Van Buren St.
Room 500
Harlingen, TX 78550
Tel: (512) 427-8533
TDD: (512) 423-0691

9301 Southwest Freeway
Suite 550
Houston, TX 77074-1591
Tel: (713) 773-6500
TDD: (713) 773-6568

1611 10th St.
Suite 200
Lubbock, TX 79401
Tel: (806) 743-7462
TDD: (806) 743-7474

7400 Blanco Road
Suite 200
San Antonio, TX 78216
Tel: (512) 229-4535
TDD: (512) 229-4555

606 N. Carancahua
Suite 1200
Corpus Christi, TX 78476
Tel: (512) 888-3331
TDD: (512) 888-3188

819 Taylor St.
Room 8A-27
Ft. Worth, TX 76102
Tel: (817) 334-3777
TDD: None Listed

300 E. Eighth St.
Room 520
Austin, TX 78701
Tel: (512) 482-5288
TDD: None Listed

505 E. Travis
Room 103
Marshall, TX 75670
Tel: (903) 935-5257
TDD: None Listed

UTAH
125 S. State St.
Room 2237
Salt Lake City, UT 84138-1195
Tel: (801) 524-5804
TDD: (801) 524-4040

VERMONT
87 State St.
Room 205
Montpelier, VT 05602
Tel: (802) 828-4422
TDD: (802) 828-4552

VIRGINIA
400 N. Eighth St.
Room 3015
Richmond, VA 23240
Tel: (804) 771-2400
TDD: (804) 771-8078

VIRGIN ISLANDS
4200 United Shopping Plaza
Suite 7
Christiansted
St. Croix, VI 00820-4487
Tel: (809) 778-5380
TDD: None Listed

Veterans Drive
Room 210
St. Thomas, VI 00802
Tel: (809) 774-8530
TDD: None Listed

WASHINGTON
915 Second Ave.
Room 1792
Seattle, WA 98174-1088
Tel: (206) 553-1420
TDD: (206) 553-6809

W. 601 First Ave.
10th Floor E.
Spokane, WA 99204-0317
Tel: (509) 353-2800
TDD: (509) 353-2424

WEST VIRGINIA
168 W. Main St.
Fifth Floor
Clarksburg, WV 26301
Tel: (304) 623-5631
TDD: (304) 623-5616

550 Eagan St.
Room 309
Charleston, WV 25301
Tel: (304) 347-5220
TDD: (304) 347-5438

WISCONSIN
212 E. Washington Ave.
Room 213
Madison, WI 53703
Tel: (608) 264-5261
TDD: (608) 264-5333

310 W. Wisconsin Ave.
Suite 400
Milwaukee, WI 53203
Tel: (414) 297-3941
TDD: (414) 297-1095

WYOMING
100 E. B St.
Room 4001
Casper, WY 82602-2839
Tel: (307) 261-5761
TDD: (307) 261-5806

Small Business Development Centers (SBDCs)

SBDCs, sponsored by SBA in partnership with state and local governments, the educational community and the private sector, provide high-quality, low-cost assistance, counseling and training to prospective and existing small business owners.

The following list of lead SBDCs is arranged by regions.

REGION I

State Director
Small Business Development Center
University of Southern Maine
15 Surrenden Street
Portland, ME 04103
Tel: 207-780-4420
Fax: 207-780-4810

State Director
Small Business Development Center
University of Massachusetts
School of Management
Amherst, MA 01003-4935
Tel: 413-545-6301
Fax: 413-545-1273

State Director
Small Business Development Center
University of Connecticut
Box U-41
368 Fairfield Road
Storrs, CT 06269-2041
Tel: 203-486-4135
Fax: 203-486-1576

State Director
Small Business Development Center
Bryant College
1150 Douglas Pike
Smithfield, RI 02917
Tel: 401-232-6111
Fax: 401-232-6407

State Director
Small Business Development Center
Vermont Technical College
P.O. Box 422
Randolph Center, VT 05060
Tel: 802-728-9101
Fax: 802-728-3026

State Director
Small Business Development Center
University of New Hampshire
108 McConnell Hall
Durham, NH 03824
Tel: 603-862-2200
Fax: 603-862-4468

REGION II

State Director
Small Business Development Center
Rutgers University
University Heights
180 University Street
Newark, NJ 07102
Tel: 201-648-5950
Fax: 201-648-1110

State Director
Small Business Development Center
State University of New York
SUNY Upstate
SUNY Plaza, S-523
Albany, NY 12246
Tel: 518-443-5398
Fax: 518-465-4992

State Director
Small Business Development Center
State University of New York
SUNY Downstate
SUNY Plaza, S-523
Albany, NY 12246
Tel: 518-443-5398
Fax: 518-465-4992

Director
Small Business Development Center
University of the Virgin Islands
8000 Nisky Center
Charlotte Amalie
St. Thomas, Virgin Islands 00802-5804
Tel: 809-776-3206
Fax: 809-775-3756

Director
Small Business Development Center
University of Puerto Rico
Box 5253—College Station
Building B
Mayaguez, PR 00681
Tel: 809-834-3590
Fax: 809-834-3790

REGION III

State Director
Small Business Development Center
University of Pennsylvania
The Wharton School
444 Vance Hall
3733 Spruce Street
Philadelphia, PA 19104
Tel: 215-898-1219
Fax: 215-898-1299

Regional Director
Small Business Development Center
Howard University
2600 6th Street, N.W.
Washington, D.C. 20059
Tel: 202-806-1550
Fax: 202-806-1777

State Director
Small Business Development Center
University of Delaware
Purnell Hall
Newark, DE 19716
Tel: 302-831-2747
Fax: 302-831-1423

State Director
Small Business Development Center
Governor's Office of Community and
    Industrial Development
1115 Virginia Street, East
Charleston, WV 25301
Tel: 304-558-2960
Fax: 304-558-0127

State Director
Small Business Development Center
Department of Economic and
    Employment Development
217 East Redwood Street
Baltimore, MD 21202
Tel: 410-333-6995
Fax: 410-333-4460

State Coordinator
Small Business Development Center
Department of Economic Development
1021 East Cary Street
Richmond, VA 23206
Tel: 804-371-8258
Fax: 804-371-8185

REGION IV

State Director
Small Business Development Center
University of South Carolina
College of Business Administration
1710 College Street
Columbia, SC 29208
Tel: 803-777-4907
Fax: 803-777-4403

State Director
Small Business Development Center
University of West Florida
19 West Garden Street
Pensacola, FL 32501
Tel: 904-444-2060
Fax: 904-444-2070

State Director
Small Business Development Center
University of Alabama
1717 11th Avenue South
Birmingham, AL 35294
Tel: 205-934-7260
Fax: 205-934-7645

State Director
Small Business Development Center
University of Georgia
Chicopee Complex
1180 East Broad Street
Athens, GA 30601
Tel: 706-542-6761-5412
Fax: 706-542-5760

State Director
Small Business Development Center
University of Kentucky
College of Business and Economics
225 Business and Economics Building
Lexington, KY 40506-0034
Tel: 606-257-7668
Fax: 606-258-1907

State Director
Small Business Development Center
University of Mississippi
Old Chemistry Building
University, MS 38677
Tel: 601-232-5001
Fax: 601-232-5650

State Director
Small Business Development Center
Memphis State University
South Campus
Getwell Road, Building #1
Memphis, TN 38152
Tel: 901-678-2500
Fax: 901-678-4072

State Director
Small Business Development Center
University of North Carolina
4509 Creedmoor Road
Raleigh, NC 27612
Tel: 919-571-4154
Fax: 919-571-4161

REGION V

State Director
Small Business Development Center
University of Wisconsin
432 North Lake Street
Madison, WI 53706
Tel: 608-263-7794
Fax: 608-262-3878

State Director
Small Business Development Center
Department of Trade and Economic
    Development
500 Metro Square
121 Seventh Place East
St. Paul, MN 55101-2146
Tel: 612-297-5770
Fax: 612-296-1290

State Director
Small Business Development Center
Wayne State University
2727 Second Avenue
Detroit, MI 48201
Tel: 313-577-4848
Fax: 313-577-4422

State Director
Small Business Development Center
Department of Commerce and
    Community Affairs
620 East Adams Street
Springfield, IL 62701
Tel: 217-524-5856
Fax: 217-785-6328

State Director
Small Business Development Center
Economic Development Council
One North Capitol
Indianapolis, IN 46204-2248
Tel: 317-264-6871
Fax: 317-264-3102

State Director
Small Business Development Center
Department of Development
77 South High Street
Columbus, OH 43226-1001
Tel: 614-466-2711
Fax: 614-466-0829

REGION VI

Acting State Director
Small Business Development Center
University of Arkansas
Little Rock Technology Center Building
100 South Main
Little Rock, AR 72201
Tel: 501-324-9043
Fax: 501-324-9049

State Director
Small Business Development Center
Northeast Louisiana University
College of Business Administration
700 University Avenue
Monroe, LA 71209-6435
Tel: 318-342-5506
Fax: 318-342-5510

State Director
Small Business Development Center
SE Oklahoma State University
Station A, Box 2584
Durant, OK 74701
Tel: 405-924-0277
Fax: 405-924-8531

Region Director
Small Business Development Center
University of Houston
601 Jefferson
Houston, TX 77002
Tel: 713-752-8444
Fax: 713-752-8400

Region Director
South Texas-Border
Small Business Development Center
University of Texas at San Antonio
College of Business
801 Bowie
San Antonio, TX 78205
Tel: 210-224-0791
Fax: 210-224-9834

Region Director
Northwest Texas
Small Business Development Center
Texas Tech University
Center for Innovation
2579 South Loop 289
Lubbock, TX 79423-1637
Tel: 806-745-3973
Fax: 806-745-6207

Region Director
North Texas
Small Business Development Center
Dallas County Community College
1402 Corinth Street
Dallas, TX 75215
Tel: 214-565-5831
Fax: 214-565-5857

State Director
Small Business Development Center
Santa Fe Community College
P.O. Box 4187
Santa Fe, NM 87502-4187
Tel: 505-438-1362
Fax: 505-438-1237

REGION VII

State Director
Small Business Development Center
University of Nebraska at Omaha
60th & Dodge Streets
Omaha, NE 68182
Tel: 402-554-2521
Fax: 402-554-3747

State Director
Small Business Development Center
Iowa State University
137 Lynn Avenue
Ames, IA 50010
Tel: 515-292-6351
Fax: 515-292-0020

State Director
Small Business Development Center
University of Missouri
300 University Place
Columbia, MO 65211
Tel: 314-882-0344
Fax: 314-884-4297

State Director
Small Business Development Center
Wichita State University
1845 Fairmount
Wichita, KS 67260-0148
Tel: 316-689-3193
Fax: 316-689-3647

REGION VIII

Executive Director
Small Business Development Center
University of Utah
102 West 500 South
Salt Lake City, UT 84101
Tel: 801-581-7905
Fax: 801-581-7814

State Director
Small Business Development Center
University of South Dakota
School of Business
414 East Clark
Vermillion, SD 57069
Tel: 605-677-5498
Fax: 605-677-5272

State Director
Small Business Development Center
University of North Dakota
Gamble Hall, University Station
Grand Forks, ND 58202-7308
Tel: 701-777-3700
Fax: 701-777-3225

State Director
Small Business Development Center
Department of Commerce
1424 Ninth Avenue
Helena, MT 59620
Tel: 406-444-4780
Fax: 406-444-2808

State Director
Small Business Development Center
Office of Business Development
1625 Broadway
Denver, CO 80202
Tel: 303-892-3809
Fax: 303-892-3848

REGION IX

State Director
Small Business Development Center
University of Nevada in Reno
College of Business Administration
Reno, NV 89557-0100
Tel: 702-784-1717
Fax: 702-784-4337

State Director
Small Business Development Center
Maricopa County Community College
2411 West 14th Street
Tempe, AZ 85281-6941
Tel: 602-731-8720
Fax: 602-731-8729

State Director
Small Business Development Center
University of Hawaii at Hilo
523 West Lanikaula Street
Hilo, HI 96720-4091
Tel: 808-933-3515
Fax: 808-933-3683

State Director
Small Business Development Center
California Trade and Commerce Agency
801 K Street
Sacramento, CA 95814
Tel: 916-324-5068
Fax: 916-322-5084

REGION X

State Director
Small Business Development Center
Washington State University
College of Business and Economics
144 Todd Hall
Pullman, WA 99164-4740
Tel: 509-335-1576
Fax: 509-335-0949

State Director
Small Business Development Center
Lane Community College
99 West 10th Avenue
Eugene, OR 97401
Tel: 503-726-2250
Fax: 503-345-6006

State Director
Small Business Development Center
Boise State University
1910 University Drive
Boise, ID 83725
Tel: 208-385-1640
Fax: 208-385-3877

Director
Small Business Development Center
University of the Virgin Islands
8000 Nicky Center
Charlotte Amalie
St. Thomas
U.S. Virgin Islands 0082-5804
Tel: 809-776-3206
Fax: 809-776-3756

State Director
Small Business Development Center
University of Alaska/Anchorage
430 West 7th Avenue
Anchorage, AK 99501
Tel: 907-274-7232
Fax: 907-274-9524

Returns on Various Types of Investments

TANGIBLE/FINANCIAL RETURNS
PERIOD ENDING 6/1/95

Asset	Av. Return 1 yr.	Av. Return 5 yrs.	Av. Return 10 yrs.	Av. Return 20 yrs.
Stocks	20.1%	11.4%	14.6%	13.8%
Forex	19.8	6.4	9.1	4.4
Bonds	15.8	11.4	11.7	10.5
T-Bills	5.5	4.8	6.2	8.1
Oil	3.5	1.6	−3.8	2.7
Stamps	0.8	1.3	−0.5	8.2
Gold	0.1	1.1	2.0	4.4
Diamonds	0.0	0.2	5.9	7.7
Sotheby's Stock (Proxy for Art Investment)	0.0	−6.2		
Silver	−0.1	1.1	−1.5	0.9
Housing	−1.4	2.5	3.8	5.8
CPI	2.9	3.3	3.5	5.4

Source: R. S. Salomon, Jr., Principal, STI Management.

Stock Market: U.S. and Foreign

Investment Returns on Stocks, Bonds, and Bills

Roger G. Ibbotson* and Carl G. Gargula**

Our look at history consists of examining the returns of five capital market sectors. We measure total returns (capital gains plus income) on large company stocks, long-term corporate bonds, long-term government bonds, U.S. Treasury bills, and rates of inflation on consumer goods. Comparing the returns from the various sectors gives us insights into the returns available from taking risk and the relationships between capital market returns and inflation.

THE RISKS AND REWARDS

We display graphically the rewards and risks available from the U.S. capital markets over the past 69 years. Exhibit 1 shows the growth of an investment in large company stocks, long-term government bonds, and Treasury bills as well as the increase in the inflation index over the 69-year period. Each of the series is initiated at $1 at year-end 1925. The vertical scale is logarithmic so that equal distances represent equal percentage changes anywhere along the axis. The graph vividly portrays that despite setbacks such as that of October 1987, large company stocks were the big winner over the entire period. If $1 were invested in stocks at year-end 1925 and all dividends reinvested, the dollar investment would have grown to $810.54 by year-end 1994. This phenomenal growth was not without substantial risk, especially during the earlier portion of the period. In contrast, long-term government bonds (with a constant 20-year maturity) exhibited much less risk, but grew to only $25.86.

A virtually riskless strategy (for those with short-term time horizons) has been to buy U.S. Treasury bills. However, Treasury bills have had a marked tendency to track inflation, with the result that their real (inflation adjusted) return is near zero for the entire 1926–1994 period. Note that the tracking is only prevalent over the latter portion of the period. During periods of deflation (such as the late 1920s and early 1930s) the Treasury bill returns were near zero, but not negative, since no one intentionally buys securities with negative yields. Beginning in the early 1940s, the yields (returns) on Treasury bills were pegged by the government at low rates while high inflation was experienced. The government pegging ended with the U.S. Treasury-Federal Reserve Accord in March 1951.

We summarize the investment returns in Exhibit 2 by presenting the average annual returns over the 1926–1994 period. Large company stocks returned a compounded (geometric mean) total return of 10.2 percent per year. The annual compound return from capital appreciation alone was 5.3 percent. After adjusting for inflation, annual compounded total returns were 6.9 percent per year.

The average total return over any single year (arithmetic mean) for stocks was 12.2 percent, with positive returns recorded in more than two-thirds of the years (49 out of 69 years). The risk or degree of return fluctuation is measured by standard deviation as 20.3 percent. The frequency distribution (histogram) counts the number of years the returns fell in each 5 percent return increment. Note the wide variations in large company stock returns relative to the other capital market sectors. Annual stock returns ranged from 54.0 percent in 1933 to −43.3 percent in 1931.

A simple example illustrates the difference between geometric and arithmetic means. Suppose $1 was invested in a large company stock portfolio that experiences successive annual returns of +50 percent and −50 percent. At the end of the first year, the portfolio is worth $1.50. At the end of the second year, the portfolio is worth $0.75. The annual arithmetic mean is 0 percent, whereas the annual geometric mean (compounded return) is −13.4 percent. Naturally, it is the geometric mean that more directly measures the change in wealth over more than one period. On the other hand, the arithmetic mean is a better representation of typical performance over any single annual period.

The other capital market sectors also had returns commensurate with their risks. Long-term corporate bonds outperformed the default-free, long-term government bonds, which in turn outperformed the essentially riskless U.S. Treasury bills. Over the entire period the riskless U.S. Treasury bills had a

---

* Professor, Yale School of Management, New Haven, Connecticut and President of Ibbotson Associates.

** Managing Director and General Counsel, Ibbotson Associates, Chicago.

EXHIBIT 1: WEALTH INDICES OF INVESTMENTS IN THE U.S. CAPITAL MARKETS, 1925–1994 (Year-End 1925 = $1.00)

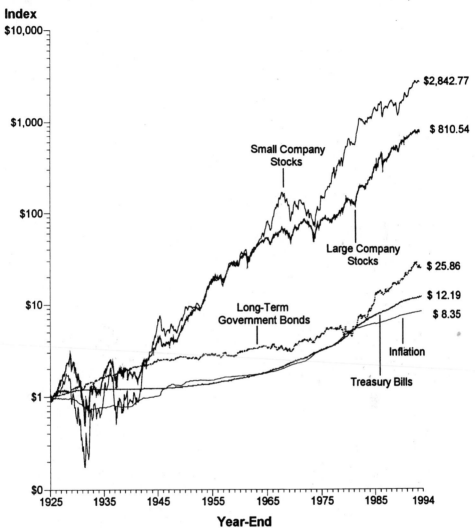

return almost identical with the inflation rate. Thus, we again note that the real rate of interest (the inflation-adjusted riskless rate) has been on average very near 0 percent historically.

MEASUREMENT OF THE FIVE SERIES

The returns were computed by compounding monthly returns, with no adjustments made for transactions costs or taxes. We describe each of the five total return series which are listed annually in Exhibit 3. The index numbers in Exhibit 3 are dollar values of a $1 investment made on December 31, 1925. They can be converted to yearly returns by taking the ratio of a given year-end index value to the previous year-end value, then subtracting one (1). For example, the return for large company stocks for 1994 equals $(810.538 \div 800.078) - 1 = .0131 = 1.31$ percent.

Large Company Stocks

The total return index is based upon Standard & Poor's (S&P) Composite Index with dividends reinvested monthly. To the extent that the 500 stocks currently included in the

EXHIBIT 2: BASIC SERIES: SUMMARY STATISTICS OF ANNUAL TOTAL RETURNS, 1926–1994

Series	Geometric Mean	Arithmetic Mean	Standard Deviation	Distribution
Large Company Stocks	10.2%	12.2%	20.3%	
Small Company Stocks	12.2	17.4	34.6	*
Long-Term Corporate Bonds	5.4	5.7	8.4	
Long-Term Government Bonds	4.8	5.2	8.8	
Intermediate-Term Government Bonds	5.1	5.2	5.7	
U.S. Treasury Bills	3.7	3.7	3.3	
Inflation	3.1	3.2	4.6	

-90%   0%   90%

* The 1933 Small Company Stock Total Return was 142.9 percent.

Source: *Stocks, Bonds, Bills and Inflation: 1995 Yearbook*, published by Ibbotson Associates, Inc., 225 North Michigan Avenue, Suite 700, Chicago, IL 60601-7676, telephone 312-616-1620. Used with permission. All rights reserved.

S&P Composite Index (prior to March 1957, there were 90 stocks) are representative of all stocks in the United States, the market value weighting scheme allows the returns of the index to correspond to the aggregate stock market returns in the U.S. economy.

Long-Term Corporate Bonds

We measure the total returns of a corporate bond index with approximately 20 years to maturity. We use Salomon Brothers' High-Grade Long-Term Corporate Bond Index from its beginning in 1969 through 1994. For the period 1946–68 we backdate Salomon Brothers' index using Salomon Brothers' monthly yield data and similar methodology. For the period 1926–45 we compute returns using Standard & Poor's monthly high-grade corporate composite bond yield data, assuming a 4 percent coupon and a 20-year maturity.

Long-Term Government Bonds

To measure the total returns of long-term U.S. government bonds, we use the bond data obtained from the U.S. Government Bond File (constructed by Lawrence

Fisher) at the Center for Research in Security Prices (CRSP) at the University of Chicago. We attempt to maintain a 20-year bond portfolio whose returns do not reflect the potential tax benefits, impaired negotiability, or the special redemption or call privileges frequently characterizing government bond prices and yields.

U.S. Treasury Bills

For the U.S. Treasury bill index, we again use the data in the CRSP U.S. Government Bond File. We measure one-month holding period returns for the shortest-term bills not less than one month in maturity. Since U.S. Treasury bills were not initiated until 1929, we use short-term coupon bonds whenever bill quotes are unavailable.

Consumer Price Index

We utilize the Consumer Price Index for All Urban Consumers (CPI-U), not seasonally adjusted, to measure inflation. The CPI-U, and its predecessor, the CPI (which we use prior to January 1978) is constructed by the Bureau of Labor Statistics, U.S. Department of Labor, Washington, D.C.

EXHIBIT 3: BASIC SERIES, INDICES OF YEAR-END CUMULATIVE WEALTH, 1925–1994 (December 1925 = $1.00)

Year	Large Stocks Total Returns	Large Stocks Capital Apprec	Small Stocks Total Returns	Long-Term Corp Bonds Total Returns	Long-Term Government Bonds Total Returns	Long-Term Government Bonds Capital Apprec	Intermediate-Term Government Bonds Total Returns	Intermediate-Term Government Bonds Capital Apprec	U.S. T-Bills Total Returns	Inflation
1925	1.000	1.000	1.000	1.000	1.000	1.000	1.000	1.000	1.000	1.000
1926	1.116	1.057	1.003	1.074	1.078	1.039	1.054	1.015	1.033	0.985
1927	1.535	1.384	1.224	1.154	1.174	1.095	1.101	1.025	1.065	0.965
1928	2.204	1.908	1.710	1.186	1.175	1.061	1.112	0.997	1.103	0.955
1929	2.018	1.681	0.832	1.225	1.215	1.059	1.178	1.014	1.155	0.957
1930	1.516	1.202	0.515	1.323	1.272	1.072	1.258	1.048	1.183	0.899
1931	0.859	0.636	0.259	1.299	1.204	0.982	1.228	0.991	1.196	0.814
1932	0.789	0.540	0.245	1.439	1.407	1.109	1.337	1.041	1.207	0.730
1933	1.214	0.792	0.594	1.588	1.406	1.074	1.361	1.031	1.211	0.734
1934	1.197	0.745	0.738	1.808	1.547	1.146	1.483	1.092	1.213	0.749
1935	1.767	1.053	1.035	1.982	1.624	1.171	1.587	1.146	1.215	0.771
1936	2.367	1.346	1.705	2.116	1.746	1.225	1.636	1.165	1.217	0.780
1937	1.538	0.827	0.716	2.174	1.750	1.195	1.661	1.165	1.221	0.804
1938	2.016	1.035	0.951	2.307	1.847	1.229	1.765	1.216	1.221	0.782
1939	2.008	0.979	0.954	2.399	1.957	1.272	1.845	1.255	1.221	0.778
1940	1.812	0.829	0.905	2.480	2.076	1.319	1.899	1.280	1.221	0.786
1941	1.602	0.681	0.823	2.548	2.096	1.306	1.909	1.278	1.222	0.862
1942	1.927	0.766	1.190	2.614	2.163	1.316	1.946	1.293	1.225	0.942
1943	2.427	0.915	2.242	2.688	2.208	1.311	2.000	1.309	1.229	0.972
1944	2.906	1.041	3.446	2.815	2.270	1.315	2.036	1.314	1.233	0.993
1945	3.965	1.361	5.983	2.930	2.514	1.424	2.082	1.327	1.237	1.015
1946	3.645	1.199	5.287	2.980	2.511	1.393	2.102	1.326	1.242	1.199
1947	3.853	1.199	5.335	2.911	2.445	1.328	2.122	1.322	1.248	1.307
1948	4.065	1.191	5.223	3.031	2.529	1.341	2.161	1.326	1.258	1.343
1949	4.829	1.313	6.254	3.132	2.692	1.396	2.211	1.338	1.272	1.318
1950	6.360	1.600	8.677	3.198	2.693	1.367	2.227	1.329	1.287	1.395
1951	7.888	1.863	9.355	3.112	2.587	1.282	2.235	1.307	1.306	1.477
1952	9.336	2.082	9.638	3.221	2.617	1.263	2.271	1.300	1.328	1.490
1953	9.244	1.944	9.013	3.331	2.713	1.271	2.345	1.308	1.352	1.499
1954	14.108	2.820	14.473	3.511	2.907	1.326	2.407	1.322	1.364	1.492
1955	18.561	3.564	17.431	3.527	2.870	1.272	2.392	1.281	1.385	1.497
1956	19.778	3.658	18.177	3.287	2.710	1.165	2.382	1.237	1.419	1.540
1957	17.646	3.134	15.529	3.573	2.912	1.209	2.568	1.287	1.464	1.587
1958	25.298	4.327	25.605	3.494	2.734	1.098	2.535	1.233	1.486	1.615
1959	28.322	4.694	29.804	3.460	2.673	1.030	2.525	1.177	1.530	1.639
1960	28.455	4.554	28.823	3.774	3.041	1.125	2.822	1.264	1.571	1.663

(continued)

EXHIBIT 3: BASIC SERIES, INDICES OF YEAR-END CUMULATIVE WEALTH, 1925–1994 (December 1925 = $1.00) *(concluded)*

Year	Large Stocks		Small Stocks	Long-Term Corp Bonds	Long-Term Government Bonds		Intermediate-Term Government Bonds		U.S. T-Bills	Inflation
	Total Returns	Capital Apprec	Total Returns	Total Returns	Total Returns	Capital Apprec	Total Returns	Capital Apprec	Total Returns	
1961	36.106	5.607	38.072	3.956	3.070	1.093	2.874	1.243	1.604	1.674
1962	32.954	4.945	33.540	4.270	3.282	1.124	3.034	1.264	1.648	1.695
1963	40.469	5.879	41.444	4.364	3.322	1.093	3.084	1.237	1.700	1.723
1964	47.139	6.642	51.193	4.572	3.438	1.085	3.209	1.237	1.760	1.743
1965	53.008	7.244	72.567	4.552	3.462	1.048	3.242	1.199	1.829	1.777
1966	47.674	6.295	67.479	4.560	3.589	1.037	3.394	1.194	1.916	1.836
1967	59.104	7.560	123.870	4.335	3.259	0.896	3.428	1.148	1.997	1.892
1968	65.642	8.139	168.429	4.446	3.251	0.847	3.583	1.136	2.101	1.981
1969	60.059	7.210	126.233	4.086	3.086	0.755	3.557	1.054	2.239	2.102
1970	62.465	7.222	104.226	4.837	3.460	0.792	4.156	1.145	2.385	2.218
1971	71.406	8.001	121.423	5.370	3.917	0.844	4.519	1.177	2.490	2.292
1972	84.956	9.252	126.807	5.760	4.140	0.841	4.752	1.168	2.585	2.371
1973	72.500	7.645	87.618	5.825	4.094	0.777	4.971	1.142	2.764	2.579
1974	53.311	5.373	70.142	5.647	4.272	0.750	5.254	1.120	2.986	2.894
1975	73.144	7.068	107.189	6.474	4.665	0.755	5.665	1.121	3.159	3.097
1976	90.584	8.422	168.691	7.681	5.447	0.816	6.394	1.180	3.319	3.246
1977	84.077	7.453	211.500	7.813	5.410	0.752	6.484	1.119	3.489	3.466
1978	89.592	7.532	261.120	7.807	5.346	0.684	6.710	1.069	3.740	3.778
1979	106.113	8.459	374.614	7.481	5.280	0.617	6.985	1.015	4.128	4.281
1980	140.514	10.639	523.992	7.274	5.071	0.530	7.258	0.946	4.592	4.812
1981	133.616	9.605	596.717	7.185	5.166	0.476	7.944	0.903	5.267	5.242
1982	162.223	11.023	763.829	10.242	7.251	0.589	10.256	1.031	5.822	5.445
1983	198.745	12.926	1066.828	10.883	7.298	0.532	11.015	0.997	6.335	5.652
1984	211.199	13.106	995.680	12.718	8.427	0.544	12.560	1.009	6.959	5.875
1985	279.117	16.559	1241.234	16.546	11.037	0.641	15.113	1.100	7.496	6.097
1986	330.671	18.981	1326.275	19.829	13.745	0.737	17.401	1.177	7.958	6.166
1987	347.967	19.366	1202.966	19.776	13.372	0.658	17.906	1.121	8.393	6.438
1988	406.458	21.769	1478.135	21.893	14.665	0.661	18.999	1.096	8.926	6.722
1989	534.455	27.703	1628.590	25.447	17.322	0.718	21.524	1.143	9.673	7.034
1990	517.499	25.886	1277.449	27.173	18.392	0.699	23.618	1.155	10.429	7.464
1991	675.592	32.695	1847.629	32.577	21.942	0.769	27.270	1.240	11.012	7.693
1992	727.412	34.155	2279.039	35.637	23.709	0.772	29.230	1.248	11.398	7.916
1993	800.078	36.565	2757.147	40.336	28.034	0.855	32.516	1.317	11.728	8.133
1994	810.538	36.002	2842.773	38.012	25.856	0.733	30.843	1.170	12.186	8.351

THE CONSTANT DOLLAR DOW

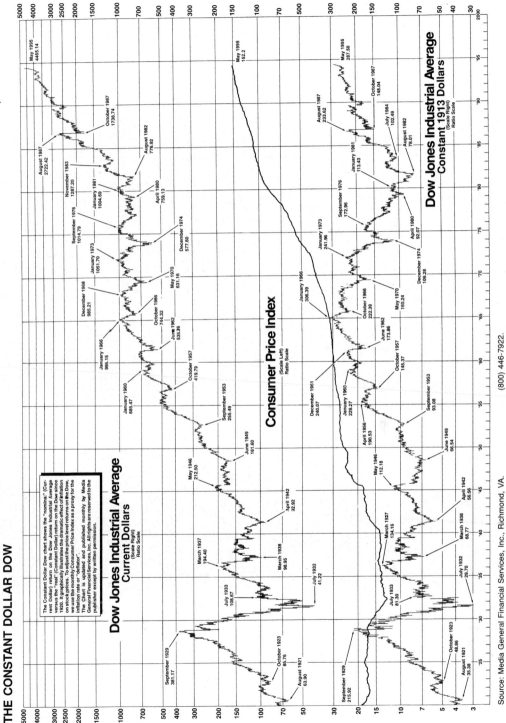

The Constant Dollar Dow chart shows the "nominal" (Current Dollar) return on the Dow Jones Industrial Average versus the "real" (Constant Dollar) return on the Dow since 1920. It graphically illustrates the dramatic effect of inflation on stock prices. To adjust the price level returns on the Dow, we use the monthly Consumer Price Index as a proxy for the inflation rate or "deflator".
The Chart is updated and published monthly by Media General Financial Services, Inc. All rights are reserved to the publisher except by written permission.

Dow Jones Industrial Average
Current Dollars
(Scale Right)
Ratio Scale

Consumer Price Index
(Scale Left)
Ratio Scale

Dow Jones Industrial Average
Constant 1913 Dollars
(Scale Right)
Ratio Scale

Source: Media General Financial Services, Inc., Richmond, VA.

(800) 446-7922.

Cash dividends on NYSE-listed common stocks

	Common stocks		
	Number of issues listed at year-end	Number paying cash dividends during year	Estimated aggregate cash payments (millions)
1940	829	577	$2,099
1945	881	746	2,275
1950	1,039	930	5,404
1951	1,054	961	5,467
1952	1,067	975	5,595
1953	1,069	964	5,874
1954	1,076	968	6,439
1955	1,076	982	7,488
1956	1,077	975	8,341
1957	1,098	991	8,807
1958	1,086	961	8,711
1959	1,092	953	9,337
1960	1,126	981	9,872
1961	1,145	981	10,430
1962	1,168	994	11,203
1963	1,194	1,032	12,096
1964	1,227	1,066	13,555
1965	1,254	1,111	15,302
1966	1,267	1,127	16,151
1967	1,255	1,116	16,866
1968	1,253	1,104	18,124
1969	1,290	1,121	19,404
1970	1,330	1,120	19,781
1971	1,399	1,132	20,256
1972	1,478	1,195	21,490
1973	1,536	1,276	23,627
1974	1,543	1,308	25,662
1975	1,531	1,273	26,901
1976	1,550	1,304	30,608
1977	1,549	1,360	36,270
1978	1,552	1,373	41,151
1979	1,536	1,359	46,937
1980	1,540	1,361	53,072
1981	1,534	1,337	60,628
1982	1,499	1,287	62,224
1983	1,518	1,259	67,102
1984	1,511	1,243	68,215
1985	1,503	1,206	74,237
1986	1,536	1,180	76,161
1987	1,606	1,219	84,377
1988	1,643	1,270	102,190
1989	1,683	1,303	101,778
1990	1,741	N/A	103,150 *
1991	1,860	N/A	123,385 *
1992	2,068	N/A	109,696 *
1993	2,331	N/A	120,206 *
1994	2,501	N/A	129,984 *

* Estimate based on average annual yield of the NYSE Composite Index.
N/A - Not available.

Source: New York Stock Exchange *Fact Book*.

NYSE Composite Index (Dec. 31, 1965=50) (closing prices)

	High	Date	Low	Date	Year-end
1950	12.01	12/30	9.85	1/14	12.01
1951	13.89	9/14, 10/6, 10/13	12.28	1/6	13.60
1952	14.49	12/26	13.31	10/24	14.49
1953	14.65	1/2	12.62	9/18	13.60
1954	19.40	12/31	13.70	1/8	19.40
1955	23.71	12/9, 12/30	19.05	1/7, 1/14	23.71
1956	25.90	8/3	22.55	1/20	24.35
1957	26.30	7/12	20.92	12/20	21.11
1958	28.85	12/24	21.45	1/10	28.85
1959	32.39	7/31	28.94	2/6	32.15
1960	31.99	1/8	28.38	10/21	30.94
1961	38.60	12/8, 12/15	31.17	1/6	38.39
1962	38.02	3/16	28.20	6/22	33.81
1963	39.92	12/27	34.41	1/4, 3/1	39.92
1964	46.49	11/18, 11/20	40.47	1/3	45.65
1965	50.00	12/31	43.64	6/28	50.00
1966	51.06	2/9	39.37	10/7	43.72
1967	54.16	10/9	43.74	1/3	53.83
1968	61.27	11/29	48.70	3/5	58.90
1969	59.32	5/14	49.31	7/29	51.53
1970	52.36	1/5	37.69	5/26	50.23
1971	57.76	4/28	49.60	11/23	56.43
1972	65.14	12/11	56.23	1/3	64.48
1973	65.48	1/11	49.05	12/5	51.82
1974	53.37	3/13	32.89	10/3	36.13
1975	51.24	7/15	37.06	1/2	47.64
1976	57.88	12/31	48.04	1/2	57.88
1977	57.69	1/3	49.78	11/2	52.50
1978	60.38	9/11, 9/12	48.37	3/6	53.62
1979	63.39	10/5	53.88	2/27	61.95
1980	81.02	11/28	55.30	3/27	77.86
1981	79.14	1/6	64.96	9/25	71.11
1982	82.35	11/9	58.80	8/12	81.03
1983	99.63	10/10	79.79	1/3	95.18
1984	98.12	11/6	85.13	7/24	96.38
1985	121.90	12/16	94.60	1/4	121.58
1986	145.75	9/4	117.75	1/22	138.58
1987	187.99	8/25	125.91	12/4	138.23
1988	159.42	10/21	136.72	1/20	156.26
1989	199.34	10/9	154.98	1/3	195.04
1990	201.13	7/16	162.20	10/11	180.49
1991	229.44	12/31	170.97	1/9	229.44
1992	242.08	12/18	217.92	4/8	240.21
1993	260.67	12/29	236.21	1/8	259.08
1994	267.71	2/2	243.14	4/4	250.94

Series records

High	267.71	2/2/94	Low	4.64	4/25/42

Source: New York Stock Exchange *Fact Book*.

NYSE Program trading participation in NYSE volume, 1994

	Total program trading as % of NYSE volume	Buy programs as % of NYSE volume	Sell programs as % of NYSE volume	Total program trading as % of twice (TTV) NYSE volume
January	10.3 %	4.8 %	5.5 %	5.1 %
February	8.5	3.7	4.8	4.2
March	15.3	6.8	8.5	7.7
April	11.9	4.5	7.4	5.9
May	9.3	3.5	5.8	4.7
June	13.3	6.1	7.2	6.7
July	10.4	4.5	5.9	5.2
August	9.3	3.7	5.6	4.7
September	12.6	5.4	7.2	6.3
October	11.6	5.8	5.8	5.8
November	11.6	5.3	6.3	5.8
December	14.5	8.5	6.0	7.2
1994	**11.6 %**	**5.3 %**	**6.3 %**	**5.8 %**
1993	11.9	6.5	5.4	6.0
1992	11.5	5.8	5.7	5.8
1991	11.0	5.9	5.1	5.5
1990	10.7	5.2	5.5	5.3
1989	9.9	5.4	4.5	5.0

Note: Starting June 13, 1991 percentages include Crossing Session II volume.

Source: New York Stock Exchange *Fact Book*.

Compounded growth rates in NYSE Composite Index (percent)

	'79	'80	'81	'82	'83	'84	'85	'86	'87	'88	'89	'90	'91	'92	'93	Index at year end
'79																61.95
'80	25.7															77.86
'81	7.1	-8.7														71.11
'82	9.4	2.0	14.0													81.03
'83	11.3	6.9	15.7	17.5												95.18
'84	9.2	5.5	10.7	9.1	1.3											96.38
'85	11.9	9.3	14.3	14.5	13.0	26.1										121.58
'86	12.2	10.1	14.3	14.4	13.3	19.9	14.0									138.58
'87	10.6	8.5	11.7	11.3	9.8	12.8	6.6	-0.3								138.23
'88	10.8	9.1	11.9	11.6	10.4	12.8	8.7	6.2	13.0							156.26
'89	12.2	10.7	13.4	13.4	12.7	15.1	12.5	12.1	18.8	24.8						195.04
'90	10.2	8.8	10.9	10.5	9.6	11.0	8.2	6.8	9.3	7.5	-7.5					180.49
'91	11.5	10.3	12.4	12.3	11.6	13.2	11.2	10.6	13.5	13.7	8.5	27.1				229.44
'92	11.0	9.8	11.7	11.5	10.8	12.1	10.2	9.6	11.7	11.3	7.2	15.4	4.7			240.21
'93	10.8	9.7	11.4	11.1	10.5	11.6	9.9	9.4	11.0	10.6	7.4	12.8	6.3	7.9		259.08
'94	9.8	8.7	10.2	9.9	9.2	10.0	8.4	7.7	8.9	8.2	5.2	8.6	3.0	2.2	-3.1	250.94

Initial year — Index figures taken at year end.

The table on this page presents annual growth rates in the NYSE Composite Index from 1979–94. Growth rate is a term referring to the average rate of increase or decrease, compounded annually, between two periods.

To obtain the growth rate, for example, between 1983 and 1994 go down the vertical column under 1983 to the horizontal row opposite 1994 which shows a 9.2% rate. This means that stock prices, as measured by the NYSE Composite Index, increased at a yearly rate of 9.2%, compounded annually, between the ends of those years. Stock prices showed a decrease of −3.1% in 1994.

The price appreciation on stocks is only a partial measure of the return on money invested in stock. To compute a total return, it is necessary to add the dividends received each year—a calculation not included in this table.

Source: New York Stock Exchange *Fact Book*.

NYSE Composite Index — yield and P/E ratio

End of period	Yield ◆	Price/ earnings ratio ★	End of period	Yield ◆	Price/ earnings ratio ★
1994			**1985**		
December	2.9 %	18.2	December	3.6 %	13.5
September	3.0	19.6	September	4.2	10.7
June	3.1	20.7	June	4.2	12.6
March	2.9	21.2	March	4.4	11.3
1993			**1984**		
December	2.5	23.4	December	4.5	10.4
September	2.9	23.8	September	4.5	10.6
June	3.0	22.8	June	4.9	10.1
March	2.8	23.3	March	4.5	11.6
1992			**1983**		
December	3.0	22.7	December	4.4	13.0
September	2.9	25.4	September	4.2	13.9
June	2.9	26.3	June	4.1	13.9
March	2.6	27.1	March	4.9	14.7
1991			**1982**		
December	2.4	25.8	December	5.2	14.7
September	3.4	19.7	September	6.1	12.5
June	3.4	17.6	June	7.0	11.3
March	3.6	17.1	March	7.2	10.3
1990			**1981**		
December	3.7	14.8	December	6.7	11.3
September	4.5	13.6	September	7.1	9.9
June	3.5	15.5	June	6.0	11.9
March	3.7	14.9	March	5.7	12.5
1989			**1980**		
December	3.2	15.0	December	5.4	13.1
September	3.4	14.2	September	5.7	12.7
June	3.5	13.3	June	6.0	9.8
March	3.9	12.5	March	6.8	9.4
1988			**1979**		
December	3.6	12.7	December	6.2	10.1
September	3.7	13.1	September	6.0	9.9
June	3.4	15.4	June	6.4	9.9
March	3.9	15.4	March	5.7	10.5
1987			**1978**		
December	3.4	15.5	December	5.9	10.3
September	2.9	22.0	September	5.3	10.9
June	2.7	21.1	June	5.5	11.8
March	2.8	20.2	March	6.0	10.7
1986			**1977**		
December	3.4	16.1	December	5.7	11.6
September	3.3	16.6	September	5.5	11.3
June	3.3	16.6	June	5.3	12.7
March	3.5	15.5	March	5.2	12.6

◆ Latest quarterly dividend divided by closing index value at end of period.

★ Latest closing index value divided by trailing 12 months of earnings.

Source: New York Stock Exchange *Fact Book*.

NASDAQ INDEX PERFORMANCES: 10 Years

Year	Value	Composite	Bank	Bio-technology[a]	Computer[a]	Industrial	Insurance	Other Finance	Telecommuni-cations[b]	Trans-portation
1994	High	803.93	787.92	209.70	235.62	851.80	949.10	966.19	184.37	808.09
	Low	693.79	662.57	143.11	182.82	686.46	858.96	831.79	149.51	621.31
	Close	751.96	697.07	161.40	233.99	753.81	925.87	863.42	155.29	660.03
	% Chg.	-3.2	1.11	-18.44	15.62	-6.46	0.57	-3.27	-16.07	-11.55
1993	High	787.42	725.65	–	–	809.72	956.91	921.28	205.94	746.26
	Low	645.87	530.03	–	–	660.17	787.80	775.76	126.05	624.44
	Close	776.8	689.43	–	–	805.84	920.59	892.64	185.02	746.26
	% Chg.	14.8	29.37	–	–	11.16	14.51	13.16	44.85	17.69
1992	High	676.95	532.93	–	–	741.92	803.91	788.81	734.18	634.10
	Low	547.84	352.81	–	–	581.60	589.03	558.38	610.08	530.06
	Close	676.95	532.93	–	–	724.94	803.91	788.81	734.18	634.10
	% Chg.	15.5	52.0	–	–	8.4	33.7	40.7	16.6	11.0
1991	High	586.34	350.56	–	–	668.95	601.09	560.79	629.53	571.39
	Low	355.75	246.07	–	–	387.47	434.23	340.72	447.48	405.00
	Close	586.34	350.56	–	–	668.95	601.09	560.79	629.53	571.39
	% Chg.	56.8	37.5	–	–	64.7	33.0	56.2	30.3	37.0
1990	High	469.60	400.19	–	–	510.61	554.21	512.55	739.56	509.93
	Low	325.44	235.25	–	–	344.11	379.36	323.14	442.34	360.34
	Close	373.84	254.91	–	–	406.05	451.84	359.13	483.01	417.07
	% Chg.	-17.8	-34.8	–	–	-9.4	-17.2	-29.0	-34.5	-16.3
1989	High	485.73	491.16	–	–	472.42	561.34	567.23	788.51	498.20
	Low	378.56	375.38	–	–	374.93	424.74	457.79	87.13	394.62
	Close	454.82	391.02	–	–	447.99	546.01	505.64	128.25	498.20
	% Chg.	19.3	-10.2	–	–	18.2	27.2	10.1	47.1	25.9
1988	High	396.11	464.91	–	–	413.09	435.80	477.88	501.13	403.68
	Low	331.97	396.44	–	–	334.85	339.41	410.75	349.68	320.91
	Close	381.38	435.31	–	–	378.95	429.14	459.34	501.13	395.81
	% Chg.	15.4	11.4	–	–	11.8	22.2	12.9	41.0	24.0
1987	High	455.26	526.64	–	–	488.92	475.78	542.04	441.61	436.53
	Low	291.88	366.75	–	–	288.30	333.66	382.43	301.51	276.03
	Close	330.47	390.66	–	–	338.94	351.06	406.96	355.30	319.21
	% Chg.	-5.3	-5.3	–	–	-3.0	-13.1	-11.7	12.4	-8.5
1986	High	411.16	457.59	–	–	414.45	467.05	553.42	362.86	365.81
	Low	323.01	346.35	–	–	326.56	381.59	424.52	295.97	288.13
	Close	348.83	412.53	–	–	349.33	404.14	460.64	316.09	348.84
	% Chg.	7.4	18.1	–	–	5.8	5.8	8.8	4.8	19.6
1985	High	325.16	350.08	–	–	330.17	385.45	423.52	303.84	296.91
	Low	245.91	230.23	–	–	258.85	276.33	298.20	234.87	236.20
	Close	324.93	349.36	–	–	330.17	382.07	423.49	301.57	291.59
	% Chg.	31.4	52.0	–	–	26.6	35.0	41.8	26.4	21.9

Note: The Nasdaq Composite Index and its subindexes started on February 5, 1971, when Nasdaq itself began operation. The Industrial Index, also begun in February 1971, is Nasdaq's largest subindex, with 3,019 securities represented in its calculation.

a. Index began on November 1, 1993.

b. On November 1, 1993, the Utility Index was renamed Telecommunications Index, and reset to a base of 200, using a factor of 5.74805.

TEN-YEAR COMPARISONS OF NASDAQ, NYSE, AND AMEX

Year	Companies			Issues			Share Volume (millions)		
	Nasdaq	NYSE	Amex	Nasdaq	NYSE	Amex	Nasdaq	NYSE	Amex
1994	4,902	2,570	824	5,761	3,150	983	74,353	73,420	4,523
1993	4,611	2,362	869	5,393	2,927	1,010	66,540	66,923	4,582
1992	4,113	2,089	814	4,764	2,658	942	48,455	51,376	3,600
1991	4,094	1,885	860	4,684	2,426	1,058	41,311	45,266	3,367
1990	4,132	1,769	859	4,706	2,284	1,063	33,380	39,665	3,329
1989	4,293	1,719	859	4,963	2,241	1,069	33,530	41,699	3,125
1988	4,451	1,681	896	5,144	2,234	1,101	31,070	40,850	2,515
1987	4,706	1,647	869	5,537	2,244	1,077	37,890	47,801	3,506
1986	4,417	1,573	796	5,189	2,257	957	28,737	35,680	2,979
1985	4,136	1,540	783	4,784	2,298	940	20,699	27,511	2,101
1984	4,097	1,543	792	4,728	2,319	930	15,159	23,071	1,545

50 MOST ACTIVE NASDAQ NATIONAL MARKET SECURITIES: 1994

Symbol	Company Name	Closing Price (12/31/93)	Share Volume (thousands)
1. INTC	Intel Corporation	$63.875	1,184,123
2. CSCO	Cisco Systems, Inc.	35.125	1,007,533
3. MSFT	Microsoft Corporation	61.125	841,594
4. NOVL	Novell, Inc.	17.125	836,027
5. MCIC	MCI Communications Corporation	18.375	772,992
6. TCOMA	Tele-Communications, Inc.	21.750	663,001
7. ORCL	Oracle Systems Corporation	44.125	565,516
8. AAPL	Apple Computer, Inc.	39.000	510,234
9. LOTS	Lotus Development Corporation	41.000	434,852
10. DIGI	DSC Communications Corporation	35.875	424,935
11. COMS	3Com Corporation	51.563	413,644
12. DELL	Dell Computer Corporation	41.000	395,595
13. BNET	Bay Networks, Inc.	29.500	382,926
14. USHC	U.S. Healthcare, Inc.	41.250	376,291
15. SUNW	Sun Microsystems, Inc.	35.500	366,444
16. AMGN	Amgen Inc.	59.000	350,045
17. ERTS	Electronic Arts Inc.	19.250	327,514
18. IDBX	IDB Communications Group, Inc.	9.188	324,219
19. SYBS	Sybase, Inc.	52.000	314,937
20. IFMX	Informix Corporation	32.125	312,963
21. AMAT	Applied Materials, Inc.	42.250	307,482
22. PCCW	Price/Costco, Inc.	12.875	303,307
23. CALL	NEXTEL Communications, Inc.	14.375	297,047
24. CMCSK	Comcast Corporation	15.563	295,438
25. IDTI	Integrated Device Technology, Inc.	29.625	294,050
26. QNTM	Quantum Corporation	15.125	282,420
27. AKLM	Acclaim Entertainment, Inc.	14.375	272,456
28. MEOHF	Methanex Corporation	13.000	264,263
29. COTTF	Cott Corporation	9.813	260,141
30. ASTA	AST Research, Inc.	14.625	257,077
31. APCC	American Power Conversion Corporation	16.375	256,258
32. LDDS	LDDS Communications, Inc.	19.438	252,625
33. SPCL	Spectrum Information Technologies, Inc.	1.750	239,127
34. ADBE	Adobe Systems Incorporated	29.750	236,692
35. BGEN	Biogen, Inc.	41.750	229,863
36. CRUS	Cirrus Logic, Inc.	22.500	227,774
37. CHIR	Chiron Corporation	80.375	208,783
38. PMTC	Parametric Technology Corporation	34.500	204,127
39. PYXS	Pyxis Corporation	19.000	193,102
40. ALTR	Altera Corporation	41.875	192,740
41. ERICY	LM Ericsson Telephone Company	55.125	179,530
42. PRGO	Perrigo Company	12.500	176,692
43. GNPT	GP Financial Corp.	20.625	173,583
44. ADPT	Adaptec, Inc.	23.625	165,327
45. ATML	Atmel Corporation	33.500	157,284
46. GATE	Gateway 2000, Inc.	21.625	155,048
47. BMCS	BMC Software, Inc.	56.875	151,963
48. CNTO	Centocor, Inc.	16.250	151,279
49. NOBE	Nordstrom, Inc.	42.000	151,003
50. CREAF	Creative Technology Ltd.	14.250	150,935

Note: This list includes only securities that had a 1994 closing price of $3 or more.

QUARTERLY DOW JONES INDUSTRIAL STOCK AVERAGE

The table below lists the total earnings (losses) of the Dow Jones Industrial Average component stocks of record based on generally accepted accounting principles as reported by the company and adjusted by the Dow Divisor in effect at quarter end and the total dividends of the component stocks based upon the record date and adjusted by the Dow Divisor in effect at quarter end. The payout ratio is the reciprocal of the latest 12 — months dividends divided by the latest 12-months earnings.— N.A.-Not available. d-Indicates deficit/negative earnings for the quarter.

Year Ended	Quarter Ended	Clos. Avg.	Qtrly Chg.	% Chg.	Qtrly Earns	12-Mth Earns	P/E Ratio	Qtrly Divs	12-Mth Divs	Divs Yield	Payout Ratio
1995	Mar. 31	4147.69	+ 313.25	+ 8.16	81.31	289.97	14.3	28.15	108.14	2.60	.3739
1994	Dec. 30	3834.44	− 8.75	− 0.22	82.68	256.13	15.0	27.37	105.66	2.75	.4125
	Sept. 30	3843.19	+ 218.23	+ 6.02	62.79	213.87	18.0	26.96	103.47	2.69	.4837
	June 30	3624.96	− 11.00	− 0.30	63.19	194.81	18.6	25.66	101.31	2.79	.5200
	Mar. 31	3635.96	− 118.13	− 2.89	47.47	150.22	24.2	25.67	100.71	2.76	.6704
1993	Dec. 31	3754.09	+ 198.97	+ 5.59	40.42	146.84	25.6	25.18	99.66	2.65	.6786
	Sept. 30	3555.12	+ 39.04	+ 1.11	43.73	104.52	34.0	24.80	100.61	2.83	.9625
	June 30	3516.08	+ 80.97	+ 2.36	18.60	84.65	41.5	25.06	101.84	2.90	1.2030
	Mar. 31	3435.11	+ 134.00	+ 4.06	44.09	113.43	30.3	24.62	102.29	2.98	.9017
1992	Dec. 31	3301.11	+ 29.45	+ 0.90	d1.90	108.25	30.5	26.13	100.72	3.05	.9304
	Sept. 30	3271.66	− 46.86	− 1.41	23.86	84.35	38.8	26.03	97.99	3.00	1.1617
	June 30	3318.52	+ 83.05	+ 2.57	47.38	71.60	46.3	25.51	95.52	2.88	1.3341
	Mar. 31	3235.47	+ 66.64	+ 2.10	38.91	60.62	53.4	23.05	93.28	2.88	1.5388
1991	Dec. 31	3168.83	+ 152.06	+ 5.04	d25.80	49.27	64.3	23.40	95.18	3.00	1.9318
	Sept. 30	3016.77	+ 110.02	+ 3.78	11.11	100.91	29.9	23.56	97.58	3.23	.9670
	June 28	2906.75	− 7.11	− 0.24	36.40	131.42	22.1	23.27	99.37	3.42	.7561
	Mar. 28	2913.86	+ 280.20	+ 10.64	27.56	154.17	18.9	24.95	102.32	3.51	.6637
1990	Dec. 31	2633.66	+ 181.18	+ 7.39	25.84	172.05	15.3	25.80	103.70	3.94	.6027
	Sept. 28	2452.48	− 428.21	− 14.86	41.62	193.17	12.7	25.35	101.40	4.13	.5249
	June 29	2880.69	+ 173.48	+ 6.41	59.15	207.78	13.9	26.22	104.75	3.64	.5041
	Mar. 30	2707.21	− 45.99	− 1.67	45.44	205.60	13.2	26.33	106.67	3.94	.5188
1989	Dec. 29	2753.20	+ 60.38	+ 1.69	46.96	221.48	12.4	23.50	103.00	3.74	.4651
	Sept. 29	2692.82	+ 252.76	+ 10.35	56.23	225.48	11.9	28.70	100.29	3.72	.4447
	June 30	2440.06	+ 146.44	+ 6.38	56.97	226.52	10.8	28.14	92.13	3.77	.4067
	Mar. 31	2293.62	+ 125.05	+ 5.77	61.32	229.75	10.0	22.66	84.17	3.67	.3663
1988	Dec. 30	2168.57	+ 55.66	+ 2.63	50.96	215.46	10.1	20.79	79.53	3.67	.3691
	Sept. 30	2112.91	− 28.80	− 1.34	57.27	181.04	11.7	20.54	76.41	3.62	.4221
	June 30	2141.71	+ 153.65	+ 7.73	60.20	168.54	12.7	20.18	73.92	3.45	.4386
	Mar. 31	1988.06	+ 49.23	+ 2.54	47.03	144.45	13.8	18.02	71.85	3.61	.4974
1987	Dec. 31	1938.83	− 657.45	− 25.32	16.54	133.05	14.6	17.67	71.20	3.67	.5351
	Sept. 30	2596.28	+ 177.75	+ 7.34	44.77	137.99	18.8	18.05	70.62	2.72	.5117
	June 30	2418.53	+ 113.84	+ 4.94	36.11	126.23	19.2	18.11	69.41	2.87	.5494
	Mar. 31	2304.69	+ 408.74	+ 21.56	35.63	126.49	18.2	17.37	68.19	2.96	.5391
1986	Dec. 31	1895.95	+ 128.37	+ 7.26	21.48	115.59	16.4	17.09	67.04	3.54	.5800
	Sept. 30	1767.58	− 125.14	− 6.61	33.01	118.80	14.9	16.79	67.14	3.80	.5652
	June 30	1892.72	+ 74.11	+ 4.08	36.37	103.39	18.3	16.94	65.37	3.45	.6323
	Mar. 31	1818.61	+ 271.94	+ 17.58	24.73	96.43	18.9	16.22	63.38	3.49	.6573
1985	Dec. 31	1546.67	+ 218.04	+ 16.41	24.69	96.11	16.1	17.19	62.03	4.01	.6454
	Sept. 30	1328.63	− 6.83	− 0.51	17.60	90.78	14.6	15.02	61.83	4.65	.6811
	June 28	1335.46	+ 68.68	+ 5.14	29.41	102.26	13.1	14.95	61.53	4.61	.6017
	Mar. 29	1266.78	+ 55.21	+ 4.56	24.41	107.87	11.7	14.87	61.56	4.86	.5707
1984	Dec. 31	1211.57	+ 4.86	+ 0.40	19.36	113.58	10.7	16.99	60.63	5.00	.5338
	Sept. 28	1206.71	+ 74.31	+ 6.56	29.08	108.11	11.2	14.72	58.41	4.84	.5403
	June 29	1132.40	− 32.49	− 2.79	35.02	102.07	11.1	14.98	57.67	5.09	.5650
	Mar. 30	1164.89	− 93.75	− 7.45	30.12	87.38	13.3	13.94	56.39	4.84	.6453
1983	Dec. 30	1258.64	+ 25.51	+ 2.07	13.89	72.45	17.4	14.77	56.33	4.47	.7775
	Sept. 30	1233.13	+ 11.17	+ 0.91	23.04	56.12	22.0	13.98	54.59	4.43	.9727
	June 30	1221.96	+ 91.93	+ 8.13	20.33	11.59	105.4	13.70	54.05	4.42	4.6635
	Mar. 31	1130.03	+ 83.49	+ 7.98	15.19	9.52	118.7	13.88	54.10	4.79	5.6828
1982	Dec. 31	1046.54	+ 150.29	+ 16.77	d2.44	9.15	114.4	13.03	54.14	5.17	5.9169
	Sept. 30	896.25	+ 84.32	+ 10.38	d21.49	35.15	25.5	13.44	55.55	6.20	1.5804
	June 30	811.93	− 10.84	− 1.32	18.26	79.90	10.2	13.75	55.84	6.88	.6989
	Mar. 31	822.77	− 52.23	− 5.97	14.82	97.13	8.5	13.92	56.28	6.84	.5794
1981	Dec. 31	875.00	+ 25.02	+ 2.94	23.56	113.71	7.7	14.44	56.22	6.42	.4944
	Sept. 30	849.98	− 126.90	− 12.99	23.26	123.32	6.9	13.73	56.18	6.61	.4539
	June 30	976.88	− 26.99	− 2.69	35.49	128.91	7.6	14.19	55.98	5.73	.4266
	Mar. 31	1003.87	+ 39.88	+ 4.14	31.40	123.60	8.1	13.86	54.99	5.48	.4449
1980	Dec. 31	963.99	+ 31.57	+ 3.39	33.17	121.86	7.9	14.40	54.36	5.64	.4461
	Sept. 30	932.42	+ 64.50	+ 7.43	28.85	111.58	8.4	13.53	53.83	5.77	.4824
	June 30	867.92	+ 82.17	+ 10.46	30.18	116.40	7.5	13.20	52.81	6.08	.4537
	Mar. 31	785.75	− 52.99	− 6.32	29.66	120.77	6.5	13.23	52.10	6.63	.4314

THE MAJOR MARKET AVERAGES

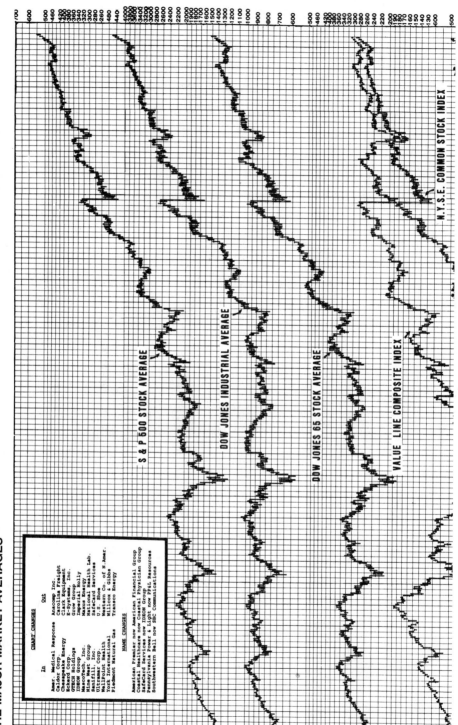

CHART CHANGES

In	Out
Amer. Medical Response	Anacomp Inc.
Caldor Corp.	Carolina Freight
Chesapeake Energy	Clark Equipment
Echard Corp.	E-Systems, Inc.
GTECH Holdings	Grow Group
IBEAM Group	Imperial Holly
ManorCare, Inc.	Marcus Energy
Mine West Group	National Health Lab.
Sanifill, Inc.	SafeCard Services
Ultramar Corp.	U.S. Shoe
WellPoint Health	Western Co. of N.Amer.
York International	Willcox & Gibbs
Piedmont Natural Gas	Transco Energy

NAME CHANGES

American Premier now American Financial Group
Coastal Healthcare now Coastal Physician Group
SafetyKleen Service now IBEAM Group
Pennsylvania Power & Light now PP&L Resources
Southwestern Bell now SBC Communications

S & P 500 STOCK AVERAGE

DOW JONES INDUSTRIAL AVERAGE

DOW JONES 65 STOCK AVERAGE

VALUE LINE COMPOSITE INDEX

N.Y.S.E. COMMON STOCK INDEX

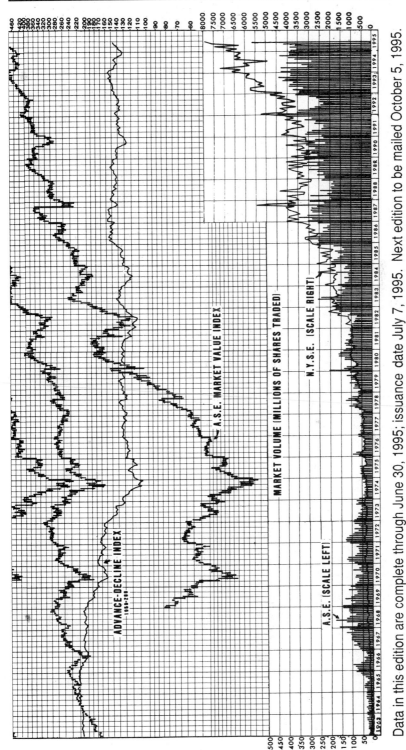

Data in this edition are complete through June 30, 1995; issuance date July 7, 1995. Next edition to be mailed October 5, 1995.

Source: Chart courtesy of Securities Research Company, a division of Babson-United Investment Advisors, Inc., 101 Prescott St., Wellesley Hills, MA 02181-7528.

STOCK MARKET AVERAGES BY INDUSTRY GROUP

The charts in this quarterly publication provide the investor with easy-to-read factual portrayals of both the market record and the underlying investment record of a large number of listed stocks which are traded on the New York and American Stock Exchanges. They represent a broadly diversified list of industrial, transportation, and utility enterprises. Each chart depicts the latest 12 years of monthly PRICE RANGES, EARNINGS, RATIO-CATOR (relative performance), and TRADING VOLUMES plotted against the running background of per share EARNINGS and DIVIDEND trends. All data have been fully adjusted for all stock dividends and splits and are drawn on uniform semi-logarithmic (ratio) scale grids.

All Capitalization figures are based on company's *latest annual* report.

Bonds include other long term debt.

Stocks included in the Dow-Jones Averages are designated by a star ''★'' placed *before the heading*.

Unless prefaced by a ''●'' for American Stock Exchange issues, all stocks charted are traded on the New York Stock Exchange.

Earnings and Dividends are read from the left-hand scale of each chart.

Earnings Lines — on a per share 12 months ended basis — are represented by the solid black line. Dots show whether company issues quarterly, semi-annual or only annual earnings reports. Earnings off the range of the charts, and deficits are shown by typed notations.

Dividend Lines — representing the annual rate of interim dividend payments — are shown by the dashed lines. The small circles show the month in which dividend payments are made. Dividends off the range of the charts as well as extra or irregular payments of each year are shown in typed figures.

Monthly Price Ranges represented by the solid vertical bars show the highest and lowest point of each month's transactions. Crossbars indicate the month's closing price.

The charted trends reflect relative, or percentage changes. Thus, in this scale, the vertical linear distance for a 100% move is the same any place on the chart — irrespective of whether the rise is from $5 to $10, $20 to $40 etc. This permits an accurate comparison from one chart to any other with the exception of those charts that have a special scale reduction. However, the comparability still exists within each of those charts.

These long-range charts complement the graphs found in the weekly-plotted and monthly published SRC Red Book of 5-Trend SECURITY CHARTS, which provide the latest short-term trends of the stocks charted herein.

Price Scale — The price ranges are always read from the scale at the right side of each chart. This scale is equal to 15 times the Earnings and Dividend scale at the left, so when the Price Range bars and the Earnings line coincide, it shows the price is at 15 times earnings. When the price is above the earnings line, the ratio of price to earnings is greater than 15 times earnings; when below, it is less.

Monthly Ratio-Cator: The plottings for this line are obtained by dividing the closing price of the stock by the closing price of the Dow-Jones Industrial Average for the same day. The resulting percentage is then multiplied by a factor of 750 to bring the price closer to the price bars for easier comparison. This line is plotted and read from the right scale. The plotting indicates whether the stock has kept pace, outperformed, or lagged the general market as represented by the DJIA.

Moving Average: This line represents the average of closing prices for the most recent 48-month period. Since our database starts in 1978, the majority of the moving averages begin in 1982. For those companies with shorter records the line begins when there is 48-months of price history.

Volume: The number of shares traded each month is shown by vertical bars at the bottom of each chart on an arithmetic scale. Thousands are indicated by a T at the top of the right volume scale and millions by an M.

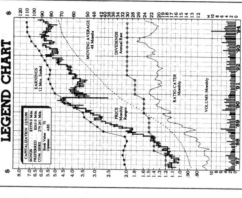

Study the Typical Patterns of these Charts and Read these Briefed ''Case Studies''

The importance of the factors of stock ''selection'' and ''timing'' in the development of a successful investment program is vividly portrayed in these CYCLI-GRAPH charts. Each graph presents the stirring pattern of a stock's market fluctuations throughout the advance and decline phases of the market cycles of the last 12 years. In this moving panorama, individual stocks are often cast in distinct roles in widely varying ''personalities'' which prosaic statistics fail to dramatize. And, in addition to facilitating the study of longer term characteristics described below, they spotlight the current ''point of cycle'' position from a historic standpoint (whether relatively in depression, mid-recovery, or advanced stages).

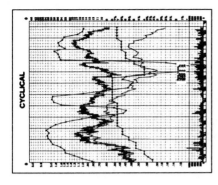

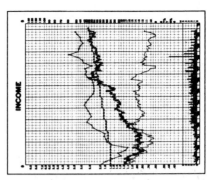

This chart portrays the record of a typical cyclical stock, demonstrating the wide fluctuations which characteristically occur in earnings, dividends, and prices. This is the type of company which benefits greatly from the upside of an economic boom and suffers substantially on the downslope. The chart also shows the tendency of these stocks to exaggerate the swings of the general market. In reflection of the risks involved in such issues, the price / earnings ratio is usually lower than the market average. With this record of wide price movement, cyclical stocks made good trading vehicles but obviously, timing is of the utmost importance.

Here is the picture of a successful company. It shows steadily rising earnings which have been reflected in higher stock market prices and a greater market evaluation of those earnings. It also shows that the performance has consistently been better than the market generally. Along with rising profits, dividends have been increased almost annually. Altogether, a gratifying long term growth investment. On the other hand, the record is not a straight upward line, for even the most outstanding companies are subject to some extent to the business cycles and market fluctuations.

Of much less interest from a capital gains viewpoint than growth issues are those classified in the "income" category. Relative to the market, such stocks often have a less than attractive record. But they are not to be disregarded since they do have appeal for the investor mainly seeking a good yield and the likelihood of gradual dividend boosts, along with some moderate appreciation. They are generally less vulnerable to cyclical changes than other groups, though they may be importantly affected by money rate fluctuations.

This chart portrays the record of a stock with a declining pattern. It is not a straight line, but one interrupted by successive rallies under favorable market conditions. But the trend is persistently down, possibly reflecting a declining industry, weak management, obsolete products, loss of competitive position — all resulting in lower earnings and dividends. This type of company "with few friends" is often sought out by bargain hunters who see in it a possible turnaround situation.

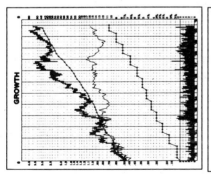

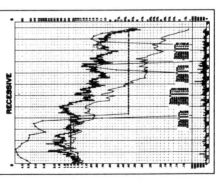

Source: Chart courtesy of Securities Research Company, a division of Babson-United Investment Advisors, Inc., 101 Prescott St., Wellesley Hills, MA 02181-7528.

STOCK MARKET AVERAGES BY INDUSTRY GROUP (continued)

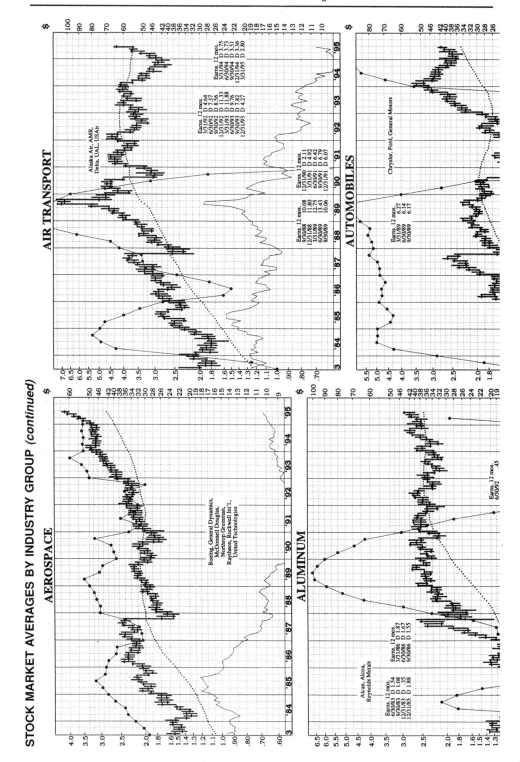

AIR TRANSPORT

Alaska Air, AMR,
Delta, UAL, USAir

Earns. 12 mos.
3/1/92   D 4.64
6/30/92 D 7.37
12/31/92 D 8.56
3/31/93 D 11.33
6/30/93 D 11.88
9/30/93 D 9.76
12/31/93 D 7.82
         D 4.27

Earns. 12 mos.
6/30/94 D 3.75
9/30/94 D 3.73
12/31/94 D 3.51
3/31/95 D 3.36
         D 2.80

Earns. 12 mos.
12/31/90 D 2.11
3/31/90 D 4.92
6/30/91 D 6.42
9/30/91 D 6.79
12/31/91 D 6.07

Earns. 12 mos.
9/30/88 10.08
12/31/88 11.80
3/31/89 12.75
6/30/89 13.43
9/30/89 10.06

AEROSPACE

Boeing, General Dynamics,
McDonnell Douglas,
Northrop Grumman,
Raytheon, Rockwell Int'l.,
United Technologies

AUTOMOBILES

Chrysler, Ford, General Motors

Earns. 12 mos.
3/31/89 6.27
6/30/89 6.14
9/30/89 6.17

ALUMINUM

Alcan, Alcoa,
Reynolds Metals

Earns. 12 mos.
6/30/83 D 1.54
9/30/83 D 1.08
12/31/83 D 2.35
12/31/85 D 1.88

Earns. 12 mos.
3/31/86 D 1.87
6/30/86 D 1.55

Earns. 12 mos.
6/30/92 .45

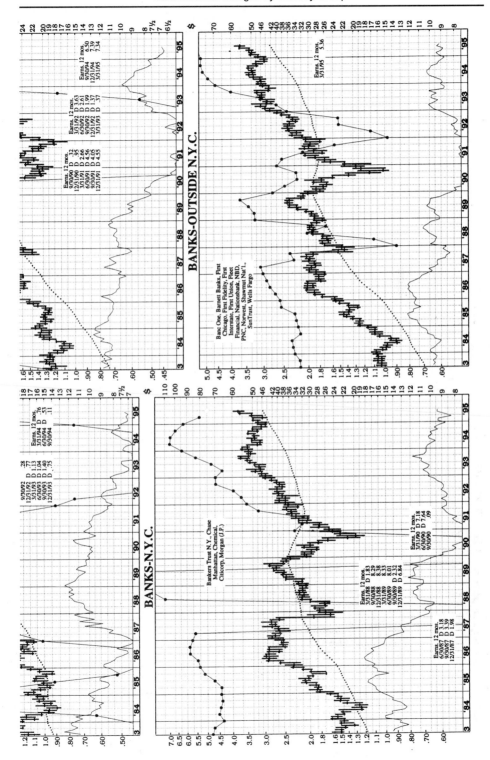

BANKS-OUTSIDE N.Y.C.

Banc One, Barnett Banks, First Chicago, First Fidelity, First Interstate, First Union, Fleet Financial, Nationsbank, NBD, PNC, Norwest, Shawmut Nat'l., SunTrust, Wells Fargo

BANKS-N.Y.C.

Bankers Trust N.Y., Chase Manhattan, Chemical, Citicorp, Morgan (J.P.)

STOCK MARKET AVERAGES BY INDUSTRY GROUP (continued)

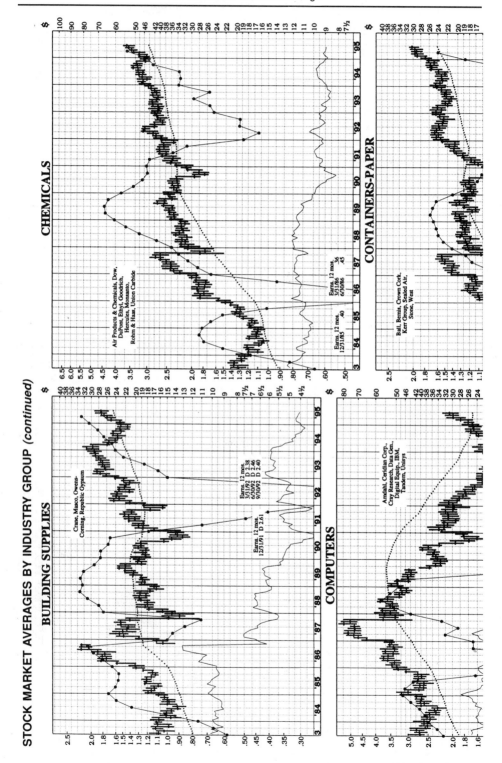

CHEMICALS

Air Products & Chemicals, Dow, DuPont, Ethyl, Goodrich, Hercules, Monsanto, Rohm & Haas, Union Carbide

Earns. 12 mos.
12/31/85   40

Earns. 12 mos.   .36
3/31/86   .45
6/30/86

CONTAINERS-PAPER

Ball, Bemis, Crown Cork, Kerr Group, Sealed Air, Stone, West

BUILDING SUPPLIES

Crane, Masco, Owens-Corning, Republic Gypsum

Earns. 12 mos.
3/31/92   D 2.38
6/30/92   D 2.46
9/30/92   D 2.40

Earns. 12 mos.
12/31/91 D 2.61

COMPUTERS

Amdahl, Ceridian Corp., Cray Research, Data Gen., Digital Equip., IBM, Tandem, Unisys

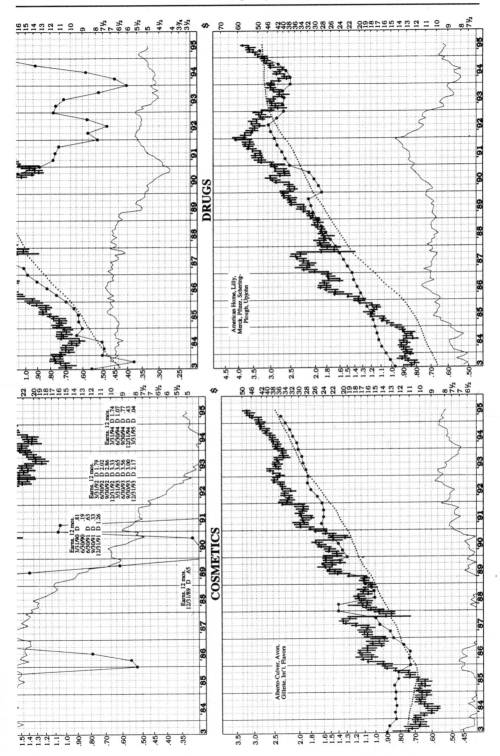

DRUGS

American Home, Lilly,
Merck, Pfizer, Schering-
Plough, Upjohn

COSMETICS

Alberto-Culver, Avon,
Gillette, Int'l. Flavors

Earns. 12 mos.
12/31/89 D .65

Earns. 12 mos.
3/31/90   D .81
6/30/90   D .19
9/30/91   D .63
12/31/91 D 1.26

Earns. 12 mos.
3/31/92   D 1.79
6/30/92   D 2.02
9/30/92   D 2.86
3/31/93   D 3.33
6/30/93   D 3.65
9/30/93   D 3.56
12/31/93 D 3.00
12/31/93 D 2.17

Earns. 12 mos.
3/31/94   D 1.74
6/30/94   D 1.07
9/30/94   D .77
12/31/94 D .43
3/31/95   D .04

STOCK MARKET AVERAGES BY INDUSTRY GROUP *(continued)*

FOODS PACKAGED

Archer Daniels, CPC Int'l,
Campbell Soup, ConAgra,
General Mills, Gerber Prod.,
Heinz, Hershey, Kellogg,
Quaker Oats, Ralston-Purina,
Sara Lee, Wrigley

ELECTRICAL EQUIPMENT

AMP, Emerson, General
Electric, Grainger, Raychem,
Thomas & Betts, Westinghouse

GOLD MINING

ASA Ltd., Coeur d'Alene,
Homestake, Newmont,
Placer Dome

ELECTRONICS

Advanced Micro, BG & G,
Hewlett-Packard, Honeywell,
Loral, Nat'l Semiconductor,
Perkin-Elmer, Tektronix,
Texas Instruments

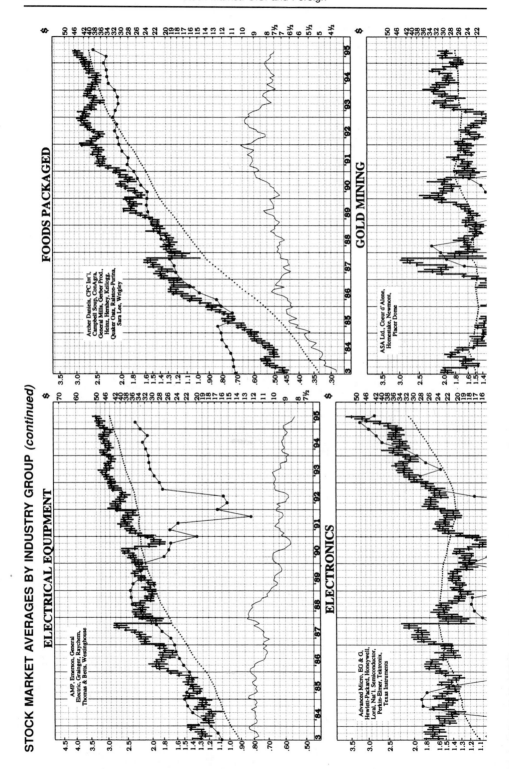

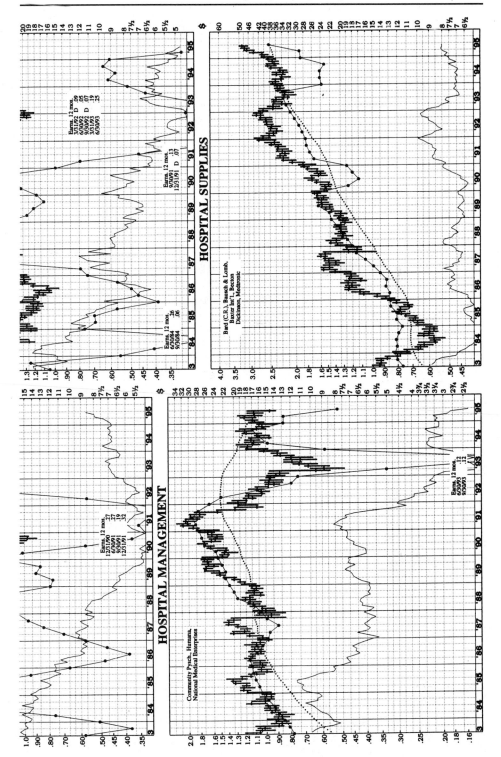

HOSPITAL SUPPLIES

Bard (C.R.), Bausch & Lomb,
Baxter Int'l, Becton
Dickinson, Medtronic

HOSPITAL MANAGEMENT

Community Psych., Humana,
National Medical Enterprises

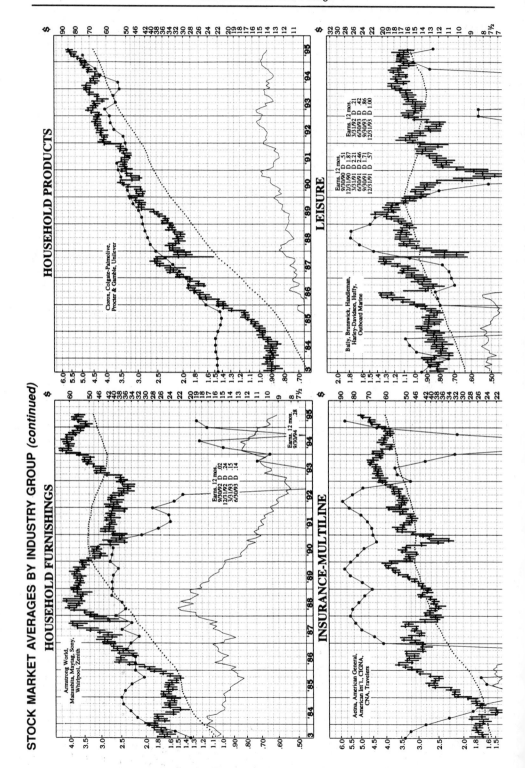

STOCK MARKET AVERAGES BY INDUSTRY GROUP *(continued)*

HOUSEHOLD PRODUCTS

Clorox, Colgate-Palmolive,
Procter & Gamble, Unilever

HOUSEHOLD FURNISHINGS

Armstrong World,
Matsushita, Maytag, Sony,
Whirlpool, Zenith

Earns. 12 mos.
9/30/92 D .02
12/31/92 D .24
3/31/93 D .15
6/30/93 D .14

Earns. 12 mos.
9/30/94 .28

LEISURE

Bally, Brunswick, Handleman,
Harley-Davidson, Huffy,
Outboard Marine

Earns. 12 mos.
9/30/90 D .51
12/31/90 D 1.87
3/31/91 D 2.21
6/30/91 D 2.46
12/31/91 D .57

Earns. 12 mos.
3/31/92 D .21
9/30/93 D .42
9/30/93 D .86
12/31/93 D 1.00

INSURANCE-MULTILINE

Aetna, American General,
American Int'l, CIGNA,
CNA, Travelers

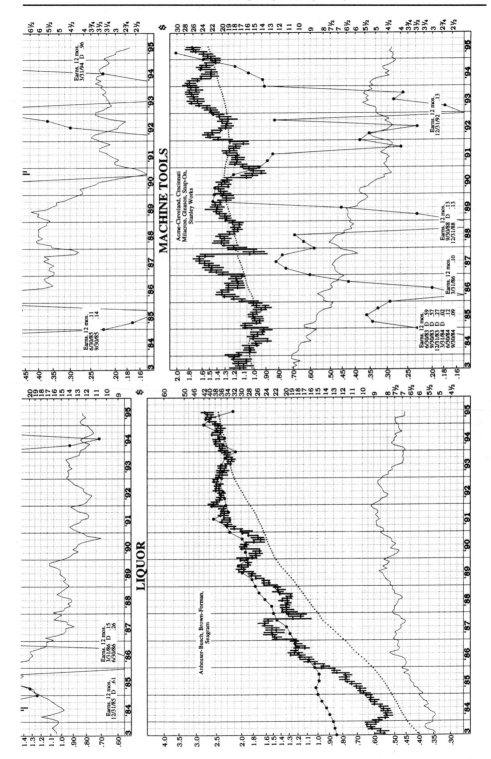

MACHINE TOOLS

Acme-Cleveland, Cincinnati
Milacron, Gleason, Snap-On,
Stanley Works

Earns. 12 mos.
3/1/94 D .96

Earns. 12 mos.
6/30/85 .11
9/30/85 .14

Earns. 12 mos.
12/31/92 .13

Earns. 12 mos.
9/30/88 D .13
12/31/88 .13

Earns. 12 mos.
3/31/86 .10

Earns. 12 mos.
6/30/83 D .59
9/30/83 D .57
12/31/83 D .27
3/31/84 D .02
6/30/84 .12
9/30/84 .09

LIQUOR

Anheuser-Busch, Brown-Forman,
Seagram

Earns. 12 mos.
3/1/86 D .15
6/30/86 .26

Earns. 12 mos.
12/31/85 D .61

STOCK MARKET AVERAGES BY INDUSTRY GROUP (*continued*)

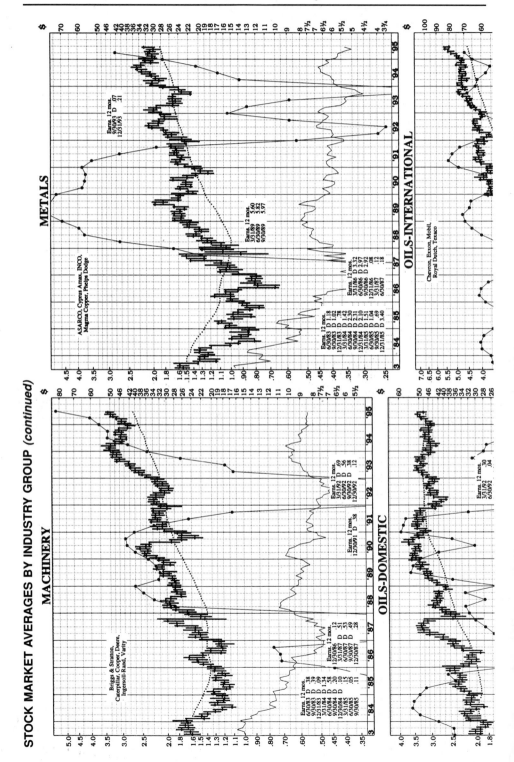

MACHINERY

Briggs & Stratton,
Caterpillar, Cooper, Deere,
Ingersoll-Rand, Varity

Earns. 12 mos.
6/30/83   D .38
9/30/83   D .39
12/31/83   D .09
3/31/84   D .34
6/30/84   D .58
9/30/84   D .20
12/30/84   D .10
3/31/85   .15
6/30/85   .05
9/30/85   .11

Earns. 12 mos.
12/30/86   D .12
3/31/87   D .51
6/30/87   D .53
9/30/87   D .49
12/30/87   .28

Earns. 12 mos.
12/30/91   D .38

Earns. 12 mos.
3/31/92   D .69
6/30/92   D .56
9/30/92   D .38
12/30/92   .12

METALS

ASARCO, Cyrus Amax, INCO,
Magma Copper, Phelps Dodge

Earns. 12 mos.
6/30/83   D 1.18
9/30/83   D 1.02
12/31/83   D .78
3/31/84   D 1.42
6/30/84   D 2.10
9/30/84   D 2.31
12/31/84   D 2.51
3/31/85   D 1.51
6/30/85   D 1.04
9/30/85   D .69
12/31/85   D 3.40

Earns. 12 mos.
3/31/86   D 3.32
6/30/86   D 2.97
9/30/86   D 2.92
12/31/86   .08
6/30/87   .18

Earns. 12 mos.
3/31/89   .60
6/30/89   5.82
9/30/89   5.97

Earns. 12 mos.
9/30/93   D .07
12/31/93   .21

OILS-DOMESTIC

Earns. 12 mos.
3/31/92   .30
6/30/92   .04

OILS-INTERNATIONAL

Chevron, Exxon, Mobil,
Royal Dutch, Texaco

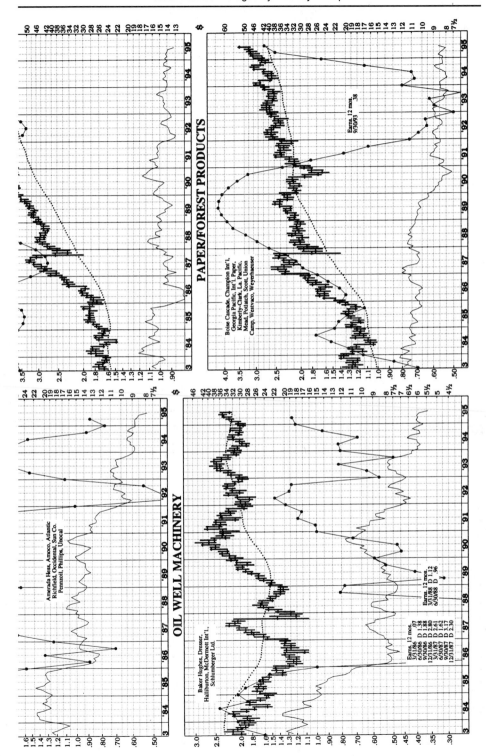

PAPER/FOREST PRODUCTS

Boise Cascade, Champion Int'l,
Georgia Pacific, Int'l. Paper,
Kimberly-Clark, La Pacific,
Mead, Potlatch, Scott, Union
Camp, Westvaco, Weyerhaeuser

Earns. 12 mos.
9/30/93 .38

OIL WELL MACHINERY

Amerada Hess, Amoco, Atlantic
Richfield, Occidental, Sun Co.
Pennzoil, Phillips, Unocal

Baker Hughes, Dresser,
Halliburton, McDermott Int'l.,
Schlumberger Ltd.

Earns. 12 mos.
3/31/86   .07
6/30/86   D .38
9/30/86   D 1.88
12/31/86 D 2.80
3/31/87   D 1.61
9/30/87   D 3.17
12/31/87 D 2.30

Earns. 12 mos.
3/31/88   D 1.12
6/30/88   D .96

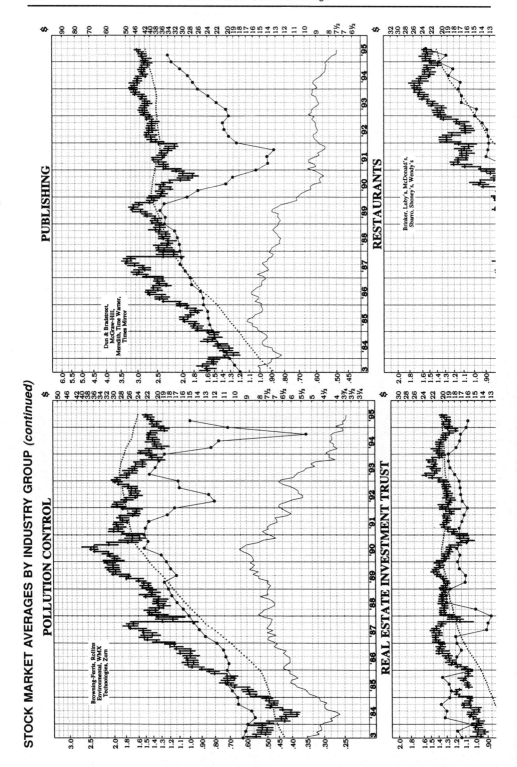

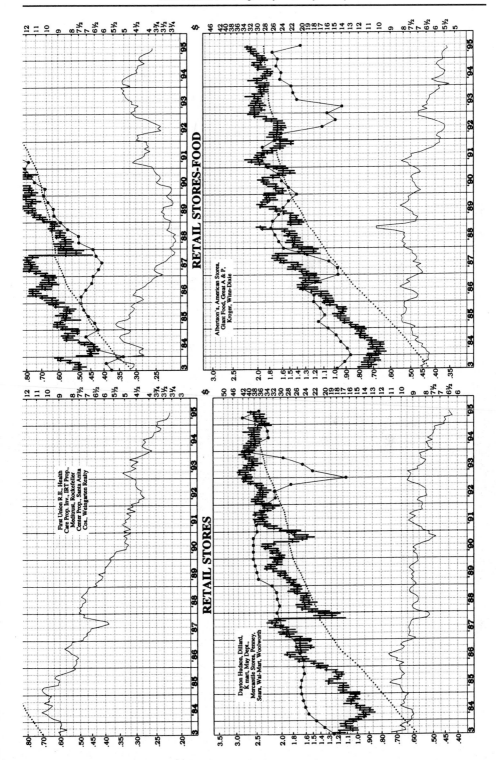

RETAIL STORES-FOOD

Albertson's, American Stores,
Giant Food, Great A & P,
Kroger, Winn-Dixie

RETAIL STORES

Dayton Hudson, Dillard,
K mart, May Dept.,
Mercantile Stores, Penney,
Sears, Wal-Mart, Woolworth

First Union R.E., Health
Care Prop. Inv., IRT Prop.,
Mediplex, New Plan Realty,
Center Prop., Santa Anita
Cos., Weingarten Realty

STOCK MARKET AVERAGES BY INDUSTRY GROUP *(continued)*

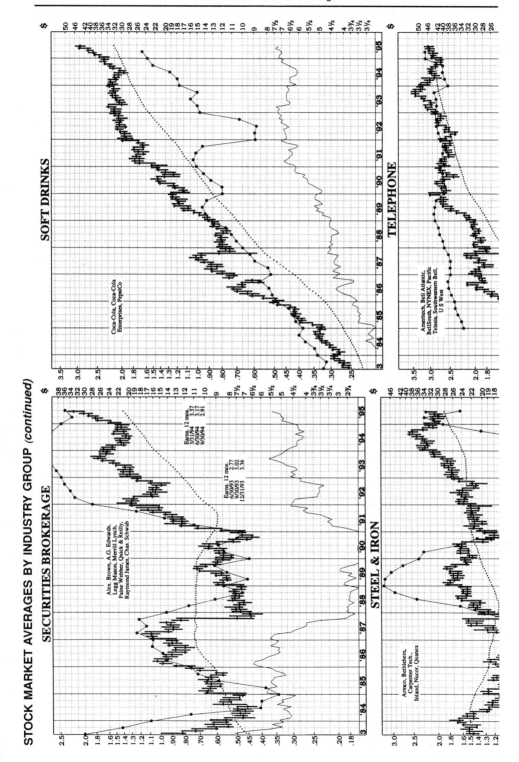

SOFT DRINKS

Coca-Cola, Coca-Cola Enterprises, PepsiCo

TELEPHONE

Ameritech, Bell Atlantic, BellSouth, NYNEX, Pacific Telesis, Southwestern Bell, U S West

SECURITIES BROKERAGE

Alex. Brown, A.G. Edwards, Legg Mason, Merrill Lynch, Paine Webber, Quick & Reilly, Raymond James, Chas. Schwab

STEEL & IRON

Armco, Bethlehem, Carpenter Tech., Inland, Nucor, Quanex

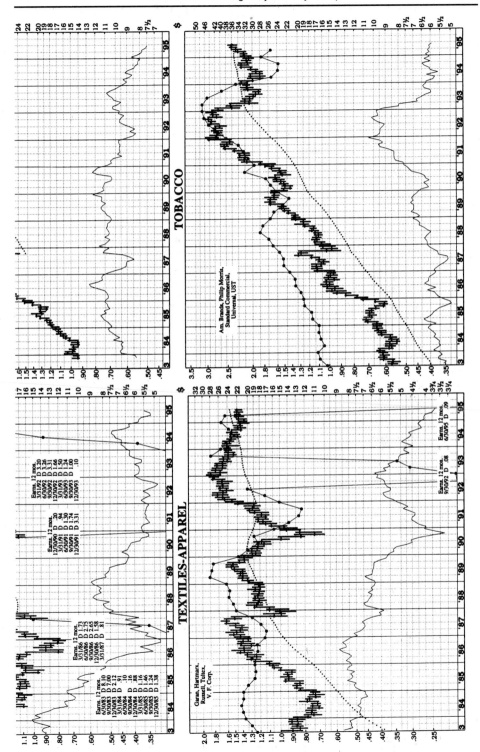

TOBACCO

Am. Brands, Philip Morris,
Standard Commercial,
Universal, UST

TEXTILES-APPAREL

Garan, Hartmarx,
Russell, Tultex,
V. F. Corp.

STOCK MARKET AVERAGES BY INDUSTRY GROUP *(concluded)*

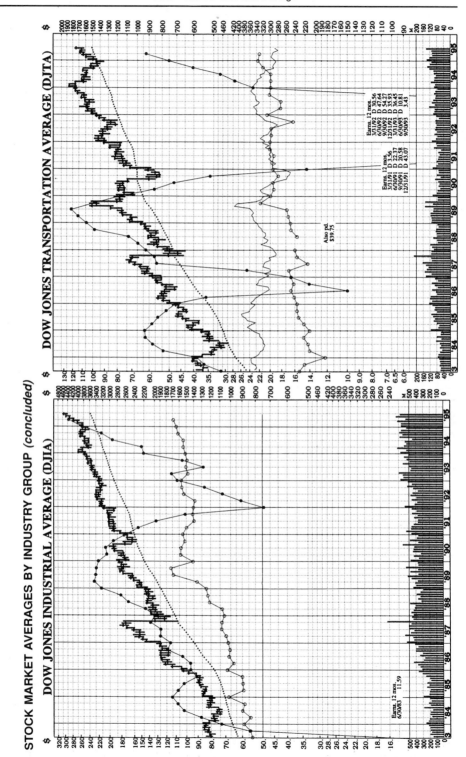

DOW JONES TRANSPORTATION AVERAGE (DJTA)

DOW JONES INDUSTRIAL AVERAGE (DJIA)

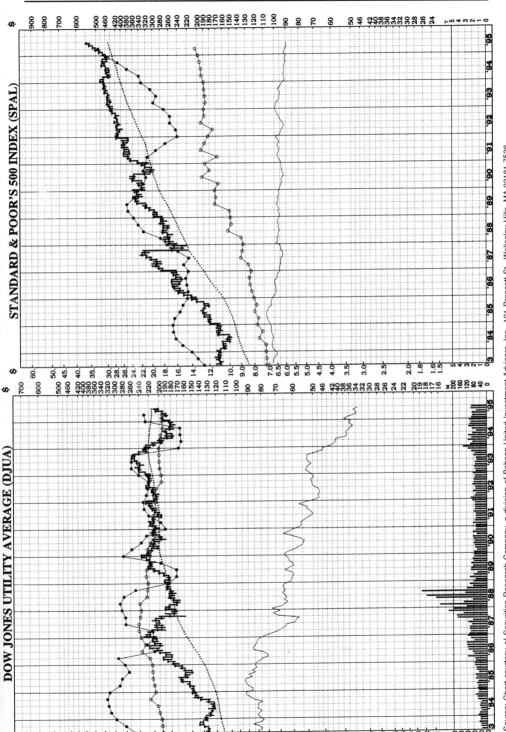

STANDARD & POOR'S 500 INDEX (SPAL)

DOW JONES UTILITY AVERAGE (DJUA)

Source: Chart courtesy of Securities Research Company, a division of Babson-United Investment Advisors, Inc., 101 Prescott St., Wellesley Hills, MA 02181-7528.

Components—Dow Jones 65 Stock Averages

The Dow Jones Stock Averages are compiled by using the New York Stock Exchange only closing prices and adjusting by the then current appropriate divisor. The divisors appear under the Dow Jones Half-Hourly Averages. A list of the stocks on which these averages are based follows:

Industrials

AT&T	Goodyear
AlliedSig	IBM
Alcoa	Int Paper
Am Exp	McDonalds
Beth Steel	Merck Co
Boeing	Minn M M
Caterpillar	Morgan (JP)
Chevron	Philip Mor
Coca Cola	Proc Gam
Disney Walt	Sears
Du Pont	Texaco
East Kodak	Un Carbide
Exxon	Utd Tech
Gen Elec	Westingh
GM	Woolworth

Transportation

AMR	Fed Ex
Airborne	Norf So
Alaska A	Roadway
Am Pres	Ryder Sys
Burl North	Sante Fe
CSX Corp	Sthwst Air
Carolina F	UAL
Consol Frt	USAir
Conrail	Un Pac
Delta Air	Xtra

Utilities

Am Elec	Pac G&E
Centerior	Panh East
Con Ed	Peco
Cons N Gas	Peoples En
Detroit Ed	Pub Sv Ent
Houston Ind	SCEcorp
Niag Moh	UnicomCp
NorAm Energy	

NEW SECURITY ISSUES U.S. CORPORATIONS
Millions of dollars

Type of issue, offering, or issuer	1992	1993	1994	1994						1995	
				July	Aug.	Sept.	Oct.	Nov.	Dec.	Jan.[r]	Feb.
1 All issues[1]	559,827	754,969	n.a.	29,818	37,871	29,416	34,481[r]	38,811[r]	22,999	30,979	32,829
2 Bonds[2]	471,502	641,498	n.a.	26,159	34,495	25,983	30,909[r]	33,286[r]	20,493	28,000	28,000
By type of offering											
3 Public, domestic	378,058	486,879	365,050[r]	22,441	30,088	22,736	25,192[r]	27,278[r]	17,809	20,000	23,000
4 Private placement, domestic[3]	65,853	116,240	n.a.	n.a.	n.a.	n.a.	n.a.	n.a.	n.a.	n.a.	n.a.
5 Sold abroad	27,591	38,379	56,238[r]	3,718	4,406	3,248	5,718	6,008	2,684	8,000	5,000
By industry group											
6 Manufacturing	82,058	88,002	31,981[r]	2,316	2,596	2,167	2,498	2,491[r]	1,508	2,000	4,000
7 Commercial and miscellaneous	43,111	60,293	27,900[r]	997	3,570	2,112	2,204	1,578	2,469	2,115	2,600
8 Transportation	9,979	10,756	4,573	248	315	229	227	239	269	0	199
9 Public utility	48,055	56,272	11,713	487	575	707	695	744	273	1,089	810
10 Communication	15,394	31,950	11,986	429	345	526	279	333	419	911	991
11 Real estate and financial	272,904	394,226	333,135[r]	21,682	27,094	20,242	25,007[r]	27,902	15,556	21,885	19,400
12 Stocks[2]	88,325	113,472	n.a.	3,700[r]	3,375[r]	3,424[r]	3,572	5,525	2,768[r]	2,979	4,829
By type of offering											
13 Public preferred	21,339	18,897	12,504[r]	625[r]	710	555	713[r]	279	178	505	296
14 Common	57,118	82,657	48,317[r]	3,075	2,665[r]	2,868[r]	2,859[r]	5,246	2,495[r]	2,474	4,532
15 Private placement[3]	9,867	11,917	n.a.	n.a.	n.a.	n.a.	n.a.	n.a.	n.a.	n.a.	n.a.
By industry group											
16 Manufacturing	22,723	22,271		492	569	904	745	1,963	1,203[r]	1,086	1,577
17 Commercial and miscellaneous	20,231	25,761		701	838[r]	821	1,105	1,783	848[r]	392	1,415
18 Transportation	2,595	2,237		75	50	154[r]	79	76	0	19	15
19 Public utility	6,532	7,050		0	180	78	4	333	165	209	258
20 Communication	2,366	3,439		0	0	0	0	0	21[r]	496	0
21 Real estate and financial	33,879	52,021		2,427[r]	1,734[r]	1,466[r]	1,639	1,351	531[r]	776	1,564

1. Figures represent gross proceeds of issues maturing in more than one year; they are the principal amount or number of units calculated by multiplying by the offering price. Figures exclude secondary offerings, employee stock plans, investment companies other than closed-end, intracorporate transactions, equities sold abroad, and Yankee bonds. Stock data include ownership securities issued by limited partnerships.

2. Monthly data cover only public offerings.
3. Monthly data are not available.
SOURCES. Beginning July 1993, Securities Data Company and the Board of Governors of the Federal Reserve System.

Source: *Federal Reserve Bulletin*, Board of Governors of the Federal Reserve System.

COMMON STOCK PRICES AND YIELDS

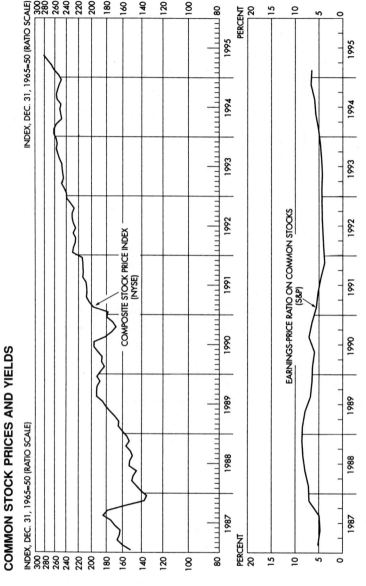

INDEX, DEC. 31, 1965=50 (RATIO SCALE)

INDEX, DEC. 31, 1965=50 (RATIO SCALE)

COMPOSITE STOCK PRICE INDEX
(NYSE)

EARNINGS-PRICE RATIO ON COMMON STOCKS
(S&P)

PERCENT

PERCENT

1987 1988 1989 1990 1991 1992 1993 1994 1995

COUNCIL OF ECONOMIC ADVISERS

SOURCES: NEW YORK STOCK EXCHANGE AND STANDARD & POOR'S CORPORATION

Period	Common stock prices [1] New York Stock Exchange indexes (Dec. 31, 1965=50, except as noted) [2]					Dow-Jones industrial average [4]	Standard & Poor's composite index (1941–43=10) [5]	Common stock yields (percent) [6]	
	Composite	Industrial	Transportation	Utility [3]	Finance			Dividend-price ratio	Earnings-price ratio
1985	108.09	123.79	104.11	113.49	114.21	1,328.23	186.84	4.25	8.12
1986	136.00	155.85	119.87	142.72	147.20	1,792.76	236.34	3.49	6.09
1987	161.70	195.31	140.39	148.59	146.48	2,275.99	286.83	3.08	5.48
1988	149.91	180.95	134.12	143.53	127.26	2,060.82	265.79	3.64	8.01
1989	180.02	216.23	175.28	174.87	151.88	2,508.91	322.84	3.45	7.41
1990	183.46	225.78	158.62	181.20	133.26	2,678.94	334.59	3.61	6.47
1991	206.33	258.14	173.99	185.32	150.82	2,929.33	376.18	3.24	4.79
1992	229.01	284.62	201.09	198.91	179.26	3,284.29	415.74	2.99	4.22
1993	249.58	299.99	242.49	228.90	216.42	3,522.06	451.41	2.78	4.46
1994	254.12	315.25	247.29	209.06	209.73	3,793.77	460.33	2.82	5.84
1994: May	249.56	307.58	244.75	205.77	211.30	3,707.99	450.90	2.89	5.67
June	251.21	308.66	246.64	206.54	215.89	3,737.58	454.83	2.84	
July	249.29	307.34	244.21	205.46	210.91	3,718.30	451.40	2.87	
Aug	256.00	316.55	244.67	211.26	214.77	3,797.48	464.24	2.78	5.91
Sept	257.61	322.19	239.10	204.60	211.90	3,880.60	466.96	2.80	
Oct	255.22	321.53	230.71	203.35	203.33	3,868.10	463.81	2.82	
Nov	252.48	319.33	227.45	200.13	198.38	3,792.43	461.01	2.86	
Dec	248.65	313.92	218.93	200.02	195.25	3,770.31	455.19	2.91	6.67
1995: Jan	253.56	319.93	230.25	201.16	201.05	3,872.46	465.25	2.87	
Feb	261.86	328.98	237.29	207.73	211.76	3,953.72	481.92	2.81	
Mar	266.81	337.96	244.45	204.16	213.29	4,062.78	493.15	2.76	6.52
Apr	274.37	347.69	254.36	208.93	219.38	4,230.66	507.91	2.68	
May	281.81	357.01	254.69	211.58	228.55	4,391.57	523.81	2.60	
Week ended:									
1995: May 6	278.86	353.96	255.30	211.07	222.65	4,344.23	518.05	2.63	
13	282.24	357.32	254.11	212.79	229.00	4,404.20	524.36	2.61	
20	282.22	357.40	256.14	210.91	229.89	4,395.42	524.35	2.60	
27	282.96	358.51	253.58	210.49	231.12	4,410.29	526.62	2.60	
June 3	285.39	360.57	253.20	214.86	234.28	4,440.24	530.75	2.58	

[1] Average of daily closing prices.
[2] Includes all the stocks (more than 2,000 in 1992) listed on the NYSE.
[3] Dec. 31, 1965=100. Effective April 27, 1993 the NYSE doubled the value of the utility index to facilitate trading of options and futures on the index. All indexes shown here reflect the doubling.
[4] Includes 30 stocks.
[5] Includes 500 stocks.
[6] Standard & Poor's series. Dividend-price ratios based on Wednesday closing prices. Earnings-price ratios based on prices at end of quarter.

NOTE.—All data relate to stocks listed on the New York Stock Exchange (NYSE).

Sources: New York Stock Exchange, Dow-Jones & Company, Inc., and Standard & Poor's Corporation.

Source: *Economic Indicators*, Council of Economic Advisers.

SEC Filings: Summary[1]

Important information about publicly traded companies is contained in the SEC filings required by the Securities Acts of 1933, 1934, and 1940. Brief descriptions of the filings are given below.

Annual Report to Shareholders

The Annual Report to Shareholders is the principal document used by most public companies to disclose corporate information to shareholders. Although they are not required SEC filings, in some circumstances they are required to be "furnished" to the Commission. They are usually state-of-the-company reports including an opening letter from the Chief Executive Officer, financial data, results of continuing operations, market segment information, new product plans, subsidiary activities and research and development activities on future programs.

Prospectus

The preliminary prospectus constitutes Part I of the Securities Act registration statements. It contains the basic business and financial information on an issuer with respect to a particular securities offering. Investors may use the prospectus to help appraise the merits of the offering and make educated investment decisions.

A prospectus in its preliminary form is frequently called a "red herring" prospectus and is subject to completion or amendment before the registration statement becomes effective, after which a final prospectus is issued and sales can be consummated.

Proxy Solicitation Materials

A proxy statement is a document which is intended to provide security holders with the information necessary to enable them to vote in an informed manner on matters intended to be acted upon at security holders' meetings, whether the traditional annual meeting or a special meeting. Typically a security holder is also provided with a proxy to authorize designated persons to vote his or her securities in the event the holder does not attend the meeting. Generally speaking, preliminary proxy materials are available for review by members of the public when they are filed. Definitive (final) copies of proxy materials are filed with the Commission at or before the time they are sent to security holders, and are also available for review.

Form ADV

This form is used to apply for registration as an investment adviser or to amend a registration. It consists of two parts. Part I contains general and personal information about the applicant. Part II contains information relating to the nature of the applicant's business, including basic operations, services offered, fees charged, types of clients advised, educational and business backgrounds of associates and other business activities of the applicant.

Form ADV-S

This is an annual supplement required to be filed by persons registered as investment advisers with the Commission. It must be filed not later than 90 days after the end of the registrant's fiscal year.

Form BD

This form is used to apply for registration as a broker or dealer of securities, or as a government securities broker or dealer, and to amend a registration. It provides background information on the applicant and the nature of its business. It includes lists of the executive officers and general partners of the company. It also contains information on any past securities violations.

Form D

Companies selling securities pursuant to a Regulation D exemption or a Section 4(6) exemption from the registration provisions of the Securities Act of 1933 (the "Securities Act") must file a Form D as notice of such a sale. The form must be filed no later than 15 days after the first sale of securities.

---

[1] For further filing information see the *General Records Information Manual* and *A User's Guide to the Facilities of the Public Reference Room* published by the Securities and Exchange Commission.

Form MSD

This report is used by a bank or a separately identifiable department or division of a bank to apply for registration as a municipal securities dealer with the SEC, or to amend such registration.

Form N-SAR

This is a semi-annual report filed by registered investment management companies. Unit investment trusts are required to file this form at the end of the calendar year. It shows names of various entities providing services to the investment company as well as information about sales of shares, 12b-1 plans, contracts, type of fund, portfolio turnover rate, financial information and fidelity bonds. This form replaces forms N-1Q, N-1R, N-30A-2, N-30A-3 and N-27D-1.

Securities Act Registration Statements

One of the major roles of the SEC is to require companies making a public issuance of securities to disclose material business and financial information in order that investors may make informed investment decisions. The Securities Act requires issuers to file registration statements with the Commission, setting forth such information, before offering their securities to the public. (See **Section 6** of the Securities Act for information concerning the "Registration of Securities and Signing of Registration Statement"; **Section 8** of the Securities Act for information on "Taking Effect of Registration Statements and Amendments Thereto."

The registration statement is divided into two parts. Part I is the preliminary prospectus. It is distributed to interested investors and others. It contains data to assist in evaluating the securities and make informed investment decisions.

Part II of the registration statement contains information not required to be filed in the prospectus. This includes information concerning the registrants' expenses of issuance and distribution, indemnification of directors and officers, and recent sales of unregistered securities as well as undertakings, copies of material contracts, and financial statement schedules.

The most widely used Securities Act registration forms are:

S-1 This is the basic registration form. It can be used to register securities for which no other form is authorized or prescribed, except securities of foreign governments or political subdivisions thereof.

S-2 This is a simplified optional registration form that may be used by companies which have reported under the Exchange Act for a minimum of three years and have timely filed all required reports during the 12 calendar months and any portion of the month immediately preceding the filing of the registration statement. It is unlike Form S-1 because it permits incorporation by reference from and delivery of the company's annual report to stockholders.

S-3 This is usually the most simplified registration form and it may only be used by companies which have reported under the Exchange Act for a minimum of three years and meet the timely filing requirements set forth under Form S-2. The form may only be used for certain specified transactions and may only be used by issuers who meet certain qualitative tests.

S-4 This form is used to register securities in connection with business combinations and applies the principles of the integrated disclosure system to disclosure in the context of mergers and exchange offers.

S-6 This form is used to register securities issued by unit investment trusts registered under the Investment Company Act of 1940 on Form N-8B-2.

S-8 This form is used for the registration of securities to be offered solely to an issuer's employees and to certain other persons pursuant to an issuer's employee benefit plans.

S-11 This form is used to register securities of certain real estate companies including real estate investment trusts.

S-20 This form may be used to register standardized options where the issuer undertakes not to issue, clear, guarantee or accept an option registered on Form S-20 unless there is a definitive options disclosure document meeting the requirements of Rule 9b-1 of the Exchange Act.

SB-1 Companies that qualify as "small business issuers" may use this form to register up to $10,000,000 of securities to be sold for cash, if they have not registered more than $10,000,000 in securities offerings in any continuous 12-month period, including the transaction being registered.

SB-2 Companies that qualify as "small business issuers" may use this form to register additional securities to be sold for cash.

F-1 This is the basic registration form authorized for certain private issuers. It is used to register the securities of those eligible foreign issuers for which no other more specialized form is authorized or prescribed.

F-2 This is an optional registration form that may be used by certain foreign private issuers which are world class issuers (i.e., they have an equity float of at least $300 million worldwide or are registering non-convertible investment grade debt securities) or have reported under the Exchange Act for a minimum of three years. The form is somewhat shorter than Form F-1 because it utilizes filings made by the issuer under the Exchange Act, particularly Form 20-F.

F-3 This form may only be used by certain foreign private issuers which are both world class issuers and have reported under the Exchange Act for a minimum of three years. The form makes maximum use of Exchange Act filings.

F-4 This form is used to register securities in connection with business combinations involving foreign private registrants and applies the principles of the integrated disclosure system to disclosure in the context of mergers and exchange offers.

F-6 This form is used to register depository shares represented by American Depositary Receipts issued by a depositary against the deposit of the securities of a foreign issuer.

F-7 Qualifying Canadian issuers may use this form to register securities offered for cash upon the exercise of rights to purchase or subscribe for such securities that are granted to its existing securityholders in proportion to the number of securities held by them as of the record date for the rights offer.

F-8 Qualifying Canadian issuers may use this form to register securities to be issued in an exchange offer or in connection with a statutory amalgamation, merger, arrangement, or other reorganization requiring the vote of shareholders of the participating companies.

F-9 This form may be used to register certain investment grade debt or investment grade preferred securities of certain Canadian issuers.

F-10 This form may be used for the registration of securities to be issued in an exchange offer or in connection with a statutory amalgamation, merger, arrangement or other reorganization requiring the vote of shareholders of the participating companies.

F-80 This form may be used for the registration of securities of certain Canadian issuers to be issued in exchange offers or a business combination.

SR First-time registrants under the Securities Act file this form to report sales of registered securities and the use of proceeds therefrom. The forms are required to be filed at specified periods of time throughout the offering period; a final report is required after the termination of the offering.

OTHER SECURITIES ACT FORMS

Form 144

This form must be filed as notice of the proposed sale of restricted securities or securities held by an affiliate of the issuer in reliance on Rule 144 when the amount to be sold during any three-month period exceeds 500 shares or units or has an aggregate sales price in excess of $10,000.

Exchange Act Registration Statements

All companies whose securities are registered on a national securities exchange pursuant to Section 12 of the Exchange Act and, in general, companies whose assets exceed $5,000,000 with a class of equity securities held by 500 or more persons, must register such securities under the Exchange Act.

This registration establishes a public file containing material financial and business information on the company for use by investors and others, and also creates an obligation on the part of the company to keep such public information current by filing periodic reports on Forms 10-Q and 10-K, and on current event Form 8-K, as applicable.

The periodic reports must be filed by a company for the year in which a public offering of its securities was made, and, in subsequent years if such securities are held by more than 300 persons.

The most widely used Exchange Act registration forms are:

10 This is the general form for registration of securities pursuant to section 12(b) or (g) of the Exchange Act of classes of securities of issuers for which no other form is prescribed.

8-A This optional short form may be used by companies already required to file reports under the Exchange Act to register a class of securities under that Act.

8-B This specialized registration form may be used by an issuer with no securities registered under the Exchange Act which is the successor to another issuer which had securities so registered at the time of succession.

20-F This is an integrated form used both as a registration statement for purposes of registering securities of qualified foreign registrants under Section 12 of the or as an annual report under section 13(a) or 15(d) of the Exchange Act.

OTHER EXCHANGE ACT FORMS

Form TA-1

This form is used to apply for registration as a transfer agent or to amend such registration. It provides information on the company's activities and operation.

Form X-17A-5

Every broker or dealer registered pursuant to Section 15 of the Exchange Act must file annually, on a calendar or fiscal year basis, a report audited by an independent public accountant.

Forms 3, 4, and 5

Generally speaking, owners of more than ten percent of any class of equity securities that is registered pursuant to section 12 of the Exchange Act, and every director and officer of an issuer with a class of equity securities so registered must report all transactions in such securities. Forms 3 are used to make an initial statement of ownership, Forms 4 are used to report changes in ownership, and Forms 5 are used for annual statements. The forms contain information on the reporting person's relationship to the company and on transactions in the company's securities.

Form 6-K

This report is used by certain foreign private issuers to furnish information: (i) required to be made public in the country of its domicile; (ii) filed with and made public by a foreign stock exchange on which its securities are traded; or (iii) distributed to security holders. The report must be furnished promptly after such material is made public. The form is not considered "filed" for Section 18 purposes. This is the only information furnished by foreign private issuers between annual reports, since such issuers are not required to file on Forms 10-Q or 8-K.

Form 8-K

This is the "current report" which is used to report the occurrence of any material events or corporate changes which are of importance to investors and have not previously been reported by the registrant. It provides more current information on certain specified events than would Forms 10-Q or 10-K. Forms 8-K are due at different times, depending on the nature of the event being reported.

Form 10-C

This form must be filed by an issuer whose securities are quoted on the NASDAQ interdealer quotation system. Reported on the form is any change that exceeds five percent in the number of shares of the class outstanding and any change in the name of the issuer. The report must be filed within ten days of such change.

Form 10-K

This is the annual report which most reporting companies file with the Commission. It provides a comprehensive overview of the registrant's business during the last fiscal year. The report must be filed within 90 days after the end of the company's fiscal year.

Form 10-Q

Form 10-Q is a report filed quarterly by most registered companies. The first part of the report includes unaudited financial statements and provides a continuing view of the company's financial position during the year. The second part includes a discussion of other information regarding the issuer including legal proceedings, changes in the rights of the holders of any class of registered securities, defaults upon senior securities, submissions of matters to a vote of securities holders, and other information. Forms 10-Q must be filed for each of the issuer's first three fiscal quarters and are due within 45 days of the close of the quarter.

Form 13-F

This is a quarterly report of equity holdings by institutional investment managers having equity assets under management of $100 million or more. Included in this category are certain banks, insurance companies, investment advisers, investment companies, foundations and pension funds.

Form 15

This form is filed by a company as notice of termination of registration under Section 12(g) of the Exchange Act, or suspension of the duty to file periodic reports under Section 15(d) of the Exchange Act.

Form 18

This form is used for the registration on a national securities exchange of securities of foreign governments and political subdivisions thereof.

Form 18-K

This form is used for the annual reports of foreign governments or political subdivisions thereof.

Schedule 13D

This Schedule discloses beneficial ownership of certain registered equity securities. Any person or group of persons who acquire a beneficial ownership of more than 5% of a class of registered equity securities of certain issuers must file a Schedule 13D reporting such acquisition together with certain other information within ten days after such acquisition. Moreover, any material changes in the facts set forth in the Schedule precipitates a duty to promptly file an amendment.

The Commission's rules define the term "beneficial owner" to be any person who directly or indirectly shares voting power or investment power (the power to sell the security).

Schedule 13E-3

This schedule must be filed by certain companies and their affiliates (such as companies with any equity securities registered under Section 12 of the Exchange Act) whenever they engage in a transaction to "take the company private," for example, when the transaction would decrease the number of shareholders to such a point that the company would no longer be required to file reports with the SEC. The transaction could take the form of a merger, tender offer, sale of assets or a reverse stock split.

Schedule 13E-4

This schedule (called an Issuer Tender Offer Statement) must be filed by certain issuers (such as companies with securities registered under Section 12 of the Exchange Act) when they are making a tender offer for their own securities.

Schedule 13G

Schedule 13G is a much abbreviated version of Schedule 13D that is only available for use by a limited category of "persons" (such as banks, broker/dealers, and insurance companies) and even then only when the securities were acquired in the ordinary course of business and not with the purpose nor effect of changing or influencing the control of the issuer.

Schedule 14D-1

Any person, other than the issuer itself (See Schedule 13E-4), making a tender offer for certain equity securities (such as equity securities registered pursuant to Section 12 of the Exchange Act), which offer, if accepted, would cause that person to own over 5 percent of that class of the securities, must at the time of the offer file a Schedule 14D-1. This schedule must be filed with the Commission and sent to certain other parties, such as the issuer and any competing bidders.

Schedule 14D-9

This schedule must be filed with the Commission when an interested party, such as an issuer, a beneficial owner of securities, or a representative of either, makes a solicitation or recommendation to an issuer's shareholders with respect to a particular tender offer which is subject to Regulation 14D.

Trust Indenture Act of 1939 Forms

T-1   This form is a statement of eligibility and qualification of a corporation to act as a trustee under the Trust Indenture Act of 1939.
T-2   This form is similar to Form T-1 except it is to be used for individual, rather than corporate trustees.
T-3   This form is used as an application for qualification of indentures pursuant to the Trust Indenture Act of 1939, but only when securities to be issued

thereunder are not required to be registered under the Securities Act.
T-4   This form is used to apply for an exemption from certain provisions of the Trust Indenture Act.

1940 Act Investment Company Registration Statements

Mutual funds, the most common type of registered investment company, make a continuous offering of their securities and register on simplified, *three-part forms*. The prospectus, or **Part A,** provides a concise description of the fundamental characteristics of the initial fund in a way that will assist investors in making informed decisions about whether to purchase the securities of the fund. The statement of additional information, **Part B,** contains additional information about the fund which may be of interest to some investors but need not be included in the prospectus. **Part C** contains other required information and exhibits. Unit investment trusts, insurance company separate accounts, business development companies and other registered investment companies register their shares and provide essential information about them on other registration forms. See the following:

N-1A   This form is used to register open-end management investment companies ("mutual funds").
N-2   This form is used to register closed-end management investment companies.
N-3   This form is used to register insurance company separate accounts organized as management investment companies offering variable annuity contracts.
N-4   This form is used to register insurance company separate accounts organized as unit investment trusts offering variable annuity contracts.

How to Read the New York Stock Exchange and American Stock Exchange Quotations

(1) (2) 52 Weeks		(3)	(4)	(5)	(6)	(7)	(8)	(9)	(10)	(11)	(12)
Hi	Lo	Stock	Sym	Div	Yld %	P-E	Vol 100s	Hi	Lo	Close	Net Chg
42¾	23⅝	WestPtPepri	WPM	...	13		47	30¼	29⅝	30¼ +	⅝
18¾	15¾	WestcstEngy	g WE	.80	5.0	15	9	15⅞	15¾	15⅞ +	⅛
17¼	3⅞	WestnCoNA	WSN	...	...		1026	4¼	4⅛	4¼ −	⅛

The composite quotations take into account prices paid for a stock on the New York or American Exchanges, plus those prices paid on regional exchanges, Over-the-Counter (OTC) and elsewhere, as shown in the example from the *Wall Street Journal*. The stock market quotations are explained below:

(1) The highest price per share paid in the past 52 weeks in terms of ⅛ of a dollar, i.e., 10⅛ means $10.125.

(2) The lowest price paid per share in the last 52 weeks.

(3) The name of the company in abbreviated form.

(4) The Stock Exchange symbol used to identify the stock.

(5) The regular annual dividend paid. Special or extra dividends are specified by letters given in the footnotes in the Explanatory Notes shown below.

(6) The yield, that is, the annual dividend divided by the current price of the stock expressed in percent. For example, a stock that sells for $20.00 per share and pays a dividend of $2.00 per share has a yield of 10 percent (2/20).

(7) The P/E ratio is the current price of the stock divided by the company's last reported annual earnings per share. The P/E ratio is generally high for companies which are thought to have a relatively large and persistent earning's growth rate. The average P/E ratio for the Dow Jones stocks varied from 9.8 to 39.5 during the last five years.

(8) The number of shares sold on the day reported in 100s of shares.

(9) The highest price paid per share on the day reported.

(10) The lowest price paid per share on the day reported.

(11) The last price paid per share on the day reported.

(12) The change in the closing price from the previous day's closing price.

EXPLANATORY NOTES

The following explanations apply to New York and American exchange listed issues and the National Association of Securities Dealers Automated Quotations system's over-the-counter securities. Exchange prices are composite quotations that include trades on the Midwest, Pacific, Philadelphia, Boston and Cincinnati exchanges and reported by the NASD and Instinet.

Boldfaced quotations highlight those issues whose price changed by 5% or more from their previous closing price.

Underlined quotations are those stocks with large changes in volume, per exchange, compared with the issue's average trading volume. The calculation includes common stocks of $5 a share or more with an average volume over 65 trading days of at least 5,000 shares. The underlined quotations are for the 40 largest volume percentage leaders on the NYSE and the NASD's National Market System. It includes the 20 largest volume percentage gainers on the Amex.

The 52-week high and low columns show the highest and lowest price of the issue during the preceding 52 weeks plus the current week, but not the latest trading day. These ranges are adjusted to reflect stock payouts of 1% or more, and cash dividends of 10% or more.

Dividend rates, unless noted, are annual disbursements based on the last quarterly, semiannual, or annual declaration. Special or extra dividends, special situations or payments not designated as regular are identified by footnotes.

Yield is defined as the dividends paid by a company on its securities, expressed as a percentage of price.

The P/E ratio is determined by dividing the price of a share of stock by its company's earnings per share of that stock. These earnings are the primary per-share earnings reported by the company for the most recent four quarters. Extraordinary items are usually excluded.

Sales figures are the unofficial daily total of shares traded, quoted in hundreds (two zeros omitted).

Exchange ticker symbols are shown for all New York and American exchange common stocks, and Dow Jones News/Retrieval symbols are listed for Class A and Class B shares listed on both markets. Nasdaq symbols are listed for all Nasdaq NMS issues. A more detailed explanation of Nasdaq ticker symbols appears with the NMS listings.

FOOTNOTES: ▲—New 52-week high. **▼**—New 52-week low. **a**—Extra dividend or extras in addition to the regular dividend. **b**—Indicates annual rate of the cash dividend and that a stock dividend was paid. **c**—Liquidating dividend. **e**—Indicates a dividend was declared or paid in the preceding 12 months, but that there isn't a regular rate. **g**—Indicates the dividend and earnings are expressed in Canadian money. The stock trades in U.S. dollars. No yield or P/E ratio is shown. **h**—Indicates a temporary exception to Nasdaq qualifications. **i**—Indicates amount declared or paid after a stock dividend or split. **j**—Indicates dividend was paid this year, and that at the last dividend meeting a dividend was omitted or deferred. **k**—Indicates dividend declared or paid this year on cumulative issues with dividends in arrears. **n**—Newly issued in the past 52 weeks. The high-low range begins with the start of trading and doesn't cover the entire period. **pf**—Preferred. **pp**—Holder owes installment(s) of purchase price. **pr**—Preference. **r**—Indicates a cash dividend declared or paid in the preceding 12 months, plus a stock dividend. **rt**—Rights. **s**—Stock split or stock dividend amounting to 25% or more in the past 52 weeks. The high-low price is adjusted from the old stock. Dividend calculations begin with the date the split was paid or the stock dividend occurred. **t**—Paid in stock in the preceding 12 months, estimated cash value on ex-dividend or ex-distribution date, except Nasdaq listings where payments are in stock. **un**—Units. **v**—Trading halted on primary market. **vj**—In bankruptcy or receivership or being reorganized under the Bankruptcy Code, or securities assumed by such companies. **wd**—When distributed. **wi**—When issued. **wt**—Warrants. **ww**—With warrants. **x**—Ex-dividend or ex-rights. **xw**—Without warrants. **y**—Ex-dividend and sales in full, not in hundreds. **z**—Sales in full, not in hundreds.

How to Read Over-the-Counter NASDAQ Listings

The notation is the same as that for the New York and American Stock Exchanges on page 264.

(1)	(2)	(3)	(4)	(5)	(6)	(7)	(8)	(9)	(10)	(11)	(12)
52 Weeks					Yld		Vol				Net
Hi	Lo	Stock	Sym	Div	%	P-E	100s	Hi	Lo	Close	Chg
4¾	1⅛	HuntrEnvr	HESI		...	...	158	4⅛	3⅞	4⅛ +	¼
22	14⅜	HuntgBcshr	HBAN	.80b	3.8	11	1231	21¾	21	21¼ −	¼
14¾	7¼	Hurco	HURC	.20	1.8	28	66	11¾	10¾	11 −	¾
32½	8¼	HutchTech	HTCH		...	21	282	28	27¼	27¼ −	¾
8⅜	3⅞	HycorBio	HYBD		...	675	265	6⅞	6½	6¾ −	⅟₁₆
3½	⅟₁₆	HycorBio wt			...	...	10	3	2¾	3 −	⅛
6⅞	4	HydeAthl	HYDE		...	19	62	5½	4¾	5 +	¼

NASDAQ SYMBOL EXPLANATION

All securities listed in the Nasdaq system are identified by a four letter or five letter symbol. The fifth letter indicates the issues that aren't common or capital shares, or are subject to restrictions or special conditions. Below is a rundown of fifth letter identifiers and a description of what they represent:

A—Class A. **B**—Class B. **C**—Exempt from Nasdaq listing qualifications for a limited period. **D**—New issue. **E**—Delinquent in required filings with SEC, as determined by the NASD. **F**—Foreign. **G**—First convertible bond. **H**—Second convertible bond, same company. **I**—Third convertible bond, same company. **J**—Voting. **K**—Non-voting. **L**—Miscellaneous situations, including second class units, third class of warrants or sixth class of preferred stock. **M**—Fourth preferred, same company. **N**—Third preferred, same company. **O**—Second preferred, same company. **P**—First preferred, same company. **Q**—In bankruptcy proceedings. **R**—Rights. **S**—Shares of beneficial interest. **T**—With warrants or rights. **U**—Units. **V**—When issued and when distributed. **W**—Warrants. **Y**—American Depository Receipt (ADR). **Z**—Miscellaneous situations, including second class of warrants, fifth class of preferred stock and any unit, receipt or certificate representing a limited partnership interest.

The Ex-dividend Explained

The ex-dividend status of a stock is indicated by an *x* in the newspaper quotation or *xd* on the ticker tape. This is an abbreviation for *without dividend*.

A stock that is purchased during the ex-dividend period will not pay a previously declared dividend to its new owner. The ex-dividend period spans four business days before the so-called record date—the date a dividend issuing corporation uses to tally its shareowners. An ex-dividend stock buyer is not entitled to a dividend because his name is not recorded with the dividend issuing corporation until after the record date.

The New York Stock Exchange requires that the buyer in every transaction be recorded with the issuing corporation on the fifth business day following a trade. A stock buyer, therefore, must purchase his shares at least five business days before the record date in order for the corporation to record

his name in time for him to receive his dividend. A purchase one day later disqualifies a buyer from a dividend because the transfer of ownership cannot be completed by the record date. Therefore, on the fourth business day prior to the record date, a stock is sold ex-dividend.

In the following example, the corporation's Board has decided to pay a 50% dividend to shareholders of record on Monday, the 10th. A person buying shares up to the close of business on Monday, the 3rd, would be eligible for the dividend because normal settlement (5 business days) will be made on Monday the 10th. On Tuesday, the 4th, however, the stock would begin selling ex-dividend because a stock purchaser as of that date could not settle till after the record date.

On the ex-dividend date, the Exchange specialist will reduce all open buy orders and open sell stop orders by the amount of the dividend. This is done to more equitably reflect the stock's value since purchasers of stock on or after the ex-dividend date are ineligible for a dividend.

EX-DIVIDEND EXPLANATION

Any Month	Date	Calendar Day	Status
	3.	Monday	With/Dividend
	4.	Tuesday.	Ex-Dividend (Without Dividend)
	5.	Wednesday	" "
	6.	Thursday	" "
	7.	Friday	" "
	8.	Saturday	Not a trading day
	9.	Sunday	Not a trading day
	10.	Monday	Record Date/Business Day
	11.	Tuesday.	Business Day

Source: *Taking the Mystery Out of Ex-Dividend*, The New York Stock Exchange, Inc.

Margin Accounts Explained

Stocks may be purchased by paying the purchase price in full (plus commissions and taxes) or on a margin account. With the margin account, the investors put up part of the purchase price in cash or securities, and the broker lends the remainder. The margin investor must pay the usual commissions as well as interest on the broker's loan. The stocks purchased on margin are held by the broker as collateral on the loan. Dividends are applied to the margin account and help offset the interest payments.

Margin (M) is defined as the market value (V) of the securities less the broker's loan (L), divided by the market value of the securities. The ratio is expressed as a percentage:

$$M = \frac{V - L}{V} \times 100$$

Example: You buy 100 shares of a stock at $20 per share at a total cost (V) of $2,000. You put up $1,200 in cash and borrow (L) $800 from the broker. The margin at the time of purchase is

$$M = \frac{\$2,000 - \$800}{\$2,000} \times 100 = 60\%$$

The margin at the time of purchase is called *initial margin*. The smallest allowed value of initial margin (set by the Federal Reserve) is currently 50%. Thus, with the above stock, if you buy 100 shares at $20 per share on 50% initial margin, you put up $1,000 (.5 × $2,000), and the broker's loan is $1,000.

After the purchase there is a *maintenance margin* (set by the Exchange) below which the margin is not permitted to decrease. The maintenance margin on the New York Stock Exchange is 25%. Some brokers, however, require a higher maintenance margin of about 30%. Thus, if the 100 shares of stocks discussed above decrease in price from $20 to $13 per share, then the margin is

$$M = \left(\frac{\$1,300 - \$1,000}{\$1,300}\right) \times 100 = 23\%$$

The margin of 23% is now below the maintenance margin of 25% set by the Exchange. The securities are said to be *under margined*, and a call for additional cash (or securities) is issued by the broker in order to bring up the margin to 25%. If the investor does not meet the call for additional cash (margin call) within a specified time, the stocks in the margin account are immediately sold.

MARGIN REQUIREMENTS (percent of market value and effective date)

	Mar. 11, 1968	June 8, 1968	May 6, 1970	Dec. 6, 1971	Nov. 24, 1972	Jan. 3, 1974
Margin stocks	70	80	65	55	65	50
Convertible bonds	50	60	50	50	50	50
Short sales	70	80	65	55	65	50

Note: Margin requirements, stated in regulations adopted by the Board of Governors pursuant to the Securities Exchange Act of 1934, limit the amount of credit that can be used to purchase and carry "margin securities" (as defined in the regulations) when such credit is collateralized by securities. Margin requirements on securities other than options are the difference between the market value (100 percent) and the maximum loan value of collateral as prescribed by the Board. Regulation T was adopted effective Oct. 15, 1934; Regulation U, effective May 1, 1936; Regulation G, effective Mar. 11, 1968; and Regulation X, effective Nov. 1, 1971.

On Jan. 1, 1977, the Board of Governors for the first time established in Regulation T the initial margin required for writing options on securities, setting it at 30 percent of the current market value of the stock underlying the option. On Sept. 30, 1985, the Board changed the required initial margin, allowing it to be the same as the option maintenance margin required by the appropriate exchange or self-regulatory organization; such maintenance margin rules must be approved by the Securities and Exchange Commission. Effective Jan. 31, 1986, the SEC approved new maintenance margin rules, permitting margins to be the price of the option plus 15 percent of the market value of the stock underlying the option.

Effective June 8, 1988, margins were set to be the price of the option plus 20 percent of the market value of the stock underlying the option (or 15 percent in the case of stock-index options).

Source: *Federal Reserve Bulletin.*

Short Selling Explained

Short selling provides an opportunity to profit from a decline in the price of a stock. If you believe that a stock is due for a substantial decline, you arrange to have your broker borrow the stock from another investor who owns the shares. The borrowed stock is then sold. This cash is held as collateral against the borrowed shares. When (and if) the stock price declines, you purchase the stock at the market price and use it to replace the borrowed shares. The broker arranges the return of your cash collateral less the cost of the repurchased stock. Your profit per share is the price received on the sale of the stock less the purchase price.

There are certain cash outlays and costs associated with the short sale. Generally there is no charge for borrowing the stock, although occasionally stock lenders may charge a premium over the market price. You must deposit $2,000 or the required initial margin, whichever is the greater, at the time the stock is borrowed. Thus, if you borrow 100 shares of a stock priced at $50 per share and the margin required is 50%, you must put up $2,500 (.5 × $50 × 100) in cash or securities. The margin deposit is returned when you close out the short sale. You pay commission when the stock is sold and when it is repurchased. In addition, you must pay the stock lender any dividends which are declared during the period you are short the stock. It is well to remember that if cash is used for the deposit, there is a loss of the interest which you would have obtained if the cash had been invested.

The dividend payments and interest loss can be reduced or eliminated if you short stocks which pay little or no dividends and use interest-bearing securities (such as T-bills or negotiable certificates of deposit) as the margin deposit.

An increase in the price of the stock can result in substantial losses since you may be forced to repurchase at a higher price than you sold. If there are many short sellers seeking to purchase the stock in order to close out their position, prices may be driven to very high levels.

The short sale cannot be executed while the stock price is declining on the exchange. According to the rules of the SEC, the stock must undergo an increase in price prior to the execution of a short sale.

Investing in Foreign Securities

Sumner N. Levine

How to Invest Internationally

Interest in international investing has grown rap dly in recent years. One reason is apparent: the size of the non-U.S. securities markets has expanded from about 35% of the total in 1970 to about 62% in 1991. It is evident that focusing exclusively on the U.S. market eliminates nearly two-thirds of the available opportunities—many of which may be very attractive.

Another reason for including foreign securities in investment portfolios is the possible risk reduction resulting from country diversification. The securities markets of most countries are only weakly interdependent. Frequently when one market is decreasing in value, that of another country is increasing. The net effect of increasing markets in a portfolio is to offset effects of the decreasing markets. For example, from mid-1991 to mid-1992, the Tokyo stock market fell 27%. However, over the same 52-week period, the Mexican market rose 81%. Clearly, including Mexican equities in a portfolio equally weighted with Japanese securities would have resulted in a net increase in portfolio value. It should be mentioned that while most markets intend to be only weakly interrelated much of the time, certain events with global impact (such as the Persian Gulf War) can cause all major markets to move together. The extent and duration of such co-movements will, of course, differ from country to country.

A quantitative measure of the extent by which two markets move together is the correlation coefficient. Two perfectly related markets are assigned a correlation coefficient of one. If the two markets are totally unrelated in their movements, the correlation coefficient has a value of zero. Some coefficients with the U.S. market over the period 1970–1989 are given in Table 1.

TABLE 1

Canada	.82
France	.45
Germany	.44
Italy	.32
Japan	.46
Netherlands	.67
United Kingdom	.59

Source: Ennis, Knupp & Associates.

Source: *The Business One Irwin International Almanac: Business and Investments*, edited by Sumner N. Levine and Caroline Levine, **IRWIN** Professional Publishing, Burr Ridge, Illinois.

Problems with International Investing

Investors should be aware of certain problems often associated with international investing. These are briefly summarized below. Further details may be found in the references given at the end of this article:

- difficulty of obtaining high quality financial information about companies in a timely manner
- language problems
- political instability
- unfamiliar financial reporting practices
- currency risks resulting from fluctuations in conversion rates
- possible restrictions on repatriating foreign earnings
- high brokerage and other transaction fees
- leveling of withholding and other taxes on gains and dividends
- delays in the delivery of stock certificates and settlements
- smaller markets may present liquidity problems
- lax oversight and regulation of many foreign markets
- dividends and interest may only be paid semiannually or even annually

How to Invest

Foreign securities may be purchased in several ways as discussed in the following:

ADRs

Several hundred foreign issues are traded as stocks or American Depository Receipts (ADRs) on the New York and American Exchanges or over the counter (OTC), and so may be purchased through the usual channels.

ADRs are receipts issued by American banks for foreign stock. The actual foreign stock certificates are held by a custodial foreign bank. It is important to note that an ADR may not represent just one foreign stock certificate. Depending on the stock, an ADR may represent several foreign stock certificates or only a fraction of a stock certificate.

Most people are unaware that there are two kinds of ADRs, sponsored and unsponsored, with different investment implications. With a sponsored ADR, a foreign company approaches a U.S. bank to issue an ADR in the U.S. Unsponsored ADRs are set up by a U.S. broker who approaches a U.S. bank with evidence of a market sufficient to warrant the issuance of an ADR. The U.S. bank then contacts the foreign company for a "no objection" letter. Stock certificates are then purchased and deposited in a foreign bank. The difference between the two types of ADRs from the viewpoint of the investor is that holders of sponsored ADRs are assured of receiving the full amount of the dividend and annual reports. Since unsponsored ADRs are set up on the initiative of a broker and not the company, the cost of distributing the dividend is taken out of the dividend by the bank, and annual reports are usually sent only on request.

Reports must be filed with the SEC for all companies listed on the exchanges or quoted on the NASDAQ. However, for those ADRs quoted on the OTC "pink sheets," SEC filings are not required, and information may be difficult to find.

Investors should also be aware that many ADRs are very thinly traded with wide spreads between the bid and ask prices.

Open-End Funds

A second approach to investing—particularly for investors with limited resources—is that of buying open-ended mutual funds. With mutual funds, investors are buying access to the expertise of the fund managers as well as all the other substantial resources often available to mutual funds.

Two categories of funds invest in foreign securities. Global funds have a portfolio that includes securities from both the U.S. and non-U.S. countries. International funds hold only non-U.S. securities. These include country funds which hold securities of companies within a given country and regional funds with portfolios consisting of companies within a geographic region (i.e., South America, etc.).

Load funds can be purchased through the management company or sponsoring broker. No-load funds must be purchased through the management company.

Closed-End Funds

Purchasing closed-end funds is yet another way for investors to participate in the foreign securities market. These funds are all traded on the exchanges so that buying them only requires a phone call to your broker. Since closed-end funds often trade at a discount from their net asset value, it is best to avoid purchasing them at a premium.

Fund Evaluation Services

Many open- and closed-end funds are evaluated by the *Morningstar Services* (53

West Jackson Boulevard, Chicago, IL. 60604-3608, phone 800-876-5005). The *No-Load Fund Investor* (P.O. Box 283, Hastings-on-the-Hudson, N.Y. 10706, phone 800-252-2042) and the *CDA/Weisenberger Financial Service* (1355 Piccard Drive, Rockville, MD. 20850, phone 301-590-1398) emphasize open-end funds. A service focusing on closed-end funds is provided by Thomas J. Herzfeld Advisors (The Herzfeld Building, Miami, Florida).

Direct Purchase

Finally, foreign securities can be purchased directly through several large U.S. brokerage firms (Merrill Lynch, Goldman Sacks, Morgan Stanley, etc.); U.S. branches of foreign banks or foreign brokerage houses.

Many foreign banks and brokerage houses make available company research reports to their clients.

For information on foreign securities consult the following:

The Wall Street Journal
The Asian Wall Street Journal
Dow Jones & Company
22 Cortlandt Street
New York, NY 10007

The Asian Wall Street Journal, a weekly, is particularly helpful for the Asian region, including stock market coverage.

Barron's
World Financial Center
200 Liberty Street
New York, NY 10281

The weekly *International Trader* section is of special interest.

Capital International Perspectives
3 Place Des Bergues
1201 Geneva, Switzerland

Capital International Perspectives is a leading monthly publication dealing with international investments.

Datastream International
299 Park Avenue
New York, NY 10171
Tel: 212-593-6500

Provides comprehensive online financial and market information worldwide.

Disclosure
5161 River Road
Bethesda, MD 20816
Tel: 301-951-1300

This service also provides annual reports and filings on foreign firms. The *Worldscope* service provides company financial information in published and compact disk formats.

This service is available online through Dow Jones Retrieval.

Contact: Wright Investor Service
P.O. Box 428
Bridgeport, CT 06601
Tel: 203-333-6666

The Financial Times
Bracken House
10 Cannon Street
London EC4P 4BY, England

The Financial Times provides comprehensive coverage of European businesses and securities markets and is published daily.

Moody's Investor Services, International Manual
Moody's Investor Services
99 Church Street
New York, NY 10007
Tel: 212-553-0300

The International Manual provides financial information on about 5,000 major foreign corporations.

Reuters, based in London, is one of the largest international news agencies. Online services include Newsline which gives current international news, and Company News Year which provides access to one year of news items concerning specific companies.

Contact: Reuters Information Services
1700 Broadway
New York, NY 10019

For Further Reading

General Texts:

1. N. Berryessa and E. Kirzner. *Global Investing*. Business One Irwin, Homewood, Illinois (1988).
2. R. Keyes and D. Miller. *The Global Investor*. Longman, Chicago, Illinois (1990).
3. J. Lederman and K. Park. *The Global Equity Market*. Probus, Chicago, Illinois (1991).
4. Ibid., *The Global Bond Market*. Probus, Chicago, Illinois (1991).

5. S. Levine. *Global Investing*. Harper-Collins, New York, New York (1992).
6. S. Levine and C. Levine (eds.). *International Almanac: Business and Investments*. Business One Irwin, Homewood, Illinois.
7. G. Warfield. *How to Buy Foreign Stocks*. Harper Row, New York, New York (1985).

Directories:

8. S. Allen and S. O'Connor. *Guide to World Equity Markets*. Euromoney London (annual).
9. *Handbook of World Stock and Commodity Exchanges*. Basil Blackwell, Oxford (annual).

How to Check up on Your Investment Advisor

If you are considering investing with a firm that you know little about, check out the firm's background in the following three areas:

Disciplinary history records can be obtained from the National Association of Securities Dealers 800-289-9999. Also check the State regulator of the State in which the firm is located. To obtain the regulator's phone number call 202-737-0900.

For information about financial planners contact the Institute of Certified Financial Planners at 303-751-7600 or the International Association for Financial Planning at 404-395-1605.

Credit background information can be obtained, for a fee, from Dun and Bradstreet at (800-362-2255).

Litigation information, past or pending, is available from the State or Federal court house where the company has its headquarters. Mead Data Central will do a search, for a fee, of newspapers and periodicals. Telephone: 808-843-6476.

PERFORMANCES OF FOREIGN SECURITIES MARKETS

主要国の株価指数　Stock Price Indices

東証株価指数（日本）
Tokyo Stock Price Index (Japan)

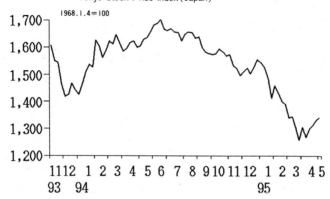

ダウ工業株30種（米国）
Dow Jones Average 30 Industrials (U.S.)

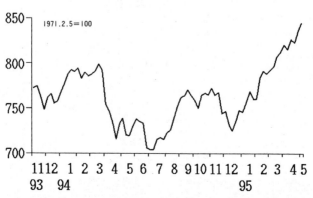

ナスダック総合指数（米国）
NASDAQ Composite Index (U.S.)

(continued)

FT工業株指数（英国）
Financial Times Index of Industrial Ordinary Shares (U.K.)

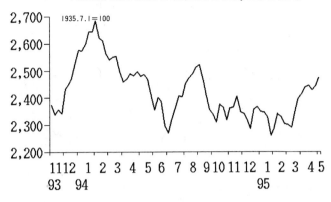

DAX株価指数（ドイツ）
DAX Index (Germany)

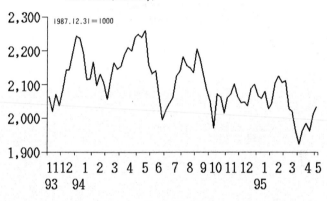

オーストラリア証券取引所全普通株指数
Australia Stock Exchange All Ordinaries Index

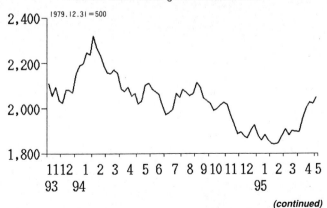

(continued)

PERFORMANCES OF FOREIGN SECURITIES MARKETS
(concluded)

ハンセン指数(香港)
Hang Seng Index(Hong Kong)

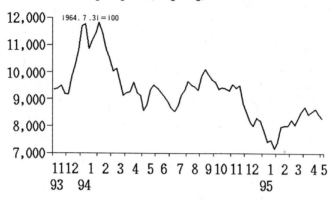

シンガポール証券取引所全上場株指数
Stock Exchange of Singapore All Singapore Index

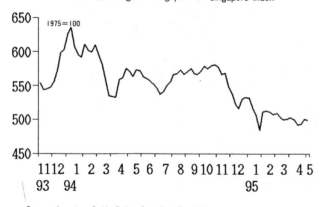

Source: *Investors Guide,* Daiwa Securities Co., Ltd.

Stocks of non-U.S. corporate issuers, December 30, 1994 (NYSE)

Country	Company	Symbol	Date Admitted
Argentina	BAESA - Buenos Aires Embotelladora, S.A.*	BAE	5/5/93
	Banco Frances del Rio de la Plata*	BFR	11/24/93
	IRSA-Inversiones y Representaciones, S.A.***	IRS	12/20/94
	MetroGas, S.A.*	MGS	11/17/94
	Telecom Argentina STET-France Telecom, S.A.*	TEO	12/9/94
	Telefonica de Argentina, S.A.*	TAR	3/8/94
	Transportadora de Gas del Sur, S.A.*	TGS	11/17/94
	YPF Sociedad Anonima*	YPF	6/29/93
Australia	Australia and New Zealand Banking Group Limited*	ANZ	12/6/94
	Australia and New Zealand Banking Group Ltd. (PFD)	ANZPR	3/2/93
	Broken Hill Proprietary Company Limited*	BHP	5/28/87
	Coles Myer Ltd.*	CM	10/31/88
	FAI Insurances Limited*	FAI	9/28/88
	National Australia Bank Limited*	NAB	6/24/88
	NewsCorporation Ltd.*	NWS	5/20/86
	Orbital Engine Corporation Limited*	OE	12/4/91
	The News Corporation Limited* (PFD)	NWSPR	11/3/94
	Western Mining Corp. Holdings Ltd.*	WMC	1/2/90
	Westpac Banking Corporation*	WBK	3/17/89
Bermuda	ACE Limited	ACL	3/25/93
	Sphere Drake Holdings Limited	SD	9/22/93
Brazil	Aracruz Celulose, S.A.*	ARA	5/27/92
British W.I.	Club Med, Inc.	CMI	9/25/84
Canada	Abitibi-Price Inc.	ABY	7/1/87
	Agnico-Eagle Mines Limited	AEM	11/22/94
	Alcan Aluminium Ltd.	AL	5/31/50
	American Barrick Resources Corp.	ABX	2/25/87
	Bank of Montreal	BMO	10/27/94
	BCE Inc.	BCE	8/18/76
	Campbell Resources Inc.	CCH	6/13/83
	Canadian Pacific Limited	CP	1/24/1883
	Cineplex Odeon Corporation	CPX	5/14/87
	Domtar Inc.	DTC	9/22/87
	Glamis Gold Ltd.	GLG	1/20/93
	Horsham Corporation	HSM	1/15/90
	Inco Limited	N	12/20/28
	International Colin Energy Corp.	KCN	3/23/94
	InterTAN Inc.	ITN	11/1/88
	Kinross Gold Corporation	KGC	10/17/94
	Laidlaw Inc. (Class A)	LDWA	12/10/90
	Laidlaw Inc. (Class B)	LDWB	12/10/90
	Magna International Inc.	MGA	10/9/92
	Mitel Corporation	MLT	5/18/81
	Moore Corporation Limited	MCL	11/13/80
	Newbridge Networks Corporation	NN	9/14/94
	Northern Telecom Limited	NT	11/10/75
	Northgate Exploration Limited	NGX	2/3/70

(continued)

Stocks of non-U.S. corporate issuers, December 30, 1994 (NYSE) *(continued)*

Country	Company	Symbol	Date Admitted
Canada (cont'd)	NOVA Corporation of Alberta	NVA	6/13/88
	Placer Dome Inc.	PDG	8/13/87
	Potash Corporation of Saskatchewan Inc.	POT	11/2/89
	Premdor Inc.	PI	4/2/93
	Ranger Oil Limited	RGO	1/28/83
	Seagram Company Ltd.	VO	12/2/35
	TransCanada Pipelines Limited	TRP	5/30/85
	TVX Gold, Inc.	TVX	8/10/94
	United Dominion Industries Limited	UDI	12/6/83
	Westcoast Energy Inc.	WE	8/15/64
Cayman Is.	Elf Overseas Ltd. Ser. A (PFD)	EOLPRA	2/11/93
	Elf Overseas Ltd. Ser. B (PFD)	EOLPRB	7/8/93
	Espirito Santo Overseas (PFD)	ESBPRA	12/17/93
	Extecapital Ltd. (PFD)	BEXPR	12/23/92
	NewsCorp. Overseas Ltd. Ser. A (PFD)	NOPPRA	8/30/93
	Santander Finance Ltd. Ser. A (PFD)	BSFPRA	11/4/93
	Santander Finance Ltd. Ser. B (PFD)	BSFPRB	3/24/94
Chile	Administradora de Fondos de Pensiones-Provida, S.A.*	PVD	11/16/94
	Banco O'Higgins*	OHG	5/18/94
	Banco Osorno y La Union*	BOU	11/4/94
	Chilgener, S.A.*	CHR	7/19/94
	Compania de Telefonos de Chile, S.A.*	CTC	7/20/90
	Cristalerias de Chile, S.A.*	CGW	1/25/94
	Embotelladora Andina, S.A.*	AKO	7/6/94
	Empresa Nacional de Electricidad, S.A. (Chile)*	EOC	7/27/94
	Enersis, S.A.*	ENI	10/20/93
	Laboratorio Chile, S.A.*	LBC	6/29/94
	Madeco, S.A.*	MAD	5/28/93
	MASISA - Maderas y Sinteticos Sociedad Anonima*	MYS	6/17/93
	SQM - Sociedad Quimica y Minera de Chile, S.A.*	SQM	9/21/93
	Telex-Chile, S.A.*	TL	10/14/94
	Vina Concha y Toro, S.A.*	VCO	10/14/94
Colombia	Banco Ganadero, S.A.*	BGA	11/15/94
	Banco Ganadero, S.A.* (PFD)	BGAPR	12/15/94
Denmark	ISS-International Service System A/S*	ISG	10/27/94
	Novo-Nordisk A/S*	NVO	7/9/81
	Tele Danmark A/S*	TLD	4/28/94
Finland	Nokia Corporation*	NOKPR	7/1/94
France	Alcatel Alsthom Compagnie Generale d'Electricite*	ALA	5/20/92
	Rhone-Poulenc, S.A.* Ord. A	RP	1/26/93
	Rhone-Poulenc Overseas (PFD)	RPOPRA	7/13/93
	Rhone-Poulenc, S.A.* 1/4A (PFD)	RPPRA	11/10/89
	SGS-THOMSON Microelectronics N.V.	STM	12/8/94
	Société National Elf Aquitaine*	ELF	6/14/91
	TOTAL*	TOT	10/25/91

Country	Company	Symbol	Date Admitted
Germany	Daimler - Benz AG*	DAI	10/5/93
Hong Kong	Amway Asia Pacific Ltd.	AAP	12/15/93
	Brilliance China Automotive Holdings Limited	CBA	10/9/92
	China Tire Holdings Limited	TIR	7/15/93
	Ek Chor China Motorcycle Co., Ltd.	EKC	6/29/93
	Hong Kong Telecommunications Ltd.*	HKT	12/8/88
	Tommy Hilfiger Corporation	TOM	9/23/92
Indonesia	Indonesian Satellite Corporation*	IIT	10/18/94
Ireland	Allied Irish Banks PLC*	AIB	9/12/89
	Allied Irish Banks PLC* (PFD)	AIBPR	9/12/89
Israel	Elscint Limited	ELT	9/20/84
	Tadiran Limited	TAD	8/6/92
Italy	Benetton Group, S.p.A.*	BNG	6/9/89
	Fiat, S.p.A.* 5 Ord.	FIA	2/14/89
	Fiat, S.p.A.* 5 (PFD)	FIAPR	2/14/89
	Fiat, S.p.A.* 5 Svg. (PFD)	FIAPRA	2/14/89
	Fila Holdings, S.p.A.*	FLH	5/27/93
	Industrie Natuzzi, S.p.A.*	NTZ	5/13/93
	Instituto Mobiliare Italiano, S.p.A.*	IMI	2/9/94
	Instituto Nazionale delle Assicurazioni, S.p.A.*	INZ	7/6/94
	Luxottica Group, S.p.A.*	LUX	1/24/90
	Montedison, S.p.A.*	MNT	7/16/87
	Montedison, S.p.A.* (PFD)	MNTPR	7/16/87
Japan	Amway Japan Limited*	AJL	6/29/94
	Hitachi, Ltd.*	HIT	4/14/82
	Honda Motor Co., Ltd.*	HMC	2/11/77
	Kubota Corporation*	KUB	11/9/76
	Kyocera Corporation*	KYO	5/23/80
	Matsushita Electric Industrial Co., Ltd.*	MC	12/13/71
	Mitsubishi Bank Ltd.*	MBK	9/19/89
	Nippon Telegraph and Telephone Corporation*	NTT	9/29/94
	Pioneer Electronic Corporation*	PIO	12/13/76
	Sony Corporation*	SNE	9/17/70
	TDK Corporation*	TDK	5/15/82
Korea	Korea Electric Power Corporation*	KEP	10/27/94
	Pohang Iron & Steel Co., Ltd.*	PKX	10/14/94
Liberia	Royal Caribbean Cruises Ltd.	RCL	4/28/93
Luxembourg	Espirito Santo Financial Holdings, S.A.*	ESF	6/30/93
Mexico	Banpais, S.A.*	BPS	6/30/94
	Bufete Industrial, S.A.*	GBI	11/4/93
	Coca-Cola Femsa, S.A. de C.V.*	KOF	9/14/93
	Consorcio G Grupo Dina, S.A. de C.V.*	DIN	3/31/93

(continued)

Stocks of non-U.S. corporate issuers, December 30, 1994 (NYSE) *(continued)*

Country	Company	Symbol	Date Admitted
Mexico (cont'd)	Consorcio G Grupo Dina, S.A. de C.V.* (Ser. L)	DINL	8/8/94
	Desc, S.A. de C.V.*	DES	7/14/94
	Empresas ICA Sociedad Controladora, S.A. de C.V.*	ICA	4/9/92
	Empresas la Moderna, S.A. de C.V.*	ELM	2/2/94
	Grupo Casa Autrey, S.A. de C.V.*	ATY	12/7/93
	Grupo Elektra, S.A. de C.V.***	EKT	12/5/94
	Grupo Embotellador de Mexico, S.A. de C.V.***	GEM	3/29/94
	Grupo Financiero Serfin, S.A. de C.V.*	SFN	12/1/93
	Grupo Industrial Durango, S.A. de C.V.*	GID	7/15/94
	Grupo Industrial Maseca, S.A. de C.V.*	MSK	5/17/94
	Grupo Iusacell, S.A. de C.V.* (Ser. D)	CELD	6/15/94
	Grupo Iusacell, S.A. de C.V.* (Ser. L)	CEL	6/15/94
	Grupo Mexicano de Desarrollo, S.A. de C.V.* (Ser. B)	GMDB	12/14/93
	Grupo Mexicano de Desarrollo, S.A. de C.V.* (Ser. L)	GMD	12/14/93
	Grupo Radio Centro, S.A. de C.V.*	RC	7/1/93
	Grupo Sidek, S.A. de C.V.* (Ser. L)	SDK	7/12/94
	Grupo Sidek, S.A. de C.V.* (Ser. B)	SDKB	10/27/94
	Grupo Televisa, S.A.***	TV	12/14/93
	Grupo Tribasa, S.A. de C.V.*	GTR	9/22/93
	Internacional de Ceramica, S.A. de C.V.*	ICM	12/8/94
	Telefonos de Mexico, S.A. de C.V.*	TMX	5/14/91
	Transportacion Maritima Mexicana, S.A. de C.V.* (Ser. L)	TMM	6/10/92
	Transportacion Maritima Mexicana, S.A. de C.V.* Ord.	TMMA	6/10/92
	Vitro, S.A.*	VTO	11/19/91
Netherlands	AEGON N.V.**	AEG	11/5/91
	Elsag Bailey Process Automation N.V.	EBY	11/19/93
	Elsevier N.V.*	ENL	10/6/94
	KLM Royal Dutch Airlines**	KLM	5/22/57
	Koninklijke Ahold N.V.*	AHO	11/15/93
	Philips N.V.**	PHG	4/14/87
	Polygram N.V.**	PLG	12/14/89
	Royal Dutch Petroleum Co.**	RD	7/20/54
	Unilever N.V.**	UN	12/12/61
Netherlands Antilles	Schlumberger Limited	SLB	2/2/62
	Singer Company N.V.	SEW	8/2/91
New Zealand	Fletcher Challenge Ltd.*	FLC	12/13/93
	Fletcher Challenge Ltd. Forest Division Shares*	FFS	12/13/93
	Telecom Corporation of New Zealand Ltd.*	NZT	7/17/91
Norway	A/S Eksportfinans (PFD)	EKPPR	1/14/93
	Hafslund Nycomed AS*	HN	6/24/92
	Norsk Hydro a.s.*	NHY	6/25/86
Panama	Banco Latinoamericano de Exportaciones, S.A.	BLX	9/24/92
	Panamerican Beverages, Inc.	PB	9/22/93
People's Rep. of China	Huaneng Power International, Inc.*	HNP	10/6/94
	Shandong Huaneng Power Development Co. Ltd.*	SH	8/4/94
	Shanghai Petrochemical Company, Ltd.*	SHI	7/26/93

Country	Company	Symbol	Date Admitted
Peru	Banco Wiese Limitado*	BWP	9/21/94
Philippines	Benguet Corporation	BE	6/27/49
	Philippine Long Distance Telephone Company*	PHI	10/19/94
	Philippine Long Distance Telephone Company*** (PFD)	PHIPRA	11/22/94
Portugal	Banco Comercial Portugues, S.A.*	BPC	6/12/92
Singapore	China Yuchai International Ltd.	CYD	12/16/94
South Africa	ASA Limited	ASA	12/8/58
Spain	ARGENTARIA - Corporacion Bancaria de Espana, S.A.*	AGR	5/12/93
	Banco Bilbao Vizcaya, S.A.*	BBV	12/14/88
	Banco Bilbao Vizcaya Int. (Gibraltar)* (PFD)	BVGPR	12/12/91
	Banco Bilbao Vizcaya Int. (Gibraltar)* (PFD)	BVGPRB	12/15/92
	Banco Bilbao Vizcaya Int. (Gibraltar)* (PFD)	BVGPRC	7/1/93
	Banco Central, S.A.*	BCH	7/20/83
	Banco de Santander, S.A.*	STD	7/30/87
	Central Hispano Capital Limited (Puerto Rico) (PFD)	HCLPR	12/29/94
	Central Hispano International, Inc. (Cayman Islands) (PFD)	HPNPR	12/29/94
	Empresa Nacional de Electricidad, S.A.*	ELE	6/1/88
	Repsol, S.A.*	REP	5/11/89
	Telefonica de Espana, S.A.*	TEF	6/12/87
Sweden	Aktiebolaget Svensk Exportkredit (PFD)	SEPPR	9/20/93
Turks and Caicos	Capital Re LLC Ser. A (PFD)	KREPRL	1/28/94
United Kingdom	Attwoods PLC*	A	4/12/91
	Automated Security (Holdings) PLC*	ASI	7/22/92
	Barclays Bank PLC* (PFD)	BCBPR	5/5/93
	Barclays Bank PLC* (PFD)	BCBPRC	7/23/90
	Barclays Bank PLC* (PFD)	BCBPRD	3/28/91
	Barclays Bank PLC*	BCS	9/9/86
	Bass PLC*	BAS	2/8/90
	BET Public Limited Company*	BEP	8/6/87
	British Airways PLC*	BAB	2/11/87
	British Gas PLC*	BRG	12/8/86
	British Petroleum Co. PLC*	BP	3/23/70
	British Sky Broadcasting Group PLC*	BSY	12/8/94
	British Steel PLC*	BST	12/5/88
	British Telecommunications PLC*	BTY	12/3/84
	Cable and Wireless Public Limited Co.*	CWP	9/27/89
	Carlton Communications PLC (PFD)	CCMPR	10/19/93
	English China Clays PLC*	ENC	4/30/92
	Enterprise Oil PLC*	ETP	10/16/92
	Enterprise Oil PLC Ser. A* (PFD)	ETPPR	7/20/92
	Enterprise Oil PLC Ser. B* (PFD)	ETPPRB	10/12/92
	Glaxo Holdings PLC*	GLX	6/10/87
	Grand Metropolitan PLC*	GRM	3/13/91
	Hanson PLC*	HAN	11/3/86

(continued)

Stocks of non-U.S. corporate issuers, December 30, 1994 (NYSE) *(concluded)*

Country	Company	Symbol	Date Admitted
United Kingdom	Huntingdon International Holdings PLC*	HTD	2/16/89
(cont'd)	Imperial Chemical Industries PLC*	ICI	11/1/83
	Lasmo PLC*	LSO	6/8/93
	Lasmo PLC Ser. A* (PFD)	LSOPRA	7/12/93
	Midland Bank PLC* (PFD)	MIBPRA	11/4/93
	National Westminster Bank PLC*	NW	10/22/86
	National Westminster Bank PLC* (PFD)	NWPRA	10/25/91
	National Westminster Bank PLC* (PFD)	NWPRB	6/14/93
	National Westminster Bank PLC (PFD)	NWXPRA	11/29/93
	Reed International PLC*	RUK	10/6/94
	Royal Bank of Scotland Group PLC*	RBSPR	10/16/89
	Royal Bank of Scotland Group PLC* (PFD)	RBSPRB	8/12/91
	Royal Bank of Scotland Group PLC* (PFD)	RBSPRC	9/28/92
	RTZ Corporation PLC*	RTZ	6/28/90
	Saatchi & Saatchi Company PLC*	SAA	12/8/87
	Shell Transport & Trading Co., PLC**	SC	3/13/57
	SmithKline Beecham PLC* (Class A)	SBH	7/27/89
	SmithKline Beecham PLC* (Class B)	SBE	7/27/89
	Tiphook PLC*	TPH	10/1/91
	Unilever PLC*	UL	12/12/61
	Vodafone Group PLC*	VOD	10/26/88
	Willis Corroon PLC*	WCG	10/9/90
	Wellcome PLC*	WEL	7/27/92
	Waste Management International PLC*	WME	4/7/92
	Zeneca Group PLC*	ZEN	5/12/93
Venezuela	Corimon C.A.*	CRM	3/23/93

*   American Depositary Receipts/Shares
** NY Shares and/or Guilder Shares
*** Global Depositary Shares

Source: New York Stock Exchange *Fact Book.*

TOPIX (Tokyo Stock Price Index)

(Jan. 4, 1968 = 100)

	Year-end	High		Low	
		Index	Date	Index	Date
1949	12.85	22.06	5/16	11.95	12/14
1950	11.57	13.24	8/21	9.59	7/3
1951—55	39.06	42.18	2/4/53	11.58	1/4/51
1956	51.21	52.95	12/6	38.81	1/25
1957	43.40	54.82	1/21	43.18	12/27
1958	60.95	60.95	12/27	43.48	1/4
1959	80.00	90.14	11/30	61.11	1/9
1960	109.18	112.53	11/15	79.46	1/4
1961	101.66	126.59	7/14	90.86	12/19
1962	99.67	111.45	2/14	83.39	10/30
1963	92.87	122.96	5/10	91.21	12/18
1964	90.68	103.77	7/3	87.94	11/11
1965	105.68	105.68	12/28	81.29	7/15
1966	111.41	114.51	3/24	105.21	1/19
1967	100.89	117.60	5/31	99.17	12/11
1968	131.31	142.95	10/2	100.00	1/4
1969	179.30	179.30	12/27	132.62	1/4
1970	148.35	185.70	4/8	147.08	12/9
1971	199.45	209.00	8/14	148.05	1/6
1972	401.70	401.70	12/28	199.93	1/4
1973	306.44	422.48	1/24	284.69	12/18
1974	278.34	342.47	6/5	251.96	10/9
1975	323.43	333.11	7/2	268.24	1/10
1976	383.88	383.88	12/28	326.28	1/5
1977	364.08	390.93	9/29	350.49	11/24
1978	449.55	452.60	12/13	364.04	1/4
1979	459.61	465.24	9/29	435.13	7/13
1980	494.10	497.96	10/20	449.01	3/10
1981	570.31	603.92	8/17	495.79	1/5
1982	593.72	593.72	12/28	511.52	8/17
1983	731.82	731.82	12/28	574.51	1/25
1984	913.37	913.37	12/28	735.45	1/4
1985	1,049.40	1,058.35	7/27	916.93	1/4
1986	1,556.37	1,583.35	8/20	1,025.85	1/21
1987	1,725.83	2,258.56	6/11	1,557.46	1/13
1988	2,357.03	2,357.03	12/28	1,690.44	1/4
1989	2,881.37	2,884.80	12/18	2,364.33	3/27
1990	1,733.83	2,867.70	1/4	1,523.43	10/1
1991	1,714.68	2,028.85	3/18	1,638.06	12/24
1992	1,307.66	1,763.43	1/6	1,102.50	8/18
1993	1,439.31	1,698.67	9/3	1,250.06	1/25
1994	1,559.09	1,712.73	6/13	1,445.97	1/4

Source: Tokyo Stock Exchange *1995 Fact Book*.

TOKYO STOCK EXCHANGE (TOPIX): 30 Most Active Stocks (Volume and Value), 1994

	(mils. of shares)				(¥ bils.)
Rank	Stocks	Volume	Rank	Stocks	Value
1	NIPPON STEEL	1,628	1	NIPPON TELEGRAPH AND TELEPHONE	2,015
2	Mitsubishi Heavy Industries	1,165	2	SONY	1,152
3	Kawasaki Steel	1,128	3	The Nomura Securities	1,098
4	Hitachi	1,003	4	East Japan Railway	982
5	NKK	927	5	Hitachi	977
6	FUJITSU	861	6	Matsushita Electric Industrial	920
7	TOSHIBA	851	7	FUJITSU	888
8	Sumitomo Metal Industries	835	8	DDI	883
9	Oki Electric Industry	734	9	Mitsubishi Heavy Industries	876
10	NEC	704	10	TOYOTA MOTOR	856
11	SANYO ELECTRIC	595	11	NEC	796
12	Mitsubishi Electric	549	12	Sharp	767
13	MITSUBISHI OIL	542	13	KYOCERA	671
14	Matsushita Electric Industrial	541	14	TOSHIBA	652
15	Kobe Steel	529	15	CANON	633
16	NISSAN MOTOR	528	16	The Sumitomo Bank	622
17	ISUZU MOTORS	513	17	Ito-Yokado	616
18	ITOCHU	501	18	NIPPON STEEL	591
19	The Nomura Securities	497	19	MITSUBISHI OIL	587
20	Kawasaki Heavy Industries	450	20	SEVEN-ELEVEN JAPAN	581
21	Sharp	443	21	Daiwa Securities	566
22	TOYOTA MOTOR	415	22	The Mitsubishi Bank	558
23	TORAY INDUSTRIES	413	23	Oki Electric Industry	520
24	TOKYO GAS	406	24	NITSUKO	509
25	The Furukawa Electric	392	25	The Tokyo Electric Power	502
26	RICOH	390	26	SEGA ENTERPRISES	502
27	SUMITOMO CHEMICAL	390	27	The Industrial Bank of Japan	499
28	Sumitomo Metal Mining	374	28	Sumitomo Electric Industries	496
29	CANON	372	29	The Sanwa Bank	459
30	Marubeni	367	30	Kawasaki Steel	447

Total Trading Volume of the 30 stocks (A)	19,044	A/B	Total Trading Value of the 30 stocks (C)	22,222	C/D
Total Trading Volume of all stocks (B)	84,514	22.5%	Total Trading Value of all stocks (D)	87,355	25.4%

Source: Tokyo Stock Exchange *1995 Fact Book.*

TOKYO STOCK EXCHANGE (TOPIX): Yields and Dividends

	All 1st Section Stocks	1st Section Dividend-Paying Stocks		
	Weighted Average Yields (%)	Average Dividend per Share (¥)	Total Amount of Dividends (¥ bil.)	Simple Average Yields (%)
1949	...	6.09	2	6.77
1950	...	6.97	12	9.53
1955	...	8.70	70	7.96
1956	...	8.27	85	6.68
1957	...	7.71	113	7.14
1958	...	7.14	123	6.66
1959	4.68	6.76	138	4.54
1960	4.27	6.71	174	3.93
1961	4.47	6.63	231	3.24
1962	5.82	6.47	307	3.86
1963	5.08	6.26	349	4.24
1964	6.01	6.26	392	5.69
1965	6.01	6.08	409	5.92
1966	4.76	5.92	408	4.44
1967	4.96	5.97	457	4.74
1968	5.00	6.09	507	4.36
1969	4.19	6.28	569	3.37
1970	4.30	6.55	647	3.52
1971	4.01	6.65	711	3.41
1972	2.42	6.55	718	2.24
1973	2.02	6.75	850	2.09
1974	2.55	6.88	912	2.53
1975	2.54	6.51	881	2.31
1976	2.27	6.25	995	1.91
1977	2.16	6.34	1,040	1.82
1978	2.00	6.45	1,090	1.60
1979	1.87	6.49	1,192	1.57
1980	1.79	6.58	1,201	1.63
1981	1.65	6.69	1,499	1.55
1982	1.80	6.80	1,526	1.68
1983	1.55	6.88	1,595	1.39
1984	1.24	7.11	1,710	1.09
1985	1.05	7.25	1,829	0.99
1986	0.83	7.33	1,850	0.78
1987	0.56	7.36	2,042	0.63
1988	0.52	7.52	2,298	0.55
1989	0.46	7.78	2,495	0.47
1990	0.61	8.04	2,826	0.52
1991	0.73	8.21	2,906	0.64
1992	0.99	8.21	2,297	0.90
1993	0.86	8.16	2,691	0.82
1994	0.77	8.03	2,504	0.76

Note: Total amount of dividends for 1994 is that of the sum from Jan. to Nov.

Source: Tokyo Stock Exchange *1995 Fact Book*.

TOPIX Average Dividend Yields
(All 1st Section Stocks)

Dividend Yields

Yields on stocks, obtained by dividing annual cash dividends by the stock price, are yardsticks for measuring the rate of return in the form of dividends of stock investment.

The simple average yields and the weighted average yields are often used as general indicators of the dividend return of the stock market.

When seen from a long-term point of view, the simple average yields of all 1st Section stocks (monthly average) have almost consistently been dropping since 1975. In recent years, the yields increased for 3 consecutive years to 0.88% in 1992, then turned to show a downward trend in 1993 and 1994.

AVERAGE DIVIDEND YIELDS
(All 1st Section Stocks)

During	Simple Average (%)
1990	0.49
1991	0.62
1992	0.88
1993	0.79
1994	0.71
Jan.	0.78
Feb.	0.74
Mar.	0.72
Apr.	0.72
May	0.71
June	0.68
July	0.65
Aug.	0.66
Sept.	0.70
Oct.	0.71
Nov.	0.74
Dec.	0.74

AVERAGE DIVIDEND YIELDS (All 1st Section Stocks)

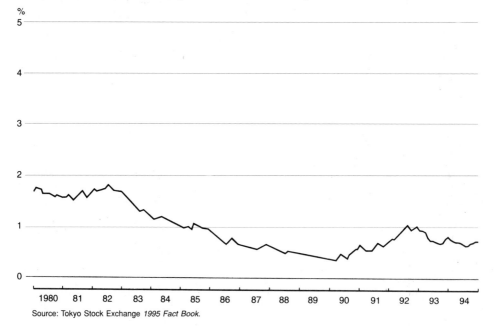

Source: Tokyo Stock Exchange *1995 Fact Book.*

Rates of Return on Common Stocks

The table below shows average compound annual rates of return on common stocks on the assumption that an investor bought all common stocks listed on the 1st Section of the Tokyo Stock Exchange in proportion to their market value and redistributed the holdings each year in order to preserve the proportionality. For example, if an investor bought all 1st-Section-listed common stocks in 1984 and sold them in 1994, the average annual rate of return on his investments over the 10-year holding period was 9.5%.

The annual rate of return between 1993 and 1994 was 6.4%.

Source: Tokyo Stock Exchange *1995 Fact Book.*

TOPIX: Average Compound Annual Rates of Return on Common Stocks (1st Section)

(%)

To	From									
	1984	1985	1986	1987	1988	1989	1990	1991	1992	1993
1985	27.0									
1986	33.4	40.1								
1987	37.5	43.1	46.2							
1988	31.4	32.9	29.4	14.6						
1989	29.6	30.2	27.1	18.5	22.4					
1990	20.5	19.3	14.6	5.7	1.4	−15.9				
1991	15.4	13.5	8.9	1.1	−3.0	−13.6	−11.3			
1992	9.4	7.1	2.4	−4.7	−9.0	−17.5	−18.3	−24.8		
1993	9.8	7.9	3.9	−1.8	−4.8	−10.6	−8.8	−7.5	13.7	
1994(P)	9.5	7.7	4.2	−0.7	−3.0	−7.5	−5.2	−3.1	10.0	6.4

Source: Japan Securities Research Institute

Source: Tokyo Stock Exchange *1995 Fact Book.*

Note: The Tokyo Stock Exchange is divided into three sections. Sections 1 and 2 are made up of Japanese companies. Section 3, known as the foreign section is comprised of non-Japanese stocks.

NASDAQ ADRS AND FOREIGN SECURITIES' ISSUES, SHARE VOLUME, AND DOLLAR VOLUME

	American Depositary Receipts				Foreign Securities		
	Issues	Share Volume (millions)	Dollar Volume (millions)		Issues	Share Volume (millions)	Dollar Volume (millions)
1994	106	1,573.0	$33,835.5		244	3,410.5	$46,989.6
1993	100	1,608.5	28,472.4		222	2,760.7	44,165.7
1992	88	961.1	12,010.5		187	1,581.2	19,610.2
1991	83	2,182.8	16,969.6		185	1,143.7	10,700.4
1990	87	2,219.2	21,313.1		184	841.6	7,069.9
1989	92	1,800.1	17,391.1		194	879.9	5,888.4
1988	96	1,078.4	9,903.8		196	1,498.0	4,672.0
1987	97	1,822.1	18,864.6		204	1,111.0	8,465.0
1986	88	1,576.1	20,026.5		178	826.7	4,859.1
1985	86	911.7	9,828.2		196	473.6	2,649.4

Source: Reprinted with permission from the *1995 Nasdaq Fact Book and Company Directory.* © National Association of Securities Dealers, Inc. All rights reserved.

FOREIGN COMPANIES AND ADR ISSUERS—NASDAQ, NYSE, AND AMEX: 1994

Number Of
Companies/Issuers

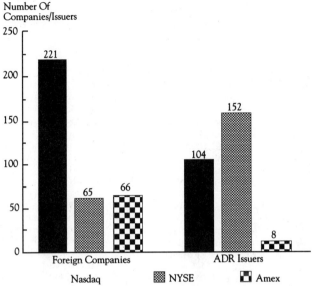

Nasdaq   NYSE   Amex

DOLLAR VOLUME OF EQUITY TRADING IN MAJOR WORLD MARKETS: 1994

Value (Billions Of Dollars)

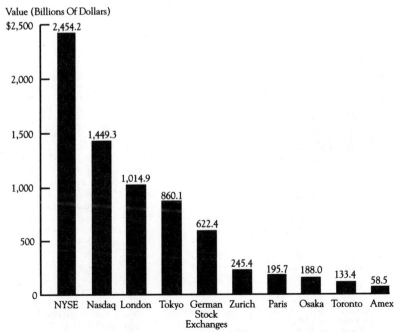

Securities Markets: Notable Dates

1792 Original brokers' agreement subscribed to by 24 brokers (May 17).

1817 Constitution and the name "New York Stock Exchange Board" adopted (March 8).

1830 Dullest day in history of exchange—31 shares traded (March 16).

1840s Outdoor trading in unlisted securities begins at Wall and Hanover Streets, moves to Wall and Broad, then shifts south along Broad Street.°

1863 Name changed to "New York Stock Exchange" (NYSE) (January 29).

1867 Stock tickers first introduced (November 15).

1868 Membership made salable (October 23).

1869 Exchange required registering of securities by listed companies to prevent their over-issuance (February 1).

NYSE and Open Board of Brokers adopted plan of consolidation (May 8).

Gold speculation resulted in "Black Friday" (September 24).

1871 Continuous markets in stocks established.

1873 NYSE closed September 18–29.

Failure of Jay Cooke & Co. and others (September 18).

Trading hours set at 10 A.M. to 3 P.M.; Saturdays, 10 A.M. to noon (December 1).

1878 First telephones introduced in the exchange (November 13).

1881 Annunciator board installed for paging members (January 29).

1885 Unlisted Securities Department established (March 25).

1886 First million share day—1,200,000 shares traded (December 15).

1895 Exchange recommended that companies listed or traded publish and distribute to stockholders annual statements showing income and balance sheet (January 23).

Exchange occupied new building with present trading floor at 18 Broad Street (April 23).

Call money loaned as high as 125%, following suspension of payments

by Knickerbocker Trust Company on previous day. This period was generally known as panic of 1907 (October 23).

1908 E. S. Mendels forms New York Curb Agency in first departure from informal trading.°

1910 Unlisted Securities Department abolished (March 31).

1911 Trading rules established with formation of New York Curb Market Association.°

1914 Exchange closed from July 31 through December 11—World War I.

1915 Stock prices quoted in dollars as against percent of par value (October 13).

1919 Separate ticker system installed for bonds (January 2).

1920 Stock Clearing Corporation established (April 26).

1921 New York Curb Market association moves indoors at 86 Trinity Place; name shortened to New York Curb Market and ticker service initiated (June 21).°

1924 Sliding scale of commission rates adopted.

1927 Start of ten-share unit of trading for inactive stocks (January 3).

1929 Stock market crash; 16,410,000 shares traded (October 29).

New York Curb Market modifies its name to New York Curb Exchange.°

1930 Faster ticker—500 characters per minute—installed (September 2).

1931 Exchange building expanded; Telephone Quotation Department formed to send stock quotes to member firm offices.°

1933 Exchange announced formal adoption of rule requiring independent audit of statements of listed companies (January 6).

New York Stock Exchange closed for bank holiday, March 4–14.

Securities Act of 1933 enacted. Its two basic purposes: to provide full disclosure to investors and to prohibit fraud in connection with the sale of securities (May 27).

1934 Enactment of Securities Exchange Act of 1934 (June 6).

1938 First salaried president elected—Wm. McChesney Martin, Jr. (June 30).

1946 Listed stocks outnumber unlisted stocks for first time since the 1934 act imposed restrictions on unlisted trading.°

1952 Trading hours changed: weekdays, 10 A.M. to 3:30 P.M. Closed Saturdays (September 29).

1953 Name of New York Curb Exchange

° Refers to American Exchange (AMEX).

† Applies to both the New York Stock Exchange and the American Exchange.

Sources: New York Stock Exchange *Fact Book*, American Stock Exchange *Data Book* and *The Wall Street Journal.*

changed to American Stock Exchange.°

1958 First member corporation—Woodcock, Hess & Co. (June 4).

Mary C. Roebling becomes first woman governor.°

1962 Committee system of administration replaced by expanded paid staff reporting to president. Specialist system strengthened, surveillance of trading increased, listing and delisting standards introduced, and board restructured to give greater representation to commission and out-of-town brokers.°

1964 New member classification—Registered Trader (August 3).

New ticker—900 characters per minute—put into service (December 1).†

Am-Quote computerized telephone-quotation service was completed as first step in major automation program.°

1965 Fully automated quotation service introduced (March 8).

Electronic Systems Center created (October 15).

First women, Phyllis S. Peterson and Julia Montgomery Walsh, elected to regular membership.°

1966 New NYSE Composite Index inaugurated (July 14).

AMEX Price Change Index System introduced; computer complex installed for ticker, surveillance, and compared-clearance operations.°

1967 First woman member admitted—Muriel F. Siebert (December 28).

1968 Ticker speed increased to maximum 900 characters per minute; transmission begun to six European countries. Trading floor modernized; line capacity for communications doubled. Visitors gallery expanded.°

1969 Central Certificate Service fully activated (February 26).

1970 Public ownership of member firms approved (March 26).

Securities Investor Protection Corporation Act signed (December 30).

1971 New York Stock Exchange Incorporated (February 18).

First negotiated commission rates effective (April 5).

First member organization listed—Merrill Lynch (July 27).

AMEX incorporates and marks 50th anniversary of move indoors; Listed Company Advisory Committee formed, composed of nine chief executives of AMEX-listed companies.

1972 NYSE reorganization, based on Martin Report, approved (January 20).

Board of Directors, with ten public members, replaced Board of Governors (July 13).

Securities Industry Automation Corporation established with AMEX to consolidate facilities of both exchanges (July 17).°

First salaried chairman took office—James J. Needham (August 28).

Board of Governors reorganized to include ten public and ten industry representatives plus full-time salaried chairman as chief executive officer.°

1973 Depository Trust Company succeeded Central Certificate Service (May 11).

Chicago Board of Options Exchange opened with trading in 16 classes of call options (April 26).

AMEX formally adopts affirmative action employment plan; Market Value Index System introduced to replace Price Change Index.

1974 Trading hours extended to 4 P.M. (October 1).

Consolidated tape begun; 15 stocks reported (October 18).

1975 Fixed commission system abolished (April 30).

Full consolidated tape begun (June 16).

AMEX trades call options.

Trading begins in call options and odd lots of U.S. government instruments.°

1976 New data line installed, handling 36,000 characters per minute (January 19).

Specialists began handling odd lots in their stocks (May 24).

Varo, Inc.—first stock traded on both NYSE and AMEX (August 23).

Competition between specialists begun (October 11).

1977 Independent audit committee on listed companies' boards required (January 6).

Competitive Trader category for members approved (January 19).

National Securities Clearing Corporation (NSCC) began merging the clearing operations of the Stock Clearing Corporation of NYSE with American Stock Exchange Clearing Corporation and National Clearing Corporation of the NASD (January 20).

Foreign broker/dealers permitted to obtain membership (February 3).

Full Automated Bond System in effect (July 27).

1978 First 60 million share day in history (63,493,000 shares) (April 17).

Intermarket Trading System (ITS) began.

Registered Competitive Market-Maker category for members approved (May 2).

First 65 million share day in history (66,370,000 shares) (August 3).

Trading in Ginnie Maes inaugurated on the AMEX Commodities Exchange (ACE) (September 12).

AMEX reached an index high of 176.87 (September 13).

1979 Trading began at pilot post on the exchange floor. First stage in a $12-million upgrading of exchange facilities (January 29).

Board of Directors of NYSE approved plan for the creation of the New York Futures Exchange, a wholly owned subsidiary of NYSE. Futures contracts in seven financial instruments will be traded on the NYSE (March 1).

New York Commodities Exchange and NYSE terminated merger talks (March 15).

81,619,000 shares were traded on the NYSE, making it the heaviest trade day in exchange history (October 10).

1980 American Stock Exchange reached an all-time daily stock volume record of 14,980,680 shares sold (January 15).

NYSE volume of 67,752,000 shares traded was second largest volume on record to date (January 16).

NYSE Futures Exchange opened (August 7).

Option seat on the American Stock Exchange sold at an all-time high of $160,000 (December 24).

NYSE index reached an all-time high of 81.02 (November 28).

1981 First 90 million share day in the history of the Exchange, 92,881,000 (January 7).

The New York Stock Exchange subsidiary, the New York Futures Exchange, started trading futures in Domestic Bank Certificates of Deposit.

1982 A new AMEX subsidiary, The American Gold Coin Exchange (AGCE), began trading in the Canadian Maple Leaf (January 21).

Trading in NYSE Composite Index Futures began on the New York Futures Exchange (May 6).

Trading started through experimental linkage between ITS operated by NYSE and six other exchanges and Computer Assisted Execution Service (CAES) operated by NASD, in

30 stocks exempted from exchange off-board trading rules under SEC Rule 19c-3 (May 17).

Record advance of 38.81 points reached in NYSE trading as measured by Dow Jones Industrial Average (August 17).

First 100 million share day (132,681,120 shares) (August 18).

Trading in Interest Rate Options on U.S. Treasury Bills & Notes started in May on the AMEX.

Trading soared to an all-time high of 147,081,070 shares on the NYSE (October 7).

All-time options high of 340,550 contracts were traded on the AMEX (October 7).

Dow Jones Industrial Average plunged 36.33 points, the largest one-day loss since the record plunge of 38.33 points on October 28, 1929 (October 25).

1983 Trading in options on NYSE Common Stock Index Futures started on New York Futures Exchange (January 28).

NYSE started trading options on the NYSE Common Stock Index (September 23).

Dow Jones Industrial Average reached an all-time high of 1260.77 (September 26).

New shares of common stocks of seven regional telephone companies and shares of the "new" AT&T began trading on a "when issued" basis. Divestiture of AT&T effective January 1, 1984 (November 21).

AMEX stock trading went over the two billion share mark for the first time.°

The AMEX list of stock options increased by four index options, two on specific industry groups, one on the AMEX Market Value Index.°

1984 Largest NYSE trading day of 159,999,031 shares traded (January 5).

CBOT (Chicago Board of Trade) began trading a futures contract on the Major Market Index (July 23).

Trading began in NYSE Double Index Options (July 23).

NYSE volume soared to a record 236,565,110 shares traded (August 3).

NYSE opened on Presidential Election Day for first time ever.

Super DOT 250 (electronic order-routing system) launched on NYSE (November 16).

1985 For the first time the NYSE index

went over 100, closing at 101.12 (January 21).

19,091,950 shares were traded on the AMEX, the highest single day volume ever (February 6).

Ronald Reagan visited the NYSE, the first President to do so while in office (March 28).

Trading in options on gold bullion started on AMEX (April 26).

50 billionth share listed in NYSE (May 30).

NYSE began trading options in three over-the-counter stocks (June 3).

NYSE reached an all-time index high of 113.49 (July 17).

AMEX and Toronto Stock Exchange linked together as part of the first two-way electronic hookup between primary equity markets in different countries (September 24).

Instinet Corporation and the AMEX reached an agreement enabling European institutional investors to have access to the AMEX options market via Reuter's electronic terminals.

The opening trading time on both the NYSE and AMEX went from 10:00 A.M. to 9:30 A.M. (September 30).

The Dow Jones Industrial Average reached an all-time high of 1368.50 (October 16).

Options traded on two listed stocks on the NYSE (October 21).

Tokyo Stock Exchange admitted its first foreign member firms (December 1).

A daily record of 119,969 contracts traded on the AMEX Major Markets Index Option (December 13).

1986   The Dow Jones Industrial Average for the first time closed above 1600 at 1600.69 (February 6).

The Dow Jones Industrial Average for the first time closed above 1700 at 1713.99 (February 27).

The Dow Jones Industrial Average for the first time closed above 1800 at 1804.24 (March 20).

NYSE began trading the NYSE Beta Index Option (May 22).

NYSE Board of Directors expanded to 24 outside directors: 12 public members and 12 industry members (June 5).

New York Futures Exchange (NYFE) began trading the Commodity Research Bureau (CRB) index futures contract (June 12).

The Dow Jones Industrial Average for the first time closed above 1900 at 1903.54 (July 1).

The Directors of the NYSE voted to abandon the one-share-one-vote rule which gives common shareholders equal voting rights (July 3).

The Dow Jones Industrials nosedived a record 86.61 points on a record volume of 237,600,000 shares traded (September 11).

$600,000.00 (the highest price ever) was paid for membership in the NYSE (December 1).

1987   The Dow Jones Industrials passed the 2000 mark, closing at 2000.25 (January 8).

The Dow Jones Industrials closed above 2300 for the first time, up 33.95 points to 2333.52 (March 20).

The Dow Jones Industrials climbed above 2400 for the first time to close at 2405.54 (April 7).

Foreign currency warrants began trading (June 11).

The Chicago Board of Trade and the Chicago Board Options Exchange agreed to permit members of both exchanges to trade financial futures and options contracts side by side (June 25).

For the first time the Dow Jones Industrials closed over 2500 at 2510.04 (July 16).

AMEX Market Value closed at the all-time high of 365.0 (August 13).

A gain of 15.14 points brought the Dow Jones Industrials above 2700 points for the first time with the market closing at 2700.52 (August 17).

Dow Jones Industrial Average set a record at 2722.42 (August 25).

New York Futures Exchange began to trade the Russell 2000 and Russell 3000® Stock Index futures contracts (September 10).

A price of $1,150,000 was paid for a member of the NYSE, the highest ever (September 21).

The stock market 'crashed' with the Dow Jones Industrials down 508.00 points or 22% to close at 1738.74 on a record volume of 604.3 shares. Other record declines were: Dow Jones transportations off 164.78; utilities off 29.16; the S & P 500 stock index off 57.86; the AMEX index down 41.05; the NYSE down 30.51; and the NASDAQ composite of over-the-counter stocks off 46.12 (October 19).

A record volume of 608,148,710 shares traded on the NYSE and 43,432,760 on the AMEX (October 20).

The Dow Jones Industrials rocketed 186.84 points, the highest ever, on a volume of 449,350,000 shares (October 21).

The AMEX Market Value Index registered its largest increase ever, 23.81 (October 21).

1988   343,949,330 shares were traded on the NYSE, making it the highest volume day to date since the 'crash' of 1987 (June 17).

The SEC approved a series of initiatives by the NYSE and the Chicago Mercantile Exchange to coordinate procedures between the equities and futures markets, including coordinated circuit breakers; a joint effort against front-running; interexchange communications; and shared audit trail and surveillance information (October 19).

The NYSE opened an office in London to assist European companies in gaining access to the U.S. capital markets and listing on the NYSE (November 7).

1989   Dow Jones Industrials established a record high of 2734.64 (August 25).

The Dow Jones Iindustrials plunged 190.58 points to 2569.26 (October 13).

The NYSE launched a new trading vehicle, the Exchange Stock Portfolio, which enables the trading of a standardized basket of stocks in a single execution (October 26).

The NYSE created a blue-ribbon panel to study market volatility and investor confidence (December 7).

The DJIA peaked to a record 2810.12 (December 29).

1990   The Dow Jones Industrials closed above 2900 for the first time (June 4).

NYSE Market Volatility and Investor Confidence Panel released a study recommending initiatives for reducing market volatility and enhancing investor confidence.

The NYSE implemented a new rule requiring Trade Date + 1 (T + 1) for the completion of transactions effected on the NYSE (August 6).

NYSE approved two crossing sessions which will extend trading hours to 5:15 P.M. (September 11).

1991   For the first time the Dow Jones industrials closed above 3,000 at 3,0004.46 on a volume of 246.9 million shares (April 17).

Dow Jones Industrials rose to a record 3035.33 (June 4).

NYSE extended trading hours to 5:15 P.M. with two crossing sessions (June 13).

1992   For the first time the Dow Jones In-

dustrials closed over 3400 to reach a high of 3413.21 (June 1).

Globex, an after hours electronic system for trading options and futures on the Chicago Board of Trade and the Chicago Mercantile Exchange went into operation (June 25).

The New York Stock Exchange's "clean cross" rule allows large institutional investors to bypass floor trades by "crossing" trades of 25,000 shares or more between customers while ignoring orders placed at the same price by investors on the floor. A broker will have to accept a floor order if it is at a better price (October 26).

AMEX launched Emerging Company Marketplace.°

1993   Dow Jones Industrials plunged 82.94 to 3309.49, the biggest one day decline since November 15, 1991 (February 16).

The NASDAQ Composite Index had its worst decline since October 26, 1987 and closed at 665.39 (February 16).

The Dow Jones Industrials soared 55.65 points to reach a record of 3500.03 on the ninth heaviest trading day on the "Big Board" to date (May 19).

The Dow Jones Industrial Average hit a record high of 3604.83 (August 18).

The AMEX Market Value Index hit a record high of 484.28 (November 2).°

The Dow Jones Industrial Average closed above the 3700 mark at 3710.77 for the first time (November 17).

1994   The Dow Jones Industrial Average broke through the 3800 level and closed at 3803.88 (January 7).

Closing above the 3900 level for the first time, the Dow Jones Industrial Average reached 3914.48 (January 23).

There are now a record of 204 non-U.S. listed companies on the NYSE (December 31).

1995   The Dow Jones Industrial Average closed above 4000 for the first time (February 23).

Surpassing its previous high, the Dow Jones Industrials closed above 4200 (April 21).

An all time high of more than 4300 was reached by the Dow Jones Industrials (April 24).

Stocks soared to a record high of 4465.14 with an 86.46 one day advance (May 31).

Investment and Financial Terms

Accelerated Cost Recovery System (ACRS) A system that specifies the allowable depreciation recovery period for different types of assets. The normal recovery period is generally shorter than that allowed before the passage of the 1981 Economic Recovery Tax Act.°

Accruals Recurring continuous short-term liabilities. Examples are accrued wages and accrued interest.

Accrued interest Interest accrued on a bond since the last interest payment was made. The buyer of the bond pays the market price plus accrued interest. Exceptions include bonds that are in default and income bonds. (See: *Flat income bond.*)†

Acquisition The acquiring of control of one corporation by another. In "unfriendly" takeover attempts, the potential buying company may offer a price well above current market values, new securities and other inducements to stockholders. The management of the subject company might ask for a better price or try to join up with a third company. (See: *Merger, Proxy.*)††

Ad valorem tax A tax based on the value (or assessed value) of property. °°

Aging of accounts receivable Analyzing accounts by the amount of time they have been on the books.°

American Depository Receipt (ADR) Issued by American banks, an ADR is a certificate which serves as a proxy for a foreign stock deposited in a foreign bank. For all practical purposes, trading an ADR is equivalent to trading the foreign stock. Hundreds of ADRs are traded on the U.S. stock exchange.

Amortization Accounting for expenses or charges as applicable rather than as paid. Includes such practices as depreciation, deple-

tion, write-off of intangibles, prepaid expenses, and deferred charges.†

Annual report The formal financial statement issued yearly by a corporation. The annual report shows assets, liabilities, earnings—how the company stood at the close of the business year, how it fared profitwise during the year and other information of interest to shareowners.†

Arbitrage A technique employed to take advantage of differences in price. If, for example, ABC stock can be bought in New York for $10 a share and sold in London at $10.50, an arbitrageur may simultaneously purchase ABC stock here and sell the same amount in London, making a profit of 50 cents a share, less expenses. Arbitrage may also involve the purchase of rights to subscribe to a security, or the purchase of a convertible security—and the sale at or about the same time of the security obtainable through exercise of the rights or of the security obtainable through conversion.

Arrearage Overdue payment; frequently omitted dividend on preferred stock.

Assessed valuation The valuation placed on property for purposes of taxation.°°

Asset-based public offerings Public offerings backed by receivables as collateral. Essentially, a firm factors (sells) its receivables in the securities markets.°

Assets Everything a corporation owns or due to it: Cash, investments, money due it, materials and inventories, which are called current assets; buildings and machinery, which are known as fixed assets; and patents and good will, called intangible assets. (See: *Liabilities.*)†

Asset utilization ratios A group of ratios that measures the speed at which the firm is turning over or utilizing its assets. We measure inventory turnover, fixed asset turnover, total asset turnover, and the average time it takes to collect accounts receivable.°

Assignment The liquidation of assets without going through formal court procedures. In order to affect an assignment, creditors must agree on liquidation values and the relative priority of claims.°

Assignment Notice to an option writer that an option holder has exercised the option and that the writer will now be required to deliver (receive) under the terms of the contract.††

Ask (See: *Bid and asked.*)†

Auction market The system of trading securities through brokers or agents on an exchange such as the New York Stock Exchange. Buyers compete with other

---

° Entries from *Foundations of Financial Management.*

† Entries from *The Language of Investing Glossary.*

°° Entries from *Tax-Exempt Securities & the Investor.*

†† Entries from the *Glossary.*

¶ Entries from the Federal Reserve *Glossary.*

Source: *Foundations of Financial Management*, 5th edition by Stanley B. Block and Geoffrey A. Hirt, Irwin, Homewood, IL 1989.

The *Language of Investing Glossary* published by the New York Stock Exchange, Inc.

The *Glossary* published by the New York Stock Exchange.

Tax-Exempt Securities & the Investor published by the Securities Industry Association.

The *Glossary* published by the Board of Governors of the Federal Reserve System.

buyers while sellers compete with other sellers for the most advantageous price.††

Auditor's report   Often called the accountant's opinion, it is the statement of the accounting firm's work and its opinion of the corporation's financial statements, especially if they conform to the normal and generally accepted practices of accountancy.††

Automated clearinghouse (ACH)   An ACH transfers information between one financial institution and another and from account to account via computer tape. There are approximately 30 regional clearinghouses throughout the United States that claim the membership of over 10,000 financial institutions.°

Average collection period   The average amount of time accounts receivable have been on the books. It may be computed by dividing accounts receivable by average daily credit sales.°

Averages   Various ways of measuring the trend of securities prices, one of the most popular of which is the Dow-Jones average of 30 industrial stocks listed on the New York Stock Exchange. The prices of the 30 stocks are totaled and then divided by a divisor which is intended to compensate for past stock splits and stock dividends and which is changed from time to time. As a result point changes in the average have only the vaguest relationship to dollar price changes in stocks included in the average. (See: *NYSE composite index.*)††

Balance of payments   The term refers to a system of government accounts that catalogs the flow of economic transactions between countries.°

Balance sheet   A condensed financial statement showing the nature and amount of a company's assets, liabilities and capital on a given date. In dollar amounts the balance sheet shows what the company owned, what it owed, and the ownership interest in the company of its stockholders. (See: *Assets, Earnings report.*)†

Bankers acceptance   Bankers acceptances are negotiable time drafts, or bills of exchange, that have been accepted by a bank which, by accepting, assumes the obligation to pay the holder of the draft the face amount of the instrument on the maturity date specified. They are used primarily to finance the export, import, shipment, or storage of goods.¶

Bankruptcy   The market value of a firm's assets are less than its liabilities, and the firm has a negative net worth. The term is also used to describe in-court procedures associated with the reorganization or liquidation of a firm.°

Basis book   A book of mathematical tables used to convert yields to equivalent dollar prices.°°

Basis point   One gradation on a 100-point scale representing one percent, used especially in expressing variations in the yields of bonds. Fixed income yields vary often and slightly within one percent and the basis point scale easily expresses these changes in hundredths of one percent. For example, the difference between 12.83% and 12.88% is 5 basis points.††

Basis price   The price expressed in yield or percentage of return on the investment.°°

Bear market   A declining market. (See: *Bull market.*)†

Bearer bond   A bond which does not have the owner's name registered on the books of the issuer and which is payable to the holder. (See: *Coupon bond, Registered bond.*)†

Bearer security   A security that has no identification as to owner. It is presumed to be owned, therefore, by the bearer or the person who holds it. Bearer securities are freely and easily negotiable since ownership can be quickly transferred from seller to buyer.°°

Beta   A measure of the volatility of returns on an individual stock relative to the market. Stocks with a beta of 1.0 are said to have risk equal to that of the market (equal volatility). Stocks with betas greater than 1.0 have more risk than the market, while those with betas of less than 1.0 have less risk than the market.°

Bid and asked   Often referred to as a quotation or quote. The bid is the highest price anyone has declared that he wants to pay for a security at a given time, the asked is the lowest price anyone will take at the same time. (See: *Quote.*)†

Blanket inventory liens   A secured borrowing arrangement in which the lender has a general claim against the inventory of the borrower.°

Block   A large holding or transaction of stock—popularly considered to be 10,000 shares or more.†

Blue chip   A company known nationally for the quality and wide acceptance of its products or services, and for its ability to make money and pay dividends.†

Blue-sky laws   A popular name for laws various states have enacted to protect the public against securities frauds. The term is believed to have originated when a judge ruled that a particular stock had about the same value as a patch of blue sky.†

Board room   A room for registered representatives and customers in a broker's office where opening, high, low, and last prices of leading stocks used to be posted on a board throughout the market day. Today such price displays are normally electronically controlled although most board rooms have replaced the board with the ticker and/or individual quotation machines.†

Bond   Basically an IOU or promissory note of a corporation, usually issued in multiples of $1,000 or $5,000, although $100 and $500 denominations are not unknown. A bond is evidence of a debt on which the issuing company usually promises to pay the bondholders a specified amount of interest for a specified length of time, and to repay the loan on the expiration date. In every case a bond represents debt—its holder is a creditor of the corporation and not a part owner as is the shareholder. (See: *Collateral, Convertible security, Debenture, General Mortgage Bond, Income Bond*.)††

Bond ratings   Bonds are rated according to risk by Standard & Poor's and Moody's Investor Service. A bond that is rated Aaa by Moody's has the lowest risk, while a bond with a C rating has the highest risk. Coupon rates are greatly influenced by a corporation's bond rating.°

Book   A notebook the specialist in a stock uses to keep a record of the buy and sell orders at specified prices, in sequence of receipt, which are left with him by other brokers. (See: *Specialist*.)†

Book value   (See: *Net worth*.)

Break-even analysis   A numerical and graphical technique that is used to determine at what point the firm will break even (revenue = cost). To compute the break-even point, we divide fixed costs by price minus variable cost per unit.°

Broker   An agent, who handles the public's orders to buy and sell securities, commodities, or other property. For this service a commission is charged. (See: *Commission broker, Dealer*.)†

Brokers' loans   Money borrowed by brokers from banks or other brokers for a variety of uses. It may be used by specialists and to help finance inventories of stock they deal in; by brokerage firms to finance the underwriting of new issues of corporate and municipal securities; to help finance a firm's own investments; and to help finance the purchase of securities for customers who prefer to use the broker's credit when they buy securities. (See: *Margin*.)†

Bull market   An advancing market. (See: *Bear market*.)††

Call   (1) The right (option) to buy a share of stock at a specified price within a given time period (see options). (2) The redemption of a bond or preferred stock before its normal maturity.

Call feature   Used for bonds and some preferred stock. A call allows the corporation to retire securities before maturity by forcing the bondholders to sell bonds back to it at a set price. The call provisions are included in the bond indenture.°

Call premium   The premium paid by a corporation to call in a bond issue before the maturity date.°

Callable   A bond issue, all or part of which may be redeemed by the issuing corporation under definite conditions before maturity. The term also applies to preferred shares which may be redeemed by the issuing corporation.†

Capital   Sources of long-term financing that are available to the business firm.°

Capital asset pricing model   A model that relates the risk-return trade offs of individual assets to market returns. A security is presumed to receive a risk-free rate of return plus a premium for risk.°

Capital gain or capital loss   Profit or loss from the sale of a capital asset. A capital gain, under current federal income tax laws, may be either short-term (12 months or less) or long-term (more than 12 months). A short-term capital gain is taxed at the reporting individual's full income tax rate. A long-term capital gain is subject to a lower tax. The capital gains provisions of the tax law are complicated. You should consult your tax advisor for specific information.†

Capital lease   A long-term, noncancelable lease that has many of the characteristics of debt. Under FASB *Statement No. 13*, the lease obligation must be shown directly on the balance sheet.°

Capital markets   Competitive markets for equity securities or debt securities with maturities of more than one year. The best examples of capital market securities are common stock, bonds, and preferred stock.°

Capital rationing   Occurs when a corporation has more dollars of capital budgeting projects with positive net present values than it has money to invest in them. Therefore, some projects that should be accepted are excluded because financial capital is rationed.°

Capital stock   All shares representing ownership of a business, including preferred and common. (See: *Common stock, Preferred stock*.)†

Capitalization   Total amount of the various securities issued by a corporation. Capitalization may include bonds, debentures, preferred and common stock, and surplus.

Bonds and debentures are usually carried on the books of the issuing company in terms of their par or face value. Preferred and common shares may be carried in terms of par or stated value. Stated value may be an arbitrary figure decided upon by the directors or may represent the amount received by the company from the sale of the securities at the time of issuance. (See: *Par*.)†

Carrying costs   The cost to hold an asset, usually inventory. For inventory, carrying costs include such items as interest, warehousing costs, insurance, and material-handling expenses.°

Cash budget   A series of monthly or quarterly budgets that indicate cash receipts, cash payments, and the borrowing requirements for meeting financial requirements. It is constructed from the pro forma income statement and other supportive schedules.°

Cash flow   Reported net income of a corporation *plus* amounts charged off for depreciation, depletion, amortization, extraordinary charges to reserves, which are bookkeeping deductions and not paid out in actual dollars and cents. (See: *Amortization, Depreciation*.)††

Cash sale   A transaction on the floor of the Stock Exchange which calls for delivery of the securities the same day. In "regular way" trades, the seller is to deliver on the fifth business day except for bonds, which is the next day.

Certificate   The actual piece of paper which is evidence of ownership of stock in a corporation. Watermarked paper is finely engraved with delicate etchings to discourage forgery.††

Certificate of Deposit (CD)   A money market instrument issued by banks. The time CD is characterized by its set date of maturity and interest rate and its wide acceptance among investors, companies and institutions as a highly negotiable short-term investment vehicle.††

CFTC   The Commodity Futures Trading Commission, created by Congress in 1974 to regulate exchange trading in futures.††

Clientele effect   The effect of investor preferences for dividends or capital gains. Investors tend to purchase securities that meet their needs.°

Coefficient of correlation   The degree of associated movement between two or more variables. Variables that move in the same direction are said to be positively correlated, while negatively correlated variables move in opposite directions.°

Coefficient of variation   A measure of risk determination that is computed by dividing the standard deviation for a series of numbers by the expected value. Generally, the larger the coefficient of variation, the greater the risk.°

Collateral trust bond   A bond secured by collateral deposited with a trustee. The collateral is often the stocks or bonds of companies controlled by the issuing company but may be other securities.†

Combined leverage   The total or combined impact of operating and financial leverage.

Commercial paper   An unsecured promissory note that large corporations issue to investors. The minimum amount is usually $25,000.°

Commission   The broker's basic fee for purchasing or selling securities or property as an agent.†

Commission broker   An agent who executes the public's order for the purchase or sale of securities or commodities.†

Commodities   (See: *Futures*.)

Common equity   The common stock or ownership capital of the firm. Common equity may be supplied through retained earnings or the sale of new common stock.°

Common stock   Securities which represent an ownership interest in a corporation. If the company has also issued preferred stock, both common and preferred have ownership rights. Common stockholders assume the greater risk, but generally exercise the greater control and may gain the greater reward in the form of dividends and capital appreciation. The terms of common stock and capital stock are often used interchangeably when the company has no preferred stock.†

Common stock equivalent   Warrants, options, and any convertible securities that pay less than two thirds of the average Aa bond yield at the time of issue.°

Common stockholder   Holders of common stock are the owners of the company. Common stockholders elect the members of the board of directors, who in turn help select the top management.°

Compensating balances   A bank requirement that business customers maintain a minimum average balance. The required amount is usually computed as a percentage of customer loans outstanding or as a percentage of the future loans to which the bank has committed itself.°

Competitive trader   A member of the Exchange who trades in stocks on the Floor for an account in which he has an interest. Also known as a Registered Trader.†

Composition An out-of-court settlement in which creditors agree to accept a fractional settlement on their original claim.°

Compound sum The future value of a single amount or an annuity when compounded at a given interest rate for a specified time period.°

Conglomerate A corporation that has diversified its operations, usually by acquiring enterprises in widely varied industries.†

Consolidated balance sheet A balance sheet showing the financial condition of a corporation and its subsidiaries. (See: *Balance sheet.*)†

Consolidated tape The ticket tape reporting transactions in NYSE listed securities that take place on the NYSE or any of the participating regional stock exchanges and other markets. Similarly, transactions in AMEX-listed securities, and certain other securities listed on regional stock exchanges, are reported and identified on a separate tape.††

Consolidation The combination of two or more firms, generally of equal size and market power, to form an entirely new entity.°

Constant dollar accounting One of two methods of inflation-adjusted accounting that have been approved by the Financial Accounting Standards Board. Financial statements are adjusted to present prices, using the consumer price index. This is shown as supplemental information in the firm's annual report.°

Consumer price index An economic indicator published monthly by the U.S. Commerce Department. It measures the rate of inflation for consumer goods.°

Contribution margin The contribution to fixed costs from each unit of sales. The margin may be computed as price minus variable cost per unit.°

Conversion premium The market price of a convertible bond or preferred stock minus the security's conversion value.°

Conversion price The conversion ratio divided into the par value. The price of the common stock at which the security is convertible. An investor would usually not convert the security into common stock unless the market price were greater than the conversion price.°

Conversion ratio The number of shares of common stock an investor will receive if he exchanges a convertible bond or convertible preferred stock for common stock.°

Conversion value The conversion ratio multiplied by the market price per share of common stock.°

Convertible security A security that may be traded into the company for a different form or type of security. Convertible securities are usually bonds or preferred stock that may be exchanged for common stock.°

Corporate stock repurchase A corporation may repurchase its shares in the market as an alternative to paying a cash dividend. Earnings per share will go up, and if the price-earnings ratio remains the same, the stockholder will receive the same dollar benefit as through a cash dividend. Furthermore, the increase in stock price is a capital gain, whereas the cash dividend would be taxed as ordinary income. A corporation may also justify the repurchase of its stock because it is at a very low price or to maintain constant demand for the shares. Reacquired shares may be used for employee options or as part of a tender offer in a merger or acquisition. Firms may also reacquire part of their shares as a protective device against being taken over as a merger candidate.°

Corporation A form of ownership in which a separate, legal entity is created. A corporation may sue or be sued, engage in contracts and acquire property. It has a continual life and is not dependent on any one stockholder for maintaining its legal existence. A corporation is owned by stockholders who enjoy the privilege of limited liability. There is, however, the potential for double taxation in the corporate form of organization: the first time at the corporate level in the form of profits, and again at the stockholder level in the form of dividends.°

Correlation coefficient Measures the degree of relationship between two variables.°

Correspondent A securities firm, bank, or other financial organization which regularly performs services for another in a place or market to which the other does not have direct access. Securities firms may have correspondents in foreign countries or on exchanges of which they are not members. Correspondents are frequently linked by private wires. Member organizations of the N.Y.S.E. with offices in New York City may also act as correspondents for out-of-town member organizations which do not maintain New York City offices.†

Cost-benefit analysis A study of the incremental costs and benefits that can be derived from a given course of action.°

Cost of capital The cost of alternative sources of financing to the firm. (See: *Weighted average cost of capital.*)°

Cost of goods sold The cost specifically associated with units sold during the time period under study.°

Coupon bond Bond with interest coupons attached. The coupons are clipped as they come due and are presented by the holder for payment of interest. (See: *Bearer bond, Registered bond.*)†

Coupon rate The actual interest rate on the bond, usually payable in semiannual installments. The coupon rate normally stays constant during the life of the bond and indicates what the bondholder's annual dollar income will be.°

Coverage A term usually connected with revenue bonds. It is a ratio of net revenues pledged to principal and interest payments to debt service requirements. It is one of the factors used in evaluating the quality of an issue.°°

Covered option An option position that is offset by an equal and opposite position in the underlying security.††

Covering Buying a security previously sold short. (See: *Short sale, Short covering.*)†

Credit terms The repayment provisions that are part of a credit arrangement. An example would be a 2/10, net 30 arrangement in which the customer may deduct 2 percent from the invoice price if payment takes place in the first ten days. Otherwise the full amount is due.°

Cumulative preferred A stock having a provision that if one or more dividends are omitted, the omitted dividends must be paid before dividends may be paid on the company's common stock.†

Cumulative voting A method of voting for corporate directors which enables the shareholder to multiply the number of his shares by the number of directorships being voted on and cast the total for one director or a selected group of directors. A 10-share holder normally casts 10 votes for each of, say 12 nominees to the board of directors. He thus has 120 votes. Under the cumulative voting principle he may do that or he may cast 120 (10×12) votes for only one nominee, 60 for two, 40 for three, or any other distribution he chooses. Cumulative voting is required under the corporate laws of some states, is permitted in most others.†

Currency futures contract A futures contract that may be used for hedging or speculation in foreign exchange.°

Current assets Those assets of a company which are reasonably expected to be realized in cash, or sold, or consumed during the normal operating cycle of the business. These include cash, U.S. government bonds, receivables and money due usually within one year, and inventories.†

Current cost accounting One of two methods of inflation-adjusted accounting approved by the Financial Accounting Standards Board in 1979. Financial statements are adjusted to the present, using current cost data rather than an index. This is shown as supplemental information in the firm's annual report.

Current liabilities Money owed and payable by a company, usually within one year.†

Current return (See: *Yield.*)

Current yield A relation stated as a percent of the annual interest to the actual market price of the bond.°°

Day order An order to buy or sell which, if not executed expires at the end of the trading day on which it was entered.†

Dealer An individual or firm in the securities business who buys and sells stocks and bonds as a principal rather than as an agent. The dealer's profit or loss is the difference between the price paid and the price received for the same security. The dealer's confirmation must disclose to the customer that the principal has been acted upon. The same individual or firm may function, at different times, either as broker or dealer. (See: *NASD, Specialist.*)††

Debenture A long-term unsecured corporate bond. Debentures are usually issued by large, prestigious firms having excellent credit ratings in the financial community.°

Debit balance In a customer's margin account that portion of purchase price of stock, bonds, or commodities covered by credit extended by the broker to the margin customer.†

Debt limit The statutory or constitutional maximum debt that a municipality can legally incur.°°

Debt service Refers to the payments required for interest and retirement of the principal amount of a debt.°°

Debt utilization ratios A group of ratios that indicates to what extent debt is being used and the prudence with which it is being managed. Calculations include debt to total assets, times interest earned, and fixed charge coverage.°

Degree of financial leverage A measure of the impact of debt on the earnings capability of the firm. The percentage change in earnings per share is divided by the percentage change in earnings before interest and taxes at a given level of operation. Other algebraic statements are also used.°

Degree of operating leverage A measure of the impact of fixed costs on the operating earnings of the firms. The percentage change in operating income is divided by the percentage change in volume at a given level of operation. Other algebraic statements are also used.°

Denomination The face amount or par value of a security which the issuer promises to pay on the maturity date. Most municipal bonds are issued with a minimum denomination of $5,000, although a few older issues are available in $1,000 denominations.°°

Depletion accounting Natural resources, such as metals, oil and gas, and timber, which conceivably can be reduced to zero over the years, present a special problem in capital management. Depletion is an accounting practice consisting of charges against earnings based upon the amount of the asset taken out of the total reserves in the period for which accounting is made. A bookkeeping entry, it does not represent any cash outlay nor are any funds earmarked for the purpose.†

Depository trust company (DTC) A central securities certificate depository through which members effect security deliveries between each other via computerized bookkeeping entries thereby reducing the physical movement of stock certificates.†

Depreciation Normally, charges against earnings to write off the cost, less salvage value, of an asset over its estimated useful life. It is a bookkeeping entry and does not represent any cash outlay nor are any funds earmarked for the purpose.†

Dilution of earnings This occurs when additional shares of stock are sold without creating an immediate increase in income. The result is a decline in earnings per share until earnings can be generated from the funds raised.°

Director Person elected by shareholders to establish company policies. The directors appoint the president, vice presidents, and all other operating officers. Directors decide, among other matters, if and when dividends shall be paid. (See: *Management, Proxy*.)†

Discount The amount by which a preferred stock or bond may sell below its par value. Also used as a verb to mean "takes into account" as the price of the stock has discounted the expected dividend cut. (See: *Premium*.)†

Discount rate The interest rate at which future sums or annuities are discounted back to the present.°

   The interest rate at which eligible depository institutions may borrow funds, usually for short periods, directly from the Federal Reserve Banks. The law requires the board of directors of each Reserve Bank to estab-

lish the discount rate every 14 days subject to the approval of the Board of Governors.¶

Discounted loan A loan in which the calculated interest payment is subtracted or discounted in advance. Because this lowers the amount of available funds, the effective interest rate is increased.°

Discretionary account An account in which the customer gives the broker or someone else discretion, which may be complete or within specific limits, either to the purchases, or sale of securities or commodities including selection, timing, amount, and price to be paid or received.†

Diversification Spreading investments among different companies in different fields. Another type of diversification is also offered by the securities of many individual companies because of the wide range of their activities. (See: *Investment trust*.)†

Dividend The payment designed by the board of directors to be distributed pro rata among the shares outstanding. On preferred shares, it is generally a fixed amount. On common shares, the dividend varies with the fortunes of the company and the amount of cash on hand, and may be omitted if business is poor or the directors determine to withhold earnings to invest in plant and equipment. Sometimes a company will pay a dividend out of past earnings even if it is not currently operating at a profit.†

Dividend information content This theory of dividends assumes that dividends provide information about the financial health and economic expectations of the company. If this is true, corporations must actively manage their dividends to provide the market with information.°

Dividend payment date The day on which a stockholder of record will receive his or her dividend.°

Dividend payout The percentage of dividends to earnings after taxes. It can be computed by dividing dividends per share by earnings per share.°

Dividend record date Stockholders owning the stock on the holder-of-record date are entitled to receive a dividend. In order to be listed as an owner on the corporate books, the investor must have bought the stock before it went ex-dividend.°

Dividend reinvestment plans Plans that provide the investor with an opportunity to buy additional shares of stock with the cash dividends paid by the company.°

Dividend valuation model A model for determining the value of a share of stock by taking the present value of an expected stream of future dividends.°

Dividend yield Dividends per share divided by market price per share. Dividend yield indicates the percentage return that a stockholder will receive on dividends alone.°

Dollar bond A bond that is quoted and traded in dollars rather than in terms of yield.°°

Dollar cost averaging A system of buying securities at regular intervals with a fixed dollar amount. Under this system the investor buys by the dollars' worth rather than by the number of shares. If each investment is of the same number of dollars, payments buy more when the price is low and fewer when it rises. Thus temporary downswings in price benefit the investor if he continues periodic purchases in both good times and bad and the price at which the shares are sold is more than their average cost. (See: *Formula investing*.)†

Double-barrelled bond A bond secured by the pledge of two or more sources of repayment, e.g., secured by taxes as well as revenues.°°

Double exemption Refers to securities that are exempt from state as well as Federal income taxes.°°

Double taxation Short for *double taxation of dividends*. The federal government taxes corporate profits once as corporate income; any part of the remaining profits distributed as dividends to stockholders may be taxed again as income to the recipient stockholder.†

Dow theory A theory of market analysis based upon the performance of the Dow-Jones industrial and transportation stock price averages. The theory says that the market is in a basic upward trend if one of these averages advances above a previous important high, accompanied or followed by a similar advance in the other. When the averages both dip below previous important lows, this is regarded as confirmation of a basic downward trend. The theory does not attempt to predict how long either trend will continue, although it is widely misinterpreted as a method of forecasting future action.†

Down tick (See: *Up tick*.)

Dual trading Exists when one security, such as General Motors common stock, is traded on more than one stock exchange. This practice is quite common between NYSE-listed companies and regional exchanges.°

Dun & Bradstreet A credit-rating agency that publishes information on over 3 million business establishments through its *Reference Book*.°

Du Pont System of Ratio Analysis An analysis of profitability that breaks down return on assets between the profit margin and asset turnover. The second, or modified, version shows how return on assets is translated into return on equity through the amount of debt that the firm has. Actually return on assets is divided by $(1 - \text{debt/assets})$ to arrive at return on equity.°

Earnings per share The earnings available to common stockholders divided by the number of common stock shares outstanding.°

Earnings report A statement—also called an *income statement*—issued by a company showing its earnings or losses over a given period. The earnings report lists the income earned, expenses, and the net result. (See: *Balance sheet*.)†

Economic indicators Hundreds of indicators exist. Each is a specialized series of data. The data are analyzed for their relationship to economic activity, and the indicator is classified as either a lagging indicator, a leading indicator, or a coincident indicator of economic activity.°

Economic ordering quantity (EOQ) The most efficient ordering quantity for the firm. The EOQ will allow the firm to minimize the total ordering and carrying costs associated with inventory.°

Efficient frontier A line drawn through the optimum point selections in a risk-return trade-off diagram. Each point represents the best possible trade-off between risk and return (the highest return at a given risk level or the lowest risk at a given return level).°

Efficient market hypothesis Hypothesis which suggests that markets adjust very quickly to new information and that it is very difficult for investors to select portfolios of securities that outperform the market.

Electronic funds transfer A system in which funds are moved between computer terminals without the use of written checks.°

Employment Act of 1946 An act which specifies the four goals that the Federal Reserve Board should strive to achieve: economic growth, stable prices, high employment, and a balance of trade.°

Equipment trust certificate A type of security, generally issued by a railroad, to pay for new equipment. Title to the equipment, such as a locomotive, is held by a trustee until the notes are paid off. An equipment trust certificate is usually secured by a first claim on the equipment.†

Equity The net worth of a business, consisting of capital stock, capital (or paid-in) surplus, earned surplus (or retained earnings), and occasionally, certain net worth reserves. *Common equity* is that part of the total net worth belonging to the common stockholders. *Total equity* would include preferred stockholders. The terms *common stock, net worth,* and *common equity* are frequently used interchangeably.†

Eurobonds Bonds payable or denominated in the borrower's currency, but sold outside the country of the borrower, usually by an international syndicate.°

Eurodollar loan A loan from a foreign bank denominated in dollars.°

Eurodollars U.S. dollars held on deposit by foreign banks and loaned out by those banks to anyone seeking dollars.°

Exchange acquisition A method of filling an order to buy a large block of stock on the floor of the exchange. Under certain circumstances, a member-broker can facilitate the purpose of a block by soliciting orders to sell. All orders to sell the security are lumped together and crossed with the buy order in the regular auction market. The price to the buyer may be on a net basis or on a commission basis.†

Exchange distribution A method of selling large blocks of stock on the floor of the exchange. Under certain circumstances, a member-broker can facilitate the sale of a block of stock by soliciting and getting other member-brokers to solicit orders to buy. Individual buy orders are lumped together and crossed with the sell order in the regular auction market. A special commission is usually paid by the seller; ordinarily the buyer pays no commission.†

Ex-dividend A synonym for "without dividend." The buyer of a stock selling ex-dividend does not receive the recently declared dividend. Every dividend is payable on a fixed date to all shareholders recorded on the books of the company as of a previous date of record. For example, a dividend may be declared as payable to holders of record on the books of the company on a given Friday. Since five business days are allowed for delivery of stock in a "regular way" transaction on the New York Stock Exchange, the Exchange would declare the stock "ex-dividend" as of the opening of the market on the preceding Monday. That means anyone who bought in on and after Monday would not be entitled to that dividend. When stocks go ex-dividend, the stock tables include the symbol "x" following the name. (See: *Cash sale, Net change, Transfer*.)†

Ex-dividend date Four business days before the holder-of-record date. On the ex-dividend date the purchase of the stock no longer carries with it the right to receive the dividend previously declared.°

Expectations theory of interest rates This theory explains the shape of the term structure relative to expectations for future short-term interest rates. It is thought that long-term rates are an average of the expected short-term rates. Therefore, an upward-sloping yield curve would indicate that short-term rates will rise.°

Expected value A representative value from a probability distribution arrived at by multiplying each outcome by the associated probability and summing up the values.°

Export-Import Bank (Eximbank) An agency of the United States government that facilitates the financing of United States exports through its miscellaneous programs. In its direct loan program, the Eximbank lends money to foreign purchasers of U.S. products—such as aircraft, electrical equipment, heavy machinery, computers, and the like. The Eximbank also purchases eligible medium-term obligations of foreign buyers of U.S. goods at a discount from face value. In this discount program, private banks and other lenders are able to rediscount (sell at a lower price) promissory notes and drafts acquired from foreign customers of U.S. firms.°

Expropriation The action of a country in taking away or modifying the property rights of a corporation or individual.°

Ex-rights The situation in which the purchase of common stock during a rights offering no longer includes rights to purchase additional shares of common stock.°

Extension An out-of-court settlement in which creditors agree to allow the firm more time to meet its financial obligations. A new repayment schedule will be developed, subject to the acceptance of creditors.°

External corporate funds Corporate financing raised through sources outside of the firm. Bonds, common stock, and preferred stock fall in this category.°

External reorganization A reorganization under the formal bankruptcy laws in which a merger partner is found for the distressed firm. Ideally, the firm should be merged with a strong firm in its own industry, although this is not always possible.°

Factoring receivables Selling accounts receivable to a finance company or a bank.°

Federal budget deficit Government expenditures are greater than government tax revenues, and the government must borrow to balance revenues and expenditures. These deficits act as an economic stimulus.°

Federal budget surplus Government tax receipts are greater than government expenditures. A rarity during the last 20 years. These surpluses have a dampening effect on the economy.°

Federal National Mortgage Association A government agency that provides a secondary market in mortgages.°

Federal Reserve discount rate The rate of interest that the Fed charges on loans to the banking system. A monetary tool for management of the money supply.°

Federally sponsored agency securities Securities issued by federal agencies such as the Federal Land Bank and Federal Home Loan Board.°

Field warehousing An inventory financing arrangement in which collateralized inventory is stored on the premises of the borrower but is controlled by an independent warehousing company.°

FIFO A system of writing off inventory into cost of goods sold in which the items purchased first are written off first. Referred to as first-in, first-out.°

Financial Accounting Standards Board A privately supported rulemaking body for the accounting profession.°

Financial capital Common stock, preferred stock, bonds, and retained earnings. Financial capital appears on the corporate balance sheet under long-term liabilities and equity.°

Financial disclosure Presentation of financial information to the investment community.°

Financial futures market A market that allows for the trading of financial instruments related to a future point in time. A purchase or sale takes place in the present, with a reversal necessitated in the future to close out the position. If a purchase (sale) takes place initially, then a sale (purchase) will be necessary in the future. The market provides for futures contracts in Treasury bonds, Treasury bills, certificates of deposits, GNMA certificates, and many other instruments. Financial futures contracts may be executed on the Chicago Board of Trade, the Chicago Mercantile Exchange, the New York Futures Exchange, and other exchanges.°

Financial intermediary A financial institution such as a bank or a life insurance company that directs other people's money into such investments as government and corporate securities.°

Financial lease A long-term noncancelable lease. The financial lease has all the characteristics of long-term debt except that the lease payments are a combination of interest expense and amortization of the cost of the asset.°

Financial leverage A measure of the amount of debt used in the capital structure of the firm.°

Financial sweetener Usually refers to equity options, such as warrants or conversion privileges, attached to a debt security. The sweetener lowers the interest cost to the corporation.°

Fiscal policy The tax policies of the federal government and the spending associated with its tax revenues.°

Fixed costs Costs that remain relatively constant regardless of the volume of operations. Examples are rent, depreciation, property taxes, and executive salaries.°

Float The difference between the corporation's recorded cash balance on its books and the amount credited to the corporation by the bank.°

Floating rate bond The interest payment on the bond changes with market conditions rather than the price of the bond.°

Floating rate preferred stock The quarterly dividend on the preferred stock changes with market conditions. The market price is considerably less volatile than it is with regular preferred stock.°

Floor price Usually equal to the pure bond value. A convertible bond will not sell at less than its pure bond value even when its conversion value is below the pure bond value.°

Flotation cost The distribution cost of selling securities to the public. The cost includes the underwriter's spread and any associated fees.°

Forced conversion Occurs when a company calls a convertible security that has a conversion value greater than the call price. Investors will take the higher of the two values and convert the security to common stock rather than take a lower cash call price.°

Foreign Credit Insurance Association (FCIA) An agency established by a group of 60 U.S. insurance companies. It sells credit export insurance to interested exporters. The FCIA promises to pay for the exported merchandise if the foreign importer defaults on payment.°

Foreign exchange rate The relationship between the value of two or more currencies. For example, the exchange rate between U.S. dollars and French francs is stated as dollars per francs or francs per dollar.°

Foreign exchange risk A form of risk that refers to the possibility of experiencing a drop in revenue or an increase in cost in an international transaction due to a change in foreign exchange rates. Importers, exporters, investors, and multinational firms alike are exposed to this risk.°

Formula investing An investment technique. One formula calls for the shifting of funds from common shares to preferred shares or bonds as the market, on average, rises above a certain predetermined point—and the return of funds to common share investments as the market average declines. (See: *Dollar cost averaging*.)†

Founders' stock Stock owned by the original founders of a company. It often carries special voting rights that allow the founders to maintain voting privileges in excess of their proportionate ownership.°

Fourth market A market of stocks and bonds in which there is direct dealing between financial institutions, such as investment bankers, insurance companies, pension funds, and mutual funds.°

Free and open market A market in which supply and demand are freely expressed in terms of price. Contrasts with a controlled market in which supply, demand, and price may all be regulated.†

Fronting loan A parent company's loan to a foreign subsidiary is channeled through a financial intermediary, usually a large international bank. The bank fronts for the parent in extending the loan to the foreign affiliate.°

Fully diluted earnings per share Equals adjusted earnings after taxes divided by shares outstanding, plus common stock equivalents, plus all convertible securities.°

Fundamental research Analysis of industries and companies based on factors such as sales, assets, earnings, products or services, markets, and management. As supplied to the economy, fundamental research includes consideration of gross national product, interest rates, unemployment, inventories, savings, and so on. (See: *Technical research*.)†

Funded debt Usually long-term, interest-bearing bonds or debentures of a company. Could include long-term bank loans. Does *not* include short-term loans, preferred, or common stock.†

Futures contract A contract to buy or sell a commodity at some specified price in the future.°

General mortgage bond A bond which is secured by a blanket mortgage on the company's property, but which may be outranked by one or more other mortgages.†

General obligation bond A bond secured by the pledge of the issuer's full faith, credit and taxing power.°°

Gilt-edged High-grade bond issued by a company which has demonstrated its ability to earn a comfortable profit over a period of years and pay its bondholders their interest without interruption.†

Give up A term with many different meanings. For one, a member of the exchange on the floor may act for a second member by executing an order for him with a third member. The first member tells the third member that he is acting on behalf of the second member and "gives up" the second member's name rather than his own.††

Going private The process by which all publicly owned shares of common stock are repurchased or retired, thereby eliminating listing fees, annual reports, and other expenses involved with publicly owned companies.°

Gold fix The setting of the price of gold by dealers (especially in a twice-daily London meeting at the central bank); the fix is the fundamental worldwide price for setting prices of gold bullion and gold-related contracts and products.††

Golden parachute Highly attractive termination payments made to current management in the event of a takeover of the company.°

Good delivery Certain basic qualifications must be met before a security sold on the exchange may be delivered. The security must be in proper form to comply with the contract of sale and to transfer title to the purchaser.†

Good 'til cancelled order (GTC) or open order An order to buy or sell which remains in effect until it is either executed or cancelled.†

Goodwill An intangible asset that reflects value above that generally recognized in the tangible assets of the firm.°

Government bonds Obligations of the U.S. government, regarded as the highest grade issues in existence.†

Growth stock Stock of a company with a record of growth in earnings at a relatively rapid rate.†

Guaranteed bond A bond which has interest or principal, or both, guaranteed by a company other than the issuer. Usually found in the railroad industry when large roads, leasing sections of trackage owned by small railroads, may guarantee the bonds of the smaller road.†

Guaranteed stock Usually preferred stock on which dividends are guaranteed by another company; under much the same circumstances as a bond is guaranteed.†

Hedge   (See: *Arbitrage, Option, Short sale.*)

Hedging   The purchase or sale of a derivative security (such as options or futures) in order to reduce or neutralize all or some portion of the risk of holding another security.††

Holding company   A corporation which owns the securities of another, in most cases with voting control.†

Hurdle rate   The minimum acceptable rate of return in a capital budgeting decision.°

Hypothecation   The pledging of securities as collateral—for example, to secure the debit balance in a margin account.†

Inactive stock   An issue traded on an exchange or in the over-the-counter market in which there is a relatively low volume of transactions. Volume may be no more than a few hundred shares a week or even less. On the New York Stock Exchange many inactive stocks are traded in 10-share units rather than the customary 100. (See: *Round lot.*)†

In-and-out   Purchase and sale of the same security within a short period—a day, a week, even a month. An in-and-out trader is generally more interested in day-to-day price fluctuations than dividends or long-term growth.†

Income bond   Generally income bonds promise to repay principal but to pay interest only when earned. In some cases unpaid interest on an income bond may accumulate as a claim against the corporation when the bond becomes due. An income bond may also be issued in lieu of preferred stock.†

Income statement   A financial statement that measures the profitability of the firm over a period of time. All expenses are subtracted from sales to arrive at net income.°

Indenture   A written agreement under which bonds and debentures are issued, setting forth maturity date, interest rate, and other terms.†

Independent broker   Members on the floor of the NYSE who execute orders for other brokers having more business at that time than they can handle themselves, or for firms who do not have their Exchange member on the floor. Formerly known as *two-dollar brokers* from the time when these independent brokers received $2 per hundred shares for executing such orders. Their fees are paid by the commission brokers. (See: *Commission broker.*)†

Index   A statistical yardstick expressed in terms of percentages of a base year or years. For instance, the Federal Reserve Board's index of industrial production is based on 1967 as 100. An index is not an average. (See: *Averages.*)†

Industrial revenue bond   A security backed by private enterprises that have been financed by a municipal issue.°°

Inflation   The phenomenon of price increase with the passage of time.°

Inflation premium   A premium to compensate the investor for the eroding effect of inflation on the value of the dollar. In the 1980s the inflation premium has been 3 to 4 percent. In the late 1970s it was in excess of 10 percent.°

Installment loan   A borrowing arrangement in which a series of equal payments are used to pay off the loan.°

Institutional Investor   An organization whose primary purpose is to invest its own assets or those held in trust by it for others. Includes pension funds, investment companies, insurance companies, universities, and banks.†

Interest   Payments a borrower pays a lender for the use of his money. A corporation pays interest on its bonds to its bondholders. (See: *Bond, dividend.*)†

Interest factor *(IF)*   The tabular value to insert into the various formulas. It is based on the number of periods *(n)* and the interest rate *(i)*.°

Interest rate parity theory   A theory based on the interplay between interest rate differentials and exchange rates. If one country has a higher interest rate than another country after adjustments for inflation, interest rates and foreign exchange rates will adjust until the foreign exchange rates and money market rates reach equilibrium (are properly balanced between the two countries).°

Intermarket Trading System (ITS)   An electronic communications network now linking the trading floor of seven registered exchanges to foster competition among them in stocks listed on either the NYSE or AMEX and one or more regional exchanges. Through ITS, any broker or market-maker on the floor of any participating market can reach out to other participants for an execution whenever the nationwide quote shows a better price is available.††

Internal corporate funds   Funds generated through the operations of the firm. The principal sources are retained earnings and cash flow added back from depreciation and other noncash deductions.°

Internal financing   Funds made available for capital budgeting and working-capital expansion through the normal operations of the firm; internal financing is approximately equal to retained earnings plus depreciation.°

Internal rate of return (IRR)   A discounted cash flow method for evaluating capital budgeting projects. The IRR is a discount rate which makes the present value of the cash inflows equal to the present value of the cash outflows.°

Internal reorganization A reorganization under the formal bankruptcy laws. New management may be brought in and a redesign of the capital structure may be implemented.°

International diversification Achieving diversification through many different foreign investments that are influenced by a variety of factors.°

International Finance Corporation (IFC) An affiliate of the World Bank established with the sole purpose of providing partial seed capital for private ventures around the world. Whenever a multinational company has difficulty raising equity capital due to lack of adequate private risk capital, the firm may explore the possibility of selling equity or debt (totaling up to 25 percent) to the International Finance Corporation.°

Intrinsic value The dollar amount of the difference between the exercise price of an option and the current cash value of the underlying security. Intrinsic value and time value are the two components of an option premium, or price.††

Inventory profits Profits generated as a result of an inflationary economy in which old inventory is sold at large profits because of increasing prices. This is particularly prevalent under FIFO accounting.°

Inverted yield curve A downward-sloping yield curve. Short-term rates are higher than long-term rates.°

Investment The use of money for the purpose of making more money, to gain income or increase capital, or both.††

Investment banker A financial organization that specializes in selling primary offerings of securities. Investment bankers can also perform other financial functions, such as advising clients, negotiating mergers and takeovers, and selling secondary offerings.°

Investment company A company or trust which uses its capital to invest in other companies. There are two principal types: the closed-end and the open-end, or mutual fund. Shares in closed-end investment companies, some of which are listed on the New York Stock Exchange, are readily transferable in the open market and are bought and sold like other shares. Capitalization of these companies remains the same unless action is taken to change, which is seldom. Open-end funds sell their own new shares to investors, stand ready to buy back their old shares, and are not listed.

Open-end funds are so called because their capitalization is not fixed; they issue more shares as people want them.†

Investment counsel One whose principal business consists of acting as investment adviser and a substantial part of his business consists of rendering investment supervisory services.†

Investment tax credit (ITC) A percentage of the purchase price that may be deducted directly from tax obligations.

IRA Individual Retirement Account. A pension plan with major tax advantages. Any worker can begin an IRA by a cash contribution up to $2,000 annually which is not tax deductible; however, the investment return on which is tax deferred. (See: *Keogh Plan*.)

Issue Any of a company's securities, or the act of distributing such securities.†

Issuer A municipal unit that borrows money through the sale of bonds or notes.°°

Keogh Plan Tax advantaged personal retirement program that can be established by a self-employed individual. Currently, annual contributions to a plan can be up to $15,000. Such contributions and reinvestments are not taxed as they accumulate but will be when withdrawn (presumably at retirement when taxable income may be less). (See: *IRA*.)††

Leading indicators The most commonly followed series of economic indicators (a series of the 12 leading indicators). These are used to help forecast economic activity.°

Lease A contractual arrangement between the owner of equipment (lessor) and the user of equipment (lessee) which calls for the lessee to pay the lessor an established lease payment. There are two kinds of leases, financial leases and operating leases.°

Legal list A list of investments selected by various states in which certain institutions and fiduciaries, such as insurance companies and banks, may invest. Legal lists are often restricted to high quality securities meeting certain specifications. (See: *Prudent man rule*.)††

Legal opinion An opinion concerning the legality of a bond issue usually written by a recognized law firm specializing in public borrowings.°°

Letter of credit A credit letter normally issued by the importer's bank in which the bank promises to pay out the money for the merchandise when delivered.°

Level production Equal monthly production used to smooth out production schedules and employ manpower and equipment more efficiently and at a lower cost.°

Leverage   The effect on a company when the company has bonds, preferred stock, or both outstanding. Example: If the earnings of a company with 1,000,000 common shares increases from $1,000,000 to $1,500,000—earnings per share would go from $1 to $1.50, or an increase of 50 percent. But if earnings of a company that had to pay $500,000 in bond interest increased that much—earnings per common share would jump from 50 cents to $1 a share, or 100 percent.††

Leveraged buy-out   Existing management or an outsider makes an offer to "go private" by retiring all the shares of the company. The buying group borrows the necessary money, using the assets of the acquired firm as collateral. The buying group then repurchases all the shares and expects to retire the debt over time with the cash flow from operations or the sale of corporate assets.°

Liabilities   All the claims against a corporation. Liabilities include accounts and wages and salaries payable, dividends declared payable, accrued taxes payable, fixed or long-term liabilities such as mortgage bonds, debentures, and bank loans. (See: *Assets, Balance sheet.*)†

LIBOR   (See: *London Interbank Offered Rate.*)°

Life cycle curve   A curve illustrating the growth phases of a firm. The dividend policy most likely to be employed during each phase is often illustrated.°

LIFO   A system of writing off inventory into cost of goods sold in which the items purchased last are written off first. Referred to as last-in, first-out.°

Limit, limited order, or limited price order   An order to buy or sell a stated amount of a security at a specified price, or at a better price, if obtainable after the order is represented in the Trading Crowd.†

Limited partnership   A special form of partnership to limit liability for most of the partners. Under this arrangement, one or more partners are designated as general partners and have unlimited liability for the debts of the firm, while the other partners are designated as limited partners and are only liable for their initial contribution.°

Limited tax bond   A bond secured by a pledge of a tax or group of taxes limited as to rate or amount.°°

Liquidation   The process of converting securities or other property into cash. The dissolution of a company, with cash remaining after sale of its assets and payment of all indebtedness being distributed to the shareholders.†

Liquidity   The ability of the market in a particular security to absorb a reasonable amount of buying or selling at reasonable price changes. Liquidity is one of the most important characteristics of a good market.†

Liquidity ratios   A group of ratios that allows one to measure the firm's ability to pay off short-term obligations as they come due. Primary attention is directed to the current ratio and the quick ratio.°

Listed stock   The stock of a company which is traded on a securities exchange. The various stock exchanges have different standards for listing. Some of the guides used by the New York Stock Exchange for an original listing are national interest in the company, a minimum of 1.1-million shares publicly held among not less than 2,000 round-lot stockholders. The publicly held common shares should have a minimum aggregate market value of $18 million. The company should have net income in the latest year of over $2.5-million before federal income tax and $2-million in each of the preceding two years.††

Listing requirements   Financial standards that corporations must meet before their common stock can be traded on a stock exchange. Listing requirements are not standard, but are set by each exchange. The requirements for the NYSE are the most stringent.°

Load   The portion of the offering price of shares of open-end investment companies in excess of the value of the underlying assets which cover sales commissions and all other costs of distribution. The load is usually incurred only on purchase, there being, in most cases, no charge when the shares are sold (redeemed).†

Lockbox system   A procedure used to expedite cash inflows to a business. Customers are requested to forward their checks to a post-office box in their geographic region, and a local bank picks up the checks and processes them for rapid collection. Funds are then wired to the corporate home office for immediate use.°

London Interbank Offered Rate (LIBOR)   An interbank rate applicable for large deposits in the London market. It is a benchmark rate just like the prime interest rate in the United States. Interest rates on Eurodollar loans are determined by adding premiums to this basic rate. Most often LIBOR is lower than the U.S. prime rate.°

Long   Signifies ownership of securities: "I am long 100 U.S. Steel" means the speaker owns 100 shares. (See: *Short position, Short sale.*)†

Majority voting All directors must be elected by a vote of more than 50 percent. Minority shareholders are unable to achieve any representation on the board of directors.°

Management The board of directors, elected by the stockholders, and the officers of the corporation, appointed by the board of directors.†

Managing underwriter An investment banker who is responsible for the pricing, prospectus development, and legal work involved in the sale of a new issue of securities.°

Manipulation An illegal operation. Buying or selling a security for the purpose of creating a false or misleading appearance of active trading or for the purpose of raising or depressing the price to induce purchase or sale by others.†

Margin The amount paid by the customer when using a broker's credit to buy or sell a security. Under Federal Reserve regulations, the initial margin required since 1945 has ranged from the current rate of 50 percent of the purchase price up to 100 percent. (See: *Brokers' loans, Equity, Margin call*.)††

Margin call A demand upon a customer to put up money or securities with the broker. The call is made when a purchase is made; also if a customer's equity in a margin account declines below a minimum standard set by the exchange or by the firm. (See: *Margin*.)†

Margin requirement A rule that specifies the amount of cash or equity that must be deposited with a brokerage firm or bank, with the balance of funds eligible for borrowing. Margin is set by the Board of Governors of the Federal Reserve Board. For example, margin of 60 percent would mean that a $10,000 purchase would allow the buyer to borrow $4,000 toward the purchase.°

Marginal corporate tax rate The rate that applies to each new dollar of taxable income. For a corporation, the rate in 1986 is 15 percent on the first $25,000, 18 percent on the second $25,000, 30 percent on the third $25,000, 40 percent on the fourth $25,000, and 46 percent on all larger amounts.°

Marginal cost of capital The cost of the last dollar of funds raised. It is assumed that each dollar is financed in proportion to the firm's optimum capital structure.°

Marginal principle of retained earnings The corporation must be able to earn a higher return on its retained earnings than a stockholder would receive after paying taxes on the distributed dividends.°

Market efficiency Markets are considered to be efficient when (1) prices adjust rapidly to new information; (2) there is a continuous market in which each successive trade is made at a price close to the previous price (the faster the price responds to new information and the smaller the differences in price changes, the more efficient the market); and (3) the market can absorb large dollar amounts of securities without destabilizing the prices.°

Market maker (See: *Dealer*.)

Market order An order to buy or sell a stated amount of a security at the most advantageous price obtainable after the order is represented in the trading crowd. (See: *Good 'til cancelled order, Limit order, Stop order*.)††

Market price In the case of a security, market price is usually considered the last reported price at which the stock or bond sold.†

Market risk premium A premium over and above the risk-free rate. It is represented by the difference between the market return (K^m) and the risk-free rate (R^f), and it may be multiplied by the beta coefficient to determine additional risk-adjusted return on a security.°

Market stabilization Intervention in the secondary markets by an investment banker to stabilize the price of a new security offering during the offering period. The purpose of market stabilization is to provide an orderly market for the distribution of the new issue.°

Market value maximization The concept of maximizing the wealth of shareholders. This calls for a recognition not only of earnings per share but also how they will be valued in the marketplace.°

Marketability The measure of the ease with which a security can be sold in the secondary market.°°

Maturity The date on which a loan or a bond or debenture comes due and is to be paid off.†

Member corporation A securities brokerage firm, organized as a corporation, with at least one member of the New York Stock Exchange, who is an officer or an employee of the corporation.††

Member firm A securities brokerage firm organized as a partnership and having at least one general partner who is a member of the New York Stock Exchange, Inc. (See: *Member corporation*.)†

Member organization This term includes New York Stock Exchange Member Firm *and* Member Corporation. (See: *Member corporation, Member firm.*)†

Merger The combination of two or more companies in which the resulting firms maintain the identity of the acquiring company.°

Merger arbitrageur A specialist in merger investments who attempts to capitalize on the difference between the value offered and the current market value of the acquisition candidate.°

Merger premium The part of a buy-out or exchange offer which represents a value over and above the market value of the acquired firm.°

Minimum warrant value The market value of the common stock minus the option price of the warrant multiplied by the number of shares of the common stock that each warrant entitles the holder to purchase.°

Monetary policy Management by the Federal Reserve Board of the money supply and the resultant interest rates.°

Money market accounts Accounts at banks, savings and loans, and credit unions in which the depositor receives competitive money market rates on a typical minimum deposit of $1,000. These accounts may generally have three deposits and three withdrawals per month, and are not meant to be transaction accounts, but a place to keep minimum and excess cash balances. These accounts are insured by various appropriate governmental agencies up to $100,000.°

Money market funds A fund in which investors may purchase shares for as little as $500 or $1,000. The fund then reinvests the proceeds in high-yielding $100,000 bank CDs, $25,000–$100,000 commercial paper, and other large-denomination, high-yielding securities. Investors receive their pro rata portion of the interest proceeds daily as a credit to their shares.°

Money markets Competitive markets for securities with maturities of one year or less. The best examples of money market instruments would be Treasury bills, commercial paper, and negotiable certificates of deposit.°

Mortgage agreement A loan which requires real property (plant and equipment) as collateral.°

Mortgage bond A bond secured by a mortgage on a property. The value of the property may or may not equal the value of the bonds issued against it. (See: *Bond, Debenture.*)††

Multinational corporation A firm doing business across its national borders is considered a multinational enterprise. Some definitions require a minimum percentage (often 30 percent or more) of a firm's business activities to be carried on outside its national borders.°

Municipal bond A bond issued by a state or a political subdivision, such as county, city, town, or village. The term also designates bonds issued by state agencies and authorities. In general, interest paid on municipal bonds is exempt from federal income taxes and state and local income taxes within the state of issue.†

Municipal securities Securities issued by state and local government units. The income from these securities is exempt from federal income taxes.°

Mutual fund (See: *Investment company.*)

Mutually exclusive The selection of one choice precludes the selection of any competitive choice. For example, several machines can do an identical job in capital budgeting. If one machine is selected, the other machines will not be used.°

Naked option An option position that is *not* offset by an equal and opposite position in the underlying security.††

NASD The National Association of Securities Dealers, Inc. An association of brokers and dealers in the over-the-counter securities business.††

NASDAQ An automated information network which provides brokers and dealers with price quotations on securities traded over-the-counter. NASDAQ is an acronym for National Association of Securities Dealers Automated Quotations.†

National Market List The list of the best-known and most widely traded securities in the over-the-counter market.°

National market system A system mandated by the Securities Acts Amendments of 1975. The national market system that is envisioned will include computer processing and computerized competitive prices for all markets trading similar stocks. The exact form of the system is yet to be determined.°

Negotiable Refers to a security, title to which is transferable by delivery. (See: *Good delivery.*)†

Negotiable Order of Withdrawal account An interest earning account on which checks may be drawn. Withdrawals from NOW accounts may be subject to a 14-day or more notice requirement although such is rarely imposed. NOW accounts may be offered by commercial banks, mutual savings banks, and savings and loan associations and may be owned only by individuals and certain nonprofit organizations and governmental units.¶

Net asset value Usually used in connection with investment companies to mean net asset value per share. An investment company computes its assets daily, or even twice daily, by totaling the market value of all securities owned. All liabilities are deducted, and the balance divided by the number of shares outstanding. The resulting figure is the net asset value per share. (See: *Assets, Investment company.*)††

Net change The change in the price of a security from the closing price on one day and the closing price on the following day on which the stock is traded. The net change is ordinarily the last figure on the stock price list. The mark + 1⅛ means up $1.125 a share from the last sale on the previous day the stock traded.†

Net debt Gross debt less sinking fund accumulations and all self-supporting debt.°°

Net present value (NPV) The NPV equals the present value of the cash inflows minus the present value of the cash outflows with the cost of capital used as a discount rate. This method is used to evaluate capital budgeting projects. If the NPV is positive, a project should be accepted.°

Net present value profile A graphical presentation of the potential net present values of a project at different discount rates. It is very helpful in comparing the characteristics of two or more investments.°

Net trade credit A measure of the relationship between the firm's accounts receivable and accounts payable. If accounts receivable exceed accounts payable, the firm is a net provider of trade credit; otherwise, it is a net user.°

Net worth, or book value Stockholders' equity minus preferred stock ownership. Basically, net worth is the common stockholders' interest as represented by common stock par value, capital paid in excess of par, and retained earnings. If you take all the assets of the firm and substract its liabilities and preferred stock, you arrive at net worth.°

New housing authority bonds A bond issued by a local public housing authority to finance public housing. It is backed by Federal funds and the solemn pledge of the U.S. Government that payment will be made in full.°°

New issue A stock or bond sold by a corporation for the first time. Proceeds may be issued to retire outstanding securities of the company, for new plant or equipment, or for additional working capital, or to acquire a public ownership interest in the company for private owners.††

New issue market Market for new issues of municipal bonds and notes.°°

New York Futures Exchange (NYFE) A subsidiary of the New York Stock Exchange devoted to the trading of futures products.††

New York Stock Exchange (NYSE) The largest organized securities market in the United States, founded in 1792. The Exchange itself does not buy, sell, own, or set the prices of securities traded there. The prices are determined by public supply and demand. The Exchange is a not-for-profit corporation of 1,366 individual members, governed by a Board of Directors consisting of 10 public representatives, 10 Exchange members or allied members and a full-time chairman, executive vice chairman and president.††

Nominal GNP GNP (gross national product) in current dollars without any adjustments for inflation.°

Nominal yield A return equal to the coupon rate.°

Noncumulative A type of preferred stock on which unpaid dividends do not accrue. Omitted dividends are, as a rule, gone forever. (See: *Cumulative preferred.*)††

Nonfinancial corporation A firm not in the banking or financial services industry. The term would primarily apply to manufacturing, wholesaling, and retail firms.°

Nonlinear break-even analysis Break-even analysis based on the assumption that cost and revenue relationships to quantity may vary at different levels of operation. Most of our analysis is based on *linear* break-even analysis.°

Normal recovery period The depreciation recovery period (3, 5, 10, 15 years) under the Accelerated Cost Recovery System of the 1981 Economic Recovery Tax Act.°

Normal yield curve An upward-sloping yield curve. Long-term interest rates are higher than short-term rates.°

Notes Short-term unsecured promises to pay specified amounts of money. For municipal notes maturities generally range from six to twelve months.°°

NYSE composite index A composite index covering price movements of all common stocks listed on the "Big Board." It is based on the close of the market December 31, 1965 as 50.00 and is weighted according to the number of shares listed for each issue. The index is computed continuously and printed on the ticker tape each half hour. Point changes in the index are converted to dollars and cents so as to provide a meaningful measure of changes in the average price of listed stocks. The composite index is supplemented by separate indexes for four industry groups: industries, transportation, utilities, and finances. (See: *Averages*.)††

Odd lot   An amount of stock less than the established 100-share unit. (See: *Round lot*.)††

Off-board   This term may refer to transactions over-the-counter in unlisted securities, or to a transaction involving listed shares that is not executed on a national securities exchange.††

Offer   The price at which a person is ready to sell. Opposed to bid, the price at which one is ready to buy. (See: *Bid and asked*.)†

Official statement   Document prepared by or for the issuer that gives in detail the security and financial information about the issue.°°

Open-end investment company   (See: *Investment company*.)

Open interest   In options and futures trading, the number of outstanding option contracts, at a given point in time, which have not been exercised and have not yet reached expiration.††

Open-market operations   The purchase and sale of government securities in the open market by the Federal Reserve Board for its own account. The most common method for managing the money supply.°

Open order   (See: *Good 'til cancelled order*.)

Operating lease   A short-term, nonbinding obligation that is easily cancelable.°

Operating leverage   A reflection of the extent to which fixed assets and fixed costs are utilized in the business firm.°

Optimum capital structure   A capital structure that has the best possible mix of debt, preferred stock, and common equity. The optimum mix should provide the lowest possible cost of capital to the firm.°

Option   A right to buy (call) or sell (put) a fixed amount of a given stock at a specified price within a limited period of time. The purchaser hopes that the stock's price will go up (a call) or down (a put) by an amount sufficient to provide a profit when the stock is sold. If the stock price holds steady or moves in the opposite direction, the price paid for the option is lost entirely. There are several other types of options available to the public but these are basically combinations of puts and calls. Individuals may write (sell) as well as purchase options. Options are also traded on stock indexes, futures, and debt instruments.††

Orders good until a specified time   A market or limited price order which is to be represented in the Trading Crowd until a specified time, after which such order or the portion thereof not executed is to be treated as cancelled.†

Overbought   An opinion as to price levels. May refer to a security which has had a sharp rise or to the market as a whole after a period of vigorous buying, which it may be argued, has left prices "too high."†

Overseas Private Investment Corporation (OPIC)   A government agency that sells insurance policies to qualified firms. This agency insures against losses due to inconvertibility into dollars of amounts invested in a foreign country. Policies are also available from OPIC to insure against expropriation and against losses due to war or revolution.°

Oversold   The reverse of overbought. A single security or a market which, it is believed, has declined to an unreasonable level.††

Over-the-counter   A market for securities made up of securities dealers who may or may not be members of a securities exchange. The over-the-counter market is conducted over the telephone and deals mainly with stocks of companies without sufficient shares, stockholders, or earnings to warrant listing on an exchange. Over-the-counter dealers may act either as principals or as brokers for customers. The over-the-counter market is the principal market for bonds of all types. (See: *NASD, NASDAQ*.)††

Paper profit (LOSS)   An unrealized profit or loss on a security still held. Paper profits and losses become realized profits only when the security is sold. (See: *Profit-taking*.)††

Par   In the case of a common share, par means a dollar amount assigned to the share by the company's charter. Par value may also be used to compute the dollar amount of the common shares on the balance sheet. Par value has little relationship to the market value of common stock. Many companies issue no-par stock but give a stated per share value on the balance sheet. In the case of preferred stocks, it signifies the dollar value upon which dividends are figured. With bonds, par value is the face amount, usually $1,000.††

Parallel loan   A U.S. firm that wishes to lend funds to a foreign affiliate (such as a Dutch affiliate) locates a foreign parent firm (such as a Dutch parent firm) that wishes to loan money to a U.S. affiliate. Avoiding the foreign exchange markets entirely, the U.S. parent lends dollars to the Dutch affiliate in the United States, while the Dutch parent lends guilders to the American affiliate in the Netherlands. At maturity, the two loans would each be repaid to the original lender.

Notice that neither loan carries any foreign exchange risk in this arrangement.°

Participating preferred A preferred stock which is entitled to its stated dividend and, also, to additional dividends on a specified basis upon payment of dividends on the common stock.†

Partnership A form of ownership in which two or more partners are involved. Like the sole proprietorship, a partnership arrangement carries unlimited liability for the owners. However, there is only single taxation for the partners, an advantage over the corporate form of ownership.°

Passed dividend Omission of a regular or scheduled dividend.†

Payback A value that indicates the time period required to recoup an initial investment. The payback does not include the time-value-of-money concept.°

Paying agent Place where principal and interest is payable. Usually a designated bank or the treasurer's office of the issuer.°°

Penny stocks Low-priced issues often highly speculative, selling at less than $1 a share. Frequently used as a term of disparagement, although a few penny stocks have developed into investment-caliber issues.†

Percent-of-sales method A method of determining future financial needs that is an alternative to the development of pro forma financial statements. We first determine the percentage relationship of various asset and liability accounts to sales, and then we show how that relationship changes as our volume of sales changes.°

Permanent current assets Current assets that will not be reduced or converted to cash within the normal operating cycle of the firm. Though from a strict accounting standpoint the assets should be removed from the current assets category, they generally are not.°

Perpetuity An investment without a maturity date.°

Planning horizon The length of time it takes to conceive, develop, and complete a project and to recover the cost of the project on a discounted cash flow basis.°

Pledging receivables Using accounts receivable as collateral for a loan. The firm usually may borrow 60 to 80 percent of the value of acceptable collateral.°

Point In the case of shares of stock, a point means $1. If ABC shares rises 3 points, each share has risen $3. In the case of bonds a point means $10, since a bond is quoted as a percentage of $1,000. A bond which rises 3 points gains 3 percent of $1,000, or $30 in

value. An advance from 87 to 90 would mean an advance in dollar value from $870 to $900. In the case of market averages, the word point means merely that and no more. If, for example, the NYSE Composite Index rises from 90.25 to 91.25, it has risen a point. A point in this average, however, is not equivalent to $1. (See: *Index*.)††

Point-of-sales terminals Computer terminals in retail stores that either allow digital input or use optical scanners. The terminals may be used for inventory control or other purposes.°

Pooling of interests A method of financial recording for mergers in which the financial statements of the firms are combined, subject to minor adjustments, and goodwill is *not* created.°

Portfolio Holdings of securities by an individual or institution. A portfolio may contain bonds, preferred stocks, common stocks and other securities.††

Portfolio effect The impact of a given investment on the overall risk-return composition of the firm. A firm must consider not only the individual investment characteristics of a project, but also how the project relates to the entire portfolio of undertakings.°

Preemptive right The right of current common stockholders to maintain their ownership percentage on new issues of common stock.°

Preferred stock A class of stock with a claim on the company's earnings before payment may be made on the common stock and usually entitled to priority over common stock if the company liquidates. Usually entitled to dividends at a specified rate—when declared by the board of directors and before payment of a dividend on the common stock—depending upon the terms of the issue. (See: *Cumulative preferred, Participating preferred*.)†

Premium The amount by which a bond or preferred stock, may sell above its par value. For options, the price that the buyer pays the writer for an option contract ("option premium") is synonymous with "the price of an option." (See: *Discount*.)††

Present value The current or discounted value of a future sum or annuity. The value is discounted back at a given interest rate for a specified time period.°

Price-earnings ratio A popular way to compare stocks selling at various price levels. The PE ratio is the price of a share of stock divided by earnings per share for a twelve-month period. For example, a stock selling for $50 a share and earning $5 a share is said to be selling at a price-earnings ratio of 10.††

Primary distribution   Also called primary offering. The original sale of a company's securities. (See: *Investment banker*.)††

Primary earnings per share   Adjusted earnings after taxes divided by shares outstanding plus common stock equivalents.°

Primary market   Market for new issues of securities.

Prime rate   The lowest interest rate charged by commercial banks to their most creditworthy and largest corporate customers; other interest rates, such as personal, automobile, commercial and financing loans are often pegged to the prime.††

Principal   The person for whom a broker executes an order, or dealers buying or selling for their own accounts. The term *principal* may also refer to a person's capital or to the face amount of a bond.††

Private placement   The sale of securities directly to a financial institution by a corporation. This eliminates the middleman and reduces the cost of issue to the corporation.°

Productivity   The amount of physical output for each unit of productive input.¶

Profitability ratios   A group of ratios that indicates the return on sales, total assets, and invested capital. Specifically, we compute the profit margin (net income to sales), return on assets, and return on equity.°

Profit-taking   Selling stock which has appreciated in value since purchase, in order to realize the profit. The term is often used to explain a downturn in the market following a period of rising prices. (See: *Paper profit*.)††

Pro forma balance sheet   A projection of future asset, liability, and stockholders' equity levels. Notes payable or cash is used as a plug or balancing figure for the statement.°

Pro forma financial statements   A series of projected financial statements. Of major importance are the pro forma income statement, the pro forma balance sheet, and the cash budget.°

Pro forma income statement   A projection of anticipated sales, expenses, and income.°

Prospectus   The official selling circular that must be given to purchasers of new securities registered with the Securities and Exchange Commission. It highlights the much longer Registration Statement filed with the commission.††

Proxy   Written authorization given by a shareholder to someone else to represent him and vote his shares at a shareholders' meeting.††

Proxy statement   Information given to stockholders in conjunction with the solicitation of proxies.††

Prudent man rule   An investment standard. In some states, the law requires that a fiduciary, such as a trustee, may invest the fund's money only in a list of securities designated by the state—the so-called legal list. In other states, the trustee may invest in a security if it is one that would be bought by a prudent man of discretion and intelligence, who is seeking a reasonable income and preservation of capital.††

Public Offering   (See: *Primary distribution*.)

Public placement   The sale of securities to the public through the investment banker-underwriter process. Public placements must be registered with the Securities and Exchange Commission.°

Public warehousing   An inventory financing arrangement in which inventory, used as collateral, is stored with and controlled by an independent warehousing company.°

Purchase of assets   A method of financial recording for mergers in which the difference between the purchase price and the adjusted book value is recognized as goodwill and amortized over a maximum time period of 40 years.°

Purchasing power parity theory   A theory based on the interplay between inflation and exchange rates. A parity between the purchasing powers of two countries establishes the rate of exchange between the two currencies. Currency exchange rates, therefore, tend to vary inversely with their respective purchasing powers in order to provide the same or similar purchasing power.°

Pure bond value   The value of the convertible bond if its present value is computed at a discount rate equal to interest rates on straight bonds of equal risk, without conversion privileges.°

Quote   The highest bid to buy and the lowest offer to sell a security in a given market at a given time. If you ask your broker for a "quote" on a stock, he may come back with something like "45¼ to 45½." This means that $45.25 is the highest price any buyer wanted to pay at the time the quote was given on the floor of the exchange and that $45.50 was the lowest price which any seller would take at the same time. (See: *Bid and asked*.)††

Rally   A brisk rise following a decline in the general price level of the market, or in an individual stock.†

Ratings   Designations used by investors' services to give relative indications of quality.°°

Real capital Long-term productive assets (plant and equipment).°

Real GNP GNP (gross national product) in current dollars adjusted for inflation.°

Real rate of return The rate of return that an investor demands for giving up the current use of his or her funds on a noninflation-adjusted basis. It is payment for forgoing current consumption. Historically, the real rate of return demanded by investors has been of the magnitude of 2 to 3 percent. However, throughout the 1980s the real rate of return has been much higher; that is, 5 to 7 percent.°

Record date The date on which you must be registered as a shareholder of a company in order to receive a declared dividend or, among other things, to vote on company affairs. (See: *Ex-dividend, Transfer*.)††

Redemption price The price at which a bond may be redeemed before maturity, at the option of the issuing company. Redemption value also applies to the price the company must pay to call in certain types of preferred stock. (See: *Callable*.)††

Red Herring (See: *Prospectus*.)

Refunding The process of retiring an old bond issue before maturity and replacing it with a new issue. Refunding will occur when interest rates have fallen and new bonds may be sold at lower interest rates.°

Registered bond A bond which is registered on the books of the issuing company in the name of the owner. It can be transferred only when endorsed by the registered owner. (See: *Bearer bond, Coupon bond*.)†

Registered representative The man or woman who serves the investor customers of a broker/dealer. In a New York Stock Exchange Member Organization, a Registered Representative must meet the requirements of the exchange as to background and knowledge of the securities business. Also known as an Account Executive or Customer's broker.††

Registrar Usually a trust company or bank charged with the responsibility of keeping a record of the owners of corporation's securities and preventing the issuance of more than the authorized amount. (See: *Transfer*.)††

Registration Before a public offering may be made of new securities by a company, or of outstanding securities by controlling stockholders—through the mails or in interstate commerce—the securities must be registered under the Securities Act of 1933. A statement is filed with the SEC by the issuer. It must disclose pertinent information relating to the company's operations, securities, management and purpose of the public offering.

Before a security may be admitted to dealings on a national securities exchange, it must be registered under the Securities Exchange Act of 1934. The application for registration must be filed with the exchange and the SEC by the company issuing the securities.††

Regional stock exchanges Organized exchanges outside of New York that list securities. Regional exchanges exist in San Francisco, Philadelphia, and a number of other U.S. cities.°

Regulation T The federal regulation governing the amount of credit which may be advanced by brokers and dealers to customers for the purchase of securities. (See: *Margin*.)†

Regulation U The federal regulation governing the amount of credit which may be advanced by a bank to its customers for the purchase of listed stocks. (See: *Margin*.)†

Reinvestment assumption An assumption must be made concerning the rate of return that can be earned on the cash flows generated by capital budgeting projects. The NPV method assumes the rate of reinvestment to be the cost of capital, while the IRR method assumes the rate to be the actual internal rate of return.°

REIT Real Estate Investment Trust, an organization similar to an investment company in some respects but concentrating its holdings in real estate investments. The yield is generally liberal since REIT's are required to distribute as much as 90 percent of their income. (See: *Investment company*.)†

Repatriation of earnings Returning earnings to the multinational parent company in the form of dividends.°

Replacement cost The cost of replacing the existing asset base at current prices as opposed to original cost.°

Replacement cost accounting Financial statements based on the present cost of replacing assets.°

Repurchase agreements When the Federal Reserve makes a repurchase agreement with a government securities dealer, it buys a security for immediate delivery with an agreement to sell the security back at the same price by a specific date (usually within 15 days) and receives interest at a specific rate. This arrangement allows the Federal Reserve to inject reserves into the banking system on a temporary basis to meet a temporary need and to withdraw these reserves as soon as that need has passed.¶

Required rate of return The rate of return that investors demand from an investment (securities) to compensate them for the amount of risk involved.°

Reserve requirements The amount of funds that commercial banks must hold in reserve for each dollar of deposits. Reserve requirements are set by the Federal Reserve Board and are different for savings and checking accounts. Low reserve requirements are stimulating; high reserve requirements are restrictive.°

Residual dividends This theory of dividend payout states that a corporation will retain as much earnings as it may profitably invest. If any income is left after investments, it will pay dividends. This theory assumes that dividends are a passive decision variable.°

Restructuring Redeploying the asset and liability structure of the firm. This can be accomplished through repurchasing shares with cash or borrowed funds, acquiring other firms, or selling off unprofitable or unwanted divisions.°

Revenue bond A bond payable from revenues derived from tolls, charges, or rents paid by users of the facility constructed from the proceeds of the bond issue.°°

Rights When a company wants to raise more funds by issuing additional securities, it may give its stockholders the opportunity, ahead of others, to buy the new securities in proportion to the number of shares each owns. The piece of paper evidencing this privilege is called a right. Because the additional stock is usually offered to stockholders below the current market price, rights ordinarily have a market value of their own and are actively traded. In most cases they must be exercised within a relatively short period. Failure to exercise or sell rights may result in actual loss to the holder. (See: *Warrant*.)†

Rights offering A sale of new common stock through a preemptive rights offering. Usually one right will be issued for every share held. A certain number of rights may be used to buy shares of common stock from the company at a set price that is lower than the market price.°

Rights-on The situation in which the purchase of a share of common stock includes a right attached to the stock.°

Risk A measure of uncertainty about the outcome from a given event. The greater the variability of possible outcomes, on both the high side and the low side, the greater the risk.°

Risk-adjusted discount rate A discount rate used in the capital budgeting process that has been adjusted upward or downward from the basic cost of capital to reflect the risk dimension of a given project.°

Risk averse An aversion or dislike for risk. In order to induce most people to take larger risks, there must be increased potential for return.°

Risk-free rate of interest Rate of return on an asset that carries no risk. U.S. Treasury bills are often used to represent this measure, although longer-term government securities have also proved appropriate in some studies.°

Risk premium A premium associated with the special risks of an investment. Of primary interest are two types of risk, business risk and financial risk. Business risk relates to the inability of the firm to maintain its competitive position and sustain stability and growth in earnings. Financial risk relates to the inability of the firm to meet its debt obligations as they come due. The risk premium will also differ (be greater or less) for different types of investments (bonds, stocks, etc.).°

Risk-return trade-off function (See *Security market line*.)

Round lot A unit of trading or a multiple thereof. On the NYSE the unit of trading is generally 100 shares in stocks and $1,000 or $5,000 par value in the case of bonds. In some inactive stocks, the unit of trading is ten shares. (See: *Odd lot*.)††

Scale order An order to buy (or sell) a security which specifies the total amount to be bought (or sold) and the amount to be bought (or sold) at specified price variations.†

Seat A traditional figure-of-speech for a membership on an exchange.

SEC The Securities and Exchange Commission, established by Congress to help protect investors. The SEC administers the Securities Act of 1933, the Securities Exchange Act of 1934, the Securities Act Amendments of 1975, the Trust Indenture Act, the Investment Company Act, the Investment Advisers Act, and the Public Utility Holding Company Act.†

Secondary offering The sale of a large block of stock in a publicly traded company, usually by estates, foundations, or large individual stockholders. Secondary offerings must be registered with the SEC and will usually be distributed by investment bankers.°

Secondary trading The buying and selling of publicly owned securities in secondary markets such as the New York Stock Exchange and the over-the-counter markets.°

Secured debt A general category of debt which indicates that the loan was obtained by pledging assets as collateral. Secured debt has many forms and usually offers some protective features to a given class of bondholders.°

Securities Act of 1933 An act that is sometimes referred to as the truth in securities act because it requires detailed financial disclosures before securities may be sold to the public.°

Securities Act Amendments of 1975 The major feature of this act was to mandate a national securities market. (See: *National market system*.)°

Securities Exchange Act of 1934 Legislation that established the Securities and Exchange Commission (SEC) to supervise and regulate the securities markets.°

Security market line A line or equation that depicts the risk-related return of a security based on a risk-free rate plus a market premium related to the beta coefficient of the security.°

Self-liquidating assets Assets that are converted to cash within the normal operating cycle of the firm. An example is the purchase and sell-off of seasonal inventory.°

Semiannual compounding A compounding period of every six months. For example, a five-year investment in which interest is compounded semiannually would indicate an *n* value equal to 10 and an *i* value at one half the annual rate.°

Semivariable costs Costs that are partially fixed but still change somewhat as volume changes. Examples are utilities and "repairs and maintenance."°

Serial bond An issue which matures in part at periodic stated intervals.†

Settlement Conclusion of a securities transaction when a customer pays a broker/dealer for securities purchased or delivers securities sold and receives from the broker the proceeds of a sale. (See: *Cash sale*.)††

Shelf registration A process which permits large companies to file one comprehensive registration statement (under SEC Rule 415), which outlines the firm's plans for future long-term financing. Then, when market conditions appear to be appropriate, the firm can issue the securities without further SEC approval.°

Short covering Buying stock to return stock previously borrowed to make delivery on a short sale.†

Short position Stocks, options, or futures sold short and not covered as of a particular date. On the NYSE, a tabulation is issued once a month listing all issues on the Exchange in which there was a short position of 5,000 or more shares and issues in which the short position had changed by 2,000 or more shares in the preceding month. Short position also means the total amount of stock an individual has sold short and has not covered, as of a particular date.††

Short sale A transaction by a person who believes a security will decline and sells it, though the person does not own any. For instance: You instruct your broker to sell short 100 shares of XYZ. Your broker borrows the stock so delivery of the 100 shares can be made to the buyer. The money value of the shares borrowed is deposited by your broker with the lender. Sooner or later you must cover your short sale by buying the same amount of stock you borrowed for return to the lender. If you are able to buy XYZ at a lower price than you sold it for, your profit is the difference between the two prices—not counting commissions and taxes. But if you have to pay more for the stock than the price you received, that is the amount of your loss. Stock exchange and federal regulations govern and limit the conditions under which a short sale may be made on a national securities exchange. Sometimes people will sell short a stock they already own in order to protect a paper profit. This is known as selling short against the box.†

Simulation A method of dealing with uncertainty in which future outcomes are anticipated. The model may use random variables for inputs. By programming the computer to randomly select inputs from probability distributions, the outcomes generated by a simulation are distributed about a mean, and instead of generating one return or net present value, a range of outcomes with standard deviations is provided.°

Sinking fund Money regularly set aside by a company to redeem its bonds, debentures or preferred stock from time to time as specified in the indenture or charter.††

SIPC Securities Investor Protection Corporation, which provides funds for use, if necessary, to protect customers' cash and securities which may be on deposit with an SIPC member firm in the event the firm fails and is liquidated under the provisions of the SIPC Act. SIPC is not a government agency. It is a nonprofit membership corporation created, however, by an act of Congress.

Special bid A method of filling an order to buy a large block of stock on the floor of the New York Stock Exchange. In a special bid, the bidder for the block of stock—a pension fund, for instance, will pay a special commission to the broker who represents him in making the purchase. The seller does not pay a commission. The special bid is made on the floor of the exchange at a fixed price which may not be below the last sale of the security or the current bid in the regular market, whichever is higher. Member firms may sell this stock for customers directly to the buyer's broker during trading hours.†

Special offering Opposite of special bid. A notice is printed on the ticker tape announcing the stock sale at a fixed price usually based on the last transaction in the regular auction market. If there are more buyers than stock, allotments are made. Only the seller pays the commission.†

Special tax bond A bond secured by a special tax, such as a gasoline tax.°°

Specialist A member of the New York Stock Exchange, Inc., who has two functions: First, to maintain an orderly market in the securities registered to the specialist. In order to maintain an orderly market, the Exchange expects specialists to buy or sell for their own account, to a reasonable degree, when there is a temporary disparity between supply and demand. Second, the specialist acts as a broker's broker. When a commission broker on the Exchange floor receives a limit order, say, to buy at $50 a stock then selling at $60—he cannot wait at the post where the stock is traded to see if the price reaches the specified level. So he leaves the order with the specialist, who will try to execute it in the market if and when the stock declines to the specified price. At all times the specialist must put his customers' interests above his own. There are about 400 specialists on the NYSE. (See: *Limited order*.)††

Speculation The employment of funds by a speculator. Safety of principal is a secondary factor. (See: *Investment*.)†

Speculative warrant premium The market price of the warrant minus the warrant's intrinsic value.°

Speculator One who is willing to assume a relatively large risk in the hope of gain.††

Spin off The separation of a subsidiary or division of a corporation from its parent by issuing shares in a new corporate entity. Shareowners in the parent receive shares in the new company in proportion to their original holding and the total value remains approximately the same.††

Split The division of the outstanding shares of a corporation into a larger number of shares. A 3-for-1 split by a company with 1 million shares outstanding results in 3 million shares outstanding. Each holder of 100 shares before the 3-for-1 split would have 300 shares, although his proportionate equity in the company would remain the same; 100

parts of 1 million are the equivalent of 300 parts of 3 million. Ordinarily splits must be voted by directors and approved by shareholders. (See: *Stock dividend*.)

Spontaneous sources of funds Funds arising through the normal course of business, such as accounts payable generated from the purchase of goods for resale.°

Standard deviation A measure of the spread or dispersion of a series of numbers around the expected value. The standard deviation tells us how well the expected value represents a series of values.°

Step-up in conversion A feature that is sometimes written into the contract which allows the conversion ratio to decline in steps over time. This feature encourages early conversion when the conversion value is greater than the call price.°

Stock ahead Sometimes an investor who has entered an order to buy or sell a stock at a certain price will see transactions at that price reported on the ticker tape while his own order has not been executed. The reason is that other buy and sell orders at the same price came in to the specialist ahead of his and had priority. (See: *Book, Specialist*.)†

Stock dividend A dividend paid in securities rather than cash. The dividend may be additional shares of the issuing company, or shares of another company (usually a subsidiary) held by the company.††

Stock Index Futures Futures contracts based on market indexes, e.g., NYSE Composite Index Futures Contracts.††

Stock split A division of shares by a ratio set by the board of directors-2 for 1, 3 for 1, 3 for 2, and so on. Stock splits usually indicate that the company's stock has risen in price to a level that the directors feel limits the trading appeal of the stock. The par value is divided by the ratio set, and new shares are issued to the current stockholders of record to increase their shares to the stated level. For example, a two-for-one split would increase your holdings from one share to two shares.°

Stockholder of record A stockholder whose name is registered on the books of the issuing corporation.†

Stockholder wealth maximization Maximizing the wealth of the firm's shareholders through achieving the highest possible value for the firm in the marketplace. It is the overriding objective of the firm and should influence all decisions.°

Stockholders' equity The total ownership position of preferred and common stockholders.°

Stop limit order   A stop order which becomes a limit order after the specified stop price has been reached. (See: *Limit order, Stop order.*)†

Stop order   An order to buy at a price above or sell at a price below the current market. Stop buy orders are generally used to limit loss or protect unrealized profits on a short sale. Stop sell orders are generally used to protect unrealized profits or limit loss on a holding. A stop order becomes a market order when the stock sells at or beyond the specified price and, thus, may not necessarily be executed at that price.†

Stopped stock   A service performed—in most cases by the specialist—for an order given him by a commission broker. Let's say XYZ just sold at $50 a share. Broker A comes along with an order to buy 100 shares at the market. The lowest offer is $50.50. Broker A believes he can do better for his client than $50.50, perhaps might get the stock at $50.25. But he doesn't want to take a chance that he'll miss the market—that is, the next sale might be $50.50 and the following one even higher. So he asks the specialist if he will stop 100 at ½ ($50.50). The specialist agrees. The specialist guarantees Broker A he will get 100 shares at 50½ if the stock sells at that price. In the meantime, if the specialist or broker A succeeds in executing the order at $50.25, the stop is called off. (See: *Specialist.*)†

Street name   Securities held in the name of a broker instead of his customer's name are said to be carried in a *street name*. This occurs when the securities have been bought on margin or when the customer wishes the security to be held by the broker.†

Subchapter S corporation   A special corporate form of ownership in which profit is taxed as direct income to the stockholders and thus is only taxed once as would be true of a partnership. The stockholders still receive all the organizational benefits of a corporation, including limited liability. The Subchapter S designation can only apply to corporations with up to 35 stockholders.°

Subdivision   Any legal and authorized political entity under a state's jurisdiction (county, city, water district, school district, etc.).°°

Subordinated debenture   An unsecured bond in which payment to the holder will take place only after designated senior debenture holders are satisfied.°

Swapping   Selling one security and buying a similar one almost at the same time to take a loss, usually for tax purposes.††

Switch order or contingent order   An order for the purchase (sale) of one stock and the sale (purchase) of another stock at a stipulated price difference.†

Switching   Selling one security and buying another.†

Syndicate   A group of investment bankers who together underwrite and distribute a new issue of securities or a large block of an outstanding issue.†

Synergy   The recognition that the whole may be equal to more than the sum of the parts. The "2 + 2 = 5" effect.

Take-over   The acquiring of one corporation by another—usually in a friendly merger but sometimes marked by a "proxy fight." In "unfriendly" take-over attempts, the potential buying company may offer a price well above current market values, new securities, and other inducements to stockholders. The management of the subject company might ask for a better price or fight the take-over or merger with another company. (See: *Proxy.*)†

Tax base   The total resources available for taxation.°°

Tax-exempt bond   Another name for a municipal bond. The interest on a municipal bond is presently exempt from Federal income tax.°°

Tax loss carry-forward   A loss that can be carried forward for a number of years to offset future taxable income and perhaps be utilized by another firm in a merger or an acquisition.°

Tax shelter   A medium or process intended to reduce or eliminate the tax burden of an individual. They range from such conventional ones as tax-exempt municipal securities and interest or dividend exclusion to sophisticated limited partnerships in real estate, cattle raising, equipment leasing, oil drilling, research and development activities and motion picture production.††

Technical insolvency   A firm is unable to pay its bills as they come due.°

Technical research   Analysis of the market and stocks based on supply and demand. The technician studies price movements, volume, and trends and patterns which are revealed by charting these factors, and attempts to assess the possible effect of current market action on future supply and demand for securities and individual issues. (See: *Fundamental research.*)†

Temporary current assets   Current assets that will be reduced or converted to cash within the normal operating cycle of the firm.°

Tender offer   A public offer to buy shares from existing stockholders of one public corporation by another company or other organization under specified terms good for a certain time period. Stockholders are asked to "tender" (surrender) their holdings for stated value, usually at a premium above current market price, subject to the tendering of a minimum and maximum number of shares.††

Term issue An issue that has a single maturity.°°

Term loan An intermediate-length loan in which credit is generally extended from one to seven years. The loan is usually repaid in monthly or quarterly installments over its life rather than the one single period.°

Term structure of interest rates The relationship between interest rates and maturities for securities of equal risk. Usually government securities are used for the term structure.°

Terms of exchange The buy-out ratio or terms of trade in a merger or an acquisition.°

Thin market A market in which there are comparatively few bids to buy or offers to sell, or both. The phrase may apply to a single security or to the entire stock market. In a thin market, price fluctuations between transactions are usually larger than when the market is liquid. A thin market in a particular stock may reflect lack of interest in that issue or a limited supply of or demand for stock in the market. (See: *Bid and asked, Liquidity, Offer*.)†

Third market Trading of stock exchange listed securities in the over-the-counter market by non-exchange-member brokers.††

Tight money A term to indicate time periods in which financing may be difficult to find and interest rates may be quite high by normal standards.°

Time order An order which becomes a market or limited price order at a specified time.†

Time value The part of an option premium that is in excess of the intrinsic value.††

Tips Supposedly "inside" information on corporate affairs.†

Trade credit Credit provided by sellers or suppliers in the normal course of business.°

Trader Individuals who buy and sell for their own accounts for short-term profit. Also, an employee of a broker/dealer or financial institution who specializes in handling purchases and sales of securities for the firm and/or its clients. (See: *Investor, Speculator*.)††

Trading market The secondary market for outstanding securities.°

Trading post One of 23 trading locations on the floor of the New York Stock Exchange at which stocks assigned to that location are bought and sold. About 75 stocks are traded at each post.†

Transaction exposure Foreign exchange gains and losses resulting from *actual* international transactions. These may be hedged through the foreign exchange market, the money market, or the currency futures market.°

Transfer This term may refer to two different operations. For one, the delivery of a stock certificate from the seller's broker to the buyer's broker and legal change of ownership, normally accomplished within a few days. For another, to record the change of ownership on the books of the corporation by the transfer agent. When the purchaser's name is recorded, dividends, notices of meetings, proxies, financial reports, and all pertinent literature sent by the issuer to its securities holders are mailed direct to the new owner. (See: *Registrar, Street name*.)††

Transfer agent A transfer agent keeps a record of the name of each registered shareowner, his or her address, the number of shares owned, and sees that certificates presented for transfer are properly cancelled and new certificates issued in the name of the new owner. (See: *Registrar*.)††

Translation exposure The foreign-located assets and liabilities of a multinational corporation, which are denominated in foreign currency units, and are exposed to losses and gains due to changing exchange rates. This is called accounting, or translation, exposure.°

Treasury bills Short-term U.S. Treasury securities issued in minimum denominations of $10,000 and usually having original maturities of 3, 6, or 12 months. Investors purchase bills at prices lower than the face value of the bills; the return to the investors is the difference between the price paid for the bills and the amount received when the bills are sold or when they mature. Treasury bills are the type of security used most frequently in open market operations.¶

Treasury bonds Long-term U.S. Treasury securities usually having initial maturities of more than 10 years and issued in denominations of $1,000 or more, depending on the specific issue. Bonds pay interest semiannually, with principal payable at maturity.¶

Treasury notes Intermediate-term coupon-bearing U.S. Treasury securities having initial maturities from 1 to 10 years and issued in denominations of $1,000 or more, depending on the maturity of the issue. Notes pay interest semiannually, and the principal is payable at maturity.¶

Treasury stock Stock issued by a company, but later reacquired. It may be held in the company's treasury indefinitely, reissued to the public, or retired. Treasury stock receives no dividends, and has no vote while held by the company.††

Trend analysis An analysis of performance that is made over a number of years in order to ascertain significant patterns.°

Trust receipt An instrument acknowledging that the borrower holds the inventory and proceeds for sale in trust for the lender.°

Two-step buy-out An acquisition plan in which the acquiring company attempts to gain control by offering a very high cash price for 51 percent of the shares of the target company. At the same time the acquiring company announces a second lower price that will be paid, either in cash, stock or bonds, at a subsequent point in time.°

Underwriter (See: *Investment banker*.)

Underwriting The process of selling securities and, at the same time, assuring the seller a specified price. Underwriting is done by investment bankers and represents a form of risk taking.°

Underwriting spread The difference between the price that a selling corporation receives for an issue of securities and the price at which the issue is sold to the public. The spread is the fee that investment bankers and others receive for selling securities.°

Underwriting syndicate A group of investment bankers that is formed to share the risk of a security offering and also to facilitate the distribution of the securities.°

Unlimited tax bond A bond secured by pledge of taxes that are not limited by rate or amount.°°

Unlisted A security not listed on a stock exchange. (See: *Over-the-counter*.)†

Unsecured debt A loan which requires no assets as collateral, but allows the bondholder a general claim against the corporation rather than a lien against specific assets.°

Up tick A term used to designate a transaction made at a price higher than the preceding transaction. Also called a *plus-tick*. A *zero-plus* tick is a term used for a transaction at the same price as the preceding trade but higher than the preceding different price.

Conversely, a *down tick*, or *minus* tick, is a term used to designate a transaction made at a price lower than the preceding trade.

A plus sign, or a minus sign, is displayed throughout the day next to the last price of each company's stock traded at each trading

post on the floor of the New York Stock Exchange. (See: *Short sale*.)†

Variable annuity A life insurance policy where the annuity premium (a set amount of dollars) is immediately turned into units of a portfolio of stocks. Upon retirement, the policyholder is paid according to accumulated units, the dollar value of which varies according to the performance of the stock portfolio. Its objective is to preserve, through stock investment, the purchasing value of the annuity which otherwise is subject to erosion through inflation.††

Variable costs Costs that move directly with a change in volume. Examples are raw materials, factory labor, and sales commissions.°

Volume The number of shares traded in a security or an entire market during a given period. Volume is usually considered on a daily basis and a daily average is computed for longer periods.†

Voting right The common stockholder's right to vote their stock in the affairs of a company. Preferred stock usually has the right to vote when preferred dividends are in default for a specified period. The right to vote may be delegated by the stockholder to another person. (See: *Cumulative voting, Proxy*.)††

Warrant A certificate giving the holder the right to purchase securities at a stipulated price within a specified time limit or perpetually. Sometimes a warrant is offered with securities as an inducement to buy. (See: *Rights*.)††

Warrant intrinsic value (See: *Minimum warrant value*.)°

Weighted average cost of capital The computed cost of capital determined by multiplying the cost of each item in the optimal capital structure by its weighted representation in the overall capital structure and summing up the results.°

When issued A short form of "when, as, and if issued." The term indicates a conditional transaction in a security authorized for issuance but not as yet actually issued. All "when issued" transactions are on an "if" basis, to be settled if and when the actual security is issued and the exchange or National Association of Securities Dealers rules the transactions are to be settled.†

Wire house A member firm of an exchange maintaining a communications network linking either its own branch offices, offices of correspondent firms, or a combination of such offices.†

Working capital management The financing and management of the current assets of the firm. The financial manager determines the mix between temporary and permanent "current assets" and the nature of the financing arrangement.°

Working control Theoretically, ownership of 51 percent of a company's voting stock is necessary to exercise control. In practice— and this is particularly true in the case of a large corporation—effective control sometimes can be exerted through ownership, individually or by a group acting in concert, of less than 50 percent.†

Yield Also known as return. The dividends or interest paid by a company expressed as a percentage of the current price. A stock with a current market value of $3.20 is said to return 8 percent ($3.20 ÷ by $40.00). The current yield on a bond is figured the same way.††

Yield curve A curve that shows interest rates at a specific point in time for all securities having equal risk but different maturity dates. Usually government securities are used to construct such curves. The yield curve is also referred to as the term structure of interest rates.°

Yield to maturity The yield of a bond to maturity takes into account the price discount from or premium over the face amount. It is greater than the current yield when the bond is selling at a discount and less than the current yield when the bond is selling at a premium.†

Zero coupon bonds Bonds which do not convey a coupon (i.e., do not pay interest) but which are offered at a substantial discount from par value and appreciate to their full value (usually $1,000) at maturity. However, under U.S. tax law, the imputed interest is taxed as it accrues. The appeal of Zero coupon bonds is primarily for IRA and other tax sheltered retirement accounts.

Acquisition Takeover Glossary

Asset Play[1] A firm whose underlying assets are worth substantially more (after paying off the firm's liabilities) than the market value of its stock.

Bear hug An unnegotiated offer, in the form of a letter made directly to the board of directors of the target company. The price and terms are sufficiently detailed so that the directors are obliged to make the offer public. The offer states a time limit for a response and may threaten a tender offer or other action if it is not accepted.

Breakup value[1] The sum of the values of the firm's assets if sold off separately.

Crown jewel option[1] The strategem of selling off or spinning off the asset that makes the firm an attractive takeover candidate.

Four-nine position[1] A holding of approximately 4.9% of the outstanding shares of a company. At 5%, the holder must file a form [13d] with the SEC, revealing his position. Thus, a four-nine position is about the largest position that one can quietly hold.

Black knight[1] A potential acquirer that management opposes and would prefer to find an alternative to (i.e. a *white knight*).

Going private[1] The process of buying back the publicly held stock so that what was heretofore a public firm becomes private.

Golden handcuffs[1] Employment agreement that makes the departure of upper level managers very costly to them. For instance, such managers may lose very attractive stock option rights by leaving prior to their normal retirement age.

Golden handshake[1] A provision in a preliminary agreement to be acquired in which the target firm gives the acquiring firm an option to purchase its shares or assets at attractive prices or to receive a substantial bonus if the proposed takeover does not occur.

Golden parachute[1] Extremely generous separation payments for upper level executives that are required to be fulfilled if the firm's control shifts.

Greenmail[1] Incentive payments to dissuade the interest of outsiders who may otherwise seek control of a firm. The payment frequently takes the form of a premium price for the outsiders' shares, coupled with an agreement from them to avoid buying more stock for a set period of time.

The firm bears the cost of the payment. The stock price generally falls after the payment and the removal of the outside threat.

In play[1] The status of being a recognized takeover candidate.

Junk bonds[1] High-risk, high-yield bonds that are often used to finance takeovers.

LBO[1] A leveraged buyout. A purchase of a company financed largely by debt that is backed by the firm's own assets.

Loaded laggard[1] A stock of a company whose assets, particularly its liquid assets, have high values relative to the stock's price.

Lockup agreement[1] An agreement between an acquirer and target that makes the

———
[1] Source: From the *AAII Journal*, American Association of *Individual Investors*, 612 North Michigan Avenue, Chicago, IL 60611. Excerpted from Ben Branch "White Knight Rescues Investors From Terminology."

target very unattractive to any other acquirer; similar to a *golden handshake*.

Mezzanine financing Debt financing subordinate to the claims of the senior debt. This financing often has equity participation in the form of stock options, warrants or conversion to cheap stock.

Nibble strategy A takeover approach involving the purchase in the public market of minority stock position in the target company and a subsequent tender offer for the rest of the target stock.

PacMan defense[1] The tactic of seeking to acquire the firm that has targeted your own firm as a takeover prospect.

Poison pill[1] A provision in the corporate by-laws or other governance documents providing for a very disadvantageous result for a potential acquirer should its ownership position be allowed to exceed some preassigned threshold. For example, if anyone acquires more than 20% of Company A's stock, the acquirer might then have to sell $100 worth of its own stock to other shareholders at $50.

Raider A hostile outside party that seeks to take over other companies.

Saturday night special A seven day cash tender offer for all of the target firm's stock. It is usually launched on a Saturday on the assumption that the target company will have difficulty mobilizing its key advisors in reaction to the offer.

Scorched earth defense[1] A tactic in which the defending company's management engages in practices that reduce their company's value to such a degree that it is no longer attractive to the potential acquirer. This approach is more often threatened than actually employed.

Senior debt financing The issuance of debt instruments having first claim on a firm's assets (secured debt) or cash flow (unsecured debt).

Shark repellant[1] Anti-takeover provisions such as the poison pill.

Short swing profit[1] A gain made by an insider (including anyone with more than 10% of the stock) who holds stock for less than six months. Such gains must be paid back to the company whose shares were sold.

Standstill agreement[1] A reciprocal understanding between a company's management and an outside party that usually owns a significant minority position. Each party gives up certain rights in exchange for corresponding concessions by the other party. For example, the outside group may agree to limit its stock purchases to keep its ownership percentage below some level (for instance, 20%). In exchange, management may agree to a minority board representation by the outsider.

Swipe An unnegotiated offer to purchase the shares of a target company's stock made after the target's board has announced its intention to sell the company (usually in a leveraged buyout to management). The swipe price is higher than that initially proposed by the board of directors.

Tender offer An offer by a firm to buy the stock of another firm (target) by going directly to the stockholders of the target. The offer is often made over the opposition of the management of the target firm.

13d[1] A form that must be filed with the SEC when a single investor or an associated group owns 5% or more of a company's stock. The form reveals the size of the holding and the investor's intentions.

Two-tier offer[1] A takeover device in which a relatively high per share price is paid for controlling interest in a target and a lesser per share price is paid for the remainder.

White knight defense[1] Finding an alternative and presumably more friendly acquirer than the present takeover threat.

White squire defense[1] Finding an important ally to purchase a strong minority position (for example, 25%) of the potential acquisition's stock. Presumably this ally (the "white squire") will oppose and hopefully block the efforts of any hostile firm seeking to acquire the vulnerable firm.

Stock Exchanges*

Common Stocks (shares of ownership in a corporation) are traded on several exchanges. The best known are the New York Stock Exchange and the American Stock Exchange, both located in Manhattan's financial district. Generally, the stocks of the largest companies are traded on the New York Stock Exchange, while somewhat smaller companies are traded on the American Exchange. There are also a number of regional exchanges such as the Midwest Exchange in Chicago and the Pacific Exchange in San Francisco. These exchanges trade stocks of local corporations as well as stocks listed on the New York and American Exchanges.

In addition, there is the Over-The-Counter-Market (OTC) which, unlike the exchanges previously mentioned, does not have a specific location but consists of a network of brokers and dealers linked by telephone and private wires. Smaller or relatively new companies are traded on the OTC. Trading information for many (but far from all) stocks on the OTC market is collected and displayed on a computerized system, the National Association of Security Dealers Automatic Quote System (NASDAQ).

Large institutional traders (mutual and pension funds, insurance companies, etc.) often trade blocks of stocks directly with one another. This information is collected and displayed on the Instinet System.

Major Stock Exchanges

UNITED STATES

AMERICAN STOCK EXCHANGE, INC.
86 Trinity Place
New York, New York 10006

BOSTON STOCK EXCHANGE, INC.
One Boston Place
Boston, Massachusetts 02109

THE CINCINNATI STOCK EXCHANGE, INC.
205 Dixie Terminal Building
Cincinnati, Ohio 45202

MIDWEST STOCK EXCHANGE, INC.
440 South LaSalle Street
Chicago, Illinois 60603

---

* See page 552 for a listing of futures and options exchanges.

NEW YORK STOCK EXCHANGE, INC.
11 Wall Street
New York, New York 10005

PACIFIC STOCK EXCHANGE, INC.
618 South Spring Street
Los Angeles, California 90014

301 Pine Street
San Francisco, California 94104

PHILADELPHIA STOCK EXCHANGE, INC.
1900 Market Street
Philadelphia, Pennsylvania 19103

SPOKANE STOCK EXCHANGE, INC.
206 Radio Central Building
Spokane, Washington 99201

FOREIGN

AUSTRALIA

SYDNEY STOCK EXCHANGE
Exchange Centre
20 Bond Street
Australia Square
P.O. Box H224
Sydney, 2000

BELGIUM

BRUSSELS STOCK EXCHANGE
Palais de la Bourse
1000 Brussels

CANADA

ALBERTA STOCK EXCHANGE
300–5th Avenue S.W.
Calgary, Alberta T2P 3C4

BOURSE DE MONTRÉAL
The Stock Exchange Tower
800 Victoria Square
Montreal, Quebec H4Z 1A9

TORONTO STOCK EXCHANGE
2 First Canadian Place
Toronto, Ontario M5X 1J2

VANCOUVER STOCK EXCHANGE
Stock Exchange Tower
P.O. Box 10333
609 Granville Street
Vancouver, B.C. V7Y 1H1

WINNIPEG STOCK EXCHANGE
500 Commodity Exchange Tower
360 Main Street
Winnipeg, Manitoba R3C 324

FRANCE

BOURSE DE PARIS—PARIS STOCK
EXCHANGE
4, Place de la Bourse
F-75080 Paris Cedex 02

GERMANY

FRANKFURTER WERTPAPIERBORE—
FRANKFORT EXCHANGE
Börsenplatz 6, P.O. 100811
D-6000 Frankfurt am Main 1

HONG KONG

STOCK EXCHANGE OF HONG KONG
One and Two Exchange Square
Central Hong Kong

JAPAN

TOKYO STOCK EXCHANGE
2–1 Nihombashi Kayuto-Cho
Cho-Ku, Tokyo 103

THE NETHERLANDS

AMSTERDAMSE EFFECTENBEURS—
AMSTERDAM STOCK EXCHANGE
Beursplein 5
1012 JW Amsterdam

SWITZERLAND

GENEVA STOCK EXCHANGE
Rue de la Confédération 8
CH-1204 Geneva

ZÜRICH STOCK EXCHANGE
Bleicherweg 5
P.O. Box CH-8021
Zürich

UNITED KINGDOM

THE INTERNATIONAL STOCK
EXCHANGE OF THE UNITED
KINGDOM AND THE REPUBLIC
OF IRELAND LIMITED
Old Broad Street
London, England EC 2N 1HP

Securities and Exchange Commission

JUDICIARY PLAZA
450 FIFTH STREET, NW
WASHINGTON, DC 20549
PUBLIC AFFAIRS: 202-942-0020
FREEDOM OF INFORMATION ACT:
202-942-4320
PUBLICATIONS
202-942-4040
PUBLIC REFERENCE ROOM
202-942-8090

FULL AND FAIR DISCLOSURE

The Securities Act of 1933 requires issuers of securities and their controlling persons making public offerings of securities in interstate commerce or through the mails, directly or by others on their behalf, to file with the Commission registration statements containing financial and other pertinent data about the issuer and the securities being offered. It is unlawful to sell such securities unless a registration statement is in effect. There are limited exemptions, such as government securities, nonpublic offerings, and intrastate offerings, as well as certain offerings not exceeding $1,500,000. The effectiveness of a registration statement may be refused or suspended after a public hearing, if the statement contains material misstatements or omissions, thus barring sale of the securities until it is appropriately amended.

Registration of securities does not imply approval of the issue by the Commission or that the Commission has found the registration disclosures to be accurate. It does not insure investors against loss in their purchase but serves rather to provide information upon which investors may make an informed and realistic evaluation of the worth of the securities.

Persons responsible for filing false information with the Commission subject themselves to the risk of fine or imprisonment or both. Persons connected with the public offering may be liable for damages to purchasers of the securities if the disclosures in the registration statement and prospectus are materially defective. Also, the above act contains antifraud provisions which apply generally to the sale of securities, whether or not registered (48 Stat. 74; 15 U.S.C. 77a et seq.).

REGULATION OF SECURITIES MARKETS

The Securities Exchange Act of 1934 assigns to the Commission board regulatory responsibilities over the securities markets, the self-regulatory organizations within the securities industry, and persons conducting a business in securities. Persons who execute transactions in securities generally are required to register with the Commission as broker-dealers. Securities exchanges and certain clearing agencies are required to register with the Commission, and associations of brokers or dealers are permitted to register with the Commission. The Act also provides

---

Source: This material was abstracted from the United States Government Manual.

for the establishment of the Municipal Securities Rulemaking Board to formulate rules for the municipal securities industry.

The Commission oversees the self-regulatory activities of the national securities exchanges and associations, registered clearing agencies, and the Municipal Securities Rulemaking Board. In addition, the Commission regulates industry professionals, such as securities brokers and dealers, certain municipal securities professionals, and transfer agents.

The Securities Exchange Act authorizes national securities exchanges, national securities associations, clearing agencies, and the Municipal Securities Rulemaking Board to adopt rules that are designed, among other things to promote just and equitable principles of trade and to protect investors. The Commission is required to approve or disapprove most proposed rules of these self-regulatory organizations and has the power to abrogate or amend existing rules of the national securities exchanges, national securities associations, and the Municipal Securities Rulemaking Board.

In addition, the Commission has broad rulemaking authority over the activities of brokers, dealers, municipal securities dealers, securities information processors, and transfer agents. The Commission may regulate such securities trading practices as short sales and stabilizing transactions. It may regulate the trading of options on national securities exchanges and the activities of members of exchanges who trade on the trading floors and may adopt rules governing broker-dealer sales practices in dealing with investors. The Commission also is authorized to adopt rules concerning the financial responsibility of brokers and dealers and reports to be made by them.

The Securities Exchange Act also requires the filing of registration statements and annual and other reports with national securities exchanges and the Commission by companies whose securities are listed upon the exchanges, and by companies that have assets of $5 million or more and 500 or more shareholders of record. In addition, companies that distributed securities pursuant to a registration statement declared effective by the Commission under the Securities Act of 1933, must also file annual and other reports with the Commission. Such applications and reports must contain financial and other data prescribed by the Commission as necessary or appropriate for the protection of investors and to issue fair dealing. In addition, the solicitation of proxies, authorizations, or consents from holders of such registered securities must be made in accordance with rules and regulations prescribed by the Commission. These rules provide for disclosures to securities holders of information relevant to the subject matter of the solicitation.

Disclosure of the holdings and transactions by officers, directors, and large (10 percent) holders of equity securities of companies is also required, and any and all persons who acquire more than 5 percent of certain equity securities are required to file detailed information with the Commission and any exchange upon which such securities may be traded. Moreover, any person making a tender offer for certain classes of equity securities is required to file reports with the Commission, if as a result of the tender offer such person would own more than 5 percent of the outstanding shares of the particular class of equity involved. The Commission also is authorized to promulgate rules governing the repurchase by a corporate issuer of its own securities.

REGULATION OF MUTUAL FUNDS AND OTHER INVESTMENT COMPANIES

The Investment Company Act of 1940 (15 U.S.C. 80a-1–80a-64) requires investment companies to register with the Commission and regulates their activities to protect investors. The regulation covers sales and management fees, composition of boards of directors, and capital structure. The act prohibits investment companies from engaging in various transactions, including transactions with affiliated persons unless the Commission first determines that such transactions are fair. In addition, the act provides a somewhat parallel but less stringent regulation of business development companies. Under the act, the Commission may institute court action to enjoin the consummation of mergers and other plans for reorganization of investment companies if such plans are unfair to security holders. It also may impose sanctions by administrative proceedings against investment company managements for violations of the act and other federal securities laws, and file court actions to enjoin acts and practices of management officials involving breaches of fiduciary duty involving personal misconduct and to disqualify such officials from office.

REGULATION OF COMPANIES CONTROLLING UTILITIES

The Public Utility Holding Company Act of 1935 (15 U.S.C. 79–79z-6) provides for regulation by the Commission of the purchase and sale of securities and assets by companies in electric and gas utility holding company systems, their intra-system transactions and service and management arrangements. It limits holding companies to a single coordinated utility system and requires simplification of complex corporate and capital structures and elimination of unfair distribution of voting power among holders of system securities.

The issuance and sale of securities by holding companies and their subsidiaries, unless exempt (subject to conditions and terms which the Commission is empowered to impose) as an issue expressly authorized by the state commission in the state in which the issuer is incorporated, must be found by the Commission to meet statutory standards.

The purchase and sale of utility properties and other assets may not be made in contravention of rules, regulations, or orders of the Commission regarding the consideration to be received, maintenance of competitive conditions, fees and commissions, accounts, disclosure of interest, and similar matters. In passing upon proposals for reorganization, merger, or consolidation, the Commission must be satisfied that the objectives of the act generally are complied with and that the terms of the proposal are fair and equitable to all classes of security holders affected.

REGULATION OF INVESTMENT ADVISERS

The Investment Advisers Act of 1940 (15 U.S.C. 80b-1–80b-21) provides that persons who, for compensation, engage in the business of advising others with respect to their security transactions must register with the Commission. The act prohibits certain types of fee arrangements, makes fraudulent or deceptive practices on the part of investment advisers unlawful, and requires, among other things, disclosure of any adverse interests the advisers may have in transactions executed for clients. The act authorizes the Commission, by rule, to define fraudulent and deceptive practices and prescribe means to prevent those practices.

REHABILITATION OF FAILING CORPORATIONS

Chapter 11, section 1109(a), of the Bankruptcy Code (11 U.S.C. 1109) provides for Commission participation as a statutory party in corporate reorganization proceedings administered in Federal courts. The principal functions of the Commission are to protect the interests of public investors involved in such cases through efforts to ensure their adequate representation and to participate on legal and policy issues which are of concern to public investors generally.

REPRESENTATION OF DEBT SECURITIES HOLDERS

The interests of purchasers of publicly offered debt securities issued pursuant to trust indentures are safeguarded under the provisions of the Trust Indenture Act of 1939 (15 U.S.C. 77aaa–77bbb). This act, among other things, requires the exclusion from such indentures of certain types of exculpatory clauses and the inclusion of certain protective provisions. The independence of the indenture trustee, who is a representative of the debt holder, is assured by proscribing certain relationships that might conflict with the proper exercise of his duties.

ENFORCEMENT ACTIVITIES

The Commission's enforcement activities are designed to secure compliance with the federal securities laws administered by the Commission and the rules and regulations adopted thereunder. These activities include measures to compel obedience to the disclosure requirements of the registration and other provisions of the acts; to prevent fraud and deception in the purchase and sale of securities; to obtain court orders enjoining acts and practices that operate as a fraud upon investors or otherwise violate the laws; to suspend or revoke the registrations of brokers, dealers, investment companies and investment advisers who willfully engage in such acts and practices; to suspend or bar from association persons associated with brokers, dealers, investment companies and investment advisers who have violated any provision of the federal securities laws; and to prosecute persons who have engaged in fraudulent activities, or other willful violations of those laws. In addition, attorneys, accountants, and other professionals who violate the securities laws face possible loss of their privilege to practice before the Commission. To this end, private investigations are conducted into complaints or other evidences of securities violations. Evidence thus established of law violations is used in appropriate administrative proceedings to revoke registration or in actions instituted in federal courts to restrain or enjoin such activities. Where the evidence tends to establish fraud or other willful violation of the securities laws, the facts are referred to the Attorney General for criminal prosecution of the offenders. The Commission may assist in such prosecutions.

SOURCES OF INFORMATION

Consumer Activities Publications detailing the Commission's activities, which include material of assistance to the potential investor, are available from the Publications Unit. In addition, the Office of Filings, Information and Consumer Services answers questions from investors, assists investors with specific problems regarding their relations with broker-dealers and companies, and advises the Commission and other offices and divisions regarding problems frequently encountered by investors and possible regulatory solutions to such problems. Phone, 202-942-9040.

INVESTOR INFORMATION AND PROTECTION

Complaints and inquiries may be directed to headquarters or to any regional office. Registration statements and other public documents filed with the Commission are available for public inspection in the public reference room at the home office. Much of the information also is available at the Northeast and Midwest regional offices. Copies of the public material may be purchased from the Commission's contract copying service at prescribed rates.

Small Business Activities Information on security laws which pertain to small businesses in relation to securities offerings may be obtained from the Commission. Phone, 202-942-2950.

Reading Rooms The Commission maintains a public reference room (phone, 202-272-7450) and also a library (phone, 202-272-2618) where additional information may be obtained.

REGIONAL/DISTRICT OFFICES (Securities and Exchange Commission)

Region/District	Address	Telephone
1. NORTHEAST		
(NEW YORK, NY)	Suite 1300, 7 World Trade Ctr., 10048	212-748-8000
Boston, MA	Suite 600, 73 Tremont St., 02108-3912	617-424-5900
Philadelphia, PA	Suite 1005 E., Curtis Ctr., 601 Walnut St., 19106-3322	215-597-3100
2. SOUTHEAST		
(MIAMI, FL)	Suite 200, 1401 Brickell Ave., 33131	305-536-4700
Atlanta, GA	Suite 1000, 3475 Lenox Rd. NE., 30326-1232	404-842-7600
3. MIDWEST		
(CHICAGO, IL)	Suite 1400, Northwestern Atrium Ctr., 500 W. Madison St., 60661-2511	312-353-7390
4. CENTRAL		
(DENVER, CO)	Suite 4800, 1801 California St., 80202-2648	303-391-6800
Fort Worth, TX	Suite 1900, 801 Cherry St., 76102	817-334-3821
Salt Lake City, UT	500 Key Bank Twr., 50 S. Main St., 84144-0402	801-524-5796
5. PACIFIC		
(LOS ANGELES, CA)	Suite 1100, 5670 Wilshire Blvd., 90036-3648	213-965-3998
San Francisco, CA	11th Fl., 44 Montgomery St., 94104	415-705-2500

Mutual Funds

Mutual Fund Reporting Regulations

Current SEC regulations concerning mutual fund reporting practices which went into effect May 1988 require that an easy-to-read table giving all fund charges must appear near the front of all prospectuses. Included must be such items as front end and back end loads, 12b-1 plans to recover marketing and distribution costs, and sales loads imposed on reinvested dividends applied everytime the fund reinvests dividends. Typically, fund expense ratios (annual operating expenses to assets) range from .7% to 1%.

Advertisements that contain yields must calculate yields (capital gains plus dividends) on a consistent basis prescribed by the SEC, taking into account any front end or redemption sales charges. To put the yield figure into perspective, ads must provide one, five and ten year total return information. Returns assume that all distributions are reinvested.

The SEC has tightened up on advertisements quoting a fund's ranking. Regulations now require that ranking information includes such items as the name of the organization providing the ranking, the ranking time period, the types and number of funds included in the ranking, and whether any fees or loads have been waived during the ranking period.

Fund fees are often shown in the newspaper listing by means of letters after the fund's name, for example:

r   indicates a back end load or redemption fee

p   indicates a 12b-1 plan is in effect

t   indicates both a back end and a 12b-1 fee

N.L.   indicates there is no front end or back end load

How to Read Mutual Fund Quotations

The reporting of mutual fund information in the financial press has been expanded considerably during the last year or so.

The Wall Street Journal has recast its statistical presentation of mutual fund performance. Monday through Thursday data present the net asset value per share, daily price change and year to date percentage gain or loss. Friday's presentations have been greatly expanded. In addition to daily and year to date returns, Friday's tables include the latest four weeks and the most recent one, three and five year returns as well as rankings and fee data, as shown in the accompanying figure.

The Sunday *New York Times* financial section provides the *Morningstar* risk/return rating, the weekly percent return as well as the year to date, the one year and three year returns. The toll free phone numbers of the mutual fund families are also given.

Both of the above publications provide tables on the performance of the various mutual fund categories.

Extensive mutual fund quotations are also given in the *Investor's Business Daily*. The latter also provides toll free phone numbers and dollar size of the fund families. Rankings of a fund's total return are provided for performance over the prior three year period versus all other mutual funds ranking from A+ for the top 5%, A for the top 10%, B+ for the top 20%, to E below the top 70%. Note that the rankings are against all mutual funds, whereas in *The Wall Street Journal* funds are ranked against other funds with the same investment objective as defined in the table included here.

How to Read These Tables

Data come from two sources. The daily Net Asset Value (NAV) and Net Change calculations are supplied by the National Association of Securities Dealers (NASD). Performance and cost data come from **Lipper Analytical Services Inc.**

Though verified, the data cannot be guaranteed by Lipper or its data sources. Double-check with funds before investing.

Performance calculations assume reinvestment of all distribu-tions, and are after subtracting annual expenses. But figures don't reflect sales charges ("loads") or redemption fees.

These expanded tables appear Fridays. Other days, you'll find net asset value and its daily and year-to-date performance.

● **NET ASSET VALUE CHANGE**
Gain or loss, based on prior day's NAV.

● **NET ASSET VALUE**
Per-share value calculated by the fund.

● **COMPANY**
Fund families in bold face

● **TOTAL RETURN**
NAV change plus accumulated income for the period, in percent. Assumes reinvestment of all distributions. Percentages are annualized for periods exceeding one year. Calculations are based on latest data from fund.

● **MAXIMUM INITIAL SALES COMMISSION**
In percent. Based on prospectus.

			4 weeks		Three years				
		Year-to-date		Latest 12 months		Five years			
XYZ Mutual:									
8.43	−0.09	Bond p	IB	+16.4	+2.8	+16.4 B	+12.6 C	+11.6 B	5.50	1.17
8.43	−0.09	Growth	GR	+16.4	+2.8	+16.4 B	+12.6 C	+11.6 B	5.50	1.17
8.43	−0.09	Midcap Stock	MC	+16.4	+2.8	+16.4 B	+12.6 C	+11.6 B	5.50	1.17

● **FUND OBJECTIVE**
(See list on next page.)

● **FUND NAME**

● **ANNUAL EXPENSES**
Shown as a percentage, based on fund annual report. Covers all asset-based charges including distribution (12b-1) fees.

— Quotations Footnotes —

e–Ex-distribution. **f**–Previous day's quotation. **g**–Footnotes x and s apply. **i**–No valid comparison with other funds because of expense structure. **j**–Footnotes e and s apply. **k**–Recalculated by Lipper, using updated data. **p**–Distribution costs apply, 12b-1 **r**–Redemption charge may apply. **s**–Stock split or dividend. **t**–Footnotes p and r apply.

v–Footnotes x and e apply. **x**–Ex-dividend. **z**–Footnotes x, e and s apply.

NA–Not available due to incomplete price, performance or cost data. **NE**–Deleted by Lipper editor; data in question. **NL**–No Load (sales commission). **NN**–Fund doesn't wish to be tracked. **NS**–Fund didn't exist at start of period.

● **RANKING**
Compares performance among funds with same investment objectives and then ranked for time periods listed. Performance is measured from either the closest Thursday or month-end for periods of more than one year. **A**=top 20%; **B**=next 20%; **C**=middle 20%; **D**=next 20%; **E**=bottom 20%.

MUTUAL FUND OBJECTIVES

Categories compiled by The Wall Street Journal, based on classifications by Lipper Analytical Services Inc.

STOCK FUNDS

Capital Appreciation (CP): Seeks rapid capital growth, often through high portfolio turnover.

Growth (GR): Invests in companies expecting higher than average revenue and earnings growth.

Growth & Income (GI): Pursues both price and dividend growth. Category includes S&P 500 Index funds.

Equity Income (EI): Tends to favor stock with the highest dividends.

Small Company Growth (SC): Stocks of lesser-known, small companies.

MidCap (MC): Shares of middle-sized companies.

Sector (SE): Health/Biotechnology; Natural Resources; Environmental; Science & Technology; Specialty & Miscellaneous; Utility; Financial Services; Real Estate; Gold Oriented funds.

Global Stock (GL): Includes small company global; global flexible. Can invest in U.S.

International Stock (IL) (non-U.S.): International; European region; Pacific region; Japanese; Latin American; Canadian; Emerging Markets; International small company.

TAXABLE BOND FUNDS

Short-Term (SB): Ultrashort obligation and short investment grade corporate debt.

Short-Term U.S. (SG): Short-term U.S. Treasury; some funds can also hold agency debt.

Intermediate (Ib): Investment grade corporate debt of up to 10-year maturity.

Intermediate U.S. (IG): U.S. Treasury and government agency debt.

Long-Term (AB): Corporate A-rated; Corporate BBB-rated.

Long-Term U.S. (LG): U.S. Treasury; U.S. government; zero coupon.

General U.S. Taxable (GT): Can invest in different types of bonds.

High Yield Taxable (HC): High yield high-risk bonds.

Mortgage (MG): Ginnie Mae and general mortgage; Adjustable-Rate Mortgage.

World (WB): Short world multi-market; short world single-market and general world income foreign bonds.

MUNICIPAL BOND FUNDS

Short-Term Muni (SM): Short municipal debt; Short term California; single-states short municipal debt.

Intermediate Muni (IM): Intermediate-term municipal debt including single-state funds.

General Muni (GM): A variety of municipal debt.

Single-State Municipal (SS): Funds that invest in debt of individual states.

High Yield Municipal (HM): High yield low credit quality.

Insured (NM): California insured, New York insured, all other insured.

STOCK & BOND FUNDS

Multi-Purpose (MP): Balanced; convertible securities; income; flexible income; flexible portfolio and other multi-purpose fund that invest in both stocks and bonds.

TOP 50 NO- AND LOW-LOAD MUTUAL FUNDS *(Based on Five- and 10-Year Performance)*

What $10,000 Grew to in 5 years (1990 - 1994)*

Fidelity Select Computers	29,307
Fidelity Select Home Finance	28,824
Fidelity Select Electronics	28,232
INVESCO Strategic—Technology	27,633
PBHG Growth Fund	27,339
Fidelity Select Technology	27,308
Twentieth Century Giftrust Investors	27,023
T Rowe Price Science & Technology Fund	26,999
Fidelity Select Software & Computer	26,566
MFS Emerging Growth Fund/Class B	26,349
Thomson Opportunity Fund/Class B	25,951
Crabbe Huson Special Fund	24,368
Twentieth Century Ultra Investors	24,246
Kaufmann Fund	24,149
Strong Common Stock Fund	23,872
CGM Capital Development Fund (c)	23,542
Fidelity Select Health Care	23,441
Fidelity Blue Chip Growth Fund	23,266
John Hancock Freedom Regional Bank/Class B	23,065
INVESCO Strategic—Financial Services	22,840
Fidelity Select Medical Delivery	22,694
Oberweis Emerging Growth	22,611
Keystone Custodian Series/S-4	22,417
Fidelity Contrafund	22,405
Wasatch Aggressive Equity Fund	21,963
Berger One Hundred Fund	21,888
Fidelity Select Regional Banks	21,767
Parkstone Small Captlzn/Institutional C	21,693
Founders Discovery Fund	21,647
INVESCO Strategic—Leisure	21,637
Parnassus Fund	21,615
Westcore MIDCO Growth Fund/Institutional	21,593
Meridian Fund	21,544
Fidelity Select Automotive	21,426
State Street Research Capital Fund/Class C	21,327
Heartland Value Fund	21,311
Brandywine Fund	21,276
Fidelity Select Biotechnology	21,226
Fidelity Select Retailing	20,928
MAS Funds—Small Captlzn Value Portfolio	20,775
INVESCO Dynamics Fund	20,665
Alliance Growth Fund/Class B	20,665
Vanguard Specialized Ports—Health Care	20,602
Fidelity Select Transportation	20,094
Fidelity Select Brokerage & Invmt Mgmt	19,840
Crabbe Huson Equity Fund	19,813
Fidelity Select Financial Services	19,787
Robertson Stephens Emerging Growth	19,615
MIM Stock Appreciation FUnd	19,479
Harbor Capital Appreciation Fund	19,373

What $10,000 Grew to in 10 years (1985 - 1994)*

Twentieth Century Giftrust Investors	97,491
Fidelity Select Health Care	70,242
INVESCO Strategic—Health Sciences	64,858
Vanguard Specialized Ports—Health Care	61,935
INVESCO Strategic—Leisure	60,851
CGM Capital Development Fund (c)	60,265
Fidelity Overseas Fund	57,726
Berger One Hundred Fund	57,652
INVESCO Strategic—Technology	56,315
Twentieth Century Ultra Investors	55,844
Thomson Opportunity Fund/Class B	55,820
Fidelity Contrafund	54,827
Fidelity OTC Portfolio	52,629
T Rowe Price International Stock	52,280
Fidelity Magellan Fund	52,130
State Street Research Capital Fund/Class C	52,118
Fidelity Select Leisure	49,426
Fidelity Growth Company Fund	48,156
Vanguard/Trustees' Equity—International	47,436
Acorn Fund (c)	46,241
Scudder International Fund	44,880
SAFECO Equity Fund	44,740
IAI Regional Fund	43,488
SteinRoe Special Fund	42,991
Fidelity Retirement Growth	42,837
Scudder Japan Fund	42,702
Sit Growth Fund	42,524
Vanguard/PRIMECAP Fund	42,387
Twentieth Century Growth Investors	42,110
Founders Growth Fund	42,055
Mutual Beacon Fund	41,890
Dodge & Cox Stock Fund	41,873
Heartland Value Fund	41,443
Special Portfolios—Stock	41,370
State Farm Balanced Fund	41,324
SoGen International Fund (c)	41,221
Thomson Growth Fund/Class B	40,994
Janus Fund	40,909
Mutual Qualified Fund (c)	40,898
Twentieth Century Vista Investors	40,444
Meridian Fund	40,288
INVESCO Industrial Fund	39,960
CGM Mutual Fund	39,905
Founders Special Fund	39,774
Babson Enterprise Fund (c)	39,758
Keystone Custodian Series/S-4	39,661
Mutual Shares Fund (c)	39,647
INVESCO Dynamics Fund	39,407
MAS Funds—Value Portfolio	39,406
Lexington Corporate Leaders Trust	39,405

* Does not take into account sales commissions or income taxes that would have to be paid. Includes reinvestment of all dividends and capital gains.
(c) *Fund closed to new investors.*

Source: 1995 IBC/Donoghue's *Mutual Funds Almanac.*

TOP 10 NO- AND LOW-LOAD MUTUAL FUNDS LISTED BY FUND TYPE

Taxable Bond Funds

Funds	1994 Annual % Gain	Assets ($ Millions) as of 11/30/94
Benchmark Short Duration Portfolio	3.8%	$ 89.8
Strong Advantage Fund	3.6	878.3
Goldman Sachs Adj Rate Mortgage Fund	3.5	16.9
Eaton Vance Short-Term Treasury Fund	3.5	6.1
Pillar Short Term Fund/Class A	3.2	29.3
Fidelity Spartan High Income Fund	3.2	623.9
PRA Secs Tr—PRA Real Estate Secs Fund	3.0	103.4
SEI Daily Income Tr Corpt Daily Incm/Cl A	2.9	48.0
Pillar Short Term Fund/Class B	2.9	0.8
PIMCO Short-Term	2.9	89.9

Balanced Funds

Funds	1994 Annual % Gain	Assets ($ Millions) as of 11/30/94
State Farm Balanced Fund	4.8%	$ 370.5
Quest for Value Opportunity/Class C	4.4	8.0
Dreyfus Balanced Fund	4.0	89.0
Pax World Fund	2.6	386.4
INVESCO Value Trust—Total Return	2.5	301.1
Dodge & Cox Balanced Fund	2.0	708.4
Fidelity Puritan Fund	1.8	11,532.0
Columbia Balanced Fund	0.1	247.5
Westwood Balanced Fund/Institutional Class	0.0	3.4
Janus Balanced Fund	0.0	93.2

Tax-Exempt Bond Funds

Funds	1994 Annual % Gain	Assets ($ Millions) as of 11/30/94
Calvert T-F Reserves Limited-Term	2.4%	$ 600.0
Venture Municipal (+) Plus	2.3	182.0
Twentieth Century Tax-Exempt Short-Term	2.2	60.3
Vanguard Muni Bond—Short-Term	1.6	1,543.5
Merrill Lynch Muni Bond—Ltd Maturity/Cl A	1.4	684.7
Hough/The FL Tax-Free Short Term Fund	1.2	9.9
Colonial Short-Term T-E Fund/A Shares	1.2	13.7
Pacifica Short Term CA Tax-Free Fund	1.1	26.5
USAA Tax-Exempt Short-Term Fund	0.8	862.7
T Rowe Price MD S-T Tax-Free Bond Fund	0.6	78.4

Growth & Income Funds

Funds	1994 Annual % Gain	Assets ($ Millions) as of 11/30/94
Crabbe Huson Special Fund	11.7%	$ 346.2
SAFECO Equity Fund	9.9	438.2
The Yacktman Fund	8.8	280.1
Warburg, Pincus Growth and Income	7.6	606.4
Mutual Qualified Fund (c)	5.7	1,766.2
Norwest Income Stock Fund/Trust	5.6	30.9
Norwest Income Stock Fund/Investor A	5.6	11.0
Mutual Beacon Fund	5.6	2,017.9
Gateway Index Plus Fund	5.6	161.1
Dodge & Cox Stock Fund	5.2	529.4

Growth Funds

Funds	1994 Annual % Gain	Assets ($ Millions) as of 11/30/94
Seligman Communication and Info/Cl D	33.9%	$ 84.8
Alliance Technology Fund/Class C	27.7	7.5
Merrill Lynch Technology/Class B	25.5	572.0
PBHG Emerging Growth	23.8	142.7
Robertson Stephens Value Plus Fund	23.1	102.7
Fidelity Select Health Care	21.4	748.2
Montgomery Growth Fund	20.9	496.3
Fidelity Select Computers	20.5	163.4
Fidelity Select Medical Delivery	19.8	263.5
Strong Growth Fund	17.3	91.7

International Bond Funds

Funds	1994 Annual % Gain	Assets ($ Millions) as of 11/30/94
MetLife Ports—Intl Fixed Income/Class C	4.2%	$ 22.4
SEI Daily Income Tr Intl Fxd Income/Cl A	3.6	40.3
Pilgrim S-T Multi-Market Income Fund	2.9	16.2
Flex-funds Short-Term Global Income Fund	2.1	4.0
Benham European Government Bond Fund	1.5	200.9
Pilgrim S-T Multi-Market Income Fund II	0.7	5.4
Dean Witter Global Short-Term Income	0.2	160.1
Waddell & Reed Global Income Fund	0.1	11.2
Scudder Short Term Global Income Fund	-1.1	537.7
JH Freedom Global Income Fund/Class B	-1.1	113.2

International Stock Funds

Funds	1994 Annual % Gain	Assets ($ Millions) as of 11/30/94
DFA Japanese Small Company Portfolio	29.5%	$ 331.0
Fidelity Japan Fund	16.5	399.8
T Rowe Price Japan Fund	15.1	177.8
Vanguard Intl Equity Index—Pacific	12.9	688.6
DFA Continental Small Company Portfolio	11.0	341.0
Scudder Japan Fund	10.0	600.8
Seligman Henderson Global Emrg Co/Cl D	9.2	38.3
Quantitative International Equity/Ordinary	9.0	29.2
DFA Intl High Book to Market Portfolio	8.8	113.0
MetLife Ports—Intl Equity/Class C	8.5	46.1

Precious Metals/Gold Funds

Funds	1994 Annual % Gain	Assets ($ Millions) as of 11/30/94
SoGen Gold Fund	-0.8%	$ 45.1
Fidelity Select Precious Metals & Minerals	-1.1	437.7
United Services Gold Shares Fund	-2.7	243.7
Vanguard Splzd—Gold & Precious Metals	-5.4	637.2
Lexington Goldfund	-7.3	151.2
Scudder Gold Fund	-7.4	125.7
USAA Gold Fund	-9.4	150.3
Thomson Precious Metals/Class B	-9.7	52.4
Keystone Precious Metals Holdings	-13.3	199.5
Bull & Bear Gold Investors Fund	-13.8	31.4

Annual Percentage Gain includes reinvestment of income and capital gain distribution.

Source: 1995 IBC/Donoghue's *Mutual Funds Almanac*.

A Guide to Mutual Fund Investing[1]

Sumner Levine

The essentials of good mutual fund investing are not very complicated and are summarized in the following.

1. *Determine Your Goals*

Begin by estimating the amount of cash you will need and when you will need it. Are you investing to purchase a home, to send the kids to college, for retirement—all of these and more? Your estimate must, of course, include the effects of inflation. How to calculate the effects of inflation on costs and hence the future purchasing power of your investments is explained below. The worksheet (Exhibit 1) given below should be helpful in formulating your thoughts.

2. *List Your Current Investments and Estimate Your Savings*

Take inventory of your current cash and investments by identifying and evaluating such items as:

bonds
certificates of deposit
checking accounts
money market funds
mutual funds
savings accounts
stocks

Also list your current and anticipated incomes, including those from salaries, self employment, rentals, royalties, trusts, social security, pensions, and other retirement plans. How much do you expect to save each year?

Using the above information and assuming plausible rates of return, estimate the future resources you expect to have available to meet your goals. The calculation is described below (see *Estimating the Future Value of Your Investments*).

3. *Understand the Risk-Return Characteristics of Investments*

Different types of investments exhibit different risk return characteristics as shown in the Basic Series Exhibit on page 223. Risk refers to the extent by which the price of an investment fluctuates and is measured by the standard deviation (SD). The larger the SD, the greater the risk. For example, funds con-

sisting of small company growth stocks with an SD of 35.3% are considerably riskier than, say, a Government bond fund with an SD of 8.6%. It is also evident from the Basic Series Exhibit that the greater the risk the greater the return. Over long time periods the greater return provided by more risky investments offsets the fluctuation in value associated with the risk. However, over relatively short time intervals investors in risky assets may experience substantial losses. Hence, it is generally best to reserve investments in riskier (aggressive) assets to money that will not be needed for several years (say, five years or more).

4. *Determine Your Risk Tolerance*

Your risk tolerance and hence the extent to which you elect to expose your portfolio to aggressive investments depend on several considerations. These include where you are in your career cycle (starting out, preparing for retirement, etc.), the number and age of your dependents, and your psychological makeup. The Worksheet provides some helpful guidance in these regards. Generally, as investors approach retirement age, investments are shifted from the more aggressive (riskier) assets to those that are less so, as discussed in the following.

5. *Select a Diversified Investment Portfolio Consistent With Your Risk Tolerance*

The importance of investment diversification in reducing risk for a given return is now well established. No one knows what type of investment will flourish or decline in the future so that a portfolio should have a broad exposure to different types of investments to reduce risk. An important requirement for effective diversification is that the investments composing your portfolio should tend to fluctuate (in price) oppositely to one another—or, at least, independently of one another. Hopefully as one investment decreases another will increase in value. In practice, diversification is achieved by including in your portfolio funds with different investment philosophies; for example, aggressive, growth, growth-income, fixed income, and foreign equity funds (see page 344 for definitions).

As discussed, the proportion of each fund type in your portfolio will depend on your risk tolerance. Since most investors are risk adverse the proportion of aggressive (riskier) funds in most portfolios is usually smaller than that of the more conservative funds.

---

[1] The material in this section is for informational purposes only. Any portfolio decisions you make should be discussed with your tax and financial advisers.

EXHIBIT 1

YOUR INVESTMENT PROFILE

Before you launch your investment plan, make a realistic analysis of your financial circumstances and your feelings about risk. Answering the following questions will give you a starting point.

Do you have a sufficient financial "safety net" in place?

❑ Do you have 3 to 6 months' salary in a liquid investment that can be converted to cash easily, in case of an emergency?

❑ Do you have adequate insurance coverage for yourself and your family?

How will your personal circumstances affect your investing approach? How aggressively — or conservatively — you pursue your investing goals will depend on such factors as:

Your age	_____
Number of dependents	_____
Your current net worth	_____
Your annual income	_____
Amount you have to invest	_____

Your investing experience: ❑ None ❑ Limited ❑ Good ❑ Extensive

What specific investing goals do you have?   How long do you have to achieve them?

❑ College savings for your children _____
❑ Home purchase _____
❑ Retirement savings _____
❑ Business investment _____
❑ Wealth building _____
❑ Other _____

What is your primary investment objective?

❑ Maximum growth   ❑ Growth   ❑ Income   ❑ Preservation of principal/safety

Should you consider tax-advantaged investments?

Are you in a tax bracket where you could keep more of your earnings if invested in tax-free investments? (Consult your tax advisor if you're unsure.)

How do you feel about investment risk?

For example, which of these descriptions fit you best:

❑ You want maximum investment growth. You're willing to risk the loss of some — or even most — of your principal in exchange for the chance to receive higher returns on your money.

❑ You seek high returns but not at the expense of too much risk. You're investing primarily for growth, but want to keep some portion of your money in more "secure" investments.

❑ You want good investment returns but only moderate exposure to risk. You're willing to accept slower growth of your investments in exchange for somewhat less portfolio risk.

❑ You want your returns to keep pace with inflation but keep risk to a minimum. You're still looking out for the future, but you have a low tolerance for risk and would limit your "growth investments."

❑ You want to safeguard your principal at all costs. You're extremely averse to risk and don't want to take any more chances than necessary to maintain the value of your portfolio and/or receive the steady income it generates.

Source: The Charles Schwab Guide to *Investing Made Easy*, Charles Schwab & Co., Inc.

The shift into more conservative investments is usually more pronounced as the investor approaches retirement. Representative portfolios illustrating this point are shown below:

	Amount (%)
EARLY TO MID-CAREER	
Aggressive Growth	15–20
Growth	50–30
Fixed Income (Bond) Funds	25–35
International	10–15
PRE-RETIREMENT	
Aggressive Growth	10–
Growth	35–30
Fixed Income	45–50
International	10–
RETIREMENT	
Growth	30–35
Fixed Income	50–45
International	10–
Money Market	10–

For those in the higher tax brackets, tax free (municipal) funds should be considered. Investors with a greater risk tolerance might prefer a somewhat different allocation: for example, a greater proportion in aggressive growth funds. As a rule of thumb, the percentage of your portfolio in equity funds is given by 100 minus your age. Thus, a 65 year old would have 35% in equities.

Selection of funds for inclusion in the portfolio can be made by examining the year to year return of funds with different investment philosophies and picking those with a consistently superior performance (say, among the top 20% over the last 5 years). A simpler and perhaps a more satisfactory approach is to refer to a good service such as Morningstar, which specializes in evaluating fund performance. Several helpful references for selecting funds are given below. Be sure that the same management which achieved the superior performance is still in place. If a management change has occurred then it might be prudent to defer inclusion until the new management has proven itself.

As to the choice between a load fund (which charges a fee for purchasing and/or selling the fund) or a no-load fund, our preference is for a no-load fund since there is no evidence that load funds, as a group, out perform no-load funds. With a no-load fund the full amount of your investment goes to work for you at the outset.

Another item to check is the annual expense ratio charged by the fund. This should be at least consistent (or preferably lower) with that of other funds of the same type.

There are no hard and fast rules concerning the number of funds to own. The number will depend on your need for diversification, the size of your assets, and your tolerance for the paper work involved in keeping tax records and monitoring performance. Typically, a modest portfolio, of say, $50,000.00 to $100,000.00 might consist of two aggressive growth funds, two international equity funds, one conservative growth fund or growth-income fund, and a fixed income fund, giving a total of six funds. Larger portfolios of about one million dollars or more might consist of fifteen to twenty funds.

6. *Time Average Your Purchases*

The market constantly fluctuates; sometime it is up, sometime down. A simple way to average out this effect is to make constant dollar purchases on a monthly basis. Thus every month a fixed amount, say $200.00 is invested. To take inflation into account, the monthly purchase might be increased by the inflation rate. If the inflation rate is, say 4%, the $200.00 purchase would become $208.00.

A second approach to time averaging requires the value of your portfolio to increase by a fixed amount, say $200.00 per month. The amount of your monthly investment contribution would be the difference between the target value you set and the actual increase. Thus, if the value of the portfolio increased $100.00, then you would invest $100.00 assuming a target value of $200.00. If your portfolio increased $200.00 or more, you add nothing.

Another version of this approach requires that you sell shares for portfolio increases over $200.00 and reinvest the cash at a later time when the gain is less than $200.00. However, this approach usually incurs large capital gains taxes.

With this approach, if your portfolio lost money, say $20.00, you would contribute $220.00 to achieve a net increase of $200.00. In this way, you invest more in a weak market and less in a strong one.

7. *Monitor Your Portfolio and Keep Abreast of Developments*

The performance of your portfolio should be reviewed at least twice a year and preferably more often. Determine how well your funds have performed relative to others of the same type. Check to see if there has been a change in investment manager or philosophy.

The total returns on your portfolio should also be calculated. This is done by multiplying the return of each fund over the period in question by the fractional amount of the fund in the portfolio. Add up the results for all the funds to obtain the over all portfolio return.

Alas, the vicissitudes of the Government are such that even the most prudent investor cannot anticipate the changes in the tax law and it is essential therefore to keep informed by reading the financial press and consulting with your tax adviser.

INFORMATION SOURCES

The following is a selected list of information sources to help you evaluate and monitor funds.

1. *The Wall Street Journal*

Probably the most complete daily source of information. For details see page 328.

2. *Morningstar Mutual Funds*

An excellent detailed source of information. This loose leaf service provides updates every two weeks. Over 1240 funds are followed. Try your library or take a trial subscription. Also publishes a newsletter on closed-end funds (i.e., funds traded on one of the Stock Exchanges).

Screening thousands of mutual funds to identify those that meet certain return, risk, expense, or style criteria is greatly facilitated with the Morningstar floppy disk service. Considerable data on the characteristics of individual funds are provided, including performance graphs. However, the information provided by the disks is not as extensive as that given in the published version of the Morningstar service. Monthly and quarterly updates are available.

Morningstar
53 West Jackson Boulevard
Chicago, IL 60604
Telephone: 800-876-5005

3. Value Line publishes a *Mutual Fund Survey* which includes several hundred more funds than the Morningstar directory. The coverage is comparable to that of Morningstar.

Value Line Mutual Fund Survey
220 East 42nd Street
New York, NY 10017-5891
Telephone: 800-284-7607

4. *Mutual Fund Buyer's Guide*

This inexpensive monthly publication is a compact information source on safety ratings, performance, fees, asset size, and more. Covers over 1500 funds.

The Institute for Econometric Research
3471 N. Federal
Fort Lauderdale, FL 33306
Telephone: 800-442-9000

5. *No-Load Fund Investor*

A monthly publication covering 664 no-load and low-load funds. Contains information on returns, risk, asset size, and gives fund fixed diversification suggestions. Also available is the useful publication *Handbook For No-Load Fund Investors*.

The No-Load Fund Investor, Inc.
P.O. Box 283
Hastings-on-Hudson, NY 10706
Telephone: 800-252-2042

6. *Barron's*

This well-known weekly provides information on 52 week high and low prices, latest dividend payouts, and 12 month payouts. Quarterly reports are published on most funds summarizing extensive data provided by the Lipper organization. Available on most news stands and by subscription.

Barron's
200 Burnett Road
Chicopee, MA 01020

HELPFUL CALCULATIONS

How Inflation Affects Future Costs

Estimating future cash needs is an important aspect of investment planning. The effect of inflation on future costs can be calculated from the expression.

$$F = P (1 + I)^n$$
F is the cost n years from now
P is the present cost
I is the estimated inflation rate

Example:

You want to estimate the cost ten years from now for sending your child to college. The present cost is $6000.00 per year and you estimate the inflation of college costs to be about 6% per year.

Here $P = $6000.00 per year
$I = .06$
$n = 10$ years
so that your future cost estimate is
$F = 6.00 \ (1.06) = $10,745/\text{yr}$

Estimating the Portfolio Return Required to Maintain Current Purchasing Power

The return on your portfolio will be decreased by income taxes and the purchasing power of your investment will be reduced by inflation. It is often important to know the before tax return which will just maintain the current purchasing power of your portfolio.

The appropriate expression for the calculation is

$$i = \frac{I}{1-t}$$

Where

i is the before tax return
t is your income tax bracket
I is the inflation rate

Example:

You want to determine the rate of return on your portfolio required to maintain the current purchasing power of the assets. You are in the 35% tax bracket (Federal and State) and you estimate future inflation to be 4% per year.

The required before tax return is

$$i = \frac{.04}{1 - .35} = 6.15\%$$

Under these assumptions this return will just maintain the purchasing power of your investments over time. The purchasing power will increase if the investment return is greater and decrease if it is less than the calculated rate.

Return Required to Maintain Purchasing Power When Funds Are Withdrawn

In the above example it was assumed that no funds were withdrawn from the portfolio. We now assume that a percentage of the portfolio is withdrawn for, say, living expenses.

The before tax return required to maintain the purchasing power of the remaining portfolio is given by

$$i = \frac{I + w}{1 - t}$$

Where w is the percentage of the portfolio withdrawn.

Example:

Assume the same tax brackets and inflation rate as in the above example. You desire to withdraw 5% of the portfolio each year for living expenses. The required before tax return (i) is

$$i = \frac{.04 + .05}{1 - .35} = 13.8\%$$

At the calculated rate the purchasing power of the remaining portfolio will be preserved. If the rate of return is smaller, the purchasing power will decrease.

Estimating the Future Value of Your Investments

You often want to know how much your portfolio will grow if you invest a fixed amount each month (or other period) and the funds generated by the portfolio investments are reinvested.

The required expression for the size of the portfolio n months from now

$$F = P(1 + i)^n + A\left[\frac{(1 + i)^n - 1}{i}\right]$$

Where

P is the current value of the portfolio
A is the fixed amount invested each period (month, year, etc.)
n is the number of months from now at which it is desired to evaluate the portfolio
i is the after tax return per month (the annual after tax return divided by twelve)

Example:

Your current portfolio is valued at $50,000.00. You want to know how much the portfolio will grow 10 years from now if you deposit $200.00 per month over that time period. You assume a before tax return of 12% per year. If you are in the 35% tax bracket, your after tax return will be 7.8% [12 (1 − .35)] per year. The *monthly return* is just the annual return divided by 12 or .65% per month. Ten years corresponds to 120 months so that at ten years the portfolio will have grown to

$$F = 50,000(1.0065)^{120}\left[\frac{(1.0065)^{120} - 1}{1.0065}\right]$$

$$F = \$144,982$$

Calculations of this type are helpful in forming realistic expectations of portfolio growth possibilities.

Maximum Amount that Can Be Withdrawn Annually from a Portfolio During Retirement

You are now retired and have accumulated a portfolio valued at P dollars. It is invested at a return of i (after income taxes). You want to know the maximum amount you can withdraw each year over your remaining life so that nothing will remain at the end.

The appropriate expression is

$$A = P\left[\frac{i(1 + i)^n}{(1 + i)^n - 1}\right]$$

Where

A is the maximum amount that can be withdrawn each year over n years
P is the value of the portfolio at retirement
i is the after tax return
n is the number of years you expect to live after retirement

Example:

You are retired at the age of 68 with a portfolio of $500,000.00. Life expectancy tables indicate that your remaining expected life is about 13 years. You estimate your after tax return to be about 6.5%. What is the most you can withdraw each year so that nothing remains when you have lived your expected life?

EXHIBIT 2: Table for Determining the Longevity of Retirement Savings

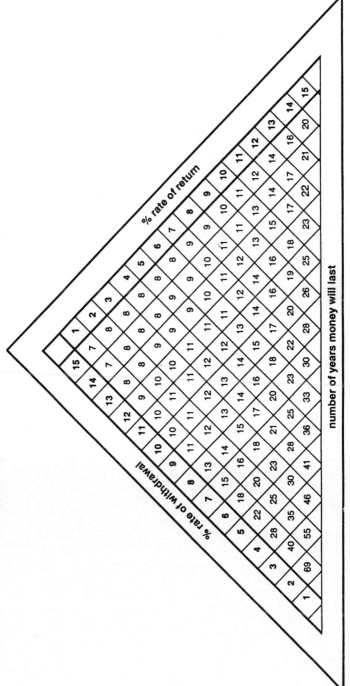

Source: Sheldon Jacobs' Guide to Successful No-Load Fund Investing, Sheldon Jacobs, The No-Load Fund Investor, Inc., P.O. Box 318, Irvington-on-Hudson, New York 10533.

$$A = \frac{500,000(.065)(1.065)^{13}}{(1.065)^{13} - 1} = \$58,151$$

How Long Will My Savings Last

You want to determine how long your investment savings will last given the after tax rate of return on your investments and a withdrawal rate.

The expression to use is:

$$n = -\frac{\ln\left(1 - \frac{Pi}{A}\right)}{\ln(1 + i)}$$

Where

ln designates the logarithm
n is the years required to use up all of your investment
P = the size of your investment when you start to withdraw
A = the amount to be withdrawn each year
i = the after tax rate of return

An alternative approach is to use Exhibit 2 based on the above equation. Find the rate of withdrawal on the left side and the rate of return on the right. The intersection of the two rows gives the number of years the money will last.

Example:

At retirement your investment savings are $200,000.00 and you want to start withdrawing $20,000.00 each year. You estimate an after tax return of 7%. How long will your savings last?

Here

$$i = .07$$
$$A = \$20,000.$$
$$P = \$200,000.$$

Therefore

$$n = -\frac{\ln\left(1 - \frac{200,000}{20,000} \times .07\right)}{\ln(1.07)} = 17.7 \text{ years}$$

Note if the withdrawal rate (A/P) is less than the rate of return (i), your savings will last indefinitely.

Understanding Mutual Fund Statements

One of the advantages of mutual fund investing is the wealth of information that mutual funds provide to fund investors and prospective investors. Taken together, the various reports provide investors with vital information concerning financial matters and how the fund is managed, both key elements in the selection process. In fact, mutual fund prospectuses, annual reports, and performance statistics are key sources of information most investors will need in the selection and monitoring process.

To new mutual fund investors, the information may seem overwhelming. However, regulations governing the industry have standardized the reports: Once you know where to look for information, the location will hold true for almost all funds.

There are basically five types of statements produced by the mutual fund: the prospectus; the statement of additional information; annual, semiannual, and quarterly reports; marketing brochures; and account statements. Actually, the second report—the statement of additional information—is part of the prospectus. However, the Securities and Exchange Commission allows mutual funds to simplify and streamline the prospectus, if they choose, by dividing it into two parts: Part A, which all prospective investors must receive if requested, and Part B—the statement of additional information—which the fund must send investors if they specifically request it. In practice, when most people (including the funds) refer to the prospectus, they are referring to Part A. For simplicity, that is what we will do here as well.

THE PROSPECTUS

The prospectus is the single most important document produced by the mutual fund, and it is must-reading for investors before investing. Current shareholders must be sent new prospectuses when they are updated, at least once every 14 months.

The prospectus is generally organized into sections, and although it must cover specific topics, the overall structure may differ somewhat among funds. The cover usually gives a quick synopsis of the fund: investment category, sales or redemption charges, minimum investment, retirement plans available, address and telephone number. More detailed descriptions are in the body of the prospectus.

Fee Table: All mutual fund prospectuses must include a table near the front that delineates all fees and charges to the investor. The table contains three sections: The first section lists all transaction charges to the investor, including all front-end and back-end loads and redemption fees; the second section lists all annual fund operating expenses, including management fees and any 12b-1 charges, as a percentage of net assets; and the third section is an illustration of the total cost of these fees and charges to an investor over time. The illustration assumes an initial investment of $1,000 and a 5% growth rate for the fund, and states the total dollar cost to an investor if he were to redeem his shares at the end of one year, three years, five years, and 10 years.

Selected Per Share Data and Ratios: One of the most important sections of the prospectus contains the selected per share data and ratios, which provides statistics on income and capital changes per share of the fund. The per share figures are given for the life of the fund or 10 years, whichever is less. Also included are important statistical summaries of investment activities throughout each period. Occasionally these financial statements are only referred to in the prospectus and are actually contained in the annual report, which in this instance would accompany the prospectus.

The per share section summarizes the financial activity over the fund's fiscal year, which may or may not correspond to the calendar year, to arrive at the end-of-year net asset value for the fund. The financial activity summarized includes increases in net asset value due to dividend and interest payments received and capital gains from investment activity. Decreases in net asset value are due to capital losses from investment activity, investment expenses, and payouts to fund shareholders in the form of distributions.

Potential investors may want to note the line items in this section. *Investment income* represents the dividends and interest earned by the fund during its fiscal year. *Expenses* reflect such fund costs as the management fee, legal fees, and transfer agent fees. These expenses are given in detail in the statement of operations section of the annual report.

Net investment income is investment income less expenses. This line is important for investors to note because it reflects the level and stability of net income over the time period. A high net investment income

Reprinted from *The Individual Investor's Guide to Low-Load Mutual Funds*, 14th edition, 1995, published by the American Association of Individual Investors, 625 N. Michigan Avenue, Suite 1900, Chicago, Illinois 60611.

would most likely be found in funds that have income rather than growth as their investment category. Since net investment income must be distributed to shareholders to avoid direct taxation of the fund, a high net investment income has the potential of translating into a high tax liability for the investor.

Net realized and unrealized gain (loss) on investments is the change in the value of investments that have been sold (realized) during the year or that continue to be held (unrealized) by the fund.

Distributions to fund shareholders are also detailed. These distributions will include dividends from net investment income for the current fiscal period. Tax law requires that income earned must be distributed in the calendar year earned. Also included in distributions will be any realized net capital gains.

The last line in the per share section will be the *net asset value* at the end of the year,

which reflects the value of one share of the fund. It is calculated by determining the total assets of the fund and dividing by the number of mutual fund shares outstanding. The figure will change for a variety of reasons, including changes in investment income, expenses, gains, losses, and distributions. Depending upon the source of change, a decline in net asset value may or may not be due to poor performance. For instance, a decline in net asset value may be due to a distribution of net realized gains on securities.

The financial ratios at the bottom of the per share financial data are important indicators of fund performance and strategy. The *expense ratio* relates expenses incurred by the fund to average net assets. These expenses include the investment advisory fee, legal and accounting fees, and 12b-1 charges to the fund; they do not include fund brokerage costs, loads, or redemption fees. A high expense ratio detracts from your investment return. In general, common stock

The Prospectus Fee Table: An Example

Expenses

The following tables are intended to assist you in understanding the various costs and expenses that an investor in the Funds may bear directly or indirectly. For a more complete explanation of the fees and expenses borne by the Funds, see the discussions under the prospectus headings "How to Purchase Shares" and "Management of the Funds", as well as the Statement of Additional Information incorporated by reference into this prospectus.

Shareholder Transaction Expenses

	Oakmark Fund	Oakmark International
Sales commissions to purchase shares (sales load)	None	None
Commissions to reinvest dividends	None	None
Deferred sales load	None	None
Redemption fees*	None	None
Fees to exchange shares**	None	None

Annual Fund Operating Expenses
(as a percentage of net assets)

	Oakmark Fund	Oakmark International
Investment management fees	1.00%	1.00%
12b-1 Fees	None	None
Other Expenses	0.32%	0.26%
Total Fund operating expenses	1.32%	1.26%

* If you request payment of redemption proceeds by wire, you must pay the cost of the wire (currently $5).

** There is no fee for an exchange between the Funds. There is a charge of $5 for an exchange from either Fund to Goldman Sachs - Institutional Liquid Assets Government Portfolio.

The following example illustrates the expenses that you would pay on a $1,000 investment in each Fund over various time periods assuming (1) a 5% annual rate of return, (2) the operating expense percentages listed in the table above remain the same through each of the periods, (3) reinvestment of all dividends and capital gain distributions, and (4) redemption at the end of each time period.

	1 Year	3 Years	5 Years	10 Years
Oakmark Fund	$13	$42	$72	$159
Oakmark International	13	40	69	152

This example should not be considered a representation of past or future expenses or performance. Actual expenses may be greater or less than those shown.

Source: Oakmark prospectus, March 1, 1994.

funds have higher expense ratios than bond funds, and smaller funds have higher expense ratios than larger funds. International funds also tend to have higher expense ratios than domestic funds. Index funds usually have the lowest expense ratios. The average expense ratio for common stock funds is 1.20%, and for bond funds about 0.75%.

The *ratio of net investment income to average net assets* is very similar to a dividend yield. This, too, should reflect the investment category of the fund. Common stock funds with income as a significant part of their investment objective would be expected to have a ratio in the 2% to 4% range under current market conditions, and aggressive growth funds would have a ratio closer to 0%. Bond funds would normally have ratios more than twice those of common stock funds.

The *portfolio turnover rate* is the lower of purchases or sales divided by average net assets. It reflects how frequently securities are bought and sold by the fund. For purposes of determining the turnover rate for common stock funds, fixed-income securities with a maturity of less than a year are excluded, as are all government securities, short- and long-term. For bond funds, however, long-term U.S. government bonds are included.

Investors should take note of the portfolio turnover rate, because the higher the turnover, the greater the brokerage costs incurred by the fund. Brokerage costs are not reflected in the expense ratio but instead are directly reflected as a decrease in net asset value. In addition, mutual funds with high turnover rates generally have higher capital gains distributions—a potential tax liability. Aggressive growth mutual funds are most likely to have high turnover rates. Some bond funds also have very high portfolio turnover rates. A 100% portfolio turnover rate indicates that the value of the portfolio was completely turned over in a year; a 200% portfolio turnover indicates that the value of the portfolio was completely turned over twice in a year. The portfolio turnover rate for the average mutual fund is around 100% but varies with market conditions and investment category.

Investment Objective/Policy: The investment objective section of the prospectus elaborates on the brief sentence or two from the prospectus cover. In this section, the fund describes the types of investments it will make—whether it is bonds, stocks, convertible securities, options, etc.—along with some general guidelines as to the proportions these securities will represent in the fund's portfolio. The investment objective statement usually indicates whether it will be oriented toward capital gains or income. In this section, the management will also briefly discuss its approach to market timing, risk assumption, and the anticipated level of portfolio turnover. Some prospectuses may indicate any investment restrictions they have placed on the fund, such as purchasing securities on margin, selling short, concentrating in firms or industries, trading foreign securities, and lending securities; this section may also state the allowable proportions in certain investment categories. The restrictions section is usually given in more detail in the statement of additional information.

Selected Per Share Data and Ratios: an Example

	500 PORTFOLIO									
	Year Ended December 31,									
	1993	1992	1991	1990	1989	1988	1987	1986	1985	1984
Net Asset Value, Beginning of Year	$40.97	$39.32	$31.24	$33.64	$27.18	$24.65	$24.27	$22.99	$19.52	$19.70
Investment Operations										
Net Investment Income	1.13	1.12	1.15	1.17	1.20	1.08	.88	.89	.91	.88
Net Realized and Unrealized Gain (Loss) on Investments	2.89	1.75	8.20	(2.30)	7.21	2.87	.36	3.30	5.08	.30
Total from Investment Operations	4.02	2.87	9.35	(1.13)	8.41	3.95	1.24	4.19	5.99	1.18
Distributions										
Dividends from Net Investment Income	(1.13)	(1.12)	(1.15)	(1.17)	(1.20)	(1.10)	(.69)	(.89)	(.91)	(.88)
Distributions from Realized Capital Gains	(.03)	(.10)	(.12)	(.10)	(.75)	(.32)	(.17)	(2.02)	(1.61)	(.48)
Total Distributions	(1.16)	(1.22)	(1.27)	(1.27)	(1.95)	(1.42)	(.86)	(2.91)	(2.52)	(1.36)
Net Asset Value, End of Year	$43.83	$40.97	$39.32	$31.24	$33.64	$27.18	$24.65	$24.27	$22.99	$19.52
Total Return*	9.89%	7.42%	30.22%	(3.32)%	31.36%	16.22%	4.71%	18.06%	31.23%	6.21%
Ratios/Supplemental Data										
Net Assets, End of Year (Millions)	$8,273	$6,547	$4,345	$2,173	$1,804	$1,055	$826	$485	$394	$290
Ratio of Expenses to Average Net Assets	.19%	.19%	.20%	.22%	.21%	.22%	.26%	.28%	.28%	.27%
Ratio of Net Investment Income to Average Net Assets	2.65%	2.81%	3.07%	3.60%	3.62%	4.08%	3.15%	3.40%	4.09%	4.53%
Portfolio Turnover Rate	6%†	4%†	5%†	23%†	8%	10%	15%	29%	36%	14%

*Total return figures do not reflect the annual account maintenance fee of $10 or applicable portfolio transaction fees.
†Portfolio turn over rates excluding in-kind redemptions were 2%, 1%, 1% and 6%, respectively.

Source: Vanguard Index Trust—500 prospectus, April 4, 1994.

Fund Management: The fund management section names the investment adviser
and gives the advisory fee schedule. Most advisers charge a management fee on a sliding
scale that decreases as assets under management increase. Occasionally, some portion of
the fund adviser's fees are subject to the
fund's performance relative to the market.

Some prospectuses will describe the
fund's officers and directors with a short bi-
ography of affiliations and relevant experience. For most funds, however, this
information is provided in more detail in the
statement of additional information. The
board of directors is elected by fund shareholders; the fund adviser is selected by the
board of directors. The adviser is usually a
firm operated by or affiliated with officers of
the fund. Information on fund officers and
directors is not critical to fund selection. In
the prospectus the portfolio manager for the
fund is named. The portfolio manager is responsible for the day-to-day investment decisions of the fund and is employed by the
fund adviser. Who the portfolio manager is
and how long the manager has been in the
position can be useful in judging historical
performance.

Other Important Sections: There are
several other sections in a mutual fund
prospectus that investors should be aware of.
They will appear under various headings, depending upon the prospectus, but they are
not difficult to find.

Mutual funds that have 12b-1 plans must
describe them in the prospectus. Under SEC
rules, a description of these plans must be
prominently and clearly placed in the
prospectus, usually in a section titled "Distribution Plan." The distribution plan details
the marketing aspects of the fund and how it
relates to fund expenses. For instance, advertising, distribution of fund literature, and
any arrangements with brokers would be included in the marketing plan; the 12b-1 plan
pays for these distribution expenses. The distribution plan section specifies the maximum
annual 12b-1 charge that can be made.
Funds often charge less than the maximum.
The actual charge to the fund of a 12b-1
plan is listed at the front of the prospectus in
the fee table.

The capital stock section, or fund share
characteristics section, provides shareholders
with a summary of their voting rights, participation in dividends and distributions, and
the number of authorized and issued shares
of the fund. Often, a separate section will
discuss the tax treatment that will apply to
fund distributions, which may include dividends, interest, and capital gains.

The how-to-buy-shares section gives the
minimum initial investment and any subse-

quent minimums; it will also list load charges
or fees. In addition, information on mail,
wire, and telephone purchases is provided,
along with distribution reinvestment options,
automatic exchange, investment and withdrawal plans, and retirement options.

The how-to-redeem-shares section discusses telephone, written, and wire redemption options, including automatic withdrawal
plans, with a special section on signature
guarantees and other documents that may be
needed. Also detailed are any fees for reinvestment or redemption. Shareholder services are usually outlined here, with emphasis
on exchanges among funds in a family of
funds. This will include any fees for exchang-
ing, any limits on the number of exchanges
allowed, and any exchange restrictions.

STATEMENT OF ADDITIONAL INFORMATION

This document elaborates on the prospectus. The investment objectives section is
more in-depth, with a list and description of
investment restrictions. The management
section gives brief biographies of directors
and officers, and provides the number of
fund shares owned beneficially by the officers and directors named. The investment
adviser section, while reiterating the major
points made in the prospectus, gives all the
expense items and contract provisions of the
agreement between the adviser and the fund.
If the fund has a 12b-1 plan, further details
will likely be in the statement of additional
information.

Many times, the statement of additional
information will include much more information on the tax consequences of mutual
fund distributions and investment. Conditions under which withholding for federal income tax will take place are also provided.
The fund's financial statements are incorporated by reference to the annual report to
shareholders and generally do not appear in
the statement of additional information. Finally, the independent auditors give their
opinion on the accuracy of the fund's financial statements.

ANNUAL, SEMIANNUAL, AND QUARTERLY REPORTS

All funds must send their shareholders
audited annual and semiannual reports.
Mutual funds are allowed to combine their
prospectus and annual report; some do this,
but many do not.

The annual report describes the fund
activities over the past year and provides a
listing of all investments of the fund at market

value as of the end of the fiscal year. Sometimes the cost basis of each investment is also given. Looking in-depth at the individual securities held by the fund is probably a waste of time. However, it is helpful to be aware of the overall investment categories. For instance, investors should look at the percentage invested in common stocks, bonds, convertible bonds, and any other holdings. In addition, a look at the types of common stocks held and the percentage of fund assets by industry classification gives the investor some indication of how the portfolio will fare in various market environments.

The annual report will also have a balance sheet, which lists all assets and liabilities of the fund by general category. This holds little interest for investors.

The statement of operations, similar to an income statement, is of interest only in that the fund expenses are broken down. For most funds, the management fee is by far the largest expense; the expense ratio in the prospectus conveys much more useful information. The statement of changes in net assets is very close to the financial information provided in the prospectus, but the information is not on a per share basis. Per share information will, however, frequently be detailed in the annual report in a separate section. Footnotes to the financial statements elaborate on the entries, but other than any pending litigation against the fund, they are most often routine.

The quarterly or semiannual reports are current accounts of the investment portfolio and provide more timely views of the fund's investments than does the annual report.

MARKETING BROCHURES AND ADVERTISEMENTS

These will generally provide a brief description of the fund. However, the most important bit of information will be the telephone number to call to receive the fund prospectus and annual report, if you have not received them already.

The SEC has tightened and standardized the rules regarding mutual fund advertising. All mutual funds that use performance figures in their ads must now include one-, three-, five-, and 10-year total return figures. Bond funds that quote yields must use a standardized method for computing yield, and they must include total return figures as well. Finally, any applicable sales commissions must be mentioned in the advertisement.

ACCOUNT STATEMENTS

Mutual funds send out periodic account statements detailing reinvestment of dividend and capital gains distributions, new purchases or redemptions, and any other account activity such as service fees. This statement provides a running account balance by date with share accumulations, an account value to date, and a total of distributions made to date. These statements are invaluable for tax purposes and should be saved. The fund will also send out, in January, a Form 1099-DIV for any distributions made in the previous year and a Form 1099-B if any mutual fund shares were sold.

About Our Listings

YOU ASKED FOR IT, YOU got it. For some time, readers have been lobbying for a change in the way *Barron's* mutual-fund quarterly presents data on the fees charged for managing mutual funds.

We've now eliminated the column in our open-end mutual fund listings that used to report 12(b)-1 fees. Instead, we're reporting each fund's expense ratio. It's a more encompassing measure of how much your fund takes off the top—the hurdle a manager faces before investors break even. The total reflects not just 12(b)-1 fees (levies intended to offset marketing costs), but also management fees and operating expenses. We continue to present sales charges and redemption fees separately.

Particularly over the long run, differences in expenses can play a big part in determining a fund's relative performance. High annual fees are in large part responsible for the historically abysmal performance of the Steadman funds, for instance. In contrast, consistently low fees have helped provide the

edge index funds have over actively controlled portfolios over most time periods.

In this edition of the quarterly, we provide data on 6,832 open-end stock and bond funds, almost 400 more than our previous report. There's information, too, on more than 500 closed-end funds, and 3,000-plus variable annuity and variable life subaccounts.

The stock and taxable bond funds, listed alphabetically, begin on page 346. Tax-exempt funds begin on page 454. You'll find closed-end funds starting on page F911, and data for variable annuities and variable life contracts on page F97[1].

And, a brief confession: to compensate for the ever-expanding roster of funds, we've used a slightly smaller typesize in the listings. Sorry about that.

We continue to look for ways to improve the section, and would love to hear what you think. Send comments, suggestions or complaints to Eric J. Savitz, *Barron's* Mutual Funds Editor, 200 Liberty St, New York, N.Y. 10281, or via e-mail to savitz@barronsmag.com.

A GUIDE TO OBJECTIVES

DEBT AND EQUITY FUNDS

Balanced: Goal is preserving principal; often maintains a roughly 60%/40% ratio of stocks to bonds.

Balanced Target: Invests to provide a guaranteed return of principal at maturity. Some assets in zero-coupon Treasury bonds, the remainder in long-term growth stocks.

Canadian: Invests primarily in securities traded in Canadian markets.

Capital Appreciation: Seeks maximum capital appreciation through strategies such as 100% or more portfolio turnover, leveraging, purchasing unregistered shares or options. May market-time, sometimes taking large cash positions.

Convertibles: Primarily in convertible bonds and preferreds.

Dual-Purpose Capital: Closed-end fund that seeks capital appreciation and preservation of capital as well as current income and income growth, primarily by investing in dividend-paying common stocks and interest-bearing securities. Capital shares incur no manage-

ment fees or expenses, receive no income, and bear all gains and losses of capital.

Dual-Purpose Income: Closed-end fund that seeks capital appreciation and preservation of capital as well as current income and income growth, primarily by investing in dividend-paying common stocks and interest-bearing securities. Unlike capital shares, income shares have a priority on redemption at NAV, bear all management expenses, and receive all net investment income.

Emerging Markets: Invests at least 65% of its assets in securities of emerging markets.

Environmental: Invests at least 65% of assets in stocks of companies engaged in contributing to a cleaner and healthier environment.

Equity Income: Normally has more than 60% of its assets in equities and seeks high income.

European Region: Focuses on one European stock market or several.

Financial Services: Invests at least 65% of assets in financial-service companies, including banks, thrifts, insurers and securities firms.

Fixed Income: Typically has more than 75% of assets in fixed-income securities, such as bonds, preferred stocks and money-market instruments.

Flexible: Aims for high total return by allocating its portfolio among a wide range of asset classes.

Global: At least 25% of assets in non-U.S. securities.

Global Flexible: Similar to flexible, with at least 25% of assets in securities of non-U.S. issuers.

Global Small-Company: Invests at least a quarter of its assets outside the U.S.; limits 65% of its holdings on the basis of market cap.

Gold: Has at least 65% of its assets in gold-mining or gold-oriented mining finance shares, gold coins or bullion.

Growth: Invests in companies whose long-term earnings it expects to grow faster than those of the stocks in the major market indexes.

Growth & Income: Seeks earnings growth as well as dividend income.

Health/Biotech: Has 65% of its portfolio in health-care, pharmaceutical and biotechnology companies.

Income: Seeks high current income through stocks, bonds and money-market instruments; has a maximum equity exposure of 60% and maximum fixed-income exposure of 75%.

International: Invests in securities traded primarily outside the U.S.

International Small-Cap: Invests in equities of non U.S. companies with market caps below $1 billion.

Japanese: Concentrates on securities trading in Tokyo.

Latin American: Invests primarily in securities in Mexico, Brazil, Chile and other Latin American countries.

Mid-Cap: Invests in companies with market caps and/or revenues between $800 million and the average market cap of the Wilshire 4500 Index.

Natural Resource: Usually invests more than 65% of its holdings in natural-resource stocks.

Pacific Region: Concentrates on stocks trading in one or more of the Pacific Basin markets.

Real Estate: Puts 65% of its assets into real-estate company securities.

S&P 500 Index: Designed to replicate the performance of the Standard & Poor's 500 Index on a reinvested basis; passively managed, with adviser fee no higher than 0.5%.

Science & Technology: At least 65% invested in science and technology stocks.

Small-Company Growth: Limits investment to companies on the basis of size.

Specialty: Limits its investments to a specific industry such as retailing, transportation, or paper, or falls outside other classifications.

Utility: Utilities comprise 65% of its equity portfolio.

World Fixed-Income: May own common and preferred, but invests primarily in U.S. and foreign debt.

MUNICIPAL BOND FUNDS

General Muni: Invests at least 65% of its assets in municipal bonds carrying the top four credit ratings.

Insured Muni: At least 65% of its holdings have been insured for timely payment of interest.

Intermediate Muni: Tax-exempt debt holdings have an average maturity of five to 10 years.

High-Yield Muni: Can put 50%-plus of assets in low-rated credits.

Short Muni: Invests in tax-exempt debt maturing, on average, in less than five years.

Single-State Muni: Limits investments to securities exempt from taxation in a particular state. States with only a few such funds are lumped together in the Single State category; the following state funds are identified separately:

Ala.; Ariz.; Calif.; Colo.; Conn.; Fla.; Ga.; Kan.; Ky.; La.; Md.; Mass.; Mich.; Minn.; Mo.; N.J.; N.Y.; N.C.; Ohio; Ore.; Pa.; S.C.; Texas; Va.

QUESTIONS? COMPLAINTS?

Queries about the data in these pages should be directed to:

Mutual Fund Profiles Dept.
Lipper Analytical Services
1380 Lawrence St., Suite 950
Denver, Colo. 80204
(303) 534-3472

FOOTNOTES

▢ means the funds availability is limited. AHA Investment Funds, for example, are open only to participants in the American Hospital Associations Investment Program.

⊠ means the fund is closed to new investors.

▥ means the fund is open only to institutions.

✳ means the fund is designed for retirement plans.

➧ means the fund has waived some fees.

★ means something unusual is going on that may affect the fund's performance or operation. Check the footnotes for details.

[1]This page number refers to *Barron's National Business and Financial Weekly*, July 10, 1995.
Source: Lipper Analytical Services, Inc. Reprinted by permission of *Barron's National Business and Financial Weekly*, © 1995 Dow Jones & Company, Inc. ALL RIGHTS RESERVED WORLDWIDE.

BARRON'S LIPPER FUND LISTINGS

BENCHMARKS

Objective	Quarter	1 Year	Annualized Return		
			3 Years	5 Years	10 Years
Growth & Income	8.11%	19.74%	11.90%	11.17%	12.60%
Fixed Income	4.93	9.30	6.36	8.93	9.14
Small-Company Growth	9.01	24.79	17.11	14.11	13.66
Gold	3.29	-0.15	11.31	4.55	6.18
International	4.04	1.19	9.67	5.83	15.01
Emerging Markets	8.56	-3.85	11.76	8.28	N/A

DEBT AND EQUITY FUNDS

FUND NAME	OBJECTIVE	ASSETS ($ MIL) 5/31/95	NAV ($/SHR) 6/30/95	QTR	1YR	3YRS	5YRS	10YRS (Annualized)	DIV YLD %	P/E RATIO	800	In-State	Load	Exp. Ratio	Redemption	MANAGER	SINCE
A-F LARGE-CAP FUND	Growth Income	47.2	11.59	12.18	23.11	☆	☆	☆	1.8	14.7	932-7781	215-989-6611	None	0.70	None	Paul Dodge	'95
AAL BOND	Fixed Income	438.9	9.87	5.07	9.75	5.80	8.24	☆	6.0	☐	553-6319	414-734-7633	4.75	1.02	None	T. Brooks Beittel	'87
AAL CAPITAL GROWTH	Growth	1,069.7	16.19	8.06	22.37	9.11	10.29	☆	1.5	18.2	553-6319	414-734-7633	4.75	1.18	None	Clyde Bartter	'87
AAL SMALLER CO STK	Midcap	224.0	12.12	10.68	35.27	☆	☆	☆	0.0	31.0	553-6319	414-734-7633	4.75	1.72	None	Bruce Muzina	'93
AAL TARGET 2001	Fixed Income	1.8	10.97	8.51	14.96	10.06	☆	☆	6.0	☐	553-6319	414-734-7633	4.75	1.00	None	T. Brooks Beittel	'90
AAL TARGET 2006	Fixed Income	1.5	12.01	13.20	23.31	13.82	☆	☆	6.0	☐	553-6319	414-734-7633	4.75	1.00	None	T. Brooks Beittel	'90
AAL UTILITIES	Utility	74.9	9.94	8.09	9.16	☆	☆	☆	3.2	14.2	553-6319	414-734-7633	4.75	None	None	Richard Spletzer	'94
AARP BAL STOCK & BOND	Balanced	204.1	15.82	7.18	15.11	☆	☆	☆	3.6	15.6	322-2282	617-439-4640	None	1.31	None	Hoffman/Hutchinson	'94/'94
AARP CAPITAL GROWTH	Growth	636.4	35.51	10.76	19.92	11.11	9.65	12.58	0.0	12.9	322-2282	617-439-4640	None	0.97	None	Gadsden/Beaty	'89/'94
AARP GNMA	Fixed Income	5,289.6	15.16	4.00	9.16	5.11	7.70	8.26	6.6	☐	322-2282	617-439-4640	None	0.66	None	Glen/Boyadjian	'84/'95
AARP GROWTH & INC	Growth Income	2,678.0	36.11	8.76	19.01	13.71	13.33	13.50	2.9	15.7	322-2282	617-439-4640	None	0.76	None	Hoffman/Millard/Thorndike '91/'91/'86	
AARP HIGH QUAL BOND	Fixed Income	537.7	15.93	5.61	10.74	6.91	8.55	8.59	5.8	☐	322-2282	617-439-4640	None	0.95	None	Glen/Hutchinson/Wohler '95/'87/'94	
ABT EMERGING GROWTH	Capital Appreciation	63.0	15.53	12.05	24.74	16.80	17.64	14.68	0.0	27.1	553-7838	407-655-7255	4.75	1.25	None	Harold Ireland	'83
ABT GROWTH & INCOME TR	Growth Income	63.8	11.51	6.66	14.86	7.10	6.15	9.83	1.8	19.7	553-7838	407-655-7255	4.75	0.94	None	Philip Keating	'94
ABT UTILITY INCOME FD	Utility	102.2	11.55	6.51	10.76	5.71	6.46	9.18	5.2	12.8	553-7838	407-655-7255	4.75	1.05	None	Philip Keating	'94

ACADEMY VALUE FUND	Growth	1.9	11.19	8.01	☆	☆	☆	☆	0.0	N/A	424-2295	None	None	None	None	Joel Adam	'94
ACCESSOR GROWTH	Growth	29.9	17.35	11.53	30.58	☆	☆	☆	0.8	17.2	759-3504	206-224-7420	None	1.76	None	State Street Bank & Trust	'92
ACCESSOR INT FXD-INC	Fixed Income	35.4	11.87	6.12	10.73	6.09	☆	☆	5.9	☐	759-3504	206-224-7420	None	1.24	None	Smith Barney Cap Mgmt	'92
ACCESSOR INTL EQUITY	International	26.8	11.31	0.89	☆	☆	☆	☆	0.0	☐	759-3504	206-224-7420	None	None	None	Laura DeMarco	'94
ACCESSOR MORTGAGE SEC	Fixed Income	35.4	12.13	5.04	11.24	6.19	☆	☆	6.1	☐	759-3504	206-224-7420	None	1.31	None	Blackrock Financial Mgt	'92
ACCESSOR SHT-INT FXD-INC	Fixed Income	33.8	12.15	3.50	7.44	4.76	☆	☆	4.7	☐	759-3504	206-224-7420	None	1.18	None	Bankers Trust Company	'92
ACCESSOR SMALL CAP	Small Company Growth	35.8	15.97	9.11	18.21	☆	☆	☆	0.2	15.7	759-3504	206-224-7420	None	1.98	None	Wells Fargo Nikko Adv.	'92
ACCESSOR VALUE & INCOME	Growth Income	23.1	15.20	8.25	20.08	☆	☆	☆	1.9	14.4	759-3504	206-224-7420	None	1.77	None	Martingale Asset Mgmt	'92
ACCOLADE BONNEL GROWTH	Midcap	11.5	12.64	15.86	☆	☆	☆	☆	0.0	N/A	873-8637	210-308-1234	None	None	None	Arthur Bonnel	'94
ACHIEVEMENT BAL; INST	Balanced	126.9	11.18	7.17	☆	☆	☆	☆	0.0	N/A	472-0577	None	None	None	None	Curtis Anderson	'94
ACHIEVEMENT EQUITY; INST	Growth	115.7	11.81	9.67	☆	☆	☆	☆	0.0	N/A	472-0577	None	None	None	None	Sterling Jensen	'94
ACHIEVEMENT INT BD; INST	Fixed Income	78.0	10.55	4.77	☆	☆	☆	☆	0.0	☐	472-0577	None	None	None	None	Mark Anderson	'95
ACHIEVEMENT SH BD; INST	Fixed Income	79.6	10.14	2.42	☆	☆	☆	☆	0.0	☐	472-0577	None	None	None	None	Mark Anderson	'94
ACORN FUND ⊠	Small Company Growth	2,139.6	13.64	8.43	13.38	18.06	14.84	15.66	0.8	16.9	922-6769	312-634-9200	None	0.62	2.00	Wanger/McQuaid/Hogan'70/'95/'95	
ACORN INV INTL ⊠	Intl Small Company	1,284.9	15.63	6.18	1.14	☆	☆	☆	0.6	☐	922-6769	312-634-9200	None	1.20	2.00	Wanger/Zell	'92/'95
ADDISON CAPITAL	Growth Income	37.4	22.92	9.98	21.11	12.55	10.55	☆	0.9	15.9	526-6397	215-665-6000	3.00	1.93	None	Cheston/Kelly/Thomas	'86/'90/'89
ADV INNR CIR HGK FXD INC	Fixed Income	8.7	10.79	6.31	☆	☆	☆	☆	0.0	☐	932-7781	215-989-6611	None	None	None	Harris/Lobo	'94/'94
ADV INNR CIR PIN OAK	Small Company Growth	11.1	14.67	14.79	56.73	☆	☆	☆	0.0	N/A	932-7781	215-989-6611	None	0.96	None	James D. Oelshlager	'92
ADV INNR CIR WHITE OAK	Growth	7.1	15.02	17.71	44.66	☆	☆	☆	0.9	N/A	932-7781	215-989-6611	None	0.97	None	James D. Oelshlager	'92
ADVANCE CAP I BALANCED	Balanced	50.1	11.50	8.56	20.90	9.51	6.73	☆	2.9	18.3	345-4783	810-350-8543	None	1.10	None	Multiple Managers	N/A
ADVANCE CAP I BOND ☚	Fixed Income	4.5	10.44	7.28	13.96	7.88	9.14	☆	6.8	☐	345-4783	810-350-8543	None	0.60	None	Shoemaker/Cappelli	'87/'91
ADVANCE CAP I EQTY GROW	Midcap	18.5	10.87	9.03	28.79	9.59	5.09	☆	0.0	23.3	345-4783	810-350-8543	None	1.21	None	Multiple Managers	N/A
ADVANCE CAP I LG TM INC ☚	Fixed Income	1.3	10.29	9.32	17.94	☆	☆	☆	7.0	☐	345-4783	810-350-8543	None	0.63	None	Shoemaker/Cappelli	'92/'93
ADVANCE CAP I RETIRE INC	Fixed Income	123.6	10.16	8.55	15.64	☆	☆	☆	7.6	☐	345-4783	810-350-8543	None	0.88	None	Shoemaker/Cappelli	'92/'93
ADVANTUS BOND; A	Fixed Income	14.9	10.18	7.20	13.04	7.45	9.10	☆	6.2	☐	443-3677	None	5.00	1.00	None	Wayne Schmidt	'91
ADVANTUS HORIZON; A	Growth Income	33.7	19.34	7.44	23.80	10.08	10.42	10.53	0.0	69.4	443-3677	None	5.00	1.43	None	Jim Tatera	'85
ADVANTUS HORIZON; B	Growth Income	1.6	19.20	7.20	☆	☆	☆	☆	0.0	N/A	443-3677	None	None	None	5.00	Jim Tatera	'94
ADVANTUS HORIZON; C	Growth Income	0.1	19.20	7.20	☆	☆	☆	☆	0.0	N/A	443-3677	None	None	None	None	Jim Tatera	'95
ADVANTUS MORTGAGE; A	Fixed Income	27.8	10.32	5.72	12.25	6.63	8.72	9.04	5.8	☐	443-3677	None	5.00	1.24	None	Kent Weber	'90
ADVANTUS SPECTRUM; A	Flexible	56.5	14.25	6.81	18.56	8.51	9.82	☆	3.5	58.5	443-3677	None	5.00	1.27	None	Thomas Gunderson	'89
ADVANTUS SPECTRUM; B	Flexible	1.3	14.21	6.67	☆	☆	☆	☆	0.0	58.5	443-3677	None	None	None	5.00	Thomas Gunderson	'94
ADVANTUS SPECTRUM; C	Flexible	0.1	14.21	6.65	☆	☆	☆	☆	0.0	N/A	443-3677	None	None	None	None	Thomas Gunderson	'95
AETNA AETNA FUND; ADV	Flexible	0.8	11.60	8.26	14.91	☆	☆	☆	1.7	15.5	238-6263	203-273-0121	None	1.87	1.00	John Kim	'94
AETNA AETNA FUND; SEL	Flexible	84.4	11.60	8.52	16.07	8.27	☆	☆	2.7	15.5	238-6263	203-273-0121	None	1.09	None	John Kim	'94
AETNA ASIAN GROWTH; ADV	Pacific Region	0.5	8.66	9.76	6.30	☆	☆	☆	0.2	☐	238-6263	203-273-0121	None	1.42	1.00	Anna Tong	'94
AETNA ASIAN GROWTH; SEL	Pacific Region	24.8	8.70	9.99	7.02	☆	☆	☆	0.4	☐	238-6263	203-273-0121	None	1.25	None	Anna Tong	'94
AETNA BOND; ADV	Fixed Income	14.9	10.13	5.52	10.34	☆	☆	☆	5.1	☐	238-6263	203-273-0121	None	1.49	1.00	Jeanne Wong-Boehm	'94
AETNA BOND; SEL	Fixed Income	31.7	10.14	5.78	11.27	7.02	☆	☆	5.8	☐	238-6263	203-273-0121	None	0.76	None	Jeanne Wong-Boehm	'92
AETNA GOVT; ADV	Fixed Income	0.3	9.94	4.97	9.81	☆	☆	☆	5.2	☐	238-6263	203-273-0121	None	1.28	1.00	Jeanne Wong-Boehm	'94
AETNA GOVT; SEL	Fixed Income	19.9	9.95	5.12	10.68	☆	☆	☆	5.8	☐	238-6263	203-273-0121	None	0.41	None	Jeanne Wong-Boehm	'94
AETNA GRO & INC; ADV	Growth Income	1.3	12.46	8.80	18.60	☆	☆	☆	0.5	16.5	238-6263	203-273-0121	None	2.32	1.00	Martin J. Duffy	'94
AETNA GRO & INC; SEL	Growth Income	333.8	12.46	9.06	19.21	9.99	☆	☆	1.0	16.5	238-6263	203-273-0121	None	0.92	None	Martin J. Duffy	'92
AETNA GROWTH; ADV	Growth	1.0	12.49	11.62	27.27	☆	☆	☆	0.5	19.6	238-6263	203-273-0121	None	1.72	1.00	Peter Canoni	'94
AETNA GROWTH; SEL	Growth	33.3	12.57	11.83	28.10	☆	☆	☆	0.7	19.6	238-6263	203-273-0121	None	0.92	None	Peter Canoni	'94
AETNA INTL GROWTH; ADV	International	28.6	10.15	0.89	-1.67	☆	☆	☆	0.5	☐	238-6263	203-273-0121	None	2.27	1.00	Douglas Thomson	'94
AETNA INTL GROWTH; SEL	International	27.6	10.20	1.19	-0.75	6.45	☆	☆	1.1	☐	238-6263	203-273-0121	None	1.66	None	Douglas Thomson	'94
AETNA SMALL CO GRO; ADV	Small Company Growth	0.7	12.41	12.00	28.87	☆	☆	☆	0.0	N/A	238-6263	203-273-0121	None	1.78	1.00	Thomas Dibella	'94
AETNA SMALL CO GRO; SEL	Small Company Growth	30.1	12.50	12.21	29.79	☆	☆	☆	0.2	N/A	238-6263	203-273-0121	None	1.15	None	Thomas Dibella	'94
AFFILIATED FUND	Growth Income	4,635.8	11.49	7.31	23.32	13.97	12.19	13.24	2.6	15.7	426-1130	212-848-1800	5.75	0.63	None	Thomas S. Henderson	'91
AHA INV BALANCED ◪	Balanced	46.2	12.63	7.99	15.84	10.05	10.46	☆	2.5	15.7	332-2111	708-295-5000	None	0.26	None	Avatar/Criterion/Cambiar'88/'91/'91	

PERFORMANCE OF MUTUAL FUNDS (continued)

FUND NAME	OBJECTIVE	ASSETS ($ MIL) 5/31/95	NAV ($/SHR) 6/30/95	QTR	1YR	3YRS	5YRS	10YRS	DIV YLD %	P/E RATIO	800	In-State	Load	Exp. Ratio	Redemption	MANAGER	SINCE
AHA INV DVSD EQUITY ◨	Growth	37.4	14.76	8.64	21.01	13.57	12.00	☆	1.9	15.8	332-2111	708-295-5000	None	0.40	None	Cambiar/Invt Research Co	'88/'91
AHA INV FULL MAT FXD INC ◨	Fixed Income	52.4	9.88	5.94	11.47	7.53	9.02	☆	6.5		332-2111	708-295-5000	None	0.24	None	Bankers Tr/Criterion	'90/'88
AHA INV LTD MAT FXD INC ◨	Fixed Income	207.3	10.22	3.12	7.73	5.09	7.03	☆	6.1		332-2111	708-295-5000	None	0.14	None	Patterson/Neuberger Berman	'88/'92
AIM EQ AGGRESS GRO ⊠	Small Company Growth	883.7	35.59	14.00	50.36	37.68	26.89	16.95	0.0	22.9	347-1919	713-626-1919	5.50	1.07	None	Team Managed	N/A
AIM EQ CHARTER; RTL	Growth Income	1,667.8	9.79	11.08	21.44	10.81	12.12	14.57	2.0	16.7	347-1919	713-626-1919	5.50	1.17	None	Team Managed	N/A
AIM EQ CONSTELTN; RTL	Midcap	4,856.0	21.24	14.13	36.13	23.04	19.16	20.32	0.0	22.6	347-1919	713-626-1919	5.50	1.20	None	Team Managed	N/A
AIM EQ WEINGARTEN; RTL	Growth	4,012.1	18.58	12.47	29.28	11.05	10.92	15.44	0.4	19.3	347-1919	713-626-1919	5.50	1.20	None	Team Managed	N/A
AIM INTL EQUITY; A	International	619.9	13.04	7.33	7.89	13.03	☆	☆	0.3		347-1919	713-626-1919	5.50	1.64	None	Team Managed	N/A
AIM INTL EQUITY; B	International	20.5	12.97	7.10	☆	☆	☆	☆	0.0		347-1919	713-626-1919	None	None	5.00	Team Managed	N/A
AIM INTL GLBL AGG GR; A	Global Small Company	74.6	11.98	14.75	☆	☆	☆	☆	0.0		347-1919	713-626-1919	4.75	None	None	Team Managed	N/A
AIM INTL GLBL AGG GR; B	Global Small Company	37.0	11.94	14.59	☆	☆	☆	☆	0.0		347-1919	713-626-1919	None	None	5.00	Team Managed	N/A
AIM INTL GLBL GROWTH; A	Global	8.8	11.37	10.71	☆	☆	☆	☆	0.0		347-1919	713-626-1919	4.75	None	None	Team Managed	N/A
AIM INTL GLBL GROWTH; B	Global	6.9	11.33	10.64	☆	☆	☆	☆	0.0		347-1919	713-626-1919	None	None	5.00	Team Managed	N/A
AIM INTL GLBL INCOME; A	World Income	6.0	10.43	4.08	☆	☆	☆	☆	0.0		347-1919	713-626-1919	4.75	None	None	Team Managed	N/A
AIM INTL GLBL INCOME; B	World Income	2.1	10.42	4.07	☆	☆	☆	☆	0.0		347-1919	713-626-1919	None	None	5.00	Team Managed	N/A
AIM INV LTD TREAS; AIM	Fixed Income	275.0	10.04	2.74	6.73	4.57	6.44	☆	5.3		347-1919	713-626-1919	1.00	0.47	None	Team Managed	N/A
AIM INV LTD TREAS; INSTL	Fixed Income	122.2	10.04	2.80	6.98	4.80	6.66	☆	5.5		347-1919	713-626-1919	None	0.25	None	Team Managed	N/A
AIM SUMMIT FUND ★	Growth	873.7	11.02	13.84	30.56	13.76	13.05	13.57	0.9	18.2	347-1919	713-626-1919	8.50	0.72	None	Team Managed	N/A
AIM BALANCED FUND; A	Balanced	46.0	16.98	10.87	18.34	14.24	12.42	9.06	2.5	16.3	347-1919	713-626-1919	4.75	1.25	None	Team Managed	N/A
AIM BALANCED FUND; B	Balanced	30.3	16.98	10.64	17.32	☆	☆	☆	1.8	16.3	347-1919	713-626-1919	None	1.98	5.00	Team Managed	N/A
AIM GLOBAL UTILITIES; A	Utility	160.3	13.07	8.67	13.23	6.58	8.50	☆	4.4	13.3	347-1919	713-626-1919	5.50	1.18	None	Team Managed	N/A
AIM GLOBAL UTILITIES; B	Utility	51.1	13.06	8.45	12.16	☆	☆	☆	3.5	13.3	347-1919	713-626-1919	None	2.07	5.00	Team Managed	N/A
AIM GOVERNMENT SECS; A	Fixed Income	157.9	9.48	5.49	9.95	5.27	7.57	☆	7.6		347-1919	713-626-1919	4.75	1.04	None	Team Managed	N/A
AIM GOVERNMENT SECS; B	Fixed Income	33.5	9.47	5.28	8.92	☆	☆	☆	6.8		347-1919	713-626-1919	None	1.82	5.00	Team Managed	N/A
AIM GROWTH; A	Growth	137.6	12.72	13.27	32.03	10.10	7.80	11.24	0.0	21.3	347-1919	713-626-1919	5.50	1.22	None	Team Managed	N/A
AIM GROWTH; B	Growth	65.0	12.52	13.00	30.79	☆	☆	☆	0.0	21.3	347-1919	713-626-1919	None	2.18	5.00	Team Managed	N/A
AIM HIGH YIELD; A	Fixed Income	697.7	9.37	4.79	9.59	10.84	14.17	11.75	10.3		347-1919	713-626-1919	4.75	1.00	None	Team Managed	N/A
AIM HIGH YIELD; B	Fixed Income	313.9	9.36	4.58	8.68	☆	☆	☆	9.5		347-1919	713-626-1919	None	1.80	5.00	Team Managed	N/A
AIM INCOME; A	Fixed Income	218.1	7.81	6.88	13.81	8.00	9.41	9.93	7.7		347-1919	713-626-1919	4.75	0.98	None	Team Managed	N/A
AIM INCOME; B	Fixed Income	20.2	7.79	6.67	12.85	☆	☆	☆	6.9		347-1919	713-626-1919	None	1.83	5.00	Team Managed	N/A
AIM VALUE; A	Growth	2,051.8	25.98	12.22	30.62	20.80	17.53	17.64	0.6	16.4	347-1919	713-626-1919	5.50	0.98	None	Team Managed	N/A
AIM VALUE; B	Growth	1,322.3	25.86	12.00	29.44	☆	☆	☆	0.0	16.4	347-1919	713-626-1919	None	1.90	5.00	Team Managed	N/A
ALGER DEFINED ALLCAP ✿	Capital Appreciation	10.7	11.36	26.24	66.46	☆	☆	☆	0.0	29.1	992-3863	201-547-3600	None	2.87	5.00	David Alger	'93
ALGER DEFINED GROWTH ✿	Growth	8.0	10.59	19.33	42.62	☆	☆	☆	0.0	24.7	992-3863	201-547-3600	None	1.26	None	David Alger	'93
ALGER DEFINED MID CAP ✿	Midcap	8.0	13.57	19.95	58.57	☆	☆	☆	0.0	25.7	992-3863	201-547-3600	None	1.53	None	David Alger	'93
ALGER DEFINED SM CAP ✿	Small Company Growth	15.1	15.24	26.30	66.20	☆	☆	☆	0.0	N/A	992-3863	201-547-3600	None	1.47	None	David Alger	'93
ALGER BALANCED	Balanced	3.5	12.48	14.18	23.32	9.21	☆	☆	0.0	23.1	992-3863	201-547-3600	None	3.18	5.00	David Alger	'92
ALGER CAPITAL APPREC ★	Capital Appreciation	3.9	15.99	29.47	74.37	☆	☆	☆	0.0	29.1	992-3863	201-547-3600	None	5.53	5.00	David Alger	'93
ALGER GROWTH	Growth	97.4	25.15	17.58	37.24	22.06	16.82	☆	0.0	22.6	992-3863	201-547-3600	None	2.20	5.00	David Alger	'86
ALGER MIDCAP GROWTH	Midcap	28.6	16.39	18.68	49.95	☆	☆	☆	0.0	26.9	992-3863	201-547-3600	None	3.20	5.00	David Alger	'93
ALGER SMALL CAPITAL	Small Company Growth	357.5	29.73	22.75	49.41	22.14	16.13	☆	0.0	29.9	992-3863	201-547-3600	None	2.18	5.00	David Alger	'86
ALLIANCE ALL-ASIA; A	Pacific Region	2.4	10.64	3.10	3.10	☆	☆	☆	0.0		227-6618	201-319-4000	4.25	None	None	A. Rama Krishna	'94
ALLIANCE ALL-ASIA; B	Pacific Region	3.4	10.61	2.91	☆	☆	☆	☆	0.0		227-6618	201-319-4000	None	4.00	4.00	A. Rama Krishna	'94
ALLIANCE ALL-ASIA; C	Pacific Region	0.2	10.62	3.11	☆	☆	☆	☆	0.0		227-6618	201-319-4000	None	None	None	A. Rama Krishna	'94
ALLIANCE BALANCED; A	Balanced	156.5	14.74	8.49	15.80	8.66	9.00	10.53	2.5	16.1	227-6618	201-319-4000	4.25	1.27	None	Bruce Calvert	'90
ALLIANCE BALANCED; B	Balanced	14.6	14.55	8.22	14.86	7.81	☆	☆	1.9	16.1	227-6618	201-319-4000	None	2.05	4.00	Bruce Calvert	'91
ALLIANCE BALANCED; C	Balanced	5.1	14.57	8.37	14.93	☆	☆	☆	1.9	16.1	227-6618	201-319-4000	None	2.03	None	Bruce Calvert	'93
ALLIANCE BD CORP BD; A	Fixed Income	231.9	12.92	15.61	13.27	12.61	12.96	11.21	8.8		227-6618	201-319-4000	4.25	1.30	None	Wayne Lyski	'86

Fund	Objective	Net Assets ($Mil)	NAV	(2)	(3)	(4)	(5)	(6)	Yield %	Risk	Phone	Phone	Load	Exp.	Redmp.	Portfolio Manager	Year
ALLIANCE BD CORP BD; B	Fixed Income	238.6	12.92	15.41	12.54		☆	☆	8.1	□	227-4618	201-319-4000	None	2.00	3.00	Wayne Lyski	93
ALLIANCE BD CORP BD; C	Fixed Income	51.0	12.93	15.50	12.62		☆	☆	8.1	□	227-4618	201-319-4000	None	1.99	None	Wayne Lyski	93
ALLIANCE BD US GOVT; A	Fixed Income	468.3	7.96	5.73	10.37	6.70	8.48	☆	8.1	□	227-4618	201-319-4000	4.25	1.02	None	Paul DeNoon	92
ALLIANCE BD US GOVT; B	Fixed Income	778.1	7.96	5.53	9.52	5.93	☆	☆	7.4	□	227-4618	201-319-4000	None	1.72	3.00	Paul DeNoon	92
ALLIANCE BD US GOVT; C	Fixed Income	188.1	7.96	5.67	9.67		☆	☆	7.4	□	227-4618	201-319-4000	None	1.70	None	Paul DeNoon	93
ALLIANCE COUNTERPT; A	Growth Income	39.0	17.31	9.84	25.05	10.40	11.61	13.46	0.0	15.1	227-4618	201-319-4000	4.25	1.94	None	Dutch Handke	85
ALLIANCE COUNTERPT; B	Growth Income	1.5	16.97	9.63	24.19		☆	☆	0.0	15.1	227-4618	201-319-4000	None	2.73	4.00	Dutch Handke	93
ALLIANCE COUNTERPT; C	Growth Income	0.5	16.99	9.68	24.17		☆	☆	0.0	15.1	227-4618	201-319-4000	None	2.66	None	Dutch Handke	93
ALLIANCE FUND; A	Growth	812.4	6.89	13.51	26.48	16.58	13.90	14.67	0.2	14.4	227-4618	201-319-4000	4.25	1.05	None	Harrison/Jenkel	90/85
ALLIANCE FUND; B	Growth	22.6	6.71	13.34	25.67	15.64	☆	☆	0.0	14.4	227-4618	201-319-4000	None	1.89	4.00	Harrison/Jenkel	91/91
ALLIANCE FUND; C	Growth	6.8	6.71	13.34	25.47		☆	☆	0.0	14.4	227-4618	201-319-4000	None	1.87	None	Harrison/Jenkel	93/93
ALLIANCE GLBL DOLLAR; A	World Income	11.8	7.96	26.16	5.32		☆	☆	11.3	□	227-4618	201-319-4000	4.25	0.75	None	Wayne Lyski	94
ALLIANCE GLBL DOLLAR; B	World Income	57.5	7.96	25.86	4.23		☆	☆	10.4	□	227-4618	201-319-4000	None	1.45	3.00	Wayne Lyski	94
ALLIANCE GLBL DOLLAR; C	World Income	9.6	7.96	25.87	4.27		☆	☆	10.4	□	227-4618	201-319-4000	None	1.45	None	Wayne Lyski	94
ALLIANCE GLBL SM CAP; A	Global Small Company	55.0	9.65	6.87	9.91	7.39	2.21	8.16	0.0	□	227-4618	201-319-4000	4.25	2.42	None	Stewart/Rissman	94/94
ALLIANCE GLBL SM CAP; B	Global Small Company	4.7	9.25	6.57	9.04	6.60	☆	☆	0.0	□	227-4618	201-319-4000	None	3.15	4.00	Stewart/Rissman	94/94
ALLIANCE GLBL SM CAP; C	Global Small Company	1.1	9.26	6.56	9.03		☆	☆	0.0	□	227-4618	201-319-4000	None	3.13	None	Stewart/Rissman	94/94
ALLIANCE GRO & INC; A	Growth Income	425.3	2.54	11.46	21.69	10.92	9.96	12.88	1.9	14.2	227-4618	201-319-4000	4.25	1.03	None	Paul Rissman	94
ALLIANCE GRO & INC; B	Growth Income	113.5	2.54	11.73	21.23	10.10	☆	☆	1.2	14.2	227-4618	201-319-4000	None	1.85	4.00	Paul Rissman	94
ALLIANCE GRO & INC; C	Growth Income	25.5	2.54	11.73	21.23		☆	☆	1.2	14.2	227-4618	201-319-4000	None	1.84	None	Paul Rissman	94
ALLIANCE INC BUILDER; A	Specialty	1.3	10.21	9.73	11.96	5.10	☆	☆	5.0	17.0	227-4618	201-319-4000	4.25	2.52	None	Aran/Perkins	94/94
ALLIANCE INC BUILDER; B	Specialty	3.1	10.22	9.54	11.17		☆	☆	4.3	17.0	227-4618	201-319-4000	None	3.09	4.00	Aran/Perkins	94/94
ALLIANCE INC BUILDER; C	Specialty	52.9	10.19	9.46	10.97		☆	☆	4.3	17.0	227-4618	201-319-4000	None	2.67	None	Aran/Perkins	94/94
ALLIANCE INTL; A	International	168.2	16.81	2.94	0.59	8.79	2.23	14.14	0.0	□	227-4618	201-319-4000	4.25	1.90	None	A. Rama Krishna	93
ALLIANCE INTL; B	International	48.9	16.19	2.79	-0.22	7.89	☆	☆	0.0	□	227-4618	201-319-4000	None	2.78	4.00	A. Rama Krishna	93
ALLIANCE INTL; C	International	19.8	16.20	2.79	-0.22		☆	☆	0.0	□	227-4618	201-319-4000	None	2.78	None	A. Rama Krishna	93
ALLIANCE MTGE INC; A	Fixed Income	541.0	8.60	5.04	9.21	5.80	8.69	8.79	6.9	□	227-4618	201-319-4000	4.25	1.29	None	Ullman/Young	92/92
ALLIANCE MTGE INC; B	Fixed Income	867.7	8.61	4.84	8.51	5.16	☆	☆	6.1	□	227-4618	201-319-4000	None	2.00	3.00	Ullman/Young	92/92
ALLIANCE MTGE INC; C	Fixed Income	54.3	8.61	4.84	8.64		☆	☆	6.1	□	227-4618	201-319-4000	None	1.97	None	Ullman/Young	93/93
ALLIANCE MTGE STR; A	Fixed Income	34.1	9.48	2.07	3.69	4.17	☆	☆	5.5	□	227-4618	201-319-4000	4.25	1.34	None	Ullman/Young	92/92
ALLIANCE MTGE STR; B	Fixed Income	109.7	9.49	1.89	2.96	3.48	☆	☆	4.8	□	227-4618	201-319-4000	None	2.08	3.00	Ullman/Young	92/92
ALLIANCE MTGE STR; C	Fixed Income	92.9	9.49	1.89	2.97		☆	☆	4.8	□	227-4618	201-319-4000	None	2.04	None	Ullman/Young	93/93
ALLIANCE MU-MK STR; A	World Income	91.2	6.74	5.46	-8.14	-3.33	☆	☆	9.9	□	227-4618	201-319-4000	4.25	1.41	None	Doug Peebles	94
ALLIANCE MU-MK STR; B	World Income	137.4	6.74	5.06	-8.92	-4.07	☆	☆	9.0	□	227-4618	201-319-4000	None	2.11	3.00	Doug Peebles	94
ALLIANCE MU-MK STR; C	World Income	0.7	6.74	5.22	-8.90		☆	☆	9.0	□	227-4618	201-319-4000	None	2.08	None	Doug Peebles	94
ALLIANCE N AM GV INC; A	World Income	236.4	6.68	17.24	-10.02	-0.98	☆	☆	14.5	□	227-4618	201-319-4000	4.25	1.70	None	Wayne Lyski	92
ALLIANCE N AM GV INC; B	World Income	1,157.6	6.68	16.93	-10.91	-1.78	☆	☆	13.5	□	227-4618	201-319-4000	None	2.41	3.00	Wayne Lyski	92
ALLIANCE N AM GV INC; C	World Income	232.6	6.68	16.93	-10.90		☆	☆	13.5	□	227-4618	201-319-4000	None	2.39	None	Wayne Lyski	93
ALLIANCE NEW EUROPE; A	European Region	81.1	14.39	6.99	20.19	12.38	6.30	☆	0.6	□	227-4618	201-319-4000	4.25	2.30	None	Eric Perkins	93
ALLIANCE NEW EUROPE; B	European Region	30.9	14.02	6.78	19.40	11.58	☆	☆	0.7	□	227-4618	201-319-4000	None	3.02	4.00	Eric Perkins	92
ALLIANCE NEW EUROPE; C	European Region	7.5	14.03	6.77	19.38		☆	☆	0.7	□	227-4618	201-319-4000	None	3.00	None	Eric Perkins	92
ALLIANCE PORT CONSV; A	Flexible	16.8	10.85	6.53	11.17	6.72	☆	☆	4.2	17.4	227-4618	201-319-4000	4.25	1.40	None	Franklin Kennedy III	92
ALLIANCE PORT CONSV; B	Flexible	31.2	10.99	6.26	10.42	5.96	☆	☆	3.2	17.4	227-4618	201-319-4000	None	2.11	4.00	Franklin Kennedy III	92
ALLIANCE PORT CONSV; C	Flexible	4.5	11.00	6.36	10.41		☆	☆	3.2	17.4	227-4618	201-319-4000	None	2.10	None	Franklin Kennedy III	92
ALLIANCE PORT GR INV; A	Flexible	23.0	12.89	8.05	15.13	11.07	☆	☆	1.2	18.6	227-4618	201-319-4000	4.25	1.40	None	Franklin Kennedy III	92
ALLIANCE PORT GR INV; B	Flexible	45.6	12.89	7.87	14.32	10.32	☆	☆	0.8	18.6	227-4618	201-319-4000	None	2.11	4.00	Franklin Kennedy III	92
ALLIANCE PORT GR INV; C	Flexible	4.4	12.90	7.95	14.40		☆	☆	0.8	18.6	227-4618	201-319-4000	None	2.10	None	Franklin Kennedy III	93

★ AIM SUMMIT--Contractual plan fund.

★ ALGER CAPITAL APPREC--Fund has been reclassified from Growth to Capital Appreciation.

© Copyright Lipper Analytical Services, Inc.

PERFORMANCE OF MUTUAL FUNDS (continued)

FUND NAME	OBJECTIVE	ASSETS ($ MIL) 5/31/95	NAV ($/SHR) 6/30/95	RETURN THROUGH 6/30 — QTR	1YR	3YRS (Ann.)	5YRS (Ann.)	10YRS (Ann.)	DIV YLD %	P/E RATIO	Phone 800	Phone In-State	FEES Load	FEES Exp. Ratio	FEES Redemption	MANAGER	SINCE
ALLIANCE PORT GROWTH; A	Growth	226.8	27.97	10.90	21.43	18.85	☆		0.4	14.9	227-4618	201-319-4000	4.25	1.40	None	Tyler Smith	'90
ALLIANCE PORT GROWTH; B	Growth	1,140.7	23.57	10.71	20.61	18.06	17.94		0.0	14.9	227-4618	201-319-4000	None	2.10	4.00	Tyler Smith	'87
ALLIANCE PORT GROWTH; C	Growth	167.9	23.58	10.70	20.60	☆			0.0	14.9	227-4618	201-319-4000	None	2.10	None	Tyler Smith	'93
ALLIANCE PORT SH GOV; A	Fixed Income	3.1	9.70	1.91	5.25	3.77	☆		4.7	□	227-4618	201-319-4000	4.25	1.27	None	Paul DeNoon	'93
ALLIANCE PORT SH GOV; B	Fixed Income	5.7	9.80	1.71	4.33	3.05	☆		3.9	□	227-4618	201-319-4000	None	2.05	3.00	Paul DeNoon	'93
ALLIANCE PORT SH GOV; C	Fixed Income	4.9	9.80	1.81	4.44	☆			3.9	□	227-4618	201-319-4000	None	2.10	None	Paul DeNoon	'93
ALLIANCE PORT STRAT; A	Balanced	10.0	17.60	7.51	12.02	7.54	☆		1.3	N/A	227-4618	201-319-4000	4.25	1.40	None	Bruce Calvert	'95
ALLIANCE PORT STRAT; B	Balanced	36.4	15.24	7.32	11.22	6.74	9.09		0.8	N/A	227-4618	201-319-4000	None	2.10	4.00	Bruce Calvert	'95
ALLIANCE PORT STRAT; C	Balanced	3.9	15.25	7.32	11.21	☆			0.8	N/A	227-4618	201-319-4000	None	2.10	None	Bruce Calvert	'95
ALLIANCE PREMIER GR; A	Growth	41.9	13.85	18.38	31.26	☆			0.0	12.7	227-4618	201-319-4000	4.25	1.96	None	Al Harrison	'92
ALLIANCE PREMIER GR; B	Growth	157.1	13.66	18.27	30.60	☆			0.0	12.7	227-4618	201-319-4000	None	2.47	4.00	Al Harrison	'93
ALLIANCE PREMIER GR; C	Growth	8.6	13.67	18.25	30.57	☆			0.0	12.7	227-4618	201-319-4000	None	2.47	None	Al Harrison	'95
ALLIANCE QUASAR; A	Small Company Growth	126.8	21.00	9.38	21.81	12.11	10.50		0.0	14.8	227-4618	201-319-4000	4.25	1.67	None	Al Stewart	'94
ALLIANCE QUASAR; B	Small Company Growth	12.5	20.06	9.20	20.93	11.19	5.81		0.0	14.8	227-4618	201-319-4000	None	2.50	4.00	Al Stewart	'94
ALLIANCE QUASAR; C	Small Company Growth	1.1	20.08	9.19	20.98	☆			0.0	14.8	227-4618	201-319-4000	None	2.48	None	Al Stewart	'94
ALLIANCE SH-TM MU-MK; A	World Income	365.4	7.42	4.42	-7.29	-1.61	2.42		9.3	□	227-4618	201-319-4000	4.25	1.13	None	Sinche/Peebles	'89/'94
ALLIANCE SH-TM MU-MK; B	World Income	611.1	7.42	4.06	-8.01	-2.34	1.69		8.5	□	227-4618	201-319-4000	None	1.85	3.00	Sinche/Peebles	'90/'94
ALLIANCE SH-TM MU-MK; C	World Income	4.1	7.42	4.06	-8.00	☆			8.5	□	227-4618	201-319-4000	None	1.83	None	Sinche/Peebles	'93/'94
ALLIANCE TECHNOLOGY; A	Science & Technology	255.1	41.15	25.50	82.40	41.01	24.66	23.05	0.0	25.9	227-4618	201-319-4000	4.25	1.73	None	Anastos/Malone	'92/'92
ALLIANCE TECHNOLOGY; B	Science & Technology	88.3	40.46	25.22	81.09	☆			0.0	25.9	227-4618	201-319-4000	None	2.57	4.00	Anastos/Malone	'93/'93
ALLIANCE TECHNOLOGY; C	Science & Technology	16.5	40.46	25.22	81.09	☆			0.0	25.9	227-4618	201-319-4000	None	2.52	None	Anastos/Malone	'93/'93
ALLIANCE UTILITY INC; A	Utility	2.5	9.57	7.33	14.04	☆			4.8	12.5	227-4618	201-319-4000	4.25	1.50	None	Levi/Alison	'95/'95
ALLIANCE UTILITY INC; B	Utility	5.6	9.57	7.16	13.21	☆			4.1	12.5	227-4618	201-319-4000	None	2.20	4.00	Levi/Alison	'95/'95
ALLIANCE UTILITY INC; C	Utility	3.5	9.58	7.15	13.19	☆			4.1	12.5	227-4618	201-319-4000	None	2.20	None	Levi/Alison	'95/'95
ALLIANCE WORLD INCOME	World Income	61.2	1.66	3.43	-6.17	-1.04	☆		5.9	□	227-4618	201-319-4000	None	1.70	None	Sinche/Peebles	'90/'92
ALLIANCE WRLWDE PRVT; A	International	13.8	10.18	7.84	4.41	☆			0.0	□	227-4618	201-319-4000	4.25		None	Mark Breedon	'94
ALLIANCE WRLWDE PRVT; B	International	79.4	10.10	7.56	3.70	☆			0.0	□	227-4618	201-319-4000	None		4.00	Mark Breedon	'94
ALLIANCE WRLWDE PRVT; C	International	0.2	10.10	7.56	☆				0.0	□	227-4618	201-319-4000	None		None	Mark Breedon	'95
AMANA INCOME FUND	Equity Income	10.7	13.04	3.68	13.41	6.65	6.82	☆	1.8	16.0	728-8762	206-734-9900	None	1.58	None	Nicholas Kaiser	'86
AMBASSADOR ESTBL; FID ■	Growth	73.8	N/A	N/A	N/A	N/A			0.0	N/A	892-4366	None	None	0.95	None	Leonard J. Barr	'95
AMBASSADOR ESTBL; INV	Growth	102.0	N/A	N/A	N/A	N/A			0.0	N/A	892-4366	None	None	1.20	None	Leonard J. Barr	'95
AMBASSADOR ESTBL; RET A	Growth	5.9	N/A	N/A	N/A	N/A			0.0	N/A	892-4366	None	3.75	1.20	None	Leonard J. Barr	N/A
AMCAP FUND	Growth	3,139.4	13.40	9.57	21.75	12.62	11.26	13.35	1.2	17.5	421-4120	714-671-7000	5.75	0.71	None	Multiple Managers	'92
AMCORE VINTAGE EQUITY	Growth	158.5	12.39	8.64	24.90	☆			0.9	17.5	438-6375	None	None	0.54	None	Darrell Thompson	'92
AMCORE VINTAGE FXD INC	Fixed Income	84.9	9.98	4.64	9.64	☆			5.9	□	438-6375	None	None	0.51	None	Dean Countryman	'92
AMELIA EARHART EAGLE EQ	Growth	1.1	16.07	17.38	39.01	☆			0.0	N/A	525-3863	919-972-9922	4.50	1.86	None	Jill H. Travis	'93
AMER AADV BALANCED; INST	Balanced	243.4	13.23	6.78	16.14	11.27	11.48		3.9	14.3	645-3795	None	None	0.36	None	Multiple Managers	N/A
AMER AADV BALANCED; MILE	Balanced	0.8	13.20	6.71	☆				0.0	14.3	645-3794	None	None	None	None	Multiple Managers	N/A
AMER AADV BALANCED; PLAN	Balanced	1.2	13.19	6.63	☆				0.0	14.3	423-7526	817-967-3509	None	None	None	Multiple Managers	N/A
AMER AADV GRO & INC; INST	Growth Income	57.7	14.99	7.07	18.73	13.05	12.53		2.8	N/A	645-3795	None	None	0.33	None	Multiple Managers	N/A
AMER AADV GRO & INC; MILE	Growth Income	1.6	14.94	7.02	☆				0.0	N/A	645-3794	None	None	None	None	Multiple Managers	N/A
AMER AADV GRO & INC; PLAN	Growth Income	0.7	14.91	6.73	☆				0.0	N/A	423-7526	817-967-3509	None	None	None	Multiple Managers	N/A
AMER AADV INTL EQTY; INST	International	24.4	12.86	7.26	12.54	12.95	☆		1.6	□	645-3794	None	None	0.61	None	Multiple Managers	N/A
AMER AADV INTL EQTY; MILE	International	1.2	12.80	7.11	☆				0.0	□	645-3795	None	None	None	None	Multiple Managers	N/A
AMER AADV INTL EQTY; PLAN	International	0.9	12.80	7.11	☆				0.0	□	423-7526	817-967-3509	None	None	None	Multiple Managers	N/A

Fund	Objective	Net Assets ($mil)	NAV	Ret (YTD)	Ret (1-Yr)	3-Yr	5-Yr	10-Yr	Yield %		Phone	Phone	Max Load	CDSC	Exp.	Manager	Mgr. Since
AMER AADV LTD TERM; INST	Fixed Income	86.4	9.79	3.29	6.76	5.35	7.41	☆	6.0	☐	817-967-3509	645-3795	None	None	0.31	Fields/Samples	'87/'95
AMER AADV LTD TERM; MILE	Fixed Income	0.6	9.79	3.23	☆	☆	☆	☆	0.0	☐	None	645-3794	None	None	None	Fields/Samples	'94/'95
AMER AADV LTD TERM; PLAN	Fixed Income	0.4	9.80	3.23	☆	☆	☆	☆	0.0	☐	817-967-3509	423-7526	None	None	None	Fields/Samples	'94/'95
AMER CAP COMSTOCK; A	Growth Income	973.7	14.40	8.46	21.54	11.42	10.50	11.81	2.0	16.7	713-993-0500	421-5666	5.75	None	1.01	Bob Baker	'94
AMER CAP COMSTOCK; B	Growth Income	31.5	14.42	8.22	20.55	☆	☆	☆	1.2	16.7	713-993-0500	421-5666	None	5.00	1.84	Bob Baker	'94
AMER CAP COMSTOCK; C	Growth Income	2.6	14.41	8.22	20.55	☆	☆	☆	1.2	16.7	713-993-0500	421-5666	None	1.00	1.85	Bob Baker	'94
AMER CAP CORP BOND; A	Fixed Income	169.2	6.92	7.35	13.46	8.08	9.87	9.58	6.9	☐	713-993-0500	421-5666	4.75	None	1.09	David R. Troth	'79
AMER CAP CORP BOND; B	Fixed Income	17.6	6.92	7.17	12.39	☆	☆	☆	6.2	☐	713-993-0500	421-5666	None	4.00	1.90	David R. Troth	'92
AMER CAP EMERG GRO; A	Midcap	802.9	28.44	12.46	28.48	20.62	17.63	13.64	0.0	N/A	713-993-0500	421-5666	5.75	None	1.18	Gary Lewis	'89
AMER CAP EMERG GRO; B	Midcap	360.7	27.63	12.23	27.43	19.63	☆	☆	0.0	N/A	713-993-0500	421-5666	None	5.00	2.01	Gary Lewis	'92
AMER CAP EMERG GRO; C	Midcap	32.8	27.97	12.19	27.41	☆	☆	☆	0.0	N/A	713-993-0500	421-5666	None	1.00	2.02	Gary Lewis	'93
AMER CAP ENTERPRISE; A	Growth	864.9	13.69	11.57	27.34	14.94	13.12	13.31	0.6	18.6	713-993-0500	421-5666	5.75	None	1.05	Stephen Boyd	'89
AMER CAP ENTERPRISE; B	Growth	129.6	13.57	11.41	26.35	13.97	☆	☆	0.0	18.6	713-993-0500	421-5666	None	5.00	1.89	Stephen Boyd	'91
AMER CAP ENTERPRISE; C	Growth	9.5	13.64	11.53	26.41	☆	☆	☆	0.0	18.6	713-993-0500	421-5666	None	1.00	1.90	Stephen Boyd	'93
AMER CAP EQUITY INC; A	Equity Income	284.3	5.96	8.15	19.53	13.24	11.61	12.02	3.1	17.4	713-993-0500	421-5666	5.75	None	1.02	Jim Gilligan	'90
AMER CAP EQUITY INC; B	Equity Income	297.3	5.96	7.97	18.68	☆	☆	☆	2.4	17.4	713-993-0500	421-5666	None	5.00	1.82	Jim Gilligan	'92
AMER CAP EQUITY INC; C	Equity Income	31.0	5.96	7.97	18.68	☆	☆	☆	2.4	17.4	713-993-0500	421-5666	None	1.00	1.82	Jim Gilligan	'93
AMER CAP EXCHANGE ☒	Growth	44.0	144.46	11.83	34.82	12.34	13.08	13.42	0.0	24.2	713-993-0500	421-5666	2.25	None	0.89	Stephen Boyd	'90
AMER CAP FED MTGE; A	Fixed Income	43.2	12.28	2.86	6.82	3.41	5.81	☆	4.9	☐	713-993-0500	421-5666	None	None	1.15	Ted Mundy	'94
AMER CAP FED MTGE; B ☒	Fixed Income	15.6	12.30	2.74	5.97	2.64	☆	☆	4.1	☐	713-993-0500	421-5666	None	3.00	1.91	Ted Mundy	'94
AMER CAP FED MTGE; C	Fixed Income	5.8	12.28	2.66	5.98	☆	☆	☆	4.1	☐	713-993-0500	421-5666	None	1.00	1.90	Ted Mundy	'94
AMER CAP GLBL MGD; A	Global Flexible	13.6	9.78	4.89	6.39	15.42	☆	☆	0.9	☐	713-993-0500	421-5666	4.75	None	2.75	Team Managed	N/A
AMER CAP GLBL MGD; B	Global Flexible	8.0	9.76	4.69	5.51	☆	☆	☆	0.3	☐	713-993-0500	421-5666	None	4.00	3.92	Team Managed	N/A
AMER CAP GLBL MGD; C	Global Flexible	1.6	9.79	4.67	5.83	☆	☆	☆	0.3	☐	713-993-0500	421-5666	None	1.00	3.36	Team Managed	N/A
AMER CAP GOVERNMENT; A	Fixed Income	2,647.1	10.31	4.99	10.92	5.24	8.74	8.35	6.5	17.3	713-993-0500	421-5666	4.75	None	1.02	Jack Reynoldson	'88
AMER CAP GOVERNMENT; B	Fixed Income	286.3	10.32	4.70	10.16	☆	☆	☆	5.8	17.3	713-993-0500	421-5666	None	4.00	1.78	Jack Reynoldson	'91
AMER CAP GOVERNMENT; C	Fixed Income	30.0	10.30	4.70	10.07	☆	☆	☆	5.8	17.3	713-993-0500	421-5666	None	1.00	1.78	Jack Reynoldson	'93
AMER CAP GROW & INC; A	Growth Income	244.4	13.37	8.81	21.33	14.17	12.21	12.26	2.1	☐	713-993-0500	421-5666	5.75	None	1.16	Jim Gilligan	'90
AMER CAP GROW & INC; B	Growth Income	30.8	13.37	8.65	20.36	☆	☆	☆	1.5	☐	713-993-0500	421-5666	None	5.00	2.02	Jim Gilligan	'93
AMER CAP GROW & INC; C	Growth Income	5.1	13.38	8.64	20.35	☆	☆	☆	1.5	☐	713-993-0500	421-5666	None	1.00	2.01	Jim Gilligan	'93
AMER CAP HARBOR; A	Convertible Securities	382.8	14.50	6.47	12.21	9.20	9.08	10.21	4.3	☐	713-993-0500	421-5666	5.75	None	1.04	James Behrmann	'84
AMER CAP HARBOR; B	Convertible Securities	75.0	14.46	6.27	11.37	☆	☆	☆	3.5	☐	713-993-0500	421-5666	None	5.00	1.84	James Behrmann	'91
AMER CAP HARBOR; C	Convertible Securities	3.4	14.52	6.17	11.32	☆	☆	☆	3.4	☐	713-993-0500	421-5666	None	1.00	1.84	James Behrmann	'93
AMER CAP HIGH YIELD; A	Fixed Income	407.6	6.10	4.76	7.28	8.34	12.29	7.85	9.3	18.6	713-993-0500	421-5666	4.75	None	1.10	Ellis Bigelow	'89
AMER CAP HIGH YIELD; B	Fixed Income	85.2	6.11	4.55	6.42	☆	☆	☆	8.5	18.6	713-993-0500	421-5666	None	4.00	1.90	Ellis Bigelow	'92
AMER CAP HIGH YIELD; C	Fixed Income	13.6	6.09	4.56	6.44	☆	☆	☆	8.6	N/A	713-993-0500	421-5666	None	1.00	1.91	Ellis Bigelow	'93
AMER CAP PACE; A	Growth	2,214.3	11.62	10.46	20.62	9.46	9.75	11.35	1.0	☐	713-993-0500	421-5666	5.75	None	1.02	Stephen Boyd	'94
AMER CAP PACE; B	Growth	45.4	11.53	10.23	19.73	11.35	☆	☆	0.3	☐	713-993-0500	421-5666	None	5.00	1.79	Stephen Boyd	'94
AMER CAP REAL ESTATE; A	Real Estate	6.2	9.27	4.64	2.45	☆	☆	☆	0.4	☐	713-993-0500	421-5666	4.75	None	None	Mary Jane Maly	'94
AMER CAP REAL ESTATE; B	Fixed Income	10.8	9.27	4.30	1.64	☆	☆	☆	3.6	☐	713-993-0500	421-5666	None	4.00	None	Mary Jane Maly	'94
AMER CAP REAL ESTATE; C	Real Estate	1.7	9.27	4.41	1.84	☆	☆	☆	3.8	☐	713-993-0500	421-5666	None	1.00	1.58	Mary Jane Maly	'94
AMER CAP TGT PORT '97 ☒	Fixed Income	17.2	13.88	2.51	6.20	10.42	☆	☆	0.0	N/A	713-993-0500	421-5666	3.00	None	1.07	Jack Reynoldson	'90
AMER CAP US GOVT INC; A	Fixed Income	72.9	8.42	4.54	10.16	4.71	☆	☆	7.7	13.6	713-993-0500	421-5666	4.75	None	1.82	Ted Mundy	'94
AMER CAP US GOVT INC; B	Fixed Income	208.7	8.41	4.24	9.18	☆	☆	☆	6.9	13.6	713-993-0500	421-5666	None	4.00	1.82	Ted Mundy	'94
AMER CAP US GOVT INC; C	Fixed Income	30.5	8.41	4.24	9.18	☆	☆	☆	6.9	13.6	713-993-0500	421-5666	None	1.00	1.82	Ted Mundy	'94
AMER CAP UTIL INCOME; A	Utility	9.2	9.18	6.76	14.52	8.08	☆	☆	5.1	☐	713-993-0500	421-5666	4.75	None	1.06	Mary Jane Maly	'94
AMER CAP UTIL INCOME; B	Utility	15.4	9.16	6.35	13.56	☆	☆	☆	4.4	☐	713-993-0500	421-5666	None	4.00	1.82	Mary Jane Maly	'94
AMER CAP UTIL INCOME; C	Utility	2.5	9.16	6.51	13.60	☆	☆	☆	4.4	☐	713-993-0500	421-5666	None	1.00	1.79	Mary Jane Maly	'94
AMER CAP WRLD GL EQ; A	Global	59.1	11.95	5.75	5.39	7.19	☆	☆	0.0	☐	713-993-0500	421-5666	5.75	None	2.46	New/Kysel	'94/'94
AMER CAP WRLD GL EQ; B	Global	61.7	11.66	5.62	4.69	☆	☆	☆	0.0	☐	713-993-0500	421-5666	None	5.00	3.21	New/Kysel	'94/'94

PERFORMANCE OF MUTUAL FUNDS (continued)

FUND NAME	OBJECTIVE	ASSETS ($ MIL) 5/31/95	NAV ($/SHR) 6/30/95	RETURN THROUGH 6/30 (Annualized) QTR	1YR	3YRS	5YRS	10YRS	DIV YLD %	P/E RATIO	PHONE 800	PHONE In-State	FEES Load	Exp. Ratio	Redemption	MANAGER	SINCE
AMER CAP WRLD GL EQ; C	Global	6.6	11.77	5.56	4.65	☆	☆	☆	0.0	□	421-5666	713-993-0500	None	3.21	1.00	New/Kysel	'94/'94
AMER CAP WRLD GL GOV; A	World Income	47.7	8.20	3.88	7.93	5.84	☆	☆	7.3	□	421-5666	713-993-0500	4.75	1.45	None	Reynoldson/Doyle	'91/'94
AMER CAP WRLD GL GOV; B	World Income	123.2	8.24	3.68	7.10	5.04	☆	☆	6.5	□	421-5666	713-993-0500	None	2.22	4.00	Reynoldson/Doyle	'91/'94
AMER CAP WRLD GL GOV; C	World Income	18.5	8.18	3.57	7.02	☆	☆	☆	6.6	□	421-5666	713-993-0500	None	2.22	1.00	Reynoldson/Doyle	'93/'94
AMER FDS INC US GOVT	Fixed Income	1,358.0	13.32	4.77	9.63	6.61	8.39	☆	7.7	□	421-4120	714-671-7000	4.75	0.78	None	Multiple Managers	N/A
AMER PERFORM AGGR GROWTH	Small Company Growth	26.5	14.55	13.41	31.20	20.24	☆	☆	0.0	25.2	762-7085	None	4.00	1.35	None	Joe Sing	'92
AMER PERFORM BOND	Fixed Income	34.6	9.31	5.40	9.16	6.61	☆	☆	5.9	□	762-7085	None	4.00	1.05	None	Brian Henderson	'90
AMER PERFORM EQUITY	Growth	71.5	11.81	9.43	22.73	10.54	☆	☆	1.6	15.4	762-7085	None	4.00	1.12	None	Gratton Potter	'90
AMER PERFORM INTMDT BOND	Fixed Income	76.9	10.27	3.75	7.26	5.48	☆	☆	5.8	□	762-7085	None	3.00	0.98	None	Brian Henderson	'93
AMERICA'S UTILITY FUND	Utility	143.4	21.59	6.13	16.32	7.06	☆	☆	5.6	N/A	487-3863	804-649-1315	None	1.21	None	Julie M. Cannell	'92
AMERICAN BALANCED FUND	Balanced	2,453.2	13.35	5.84	17.45	10.52	11.16	12.31	4.2	15.4	421-4120	714-671-7000	5.75	0.68	None	Multiple Managers	N/A
AMERICAN GROWTH	Growth	79.3	8.41	9.65	11.76	14.52	13.13	10.39	1.3	16.3	525-2406	303-623-6137	5.75	1.34	None	Robert Brody	'58
AMERICAN HERITAGE FUND	Capital Appreciation	31.0	0.65	-14.47	-30.58	-8.76	2.62	-4.37	21.2	8.2	828-5050	212-397-3900	None	2.41	None	Heiko Thieme	'90
AMERICAN HERITAGE GROWTH	Growth	4.4	3.77	6.80	26.50	☆	☆	☆	62.6	6.5	828-5050	212-397-3900	None		None	Heiko Thieme	'94
AMERICAN HIGH-INCOME TR	Fixed Income	988.5	14.15	7.46	10.61	10.34	12.68	☆	9.3	□	421-4120	714-671-7000	4.75	0.86	None	Multiple Managers	N/A
AMERICAN LEADERS; A	Growth Income	291.5	16.80	8.87	20.23	13.14	12.88	12.08	1.3	15.0	245-4770	412-288-1900	5.50	1.18	None	Peter R. Anderson	'89
AMERICAN LEADERS; B	Growth Income	66.3	16.81	8.70	8.64	☆	☆	☆	1.0	N/A	245-4770	412-288-1900	None	2.11	5.50	Peter R. Anderson	'94
AMERICAN LEADERS; C	Growth Income	22.6	16.79	8.60	19.14	☆	☆	☆	0.6	15.0	245-4770	412-288-1900	1.00	1.35	1.00	Peter R. Anderson	'93
AMERICAN LEADERS; FORT	Growth Income	31.8	16.79	8.80	20.36	☆	☆	☆	1.3	15.0	245-4770	412-288-1900	1.00	1.35	1.00	Peter R. Anderson	'93
AMERICAN MUTUAL	Growth Income	6,043.6	22.91	6.99	17.84	11.72	11.07	12.84	3.6	N/A	421-4120	714-671-7000	5.75	0.60	None	Multiple Managers	N/A
AMERICAN NATIONAL GROWTH	Growth	126.2	4.34	5.96	21.85	12.00	10.29	12.11	1.6	18.6	231-4639	409-763-2767	5.75	0.97	None	Gordon D. Dixon	'93
AMERICAN NATIONAL INCOME	Equity Income	126.5	21.48	6.61	18.24	10.76	11.34	11.51	2.7	15.2	231-4639	409-763-2767	5.75	1.12	None	David Zimansky	'91
AMSOUTH BALANCED	Balanced	288.0	12.59	6.64	16.09	11.23	☆	☆	3.6	18.3	451-8379	205-326-4732	4.50	0.83	None	AmSouth Bank	'88
AMSOUTH BOND FUND	Fixed Income	105.3	10.92	6.55	11.96	7.60	9.05	☆	6.4	□	451-8379	205-326-4732	3.00	0.78	None	AmSouth Bank	'88
AMSOUTH EQUITY FUND	Capital Appreciation	262.1	16.26	6.86	18.88	13.91	11.38	☆	1.9	18.0	451-8379	205-326-4732	4.50	0.94	None	AmSouth Bank	'88
AMSOUTH GOVT INCOME	Fixed Income	16.4	9.59	4.54	9.68	☆	☆	☆	7.3	□	451-8379	205-326-4732	3.00	0.37	None	AmSouth Bank	'93
AMSOUTH LTD MATURITY	Fixed Income	50.1	10.43	4.03	8.64	5.34	7.27	☆	5.5	□	451-8379	205-326-4732	3.00	0.79	None	AmSouth Bank	'89
AMSOUTH REGIONAL EQUITY	Capital Appreciation	65.5	18.23	3.31	12.18	12.32	12.37	☆	1.3	15.2	451-8379	205-326-4732	4.50	0.79	None	AmSouth Bank	'88
AMTRUST VALUE FUND	Small Company Growth	0.7	10.84	10.05	17.44	☆	☆	☆	0.0	19.8	532-1146	512-578-7778	None	0.80	None	James Baker	'93
AMWAY MUTUAL FUND	Growth	70.6	7.82	6.68	17.51	10.47	10.21	12.92	0.4	18.0	346-2670	616-676-6288	3.00	1.10	None	C. Charles Hetzel	'95
ANALYSTS INV FXD INC.	Fixed Income	1.4	13.61	6.23	9.84	☆	☆	☆	5.7	□	None	513-984-3377	None	1.50	None	Lee Manzler	'93
ANALYSTS INV STOCK	Growth	2.3	17.26	6.62	15.19	☆	☆	☆	1.6	N/A	None	513-984-3377	None	2.00	None	Lee Manzler	'93
ANALYTIC OPTIONED EQU	Equity Income	45.9	12.43	6.38	16.58	8.69	8.20	9.69	2.4	16.1	374-2633	714-833-0294	None	1.10	None	Chuck Dobson	'78
ANALYTIC ENHANCED EQUITY	Growth	1.6	11.67	10.04	21.73	☆	☆	☆	2.2	19.2	374-2633	714-833-0294	None	0.24	None	Steve Huntsinger	'93
ANALYTIC MASTER FXD INC	Fixed Income	6.2	10.12	5.40	12.00	☆	☆	☆	6.1	□	374-2633	714-833-0294	None	0.60	None	John Flom	'93
ANALYTIC SH-TERM GOVT	Fixed Income	26.2	9.89	2.98	7.61	☆	☆	☆	5.2	□	374-2633	714-833-0294	None	0.45	None	John Flom	'93
ANCHOR CAP ACCUM ➹	Midcap	10.3	21.58	0.70	12.80	5.56	5.92	7.59	2.1	17.1	None	610-458-9599	4.00	1.10	None	Paul Jaspard	'83
ANCHOR INTL BOND ➹	World Income	28.8	9.40	1.95	N/A	☆	☆	☆	4.1	□	None	610-458-9599	4.00	1.09	None	Paul Jaspard	'87
ANCHOR RES & COMMODITY ➹ ☒	Natural Resources	7.0	9.87	2.07	☆	☆	☆	☆	0.0	N/A	None	610-458-9599	4.00	None	None	Paul Jaspard	'95
ANTHEM AGGRESS GROWTH ☒	Midcap	0.1	11.33	1.61	☆	☆	☆	☆	0.1	N/A	273-3936	317-692-3900	None	None	None	Steven W. Voss	'95
ANTHEM BALANCED ☒	Balanced	1.2	11.43	2.33	12.73	6.49	☆	☆	2.7	17.0	273-3936	317-692-3900	None	1.42	None	Stephen L. Tufts	'95
ANTHEM EQUITY INCOME ☒	Equity Income	0.1	10.82	1.88	☆	☆	☆	☆	2.0	N/A	273-3936	317-692-3900	None	1.18	None	Nancy E. Dobras	'95
ANTHEM GOVT SECS ☒	Fixed Income	0.1	10.22	2.08	6.60	5.57	☆	☆	5.8	□	273-3936	317-692-3900	None	1.18	None	Baird A. Blake	'95
ANTHEM GROWTH & INCOME ☒	Growth Income	1.5	11.65	0.43	11.96	4.74	☆	☆	1.0	18.0	273-3936	317-692-3900	None	1.55	None	Steven W. Voss	'95
ANTHEM INCOME ☒	Fixed Income	0.1	9.95	2.03	☆	☆	☆	☆	5.9	□	273-3936	317-692-3900	None	None	None	Stephen L. Tufts	'94

Fund	Objective	Net Assets	NAV	YTD %	Total Returns / Rank	Yield %	5-Yr / NA	Local Phone	Toll-Free Phone	Load	Expense	Manager	Yr
ANTHEM INTMDT GOVT SEC ⊠	Fixed Income	0.1	9.93	1.93	—	5.9	□	273-3936	317-692-3900	None	None	Stephen L. Tufts	'94
ANTHEM VALUE ⊠	Growth	0.1	10.57	0.48	★	1.5	N/A	273-3936	317-692-3900	None	None	Steven W. Voss	'94
AON FLEXIBLE ASSET ALLO	Flexible	32.4	11.42	9.69	21.42	2.5	N/A	None	804-281-6049	None	2.24	Rimas Milaitis	'85
API TRUST GROWTH FUND	Capital Appreciation	60.1	12.86	8.25	19.51 13.74 11.85 11.76	0.0	N/A	544-6060	804-846-1361	None	None	David Basten	'94
API TRUST T-1 TREASURY	Fixed Income	4.1	4.71	1.50	—	0.0	□	544-6060	804-846-1361	None	None	David Basten	'92
API TRUST YORKTOWN VAL	Growth	6.5	12.94	7.39	35.24	0.5	N/A	544-6060	None	None	2.00	David Greer	'94
AQUILA ROCKY MTN EQTY	Growth	1.0	12.62	6.41	★	0.0	N/A	872-6734	212-697-6666	4.75	None	Randy Greer	N/A
AQUINAS BALANCED	Balanced	30.6	10.50	6.27	★	2.8	20.4	423-6369	214-233-6655	None	1.49	Multiple Managers	N/A
AQUINAS EQ GRO	Growth	11.1	10.81	7.78	★	0.1	22.3	423-6369	214-233-6655	None	1.50	Multiple Managers	N/A
AQUINAS EQ INC	Equity Income	36.9	11.12	8.25	★	2.5	16.0	423-6369	214-233-6655	None	1.45	Multiple Managers	N/A
AQUINAS FXD INC	Fixed Income	36.1	9.89	5.53	★	5.2	□	423-6369	214-233-6655	None	1.00	Multiple Managers	'93
ARBOR GOLDENOAK DVSFD; A ▦	Growth Income	38.1	11.22	8.12	★	0.8	N/A	545-6331	None	5.75	1.10	Dave Finger	'93
ARBOR GOLDENOAK DVSFD; B ▦	Growth Income	30.1	11.18	8.09	★	0.6	N/A	545-6331	None	None	1.35	Dave Finger	'93
ARBOR GOLDENOAK INTMDT; A ▦	Fixed Income	92.2	9.92	4.45	★	5.6	N/A	545-6331	None	4.50	0.65	Richard Ranville Jr.	'93
ARBOR GOLDENOAK INTMDT; B ▦	Fixed Income	0.3	9.92	4.37	★	5.3	□	545-6331	None	None	0.90	Richard Ranville Jr.	'93
ARBOR OVB CAP APP; A	Growth	83.2	11.59	13.66	27.88 ★ ★ ★	0.2	N/A	545-6331	None	4.50	1.02	Dave Nolan	'93
ARBOR OVB CAP APP; B	Growth	0.7	11.55	13.46	27.49 ★	0.1	N/A	545-6331	None	None	1.27	Dave Nolan	'94
ARBOR OVB EMRG GRO; A	Small Company Growth	40.3	10.37	14.97	30.11 ★	0.0	N/A	545-6331	None	4.50	1.15	Dave Nolan	'93
ARBOR OVB EMRG GRO; B	Small Company Growth	1.1	10.33	14.91	29.77 ★	0.0	N/A	545-6331	None	None	1.40	Dave Nolan	'93
ARBOR OVB GOVT SECS; A	Fixed Income	58.7	9.74	6.36	11.95 ★	5.5	□	545-6331	None	4.50	0.83	Jay Thomas	'93
ARBOR OVB GOVT SECS; B	Fixed Income	0.6	9.75	6.29	11.78 ★	5.3	N/A	545-6331	None	None	1.08	Jay Thomas	'93
ARCH BALANCED; INSTL	Balanced	27.9	10.85	6.50	16.18 ★	2.8	17.9	452-2724	617-722-7868	None	1.27	Gene Gillespie	'94
ARCH BALANCED; INV A	Balanced	7.7	10.87	6.59	16.39 ★	2.8	17.9	452-2724	617-722-7868	4.50	1.27	Gene Gillespie	'93
ARCH BALANCED; TR	Balanced	69.8	13.01	6.57	16.64 28.65 ★	3.0	17.9	452-2724	617-722-7868	None	0.97	Gene Gillespie	'93
ARCH EMERG GRO; INSTL	Small Company Growth	9.8	13.04	7.41	28.93 ★	0.0	20.2	452-2724	617-722-7868	None	1.25	R. Anthony	'94
ARCH EMERG GRO; INV A	Small Company Growth	13.6	13.09	7.47	29.39 ★	0.0	20.2	452-2724	617-722-7868	4.50	1.25	R. Anthony	'92
ARCH EMERG GRO; TR ▦	Small Company Growth	98.5	13.09	7.43	28.65 ★	0.0	□	452-2724	617-722-7868	None	0.95	R. Anthony	'92
ARCH GOVT & CORP; INSTL	Fixed Income	7.0	10.33	5.62	11.35 6.66 ★	6.0		452-2724	617-722-7868	None	0.96	David Bethke	'94
ARCH GOVT & CORP; INV A	Fixed Income	5.1	10.33	5.62	11.46 8.26 ★	6.0		452-2724	617-722-7868	4.50	0.95	David Bethke	'88
ARCH GOVT & CORP; TR	Fixed Income	142.7	10.33	5.70	11.79 8.58 ★	6.2		452-2724	617-722-7868	None	0.65	David Bethke	'93
ARCH GR & INC EQ; INSTL	Growth Income	26.8	14.79	7.73	21.15 ★	1.5	17.9	452-2724	617-722-7868	None	1.05	Gene Gillespie	'94
ARCH GR & INC EQ; INV A	Growth Income	20.6	14.81	7.79	21.30 12.55 11.16	1.7	17.9	452-2724	617-722-7868	4.50	1.05	Gene Gillespie	'88
ARCH GR & INC EQ; TR ▦	Growth Income	274.7	14.81	7.79	21.46 12.66 11.23	1.7	17.9	452-2724	617-722-7868	None	0.75	Gene Gillespie	'88
ARCH INTL EQUITY; INSTL	International	1.6	10.23	4.28	1.57 ★	0.0	□	452-2724	617-722-7868	None	1.70	Dana Bruce	'94
ARCH INTL EQUITY; INV A	International	1.1	10.24	4.38	1.67 ★	0.0	□	452-2724	617-722-7868	4.50	1.55	Clay Finley	'94
ARCH INTL EQUITY; TR	International	29.0	10.26	4.37	1.87 ★	0.0	□	452-2724	617-722-7868	None	1.23	Dana Bruce	'94
ARCH US GOVT SEC; INSTL	Fixed Income	0.5	10.72	5.41	10.94 6.53 ★	6.0		452-2724	617-722-7868	4.50	0.96	David Bethke	'88
ARCH US GOVT SEC; INV A	Fixed Income	9.2	10.75	5.40	11.28 6.85 ★	6.0		452-2724	617-722-7868	None	0.66	David Bethke	'88
ARCH US GOVT SEC; TR	Fixed Income	36.0	10.75	5.48	11.61 7.49 8.51 8.79 7.75	6.3	15.4	452-2724	617-722-7868	None	1.35	Eric McKissack	'90
ARIEL APPRECIATION	Midcap	132.0	21.32	2.06	5.60 6.79 ★	0.3	15.2	292-7435	312-726-0140	4.50	1.25	Eric McKissack	'86
ARIEL GROWTH ⊠	Small Company Growth	129.1	28.98	2.04	9.32 7.86 ★	0.8	19.3	292-7435	312-726-0140	None	0.87	John W. Rogers	'93
ARK FDS CAP GROWTH; INSTL	Growth	44.1	11.05	11.87	17.17 ★	1.2		842-2265	None	None	0.96	First Natl Bk of Maryland	'94
ARK FDS CAP GROWTH; RET	Growth	0.5	11.03	11.58	16.63 ★	0.8	18.8	842-2265	None	None	0.81	First Natl Bk of Maryland	'93
ARK FDS GRO & INC; INSTL ➤	Flexible	94.5	10.53	8.34	12.38 8.26 ★	3.9	N/A	842-2265	None	None		First Natl Bk of Maryland	'94
ARK FDS GRO & INC; RET	Flexible	0.6	10.52	8.14	11.82 ★	3.3	N/A	842-2265	None	None	0.77	First Natl Bk of Maryland	'94
ARK FDS INCOME; INSTL ➤	Fixed Income	70.1	9.95	6.67	11.99 ★	6.2	□	842-2265	None	None		First Natl Bk of Maryland	'93
ARK FDS INCOME; RET	Fixed Income	0.4	10.07	6.58	11.95 ★	5.3		842-2265	None	None		First Natl Bk of Maryland	'94
ARMADA ENHANCD; INSTL	Fixed Income	60.5	10.05	2.14	★	0.0		622-3863	None	2.75		National Asset Management	'94
ARMADA ENHANCD; RET	Fixed Income	2.5	10.07	2.04	★	0.0		622-3863	None	None		National Asset Management	'94
ARMADA EQTY INC; INSTL	Equity Income	35.8	11.05	5.33	★	2.5	N/A	622-3863	None	None		Tony Zimmerer	'94

353

PERFORMANCE OF MUTUAL FUNDS (continued)

FUND NAME	OBJECTIVE	ASSETS ($ MIL) 5/31/95	NAV ($/SHR) 6/30/95	QTR	1YR	3YRS	5YRS	10YRS (Annualized)	DIV YLD %	P/E RATIO	Load	Exp. Ratio	Redemption	800	In-State	MANAGER	SINCE
ARMADA EQTY INC; RET	Equity Income	0.1	11.04	5.27	☆	☆	☆	☆	0.0	N/A	3.75	None	None	622-3863	None	Tony Zimmerer	'94
ARMADA EQUITY; INSTL	Growth	123.3	15.21	8.00	16.68	8.15	9.61	☆	1.3	17.6	None	1.07	None	622-3863	None	Gerald Gray	'89
ARMADA EQUITY; RET	Growth	6.0	15.23	7.92	16.39	7.88	9.44	☆	1.1	17.6	3.75	1.32	None	622-3863	None	Gerald Gray	'89
ARMADA FXD INC; INSTL	Fixed Income	90.6	10.54	5.41	10.30	6.51	9.19	☆	6.0	☐	None	0.83	None	622-3863	None	Larry Kekst	'89
ARMADA FXD INC; RET	Fixed Income	5.5	10.60	5.33	10.12	6.01	☆	☆	5.8	☐	3.75	1.08	None	622-3863	None	Larry Kekst	'91
ARMADA MID CAP; INSTL	Midcap	50.9	11.57	6.05	☆	☆	☆	☆	0.0	N/A	None	None	None	622-3863	None	Larry Baumgartner	'94
ARMADA MID CAP; RET	Midcap	3.5	11.44	5.93	☆	☆	☆	☆	0.0	N/A	3.75	None	None	622-3863	None	Larry Baumgartner	'94
ARMADA TOT RTN; INSTL	Fixed Income	261.4	10.45	6.93	☆	☆	☆	☆	0.0	☐	None	None	None	622-3863	None	National Asset Management	'94
ARMADA TOT RTN; RET	Fixed Income	0.1	10.44	6.29	☆	☆	☆	☆	0.4	☐	3.75	None	None	622-3863	None	National Asset Management	'94
ARMSTRONG ASSOCIATES	Growth	11.6	9.70	8.62	27.32	14.67	9.58	9.64	0.4	N/A	None	1.90	None	None	214-720-9101	C.K. Lawson	'68
ARROW EQUITY	Growth	33.8	12.19	12.54	29.51	☆	☆	☆	0.8	N/A	3.50	1.36	None	None	314-889-0715	Carlo Enloe	'93
ARROW FIXED INCOME	Fixed Income	30.1	10.24	6.78	12.76	☆	☆	☆	6.0	N/A	3.50	1.15	None	None	314-889-0715	Carlo Enloe	'95
ARTISAN SMALL CAP	Small Company Growth	48.9	11.52	14.63	☆	☆	☆	☆	0.0	N/A	None	None	None	344-1770	414-390-6100	Carlene Murphy-Ziegler	'95
ASIA HOUSE ASEAN	Pacific Region	1.1	8.85	4.12	-9.75	☆	☆	☆	0.9		None	None	None	416-7204	None	John Vail	'94
ASIA HOUSE FAR EAST	Pacific Region	1.8	9.25	-2.84	-5.90	☆	☆	☆	0.1		None	None	None	416-7204	None	John Vail	'94
ASM FUND	Growth Income	5.7	11.00	8.02	20.93	9.79	☆	☆	2.6	17.8	None	0.75	None	445-2763	813-963-3150	Steven H. Adler	'91
ASSET MGMT ARM	Fixed Income	840.1	9.94	2.39	7.00	4.64	☆	☆	5.6	☐	None	0.47	None	527-3713	312-856-0715	Edward Sammons, Jr.	'91
ASSET MGMT GOVT MTGE SEC	Fixed Income	61.4	10.61	4.49	9.64	5.58	8.13	9.06	7.1	☐	None	0.51	None	527-3713	312-856-0715	Edward Sammons, Jr.	'84
ASSET MGMT INTMDT MTGE	Fixed Income	186.2	9.64	4.14	9.04	5.67	8.13	☆	6.2	☐	None	0.39	None	527-3713	312-856-0715	Edward Sammons, Jr.	'86
ASSET MGMT SH GOVT SECS	Fixed Income	150.5	10.66	3.44	7.67	5.45	7.43	7.95	6.1	☐	None	0.47	None	527-3713	312-856-0715	Edward Sammons, Jr.	'82
ASTRA ADJ GOVT I ⊠	Fixed Income	133.7	5.72	1.31	-10.68	-2.52	☆	☆	5.9	☐	None	1.84	4.00	334-3444	310-551-0543	Brian Carrico	'91
ASTRA ADJ GOVT I-A	Fixed Income	86.1	5.73	1.29	-11.27	-2.64	☆	☆	5.6	☐	None	2.04	4.00	334-3444	310-551-0543	Brian Carrico	'92
ASTRA ADJ GOVT II	Fixed Income	6.5	5.81	1.22	-11.01	-2.11	☆	☆	5.9	☐	3.00	1.38	None	334-3444	310-551-0543	Brian Carrico	'91
ASTRA ADJ GOVT III	Fixed Income	3.5	5.83	1.22	-10.71	-1.83	☆	☆	5.9	☐	5.00	1.24	None	334-3444	310-551-0543	Brian Carrico	'92
ASTRA ADJ GOVT IV	Fixed Income	4.8	5.82	1.05	-11.74	☆	☆	☆	5.9	☐	None	1.47	0.25	334-3444	310-551-0543	Brian Carrico	'93
ASTRA ADJ RT I ⊠	Fixed Income	9.6	4.21	-7.60	-34.51	-10.52	☆	☆	9.7	☐	None	2.10	4.00	334-3444	310-551-0543	Brian Carrico	'91
ASTRA ADJ RT I-A	Fixed Income	30.0	4.18	-7.98	-35.48	-10.93	☆	☆	9.4	☐	None	2.19	4.00	334-3444	310-551-0543	Brian Carrico	'92
ASTRA ADJ RT II	Fixed Income	6.8	4.27	-7.83	-34.87	-10.26	☆	☆	10.0	☐	3.00	1.35	None	334-3444	310-551-0543	Brian Carrico	'91
ASTRA ADJ RT III	Fixed Income	0.6	4.15	-9.76	-35.82	-10.64	☆	☆	11.3	☐	5.00	1.07	None	334-3444	310-551-0543	Brian Carrico	'92
ASTRA ADJ RT IV	Fixed Income	12.1	4.30	-7.78	-35.29	☆	☆	☆	9.7	☐	None	1.43	0.25	334-3444	310-551-0543	Brian Carrico	'93
ASTRA GL SH MU-MKT	World Income	12.8	6.78	1.41	5.56	-3.53	-0.65	☆	5.2	☐	3.00	1.68	None	334-3444	310-551-0543	S.G. Warburg & Co.	'92
ASTRA GL SH MU-MKT II	World Income	4.8	7.43	1.09	4.05	-2.77	☆	☆	4.4	☐	None	2.66	4.00	334-3444	310-551-0543	S.G. Warburg & Co.	'92
ASTRA INSTL ALL-AMER; A	World Income	0.3	5.89	9.44	-5.58	☆	☆	☆	9.1	☐	3.50	3.24	None	334-3444	310-551-0543	Team Managed	N/A
ASTRA INSTL ALL-AMER; B	World Income	16.3	5.67	9.05	-5.69	☆	☆	☆	9.4	☐	None	3.44	4.00	334-3444	310-551-0543	Team Managed	N/A
ASTRA INSTL ALL-AMER; C	World Income	3.4	5.66	9.27	-5.70	☆	☆	☆	9.4	☐	None	3.56	1.50	334-3444	310-551-0543	Team Managed	N/A
ATLANTA GROWTH FUND	Specialty	4.9	11.65	7.08	13.93	8.07	☆	☆	0.0	17.5	3.75	4.82	None	899-4742	404-875-1200	Astrop/Lucas	'92-'94
ATLAS BALANCED; A	Balanced	10.6	10.42	6.44	14.76	☆	☆	☆	3.3	10.5	3.00	0.80	None	933-2852	None	John Doney	'93
ATLAS BALANCED; B	Balanced	0.8	10.41	6.44	☆	☆	☆	☆	3.0	10.5	None	1.48	3.00	933-2852	None	John Doney	'94
ATLAS GOVT&MTGE SEC; A	Fixed Income	252.2	10.13	4.64	11.04	5.86	8.70	☆	7.0	☐	3.00	0.80	None	933-2852	None	Roberta Conger	'90
ATLAS GOVT&MTGE SEC; B	Fixed Income	1.9	10.13	4.51	☆	☆	☆	☆	6.4	☐	None	1.43	3.00	933-2852	None	Roberta Conger	'94
ATLAS GRO & INC; A	Growth Income	74.4	15.63	7.26	22.52	10.70	☆	☆	1.0	17.4	3.00	1.04	None	933-2852	None	John Wallace	'93
ATLAS GRO & INC; B	Growth Income	2.0	15.62	7.14	☆	☆	☆	☆	0.6	17.4	None	1.66	3.00	933-2852	None	John Wallace	'94
ATLAS STRAT GROWTH; A ➧	Growth	7.7	11.70	8.84	19.26	☆	☆	☆	1.0	17.6	3.00	1.17	None	933-2852	None	Robert Doll, Jr.	'93
ATLAS STRAT GROWTH; B ➧	Growth	-0.6	11.65	8.78	☆	☆	☆	☆	0.8	17.6	None	1.80	3.00	933-2852	None	Robert Doll, Jr.	'94
ATLAS US TREAS INT; A ➧	Fixed Income	9.5	9.67	3.08	7.04	☆	☆	☆	4.7	☐	3.00	0.43	None	933-2852	None	Roberta Conger	'92

Fund	Objective	Assets ($Mil)	NAV	Yield %	Telephone	Telephone (800)	Front Load	Def. Load	Exp %	Manager	Since
ATLAS US TREAS INT; B	Fixed Income	0.4	9.67	4.2	None	933-2852	None	3.00	1.08	Roberta Conger	'94
AVESTA TR BALANCED	Balanced	20.9	19.56	0.0	713-216-4643	216-3291	None	None	1.00	Lartigue/Miller	'94/'94
AVESTA TR CORE EQUITY	Capital Appreciation	22.1	11.63	0.0	713-216-4643	216-3291	None	None	1.00	Theodore Davis	'93
AVESTA TR EQUITY GROWTH	Growth	39.3	21.37	0.0	713-216-4643	216-3291	None	None	1.00	Henry Lartigue	'88
AVESTA TR EQUITY INCOME	Equity Income	43.3	20.87	0.0	713-216-4643	216-3291	None	None	1.00	Robert Heintz	'94
AVESTA TR INCOME	Fixed Income	54.2	16.95	0.0	713-216-4643	216-3291	None	None	0.84	John Miller	'93
AVESTA TR SH-INT GOVT	Fixed Income	24.0	10.91	0.0	713-216-4643	216-3291	None	None	0.75	Guy Barba	'93
AVESTA TR SMALL CAP	Small Company Growth	9.7	11.45	0.0	713-216-4643	216-3291	None	None	1.06	Juliet Ellis	'93
AVESTA TR US GOVT SECS	Fixed Income	2.5	11.75	0.0	713-216-4643	216-3291	None	None	0.80	Jan Koenig	'94
AVONDALE TOTAL RETURN	Balanced	7.2	26.18	0.9	817-761-3777	424-2295	None	None	1.77	Herbert R. Smith, Inc.	'88
B STEARNS EMERG MKT DEBT	World Income	29.4	7.88	10.7	212-272-6404	432-8224	None	None	2.00	E.D. Vaimberg	'95
B STEARNS LG CAP VAL; A	Growth	1.6	12.84	0.0	212-272-6404	432-8224	4.75	None	—	Neil T. Eigen	'95
B STEARNS LG CAP VAL; C	Growth	17.0	12.82	0.0	212-272-6404	432-8224	None	1.00	—	Neil T. Eigen	'95
B STEARNS S&P STARS; A	Growth	18.9	13.32	0.0	212-272-6404	432-8224	4.75	None	—	Robert S. Reitzes	'95
B STEARNS S&P STARS; C	Growth	3.6	13.30	0.0	212-272-6404	432-8224	None	1.00	—	Robert S. Reitzes	'95
B STEARNS SM CAP VAL; A	Small Company Growth	1.8	13.03	0.0	212-272-6404	432-8224	4.75	None	—	Neil T. Eigen	'95
B STEARNS SM CAP VAL; C	Small Company Growth	3.8	13.01	0.0	212-272-6404	432-8224	None	1.00	—	Neil T. Eigen	'95
B STEARNS TOT RET BD; A	Fixed Income	1.4	12.35	0.0	212-272-6404	432-8224	3.75	None	—	J.D. Knox	'95
B STEARNS TOT RET BD; C	Fixed Income	—	12.35	6.9	212-272-6404	432-8224	None	1.00	—	J.D. Knox	'95
BABSON BOND PORTFOLIO L	Fixed Income	153.5	1.56	7.2	816-471-5200	422-2766	None	None	0.97	Edward L. Martin	'84
BABSON BOND PORTFOLIO S	Fixed Income	30.0	9.84	1.3	816-471-5200	422-2766	None	None	0.67	Edward L. Martin	'88
DAVID L BABSON GROWTH	Growth	242.2	13.43	0.2	816-471-5200	422-2766	None	None	0.86	David G. Kirk	'85
BABSON ENTERPRISE	Small Company Growth	200.2	16.57	0.1	816-471-5200	422-2766	None	None	1.08	Peter C. Schliemann	'85
BABSON ENTERPRISE II	Small Company Growth	37.9	17.78	0.1	816-471-5200	422-2766	None	None	1.50	Schliemann/James	'91/'91
BABSON VALUE	Growth Income	202.5	28.99	1.8	816-471-5200	422-2766	None	None	0.99	Nick Whitridge	'84
BABSON-STEWART IVORY	International	64.3	15.95	1.0	816-471-5200	422-2766	None	None	1.32	John Wright	'88
BAIRD ADJ RATE INCOME	Fixed Income	N/A	9.59	6.0	414-765-3500	792-2473	None	None	0.50	Jim Kochan	'92
BAIRD BLUE CHIP	Growth Income	66.4	22.32	0.5	414-765-3500	792-2473	3.25	None	1.40	Evans/Bosworth	'87/'87
BAIRD CAP DEVELOPMENT	Midcap	55.2	24.90	0.1	414-765-3500	792-2473	5.75	None	1.40	Kellner/Wilson	'86/'86
BAIRD QUALITY BOND	Fixed Income	28.8	9.43	6.9	414-765-3500	792-2473	4.00	None	0.60	Jim Kochan	'92
BARON ASSET FUND	Small Company Growth	181.2	25.79	0.0	212-759-7700	992-2766	None	None	1.60	Ronald Baron	'87
BARON GROWTH & INCOME	Growth Income	4.5	13.08	0.0	212-759-7700	992-2766	None	None	1.20	Ronald Baron	'95
BARTLETT BASIC VALUE	Growth Income	109.0	16.40	1.7	513-621-4612	800-4612	None	None	1.00	Miller/Uible	'90/'93
BARTLETT FIXED INCOME	Fixed Income	91.9	9.97	5.7	513-621-4612	800-4612	None	None	0.85	Dale H. Rabiner	'86
BARTLETT SHORT TERM BOND	Fixed Income	22.4	9.78	5.7	513-621-4612	800-4612	None	None	—	Dale H. Rabiner	'94
BARTLETT VALUE INTL	International	65.2	12.09	0.7	513-621-4612	800-4612	None	None	1.83	Madelynn M. Matlock	'89
BASCOM HILL BALANCED	Balanced	10.3	22.27	4.5	608-273-2020	767-0300	None	None	1.34	Frank Burgess	'86
BASCOM HILL INVESTORS	Growth Income	10.8	17.80	3.9	608-273-2020	767-0300	None	None	1.20	Frank Burgess	'78
BAYFUNDS BOND; INST	Fixed Income	54.7	10.01	5.7	None	229-3863	None	None	0.99	Todd Finkelstein	'95
BAYFUNDS BOND; INV	Fixed Income	6.1	10.01	5.4	None	229-3863	None	None	1.19	Todd Finkelstein	'95
BAYFUNDS EQUITY; INST	Growth	80.8	12.28	0.9	None	229-3863	None	None	1.02	Lisa Austin	'95
BAYFUNDS EQUITY; INV	Growth	28.2	12.28	0.7	None	229-3863	None	None	1.26	Lisa Austin	'95
BAYFUNDS SH TM YLD; INST	Fixed Income	46.9	9.20	5.6	None	229-3863	None	None	0.80	Barbara Cummings	'95
BAYFUNDS SH TM YLD; INV	Fixed Income	25.7	9.20	5.4	None	229-3863	None	None	1.04	Barbara Cummings	'95
BB&T BALANCED; INV	Balanced	8.5	10.73	4.1	614-899-4668	228-1872	4.00	None	0.98	BB&T	'95
BB&T BALANCED; TR	Balanced	42.3	10.71	4.3	614-899-4668	228-1872	None	None	0.73	Branch Banking & Trust Co	'93
BB&T GRO & INC; INV	Growth Income	9.1	12.38	2.0	614-899-4668	228-1872	4.00	None	0.92	Branch Banking & Trust Co	'93
BB&T GRO & INC; TR	Growth Income	113.0	12.40	2.3	614-899-4668	228-1872	None	None	0.66	Branch Banking & Trust Co	'92
BB&T INTMDT GOVT; INV	Fixed Income	5.8	9.89	6.0	614-899-4668	228-1872	2.00	None	0.96	Branch Banking & Trust Co	'93
BB&T INTMDT GOVT; TR	Fixed Income	76.2	9.90	6.3	614-899-4668	228-1872	None	None	0.70	Branch Banking & Trust Co	'92

PERFORMANCE OF MUTUAL FUNDS (continued)

FUND NAME	OBJECTIVE	ASSETS ($ MIL) 5/31/95	NAV ($/SHR) 6/30/95	QTR	1YR	3YRS	5YRS	10YRS	DIV YLD %	P/E RATIO	800	In-State	Load	Exp. Ratio	Redemption	MANAGER	SINCE
BB&T SH-INTMDT GOVT; INV	Fixed Income	7.5	9.90	4.06	8.03	☆	☆	☆	5.3	□	228-1872	614-899-4668	2.00	0.89	None	Branch Banking & Trust Co	'93
BB&T SH-INTMDT GOVT; TR	Fixed Income	47.1	9.91	4.23	8.30	☆	☆	☆	5.5	□	228-1872	614-899-4668	None	0.71	None	Branch Banking & Trust Co	'92
BB&T SMALL CO GROWTH; INV	Small Company Growth	0.5	12.76	11.54	☆				0.0	N/A	228-1872	614-899-4668	None	None	None	Branch Banking & Trust Co	'95
BB&T SMALL CO GROWTH; TR	Small Company Growth	7.2	12.75	11.55	☆				0.0	N/A	228-1872	614-899-4668	4.00	None	None	Branch Banking & Trust Co	'95
BBK GRP DIVERSA	Global Flexible	42.5	12.85	6.02	9.62	9.04	5.80	11.02	2.3		882-8383	415-571-5800	None	1.82	None	Holbrook/Micheletti	'86/'86
BBK INTL INTL EQUITY	International	82.2	5.81	5.28	0.88	5.97	-0.62		0.0	□	882-8383	415-571-5800	None	1.39	None	Richard Holbrook	'93
BBK INTL INTL FXD INC	World Income	93.4	8.77	3.90	13.10	2.90	6.61	8.94	6.6		882-8383	415-571-5800	None	1.12	None	Arthur Micheletti	'92
BEACON HILL MUTUAL	Growth	4.2	32.86	9.61	28.25	5.75			0.0	19.5	343-0529	617-482-0795	None	2.70	None	Bernard Zimmerman	'94
BENCHMARK BALANCED; A	Balanced	37.3	10.39	5.25	11.71	☆			2.9	N/A	621-2550	312-630-6000	None	0.61	None	Zielinski/Memler	'93/'93
BENCHMARK BOND; A	Fixed Income	266.8	20.20	7.65	14.07	☆			5.9	N/A	621-2550	312-630-6000	None	0.36	None	Mark Wirth	'93
BENCHMARK DVSD GRO; A	Growth	156.6	11.00	5.77	13.24	☆	☆		0.8	N/A	621-2550	312-630-6000	None	0.67	None	Bill Proskow	'93
BENCHMARK EQ INDEX; A	S&P Index	399.0	12.50	9.46	25.76	☆	☆		2.8	N/A	621-2550	312-630-6000	None	0.23	None	Judy Bednar	'93
BENCHMARK FOCUSED GR; A	Growth	77.1	11.39	7.35	18.70	☆			0.2	N/A	621-2550	312-630-6000	None	0.91	None	Tom Kirkenmeier	'94
BENCHMARK INTL BOND; A	World Income	34.3	22.13	4.23	17.34	☆			6.9	□	621-2550	312-630-6000	None	0.96	None	Michael Lannan	'94
BENCHMARK INTL GRO; A	International	156.5	9.80	1.98	-4.15	☆			1.0	□	621-2550	312-630-6000	None	1.04	None	Robert LaFleur	'95
BENCHMARK SH INT BD; A	Fixed Income	111.8	20.47	3.98	9.15	☆			4.7		621-2550	312-630-6000	None	0.36	None	Mark Wirth	'93
BENCHMARK SHORT DURATION	Fixed Income	65.0	9.99	1.58	5.59	☆			5.5		621-2550	312-630-6000	None	0.25	None	Pearson/Flynn	'94/'94
BENCHMARK SM CO IDX; A	Small Company Growth	83.3	11.90	9.17	19.31	☆			1.4		621-2550	312-630-6000	None	0.33	None	Susan French	'93
BENCHMARK TREAS IDX; A	Fixed Income	47.6	20.42	6.22	11.78	☆			5.1		621-2550	312-630-6000	None	0.26	None	Richard Steck	'93
BENCHMARK US GOVT SECS; A	Fixed Income	31.5	19.83	3.51	7.82	☆			5.0		621-2550	312-630-6000	None	0.36	None	Steven Schafer	'95
BENHAM EQ EQ GROWTH	Growth	139.2	13.70	9.64	23.69	14.27	☆		2.1	15.8	331-8331	415-965-4274	None	0.75	None	Steve Colton	'91
BENHAM EQ GLBL NAT RES	Natural Resources	26.7	10.18	2.39	☆	☆			0.2	N/A	331-8331	415-965-4274	None	0.61	None	Bill Martin	'94
BENHAM EQ GOLD EQ INDEX	Gold	607.0	12.44	1.72	6.16	15.60	5.00		0.2	N/A	331-8331	415-965-4274	None	0.73	None	Bill Martin	'91
BENHAM EQ INC & GROWTH	Growth Income	260.7	16.34	9.43	23.29	13.74			2.6	15.6	331-8331	415-965-4274	None	0.75	None	Steve Colton	'91
BENHAM EQ UTILITIES INC	Utility	170.3	9.74	6.90	12.69	☆			4.5	13.6	331-8331	415-965-4274	None	0.51	None	Steve Colton	'93
BENHAM GOVT ADJ RATE	Fixed Income	376.9	9.49	2.20	4.98	3.42			5.5	□	331-8331	415-965-4274	None	0.54	None	Merk/Rankin	'91/'94
BENHAM GOVT GNMA	Fixed Income	1,017.8	10.49	4.95	11.23	6.30	8.82		7.0	□	331-8331	415-965-4274	None	0.57	None	Tyler/Colton	'87/'94
BENHAM GOVT LG TREAS/AGY	Fixed Income	43.4	9.84	10.48	18.15				6.2	□	331-8331	415-965-4274	None	0.58	None	David W. Schroeder	'92
BENHAM GOVT SH TREAS/AGY	Fixed Income	61.6	9.87	2.90	6.89				5.4	□	331-8331	415-965-4274	None	0.51	None	David W. Schroeder	'92
BENHAM GOVT TREAS NOTE	Fixed Income	313.8	10.28	4.42	8.92	5.97	8.07	8.49	5.4	□	331-8331	415-965-4274	None	0.86	None	David W. Schroeder	'90
BENHAM INTL EURO GOVT	World Income	231.4	11.80	2.66	18.63	9.79	☆		5.9		331-8331	415-965-4274	None	None	None	Tyler/Paul	'92/'92
BENHAM MGR CAPITAL MGR	Flexible	34.7	11.16	5.73	☆	☆			0.0	N/A	331-8331	415-965-4274	None	0.61	None	Jeff Tyler	'94
BENHAM TARGET 1995	Fixed Income	83.6	99.23	1.78	5.50	5.42	8.53	10.45	0.0		331-8331	415-965-4274	None	0.59	None	David W. Schroeder	'90
BENHAM TARGET 2000	Fixed Income	308.4	75.98	7.80	13.79	9.86	11.44	13.17	0.0		331-8331	415-965-4274	None	0.64	None	David W. Schroeder	'90
BENHAM TARGET 2005	Fixed Income	138.7	55.52	12.46	21.51	13.91	13.57	15.54	0.0		331-8331	415-965-4274	None	0.68	None	David W. Schroeder	'90
BENHAM TARGET 2010	Fixed Income	75.7	41.04	15.87	27.26	16.06	14.20	16.48	0.0		331-8331	415-965-4274	None	0.68	None	David W. Schroeder	'90
BENHAM TARGET 2015	Fixed Income	120.5	30.94	18.27	31.77	17.48	14.59		0.0		331-8331	415-965-4274	None	0.70	None	David W. Schroeder	'90
BENHAM TARGET 2020	Fixed Income	245.2	21.52	21.44	34.08	18.26	14.14		0.0		331-8331	415-965-4274	None	2.05	None	William Keithler	'90
BERGER INV SMALL CO GR	Small Company Growth	375.7	3.10	5.80	31.51	☆			0.1	30.0	333-1001	303-329-0200	None	1.70	None	Rodney Linafelter	'91
BERGER ONE HUNDRED	Growth	2,030.2	17.23	8.09	20.24	15.79	17.96	18.29	0.0	26.4	333-1001	303-329-0200	None	1.81	None	Rodney Linafelter	'91
BERGER ONE HUNDRED & ONE	Growth Income	349.5	11.91	9.01	11.64	10.65	13.94	11.72	1.2	15.7	333-1001	303-329-0200	None	1.33	None	Rodney Linafelter	'91
BERWYN FUND	Growth Income	70.9	20.29	12.53	22.74	17.40	15.16	13.42	1.3	11.1	824-2249	302-324-4495	None	0.93	1.00	Robert Killen	'84
BERWYN INCOME FUND	Income	91.8	11.94	6.41	13.89	11.75	14.06		6.2		824-2249	302-324-4495	None	0.55	None	Edward Killen	'94
BFM INSTL CORE FIXED INC	Fixed Income	25.8	9.85	5.87	12.43	☆			6.4	□	227-7236	None	None	0.57	None	Team Managed	N/A
BFM INSTL SHORT DURATION	Fixed Income	44.1	9.83	2.84	7.55	☆			6.0	□	227-7236	None	None		None	Team Managed	N/A

Fund	Objective	Assets ($M)	NAV	Yld	1-Yr	3-Yr	5-Yr	10-Yr	Cur Yld	Risk	Phone	Toll-Free	Load	Exp	CDSC	Manager	Since
BHIRUD MID CAP GROWTH	Midcap	7.2	9.32	7.50	8.96	☆	☆	☆	7.4	N/A	424-2295	None	5.75	2.71	None	Suresh L. Bhirud	'92
BILTMORE BALANCED	Balanced	193.2	11.00	7.32	17.57	☆	☆	☆	3.3	16.5	462-7538	919-725-0036	4.50	0.75	None	Emery Pike	'94
BILTMORE EMERG MKTS	Emerging Markets	35.0	11.04	8.77	20.64	☆	☆	☆	0.0		462-7538	919-725-0036	4.50	None	None	Scott Sadler	'95
BILTMORE EQUITY FUND	Growth Income	112.6	11.63	7.04	25.25	☆	☆	☆	2.0	16.5	462-7538	919-725-0036	4.50	0.87	None	Doris Burnett	'94
BILTMORE EQUITY INDEX FD	S&P Index	190.3	12.21	9.32	25.25	☆	☆	☆	2.2	17.2	462-7538	919-725-0036	4.50	0.46	None	Doris Burnett	'94
BILTMORE FIXED INCOME	Fixed Income	164.2	9.69	5.97	11.86	☆	☆	☆	5.8		462-7538	919-725-0036	4.50	0.71	None	Sam Gibb	'94
BILTMORE QUANT EQUITY	Growth	103.1	11.48	10.12	23.46	☆	☆	☆	1.8	13.8	462-7538	919-725-0036	4.50	0.90	None	Doris Burnett	'94
BILTMORE SH-TM FXD INC	Fixed Income	142.2	9.84	2.65	6.91	☆	☆	☆	4.9		462-7538	919-725-0036	2.50	0.60	None	Sam Gibb	'94
BILTMORE SPECIAL VALUES	Small Company Growth	21.0	11.53	10.87	20.24	☆	☆	☆	0.3	11.4	462-7538	919-725-0036	4.50	1.13	None	Scott Sutterwhile	'95
BJB GLOBAL INCOME; A	World Income	19.1	11.82	3.64	11.12	6.15	☆	☆	4.5		362-2863	None	4.00	1.66	None	Avril Griffiths	'92
BJB GLOBAL INCOME; B	World Income	0.1	11.82	3.54	10.45	☆	☆	☆	3.9		362-2863	None	None	2.38	4.00	Avril Griffiths	'93
BJB INTL EQUITY; A	International	8.1	9.86	5.34	-9.73	☆	☆	☆	0.3		362-2863	None	4.00	2.16	None	Richard Pell	'95
BJB INTL EQUITY; B	International	0.1	9.82	5.03	-10.09	☆	☆	☆	0.3		362-2863	None	None	2.86	4.00	Richard Pell	'95
BLACKROCK GOVT INC; A	Fixed Income	47.5	9.37	2.17	6.52	3.32	☆	☆	5.5		225-1852	None	3.00	1.17	None	Team Managed	N/A
BLACKROCK GOVT INC; B	Fixed Income	2.5	9.37	2.15	6.13	☆	☆	☆	5.2		225-1852	None	None	2.05		Team Managed	N/A
BLACKROCK GOVT INC; C	Fixed Income	0.1	9.37	2.00	☆	☆	☆	☆	0.0	N/A	922-7771	None	None		1.00	Team Managed	N/A
BLANCHARD PREC METALS	Gold	78.4	7.38	5.13	-1.47	15.60	7.31	☆	0.0	23.2	922-7771	212-279-7979	None	2.46	1.00	Peter Cavelti	'88
BLANCHARD AMER EQUITY	Growth	10.0	10.78	10.11	22.01	☆	☆	☆	1.9	N/A	922-7771	212-279-7979	None	3.00	None	Jeff Miller	'92
BLANCHARD CAP GROWTH	Midcap	1.6	7.53	3.86	☆	☆	☆	☆	0.0		922-7771	212-279-7979	None	None	None	Chase Manhattan Bank	'94
BLANCHARD EMRG MKTS	Emerging Markets	12.4	6.57	7.70	-15.12	☆	☆	☆	0.0		922-7771	212-279-7979	None	None	None	James Fairweather	'94
BLANCHARD FLEX INCOME	Fixed Income	263.9	4.81	4.77	8.09	☆	☆	☆	6.4		922-7771	212-279-7979	None	1.30	None	Jack Burks	'92
BLANCHARD GLBL GRO	Global Flexible	86.7	10.05	6.35	4.83	7.38	5.12	☆	1.9		922-7771	212-279-7979	None	2.61	None	Team Managed	N/A
BLANCHARD GRO & INC	Growth Income	4.0	7.80	6.85	6.73	7.38	☆	☆	0.0		922-7771	212-279-7979	None	0.63	None	Chase Manhattan Bank	'94
BLANCHARD SH-TERM BOND	Fixed Income	23.0	2.97	2.58	0.81	2.33	☆	☆	4.7		922-7771	212-279-7979	None	1.44	None	Jack Burks	'93
BLANCHARD SH-TM GLBL INC	World Income	229.0	1.67	2.09	☆	☆	☆	☆	6.2	N/A	922-7771	212-279-7979	None		None	McHenry/Abberly	'91/'93
BNY HAMILTON EQ INC ★	Equity Income	152.6	11.94	6.95	16.71	☆	☆	☆	2.6	16.4	426-9363	None	3.00	1.04	None	Robert G. Knott, Jr.	'92
BNY HAMILTON INTMDT GOVT ★	Fixed Income	62.3	9.75	5.48	10.11	10.22	10.31	☆	5.2		426-9363	None	3.00	1.07	None	Team Managed	N/A
BOND FUND OF AMERICA	Fixed Income	5,608.1	13.49	6.07	10.84	8.33	10.02	☆	7.8		421-4120	714-671-7000	4.75	0.69	None	Multiple Managers	N/A
BOND PORT FOR ENDOW ☑	Fixed Income	45.9	16.84	4.45	9.66	7.16	9.66	☆	7.4		421-4120	714-671-7000	None	0.77	None	Multiple Managers	N/A
BRAMWELL GROWTH FUND	Growth	53.6	12.30	10.91	☆	☆	☆	☆	0.0	N/A	272-6227	212-308-0505	None	None	None	Elizabeth R. Bramwell	'94
BRANDES INTL; A	International	1.4	13.24	4.17	☆	☆	☆	☆	0.0	N/A	331-2979	619-755-0239	4.75	None	None	Brandes Investment Ptns.	'95
BRANDES INTL; C	International	2.2	13.23	4.09	☆	☆	☆	☆	0.0	N/A	331-2979	619-755-0239	None	1.90	1.00	Brandes Investment Ptns.	'95
BRANDYWINE BLUE FUND	Growth	69.7	21.49	15.91	35.67	26.95	☆	☆	0.0	20.7	338-1579	302-656-6200	None	1.10	None	Friess Associates	'91
BRANDYWINE FUND	Growth	2,922.6	29.77	17.30	34.97	25.46	17.93	☆	0.0	20.1	338-1579	302-656-6200	None		None	Friess Associates	'85
BRENTON INTMDT GOVT SECS	Fixed Income	18.4	10.25	4.17	☆	☆	☆	☆	0.0		706-3863	None	3.50		None	Wright/Muenzenmay	'94/'94
BRENTON VALUE EQUITY	Growth	18.1	11.69	8.17	19.73	10.08	9.22	10.90	0.0	N/A	661-3550	402-397-4700	4.00	0.90	None	Wright/Muenzenmay	'94/'94
BRIDGES INVESTMENT FD	Growth Income	20.9	19.90	8.37	☆	☆	☆	☆	3.0	N/A	None	None	None	None	None	Edson L. Bridges II	'63
BRIDGEWAY AGGRESS GROWTH	Capital Appreciation	0.2	11.71	9.64	☆	☆	☆	☆	0.0	N/A	661-3550	713-661-3500	None	1.90	None	John N.R. Montgomery	'94
BRIDGEWAY SOCIAL RESP	Growth	0.1	11.55	5.29	☆	☆	☆	☆	0.0	N/A	661-3550	713-661-3500	None	None	None	John N.R. Montgomery	'94
BRIDGEWAY ULTRA-SMALL CO	Small Company Growth	0.6	11.35	7.79	☆	☆	☆	☆	0.0	N/A	661-3550	713-661-3500	None	1.00	None	John N.R. Montgomery	'94
BRINSON GLOBAL	Global Flexible	358.0	11.35	6.19	12.57	☆	☆	☆	2.4		448-2430	312-220-7100	None	None	None	Brinson Partners Inc.	'92
BRINSON GLOBAL BOND	World Income	50.6	10.39	5.80	11.34	☆	☆	☆	2.3		448-2430	312-220-7100	None		None	Brinson Partners Inc.	'93
BRINSON GLOBAL EQUITY	Global	20.5	9.93	4.68	6.06	☆	☆	☆	0.4		448-2430	312-220-7100	None	1.16	None	Brinson Partners Inc.	'94
BRINSON NON-US EQUITY	International	146.5	9.68	2.33	-0.10	☆	☆	☆	0.0		448-2430	312-220-7100	None	0.90	None	Brinson Partners Inc.	'93
BRINSON US BALANCED	Balanced	138.8	11.23	7.06	☆	☆	☆	☆	0.0	N/A	448-2430	312-220-7100	None	1.00	None	Brinson Partners Inc.	'94
BRINSON US EQUITY FUND	Growth Income	33.4	11.53	9.46	21.45	☆	☆	☆	1.2	14.9	448-2430	312-220-7100	None	None	None	Brinson Partners Inc.	'94
BROWN CAP BALANCED	Flexible	2.4	12.72	9.99	20.23	☆	☆	☆	0.6	20.1	525-3863	919-972-9922	None	2.01	None	Brown Capital Management	'92
BROWN CAP EQUITY	Capital Appreciation	1.3	13.66	10.49	24.73	☆	☆	☆	0.0	20.0	525-3863	919-972-9922	None	2.04	None	Brown Capital Management	'92
BROWN CAP SMALL COMPANY	Small Company Growth	2.7	13.22	8.04	34.73	25.77	☆	☆	0.0	23.7	525-3863	919-972-9922	None	2.03	None	Brown Capital Management	'92
BRUCE FUND	Capital Appreciation	2.2	13.94	15.15	25.77	12.91	3.42	8.82	3.1	6.0	872-7823	312-236-9160	None	1.90	None	Robert Bruce	'83

★ BNY HAMILTON EQ INC--12b-1 fee has been adopted by the fund but is not currently being charged.

★ BNY HAMILTON INTMDT GOVT--12b-1 has been adopted by the fund but is not currently being charged.

© Copyright Lipper Analytical Services, Inc.

PERFORMANCE OF MUTUAL FUNDS (continued)

FUND NAME	OBJECTIVE	ASSETS ($ MIL) 5/31/95	NAV ($/SHR) 6/30/95	QTR	1YR	3YRS	5YRS	10YRS	DIV YLD %	P/E RATIO	PHONE 800	PHONE In-State	Load	Exp. Ratio	Redemption	MANAGER	SINCE
BSR TR GROWTH & INCOME	Growth & Income	21.3	13.42	5.08	18.15	9.61	☆	☆	0.5	17.2	543-8721	513-629-2000	None	1.50	None	Brandon Reid	'91
BSR TR SH/INTMDT FXD INC	Fixed Income	36.2	10.57	5.01	10.11	6.30	☆	☆	6.1		543-8721	513-629-2000	None	0.50	None	H. Dean Benner	'91
BT INSTL EQ 500 INDEX	S&P Index	446.5	12.47	9.60	26.12	☆	☆	☆	2.3	17.3	545-1074	None	None	0.10	None	Frank Salerno	'93
BT INSTL SH/INT US GOVT	Fixed Income	2.1	9.85	3.22	6.62	☆	☆	☆	5.4		545-1074	None	None		None	Louis Hudson	'94
BT INV CAPITAL APPREC	Growth	43.8	14.27	10.88	33.24	☆	☆	☆	0.0	26.8	545-1074	None	None	1.25	None	Mary Lisanti	'93
BT INV GLOBAL HIGH-YIELD	World Income	20.6	9.53	11.81	5.10	☆	☆	☆	7.0		545-1074	None	None	None	None	Jim Tucker	'93
BT INV INTL EQUITY FD	International	66.9	14.56	6.51	12.77	☆	☆	☆	0.6		545-1074	None	None	1.50	None	Francis Ledwidge	'92
BT INV LATIN AMERICAN	Latin American	13.2	8.36	15.31	-22.37	☆	☆	☆	0.0		545-1074	None	None	None	None	Maria Carrion	'93
BT INV LIFECYCLE LONG	Flexible	25.2	10.66	6.60	15.37	☆	☆	☆	2.7	18.4	545-1074	None	None	None	None	Phil Green	'94
BT INV LIFECYCLE MID	Flexible	30.2	10.04	5.49	12.12	☆	☆	☆	3.6	N/A	545-1074	None	None	None	None	Phil Green	'94
BT INV LIFECYCLE SHORT	Flexible	23.2	9.82	4.50	9.07	☆	☆	☆	4.2	17.9	545-1074	None	None	None	None	Phil Green	'94
BT INV LTD TERM GOVT SEC	Fixed Income	33.2	9.90	2.79	6.12	☆	☆	☆	5.0		545-1074	None	None	None	None	Louis Hudson	'94
BT INV PACIFIC BASIN	Pacific Region	23.2	10.88	9.68	4.74	☆	☆	☆	0.0		545-1074	None	None	None	None	Paul Durham	'93
BT INV SH/INT US GOVT FD	Fixed Income	20.8	9.90	3.01	6.27	☆	☆	☆	5.1		545-1074	None	None	0.85	None	Louis Hudson	'92
BT INV SMALL CAP	Small Company Growth	66.4	16.11	12.74	59.82	☆	☆	☆	0.0	N/A	545-1074	None	None	None	None	Mary Lisanti	'93
BT INV UTILITY FUND	Utility	15.8	9.72	4.07	7.75	☆	☆	☆	4.9	11.3	545-1074	None	None	1.25	None	Sarah Blair	'94
BT PYRAMID EQTY APPREC	Midcap	45.4	11.98	10.93	33.71	☆	☆	☆	1.0	N/A	545-1074	None	None	1.00	None	Mary Lisanti	'94
BT PYRAMID INST ASST MGT	Flexible	94.9	10.55	6.63	15.87	☆	☆	☆	3.4	N/A	545-1074	None	None	0.60	None	Phil Green	'94
BT PYRAMID II EQ 500	S&P Index	218.5	12.37	9.54	25.76	☆	☆	☆	2.2	17.3	545-1074	None	None	0.25	None	Frank Salerno	'93
BT PYRAMID LTD GOVT SECS	Fixed Income	28.2	9.90	4.87	8.27	☆	☆	☆	7.0	N/A	545-1074	None	None	0.60	None	Louis Hudson	'92
BUFFALO BALANCED	Balanced	40.2	10.34	7.16	☆	☆	☆	☆	0.0	N/A	422-2766	816-471-5200	None	1.06	None	Kent Gasaway	'94
BULL&BEAR GOLD INVESTORS	Gold	30.8	13.13	0.69	-8.01	7.76	1.85	1.76	0.0	N/A	847-4200	212-363-1100	None	2.57	None	Bassett S. Winmill	'94
BULL&BEAR I QUAL GROWTH	Growth Income	4.5	15.09	9.59	15.54	☆	☆	☆	0.0		847-4200	212-363-1100	None	3.60	None	Bassett S. Winmill	'94
BULL&BEAR I US & OVERSEA	Global	9.0	8.32	14.13	16.24	8.45	6.01		0.0	17.3	847-4200	212-363-1100	None	3.53	None	Brett B. Sneed	'94
BULL&BEAR II GLBL INC	World Income	39.0	8.00	7.28	4.52	5.79	7.27	4.74	7.5		847-4200	212-363-1100	None	1.98	None	Steven Landis	'95
BULL&BEAR II US GOVT SEC	Fixed Income	16.5	15.20	5.86	9.41	5.97	8.04		5.0		847-4200	212-363-1100	None	1.85	None	Steven Landis	'95
BULL&BEAR SPL EQUITIES	Capital Appreciation	50.0	23.32	12.39	31.68	14.70	1.44		0.0	18.0	847-4200	212-363-1100	None	2.92	None	Brett B. Sneed	'88
BURNHAM FUND; A	Growth Income	105.4	21.39	6.84	16.41	9.72	8.97	11.79	3.6	15.4	874-3863	212-262-3100	5.00	1.50	None	I.W. Burnham II	'61
BURNHAM FUND; B	Growth Income	0.5	21.56	6.57	15.24	☆	☆	☆	1.8	15.4	874-3863	212-262-3100	None	2.30	5.00	I.W. Burnham II	'93
BURNHAM FUND; C	Growth Income	N/A	21.39	6.79	16.58	☆	☆	☆	3.4	15.4	874-3863	212-262-3100	None	1.50	1.00	I.W. Burnham II	'93
CA INV TR II S&P 500	S&P Index	18.4	12.86	9.22	25.67	12.79	☆	☆	3.5	17.3	225-8778	415-398-2727	None	0.20	None	Bank of America	'92
CA INV TR II S&P MIDCAP	Midcap	23.6	12.92	8.67	22.16	13.59	☆	☆	2.3	18.6	225-8778	415-398-2727	None	0.40	None	Bank of America	'92
CA INV TR II US GOVT SEC	Fixed Income	27.9	10.65	6.67	12.09	8.76	☆	☆	7.1		225-8778	415-398-2727	None	0.62	None	Philip McClanahan	'85
CALDWELL & ORKIN AGG GRO	Small Company Growth	32.4	11.58	1.49	-0.38	12.03	10.14	N/A	5.4	N/A	237-7073	404-842-7858	None	1.21	None	Michael B. Orkin	'92
CALDWELL FUND	Growth Income	3.8	N/A	N/A	N/A	N/A	N/A	N/A	0.0	N/A	None	N/A	None	1.83	None	Roland Caldwell	'85
CALDWELL GROWTH	Growth	1.6	N/A	N/A	N/A	☆	☆	☆	0.0	N/A	None	None	None	1.87	None	Roland Caldwell	'92
CALVERT FD INCOME; A	Fixed Income	45.0	16.79	7.04	12.90	7.52	9.12	9.71	6.8		368-2748	301-951-4820	3.75	1.07	None	Patterson/Gilkison	'82/'82
CALVERT FD INCOME; C	Fixed Income	0.7	16.59	6.47	10.81	☆	☆	☆	6.2		368-2748	301-951-4820	None	2.65	None	Patterson/Gilkison	'94/'94
CALVERT FD STRAT GRO; A	Growth	121.5	16.40	-3.24	17.60	☆	☆	☆	0.2		368-2748	301-951-4820	4.75	None	None	Cedd Moses	'94
CALVERT FD STRAT GRO; C	Growth	23.1	16.27	-3.50	16.75	☆	☆	☆	0.2		368-2748	301-951-4820	None	None	None	Cedd Moses	'94
CALVERT FD US GOVT; A	Fixed Income	9.5	14.63	6.18	11.35	5.69	7.38		5.4		368-2748	301-951-4820	3.75	1.02	None	Van Order/Denzler	'93/'93
CALVERT FD US GOVT; C	Fixed Income	0.4	14.51	5.59	9.49	☆	☆	☆	4.5		368-2748	301-951-4820	None	2.41	None	Van Order/Denzler	'94/'94
CALVERT N WLD AFRICA	International	0.6	11.71	☆	☆	☆	☆	☆	0.0		368-2748	301-951-4820	2.50		2.00	Calvert/Slone	'95/'95
CALVERT SOCIAL INV BD; A	Fixed Income	63.5	16.30	5.76	10.41	7.23	9.01		5.8		368-2748	301-951-4820	3.75	1.10	None	Domenic Colasacco	'87
CALVERT SOCIAL INV BD; C	Fixed Income	0.6	16.18	5.45	8.99	☆	☆	☆	5.1		368-2748	301-951-4820	None	2.41	None	Domenic Colasacco	'94

Fund	Objective	Assets ($mil)	NAV	%	%	%	%	%	Yield		Tel 1	Tel 2	Load	Fee	Manager	Begun
CALVERT SOCIAL INV EQ; A	Growth	89.1	19.90	8.86	6.52	4.33	4.52	☆	0.2	15.8	368-2748	301-951-4820	4.75	1.27	Domenic Colasacco	'87
CALVERT SOCIAL INV EQ; C	Growth	1.3	19.53	8.62	5.14	☆	☆	☆	0.4	15.8	368-2748	301-951-4820	None	2.75	Domenic Colasacco	'94
CALVERT SOCIAL INV GRO; A	Balanced	527.2	31.47	7.24	14.98	8.11	8.09	10.03	2.8	17.8	368-2748	301-951-4820	4.75	1.24	Colasacco/Trosko	'82/'86
CALVERT SOCIAL INV GRO; C	Balanced	3.1	31.29	6.88	13.57	☆	☆	☆	1.9	17.8	368-2748	301-951-4820	4.75	2.47	Colasacco/Trosko	'94/'94
CALVERT WRLD CAP ACC; A	Midcap	5.7	19.04	14.77	☆	☆	☆	☆	0.0	N/A	368-2748	301-951-4820	4.75	None	Calvert Asset Mgmt	'94
CALVERT WRLD CAP ACC; C	Midcap	0.3	19.14	14.47	☆	☆	☆	☆	0.0	N/A	368-2748	301-951-4820	4.75	None	Calvert Asset Mgmt	'94
CALVERT WRLD GLBL EQ; A	Global	187.3	16.91	4.45	1.33	7.18	☆	☆	0.0	16.5	368-2748	301-951-4820	None	1.96	Murray Johnston Intl Ltd	'92
CALVERT WRLD GLBL EQ; C	Global	5.4	16.65	4.32	0.12	☆	☆	☆	0.0	16.5	368-2748	301-951-4820	None	3.32	Murray Johnston Intl Ltd	'94
CAMCO INTMDT TM	Fixed Income	0.1	9.98	2.19	5.34	4.14	☆	☆	4.9	N/A	352-7507	610-832-1075	None	0.75	Daryl L. Hudson	'92
CAMCO SH TM	Fixed Income	0.1	10.02	1.75	5.19	3.84	☆	☆	4.9	N/A	352-7507	610-832-1075	None	0.60	Daryl L. Hudson	'92
CAMCO TOTAL RETURN	Fixed Income	0.1	10.10	3.96	7.35	5.16	☆	☆	5.0	N/A	352-7507	610-832-1075	None	0.75	Daryl L. Hudson	'92
CANANDAIGUA CIT BOND ✸	Fixed Income	0.1	11.53	7.46	15.88	☆	☆	☆	0.0	N/A	724-2621	716-394-4260	None	0.77	Gregory MacKay	'92
CANANDAIGUA CIT EQUITY ✸	Growth Income	6.7	12.58	9.58	18.01	☆	☆	☆	0.0	18.6	724-2621	716-394-4260	None	1.09	Robert Swartout	'92
CAPITAL EXCHANGE ⊠	Growth	103.2	213.79	10.00	32.24	14.24	13.17	☆	1.2	17.7	225-6265	617-482-8260	None	0.76	Duncan Richardson	'90
CAPITAL INCOME BUILDER	Equity Income	4,078.5	34.03	5.85	13.93	9.51	12.37	14.16	5.0	11.9	421-4120	714-671-7000	5.75	0.73	Multiple Managers	N/A
CAPITAL MGMT EQUITY; INST	Midcap	1.5	11.53	4.44	☆	☆	☆	☆	0.0	N/A	525-3863	919-972-9922	None	None	Capital Management Assoc	'95
CAPITAL VAL EQTY; INL	Growth	5.4	11.29	6.41	16.31	☆	☆	☆	1.5	16.5	798-1819	515-244-5426	None	4.00	James Richards	'93
CAPITAL VAL EQTY; SEL	Growth	14.1	11.28	6.42	16.71	☆	☆	☆	1.8	16.5	798-1819	515-244-5426	None	None	James Richards	'93
CAPITAL VAL FIXED; INL	Fixed Income	1.5	10.16	6.83	12.85	☆	☆	☆	5.6	N/A	798-1819	515-244-5426	None	4.00	Jeff Lorenzen	'93
CAPITAL VAL FIXED; SEL	Fixed Income	7.1	10.07	6.91	13.64	☆	☆	☆	6.1	N/A	798-1819	515-244-5426	None	None	Jeff Lorenzen	'93
CAPITAL VAL SH GVT; INL	Fixed Income	0.2	9.83	3.32	7.60	☆	☆	☆	5.4	N/A	798-1819	515-244-5426	None	4.00	Kathy Beyer	'93
CAPITAL VAL SH GVT; SEL	Fixed Income	3.9	9.96	3.40	7.88	☆	☆	☆	5.6	N/A	798-1819	515-244-5426	None	None	Kathy Beyer	'93
CAPITAL VAL TOT RT; INL	Balanced	2.9	10.69	5.74	12.27	☆	☆	☆	2.8	17.4	798-1819	515-244-5426	None	4.00	Beyer/Richards	'93/'93
CAPITAL VAL TOT RT; SEL	Balanced	15.1	10.50	5.74	11.96	☆	☆	☆	2.6	17.4	798-1819	515-244-5426	4.75	None	Beyer/Richards	'93/'93
CAPITAL WORLD BOND	World Income	630.1	16.67	5.43	16.98	☆	☆	10.78	5.8	17.4	421-4120	714-671-7000	5.75	1.11	Multiple Managers	'93
CAPITAL WORLD GRO & INC	Global	3,194.0	18.88	7.13	15.56	☆	☆	☆	3.2	N/A	421-4120	714-671-7000	None	0.62	Multiple Managers	N/A
CAPP-RUSH EMERG GRO	Small Company Growth	32.1	14.96	11.73	44.12	☆	☆	☆	0.0	16.8	621-7874	301-657-1517	None	1.50	Frank Cappiello	'92
CAPP-RUSH GOLD	Gold	6.9	9.89	3.34	3.89	☆	☆	☆	0.0	N/A	621-7874	301-657-1517	None	1.50	Frank Cappiello	'94
CAPP-RUSH GROWTH	Growth	15.8	14.64	13.40	32.64	☆	☆	☆	0.1	19.2	621-7874	301-657-1517	None	1.05	Frank Cappiello	'92
CAPP-RUSH UTIL INC	Utility	18.0	9.24	7.45	16.61	☆	☆	☆	5.5	11.4	621-7874	301-657-1517	None	None	Frank Cappiello	'92
CAPSTONE GOVT INCOME FD	Fixed Income	273.9	4.88	1.67	4.35	3.16	2.97	6.18	2.6	N/A	262-6631	713-260-9000	4.75	0.87	Jaroski/Potter	'87/'91
CAPSTONE GROWTH	Growth	79.8	13.05	6.53	17.34	6.47	7.37	10.73	1.1	18.3	262-6631	713-260-9000	4.75	1.28	Dan Watson	'86
CAPSTONE MED RESEARCH	Health/Biotechnology	14.2	20.61	12.68	30.07	15.82	15.03	☆	0.0	N/A	262-6631	713-260-9000	4.75	2.50	Samuel D. Isaly	'89
CAPSTONE NEW ZEALAND	Pacific Region	3.5	10.02	0.80	-2.71	3.30	-5.37	☆	2.1	N/A	262-6631	713-260-9000	4.75	2.50	Rob Scharar	'91
CAPSTONE NIKKO JAPAN	Japanese	2.8	6.36	-9.92	-25.18	7.71	☆	☆	0.0	N/A	262-6631	713-260-9000	4.75	3.25	Toshihiko Tsuyusaki	'91
CARDINAL FUND	Growth Income	235.4	12.65	6.31	13.89	7.95	9.46	11.75	2.7	N/A	848-7734	614-464-5511	4.50	0.72	John Schlater	'84
CARDINAL GOVT OBLIGATION	Fixed Income	157.1	8.13	3.79	9.21	4.99	7.40	☆	8.0	N/A	848-7734	614-464-5511	4.50	0.75	John R. Carle	'86
CARDINAL AGGRESSIVE GRO	Capital Appreciation	9.2	11.52	8.58	28.57	☆	☆	☆	0.0	N/A	848-7734	614-464-5511	4.50	None	Timothy McCombs	'93
CARDINAL BALANCED FUND	Balanced	13.5	10.89	7.24	16.85	☆	☆	☆	3.1	N/A	848-7734	614-464-5511	4.50	2.07	Barry McMahon	'93
CARILLON INVST CAPITAL	Flexible	44.2	12.38	4.03	10.67	9.37	10.49	☆	4.6	N/A	999-1840	513-595-2600	5.00	1.05	George L. Clucas	'88
CAROLINAS FUND; INV	Growth	0.8	11.03	5.24	23.70	☆	☆	☆	0.0	N/A	525-3863	919-972-9922	3.50	None	Moorehead Capital Advisor	'95
CENTURA EQTY GROWTH; A	Midcap	1.2	11.50	10.94	23.02	☆	☆	☆	0.6	N/A	442-3688	None	4.50	None	Carlisle Whitlock	'94
CENTURA EQTY GROWTH; B	Midcap	1.6	11.48	10.61	23.69	☆	☆	☆	0.3	N/A	442-3688	None	None	4.50	Carlisle Whitlock	'94
CENTURA EQTY GROWTH; C	Midcap	86.5	11.49	10.88	☆	☆	☆	☆	0.7	N/A	442-3688	None	None	None	Carlisle Whitlock	'94
CENTURA FEDERAL SECS; A	Fixed Income	0.3	10.18	4.09	8.29	☆	☆	☆	5.6	N/A	442-3688	None	2.75	None	Larry Allen	'95
CENTURA FEDERAL SECS; B	Fixed Income	0.1	10.18	3.89	7.47	☆	☆	☆	4.8	N/A	442-3688	None	None	4.50	Larry Allen	'95
CENTURA FEDERAL SECS; C	Fixed Income	96.3	10.18	4.16	8.56	☆	☆	☆	5.8	N/A	442-3688	None	None	None	Larry Allen	'95
CENTURION TAA FUND	Growth	0.9	3.28	-4.37	-13.46	-10.39	☆	-0.16	0.0	N/A	None	619-673-8536	None	6.00	Jack Heilbron	'91
CENTURY SHARES TRUST	Financial Services	223.5	24.54	3.86	15.36	9.45	11.30	11.99	1.8	N/A	321-1928	617-482-3060	None	1.01	Allan W. Fulkerson	'76
CFS CALAMOS CONVERTIBLE	Convertible Securities	17.5	13.54	9.83	16.81	11.57	12.26	10.15	2.7	N/A	323-9943	708-245-7200	4.50	1.60	Calamos/Calamos	'85/'88

FUND NAME	OBJECTIVE	ASSETS ($ MIL) 5/31/95	NAV ($/SHR) 6/30/95	RETURN THROUGH 6/30 (Annualized) QTR	1YR	3YRS	5YRS	10YRS	DIV YLD %	P/E RATIO	PHONE 800	PHONE In-State	FEES Load	FEES Exp. Ratio	FEES Redemption	MANAGER	SINCE
CFS CALAMOS GRO & INC	Convertible Securities	4.0	13.61	8.51	15.83	11.66	11.90	☆	2.7		323-9943	708-245-7200	4.50	2.00	None	Calamos/Calamos	'88/'88
CFS CALAMOS GROWTH	Growth	2.0	15.52	10.51	12.33	7.44	☆	☆	0.5	18.7	323-9943	708-245-7200	4.50	2.00	None	Calamos/Calamos	'90/'94
CFS CALAMOS STRAT INCOME	Fixed Income	2.2	10.55	5.33	7.33	6.64	☆	☆	4.6		323-9943	708-245-7200	4.50	2.20	None	Calamos/Calamos	'90/'94
CG CAP MKTS BALANCED ■	Balanced	21.0	9.17	7.04	16.50	☆	☆	☆	3.0		None	212-816-8725	None	1.00	None	Roger Palley	'93
CG CAP MKTS EMERG MKTS ■	Emerging Markets	54.0	7.77	7.92	0.83	☆	☆	☆	0.0	14.2	None	212-816-8725	None	None	None	Rachael Maunder	'94
CG CAP MKTS INTL EQUITY ■	International	596.8	9.81	0.72	-2.82	10.27		☆	0.0		None	212-816-8725	None	1.19	None	Oechsle/Leary/Davis	'91/'95/'95
CG CAP MKTS INTL FXD ■	World Income	108.8	9.16	4.41	19.48	11.02		☆	6.1		None	212-816-8725	None	0.95	None	Edward Dove	'92
CG CAP MKTS INTMDT FXD	Fixed Income	222.5	8.12	4.73	9.70	6.66		☆	5.9		None	212-816-8725	None	0.80	None	Richard Doll	'91
CG CAP MKTS LONG TM BD	Fixed Income	141.6	8.22	5.89	11.19	6.63		☆	5.4		None	212-816-8725	None	0.80	None	Munsch/Lunsford	'91/'91
CG CAP MKTS LRG CAP GRO ■	Growth	684.3	11.67	10.41	27.43	11.55		☆	0.7	20.1	None	212-816-8725	None	0.98	None	Blacher/Samuelson	'91/'93
CG CAP MKTS LRG CAP VAL ■	Growth Income	951.5	9.96	8.03	17.52	7.92	☆	☆	2.4	15.0	None	212-816-8725	None	0.88	None	Taylor/Wate	'91/'93
CG CAP MKTS MORTGAGE ■	Fixed Income	105.0	7.91	4.95	10.88	5.75	☆	☆	6.5		None	212-816-8725	None	0.80	None	Trent Williams	'94
CG CAP MKTS SM CAP GRO ■	Small Company Growth	245.6	15.61	8.63	42.82	25.04	☆	☆	0.0	32.3	None	212-816-8725	None	1.20	None	John S Force	'93
CG CAP MKTS SM CAP VAL ■	Small Company Growth	297.8	9.35	7.72	11.25	5.27	☆	☆	1.3	12.6	None	212-816-8725	None	1.06	None	Team Managed	N/A
CGM CAP DEVELOPMENT ☒	Growth	417.8	24.25	13.90	7.06	13.85	18.92	18.45	0.3	8.5	345-4048	617-859-7714	None	0.84	None	G. Kenneth Heebner	'76
CGM TR FIXED INCOME	Fixed Income	30.2	10.88	9.93	13.97	10.35	☆	☆	6.9		345-4048	617-859-7714	None	0.85	None	Heebner/Saul	'93/'93
CGM TR MUTUAL FUND	Balanced	1,088.8	28.64	12.51	12.08	11.40	12.78	14.72	3.6	11.1	345-4048	617-859-7714	None	0.92	None	G. Kenneth Heebner	'81
CGM TR REALTY FUND	Real Estate	37.5	10.05	4.36	5.46	☆	☆	☆	4.6	12.4	345-4048	617-859-7714	None	1.00	None	G. Kenneth Heebner	'94
CHARTER CAP BLUE CHIP	Growth	4.8	14.04	7.83	10.48	7.45	8.28	6.44	1.3	21.4	None	414-257-1842	None	2.26	None	Toll/Mirek	'90/'93
CHESAPEAKE GROWTH FUND ☒	Growth	353.3	18.03	17.77	47.67	☆	☆	☆	0.0	N/A	525-3863	919-972-9922	3.00	1.49	None	Gardner/Lewis Asset Mgt.	'93/'93
CHESTNUT ST EXCH LP ☒■	Growth	228.3	178.89	11.82	32.53	16.01	14.74	N/A	1.8	N/A	852-4750	302-791-1043	None	0.54	None	Gayland Gee	'90
CHUBB INV GOVERNMENT SEC	Fixed Income	14.1	10.49	5.53	11.62	7.45	9.19	☆	6.1		258-3648	603-226-5000	3.00	1.00	None	Ned Gerstman	'87
CHUBB INV GROWTH & INC	Growth Income	24.1	18.05	12.74	21.83	13.27	11.93	☆	1.4	14.1	258-3648	603-226-5000	5.00	1.00	None	David Schafer	'93
CHUBB INV TOTAL RETURN	Balanced	19.5	15.46	10.16	17.68	11.59	11.25	☆	2.5	14.7	258-3648	603-226-5000	5.00	1.00	None	O'Reilly/Schafer	'87/'93
CIGNA INSTL INTL STOCK	International	7.0	11.21	1.63	-6.91	☆	☆	☆	16.1		528-6718	None	None	1.25	None	Lee Mickelburough	'94
CLIPPER FUND	Growth	335.9	58.21	12.74	29.06	15.47	14.76	14.33	1.2	15.7	776-5033	310-247-3940	None	1.11	None	Gipson/Sandler	'84/'94
CLOVER EQUITY VALUE	Growth	39.4	14.88	6.65	27.90	16.47	☆	☆	1.3	16.8	932-7781	215-989-6611	None	1.14	None	Paul W. Spindler	'91
CLOVER FIXED INCOME	Fixed Income	11.6	9.81	5.85	11.81	8.33	☆	☆	5.8		932-7781	215-989-6611	None	0.80	None	Paul W. Spindler	'91
COHEN & STEERS REALTY	Real Estate	530.9	32.70	4.47	2.91	14.83	☆	☆	5.2	20.8	437-9912	212-832-3232	3.25	1.14	None	Cohen/Steers	'92/'93
COLONIAL ADJ RATE; A	Fixed Income	13.3	9.86	2.41	7.11	☆	☆	☆	4.7		426-3750	617-426-3750	None	0.50	None	Finnemore/Peterson	'93/'93
COLONIAL ADJ RATE; B	Fixed Income	4.1	9.86	2.24	6.42		☆	☆	4.1		426-3750	617-426-3750	4.75	1.15	4.00	Finnemore/Peterson	'92/'95
COLONIAL FED SEC; A	Fixed Income	1,276.9	10.71	6.86	13.11	7.69	9.06	9.29	7.1		426-3750	617-426-3750	4.75	1.16	None	Peters/Finnemore	'92/'95
COLONIAL FED SEC; B	Fixed Income	78.0	10.71	6.66	12.27	6.87		☆	6.4		426-3750	617-426-3750	None	1.91	5.00	Peters/Finnemore	'93/'93
COLONIAL FUND; A	Growth Income	637.7	8.51	9.04	19.64	12.35	11.67	13.17	2.4	12.2	426-3750	617-426-3750	5.75	1.14	None	Rie/Palmer	'93/'93
COLONIAL FUND; B	Growth Income	308.2	8.51	8.85	18.77	11.67		☆	1.7	12.2	426-3750	617-426-3750	None	1.89	5.00	Rie/Palmer	'93/'93
COLONIAL GL EQUITY; A	Global	11.0	12.16	6.69	12.16	12.12	☆	☆	1.6		426-3750	617-426-3750	5.75	1.25	None	Betsy Palmer	'92
COLONIAL GL EQUITY; B	Global	60.4	12.13	6.41	11.34	11.24	☆	☆	0.9		426-3750	617-426-3750	None	2.00	5.00	Betsy Palmer	'92
COLONIAL GL NAT RES; A	Natural Resources	33.6	12.79	5.65	5.89	10.38	☆	☆	0.8	14.8	426-3750	617-426-3750	5.75	1.70	None	Cordes	'93
COLONIAL GL NAT RES; B	Natural Resources	23.0	12.77	5.45	5.17	9.59	☆	☆	0.2	14.8	426-3750	617-426-3750	None	2.45	5.00	Cordes	'93
COLONIAL GL UTIL; A	Utility	N/A	10.94	5.75	9.20	8.27	☆	☆	4.9	N/A	426-3750	617-426-3750	5.75	1.20	None	Robert A. Christensen	'93
COLONIAL GROWTH; A	Growth	168.9	14.65	11.38	23.08	14.42	11.00	13.51	1.1	14.2	426-3750	617-426-3750	5.75	1.22	None	Daniel Rie	'86
COLONIAL GROWTH; B	Growth	60.5	14.59	11.14	22.20	13.61	☆	☆	0.4	14.2	426-3750	617-426-3750	None	1.97	5.00	Daniel Rie	'92
COLONIAL HI YLD SEC; A	Fixed Income	445.3	6.58	5.12	9.63	11.51	14.18	11.12	9.5		426-3750	617-426-3750	4.75	1.23	None	Peters/Feingold	'93/'93
COLONIAL HI YLD SEC; B	Fixed Income	293.7	6.58	4.87	8.76	10.61	☆	☆	8.7		426-3750	617-426-3750	None	1.98	5.00	Peters/Feingold	'92/'93
COLONIAL INCOME; A	Fixed Income	141.8	6.43	6.71	13.71	8.09	9.56	9.16	7.7		426-3750	617-426-3750	4.75	1.11	None	Carl C. Ericson	'91

Fund	Objective	Assets ($Mil)	NAV	13-Wk %	1-Yr %	3-Yr %	5-Yr %	Yield %	Phone 1	Phone 2	Max Load %	Exp %	Def Load %	Manager	Since
COLONIAL INCOME; B	Fixed Income	29.1	6.43	6.52	12.87	7.29	☆	7.0	617-426-3750	426-3750	None	1.86	5.00	Carl C. Ericson	'92
COLONIAL INTL FD GRO; A	International	48.2	9.22	2.33	-8.35	☆	☆	0.0	617-426-3750	426-3750	5.75	1.71	None	Fleming/Rie	'95/95
COLONIAL INTL FD GRO; B	International	82.7	9.12	2.24	-8.98	☆	☆	0.0	617-426-3750	426-3750	None	2.46	5.00	Fleming/Rie	'95/95
COLONIAL INTL FD GRO; D	International	0.6	9.16	2.12	-8.95	☆	☆	0.0	617-426-3750	426-3750	None	None	1.00	Fleming/Rie	'95/95
COLONIAL NEWPORT TGR; T	Pacific Region	214.9	11.99	10.41	15.00	20.86	16.26	1.3	617-426-3750	426-3750	5.75	1.29	None	John Mussey	'89
COLONIAL SMALL STOCK; A	Small Company Growth	35.3	22.27	12.53	33.59	21.78	10.52	0.0	617-426-3750	426-3750	5.75	1.56	None	Haynie	'93
COLONIAL SMALL STOCK; B	Small Company Growth	25.2	21.85	12.34	32.67	☆	☆	0.0	617-426-3750	426-3750	None	2.31	5.00	Haynie	'93
COLONIAL STRAT BAL; A	Balanced	12.8	10.88	8.24	☆	☆	☆	0.0	617-426-3750	426-3750	4.75	None	None	Ericson/Hayne	'94/94
COLONIAL STRAT BAL; B	Balanced	13.5	10.87	8.14	☆	☆	☆	0.0	617-426-3750	426-3750	None	None	5.00	Ericson/Hayne	'94/94
COLONIAL STRAT BAL; D	Balanced	3.4	10.88	8.23	☆	☆	☆	0.0	617-426-3750	426-3750	1.00	None	1.00	Ericson/Hayne	'94/94
COLONIAL STRAT INC; A	Fixed Income	681.2	6.96	5.46	11.50	8.16	9.97	8.4	617-426-3750	426-3750	4.75	1.21	None	Carl C. Ericson	'91
COLONIAL STRAT INC; B	Fixed Income	658.5	6.96	5.26	10.67	7.41	☆	7.7	617-426-3750	426-3750	None	1.96	5.00	Carl C. Ericson	'92
COLONIAL US FD GRO; A	Growth	120.4	13.26	8.37	24.84	☆	☆	1.2	617-426-3750	426-3750	5.75	1.49	None	Holmes/Rie	'95/95
COLONIAL US FD GRO; B	Growth	210.8	13.18	8.24	23.94	☆	☆	0.5	617-426-3750	426-3750	None	2.24	5.00	Holmes/Rie	'95/95
COLONIAL US FD GRO; D	Growth	2.6	13.24	8.27	24.01	☆	☆	0.7	617-426-3750	426-3750	1.00	None	1.00	Holmes/Rie	'95/95
COLONIAL US GOVT; A	Fixed Income	1,239.9	6.56	4.49	9.57	4.96	6.86	6.4	617-426-3750	426-3750	4.75	1.11	None	Finnemore/Peters	'87/93
COLONIAL US GOVT; B	Fixed Income	728.5	6.56	4.30	8.76	4.18	☆	5.6	617-426-3750	426-3750	None	1.86	5.00	Finnemore/Peters	'92/93
COLONIAL UTILITIES; A	Utility	391.4	12.96	7.02	16.84	6.49	10.58	5.1	617-426-3750	426-3750	4.75	1.23	None	J.E. Lennon	'92
COLONIAL UTILITIES; B	Utility	793.1	12.96	6.82	15.98	5.74	☆	4.4	617-426-3750	426-3750	None	1.98	5.00	J.E. Lennon	'91
COLUMBIA BALANCED	Balanced	353.6	19.13	6.15	16.22	11.18	9.46	3.7	503-222-3606	547-1707	None	0.72	None	Mike Powers	'91
COLUMBIA COMMON STOCK	Growth Income	181.9	17.08	5.93	18.92	13.84	13.71	1.5	503-222-3606	547-1707	None	0.84	None	Terry Chambers	'83
COLUMBIA FIXED INCOME	Fixed Income	282.7	13.11	6.36	12.43	7.61	9.68	6.7	503-222-3606	547-1707	None	0.66	None	Tom Thomsen	'92
COLUMBIA GROWTH	Growth	689.6	29.11	7.62	23.60	15.77	12.65	0.9	503-222-3606	547-1707	None	0.81	None	Alec Macmillan	'92
COLUMBIA HIGH YIELD	Fixed Income	16.8	9.59	5.56	12.78	☆	9.65	8.6	503-222-3606	547-1707	None	1.00	None	Tom Thomsen	'92
COLUMBIA INTL STOCK	International	102.0	11.78	0.60	-9.18	☆	☆	0.0	503-222-3606	547-1707	None	1.52	None	James McAlear	'94
COLUMBIA REAL ESTATE EQ	Real Estate	18.0	11.77	5.92	4.15	18.84	14.44	6.4	503-222-3606	547-1707	None	1.14	None	David Jellison	'95
COLUMBIA SPECIAL	Midcap	1,094.5	21.21	7.94	20.34	4.99	7.22	0.3	503-222-3606	547-1707	None	1.05	None	Chad Fleischman	'86
COLUMBIA US GOVT SEC	Fixed Income	36.9	8.22	2.94	6.63	☆	☆	5.4	503-222-3606	547-1707	None	0.81	None	Tom Thomsen	'94
COMMERCE AGGRESS GROWTH	Midcap	24.2	23.26	9.10	☆	☆	☆	0.0	None	305-2140	3.50	None	None	Paul Cox	'94/94
COMMERCE BALANCED	Balanced	39.3	20.92	9.20	☆	☆	☆	0.0	None	305-2140	3.50	None	None	Williams/Colbert	'94
COMMERCE BOND	Fixed Income	88.8	19.40	6.80	☆	☆	☆	0.0	None	305-2140	3.50	1.56	None	Scott Colbert	N/A
COMMERCE GROWTH	Growth	120.6	22.51	11.42	☆	☆	☆	0.0	None	305-2140	3.50	None	None	Joe Williams	'94
COMMERCE INTL EQUITY	International	13.6	18.17	3.83	☆	☆	☆	0.0	None	305-2140	3.50	None	None	Team Managed	'94
COMMERCE SHORT-TERM GOVT	Fixed Income	16.1	18.79	4.13	☆	☆	☆	1.3	None	305-2140	5.50	None	None	Scott Colbert	'94
COMMON SENSE II G&I; A	Growth Income	7.9	13.25	8.72	16.79	☆	☆	0.7	404-381-1000	544-5445	4.75	3.37	None	James Gilligan	'94
COMMON SENSE II G&I; B	Growth Income	10.6	13.22	8.49	15.83	☆	☆		404-381-1000	544-5445	None	4.42	5.00	James Gilligan	'94
COMMON SENSE II GOVT; A	Fixed Income	6.7	12.09	3.85	7.77	☆	☆	4.7	404-381-1000	544-5445	4.75	2.32	None	Jack Reynoldson	'94
COMMON SENSE II GOVT; B	Fixed Income	5.9	12.09	3.66	7.02	☆	☆	4.0	404-381-1000	544-5445	None	3.25	4.00	Jack Reynoldson	'94
COMMON SENSE II GRO; A	Growth	12.5	13.63	10.10	17.20	☆	☆	0.0	404-381-1000	544-5445	5.50	4.89	None	Stephen Boyd	'94
COMMON SENSE II GRO; B	Growth	19.1	13.52	10.01	16.35	☆	☆	0.0	404-381-1000	544-5445	None	5.79	5.00	Stephen Boyd	
COMMON SENSE II GROW; A	Capital Appreciation	44.1	13.36	8.08	15.14	☆	☆	0.8	404-381-1000	544-5445	5.50	2.64	None	Harvey Eisen	
COMMON SENSE II GROW; B	Capital Appreciation	21.7	13.36	7.84	14.32	☆	☆	0.1	404-381-1000	544-5445	None	3.40	5.00	Harvey Eisen	
COMMON SENSE GOVERNMENT	Fixed Income	334.3	10.60	5.14	10.99	8.43	☆	6.5	404-381-1000	544-5445	6.75	0.89	None	Jack Reynoldson	'88
COMMON SENSE GRO & INC	Growth Income	776.9	16.05	8.90	21.71	10.45	☆	1.8	404-381-1000	544-5445	8.50	1.02	None	James Gilligan	'94
COMMON SENSE GROWTH FUND	Growth	2,385.8	16.28	10.52	20.44	11.49	☆	0.9	404-381-1000	544-5445	8.50	1.09	None	Stephen Boyd	'89
COMPASS CAP BALANCED	Balanced	29.6	10.98	6.44	18.94	14.02	☆	3.7	215-254-1000	451-8371	3.75	0.93	None	DiMatties/Krieck	'95/95
COMPASS CAP EQU INCOME	Equity Income	316.1	13.26	9.40	11.75	13.90	☆	2.1	215-254-1000	451-8371	3.75	0.83	None	Arnold C. Schneider	'93
COMPASS CAP FIX INCOME	Fixed Income	253.3	10.54	6.29	7.80	9.41	☆	5.9	215-254-1000	451-8371	3.75	0.94	None	Bill Cevallos	'92
COMPASS CAP GROWTH	Growth	148.6	12.50	9.01	23.47	8.70	☆	0.6	215-254-1000	451-8371	3.75	1.59	None	Matthew E. Megargel	'93
COMPASS CAP INTL EQ	International	38.3	12.71	3.08	0.27	9.51	☆	0.0	215-254-1000	451-8371	3.75		None	Ian Clark	'91

FUND NAME	OBJECTIVE	ASSETS ($ MIL) 5/31/95	NAV ($/SHR) 6/30/95	QTR	1YR	3YRS	5YRS	10YRS	DIV YLD %	P/E RATIO	PHONE 800	PHONE In-State	Load	Exp. Ratio	Redemption	MANAGER	SINCE
COMPASS CAP INTL FIX INC	World Income	48.4	11.34	3.76	12.86	8.48	☆	☆	0.7	□	451-8371	215-254-1000	3.75	1.38	None	Martin Hall	'91
COMPASS CAP SHT/INTMDT	Fixed Income	201.8	10.31	3.34	7.53	5.49	7.46	☆	5.7	□	451-8371	215-254-1000	3.75	0.84	None	Bill Cevallos	'92
COMPASS CAP SMALL CAP	Small Company Growth	23.1	11.67	7.81	11.14	11.14	☆	☆	0.8	N/A	451-8371	215-254-1000	3.75	1.31	None	Jeff Silk	'91
COMPOSITE BOND & STK; A	Balanced	192.6	12.74	8.21	18.72	9.90	10.44	10.03	3.8	16.1	543-8072	509-353-3550	4.50	1.06	None	Team Managed	N/A
COMPOSITE BOND & STK; B	Balanced	4.6	12.75	8.02	17.80	☆	☆	☆	3.1	16.1	543-8072	509-353-3550	None	1.77	3.00	Team Managed	N/A
COMPOSITE GOVT SEC; A	Fixed Income	188.5	10.52	6.48	12.92	6.22	8.48	8.57	6.0	□	543-8072	509-353-3550	4.00	0.97	None	Team Managed	N/A
COMPOSITE GOVT SEC; B	Fixed Income	1.4	10.52	6.25	12.00	☆	☆	☆	5.2	□	543-8072	509-353-3550	None	1.76	3.00	Team Managed	N/A
COMPOSITE GRO & INC; A	Growth Income	116.2	13.70	7.05	19.71	11.10	11.01	11.05	1.4	51.0	543-8072	509-353-3550	4.50	1.10	None	Team Managed	N/A
COMPOSITE GRO & INC; B	Growth Income	5.4	13.66	6.74	18.79	☆	☆	☆	0.9	51.0	543-8072	509-353-3550	None	1.85	3.00	Team Managed	N/A
COMPOSITE INCOME FD; A	Fixed Income	94.1	9.11	8.04	14.20	7.70	9.65	8.79	6.5	□	543-8072	509-353-3550	4.00	1.04	None	Team Managed	N/A
COMPOSITE INCOME FD; B	Fixed Income	3.1	9.12	7.82	13.28	☆	☆	☆	5.8	□	543-8072	509-353-3550	None	1.80	3.00	Team Managed	N/A
COMPOSITE NRTHWST 50; A	Growth	146.8	16.35	8.94	16.12	9.01	8.90	☆	0.4	17.3	543-8072	509-353-3550	4.50	1.09	None	Team Managed	N/A
COMPOSITE NRTHWST 50; B	Growth	5.2	16.30	8.74	15.23	☆	☆	☆	0.0	17.3	543-8072	509-353-3550	None	1.96	3.00	Team Managed	N/A
COMSTOCK PRTNRS STRT; A	Fixed Income	63.3	8.88	-2.16	-0.35	5.43	☆	☆	5.2	□	334-6899	201-332-1600	4.50	1.40	None	Team Managed	N/A
COMSTOCK PRTNRS STRT; O ⊠	Fixed Income	313.3	8.89	-1.97	0.19	5.43	6.92	☆	5.5	□	334-6899	201-332-1600	4.50	1.07	None	Team Managed	N/A
CONCORDE VALUE FUND	Growth Income	11.5	12.48	9.19	10.13	9.49	8.03	☆	0.5	18.0	338-1579	214-387-8258	None	1.69	None	Gary B. Wood	'87
CONESTOGA BOND; INSTL	Fixed Income	188.8	10.45	5.64	☆	☆	☆	☆	0.0	□	344-2716	None	None	1.01	None	Dintino/Moyer	'95/'95
CONESTOGA BOND; RTL	Fixed Income	1.4	10.44	5.74	10.40	6.12	8.44	☆	5.3	□	344-2716	None	2.00	1.01	None	Dintino/Moyer	'90/'90
CONESTOGA EQUITY; INSTL	Growth	363.3	16.01	9.06	☆	☆	☆	☆	0.9	N/A	344-2716	None	None	1.49	None	Joe Stocke	'95
CONESTOGA EQUITY; RTL	Growth	6.0	16.02	9.16	21.16	11.52	12.55	☆	0.9	15.4	344-2716	None	2.00	1.49	None	Joe Stocke	'90
CONESTOGA INT INC; INSTL	Fixed Income	140.3	10.62	3.66	☆	☆	☆	☆	0.0	□	344-2716	None	None	0.90	None	Craig Moyer	'95
CONESTOGA INT INC; RTL	Fixed Income	1.3	10.62	3.80	7.77	5.21	7.61	☆	4.9	□	344-2716	None	2.00	0.90	None	Craig Moyer	'90
CONESTOGA SPEC EQ; INSTL	Capital Appreciation	52.0	10.30	11.47	☆	☆	☆	☆	0.0	N/A	344-2716	None	None	☆	None	Joe Stocke	'90
CONESTOGA SPEC EQ; RTL	Capital Appreciation	0.5	10.30	11.47	22.26	☆	☆	☆	1.0	N/A	344-2716	None	2.00	☆	None	Joe Stocke	'94
CONN MUTUAL GOVT ACCT ☞	Fixed Income	53.5	10.44	5.91	11.65	6.62	8.71	☆	6.9	□	322-2642	None	4.00	0.91	None	Steve Libera	'85
CONN MUTUAL GROWTH ACCT	Growth	95.1	16.63	8.48	22.43	16.55	14.06	☆	1.4	15.0	322-2642	None	5.00	1.02	None	Peter Antos	'89
CONN MUTUAL INCOME ACCT ☞	Fixed Income	49.4	9.44	4.05	8.06	5.78	7.48	☆	7.2	N/A	322-2642	None	4.00	0.63	None	Steve Libera	'85
CONN MUTUAL LFSPN BAL	Flexible	33.9	10.31	☆	☆	☆	☆	☆	0.0	N/A	322-2642	None	5.00	None	None	Team Managed	'95
CONN MUTUAL LFSPN CAP AP	Flexible	25.4	10.37	☆	☆	☆	☆	☆	0.0	N/A	322-2642	None	5.00	None	None	Team Managed	'95
CONN MUTUAL LFSPN DV INC	Flexible	20.6	10.25	☆	☆	☆	☆	☆	0.0	N/A	322-2642	None	5.00	None	None	Team Managed	'95
CONN MUTUAL TOT RTN ACCT	Balanced	199.4	14.89	6.54	15.53	11.39	11.86	☆	4.1	15.2	322-2642	None	5.00	0.96	None	Peter Antos	'89
COPLEY FUND	Growth Income	76.1	21.50	4.62	12.15	9.07	9.15	9.44	0.0	N/A	None	508-674-8459	None	1.09	None	Irving Levine	'78
COREFUND BALANCED; A	Balanced	59.1	11.06	7.98	16.21	☆	☆	☆	3.2	19.0	252-1784	None	4.50	0.62	None	Steve Dalton	'93
COREFUND BALANCED; B	Balanced	2.3	11.06	7.92	15.84	☆	☆	☆	3.0	19.0	252-1784	None	4.50	0.87	None	Steve Dalton	'93
COREFUND EQUITY INDEX	S&P Index	108.3	23.79	9.04	24.45	12.04	11.17	12.91	2.1	17.3	252-1784	None	None	0.35	None	Larry Aasheim	'91
COREFUND GLOBAL BOND; A	World Income	27.4	9.62	4.28	9.70	☆	☆	☆	3.1	□	252-1784	None	None	0.73	None	George McNeill	'93
COREFUND GLOBAL BOND; B	World Income	0.2	9.61	4.22	9.57	☆	☆	☆	2.9	□	252-1784	None	4.50	0.98	None	George McNeill	'93
COREFUND GOVT INC; A	Fixed Income	10.9	9.83	4.43	10.26	☆	☆	☆	6.4	□	252-1784	None	None	0.50	None	William T. Lawrence	'93
COREFUND GOVT INC; B	Fixed Income	1.4	9.84	4.48	10.23	☆	☆	☆	6.2	□	252-1784	None	4.50	0.75	None	William T. Lawrence	'93
COREFUND GROWTH EQ; A	Growth	85.5	11.18	10.97	23.72	9.31	☆	☆	0.7	20.6	252-1784	None	None	0.69	None	Timothy R. Stives	'94
COREFUND GROWTH EQ; B	Growth	1.9	11.17	10.91	23.44	☆	☆	☆	0.5	20.6	252-1784	None	4.50	0.94	None	Timothy R. Stives	'94
COREFUND INTL GROWTH; A	International	111.8	12.29	3.36	-0.21	9.16	5.83	☆	0.3	□	252-1784	None	None	0.99	None	Michael J. Gibson	'90
COREFUND INTL GROWTH; B	International	1.8	12.27	3.20	-0.48	☆	☆	☆	0.1	□	252-1784	None	4.50	1.24	None	Michael J. Gibson	'93
COREFUND INTMDT BD; A	Fixed Income	53.5	9.84	3.53	8.22	5.19	☆	☆	5.6	□	252-1784	None	None	0.58	None	William T. Lawrence	'93
COREFUND INTMDT BD; B	Fixed Income	2.0	9.84	3.46	7.95	☆	☆	☆	5.4	□	252-1784	None	4.50	0.83	None	William T. Lawrence	'94

Fund	Objective	Net Assets	NAV	Return A	Return B	Return C	Return D	Rating	Yld	3-Yr	Phone 1	Phone 2	Load	Expense	Manager	Started
COREFUND VALUE EQ; A	Growth Income	30.4	14.27	8.90	17.29	10.97	9.18	☆	1.0	15.6	None	252-1784	None	0.80	Doug Pyle	'90
COREFUND VALUE EQ; B	Growth Income	4.8	14.29	8.80	16.96			☆	0.8	15.6	None	252-1784	4.50	1.05	Doug Pyle	'93
CORNERSTONE GROWTH	Capital Appreciation	7.7	8.82	2.44	12.36	8.66	6.31	8.91	0.2		404-240-0666	728-0670	None	2.00	Thomas E. Quinn	'95
CORP FUND ACCUM PROGRAM ▣	Small Company Growth	84.7	20.85	6.55	11.85	7.26	8.86	☆	5.4		609-282-2800	None	None	1.10	Jay Harbeck	'92
COWEN OPPTY; A	Small Company Growth	37.5	13.22	1.77	17.33	20.68	14.99	☆	0.0	N/A	262-7116	262-7116	5.00	1.47	William Church	'88
COWEN OPPTY; B	Small Company Growth	5.2	13.06	1.32	16.15			☆	0.0	N/A	212-495-6000	262-7116	None	1.32	William Church	'94
COWEN OPPTY; C ▥	Small Company Growth	12.7	13.27	2.00	17.77			☆	4.2	N/A	212-495-6000	262-7116	None	0.75	William Church	
COWEN INCOME+GROWTH; A	Equity Income	44.7	11.82	5.66	15.33	8.32	9.59	☆	3.6	N/A	212-495-6000	262-7116	4.75	1.26	William Rechter	'94
COWEN INCOME+GROWTH; B	Equity Income	1.0	11.79	5.40	14.43			☆	4.3	N/A	212-495-6000	262-7116	None	None	William Rechter	'86
COWEN INCOME+GROWTH; C ▥	Equity Income	8.0	11.84	5.79	15.73			☆		N/A	212-495-6000	262-7116	None	None	William Rechter	'94
CRABBE HUSON ASST ALLOC	Flexible	124.4	13.54	5.47	14.94	12.24	11.91	☆	2.4	15.9	503-295-0919	541-9732	None	1.44	Huson/Maack	'89/'90
CRABBE HUSON EQUITY	Growth	300.9	18.00	6.70	18.50	17.48	16.95	☆	0.8	15.3	503-295-0919	541-9732	None	1.45	Huson/Maack	'89/'95
CRABBE HUSON GOVT INCOME	Fixed Income	8.6	10.54	3.11	6.84	4.56	6.66	☆	4.8	□	503-295-0919	541-9732	None	0.75	Huson/Nesbit	'89/'95
CRABBE HUSON FIXED INCOME	Fixed Income	6.5	9.99	4.42	7.73	4.99	7.01	☆	5.8	□	503-295-0919	541-9732	None	0.80	Huson/Nesbit	'94/'94
CRABBE HUSON REAL ESTATE	Real Estate	20.5	9.93	6.50	0.27			☆	2.4	20.3	503-295-0919	541-9732	None	1.01	Huson/Maack	'95/'95
CRABBE HUSON SPECIAL	Midcap	791.9	14.35	1.13	17.52	25.00	19.66	☆	0.3	18.1	503-295-0919	541-9732	None	1.44	Crabbe/Kinnucan	'93
CRESCENT FUND	Balanced	16.7	11.94	6.65	14.53			☆	1.6	13.3	310-201-2773	424-2295	4.50	1.65	Matthew Kallis	'93
CRESTFDS CAP APP; INV A ▰	Growth	2.2	11.70	11.96	28.13			☆	0.2	N/A	273-7827	273-7827	None	1.06	David A. Halloran	'93/'93
CRESTFDS CAP APP; TR	Growth	15.8	11.80	11.85	28.38			☆	0.2	N/A	273-7827	273-7827	3.00	1.05	David A. Halloran	
CRESTFDS INT BD; INV A ▰	Fixed Income	1.2	9.90	6.41	12.02			☆	5.6		273-7827	273-7827	None	0.89	Reid/Constine	'92/'92
CRESTFDS INT BD; TR	Fixed Income	74.5	9.90	6.42	12.01			☆	5.6		273-7827	273-7827	2.00	0.88	Reid/Constine	'93/'93
CRESTFDS LTD BD; INV A ▰	Fixed Income	0.7	9.94	4.07	8.52			☆	5.1		273-7827	273-7827	None	0.77	Reid/Constine	'92/'92
CRESTFDS LTD BD; TR	Fixed Income	83.3	9.92	4.08	8.42			☆	5.1		273-7827	273-7827	4.50	0.76	Reid/Constine	'93
CRESTFDS SPEC EQ; INV A ▰	Small Company Growth	4.0	11.54	10.43	14.98			☆	0.5	14.7	273-7827	273-7827	None	1.04	Jeffrey E. Markunas	'92
CRESTFDS SPEC EQ; TR	Small Company Growth	45.6	11.54	10.43	14.98			☆	0.5	14.7	273-7827	273-7827	4.50	1.03	Jeffrey E. Markunas	
CRESTFDS VALUE; INV A ▰	Growth Income	10.4	11.59	5.89	17.20			☆	2.3	N/A	273-7827	273-7827	None	1.02	Jeffrey E. Markunas	'93
CRESTFDS VALUE; TR	Growth Income	195.5	11.54	6.01	17.50	7.63	4.92	☆	2.3	N/A	273-7827	273-7827	None	1.01	Jeffrey E. Markunas	'92
CROWLEY GROWTH	Growth	6.2	10.89	3.81	11.83			☆	1.1	14.5	None	302-529-1717	None	1.85	Robert A. Crowley	'89
CROWLEY INCOME	Fixed Income	8.1	N/A	N/A	N/A	N/A	N/A	N/A	0.0	N/A	302-529-1717	None	1.37	Robert A. Crowley	'89
CT&T GROWTH & INCOME	Growth Income	15.2	11.79	9.28	23.44			☆	0.7	N/A	None	992-8151	None	1.20	Jerrold Stodden	'93
CT&T INTMDT FXD INC	Fixed Income	17.8	9.80	5.55	11.60			☆	6.1	N/A	992-8151	992-8151	None	0.80	Thomas Marthaler	'94
CT&T M&C BALANCED	Balanced	9.7	11.52	10.76				☆	0.0	N/A	992-8151	992-8151	None		Ron Canakaris	'92
CT&T M&C GROWTH	Growth	16.8	12.08	13.83				☆	0.0	N/A	992-8151	992-8151	None		Ron Canakaris	'94
CT&T TALON FUND	Midcap	9.1	11.63	8.23				☆	0.0	N/A	992-8151	992-8151	None		Terry Diamond	'93
CUFUND ADJ RATE ▥	Fixed Income	162.1	9.94	1.86	5.54		14.92		5.5	N/A	538-9683	538-9683	None	0.38	Linda Bowers	
CUFUND SHORT-TERM ▥	Fixed Income	35.0	9.74	2.82	6.95	3.89		☆	5.2	N/A	538-9683	538-9683	None	0.38	Bruce Fox	'94
CUTLER TR APPROVED LIST	Growth	21.3	11.71	6.88	22.33			☆	2.0	16.8	503-770-9000	228-8537	None	1.00	Kenneth R. Cutler	'92
CUTLER TR EQUITY INCOME	Equity Income	41.4	10.96	5.44	18.63			☆	3.0	14.2	503-770-9000	228-8537	None	1.00	Kenneth R. Cutler	'92
CUTLER TR GOVT SECS	Fixed Income	6.8	10.10	3.73	7.83	4.76	7.00	☆	4.5		503-770-9000	228-8537	None	0.74	Anita Kolleeny	'87
DEAN WITTER AMER VALUE	Growth	1,707.4	25.48	12.71	25.65	15.38	15.60	14.92	0.0	25.2	610-989-6611	869-3863	5.00	1.71	Vance/Gupta	'95/'95
DEAN WITTER BALANCED GRO	Balanced	11.6	10.62	7.11				☆	0.0	N/A	212-392-2550	869-3863	None		Vance/Gupta	'95/'95
DEAN WITTER BALANCED INC	Income	8.1	10.45	5.29				☆	0.0	N/A	212-392-2550	869-3863	None		Vance/Gupta	'90
DEAN WITTER CAP GROWTH	Growth	181.5	13.58	4.22	17.78	4.76	7.00	☆	0.0	20.4	212-392-2550	869-3863	5.00	1.87	Paul Vance	'92/'94
DEAN WITTER CONVERT	Convertible Securities	178.1	11.09	6.26	12.81	11.94	8.76	☆	4.2		212-392-2550	869-3863	5.00	1.93	Worobel/Knox	'92/'94
DEAN WITTER DEV GRO	Small Company Growth	370.5	21.80	16.02	40.76	24.60	10.99	10.99	0.0	24.5	212-392-2550	869-3863	5.00	1.78	Worobel/Stevingson	'81
DEAN WITTER DIVID GRO	Growth Income	7,853.5	34.25	8.36	20.08	11.31	11.11	13.34	1.9	16.8	212-392-2550	869-3863	5.00	1.42	Paul Vance	'92/'92/'92
DEAN WITTER DVSD INC	Fixed Income	488.4	9.64	4.28	8.27	6.37		☆	7.5	□	212-392-2550	869-3863	5.00	1.51	Gupta/Avelar/Tran	'94/'95
DEAN WITTER EURO GROW	European Region	780.0	13.68	10.53	23.50	16.35	9.86	☆	0.0	□	212-392-2550	869-3863	5.00	2.27	Lodwick/Reilly	'87
DEAN WITTER FED SEC	Fixed Income	847.3	9.36	6.34	11.61	6.33	8.13	☆	6.5	□	212-392-2550	869-3863	5.00	1.52	Rajesh Gupta	'95/'95
DEAN WITTER GLBL ASSET	Global Flexible	25.1	10.79	5.37				☆	0.0	□	212-392-2550	869-3863	5.00	None	Bavoso/Bullock	

PERFORMANCE OF MUTUAL FUNDS (continued)

FUND NAME	OBJECTIVE	ASSETS ($ MIL) 5/31/95	NAV ($/SHR) 6/30/95	QTR	1YR	3YRS	5YRS	10YRS	DIV YLD %	P/E RATIO	800	In-State	Load	Exp. Ratio	Redemption	MANAGER	SINCE
						(Annualized)											
DEAN WITTER GLBL DIV	Global	1,959.7	11.64	4.80	12.23	☆	☆	☆	1.2	□	869-3863	212-392-2550	None	2.03	5.00	Paul Vance	'93
DEAN WITTER GLBL SH-TM	World Income	124.4	8.92	3.61	8.17	3.87	☆	☆	6.1	□	869-3863	212-392-2550	None	1.63	3.00	Tran/Pickrell	'90/'94
DEAN WITTER GLBL UTIL	Utility	344.9	10.59	7.26	8.40	☆	☆	☆	1.8	N/A	869-3863	212-392-2550	None	None	5.00	Edward Gaylor	'94
DEAN WITTER HEALTH SCI	Health/Biotechnology	238.0	11.88	4.30	29.27	☆	☆	☆	0.0	24.0	869-3863	212-392-2550	None	2.30	5.00	Ronald Worobel	'92
DEAN WITTER HI INC SEC	Fixed Income	228.3	9.98	4.65	9.98	☆	☆	☆	9.4	□	869-3863	212-392-2550	None	None	4.00	Peter Avelar	'94
DEAN WITTER HIGH YIELD ⊠	Fixed Income	453.8	6.72	5.66	5.25	11.23	13.07	7.26	11.9	□	869-3863	212-392-2550	5.50	0.69	None	Peter Avelar	'90
DEAN WITTER INTL SM CP	Intl Small Company	93.7	8.53	0.47	☆	☆	☆	☆	0.0		869-3863	212-392-2550	None	1.63	5.00	Graham Bamping	'94
DEAN WITTER INTMDT INC	Fixed Income	236.5	9.71	4.76	9.33	5.61	7.37	☆	6.0		869-3863	212-392-2550	None	1.63	5.00	Rochelle Siegel	'94
DEAN WITTER MGD ASSETS	Flexible	421.3	10.39	1.30	4.92	6.38	8.13	☆	3.5	N/A	869-3863	212-392-2550	None	1.79	5.00	Kenton Hinchliffe	'89
DEAN WITTER MID-CAP	Midcap	115.2	11.66	10.10	☆	☆	☆	☆	0.0	N/A	869-3863	212-392-2550	None	None	5.00	Kolleeny/Hermann	'94
DEAN WITTER NTRL RES	Natural Resources	143.6	11.77	3.95	10.12	☆	☆	☆	0.4	19.6	869-3863	212-392-2550	None	1.90	5.00	Konrad Krill	'95
DEAN WITTER PACIFIC GR	Pacific Region	1,472.2	18.97	7.48	1.74	16.64	6.29	10.09	0.0	□	869-3863	212-392-2550	None	2.41	5.00	Graham Bamping	'90
DEAN WITTER PREC MTLS	Gold	67.7	10.65	1.45	0.90	9.34	☆	☆	0.0	N/A	869-3863	212-392-2550	None	2.28	5.00	Konrad Krill	'94
DEAN WITTER PREMIER INC ❉	Fixed Income	34.4	8.79	2.60	7.57	3.11	☆	☆	7.3	□	869-3863	212-392-2550	3.00	1.58	None	Scott Amero	'91
DW RET SRS AMER VALUE ❉	Growth	17.6	12.28	12.15	28.35	☆	☆	☆	1.0	24.5	869-3863	212-392-2550	None	None	None	Anita Kolleeny	'93
DW RET SRS CAP GROWTH ❉	Growth	0.5	10.91	4.20	19.44	☆	☆	☆	1.1	20.4	869-3863	212-392-2550	None	None	None	Paul Vance	'93
DW RET SRS DIV GROWTH ❉	Growth Income	30.5	12.67	10.13	23.24	☆	☆	☆	2.4	15.1	869-3863	212-392-2550	None	None	None	Paul Vance	'93
DW RET SRS GLOBAL EQUITY ❉	Global	6.2	10.56	4.87	1.52	☆	☆	☆	1.1	□	869-3863	212-392-2550	None	None	None	Thomas Connelly	'93
DW RET SRS INTMDT INC ❉	Fixed Income	0.7	9.68	5.24	10.60	☆	☆	☆	6.3	□	869-3863	212-392-2550	None	None	None	Rochelle Siegel	'93
DW RET SRS STRATEGIST ❉	Flexible	6.0	11.00	7.84	18.07	☆	☆	☆	1.6	21.6	869-3863	212-392-2550	None	None	None	Mark Bavoso	'93
DW RET SRS US GOVT SECS ❉	Fixed Income	3.7	9.78	4.06	9.62	☆	☆	☆	5.7	□	869-3863	212-392-2550	None	None	None	Rajesh Gupta	'93
DW RET SRS UTILITIES ❉	Utility	4.8	10.94	5.36	14.11	☆	☆	☆	3.4	15.6	869-3863	212-392-2550	None	None	None	Edward Gaylor	'93
DW RET SRS VALUE ADDED ❉	Growth Income	6.7	12.40	8.20	22.67	☆	☆	☆	2.1	16.6	869-3863	212-392-2550	None	None	None	Kenton Hinchliffe	'93
DEAN WITTER SH-TM BOND	Fixed Income	30.5	9.61	3.73	7.42	☆	☆	☆	6.2	□	869-3863	212-392-2550	None	None	None	Rochelle Siegel	'94
DEAN WITTER SH-TM TREAS	Fixed Income	273.9	9.99	3.19	6.69	4.16	☆	☆	5.0	□	869-3863	212-392-2550	None	0.79	None	Rajesh Gupta	'91
DEAN WITTER STRATEGIST	Flexible	843.6	15.50	6.39	16.66	9.29	9.67	☆	1.9	N/A	869-3863	212-392-2550	None	1.62	5.00	Mark Bavoso	'88
DEAN WITTER US GOVT	Fixed Income	8,302.5	9.01	5.48	11.58	5.81	7.21	7.58	6.4	□	869-3863	212-392-2550	None	1.22	5.00	Rajesh Gupta	'92
DEAN WITTER UTILITIES	Utility	3,048.2	13.57	7.31	13.58	7.57	8.84	☆	4.5	N/A	869-3863	212-392-2550	None	1.64	5.00	Edward Gaylor	'88
DEAN WITTER VAL-ADD EQ	Growth	613.5	23.06	7.91	21.41	13.74	11.73	☆	0.4	N/A	869-3863	212-392-2550	None	1.68	5.00	Kenton Hinchliffe	'93
DEAN WITTER WRLDWD INC	World Income	156.2	9.04	4.19	11.24	5.51	5.89	☆	5.3	□	869-3863	212-392-2550	None	1.91	5.00	Tran/Seely	'89/'94
DEAN WITTER WRLDWD INV ✔	Global	526.6	16.63	5.86	-4.49	7.41	5.13	11.70	0.1	□	869-3863	212-392-2550	None	2.40	5.00	Thomas Connelly	'83
DEKALB SHORT DUR GOVT	Growth	14.3	9.38	0.93	4.77	☆	☆	☆	5.7	□	346-3312	718-403-7770	None	1.10	None	Art Gandolfi	'92
DELAFIELD FUND	Equity Income	14.1	12.02	4.61	19.21	☆	☆	☆	0.8	12.9	221-3079	212-476-5055	None	1.78	None	Dennis Delafield	'93
DELAWARE DECATUR INC; A	Equity Income	1,287.5	17.55	6.70	18.09	12.58	9.93	11.93	3.9	N/A	523-4640	215-988-1333	5.75	0.81	None	John B. Fields	'93
DELAWARE DECATUR INC; B	Equity Income	9.2	17.51	6.37	☆	☆	☆	☆	0.0	N/A	523-4640	215-988-1333	None	None	4.00	John B. Fields	'94
DELAWARE DECATUR TOT; A	Equity Income	478.9	14.03	7.22	19.89	12.77	10.97	☆	2.7	N/A	523-4640	215-988-1333	5.75	1.26	None	John B. Fields	'92
DELAWARE DECATUR TOT; B	Equity Income	5.8	14.01	7.08	20.79	☆	☆	☆	0.0	N/A	523-4640	215-988-1333	None	None	4.00	John B. Fields	'94
DELAWARE DELCAP; A	Midcap	813.0	26.05	5.94	13.29	☆	9.61	☆	0.0	21.8	523-4640	215-988-1333	5.75	1.35	None	Edward N. Antoian	'86
DELAWARE DELCAP; B	Midcap	1.7	25.93	5.75	☆	☆	☆	☆	0.0	21.8	523-4640	215-988-1333	None	None	4.00	Edward N. Antoian	'94
DELAWARE DELCHESTER; A	Fixed Income	1,016.9	6.23	4.18	5.15	8.09	12.33	10.42	10.9	□	523-4640	215-988-1333	4.75	1.05	None	Matlack/Nichols/Raith	'92/'92/'94
DELAWARE DELCHESTER; B	Fixed Income	103.2	6.23	3.98	4.36	☆	☆	☆	10.2	□	523-4640	215-988-1333	None	1.25	4.00	Matlack/Nichols/Raith	'94/'94/'94
DELAWARE DIV GROWTH; A	Equity Income	7.4	11.61	6.20	19.07	☆	☆	☆	1.8	17.4	523-4640	215-988-1333	5.75	1.25	None	George Burwell	'93
DELAWARE DIV GROWTH; B	Equity Income	0.5	11.58	6.03	☆	☆	☆	☆	0.0	17.4	523-4640	215-988-1333	None	None	4.00	George Burwell	'94
DELAWARE FUND; A	Balanced	478.8	18.99	5.40	12.95	9.65	9.50	11.15	3.3	18.1	523-4640	215-988-1333	5.75	0.97	None	Burwell/Dutton	'92/'88
DELAWARE FUND; B	Balanced	1.9	18.97	5.18	☆	☆	☆	☆	0.0	18.1	523-4640	215-988-1333	None	None	4.00	Burwell/Dutton	'94/'94

DELAWARE GL ASSETS; A	Global Flexible	0.3	11.18	5.37	☆	☆	☆	☆	0.0	□	523-4640	215-988-1333	5.75	None	None	Clive A. Gillmore	'94
DELAWARE GL ASSETS; B	Global Flexible	0.1	11.18	5.37	☆	☆	☆	☆	0.0	□	523-4640	215-988-1333	None	None	4.00	Clive A. Gillmore	'94
DELAWARE GL BOND; A	World Income	0.3	10.54	5.74	☆	☆	☆	☆	0.0	□	523-4640	215-988-1333	4.75	None	None	Ian Sims	'94
DELAWARE GL BOND; B	World Income	0.1	10.55	5.66	☆	☆	☆	☆	0.0	□	523-4640	215-988-1333	None	None	4.00	Ian Sims	'94
DELAWARE INTL EQ; A	International	58.5	11.74	1.64	2.88	8.71	☆	☆	1.5	□	523-4640	215-988-1333	5.75	1.56	None	Clive A. Gillmore	'91
DELAWARE INTL EQ; B	International	1.6	11.70	1.38	☆	☆	☆	☆	0.0	□	523-4640	215-988-1333	None	None	4.00	Clive A. Gillmore	'94
DELAWARE TREAS RSVS; A	Fixed Income	747.7	9.13	2.80	6.49	3.97	6.61	☆	7.8	□	523-4640	215-988-1333	3.00	0.91	None	Roger A. Early	'94
DELAWARE TREAS RSVS; B	Fixed Income	10.1	9.13	2.58	5.59	☆	☆	☆	7.0	□	523-4640	215-988-1333	None	1.76	2.00	Roger A. Early	'94
DELAWARE TREND; A	Capital Appreciation	287.7	14.21	11.19	24.40	19.17	15.81	15.64	0.0	18.3	523-4640	215-988-1333	5.75	1.37	None	Edward N. Antoian	'84
DELAWARE TREND; B	Capital Appreciation	3.7	14.13	10.91	☆	☆	☆	☆	0.0	18.3	523-4640	215-988-1333	None	None	4.00	Edward N. Antoian	'94
DELAWARE US GOVT; A	Fixed Income	210.0	7.92	4.08	8.44	4.43	7.26	☆	8.3	□	523-4640	215-988-1333	4.75	1.23	None	Roger A. Early	'94
DELAWARE US GOVT; B	Fixed Income	7.1	7.92	3.89	7.69	☆	☆	☆	7.6	□	523-4640	215-988-1333	None	None	4.00	Roger A. Early	'94
DELAWARE VALUE; A	Capital Appreciation	173.2	20.64	6.17	7.34	11.89	13.38	☆	0.8	13.7	523-4640	215-988-1333	5.75	1.46	None	Edward A. Trumpbour	'87
DELAWARE VALUE; B	Capital Appreciation	3.4	20.55	5.98	☆	☆	☆	☆	0.0	13.7	523-4640	215-988-1333	None	None	4.00	Edward A. Trumpbour	'94
DEPOSITORS BOSTON ⊠	Growth	63.6	103.67	9.26	29.33	10.23	10.18	12.55	1.1	16.9	225-6265	617-482-8260	None	0.81	None	Thomas E. Faust, Jr.	'91
DFA GRP 1 YEAR FIXED INC ▮	Fixed Income	614.0	102.05	2.29	6.64	4.72	6.05	7.12	5.4	□	None	310-395-8005	None	0.21	None	Team Managed	N/A
DFA GRP 5 YEAR GOVT ▮	Fixed Income	270.1	100.39	3.19	6.11	5.02	7.80	☆	5.5	□	None	310-395-8005	None	0.31	None	Team Managed	N/A
DFA GRP CONTL SMALL CO ▮	European Region	376.1	15.82	5.05	5.05	6.22	-0.17	☆	1.1	□	None	310-395-8005	None	0.77	None	Team Managed	N/A
DFA GRP DFA/AEW RE SECS ▮	Real Estate	36.5	10.33	5.62	2.64	☆	☆	☆	4.0	N/A	None	310-395-8005	None	0.90	None	Team Managed	N/A
DFA GRP GLOBAL FIXED INC ▮	World Income	177.3	103.55	4.04	10.83	6.38	☆	☆	3.9	□	None	310-395-8005	None	0.49	None	Team Managed	N/A
DFA GRP INTL HIGH BK-MKT ▮	International	140.4	11.83	1.46	1.98	☆	☆	☆	1.2	□	None	310-395-8005	None	0.69	None	Team Managed	N/A
DFA GRP INTL VAL ▮	International	198.3	10.30	1.42	2.00	☆	☆	☆	1.8	□	None	310-395-8005	None	None	None	Team Managed	N/A
DFA GRP INTMDT GOVT ▮	Fixed Income	72.8	111.46	6.86	12.52	7.91	☆	☆	6.2	□	None	310-395-8005	None	0.29	None	Team Managed	N/A
DFA GRP JAPAN SMALL CO ▮	Japanese	314.9	21.16	-12.13	-25.80	6.47	-5.78	☆	0.1	□	None	310-395-8005	None	0.76	None	Team Managed	N/A
DFA GRP LRG CAP INTL ▮	International	57.6	12.22	0.74	3.84	10.82	☆	☆	0.7	□	None	310-395-8005	None	0.66	None	Team Managed	N/A
DFA GRP LRG CAP VAL ▮	Growth	211.6	12.11	11.36	25.45	☆	☆	☆	2.5	13.0	None	310-395-8005	None	0.44	None	Team Managed	N/A
DFA GRP PAC RIM SMALL CO ▮	Pacific Region	207.8	14.69	2.23	-2.05	☆	☆	☆	1.5	□	None	310-395-8005	None	0.95	None	Team Managed	N/A
DFA GRP SMALL CAP VALUE ▮	Small Company Growth	486.6	13.14	10.61	17.93	☆	☆	☆	1.0	11.3	None	310-395-8005	None	0.66	None	Team Managed	N/A
DFA GRP UK SMALL COMPANY ▮	European Region	237.8	24.83	5.79	9.13	5.58	5.15	☆	1.9	□	None	310-395-8005	None	0.74	None	Team Managed	N/A
DFA GRP US 6-10 SMALL CO ▮	Small Company Growth	155.9	12.01	10.69	22.86	17.67	☆	☆	2.1	14.9	None	310-395-8005	None	0.53	None	Team Managed	N/A
DFA GRP US 9-10 SMALL CO ▮	Small Company Growth	792.8	10.23	12.67	25.44	21.50	15.62	11.73	0.2	13.6	None	310-395-8005	None	0.65	None	Team Managed	N/A
DFA GRP US LARGE CO ▮	Growth	77.8	16.35	9.47	25.92	12.92	☆	☆	2.3	17.3	None	310-395-8005	None	0.24	None	Team Managed	N/A
DG INV EQUITY	Growth	315.4	12.55	8.09	26.91	☆	☆	☆	1.4	18.8	344-2488	None	3.50	0.96	None	Ron Lindquist	'92
DG INV GOVT INCOME	Fixed Income	149.0	9.88	5.79	11.40	☆	☆	☆	5.6	□	344-2488	None	2.00	0.70	None	John Mark McKenzie	'92
DG INV LTD TM GOVT INC	Fixed Income	99.3	9.81	2.99	7.04	☆	☆	☆	5.0	□	344-2488	None	2.00	0.63	None	John Mark McKenzie	'92
DG INV OPPORTUNITY	Small Company Growth	42.5	12.71	11.69	☆	☆	☆	☆	0.0	N/A	344-2488	None	3.50	None	None	William Womack	'94
DIAZ-VERSON AMERICAS EQ	Global	5.4	8.87	5.85	-11.49	☆	☆	☆	0.0	□	343-5133	None	None	2.44	None	Salvador Diaz-Verson	'93
DIVERSIFICATION FUND ⊠	Growth	72.9	207.40	10.99	29.32	12.62	10.86	12.68	1.1	17.1	225-6265	617-482-8260	None	0.78	None	Robert S. Goodof	'87
DVSFD INV BALANCED ✲	Flexible	N/A	11.83	9.74	19.66	☆	☆	☆	0.6	N/A	None	914-697-8000	None	0.99	None	Institutional Capital	'94
DVSFD INV EQTY GRO ✲	Growth	N/A	12.49	7.86	25.46	☆	☆	☆	0.0	26.6	None	914-697-8000	None	1.17	None	Jundt Associates Inc.	'94
DVSFD INV EQTY INC ✲	Equity Income	N/A	11.51	7.77	16.34	☆	☆	☆	0.8	17.5	None	914-697-8000	None	0.92	None	Asset Mgmt Group	'94
DVSFD INV GOVT/CORP BD ✲	Fixed Income	N/A	11.16	8.14	13.83	☆	☆	☆	1.8	□	None	914-697-8000	None	0.94	None	Capital Management Grp	'94
DVSFD INV GRO & INC ✲	Growth Income	N/A	11.74	6.44	18.34	☆	☆	☆	0.3	18.8	None	914-697-8000	None	1.08	None	Munder Capital Mgmt Inc.	'94
DVSFD INV HIGH QUAL BD ✲	Fixed Income	N/A	10.56	4.14	7.75	☆	☆	☆	1.9	□	None	914-697-8000	None	0.95	None	Merganser Capital Mgmt	'94
DVSFD INV SPECIAL EQ ✲	Small Company Growth	N/A	12.63	10.89	27.94	☆	☆	☆	0.0	20.4	None	914-697-8000	None	1.39	None	Multiple Managers	N/A
DODGE & COX BALANCED	Balanced	1,132.1	51.63	8.02	20.46	13.62	12.48	14.06	3.6	15.8	621-3979	415-434-0311	None	0.58	None	Team Managed	N/A
DODGE & COX INCOME	Fixed Income	217.8	11.72	7.01	14.02	8.55	10.36	☆	6.6	□	621-3979	415-434-0311	None	0.54	None	Team Managed	N/A
DODGE & COX STOCK	Growth Income	782.5	63.38	8.54	25.20	16.91	13.01	15.64	2.0	15.9	621-3979	415-434-0311	None	0.61	None	Team Managed	N/A
DOMINI SOCIAL EQUITY	Growth	48.4	14.41	9.28	24.58	12.92	☆	☆	1.4	17.1	762-6814	None	None	0.75	None	Amy Domini	'91
DOMINION INSIGHT GROWTH	Growth	7.2	13.53	23.56	42.41	☆	☆	☆	0.0	26.2	880-1095	214-385-9595	3.50	2.37	None	Jim Collins	'92

PERFORMANCE OF MUTUAL FUNDS (continued)

FUND NAME	OBJECTIVE	ASSETS ($MIL) 5/31/95	NAV ($/SHR) 6/30/95	QTR	1YR	3YRS	5YRS	10YRS	DIV YLD %	P/E RATIO	800	In-State	Load	Exp. Ratio	Redemption	MANAGER	SINCE
DREMAN CONTRARIAN PORT	Growth Income	13.2	14.37	9.48	20.79	12.90	10.56	☆	1.8	11.8	533-1608	201-332-8228	None	1.25	None	David N. Dreman	'88
DREMAN FIXED INCOME PORT	Fixed Income	2.6	9.83	3.52	7.56	4.76	6.87	☆	5.5		533-1608	201-332-8228	None	0.75	None	William F Coughlin	'88
DREMAN HIGH RETURN PORT	Equity Income	43.4	17.99	10.20	17.58	13.78	15.51	☆	1.4	11.5	533-1608	201-332-8228	None	1.25	None	David N. Dreman	'88
DREMAN SMALL CAP VALUE	Small Company Growth	10.0	13.90	16.42	30.15	16.21	☆	☆	0.0	13.5	533-1608	201-332-8228	None	1.25	None	Holmes/Schuss/Dreman '93/'94/'95	'93/'94/'95
DREY-LRL INV CONTR; INV	Growth	0.8	N/A	N/A	N/A	N/A	N/A	N/A	0.0	N/A	554-4611	None	None	1.83	None	Guy Scott	'91
DREY-LRL INV SHTM; INV	Fixed Income	3.6	11.99	2.57	7.11	4.13	6.41	☆	5.7		554-4611	None	None	0.95	None	Roberta Shea	'89
DREY-LRL BD INDEX; INV	Fixed Income	0.2	9.81	6.24	11.48	☆	☆	☆	5.4		554-4611	None	None	0.65	None	Laurie Carroll	'94
DREY-LRL BD INDEX; R	Fixed Income	6.1	9.81	6.30	11.74	☆	☆	☆	5.6		554-4611	None	None	0.40	None	Laurie Carroll	'93
DREY-LRL CORE VAL; INST	Growth	70.2	29.11	9.52	20.68	13.95	9.28	12.64	1.5	N/A	554-4611	None	None	1.02	None	Guy Scott	'93
DREY-LRL CORE VAL; INV	Growth	359.3	29.11	9.54	20.56	☆	☆	☆	1.4	N/A	554-4611	None	None	1.11	None	Guy Scott	'91
DREY-LRL CORE VAL; R	Growth	4.7	29.11	9.52	☆	☆	☆	☆	0.0	N/A	554-4611	None	None	None	None	Guy Scott	'94
DREY-LRL DISC MIDCAP; INV	Midcap	0.6	10.87	8.72	16.77	☆	☆	☆	0.8	N/A	554-4611	None	None	1.40	None	John O'Toole	'94
DREY-LRL DISC MIDCAP; R	Midcap	19.2	10.87	8.81	17.06	☆	☆	☆	1.0	N/A	554-4611	None	None	1.16	None	John O'Toole	'94
DREY-LRL DISC STK; INV	Growth Income	28.2	20.50	9.61	22.48	☆	☆	☆	1.2	N/A	554-4611	None	None	1.15	None	Bert Mullins	'94
DREY-LRL DISC STK; R	Growth Income	292.6	20.50	9.64	22.79	13.17	12.45	☆	1.4	N/A	554-4611	None	None	0.90	None	Bert Mullins	'87
DREY-LRL EQUITY INC; INV	Equity Income	0.8	11.19	8.05	☆	☆	☆	☆	0.0	N/A	554-4611	None	None	None	None	Bert Mullins	'94
DREY-LRL EQUITY INC; R	Equity Income	4.8	11.19	8.14	☆	☆	☆	☆	0.0	N/A	554-4611	None	None	None	None	Bert Mullins	'94
DREY-LRL EURO; INV	European Region	0.4	11.39	6.75	13.29	☆	☆	☆	0.6		554-4611	None	None	2.00	None	Catherine Adibi	'89
DREY-LRL EURO; R	European Region	10.6	11.37	6.86	13.42	4.67	5.65	☆	0.9		554-4611	None	None	1.75	None	Catherine Adibi	'89
DREY-LRL INST SHTM BD; I	Fixed Income	0.8	9.94	1.83	5.67	☆	☆	☆	5.1		554-4611	None	None	0.21	None	Laurie Carroll	'93
DREY-LRL INTL ALLOC; INV	International	4.6	9.68	0.41	☆	☆	☆	☆	0.0		554-4611	None	None	None	None	Patrice Conxicouer	'94
DREY-LRL INTL ALLOC; R	International	16.3	9.68	0.41	☆	☆	☆	☆	0.0		554-4611	None	None	None	None	Patrice Conxicouer	'94
DREY-LRL PRM BAL; A	Balanced	1.0	11.17	8.74	18.27	☆	☆	☆	2.1	N/A	554-4611	None	4.50	1.29	None	Carroll/Gala	'94/'94
DREY-LRL PRM BAL; R	Balanced	88.2	11.17	8.83	18.57	☆	☆	☆	2.4	N/A	554-4611	None	None	1.04	None	Carroll/Gala	'93/'93
DREY-LRL PRM LTD GVT; A	Fixed Income	15.9	12.66	5.81	10.07	6.00	7.62	☆	5.9		554-4611	None	3.00	1.02	None	Almond Goduti	'90
DREY-LRL PRM LTD INC; A	Fixed Income	1.1	10.74	4.85	9.48	☆	☆	☆	5.0		554-4611	None	3.00	0.83	None	Laurie Carroll	'94
DREY-LRL PRM LTD INC; B	Fixed Income	0.1	10.74	4.72	☆	☆	☆	☆	0.0		554-4611	None	None	None	3.00	Laurie Carroll	'95
DREY-LRL PRM LTD INC; R	Fixed Income	70.2	10.74	4.92	9.76	6.15	☆	☆	5.3		554-4611	None	None	0.60	None	Laurie Carroll	'91
DREY-LRL PRM MGD INC; A	Fixed Income	81.6	10.79	6.79	11.01	7.64	9.35	8.98	6.6		554-4611	None	4.50	1.14	None	Goduti/MacBride	'89/'89
DREY-LRL PRM MGD INC; B	Fixed Income	0.5	10.79	6.60	☆	☆	☆	☆	0.0		554-4611	None	None	None	4.00	Goduti/MacBride	'95/'95
DREY-LRL PRM MGD INC; R	Fixed Income	10.8	10.79	6.86	11.29	☆	☆	☆	6.9	N/A	554-4611	None	None	None	None	Goduti/MacBride	'93/'93
DREY-LRL PRM SM CO; A	Small Company Growth	0.7	12.07	12.78	☆	☆	☆	☆	0.0	N/A	554-4611	None	4.50	None	None	James Wadsworth	'94
DREY-LRL PRM SM CO; B	Small Company Growth	0.3	12.06	12.82	☆	☆	☆	☆	0.0	N/A	554-4611	None	None	None	4.00	James Wadsworth	'94
DREY-LRL PRM SM CO; R	Small Company Growth	21.2	12.07	12.77	25.16	☆	☆	☆	0.0	N/A	554-4611	None	None	None	None	James Wadsworth	'94
DREY-LRL S&P 500; INV	S&P Index	7.0	11.94	9.40	25.48	☆	☆	☆	1.9	N/A	554-4611	None	None	0.40	None	John O'Toole	'93
DREY-LRL S&P 500; R	S&P Index	156.3	11.94	9.39	25.48	☆	☆	☆	2.1	N/A	554-4611	None	None	None	None	John O'Toole	'93
DREY-LRL SHTM GOVT; INV	Fixed Income	0.1	10.09	2.22	5.44	☆	☆	☆	4.4		554-4611	None	None	0.80	None	Laurie Carroll	'94
DREY-LRL SHTM GOVT; R	Fixed Income	0.8	10.09	2.29	5.70	☆	☆	☆	4.6		554-4611	None	None	0.55	None	Laurie Carroll	'94
DREY-LRL SPEC GRO; INV	Growth	64.7	16.73	7.24	5.62	13.19	11.97	11.14	0.0	N/A	554-4611	None	None	1.73	None	Guy Scott	'90
DREY-LRL SPEC GRO; R	Growth	6.1	16.90	7.30	5.89	☆	☆	☆	0.0	N/A	554-4611	None	None	1.19	None	Guy Scott	'93
DREY-WILSH LG CO GRO	Growth	19.0	15.86	10.22	30.32	☆	☆	☆	0.6	19.9	554-4611	None	None	0.68	1.00	Wilshire Associates Inc.	'92
DREY-WILSH LG CO VAL	Growth	18.6	15.24	8.32	19.05	☆	☆	☆	2.6	12.9	554-4611	None	None	0.58	1.00	Wilshire Associates Inc.	'92
DREY-WILSH SM CO GRO	Small Company Growth	17.6	14.74	6.23	28.35	☆	☆	☆	0.0	22.8	554-4611	None	None	0.74	1.00	Wilshire Associates Inc.	'92
DREY-WILSH SM CO VAL	Small Company Growth	28.8	14.74	6.73	11.41	☆	☆	☆	3.0	12.0	554-4611	None	None	0.50	1.00	Wilshire Associates Inc.	'92
DREYFUS 100% TREAS INT	Fixed Income	184.9	12.93	5.81	9.63	7.25	9.02	☆	7.0		554-4611	None	None	0.89	None	Gerald Thunelius	'94

DREYFUS 100% TREAS LONG	Fixed Income	135.3	14.75	9.96	12.60	9.26	10.48	☆	6.7	□	554-4611	None	None	0.98	None	Gerald Thunelius	'94
DREYFUS 100% TREAS SHORT	Fixed Income	175.5	15.04	3.57	7.50	5.87	7.59	☆	7.2	□	554-4611	None	None	0.35	None	Gerald Thunelius	'94
DREYFUS A BONDS PLUS	Fixed Income	582.2	14.51	7.36	12.96	8.69	10.18	9.90	6.5	□	554-4611	None	None	0.99	None	Garitt Kono	'94
DREYFUS APPRECIATION FD	Growth	286.3	18.05	9.73	29.46	10.41	10.79	14.45	1.5	17.7	554-4611	None	None	0.96	None	Fayez Sarofim & Co.	'90
DREYFUS ASSET GROWTH	Flexible	1.5	14.04	7.67	☆	☆	☆	☆	0.0	16.9	554-4611	None	None	None	None	Ernest Wiggins	'94
DREYFUS ASSET INCOME	Flexible	1.5	14.76	9.74	☆	☆	☆	☆	0.0	17.5	554-4611	None	None	None	None	Ernest Wiggins	'94
DREYFUS ASSET TOT RETURN	Flexible	59.4	14.79	9.64	22.82	☆	☆	☆	2.5	17.5	554-4611	None	None	0.16	None	Ernest Wiggins	'94
DREYFUS BALANCED	Balanced	137.5	15.13	8.05	20.91	☆	☆	☆	4.1	19.3	554-4611	None	None	0.69	None	Ernest Wiggins	'94
DREYFUS CAP VALUE; A	Capital Appreciation	302.8	10.74	-5.04	-6.28	-2.02	1.41	☆	2.4	41.5	554-4611	None	4.50	1.21	None	Comstock Partners	'87
DREYFUS CAP VALUE; B	Capital Appreciation	93.5	10.56	-5.21	-6.93	☆	☆	☆	1.9	41.5	554-4611	None	None	1.99	4.00	Comstock Partners	'93
DREYFUS CAPITAL GROWTH	Capital Appreciation	584.8	16.07	3.48	11.46	7.82	9.23	11.59	2.7	13.1	554-4611	None	3.00	1.12	None	Howard Stein	'69
DREYFUS EDISON ELEC INDX	Utility	76.6	12.35	8.26	20.65	5.47	☆	☆	7.6	12.3	554-4611	None	None	0.74	None	Wells Fargo Nikko Adv.	'91
DREYFUS FOCUS LG CO GR	Growth	5.5	13.84	8.46	18.61	☆	☆	☆	1.5	N/A	554-4611	None	None	None	None	Ernest Wiggins	'93
DREYFUS FOCUS LG CO VAL	Growth	6.0	14.41	9.58	21.82	☆	☆	☆	2.2	N/A	554-4611	None	None	None	None	Ernest Wiggins	'93
DREYFUS FOCUS SM CO GR	Small Company Growth	5.2	13.31	10.73	17.25	☆	☆	☆	0.9	N/A	554-4611	None	None	None	None	Ernest Wiggins	'93
DREYFUS FOCUS SM CO VAL	Small Company Growth	5.6	12.98	7.36	15.05	☆	☆	☆	2.5	N/A	554-4611	None	None	None	None	Ernest Wiggins	'93
DREYFUS FUND	Growth Income	2,673.5	13.64	7.79	18.28	9.47	8.43	11.10	1.5	N/A	554-4611	None	None	0.74	None	Ernest Wiggins	'95
DREYFUS GLOBAL BOND	World Income	16.4	13.00	5.69	15.13	☆	☆	☆	7.2	□	554-4611	None	None	None	None	M&G Investment Mgmt Ltd	'94
DREYFUS GLOBAL GROWTH	Global Flexible	121.7	35.21	4.70	4.76	4.88	6.61	☆	0.0	□	554-4611	None	3.00	1.40	None	Kelly McDermott	'94
DREYFUS GNMA	Fixed Income	1,459.8	14.62	4.64	9.32	5.84	7.99	8.23	6.6	□	554-4611	None	None	0.95	None	Garitt Kono	'92
DREYFUS GRO OPPORTUNITY	Growth	389.7	9.74	8.10	19.41	8.83	8.39	11.71	0.8	20.0	554-4611	None	None	1.10	None	Ernest Wiggins	'94
DREYFUS GROWTH & INCOME	Growth Income	1,707.0	17.63	7.52	15.26	13.01	☆	☆	3.0	16.6	554-4611	None	None	1.14	None	Richard Hoey	'91
DREYFUS INSTL SH TREAS; A	Fixed Income	50.1	2.00	3.31	8.31	☆	☆	☆	6.4	□	554-4611	None	None	0.20	None	Gerald Thunelius	'94
DREYFUS INSTL SH TREAS; B	Fixed Income	8.1	2.01	3.24	8.04	☆	☆	☆	6.2	□	554-4611	None	None	0.45	None	Gerald Thunelius	'94
DREYFUS INTL EQUITY	International	129.5	13.66	1.86	-6.63	☆	☆	☆	0.2	□	554-4611	None	None	1.87	None	M&G Investment Ltd	'93
DREYFUS INVSTRS GNMA FD	Fixed Income	48.5	15.04	5.43	11.16	7.44	8.52	☆	7.2	□	554-4611	None	None	0.06	None	Garitt Kono	'92
DREYFUS NEW LEADERS	Small Company Growth	447.0	35.76	8.40	18.05	15.20	12.72	14.55	0.2	19.8	554-4611	None	None	1.16	1.00	Thomas Frank	'85
DREYFUS PREM GL INV; A	Global	71.6	15.76	4.72	5.59	7.96	☆	☆	0.9	□	554-4611	None	4.50	1.38	None	Kelly McDermott	'94
DREYFUS PREM GL INV; B	Global	75.0	15.60	4.56	4.82	☆	☆	☆	0.3	□	554-4611	None	None	2.15	4.00	Kelly McDermott	'94
DREYFUS PREM GNMA; A	Fixed Income	141.4	14.33	5.19	9.37	6.13	8.50	☆	6.4	□	554-4611	None	4.50	0.94	None	Garitt Kono	'93
DREYFUS PREM GNMA; B	Fixed Income	38.8	14.34	5.05	8.77	☆	☆	☆	5.8	□	554-4611	None	None	1.51	3.00	Garitt Kono	'93
DREYFUS PREM GROWTH; A	Global	13.5	15.65	8.01	21.97	☆	☆	☆	1.3	□	554-4611	None	4.50	1.33	None	Fayez Sarofim & Co.	'93
DREYFUS PREM GROWTH; B	Global	21.1	15.51	7.78	21.00	☆	☆	☆	0.8	□	554-4611	None	None	2.07	4.00	Fayez Sarofim & Co.	'93
DREYFUS SHT-INTMDT GOVT	Fixed Income	526.3	10.99	4.29	8.36	6.13	8.19	☆	6.9	□	554-4611	None	None	0.47	None	Gerald Thunelius	'94
DREYFUS SHT-TERM INCOME	Fixed Income	219.9	11.93	4.15	7.73	☆	☆	☆	7.1	□	554-4611	None	None	0.24	None	Gerald Thunelius	'94
DREYFUS STRAT GROWTH LP	Flexible	81.7	38.23	-2.47	-8.28	5.91	5.80	☆	0.0	12.9	554-4611	None	3.00	1.62	None	Howard Stein	'88
DREYFUS STRAT INCOME	Fixed Income	324.4	14.04	7.44	13.77	8.64	10.60	☆	6.7	□	554-4611	None	3.00	0.94	None	Garitt Kono	'94
DREYFUS STRAT INVEST; A	Flexible	213.6	20.69	5.89	10.88	7.32	8.60	☆	0.2	18.4	554-4611	None	4.50	1.54	None	Richard Hoey	'95
DREYFUS STRAT INVEST; B	Flexible	41.8	20.33	5.61	10.00	☆	☆	☆	0.1	18.4	554-4611	None	None	2.08	4.00	Richard Hoey	'95
DREYFUS THIRD CENTURY	Growth	366.5	7.74	11.05	19.54	9.16	8.84	11.17	0.8	18.6	554-4611	None	None	1.17	None	Diane Coffey	'90
DUFF & PHELPS ENHANCED	Fixed Income	115.3	10.03	2.05	6.11	☆	☆	☆	5.6	□	500-3833	303-623-2577	None	0.34	None	Robert Moore	'94
DUPREE INTMDT GOVT BOND	Fixed Income	7.8	10.15	6.01	12.87	☆	☆	☆	6.8	□	866-0614	606-254-7741	None	0.40	None	Bill Griggs	'92
EAGLE GROWTH SHARES	Growth	2.5	11.88	4.49	5.87	0.73	2.16	6.40	0.0	22.0	749-9933	407-395-2155	8.50	3.71	None	Donald Baxter	'87
EASTCLIFF TOTAL RETURN	Balanced	14.9	11.96	6.69	12.09	8.77	9.31	☆	1.1	16.3	338-1579	414-765-3500	None	2.00	None	Tom Keresey	'95
EBI FDS EQUITY	Growth Income	93.9	64.77	7.20	22.94	11.21	11.45	11.60	0.7	15.5	972-9030	404-892-0666	None	2.25	None	Michael Harhai	'93
EBI FDS FLEX	Flexible	305.0	57.91	7.77	20.68	10.88	11.18	☆	2.4	15.4	972-9030	404-892-0666	None	2.25	None	Edward Mitchell	'88
EBI FDS INCOME	Fixed Income	27.8	50.03	7.69	14.03	7.22	8.27	7.78	4.9	□	972-9030	404-892-0666	None	2.25	None	James Baker	'93
EBI FDS MULTIFLEX	Flexible	135.9	42.94	6.99	12.39	☆	☆	☆	1.7	16.0	972-9030	404-892-0666	None	2.49	None	Robert Slotpole	'94
ECLIPSE BALANCED	Balanced	31.9	19.63	6.75	15.72	12.79	12.23	☆	2.8	18.2	872-2710	404-631-0414	None	0.80	None	Wesley G. McCain	'89
ECLIPSE EQUITY FUND	Small Company Growth	193.9	12.86	6.11	12.11	13.42	10.10	☆	0.2	14.6	872-2710	404-631-0414	None	1.12	None	Wesley G. McCain	'87

PERFORMANCE OF MUTUAL FUNDS (continued)

FUND NAME	OBJECTIVE	ASSETS ($ MIL) 5/31/95	NAV ($/SHR) 6/30/95	QTR	1YR	3YRS	5YRS	10YRS	DIV YLD %	P/E RATIO	800	In-State	Load	Exp. Ratio	Redemption	MANAGER	SINCE
						(Annualized)											
ECLIPSE GROWTH & INCOME	Growth Income	4.4	11.27	7.74	☆	☆	☆	☆	0.0	N/A	872-2710	404-631-0414	None	None	None	Westley McCain	'94
ECLIPSE ULTRA SHT TM INC	Fixed Income	2.5	2.04	2.48	☆	☆	☆	☆	0.0	N/A	872-2710	404-631-0414	None	None	None	Wesley G. McCain	'94
EHRENKRANTZ GROWTH	Growth	6.6	5.77	4.72	15.18	9.86	6.44	☆	0.7	N/A	424-8570	212-508-4700	None	2.30	None	Ehrenkrantz/King/Nussbaum	'87
ELFUN DIVERSIFIED FUND ◪	Balanced	66.0	15.24	7.55	18.42	10.67	10.40	9.38	3.0	18.4	242-0134	203-326-4040	None	0.39	None	MacDougall/Carlson	'88/'88
ELFUN GLOBAL FUND ◪	Global	135.0	17.43	8.60	11.24	13.32	☆	☆	1.1	18.4	242-0134	203-326-4040	None	0.38	None	Ralph R. Layman	'91
ELFUN INCOME FUND	Fixed Income	202.3	11.30	6.29	12.09	7.37	9.45	9.77	6.7		242-0134	203-326-4040	None	0.30	None	Robert A. MacDougall	'84
ELFUN TRUSTS ◪	Growth	1,047.1	37.19	9.32	25.03	13.05	11.23	14.31	2.0	18.2	242-0134	203-326-4040	None	0.17	None	David Carlson	'88
ELITE GROUP GROWTH & INC	Growth Income	27.4	15.42	9.34	18.00	13.55	10.37	☆	1.2	N/A	423-1068	206-624-5863	None	1.42	None	Richard McCormick	'87
ELITE GROUP INCOME	Fixed Income	11.9	10.03	5.94	10.95	6.97	7.75	☆	6.2		423-1068	206-624-5863	None	1.11	None	William Church	'93
EMERALD BALANCED; A	Flexible	0.6	11.22	9.16	17.56	☆	☆	☆	3.2	18.3	637-6336	None	4.50	0.68	None	Creighten/Cantor	'94/'95
EMERALD BALANCED; B	Flexible	1.5	11.10	8.85	16.62	☆	☆	☆	2.6	18.3	637-6336	None	None	1.43	4.50	Creighten/Cantor	'94/'95
EMERALD BALANCED; INSTL	Flexible	55.6	11.12	9.24	17.97	☆	☆	☆	3.5	18.3	637-6336	None	None	0.28	None	Creighten/Cantor	'94/'95
EMERALD EQUITY; A	Growth	19.0	13.05	11.09	21.60	9.46	☆	☆	0.4	18.3	637-6336	None	4.50	1.07	None	Russell Creighten	'93
EMERALD EQUITY; B	Growth	1.6	12.91	10.82	20.02	☆	☆	☆	0.1	18.3	637-6336	None	None	2.50	4.50	Russell Creighten	'94
EMERALD EQUITY; INSTL	Growth	172.7	13.09	11.21	22.29	☆	☆	☆	0.9	18.3	637-6336	None	None	0.79	None	Russell Creighten	'94
EMERALD GOVT SECS; A	Fixed Income	28.3	10.30	4.25	9.54	6.40	☆	☆	6.0		637-6336	None	4.50	0.98	None	Andrew Cantor	'91
EMERALD GOVT SECS; B	Fixed Income	1.2	10.29	4.05	8.84	☆	☆	☆	5.6		637-6336	None	None	1.55	4.50	Andrew Cantor	'94
EMERALD GOVT SECS; INSTL	Fixed Income	70.4	10.28	4.25	9.75	☆	☆	☆	6.4		637-6336	None	None	0.68	None	Andrew Cantor	'94
EMERALD MGD BOND; A	Fixed Income	1.2	10.55	6.90	12.91	☆	☆	☆	6.5		637-6336	None	4.50	0.65	None	Andrew Cantor	'94
EMERALD MGD BOND; B	Fixed Income	0.5	10.28	6.09	11.21	☆	☆	☆	5.8		637-6336	None	None	1.34	4.50	Andrew Cantor	'94
EMERALD MGD BOND; INSTL	Fixed Income	65.1	10.31	6.59	12.80	☆	☆	☆	6.9		637-6336	None	None	0.27	None	Andrew Cantor	'94
EMERALD SH-TM INC; A	Fixed Income	0.3	10.08	3.49	7.69	☆	☆	☆	5.4		637-6336	None	2.50	0.67	None	Jacqueline Lunsford	'94
EMERALD SH-TM INC; B	Fixed Income	0.1	10.03	3.31	6.37	☆	☆	☆	4.7		637-6336	None	None	1.43	4.50	Jacqueline Lunsford	'94
EMERALD SH-TM INC; INSTL	Fixed Income	20.7	10.09	3.59	8.19	☆	☆	☆	5.8		637-6336	None	None	0.28	None	Jacqueline Lunsford	'94
EMERALD SMALL CAP; A	Small Company Growth	1.8	11.48	11.35	28.70	☆	☆	☆	0.0	18.1	637-6336	None	4.50	1.54	None	Dean McQuiddy	'94
EMERALD SMALL CAP; B	Small Company Growth	1.9	11.33	11.19	27.73	☆	☆	☆	0.0	18.1	637-6336	None	None	2.32	4.50	Dean McQuiddy	'94
EMERALD SMALL CAP; INSTL	Small Company Growth	65.3	11.49	11.45	28.96	☆	☆	☆	0.0	18.1	637-6336	None	None	1.29	None	Dean McQuiddy	'94
ENDOWMENTS INC ◪	Growth Income	59.1	17.52	6.11	18.47	10.53	11.29	12.54	3.3	14.5	421-4120	714-671-7000	None	0.73	None	Multiple Managers	N/A
ENTERPRISE CAPITAL APPR	Capital Appreciation	109.1	33.78	11.19	23.64	13.24	13.24	☆	0.0	23.1	432-4320	404-261-1116	4.75	1.66	None	Jeff Miller	'87
ENTERPRISE GOVT SEC	Fixed Income	87.4	11.53	5.92	12.46	6.19	8.20	☆	7.1		432-4320	404-261-1116	4.75	1.30	None	Barach/Gundlach	'92/'92
ENTERPRISE GROWTH	Growth	101.9	9.70	14.79	31.90	16.32	13.95	14.95	0.0	21.4	432-4320	404-261-1116	4.75	1.60	None	Ron Canakaris	'80
ENTERPRISE GROWTH & INC	Growth Income	55.2	18.67	6.88	15.47	10.85	10.04	☆	2.3	17.5	432-4320	404-261-1116	4.75	1.50	None	John Rock	'87
ENTERPRISE HIGH YLD BOND	Fixed Income	50.4	11.27	5.29	11.48	11.13	12.01	☆	9.0		432-4320	404-261-1116	4.75	1.30	None	Jim Caywood	'87
ENTERPRISE INTL GROWTH	International	26.6	14.69	2.80	-0.37	7.63	4.62	☆	0.0		432-4320	404-261-1116	4.75	2.00	None	Richard Carr	'94
ENTERPRISE MANAGED	Flexible	22.9	6.13	12.27	☆	☆	☆	☆	0.0	N/A	432-4320	404-261-1116	4.75	None	None	Richard Glasebrook II	'94
ENTERPRISE SMALL COMPANY	Small Company Growth	21.6	5.40	3.45	7.65	☆	☆	☆	0.5	12.0	432-4320	404-261-1116	4.75	1.75	None	Kenneth Fisher	'93
ESC STRATEGIC ASSET PRES	Fixed Income	12.2	10.05	3.02	6.88	☆	☆	☆	5.3		261-3863	None	None	None	None	Equitable Asset Mgmt	'94
ESC STRATEGIC GLBL EQ; A	Global	10.4	10.46	5.66	8.27	☆	☆	☆	0.0		261-3863	None	4.50	None	None	Multiple Managers	N/A
ESC STRATEGIC GLBL EQ; B	Global	3.5	10.37	5.60	7.45	☆	☆	☆	0.0		261-3863	None	4.50	None	None	Multiple Managers	N/A
ESC STRATEGIC INCOME; A	Fixed Income	34.9	10.25	4.75	10.83	☆	☆	☆	6.2		261-3863	None	4.50	None	None	Multiple Managers	N/A
ESC STRATEGIC INCOME; B	Fixed Income	1.2	10.25	4.62	10.26	☆	☆	☆	5.7		261-3863	None	None	None	None	Multiple Managers	N/A
ESC STRATEGIC SM CAP; A	Small Company Growth	11.4	12.14	7.91	25.89	☆	☆	☆	0.0	N/A	261-3863	None	4.50	None	None	Equitable Asset Mgmt	'94
ESC STRATEGIC SM CAP; B	Small Company Growth	3.7	12.08	7.66	25.28	☆	☆	☆	0.0	N/A	261-3863	None	None	None	None	Multiple Managers	N/A
EUROPACIFIC GROWTH	International	9,320.9	22.21	6.94	8.76	12.08	10.10	17.36	1.6		421-4120	714-671-7000	5.75	0.97	None	Multiple Managers	N/A
EV CLASSIC GOVT OBLIG	Fixed Income	43.4	9.39	3.95	8.35	☆	☆	☆	7.0		225-6265	617-482-8260	None	2.72	1.00	Susan Schiff	'93

Fund	Objective	Net Assets	NAV	%Ret 1	%Ret 2	%Ret 3	%Ret 4	%Ret 5	Yield	Rtg	Tel 1	Tel 2	Load	Exp	CDSC	Manager	Yr
EV CLASSIC GREAT CHINA ★	Pacific Region	N/A	8.24	5.64	4.57	☆	☆	☆	0.2	☐	617-482-8260	225-6265	None	2.75	1.00	Robert Lloyd George Mgt	'93
EV CLASSIC GROWTH	Growth	0.8	11.25	5.73	☆	☆	☆	☆	0.0	N/A	617-482-8260	225-6265	None	None	1.00	Peter Kiely	'94
EV CLASSIC HIGH INCOME	Fixed Income	3.4	9.65	4.66	7.66	☆	☆	☆	10.4	☐	617-482-8260	225-6265	None	2.04	1.00	Hooker Talcott Jr.	'94
EV CLASSIC INVESTORS	Balanced	4.1	10.81	7.44	15.27	☆	☆	☆	1.9	15.1	617-482-8260	225-6265	None	3.23	1.00	Thomas E. Faust, Jr.	'93
EV CLASSIC SPECIAL EQ	Growth	1.0	10.59	2.72	☆	☆	☆	☆	0.0	☐	617-482-8260	225-6265	None	None	1.00	Clifford Krauss	'94
EV CLASSIC STOCK FUND	Growth Income	1.0	11.37	7.87	☆	☆	☆	☆	0.0	N/A	617-482-8260	225-6265	None	None	1.00	Duncan Richardson	'94
EV CLASSIC TOT RETURN	Utility	6.4	8.94	6.46	7.48	4.00	☆	☆	3.2	14.3	617-482-8260	225-6265	None	2.66	1.00	Timothy O'Brien	'95
EATON VANCE EQUITY-INC	Equity Income	25.5	10.79	6.88	9.53	3.69	3.92	☆	3.3	15.6	617-482-8260	225-6265	None	2.18	5.00	Timothy O'Brien	'95
EATON VANCE GOVT SH TREA	Fixed Income	54.4	59.68	1.72	5.87	3.69	☆	☆	0.0	☐	617-482-8260	225-6265	None	0.60	None	Michael Terry	'91
EATON VANCE INC OF BOSTN	Fixed Income	102.8	7.97	5.51	8.25	9.95	13.26	11.11	10.3	☐	617-482-8260	225-6265	3.75	1.04	None	Hooker Talcott Jr.	'86
EV MRTHN EMERGING MKTS ★	Emerging Markets	N/A	10.45	8.40	☆	☆	☆	☆	0.0	N/A	617-482-8260	225-6265	None	None	5.00	Robert Lloyd George Mgt	'94
EV MRTHN GOLD&NAT RES	Natural Resources	13.4	15.60	7.66	16.24	11.62	8.24	☆	0.0	☐	617-482-8260	225-6265	None	2.64	5.00	Titman/Burt	'95/95
EV MRTHN GOVT OBLIG	Fixed Income	103.3	9.39	3.91	8.74	☆	☆	☆	7.3	☐	617-482-8260	225-6265	None	2.43	5.00	Susan Schiff	'93
EV MRTHN GREATER CHINA ★	Pacific Region	N/A	12.06	5.79	5.74	☆	☆	☆	0.5	☐	617-482-8260	225-6265	None	2.38	5.00	Robert Lloyd George Mgt	'93
EV MRTHN GREATER INDIA ★	Pacific Region	N/A	8.12	-2.99	-19.52	☆	☆	☆	0.0	☐	617-482-8260	225-6265	None	2.54	5.00	Robert Lloyd George Mgt	'94
EV MRTHN GROWTH	Growth	1.5	11.25	6.33	8.03	8.97	11.60	☆	0.0	N/A	617-482-8260	225-6265	None	1.82	5.00	Peter Kiely	'94
EV MRTHN HIGH INCOME	Fixed Income	468.8	7.10	5.00	17.09	☆	☆	☆	9.6	☐	617-482-8260	225-6265	None	2.41	5.00	Hooker Talcott Jr.	'86
EV MRTHN INVESTORS	Balanced	18.4	10.79	7.83	☆	☆	☆	☆	2.3	15.1	617-482-8260	225-6265	None	None	5.00	Thomas E. Faust, Jr.	'93
EV MRTHN SPECIAL EQ	Growth	0.6	10.58	2.72	☆	☆	☆	☆	0.0	N/A	617-482-8260	225-6265	None	None	5.00	Clifford Krauss	'94
EV MRTHN STOCK FUND	Growth Income	2.7	11.12	7.96	☆	☆	☆	☆	0.0	N/A	617-482-8260	225-6265	None	None	5.00	Duncan Richardson	'94
EV MRTHN STRAT INC	World Income	172.0	8.30	7.37	8.05	1.67	☆	☆	8.1	☐	617-482-8260	225-6265	None	2.00	5.00	Mark S. Venezia	'90
EV MRTHN TOTAL RETURN	Utility	29.8	8.86	6.93	8.37	7.11	8.14	☆	3.8	14.3	617-482-8260	225-6265	None	2.07	5.00	Timothy O'Brien	'94
EV TRAD EMERGING MKTS ★	Emerging Markets	N/A	10.50	8.58	☆	☆	☆	☆	0.0	☐	617-482-8260	225-6265	4.75	None	None	Robert Lloyd George Mgt	'94
EV TRAD GOVT OBLIG	Fixed Income	384.2	10.90	4.26	9.53	6.56	7.63	☆	7.6	☐	617-482-8260	225-6265	3.75	1.73	None	Susan Schiff	'92
EV TRAD GREATER CHINA ★	Pacific Region	N/A	14.43	5.95	6.02	☆	☆	☆	0.4	☐	617-482-8260	225-6265	4.75	1.02	None	Robert Lloyd George Mgt	'92
EV TRAD GREATER INDIA ★	Pacific Region	N/A	8.12	-3.10	-19.60	☆	☆	☆	0.0	☐	617-482-8260	225-6265	4.75	0.98	None	Duncan Richardson	'94
EV TRAD GROWTH	Growth	125.2	7.96	6.42	19.02	6.58	11.27	☆	0.6	20.9	617-482-8260	225-6265	4.75	2.46	None	Peter Kiely	'90
EV TRAD INVESTORS	Balanced	217.1	7.72	8.07	19.01	10.33	10.82	☆	3.5	15.1	617-482-8260	225-6265	4.75	0.95	None	Thomas E. Faust, Jr.	'93
EV TRAD SPECIAL EQ	Growth	65.0	7.52	3.44	16.66	5.89	9.14	☆	0.0	19.8	617-482-8260	225-6265	4.75	0.91	None	Clifford Krauss	'87
EV TRAD STOCK FUND	Growth Income	91.8	12.64	8.59	16.45	8.29	11.52	☆	2.0	18.2	617-482-8260	225-6265	4.75	0.98	None	Duncan Richardson	'94
EV TRAD TOTAL RETURN	Utility	443.0	8.15	7.15	9.44	4.62	10.40	☆	4.4	14.3	617-482-8260	225-6265	4.75	1.18	None	Timothy O'Brien	'94
EVERGREEN AMER RET; A	Balanced	0.1	11.67	5.41	☆	☆	☆	☆	0.0	15.2	914-694-2020	807-2940	4.75	None	None	Irene O'Neill	'95
EVERGREEN AMER RET; B	Balanced	0.8	11.65	5.41	☆	☆	☆	☆	0.0	15.2	914-694-2020	807-2940	None	None	5.00	Irene O'Neill	'95
EVERGREEN AMER RET; C	Balanced	0.1	11.66	5.31	☆	☆	☆	☆	0.0	15.2	914-694-2020	807-2940	None	None	1.00	Irene O'Neill	'95
EVERGREEN AMER RET; Y	Balanced	38.2	11.67	5.60	12.77	9.91	☆	☆	6.0	15.2	914-694-2020	807-2940	None	1.28	None	Irene O'Neill	'88
EVERGREEN FOUNDATION; A	Balanced	31.1	13.95	9.44	☆	☆	☆	☆	0.0	15.9	914-694-2020	807-2940	4.75	None	None	Stephen Lieber	'95
EVERGREEN FOUNDATION; B	Balanced	92.2	13.92	9.22	☆	☆	☆	☆	0.0	15.9	914-694-2020	807-2940	None	None	5.00	Stephen Lieber	'95
EVERGREEN FOUNDATION; C	Balanced	4.2	13.93	9.31	☆	☆	☆	☆	0.0	15.9	914-694-2020	807-2940	None	None	1.00	Stephen Lieber	'95
EVERGREEN FOUNDATION; Y	Growth	390.5	13.96	9.48	20.01	14.21	☆	☆	4.2	15.9	914-694-2020	807-2940	4.75	1.14	None	Stephen Lieber	'90
EVERGREEN FUND; A	Growth	11.7	14.45	7.76	☆	☆	☆	☆	0.0	17.2	914-694-2020	807-2940	4.75	None	None	Stephen Lieber	'95
EVERGREEN FUND; B	Growth	29.4	14.41	7.62	☆	☆	☆	☆	0.0	17.2	914-694-2020	807-2940	None	None	5.00	Stephen Lieber	'95
EVERGREEN FUND; C	Growth	0.6	14.41	7.62	☆	☆	☆	☆	0.0	17.2	914-694-2020	807-2940	None	None	1.00	Stephen Lieber	'95
EVERGREEN FUND; Y	Growth	495.3	14.47	7.82	23.33	13.08	11.77	☆	0.5	17.2	914-694-2020	807-2940	4.75	1.22	None	Stephen Lieber	'71
EVERGREEN FXD GOVT; A	Fixed Income	0.4	9.17	5.94	☆	☆	☆	☆	0.0	N/A	914-694-2020	807-2940	4.75	None	None	James Colby III	'95
EVERGREEN FXD GOVT; B	Fixed Income	2.4	9.17	5.74	☆	☆	☆	☆	0.0	N/A	914-694-2020	807-2940	None	None	5.00	James Colby III	'95
EVERGREEN FXD GOVT; C	Fixed Income	0.1	9.16	5.62	☆	☆	☆	☆	0.0	N/A	914-694-2020	807-2940	None	None	1.00	James Colby III	'95
EVERGREEN FXD GOVT; Y	Fixed Income	2.2	9.17	5.88	8.45	☆	☆	☆	5.9	N/A	914-694-2020	807-2940	None	None	None	James Colby III	'95
EVERGREEN GL RE; A	Real Estate	0.6	11.90	11.01	☆	☆	☆	☆	0.0	14.7	914-694-2020	807-2940	4.75	None	None	Sam Lieber	'93
EVERGREEN GL RE; B	Real Estate	0.1	11.87	10.83	☆	☆	☆	☆	0.0	14.7	914-694-2020	807-2940	None	None	5.00	Sam Lieber	'93
EVERGREEN GL RE; C	Real Estate	0.1	11.87	10.83	☆	☆	☆	☆	0.0	14.7	914-694-2020	807-2940	None	None	1.00	Sam Lieber	'95

★ EATON VANCE FUNDS--Fund does not disclose total net assets.

PERFORMANCE OF MUTUAL FUNDS (continued)

FUND NAME	OBJECTIVE	ASSETS ($ MIL) 5/31/95	NAV ($/SHR) 6/30/95	QTR	1YR	3YRS	5YRS	10YRS	DIV YLD %	P/E RATIO	800	In-State	Load	Exp. Ratio	Redemption	MANAGER	SINCE
					RETURN THROUGH 6/30 (Annualized)						PHONE NUMBER		FEES				
EVERGREEN GL RE; Y	Real Estate	77.1	11.90	11.01	-6.16	13.94	4.90	☆	0.8	14.7	807-2940	914-694-2020	None	1.54	None	Sam Lieber	'89
EVERGREEN GRO & INC; A	Growth Income	6.6	17.12	7.12	☆	☆	☆	☆	0.0	15.1	807-2940	914-694-2020	4.75	None	None	Edmund Nicklin	'95
EVERGREEN GRO & INC; B	Growth Income	15.9	17.10	6.99	☆	☆	☆	☆	0.0	15.1	807-2940	914-694-2020	None	None	5.00	Edmund Nicklin	'95
EVERGREEN GRO & INC; C	Growth Income	0.4	17.10	6.98	☆	☆	☆	☆	0.0	15.1	807-2940	914-694-2020	None	None	1.00	Edmund Nicklin	'95
EVERGREEN GRO & INC; Y	Growth Income	91.1	17.13	7.18	24.48	16.11	13.36	☆	1.2	15.1	807-2940	914-694-2020	None	1.33	None	Edmund Nicklin	'86
EVERGREEN LTD MKT; A	Small Company Growth	1.0	16.93	3.23	☆	☆	☆	☆	0.0	10.8	807-2940	914-694-2020	4.75	None	None	Lieber/Wenger	'95/'95
EVERGREEN LTD MKT; B	Small Company Growth	1.9	16.86	2.99	☆	☆	☆	☆	0.0	10.8	807-2940	914-694-2020	None	None	5.00	Lieber/Wenger	'95/'95
EVERGREEN LTD MKT; C	Small Company Growth	0.1	16.87	3.05	☆	☆	☆	☆	0.0	10.8	807-2940	914-694-2020	None	None	1.00	Lieber/Wenger	'95/'95
EVERGREEN LTD MKT; Y	Small Company Growth	71.5	16.93	3.23	1.86	7.31	8.65	11.47	0.0	10.8	807-2940	914-694-2020	None	1.26	None	Lieber/Wenger	'83/'93
EVERGREEN RET SM CAP; A	Small Company Growth	0.1	10.47	5.30	☆	☆	☆	☆	0.0	N/A	807-2940	914-694-2020	4.75	None	None	Nola M. Falcone	'95
EVERGREEN RET SM CAP; B	Small Company Growth	0.1	10.47	5.13	☆	☆	☆	☆	0.0	N/A	807-2940	914-694-2020	None	None	5.00	Nola M. Falcone	'95
EVERGREEN RET SM CAP; C	Small Company Growth	0.1	10.46	5.10	☆	☆	☆	☆	0.0	N/A	807-2940	914-694-2020	None	None	1.00	Nola M. Falcone	'95
EVERGREEN RET SM CAP; Y	Small Company Growth	4.1	10.47	5.37	13.40	☆	☆	☆	4.2	11.1	807-2940	914-694-2020	None	1.48	None	Nola M. Falcone	'93
EVERGREEN TAX-STRAT; A	Balanced	0.5	11.35	7.44	☆	☆	☆	☆	0.0	N/A	807-2940	914-694-2020	4.75	None	5.00	Lieber/Colby	'95/'95
EVERGREEN TAX-STRAT; B	Balanced	0.1	11.34	7.20	☆	☆	☆	☆	0.0	N/A	807-2940	914-694-2020	None	None	5.00	Lieber/Colby	'95/'95
EVERGREEN TAX-STRAT; Y	Balanced	11.7	11.36	7.48	18.67	☆	☆	☆	3.4	18.0	807-2940	914-694-2020	None	None	None	Lieber/Colby	'93/'93
EVERGREEN TOT RTN; A	Equity Income	1.2	18.66	6.88	☆	☆	☆	☆	0.0	13.4	807-2940	914-694-2020	4.75	None	None	Nola M. Falcone	'95
EVERGREEN TOT RTN; B	Equity Income	3.3	18.63	6.69	☆	☆	☆	☆	0.0	13.4	807-2940	914-694-2020	None	None	5.00	Nola M. Falcone	'95
EVERGREEN TOT RTN; C	Equity Income	0.1	18.63	6.73	☆	☆	☆	☆	0.0	13.4	807-2940	914-694-2020	None	None	1.00	Nola M. Falcone	'95
EVERGREEN TOT RTN; Y	Equity Income	943.4	18.66	6.89	14.15	8.91	9.11	9.66	7.2	13.4	807-2940	914-694-2020	None	1.24	None	Nola M. Falcone	'78
EVERGREEN US RE; A	Real Estate	0.1	10.41	11.94	☆	☆	☆	☆	0.0	N/A	807-2940	914-694-2020	4.75	None	None	Sam Lieber	'95
EVERGREEN US RE; B	Real Estate	0.1	10.38	11.73	☆	☆	☆	☆	0.0	N/A	807-2940	914-694-2020	None	None	5.00	Sam Lieber	'95
EVERGREEN US RE; Y	Real Estate	8.4	10.42	11.92	7.14	☆	☆	☆	1.9	18.2	807-2940	914-694-2020	None	None	None	Sam Lieber	'93
EXCEL MIDAS GOLD SHARES	Gold	8.7	4.51	27.76	23.69	28.64	14.01	☆	0.0	N/A	783-3444	619-485-9400	4.50	2.18	None	Kgeld Thygesen	'92
EXCELSIOR INSTL BALANCED	Balanced	74.5	7.71	7.42	☆	9.77	9.25	N/A	0.0	N/A	None	None	None	None	None	N/A	N/A
EXCELSIOR INSTL BD INDEX	Fixed Income	16.2	7.27	5.91	☆	☆	☆	☆	0.0	N/A	None	None	None	None	None	N/A	N/A
EXCELSIOR INSTL EQ GRO	Growth	52.4	8.11	9.32	☆	☆	☆	☆	0.0	N/A	None	None	None	None	None	N/A	N/A
EXCELSIOR INSTL EQ INDEX	S&P Index	13.6	8.47	9.29	☆	☆	☆	☆	0.0	N/A	None	None	None	None	None	N/A	N/A
EXCELSIOR INSTL EQUITY	Growth	15.3	8.47	15.55	☆	☆	☆	☆	0.0	□	None	None	None	None	None	N/A	N/A
EXCELSIOR INSTL INCOME	Fixed Income	33.2	7.32	4.89	☆	☆	☆	☆	0.0	N/A	None	None	None	None	None	N/A	N/A
EXCELSIOR INSTL INTL EQ	International	8.8	7.93	9.08	☆	☆	☆	☆	0.0	N/A	None	None	None	None	None	N/A	N/A
EXCELSIOR INSTL SM CAP	Small Company Growth	13.7	8.04	9.84	☆	☆	☆	☆	0.0	N/A	None	None	None	None	None	N/A	N/A
EXCELSIOR INSTL TOT RET	Flexible	24.9	7.50	7.07	☆	☆	☆	☆	0.0	N/A	None	None	None	None	None	N/A	N/A
EXCELSIOR INSTL VAL EI	Equity Income	17.5	7.89	5.06	☆	☆	☆	☆	0.0	N/A	None	None	None	None	None	N/A	N/A
EXCHANGE FUND BOSTON ⊠	Growth	69.5	238.23	7.66	26.01	9.77	9.25	N/A	1.3	16.7	225-6265	617-482-8260	None	0.79	None	Thomas E. Faust, Jr.	'91
EXECUTIVE INV BLUE CHIP	Growth Income	1.1	15.07	8.93	20.57	10.99	10.24	☆	1.5	17.7	423-4026	212-858-8000	4.75	0.50	None	Patricia Poitra	'94
EXECUTIVE INV HIGH YIELD	Fixed Income	15.4	7.39	5.73	10.12	10.06	11.28	☆	9.4	□	423-4026	212-858-8000	4.75	1.33	None	George Ganter	'89
FAHNESTOCK HUD CAP APPRE	Growth	15.0	12.16	4.83	9.61	9.57	☆	☆	0.0	N/A	221-5588	None	4.50	2.49	None	Howard Shawn	'91
FAIRMONT FUND	Capital Appreciation	23.4	27.48	12.16	14.36	14.16	14.03	8.48	0.0	15.7	262-9936	502-636-5633	None	1.74	None	Morton H. Sachs	'81
FAM VALUE	Growth Income	229.8	22.86	8.39	19.35	10.83	14.02	☆	0.5	14.0	932-3271	518-234-7400	None	1.39	None	Thomas Putnam	'87
FASCIANO FUND	Midcap	20.0	20.17	7.80	24.11	12.74	11.87	☆	0.0	18.6	848-6050	312-444-6050	None	1.70	None	Michael Fasciano	'88
FBL SERIES BLUE CHIP	Growth Income	9.0	22.19	9.26	23.92	11.60	10.14	☆	0.6	17.6	247-4170	515-225-5586	4.75	1.83	5.00	Team Managed	N/A
FBL SERIES GRO COM STK	Growth Income	68.4	12.88	4.46	8.35	12.40	11.56	9.19	6.5	18.1	247-4170	515-225-5586	4.75	1.60	5.00	Roger Grefe	'86
FBL SERIES HI GRADE BD	Fixed Income	8.3	10.29	4.01	9.23	6.47	8.60	☆	5.5	□	247-4170	515-225-5586	None	1.90	5.00	Bob Rummelhart	'87
FBL SERIES HI YLD BD	Fixed Income	6.6	9.99	4.04	8.26	7.84	10.35	☆	7.2	□	247-4170	515-225-5586	None	2.00	5.00	Bob Rummelhart	'87

Fund	Objective	Assets	NAV						Yield		Phone	Phone		Exp.	Load	Manager	Since
FBL SERIES MANAGED	Flexible	20.4	11.92	6.11	9.81	11.14	10.57	★	5.5	16.4	515-225-5586	247-4170	None	1.96	5.00	Roger Grefe	'87
FBP CONTRARIAN BALANCED	Balanced	27.9	13.68	7.70	18.90	11.06	11.11	★	2.9	13.0	513-629-2000	443-4249	None	1.25	None	John Bruce	'89
FBP CONTRARIAN EQUITY	Growth	5.5	12.19	8.74	22.60	4.03	7.00	★	1.4	12.7	513-629-2000	443-4249	None	1.25	None	John Bruce	'93
FEDERATED ARMS; INSTL	Fixed Income	901.1	9.65	1.97	5.80	3.76	★	N/A	5.6	□	412-288-1900	245-4770	None	0.55	None	Gary Madich	'92
FEDERATED ARMS; INSTL SV	Fixed Income	146.4	9.65	1.91	5.53	★	★	★	5.4	□	412-288-1900	245-4770	None	0.80	None	Gary Madich	'92
FEDERATED EXCHANGE ☒	Growth	91.0	80.77	8.73	19.58	12.59	11.48	N/A	1.6	14.6	412-288-1900	245-4770	None	1.15	None	Peter R. Anderson	'89
FEDERATED GNMA; INSTL	Fixed Income	1,463.0	11.13	4.99	11.37	5.86	8.48	9.29	7.2	□	412-288-1900	245-4770	None	0.51	None	Gary Madich	'87
FEDERATED GNMA; INT SV	Fixed Income	123.7	11.13	4.94	11.15	5.62	★	★	7.2	□	412-288-1900	245-4770	None	0.76	None	Gary Madich	'92
FEDERATED GOV 1-3; INSTL	Fixed Income	703.7	10.36	2.68	6.78	4.55	6.38	7.18	5.8	□	412-288-1900	245-4770	None	0.51	None	Susan M. Nason	'91
FEDERATED GOV 1-3; INT SV	Fixed Income	34.6	10.36	2.62	6.51	4.30	★	★	5.4	□	412-288-1900	245-4770	None	0.76	None	Susan M. Nason	'92
FEDERATED GROWTH TRUST	Growth	239.0	23.84	10.58	18.76	6.65	7.77	13.48	1.1	16.0	412-288-1900	245-4770	None	0.99	None	Gregory M. Melvin	'87
FEDERATED HIGH YIELD TR	Fixed Income	553.9	8.80	5.09	10.20	9.55	13.90	10.90	9.5	□	412-288-1900	245-4770	None	0.85	None	Mark E. Durbiano	'84
FEDRTD IDX MAX; INSTL	S&P Index	602.3	13.80	9.34	25.68	12.79	★	★	2.3	17.3	412-288-1900	245-4770	None	0.32	None	Fred L. Plautz	'94
FEDRTD IDX MAX; INSTL SVC	S&P Index	26.3	13.79	9.20	25.17	★	★	★	2.1	17.3	412-288-1900	245-4770	None	0.62	None	Fred L. Plautz	'94
FEDRTD IDX MID-CAP	Midcap	53.2	12.05	8.57	21.34	★	★	★	1.5	18.5	412-288-1900	245-4770	None	0.54	None	Fred L. Plautz	'94
FEDRTD IDX MINI-CAP	Small Company Growth	95.5	12.83	8.87	18.73	★	★	★	1.0	17.0	412-288-1900	245-4770	None	0.73	None	Fred L. Plautz	'94
FEDERATED INC; INSTL	Fixed Income	1,079.6	10.16	4.75	10.30	5.49	7.88	8.44	6.9	□	412-288-1900	245-4770	None	0.56	None	Kathy Malus	'90
FEDERATED INC; INT SV	Fixed Income	45.6	10.16	4.69	10.07	5.24	★	★	6.7	□	412-288-1900	245-4770	None	0.78	None	Kathy Malus	'92
FEDERATED INT GOV; INSTL	Fixed Income	785.0	10.52	4.26	8.70	5.70	7.97	8.21	5.9	□	412-288-1900	245-4770	None	0.54	None	Susan M. Nason	'91
FEDERATED INT GOV; INT SV	Fixed Income	35.3	10.52	4.20	8.43	5.45	★	★	5.7	□	412-288-1900	245-4770	None	0.79	None	Susan M. Nason	'92
FEDERATED INT INC; SVC	Fixed Income	0.3	9.93	6.61	13.17	★	★	★	6.5	N/A	412-288-1900	245-4770	None	None	None	Joe Balestrino	'93
FEDERATED MGD AGG; INT SV ▥	Flexible	18.1	10.87	6.22	13.76	★	★	★	2.9	N/A	412-288-1900	245-4770	None	None	None	Charles A. Ritter	'94
FEDERATED MGD AGG; SEL	Flexible	4.3	10.86	6.04	13.12	★	★	★	2.3	N/A	412-288-1900	245-4770	None	None	None	Charles A. Ritter	'94
FEDERATED MGD G&I; INT SV ▥	Flexible	67.2	10.66	5.49	12.26	★	★	★	4.4	N/A	412-288-1900	245-4770	None	0.88	None	Charles A. Ritter	'94
FEDERATED MGD G&I; SEL	Flexible	9.5	10.65	5.31	11.39	★	★	★	3.7	N/A	412-288-1900	245-4770	None	1.64	None	Charles A. Ritter	'94
FEDERATED MGD GRO; INT SV ▥	Flexible	47.2	10.88	6.20	13.88	★	★	★	3.5	N/A	412-288-1900	245-4770	None	None	None	Charles A. Ritter	'94
FEDERATED MGD INC; INT SV ▥	Fixed Income	38.2	10.38	4.25	10.49	★	★	★	5.8	□	412-288-1900	245-4770	None	0.67	None	Charles A. Ritter	'94
FEDERATED MGD INC; SEL	Fixed Income	7.0	10.38	4.06	9.66	★	★	★	5.1	□	412-288-1900	245-4770	None	1.42	None	Charles A. Ritter	'92
FEDERATED SHT INC; INSTL	Fixed Income	216.1	8.76	3.83	6.87	4.87	6.05	★	6.3	□	412-288-1900	245-4770	None	0.56	None	Deborah Cunningham	'92
FEDERATED SHT INC; INT SV	Fixed Income	16.3	8.76	3.77	6.61	4.62	★	★	6.1	□	412-288-1900	245-4770	None	0.81	None	Deborah Cunningham	'92
FEDERATED STOCK TRUST	Growth Income	579.7	28.48	9.23	19.67	13.17	12.27	11.90	1.7	14.7	412-288-1900	245-4770	None	0.97	None	Peter R. Anderson	'82
FEDERATED US GOVT BOND ▣	Fixed Income	154.5	10.49	9.28	16.37	9.40	9.99	★	5.6	□	412-288-1900	245-4770	None	0.83	None	Gary Madich	'93
FFB LEXICON CAP APPREC ▣	Growth	140.5	12.75	11.46	21.51	10.37	★	★	1.0	18.8	None	833-8974	None	0.55	None	Art Fitlis	'94
FFB LEXICON FXD INC ▣	Fixed Income	94.3	10.15	5.41	11.01	7.47	★	★	5.4	□	None	833-8974	None	0.55	None	Mander/Besecker	'91/'91
FFB LEXICON INTMDT GOVT ▣	Fixed Income	106.2	10.15	3.94	8.59	5.62	★	★	5.4	□	None	833-8974	None	0.55	None	Robert Cheshire	'91
FFB LEXICON SELECT VALUE ▣	Growth Income	79.4	13.40	13.73	28.96	★	★	★	2.0	16.5	None	833-8974	None	0.44	None	Tim O'Grady	'92
FFB LEXICON SMALL CO GRO ▣	Small Company Growth	24.6	12.57	8.65	18.42	★	★	★	0.7	17.5	None	833-8974	None	0.45	None	Don Jones	'93
FFB EQUITY	Capital Appreciation	11.2	12.75	13.03	29.72	10.37	10.32	★	1.0	19.0	None	437-8790	None	1.12	4.50	Richard Vivona	'93
FFTW STABLE RETURN	Fixed Income	4.8	9.90	3.38	8.00	★	★	★	5.6	□	None	762-4848	None	1.74	None	Stewart Russell	'94
FFTW US SH TM FXD INC	Fixed Income	411.6	9.89	1.36	5.28	3.75	4.76	★	5.7	□	212-308-4848	762-4848	None	0.43	None	Marmon/Russell	'94/'94
FFTW WORLDWIDE FXD INC	World Income	34.9	9.69	4.09	10.16	9.45	★	★	6.0	□	212-308-4848	762-4848	None	0.63	None	Liaquat Ahamed	'92
FGIC SH-TM US GOVT INC	Fixed Income	42.2	9.99	1.62	5.27	★	★	★	5.1	□	303-623-2577	298-3442	None	None	None	James McCullough	'94
FIDELITY ADV EMERG; A	World Income	40.3	8.37	15.71	-3.81	★	★	★	8.9	N/A	None	522-7297	None	1.50	4.75	John H. Carlson	'95
FIDELITY ADV EMERG; B	World Income	7.2	8.39	15.60	-4.44	★	★	★	7.9	N/A	None	522-7297	4.00	2.25	None	John H. Carlson	'95
FIDELITY ADV EQ GRO; A	Growth	1,276.6	35.18	16.14	30.06	★	★	★	0.2	N/A	None	522-7297	None	1.70	4.75	Robert Stansky	'92
FIDELITY ADV EQ INC; A	Equity Income	449.1	17.99	6.99	22.57	★	★	★	1.7	N/A	None	522-7297	None	1.64	4.75	Bettina Doulton	'93
FIDELITY ADV EQ INC; B	Equity Income	123.2	17.95	6.93	21.64	★	★	★	1.2	N/A	None	522-7297	4.00	None	None	Bettina Doulton	'94
FIDELITY ADV GLBL RES	Natural Resources	231.2	18.84	8.53	15.82	17.44	13.21	★	0.0	N/A	None	522-7297	None	2.07	4.75	Malcolm MacNaught	'87
FIDELITY ADV GOVT; A	Fixed Income	176.0	9.56	5.86	11.95	6.68	8.21	★	6.1	14.3	None	522-7297	None	0.74	4.75	Bob Ives	'95
FIDELITY ADV GOVT; B	Fixed Income	7.6	9.55	5.66	10.95	★	★	★	5.3	□	None	522-7297	4.00	None	None	Bob Ives	'95

PERFORMANCE OF MUTUAL FUNDS (continued)

FUND NAME	OBJECTIVE	ASSETS ($ MIL) 5/31/95	NAV ($/SHR) 6/30/95	QTR	RETURN THROUGH 6/30 1YR	(Annualized) 3YRS	5YRS	10YRS	DIV YLD %	P/E RATIO	PHONE NUMBER 800	In-State	FEES Load	Redemption	Exp. Ratio	MANAGER	SINCE
FIDELITY ADV GROWTH OPP	Growth	7,158.9	28.94	-11.35	22.09	17.45	17.79	☆	0.9	N/A	522-7297	None	4.75	None	1.62	George Vanderheiden	87
FIDELITY ADV HI YLD; A	Fixed Income	971.2	11.56	5.32	10.48	11.69	16.86	☆	7.5	☐	522-7297	None	4.75	None	1.20	Margaret Eagle	87
FIDELITY ADV HI YLD; B	Fixed Income	82.5	11.55	5.12	9.56	☆	☆	☆	6.8	☐	522-7297	None	None	4.00	None	Margaret Eagle	94
FIDELITY ADV INC & GRO	Balanced	3,478.2	15.20	-4.30	7.80	8.54	11.86	☆	2.6	13.0	522-7297	None	4.75	None	1.58	Robert Haber	87
FIDELITY ADV INST EQ GRO	Growth	574.2	35.56	16.32	31.09	19.55	19.86	19.96	0.8	N/A	522-7297	None	None	None	0.84	Robert Stansky	87
FIDELITY ADV INST EQ INC	Equity Income	248.4	18.08	7.13	23.55	17.34	14.73	13.34	2.4	N/A	522-7297	None	None	None	0.71	Bettina Doulton	93
FIDELITY ADV INST LTD TM	Fixed Income	186.0	10.66	4.13	8.54	7.22	8.94	9.13	6.0	☐	522-7297	None	None	None	0.64	Michael Gray	87
FIDELITY ADV LTD TM; A	Fixed Income	195.9	10.65	4.06	8.26				5.7		522-7297	None	4.75	None	1.02	Michael Gray	92
FIDELITY ADV LTD TM; B	Fixed Income	8.4	10.65	3.97	7.36				4.9		522-7297	None	None	4.00	None	Michael Gray	94
FIDELITY ADV OVERSEAS	International	696.6	13.85	4.84	1.78	10.09	5.93	☆	0.0		522-7297	None	4.75	None	2.12	John Hickling	93
FIDELITY ADV SHT FXD INC	Fixed Income	620.4	9.44	3.11	5.51	4.91	6.96	☆	6.0		522-7297	None	1.50	None	0.97	Charles Morrison	95
FIDELITY ADV STR INC; A	Fixed Income	23.7	10.88	8.31	☆	☆	☆	☆	0.0		522-7297	None	4.75	None	None	Donald Taylor	94
FIDELITY ADV STR INC; B	Fixed Income	19.1	10.89	8.11	☆	☆	☆	☆	0.0		522-7297	None	None	4.00	None	Donald Taylor	94
FIDELITY ADV STR OP; A	Capital Appreciation	461.8	22.31	10.34	17.23	12.87	12.87	☆	1.6	10.5	522-7297	None	4.75	None	1.84	Daniel Frank	86
FIDELITY ADV STR OP; B	Capital Appreciation	37.1	22.08	10.23	16.79	☆	☆	☆	2.1	10.5	522-7297	None	None	4.00	None	Daniel Frank	94
FIDELITY ADV STR OP; IN ⊠	Capital Appreciation	19.5	22.54	10.54	18.00	13.56	13.52	15.09	2.2	10.5	544-8888	None	4.75	None	1.14	Daniel Frank	83
FIDELITY ASSET MANAGER	Flexible	11,093.7	14.80	5.91	7.95	9.95	12.26	☆	2.4	N/A	544-8888	None	None	None	1.04	Bob Beckwitt	88
FIDELITY ASSET MGR GRO	Flexible	2,786.1	13.97	7.54	7.88	12.78	☆	☆	1.4	N/A	544-8888	None	None	None	1.15	Bob Beckwitt	91
FIDELITY ASSET MGR INC	Income	540.6	11.13	4.78	9.32	☆	☆	☆	4.3	18.2	544-8888	None	None	None	0.71	Bob Beckwitt	92
FIDELITY BALANCED	Balanced	5,213.7	13.01	4.05	7.67	8.36	10.69	☆	3.5	12.9	544-8888	None	None	None	1.01	Robert Haber	88
FIDELITY BLUE CHIP GROW	Growth	5,134.4	30.48	11.89	27.18	21.51	19.65	☆	0.0	22.0	544-8888	None	3.00	None	1.22	Michael Gordon	93
FIDELITY CANADA	Canadian	384.4	17.73	7.72	7.52	6.40	6.26	☆	0.1	☐	544-8888	None	None	None	1.57	George Domolky	87
FIDELITY CAPITAL & INC	Fixed Income	2,299.7	9.08	4.74	8.45	12.13	16.10	11.74	9.2	☐	544-8888	None	3.00	1.50	0.97	David Breazzano	90
FIDELITY CAPITAL APPREC	Capital Appreciation	1,677.3	16.97	5.67	17.22	15.53	10.78	15.66	1.0	N/A	544-8888	None	3.00	None	1.17	Thomas Sweeney	86
FIDELITY CONGRESS ST ⊠	Growth Income	70.8	183.53	10.14	33.41	12.79	11.65	☆	2.5	N/A	544-8888	None	None	None	0.60	Jonathan Weed	95
FIDELITY CONTRAFUND	Growth	10,701.2	36.56	13.82	25.42	17.72	20.08	19.36	0.0	19.6	544-8888	None	3.00	None	1.00	Will Danoff	90
FIDELITY CONVERTIBLE	Convertible Securities	957.1	16.77	5.97	15.91	13.01	15.38	☆	4.4	☐	544-8888	None	None	None	0.85	Charles Magnum	95
FIDELITY D-MARK PERFORM	World Income	13.5	18.60	0.27	18.62	8.46	10.04	☆	0.0	☐	544-8888	None	0.40	None	1.50	Scott Kuldell	94
FIDELITY DESTINY I ★	Growth	3,703.1	17.61	12.31	25.05	20.34	18.58	18.26	1.8	15.7	752-2347	None	8.24	None	0.70	George Vanderheiden	80
FIDELITY DESTINY II ★	Growth	1,794.8	29.78	11.95	24.67	20.22	19.10	☆	1.6	15.6	752-2347	None	8.24	None	0.80	George Vanderheiden	85
FIDELITY DISCPLN EQU	Growth	1,525.5	20.98	10.48	23.03	14.45	14.56	☆	1.2	16.1	544-8888	None	None	None	1.05	Brad Lewis	88
FIDELITY DIVIDEND GROWTH	Growth	300.8	15.33	14.23	39.06	☆	☆	☆	0.1	17.3	544-8888	None	None	None	1.40	Steve Wymer	95
FIDELITY DVSD INTL	International	283.4	12.08	5.59	5.52	10.31	☆	☆	0.2		544-8888	None	None	None	1.25	Greg Fraser	91
FIDELITY EMERGING GROW	Midcap	784.4	21.57	19.57	45.71	24.05	☆	☆	0.0	25.7	544-8888	None	3.00	None	1.02	Larry Greenberg	93
FIDELITY EMERGING MKTS	Emerging Markets	1,363.9	15.68	13.71	-1.03	11.61	☆	☆	0.3		544-8888	None	3.00	1.50	1.52	Richard Hazelwood	93
FIDELITY EQUITY-INC	Equity Income	8,637.2	34.69	8.26	17.52	15.10	13.36	12.64	2.9	15.7	544-8888	None	None	None	0.66	Steve Peterson	93
FIDELITY EQUITY-INC II	Equity Income	9,820.6	19.89	6.16	15.16	15.16	☆	☆	2.0	18.2	544-8888	None	None	None	0.81	Brian Posner	92
FIDELITY EUROPE	European Region	466.0	22.12	8.43	18.14	10.24	5.62	☆	0.9	☐	544-8888	None	3.00	None	1.35	Sally Walden	92
FIDELITY EUROPE CAP APP	European Region	246.7	12.00	7.91	9.79	☆	☆	☆	0.0		544-8888	None	3.00	None	1.54	Kevin McCarey	93
FIDELITY EXCHANGE ⊠	Growth Income	207.7	119.23	9.33	30.05	12.56	11.16	14.42	2.2	N/A	544-8888	None	None	None	0.58	Jonathan Weed	95
FIDELITY EXPORT	Growth	171.3	12.96	20.78	☆	☆	☆	☆	0.0	N/A	544-8888	None	None	None	None	Arieh Coll	94
FIDELITY FIFTY	Capital Appreciation	105.4	13.10	11.49	30.26	☆	☆	☆	0.2	19.8	544-8888	None	None	None	1.58	Scott Stewart	93
FIDELITY FUND	Growth Income	2,318.6	21.04	7.48	21.09	14.27	11.73	13.72	1.7	16.9	544-8888	None	None	None	0.65	Beth Terrana	93
FIDELITY GLOBAL BALANCED	Global Flexible	161.0	11.91	1.88	1.19	☆	☆	☆	0.0	☐	544-8888	None	None	None	1.67	Robert Haber	93
FIDELITY GLOBAL BOND	World Income	290.3	10.10	5.73	5.21	2.61	6.58	☆	6.4		544-8888	None	None	None	1.14	Jonathan Kelly	94

Fund	Objective	Net Assets ($mil)	NAV	YTD %	1-Yr %	3-Yr %	5-Yr %	10-Yr %	Yield %	P/E	Phone	Deferred	Load	Expense	Redem	Manager	Since
FIDELITY GOVT SECURITIES	Fixed Income	874.2	9.88	6.02	11.53	7.73	9.66	9.37	6.2		544-8888	None	None	0.69	None	Bob Ives	'95
FIDELITY GROWTH & INCOME	Growth & Income	11,267.5	24.18	7.63	20.86	15.21	15.38	17.24	1.6	17.4	544-8888	None	3.00	0.82	None	Steven Kaye	'93
FIDELITY GROWTH COMPANY	Growth	4,264.9	33.86	16.04	30.66	18.57	15.89		0.6	19.7	544-8888	None	None	1.05	None	Robert Stansky	'87
FIDELITY INC GNMA	Fixed Income	761.2	10.67	5.07	12.16	5.91	8.35	9.06	6.6		544-8888	None	None	0.82	None	Kevin Grant	'95
FIDELITY INC MORTGAGE	Fixed Income	413.5	10.93	5.57	12.40	6.97	8.98		6.6		544-8888	None	None	0.79	None	Kevin Grant	'93
FIDELITY INST SH-IN GOV1	Fixed Income	350.5	9.54	3.84	8.78	5.37	7.40		7.0		522-7297	None	None	0.45	None	Curt Hollingsworth	'87
FIDELITY INST SH-IN GOV2	Fixed Income	0.1	9.54	3.77	8.51	★	★		6.8		522-7297	None	None	0.70	None	Curt Hollingsworth	'94
FIDELITY INTERMEDIATE BD	Fixed Income	2,541.5	10.24	4.10	8.68	6.98	8.54		6.1		544-8888	None	None	0.64	None	Michael Gray	'87
FIDELITY INTL GRO & INC	International	865.6	17.13	0.76	2.17	7.93	5.77		0.0		544-8888	None	None	1.21	None	Rick Mace	'94
FIDELITY INTL VALUE FD	International	50.5	10.04	0.40	★	★	★		0.0		544-8888	None	None	None	None	Rick Mace	'94
FIDELITY INV GRADE BOND	Fixed Income	1,141.4	7.20	5.74	9.50	8.08	9.88	9.61	6.7		544-8888	None	None	0.74	None	Michael Gray	'87
FIDELITY JAPAN	Japanese	285.2	11.66	-5.82	-19.54	★	★		0.0		544-8888	None	None	1.42	1.00	Shigeki Makino	'94
FIDELITY LATIN AMERICA	Latin American	581.9	10.04	14.48	-23.71	★	★		0.0		544-8888	None	3.00	1.48	1.50	Patti Satterthwaite	'93
FIDELITY LOW-PRICE	Small Company Growth	2,611.9	18.12	9.42	19.18	18.39	19.75		0.5	10.1	544-8888	None	3.00	1.13	1.50	Joel Tillinghast	'89
FIDELITY MAGELLAN FUND	Growth	43,208.4	83.50	15.77	31.16	18.06	16.24	18.28	0.4	17.8	544-8888	None	3.00	0.96	None	Jeff Vinik	'92
FIDELITY MARKET INDEX	S&P Index	419.1	40.36	9.40	25.59	12.84	11.77		2.1	17.2	544-8888	None	None	0.45	0.50	Jennifer Farrelly	'94
FIDELITY MID-CAP STOCK	Midcap	631.5	12.61	9.48	34.00	★	★		0.1	16.1	544-8888	None	None	1.61	None	Jennifer Uhrig	'94
FIDELITY NC CASH MGT TRM	Fixed Income	69.8	9.91	1.84	5.87	3.96	5.49		5.1		544-8888	None	None	0.41	None	Duby	'94
FIDELITY NEW MILLENNIUM	Capital Appreciation	307.6	14.91	16.76	34.65	★	★		0.0	21.6	544-8888	None	3.00	1.29	1.00	Neal Miller	'92
FIDELITY NEW MKTS INC	World Income	188.3	8.96	15.70	1.86	★	★		7.7		544-8888	None	None	1.28	1.00	Jonathan Kelly	'95
FIDELITY OTC	Midcap	1,722.9	29.17	15.48	34.21	15.96	16.00	16.37	0.7	N/A	544-8888	None	3.00	0.88	None	Abigail Johnson	'94
FIDELITY OVERSEAS	International	2,298.2	28.30	5.09	2.15	7.50	4.26	16.75	0.0		544-8888	None	None	1.24	None	John Hickling	'93
FIDELITY PACIFIC BASIN	Pacific Region	377.8	14.85	-0.40	-11.84	12.57	3.41		0.1	19.3	544-8888	None	None	1.54	1.00	Simon Fraser	'93
FIDELITY PURITAN	Equity Income	13,577.5	16.15	5.39	12.12	12.63	13.12	13.03	3.0	N/A	544-8888	None	None	0.79	None	Richard Fentin	'87
FIDELITY REAL ESTATE	Real Estate	514.6	13.08	4.18	1.17	10.43	12.68		5.4	N/A	544-8888	None	None	1.03	None	Barry Greenfield	'86
FIDELITY RETIREMENT GR ★	Capital Appreciation	3,594.9	17.88	6.05	15.38	13.33	15.55		1.2	16.1	544-8888	None	None	1.07	None	Harris Leviton	'92
FIDELITY SEL AIR TRANS	Specialty	53.1	18.34	23.67	32.56	12.19			0.0	9.2	544-8888	None	3.00	2.50	0.75	Jason Weiner	'94
FIDELITY SEL AMER GOLD	Gold	356.2	21.93	3.10	4.03	7.19			0.0	N/A	544-8888	None	3.00	1.41	0.75	Malcolm MacNaught	'85
FIDELITY SEL AUTOMOTIVE	Specialty	55.7	20.58	4.26	2.33	15.35			0.2	11.5	544-8888	None	3.00	1.80	0.75	Brenda Reed	'94
FIDELITY SEL BIO TECH	Health/Biotechnology	404.0	27.72	7.82	20.47	14.04			0.0	N/A	544-8888	None	3.00	1.59	0.75	Karen Firestone	'92
FIDELITY SEL BROKERAGE	Financial Services	37.9	17.46	14.93	8.36	20.58	17.90		0.0	6.1	544-8888	None	3.00	2.54	0.75	Jeff Feinberg	'95
FIDELITY SEL CHEMICALS	Specialty	85.3	36.10	4.91	15.54	14.40	15.14		0.8	18.6	544-8888	None	3.00	1.51	0.75	David Felman	'95
FIDELITY SEL CNSMR PRDCT	Specialty	22.6	14.80	4.00	15.59	11.67	13.32		0.0	17.5	544-8888	None	3.00	2.49	0.75	Mary English	'94
FIDELITY SEL COMPUTER	Science & Technology	391.4	40.98	25.66	70.32	40.69	26.19		0.0	14.6	544-8888	None	3.00	1.69	0.75	Harry Lange	'92
FIDELITY SEL CONST&HOUSE	Specialty	57.9	18.12	6.03	8.74	12.63	12.95		0.0	15.4	544-8888	None	3.00	1.74	0.75	Bill Bower	'94
FIDELITY SEL DEFENSE	Specialty	26.0	23.79	16.16	33.65	24.51	14.77	7.36	0.0	15.4	544-8888	None	3.00	2.49	0.75	Bill Rubin	'94
FIDELITY SEL DVLP COMM	Science & Technology	252.7	22.65	19.38	60.74	31.10	25.71		0.0	19.1	544-8888	None	3.00	1.56	0.75	Paul Antico	'93
FIDELITY SEL ELECTRONIC	Science & Technology	698.6	29.76	36.26	80.91	27.13	27.13	8.26	0.0	17.3	544-8888	None	3.00	1.71	0.75	Marc Kaufman	'94
FIDELITY SEL ENERGY	Natural Resources	130.5	17.37	2.66	5.18	9.41	4.43		0.6	23.6	544-8888	None	3.00	1.85	0.75	Albert Ruback	'94
FIDELITY SEL ENERGY SER	Natural Resources	194.9	13.28	5.15	13.89	13.34	0.69		0.1	19.1	544-8888	None	3.00	1.79	0.75	Dan Pickering	'94
FIDELITY SEL ENVIRONMENT	Environmental	36.0	12.19	13.29	17.89	6.33	0.39		0.0	16.1	544-8888	None	3.00	2.01	0.75	Philip Barton	'93
FIDELITY SEL FINANCIAL	Financial Services	147.8	53.68	9.37	15.57	18.25	20.93	13.55	1.0	9.7	544-8888	None	3.00	1.54	0.75	Louis Salemy	'94
FIDELITY SEL FOOD	Specialty	209.3	35.46	8.35	29.41	15.13	13.94		0.3	13.1	544-8888	None	3.00	1.68	0.75	Bill Mankivsky	'94
FIDELITY SEL HEALTH	Health/Biotechnology	798.5	83.67	7.55	43.39	14.90	19.50	18.95	0.6	18.0	544-8888	None	3.00	1.36	0.75	Karen Firestone	'95
FIDELITY SEL HOME FIN	Financial Services	337.2	26.90	12.65	14.93	26.23	29.23		0.4	4.3	544-8888	None	3.00	1.45	0.75	David Ellison	'85
FIDELITY SEL INDUS EQUIP	Specialty	118.1	24.05	10.88	35.71	23.74	13.70		0.0	11.8	544-8888	None	3.00	1.78	0.75	Bob Bertleson	'94
FIDELITY SEL INDUS MAT	Specialty	117.1	24.54	3.89	13.51	13.93	14.58		0.7	20.2	544-8888	None	3.00	1.53	0.75	Doug Chase	'94
FIDELITY SEL INSURANCE	Financial Services	13.7	22.99	6.38	18.42	14.35	13.68		0.2	14.2	544-8888	None	3.00	2.34	0.75	Michael Tempero	'95
FIDELITY SEL LEISURE	Specialty	67.6	44.32	6.81	21.56	19.31	15.08		0.0	21.4	544-8888	None	3.00	1.62	0.75	Deborah Wheeler	'92
FIDELITY SEL MEDICAL	Health/Biotechnology	153.7	23.37	-4.92	27.15	13.29	17.09	15.44	0.3	22.4	544-8888	None	3.00	1.45	0.75	Steve Binder	'94

★ FIDELITY DESTINY I and FIDELITY DESTINY II—Sold through a contractual plan.

PERFORMANCE OF MUTUAL FUNDS (continued)

FUND NAME	OBJECTIVE	ASSETS ($ MIL) 5/31/95	NAV ($/SHR) 6/30/95	QTR	1YR	3YRS	5YRS	10YRS	DIV YLD %	P/E RATIO	800	In-State	Load	Exp. Ratio	Redemption	MANAGER	SINCE
FIDELITY SEL MULTIMEDIA	Specialty	149.7	25.39	6.82	30.47	24.05	19.62	☆	0.0	15.7	544-8888	None	3.00	2.03	0.75	Stephen Dufour	'93
FIDELITY SEL NAT GAS	Natural Resources	76.7	9.79	3.05	0.03	☆	☆	☆	0.3	20.6	544-8888	None	3.00	1.66	0.75	Dan Pickering	'95
FIDELITY SEL PAPER&FRS	Specialty	58.4	23.47	11.32	40.01	19.66	18.26	☆	0.0	10.9	544-8888	None	3.00	1.87	0.75	Scott Offen	'93
FIDELITY SEL PREC MTLS	Gold	392.1	16.95	0.77	2.22	18.66	8.63	6.68	1.3	N/A	544-8888	None	3.00	1.46	0.75	Malcolm MacNaught	'85
FIDELITY SEL REGL BANKS	Financial Services	160.6	20.08	10.57	13.37	17.34	24.52	☆	1.2	9.1	544-8888	None	3.00	1.56	0.75	Louis Salemy	'94
FIDELITY SEL RETAILING	Specialty	30.3	25.16	4.05	6.21	10.92	14.13	☆	0.0	18.5	544-8888	None	3.00	1.96	0.75	Erin Sullivan	'95
FIDELITY SEL SOFTWARE	Science & Technology	256.6	35.43	15.29	68.71	29.99	23.85	☆	0.0	24.9	544-8888	None	3.00	1.50	0.75	John Hurley	'94
FIDELITY SEL TECHNOLOGY	Science & Technology	302.1	52.82	22.06	56.06	31.65	25.01	14.05	0.0	18.1	544-8888	None	3.00	1.56	0.75	Harry Lange	'93
FIDELITY SEL TELECOMM	Science & Technology	379.7	42.21	11.02	23.92	22.32	16.19	☆	1.2	14.8	544-8888	None	3.00	1.55	0.75	David Felman	'94
FIDELITY SEL TRANSPORT	Specialty	9.8	20.26	-2.60	7.23	18.85	16.18	☆	0.0	16.2	544-8888	None	3.00	2.36	0.75	Stephen Dufour	'94
FIDELITY SEL UTILITIES	Utility	221.2	37.11	6.12	10.19	8.64	10.33	12.11	2.6	13.9	544-8888	None	3.00	1.42	0.75	John Muresianu	'92
FIDELITY SH-INT GOVT FD	Fixed Income	170.2	9.52	3.78	8.40	4.51	☆	☆	6.5		544-8888	None	None	0.95	None	Curt Hollingsworth	'91
FIDELITY SHORT WORLD	World Income	158.2	8.89	3.35	2.92	3.21	☆	☆	7.4		544-8888	None	None	1.01	None	Scott Kuldell	'94
FIDELITY SHORT-TERM BOND	Fixed Income	1,294.8	8.84	3.38	5.00	4.45	6.82	☆	6.1		544-8888	None	None	0.80	None	Charles Morrison	'95
FIDELITY SM CAP STOCK	Small Company Growth	374.0	12.31	15.77	26.15	☆	☆	☆	0.6	17.8	544-8888	None	3.00	0.90	None	Brad Lewis	'93
FIDELITY SOEAST ASIA	Pacific Region	677.4	14.06	11.23	11.41	☆	☆	☆	0.0		544-8888	None	3.00	1.47	1.50	Alan Liu	'93
FIDELITY SPARTAN GNMA	Fixed Income	414.5	9.96	5.19	12.40	5.93	8.54	☆	7.0		544-8888	None	None	0.65	None	Kevin Grant	'95
FIDELITY SPARTAN GOV INC	Fixed Income	245.9	10.30	6.05	12.47	6.20	☆	☆	7.3		544-8888	None	None	0.65	None	Bob Ives	'95
FIDELITY SPARTAN HIINC	Fixed Income	844.2	12.00	5.91	14.25	13.76	☆	☆	9.0		544-8888	None	None	0.75	1.00	David Glancy	'93
FIDELITY SPARTAN INV GRD	Fixed Income	162.0	10.14	6.28	13.01	☆	☆	☆	6.7		544-8888	None	None	0.65	None	Michael Gray	'92
FIDELITY SPARTAN LG GOVT	Fixed Income	82.2	11.71	11.13	18.92	8.70	☆	☆	5.0		544-8888	None	None	0.65	None	Curt Hollingsworth	'93
FIDELITY SPARTAN LTD MAT	Fixed Income	829.9	9.79	4.43	9.01	5.53	7.32	☆	6.1		544-8888	None	None	0.65	None	Curt Hollingsworth	'88
FIDELITY SPARTAN S-I GOV	Fixed Income	100.4	9.59	3.84	9.42	☆	☆	☆	7.0		544-8888	None	None	0.10	None	Curt Hollingsworth	'92
FIDELITY SPARTAN SH-TM	Fixed Income	566.3	9.13	3.32	4.38	☆	☆	☆	6.5		544-8888	None	None	0.54	None	Charles Morrison	'95
FIDELITY SPARTAN STRT	Fixed Income	18.9	9.31	2.70	8.20	☆	☆	☆	5.2		544-8888	None	None	0.70	0.50	George Fischer	'93
FIDELITY STOCK SELECTOR	Growth	798.5	21.66	13.46	23.72	15.99	☆	☆	0.7	14.1	544-8888	None	None	1.09	None	Brad Lewis	'90
FIDELITY STRLING PERFORM	World Income	1.2	15.39	-0.65	7.47	-1.16	5.23	☆	0.0		544-8888	None	0.40	1.50	None	Scott Kuldell	'94
FIDELITY TREND	Growth	1,203.6	56.68	6.90	12.82	13.30	11.55	13.00	0.3	N/A	544-8888	None	None	1.04	None	Fergus Shiel	'95
FIDELITY US BOND INDEX ▦	Fixed Income	388.5	10.67	6.10	12.17	7.68	9.71	☆	7.2		544-8888	None	None	0.32	None	Christine Thompson	'90
FIDELITY US EQUITY INDEX	S&P Index	2,637.8	20.06	9.46	25.76	12.98	11.75	☆	2.1	N/A	544-8888	None	None	0.28	None	Jennifer Farrelly	'94
FIDELITY UTILITIES	Utility	1,326.5	14.29	6.05	9.79	10.15	11.71	☆	4.0	13.8	544-8888	None	None	0.87	None	John Muresianu	'92
FIDELITY VALUE FUND	Capital Appreciation	4,580.8	45.22	5.75	14.83	17.33	15.34	13.42	0.4	N/A	544-8888	None	None	1.08	None	Bettina Doulton	'95
FIDELITY WORLDWIDE	Global	699.6	13.46	4.91	6.36	14.06	8.14	☆	0.5		544-8888	None	None	1.32	None	Penelope Dobkin	'95
FIDELITY YEN PERFORM	World Income	5.8	19.95	2.05	16.60	15.14	15.30	☆	0.0		544-8888	None	0.40	1.50	None	Scott Kuldell	'94
FIDUCIARY CAPITAL GROWTH	Growth	42.0	20.15	7.07	21.84	13.84	11.66	9.58	0.2	15.9	338-1579	414-765-3500	None	1.20	None	Kellner/Wilson	'81/81
FIDUCIARY EXCHANGE ⊠	Growth	56.4	174.31	11.62	28.72	10.11	11.09	13.10	1.2	18.7	225-6265	617-482-8260	None	0.83	None	Duncan Richardson	'90
59 WALL ST EUROPEAN	European Region	110.2	30.76	3.85	14.99	10.54	☆	☆	0.0		None	212-493-8100	None	1.37	None	Henry Frantzen	'92
59 WALL ST PAC BASIN	Pacific Region	107.6	29.59	2.25	-7.15	11.98	☆	☆	0.0		None	212-493-8100	None	1.29	None	Henry Frantzen	'92
59 WALL ST SMALL CO	Small Company Growth	29.3	11.99	6.58	8.79	9.59	☆	☆	0.6	19.6	None	212-493-8100	None	1.10	None	Team Managed	N/A
59 WALL ST US EQUITY	Growth	26.6	33.41	7.15	21.58	☆	☆	☆	0.4	N/A	None	212-493-8100	None	1.20	None	Donald B. Murphy	'92
FINL HRZNS GOVT BOND	Fixed Income	71.0	10.93	7.02	12.86	7.17	9.57	☆	6.1		533-5622	None	None	1.28	5.00	Wayne Frisbee	'89
FINL HRZNS GROWTH	Growth	7.3	17.36	9.32	27.73	13.61	12.81	☆	0.1	17.1	533-5622	None	None	1.59	5.00	John Schaffner	'89
FIRST AMER ASST ALL; A	Flexible	0.8	11.25	6.58	17.68	☆	☆	☆	3.0	17.6	637-2548	612-973-4069	4.50	0.75	None	Cori Johnson	'92
FIRST AMER ASST ALL; B	Flexible	0.3	11.22	6.42	☆	☆	☆	☆	0.0	17.6	637-2548	612-973-4069	None	None	5.00	Cori Johnson	'94
FIRST AMER ASST ALL; C ▦	Flexible	40.9	11.25	6.65	17.86	☆	☆	☆	3.2	17.6	637-2548	612-973-4069	None	0.75	None	Cori Johnson	'94

Fund	Objective	Assets	NAV	%	%	%	%	Rtg	Yld	Risk	Phone 1	Phone 2	Load	Exp	CDSC	Manager	Since
FIRST AMER BALANCED; A	Balanced	14.3	11.70	6.88	18.22	☆		☆	3.1	N/A	612-973-4069	637-2548	4.50	0.77	None	Jim Rovner	'92
FIRST AMER BALANCED; B	Balanced	1.4	11.68	6.63	18.49	☆		☆	0.0	N/A	612-973-4069	637-2548	None	None	5.00	Jim Rovner	'94
FIRST AMER BALANCED; C ▥	Balanced	163.1	11.71	6.94	28.04	☆		☆	3.3	N/A	612-973-4069	637-2548	None	0.75	None	Jim Rovner	'94
FIRST AMER DVSFD GR; A	Growth Income	2.1	11.00	11.12	☆	☆		☆	1.3	N/A	612-973-4069	637-2548	4.50	0.90	None	Bren/Dubiak	'94/'94
FIRST AMER DVSFD GR; B	Growth Income	0.2	10.98	10.94	☆	☆		☆	0.0	N/A	612-973-4069	637-2548	None	None	5.00	Bren/Dubiak	'94/'94
FIRST AMER EMRG GRO; C ▥	Small Company Growth	96.0	11.02	11.25	27.06	☆		☆	0.0	N/A	612-973-4069	637-2548	None	None	None	Bren/Dubiak	'94/'94
FIRST AMER EMRG GRO; A	Small Company Growth	0.2	12.13	7.73	☆	☆		☆	0.2	N/A	612-973-4069	637-2548	4.50	0.79	None	Bren/Dubiak	'94/'94
FIRST AMER EMRG GRO; B	Small Company Growth	0.1	12.04	7.40	27.22	☆		☆	0.0	N/A	612-973-4069	637-2548	None	None	5.00	Bren/Dubiak	'94/'94
FIRST AMER EMRG GRO; C ▥	Growth Income	25.5	12.12	7.64	25.37	☆		☆	0.2	N/A	612-973-4069	637-2548	None	0.80	None	Bren/Dubiak	'94/'94
FIRST AMER EQ INDEX; A	Growth Income	1.6	12.45	9.33	☆	☆		☆	2.1	17.2	612-973-4069	637-2548	4.50	0.35	None	Jim Rovner	'92
FIRST AMER EQ INDEX; B	Growth Income	0.5	12.41	9.21	25.44	☆		☆	0.0	17.2	612-973-4069	637-2548	None	0.35	5.00	Jim Rovner	'94
FIRST AMER EQ INDEX; C ▥	Growth Income	187.2	12.44	9.40	14.73	☆		☆	2.2	N/A	612-973-4069	637-2548	4.50	None	None	Jim Rovner	'94
FIRST AMER EQTY INC; A	Equity Income	1.9	10.73	4.84	☆	☆		☆	3.7	N/A	612-973-4069	637-2548	4.50	0.88	None	Bren/Dubiak	'94/'94
FIRST AMER EQTY INC; B	Equity Income	0.4	10.69	4.63	☆	☆		☆	0.0	N/A	612-973-4069	637-2548	None	None	5.00	Bren/Dubiak	'94/'94
FIRST AMER EQTY INC; C ▥	Equity Income	46.5	10.73	4.90	☆	☆		☆	0.0	N/A	612-973-4069	637-2548	None	None	None	Bren/Dubiak	'94/'94
FIRST AMER FXD INC; A	Fixed Income	7.1	11.01	6.06	11.50	7.43	8.85	☆	5.8	□□□□□	612-973-4069	637-2548	3.75	0.68	None	Martin Jones	'87
FIRST AMER FXD INC; B	Fixed Income	3.4	10.97	5.83	11.61	☆		☆	5.0	□□□□□	612-973-4069	637-2548	None	None	5.00	Martin Jones	'94
FIRST AMER FXD INC; C ▥	Fixed Income	220.0	11.00	6.13	8.86	4.97	6.65	☆	5.9	□□□□□	612-973-4069	637-2548	None	0.61	None	Martin Jones	'94
FIRST AMER INT GOV; A ➜	Fixed Income	2.2	9.30	4.41	8.75	☆		☆	5.5	□□□□□	612-973-4069	637-2548	3.00	0.53	None	Chris Drahn	'94
FIRST AMER INT GOV; C ▥	Fixed Income	94.7	9.29	4.42	☆	☆		☆	5.5	□□□□□	612-973-4069	637-2548	None	0.36	None	Chris Drahn	'94
FIRST AMER INT TERM; A ➜	Fixed Income	2.6	9.96	4.71	9.73	16.66	13.79	☆	5.6	□□□□□	612-973-4069	637-2548	3.75	0.69	None	Martin Jones	'92
FIRST AMER INT TERM; C ▥	Fixed Income	84.6	9.96	4.71	9.73	☆		☆	5.6	□□□□□	612-973-4069	637-2548	None	0.58	None	Martin Jones	'94
FIRST AMER INTL; A	International	0.5	9.27	8.93	-6.46	☆		☆	0.0	□□□□□	612-973-4069	637-2548	4.50	1.75	None	Marvin & Palmer Assoc.	'94
FIRST AMER INTL; B	International	0.1	9.20	8.75	☆	☆		☆	0.0	□□□□□	612-973-4069	637-2548	None	None	5.00	Marvin & Palmer Assoc.	'94
FIRST AMER INTL; C ▥	International	74.0	9.28	8.92	-6.36	☆		☆	0.0	N/A	612-973-4069	637-2548	None	1.75	None	Marvin & Palmer Assoc.	'94
FIRST AMER LTD TERM; A ➜	Fixed Income	10.0	9.92	2.47	6.47	☆		☆	5.3	□□□□□	612-973-4069	637-2548	2.00	0.60	None	Martin Jones	'92
FIRST AMER LTD TERM; C ▥	Fixed Income	114.0	9.92	2.47	6.48	☆		☆	5.3	□□□□□	612-973-4069	637-2548	None	0.60	None	Martin Jones	'94
FIRST AMER MTGE SEC; A ➜	Fixed Income	0.3	10.17	5.08	10.28	☆		☆	5.9	□□□□□	612-973-4069	637-2548	3.75	0.70	None	Martin Jones	'94
FIRST AMER MTGE SEC; C ▥	Fixed Income	26.8	10.17	5.08	10.29	☆		☆	5.9	□□□□□	612-973-4069	637-2548	None	0.56	None	Martin Jones	'94
FIRST AMER REGNL EQ; A	Small Company Growth	10.7	14.97	12.16	33.47	☆		☆	0.6	N/A	612-973-4069	637-2548	4.50	0.82	None	Rick Rinkoff	'92
FIRST AMER REGNL EQ; B	Small Company Growth	2.8	14.89	11.96	☆	☆		☆	0.0	N/A	612-973-4069	637-2548	None	None	5.00	Rick Rinkoff	'94
FIRST AMER REGNL EQ; C ▥	Small Company Growth	140.5	14.98	12.30	33.73	☆		☆	0.7	N/A	612-973-4069	637-2548	None	0.80	None	Rick Rinkoff	'94
FIRST AMER SPEC EQ; A	Capital Appreciation	9.5	17.04	5.72	18.14	14.10	11.55	☆	2.0	16.6	612-973-4069	637-2548	4.50	0.81	None	Larry Smith	'94
FIRST AMER SPEC EQ; B	Capital Appreciation	3.2	16.99	5.57	☆	☆		☆	0.0	16.6	612-973-4069	637-2548	None	None	5.00	Larry Smith	'94
FIRST AMER SPEC EQ; C ▥	Capital Appreciation	181.2	17.04	5.78	18.38	☆		☆	2.1	16.6	612-973-4069	637-2548	None	0.79	None	Larry Smith	'94
FIRST AMER STOCK; A	Growth Income	10.5	18.48	7.28	22.47	☆		☆	1.8	15.3	612-973-4069	637-2548	4.50	0.76	None	Jim Doak	'87
FIRST AMER STOCK; B	Growth Income	3.3	18.41	7.04	☆	☆		☆	0.0	15.3	612-973-4069	637-2548	None	None	5.00	Jim Doak	'94
FIRST AMER STOCK; C ▥	Growth Income	257.4	18.47	7.35	22.57	☆		☆	1.9	15.3	612-973-4069	637-2548	None	0.75	None	Jim Doak	'94
FIRST AMER TECH; A	Science & Technology	0.4	15.92	22.74	78.79	☆		☆	0.0	N/A	612-973-4069	637-2548	4.50	0.80	None	Bren/Whitcomb	'94/'94
FIRST AMER TECH; B	Science & Technology	0.5	15.79	22.59	☆	☆		☆	0.0	N/A	612-973-4069	637-2548	None	None	5.00	Bren/Whitcomb	'94/'94
FIRST AMER TECH; C ▥	Science & Technology	18.5	15.94	22.80	79.02	☆		☆	0.0	N/A	612-973-4069	637-2548	None	0.80	None	Bren/Whitcomb	'94/'94
FIRST BOS INSTL GOVT; A	Fixed Income	23.0	9.45	4.71	10.74	☆		☆	6.5	N/A	None	545-5799	2.50	0.96	None	Mark Silverstein	'95
FIRST EAGLE FD OF AMER	Capital Appreciation	119.0	14.68	6.84	17.10	16.77	12.37	☆	0.0	12.8	212-943-9200	451-3623	None	1.90	None	Levy/Cohen	'87/'89
FIRST EAGLE INTL FD	International	20.6	12.25	3.03	1.58	☆		☆	0.0	□□□□□	212-943-9200	451-3623	None	None	None	Raphael/Lerner	'94/'94
FIRST TOT EQ; I	Growth Income	109.4	12.22	8.50	24.20	☆		☆	1.9	17.8	None	442-1941	None	0.34	None	Pruett/Ratiff	'93/'93
FIRST TOT EQ; III	Growth Income	17.2	12.24	8.20	22.70	☆		☆	0.5	17.8	None	442-1941	None	1.83	None	Pruett/Ratiff	'93/'93
FIRST TOT FXD; I	Fixed Income	89.3	9.91	6.54	11.87	☆		☆	5.8	□□□□□	None	442-1941	None	0.36	None	Stephen T. Ashby	'93
FIRST TOT FXD; III	Fixed Income	1.6	9.89	6.06	10.12	☆		☆	4.4	□□□□□	None	442-1941	None	1.82	None	Stephen T. Ashby	'93
FIRST INV FD FOR INC; A	Fixed Income	420.1	4.01	5.15	11.95	11.32	12.58	☆	9.1	□□□□□	212-858-8000	423-4026	6.25	1.22	None	Nancy Jones	'89
FIRST INV FD FOR INC; B	Fixed Income	0.1	3.97	5.59	☆	3.45		☆	0.0	□□□□□	212-858-8000	423-4026	None	None	4.00	Nancy Jones	'95

375

PERFORMANCE OF MUTUAL FUNDS (continued)

FUND NAME	OBJECTIVE	ASSETS ($ MIL) 5/31/95	NAV ($/SHR) 6/30/95	QTR	1YR	3YRS	5YRS	10YRS	DIV YLD %	P/E RATIO	800	In-State	Load	Exp. Ratio	Redemption	MANAGER	SINCE
FIRST INV GLOBAL FD; A	Global	220.0	6.29	5.36	9.21	7.53	3.31	14.05	0.4	□	423-4026	212-858-8000	6.25	1.84	None	Wellington Mgmt. Co.	'89
FIRST INV GLOBAL FD; B	Global	0.1	6.27	5.20	☆	☆	☆	☆	0.1		423-4026	212-858-8000	None		4.00	Wellington Mgmt. Co.	'95
FIRST INV GOV PLUS III ☒	Balanced Target	1.1	12.12	6.22	10.87	8.33	9.19	☆	5.0	N/A	423-4026	212-858-8000	8.00	1.74	None	Patricia Poitra	'94
FIRST INV GOVT PLUS I ☒	Balanced Target	1.4	11.62	10.77	18.15	11.12	11.37	☆	5.8	N/A	423-4026	212-858-8000	8.00	1.60	None	Patricia Poitra	'86
FIRST INV GOVT PLUS II ☒	Balanced Target	2.5	11.68	6.09	10.02	7.43	9.24	☆	5.7	N/A	423-4026	212-858-8000	8.00	1.78	None	Patricia Poitra	'94
FIRST INV GOVT; A	Fixed Income	222.9	11.11	5.08	10.10	4.73	7.24	7.90	6.5	□	423-4026	212-858-8000	6.25	1.40	None	John Tomasulo	'95
FIRST INV GOVT; B	Fixed Income	0.1	11.11	4.71	☆	☆	☆	☆	0.1		423-4026	212-858-8000	None		4.00	John Tomasulo	'95
FIRST INV HIGH YIELD; A	Fixed Income	182.2	5.15	6.28	12.49	11.69	12.00	☆	9.3	□	423-4026	212-858-8000	6.25	1.56	None	George Ganter	'89
FIRST INV HIGH YIELD; B	Fixed Income	0.1	5.15	6.10	☆	☆	☆	☆	0.7		423-4026	212-858-8000	None		4.00	George Ganter	'95
FIRST INV SRS BLUE CHIP	Growth Income	142.2	15.81	8.47	19.31	10.66	8.71	☆	0.7	17.9	423-4026	212-858-8000	6.25	1.54	None	Patricia Poitra	'94
FIRST INV SRS INV GRADE	Fixed Income	48.5	10.04	6.72	13.09	7.86	☆	☆	6.3	□	423-4026	212-858-8000	6.25	0.95	None	Nancy Jones	'91
FIRST INV SRS SP SIT; A	Small Company Growth	100.3	18.76	8.38	22.07	17.00	☆	☆	0.0	17.0	423-4026	212-858-8000	6.25	1.65	None	Patricia Poitra	'90
FIRST INV SRS TOT RTN	Flexible	52.0	12.36	8.18	16.64	8.17	7.47	N/A	1.7	16.5	423-4026	212-858-8000	6.25	1.63	None	Team Managed	N/A
FIRST INV SRSII GR & INC	Growth Income	49.5	7.58	9.22	20.49	☆	☆	☆	1.9	N/A	423-4026	212-858-8000	6.25	0.67	None	Wellington Mgmt. Co.	'93
FIRST INV SRSII MADE USA	Growth	8.0	13.87	6.77	28.33	☆	☆	☆	0.6	22.3	423-4026	212-858-8000	6.25	0.90	None	Patricia Poitra	'94
FIRST INV SRSII UTIL	Utility	75.0	5.50	6.13	13.41	☆	☆	☆	4.3	14.1	423-4026	212-858-8000	6.25	0.80	None	Margaret Haggerty	'93
FIRST MUTUAL FUND	Capital Appreciation	18.6	10.03	11.57	25.04	10.46	6.84	☆	0.0	N/A	257-4414	None	None	1.97	None	David P. Como	'82
FIRST OMAHA EQUITY ➜	Growth Income	172.6	12.00	6.40	23.27	☆	☆	☆	2.2	16.3	273-3936	317-692-3900	None	1.04	None	Vicki Hohenstein	'92
FIRST OMAHA FXD INCOME ➜	Fixed Income	70.4	10.09	6.66	12.67	☆	☆	☆	6.3	□	273-3936	317-692-3900	None	0.86	None	Dick Chapman	'92
FIRST OMAHA SH-INTMDT	Fixed Income	22.6	9.89	3.84	8.53	☆	☆	☆	5.3	□	273-3936	317-692-3900	None	0.83	None	Dick Chapman	'92
1ST PRIORITY BALANCED	Balanced	46.1	10.98	6.52	☆	☆	☆	☆	0.0	N/A	433-2829	205-326-7041	2.00	None	None	Ken Alderman	'94
1ST PRIORITY EQUITY	Growth Income	145.0	11.31	7.80	18.25	8.61	☆	☆	1.9	17.4	433-2829	205-326-7041	2.00	1.09	None	Charles Murray	'92
1ST PRIORITY EQUITY INC	Equity Income	38.1	11.10	6.36	11.31	6.33	☆	☆	5.2	N/A	433-2829	205-326-7041	2.00	None	None	Ken Alderman	'94
1ST PRIORITY FXD INCOME	Fixed Income	163.9	10.20	6.26	7.76	☆	☆	☆	4.8	□	433-2829	205-326-7041	2.00	1.09	None	Jerry Harris	'92
1ST PRIORITY LTD GOVT	Fixed Income	61.5	9.94	3.38	☆	☆	☆	☆	3.8	□	433-2829	205-326-7041	2.00	0.38	None	John Haigler	'93
FIRST UN BAL; INV A	Balanced	41.3	12.50	7.08	15.40	9.71	☆	☆	3.1	14.1	326-3241	704-374-4343	4.75	0.91	None	Dean Hawes	'91
FIRST UN BAL; INV B	Balanced	105.6	12.51	6.89	14.58	☆	☆	☆	0.0	14.1	326-3241	704-374-4343	None	1.41	5.00	Dean Hawes	'93
FIRST UN BAL; INV C	Balanced	0.2	12.49	6.90	☆	☆	☆	☆	4.0	14.1	326-3241	704-374-4343	None	None	1.00	Dean Hawes	'94
FIRST UN BAL; Y	Balanced	850.5	12.50	7.15	15.69	☆	☆	☆	0.0	14.1	326-3241	704-374-4343	None	0.66	None	Dean Hawes	'91
FIRST UN EMRG GR; INV A	Emerging Markets	1.1	7.97	11.16	☆	☆	☆	☆	0.0	□	326-3241	704-374-4343	4.75	None	None	Richard Wagoner	'95
FIRST UN EMRG GR; INV B	Emerging Markets	1.8	7.94	10.89	☆	☆	☆	☆	0.0	□	326-3241	704-374-4343	None	None	5.00	Richard Wagoner	'95
FIRST UN EMRG GR; INV C	Emerging Markets	0.1	7.93	10.91	☆	☆	☆	☆	0.0	□	326-3241	704-374-4343	None	None	1.00	Richard Wagoner	'95
FIRST UN EMRG GR; Y	Emerging Markets	7.9	7.98	11.14	☆	☆	☆	☆	0.0	□	326-3241	704-374-4343	None	None	None	Richard Wagoner	'95
FIRST UN FXD INC; INV A	Fixed Income	19.5	10.02	4.68	9.22	5.84	8.02	☆	6.3	□	326-3241	704-374-4343	4.75	0.75	None	Tom Ellis	'89
FIRST UN FXD INC; INV B	Fixed Income	17.2	10.04	4.45	8.28	☆	☆	☆	5.5	□	326-3241	704-374-4343	None	1.50	5.00	Tom Ellis	'93
FIRST UN FXD INC; INV C	Fixed Income	0.5	10.05	4.40	☆	☆	☆	☆	0.5	□	326-3241	704-374-4343	None	None	1.00	Tom Ellis	'94
FIRST UN FXD INC; Y	Fixed Income	345.6	10.02	4.68	9.31	6.03	☆	☆	6.4	□	326-3241	704-374-4343	None	0.75	None	Tom Ellis	'93
FIRST UN INTL EQ; INV A	International	3.0	9.79	3.59	☆	☆	☆	☆	0.0	□	326-3241	704-374-4343	4.75	None	None	Richard Wagoner	'95
FIRST UN INTL EQ; INV B	International	6.7	9.76	3.39	☆	☆	☆	☆	0.0	□	326-3241	704-374-4343	None	0.65	5.00	Richard Wagoner	'95
FIRST UN INTL EQ; INV C	International	0.3	9.76	3.39	☆	☆	☆	☆	0.0	□	326-3241	704-374-4343	None	None	1.00	Richard Wagoner	'95
FIRST UN INTL EQ; Y	International	32.7	9.80	3.69	☆	☆	☆	☆	0.0	□	326-3241	704-374-4343	None	None	None	Richard Wagoner	'95
FIRST UN MGD BD; Y	Fixed Income	73.5	10.05	6.48	11.98	6.84	☆	☆	6.5	□	326-3241	704-374-4343	None	0.70	None	Glen Insley	'93
FIRST UN US GOVT; INV A	Fixed Income	22.2	9.65	5.35	11.02	☆	☆	☆	6.9	□	326-3241	704-374-4343	4.75	0.96	None	Rollin Williams	'93
FIRST UN US GOVT; INV B	Fixed Income	192.9	9.65	5.16	10.25	☆	☆	☆	6.2	□	326-3241	704-374-4343	None	1.54	5.00	Rollin Williams	'93
FIRST UN US GOVT; INV C	Fixed Income	0.4	9.65	5.15	☆	☆	☆	☆	0.0	□	326-3241	704-374-4343	None	None	1.00	Rollin Williams	'94

RETURN THROUGH 6/30 columns (QTR, 1YR, 3YRS, 5YRS, 10YRS) are annualized.

Fund	Objective	Net Assets ($mil)	NAV	Col 2	1-Yr %	Rtg 1	Rtg 2	Rtg 3	Yield %	5-Yr %	Phone 1	Phone 2	Max Sales Chg	Exp/12b-1	CDSC	Manager	Since
FIRST UN US GOVT; Y	Fixed Income	16.3	9.65	5.42	11.30	☆	☆	☆	7.1	□	326-3241	704-374-4343	None	0.71	None	Rollin Williams	'93
FIRST UN UTILITY; INV A	Utility	4.5	9.76	5.91	12.21	☆	☆	☆	4.4	13.7	326-3241	704-374-4343	4.75	None	None	Brad Donovan	'94
FIRST UN UTILITY; INV B	Utility	30.7	9.77	5.84	11.61	☆	☆	☆	3.8	13.7	326-3241	704-374-4343	None	None	5.00	Brad Donovan	'94
FIRST UN UTILITY; INV C	Utility	0.2	9.77	5.70	☆	☆	☆	☆	0.0	13.7	326-3241	704-374-4343	None	None	1.00	Brad Donovan	'94
FIRST UN UTILITY; Y	Utility	6.5	9.77	6.08	12.60	☆	12.86	12.86	4.7	13.7	326-3241	704-374-4343	None	0.99	None	Brad Donovan	'94
FIRST UN VALUE; INV A	Growth	210.3	19.26	6.45	21.50	12.02	11.04	12.86	2.7	14.8	326-3241	704-374-4343	4.75	1.48	None	Bill Davis	'91
FIRST UN VALUE; INV B	Growth	120.2	19.26	6.21	20.59	☆	☆	☆	2.0	14.8	326-3241	704-374-4343	None	None	5.00	Bill Davis	'93
FIRST UN VALUE; INV C	Growth	0.6	19.24	6.21	☆	12.31	☆	☆	0.0	14.8	326-3241	704-374-4343	None	0.65	1.00	Bill Davis	'94
FIRST UN VALUE; Y	Growth	661.5	19.26	6.51	21.71	11.12	☆	☆	2.8	14.8	326-3241	704-374-4343	None	1.50	None	Bill Davis	'91
FLAG INV EMERGING GROWTH	Small Company Growth	29.2	15.36	9.56	43.76	☆	6.04	6.04	0.0	29.6	645-3923	410-637-6819	4.50	1.50	None	Fred Meserve	'93
FLAG INV INTL; FLAG	International	13.2	12.44	3.75	-4.31	9.27	0.43	☆	0.0	□	645-3923	410-637-6819	4.50	0.70	None	Glenmede Trust/Williams	'93/'93
FLAG INV INTMDT-TM INC	Fixed Income	73.5	10.25	4.98	9.24	6.02	6.02	☆	5.9	□	645-3923	410-637-6819	1.50	0.92	None	Randolph/Corbin	'91/'91
FLAG INV TPHONE INC; A	Equity Income	444.7	13.71	8.06	13.19	13.08	11.25	14.87	3.2	15.2	645-3923	410-637-6819	4.50	1.27	None	Behrens/Buppert	'84/'84
FLAG INV TPHONE INC; D ⊠	Equity Income	30.9	13.69	7.98	13.36	☆	☆	☆	3.2	15.2	645-3923	410-637-6819	None	1.35	1.00	Behrens/Buppert	'93/'93
FLAG INV VALUE BLDR; A	Balanced	155.1	12.96	8.54	20.66	11.89	6.04	☆	2.7	14.7	645-3923	410-637-6819	4.50	1.70	None	Buppert/Owen	'92/'92
FLAG INV VALUE BLDR; D ⊠	Balanced	12.1	12.95	8.45	20.25	☆	☆	☆	2.4	□	645-3923	410-637-6819	None	None	1.00	Buppert/Owen	'92/'92
FLAGSHIP ADM INT GOV; A	Fixed Income	0.9	9.68	7.94	14.41	☆	☆	☆	6.1	□	227-4648	513-461-0332	3.00	1.00	None	Jan Terbrueggen	'94
FLAGSHIP ADM INT GOV; C	Fixed Income	2.3	9.69	7.74	13.57	☆	☆	☆	5.4	□	227-4648	513-461-0332	None	1.00	1.00	Jan Terbrueggen	'94
FLAGSHIP ADM LTD GOV; A	Fixed Income	1.2	9.60	5.09	9.06	☆	☆	☆	6.0	□	227-4648	513-461-0332	2.50	1.09	None	Jan Terbrueggen	'94
FLAGSHIP ADM LTD GOV; C	Fixed Income	2.0	9.61	5.07	8.64	☆	☆	☆	5.5	□	227-4648	513-461-0332	None	0.94	1.00	Jan Terbrueggen	'94
FLAGSHIP ADM UTILITY; A	Utility	25.2	10.24	5.91	12.73	☆	☆	☆	6.2	13.6	227-4648	513-461-0332	4.20	1.46	None	Bedford/Huber	'92/'92
FLAGSHIP ADM UTILITY; C	Utility	5.5	10.24	5.89	12.15	☆	☆	☆	5.7	13.6	227-4648	513-461-0332	None	1.00	1.00	Bedford/Huber	'93/'93
FLEX-FUNDS BOND	Fixed Income	14.6	20.86	7.60	13.74	7.54	8.24	☆	4.6	N/A	325-3539	614-766-7000	None	1.63	None	G. Robert Kincheloe	'92
FLEX-FUNDS GROWTH	Flexible	23.6	14.49	6.72	15.15	8.01	9.81	7.42	3.4	N/A	325-3539	614-766-7000	None	1.22	None	Robert Meeder, Jr.	'88
FLEX-FUNDS MUIRFIELD	Flexible	91.4	6.03	8.45	16.03	11.01	11.41	7.97	2.1	□	325-3539	614-766-7000	None	1.08	None	Robert Meeder, Jr.	'92
FLEX-FUNDS SHT GLBL INC	World Income	3.9	9.45	2.38	5.39	1.98	☆	☆	4.0	□	325-3539	614-766-7000	4.00	1.61	None	Joseph Zarr	'93
FMB DVSD EQ; CNSMR	Growth	5.2	13.18	7.39	19.15	8.21	☆	☆	0.8	19.0	453-4234	None	4.00	1.61	None	Dan Van Timmeren	'93
FMB DVSD EQ; INSTL	Growth	49.1	13.18	7.39	19.15	8.22	☆	☆	0.8	19.0	453-4234	None	None	0.83	None	Dan Van Timmeren	'93
FMB INTMDT GOVT; CNSMR	Fixed Income	8.4	10.14	4.10	8.81	5.99	☆	☆	5.9	□	453-4234	None	3.00	0.83	None	Duane Carpenter	'91
FMB INTMDT GOVT; INSTL	Fixed Income	155.2	10.14	4.10	8.81	6.02	☆	☆	5.9	□	453-4234	None	None	None	None	Duane Carpenter	'91
FOCUS TRUST INC	Growth	N/A	10.14	☆	☆	☆	☆	☆	0.0	N/A	665-2550	None	None	1.50	None	Robert Hagstrom	'95
FONTAINE CAPITAL APPREC	Capital Appreciation	5.4	11.93	0.85	18.42	6.85	6.75	☆	0.6	17.7	247-1550	410-825-7890	None	1.45	2.00	Richard H. Fontaine	'89
FONTAINE GLBL GROWTH	Global	0.4	10.50	1.94	15.35	5.08	☆	☆	1.5	□	247-1550	410-825-7890	None	1.21	None	Richard H. Fontaine	'92
FONTAINE GLBL INCOME	World Income	0.8	10.70	1.22	10.44	7.15	10.85	☆	4.0	□	247-1550	410-825-7890	None	1.55	None	Richard H. Fontaine	'92
FORTIS ADVTG ASSET; A	Flexible	125.0	15.86	7.97	22.10	10.91	☆	☆	3.1	21.9	800-2638	612-738-4000	4.50	None	None	Poling/Ott	'88/'88
FORTIS ADVTG ASSET; B	Flexible	0.3	15.82	7.89	☆	☆	☆	☆	0.0	21.9	800-2638	612-738-4000	None	1.00	4.00	Poling/Ott	'94/'94
FORTIS ADVTG ASSET; C	Flexible	0.4	15.78	7.91	☆	☆	☆	☆	0.0	21.9	800-2638	612-738-4000	None	1.00	4.00	Poling/Ott	'94/'94
FORTIS ADVTG ASSET; H	Flexible	2.3	15.80	7.83	☆	☆	☆	☆	0.0	26.4	800-2638	612-738-4000	None	1.62	None	Poling/Ott	'94
FORTIS ADVTG CAP APP; A	Small Company Growth	73.2	26.99	11.58	30.45	17.05	10.10	☆	0.0	26.4	800-2638	612-738-4000	4.50	None	4.00	Stephen Poling	'94
FORTIS ADVTG CAP APP; B	Small Company Growth	0.3	26.97	11.72	☆	☆	☆	☆	0.0	□	800-2638	612-738-4000	None	1.00	4.00	Stephen Poling	'94
FORTIS ADVTG CAP APP; C	Small Company Growth	0.1	26.92	11.47	☆	☆	☆	☆	0.0	□	800-2638	612-738-4000	None	None	1.00	Stephen Poling	'94
FORTIS ADVTG CAP APP; H	Small Company Growth	1.2	26.93	11.47	9.03	4.47	6.18	☆	0.0	□	800-2638	612-738-4000	None	1.28	4.00	Stephen Poling	'94
FORTIS ADVTG GOVT; A	Fixed Income	65.8	8.10	5.28	☆	☆	☆	☆	7.3	□	800-2638	612-738-4000	4.50	None	None	Dennis M. Ott	'86
FORTIS ADVTG GOVT; B	Fixed Income	0.1	8.07	4.99	☆	☆	☆	☆	0.0	□	800-2638	612-738-4000	None	None	4.00	Dennis M. Ott	'88
FORTIS ADVTG GOVT; C	Fixed Income	0.1	8.08	5.12	☆	☆	☆	☆	0.0	□	800-2638	612-738-4000	None	None	1.00	Dennis M. Ott	'94
FORTIS ADVTG HI YLD; A	Fixed Income	109.6	8.06	4.86	☆	☆	☆	☆	11.4	□	800-2638	612-738-4000	4.50	1.23	None	Dennis M. Ott	'94
FORTIS ADVTG HI YLD; B	Fixed Income	2.2	7.87	3.42	5.59	10.34	14.50	☆	0.0	□	800-2638	612-738-4000	None	None	4.00	Dennis M. Ott	'88
FORTIS ADVTG HI YLD; C	Fixed Income	1.0	7.86	3.12	☆	☆	☆	☆	0.0	□	800-2638	612-738-4000	None	None	4.00	Dennis M. Ott	'88
FORTIS ADVTG HI YLD; H	Fixed Income	11.3	7.86	3.26	☆	☆	☆	☆	0.0	□	800-2638	612-738-4000	None	None	4.00	Dennis M. Ott	'94

PERFORMANCE OF MUTUAL FUNDS (continued)

FUND NAME	OBJECTIVE	ASSETS ($ MIL) 5/31/95	NAV ($/SHR) 6/30/95	QTR	1YR	3YRS	5YRS	10YRS	DIV YLD %	P/E RATIO	800	In-State	Load	Exp. Ratio	Redemption	MANAGER	SINCE
						RETURN THROUGH 6/30 (Annualized)					PHONE NUMBER		FEES				
FORTIS EQ CAPITAL; A	Growth Income	260.0	20.05	10.74	27.89	12.15	11.56	13.80	0.4	23.5	800-2638	612-738-4000	4.75	1.21	None	Stephen Poling	83
FORTIS EQ CAPITAL; B	Growth Income	1.0	20.01	10.55	☆	☆	☆	☆	0.0	23.5	800-2638	612-738-4000	None	None	4.00	Stephen Poling	94
FORTIS EQ CAPITAL; C	Growth Income	0.2	20.00	10.56	☆	☆	☆	☆	0.0	23.5	800-2638	612-738-4000	None	None	1.00	Stephen Poling	94
FORTIS EQ CAPITAL; H	Growth Income	2.0	20.00	10.56	☆	☆	☆	☆	0.0	23.5	800-2638	612-738-4000	None	None	4.00	Stephen Poling	94
FORTIS FIDUCIARY FD; A	Growth	55.1	33.68	11.41	30.88	13.24	12.01	14.41	0.0	22.8	800-2638	612-738-4000	4.75	1.45	None	Stephen Poling	83
FORTIS GROWTH FD; A	Capital Appreciation	583.0	30.31	13.86	30.41	12.19	12.21	14.66	0.0	26.5	800-2638	612-738-4000	4.75	1.09	None	Stephen Poling	83
FORTIS GROWTH FD; B	Capital Appreciation	1.5	30.18	13.63	☆	☆	☆	☆	0.0	26.5	800-2638	612-738-4000	None	None	4.00	Stephen Poling	94
FORTIS GROWTH FD; C	Capital Appreciation	0.1	30.16	13.64	☆	☆	☆	☆	0.0	26.5	800-2638	612-738-4000	None	None	1.00	Stephen Poling	94
FORTIS GROWTH FD; H	Capital Appreciation	3.5	30.17	13.63	☆	☆	☆	☆	0.0	26.5	800-2638	612-738-4000	None	None	4.00	Stephen Poling	94
FORTIS INC US GOVT; A	Fixed Income	3.7	9.09	4.76	☆	☆	☆	☆	0.0	☐	800-2638	612-738-4000	4.50	None	None	Dennis M. Ott	94
FORTIS INC US GOVT; B	Fixed Income	0.4	9.09	4.57	☆	☆	☆	☆	0.0	☐	800-2638	612-738-4000	None	None	4.00	Dennis M. Ott	94
FORTIS INC US GOVT; C	Fixed Income	0.2	9.09	4.57	☆	☆	☆	☆	0.0	☐	800-2638	612-738-4000	None	None	1.00	Dennis M. Ott	94
FORTIS INC US GOVT; E	Fixed Income	485.6	9.10	4.94	9.83	4.98	7.58	8.75	7.4	☐	800-2638	612-738-4000	4.50	0.77	None	Dennis M. Ott	85
FORTIS INC US GOVT; H	Fixed Income	3.4	9.09	4.57	☆	☆	☆	☆	0.0	☐	800-2638	612-738-4000	None	None	4.00	Dennis M. Ott	91
FORTIS WORLD GLBL GR; A	Global	56.7	16.53	14.47	24.01	14.68	☆	☆	0.0	☐	800-2638	612-738-4000	4.75	1.72	None	James Byrd	91
FORTIS WORLD GLBL GR; B	Global	0.4	16.46	14.31	☆	☆	☆	☆	0.0	☐	800-2638	612-738-4000	None	None	4.00	James Byrd	94
FORTIS WORLD GLBL GR; C	Global	0.1	16.47	14.38	☆	☆	☆	☆	0.0	☐	800-2638	612-738-4000	None	None	1.00	James Byrd	94
FORTIS WORLD GLBL GR; H	Global	0.7	16.47	14.30	☆	☆	☆	☆	0.0	☐	800-2638	612-738-4000	None	None	4.00	James Byrd	94
FORTRESS ADJ RT GOVT	Fixed Income	379.1	9.51	1.75	4.83	3.33	☆	☆	5.5	☐	245-4770	412-288-1900	1.00	1.02	1.00	Gary Madich	91
FORTRESS BOND FUND	Fixed Income	171.2	9.61	6.09	12.97	9.86	12.97	☆	7.8	☐	245-4770	412-288-1900	1.00	1.05	1.00	Joe Balestrino	93
FORTRESS UTILITY	Utility	778.9	12.68	5.65	12.01	8.45	10.63	☆	4.7	15.1	245-4770	412-288-1900	1.00	1.11	1.00	Christopher H. Wiles	90
44 WALL STREET EQUITY	Capital Appreciation	8.5	6.88	11.51	19.36	17.56	12.70	8.86	0.0	17.4	543-2620	212-248-8080	None	5.01	None	Mark D. Beckerman	88
FORUM INVESTORS BOND	Fixed Income	26.2	10.20	3.60	9.55	7.22	9.47	☆	7.9	☐	None	207-879-0001	3.75	0.75	None	Forum Advisors	89
FORUM PAYSON BALANCED	Balanced	14.8	12.42	5.29	15.06	10.80	☆	☆	3.6	14.5	None	207-879-0001	None	1.15	None	H.M. Payson & Co.	93
FORUM PAYSON VALUE	Growth Income	8.1	13.35	5.51	15.63	☆	☆	☆	1.5	15.7	None	207-879-0001	None	1.46	None	H.M. Payson & Co.	93
FOUNDERS BALANCED	Balanced	103.5	9.58	7.12	12.59	13.49	11.14	11.06	2.4	18.8	525-2440	303-394-4404	None	1.26	None	Patrick S. Adams	93
FOUNDERS BLUE CHIP FUND	Growth Income	334.2	7.13	8.52	20.54	12.94	10.07	13.46	0.7	18.2	525-2440	303-394-4404	None	1.21	None	Patrick S. Adams	93
FOUNDERS DISCOVERY FUND	Small Company Growth	181.3	23.37	11.23	29.76	14.93	16.65	☆	0.0	21.5	525-2440	303-394-4404	None	1.67	None	Haines/Kern	'89/'95
FOUNDERS FRONTIER FUND	Small Company Growth	274.3	30.92	9.03	29.63	15.88	13.87	☆	0.0	23.1	525-2440	303-394-4404	None	1.62	None	Michael K. Haines	87
FOUNDERS GOVERNMENT SEC ☛	Fixed Income	21.1	9.13	3.79	5.82	3.78	6.50	☆	5.0	☐	525-2440	303-394-4404	None	1.34	None	Team Managed	N/A
FOUNDERS GROWTH FUND	Growth	428.7	14.21	12.87	32.67	19.85	15.23	15.70	0.0	23.6	525-2440	303-394-4404	None	1.33	None	Edward Keely	93
FOUNDERS OPPTY BOND	Fixed Income	3.8	8.71	5.03	4.72	☆	☆	☆	6.1	☐	525-2440	303-394-4404	None	1.22	None	Team Managed	N/A
FOUNDERS PASSPORT FUND	Intl Small Company	17.9	10.57	10.45	9.42	☆	☆	☆	0.2	☐	525-2440	303-394-4404	None	1.88	None	Michael W. Gerding	93
FOUNDERS SPECIAL FUND	Capital Appreciation	375.9	8.43	10.63	29.56	15.38	16.50	15.48	0.0	19.6	525-2440	303-394-4404	None	1.36	None	Charles Hooper	91
FOUNDERS WORLDWIDE GROW	Global	136.6	19.11	9.14	17.18	13.76	13.42	☆	0.0	☐	525-2440	303-394-4404	None	1.66	None	Michael W. Gerding	90
FOUNTAIN SQ BALANCED	Balanced	54.4	10.99	6.56	19.26	☆	☆	☆	2.4	N/A	654-5372	513-579-5452	4.50	1.00	None	Tom Atteberry	93
FOUNTAIN SQ INTL EQTY	International	80.8	9.30	1.31	☆	☆	☆	☆	0.6	N/A	654-5372	513-579-5452	4.50	1.00	None	Paul Jackson	94
FOUNTAIN SQ MID CAP	Midcap	42.6	12.06	8.47	23.09	☆	☆	☆	0.0	☐	654-5372	513-579-5452	4.50	1.00	None	Steve Folker	94
FOUNTAIN SQ QUALITY BD	Fixed Income	52.5	9.84	5.76	11.54	☆	☆	☆	6.4	N/A	654-5372	513-579-5452	4.50	0.75	None	Tom Atteberry	93
FOUNTAIN SQ QUALITY GRO	Growth	75.0	11.39	6.59	22.30	☆	☆	☆	1.2	N/A	654-5372	513-579-5452	4.50	1.00	None	Steve Folker	93
FOUNTAIN SQ US GOVT SECS	Fixed Income	23.4	9.84	4.49	9.00	☆	☆	☆	5.8	N/A	654-5372	513-579-5452	4.50	0.75	None	Tom Atteberry	93
FPA CAPITAL ☒	Growth	288.2	26.01	16.12	42.31	26.72	21.10	19.33	0.3	15.6	982-4372	310-996-5425	6.50	0.95	None	Robert L. Rodriguez	84
FPA NEW INCOME	Fixed Income	167.0	10.99	5.16	11.18	8.87	11.16	10.78	6.4	☐	982-4372	310-996-5425	4.50	0.74	None	Robert L. Rodriguez	84
FPA PARAMOUNT ☒	Growth Income	567.8	14.31	3.10	16.25	14.64	13.66	14.51	1.6	12.9	982-4372	310-996-5425	6.50	0.90	None	William M. Sams	81
FPA PERENNIAL FUND	Growth Income	48.8	21.20	4.18	13.82	7.47	8.94	11.03	2.0	15.3	982-4372	310-996-5425	6.50	1.13	None	Christopher Linden	84

Fund	Objective	Net Assets									Tel A	Tel B	Load	12b-1	Redem	Portfolio Manager	Mgr Since
FRANKLIN AGE HI INC	Fixed Income	1,908.9	2.77	5.90	14.16	10.95	13.92	9.93	9.5	□	342-5236	415-312-3200	4.25	0.59	None	Wiskemann/Molumphy	'72/'91
FRANKLIN BALANCE SHEET	Capital Appreciation	262.3	25.48	7.89	19.22	19.96	16.02	☆	1.0	7.8	342-5236	415-312-3200	1.50	1.19	None	Lippman/Baughman	'90/'90
FRANKLIN CUST DYNATECH	Science & Technology	79.0	12.13	15.52	34.84	14.24	11.84	12.13	0.4	20.1	342-5236	415-312-3200	4.50	1.00	None	Johnson/Costa	'68/'83
FRANKLIN CUST GRO;1	Growth	618.7	17.92	9.20	27.64	12.18	10.50	13.87	0.8	18.0	342-5236	415-312-3200	4.50	0.77	None	Palmeieri/Herrmann	'65/'93
FRANKLIN CUST INC;1	Income	5,432.6	2.25	7.33	12.06	9.28	13.28	11.48	8.0	12.2	342-5236	415-312-3200	4.50	0.64	None	Johnson/Avery	'57/'90
FRANKLIN CUST GOVT;1	Fixed Income	11,286.4	6.85	5.37	12.04	6.20	8.49	9.10	7.0	12.8	342-5236	415-312-3200	4.25	0.55	None	Jack Lemein	'70
FRANKLIN CUST UTIL;1	Utility	2,752.3	9.27	8.06	19.25	6.06	9.44	9.85	5.7	16.6	342-5236	415-312-3200	4.25	0.64	None	Johnson/Edwards	'57/'91
FRANKLIN EQUITY FD;1	Growth	301.5	7.24	12.01	23.83	11.59	8.55	11.79	1.1	N/A	342-5236	415-312-3200	4.50	0.79	None	Conrad Herrmann	'93
FRANKLIN GOLD FUND;1	Gold	389.6	14.66	0.21	2.88	9.95	5.18	8.94	1.8	□	342-5236	415-312-3200	4.50	0.81	None	Wiskemann/Killea	'94/'94
FRANKLIN INTL INTL EQU	International	50.1	13.11	9.39	7.65	11.74	☆	☆	1.4	□	342-5236	415-312-3200	4.50	1.22	None	Templeton Invt Council	'93
FRANKLIN INTL PAC GROWTH	Pacific Region	54.5	14.09	3.15	-2.43	10.89	☆	☆	1.1	□	342-5236	415-312-3200	4.50	1.22	None	Templeton Invt Council	'93
FRANKLIN INV ADJ RATE	Fixed Income	19.1	9.79	2.62	6.07	4.36	☆	☆	5.8	□	342-5236	415-312-3200	2.25	0.45	None	Lemein/Coffey/Bayston	'91/'91/'91
FRANKLIN INV ADJ US GOVT	Fixed Income	572.7	9.31	2.70	4.16	1.94	4.40	☆	5.0	□	342-5236	415-312-3200	2.25	0.42	None	Lemein/Coffey/Bayston	'87/'89/'91
FRANKLIN INV CONV SEC	Convertible Securities	128.7	12.35	8.84	14.77	14.86	13.70	☆	4.5	□	342-5236	415-312-3200	4.50	0.84	None	Jamieson/Nori	'87/'92
FRANKLIN INV EQUITY INC	Equity Income	128.7	14.68	4.89	14.59	11.80	11.86	☆	4.1	14.5	342-5236	415-312-3200	4.50	0.77	None	Frank Felicelli	'88
FRANKLIN INV GL GVT;1	World Income	171.7	8.15	5.49	10.40	4.87	7.07	☆	9.0	□	342-5236	415-312-3200	4.25	0.89	None	Devlin/Perin	'94/'93
FRANKLIN INV SH-INT USG	Fixed Income	210.3	10.32	3.38	7.56	5.60	7.27	☆	5.1	N/A	342-5236	415-312-3200	2.25	0.65	None	Jack Lemein	'87
FRANKLIN MGD CORP QUAL	Income	28.3	23.72	1.75	3.93	4.71	9.78	☆	4.6	□	342-5236	415-312-3200	1.50	1.00	None	Lippman/Smith	'87/'87
FRANKLIN MGD INV GRADE	Fixed Income	29.2	9.03	3.67	7.72	6.09	8.20	☆	5.2	□	342-5236	415-312-3200	4.25	1.05	None	Lippman/Smith	'87/'87
FRANKLIN MGD RS DIV;1	Growth Income	252.5	16.14	5.51	14.83	4.79	9.19	☆	1.8	13.4	342-5236	415-312-3200	4.50	1.43	None	Lippman/Baughman	'87/'87
FRANKLIN PREMIER RET	Flexible	29.2	6.74	4.71	12.91	12.86	10.84	10.50	2.2	18.3	342-5236	415-312-3200	4.50	1.27	None	Costa/Wiskemann	'87/'72
FRANKLIN PRT TX-AD HY	Fixed Income	98.9	8.69	6.45	16.22	11.29	14.66	☆	9.2	□	342-5236	415-312-3200	4.25	0.81	None	Wiskemann/Hofman-Schwab	'87/'37
FRANKLIN PRT TX-AD INTL	World Income	23.2	11.42	5.09	14.87	6.53	9.64	☆	7.9	□	342-5236	415-312-3200	4.25	0.29	None	Devlin/Perin	'94/'93
FRANKLIN PRT TX-AD USG	Fixed Income	444.6	10.56	6.13	13.16	6.64	8.78	☆	6.7	□	342-5236	415-312-3200	4.25	0.61	None	Jack Lemein	'87
FRANKLIN REAL EST;1	Real Estate	18.9	11.18	5.47	5.59	☆	☆	☆	2.5	17.1	342-5236	415-312-3200	4.50	None	None	Matt Avery	'93
FRANKLIN STR CA GROWTH	Growth	17.2	15.03	13.58	46.76	26.00	☆	☆	1.1	24.1	342-5236	415-312-3200	4.50	0.09	None	Conrad Herrmann	'93
FRANKLIN STR GL UTL;1	Utility	124.5	12.53	7.96	12.85	☆	☆	☆	3.0	12.3	342-5236	415-312-3200	4.50	0.84	None	Johnson/Edwards	'92/'92
FRANKLIN STR GLBL HLTH	Health/Biotechnology	13.1	12.09	1.43	27.86	15.66	☆	☆	4.1	15.1	342-5236	415-312-3200	4.50	0.10	None	Johnson/Von Ernster	'92/'92
FRANKLIN STR INCOME	Fixed Income	7.1	10.38	5.87	13.56	☆	☆	☆	5.8	□	342-5236	415-312-3200	4.25	None	None	C. Molumphy	'94
FRANKLIN STR SM CAP GR	Small Company Growth	76.6	16.04	12.60	48.20	26.16	☆	☆	0.1	21.5	342-5236	415-312-3200	4.50	0.30	None	Ed Jamieson	'92
FRANKLIN STRAT MTGE	Fixed Income	5.8	9.89	5.26	11.85	☆	☆	☆	6.9	□	342-5236	415-312-3200	4.25	None	None	Roger Bayston	'93
FRANKLIN/TEMP GERMAN GVT	World Income	19.9	14.27	1.81	22.32	☆	☆	☆	8.4	□	342-5236	415-312-3200	3.00	1.04	None	Templeton Invt Council	'93
FRANKLIN/TEMP GL CURR	World Income	60.0	14.24	1.36	10.48	7.50	8.78	☆	8.6	□	342-5236	415-312-3200	3.00	1.04	None	Templeton Invt Council	'93
FRANKLIN/TEMP HARD CURR	World Income	111.6	13.85	0.65	17.04	10.49	11.54	☆	11.9	□	342-5236	415-312-3200	3.00	1.05	None	Templeton Invt Council	'93
FRANKLIN/TEMP HIGH INC	World Income	12.3	11.52	1.02	10.78	1.89	6.45	☆	8.6	□	342-5236	415-312-3200	3.00	1.04	None	Templeton Invt Council	'93
FRANKLIN/TEMP JAPAN	Japanese	N/A	9.56	-3.73	☆	☆	☆	☆	0.0	□	342-5236	415-312-3200	5.75	0.66	None	William Howard	'94
FREMONT BOND	Fixed Income	70.0	9.98	6.38	12.71	9.77	8.81	☆	6.2	□	548-4539	415-284-8900	None	0.95	None	William Gross	'94
FREMONT GLOBAL	Global Flexible	450.4	13.85	7.01	11.49	☆	☆	☆	1.9	□	548-4539	415-284-8900	None	0.94	None	Redo/Landini	'88/'88
FREMONT GROWTH	Growth	40.5	11.91	10.69	27.05	☆	☆	☆	1.6	□	548-4539	415-284-8900	None	1.50	None	Pang/Sit	'92/'92
FREMONT INTL GROWTH	International		9.72	8.24	7.08	☆	☆	☆	0.0	19.8	548-4539	415-284-8900	None		None	Andrew B. Kim	'94
FREMONT INTL SMALL CAP	Intl Small Company	2.7	9.09	5.09	-9.10	☆	☆	☆	0.0	□	548-4539	415-284-8900	None	None	None	Gary L. Bergstrom	'94
FREMONT US MICRO-CAP	Small Company Growth	3.3	12.47	12.34	24.70	☆	☆	☆	0.0	14.7	548-4539	415-284-8900	None	None	None	Robert E. Kern	'94
FRONTIER EQUITY FUND	Growth	1.1	6.38	13.93	-1.24	-10.84	☆	☆	0.0	N/A	231-2901	414-691-1196	8.00	9.55	None	James Fay	'92
FUND FOR US GOVT SEC; A	Fixed Income	1,385.9	7.85	4.25	9.76	4.70	7.22	8.07	7.2	□	245-4770	412-288-1900	4.50	0.88	None	Gary Madich	'87
FUND FOR US GOVT SEC; B	Fixed Income	46.9	7.85	4.05	☆	☆	☆	☆	0.0	□	245-4770	412-288-1900	None	5.50	5.50	Gary Madich	'94
FUND FOR US GOVT SEC; C	Fixed Income	80.0	7.85	4.05	8.87	☆	☆	☆	6.4	□	245-4770	412-288-1900	None	1.81	1.00	Gary Madich	'93
FUNDAMENTAL INVESTORS	Growth Income	3,437.8	20.36	9.49	23.31	15.89	12.85	15.36	2.1	14.7	421-4120	714-671-7000	5.75	0.68	None	Multiple Managers	N/A
FUNDAMENTAL GOVT STRAT	Fixed Income	16.4	1.38	1.48	-4.15	-5.38	11.38	11.68	6.9	N/A	322-6864	212-635-3005	None	2.28	None	Team Managed	N/A
FUNDMANAGER TR AGG GRO	Capital Appreciation	36.7	17.09	10.19	22.05	13.71	10.50	10.68	0.2	N/A	638-1896	212-644-1400	None	1.70	None	Michael Hirsch	'84
FUNDMANAGER TR GRO & INC	Growth Income	46.8	17.08	7.52	19.01	11.88	☆	☆	1.7	N/A	638-1896	212-644-1400	None	1.55	None	Michael Hirsch	'84

FUND NAME	OBJECTIVE	ASSETS ($ MIL) 5/31/95	NAV ($/SHR) 6/30/95	QTR	1YR	3YRS	5YRS	10YRS	DIV YLD %	P/E RATIO	800	In-State	Load	Exp. Ratio	Redemption	MANAGER	SINCE
FUNDMANAGER TR GROWTH	Growth	31.6	15.17	8.13	19.35	12.78	11.21	11.12	0.3	N/A	638-1896	212-644-1400	None	1.71	None	Michael Hirsch	'84
FUNDMANAGER TR INCOME	Fixed Income	66.2	10.14	4.81	9.63	6.68	8.06	7.26	4.9	N/A	638-1896	212-644-1400	None	1.43	None	Michael Hirsch	'84
FUNDMANAGER TR MGD T RET	Flexible	14.7	11.21	5.36	11.50	7.63	8.17	☆	2.2	N/A	638-1896	212-644-1400	None	1.94	None	Michael Hirsch	'88
FUNDS IV AGGR STOCK; SVC	Capital Appreciation	42.0	10.87	7.73	☆	☆	☆	☆	0.0		557-3768	212-309-8400	None	None	None	Paul Worth	'94
FUNDS IV BOND INCOME; SVC	Fixed Income	12.4	10.35	6.24	☆	☆	☆	☆	0.0		557-3768	212-309-8400	None	None	None	Brad Eppard	'94
FUNDS IV INTMDT BOND; SVC	Fixed Income	127.8	10.19	4.73	☆	☆	☆	☆	0.0		557-3768	212-309-8400	None	None	None	Brad Eppard	'94
FUNDS IV SH-TM TREAS; SVC	Fixed Income	15.0	10.20	3.79	☆	☆	☆	☆	0.0		557-3768	212-309-8400	None	None	None	Janet Mullen	'94
FUNDS IV STOCK APPR; SVC	Growth	126.4	11.05	8.22	☆	☆	☆	☆	0.0		557-3768	212-309-8400	None	None	None	Paul Worth	'94
FXD INC LTD; A	Fixed Income	151.9	9.88	4.03	7.57	5.52	☆	☆	5.4	N/A	245-4770	412-288-1900	1.00	1.10	None	Deborah Cunningham	'94
FXD INC LTD; FORT	Fixed Income	10.9	9.88	4.06	7.68	☆	☆	☆	5.5		245-4770	412-288-1900	1.00	0.99	1.00	Deborah Cunn~gham	'93
FXD INC STRAT INC; A	Fixed Income	3.6	9.92	4.78	10.12	☆	☆	☆	8.7		245-4770	412-288-1900	4.50	None	None	Bauer/Durbiano/Malus	'94/'94/'94
FXD INC STRAT INC; C	Fixed Income	2.0	9.92	4.48	9.32	☆	☆	☆	7.9		245-4770	412-288-1900	None	None	1.00	Bauer/Durbiano/Malus	'94/'94/'94
FXD INC STRAT INC; FORT	Fixed Income	3.3	9.92	4.55	9.59	☆	☆	☆	8.2		245-4770	412-288-1900	1.00	None	1.00	Bauer/Durbiano/Malus	'94/'94/'94
GABELLI ASSET	Growth	1,068.7	25.10	5.29	17.56	14.47	14.73	☆	1.0	14.7	422-3554	914-921-5100	4.50	1.28	None	Mario J. Gabelli	'86
GABELLI EQ EQ INCOME	Equity Income	53.1	11.99	4.33	17.87	12.24	☆	☆	2.5	N/A	422-3554	914-921-5100	4.50	1.81	None	Mario J. Gabelli	'92
GABELLI EQ SM CAP GRO	Small Company Growth	215.1	17.88	4.99	16.61	13.78	☆	☆	0.0	14.5	422-3554	914-921-5100	4.50	1.54	None	Mario J. Gabelli	'91
GABELLI GL CONVERTIBLE	Convertible Securities	17.9	10.64	5.35	4.26	☆	☆	☆	1.5		422-3554	914-921-5100	None	2.49	None	Hartswell Woodson III	'94
GABELLI GL COUCH POTATO	Global	27.7	11.28	6.21	13.14	☆	☆	☆	0.0		422-3554	914-921-5100	None	None	None	Mario J. Gabelli	'94
GABELLI GL GL TELECOM	Global	127.4	11.29	5.32	8.01	☆	☆	☆	0.6		422-3554	914-921-5100	None	None	None	Team Managed	N/A
GABELLI GOLD FUND	Gold	20.6	11.96	8.73	☆	☆	☆	☆	0.0	N/A	422-3554	914-921-5100	None	None	None	Caesar Bryan	'94
GABELLI GROWTH	Growth	480.8	22.99	10.21	23.64	12.29	10.62	☆	0.5	18.2	422-3554	914-921-5100	None	1.36	None	Howard F. Ward	'95
GABELLI INV ABC FUND	Growth	22.2	10.14	2.01	9.86	☆	☆	☆	3.2	N/A	422-3554	914-921-5100	2.00	2.09	None	Mario J. Gabelli	'93
GABELLI VALUE FUND	Capital Appreciation	465.1	11.75	2.98	17.25	19.25	14.13	☆	0.7	12.8	422-3554	914-921-5100	5.50	1.50	None	Mario J. Gabelli	'89
GALAXY ASSET ALLOC; RTL	Flexible	67.4	12.17	9.41	20.33	10.55	☆	☆	2.5	18.7	628-0414	None	None	1.21	None	Fred Thompson	'91
GALAXY ASSET ALLOC; TR	Flexible	69.3	12.18	9.45	☆	☆	☆	☆	0.0	18.7	628-0414	None	None	None	None	Fred Thompson	'94
GALAXY EQUITY GROWTH; RTL	Growth	80.6	16.17	10.26	24.47	11.68	☆	☆	0.9	19.8	628-0414	None	None	0.98	None	Bob Armknecht	'90
GALAXY EQUITY GROWTH; TR	Growth	383.1	16.17	10.38	☆	☆	☆	☆	0.9	19.8	628-0414	None	None	None	None	Bob Armknecht	'94
GALAXY EQUITY INCOME; RTL	Equity Income	69.1	14.01	6.83	19.22	10.60	☆	☆	2.1	18.0	628-0414	None	None	1.11	None	Edward Kliesziewicz	'90
GALAXY EQUITY INCOME; TR	Equity Income	84.8	14.01	6.96	☆	☆	☆	☆	0.0	18.0	628-0414	None	None	None	None	Edward Kliesziewicz	'94
GALAXY EQUITY VALUE; RTL	Growth Income	83.7	13.66	8.50	22.62	13.44	11.81	☆	1.6	14.9	628-0414	None	None	1.08	None	G. Jay Evans	'92
GALAXY EQUITY VALUE; TR	Growth Income	161.3	13.66	8.72	☆	☆	☆	☆	0.0	14.9	628-0414	None	None	None	None	G. Jay Evans	'94
GALAXY HI QUAL BOND; RTL	Fixed Income	27.0	10.44	7.54	12.76	7.72	☆	☆	6.1		628-0414	None	None	0.81	None	Ken Thomae	'90
GALAXY HI QUAL BOND; TR	Fixed Income	123.8	10.44	7.59	☆	☆	☆	☆	0.0		628-0414	None	None	None	None	Ken Thomae	'94
GALAXY INTL EQU; RTL	International	32.2	12.59	3.20	0.79	7.68	☆	☆	0.2		628-0414	None	None	1.49	None	James Knauf	'91
GALAXY INTL EQU; TR	International	78.8	12.62	3.27	☆	☆	☆	☆	0.0		628-0414	None	None	None	None	James Knauf	'94
GALAXY INTMDT BOND; RTL	Fixed Income	81.0	10.22	5.34	10.86	5.29	7.57	☆	5.8		628-0414	None	None	0.78	None	Bruce R. Barton	'92
GALAXY INTMDT BOND; TR	Fixed Income	200.2	10.22	5.43	☆	☆	☆	☆	0.0		628-0414	None	None	None	None	Bruce R. Barton	'94
GALAXY SHT-TM BOND; RTL	Fixed Income	29.4	10.00	3.68	7.37	5.15	☆	☆	5.2		628-0414	None	None	0.93	None	Ken Thomae	'91
GALAXY SHT-TM BOND; TR	Fixed Income	34.4	10.00	3.76	☆	☆	☆	☆	0.0		628-0414	None	None	None	None	Ken Thomae	'94
GALAXY SM CO EQUITY; RTL	Small Company Growth	31.5	14.56	12.87	34.56	23.25	☆	☆	0.0	22.2	628-0414	None	None	1.31	None	Steve Barbaro	'91
GALAXY SM CO EQUITY; TR	Small Company Growth	71.1	14.62	13.16	☆	☆	☆	☆	0.0	22.2	628-0414	None	None	None	None	Steve Barbaro	'94
GALAXY II LARGE CO INDEX	S&P Index	167.0	17.15	9.43	25.41	12.75	☆	☆	2.2	N/A	628-0414	None	None	0.40	None	IBM Credit Invt Mgt	'90
GALAXY II SMALL CO INDEX	Small Company Growth	238.9	19.72	8.51	20.91	12.87	☆	☆	1.4	N/A	628-0414	None	None	0.40	None	IBM Credit Invt Mgt	'90
GALAXY II TREAS INDEX	Fixed Income	110.6	10.35	6.15	11.71	7.30	☆	☆	6.4		628-0414	None	None	0.40	None	IBM Credit Invt Mgt	'91
GALAXY II UTILITY INDEX	Utility	53.0	10.43	6.72	12.25	☆	☆	☆	5.2	N/A	628-0414	None	None	0.40	None	IBM Credit Invt Mgt	'93

Fund	Objective	Net Assets	NAV	Ret 1	Ret 2	Ret 3	Ret 4	Ret 5	Yield %		Phone 1	Phone 2	Load	Exp.	Def.	Manager	Year
GAM EUROPE	European Region	11.2	95.17	6.00	9.32	7.00	-0.71	☆	0.0		426-4685	212-407-4700	5.00	2.35	None	Bennett/Houston	'93/'93
GAM GLOBAL	Global	20.1	132.92	3.75	21.23	19.78	10.01	☆	4.6		426-4685	212-407-4700	5.00	2.29	None	John Horseman	'90
GAM INTERNATIONAL	International	259.4	206.30	2.01	19.21	22.69	15.24	☆	4.5		426-4685	212-407-4700	5.00	1.60	None	John Horseman	'90
GAM JAPAN CAPITAL	Japanese	2.1	83.33	-2.80	☆	6.92	21.72	☆	0.0		426-4685	212-407-4700	5.00	2.19	None	Paul Kirkby	'94
GAM NORTH AMERICA	Capital Appreciation	3.3	104.65	6.97	25.38	9.52	☆	☆	0.4	18.2	426-4685	212-407-4700	5.00	2.54	None	Fayez Sarofim & Co.	'90
GAM PACIFIC BASIN	Pacific Region	33.3	168.31	6.12	-3.93	16.36	10.36	☆	0.0	N/A	426-4685	212-407-4700	5.00	1.78	None	Michael Bunker	'87
GATEWAY CINCINNATI FUND	Growth	4.5	11.65	9.70	☆	☆	☆	☆	0.0	16.6	354-6339	513-248-2700	None	None	None	J. Patrick Rogers	'94
GATEWAY INDEX PLUS FUND	Growth Income	172.3	16.29	1.87	13.48	7.18	9.16	☆	1.6	18.3	354-6339	513-248-2700	None	1.21	None	Thayer/Rogers	'77/'95
GATEWAY MID CAP INDEX	Midcap	5.1	11.08	7.36	18.99	☆	10.10	☆	0.5	16.6	354-6339	513-248-2700	None	1.50	None	Thayer/Rogers	'92/'95
GATEWAY SM CAP INDEX	Small Company Growth	9.5	10.82	7.88	14.72	☆	☆	☆	0.5	16.6	354-6339	513-248-2700	None	2.00	None	Thayer/Rogers	'93/'95
GE FXD INC; A	Fixed Income	4.1	11.90	5.81	11.36	☆	☆	☆	6.1		242-0134	203-326-4040	4.25	1.10	None	Robert A. MacDougall	'93
GE FXD INC; B	Fixed Income	0.2	11.90	5.77	10.91	☆	☆	☆	5.6		242-0134	203-326-4040	None	1.58	3.00	Robert A. MacDougall	'93
GE FXD INC; C	Fixed Income	18.6	11.91	5.96	11.73	☆	☆	☆	6.3		242-0134	203-326-4040	None	0.79	None	Robert A. MacDougall	'93
GE FXD INC; D	Fixed Income	1.1	11.91	6.03	12.02	☆	☆	☆	6.5		242-0134	203-326-4040	None	0.58	None	Robert A. MacDougall	'93
GE GLBL EQTY; A	Global	2.2	19.72	8.17	9.35	☆	☆	☆	0.5		242-0134	203-326-4040	4.75	1.60	None	Ralph R. Layman	'93
GE GLBL EQTY; B	Global	0.3	19.70	8.00	8.74	☆	☆	☆	0.1		242-0134	203-326-4040	None	2.10	4.00	Ralph R. Layman	'93
GE GLBL EQTY; C	Global	22.7	19.83	8.18	9.62	☆	☆	☆	0.4		242-0134	203-326-4040	None	1.31	None	Ralph R. Layman	'93
GE GLBL EQTY; D	Global	9.0	19.88	8.28	9.92	☆	☆	☆	0.7		242-0134	203-326-4040	None	1.10	None	Ralph R. Layman	'94
GE INTL EQTY; A	International	3.6	15.40	6.35	5.59	☆	☆	☆	0.3		242-0134	203-326-4040	4.75	1.60	None	Ralph R. Layman	'94
GE INTL EQTY; B	International	0.1	15.32	6.17	4.96	☆	☆	☆	0.1		242-0134	203-326-4040	None	2.10	4.00	Ralph R. Layman	'94
GE INTL EQTY; C	International	0.9	15.39	6.36	5.74	☆	☆	☆	0.6		242-0134	203-326-4040	None	1.35	None	Ralph R. Layman	'94
GE INTL EQTY; D	International	24.5	15.43	6.41	5.98	☆	☆	☆	0.6		242-0134	203-326-4040	None	1.10	None	Ralph R. Layman	'94
GE SH-TM GOVT; A	Fixed Income	0.1	11.90	3.11	7.10	☆	☆	☆	5.5		242-0134	203-326-4040	2.50	0.95	None	Robert A. MacDougall	'94
GE SH-TM GOVT; B	Fixed Income	0.1	11.90	3.02	6.64	☆	☆	☆	5.2		242-0134	203-326-4040	None	1.30	3.00	Robert A. MacDougall	'94
GE SH-TM GOVT; C	Fixed Income	1.7	11.91	3.18	7.36	☆	☆	☆	5.8		242-0134	203-326-4040	None	0.70	None	Robert A. MacDougall	'94
GE SH-TM GOVT; D	Fixed Income	7.9	11.90	3.24	7.54	☆	☆	☆	6.0		242-0134	203-326-4040	None	0.45	None	Robert A. MacDougall	'94
GE STRAT INV; A	Balanced	7.0	17.53	7.28	17.54	☆	☆	☆	2.1	16.8	242-0134	203-326-4040	4.75	1.15	None	Carlson/MacDougall	'93/'93
GE STRAT INV; B	Balanced	0.4	17.39	7.15	16.99	☆	☆	☆	2.0	16.8	242-0134	203-326-4040	None	1.65	4.00	Carlson/MacDougall	'93/'93
GE STRAT INV; C	Balanced	16.0	17.55	7.34	17.86	☆	☆	☆	2.2	16.8	242-0134	203-326-4040	None	0.85	None	Carlson/MacDougall	'93/'93
GE STRAT INV; D	Balanced	15.3	17.57	7.46	18.15	☆	☆	☆	2.4	16.8	242-0134	203-326-4040	None	0.65	None	Carlson/MacDougall	'93/'93
GE US EQUITY; A	Growth Income	10.2	18.88	9.45	22.34	☆	☆	☆	0.0	16.4	242-0134	203-326-4040	4.75	1.00	None	Eugene Bolton	'93
GE US EQUITY; B	Growth Income	0.5	18.37	9.28	21.60	☆	☆	☆	1.5	16.4	242-0134	203-326-4040	None	1.50	4.00	Eugene Bolton	'93
GE US EQUITY; C	Growth Income	21.5	18.59	9.55	22.59	☆	☆	☆	1.5	16.4	242-0134	203-326-4040	None	0.62	None	Eugene Bolton	'93
GE US EQUITY; D	Growth Income	111.7	18.58	9.62	22.86	☆	☆	☆	1.9	16.4	242-0134	203-326-4040	None	0.50	None	Eugene Bolton	'93
GE S&S PRGRM LG-TM INTST	Fixed Income	3,012.6	11.28	6.26	12.35	7.44	9.58	10.13	7.0	16.4	242-0134	203-326-4040	None	0.11	None	Robert A. MacDougall	'87
GE S&S PRGRM MUTUAL FUND	Growth Income	1,997.2	40.43	9.69	23.66	12.80	11.73	13.31	2.4	16.1	242-0134	203-326-4040	None	0.13	None	Eugene Bolton	'90
GENERAL SECURITIES	Capital Appreciation	30.3	14.60	10.66	24.97	11.38	12.90	13.20	1.1	15.7	577-9217	612-927-6799	None	1.50	None	Jack Robinson	'51
GIBRALTAR EQUITY GROWTH	Growth Income	0.7	15.23	9.33	26.56	4.96	5.17	8.49	0.0	N/A	None	215-525-5102	None	5.03	None	Norman McAvoy	'90
GIBRALTAR US GOVT	Fixed Income	1.5	9.70	1.93	4.10	☆	2.43	☆	5.5	N/A	None	215-525-5102	4.50	3.37	None	Tim Hutchinson	'95
GINTEL ERISA	Growth Income	27.4	26.17	4.72	9.36	1.75	☆	8.83	1.7	15.0	243-5808	203-622-6400	None	2.60	None	Gintel/Godman	'82/'92
GINTEL FUND	Growth	92.7	14.60	10.11	13.25	4.03	5.30	9.37	0.3	15.0	243-5808	703-528-6500	None	2.40	None	Gintel/Godman	'81/'92
GIT EQUITY EQUITY INCOME	Equity Income	3.5	16.28	6.24	11.98	7.12	7.32	9.36	2.3	15.6	336-3063	703-528-6500	None	2.17	None	Charles Tennes	'93
GIT EQUITY SELECT GROWTH	Growth	4.8	18.56	11.07	21.91	7.58	6.76	11.08	0.8	14.6	336-3063	703-528-6500	None	2.02	None	Charles Tennes	'93
GIT EQUITY SPEC GROWTH	Small Company Growth	31.9	19.10	5.58	10.06	10.55	6.65	10.93	0.8	18.3	336-3063	703-528-6500	None	1.45	None	Richard Carney	'83
GIT EQUITY WORLDWIDE GRO	Emerging Markets	3.7	9.39	10.47	-11.75	☆	☆	☆	0.1		336-3063	703-528-6500	None	1.81	None	Charles Tennes	'93
GIT INCOME GOVERNMENT	Fixed Income	7.6	9.90	4.98	8.95	6.68	7.83	8.35	4.4		336-3063	703-528-6500	None	1.54	None	John Edwards	'89
GIT INCOME MAXIMUM INC	Fixed Income	7.0	7.11	4.64	10.02	8.14	9.22	7.57	8.6		336-3063	703-528-6500	None	1.54	None	John Edwards	'88
GLENMEDE EQUITY FUND	Growth	69.9	14.57	10.96	23.71	13.78	11.94	☆	2.1	14.3	336-3063	None	None	0.16	None	John Church	'93
GLENMEDE INSTL INTERNATL	International	17.9	12.49	5.46	4.81	☆	☆	☆	1.3		441-7379	None	None	1.00	None	Andrew B. Williams	'92
GLENMEDE INTERNATIONAL	International	309.7	13.06	5.70	6.76	11.73	9.52	☆	2.0		441-7379	None	None	0.16	None	Andrew B. Williams	'88

PERFORMANCE OF MUTUAL FUNDS (continued)

FUND NAME	OBJECTIVE	ASSETS ($ MIL) 5/31/95	NAV ($/SHR) 6/30/95	QTR	1YR	3YRS	5YRS	10YRS	DIV YLD %	P/E RATIO	800	In-State	Load	Exp. Ratio	Redemption	MANAGER	SINCE
GLENMEDE INTL FIXED INC	World Income	29.6	11.41	4.48	18.97	☆	☆	☆	10.0		441-7379	None	None	0.24	None	Sheryl Durham	'93
GLENMEDE INTMDT GOVT	Fixed Income	339.0	10.28	4.54	9.84	6.00	8.46	☆	6.5		441-7379	None	None	0.14	None	Sheryl Durham	'93
GLENMEDE MODEL EQUITY	Growth	18.3	11.85	9.87	16.18	☆	☆	☆	2.1	13.7	441-7379	None	None	0.24	None	Andrew B. Williams	'93
GLENMEDE SMALL CAP EQU	Small Company Growth	139.4	15.51	6.16	18.78	19.64	☆	☆	1.4	13.2	441-7379	None	None	0.14	None	Williams/Mancuso	'92/'93
GLOBAL UTILITY FUND; A	Utility	127.3	13.98	7.38	11.05	9.91	12.49	☆	3.3	12.0	225-1852	None	5.00	1.25	None	William Hicks	'90
GLOBAL UTILITY FUND; B	Utility	230.8	13.98	7.19	10.23	9.06	☆	☆	2.6	12.0	225-1852	None	None	2.02	5.00	William Hicks	'91
GLOBAL UTILITY FUND; C	Utility	0.5	13.98	7.19	☆	☆	☆	☆		12.0	None	None	None	0.79	0.75	William Hicks	'94
GMO CORE II SECOND	Small Company Growth	136.2	14.79	6.94	22.97	16.83	☆	☆	1.4	17.5	None	617-330-7500	None		None	Jeremy Grantham	'91
GMO CURRENCY HGD INTL BD	World Income	249.9	11.00	8.70	☆	☆	☆	☆	0.0		None	617-330-7500	None		None	Bill Nemerever	'94
GMO DOMESTIC BOND	Fixed Income	255.4	10.71	6.35	☆	☆	☆	☆	0.0		None	617-330-7500	None		None	Bill Nemerever	'94
GMO EMERG COUNTRY DEBT	World Income	455.0	10.59	26.52	13.91	☆	☆	☆	3.7		None	617-330-7500	None		None	Bill Nemerever	'94
GMO EMERGING MKTS	Emerging Markets	489.9	10.62	11.67	-1.08	☆	☆	☆	0.7		None	617-330-7500	None		0.40	Arjun Divecha	'93
GMO GROWTH ALLOCATION	Growth	321.1	4.99	9.07	29.73	12.61	11.54	☆	1.2	17.8	None	617-330-7500	None	0.48	None	Jeremy Grantham	'88
GMO INTL BOND	World Income	184.8	11.15	8.36	23.70	11.66	☆	☆	6.6		None	617-330-7500	None		None	Bill Nemerever	'93
GMO INTL CORE	International	2,933.3	24.03	4.39	1.33	☆	8.63	☆	1.3		None	617-330-7500	None	0.71	None	Forrest Berkley	'87
GMO INTL SMALL CO	Intl Small Company	197.9	12.27	2.68	-7.24	12.64	☆	☆	1.6		None	617-330-7500	None	0.75	None	Forrest Berkley	'91
GOLDEN RNBOW A JAMES ADV	Growth Income	195.2	18.27	7.20	16.55	10.67	☆	☆	3.7	14.2	227-4648	513-461-0332	None	0.96	0.75	Team Managed	N/A
GOLDMAN EQ ASIA GR	Pacific Region	157.6	15.33	8.65	☆	☆	☆	☆	0.0	N/A	526-7384	212-902-0800	5.50	1.90	None	Warwik Negus	'94
GOLDMAN EQ BALANCE	Balanced	19.9	16.14	8.05	☆	☆	☆	☆	0.0	N/A	526-7384	212-902-0800	5.50	1.38	None	Team Managed	N/A
GOLDMAN EQ CAP GRO	Growth	987.9	16.43	9.68	18.72	15.54	14.85	☆	0.1	N/A	526-7384	212-902-0800	5.50	1.38	None	Team Managed	N/A
GOLDMAN EQ G&I	Growth Income	273.3	18.39	7.42	21.27	☆	☆	☆	1.6	N/A	526-7384	212-902-0800	5.50	1.25	None	Team Managed	N/A
GOLDMAN EQ INTL	International	278.0	16.45	5.65	6.29	☆	☆	☆	0.0		526-7384	212-902-0800	5.50	1.73	None	Team Managed	N/A
GOLDMAN EQ SEL EQU	Growth	110.2	17.35	11.36	24.48	13.99	☆	☆	1.1	N/A	526-7384	212-902-0800	5.50	1.38	None	Team Managed	N/A
GOLDMAN EQ SM CAP	Small Company Growth	319.4	16.88	-1.86	-8.14	4.05	☆	☆	0.0	N/A	526-7384	212-902-0800	5.50	1.53	None	Team Managed	N/A
GOLDMAN ADJ AGY; INSTL	Fixed Income	714.5	9.77	1.70	5.50	☆	☆	☆	5.8		526-7384	212-902-0800	None	0.46	None	Team Managed	N/A
GOLDMAN CORE; INSTL	Fixed Income	42.4	9.88	5.98	12.62	☆	☆	☆	6.6		526-7384	212-902-0800	None	0.45	None	Team Managed	N/A
GOLDMAN GLBL INC	World Income	305.5	14.16	3.91	10.35	6.67	☆	☆	6.4		526-7384	212-902-0800	4.50	1.28	None	Team Managed	N/A
GOLDMAN GOVT INC	Fixed Income	19.5	14.34	5.66	11.82	☆	☆	☆	6.6		526-7384	212-902-0800	4.50	0.11	None	Gary Madich	'87
GOVERNMENT INCOME SEC	Fixed Income	2,504.9	8.74	4.33	9.79	4.89	7.35	☆	7.0		245-4770	412-288-1900	1.00	0.97	1.00	Tom Leavell	'91
GOVERNMENT STREET BOND	Fixed Income	29.4	21.06	5.24	10.37	6.46	☆	☆	6.5		443-4249	513-629-2000	None	0.88	None	Tom Leavell	'91
GOVERNMENT STREET EQUITY	Growth	33.6	25.46	7.18	18.25	7.82	☆	☆	1.6	20.9	443-4249	513-629-2000	None	1.00	None	Tom Leavell	'91
GOVETT DEV MKTS BOND; A	World Income	1.0	N/A	N/A	N/A	☆	☆	☆	0.0		634-6838	415-274-2700	4.95	2.35	None	Alan Doyle	'94
GOVETT DEV MKTS BOND; B	World Income	0.1	N/A	N/A	☆	☆	☆	☆	0.0		634-6838	415-274-2700	None	None	4.00	Alan Doyle	'95
GOVETT DEV MKTS BOND; C	World Income	0.1	N/A	N/A	☆	☆	☆	☆	0.0		634-6838	415-274-2700	None	None	1.00	Alan Doyle	'95
GOVETT EMERGING MKTS; A	Emerging Markets	78.4	12.61	5.88	-4.93	13.13	☆	☆	0.0		634-6838	415-274-2700	4.95	2.50	None	Rachael Maunder	'92
GOVETT EMERGING MKTS; B	Emerging Markets	0.1	12.66	6.12	☆	☆	☆	☆	0.0		634-6838	415-274-2700	None	None	4.00	Rachael Maunder	'95
GOVETT EMERGING MKTS; C	Emerging Markets	0.1	12.66	6.12	☆	☆	☆	☆	0.0		634-6838	415-274-2700	None	None	1.00	Rachael Maunder	'95
GOVETT GLBL INCOME; A	World Income	46.3	8.90	4.55	9.20	6.96	☆	☆	7.4		634-6838	415-274-2700	4.95	1.75	None	Alan Doyle	'95
GOVETT GLBL INCOME; B	World Income	0.1	8.90	4.26	☆	☆	☆	☆	0.0		634-6838	415-274-2700	None	None	4.00	Alan Doyle	'94
GOVETT GLBL INCOME; C	World Income	0.1	8.90	4.26	☆	☆	☆	☆	0.0		634-6838	415-274-2700	None	None	1.00	Alan Doyle	'95
GOVETT INTL EQUITY; A	International	31.4	10.55	4.04	-0.49	11.29	☆	☆	0.0		634-6838	415-274-2700	4.95	2.50	None	Gareth Watts	'92
GOVETT INTL EQUITY; B	International	0.1	10.59	4.23	☆	☆	☆	☆	0.0		634-6838	415-274-2700	None	None	4.00	Gareth Watts	'95
GOVETT INTL EQUITY; C	International	0.1	10.59	4.23	☆	☆	☆	☆	0.0		634-6838	415-274-2700	None	None	1.00	Gareth Watts	'95
GOVETT LATIN AMERICA; A	Latin American	5.6	6.33	14.05	-20.02	☆	☆	☆	0.0		634-6838	415-274-2700	4.95	2.50	None	Caroline Lane	'94
GOVETT LATIN AMERICA; B	Latin American	0.1	6.34	14.03	☆	☆	☆	☆	0.0		634-6838	415-274-2700	None	None	4.00	Caroline Lane	'95

Fund	Objective	Net Assets ($Mil)	NAV	YTD %	1-Yr %	3-Yr %	5-Yr %	10-Yr %	Yield %	Turn %	Phone 1	Phone 2	Load	Exp %	Redemp	Manager	Year
GOVETT LATIN AMERICA; C	Latin American	0.1	6.34	14.03	☆	☆	☆	☆	0.0		415-274-2700	634-6838	None	None	1.00	Caroline Lane	'95
GOVETT PACIFIC STRAT; A	Pacific Region	13.5	8.41	3.70	-6.24	☆	☆	☆	0.0		415-274-2700	634-6838	4.95	2.50	None	Peter Robson	'94
GOVETT PACIFIC STRAT; B	Pacific Region	0.1	8.45	3.94	☆	☆	☆	☆	0.0		415-274-2700	634-6838	None	None	4.00	Peter Robson	'95
GOVETT PACIFIC STRAT; C	Pacific Region	0.1	8.45	3.94	☆	☆	☆	☆	0.0		415-274-2700	634-6838	None	None	1.00	Peter Robson	'95
GOVETT SMALLER CO; A	Small Company Growth	213.9	25.04	13.56	70.12	☆	☆	☆	0.0	31.9	415-274-2700	634-6838	4.95	1.95	None	Garett Van Wagoner	'93
GOVETT SMALLER CO; B	Small Company Growth	0.1	25.10	13.78	☆	☆	☆	☆	0.0	N/A	415-274-2700	634-6838	None	None	4.00	Garett Van Wagoner	'95
GOVETT SMALLER CO; C	Small Company Growth	0.1	25.10	13.78	☆	☆	☆	☆	0.0	N/A	415-274-2700	634-6838	None	None	1.00	Garett Van Wagoner	'95
GRADISON GR TR ESTAB VAL	Growth	300.0	24.66	8.39	21.28	17.17	12.17	13.49	1.8	N/A	513-579-5700	869-5999	None	1.22	None	William Leugers	'83
GRADISON GR TR GRO & INC	Growth Income	3.7	15.91	4.74	☆	☆	☆	☆	0.0	N/A	513-579-5700	869-5999	None	None	None	Julian Ball	'95
GRADISON GR TR OPPTY VAL	Small Company Growth	86.2	19.07	8.76	☆	☆	☆	☆	0.9	N/A	513-579-5700	869-5999	None	1.38	None	William Leugers	'83
GRADISON-MCDONALD GOVT	Fixed Income	186.6	12.91	5.33	12.06	8.28	6.37	☆	6.6		513-579-5700	869-5999	2.00	0.90	None	Michael Link	'87
PETER GRANDICH CONTRN	Growth	2.3	9.08	-2.89	☆	☆	☆	☆	0.0	N/A	708-564-5764	957-4386	3.50	None	None	Peter Grandich	'94
GREATER CINCINNATI; INV	Growth	0.5	10.80	5.46	☆	☆	☆	☆	0.0	N/A	919-972-9922	525-3863	None	None	None	John Ramsey	'95
GREEN CENTURY BALANCED	Balanced	3.2	11.03	7.40	15.00	4.67	☆	☆	0.9	N/A	212-986-2600	934-7336	None	2.50	None	Team Managed	N/A
GREENFIELD FUND	Flexible	0.7	N/A	N/A	N/A	N/A	N/A	N/A	0.0	N/A	None	None	None	1.50	1.00	R.F. Nichols Jr.	'81
GREENSPRING FUND	Growth Income	65.7	15.09	6.87	13.42	14.01	10.97	11.76	3.3	N/A	410-823-5353	366-3863	None	1.27	None	C. Carlson	'87
GRIFFIN BOND; A	Fixed Income	9.6	8.94	6.12	11.63	☆	☆	☆	6.5		None	676-4450	4.50	0.09	None	Matthew Fountaine	'95
GRIFFIN BOND; B	Fixed Income	0.1	8.93	5.85	☆	☆	☆	☆	0.0	N/A	None	676-4450	None	None	5.00	Matthew Fountaine	'95
GRIFFIN GRO & INC; A	Growth Income	27.8	13.15	9.52	25.59	☆	☆	☆	2.2	17.6	None	676-4450	4.50	0.25	None	Quinn Stills	'95
GRIFFIN GRO & INC; B	Growth Income	0.7	13.14	9.37	☆	☆	☆	☆	0.0	N/A	None	676-4450	None	None	5.00	Quinn Stills	'95
GRIFFIN US GOVT INC; A	Fixed Income	26.9	9.21	5.18	☆	☆	☆	☆	6.6		None	676-4450	4.50	0.09	None	Scott King	'93
GRIFFIN US GOVT INC; B	Fixed Income	0.3	9.21	5.03	☆	☆	☆	☆	0.0	N/A	None	676-4450	None	None	5.00	Scott King	'94
GROWTH FD OF WASHINGTON	Growth	38.8	16.06	8.39	12.81	13.25	9.32	☆	1.1	13.5	714-671-7000	348-4782	4.75	1.50	None	Prabha S. Carpenter	'86
GROWTH FUND OF AMERICA	Growth	6,443.5	31.32	12.58	18.18	16.38	15.32	13.38	0.5	15.7	212-902-0800	421-4120	5.75	0.78	None	Multiple Managers	N/A
GS SH-TM GOVT AGCY; INSTL	Fixed Income	107.1	9.82	3.27	7.84	5.04	6.65	☆	6.3		None	526-7384	None	0.45	None	Team Managed	N/A
GT GLOBAL AMERICA; A	Growth	336.3	21.93	13.04	32.54	27.85	14.37	☆	0.1	N/A	415-392-6181	824-1580	4.75	1.58	None	Team Managed	N/A
GT GLOBAL AMERICA; B	Growth	232.8	21.62	12.84	31.74	☆	☆	☆	0.0	N/A	415-392-6181	824-1580	None	2.20	5.00	Team Managed	N/A
GT GLOBAL CNSMR PROD; A	Specialty	1.7	12.61	6.59	☆	☆	☆	☆	0.0	N/A	415-392-6181	824-1580	4.75		None	Derek Webb	'95
GT GLOBAL CNSMR PROD; B	Specialty	0.6	12.59	6.51	☆	☆	☆	☆	0.0	N/A	415-392-6181	824-1580	None	2.06	5.00	Derek Webb	N/A
GT GLOBAL EMERG MKTS; A	Emerging Markets	307.4	14.49	6.54	-0.09	11.39	☆	☆	0.0		415-392-6181	824-1580	4.75	2.56	None	Team Managed	N/A
GT GLOBAL EMERG MKTS; B	Emerging Markets	254.1	14.34	6.38	☆	☆	☆	☆	0.0		415-392-6181	824-1580	None	1.73	5.00	Team Managed	N/A
GT GLOBAL EUROPE; A	European Region	576.6	10.42	8.65	-0.63	4.41	2.96	☆	0.5		415-392-6181	824-1580	4.75	2.38	None	Team Managed	N/A
GT GLOBAL EUROPE; B	European Region	77.5	10.33	8.51	3.83	☆	☆	☆	0.0		415-392-6181	824-1580	None	None	5.00	Team Managed	N/A
GT GLOBAL FINL SVCS; A	Financial Services	5.0	11.28	11.79	-1.31	☆	☆	☆	0.0	11.9	415-392-6181	824-1580	4.75	None	None	Team Managed	N/A
GT GLOBAL FINL SVCS; B	Financial Services	3.4	11.22	11.64	-1.84	☆	☆	☆	0.0	11.9	415-392-6181	824-1580	None	1.33	5.00	Team Managed	N/A
GT GLOBAL GOVT INC; A	World Income	448.4	8.89	4.22	8.72	8.18	6.59	☆	6.7		415-392-6181	824-1580	4.75	1.98	None	Team Managed	N/A
GT GLOBAL GOVT INC; B	World Income	260.2	8.89	4.05	7.97	☆	☆	☆	6.0		415-392-6181	824-1580	None	1.67	5.00	Team Managed	N/A
GT GLOBAL GRO & INC; A	Global	300.3	6.15	4.50	8.69	7.51	☆	☆	3.7		415-392-6181	824-1580	4.75	2.32	None	Team Managed	N/A
GT GLOBAL GRO & INC; B	Global	362.3	6.16	4.33	6.80	☆	☆	☆	3.1		415-392-6181	824-1580	None	1.57	5.00	Team Managed	N/A
GT GLOBAL HIGH INC; A	World Income	145.5	11.54	18.61	7.29	☆	☆	☆	9.0		415-392-6181	824-1580	4.75	2.22	None	Team Managed	N/A
GT GLOBAL HIGH INC; B	World Income	210.1	11.53	18.31	☆	☆	☆	☆	8.3		415-392-6181	824-1580	None	2.00	5.00	Team Managed	N/A
GT GLOBAL HLTH CARE; A	Health/Biotechnology	377.1	18.96	-1.30	19.24	8.80	5.45	☆	0.0		415-392-6181	824-1580	4.75	2.50	None	Team Managed	N/A
GT GLOBAL HLTH CARE; B	Health/Biotechnology	52.8	18.76	-1.42	18.67	☆	☆	☆	0.0		415-392-6181	824-1580	None	None	5.00	Team Managed	N/A
GT GLOBAL INFRA; A	Global	40.4	12.35	12.68	7.58	☆	☆	☆	0.0	18.0	415-392-6181	824-1580	4.75	None	None	Team Managed	N/A
GT GLOBAL INFRA; B	Global	50.2	12.29	12.55	7.06	☆	☆	☆	0.0	18.0	415-392-6181	824-1580	None	1.70	5.00	Team Managed	N/A
GT GLOBAL INTL GROW; A	International	343.0	8.59	4.00	-8.99	1.60	0.90	☆	0.0		415-392-6181	824-1580	4.75	2.35	None	Team Managed	N/A
GT GLOBAL INTL GROW; B	International	66.7	8.46	3.68	-9.58	☆	☆	☆	0.0		415-392-6181	824-1580	None	1.91	5.00	Team Managed	N/A
GT GLOBAL JAPAN GROW; A	Japanese	72.7	10.75	-2.18	-20.39	6.55	-6.87	☆	0.0		415-392-6181	824-1580	4.75	2.56	None	Team Managed	N/A
GT GLOBAL JAPAN GROW; B	Japanese	21.1	10.60	-2.39	-20.91	☆	☆	☆	0.0		415-392-6181	824-1580	None	2.04	5.00	Team Managed	N/A
GT GLOBAL LATIN AMER; A	Latin American	222.4	16.35	16.95	-15.00	2.73	☆	☆	0.0		415-392-6181	824-1580	4.75		None	Team Managed	N/A

PERFORMANCE OF MUTUAL FUNDS (continued)

FUND NAME	OBJECTIVE	ASSETS ($ MIL) 5/31/95	NAV ($/SHR) 6/30/95	RETURN THROUGH 6/30 QTR	1YR	3YRS (Ann.)	5YRS (Ann.)	10YRS (Ann.)	DIV YLD %	P/E RATIO	PHONE 800	In-State	Load	Redemption	Exp. Ratio	MANAGER	SINCE
GT GLOBAL LATIN AMER; B	Latin American	155.9	16.20	16.88	-15.37	☆	☆	☆	0.0	☐	824-1580	415-392-6181	None	5.00	2.54	Team Managed	N/A
GT GLOBAL NAT RES; A	Natural Resources	15.0	11.52	6.67	2.84	☆	☆	☆	0.3	4.3	824-1580	415-392-6181	4.75	None	None	Team Managed	N/A
GT GLOBAL NAT RES; B	Natural Resources	15.3	11.46	6.51	2.25	☆	☆	☆	0.2	4.3	824-1580	415-392-6181	None	5.00	None	Team Managed	N/A
GT GLOBAL PACIFIC GR; A	Pacific Region	448.0	12.69	8.37	2.07	7.00	4.14	☆	0.1	☐	824-1580	415-392-6181	4.75	None	1.81	Team Managed	N/A
GT GLOBAL PACIFIC GR; B	Pacific Region	128.2	12.49	8.14	1.25	☆	☆	16.30	0.0	☐	824-1580	415-392-6181	None	5.00	2.46	Team Managed	N/A
GT GLOBAL STRAT INC; A	World Income	216.3	10.25	9.35	3.43	7.80	9.48	☆	8.0	☐	824-1580	415-392-6181	4.75	None	1.50	Team Managed	N/A
GT GLOBAL STRAT INC; B	World Income	384.1	10.26	9.28	2.86	☆	☆	☆	7.3	☐	824-1580	415-392-6181	None	5.00	2.15	Team Managed	N/A
GT GLOBAL TELECOMM; A	Global	1,369.0	16.13	11.63	5.61	16.03	☆	☆	0.0	☐	824-1580	415-392-6181	4.75	None	1.80	Team Managed	N/A
GT GLOBAL TELECOMM; B	Global	1,068.2	15.95	11.54	5.13	☆	☆	☆	0.0	☐	824-1580	415-392-6181	None	5.00	2.30	Team Managed	N/A
GT GLOBAL WORLDWIDE; A	Global	151.7	15.80	9.27	0.37	6.78	5.08	☆	0.0	☐	824-1580	415-392-6181	4.75	None	1.81	Team Managed	N/A
GT GLOBAL WORLDWIDE; B	Global	49.8	15.55	9.05	-0.38	☆	☆	☆	0.0	☐	824-1580	415-392-6181	None	5.00	2.46	Team Managed	N/A
GUARDIAN ASSET ALLOC	Flexible	59.9	11.70	6.17	17.73	☆	☆	☆	2.4	☐	824-1580	415-392-6181	4.50	None	1.30	Frank J. Jones	'93
GUARDIAN BAIL GIFF INTL	International	42.3	13.09	2.83	-0.17	☆	☆	☆	0.1	15.5	221-3253	None	4.50	None	1.91	R. Robin Menzies	'93
GUARDIAN INV QUAL BOND	Fixed Income	52.0	9.73	5.20	10.44	☆	☆	☆	5.6	☐	221-3253	None	4.50	None	1.46	Michelle Babakian	'93
GUARDIAN PARK AVENUE FD	Growth	782.1	32.41	10.50	23.77	19.38	15.50	15.34	1.0	15.7	221-3253	None	4.50	None	0.84	Charles E. Albers	'72
GUINNESS FLIGHT CHINA	Pacific Region	9.6	12.40	8.27	0.40	☆	☆	☆	0.9	☐	915-6565	None	None	None	2.00	Lynda Johnstone	'94
GUINNESS FLIGHT GL GOVT	World Income	0.9	12.71	5.39	6.38	☆	☆	☆	4.4	☐	915-6565	None	None	None	1.75	Philip Saunders	'94
J HANCOCK AV&T; A	Science & Technology	65.5	10.06	20.62	34.89	18.25	8.81	10.85	0.0	N/A	225-5291	617-375-1500	5.00	None	1.60	Barry Gordon	'73
J HANCOCK AV&T; B	Science & Technology	0.5	9.89	20.32	33.43	☆	☆	☆	0.0	N/A	225-5291	617-375-1500	None	5.00	2.59	Barry Gordon	'94
J HANCOCK BD ADJ GVT; A	Fixed Income	11.7	9.88	2.49	6.45	4.06	☆	☆	5.4	☐	225-5291	617-375-1500	3.00	None	0.75	Team Managed	N/A
J HANCOCK BD ADJ GVT; B	Fixed Income	9.5	9.88	2.32	5.77	☆	☆	☆	4.8	☐	225-5291	617-375-1500	None	5.00	1.40	Team Managed	N/A
J HANCOCK BD GVT SEC; A	Fixed Income	498.0	7.87	6.25	11.68	7.16	8.81	7.90	7.6	☐	225-5291	617-375-1500	4.50	None	1.16	Team Managed	N/A
J HANCOCK BD GVT SEC; B	Fixed Income	2.0	7.86	5.92	☆	☆	☆	☆	7.0	☐	225-5291	617-375-1500	None	5.00	2.00	Team Managed	N/A
J HANCOCK BD IN QUAL; A	Fixed Income	84.4	8.52	6.34	10.24	8.49	8.49	8.58	7.7	☐	225-5291	617-375-1500	4.50	None	1.25	James Ho	'95
J HANCOCK BD IN QUAL; B	Fixed Income	7.7	8.52	6.12	9.33	☆	☆	☆	6.9	☐	225-5291	617-375-1500	None	5.00	2.00	James Ho	'95
J HANCOCK BD INT GVT; A	Fixed Income	7.7	9.53	4.52	8.46	4.62	6.00	☆	6.6	☐	225-5291	617-375-1500	4.50	None	1.30	Team Managed	N/A
J HANCOCK BD INT GVT; B	Fixed Income	0.4	9.53	4.31	☆	☆	☆	☆	6.6	☐	225-5291	617-375-1500	None	5.00	1.41	Team Managed	N/A
J HANCOCK BD US GOVT; A	Fixed Income	16.5	7.91	4.73	10.11	7.82	7.74	☆	7.0	☐	225-5291	617-375-1500	4.50	None	1.46	Team Managed	N/A
J HANCOCK BD US GOVT; B	Fixed Income	0.3	7.91	4.54	☆	☆	☆	☆	7.0	N/A	225-5291	617-375-1500	None	5.00	2.00	Team Managed	N/A
J HANCOCK CAP GROW; A	Growth	68.8	12.34	8.34	14.58	16.50	15.76	13.56	0.0	N/A	225-5291	617-375-1500	5.00	None	1.30	Ben A. Hock, Jr.	'93
J HANCOCK CAP GROW; B	Growth	13.1	12.14	8.10	13.68	☆	☆	☆	0.0	N/A	225-5291	617-375-1500	None	5.00	2.01	Ben A. Hock, Jr.	'93
J HANCOCK DISCOVERY; A	Small Company Growth	3.7	11.28	20.26	36.02	☆	☆	☆	0.0	N/A	225-5291	617-375-1500	5.00	None	2.01	Bernice Behar	'94
J HANCOCK DISCOVERY; B	Small Company Growth	24.6	10.93	20.11	35.24	☆	☆	☆	0.0	N/A	225-5291	617-375-1500	None	5.00	2.62	Bernice Behar	'94
J HANCOCK DIVERSIFIED	Growth Income	101.4	14.32	9.13	21.68	☆	☆	☆	2.5	26.6	225-5291	617-375-1500	5.00	None	0.70	Paul McManus	'91
J HANCOCK GL RETAIL; A	Global	0.6	10.27	10.79	☆	☆	☆	☆	0.0	N/A	225-5291	617-375-1500	5.00	None	1.46	Bernice Behar	'83
J HANCOCK GL TECH; A	Science & Technology	64.9	24.72	24.72	63.91	32.87	17.12	13.33	0.0	N/A	225-5291	617-375-1500	5.00	None	2.16	Barry Gordon	'94
J HANCOCK GL TECH; B	Science & Technology	15.9	24.40	24.49	62.69	☆	☆	☆	0.0	N/A	225-5291	617-375-1500	None	5.00	2.90	Barry Gordon	'94
J HANCOCK GLB INC; A	World Income	10.7	9.17	2.61	11.58	3.61	☆	☆	6.7	N/A	225-5291	617-375-1500	5.00	None	1.59	Goodchild/Daley	'94/'94
J HANCOCK GLB INC; B	World Income	100.3	9.17	2.44	11.01	3.07	☆	☆	6.1	N/A	225-5291	617-375-1500	None	5.00	2.17	Goodchild/Daley	'94/'94
J HANCOCK GLBL RX; A	Health/Biotechnology	20.8	19.02	-3.21	29.21	14.71	6.46	☆	0.0	26.6	225-5291	617-375-1500	5.00	None	2.55	Benjamin Williams	'92
J HANCOCK GLBL RX; B	Health/Biotechnology	4.8	18.82	-3.44	28.11	☆	☆	☆	0.0	N/A	225-5291	617-375-1500	None	5.00	3.34	Benjamin Williams	'94
J HANCOCK GLD&GOV; A	Gold	13.5	14.13	5.10	0.11	2.44	3.98	6.56	3.9	N/A	225-5291	617-375-1500	5.00	None	1.53	Anne McDonley	'94
J HANCOCK GLD&GOV; B	Gold	29.9	14.12	4.91	-0.56	1.88	☆	☆	3.0	N/A	225-5291	617-375-1500	None	5.00	2.18	Anne McDonley	'93
J HANCOCK GLOBAL; A	Global	92.5	12.32	4.14	6.42	10.19	3.98	☆	0.0	☐	225-5291	617-375-1500	5.00	None	1.98	Beckwith/Wills	'93/'94
J HANCOCK GLOBAL; B	Global	28.8	12.05	3.97	5.68	9.58	5.51	☆	0.0	☐	225-5291	617-375-1500	None	5.00	2.59	Beckwith/Wills	'93/'94

Fund	Objective	Net Assets ($Mil)	NAV	%Ret A	%Ret B	%Ret C	%Ret D	%Ret E	Yield %	Rating	Phone	Phone	Chg 1	Chg 2	Chg 3	Exp	Manager	Since
J HANCOCK GROWTH; A	Growth	156.0	18.69	8.92	27.89	13.75	9.96	12.69	0.0	N/A	225-5291	617-375-1500	5.00	5.00	None	1.65	Benjamin Williams	94
J HANCOCK GROWTH; B	Growth	5.0	18.53	8.62	26.88	☆	☆	☆	0.0	N/A	225-5291	617-375-1500	None	None	5.00	2.38	Benjamin Williams	94
J HANCOCK INTL; A	International	4.4	8.03	3.61	0.24	☆	☆	☆	0.3	□	225-5291	617-375-1500	5.00	None	5.00	1.50	Wills/Beckwith	94/94
J HANCOCK INTL; B	International	3.5	7.97	3.24	-0.59	☆	☆	☆		□	225-5291	617-375-1500	5.00	None	5.00	2.22	Wills/Beckwith	94/94
J HANCOCK INV GR&INC; A	Growth Income	126.4	12.73	9.99	20.50	9.14	9.74	10.75	1.6	16.5	225-5291	617-375-1500	5.00	5.00	None	1.31	Brian Grove	94
J HANCOCK INV GR&INC; B	Growth Income	115.1	12.77	9.86	19.66	8.27	☆	☆	0.9	16.5	225-5291	617-375-1500	None	None	5.00	2.06	Brian Grove	94
J HANCOCK LTD GOVT; A	Fixed Income	207.7	8.67	3.47	6.88	5.35	6.98	7.76	5.2	□	225-5291	617-375-1500	3.00	None	5.00	1.41	Anne McDonley	94
J HANCOCK LTD GOVT; B	Fixed Income	8.3	8.67	3.46	6.22	☆	☆	☆	4.6	N/A	225-5291	617-375-1500	None	None	3.00	2.12	Anne McDonley	94
J HANCOCK PAC BSN; A	Pacific Region	40.8	13.83	2.52	-3.72	16.75	☆	9.97	0.0	N/A	225-5291	617-375-1500	5.00	None	5.00	2.43	Li/Wills/Behar	94/94/94
J HANCOCK PAC BSN; B	Pacific Region	13.7	13.70	2.32	-4.48	☆	☆	☆	0.0	N/A	225-5291	617-375-1500	None	None	5.00	3.00	Li/Wills/Behar	94/94/94
J HANCOCK REG BNK; A	Financial Services	264.0	24.15	10.60	13.92	22.07	24.23	☆	2.3	N/A	225-5291	617-375-1500	5.00	5.00	None	1.34	Jim Schmidt	92
J HANCOCK REG BNK; B	Financial Services	676.3	24.06	10.39	13.12	21.31	☆	☆	1.5	N/A	225-5291	617-375-1500	None	None	5.00	2.06	Jim Schmidt	85
J HANCOCK S-T STRAT; A	Fixed Income	16.7	8.43	5.17	8.64	4.72	☆	☆	9.1	□	225-5291	617-375-1500	3.00	None	5.00	1.26	Goodchild/Daley	94/94
J HANCOCK S-T STRAT; B	Fixed Income	89.5	8.42	4.98	7.86	3.92	☆	☆	8.4	□	225-5291	617-375-1500	None	None	3.00	1.99	Goodchild/Daley	94/94
J HANCOCK SOVER ACHV; A	Growth	23.4	12.56	4.74	15.28	10.07	☆	☆	1.2	N/A	225-5291	617-375-1500	5.00	5.00	None	1.53	John Snyder	92
J HANCOCK SOVER ACHV; B	Growth	94.2	12.51	4.61	14.48	☆	☆	☆	0.3	N/A	225-5291	617-375-1500	None	None	5.00	2.10	John Snyder	92/92
J HANCOCK SOVER BAL; A	Balanced	65.8	10.89	5.52	14.88	☆	☆	☆	5.4	□	225-5291	617-375-1500	5.00	5.00	None	1.23	Snyder/Evans	92/92
J HANCOCK SOVER BAL; B	Balanced	83.2	10.89	5.28	14.10	☆	☆	☆	4.7	N/A	225-5291	617-375-1500	None	None	5.00	1.87	Snyder/Evans	92/92
J HANCOCK SOVER BOND; A	Fixed Income	1,414.8	15.01	6.58	13.69	8.54	9.87	☆	7.5	□	225-5291	617-375-1500	4.50	None	5.00	1.26	James Ho	88
J HANCOCK SOVER BOND; B	Fixed Income	57.1	15.01	6.34	13.05	☆	☆	☆	6.9	□	225-5291	617-375-1500	None	None	5.00	1.78	James Ho	93
J HANCOCK SOVER GOVT; A	Fixed Income	321.3	9.94	6.73	11.75	6.40	8.06	☆	6.5	N/A	225-5291	617-375-1500	4.50	None	None	1.23	Barry Evans	95
J HANCOCK SOVER GOVT; B	Fixed Income	191.4	9.93	6.59	11.22	6.01	☆	☆	6.0	N/A	225-5291	617-375-1500	None	5.00	None	1.64	Barry Evans	95
J HANCOCK SOVER INV; A	Growth Income	1,188.3	16.17	5.95	18.87	8.76	10.77	12.54	3.5	N/A	225-5291	617-375-1500	5.00	5.00	None	1.16	John Snyder	92
J HANCOCK SOVER INV; B	Growth Income	182.9	16.17	5.78	17.97	☆	☆	☆	2.7	N/A	225-5291	617-375-1500	None	None	5.00	1.86	John Snyder	94
J HANCOCK SOVER INV; C	Growth Income	15.8	16.17	6.10	19.28	☆	☆	☆	3.9	N/A	225-5291	617-375-1500	None	None	5.00	0.81	John Snyder	93
J HANCOCK SPEC EQ; A	Small Company Growth	344.1	19.00	11.11	41.05	27.28	24.20	16.20	0.0	88	225-5291	617-375-1500	5.00	5.00	None	1.62	Michael DiCarlo	88
J HANCOCK SPEC EQ; B	Small Company Growth	257.2	18.74	10.82	40.16	☆	☆	☆	0.0	93	225-5291	617-375-1500	None	None	5.00	2.25	Michael DiCarlo	93
J HANCOCK SPEC EQ; C	Small Company Growth	9.3	19.18	11.19	41.97	☆	☆	☆	0.0	93	225-5291	617-375-1500	None	5.00	None	1.11	Michael DiCarlo	93
J HANCOCK SPEC OPPTY; A	Capital Appreciation	96.6	8.79	7.46	17.36	☆	☆	☆	0.0	93	225-5291	617-375-1500	5.00	5.00	None	1.50	Michael DiCarlo	93
J HANCOCK SPEC OPPTY; B	Capital Appreciation	130.5	8.70	7.41	16.78	☆	☆	☆	0.0	93	225-5291	617-375-1500	None	None	5.00	2.22	Michael DiCarlo	93
J HANCOCK SPEC VALUE; A	Growth Income	8.5	9.95	7.69	18.49	☆	☆	☆	2.4	N/A	225-5291	617-375-1500	5.00	5.00	None	0.99	Team Managed	N/A
J HANCOCK SPEC VALUE; B	Growth Income	9.1	9.95	7.50	17.45	☆	☆	☆	1.5	N/A	225-5291	617-375-1500	None	None	5.00	1.72	Team Managed	N/A
J HANCOCK STRAT INC; A	Fixed Income	327.9	7.13	5.29	10.56	6.98	10.22	☆	9.0	□	225-5291	617-375-1500	4.50	None	None	1.32	Frederick L. Cavanaugh	86
J HANCOCK STRAT INC; B	Fixed Income	134.5	7.13	5.12	9.81	☆	☆	☆	8.3	□	225-5291	617-375-1500	None	5.00	None	1.91	Frederick L. Cavanaugh	93
J HANCOCK UTILITIES; A	Utility	19.2	8.42	5.18	10.82	☆	☆	☆	5.2	N/A	225-5291	617-375-1500	5.00	5.00	None	1.44	Andrew St. Pierre	94
J HANCOCK UTILITIES; B	Utility	38.3	8.40	4.98	10.09	☆	☆	☆	4.6	N/A	225-5291	617-375-1500	None	None	5.00	2.19	Andrew St. Pierre	94
J HANCOCK EMERG GR; A	Small Company Growth	131.8	32.23	14.01	37.38	21.36	16.18	☆	0.0	91	225-5291	617-375-1500	5.00	None	5.00	2.54	Edgar Larsen	91
J HANCOCK EMERG GR; B	Small Company Growth	308.6	31.16	13.85	36.43	20.38	☆	☆	0.0	87	225-5291	617-375-1500	5.00	None	5.00	1.94	Edgar Larsen	87
J HANCOCK GLBL RES; A	Natural Resources	2.7	15.16	9.30	3.84	☆	☆	☆	0.0	94	225-5291	617-375-1500	5.00	None	5.00	1.16	B. J. Willingham	94
J HANCOCK GLBL RES; B	Natural Resources	32.3	15.04	9.14	3.08	8.15	☆	☆	0.0	94	225-5291	617-375-1500	None	None	5.00	1.91	B. J. Willingham	94
J HANCOCK GOVT INC; A	Fixed Income	0.5	9.28	6.59	11.07	☆	7.66	☆	0.0	N/A	225-5291	617-375-1500	4.50	None	None	1.00	Team Managed	N/A
J HANCOCK GOVT INC; B	Fixed Income	238.3	9.28	6.40	2.46	☆	☆	☆	7.1	N/A	225-5291	617-375-1500	None	5.00	None	0.85	Team Managed	N/A
J HANCOCK HIGH YIELD; A	Fixed Income	173.8	7.13	4.82	5.64	5.64	11.34	☆	10.6	N/A	225-5291	617-375-1500	4.50	None	None	0.65	Team Managed	N/A
J HANCOCK HIGH YIELD; B	Fixed Income	6.8	7.14	4.73	1.77	8.20	☆	☆	9.8	N/A	225-5291	617-375-1500	None	5.00	None	1.04	Team Managed	N/A
HANOVER AMER VALUE; INV	Growth Income	0.1	10.83	4.84	☆	☆	☆	☆	0.0	N/A	821-2371	None	None	None	None		Henderson/Trautwein	95/95
HANOVER BLUE CHIP; ADV	Growth	50.0	11.64	10.75	20.13	☆	☆	☆	0.0	19.1	821-2371	None	3.00	None	None		Karen Shapiro	95
HANOVER BLUE CHIP; INV	Growth	83.3	11.64	10.75	20.13	☆	☆	☆	1.0	19.1	821-2371	None	None	None	None	1.00	Karen Shapiro	95
HANOVER GOVT SECS; INV	Fixed Income	9.6	9.91	6.16	10.76	☆	☆	☆	5.6	N/A	821-2371	None	None	None	None	0.85	Pam Wooster	93
HANOVER SH-TM GOVT; INV	Fixed Income	20.2	9.78	3.33	7.50	☆	☆	☆	5.3	N/A	821-2371	None	None	None	None	0.65	Guy Barba	93
HANOVER SM CAP GRO; CBC	Small Company Growth		10.53	3.85	13.96	☆	☆	☆	0.0	23.0	821-2371	None	None	None	None	1.04	Francis Lane	94

PERFORMANCE OF MUTUAL FUNDS (continued)

Return figures are through 6/30; 3YRS, 5YRS and 10YRS are annualized. PHONE NUMBER columns are 800 / In-State. FEES columns are Load / Exp. Ratio / Redemption.

FUND NAME	OBJECTIVE	ASSETS ($ MIL) 5/31/95	NAV ($/SHR) 6/30/95	QTR	1YR	3YRS	5YRS	10YRS	DIV YLD %	P/E RATIO	800	In-State	Load	Exp. Ratio	Redemption	MANAGER	SINCE
HANOVER SM CAP GRO; INV	Small Company Growth	13.4	10.50	3.75	13.60	☆	☆	☆	0.0	23.0	821-2371	None	None	1.30	None	Francis Lane	'93
HARBOR BOND	Fixed Income	198.4	10.91	5.33	10.60	7.77	10.37	☆	5.9		422-1050	419-247-1940	None	0.77	None	William Gross	'87
HARBOR CAPITAL APPREC	Growth	529.5	21.33	15.86	42.67	20.58	17.57	☆	0.2	23.8	422-1050	419-247-1940	None	0.81	None	Spiros Segalas	'90
HARBOR GROWTH	Growth	132.0	14.03	9.35	20.39	9.90	9.02	☆	0.0	23.4	422-1050	419-247-1940	None	0.93	None	Nicholas/Marshall	'93/'93
HARBOR INTERNATIONAL ⊠	International	3,170.2	26.01	4.92	15.14	14.85	10.76	☆	0.9	23.4	422-1050	419-247-1940	None	1.10	None	Hakan Castegren	'87
HARBOR INTL GROWTH	International	87.1	11.44	12.62	14.01	☆	☆	☆	0.7		422-1050	419-247-1940	None	1.32	None	Howard B. Moss	'93
HARBOR SHORT DURATION	Fixed Income	110.3	8.86	2.46	6.83	4.82	☆	☆	6.9		422-1050	419-247-1940	None	1.64	None	Stewart Russell	'94
HARBOR VALUE	Growth Income	71.6	13.80	7.16	20.93	10.13	9.11	☆	2.6	15.7	422-1050	419-247-1940	None	1.04	None	DePrince/Tierney	'94/'94
HARRIS INSIGHT CONVERT	Convertible Securities	1.3	9.62	8.30	13.14	10.25	9.66	☆	8.3		982-8782	302-792-6400	4.50	0.80	None	Tom Corkill	'94
HARRIS INSIGHT EQUITY; A	Growth Income	52.1	13.34	10.45	21.77	14.92	12.11	☆	1.9	15.3	982-8782	302-792-6400	4.50	0.90	None	James Depies	'94
HARRIS INSIGHT MGD FI; A	Fixed Income	45.4	10.19	4.48	9.90	6.39	☆	☆	5.8		982-8782	302-792-6400	4.50	0.60	None	Fred Duda	'94
HARTWELL EMRG GRO; A	Small Company Growth	99.1	24.56	5.91	35.49	10.85	10.47	16.07	0.0	36.4	343-2898	617-621-6100	5.75	1.80	None	John M. Hartwell	'68
HARTWELL EMRG GRO; B	Small Company Growth	4.5	24.11	5.65	33.97	☆	☆	☆	0.0	36.4	343-2898	617-621-6100	None	2.49	3.00	John M. Hartwell	'93
HARTWELL EMRG GRO; C	Small Company Growth	1.7	24.21	5.67	34.22	☆	☆	☆	0.0	36.4	343-2898	617-621-6100	None	2.47	1.00	John M. Hartwell	'93
HARTWELL GROWTH; A	Capital Appreciation	19.0	21.66	11.13	25.48	8.60	9.15	13.88	0.0	16.7	343-2898	617-621-6100	5.75	2.05	None	William Miller	'84
HARTWELL GROWTH; B	Capital Appreciation	0.8	21.32	10.87	24.29	☆	☆	☆	0.0	16.7	343-2898	617-621-6100	None	3.04	3.00	William Miller	'93
HARTWELL GROWTH; C	Capital Appreciation	0.6	21.19	10.71	24.18	☆	☆	☆	0.0	16.7	343-2898	617-621-6100	None	3.11	1.00	William Miller	'93
HAVEN CAPITAL HAVEN FUND	Growth	51.3	11.29	5.87	17.95	6.20	☆	☆	1.3	36.4	850-7163	None	None	0.84	None	Colin Ferenback	'94
HAWTHORNE INV BOND	Fixed Income	N/A	7.99	1.50	4.46	☆	☆	☆	4.6	N/A	272-4548	617-227-4800	None	1.42	None	Charles G. Dyer	'93
HAWTHORNE INV SEA FUND	Growth	N/A	10.02	13.22	21.49	5.95	5.84	☆	2.2	N/A	272-4548	617-227-4800	None		None	Charles G. Dyer	'90
HEARTLAND SM CAP CONTR	Small Company Growth	N/A	11.22	☆	☆	☆	☆	☆	0.0	N/A	432-7856	414-347-7777	None		None	William Nasgovitz	'95
HEARTLAND US GOVT SECS	Fixed Income	67.6	9.56	4.55	9.35	8.29	10.12	☆	6.2	N/A	432-7856	414-347-7777	None	1.07	None	Retzer/Nasgovitz	'89/'87
HEARTLAND SM CAP VALUE	Small Company Growth	809.1	27.11	9.80	19.16	23.01	18.95	14.86	0.0	11.9	432-7856	414-347-7777	None	1.39	None	Nasgovitz/Denison	'85/'88
HEARTLAND VALUE & INC	Growth Income	12.9	11.01	10.51	16.16	☆	☆	☆	3.9	11.1	432-7856	414-347-7777	None	1.80	None	William Nasgovitz	'94
HENLOPEN FUND	Growth	10.7	14.68	14.06	27.77	☆	☆	☆	0.0	12.8	338-1579	302-654-3131	None	2.00	None	Michael Hershey	'92
HERCULES EURO VALUE	European Region	18.0	11.10	5.21	13.52	☆	☆	☆	0.2		584-1317	612-342-1100	None	2.00	None	Pictet Intl Mgmt	'93
HERCULES GLOBAL SH-TM	World Income	0.3	10.00	0.20	1.89	☆	☆	☆	1.0		584-1317	612-342-1100	None	1.25	None	Salomon Bros. Asset Mgt	'93
HERCULES LATIN AMER VAL	Latin American	22.8	7.20	15.02	-21.23	☆	☆	☆	0.0		584-1317	612-342-1100	None	2.00	None	Bankers Trust Company	'93
HERCULES N AMER GR & INC	Growth	13.9	9.92	11.59	5.36	☆	☆	☆	0.4	17.0	584-1317	612-342-1100	None	2.00	None	Multiple Managers	N/A
HERCULES PAC BASIN VALUE	Pacific Region	33.9	9.06	-3.82	-14.25	☆	☆	☆	0.0		584-1317	612-342-1100	None	2.00	None	Edinburgh Fund Managers	'93
HERITAGE WORLD BOND	World Income	16.0	9.82	3.76	7.24	☆	☆	☆	2.1		584-1317	612-342-1100	4.75	1.80	None	Salomon Bros. Asset Mgt	'93
HERITAGE CAP APPREC; A	Capital Appreciation	70.7	14.88	4.57	13.08	13.12	11.29	☆	0.4	16.5	421-4184	813-573-8143	4.75	1.55	None	Herb Ehlers	'85
HERITAGE CAP APPREC; C	Capital Appreciation	0.2	14.80	☆	☆	☆	☆	☆	0.4	N/A	421-4184	813-573-8143	None	1.64	1.00	Herb Ehlers	'85
HERITAGE INC-GRO; A	Equity Income	32.6	11.72	5.36	14.14	11.24	11.22	☆	2.7	16.7	421-4184	813-573-8143	4.75		None	Lou Kirschbaum	'90
HERITAGE INC-GRO; C	Equity Income	0.1	11.68	☆	☆	☆	☆	☆	0.0	N/A	421-4184	813-573-8143	None		1.00	Lou Kirschbaum	'95
HERITAGE INC DVRSFD; A	Fixed Income	32.0	9.97	5.19	10.04	6.52	9.38	☆	7.4		421-4184	813-573-8143	3.75	1.25	None	Blount/Wallace	'93/'94
HERITAGE INC DVRSFD; C	Fixed Income	0.1	9.94	☆	☆	☆	☆	☆	0.0		421-4184	813-573-8143	None	None	1.00	Blount/Wallace	'95/'95
HERITAGE INC INST GV; A	Fixed Income	2.6	9.84	2.36	5.59	☆	☆	☆	5.4		421-4184	813-573-8143	3.75	0.75	None	H. Peter Wallace	'93
HERITAGE INC INST GV; C	Fixed Income	0.1	9.84	☆	☆	☆	☆	☆	5.4		421-4184	813-573-8143	None	None	1.00	H. Peter Wallace	'95
HERITAGE INC LTD GVT; A	Fixed Income	26.6	9.30	3.97	7.63	3.34	5.43	☆	5.7		421-4184	813-573-8143	3.75	0.95	None	H. Peter Wallace	'95
HERITAGE INC LTD GVT; C	Fixed Income	0.1	9.29	☆	☆	☆	☆	☆	0.0		421-4184	813-573-8143	None	None	1.00	H. Peter Wallace	'93
HERITAGE EAGLE INTL EQ	International	4.6	20.08	9.24	☆	☆	☆	☆	0.0	17.5	421-4184	813-573-8143	4.75	1.91	None	Martin Currie, Inc.	'95
HERITAGE SM CAP STK; A	Small Company Growth	44.4	17.15	9.24	19.91	☆	☆	☆	0.1		421-4184	813-573-8143	4.75	None	None	Awad/Henwood	'93/'93
HERITAGE SM CAP STK; C	Small Company Growth	0.5	17.09	☆	☆	☆	☆	☆	0.1		421-4184	813-573-8143	None	None	1.00	Awad/Henwood	'95/'95
HERITAGE VALUE EQTY; A	Growth Income	5.6	16.88	10.76	☆	☆	☆	☆	0.0	N/A	421-4184	813-573-8143	4.75	None	None	Christian Bertelsen	'95

Fund	Objective											Phone	Phone 2	Load	12b-1	Manager	Since
HERITAGE VALUE EQTY; C	Growth Income	0.7	16.85	☆	☆	☆	☆	0.0	N/A	421-4184	813-573-8143	None	1.00	Christian Bertelsen	'95
HIGHMARK BALANCED; FID	Balanced	26.8	16.70	7.15	16.43	☆	☆	3.7	17.0	433-6884	None	None	None	Freeman/Montgomery	'93/'93
HIGHMARK BALANCED; INV	Balanced	0.1	10.63	7.09	16.06	☆	☆	3.7	17.0	433-6884	None	4.50	0.87	Freeman/Montgomery	'94/'94
HIGHMARK BOND; FID	Fixed Income	60.3	10.48	6.25	11.69	6.18	8.28	6.1		433-6884	None	None	0.86	Jack Montgomery	'94
HIGHMARK BOND; INV	Fixed Income	0.5	10.39	6.31	11.00			6.1		433-6884	None	3.00		Jack Montgomery	'94
HIGHMARK GOVT BOND; FID	Fixed Income	4.1	9.53	4.10	8.25	☆	☆	6.3		433-6884	None	None	0.85	William Howard	'93
HIGHMARK GOVT BOND; INV	Fixed Income	0.1	9.45	4.02	7.74	☆	☆	6.4		433-6884	None	3.00	None	William Howard	'94
HIGHMARK GROWTH; FID	Growth	22.5	11.50	10.06	25.43	☆	☆	1.3	17.8	433-6884	None	None	0.77	Scott Chapman	'93
HIGHMARK GROWTH; INV	Growth	0.9	11.50	10.06	25.30	☆	☆	1.3	17.0	433-6884	None	4.50		Scott Chapman	'93
HIGHMARK INC & GRO; FID	Growth Income	6.9	11.40	7.54	20.95	☆	☆	2.2	17.0	433-6884	None	None	0.95	David Freeman	'93
HIGHMARK INC & GRO; INV	Growth Income	0.1	11.41	7.63	20.93	☆	☆	2.2	17.0	433-6884	None	4.50		David Freeman	'94
HIGHMARK INCOME EQTY; FID	Equity Income	213.0	12.81	6.17	18.44	11.19	11.07	3.3	17.0	433-6884	None	None	1.06	Tom Arrington	'88
HIGHMARK INCOME EQTY; INV	Equity Income	2.8	12.84	6.24	18.50	☆	☆	3.1	15.4	433-6884	None	4.50		Tom Arrington	'94
HILLIARD LYONS GROWTH	Growth	23.3	18.52	7.05	23.15	9.98	☆	0.6	15.4	444-1854	502-588-8400	4.75	1.75	Samuel C. Harvey	'92
HODGES FUND	Capital Appreciation	9.8	12.00	6.87	26.09	☆	☆	0.0	18.3	388-8513	214-954-1954	2.50	2.31	Donald Hodges	'92
HOMESTATE PA GROWTH	Growth	18.4	15.68	16.67	28.96	☆	☆	0.0	N/A	232-0224	717-396-7864	5.00	2.23	Kenneth G. Mertz II	'92
HOMESTEAD SHORT-TERM BD	Fixed Income	58.7	5.15	3.58	7.85	5.64	☆	5.1		254-3948	None	None	0.75	Doug Kern	'91
HOMESTEAD SHORT-TERM GVT	Fixed Income	0.7	5.05	☆	☆	☆	☆	0.0		254-3948	None	None	1.15	Stuart Teach	'95
HOMESTEAD VALUE	Growth Income	116.2	16.88	7.93	19.03	15.15	☆	2.1	16.2	254-3948	None	None	1.00	DeBard/Landmann/Rivelle'85/'94/'94	'87/'94
HOTCHKIS & WILEY BAL INC	Balanced	31.3	16.74	6.53	16.34	9.91	10.84	4.7	16.2	346-7301	213-362-8900	None	1.00	Wiley/Bardin	
HOTCHKIS & WILEY EQ INC	Equity Income	120.3	17.24	8.34	20.55	11.66	12.18	2.5	13.1	346-7301	213-362-8900	None	1.00	Bouwer/Ketterer/Hartford'90/'90/'94	'90/'94
HOTCHKIS & WILEY INTL	International	42.1	17.70	6.48	11.12	11.66	☆	2.5		346-7301	213-362-8900	None	1.00	Rivelle/Landmann	'93/'93
HOTCHKIS & WILEY LOW DUR	Fixed Income	118.7	10.15	4.03	10.25	☆	☆	7.3		346-7301	213-362-8900	None	0.58	Rivelle/Landmann	'93/'93
HOTCHKIS & WILEY S-T INV	Fixed Income	19.5	10.12	1.65	5.78	☆	☆	6.5		346-7301	213-362-8900	None	0.48	Hitchman/Miles	'94/'95
HOTCHKIS & WILEY SM CAP	Small Company Growth	20.2	21.53	5.80	14.79	12.58	12.40	0.0	16.4	346-7301	213-362-8900	None	1.00		
HYPRN I HYPRN TOT RET	Fixed Income	14.8	12.94	6.58	☆	☆	☆	0.0		497-3746	213-362-8900	None	None	Tad Rivelle	'94
HYPRN II HYPRN SHDUR 2	Fixed Income	26.4	9.11	1.80	4.12	1.21	☆	4.7		497-3746	212-980-8400	None	2.16	L. David Ricci	'93
HYPRN HYPRN SH DUR I	Fixed Income	10.2	8.76	1.54	4.20	1.82	☆	5.5		245-2100	212-980-8400	3.00	1.60	L. David Ricci	'93
IAA TRUST ASSET ALLOC	Flexible	9.3	12.29	8.11	16.29	8.67	9.39	2.8		245-2100	610-834-3500	3.00	1.78	Jacobs/Marks	'78/'93
IAA TRUST GROWTH	Growth	69.0	17.23	9.47	26.68	11.36	11.30	1.0		245-2100	610-834-3500	3.00	1.24	Bruce Finks	'92
IAI INV I BALANCED	Fixed Income	84.7	9.18	4.04	10.93	7.61	9.35	6.6		945-3863	612-376-2700	None	1.10	Hill/Bettin/Douglas	'84/'95/'95
IAI INV I INSTL BOND	Fixed Income	94.7	9.40	4.18	11.26	☆	☆	6.6		945-3863	612-376-2700	None	None	Team Managed	N/A
IAI INV II GROWTH	Growth	25.6	11.51	5.37	22.17	☆	☆	0.5		945-3863	612-376-2700	None	1.25	Twele/McDonald	'94/'94
IAI INV III DEV CNTRIES	Emerging Markets	2.9	10.77	8.79	☆	☆	☆	0.0		945-3863	612-376-2700	None	None	Roy Gillson	'95
IAI INV III INTL	International	147.2	12.60	0.53	-0.03	☆	6.92	0.1		945-3863	612-376-2700	None	1.72	Roy Gillson	'95
IAI INV VI BALANCED	Balanced	41.2	10.83	4.09	16.09	8.06	☆	3.2	20.9	945-3863	612-376-2700	None	1.25	Simenstad/Twele/McDonald'93/'94/'94	'93/'94/'94
IAI INV VI EMERG GROWTH	Small Company Growth	338.1	17.28	9.16	39.35	22.61	☆	0.0	N/A	945-3863	612-376-2700	None	1.25	Rick Leggott	'91
IAI INV VI GOVERNMENT	Fixed Income	41.4	9.91	2.61	7.46	5.23	☆	5.8		945-3863	612-376-2700	None	1.10	Scott Bettin	'91
IAI INV VII GRO & INC	Capital Appreciation	100.9	14.96	4.84	16.60	9.29	7.39	0.9		945-3863	612-376-2700	None	1.25	Todd McCallister	'93
IAI REGIONAL FUND	Growth	524.5	22.63	7.80	22.28	10.98	10.33	0.8		945-3863	612-376-2700	None	1.23	Carlin/Hoonsbeen	'80/'94
IAI RESERVE FUND	Fixed Income	80.3	9.98	1.99	5.78	3.86	5.12	5.2		945-3863	612-376-2700	None	0.85	Tim Palmer	'91
IAI VALUE FUND	Growth	41.7	11.85	7.02	11.89	11.47	8.29	0.3	N/A	945-3863	612-376-2700	None	1.25	Douglas Platt	'91
IAI MIDCAP GROWTH FUND	Midcap	89.9	15.39	5.08	26.88	20.26	☆	0.0	N/A	994-2533	None	None	1.10	Suzanne Zak	'95
IBJ FDS TR BOND; SRVC	Fixed Income	N/A	10.53	4.46	☆	☆	☆	0.0		994-2533	None	None	1.25	Martin Liebgott	'95
IBJ FDS TR CORE EQ; SRVC	Growth	N/A	11.39	6.15	☆	☆	☆	0.0	N/A	994-2533	None	None	1.23	Christian Kaefer	'95
ICAP EQUITY	Growth Income	N/A	10.98	5.22	☆	☆	☆	0.0	N/A	994-2533	317-692-3900	None	None	Keafer/Liebgott	'95/'95
ICAP DISCRETIONARY EQTY	Growth Income	16.5	24.33	11.81	☆	☆	☆	0.0	N/A	273-3936	317-692-3900	None	None	Team Managed	N/A
IDEX FUND	Growth	17.9	24.65	13.37	24.11	9.40	11.37	0.6	17.8	851-9777	813-585-6565	8.50	1.29	Thomas F. Marsico	'85
IDEX FUND 3 ⊠	Growth	142.1	17.33	17.46	25.85	10.58	11.59	0.4	18.1	851-9777	813-585-6565	8.50	1.25	Thomas F. Marsico	'87

© Copyright Lipper Analytical Services, Inc.

387

PERFORMANCE OF MUTUAL FUNDS (continued)

Note: Under "RETURN THROUGH 6/30", the 3YRS, 5YRS, and 10YRS columns are annualized. ☆ indicates a star mark printed in the cell (no data / rating). Blank cells in P/E RATIO were shown as empty boxes in the source.

FUND NAME	OBJECTIVE	ASSETS ($MIL) 5/31/95	NAV ($/SHR) 6/30/95	QTR	1YR	3YRS	5YRS	10YRS	DIV YLD %	P/E RATIO	PHONE 800	PHONE In-State	Load	Exp. Ratio	Redemption	MANAGER	SINCE
IDEX II AGG GROWTH; A	Capital Appreciation	7.6	14.87	22.79	☆	☆	☆	☆	0.0	30.6	851-9777	813-585-6565	5.50	None	None	David Alger	'94
IDEX II AGG GROWTH; C	Capital Appreciation	0.2	14.84	22.75	☆	☆	☆	☆	0.0	30.6	851-9777	813-585-6565	None	None	None	David Alger	'94
IDEX II BALANCED; A	Balanced	2.4	10.98	5.48	☆	☆	☆	☆	0.0	16.1	851-9777	813-585-6565	5.50	None	None	James P. Craig	'94
IDEX II BALANCED; C	Balanced	2.2	10.98	5.48	☆	☆	☆	☆	0.0	16.1	851-9777	813-585-6565	None	None	None	James P. Craig	'94
IDEX II CAP APP; A	Midcap	4.6	11.88	7.90	☆	☆	☆	☆	0.0	24.5	851-9777	813-585-6565	5.50	None	None	James P. Goff	'94
IDEX II CAP APP; C	Midcap	1.3	11.85	7.83	☆	☆	☆	☆	0.0	24.5	851-9777	813-585-6565	None	None	None	James P. Goff	'94
IDEX II EQUITY INC; A	Equity Income	3.4	11.12	3.35	☆	☆	☆	☆	0.0	17.3	851-9777	813-585-6565	5.50	None	None	King/Hollmann/Clegg	'94/'94/'94
IDEX II EQUITY INC; C	Equity Income	0.2	11.11	3.25	☆	☆	☆	☆	0.0	17.3	851-9777	813-585-6565	None	None	None	King/Hollmann/Clegg	'94/'94/'94
IDEX II FLEX INC; A	Fixed Income	20.0	9.13	6.37	9.57	8.07	☆	☆	6.9		851-9777	813-585-6565	4.75	1.85	None	Ronald V. Speaker	'87
IDEX II FLEX INC; C	Fixed Income	0.6	9.13	6.22	8.97	☆	☆	☆	6.4		851-9777	813-585-6565	None	2.40	None	Ronald V. Speaker	'93
IDEX II GLOBAL; A	Global	80.5	16.47	10.61	13.74	☆	☆	☆	0.0		851-9777	813-585-6565	5.50	2.14	None	Helen Young-Hayes	'92
IDEX II GLOBAL; C	Global	3.5	16.23	10.63	13.27	☆	☆	☆	0.0		851-9777	813-585-6565	None	4.04	None	Helen Young-Hayes	'93
IDEX II GROWTH; A	Growth	416.0	20.13	16.70	23.73	☆	☆	☆	0.0	17.9	851-9777	813-585-6565	5.50	1.76	None	Thomas F. Marsico	'86
IDEX II GROWTH; C	Growth	4.3	19.96	16.73	23.21	☆	☆	☆	0.0	17.9	851-9777	813-585-6565	None	3.48	None	Thomas F. Marsico	'93
IDEX II INCOME PLUS; A	Fixed Income	67.4	10.36	6.75	13.80	8.86	10.80	11.05	7.4		851-9777	813-585-6565	4.75	1.33	None	David Halfpap	'85
IDEX II INCOME PLUS; C	Fixed Income	1.8	10.36	6.60	12.79	☆	☆	☆	6.5		851-9777	813-585-6565	None	3.52	None	David Halfpap	'93
IDS BLUE CHIP ADVNTG; A	Growth Income	162.9	6.79	8.00	21.79	☆	☆	☆	1.6	17.4	328-8300	612-671-3733	5.00	1.03	None	Guru Baliga	'94
IDS BLUE CHIP ADVNTG; B	Growth Income	5.6	6.78	7.76	☆	☆	☆	☆	0.0	N/A	328-8300	612-671-3733	None	None	5.00	Guru Baliga	'95
IDS BLUE CHIP ADVNTG; Y	Growth Income	19.9	6.79	8.05	☆	☆	☆	☆	0.0	N/A	328-8300	612-671-3733	None	0.68	None	Guru Baliga	'85
IDS BOND FUND; A	Fixed Income	2,302.8	5.06	7.83	14.18	11.51	11.66	10.85	7.4		328-8300	612-671-3733	5.00	0.97	None	Frederick C. Quirsfeld	'95
IDS BOND FUND; B	Fixed Income	726.6	5.06	7.65	☆	☆	☆	☆	0.0		328-8300	612-671-3733	None	None	5.00	Frederick C. Quirsfeld	'95
IDS BOND FUND; Y	Fixed Income	59.1	5.06	7.51	☆	☆	☆	☆	0.0		328-8300	612-671-3733	None	None	None	Frederick C. Quirsfeld	'95
IDS DISCOVERY FUND; A	Midcap	661.5	12.33	8.35	21.16	11.92	10.16	11.68	0.0	27.1	328-8300	612-671-3733	5.00	0.88	None	Kurt Winters	'95
IDS DISCOVERY FUND; B	Midcap	5.0	12.30	8.27	☆	☆	☆	☆	0.0	N/A	328-8300	612-671-3733	None	None	5.00	Kurt Winters	'95
IDS DISCOVERY FUND; Y	Midcap	32.6	12.33	8.35	☆	☆	☆	☆	0.0	N/A	328-8300	612-671-3733	None	0.71	None	Kurt Winters	'95
IDS DVSD EQUITY INC; A	Equity Income	1,024.4	7.48	5.07	9.56	12.23	9.75	10.04	3.9	15.1	328-8300	612-671-3733	5.00	0.79	None	Keith Tufte	'94
IDS EQUITY SELECT; A	Growth Income	611.5	11.15	6.58	14.09	9.93	13.25	13.97	1.0	17.4	328-8300	612-671-3733	5.00	0.71	None	Joseph M. Barsky III	'83
IDS EQUITY SELECT; B	Growth Income	0.7	11.14	6.39	☆	☆	☆	☆	0.0	N/A	328-8300	612-671-3733	None	None	5.00	Joseph M. Barsky III	'95
IDS EQUITY SELECT; Y	Growth Income	3.6	11.15	6.62	☆	☆	☆	☆	0.0	N/A	328-8300	612-671-3733	None	0.79	None	Joseph M. Barsky III	'83
IDS EXTRA INCOME; A	Fixed Income	1,746.9	4.11	6.74	9.00	9.79	7.40	10.04	9.7		328-8300	612-671-3733	5.00	0.76	None	John A. Utter	'95
IDS EXTRA INCOME; B	Fixed Income	28.4	4.11	6.54	☆	☆	☆	☆	0.0		328-8300	612-671-3733	None	None	5.00	John A. Utter	'95
IDS EXTRA INCOME; Y	Fixed Income	1.2	4.11	6.78	☆	☆	☆	☆	0.0		328-8300	612-671-3733	None	None	None	John A. Utter	'93
IDS FEDERAL INCOME; A	Fixed Income	972.2	4.97	4.08	9.38	5.81	7.40	☆	6.3		328-8300	612-671-3733	5.00	None	None	James Synder	'95
IDS FEDERAL INCOME; B	Fixed Income	265.4	4.97	3.89	☆	☆	☆	☆	0.0		328-8300	612-671-3733	None	None	5.00	James Synder	'95
IDS FEDERAL INCOME; Y	Fixed Income	83.0	4.97	4.12	☆	☆	☆	☆	0.0		328-8300	612-671-3733	None	None	None	James Synder	'95
IDS GLOBAL BOND; A	World Income	506.8	6.17	7.09	14.62	11.45	6.73	☆	5.1		328-8300	612-671-3733	5.00	None	None	Ray S. Goodner	'89
IDS GLOBAL GROWTH; A	Global	678.1	6.48	8.36	1.72	6.73	☆	☆	0.7	23.1	328-8300	612-671-3733	5.00	1.26	None	Edward Korff	'90
IDS GLOBAL GROWTH; B	Global	5.8	6.47	8.19	☆	☆	☆	☆	0.0	N/A	328-8300	612-671-3733	None	1.38	5.00	Edward Korff	'95
IDS GLOBAL GROWTH; Y	Global	22.3	6.49	8.53	☆	☆	☆	☆	0.0	N/A	328-8300	612-671-3733	None	None	None	Edward Korff	'95
IDS GROWTH FUND; A	Growth	1,191.9	20.24	11.95	32.67	13.41	13.85	15.50	0.2	23.1	328-8300	612-671-3733	5.00	0.83	None	Mary J. Malevich	'92
IDS GROWTH FUND; B	Growth	17.9	20.20	11.79	☆	☆	☆	☆	0.0		328-8300	612-671-3733	None	None	5.00	Mary J. Malevich	'95
IDS GROWTH FUND; Y	Growth	6.2	20.25	7.83	☆	☆	☆	☆	0.0		328-8300	612-671-3733	None	None	None	Mary J. Malevich	'95
IDS INTERNATIONAL; A	International	740.5	9.53	3.03	-1.26	3.70	☆	☆	0.2	N/A	328-8300	612-671-3733	5.00	1.33	None	Paul Hopkins	'95
IDS INTERNATIONAL; B	International	332.2	9.50	2.70	☆	☆	☆	☆	0.0	N/A	328-8300	612-671-3733	None	None	5.00	Paul Hopkins	'95
IDS INTERNATIONAL; Y	International	54.5	9.53	3.03	☆	☆	☆	☆	0.0	N/A	328-8300	612-671-3733	None	None	None	Paul Hopkins	'95

Fund	Objective	Net Assets ($Mil)	NAV						Yield %		Tel 1	Tel 2	Max Chg	12b-1	Redem	Portfolio Manager	Since
IDS MGD RETIREMENT; A	Flexible	2,386.3	11.44	8.18	14.73	11.46	11.72	15.46	1.3	16.9	328-8300	612-671-3733	5.00	0.85	None	Richard Lazarchic	'93
IDS MGD RETIREMENT; B	Flexible	19.7	11.43	7.98	☆	☆	☆	☆	0.0	N/A	328-8300	612-671-3733	None	None	5.00	Richard Lazarchic	'95
IDS MGD RETIREMENT; Y	Flexible	97.2	11.44	8.22	☆	☆	☆	☆	0.0	N/A	328-8300	612-671-3733	None	None	None	Richard Lazarchic	'95
IDS MUTUAL; A	Balanced	2,502.7	12.23	5.75	13.50	10.60	11.16	12.35	4.5	15.8	328-8300	612-671-3733	5.00	0.79	None	Medcalf/Labenski	'83/87
IDS MUTUAL; B	Balanced	9.2	12.22	5.66	☆	☆	☆	☆	0.0	N/A	328-8300	612-671-3733	None	None	5.00	Medcalf/Labenski	'95/95
IDS MUTUAL; Y	Balanced	789.7	12.23	5.78	☆	☆	☆	☆	0.0	N/A	328-8300	612-671-3733	None	None	None	Medcalf/Labenski	
IDS NEW DIMENSIONS; A	Growth	3,952.5	15.84	11.00	23.29	14.72	14.74	16.82	0.7	19.6	328-8300	612-671-3733	5.00	0.90	None	Gordon Fines	'91
IDS NEW DIMENSIONS; B	Growth	46.8	15.80	10.72	☆	☆	☆	☆	0.0	N/A	328-8300	612-671-3733	None	None	5.00	Gordon Fines	'95
IDS NEW DIMENSIONS; Y	Growth	1,387.8	15.84	11.00	☆	☆	☆	☆	0.0	N/A	328-8300	612-671-3733	None	None	None	Gordon Fines	'95
IDS PRECIOUS METALS; A	Gold	74.3	8.97	12.27	15.23	18.55	8.71	9.75	0.4	N/A	328-8300	612-671-3733	5.00	1.51	None	Richard Warden	'91
IDS PRECIOUS METALS; B	Gold	0.3	8.95	12.02	☆	☆	☆	☆	0.0	N/A	328-8300	612-671-3733	None	None	5.00	Richard Warden	'95
IDS PRECIOUS METALS; Y	Gold	0.1	8.97	12.27	☆	☆	☆	☆	0.0	N/A	328-8300	612-671-3733	None	None	None	Richard Warden	'95
IDS PROGRESSIVE FUND; A	Capital Appreciation	310.8	7.23	4.48	17.59	12.42	9.49	10.33	1.7	13.6	328-8300	612-671-3733	5.00	0.99	None	Michael W. Garbisch	'91
IDS PROGRESSIVE FUND; B	Capital Appreciation	0.1	7.21	4.34	☆	☆	☆	☆	0.0	N/A	328-8300	612-671-3733	None	None	5.00	Michael W. Garbisch	'95
IDS PROGRESSIVE FUND; Y	Capital Appreciation	1.2	7.23	3.73	☆	☆	☆	☆	0.0	N/A	328-8300	612-671-3733	None	None	None	Michael W. Garbisch	'95
IDS SELECTIVE FUND; A	Fixed Income	1,414.9	9.25	7.33	13.69	9.09	10.53	10.50	6.3		328-8300	612-671-3733	5.00	0.72	None	Ray S. Goodner	'85
IDS SELECTIVE FUND; B	Fixed Income	117.5	9.25	7.12	☆	☆	☆	☆	0.0	N/A	328-8300	612-671-3733	None	None	5.00	Ray S. Goodner	'95
IDS SELECTIVE FUND; Y	Fixed Income	1,884.2	9.25	7.36	☆	☆	☆	☆	2.6	N/A	328-8300	612-671-3733	None	None	None	Ray S. Goodner	'95
IDS STOCK FUND; A	Growth Income	7.8	19.21	6.57	14.94	12.09	11.52	14.11	0.0	15.8	328-8300	612-671-3733	5.00	0.76	None	Richard Warden	'95
IDS STOCK FUND; B	Growth Income		19.19	6.42	☆	☆	☆	☆	0.0	N/A	328-8300	612-671-3733	None	None	5.00	Richard Warden	'95
IDS STOCK FUND; Y	Growth Income	665.8	19.21	6.60	☆	☆	☆	☆	0.0	N/A	328-8300	612-671-3733	None	None	None	Richard Warden	'95
IDS STR AGGR EQUITY; A	Capital Appreciation	10.2	16.27	9.19	23.65	9.80	8.90	12.92	0.0	26.6	328-8300	612-671-3733	5.00	1.71	None	David Bayer	'95
IDS STR AGGR EQUITY; B	Capital Appreciation	780.3	16.23	8.93	☆	☆	☆	☆	0.0	N/A	328-8300	612-671-3733	None	None	5.00	David Bayer	'95
IDS STR AGGR EQUITY; Y	Capital Appreciation	0.1	16.26	9.20	☆	☆	☆	☆	0.0	N/A	328-8300	612-671-3733	None	None	None	David Bayer	'95
IDS STR EQUITY; A	Growth Income	8.1	9.71	6.12	☆	☆	☆	☆	1.9	N/A	328-8300	612-671-3733	5.00	1.56	None	Tom Medcalf	'89
IDS STR EQUITY; B	Growth Income	1,372.8	9.71	5.92	14.25	10.64	11.39	12.93	5.0	14.4	328-8300	612-671-3733	None	None	5.00	Tom Medcalf	'95
IDS STR EQUITY; Y	Growth Income	0.1	9.71	6.16	☆	☆	☆	☆	5.0	14.9	328-8300	612-671-3733	None	None	None	Tom Medcalf	'93
IDS UTILITIES INCOME; A	Utility	596.2	6.26	5.69	8.64	8.64	10.41	☆	0.0	N/A	328-8300	612-671-3733	5.00	0.82	None	Richard Warden	'95
IDS UTILITIES INCOME; B	Utility	4.1	6.26	5.47	☆	☆	☆	☆	0.0	N/A	328-8300	612-671-3733	None	None	5.00	Richard Warden	'95
IDS UTILITIES INCOME; Y	Utility	0.1	6.26	5.73	☆	☆	☆	☆	0.0	N/A	328-8300	612-671-3733	None	None	None	Richard Warden	
IFT FR INST ADJ RATE	Fixed Income	8.6	9.78	2.66	6.35	4.59	☆	☆	6.0		342-5236	415-312-3200	None	0.25	None	Lemein/Coffey/Bayston	'92/92/92
IFT FR INST ADJ USG	Fixed Income	25.7	9.25	2.77	4.41	2.27	☆	☆	5.9		342-5236	415-312-3200	None	0.07	None	Lemein/Coffey/Bayston	'91/91/91
IMG INSTL FIXED INCOME	Fixed Income	27.9	13.46	6.70	☆	☆	☆	☆	0.0		798-1819	515-244-5426	None	None	None	Hance West	'94
IMG INSTL INTMDT DUR	Fixed Income	11.3	13.18	5.18	☆	☆	☆	☆	0.0	N/A	798-1819	515-244-5426	None	None	None	Hance West	N/A
INCOME FUND OF AMERICA	Equity Income	11,967.5	14.67	7.13	16.29	10.82	11.90	11.88	5.6	N/A	421-4120	714-671-7000	5.75	0.63	None	Multiple Manager	'95
INDEPND ONE US GOVT; TR	Fixed Income	64.1	10.16	6.17	11.26	☆	☆	☆	6.0		None	934-3883	None	0.31	None	Bruce Beaumont	'94
INFINITY BEA SH DUR; CLT	Fixed Income	79.8	4.96	2.52	6.36	☆	☆	☆	5.7		None	852-9730	None	0.50	None	Mark Silverstein	'94
INFINITY BEA SH DUR; INV	Fixed Income	31.9	4.96	2.52	6.26	☆	☆	☆	5.6		None	852-9730	None	None	None	Mark Silverstein	'94
INFINITY BEA SH DUR; SVC	Fixed Income	2.4	4.96	2.64	6.07	☆	☆	☆	5.3		None	852-9730	None	0.93	None	Mark Silverstein	'89
INSTL INTL FOREIGN EQU	International	1,255.6	13.57	4.95	4.27	☆	☆	☆	0.9	N/A	410-547-2308	638-5660	None	0.86	None	Martin G. Wade	'89
INSTL INVSTRS CAP APPREC	Growth Income	47.8	125.35	4.07	14.75	12.43	9.03	11.07	1.2	15.8	631-6364	212-551-1920	None	1.06	None	McCabe/Trautman	'93/93
INSTL INVSTRS TX-ADV INC	Income	19.0	99.85	0.99	2.36	3.19	7.18	☆	3.2	N/A	631-6364	212-551-1920	None	1.23	None	Trautman/Keasler	'93/93
INSTL SRS ADJ RT; FINL	Fixed Income	0.1	11.85	1.69	4.22	☆	☆	☆	5.5		647-1568	None	None	None	None	Singh/McCauley	'94/94
INSTL SRS ADJ-RT; INSTL	Fixed Income	5.4	11.85	1.75	4.47	☆	☆	☆	5.5		647-1568	None	None	None	None	Singh/McCauley	'94/94
INTEGRITY FUND OF FDS	Growth	1.4	11.42	8.87	☆	☆	☆	☆	0.0		562-6637	701-852-5292	1.50	0.83	None	W. Dan Korgel	'95
INTERMEDIATE BD FD AMER	Fixed Income	1,501.5	13.57	4.29	9.23	6.23	8.06	14.17	6.8		421-4120	714-671-7000	4.75	1.61	None	Multiple Managers	N/A
INTL SRS INTL EQ; A	International	220.0	17.75	5.65	0.48	6.73	3.09	☆	0.0		245-4770	412-288-1900	5.50	None	None	Randall S. Bauer	'92
INTL SRS INTL EQ; B	International	3.5	17.63	5.38	-0.48	☆	☆	☆	0.0		None	245-4770	None	2.55	5.50	Randall S. Bauer	'93
INTL SRS INTL EQ; C	International	7.7	17.42	5.38	☆	☆	☆	☆	0.0		None	245-4770	1.00	1.30	1.00	Randall S. Bauer	
INTL SRS INTL INC; A	World Income	184.8	11.09	2.91	15.63	9.78	☆	☆	5.3		None	245-4770	4.50	None	None	Randall S. Bauer	'91

389

PERFORMANCE OF MUTUAL FUNDS (continued)

FUND NAME	OBJECTIVE	ASSETS ($ MIL) 5/31/95	NAV ($/SHR) 6/30/95	QTR	RETURN THROUGH 6/30 1YR	3YRS (Annualized)	5YRS	10YRS	DIV YLD %	P/E RATIO	PHONE NUMBER 800	In-State	FEES Load	Exp. Ratio	Redemption	MANAGER	SINCE
INTL SRS INTL INC; B	World Income	0.5	11.08	2.74	☆	☆	☆	☆	0.0	□	245-4770	412-288-1900	None	None	5.50	Randall S. Bauer	'94
INTL SRS INTL INC; C	World Income	8.2	11.08	2.73	14.79	☆	☆	☆	4.6	□	245-4770	412-288-1900	None	2.05	1.00	Randall S. Bauer	'93
INVENTOR EQUITY GROW; A ➤	Growth	47.7	11.34	7.26	☆	☆	☆	☆	0.0	N/A	342-5734	610-254-1000	4.00	None	None	Anthony Gray	'94
INVENTOR GNMA; A ➤	Fixed Income	48.9	10.39	4.94	☆	☆	☆	☆	0.0	□	342-5734	610-254-1000	4.00	None	None	Thomas Pappas	'94
INVENTOR INTMDT GOVT; A	Fixed Income	84.2	10.25	4.67	☆	☆	☆	☆	0.0	□	342-5734	610-254-1000	4.00	None	None	Thomas Pappas	'94
INVESCO DVSFD SMALL CO	Small Company Growth	24.4	11.21	8.31	17.34	☆	☆	☆	0.5	16.3	525-8085	303-930-6300	None	1.00	None	Robert Slotpole	'94
INVESCO DYNAMICS	Capital Appreciation	449.9	12.17	9.53	27.08	20.18	17.84	14.82	0.3	23.5	525-8085	303-930-6300	None	1.17	None	Tim Miller	'93
INVESCO EMERGING GROWTH	Small Company Growth	153.7	10.02	5.87	12.36	20.94	☆	☆	0.4	14.4	525-8085	303-930-6300	None	1.37	None	John Schroer	'95
INVESCO GROWTH FUND	Growth	475.6	5.11	7.66	13.99	10.61	9.81	11.55	1.0	16.4	525-8085	303-930-6300	None	1.03	None	Sim/Pratt	'88/'95
INVESCO INC HIGH YIELD	Fixed Income	304.6	6.70	5.38	9.84	9.06	10.30	9.68	10.1		525-8085	303-930-6300	None	0.97	None	Jerry Paul	'94
INVESCO INC SELECT INC	Fixed Income	204.8	6.52	6.75	14.14	9.16	10.53	10.20	7.2	□	525-8085	303-930-6300	None	1.11	None	Jerry Paul	'94
INVESCO INC SH-TM BOND	Fixed Income	9.1	9.54	2.73	7.68	☆	☆	☆	6.2	□	525-8085	303-930-6300	None	0.46	None	Richard Hinderlie	'94
INVESCO INC US GOVT SECS	Fixed Income	52.8	7.52	7.68	14.37	7.12	8.63	☆	6.0	□	525-8085	303-930-6300	None	1.32	None	Richard Hinderlie	'94
INVESCO INDUST INCOME	Equity Income	3,976.7	11.92	7.72	14.79	11.07	12.65	14.95	3.4	□	525-8085	303-930-6300	None	0.92	None	Paul/Mayer	'94/'93
INVESCO INTL EUROPEAN	European Region	244.0	13.66	6.39	12.22	5.92	4.24	☆	1.2	16.0	525-8085	303-930-6300	None	1.20	None	Chamberlain/Grossi	'90/'95
INVESCO INTL INTL GROWTH	International	87.5	15.32	2.75	-1.37	7.39	1.04	☆	0.5	□	525-8085	303-930-6300	None	1.50	None	Davidson/Ehrman	'87/'93
INVESCO INTL PACIFIC	Pacific Region	196.9	13.42	-0.89	-8.19	10.80	1.70	12.82	0.3	□	525-8085	303-930-6300	None	1.24	None	Morris/Pickstone	'94/'93
INVESCO MULT ASSET ALLO	Flexible	7.3	10.63	7.01	13.95	☆	☆	☆	2.5	15.8	525-8085	303-930-6300	None	1.50	None	Robert Slotpole	'94
INVESCO MULT BALANCED	Balanced	32.3	11.68	6.26	19.80	☆	☆	☆	2.7	17.5	525-8085	303-930-6300	None	1.25	None	Kelly/Paul	'94/'94
INVESCO SPEC EURO SM CO	European Region	1.7	10.95	7.35	☆	☆	☆	☆	0.0	16.0	525-8085	303-930-6300	None	None	None	Team Managed	'95
INVESCO SPEC LT AM GRO	Latin American	5.7	11.50	13.30	☆	☆	☆	☆	0.0	□	525-8085	303-930-6300	None	1.50	None	Phillip Ehrmann	'95
INVESCO SPEC WRLD CAP GD	Global	8.5	9.35	9.36	☆	☆	☆	☆	0.0	□	525-8085	303-930-6300	None	1.24	2.00	Al Grossi	'95
INVESCO SPEC WRLD COMMUN	Global	24.9	11.86	8.91	☆	☆	☆	☆	0.0	25.2	525-8085	303-930-6300	None	1.50	None	Brian Kelly	'94
INVESCO STRAT ENERGY	Natural Resources	79.4	10.27	4.37	-2.90	6.64	☆	-2.90	0.5	18.0	525-8085	303-930-6300	None	1.35	None	Tom Samuelson	'95
INVESCO STRAT ENVIRON	Environmental	38.5	7.94	14.41	26.16	0.27	☆	4.78	0.7		525-8085	303-930-6300	None	1.29	None	Jeff Morris	'95
INVESCO STRAT FINANCIAL	Financial Services	281.4	17.06	8.46	14.19	14.94	21.47	☆	2.0	10.4	525-8085	303-930-6300	None	1.18	None	Doug Pratt	'92
INVESCO STRAT GOLD	Gold	219.3	5.46	13.04	-4.71	9.40	1.96	2.17	0.0	N/A	525-8085	303-930-6300	None	1.07	None	Dan Leonard	'89
INVESCO STRAT HEALTH	Health/Biotechnology	529.6	42.03	5.02	34.24	6.37	14.15	19.98	0.0	23.5	525-8085	303-930-6300	None	1.19	None	Kurokawa/Schroer	'92/'94
INVESCO STRAT LEISURE	Specialty	267.9	23.67	4.46	18.69	20.83	18.40	18.85	0.0	20.4	525-8085	303-930-6300	None	1.17	None	Tim Miller	'92
INVESCO STRAT TECH	Science & Technology	454.6	30.24	14.98	44.48	25.53	21.94	20.39	0.0	21.1	525-8085	303-930-6300	None	1.17	None	Daniel B. Leonard	'85
INVESCO STRAT UTILITIES	Utility	156.5	10.04	5.89	8.57	9.80	10.37	☆	2.8	12.4	525-8085	303-930-6300	None	1.13	None	Brian Kelly	'93
INVESCO VALUE EQUITY	Growth Income	156.0	19.16	7.45	23.93	12.22	12.32	☆	1.9	15.5	525-8085	303-930-6300	None	1.01	None	Harhai/Irrgang	'93/'94
INVESCO VALUE INTMDT GVT	Fixed Income	38.5	12.70	5.92	11.11	7.15	8.85	☆	5.7		525-8085	303-930-6300	None	1.07	None	Baker/Jenkins	'93/'94
INVESCO VALUE TOTAL RET	Flexible	458.1	20.60	7.90	21.34	12.59	12.54	☆	3.3	15.7	525-8085	303-930-6300	None	0.96	None	Mitchell/Griffin	'87/'94
INVESTMENT CO OF AMERICA	Growth Income	22,043.2	20.28	8.70	19.50	11.69	11.33	14.30	2.4	15.1	421-4120	714-671-7000	5.75	0.60	None	Multiple Managers	N/A
INVESTORS RESEARCH	Capital Appreciation	35.2	4.08	4.88	9.07	6.03	6.44	9.23	1.8	15.0	732-1733	805-569-3253	5.75	1.47	None	Richard W. Arms, Jr.	'94
INVESTORS TR ADJ RT; A	Fixed Income	5.5	6.35	3.08	7.93	7.93	☆	☆	4.8	□	656-6626	206-625-1755	4.50	0.95	None	Delores Driscoll	'93
INVESTORS TR ADJ RT; B	Fixed Income	2.0	6.35	2.81	7.05	☆	☆	☆	4.0	□	656-6626	206-625-1755	None	1.70	5.00	Delores Driscoll	'93
INVESTORS TR GOVT; A	Fixed Income	23.2	8.71	5.08	7.42	☆	☆	☆	8.4	□	656-6626	206-625-1755	4.50	0.99	None	Anderson/Fisher	'95/'95
INVESTORS TR GOVT; B	Fixed Income	1,180.2	8.72	4.89	6.84	3.18	6.20	☆	7.6	□	656-6626	206-625-1755	None	1.76	5.00	Anderson/Fisher	'95/'95
INVESTORS TR GROWTH; A	Growth	4.7	10.42	11.44	31.02	☆	☆	☆	0.0	17.3	656-6626	206-625-1755	4.50	1.34	None	John Moore	'93
INVESTORS TR GROWTH; B	Growth	9.5	10.28	11.26	29.91	☆	☆	☆	0.0	17.3	656-6626	206-625-1755	None	2.09	5.00	John Moore	'93
INVESTORS TR VALUE; A	Growth Income	3.4	8.40	7.32	20.03	☆	☆	☆	1.6	18.3	656-6626	206-625-1755	4.50	1.35	None	Carl Faust	'93
INVESTORS TR VALUE; B	Growth Income	11.6	8.39	7.13	19.06	☆	☆	☆	1.0	18.3	656-6626	206-625-1755	None	2.10	5.00	Carl Faust	'93
INVMNT SRS CAP GR; A	Capital Appreciation	9.9	12.98	10.36	16.99	6.28	☆	☆	1.3	N/A	245-4770	412-288-1900	5.50	1.25	None	Gregory M. Melvin	'92

The following is a mutual-fund data table. No column headers are printed on the page; the columns are, left to right: Fund Name, Investment Objective, Net Assets ($ mil), NAV, and five total-return columns (a ☆ indicates no figure/unrated), Yield %, a ratio/indicator column (☐ = marker), Toll-Free Phone, Direct Phone, Front Load, Expense/12b-1, Deferred Load, Portfolio Manager, and Inception date(s).

Fund	Objective	Net Assets	NAV	Ret1	Ret2	Ret3	Ret4	Ret5	Yld%	Ratio	Toll-Free	Phone	Load	Exp	Def	Manager	Date
IPS MILLENNIUM	Growth Income	0.7	13.46	8.27	☆	☆	☆	☆	0.0	N/A	None	615-524-1676	None	None	None	Loest/D'Amilo	'95/95
ISRAEL GROWTH FUND	Emerging Markets	0.1	6.71	-2.61	7.70	8.91	9.79	☆	0.0	☐	708-7228	None	4.75	None	None	Israel Growth Inv. Adv.	'94
IVY BOND FUND; A	Fixed Income	112.3	9.51	8.20	11.08	12.23	1.90	☆	7.9		456-5111	None	5.75	1.45	None	Leslie Ferris	93
IVY CANADA FUND; A	Canadian	18.4	9.31	9.54	-4.90	☆	☆	☆	0.6		456-5111	None	5.75	2.05	None	Sturm/Christ	'87/'87
IVY CHINA REGION; A	Pacific Region	13.6	8.75	5.35	-6.18	☆	☆	☆	0.8	25.3	456-5111	None	5.75	2.20	None	Trebbi-Longa/Landry	'93/'93
IVY CHINA REGION; B	Pacific Region	7.3	8.75	5.17	-6.91	☆	☆	☆	0.0	25.3	456-5111	None	None	2.95	5.00	Trebbi-Longa/Landry	'93/'93
IVY EMERGING GROWTH; A	Small Company Growth	24.3	21.64	8.65	41.44	☆	☆	☆	0.0	25.3	456-5111	None	5.75	2.20	None	James Broadfoot	93
IVY EMERGING GROWTH; B	Small Company Growth	7.6	21.64	8.47	40.52	☆	☆	☆	0.0	☐	456-5111	None	None	2.20	5.00	James Broadfoot	93
IVY GLOBAL FUND; A	Global	21.0	11.88	6.45	5.23	8.69	10.85	11.75	0.7	17.2	456-5111	None	5.75	1.38	None	Landry/Trebbi-Longa	'91/'91
IVY GROWTH FUND; A	Growth	269.1	15.87	8.48	19.03	☆	☆	☆	0.9	17.1	456-5111	None	5.75	2.34	None	Team Managed	N/A
IVY GROWTH FUND; B	Growth	2.1	15.87	8.25	17.89	☆	☆	☆	0.0	17.1	456-5111	None	None	1.84	5.00	Team Managed	N/A
IVY GROWTH WITH INC; A	Growth Income	58.6	10.17	8.75	16.34	11.84	10.55	13.62	1.7		456-5111	None	5.75	2.70	None	James Broadfoot	'92
IVY GROWTH WITH INC; B	Growth Income	7.3	10.17	8.57	15.42	☆	☆	☆	1.0	☐	456-5111	None	None	1.58	5.00	James Broadfoot	93
IVY INTL FUND; A	International	314.1	29.02	4.96	11.95	14.36	9.52	☆	0.9		456-5111	None	5.75	2.50	None	Hakan Castegren	'86
IVY INTL FUND; B	International	42.7	29.02	4.73	10.94	☆	☆	☆	0.0		456-5111	None	None		5.00	Hakan Castegren	'92
IVY LATIN AMERICA; A	Latin American	0.8	6.59	5.97	☆	☆	☆	☆	0.0		456-5111	None	5.75		None	Landry/Dominguez	'94/'94
IVY LATIN AMERICA; B	Latin American	0.3	6.59	5.78	☆	☆	☆	☆	0.0		456-5111	None	None	5.00	5.00	Landry/Dominguez	'94/'94
IVY NEW CENTURY; A	Emerging Markets	1.0	8.83	6.19	☆	☆	☆	☆	0.0		456-5111	None	5.75		None	Landry/Trebbi-Longa	'94/'94
IVY NEW CENTURY; B	Emerging Markets	0.4	8.83	6.00	☆	☆	☆	☆	5.2		456-5111	None	None	5.00	5.00	Landry/Trebbi-Longa	'94/'94
IVY SHORT TERM BOND; A	Fixed Income	7.2	9.62	3.62	☆	3.34	4.40	☆			456-5111	None	3.50	0.92	None	Leslie Ferris	95
JACKSON NATL GROWTH	S&P Index	11.4	12.94	9.38	25.43	☆	☆	☆	2.0	17.2	888-3863	None	4.75	0.46	None	PPM America	'92
JACKSON NATL INCOME	Fixed Income	21.3	10.01	5.16	10.64	☆	☆	☆	5.9		888-3863	None	4.75	0.97	None	PPM America	92
JACKSON NATL TOTAL RET	Flexible	21.7	11.86	6.56	17.75	☆	☆	☆	3.4	15.3	888-3863	None	4.75	1.16	None	PPM America	92
JANUS BALANCED	Balanced	111.6	13.03	6.16	14.16	☆	☆	☆	4.4	16.5	525-8983	303-333-3863	None	1.42	None	James P. Craig	93
JANUS ENTERPRISE	Midcap	390.8	24.37	5.41	23.69	☆	☆	☆	2.1	21.4	525-8983	303-333-3863	None	1.25	None	James P. Goff	92
JANUS FLEXIBLE INCOME	Fixed Income	491.4	9.38	7.35	11.26	9.63	11.97	☆	7.8		525-8983	303-333-3863	None	0.93	None	Ronald V. Speaker	'91
JANUS FUND	Capital Appreciation	10,742.1	21.88	8.96	19.73	11.82	12.33	15.40	0.0	16.7	525-8983	303-333-3863	None	0.91	None	James P. Craig	'86
JANUS GROWTH AND INCOME	Growth Income	487.4	16.36	11.50	20.19	11.11	☆	☆	0.6	16.4	525-8983	303-333-3863	None	1.22	None	Thomas F. Marsico	'91
JANUS INTMDT GOVT SECS	Fixed Income	36.3	4.96	4.72	8.46	3.68	☆	☆	6.2		525-8983	303-333-3863	None	0.65	None	Ronald V. Speaker	'91
JANUS MERCURY	Capital Appreciation	1,162.9	16.23	13.81	39.91	☆	☆	☆	1.0	12.9	525-8983	303-333-3863	None	1.33	None	Warren B. Lammert	'93
JANUS OVERSEAS	International	74.6	10.79	8.99	10.10	☆	☆	☆	0.0		525-8983	303-333-3863	None	2.16	None	Helen Y. Hayes	'94
JANUS SHORT-TERM BOND	Fixed Income	48.8	2.84	2.29	4.62	☆	☆	☆	6.7		525-8983	303-333-3863	None	0.65	None	Ronald V. Speaker	'92
JANUS TWENTY ☒	Capital Appreciation	2,667.3	27.74	14.25	26.46	10.25	12.64	14.79	0.2	19.6	525-8983	303-333-3863	None	1.02	None	Thomas F. Marsico	'88
JANUS VENTURE	Small Company Growth	1,577.4	55.27	9.27	27.04	14.01	13.99	16.93	0.1	16.9	525-8983	303-333-3863	None	0.96	None	Lammert/Goff	'93/'93
JANUS WORLDWIDE	Global	1,563.3	26.40	9.45	14.39	15.46	☆	☆	2.0		525-8983	303-333-3863	None	1.12	None	Helen Y. Hayes	'91
THE JAPAN FUND	Japanese	448.6	8.44	-6.64	-27.29	3.00	☆	12.21	0.0		535-2726	617-439-4640	4.50	1.08	None	Kwak/Allan/Gerspach	'88/'90/'95
JEFFERSON-PILOT CAP APP	Growth	34.9	14.66	8.19	19.54	10.82	9.21	11.29	1.8		458-4498	910-691-3448	4.50	0.83	None	Gregory D. Walker	'94
JEFFERSON-PILOT INV GRD	Fixed Income	22.4	9.54	6.45	11.61	6.38	7.87	9.31	6.3		458-4498	910-691-3448	4.50	0.85	None	H. Lusby Brown	'94
JENSEN PORTFOLIO	Growth Income	9.9	10.27	6.46	21.38	☆	☆	☆	1.6		221-4384	503-274-2044	None	1.13	None	Val E. Jensen	'92
JHAVERI VALUE FUND	Growth	N/A	12.50	☆	☆	☆	☆	☆	0.0	N/A	977-8778	216-331-0703	None	None	None	Ramesch Jhaveri	95
JOSHUA MEDIA FUND	Specialty	N/A	14.95	☆	☆	☆	☆	☆	0.0	N/A	352-7507	610-832-1075	None	0.50	None	David Butterworth	'95
JPM INSTL BOND	Fixed Income	343.0	9.86	6.30	12.26	☆	☆	☆	6.3		521-5412	212-826-1303	None	0.65	None	Bill Tennille	'94
JPM INSTL DIVERSIFIED	Balanced	161.8	11.26	7.03	17.36	☆	☆	☆	2.3		521-5412	212-826-1303	None	1.46	None	Gerald H. Osterberg	93
JPM INSTL EMRG MKTS EQTY	Emerging Markets	175.1	10.16	8.20	-4.68	☆	☆	☆	0.5		521-5412	212-826-1303	None	1.00	None	Doug Dooley	93
JPM INSTL INTL EQUITY	International	376.1	10.14	-1.46	-4.29	☆	☆	☆	0.0		521-5412	212-826-1303	None	0.60	None	Paul Quinsee	93
JPM INSTL SELECTED US EQ	Growth Income	172.5	12.29	7.62	20.75	☆	☆	☆	1.2	N/A	521-5412	212-826-1303	None	0.45	None	William Peterson	'93
JPM INSTL SH TM BOND	Fixed Income	53.6	9.81	3.36	7.54	☆	☆	☆	6.0	N/A	521-5412	212-826-1303	None	0.80	None	Connie Plaehn	'93/'93
JPM INSTL US SMALL CO	Small Company Growth	149.3	11.74	9.11	22.61	15.32	☆	☆	0.7	N/A	521-5412	212-826-1303	None	1.63	None	Otness/Kittler	'92
JURIKA & VOYLES BALANCED	Balanced	38.1	13.96	10.12	17.88	☆	☆	☆	2.1	N/A	584-6878	None	None	None	None	Jurika & Voyles, Inc.	'93/'93
JURIKA & VOYLES MINI-CAP	Small Company Growth	7.8	14.12	12.56	☆	☆	☆	☆	0.0	N/A	584-6878	None	None	None	None	Jurika & Voyles, Inc.	'94

PERFORMANCE OF MUTUAL FUNDS (continued)

FUND NAME	OBJECTIVE	ASSETS ($ MILL) 5/31/95	NAV ($/SHR) 6/30/95	QTR	1YR	3YRS	5YRS	10YRS	DIV YLD %	P/E RATIO	800	In-State	Load	Exp. Ratio	Redemption	MANAGER	SINCE
					RETURN THROUGH 6/30 (Annualized)						PHONE NUMBER		FEES				
JURIKA & VOYLES VAL + GR	Growth	7.4	12.82	14.57	☆	☆	☆	☆	0.0	N/A	584-6878	None	None	None	None	Jurika & Voyles, Inc.	'94
KAUFMANN FUND	Small Company Growth	2,049.5	4.39	10.58	37.19	24.84	20.06	☆	0.0	25.9	666-4943	212-922-0123	None	2.29	0.20	Utsch/Auriana	'86/'86
KEELEY SMALL CAP VALUE	Small Company Growth	5.9	11.36	7.78	17.48	☆	☆	☆	0.0	12.9	533-5344	312-786-5050	4.50	2.49	None	John Keeley	'93
KEMPER ADJ RATE GOVT; A	Fixed Income	143.4	8.31	2.14	5.06	4.26	7.08	☆	5.5	☐☐	621-1048	312-781-1121	3.50	0.93	None	Sloan/Byrnes	'95/'94
KEMPER ADJ RATE GOVT; B	Fixed Income	5.0	8.31	1.91	3.98	☆	☆	☆	4.6		621-1048	312-781-1121	None		4.00	Sloan/Byrnes	'95/'94
KEMPER ADJ RATE GOVT; C	Fixed Income	0.7	8.32	1.92	4.29	☆	☆	☆	4.7		621-1048	312-781-1121	None		None	Sloan/Byrnes	'95/'94
KEMPER BLUE CHIP; A	Growth Income	146.1	13.87	8.23	20.55	8.12	8.79	☆	1.4	N/A	621-1048	312-781-1121	5.75	1.48	None	Tracy McCormick Chester	'94
KEMPER BLUE CHIP; B	Growth Income	8.7	13.87	8.05	19.50	☆	☆	☆	0.7	N/A	621-1048	312-781-1121	None		4.00	Tracy McCormick Chester	'94
KEMPER BLUE CHIP; C	Growth Income	0.6	13.92	8.04	20.01	☆	☆	☆	0.8	N/A	621-1048	312-781-1121	None		None	Tracy McCormick Chester	'94
KEMPER DVSFD INCOME; A	Fixed Income	496.2	5.97	5.67	10.74	10.66	14.28	9.97	8.4		621-1048	312-781-1121	4.50	1.12	None	Team Managed	N/A
KEMPER DVSFD INCOME; B	Fixed Income	270.1	5.97	5.42	9.73	☆	☆	☆	7.5		621-1048	312-781-1121	None		4.00	Team Managed	N/A
KEMPER DVSFD INCOME; C	Fixed Income	2.1	5.99	5.62	9.98	☆	☆	☆	7.6		621-1048	312-781-1121	None		None	Team Managed	N/A
KEMPER GLOBAL INCOME; A	World Income	117.9	9.63	4.73	19.35	8.47	9.09	☆	6.3	☐☐☐☐☐	621-1048	312-781-1121	4.50	1.53	None	Johns/Beimford	'89/'93
KEMPER GLOBAL INCOME; B	World Income	53.7	9.65	4.52	18.54	☆	☆	☆	5.5		621-1048	312-781-1121	None	2.27	4.00	Johns/Beimford	'94/'94
KEMPER GLOBAL INCOME; C	World Income	0.1	9.65	4.64	18.45	☆	☆	☆	5.6		621-1048	312-781-1121	None	2.23	None	Johns/Beimford	'94/'94
KEMPER GROWTH FUND; A	Growth	1,560.7	14.75	7.66	22.33	8.38	11.24	13.83	0.0	N/A	621-1048	312-781-1121	5.75	1.09	None	C. Beth Cotner	'94
KEMPER GROWTH FUND; B	Growth	704.9	14.58	7.36	21.03	☆	☆	☆	0.0	N/A	621-1048	312-781-1121	None		4.00	C. Beth Cotner	'94
KEMPER GROWTH FUND; C	Growth	3.5	14.61	7.51	21.18	☆	☆	☆	0.0	N/A	621-1048	312-781-1121	None		None	C. Beth Cotner	'94
KEMPER HIGH YIELD; A	Fixed Income	2,434.2	7.93	4.82	11.18	10.47	13.75	11.90	9.6	☐☐☐☐☐	621-1048	312-781-1121	4.50	0.86	None	McNamara/Resis	'90/'92
KEMPER HIGH YIELD; B	Fixed Income	1,042.5	7.92	4.59	10.05	☆	☆	☆	8.7		621-1048	312-781-1121	None		4.00	McNamara/Resis	'94/'94
KEMPER HIGH YIELD; C	Fixed Income	12.8	7.94	4.59	10.22	☆	☆	☆	8.8		621-1048	312-781-1121	None		None	McNamara/Resis	'94
KEMPER INC&CAP PRES; A	Fixed Income	514.9	8.52	7.41	13.54	8.50	9.88	9.69	7.3		621-1048	312-781-1121	4.50	0.94	None	Robert Cessine	'94
KEMPER INC&CAP PRES; B	Fixed Income	32.4	8.50	7.17	12.36	☆	☆	☆	6.4		621-1048	312-781-1121	None		4.00	Robert Cessine	'94
KEMPER INC&CAP PRES; C	Fixed Income	0.8	8.50	7.05	12.26	☆	☆	☆	6.4		621-1048	312-781-1121	None		None	Robert Cessine	'94
KEMPER INTL FUND; A	International	332.6	10.04	4.26	2.88	8.31	4.23	14.87	0.0	☐☐☐☐☐	621-1048	312-781-1121	5.75	1.54	None	Dennis Ferro	'94
KEMPER INTL FUND; B	International	34.4	9.95	4.08	1.80	☆	☆	☆	3.1		621-1048	312-781-1121	None		4.00	Dennis Ferro	'94
KEMPER INTL FUND; C	International	1.5	9.95	4.08	1.99	☆	☆	☆	3.1	N/A	621-1048	312-781-1121	None		None	Dennis Ferro	'94
KEMPER RETIRE SRS I ⊠	Balanced Target	105.3	11.19	7.39	17.03	9.78	11.74	☆	3.6	N/A	621-1048	312-781-1121	5.00	0.91	4.00	Tracy McCormick Chester	'94
KEMPER RETIRE SRS II ⊠	Balanced Target	172.4	12.94	7.74	16.52	9.73	☆	☆	4.3	N/A	621-1048	312-781-1121	5.00	0.90	None	Tracy McCormick Chester	'94
KEMPER RETIRE SRS III ⊠	Balanced Target	123.2	10.75	8.70	18.37	10.59	☆	☆	3.9	N/A	621-1048	312-781-1121	5.00	0.95	None	Tracy McCormick Chester	'94
KEMPER RETIRE SRS IV ⊠	Balanced Target	151.5	10.07	9.34	18.95	☆	☆	☆	3.7	N/A	621-1048	312-781-1121	5.00	0.97	None	Tracy McCormick Chester	'94
KEMPER RETIRE SRS V ⊠	Balanced Target	134.1	9.53	9.79	19.97	☆	☆	☆	2.2	N/A	621-1048	312-781-1121	5.00	None	None	Tracy McCormick Chester	'93
KEMPER SH-INT GOVT; A	Fixed Income	28.5	8.13	3.86	7.20	4.96	6.02	☆	6.5	☐☐☐☐	621-1048	312-781-1121	3.50	1.06	None	Sloan/Keeley	'95/'94
KEMPER SH-INT GOVT; B	Fixed Income	219.4	8.10	3.65	6.42	4.07	☆	☆	5.6		621-1048	312-781-1121	None	1.93	4.00	Sloan/Keeley	'95/'94
KEMPER SH-INT GOVT; C	Fixed Income	2.2	8.10	3.66	6.35	☆	☆	☆	5.7		621-1048	312-781-1121	None		None	Sloan/Keeley	'95/'94
KEMPER SM CAP EQTY; A ★★	Small Company Growth	480.8	6.27	9.04	25.76	14.64	14.78	13.58	0.0	N/A	621-1048	312-781-1121	5.75	1.34	None	Karen Hussey	'94
KEMPER SM CAP EQTY; B ★★	Small Company Growth	172.2	6.19	8.79	24.21	☆	☆	☆	0.0	N/A	621-1048	312-781-1121	None		4.00	Karen Hussey	'94
KEMPER SM CAP EQTY; C ★★	Small Company Growth	1.8	6.18	8.80	23.56	☆	☆	☆	0.0	N/A	621-1048	312-781-1121	None		None	Karen Hussey	'94
KEMPER TECHNOLOGY FD; A	Science & Technology	764.5	12.68	18.73	56.03	23.45	15.29	15.03	0.0	N/A	621-1048	312-781-1121	5.75	0.89	None	Goers/Korth	'91/'94
KEMPER TECHNOLOGY FD; B	Science & Technology	20.9	12.52	18.45	54.03	☆	☆	☆	0.0	N/A	621-1048	312-781-1121	None		4.00	Goers/Korth	'94/'94
KEMPER TECHNOLOGY FD; C	Science & Technology	0.7	12.56	18.71	54.83	☆	☆	☆	0.0	N/A	621-1048	312-781-1121	None		None	Goers/Korth	'94/'94
KEMPER TOTAL RETURN; A	Balanced	1,729.3	10.05	7.89	16.83	8.33	10.15	11.20	2.5	21.8	621-1048	312-781-1121	5.75	1.13	None	Gary Langbaum	'95
KEMPER TOTAL RETURN; B	Balanced	1,109.0	10.04	7.56	15.73	☆	☆	☆	1.7	21.8	621-1048	312-781-1121	None		4.00	Gary Langbaum	'95
KEMPER TOTAL RETURN; C	Balanced	3.7	10.05	7.71	15.81	☆	☆	☆	1.7	21.8	621-1048	312-781-1121	None		None	Gary Langbaum	'95
KEMPER US GOVT SEC; A	Fixed Income	4,850.8	8.87	5.84	11.50	5.72	8.69	9.39	7.4	☐	621-1048	312-781-1121	4.50	0.75	None	Beimford/Sloan	'81/'95

Fund	Objective	Net Assets ($Mil)				Rating			Yield %	M*	Phone 1	Phone 2	Load	12b-1	CDSC	Manager	Since
KEMPER US GOVT SEC; B	Fixed Income	36.1	8.86	5.71	10.59	☆	☆	☆	6.5		621-1048	312-781-1121	None	None	4.00	Beimford/Sloan	'94/95
KEMPER US GOVT SEC; C	Fixed Income	2.1	8.88	5.71	10.75	☆	☆	☆	6.5		621-1048	312-781-1121	None	0.99	None	Beimford/Sloan	'94/95
KEMPER US MTGE; A	Fixed Income	2,034.1	7.13	5.74	11.17	5.43	7.64	7.40	7.3		621-1048	312-781-1121	4.50	1.79	None	Beimford/Sloan	'92/95
KEMPER US MTGE; B	Fixed Income	1,617.2	7.12	5.38	10.28	4.59	☆	☆	6.5		621-1048	312-781-1121	None	None	4.00	Beimford/Sloan	'94/95
KEMPER US MTGE; C	Fixed Income	1.1	7.12	5.55	10.34	☆	☆	☆	6.6		621-1048	312-781-1121	None	None	None	Beimford/Sloan	
KENILWORTH FUND	Balanced Target	29.9	9.96	8.14	11.91	☆	☆	☆	1.2	N/A	None	312-236-5388	5.00	None	None	Dennis Ferro	'94
KENT FDS GRO & INC; INST	Growth	4.3	11.82	12.36	27.16	☆	☆	☆	0.5	N/A	633-5368	None	None	0.98	None	B. Padmanabha Pai	'93
KENT FDS GRO & INC; INV	Growth	317.7	12.19	8.11	25.02	☆	☆	☆	2.7	16.2	633-5368	None	4.00	0.98	None	Old Kent Bank	'92
KENT FDS INCOME; INST	Fixed Income	8.7	12.14	8.09	24.91	☆	☆	☆	2.7	16.2	633-5368	None	None	None	Old Kent Bank	'92
KENT FDS INCOME; INV	Fixed Income	137.9	10.51	7.61	☆	☆	☆	☆	0.0		633-5368	None	4.00	0.58	None	Mitch Stapley	'95
KENT FDS INDEX EQ; INST	S&P Index	0.7	10.49	7.35	25.07	☆	☆	☆	0.0	17.3	633-5368	None	None	0.60	None	Mitch Stapley	'95
KENT FDS INDEX EQ; INV	S&P Index	232.4	12.04	9.28	24.81	☆	☆	☆	2.3	17.3	633-5368	None	4.00	1.22	None	Old Kent Bank	'92
KENT FDS INTL GRO; INST	International	5.1	12.05	9.12	-2.33	☆	☆	☆	2.2		633-5368	None	None	1.25	None	Old Kent Bank	'92
KENT FDS INTL GRO; INV	International	183.1	12.54	2.45	-2.41	☆	☆	☆	1.0		633-5368	None	4.00	0.80	None	Old Kent Bank	'92
KENT FDS INTMDT BD; INST	Fixed Income	6.2	12.48	2.46	11.13	☆	☆	☆	1.0		633-5368	None	None	0.81	None	Old Kent Bank	'92
KENT FDS INTMDT BD; INV	Fixed Income	865.6	9.96	5.56	10.99	☆	☆	☆	6.1		633-5368	None	4.00	0.73	None	Old Kent Bank	'92
KENT FDS SH TM BD; INST	Fixed Income	6.5	9.98	5.48	7.25	☆	☆	☆	6.0		633-5368	None	None	0.74	None	Old Kent Bank	'92
KENT FDS SH TM BD; INV	Fixed Income	170.6	9.85	3.16	7.20	☆	☆	☆	5.9		633-5368	None	4.00	0.98	None	Old Kent Bank	'92
KENT FDS SM CO GRO; INST	Small Company Growth	1.7	12.91	3.24	15.58	☆	☆	☆	5.8	14.4	633-5368	None	None	0.86	None	Old Kent Bank	'92
KENT FDS SM CO GRO; INV	Small Company Growth	299.7	12.90	8.15	15.56	22.59	16.36	☆	0.8	14.4	633-5368	None	4.00	1.50	None	Old Kent Bank	'91
KEYSTONE AM CAP P&I; A	Fixed Income	8.9	9.70	8.17	5.86	3.94	☆	☆	0.7		343-2898	617-621-6100	3.00	1.50	None	Christopher Conkey	'91
KEYSTONE AM CAP P&I; B	Fixed Income	21.0	9.70	1.86	4.87	3.03	☆	☆	5.3		343-2898	617-621-6100	None	2.85	3.00	Christopher Conkey	'93
KEYSTONE AM CAP P&I; C	Fixed Income	70.2	9.69	1.70	4.98	☆	☆	☆	4.6		343-2898	617-621-6100	1.00	1.00	1.00	Christopher Conkey	'95
KEYSTONE AM GLBL OPP; A	Global Small Company	2.7	21.18	1.71	17.99	☆	☆	☆	4.6		343-2898	617-621-6100	5.75	1.75	1.00	Christopher Ely	'95
KEYSTONE AM GLBL OPP; B	Global Small Company	74.3	20.83	10.49	17.15	☆	☆	☆	0.0		343-2898	617-621-6100	None	1.75	1.00	Christopher Ely	'95
KEYSTONE AM GLBL OPP; C	Global Small Company	170.2	20.89	10.33	17.16	7.04	8.52	☆	0.0		343-2898	617-621-6100	None	1.00	3.00	Christopher Ely	'95
KEYSTONE AM GOVT SEC; B	Fixed Income	64.8	9.68	10.35	10.83	☆	☆	☆	0.0		343-2898	617-621-6100	None	1.75	1.00	Christopher Conkey	'88
KEYSTONE AM GOVT SEC; C	Fixed Income	30.1	9.69	5.32	9.98	☆	☆	☆	6.7		343-2898	617-621-6100	None	1.75	1.00	Christopher Conkey	'93
KEYSTONE AM INT BD; A	Fixed Income	11.2	8.95	5.13	10.09	6.61	8.67	☆	6.0		343-2898	617-621-6100	4.75	1.41	3.00	Christopher Conkey	'88
KEYSTONE AM INT BD; B	Fixed Income	15.2	8.96	5.12	9.46	☆	☆	☆	5.9		343-2898	617-621-6100	None	2.30	1.00	Christopher Conkey	'93
KEYSTONE AM INT BD; C	Fixed Income	17.5	8.96	4.57	8.55	☆	☆	☆	6.8		343-2898	617-621-6100	None	2.30	3.00	Christopher Conkey	'93
KEYSTONE AM OMEGA; A	Capital Appreciation	10.7	18.02	4.35	8.55	13.08	13.53	15.32	6.0		343-2898	617-621-6100	5.75	1.32	None	Maureen E. Cullinane	'89
KEYSTONE AM OMEGA; B	Capital Appreciation	104.2	17.71	4.47	20.91	☆	☆	☆	6.0		343-2898	617-621-6100	None	2.07	1.00	Maureen E. Cullinane	'93
KEYSTONE AM OMEGA; C	Capital Appreciation	39.9	9.24	9.54	19.80	☆	☆	☆	0.0		343-2898	617-621-6100	None	2.07	1.00	Maureen E. Cullinane	'93
KEYSTONE AM STR DEV; A	Global	10.5	9.69	9.25	19.77	☆	☆	☆	0.0	24.9	343-2898	617-621-6100	4.75	1.59	None	John C. Madden	'94
KEYSTONE AM STR DEV; B	Global	5.0	9.64	7.43	☆	☆	☆	☆	0.0	24.9	343-2898	617-621-6100	None	2.31	1.00	John C. Madden	'94
KEYSTONE AM STR DEV; C	Global	15.3	7.23	7.23	☆	☆	☆	☆	0.0	24.9	343-2898	617-621-6100	None	2.34	3.00	John C. Madden	'94
KEYSTONE AM STR INC; A	Fixed Income	1.5	6.82	6.46	1.01	9.16	10.98	☆	9.6		343-2898	617-621-6100	4.75	2.20	None	Cryan/Gunn/Conkey	'95/'87/'87
KEYSTONE AM STR INC; B	Fixed Income	88.1	6.86	6.37	0.43	9.36	9.43	☆	8.7		343-2898	617-621-6100	None	2.95	3.00	Cryan/Gunn/Conkey	'95/'93/'93
KEYSTONE AM STR INC; C	Fixed Income	146.7	6.85	6.21	0.30	☆	☆	☆	8.7		343-2898	617-621-6100	None	1.71	1.00	Cryan/Gunn/Conkey	'95/'93/'93
KEYSTONE AM TOT RTN; B	Equity Income	47.2	13.19	6.77	12.27	☆	☆	☆	2.1		343-2898	617-621-6100	None	1.75	None	Walter McCormick	'93
KEYSTONE AM TOT RTN; C	Equity Income	24.9	13.20	6.59	11.40	☆	☆	☆	1.4		343-2898	617-621-6100	None	2.07	1.00	Walter McCormick	'92
KEYSTONE AM WORLD BD; A	World Income	13.0	8.21	6.59	3.42	4.00	☆	☆	7.3		343-2898	617-621-6100	4.75	2.20	None	Gilman Gunn	'93
KEYSTONE AM WORLD BD; B	World Income	8.4	8.25	6.65	2.73	☆	☆	☆	6.5		343-2898	617-621-6100	None	2.95	3.00	Gilman Gunn	'93
KEYSTONE AM WORLD BD; C	World Income	10.8	8.21	6.56	2.73	☆	☆	☆	6.5		343-2898	617-621-6100	None	1.71	1.00	Gilman Gunn	'84/'84
KEYSTONE BALANCED	Income	1,350.1	10.09	6.70	14.20	7.61	8.42	10.34	3.3		343-2898	617-621-6100	None	1.75	4.00	McCormick/McCue	'95
KEYSTONE DVSFD BOND	Fixed Income	769.7	15.22	5.00	7.84	6.63	8.19	7.93	7.6		343-2898	617-621-6100	None			Christopher Conkey	

★ KEMPER SM CAP EQTY; A,B,C–Fund has been reclassified from Midcap to Small Company.

© Copyright Lipper Analytical Services, Inc.

FUND NAME	OBJECTIVE	ASSETS ($ MIL) 5/31/95	NAV ($/SHR) 6/30/95	QTR	1YR	3YRS	5YRS	10YRS	DIV YLD %	P/E RATIO	800	In-State	Load	Exp. Ratio	Redemption	MANAGER	SINCE
						(Annualized)											
KEYSTONE FUND AMER; A	Global	17.3	9.84	13.91	9.15	☆	☆		4.1	□	343-2898	617-621-6100	5.75	1.79	None	Gilman Gunn	'93
KEYSTONE FUND AMER; B	Global	112.3	9.77	13.69	8.52	☆	☆		3.8	□	343-2898	617-621-6100	None	2.54	3.00	Gilman Gunn	'93
KEYSTONE FUND AMER; C	Global	13.4	9.77	13.69	8.40	☆	☆		3.8	□	343-2898	617-621-6100	None	2.54	1.00	Gilman Gunn	'93
KEYSTONE GRO & INC	Growth Income	194.5	23.80	9.36	15.89	7.42	7.48	10.52	1.5	31.0	343-2898	617-621-6100	None	2.07	4.00	Judith Warners	'95
KEYSTONE HIGH INCOME	Fixed Income	745.6	4.29	4.73	0.46	7.43	9.67	6.63	10.6		343-2898	617-621-6100	None	1.84	4.00	Team Managed	N/A
KEYSTONE INSTL ADJ RATE	Fixed Income	23.3	9.67	2.00	5.90	4.36			5.8	□	343-2898	617-621-6100	None	0.30	None	Christopher Conkey	'91
KEYSTONE INTERNATIONAL	International	128.8	6.75	5.30	1.73	8.16	10.77		0.5	20.7	343-2898	617-621-6100	None	2.54	4.00	Gilman Gunn	'91
KEYSTONE MIDCAP GRO	Growth	250.8	9.53	10.17	18.53	10.53	9.84	11.43	0.6		343-2898	617-621-6100	None	1.35	4.00	Margery Parker	'95
KEYSTONE PREC METALS	Gold	187.8	21.95	4.37	-3.31	12.73	7.89	7.25	0.3	N/A	343-2898	617-621-6100	None	2.33	4.00	Pirnie/Thorne	'79/'74
KEYSTONE QUALITY BOND	Fixed Income	312.9	15.33	5.69	10.81	5.26	7.33	7.72	6.1	□	343-2898	617-621-6100	None	1.86	4.00	Christopher Conkey	'95
KEYSTONE SM CO GROWTH	Small Company Growth	1,459.9	9.08	15.33	41.01	24.69	19.56	15.18	0.0	24.1	343-2898	617-621-6100	None	1.73	4.00	Christopher Ely	'95
KEYSTONE STRAT GROWTH	Growth	455.6	8.07	9.20	17.30	13.03	11.57	12.85	0.0	16.9	343-2898	617-621-6100	None	1.73	4.00	Walter McCormick	'89
KIDDER GOVT INCOME; A	Fixed Income	41.3	14.22	5.14	9.34	4.67	6.56		5.8		647-1568	None	2.25	1.23	None	Singh/McCauley	'94/'94
KIDDER GOVT INCOME; B	Fixed Income	1.3	14.21	5.08	9.07	☆	☆		5.6		647-1568	None	None	None	None	Singh/McCauley	'94/'94
KIDDER GOVT INCOME; C	Fixed Income	3.3	14.21	5.28	9.90	☆	☆		6.3		647-1568	None	None	None	None	Singh/McCauley	'94/'94
KIDDER INV II EMERG; A	Emerging Markets	33.2	9.73	7.99	-9.38	☆	☆		0.5	□	647-1568	None	5.75	None	None	Antoine W. Van Agtmael	'94
KIDDER INV II EMERG; B	Emerging Markets	18.2	9.67	7.68	-10.10	☆	☆		0.0	□	647-1568	None	None	None	1.00	Antoine W. Van Agtmael	'94
KIDDER INV II EMERG; C	Emerging Markets	12.3	9.75	8.09	-9.12	☆	☆		0.7	□	647-1568	None	None	None	None	Antoine W. Van Agtmael	'94
KIDDER INV III SM CP; A	Small Company Growth	27.6	12.32	8.26	24.95	☆	☆		0.0	N/A	647-1568	None	5.75	1.68	None	Owen T. Barry III	'93
KIDDER INV III SM CP; B	Small Company Growth	13.6	12.17	8.08	24.06	☆	☆		0.0	N/A	647-1568	None	None	2.43	None	Owen T. Barry III	'93
KIDDER INV III SM CP; C	Small Company Growth	5.4	12.37	8.32	25.20	☆	☆		0.0	N/A	647-1568	None	None	1.43	None	Owen T. Barry III	'93
KIDDER INV ADJ RATE; A	Fixed Income	25.8	11.56	2.19	2.45	☆	☆		4.9		647-1568	None	2.25	0.88	None	Singh/McCauley	'94/'94
KIDDER INV ADJ RATE; B	Fixed Income	2.7	11.56	2.07	1.95	☆	☆		4.4		647-1568	None	None	1.38	None	Singh/McCauley	'94/'94
KIDDER INV ADJ RATE; C	Fixed Income	0.6	11.56	2.17	2.62	☆	☆		5.2		647-1568	None	None	0.63	None	Singh/McCauley	'95/'95
KIDDER INV ASST ALLO; A	Flexible	1.8	14.36	8.94	22.83	☆	☆		1.5	N/A	647-1568	None	5.75	None	None	Kirk Barneby	'94
KIDDER INV ASST ALLO; B	Flexible	47.3	14.39	8.78	21.91	☆	☆		0.8	N/A	647-1568	None	None	None	None	Kirk Barneby	'94
KIDDER INV ASST ALLO; C	Flexible	2.5	14.38	9.07	23.10	☆	☆		1.7	N/A	647-1568	None	None	None	None	Kirk Barneby	'94
KIDDER INV GLBL EQ; A	Global	146.7	15.94	7.78	9.16	☆	11.48		0.0	□	647-1568	None	5.75	1.58	None	Ralph R. Layman	'91
KIDDER INV GLBL EQ; B	Global	28.7	15.66	7.55	8.31	☆	☆		0.0	□	647-1568	None	None	2.33	None	Ralph R. Layman	'93
KIDDER INV GLBL EQ; C	Global	28.8	16.03	7.87	9.46	☆	☆		0.0	□	647-1568	None	None	1.33	None	Ralph R. Layman	'93
KIDDER INV GLBL FXD; A	World Income	98.3	13.07	4.41	16.46	☆	☆		6.9		647-1568	None	2.25	1.19	None	Kenneth A. Windheim	'92
KIDDER INV GLBL FXD; B	World Income	20.1	13.07	4.28	16.08	☆	☆		6.4		647-1568	None	None	1.68	None	Kenneth A. Windheim	'93
KIDDER INV GLBL FXD; C	World Income	11.0	13.08	4.47	17.02	☆	☆		7.1		647-1568	None	None	0.94	None	Kenneth A. Windheim	'93
KIDDER INV INTMDT; A	Fixed Income	18.2	12.14	5.99	11.03	5.96	☆		5.3		647-1568	None	2.25	1.46	None	Robert Aufiero	'93
KIDDER INV INTMDT; B	Fixed Income	2.0	12.14	5.87	10.49	☆	☆		4.9		647-1568	None	None	1.96	None	Robert Aufiero	'94
KIDDER INV INTMDT; C	Fixed Income	1.1	12.14	6.07	11.32	☆	☆		5.6		647-1568	None	None	1.21	None	Robert Aufiero	'94
KIEWIT EQUITY	Growth	12.6	14.04	8.92	☆	☆	☆		0.0	N/A	254-3948	None	None	None	None	Robert Aufiero	'94
KIEWIT INT-TM BOND	Fixed Income	96.4	2.05	4.17	☆	☆	☆		0.0		254-3948	None	None	None	None	P. Greggory Williams	'95
KIEWIT SH-TM GOVT	Fixed Income	103.9	2.03	2.62	☆	☆	☆		0.0		254-3948	None	None	None	None	P. Greggory Williams	'94
KPM EQUITY	Growth	12.8	12.00	8.20	☆	☆	☆		0.0	N/A	776-5777	402-392-7976	None	None	None	Thomas J Sudyka	'94
KPM FIXED INCOME	Fixed Income	4.2	10.47	5.33	☆	☆	☆		0.0		776-5777	402-392-7976	None	None	None	Patrick M Miner	'94
LAIDLAW COVENANT FUND	Growth Income	4.3	14.92	5.22	22.50	11.03	☆		0.1	17.2	275-2683	None	4.50	2.50	None	Fingerhood/Carfang	'92/'92
LAKE FOREST CORE EQUITY	Growth Income	0.1	15.28	1.46	☆	☆	☆		0.0	N/A	592-7722	None	None	None	None	Irving Boberski	'95
LANDMRK FXD INTMDT INC	Fixed Income	49.9	9.67	6.49	12.05	☆	☆		5.7		223-4447	212-564-3456	4.00	0.90	None	Mark Lindbloom	'93
LANDMRK FXD US GOVT INC	Fixed Income	52.0	9.73	3.89	8.02	4.85	7.42		5.0		223-4447	212-564-3456	1.50	0.80	None	Tom Halley	'88

Fund	Objective	10 Yr	5 Yr	3 Yr	1 Yr	Curr	Rating	Yield	Net Assets	Phone (local)	Phone (toll)	Load	Other	Mgmt Fee	Risk	Portfolio Manager	Tenure
LANDMRK I BALANCED	Balanced	15.06	6.16	15.33	9.52	9.86	☆	2.8	N/A	237.7	223-4447	212-564-3456	4.75	None	1.02	Lindbloom/Hyde	'90/'90
LANDMRK II EQUITY	Growth	15.83	5.96	16.35	-12.65	9.00	☆	1.2	N/A	193.6	223-4447	212-564-3456	4.75	None	1.05	Dwight Hyde	'92
LANDMRK INTL EQUITY	International	12.59	7.61	6.41	6.04		☆	0.1		28.8	223-4447	212-564-3456	4.75	None	1.75	Henry de Vismes	'91
LAZARD BOND	Fixed Income	9.91	6.16	10.29	5.99		☆	6.2	15.2	31.6	228-0203	212-632-6000	None	None	0.80	Dunn/O'Grady	'95/'91
LAZARD EMERGING MKTS	Emerging Markets	9.14	8.81					0.0		22.2	228-0203	212-632-6000	None	None		Pablo Salas	'94
LAZARD EQUITY	Capital Appreciation	16.51	10.41	26.06	17.78	13.49	☆	1.1		121.1	228-0203	212-632-6000	None	None	1.05	Gulliquist/Rome	'87/'91
LAZARD INTL EQUITY	International	11.66	6.97	1.50	6.72		☆	1.1		1,015.4	228-0203	212-632-6000	None	None	0.94	John Reinsberg	'92
LAZARD INTL FXD INC	World Income	11.86	5.83	21.43	13.40		☆	5.8		44.4	228-0203	212-632-6000	None	None	1.05	Dunn/O'Grady	'95/'92
LAZARD INTL SMALL CAP	Intl Small Company	10.36	5.93	-3.27	☆			0.0		92.6	228-0203	212-632-6000	None	None	1.05	John Reinsberg	'93
LAZARD SMALL CAP	Small Company Growth	16.76	9.83	21.81	22.69		☆	0.2	15.9	518.4	228-0203	212-632-6000	None	None	0.85	Multiple Managers	N/A
LAZARD SPECIAL EQUITY	Capital Appreciation	12.98	5.10	8.68	9.04	10.68	☆	1.1	12.1	61.0	228-0203	212-632-6000	None	None	1.71	Charles Dreifus	'86
LAZARD STRATEGIC YIELD	World Income	9.27	5.69	8.16	7.04		☆	9.0		68.7	228-0203	212-632-6000	None	None	1.05	Multiple Managers	N/A
LEEB INV PERSONAL FIN	Growth	11.17	7.04	12.20	5.67		☆	2.5	14.6	34.1	543-8721	513-629-2000	3.00	None	1.50	Stephen Leeb	'92
LEGACY EQUITY FUND	Growth	11.65	10.95	☆	☆			0.0	N/A	1.0	525-3863	919-972-9922	None	None		Legacy Advisors, Inc.	'95
LEGG MASON AM LEAD CO TR	Growth	10.68	5.31	11.89			☆	1.1	20.9	64.5	822-5544	410-539-0000	None	None	1.95	J. Eric Leo	'93
LEGG MASON GL GLBL EQTY	Global	10.40	3.07	☆	☆			0.0		16.9	822-5544	410-539-0000	None	None		Charles F. Lovejoy	'95
LEGG MASON GL GLBL GOVT	World Income	10.69	6.70	16.43			☆	5.8		153.8	822-5544	410-539-0000	None	None	1.30	Keith J. Gardner	'94
LEGG MASON INC GOVT; NAV	Fixed Income	10.29	4.90	☆	☆			0.0		3.3	822-5544	410-539-0000	None	None		Carl L. Eichstaedt	'94
LEGG MASON INC GOVT; PRM	Fixed Income	10.29	4.76	9.02	7.96		☆	5.1		237.6	822-5544	410-539-0000	None	None	0.90	Carl L. Eichstaedt	'94
LEGG MASON INC HIGH YLD	Fixed Income	14.22	5.48	8.95	☆			8.6		65.7	822-5544	410-539-0000	None	None	None	Trudie Whitehead	'94
LEGG MASON INC INV GRADE	Fixed Income	10.11	6.26	12.92	7.38	8.89	☆	6.2		75.2	822-5544	410-539-0000	None	None	0.85	Kent S. Engel	'87
LEGG MASON SPEC INV; NAV	Midcap	21.49	8.00	☆	☆			0.0	N/A	26.6	822-5544	410-539-0000	None	None	1.94	William H. Miller III	'94
LEGG MASON SPEC INV; PRM	Midcap	21.35	7.65	8.85	12.83	13.04	☆	0.0	12.8	649.1	822-5544	410-539-0000	None	None	1.94	William H. Miller III	'85
LEGG MASON TOTAL RET; NAV	Growth Income	14.07	10.85	☆	☆			0.0	N/A	5.4	822-5544	410-539-0000	None	None	1.94	Miller/Dennin	'94/'94
LEGG MASON TOTAL RET; PRM	Growth Income	14.04	10.64	11.83	10.31	11.46	☆	2.3	13.6	218.6	822-5544	410-539-0000	None	None	1.94	Miller/Dennin	'90/'92
LEGG MASON VALUE TR; NAV	Growth	22.34	14.75	14.75	15.09		☆	0.0	N/A	39.9	822-5544	410-539-0000	None	None	1.82	William H. Miller III	'94
LEGG MASON VALUE TR; PRM	Growth	22.28	14.47	27.59	☆	11.34		0.4	N/A	1,126.2	822-5544	410-539-0000	None	None		William H. Miller III	'82
LEHMAN BROS SEL GR STK	Midcap	12.38	10.34	28.19	☆		☆	0.1	N/A	35.1	368-5556	617-722-7868	None	None	2.00	Susan Hirsch	'94
LEHMAN INST FLT RATE; PRM	Fixed Income	10.00	2.80	6.65			☆	5.8		32.1	368-5556	617-722-7868	None	None	0.10	Kirk Hartman	'94
LEHMAN INST FLT RATE; SEL	Fixed Income	10.00	2.74	6.38			☆	5.5		N/A	368-5556	617-722-7868	None	None	None	Kirk Hartman	'94
LEHMAN INST SH DUR; PRM	Fixed Income	9.98	2.32	6.40	☆			5.8		24.4	368-5556	617-722-7868	None	None	0.10	Kirk Hartman	'94
LEHMAN INST SH DUR; SEL	Fixed Income	9.98	2.29	6.17	☆			5.6		2.0	368-5556	617-722-7868	None	None	0.35	Kirk Hartman	'94
LEPERCQ-ISTEL TR L-I FD	Growth Income	15.52	10.23	14.80	11.52	8.35	☆	0.7		18.3	338-1579	212-698-0749	None	None	1.56	Hanson/Ngudu	'93/'93
LEXINGTON CONVERTIBLE	Convertible Securities	12.39	1.64	12.68	11.00	10.99	☆	0.9		9.5	526-0056	201-845-7300	None	None	2.75	Van Eck	'88
LEXINGTON CORP LEADERS	Growth Income	12.21	7.24	23.07	14.46	11.70	14.96	4.8	16.6	195.9	526-0056	201-845-7300	None	None	0.62	Team Managed	N/A
LEXINGTON GLOBAL	Global	11.37	2.90	0.98	10.27	5.66	☆	0.0		62.7	526-0056	201-845-7300	None	None	1.61	Wapnick/Saler	'94/'94
LEXINGTON GNMA INCOME	Fixed Income	8.04	4.09	11.14	6.19	8.55	☆	7.2		125.3	526-0056	201-845-7300	None	None	0.98	Denis P. Jamison	'81
LEXINGTON GOLDFUND	Gold	6.04	1.34	-1.20	10.27	3.40	8.99	0.5	N/A	154.7	526-0056	201-845-7300	None	None	1.54	Robert W. Radsch	'94
LEXINGTON GROWTH & INC	Growth Income	15.69	4.38	10.45	10.49	8.76	7.06	1.2	20.7	130.8	526-0056	201-845-7300	None	None	1.15	Alan Wapnick	'94
LEXINGTON INTERNATIONAL	International	10.12	1.20	-3.08	☆	☆	10.85	0.0		17.6	526-0056	201-845-7300	None	None	2.39	Richard Saler	'94
LEXINGTON RAMIREZ GL INC	World Income	10.42	8.76	9.60	5.78	6.94	☆	5.7		9.6	526-0056	201-845-7300	None	None	1.44	Jamison/Ramirez	'86/'95
LEXINGTON SH-INTMDT GOVT	Fixed Income	9.96	2.39	8.06	☆	☆		4.8		5.4	526-0056	201-845-7300	None	None	1.00	Denis P. Jamison	'93
LEXINGTON STRAT INVMENTS	Gold	2.51	-2.71	2.47	26.90	0.34	-4.89	1.5		92.9	526-0056	201-845-7300	5.75	None	1.76	Robert W. Radsch	'94
LEXINGTON STRAT SILVER	Specialty	4.00	10.50	2.04	-2.41	-1.84		0.0		60.6	526-0056	201-845-7300	5.75	None	1.84	Robert W. Radsch	'94
LEXINGTON WRLDWD EMERG	Emerging Markets	11.15	8.46	-3.18	10.68	8.32	10.94	0.0	11.0	325.9	526-0056	201-845-7300	None	None	1.65	Richard Saler	'94
LIBERTY EQTY INC; A	Equity Income	12.32	7.93	16.44	12.95	13.27	☆	3.6	15.0	118.8	245-4770	412-288-1900	5.50	1.00	1.00	Christopher H. Wiles	'91
LIBERTY EQTY INC; B	Equity Income	12.32	7.74	☆	☆	☆		0.0	N/A	9.9	245-4770	412-288-1900	None	5.50	None	Christopher H. Wiles	'94
LIBERTY EQTY INC; C	Equity Income	12.32	7.74	15.59	☆	☆		2.9		31.9	245-4770	412-288-1900	None	1.79	1.00	Christopher H. Wiles	'94
LIBERTY EQTY INC; FORT	Equity Income	12.32	7.89	16.19	☆	☆		3.4	15.0	37.6	245-4770	412-288-1900	1.00	None	None	Christopher H. Wiles	'93
LIBERTY HIGH INCOME; A	Fixed Income	10.82	5.11	10.89	10.40	15.60	11.34	9.5	15.0	471.2	245-4770	412-288-1900	4.50	None	1.18	Mark E. Durbiano	'89

PERFORMANCE OF MUTUAL FUNDS (continued)

FUND NAME	OBJECTIVE	ASSETS ($ MIL) 5/31/95	NAV ($/SHR) 6/30/95	RETURN THROUGH 6/30 QTR	1YR	3YRS (Annualized)	5YRS	10YRS	DIV YLD %	P/E RATIO	PHONE NUMBER 800	In-State	FEES Load	Exp. Ratio	Redemption	MANAGER	SINCE
LIBERTY HIGH INCOME; B	Fixed Income	62.0	10.82	4.91		☆			0.0	☐	245-4770	412-288-1900	None	None	5.50	Mark E. Durbiano	'94
LIBERTY HIGH INCOME; C	Fixed Income	36.2	10.82	4.94	10.14	☆			8.8		245-4770	412-288-1900	None	1.99	1.00	Mark E. Durbiano	'93
LIBERTY UTILITY; A	Utility	761.9	11.40	5.49	11.74	8.49		10.70	4.6	14.7	245-4770	412-288-1900	5.50	1.10	None	Christopher H. Wiles	'90
LIBERTY UTILITY; B	Utility	35.5	11.40	5.33		☆			0.0	N/A	245-4770	412-288-1900	None	None	5.50	Christopher H. Wiles	'94
LIBERTY UTILITY; C	Utility	60.1	11.40	5.32	10.82	☆			3.9	14.7	245-4770	412-288-1900	None	1.86	1.00	Christopher H. Wiles	'93
LINCOLN ADV CORP INC; A	Fixed Income	10.9	9.62	7.41	13.60	☆			6.0	☐	923-8476	219-455-3361	4.50	None	None	Team Managed	N/A
LINCOLN ADV CORP INC; B	Fixed Income	0.3	10.28	7.19	12.77	☆			8.4		923-8476	219-455-3361	None	None	5.00	Team Managed	N/A
LINCOLN ADV CORP INC; C	Fixed Income	0.1	10.28	6.62	☆				0.0		923-8476	219-455-3361	None	None	None	Team Managed	N/A
LINCOLN ADV CORP INC; D	Fixed Income	2.8	9.36	7.46	13.98	☆			9.4		923-8476	219-455-3361	None	None	1.00	Team Managed	N/A
LINCOLN ADV ENTRPRSE; A	Midcap	12.3	10.33	6.28	25.52	☆			0.0	N/A	923-8476	219-455-3361	5.50	None	None	Team Managed	N/A
LINCOLN ADV ENTRPRSE; B	Midcap	1.3	10.96	6.10	24.69	☆			0.0	N/A	923-8476	219-455-3361	None	None	5.00	Team Managed	N/A
LINCOLN ADV ENTRPRSE; C	Midcap	0.1	11.20	6.16	24.72	☆			0.0	N/A	923-8476	219-455-3361	None	None	1.00	Team Managed	N/A
LINCOLN ADV ENTRPRSE; D	Midcap	0.4	10.38	6.35	25.97	☆			0.0	N/A	923-8476	219-455-3361	4.50	None	None	Team Managed	N/A
LINCOLN ADV GOVT INC; A	Fixed Income	10.7	9.71	5.80	10.41	☆			5.7	☐	923-8476	219-455-3361	None	None	5.00	Team Managed	N/A
LINCOLN ADV GOVT INC; B	Fixed Income	0.3	10.14	5.60		☆			0.0		923-8476	219-455-3361	None	None	5.00	Team Managed	N/A
LINCOLN ADV GOVT INC; C	Fixed Income	0.1	10.27	5.66	10.57	☆			0.0	☐	923-8476	219-455-3361	None	None	1.00	Team Managed	N/A
LINCOLN ADV GOVT INC; D	Fixed Income	0.7	9.51	5.80	19.00	☆			8.0		923-8476	219-455-3361	5.50	None	None	Team Managed	N/A
LINCOLN ADV GRO&INC; A	Growth Income	12.5	11.00	10.32	18.30	☆			0.6	N/A	923-8476	219-455-3361	None	None	5.00	Team Managed	N/A
LINCOLN ADV GRO&INC; B	Growth Income	1.1	10.64	10.13	☆				0.7	N/A	923-8476	219-455-3361	None	None	5.00	Team Managed	N/A
LINCOLN ADV GRO&INC; C	Growth Income	0.1	11.19	10.13	18.24	☆			0.6	N/A	923-8476	219-455-3361	None	None	1.00	Team Managed	N/A
LINCOLN ADV GRO&INC; D	Growth Income	5.0	11.00	10.43	19.30	☆			0.9	N/A	923-8476	219-455-3361	None	None	None	Team Managed	N/A
LINCOLN ADV NEW PAC; A	Pacific Region	10.3	8.82	3.28	-6.84	☆			0.0		923-8476	219-455-3361	5.50	None	None	Team Managed	N/A
LINCOLN ADV NEW PAC; B	Pacific Region	0.6	9.14	3.04	-7.27	☆			0.0		923-8476	219-455-3361	None	None	5.00	Team Managed	N/A
LINCOLN ADV NEW PAC; C	Pacific Region	0.1	8.96	2.99	☆				0.0		923-8476	219-455-3361	None	None	5.00	Team Managed	N/A
LINCOLN ADV NEW PAC; D	Pacific Region	0.1	8.87	3.38	-6.41	☆			0.0	N/A	923-8476	219-455-3361	None	None	1.00	Team Managed	N/A
LINCOLN ADV US GRO; A	Growth	11.4	11.34	10.85	22.33	☆			0.0	N/A	923-8476	219-455-3361	5.50	None	None	Team Managed	N/A
LINCOLN ADV US GRO; B	Growth	0.4	11.27	10.71	21.57	☆			0.0	N/A	923-8476	219-455-3361	None	None	5.00	Team Managed	N/A
LINCOLN ADV US GRO; C	Growth	0.1	11.74	10.65	21.53	☆			0.0	N/A	923-8476	219-455-3361	None	None	1.00	Team Managed	N/A
LINCOLN ADV US GRO; D	Growth	3.3	11.39	11.01	22.87	☆			0.0		923-8476	219-455-3361	5.50	None	None	Team Managed	N/A
LINCOLN ADV WRLD GRO; A	International	12.0	10.86	3.67	0.87	☆			0.3		923-8476	219-455-3361	None	None	None	Team Managed	N/A
LINCOLN ADV WRLD GRO; B	International	0.9	10.21	3.44	-0.04	☆			0.4		923-8476	219-455-3361	5.00	None	None	Team Managed	N/A
LINCOLN ADV WRLD GRO; C	International	0.1	10.24	3.54	0.03	☆			0.4		923-8476	219-455-3361	None	None	1.00	Team Managed	N/A
LINCOLN ADV WRLD GRO; D	Equity Income	0.1	10.88	3.73	1.20	☆			0.6	12.0	923-8476	219-455-3361	5.00	None	None	Team Managed	N/A
LINDNER DIVIDEND	Equity Income	1,880.2	26.00	6.71	11.81	12.88	11.86		9.1	12.0	None	314-727-5305	None	0.61	2.00	Eric Ernest Ryback	'82
LINDNER FUND	Growth	1,436.4	23.33	8.41	14.90	11.43	10.17	12.19	1.5	11.6	None	314-727-5305	None	0.65	2.00	Lange/Ryback/Callahan	'77/'82/'93
LINDNER INV BULWARK	Capital Appreciation	70.6	7.09	2.40	0.10	☆			1.3	11.8	None	314-727-5305	None	None	2.00	Larry Callahan	'94
LINDNER INV INTL	International	0.2	9.09	0.44		☆			0.0		None	314-727-5305	None	None	2.00	Robert Lange	'95
LINDNER INV L/R SM CAP	Small Company Growth	7.9	5.46	8.98	14.33	☆			0.2	11.2	None	314-727-5305	None	None	2.00	Eric Ernest Ryback	'94
LINDNER INV UTILITY	Utility	18.1	10.77	9.50	12.50	☆			3.6	10.0	None	314-727-5305	None	1.30	2.00	Eric Ernest Ryback	'93
LKCM SMALL CAP EQUITY	Small Company Growth	71.2	12.17	7.41		☆			0.0	N/A	None	817-332-3235	None	None	None	Luther King	'94
LMH FUND	Growth Income	6.0	20.98	3.81	20.46	9.03	5.98	7.04	1.9	18.3	847-6002	203-226-4768	None	2.50	None	Heine/Wayne	'83/'91
LONGLEAF PARTNERS FUND	Growth	1,318.5	20.09	5.24	17.51	21.17	17.88	☆	0.8	19.4	445-9469	901-761-2474	None	1.17	None	Hawkins/Cates	'87/'94
LONGLEAF PARTNERS SM-CAP	Small Company Growth	110.0	14.18	3.43	13.34	13.45	5.90		0.0	N/A	445-9469	901-761-2474	None	1.38	None	Hawkins/Cates	'91/'91
LOOMIS SAYLES BOND	Fixed Income	134.1	11.75	10.72	19.19	13.73			7.3	☐	633-3330	617-482-2450	None	0.84	None	Daniel J. Fuss	'91
LOOMIS SAYLES GLBL BOND	World Income	15.3	10.44	9.55	7.52	2.86	☆		1.3	N/A	633-3330	617-482-2450	None	1.30	None	John de Beer	'91

LOOMIS SAYLES GRO & INC	Growth Income	31.6	14.33	9.81	22.13	14.18	☆	☆	1.0	14.1	633-3330	617-482-2450	None	1.33	None	Jeffrey W. Wardlow	'91
LOOMIS SAYLES GROWTH	Growth	39.6	14.85	11.32	23.89	13.83	☆	☆	0.0	25.2	633-3330	617-482-2450	None	1.16	None	Jerome A. Castellini	'91
LOOMIS SAYLES INTL EQU	International	77.2	12.80	7.93	10.02	9.59	☆	☆	1.1	□	633-3330	617-482-2450	None	1.50	None	Frank E. Jedlicka	'91
LOOMIS SAYLES SH-TM BOND	Fixed Income	25.0	9.74	3.11	8.58	☆	☆	☆	6.9	□	633-3330	617-482-2450	None	1.00	None	John Hyll	'92
LOOMIS SAYLES SMALL CAP	Small Company Growth	79.3	14.41	5.11	14.13	14.93	☆	☆	0.0	16.1	633-3330	617-482-2450	None	1.27	None	Friedman/Petherick	'91/'93
LOOMIS SAYLES US GOVT	Fixed Income	16.1	10.28	7.29	15.28	9.87	☆	☆	6.3	□	633-3330	617-482-2450	None	1.00	None	Kent P. Newmark	'91
LORD ABBETT BOND-DEB	Fixed Income	1,112.4	9.14	5.69	8.72	9.37	12.33	10.14	9.6	□	426-1130	212-848-1800	4.75	0.88	None	Morais A. Taylor	'92
LORD ABBETT DEVEL GROWTH	Midcap	149.6	12.39	19.02	45.56	20.27	13.69	10.62	0.0	N/A	426-1130	212-848-1800	5.75	1.31	None	Steve McGruder	'95
LORD ABBETT EQU 1990 ⊠	Balanced Target	54.7	16.61	6.75	20.10	12.68	11.92	☆	0.0	15.3	426-1130	212-848-1800	5.50	1.80	None	John Walsh	'90
LORD ABBETT FUNDMNTL VAL	Growth Income	37.9	13.60	6.33	20.18	12.91	11.01	☆	1.4	15.9	426-1130	212-848-1800	5.75	1.28	None	Thomas Hudson	'89
LORD ABBETT GLBL EQUITY	Global	82.9	11.62	2.38	0.25	8.52	5.15	☆	0.8	□	426-1130	212-848-1800	5.75	1.56	None	E. Wayne Nordberg	'88
LORD ABBETT GLBL INCOME	World Income	254.5	8.60	3.86	13.58	6.93	9.72	☆	7.9	□	426-1130	212-848-1800	4.75	1.02	None	Zane Brown	'92
LORD ABBETT INV BAL	Balanced	3.7	10.49	5.86	☆	☆	☆	☆	0.0	N/A	426-1130	212-848-1800	4.75	None	None	Dow/Nordberg	'94/'94
LORD ABBETT INV LTD DUR	Fixed Income	7.6	4.54	2.82	6.74	☆	☆	☆	5.8	□	426-1130	212-848-1800	3.00	None	None	Dow/Seto	'93/'93
LORD ABBETT SEC BAL	Balanced	1.6	11.09	6.24	☆	☆	☆	☆	0.0	N/A	426-1130	212-848-1800	None	None	1.00	Dow/Nordberg	'94/'94
LORD ABBETT SEC BD-DEB	Fixed Income	89.9	4.77	5.34	9.92	☆	☆	☆	8.8	□	426-1130	212-848-1800	None	1.23	1.00	Morais A. Taylor	'94
LORD ABBETT SEC GL INC	World Income	7.2	4.86	4.10	14.36	☆	☆	☆	7.4	□	426-1130	212-848-1800	None	1.09	1.00	Zane Brown	'94
LORD ABBETT SEC GR&INC	Growth Income	20.7	5.73	6.88	20.92	☆	☆	☆	2.1	14.9	426-1130	212-848-1800	None	0.61	1.00	Thomas Hudson	'94
LORD ABBETT SEC LTD GV	Fixed Income	12.9	4.75	2.85	6.63	☆	☆	☆	5.6	□	426-1130	212-848-1800	None	1.31	1.00	David Seto	'93
LORD ABBETT SEC US GVT	Fixed Income	335.5	4.58	4.66	9.16	☆	☆	☆	8.2	□	426-1130	212-848-1800	None	1.64	1.00	David Seto	'93
LORD ABBETT US GOVT	Fixed Income	3,304.9	2.70	4.45	9.78	6.33	8.73	9.24	8.8	□	426-1130	212-848-1800	4.75	0.90	None	Robert S. Dow	'92
LORD ABBETT VALUE APPREC	Midcap	208.1	11.09	6.63	15.18	12.18	11.61	12.17	1.4	16.8	426-1130	212-848-1800	5.75	1.12	None	John Walsh	'94
LUTHERAN BRO FUND ◪	Growth Income	587.8	19.78	9.80	20.34	10.75	10.07	10.79	1.1	20.8	328-4552	612-339-8091	5.00	1.04	None	James Walline	'94
LUTHERAN BRO HI YLD ◪	Fixed Income	556.0	8.86	5.06	7.28	10.49	14.05	☆	9.5	□	328-4552	612-339-8091	5.00	0.95	None	Tom Haag	'92
LUTHERAN BRO INCOME ◪	Fixed Income	947.1	8.65	6.69	12.90	7.08	9.08	8.98	6.6	□	328-4552	612-339-8091	5.00	0.82	None	Charles E. Heeren	'86
LUTHERAN BRO OPPTY GRO ◪	Small Company Growth	125.5	12.74	12.84	40.31	☆	☆	☆	0.0	27.1	328-4552	612-339-8091	5.00	1.66	None	Mike Binger	'94
MADISON BOND FUND	Fixed Income	6.0	21.09	4.34	9.43	5.36	6.95	☆	5.5	□	767-0300	608-273-2020	2.50	1.18	2.00	Frank Burgess	'90
MAGNA GROWTH & INCOME	Growth Income	N/A	13.67	8.26	☆	☆	☆	☆	0.0	N/A	621-6004	None	4.00	None	None	Gary Gutherie	'94
MAGNA INTMDT GOVT BOND	Fixed Income	N/A	12.78	4.65	☆	☆	☆	☆	0.0	□	621-6004	None	4.00	None	None	Louis Zedric	'94
MNSTY INSTL BOND; INST	Fixed Income	192.0	9.90	6.00	11.67	7.00	☆	☆	7.3	□	695-2126	None	None	0.75	None	Ravi Akhoury	'91
MNSTY INSTL BOND; SERV	Fixed Income	0.2	9.89	6.00	☆	☆	☆	☆	0.0	□	695-2126	None	None	None	None	Ravi Akhoury	'95
MNSTY INSTL EAFE; INST	International	81.7	12.85	0.16	0.04	11.15	☆	☆	0.7	□	695-2126	None	None	1.26	None	James Mehling	'91
MNSTY INSTL EAFE; SERV	International	0.1	12.85	0.08	☆	☆	☆	☆	0.0	□	695-2126	None	None	None	None	James Mehling	'95
MNSTY INSTL GRO EQ; INST	Growth	330.7	16.45	10.18	28.16	17.05	☆	☆	0.0	19.3	695-2126	None	None	0.92	None	Spelman/Carryl	'91/'92
MNSTY INSTL GRO EQ; SERV	Growth	0.2	16.43	10.12	☆	☆	☆	☆	0.0	19.3	695-2126	None	None	None	None	Spelman/Carryl	'95/'95
MNSTY INSTL INDX BD; INST	Fixed Income	172.0	11.18	5.97	11.96	7.12	☆	☆	5.7	□	695-2126	None	None	0.50	None	James Mehling	'91
MNSTY INSTL INDX BD; SERV	Fixed Income	0.7	11.20	5.96	☆	☆	☆	☆	0.0	□	695-2126	None	None	None	None	James Mehling	'94
MNSTY INSTL INDX EQ; INST	S&P Index	283.4	16.23	9.37	25.66	12.70	☆	☆	2.0	17.2	695-2126	None	None	0.50	None	James Mehling	'91
MNSTY INSTL INDX EQ; SERV	S&P Index	0.1	16.22	9.30	☆	☆	☆	☆	0.0	17.2	695-2126	None	None	None	None	James Mehling	'95
MNSTY INSTL INTL BD; INST	World Income	41.3	11.13	3.15	☆	☆	☆	☆	0.0	□	695-2126	None	None	None	None	Perelstein/Portera	'95/'95
MNSTY INSTL INTL BD; SERV	World Income	0.1	11.13	3.15	☆	☆	☆	☆	0.0	□	695-2126	None	None	None	None	Perelstein/Portera	'95/'95
MNSTY INSTL INTL EQ; INST	International	84.6	9.49	-3.46	☆	☆	☆	☆	0.0	□	695-2126	None	None	None	None	Perelstein/Takagl	'95/'95
MNSTY INSTL INTL EQ; SERV	International	0.5	9.48	-3.56	☆	☆	☆	☆	0.0	□	695-2126	None	None	None	None	Perelstein/Takagl	'95/'95
MNSTY INSTL MLT-AST; INST	Flexible	243.2	12.05	6.35	15.73	8.89	☆	☆	3.7	16.9	695-2126	None	None	0.70	None	James Mehling	'91
MNSTY INSTL MLT-AST; SERV	Flexible	0.7	12.05	6.26	☆	☆	☆	☆	0.0	16.9	695-2126	None	None	None	None	James Mehling	'95
MNSTY INSTL S-T BD; INST	Fixed Income	52.4	9.96	2.89	7.14	4.99	☆	☆	9.8	□	695-2126	None	None	0.60	None	Akhoury/Munshower	'91/'93
MNSTY INSTL S-T BD; SERV	Fixed Income	0.5	9.95	2.79	☆	☆	☆	☆	0.0	□	695-2126	None	None	None	None	Akhoury/Munshower	'95/'95
MNSTY INSTL VAL EQ; INST	Growth Income	507.0	13.40	6.35	16.38	14.88	☆	☆	1.2	14.8	695-2126	None	None	0.92	None	Laplaige/Kolefas	'91/'91
MNSTY INSTL VAL EQ; SERV	Growth Income	0.3	13.41	6.34	☆	☆	☆	☆	0.0	14.8	695-2126	None	None	None	None	Laplaige/Kolefas	'95/'95
MAINSTAY CAP APPREC; A	Capital Appreciation	15.3	22.82	9.66	☆	☆	☆	☆	0.0	19.7	522-4202	None	5.50	None	None	Team Managed	N/A

© Copyright Lipper Analytical Services, Inc.

PERFORMANCE OF MUTUAL FUNDS (continued)

FUND NAME	OBJECTIVE	ASSETS ($ MIL) 5/31/95	NAV ($/SHR) 6/30/95	RETURN THROUGH 6/30 QTR	1YR	3YRS	5YRS (Annualized)	10YRS	DIV YLD %	P/E RATIO	PHONE NUMBER 800	In-State	FEES Load	Exp. Ratio	Redemption	MANAGER	SINCE
MAINSTAY CAP APPREC; B	Capital Appreciation	607.0	22.76	9.48	26.75	18.90	18.88	☆	0.0	19.7	522-4202	None	None	1.80	5.00	Team Managed	N/A
MAINSTAY CONVERTBL; A	Convertible Securities	7.2	13.13	5.17	☆	☆	☆	☆	0.0	□	522-4202	None	5.50	None	5.00	Team Managed	N/A
MAINSTAY CONVERTBL; B	Convertible Securities	240.4	13.13	5.02	15.18	16.55	17.12	☆	4.8	□	522-4202	None	None	1.90	5.00	Team Managed	N/A
MAINSTAY EQUITY INDEX	S&P Index	76.0	16.84	9.21	24.83	12.11	☆	☆	0.0	N/A	522-4202	None	3.00	0.90	None	James Mehling	'91
MAINSTAY GLOBAL; B	Global	11.4	10.74	7.08	☆	☆	☆	☆	0.0	□	522-4202	None	5.50	None	None	Stokes/Tapley	'95/'95
MAINSTAY GLOBAL; B	Global	28.1	10.71	6.99	-1.76	5.22	1.78	☆	0.0	□	522-4202	None	None	2.40	5.00	Stokes/Tapley	'91/'91
MAINSTAY GOVT; A	Fixed Income	5.4	8.24	5.38	☆	☆	☆	☆	0.0	□	522-4202	None	4.50	None	None	Team Managed	N/A
MAINSTAY GOVT; B	Fixed Income	1,043.0	8.24	5.32	10.02	5.10	7.14	☆	6.5	□	522-4202	None	None	1.70	5.00	Team Managed	N/A
MAINSTAY HI YLD CORP; A	Fixed Income	18.2	7.96	5.61	☆	☆	☆	☆	0.0	□	522-4202	None	4.50	None	None	Team Managed	N/A
MAINSTAY HI YLD CORP; B	Fixed Income	1,319.0	7.96	5.45	12.06	13.61	15.35	☆	8.4	□	522-4202	None	None	1.60	5.00	Team Managed	N/A
MAINSTAY INTL BOND; A	World Income	11.0	10.67	2.91	☆	☆	☆	☆	0.0	□	522-4202	None	4.50	None	None	Team Managed	N/A
MAINSTAY INTL BOND; B	World Income	9.9	10.68	2.61	☆	☆	☆	☆	0.0	□	522-4202	None	None	5.00	5.00	Team Managed	N/A
MAINSTAY INTL EQTY; A	International	10.6	9.22	-3.76	☆	☆	☆	☆	0.0	□	522-4202	None	5.50	None	None	Team Managed	N/A
MAINSTAY INTL EQTY; B	International	16.1	9.18	-3.97	☆	☆	☆	☆	0.0	□	522-4202	None	None	5.00	5.00	Team Managed	N/A
MAINSTAY NAT RS/GOLD; A	Natural Resources	5.4	10.33	2.99	☆	☆	☆	☆	0.0	15.1	522-4202	None	5.50	None	None	Stokes/Tapley	'95/'95
MAINSTAY NAT RS/GOLD; B	Natural Resources	15.6	10.30	2.90	4.59	9.35	3.67	☆	0.0	15.1	522-4202	None	None	2.20	5.00	Stokes/Tapley	'91/'91
MAINSTAY TOTAL RTN; A	Balanced	7.8	16.90	8.32	☆	☆	☆	☆	0.0	19.7	522-4202	None	5.50	None	None	Team Managed	N/A
MAINSTAY TOTAL RTN; B	Balanced	730.0	16.90	8.17	20.18	11.70	11.65	☆	2.3	19.7	522-4202	None	None	1.70	5.00	Team Managed	N/A
MAINSTAY VALUE; A	Growth Income	10.3	16.79	6.14	☆	☆	☆	☆	2.8	15.1	522-4202	None	5.50	None	None	Team Managed	N/A
MAINSTAY VALUE; B	Growth Income	568.7	16.79	5.99	14.66	13.49	15.35	☆	0.8	15.1	522-4202	None	None	1.90	5.00	Team Managed	N/A
MAIRS & POWER GROWTH	Growth	51.3	48.31	10.94	31.83	17.71	16.68	14.97	1.3	N/A	None	612-222-8478	None	0.99	None	George A. Mairs III	'80
MANAGERS BOND	Fixed Income	26.7	21.88	9.49	18.94	9.31	10.86	10.79	8.1	N/A	835-3879	203-857-5321	None	1.20	None	Multiple Managers	N/A
MANAGERS CAPITAL APPREC	Capital Appreciation	74.3	27.66	10.46	23.64	14.90	13.37	14.20	0.4	18.1	835-3879	203-857-5321	None	1.29	None	Multiple Managers	N/A
MANAGERS INCOME EQUITY	Equity Income	39.0	28.60	7.15	19.64	12.28	10.87	12.33	2.8	15.4	835-3879	203-857-5321	None	1.33	None	Multiple Managers	N/A
MANAGERS INTL EQUITY	International	97.7	39.16	6.85	9.95	14.64	10.10	☆	0.2	□	835-3879	203-857-5321	None	1.49	None	Multiple Managers	N/A
MANAGERS INTMDT MTGE	Fixed Income	48.3	15.25	5.90	7.49	-0.09	5.33	☆	7.6	□	835-3879	203-857-5321	None	0.85	None	Multiple Managers	N/A
MANAGERS SH & INT BD	Fixed Income	25.8	19.03	4.86	6.56	4.64	7.26	7.68	7.3	□	835-3879	203-857-5321	None	1.05	None	Multiple Managers	N/A
MANAGERS SHORT GOVT	Fixed Income	8.7	17.55	2.90	7.10	1.46	4.32	☆	5.4	□	835-3879	203-857-5321	None	0.97	None	Multiple Managers	N/A
MANAGERS SPECIAL EQUITY	Small Company Growth	98.3	41.55	7.81	18.85	15.66	14.91	14.69	0.0	20.2	835-3879	203-857-5321	None	1.37	None	Multiple Managers	N/A
MANNING & NAPIER BLD SR1	Flexible	6.2	11.12	8.28	19.72	☆	☆	☆	1.9	N/A	466-3863	None	None	None	None	Team Managed	N/A
MANNING & NAPIER BLD SR2	Flexible	11.7	12.29	10.96	30.63	☆	☆	☆	1.5	N/A	466-3863	None	None	None	None	Team Managed	N/A
MANNING & NAPIER SM CAP	Small Company Growth	115.6	14.76	8.21	36.23	23.03	☆	☆	0.0	N/A	466-3863	None	None	None	None	Team Managed	N/A
MAP-EQUITY FUND	Growth Income	51.4	18.84	6.92	17.74	17.74	10.80	14.06	1.9	17.2	559-5555	201-268-4549	None	1.07	None	Markston Inv. Mgt.	'81
MARINER FDS GOVT SECS	Fixed Income	13.3	9.81	5.78	10.52	10.86	☆	☆	5.7	□	634-2536	None	4.75	None	None	David Fox	'94
MARINER FIXED INCOME FD	Fixed Income	83.9	10.03	6.04	11.38	☆	☆	☆	5.9	□	634-2536	None	4.75	None	None	David Fox	'94
MARINER SH-TM FXD INC	Fixed Income	13.0	9.88	3.80	8.13	☆	☆	☆	5.3	□	634-2536	None	2.00	0.78	None	David Fox	'94
MARINER SMALL CAP	Small Company Growth	23.0	14.21	15.59	35.24	☆	☆	☆	0.2	26.5	634-2536	None	5.00	1.23	None	Joseph Sing	'93
MARINER TOTAL RETURN EQ	Growth Income	64.8	14.06	8.07	19.46	19.46	11.39	☆	2.1	16.7	634-2536	None	5.00	0.78	None	Leo Grohowski	'87
MARKETWATCH FLEX INC	Fixed Income	113.9	11.62	6.64	20.68	20.68	☆	☆	1.7	17.1	232-9091	None	4.50	1.35	None	Team Managed	N/A
MARKETWATCH FLEX INC	Fixed Income	23.4	9.91	2.59	6.35	☆	☆	☆	4.1	□	232-9091	None	4.50	1.13	None	Team Managed	N/A
MARKETWATCH INT FXD INC	Fixed Income	39.5	9.91	5.25	10.54	☆	☆	☆	5.1	□	232-9091	None	4.50	1.09	None	Team Managed	N/A
MARKMAN MULTI AGGR GRO	Growth	15.3	11.79	12.72	☆	☆	☆	☆	0.0	N/A	443-4249	513-629-2000	None	None	None	Bob Markman	'95
MARKMAN MULTI CONSRV GRO	Balanced	4.9	10.90	6.24	☆	☆	☆	☆	0.0	N/A	443-4249	513-629-2000	None	None	None	Bob Markman	'95
MARKMAN MULTI MOD GRO	Equity Income	22.7	11.21	7.27	☆	☆	☆	☆	0.0	N/A	443-4249	513-629-2000	None	None	None	Bob Markman	'95
MARQUIS GOVT SEC; A	Fixed Income	106.0	9.84	4.58	9.83	☆	☆	☆	5.4	□	462-9511	None	3.50	None	None	Kevin Reed	'93

MARQUIS GOVT SEC; B	Fixed Income	0.2	9.89	4.37	9.11	☆	☆	☆	4.7	□	462-9511	None	None	None	3.50	Kevin Reed	'93
MARQUIS GRO & INC; A	Flexible	81.4	10.45	6.60	14.14	☆	☆	☆	3.5	14.8	462-9511	None	3.50	None	None	James McElroy	'94
MARQUIS GRO & INC; B	Flexible	1.0	10.51	6.47	13.29	☆	☆	☆	2.7	14.8	462-9511	None	None	None	3.50	James McElroy	'94
MARQUIS VALUE EQTY; A	Growth	50.7	10.99	8.90	20.07	☆	☆	☆	2.1	14.8	462-9511	None	3.50	None	None	James McElroy	'94
MARQUIS VALUE EQTY; B	Growth	0.8	11.04	8.69	19.23	☆	☆	☆	1.4	14.8	462-9511	None	None	None	3.50	James McElroy	'94
MARSHALL EQUITY INCOME	Equity Income	103.5	10.86	6.41	18.87	☆	☆	☆	3.1	15.2	236-8560	414-287-8500	None	1.01	None	Bruce Hutson	'93
MARSHALL GOVT INC	Fixed Income	100.9	9.51	4.92	10.77	☆	☆	☆	6.5	□	236-8560	414-287-8500	None	0.86	None	Larry Pavelec	'93
MARSHALL INTL STOCK	International	83.2	10.02	8.09	☆	☆	☆	☆	0.0	□	236-8560	414-287-8500	None	None	None	Al Schwartz	'94
MARSHALL INTMDT BD	Fixed Income	353.8	9.52	4.68	9.05	☆	☆	☆	6.4	□	236-8560	414-287-8500	None	0.71	None	Larry Pavelec	'93
MARSHALL MID-CAP STOCK	Midcap	87.0	11.24	9.77	26.41	☆	☆	☆	0.1	20.9	236-8560	414-287-8500	None	1.01	None	Steve Hayward	'94
MARSHALL SHORT-TERM INC	Fixed Income	79.9	9.74	2.48	6.26	☆	☆	☆	5.7	□	236-8560	414-287-8500	None	0.50	None	Mark Pittman	'95
MARSHALL STOCK	Growth Income	260.8	11.30	7.58	20.89	☆	☆	☆	0.8	19.0	236-8560	414-287-8500	None	0.99	None	Charles Mehlhouse	'93
MARSHALL VALUE EQUITY	Growth Income	212.5	11.62	6.26	19.50	☆	☆	☆	1.7	15.1	236-8560	414-287-8500	None	1.00	None	Gerry Sandel	'93
MAS BALANCED	Balanced	322.9	12.47	7.77	17.58	☆	☆	☆	3.7	16.8	354-8185	610-940-5000	None	0.58	None	Team Managed	N/A
MAS DOM FXD INC	Fixed Income	32.6	10.87	6.05	12.07	9.11	11.28	☆	2.8	□	354-8185	610-940-5000	None	0.50	None	Team Managed	N/A
MAS EQUITY	Growth	1,474.4	22.94	9.03	22.15	12.14	12.59	14.79	2.2	16.8	354-8185	610-940-5000	None	0.60	None	Team Managed	N/A
MAS FXD INC	Fixed Income	1,412.0	11.59	5.64	11.03	7.99	10.55	10.80	5.1	□	354-8185	610-940-5000	None	0.49	None	Team Managed	N/A
MAS FXD INC II	Fixed Income	166.1	11.16	5.67	11.30	7.78	☆	☆	4.8	□	354-8185	610-940-5000	None	0.51	None	Team Managed	N/A
MAS GLBL FXD INC	World Income	56.4	11.15	5.88	16.11	☆	☆	☆	5.0	□	354-8185	610-940-5000	None	0.57	None	Team Managed	N/A
MAS HIGH YIELD	Fixed Income	216.7	8.92	10.60	11.49	12.65	14.63	☆	8.8	□	354-8185	610-940-5000	None	0.50	None	Team Managed	N/A
MAS INTL EQUITY	International	1,093.0	12.18	3.31	-3.72	7.05	5.32	☆	0.0	□	354-8185	610-940-5000	None	0.64	None	Team Managed	N/A
MAS INTL FXD INC	World Income	144.3	11.31	5.69	18.85	☆	☆	☆	4.2	□	354-8185	610-940-5000	None	None	None	Team Managed	N/A
MAS LTD DURATION	Fixed Income	71.5	10.38	2.97	7.34	5.14	☆	☆	6.1	□	354-8185	610-940-5000	None	0.41	None	Team Managed	N/A
MAS MID CAP GRO	Midcap	281.9	16.42	8.10	25.51	14.45	15.42	☆	0.2	21.9	354-8185	610-940-5000	None	0.60	None	Team Managed	N/A
MAS MTGE SECS	Fixed Income	72.1	10.39	4.40	9.85	6.18	☆	☆	5.6	□	354-8185	610-940-5000	None	0.50	None	Team Managed	N/A
MAS MULTI ASSET	Global Flexible	76.0	10.93	7.78	☆	☆	☆	☆	0.0	□	354-8185	610-940-5000	None	None	None	Team Managed	N/A
MAS SEL EQUITY ⊠	Growth	23.9	11.06	9.27	23.08	12.21	12.92	☆	4.7	N/A	354-8185	610-940-5000	None	0.62	None	Team Managed	N/A
MAS SM CAP VAL ⊠	Small Company Growth	361.3	16.49	6.59	13.20	17.86	16.57	☆	0.8	14.6	354-8185	610-940-5000	None	0.88	None	Team Managed	N/A
MAS SPEC PURP FXD	Fixed Income	462.3	12.32	5.83	11.70	8.79	☆	☆	4.8	□	354-8185	610-940-5000	None	0.50	None	Team Managed	N/A
MAS VALUE	Growth Income	1,056.5	13.86	11.68	28.18	17.85	16.77	15.27	2.2	13.9	354-8185	610-940-5000	None	0.61	None	Team Managed	N/A
MASS INVESTORS GRO; A	Growth	1,010.9	11.16	12.61	25.89	13.42	11.54	13.20	0.0	20.4	637-2929	617-954-5000	5.75	0.72	None	Bennett/Felipe	'93/'95
MASS INVESTORS GRO; B	Growth	11.6	10.98	12.38	25.19	☆	☆	☆	0.0	20.4	637-2929	617-954-5000	None	1.60	4.00	Bennett/Felipe	'93/'95
MASS INVESTORS TRUST; A	Growth Income	1,783.7	11.84	8.80	20.48	12.43	10.89	14.23	2.0	16.1	637-2929	617-954-5000	5.75	0.71	None	Laupheimer/Parke/Dynan	'93/'92/'95
MASS INVESTORS TRUST; B	Growth Income	101.1	11.78	8.56	19.34	☆	☆	☆	1.3	16.1	637-2929	617-954-5000	None	1.61	4.00	Laupheimer/Parke/Dynan	'93/'93/'95
MASSMUTUAL INST BAL; 1	Balanced	0.1	11.02	5.35	☆	☆	☆	☆	0.0	N/A	None	413-788-8411	None	None	None	Salerno/Wilson/Wilson	'94/'94/'94
MASSMUTUAL INST BAL; 2	Balanced	0.1	11.05	5.44	☆	☆	☆	☆	0.0	N/A	None	413-788-8411	None	None	None	Salerno/Wilson/Wilson	'94/'94/'94
MASSMUTUAL INST BAL; 3	Balanced	0.1	11.08	5.52	☆	☆	☆	☆	0.0	N/A	None	413-788-8411	None	None	None	Salerno/Wilson/Wilson	'94/'94/'94
MASSMUTUAL INST BAL; 4	Balanced	392.5	11.06	5.64	☆	☆	☆	☆	0.0	N/A	None	413-788-8411	None	None	None	Salerno/Wilson/Wilson	'94/'94/'94
MASSMUTUAL INST CORE; 1	Fixed Income	0.1	11.01	6.27	☆	☆	☆	☆	0.0	□	None	413-788-8411	None	None	None	Mary Wilson	'94
MASSMUTUAL INST CORE; 2	Fixed Income	0.1	11.05	6.56	☆	☆	☆	☆	0.0	□	None	413-788-8411	None	None	None	Mary Wilson	'94
MASSMUTUAL INST CORE; 3	Fixed Income	0.1	11.07	6.65	☆	☆	☆	☆	0.0	□	None	413-788-8411	None	None	None	Mary Wilson	'94
MASSMUTUAL INST CORE; 4	Fixed Income	207.4	11.01	6.58	☆	☆	☆	☆	0.0	□	None	413-788-8411	None	None	None	Mary Wilson	'94
MASSMUTUAL INST INTL; 1	International	0.1	9.42	3.29	☆	☆	☆	☆	0.0	□	None	413-788-8411	None	None	None	William Wilby	'94
MASSMUTUAL INST INTL; 2	International	0.1	9.46	3.50	☆	☆	☆	☆	0.0	□	None	413-788-8411	None	None	None	William Wilby	'94
MASSMUTUAL INST INTL; 3	International	0.1	9.48	3.61	☆	☆	☆	☆	0.0	□	None	413-788-8411	None	None	None	William Wilby	'94
MASSMUTUAL INST INTL; 4	International	181.8	9.51	3.71	☆	☆	☆	☆	0.0	□	None	413-788-8411	None	None	None	William Wilby	'94
MASSMUTUAL INST PRIME; 1	Fixed Income	0.1	153.87	1.15	☆	☆	☆	☆	0.0	□	None	413-788-8411	None	None	None	Mary Wilson	'94
MASSMUTUAL INST PRIME; 2	Fixed Income	0.1	154.46	1.29	☆	☆	☆	☆	0.0	□	None	413-788-8411	None	None	None	Mary Wilson	'94
MASSMUTUAL INST PRIME; 3	Fixed Income	0.1	154.78	1.38	☆	☆	☆	☆	0.0	□	None	413-788-8411	None	None	None	Mary Wilson	'94
MASSMUTUAL INST PRIME; 4	Fixed Income	228.6	154.71	1.44	☆	☆	☆	☆	0.0	□	None	413-788-8411	None	None	None	Mary Wilson	'94

PERFORMANCE OF MUTUAL FUNDS (continued)

FUND NAME	OBJECTIVE	ASSETS ($ MIL) 5/31/95	NAV ($/SHR) 6/30/95	QTR	1YR	3YRS	5YRS	10YRS	DIV YLD %	P/E RATIO	PHONE 800	PHONE In-State	Load	Exp. Ratio	Redemption	MANAGER	SINCE
MASSMUTUAL INST S-T BD; 1	Fixed Income	0.1	10.63	3.81	☆	☆	☆	☆	0.0		None	413-788-8411	None	None	None	Ronald E. Desautels	94
MASSMUTUAL INST S-T BD; 2	Fixed Income	0.1	10.66	4.00	☆	☆	☆	☆	0.0		None	413-788-8411	None	None	None	Ronald E. Desautels	94
MASSMUTUAL INST S-T BD; 3	Fixed Income	0.1	10.69	3.99	☆	☆	☆	☆	0.0		None	413-788-8411	None	None	None	Ronald E. Desautels	94
MASSMUTUAL INST S-T BD; 4	Fixed Income	116.2	10.64	4.11	☆	☆	☆	☆	0.0		None	413-788-8411	None	None	None	Ronald E. Desautels	94
MASSMUTUAL INST SM CAP; 1	Small Company Growth	0.1	10.40	4.21	☆	☆	☆	☆	0.0	N/A	None	413-788-8411	None	None	None	George P. Ulrich	94
MASSMUTUAL INST SM CAP; 2	Small Company Growth	0.1	10.44	4.40	☆	☆	☆	☆	0.0	N/A	None	413-788-8411	None	None	None	George P. Ulrich	94
MASSMUTUAL INST SM CAP; 3	Small Company Growth	0.1	10.46	4.50	☆	☆	☆	☆	0.0	N/A	None	413-788-8411	None	None	None	George P. Ulrich	94
MASSMUTUAL INST SM CAP; 4	Small Company Growth	339.4	10.46	4.39	☆	☆	☆	☆	0.0	N/A	None	413-788-8411	None	None	None	George P. Ulrich	94
MASSMUTUAL INST VAL EQ; 1	Growth Income	0.1	11.46	7.30	☆	☆	☆	☆	0.0	N/A	None	413-788-8411	None	None	None	David Salerno	94
MASSMUTUAL INST VAL EQ; 2	Growth Income	0.1	11.51	7.47	☆	☆	☆	☆	0.0	N/A	None	413-788-8411	None	None	None	David Salerno	94
MASSMUTUAL INST VAL EQ; 3	Growth Income	0.1	11.53	7.56	☆	☆	☆	☆	0.0	N/A	None	413-788-8411	None	None	None	David Salerno	94
MASSMUTUAL INST VAL EQ; 4	Growth Income	1,826.3	11.52	7.66	☆	☆	☆	☆	0.0	N/A	None	413-788-8411	None	None	None	David Salerno	94
MATHERS FUND	Growth	278.0	14.45	4.03	5.35	2.21	3.73	9.84	4.7	7.3	962-3863	708-295-7400	None	0.93	None	Henry G. Van der Eb, Jr	75
MATRIX GROWTH FUND	Growth	16.7	15.10	4.28	14.68	9.58	8.73	☆	0.3	17.1	424-2295	None	None	1.84	None	Williams/Osborn	'86/'95
MATTHEWS INTL ASIAN CV	Convertible Securities	1.0	10.01	5.47	☆	☆	☆	☆		17.7	789-2472	None	None	None	1.00	Matthews/Chuang	'94/'94
MATTHEWS INTL KOREA	Pacific Region	0.5	9.09	-3.61	☆	☆	☆	☆	0.0		789-2472	None	5.00	None	None	G. Paul Mathews	'95
MATTHEWS INTL PC TIGER	Pacific Region	0.7	9.72	6.11	☆	☆	☆	☆	0.0	14.2	789-2472	None	None	2.00	1.00	Matthews/Chuang	'94/'94
MAXUS EQUITY	Flexible	24.4	15.05	7.96	20.85	16.10	14.93	☆	1.5		446-2987	216-292-3434	None	2.00	None	Richard Barone	'89
MAXUS INCOME FUND	Fixed Income	35.6	10.45	4.05	9.80	5.62	8.05	7.48	6.9		446-2987	216-292-3434	None	1.81	None	Richard Barone	'85
MAXUS LAUREATE FUND	Capital Appreciation	1.8	10.22	2.82	6.46	☆	☆	☆	0.0	N/A	446-2987	216-292-3434	None	3.60	None	Alan Miller	'95
MEGY FD INCOME	World Income	N/A	N/A	N/A	N/A	N/A	☆	☆	0.0		933-8637	407-832-7733	2.87	2.00	1.00	Hector Megy	'91
MENTOR/CAMBRIDGE GRO; A	Growth	12.4	16.63	6.33	19.73	6.53	☆	☆	0.0	22.8	382-0016	None	5.75	1.81	None	John Davenport	'95
MENTOR/CAMBRIDGE GRO; B	Growth	22.9	16.36	6.10	18.81	5.89	☆	☆	0.0	22.8	382-0016	None	None	2.56	1.00	John Davenport	'95
MENTOR CAP GROWTH; A	Growth	18.9	16.48	5.44	17.22	7.60	☆	☆	0.0	17.2	382-0016	None	5.75	1.70	None	John Davenport	'95
MENTOR CAP GROWTH; B	Growth	36.7	16.28	5.24	16.38	6.84	☆	☆	0.0	17.2	382-0016	None	None	2.46	1.00	John Davenport	'95
MENTOR GLOBAL; A	Global	6.8	14.59	4.44	3.70	☆	☆	☆	0.0	N/A	382-0016	None	5.75	2.09	None	McGlashan	'95
MENTOR GLOBAL; B	Global	8.9	14.43	4.26	3.00	☆	☆	☆	0.0	N/A	382-0016	None	None	2.79	1.00	McGlashan	'95
MENTOR GROWTH	Midcap	207.4	14.08	8.14	20.29	15.21	14.06	11.80	0.0	13.6	382-0016	None	5.75	2.01	None	Price/Ziglar/Drummond	'85/'91/'93
MENTOR INC & GRO; A	Balanced	19.8	16.47	7.93	15.65	☆	☆	☆	2.0	13.6	472-0090	804-782-3207	5.75	1.75	5.00	Kaplan/Schneider	'93/'93
MENTOR INC & GRO; B	Balanced	42.9	16.48	7.85	15.02	☆	☆	☆	1.5	13.6	382-0016	None	None	2.44	1.00	Kaplan/Schneider	'93/'93
MENTOR QUALITY INC; A	Fixed Income	26.9	13.33	5.97	11.26	4.53	☆	☆	6.6		382-0016	None	4.75	1.38	None	Jones/Grant/Henderson	'95/'95/'95
MENTOR QUALITY INC; B	Fixed Income	64.5	13.35	5.92	10.68	4.02	☆	☆	6.1		382-0016	None	None	1.88	1.00	Jones/Grant/Henderson	'95/'95/'95
MENTOR SH-DUR INCOME	Fixed Income	16.8	12.75	4.28	8.64	☆	☆	☆	6.2		472-0090	804-782-3207	None	1.29	None	Jones/Grant	'94/'94
MENTOR STRATEGY FUND	Flexible	194.5	13.99	8.20	23.91	☆	☆	☆	0.0	N/A	472-0090	None	None	2.19	5.00	Hays/Graves	'93/'94
MERGER FUND	Capital Appreciation	196.8	13.90	1.68	9.03	11.54	10.01	8.96	0.0	7.9	343-8959	None	None	1.58	None	Green/Smith	'89/'89
MERIDIAN FUND	Midcap	308.1	27.29	4.60	16.44	16.03	14.83	14.38	0.6	21.8	446-6662	415-461-6237	None	1.22	None	Richard Aster Jr	'84
MERIDIAN VALUE FUND	Growth	0.7	10.27	4.90	4.05	☆	☆	☆	0.0	32.4	446-6662	415-461-6237	None	None	None	Richard Aster Jr	'94
MERRILL ADJ RATE SEC; A ⊠	Fixed Income	0.3	9.53	2.38	☆	☆	☆	☆	5.1		None	609-282-2800	4.00	None	None	Maunz/Hewson	'94/'94
MERRILL ADJ RATE SEC; B	Fixed Income	202.3	9.53	2.08	5.53	2.72	☆	☆	5.1		None	609-282-2800	None	1.46	4.00	Maunz/Hewson	'91/'91
MERRILL ADJ RATE SEC; C	Fixed Income	1.4	9.53	2.06	☆	☆	☆	☆	5.1		None	609-282-2800	None	None	1.00	Maunz/Hewson	'94/'94
MERRILL ADJ RATE SEC; D	Fixed Income	17.0	9.53	2.32	6.19	3.21	☆	☆	5.7		None	609-282-2800	4.00	1.97	None	Maunz/Hewson	'91/'91
MERRILL AMERICAS INC; A ⊠	World Income	1.1	8.59	19.49	☆	☆	☆	☆	9.5		None	609-282-2800	4.00	0.96	None	Paolo Valle	'94
MERRILL AMERICAS INC; B	World Income	92.8	8.55	19.20	6.92	☆	☆	☆	9.5		None	609-282-2800	None	2.49	4.00	Paolo Valle	'93
MERRILL AMERICAS INC; C	World Income	0.3	8.55	19.18	☆	☆	☆	☆	9.5		None	609-282-2800	None	None	1.00	Paolo Valle	'93
MERRILL AMERICAS INC; D	World Income	22.1	8.55	19.35	7.47	☆	☆	☆	10.0		None	609-282-2800	4.00	1.97	None	Paolo Valle	'93

Listing of Merrill Lynch mutual funds (Lipper Analytical Services). Columns, left to right: Fund, Objective, Net Assets ($Mil), NAV, %, 1-Yr, 3-Yr, 5-Yr, 10-Yr, %, (col), Min, Phone, Max Chg, 12b-1, Redemp, Manager, Year.

Fund	Objective	Net Assets	NAV	%	1-Yr	3-Yr	5-Yr	10-Yr	%	(col)	Min	Phone	Max Chg	12b-1	Redemp	Manager	Yr
MERRILL ASSET GROWTH; A ☒	Global Flexible	2.0	9.55	3.58	☆	☆	☆	☆	0.0	□	None	609-282-2800	5.25	None	None	Joel Heymsfeld	'94
MERRILL ASSET GROWTH; B	Global Flexible	13.3	9.50	3.37	☆	☆	☆	☆	0.0	□	None	609-282-2800	None	None	4.00	Joel Heymsfeld	'94
MERRILL ASSET GROWTH; C	Global Flexible	0.7	9.49	3.38	☆	☆	☆	☆	0.0	□	None	609-282-2800	None	None	1.00	Joel Heymsfeld	'94
MERRILL ASSET GROWTH; D	Global Flexible	1.6	9.54	3.58	☆	☆	☆	☆	0.0	□	None	609-282-2800	5.25	None	None	Joel Heymsfeld	'94
MERRILL ASSET INC; A ☒	Fixed Income	1.3	10.35	5.68	☆	☆	☆	☆	0.0	□	None	609-282-2800	4.00	None	None	Joel Heymsfeld	'94
MERRILL ASSET INC; B	Fixed Income	8.4	10.35	5.49	☆	☆	☆	☆	0.0	□	None	609-282-2800	None	None	4.00	Joel Heymsfeld	'94
MERRILL ASSET INC; C	Fixed Income	0.3	10.35	5.47	☆	☆	☆	☆	2.6	13.3	None	609-282-2800	None	None	1.00	Joel Heymsfeld	'94
MERRILL ASSET INC; D	Fixed Income	0.5	10.35	5.62	☆	☆	☆	☆	1.8	13.3	None	609-282-2800	4.00	None	None	Joel Heymsfeld	'94
MERRILL BASIC VALUE; A ☒	Growth Income	2,785.1	26.44	8.94	21.67	15.24	13.17	13.42	0.0	N/A	None	609-282-2800	5.25	0.53	None	Paul F. Hoffmann	'77
MERRILL BASIC VALUE; B	Growth Income	2,395.0	26.08	8.67	20.45	14.07	12.02	☆	0.0	N/A	None	609-282-2800	None	1.55	4.00	Paul F. Hoffmann	'88
MERRILL BASIC VALUE; C	Growth Income	64.0	25.98	8.66	☆	☆	☆	☆	3.0	17.6	None	609-282-2800	None	0.83	1.00	Paul F. Hoffmann	'94
MERRILL BASIC VALUE; D	Growth Income	185.4	26.41	8.86	☆	☆	☆	☆	1.5	17.6	None	609-282-2800	5.25	1.86	None	Paul F. Hoffmann	'94
MERRILL BL INV & RET; A ☒	Balanced	31.1	11.16	6.59	11.08	8.25	8.73	☆	0.0	N/A	None	609-282-2800	5.25	None	None	Denis Cummings	'91
MERRILL BL INV & RET; B	Balanced	189.4	11.29	6.31	9.93	7.15	7.63	☆	5.4	15.1	None	609-282-2800	None	None	4.00	Denis Cummings	'91
MERRILL BL INV & RET; C	Balanced	0.7	11.19	6.27	☆	☆	☆	☆	4.2	15.1	None	609-282-2800	None	None	1.00	Denis Cummings	'94
MERRILL BL INV & RET; D	Balanced	436.2	11.13	6.41	☆	☆	☆	☆	0.0	N/A	None	609-282-2800	5.25	None	None	Denis Cummings	'94
MERRILL CAPITAL; A ☒	Growth Income	2,708.3	29.30	8.50	18.82	12.13	11.69	13.46	0.0	□	None	609-282-2800	5.25	0.53	None	Ernest S. Watts	'83
MERRILL CAPITAL; B	Growth Income	4,017.6	28.83	8.20	17.56	10.98	10.55	☆	1.2	□	None	609-282-2800	None	1.55	4.00	Ernest S. Watts	'88
MERRILL CAPITAL; C	Growth Income	77.2	28.67	8.23	☆	☆	☆	☆	10.6	□	None	609-282-2800	None	None	1.00	Ernest S. Watts	'88
MERRILL CAPITAL; D	Growth Income	248.6	29.28	8.44	☆	☆	☆	☆	9.3	□	None	609-282-2800	5.25	None	None	Ernest S. Watts	'94
MERRILL CONSULTS INTL	International	205.8	11.34	0.71	-8.71	☆	☆	☆	0.0	□	None	609-282-2800	4.00	2.27	None	James Boller	'92
MERRILL CORP HI INC; A ☒	Fixed Income	892.1	7.74	5.36	10.56	10.64	14.23	11.88	7.0	□	None	609-282-2800	4.00	0.53	None	Vincent T. Lathbury III	'82
MERRILL CORP HI INC; B	Fixed Income	2,876.6	7.74	5.16	9.71	9.81	13.37	13.37	6.5	□	None	609-282-2800	None	1.29	4.00	Vincent T. Lathbury III	'88
MERRILL CORP HI INC; C	Fixed Income	70.0	7.75	5.15	☆	☆	☆	☆	0.0	□	None	609-282-2800	None	None	1.00	Vincent T. Lathbury III	'94
MERRILL CORP HI INC; D	Fixed Income	61.3	7.75	5.29	☆	☆	☆	☆	0.0	□	None	609-282-2800	4.00	None	None	Vincent T. Lathbury III	'94
MERRILL CORP INTMDT; A ☒	Fixed Income	167.8	11.49	6.51	12.02	7.85	9.34	9.30	7.0	□	None	609-282-2800	1.00	0.53	None	Jay Harbeck	'92
MERRILL CORP INTMDT; B	Fixed Income	154.8	11.49	6.37	11.45	☆	☆	☆	6.3	□	None	609-282-2800	None	1.04	4.00	Jay Harbeck	'92
MERRILL CORP INTMDT; C	Fixed Income	0.7	11.50	6.36	☆	☆	☆	☆	0.0	□	None	609-282-2800	None	None	1.00	Jay Harbeck	'94
MERRILL CORP INTMDT; D	Fixed Income	6.0	11.50	6.57	☆	☆	☆	☆	0.0	□	None	609-282-2800	1.00	None	None	Jay Harbeck	'94
MERRILL CORP INV GRD; A ☒	Fixed Income	415.2	11.47	6.94	12.63	8.03	9.60	9.59	7.0	□	None	609-282-2800	4.00	0.53	None	Jay Harbeck	'92
MERRILL CORP INV GRD; B	Fixed Income	549.7	11.47	6.74	11.78	7.21	8.78	8.78	6.3	□	None	609-282-2800	None	1.29	4.00	Jay Harbeck	'92
MERRILL CORP INV GRD; C	Fixed Income	10.0	11.48	6.82	☆	☆	☆	☆	0.0	□	None	609-282-2800	None	None	1.00	Jay Harbeck	'94
MERRILL CORP INV GRD; D	Fixed Income	14.2	11.48	6.97	☆	☆	☆	☆	0.0	□	None	609-282-2800	4.00	None	None	Jay Harbeck	'94
MERRILL DEVLP CP MKT; A ☒	Emerging Markets	353.2	13.35	4.13	-1.67	10.01	8.28	8.28	3.3	□	None	609-282-2800	5.25	None	None	Grace Pineda	'89
MERRILL DEVLP CP MKT; B	Emerging Markets	150.9	13.24	3.92	☆	☆	☆	☆	3.0	□	None	609-282-2800	None	None	4.00	Grace Pineda	'94
MERRILL DRAGON FUND; A ☒	Pacific Region	17.0	13.22	3.85	☆	☆	☆	☆	0.0	□	None	609-282-2800	None	None	1.00	Grace Pineda	'94
MERRILL DRAGON FUND; B	Pacific Region	20.0	13.33	4.06	☆	☆	☆	☆	0.0	□	None	609-282-2800	5.25	None	None	Grace Pineda	'94
MERRILL DRAGON FUND; C	Pacific Region	15.4	15.88	9.90	17.39	☆	☆	☆	0.8	□	None	609-282-2800	None	1.46	None	Kara Tan Bhala	'94
MERRILL DRAGON FUND; D	Pacific Region	926.2	15.79	9.81	☆	☆	☆	☆	1.3	□	None	609-282-2800	None	None	4.00	Kara Tan Bhala	'92
MERRILL EUROFUND; A ☒	European Region	10.0	15.68	9.80	5.80	☆	☆	☆	5.8	□	None	609-282-2800	5.25	2.40	None	Kara Tan Bhala	'94
MERRILL EUROFUND; B	European Region	295.1	15.91	9.95	13.45	11.70	8.05	☆	6.1	□	None	609-282-2800	5.25	1.63	None	Adrian Holmes	'88
MERRILL EUROFUND; C	European Region	195.4	14.97	9.09	12.32	10.57	6.95	☆	0.0	□	None	609-282-2800	None	1.03	None	Adrian Holmes	'84
MERRILL EUROFUND; D	European Region	829.5	14.16	8.81	☆	☆	☆	☆	1.6	□	None	609-282-2800	4.00	2.06	None	Adrian Holmes	'94
MERRILL FD TOMORROW; A ☒	Growth	2.6	14.15	8.82	☆	☆	☆	☆	1.5	□	None	609-282-2800	1.00	None	None	Adrian Holmes	'94
MERRILL FD TOMORROW; B	Growth	75.7	14.94	9.03	☆	☆	☆	☆	0.0	□	None	609-282-2800	5.25	None	None	Adrian Holmes	'94
MERRILL FD TOMORROW; C	Growth	8.5	16.26	14.43	24.79	10.09	10.48	10.61	1.6	14.5	None	609-282-2800	5.25	0.98	None	Vincent P. Dileo	'88
MERRILL FD TOMORROW; D	Growth	82.8	15.94	14.18	23.53	8.98	9.35	☆	1.5	14.5	None	609-282-2800	None	1.99	None	Vincent P. Dileo	'84
MERRILL FDMNTL GRO; A ☒	Growth	0.1	15.87	14.17	☆	☆	☆	☆	0.0	14.5	None	609-282-2800	None	None	None	Vincent P. Dileo	'94
	Growth	195.6	16.24	14.37	☆	☆	☆	☆	0.0	14.5	None	609-282-2800	5.25	None	None	Vincent P. Dileo	'94
	Growth	10.0	11.11	8.71	☆	☆	☆	☆	0.0	20.8	None	609-282-2800	5.25	None	None	Lawrence Fuller	'94

PERFORMANCE OF MUTUAL FUNDS (continued)

FUND NAME	OBJECTIVE	ASSETS ($ MIL) 5/31/95	NAV ($/SHR) 6/30/95	QTR	1YR	3YRS	5YRS	10YRS	DIV YLD %	P/E RATIO	PHONE 800	PHONE In-State	Load	Exp. Ratio	Redemption	MANAGER	SINCE
MERRILL FDMNTL GRO; B	Growth	46.1	10.88	8.47	21.41	☆	☆	☆	0.0	20.8	None	609-282-2800	None	None	4.00	Lawrence Fuller	'94
MERRILL FDMNTL GRO; C	Growth	40.3	10.88	8.47	22.35	☆	☆	☆	0.0	20.8	None	609-282-2800	None	2.35	1.00	Lawrence Fuller	'92
MERRILL FDMNTL GRO; D	Growth	11.2	11.10	8.72	☆	☆	☆	☆	0.0	20.8	None	609-282-2800	5.25	1.58	None	Lawrence Fuller	'92
MERRILL FEDERAL SEC; A ☒	Fixed Income	212.0	9.61	4.61	☆	☆	☆	☆	0.0	□	None	609-282-2800	4.00	None	None	Maunz/Hewson	'94/'94
MERRILL FEDERAL SEC; B	Fixed Income	1,298.9	9.61	4.41	9.54	4.74	6.88	☆	6.1	□	None	609-282-2800	None	1.33	4.00	Maunz/Hewson	'91/'92
MERRILL FEDERAL SEC; C	Fixed Income	9.8	9.61	4.40	☆	☆	☆	☆	0.0	□	None	609-282-2800	None	None	1.00	Maunz/Hewson	'94/'94
MERRILL FEDERAL SEC; D	Fixed Income	1,024.5	9.61	4.55	10.11	5.30	7.79	8.75	6.6	□	None	609-282-2800	4.00	0.83	None	Maunz/Hewson	'89/'92
MERRILL GL INV & RET; A ☒	World Income	104.8	9.42	3.18	9.42	6.25	10.10	☆	6.1	□	None	609-282-2800	4.00	0.84	4.00	Robert Parish	'93
MERRILL GL INV & RET; B	World Income	676.2	9.42	2.98	8.58	5.44	9.26	☆	5.3	□	None	609-282-2800	None	1.61	1.00	Robert Parish	'93
MERRILL GL INV & RET; C	World Income	9.6	9.42	2.96	☆	☆	☆	☆	0.0	□	None	609-282-2800	None	None	None	Robert Parish	'94
MERRILL GL INV & RET; D	World Income	3.8	9.42	3.11	☆	☆	☆	☆	0.0	□	None	609-282-2800	4.00	None	4.00	Robert Parish	'89/'94
MERRILL GLBL ALLOC; A ☒	Global Flexible	1,437.8	13.42	8.78	8.88	11.38	13.20	☆	5.7		None	609-282-2800	5.25	0.89	None	Ison/Stattman	'89/'94
MERRILL GLBL ALLOC; B	Global Flexible	6,406.3	13.28	8.48	7.75	10.23	12.06	☆	4.4		None	609-282-2800	None	1.91	4.00	Ison/Stattman	'94/'94
MERRILL GLBL ALLOC; C	Global Flexible	57.6	13.21	8.50	☆	☆	☆	☆	0.0		None	609-282-2800	None	None	1.00	Ison/Stattman	'94/'94
MERRILL GLBL ALLOC; D	Global Flexible	184.7	13.42	8.78	☆	☆	☆	☆	0.0		None	609-282-2800	5.25	None	None	Ison/Stattman	'88
MERRILL GLBL CONV; A ☒▥	Convertible Securities	34.5	10.97	3.82	5.92	9.17	8.13	☆	2.3		None	609-282-2800	5.25	1.66	None	Harry Dewdney	'88
MERRILL GLBL CONV; B	Convertible Securities	106.4	11.00	3.57	4.84	8.06	7.01	☆	1.4		None	609-282-2800	None	2.69	4.00	Harry Dewdney	'94
MERRILL GLBL CONV; C	Convertible Securities	8.1	10.98	3.54	☆	☆	☆	☆	0.0		None	609-282-2800	None	1.00	1.00	Harry Dewdney	'94
MERRILL GLBL CONV; D	Convertible Securities	3.8	10.98	3.87	☆	☆	☆	☆	0.0		None	609-282-2800	5.25	None	None	Harry Dewdney	'94
MERRILL GLBL HOLDNGS; A ☒	Global	326.5	13.03	6.11	4.53	10.38	6.90	12.70	0.1	17.8	None	609-282-2800	5.25	1.44	None	Peter Lehman	'94
MERRILL GLBL HOLDNGS; B	Global	44.7	12.63	5.87	3.53	9.29	5.80	☆	0.0	17.8	None	609-282-2800	None	2.48	4.00	Peter Lehman	'94
MERRILL GLBL HOLDNGS; C	Global	0.3	12.63	5.87	☆	☆	☆	☆	0.0		None	609-282-2800	None	None	1.00	Peter Lehman	'94
MERRILL GLBL HOLDNGS; D	Global	3.3	13.02	6.11	☆	☆	☆	☆	0.0		None	609-282-2800	5.25	None	None	Peter Lehman	'94
MERRILL GLBL RES; A ☒	Natural Resources	34.5	16.14	4.06	7.60	7.03	4.98	☆	1.5	17.8	None	609-282-2800	5.25	0.92	None	Peter Lehman	'94
MERRILL GLBL RES; B	Natural Resources	178.7	16.08	3.81	6.51	5.95	3.89	☆	0.2	17.8	None	609-282-2800	None	1.95	4.00	Peter Lehman	'94
MERRILL GLBL RES; C	Natural Resources	4.6	16.01	3.76	☆	☆	☆	☆	0.0		None	609-282-2800	None	None	1.00	Peter Lehman	'94
MERRILL GLBL RES; D	Natural Resources	94.5	16.12	4.00	☆	☆	☆	☆	0.0		None	609-282-2800	5.25	None	None	Peter Lehman	'94/'94
MERRILL GLBL SM CAP; A ☒	Global Small Company	5.5	8.92	2.53	☆	☆	☆	☆	0.0		None	609-282-2800	5.25	None	None	Bascard/Stattman	'94/'94
MERRILL GLBL SM CAP; B	Global Small Company	136.8	8.84	2.31	☆	☆	☆	☆	0.0		None	609-282-2800	None	None	4.00	Bascard/Stattman	'94/'94
MERRILL GLBL SM CAP; C	Global Small Company	4.9	8.84	2.31	☆	☆	☆	☆	0.0		None	609-282-2800	None	None	1.00	Bascard/Stattman	'94/'94
MERRILL GLBL SM CAP; D	Global Small Company	24.9	8.91	2.53	☆	☆	☆	☆	0.0		None	609-282-2800	5.25	None	None	Bascard/Stattman	'94/'94
MERRILL GLBL UTILITY; A ☒	Utility	51.5	13.02	7.69	10.34	9.55	☆	☆	3.6	11.1	None	609-282-2800	5.25	0.86	None	Walter D. Rogers	'90
MERRILL GLBL UTILITY; B	Utility	426.9	12.96	7.37	9.40	8.68	☆	☆	2.8	11.1	None	609-282-2800	None	1.63	4.00	Walter D. Rogers	'90
MERRILL GLBL UTILITY; C	Utility	1.7	12.96	7.46	☆	☆	☆	☆	0.0	11.1	None	609-282-2800	None	None	1.00	Walter D. Rogers	'94
MERRILL GLBL UTILITY; D	Utility	1.4	13.04	7.59	☆	☆	☆	☆	0.0	11.1	None	609-282-2800	5.25	None	None	Walter D. Rogers	'94
MERRILL GR INV & RET; A ☒	Growth Income	548.5	21.63	11.27	23.88	26.38	15.76	☆	0.0	22.7	None	609-282-2800	5.25	0.82	None	Stephen C. Johnes	'88
MERRILL GR INV & RET; B	Growth Income	1,525.4	20.27	11.01	22.70	25.09	14.57	☆	0.0	22.7	None	609-282-2800	None	1.84	4.00	Stephen C. Johnes	'87
MERRILL GR INV & RET; C	Growth Income	36.1	20.27	11.01	☆	☆	☆	☆	0.0	22.7	None	609-282-2800	None	None	1.00	Stephen C. Johnes	'94
MERRILL GR INV & RET; D	Growth Income	432.2	21.59	11.23	☆	☆	☆	☆	0.0	22.7	None	609-282-2800	5.25	None	None	Stephen C. Johnes	'94
MERRILL HEALTHCARE; A ☒	Health/Biotechnology	72.0	4.10	7.61	24.20	5.78	☆	☆	0.0	16.0	None	609-282-2800	5.25	1.55	None	Jordan Schreiber	'92
MERRILL HEALTHCARE; B	Health/Biotechnology	78.7	3.68	7.29	23.01	4.74	☆	☆	0.0	16.0	None	609-282-2800	None	2.56	4.00	Jordan Schreiber	'92
MERRILL HEALTHCARE; C	Health/Biotechnology	2.1	3.68	6.98	☆	☆	☆	☆	0.0	16.0	None	609-282-2800	None	None	1.00	Jordan Schreiber	'94
MERRILL HEALTHCARE; D	Health/Biotechnology	4.8	4.00	7.53	☆	☆	☆	☆	0.0		None	609-282-2800	5.25	None	None	Jordan Schreiber	'94
MERRILL INSTL INTMDT	Fixed Income	66.3	9.82	4.02	7.57	5.37	7.69	☆	6.2	□	None	609-282-2800	5.25	0.83	None	Jay Harbeck	'92
MERRILL INTL EQUITY; A ☒	International	74.5	10.17	2.42	☆	☆	☆	☆	0.0	□	None	609-282-2800	5.25	None	None	Pineda/Silverman/Bascard	'94/'94/'94

(Returns through 6/30 — 3YRS, 5YRS, 10YRS figures are annualized.)

Lipper/Merrill Lynch mutual fund data table.

Fund	Objective	Net Assets ($Mil)	NAV	Ret %	1-Yr	3-Yr	5-Yr	Yield %	P/E		Phone		Init Chg	Exp	CDSC	Manager	Started
MERRILL INTL EQUITY; B	International	962.3	10.10	2.12	-5.42	☆	☆	4.8		None	609-282-2800	None	None	2.07	4.00	Pineda/Silverman/Bascard'93/'93/'93	'93
MERRILL INTL EQUITY; C	International	25.7	10.01	2.14	☆	☆	☆	0.0		None	609-282-2800	None	None	None	1.00	Pineda/Silverman/Bascard'94/'94/'94	'93
MERRILL INTL EQUITY; D	International	189.1	10.18	2.31	-4.70	☆	☆	5.5		None	609-282-2800	None	5.25	1.31	None	Pineda/Silverman/Bascard'93/'93/'93	'93
MERRILL LATIN AMER; A ☒	Latin American	19.5	10.76	1.97	☆	☆	☆	0.0		None	609-282-2800	None	5.25	None	None	Grace Pineda	'94
MERRILL LATIN AMER; B ☒	Latin American	571.3	10.60	1.58	-25.67	☆	2.18	1.1		None	609-282-2800	None	None	2.51	4.00	Grace Pineda	'91
MERRILL LATIN AMER; C	Latin American	11.5	10.61	11.68	☆	☆	☆	0.0		None	609-282-2800	None	None	None	1.00	Grace Pineda	'94
MERRILL LATIN AMER; D ☒	Latin American	138.2	10.74	11.76	-25.07	3.00	☆	1.1		None	609-282-2800	None	5.25	1.73	None	Grace Pineda	'91
MERRILL MIDEAST/AFR; A ☒	International	N/A	11.02	1.94	☆	☆	☆	0.0		None	609-282-2800	None	5.25	None	None	Grace Pineda	'94
MERRILL MIDEAST/AFR; B	International	N/A	10.96	1.67	☆	☆	☆	0.0		None	609-282-2800	None	None	None	4.00	Grace Pineda	'94
MERRILL MIDEAST/AFR; C	International	N/A	10.96	1.67	☆	☆	☆	0.0		None	609-282-2800	None	None	None	1.00	Grace Pineda	'94
MERRILL MIDEAST/AFR; D ☒	International	N/A	11.00	1.85	☆	☆	☆	0.0		None	609-282-2800	None	5.25	None	None	Grace Pineda	'94
MERRILL PACIFIC; A ☒	Pacific Region	570.4	20.67	0.15	-8.29	9.89	16.71	1.1		None	609-282-2800	None	5.25	0.91	None	Stephen I. Silverman	'83
MERRILL PACIFIC; B	Pacific Region	896.4	19.74	-0.10	-9.20	8.76	7.96	0.2		None	609-282-2800	None	None	1.94	4.00	Stephen I. Silverman	'88
MERRILL PACIFIC; C	Pacific Region	18.1	19.59	-0.15	☆	☆	6.74	0.0		None	609-282-2800	None	None	None	1.00	Stephen I. Silverman	'88
MERRILL PACIFIC; D	Pacific Region	40.1	20.64	0.05	☆	☆	☆	0.0		None	609-282-2800	None	5.25	None	None	Stephen I. Silverman	'94
MERRILL PHOENIX; A ☒	Growth Income	263.9	12.93	8.47	12.64	16.34	14.70	5.9	12.3	None	609-282-2800	None	5.25	1.22	None	Robert J. Martorelli	'86
MERRILL PHOENIX; B	Growth Income	380.2	12.63	8.13	11.52	15.13	13.68	5.1	12.3	None	609-282-2800	None	None	2.24	4.00	Robert J. Martorelli	'88
MERRILL PHOENIX; C	Growth Income	9.4	12.59	8.25	☆	☆	12.50	0.0	12.3	None	609-282-2800	None	None	None	1.00	Robert J. Martorelli	'94
MERRILL PHOENIX; D	Growth Income	31.2	12.93	8.47	☆	☆	☆	0.0	12.3	None	609-282-2800	None	5.25	None	None	Robert J. Martorelli	'94
MERRILL RET GLBL OPP; A ☒★	Global Flexible	8.5	10.47	3.77	☆	☆	☆	0.0		None	609-282-2800	None	4.00	None	None	Joel Heymsfeld	'95
MERRILL RET GLBL OPP; B	Global Flexible	7.9	10.42	3.48	☆	☆	☆	0.0		None	609-282-2800	None	None	None	4.00	Joel Heymsfeld	'95
MERRILL RET GLBL OPP; C	Global Flexible	1.9	10.42	3.48	☆	☆	☆	0.0		None	609-282-2800	None	None	None	1.00	Joel Heymsfeld	'95
MERRILL RET GLBL OPP; D	Global Flexible	0.6	10.45	3.67	☆	☆	☆	0.0		None	609-282-2800	None	4.00	None	None	Joel Heymsfeld	'95
MERRILL RET GOVT SEC; A ☒	Fixed Income	5.4	10.51	5.25	☆	☆	☆	0.0		None	609-282-2800	None	4.00	None	None	Gregory Maunz	'95
MERRILL RET GOVT SEC; B	Fixed Income	1.3	10.51	5.04	☆	☆	☆	0.0		None	609-282-2800	None	None	None	4.00	Gregory Maunz	'95
MERRILL RET GOVT SEC; C	Fixed Income	0.4	10.51	5.02	☆	☆	☆	0.0		None	609-282-2800	None	None	None	1.00	Gregory Maunz	'95
MERRILL RET GOVT SEC; D	Fixed Income	1.0	10.52	5.18	☆	☆	☆	0.0		None	609-282-2800	None	4.00	None	None	Gregory Maunz	'95
MERRILL RET QUAL BD; A ☒	Fixed Income	2.0	9.98	1.28	☆	☆	☆	0.0		None	609-282-2800	None	4.00	None	None	Jay Harbeck	'95
MERRILL RET QUAL BD; B	Fixed Income	1.6	9.98	1.17	☆	☆	☆	0.0		None	609-282-2800	None	None	None	4.00	Jay Harbeck	'95
MERRILL RET QUAL BD; C	Fixed Income	0.5	9.98	1.16	☆	☆	☆	0.0		None	609-282-2800	None	None	None	1.00	Jay Harbeck	'95
MERRILL RET QUAL BD; D	Fixed Income	0.1	9.98	1.31	☆	☆	☆	0.0		None	609-282-2800	None	4.00	None	None	Jay Harbeck	'95
MERRILL RET VALUE; A ☒	Growth Income	2.3	11.27	7.95	☆	☆	☆	0.0		None	609-282-2800	None	5.25	None	None	Kevin Rendino	'94
MERRILL RET VALUE; B	Growth Income	10.9	11.22	7.68	☆	☆	☆	5.9		None	609-282-2800	None	None	1.49	4.00	Kevin Rendino	'92
MERRILL RET VALUE; C	Growth Income	3.4	11.22	7.68	☆	☆	☆	6.5		None	609-282-2800	None	None	0.98	1.00	Kevin Rendino	'94
MERRILL RET VALUE; D	Growth Income	1.3	11.25	7.86	☆	☆	☆	5.7	12.9	None	609-282-2800	None	5.25	1.17	None	Kevin Rendino	'92
MERRILL SH-TM GLBL; A ☒	World Income	0.1	7.87	1.83	1.86	-0.57	☆	4.7	N/A	None	609-282-2800	None	4.00	None	None	Alex Bouzakis	'89
MERRILL SH-TM GLBL; B	World Income	490.7	7.87	1.63	☆	☆	☆	0.0	N/A	None	609-282-2800	None	None	None	4.00	Alex Bouzakis	'95
MERRILL SH-TM GLBL; C	World Income	0.1	7.69	1.10	2.27	-0.06	☆	0.0	N/A	None	609-282-2800	None	None	None	1.00	Alex Bouzakis	'92
MERRILL SH-TM GLBL; D	World Income	32.6	7.87	1.76	☆	☆	☆	3.5	N/A	None	609-282-2800	None	4.00	None	None	Alex Bouzakis	'94
MERRILL SPEC VALUE; A ☒	Growth	128.2	15.84	4.54	15.02	14.64	11.77	2.5	12.9	None	609-282-2800	None	5.25	2.19	None	Dennis Stattman	'92
MERRILL SPEC VALUE; B	Growth	257.4	15.38	4.31	13.88	13.47	10.63	0.0		None	609-282-2800	None	None	None	4.00	Dennis Stattman	'89
MERRILL SPEC VALUE; C	Growth	14.1	15.29	4.27	☆	☆	☆	0.0		None	609-282-2800	None	None	None	1.00	Dennis Stattman	'94
MERRILL SPEC VALUE; D	Growth	15.3	15.83	4.51	☆	☆	☆	0.0		None	609-282-2800	None	5.25	0.85	None	Dennis Stattman	'94
MERRILL STRAT DIV; A ☒	Equity Income	19.0	12.11	5.58	15.71	9.21	8.36	8.2	16.5	None	609-282-2800	None	5.25	1.88	None	Walter D. Rogers	'88
MERRILL STRAT DIV; B	Equity Income	134.4	12.08	5.32	14.46	8.09	7.24	7.7	16.5	None	609-282-2800	None	None	None	4.00	Walter D. Rogers	'87
MERRILL STRAT DIV; C	Equity Income	0.7	12.05	5.24	6.37	☆	☆	0.0		None	609-282-2800	None	None	None	1.00	Walter D. Rogers	'89
MERRILL STRAT DIV; D	Equity Income	13.6	12.11	5.58	5.35	☆	☆	0.0		None	609-282-2800	None	5.25	None	None	Walter D. Rogers	'94
MERRILL TECHNOLOGY; A ☒	Science & Technology	249.6	5.37	9.82	27.75	☆	6.44	0.0	22.0	None	609-282-2800	None	5.25	None	None	Jim Renck	'94
MERRILL TECHNOLOGY; B	Science & Technology	605.8	5.24	9.62	26.48	☆	☆	0.0	22.0	None	609-282-2800	None	None	None	4.00	Jim Renck	'92
MERRILL TECHNOLOGY; C	Science & Technology	25.8	5.22	9.66	☆	☆	☆	0.0	N/A	None	609-282-2800	None	None	None	1.00	Jim Renck	'94

★ MERRILL RET GLBL OPP; A–Fund has been reclassified from Global to Global Flexible.

© Copyright Lipper Analytical Services, Inc.

PERFORMANCE OF MUTUAL FUNDS (continued)

FUND NAME	OBJECTIVE	ASSETS ($ MIL) 5/31/95	NAV ($/SHR) 6/30/95	QTR	1YR	3YRS	5YRS (Annualized)	10YRS	DIV YLD %	P/E RATIO	800	In-State	Load	Exp. Ratio	Redemption	MANAGER	SINCE
MERRILL TECHNOLOGY; D	Science & Technology	35.8	5.37	9.82	☆	☆	☆	☆	0.0	N/A	None	609-282-2800	5.25	None	None	Jim Renck	'94
MERRILL UTILITY INC; A ⊠	Utility	3.4	9.01	7.37	17.50	☆	☆	☆	5.5	12.2	None	609-282-2800	4.00	None	None	Walter D. Rogers	'93
MERRILL UTILITY INC; B	Utility	39.3	9.01	7.08	16.52	☆	☆	☆	4.7	12.2	None	609-282-2800	None	None	4.00	Walter D. Rogers	'93
MERRILL UTILITY INC; C	Utility	1.4	9.00	7.06	☆	☆	☆	☆	0.0	12.2	None	609-282-2800	None	None	1.00	Walter D. Rogers	'94
MERRILL UTILITY INC; D	Utility	0.6	9.01	7.15	☆	☆	☆	☆	0.0	12.2	None	609-282-2800	4.00	None	None	Walter D. Rogers	'94
MERRILL WORLD INC; A ⊠	World Income	291.2	8.47	5.15	8.45	5.48	9.22	☆	8.6	□	None	609-282-2800	4.00	0.77	None	Parish/Lathbury	'93/'88
MERRILL WORLD INC; B	World Income	1,371.9	8.46	4.83	7.62	4.64	☆	☆	7.8		None	609-282-2800	None	1.54	4.00	Parish/Lathbury	'93/'91
MERRILL WORLD INC; C	World Income	3.8	8.46	4.93	☆	☆	☆	☆	0.0	□	None	609-282-2800	None	1.00	1.00	Parish/Lathbury	'94/'94
MERRILL WORLD INC; D	World Income	2.2	8.47	5.09	☆	☆	☆	☆	0.0		None	609-282-2800	4.00		None	Parish/Lathbury	'94/'94
MERRIMAN ASSET ALLOC	Global Flexible	23.7	10.95	4.58	8.31	8.34	7.11	☆	1.6	21.5	423-4893	206-285-5877	None	1.56	None	Merriman/Notaro	'89/'89
MERRIMAN CAP APPREC	Growth	21.9	10.89	5.93	11.27	6.10	7.55	☆	1.3	N/A	423-4893	206-285-5877	None	1.58	None	Merriman/Notaro	'89/'89
MERRIMAN FLEXIBLE BOND	Fixed Income	9.0	10.24	4.84	7.38	7.38	8.27	☆	4.9		423-4893	206-285-5877	None	1.50	None	Merriman/Notaro	'88/'88
MERRIMAN GRWOTH & INCOME	Growth Income	9.5	10.72	4.48	8.63	4.65	5.88	☆	1.4	N/A	423-4893	206-285-5877	None	1.90	None	Merriman/Notaro	'88/'88
MERRIMAN LVGD GROWTH	Capital Appreciation	7.7	11.14	6.20	13.32	5.52	☆	☆	1.1	N/A	423-4893	206-285-5877	None	2.06	None	Merriman/Notaro	'92/'92
METLIFE SS CAP APP; A	Capital Appreciation	275.3	11.52	12.94	32.56	21.52	17.52	☆	0.0	21.5	882-3302	617-348-2000	4.50	1.50	None	Fredrick R. Kobrick	'86
METLIFE SS CAP APP; B	Capital Appreciation	83.5	11.38	12.67	31.86	☆	☆	☆	0.0	21.5	882-3302	617-348-2000	None	2.00	5.00	Fredrick R. Kobrick	'93
METLIFE SS CAP APP; C	Capital Appreciation	96.1	11.63	12.91	33.06	☆	☆	☆	0.0	21.5	882-3302	617-348-2000	None	1.00	None	Fredrick R. Kobrick	'93
METLIFE SS CAP APP; D	Capital Appreciation	3.6	11.40	12.65	31.79	☆	☆	☆	0.0	21.5	882-3302	617-348-2000	None	2.00	1.00	Fredrick R. Kobrick	'93
METLIFE SS EQ INC; A	Equity Income	36.9	11.71	7.38	16.13	13.84	9.62	☆	2.4	15.1	882-3302	617-348-2000	4.50	1.50	None	Bartlett R. Geer	'92
METLIFE SS EQ INC; B	Equity Income	15.5	11.68	7.12	15.43	☆	☆	☆	2.0	15.1	882-3302	617-348-2000	None	2.00	5.00	Bartlett R. Geer	'93
METLIFE SS EQ INC; C	Equity Income	33.3	11.70	7.45	16.66	☆	☆	☆	2.8	15.1	882-3302	617-348-2000	None	1.00	1.00	Bartlett R. Geer	'93
METLIFE SS EQ INC; D	Equity Income	1.4	11.67	7.13	15.34	☆	☆	☆	2.0	15.1	882-3302	617-348-2000	None	2.00	5.00	Bartlett R. Geer	'93
METLIFE SS EQ INVMT; A	Growth Income	30.6	14.28	8.98	18.34	12.86	9.81	☆	0.4	17.9	882-3302	617-348-2000	4.50	1.50	None	Peter Bennett	'89
METLIFE SS EQ INVMT; B	Growth Income	5.6	14.16	8.76	17.70	☆	☆	☆	0.0	17.9	882-3302	617-348-2000	None	2.00	5.00	Peter Bennett	'93
METLIFE SS EQ INVMT; C ▥	Growth Income	46.5	14.27	9.03	18.83	☆	☆	☆	1.2	17.9	882-3302	617-348-2000	None	1.00	1.00	Peter Bennett	'93
METLIFE SS EQ INVMT; D	Growth Income	0.7	14.15	8.76	17.53	☆	☆	☆	0.0	17.9	882-3302	617-348-2000	None	2.00	1.00	Peter Bennett	'93
METLIFE SS HIGH INC; A	Fixed Income	629.7	5.81	2.69	5.27	11.21	12.41	☆	11.2		882-3302	617-348-2000	4.50	1.16	None	Bartlett R. Geer	'87
METLIFE SS HIGH INC; B	Fixed Income	128.4	5.79	2.51	4.51	☆	☆	☆	10.5		882-3302	617-348-2000	None	1.93	5.00	Bartlett R. Geer	'93
METLIFE SS HIGH INC; C ▥	Fixed Income	2.9	5.79	2.94	5.54	☆	☆	☆	11.5		882-3302	617-348-2000	None	0.93	None	Bartlett R. Geer	'93
METLIFE SS HIGH INC; D	Fixed Income	8.6	5.80	2.67	4.49	☆	☆	☆	10.5		882-3302	617-348-2000	None	1.93	1.00	Bartlett R. Geer	'93
METLIFE SS MGD ASSTS; A	Flexible	187.3	9.37	7.53	12.50	11.89	9.72	☆	1.8	16.8	882-3302	617-348-2000	4.50	1.25	None	Michael Yogg	'91
METLIFE SS MGD ASSTS; B	Flexible	159.9	9.34	7.24	11.61	☆	☆	☆	1.2	16.8	882-3302	617-348-2000	None	2.00	5.00	Michael Yogg	'93
METLIFE SS MGD ASSTS; C ▥	Flexible	27.2	9.37	7.48	12.78	☆	☆	☆	2.1	16.8	882-3302	617-348-2000	None	1.00	None	Michael Yogg	'93
METLIFE SS MGD ASSTS; D	Flexible	12.9	9.35	7.23	11.59	☆	☆	☆	1.1	16.8	882-3302	617-348-2000	None	2.00	1.00	Michael Yogg	'93
MFS BOND; A	Fixed Income	499.4	13.26	7.74	15.17	8.27	10.13	10.18	6.6		637-2929	617-954-5000	4.75	0.96	None	Geoff Kurinsky	'89
MFS BOND; B	Fixed Income	80.2	13.23	7.45	14.20	☆	☆	☆	6.0		637-2929	617-954-5000	None	1.83	4.00	Geoff Kurinsky	'93
MFS BOND; C	Fixed Income	9.8	13.23	7.52	14.30	☆	☆	☆	6.0		637-2929	617-954-5000	None	None	None	Geoff Kurinsky	'94
MFS CAP GROWTH; A	Capital Appreciation	26.4	15.38	8.16	20.09	☆	☆	☆	1.4	15.6	637-2929	617-954-5000	5.75	1.12	None	John Brennan	'94
MFS CAP GROWTH; B	Capital Appreciation	431.1	15.34	7.88	18.74	11.07	10.42	☆	0.3	15.6	637-2929	617-954-5000	None	2.18	4.00	John Brennan	'95
MFS EMERG GRO; A	Midcap	749.6	22.12	5.94	34.22	☆	☆	☆	0.0	26.7	637-2929	617-954-5000	5.75	1.33	None	John Ballen	'95
MFS EMERG GRO; B	Midcap	1,226.8	22.00	5.77	33.22	23.12	21.37	☆	0.0	26.7	637-2929	617-954-5000	None	2.14	4.00	John Ballen	'86
MFS EMERGING EQUITIES ▥	Small Company Growth	101.7	16.42	7.67	43.21	☆	☆	☆	0.0	N/A	637-2262	617-954-5000	None	0.78	None	Felipe/Ballen	'93/'93
MFS GOLD & NATL RES; A	Gold	5.1	5.78	-2.03	-7.22	☆	☆	☆	0.0	N/A	637-2929	617-954-5000	5.75	1.42	4.00	Constantine Mokas	'94
MFS GOLD & NATL RES; B	Gold	26.4	5.66	-2.41	-8.12	4.53	0.72	☆	0.0	N/A	637-2929	617-954-5000	None	2.49	4.00	Constantine Mokas	'94
MFS GOVT LTD MAT; A	Fixed Income	244.4	8.59	2.71	6.50	5.18	6.17	☆	6.5	□	637-2929	617-954-5000	2.50	0.89	None	Steve Nothern	'88

MFS GOVT LTD MAT; B	Fixed Income	28.7	8.57	2.39	5.45	☆	☆	☆	5.6	☐	637-2929	617-954-5000	None	1.79	4.00	Steve Nothern	'93
MFS GOVT LTD MAT; C	Fixed Income	5.8	8.56	2.49	☆	☆	☆	☆	0.0	☐	637-2929	617-954-5000	None	None	None	Steve Nothern	'94
MFS GOVT MTGE; A	Fixed Income	454.7	6.70	5.60	11.49	6.61	7.73	☆	6.5	☐	637-2929	617-954-5000	4.75	1.27	None	James Calmas	'93
MFS GOVT MTGE; B	Fixed Income	938.5	6.69	5.41	10.69	☆	☆	☆	5.8	☐	637-2929	617-954-5000	None	1.94	4.00	James Calmas	'93
MFS GOVT SEC; A	Fixed Income	324.4	9.66	6.42	12.36	7.55	8.84	8.32	7.0	☐	637-2929	617-954-5000	4.75	0.79	None	Steve Nothern	'91
MFS GOVT SEC; B	Fixed Income	113.6	9.64	6.19	11.50	☆	☆	☆	6.3	☐	637-2929	617-954-5000	None	1.51	4.00	Steve Nothern	'93
MFS GROWTH OPPTY; A	Growth	639.7	12.20	10.51	26.46	13.82	10.65	10.77	0.3	20.0	637-2929	617-954-5000	5.75	0.86	None	Paul McMahon	'92
MFS GROWTH OPPTY; B	Growth	4.2	12.03	10.16	25.14	☆	☆	☆	0.0	20.0	637-2929	617-954-5000	None	1.81	4.00	Paul McMahon	'93
MFS HIGH INCOME; A	Fixed Income	584.0	5.08	5.08	11.09	10.18	13.49	9.75	8.5	☐	637-2929	617-954-5000	4.75	0.99	None	Robert Manning	'94
MFS HIGH INCOME; B	Fixed Income	310.6	5.08	4.85	10.16	☆	☆	☆	7.7	☐	637-2929	617-954-5000	None	1.85	4.00	Robert Manning	'94
MFS HIGH INCOME; C	Fixed Income	8.3	5.09	5.07	10.45	☆	☆	☆	7.8	☐	637-2929	617-954-5000	None	1.79	None	Robert Manning	'94
MFS INTMDT INCOME; A	World Income	6.7	8.42	3.73	10.50	☆	☆	☆	5.9	☐	637-2929	617-954-5000	4.75	1.18	None	Nothen/Hawkins	'93/'93
MFS INTMDT INCOME; B	World Income	268.2	8.42	3.62	9.35	3.63	6.20	☆	5.0	☐	637-2929	617-954-5000	None	2.22	4.00	Nothen/Hawkins	'88/'92
MFS LTD MAT; A	Fixed Income	88.7	7.22	4.01	8.93	5.65	☆	☆	6.5	☐	637-2929	617-954-5000	2.50	0.85	None	Geoff Kurinsky	'95
MFS LTD MAT; B	Fixed Income	18.2	7.22	3.98	8.05	☆	☆	☆	5.7	☐	637-2929	617-954-5000	None	1.74	4.00	Geoff Kurinsky	'95
MFS LTD MAT; C	Fixed Income	4.4	7.23	3.94	8.06	☆	☆	☆	5.6	☐	637-2929	617-954-5000	None	None	None	Geoff Kurinsky	'95
MFS MGD SECTORS; A	Specialty	140.5	14.47	11.31	28.47	☆	☆	☆	0.0	16.6	637-2929	617-954-5000	5.75	1.52	None	Ken Enright	'93
MFS MGD SECTORS; B	Specialty	210.2	14.41	11.10	27.59	13.80	11.64	☆	0.0	16.6	637-2929	617-954-5000	None	2.26	4.00	Ken Enright	'93
MFS OTC FUND; A	Small Company Growth	25.1	9.11	3.29	26.11	☆	☆	☆	0.0	19.1	637-2929	617-954-5000	5.75	1.50	None	Mark Regan	'94
MFS OTC FUND; B	Small Company Growth	51.4	8.99	3.10	25.01	☆	☆	☆	0.0	19.1	637-2929	617-954-5000	None	2.57	4.00	Mark Regan	'94
MFS OTC FUND; C	Small Company Growth	1.8	8.98	3.34	☆	☆	☆	☆	0.0	19.1	637-2929	617-954-5000	None	None	None	Mark Regan	'94
MFS RESEARCH; A	Growth Income	389.7	14.12	8.87	22.46	17.81	14.00	13.77	1.6	20.2	637-2929	617-954-5000	5.75	0.91	None	Bill McAdams	'93
MFS RESEARCH; B	Growth Income	89.6	13.96	8.72	21.46	☆	☆	☆	1.5	20.2	637-2929	617-954-5000	None	1.82	4.00	Bill McAdams	'93
MFS RESEARCH; C	Growth Income	13.6	13.97	8.72	21.52	☆	☆	☆	1.5	20.2	637-2929	617-954-5000	None	1.74	None	Bill McAdams	'94
MFS STRATEGIC INCOME; A	Fixed Income	42.3	8.11	10.05	16.03	7.06	9.47	☆	6.2	☐	637-2929	617-954-5000	4.75	1.71	None	James Swanson	'92
MFS STRATEGIC INCOME; B	Fixed Income	8.9	8.07	9.91	15.04	☆	☆	☆	6.2	☐	637-2929	617-954-5000	None	2.43	4.00	James Swanson	'93
MFS STRATEGIC INCOME; C	Fixed Income	0.7	8.04	9.74	☆	☆	☆	☆	0.0	☐	637-2929	617-954-5000	None	None	None	James Swanson	'94
MFS TOTAL RETURN; A	Balanced	2,065.6	13.85	7.35	14.46	10.56	10.54	12.58	4.2	15.9	637-2929	617-954-5000	4.75	0.85	None	Richard Dahlberg	'84
MFS TOTAL RETURN; B	Balanced	942.4	13.85	7.13	13.51	☆	☆	☆	3.4	15.9	637-2929	617-954-5000	None	1.70	4.00	Richard Dahlberg	'93
MFS TOTAL RETURN; C	Balanced	10.2	13.88	7.20	☆	☆	☆	☆	0.0	15.9	637-2929	617-954-5000	None	None	None	Richard Dahlberg	'94
MFS UNION STD EQUITY	Growth	34.6	11.05	9.19	20.83	☆	☆	☆	0.9	16.9	637-2929	617-954-5000	None	None	None	Bill Harris	'94
MFS UTILITIES; A	Utility	43.4	7.49	8.87	13.90	11.81	☆	☆	4.4	13.4	637-2929	617-954-5000	4.75	0.65	None	Maura Shaughnhessy	'92
MFS UTILITIES; B	Utility	26.8	7.47	8.69	12.66	☆	☆	☆	3.5	13.4	637-2929	617-954-5000	None	1.72	4.00	Maura Shaughnhessy	'93
MFS UTILITIES; C	Utility	4.0	7.48	8.61	12.62	☆	☆	☆	3.5	13.4	637-2929	617-954-5000	None	1.65	None	Maura Shaughnhessy	'94
MFS VALUE; A	Capital Appreciation	165.1	10.51	10.17	20.69	19.37	13.21	13.91	0.0	15.9	637-2929	617-954-5000	5.75	1.37	None	John Brennan	'91
MFS VALUE; B	Capital Appreciation	26.7	10.34	9.88	19.73	☆	☆	☆	0.0	15.9	637-2929	617-954-5000	None	2.25	4.00	John Brennan	'93
MFS WORLD ASSET ALLO; A	Global Flexible	54.5	16.11	6.07	☆	☆	☆	☆	0.0	☐	637-2929	617-954-5000	4.75	None	None	Multiple Managers	N/A
MFS WORLD ASSET ALLO; B	Global Flexible	75.3	16.09	5.95	☆	☆	☆	☆	0.0	☐	637-2929	617-954-5000	None	None	4.00	Multiple Managers	N/A
MFS WORLD ASSET ALLO; C	Global Flexible	17.4	16.08	5.98	☆	☆	☆	☆	0.0	☐	637-2929	617-954-5000	None	None.	None	Multiple Managers	N/A
MFS WORLD EQUITY; A	Global	34.4	15.80	6.47	10.13	☆	☆	☆	0.0	☐	637-2929	617-954-5000	5.75	1.54	None	David Mannheim	'93
MFS WORLD EQUITY; B	Global	163.7	15.72	6.22	8.99	11.38	6.33	☆	0.0	☐	637-2929	617-954-5000	None	2.58	4.00	David Mannheim	'92
MFS WORLD EQUITY; C	Global	2.1	15.70	6.22	9.11	☆	☆	☆	0.0	☐	637-2929	617-954-5000	None	2.55	None	David Mannheim	'94
MFS WORLD GOVTS; A	World Income	358.5	12.23	2.86	14.44	6.96	9.85	13.88	0.0	☐	637-2929	617-954-5000	4.75	1.54	None	Leslie Nanberg	'84
MFS WORLD GOVTS; B	World Income	85.3	12.09	2.63	13.46	☆	☆	☆	0.0	☐	637-2929	617-954-5000	None	2.38	4.00	Leslie Nanberg	'93
MFS WORLD GOVTS; C	World Income	9.8	12.09	2.63	13.57	☆	☆	☆	0.0	☐	637-2929	617-954-5000	None	2.32	None	Leslie Nanberg	'94
MFS WORLD GROWTH; A	Global	133.2	17.12	5.88	8.57	☆	☆	☆	0.0	☐	637-2929	617-954-5000	5.75	1.57	None	Shimura/Mannheim	'93/'93
MFS WORLD GROWTH; B	Global	236.8	16.98	5.78	7.80	☆	☆	☆	0.1	☐	637-2929	617-954-5000	None	2.39	4.00	Shimura/Mannheim	'93/'93
MFS WORLD GROWTH; C	Global	12.4	16.96	5.67	7.74	☆	☆	☆	0.0	☐	637-2929	617-954-5000	None	2.31	None	Shimura/Mannheim	'94/'94
MFS WORLD TOT RTN; A	Global Flexible	107.3	11.18	4.52	11.94	10.16	☆	☆	0.7	☐	637-2929	617-954-5000	4.75	1.76	None	Frederick Simmons	'91
MFS WORLD TOT RTN; B	Global Flexible	55.0	11.17	4.37	11.12	☆	☆	☆	0.3	☐	637-2929	617-954-5000	None	2.49	4.00	Frederick Simmons	'93

PERFORMANCE OF MUTUAL FUNDS (continued)

FUND NAME	OBJECTIVE	ASSETS ($ MIL) 5/31/95	NAV ($/SHR) 6/30/95	RETURN THROUGH 6/30 (Annualized) QTR	1YR	3YRS	5YRS	10YRS	DIV YLD %	P/E RATIO	FEES Load	Exp. Ratio	Redemption	PHONE 800	In-State	MANAGER	SINCE
MFS WORLD TOT RTN; C	Global Flexible	11.0	11.17	4.37	11.22	☆	☆		0.3	□□	None	None	None	637-2929	617-954-5000	Frederick Simmons	'94
MFS WRLDWDE FXD INC ▦	World Income	75.6	10.13	2.74	15.10	☆	☆		2.2	□	None	0.75	None	637-2262	617-954-5000	Leslie Nanberg	'92
MIDWEST STRT EQUITY; A	Capital Appreciation	4.4	10.45	6.20	19.36	☆	☆		1.2	N/A	4.00	1.24	1.00	443-4299	513-629-2000	Susan Flischel	'95
MIDWEST STRT EQUITY; C	Capital Appreciation	1.9	10.47	6.19	18.75	☆	☆		0.6	N/A	None	1.94	1.00	443-4299	513-629-2000	Susan Flischel	'95
MIDWEST STRT GOVT SEC	Fixed Income	25.7	9.54	5.10	9.51	4.26	6.87	7.56	6.1		2.00	1.20	None	443-4299	513-629-2000	Bruce Chaiken	'94
MIDWEST STRT TOT RTN; A	Fixed Income	25.0	8.37	1.36	2.95	3.76	5.85	☆	5.2	□	4.00	1.25	None	443-4299	513-629-2000	Robert Leshner	'95
MIDWEST STRT UTIL; A	Utility	40.7	10.87	5.03	9.82	7.18	9.39	☆	4.2	N/A	4.00	1.25	None	443-4299	513-629-2000	Susan Flischel	'93
MIDWEST STRT UTIL; C	Utility	3.5	10.86	4.85	8.98	☆	☆		3.5	N/A	None	2.00	1.00	443-4299	513-629-2000	Susan Flischel	'93
MIDWEST ADJ GOVT SEC	Fixed Income	21.2	9.79	2.01	4.12	☆	☆		5.3		2.00	0.68	None	443-4299	513-629-2000	Tavares/Goetz/Chaiken	'93/'93/'94
MIDWEST GLOBAL BOND; A	World Income	7.4	10.85	1.02	☆	☆	☆		0.0		4.00	None	None	443-4299	513-629-2000	Rogge Global Partners plc	'95
MIDWEST GLOBAL BOND; C	World Income	0.1	10.81	0.75	☆	☆	☆		0.0	□□	None	None	1.00	443-4299	513-629-2000	Rogge Global Partners plc	'95
MIDWEST INTMDT GOVT; A	Fixed Income	58.9	10.76	5.94	10.91	6.39	8.30	7.86	5.8		2.00	0.99	None	443-4299	513-629-2000	Bruce Chaiken	'94
MIDWEST INTMDT GOVT; C	Fixed Income	0.6	10.76	5.82	10.36	☆	☆		5.4		None	1.46	1.00	443-4299	513-629-2000	Bruce Chaiken	'94
MIM MUTUAL AFA EQU INC	Equity Income	0.9	11.55	6.01	16.49	5.23	☆		2.0	16.8	None	3.19	None	233-1240	216-642-3000	AFA Financial, Inc.	'91
MIM MUTUAL BOND INCOME	Income	1.9	10.45	6.52	16.37	5.56	6.85		0.0	15.9	None	3.02	None	233-1240	216-642-3000	Harvey M. Salkin	'86
MIM MUTUAL STOCK APPREC	Capital Appreciation	36.2	15.80	10.88	18.26	8.01	13.16		0.0	23.1	None	2.44	None	233-1240	216-642-3000	Martin A. Weisberg	'94
MIM MUTUAL STOCK GROWTH	Growth	6.8	11.01	4.66	10.06	1.60	3.01		0.0	17.7	None	2.80	None	233-1240	216-642-3000	Martin A. Weisberg	'93
MIM MUTUAL STOCK INCOME	Growth	5.7	11.82	6.87	20.61	5.51	5.73		0.0	18.7	None	2.75	None	233-1240	216-642-3000	Harvey M. Salkin	'86
MINERVA EQUITY	Growth	11.8	11.56	7.64	20.69	☆	☆		1.3	N/A	None	1.00	None	393-9998	None	Katsunari Yamaguchi	'93
MINERVA FIXED INCOME	Fixed Income	3.2	9.40	6.59	11.81	☆	☆		8.6	18.6	None	0.91	None	393-9998	None	Akihito Sakata	'93
MITCH/KIDDER EQTY INC; A	Equity Income	56.8	21.75	9.17	21.94	7.22	9.69		1.7	N/A	5.75	1.63	None	647-1568	None	Kirk Barneby	'94
MITCH/KIDDER EQTY INC; B	Equity Income	1.6	21.63	9.09	21.39	☆	☆		1.3	N/A	None	2.13	None	647-1568	None	Kirk Barneby	'94
MITCH/KIDDER EQTY INC; C	Equity Income	3.5	21.73	9.32	22.63	☆	☆		2.2	N/A	None	1.13	None	647-1568	None	Kirk Barneby	'94
MMA PRAXIS GROWTH	Growth Income	23.3	11.58	8.96	23.62	☆	☆		0.8	18.6	5.00	1.75	5.00	977-2947	614-897-4600	Keith Yonder	'93
MMA PRAXIS INTMDT INC	Fixed Income	22.0	9.91	6.29	11.77	☆	☆		5.1	□	5.00	1.10	5.00	977-2947	614-897-4600	Delmar King	'93
MONETTA FUND ⊠	Growth Income	335.8	17.02	6.91	19.39	7.35	11.42	☆	0.4	21.8	None	1.35	None	666-3882	708-462-9800	Robert S. Bacarella	'86
MONETTA INTMDT BOND	Fixed Income	3.2	10.32	5.29	13.07	☆	☆		6.5	□□	None	0.28	None	666-3882	708-462-9800	Alogna/Grossman	'93/'93
MONETTA MID-CAP EQUITY	Midcap	12.8	14.58	11.47	26.13	☆	☆		1.8	21.3	None	1.30	None	666-3882	708-462-9800	John M. Alogna	'93
MONITOR FIXED INC; INV	Fixed Income	2.1	21.22	6.17	11.49	6.80	☆		6.1		2.00	1.00	None	253-0412	614-463-5580	Stephen Geis	'91
MONITOR FIXED INC; TR	Fixed Income	134.7	21.22	6.21	11.75	7.07	8.97		6.3		None	0.75	None	253-0412	614-463-5580	Stephen Geis	'89
MONITOR GROWTH; INV	Growth	3.5	30.49	6.99	23.01	9.62	9.65	☆	1.0	N/A	4.00	1.13	None	253-0412	614-463-5580	Gibboney/Sauer/Farrington	'94/'94/'94
MONITOR GROWTH; TR	Growth	126.8	30.49	7.05	23.30	9.90	8.79	☆	1.2	N/A	None	0.88	None	253-0412	614-463-5580	Gibboney/Sauer/Farrington	'94/'94/'94
MONITOR INC EQUITY; TR	Equity Income	126.7	24.19	5.22	16.58	8.98			4.0	N/A	4.00	0.84	None	253-0412	614-463-5580	James Buskirk	'89
MONITOR MTGE SEC; INV	Fixed Income	2.1	7.80	10.89	14.89	3.40			9.4		2.00	1.13	None	253-0412	614-463-5580	Marijo Goldstein	'94
MONITOR MTGE SEC; TR	Fixed Income	59.1	7.77	10.82	14.91	3.54			9.6		None	0.88	None	253-0412	614-463-5580	Marijo Goldstein	'94
MONITOR SHT/INT FXD; TR	Fixed Income	134.5	20.05	4.19	8.67	5.90	7.80	☆	6.0	□	None	0.72	None	253-0412	614-463-5580	Stephen Geis	'89
MONITREND GAMING & LEISR	Growth	0.7	7.37	6.97	19.64	☆	☆		0.0	17.8	4.50	2.89	None	251-1970	615-298-1000	Team Managed	N/A
MONITREND GOLD FUND	Gold	0.4	5.73	3.24	-27.10	-24.05	-19.77		0.0	N/A	4.50	2.45	None	251-1970	615-298-1000	Lion Resources	'94
MONITREND GOVERNMENT	Fixed Income	1.0	13.66	5.27	11.41	5.86	5.65		6.4	N/A	4.50	1.10	None	251-1970	615-298-1000	Pacific Income Advisors	'92
MONITREND GROWTH FUND	Growth	0.5	12.13	9.87	13.58	0.33	☆		0.0	28.7	4.50	2.44	None	251-1970	615-298-1000	Robert Bender	'92
MONITREND SUMMATION FUND	Growth Income	1.5	19.35	7.74	17.19	0.28	1.25		0.5	17.4	4.50	2.44	None	251-1970	615-298-1000	MidCap Associates	'95
MONITREND TECHNOLOGY	Science & Technology	0.2	17.29	17.86	35.00	☆	☆		0.0	30.1	4.50	2.44	None	251-1970	615-298-1000	Michaal Murphy	'93
MONTGOMERY II ASSET ALLO	Flexible	47.2	16.33	7.72	35.99	☆	☆		1.0	N/A	None	2.44	None	572-3863	415-627-2400	Stevens/Honour/Pratt	'94/'94/'94
MONTGOMERY INSTL EMERG	Emerging Markets	158.6	44.65	9.30	2.18	☆	☆		0.0	□	None	1.40	0.75	572-3863	415-627-2400	Jimenez/Sudweeks	'93/'93
MONTGOMERY INSTL INTL SC	Intl Small Company	1.9	48.39	4.49	-0.97	☆	☆		0.6	□	None	None	0.75	572-3863	415-627-2400	Castro/Boich	'94

Fund	Objective	Net Assets	NAV	%R1	%R2	%R3	%R4	Rtg	Yld%	Turn	Phone	Toll	Init Chg	Exp	Manager	Since
MONTGOMERY EMERG MKTS	Emerging Markets	978.2	13.18	8.21	1.48	12.50	☆	☆	0.0	□	572-3863	415-627-2400	None	1.85	Jimenez/Sudweeks	'92/'92
MONTGOMERY EQTY INC	Equity Income	6.1	13.38	5.56	☆	☆	☆	☆	0.0	N/A	572-3863	415-627-2400	None	None	John Brown	'94
MONTGOMERY GLBL COMMUN	Global	205.4	15.46	14.86	9.11	☆	☆	☆	0.0	□	572-3863	415-627-2400	None	1.94	Castro/Boich	'94/'93
MONTGOMERY GLBL OPPTY	Global	13.2	13.27	10.95	6.59	☆	☆	☆	0.0	□	572-3863	415-627-2400	None	1.99	Castro/Boich	'93/'93
MONTGOMERY GROWTH	Growth	838.4	19.16	7.04	26.53	☆	☆	☆	0.4	N/A	572-3863	415-627-2400	None	1.49	Roger W. Honour	'93
MONTGOMERY INTL SM CAP	Intl Small Company	29.3	11.79	5.65	-1.90	☆	☆	☆	0.0	□	572-3863	415-627-2400	None	1.99	Castro/Boich	'93/'93
MONTGOMERY MICRO CAP	Small Company Growth	112.4	13.75	8.52	☆	☆	☆	☆	0.0	N/A	572-3863	415-627-2400	None	None	Honour/Pratt	'94/'94
MONTGOMERY SHORT GOVT BD	Fixed Income	16.2	9.95	3.29	8.28	☆	☆	☆	6.3	□	572-3863	415-627-2400	None	0.71	William Stevens	'92
MONTGOMERY SMALL CAP [☒]	Small Company Growth	196.7	17.15	8.07	20.40	15.63	☆	☆	0.0	□	572-3863	415-627-2400	None	1.35	Stuart O. Roberts	'90
MORG STAN FDS AM VAL; A	Small Company Growth	18.8	12.89	5.92	14.47	☆	☆	☆	1.7	□	282-2404	None	4.75	1.50	Crowe/Stadlinger	'93/'93
MORG STAN FDS AM VAL; C	Small Company Growth	12.9	12.89	5.92	13.79	☆	☆	☆	1.1	25.0	282-2404	None	None	2.25	Crowe/Stadlinger	'93/'93
MORG STAN FDS ASIAN; A	Pacific Region	180.1	16.41	9.77	9.43	☆	☆	☆	0.0	□	282-2404	None	4.75	1.90	Cheng/Chin/Seng	'93/'93/'93
MORG STAN FDS ASIAN; C	Pacific Region	141.1	16.18	9.55	8.64	☆	☆	☆	0.0	□	282-2404	None	None	2.65	Cheng/Chin/Seng	'93/'93/'93
MORG STAN FDS EMERG; A	Emerging Markets	26.9	10.61	11.22	☆	☆	☆	☆	0.0	□	282-2404	None	4.75		Madhav Dhar	'94
MORG STAN FDS EMERG; C	Emerging Markets	21.1	10.53	10.96	☆	☆	☆	☆	0.0	□	282-2404	None	None		Madhav Dhar	'94
MORG STAN FDS GL EQ; A	Global	42.7	12.60	3.62	6.69	☆	☆	☆	0.4	□	282-2404	None	4.75	1.70	Paul Jackson	'94
MORG STAN FDS GL EQ; C	Global	40.7	12.42	3.33	5.75	☆	☆	☆	0.2	□	282-2404	None	None	2.45	Paul Jackson	'94
MORG STAN FDS GL FXD; A	World Income	11.0	10.23	4.05	10.64	☆	☆	☆	2.8	□	282-2404	None	4.75	1.45	Smith/Akerman	'93/'95
MORG STAN FDS GL FXD; C	World Income	6.0	10.20	3.86	9.58	☆	☆	☆	2.3	□	282-2404	None	None	2.20	Smith/Akerman	'93/'95
MORG STAN FDS LATIN; A	Latin American	8.8	9.08	19.79	☆	☆	☆	☆	0.0	□	282-2404	None	4.75		Robert Meyer	'94
MORG STAN FDS LATIN; C	Latin American	4.1	8.99	19.55	☆	☆	☆	☆	0.0	□	282-2404	None	None		Robert Meyer	'94
MORG STAN FDS WORLD; A	World Income	19.1	11.57	13.10	4.97	☆	☆	☆	8.7	□	282-2404	None	4.75		Angevine/Ghaffari	'94/'94
MORG STAN FDS WORLD; C	World Income	11.2	11.57	12.78	4.27	☆	☆	☆	8.1	□	282-2404	None	None		Angevine/Ghaffari	'94/'94
MORG STAN INSTL ACTIVE	International	143.3	11.00	2.33	-2.48	6.81	☆	☆	0.0	□	548-7786	617-557-8000	None	0.80	Paul Jackson	'92
MORG STAN INSTL ASIAN EQ	Pacific Region	298.4	20.46	9.94	9.64	22.90	☆	☆	0.7	□	548-7786	617-557-8000	None	1.00	Chin/Cheng	'91/'91
MORG STAN INSTL BALANCED	Balanced	21.5	9.73	6.68	13.86	9.80	9.98	☆	4.2	14.8	548-7786	617-557-8000	None	0.70	Crowe/Sexauer/Zick	'92/'90/'90
MORG STAN INSTL EMRG DEBT	World Income	210.7	9.02	29.97	17.33	7.14	9.24	☆	5.4	27.6	548-7786	617-557-8000	None	1.49	Paul Ghaffari	'94
MORG STAN INSTL EMRG GRO	Small Company Growth	127.9	18.24	6.17	18.18	☆	☆	☆	0.0	□	548-7786	617-557-8000	None	1.25	Dennis Sherva	'89
MORG STAN INSTL EMRG MKT	Emerging Markets	945.9	14.21	11.45	-6.95	☆	☆	☆	0.0	□	548-7786	617-557-8000	None	1.75	Dhar/Hay	'92/'94
MORG STAN INSTL EQ GR	Growth	136.5	14.16	11.93	30.74	13.70	☆	☆	1.3	16.4	548-7786	617-557-8000	None	0.80	Feuerman/Johnson	'93/'91
MORG STAN INSTL EURO EQ	European Region	47.3	14.12	9.29	12.15	7.18	☆	☆	0.0	N/A	548-7786	617-557-8000	None	1.00	Robert Sargent	'93
MORG STAN INSTL FXD INC	Fixed Income	176.4	10.54	6.30	12.50	☆	☆	☆	6.0	□	548-7786	617-557-8000	None	0.45	Warren Akerman	'93
MORG STAN INSTL GLBL EQ	Global	82.0	14.75	8.54	12.95	☆	☆	☆	0.4	□	548-7786	617-557-8000	None	1.00	Michael Cowan	'92
MORG STAN INSTL GLBL FXD	World Income	93.6	11.15	5.57	13.22	6.83	☆	☆	5.0	□	548-7786	617-557-8000	None	0.50	Smith/Akerman	'94/'93
MORG STAN INSTL GOLD	Gold	29.4	9.53	3.36	10.37	☆	☆	☆	0.1	□	548-7786	617-557-8000	None	1.25	Peter Palmedo	'94
MORG STAN INSTL HI YLD	Fixed Income	67.6	10.29	7.74	11.89	15.66	☆	☆	10.3	□	548-7786	617-557-8000	None	0.75	Robert Angevine	'92
MORG STAN INSTL INT EQ [☒]	International	1,387.2	15.25	6.05	7.76	☆	9.08	☆	0.0	□	548-7786	617-557-8000	None	1.00	Dominic Caldecott	'89
MORG STAN INSTL INTL SM	Intl Small Company	183.9	15.43	4.68	-5.17	☆	☆	☆	0.2	□	548-7786	617-557-8000	None	1.15	Margaret Naylor	'92
MORG STAN INSTL JAPANESE	Japanese	29.3	8.19	-8.49	-21.33	☆	☆	☆	0.0	□	548-7786	617-557-8000	None	1.00	Kunihiko Sugio	'94
MORG STAN INSTL LATIN AM	Latin American	12.9	8.80	21.21	☆	☆	☆	☆	0.0	□	548-7786	617-557-8000	None	None	Robert Meyer	'95
MORG STAN INSTL SM CAP	Small Company Growth	46.7	11.51	6.67	15.59	13.34	☆	☆	2.4	13.1	548-7786	617-557-8000	None	1.00	Crowe/Stadlinger	'92/'92
MORG STAN INSTL VALUE EQ	Growth Income	102.1	13.06	8.64	18.77	☆	11.32	☆	2.9	14.7	548-7786	617-557-8000	None	0.70	Crowe/Sexauer/Zick	'92/'90/'90
MORGAN GRENFELL EMERG EQ	Emerging Markets	67.0	8.38	8.83	1.35	☆	☆	☆	0.3	□	932-7781	215-989-6611	None	1.36	Lamb/Getley	'94/'94
MORGAN GRENFELL EMERG FI	World Income	60.1	10.19	16.99	☆	☆	☆	☆	0.0	□	932-7781	215-989-6611	None	None	Geoffrey Blanning	'94
MORGAN GRENFELL EURO SM	European Region	8.7	10.86	6.78	☆	☆	☆	☆	0.0	□	932-7781	215-989-6611	None	None	Curling/Turner	'94/'94
MORGAN GRENFELL FXD INC	Fixed Income	397.2	10.47	5.35	11.52	☆	9.47	☆	6.6	□	932-7781	215-989-6611	None	0.54	David Baldt	'92
MORGAN GRENFELL GLBL FXD	World Income	83.2	10.91	4.00	14.10	☆	☆	☆	1.8	□	932-7781	215-989-6611	None	0.85	Kelson/Hall	'93/'93
MORGAN GRENFELL INTL FXD	World Income	26.0	11.08	3.84	13.08	☆	☆	☆	0.5	□	932-7781	215-989-6611	None	0.85	Kelson/Hall	'94/'94
MORGAN GRENFELL INTL SM	Intl Small Company	6.1	8.75	0.81	-15.88	☆	☆	☆	0.5	□	932-7781	215-989-6611	None	1.25	Bamping/Freeze	'93/'93
MORGAN KEEGAN SOUTHERN	Growth	27.4	14.34	7.17	13.81	9.00	9.47	☆	0.6	18.4	366-7426	901-524-4100	3.00	2.00	Elkan Scheidt	'94

PERFORMANCE OF MUTUAL FUNDS (continued)

FUND NAME	OBJECTIVE	ASSETS ($ MIL) 5/31/95	NAV ($/SHR) 6/30/95	QTR	1YR	3YRS	5YRS	10YRS	DIV YLD %	P/E RATIO	800	In-State	Load	Exp. Ratio	Redemption	MANAGER	SINCE
						RETURN THROUGH 6/30 (Annualized)					PHONE NUMBER		FEES				
MSB FUND	Growth Income	35.4	14.62	4.20	14.77	12.33	9.20	11.33	2.5	15.6	631-6364	212-551-1920	None	1.28	None	McCabe/Trautman	'93/'93
MUHLENKAMP FUND	Flexible	19.7	19.02	11.03	14.74	12.99	12.28	☆	0.4	N/A	860-3863	412-935-5520	None	1.57	None	Ronald Muhlenkamp	'88
MUNDER ACCEL GROWTH; Y	Growth	181.0	14.88	12.73	28.79	15.94	☆	☆	0.0	19.2	892-4366	None	None	0.93	None	Ann Conrad	'91
MUNDER ACCEL GROWTH; K	Growth	78.3	14.82	12.61	28.49	☆	☆	☆	0.0	19.2	892-4366	None	None	1.18	None	Ann Conrad	'92
MUNDER ACCEL GROWTH; A	Growth	4.3	14.82	12.61	28.48	☆	☆	☆	0.0	19.2	892-4366	None	3.75	1.18	None	Ann Conrad	'92
MUNDER BALANCED; Y	Balanced	47.4	10.77	7.55	17.68	☆	☆	☆	2.7	18.7	892-4366	None	None	0.97	None	Barr/Chatain/Conrad	'95/'95/'95
MUNDER BALANCED; K	Balanced	0.2	10.78	7.38	17.36	☆	☆	☆	2.3	18.7	892-4366	None	None	1.22	None	Barr/Chatain/Conrad	'95/'95/'95
MUNDER BALANCED; A	Balanced	0.3	10.77	7.49	17.33	☆	☆	☆	2.4	18.7	892-4366	None	3.75	1.22	None	Barr/Chatain/Conrad	'95/'95/'95
MUNDER BOND; Y	Fixed Income	145.7	9.70	5.88	11.03	5.19	☆	☆	6.7	☐	892-4366	None	None	0.67	None	Stephen Chatain	'91
MUNDER BOND; K	Fixed Income	35.8	9.69	5.70	10.62	☆	☆	☆	6.5	☐	892-4366	None	None	0.92	None	Stephen Chatain	'92
MUNDER BOND; A	Fixed Income	0.9	9.70	5.81	10.73	☆	☆	☆	6.5		892-4366	None	3.75	0.92	None	Stephen Chatain	'92
MUNDER GOVT INC; K	Fixed Income	174.2	10.30	5.91	☆	☆	☆	☆	6.7		892-4366	None	None	0.95	None	Robinson/Root	'95/'95
MUNDER INDEX 500; Y	S&P Index	119.4	13.81	9.39	25.82	12.89	☆	☆	2.9	17.2	892-4366	None	None	0.25	None	Todd Johnson	'91
MUNDER INDEX 500; K	S&P Index	2.5	13.80	9.34	25.39	☆	☆	☆	2.7	17.2	892-4366	None	None	0.50	None	Todd Johnson	'92
MUNDER INDEX 500; A	S&P Index	0.6	13.80	9.34	25.37	☆	☆	☆	2.6	17.2	892-4366	None	3.75	0.50	None	Todd Johnson	'92
MUNDER INTMDT BOND; Y	Fixed Income	162.9	9.51	4.56	9.11	5.62	☆	☆	6.9		892-4366	None	None	0.68	None	Kennedy/Robinson	'95/'95
MUNDER INTMDT BOND; K	Fixed Income	298.5	9.51	4.50	8.86	☆	☆	☆	6.7		892-4366	None	None	0.93	None	Kennedy/Robinson	'95/'95
MUNDER INTMDT BOND; A	Fixed Income	5.5	9.52	4.50	8.97	☆	☆	☆	6.7		892-4366	None	3.75	0.93	None	Kennedy/Robinson	'95/'95
MUNDER INTL EQTY; Y	International	76.0	13.44	6.33	8.26	8.46	☆	☆	0.8		892-4366	None	None	0.93	None	Richardson/Hollinshead	'93/'95
MUNDER INTL EQTY; K	International	69.8	13.41	6.26	8.03	☆	☆	☆	0.7		892-4366	None	None	1.18	None	Richardson/Hollinshead	'93/'95
MUNDER INTL EQTY; A	International	1.3	13.42	6.25	8.04	☆	☆	☆	0.6	18.9	892-4366	None	3.75	1.18	None	Richardson/Hollinshead	'95/'95
MUNDER MULTI-SEASON; A	Growth	3.3	12.02	6.84	19.68	☆	☆	☆	0.0	18.9	239-3334	810-901-0770	5.50	1.75	None	Munder/Barr	'93/'93
MUNDER MULTI-SEASON; B	Growth	53.2	11.85	6.56	18.82	☆	☆	☆	0.0	18.9	239-3334	810-901-0770	None	2.50	5.00	Munder/Barr	'93/'93
MUNDER MULTI-SEASON; Y	Growth	9.3	12.10	6.89	20.12	☆	☆	☆	0.0	18.9	239-3334	810-901-0770	None	1.50	None	Munder/Barr	'93/'93
MUNDER MULTI-SEASON; C	Growth	2.9	11.86	6.56	18.80	☆	☆	☆	0.0	18.9	239-3334	810-901-0770	None	2.50	1.00	Munder/Barr	'93/'93
MUNDER REAL ESTATE; A	Real Estate	0.2	10.09	4.60	☆	☆	☆	☆	0.0	N/A	239-3334	810-901-0770	5.00	None	None	Lee Munder	'94
MUNDER REAL ESTATE; B	Real Estate	1.4	10.09	4.40	☆	☆	☆	☆	0.0	N/A	239-3334	810-901-0770	None	None	5.00	Lee Munder	'94
MUNDER REAL ESTATE; Y	Real Estate	3.9	10.09	4.66	☆	☆	☆	☆	0.0	N/A	239-3334	810-901-0770	None	None	None	Lee Munder	'94
MUNDER REAL ESTATE; C	Real Estate	0.1	10.12	4.13	☆	☆	☆	☆	0.0	N/A	239-3334	810-901-0770	None	None	1.00	Lee Munder	'94
MUNDER SM CO GROWTH; Y	Small Company Growth	75.7	15.33	6.16	22.51	15.00	☆	☆	0.0	22.2	892-4366	None	None	0.98	None	Stalzer/Harris	'92/'93
MUNDER SM CO GROWTH; K	Small Company Growth	48.1	15.28	6.11	22.21	☆	☆	☆	0.0	22.2	892-4366	None	None	1.23	None	Stalzer/Harris	'92/'93
MUNDER SM CO GROWTH; A	Small Company Growth	2.6	15.28	6.11	22.21	☆	☆	☆	0.0	22.2	892-4366	None	3.75	1.23	None	Stalzer/Harris	'92/'93
MUTUAL BEACON	Growth Income	2,886.3	35.15	6.61	16.34	17.78	14.12	15.93	1.2	12.1	448-3863	201-912-2100	None	0.75	None	Michael F. Price	'85
MUTUAL DISCOVERY ☒	Small Company Growth	823.5	14.50	9.10	15.82	17.92	☆	☆	1.1	10.1	448-3863	201-912-2100	None	0.99	None	Michael F. Price	'92
MUTUAL QUALIFIED	Growth Income	2,360.4	30.33	6.12	19.88	17.92	14.89	15.34	1.4	13.3	448-3863	201-912-2100	None	0.73	None	Michael F. Price	'80
MUTUAL SHARES	Growth Income	4,474.6	90.09	6.19	20.56	17.07	14.17	14.89	1.5	14.2	448-3863	201-912-2100	None	0.72	None	Michael F. Price	'75
N&B ADV MGT TR BALANCED ✱	Flexible	192.4	16.41	7.47	20.40	8.79	9.19	☆	1.7	17.2	877-9700	212-476-8800	None	0.91	None	Havell/Goldstein	'89/'94
N&B FOCUS TRUST P	Growth	797.3	26.64	12.45	26.38	19.28	15.48	14.03	0.7	12.4	877-9700	212-476-8800	None	0.85	None	Marx/Simons	'88/'88
N&B FOCUS TRUST	Growth	5.1	13.23	11.93	25.75	20.22	16.03	14.30	0.4	12.4	877-9700	212-476-8800	None	0.85	None	Marx/Simons	'93/'93
N&B GENESIS FUND	Small Company Growth	108.5	8.81	9.03	16.39	12.69	11.41	☆	0.0	14.4	877-9700	212-476-8800	None	1.36	None	Milman/Vale	'88/'94
N&B GENESIS TRUST P	Small Company Growth	27.0	11.72	9.02	16.33	12.90	11.54	☆	0.0	14.4	877-9700	212-476-8800	None	1.36	None	Milman/Vale	'93/'94
N&B GOVT INCOME FUND	Fixed Income	10.8	9.48	4.34	8.14	☆	☆	☆	7.1		877-9700	212-476-8800	None	0.75	None	Havell/White	'93/'93
N&B GOVT INCOME TRUST P	Fixed Income	0.1	9.37	4.19	8.01	☆	☆	☆	7.0		877-9700	212-476-8800	None	None	None	Havell/White	'93/'93
N&B GUARDIAN FUND	Growth Income	3,226.1	22.19	11.42	24.92	17.57	16.17	14.94	1.1	14.4	877-9700	212-476-8800	None	0.80	None	Simons/Marx	'32/'88
N&B GUARDIAN TRUST P	Growth Income	433.1	13.00	11.46	24.88	17.57	16.17	14.95	0.9	14.4	877-9700	212-476-8800	None	0.80	None	Simons/Marx	'93/'93

Mutual fund data table (columns: Fund | Objective | Net Assets ($mil) | NAV | 13-wk | 52-wk | 3-yr | 5-yr | 10-yr | Yield | Risk | Phone 1 | Phone 2 | Load | 12b-1 | Manager | Since). Ratings shown as ☆ where unrated; □ denotes no rating; blank cells left empty.

Fund	Objective	Assets	NAV	13wk	52wk	3yr	5yr	10yr	Yld	Risk	Phone 1	Phone 2	Load	12b-1	Manager	Since
N&B INTERNATIONAL	International	23.9	10.21	7.02	3.13	☆	☆	☆	0.3	□	212-476-8800	877-9700	None	None	Felix Rovelli	'94
N&B LTD MATURITY FUND	Fixed Income	298.9	10.02	3.02	7.07	5.06	6.84	☆	6.0		212-476-8800	877-9700	None	0.69	Havel/Weinblatt	'86/'93
N&B LTD MATURITY TRUST P	Fixed Income	9.2	9.56	2.84	6.86	5.05	6.83	☆	6.0		212-476-8800	877-9700	None	None	Havel/Weinblatt	'93/'93
N&B MANHATTAN FUND	Capital Appreciation	530.5	12.18	10.23	28.39	16.56	12.56	13.98	0.1	17.3	212-476-8800	877-9700	None	0.96	Goldstein/Switzer	'92/'94
N&B MANHATTAN TRUST P	Capital Appreciation	28.3	11.93	10.26	28.38	16.61	12.59	13.99	0.1	17.3	212-476-8800	877-9700	None	0.96	Goldstein/Switzer	'92/'94
N&B NYCDC SOCIALLY RESP	Growth	78.6	11.70	9.45	20.84	☆	☆	☆	0.9	14.8	212-476-8800	877-9700	None	None	Prindle/Haboucha	'94/'94
N&B PARTNERS FUND	Growth	1,413.6	22.15	9.38	23.95	16.02	13.21	13.57	0.5	12.5	212-476-8800	877-9700	None	0.81	Michael Kassen	'90
N&B PARTNERS TRUST P	Growth	51.3	11.84	9.33	23.93	16.04	13.22	13.58	0.2	12.5	212-476-8800	877-9700	None	0.81	Michael Kassen	'93
N&B SOCIALLY RESP FUND	Growth	6.1	11.32	9.16	19.91	3.57	4.92	☆	0.2	N/A	212-476-8800	877-9700	None	None	Prindle/Haboucha	'94/'94
N&B ULTRA FUND	Fixed Income	84.7	9.52	1.76	5.49	☆	☆	☆	4.9		212-476-8800	877-9700	None	0.65	Havel/Mahaney	'86/'93
N&B ULTRA TRUST P	Fixed Income	1.5	9.84	1.72	5.33	3.56	4.91	☆	4.9	N/A	212-476-8800	877-9700	None	1.64	Havel/Mahaney	'93/'93
NATIONAL INDUSTRIES	Growth Income	32.8	13.56	8.65	18.98	6.47	7.57	9.99	0.5	N/A	367-7814	303-220-8500	3.25	0.73	Richard Barrett	'84
NATIONS ADJ RT; INV A	Fixed Income	6.1	9.66	2.68	5.54	☆	☆	☆	5.3		None	321-7854	None	0.73	John Swaim	'92
NATIONS ADJ RT; INV C	Fixed Income	2.0	9.66	2.64	5.38	☆	☆	☆	5.2		None	321-7854	None	1.03	John Swaim	'92
NATIONS ADJ RT; INV N	Fixed Income	4.8	9.66	2.60	5.23	☆	☆	☆	5.1		None	321-7854	4.00	1.05	John Swaim	'93
NATIONS ADJ RT; TR A	Fixed Income	32.0	9.66	2.73	5.75	☆	☆	☆	5.5		None	321-7854	None	0.55	John Swaim	'92
NATIONS BALANCED; INV A	Balanced	5.0	11.75	8.28	18.03	☆	☆	☆	2.3	20.6	None	321-7854	5.75	1.23	Steve Hoeft	'92
NATIONS BALANCED; INV C	Balanced	0.8	11.71	8.02	17.06	☆	☆	☆	1.6	20.6	None	321-7854	1.00	1.98	Steve Hoeft	'92
NATIONS BALANCED; INV N	Balanced	57.1	11.73	8.07	17.37	☆	☆	☆	1.8	20.6	None	321-7854	5.00	1.73	Steve Hoeft	'93
NATIONS BALANCED; TR A	Balanced	165.1	11.76	8.24	18.30	☆	☆	☆	2.5	20.6	None	321-7854	None	0.98	Steve Hoeft	'92
NATIONS CAP GRO; INV A	Growth	13.4	12.86	10.94	23.48	☆	☆	☆	0.8	20.3	None	321-7854	5.75	1.15	Edwin Riley	'92
NATIONS CAP GRO; INV C	Growth	2.9	12.77	10.47	22.18	☆	☆	☆	0.0	20.3	None	321-7854	1.00	1.90	Edwin Riley	'92
NATIONS CAP GRO; INV N	Growth	30.9	12.82	10.52	22.31	☆	☆	☆	0.0	20.3	None	321-7854	5.00	1.90	Edwin Riley	'93
NATIONS CAP GRO; TR A	Growth	796.4	12.87	10.95	23.80	☆	☆	☆	1.0	20.3	None	321-7854	None	0.90	Edwin Riley	'92
NATIONS DISCPLN EQ; TR A	Small Company Growth	47.6	15.07	12.65	21.02	☆	☆	☆	0.3	25.3	None	321-7854	None	1.13	Gil Knight	'92
NATIONS DVSD INC; INV A	Fixed Income	12.6	10.58	7.42	14.71	☆	☆	☆	6.9		None	321-7854	4.75	0.96	Mark Ahrnud	'92
NATIONS DVSD INC; INV C	Fixed Income	3.2	10.58	7.29	14.15	☆	☆	☆	6.4		None	321-7854	1.00	1.49	Mark Ahrnud	'92
NATIONS DVSD INC; INV N	Fixed Income	73.6	10.58	7.29	14.15	☆	☆	☆	6.4		None	321-7854	5.00	1.49	Mark Ahrnud	'93
NATIONS DVSD INC; TR A	Small Company Growth	24.6	10.58	7.48	15.00	☆	☆	☆	7.1		None	321-7854	None	0.74	Mark Ahrnud	'92
NATIONS EMERG GR; INV A	Small Company Growth	4.2	12.59	8.72	29.71	☆	☆	☆	0.0	23.2	None	321-7854	5.75	1.26	Edward Smiley	'92
NATIONS EMERG GR; INV C	Small Company Growth	0.6	12.36	8.52	28.81	☆	☆	☆	0.0	23.2	None	321-7854	1.00	2.01	Edward Smiley	'93
NATIONS EMERG GR; INV N	Small Company Growth	22.3	12.41	8.48	28.80	☆	☆	☆	0.0	23.2	None	321-7854	5.00	2.01	Edward Smiley	'93
NATIONS EMERG GR; TR A	S&P Index	209.9	12.68	8.84	30.10	☆	☆	☆	2.3	17.3	None	321-7854	None	1.01	Edward Smiley	'91
NATIONS EQ INDEX; TR A	Equity Income	137.8	11.60	9.48	25.73	☆	☆	☆	3.4	15.5	None	321-7854	None	0.35	Greg Golden	'92
NATIONS EQU INC; INV A	Equity Income	35.6	11.76	6.02	16.13	11.27	☆	☆	2.6	15.5	None	321-7854	5.75	1.19	Eric Williams	'93
NATIONS EQU INC; INV C	Equity Income	4.3	11.83	5.80	15.18	10.57	☆	☆	2.9	15.5	None	321-7854	1.00	1.94	Eric Williams	'91
NATIONS EQU INC; INV N	Equity Income	75.3	11.75	5.82	15.42	☆	☆	☆	3.6	15.5	None	321-7854	5.00	1.69	Eric Williams	'92
NATIONS EQU INC; TR A	Equity Income	294.8	11.78	5.98	16.39	11.55	☆	☆	6.2		None	321-7854	None	0.94	William Brown	'93
NATIONS GOVT SEC; INV N	Fixed Income	10.9	9.86	4.57	9.03	4.76	☆	☆	5.7		None	321-7854	4.75	0.90	William Brown	'91
NATIONS GOVT SEC; INV C	Fixed Income	2.9	9.86	4.44	8.49	☆	☆	☆	5.8		None	321-7854	1.00	1.48	William Brown	'92
NATIONS INTL EQU; INV A	International	56.0	9.86	4.47	8.60	4.97	☆	☆	6.5		None	321-7854	5.75	1.38	William Brown	'93
NATIONS INTL EQU; INV N	International	40.0	9.86	4.64	9.30	5.79	☆	☆	0.0		None	321-7854	None	0.73	Richard Williams	'92
NATIONS INTL EQU; INV C	International	4.9	11.55	2.21	-1.58	4.98	☆	☆	0.0		None	321-7854	5.75	1.42	Richard Williams	'92
NATIONS INTL EQU; TR A	International	0.5	11.32	1.98	-2.29	☆	☆	☆	0.0		None	321-7854	1.00	2.17	Richard Williams	'93
NATIONS INTL EQU; TR A	International	31.4	11.44	2.05	-2.10	☆	☆	☆	0.0		None	321-7854	5.00	1.92	Richard Williams	'91
NATIONS MGD BOND; INV C	Fixed Income	571.4	11.64	2.28	-1.32	6.10	8.74	☆	5.5	□	None	321-7854	3.25	1.17	Richard Williams	'93
NATIONS MGD BOND; INV N	Fixed Income	4.2	10.44	6.17	11.62	7.28	☆	☆	5.3	□	None	321-7854	None	0.90	Mark Ahrnud	'93
NATIONS MGD BOND; INV A	Fixed Income	0.1	10.44	6.09	11.29	6.70	8.86	☆	5.7	□	None	321-7854	1.00	1.30	Mark Ahrnud	'93
NATIONS MGD BOND; TR A	Fixed Income	140.3	10.44	6.22	11.85	7.46	☆	☆	6.8	□	None	321-7854	None	0.72	Mark Ahrnud	'93
NATIONS MTGE SEC; TR A	Fixed Income	58.5	9.55	4.60	10.60	☆	☆	☆		□	None	321-7854	None	0.75	John Swaim	'92

© Copyright Lipper Analytical Services, Inc.

409

PERFORMANCE OF MUTUAL FUNDS (continued)

FUND NAME	OBJECTIVE	ASSETS ($ MIL) 5/31/95	NAV ($/SHR) 6/30/95	QTR	1YR	3YRS	5YRS	10YRS	DIV YLD %	P/E RATIO	PHONE 800	PHONE In-State	Load	Exp. Ratio	Redemption	MANAGER	SINCE
NATIONS S-I GOVT; INV A	Fixed Income	64.4	4.10	3.71	7.83	5.11	☆	☆	5.7	□	321-7854	None	3.25	0.77	None	William Brown	'92
NATIONS S-I GOVT; INV C	Fixed Income	13.7	4.10	3.63	7.51	4.61	☆	☆	5.4	□	321-7854	None	None	1.17	1.00	William Brown	'92
NATIONS S-I GOVT; INV N	Fixed Income	10.7	4.10	3.61	7.41	☆	☆	☆	5.3	□	321-7854	None	None	1.19	4.00	William Brown	'93
NATIONS S-I GOVT; TR A	Fixed Income	N/A	4.10	3.76	8.05	5.29	☆	☆	5.9	□	321-7854	None	None	0.59	None	William Brown	'91
NATIONS SHTM INC; INV A	Fixed Income	2.5	9.78	3.47	7.73	☆	☆	☆	5.8	□	321-7854	None	1.50	0.71	None	Greg Cobb	'94
NATIONS SHTM INC; INV C	Fixed Income	6.9	9.78	3.39	7.54	☆	☆	☆	5.6	□	321-7854	None	None	0.89	None	Greg Cobb	'94
NATIONS SHTM INC; INV N	Fixed Income	10.5	9.78	3.40	7.56	☆	☆	☆	5.7	□	321-7854	None	None	0.85	None	Greg Cobb	'94
NATIONS SHTM INC; TR A	Fixed Income	169.4	9.78	3.49	7.93	☆	☆	☆	6.0	□	321-7854	None	None	0.50	None	Greg Cobb	'94
NATIONS STR INC; INV A	Fixed Income	1.5	10.04	5.90	11.30	☆	☆	☆	5.5	□	321-7854	None	3.25	0.86	None	Mark Ahnrud	'94
NATIONS STR INC; INV C	Fixed Income	0.1	10.04	5.82	10.97	☆	☆	☆	5.2	□	321-7854	None	None	1.43	1.00	Mark Ahnrud	'93
NATIONS STR INC; INV N	Fixed Income	2.2	10.04	5.78	10.80	☆	☆	☆	5.0	□	321-7854	None	None	1.33	5.00	Mark Ahnrud	'93
NATIONS STR INC; TR A	Fixed Income	606.8	10.04	5.95	11.52	☆	☆	☆	5.7	□	321-7854	None	None	0.68	None	Mark Ahnrud	'93
NATIONS VALUE; INV A	Growth Income	40.1	14.70	10.00	20.60	12.73	12.24	☆	1.6	15.0	321-7854	None	5.75	1.18	None	Sharon Herrmann	'89
NATIONS VALUE; INV C	Growth Income	3.6	14.62	10.14	20.00	11.89	☆	☆	1.1	15.0	321-7854	None	None	1.93	1.00	Sharon Herrmann	'92
NATIONS VALUE; INV N	Growth Income	59.2	14.66	10.24	20.27	☆	☆	☆	1.5	15.0	321-7854	None	None	1.68	5.00	Sharon Herrmann	'93
NATIONS VALUE; TR A	Growth Income	873.7	14.70	10.14	20.89	12.96	12.38	☆	1.8	15.0	321-7854	None	None	0.93	None	Sharon Herrmann	'89
NATIONWIDE II GOVT INC	Fixed Income	39.5	10.03	6.83	12.57	6.91	☆	☆	5.8	□	848-0920	614-249-7855	4.50	1.09	5.00	Wayne Frisbee	'92
NATIONWIDE BOND	Fixed Income	132.5	9.33	8.69	13.72	7.10	9.05	8.90	6.8	17.4	848-0920	614-249-7855	4.50	0.71	None	Mike Groseclose	'80
NATIONWIDE FUND	Growth Income	736.0	16.05	5.53	17.03	8.61	9.65	13.29	1.8	16.0	848-0920	614-249-7855	4.50	0.63	None	Charles Bath	'85
NATIONWIDE GROWTH	Growth	512.7	12.61	9.23	24.28	12.85	12.65	13.09	1.6	□	848-0920	614-249-7855	4.50	0.68	None	John Schaffner	'81
NAVELLIER AGGR SM CAP EQ	Small Company Growth	37.1	13.50	20.54	48.51	☆	☆	☆	0.0	N/A	887-8671	702-831-7800	3.00	1.68	None	Louis Navellier	'94
NEW ALTERNATIVES FUND	Environmental	30.4	31.67	6.17	14.11	7.43	6.09	10.76	1.0	19.0	423-5383	516-423-7373	4.75	1.30	None	Schoenwald/Schoenwald	'82/'82
NEW ECONOMY FUND	Growth	2,964.7	15.39	8.75	15.06	15.98	12.90	14.50	1.1	13.9	421-4120	714-671-7000	5.75	0.85	None	Multiple Managers	N/A
NEW ENGLAND ADJ RATE; A	Fixed Income	411.5	7.36	1.87	5.95	4.06	☆	☆	5.2	□	888-4823	None	1.00	0.60	None	Scott Nicholson	'91
NEW ENGLAND ADJ RATE; B	Fixed Income	2.2	7.36	1.68	5.16	☆	☆	☆	4.5	□	888-4823	None	None	1.35	4.00	Scott Nicholson	'93
NEW ENGLAND BALANCED; A	Balanced	177.6	12.90	8.65	17.24	12.07	11.43	10.68	2.9	14.5	888-4823	None	5.75	1.40	None	Ramos/Beck	'90/'90
NEW ENGLAND BALANCED; B	Balanced	28.6	12.85	8.41	16.34	☆	☆	☆	2.3	14.5	888-4823	None	None	2.15	4.00	Ramos/Beck	'93/'93
NEW ENGLAND BALANCED; C	Balanced	N/A	N/A	N/A	☆	☆	☆	☆	0.0	N/A	888-4823	None	None	None	None	Ramos/Beck	'95/'95
NEW ENGLAND BALANCED; Y	Balanced	47.8	12.90	8.74	17.79	☆	☆	☆	3.3	14.5	888-4823	None	None	0.99	None	Ramos/Beck	'94/'94
NEW ENGLAND BOND INC; A	Fixed Income	188.5	11.96	7.41	14.32	8.29	☆	9.60	6.2	□	888-4823	None	4.50	1.04	None	Catherine Bunting	'89
NEW ENGLAND BOND INC; B	Fixed Income	15.6	11.96	7.22	13.48	☆	☆	☆	5.5	□	888-4823	None	None	1.83	4.00	Catherine Bunting	'93
NEW ENGLAND BOND INC; C	Fixed Income	0.1	11.94	7.29	☆	☆	☆	☆	0.0	□	888-4823	None	None	None	None	Catherine Bunting	'95
NEW ENGLAND BOND INC; Y	Fixed Income	1.9	11.94	7.29	☆	☆	☆	☆	0.0	□	888-4823	None	None	None	None	Catherine Bunting	'95
NEW ENGLAND CAP GRO; A	Growth	104.2	18.10	11.32	30.97	☆	☆	☆	0.0	22.0	888-4823	None	5.75	1.63	None	Hurckes/Pape	'92/'92
NEW ENGLAND CAP GRO; B	Growth	19.0	17.87	11.13	29.96	☆	☆	☆	0.0	22.0	888-4823	None	None	2.38	4.00	Hurckes/Pape	'93/'93
NEW ENGLAND CAP GRO; C	Growth	N/A	17.87	11.13	☆	☆	☆	☆	0.0	N/A	888-4823	None	None	None	None	Hurckes/Pape	'95/'95
NEW ENGLAND GOVT SEC; A	Fixed Income	150.3	11.32	7.21	11.67	6.44	8.48	☆	6.2	□	888-4823	None	4.50	1.29	None	Eric Gutterson	'94
NEW ENGLAND GOVT SEC; B	Fixed Income	3.7	11.32	7.11	10.81	☆	☆	☆	5.5	□	888-4823	None	None	2.04	4.00	Eric Gutterson	'94
NEW ENGLAND GOVT SEC; Y	Fixed Income	4.7	11.33	7.37	12.01	☆	☆	☆	6.5	□	888-4823	None	None	0.93	None	Eric Gutterson	'94
NEW ENGLAND GR OPPTY; A	Growth Income	117.3	14.59	8.88	23.58	11.83	11.48	11.94	1.4	16.9	888-4823	None	5.75	1.28	None	Gerald Scriver	'94
NEW ENGLAND GR OPPTY; B	Growth Income	7.9	14.60	8.87	23.04	☆	☆	☆	0.8	16.9	888-4823	None	None	1.93	4.00	Gerald Scriver	'94
NEW ENGLAND GROWTH ☒	Growth	1,096.3	11.30	20.83	25.70	10.98	12.66	14.49	1.0	15.1	888-4823	None	6.50	1.19	None	G. Kenneth Heebner	'76
NEW ENGLAND HIGH INC; A	Fixed Income	37.6	9.12	3.73	5.40	8.26	10.09	7.61	9.9	□	888-4823	None	4.50	1.60	None	Charles Glueck	'88
NEW ENGLAND HIGH INC; B	Fixed Income	8.7	9.10	3.46	4.61	☆	☆	☆	9.3	□	888-4823	None	None	2.25	4.00	Charles Glueck	'93
NEW ENGLAND INTL EQ; A	International	141.3	15.58	1.43	0.06	10.72	☆	☆	0.0	□	888-4823	None	5.75	1.75	None	Nick Carn	'92

NEW ENGLAND INTL EQ; B	International	47.8	15.38	1.25	-0.64	☆	☆	☆	0.0	□	888-4823	None	None	2.50	4.00	Nick Carn	'93
NEW ENGLAND INTL EQ; C	International	N/A	15.40	1.38	☆	☆	☆	☆	0.0	□	888-4823	None	None	None	None	Nick Carn	'95
NEW ENGLAND INTL EQ; Y	International	68.3	15.79	1.67	0.88	☆	☆	☆	0.0	□	888-4823	None	None	1.00	None	Nick Carn	'93
NEW ENGLAND LTD GOVT; A	Fixed Income	387.2	11.95	4.27	7.52	5.02	7.38	☆	6.3	□	888-4823	None	3.00	1.18	None	Eric Gutterson	'94
NEW ENGLAND LTD GOVT; B	Fixed Income	14.2	11.94	4.10	6.85	☆	☆	☆	5.7	□	888-4823	None	None	1.83	4.00	Eric Gutterson	'94
NEW ENGLAND LTD GOVT; Y	Fixed Income	5.3	11.95	4.25	7.84	☆	☆	☆	6.6	□	888-4823	None	None	0.83	None	Eric Gutterson	'94
NEW ENGLAND STAR ADV; A	Growth	151.2	15.26	9.00	☆	☆	☆	☆	0.0	N/A	888-4823	None	5.75	None	None	Multiple Managers	N/A
NEW ENGLAND STAR ADV; B	Growth	129.8	15.19	8.89	☆	☆	☆	☆	0.0	N/A	888-4823	None	None	None	4.00	Multiple Managers	N/A
NEW ENGLAND STAR ADV; C	Growth	29.5	15.19	8.81	☆	☆	☆	☆	0.0	N/A	888-4823	None	None	None	None	Multiple Managers	N/A
NEW ENGLAND STAR ADV; Y	Growth	1.8	15.28	9.14	☆	☆	☆	☆	0.0	N/A	888-4823	None	None	None	None	Multiple Managers	N/A
NEW ENGLAND STR INC; A	Fixed Income	9.7	12.33	☆	☆	☆	☆	☆	0.0	□	888-4823	None	4.50	None	None	Daniel J. Fuss	'95
NEW ENGLAND STR INC; B	Fixed Income	9.7	12.33	☆	☆	☆	☆	☆	0.0	□	888-4823	None	None	None	4.00	Daniel J. Fuss	'95
NEW ENGLAND STR INC; C	Fixed Income	4.3	12.32	☆	☆	☆	☆	☆	0.0	□	888-4823	None	None	None	None	Daniel J. Fuss	'95
NEW ENGLAND VALUE; A	Growth Income	218.5	8.65	10.19	20.82	14.47	11.80	12.68	0.8	14.3	888-4823	None	5.75	1.37	None	Ramos/McMurtrie/Mills	'93/'93/'93
NEW ENGLAND VALUE; B	Growth Income	19.6	8.56	9.88	19.75	☆	☆	☆	0.6	14.3	888-4823	None	None	2.12	4.00	Ramos/McMurtrie/Mills	'93/'93/'93
NEW ENGLAND VALUE; C	Growth Income	N/A	8.56	9.88	☆	☆	☆	☆	0.0	N/A	888-4823	None	None	None	None	Ramos/McMurtrie/Mills	'95/'95/'95
NEW ENGLAND VALUE; Y	Growth Income	5.1	8.62	10.23	20.82	☆	☆	☆	1.0	14.3	888-4823	None	None	1.54	None	Ramos/McMurtrie/Mills	'94/'94/'94
NEW PERSPECTIVE FUND	Global	7,812.5	16.25	9.03	19.83	14.18	11.72	16.38	1.4	□	421-4120	714-671-7000	5.75	0.84	None	Multiple Managers	N/A
NEW YORK VENTURE; A	Growth	1,415.0	13.86	12.32	24.50	18.07	15.94	17.10	0.9	14.5	279-0279	505-983-4335	4.75	0.87	None	Shelby M.C. Davis	'69
NEW YORK VENTURE; B	Growth	23.1	13.74	11.89	☆	☆	☆	☆	0.0	14.5	279-0279	505-983-4335	None	None	4.00	Shelby M.C. Davis	'94
NEW YORK VENTURE; C	Growth	4.5	13.78	11.94	☆	☆	☆	☆	0.0	14.5	279-0279	505-983-4335	None	None	None	Shelby M.C. Davis	'94
NEWPOINT EQUITY	Growth Income	20.9	11.54	9.22	☆	☆	☆	☆	0.0	N/A	245-4770	412-288-1900	4.50	None	None	Wes Meinerding	'94
NICH-APP BALANCED INSTL	Balanced	0.3	13.09	9.82	20.75	☆	☆	☆	2.2	N/A	551-8045	619-687-8000	None	0.99	None	John Wylie	'93
NICH-APP BALANCED; A	Balanced	5.1	14.92	9.24	19.86	☆	☆	☆	1.7	N/A	551-8045	619-687-8000	5.25	1.59	None	John Wylie	'93
NICH-APP BALANCED; C	Balanced	15.5	14.95	9.16	19.12	☆	☆	☆	1.1	N/A	551-8045	619-687-8000	None	2.24	1.00	John Wylie	'93
NICH-APP CORE GR INSTL	Growth	80.5	14.03	11.17	21.87	☆	☆	☆	0.0	N/A	551-8045	619-687-8000	None	0.97	None	John Marshall, Jr.	'93
NICH-APP CORE GR QUAL	Growth	2.3	15.17	11.05	21.36	☆	☆	☆	0.0	N/A	551-8045	619-687-8000	None	None	None	John Marshall, Jr.	'94
NICH-APP CORE GR; A	Growth	63.1	15.10	11.03	21.10	☆	☆	☆	0.0	N/A	551-8045	619-687-8000	5.25	1.57	None	John Marshall, Jr.	'93
NICH-APP CORE GR; C	Growth	143.0	14.90	10.78	20.36	☆	☆	☆	0.0	N/A	551-8045	619-687-8000	None	2.17	1.00	John Marshall, Jr.	'93
NICH-APP EMERG GR INSTL	Small Company Growth	208.5	12.91	11.49	30.84	☆	☆	☆	0.0	N/A	551-8045	619-687-8000	None	None	None	Catherine Avery	'93
NICH-APP EMERG GR; A	Small Company Growth	105.7	14.53	11.26	29.85	☆	☆	☆	0.0	N/A	551-8045	619-687-8000	5.25	None	None	Catherine Avery	'93
NICH-APP EMERG GR; C	Small Company Growth	155.3	14.40	11.11	29.15	☆	☆	☆	0.0	N/A	551-8045	619-687-8000	None	None	1.00	Catherine Avery	'93
NICH-APP GOVT INCOME; A	Fixed Income	0.9	12.85	6.13	11.07	☆	☆	☆	6.0	□	551-8045	619-687-8000	4.75	1.10	None	John Wylie	'93
NICH-APP GOVT INCOME; C	Fixed Income	4.1	12.81	5.96	10.41	☆	☆	☆	5.9	□	551-8045	619-687-8000	None	1.50	1.00	John Wylie	'93
NICH-APP GR EQUITY; A	Midcap	101.3	13.93	8.57	19.57	15.93	12.97	☆	0.0	N/A	225-1852	None	5.00	1.49	None	Jack Marshall	'91
NICH-APP GR EQUITY; B	Midcap	251.3	13.38	8.43	18.72	14.97	☆	☆	0.0	N/A	225-1852	None	None	2.32	5.00	Jack Marshall	'91
NICH-APP GR EQUITY; C	Midcap	2.5	13.38	8.43	☆	☆	☆	☆	0.0	N/A	225-1852	None	None	None	1.00	Jack Marshall	'94
NICH-APP INC & GR INSTL	Equity Income	12.5	12.56	7.07	9.93	☆	☆	☆	4.3	N/A	551-8045	619-687-8000	None	0.99	None	John Wylie	'93
NICH-APP INC & GR; A	Equity Income	29.9	13.62	6.94	9.33	☆	☆	☆	3.7	N/A	551-8045	619-687-8000	5.25	1.59	None	John Wylie	'93
NICH-APP INC & GR; C	Equity Income	60.2	13.81	6.85	8.66	☆	☆	☆	3.1	N/A	551-8045	619-687-8000	None	2.22	1.00	John Wylie	'93
NICH-APP INTL GR INSTL	International	17.4	13.29	1.53	-3.68	☆	☆	☆	0.5	□	551-8045	619-687-8000	None	None	None	Loretta Morris	'94
NICH-APP WRLDWD GR INSTL	Global	4.0	13.82	5.82	7.25	☆	☆	☆	0.3	□	551-8045	619-687-8000	None	1.34	None	Art Nicholas	'93
NICH-APP WRLDWD GR; A	Global	17.4	15.11	5.74	6.65	☆	☆	☆	1.0	□	551-8045	619-687-8000	5.25	1.85	None	Art Nicholas	'93
NICH-APP WRLDWD GR; C	Global	70.7	15.23	5.47	5.97	☆	☆	☆	0.3	□	551-8045	619-687-8000	None	2.44	1.00	Art Nicholas	'93
NICHOLAS EQUITY INCOME	Equity Income	13.1	10.58	0.91	8.52	☆	☆	☆	2.9	14.2	None	414-272-6133	None	None	None	Albert O. Nicholas	'93
NICHOLAS FUND	Growth	3,055.4	53.74	5.63	16.22	10.31	11.37	12.00	1.2	N/A	None	414-272-6133	None	0.77	None	Albert O. Nicholas	'69
NICHOLAS II	Midcap	631.6	27.46	3.19	17.25	11.18	10.64	11.85	0.7	19.5	None	414-272-6133	None	0.67	None	David O. Nicholas	'93
NICHOLAS INCOME	Fixed Income	152.0	3.43	4.97	10.80	8.88	10.09	9.07	8.8	□	None	414-272-6133	None	0.59	None	Albert O. Nicholas	'77
NICHOLAS LTD EDITION	Small Company Growth	155.1	19.31	3.37	16.01	13.07	12.96	☆	0.5	N/A	None	414-272-6133	None	0.90	None	David O. Nicholas	'93
NOMURA PACIFIC BASIN	Pacific Region	43.0	15.55	3.19	-8.57	11.93	4.43	☆	0.0	□	833-0018	212-509-7893	None	1.39	None	Iwao Komatsu	'95

PERFORMANCE OF MUTUAL FUNDS (continued)

FUND NAME	OBJECTIVE	ASSETS ($ MIL.) 5/31/95	NAV ($/SHR) 6/30/95	RETURN THROUGH 6/30 QTR	1YR	3YRS (Annualized)	5YRS	10YRS	DIV YLD %	P/E RATIO	PHONE 800	PHONE In-State	Load	Exp. Ratio	Redemption	MANAGER	SINCE
NORTH AM GOVT BD; ISI	World Income	68.8	8.61	9.16	1.56	☆	☆	☆	8.4		645-3923	410-637-6819	3.00	1.25	None	R. Alan Medaugh	'93
NORTHEAST INV GROWTH	Growth	39.8	29.52	11.48	27.23	10.45	10.62	13.39	0.6	16.1	225-6704	617-523-3588	None	1.53	None	William A. Oates	'80
NORTHEAST INV TRUST	Fixed Income	736.7	10.13	4.20	10.01	13.47	14.25	11.13	9.5		225-6704	617-523-3588	None	1.06	None	Ernest E. Monrad	'60
NORTHERN FDS FXD INCOME	Fixed Income	80.8	10.26	6.55	12.67	☆	☆	☆	6.2		595-9111	414-271-5885	None	0.90	None	Michael Lannan	'94
NORTHERN FDS GROWTH EQTY	Growth	133.2	11.37	7.44	15.23	☆	☆	☆	0.8	19.7	595-9111	414-271-5885	None	1.00	None	Ted Breckel	'95
NORTHERN FDS INCOME EQTY	Equity Income	41.1	10.34	5.00	9.29	☆	☆	☆	3.0	15.9	595-9111	414-271-5885	None	1.00	None	William Hyatt	'94
NORTHERN FDS INTL EQTY	International	78.3	10.18	4.09	0.06	☆	☆	☆	0.3		595-9111	414-271-5885	None	1.25	None	Robert LaFleur	'94
NORTHERN FDS INTL FXD	World Income	14.8	10.91	3.98	16.60	☆	☆	☆	5.7		595-9111	414-271-5885	None	1.15	None	Michael Lannan	'94
NORTHERN FDS INTL GRO EQ	International	140.2	9.80	1.98	-3.94	☆	☆	☆	0.3		595-9111	414-271-5885	None	1.25	None	Robert LaFleur	'94
NORTHERN FDS SELECT EQTY	Growth	17.3	11.59	7.61	20.52	☆	☆	☆	0.4	22.4	595-9111	414-271-5885	None	1.00	None	Robert Streed	'94
NORTHERN FDS SMALL CAP	Small Company Growth	91.1	10.90	9.44	13.74	☆	☆	☆	0.7	13.1	595-9111	414-271-5885	None	1.00	None	Susan French	'94
NORTHERN FDS US GOVT	Fixed Income	123.2	10.09	3.87	8.18	☆	☆	☆	5.1		595-9111	414-271-5885	None	0.90	None	Monty Memler	'94
NORTHSTAR ADV GOVT; T	Fixed Income	153.4	9.28	5.37	10.56	8.00	9.38	☆	6.3		243-8115	203-525-1421	None	1.29	4.00	Margaret D. Patel	'88
NORTHSTAR ADV GROWTH; T	Growth	76.8	18.18	10.51	17.13	9.76	10.15	☆	0.5	17.9	243-8115	203-525-1421	4.75	2.00	4.00	Robert Thomas	'89
NORTHSTAR ADV HI YLD; A	Fixed Income	68.8	4.41	3.67	4.02	☆	☆	☆	10.7		595-7827	203-863-6200	None	None	None	Thomas Ole Dial	'93
NORTHSTAR ADV HI YLD; B	Fixed Income	61.3	4.41	3.74	3.29	☆	☆	☆	10.0		595-7827	203-863-6200	None	1.34	5.00	Thomas Ole Dial	'94
NORTHSTAR ADV HI YLD; T	Fixed Income	147.1	8.57	4.00	7.83	11.46	15.53	☆	9.7	13.7	243-8115	203-525-1421	4.75	None	4.00	Patel/Crocker	'89/'93
NORTHSTAR ADV INC&GR; A	Balanced	74.5	10.52	7.34	11.61	☆	☆	☆	3.1	13.7	595-7827	203-863-6200	None	None	None	Mysogland/Wadsworth	'93/'93
NORTHSTAR ADV INC&GR; B	Balanced	51.9	10.51	7.21	10.90	☆	☆	☆	2.6	13.7	595-7827	203-863-6200	None	1.69	5.00	Mysogland/Wadsworth	'94/'94
NORTHSTAR ADV INCOME; T	Income	73.2	12.56	5.34	10.17	8.85	9.54	☆	4.7	16.0	243-8115	203-525-1421	4.75	None	4.00	Susann Stauffer	'86
NORTHSTAR ADV MLT-BD; A	Fixed Income	28.0	4.48	4.77	7.21	☆	☆	☆	8.6		595-7827	203-863-6200	4.75	None	5.00	Dial	'93
NORTHSTAR ADV MLT-BD; B	Fixed Income	15.4	4.47	4.35	6.19	☆	☆	☆	7.9		595-7827	203-863-6200	None	None	5.00	Dial	'94
NORTHSTAR ADV SPEC; T	Small Company Growth	35.6	21.01	6.22	12.25	14.81	12.34	☆	0.0	19.4	243-8115	203-525-1421	None	2.16	4.00	Robert Thomas	'89
NORTHSTAR ADV ST INC; T	Fixed Income	30.9	12.15	3.95	☆	☆	☆	☆	8.1		243-8115	203-525-1421	None	1.90	4.00	Prescott B. Crocker	'94
NORTHWEST NORTHWEST GRO	Growth	0.9	7.18	8.95	19.47	6.22	8.44	☆	0.0	17.7	728-8762	206-734-9900	None	1.50	None	Nicholas Kaiser	'90
NORWEST ADJ US GOVT; A ★	Fixed Income	41.7	9.39	2.20	3.42	3.25	☆	☆	5.9		338-1348	612-667-6833	1.50	0.82	None	Karl P. Tourville	'95
NORWEST ADJ US GOVT; B	Fixed Income	0.4	9.35	2.01	2.64	☆	☆	☆	5.2		338-1348	612-667-6833	None	1.51	1.50	Karl P. Tourville	'95
NORWEST ADJ US GOVT; TR	Fixed Income	21.5	9.39	2.20	3.41	☆	☆	☆	5.9		338-1348	612-667-6833	None	0.85	None	Karl P. Tourville	'95
NORWEST CONSRV BAL; ADV ✹	Balanced	125.1	17.60	4.64	☆	☆	☆	☆	0.0	N/A	338-1348	612-667-6833	None	None	None	Multiple Managers	N/A
NORWEST CONTR STK; A ★	Growth Income	0.6	11.26	6.49	17.40	☆	☆	☆	0.9	18.7	338-1348	612-667-6833	4.50	None	None	James C. Peery	'93
NORWEST CONTR STK; B	Growth Income	0.5	11.18	6.27	16.48	☆	☆	☆	0.6	18.7	338-1348	612-667-6833	None	None	None	James C. Peery	'93
NORWEST CONTR STK; TR	Growth Income	45.8	11.26	6.49	17.52	☆	☆	☆	0.9	18.7	338-1348	612-667-6833	None	None	None	James C. Peery	'93
NORWEST DVSFD EQTY; ADV ✹	Growth Income	606.2	25.75	9.16	☆	☆	☆	☆	0.0	N/A	338-1348	612-667-6833	3.75	None	4.00	Multiple Managers	N/A
NORWEST GOVT INC; A ★	Fixed Income	18.3	8.77	4.63	6.56	4.35	7.63	☆	7.1		338-1348	612-667-6833	None	0.60	None	Margie Grace	'95
NORWEST GOVT INC; B	Fixed Income	10.7	8.76	4.44	5.76	☆	☆	☆	6.3		338-1348	612-667-6833	None	1.31	None	Margie Grace	'93
NORWEST GOVT INC; TR	Fixed Income	94.3	8.77	4.63	6.56	☆	☆	☆	7.1		338-1348	612-667-6833	None	0.61	3.00	Margie Grace	'95
NORWEST GROWTH BAL; ADV ✹	Balanced	335.4	20.13	7.07	☆	☆	☆	☆	0.0	N/A	338-1348	612-667-6833	None	None	None	Multiple Managers	N/A
NORWEST GROWTH EQTY; ADV ✹	Growth	464.6	25.32	9.04	27.24	☆	☆	☆	0.0	N/A	338-1348	612-667-6833	4.50	None	None	Multiple Managers	N/A
NORWEST INC STOCK; A ★	Growth Income	14.3	11.55	7.54	26.18	☆	☆	☆	2.3	16.2	338-1348	612-667-6833	4.50	0.67	None	Dave Roberts	'93
NORWEST INC STOCK; B	Growth Income	3.1	11.49	7.21	26.18	☆	☆	☆	1.9	16.2	338-1348	612-667-6833	None	1.65	4.00	Dave Roberts	'93
NORWEST INC STOCK; TR	Growth Income	58.9	11.56	7.53	27.21	☆	☆	☆	2.3	16.2	338-1348	612-667-6833	None	0.86	None	Dave Roberts	'93
NORWEST INCOME EQTY; ADV ✹	Equity Income	40.5	22.25	7.70	☆	☆	☆	☆	0.0	N/A	338-1348	612-667-6833	None	0.60	None	Dave Roberts	'94
NORWEST INCOME; A ★	Fixed Income	6.2	9.62	6.05	9.40	5.66	8.55	☆	6.8		338-1348	612-667-6833	3.75	1.33	None	Mark Karstom	'87
NORWEST INCOME; B	Fixed Income	3.3	9.60	5.86	8.47	☆	☆	☆	6.0		338-1348	612-667-6833	None	0.61	3.00	Mark Karstom	'93
NORWEST INCOME; TR	Fixed Income	110.0	9.60	5.95	9.29	☆	☆	☆	6.8		338-1348	612-667-6833	None	None	None	Mark Karstom	'93
NORWEST INDEX FUND; ADV ✹	S&P Index	148.4	25.84	9.31	☆	☆	☆	☆	0.0	N/A	338-1348	612-667-6833	None	None	None	Multiple Managers	N/A
NORWEST INTL; ADV ✹	International	85.6	17.55	5.47	☆	☆	☆	☆	0.0		338-1348	612-667-6833	None	None	None	Mark J. Smith	'94
NORWEST INTMDT GOVT; ADV ✹	Fixed Income	48.3	60.72	4.71	☆	☆	☆	☆	0.0		338-1348	612-667-6833	None	None	None	Karl P. Tourville	'94

Fund	Objective	Net Assets	NAV	Ret	Rk1	Rk2	Yld %	5-Yr	Phone (toll-free)	Phone	Fee A	Fee B	Fee C	Manager	Since
NORWEST LARGE CO; ADV ❀	Growth	53.3	22.06	13.48	☆	☆	0.0	N/A	338-1348	612-667-8833	None	None	None	John S. Dale	'94
NORWEST MGD FXD INC; ADV ❀	Fixed Income	188.5	27.15	4.30	☆	☆	0.0	□	338-1348	612-667-8833	None	None	None	William D. Giese	'94
NORWEST MOD BAL; ADV ❀	Balanced	342.4	18.99	5.68	☆	☆	0.0	N/A	338-1348	612-667-8833	None	None	None	Multiple Managers	N/A
NORWEST SMALL CO GR; ADV ❀	Small Company Growth	214.5	26.67	10.71	☆	☆	0.0	N/A	338-1348	612-667-8833	None	None	None	Paul Von Kuster	'94
NORWEST SMALL CO STK; A ★	Small Company Growth	1.5	11.14	9.76	☆	☆	0.7	18.7	338-1348	612-667-8833	4.50	4.00	None	Kirk McCown	'93
NORWEST SMALL CO STK; B	Small Company Growth	1.0	11.06	9.66	☆	☆	1.0	18.7	338-1348	612-667-8833	None	None	None	Kirk McCown	'93
NORWEST SMALL CO STK; TR	Small Company Growth	52.2	11.09	9.81	☆	☆	1.0	18.7	338-1348	612-667-8833	None	None	None	Kirk McCown	'93
NORWEST STABLE INC; ADV ❀	Fixed Income	36.6	10.51	2.24	☆	☆	6.9		338-1348	612-667-8833	None	None	None	Karl P. Tourville	'94
NORWEST TOT RT BD; A ★	Fixed Income	0.6	9.74	4.65	☆	☆	6.1	□	338-1348	612-667-8833	3.75	3.00	None	David B. Kinney	'93
NORWEST TOT RT BD; B	Fixed Income	0.9	9.75	4.55	☆	☆	6.9		338-1348	612-667-8833	None	None	None	David B. Kinney	'93
NORWEST TOT RT BD; TR	Fixed Income	96.2	9.74	4.65	☆	☆	0.9		338-1348	612-667-8833	None	None	None	David B. Kinney	'93
NORWEST VALUGROWTH; A ★	Growth	12.1	19.37	6.90	9.20	9.19	0.7	21.3	338-1348	612-667-8833	4.50	4.50	1.20	David Beeck	'88
NORWEST VALUGROWTH; B	Growth	3.6	19.19	6.71	☆	☆	0.9	21.3	338-1348	612-667-8833	None	None	1.95	David Beeck	'93
NORWEST VALUGROWTH; TR	Growth	136.6	19.36	6.66	☆	☆	1.4	21.3	338-1348	612-667-8833	None	None	1.20	David Beeck	'93
NOTTINGHAM II CAP VALUE	Balanced	6.9	11.55	7.44	10.20	10.20	6.1	N/A	525-3863	919-972-9922	4.50	4.50	2.43	Capital Investmt Counsel	'91
NOTTINGHAM II INVSTK FXD	Fixed Income	15.5	10.20	6.40	7.25	7.25	2.7	13.4	525-3863	919-972-9922	4.75	None	0.77	Investek Cap. Mgmt.	'91
NTH AM FDS ASSET ALL; A	Flexible	8.2	11.53	6.66	☆	☆	2.4	13.4	334-0575	203-698-0068	4.75	None	1.34	Goldman Sachs Asset Mgt.	'94
NTH AM FDS ASSET ALL; B	Flexible	8.5	11.52	6.57	☆	☆	2.1	13.4	334-0575	203-698-0068	None	5.00	1.99	Goldman Sachs Asset Mgt.	'92
NTH AM FDS ASSET ALL; C	Flexible	82.4	11.56	6.54	8.13	8.13	0.0		334-0575	203-698-0068	None	None	1.99	Goldman Sachs Asset Mgt.	'94
NTH AM FDS GLBL GRO; A	Global	21.5	13.46	2.36	☆	☆	0.0		334-0575	203-698-0068	4.75	None	1.75	Walter Oechsle	'94
NTH AM FDS GLBL GRO; B	Global	20.6	13.39	2.21	☆	☆	0.0		334-0575	203-698-0068	none	5.00	2.40	Walter Oechsle	'94
NTH AM FDS GLBL GRO; C	Global	90.6	13.39	2.21	8.34	8.13	0.0		334-0575	203-698-0068	None	None	2.40	Walter Oechsle	'90
NTH AM FDS GOVT SECS; A	Fixed Income	85.6	9.96	5.42	☆	☆	6.2	21.3	334-0575	203-698-0068	4.75	None	1.25	Salomon Bros. Asset Mgt	'91
NTH AM FDS GOVT SECS; B	Fixed Income	7.8	9.95	5.15	☆	☆	5.6	21.3	334-0575	203-698-0068	None	5.00	1.90	Salomon Bros. Asset Mgt	'94
NTH AM FDS GOVT SECS; C	Fixed Income	18.4	9.95	5.15	6.48	6.48	5.6	15.2	334-0575	203-698-0068	None	None	1.90	Salomon Bros. Asset Mgt	'94
NTH AM FDS GR & INC; A	Growth Income	8.9	14.04	8.09	☆	☆	1.6	15.2	334-0575	203-698-0068	4.75	None	1.34	Wellington Mgmt. Co.	'94
NTH AM FDS GR & INC; B	Growth Income	12.1	14.03	7.91	☆	☆	1.3	15.2	334-0575	203-698-0068	None	5.00	1.99	Wellington Mgmt. Co.	'91
NTH AM FDS GR & INC; C	Growth Income	56.8	14.06	6.23	12.54	☆	1.1		334-0575	203-698-0068	None	None	1.99	Goldman Sachs Asset Mgt.	'94
NTH AM FDS GROWTH; A	Growth	19.8	15.90	6.08	☆	☆	0.0		334-0575	203-698-0068	4.75	None	1.34	Goldman Sachs Asset Mgt.	'94
NTH AM FDS GROWTH; C	Growth	13.3	15.83	6.23	10.46	13.07	0.0		334-0575	203-698-0068	None	5.00	1.99	Wellington Mgmt. Co.	'91
NTH AM FDS INV QUAL; A	Fixed Income	79.4	10.42	6.08	☆	☆	6.1	21.3	334-0575	203-698-0068	4.75	None	1.99	Wellington Mgmt. Co.	'91
NTH AM FDS INV QUAL; B	Fixed Income	10.3	10.42	8.22	☆	☆	5.5	21.2	334-0575	203-698-0068	None	5.00	1.25	Wellington Mgmt. Co.	'91
NTH AM FDS INV QUAL; C	Fixed Income	2.3	10.42	8.07	11.26	11.26	5.5	21.8	334-0575	203-698-0068	None	None	1.90	Wellington Mgmt. Co.	'91
NTH AM FDS STRAT INC; A	Fixed Income	4.4	9.03	8.22	☆	☆	9.1	13.8	334-0575	203-698-0068	4.75	None	1.90	Salomon Bros. Asset Mgt	'94
NTH AM FDS STRAT INC; B	Fixed Income	9.9	9.03	8.07	☆	☆	8.5	21.3	334-0575	203-698-0068	None	5.00	0.41	Salomon Bros. Asset Mgt	'94
NTH AM FDS STRAT INC; C	Fixed Income	16.2	9.03	8.07	6.61	☆	8.5		334-0575	203-698-0068	None	None	1.00	Salomon Bros. Asset Mgt	'93
OAK HALL EQUITY	Capital Appreciation	17.4	11.33	3.94	☆	☆	0.0	8.7	625-4255	207-879-0001	None	5.00	1.00	John Hathaway	'94
OAK VALUE FUND	Growth	10.0	12.19	1.33	12.82	☆	0.0	21.2	680-4199	513-629-2000	None	None	2.01	David R. Carr	'94
OAKMARK	Growth	2,335.4	26.63	6.18	21.45	☆	0.8	13.8	625-6275	312-621-0600	None	None	1.89	Robert Sanborn	'92
OAKMARK INTERNATIONAL	International	929.1	13.05	8.75	2.78	25.78	0.0		625-6275	312-621-0600	4.75	None	1.22	David Herro	'93
OBERWEIS EMERGING GROWTH	Small Company Growth	102.3	26.87	14.24	47.96	21.35	0.0	21.3	323-6166	708-897-7100	None	None	1.37	James Oberweis	'87
OFFITBANK EMERGING MKTS	World Income	34.1	9.14	9.43	3.60	☆	10.1		618-9510	None	None	None	1.78	Rick Johnston	'94
OFFITBANK HIGH YIELD	Fixed Income	341.5	9.75	7.86	12.26	☆	8.9	21.2	618-9510	None	None	None	2.01	Stephen T. Shapiro	'94
OLD DOMINION INVESTRS TR	Equity Income	7.0	20.95	9.07	17.32	9.28	4.1	13.5	441-6580	804-539-2396	4.00	None	1.33	Birdsong/Hollingsworth	'64/'93
OLD WESTBURY INTL FUND ⬛	International	96.8	9.86	2.72	2.72	9.28	0.8		545-1074	None	4.50	4.59	1.89	John Trott	'93
OMNI INVESTMENT	Capital Appreciation	27.6	14.58	4.13	15.13	18.07	14.21	0.0	N/A	223-9790	312-922-0431	None	None	1.43	Robert Perkins	'85

★ NORWEST ADJ US GOVT; A—The maximum load is currently reduced to 1.50%.
★ NORWEST CONTR STK; A—The maximum load is currently reduced to 4.00%.
★ NORWEST GOVT INC; A—The maximum load is currently reduced to 3.25%.
★ NORWEST INC STOCK; A—The maximum load is currently reduced to 4.00%.

★ NORWEST INCOME; A—The maximum load is currently reduced to 3.25%.
★ NORWEST SMALL CO STK; A—The maximum load is currently reduced to 4.00%.
★ NORWEST TOT RT BD; A—The maximum load is currently reduced to 3.25%.
★ NORWEST VALUGROWTH; A—The maximum load is currently reduced to 4.00%.

PERFORMANCE OF MUTUAL FUNDS (continued)

FUND NAME	OBJECTIVE	ASSETS ($ MIL) 5/31/95	NAV ($/SHR) 6/30/95	QTR	1YR	3YRS	5YRS	10YRS	DIV YLD %	P/E RATIO	800	In-State	Load	Exp. Ratio	Redemption	MANAGER	SINCE
111 CORCORAN BOND FD	Fixed Income	87.1	10.03	6.71	12.68	6.39			6.6	☐	422-2080	919-683-7277	4.50	0.50	None	Jim Agnew	'92
ONE FUND GL CONTRARIAN	Global	3.8	10.01	3.61	☆	☆			0.0	☐	578-8078	None	5.00	1.04	None	Jean-Marie Eveillard	'94
ONE FUND GROWTH	Growth	7.0	13.03	9.11	20.19	☆			0.9	N/A	578-8078	None	5.00	1.04	None	Steve Williams	'92
ONE FUND INC & GRO	Growth Income	7.6	11.57	8.53	18.50	☆			2.7	N/A	578-8078	None	5.00	0.94	None	Steve Williams	'92
ONE FUND INCOME	Fixed Income	7.1	9.78	5.83	11.58	☆			6.6	☐	578-8078	None	3.00	1.02	None	Michael Boedeker	'92
ONE FUND INTERNATIONAL	International	12.0	12.88	3.80	6.12	☆			1.1		578-8078	None	5.00	1.50	None	Jean-Marie Eveillard	'93
ONE GROUP ASSET ALLO; A	Flexible	4.2	10.74	6.77	15.79	☆			3.3	16.3	338-4345	None	4.50	1.33	None	Sexton/Jandrain/Weiner	'94/'93/'94
ONE GROUP ASSET ALLO; B	Flexible	2.9	10.76	6.57	14.37	☆			2.6	N/A	338-4345	None	None	1.06	5.00	Sexton/Jandrain/Weiner	'94/'94/'94
ONE GROUP ASSET ALLO; FID	Flexible	37.5	10.73	6.84	16.06	☆			3.5	16.3	338-4345	None	None	1.20	None	Sexton/Jandrain/Weiner	'94/'93/'94
ONE GROUP BLUE CHIP; A	Growth Income	3.6	14.32	6.67	16.74	5.15			1.4	17.8	338-4345	None	4.50	0.95	None	Scott Andrews	'92
ONE GROUP BLUE CHIP; B	Growth Income	0.4	14.40	6.42	15.19	☆			0.9	N/A	338-4345	None	None	1.18	5.00	Scott Andrews	'94
ONE GROUP BLUE CHIP; FID	Growth Income	40.7	14.33	6.71	16.90	5.37			1.5	17.8	338-4345	None	None	0.93	None	Scott Andrews	'90
ONE GROUP DISC VAL; A	Growth	12.1	13.22	5.58	15.43	10.89			1.8	14.3	338-4345	None	4.50	0.62	None	Terrence Pavlic	'92
ONE GROUP DISC VAL; B	Growth	10.8	13.19	5.32	12.29	☆			1.2	N/A	338-4345	None	None	0.46	5.00	Terrence Pavlic	'94
ONE GROUP DISC VAL; FID	Growth	433.4	13.20	5.57	16.03	11.09	10.15		2.1	14.3	338-4345	None	None	0.89	None	Terrence Pavlic	'92
ONE GROUP EQ INDEX; A	S&P Index	2.5	14.02	9.37	25.45	12.46			2.0	17.3	338-4345	None	4.50	0.65	None	Mike Weiner	'94
ONE GROUP EQ INDEX; B	S&P Index	1.0	14.05	9.24	22.87	☆			1.4	N/A	338-4345	None	None	0.92	5.00	Mike Weiner	'94
ONE GROUP EQ INDEX; FID	S&P Index	203.0	14.03	9.52	25.79	12.69			2.2	17.3	338-4345	None	None	0.68	None	Mike Weiner	'94
ONE GROUP GOVT ARM; A	Fixed Income	6.7	9.83	1.41	4.87	☆			4.9		338-4345	None	3.00	1.23	None	Beinner/Sotir	'93/'93
ONE GROUP GOVT ARM; B	Fixed Income	0.2	9.84	1.33	4.70	☆			4.6		338-4345	None	None	0.98	3.00	Beinner/Sotir	'94/'94
ONE GROUP GOVT ARM; FID	Fixed Income	51.0	9.84	1.49	5.23	☆			5.2		338-4345	None	None	0.78	None	Beinner/Sotir	'93/'93
ONE GROUP GOVT BOND; A	Fixed Income	7.1	9.81	5.65	11.88	☆			6.2		338-4345	None	4.50	0.53	None	Beinner/Sotir	'94
ONE GROUP GOVT BOND; B	Fixed Income	2.2	9.81	5.49	11.20	☆			5.6		338-4345	None	None	1.26	5.00	Jim Sexton	'95
ONE GROUP GOVT BOND; FID	Fixed Income	370.1	9.81	5.70	12.08	☆			6.3		338-4345	None	None	1.02	None	Jim Sexton	'95
ONE GROUP INCOME EQ; A	Equity Income	13.0	15.11	5.94	20.79	11.47			2.4	18.3	338-4345	None	4.50	0.32	None	Lynn Yturri	'93
ONE GROUP INCOME EQ; B	Equity Income	3.0	15.14	5.74	16.67	☆			1.8	N/A	338-4345	None	None		5.00	Lynn Yturri	'94
ONE GROUP INCOME EQ; FID	Equity Income	174.6	15.13	6.00	21.04	11.72	10.98		2.6	18.3	338-4345	None	None		None	Lynn Yturri	'93
ONE GROUP INCOME; A	Fixed Income	5.5	9.54	6.08	10.94	6.21			6.5		338-4345	None	4.50		None	Roger Craig	'93
ONE GROUP INCOME; B	Fixed Income	1.7	9.62	6.00	10.10	☆			5.9		338-4345	None	None		5.00	Roger Craig	'94
ONE GROUP INCOME; FID	Fixed Income	472.8	9.54	6.14	11.33	6.39	8.43		6.7		338-4345	None	None		None	Roger Craig	'93
ONE GROUP INTL EQ; A	International	3.9	13.93	4.03	3.95	☆			0.6		338-4345	None	4.50		None	Boston Intl Advisors	'95
ONE GROUP INTL EQ; B	International	3.6	13.73	3.78	2.85	☆			0.5		338-4345	None	None		5.00	Boston Intl Advisors	'95
ONE GROUP INTL EQ; FID	International	215.1	13.93	4.11	4.20	☆			0.6		338-4345	None	None		None	Boston Intl Advisors	'95
ONE GROUP INTMDT BD; A	Fixed Income	4.8	10.04	4.90	☆	☆			0.0		338-4345	None	4.50		None	Jim Sexton	'95
ONE GROUP INTMDT BD; FID	Fixed Income	183.0	10.01	4.95	10.18	6.57			6.6		338-4345	None	None		None	Jim Sexton	'92
ONE GROUP LG CO GRO; A	Growth Income	23.1	13.83	7.23	21.52	☆			1.2	20.8	338-4345	None	4.50		None	Lynn Yturri	'94
ONE GROUP LG CO GRO; B	Growth Income	5.3	13.63	6.99	19.74	☆			0.7	N/A	338-4345	None	None		5.00	Lynn Yturri	'94
ONE GROUP LG CO GRO; FID	Growth Income	515.2	13.47	7.33	21.85	14.47			1.5	17.1	338-4345	None	None		None	Lynn Yturri	'92
ONE GROUP LG CO VAL; A	Growth Income	2.5	12.90	7.74	22.66	8.96			2.2	N/A	338-4345	None	4.50		None	Frank Boso	'94
ONE GROUP LG CO VAL; B	Growth Income	0.7	12.96	7.42	15.52	☆			1.6	N/A	338-4345	None	None		5.00	Frank Boso	'94
ONE GROUP LG CO VAL; FID	Growth Income	346.4	12.87	7.65	23.42	10.19			2.4	N/A	338-4345	None	None		None	Frank Boso	'95
ONE GROUP LTD VOL BD; A	Fixed Income	13.1	10.53	3.40	7.81	5.39			5.4	☐	338-4345	None	3.00	0.95	None	Jim Sexton	'95
ONE GROUP LTD VOL BD; B	Fixed Income	2.8	10.60	3.27	7.18	☆			4.9	☐	338-4345	None	None		3.00	Jim Sexton	'95
ONE GROUP LTD VOL BD; FID	Fixed Income	404.0	10.53	3.37	8.00	5.63			5.7	☐	338-4345	None	None	0.50	None	Jim Sexton	'93
ONE GROUP SMALL CO; A ★	Small Company Growth	9.2	18.36	7.84	19.50	12.95			0.2	20.5	338-4345	None	4.50	1.22	None	Richard R. Jandrain	'94

ONE GROUP SMALL CO; B	Small Company Growth	2.4	18.14	7.66	14.45	☆	☆	☆	0.0	N/A	338-4345	None	None	None	5.00	Richard R. Jandrain	'94
ONE GROUP SMALL CO; FID ★	Small Company Growth	393.9	18.40	7.95	19.75	13.21	12.90	☆	0.3	20.5	338-4345	None	None	0.98	None	Richard R. Jandrain	'94
OPPENHEIMER ASST ALL; A	Flexible	255.7	12.88	6.46	16.56	11.18	10.13	☆	4.1	N/A	525-7048	303-671-3200	5.75	1.09	None	Negri/Rubenstien	'89/'91
OPPENHEIMER ASST ALL; C	Flexible	10.5	12.83	6.20	15.55	☆	☆	☆	3.4	N/A	525-7048	303-671-3200	None	2.00	1.00	Negri/Rubenstien	'93/'93
OPPENHEIMER CHMPN HY; A	Fixed Income	222.6	12.43	4.33	8.22	10.82	14.13	☆	8.4	□	525-7048	303-671-3200	4.75	1.22	None	Ralph Stellmacher	'87
OPPENHEIMER CHMPN HY; C	Fixed Income	50.1	12.42	4.13	7.29	☆	☆	☆	7.6	□	525-7048	303-671-3200	None	1.94	1.00	Ralph Stellmacher	'93
OPPENHEIMER DISCVRY; A	Small Company Growth	621.5	37.84	7.01	21.32	15.83	15.64	☆	0.0	21.8	525-7048	303-671-3200	5.75	1.32	None	Jay W. Tracey	'91
OPPENHEIMER DISCVRY; B	Small Company Growth	44.9	37.45	6.79	20.39	☆	☆	☆	0.0	21.8	525-7048	303-671-3200	None	2.36	5.00	Jay W. Tracey	'94
OPPENHEIMER EQ INC; A	Equity Income	1,900.3	10.25	7.24	15.66	10.77	9.22	11.73	4.7	N/A	525-7048	303-671-3200	5.75	0.90	None	John Doney	'92
OPPENHEIMER EQ INC; B	Equity Income	153.5	10.21	7.09	14.87	☆	☆	☆	4.0	N/A	525-7048	303-671-3200	None	1.82	5.00	John Doney	'93
OPPENHEIMER FUND; A	Growth	265.7	11.34	6.38	19.60	12.78	12.24	10.28	0.2	N/A	525-7048	303-671-3200	5.75	1.15	None	Richard Rubinstein	'90
OPPENHEIMER FUND; C	Growth	1.9	11.19	6.17	18.57	☆	☆	☆	0.0	N/A	525-7048	303-671-3200	None	None	1.00	Richard Rubinstein	'93
OPPENHEIMER GL G&I; A	Global Flexible	118.5	14.38	6.54	7.86	11.16	☆	☆	2.7	□	525-7048	303-671-3200	5.75	1.49	None	William Wilby	'91
OPPENHEIMER GL G&I; C	Global Flexible	23.8	14.32	6.31	7.00	☆	☆	☆	2.1	□	525-7048	303-671-3200	None	2.44	1.00	William Wilby	'93
OPPENHEIMER GLBL EMRG GR	Global Small Company	138.9	16.92	2.98	-6.57	-8.05	3.98	☆	0.0	□	525-7048	303-671-3200	5.75	1.77	None	James Ayer	'94
OPPENHEIMER GLBL FD; A	Global	2,033.6	34.80	6.91	9.68	11.43	7.53	18.27	0.0	□	525-7048	303-671-3200	5.75	1.15	None	William Wilby	'92
OPPENHEIMER GLBL FD; B	Global	280.2	34.23	6.67	8.72	☆	☆	☆	0.0	□	525-7048	303-671-3200	None	2.08	5.00	William Wilby	'93
OPPENHEIMER GLD & SP MIN	Gold	174.2	13.48	4.74	2.03	8.97	3.95	12.33	0.5	N/A	525-7048	303-671-3200	5.75	1.31	None	James Ayer	'94
OPPENHEIMER GROWTH; A	Growth	831.2	30.80	10.99	29.45	14.90	13.93	12.73	0.7	18.0	525-7048	303-671-3200	5.75	1.07	None	Robert Doll, Jr.	'87
OPPENHEIMER GROWTH; B	Growth	34.3	30.36	10.72	28.22	☆	☆	☆	0.4	18.0	525-7048	303-671-3200	None	1.98	5.00	Robert Doll, Jr.	'93
OPPENHEIMER HI YLD; A	Fixed Income	1,073.4	13.22	4.81	7.09	9.48	12.01	10.37	9.9	□	525-7048	303-671-3200	4.75	0.96	None	Ralph Stellmacher	'88
OPPENHEIMER HI YLD; B	Fixed Income	184.3	13.15	4.55	6.21	☆	☆	☆	9.2	□	525-7048	303-671-3200	None	1.88	5.00	Ralph Stellmacher	'93
OPPENHEIMER INV GRD; A	Fixed Income	110.8	10.81	6.24	12.27	7.16	9.01	8.92	6.5	□	525-7048	303-671-3200	4.75	1.06	None	Mary Wilson	'91
OPPENHEIMER INV GRD; B	Fixed Income	6.9	10.81	6.04	11.43	☆	☆	☆	5.8	□	525-7048	303-671-3200	None	1.78	5.00	Mary Wilson	'93
OPPENHEIMER LTD GOVT; A	Fixed Income	288.6	10.45	2.09	6.93	5.58	8.07	☆	7.3	□	525-7048	303-671-3200	3.50	0.99	None	David A. Rosenberg	'94
OPPENHEIMER LTD GOVT; B	Fixed Income	83.5	10.44	1.82	5.89	☆	☆	☆	6.6	□	525-7048	303-671-3200	None	1.79	5.00	David A. Rosenberg	'94
OPPENHEIMER LTD GOVT; C	Fixed Income	5.3	10.44	1.88	☆	☆	☆	☆	0.0	□	525-7048	303-671-3200	None	None	1.00	David A. Rosenberg	'95
OPPENHEIMER MAIN I&G; A	Growth Income	1,838.1	24.07	7.24	20.52	26.67	25.68	☆	1.9	N/A	525-7048	303-671-3200	5.75	1.28	None	John Wallace	'91
OPPENHEIMER MAIN I&G; B	Growth Income	538.1	24.00	7.00	☆	☆	☆	☆	0.0	N/A	525-7048	303-671-3200	None	None	5.00	John Wallace	'94
OPPENHEIMER MAIN I&G; C	Growth Income	448.4	23.97	7.07	19.63	☆	☆	☆	1.3	N/A	525-7048	303-671-3200	None	2.11	1.00	John Wallace	'93
OPPENHEIMER MTGE INC; A	Fixed Income	80.1	13.68	5.65	11.96	6.17	8.26	☆	8.0	□	525-7048	303-671-3200	4.75	1.22	None	Eva A. Zeff	'92
OPPENHEIMER MTGE INC; B	Fixed Income	5.7	13.67	5.45	11.14	☆	☆	☆	7.3	□	525-7048	303-671-3200	None	1.93	5.00	Eva A. Zeff	'93
OPPENHEIMER STR DVFD; C	Fixed Income	54.3	4.73	6.37	5.29	☆	☆	☆	7.8	□	525-7048	303-671-3200	None	None	1.00	Arthur Steinmetz	'94
OPPENHEIMER STR I&G; A	Fixed Income	40.7	5.19	9.20	13.59	6.80	☆	☆	5.9	□	525-7048	303-671-3200	4.75	1.43	None	Steinmetz/Negri	'92/'92
OPPENHEIMER STR I&G; B	Fixed Income	17.8	5.18	9.02	12.82	☆	☆	☆	5.2	□	525-7048	303-671-3200	None	2.17	5.00	Steinmetz/Negri	'92/'92
OPPENHEIMER STR INC; A	Fixed Income	3,139.5	4.66	5.77	6.71	7.56	9.99	☆	9.5	□	525-7048	303-671-3200	4.75	0.95	None	Steinmetz/Negri	'89/'89
OPPENHEIMER STR INC; B	Fixed Income	1,795.1	4.67	5.80	5.89	☆	☆	☆	8.7	□	525-7048	303-671-3200	None	1.71	5.00	Steinmetz/Negri	'92/'92
OPPENHEIMER STR INV; A	Fixed Income	23.8	4.92	5.73	10.40	6.76	☆	☆	6.6	□	525-7048	303-671-3200	4.75	1.33	None	Steinmetz/Negri	'92/'92
OPPENHEIMER STR INV; B	Fixed Income	16.0	4.92	5.76	9.83	☆	☆	☆	5.8	□	525-7048	303-671-3200	None	2.12	5.00	Steinmetz/Negri	'92/'92
OPPENHEIMER STR SHRT; A	Fixed Income	20.3	4.64	3.43	7.83	☆	☆	☆	6.6	□	525-7048	303-671-3200	3.50	1.17	None	Steinmetz/Negri	'92/'92
OPPENHEIMER STR SHRT; B	Fixed Income	8.6	4.63	3.24	7.02	☆	☆	☆	5.8	□	525-7048	303-671-3200	None	1.97	4.00	Steinmetz/Negri	'92/'92
OPPENHEIMER TARGET; A	Capital Appreciation	356.1	27.57	11.76	29.22	14.17	12.74	11.96	0.7	N/A	525-7048	303-671-3200	5.75	1.16	None	Robert Doll, Jr.	'88
OPPENHEIMER TARGET; C	Capital Appreciation	3.0	27.26	11.45	27.96	☆	☆	☆	0.3	N/A	525-7048	303-671-3200	None	2.18	1.00	Robert Doll, Jr.	'93
OPPENHEIMER TIME	Midcap	304.8	N/A	N/A	N/A	N/A	N/A	N/A	0.0	N/A	525-7048	303-671-3200	5.75	0.94	None	Jay W. Tracey	'94
OPPENHEIMER TOT RET; A	Growth Income	1,372.5	8.85	7.10	15.82	14.53	12.85	14.61	2.4	N/A	525-7048	303-671-3200	5.75	1.01	None	John Wallace	'90
OPPENHEIMER TOT RET; B	Growth Income	500.1	8.79	6.80	14.74	☆	☆	☆	1.7	N/A	525-7048	303-671-3200	None	1.87	5.00	John Wallace	'93
OPPENHEIMER US GOVT; A	Fixed Income	313.0	9.51	3.63	11.22	6.39	8.31	8.47	7.2	□	525-7048	303-671-3200	4.75	1.14	None	David A. Rosenberg	'94
OPPENHEIMER US GOVT; C	Fixed Income	9.0	9.50	3.42	10.31	☆	☆	☆	6.3	□	525-7048	303-671-3200	None	1.96	1.00	David A. Rosenberg	'94
OPPENHEIMER VALUE; A	Growth Income	113.1	16.24	7.44	20.13	11.29	11.48	☆	2.0	N/A	525-7048	303-671-3200	5.75	1.27	None	David Salerno	'91
OPPENHEIMER VALUE; B	Growth Income	17.6	16.14	7.18	19.12	☆	☆	☆	1.4	N/A	525-7048	303-671-3200	None	2.01	5.00	David Salerno	'93

★ ONE GROUP SMALL CO; A, FID--Fund has been reclassified from Midcap to Small Company Growth.

© Copyright Lipper Analytical Services, Inc.

PERFORMANCE OF MUTUAL FUNDS (continued)

FUND NAME	OBJECTIVE	ASSETS ($ MIL) 5/31/95	NAV ($/SHR) 6/30/95	QTR	1YR	3YRS	5YRS	10YRS	DIV YLD %	P/E RATIO	800	In-State	Load	Exp. Ratio	Redemption	MANAGER	SINCE
ORI GROWTH FUND	Growth	3.1	12.16	12.28	24.17	☆	☆	☆		15.3	407-7298	312-616-1040	None	2.00	None	David Klaskin	'94
OSTERWEIS FUND	Growth	13.2	11.00	6.49	10.11	☆	☆	☆	1.9	N/A	424-2295	415-434-4441	None	1.74	None	John Osterweis	'93
OVERLAND ASSET ALLOC; A	Flexible	47.8	12.49	9.61	23.05	12.80	12.26	☆	2.7	17.2	552-9612	415-396-0376	4.50	1.30	None	Janice Derringer	'88
OVERLAND STRAT GRO; A	Capital Appreciation	33.5	17.06	17.57	50.30	☆	☆	☆	0.0	N/A	552-9612	415-396-0376	4.50	1.20	None	Hickman/Bissell	'93/'93
OVERLAND US GOVT INC; A	Fixed Income	37.9	10.45	7.06	11.99	7.63	9.45	☆	6.7	☐	552-9612	415-396-0376	4.50	0.76	None	Niedermeyer/Thomas	'88/'94
OVERLAND VAR RT GOVT; A	Fixed Income	776.1	9.31	1.69	1.87	2.18	☆	☆	5.4	N/A	552-9612	415-396-0376	3.00	0.79	None	Single/Glessman	'90/'92
P HZN AGG GRO	Capital Appreciation	129.9	23.52	11.21	26.06	12.10	11.97	15.09	0.0	N/A	332-3863	619-456-9197	4.50	1.46	None	Scott Billeadeau	'94
P HZN ASSET ALLOCATION	Flexible	6.6	16.37	7.06	17.14	☆	☆	☆	1.0	N/A	332-3863	619-456-9197	4.50	None	None	Keith Wirtz	'94
P HZN BLUE CHIP	Growth	9.4	17.56	8.66	19.87	☆	☆	☆	1.5	20.0	332-3863	619-456-9197	4.50	None	None	Robert Pyles	'95
P HZN CAP INC	Convertible Securities	206.4	14.65	7.36	12.57	14.78	14.29	☆	4.4	☐	332-3863	619-456-9197	4.50	0.97	None	Ed Cassens	'94
P HZN CORP BOND	Fixed Income	32.2	15.97	7.66	14.13	8.83	10.55	10.18	6.8	☐	332-3863	619-456-9197	4.50	0.91	None	Steve Vielhaber	'94
P HZN FLEXIBLE BOND	Fixed Income	2.3	9.72	4.47	9.88	☆	☆	☆	6.3	☐	332-3863	619-456-9197	4.50	None	None	Steve Vielhaber	'94
P HZN US GOVT SEC	Fixed Income	85.7	9.45	3.67	8.11	4.81	7.87	☆	6.2	☐	332-3863	619-456-9197	4.50	1.15	None	Michael Kagawa	'92
PAC CAP DVSFD INC; INST	Fixed Income	49.3	11.00	7.93	☆	☆	☆	☆	0.0	☐	258-9232	617-722-7868	None	None	None	Hawaiian Trust	'94
PAC CAP DVSFD INC; RET	Fixed Income	0.1	10.91	7.82	☆	☆	☆	☆	0.0	☐	258-9232	617-722-7868	4.00	None	None	Hawaiian Trust	'94
PAC CAP GRO & INC; RET	Growth Income	0.2	11.15	6.36	☆	☆	☆	☆	0.0	N/A	258-9232	617-722-7868	4.00	None	None	Roger Khlopin	'94
PAC CAP GROWTH STK; RET	Growth	3.7	11.34	8.33	19.46	☆	☆	☆	0.9	N/A	258-9232	617-722-7868	4.00	1.41	None	Chris Labelle	'93
PAC CAP SH INT TRES; INST	Fixed Income	15.2	9.66	4.41	☆	☆	☆	☆	0.0	☐	258-9232	617-722-7868	None	1.00	None	Janet Katakura	'94
PAC CAP SH INT TRES; RET	Fixed Income	0.5	9.65	4.34	7.87	☆	☆	☆	5.0	☐	258-9232	617-722-7868	2.25	1.00	None	Janet Katakura	'94
PAC CAP TREAS SECS; INST	Fixed Income	57.7	9.61	8.79	☆	☆	☆	☆	0.0	☐	258-9232	617-722-7868	None	None	None	Janet Katakura	'94
PAC CAP TREAS SECS; RET	Fixed Income	1.0	9.60	8.73	14.66	☆	☆	☆	5.1	☐	258-9232	617-722-7868	4.00	1.15	None	Janet Katakura	'94
PACIFIC ADV BALANCED	Balanced	1.7	9.14	2.35	8.19	☆	☆	☆	0.3	15.9	282-2693	818-242-2693	5.75	1.83	None	Hamilton & Bache, Inc.	'94
PACIFIC ADV GOVT SECS	Fixed Income	5.0	9.71	7.75	13.77	☆	☆	☆	2.8	☐	282-2693	818-242-2693	4.75	1.60	None	Spectrum Asset Mgmt.	'93
PACIFIC ADV INCOME	Income	0.8	9.38	3.98	6.63	☆	☆	☆	3.1	N/A	282-2693	818-242-2693	4.75	1.75	None	Team Managed	N/A
PACIFIC ADV SMALL CAP	Small Company Growth	3.8	13.13	24.22	25.77	☆	☆	☆	0.0	10.9	282-2693	818-242-2693	5.75	2.45	None	Pacific Global Inv Mgmt	'94
PACIFICA ASSET PRES	Fixed Income	60.9	10.05	1.45	5.09	4.19	5.74	☆	5.0	☐	662-8417	212-808-3900	None	0.84	None	Michael Hughes	'95
PACIFICA BALANCED	Balanced	95.4	11.50	4.97	8.85	10.20	10.31	☆	4.2	12.2	662-8417	212-808-3900	4.50	1.09	None	Bruser/Underwood/Romano	'95/'95/'90
PACIFICA EQUITY VALUE	Growth	166.1	12.44	6.57	12.64	14.92	11.54	☆	2.1	12.2	662-8417	212-808-3900	4.50	0.99	None	Bruser/Underwood	'95/'95
PACIFICA GOVT INCOME	Fixed Income	95.8	9.84	4.60	8.90	4.87	7.30	☆	5.8	16.4	662-8417	212-808-3900	4.50	0.94	None	Michael Hughes	'95
PAINEWBR ASSET ALLOC; A	Flexible	172.9	10.62	7.45	15.34	8.34	☆	☆	2.7	16.4	647-1568	None	4.50	1.21	None	Ellen Harris	'94
PAINEWBR ASST ALLOC; B	Flexible	33.8	10.74	7.09	14.40	7.47	7.84	☆	1.4	16.4	647-1568	None	None	2.05	5.00	Ellen Harris	'94
PAINEWBR ASST ALLOC; D	Flexible	7.5	10.65	7.26	14.47	☆	☆	☆	1.5	16.4	647-1568	None	None	1.96	None	Ellen Harris	'94
PAINEWBR ATLAS GL GR; A	Global	137.1	13.71	3.01	-0.86	3.27	0.97	☆	0.0	☐	647-1568	None	4.50	1.39	None	Frank Jennings	'92
PAINEWBR ATLAS GL GR; B	Global	107.1	13.35	2.85	-1.54	2.48	☆	☆	0.0	☐	647-1568	None	None	2.19	5.00	Frank Jennings	'92
PAINEWBR ATLAS GL GR; D	Global	44.5	13.43	2.83	-1.52	☆	☆	☆	0.0	☐	647-1568	None	None	2.20	None	Frank Jennings	'92
PAINEWBR BL CHIP GR; A	Growth	49.7	15.70	5.44	18.32	12.58	☆	☆	0.0	19.3	647-1568	None	4.50	1.32	None	Ellen Harris	'95
PAINEWBR BL CHIP GR; B	Growth	31.4	15.13	5.29	17.50	11.68	8.19	☆	0.0	19.3	647-1568	None	None	2.10	5.00	Ellen Harris	'95
PAINEWBR BL CHIP GR; D	Growth	3.4	15.30	5.23	17.36	☆	☆	☆	0.0	19.3	647-1568	None	None	2.08	5.00	Ellen Harris	'95
PAINEWBR CAP APPREC; A	Midcap	61.8	13.74	7.26	25.49	16.11	☆	☆	0.0	26.4	647-1568	None	4.50	1.54	None	Todger Anderson	'92
PAINEWBR CAP APPREC; B	Midcap	134.8	14.04	7.09	24.48	15.23	☆	☆	0.0	26.4	647-1568	None	None	2.30	5.00	Todger Anderson	'92
PAINEWBR CAP APPREC; D	Midcap	24.4	13.43	7.10	24.48	☆	☆	☆	0.0	26.4	647-1568	None	None	2.28	None	Todger Anderson	'92
PAINEWBR COMM & TECH; A	Science & Technology	14.5	10.69	11.24	25.03	☆	☆	☆	0.0	19.2	647-1568	None	4.50	None	None	Ellen Harris	'93
PAINEWBR COMM & TECH; B	Science & Technology	41.7	10.56	11.04	24.09	☆	☆	☆	0.0	19.2	647-1568	None	None	None	5.00	Ellen Harris	'93
PAINEWBR COMM & TECH; D	Science & Technology	8.1	10.56	11.04	24.09	☆	☆	☆	0.0	19.2	647-1568	None	None	None	None	Ellen Harris	'93
PAINEWBR EUROPE GR; A	European Region	59.9	9.64	8.31	7.71	6.06	-0.06	☆	0.0	☐	647-1568	None	4.50	1.65	None	GE	'95

Fund	Objective	Net Assets ($Mil)	NAV	Ret 1	Ret 2	Ret 3	Ret 4	Yield %	Max Load	Def. Load	Exp.	Phone	Manager	Since
PAINEWBR EUROPE GR; B	European Region	28.5	9.40	8.17	6.94	☆	☆	0.0	None	5.00	2.40	647-1568	GE	95
PAINEWBR EUROPE GR; D	European Region	10.4	9.45	8.12	6.90	☆	☆	0.0	None	None	2.39	647-1568	GE	95
PAINEWBR GL GR&INC; A	Global Flexible	42.9	10.18	4.30	4.63	5.29	4.51	0.0	4.50	None	1.76	647-1568	Frank Jennings	89
PAINEWBR GL GR&INC; B	Global Flexible	24.4	9.96	3.97	3.66	5.42	☆	0.0	None	5.00	2.54	647-1568	Frank Jennings	91
PAINEWBR GL GR&INC; D	Global Flexible	7.3	9.98	4.07	3.76	4.59	☆	0.0	None	None	2.55	647-1568	Frank Jennings	92
PAINEWBR GLOB ENGY; A	Natural Resources	9.3	11.15	5.69	-1.33	4.03	☆	0.0	4.50	None	1.99	647-1568	Ellen Harris	91
PAINEWBR GLOB ENGY; B	Natural Resources	12.6	11.13	5.60	-1.68	3.32	2.42	0.0	None	5.00	2.82	647-1568	Ellen Harris	87
PAINEWBR GLOB ENGY; D	Natural Resources	0.7	10.98	5.48	-2.23	☆	☆	0.0	None	None	2.74	647-1568	Ellen Harris	92
PAINEWBR GLOBAL INC; A	World Income	541.2	10.18	2.45	9.05	5.03	☆	8.4	4.00	None	1.17	647-1568	Stuart Waugh	91
PAINEWBR GLOBAL INC; B	World Income	563.6	10.15	2.16	8.20	4.19	6.98	7.5	None	5.00	1.94	647-1568	Stuart Waugh	87
PAINEWBR GLOBAL INC; D	World Income	68.9	10.17	2.29	8.52	☆	☆	7.8	None	None	1.68	647-1568	Stuart Waugh	92
PAINEWBR GRO & INC; A	Growth Income	180.9	21.27	7.64	19.99	6.04	7.36	0.8	4.50	None	1.20	647-1568	Joe Joshi	94
PAINEWBR GRO & INC; B	Growth Income	240.0	21.16	7.47	18.47	5.23	☆	0.3	None	5.00	1.97	647-1568	Joe Joshi	94
PAINEWBR GRO & INC; D	Growth Income	29.6	21.22	7.44	18.47	☆	☆	0.3	None	None	1.94	647-1568	Joe Joshi	94
PAINEWBR GROWTH; A	Growth	116.7	20.79	5.11	12.23	10.21	12.90	0.0	4.50	None	1.21	647-1568	Ellen Harris	85
PAINEWBR GROWTH; B	Growth	79.5	20.13	4.95	11.37	9.35	☆	0.0	None	5.00	2.00	647-1568	Ellen Harris	91
PAINEWBR GROWTH; D	Growth	20.6	20.27	4.92	11.41	☆	☆	0.0	None	None	1.98	647-1568	Ellen Harris	92
PAINEWBR HIGH INCOME; A	Fixed Income	270.4	7.15	3.34	-1.20	8.32	14.37	11.5	4.00	None	0.91	647-1568	Tom LiBassi	84
PAINEWBR HIGH INCOME; B	Fixed Income	244.7	7.14	3.16	-1.95	7.56	☆	10.8	None	5.00	1.64	647-1568	Tom LiBassi	91
PAINEWBR HIGH INCOME; D	Fixed Income	121.6	7.16	3.22	-1.69	☆	☆	11.0	None	None	1.38	647-1568	Tom LiBassi	92
PAINEWBR INVEST GR; A	Fixed Income	271.5	10.43	6.86	13.42	7.85	9.82	7.4	4.00	None	0.97	647-1568	Mary King	84
PAINEWBR INVEST GR; B	Fixed Income	74.6	10.43	6.66	12.58	7.05	☆	6.6	None	5.00	1.72	647-1568	Mary King	91
PAINEWBR INVEST GR; D	Fixed Income	41.0	10.43	6.73	12.88	☆	☆	6.9	None	None	1.45	647-1568	Mary King	92
PAINEWBR REG FINL GR; A	Financial Services	52.5	19.04	11.28	14.15	17.05	22.57	0.7	4.50	None	1.44	647-1568	Karen Levy Finkel	86
PAINEWBR REG FINL GR; B	Financial Services	18.0	18.71	11.04	13.31	16.19	☆	0.2	None	5.00	2.16	647-1568	Karen Levy Finkel	91
PAINEWBR REG FINL GR; D	Financial Services	4.6	18.72	11.03	13.27	☆	☆	0.1	None	None	2.17	647-1568	Karen Levy Finkel	92
PAINEWBR S/T GOVT CU; A	Fixed Income	5.9	N/A	N/A	N/A	☆	☆	0.0	2.50	None	None	647-1568	Nirmal Singh	94
PAINEWBR S/T GOVT CU; D	Fixed Income	0.3	N/A	N/A	N/A	☆	☆	0.0	None	None	None	647-1568	Nirmal Singh	94
PAINEWBR S/T GOVT; A	Fixed Income	132.7	2.31	2.78	8.65	☆	9.70	5.6	3.00	None	0.84	647-1568	PIMCO-Parametric–PIMCO Adv '93	94
PAINEWBR S/T GOVT; B	Fixed Income	10.2	2.31	2.55	7.74	☆	☆	4.8	None	5.00	1.62	647-1568	PIMCO-Parametric–PIMCO Adv '93	N/A
PAINEWBR S/T GOVT; D	Fixed Income	216.4	2.31	2.63	8.04	☆	☆	5.1	None	None	1.36	647-1568	PIMCO-Parametric–PIMCO Adv '93	93
PAINEWBR SMALL CAP; A	Small Company Growth	19.8	11.05	6.45	14.48	☆	☆	0.0	4.50	None	None	647-1568	Charles M. Royce	93
PAINEWBR SMALL CAP; B	Small Company Growth	45.0	10.92	6.33	13.62	☆	☆	0.0	None	5.00	None	647-1568	Charles M. Royce	93
PAINEWBR SMALL CAP; D	Small Company Growth	13.2	10.91	6.34	13.63	☆	☆	0.0	None	None	None	647-1568	Charles M. Royce	N/A
PAINEWBR STRAT INC; A	Fixed Income	10.7	8.97	3.42	6.58	☆	☆	9.0	4.00	None	None	647-1568	Multiple Managers	N/A
PAINEWBR STRAT INC; B	Fixed Income	40.9	8.96	3.23	5.80	☆	☆	8.3	None	5.00	None	647-1568	Multiple Managers	93
PAINEWBR STRAT INC; D	Fixed Income	21.6	8.96	3.30	6.05	☆	☆	8.5	None	None	None	647-1568	Multiple Managers	93
PAINEWBR US GOVT; A	Fixed Income	405.6	8.97	5.88	7.79	2.90	6.48	6.6	4.00	None	0.95	647-1568	Nirmal Singh	94
PAINEWBR US GOVT; B	Fixed Income	91.3	8.97	5.68	6.96	2.08	☆	5.9	None	5.00	1.72	647-1568	Nirmal Singh	93
PAINEWBR US GOVT; D	Fixed Income	58.1	8.96	5.75	7.13	☆	☆	6.1	None	None	1.45	647-1568	Nirmal Singh	93
PAINEWBR UTILITY INC; A	Utility	11.7	9.12	6.65	14.31	☆	☆	5.0	4.50	None	1.58	647-1568	Karen Levy Finkel	93
PAINEWBR UTILITY INC; B	Utility	39.7	9.12	6.57	13.46	☆	☆	4.2	None	5.00	2.33	647-1568	Karen Levy Finkel	94
PAINEWBR UTILITY INC; D	Utility	13.6	9.12	6.57	13.57	☆	☆	4.2	None	None	2.32	647-1568	Karen Levy Finkel	94
PANAGORA ASSET ALLOC	Flexible	7.3	11.60	9.02	19.33	☆	☆	1.1	None	None	None	617-439-6300 / 423-6041	David Arrighini	N/A
PANAGORA GLOBAL	Global Flexible	51.3	11.27	4.64	8.93	☆	☆	0.0	None	None	None	617-439-6300 / 423-6041	Kristine Lino	94
PANAGORA INTL EQUITY	International	18.0	10.46	3.16	3.70	☆	☆	1.8	None	None	None	423-6041	Kristine Lino	94
PAPP AMERICA-ABROAD	Growth	13.3	14.80	10.60	35.92	☆	☆	0.5	None	None	1.25	602-956-0980 / 421-1004	Papp/Papp	91/91
L ROY PAPP STOCK FUND	Growth	38.6	17.34	10.52	23.73	11.29	☆	0.6	None	None	1.19	602-956-0980 / 421-1004	Papp/Papp	89/89
PARAGON GULF SOUTH GRO	Small Company Growth	87.4	16.89	6.43	12.00	☆	☆	0.0	4.50	None	1.00	504-332-5968	Don Allred	91
PARAGON INTMDT-TERM BOND	Fixed Income	314.8	10.26	5.67	11.43	8.65	☆	6.6	4.50	None	0.76	504-332-5968	Keith Mooney	89

FUND NAME	OBJECTIVE	ASSETS ($ MIL) 5/31/95	NAV ($/SHR) 6/30/95	RETURN THROUGH 6/30 (Annualized)					DIV YLD %	P/E RATIO	PHONE NUMBER		FEES			MANAGER	SINCE
				QTR	1YR	3YRS	5YRS	10YRS			800	In-State	Load	Exp. Ratio	Redemption		
PARAGON SHORT-TERM GOVT	Fixed Income	130.6	10.10	2.65	6.64	4.59	6.65	☆	5.3		None	504-332-5968	4.50	0.77	None	Keith Mooney	'89
PARAGON VALUE EQUITY INC	Equity Income	116.3	13.38	11.35	21.30	12.18	12.04	☆	2.3	14.1	None	504-332-5968	4.50	0.93	None	Richard Chauvin, Jr.	'89
PARAGON VALUE GROWTH	Growth Income	193.1	15.58	8.40	16.37	11.61	12.57	☆	1.4	18.0	None	504-332-5968	4.50	0.96	None	Don Allred	'89
PARIBAS INSTL QUANT EQ	Growth	2.8	8.68	8.50	18.16	10.57	9.01	☆	0.0	N/A	233-1137	212-841-3200	None	2.50	4.00	Paribas Asset Mgmt	'86
PARIBAS INSTL QUANTUS II	Flexible	83.4	12.00	7.82	19.05	9.59	8.47	☆	1.1	N/A	233-1137	212-841-3200	None	0.89	None	Paribas Asset Mgmt	'86
PARKSTONE BALANCED; A	Balanced	12.3	12.19	7.18	18.97	☆	☆	☆	2.3	26.3	451-8377	None	4.50	1.18	None	First of Amer Invt Corp	'93
PARKSTONE BALANCED; B	Balanced	1.1	12.18	6.90	17.93	☆	☆	☆	1.6	26.3	451-8377	None	None		4.00	First of Amer Invt Corp	'94
PARKSTONE BALANCED; C	Balanced	0.1	12.18	7.03	☆	☆	☆	☆	0.0	26.3	451-8377	None	None	1.00	1.00	First of Amer Invt Corp	'94
PARKSTONE BALANCED; INSTL	Balanced	86.0	12.19	7.15	19.22	11.40	☆	☆	2.5	□	451-8377	None	None	1.09	None	First of Amer Invt Corp	'94
PARKSTONE BOND; A	Fixed Income	17.4	9.67	6.14	10.85	☆	☆	☆	6.1		451-8377	None	4.00	0.98	None	First of Amer Invt Corp	'93
PARKSTONE BOND; B	Fixed Income	1.2	9.68	5.92	10.63	☆	☆	☆	5.4		451-8377	None	None		4.00	First of Amer Invt Corp	'94
PARKSTONE BOND; C	Fixed Income	0.1	9.67	6.02	☆	☆	☆	☆	0.0		451-8377	None	None		1.00	First of Amer Invt Corp	'94
PARKSTONE BOND; INSTL	Fixed Income	506.3	9.72	6.17	11.78	7.17	8.90	☆	6.3		451-8377	None	None	0.88	None	First of Amer Invt Corp	'88
PARKSTONE EQUITY; A	Growth	41.0	16.56	8.24	24.85	☆	☆	☆	0.0	25.5	451-8377	None	4.50	1.38	None	First of Amer Invt Corp	'88
PARKSTONE EQUITY; B	Growth	5.0	16.35	8.06	23.88	☆	☆	☆	0.0	25.5	451-8377	None	None		4.00	First of Amer Invt Corp	'93
PARKSTONE EQUITY; C	Growth	0.1	16.40	7.75	☆	☆	☆	☆	0.0	25.5	451-8377	None	4.00	1.00	1.00	First of Amer Invt Corp	'94
PARKSTONE EQUITY; INSTL	Growth	635.5	16.62	8.34	25.20	14.02	11.48	☆	0.0	25.5	451-8377	None	None	1.28	None	First of Amer Invt Corp	'94
PARKSTONE GOVT INC; A	Fixed Income	50.0	9.42	3.90	8.46	☆	☆	☆	7.9		451-8377	None	4.00	0.82	None	First of Amer Invt Corp	'92
PARKSTONE GOVT INC; B	Fixed Income	7.3	9.39	3.71	7.71	☆	☆	☆	7.2		451-8377	None	None		4.00	First of Amer Invt Corp	'93
PARKSTONE GOVT INC; C	Fixed Income	0.1	9.36	3.72	☆	☆	☆	☆	0.0		451-8377	None	None		1.00	First of Amer Invt Corp	'93
PARKSTONE GOVT INC; INSTL	Fixed Income	107.8	9.42	3.96	8.70	☆	☆	☆	8.1		451-8377	None	None	0.72	None	First of Amer Invt Corp	'94
PARKSTONE HI INC; A	Equity Income	71.3	14.49	5.40	10.32	☆	☆	☆	2.6	19.7	451-8377	None	4.50	1.40	None	First of Amer Invt Corp	'92
PARKSTONE HI INC; B	Equity Income	6.8	14.47	5.22	9.41	☆	☆	☆	1.9	19.7	451-8377	None	None		4.00	First of Amer Invt Corp	'93
PARKSTONE HI INC; C	Equity Income	0.1	14.54	5.26	☆	☆	☆	☆	0.0	19.7	451-8377	None	None		1.00	First of Amer Invt Corp	'93
PARKSTONE HI INC; INSTL	Equity Income	345.7	14.49	5.47	10.55	8.31	9.83	☆	2.8	19.7	451-8377	None	None	1.30	None	First of Amer Invt Corp	'88
PARKSTONE INT GOVT; A	Fixed Income	28.0	9.92	4.22	8.69	☆	☆	☆	5.1		451-8377	None	4.00	1.00	None	First of Amer Invt Corp	'93
PARKSTONE INT GOVT; B	Fixed Income	0.1	9.89	3.99	7.72	☆	☆	☆	4.4		451-8377	None	None		4.00	First of Amer Invt Corp	'94
PARKSTONE INT GOVT; C	Fixed Income	0.1	9.76	4.04	☆	☆	☆	☆	0.0		451-8377	None	None		1.00	First of Amer Invt Corp	'94
PARKSTONE INT GOVT; INSTL	Fixed Income	248.6	9.93	4.39	9.02	5.62	7.61	☆	5.3		451-8377	None	None	0.90	None	First of Amer Invt Corp	'88
PARKSTONE INTL DSC; A	International	33.9	12.23	6.53	-2.16	☆	☆	☆	0.0	□	451-8377	None	4.50	1.63	None	Gulfstream Global	'95
PARKSTONE INTL DSC; B	International	5.1	12.15	6.39	-3.02	☆	☆	☆	0.0	□	451-8377	None	None		4.00	Gulfstream Global	'95
PARKSTONE INTL DSC; C	International	0.1	12.42	6.34	☆	☆	☆	☆	0.0	□	451-8377	None	None		1.00	Gulfstream Global	'95
PARKSTONE INTL DSC; INSTL	International	262.5	12.33	6.66	-1.83	☆	☆	☆	0.0	□	451-8377	None	None	1.52	None	First of Amer Invt Corp	'93
PARKSTONE LTD MAT; A	Fixed Income	18.9	9.71	3.56	7.53	☆	☆	☆	5.7		451-8377	None	4.00	0.86	None	First of Amer Invt Corp	'94
PARKSTONE LTD MAT; B	Fixed Income	0.1	9.70	3.43	6.54	☆	☆	☆	4.8		451-8377	None	None		4.00	First of Amer Invt Corp	'94
PARKSTONE LTD MAT; C	Fixed Income	0.1	9.53	3.02	☆	☆	☆	☆	0.0		451-8377	None	None		1.00	First of Amer Invt Corp	'88
PARKSTONE LTD MAT; INSTL	Fixed Income	142.6	9.71	3.62	7.76	5.33	7.20	☆	5.9		451-8377	None	None	0.76	None	First of Amer Invt Corp	'93
PARKSTONE SM CAP; A	Small Company Growth	61.1	25.88	10.22	44.88	☆	☆	☆	0.0	27.8	451-8377	None	4.50	1.40	None	First of Amer Invt Corp	'93
PARKSTONE SM CAP; B	Small Company Growth	8.0	25.79	10.03	43.78	☆	☆	☆	0.0	27.8	451-8377	None	None		4.00	First of Amer Invt Corp	'94
PARKSTONE SM CAP; C	Small Company Growth	0.1	25.91	10.16	☆	☆	☆	☆	0.0	27.8	451-8377	None	None		1.00	First of Amer Invt Corp	'94
PARKSTONE SM CAP; INSTL	Small Company Growth	316.4	26.08	10.32	45.32	28.37	17.37	☆	0.0	27.8	451-8377	None	None	1.30	None	First of Amer Invt Corp	'88
PARNASSUS FUND	Growth	227.0	37.55	8.28	31.39	23.63	19.05	14.76	0.3	15.4	None	415-362-3505	None	1.14	None	Jerome L. Dodson	'85
PARNASSUS BALANCED	Balanced	20.5	17.83	8.36	20.99	☆	☆	☆	4.3	N/A	999-3505	415-362-3505	3.50	0.83	None	Jerome L. Dodson	'92
PARNASSUS FXD INC	Fixed Income	5.3	15.25	7.51	15.77	☆	☆	☆	7.5	□	999-3505	415-362-3505	None	0.81	None	Jerome L. Dodson	'92
PASADENA BALANCED; A	Balanced	52.7	24.01	8.20	20.55	7.13	9.02	☆	1.9	20.0	648-8050	818-351-9686	5.50	2.10	None	Roger Engemann	'87

Fund	Objective	Assets ($Mil)	NAV	% Chg	1-Yr	(5)	(6)	(7)	Yield	(9)	Tel 1	Tel 2	Load	Exp	Redem	Manager	Incept
PASADENA GROWTH; A	Growth	412.3	18.10	8.71	23.80	5.54	9.44		0.0	20.7	818-351-9686	648-8050	5.50	1.60	None	Roger Engemann	'86
PASADENA NIFTY FIFTY; A	Growth	117.8	20.39	8.23	26.18	8.96	☆		0.0	21.0	818-351-9686	648-8050	5.50	1.90	None	Roger Engemann	'90
PAUZE/SWANSON GOV TOTAL	Fixed Income	47.5	9.67	4.51	9.25	5.66	☆		4.2	□	210-308-1234	873-8637	None	None	None	Philip Pauze	'94
PAX WORLD FUND	World Income	419.6	15.03	5.70	18.91		7.68		3.3	16.4	603-431-8022	767-1729	None	0.98	None	Anthony S. Brown	71
PAYDEN&RYGEL GL FXD; A	Fixed Income	494.8	11.35	4.02	12.89		9.98		6.5	□□□□□	213-625-1900	572-9336	None	0.55	None	Team Managed	N/A
PAYDEN&RYGEL INT BD; A	Fixed Income	31.8	9.78	4.86	9.93				5.4		213-625-1900	572-9336	None	0.46	None	Team Managed	N/A
PAYDEN&RYGEL LTD MAT; A	Fixed Income	13.0	10.06	1.79	5.68				4.9		213-625-1900	572-9336	None	0.41	None	Team Managed	N/A
PAYDEN&RYGEL OPPTY; A	Fixed Income	7.9	9.80	6.28	11.67				5.6		213-625-1900	572-9336	None	0.49	None	Team Managed	N/A
PAYDEN&RYGEL SH BD; A	Fixed Income	15.6	10.00	3.47	8.06				5.1		213-625-1900	572-9336	None	0.48	None	Team Managed	N/A
PAYDEN&RYGEL TREAS; A	Fixed Income	6.7	10.54	5.10	☆				5.0		213-625-1900	572-9336	None		None	Team Managed	'95
PBHG EMERGING GROWTH	Small Company Growth	456.0	18.05	12.11	61.43	36.59	☆		0.0	30.8	None	809-8008	None	1.45	2.00	Pilgrim/Baxter	'93/'93
PBHG GROWTH FUND	Capital Appreciation	1,200.7	18.48	10.66	44.26	22.35	☆		0.0	27.2	None	809-8008	None	1.50	2.00	Gary Pilgrim	'85
PBHG INTERNATIONAL	International	17.1	9.43	3.29	-4.94		☆		0.3		None	809-8008	None	2.25	2.00	Akami International	'94
PC&J PERFORMANCE	Capital Appreciation	22.1	19.99	5.94	20.38	14.07	10.25	11.31	0.3	18.6	513-223-0600	None	None	1.50	None	Johnson/Carlson	'84/'84
PC&J PRESERVATION	Fixed Income	14.5	11.35	5.29	10.53	6.36	8.05	8.03	6.1		513-223-0600	None	None	1.00	None	Johnson/Carlson	'85/'85
PEACHTREE BOND	Fixed Income	85.1	9.61	3.90	8.30				5.9		282-6680	282-6680	2.50	None	None	Mack Johnston	'94
PEACHTREE EQUITY	Growth Income	114.2	11.56	10.80	24.74		☆		1.1	17.9	282-6680	282-6680	3.75	1.10	None	Shelton Prince	'94
PELICAN FUND	Growth	143.5	13.32	8.37	25.57	16.03	13.49	12.67	2.9	14.4	617-346-7512	447-3167	4.75	0.99	None	Richard Mayo	'89
PENN SQUARE MUTUAL	Growth Income	272.6	11.44	6.02	18.75	11.84	11.07	11.66	2.0	N/A	610-670-1031	523-8440	None	0.98	1.00	James E. Jordan, Jr	'86
PENNSYLVANIA MUTUAL	Small Company Growth	704.1	8.21	6.49	13.69	10.70	10.13	☆	1.3	13.9	212-355-7311	221-4268	None	1.00	None	Charles M. Royce	73
PEOPLES INDEX FUND	S&P Index	291.3	17.13	9.39	25.22	12.69	11.68		2.3	17.3	554-4611	554-4611	None	0.61		Wells Fargo Nikko Adv.	'90
PEOPLES S&P MIDCAP	Midcap	98.5	18.18	8.73	21.87	14.08	☆		1.5	18.4	554-4611	554-4611	None	0.40		World Asset Management	'91
PERFORM EQUITY; CNSMR	Growth	5.2	12.72	8.68	19.79	12.03	☆		1.7	17.0	212-808-3900	524-2276	4.70	1.08		C. Windham	'92
PERFORM EQUITY; INSTL	Growth	100.0	12.72	8.74	20.09	12.26	☆		1.9	17.0	212-808-3900	524-2276	None	0.83		C. Windham	'92
PERFORM INT GVT; CNSMR	Fixed Income	3.2	10.12	5.94	10.01	6.71	☆		5.9		212-808-3900	524-2276	2.00	0.90		P. Farnsley	'92
PERFORM INT GVT; INSTL	Fixed Income	109.9	10.12	6.00	10.29	6.92	☆		6.2	N/A	212-808-3900	524-2276	None	0.65		P. Farnsley	'92
PERFORM MID-CAP GR; CNSMR	Midcap	0.3	11.59	10.40	26.44	☆	☆		1.0	N/A	212-808-3900	524-2276	4.70	None		Donald H. Ralston	'94
PERFORM MID-CAP GR; INSTL	Midcap	48.1	11.59	10.47	26.73	☆	☆		1.2	N/A	212-808-3900	524-2276	None	0.94		Donald H. Ralston	'94
PERFORM SHT GVT; CNSMR	Fixed Income	0.7	9.83	2.80	6.24	4.37	☆		5.3		212-808-3900	524-2276	2.00	0.69		Robert H. Spaulding	'92
PERFORM SHT GVT; INSTL	Fixed Income	105.1	9.83	2.86	6.49	4.57	☆		5.5		212-808-3900	524-2276	None			Robert H. Spaulding	'92
PERKINS OPPORTUNITY FUND	Capital Appreciation	23.3	30.07	17.76	81.14	24.61	15.44	☆	0.1	19.8	612-473-8367	366-8361	4.75	2.63	None	Richard W. Perkins	'93
PERMANENT PORT AGGR GR	Capital Appreciation	7.5	39.89	18.72	39.03	8.72	6.26	7.08	0.1	N/A	707-778-1000	531-5142	None	1.23	None	Terry Coxon	'90
PERMANENT PORT PERMANENT	Global Flexible	74.4	38.40	5.75	12.49	3.15	3.99		1.2		707-778-1000	531-5142	None	1.32	None	Terry Coxon	'82
PERMANENT PORT TREASURY	Fixed Income	119.0	67.87	1.34	4.64				1.0		707-778-1000	531-5142	None	0.82	None	Terry Coxon	'87
PERMANENT PORT VERSATILE	Fixed Income	22.0	56.94	2.21	6.58	4.55			2.3		707-778-1000	531-5142	None	0.86	None	Terry Coxon	'91
PERRITT CAPITAL GROWTH	Small Company Growth	6.1	13.15	8.68	21.15	10.25	7.77	☆	0.0	16.0	312-649-6940	326-6941	None	2.00	None	Gerald W. Perritt	'88
PHILADELPHIA FUND	Growth Income	86.3	7.10	7.39	14.61	9.78	7.28	☆	1.5	10.7	407-395-2155	749-9933	None	1.67	None	Donald Baxter	'87
PHILLIPS CAPITAL INV	Growth	5.8	14.48	4.32	9.48	6.88	9.04	9.81	2.1	N/A	214-458-2448	None	2.25	1.11	1.00	Guy F. Phillips Jr.	'89
PHOENIX ASSET RSV; A	Fixed Income	10.1	4.70	5.37	7.95				6.7		203-253-1000	243-4361	None	1.00	None	David Albrycht	'93
PHOENIX ASSET RSV; B	Fixed Income	4.9	4.70	5.24	7.43				6.2		203-253-1000	243-4361	None	1.45	2.00	David Albrycht	'93
PHOENIX BALANCED; A	Balanced	2,389.6	16.18	5.70	11.24	6.28	9.14	11.98	3.1	18.0	203-253-1000	243-4361	4.75	0.96	None	Patricia Bannan	'86
PHOENIX BALANCED; B	Balanced	12.6	16.17	5.54	☆				3.0	18.0	203-253-1000	243-4361	None		5.00	Patricia Bannan	'94
PHOENIX CAP APPREC; A	Growth	435.9	19.66	9.34	18.73	15.17	☆	☆	0.6	15.6	203-253-1000	243-4361	4.75	1.36	None	Dudley/Wilson	'91/'94
PHOENIX CAP APPREC; B	Growth	5.8	19.56	9.16	☆				0.0	15.6	203-253-1000	243-4361	None		5.00	Dudley/Wilson	'94/'94
PHOENIX CONVERTIBLE; A	Convertible Securities	216.6	17.93	5.97	10.04	8.22	8.57	10.81	5.7		203-253-1000	243-4361	4.75	1.14	None	John Hamlin	'92
PHOENIX CONVERTIBLE; B	Convertible Securities	2.6	17.90	5.79	☆				0.0	N/A	203-253-1000	243-4361	None		5.00	John Hamlin	'94
PHOENIX ENDOWMENT EQTY	Growth	4.2	11.40	8.47	18.85	13.89	☆		0.9		203-253-1000	243-4361	None	0.85	None	Tom Melvin	'93
PHOENIX ENDOWMENT FXD	Fixed Income	0.3	9.34	6.14	11.37	10.77	12.55		9.9		203-253-1000	243-4361	None	0.65	None	David Albrycht	'93
PHOENIX EQUITY OPP; A	Growth	182.0	8.06	9.21	21.06				0.5	17.8	203-253-1000	243-4361	4.75	1.26	None	Michael Arends	'94
PHOENIX EQUITY OPP; B	Growth	0.5	8.04	8.94	☆				0.0	17.8	203-253-1000	243-4361	None	None	5.00	Michael Arends	'94

PERFORMANCE OF MUTUAL FUNDS (continued)

FUND NAME	OBJECTIVE	ASSETS ($ MIL) 5/31/95	NAV ($/SHR) 6/30/95	RETURN THROUGH 6/30 (Annualized)					DIV YLD %	P/E RATIO	PHONE NUMBER		FEES			MANAGER	SINCE
				QTR	1YR	3YRS	5YRS	10YRS			800	In-State	Load	Exp. Ratio	Redemption		
PHOENIX GROWTH; A	Growth	2,136.5	23.08	9.70	21.33	9.12	10.13	13.34	1.3	17.7	243-4361	203-253-1000	4.75	1.19	None	Cathy Dudley	'89
PHOENIX GROWTH; B	Growth	12.0	22.96	9.46	☆	☆	☆	☆	0.0	17.7	243-4361	203-253-1000	None	None	5.00	Cathy Dudley	'94
PHOENIX HIGH YIELD; A	Fixed Income	520.8	8.13	10.35	7.41	9.34	12.31	9.81	9.6		243-4361	203-253-1000	4.75	1.19	None	Curtiss Barrows	'85
PHOENIX HIGH YIELD; B	Fixed Income	9.8	8.14	10.16	6.64	☆	☆	☆	8.9		243-4361	203-253-1000	None	1.80	5.00	Curtiss Barrows	'94
PHOENIX INC & GRO; A	Balanced	499.2	9.20	6.88	10.73	9.01	13.55	12.57	5.1	16.5	243-4361	203-253-1000	4.75	1.23	None	John Hamlin	'93
PHOENIX INC & GRO; B	Balanced	391.7	9.21	6.63	9.96	8.25	☆	☆	4.4	16.5	243-4361	203-253-1000	None	1.91	5.00	John Hamlin	'93
PHOENIX INTL; A	International	143.3	11.82	6.78	1.92	8.41	4.26	☆	0.0		243-4361	203-253-1000	4.75	1.78	5.00	Jeanne Dorey	'93
PHOENIX INTL; B	International	2.8	11.74	6.63	☆	☆	☆	☆	0.0		243-4361	203-253-1000	None	1.78	5.00	Jeanne Dorey	'94
PHOENIX MULTI-SECT; A	Fixed Income	165.3	12.39	9.94	9.73	7.90	12.13	☆	7.6		243-4361	203-253-1000	4.75	1.13	None	David Albrycht	'94
PHOENIX MULTI-SECT; B	Fixed Income	147.6	12.38	9.74	8.97	7.08	☆	☆	6.9		243-4361	203-253-1000	None	1.78	5.00	David Albrycht	'93
PHOENIX REAL ESTATE; A	Real Estate	6.6	10.41	3.58	☆	☆	☆	☆	0.0	N/A	243-4361	203-253-1000	4.75	None	None	Rubin/Morrill	'95/'95
PHOENIX REAL ESTATE; B	Real Estate	0.4	10.39	3.49	☆	☆	☆	☆	0.0	N/A	243-4361	203-253-1000	None	None	5.00	Rubin/Morrill	'95/'95
PHOENIX TOTAL RETURN; A	Flexible	364.1	16.18	5.37	12.02	9.28	11.28	11.35	3.6	17.0	243-4361	203-253-1000	4.75	1.24	None	Robert Milnamow	'89
PHOENIX TOTAL RETURN; B	Flexible	4.3	16.11	5.13	☆	☆	☆	☆	0.0	N/A	243-4361	203-253-1000	None	None	5.00	Robert Milnamow	'94
PHOENIX US GOVT SEC; A	Fixed Income	255.8	9.49	6.09	11.81	6.85	8.55	☆	6.1	N/A	243-4361	203-253-1000	4.75	0.98	None	Christopher J. Kelleher	'89
PHOENIX US GOVT SEC; B	Fixed Income	3.0	9.47	5.77	10.69	☆	☆	☆	5.4		243-4361	203-253-1000	None	2.00	5.00	Christopher J. Kelleher	'94
PHOENIX US STOCK; A	Capital Appreciation	141.4	14.57	14.03	22.29	13.30	10.96	12.17	1.3	18.8	243-4361	203-253-1000	4.75	1.26	None	Michael Matty	'89
PHOENIX US STOCK; B	Capital Appreciation	0.9	14.48	13.73	☆	☆	☆	☆	0.0	18.8	243-4361	203-253-1000	None	None	5.00	Michael Matty	'94
PHOENIX WORLDWIDE; A	Global	126.1	9.04	8.26	6.53	14.80	8.61	7.30	0.0		243-4361	203-253-1000	4.75	1.50	None	Dorey/Wilson	'93/'94
PHOENIX WORLDWIDE; B	Global	2.7	8.98	8.19	☆	☆	☆	☆	0.0		243-4361	203-253-1000	None	None	5.00	Dorey/Wilson	'94/'94
PIC ENDEAVOR GROWTH	Growth	81.1	13.04	11.36	24.35	☆	☆	☆	0.2	N/A	576-8229	818-449-8500	None	1.00	None	Team Managed	'94
PIC INSTL BALANCED	Balanced	14.5	12.37	10.10	20.37	8.79	☆	☆	1.4	N/A	576-8229	818-449-8500	None	1.05	None	Team Managed	'93
PIC INSTL GROWTH	Growth	110.4	13.14	11.26	24.08	9.60	☆	☆	0.0	23.5	576-8229	818-449-8500	None	1.25	None	Team Managed	'94
PIC SMALL CAP GROWTH	Small Company Growth	92.1	15.20	12.43	35.23	☆	☆	☆	0.0	N/A	576-8229	818-449-8500	None	None	None	Team Managed	'94
PIERPONT BOND FUND	Fixed Income	126.9	10.29	6.25	11.87	7.32	8.62	☆	6.1	N/A	521-5412	212-826-1303	None	0.81	None	Bill Tennille	'93
PIERPONT CAP APPREC	Small Company Growth	179.1	23.16	9.09	22.56	16.47	10.42	12.47	0.9	N/A	521-5412	212-826-1303	None	0.90	None	Otness/Kittler	'93/'94
PIERPONT DIVERSIFIED	Balanced	21.8	11.02	5.25	15.19	☆	☆	☆	1.8	N/A	521-5412	212-826-1303	None	0.98	None	Gerald H. Osterberg	'93
PIERPONT EMRG MKTS EQ	Emerging Markets	50.0	10.11	8.01	-5.02	☆	☆	☆	0.3	N/A	521-5412	212-826-1303	None	1.84	None	Doug Dooley	'93
PIERPONT EQUITY	Growth Income	259.3	19.72	7.52	20.49	12.70	12.83	14.33	1.4	N/A	521-5412	212-826-1303	None	0.90	None	William Peterson	'93
PIERPONT INTL EQUITY	International	184.6	10.38	-1.52	-4.62	7.93	2.87	☆	0.0	N/A	521-5412	212-826-1303	None	1.38	None	Paul Quinsee	'93
PILGRIM SH TM BOND FUND	Fixed Income	8.6	9.81	3.41	7.40	☆	☆	☆	5.7		521-5412	212-826-1303	None	1.21	None	Connie Plaehn	'94
PILGRIM GOVT SECS INC	Fixed Income	44.0	12.97	4.38	8.96	5.27	6.80	6.98	6.5		334-3444	310-551-0543	None	1.21	None	Rob Womack	'93
PILGRIM MAGNACAP	Growth Income	208.8	14.03	5.33	20.61	12.51	10.90	12.60	1.0	32.9	334-3444	310-551-0543	5.75	1.53	None	Howard N. Kornblue	'89
PILGRIM HIGH YIELD	Fixed Income	16.2	6.15	5.18	9.63	10.00	12.21	9.27	8.9		334-3444	310-551-0543	4.75	2.00	None	Howard N. Kornblue	'95
PILLAR BALANCED GRO; A ▦	Flexible	30.5	11.27	7.57	16.06	7.86	☆	☆	3.5	15.6	932-7782	None	4.75	0.80	None	Fernando Garip	'92
PILLAR BALANCED GRO; B	Flexible	7.3	11.28	7.62	15.88	7.59	☆	☆	3.4	15.6	932-7782	None	4.00	1.05	None	Fernando Garip	'92
PILLAR EQUITY AGGR GRO; A ▦	Small Company Growth	36.0	11.90	2.34	7.74	8.81	☆	☆	1.1	17.5	932-7782	None	None	0.80	None	John Gustafson	'92
PILLAR EQUITY AGGR GRO; B	Small Company Growth	5.2	11.88	2.27	7.48	8.56	☆	☆	0.9	17.5	932-7782	None	4.00	1.05	None	John Gustafson	'92
PILLAR EQUITY GRO; A ▦	Growth	70.0	12.09	8.39	20.90	9.54	☆	☆	1.7	15.9	932-7782	None	None	0.80	None	Pete Fusco	'93
PILLAR EQUITY GRO; B	Growth	3.9	12.10	8.43	20.71	9.33	☆	☆	1.7	15.9	932-7782	None	4.00	1.05	None	Pete Fusco	'93
PILLAR EQUITY INC; A ▦	Income	38.5	11.78	6.40	15.48	9.59	☆	☆	2.6	15.3	932-7782	None	None	0.80	None	John Gustafson	'94
PILLAR EQUITY INC; B ▦	Income	6.5	11.79	6.45	15.31	9.35	☆	☆	2.4	15.3	932-7782	None	4.00	1.05	None	John Gustafson	'94
PILLAR FIXED INC; A ▦	Fixed Income	105.0	10.23	6.03	11.89	7.01	☆	☆	5.8		932-7782	None	None	0.80	None	Bob Lowe	'92
PILLAR FIXED INC; B	Fixed Income	5.4	10.22	5.86	11.62	6.74	☆	☆	5.5		932-7782	None	4.00	1.05	None	Bob Lowe	'92
PILLAR INT-TERM GOVT; A ▦	Fixed Income	29.6	10.17	4.86	9.83	5.13	☆	☆	5.2		932-7782	None	None	0.80	None	Frances Tendall	'92

PILLAR INT-TERM GOVT; B	Fixed Income	2.4	10.17	4.90	9.56	4.87	☆	☆	5.0	☐	932-7782	None	4.00	1.05	None	Frances Tendall	'92
PILLAR SHORT-TERM; A ▮	Fixed Income	30.3	10.04	1.73	5.80	3.76	☆	☆	4.7	☐	932-7782	None	None	0.80	None	Bob Lowe	'92
PILLAR SHORT-TERM; B	Fixed Income	0.8	10.06	1.67	5.53	3.55	☆	☆	4.4	☐	932-7782	None	1.00	1.05	None	Bob Lowe	'92
PILOT EQTY INC; A	Equity Income	0.1	11.14	6.67	☆	☆	☆	☆	0.0	N/A	817-4568	314-466-3368	4.50	None	None	David Papendick	'95
PILOT EQTY INC; B	Equity Income	0.2	11.13	6.51	☆	☆	☆	☆	0.0	N/A	817-4568	314-466-3368	None	None	4.50	David Papendick	'95
PILOT EQTY INC; PILOT	Equity Income	96.2	11.08	6.75	☆	☆	☆	☆	0.0	N/A	817-4568	314-466-3368	None	None	None	David Papendick	'94
PILOT GOVT SECS; A	Fixed Income	0.1	11.23	7.24	☆	☆	☆	☆	0.0	☐	817-4568	314-466-3368	4.50	None	None	Frank J. Aten	'95
PILOT GOVT SECS; B	Fixed Income	0.1	11.24	7.10	☆	☆	☆	☆	0.0	☐	817-4568	314-466-3368	None	None	4.50	Frank J. Aten	'94
PILOT GOVT SECS; PILOT	Fixed Income	136.5	11.24	7.36	☆	☆	☆	☆	0.0	☐	817-4568	314-466-3368	None	None	None	Frank J. Aten	'94
PILOT GRO & INC; A	Growth Income	0.3	11.40	7.22	☆	☆	☆	☆	0.0	N/A	817-4568	314-466-3368	4.50	None	None	Randall Yoakum	'95
PILOT GRO & INC; B	Growth Income	0.4	11.40	6.98	☆	☆	☆	☆	0.0	N/A	817-4568	314-466-3368	None	None	4.50	Randall Yoakum	'94
PILOT GRO & INC; PILOT	Growth Income	100.7	11.40	7.26	☆	☆	☆	☆	0.0	N/A	817-4568	314-466-3368	None	None	None	Randall Yoakum	'94
PILOT INTL EQ; ADMIN	International	29.5	15.36	6.22	3.80	7.56	3.71	16.00	1.3	☐	817-4568	314-466-3368	4.50	1.37	None	Team Managed	N/A
PILOT INTL EQ; PILOT	International	334.1	15.44	6.26	4.05	☆	☆	☆	1.3	☐	817-4568	314-466-3368	None	1.12	None	Team Managed	N/A
PILOT INTMDT GOVT; A	Fixed Income	0.2	10.48	4.53	☆	☆	☆	☆	0.0	☐	817-4568	314-466-3368	4.00	None	None	Frank J. Aten	'94
PILOT INTMDT GOVT; PILOT	Fixed Income	151.0	10.48	4.53	☆	☆	☆	☆	0.0	☐	817-4568	314-466-3368	None	None	None	Frank J. Aten	'94
PIMCO ADV EQUITY INC; A	Equity Income	12.8	12.96	4.66	13.47	11.16	☆	☆	2.5	14.3	227-7337	203-352-4946	5.50	1.30	None	Team Managed	N/A
PIMCO ADV EQUITY INC; C	Equity Income	166.2	12.93	4.47	12.59	10.32	9.01	☆	1.9	14.3	227-7337	203-352-4946	None	2.00	1.00	Team Managed	N/A
PIMCO ADV GOVERNMENT; A	Fixed Income	15.9	9.11	4.82	9.98	5.39	☆	☆	6.4	☐	227-7337	203-352-4946	4.75	1.00	None	Frank Rabinovitch	'94
PIMCO ADV GOVERNMENT; C	Fixed Income	301.9	9.07	4.65	9.15	4.51	6.85	☆	5.7	☐	227-7337	203-352-4946	None	1.70	1.00	Frank Rabinovitch	'94
PIMCO ADV GROWTH; A	Growth	116.3	24.12	10.74	22.22	12.23	☆	☆	0.0	18.9	227-7337	203-352-4946	5.50	1.10	None	Team Managed	N/A
PIMCO ADV GROWTH; C	Growth	1,163.7	23.42	10.58	21.28	11.40	11.18	15.22	0.0	18.9	227-7337	203-352-4946	None	1.90	1.00	Team Managed	N/A
PIMCO ADV HIGH INC; A	Fixed Income	5.5	7.83	6.03	12.00	5.92	☆	☆	8.1	☐	227-7337	203-352-4946	4.75	1.10	None	Ben Trosky	'94
PIMCO ADV HIGH INC; C	Fixed Income	156.7	7.78	5.88	11.20	5.00	6.17	7.00	7.4	☐	227-7337	203-352-4946	None	1.90	1.00	Ben Trosky	'94
PIMCO ADV INNOVATION; A	Science & Technology	13.9	12.87	18.62	☆	☆	☆	☆	0.0	N/A	227-7337	203-352-4946	5.50	None	None	Team Managed	N/A
PIMCO ADV INNOVATION; C	Science & Technology	29.4	12.82	18.37	☆	☆	☆	☆	0.0	N/A	227-7337	203-352-4946	None	None	1.00	Team Managed	N/A
PIMCO ADV INTL; A	International	19.7	11.60	3.02	-4.67	8.39	☆	☆	0.0	☐	227-7337	203-352-4946	5.50	1.40	None	Blairlogie Capital Mgmt	'92
PIMCO ADV INTL; C	International	231.5	11.20	2.75	-5.47	7.56	3.24	☆	0.0	☐	227-7337	203-352-4946	None	2.20	1.00	Blairlogie Capital Mgmt	'92
PIMCO ADV OPPTY; A ⊠	Capital Appreciation	99.8	34.96	14.77	45.91	27.95	☆	☆	0.0	20.2	227-7337	203-352-4946	5.50	1.10	None	Team Managed	N/A
PIMCO ADV OPPTY; C ⊠	Capital Appreciation	587.8	33.73	14.53	44.84	26.98	24.52	19.13	0.0	20.2	227-7337	203-352-4946	None	1.90	1.00	Team Managed	N/A
PIMCO ADV PREC MTLS; A	Gold	8.2	11.58	-1.03	-4.06	14.72	☆	☆	0.0	N/A	227-7337	203-352-4946	5.50	1.30	None	Van Eck	'91
PIMCO ADV PREC MTLS; C	Gold	46.5	11.19	-1.24	-4.85	13.86	5.36	☆	0.0	N/A	227-7337	203-352-4946	None	2.10	1.00	Van Eck	'88
PIMCO ADV SH-INTMDT; A	Fixed Income	6.4	9.57	3.85	7.47	3.92	☆	☆	5.8	☐	227-7337	203-352-4946	3.00	0.90	None	Dave Edington	'94
PIMCO ADV SH-INTMDT; C	Fixed Income	65.8	9.55	3.85	6.72	3.33	☆	☆	5.4	☐	227-7337	203-352-4946	None	1.40	1.00	Dave Edington	'94
PIMCO ADV TARGET; A	Midcap	93.7	15.02	8.53	28.38	☆	☆	☆	0.0	17.9	227-7337	203-352-4946	5.50	1.20	None	Team Managed	N/A
PIMCO ADV TARGET; C	Midcap	645.6	14.73	8.31	27.43	☆	☆	☆	0.0	17.9	227-7337	203-352-4946	None	2.00	1.00	Team Managed	N/A
PIMCO ADV TOT RET; A	Fixed Income	24.8	10.60	4.46	☆	☆	☆	☆	0.0	☐	227-7337	203-352-4946	4.75	None	None	William Gross	'94
PIMCO ADV TOT RET; C	Fixed Income	25.1	10.60	4.27	☆	☆	☆	☆	0.0	☐	227-7337	203-352-4946	None	None	1.00	William Gross	'94
PIMCO FOREIGN; INST ✿	World Income	237.9	9.76	5.83	8.42	☆	☆	☆	6.4	☐	927-4648	714-760-4880	None	0.47	None	John Hague	'92
PIMCO GLOBAL FUND; INST ✿	World Income	82.0	10.23	5.35	16.06	☆	☆	☆	9.6	☐	927-4648	714-760-4880	None	0.64	None	John Hague	'93
PIMCO GROWTH STOCK; INST ✿	Capital Appreciation	15.0	14.86	8.70	20.11	11.45	10.22	☆	1.2	18.6	927-4648	714-760-4880	None	0.50	None	Ben Ehlert	'87
PIMCO HIGH YIELD; INST ✿	Fixed Income	389.2	10.79	6.01	15.36	☆	☆	☆	9.1	☐	927-4648	714-760-4880	None	0.48	None	Ben Trosky	'92
PIMCO INST BALANCED; IN	Flexible	80.6	11.49	7.05	18.16	9.51	☆	☆	3.4	17.8	800-7674	None	None	0.70	None	PIMCO-Parametric-PIMCO Adv	'92
PIMCO INST BLR EM MK; ADM	Emerging Markets	0.8	11.86	10.84	☆	☆	☆	☆	0.0	☐	800-7674	None	None	None	None	Blairlogie Capital Mgmt	'94
PIMCO INST BLR EM MK; IN	Emerging Markets	79.3	11.86	10.63	-10.45	☆	☆	☆	0.0	☐	800-7674	None	None	1.35	None	Blairlogie Capital Mgmt	'93
PIMCO INST BLR IN AC; ADM	International	0.4	11.23	0.81	☆	☆	☆	☆	0.0	☐	800-7674	None	None	None	None	Blairlogie Capital Mgmt	'94
PIMCO INST BLR IN AC; IN	International	55.3	11.24	0.90	1.56	☆	☆	☆	0.2	☐	800-7674	None	None	1.10	None	Blairlogie Capital Mgmt	'93
PIMCO INST CAD CP AP; IN	Capital Appreciation	200.9	15.66	11.87	24.04	16.48	☆	☆	1.1	15.6	800-7674	None	None	0.70	None	Cadence Cap Mgmt Corp.	'91
PIMCO INST CAD MD CP; ADM	Midcap	0.1	16.51	12.01	☆	☆	☆	☆	0.0	N/A	800-7674	None	None	None	None	Cadence Cap Mgmt Corp.	'94
PIMCO INST CAD MD CP; IN	Midcap	138.5	16.52	12.02	26.77	16.41	☆	☆	0.4	17.9	800-7674	None	None	0.70	None	Cadence Cap Mgmt Corp.	'91

PERFORMANCE OF MUTUAL FUNDS (continued)

FUND NAME	OBJECTIVE	ASSETS ($ MIL) 5/31/95	NAV ($/SHR) 6/30/95	QTR	1YR	3YRS	5YRS	10YRS	DIV YLD %	P/E RATIO	PHONE 800	PHONE In-State	Load	Exp. Ratio	Redemption	MANAGER	SINCE
PIMCO INST CAD MICRO; IN	Small Company Growth	45.4	13.85	13.34	26.48	☆	☆	☆	0.0	15.7	800-7674	None	None	1.50	None	Cadence Cap Mgmt Corp.	'93
PIMCO INST COL CR EQ; IN	Growth	4.1	11.82	10.89	☆	☆	☆	☆	0.0	N/A	800-7674	None	None	None	None	Columbus Circle Mgt Team	'94
PIMCO INST COL MD EQ; IN	Midcap	4.3	11.70	8.94	☆	☆	☆	☆	0.0	N/A	800-7674	None	None	None	None	Columbus Circle Mgt Team	'94
PIMCO INST MGD BOND; ADM	Fixed Income	2.9	10.03	5.15	☆	☆	☆	☆	0.0	☐	800-7674	None	None	None	None	Pacific Investment Mgt Co	'94
PIMCO INST MGD BOND; IN	Fixed Income	427.6	10.01	5.27	12.09	8.37	☆	☆	6.1		800-7674	None	None	0.50	None	Pacific Investment Mgt Co	'91
PIMCO INST NFJ EQ IN; ADM	Equity Income	0.1	12.42	5.88	☆	☆	☆	☆	0.0	N/A	800-7674	None	None	None	None	NFJ Investment Grp Inc	'94
PIMCO INST NFJ EQ IN; IN	Equity Income	102.5	12.42	6.72	18.71	10.76	☆	☆	3.7	16.5	800-7674	None	None	0.70	None	NFJ Investment Grp Inc	'91
PIMCO INST NFJ LW PE; IN	Growth Income	13.2	11.64	8.49	22.06	14.25	☆	☆	2.9	16.7	800-7674	None	None	0.70	None	NFJ Investment Grp Inc	'91
PIMCO INST NFJ SM CP; IN	Small Company Growth	33.2	12.62	8.16	15.64	12.72	☆	☆	2.3	10.6	800-7674	None	None	0.85	None	NFJ Investment Grp Inc	'91
PIMCO INST PAR ENHCD; IN	Growth Income	72.5	13.56	8.81	23.38	10.96	☆	☆	1.9	17.7	800-7674	None	None	0.70	None	Parametric Port. Assoc	'91
PIMCO INST PAR IN EQ; IN	International	5.4	N/A	N/A	19.05	☆	☆	☆	0.0		800-7674	None	None	0.95	None	Parametric Port. Assoc	'90
PIMCO INST SM CAP; IN	Small Company Growth	55.0	19.21	8.23	17.28	☆	☆	☆	0.0	18.1	800-7674	None	None	1.25	None	Cadence Cap Mgmt Corp.	'90
PIMCO INST UTIL STK; IN	Utility	23.1	8.58	5.24	4.13	☆	☆	☆	4.1	12.1	800-7674	None	None	0.70	None	Pacific Fin'l Asset Mgmt	'94
PIMCO LONG-TERM GOV; INST	Fixed Income	32.6	10.72	10.76	19.94	12.85	☆	☆	6.3	☐	927-4648	714-760-4880	None	0.50	None	Frank Rabinovitch	'91
PIMCO LOW DURATN; INST	Fixed Income	2,477.8	9.94	3.63	7.61	6.32	8.13	☆	6.6	☐	927-4648	714-760-4880	None	0.41	None	William Gross	'87
PIMCO LOW DURATN II; INST	Fixed Income	194.9	9.86	2.66	8.03	5.55	☆	☆	6.5	☐	927-4648	714-760-4880	None	0.47	None	William Gross	'91
PIMCO SHORT-TERM; INST	Fixed Income	89.5	9.85	2.50	6.26	4.47	5.30	☆	6.4	☐	927-4648	714-760-4880	None	0.50	None	Dave Edington	'87
PIMCO STOCK PLUS; INST	Growth Income	51.4	11.34	10.39	29.60	☆	☆	☆	7.6	N/A	927-4648	714-760-4880	None	0.50	None	Dave Edington	'93
PIMCO TOTAL RET III; INST	Fixed Income	113.5	9.25	4.73	11.79	8.53	☆	☆	7.0	☐	927-4648	714-760-4880	None	0.50	None	William Gross	'91
PIMCO TOTAL RETURN; ADM	Fixed Income	12.4	10.32	4.80	☆	☆	☆	☆	0.0	☐	927-4648	714-760-4880	None	0.66	None	William Gross	'94
PIMCO TOTAL RETURN; INST	Fixed Income	8,036.3	10.33	4.92	11.37	8.26	10.71	☆	6.4	☐	927-4648	714-760-4880	None	0.41	None	William Gross	'87
PINNACLE FUND	Growth	14.3	22.08	9.36	23.30	9.84	7.84	12.38	0.4	19.3	None	317-633-4080	None	1.15	None	Heartland Cap. Mgmt	'85
PIONEER AMERICA INC; A	Fixed Income	162.3	9.96	4.72	10.00	6.01	☆	☆	6.8	☐	225-6292	617-742-7825	4.50	1.00	None	Sherman Russ	'88
PIONEER AMERICA INC; B	Fixed Income	3.2	9.94	4.43	9.09	☆	☆	☆	6.2	☐	225-6292	617-742-7825	None	1.78	4.00	Sherman Russ	'94
PIONEER BOND; A	Fixed Income	109.4	9.35	6.11	11.49	7.39	9.03	8.95	7.2	☐	225-6292	617-742-7825	4.50	1.05	None	Sherman Russ	'87
PIONEER BOND; B	Fixed Income	6.6	9.31	5.95	10.57	☆	☆	☆	6.7	☐	225-6292	617-742-7825	None	1.26	4.00	Sherman Russ	'94
PIONEER CAPITAL GRO; A	Growth	666.8	18.81	10.13	29.45	23.56	☆	☆	0.0	13.5	225-6292	617-742-7825	5.75	1.26	None	Warren Isabelle	'90
PIONEER CAPITAL GRO; B	Growth	174.1	18.65	9.96	28.64	☆	☆	☆	0.0	13.5	225-6292	617-742-7825	None	2.04	4.00	Warren Isabelle	'94
PIONEER EMERGING MKT; A	Emerging Markets	15.7	11.61	11.13	-6.71	☆	☆	☆	0.5	N/A	225-6292	617-742-7825	5.75	None	None	Mark Madden	'94
PIONEER EMERGING MKT; B	Emerging Markets	5.3	11.54	10.88	-7.45	☆	☆	☆	0.3	N/A	225-6292	617-742-7825	None	None	4.00	Mark Madden	'94
PIONEER EQTY-INCOME; A	Equity Income	212.2	16.89	7.04	13.10	12.10	☆	☆	3.2	N/A	225-6292	617-742-7825	5.75	1.24	None	John Carey	'90
PIONEER EQTY-INCOME; B	Equity Income	37.0	16.85	6.86	12.36	☆	☆	☆	2.8	N/A	225-6292	617-742-7825	None	1.92	4.00	John Carey	'94
PIONEER EUROPE; A	European Region	71.3	20.38	15.93	21.99	11.29	☆	☆	0.1		225-6292	617-742-7825	5.75	1.86	None	Patrick Smith	'93
PIONEER EUROPE; B	European Region	5.6	20.17	15.79	21.30	☆	☆	☆	0.0		225-6292	617-742-7825	None	2.47	4.00	Patrick Smith	'94
PIONEER FUND	Growth Income	2,231.3	24.28	6.79	17.32	12.02	10.65	12.00	2.0	16.5	225-6292	617-742-7825	5.75	0.94	None	John Carey	'86
PIONEER GOLD SHARES; A	Gold	26.0	7.47	0.81	0.95	☆	☆	☆	0.0	N/A	225-6292	617-742-7825	5.75	1.75	None	David Tripple	'90
PIONEER GOLD SHARES; B	Gold	1.5	7.41	0.68	0.41	☆	☆	☆	0.0	N/A	225-6292	617-742-7825	None	2.67	4.00	David Tripple	'94
PIONEER GROWTH SHRS; A	Growth	154.3	10.21	6.91	37.70	14.53	9.09	13.81	0.0	16.1	225-6292	617-742-7825	5.75	1.46	None	Warren Isabelle	'93
PIONEER II	Growth Income	4,764.9	19.38	8.99	19.06	13.10	10.13	11.81	1.5	13.4	225-6292	617-742-7825	5.75	0.90	None	Tripple/Boggan	'80/'91
PIONEER INCOME; A	Income	270.8	9.79	6.18	11.29	7.59	8.63	9.94	6.8	16.0	225-6292	617-742-7825	4.50	1.11	None	Carey/Russ	'93/'93
PIONEER INDIA; A	Pacific Region	9.4	9.43	0.32	-17.86	☆	☆	☆	0.2	☐☐☐☐☐	225-6292	617-742-7825	5.75	None	None	David Tripple	'94
PIONEER INDIA; B	Pacific Region	7.0	9.37	0.11	-18.47	☆	☆	☆	0.1		225-6292	617-742-7825	None	None	4.00	David Tripple	'94
PIONEER INTL GROWTH; A	International	282.8	20.24	10.24	1.66	☆	☆	☆	0.0		225-6292	617-742-7825	5.75	1.95	None	Norman Kurland	'94
PIONEER INTL GROWTH; B	International	26.6	20.05	9.98	0.93	☆	☆	☆	0.0		225-6292	617-742-7825	None	3.02	4.00	Norman Kurland	'94
PIONEER SH-TM INCOME; A	Fixed Income	54.9	3.84	2.86	6.70	☆	☆	☆	6.4		225-6292	617-742-7825	2.50	0.85	None	Richard Schlanger	'92

Fund	Objective	Net Assets ($Mil)	NAV	13-Wk %	52-Wk %	Perf D	Perf E	Perf F	Rank	Yield %	P/E	Phone 1	Phone 2	Max Load	12b-1	Min/Other	Manager	Since
PIONEER SH-TM INCOME; B	Fixed Income	3.4	3.84	2.56	5.64	12.15	11.78	11.94	☆	5.7	□15.7	617-742-7825	225-6292	None	1.41	2.00	Richard Schlanger	'94
PIONEER THREE	Growth Income	1,018.7	20.03	5.50	14.00	☆	☆	☆	☆	1.1	23.0	617-742-7825	225-6292	5.75	0.86	None	Robert W. Benson	'86
PIONEER WNTHRP REAL EST	Real Estate	25.8	11.47	7.41	1.58	☆	11.00	☆	☆	5.9	17.5	617-742-7825	225-6292	5.75	1.75	None	Robert W. Benson	'93
PIPER FDS BALANCED	Balanced	43.9	13.26	7.66	19.28	9.97	☆	☆	☆	3.4	22.8	612-342-6402	866-7778	4.00	1.32	None	Multiple Managers	N/A
PIPER FDS EMERG GROWTH	Midcap	212.5	22.40	9.38	25.98	16.52	15.84	☆	☆	3.6		612-342-6402	866-7778	4.00	1.24	None	Multiple Managers	N/A
PIPER FDS EQTY STRAT	Capital Appreciation	55.4	17.57	2.27	7.05	9.73	9.31	☆	☆	0.5	20.8	612-342-6402	866-7778	4.00	1.32	None	Ed Nicoski	'87
PIPER FDS GOVT INCOME	Fixed Income	119.0	8.96	6.11	12.56	5.18	8.33	☆	☆	7.4		612-342-6402	866-7778	4.00	1.05	None	Skele/Salvog/Stone	'95/'95/'87
PIPER FDS GRO & INC	Growth Income	68.9	12.06	8.81	24.38	☆	☆	☆	☆	2.0	17.0	612-342-6402	866-7778	4.00	1.29	None	Dow/Schonberg	'94/'94
PIPER FDS INSTL GOVT	Fixed Income	376.6	8.14	9.26	11.87	0.91	6.23	☆	☆	11.9		612-342-6402	866-7778	1.50	0.78	None	Bruntjen/Goldstein	'88/'88
PIPER FDS SH-INT BOND	Fixed Income	0.1	10.09	☆	☆	☆	☆	☆	☆	0.0		612-342-6402	866-7778	1.50	0.65	None	Skele/Salvog	'95/'95
PIPER FDS VALUE FUND	Growth	167.0	19.24	7.84	17.96	8.89	10.74	☆	☆	0.4	20.4	612-342-6402	866-7778	4.00	1.23	None	Markusen/Rossini	'94/'87
PIPER GLBL PAC-EURO GRO	International	167.2	13.34	-0.82	-4.22	10.32	6.06	☆	☆	0.0	N/A	612-342-6402	866-7778	4.00	1.81	None	Team Managed	N/A
PIPER INSTL ENHANCED 500	Growth Income	3.2	N/A	N/A	N/A	☆	☆	☆	☆	0.0		612-342-6402	866-7778	None	0.50	None	John Schonberg	'95
PIPER INSTL GOVT ADJ	Fixed Income	15.3	9.44	2.64	5.26	☆	☆	☆	☆	5.3		612-342-6402	866-7778	1.00	0.55	None	Tom McGlinch	'93
PNC BALANCED; INSTL	Flexible	22.5	13.15	7.51	15.98	☆	☆	☆	☆	3.6	18.0	None	422-6402	None	0.65	None	Daniel B. Eagan	'94
PNC BALANCED; INV A	Flexible	65.2	13.15	7.40	15.53	10.60	10.50	☆	☆	3.2	18.0	None	422-6538	4.50	1.05	None	Daniel B. Eagan	'94
PNC BALANCED; INV B	Flexible	2.5	13.12	7.16	☆	☆	☆	☆	☆	0.0	18.0	None	422-6538	None	None	5.00	Daniel B. Eagan	'94
PNC BALANCED; SERV	Flexible	79.9	13.15	7.43	15.70	☆	☆	☆	☆	3.4	18.0	None	422-6538	None	0.90	None	Daniel B. Eagan	'93
PNC CORE EQUITY; INSTL	Growth	136.1	11.12	7.26	19.62	☆	☆	☆	☆	2.0	19.9	None	422-6538	None	0.65	None	John Bye	'93
PNC CORE EQUITY; INV A	Growth	2.5	11.11	7.06	18.95	☆	☆	☆	☆	1.7	19.9	None	422-6538	4.50	1.05	None	John Bye	'93
PNC CORE EQUITY; SERV	Growth	62.2	11.11	7.09	19.21	9.21	☆	☆	☆	1.8	19.9	None	422-6538	None	0.90	None	John Bye	'93
PNC GOVT INCOME; INV A	Fixed Income	2.3	10.67	6.93	☆	☆	☆	☆	☆	0.0		None	422-6538	4.50	None	5.00	Charles F. Wills	'94
PNC GOVT INCOME; INV B	Fixed Income	8.3	10.67	6.74	☆	☆	☆	☆	☆	0.0		None	422-6538	None	0.65	None	Charles F. Wills	'94
PNC GROWTH EQTY; INSTL	Growth	183.7	11.84	8.96	23.66	☆	☆	☆	☆	1.2	21.1	None	422-6538	None	None	None	Mike Clark	'93
PNC GROWTH EQTY; SERV	Growth	7.9	11.83	8.86	23.18	8.65	7.77	☆	☆	0.7	21.1	None	422-6538	4.50	1.05	None	Mike Clark	'92
PNC INDEX EQTY; INV A	S&P Index	56.9	11.83	8.85	23.32	☆	☆	☆	☆	0.9	21.1	None	422-6538	None	0.90	None	Mike Clark	'93
PNC INDEX EQTY; SERV	S&P Index	174.4	12.69	9.57	25.60	☆	☆	☆	☆	2.7	17.2	None	422-6538	None	0.15	None	Francis X. Morris	'93
PNC INDEX EQTY; INV A	S&P Index	4.6	12.69	9.65	25.15	12.45	☆	☆	☆	2.4	17.2	None	422-6538	4.50	0.55	None	Francis X. Morris	'92
PNC INTL EMERG; INSTL	Emerging Markets	54.5	12.69	9.50	25.29	☆	☆	☆	☆	2.5	17.2	None	422-6538	None	0.40	None	Francis X. Morris	'93
PNC INTL EMERG; INV A	Emerging Markets	27.9	8.51	7.59	-12.83	☆	☆	☆	☆	0.0		None	422-6538	None	None	None	Herve Van Caloen	'95
PNC INTL EMERG; SERV	Emerging Markets	2.8	8.50	7.87	-12.93	☆	☆	☆	☆	0.0		None	422-6538	None	None	None	Herve Van Caloen	'94
PNC INTL EQUITY; INSTL	International	9.7	8.50	7.59	-12.93	☆	☆	☆	☆	0.0		None	422-6538	None	0.95	None	Herve Van Caloen	'94
PNC INTL EQUITY; INV A	International	308.1	12.88	3.62	1.57	9.67	☆	☆	☆	0.0		None	422-6538	4.50	1.35	None	Herve Van Caloen	'94
PNC INTL EQUITY; INV B	International	16.8	12.80	3.48	1.26	☆	☆	☆	☆	0.0		None	422-6538	None	None	5.00	Herve Van Caloen	'92
PNC INTL EQUITY; SERV	International	0.9	12.74	3.24	☆	☆	☆	☆	☆	0.0		None	422-6538	None	None	None	Herve Van Caloen	'94
PNC INTMDT BOND; INSTL	Fixed Income	90.9	12.83	3.47	1.26	☆	☆	☆	☆	0.9		None	422-6538	None	1.20	None	Herve Van Caloen	'93
PNC INTMDT BOND; INV A	Fixed Income	107.9	9.40	4.52	9.44	☆	☆	☆	☆	5.8		None	422-6538	None	0.45	None	Beth Wagner	'93
PNC INTMDT BOND; SERV	Fixed Income	0.5	9.40	4.44	9.13	☆	☆	☆	☆	5.5		None	422-6538	4.50	0.70	None	Beth Wagner	'93
PNC INTMDT GOVT; INSTL	Fixed Income	36.7	9.40	4.44	9.15	☆	☆	☆	☆	5.6		None	422-6538	4.50	0.40	None	Beth Wagner	'93
PNC INTMDT GOVT; INV A	Fixed Income	132.7	10.02	4.23	9.17	☆	☆	☆	☆	5.7		None	422-6538	4.50	0.40	None	Beth Wagner	'94
PNC INTMDT GOVT; SERV	Fixed Income	9.8	10.02	4.15	8.92	5.30	☆	☆	☆	5.4		None	422-6538	4.50	0.65	None	Beth Wagner	'94
PNC MGD INCOME; INSTL	Fixed Income	49.5	10.02	4.15	8.89	☆	☆	☆	☆	5.4		None	422-6538	None	0.65	None	Beth Wagner	'94
PNC MGD INCOME; INV A	Fixed Income	431.9	10.36	5.70	11.59	☆	☆	☆	☆	6.4		None	422-6538	4.50	0.55	None	Beth Wagner	'94
PNC MGD INCOME; SERV	Fixed Income	11.3	10.36	5.57	11.08	6.97	8.65	☆	☆	6.4		None	422-6538	None	1.00	None	Beth Wagner	'92
PNC SH-TM BOND; INSTL	Fixed Income	93.4	10.36	5.63	11.30	☆	☆	☆	☆	6.2		None	422-6538	None	0.80	None	Beth Wagner	'94
PNC SH-TM BOND; INV A	Fixed Income	5.3	9.69	2.77	5.73	☆	☆	☆	☆	5.2		None	422-6538	None	0.40	None	Beth Wagner	'93
PNC SH-TM BOND; INV B	Fixed Income	0.4	9.69	2.69	5.46	☆	☆	☆	☆	5.0		None	422-6538	4.50	0.65	None	Beth Wagner	'93
PNC SH-TM BOND; SERV	Fixed Income	6.3	9.69	2.70	5.46	☆	☆	☆	☆	5.0		None	422-6538	None	0.65	None	Beth Wagner	'93
PNC SM CAP GROW; INSTL	Small Company Growth	102.7	13.16	13.06	43.93	☆	☆	☆	☆	0.2	N/A	None	422-6538	None	0.48	None	Bill Wykle	'93
PNC SM CAP GROW; INV A	Small Company Growth	4.0	13.10	12.93	43.33	☆	☆	☆	☆	0.0	N/A	None	422-6538	4.50	0.86	None	Bill Wykle	'93

PERFORMANCE OF MUTUAL FUNDS (continued)

FUND NAME	OBJECTIVE	ASSETS ($MIL) 5/31/95	NAV ($/SHR) 6/30/95	RETURN QTR	1YR	3YRS	5YRS	10YRS	DIV YLD %	P/E RATIO	PHONE 800	In-State	Load	Exp. Ratio	Redemption	MANAGER	SINCE
PNC SM CAP GROW; SERV	Small Company Growth	34.8	13.14	12.98	43.77	☆	☆	☆	0.0	N/A	422-6538	None	None	0.71	None	Bill Wykle	'93
PNC SM CAP VALUE; INSTL	Small Company Growth	156.5	13.85	5.81	13.00	☆	☆	☆	0.5	14.7	422-6538	None	None	0.73	None	Susan Menzies	'94
PNC SM CAP VALUE; INV A	Small Company Growth	19.6	13.85	5.64	12.63	15.72	☆	☆	0.0	14.7	422-6538	None	4.50	1.13	None	Susan Menzies	'94
PNC SM CAP VALUE; INV B	Small Company Growth	1.1	13.80	5.50	☆	☆	☆	☆	0.0	14.7	422-6538	None	None	None	5.00	Susan Menzies	'94
PNC SM CAP VALUE; SERV	Small Company Growth	49.5	13.86	5.76	12.84	☆	☆	☆	0.2	14.7	422-6538	None	None	0.98	None	Susan Menzies	'94
PNC VALUE EQUITY; INSTL	Capital Appreciation	492.0	13.02	7.90	21.35	☆	☆	☆	2.5	N/A	422-6538	None	None	0.65	None	Earl J Gaskins	'94
PNC VALUE EQUITY; INV A	Capital Appreciation	13.9	13.02	7.78	20.98	13.87	☆	☆	2.1	N/A	422-6538	None	4.50	1.05	None	Earl J Gaskins	'94
PNC VALUE EQUITY; SERV	Capital Appreciation	137.9	13.02	7.82	21.04	☆	☆	☆	2.2	N/A	422-6538	None	None	0.90	None	Earl J Gaskins	'94
PORTICO BALANCED; INSTL	Balanced	91.3	24.48	7.02	19.55	10.30	☆	☆	2.0	23.4	982-8909	414-287-3710	None	0.75	None	Wear/Westman	'94/'92
PORTICO BD IMMDEX; INSTL	Fixed Income	270.6	27.43	6.65	12.95	8.19	9.88	☆	6.1		982-8909	414-287-3710	None	0.48	None	Stanek/Westman	'89/'92
PORTICO EQTY INDEX; INSTL	S&P Index	121.8	38.42	9.39	25.61	12.57	11.54	☆	2.1	17.3	982-8909	414-287-3710	None	0.50	None	Daniel Tranchita	'92
PORTICO GRO & INC; INSTL	Growth Income	151.1	25.73	6.72	20.13	9.65	9.74	☆	1.6	18.8	982-8909	414-287-3710	None	0.90	None	Marian Zentmyer	'93
PORTICO INT BD MKT; INSTL	Fixed Income	102.8	10.13	5.02	10.21	☆	☆	☆	5.9	□	982-8909	414-287-3710	None	0.50	None	Stanek/Westman	'93/'93
PORTICO INTL EQTY; INSTL	International	28.5	19.51	2.20	-0.25	☆	☆	☆	0.2	□	982-8909	414-287-3710	None	1.49	None	Tranchita/Peskin	'94/'94
PORTICO MIDCORE GR; INSTL	Midcap	121.1	24.26	8.06	21.33	☆	☆	☆	0.2	22.4	982-8909	414-287-3710	None	0.88	None	Bart Wear	'92
PORTICO SHTM BD MK; INSTL	Fixed Income	83.1	10.25	3.26	8.04	5.87	7.72	☆	6.0	□	982-8909	414-287-3710	None	0.50	None	Stanek/Tranchita	'89/'93
PORTICO SPEC GRO; INSTL	Small Company Growth	371.7	37.20	5.44	26.10	12.94	14.92	☆	0.0	23.9	982-8909	414-287-3710	None	0.89	None	Harkness/Docter	'89/'89
PRA REAL ESTATE	Real Estate	0.9	7.96	3.89	-1.07	☆	7.60	☆	6.6	23.9	435-1405	302-651-8448	None	1.22	5.00	Michael T. Oliver	'89
PRAIRIE BOND FUND; A	Fixed Income	0.1	10.71	6.81	☆	☆	☆	☆	0.0	N/A	370-9446	None	4.50	None	None	Annette Cole	'95
PRAIRIE BOND FUND; B	Fixed Income	0.1	10.72	6.72	☆	☆	☆	☆	0.0	N/A	370-9446	None	None	None	5.00	Annette Cole	'95
PRAIRIE BOND FUND; I	Fixed Income	118.5	10.72	6.98	☆	☆	☆	☆	0.0	N/A	370-9446	None	None	None	None	Annette Cole	'95
PRAIRIE EQTY INC; A	Equity Income	0.6	11.09	7.45	☆	☆	☆	☆	0.0	N/A	370-9446	None	4.50	None	None	Jim Moeller	'95
PRAIRIE EQTY INC; B	Equity Income	0.1	11.08	7.29	☆	☆	☆	☆	0.0	N/A	370-9446	None	None	None	5.00	Jim Moeller	'95
PRAIRIE EQTY INC; I	Equity Income	224.6	11.09	7.52	☆	☆	☆	☆	0.0	N/A	370-9446	None	None	None	None	Jim Moeller	'95
PRAIRIE GROWTH; A	Growth	1.3	11.28	6.24	☆	☆	☆	☆	0.0	N/A	370-9446	None	4.50	None	None	Jim Moeller	'95
PRAIRIE GROWTH; B	Growth	0.1	11.25	5.83	☆	☆	☆	☆	0.0	N/A	370-9446	None	None	None	5.00	Jim Moeller	'95
PRAIRIE GROWTH; I	Growth	291.2	11.28	6.26	☆	☆	☆	☆	0.0	N/A	370-9446	None	None	None	None	Jim Moeller	'95
PRAIRIE INTL BD; A	World Income	0.3	11.37	3.78	☆	☆	☆	☆	0.0	N/A	370-9446	None	4.50	None	None	Claude Erb	'95
PRAIRIE INTL BD; B	World Income	0.1	11.43	4.14	☆	☆	☆	☆	0.0	N/A	370-9446	None	None	None	5.00	Claude Erb	'95
PRAIRIE INTL BD; I	World Income	11.0	11.43	4.39	☆	☆	☆	☆	0.0	N/A	370-9446	None	None	None	None	Claude Erb	'95
PRAIRIE INTL EQTY; A	International	1.1	10.05	-2.17	☆	☆	☆	☆	0.0	N/A	370-9446	None	4.50	None	None	Peter Jankovskis	'95
PRAIRIE INTL EQTY; B	International	0.1	10.04	-2.23	☆	☆	☆	☆	0.0	N/A	370-9446	None	None	None	5.00	Peter Jankovskis	'95
PRAIRIE INTL EQTY; I	International	63.7	10.07	-1.94	☆	☆	☆	☆	0.0	N/A	370-9446	None	None	None	None	Peter Jankovskis	'95
PRAIRIE INTMDT BD; A	Fixed Income	2.2	8.14	5.55	11.37	☆	☆	☆	6.2		370-9446	None	3.00	None	None	Annette Furmanski-Cole	'93
PRAIRIE MGD ASSETS; A	Flexible	1.9	10.51	☆	☆	☆	☆	☆	0.0	N/A	224-4800	None	4.50	None	None	Krill/Erb	'95/'95
PRAIRIE MGD ASSETS; B	Flexible	0.5	10.49	☆	☆	☆	☆	☆	0.0	N/A	224-4800	None	None	None	5.00	Krill/Erb	'95/'95
PRAIRIE MGD ASSETS; I	Flexible	0.4	10.52	☆	☆	☆	☆	☆	0.0	N/A	224-4800	None	None	None	None	Krill/Erb	'95/'95
PRAIRIE MGD AST INC; A	Income	47.6	13.40	7.41	15.97	9.06	10.73	☆	5.5	N/A	224-4800	None	4.50	0.63	None	Krill/Erb	'86/'95
PRAIRIE MGD AST INC; B	Income	0.3	13.39	7.10	☆	☆	☆	☆	0.0	N/A	224-4800	None	None	None	5.00	Krill/Erb	'95/'95
PRAIRIE MGD AST INC; I	Income	0.4	13.43	7.43	☆	☆	☆	☆	0.0	N/A	224-4800	None	None	None	None	Krill/Erb	'95/'95
PRAIRIE SPEC OPPTY; A	Small Company Growth	0.3	10.64	0.43	☆	☆	☆	☆	0.0	N/A	370-9446	None	4.50	None	None	Jim Moeller	'95
PRAIRIE SPEC OPPTY; B	Small Company Growth	0.1	10.60	0.09	☆	☆	☆	☆	0.0	N/A	370-9446	None	None	None	5.00	Jim Moeller	'95
PRAIRIE SPEC OPPTY; I	Small Company Growth	66.7	10.63	0.38	☆	☆	☆	☆	0.0	N/A	370-9446	None	None	None	None	Jim Moeller	'95
PREFERRED ASSET ALLOC	Flexible	73.8	11.97	9.46	21.70	10.91	☆	☆	3.2	17.3	662-4769	None	None	1.25	None	Mellon/PanAgora	'92/'92
PREFERRED FXD INC	Fixed Income	58.7	10.30	6.06	11.48	7.65	☆	☆	5.7	□	662-4769	None	None	0.97	None	J.P. Morgan Inv Mgt Inc	'92

Fund	Objective	Net Assets	%	%	%	%	%	%	Rating	Yield	P/E	Tel 1	Tel 2	Load	Exp	Fee	Manager	Since
PREFERRED GROWTH	Growth	331.2	16.63	13.98	34.21	18.72			☆	0.1	23.4	309-675-5123	662-4769	None	0.91	None	Jennison Assoc Cap Corp	'92
PREFERRED INTL	International	112.8	12.24	8.13	6.71	9.16			☆	1.0		309-675-5123	662-4769	None	1.38	None	Mercator Invt Mgt, Inc	'92
PREFERRED SHT-TM GOVT	Fixed Income	31.4	9.80	2.94	5.71	4.27			☆	5.2		309-675-5123	662-4769	None	0.74	None	Caterpillar Inv Mgt Ltd	'92
PREFERRED VALUE	Growth Income	197.0	13.82	11.27	25.73	13.76	11.94		☆	1.5	15.7	309-675-5123	662-4769	None	0.93	None	Oppenheimer Capital	'92
T ROWE PRICE BALANCED	Balanced	496.3	12.37	7.12	17.49	10.92	12.27		☆	3.7	N/A	410-547-2308	638-5660	None	1.00	None	Richard T. Whitney	'91
T ROWE PRICE BLUE CHIP	Growth	70.4	13.33	7.67	25.41				☆	0.8	N/A	410-547-2308	638-5660	None	1.25	None	Thomas Broadus	'93
T ROWE PRICE CAP APPREC	Capital Appreciation	772.5	13.67	6.38	17.92	12.76	11.85		☆	2.5	16.3	410-547-2308	638-5660	None	1.10	None	Richard P. Howard	'89
T ROWE PRICE CAP OPPTY	Capital Appreciation		13.21	10.64					☆			410-547-2308	638-5660	None	None	None	John Wakeman	'94
T ROWE PRICE DIV GROWTH	Growth Income	65.1	12.43	5.75	19.45				☆	2.9	17.9	410-547-2308	638-5660	None	1.00	None	Bill Stromberg	'92
T ROWE PRICE EQU INCOME	Equity Income	4,002.6	17.96	6.71	21.70	13.69	13.25		☆	3.4	14.9	410-547-2308	638-5660	None	0.88	None	Brian C. Rogers	'85
T ROWE PRICE GNMA	Fixed Income	810.5	9.49	5.02	13.00	6.24	8.64		☆	7.2		410-547-2308	638-5660	None	0.77	None	Peter Van Dyke	'87
T ROWE PRICE GRO & INC	Growth Income	1,418.0	17.59	7.26	18.77	13.21	12.06		☆	3.0	16.8	410-547-2308	638-5660	None	0.81	None	Stephen W. Boesel	'87
T ROWE PRICE GROWTH STK	Growth	2,325.9	21.80	8.19	21.77	14.34	11.46	11.50	☆	0.8	16.9	410-547-2308	638-5660	None	0.85	None	John D. Gillespie	'93
T ROWE PRICE HIGH YLD	Fixed Income	1,208.5	8.12	3.44	9.19	8.96	10.76	13.55	☆	9.3		410-547-2308	638-5660	None		1.00	Catherine H. Bray	'94
T ROWE PRICE INDEX EQU *	S&P Index	313.4	15.51	9.40	25.71	12.75	11.53	9.49	☆	2.4	17.3	410-547-2308	638-5660	None	0.45	None	Richard T. Whitney	'90
T ROWE PRICE INT ASIA	Pacific Region	2,124.5	8.37	7.31	4.96	13.50	13.36		☆	0.8		410-547-2308	638-5660	None	1.22	None	Martin G. Wade	'90
T ROWE PRICE INT BOND	World Income	928.7	10.60	3.81	17.33	10.94	0.82		☆	5.4		410-547-2308	638-5660	None	0.98	2.00	Peter B. Askew	'94
T ROWE PRICE INT DISC	Intl Small Company	373.7	14.26	3.63	-10.84	4.66			☆	0.4		410-547-2308	638-5660	None	1.50	2.00	Martin G. Wade	'89
T ROWE PRICE INT EM BD	World Income	6.4	10.47	17.56					☆	0.0		410-547-2308	638-5660	None	None	None	Peter B. Askew	'94
T ROWE PRICE INT EM ST	Emerging Markets	6.3	11.05	10.50					☆	0.0		410-547-2308	638-5660	None	2.00	2.00	Martin G. Wade	'95
T ROWE PRICE INT EU STK	European Region	448.6	13.65	7.48	17.91	9.56	5.98		☆	0.9	N/A	410-547-2308	638-5660	None	1.25	None	Martin G. Wade	'90
T ROWE PRICE INT GL GVT	World Income	29.4	10.06	4.25	12.49	7.28			☆	5.7	23.8	410-547-2308	638-5660	None	1.20	None	Peter B. Askew	'94
T ROWE PRICE INT JAPAN	Japanese	134.6	9.06	-5.82	-20.05	5.26			☆	0.0	22.3	410-547-2308	638-5660	None	1.99	2.00	Martin G. Wade	'91
T ROWE PRICE INT LAT	Latin American	162.4	6.78	11.33	-20.33				☆	0.0	23.8	410-547-2308	638-5660	None	2.00	None	Martin G. Wade	'93
T ROWE PRICE INT SH GL	World Income	47.4	4.38	1.72	3.65				☆	6.6		410-547-2308	638-5660	None	1.00	None	Peter B. Askew	'94
T ROWE PRICE INT STOCK	International	6,159.9	11.73	4.73	4.47	10.67	6.94	17.38	☆	1.0	N/A	410-547-2308	638-5660	None	0.96	None	Testa/Wade	'80/'80
T ROWE PRICE MID-CAP GRO	Midcap	118.0	17.61	9.65	26.25	23.20	14.19		☆	0.0	23.8	410-547-2308	638-5660	None	1.25	None	Brian Berghuis	'92
T ROWE PRICE NEW AMER GR	Growth	724.7	30.42	8.99	23.02	16.70	8.21	11.67	☆	0.0	22.3	410-547-2308	638-5660	None	1.14	None	John H. Laporte	'85
T ROWE PRICE NEW ERA	Natural Resources	1,093.4	22.58	3.34	17.22	11.95	16.37		☆	1.7	23.8	410-547-2308	638-5660	None	0.80	None	George A. Roche	'79
T ROWE PRICE NEW HORIZON	Small Company Growth	1,933.7	18.31	12.95	37.91	23.99		12.88	☆	0.0		410-547-2308	638-5660	None	0.93	None	John H. Laporte	'87
T ROWE PRICE NEW INCOME	Fixed Income	1,565.9	8.99	5.83	12.19	7.10	8.94	9.12	☆	6.7	N/A	410-547-2308	638-5660	None	0.82	None	Charles P. Smith	'86
T ROWE PRICE OTC	Small Company Growth	227.6	15.82	9.18	19.47	16.43	11.63	10.26	☆	0.2	23.7	410-547-2308	638-5660	None	1.11	None	Greg A. McCrickard	'92
T ROWE PRICE PRS STR BAL	Flexible	13.3	11.29	7.25					☆	0.0		410-547-2308	638-5660	None	None	None	Peter Van Dyke	'94
T ROWE PRICE PRS STR GRO	Flexible	10.7	11.77	7.98					☆	0.0		410-547-2308	638-5660	None	None	None	Peter Van Dyke	'94
T ROWE PRICE PRS STR INC	Income	20.7	10.97	6.61					☆	0.0		410-547-2308	638-5660	None	None	None	Peter Van Dyke	'94
T ROWE PRICE SCI & TECH	Science & Technology	1,372.8	28.42	20.07	68.12	34.52	24.14		☆	0.0	23.7	410-547-2308	638-5660	None	1.11	None	Laporte/Morris	'87/'91
T ROWE PRICE SH-TM BOND	Fixed Income	491.5	4.72	2.48	3.95	3.82	6.05	6.90	☆	6.2		410-547-2308	638-5660	None	0.74	None	Edward A. Wiese	'95
T ROWE PRICE SH-TM GOVT	Fixed Income	112.4	4.67	3.33	6.55	3.24			☆	5.6		410-547-2308	638-5660	None	0.40	1.00	Heather Landon	'93
T ROWE PRICE SM CAP	Small Company Growth	525.6	15.58	9.87	17.06	17.30	14.25		☆	0.9		410-547-2308	638-5660	None	0.97	None	Preston G. Athey	'88
T ROWE PRICE SPCTRM GRO	Growth Income	1,063.0	12.71	7.26	20.04	15.23	11.90		☆	1.3		410-547-2308	638-5660	None	None	None	Van Dyke/Notzon	'90/'90
T ROWE PRICE SPCTRM INC	Fixed Income	833.8	10.88	4.75	13.34	8.42	10.25		☆	6.5		410-547-2308	638-5660	None	0.60	None	Van Dyke/Notzon	'90/'90
T ROWE PRICE SUM GNMA	Fixed Income	19.1	9.69	4.88	11.49				☆	7.3		410-547-2308	638-5660	None	0.55	None	Peter Van Dyke	'93
T ROWE PRICE SUM LTD TD BD	Fixed Income	23.2	4.65	2.57	6.79	6.47	8.44		☆	7.2		410-547-2308	638-5660	None	0.79	None	Edward A. Wiese	'95
T ROWE PRICE TREAS INTMD	Fixed Income	112.7	5.26	5.17	10.00	9.31	10.00		☆	6.1		410-547-2308	638-5660	None	0.80	None	Charles P. Smith	'89
T ROWE PRICE TREAS LONG	Fixed Income	65.3	10.58	10.15	17.32				☆	6.5		410-547-2308	638-5660	None	None	None	Peter Van Dyke	'89
T ROWE PRICE VALUE	Growth Income	20.9	12.49	8.47		8.77	10.36		☆	0.0	N/A	410-547-2308	638-5660	None	None	None	Brian S. Rogers	'94
PRIMARY INC INCOME	Income	4.2	12.07	5.05	14.87	5.42	7.27		☆	4.1	13.3	414-271-7870	443-6544	None	0.84	None	Barry S. Arnold	'95
PRIMARY INC US GOVT	Fixed Income	1.3	10.09	4.44	10.16		8.42		☆	5.6		414-271-7870	443-6544	None	0.75	None	David R. Austwitz	'89
PRIMARY TREND	Growth Income	21.4	12.10	8.13	17.03	8.07			☆	2.1	19.0	414-271-7870	443-6544	None	1.27	None	David R. Austwitz	'93
PRINCIPAL PRES BALANCED	Balanced	7.4	10.78	5.39	13.94				☆	3.6	18.1	414-334-5521	826-4600	None	1.20	4.50	Ralph Patek	

PERFORMANCE OF MUTUAL FUNDS (continued)

FUND NAME	OBJECTIVE	ASSETS ($ MIL) 5/31/95	NAV ($/SHR) 6/30/95	QTR	1YR	3YRS	5YRS	10YRS	Rating	DIV YLD %	P/E RATIO	800	In-State	Load	Exp. Ratio	Redemption	MANAGER	SINCE
PRINCIPAL PRES DIV ACHVR	Growth Income	21.8	15.00	8.26	17.59	7.21	9.09		☆	1.3	18.3	826-4600	414-334-5521	4.50	1.50	None	R. Douglas Ziegler	'92
PRINCIPAL PRES GOVT	Fixed Income	50.4	9.43	5.45	9.81	6.49	8.55		☆	6.5		826-4600	414-334-5521	3.50	1.10	None	Vern Van Vooren	'89
PRINCIPAL PRES S&P 100 +	Growth Income	48.1	17.90	10.14	26.82	11.98	10.86		☆	1.4	16.9	826-4600	414-334-5521	4.50	1.20	None	William Zink	'93
PRINCIPAL PRES SEL VALUE	Midcap	2.8	9.55	4.26	☆	☆	☆			0.0	N/A	826-4600	414-334-5521	4.50	None	None	Kenneth Kailin	'94
PRINCIPAL SP MKT INTL	International	16.1	11.64	9.50	5.57	☆	☆			2.4		247-4123	515-247-5711	4.50	0.90	None	Opsal/Dau	'93/'93
PRINCIPAL SP MKT MBS	Fixed Income	13.7	9.90	6.41	13.94	☆	☆			6.6	□	247-4123	515-247-5711	None	0.45	None	Schafer/Alexander	'93/'93
PRINCOR BALANCED; A	Balanced	56.3	13.31	5.84	12.16	8.06	10.38		☆	2.4	16.5	247-4123	515-247-5711	4.75	1.51	None	Vogel/Green	'93/'93
PRINCOR BALANCED; B	Balanced	0.5	13.27	5.68	☆	☆	☆			0.0	N/A	247-4123	515-247-5711	None		4.00	Vogel/Green	'94/'94
PRINCOR BLUE CHIP; A	Growth Income	31.0	13.97	6.64	23.32	9.70	☆			1.4	17.0	247-4123	515-247-5711	4.75	1.46	None	Williams/White	'91/'94
PRINCOR BLUE CHIP; B	Growth Income	0.7	13.93	6.56	☆	☆	☆			0.0	17.0	247-4123	515-247-5711	None		4.00	Williams/White	'94/'94
PRINCOR BOND; A	Fixed Income	101.6	11.30	8.54	16.18	9.11	10.18		☆	6.9	□	247-4123	515-247-5711	4.75	0.95	None	Brattebo/Bennett	'87/'95
PRINCOR BOND; B	Fixed Income	1.1	11.28	8.47	☆	☆	☆			0.0		247-4123	515-247-5711	None		4.00	Brattebo/Bennett	'94/'95
PRINCOR CAP ACCUM; A	Growth Income	316.6	22.34	6.03	18.18	10.29	10.41	11.57		1.8	16.3	247-4123	515-247-5711	4.75	0.83	None	White/Green	'69/'92
PRINCOR CAP ACCUM; B	Growth Income	1.1	22.23	5.86	☆	☆	☆			0.0	16.3	247-4123	515-247-5711	None		4.00	White/Green	'94/'94
PRINCOR EMERG GROWTH; A	Midcap	121.0	29.01	9.47	23.38	17.27	16.49		☆	0.1	17.6	247-4123	515-247-5711	4.75	1.74	None	Hamilton/Craven	'87/'93
PRINCOR EMERG GROWTH; B	Midcap	4.3	28.91	9.30	☆	☆	☆			0.0	17.6	247-4123	515-247-5711	None		4.00	Hamilton/Craven	'94/'94
PRINCOR GOVT SEC INC; A	Fixed Income	258.1	11.21	6.38	13.80	6.69	9.05	9.60		6.2	□	247-4123	515-247-5711	4.75	0.94	None	Schafer/Alexander	'85/'93
PRINCOR GOVT SEC INC; B	Fixed Income	1.2	11.19	6.21	☆	☆	☆			0.0		247-4123	515-247-5711	None		4.00	Schafer/Alexander	'94/'94
PRINCOR GROWTH; A	Growth	148.7	34.91	8.25	23.69	14.19	15.29	15.20		0.8	18.4	247-4123	515-247-5711	4.75	1.30	None	Hamilton/Craven	'87/'93
PRINCOR GROWTH; B	Growth	3.2	34.76	8.08	☆	☆	☆			0.0	18.4	247-4123	515-247-5711	None		4.00	Hamilton/Craven	'94/'94
PRINCOR HIGH YIELD; A	Fixed Income	22.1	8.12	5.34	12.07	8.30	9.82		☆	7.9		247-4123	515-247-5711	4.75	1.46	None	Hovey/Denkinger	'87/'93
PRINCOR HIGH YIELD; B	Fixed Income	0.3	8.11	5.16	☆	☆	☆			0.0		247-4123	515-247-5711	None		4.00	Hovey/Denkinger	'94/'94
PRINCOR UTILITIES; A	Utility	60.9	10.02	5.81	13.98	☆	☆			4.9	13.6	247-4123	515-247-5711	4.75	1.00	None	Green/Vogel	'93/'93
PRINCOR UTILITIES; B	Utility	1.7	10.00	5.74	☆	☆	☆			0.0	13.6	247-4123	515-247-5711	None		4.00	Green/Vogel	'93/'93
PRINCOR WORLD; A	International	119.2	7.04	8.81	3.84	10.58	8.06	11.14		0.5		247-4123	515-247-5711	4.75	1.74	None	Opsal/Dau	'93/'93
PRINCOR WORLD; B	International	2.0	7.01	8.68	☆	☆	☆			0.0		247-4123	515-247-5711	4.75		4.00	Opsal/Dau	'94/'94
PROGRESSIVE AGGR GRO ☒	Capital Appreciation	0.5	8.84	4.62	-7.05	-1.25	-1.25		☆	0.0	11.9	543-2620	212-248-8080	None	3.40	None	Mark D. Beckerman	'94/'94
PROGRESSIVE ENVIRONMNT ☒	Environmental	1.6	4.15	6.96	-3.71	-1.25	-6.72		☆	0.0	17.2	543-2620	212-248-8080	None	1.85	None	George R. Gay	'92
PROGRESSIVE VALUE ☒	Growth	0.3	10.44	5.03	7.41	8.78	-0.60		☆	0.0	26.5	543-2620	212-248-8080	4.00	2.34	None	Mark D. Beckerman	'94
PROV INSTL INTMDT DUR	Fixed Income	35.7	9.76	5.29	10.58	☆	☆			6.1		None	None	None	None	None	N/A	N/A
PROV INSTL SHORT DUR	Fixed Income	89.6	9.79	2.67	6.86	☆	☆			5.3		None	None	None	None	None	N/A	N/A
PRUDENT SPECULATOR FUND	Small Company Growth	2.2	7.64	10.09	17.00	8.26	2.07		☆	0.0	12.3	444-4778	213-252-9000	None	6.19	None	Ed Bernstein	'89
PRUDENTIAL ADJ RATE; A	Fixed Income	55.4	9.61	1.25	5.04	2.95	☆			3.7	N/A	225-1852	None	1.00	0.69	None	David Graham	'93
PRUDENTIAL ADJ RATE; B	Fixed Income	0.2	9.64	1.24	5.02	2.91	☆			3.7	N/A	225-1852	None	None	0.75	1.00	David Graham	'93
PRUDENTIAL ALL CONSV; A	Flexible	106.9	11.79	6.98	13.45	10.36	10.69		☆	2.8	N/A	225-1852	None	5.00	1.23	None	Greg Goldberg	'95
PRUDENTIAL ALL CONSV; B	Flexible	376.9	11.76	6.82	12.57	9.51	9.85		☆	2.2	N/A	225-1852	None	None	2.00	5.00	Greg Goldberg	'95
PRUDENTIAL ALL CONSV; C	Flexible	1.3	11.76	6.81	☆	☆	☆			2.0	N/A	225-1852	None	None	1.00	1.00	Greg Goldberg	'95
PRUDENTIAL ALL STRAT; A	Flexible	84.8	12.23	7.84	13.92	9.21	10.10		☆	2.4	N/A	225-1852	None	5.00	1.26	5.00	Team Managed	N/A
PRUDENTIAL ALL STRAT; B	Flexible	274.8	12.17	7.68	13.01	8.38	9.24		☆	1.7	N/A	225-1852	None	None	2.03	5.00	Team Managed	N/A
PRUDENTIAL ALL STRAT; C	Flexible	0.2	12.17	7.68	☆	☆	☆			0.0	N/A	225-1852	None	None	1.00	1.00	Team Managed	N/A
PRUDENTIAL DVSFD BD; A	Fixed Income	6.3	13.48	6.76	☆	☆	☆			0.0		225-1852	None	4.00	None	None	Richard Lynes	'95
PRUDENTIAL DVSFD BD; B	Fixed Income	35.2	13.48	6.51	☆	☆	☆			0.0		225-1852	None	None	None	5.00	Richard Lynes	'95
PRUDENTIAL DVSFD BD; C	Fixed Income	1.0	13.48	6.51	☆	☆	☆			0.0		225-1852	None	None	1.00	1.00	Richard Lynes	'95
PRUDENTIAL EQU INC; A	Equity Income	269.3	14.41	7.79	15.95	14.45	13.10		☆	3.4	16.2	225-1852	None	5.00	1.09	None	Warren Spitz	'90
PRUDENTIAL EQU INC; B	Equity Income	904.4	14.38	7.54	15.04	13.56	12.21		☆	2.7	16.2	225-1852	None	None	1.85	5.00	Warren Spitz	'87

Prudential fund family listing (continued). Columns read left-to-right; performance columns are shown as printed (☆ indicates a rating/insufficient-history placeholder).

Fund	Objective	Net Assets ($Mil)	Ret 1	Ret 2	Ret 3	Yield %	Telephone	Portfolio Manager
PRUDENTIAL EQU INC; C	Equity Income	3.5	14.38	7.54	☆	0.0	225-1852	Warren Spitz
PRUDENTIAL EQUITY; A	Growth	923.4	15.49	7.20	22.63	1.4	225-1852	Tom Jackson
PRUDENTIAL EQUITY; C	Growth	1,785.1	15.44	7.00	21.66	0.8	225-1852	Tom Jackson
PRUDENTIAL EUROPE GR; A	European Region	10.0	15.44	7.00	☆	0.0	225-1852	Dan Duane
PRUDENTIAL EUROPE GR; B	European Region	43.3	12.58	12.83	☆	0.0	225-1852	Dan Duane
PRUDENTIAL EUROPE GR; C	European Region	109.4	12.48	12.64	☆	0.0	225-1852	Dan Duane
PRUDENTIAL GL GENSIS; A	Global Small Company	7.5	12.48	12.64	☆	0.6	225-1852	Dan Duane
PRUDENTIAL GL GENSIS; B	Global Small Company	41.4	19.06	10.11	3.54	0.2	225-1852	Dan Duane
PRUDENTIAL GL GENSIS; C	Global Small Company	154.2	18.43	9.90	2.76	0.0	225-1852	Dan Duane
PRUDENTIAL GL NT RES; A	Natural Resources	1.3	18.43	9.90	☆	0.0	225-1852	Leigh Goehring
PRUDENTIAL GL NT RES; B	Natural Resources	19.7	13.75	5.93	12.24	0.0	225-1852	Leigh Goehring
PRUDENTIAL GL NT RES; C	Natural Resources	80.8	13.36	5.78	11.43	0.0	225-1852	Leigh Goehring
PRUDENTIAL GLOBAL; A	Global	0.6	13.36	5.78	☆	0.0	225-1852	Dan Duane
PRUDENTIAL GLOBAL; B	Global	210.5	14.75	10.55	9.38	0.0	225-1852	Dan Duane
PRUDENTIAL GLOBAL; C	Global	248.4	14.31	10.31	8.62	0.0	225-1852	Dan Duane
PRUDENTIAL GNMA; A	Fixed Income	2.3	14.31	10.31	☆	0.0	225-1852	David Graham
PRUDENTIAL GNMA; B	Fixed Income	101.6	14.40	5.18	11.13	6.7	225-1852	David Graham
PRUDENTIAL GNMA; C	Fixed Income	139.2	14.36	4.96	10.44	6.1	225-1852	David Graham
PRUDENTIAL GOVT INC; A	Fixed Income	0.6	14.40	5.25	☆	0.0	225-1852	Barbara Kenworthy
PRUDENTIAL GOVT INC; B	Fixed Income	918.7	9.01	6.67	12.75	6.8	225-1852	Barbara Kenworthy
PRUDENTIAL GOVT INC; C	Fixed Income	671.5	9.02	6.48	12.10	6.1	225-1852	David Graham
PRUDENTIAL GOVT INTMDT	Fixed Income	0.5	9.02	6.51	☆	0.0	225-1852	Bob Fetch
PRUDENTIAL GR OPPTY; A	Small Company Growth	213.3	9.64	4.14	8.57	5.7	225-1852	Bob Fetch
PRUDENTIAL GR OPPTY; B	Small Company Growth	210.6	13.04	7.95	20.16	0.0	225-1852	Bob Fetch
PRUDENTIAL GR OPPTY; C	Small Company Growth	320.2	12.49	7.77	19.18	0.0	225-1852	Bob Fetch
PRUDENTIAL HI YLD; A	Fixed Income	0.9	12.49	7.77	☆	0.0	225-1852	Lars Berkman
PRUDENTIAL HI YLD; B	Fixed Income	1,175.3	8.03	4.39	9.56	10.4	225-1852	Lars Berkman
PRUDENTIAL HI YLD; C	Fixed Income	2,676.8	8.03	4.38	9.05	9.8	225-1852	Lars Berkman
PRUDENTIAL INCOMVRT; A	Specialty	9.9	8.03	4.38	☆	0.0	225-1852	Greg Goldberg
PRUDENTIAL INCOMVRT; B	Specialty	156.9	12.06	8.20	16.46	3.6	225-1852	Greg Goldberg
PRUDENTIAL INCOMVRT; C	Specialty	79.4	12.08	8.10	15.85	3.0	225-1852	Greg Goldberg
PRUDENTIAL INSTL ACT BAL	Balanced	0.1	12.08	8.10	☆	0.0	824-7513	Jennison Assoc Cap Corp
PRUDENTIAL INSTL BAL	Flexible	114.9	12.02	7.32	16.05	2.4	824-7513	Prudential Invstmnt Corp
PRUDENTIAL INSTL GROWTH	Growth	75.0	11.95	6.13	13.65	2.1	824-7513	Jennison Assoc Cap Corp
PRUDENTIAL INSTL INCOME	Fixed Income	158.1	14.96	15.17	34.71	0.0	824-7513	Prudential Invstmnt Corp
PRUDENTIAL INSTL INTL ST	International	49.6	9.96	5.79	11.63	5.8	824-7513	Mercator Invt Mgt, Inc
PRUDENTIAL INSTL STK IDX	S&P Index	123.5	14.63	7.65	6.68	0.7	824-7513	Prudential Invstmnt Corp
PRUDENTIAL INT GL; A	World Income	82.3	13.19	9.28	25.35	1.6	225-1852	Barnett/Sargen
PRUDENTIAL INT GL; B	World Income	210.0	8.19	4.64	12.96	5.7	225-1852	Barnett/Sargen
PRUDENTIAL INT GL; C	World Income	19.8	8.20	4.35	12.24	5.1	225-1852	Barnett/Sargen
PRUDENTIAL MULTI-SEC; A	Capital Appreciation	0.1	8.20	4.35	☆	0.0	225-1852	Goldberg/Smith
PRUDENTIAL MULTI-SEC; B	Capital Appreciation	76.8	13.49	8.62	20.66	0.3	225-1852	Goldberg/Smith
PRUDENTIAL MULTI-SEC; C	Capital Appreciation	190.0	13.34	8.44	19.90	0.1	225-1852	Goldberg/Smith
PRUDENTIAL PAC GR; A	Pacific Region	4.1	13.34	8.44	☆	0.0	225-1852	Dan Duane
PRUDENTIAL PAC GR; C	Pacific Region	108.6	15.31	4.58	-7.42	0.0	225-1852	Dan Duane
PRUDENTIAL SH GL AST; A	World Income	358.3	14.99	4.39	☆	0.0	225-1852	Dan Duane
PRUDENTIAL SH GL GL; A	World Income	1.3	14.99	4.39	-8.13	4.9	225-1852	Brummette/Sargen
PRUDENTIAL SH GL GL; B	World Income	31.3	1.77	0.61	1.48	6.9	225-1852	Brummette/Sargen
PRUDENTIAL SH GL GL; B	World Income	19.6	8.31	1.96	1.67	6.2	225-1852	Brummette/Sargen

PERFORMANCE OF MUTUAL FUNDS *(continued)*

FUND NAME	OBJECTIVE	ASSETS ($ MIL) 5/31/95	NAV ($/SHR) 6/30/95	RETURN THROUGH 6/30 QTR	1YR	3YRS (Annualized)	5YRS (Annualized)	10YRS (Annualized)	DIV YLD %	P/E RATIO	PHONE NUMBER 800	PHONE NUMBER In-State	FEES Load	FEES Exp. Ratio	FEES Redemption	MANAGER	SINCE
PRUDENTIAL SH GL GL; C	World Income	0.1	8.34	1.78	☆	☆	☆	☆	0.0	☐	225-1852	None	None	None	1.00	Brummette/Sargen	'94/'94
PRUDENTIAL STRUC MAT; A	Fixed Income	90.3	11.45	4.41	8.45	5.73	7.80	☆	6.2	☐	225-1852	None	3.25	0.94	None	Carlucci/Rodriquez	'92/'95
PRUDENTIAL STRUC MAT; B	Fixed Income	127.0	11.45	4.33	7.84	☆	☆	☆	5.6	☐	225-1852	None	None	1.66	3.00	Carlucci/Rodriquez	'92/'95
PRUDENTIAL STRUC MAT; C	Fixed Income	0.8	11.45	4.33	☆	☆	☆	☆	0.0	☐	225-1852	None	None	None	1.00	Carlucci/Rodriquez	'94/'95
PRUDENTIAL US GOVT; A	Fixed Income	47.0	10.05	7.32	13.76	8.16	8.89	☆	6.3	☐	225-1852	None	4.00	1.09	None	Carlucci/Graham	'91/'95
PRUDENTIAL US GOVT; B	Fixed Income	82.7	10.05	7.13	12.94	7.30	8.02	☆	5.7	☐	225-1852	None	None	1.75	5.00	Carlucci/Graham	'91/'95
PRUDENTIAL US GOVT; C	Fixed Income	0.1	10.05	7.16	☆	☆	☆	☆	0.0	☐	225-1852	None	None	None	1.00	Carlucci/Graham	'94/'95
PRUDENTIAL UTILITY; A	Utility	1,588.5	9.05	7.35	11.03	8.96	9.29	☆	3.5	N/A	225-1852	None	5.00	0.88	None	Spitz/Kiefer	'90/'94
PRUDENTIAL UTILITY; B	Utility	2,371.8	9.05	7.24	10.42	8.16	8.45	12.25	2.6	N/A	225-1852	None	None	1.63	5.00	Spitz/Kiefer	'87/'94
PRUDENTIAL UTILITY; C	Utility	2.0	9.05	7.24	☆	☆	☆	☆	0.0	N/A	225-1852	None	None	None	1.00	Spitz/Kiefer	'94/'94
PUTNAM ADJ RT GOVT; A	Fixed Income	86.8	10.31	2.31	5.95	2.12	4.28	☆	4.5	☐	225-1581	617-292-1000	3.25	0.99	None	Michael Martino	'94
PUTNAM ADJ RT GOVT; B	Fixed Income	30.8	10.29	2.16	5.21	1.48	☆	☆	3.9	☐	225-1581	617-292-1000	None	1.59	3.00	Michael Martino	'94
PUTNAM AMERICAN GOVT; A	Fixed Income	2,253.3	8.61	6.40	11.87	5.57	6.98	7.65	7.1	☐	225-1581	617-292-1000	4.75	0.83	None	Michael Martino	'94
PUTNAM AMERICAN GOVT; B	Fixed Income	6.3	8.58	6.30	11.21	☆	☆	☆	6.7	☐	225-1581	617-292-1000	None	None	5.00	Michael Martino	'94
PUTNAM AMERICAN GOVT; M	Fixed Income	N/A	8.61	6.36	☆	☆	☆	☆	0.0	☐	225-1581	617-292-1000	3.25	None	None	Michael Martino	'95
PUTNAM ASIA PAC GRO; A	Pacific Region	152.7	13.13	2.02	-5.57	16.77	☆	☆	0.0	☐	225-1581	617-292-1000	5.75	1.53	None	David Thomas	'91
PUTNAM ASIA PAC GRO; B	Pacific Region	131.0	12.96	1.89	-6.25	☆	☆	☆	0.0	☐	225-1581	617-292-1000	None	2.27	5.00	David Thomas	'93
PUTNAM ASST BALANCED; A ★	Global Flexible	126.3	9.10	6.84	14.99	☆	☆	☆	2.1	☐	225-1581	617-292-1000	5.75	0.83	None	Carman/Coburn	'94/'94
PUTNAM ASST BALANCED; B ★	Global Flexible	133.1	9.07	6.68	14.07	☆	☆	☆	1.5	☐	225-1581	617-292-1000	None	1.23	5.00	Carman/Coburn	'94/'94
PUTNAM ASST BALANCED; C ★	Global Flexible	N/A	9.05	6.69	☆	☆	☆	☆	0.0	☐	225-1581	617-292-1000	None	None	1.00	Carman/Coburn	'94/'94
PUTNAM ASST BALANCED; M	Global Flexible	N/A	9.09	6.70	☆	☆	☆	☆	0.0	☐	225-1581	617-292-1000	3.50	None	None	Carman/Coburn	'95/'95
PUTNAM ASST CONSV; A ★	Global Flexible	40.4	8.88	6.31	12.70	☆	☆	☆	3.0	☐	225-1581	617-292-1000	5.75	0.75	None	Carman/Coburn	'94/'94
PUTNAM ASST CONSV; B ★	Global Flexible	57.5	8.85	6.01	11.77	☆	☆	☆	2.4	☐	225-1581	617-292-1000	None	1.21	5.00	Carman/Coburn	'94/'94
PUTNAM ASST CONSV; C ★	Global Flexible	N/A	8.84	6.06	☆	☆	☆	☆	0.0	☐	225-1581	617-292-1000	None	None	1.00	Carman/Coburn	'94/'94
PUTNAM ASST CONSV; M ★	Global Flexible	N/A	8.87	6.22	☆	☆	☆	☆	0.0	☐	225-1581	617-292-1000	3.50	None	None	Carman/Coburn	'95/'95
PUTNAM ASST GROWTH; A ★	Global Flexible	137.1	9.32	7.00	16.71	☆	☆	☆	0.8	☐	225-1581	617-292-1000	5.75	0.78	None	Carman/Coburn	'94/'94
PUTNAM ASST GROWTH; B ★	Global Flexible	91.9	9.25	6.81	15.77	☆	☆	☆	0.5	☐	225-1581	617-292-1000	None	1.21	5.00	Carman/Coburn	'94/'94
PUTNAM ASST GROWTH; C ★	Global Flexible	N/A	9.22	6.84	☆	☆	☆	☆	0.0	☐	225-1581	617-292-1000	None	None	1.00	Carman/Coburn	'94/'94
PUTNAM ASST GROWTH; M ★	Global Flexible	N/A	9.28	6.79	☆	☆	☆	☆	0.0	☐	225-1581	617-292-1000	3.50	None	None	Carman/Coburn	'95/'95
PUTNAM BALANCED RET; A ★	Balanced	455.7	9.46	7.08	16.45	11.23	11.19	10.06	5.1	15.8	225-1581	617-292-1000	5.75	1.08	None	Bousa/Taubes	'92/'94
PUTNAM BALANCED RET; B ★	Balanced	7.0	9.44	6.93	15.92	☆	☆	☆	4.7	15.8	225-1581	617-292-1000	None	1.34	5.00	Bousa/Taubes	'94/'94
PUTNAM BALANCED RET; M ★	Balanced	N/A	9.45	6.95	☆	☆	☆	☆	0.0	N/A	225-1581	617-292-1000	3.50	None	None	Bousa/Taubes	'95/'95
PUTNAM CAP APPREC; A	Growth	103.7	12.56	7.63	24.18	☆	☆	☆	0.2	16.2	225-1581	617-292-1000	5.75	0.95	None	Gerald Zukowski	'93
PUTNAM CAP APPREC; B	Growth	N/A	12.50	7.39	☆	☆	☆	☆	0.0	N/A	225-1581	617-292-1000	None	None	5.00	Gerald Zukowski	'94
PUTNAM CONV INC-GRO; A	Convertible Securities	737.2	18.91	6.69	14.55	12.96	12.86	11.09	4.9	☐	225-1581	617-292-1000	5.75	0.96	None	Mullin/Pohl	'92/'92
PUTNAM CONV INC-GRO; B	Convertible Securities	52.9	18.81	6.50	13.76	☆	☆	☆	4.3	☐	225-1581	617-292-1000	None	1.71	5.00	Mullin/Pohl	'93/'93
PUTNAM CONV INC-GRO; M	Convertible Securities	N/A	18.89	6.56	☆	☆	☆	☆	0.0	☐	225-1581	617-292-1000	3.50	None	None	Mullin/Pohl	'95/'95
PUTNAM DIVIDEND GRO; A	Growth Income	49.3	10.87	8.00	21.23	10.63	10.54	☆	2.6	15.7	225-1581	617-292-1000	5.75	1.30	None	Michael Mach	'90
PUTNAM DIVIDEND GRO; B	Growth Income	11.3	10.80	7.76	20.03	☆	☆	☆	2.0	15.7	225-1581	617-292-1000	None	2.14	5.00	Michael Mach	'93
PUTNAM DVSFD EQUITY; A	Global	106.3	9.76	8.08	☆	☆	☆	☆	0.0	☐	225-1581	617-292-1000	4.50	None	None	Bousa/Taubes/Thomsen	'94/'94/'94
PUTNAM DVSFD EQUITY; B	Global	93.4	9.72	8.00	☆	☆	☆	☆	0.0	☐	225-1581	617-292-1000	None	None	5.00	Bousa/Taubes/Thomsen	'94/'94/'94
PUTNAM DVSFD INCOME; A	Fixed Income	1,557.3	11.93	5.97	9.69	8.67	11.48	☆	8.3	☐	225-1581	617-292-1000	4.75	1.01	None	Multiple Managers	N/A
PUTNAM DVSFD INCOME; B	Fixed Income	1,718.0	11.89	5.78	8.89	☆	☆	☆	7.6	☐	225-1581	617-292-1000	None	1.76	5.00	Multiple Managers	N/A
PUTNAM DVSFD INCOME; M	Fixed Income	6.8	11.91	5.92	☆	☆	☆	☆	0.0	☐	225-1581	617-292-1000	3.25	None	None	Multiple Managers	N/A
PUTNAM EQUITY INCOME; A	Equity Income	347.6	9.84	7.95	20.94	14.26	11.18	10.02	3.3	N/A	225-1581	617-292-1000	5.75	1.04	None	Edward Bousa	'92
PUTNAM EQUITY INCOME; B	Equity Income	49.9	9.82	7.67	20.06	☆	☆	☆	2.7	N/A	225-1581	617-292-1000	None	1.78	5.00	Edward Bousa	'93
PUTNAM EQUITY INCOME; M	Equity Income	N/A	9.82	7.76	☆	☆	☆	☆	0.0	N/A	225-1581	617-292-1000	3.50	None	None	Edward Bousa	'94
PUTNAM EUROPE GROWTH; A	European Region	90.7	13.87	11.58	20.75	13.25	☆	☆	0.0	☐	225-1581	617-292-1000	5.75	1.50	None	Justin Scott	'90

Fund	Objective	Net Assets	NAV	Ret 1	Ret 2	Ret 3	Rating	Ret 4	Ret 5	Yield	Risk/PE	Phone	Service	Load	Exp	CDSC	Manager	Since
PUTNAM EUROPE GROWTH; B	European Region	44.1	13.75	11.43	19.92		☆	5.46	7.80	0.0	□	617-292-1000	225-1581	None	None	5.00	Justin Scott	'94
PUTNAM EUROPE GROWTH; M	European Region	N/A	13.89	11.39			☆			0.0	□	617-292-1000	225-1581	3.50	None	None	Justin Scott	'94
PUTNAM FEDERAL INC; A	Fixed Income	440.1	9.99	6.19	12.38		☆	5.46		6.0		617-292-1000	225-1581	4.75	1.06	None	Taubes/Senter	'92/'92
PUTNAM FEDERAL INC; B	Fixed Income	1.0	9.96	6.03	11.46		☆			5.4		617-292-1000	225-1581	None	None	5.00	Taubes/Senter	'94/'94
PUTNAM FEDERAL INC; M	Fixed Income	N/A	9.99	6.15			☆			0.0		617-292-1000	225-1581	3.25	None	None	Taubes/Senter	'95/'95
GEORGE PUTNAM BOSTON; A	Balanced	1,030.7	14.65	7.43	18.29	10.37		10.69	12.41	3.8	N/A	617-292-1000	225-1581	5.75	0.95	None	Bousa/Taubes	'93/'93
GEORGE PUTNAM BOSTON; B	Balanced	207.5	14.59	7.21	17.42	9.54				3.1	N/A	617-292-1000	225-1581	None	1.71	5.00	Bousa/Taubes	'93/'93
GEORGE PUTNAM BOSTON; M	Balanced	N/A	14.61	7.25						0.0		617-292-1000	225-1581	3.50	None	None	Bousa/Taubes	'94/'94
PUTNAM GLOBAL GOVT; A	World Income	394.9	13.56	6.22	6.53		☆	4.96	8.40	5.5		617-292-1000	225-1581	4.75	1.27	None	Turner/Francis/Kohli	'92/'94/'94
PUTNAM GLOBAL GOVT; B	World Income	27.5	13.52	6.01	5.75		☆	5.75		5.0		617-292-1000	225-1581	None	1.49	5.00	Turner/Francis/Kohli	'94/'94/'94
PUTNAM GLOBAL GOVT; M	World Income	0.2	13.54	6.04			☆			0.0		617-292-1000	225-1581	3.25	1.33	None	Turner/Francis/Kohli	'95/'95/'95
PUTNAM GLOBAL GROWTH; A	Global	1,596.3	9.63	6.53	6.32	10.10		7.02	14.89	0.0		617-292-1000	225-1581	5.75		None	Regan/Zukowski	'88/'93
PUTNAM GLOBAL GROWTH; B	Global	883.6	9.40	6.33	5.43			9.25		0.0		617-292-1000	225-1581	None	2.11	5.00	Regan/Zukowski	'92/'93
PUTNAM GRO & INC II; A	Growth Income	N/A	9.61	6.31			☆			0.0		617-292-1000	225-1581	3.50	None	None	King/Kreisel	'95/'95
PUTNAM GRO & INC; A	Growth Income	71.5	9.88	8.17	21.13	12.72		12.28	14.35	0.0	16.5	617-292-1000	225-1581	5.75	0.95	None	King/Kreisel	'93/'92
PUTNAM GRO & INC; B	Growth Income	7,054.8	14.88	8.24	20.19	11.87				2.7	16.5	617-292-1000	225-1581	5.75	1.70	5.00	King/Kreisel	'93/'93
PUTNAM GROWTH FUND; A ■	Growth	4,259.1	14.77	8.12	32.89		☆	9.30	14.97	2.0	N/A	617-292-1000	225-1581	None	0.92	None	Chuck Swanberg	'93
PUTNAM HI YLD ADVTG; A	Fixed Income	3.5	11.83	10.87	7.04		☆			1.6		617-292-1000	225-1581	4.75	1.03	None	Jin Ho	'87
PUTNAM HI YLD ADVTG; B	Fixed Income	773.3	9.39	4.99	6.27		☆	9.00	14.00	10.9		617-292-1000	225-1581	None	1.02	5.00	Jin Ho	'85/'86
PUTNAM HIGH YIELD; A	Fixed Income	130.9	9.37	4.82	6.86		☆		10.80	10.3		617-292-1000	225-1581	4.75	0.94	None	D'Alelio/Ho	'93/'93
PUTNAM HIGH YIELD; B	Fixed Income	2,957.6	11.92	5.15	6.00		☆			10.6		617-292-1000	225-1581	5.75	1.69	5.00	D'Alelio/Ho	'93/'94
PUTNAM HLTH SCIENCES; A	Health/Biotechnology	695.2	11.88	4.88	35.80	11.80		12.22	15.53	9.9	21.3	617-292-1000	225-1581		1.12	None	Soja/Giblin	'93/'94
PUTNAM HLTH SCIENCES; B	Health/Biotechnology	854.0	33.96	3.60	34.79		☆			0.8	21.3	617-292-1000	225-1581	5.75	1.87	5.00	Soja/Giblin	N/A
PUTNAM INCOME; A	Fixed Income	93.6	33.55	3.39	12.85	8.17		10.22	9.73	0.4		617-292-1000	225-1581	None	0.83	None	Multiple Managers	N/A
PUTNAM INCOME; B	Fixed Income	870.9	6.98	6.49	12.06		☆			7.1		617-292-1000	225-1581	4.75	1.59	5.00	Multiple Managers	'94
PUTNAM INCOME; M	Fixed Income	216.4	6.96	6.31			☆			6.4		617-292-1000	225-1581	5.75		None	Multiple Managers	'94
PUTNAM INT GOVT INC; A	Fixed Income	N/A	6.96	6.32	9.87		☆			0.0		617-292-1000	225-1581	3.25	1.12	None	Michael Martino	'94
PUTNAM INT GOVT INC; B	Fixed Income	50.7	4.83	5.06	9.21	8.17		12.00	13.44	5.9		617-292-1000	225-1581	None	0.99	3.00	Michael Martino	'94
PUTNAM INVESTORS; A	Growth	21.3	4.83	4.90	25.28	16.08				5.3		617-292-1000	225-1581	5.75	1.77	5.00	Cobb/Santos/Sonderling	88/'94/'94
PUTNAM INVESTORS; B	Growth	876.0	8.64	11.05	24.28		☆			0.0	18.0	617-292-1000	225-1581	None		None	Cobb/Santos/Sonderling	'93/'94/'94
PUTNAM INVESTORS; M	Growth	39.3	8.48	10.85			☆			0.0	18.0	617-292-1000	225-1581	3.50	1.24	5.00	Cobb/Santos/Sonderling	'94/'94/'94
PUTNAM NATURAL-RES; A	Natural Resources	N/A	8.62	11.08	14.40	8.69		6.27	9.61	0.0	N/A	617-292-1000	225-1581	5.75	1.11	None	Jeanne Mockard	'94
PUTNAM NATURAL-RES; B	Natural Resources	132.7	15.59	3.79	13.72		☆			1.5	18.8	617-292-1000	225-1581	None	1.23	5.00	Jeanne Mockard	'94
PUTNAM NEW OPPTY; A	Growth	23.2	15.47	3.62	36.34	28.71				1.3	18.8	617-292-1000	225-1581	5.75	2.04	None	Daniel Miller	'90
PUTNAM NEW OPPTY; B	Growth	1,184.8	29.59	6.71	35.39		☆			0.0	25.8	617-292-1000	225-1581	3.50		None	Daniel Miller	'93
PUTNAM NEW OPPTY; M	Growth	873.9	29.10	6.52			☆			0.0	25.8	617-292-1000	225-1581	5.75	1.16	5.00	Daniel Miller	'94
PUTNAM OTC EMERG GRO; A	Small Company Growth	N/A	29.51	6.57	37.62	25.69		15.90	16.91	0.0	N/A	617-292-1000	225-1581	3.50	1.94	None	Miller/Callinan	'94
PUTNAM OTC EMERG GRO; B	Small Company Growth	582.2	12.62	6.77	36.45		☆			0.0	N/A	617-292-1000	225-1581	5.75	2.17	5.00	Miller/Callinan	'94/'94
PUTNAM OTC EMERG GRO; M	Small Company Growth	109.5	12.40	6.53			☆			0.0	N/A	617-292-1000	225-1581	None		None	Miller/Callinan	'94/'94
PUTNAM OVERSEAS GRO; A	International	32.0	12.58	6.61	3.76	12.34				0.0		617-292-1000	225-1581	3.50	1.16	5.00	Justin Scott	'94/'94
PUTNAM OVERSEAS GRO; B	International	22.9	12.00	5.13	3.00		☆			7.4		617-292-1000	225-1581	3.25	0.81	None	Justin Scott	
PUTNAM OVERSEAS GRO; M	International	N/A	12.09	4.90			☆	7.67	9.99	0.0	N/A	617-292-1000	225-1581	3.50	1.94	None	Sheldon N. Simon	'92
PUTNAM PREFERRED INC; A	Equity Income	125.4	8.40	5.04	9.68		☆	7.87		7.1	N/A	617-292-1000	225-1581	2.00	0.85	None	Sheldon N. Simon	'95
PUTNAM PREFERRED INC; M	Equity Income	N/A	8.39	4.81			☆			0.0		617-292-1000	225-1581	3.25		None	Michael Martino	'94
PUTNAM US GOVT INC; A	Fixed Income	3,009.8	12.89	4.98	11.08	5.42		7.47	8.35	7.1		617-292-1000	225-1581	4.75	1.60	5.00	Michael Martino	'94
PUTNAM US GOVT INC; B	Fixed Income	1,658.0	12.85	4.72	10.28	4.64	☆			6.4		617-292-1000	225-1581	None				

★ PUTNAM ASST BALANCED; A,B,C--Fund has been reclassified from Flexible to Global Flexible.
★ PUTNAM ASST GROWTH; A,B,C,M--Fund has been reclassified from Flexible to Global Flexible.
★ PUTNAM ASST CONSV; A,B,C,M--Fund has been reclassified from Flexible to Global Flexible.
★ PUTNAM BALANCED RET; A,B,M--Fund has been reclassified from Income to Balanced.

PERFORMANCE OF MUTUAL FUNDS (continued)

FUND NAME	OBJECTIVE	ASSETS ($ MIL) 5/31/95	NAV ($/SHR) 6/30/95	RETURN THROUGH 6/30 — QTR	1YR	3YRS (Ann.)	5YRS (Ann.)	10YRS (Ann.)	DIV YLD %	P/E RATIO	PHONE 800	In-State	FEES Load	Exp. Ratio	Redemption	MANAGER	SINCE
PUTNAM US GOVT INC; M ■	Fixed Income	N/A	12.89	4.96	☆	☆	☆	☆	0.0	□	225-1581	617-292-1000	3.25	None	None	Michael Martino	'95
PUTNAM UTIL GR & INC; A	Utility	56.1	9.72	7.72	16.09	9.15	☆	☆	4.7	14.0	225-1581	617-292-1000	5.75	1.08	None	Simon/Ray	'90/'94
PUTNAM UTIL GR & INC; B	Utility	541.3	9.68	7.56	15.17	8.36	☆	☆	4.1	14.0	225-1581	617-292-1000	None	1.83	5.00	Simon/Ray	'92/'94
PUTNAM UTIL GR & INC; M	Utility	N/A	9.70	7.60	☆	☆	☆	☆	0.0	N/A	225-1581	617-292-1000	3.50	None	None	Simon/Ray	'95/'95
PUTNAM VISTA; A	Growth	729.0	8.53	9.78	25.15	15.89	24.86	14.68	0.0	N/A	225-1581	617-292-1000	5.75	1.09	None	Silver/Santosus/Mufson	'91/'94/'94
PUTNAM VISTA; B	Growth	204.2	8.40	9.66	24.34	☆	☆	☆	0.0	N/A	225-1581	617-292-1000	None	1.87	5.00	Silver/Santosus/Mufson	'92/'94/'94
PUTNAM VISTA; M	Growth	N/A	8.50	9.68	☆	☆	☆	☆	0.0	N/A	225-1581	617-292-1000	3.50	None	None	Silver/Santosus/Mufson	'94/'94/'94
PUTNAM VOYAGER; A	Capital Appreciation	4,232.2	13.49	8.27	29.86	18.06	16.79	17.48	0.0	N/A	225-1581	617-292-1000	5.75	1.10	None	Weatherbie/Swanberg	'83/'94
PUTNAM VOYAGER; B	Capital Appreciation	1,542.0	13.12	8.07	28.92	17.13	☆	☆	0.0	N/A	225-1581	617-292-1000	None	1.84	5.00	Weatherbie/Swanberg	'92/'94
PUTNAM VOYAGER; M	Capital Appreciation	N/A	13.46	8.20	☆	☆	☆	☆	0.0	N/A	225-1581	617-292-1000	3.50	None	None	Weatherbie/Swanberg	'94/'94
QUALIVEST INTMDT BD; A	Fixed Income	0.3	10.12	4.57	☆	☆	☆	☆	0.0	□	743-8637	None	3.50	None	None	Curry A. Garvin	'94
QUALIVEST INTMDT BD; C	Fixed Income	0.1	10.02	4.31	☆	☆	☆	☆	0.0	□	743-8637	None	None	1.00	1.00	Curry A. Garvin	'94
QUALIVEST INTMDT BD; Y ▨	Fixed Income	137.9	10.21	4.59	☆	☆	☆	☆	0.0	□	743-8637	None	None	None	None	Curry A. Garvin	'94
QUALIVEST LRG CO VAL; A	Growth	0.7	11.72	8.68	☆	☆	☆	☆	0.0	N/A	743-8637	None	4.50	None	None	John R. Dozier	'94
QUALIVEST LRG CO VAL; C	Growth	0.2	11.57	8.54	☆	☆	☆	☆	0.0	N/A	743-8637	None	None	1.00	1.00	John R. Dozier	'94
QUALIVEST LRG CO VAL; Y ▨	Growth	92.9	11.75	8.80	☆	☆	☆	☆	0.0	N/A	743-8637	None	None	None	None	John R. Dozier	'94
QUALIVEST SM CO VAL; A	Small Company Growth	0.9	12.52	14.27	☆	☆	☆	☆	0.0	N/A	743-8637	None	4.50	None	None	Dale E. Benson	'94
QUALIVEST SM CO VAL; C	Small Company Growth	0.2	12.45	14.12	☆	☆	☆	☆	0.0	N/A	743-8637	None	None	1.00	1.00	Dale E. Benson	'94
QUALIVEST SM CO VAL; Y ▨	Small Company Growth	184.1	12.55	14.49	☆	☆	☆	☆	0.0	N/A	743-8637	None	None	None	None	Dale E. Benson	'94
QUANT GROW & INC; INSTL	Growth & Income	2.1	14.83	8.09	22.85	☆	☆	☆	1.5	16.5	331-1244	617-259-1144	None	1.23	1.00	Holmes/Esielonis	'94/'93
QUANT GROW & INC; SHS	Growth & Income	39.2	14.81	7.94	22.32	12.44	11.09	14.22	1.1	16.5	331-1244	617-259-1144	None	1.69	1.00	Holmes/Esielonis	'94/'93
QUANT INTL EQTY; SHS	International	28.4	10.27	2.09	-2.63	9.29	0.45	☆	1.3	15.4	331-1244	617-259-1144	None	1.91	1.00	Davis/Umstead	'87/'94
QUANT NUMERIC; INSTL ⊠	Small Company Growth	40.0	17.57	9.47	31.78	☆	☆	☆	0.0	N/A	331-1244	617-259-1144	None	1.36	None	John C. Bogle, Jr.	'93
QUANT NUMERIC; SHS ⊠	Small Company Growth	56.1	17.30	9.42	31.15	☆	☆	☆	0.0	N/A	331-1244	None	None	1.84	1.00	John C. Bogle, Jr.	'92
QUEST FOR VALUE FUND; A	Capital Appreciation	263.3	13.73	10.37	24.88	14.59	13.45	12.93	0.6	15.4	232-3863	None	5.50	1.71	None	Eileen Rominger	'89
QUEST FOR VALUE FUND; B	Capital Appreciation	27.0	13.62	10.19	24.15	☆	☆	☆	0.5	15.4	232-3863	None	None	2.24	5.00	Eileen Rominger	'93
QUEST FOR VALUE FUND; C ✿	Capital Appreciation	7.3	13.61	10.29	24.25	☆	☆	☆	0.6	15.4	232-3863	None	None	2.28	1.00	Eileen Rominger	'93
QUEST VALUE GLBL EQ; A	Global	155.0	14.50	9.19	12.65	12.93	8.48	☆	0.0	□	232-3863	None	5.50	1.92	None	R.J. Glasebrook II	'90
QUEST VALUE GLBL EQ; B	Global	14.1	14.35	8.96	12.04	☆	☆	☆	0.0	□	232-3863	None	None	2.50	5.00	R.J. Glasebrook II	'93
QUEST VALUE GLBL EQ; C ✿	Global	3.8	14.32	8.90	11.81	☆	☆	☆	0.0	□	232-3863	None	None	2.66	1.00	R.J. Glasebrook II	'93
QUEST VALUE GLBL INC; A	World Income	5.4	8.90	6.52	12.09	2.77	☆	☆	6.7	□	232-3863	None	3.00	1.65	None	Robert J. Bluestone	'91
QUEST VALUE GLBL INC; B	World Income	1.2	8.90	6.33	11.25	☆	☆	☆	6.2	□	232-3863	None	None	2.41	5.00	Robert J. Bluestone	'93
QUEST VALUE GLBL INC; C	World Income	0.3	8.90	6.22	10.73	☆	☆	☆	5.7	□	232-3863	None	None	2.70	1.00	Robert J. Bluestone	'93
QUEST VALUE GOVT INC; A	Fixed Income	117.6	11.23	3.85	8.53	5.00	7.29	☆	5.7	□	232-3863	None	4.75	1.20	None	Robert J. Bluestone	'88
QUEST VALUE GOVT INC; B	Fixed Income	10.5	11.22	3.66	7.75	☆	☆	☆	5.0	□	232-3863	None	None	1.92	5.00	Robert J. Bluestone	'93
QUEST VALUE GOVT INC; C ✿	Fixed Income	1.9	11.22	3.52	7.64	☆	☆	☆	4.9	□	232-3863	None	None	1.94	1.00	Robert J. Bluestone	'93
QUEST VALUE GR & INC; A ✿	Growth Income	34.0	10.83	9.98	19.86	12.20	☆	☆	2.9	16.1	232-3863	None	4.75	1.86	None	Colin Glinsman	'93
QUEST VALUE GR & INC; B	Growth Income	5.0	10.80	9.78	19.14	☆	☆	☆	2.5	16.1	232-3863	None	None	2.47	5.00	Colin Glinsman	'93
QUEST VALUE GR & INC; C ✿	Growth Income	1.0	10.81	9.70	18.78	☆	☆	☆	2.3	16.1	232-3863	None	None	2.62	1.00	Colin Glinsman	'93
QUEST VALUE INV QUAL; A	Fixed Income	48.3	10.73	8.01	15.36	8.41	☆	☆	6.6	□	232-3863	None	4.75	1.29	None	Robert J. Bluestone	'90
QUEST VALUE INV QUAL; B	Fixed Income	10.0	10.73	7.85	14.64	☆	☆	☆	6.0	□	232-3863	None	None	1.92	5.00	Robert J. Bluestone	'93
QUEST VALUE INV QUAL; C ✿	Fixed Income	3.5	10.73	7.84	14.63	☆	☆	☆	6.0	□	232-3863	None	None	1.90	1.00	Robert J. Bluestone	'93
QUEST VALUE OPPTY; A	Flexible	261.1	23.52	14.45	31.02	17.16	18.19	☆	0.5	12.8	232-3863	None	5.50	1.78	None	R.J. Glasebrook II	'89
QUEST VALUE OPPTY; B	Flexible	125.9	23.31	14.26	30.30	☆	☆	☆	0.5	12.8	232-3863	None	None	2.34	5.00	R.J. Glasebrook II	'93
QUEST VALUE OPPTY; C ✿	Flexible	25.7	23.30	14.27	30.24	☆	☆	☆	0.5	12.8	232-3863	None	None	2.35	1.00	R.J. Glasebrook II	'93

Fund	Objective	Assets ($Mil)	NAV	(3)	(4)	(5)	(6)	Rank	Yld	P/E	Phone (local)	Phone (800)	Max Load	12b-1	Def. Load	Manager	Since
QUEST VALUE SM CAP; A	Small Company Growth	119.7	16.96	8.30	12.18	11.62	13.55	☆	0.0	18.9	None	232-3863	5.50	1.88	None	Jenny Beth Jones	'89
QUEST VALUE SM CAP; B	Small Company Growth	20.4	16.79	8.11	11.51	☆	☆	☆	0.0	18.9	None	232-3863	None	2.48	5.00	Jenny Beth Jones	'93
QUEST VALUE SM CAP; C ✷	Small Company Growth	6.4	16.79	8.11	11.43	☆	☆	☆	0.0	18.9	None	232-3863	None	2.59	1.00	Jenny Beth Jones	'93
RAINBOW FUND	Capital Appreciation	1.5	5.15	5.97	11.07	2.67	3.19	6.67	0.0	13.2	212-983-2980	None	None	3.36	None	Robert M. Furman	N/A
RAINIER BALANCED	Flexible	14.6	13.44	3.70	16.38	☆	☆	☆	2.0	N/A	None	248-6314	None	None	Team Managed	
RAINIER CORE EQTY	Growth	25.1	15.27	10.33	30.70	☆	☆	☆	0.5	N/A	None	248-6314	None	None	Margard/Veterane	'94/'94
RAINIER INTMDT FXD INC	Fixed Income	6.9	12.38	4.25	8.59	☆	☆	☆	5.0	N/A	None	248-6314	None	None	Frost/Achey	'94/'94
RAINIER SM/MID CAP EQ	Midcap	11.7	15.30	10.07	32.83	☆	☆	☆	0.4	N/A	None	248-6314	None	None	Margard/Veterane	'94/'94
RBB EMERG MKTS; BEA ∎	Emerging Markets	133.3	17.59	13.41	-10.05	☆	☆	☆	0.4	N/A	212-878-0600	888-9723	None	1.50	1.50	Emilio Bassini	'93
RBB GLBL FIXED INC; BEA ∎	World Income	19.7	15.79	5.62	10.83	☆	☆	☆	5.6	N/A	212-878-0600	888-9723	None	1.50	1.50	Robert Moore	'95
RBB GOVT SECS	Fixed Income	53.7	9.62	3.08	8.05	5.48	☆	☆	8.0	N/A	212-878-0600	888-9723	4.75	0.64	None	Robert Morgan	'92
RBB INTL EQ; BEA ∎	International	772.4	17.65	4.42	-3.97	☆	☆	☆	0.0	N/A	212-878-0600	888-9723	None	1.25	1.00	Emilio Bassini	'92
RBB LAFFER/CANTO EQUITY	Growth Income	0.5	10.99	5.77	16.51	☆	☆	☆	0.6	N/A	212-878-0600	888-9723	4.75	1.50	None	Laffer/Canto	'93/'93
RBB STRAT FXD INC; BEA ∎	Fixed Income	148.5	15.26	9.43	7.34	☆	☆	☆	8.8	N/A	212-878-0600	888-9723	None	1.00	0.50	Robert Moore	'95
RBB US CORE EQTY; BEA ∎	Growth	29.2	16.98	8.78	☆	☆	☆	☆	0.0	N/A	212-878-0600	888-9723	None	None	None	William W. Priest	'94
RBB US CORE FXD INC; BEA	Fixed Income	90.1	15.23	6.28	11.41	☆	☆	☆	5.5	N/A	212-878-0600	888-9723	None	None	None	Robert Moore	'95
REA-GRAHAM BALANCED	Global Flexible	13.8	13.82	5.34	6.72	2.71	3.47	6.06	0.7	N/A	310-208-2282	433-1998	4.75	2.37	None	Rea/Rea	'82/'82
REGIS II MJI INTL EQTY	International	6.0	9.38	1.30	☆	☆	☆	☆	0.0	N/A	617-557-8000	638-7983	None	None	None	Rodger Scullion	'94
REGIS ACADIAN EMRG MKTS	Emerging Markets	31.0	11.81	12.91	4.61	☆	☆	☆	0.0	N/A	617-557-8000	638-7983	None	2.07	None	Team Managed	N/A
REGIS ACADIAN INTL EQ	International	2.4	11.59	1.49	-1.38	☆	☆	☆	0.0	N/A	617-557-8000	638-7983	None	2.50	None	Team Managed	N/A
REGIS C&B BALANCED	Balanced	34.8	12.83	5.68	15.67	8.40	10.40	☆	3.6	17.2	617-557-8000	638-7983	None	1.00	None	Team Managed	N/A
REGIS C&B EQUITY	Equity Income	224.9	14.89	6.12	19.93	9.69	11.44	☆	2.2	18.4	617-557-8000	638-7983	None	0.82	None	Team Managed	N/A
REGIS DSI DISCIP VALUE	Fixed Income	51.1	11.10	6.32	17.81	12.53	10.57	☆	2.0	15.4	617-557-8000	638-7983	None	1.04	None	McCullough/Stephenson	'89/'89
REGIS DSI LTD MAT BOND	Fixed Income	30.7	9.60	3.33	7.99	4.57	7.38	☆	6.5	N/A	617-557-8000	638-7983	None	0.79	None	Isaac N. Frankel	
REGIS FMA SMALL COMPANY	Small Company Growth	20.7	12.41	5.98	15.90	18.86	☆	☆	0.2	N/A	617-557-8000	638-7983	None	1.03	None	Patricia Falkowski	'92
REGIS ICM EQUITY	Growth Income	6.2	11.61	8.20	19.24	☆	☆	☆	1.9	N/A	617-557-8000	638-7983	None	0.90	None	Team Managed	N/A
REGIS ICM FIXED INCOME	Fixed Income	15.1	10.36	5.71	11.42	☆	☆	☆	4.9	N/A	617-557-8000	638-7983	None	0.84	None	Team Managed	N/A
REGIS ICM SMALL COMPANY	Small Company Growth	184.2	18.36	7.94	23.23	21.12	18.27	☆	0.5	12.5	617-557-8000	638-7983	None	0.93	None	Team Managed	N/A
REGIS MCKEE INTL EQTY	International	70.8	10.09	6.66	1.51	☆	☆	☆	0.5	N/A	617-557-8000	638-7983	None		None	Walter C. Bean	'94
REGIS RHJ SMALL CAP	Small Company Growth	14.0	13.43	13.52	☆	☆	☆	☆	0.1	N/A	617-557-8000	638-7983	None		None	Thomas W. McDowell, Jr.	'92
REGIS SAMI PRFD STK INC	Utility	52.2	9.13	1.32	3.79	3.07	☆	☆	7.5	N/A	617-557-8000	638-7983	None	0.89	None	Team Managed	N/A
REGIS SIRACH FIXED INC	Fixed Income	14.9	9.88	5.89	11.53	8.40	☆	☆	5.9	17.3	617-557-8000	638-7983	None	0.75	None	Team Managed	N/A
REGIS SIRACH GROWTH	Growth	92.5	10.83	8.73	18.06	11.08	☆	☆	1.3	17.1	617-557-8000	638-7983	None	0.92	None	Team Managed	N/A
REGIS SIRACH SH-TM RSVS	Fixed Income	19.2	10.18	1.80	5.52	4.87	☆	☆	4.4	N/A	617-557-8000	638-7983	None	0.50	None	Team Managed	N/A
REGIS SIRACH SPEC EQ	Small Company Growth	499.7	16.76	7.09	19.71	15.16	14.45	☆	0.5	25.7	617-557-8000	638-7983	None	0.88	None	Team Managed	'94
REGIS SIRACH STRAT BAL	Balanced	95.4	10.40	8.33	15.98	☆	☆	☆	3.3	N/A	617-557-8000	638-7983	None	0.90	None	Team Managed	N/A
REGIS STRLG PTNR BAL	Balanced	68.3	11.59	5.65	12.05	☆	☆	☆	3.3	17.3	617-557-8000	638-7983	None	1.01	None	Team Managed	N/A
REGIS STRLG PTNR EQ	Equity Income	25.4	13.05	6.70	15.86	☆	☆	☆	1.4	17.1	617-557-8000	638-7983	None	0.99	None	Team Managed	N/A
REGIS STRLG PTNR SHT FXD	Fixed Income	22.6	9.93	2.95	7.09	☆	☆	☆	5.5	N/A	617-557-8000	638-7983	None	0.53	None	Team Managed	N/A
REGIS T&W EQUITY	Small Company Growth	52.6	12.10	4.85	18.03	☆	☆	☆	1.6	N/A	617-557-8000	638-7983	None	1.10	None	Team Managed	N/A
REGIS T&W FIXED INCOME	Fixed Income	43.1	10.29	5.91	11.63	☆	☆	☆	5.2	N/A	617-557-8000	638-7983	None	1.02	None	Team Managed	N/A
REGIS T&W INTL EQUITY	International	61.2	13.25	4.25	4.31	☆	☆	☆	0.7	N/A	617-557-8000	638-7983	None	1.38	None	Rothenberg/Davies	'92/'92
REICH & TANG EQUITY	Midcap	107.5	17.91	4.95	21.64	15.29	12.84	☆	1.3	19.8	221-3079	None	None	1.17	None	Robert Hoerle	'85
REICH & TANG GOVT SEC	Fixed Income	4.5	N/A	N/A	N/A	N/A	N/A	13.73	0.0	N/A	221-3079	None	None	0.55	None	Molly Flewnarty	'88
REMBRANDT ASIAN TIGR; INV	Pacific Region	0.8	10.22	7.24	10.13	☆	☆	☆	0.0	N/A	443-4725	None	4.50	1.90	None	Ruelse/Nijhvis	'94/'94
REMBRANDT ASIAN TIGR; TR	Pacific Region	21.8	10.24	7.34	10.43	☆	☆	☆	0.2	N/A	443-4725	None	None	1.60	None	Ruelse/Nijhvis	'94/'94
REMBRANDT BALANCED; INV	Flexible	3.4	10.36	6.03	12.29	☆	☆	☆	3.1	16.8	443-4725	None	4.50	1.24	None	Cerney/Rumas/Gidley	'93/'93/'93
REMBRANDT BALANCED; TR	Flexible	70.3	10.36	6.11	12.63	☆	☆	☆	3.4	16.8	443-4725	None	None	0.94	None	Cerney/Rumas/Gidley	'93/'93/'93
REMBRANDT GLBL FXD; INV	World Income	0.1	11.11	4.12	17.86	☆	☆	☆	4.7	N/A	443-4725	None	4.50	1.41	None	Roy Scheepe	'94
REMBRANDT GLBL FXD; TR	World Income	17.7	11.13	4.12	18.12	☆	☆	☆	5.0	N/A	443-4725	None	None	1.16	None	Roy Scheepe	'94

FUND NAME	OBJECTIVE	ASSETS ($ MIL) 5/31/95	NAV ($/SHR) 6/30/95	RETURN THROUGH 6/30 (Annualized)					DIV YLD %	P/E RATIO	PHONE NUMBER 800	In-State	FEES Load	Redemption	Exp. Ratio	MANAGER	SINCE
				QTR	1YR	3YRS	5YRS	10YRS									
REMBRANDT GROWTH; INV	Growth	2.1	11.58	10.51	20.75	☆	☆	☆	1.1	18.0	443-4725	None	4.50	None	1.33	Bonetti/Dibble/Ellefson	'93/'93/'93
REMBRANDT GROWTH; TR	Growth	82.9	11.57	10.59	21.12	☆	☆	☆	1.3	18.0	443-4725	None	None	None	1.02	Bonetti/Dibble/Ellefson	'93/'93/'93
REMBRANDT INTL EQ; INV	International	1.5	13.87	3.97	8.25	☆	☆	☆	0.0	□□□	443-4725	None	4.50	None	1.73	Gijs Dorrasteijn	'93
REMBRANDT INTL EQ; TR	International	61.5	13.92	4.04	8.30	☆	☆	☆	0.0	□□□	443-4725	None	None	None	1.43	Gijs Dorrasteijn	'93
REMBRANDT SH/INT GVT; INV	Fixed Income	3.2	9.82	4.26	8.58	☆	☆	☆	5.1		443-4725	None	4.50	None	1.02	Gidley/Pratt	'93/'93
REMBRANDT SH/INT GVT; TR	Fixed Income	78.8	9.83	4.32	8.84	☆	☆	☆	5.3	17.4	443-4725	None	None	None	0.74	Gidley/Pratt	'93/'93
REMBRANDT SMALL CAP; INV	Small Company Growth	0.3	10.62	7.38	13.70	☆	☆	☆	0.0	□□	443-4725	None	4.50	None	1.38	Barbara Knapp	'93
REMBRANDT SMALL CAP; TR	Small Company Growth	14.6	10.62	7.57	14.03	☆	☆	☆	0.3	17.4	443-4725	None	None	None	1.06	Barbara Knapp	'93
REMBRANDT TXBL FXD; INV	Fixed Income	0.5	10.02	5.85	11.19	☆	☆	☆	5.6	□□	443-4725	None	4.50	None	0.98	Gidley/Pratt	'93/'93
REMBRANDT TXBL FXD; TR	Fixed Income	112.3	9.99	5.93	11.29	☆	☆	☆	5.9		443-4725	None	None	None	0.72	Gidley/Pratt	'93/'93
REMBRANDT VALUE; INV	Growth	1.0	11.16	6.38	17.24	☆	☆	☆	2.9	16.0	443-4725	None	4.50	None	1.37	Cerney/Rumas	'93/'93
REMBRANDT VALUE; TR	Growth	91.6	11.15	6.56	17.62	☆	☆	☆	3.2	16.0	443-4725	None	None	None	1.06	Cerney/Rumas	'93/'93
REPUBLIC FDS FIXED INC	Fixed Income	17.1	10.79	5.66	☆	☆	☆	☆	0.0	N/A	638-1896	212-644-1400	None	None	None	Miller Anderson & Sherr.	'95
RESERVE SPEC BLUE CHIP ★	Growth	2.0	13.02	17.19	☆	☆	☆	☆	0.0	N/A	223-5547	212-977-9880	4.00	None	None	Charles V. Moore	'95
RESERVE SPEC EMER GROWTH ★	Small Company Growth	1.2	13.36	16.68	☆	☆	☆	☆	0.0	N/A	223-5547	212-977-9880	4.50	None	None	Edwin Vroom	'95
RESERVE SPEC INFRMD INV ★	Growth Income	6.8	14.26	33.40	☆	☆	☆	☆	0.0	N/A	223-5547	212-977-9880	4.00	None	None	Thomas Fitzgerald	'95
RET SYS CORE EQUITY	Growth Income	4.7	15.30	15.38	34.10	18.83	☆	☆	1.0	N/A	772-3615	212-503-0160	None	None	0.90	Jim Coughlin	'91
RET SYS EMERG GROWTH EQ	Small Company Growth	2.2	16.45	7.31	35.81	26.00	☆	☆	0.0	N/A	772-3615	212-503-0160	None	None	1.85	Richard Frucci	'91
RET SYS INT FXD-INC	Fixed Income	5.0	10.83	4.51	8.42	6.35	☆	☆	5.1	□□	772-3615	212-503-0160	None	None	0.90	Herb Kuhl	'91
RETIRE PLAN BOND; A	Fixed Income	21.4	5.98	3.30	☆	☆	☆	☆	0.0	□□□	279-0279	505-983-4335	4.75	None	None	Carolyn Spolidono	'95
RETIRE PLAN BOND; B	Fixed Income	16.7	5.97	3.11	6.99	3.88	6.07	6.71	7.2		279-0279	505-983-4335	None	4.00	2.38	Carolyn Spolidono	'95
RETIRE PLAN CV SEC; A	Convertible Securities	51.6	17.75	8.23	12.89	12.00	☆	☆	3.9	17.3	279-0279	505-983-4335	4.75	None	1.20	Andrew A. Davis	'94
RETIRE PLAN CV SEC; B	Convertible Securities	0.1	17.72	8.38	☆	☆	☆	☆	0.0	17.3	279-0279	505-983-4335	None	4.00	None	Andrew A. Davis	'95
RETIRE PLAN FINL VAL; A	Financial Services	65.2	13.30	12.81	24.41	18.41	☆	☆	0.3	N/A	279-0279	505-983-4335	4.75	None	1.24	Christopher C. Davis	'94
RETIRE PLAN FINL VAL; B	Financial Services	0.2	13.24	12.49	☆	☆	☆	☆	0.0	N/A	279-0279	505-983-4335	None	4.00	None	Christopher C. Davis	'94
RETIRE PLAN GROWTH; A	Growth	18.4	17.66	14.38	28.77	17.53	11.59	14.13	0.0	17.3	279-0279	505-983-4335	4.75	None	None	Graham Tanaka	'94
RETIRE PLAN GROWTH; B	Growth	33.5	17.56	14.17	☆	☆	☆	☆	0.0	17.3	279-0279	505-983-4335	None	4.00	2.15	Graham Tanaka	'87
RETIRE PLAN RE SECS; A	Real Estate	24.9	15.03	2.95	1.09	☆	☆	☆	4.1	N/A	279-0279	505-983-4335	4.75	None	1.86	Andrew A. Davis	'94
RETIRE PLAN RE SECS; B	Real Estate	0.1	15.00	1.56	☆	☆	☆	☆	0.0	N/A	279-0279	505-983-4335	None	4.00	None	Andrew A. Davis	'94
REVEST GROWTH & INCOME	Growth Income	30.8	10.55	5.95	☆	☆	☆	☆	0.0	N/A	221-4268	212-355-7511	None	1.00	None	Thomas R. Ebright	'94
REYNOLDS BLUE CHIP GRO	Growth Income	24.4	17.80	16.19	32.72	8.00	7.52	☆	0.4	19.5	338-1579	415-461-7860	None	None	1.50	Frederick L. Reynolds	'88
REYNOLDS OPPORTUNITY	Growth	7.9	12.29	12.24	38.87	10.22	☆	☆	0.0	25.4	338-1579	415-461-7860	None	None	2.00	Frederick L. Reynolds	'92
REYNOLDS US GOVT BOND	Fixed Income	2.8	9.87	4.12	7.40	4.64	☆	☆	5.6		338-1579	415-461-7860	None	None	0.86	Frederick L. Reynolds	'92
RIGHTIME BLUE CHIP FUND	Growth Income	235.8	30.75	8.85	15.33	10.14	9.99	☆	1.4	17.0	242-1421	215-887-8111	4.75	None	2.22	Rights/Soslow/Houser	'87/'88/'88
RIGHTIME FUND	Growth Income	145.5	34.85	9.80	15.31	10.86	10.53	☆	1.2	N/A	242-1421	215-887-8111	None	None	2.51	Rights/Soslow/Houser	'85/'88/'88
RIGHTIME GOVERNMENT SEC	Fixed Income	22.3	12.93	0.93	4.30	5.55	4.57	☆	4.8		242-1421	215-887-8111	4.75	None	1.90	Rights/Soslow/Houser	'86/'86/'88
RIGHTIME MIDCAP FUND	Midcap	70.6	30.93	8.49	13.44	11.27	☆	☆	1.5	18.2	242-1421	215-887-8111	4.75	None	2.28	Rights/Soslow/Houser	'92/'92/'91
RIGHTIME SOC AWARENESS	Growth	7.0	29.61	7.83	12.88	8.91	7.53	☆	1.6	N/A	242-1421	215-887-8111	4.75	None	2.56	Rights/Soslow/Houser	'90/'90/'90
RIMCO BOND	Fixed Income	48.2	9.74	6.49	10.87	7.16	☆	☆	5.9		934-3883	202-835-4280	3.50	None	0.68	Bruce Holmquist	'94
RIMCO STOCK	Growth Income	70.1	13.39	7.69	22.70	16.11	☆	☆	1.5	16.7	934-3883	202-835-4280	3.50	None	1.00	Bob Von Pentz	'94
RIVERFRONT INCOME EQUITY ☞	Equity Income	45.3	11.70	5.89	20.59	☆	☆	☆	2.5	18.1	424-2295	None	4.50	None	1.30	SunBank	'92
RIVERFRONT US GOVT INC ☞	Fixed Income	36.5	9.49	4.87	9.96	☆	☆	☆	5.7	N/A	424-2295	None	4.50	None	0.86	David Land	'92
RIVERSIDE CAP EQTY&MUNI	Balanced	1.3	9.82	2.14	☆	☆	☆	☆	0.0	□□□	874-8376	None	4.00	None	None	Alfred Jordan	'94
RIVERSIDE CAP FXD INC	Fixed Income	41.0	9.27	1.95	4.83	3.98	☆	☆	6.4		874-8376	None	3.00	None	1.37	Alfred Jordan	'91
RIVERSIDE CAP GOVT SECS	Fixed Income	7.7	10.15	4.03	8.03	☆	☆	☆	5.4		874-8376	None	2.00	None	None	Alfred Jordan	'94

Mutual fund directory data (Lipper Analytical Services). Columns are approximate readings of a very dense rotated table; performance and ratio columns carry some uncertainty.

Fund	Objective	Net Assets ($mil)	NAV	YTD %	1-yr %	3-yr %	5-yr %	Rating	Yield %	P/E	Phone	Max Load	Fee	Exp	Manager	Year
RIVERSIDE CAP GROWTH	Growth	17.8	12.14	8.92	25.27			☆	1.2	17.7	874-8376	4.50	None	None	Jay Brooks	'94
RIVERSIDE CAP VALUE EQTY	Growth	80.4	12.63	6.86	8.07	10.26		☆	1.0	N/A	874-8376	4.50	None	1.36	Alan Catmur	'95
ROBRTSN STEPH CONTRARIAN	Growth	569.9	12.58	17.57	8.68	12.92		☆	0.0	15.4	415-781-9700 / 766-3863	None	None	2.46	Paul Stephens	'93
ROBRTSN STEPH EMERG GRO	Small Company Growth	164.4	17.60	-2.00	19.59	11.45		☆	0.0	29.9	415-781-9700 / 766-3863	None	None	1.56	Robert Czepiel	'87
ROBRTSN STEPH EMERG MKTS	Emerging Markets	13.3	9.25	7.93	-5.87			☆	1.4	□	415-781-9700 / 766-3863	None	None	3.15	Michael Hoffman	'94
ROBRTSN STEPH VAL + GRO	Small Company Growth	702.2	22.26	21.97	73.90	33.05	16.21	☆	0.0	29.6	415-781-9700 / 766-3863	None	None	1.68	Ron Elijah	'92
ROCHESTER BOND FD FOR GR	Convertible Securities	161.9	13.73	8.10	15.16	17.66	16.21	☆	5.0	N/A	716-383-1708	3.25	None	1.66	Michael S. Rosen	'86
ROCKWOOD GROWTH	Capital Appreciation	0.7	17.02	-5.23	13.80	13.80	6.09	☆	0.0	N/A	208-522-5593	None	None	2.00	Ross H. Farmer	'86
ROD SQ INTL SEC INTL EQ	International	19.2	11.87	5.14	1.17	7.50	1.79	☆	0.0	N/A	336-9970	4.00	None	1.75	Multiple Managers	N/A
ROD SQ MULTI-MGR GRO&INC	Growth Income	6.8	9.50	7.32	16.39	10.41	9.37	☆	1.3	N/A	302-651-8418 / 336-9970	4.00	None	1.50	Multiple Managers	N/A
ROD SQ MULTI-MGR GROWTH	Growth	58.7	17.56	8.80	21.34	15.06	11.78	☆	0.0	N/A	302-651-8418 / 336-9970	4.00	None	1.38	Multiple Managers	N/A
ROD SQ STRAT DVSD INC	Fixed Income	30.6	13.02	5.15	10.11	6.30		☆	6.2	17.8	336-9970	3.50	None	0.65	Clayton Albright	'94
ROULSTON GROWTH & INCOME	Growth Income	21.1	11.81	5.53	16.16	☆		☆	1.8	16.0	332-6459	None	None	1.50	Joseph Harrison	'93
ROULSTON GOVT SECURITIES	Fixed Income	8.4	9.69	6.45	11.28	☆		☆	4.8	12.2	332-6459	None	None	0.90	Lockyer/Harrison	'93/'95
ROULSTON MIDWEST GROWTH	Growth	40.7	13.18	7.91	22.53	☆		☆	0.3	N/A	None	None	None	1.45	Norm Klopp	'93
ROYCE FD EQUITY INCOME	Equity Income	66.4	5.59	6.82	10.79	9.92		☆	3.2	10.4	212-355-7311 / 221-4268	None	1.00	1.27	Charles M. Royce	'90
ROYCE FD GLBL SVCS	Global	1.5	5.85	7.73	★			☆	0.0	14.4	212-355-7311 / 221-4268	None	1.00	1.00	Charles M. Royce	'94
ROYCE FD LOW-PRICED ST	Small Company Growth	2.1	5.96	10.17	25.59	★		☆	1.5	N/A	212-355-7311 / 221-4268	None	1.00	1.89	Charles M. Royce	'93
ROYCE FD MICRO-CAP	Small Company Growth	42.3	7.22	7.44	16.46	19.95		☆	0.0	14.3	212-355-7311 / 221-4268	None	1.00	1.99	Charles M. Royce	'93
ROYCE FD PREMIER	Small Company Growth	250.1	7.33	8.43	17.19	16.67		☆	0.7	17.6	212-355-7311 / 221-4268	None	1.00	1.38	Charles M. Royce	'92
ROYCE FD TOTAL RETURN	Growth Income	2.1	5.85	7.73	20.59	★		☆	2.3	21.9	212-355-7311 / 221-4268	None	1.00	1.96	Charles M. Royce	'93
ROYCE FD VALUE	Small Company Growth	165.3	10.11	6.53	13.35	10.43	9.33	☆	0.5	□	212-355-7311 / 221-4268	None	1.00	1.80	Charles M. Royce	'82
RSI TR ACTIVELY MGD BD ✱	Fixed Income	139.8	29.09	6.17	11.88	7.54	9.55	☆	0.0	□	212-355-7311	None	None	0.82	Herb Kuhl	'90
RSI TR CORE EQUITY ✱	Growth Income	165.3	43.10	12.62	27.40	14.68	10.61	☆	0.0	□	772-3615	None	None	1.01	Jim Coughlin	'83
RSI TR EMERG GROWTH EQ ✱	Small Company Growth	55.9	44.95	12.66	42.29	26.40	17.05	☆	0.0	17.0	772-3615	None	None	2.08	Chuck Adams, Jr.	'90
RSI TR INTERNATL EQUITY ✱	International	27.8	36.73	2.28	-2.80	7.98	4.17	☆	0.0	N/A	772-3615	None	None	1.96	William Thomas	'84
RSI TR INTMDT-TERM BOND ✱	Fixed Income	90.3	27.62	4.70	9.43	5.89	8.05	☆	0.0	N/A	772-3615	None	None	0.95	Herb Kuhl	'83
RSI TR SHORT-TERM INVEST ✱	Fixed Income	29.3	19.07	1.38	4.84	3.34	5.85	☆	0.0	N/A	772-3615	None	None	0.80	Retirement System Inv.	'90
RSI TR VALUE EQUITY ✱	Growth Income	39.5	30.37	6.60	20.56	10.63	8.73	☆	0.0	□	772-3615	None	None	1.41	Jim Coughlin	'95
RUSHMORE AMER GAS INDEX	Natural Resources	195.0	11.62	5.39	12.19	5.66	★	☆	3.9	22.3	621-7874	None	None	0.84	Team Managed	N/A
RUSHMORE USG INT TERM	Fixed Income	12.3	9.50	8.24	14.31	8.09	9.36	☆	6.0	N/A	301-657-1517 / 621-7874	None	None	0.80	Team Managed	N/A
RUSHMORE USG LONG TERM	Fixed Income	19.0	9.99	11.48	18.76	9.75	10.08	☆	6.1	N/A	301-657-1517 / 621-7874	None	None	0.80	Team Managed	N/A
RYDEX JUNO FUND	Specialty	1.6	9.08	-7.82	★			☆	0.0	□	820-0888	None	None	None	Mike Byrum	'95
RYDEX NOVA FUND	Capital Appreciation	44.2	11.81	12.14	32.65	★		☆	2.6	□	820-0888	None	None	1.73	Tom Michael	'94
RYDEX OTC FUND	Capital Appreciation	136.5	12.21	21.65	48.88	★		☆	2.0	□	301-652-4402 / 820-0888	None	None	None	Terry Apple	'94
RYDEX PRECIOUS METALS	Gold	52.2	8.73	-0.55	5.57	★		☆	0.8	N/A	820-0888	None	None	2.06	Mike Byrum	'93
RYDEX URSA FUND	Capital Appreciation	141.0	8.79	-6.03	-14.08	★		☆	3.1	□	820-0888	None	None	1.67	Skip Viragh	'94
RYDEX US GOVT BOND FUND	Fixed Income	1.1	9.55	13.78	18.53	★		☆	2.5	□	820-0888	None	None	3.05	Mike Byrum	'94
S BERNSTEIN GOVT SH DUR	Fixed Income	143.1	12.56	3.15	6.99	4.63		☆	5.4	N/A	212-756-4097	None	None	0.68	Investment Policy Group	'89
S BERNSTEIN INTL VALUE	International	1,673.5	15.11	2.30	-4.90	9.11		☆	0.7	N/A	None	None	None	1.39	Investment Policy Group	'92
S BERNSTEIN INTMDT DUR	Fixed Income	1,024.3	13.25	5.61	10.72	7.31		☆	5.8	□	212-756-4097	None	None	0.65	Investment Policy Group	'89
S BERNSTEIN SH DUR PLUS	Fixed Income	549.9	12.49	2.84	6.50	4.80		☆	5.5	□	None	None	None	0.65	Investment Policy Group	'88
SAFECO ADV EQUITY; A	Growth Income	2.0	11.29	9.19	★			☆	0.0	N/A	206-545-6283 / 528-6501	4.75	None	None	Richard D. Meagley	'95
SAFECO ADV EQUITY; B	Growth Income	1.9	11.29	9.19	★			☆	0.0	N/A	206-545-6283 / 528-6501	5.00	None	None	Richard D. Meagley	'95
SAFECO ADV EQUITY; C	Growth Income	1.9	11.29	9.19	★			☆	0.0	N/A	206-545-6283 / 528-6501	None	5.00	None	Richard D. Meagley	'95
SAFECO ADV GNMA; A	Fixed Income	1.8	10.39	4.55	★			☆	0.0	□	206-545-6283 / 528-6501	4.75	None	None	Paul Stevenson	'94
SAFECO ADV GNMA; B	Fixed Income	1.7	10.39	4.36	★			☆	0.0	□	206-545-6283 / 528-6501	5.00	None	None	Paul Stevenson	'94
SAFECO ADV GNMA; C	Fixed Income	1.7	10.39	4.36	★			☆	0.0	□	206-545-6283 / 528-6501	None	5.00	None	Paul Stevenson	'94
SAFECO ADV INT TREAS; A	Fixed Income	1.8	10.49	5.67	★			☆	0.0	□	206-545-6283 / 528-6501	4.75	None	None	Mike Knebel	'95
SAFECO ADV INT TREAS; B	Fixed Income	1.7	10.49	5.47	★			☆	0.0	□	206-545-6283 / 528-6501	None	5.00	None	Mike Knebel	'95

PERFORMANCE OF MUTUAL FUNDS (continued)

		ASSETS ($ MIL)	NAV ($/SHR)	RETURN THROUGH 6/30 (Annualized)					DIV YLD	P/E	PHONE NUMBER		FEES				
FUND NAME	OBJECTIVE	5/31/95	6/30/95	QTR	1YR	3YRS	5YRS	10YRS	%	RATIO	800	In-State	Load	Exp. Ratio	Redemption	MANAGER	SINCE
SAFECO ADV INT TREAS; C	Fixed Income	1.8	10.49	5.47	☆	☆	☆	☆	0.0		528-6501	206-545-6283	None	None	None	Mike Knebel	'95
SAFECO ADV NORTHWEST; A	Growth	1.8	10.84	7.43	☆	☆	☆	☆	0.0	N/A	528-6501	206-545-6283	4.75	None	None	Charles Driggs	'94
SAFECO ADV NORTHWEST; B	Growth	1.7	10.78	7.26	☆	☆	☆	☆	0.0	N/A	528-6501	206-545-6283	None	None	5.00	Charles Driggs	'94
SAFECO ADV NORTHWEST; C	Growth	1.7	10.78	7.26	☆	☆	☆	☆	0.0	N/A	528-6501	206-545-6283	None	None	None	Charles Driggs	'94
SAFECO ADV US GOVT; A	Fixed Income	1.7	10.50	5.27	☆	☆	☆	☆	0.0		528-6501	206-545-6283	4.75	None	None	Mike Knebel	'95
SAFECO ADV US GOVT; B	Fixed Income	1.7	10.50	5.08	☆	☆	☆	☆	0.0		528-6501	206-545-6283	None	None	5.00	Mike Knebel	'95
SAFECO ADV US GOVT; C	Fixed Income	1.7	10.50	5.08	☆	☆	☆	☆	0.0		528-6501	206-545-6283	None	None	None	Mike Knebel	'95
SAFECO EQUITY FUND	Growth Income	554.4	15.20	7.90	21.50	22.84	15.17	15.57	2.2	14.6	426-6730	206-545-5530	None	0.85	None	Richard D. Meagley	'94
SAFECO GROWTH FUND	Growth	160.8	20.11	10.84	23.42	17.07	10.68	12.12	0.1	18.2	426-6730	206-545-5530	None	0.95	None	Thomas Maguire	'89
SAFECO INCOME FUND	Equity Income	202.2	18.71	6.42	17.77	11.21	10.25	10.87	4.4	16.3	426-6730	206-545-5530	None	0.86	None	Arley N. Hudson	'78
SAFECO IST FXD INC	Fixed Income	4.7	8.68	5.74	9.97	☆	☆	☆	5.1		426-6730	206-545-5530	None	None	None	Ron Spaulding	'94
SAFECO NORTHWEST FUND	Growth	36.4	14.01	7.92	15.56	9.73	☆	☆	0.3	15.3	426-6730	206-545-5530	None	1.06	None	Charles Driggs	'92
SAFECO TR GNMA	Fixed Income	43.6	9.40	4.51	9.80	5.31	7.85	☆	6.4		426-6730	206-545-5530	None	0.95	None	Paul Stevenson	'88
SAFECO TR HIGH-YLD BOND	Fixed Income	37.4	8.65	5.09	8.91	9.54	10.81	☆	9.3		426-6730	206-545-5530	None	1.03	None	Kurt Havnaer	'95
SAFECO TR INTMDT US TRES	Fixed Income	N/A	10.23	5.67	9.79	6.63	8.05	☆	5.1		426-6730	206-545-5530	None	0.90	None	Mike Knebel	'95
SALOMON BROS CAPITAL	Capital Appreciation	93.4	18.30	7.27	17.66	8.70	7.66	9.44	0.2	15.7	725-6666	212-783-1301	None	1.30	None	Ross Margolies	'95
SALOMON BROS INV; A	Growth Income	0.3	15.77	7.45	☆	☆	☆	☆	0.0	N/A	725-6666	212-783-1301	4.75	None	None	Margolies/White	'95/'95
SALOMON BROS INV; B	Growth Income	0.3	15.73	7.22	☆	☆	☆	☆	0.0	N/A	725-6666	212-783-1301	None	None	5.00	Margolies/White	'95/'95
SALOMON BROS INV; C	Growth Income	0.3	15.73	7.22	☆	☆	☆	☆	0.0	N/A	725-6666	212-783-1301	None	None	1.00	Margolies/White	'95/'95
SALOMON BROS INV; O	Growth Income	385.5	15.78	7.52	20.25	13.54	11.21	12.26	1.6	16.2	725-6666	212-783-1301	None	0.69	None	Margolies/White	'94/'92
SALOMON BROS OPPORTUNITY	Capital Appreciation	122.8	33.58	8.53	19.68	13.85	12.24	12.00	1.1	13.8	725-6666	212-783-1301	None	1.22	None	Irving Brilliant	'79
SALOMON BROS HI YLD; A	Fixed Income	0.6	10.46	8.37	☆	☆	☆	☆	0.0		725-6666	212-783-1301	4.75	None	None	Peter Wilby	'95
SALOMON BROS HI YLD; B	Fixed Income	0.4	10.46	8.16	☆	☆	☆	☆	0.0		725-6666	212-783-1301	None	None	5.00	Peter Wilby	'95
SALOMON BROS HI YLD; C	Fixed Income	0.3	10.46	8.29	☆	☆	☆	☆	0.0		725-6666	212-783-1301	None	None	1.00	Peter Wilby	'95
SALOMON BROS HI YLD; O	Fixed Income	9.7	10.46	8.44	☆	☆	☆	☆	0.0		725-6666	212-783-1301	None	None	None	Peter Wilby	'95
SALOMON BROS STR BD; A	Fixed Income	0.3	10.46	7.80	☆	☆	☆	☆	0.0		725-6666	212-783-1301	4.75	None	None	Gutterman	'95
SALOMON BROS STR BD; B	Fixed Income	0.4	10.46	7.59	☆	☆	☆	☆	0.0		725-6666	212-783-1301	None	None	5.00	Gutterman	'95
SALOMON BROS STR BD; C	Fixed Income	0.3	10.46	7.60	☆	☆	☆	☆	0.0		725-6666	212-783-1301	None	None	1.00	Gutterman	'95
SALOMON BROS STR BD; O	Fixed Income	9.5	10.46	7.86	☆	☆	☆	☆	0.0		725-6666	212-783-1301	None	None	None	Gutterman	'95
SALOMON BROS US GOVT; A	Fixed Income	0.3	10.24	4.15	☆	☆	☆	☆	0.0		725-6666	212-783-1301	4.75	None	None	Gutterman/Wilby	'95/'95
SALOMON BROS US GOVT; B	Fixed Income	0.3	10.24	3.96	☆	☆	☆	☆	0.0		725-6666	212-783-1301	None	None	5.00	Gutterman/Wilby	'95/'95
SALOMON BROS US GOVT; C	Fixed Income	0.3	10.24	3.96	☆	☆	☆	☆	0.0		725-6666	212-783-1301	None	None	1.00	Gutterman/Wilby	'95/'95
SALOMON BROS US GOVT; O	Fixed Income	9.7	10.24	4.22	☆	☆	☆	☆	0.0		725-6666	212-783-1301	None	None	None	Gutterman/Wilby	'95/'95
SBSF FDS CAPITAL GROWTH	Midcap	6.4	8.75	6.97	20.03	☆	☆	☆	0.0	14.0	422-7273	212-903-1200	None	1.22	None	Charles G. Crane	'95
SBSF FDS CONVERTIBLE SEC	Convertible Securities	59.5	11.25	5.15	8.90	10.17	11.22	☆	5.5		422-7273	212-903-1200	None	1.30	None	Louis R. Benzak	'88
SBSF FDS SBSF FUND	Growth	106.1	16.01	7.22	15.39	14.08	☆	☆	1.2	15.3	422-7273	212-903-1200	None	1.23	None	Louis R. Benzak	'83
SCHAFER VALUE FUND	Growth Income	100.5	40.24	11.47	19.86	17.19	16.33	☆	0.8	14.6	343-0481	212-644-1800	None	1.48	None	David Schafer	'85
SCHOONER FUND	Small Company Growth	5.1	28.24	7.87	13.68	☆	☆	☆	0.8	14.8	776-5033	310-247-3940	None	1.50	None	Gipson/Grey	'93/'94
SCHRODER CAP INTL EQUITY	International	195.4	20.25	5.25	3.37	12.56	5.47	☆	0.9		344-8332	212-841-3848	None	0.90	None	Mark J. Smith	'89
SCHRODER CAP US EQUITY	Growth	19.3	8.91	7.09	15.82	13.62	12.43	12.15	0.6	16.8	344-8332	212-841-3848	None	1.31	None	Fariba Talebi	'91
SCHRODER CAP US SMALL CO	Small Company Growth	14.3	13.36	9.42	25.27	☆	☆	☆	0.0	N/A	344-8332	212-841-3848	None	0.90	None	Unschuld/Talebi	'93/'93
SCHWAB CAP INTL IDX	International	160.2	10.88	2.84	5.49	☆	☆	☆	1.1	N/A	838-0650	None	None	0.90	0.75	Schwab Investment	'95
SCHWAB CAP SM-CAP IDX	Small Company Growth	87.4	11.13	8.48	20.13	☆	☆	☆	0.5	17.3	838-0650	None	None	0.67	0.50	Hom/Ward	'95/'95
SCHWAB INV 1000	Growth Income	691.3	14.99	9.02	24.66	12.89	☆	☆	1.0	N/A	838-0650	None	None	0.51	0.50	Schwab Investment	'95
SCHWAB INV LONG-TM GOVT	Fixed Income	12.1	9.81	6.79	14.13	☆	☆	☆	7.0	N/A	838-0650	None	None	0.10	0.50	Regan/Ward	'93/'93

SCHWAB INV SHORT/INTMDT	Fixed Income	158.9	9.85	3.04	6.79	5.03	☆	☆	5.9	□	838-0650	None	None	0.60	None	Regan/Ward	'91/'91
SCHWARTZ VALUE FUND	Small Company Growth	49.7	20.71	6.04	14.18	☆	☆	☆	0.0	14.1	None	810-644-2701	None	None	None	George P. Schwartz	'93
SCM PORTFOLIO FUND	Flexible	0.8	10.65	3.40	9.92	5.19	5.31	☆	2.8	15.4	None	404-834-5839	None	1.59	1.00	Stephen McCutcheon	'89
SCOTTISH WIDOWS INTL	International	32.2	12.39	6.90	0.34	8.95	☆	☆	0.0	□	523-8440	610-670-1031	4.75	1.92	None	Allan McKenzie	'90
SCOUT BOND FUND	Fixed Income	76.6	11.10	4.84	9.56	5.93	7.64	8.07	5.7	□	422-2766	816-471-5200	None	0.87	None	George Root	'82
SCOUT REGIONAL FUND	Small Company Growth	31.3	9.89	5.68	13.98	8.02	7.54	☆	1.9	16.5	422-2766	816-471-5200	None	0.91	None	David Anderson	'91
SCOUT STOCK FUND	Growth	136.7	16.36	5.78	17.30	11.22	10.63	11.49	2.7	17.5	422-2766	816-471-5200	None	0.87	None	David Anderson	'82
SCOUT WORLDWIDE FUND	Global	19.3	11.56	6.34	12.12	☆	☆	☆	1.9	□	422-2766	816-471-5200	None	0.85	None	James Moffett	'94
SCUDDER BALANCED	Balanced	72.3	13.33	7.93	19.16	☆	☆	☆	2.4	18.5	225-2470	617-439-4640	None	1.00	None	Beaty/Hutchison/Shields	'93/'93/'95
SCUDDER CAP GROWTH	Growth	1,382.7	21.21	11.28	18.75	12.03	10.65	13.48	0.0	N/A	225-2470	617-439-4640	None	0.97	None	Millard/Cox/Aronoff	'95/'83/'83
SCUDDER DEVELOPMENT	Midcap	648.3	37.35	17.71	45.41	15.69	14.03	13.06	0.0	26.9	225-2470	617-439-4640	None	1.27	None	McKay/Chin	'88/'93
SCUDDER EMRG MKTS INCOME	World Income	148.4	10.32	14.64	5.78	☆	☆	☆	8.9	□	225-2470	617-439-4640	None	None	None	Saltzman/Rathman/Gray	'93/'93/'93
SCUDDER GLBL SMALLCO	Global Small Company	222.3	16.29	9.92	5.38	9.67	☆	☆	0.0	□	225-2470	617-439-4640	None	1.70	None	Moran/Allan/Franklin	'91/'94/'91
SCUDDER GLOBAL FUND	Global	1,158.6	25.64	7.64	8.93	11.84	8.63	☆	0.4	□	225-2470	617-439-4640	None	1.45	None	Holzer/Bratt/Ho	'86/'86/'94
SCUDDER GNMA FUND	Fixed Income	434.6	14.55	5.15	11.47	5.54	8.21	☆	6.6	□	225-2470	617-439-4640	None	0.87	None	Glen/Pruyne	'85/'85
SCUDDER GOLD FUND	Gold	125.4	12.87	10.28	7.50	14.70	6.32	☆	1.9	N/A	225-2470	617-439-4640	None	1.69	None	Donald/Wallace	'88/'88
SCUDDER GREATER EUROPE	European Region	30.6	13.20	10.00	☆	☆	☆	☆	0.0	□	225-2470	617-439-4640	None	None	None	Franklin/Bratt/Gregory	'94/'94/'94
SCUDDER GROWTH & INC	Growth Income	2,493.8	18.53	8.50	18.72	13.49	13.45	13.68	2.7	15.2	225-2470	617-439-4640	None	0.86	None	Hoffman/Millard/Thorndike	'91/'91/'86
SCUDDER INCOME FUND	Fixed Income	513.4	13.43	5.97	12.21	7.68	9.53	9.59	5.8	□	225-2470	617-439-4640	None	0.97	None	Hutchinson/Wohler	'86/'94
SCUDDER INTERNATIONAL	International	2,300.6	42.52	7.05	3.02	10.39	5.25	15.41	0.0	□	225-2470	617-439-4640	None	1.21	None	Franklin/Bratt/Cheng	'89/'76/'93
SCUDDER INTRN'L BOND	World Income	940.5	11.43	5.12	3.92	4.26	10.78	☆	8.6	□	225-2470	617-439-4640	None	1.27	None	Greshin/Hadzima/Craddock	'95/'95/'95
SCUDDER LATIN AMERICA	Latin American	555.3	16.43	13.31	-14.11	☆	☆	☆	0.0	□	225-2470	617-439-4640	None	2.01	2.00	Games/Truscott/Cornell	'92/'92/'93
SCUDDER MANAGED INT GOV ▮	Fixed Income	11.5	9.42	2.30	5.56	☆	☆	☆	5.2	□	225-2470	617-439-4640	None	1.01	None	Glen/Pruyne/Boyadjian	'93/'93/'95
SCUDDER PACIFIC OPPTY	Pacific Region	429.7	15.92	4.46	0.79	☆	☆	☆	0.6	□	225-2470	617-439-4640	None	1.81	None	Allan/Bratt/Cornell	'94/'92/'93
SCUDDER QUALITY GROW	Growth	140.5	17.22	9.40	23.79	10.64	☆	☆	0.8	18.5	225-2470	617-439-4640	None	1.25	None	Beaty/Shields	'91/'92
SCUDDER SHRT TRM BND	Fixed Income	1,968.9	11.19	3.86	5.19	4.69	7.27	8.39	6.6	□	225-2470	617-439-4640	None	0.73	None	Poor/Gootkind/Dolan	'89/'89/'94
SCUDDER ST GLBL INC	World Income	404.6	10.37	2.11	2.28	3.00	☆	☆	8.0	□	225-2470	617-439-4640	None	1.00	None	Craddock/Greshin/Johnson	'91/'91/'92
SCUDDER VALUE FUND	Growth	60.2	15.22	11.58	24.65	☆	☆	☆	0.8	12.0	225-2470	617-439-4640	None	1.25	None	Hall/Wallace	'92/'92
SCUDDER ZERO CP 2000	Fixed Income	27.2	11.99	6.77	11.91	9.23	10.68	☆	5.0	□	225-2470	617-439-4640	None	1.00	None	Heisler/Ross/Wohler	'86/'86/'94
SEAFIRST ASSET ALLOC ❁	Flexible	145.9	14.64	7.83	19.61	9.50	9.60	☆	3.2	N/A	852-9730	None	None	0.78	None	Keith Wirtz	'95
SEAFIRST BLUE CHIP FUND ❁	Growth	167.9	19.23	9.07	25.57	12.00	10.65	☆	1.7	N/A	852-9730	None	None	0.82	None	Robert Pyles	'94
SEAFIRST BOND FUND ❁	Fixed Income	53.4	10.81	4.64	9.72	5.72	7.73	☆	6.0	□	852-9730	None	None	0.83	None	Steve Vielhaber	'94
SECOND FID EXCHANGE ⊠	Growth	70.1	146.94	9.38	22.34	10.28	8.98	10.69	1.5	17.3	225-6265	617-482-8260	None	0.82	None	Robert S. Goodof	'87
SECURITY EQ EQUITY; A	Growth	402.6	6.08	9.95	23.94	14.27	13.16	14.69	0.4	18.1	888-2461	913-295-3127	5.75	1.06	None	Terry Millberger	'81
SECURITY EQ GLOBAL; A	Global	17.0	10.36	2.17	-0.54	☆	☆	☆	0.0	□	888-2461	913-295-3127	5.75	2.00	None	Wapnick/Sayler	'94/'94
SECURITY GRO & INC; A	Growth Income	63.9	7.52	9.43	16.71	7.60	8.09	8.50	1.7	18.7	888-2461	913-295-3127	5.75	1.28	None	John Cleland	'66
SECURITY INC CORP BD; A	Fixed Income	96.7	7.11	5.30	10.57	6.63	8.38	8.73	7.1	□	888-2461	913-295-3127	4.75	1.01	None	Jane Tedder	'85
SECURITY INC US GOVT; A	Fixed Income	8.2	4.71	7.34	11.68	6.51	8.23	☆	6.6	□	888-2461	913-295-3127	4.75	1.10	None	Jane Tedder	'85
SECURITY ULTRA; A	Capital Appreciation	52.7	7.37	6.66	19.74	11.94	4.95	6.20	0.0	24.4	888-2461	913-295-3127	5.75	1.33	None	Cindy Shields	'94
SEI DAILY CORP DAILY; A ▮	Fixed Income	61.2	1.99	2.53	6.72	☆	☆	☆	5.5	□	342-5734	610-254-1000	None	0.35	None	John Keough	'93
SEI DAILY GNMA; A ▮	Fixed Income	165.9	9.66	5.28	12.33	5.93	8.63	☆	6.9	□	342-5734	610-254-1000	None	0.47	None	Paul Kaplan	'87
SEI DAILY GNMA; B ▮	Fixed Income	0.1	9.66	5.20	☆	☆	☆	☆	0.0	□	342-5734	610-254-1000	None	0.79	None	Paul Kaplan	'94
SEI DAILY GNMA; PROV	Fixed Income	0.2	9.64	5.07	11.84	☆	☆	☆	6.6	□	342-5734	610-254-1000	4.50	0.86	None	Paul Kaplan	'93
SEI DAILY INT GOVT; A ▮	Fixed Income	189.4	9.82	5.08	9.94	5.85	8.05	☆	5.5	□	342-5734	610-254-1000	None	0.45	None	Paul Kaplan	'87
SEI DAILY INT GOVT; B ▮	Fixed Income	0.1	9.82	5.00	9.62	☆	☆	☆	5.2	□	342-5734	610-254-1000	None	0.75	None	Paul Kaplan	'94
SEI DAILY INT GOVT; PROV	Fixed Income	0.1	9.82	5.09	9.53	☆	☆	☆	5.1	□	342-5734	610-254-1000	3.50	0.84	None	Paul Kaplan	'93
SEI DAILY SHT-TM GOVT; A ▮	Fixed Income	80.4	9.99	3.13	7.59	4.79	6.69	☆	4.9	□	342-5734	610-254-1000	None	0.45	None	Paul Kaplan	'87
SEI DAILY SHT-TM GOVT; B ▮	Fixed Income	0.1	9.98	3.16	7.37	4.43	☆	☆	4.6	□	342-5734	610-254-1000	None	0.75	None	Paul Kaplan	'90
SEI DAILY SHT-TM MTGE; A ▮	Fixed Income	2.5	9.78	2.40	7.13	☆	☆	☆	6.4	□	342-5734	610-254-1000	None	0.45	None	Thomas Pappas	'94
SEI INDEX BOND ▮	Fixed Income	44.8	10.32	5.96	11.94	7.08	8.64	☆	6.2	□	342-5734	610-254-1000	None	0.38	None	Paul Greff	'93

© Copyright Lipper Analytical Services, Inc.

PERFORMANCE OF MUTUAL FUNDS (continued)

FUND NAME	OBJECTIVE	ASSETS ($ MIL) 5/31/95	NAV ($/SHR) 6/30/95	QTR	1YR	3YRS	5YRS	10YRS	DIV YLD %	P/E RATIO	PHONE 800	PHONE In-State	Load	Exp. Ratio	Redemption	MANAGER	SINCE
SEI INDEX S&P 500	S&P Index	478.8	17.86	9.48	25.78	12.97	11.81	☆	2.3	17.3	342-5734	610-254-1000	None	0.25	None	Todd Johnson	'94
SEI INSTL BALANCED; A	Flexible	68.7	12.27	6.31	13.49	8.07	☆	☆	2.5	18.2	342-5734	610-254-1000	None	0.75	None	Anthony Gray	'92
SEI INSTL BOND; A	Fixed Income	66.5	10.85	7.51	14.90	9.59	10.45	☆	6.3	□	342-5734	610-254-1000	None	0.55	None	Paul Rapponetti	'87
SEI INSTL BOND; PROV	Fixed Income	0.1	10.83	7.40	14.36	9.30	9.99	☆	5.9	□	342-5734	610-254-1000	4.50	0.95	None	Paul Rapponetti	'93
SEI INSTL CAP APP; A	Growth	366.8	15.74	7.20	15.44	☆	☆	☆	1.5	16.2	342-5734	610-254-1000	None	0.79	None	Anthony Gray	'88
SEI INSTL CAP APP; PROV	Growth	0.6	15.73	7.02	14.94	☆	☆	☆	1.0	16.2	342-5734	610-254-1000	5.00	None	None	Anthony Gray	'93
SEI INSTL CAPITAL GROWTH	Capital Appreciation	110.5	11.33	9.20	22.70	15.12	14.63	☆	1.7	20.1	342-5734	610-254-1000	None	None	None	Thomas Edgar	'90
SEI INSTL EQU INC; A	Equity Income	279.6	14.96	6.21	18.42	11.47	11.29	☆	3.6	15.5	342-5734	610-254-1000	None	0.78	None	Tom Arrington	'88
SEI INSTL CORE FXD; A	Fixed Income	437.8	10.43	6.28	13.92	6.88	8.42	☆	6.1		342-5734	610-254-1000	None	0.55	None	Kent S. Engel	'94
SEI INSTL CORE FXD; PROV	Fixed Income	0.2	10.40	6.47	13.30	☆	☆	☆	5.7		342-5734	610-254-1000	4.50	None	None	Kent S. Engel	'94
SEI INSTL LG CP GR; A	Growth	169.5	11.91	10.72	☆	☆	☆	☆	0.0	N/A	342-5734	610-254-1000	None	None	None	Multiple Managers	N/A
SEI INSTL MD-CP GR; A	Midcap	30.9	11.94	7.76	14.18	☆	☆	☆	0.0	21.0	342-5734	610-254-1000	None	0.93	None	John Marshall, Jr.	'93
SEI INSTL MD-CP GR; PROV	Midcap	0.1	11.88	7.61	13.72	☆	☆	☆	0.0	21.0	342-5734	610-254-1000	5.00	None	None	John Marshall, Jr.	'94
SEI INSTL SM CP GR; A	Small Company Growth	262.9	16.91	10.89	38.32	☆	☆	☆	0.0	28.0	342-5734	610-254-1000	None	1.01	None	Multiple Managers	N/A
SEI INSTL SM CP GR; PROV	Small Company Growth	0.4	16.83	10.80	37.77	☆	☆	☆	0.0	28.0	342-5734	610-254-1000	5.00	None	None	Multiple Managers	N/A
SEI INSTL SM CP VAL; A	Small Company Growth	63.3	11.12	5.93	☆	☆	☆	☆	0.0	N/A	342-5734	610-254-1000	None	None	None	Powell/Doyle/Guthrie	'94/'94
SEI INSTL VALUE; A	Growth Income	223.9	11.97	7.94	20.59	6.84	7.48	☆	2.5	17.5	342-5734	610-254-1000	None	0.75	None	Robert Milne	'92
SEI INTL CORE INTL; A	International	314.7	9.97	1.73	-1.42	6.55	2.93	☆	0.0		342-5734	610-254-1000	None	1.19	None	Multiple Managers	N/A
SEI INTL CORE INTL; PROV	International	0.1	9.93	1.64	-1.71	☆	☆	☆	0.0		342-5734	610-254-1000	5.00	1.47	None	Multiple Managers	N/A
SEI INTL EURO EQTY; A	European Region	45.7	10.98	9.25	14.83	☆	☆	☆	0.5		342-5734	610-254-1000	5.00	1.30	None	Julian Johnston	'94
SEI INTL INTL FXD INC; A	World Income	49.3	11.86	4.40	20.82	☆	☆	☆	5.2		342-5734	610-254-1000	None	1.00	None	Kenneth A. Windheim	'93
SEI INTL PAC BASIN; A	Pacific Region	41.0	9.06	-0.88	-12.38	☆	☆	☆	0.0	14.6	342-5734	610-254-1000	None	1.30	None	John Ayer	'94
SELECTED AMERICAN SHARES	Growth Income	708.3	15.85	10.87	22.99	11.29	12.72	13.70	1.4		279-0279	505-983-4335	None	1.26	None	Shelby M.C. Davis	'93
SELECTED CAP GOVT INC	Fixed Income	7.6	9.00	5.11	9.87	6.55	7.97	☆	5.9		279-0279	505-983-4335	None	1.42	None	Carolyn Spolidono	'95
SELECTED SPECIAL SHARES	Small Company Growth	51.4	10.60	10.42	24.37	13.19	9.13	11.56	0.0	19.4	279-0279	505-983-4335	None	1.41	None	Elizabeth R. Bramwell	'94
SELIGMAN CAPITAL; A	Capital Appreciation	170.2	15.17	9.06	24.91	9.99	12.11	12.65	0.0	22.3	221-7844	212-850-1864	4.75	1.13	None	Loris D. Muzzatti	'88
SELIGMAN CAPITAL; D	Capital Appreciation	3.8	14.68	8.74	23.31	☆	☆	☆	0.0	22.3	221-7844	212-850-1864	None	2.66	1.00	Loris D. Muzzatti	'93
SELIGMAN COMMON STK; A	Growth Income	577.8	13.93	7.27	19.20	12.45	11.60	13.48	2.6	19.6	221-7844	212-850-1864	4.75	0.85	None	Charles C. Smith	'91
SELIGMAN COMMON STK; D	Growth Income	25.2	13.89	7.12	18.02	☆	☆	☆	1.8	19.6	221-7844	212-850-1864	None	1.96	1.00	Charles C. Smith	'93
SELIGMAN COMMUNICATN; A	Science & Technology	1,046.3	24.63	29.77	107.85	50.90	31.22	25.38	0.0	N/A	221-7844	212-850-1864	4.75	1.63	None	Paul Wick	'90
SELIGMAN COMMUNICATN; D	Science & Technology	351.0	24.05	29.51	106.16	☆	19.79	☆	0.0	N/A	221-7844	212-850-1864	4.75	2.56	None	Paul Wick	'93
SELIGMAN FRONTIER; A	Small Company Growth	126.5	12.32	10.39	38.24	27.36	☆	16.24	0.0	22.9	221-7844	212-850-1864	4.75	1.34	None	Paul Wick	'91
SELIGMAN FRONTIER; D	Small Company Growth	58.9	11.96	10.03	36.87	☆	☆	☆	0.0	22.9	221-7844	212-850-1864	4.75	2.72	1.00	Paul Wick	'93
SELIGMAN GROWTH; A	Growth	546.2	5.10	7.37	18.37	11.18	9.97	12.36	0.2	21.1	221-7844	212-850-1864	4.75	0.90	None	David Watts	'92
SELIGMAN GROWTH; D	Growth	3.4	4.88	6.78	16.59	☆	☆	☆	0.0	21.1	221-7844	212-850-1864	None	2.93	1.00	David Watts	'93
SELIGMAN HEND GL INT; A	International	59.6	15.87	2.85	-0.34	11.33	☆	☆	0.0		221-7844	212-850-1864	4.75	1.63	None	Ian Clark	'92
SELIGMAN HEND GL INT; D	International	25.1	15.64	2.62	-1.27	☆	☆	☆	0.0		221-7844	212-850-1864	None	2.50	1.00	Ian Clark	'93
SELIGMAN HEND GL SM; A	Global Small Company	59.3	12.37	7.75	22.84	☆	☆	☆	0.0		221-7844	212-850-1864	4.75	1.92	None	Ian Clark	'92
SELIGMAN HEND GL SM; D	Global Small Company	50.0	12.16	7.52	21.74	☆	☆	☆	0.0		221-7844	212-850-1864	None	2.70	1.00	Ian Clark	'93
SELIGMAN HEND GL TCH; A	Science & Technology	120.3	11.41	23.75	64.46	☆	☆	☆	0.0	N/A	221-7844	212-850-1864	4.75	None	None	Brian Ashford Russell	'94
SELIGMAN HEND GL TCH; D	Science & Technology	34.6	11.30	23.50	63.11	☆	☆	☆	0.0	N/A	221-7844	212-850-1864	None	None	1.00	Brian Ashford Russell	'94
SELIGMAN HI INC BOND; A	Fixed Income	87.6	6.75	6.16	13.46	12.76	14.40	11.43	9.8	□	221-7844	212-850-1864	4.75	1.13	None	Dan Charleston	'89
SELIGMAN HI INC BOND; D	Fixed Income	28.5	6.75	5.93	12.13	☆	☆	☆	8.8	□	221-7844	212-850-1864	None	2.19	1.00	Dan Charleston	'93
SELIGMAN HI INC GOVT; A	Fixed Income	54.1	6.89	6.35	10.02	5.80	7.79	8.20	6.7	□	221-7844	212-850-1864	4.75	1.10	None	Lenord Lovito	'94
SELIGMAN HI INC GOVT; D	Fixed Income	6.6	6.90	5.96	8.87	☆	☆	☆	5.7	□	221-7844	212-850-1864	None	2.22	1.00	Lenord Lovito	'94

Fund	Objective	Net Assets ($Mil)	NAV	(a)	(b)	(c)	(d)	(e)	P/E	Yield %	Phone 1	Phone 2	Exp %	12b-1	Load %	Manager	Since
SELIGMAN INCOME; A	Income	305.7	14.36	7.31	13.21	10.11	11.77	10.61	13.1	5.3	212-850-1864	221-7844	1.02	None	4.75	Charles C. Smith	'91
SELIGMAN INCOME; D	Income	77.3	14.32	7.10	12.27	☆	☆	☆	13.1	4.6	212-850-1864	221-7844	1.82	1.00	None	Charles C. Smith	'93
SENTINEL BALANCED	Balanced	251.2	15.68	6.41	14.08	8.03	9.45	10.64	18.5	3.9	802-229-3761	233-4332	1.21	None	5.00	Rodney A. Buck	'82
SENTINEL BOND	Fixed Income	105.5	6.35	6.89	12.43	7.82	9.73	9.63	6.4	6.4	802-229-3761	233-4332	0.98	None	5.00	Richard D. Temple	'85
SENTINEL COMMON STOCK	Growth Income	989.4	31.67	8.13	20.16	10.05	11.00	12.96	17.9	2.5	802-229-3761	233-4332	1.02	None	5.00	Merrill/Lee/Pender	'94/'94/'94
SENTINEL EMERGING GROWTH	Small Company Growth	93.8	5.10	1.19	15.42	☆	☆	☆	19.2	0.0	802-229-3761	233-4332	1.58	None	5.00	Louis E. Conrad II	'93
SENTINEL GOVERNMENT SEC	Fixed Income	105.8	10.02	5.72	11.62	6.71	8.79	10.18		6.0	802-229-3761	233-4332	1.00	None	5.00	David M. Brownlee	'93
SENTINEL GROWTH	Growth	55.6	15.69	5.94	18.43	7.33	5.96	☆	21.4	0.3	802-229-3761	233-4332	1.43	None	5.00	Robert L. Lee	'93
SENTINEL WORLD FUND	International	44.0	13.30	3.34	6.14	☆	☆	☆		0.6	802-229-3761	233-4332	1.58	None	5.00	Eric Granade	'94
SENTRY FUND	Growth	82.4	15.71	6.90	15.12	9.52	10.05	12.10	N/A	1.1	None	533-7827	0.86	None	None	Keith Springer	'77
SEQUOIA FUND ⊠	Growth	1,791.9	64.66	5.65	19.66	13.98	13.30	13.75	14.4	0.5	212-832-5280	None	1.00	None	None	Ruane/Cunniff	'70/'70
SEVEN SEAS EMERG MKTS	Emerging Markets	56.9	9.98	7.66	8.92	☆	☆	☆		1.0	617-542-9049	647-7327	1.50	None	None	Team Managed	N/A
SEVEN SEAS GROWTH & INC	Growth Income	38.5	11.61	10.56	22.38	☆	☆	☆	18.7	1.5	617-542-9049	647-7327	0.95	None	None	Team Managed	N/A
SEVEN SEAS INTMDT FUND	Fixed Income	30.3	9.64	5.57	11.28	☆	☆	☆		5.7	617-542-9049	647-7327	0.60	None	None	Team Managed	N/A
SEVEN SEAS MATRIX EQUITY	Growth	186.8	13.53	8.13	23.82	☆	☆	☆	16.2	2.1	617-542-9049	647-7327	0.58	None	None	Team Managed	N/A
SEVEN SEAS S&P 500 INDEX	S&P Index	396.4	12.38	9.47	25.71	☆	☆	☆	16.7	2.4	617-542-9049	647-7327	0.15	None	None	Team Managed	N/A
SEVEN SEAS SMALL CAP	Small Company Growth	16.6	13.24	10.80	29.66	☆	☆	☆	45.1	1.1	617-542-9049	647-7327	0.30	None	None	Team Managed	N/A
SEVEN SEAS YIELD PLUS	Fixed Income	1,317.0	10.00	1.60	5.89	☆	☆	☆	N/A	5.4	617-542-9049	647-7327	0.35	None	None	Team Managed	N/A
1784 ASSET ALLOC ➤	Flexible	8.6	11.04	6.76	18.46	☆	☆	☆	N/A	2.6	None	252-1784	1.25	None	None	Ablin/Clausen	'93/'93
1784 GOVT MED TM ➤	Fixed Income	130.1	9.63	5.48	9.94	☆	☆	☆		6.0	None	252-1784	0.31	None	None	Jack Ablin	'93
1784 GRO & INC ➤	Growth Income	229.3	12.55	11.03	25.80	☆	☆	☆	22.6	0.9	None	252-1784	0.35	None	None	Takach/Ober	'93/'94
1784 INCOME FUND ➤	Fixed Income	196.5	10.39	6.30	☆	☆	☆	☆		6.5	None	252-1784	None	None	None	Jack Ablin	'94
1784 SH-TM INC ➤	Fixed Income	52.6	10.09	3.28	☆	☆	☆	☆		6.0	None	252-1784	None	None	None	Mary K. Werler	N/A
SHADOW STOCK	Small Company Growth	39.8	10.55	8.35	16.16	13.08	11.10	☆	N/A	0.9	816-471-5200	422-2766	1.28	None	None	Schliemann/Whitridge	'87/'87
SHAWMUT FXD INCOME; INV	Fixed Income	8.5	10.00	6.22	11.85	☆	☆	☆		5.6	508-626-7877	742-9688	1.19	None	2.00	Max Brenninkmeyer	'93
SHAWMUT FXD INCOME; TR	Fixed Income	81.0	10.00	6.40	11.85	☆	☆	☆		5.9	508-626-7877	742-9688	0.94	None	None	Max Brenninkmeyer	'92
SHAWMUT GRO & INC EQ; INV	Growth Income	35.6	11.93	7.67	21.54	☆	☆	☆		2.0	508-626-7877	742-9688	1.29	None	4.00	Brendan Henebry	'93
SHAWMUT GRO & INC EQ; TR	Growth Income	179.2	11.93	7.71	21.84	☆	☆	☆	16.3	2.3	508-626-7877	742-9688	1.04	None	None	Brendan Henebry	'92
SHAWMUT GROW EQTY; INV	Growth	7.0	11.67	7.87	25.25	☆	☆	☆	17.0	0.8	508-626-7877	742-9688	1.43	None	4.00	Philip Tasho	'95
SHAWMUT GROW EQTY; TR	Growth	15.9	11.67	7.92	25.56	☆	☆	☆	17.0	1.0	508-626-7877	742-9688	1.18	None	None	Philip Tasho	'95
SHAWMUT INTMDT GOVT; INV	Fixed Income	10.5	9.80	4.76	8.85	☆	☆	☆		5.3	508-626-7877	742-9688	1.26	None	2.00	Michael Spencer	'93
SHAWMUT INTMDT GOVT; TR	Fixed Income	46.1	9.80	4.82	9.13	☆	☆	☆		5.6	508-626-7877	742-9688	1.01	None	None	Michael Spencer	'94
SHAWMUT LTD TM INC INV	Fixed Income	7.1	9.75	3.90	7.79	☆	☆	☆		5.2	508-626-7877	742-9688	1.28	None	2.00	Perry Vieth	'94
SHAWMUT LTD TM INC; TR	Fixed Income	40.0	9.75		8.09	☆	☆	☆		5.5	508-626-7877	742-9688	1.03	None	None	Perry Vieth	'94
SHAWMUT QUANT EQTY; INV	Growth	0.8	10.66	1.88	☆	☆	☆	☆	N/A	0.0	508-626-7877	742-9688	None	None	4.00	Kenneth Garvey	'95
SHAWMUT QUANT EQTY; TR	Growth	3.4	10.66	1.81	8.49	☆	☆	☆	16.8	0.0	508-626-7877	742-9688	None	None	None	Kenneth Garvey	'95
SHAWMUT SMALL CAP EQ; INV	Small Company Growth	22.2	11.90	10.59	21.38	☆	☆	☆	16.8	0.1	508-626-7877	742-9688	None	None	4.00	Peter Larson	'93
SHAWMUT SMALL CAP EQ; TR	Small Company Growth	106.8	11.92	10.58	21.58	☆	☆	☆	N/A	0.5	508-626-7877	742-9688	None	None	None	Peter Larson	'92
SHELBY FUND	Growth	67.2	12.56	14.29	15.57	8.47	☆	☆	16.8	1.8	None	774-3529	1.35	None	4.50	Wells/Weder	'94/'94
SIERRA CORP INCOME; A	Fixed Income	390.5	10.52	8.86	☆	☆	☆	☆	N/A	7.7	818-725-0405	222-5852	1.31	None	4.50	James Goldberg	'90
SIERRA CORP INCOME; B	Fixed Income	14.3	10.52	8.62	☆	☆	☆	☆	N/A	7.0	818-725-0405	222-5852	None	5.00	None	James Goldberg	'94
SIERRA CORP INCOME; S	Fixed Income	8.3	10.52	8.66	☆	☆	☆	☆	N/A	7.0	818-725-0405	222-5852	1.66	None	None	James Goldberg	'94
SIERRA EMERG GROWTH; A	Midcap	159.5	15.47	7.58	21.54	☆	☆	☆	15.7	0.0	818-725-0405	222-5852	1.41	None	4.50	James P. Goff	'93
SIERRA EMERG GROWTH; B	Midcap	9.1	15.36	7.34	☆	☆	☆	☆	15.7	0.0	818-725-0405	222-5852	None	5.00	None	James P. Goff	'93
SIERRA EMERG GROWTH; S	Midcap	7.6	15.37	7.41	☆	☆	☆	☆	N/A	0.0	818-725-0405	222-5852	None	None	None	James P. Goff	'94
SIERRA GRO & INC; A	Growth Income	167.7	12.57	7.31	20.47	☆	☆	☆	16.1	1.0	818-725-0405	222-5852	1.50	None	4.50	William M. Reigel	'94
SIERRA GRO & INC; B	Growth Income	6.2	12.54	7.09	☆	☆	☆	☆	16.1	0.6	818-725-0405	222-5852	None	5.00	None	William M. Reigel	'94
SIERRA GRO & INC; S	Growth Income	13.2	12.55	7.16	☆	☆	☆	☆	N/A	0.6	818-725-0405	222-5852	None	None	None	William M. Reigel	'94
SIERRA GROWTH; A	Growth	148.3	14.18	13.53	32.33	☆	☆	☆	22.8	0.1	818-725-0405	222-5852	1.75	None	5.75	Warren B. Lammert	'93
SIERRA GROWTH; B	Growth	5.8	14.10	13.34	☆	☆	☆	☆	22.8	0.0	818-725-0405	222-5852	None	5.00	None	Warren B. Lammert	'94

PERFORMANCE OF MUTUAL FUNDS (continued)

FUND NAME	OBJECTIVE	ASSETS ($ MIL) 5/31/95	NAV ($/SHR) 6/30/95	QTR	1YR	3YRS	5YRS	10YRS	DIV YLD %	P/E RATIO	800	In-State	Load	Exp. Ratio	Redemption	MANAGER	SINCE
						RETURN THROUGH 6/30 (Annualized)					PHONE NUMBER		FEES				
SIERRA GROWTH; S ☒	Growth	16.8	14.10	13.25	☆				0.0	N/A	222-5852	818-725-0405	None	None	5.00	Warren B. Lammert	'94
SIERRA INTL GROWTH; A	International	108.1	9.78	2.95	-4.01	6.35	☆		0.4		222-5852	818-725-0405	4.50	1.69	None	Doug Dooley	'90
SIERRA INTL GROWTH; B	International	2.2	9.73	2.85	☆				0.3		222-5852	818-725-0405	None	None	5.00	Doug Dooley	'94
SIERRA INTL GROWTH; S	International	12.5	9.73	2.85	☆				0.3		222-5852	818-725-0405	None	None	5.00	Doug Dooley	'94
SIERRA SH TM HI QUAL; A	Fixed Income	44.5	2.35	3.28	4.42	☆			6.0		222-5852	818-725-0405	3.50	None	None	Thomas M. Poor	'93
SIERRA SH TM HI QUAL; B	Fixed Income	3.1	2.35	3.06	☆				5.2		222-5852	818-725-0405	None	None	4.00	Thomas M. Poor	'94
SIERRA SH TM HI QUAL; S	Fixed Income	2.2	2.35	3.09	☆				5.3		222-5852	818-725-0405	None	None	5.00	Thomas M. Poor	'94
SIERRA SHT GLBL GOVT; B	World Income	108.6	2.24	2.48	2.06	3.05	☆		6.5		222-5852	818-725-0405	3.50	0.85	None	Margaret Craddock	'92
SIERRA SHT GLBL GOVT; A	World Income	1.3	2.24	2.26	☆				5.7		222-5852	818-725-0405	None	None	4.00	Margaret Craddock	'94
SIERRA SHT GLBL GOVT; S	World Income	2.2	2.24	2.30	☆				5.8		222-5852	818-725-0405	None	None	5.00	Margaret Craddock	'94
SIERRA US GOVT; A	Fixed Income	463.1	9.67	4.63	10.17	4.60	7.39	☆	7.2		222-5852	818-725-0405	4.50	1.06	None	Keith Anderson	'94
SIERRA US GOVT; B	Fixed Income	9.8	9.67	4.40	☆				6.5		222-5852	818-725-0405	None	None	5.00	Keith Anderson	'94
SIERRA US GOVT; S	Fixed Income	6.3	9.67	4.44	☆				6.5		222-5852	818-725-0405	None	None	5.00	Keith Anderson	'94
SIFE TRUST FUND	Financial Services	499.7	4.42	10.56	15.73	15.84	17.70	13.53	3.4	10.5	524-7433	510-937-7964	5.00	0.94	None	Stead/Sloan/Edgar	'95/'91/'93
SIT BALANCED	Balanced	2.4	10.99	7.75	19.16	☆	☆		2.5	22.7	332-5580	612-334-5888	None	1.00	None	Mitchelson/Rogers	'93/'93
SIT BOND FUND	Fixed Income	4.1	9.89	5.99	11.95	☆	☆		6.3		332-5580	612-334-5888	None	None	None	Brilley/Rogers	'93/'93
SIT DEVELOPING MKTS	Emerging Markets	4.5	9.41	10.06	☆				0.0		332-5580	612-334-5888	None	0.82	None	Andrew B. Kim	'94
SIT GROWTH	Midcap	315.6	13.00	7.62	28.44	11.74	12.54	14.41	0.0	24.1	332-5580	612-334-5888	None	1.10	None	Sit/Anderson	'82/'85
SIT GROWTH & INCOME	Growth Income	42.8	28.38	10.23	26.33	10.32	10.32	12.76	0.3	21.5	332-5580	612-334-5888	None	1.65	None	Mitchelson/Sit	'82/'82
SIT INTERNATIONAL GROWTH	International	66.1	15.71	9.25	7.86	14.95	☆		0.3		332-5580	612-334-5888	None		None	Kim/Sit	'91/'91
SIT SMALL CAP GROWTH	Small Company Growth	10.7	13.49	10.03	☆				0.1	N/A	332-5580	612-334-5888	None	None	None	Eugene Sit	'94
SIT US GOVERNMENT	Fixed Income	37.9	10.43	3.26	7.89	6.00	7.98	☆	6.7		332-5580	612-334-5888	None	0.86	None	Brilley/Rogers	'87/'94
SKYLINE SPECIAL EQ ☒	Small Company Growth	191.8	16.62	4.79	9.59	18.62	17.85	☆	0.0	12.3	458-5222	312-670-6035	None	1.49	None	William Dutton	'87
SKYLINE SPECIAL EQ II	Midcap	94.8	10.84	4.23	9.12	☆			0.2	13.8	458-5222	312-670-6035	None	1.51	None	Kenneth S. Kailin	'93
SM BARNEY 1996 ☒	Balanced Target	57.9	9.08	4.25	10.97	7.61	8.68	☆	6.1	18.6	327-6748	212-723-9218	5.00	0.75	None	Hersch Cohen	'89
SM BARNEY 1998 ☒	Balanced Target	100.9	7.91	6.32	13.19	8.49	☆		4.9	18.6	327-6748	212-723-9218	5.00	1.01	None	Richard Cohen	'91
SM BARNEY 2000 ☒	Balanced Target	74.7	9.08	12.66	23.45	12.58	☆		3.0	15.3	327-6748	212-723-9218	5.00	1.15	None	Richard Freeman	'91
SM BARNEY ADJ RT; A	Fixed Income	175.0	9.84	1.48	6.11	3.98	☆		5.2	18.4	327-6748	212-723-9218	None	2.31	None	Anderson/Amero/Kapito	'92/'92/'92
SM BARNEY ADJ RT; B	Fixed Income	5.6	9.84	1.48	6.11	☆			5.2	☆	327-6748	212-723-9218	None	2.35	3.00	Anderson/Amero/Kapito	'92/'92/'92
SM BARNEY AGGR GRO; A	Capital Appreciation	185.8	29.97	14.68	32.77	18.22	12.02	16.03	0.0	19.8	327-6748	212-723-9218	5.00	1.42	None	Richard Freeman	'86
SM BARNEY AGGR GRO; B	Capital Appreciation	63.6	29.42	14.64	32.00	☆	☆		0.0	19.8	327-6748	212-723-9218	5.00	2.22	5.00	Richard Freeman	'92
SM BARNEY APPREC; A	Growth	1,816.0	11.90	7.79	18.70	10.92	10.14	13.71	1.5	18.4	327-6748	212-723-9218	5.00	1.02	None	Hersch Cohen	'79
SM BARNEY APPREC; B	Growth	865.4	11.83	7.55	17.66	☆	☆		0.8	18.4	327-6748	212-723-9218	None	1.80	5.00	Hersch Cohen	'92
SM BARNEY CONVERT; A	Convertible Securities	35.1	15.04	5.60	10.62	☆	☆		4.9	☆	None	212-723-9218	5.00	1.40	None	Bob Swab	'95
SM BARNEY CONVERT; B	Convertible Securities	45.2	15.04	5.47	10.06	8.12	9.38		4.4	☆	None	212-723-9218	None	1.88	5.00	Bob Swab	'95
SM BARNEY DVSD STRAT; A	Fixed Income	171.8	7.77	4.04	8.94	5.89	9.06	☆	8.5	☆	None	212-698-5349	4.50	1.10	None	Bianchi/Conroy/Filatov	'92/'92/'94
SM BARNEY DVSD STRAT; B	Fixed Income	2,340.9	7.78	4.03	8.49	☆	☆		7.9	☆	None	212-698-5349	None	1.57	4.50	Bianchi/Conroy/Filatov	'89/'89/'94
SM BARNEY FDMNTL VAL; A	Growth	352.6	8.23	9.30	17.28	15.51	13.05	12.39	1.5	12.2	None	212-698-5349	5.00	1.30	None	John Goode	'90
SM BARNEY FDMNTL VAL; B	Growth	484.8	8.20	9.04	16.38	☆	☆		0.9	12.2	None	212-698-5349	None	2.06	5.00	John Goode	'92
SM BARNEY GOVT SECS; A	Fixed Income	474.6	9.63	4.64	9.53	☆	☆		5.8	☆	327-6748	212-723-9218	4.50	1.26	None	James Conroy	'92
SM BARNEY GOVT SECS; B	Fixed Income	171.8	9.63	4.50	8.98	8.26	☆	7.99	5.3	☆	327-6748	212-723-9218	None	1.74	4.50	James Conroy	'84
SM BARNEY GRO & INC; A	Growth Income	99.1	10.76	7.19	16.20	☆	☆		1.6	16.9	None	212-698-5349	5.00	1.41	None	Gerken/Novello	'92/'92
SM BARNEY GRO & INC; B	Growth Income	96.4	10.79	7.04	15.68	☆			1.1	16.9	None	212-698-5349	None	1.90	5.00	Gerken/Novello	'92/'92
SM BARNEY HIGH INC; A	Fixed Income	314.4	10.95	4.58	7.73	9.79	12.03		10.2	☆	None	212-698-5349	4.50	1.11	None	John Bianchi	'92
SM BARNEY HIGH INC; B	Fixed Income	459.2	10.96	4.53	7.23	☆			9.6	☆	None	212-698-5349	None	1.60	4.50	John Bianchi	'88

Fund	Objective	Net Assets ($Mil)	NAV	Ret 1	Ret 2	Ret 3	Ret 4	Ret 5	Yield %	Rtg	Phone 1	Front Load	Exp Ratio	Def Load	Phone 2	Manager	Incept.
SM BARNEY INVMNT GRD; A	Fixed Income	207.4	12.49	12.47	22.79	10.83	☆	☆	6.9		327-6748	4.50	1.11	None	212-723-9218	George Mueller, Jr.	'92
SM BARNEY INVMNT GRD; B	Fixed Income	263.2	12.49	12.33	22.15	10.83	12.07	11.16	6.5		327-6748	None	1.57	4.50	212-723-9218	George Mueller, Jr.	'85
SM BARNEY LTD TREAS; A	Fixed Income	58.4	7.62	5.59	10.34	5.67	☆	☆	4.9		327-6748	2.00	0.99	None	212-723-9218	James Conroy	'91
SM BARNEY METALS; A	Gold	33.9	18.25	-0.87	-5.49	9.84	4.04	☆	0.0	N/A	327-6748	5.00	1.81	5.00	212-723-9218	Ailsing O'Duffy	'91
SM BARNEY METALS; B	Gold	29.7	17.91	-1.00	-6.13	☆	☆	☆	0.0	N/A	327-6748	None	2.54	5.00	212-723-9218	Ailsing O'Duffy	'92
SM BARNEY MGD GOVTS; A	Fixed Income	537.8	12.67	4.36	9.36	6.58	8.62	8.48	6.1		327-6748	4.50	1.22	None	212-723-9218	James Conroy	'90
SM BARNEY MGD GOVTS; B	Fixed Income	136.1	12.67	4.21	8.74	☆	☆	☆	5.5		327-6748	None	1.74	4.50	212-723-9218	James Conroy	'92
SM BARNEY SPEC EQTY; A	Small Company Growth	92.9	22.79	17.35	33.20	24.42	☆	☆	0.0	24.4	327-6748	5.00	1.49	None	212-723-9218	George Novello	'92
SM BARNEY SPEC EQTY; B	Small Company Growth	92.4	22.38	17.11	32.27	☆	☆	☆	0.0	24.4	327-6748	None	2.21	5.00	212-723-9218	George Novello	'90
SM BARNEY STRAT INV; A	Flexible	162.5	17.75	6.99	14.85	☆	☆	9.38	2.3	14.6	None	5.00	1.33	None	212-698-5349	William Carter	'92
SM BARNEY STRAT INV; B	Flexible	225.1	17.82	6.90	14.63	10.22	10.83	☆	1.8	14.6	327-6748	None	2.00	5.00	212-723-9218	William Carter	'87
SM BARNEY TELECOMM INC ☒	Specialty	N/A	104.27	6.09	8.16	12.65	9.47	13.70	5.3	13.8	None	None	0.95	None	212-723-9218	Guy Scott	'91
SM BARNEY TELECOMM; A	Science & Technology	76.8	12.91	9.22	13.50	18.13	12.77	13.56	1.0	14.5	327-6748	5.00	1.24	5.00	212-723-9218	Guy Scott	'91
SM BARNEY TELECOMM; B	Science & Technology	170.8	12.76	8.97	12.56	☆	☆	☆	0.3	14.5	327-6748	5.00	2.07	5.00	212-723-9218	Guy Scott	'92
SM BARNEY TOTAL RET; A	Growth Income	465.9	16.20	6.14	13.90	☆	☆	☆	7.9	13.5	None	5.00	1.19	None	212-698-5349	Fullerton/Rosenbluth	'92/'95
SM BARNEY TOTAL RET; B	Growth Income	1,607.1	16.20	5.95	13.33	10.99	12.51	☆	7.4	13.5	None	5.00	1.66	None	212-698-5349	Fullerton/Rosenbluth	'85/'95
SM BARNEY UTILITIES; A	Utility	177.7	14.18	8.74	17.59	☆	☆	☆	5.9	13.4	None	5.00	1.07	None	212-698-5349	Levande/Mueller	'92/'95
SM BARNEY UTILITIES; B	Utility	1,644.2	14.18	8.62	17.02	9.52	9.52	☆	5.4	13.4	None	5.00	1.54	None	212-698-5349	Levande/Mueller	'88/'95
SM BARNEY WLD EUROPE; A	European Region	25.3	14.07	8.73	19.64	7.09	☆	☆	5.4		None	5.00	None	5.00	212-698-5349	Maurits Edersheim	'94
SM BARNEY WLD EUROPE; B	European Region	1.5	14.00	8.61	☆	☆	☆	☆	0.0		None	None	None	5.00	212-698-5349	Maurits Edersheim	'94
SM BARNEY WLD EUROPE; C	European Region	134.0	13.95	8.64	18.93	7.07	☆	☆	0.0		None	None	1.32	1.00	212-698-5349	Maurits Edersheim	'94
SM BARNEY WLD GLBL; A	World Income	36.2	12.05	3.17	9.68	☆	☆	☆	6.5		None	4.50	None	None	212-698-5349	Team Managed	N/A
SM BARNEY WLD GLBL; B	World Income	4.6	12.01	2.97	☆	☆	☆	☆	0.0		None	None	1.80	4.50	212-698-5349	Team Managed	N/A
SM BARNEY WLD GLBL; C	World Income	3.1	11.98	2.98	8.52	☆	☆	☆	0.0		None	None	1.20	1.00	212-698-5349	Team Managed	N/A
SM BARNEY WLD GLBL; Y	World Income	18.9	11.90	3.19	8.57	☆	☆	☆	6.8		None	None	None	None	212-698-5349	Team Managed	'94
SM BARNEY WLD IN BAL; A	Global Flexible	2.2	12.30	8.67	☆	☆	☆	☆	0.0		None	5.00	None	5.00	212-698-5349	Maurits Edersheim	'94
SM BARNEY WLD IN BAL; B	Global Flexible	4.4	12.32	8.46	☆	☆	☆	☆	0.0		None	None	None	1.00	212-698-5349	Maurits Edersheim	'94
SM BARNEY WLD IN BAL; C	Global Flexible	522.5	12.30	8.48	0.87	11.35	☆	☆	0.0		None	5.00	1.35	1.00	212-698-5349	Maurits Edersheim	'94
SM BARNEY WLD INTL; A	International	99.6	17.19	8.45	11.35	☆	10.17	☆	0.7	16.6	None	None	None	5.00	212-698-5349	Maurits Edersheim	'86
SM BARNEY WLD INTL; B	International	251.9	17.24	8.29	☆	☆	☆	☆	0.0	16.6	None	5.00	2.10	1.00	212-698-5349	Maurits Edersheim	'94
SM BARNEY WLD INTL; C	International	251.9	17.00	8.28	0.15	☆	☆	☆	0.0		None	None	None	None	212-698-5349	Maurits Edersheim	'93
SM BARNEY WLD PACFIC; A	Pacific Region	5.5	10.70	0.85	-11.13	☆	☆	☆	0.0		None	5.00	None	5.00	212-698-5349	Maurits Edersheim	'94
SM BARNEY WLD PACFIC; B	Pacific Region	0.5	10.61	0.57	☆	☆	☆	☆	0.0		None	None	None	1.00	212-698-5349	Maurits Edersheim	'94
SM BARNEY WLD PACFIC; C	Pacific Region	2.4	10.59	0.67	-11.82	☆	☆	☆	0.0		None	5.00	0.96	None	212-698-5349	Maurits Edersheim	'94
SM BARNEY INC & GRO; A	Growth Income	579.3	13.91	6.78	15.76	10.26	10.08	11.78	3.2	16.6	None	5.00	2.10	None	212-698-5349	Bruce Sargent	'74
SM BARNEY INC & GRO; B	Growth Income	1.5	13.88	6.61	14.74	☆	☆	☆	0.0		None	5.00	1.75	None	212-698-5349	Bruce Sargent	'94
SM BARNEY INC & GRO; C	Growth Income	27.8	13.90	6.52	6.95	4.92	☆	7.88	2.5		None	2.00	0.56	1.00	212-698-5349	Bruce Sargent	'92
SM BARNEY INC RET; A	Fixed Income	16.8	9.58	2.65	6.54	☆	☆	☆	5.4		None	None	0.94	1.00	212-698-5349	Patrick Sheehan	'92
SM BARNEY INC RET; C	Fixed Income	2.8	9.58	2.56	6.88	☆	6.74	☆	5.0		None	None	0.69	1.00	212-698-5349	Patrick Sheehan	'92
SM BARNEY INC RET; Y	Fixed Income	1.4	9.58	2.65	☆	☆	☆	☆	5.3		None	None	None	None	212-698-5349	Patrick Sheehan	'93
SM BARNEY MTHLY GOVT; A	Fixed Income	41.4	12.67	5.08	12.08	6.49	8.84	☆	6.3		None	4.50	0.67	None	212-698-5349	Patrick Sheehan	'92
SM BARNEY MTHLY GOVT; C	Fixed Income	3.1	12.67	4.97	11.54	☆	☆	☆	5.7		None	None	1.32	1.00	212-698-5349	Patrick Sheehan	'92
SM BARNEY SH-TM TRES; A	Fixed Income	72.7	4.11	3.86	8.02	5.30	9.00	☆	4.9		None	None	0.91	None	212-698-5349	Patrick Sheehan	'92
SM BARNEY US GOVT; B	Fixed Income	367.5	13.33	5.36	12.30	6.44	9.42	☆	7.1		None	4.50	0.56	4.50	212-698-5349	Patrick Sheehan	'92
SM BARNEY US GOVT; B	Fixed Income	4.5	13.34	5.23	☆	☆	☆	☆	0.0		None	None	None	None	212-698-5349	Patrick Sheehan	'94
SM BARNEY US GOVT; C	Fixed Income	21.2	13.32	5.17	11.74	11.74	☆	☆	6.6		None	None	1.21	1.00	212-698-5349	Patrick Sheehan	'92
SM BARNEY US GOVT; Y	Fixed Income	8.0	13.33	5.28	12.31	12.31	☆	☆	7.2		None	None	0.61	None	212-698-5349	Patrick Sheehan	'93
SM BARNEY UTILITY; B	Utility	72.4	12.31	6.71	12.83	12.83	☆	☆	6.6	11.9	None	5.00	1.01	5.00	212-698-5349	Phil Miller	'90
SM BARNEY UTILITY; B	Utility	2.4	12.34	6.56	☆	☆	☆	☆	0.0	N/A	None	None	None	None	212-698-5349	Phil Miller	'94
SM BARNEY UTILITY; C	Utility	7.9	12.33	6.57	12.04	☆	☆	☆	5.7	11.9	None	None	1.77	1.00	212-698-5349	Phil Miller	'92

PERFORMANCE OF MUTUAL FUNDS (continued)

FUND NAME	OBJECTIVE	ASSETS ($MIL) 5/31/95	NAV ($/SHR) 6/30/95	RETURN THROUGH 6/30 (Annualized) QTR	1YR	3YRS	5YRS	10YRS	DIV YLD %	P/E RATIO	PHONE NUMBER 800	In-State	FEES Load	Exp. Ratio	Redemption	MANAGER	SINCE
SM BREEDEN INTMDT GOVT	Fixed Income	35.9	10.14	4.87	11.95	8.30	☆	☆	5.8	☐	221-3138	None	None	0.78	None	Daniel C. Dektar	'92
SM BREEDEN MKT TRACKING	Growth Income	2.5	11.76	9.23	27.76	15.08	☆	☆	4.8	N/A	221-3138	None	None	0.90	None	John Sprow	'92
SM BREEDEN SHORT GOVT	Fixed Income	252.3	9.83	1.02	6.92	4.95	☆	☆	6.7	☐	221-3138	None	None	0.11	None	Daniel C. Dektar	'92
SM&R AMER NATL GOVT INC	Fixed Income	19.8	10.47	6.44	10.60	7.04	☆	☆	6.5	☐	231-4639	409-763-2767	4.50	1.12	None	Terry E. Frank	'93
SM&R AMER NATL PRIMARY	Fixed Income	17.4	1.00	1.30	4.75	3.39	☆	☆	4.7	☐	231-4639	409-763-2767	None	0.79	None	Vera M. Young	'92
SMALLCAP WORLD FUND	Global Small Company	3,845.8	23.71	9.15	15.72	14.80	12.84	☆	0.7	☐	421-4120	714-671-7000	5.75	1.12	None	Multiple Managers	N/A
SMITH HAYES SMALL CAP	Small Company Growth	8.9	13.49	10.76	20.33	☆	☆	☆	0.0	18.2	279-7437	402-476-3000	None	1.91	None	Kirk McCown	'92
SOGEN INTERNATIONAL	Global	2,117.2	24.57	5.91	9.72	12.72	11.47	14.49	0.6	☐	628-0252	212-399-1141	3.75	1.28	None	Jean-Marie Eveillard	'79
SOGEN GOLD FUND	Gold	49.8	11.55	2.39	6.74	☆	☆	☆	0.3	N/A	628-0252	212-399-1141	3.75	2.27	None	Jean-Marie Eveillard	'93
SOGEN OVERSEAS FUND	International	487.9	12.32	5.75	7.12	☆	☆	☆	0.4	☐	628-0252	212-399-1141	3.75	1.72	None	Jean-Marie Eveillard	'93
SOLON SDGF 1 YEAR ▥	Fixed Income	0.1	9.98	1.75	6.34	☆	☆	☆	6.3	☐	467-6566	510-988-7110	None	None	None	James I. Midanek	'94
SOLON SDGF 3 YEAR	Fixed Income	7.5	9.96	3.22	8.45	☆	☆	☆	6.3	☐	467-6566	510-988-7110	None	None	None	James I. Midanek	'94
SOUND SHORE	Growth	65.7	18.03	8.81	19.63	15.27	12.95	13.90	1.3	13.8	551-1980	207-879-0001	None	1.22	None	Kane/Burn	'85/'85
SOUTHTRUST VULCAN BOND	Fixed Income	79.8	10.24	5.12	10.09	6.79	☆	☆	5.9	☐	239-7470	None	4.00	0.51	1.00	Dave Howell	'93
SOUTHTRUST VULCAN STK	Growth	144.2	12.11	8.96	24.03	9.73	☆	☆	1.7	17.6	239-7470	None	4.50	0.48	1.00	Bob Hardin	'93
SPECIAL PORTFOLIOS CASH ✿ ✿	Fixed Income	26.7	9.52	2.22	6.52	4.94	5.11	☆	5.7	☐	800-2638	612-738-4000	None	0.42	None	Poling/Ott	'89/'89
SPECIAL PORTFOLIOS STOCK	Capital Appreciation	84.4	39.35	13.56	29.85	12.69	12.86	14.70	0.0	26.0	800-2638	612-738-4000	None	1.15	None	Stephen Poling	'83
SS RESEARCH AGGRESS; A ▥	Flexible	37.0	10.50	7.14	13.96	☆	☆	☆	1.5	17.3	882-3302	617-348-2000	None	1.16	None	Michael Yogg	'94
SS RESEARCH AGGRESS; C ▥	Flexible	18.9	10.51	7.24	14.32	☆	☆	☆	1.7	17.3	882-3302	617-348-2000	None	2.16	None	Michael Yogg	'94
SS RESEARCH CAPITAL; A	Capital Appreciation	34.1	11.76	12.75	33.58	☆	☆	☆	0.0	21.1	882-3302	617-348-2000	4.50	1.41	None	Fredrick R. Kobrick	'93
SS RESEARCH CAPITAL; B	Capital Appreciation	122.7	11.58	12.54	32.59	☆	☆	☆	0.0	21.1	882-3302	617-348-2000	None	2.16	5.00	Fredrick R. Kobrick	'93
SS RESEARCH CAPITAL; C ▥	Capital Appreciation	24.9	11.86	12.74	33.95	24.96	19.18	18.18	0.0	21.1	882-3302	617-348-2000	None	1.16	None	Fredrick R. Kobrick	'85
SS RESEARCH CAPITAL; D	Capital Appreciation	57.6	11.60	12.51	32.67	☆	☆	☆	0.0	21.1	882-3302	617-348-2000	None	2.16	1.00	Fredrick R. Kobrick	'93
SS RESEARCH CONSERV; A	Fixed Income	26.8	10.26	5.77	12.39	☆	☆	☆	3.6	☐	882-3302	617-348-2000	None	1.16	None	Michael Yogg	'94
SS RESEARCH CONSERV; C ▥	Fixed Income	1.3	10.26	5.77	12.64	☆	☆	☆	3.8	☐	882-3302	617-348-2000	None	2.16	1.00	Michael Yogg	'94
SS RESEARCH GL ENGY; A	Natural Resources	27.9	12.16	9.55	2.70	14.88	1.73	☆	0.0	14.1	882-3302	617-348-2000	4.50	1.75	None	Dan Rice	'90
SS RESEARCH GL ENGY; B	Natural Resources	7.1	12.03	9.26	2.12	☆	☆	☆	0.0	14.1	882-3302	617-348-2000	None	2.25	5.00	Dan Rice	'93
SS RESEARCH GL ENGY; C	Natural Resources	1.7	12.27	9.55	3.11	☆	☆	☆	0.0	14.1	882-3302	617-348-2000	None	1.25	None	Dan Rice	'93
SS RESEARCH GL ENGY; D	Natural Resources	2.6	12.02	9.27	2.12	☆	☆	☆	0.0	14.1	882-3302	617-348-2000	None	2.25	1.00	Dan Rice	'93
SS RESEARCH GOVT INC; A	Fixed Income	686.5	12.50	6.15	11.77	7.49	9.38	☆	6.4	☐	882-3302	617-348-2000	4.50	1.07	None	Jack Kallis	'87
SS RESEARCH GOVT INC; B	Fixed Income	74.8	12.48	6.05	10.97	☆	☆	☆	5.7	☐	882-3302	617-348-2000	None	1.82	5.00	Jack Kallis	'93
SS RESEARCH GOVT INC; C	Fixed Income	2.3	12.50	6.30	12.15	☆	☆	☆	6.6	☐	882-3302	617-348-2000	None	0.82	None	Jack Kallis	'93
SS RESEARCH GOVT INC; D	Fixed Income	13.1	12.49	6.05	11.05	☆	☆	☆	5.7	☐	882-3302	617-348-2000	None	1.82	1.00	Jack Kallis	'93
SS RESEARCH GROWTH; A	Growth	1.0	8.82	13.80	26.64	☆	☆	☆	0.6	20.3	882-3302	617-348-2000	4.50	0.90	None	Fredrick R. Kobrick	'95
SS RESEARCH GROWTH; B	Growth	2.9	8.72	13.54	25.37	☆	☆	☆	0.0	20.3	882-3302	617-348-2000	None	1.63	5.00	Fredrick R. Kobrick	'95
SS RESEARCH GROWTH; C ▥	Growth	209.0	8.81	13.92	26.63	13.13	9.41	13.22	0.8	20.3	882-3302	617-348-2000	None	0.64	None	Fredrick R. Kobrick	'95
SS RESEARCH GROWTH; D	Growth	0.7	8.72	13.69	25.37	☆	☆	☆	0.0	20.3	882-3302	617-348-2000	None	1.63	1.00	Fredrick R. Kobrick	'95
SS RESEARCH INTL EQ; A	International	21.5	9.37	1.19	-6.51	☆	☆	☆	0.0	☐	882-3302	617-348-2000	4.50	1.90	None	Steve Bamford	'94
SS RESEARCH INTL EQ; B	International	23.9	9.28	0.98	-7.20	☆	☆	☆	0.0	☐	882-3302	617-348-2000	None	2.65	5.00	Steve Bamford	'94
SS RESEARCH INTL EQ; C ▥	International	37.3	9.42	1.29	15.75	☆	☆	☆	0.0	☐	882-3302	617-348-2000	None	1.65	None	Steve Bamford	'92
SS RESEARCH INTL EQ; D	International	3.2	9.28	1.09	-7.12	☆	☆	☆	0.0	☐	882-3302	617-348-2000	None	2.65	1.00	Steve Bamford	'94
SS RESEARCH INTL FI; A	World Income	1.3	9.13	4.29	20.42	☆	☆	☆	6.2	☐	882-3302	617-348-2000	4.50	1.69	None	Nick Sanjana	'94
SS RESEARCH INTL FI; B	World Income	2.1	9.11	4.12	19.68	☆	☆	☆	5.6	☐	882-3302	617-348-2000	None	2.43	5.00	Nick Sanjana	'94
SS RESEARCH INTL FI; C ▥	World Income	25.3	9.14	4.34	20.67	11.85	☆	☆	6.4	☐	882-3302	617-348-2000	None	1.47	None	Nick Sanjana	'94
SS RESEARCH INTL FI; D	World Income	0.7	9.11	4.12	19.46	☆	☆	☆	5.6	☐	882-3302	617-348-2000	None	2.45	1.00	Nick Sanjana	'94

Fund	Objective	Net Assets ($Mil)	NAV	YTD %	1-Yr %	5-Yr %	Yield %	%	Phone	Phone	Max Load	12b-1/Exp	Def. Load	Manager	Inception
SS RESEARCH INTMDT BD; A ▪▪	Fixed Income	10.5	9.90	4.71	9.69	☆	5.5	☐	882-3302	617-348-2000	4.50			Jack Kallis	'94
SS RESEARCH INTMDT BD; C ▪▪	Fixed Income	3.9	9.90	4.77	10.00	☆	5.7	17.2	882-3302	617-348-2000	None	1.31	1.00	Jack Kallis	'94
SS RESEARCH MODERATE; C ▪	Balanced	32.4	9.93	7.31	14.26	☆	2.7	N/A	882-3302	617-348-2000	None		1.00	Michael Yogg	'94
SS RESEARCH SC VALUE; A	Small Company Growth	5.1	10.38	6.13	☆	☆	0.0	N/A	882-3302	617-348-2000	4.50			Rudy Kluiber	'95
SS RESEARCH SC VALUE; B	Small Company Growth	0.1	10.35	5.94	☆	☆	0.0	N/A	882-3302	617-348-2000	None		5.00	Rudy Kluiber	'95
SS RESEARCH SC VALUE; C	Small Company Growth	0.1	10.39	6.24	☆	☆	0.0	N/A	882-3302	617-348-2000	None		1.00	Rudy Kluiber	'95
SS RESEARCH SC VALUE; D	Small Company Growth	0.1	10.35	5.94	☆	☆	0.0	N/A	882-3302	617-348-2000	None			Rudy Kluiber	'95
SS RESEARCH SM CAP; A ⊠	Small Company Growth	19.5	8.76	6.44	8.96	☆	0.0	24.4	882-3302	617-348-2000	4.50			Charles Glovsky	'94
SS RESEARCH SM CAP; B	Small Company Growth	23.6	8.67	6.25	8.24	☆	0.0	24.4	882-3302	617-348-2000	None		5.00	Charles Glovsky	'94
SS RESEARCH SM CAP; C ▪⊠	Small Company Growth	7.5	8.82	6.65	9.29	☆	0.0	24.4	882-3302	617-348-2000	None		1.00	Charles Glovsky	'93
SS RESEARCH SM CAP; D ⊠	Small Company Growth	7.5	8.67	6.25	8.24	☆	0.0	24.4	882-3302	617-348-2000	4.50			Charles Glovsky	'94
STAGECOACH INST ASST ALL	Flexible	324.2	10.87	9.12	21.11	☆	4.1	N/A	776-0179	None	None	0.79		Janice Deringer	'93
STAGECOACH INST BD INDEX	Fixed Income	20.8	9.64	6.50	12.49	☆	6.8	22.1	776-0179	None	None	0.31		Jonathan Tiemann	'93
STAGECOACH INST GROW STK	Growth	108.6	14.02	15.77	40.90	☆	0.0	17.0	776-0179	None	None	0.80		Jon Hickman	'93
STAGECOACH INST S&P 500	S&P Index	553.5	12.05	9.47	25.56	☆	2.4		776-0179	None	None	0.27		Tom Seto	'93
STAGECOACH INST SH-INT	Fixed Income	11.8	9.43	4.97	10.59	☆	6.8	☐	776-0179	None	None	0.65		Thomas/Glessman	'93
STAGECOACH INST TRES ALL	Fixed Income	59.6	9.33	5.11	21.21	☆	6.2	17.3	776-0179	None	None	0.78		Janice Deringer	'93
STAGECOACH AST ALLOC; A	Flexible	1,017.0	19.24	9.13	21.21	12.20	4.2	17.3	222-8222	None	4.50	0.84		Derringer/Sakamoto	'88/'91
STAGECOACH AST ALLOC; B	Flexible	4.3	11.55	8.35	☆	☆	1.6	15.6	222-8222	None	None		5.00	Derringer/Sakamoto	'95/'95
STAGECOACH CORP STOCK	S&P Index	282.5	37.23	9.20	24.71	13.20		N/A	222-8222	None	None	0.97		Horn/Seto	'84/'91
STAGECOACH DVSD INC; A	Income	57.2	12.16	6.11	16.82	☆	2.8	N/A	222-8222	None	4.50	1.06		Wisniewski/Bissell	'92/'92
STAGECOACH DVSD INC; B	Income	1.3	11.37	5.57	☆	☆	2.8	17.0	222-8222	None	None		5.00	Wisniewski/Bissell	'95/'95
STAGECOACH GNMA; A	Fixed Income	162.8	10.89	5.38	12.01	6.29	7.1	N/A	222-8222	None	4.50	0.73		Mike Niedermeyer	'91
STAGECOACH GRO & INC; A	Growth Income	145.8	16.37	8.71	22.38	12.43	1.4	☐	222-8222	None	4.50	1.11		Wisniewski/Bissell	'90/'90
STAGECOACH GRO & INC; B	Growth Income	1.2	11.66	8.36	☆	☆	0.0	N/A	222-8222	None	None		5.00	Wisniewski/Bissell	'95/'95
STAGECOACH GVT ALLOC; A	Flexible	135.6	14.73	5.02	10.02	9.60	5.8	N/A	222-8222	None	4.50	1.01		Derringer/Sakamoto	'90/'91
STAGECOACH LFPTH 2000; IN	Flexible	9.4	10.34	5.34	11.44	☆	4.0	N/A	776-0179	None	None			Wells Fargo Nikko Adv.	'94
STAGECOACH LFPTH 2000; RT	Flexible	60.8	10.31	5.22	11.19	☆	4.1	N/A	222-8222	None	None			Wells Fargo Nikko Adv.	'94
STAGECOACH LFPTH 2010; IN	Flexible	17.3	10.70	7.00	15.34	☆	3.5	N/A	776-0179	None	None			Wells Fargo Nikko Adv.	'94
STAGECOACH LFPTH 2010; RT	Flexible	41.6	10.65	6.90	15.02	☆	3.6	N/A	222-8222	None	None			Wells Fargo Nikko Adv.	'94
STAGECOACH LFPTH 2020; IN	Flexible	21.0	11.01	7.86	17.64	☆	3.0	N/A	776-0179	None	None			Wells Fargo Nikko Adv.	'94
STAGECOACH LFPTH 2020; RT	Flexible	80.1	11.01	7.72	17.32	☆	2.8	N/A	222-8222	None	None			Wells Fargo Nikko Adv.	'94
STAGECOACH LFPTH 2030; IN	Flexible	13.6	11.21	8.94	21.09	☆	2.5	N/A	776-0179	None	None			Wells Fargo Nikko Adv.	'94
STAGECOACH LFPTH 2030; RT	Flexible	51.7	11.19	8.93	20.69	☆	2.4	N/A	222-8222	None	None			Wells Fargo Nikko Adv.	'94
STAGECOACH LFPTH 2040; IN	Flexible	16.2	11.49	8.96	22.65	☆	1.8	N/A	776-0179	None	None			Wells Fargo Nikko Adv.	'94
STAGECOACH LFPTH 2040; RT	Flexible	76.1	11.49	8.93	22.40	☆	1.7	☐	222-8222	None	None			Wells Fargo Nikko Adv.	'94
STAGECOACH SH-INT GOVT	Fixed Income	13.2	9.84	3.73	6.84	☆	5.4	N/A	222-8222	None	None			Mark Kraschel	'93
STAGECOACH VAR RATE GOVT	Fixed Income	15.7	10.17	2.73	3.02	2.60	5.5	N/A	222-8222	None	None	0.25		R. Glessman	'92
STALWART AGGRESS EQUITY	Small Company Growth	6.8	11.01	8.69	☆	☆	0.0	N/A	273-3936	317-692-3900	3.00	0.77		Samuel S. Stewart Jr.	'95
STALWART CORE EQUITY	Growth	8.5	11.27	6.02	☆	☆	0.0	N/A	273-3936	317-692-3900	3.00			Robert H. Harper	'95
STALWART INCOME	Income	6.9	10.80	6.78	☆	☆	5.9	N/A	273-3936	None	None			Sheldon M. Lekin	'95
STALWART INTL EQUITY	International	4.6	10.99	8.06	☆	☆	0.0	N/A	273-3936	317-692-3900	None			Dave Loewner	'95
STALWART US GOVT SECS	Fixed Income	8.7	10.69	6.51	17.56	7.42	5.9	13.4	273-3936	317-692-3900	None			Sheldon M. Pekin	'91
STAND AYER WOOD EQUITY	Growth	106.4	34.31	11.11	22.86	☆	1.7	☐	221-4795	617-350-6100	None	0.70		David H. Cameron	'93
STAND AYER WOOD FXD INC	Fixed Income	1,969.1	20.29	5.92	11.66	☆	5.9	17.2	221-4795	617-350-6100	None	0.38		Caleb Aldrich	'93
STAND AYER WOOD GL FXD	World Income	141.3	18.97	5.20	9.62	5.69	4.2	☐	221-4795	617-350-6100	None	0.65		Richard S. Wood	'93/'93
STAND AYER WOOD INTL EQU	International	95.0	22.44	2.47	-3.75	6.90	3.1	☐	221-4795	617-350-6100	None	1.23		Clayson/Schoeck	'88/'93
STAND AYER WOOD INTL FXD	World Income	1,064.3	22.47	4.71	8.37	6.37	3.1	☐	221-4795	617-350-6100	None	0.51		Richard S. Wood	'91
STAND AYER WOOD SEC	Fixed Income	58.1	19.93	5.31	11.70	17.60	6.0	☐	221-4795	617-350-6100	None	0.45		Sweeney/Driscoll	'89/'89
STAND AYER WOOD SML CAP	Small Company Growth	128.4	45.82	2.54	13.50	16.26		17.2	221-4795	617-350-6100	None	0.79		Nicholas S. Battelle	'88

© Copyright Lipper Analytical Services, Inc.

441

PERFORMANCE OF MUTUAL FUNDS (continued)

FUND NAME	OBJECTIVE	ASSETS ($ MIL) 5/31/95	NAV ($/SHR) 6/30/95	QTR	1YR	3YRS	5YRS	10YRS	DIV YLD %	P/E RATIO	800	In-State	Load	Redemption	Exp. Ratio	MANAGER	SINCE
STAND AYER WOOD STAR	Fixed Income	273.5	19.47	2.12	6.47	4.32	6.02	☆	5.6		221-4795	617-350-6100	None	None	0.33	Jennifer Pline	'93
STAR CAP APP ●	Midcap	40.6	11.46	4.69	18.57	☆	☆	☆	0.4	N/A	677-3863	513-632-5547	4.50	None	None	Scott Dooley	'94
STAR GROWTH EQUITY	Growth	38.8	11.60	6.68				☆	0.0	N/A	677-3863	513-632-5547	None	5.00		Donald Keller	'95
STAR RELATIVE VALUE	Growth	101.8	13.61	9.79	22.84	12.75	☆	☆	2.0		677-3863	513-632-5547	4.50	None	1.15	Joseph Belew	'95
STAR STELLAR; INV	Global Flexible	50.4	11.74	5.98	9.39	7.98	☆	☆	2.9	15.9	677-3863	513-632-5547	4.50	None	1.55	Donald Keller	'94
STAR STELLAR; TR	Global Flexible	64.6	11.71	5.77	9.40	☆	☆	☆	3.2		677-3863	513-632-5547	None	None	1.43	Donald Keller	'94
STAR STRATEGIC INCOME	Fixed Income	25.9	10.50	4.29	☆	☆	☆	☆	0.0		677-3863	513-632-5547	None	5.00	None	Kirk Mentzer	'95
STAR US GOVT INC	Fixed Income	95.4	9.80	4.87	10.19	5.22	☆	☆	6.1		677-3863	513-632-5547	3.50	None	0.97	Kirk Mentzer	'93
STARBURST GOVT INC; INV	Fixed Income	66.7	9.90	4.28	8.98	5.22	☆	☆	6.0		239-6669	205-558-6702	2.50	None	1.20	Dan Davidson	'92
STATE BOND COMMON STOCK	Growth	58.3	8.86	7.22	24.91	10.66	9.49	13.62	0.9	N/A	437-6663	612-835-0097	4.75	None	1.22	Keith Martens	'84
STATE BOND DIVERSIFIED	Growth Income	41.5	9.54	6.20	17.07	9.37	10.28	12.83	2.3	15.9	437-6663	612-835-0097	4.75	None	1.17	Keith Martens	'84
STATE BOND US GOVT SEC	Fixed Income	14.4	5.07	5.26	12.25	5.82	7.99	☆	6.2		437-6663	612-835-0097	5.00	None	1.00	Keith Martens	'85
STATE FARM BALANCED ◼	Balanced	430.9	34.58	5.98	20.91	10.04	12.92	14.85	3.4	19.3	None	309-766-2029	None	None	0.17	Kurt Moser	'91
STATE FARM GROWTH ◼	Growth	913.5	26.43	6.63	28.85	10.05	11.39	14.78	2.0	17.8	None	309-766-2029	None	None	0.14	Kurt Moser	'91
STATE FARM INTERIM ◼	Fixed Income	97.1	10.09	3.89	8.46	5.75	7.68	8.16	7.1		None	309-766-2029	None	None	0.22	Kurt Moser	'91
STATE ST MSTR INVEST; A	Growth Income	105.8	9.02	8.58	19.45	☆	☆	☆	1.3	18.1	882-3302	617-348-2000	4.50	None	0.89	Steven P. Somes	'93
STATE ST MSTR INVEST; B	Growth Income	137.6	8.99	8.41	18.51	☆	☆	☆	0.6	18.1	882-3302	617-348-2000	None	5.00	1.64	Steven P. Somes	'93
STATE ST MSTR INVEST; C ◼	Growth Income	691.3	9.04	8.62	19.84	10.86	9.48	12.53	1.5	18.1	882-3302	617-348-2000	None	None	0.65	Steven P. Somes	'95
STATE ST MSTR INVEST; D	Growth Income	13.8	9.01	8.40	18.51	☆	☆	☆	1.6	18.1	882-3302	617-348-2000	None	1.00	1.64	Steven P. Somes	'95
STATE STREET EXCHANGE ⊠	Growth	217.6	241.46	9.03	26.42	12.07	10.02	13.89	1.6	18.0	882-3302	617-348-2000	None	None	0.57	Peter Woodworth	'93
STEADMAN AMER INDUSTRY ⊠	Capital Appreciation	1.3	0.89	-3.26	-26.45	-11.41	-15.86	-10.80	0.0	14.8	424-8570	202-223-1000	None	None	12.66	C.W. Steadman	'92
STEADMAN ASSOCIATED FD	Equity Income	5.4	0.73	12.31	7.35	5.03	-1.81	1.51	0.0	7.6	424-8570	202-223-1000	None	None	7.76	C.W. Steadman	'92
STEADMAN INVESTMENT ⊠	Growth	2.3	1.02	8.51	-8.11	-8.24	-5.73	-4.36	0.0	15.8	424-8570	202-223-1000	None	None	8.90	C.W. Steadman	'92
STEADMAN TECH & GROWTH ⊠	Capital Appreciation	0.8	1.43	0.70	-24.74	-14.90	-18.68	-12.31	0.0	13.8	424-8570	202-223-1000	None	None	16.34	C.W. Steadman	'92
STEINROE CAPITAL OPP	Capital Appreciation	188.6	38.28	9.37	33.42	19.86	12.59	12.29	0.1	33.7	338-2550	None	None	None	0.97	Gloria Santella	'91
STEINROE GOVT INC	Fixed Income	38.3	9.85	5.25	10.94	5.93	8.17	☆	6.3		338-2550	None	None	None	0.98	Michael T. Kennedy	'88
STEINROE GROWTH STOCK FD	Growth	326.4	23.73	9.05	23.03	10.00	10.24	12.62	0.6	21.7	338-2550	None	None	None	0.94	Gustafson/Hirschhorn	'94/'95
STEINROE INCOME FD	Fixed Income	173.4	9.79	6.52	12.79	8.70	10.11	☆	7.2		338-2550	None	None	None	0.82	Ann Benjamin	'90
STEINROE INTERNATIONAL	International	72.3	9.78	4.82	0.04	☆	☆	☆	0.5		338-2550	None	None	None	1.61	Bruno Bertocci	'94
STEINROE INTMDT BOND	Fixed Income	294.0	8.67	5.24	10.11	6.62	8.83	9.16	6.7		338-2550	None	None	None	0.70	Michael T. Kennedy	'88
STEINROE LTD MATURITY	Fixed Income	26.9	9.70	2.87	6.96	☆	☆	☆	5.7		338-2550	None	None	None	0.45	Steve Luetger	'95
STEINROE PRIME EQTY	Growth Income	127.6	15.54	8.21	16.53	12.92	11.47	☆	1.1	17.0	338-2550	None	None	None	0.90	Cantor/Christensen	'95/'95
STEINROE SPECIAL FD	Growth	1,197.4	23.61	4.05	13.38	13.36	10.94	14.77	0.6	18.0	338-2550	None	None	None	0.96	Dunn/Peterson	'91/'91
STEINROE SPECIAL VENTURE	Small Company Growth	44.7	11.40	3.83	☆	☆	☆	☆	1.0	N/A	338-2550	None	None	None	0.83	Dunn/Peterson	'94/'94
STEINROE TOTAL RETRN	Equity Income	223.4	26.61	6.10	12.27	8.89	10.19	10.66	4.5	14.7	338-2550	None	None	None		Maddox/Christensen	'95/'81
STEINROE YOUNG INVESTOR	Growth	19.3	12.63	11.47	31.17	☆	☆	☆	0.6	27.8	338-2550	None	None	None	None	Gustafson/Brady/Maddix	'94/'95/'95
STEPSTONE BALANCED; INSTL	Flexible	186.0	12.93	8.16	18.89	10.85	☆	☆	3.1	15.9	634-1100	213-236-5698	None	None	0.69	Colombo/Power	'91/'95
STEPSTONE BALANCED; INVST	Flexible	7.3	12.93	8.16	18.88	☆	☆	☆	3.1	15.9	634-1100	213-236-5698	4.50	None	0.69	Colombo/Power	'92/'95
STEPSTONE BLUE; INSTL	Growth	42.3	11.10	10.31	24.13	☆	☆	☆	1.6	N/A	634-1100	213-236-5698	None	None	0.85	Harold C. Elliott	'94
STEPSTONE CV SECS; INSTL	Convertible Securities	10.8	9.84	6.61	10.92	☆	☆	☆	4.0		634-1100	213-236-5698	None	None		Harold C. Elliott	'94
STEPSTONE EMRG GRO; INSTL	Small Company Growth	26.8	10.60	6.89	21.51	☆	☆	☆	0.9	20.8	634-1100	213-236-5698	None	None	None	Seth Shalov	'94
STEPSTONE GRO EQU; INSTL	Growth	151.6	16.63	9.22	26.38	14.35	☆	☆	0.6	N/A	634-1100	213-236-5698	None	None	0.77	Colombo/Power	'91/'95
STEPSTONE GRO EQU; INVST	Growth	1.5	16.63	9.22	26.19	14.35	☆	☆	0.6	N/A	634-1100	213-236-5698	4.50	None	0.77	Colombo/Power	'92/'95
STEPSTONE GVT SECS; INSTL	Fixed Income	42.0	9.61	5.92	11.28	☆	☆	☆	5.5		634-1100	213-236-5698	None	None	None	Stephen Blocklin	'94
STEPSTONE INT-TM; INSTL	Fixed Income	115.0	10.27	5.92	10.79	6.72	☆	☆	6.0		634-1100	213-236-5698	None	None	0.69	Jim Atkinson	'91

Note: The 3YRS, 5YRS and 10YRS returns are annualized.

STEPSTONE INT-TM; INVST	Fixed Income	6.5	10.26	5.82	10.69	6.52	☆	☆	6.0	☐	634-1100	213-236-5698	3.00	0.69	None	Jim Atkinson	'92
STEPSTONE INTL EQ; INSTL	International	N/A	35.07	1.24	☆	☆	☆	☆	0.0	☐	634-1100	213-236-5698	None	None	None	Union Capital Advisers	'95
STEPSTONE LTD GOVT; INSTL	Fixed Income	35.3	9.60	2.12	5.06	☆	☆	☆	5.3	☐	634-1100	213-236-5698	None	0.58	None	Martin Standish	'93
STEPSTONE LTD GOVT; INVST	Fixed Income	0.8	9.60	2.01	4.94	☆	☆	☆	5.3	☐	634-1100	213-236-5698	None	None	None	Martin Standish	'93
STEPSTONE VALUE; INSTL	Growth Income	172.9	15.81	10.31	23.46	13.57	☆	☆	2.1	N/A	634-1100	213-236-5698	None	0.77	None	Richard H. Earnest	'91
STEPSTONE VALUE; INVST	Growth Income	9.9	15.81	10.31	23.45	13.57	☆	☆	2.1	N/A	634-1100	213-236-5698	4.50	0.77	None	Richard H. Earnest	'92
STI CLASSIC AGGR GRO; INV	Small Company Growth	7.3	11.52	8.81	21.97	☆	☆	☆	0.3	N/A	428-6970	None	3.75	None	None	Thomas Edgar	'94
STI CLASSIC AGGR GRO; TR	Small Company Growth	125.1	11.53	8.98	22.70	☆	☆	☆	0.7	N/A	428-6970	None	None	None	None	Thomas Edgar	'94
STI CLASSIC BALANCED; INV	Balanced	3.8	10.40	6.32	13.30	☆	☆	☆	3.2	N/A	428-6970	None	3.75	None	None	Gray/Denney	'94/'94
STI CLASSIC BALANCED; TR	Balanced	89.0	10.37	6.50	13.81	☆	☆	☆	3.2	N/A	428-6970	None	None	None	None	Gray/Denney	'93/'93
STI CLASSIC CAP GRO; INV	Growth	160.9	12.52	6.63	14.12	9.48	☆	☆	0.6	17.5	428-6970	None	3.75	1.80	None	Anthony Gray	'92
STI CLASSIC CAP GRO; TR	Growth	984.3	12.51	6.80	14.77	☆	☆	☆	1.2	17.5	428-6970	None	None	1.15	None	Anthony Gray	'92
STI CLASSIC GOVT SEC; TR	Fixed Income	3.3	10.28	5.89	☆	☆	☆	☆	0.0	☐	428-6970	None	None	None	None	Charles Leonard	'94
STI CLASSIC INTL EQ; INV	International	4.0	10.11	3.06	1.99	☆	☆	☆	0.1	☐	428-6970	None	3.75	None	None	Trusco Rhodes	'94
STI CLASSIC INTL EQ; TR	International	88.3	10.16	3.25	2.50	☆	☆	☆	0.2	☐	428-6970	None	None	None	None	Trusco Rhodes	'94
STI CLASSIC INV GRD; INV	Fixed Income	33.6	10.28	6.02	10.98	6.78	☆	☆	5.7	☐	428-6970	None	3.75	1.14	None	Earl Denney	'92
STI CLASSIC INV GRD; TR	Fixed Income	540.0	10.28	6.11	11.45	☆	☆	☆	6.0	☐	428-6970	None	None	0.75	None	Earl Denney	'92
STI CLASSIC LTD FED; INV	Fixed Income	0.6	10.11	3.50	☆	☆	☆	☆	0.0	☐	428-6970	None	2.50	None	None	Earl Denney	'94
STI CLASSIC LTD FED; TR	Fixed Income	41.5	10.11	3.52	7.96	☆	☆	☆	6.2	☐	428-6970	None	None	None	None	Earl Denney	'94
STI CLASSIC S-T BOND; INV	Fixed Income	2.6	10.02	3.81	7.99	☆	☆	☆	5.2	☐	428-6970	None	2.00	0.85	None	Aki Pampush	'93
STI CLASSIC S-T BOND; TR	Fixed Income	60.5	9.99	3.76	8.04	☆	☆	☆	5.4	☐	428-6970	None	None	0.65	None	Aki Pampush	'93
STI CLASSIC S-T TRES; INV	Fixed Income	7.1	9.94	2.20	6.17	☆	☆	☆	4.8	☐	428-6970	None	1.00	0.78	None	Aki Pampush	'93
STI CLASSIC S-T TRES; TR	Fixed Income	9.7	9.94	2.33	6.35	☆	☆	☆	4.9	☐	428-6970	None	None	0.65	None	Aki Pampush	'93
STI CLASSIC SUNBELT; INV	Growth	22.2	10.41	5.36	12.62	☆	☆	☆	0.0	18.2	428-6970	None	3.75	None	None	James Foster	'94
STI CLASSIC SUNBELT; TR	Growth	258.8	10.49	5.53	13.12	☆	☆	☆	0.0	18.2	428-6970	None	None	None	None	James Foster	'94
STI CLASSIC VAL INC; INV	Equity Income	91.8	11.59	6.41	21.35	☆	☆	☆	2.5	17.5	428-6970	None	3.75	1.25	None	Gregory DePrince	'93
STI CLASSIC VAL INC; TR	Equity Income	990.6	11.60	6.49	21.75	☆	☆	☆	2.8	17.5	428-6970	None	None	0.88	None	Gregory DePrince	'93
STOCK & BOND FUND	Balanced	133.9	17.50	6.85	14.69	8.84	8.81	9.44	3.4	16.0	245-4770	412-288-1900	None	1.06	None	Mike Donnelly	'89
STRATTON GROWTH FUND	Growth Income	31.8	22.77	7.56	21.31	12.29	10.71	10.88	2.4	13.9	634-5726	610-941-0255	None	1.34	None	Stratton/Affleck	'72/'79
STRATTON MONTHLY DIV	Utility	135.5	25.16	5.15	12.02	3.91	8.85	8.26	7.6	13.8	634-5726	610-941-0255	None	1.08	None	Stratton/Heffernan	'80/'80
STRATTON SMALL-CAP YIELD	Small Company Growth	15.0	27.47	6.61	8.89	☆	☆	☆	2.2	12.7	634-5726	610-941-0255	None	2.12	None	Stratton/Reichel	'93/'93
STRONG ADVANTAGE	Fixed Income	866.0	10.02	2.20	6.32	6.33	7.49	☆	6.2	☐	368-1030	414-359-1400	None	0.80	None	Jeffrey A. Koch	'91
STRONG AMER UTILITIES	Utility	58.8	10.57	7.01	15.34	☆	☆	☆	3.7	15.5	368-1030	414-359-1400	None	0.50	None	W.H. Reaves	'93
STRONG ASIA PACIFIC	Pacific Region	57.8	9.31	4.20	-3.77	☆	☆	☆	0.5	☐	368-1030	414-359-1400	None	2.00	None	Anthony L.T. Cragg	'93
STRONG ASSET ALLOCATION	Flexible	247.7	19.39	6.59	13.26	9.09	9.47	9.47	3.9	17.6	368-1030	414-359-1400	None	1.20	None	Multiple Managers	N/A
STRONG COMMON STOCK ⊠	Growth	879.9	19.35	9.41	20.34	21.59	20.82	☆	0.4	17.1	368-1030	414-359-1400	None	1.30	None	Weiss/Carlson	'91/'93
STRONG CORP BOND	Fixed Income	174.8	10.35	7.68	18.16	11.44	10.31	☆	7.3	☐	368-1030	414-359-1400	None	1.10	None	Jeffrey A. Koch	'92
STRONG DISCOVERY FUND	Capital Appreciation	430.5	18.28	11.60	23.47	14.38	16.17	☆	3.8	21.1	368-1030	414-359-1400	None	1.50	None	Richard S. Strong	'87
STRONG GOVERNMENT	Fixed Income	335.8	10.47	6.44	13.44	9.03	10.43	☆	6.2	☐	368-1030	414-359-1400	None	0.90	None	Bradley C. Tank	'90
STRONG GROWTH	Growth	330.7	13.85	11.42	31.53	☆	☆	☆	0.0	28.1	368-1030	414-359-1400	None	1.60	None	Ronald C. Ognar	'93
STRONG INTL BOND	World Income	15.3	11.81	4.75	21.96	☆	☆	☆	7.9	☐	368-1030	414-359-1400	None	None	None	Shirish Maleker	'94
STRONG INTL STOCK	International	228.7	12.55	3.94	-1.42	11.78	☆	☆	0.4	☐	368-1030	414-359-1400	None	1.70	None	Anthony L.T. Cragg	'93
STRONG OPPORTUNITY	Growth	1,033.9	31.33	8.24	17.71	18.98	14.56	☆	0.7	15.3	368-1030	414-359-1400	None	1.40	None	Weiss/Carlson	'91/'93
STRONG SH-TM GLBL BD	World Income	15.2	10.32	3.77	8.47	☆	☆	☆	6.6	☐	368-1030	414-359-1400	None	None	None	Shirish Maleker	'94
STRONG SHORT-TERM BOND	Fixed Income	1,042.6	9.71	4.43	7.13	5.63	8.07	☆	6.9	☐	368-1030	414-359-1400	None	0.90	None	Bradley C. Tank	'90
STRONG TOTAL RETURN	Growth Income	628.5	26.70	6.79	18.23	13.72	11.67	11.35	1.5	23.6	368-1030	414-359-1400	None	1.20	None	Ognar/Rogers	'93/'94
SUMMIT HIGH YIELD	Fixed Income	27.6	10.11	6.23	10.83	☆	☆	☆	9.0	☐	272-3442	None	4.75	None	1.00	Chris Meng	'94
SUNAMER BALANCED; A	Balanced	57.3	15.37	6.35	16.73	☆	☆	☆	3.2	17.4	858-8850	212-551-5125	5.75	1.58	None	Stan Feeley	'93
SUNAMER BALANCED; B	Balanced	191.5	15.37	6.20	15.95	11.64	9.19	10.71	2.1	17.4	858-8850	212-551-5125	None	2.21	4.00	Stan Feeley	'93
SUNAMER BLUE CHIP; A	Growth	3.5	15.68	5.31	14.82	☆	☆	☆	0.0	18.0	858-8850	212-551-5125	5.75	1.64	None	Stan Feeley	'93

PERFORMANCE OF MUTUAL FUNDS (continued)

Note: Columns QTR, 1YR, 3YRS, 5YRS, 10YRS show RETURN THROUGH 6/30 (Annualized). A ☆ indicates no data.

FUND NAME	OBJECTIVE	ASSETS ($ MIL) 5/31/95	NAV ($/SHR) 6/30/95	QTR	1YR	3YRS	5YRS	10YRS	DIV YLD %	P/E RATIO	PHONE 800	PHONE In-State	Load	Exp. Ratio	Redemption	MANAGER	SINCE
SUNAMER BLUE CHIP; B	Growth	69.9	15.51	5.08	14.10	12.35	6.46	9.12	0.0	18.0	858-8850	212-551-5125	None	2.28	4.00	Stan Feeley	'92
SUNAMER DVSD INC; A	Fixed Income	14.5	4.28	5.72	2.54	1.95	☆	☆	9.6		858-8850	212-551-5125	4.75	1.42	None	Leary/Dudley	'93/'93
SUNAMER DVSD INC; B	Fixed Income	136.5	4.29	5.56	1.95	☆	☆	☆	9.0		858-8850	212-551-5125	None	2.11	4.00	Leary/Dudley	'92/'92
SUNAMER FED SECS; A	Fixed Income	6.6	10.43	6.13	11.82	☆	☆	☆	6.4	N/A	858-8850	212-551-5125	4.75	1.39	None	Christopher Leary	'93
SUNAMER FED SECS; B	Fixed Income	66.8	10.45	5.86	11.21	4.55	☆	7.72	5.8	N/A	858-8850	212-551-5125	None	1.98	4.00	Christopher Leary	'93
SUNAMER GLBL BAL; A	Global Flexible	12.3	6.86	1.93	-0.38	☆	☆	☆	0.2		858-8850	212-551-5125	5.75	None	None	Stan Feeley	'94
SUNAMER GLBL BAL; B	Global Flexible	13.9	6.81	1.64	-1.05	☆	☆	☆	0.1		858-8850	212-551-5125	None	None	4.00	Stan Feeley	'94
SUNAMER GRO & INC; A	Growth Income	3.0	7.93	3.76	☆	☆	☆	☆	3.5	N/A	858-8850	212-551-5125	5.75	None	None	Charles Dudley	'94
SUNAMER GRO & INC; B	Growth Income	1.3	7.93	3.76	1.91	☆	☆	☆	3.1	N/A	858-8850	212-551-5125	None	None	4.00	Charles Dudley	'94
SUNAMER HIGH INC; A	Fixed Income	50.8	6.89	1.70	1.91	6.31	☆	11.50	11.9		858-8850	212-551-5125	4.75	1.72	None	Charles Dudley	'90
SUNAMER HIGH INC; B	Fixed Income	169.4	6.90	1.56	1.35	☆	9.79	☆	11.3		858-8850	212-551-5125	None	2.15	4.00	Charles Dudley	'93
SUNAMER MID-CAP GRO; A	Growth	31.9	16.05	7.65	23.31	14.86	☆	☆	0.2	24.2	858-8850	212-551-5125	5.75	1.76	None	Dudley/Snell	'93/'91
SUNAMER MID-CAP GRO; B	Growth	26.8	15.88	7.44	22.56	☆	☆	☆	0.2	24.2	858-8850	212-551-5125	None	2.43	4.00	Dudley/Snell	'93/'93
SUNAMER SMALL CO GRO; A	Small Company Growth	47.3	21.60	12.27	43.56	22.74	15.24	☆	0.0	28.4	858-8850	212-551-5125	5.75	1.67	None	Audrey Snell	'91
SUNAMER SMALL CO GRO; B	Small Company Growth	56.9	21.35	12.07	42.57	☆	☆	☆	0.0	28.4	858-8850	212-551-5125	None	2.31	4.00	Audrey Snell	'93
SUNAMER US GOVT SEC; A	Fixed Income	67.3	8.49	4.72	9.64	☆	☆	☆	5.8		858-8850	212-551-5125	4.75	1.35	None	Christopher Leary	'93
SUNAMER US GOVT SEC; B	Fixed Income	581.7	8.49	4.42	8.88	4.50	6.33	☆	5.1		858-8850	212-551-5125	None	1.95	4.00	Christopher Leary	'93
SUNBURST SHRT-INT GOVT	Fixed Income	8.5	9.77	3.56	7.64	☆	☆	☆	4.5		467-2506	None	1.00	0.95	None	James Plunkett	'93
SWISSKEY SBC SH-TM WORLD	World Income	12.8	9.37	2.71	4.41	☆	☆	☆	5.1	N/A	524-9984	None	None	1.50	None	Fabio Salvoldeli	'92
SWISSKEY SBC WORLD GRO	Global	25.4	16.08	4.62	1.28	☆	☆	☆	0.0	N/A	524-9984	None	None	1.85	None	Team Managed	N/A
TARGET INTL BOND	World Income	29.7	10.73	2.71	15.39	☆	☆	☆	6.6		225-1852	None	None	1.00	None	Chong Hock Lau	'93
TARGET INTL EQ	International	176.3	12.61	6.50	4.04	☆	☆	☆	0.1		225-1852	None	None	1.07	None	Lazard Freres Asset Mgt.	'93
TARGET INTMDT-TERM BOND	Fixed Income	66.5	10.22	5.80	9.87	☆	☆	☆	5.0		225-1852	None	None	0.80	None	Pacific Investment Mgt Co	'93
TARGET LARGE CAP GROWTH	Growth	156.7	11.38	8.90	23.00	☆	☆	☆	0.9	N/A	225-1852	None	None	0.81	None	Roger Engemann Mgmt. Co.	'93
TARGET LARGE CAP VALUE	Growth Income	159.2	11.71	8.08	23.38	☆	☆	☆	2.1	N/A	225-1852	None	None	0.81	None	INVESCO MIM Inc.	'93
TARGET MTGE BACKED SECS	Fixed Income	64.4	10.05	4.50	11.36	☆	☆	☆	6.8		225-1852	None	None	0.85	None	Wellington Mgmt. Co.	'93
TARGET SMALL CAP GROWTH	Small Company Growth	98.4	12.98	7.45	21.08	☆	☆	☆	0.1		225-1852	None	None	0.93	None	Nicholas Applegate Mgmt.	'93
TARGET SMALL CAP VALUE	Small Company Growth	83.4	12.14	6.87	5.92	☆	☆	☆	0.0		225-1852	None	None	0.93	None	Oak Hall Cap Adv Inc	'93
TARGET TOTAL RETURN BOND	Fixed Income	35.3	10.30	6.34	12.03	☆	☆	☆	4.6		225-1852	None	None	0.85	None	Pacific Investment Mgt Co	'93
TCW/DW BALANCED	Balanced	113.6	10.06	9.14	10.76	11.74	☆	☆	1.0	16.4	869-3863	212-392-2550	None	2.06	None	Tilton/Goldberg	'93/'93
TCW/DW CORE EQUITY	Growth	725.7	13.59	12.22	18.59	12.56	☆	☆	0.0	16.8	869-3863	212-392-2550	None	1.96	5.00	Hanisee/Tilton	'94/'95
TCW/DW GLBL CONVERT	Convertible Securities	17.6	10.55	6.08	☆	☆	☆	☆	0.0		869-3863	212-392-2550	None	None	5.00	Hunter/Hanisee	'95/'95
TCW/DW INCOME & GROWTH	Fixed Income	53.4	10.51	5.96	11.85	☆	☆	☆	5.5		869-3863	212-392-2550	None	2.04	None	Team Managed	N/A
TCW/DW LATIN AMER GR	Latin American	267.2	8.50	12.14	-24.91	☆	☆	☆	0.0	N/A	869-3863	212-392-2550	None	2.87	5.00	David Reilly	'94
TCW/DW NTH AMER GOVT INC	World Income	736.4	8.24	5.65	-3.21	☆	☆	☆	8.2	N/A	869-3863	212-392-2550	None	1.52	None	Philip Barach	'92
TCW/DW NTH AMER INT INC	World Income	3.2	9.47	6.67	3.24	☆	☆	☆	7.2	N/A	869-3863	212-392-2550	None	0.75	None	Goldberg/Metcalf	'94/'95
TCW/DW SMALL CAP GROWTH	Small Company Growth	76.6	11.92	13.52	42.07	☆	☆	☆	0.0		869-3863	212-392-2550	None	2.57	5.00	Larsen/Foreman	'94/'94
TCW/DW TOTAL RETURN	Growth Income	31.7	11.60	10.53	☆	☆	☆	☆	0.0	23.0	869-3863	212-392-2550	None	None	None	James Tilton	'94
TEDDY ROOSEVELT TOT RET	Equity Income	2.3	10.55	7.34	6.35	☆	☆	☆	2.0	N/A	304-8333	813-823-8712	None	1.90	1.00	Craig R. Pieringer	'94
TEMPLETON AMER TR; II	Growth	44.1	14.03	7.51	14.57	11.74	☆	☆	0.3	14.9	237-0738	813-823-8712	1.00	2.47	1.00	Gary Motyl	'92
TEMPLETON CAP ACCUMULATR ★	Global Flexible	58.1	15.84	6.67	11.71	16.07	16.07	17.42	1.2		237-0738	813-823-8712	8.99	1.00	None	Gary Motyl	'93
TEMPLETON DEV MRKTS; I	Emerging Markets	2,129.4	13.60	7.17	3.07	13.03	☆	☆	0.9		237-0738	813-823-8712	5.75	2.11	None	Mark Mobius	'91
TEMPLETON FDS FOR; I	International	6,422.5	9.41	6.21	7.44	10.46	9.06	☆	1.6		237-0738	813-823-8712	5.75	1.14	None	Mark G. Holowesko	'87
TEMPLETON FDS WORLD; I	Global	5,571.3	16.10	9.00	14.54	14.86	11.75	13.29	1.7		237-0738	813-823-8712	5.75	1.04	None	Mark G. Holowesko	'87
TEMPLETON GL AMER GOVT	World Income	3.1	9.98	4.91	3.52	☆	☆	☆	3.6		237-0738	813-823-8712	4.25	None	None	Douglas Lempereur	'94
TEMPLETON GL INFRA; I	Global	20.8	10.25	8.96	3.38	☆	☆	☆	0.6		237-0738	813-823-8712	5.75	1.00	None	Gary Clemons	'95
TEMPLETON GL RISING DIVS	Global	6.5	10.22	1.59	3.36	☆	☆	☆	1.0		237-0738	813-823-8712	5.75	1.25	None	Dorian Foyil	'94
TEMPLETON GLBL OPP; I	Global	509.1	13.06	10.77	13.50	13.09	12.84	☆	0.4		237-0738	813-823-8712	5.75	1.53	None	Howard Leonard	'93

Fund	Objective	Net Assets ($Mil)	NAV	Ret A	Ret B	Ret C	Ret D	Ret E	Yield	Rank	Tel (toll)	Tel (local)	Max Chrg	Exp	Redem	Manager	Since
TEMPLETON GROWTH; I	Global	6,453.6	18.26	8.11	14.14	14.04	12.52	14.75	1.5	□□	237-0738	813-823-8712	5.75	1.10	None	Mark G. Holowesko	'87
TEMPLETON INC INC; I	World Income	199.5	9.27	5.87	11.23	4.58	7.95	11.74	6.6	□□	237-0738	813-823-8712	4.25	1.18	None	Samuel J. Forester, Jr.	'90
TEMPLETON REAL EST; I	Real Estate	133.3	12.93	6.42	1.22	8.46	8.84	☆	1.7	14.5	237-0738	813-823-8712	5.75	1.58	None	Jeffrey Everett	'92
TEMPLETON SM CO GRO; I	Global Small Company	1,348.8	8.33	10.48	11.14	11.42	10.67	☆	1.3		237-0738	813-823-8712	5.75	1.36	None	Dan Jacobs	'92
THE NEW USA FUND	Growth	161.9	14.53	15.04	31.26	11.15	☆	☆	0.0	N/A	222-2872	310-448-8856	5.00	2.12	None	David Ryan	'92
THIRD AVENUE VALUE FUND ★	Capital Appreciation	241.4	20.19	10.57	22.01	18.88	☆	☆	1.2	12.7	443-1021	212-888-6685	None	1.16	1.00	Martin J. Whitman	'90
THOMAS WHITE WORLD FD	Global	30.6	11.01	5.46	10.95	☆	☆	☆	0.8		None	312-663-3500	None	1.00	None	Thomas White	'94
THOMPSON PLUMB BALANCED	Balanced	17.2	13.51	6.71	19.57	9.27	8.60	☆	2.0	19.0	999-0887	608-831-1300	None	1.42	None	Thompson, Plumb & Assoc.	'87
THOMPSON PLUMB BOND	Fixed Income	12.4	10.41	4.24	9.79	5.81	☆	☆	5.3		999-0887	608-831-1300	None	1.00	None	Thompson, Plumb & Assoc.	'92
THOMPSON PLUMB GROWTH	Growth	7.7	23.15	9.87	32.64	12.21	☆	☆	0.0	20.2	999-0887	608-831-1300	None	2.00	None	Thompson, Plumb & Assoc.	'92
THORNBURG LTD GOVT; A	Fixed Income	142.5	12.36	3.98	8.16	5.45	7.37	☆	6.0		847-0200	505-984-0200	2.50	0.95	None	Steven Bohlin	'87
THORNBURG LTD GOVT; B	Fixed Income	0.6	12.40	3.84	☆	☆	☆	☆	0.0		847-0200	505-984-0200	None	None	None	Steven Bohlin	'94
THORNBURG LTD GOVT; C	Fixed Income	1.5	12.41	3.84	☆	☆	☆	☆	0.0		847-0200	505-984-0200	None	None	2.50	Steven Bohlin	'94
THORNBURG LTD TM INC; A	Fixed Income	21.1	11.99	4.87	7.83	8.22	☆	☆	6.2		847-0200	505-984-0200	2.50	0.66	None	Steven Bohlin	'92
THORNBURG LTD TM INC; B	Fixed Income	0.1	12.02	4.83	☆	☆	☆	☆	0.0		847-0200	505-984-0200	None	None	None	Steven Bohlin	'94
THORNBURG LTD TM INC; C	Fixed Income	0.6	11.96	4.75	☆	☆	☆	☆	0.0		847-0200	505-984-0200	None	None	2.50	Steven Bohlin	'94
TIFI EMERGING MARKETS ▥	Emerging Markets	656.2	11.28	7.63	2.81	2.91	☆	☆	1.5		237-0738	813-823-8712	4.00	1.60	None	Dr. J. Mark Mobius	'93
TIFI FOREIGN EQ (SAF) ▥	International	33.3	8.39	8.82	10.94	☆	☆	☆	2.2		237-0738	813-823-8712	None	1.00	None	James Chaney	'93
TIFI FOREIGN EQUITY ▥	International	1,398.8	13.72	7.69	9.01	8.22	☆	☆	1.4		237-0738	813-823-8712	None	0.95	None	James Chaney	'93
TIFI GLOBAL FXD INC ▥	World Income	0.1	8.15	0.99	4.98	☆	☆	☆	20.9		237-0738	813-823-8712	None	1.00	None	Tom Latta	'93
TIFI GROWTH ▥	Global	213.2	12.07	8.74	11.85	☆	☆	☆	2.4		237-0738	813-823-8712	None	0.95	None	James Chaney	'93
TOCQUEVILLE ASIA-PAC	Pacific Region	4.9	9.08	4.85	-6.13	2.91	☆	☆	0.8		697-3863	212-698-0851	4.00	2.82	None	Frederic Naveillou	'91
TOCQUEVILLE TOCQ FUND	Growth	33.7	13.76	11.33	17.03	☆	13.16	☆	0.8	N/A	697-3863	212-698-0851	None	1.54	None	Sicart/Kleinschmidt	'87/'91
TORCHMARK GOVT SECS ⊠	Fixed Income	1.4	9.69	6.09	12.00	☆	☆	☆	5.8	□	733-3863	913-236-2050	None	1.00	None	John E. Sundeen	'93
TORRAY FUND	Flexible	28.6	16.59	12.03	24.87	12.98	☆	☆	1.6	12.1	443-3036	301-493-4600	None	1.25	None	Robert E. Torray	'90
TOT RTN TREAS; INV A	Fixed Income	165.4	10.02	7.79	13.81	8.88	9.64	☆	6.4		645-5923	410-637-6819	4.50	0.77	None	R. Alan Medaugh	'88
TOT RTN TREAS; ISI	Fixed Income	205.3	10.02	7.79	13.81	8.88	9.64	☆	6.4		645-5923	410-637-6819	4.45	0.77	None	R. Alan Medaugh	'88
TOWER CAPITAL APPREC	Growth Income	140.1	15.40	9.89	23.21	12.99	10.41	☆	1.3	16.0	999-0124	504-533-5100	3.00	1.09	None	John Cain	'95
TOWER TOTAL RETURN BOND	Fixed Income	70.0	10.08	6.10	11.16	5.66	7.87	☆	5.3		999-0124	504-533-5100	3.00	1.21	None	Jeff Tanguis	'95
TOWER US GOVT INCOME	Fixed Income	46.2	10.17	5.01	10.45	☆	☆	☆	6.7		999-0124	504-533-5100	3.00	0.74	None	Jeff Tanguis	'88
TR CREDIT UN 1996 ▣⊠	Fixed Income	127.7	9.58	2.21	7.01	☆	☆	☆	5.9		526-7384	212-902-0800	None	0.38	0.50	Team Managed	N/A
TR CREDIT UN FEB 1997 ▣⊠	Fixed Income	95.6	9.73	3.04	8.40	☆	☆	☆	6.3		526-7384	212-902-0800	None	0.42	0.50	Team Managed	N/A
TR CREDIT UN GOVT ▣	Fixed Income	523.6	9.76	1.64	5.48	4.01	☆	☆	5.6		526-7384	212-902-0800	None	0.35	None	Team Managed	N/A
TR CREDIT UN MAY 1997	Fixed Income	64.0	10.02	2.89	7.50	☆	☆	☆	6.0		526-7384	212-902-0800	None	None	0.50	Team Managed	N/A
TR CREDIT UN MTGE SEC ▣	Fixed Income	268.8	9.76	3.27	8.41	4.97	☆	☆	6.5		526-7384	212-902-0800	None	0.28	None	Team Managed	'88
TR FED SEC SHT GOVT; SHS	Fixed Income	4.1	9.44	2.92	6.53	6.85	☆	☆	5.8		221-8120	None	None	0.40	None	Bruce Repasy	'92/'92
TRENT EQUITY FUND	Capital Appreciation	3.5	9.82	9.48	12.16	4.97	☆	☆	0.0	13.7	424-2295	None	None	1.85	None	Holderness/May	'93
TRIFLEX FUND	Balanced	20.6	15.94	6.29	16.82	9.37	9.49	9.15	2.9	N/A	231-4639	409-763-2767	5.75	1.25	None	William R. Berger	'92
TURNER GROWTH EQUITY	Capital Appreciation	126.8	13.44	7.90	17.36	11.65	☆	☆	0.9	19.4	932-7781	215-989-6611	None	0.95	None	Turner Invest. Partners	'94
TURNER SMALL CAP	Small Company Growth	7.6	13.68	16.03	47.89	☆	☆	☆	0.5	22.0	932-7781	215-989-6611	None	1.09	None	Turner Invest. Partners	N/A
TWEEDY BROWNE AMER VALUE	Growth	86.0	11.90	11.11	21.97	☆	☆	☆	0.0	9.3	432-4789	212-916-0600	None	1.74	None	Team Managed	N/A
TWEEDY BROWNE GLBL VALUE	Global Small Company	734.5	12.16	5.56	0.96	☆	☆	☆	0.0		432-4789	212-916-0600	None	1.65	None	Team Managed	N/A
TWEN CENTURY PR MGD BD	Fixed Income	12.5	9.95	6.82	13.15	☆	☆	☆	6.0	6.0	345-2021	816-531-5575	None	0.45	None	Team Managed	N/A
TWEN CENTURY WRLD EMRG	Intl Small Company	112.6	5.51	9.11	2.42	☆	☆	☆	0.0		345-2021	816-531-5575	None	2.00	2.00	Tyson/Strabo	'94/'94
TWEN CENTURY WRLD INTL	International	1,252.8	7.12	5.79	-0.23	9.13	9.81	☆	1.8		345-2021	816-531-5575	None	1.84	None	Tyson/Strabo	'91/'91
TWEN CENTURY BALANCED	Balanced	749.4	17.00	8.61	16.45	8.13	☆	☆	2.6	N/A	345-2021	816-531-5575	None	1.00	None	Team Managed	N/A
TWEN CENTURY EQTY INCOME	Equity Income	68.4	5.74	6.68	☆	☆	☆	☆	0.0	N/A	345-2021	816-531-5575	None	1.00	None	Zuger/Davidson	'94/'94

★ TEMPLETON CAP ACCUMULATR--Sold only on a contractual plan.

★ THIRD AVENUE VALUE--Fund has been reclassified from Specialty to Capital Appreciation.

PERFORMANCE OF MUTUAL FUNDS (continued)

FUND NAME	OBJECTIVE	ASSETS ($ MIL) 5/31/95	NAV ($/SHR) 6/30/95	RETURN THROUGH 6/30 QTR	1YR	3YRS (Ann.)	5YRS (Ann.)	10YRS (Ann.)	DIV YLD %	P/E RATIO	PHONE 800	PHONE In-State	Load	Redemption	Exp. Ratio	MANAGER	SINCE
TWEN CENTURY GIFTRUST	Small Company Growth	387.5	23.98	20.93	60.36	39.54	25.54	24.35	0.0	N/A	345-2021	816-531-5575	None	None	1.00	Team Managed	N/A
TWEN CENTURY GROWTH	Growth	4,591.7	22.26	12.08	22.70	10.06	11.19	15.51	0.2	N/A	345-2021	816-531-5575	None	None	1.00	Team Managed	N/A
TWEN CENTURY HERITAGE	Growth	863.6	10.99	9.35	19.71	15.68	11.44	☆	0.3	N/A	345-2021	816-531-5575	None	None	1.00	Team Managed	N/A
TWEN CENTURY INTMDT BD	Fixed Income	8.8	9.97	4.77	9.73	☆	☆	☆	5.6	□	345-2021	816-531-5575	None	None	0.75	Team Managed	N/A
TWEN CENTURY LIMITED BD	Fixed Income	6.3	9.91	3.20	7.21	☆	☆	☆	5.4	□	345-2021	816-531-5575	None	None	0.70	Team Managed	N/A
TWEN CENTURY LNG-TM BD	Fixed Income	138.7	9.66	7.08	13.18	7.12	9.31	☆	6.3	N/A	345-2021	816-531-5575	None	None	0.88	Team Managed	N/A
TWEN CENTURY SELECT	Growth Income	4,110.9	38.36	8.76	16.53	9.19	7.41	12.28	0.7	N/A	345-2021	816-531-5575	None	None	1.00	Team Managed	N/A
TWEN CENTURY ULTRA INV	Midcap	10,735.9	24.04	15.19	28.99	20.05	21.35	19.01	0.0	N/A	345-2021	816-531-5575	None	None	1.00	Team Managed	N/A
TWEN CENTURY US GOVT INT	Fixed Income	15.3	9.96	4.65	9.17	6.22	☆	☆	5.8	□	345-2021	816-531-5575	None	None	0.75	Team Managed	N/A
TWEN CENTURY US GOVT SHT	Fixed Income	392.5	9.47	3.04	7.15	4.14	6.81	☆	5.3	□	345-2021	816-531-5575	None	None	0.81	Team Managed	N/A
TWEN CENTURY VALUE	Growth Income	491.0	5.79	6.61	24.10	☆	☆	☆	2.0	16.0	345-2021	816-531-5575	None	None	1.00	Zuger/Davidson	'93/'93
TWEN CENTURY VISTA INV	Midcap	1,063.4	13.53	17.75	55.43	17.93	12.50	16.10	0.0	N/A	345-2021	816-531-5575	None	None	1.00	Team Managed	N/A
UNITED CONTL INCOME	Balanced	450.3	22.14	7.05	13.92	10.62	10.45	10.93	3.2	16.7	None	913-236-2000	5.75	None	0.89	Cynthia Prince-Fox	'93
UNITED GOLD & GOVERNMENT	Gold	36.4	8.45	3.67	-5.41	8.84	4.62	☆	0.6	N/A	None	913-236-2000	5.75	None	1.59	Michael L. Avery	'94
UNITED GOVERNMENT SECS	Fixed Income	153.8	5.35	6.00	12.14	7.41	9.22	9.12	6.2	□	None	913-236-2000	4.25	None	0.82	John E. Sundeen	'91
UNITED HIGH INCOME	Fixed Income	966.3	8.95	5.12	9.21	9.70	11.89	8.20	8.7	□	None	913-236-2000	5.75	None	0.84	Louise D. Rieke	'90
UNITED HIGH INCOME II	Fixed Income	368.0	4.02	4.72	8.39	9.48	12.14	☆	8.6	□	None	913-236-2000	5.75	None	0.88	Louise D. Rieke	'92
UNITED INTL GROWTH; A	International	651.3	8.68	14.03	7.98	13.89	9.96	14.51	0.5	□	None	913-236-2000	5.75	None	1.20	Mark Yockey	'90
UNITED NEW CONCEPTS	Small Company Growth	316.4	13.21	7.84	39.53	18.45	20.69	15.19	0.1	26.7	None	913-236-2000	5.75	None	1.24	Mark G. Seferovich	'89
UNITED RETIREMENT SHARES	Growth Income	518.9	8.26	7.36	15.07	11.10	10.86	11.87	2.6	18.1	None	913-236-2000	5.75	None	0.87	Cynthia Prince-Fox	'95
UNITED VANGUARD FUND	Growth	1,095.7	8.20	13.23	29.89	16.93	13.02	☆	0.4	21.0	None	913-236-2000	5.75	None	1.05	James D. Wineland	'92
UNITED ACCUMULATIVE; A	Growth	1,030.5	7.63	9.72	19.64	12.27	10.05	12.26	1.7	17.0	None	913-236-2000	5.75	None	0.71	Antonio Intagliata	'79
UNITED BOND; A	Fixed Income	552.9	6.10	6.74	12.39	8.16	10.03	☆	6.5	□	None	913-236-2000	5.75	None	0.72	James C. Cusser	'92
UNITED INCOME; A	Equity Income	3,608.3	27.97	12.29	21.33	14.08	12.24	15.74	1.2	16.9	None	913-236-2000	5.75	None	0.74	Russell E. Thompson	'79
UNITED SCIENCE & TECH; A	Science & Technology	578.5	19.46	19.09	56.39	20.41	16.30	16.73	0.0	27.1	None	913-236-2000	5.75	None	0.96	Abel Garcia	'84
UNIVERSAL CAPITAL GROWTH	Capital Appreciation	6.0	14.94	15.63	47.45	16.59	☆	☆	0.0	23.2	223-9100	708-932-3000	4.75	None	2.00	Dreher/Biscan	'91/'91
US LARGE STOCK FUND	Growth Income	137.0	5.96	6.81	23.15	☆	☆	☆	1.8	N/A	223-3332	212-908-9500	None	None	None	Joseph N. Pappo	'93
US ALL AMERICAN EQUITY	Growth Income	11.7	20.08	8.54	17.98	8.76	8.96	6.87	1.8	17.5	873-8637	210-308-1234	None	None	0.61	Ralph Aldis	'95
US CHINA REGION OPPTY	Pacific Region	20.0	6.67	1.96	-12.80	☆	☆	☆	1.4	□	873-8637	210-308-1234	None	1.00	1.88	Battenymarch, Inc.	'95
US GLOBAL RESOURCES	Natural Resources	21.1	5.76	5.11	5.94	2.78	2.26	5.33	0.0	13.7	873-8637	210-308-1234	None	None	2.43	Ralph Aldis	'92
US GOLD SHARES	Gold	217.8	2.14	-6.06	-11.22	1.81	-8.39	-4.50	3.3	N/A	873-8637	210-308-1234	None	None	1.46	Victor Flores	'92
US INCOME FUND	Utility	10.4	13.35	5.16	9.31	7.50	6.95	8.66	2.5	12.0	873-8637	210-308-1234	None	None	1.74	Frank Holmes	'93
US INTMDT TREASURY	Fixed Income	4.5	10.48	5.16	9.62	7.04	☆	☆	5.9	□	873-8637	210-308-1234	None	None	None	Creston King	'95
US REAL ESTATE	Real Estate	10.1	9.80	6.96	1.09	0.70	5.77	☆	1.6	14.2	873-8637	210-308-1234	None	None	1.59	Ralph Aldis	'95
US SPECIAL TERM GOVT	Fixed Income	6.8	9.48	1.70	1.85	☆	☆	☆	5.9	□	873-8637	210-308-1234	None	None	0.05	Aldis/King	'94/'94
US WORLD GOLD	Gold	182.2	15.81	6.04	1.36	18.63	7.96	☆	0.2	N/A	873-8637	210-308-1234	None	None	1.53	Vance/Gupta	'90/'95
USAA AGGR GROWTH	Small Company Growth	296.7	22.03	12.57	39.72	15.19	11.12	9.78	0.0	26.7	382-8722	None	None	None	0.83	Cabell/Efron	'95/'95
USAA BALANCED	Balanced	134.6	12.69	3.89	11.09	8.42	8.59	☆	3.9	14.5	382-8722	None	None	None	0.84	John W. Saunders, Jr.	'89
USAA CORNERSTONE	Global Flexible	874.9	22.88	6.92	9.25	11.44	9.24	12.00	2.5	□	382-8722	None	None	None	1.11	Harry W. Miller	'90
USAA EMERG MKTS	Emerging Markets	22.7	9.95	14.11	☆	☆	☆	☆	0.0	□	382-8722	None	None	None	None	W. Travis Selmier III	'94
USAA GNMA TRUST	Fixed Income	264.1	10.10	5.19	11.00	6.90	☆	☆	7.1	N/A	382-8722	None	None	None	0.31	Kenneth Willman	'95
USAA GOLD FUND	Gold	160.3	9.01	2.50	6.88	12.58	4.66	2.86	0.1	□	382-8722	None	None	None	1.26	Mark Johnson	'94
USAA GRO & INC	Growth Income	186.4	11.69	8.81	21.20	☆	☆	☆	2.0	16.0	382-8722	None	None	None	1.12	R. David Ullom	'93
USAA GROWTH FUND	Growth	865.6	18.46	6.89	26.34	13.77	12.37	11.75	1.5	17.8	382-8722	None	None	None	1.04	David Parsons	'94
USAA INCOME FUND	Fixed Income	1,770.8	12.19	6.92	15.07	7.61	9.99	10.04	7.0	□	382-8722	None	None	None	0.41	John W. Saunders, Jr.	'85

Fund	Objective	Net Assets	NAV	%	%	%	%	%	Yield	P/E	Phone	Local	Load	Exp	Manager	Started
USAA INCOME STOCK	Equity Income	1,356.9	14.69	7.28	19.52	10.52	12.26		5.1	14.7	382-8722	None	None	0.73	Harry W. Miller	'89
USAA INTERNATIONAL	International	347.6	15.90	7.80	4.16	11.97	7.89		0.0	□	382-8722	None	None	1.31	David Peebles	'88
USAA SH-TM BOND	Fixed Income	68.6	9.89	4.72	8.40	☆	☆		6.0	□	382-8722	None	None	0.50	Paul Lundmark	'93
USAA WORLD GROWTH	Global	201.0	13.21	8.81	7.88	☆	☆		0.0	□	382-8722	None	None	1.28	David Peebles	'92
UST MSTR AGING OF AMER	Growth	26.0	8.23	5.12	21.71	☆	☆		0.5	19.9	233-1136	None	4.50	0.99	Roger F. Schaefer	'92
UST MSTR BUS & INDUST	Growth	34.9	11.56	9.81	25.69	☆	☆		0.6	15.4	233-1136	None	4.50	0.99	David J. Williams	'92
UST MSTR COMMUN & ENTER	Growth	31.3	10.52	9.49	28.96	☆	☆		0.4	14.4	233-1136	None	4.50	0.98	John J. Apruzzese	'92
UST MSTR EARLY LIFE	Small Company Growth	49.7	10.12	8.26	31.82	☆	☆		0.0	15.1	233-1136	None	4.50	0.95	Timothy W. Evnin	'92
UST MSTR EMERGING AMER	Latin American	32.3	7.03	19.97	-8.82	☆	☆		2.4	□	233-1136	None	4.50	1.49	Harry C. Rowney	'92
UST MSTR ENVIRONMENTAL	Environmental	4.2	6.94	11.76	15.53	☆	☆		0.2	20.2	233-1136	None	4.50	0.99	Victor Sapuppo	'94
UST MSTR EQUITY	Growth	142.2	21.77	7.35	25.53	16.41	12.66	14.23	0.3	18.8	233-1136	None	4.50	1.14	David A. Tillson	'94
UST MSTR GLBL COMPETITOR	Growth	32.4	9.35	9.06	26.34	☆	☆		0.8	19.5	233-1136	None	4.50	0.99	Wendy S. Popowich	'90
UST MSTR INC & GROWTH	Growth Income	103.6	12.91	10.55	17.97	16.23	12.92		2.9	16.5	233-1136	None	4.50	1.17	Richard L. Bayles	'87
UST MSTR INTL	International	71.1	10.17	3.56	0.16	7.75	2.83		1.0	□	233-1136	None	4.50	1.53	Harry C. Rowney	'94
UST MSTR INTMDT TM MGD	Fixed Income	51.9	7.10	6.87	12.64	☆	☆		5.8	□	233-1136	None	4.50	0.69	Henry Milkewicz	'92
UST MSTR L-T SPPLY ENERG	Natural Resources	18.4	8.23	4.06	5.92	☆	10.00		1.1	19.7	233-1136	None	4.50	0.99	Richard L. Bayles	'86
UST MSTR MGD INC	Fixed Income	80.2	8.93	8.13	14.36	8.48	☆		6.0	□	233-1136	None	4.50	0.90	Henry Milkewicz	'92
UST MSTR PACIFIC/ASIA	Pacific Region	51.0	8.70	3.08	-4.78	☆	☆		3.0	□	233-1136	None	4.50	1.53	Harry C. Rowney	'92
UST MSTR PAN EUROPEAN	European Region	42.8	8.71	7.27	13.76	☆	☆		1.0	□	233-1136	None	4.50	1.61	Harry C. Rowney	'92
UST MSTR PRODUCTIVITY	Growth	20.8	9.09	13.80	32.39	☆	☆		0.0	13.3	233-1136	None	4.50	0.99	Ronald C. Steele	'92
UST MSTR SH-TM GOVT SECS	Fixed Income	25.3	7.02	3.39	7.47	10.15	7.42		5.3	□	233-1136	None	4.50	0.62	Charles E. Rabus	'92
VALLEY FORGE FD	Growth	11.0	9.90	1.85	9.11	8.76	10.76	7.36	1.8	15.6	548-1942	610-688-6839	None	1.40	Bernard B. Klawans	'72
VALUE LINE AGGR INCOME	Fixed Income	32.8	7.05	4.87	6.88	0.36	☆		9.7	□	223-0818	None	None	1.27	Team Managed	N/A
VALUE LINE ARM	Fixed Income	9.5	8.65	1.51	0.90	☆	☆		4.9	□	223-0818	None	None	1.36	Team Managed	N/A
VALUE LINE ASSET ALLOC	Flexible	29.7	12.50	7.94	24.16	☆	☆		0.5	20.4	223-0818	None	None	0.47	Team Managed	N/A
VALUE LINE CONVERTIBLE	Convertible Securities	51.6	12.18	6.99	12.70	11.96	10.65	10.21	6.2	21.1	223-0818	None	None	1.07	Team Managed	N/A
VALUE LINE FUND	Growth Income	291.0	16.68	7.05	23.31	12.23	11.55	13.49	0.8	19.8	223-0818	None	None	0.82	Team Managed	N/A
VALUE LINE INCOME	Income	135.7	6.95	6.72	15.62	7.60	9.28	10.29	3.3	20.6	223-0818	None	None	0.90	Team Managed	N/A
VALUE LINE LVGE GROWTH	Capital Appreciation	305.1	28.31	12.61	31.46	16.49	12.60	13.63	0.4	23.0	223-0818	None	None	0.89	Team Managed	N/A
VALUE LINE SM-CAP GRO	Small Company Growth	13.4	13.21	7.14	18.56	☆	☆		0.0	□	223-0818	None	None	0.61	Team Managed	N/A
VALUE LINE SPECIAL SIT	Midcap	87.6	18.84	9.22	38.16	15.65	9.37	8.11	0.0	24.5	223-0818	None	None	1.10	Team Managed	N/A
VALUE LINE US GOVT SEC	Fixed Income	267.2	11.18	4.90	7.28	4.01	7.22	8.30	6.3	□	223-0818	None	None	0.63	Donald Turk	'94
VALUESTAR SH-INT BD; INV	Fixed Income	96.4	10.02	3.35	7.82	☆	☆		5.5	□	824-3741	None	3.00	0.83	Peter Soo	'93
VAN ECK ASIA DYNSTY; A	Pacific Region	95.8	12.41	8.20	1.57	☆	☆		0.6	□	221-2220	None	4.75	1.85	Peter Soo	'93
VAN ECK ASIA DYNSTY; B ⊠	Pacific Region	34.0	12.33	8.06	1.00	☆	☆		0.2	□	221-2220	None	6.00	2.38	Peter Soo	'93
VAN ECK ASIA INFRA; A	Pacific Region	1.1	7.16	9.15	☆	☆	☆		0.0	□	221-2220	None	4.75		Peter Soo	'94
VAN ECK GL HARD ASST; A	Global	3.2	10.41	4.83	☆	☆	☆		0.0	□	221-2220	None	4.75		Derek Van Eck	'94
VAN ECK GL HARD ASST; C	Global	0.1	10.39	4.74	☆	☆	☆		0.0	□	221-2220	None	1.00		Derek Van Eck	'94
VAN ECK GLBL BAL; A	Global Flexible	12.9	9.92	5.98	9.34	☆	☆		1.1	□	221-2220	None	4.75		Hopkinson/Lau	'93/'93
VAN ECK GLBL BAL; B ⊠	Global Flexible	5.9	9.87	6.01	8.46	☆	☆		0.4	□	221-2220	None	5.00		Hopkinson/Lau	'93/'93
VAN ECK GLBL INCOME; A	World Income	133.8	9.11	3.29	19.10	3.26	8.12		5.7	N/A	221-2220	None	4.75	1.39	Madis Senner	'94
VAN ECK GLBL SM CAP; A	Global Small Company	2.6	8.67	0.35	☆	☆	☆		0.0	N/A	221-2220	None	4.75		Jonathan Neill	'94
VAN ECK GOLD OPPTY; A	Gold	0.8	9.94	-0.20	☆	☆	☆		0.0	N/A	221-2220	None	5.75		Lucille Palermo	'95
VAN ECK GOLD OPPTY; C	Gold	0.1	9.94	-0.10	☆	☆	☆		0.0	N/A	221-2220	None	1.00		Lucille Palermo	'95
VAN ECK GOLD; RES; A	Gold	187.5	5.39	5.39	-4.43	11.89	5.38		0.0	N/A	221-2220	None	5.75	1.52	L. Palermo	'92
VAN ECK INTL GOLD; A	Gold	576.2	13.60	-1.73	-1.66	13.75	5.02	6.75	1.3	N/A	221-2220	None	5.75	1.15	Harry Bingham	'93
VAN ECK WORLD TRENDS	Global	23.0	12.62	4.99	5.81	6.38	3.92	13.40	0.0	□	221-2220	None	4.75	1.85	Kenerson/Van Eck	'86/'94
VANCE SANDERS EXCHANGE ⊠	Growth	208.2	308.44	10.39	31.96	12.67	11.00		1.1	18.0	225-6265	617-482-8260	None	0.71	Thomas E. Faust, Jr.	'91
VANGUARD ADM INT TREAS	Fixed Income	496.1	10.31	7.17	13.20	☆	☆		6.3	□	662-7447	610-669-1000	None	0.15	Ian A. MacKinnon	'92
VANGUARD ADM LG TM TREAS	Fixed Income	145.7	10.45	10.62	18.79	☆	☆		6.6	□	662-7447	610-669-1000	None	0.15	Ian A. MacKinnon	'92

PERFORMANCE OF MUTUAL FUNDS (continued)

FUND NAME	OBJECTIVE	ASSETS ($ MIL) 5/31/95	NAV ($/SHR) 6/30/95	QTR	1YR	3YRS	5YRS	10YRS	DIV YLD %	P/E RATIO	800	In-State	Load	Exp. Ratio	Redemption	MANAGER	SINCE
						(Annualized)											
VANGUARD ADM SH TM TREAS	Fixed Income	364.0	10.09	3.74	8.57	☆			5.8	□	662-7447	610-669-1000	None	0.15	None	Ian A. MacKinnon	'92
VANGUARD ASSET ALLOC	Flexible	1,351.0	15.96	10.46	23.45	12.56	12.27	☆	3.6	17.3	662-7447	610-669-1000	None	0.50	None	Thomas Hazuka	'88
VANGUARD BALANCED INDEX ➤	Balanced	471.4	11.81	7.99	19.33	☆			3.4	17.1	662-7447	610-669-1000	None	0.20	None	George U. Sauter	'92
VANGUARD BD INDX INTMDT ➤	Fixed Income	149.9	10.04	7.37	13.80	☆			6.6	□	662-7447	610-669-1000	None	0.18	None	Ian A. MacKinnon	'94
VANGUARD BD INDX LONG ➤	Fixed Income	12.5	10.14	10.26	18.70	☆			6.9	□	662-7447	610-669-1000	None	0.18	None	Ian A. MacKinnon	'94
VANGUARD BD INDX SHORT	Fixed Income	144.7	9.94	3.91	8.67	☆			6.1	□	662-7447	610-669-1000	None	0.18	None	Ian A. MacKinnon	'94
VANGUARD BD INDX TOTAL	Fixed Income	2,101.6	9.85	6.01	12.30	7.40	9.20	☆	6.6	□	662-7447	610-669-1000	None	0.18	None	Ian A. MacKinnon	'86
VANGUARD CONVERTIBLE	Convertible Securities	168.9	11.40	5.69	11.54	10.22	10.87		4.4		662-7447	610-669-1000	None	0.73	None	Rohit M. Desai	'86
VANGUARD EQUITY INCOME	Equity Income	903.7	14.55	6.06	20.04	11.38	10.06		4.0	15.7	662-7447	610-669-1000	None	0.43	None	Roger Newell	'88
VANGUARD EXPLORER FUND	Small Company Growth	1,258.6	48.23	6.68	21.66	16.04	14.09	10.12	0.3	19.4	662-7447	610-669-1000	None	0.70	None	Abrams/Granahan	'94/'90
VANGUARD FXD GNMA PORT	Fixed Income	6,334.8	10.21	5.33	12.47	6.49	9.07	9.57	7.1	□	662-7447	610-669-1000	None	0.30	None	Paul Kaplan	'94
VANGUARD FXD HI YLD	Fixed Income	2,503.8	7.64	5.42	13.57	10.76	11.93	10.48	8.9	□	662-7447	610-669-1000	None	0.34	1.00	Earl E. McEvoy	'84
VANGUARD FXD INTMDT CORP	Fixed Income	239.2	9.79	7.23	13.66	13.15	☆		6.5	□	662-7447	610-669-1000	None	0.28	None	Ian A. MacKinnon	'93
VANGUARD FXD INTMDT TREA	Fixed Income	1,042.8	10.51	7.23	13.15	8.32	☆		6.2	□	662-7447	610-669-1000	None	0.28	None	Ian A. MacKinnon	'91
VANGUARD FXD LG-TM CORP	Fixed Income	3,009.3	8.96	8.56	16.57	10.01	11.55	10.85	7.0	□	662-7447	610-669-1000	None	0.32	None	Ian A. MacKinnon	'94
VANGUARD FXD LG-TM TREAS	Fixed Income	771.7	10.26	10.53	18.61	11.04	11.31		6.6	□	662-7447	610-669-1000	None	0.28	None	Ian A. MacKinnon	'86
VANGUARD FXD SHT-TM CORP	Fixed Income	3,278.2	10.75	3.61	8.60	6.01	8.03	8.43	5.9		662-7447	610-669-1000	None	0.28	None	Ian A. MacKinnon	'82
VANGUARD FXD SHT-TM FED	Fixed Income	1,493.5	10.12	3.66	8.15	5.59	7.53		5.7		662-7447	610-669-1000	None	0.28	None	Ian A. MacKinnon	'87
VANGUARD FXD SHT-TM TREA	Fixed Income	833.7	10.21	3.69	8.38	5.69	☆		5.8		662-7447	610-669-1000	None	0.28	None	Ian A. MacKinnon	'91
VANGUARD FXD INDEX 500 PORT	S&P Index	12,161.0	51.15	9.49	25.89	13.07	11.90	14.35	2.3	17.3	662-7447	610-669-1000	None	0.19	None	George U. Sauter	'87
VANGUARD INDEX EXTND MKT ➤	Midcap	1,137.4	21.68	9.00	21.98	14.77	12.90	☆	1.3	17.4	662-7447	610-669-1000	None	0.20	None	George U. Sauter	'87
VANGUARD INDEX GROWTH ➤	Growth	140.2	12.34	10.33	30.48	☆			1.7	19.3	662-7447	610-669-1000	None	0.20	None	George U. Sauter	'92
VANGUARD INDEX SM CAP ST	Small Company Growth	692.5	17.17	9.29	20.34	16.62	13.35	9.91	1.3	17.0	662-7447	610-669-1000	None	0.17	None	George U. Sauter	'89
VANGUARD INDEX TOT STOCK	Growth	1,079.0	13.43	9.23	24.74	13.25	☆		2.0	17.1	662-7447	610-669-1000	None	0.20	None	George U. Sauter	'92
VANGUARD INDEX VALUE	Growth Income	348.8	13.10	8.66	21.15	☆			2.9	14.8	662-7447	610-669-1000	None	0.20	None	George U. Sauter	'92
VANGUARD INSTL INDEX FD	S&P Index	4,396.6	51.48	9.53	26.06	13.20	☆		2.3	16.9	662-7447	610-669-1000	None	0.07	None	George U. Sauter	'90
VANGUARD INTL IDX EMRG	Emerging Markets	142.2	10.87	12.64	3.89	☆			0.6		662-7447	610-669-1000	None	0.60	1.00	George U. Sauter	'94
VANGUARD INTL IDX EURO	European Region	813.8	13.40	8.15	19.20	10.52	7.92	☆	1.9		662-7447	610-669-1000	None	0.32	None	George U. Sauter	'90
VANGUARD INTL IDX PAC	Pacific Region	717.2	10.65	-3.45	-10.65	15.24	2.46	☆	0.8		662-7447	610-669-1000	None	0.32	None	George U. Sauter	'90
VANGUARD PREFERRED STK	Fixed Income	309.4	9.29	8.25	15.60	8.72	10.96	10.59	7.0		662-7447	610-669-1000	None	0.51	None	Earl E. McEvoy	'82
VANGUARD PRIMECAP ⊠	Growth	2,460.9	24.95	13.93	38.93	23.09	16.45	16.35	0.5	17.7	662-7447	610-669-1000	None	0.64	None	Howard B. Schow	'84
VANGUARD QUANTITATIVE	Growth Income	715.3	18.44	9.42	24.69	13.94	12.34	12.24	2.1	15.9	662-7447	610-669-1000	None	0.48	None	John Nagorniak	'86
VANGUARD SPL ENERGY	Natural Resources	548.6	16.09	4.62	5.86	13.72	7.55	8.65	1.4	19.0	662-7447	610-669-1000	None	0.30	None	Ernst Von Metzsch	'84
VANGUARD SPL GOLD	Gold	588.7	11.88	2.24	-4.05	11.96	6.66	N/A	2.3	N/A	662-7447	610-669-1000	None	0.25	1.00	David Hutchins	'87
VANGUARD SPL HEALTH	Health/Biotechnology	943.8	41.55	6.37	35.26	15.91	16.74	18.86	1.3	N/A	662-7447	610-669-1000	None	0.40	1.00	Edward Owens	'84
VANGUARD SPL UTILITIES	Utility	634.2	11.07	7.49	15.22	10.31	☆		5.1	13.4	662-7447	610-669-1000	None	0.50	None	John R. Ryan	'92
VANGUARD STAR CONS GR	Balanced	110.3	11.03	7.09	☆				0.0	N/A	662-7447	610-669-1000	None	None	None	The Vanguard Group	'94
VANGUARD STAR GROWTH	Balanced	105.4	11.36	8.00	☆				0.0	N/A	662-7447	610-669-1000	None	None	None	The Vanguard Group	'94
VANGUARD STAR INCOME	Balanced	27.8	10.95	6.93	☆				0.0	N/A	662-7447	610-669-1000	None	None	None	The Vanguard Group	'94
VANGUARD STAR MOD GR	Balanced	94.6	11.23	7.88	☆				0.0	N/A	662-7447	610-669-1000	None	None	None	The Vanguard Group	'94
VANGUARD STAR STAR	Balanced	4,255.8	14.32	7.64	17.73	10.94	11.01	11.68	3.6	N/A	662-7447	610-669-1000	None	None	None	The Vanguard Group	'85
VANGUARD TX MGD BAL	Balanced	27.5	11.03	6.42	☆				0.0	N/A	662-7447	610-669-1000	None	None	2.00	Sauter/McKinnon	'94/'94
VANGUARD TX MGD CAP AP	Growth	147.2	11.95	10.04	☆				0.0	N/A	662-7447	610-669-1000	None	None	2.00	George U. Sauter	'94
VANGUARD TX MGD GR&INC	Growth Income	52.3	11.63	9.56	☆				0.0	N/A	662-7447	610-669-1000	None	None	2.00	George U. Sauter	'94
VANGUARD WELLESLEY INC	Income	6,485.7	19.24	8.50	16.73	10.83	11.65	11.92	5.7	15.8	662-7447	610-669-1000	None	0.34	None	Ryan/McEvoy	'87/'82

VANGUARD WELLINGTON FUND	Balanced	10,407.4	22.41	8.65	20.10	12.01	11.63	12.61	3.9	19.0	662-7447	610-669-1000	None	0.35	None	Bajakian/Kaplan	'72/'94
VANGUARD WINDSOR ☒	Growth Income	12,289.4	15.01	11.35	18.35	15.08	13.11	13.68	2.9	13.0	662-7447	610-669-1000	None	0.45	None	John B. Neff	'64
VANGUARD WINDSOR II	Growth Income	9,261.2	18.59	8.11	19.73	12.78	12.28	13.63	2.9	14.9	662-7447	610-669-1000	None	0.39	None	Team Managed	N/A
VANGUARD WORLD INTL GRO	International	3,123.7	14.31	7.35	7.12	12.85	5.94	16.75	1.3	☐	662-7447	610-669-1000	None	0.46	None	Richard R. Foulkes	'81
VANGUARD WORLD US GROWTH	Growth	2,769.3	18.51	10.51	28.44	10.55	11.45	12.77	1.0	N/A	662-7447	610-669-1000	None	0.52	None	J. Parker Hall, III	'87
VANGUARD/MORGAN GROWTH	Growth	1,195.1	13.65	11.79	27.99	12.95	11.05	13.33	1.0	17.3	662-7447	610-669-1000	None	0.50	None	Team Managed	N/A
VANGUARD/TRUST EQ INTL	International	1,048.4	32.00	3.28	2.12	9.35	3.93	15.74	2.0	☐	662-7447	610-669-1000	None	0.34	None	Debra Miller	'94
VANGUARD/TRUST EQ US	Growth Income	118.2	33.98	8.73	20.74	13.32	10.41	11.69	1.4	16.7	662-7447	610-669-1000	None	0.73	None	John Geewax	'92
VANKAMP ADJ RT GOVT; A	Fixed Income	5.7	9.36	1.87	4.79	☆	☆	☆	5.1	☐	225-2222	708-684-6503	3.25	0.61	None	Bob Hickey	'94
VANKAMP ADJ RT GOVT; B	Fixed Income	19.2	9.37	1.69	4.11	☆	☆	☆	4.3	☐	225-2222	708-684-6503	None	1.31	3.00	Bob Hickey	'94
VANKAMP ADJ RT GOVT; C	Fixed Income	2.9	9.37	1.80	4.12	☆	☆	☆	4.3	☐	225-2222	708-684-6503	None	1.31	1.00	Bob Hickey	'94
VANKAMP BALANCED; A	Balanced	4.7	15.39	6.00	11.49	☆	☆	☆	3.4	N/A	225-2222	708-684-6503	5.75	None	None	Dan Smith	'94
VANKAMP BALANCED; B	Balanced	6.5	15.39	5.82	10.79	☆	☆	☆	2.8	N/A	225-2222	708-684-6503	None	None	4.00	Dan Smith	'94
VANKAMP BALANCED; C	Balanced	0.7	15.39	5.82	10.79	☆	☆	☆	2.8	N/A	225-2222	708-684-6503	None	None	1.00	Dan Smith	'94
VANKAMP GRO & INC; A	Growth Income	51.4	20.38	7.32	17.51	9.87	10.33	☆	1.3	16.6	225-2222	708-684-6503	5.75	1.61	None	Dan Smith	'92
VANKAMP GRO & INC; B	Growth Income	33.5	20.38	7.21	16.73	☆	☆	☆	0.7	16.6	225-2222	708-684-6503	None	2.46	4.00	Dan Smith	'92
VANKAMP GRO & INC; C	Growth Income	1.5	20.36	7.10	16.55	☆	☆	☆	0.7	16.6	225-2222	708-684-6503	None	2.46	1.00	Dan Smith	'93
VANKAMP HIGH YIELD; A	Fixed Income	257.5	9.40	5.27	8.50	9.66	11.87	☆	10.5	☐	225-2222	708-684-6503	4.75	1.32	None	Kevin G. Mathews	'87
VANKAMP HIGH YIELD; B	Fixed Income	53.5	9.40	5.07	7.61	☆	☆	☆	9.7	☐	225-2222	708-684-6503	None	2.13	4.00	Kevin G. Mathews	'93
VANKAMP HIGH YIELD; C	Fixed Income	1.8	9.40	5.07	7.61	☆	☆	☆	9.7	☐	225-2222	708-684-6503	None	2.14	1.00	Kevin G. Mathews	'93
VANKAMP SHORT GLBL; A	World Income	77.1	7.56	3.00	0.68	-0.06	☆	☆	8.5	☐	225-2222	708-684-6503	3.25	1.13	None	Tom Slefinger	'90
VANKAMP SHORT GLBL; B	World Income	135.0	7.56	2.80	-0.14	-0.81	☆	☆	7.6	☐	225-2222	708-684-6503	None	1.85	3.00	Tom Slefinger	'91
VANKAMP SHORT GLBL; C	World Income	0.2	7.56	2.66	-0.27	☆	☆	☆	7.6	☐	225-2222	708-684-6503	None	1.84	1.00	Tom Slefinger	'93
VANKAMP STRAT INC; A ❁	Fixed Income	28.5	11.70	11.48	8.46	☆	☆	☆	10.3	☐	225-2222	708-684-6503	4.75	1.88	None	Peter Hegel	'93
VANKAMP STRAT INC; B ❁	Fixed Income	52.0	11.71	11.11	7.62	☆	☆	☆	9.3	☐	225-2222	708-684-6503	None	2.63	4.00	Peter Hegel	'93
VANKAMP STRAT INC; C ❁	Fixed Income	1.7	11.70	11.02	7.53	☆	☆	☆	9.3	☐	225-2222	708-684-6503	None	2.65	1.00	Peter Hegel	'93
VANKAMP US GOVT; A	Fixed Income	3,035.6	14.73	5.74	11.83	5.83	8.39	9.30	7.7	☐	225-2222	708-684-6503	4.75	1.00	None	J. Doyle	'84
VANKAMP US GOVT; B	Fixed Income	460.7	14.73	5.47	10.92	☆	☆	☆	6.8	☐	225-2222	708-684-6503	None	1.83	4.00	J. Doyle	'92
VANKAMP US GOVT; C	Fixed Income	11.8	14.73	5.47	11.16	☆	☆	☆	6.8	☐	225-2222	708-684-6503	None	1.84	1.00	J. Doyle	'93
VANKAMP UTILITY; A	Utility	51.1	13.39	4.94	8.70	☆	☆	☆	4.5	14.1	225-2222	708-684-6503	5.75	1.34	None	Dan Smith	'93
VANKAMP UTILITY; B	Utility	82.4	13.36	4.46	7.79	☆	☆	☆	3.7	14.1	225-2222	708-684-6503	None	2.06	4.00	Dan Smith	'93
VANKAMP UTILITY; C	Utility	1.2	13.36	4.54	7.88	☆	☆	☆	3.7	14.1	225-2222	708-684-6503	None	2.05	1.00	Dan Smith	'93
VENTURE INCOME PLUS; A	Fixed Income	57.8	4.89	3.12	9.02	11.52	9.89	6.54	9.8	☐	279-0279	505-983-4335	4.75	1.48	None	B. Clark Stamper	'90
VENTURE INCOME PLUS; B	Fixed Income	3.4	4.87	2.72	☆	☆	☆	☆	0.0	☐	279-0279	505-983-4335	None	None	4.00	B. Clark Stamper	'94
VENTURE INTL TOT RET; A	International	9.4	11.54	9.38	☆	☆	☆	☆	0.0	☐	279-0279	505-983-4335	4.75	None	None	Edward Iselin	'95
VENTURE INTL TOT RET; B	International	0.5	11.49	9.12	☆	☆	☆	☆	0.0	☐	279-0279	505-983-4335	None	None	4.00	Edward Iselin	'95
VICTORY BALANCED	Balanced	167.9	10.59	6.55	16.76	☆	☆	☆	3.9	N/A	362-5365	None	4.75	0.87	None	Coyne/Heine	'95/'93
VICTORY DVSD STOCK	Growth	344.5	12.97	8.57	25.75	14.90	12.22	☆	2.1	N/A	362-5365	None	4.75	0.89	None	Larry Babin	'89
VICTORY FD FOR INCOME	Fixed Income	25.0	9.95	5.01	9.89	5.26	7.92	☆	6.3	☐	362-5365	None	2.00	1.12	None	Robert Hennes	'87
VICTORY GOVT BOND	Fixed Income	84.6	9.78	5.49	10.04	☆	☆	☆	5.2	☐	362-5365	None	4.75	0.38	None	R. Fernald	'94
VICTORY GOVT MORTGAGE	Fixed Income	142.4	10.80	4.93	10.81	6.52	8.64	☆	6.7	☐	362-5365	None	4.75	0.76	None	R. Fernald	'94
VICTORY GROWTH FUND	Growth	44.9	11.40	8.30	20.13	☆	☆	☆	0.9	N/A	362-5365	None	4.75	0.94	None	Martha Kelly	'93
VICTORY INTL GROWTH	International	83.0	12.17	5.00	2.55	10.16	6.09	☆	0.0	☐	362-5365	None	4.75	1.48	None	Paul Danes	'95
VICTORY INTMDT INCOME	Fixed Income	143.5	9.63	4.72	9.07	☆	☆	☆	6.3	☐	362-5365	None	4.75	0.79	None	R. Fernald	'95
VICTORY INVMT QUAL BOND	Fixed Income	101.0	9.69	5.85	11.60	☆	☆	☆	6.5	☐	362-5365	None	4.75	0.79	None	Richard Heine	'93
VICTORY LTD TM INCOME	Fixed Income	168.8	10.13	3.46	7.23	4.85	6.75	☆	5.5	☐	362-5365	None	2.00	0.79	None	R. Fernald	'95
VICTORY OH REGIONAL STK	Capital Appreciation	35.7	15.65	10.83	19.56	14.83	14.41	☆	1.1	N/A	362-5365	None	4.75	1.04	None	Lynn Hamilton	'89
VICTORY SPEC VALUE FUND	Midcap	159.8	11.64	5.88	19.01	☆	☆	☆	1.3	N/A	362-5365	None	4.75	1.00	None	Anthony Aveni	'93
VICTORY SPECIAL GROWTH	Midcap	19.3	11.12	7.16	12.69	☆	☆	☆	0.2	N/A	362-5365	None	4.75	0.98	None	T. Rowe Price	'95
VICTORY STOCK INDEX	S&P Index	113.7	11.70	9.24	25.20	☆	☆	☆	2.1	N/A	362-5365	None	4.75	0.58	None	Denise Coyne	'93

PERFORMANCE OF MUTUAL FUNDS (continued)

FUND NAME	OBJECTIVE	ASSETS ($ MIL) 5/31/95	NAV ($/SHR) 6/30/95	QTR	1YR	3YRS	5YRS	10YRS	DIV YLD %	P/E RATIO	PHONE 800	PHONE In-State	Load	Exp. Ratio	Redemption	MANAGER	SINCE
VICTORY VALUE FUND	Growth Income	272.3	11.22	7.10	20.91	☆	☆	☆	2.4	N/A	362-5365	None	4.75	0.92	None	Judith Jones	'93
VIRTUS GOVT SEC; INV	Fixed Income	106.7	10.17	4.67	9.19	5.52	☆	☆	6.1	—	444-7123	None	None	0.99	2.00	E. Christian Goetz	'91
VIRTUS GOVT SEC; TR	Fixed Income	107.0	10.17	4.74	9.46	5.71	☆	☆	6.4	—	444-7123	None	None	0.74	2.00	E. Christian Goetz	'91
VIRTUS STOCK; INV	Growth Income	33.3	12.71	5.22	13.63	6.12	☆	☆	0.7	N/A	444-7123	None	None	1.20	2.00	Kevin Lewis	'95
VIRTUS STOCK; TR	Growth Income	45.2	12.71	5.29	13.91	6.30	☆	☆	0.9	N/A	444-7123	None	None	0.95	None	Kevin Lewis	'95
VISION GRO & INC	Growth Income	41.7	11.15	10.68	17.89	☆	☆	☆	1.7	20.1	836-2211	716-842-4488	4.50	None	None	Allan Fields	'94
VISION US GOVT SECS	Fixed Income	30.5	9.47	6.45	11.68	☆	☆	☆	5.8	—	836-2211	716-842-4488	4.50	None	None	Tom Pierce	'95
VISTA BALANCED; A	Balanced	24.1	11.86	6.41	15.13	☆	☆	☆	3.5	14.6	348-4782	None	4.50	0.58	None	Adams/Nelson	'92/'92
VISTA BALANCED; B	Balanced	5.0	11.78	6.24	14.36	☆	☆	☆	3.1	14.6	348-4782	None	None	1.50	5.00	Adams/Nelson	'93/'93
VISTA BOND ➧	Fixed Income	54.9	10.77	6.38	12.21	7.62	☆	☆	6.3	—	348-4782	None	None	0.31	None	Mark Buonaugurio	'91
VISTA CAPITAL GR; A	Midcap	666.3	N/A	N/A	N/A	N/A	N/A	☆	0.0	15.7	348-4782	None	4.75	1.02	None	Dave Klassen	'93
VISTA CAPITAL GR; B	Midcap	218.0	34.15	5.29	15.84	☆	☆	☆	0.3	15.7	348-4782	None	None	1.53	5.00	Dave Klassen	'93
VISTA EQUITY ➧	Growth	66.8	11.63	8.05	20.53	11.64	☆	☆	2.3	14.7	348-4782	None	None	0.31	5.00	Greg Adams	'95
VISTA EQUITY INCOME	Equity Income	11.1	12.68	7.45	14.82	☆	☆	☆	2.8	12.8	348-4782	None	4.50	1.50	None	Greg Adams	'95
VISTA GLBL FXD INC; A	World Income	1.5	10.75	3.05	11.04	☆	☆	☆	3.5	—	348-4782	None	4.50	0.70	None	Gordon Ross	'94
VISTA GLBL FXD INC; B	World Income	0.3	10.74	2.91	10.42	☆	☆	☆	3.2	—	348-4782	None	None	1.34	5.00	Gordon Ross	'94
VISTA GOVT INCOME; A	Fixed Income	101.0	11.28	5.87	10.84	6.71	☆	☆	6.3	—	348-4782	None	4.50	0.76	None	Tom Nelson	'92
VISTA GOVT INCOME; B	Fixed Income	9.1	11.25	5.65	9.96	☆	8.67	☆	5.8	—	348-4782	None	None	1.50	5.00	Tom Nelson	'93
VISTA GRO & INC; A	Growth Income	1,449.7	33.45	7.67	16.87	12.43	☆	☆	1.9	14.5	348-4782	None	4.75	0.97	None	Adams/Klassen	'95/'95
VISTA GRO & INC; B	Growth Income	227.8	33.32	7.55	16.28	15.59	☆	☆	1.5	14.5	348-4782	None	None	1.46	5.00	Adams/Klassen	'95/'95
VISTA IEEE BALANCED FUND	Balanced	9.7	10.49	6.67	16.90	☆	☆	☆	2.4	18.5	348-4782	None	None	1.12	None	Frederick Muller	'93
VISTA INTL EQUITY; A	International	28.2	11.60	3.57	-1.19	☆	☆	☆	0.0	—	348-4782	None	4.75	0.86	None	Joseph DeSantis	'93
VISTA INTL EQUITY; B	International	7.8	11.49	3.42	-1.78	☆	☆	☆	0.0	—	348-4782	None	None	1.36	5.00	Joseph DeSantis	'93
VISTA SH-TM BD ➧	Fixed Income	33.8	10.06	2.31	6.51	4.67	☆	☆	5.2	—	348-4782	None	None	0.31	5.00	Linda Struble	'90
VISTA SMALL CAP EQTY; B	Small Company Growth	N/A	13.14	14.63	☆	☆	☆	☆	0.0	N/A	348-4782	None	None	None	5.00	Dave Klassen	'95
VOLUMETRIC FUND	Growth	11.9	15.71	2.95	13.14	7.22	8.63	☆	0.0	17.9	541-3863	914-623-7637	None	1.99	None	Gabriel Gibs	'86
VOYAGEUR AGGR GROWTH; A	Growth	2.3	11.39	10.15	23.54	☆	☆	☆	0.0	N/A	553-2143	612-376-7000	4.75	None	None	Tony Elavia	'95
VOYAGEUR AGGR GROWTH; C	Growth	0.1	11.29	9.82	22.58	☆	☆	☆	0.0	N/A	553-2143	612-376-7000	None	None	1.00	Tony Elavia	'95
VOYAGEUR GROWTH STOCK	Growth	24.4	20.94	7.66	25.88	7.82	10.08	☆	0.6	18.0	553-2143	612-376-7000	4.75	1.90	None	James C. King	'90
VOYAGEUR INTL EQTY; A	International	2.1	9.38	2.51	-2.90	☆	☆	☆	0.0	—	553-2143	612-376-7000	4.75	None	None	Rodger Scullion	'94
VOYAGEUR INTL EQTY; C	International	0.1	9.31	2.53	-3.32	☆	☆	☆	0.0	—	553-2143	612-376-7000	None	None	1.00	Rodger Scullion	'94
VOYAGEUR US GOVT; A	Fixed Income	76.3	10.37	6.68	13.46	7.59	9.80	☆	6.2		553-2143	612-376-7000	4.75	0.96	None	Wyatt/Vandenberg	'90/'93
VOYAGEUR US GOVT; B	Fixed Income	0.1	10.38	6.54	12.96	☆	☆	☆	5.6		553-2143	612-376-7000	None	None	4.00	Wyatt/Vandenberg	'94/'94
VOYAGEUR US GOVT; Y	Fixed Income	53.9	10.37	6.68	13.53	☆	☆	☆	6.2		553-2143	612-376-7000	None	None	3.00	Wyatt/Vandenberg	'94/'94
WADDELL & REED AST STR	Global Flexible	0.1	10.03	☆	☆	☆	☆	☆	0.0		None	913-236-2000	None	None	3.00	James D. Wineland	'95
WADDELL & REED GROWTH	Growth	107.9	18.08	6.98	39.71	☆	☆	☆	0.0	26.9	None	913-236-2000	None	2.23	3.00	Mark G. Seferovich	'92
WADDELL & REED INTL GR	World Income	12.1	9.77	4.59	8.72	☆	☆	☆	3.0		None	913-236-2000	None	2.29	3.00	Mark Yockey	'95
WADDELL & REED LTD-TM	Fixed Income	13.1	10.03	4.51	8.24	☆	☆	☆	4.0		None	913-236-2000	None	2.17	3.00	W. Patrick Sterner	'92
WADDELL & REED TOT RTN	Growth Income	117.0	14.31	12.41	21.79	☆	☆	☆	0.0	16.8	None	913-236-2000	None	2.05	3.00	Russell E. Thompson	'92
WADE FUND	Growth	0.6	34.48	10.76	15.44	9.49	9.37	8.58	0.2	19.0	None	901-682-4613	None	2.82	None	Maury Wade	'73
WALL STREET FUND	Growth	11.6	8.66	9.90	30.17	13.41	10.39	11.11	0.0	N/A	443-4693	212-207-1660	4.00	1.96	None	Robert Morse	'84
WARBG PINCUS BALANCED	Balanced	2.4	10.19	8.37	17.03	12.14	11.53	☆	2.9	50.4	257-5614	212-878-0600	None	None	None	Orphanos/Christensen	'95/'95
WARBG PINCUS CAP APP; COM	Growth	199.4	15.01	8.57	22.80	13.99	10.96	☆	0.3	20.6	257-5614	212-878-0600	None	1.05	None	Black/Wyper	'94/'94
WARBG PINCUS CAP APP; SR2	Growth	9.1	14.92	8.43	22.12	13.47	☆	☆	0.0	20.6	257-5614	212-878-0600	None	1.55	None	Black/Wyper	'94/'94
WARBG PINCUS EMER GR; COM	Small Company Growth	300.3	26.42	12.95	32.03	19.53	16.22	☆	0.0	23.2	257-5614	212-878-0600	None	1.22	None	Dater/Lurito	'88/'93

Fund	Objective	Net Assets	NAV	R1	R2	R3	R4	R5	Rtg	%	%	Tel	Tel (800)	Load	Exp	Min	Manager	Since
WARBG PINCUS EMER GR; SR2	Small Company Growth	108.4	25.95	12.83	31.46	18.96	☆	☆	☆	0.0	23.2	257-5614	212-878-0600	None	1.72	None	Dater/Lurito	'91/'93
WARBG PINCUS EMER MK; COM	Emerging Markets	2.9	10.89	5.10	☆	☆	☆	☆	☆	0.0	□	257-5614	212-878-0600	None	None	None	King/Horsley	'94/'94
WARBG PINCUS FXD INC	Fixed Income	112.0	9.91	5.81	10.00	7.25	8.32	☆	☆	6.9	□	257-5614	212-878-0600	None	0.75	None	Christensen/Van Daalen	'92/'92
WARBG PINCUS GLBL FXD	World Income	75.7	10.58	6.16	6.21	6.31	☆	☆	☆	4.5	□	257-5614	212-878-0600	None	0.95	None	Christensen/Bhandari	'90/'93
WARBG PINCUS GRO&INC; COM	Growth Income	941.1	15.12	4.58	15.39	20.03	15.34	☆	☆	1.2	17.4	257-5614	212-878-0600	None	1.28	None	Anthony G. Orphanos	'92
WARBG PINCUS GRO&INC; SR2	Growth Income	42.4	15.12	☆	☆	☆	☆	☆	☆	0.0	N/A	257-5614	212-878-0600	None	None	None	Anthony G. Orphanos	'95
WARBG PINCUS INST INT EQ	International	383.2	14.03	2.26	-4.21	12.35	9.03	☆	☆	1.2	□	257-5614	212-878-0600	None	0.95	None	Richard King	'92
WARBG PINCUS INTL EQ; COM	International	1,839.1	17.87	1.98	-4.41	11.91	8.52	☆	☆	0.7	□	257-5614	212-878-0600	None	1.48	None	Richard King	'89
WARBG PINCUS INTL EQ; SR2	International	270.7	17.77	1.83	-4.75	☆	☆	☆	☆	0.3	□	257-5614	212-878-0600	None	1.94	None	Richard King	'91
WARBG PINCUS INTMDT GOVT	Fixed Income	53.1	10.08	4.73	9.40	6.33	☆	☆	☆	5.8	□	257-5614	212-878-0600	None	0.60	None	Christensen/Van Daalen	'89/'92
WARBG PINCUS JAPAN; COM	Japanese	25.9	7.26	-7.75	☆	☆	☆	☆	☆	0.0		257-5614	212-878-0600	None	1.00	None	King/Abe/Horsley	'94/'94/'94
WASATCH AGGRESSIVE EQU	Small Company Growth	169.8	22.23	11.04	32.34	20.04	16.37	☆	☆	0.0	19.8	551-1700	801-533-0778	None	1.50	None	Samuel S. Stewart Jr.	'87
WASATCH GROWTH	Growth	19.8	14.33	12.04	40.36	16.86	14.19	☆	☆	0.0	22.5	551-1700	801-533-0778	None	1.50	None	Samuel S. Stewart Jr.	'87
WASATCH INCOME	Fixed Income	3.4	10.38	4.01	9.74	5.90	7.68	☆	☆	5.7		551-1700	801-533-0778	None	1.00	None	Samuel S. Stewart Jr.	'87
WASATCH MID-CAP	Midcap	14.3	15.79	18.10	60.49	☆	☆	☆	☆	0.0	20.9	551-1700	801-533-0778	None	1.75	None	Samuel S. Stewart Jr.	'92
WASHINGTON MUTUAL INV	Growth Income	15,070.1	19.61	7.89	21.96	12.77	12.03	13.96	☆	3.2	14.9	421-4120	714-671-7000	5.75	0.68	None	Multiple Managers	N/A
WAYNE HUMMER GROWTH FUND	Growth	95.7	23.84	2.57	17.37	8.45	10.15	12.25	☆	1.3	20.5	621-1477	312-431-1700	None	1.07	None	Bird/Rowland	'83/'87
WAYNE HUMMER INCOME FUND	Fixed Income	26.8	15.11	4.48	10.56	☆	☆	☆	☆	6.6		621-1477	312-431-1700	None	1.13	None	David Poitras	'92
WEITZ PARTNERS VALUE	Growth Income	61.0	10.02	11.21	17.82	☆	☆	☆	☆	0.0	7.1	232-4161	402-391-1980	None	None	None	Wallace Weitz	'94
WEITZ FIXED INCOME	Fixed Income	12.5	10.96	5.05	10.72	6.10	7.50	☆	☆	6.1		232-4161	402-391-1980	None	0.75	None	Wallace	'88
WEITZ HICKORY	Growth	3.8	12.47	12.10	12.91	☆	☆	☆	☆	1.1	7.0	232-4161	402-391-1980	None	1.50	None	Richard Lawson	'93
WEITZ VALUE	Growth Income	123.6	16.99	11.29	14.86	12.09	☆	☆	☆	1.7	7.6	232-4161	402-391-1980	None	1.41	None	Wallace Weitz	'86
WESTCORE BALANCED; INSTL	Flexible	43.0	19.10	7.47	15.40	☆	☆	☆	☆	3.1	13.3	392-2673	303-623-2577	None	1.10	None	Fish/Hughes	'91/'91
WESTCORE BALANCED; RET	Flexible	3.6	19.08	7.37	15.18	☆	☆	☆	☆	3.0	13.3	392-2673	303-623-2577	4.50	1.85	None	Fish/Hughes	'93/'93
WESTCORE BASIC VAL; INSTL	Growth Income	71.0	22.12	9.78	21.14	9.36	☆	☆	☆	2.2	13.2	392-2673	303-623-2577	None	1.01	None	Charlie Fish	'87
WESTCORE BASIC VAL; RET	Growth Income	0.7	22.10	9.74	20.68	☆	☆	☆	☆	2.0	13.2	392-2673	303-623-2577	4.50	1.64	None	Charlie Fish	'93
WESTCORE BOND PLUS	Fixed Income	56.1	14.80	5.37	10.96	8.77	7.95	☆	☆	6.4		392-2673	303-623-2577	None	0.79	None	Charlie Fish	'94
WESTCORE EQ INCOME; INSTL	Equity Income	27.0	10.71	6.92	8.67	☆	☆	☆	☆	1.7	17.9	392-2673	303-623-2577	None	1.00	None	Larry Luchini	'88
WESTCORE EQ INCOME; RET	Equity Income	3.9	10.72	6.86	8.50	☆	☆	☆	☆	1.5	17.9	392-2673	303-623-2577	4.50	1.75	None	Larry Luchini	'93
WESTCORE GNMA; INSTL	Fixed Income	24.1	15.70	5.21	11.26	8.16	☆	☆	☆	6.8		392-2673	303-623-2577	None	0.79	None	Charlie Fish	'94
WESTCORE GNMA; RET	Fixed Income	9.2	15.68	5.16	10.98	☆	☆	☆	☆	6.7		392-2673	303-623-2577	4.50	1.45	None	Charlie Fish	'94
WESTCORE GROWTH; INSTL	Growth	12.6	17.69	8.95	20.93	☆	☆	☆	☆	1.4	18.1	392-2673	303-623-2577	None	0.78	None	Peter Glidden	'93
WESTCORE GROWTH; RET	Growth	0.2	17.68	8.88	20.86	☆	☆	☆	☆	1.4	18.1	392-2673	303-623-2577	4.50	1.88	None	Peter Glidden	'93
WESTCORE INT-TM BD; INSTL	Fixed Income	98.1	10.28	4.94	6.48	8.16	☆	☆	☆	5.8		392-2673	303-623-2577	None	0.67	None	John Cormey	'92
WESTCORE INT-TM BD; RET	Fixed Income	2.6	10.28	4.84	9.50	9.36	☆	☆	☆	5.6		392-2673	303-623-2577	4.50	1.20	None	John Cormey	'93
WESTCORE LONG-TERM BOND	Fixed Income	33.7	9.92	9.54	16.20	9.90	11.07	☆	☆	6.0		392-2673	303-623-2577	4.50	0.89	None	John Cormey	'92
WESTON MIDCO GRO; INSTL	Midcap	402.4	18.34	7.06	24.39	16.78	17.21	☆	☆	0.0	26.5	392-2673	303-623-2577	None	0.83	None	Todger Anderson	'86
WESTON MIDCO GRO; RET	Midcap	25.7	18.31	7.01	24.10	☆	☆	☆	☆	0.0	26.5	392-2673	303-623-2577	4.50	1.47	None	Todger Anderson	'93
WESTCORE MODERN VAL EQU	Growth Income	53.0	14.92	8.49	13.07	☆	11.81	☆	☆	1.2	14.6	392-2673	303-623-2577	4.50	1.06	None	Varilyn Schock	'91
WESTCORE SH-TM GOV; INSTL	Fixed Income	37.1	15.51	2.86	4.32	☆	6.51	☆	☆	5.3		392-2673	303-623-2577	None	0.60	None	Charlie Fish	'94
WESTCORE SH-TM GOV; RET	Fixed Income	4.5	15.50	2.84	6.82	☆	☆	☆	☆	5.2		392-2673	303-623-2577	2.00	1.01	None	Charlie Fish	'94
WESTCORE SMALL-CAP; INSTL	Small Company Growth	9.7	16.47	6.95	13.50	☆	☆	☆	☆	0.5	N/A	392-2673	303-623-2577	None	None	None	Varilyn Shock	'93
WESTCORE SMALL-CAP; RET	Small Company Growth	0.9	16.48	7.02	13.35	☆	☆	☆	☆	0.2	N/A	392-2673	303-623-2577	4.50	None	None	Varilyn Shock	'93
WESTERN FULL RANGE DUR	Fixed Income	297.5	112.18	6.94	14.10	9.00	☆	☆	☆	6.1		None	818-584-4300	None	None	None	Kent S. Engel	'90
WESTERN INTL SEC	World Income	178.8	92.10	2.08	9.00	☆	☆	☆	☆	8.3		None	818-584-4300	None	None	None	Keith J. Gardner	'95
WESTERN INTMDT DURATION	Fixed Income	17.5	107.36	5.17	☆	10.07	☆	☆	☆	2.3		None	818-584-4300	4.50	1.60	None	Walsh/Eichstaedt	'94/'94
WESTON NEW CENTURY CAP	Flexible	41.3	12.17	8.76	17.83	13.38	8.87	☆	☆	2.2	N/A	None	617-239-0445	4.50	1.73	None	Douglas Biggar	'89
WESTON NEW CENTURY I	Income	26.9	11.35	6.27	13.56	13.70	☆	☆	☆	2.4	N/A	None	617-239-0445	4.50	1.68	None	Douglas Biggar	'89
WESTWOOD BALANCED; RTL	Balanced	5.2	7.99	8.51	18.06	13.23	☆	☆	☆	2.5	16.5	937-8966	None	None	None	None	Byrne/Fraze	'91/'91
WESTWOOD BALANCED; SERV	Balanced	7.4	7.96	8.31	17.51	☆	☆	☆	☆	2.1	16.5	937-8966	None	4.00	1.17	None	Byrne/Fraze	'93/'93

PERFORMANCE OF MUTUAL FUNDS (continued)

FUND NAME	OBJECTIVE	ASSETS ($ MIL) 5/31/95	NAV ($/SHR) 6/30/95	RETURN THROUGH 6/30 (Annualized)					DIV YLD %	P/E RATIO	PHONE NUMBER		FEES			MANAGER	SINCE
				QTR	1YR	3YRS	5YRS	10YRS			800	In-State	Load	Exp. Ratio	Redemption		
WESTWOOD EQUITY; RTL	Capital Appreciation	12.3	6.08	9.16	21.41	15.92	11.20	☆	1.0	16.2	937-8966	None	None	0.71	None	Susan Byrne	'87
WESTWOOD EQUITY; SERV	Capital Appreciation	0.1	6.06	8.99	21.10	☆	☆	☆	0.7	16.2	937-8966	None	4.00	1.04	None	Susan Byrne	'94
WESTWOOD INTMDT BD; RTL	Fixed Income	4.4	9.94	5.27	9.39	6.12	☆	☆	5.2		937-8966	None	None	0.92	None	Patricia Fraze	'91
WILLIAM PENN QUALITY INC	Fixed Income	28.8	10.27	6.51	11.23	8.81	10.43	☆	6.6		523-8440	610-670-1031	4.75	0.38	None	Miller Anderson & Sherr.	'87
WILLIAM PENN US GOVT	Fixed Income	48.0	10.51	6.62	12.67	8.51	9.54	☆	6.6		523-8440	610-670-1031	4.75	1.00	None	Miller Anderson & Sherr.	'87
WINTHROP FOCUS AGG GRO	Small Company Growth	185.1	16.17	5.55	11.00	16.29	16.23	12.97	0.0	16.6	225-8011	212-504-4000	None	1.70	None	Engle/Vogel	'89/'93
WINTHROP FOCUS FIX INC	Fixed Income	47.6	10.16	5.00	9.65	6.54	8.66	☆	5.7		225-8011	212-504-4000	None	0.93	4.00	Cathy Jameson	'86
WINTHROP FOCUS GRO&INC	Growth Income	78.4	13.64	5.78	11.72	11.79	9.89	10.65	1.9	15.1	225-8011	212-504-4000	None	1.64	4.00	Engle/Vogel	'86/'93
WINTHROP FOCUS GROWTH	Growth	53.9	10.74	5.50	10.04	9.59	7.56	☆	0.1	15.4	225-8011	212-504-4000	None	1.65	4.00	Engle/Vogel	'93/'93
WM BLAIR GROWTH FUND	Growth	267.0	11.29	9.08	28.77	18.52	15.35	14.44	0.2	25.6	742-7272	312-364-8000	None	0.71	None	Barber/Fuller	'93/'93
WM BLAIR INCOME	Fixed Income	151.7	10.36	4.49	10.18	6.45	☆	☆	6.6		742-7272	312-364-8000	None	0.68	None	Bentley M. Myer	'91
WM BLAIR INTL GROWTH FD	International	78.2	12.18	3.22	-4.68	☆	☆	☆	0.2		742-7272	312-364-8000	None	1.51	None	Framlington Overseas Mgmt	'92
WOMENS EQUITY MUTUAL FD	Capital Appreciation	1.6	10.01	0.81	5.14	☆	☆	☆	0.2	N/A	424-2295	415-296-9135	None	1.50	None	Pro-Conscience Funds	'93
WOOD ISLAND GROWTH FUND	Growth	3.9	15.19	7.73	9.47	8.42	8.29	10.50	0.7	N/A	None	415-461-3850	None	2.13	None	Siebel/Kirk	'84/'84
WOODWARD BALANCED; INSTL	Balanced	57.1	10.60	6.15	14.15	☆	☆	☆	3.0	17.2	688-3350	None	None	0.85	None	Kost/Cawley	'94/'94
WOODWARD BALANCED; RTL	Balanced	9.0	10.60	6.15	14.15	☆	☆	☆	3.0	17.2	688-3350	None	5.00	0.85	None	Kost/Cawley	'94/'94
WOODWARD BOND; INSTL	Fixed Income	455.7	10.01	7.62	12.28	7.37	☆	☆	5.9		688-3350	None	None	0.74	None	Douglas Swanson	'91
WOODWARD BOND; RTL	Fixed Income	32.6	10.01	7.62	12.28	7.37	☆	☆	5.9		688-3350	None	4.75	0.74	None	Douglas Swanson	'91
WOODWARD CAP GRO; INSTL	Growth	2.8	12.14	5.47	22.05	☆	☆	☆	0.5	N/A	688-3350	None	None	0.85	None	Jeffrey Beard	'94
WOODWARD CAP GRO; RTL	Growth		12.14	5.47	22.05	☆	☆	☆	0.5	N/A	688-3350	None	5.00	0.85	None	Jeffrey Beard	'94
WOODWARD EQ INDEX; INSTL	S&P Index	390.4	12.63	9.46	25.76	☆	☆	☆	2.4	17.2	688-3350	None	None	0.17	None	F. Richard Neumann	'92
WOODWARD EQ INDEX; RTL	S&P Index	1.6	12.63	9.46	25.76	☆	☆	☆	2.4	17.2	688-3350	None	None	0.17	None	F. Richard Neumann	'92
WOODWARD GRO/VAL; INSTL	Growth Income	606.7	11.97	5.42	14.59	11.56	☆	☆	2.2	17.0	688-3350	None	None	0.84	None	George Abel	'91
WOODWARD GRO/VAL; RTL	Growth Income	45.5	11.97	5.42	14.59	11.56	☆	☆	2.2	17.0	688-3350	None	5.00	0.84	None	George Abel	'91
WOODWARD INTL EQTY; INSTL	International	61.1	10.53	3.54	☆	☆	☆	☆	0.0		688-3350	None	None	None	None	Clyde Carter	'94
WOODWARD INTL EQTY; RTL	International	0.6	10.53	3.54	☆	☆	☆	☆	0.0		688-3350	None	5.00	None	None	Clyde Carter	'91
WOODWARD INTMDT BD; INSTL	Fixed Income	407.2	10.04	6.10	9.86	5.58	☆	☆	5.7		688-3350	None	None	0.74	None	Douglas Swanson	'91
WOODWARD INTMDT BD; RTL	Fixed Income	12.4	10.04	6.10	9.86	5.58	☆	☆	5.7		688-3350	None	4.75	0.74	None	Douglas Swanson	'91
WOODWARD INTRINSIC; INSTL	Growth Income	232.3	11.80	6.70	17.11	12.08	☆	☆	2.6	14.0	688-3350	None	None	0.91	None	Christopher Gassen	'91
WOODWARD INTRINSIC; RTL	Growth Income	17.4	11.80	6.70	17.11	12.08	☆	☆	2.6	14.0	688-3350	None	5.00	0.91	None	Christopher Gassen	'91
WOODWARD OPPTY; INSTL	Small Company Growth	524.8	15.05	7.13	14.96	18.22	☆	☆	0.5	18.5	688-3350	None	None	0.90	None	Ronald L. Doyle	'91
WOODWARD OPPTY; RTL	Small Company Growth	67.4	15.05	7.13	14.96	18.22	☆	☆	0.5	18.5	688-3350	None	5.00	0.90	None	Ronald L. Doyle	'91
WOODWARD SHORT BD; INSTL	Fixed Income	86.7	10.13	3.03	☆	☆	☆	☆	0.0		688-3350	None	None	None	None	Rick Cipiccio	'94
WOODWARD SHORT BD; RTL	Fixed Income	0.6	10.13	3.03	☆	☆	☆	☆	0.0		688-3350	None	3.00	None	None	Rick Cipiccio	'94
WORKING ASSETS CIT EMERG	Midcap	9.7	11.87	8.01	23.24	☆	☆	☆	0.7	19.5	223-7010	415-989-3200	4.00	None	None	Rich Little	'94
WORKING ASSETS CIT GL EQ	Global	9.3	10.69	8.97	9.77	☆	☆	☆	0.0		223-7010	415-989-3200	4.00	None	None	Lilia Clemente	'91
WORKING ASSETS CIT INC	Fixed Income	28.0	10.38	5.03	10.52	6.76	☆	☆	6.3		223-7010	415-989-3200	2.00	None	None	Gail Seneca	'93
WORLD INV UTILITY; A	Utility	6.1	10.29	7.01	9.67	☆	☆	☆	2.7	12.9	245-4770	412-288-1900	5.50	1.25	None	Christopher H. Wiles	'94
WORLD INV UTILITY; FORT	Utility	5.5	10.28	6.95	9.38	☆	☆	☆	2.6	12.9	245-4770	412-288-1900	1.00	0.25	1.00	Christopher H. Wiles	'94
WORLD FUNDS EUROPAC	International	118.9	15.99	3.83	-1.78	7.69	6.16	5.42	0.0		527-9500	804-285-8211	None	1.54	None	Fabrizio Pierallini	'94
WORLD VNTBEL INTL BD	World Income	12.9	10.54	4.67	12.98	☆	☆	☆	6.8		527-9500	804-285-8211	None	1.62	None	Sven Rump	'94
WORLD VNTBEL US VALUE	Growth Income	36.7	12.30	8.08	19.35	12.47	11.73	☆	0.8	14.0	527-9500	804-285-8211	None	0.80	None	Ed Walczak	'90
WPG FUNDS TR GOVT SEC	Fixed Income	193.3	9.24	4.28	7.27	4.10	7.01	☆	6.7		223-3332	212-908-9500	None	1.14	None	Daniel S. Vandivort	'95
WPG FUNDS TR QUANT EQ	Growth Income	99.7	6.41	6.83	23.76	12.06	9.24	☆	1.7	17.0	223-3332	212-908-9500	None	0.95	None	Joseph N. Pappo	'93
WPG GROWTH	Small Company Growth	64.5	110.58	8.28	19.65	☆	☆	☆	0.0	20.4	223-3332	212-908-9500	None		None	John P. Callaghan	'93

Fund	Objective	Net Assets	NAV	Ret 1	Ret 2	Ret 3	Ret 4	Ret 5	Yield	Rating	Phone	Phone (alt)	Load	Exp.	Manager	Since
WPG GROWTH & INCOME	Growth Income	65.3	24.62	11.43	16.37	11.41	10.42	12.32	3.1	17.4	212-908-9500	223-3332	None	1.23	A. Roy Knutsen	'92
WPG INTERNATIONAL	International	14.2	11.37	3.74	0.19	7.52	1.68	☆	0.0	□	212-908-9500	223-3332	None	1.95	Raymond Haines	'94
WPG TUDOR FUND	Capital Appreciation	138.6	22.62	10.67	24.91	10.96	9.69	12.28	0.0	18.5	212-908-9500	223-3332	None	1.28	Melville Straus	'73
WRIGHT EQ INTL BLUE CHIP	International	221.1	14.54	5.90	11.25	8.35	7.37	☆	0.3	□	203-333-6666	232-0013	None	1.31	Team Managed	N/A
WRIGHT EQ JR BLUE CHIP	Small Company Growth	31.3	11.06	5.95	12.79	8.44	7.92	8.14	0.9	15.0	203-333-6666	232-0013	None	1.11	Team Managed	N/A
WRIGHT EQ QUAL CORE EQU	Growth Income	52.7	12.90	6.50	18.89	8.83	9.96	☆	1.2	17.6	203-333-6666	232-0013	None	0.99	Team Managed	N/A
WRIGHT EQ SEL BLUE CHIP	Growth Income	212.1	15.65	7.68	17.18	8.31	8.85	11.27	1.3	14.5	203-333-6666	232-0013	None	1.03	Team Managed	N/A
WRIGHT EQUI BELGIAN/LUX	European Region	14.1	11.89	11.64	17.15	☆	☆	☆	0.3	□	203-333-6666	888-9471	None	1.62	Team Managed	N/A
WRIGHT EQUI DUTCH	European Region	7.0	9.44	7.64	23.26	10.02	☆	☆	0.2	□	203-333-6666	888-9471	None	1.93	Team Managed	N/A
WRIGHT EQUI HONG KONG	Pacific Region	39.9	13.40	2.37	-16.14	1.00	☆	☆	1.5	□	203-333-6666	888-9471	None	1.41	Team Managed	N/A
WRIGHT EQUI ITALIAN	European Region	1.1	4.61	4.77	-11.53	-7.21	☆	☆	7.2	□	203-333-6666	888-9471	None	2.00	Team Managed	N/A
WRIGHT EQUI JAPANESE	Japanese	14.1	8.78	-6.40	-18.35	☆	☆	☆	0.0	□	203-333-6666	888-9471	None	1.83	Team Managed	N/A
WRIGHT EQUI MEXICO	Latin American	21.9	4.46	24.58	☆	☆	☆	☆	0.0	□	203-333-6666	888-9471	None	None	Team Managed	N/A
WRIGHT EQUI NORDIC	European Region	2.9	10.39	10.53	13.75	☆	☆	☆	0.0	□	203-333-6666	888-9471	None	1.78	Team Managed	N/A
WRIGHT EQUI SPANISH	European Region	2.9	6.20	10.71	-3.85	-6.68	☆	☆	0.3	□	203-333-6666	888-9471	None	2.00	Team Managed	N/A
WRIGHT EQUI SWISS	European Region	7.7	11.20	9.06	14.67	☆	☆	☆	0.5	□	203-333-6666	888-9471	None	2.00	Team Managed	N/A
WRIGHT INC CURRENT INC	Fixed Income	82.7	10.45	5.57	12.75	6.10	8.45	10.51	6.7	□	203-333-6666	232-0013	None	0.80	Team Managed	N/A
WRIGHT INC GOVT OBLIG	Fixed Income	17.5	13.85	10.36	17.86	9.86	10.61	7.99	6.4	□	203-333-6666	232-0013	None	0.90	Team Managed	N/A
WRIGHT INC NEAR TERM BD	Fixed Income	172.5	10.37	4.11	8.17	5.30	7.41	9.36	5.8	□	203-333-6666	232-0013	None	0.70	Team Managed	N/A
WRIGHT INC TOTAL RETURN	Fixed Income	126.1	12.58	7.65	13.61	7.33	8.77	☆	5.9	□	203-333-6666	232-0013	None	0.80	Team Managed	'94
WSIS WERTHEIM EQTY VALUE	Growth Income	36.3	10.70	7.32	13.91	☆	☆	☆	0.7	16.0	212-492-6000	464-3108	None	None	E. William Smethurst	'94
WSIS WERTHEIM HI YLD INC	Fixed Income	20.8	8.69	1.66	5.93	☆	☆	☆	10.2	□	212-492-6000	464-3108	None	None	Kenneth Malamed	'94
WSIS WERTHEIM INV GR INC	Fixed Income	21.0	9.85	6.50	12.58	☆	☆	☆	6.1	□	212-492-6000	464-3108	None	None	Gary Zeltzer	'94
WSIS WERTHEIM SH-TM INV	Fixed Income	34.9	9.89	1.52	4.90	☆	☆	☆	4.9	□	212-492-6000	464-3108	None	None	Gary Zeltzer	'94
WSIS WERTHEIM SMALL CAP	Small Company Growth	36.4	10.64	9.24	12.51	☆	☆	☆	0.0	17.8	212-492-6000	464-3108	None	None	Nancy Tooke	'94
YACKTMAN FUND	Growth	55.8	11.50	5.67	27.20	☆	☆	☆	1.9	17.0	None	525-8258	None	1.07	Donald Yacktman	'92
YAMAICHI FDS GLOBAL FUND	Global	19.9	9.08	7.46	4.76	11.77	5.73	☆	0.0	□	212-432-8670	327-6145	4.75	2.04	Edward Burke	'89
ZSA ASSET ALLOCATION	Flexible	10.8	11.43	6.69	11.98	☆	☆	☆	1.8	18.1	919-972-9922	525-3863	None	1.92	Zaske, Sarafa & Assoc.	'92
ZSA EQUITY	Capital Appreciation	8.4	11.20	5.75	12.91	☆	☆	☆	0.2	17.6	919-972-9922	525-3863	5.50	1.93	Zaske, Sarafa & Assoc.	'92
ZWEIG SR TR APPREC; A	Small Company Growth	249.9	14.89	8.13	10.22	11.54	☆	☆	1.0	11.8	212-635-9800	272-2700	4.75	1.70	David Katzen	'91
ZWEIG SR TR TR APPREC; C	Small Company Growth	157.9	14.76	7.97	9.49	10.70	☆	6.88	0.4	11.8	212-635-9800	272-2700	None	2.40	David Katzen	'92
ZWEIG SR TR TR GOVT SEC; A	Fixed Income	46.3	10.04	4.30	7.24	6.18	7.97	☆	5.1	□	212-635-9800	272-2700	5.50	1.28	Carlton Neel	'95
ZWEIG SR TR TR GOVT SEC; C	Fixed Income	20.0	10.03	4.18	6.80	5.54	☆	☆	4.6	□	212-635-9800	272-2700	None	1.73	Carlton Neel	'95
ZWEIG SR TR MGD ASST: A ★	Global Flexible	156.7	12.56	3.63	8.33	☆	☆	☆	3.2	□	212-635-9800	272-2700	5.50	1.68	Carlton Neel	'95
ZWEIG SR TR MGD ASST: C ★	Global Flexible	561.9	12.55	3.46	7.57	☆	☆	☆	2.4	□	212-635-9800	272-2700	None	2.38	Carlton Neel	'95
ZWEIG SR TR STRATEGY; A	Growth	460.5	14.20	11.37	17.15	14.20	12.12	☆	2.2	12.5	212-635-9800	272-2700	5.50	1.40	David Katzen	'89
ZWEIG SR TR STRATEGY; C	Growth	360.0	14.21	11.19	16.37	13.38	☆	☆	1.4	12.5	212-635-9800	272-2700	None	2.10	David Katzen	'92

★ ZWEIG SR TR MGD ASST; A,C--Fund has been reclassified from Flexible to Global Flexible.

© Copyright Lipper Analytical Services, Inc.

PERFORMANCE OF MUTUAL FUNDS (continued)

BENCHMARKS

Objective	Quarter	1 Year	Annualized Return 3 Years	5 Years	10 Years
General Muni	1.92%	7.69%	6.18%	7.77%	8.64%
High-Yield Muni	2.36	7.70	6.32	7.63	8.70
Intermediate Muni	2.17	6.81	5.99	7.16	7.49
California Muni	1.80	7.58	6.08	7.51	8.22
Insured Muni	1.78	7.94	6.08	7.45	8.31
Short-Term Muni	1.75	4.89	4.54	5.60	5.68

MUNICIPAL BOND FUNDS

FUND NAME	OBJECTIVE	ASSETS ($ MIL) 5/31/95	NAV ($/SHR) 6/30/95	RETURNS THROUGH 6/30 QTR	1YR	3YRS	5YRS	10YRS (Annualized)	DIV YLD %	PHONE NUMBER 800	In-State	FEES Load	Exp. Ratio	Redemption	MANAGER	SINCE
AAL MUNICIPAL BOND ◻	General Muni	386.7	10.82	2.65	8.87	6.29	7.61	☆	4.8	553-6319	414-734-7633	4.75	0.99	None	Duane McAllister	'94
AARP INS TF GEN BOND	Insured Muni	1,839.3	17.50	1.35	7.33	6.31	7.84	8.29	5.0	322-2282	617-439-4640	None	0.68	None	Carleton/Condon	'86/'89
ABT FL HIGH INCOME MUNI	Florida Muni	64.2	10.30	2.98	8.70	7.98	☆	☆	6.3	553-7838	407-655-7255	4.75	0.14	None	Steven Eldredge	'92
ABT FL TAX-FREE FUND	Florida Muni	163.6	10.96	2.08	9.02	7.01	8.63	☆	5.7	553-7838	407-655-7255	4.75	0.56	None	Steven Eldredge	'89
ACCESSOR MUNI INTMDT FXD	Intermediate Muni	14.1	11.55	1.82	6.51	☆	☆	☆	3.9	759-3504	206-224-7420	None	1.05	None	Lazard Freres Asset Mgt.	'94
ACHIEVEMENT ID MUNI; INST	Single State Muni	25.8	10.32	1.44	☆	☆	☆	☆	0.0	472-0577	None	None	None	None	James Schuck	'94
ACHIEVEMENT SH MUNI; INST	Short-Term Muni	31.3	10.13	1.71	☆	☆	☆	☆	0.0	472-0577	None	None	None	None	James Schuck	'94
AETNA TAX-FREE; ADV	General Muni	22.0	9.53	2.02	7.50	☆	☆	☆	3.9	238-6263	203-273-0121	None	1.27	1.00	Neil Grabowski	'94
AETNA TAX-FREE; SEL	General Muni	2.1	9.53	2.18	8.32	☆	☆	☆	4.7	238-6263	203-273-0121	None	0.30	None	Neil Grabowski	'94
AIM TXEX INTMDT; AIM	Intermediate Muni	76.7	10.76	1.97	6.14	5.82	7.04	☆	4.5	347-1919	713-626-1919	1.00	0.61	None	Team Managed	N/A
AIM TXEX TX-EX BD OF CT	Connecticut Muni	39.4	10.77	1.91	6.96	6.53	7.91	☆	5.4	347-1919	713-626-1919	4.75	0.34	None	Team Managed	N/A
AIM MUNICIPAL BOND; A	General Muni	277.4	8.11	2.30	6.74	6.32	7.99	9.21	5.8	347-1919	713-626-1919	4.75	0.89	None	Team Managed	N/A
AIM MUNICIPAL BOND; B	General Muni	13.7	8.11	2.09	5.87	☆	☆	☆	5.0	347-1919	713-626-1919	None	1.67	5.00	Team Managed	N/A
ALABAMA TAX FREE BOND	Alabama Muni	13.4	10.12	2.67	6.81	☆	☆	☆	4.4	443-4249	513-629-2000	None	0.75	None	Timothy S. Healey	'93
ALLIANCE MUNI II AZ; A	Arizona Muni	2.1	10.21	2.31	9.40	☆	☆	☆	5.6	227-4618	201-319-4000	4.25	None	None	Keenan/Dowden	'95/'95
ALLIANCE MUNI II AZ; B	Arizona Muni	2.6	10.20	2.04	8.52	☆	☆	☆	4.9	227-4618	201-319-4000	None	None	3.00	Keenan/Dowden	'95/'95
ALLIANCE MUNI II AZ; C	Arizona Muni	0.3	10.21	2.14	8.63	☆	☆	☆	4.9	227-4618	201-319-4000	None	None	None	Keenan/Dowden	'95/'95
ALLIANCE MUNI II FL; A	Florida Muni	10.5	9.38	3.23	10.64	☆	☆	☆	5.8	227-4618	201-319-4000	4.25	0.38	None	Keenan/Dowden	'95/'95
ALLIANCE MUNI II FL; B	Florida Muni	21.0	9.39	3.14	9.89	☆	☆	☆	5.1	227-4618	201-319-4000	None	1.08	3.00	Keenan/Dowden	'93/'95
ALLIANCE MUNI II FL; C	Florida Muni	34.2	9.39	3.14	9.89	☆	☆	☆	5.1	227-4618	201-319-4000	None	1.08	None	Keenan/Dowden	'95/'95

Fund	Net Assets	NAV			R1	R2	R3	Yld	Tel 1	Tel 2	Load	Exp	CDSC	Manager	Since
ALLIANCE MUNI II MA; A	0.9	10.34	2.07	8.06	☆	☆	☆	5.9	227-4618	201-319-4000	4.25	0.60	None	Keenan/Dowden	'95/'95
ALLIANCE MUNI II MA; B	0.8	10.34	1.90	7.31	☆	☆	☆	5.2	227-4618	201-319-4000	None	1.30	3.00	Keenan/Dowden	'95/'95
ALLIANCE MUNI II MA; C	2.2	10.34	1.90	7.31	☆	☆	☆	5.2	227-4618	201-319-4000	None	1.30	None	Keenan/Dowden	'95/'95
ALLIANCE MUNI II MI; A	3.0	9.97	3.68	10.99	☆	☆	☆	5.5	227-4618	201-319-4000	4.25	0.93	None	Keenan/Dowden	'95/'95
ALLIANCE MUNI II MI; B	2.2	9.97	3.50	10.18	☆	☆	☆	4.8	227-4618	201-319-4000	None	1.63	3.00	Keenan/Dowden	'95/'95
ALLIANCE MUNI II MI; C	2.3	9.97	3.40	10.18	☆	☆	☆	4.8	227-4618	201-319-4000	None	1.63	None	Keenan/Dowden	'95/'95
ALLIANCE MUNI II MN; A	2.4	9.42	1.90	7.78	☆	☆	☆	5.9	227-4618	201-319-4000	4.25	0.09	None	Keenan/Oliver	'93/'95
ALLIANCE MUNI II MN; B	6.7	9.42	1.71	6.95	☆	☆	☆	5.1	227-4618	201-319-4000	None	0.80	3.00	Keenan/Oliver	'93/'95
ALLIANCE MUNI II MN; C	7.8	9.42	1.71	6.94	☆	☆	☆	5.1	227-4618	201-319-4000	None	0.79	None	Keenan/Oliver	'93/'95
ALLIANCE MUNI II NJ; A	11.5	9.50	2.97	10.49	☆	☆	☆	5.8	227-4618	201-319-4000	4.25	0.20	None	Keenan/Oliver	'93/'95
ALLIANCE MUNI II NJ; B	32.7	9.51	2.89	9.73	☆	☆	☆	5.0	227-4618	201-319-4000	None	0.91	3.00	Keenan/Oliver	'93/'94
ALLIANCE MUNI II NJ; C	22.2	9.51	2.78	9.51	☆	☆	☆	5.0	227-4618	201-319-4000	None	0.90	None	Keenan/Oliver	'93/'94
ALLIANCE MUNI II OH; A	3.7	9.43	2.00	8.94	☆	☆	☆	5.8	227-4618	201-319-4000	4.25	0.04	None	Keenan/Oliver	'93/'94
ALLIANCE MUNI II OH; B	21.5	9.43	1.80	8.09	☆	☆	☆	5.1	227-4618	201-319-4000	None	0.74	3.00	Keenan/Oliver	'93/'94
ALLIANCE MUNI II OH; C	20.9	9.43	1.80	8.09	☆	☆	☆	5.1	227-4618	201-319-4000	None	0.74	None	Keenan/Oliver	'93/'94
ALLIANCE MUNI II PA; A	8.4	9.52	2.44	9.00	☆	☆	☆	5.9	227-4618	201-319-4000	4.25	0.45	None	Keenan/Oliver	'93/'94
ALLIANCE MUNI II PA; B	28.6	9.52	2.25	8.16	☆	☆	☆	5.1	227-4618	201-319-4000	None	1.16	3.00	Keenan/Oliver	'93/'94
ALLIANCE MUNI II PA; C	15.3	9.52	2.25	8.16	☆	☆	☆	5.1	227-4618	201-319-4000	None	1.15	None	Keenan/Oliver	'93/'94
ALLIANCE MUNI II VA; A	1.3	10.13	2.11	9.19	☆	☆	☆	5.6	227-4618	201-319-4000	4.25	None	None	Keenan/Dowden	'94/'95
ALLIANCE MUNI II VA; B	0.9	10.13	1.94	8.42	☆	☆	☆	4.9	227-4618	201-319-4000	None	None	3.00	Keenan/Oliver	'94/'95
ALLIANCE MUNI II VA; C	0.1	10.13	1.94	8.42	☆	☆	☆	4.9	227-4618	201-319-4000	None	None	None	Keenan/Dowden	'86
ALLIANCE MUNI CA; A	485.0	10.10	1.75	8.67	6.20	7.66	☆	5.8	227-4618	201-319-4000	4.25	0.64	None	Susan P. Keenan	'93
ALLIANCE MUNI CA; B	168.9	10.11	1.66	7.83	☆	☆	☆	5.1	227-4618	201-319-4000	None	1.35	3.00	Susan P. Keenan	'86
ALLIANCE MUNI CA; C	90.4	10.11	1.66	7.82	6.17	7.67	☆	5.1	227-4618	201-319-4000	None	1.34	None	Susan P. Keenan	'93
ALLIANCE MUNI INS CA; A	106.5	12.88	1.89	10.07	☆	☆	☆	5.4	227-4618	201-319-4000	4.25	0.82	None	Susan P. Keenan	'86
ALLIANCE MUNI INS CA; B	26.3	12.88	1.69	9.18	6.38	8.07	☆	4.6	227-4618	201-319-4000	None	1.53	3.00	Susan P. Keenan	'93
ALLIANCE MUNI INS CA; C	13.1	12.88	1.80	9.29	☆	☆	☆	4.6	227-4618	201-319-4000	None	1.52	None	Susan P. Keenan	'86
ALLIANCE MUNI INS NA; A	167.9	9.78	1.76	9.33	☆	☆	☆	5.4	227-4618	201-319-4000	4.25	0.66	None	Susan P. Keenan	'93
ALLIANCE MUNI INS NA; B	59.5	9.78	1.60	8.57	5.98	7.86	☆	4.7	227-4618	201-319-4000	None	1.37	3.00	Susan P. Keenan	'93
ALLIANCE MUNI INS NA; C	23.6	9.79	1.70	8.68	☆	☆	☆	4.7	227-4618	201-319-4000	None	1.36	None	Susan P. Keenan	'93
ALLIANCE MUNI NATL; A	347.7	10.13	2.65	9.38	6.34	8.24	☆	5.8	227-4618	201-319-4000	4.25	0.62	None	Susan P. Keenan	'86
ALLIANCE MUNI NATL; B	261.1	10.13	2.47	8.61	☆	☆	☆	5.1	227-4618	201-319-4000	None	1.32	3.00	Susan P. Keenan	'93
ALLIANCE MUNI NATL; C	113.5	10.13	2.48	8.62	☆	☆	☆	5.1	227-4618	201-319-4000	None	1.31	None	Susan P. Keenan	'93
ALLIANCE MUNI NY; A	188.2	9.39	2.89	8.34	☆	☆	☆	5.9	227-4618	201-319-4000	4.25	0.66	None	Susan P. Keenan	'86
ALLIANCE MUNI NY; B	92.0	9.40	2.69	7.60	☆	☆	☆	5.1	227-4618	201-319-4000	None	1.36	3.00	Susan P. Keenan	'93
ALLIANCE MUNI NY; C	33.0	9.40	2.69	7.60	☆	☆	8.41	5.1	227-4618	201-319-4000	None	1.36	None	Susan P. Keenan	'93
AMCORE VINTAGE INT TX-FR	31.4	10.13	2.69	7.54	6.61	7.90	☆	4.3	438-6375		None	0.57	None	Dean Countryman	'95
AMER CAP MUNI BOND; A	309.5	10.06	2.31	7.98	☆	☆	☆	5.9	421-5666	713-993-0500	4.75	0.93	None	David Johnson	'95
AMER CAP MUNI BOND; B	40.0	10.06	2.13	7.15	☆	☆	☆	5.1	421-5666	713-993-0500	None	1.72	4.00	David Johnson	'95
AMER CAP MUNI BOND; C	7.3	10.07	2.13	7.14	☆	☆	☆	5.1	421-5666	713-993-0500	1.00	1.72	1.00	David Johnson	'95
AMER CAP TEXAS MUNI; A	11.8	9.95	1.88	8.32	6.97	☆	☆	5.4	421-5666	713-993-0500	4.75	1.03	None	Joseph Piraro	'95
AMER CAP TEXAS MUNI; B	7.5	9.95	1.69	7.46	☆	☆	☆	4.7	421-5666	713-993-0500	None	1.80	4.00	Joseph Piraro	'95
AMER CAP TEXAS MUNI; C	1.3	9.96	1.69	12.63	7.22	7.97	☆	4.6	421-5666	713-993-0500	None	1.79	1.00	Joseph Piraro	'90
AMER CAP TX-EX HI YD; A	482.0	10.92	1.82	8.80	☆	☆	☆	6.9	421-5666	713-993-0500	4.75	1.02	None	Wayne Godlin	'92
AMER CAP TX-EX HI YD; B	212.5	10.92	1.62	8.06	☆	☆	☆	6.1	421-5666	713-993-0500	None	1.77	4.00	Wayne Godlin	'93
AMER CAP TX-EX HI YD; C	26.6	10.91	1.62	7.97	5.48	6.76	☆	6.1	421-5666	713-993-0500	None	1.75	1.00	Wayne Godlin	'95
AMER CAP TX-EX INS; A	68.3	11.17	2.08	6.95	☆	☆	☆	5.4	421-5666	713-993-0500	4.75	1.15	None	Joseph Piraro	'95
AMER CAP TX-EX INS; B	37.0	11.16	1.80	6.04	☆	☆	☆	4.6	421-5666	713-993-0500	None	1.91	4.00	Joseph Piraro	'95
AMER FDS TX-EX SR I MD	74.8	15.22	2.56	8.23	6.16	7.25	☆	5.2	421-4120	714-671-7000	4.75	0.75	None	Multiple Managers	N/A
AMER FDS TX-EX SR I VA	92.3	15.73	2.37	8.40	6.51	7.44	☆	5.2	421-4120	714-671-7000	4.75	0.78	None	Multiple Managers	N/A

PERFORMANCE OF MUTUAL FUNDS (continued)

FUND NAME	OBJECTIVE	ASSETS ($ MIL) 5/31/95	NAV ($/SHR) 6/30/95	QTR	1YR	3YRS (Ann.)	5YRS (Ann.)	10YRS (Ann.)	DIV YLD %	800	In-State	Load	Redemption	Exp. Ratio	MANAGER	SINCE
AMER FDS TX-EX SR II CA	California Muni	232.5	15.61	2.34	8.37	7.15	7.86	☆	5.5	421-4120	714-671-7000	4.75	None	0.71	Multiple Managers	N/A
AMER PERFORM INTMDT TXFR	Intermediate Muni	28.1	10.54	2.34	7.63	6.87	☆	☆	4.9	762-7085	None	3.00	None	0.25	Bill Bequette	'92
AMERICAN HI-INC MUNI BD	High-Yield Muni	145.5	15.08	3.05	☆	☆	☆	☆	0.0	421-4120	714-671-7000	4.75	None	None	Multiple Managers	N/A
AMSOUTH FL TAX-FREE	Florida Muni	47.8	10.28	2.36	☆	☆	☆	☆	0.0	451-8379	205-326-4732	3.00	None	None	Gerald Canopari	'94
ANTHEM MUNICIPAL SECS ⊠	General Muni	0.1	10.14	0.00	☆	☆	☆	☆	4.3	273-3936	317-692-3900	None	None	None	Kent A. Deeter	'95
ARBOR OVB WV TX-EX; A	Single State Muni	34.3	9.72	1.99	8.29	☆	☆	☆	4.9	545-6331	None	None	None	0.75	Jay Thomas	'93
ARBOR OVB WV TX-EX; B	Single State Muni	2.7	9.71	1.83	8.03	☆	☆	☆	4.7	545-6331	None	None	None	1.00	Jay Thomas	'93
ARCH TX-EX MO; INV	Missouri Muni	24.3	11.36	2.09	8.61	6.37	☆	☆	4.8	452-2724	617-722-7868	4.50	None	0.65	Peter Merzian	'93
ARCH TX-EX MO; TR	Missouri Muni	44.3	11.36	2.14	8.82	6.58	7.87	☆	5.0	452-2724	617-722-7868	None	None	0.45	Peter Merzian	'93
ARMADA OH; INSTL	Ohio Muni	72.0	10.68	2.42	6.94	5.81	6.23	☆	4.7	622-3863	None	None	None	0.33	Stephen P. Carpenter	'90
ARMADA OH; RET	Ohio Muni	3.2	10.64	2.43	6.97	5.67	☆	☆	4.7	622-3863	None	3.00	None	0.33	Stephen P. Carpenter	'91
ARROW MUNI INCOME	General Muni	17.9	10.12	1.96	6.88	☆	☆	☆	4.6	None	314-889-0715	3.50	None	0.85	Larry Kaestner	'93
ATLAS CA INS INTMDT; A ➜	California Muni	24.7	10.17	2.59	6.89	☆	☆	☆	4.0	933-2852	None	3.00	None	0.40	John Poole	'94
ATLAS CA INS INTMDT; B	California Muni	0.3	10.17	2.46	☆	☆	☆	☆	3.4	933-2852	None	None	None	1.08	John Poole	'94
ATLAS CA MUNI BOND; A	California Muni	184.1	10.84	1.81	6.39	6.20	8.02	☆	5.2	933-2852	None	3.00	None	0.57	John Poole	'94
ATLAS CA MUNI BOND; B	California Muni	1.9	10.84	1.68	☆	☆	☆	☆	4.6	933-2852	None	None	None	1.28	John Poole	'94
ATLAS NATL INS INT; A	Intermediate Muni	16.3	10.17	2.73	6.97	☆	☆	☆	4.1	933-2852	None	3.00	None	0.43	John Poole	'94
ATLAS NATL INS INT; B	Intermediate Muni	0.2	10.18	2.60	☆	☆	☆	☆	3.5	933-2852	None	None	None	1.09	John Poole	'94
ATLAS NATL MUNI BOND; A	General Muni	52.8	10.93	1.86	6.89	6.44	8.35	☆	5.0	933-2852	None	3.00	None	0.57	John Poole	'94
ATLAS NATL MUNI BOND; B	General Muni	0.7	10.94	1.82	☆	☆	☆	☆	4.4	933-2852	None	None	None	1.28	John Poole	'94
BABSON TX-FR INC LONG	General Muni	28.5	8.67	2.27	7.21	5.62	7.45	8.24	4.9	422-2766	816-471-5200	None	None	1.02	Joel Vernick	'86
BABSON TX-FR INC SHORT	Short-Term Muni	28.6	10.71	1.92	5.32	4.48	6.00	6.28	4.2	422-2766	816-471-5200	None	None	1.02	Joel Vernick	'86
BB&T NC NTMDT TX-FR; INV	Single State Muni	8.7	10.01	1.91	5.82	☆	☆	☆	3.6	228-1872	614-899-4668	2.00	None	0.75	Branch Banking & Trust Co	'93
BB&T NC NTMDT TX-FR; TR ▥	Single State Muni	29.9	10.01	1.95	5.98	☆	☆	☆	3.7	228-1872	614-899-4668	None	None	0.63	Branch Banking & Trust Co	'92
BENHAM CA TX-FR HIGH YLD ➜	California Muni	113.0	9.05	1.99	7.54	6.77	7.64	☆	6.2	331-8331	415-965-4274	None	None	0.51	Steve Permut	'88
BENHAM CA TX-FR INSURED	California Muni	179.6	9.80	1.96	8.45	6.59	7.98	☆	5.4	331-8331	415-965-4274	None	None	0.49	David MacEwen	'91
BENHAM CA TX-FR INTMDT	California Muni	417.4	10.93	2.09	6.89	6.01	7.11	6.96	4.9	331-8331	415-965-4274	None	None	0.48	David MacEwen	'91
BENHAM CA TX-FR LONG	California Muni	281.5	10.81	1.72	7.39	6.42	7.87	8.06	5.7	331-8331	415-965-4274	None	None	0.48	David MacEwen	'91
BENHAM CA TX-FR SHT-TM	Single State Muni	103.9	10.19	2.02	5.27	4.57	☆	☆	4.0	331-8331	415-965-4274	None	None	0.51	David MacEwen	'92
BENHAM MUNI AZ INTMDT	Single State Muni	19.6	10.31	2.77	7.86	☆	☆	☆	5.0	331-8331	415-965-4274	None	None	None	David MacEwen	'94
BENHAM MUNI FL INTMDT	Florida Muni	9.4	10.24	2.58	7.53	☆	☆	☆	5.1	331-8331	415-965-4274	None	None	None	David MacEwen	'94
BENHAM MUNI NATL TF INT	Intermediate Muni	64.7	10.67	2.64	6.71	5.91	7.25	7.49	4.7	331-8331	415-965-4274	None	None	0.67	David MacEwen	'91
BENHAM MUNI NATL TF LONG	General Muni	46.5	11.28	1.84	7.65	6.80	8.34	8.31	5.5	331-8331	415-965-4274	None	None	0.67	Michael Peters	'91
BILTMORE MUNI GA	Georgia Muni	8.6	10.60	2.28	☆	☆	☆	☆	0.0	462-7538	919-725-0036	4.50	None	None	Michael Peters	'95
BILTMORE MUNI NC	North Carolina Muni	11.7	10.59	1.99	☆	☆	☆	☆	0.0	462-7538	919-725-0036	4.50	None	None	Michael Peters	'95
BILTMORE MUNI SC	South Carolina Muni	87.0	10.71	2.28	8.23	6.82	☆	☆	5.2	462-7538	919-725-0036	4.50	None	0.60	Michael J. Peters	'93
BLANCHARD FLEX TAX-FREE ★	General Muni	20.1	5.12	2.49	12.58	☆	☆	☆	4.5	922-7771	212-779-7979	None	None	None	Ken McAlley	'93
BNY HAMILTON INTMDT NY	New York Muni	44.1	10.14	2.70	6.35	☆	☆	☆	3.9	426-9363	None	3.00	None	0.85	Colleen M. Frey	'92
BRENTON INTMDT TX-FR ➜	Intermediate Muni	6.6	10.05	1.55	☆	☆	☆	☆	0.0	706-3863	None	3.50	None	None	Wright/Muenzenmay	'94/'95
BT INV INTMDT TAX FREE	Intermediate Muni	24.6	10.27	2.47	7.53	☆	☆	☆	4.4	545-1074	None	None	None	0.85	Gary Pollack	'92
BULL&BEAR MUNI INCOME	General Muni	17.6	16.21	1.77	7.23	3.80	6.01	7.87	4.1	847-4200	212-363-1100	None	None	1.60	Steven Landis	'95
CA INV TR CA INS TX-FR	California Muni	23.0	10.31	2.28	6.61	☆	☆	☆	4.5	225-8778	415-398-2727	None	None	0.46	Philip McClanahan	'92
CA INV TR CA TX-FR INC	California Muni	196.8	12.13	2.00	8.87	6.58	8.04	☆	5.4	225-8778	415-398-2727	None	None	0.60	Philip McClanahan	'85
CALVERT MUNI AZ INTMDT; A	Single State Muni	2.2	4.95	2.52	6.82	☆	☆	☆	4.3	368-2748	301-951-4820	2.75	None	0.38	Reno Martini	'93
CALVERT MUNI AZ INTMDT; C	Single State Muni	0.8	4.94	2.34	5.98	☆	☆	☆	3.5	368-2748	301-951-4820	None	None	1.43	Reno Martini	'94
CALVERT MUNI CA INTMDT; A	California Muni	36.1	10.22	1.71	5.98	5.55	☆	☆	4.6	368-2748	301-951-4820	2.75	None	0.76	Reno Martini	'92
CALVERT MUNI CA INTMDT; C	California Muni	3.5	10.19	1.53	4.96	☆	☆	☆	3.8	368-2748	301-951-4820	None	None	1.86	Reno Martini	'94
CALVERT MUNI FL INTMDT; A	Florida Muni	3.1	4.91	2.04	7.30	☆	☆	☆	4.7	368-2748	301-951-4820	2.75	None	0.21	Reno Martini	'93
CALVERT MUNI FL INTMDT; C	Florida Muni	0.5	4.91	1.82	6.41	☆	☆	☆	3.9	368-2748	301-951-4820	None	None	1.32	Reno Martini	'94
CALVERT MUNI MD INTMDT; A ➜	Single State Muni	8.6	4.92	2.45	8.26	☆	☆	☆	4.9	368-2748	301-951-4820	2.75	None	0.17	Reno Martini	'93

Fund	Objective	Net Assets	NAV	'95	'94	3-Yr	5-Yr	10-Yr	Yield	Tel 1	Tel 2	Max Chg	12b-1	Manager	Since
CALVERT MUNI MD INTMDT; C	Single State Muni	2.2	4.90	2.25	7.03	☆	☆	☆	4.2	368-2748	301-951-4820	None	1.17	Reno Martini	'94
CALVERT MUNI MI INTMDT; C	Michigan Muni	4.9	4.98	2.38	7.29	☆	☆	☆	4.7	368-2748	301-951-4820	2.75	0.18	Reno Martini	'93
CALVERT MUNI MI INTMDT; C	Michigan Muni	1.4	4.98	2.39	6.45	☆	☆	☆	3.9	368-2748	301-951-4820	None	1.15	Reno Martini	'93
CALVERT MUNI NATL INT; A	Intermediate Muni	40.1	10.30	2.32	7.94	☆	☆	☆	4.9	368-2748	301-951-4820	2.75	0.69	Reno Martini	'92
CALVERT MUNI NATL INT; C	Intermediate Muni	6.5	10.28	2.12	7.01	☆	☆	☆	4.1	368-2748	301-951-4820	None	1.71	Reno Martini	'94
CALVERT MUNI NY INTMDT; A	New York Muni	3.0	4.96	2.51	6.91	☆	☆	☆	4.5	368-2748	301-951-4820	2.75	0.18	Reno Martini	'93
CALVERT MUNI NY INTMDT; C	New York Muni	1.7	4.95	2.32	5.90	☆	☆	☆	3.8	368-2748	301-951-4820	None	1.22	Reno Martini	'94
CALVERT MUNI PA INTMDT; A	Pennsylvania Muni	2.2	4.95	2.24	8.62	☆	☆	☆	4.9	368-2748	301-951-4820	2.75	0.26	Reno Martini	'93
CALVERT MUNI PA INTMDT; C	Pennsylvania Muni	1.4	4.97	2.22	7.94	☆	☆	☆	4.0	368-2748	301-951-4820	None	1.22	Reno Martini	'94
CALVERT MUNI VA INTMDT; A	Single State Muni	7.0	5.00	2.43	8.31	☆	☆	☆	4.8	368-2748	301-951-4820	2.75	0.19	Reno Martini	'93
CALVERT MUNI VA INTMDT; C	Single State Muni	2.8	5.01	2.22	7.68	6.71	☆	☆	4.0	368-2748	301-951-4820	None	0.94	Reno Martini	'94
CALVERT TX-FR RSVS L-T; A	General Muni	50.8	16.64	2.00	9.40	☆	7.85	8.05	5.6	368-2748	301-951-4820	3.75	0.81	Reno Martini	'83
CALVERT TX-FR RSVS L-T; C	General Muni	1.2	16.50	1.71	7.90	4.03	☆	☆	4.7	368-2748	301-951-4820	None	2.55	Reno Martini	'93
CALVERT TX-FR RSVS LTD; A	Short-Term Muni	498.9	10.70	1.55	4.53	☆	4.88	5.60	4.0	368-2748	301-951-4820	2.00	0.66	Reno Martini	'81
CALVERT TX-FR RSVS LTD; C	Short-Term Muni	31.1	10.66	1.31	3.78	☆	☆	☆	3.5	368-2748	301-951-4820	None	1.38	Reno Martini	'94
CALVERT TX-FR RSVS VT; A	Single State Muni	63.6	16.06	2.49	7.85	6.38	☆	☆	5.3	368-2748	301-951-4820	3.75	0.73	Reno Martini	'91
CALVERT TX-FR RSVS VT; C	Single State Muni	0.6	15.94	2.11	6.24	☆	☆	☆	4.4	368-2748	301-951-4820	None	2.41	Reno Martini	'94
CARNEGIE TX-EX OH MUNI	Ohio Muni	11.5	9.46	2.18	5.76	5.71	7.00	☆	5.8	321-2322	216-781-4440	4.50	0.93	Roy Wallace	'86
CASCADES TX-FR TR OF OR	Oregon Muni	312.2	10.42	1.81	7.50	5.82	7.32	☆	5.3	872-6734	872-6734	4.00	0.68	Edward Potts	'86
CENTURA NC TAX-FREE; A	Single State Muni	0.6	10.08	1.82	6.51	☆	☆	☆	4.3	442-3688	None	2.75	None	Bob Marsh	'95
CENTURA NC TAX-FREE; B	Single State Muni	0.3	10.08	1.63	5.67	☆	☆	☆	3.6	442-3688	None	None	None	Bob Marsh	'95
CENTURA NC TAX-FREE; C	Single State Muni	35.8	10.08	1.89	6.78	☆	☆	☆	4.6	442-3688	None	None	None	Bob Marsh	'95
CG CAP MKTS MUNI BOND ☐	General Muni	47.1	8.18	1.59	8.17	5.37	☆	☆	4.9	None	212-816-8725	None	0.80	John Pandolfino	'91
CGM TR AMERICAN TAX FREE	General Muni	11.0	9.34	2.40	8.48	☆	☆	☆	6.6	345-4048	617-859-7714	None	None	Janice H. Saul	'93
CHUBB INV TAX EXEMPT FD	General Muni	15.1	11.92	2.25	7.57	6.39	7.67	☆	5.3	258-3648	603-226-5000	3.00	1.00	Frederick Gaertner	'89
CHURCHILL TX-FR FD OF KY	Kentucky Muni	247.1	10.42	1.75	7.31	6.14	7.68	☆	5.8	872-5859	212-697-6666	4.00	0.72	William Frey Jr.	'95
COLONIAL CA TAX-EX; A	California Muni	313.9	7.08	1.10	7.36	5.15	6.80	☆	5.7	426-3750	617-426-3750	4.75	0.77	William Loring	'86
COLONIAL CA TAX-EX; B	California Muni	104.9	7.08	0.92	6.57	☆	☆	☆	5.0	426-3750	617-426-3750	5.00	1.52	William Loring	'92
COLONIAL CT TAX-EX; A	Connecticut Muni	79.3	7.27	1.14	6.88	5.89	☆	☆	5.7	426-3750	617-426-3750	4.75	0.32	Jeffrey Augustine	'91
COLONIAL CT TAX-EX; B	Connecticut Muni	79.8	7.27	0.95	6.09	5.11	☆	☆	5.0	426-3750	617-426-3750	5.00	1.07	Jeffrey Augustine	'92
COLONIAL FL TAX-EX; A	Florida Muni	29.5	7.26	0.51	6.83	☆	☆	☆	5.8	426-3750	617-426-3750	4.75	0.22	Jeffrey Augustine	'93
COLONIAL FL TAX-EX; B	Florida Muni	33.5	7.26	0.32	6.03	☆	☆	☆	5.1	426-3750	617-426-3750	5.00	0.97	Jeffrey Augustine	'93
COLONIAL HY MUNI; B	High-Yield Muni	11.0	9.91	2.64	☆	☆	☆	☆	0.0	426-3750	617-426-3750	5.00	None	Bonny Boatman	'94
COLONIAL HY MUNI; B ☒	High-Yield Muni	128.8	9.91	2.45	8.11	5.70	☆	☆	6.0	426-3750	617-426-3750	5.00	1.90	Bonny Boatman	'93
COLONIAL INT TAX-FREE; B	Intermediate Muni	13.1	7.58	1.85	6.05	☆	☆	☆	5.2	426-3750	617-426-3750	3.25	0.20	William Loring	'93
COLONIAL INT TAX-EX; B	Intermediate Muni	14.8	7.58	1.68	5.36	☆	☆	☆	4.5	426-3750	617-426-3750	4.00	0.85	William Loring	'93
COLONIAL MA TAX-EX; A	Massachusetts Muni	206.5	7.59	1.42	7.07	6.49	8.08	☆	5.8	426-3750	617-426-3750	4.75	0.72	Jeffrey Augustine	'88
COLONIAL MA TAX-EX; B	Massachusetts Muni	59.1	7.59	1.23	6.27	5.71	☆	☆	5.1	426-3750	617-426-3750	5.00	1.47	Jeffrey Augustine	'92
COLONIAL MI TAX-EX; A	Michigan Muni	43.4	6.73	-0.19	5.69	5.61	6.95	☆	6.0	426-3750	617-426-3750	4.75	0.62	Brian Hartford	'92
COLONIAL MI TAX-EX; B	Michigan Muni	14.4	6.73	-0.38	4.90	☆	☆	☆	5.2	426-3750	617-426-3750	5.00	1.37	Brian Hartford	'93
COLONIAL MN TAX-EX; A	Minnesota Muni	36.8	6.95	0.13	6.02	5.36	6.60	☆	5.8	426-3750	617-426-3750	4.75	0.72	Brian Hartford	'93
COLONIAL MN TAX-EX; B	Minnesota Muni	16.2	6.95	-0.06	5.23	☆	☆	☆	5.1	426-3750	617-426-3750	5.00	1.47	Brian Hartford	'93
COLONIAL NC TAX-EX; B	North Carolina Muni	15.6	6.90	0.98	7.71	☆	☆	☆	5.7	426-3750	617-426-3750	5.00	0.12	Jeffrey Augustine	'93
COLONIAL NC TAX-EX; B	North Carolina Muni	19.2	6.90	0.79	6.92	☆	☆	☆	5.0	426-3750	617-426-3750	5.00	0.87	Brian Hartford	'93
COLONIAL NY TAX-EX; A	New York Muni	56.9	6.86	0.92	6.96	5.56	7.30	☆	6.1	426-3750	617-426-3750	4.75	0.42	Jeffrey Augustine	'87
COLONIAL NY TAX-EX; B	New York Muni	48.6	6.86	0.73	6.16	☆	☆	☆	5.3	426-3750	617-426-3750	5.00	1.17	Jeffrey Augustine	'92
COLONIAL OH TAX-EX; A	Ohio Muni	74.0	7.08	0.65	6.18	5.34	7.05	☆	5.5	426-3750	617-426-3750	4.75	0.72	Brian Hartford	'93
COLONIAL OH TAX-EX; B	Ohio Muni	56.5	7.08	0.46	5.39	☆	☆	☆	4.8	426-3750	617-426-3750	5.00	1.47	Brian Hartford	'93
COLONIAL SH-TM TAX-EX; A	Short-Term Muni	11.9	7.50	1.41	4.01	☆	☆	☆	3.4	426-3750	617-426-3750	1.00	0.50	William Loring	'93
COLONIAL TAX-EX INS; A	Insured Muni	250.2	8.01	1.08	6.81	5.45	7.06	☆	5.4	426-3750	617-426-3750	4.75	1.05	William Loring	'87

★ BNY HAMILTON INTMDT NY--12b-1 fee has been adopted by the fund but is not currently being charged.

© Copyright Lipper Analytical Services, Inc.

PERFORMANCE OF MUTUAL FUNDS (continued)

FUND NAME	OBJECTIVE	ASSETS ($ MIL) 5/31/95	NAV ($/SHR) 6/30/95	QTR	1YR	3YRS	5YRS (Annualized)	10YRS	DIV YLD %	800	In-State	Load	Redemption	Exp. Ratio	MANAGER	SINCE
COLONIAL TAX-EX INS; B	Insured Muni	49.7	8.01	0.89	6.02	4.67	☆	8.15	4.6	426-3750	617-426-3750	None	5.00	1.80	William Loring	'92
COLONIAL TAX-EX; A	General Muni	3,220.4	13.21	1.45	7.80	5.71	7.31	☆	5.9	426-3750	617-426-3750	4.75	None	1.01	Bonny Boatman	'93
COLONIAL TAX-EX; B	General Muni	495.6	13.21	1.26	7.00	4.98	☆	☆	5.1	426-3750	617-426-3750	None	5.00	1.76	Bonny Boatman	'93
COLORADO BOND; A	Colorado Muni	42.8	9.11		7.42	7.70	7.11	☆	6.7	572-0069	303-572-6990	4.75	None	0.74	Fred Kelly Jr.	'90
COLUMBIA MUNI BOND	Oregon Muni	372.6	12.03	1.75	7.18	5.73	7.10	8.10	5.3	547-1707	503-222-3606	None	None	0.57	Tom Thomsen	'84
COMMERCE MO TX-FR BD	Missouri Muni	4.5	18.09	1.22	☆	☆	☆	☆	0.0	305-2140	None	3.50	None	None	Craig Mac Pherson	'95
COMMERCE NATL TX-FR BD	Intermediate Muni	5.9	18.18	1.70	☆	☆	☆	☆	0.0	305-2140	None	3.50	None	None	Craig Mac Pherson	'95
COMMON SENSE MUNI BOND	General Muni	115.4	13.47	2.27	7.63	6.36	7.57	☆	5.3	544-5445	404-381-1000	4.75	None	0.99	Robert B. Evans	'88
COMPASS CAP MUNI BOND	Intermediate Muni	28.7	10.43	2.02	7.45	5.60	6.94	☆	4.6	451-8371	215-254-1000	3.75	None	0.69	S. Robert Cembor	'93
COMPASS CAP NJ MUNI BD	New Jersey Muni	97.8	11.09	1.96	7.59	6.28	☆	☆	4.6	451-8371	215-254-1000	3.75	None	0.38	S. Robert Cembor	'93
COMPASS CAP PA MUNI BD	Pennsylvania Muni	17.6	9.75	1.96	7.85	☆	☆	☆	4.5	451-8371	215-254-1000	3.75	None	0.22	S. Robert Cembor	'94
COMPOSITE TX-EX BD; A	General Muni	229.7	7.64	2.46	8.98	6.68	7.88	8.55	5.1	543-8072	509-353-3550	4.00	None	0.79	Team Managed	N/A
COMPOSITE TX-EX BD; B	General Muni	1.9	7.64	2.25	8.10	☆	☆	☆	4.3	543-8072	509-353-3550	None	3.00	1.58	Team Managed	N/A
CONESTOGA PA TX-FR; INSTL	Pennsylvania Muni	5.2	10.04	1.37	☆	☆	☆	☆	0.0	344-2716	None	None	None		Craig Moyer	'95
CONESTOGA PA TX-FR; RTL	Pennsylvania Muni	0.8	10.04	1.36	7.41	☆	☆	☆	4.8	344-2716	None	2.00	None	0.38	Craig Moyer	'92
➤➤ CONN MUTUAL CA MUNI ACCT	California Muni	0.5	10.13	1.09	☆	☆	☆	☆	0.0	322-2642	None	4.00	None	None	Robert Macintosh	'94
CONN MUTUAL MA MUNI ACCT	Massachusetts Muni	0.1	10.18	0.80	☆	☆	☆	☆	0.0	322-2642	None	4.00	None	None	Robert Macintosh	'94
CONN MUTUAL NATL MUNI ACCT	General Muni	2.4	10.66	2.90	☆	☆	☆	☆	0.0	322-2642	None	4.00	None	None	Thomas M. Metzold	'94
➤➤ CONN MUTUAL NY MUNI ACCT	New York Muni	0.4	10.27	1.40	☆	☆	☆	☆	0.0	322-2642	None	4.00	None	None	Nicole Anders	'94
CONN MUTUAL OH MUNI ACCT	Ohio Muni	0.4	10.40	1.90	☆	☆	☆	☆	0.0	322-2642	None	4.00	None	None	Thomas J. Fetter	'94
COREFUND INTMDT MUNI; A	Intermediate Muni	0.4	9.83	1.97	5.58	☆	☆	☆	3.8	252-1784	None	None	None	0.63	Joseph R. Baxter	'93
COREFUND INTMDT MUNI; B	Intermediate Muni	1.0	9.83	2.01	5.42	☆	☆	☆	3.6	252-1784	None	4.50	None	0.88	Joseph R. Baxter	'93
COREFUND NJ MUNI BD; A	New Jersey Muni	1.6	10.12	2.11	7.25	☆	☆	☆	5.1	252-1784	None	None	None	None	Joseph R. Baxter	'94
COREFUND NJ MUNI BD; B	New Jersey Muni	0.1	10.12	2.05	6.84	☆	☆	☆	4.8	252-1784	None	4.50	None	None	Joseph R. Baxter	'94
COREFUND PA MUNI BD; A	Pennsylvania Muni	2.3	10.16	1.76	7.50	☆	☆	☆	5.0	252-1784	None	None	None	None	Joseph R. Baxter	'94
➤ COREFUND PA MUNI BD; B	Pennsylvania Muni	0.3	10.16	1.70	7.25	☆	☆	☆	4.8	252-1784	None	4.50	None	None	Joseph R. Baxter	'94
CRESTFDS VA INT; INV A	Single State Muni	8.5	9.93	2.12	7.31	☆	☆	☆	4.4	273-7827	None	3.50	None	0.66	Reid/Page	'93/'93
CRESTFDS VA INT; TR	Single State Muni	40.2	9.93	2.13	7.21	☆	☆	☆	4.4	273-7827	None	None	None	0.65	Reid/Page	'93/'93
CT&T INTMDT MUNI	Intermediate Muni	11.2	9.91	2.10	6.05	☆	☆	☆	3.4	992-8151	None	None	None	0.90	Lois Pasquale	'93
DEAN WITTER CAL TAX FR	California Muni	1,068.5	12.48	1.56	6.59	5.27	6.64	7.71	5.0	869-3863	212-392-2550	None	5.00	1.32	James Willison	'84
DEAN WITTER LTD MUNI TR	Intermediate Muni	84.5	9.75	3.08	6.82	☆	☆	☆	4.3	869-3863	212-392-2550	None	5.00	0.31	Katherine H. Stromberg	'93
DEAN WITTER MUNI AZ	Arizona Muni	50.6	10.26	1.92	8.27	6.35	☆	☆	5.3	869-3863	212-392-2550	4.00	None	0.62	James Willison	'91
DEAN WITTER MUNI CA	California Muni	120.1	10.23	1.36	8.20	6.02	☆	☆	5.5	869-3863	212-392-2550	4.00	None	0.58	James Willison	'91
DEAN WITTER MUNI FL	Florida Muni	73.2	10.48	1.83	8.07	6.50	☆	☆	5.3	869-3863	212-392-2550	4.00	None	0.61	James Willison	'91
DEAN WITTER MUNI MA	Massachusetts Muni	17.2	10.54	1.82	9.02	6.82	☆	☆	5.3	869-3863	212-392-2550	4.00	None	0.50	James Willison	'91
DEAN WITTER MUNI MI	Michigan Muni	21.5	10.36	1.85	8.55	6.54	☆	☆	5.4	869-3863	212-392-2550	4.00	None	0.50	James Willison	'91
DEAN WITTER MUNI MN	Minnesota Muni	11.0	10.22	2.54	8.20	6.40	☆	☆	5.4	869-3863	212-392-2550	4.00	None	0.50	James Willison	'91
DEAN WITTER MUNI NJ	New Jersey Muni	48.2	10.36	2.24	8.47	6.39	☆	☆	5.3	869-3863	212-392-2550	4.00	None	0.64	James Willison	'91
DEAN WITTER MUNI NY	New York Muni	15.5	10.38	2.15	7.74	6.05	☆	☆	5.3	869-3863	212-392-2550	4.00	None	0.50	James Willison	'91
DEAN WITTER MUNI OH	Ohio Muni	22.2	10.36	2.03	8.60	6.70	☆	☆	5.4	869-3863	212-392-2550	4.00	None	0.50	James Willison	'91
DEAN WITTER MUNI PA	Pennsylvania Muni	52.4	10.45	1.90	8.75	6.58	☆	☆	5.2	869-3863	212-392-2550	None	None	0.64	James Willison	'91
DEAN WITTER NATL MUNI	General Muni	51.4	10.23	1.47	7.13	☆	☆	☆	4.3	869-3863	212-392-2550	None	3.00	1.40	James Willison	'94
DEAN WITTER NY TXFR IN	New York Muni	218.4	11.52	1.88	7.04	5.37	7.22	7.89	4.8	869-3863	212-392-2550	None	5.00	0.96	James Willison	'85
DW SELECT MUNI REINVEST	General Muni	92.1	11.97	1.91	7.61	5.96	7.63	8.25	5.6	869-3863	212-392-2550	None	None		James Willison	'83
DEAN WITTER TAX-EXEMPT ⊠	General Muni	1,351.7	11.67	2.08	8.38	6.16	7.91	9.03	5.8	869-3863	212-392-2550	4.00	None	0.47	James Willison	'80
DELAWARE TX-FR INS; A	Insured Muni	88.5	10.98	1.74	6.35	5.59	7.02	8.23	5.8	523-4640	215-988-1333	4.75	None	0.98	Patrick P. Coyne	'94
DELAWARE TX-FR INS; B	Insured Muni	2.4	10.98	1.54	5.48	☆	☆	☆	5.0	523-4640	215-988-1333	None	4.00	0.98	Patrick P. Coyne	'94
DELAWARE TX-FR INT; A	Intermediate Muni	21.2	10.29	2.34	5.99	☆	☆	☆	5.3	523-4640	215-988-1333	3.00	None	0.25	Patrick P. Coyne	'93
DELAWARE TX-FR INT; B	Intermediate Muni	1.8	10.29	2.13	5.12	☆	☆	☆	4.5	523-4640	215-988-1333	None	2.00		Patrick P. Coyne	'94
DELAWARE TX-FR PA; A	Pennsylvania Muni	1,001.4	8.33	2.56	7.07	6.48	7.87	8.58	5.9	523-4640	215-988-1333	4.75	None	0.88	J. Michael Pokorny	'80

Fund	Objective	Net Assets ($mil)	NAV						Yield %	Telephone		Load	Exp	Redem	Portfolio Manager	Since
DELAWARE TX-FR PA; B	Pennsylvania Muni	14.1	8.33	2.35	6.21	☆	☆	☆	5.1	523-4640	215-988-1333	None	None	4.00	J. Michael Pokorny	'94
DELAWARE TX-FR USA; A	General Muni	757.0	12.00	2.23	6.39	6.69	8.04	9.33	6.2	523-4640	215-988-1333	4.75	0.89	None	Patrick P. Coyne	'94
DELAWARE TX-FR USA; B	General Muni	14.0	12.00	2.02	5.53	☆	☆	☆	5.4	523-4640	215-988-1333	None	0.74	4.00	Patrick P. Coyne	'94
DG INV MUNI INC	General Muni	42.9	10.29	2.10	8.31	6.28	7.57	☆	4.7	344-2488	None	2.00	0.58	None	William Womack	'94
DREY-LRL TF PRM CA LTD; A	California Muni	8.8	12.81	1.91	6.57	☆	☆	☆	4.6	554-4611	None	3.00	0.42	None	David Holmes	'94
DREY-LRL TF PRM CA LTD; R	California Muni	8.9	12.81	1.97	6.83	☆	☆	☆	4.9	554-4611	None	None	0.76	None	David Holmes	'94
DREY-LRL TF PRM LTD; A	Intermediate Muni	21.5	11.82	1.99	6.38	6.02	7.57	☆	4.5	554-4611	None	3.00	None	John Flahive	'94
DREY-LRL TF PRM LTD; B	Intermediate Muni	0.1	11.82	1.87	☆	☆	☆	☆	0.0	554-4611	None	None	0.50	3.00	John Flahive	'94
DREY-LRL TF PRM LTD; R	Intermediate Muni	16.6	11.82	2.06	6.64	☆	☆	☆	4.8	554-4611	None	None	0.76	None	John Flahive	'94
DREY-LRL TF PRM MA LTD; A	Massachusetts Muni	16.5	11.91	2.11	6.60	6.03	7.66	☆	4.6	554-4611	None	3.00	0.62	Kristen Lindquist	'94
DREY-LRL TF PRM MA LTD; R	Massachusetts Muni	20.2	11.91	2.18	6.87	☆	☆	☆	4.8	554-4611	None	None	0.57	None	Kristen Lindquist	'94
DREY-LRL TF PRM NY LTD; A	New York Muni	2.5	12.71	2.34	6.40	5.89	7.11	☆	4.8	554-4611	None	3.00	0.29	Kristen Lindquist	'94
DREY-LRL TF PRM NY LTD; R	New York Muni	3.3	12.71	2.40	6.69	☆	☆	☆	5.0	554-4611	None	None	None	None	Kristen Lindquist	'94
DREYFUS BASIC INT MUNI	Intermediate Muni	41.8	12.77	2.65	8.11	☆	☆	☆	5.4	554-4611	None	None	None	None	Joseph Darcy	'94
DREYFUS BASIC MUNI BOND	General Muni	41.1	12.88	2.11	8.53	☆	☆	☆	5.9	554-4611	None	None	0.04	None	Joseph Darcy	'94
DREYFUS CA INTMDT MUNI	California Muni	244.2	13.19	2.54	6.38	6.80	☆	☆	5.0	554-4611	None	None	0.70	None	Lawrence Troutman	'92
DREYFUS CA TAX EX BOND	California Muni	1,552.6	14.23	1.33	4.80	4.95	6.41	7.45	5.7	554-4611	None	None	0.01	None	Lawrence Troutman	'87
DREYFUS CT INTMDT MUNI	Single State Muni	133.6	13.24	2.79	7.76	6.66	☆	☆	4.8	554-4611	None	None	0.48	None	Stephen Kris	'92
DREYFUS FL INTMDT MUNI	Florida Muni	422.8	13.25	2.35	7.13	7.02	☆	☆	4.8	554-4611	None	None	0.76	None	Stephen Kris	'92
DREYFUS GEN CA MUNI BD	California Muni	329.6	13.15	1.94	7.55	6.37	7.69	☆	5.6	554-4611	None	None	0.87	None	Paul Disdier	'89
DREYFUS GEN MUNI BOND	General Muni	928.4	14.65	2.31	8.22	6.26	8.57	8.96	5.8	554-4611	None	None	0.76	None	Paul Disdier	'88
DREYFUS GEN NY MUNI BD	New York Muni	332.8	19.44	1.61	6.07	6.29	8.35	7.77	5.6	554-4611	None	None	0.93	None	Monica Wieboldt	'88
DREYFUS INSURED MUNI BD	Insured Muni	233.1	17.47	2.08	6.40	5.20	6.96	7.75	5.4	554-4611	None	None	0.70	None	Lawrence Troutman	'85
DREYFUS INTMDT MUNI	Intermediate Muni	1,564.2	13.90	2.59	7.38	6.45	7.76	8.04	5.4	554-4611	None	None	0.06	None	Monica Wieboldt	'85
DREYFUS MA INTMDT MUNI	Massachusetts Muni	70.0	13.04	2.97	6.61	6.34	8.04	☆	4.6	554-4611	None	None	0.80	None	Lawrence Troutman	'92
DREYFUS MA TAX EX BOND	Massachusetts Muni	160.2	15.99	1.94	7.02	5.87	7.42	7.62	5.7	554-4611	None	None	0.68	None	Lawrence Troutman	'85
DREYFUS MUNICIPAL BOND	General Muni	3,946.1	12.35	2.44	7.58	5.99	7.55	8.36	5.5	554-4611	None	None	0.06	None	Richard Moynihan	'76
DREYFUS NJ INTMDT MUNI	Single State Muni	225.9	13.32	2.71	7.29	7.43	☆	☆	4.8	554-4611	None	None	0.77	None	Stephen Kris	'93
DREYFUS NJ MUNI BOND	New Jersey Muni	620.2	13.11	2.70	7.30	6.39	8.04	☆	5.8	554-4611	None	None	0.98	None	Samuel Weinstock	'87
DREYFUS NY INS TAX EX BD	New York Muni	162.2	11.23	1.78	6.79	5.37	7.41	☆	5.3	554-4611	None	None	0.89	None	Lawrence Troutman	'87
DREYFUS NY INTMDT TAX EX	New York Muni	359.2	17.87	2.55	6.44	6.19	7.68	☆	4.8	554-4611	None	None	0.71	None	Monica Wieboldt	'87
DREYFUS NY TAX EX BOND	New York Muni	1,874.5	14.88	1.84	6.46	5.80	7.54	7.95	5.6	554-4611	None	None	0.90	None	Monica Wieboldt	'85
DREYFUS PA INTMDT MUNI	Pennsylvania Muni	31.8	12.78	2.70	8.27	☆	☆	☆	5.2	554-4611	None	None	1.42	None	Monica Wieboldt	'93
DREYFUS PREM CA MUNI; A	California Muni	197.2	12.65	1.72	7.30	6.53	7.74	☆	5.5	554-4611	None	4.50	0.50	None	Paul Disdier	'88
DREYFUS PREM CA MUNI; B	California Muni	20.4	12.65	1.59	6.66	☆	☆	☆	5.0	554-4611	None	None	None	3.00	Paul Disdier	'93
DREYFUS PREM INS CA; A	California Muni	3.4	11.56	1.68	8.14	☆	☆	☆	5.5	554-4611	None	4.50	None	None	Stephen Kris	'93
DREYFUS PREM INS CA; B	California Muni	3.5	11.57	1.55	7.69	☆	☆	☆	5.0	554-4611	None	None	None	3.00	Stephen Kris	'93
DREYFUS PREM INS CT; A	Connecticut Muni	11.7	12.93	2.36	8.98	☆	☆	☆	5.0	554-4611	None	4.50	None	None	Lawrence Troutman	'94
DREYFUS PREM INS CT; B	Connecticut Muni	15.4	12.94	2.22	8.41	☆	☆	☆	5.0	554-4611	None	None	None	3.00	Lawrence Troutman	'94
DREYFUS PREM INS FL; A	Florida Muni	19.3	13.07	1.82	10.25	☆	☆	☆	5.6	554-4611	None	4.50	None	None	Lawrence Troutman	'94
DREYFUS PREM INS FL; B	Florida Muni	21.1	13.07	1.69	9.69	☆	☆	☆	5.1	554-4611	None	None	None	3.00	Lawrence Troutman	'94
DREYFUS PREM INS FL NAT; A	Insured Muni	7.8	13.02	2.61	9.54	☆	☆	☆	5.9	554-4611	None	4.50	None	None	Lawrence Troutman	'94
DREYFUS PREM INS NAT; B	Insured Muni	8.7	13.02	2.40	8.90	☆	☆	☆	5.4	554-4611	None	None	None	3.00	Lawrence Troutman	'94
DREYFUS PREM MUNI NJ; A	New Jersey Muni	4.2	12.69	2.16	9.07	☆	☆	☆	5.6	554-4611	None	4.50	None	None	Lawrence Troutman	'94
DREYFUS PREM MUNI NJ; B	New Jersey Muni	6.2	12.68	1.95	8.44	☆	☆	☆	5.2	554-4611	None	None	None	3.00	Lawrence Troutman	'94
DREYFUS PREM INS NY; A	New York Muni	3.7	12.70	1.86	7.24	☆	☆	☆	5.6	554-4611	None	4.50	None	None	Lawrence Troutman	'94
DREYFUS PREM INS NY; B	New York Muni	6.3	12.71	1.73	6.69	☆	☆	☆	5.1	554-4611	None	None	None	3.00	Lawrence Troutman	'94
DREYFUS PREM MUNI BD; A	General Muni	503.2	14.10	3.06	9.19	6.89	8.85	☆	6.0	554-4611	None	4.50	0.85	None	Samuel Weinstock	'87
DREYFUS PREM MUNI BD; B	General Muni	101.3	14.11	3.00	8.71	☆	☆	☆	5.5	554-4611	None	None	1.40	3.00	Samuel Weinstock	'93
DREYFUS PREM MUNI AZ; A	Arizona Muni	11.4	12.91	1.97	9.85	☆	☆	☆	5.8	554-4611	None	4.50	None	None	Stephen Kris	'92

PERFORMANCE OF MUTUAL FUNDS (continued)

FUND NAME	OBJECTIVE	ASSETS ($ MIL) 5/31/95	NAV ($/SHR) 6/30/95	QTR	1YR	3YRS	5YRS	10YRS	DIV YLD %	PHONE 800	PHONE In-State	Load	Exp. Ratio	Redemption	MANAGER	SINCE
DREYFUS PREM MUNI AZ; B	Arizona Muni	8.8	12.93	1.92	9.38	☆			5.3	554-4611	None	None	0.50	3.00	Stephen Kris	'93
DREYFUS PREM MUNI CO; A	Colorado Muni	1.0	12.60	2.29	7.61	☆			6.0	554-4611	None	4.50	None	None	Stephen Kris	'94
DREYFUS PREM MUNI CO; B	Colorado Muni	3.2	12.61	2.25	7.21	☆			5.5	554-4611	None	None	None	3.00	Stephen Kris	'94
DREYFUS PREM MUNI CT; A	Connecticut Muni	342.2	11.93	2.43	7.33	6.63	7.73		5.6	554-4611	None	4.50	0.80	None	Samuel Weinstock	'87
DREYFUS PREM MUNI CT; B	Connecticut Muni	37.1	11.93	2.39	6.86	☆			5.1	554-4611	None	None	1.36	3.00	Samuel Weinstock	'93
DREYFUS PREM MUNI FL; A	Florida Muni	258.0	14.77	2.49	8.59	7.12	8.50		5.5	554-4611	None	4.50	0.80	None	Paul Disdier	'88
DREYFUS PREM MUNI FL; B	Florida Muni	26.1	14.76	2.28	7.96	☆			5.0	554-4611	None	None	1.34	3.00	Paul Disdier	'93
DREYFUS PREM MUNI GA; A	Georgia Muni	9.2	12.98	2.18	9.33	☆			5.6	554-4611	None	4.50	0.07	None	Stephen Kris	'92
DREYFUS PREM MUNI GA; B	Georgia Muni	21.0	12.98	2.06	8.69	☆			5.1	554-4611	None	None	0.58	3.00	Stephen Kris	'93
DREYFUS PREM MUNI MA; A	Massachusetts Muni	73.9	11.68	2.67	7.57	6.64	8.13		5.8	554-4611	None	4.50	0.82	None	Samuel Weinstock	'87
DREYFUS PREM MUNI MA; B	Massachusetts Muni	4.4	11.67	2.53	7.01	☆			5.3	554-4611	None	None	1.36	3.00	Samuel Weinstock	'93
DREYFUS PREM MUNI MD; A	Maryland Muni	304.3	12.74	2.60	8.49	6.41	8.01		5.5	554-4611	None	4.50	0.80	None	Paul Disdier	'88
DREYFUS PREM MUNI MD; B	Maryland Muni	36.4	12.74	2.47	7.90	☆			4.9	554-4611	None	None	1.37	3.00	Paul Disdier	'93
DREYFUS PREM MUNI MI; A	Michigan Muni	180.1	15.30	2.03	8.08	7.36	8.66		5.5	554-4611	None	4.50	0.81	None	Joseph Darcy	'94
DREYFUS PREM MUNI MI; B	Michigan Muni	17.2	15.30	1.90	7.52	☆			5.0	554-4611	None	None	1.38	3.00	Joseph Darcy	'94
DREYFUS PREM MUNI MN; A	Minnesota Muni	147.7	15.04	2.25	8.42	6.74	8.12		5.5	554-4611	None	4.50	0.80	None	Joseph Darcy	'94
DREYFUS PREM MUNI MN; B	Minnesota Muni	23.7	15.06	2.04	7.84	☆			5.0	554-4611	None	None	1.38	3.00	Joseph Darcy	'94
DREYFUS PREM MUNI NC; A	North Carolina Muni	52.2	12.88	2.05	7.64	6.20			5.4	554-4611	None	4.50	0.44	None	Samuel Weinstock	'91
DREYFUS PREM MUNI NC; B	North Carolina Muni	43.6	12.87	1.92	7.08	☆			4.9	554-4611	None	None	1.00	3.00	Samuel Weinstock	'93
DREYFUS PREM MUNI OH; A	Ohio Muni	276.6	12.74	1.99	6.78	6.74	8.25		5.7	554-4611	None	4.50	0.81	None	Joseph Darcy	'94
DREYFUS PREM MUNI OH; B	Ohio Muni	34.1	12.75	1.85	6.30	☆			5.2	554-4611	None	None	1.38	3.00	Joseph Darcy	'94
DREYFUS PREM MUNI OR; A	Oregon Muni	2.9	13.04	1.70	9.70	☆			5.8	554-4611	None	4.50	None	3.00	Stephen Kris	'94
DREYFUS PREM MUNI OR; B	Oregon Muni	1.8	13.04	1.49	9.15	☆			5.3	554-4611	None	None	0.81	3.00	Stephen Kris	'94
DREYFUS PREM MUNI PA; A	Pennsylvania Muni	224.5	16.33	2.18	8.53	7.03	8.57		5.6	554-4611	None	4.50	0.81	None	Paul Disdier	'88
DREYFUS PREM MUNI PA; B	Pennsylvania Muni	72.0	16.32	2.05	7.90	☆			5.1	554-4611	None	None	1.38	3.00	Paul Disdier	'93
DREYFUS PREM MUNI TX; B	Texas Muni	69.7	21.00	2.48	9.45	7.55	9.10		5.8	554-4611	None	4.50	0.39	None	Paul Disdier	'88
DREYFUS PREM MUNI TX; B	Texas Muni	17.3	20.99	2.30	8.82	☆			5.3	554-4611	None	None	0.94	3.00	Paul Disdier	'93
DREYFUS PREM MUNI VA; A	Virginia Muni	63.9	16.33	2.87	9.27	7.07			5.7	554-4611	None	4.50	0.46	None	Samuel Weinstock	'91
DREYFUS PREM MUNI VA; B	Virginia Muni	30.1	16.33	2.74	8.71	☆			5.2	554-4611	None	None	1.01	3.00	Samuel Weinstock	'93
DREYFUS PREM NY MUNI; A	New York Muni	147.3	14.33	2.44	7.59	6.95	8.75		5.3	554-4611	None	4.50	0.89	None	Paul Disdier	'88
DREYFUS PREM NY MUNI; B	New York Muni	62.1	14.33	2.31	7.02	☆			4.8	554-4611	None	None	1.44	3.00	Paul Disdier	'93
DREYFUS SHT-INT MUNI	Short-Term Muni	368.5	12.95	2.14	4.39	4.57	5.81		4.4	554-4611	None	None	0.70	None	Samuel Weinstock	'87
DUPREE KY TX-FR INC	Kentucky Muni	274.5	7.34	1.92	7.61	6.85	7.97	8.44	5.5	866-0614	606-254-7741	None	0.69	None	Bill Griggs	'89
DUPREE KY TX-FR SHT-MED	Single State Muni	57.9	5.19	1.99	4.45	4.34	5.53		4.0	866-0614	606-254-7741	None	0.72	None	Bill Griggs	'87
DUPREE TN TX-FR INC	Tennessee Muni	4.7	10.05	2.61	11.65	☆			5.4	866-0614	606-254-7741	None	0.12	None	Bill Griggs	'93
DUPREE TN TX-FR SHT-MED	Single State Muni	1.3	10.20	2.08	☆				0.0	866-0614	606-254-7741	None	None	None	Bill Griggs	'94
ELFUN TAX-EX INCOME FUND ■	General Muni	1,263.5	11.48	2.01	8.57	6.30	7.78	9.18	5.9	242-0134	203-326-4040	None	0.13	None	Robert R. Kaelin	'84
EMERALD FL TX-EX; A	General Muni	102.4	10.67	1.26	6.84	6.40			5.0	637-6336	None	4.50	0.96	None	Doug Byrne	'91
EMERALD FL TX-EX; B	Florida Muni	7.8	10.65	1.16	6.17	☆			4.6	637-6336	None	None	1.36	4.50	Doug Byrne	'94
EMERALD FL TX-EX; INSTL	Florida Muni	31.5	10.68	1.44	7.16	☆			5.3	637-6336	None	None	0.71	None	Doug Byrne	'94
EMPIRE BUILDER TAX FR BD	New York Muni	13.5	17.54	1.84	6.95	6.29	7.40	8.03	5.0	847-5886	212-309-8400	None	0.93	None	James Vaccacio	'94
ENTERPRISE TAX-EX INCOME	General Muni	35.0	13.58	1.81	7.55	5.74	7.08		5.0	432-4320	404-261-1116	4.75	1.25	None	Gerald Barth	'92
EV CLASSIC AL TAX FREE	Alabama Muni	10.3	9.41	1.10	7.53	☆			4.8	225-6265	617-482-8260	None	1.49	1.00	Timothy Browse	'93
EV CLASSIC AR TAX FREE	Single State Muni	0.5	9.47	1.01	6.63	☆			4.8	225-6265	617-482-8260	None	1.59	1.00	Timothy Browse	'94
EV CLASSIC AZ TAX FREE	Arizona Muni	2.7	9.49	1.57	8.21	☆			4.9	225-6265	617-482-8260	None	1.75	1.00	Cynthia J. Clemson	'93
EV CLASSIC CA LTD MAT	California Muni	7.6	9.58	1.56	4.71	☆			4.0	225-6265	617-482-8260	None	None	1.00	Raymond E. Hender	'93
EV CLASSIC CA MUNI	California Muni	2.8	9.25	1.23	6.77	☆			5.3	225-6265	617-482-8260	None	1.73	1.00	Robert MacIntosh	'93
EV CLASSIC CO TAX FREE	Colorado Muni	2.1	9.22	0.97	7.82	☆			5.1	225-6265	617-482-8260	None	1.38	1.00	Cynthia J. Clemson	'93
EV CLASSIC CT LTD MAT	Single State Muni	1.3	9.52	1.54	5.14	☆			3.9	225-6265	617-482-8260	None	None	1.00	William H. Ahern, Jr	'94
EV CLASSIC CT TAX FREE	Connecticut Muni	4.6	9.13	0.96	5.55	☆			5.1	225-6265	617-482-8260	None	1.64	1.00	Nicole Anderes	'93

Fund	Category													Manager	Year
EV CLASSIC FL INS TXFR	Florida Muni	1.5	9.99	0.31	6.93	☆	☆	5.5	225-6265	617-482-8260	None	0.95	1.00	Thomas J. Fetter	'94
EV CLASSIC FL LTD MAT	Florida Muni	10.2	9.61	1.88	5.60	☆	☆	4.0	225-6265	617-482-8260	None	None	1.00	Raymond E. Hender	'93
EV CLASSIC FL TAX FREE	Florida Muni	5.6	9.23	0.88	6.96	☆	☆	5.2	225-6265	617-482-8260	None	1.63	1.00	Thomas J. Fetter	'93
EV CLASSIC GA TAX FREE	Georgia Muni	2.5	9.11	0.59	5.04	☆	☆	4.9	225-6265	617-482-8260	None	1.64	1.00	David Reilly	'93
EV CLASSIC HI TAX-FREE	Hawaii Muni	0.3	9.36	1.12	5.62	☆	☆	5.4	225-6265	617-482-8260	None	1.01	1.00	Robert McIntosh	'94
EV CLASSIC KS TAX FREE	Kansas Muni	0.7	9.84	0.85	6.08	☆	☆	5.1	225-6265	617-482-8260	None	0.95	1.00	Nicole Anderes	'94
EV CLASSIC KY TAX FREE	Kentucky Muni	1.9	9.22	1.16	6.77	☆	☆	4.9	225-6265	617-482-8260	None	1.69	1.00	Timothy Browse	'93
EV CLASSIC LA TAX FREE	Louisiana Muni	2.6	9.35	-0.07	5.16	☆	☆	5.2	225-6265	617-482-8260	None	1.57	1.00	Nicole Anderes	'94
EV CLASSIC MA LTD MAT	Massachusetts Muni	5.7	9.61	1.48	5.36	☆	☆	4.1	225-6265	617-482-8260	None	None	1.00	Raymond E. Hender	'93
EV CLASSIC MA TAX FREE	Massachusetts Muni	2.9	9.14	0.48	6.06	☆	☆	5.4	225-6265	617-482-8260	None	1.61	1.00	Robert MacIntosh	'93
EV CLASSIC MD TAX FREE	Maryland Muni	0.9	9.25	0.59	7.41	☆	☆	4.9	225-6265	617-482-8260	None	1.64	1.00	Timothy Browse	'93
EV CLASSIC MI LTD MAT	Michigan Muni	5.1	9.53	1.47	4.63	☆	☆	4.1	225-6265	617-482-8260	None	None	1.00	William H. Ahern, Jr	'94
EV CLASSIC MI TAX FREE	Michigan Muni	4.8	9.24	1.13	6.96	☆	☆	4.9	225-6265	617-482-8260	None	1.69	1.00	Timothy Browse	'93
EV CLASSIC MN TAX FREE	Minnesota Muni	3.8	9.29	0.52	5.73	☆	☆	5.1	225-6265	617-482-8260	None	1.51	1.00	Robert MacIntosh	'93
EV CLASSIC MO TAX FREE	Missouri Muni	3.5	9.39	1.87	7.71	☆	☆	4.8	225-6265	617-482-8260	None	1.61	1.00	Cynthia J. Clemson	'93
EV CLASSIC MS TAX FREE	Single State Muni	2.4	9.20	1.15	7.07	☆	☆	5.0	225-6265	617-482-8260	None	1.24	1.00	Cynthia J. Clemson	'93
EV CLASSIC NAT LTD MAT	Intermediate Muni	17.1	9.56	1.30	4.82	☆	☆	4.3	225-6265	617-482-8260	None	1.57	1.00	Raymond E. Hender	'93
EV CLASSIC NATL MUNI	General Muni	38.3	9.28	2.99	8.39	☆	☆	6.0	225-6265	617-482-8260	None	1.60	1.00	Thomas M. Metzold	'93
EV CLASSIC NC TAX FREE	North Carolina Muni	6.1	9.23	0.39	5.70	☆	☆	4.9	225-6265	617-482-8260	None	1.56	1.00	David Reilly	'93
EV CLASSIC NJ LTD MAT	Single State Muni	3.1	9.62	1.23	4.85	☆	☆	4.0	225-6265	617-482-8260	None	None	1.00	William H. Ahern, Jr	'94
EV CLASSIC NJ TAX FREE	New Jersey Muni	3.4	9.28	1.44	6.38	☆	☆	5.2	225-6265	617-482-8260	None	1.64	1.00	Robert MacIntosu	'93
EV CLASSIC NY LTD MAT	New York Muni	5.7	9.56	1.68	4.96	☆	☆	4.0	225-6265	617-482-8260	None	None	1.00	Raymond E. Hender	'93
EV CLASSIC NY TAX FREE	New York Muni	6.1	9.30	1.10	6.73	☆	☆	5.2	225-6265	617-482-8260	None	1.64	1.00	Nicole Anderes	'93
EV CLASSIC OH LTD MAT	Ohio Muni	4.9	9.57	1.34	4.77	☆	☆	4.0	225-6265	617-482-8260	None	None	1.00	William H. Ahern, Jr	'94
EV CLASSIC OH TAX FREE	Ohio Muni	2.1	9.20	1.63	7.24	☆	☆	5.1	225-6265	617-482-8260	None	1.60	1.00	Thomas J. Fetter	'93
EV CLASSIC OR TAX FREE	Oregon Muni	1.0	9.34	1.21	7.49	☆	☆	4.7	225-6265	617-482-8260	None	1.65	1.00	Cynthia J. Clemson	'93
EV CLASSIC PA LTD MAT	Pennsylvania Muni	8.7	9.61	1.59	5.25	☆	☆	4.1	225-6265	617-482-8260	None	None	1.00	Raymond E. Hender	'93
EV CLASSIC PA TAX FREE	Pennsylvania Muni	2.7	9.17	1.65	6.48	☆	☆	5.2	225-6265	617-482-8260	None	1.66	1.00	David Reilly	'93
EV CLASSIC RI TAX FREE	Single State Muni	3.4	9.05	-0.12	5.88	☆	☆	5.2	225-6265	617-482-8260	None	1.23	1.00	Nicole Anderes	'93
EV CLASSIC SC TAX FREE	South Carolina Muni	1.0	9.35	0.89	6.05	☆	☆	4.8	225-6265	617-482-8260	None	1.76	1.00	David Reilly	'94
EV CLASSIC TN TAX FREE	Tennessee Muni	1.2	9.21	0.73	6.68	☆	☆	4.9	225-6265	617-482-8260	None	1.59	1.00	Cynthia J. Clemson	'93
EV CLASSIC TX TAX FREE	Texas Muni	0.5	9.19	1.04	7.17	☆	☆	5.4	225-6265	617-482-8260	None	1.08	1.00	Timothy Browse	'93
EV CLASSIC VA TAX FREE	Virginia Muni	1.5	9.25	0.95	7.01	☆	☆	5.0	225-6265	617-482-8260	None	1.54	1.00	David Reilly	'93
EV CLASSIC WV TAX FREE	Single State Muni	1.3	9.23	1.05	7.33	☆	☆	5.0	225-6265	617-482-8260	None	1.28	1.00	Timothy Browse	'93
EV MRTHN AL TAX FREE	Alabama Muni	109.9	10.33	1.15	7.85	5.74	5.78	4.9	225-6265	617-482-8260	None	1.43	5.00	Timothy Browse	'92
EV MRTHN AR TAX FREE	Single State Muni	82.2	10.13	1.06	6.80	☆	☆	4.9	225-6265	617-482-8260	None	1.17	5.00	Timothy Browse	'92
EV MRTHN AZ LTD MAT	Single State Muni	0.5	10.29	1.38	5.38	☆	☆	0.0	225-6265	617-482-8260	None	None	3.00	Raymond E. Hender	'94
EV MRTHN AZ TAX FREE	Arizona Muni	148.2	10.52	1.55	8.24	6.19	☆	5.0	225-6265	617-482-8260	None	1.46	5.00	Cynthia J. Clemson	'93
EV MRTHN CA LTD MAT	California Muni	71.4	10.00	1.47	4.48	4.58	☆	4.2	225-6265	617-482-8260	None	1.40	3.00	Raymond E. Hender	'92
EV MRTHN CA MUNI	California Muni	423.3	9.33	1.07	6.66	4.40	☆	5.5	225-6265	617-482-8260	None	1.63	5.00	Robert MacIntosh	'92
EV MRTHN CO TAX FREE	Colorado Muni	45.6	10.01	0.93	7.43	☆	☆	4.9	225-6265	617-482-8260	None	1.09	5.00	Cynthia J. Clemson	'92
EV MRTHN CT LTD MAT	Single State Muni	15.4	10.29	1.66	5.38	☆	☆	4.0	225-6265	617-482-8260	None	0.86	3.00	William H. Ahern, Jr	'94
EV MRTHN CT TAX FREE	Connecticut Muni	193.4	9.93	1.11	5.74	4.64	☆	5.2	225-6265	617-482-8260	None	1.43	5.00	Nicole Anderes	'94
EV MRTHN FL LTD MAT	Florida Muni	144.4	10.17	1.85	5.52	5.26	☆	4.1	225-6265	617-482-8260	None	1.42	3.00	Raymond E. Hender	'92
EV MRTHN FL TAX FREE	Florida Muni	738.5	10.56	0.84	7.01	5.20	☆	5.3	225-6265	617-482-8260	None	1.44	5.00	Thomas J. Fetter	'90
EV MRTHN GA TAX FREE	Georgia Muni	124.6	9.71	0.64	5.43	4.38	☆	4.9	225-6265	617-482-8260	None	1.41	5.00	David Reilly	'91
EV MRTHN HI TAX FREE	Hawaii Muni	14.5	9.49	0.96	5.68	☆	☆	5.7	225-6265	617-482-8260	None	None	5.00	Robert McIntosh	'94
EV MRTHN KY TAX FREE	Kentucky Muni	146.3	9.88	1.18	7.07	5.01	☆	5.0	225-6265	617-482-8260	None	1.44	5.00	Timothy Browse	'92
EV MRTHN LA TAX FREE	Louisiana Muni	31.9	9.88	0.13	5.29	☆	☆	5.3	225-6265	617-482-8260	None	1.08	5.00	Nicole Anderes	'94
EV MRTHN MA LTD MAT	Massachusetts Muni	112.6	10.03	1.48	5.48	4.79	☆	4.2	225-6265	617-482-8260	None	1.46	3.00	Raymond E. Hender	'92

PERFORMANCE OF MUTUAL FUNDS (continued)

FUND NAME	OBJECTIVE	ASSETS ($ MIL) 5/31/95	NAV ($/SHR) 6/30/95	RETURNS THROUGH 6/30 QTR	1YR	3YRS (Annualized)	5YRS	10YRS	DIV YLD %	PHONE NUMBER 800	In-State	FEES Load	Exp. Ratio	Redemption	MANAGER	SINCE
EV MRTHN MA TAX FREE	Massachusetts Muni	297.2	10.14	0.67	5.94	4.60	☆	☆	5.4	225-6265	617-482-8260	None	1.50	5.00	Robert MacIntosh	'91
EV MRTHN MD TAX FREE	Maryland Muni	117.2	10.09	0.66	7.16	5.01	☆	☆	4.9	225-6265	617-482-8260	None	1.43	5.00	Timothy Browse	'92
EV MRTHN MI LTD MAT	Michigan Muni	25.6	9.68	1.48	4.80	☆			4.1	225-6265	617-482-8260	None	0.91	3.00	William H. Ahern, Jr	'94
EV MRTHN MI TAX FREE	Michigan Muni	192.5	10.23	0.99	7.11	4.93	☆	☆	5.0	225-6265	617-482-8260	None	1.49	5.00	Timothy Browse	'92
EV MRTHN MN TAX FREE	Minnesota Muni	81.4	9.94	0.60	5.71	4.45	☆	☆	5.2	225-6265	617-482-8260	None	1.54	5.00	Robert MacIntosh	'91
EV MRTHN MO TAX FREE	Missouri Muni	93.3	10.40	2.03	8.09	6.06	☆	☆	4.9	225-6265	617-482-8260	None	1.49	5.00	Cynthia J. Clemson	'92
EV MRTHN MS TAX FREE	Single State Muni	27.9	9.37	1.08	6.94	☆	☆		5.1	225-6265	617-482-8260	None	0.99	5.00	Cynthia J. Clemson	'93
EV MRTHN NATL LTD MAT	Intermediate Muni	138.5	10.16	1.31	4.95	5.09	☆		4.4	225-6265	617-482-8260	None	1.46	3.00	Raymond E. Hender	'92
EV MRTHN NATL MUNI	General Muni	2,246.8	9.76	3.04	8.65	6.67	8.03	☆	6.1	225-6265	617-482-8260	None	1.51	5.00	Thomas M. Metzold	'93
EV MRTHN NC LTD MAT	Single State Muni	0.1	10.24	1.28	☆	☆			0.0	225-6265	617-482-8260	None	None	3.00	William H. Ahern, Jr	'94
EV MRTHN NC TAX FREE	North Carolina Muni	193.0	9.92	0.47	5.88	4.24	☆	☆	5.0	225-6265	617-482-8260	None	1.42	5.00	David Reilly	'91
EV MRTHN NJ LTD MAT	Single State Muni	92.3	10.05	1.26	4.96	4.79	☆		4.1	225-6265	617-482-8260	None	1.51	3.00	William H. Ahern, Jr	'94
EV MRTHN NJ TAX FREE	New Jersey Muni	416.8	10.36	1.44	6.20	5.27	☆	☆	5.3	225-6265	617-482-8260	None	1.48	5.00	Robert MacIntosh	'91
EV MRTHN NY LTD	New York Muni	162.7	10.10	1.66	4.94	5.03	☆		4.1	225-6265	617-482-8260	None	1.40	3.00	Raymond E. Hender	'92
EV MRTHN NY TAX FREE	New York Muni	658.6	10.69	1.16	6.50	5.48	☆	☆	5.4	225-6265	617-482-8260	None	1.46	5.00	Nicole Anderes	'94
EV MRTHN OH LTD MAT	Ohio Muni	33.5	9.78	1.47	4.87	☆	☆		4.1	225-6265	617-482-8260	None	1.03	3.00	William H. Ahern, Jr	'94
EV MRTHN OH TAX FREE	Ohio Muni	325.2	10.37	1.59	7.22	5.53	☆	☆	5.1	225-6265	617-482-8260	None	1.50	5.00	Thomas J. Fetter	'91
EV MRTHN OR TAX FREE	Oregon Muni	148.7	10.16	1.42	7.38	5.53	☆	☆	4.8	225-6265	617-482-8260	None	1.43	5.00	Cynthia J. Clemson	'91
EV MRTHN PA LTD MAT	Pennsylvania Muni	101.2	10.16	1.67	5.24	5.02	☆		4.2	225-6265	617-482-8260	None	1.45	3.00	Raymond E. Hender	'91
EV MRTHN PA TAX FREE	Pennsylvania Muni	511.3	10.30	1.62	6.30	4.90	☆	☆	5.2	225-6265	617-482-8260	None	1.46	5.00	David Reilly	'91
EV MRTHN RI TAX FREE	Single State Muni	39.4	9.24	-0.16	5.65	☆	☆		5.3	225-6265	617-482-8260	None	1.02	5.00	Nicole Anderes	'94
EV MRTHN SC TAX FREE	South Carolina Muni	60.5	9.92	0.85	6.18	☆	☆		4.9	225-6265	617-482-8260	None	1.36	5.00	David Reilly	'92
EV MRTHN TN TAX FREE	Tennessee Muni	57.8	9.98	0.78	6.67	☆	☆		5.1	225-6265	617-482-8260	None	1.37	5.00	Cynthia J. Clemson	'93
EV MRTHN TX TAX FREE	Texas Muni	28.1	10.28	0.97	8.30	5.64	☆		5.4	225-6265	617-482-8260	None	0.82	5.00	Timothy Browse	'94
EV MRTHN VA LTD MAT	Single State Muni	0.1	10.18	-0.59	☆	☆			0.0	225-6265	617-482-8260	None	None	3.00	William H. Ahern, Jr	'94
EV MRTHN VA TAX FREE	Virginia Muni	197.3	10.18	1.08	6.97	4.74	☆	☆	5.1	225-6265	617-482-8260	None	1.44	5.00	David Reilly	'93
EV MRTHN WV TAX FREE	Single State Muni	40.1	9.38	1.08	7.27	☆	☆		5.1	225-6265	617-482-8260	None	0.95	5.00	Timothy Browse	'93
EATON VANCE MUNI BOND LP	General Muni	97.2	9.81	1.79	7.81	6.26	8.23	9.31	6.3	225-6265	617-482-8260	3.75	0.80	None	Thomas J. Fetter	'86
EV TRAD CA MUNI	California Muni	4.0	10.09	1.26	8.12	☆	☆		6.0	225-6265	617-482-8260	3.75	None	None	Robert MacIntosh	'94
EV TRAD CT TAX FREE	Connecticut Muni	0.9	10.06	1.60	7.39	☆	☆		5.7	225-6265	617-482-8260	3.75	None	None	Nicole Anderes	'94
EV TRAD FL INS TAX FREE	Florida Muni	1.3	10.65	0.11	6.92	☆	☆		5.5	225-6265	617-482-8260	3.75	0.01	None	Thomas J. Fetter	'94
EV TRAD FL LTD MAT	Florida Muni	0.2	10.14	1.84	☆	☆			0.0	225-6265	617-482-8260	2.50	None	None	Raymond E. Hender	'94
EV TRAD FL TAX FREE	Florida Muni	2.3	10.31	1.21	7.65	☆	☆		5.8	225-6265	617-482-8260	3.75	None	None	Thomas J. Fetter	'94
EV TRAD NATL LTD MAT	Intermediate Muni	8.3	9.96	1.54	5.97	☆	☆		5.0	225-6265	617-482-8260	2.50	None	None	Raymond E. Hender	'94
EV TRAD NATL MUNI	General Muni	18.3	10.43	3.12	10.44	☆	☆		6.7	225-6265	617-482-8260	3.75	0.43	None	Thomas M. Metzold	'94
EV TRAD NJ TAX FREE	New Jersey Muni	1.4	9.98	1.65	7.81	☆	☆		5.9	225-6265	617-482-8260	3.75	None	None	Robert MacIntosh	'94
EV TRAD NY LTD MAT	New York Muni	0.8	10.11	1.97	☆	☆			0.0	225-6265	617-482-8260	2.50	None	None	Raymond E. Hender	'94
EV TRAD NY TAX FREE	New York Muni	3.7	10.03	1.49	7.72	☆	☆		6.0	225-6265	617-482-8260	3.75	None	None	Nicole Anderes	'94
EV TRAD PA TAX FREE	Pennsylvania Muni	1.3	9.97	2.05	6.79	☆	☆		5.9	225-6265	617-482-8260	3.75	None	None	David Reilly	'94
EVERGREEN MUN NATL, A	Insured Muni	0.9	10.10	1.89	☆	☆			0.0	807-2940	914-694-2020	4.75	None	None	James Colby III	'95
EVERGREEN MUN NATL, B	Insured Muni	2.3	10.11	1.82	☆	☆			0.0	807-2940	914-694-2020	None	None	5.00	James Colby III	'95
EVERGREEN MUN NATL, Y	Insured Muni	22.4	10.11	2.05	8.29	☆	☆		0.0	807-2940	914-694-2020	None	0.29	None	James Colby III	'95
EVERGREEN MUN SH CA; Y	California Muni	22.3	10.03	1.96	4.43	☆	☆		4.1	807-2940	914-694-2020	None	0.52	None	Steven Shachat	'92
EVERGREEN MUN SH-INT; A	Short-Term Muni	8.3	10.14	1.86	☆	☆			0.0	807-2940	914-694-2020	4.75	None	None	Steven Shachat	'95
EVERGREEN MUN SH-INT; B	Short-Term Muni	5.4	10.13	1.53	☆	☆			0.0	807-2940	914-694-2020	None	None	5.00	Steven Shachat	'95
EVERGREEN MUN SH-INT; Y	Short-Term Muni	42.3	10.13	1.75	4.12	4.48	☆	☆	4.5	807-2940	914-694-2020	None	0.58	None	Steven Shachat	'91
EXECUTIVE INV INS TAX EX	Insured Muni	12.0	13.48	2.26	10.45	8.91	☆	☆	5.2	423-4026	212-858-8000	4.75	0.50	None	Clark Wagner	N/A
FD T-F INV RUSHMORE MD	Maryland Muni	47.6	10.65	2.21	7.31	6.01	6.87	7.11	5.3	621-7874	301-657-1517	None	0.55	None	Team Managed	N/A
FD T-F INV RUSHMORE VA	Virginia Muni	30.8	10.89	2.00	7.15	6.17	7.21	6.88	5.3	621-7874	301-657-1517	None	0.55	None	Team Managed	N/A
FFB NJ TAX-FREE	New Jersey Muni	36.0	10.67	2.08	7.90	6.53	☆	☆	5.5	437-8790	None	4.50	0.25	None	Jocelyn Turner	'92

Fund	Objective	Net Assets ($Mil)	NAV	% Yr	1-Yr	5-Yr	10-Yr	Yield %	Fee/12b-1	Expense	Max Load	Phone	Toll-Free	Manager	Since
FIDELITY ADV HI MUNI; A	High-Yield Muni	566.9	11.70	2.73	7.17	6.52	8.71	6.0	None	0.89	4.75	None	522-7297	Guy Wickwire	'94
FIDELITY ADV HI MUNI; B	High-Yield Muni	24.7	11.68	2.45	6.03	★	★	5.2	4.00	None	None	None	522-7297	Guy Wickwire	'94
FIDELITY ADV INST LTD TX TX	Intermediate Muni	10.0	10.07	1.77	6.94	5.19	6.56	4.8	None	0.65	None	None	522-7297	David Murphy	'95
FIDELITY ADV LTD TX; A	Intermediate Muni	57.9	10.07	1.71	6.67	★	★	4.6	None	0.90	4.75	None	522-7297	David Murphy	'95
FIDELITY ADV LTD TX; B	Intermediate Muni	3.8	10.07	1.51	5.90	★	★	3.8	4.00	None	None	None	522-7297	David Murphy	'95
FIDELITY ADV SH-INT TXEX	Short-Term Muni	17.7	10.07	1.53	5.60	★	★	4.2	None	None	1.50	None	522-7297	David Murphy	'94
FIDELITY AGGRESSIVE TX	High-Yield Muni	908.8	11.31	2.20	6.64	6.50	8.09	6.6	1.00	0.63	None	None	544-8888	Anne Punzak	'86
FIDELITY CA TX FR HI YLD	California Muni	490.8	11.25	2.04	7.56	5.89	7.93	5.9	None	0.56	None	None	544-8888	Jonathan Short	'95
FIDELITY CA TX FR INSURD	California Muni	217.6	9.88	1.44	6.89	5.43	7.29	5.5	None	0.59	None	None	544-8888	Jonathan Short	'95
FIDELITY HIGH YLD TAX-FR	High-Yield Muni	1,822.7	11.84	1.58	6.13	5.49	8.65	6.1	None	0.56	None	None	544-8888	Anne Punzak	'93
FIDELITY INSURED TAX FR	Insured Muni	357.7	11.49	1.67	9.22	6.47	7.85	5.4	None	0.58	None	None	544-8888	Guy Wickwire	'93
FIDELITY LTD TERM MUNI	Intermediate Muni	953.6	9.47	1.99	7.68	6.50	7.80	5.4	None	0.56	None	None	544-8888	David Murphy	'89
FIDELITY MA TX-FR HI YLD	Massachusetts Muni	1,120.9	11.15	1.59	7.76	6.57	8.12	6.1	None	0.54	None	None	544-8888	Guy Wickwire	'83
FIDELITY MI TX-FR HI YLD	Michigan Muni	482.1	11.04	2.22	4.98	5.86	8.46	6.0	None	0.57	None	None	544-8888	Maureen Newman	'94
FIDELITY MN TX-FR	Minnesota Muni	306.9	10.74	2.01	7.88	5.99	7.15	5.9	None	0.59	None	None	544-8888	Steven Harvey	'93
FIDELITY MUNICIPAL BOND	General Muni	1,103.8	7.92	2.21	7.66	6.10	8.70	5.5	None	0.53	None	None	544-8888	Tanya Roy	'95
FIDELITY NY TX-FR HI YLD	New York Muni	423.2	11.93	2.55	9.09	6.44	8.36	5.5	None	0.58	None	None	544-8888	Norman Lind	'93
FIDELITY NY TX-FR INSURD	New York Muni	329.4	11.33	2.54	8.70	6.23	7.79	5.3	None	0.58	None	None	544-8888	Norman Lind	'94
FIDELITY OH TX-FR HI YLD	Ohio Muni	393.0	11.18	2.26	8.08	6.65	8.14	5.8	None	0.57	None	None	544-8888	Steven Harvey	'94
FIDELITY SPARTAN AGGR	High-Yield Muni	71.3	9.86	2.56	8.67	★	★	6.1	1.00	0.60	None	None	544-8888	Maureen Newman	'94
FIDELITY SPARTAN CA HY	California Muni	406.6	10.11	1.92	7.31	5.90	7.77	5.9	0.50	0.55	None	None	544-8888	Jonathan Short	'95
FIDELITY SPARTAN CA INT	California Muni	49.3	9.55	2.22	7.12	★	★	5.1	0.05	0.05	None	None	544-8888	Jonathan Short	'95
FIDELITY SPARTAN CT HY	Connecticut Muni	348.6	10.84	2.30	8.00	6.45	7.63	5.9	0.50	0.55	None	None	544-8888	Maureen Newman	'94
FIDELITY SPARTAN FL	Florida Muni	371.4	10.74	2.19	8.91	7.48	★	5.4	0.50	0.54	None	None	544-8888	Anne Punzak	'92
FIDELITY SPARTAN IN MUNI	Intermediate Muni	217.6	9.92	2.03	7.19	★	★	5.0	None	0.20	None	None	544-8888	David Murphy	'93
FIDELITY SPARTAN MD	Maryland Muni	43.7	9.70	2.29	7.63	★	★	5.7	0.50	0.03	None	None	544-8888	Steven Harvey	'93
FIDELITY SPARTAN MUNI	General Muni	586.8	10.06	2.33	8.30	6.46	8.12	5.4	0.50	0.55	None	None	544-8888	Norman Lind	'91
FIDELITY SPARTAN NJ HY	New Jersey Muni	361.3	11.11	1.95	8.24	6.62	8.15	5.7	0.50	0.55	None	None	544-8888	David Murphy	'93
FIDELITY SPARTAN NY HY	New York Muni	321.2	10.25	2.86	8.87	6.35	8.22	5.7	0.50	0.55	None	None	544-8888	Norman Lind	'93
FIDELITY SPARTAN NY INT	New York Muni	48.7	9.56	1.43	6.37	★	★	5.0	None	0.04	None	None	544-8888	David Murphy	'93
FIDELITY SPARTAN PA HY	Pennsylvania Muni	275.3	10.25	1.97	8.73	7.28	8.71	6.2	0.50	0.55	None	None	544-8888	Steven Harvey	'93
FIDELITY SPARTAN S-I MUN	Short-Term Muni	915.2	9.90	1.70	5.66	4.96	6.82	4.4	0.55	0.55	None	None	544-8888	David Murphy	'89
59 WALL ST TX FR SH/INT	Short-Term Muni	27.1	10.27	1.90	5.38	5.32	★	3.6	0.70	0.70	None	212-493-8100	533-5622	Barbara Brinkley	'92
FINL HRZNS MUNI BOND	General Muni	1,367.9	10.58	2.00	8.38	★	7.19	4.6	5.00	1.27	3.00	None	637-2548	Randy Baney	'89
FIRST AMER CO INT; A ➤	Single State Muni	49.1	10.40	1.77	6.76	★	★	4.5	None	0.69	None	612-973-4069	637-2548	Richard Stanley	'94
FIRST AMER CO INT; C ▥	Single State Muni	0.7	10.59	2.11	7.16	★	6.15	4.4	3.00	0.69	3.00	612-973-4069	637-2548	Richard Stanley	'87
FIRST AMER INT TXFR; A ➤	Intermediate Muni	34.1	10.58	2.11	7.16	5.25	★	4.4	None	0.59	None	612-973-4069	637-2548	Richard Stanley	'94
FIRST AMER INT TXFR; C ▥	Intermediate Muni	1.3	10.03	1.35	5.92	★	★	3.7	2.00	0.45	2.00	612-973-4069	637-2548	Stanley/Drahn	'94/94
FIRST AMER LTD TXFR; A ➤	Short-Term Muni	13.0	10.03	1.35	★	★	★	3.0	None	0.90	None	612-973-4069	637-2548	Stanley/Drahn	'94/95
FIRST AMER LTD TXFR; C ▥	Short-Term Muni	2.0	9.82	1.76	7.15	★	★	4.5	None	None	3.00	612-973-4069	637-2548	Richard Stanley	'94
FIRST AMER MN INTMDT; A ➤	Single State Muni	63.4	9.82	1.76	7.03	★	★	4.5	None	0.67	None	612-973-4069	637-2548	Richard Stanley	'94
FIRST AMER MN INTMDT; C ▥	Single State Muni	1,367.9	9.92	1.65	7.54	5.17	7.82	5.4	6.25	0.67	6.25	612-973-4069	637-2548	Richard Stanley	'91
FIRST INV INS TAX EX; A	Insured Muni	0.1	9.93	1.57	★	★	6.78	5.4	None	1.18	None	212-858-8000	423-4026	Clark Wagner	'95
FIRST INV INS TAX EX; B	Insured Muni	9.4	12.58	2.15	10.17	★	★	0.0	4.00	None	4.00	212-858-8000	423-4026	Clark Wagner	'91
FIRST INV INS TAX AZ	Arizona Muni	17.2	11.42	1.50	7.69	8.02	8.02	5.4	None	0.30	6.25	212-858-8000	423-4026	Clark Wagner	'91
FIRST INV MULTI INS CA	California Muni	3.4	12.01	1.91	9.49	6.79	8.05	5.5	None	0.97	6.25	212-858-8000	423-4026	Clark Wagner	'91
FIRST INV MULTI INS CO	Colorado Muni	16.0	12.36	2.00	8.26	7.62	★	5.0	None	0.20	6.25	212-858-8000	423-4026	Clark Wagner	'92
FIRST INV MULTI INS CT	Connecticut Muni	21.8	12.64	2.41	9.69	7.03	★	5.0	None	0.87	6.25	212-858-8000	423-4026	Clark Wagner	'91
FIRST INV MULTI INS FL	Florida Muni	2.7	12.07	2.01	9.30	7.73	★	5.1	None	0.62	6.25	212-858-8000	423-4026	Clark Wagner	'91
FIRST INV MULTI INS GA	Georgia Muni					7.71	★	5.0	None	0.20	6.25	212-858-8000	423-4026	Clark Wagner	'92

PERFORMANCE OF MUTUAL FUNDS (continued)

FUND NAME	OBJECTIVE	ASSETS ($ MIL) 5/31/95	NAV ($/SHR) 6/30/95	RETURNS THROUGH 6/30 QTR	1YR	3YRS (Annualized)	5YRS	10YRS	DIV YLD %	PHONE NUMBER 800	In-State	FEES Load	Exp. Ratio	Redemption	MANAGER	SINCE
FIRST INV MULTI INS MA	Massachusetts Muni	22.1	11.66	2.09	7.88	6.58	8.01		5.3	423-4026	212-858-8000	6.25	0.95	None	Clark Wagner	'95
FIRST INV MULTI INS MD	Maryland Muni	8.1	12.51	1.98	8.77	7.50	☆		5.2	423-4026	212-858-8000	6.25	0.45	None	Clark Wagner	'91
FIRST INV MULTI INS MI	Michigan Muni	33.9	12.29	2.31	9.01	7.42	8.54		5.1	423-4026	212-858-8000	6.25	0.93	None	Clark Wagner	'91
FIRST INV MULTI INS MN	Minnesota Muni	7.8	11.10	1.79	7.93	6.03	7.43		5.4	423-4026	212-858-8000	6.25	0.65	None	Clark Wagner	'91
FIRST INV MULTI INS MO	Missouri Muni	1.7	11.90	2.11	9.01	7.28	☆		5.4	423-4026	212-858-8000	6.25	0.20	None	Clark Wagner	'92
FIRST INV MULTI INS NC	North Carolina Muni	4.3	11.66	1.83	9.20	6.68	8.13		5.2	423-4026	212-858-8000	6.25	0.20	None	Clark Wagner	'92
FIRST INV MULTI INS NJ	New Jersey Muni	58.4	12.79	2.01	7.66	6.82	8.26		5.1	423-4026	212-858-8000	6.25	0.99	None	Clark Wagner	'91
FIRST INV MULTI INS OH	Ohio Muni	19.6	12.03	1.83	8.29	6.90	☆		5.2	423-4026	212-858-8000	6.25	0.85	None	Clark Wagner	'91
FIRST INV MULTI INS OR	Oregon Muni	5.6	11.61	1.98	9.08	6.29	☆		5.4	423-4026	212-858-8000	6.25	0.20	None	Clark Wagner	'92
FIRST INV MULTI INS PA	Pennsylvania Muni	37.1	12.53	1.84	8.42	7.27	8.19		5.0	423-4026	212-858-8000	6.25	0.88	None	Clark Wagner	'91
FIRST INV MULTI INS VA	Virginia Muni	24.7	12.46	2.24	8.94	7.00	7.99		4.9	423-4026	212-858-8000	6.25	0.85	None	Clark Wagner	'91
FIRST INV NY INS TAX FR	New York Muni	211.7	14.46	1.94	7.20	5.73	7.38	7.83	5.2	423-4026	212-858-8000	6.25	1.28	None	Clark Wagner	'91
FIRST INV SRS INS INT TE	Intermediate Muni	6.2	5.73	2.75	8.82	☆	☆		4.8	423-4026	212-858-8000	6.25	0.14	None	Clark Wagner	'93
FIRST PACIFIC HAWAII	Hawaii Muni	50.6	10.73	2.01	5.74	5.54	6.89		5.1	None	808-988-8088	None	0.95	None	Louis D'Avanzo	'94
FIRST UN FL MUNI; INV A	Florida Muni	8.8	9.67	2.21	10.27	☆	☆		5.1	326-3241	704-374-4343	4.75	0.64	None	Bob Drye	'93
FIRST UN FL MUNI; INV B	Florida Muni	26.6	9.67	2.02	9.51	☆	☆		4.4	326-3241	704-374-4343	None	1.22	5.00	Bob Drye	'94
FIRST UN FL MUNI; Y	Florida Muni	3.1	9.67	2.27	10.55	☆	☆		5.3	326-3241	704-374-4343	None	0.39	None	Bob Drye	'94
FIRST UN GA MUNI; INV A	Georgia Muni	1.8	9.38	1.55	9.31	☆	☆		5.3	326-3241	704-374-4343	4.75	0.53	None	Rick Marrone	'93
FIRST UN GA MUNI; INV B	Georgia Muni	8.1	9.38	1.36	8.55	☆	☆		4.6	326-3241	704-374-4343	None	1.13	5.00	Rick Marrone	'93
FIRST UN HI GRD; INV A	Insured Muni	58.3	10.57	2.07	8.94	6.55	☆		4.9	326-3241	704-374-4343	4.75	1.01	None	Bob Drye	'92
FIRST UN HI GRD; INV B	Insured Muni	33.6	10.57	1.88	8.18	☆	☆		4.3	326-3241	704-374-4343	None	1.58	5.00	Bob Drye	'93
FIRST UN HI GRD; Y	Insured Muni	5.1	10.57	2.13	9.20	☆	☆		5.2	326-3241	704-374-4343	None	0.76	None	Bob Drye	'93
FIRST UN NC MUNI; INV A	North Carolina Muni	8.3	9.86	1.34	9.55	☆	☆		5.1	326-3241	704-374-4343	4.75	0.79	None	Rick Marrone	'93
FIRST UN NC MUNI; INV B	North Carolina Muni	49.9	9.86	1.15	8.80	☆	☆		4.4	326-3241*	704-374-4343	None	1.37	5.00	Rick Marrone	'93
FIRST UN SC MUNI; INV A	South Carolina Muni	0.5	9.46	2.65	10.77	☆	☆		5.4	326-3241	704-374-4343	4.75	0.25	None	Bob Drye	'94
FIRST UN SC MUNI; INV B	South Carolina Muni	3.3	9.46	2.46	10.00	☆	☆		4.7	326-3241	704-374-4343	None	0.87	5.00	Bob Drye	'94
FIRST UN VA MUNI; INV A	Virginia Muni	2.0	9.57	1.61	10.23	☆	☆		5.1	326-3241	704-374-4343	4.75	0.53	None	Chuck Jeanne	'93
FIRST UN VA MUNI; INV B	Virginia Muni	4.9	9.57	1.42	9.47	☆	☆		4.4	326-3241	704-374-4343	None	1.12	5.00	Chuck Jeanne	'93
FIRST UN VA MUNI; Y	Virginia Muni	0.6	9.57	1.71	10.55	☆	☆		5.4	326-3241	704-374-4343	None	0.28	None	Chuck Jeanne	'94
FLAG INV MD INTMDT	Single State Muni	13.3	9.71	3.20	7.75	☆	☆		4.6	645-5923	410-637-6819	1.50	0.29	None	Randolph/Corbin	'93/'93
FLAGSHIP PA TRI TXEX; A	Pennsylvania Muni	42.6	10.06	2.02	7.48	6.29	7.86		6.0	227-4648	513-461-0352	4.20	0.91	None	Michael Davern	'92
FLAGSHIP PA TRI TXEX; C	Pennsylvania Muni	3.1	10.05	1.78	6.99	☆	☆		5.7	227-4648	513-461-0352	None	None	1.00	Michael Davern	'94
FLAGSHIP TXEX AMER; C	General Muni	185.4	10.64	2.23	7.61	7.25	8.92		5.9	227-4648	513-461-0352	4.20	0.62	None	Richard Huber	'94
FLAGSHIP TXEX AMER; C	General Muni	45.2	10.64	2.19	7.12	☆	☆		5.4	227-4648	513-461-0352	4.20	1.09	1.00	Richard Huber	'95
FLAGSHIP TXEX AL DBL; A	Alabama Muni	1.9	9.72	1.88	6.80	☆	☆		5.5	227-4648	513-461-0352	4.20	None	None	Michael Davern	'94
FLAGSHIP TXEX AZ DBL; A	Arizona Muni	80.3	10.60	1.55	8.73	6.91	8.31		5.5	227-4648	513-461-0352	4.20	0.64	None	Jan Terbrueggen	'92
FLAGSHIP TXEX AZ DBL; C	Arizona Muni	1.6	10.60	1.53	8.10	☆	☆		5.0	227-4648	513-461-0352	None	None	1.00	Jan Terbrueggen	'94
FLAGSHIP TXEX CO DBL; A	Colorado Muni	34.8	9.78	3.24	9.12	6.83	8.01		5.8	227-4648	513-461-0352	4.20	0.37	None	Jan Terbrueggen	'92
FLAGSHIP TXEX CT DBL; A	Connecticut Muni	203.3	10.24	2.33	7.91	6.39	7.62		5.7	227-4648	513-461-0352	4.20	0.65	None	Rick Huber	'92
FLAGSHIP TXEX CT DBL; C	Connecticut Muni	5.5	10.23	2.19	7.32	☆	☆		5.2	227-4648	513-461-0352	None	None	1.00	Rick Huber	'93
FLAGSHIP TXEX FL DBL; A	Florida Muni	341.8	10.47	2.16	8.03	6.43	8.23		5.6	227-4648	513-461-0352	4.20	0.58	None	Michael Davern	'92
FLAGSHIP TXEX FL INT; A	Florida Muni	3.9	9.94	2.46	7.66	☆	☆		4.0	227-4648	513-461-0352	3.00	None	None	Michael Davern	'95
FLAGSHIP TXEX FL INT; C	Florida Muni	1.8	9.94	2.32	7.07	☆	☆		3.5	227-4648	513-461-0352	None	None	1.00	Michael Davern	'95
FLAGSHIP TXEX GA DBL; A	Georgia Muni	113.4	10.30	2.10	7.80	5.88	7.49		5.6	227-4648	513-461-0352	4.20	0.70	None	Michael Davern	'92
FLAGSHIP TXEX GA DBL; C	Georgia Muni	7.0	10.28	1.96	7.22	☆	☆		5.1	227-4648	513-461-0352	None	None	1.00	Michael Davern	'94

Fund	Objective	Net Assets	NAV					Rating	Yield	Tel	Tel	Load			Manager	Since
FLAGSHIP TXEX INTMDT; A	Intermediate Muni	42.0	10.20	2.67	6.53	☆	☆	☆	5.0	227-4648	513-461-0332	3.00	0.40	None	Jan Terbrueggen	'95
FLAGSHIP TXEX KS TRI; A	Kansas Muni	83.7	9.86	2.00	7.81	6.24	☆	☆	5.6	227-4648	513-461-0332	4.20	0.26	None	Michael Davern	'92
FLAGSHIP TXEX KY TRI; A	Kentucky Muni	394.5	10.83	2.37	8.93	6.77	8.23	☆	5.7	227-4648	513-461-0332	4.20	0.58	None	Rick Huber	'93
FLAGSHIP TXEX KY TRI; C	Kentucky Muni	15.9	10.82	2.14	8.24	☆	☆	☆	5.2	227-4648	513-461-0332	None	1.08	1.00	Rick Huber	'93
FLAGSHIP TXEX LA DBL; A	Louisiana Muni	68.1	10.61	2.18	8.40	6.72	8.60	☆	5.7	227-4648	513-461-0332	4.20	0.66	None	Jan Terbrueggen	'92
FLAGSHIP TXEX LA DBL; C	Louisiana Muni	3.2	10.61	2.04	7.81	☆	☆	☆	5.1	227-4648	513-461-0332	None	None	1.00	Jan Terbrueggen	'94
FLAGSHIP TXEX LTD; A	Short-Term Muni	569.3	10.62	2.54	5.61	5.77	7.06	☆	4.7	227-4648	513-461-0332	2.50	0.70	None	Richard Huber	'95
FLAGSHIP TXEX MI TRI; A	Michigan Muni	250.4	11.40	2.04	7.73	6.34	7.79	☆	5.7	227-4648	513-461-0332	4.20	0.75	None	Michael Davern	'87
FLAGSHIP TXEX MI TRI; C	Michigan Muni	37.1	11.39	1.90	7.14	☆	☆	☆	5.1	227-4648	513-461-0332	None	1.25	1.00	Michael Davern	'93
FLAGSHIP TXEX MO DBL; A	Missouri Muni	205.1	10.55	2.08	7.59	6.57	8.02	☆	5.7	227-4648	513-461-0332	4.20	0.62	None	Michael Davern	'92
FLAGSHIP TXEX MO DBL; C	Missouri Muni	4.0	10.54	1.94	7.00	☆	☆	☆	5.1	227-4648	513-461-0332	None	None	1.00	Michael Davern	'94
FLAGSHIP TXEX NC TRI; A	North Carolina Muni	191.9	10.08	1.80	7.14	5.68	7.33	☆	5.6	227-4648	513-461-0332	4.20	0.89	None	Jan Terbrueggen	'95
FLAGSHIP TXEX NC TRI; C	North Carolina Muni	6.0	10.07	1.67	6.66	☆	☆	☆	5.1	227-4648	513-461-0332	None	None	1.00	Jan Terbrueggen	'95
FLAGSHIP TXEX NJ DBL; A	New Jersey Muni	7.8	9.89	1.71	8.43	☆	☆	☆	5.6	227-4648	513-461-0332	4.20	0.01	None	Rick Huber	'92
FLAGSHIP TXEX NJ INT; A	Single State Muni	9.2	10.14	2.15	7.22	☆	☆	☆	5.0	227-4648	513-461-0332	3.00	0.16	None	Rick Huber	'92
FLAGSHIP TXEX NM DBL; A	Single State Muni	52.1	9.79	1.86	8.52	☆	☆	☆	5.4	227-4648	513-461-0332	4.20	0.40	None	Jan Terbrueggen	'92
FLAGSHIP TXEX NY; A	New York Muni	49.1	10.42	2.66	7.72	7.52	☆	☆	5.9	227-4648	513-461-0332	4.20	0.30	None	Rick Huber	'92
FLAGSHIP TXEX OH DBL; A	Ohio Muni	445.4	11.27	1.95	7.43	6.13	7.70	☆	5.6	227-4648	513-461-0332	4.20	0.93	None	Michael Davern	'95
FLAGSHIP TXEX OH DBL; C	Ohio Muni	27.3	11.26	1.73	6.75	☆	☆	☆	5.1	227-4648	513-461-0332	None	1.46	1.00	Michael Davern	'92
FLAGSHIP TXEX SC DBL; A	South Carolina Muni	9.2	9.29	1.89	7.62	☆	☆	☆	5.4	227-4648	513-461-0332	4.20	0.40	None	Jan Terbrueggen	'92
FLAGSHIP TXEX TN DBL; A	Tennessee Muni	242.0	10.87	2.03	7.76	6.22	7.67	☆	5.5	227-4648	513-461-0332	4.20	0.76	None	Jan Terbrueggen	'95
FLAGSHIP TXEX TN DBL; C	Tennessee Muni	12.5	10.87	1.89	7.27	☆	☆	☆	5.0	227-4648	513-461-0332	None	1.23	1.00	Jan Terbrueggen	'95
FLAGSHIP TXEX VA DBL; A	Virginia Muni	112.6	10.40	2.10	7.90	6.54	7.93	☆	5.6	227-4648	513-461-0332	4.20	0.64	None	Rick Huber	'92
FLAGSHIP TXEX VA DBL; C	Virginia Muni	6.4	10.40	1.96	7.33	☆	☆	☆	5.1	227-4648	513-461-0332	None	None	1.00	Rick Huber	'93
FLAGSHIP TXEX WI DBL; A	Single State Muni	8.2	9.61	2.06	5.81	☆	☆	☆	5.3	227-4648	513-461-0332	4.20	None	None	Michael Davern	'94
FMB MI BD; CNSMR	Michigan Muni	13.6	10.53	2.13	7.57	6.01	☆	☆	4.5	453-4234	None	3.00	0.51	None	Dan Van Timmeren	'91
FMB MI BD; INSTL	Michigan Muni	17.3	10.53	2.13	7.58	6.03	☆	☆	4.5	453-4234	None	4.50	0.51	None	Dan Van Timmeren	'91
FORTIS TAX-FREE MN; A	Minnesota Muni	0.4	10.23	1.75	☆	☆	☆	☆	0.0	800-2638	612-738-4000	4.50	None	4.00	Dennis M. Ott	'94
FORTIS TAX-FREE MN; B	Minnesota Muni	0.1	10.21	1.67	☆	☆	☆	☆	0.0	800-2638	612-738-4000	None	None	1.00	Dennis M. Ott	'94
FORTIS TAX-FREE MN; C	Minnesota Muni	0.1	10.22	1.47	☆	☆	☆	☆	0.0	800-2638	612-738-4000	None	None	1.00	Dennis M. Ott	'94
FORTIS TAX-FREE MN; E	Minnesota Muni	54.0	10.25	1.81	6.90	6.15	7.49	☆	5.6	800-2638	612-738-4000	4.50	0.85	None	Dennis M. Ott	'86
FORTIS TAX-FREE MN; H	Minnesota Muni	0.6	10.23	1.57	☆	☆	☆	☆	0.0	800-2638	612-738-4000	None	None	4.00	Dennis M. Ott	'94
FORTIS TAX-FREE NATL; A	General Muni	1.1	10.61	1.55	☆	☆	☆	☆	0.0	800-2638	612-738-4000	4.50	None	4.00	Dennis M. Ott	'94
FORTIS TAX-FREE NATL; B	General Muni	0.2	10.59	1.27	☆	☆	☆	☆	0.0	800-2638	612-738-4000	None	None	None	Dennis M. Ott	'94
FORTIS TAX-FREE NATL; C	General Muni	0.1	10.60	1.36	☆	☆	☆	☆	0.0	800-2638	612-738-4000	None	None	1.00	Dennis M. Ott	'94
FORTIS TAX-FREE NATL; E	General Muni	72.7	10.61	1.61	7.35	6.16	7.86	☆	5.5	800-2638	612-738-4000	4.50	0.87	None	Dennis M. Ott	'86
FORTIS TAX-FREE NATL; H	General Muni	0.8	10.61	1.46	☆	☆	☆	☆	0.0	800-2638	612-738-4000	None	None	4.00	Dennis M. Ott	'94
FORTIS TAX-FREE NY; A	New York Muni	0.1	10.83	1.74	☆	☆	☆	☆	0.0	800-2638	612-738-4000	4.50	None	4.00	Dennis M. Ott	'94
FORTIS TAX-FREE NY; B	New York Muni	0.2	10.81	1.55	☆	☆	☆	☆	0.0	800-2638	612-738-4000	None	None	None	Dennis M. Ott	'94
FORTIS TAX-FREE NY; C	New York Muni	0.1	10.80	1.45	☆	☆	☆	☆	0.0	800-2638	612-738-4000	None	None	1.00	Dennis M. Ott	'94
FORTIS TAX-FREE NY; E	New York Muni	12.1	10.83	1.79	6.28	6.26	7.71	☆	5.7	800-2638	612-738-4000	4.50	0.99	None	Dennis M. Ott	'88
FORTIS TAX-FREE NY; H	New York Muni	N/A	10.79	1.36	☆	☆	☆	☆	0.0	800-2638	612-738-4000	None	None	4.00	Dennis M. Ott	'94
FORTRESS MUNI INC FD	General Muni	434.6	10.62	2.46	7.78	5.78	7.43	☆	5.8	245-4770	412-288-1900	1.00	1.09	1.00	Jonathan C. Conley	'87
FORUM MAINE MUNI	Single State Muni	26.2	10.63	2.75	8.46	6.76	☆	☆	4.9	None	207-879-0001	3.75	0.50	None	Forum Advisors	'91
FORUM NH BOND FUND	Single State Muni	5.6	10.24	2.82	8.46	☆	☆	☆	4.8	None	207-879-0001	3.75	0.46	None	Forum Advisors	'92
FORUM TAXSAVER BOND	General Muni	17.0	10.48	2.24	8.06	7.11	7.92	☆	5.5	None	207-879-0001	3.75	0.60	None	Forum Advisors	'89
FOUNTAIN SQ OH TX FR	Ohio Muni	26.5	9.92	2.84	7.36	☆	☆	☆	4.2	654-5372	513-579-5452	4.50	None	None	Carla Sanders	'93
FRANKLIN CA TF INC; I	California Muni	13,232.6	7.14	2.00	7.59	6.42	7.47	☆	6.2	342-5236	415-312-3200	4.25	0.55	None	Bernie Schroer	'87
FRANKLIN CA TF INS; I	California Muni	1,487.9	11.95	1.74	7.80	6.70	7.61	8.20	5.6	342-5236	415-312-3200	4.25	0.54	None	Don Duerson	'86
FRANKLIN CA TF INTMDT	California Muni	91.6	10.38	1.96	7.19	☆	☆	☆	5.1	342-5236	415-312-3200	2.25	0.25	None	Bernie Schroer	'92

PERFORMANCE OF MUTUAL FUNDS (continued)

FUND NAME	OBJECTIVE	ASSETS ($MIL) 5/31/95	NAV ($/SHR) 6/30/95	QTR	1YR	3YRS	5YRS	10YRS	DIV YLD %	800	In-State	Load	Exp. Ratio	Redemption	MANAGER	SINCE
					RETURNS THROUGH 6/30 (Annualized)					PHONE NUMBER		FEES				
FRANKLIN FED TF INC; I	General Muni	7,043.6	11.84	2.37	7.98	6.70	8.15	8.86	6.5	342-5236	415-312-3200	4.25	0.52	None	Andrew Jennings, Sr.	'90
FRANKLIN MUNI AR	Single State Muni	4.1	10.17	2.02	N/A	☆	☆	☆	4.8	342-5236	415-312-3200	4.25	None	None	Team Managed	N/A
FRANKLIN MUNI CA HI YLD	California Muni	51.1	9.78	2.25	9.12	☆	☆	☆	6.5	342-5236	415-312-3200	4.25	0.07	None	Bernie Schroer	'93
FRANKLIN MUNI HI	Hawaii Muni	36.8	10.47	2.40	8.47	6.75	☆	☆	6.5	342-5236	415-312-3200	4.25	0.05	None	Amoroso/Schubert/Jennings'92/'94/'92	N/A
FRANKLIN MUNI TN	Tennessee Muni	6.0	10.38	2.30	N/A	☆	☆	☆	4.9	342-5236	415-312-3200	4.25	None	None	Team Managed	N/A
FRANKLIN MUNI WA	Washington Muni	5.7	9.71	2.64	9.62	☆	☆	☆	5.9	342-5236	415-312-3200	4.25	0.05	None	Amoroso/Schubert/Jennings'93/'94/'93	'93
FRANKLIN NY TF INC; I	New York Muni	4,725.1	11.59	2.09	6.46	6.72	8.32	8.96	6.5	342-5236	415-312-3200	4.25	0.52	None	John Pinkham	'85
FRANKLIN NY TF INS; I	New York Muni	245.6	10.98	2.17	8.67	6.70	☆	☆	5.4	342-5236	415-312-3200	4.25	0.56	None	Don Duerson	'91
FRANKLIN NY TF INTMDT	New York Muni	39.8	10.06	2.39	5.34	☆	☆	☆	5.3	342-5236	415-312-3200	2.25	0.05	None	John Pinkham	'92
FRANKLIN TF AL; I	Alabama Muni	178.1	11.46	2.31	7.84	6.79	7.82	☆	5.7	342-5236	415-312-3200	4.25	0.72	None	J. Pomeroy	'87
FRANKLIN TF AZ INSURED	Arizona Muni	26.8	9.96	2.08	10.29	☆	☆	☆	5.5	342-5236	415-312-3200	4.25	0.10	None	Don Duerson	'93
FRANKLIN TF AZ; I	Arizona Muni	739.5	11.24	2.08	7.61	6.87	7.81	☆	5.7	342-5236	415-312-3200	4.25	0.60	None	Shelia Amoroso	'87
FRANKLIN TF CO; I	Colorado Muni	203.4	11.51	2.24	8.31	7.03	7.97	☆	5.8	342-5236	415-312-3200	4.25	0.70	None	Shelia Amoroso	'87
FRANKLIN TF CT; I	Connecticut Muni	160.9	10.71	1.90	6.58	6.13	6.90	☆	5.7	342-5236	415-312-3200	4.25	0.71	None	John Pinkham	'88
FRANKLIN TF FED INTMDT	Intermediate Muni	76.7	10.63	2.23	7.57	☆	☆	☆	5.0	342-5236	415-312-3200	2.25	0.56	None	Stella Wong	'92
FRANKLIN TF FL INSURED	Florida Muni	51.8	9.66	2.32	9.95	☆	☆	☆	5.5	342-5236	415-312-3200	4.25	0.35	None	Don Duerson	'93
FRANKLIN TF FL; I	Florida Muni	1,299.9	11.50	2.56	8.21	7.15	8.17	☆	5.9	342-5236	415-312-3200	4.25	0.59	None	Jennings/Amoroso	'90/'93
FRANKLIN TF GA; I	Georgia Muni	121.4	11.68	2.20	8.07	6.79	7.78	☆	5.7	342-5236	415-312-3200	4.25	0.76	None	Pomeroy/Noug	'87/'90
FRANKLIN TF HI YLD; I	High-Yield Muni	3,422.7	10.96	3.00	9.10	8.17	8.54	☆	6.7	342-5236	415-312-3200	4.25	0.60	None	Jennings/Amoroso	'90/'92
FRANKLIN TF IN	Single State Muni	47.0	11.52	2.14	6.85	6.65	7.78	☆	5.8	342-5236	415-312-3200	4.25	0.81	None	Stella Wong	'87
FRANKLIN TF INSURED; I	Insured Muni	1,696.1	12.07	1.98	7.63	6.69	7.93	8.62	5.9	342-5236	415-312-3200	4.25	0.59	None	Don Duerson	'86
FRANKLIN TF KY	Kentucky Muni	34.9	10.69	2.19	8.74	6.83	☆	☆	5.7	342-5236	415-312-3200	4.25	0.29	None	Shelia Amoroso	'91
FRANKLIN TF LA; I	Louisiana Muni	105.9	11.09	2.01	7.04	6.17	7.53	☆	5.8	342-5236	415-312-3200	4.25	0.75	None	Stella Wong	'87
FRANKLIN TF MA INS; I	Massachusetts Muni	291.9	11.43	1.98	7.67	6.62	7.74	7.92	5.8	342-5236	415-312-3200	4.25	0.67	None	Don Duerson	'86
FRANKLIN TF MD; I	Maryland Muni	160.2	11.03	1.97	8.39	6.77	7.75	☆	5.6	342-5236	415-312-3200	4.25	0.73	None	J. Pomeroy	'88
FRANKLIN TF MI INS; I	Michigan Muni	1,071.4	11.86	1.96	7.41	6.61	7.71	8.42	5.8	342-5236	415-312-3200	4.25	0.61	None	Don Duerson	'86
FRANKLIN TF MN !NS; I	Minnesota Muni	484.5	11.96	1.75	7.08	6.15	7.31	8.14	5.7	342-5236	415-312-3200	4.25	0.66	None	Don Duerson	'86
FRANKLIN TF MO; I	Missouri Muni	235.8	11.60	2.43	7.96	7.07	8.06	☆	5.5	342-5236	415-312-3200	4.25	0.70	None	Shelia Amoroso	'87
FRANKLIN TF NC; I	North Carolina Muni	227.4	11.51	1.94	7.91	6.59	7.53	☆	5.7	342-5236	415-312-3200	4.25	0.70	None	Stella Wong	'87
FRANKLIN TF NJ; I	New Jersey Muni	552.6	11.42	2.20	7.89	6.24	7.77	☆	5.6	342-5236	415-312-3200	4.25	0.63	None	Stella Wong	'88
FRANKLIN TF OH INS; I	Ohio Muni	666.8	12.00	1.94	7.53	6.67	7.73	8.36	5.7	342-5236	415-312-3200	4.25	0.63	None	Don Duerson	'86
FRANKLIN TF OR; I	Oregon Muni	359.5	11.33	1.92	7.76	6.21	7.50	☆	5.5	342-5236	415-312-3200	4.25	0.65	None	Shelia Amoroso	'89
FRANKLIN TF P RICO; I	Single State Muni	184.7	11.37	1.93	7.42	6.32	7.50	8.16	6.0	342-5236	415-312-3200	4.25	0.73	None	Shelia Amoroso	'87
FRANKLIN TF PA; I	Pennsylvania Muni	606.3	10.27	2.22	7.89	7.13	8.07	☆	6.0	342-5236	415-312-3200	4.25	0.63	None	Stella Wong	'86
FRANKLIN TF TX; I	Texas Muni	131.5	11.40	2.47	7.15	6.75	7.89	☆	5.8	342-5236	415-312-3200	4.25	0.73	None	Stella Wong	'87
FRANKLIN TF VA; I	Virginia Muni	263.0	11.46	2.13	8.04	6.92	7.96	☆	5.7	342-5236	415-312-3200	4.25	0.69	None	Stella Wong	'87
FREMONT CA INTMDT	California Muni	57.9	10.64	2.22	7.37	5.79	☆	☆	5.0	548-4539	415-284-8900	None	0.51	None	William M. Feeney	'90
FUNDAMENTAL CALIF MUNI	California Muni	14.1	8.35	5.72	11.11	5.38	6.07	7.14	5.5	322-6864	212-635-3005	None	3.48	None	Lance Brofman	'84
FUNDAMENTAL HI-YLD MUNI	High-Yield Muni	1.2	6.56	4.69	9.30	2.52	3.30	☆	5.5	322-6864	212-635-3005	None	2.50	None	David Wieder	'87
FUNDAMENTAL NY MUNI	New York Muni	163.3	0.94	1.95	-2.76	0.83	4.44	6.05	4.4	322-6864	212-635-3005	None	3.21	None	Lance Brofman	'81
FXD INC LTD MUNI; A	Short-Term Muni	26.9	9.78	2.30	5.02	☆	☆	☆	4.7	245-4770	412-288-1900	1.00	0.63	None	Mary Jo Ochson	'93
FXD INC LTD MUNI; FORT	Short-Term Muni	14.5	9.78	2.32	5.15	☆	☆	☆	4.8	245-4770	412-288-1900	1.00	0.44	1.00	Mary Jo Ochson	'93
GALAXY CT MUNI BOND; RTL	Connecticut Muni	17.0	9.83	2.22	7.92	☆	☆	☆	4.5	628-0414	None	None	0.25	None	Steve Woodruff	'93
GALAXY CT MUNI BOND; TR	Connecticut Muni	3.9	9.83	2.28	☆	☆	☆	☆	0.0	628-0414	None	None	None	None	Steve Woodruff	'94
GALAXY MA MUNI BOND; RTL	Massachusetts Muni	14.7	9.69	2.04	7.97	☆	☆	☆	4.6	628-0414	None	None	0.33	None	Dave Lindsay	'93

Lipper fund data table (municipal bond funds). Columns transcribed where legibly readable: Fund | Objective | Net Assets ($Mil) | NAV | 4-Wk % | 1-Yr Total Return % | Yield % | Telephone | Phone | Max Sales Chg | Expense | Deferred/12b-1 | Manager | Mgr. Since. The two intermediate Lipper rating columns appear largely as ☆ symbols with scattered longer-period return figures; they are rendered ☆ here.

Fund	Objective	Net Assets ($Mil)	NAV	4-Wk %	1-Yr %	☆	☆	Yield %	Telephone	Phone	Max Chg	Exp	Def	Manager	Since
GALAXY MA MUNI BOND; TR	Massachusetts Muni	7.2	9.69	2.10	☆	☆	☆	0.0	628-0414	None	None	None	None	Dave Lindsay	'94
GALAXY NY MUNI BOND; RTL	New York Muni	40.8	10.52	2.22	7.63	☆	☆	4.7	628-0414	None	None	0.87	None	Maria C. Schwenzer	'91
GALAXY NY MUNI BOND; TR	New York Muni	23.9	10.52	2.28	☆	☆	☆	0.0	628-0414	None	None	None	None	Maria C. Schwenzer	'94
GALAXY RI MUNI BOND; RTL	Single State Muni	6.9	10.44	1.87	☆	☆	☆	0.0	628-0414	None	None	None	None	Patricia Galuska	'94
GALAXY TAX-EXEMPT BD; RTL	General Muni	31.0	10.54	1.90	7.70	☆	☆	5.0	628-0414	None	None	0.80	None	Mary McGoldrick	'91
GALAXY TAX-EXEMPT BD; TR	General Muni	88.0	10.54	1.96	☆	☆	☆	0.0	628-0414	None	None	None	None	Mary McGoldrick	'94
GALAXY II MUNICIPAL BOND	Intermediate Muni	24.4	10.05	2.28	7.11	☆	☆	4.6	628-0414	None	None	0.60	None	IBM Credit Invt Mgt	'93
GE TX-EX; A	General Muni	0.1	11.67	1.81	7.17	☆	☆	4.6	242-0134	203-326-4040	4.25	1.10	None	Robert R. Kaelin	'93
GE TX-EX; B	General Muni	0.1	11.67	1.68	6.63	☆	☆	4.1	242-0134	203-326-4040	None	1.60	None	Robert R. Kaelin	'93
GE TX-EX; C	General Muni	6.5	11.67	1.87	7.43	☆	☆	4.8	242-0134	203-326-4040	None	0.79	3.00	Robert R. Kaelin	'93
GE TX-EX; D	General Muni	3.9	11.67	1.93	7.70	☆	☆	5.1	242-0134	203-326-4040	None	0.60	None	Robert R. Kaelin	'93
GIT TAX-FREE ARIZONA	Arizona Muni	10.6	10.01	1.72	7.05	4.95	☆	4.4	336-3063	703-528-6500	None	1.29	None	Dan Gillespie	'94
GIT TAX-FREE MARYLAND	Maryland Muni	3.2	9.62	1.61	6.67	☆	6.55	4.5	336-3063	703-528-6500	None	0.64	None	Dan Gillespie	'94
GIT TAX-FREE MISSOURI	Missouri Muni	11.5	10.06	1.75	6.62	4.91	6.41	4.4	336-3063	703-528-6500	None	1.29	None	Dan Gillespie	'94
GIT TAX-FREE NATIONAL	General Muni	33.1	10.13	2.01	7.04	4.73	6.44	4.4	336-3063	703-528-6500	None	1.23	None	Dan Gillespie	'94
GIT TAX-FREE VIRGINIA	Virginia Muni	33.4	10.96	1.61	7.13	5.12	6.49	4.6	336-3063	703-528-6500	None	1.18	None	Dan Gillespie	'94
GLENMEDE MUNI INTMDT	Intermediate Muni	18.7	10.19	2.42	7.25	5.31	☆	5.3	441-7379	None	None	0.25	None	Laura LaRosa	'94
GLENMEDE NJ MUNI	New Jersey Muni	5.0	9.82	3.39	7.32	☆	☆	3.5	441-7379	None	None	0.60	None	Laura LaRosa	'94
GOLDMAN MUNI INC	General Muni	52.7	13.78	1.91	7.71	5.74	☆	5.0	526-7384	212-902-0800	4.50	0.45	None	Mark Muller	'93
GOLDMAN SH DUR; INSTL	Short-Term Muni	61.9	9.86	1.92	4.41	☆	☆	4.4	526-7384	212-902-0800	None	0.45	None	Team Managed	N/A
GRADISON-MCDONALD MUN OH	Ohio Muni	71.4	12.77	1.93	8.03	5.74	☆	5.1	869-5999	513-579-5700	2.00	0.90	None	Steve Dilbone	'92
GREAT HALL MN INSURED	Minnesota Muni	29.6	9.86	1.76	7.75	5.74	7.22	5.0	934-6674	612-371-7970	4.50	0.80	None	Hippen/Kanzenbach	'86/'86
GREAT HALL NATIONAL	High-Yield Muni	68.0	10.16	2.30	8.29	7.22	8.35	6.3	934-6674	612-371-7970	4.50	0.91	None	Hippen/Kanzenbach	'86/'86
GRIFFIN CA TAX-FREE; A	California Muni	18.7	7.75	0.99	7.27	☆	☆	5.3	676-4450	None	4.50	0.25	None	Scott King	'93
GRIFFIN CA TAX-FREE; B	California Muni	0.2	7.75	0.85	☆	☆	☆	0.0	676-4450	None	None	None	5.00	Scott King	'94
GRIFFIN MUNI BOND; A	General Muni	5.1	8.82	1.34	7.41	☆	☆	5.3	676-4450	None	4.50	0.25	None	Scott King	'94
GRIFFIN MUNI BOND; B	General Muni	0.1	8.82	1.20	☆	☆	☆	0.0	676-4450	None	None	None	5.00	Scott King	'94
GUARDIAN TAX-EXEMPT FUND	General Muni	17.0	9.27	0.98	6.46	☆	8.05	4.8	221-3253	None	4.50	1.09	None	Alex Grant	'93
J HANCOCK CA T-F INC; A	California Muni	258.0	10.08	2.35	8.16	6.26	☆	5.8	225-5291	617-375-1500	4.50	0.69	None	Team Managed	N/A
J HANCOCK CA T-F INC; B	California Muni	84.8	10.08	2.15	7.36	5.51	☆	5.1	225-5291	617-375-1500	None	1.44	5.00	Team Managed	N/A
J HANCOCK MGD TAX; A	General Muni	20.4	11.34	1.64	7.48	6.37	7.35	5.6	225-5291	617-375-1500	4.50	0.95	None	Frank Lucibella	'93
J HANCOCK MGD TAX; B	General Muni	209.4	11.34	1.46	6.75	5.73	☆	4.9	225-5291	617-375-1500	None	1.62	5.00	Frank Lucibella	'93
J HANCOCK TX-EXEMPT; A	General Muni	492.1	10.49	1.74	6.89	5.73	7.49	5.5	225-5291	617-375-1500	4.50	1.11	None	Frank Lucibella	'88
J HANCOCK TX-EXEMPT; B	General Muni	6.0	10.48	1.43	6.08	☆	☆	4.8	225-5291	617-375-1500	None	1.83	5.00	Frank Lucibella	'94
J HANCOCK TX-EX SRS CA	California Muni	48.4	11.54	2.15	8.69	6.56	7.78	5.5	225-5291	617-375-1500	4.50	0.70	None	Diane Sales-Singer	'93
J HANCOCK TX-EX SRS MA	Massachusetts Muni	55.0	11.64	1.80	7.88	6.52	8.12	5.6	225-5291	617-375-1500	4.50	0.70	None	Diane Sales-Singer	'93
J HANCOCK TX-EX SRS NY	New York Muni	56.1	11.75	2.07	7.12	6.46	8.20	5.6	225-5291	617-375-1500	4.50	0.70	None	Team Managed	'93
J HANCOCK TX-FR BD; A	General Muni	119.6	10.05	1.22	6.78	6.43	8.54	5.8	225-5291	617-375-1500	4.50	0.78	None	Team Managed	'93
J HANCOCK TX-FR BD; B	General Muni	75.3	10.05	1.01	5.96	5.63	☆	5.0	225-5291	617-375-1500	None	1.53	5.00	Team Managed	N/A
J HANCOCK HI YLD TF; A	High-Yield Muni	14.7	9.35	3.10	8.64	☆	☆	6.9	225-5291	617-375-1500	4.50	0.96	None	Team Managed	N/A
J HANCOCK HI YLD TF; B	High-Yield Muni	160.0	9.36	3.02	7.92	6.72	7.49	6.2	225-5291	617-375-1500	4.00	1.85	5.00	Team Managed	'93
HAWAIIAN TX-FR TR	Hawaii Muni	661.6	11.23	2.28	7.63	5.89	7.16	5.5	228-4227	212-447-6666	None	0.74	None	Lorene Okimoto	'91
HEARTLAND NE TAX FREE	Single State Muni	13.5	8.86	1.95	8.32	☆	7.98	5.0	432-7856	414-347-7777	None	0.81	None	Patrick Retzer	'93
HEARTLAND WI TAX FREE	Single State Muni	113.6	9.83	1.92	7.93	5.39	☆	5.2	432-7856	414-347-7777	None	0.85	None	Patrick Retzer	'92
HOUGH FL TXFR SHORT TERM	Single State Muni	12.0	9.93	1.69	5.23	☆	☆	4.3	557-7555	813-825-7730	None	0.05	None	Team Managed	N/A
IAI INV VI MN TAX FREE	Minnesota Muni	7.4	10.06	1.73	4.66	5.07	7.49	5.3	945-3863	612-376-2700	None	0.25	None	Coleman/Douglas	'92/'95
IDEX II TAX-EXEMPT; A	General Muni	28.3	11.31	1.60	6.89	5.49	6.82	4.8	851-9777	813-585-6565	4.75	1.00	None	Rachel Dennis	'85
IDEX II TAX-EXEMPT; C	General Muni	0.3	11.31	1.62	6.63	☆	☆	4.6	851-9777	813-585-6565	None	1.25	None	Rachel Dennis	'93
IDS CA TAX-EX; A	California Muni	244.0	5.16	0.22	6.67	5.80	7.31	5.8	328-8300	612-671-3733	5.00	0.61	None	Paul Hylle	'93
IDS HIGH YLD TAX-EX; A	High-Yield Muni	6,204.7	4.49	2.25	8.21	5.72	7.45	6.4	328-8300	612-671-3733	5.00	0.59	None	Kurt Larson	'79

PERFORMANCE OF MUTUAL FUNDS (continued)

FUND NAME	OBJECTIVE	ASSETS ($ MIL) 5/31/95	NAV ($/SHR) 6/30/95	RETURNS THROUGH 6/30 (Annualized)					DIV YLD %	PHONE NUMBER		FEES			MANAGER	SINCE
				QTR	1YR	3YRS	5YRS	10YRS		800	In-State	Load	Exp. Ratio	Redemption		
IDS INSURED TAX-EX; A	Insured Muni	517.7	5.40	-0.15	6.81	6.11	7.76	★	5.6	328-8300	612-671-3733	5.00	0.65	None	Paul Hylle	'93
IDS MA TAX-EX; A	Massachusetts Muni	69.2	5.27	0.41	6.51	6.19	7.66	★	5.7	328-8300	612-671-3733	5.00	0.69	None	Paul Hylle	'93
IDS MI TAX-EX; A	Michigan Muni	80.0	5.39	0.25	6.72	6.32	7.84	★	5.7	328-8300	612-671-3733	5.00	0.65	None	Paul Hylle	'93
IDS MN TAX-EX; A	Minnesota Muni	410.0	5.19	0.31	6.80	5.85	7.33	★	6.0	328-8300	612-671-3733	5.00	0.66	None	Paul Hylle	'93
IDS NY TAX-EX; A	New York Muni	122.0	5.09	-0.08	5.53	5.67	7.45	★	6.0	328-8300	612-671-3733	5.00	0.65	None	Paul Hylle	'93
IDS OH TAX-EX; A	Ohio Muni	74.7	5.28	0.05	6.26	5.79	7.47	★	5.7	328-8300	612-671-3733	5.00	0.66	None	Paul Hylle	'93
IDS TAX-EX BOND; A	General Muni	1,152.4	3.84	0.57	6.80	5.52	6.84	8.31	5.7	328-8300	612-671-3733	5.00	0.61	None	Terry Seierstad	'93
INTMDT MUNI TR OH; INSTL	Ohio Muni	6.6	9.73	3.04	8.13	★	★	★	4.9	245-4770	412-288-1900	None	0.24	None	Scott Albrecht	'93
INTMDT MUNI TR PA; INSTL	Pennsylvania Muni	8.3	9.99	2.39	7.75	★	★	★	4.9	245-4770	412-288-1900	None	0.25	None	Scott Albrecht	'93
INTMDT-MUNI TR; INSTL	Intermediate Muni	229.2	10.49	2.20	5.99	5.50	6.91	★	5.2	245-4770	412-288-1900	None	0.61	None	Jonathan C. Conley	'85
INVENTOR PA MUNI BD; A ►	Pennsylvania Muni	35.9	10.12	1.74	★	★	★	★	0.0	342-5734	610-254-1000	4.00	None	None	Blake Miller	'94
INVESCO TAX-FR LG-TM	General Muni	263.7	15.07	1.00	6.16	5.71	7.65	9.32	5.3	525-8085	303-930-6300	None	1.00	None	Jim Grabovac	'95
INVESCO TAX-FR INTMDT BD	Intermediate Muni	5.1	9.70	2.17	6.67	★	★	★	4.5	525-8085	303-930-6300	None	0.70	None	Jim Grabovac	'95
INVESTORS TR TX FR; A	Intermediate Muni	15.8	11.14	1.79	8.35	★	★	★	5.0	656-6626	206-625-1755	4.50	0.77	None	Barbara Brinkley	'93
INVESTORS TR TX FR; B	Intermediate Muni	6.7	11.16	1.87	8.39	★	★	★	4.9	656-6626	206-625-1755	None	1.14	5.00	Barbara Brinkley	'93
JACKSON NATL TAX-EXEMPT	General Muni	21.0	10.17	1.75	6.12	★	★	★	4.7	888-3863	None	4.75	0.90	None	PPM America	'92
JANUS FEDERAL TAX-EXEMPT	General Muni	30.8	6.72	1.36	6.16	★	★	★	5.5	525-8983	303-333-3863	None	0.65	None	Ronald V. Speaker	'93
JPM INSTL NY TOT RTN BD	New York Muni	26.8	10.26	2.72	7.45	★	★	★	4.6	521-5412	212-826-1303	None	0.50	None	Ebby Gerry	'95
JPM INSTL TAX EX BOND	Intermediate Muni	53.4	9.90	2.51	7.55	★	★	★	4.9	521-5412	212-826-1303	None	0.77	None	Ebby Gerry	'93
KEMPER INTMDT MUNI; A	Intermediate Muni	10.2	10.02	2.28	★	★	★	★	0.0	621-1048	312-781-1121	2.75	1.14	None	Mier/Beimford	'94/'94
KEMPER INTMDT MUNI; B	Intermediate Muni	2.1	10.00	1.85	★	★	★	★	0.0	621-1048	312-781-1121	None	None	4.00	Mier/Beimford	'94/'94
KEMPER INTMDT MUNI; C	Intermediate Muni	0.7	10.03	2.19	★	★	★	★	0.0	621-1048	312-781-1121	None	None	None	Mier/Beimford	'94/'94
KEMPER MUNI BOND; A	General Muni	3,603.3	10.02	2.09	8.24	6.87	8.46	9.34	5.5	621-1048	312-781-1121	4.50	0.60	None	Beimford/Mier	'83/'91
KEMPER MUNI BOND; B	General Muni	30.1	10.00	1.86	7.26	★	★	★	4.6	621-1048	312-781-1121	None	None	4.00	Beimford/Mier	'94/'94
KEMPER MUNI BOND; C	General Muni	0.9	10.03	1.88	7.31	★	★	★	4.7	621-1048	312-781-1121	None	None	None	Beimford/Mier	'94/'94
KEMPER TX-FR INC CA; A	California Muni	1,128.7	7.29	1.89	8.16	6.64	7.93	8.97	5.4	621-1048	312-781-1121	4.50	0.74	None	Beimford/Mier	'83/'89
KEMPER TX-FR INC CA; B	California Muni	10.2	7.29	1.68	7.20	★	★	★	4.6	621-1048	312-781-1121	None	None	4.00	Beimford/Mier	'94/'94
KEMPER TX-FR INC CA; C	California Muni	0.2	7.29	1.69	7.28	★	★	★	4.7	621-1048	312-781-1121	None	None	None	Beimford/Mier	'94/'94
KEMPER TX-FR INC FL; A	Florida Muni	121.0	10.22	2.08	9.07	7.52	★	★	5.2	621-1048	312-781-1121	4.50	0.79	None	Beimford/Mier	'91/'91
KEMPER TX-FR INC FL; B	Florida Muni	1.9	10.21	1.95	8.19	★	★	★	4.4	621-1048	312-781-1121	None	None	4.00	Beimford/Mier	'94/'94
KEMPER TX-FR INC FL; C	Florida Muni	0.1	10.21	1.90	8.28	★	★	★	4.5	621-1048	312-781-1121	None	None	None	Beimford/Mier	'94/'94
KEMPER TX-FR INC NY; A	New York Muni	325.7	10.70	2.08	7.24	6.81	8.45	★	5.4	621-1048	312-781-1121	4.50	0.76	None	Beimford/Mier	'85/'89
KEMPER TX-FR INC NY; B	New York Muni	3.3	10.70	1.87	6.00	★	★	★	4.6	621-1048	312-781-1121	None	None	4.00	Beimford/Mier	'94/'94
KEMPER TX-FR INC NY; C	New York Muni	0.2	10.69	1.88	6.25	★	★	★	4.6	621-1048	312-781-1121	None	None	None	Beimford/Mier	'94/'94
KEMPER TX-FR INC OH; A	Ohio Muni	26.4	9.73	1.75	8.77	★	★	★	5.2	621-1048	312-781-1121	4.50	0.02	None	Beimford/Mier	'93/'93
KEMPER TX-FR INC OH; B	Ohio Muni	4.2	9.72	1.45	7.91	★	★	★	4.9	621-1048	312-781-1121	None	None	4.00	Beimford/Mier	'94/'94
KEMPER TX-FR INC OH; C	Ohio Muni	0.2	9.73	1.55	8.29	★	★	★	4.9	621-1048	312-781-1121	None	None	None	Beimford/Mier	'94/'94
KEMPER TX-FR INC TX; A	Texas Muni	14.7	10.33	2.16	9.38	8.17	★	★	5.3	621-1048	312-781-1121	4.50	0.36	None	Beimford/Mier	'91/'91
KEMPER TX-FR INC TX; B	Texas Muni	0.4	10.33	1.97	8.26	★	★	★	4.5	621-1048	312-781-1121	None	None	4.00	Beimford/Mier	'94/'94
KEMPER TX-FR INC TX; C	Texas Muni	0.5	10.33	1.96	8.36	★	★	★	4.6	621-1048	312-781-1121	None	None	None	Beimford/Mier	'94/'94
KENT FDS INT TX-FR; INST	Intermediate Muni	300.4	10.23	1.91	7.52	★	★	★	4.4	633-5368	None	None	0.78	None	Old Kent Bank	'92
KENT FDS INT TX-FR; INV	Intermediate Muni	4.0	10.23	1.85	7.31	★	★	★	4.3	633-5368	None	None	0.79	None	Old Kent Bank	'92
KENT FDS MI MUNI; INST	Michigan Muni	123.8	9.96	1.54	5.15	★	★	★	4.0	633-5368	None	None	0.49	None	Old Kent Bank	'93
KENT FDS MI MUNI; INV	Michigan Muni	1.9	9.96	1.51	5.09	★	★	★	3.9	633-5368	None	4.00	0.49	None	Old Kent Bank	'93
KEYSTONE AM TXFR INC; A	General Muni	98.4	9.72	2.38	8.10	5.30	6.88	★	5.4	343-2898	617-621-6100	4.75	1.13	None	Betsy Blacher	'88

Fund	Objective	Net Assets	NAV	(1)	(2)	(3)	(4)	(5)	Yield	Tel 1	Tel 2	Load	12b-1	Red	Manager	Since
KEYSTONE AM TXFR INC; B	General Muni	32.2	9.65	2.16	7.26	★	★	★	5.1	343-2898	617-621-6100	None	1.88	3.00	Betsy Blacher	'93
KEYSTONE AM TXFR INC; C	General Muni	22.1	9.65	2.16	7.26	★	★	★	5.1	343-2898	617-621-6100	None	1.89	1.00	Betsy Blacher	'93
KEYSTONE AM TXFR2 CA; A	California Muni	3.7	9.33	1.68	6.77	★	★	★	5.5	343-2898	617-621-6100	4.75	None	None	Betsy Blacher	'94
KEYSTONE AM TXFR2 CA; B	California Muni	13.4	9.30	1.47	5.96	★	★	★	5.3	343-2898	617-621-6100	None	None	3.00	Betsy Blacher	'94
KEYSTONE AM TXFR2 CA; C	California Muni	2.6	9.29	1.47	5.67	★	★	★	5.2	343-2898	617-621-6100	None	None	1.00	Betsy Blacher	'94
KEYSTONE AM TXFR2 MO; A	Missouri Muni	3.1	9.50	2.63	7.18	★	★	★	5.4	343-2898	617-621-6100	4.75	None	None	Daniel A Rabasco	'94
KEYSTONE AM TXFR2 MO; B	Missouri Muni	16.9	9.40	2.34	6.20	★	★	★	5.3	343-2898	617-621-6100	None	None	3.00	Daniel A Rabasco	'94
KEYSTONE AM TXFR2 MO; C	Missouri Muni	1.6	9.40	2.45	6.02	★	★	★	5.2	343-2898	617-621-6100	None	None	1.00	Daniel A Rabasco	'93
KEYSTONE AM TXFR FL; A	Florida Muni	42.0	10.45	2.53	8.49	5.94	★	★	5.6	343-2898	617-621-6100	4.75	0.75	None	Betsy Blacher	'90
KEYSTONE AM TXFR FL; B	Florida Muni	52.9	10.36	2.46	7.78	★	★	★	5.4	343-2898	617-621-6100	None	1.50	3.00	Betsy Blacher	'93
KEYSTONE AM TXFR FL; C	Florida Muni	12.8	10.38	2.45	7.81	★	★	★	5.3	345-2898	617-621-6100	None	1.50	1.00	Betsy Blacher	'93
KEYSTONE AM TXFR MA; A	Massachusetts Muni	2.2	9.23	1.81	7.78	★	★	★	5.6	343-2898	617-621-6100	4.75	None	None	Daniel A Rabasco	'94
KEYSTONE AM TXFR MA; B	Massachusetts Muni	6.4	9.18	1.60	6.94	★	★	★	5.4	343-2898	617-621-6100	None	None	3.00	Daniel A Rabasco	'94
KEYSTONE AM TXFR MA; C	Massachusetts Muni	2.0	9.18	1.72	6.88	★	★	★	5.4	343-2898	617-621-6100	None	None	1.00	Daniel A Rabasco	'94
KEYSTONE AM TXFR NY; A	New York Muni	3.7	9.52	2.15	7.75	★	★	★	5.3	343-2898	617-621-6100	4.75	None	None	Daniel A Rabasco	'94
KEYSTONE AM TXFR NY; B	New York Muni	13.3	9.45	1.97	6.98	★	★	★	5.1	343-2898	617-621-6100	None	None	3.00	Daniel A Rabasco	'94
KEYSTONE AM TXFR NY; C	New York Muni	2.6	9.45	2.08	7.03	★	★	★	5.1	343-2898	617-621-6100	None	0.75	1.00	Daniel A Rabasco	'94
KEYSTONE AM TXFR PA; A	Pennsylvania Muni	31.4	11.05	2.64	7.03	6.22	★	★	5.5	343-2898	617-621-6100	4.75	1.50	None	Daniel A Rabasco	'94
KEYSTONE AM TXFR PA; B	Pennsylvania Muni	32.5	10.93	2.38	6.19	★	★	★	5.3	343-2898	617-621-6100	None	1.50	3.00	Daniel A Rabasco	'94
KEYSTONE AM TXFR PA; C	Pennsylvania Muni	10.1	10.96	2.47	6.21	★	★	★	5.3	343-2898	617-621-6100	None	None	1.00	Daniel A Rabasco	'94
KEYSTONE AM TXFR TX; A	Texas Muni	1.7	10.26	2.45	7.41	5.97	★	★	5.3	343-2898	617-621-6100	4.75	0.29	None	Daniel A Rabasco	'94
KEYSTONE AM TXFR TX; B	Texas Muni	2.1	10.14	2.15	6.65	★	★	★	5.1	343-2898	617-621-6100	None	1.47	3.00	Daniel A Rabasco	'94
KEYSTONE AM TXFR TX; C	Texas Muni	0.3	10.13	2.26	6.81	★	★	★	5.0	343-2898	617-621-6100	None	1.84	1.00	Daniel A Rabasco	'88
KEYSTONE TAX EXEMPT TR	General Muni	713.0	10.50	2.10	7.58	5.03	6.67	★	5.5	343-2898	617-621-6100	4.00	1.65	4.00	Betsy Blacher	'88
KEYSTONE TAX FREE FUND	General Muni	1,251.0	7.54	2.28	7.63	5.16	6.87	8.15	5.6	343-2898	617-621-6100	4.00	1.55	4.00	Betsy Blacher	'88
KIDDER INV II MUNI; A	General Muni	9.7	11.11	1.30	8.42	★	★	★	5.5	647-1568	None	2.25	None	None	Gregory Serbe	'94
KIDDER INV II MUNI; B	General Muni	3.8	11.11	1.30	7.90	★	★	★	5.0	647-1568	None	None	None	None	Gregory Serbe	'94
KIDDER INV II MUNI; C	General Muni	0.4	11.11	1.30	8.48	★	★	★	5.6	647-1568	None	None	None	None	Gregory Serbe	'94
KIEWIT TAX-EX	General Muni	135.4	2.02	2.15	*	*	*	*	0.0	254-3948	None	None	None	None	P. Gregory Williams	'95
LANDMRK TXFR NY INC; A	New York Muni	90.4	10.75	2.44	8.07	5.62	7.44	★	5.7	223-4447	212-564-3456	4.00	0.80	None	Carla Wracklage	'95
LEAHI TR TAX FREE INCOME	Hawaii Muni	44.3	13.62	2.74	7.66	6.49	7.75	★	5.2	None	808-522-7777	None	0.85	None	Leahi Management Co.	'87
LEBENTHAL NY MUNI	New York Muni	91.6	7.71	3.47	10.30	6.87	★	★	5.6	221-5822	212-425-6116	4.50	0.64	None	James L. Gammon	'94
LEGG MASON TX-FR PA	Pennsylvania Muni	65.8	16.16	2.22	8.51	7.24	★	★	5.3	822-5544	410-539-0000	2.75	0.40	None	Victoria M. Schwatka	'91
LEGG MASON TX-FR INTMDT	Intermediate Muni	49.9	15.24	2.36	7.24	6.97	★	★	4.7	822-5544	410-539-0000	2.00	0.30	None	Victoria M. Schwatka	'92
LEGG MASON TX-FR MD	Maryland Muni	146.3	16.01	2.23	8.03	★	★	★	5.2	822-5544	410-539-0000	2.75	0.46	None	Victoria M. Schwatka	'91
LIBERTY MUNI SECS; A	General Muni	711.0	10.98	2.08	7.30	5.96	7.64	8.74	6.1	245-4770	412-288-1900	4.50	0.84	None	Jonathan C. Conley	'76
LIBERTY MUNI SECS; B	General Muni	24.6	10.98	1.86	6.36	★	★	★	0.0	245-4770	412-288-1900	None	None	5.50	Jonathan C. Conley	'94
LIBERTY MUNI SECS; C	General Muni	22.0	10.98	1.86	8.21	★	★	★	5.2	245-4770	412-288-1900	None	1.80	1.00	Jonathan C. Conley	'93
LINCOLN ADV TXFR INC; A	General Muni	10.6	9.54	2.15	7.56	★	★	★	4.3	923-8476	219-455-3361	4.50	None	None	Team Managed	N/A
LINCOLN ADV TXFR INC; B	General Muni	0.1	10.11	1.87	*	★	★	★	5.5	923-8476	219-455-3361	None	None	5.00	Team Managed	N/A
LINCOLN ADV TXFR INC; C	General Muni	0.1	9.91	1.92	*	*	★	★	0.0	923-8476	219-455-3361	None	None	1.00	Team Managed	N/A
LOOMIS SAYLES MUNI	General Muni	7.6	11.03	1.83	7.30	★	★	★	4.7	633-3330	617-482-2450	4.75	1.00	None	Martha F. Hodgman	'93
LORD ABBETT CA TX-FR INC	California Muni	310.7	10.36	2.21	6.66	6.30	7.67	★	5.8	426-1130	212-848-1800	None	0.66	1.00	Dow/Grummel	'85/'91
LORD ABBETT SEC CA TF	California Muni	20.6	4.46	1.99	6.11	5.31	★	★	5.7	426-1130	212-848-1800	4.75	0.99	1.00	Barbara Grummel	'93
LORD ABBETT SEC FL TF	Florida Muni	10.1	4.51	2.20	6.71	★	★	★	5.6	426-1130	212-848-1800	4.75	0.89	1.00	Barbara Grummel	'93
LORD ABBETT SEC NATL	General Muni	42.3	4.62	2.46	8.09	★	★	★	5.8	426-1130	212-848-1800	None	0.91	1.00	Mousseau/Dow	'93/'93
LORD ABBETT SEC NY TF	New York Muni	8.9	4.59	2.39	7.86	★	★	★	5.6	426-1130	212-848-1800	None	0.84	1.00	Barbara Grummel	'91/'91
LORD ABBETT TX-FR CT	Connecticut Muni	112.9	10.01	2.25	8.31	6.37	★	★	5.8	426-1130	212-848-1800	4.75	0.49	None	Dow/Fang	'91/'91
LORD ABBETT TX-FR FL	Florida Muni	182.0	4.77	2.24	8.15	6.33	★	★	5.6	426-1130	212-848-1800	4.75	0.32	None	Dow/Grummel	'94
LORD ABBETT TX-FR GA	Georgia Muni	3.4	5.02	2.30	*	*	*	*	0.0	426-1130	212-848-1800	4.75	None	None	Barbara Grummel	'94

FUND NAME	OBJECTIVE	ASSETS ($ MIL) 5/31/95	NAV ($/SHR) 6/30/95	QTR	1YR	3YRS	5YRS	10YRS	DIV YLD %	PHONE 800	PHONE In-State	Load	Exp. Ratio	Redemption	MANAGER	SINCE
LORD ABBETT TX-FR HI	Hawaii Muni	87.8	4.88	2.67	8.58	6.46	☆	☆	5.8	426-1130	212-848-1800	4.75	0.41	None	Dow/Fang	'91/'91
LORD ABBETT TX-FR MI	Michigan Muni	52.3	4.84	2.48	8.68	☆	☆	☆	5.9	426-1130	212-848-1800	4.75	0.34	None	Dow/Fang	'92/'92
LORD ABBETT TX-FR MN	Minnesota Muni	3.1	4.97	2.75	☆	☆	☆	☆	0.0	426-1130	212-848-1800	4.75	None	None	Barbara Grummel	'94
LORD ABBETT TX-FR MO	Missouri Muni	130.7	5.04	2.41	7.69	6.04	☆	☆	5.7	426-1130	212-848-1800	4.75	0.60	None	Dow/Grummel	'91/'91
LORD ABBETT TX-FR NATL	General Muni	665.2	10.86	1.62	7.45	5.70	7.67	8.97	5.9	426-1130	212-848-1800	4.75	0.86	None	Dow/Mousseau	'84/'91
LORD ABBETT TX-FR NJ	New Jersey Muni	194.0	5.10	2.21	7.92	6.90	☆	☆	5.7	426-1130	212-848-1800	4.75	0.51	None	Dow/Mousseau	'90/'91
LORD ABBETT TX-FR NY	New York Muni	339.3	10.79	2.56	7.01	5.38	7.58	8.64	5.8	426-1130	212-848-1800	4.75	0.83	None	Dow/Grummel	'84/'91
LORD ABBETT TX-FR PA	Pennsylvania Muni	91.9	4.94	2.70	8.80	6.90	☆	☆	5.8	426-1130	212-848-1800	4.75	0.33	None	Dow/Fang	'92/'92
LORD ABBETT TX-FR TX	Texas Muni	102.9	9.92	1.93	8.63	6.09	8.20	☆	5.8	426-1130	212-848-1800	4.75	0.50	None	Dow/Grummel	'87/'91
LORD ABBETT TX-FR WA	Washington Muni	74.5	4.85	2.32	8.24	6.21	☆	☆	5.9	426-1130	212-848-1800	4.75	0.29	None	Dow/Mousseau	'92/'92
LTD TM TXEX BOND OF AMER	Intermediate Muni	190.9	14.23	2.81	6.67	☆	☆	☆	4.8	421-4120	714-671-7000	4.75	0.51	None	Multiple Managers	N/A
LUTHERAN BRO MUNI BOND ☒	General Muni	632.1	8.36	2.09	8.76	6.62	8.15	9.11	5.5	328-4552	612-339-8091	5.00	0.75	None	Janet Grangaard	'94
MACKENZIE CA MUNI; A	California Muni	38.5	10.08	2.29	7.47	5.89	7.19	☆	5.4	456-5111	None	4.75	1.10	None	Team Managed	N/A
MACKENZIE FL LTD TM; A	Florida Muni	4.5	10.16	2.67	6.97	☆	☆	☆	5.3	456-5111	None	3.00	None	None	Team Managed	N/A
MACKENZIE FL LTD TM; B	Florida Muni	2.3	10.16	2.55	6.38	☆	☆	☆	4.7	456-5111	None	None	None	3.00	Team Managed	N/A
MACKENZIE LTD MUNI; A	Intermediate Muni	117.3	10.11	2.37	6.42	4.95	☆	☆	5.2	456-5111	None	3.00	0.88	None	Team Managed	N/A
MACKENZIE NATL MUNI; A	General Muni	30.9	9.76	2.69	7.54	5.86	7.17	☆	5.5	456-5111	None	4.75	1.10	None	Team Managed	N/A
MACKENZIE NY MUNI; A	New York Muni	41.6	9.72	2.91	8.26	6.23	7.66	☆	5.5	456-5111	None	4.75	1.10	None	Team Managed	N/A
MAINSTAY CA; A	California Muni	17.5	9.51	1.36	5.94	6.17	☆	☆	5.4	522-4202	None	4.50	0.99	None	Team Managed	N/A
MAINSTAY CA; B	California Muni	0.7	9.50	1.19	☆	☆	☆	☆	0.0	522-4202	None	None	None	5.00	Team Managed	N/A
MAINSTAY NY; A	New York Muni	17.7	9.62	1.90	6.60	6.16	☆	☆	5.5	522-4202	None	4.50	0.99	None	Team Managed	N/A
MAINSTAY NY; B	New York Muni	0.2	9.62	1.84	☆	☆	☆	☆	0.0	522-4202	None	None	None	5.00	Team Managed	N/A
MAINSTAY TAX FREE BD; A	General Muni	7.5	9.64	1.27	☆	☆	☆	☆	0.0	522-4202	None	4.50	None	5.00	Team Managed	N/A
MAINSTAY TAX FREE BD; B	General Muni	534.0	9.65	1.31	5.75	5.11	6.79	☆	5.2	522-4202	None	None	1.20	None	Team Managed	N/A
MANAGERS MUNI BOND	General Muni	6.3	22.70	1.81	7.33	5.43	6.85	7.99	5.6	835-3879	203-857-5321	None	1.12	None	Multiple Managers	N/A
MANAGERS SHORT MUNI	Short-Term Muni	1.2	19.56	0.72	2.33	2.85	3.76	4.47	2.9	835-3879	203-857-5321	None	1.47	None	Multiple Managers	'90
MARINER NY TAX FREE BD	New York Muni	52.9	10.68	2.35	4.92	5.84	7.87	☆	5.1	634-2536	None	4.75	0.84	None	Lucia Dunbar	N/A
MARKETWATCH VA MUNI	Virginia Muni	44.0	9.85	1.67	5.85	☆	☆	☆	4.0	232-9091	None	4.50	1.04	None	Team Managed	N/A
MARQUIS LA TXFR INC; A	Louisiana Muni	11.3	9.63	1.76	6.79	☆	☆	☆	4.4	462-9511	None	3.50	0.99	None	Kevin Reed	'93
MARQUIS LA TXFR INC; B	Louisiana Muni	0.6	9.64	1.57	6.00	☆	☆	☆	3.6	462-9511	None	None	None	3.50	Kevin Reed	'93
MARSHALL INTMDT TX FR	Intermediate Muni	43.9	9.79	1.83	5.96	☆	☆	☆	4.2	236-8560	414-287-8500	None	0.62	None	John D. Boritzke	'94
MARSHALL SHRT TAX FREE	Short-Term Muni	20.1	9.99	1.54	4.87	☆	☆	☆	3.8	236-8560	414-287-8500	None	0.52	None	John D. Boritzke	'94
MAS MUNICIPAL	General Muni	43.7	10.41	-0.49	8.98	☆	☆	☆	5.6	354-8185	610-940-5000	None	0.50	None	Team Managed	N/A
MAS PA MUNICIPAL	Pennsylvania Muni	15.4	10.52	0.08	9.40	☆	☆	☆	5.8	354-8185	610-940-5000	None	0.50	None	Team Managed	N/A
MENTOR MUNI INC; A	General Muni	21.4	14.83	2.24	8.04	6.64	☆	☆	5.5	382-0016	None	4.75	1.24	None	William Grady	'93
MENTOR MUNI INC; B	General Muni	41.0	14.86	2.11	7.50	6.14	☆	☆	4.9	382-0016	None	None	1.74	1.00	William Grady	'93
MERRILL CA MUNI BOND; A ☒	California Muni	50.8	11.33	1.83	7.68	6.26	7.55	☆	5.8	None	609-282-2800	4.00	0.62	None	Walter O'Connor	'91
MERRILL CA MUNI BOND; B	California Muni	650.5	11.33	1.71	7.14	5.70	7.00	☆	5.3	None	609-282-2800	None	1.13	4.00	Walter O'Connor	'91
MERRILL CA MUNI BOND; C	California Muni	2.8	11.33	1.68	☆	☆	☆	☆	0.0	None	609-282-2800	None	None	1.00	Walter O'Connor	'94
MERRILL CA MUNI BOND; D	California Muni	3.4	11.33	1.80	☆	☆	☆	☆	0.0	None	609-282-2800	4.00	None	None	Walter O'Connor	'94
MERRILL CA MUNI INS; A ☒	California Muni	14.7	9.56	1.74	7.76	☆	☆	☆	5.5	None	609-282-2800	4.00	0.33	None	Walter O'Connor	'93
MERRILL CA MUNI INS; B	California Muni	73.2	9.56	1.61	7.21	☆	☆	☆	5.0	None	609-282-2800	None	0.83	4.00	Walter O'Connor	'93
MERRILL CA MUNI INS; C	California Muni	1.3	9.55	1.59	☆	☆	☆	☆	0.0	None	609-282-2800	None	None	1.00	Walter O'Connor	'94
MERRILL CA MUNI INS; D	California Muni	1.1	9.57	1.71	☆	☆	☆	☆	0.0	None	609-282-2800	4.00	None	None	Walter O'Connor	'94
MERRILL MULTI LTD AZ; A ☒	Single State Muni	1.0	10.12	1.71	6.28	☆	☆	☆	4.2	None	609-282-2800	1.00	None	None	Helen Marie Sheehan	'93

Fund	Objective	Net Assets	NAV			★		★	Yield		Telephone	Load	Fee	Redemp	Manager	Yr
MERRILL MULTI LTD AZ; B	Single State Muni	5.2	10.12	1.62	5.90	★	★	★	3.9	None	609-282-2800	None	None	1.00	Helen Marie Sheehan	'93
MERRILL MULTI LTD AZ; C	Single State Muni	0.1	10.12	1.55	★	★	★	★	0.0	None	609-282-2800	None	None	1.00	Helen Marie Sheehan	'94
MERRILL MULTI LTD AZ; D	Single State Muni	0.1	10.12	1.68	★	★	★	★	0.0	None	609-282-2800	None	None	None	Helen Marie Sheehan	'94
MERRILL MULTI LTD CA; A ⊠	California Muni	3.4	9.95	1.92	5.74	★	★	★	4.3	None	609-282-2800	1.00	None	None	Edward Andrews	'93
MERRILL MULTI LTD CA; B	California Muni	10.2	9.95	1.83	5.37	★	★	★	4.0	None	609-282-2800	None	None	1.00	Edward Andrews	'93
MERRILL MULTI LTD CA; C	California Muni	0.1	9.95	1.87	★	★	★	★	0.0	None	609-282-2800	None	None	1.00	Edward Andrews	'94
MERRILL MULTI LTD CA; D	California Muni	1.7	9.95	1.90	★	★	★	★	0.0	None	609-282-2800	None	None	None	Edward Andrews	'94
MERRILL MULTI LTD FL; A ⊠	Single State Muni	10.7	9.97	2.13	5.97	★	★	★	4.3	None	609-282-2800	1.00	None	None	Edward Andrews	'93
MERRILL MULTI LTD FL; B	Single State Muni	16.7	9.97	2.04	5.60	★	★	★	4.0	None	609-282-2800	None	None	1.00	Edward Andrews	'93
MERRILL MULTI LTD FL; C	Single State Muni	0.1	9.96	1.88	★	★	★	★	0.0	None	609-282-2800	None	None	1.00	Edward Andrews	'94
MERRILL MULTI LTD FL; D	Single State Muni	2.2	9.96	2.00	★	★	★	★	0.0	None	609-282-2800	None	None	None	Edward Andrews	'94
MERRILL MULTI LTD MA; A ⊠	Single State Muni	4.2	9.92	2.13	4.61	★	★	★	4.5	None	609-282-2800	1.00	None	None	Peter Hayes	'93
MERRILL MULTI LTD MA; B	Single State Muni	4.8	9.92	1.04	4.23	★	★	★	4.1	None	609-282-2800	None	None	1.00	Peter Hayes	'93
MERRILL MULTI LTD MA; C	Single State Muni	0.4	9.92	1.21	★	★	★	★	0.0	None	609-282-2800	None	None	1.00	Peter Hayes	'94
MERRILL MULTI LTD MA; D	Single State Muni	0.2	9.92	1.21	★	★	★	★	0.0	None	609-282-2800	None	None	None	Peter Hayes	'94
MERRILL MULTI LTD MI; A ⊠	Single State Muni	2.4	9.92	1.76	5.28	★	★	★	4.4	None	609-282-2800	1.00	None	None	Edward Andrews	'94
MERRILL MULTI LTD MI; B	Single State Muni	2.4	9.92	1.66	4.90	★	★	★	4.0	None	609-282-2800	None	None	1.00	Edward Andrews	'93
MERRILL MULTI LTD MI; C	Single State Muni	0.1	9.94	1.81	★	★	★	★	0.0	None	609-282-2800	None	None	1.00	Edward Andrews	'93
MERRILL MULTI LTD MI; D	Single State Muni	0.2	9.93	1.94	★	★	★	★	0.0	None	609-282-2800	None	None	None	Edward Andrews	'94
MERRILL MULTI LTD NJ; A ⊠	Single State Muni	2.3	10.10	2.01	6.37	★	★	★	4.1	None	609-282-2800	1.00	None	None	Helen Marie Sheehan	'93
MERRILL MULTI LTD NJ; B	Single State Muni	7.1	10.10	1.92	5.99	★	★	★	3.8	None	609-282-2800	None	None	1.00	Helen Marie Sheehan	'94
MERRILL MULTI LTD NJ; C	Single State Muni	0.1	9.15	1.92	★	★	★	★	0.0	None	609-282-2800	None	None	1.00	Helen Marie Sheehan	'93
MERRILL MULTI LTD NJ; D	Single State Muni	0.3	10.10	1.98	★	★	★	★	0.0	None	609-282-2800	None	None	None	Edward Andrews	'93
MERRILL MULTI LTD NY; A ⊠	Single State Muni	4.9	10.02	2.27	6.15	★	★	★	4.4	None	609-282-2800	1.00	None	None	Edward Andrews	'94
MERRILL MULTI LTD NY; B	Single State Muni	8.7	10.02	2.18	5.77	★	★	★	4.0	None	609-282-2800	None	None	1.00	Edward Andrews	'94
MERRILL MULTI LTD NY; C	Single State Muni	0.1	10.01	2.03	★	★	★	★	0.0	None	609-282-2800	None	None	1.00	Edward Andrews	'93
MERRILL MULTI LTD NY; D	Single State Muni	0.9	10.02	2.24	★	★	★	★	0.0	None	609-282-2800	None	None	None	Edward Andrews	'93
MERRILL MULTI LTD PA; A ⊠	Single State Muni	1.1	10.06	1.92	5.90	★	★	★	4.2	None	609-282-2800	1.00	None	None	Helen Marie Sheehan	'94
MERRILL MULTI LTD PA; B	Single State Muni	7.6	10.06	1.83	5.53	★	★	★	3.8	None	609-282-2800	None	None	1.00	Helen Marie Sheehan	'94
MERRILL MULTI LTD PA; C	Single State Muni	0.1	10.06	1.78	★	★	★	★	0.0	None	609-282-2800	None	None	1.00	Helen Marie Sheehan	'93
MERRILL MULTI LTD PA; D	Single State Muni	0.3	10.06	1.90	★	★	★	★	0.0	None	609-282-2800	None	None	None	Helen Marie Sheehan	'94
MERRILL MUN AR; A ⊠	Single State Muni	2.2	10.27	2.71	★	★	★	★	0.0	None	609-282-2800	4.00	None	None	Vincent Giordano	'94
MERRILL MUN AR; B	Single State Muni	7.9	10.27	2.58	★	★	★	★	0.0	None	609-282-2800	None	None	4.00	Vincent Giordano	'91
MERRILL MUN AR; C	Single State Muni	0.4	10.27	2.55	★	★	★	★	0.0	None	609-282-2800	None	None	4.00	Vincent Giordano	'94
MERRILL MUN AR; D	Single State Muni	0.6	10.27	2.68	★	★	★	★	0.0	None	609-282-2800	None	None	None	Vincent Giordano	'94
MERRILL MUN AZ; A ⊠	Arizona Muni	16.1	10.40	1.69	7.87	★	6.92	★	5.4	None	609-282-2800	4.00	0.56	None	Walter O'Connor	'93
MERRILL MUN AZ; B	Arizona Muni	74.4	10.40	1.57	7.32	★	6.39	★	4.9	None	609-282-2800	None	1.07	4.00	Walter O'Connor	'93
MERRILL MUN AZ; C	Arizona Muni	0.5	10.39	1.54	★	★	★	★	0.0	None	609-282-2800	None	None	4.00	Walter O'Connor	'94
MERRILL MUN AZ; D	Arizona Muni	0.6	10.39	1.67	★	★	★	★	0.0	None	609-282-2800	None	None	None	Walter O'Connor	'93
MERRILL MUN CO; A ⊠	Colorado Muni	10.0	9.35	2.28	7.39	★	★	★	5.6	None	609-282-2800	4.00	0.54	None	Hugh Hurley	'93
MERRILL MUN CO; B	Colorado Muni	16.9	9.35	2.15	6.84	★	★	★	5.1	None	609-282-2800	None	0.03	4.00	Hugh Hurley	'94
MERRILL MUN CO; C	Colorado Muni	0.1	9.35	2.12	★	★	★	★	0.0	None	609-282-2800	None	None	4.00	Hugh Hurley	'94
MERRILL MUN CO; D	Colorado Muni	1.3	9.34	2.26	★	★	★	★	0.0	None	609-282-2800	None	None	None	Hugh Hurley	'94
MERRILL MUN CT; A ⊠	Connecticut Muni	8.1	10.22	2.28	★	★	★	★	5.9	None	609-282-2800	4.00	None	None	Vincent Giordano	'93
MERRILL MUN CT; B	Connecticut Muni	29.4	10.22	2.15	★	★	★	★	5.4	None	609-282-2800	None	None	4.00	Vincent Giordano	'94
MERRILL MUN CT; C	Connecticut Muni	0.8	10.22	2.03	★	★	★	★	0.0	None	609-282-2800	None	None	4.00	Vincent Giordano	'94
MERRILL MUN CT; D	Connecticut Muni	1.1	10.22	2.26	★	★	★	★	0.0	None	609-282-2800	None	None	None	Vincent Giordano	'93
MERRILL MUN FL; A ⊠	Florida Muni	57.5	9.87	1.88	7.26	★	5.71	★	5.5	None	609-282-2800	4.00	0.68	None	Michael Rubashkin	'94
MERRILL MUN FL; B	Florida Muni	215.8	9.87	1.75	6.71	★	5.14	★	5.0	None	609-282-2800	None	1.18	4.00	Michael Rubashkin	'93
MERRILL MUN FL; C	Florida Muni	1.6	9.86	1.83	★	★	★	★	0.0	None	609-282-2800	None	None	4.00	Michael Rubashkin	'94

PERFORMANCE OF MUTUAL FUNDS (continued)

FUND NAME	OBJECTIVE	ASSETS ($ MIL) 5/31/95	NAV ($/SHR) 6/30/95	QTR	1YR	3YRS	5YRS	10YRS	DIV YLD %	800	In-State	Load	Exp. Ratio	Redemption	MANAGER	SINCE
MERRILL MULTI MUN FL; D	Florida Muni	8.3	9.86	1.96	☆	☆	☆	☆	0.0	None	609-282-2800	4.00	None	None	Michael Rubashkin	'94
MERRILL MULTI MUN MA; A ☒	Massachusetts Muni	7.4	10.45	1.51	7.35	6.78	☆	☆	5.4	None	609-282-2800	4.00	0.62	None	Roberto Roffo	'93
MERRILL MULTI MUN MA; B	Massachusetts Muni	70.4	10.45	1.38	6.81	6.24	☆	☆	4.9	None	609-282-2800	None	1.12	4.00	Roberto Roffo	'93
MERRILL MULTI MUN MA; C	Massachusetts Muni	0.4	10.45	1.35	☆	☆	☆	☆	0.0	None	609-282-2800	None	None	1.00	Roberto Roffo	'94
MERRILL MULTI MUN MA; D	Massachusetts Muni	0.7	10.45	1.48	☆	☆	☆	☆	0.0	None	609-282-2800	4.00	None	None	Roberto Roffo	'94
MERRILL MULTI MUN MD; A ☒	Maryland Muni	1.5	9.13	2.09	7.06	☆	☆	☆	5.7	None	609-282-2800	4.00	0.03	None	Michael Rubashkin	'93
MERRILL MULTI MUN MD; B	Maryland Muni	17.8	9.13	1.96	6.51	☆	☆	☆	5.2	None	609-282-2800	None	0.53	4.00	Michael Rubashkin	'93
MERRILL MULTI MUN MD; C	Maryland Muni	0.7	9.13	1.94	☆	☆	☆	☆	0.0	None	609-282-2800	None	None	1.00	Michael Rubashkin	'94
MERRILL MULTI MUN MD; D	Maryland Muni	0.5	9.13	2.07	☆	☆	☆	☆	0.0	None	609-282-2800	4.00	None	None	Michael Rubashkin	'94
MERRILL MULTI MUN MI; A ☒	Michigan Muni	12.7	9.84	1.57	7.57	☆	☆	☆	5.4	None	609-282-2800	4.00	0.31	None	Fred Stuebe	'93
MERRILL MULTI MUN MI; B	Michigan Muni	62.5	9.84	1.45	7.02	☆	☆	☆	4.9	None	609-282-2800	None	0.81	4.00	Fred Stuebe	'93
MERRILL MULTI MUN MI; C	Michigan Muni	0.9	9.84	1.42	☆	☆	☆	☆	0.0	None	609-282-2800	None	None	1.00	Fred Stuebe	'94
MERRILL MULTI MUN MI; D	Michigan Muni	0.9	9.83	1.45	☆	☆	☆	☆	0.0	None	609-282-2800	4.00	None	None	Fred Stuebe	'94
MERRILL MULTI MUN MN; A ☒	Minnesota Muni	7.0	10.31	2.11	6.94	6.52	☆	☆	5.4	None	609-282-2800	4.00	0.69	None	Hugh Hurley	'93
MERRILL MULTI MUN MN; B	Minnesota Muni	53.8	10.31	1.98	6.40	5.99	☆	☆	4.9	None	609-282-2800	None	1.21	4.00	Hugh Hurley	'93
MERRILL MULTI MUN MN; C	Minnesota Muni	0.4	10.31	1.96	☆	☆	☆	☆	0.0	None	609-282-2800	None	None	1.00	Hugh Hurley	'94
MERRILL MULTI MUN MN; D	Minnesota Muni	0.6	10.31	2.09	☆	☆	☆	☆	0.0	None	609-282-2800	4.00	None	None	Hugh Hurley	'94
MERRILL MULTI MUN NC; A ☒	North Carolina Muni	9.7	10.26	1.80	8.37	☆	☆	☆	5.3	None	609-282-2800	4.00	0.50	None	Hugh Hurley	'93
MERRILL MULTI MUN NC; B	North Carolina Muni	52.0	10.26	1.67	7.81	☆	☆	☆	4.8	None	609-282-2800	None	1.01	4.00	Hugh Hurley	'93
MERRILL MULTI MUN NC; C	North Carolina Muni	0.4	10.26	1.65	☆	☆	☆	☆	0.0	None	609-282-2800	None	None	1.00	Hugh Hurley	'94
MERRILL MULTI MUN NC; D	North Carolina Muni	1.1	10.27	1.88	☆	☆	☆	☆	0.0	None	609-282-2800	4.00	None	None	Hugh Hurley	'94
MERRILL MULTI MUN NJ; A ☒	New Jersey Muni	41.2	10.69	2.50	7.77	☆	5.75	☆	5.5	None	609-282-2800	4.00	0.69	None	Mike Petty	'93
MERRILL MULTI MUN NJ; B	New Jersey Muni	167.7	10.69	2.28	7.22	☆	5.20	☆	5.0	None	609-282-2800	None	1.20	4.00	Mike Petty	'93
MERRILL MULTI MUN NJ; C	New Jersey Muni	1.2	10.69	2.25	☆	☆	☆	☆	0.0	None	609-282-2800	None	None	1.00	Mike Petty	'94
MERRILL MULTI MUN NJ; D	New Jersey Muni	2.1	10.69	2.38	☆	☆	☆	☆	0.0	None	609-282-2800	4.00	None	None	Mike Petty	'94
MERRILL MULTI MUN NM; A ☒	Single State Muni	8.1	10.30	2.15	8.04	☆	☆	☆	5.8	None	609-282-2800	4.00	None	None	Vincent Giordano	'93
MERRILL MULTI MUN NM; B	Single State Muni	11.5	10.30	2.02	7.49	☆	☆	☆	5.3	None	609-282-2800	None	None	4.00	Vincent Giordano	'93
MERRILL MULTI MUN NM; C	Single State Muni	0.1	10.30	1.99	☆	☆	☆	☆	0.0	None	609-282-2800	None	None	1.00	Vincent Giordano	'94
MERRILL MULTI MUN NM; D	Single State Muni	1.4	10.31	2.22	☆	☆	☆	☆	0.0	None	609-282-2800	4.00	None	None	Vincent Giordano	'94
MERRILL MULTI MUN NY; A ☒	New York Muni	23.7	10.95	1.36	5.32	5.15	7.46	☆	5.7	None	609-282-2800	4.00	0.63	None	Michael Rubashkin	'93
MERRILL MULTI MUN NY; B	New York Muni	595.0	10.95	1.24	4.69	4.57	6.88	☆	5.2	None	609-282-2800	None	1.14	4.00	Michael Rubashkin	'93
MERRILL MULTI MUN NY; C	New York Muni	2.5	10.95	1.12	☆	☆	☆	☆	0.0	None	609-282-2800	None	None	1.00	Michael Rubashkin	'94
MERRILL MULTI MUN NY; D	New York Muni	1.7	10.95	1.34	☆	☆	☆	☆	0.0	None	609-282-2800	4.00	None	None	Michael Rubashkin	'94
MERRILL MULTI MUN OH; A ☒	Ohio Muni	7.5	10.51	1.78	7.20	6.65	☆	☆	5.2	None	609-282-2800	4.00	0.65	None	Hugh Hurley	'93
MERRILL MULTI MUN OH; B	Ohio Muni	66.0	10.51	1.65	6.66	6.14	☆	☆	4.7	None	609-282-2800	None	1.16	4.00	Hugh Hurley	'93
MERRILL MULTI MUN OH; C	Ohio Muni	0.7	10.51	1.63	☆	☆	☆	☆	0.0	None	609-282-2800	None	None	1.00	Hugh Hurley	'94
MERRILL MULTI MUN OH; D	Ohio Muni	3.2	10.51	1.85	☆	☆	☆	☆	0.0	None	609-282-2800	4.00	None	None	Hugh Hurley	'94
MERRILL MULTI MUN OR; A ☒	Oregon Muni	4.4	9.35	1.85	6.98	☆	☆	☆	5.5	None	609-282-2800	4.00	0.08	None	Michael Rubashkin	'93
MERRILL MULTI MUN OR; B	Oregon Muni	26.9	9.35	1.72	6.44	☆	☆	☆	5.0	None	609-282-2800	None	0.58	4.00	Michael Rubashkin	'93
MERRILL MULTI MUN OR; C	Oregon Muni	0.7	9.35	1.59	☆	☆	☆	☆	0.0	None	609-282-2800	None	None	1.00	Michael Rubashkin	'94
MERRILL MULTI MUN OR; D	Oregon Muni	0.2	9.36	1.93	☆	☆	☆	☆	0.0	None	609-282-2800	4.00	None	None	Michael Rubashkin	'94
MERRILL MULTI MUN PA; A ☒	Pennsylvania Muni	24.3	11.08	2.79	8.25	7.07	☆	☆	5.6	None	609-282-2800	4.00	0.75	None	Mike Petty	'90
MERRILL MULTI MUN PA; B	Pennsylvania Muni	126.8	11.08	2.66	7.70	6.53	☆	☆	5.1	None	609-282-2800	None	1.25	4.00	Mike Petty	'93
MERRILL MULTI MUN PA; C	Pennsylvania Muni	1.7	11.08	2.63	☆	☆	☆	☆	0.0	None	609-282-2800	None	None	1.00	Mike Petty	'94
MERRILL MULTI MUN PA; D	Pennsylvania Muni	2.5	11.09	2.76	☆	☆	☆	☆	0.0	None	609-282-2800	4.00	None	None	Mike Petty	'94

Fund	Category	Assets ($M)	NAV	Col1	Ret	5-Yr	Rating	Yield %	Local	Toll Phone	Max Load	12b-1	CDSC	Manager	Yr
MERRILL MULTI MUN TX; A ⊠	Texas Muni	11.8	10.57	2.04	8.00	7.07	☆☆☆	5.6	None	609-282-2800	4.00	0.67	None	Roberto Roffo	93
MERRILL MULTI MUN TX; B	Texas Muni	74.7	10.57	1.91	7.45	6.53	☆☆☆	5.1	None	609-282-2800	None	1.17	4.00	Roberto Roffo	93
MERRILL MULTI MUN TX; C	Texas Muni	0.4	10.57	1.88	☆	☆	☆☆	0.0	None	609-282-2800	None	None	1.00	Roberto Roffo	94
MERRILL MULTI MUN TX; D	Texas Muni	0.8	10.59	2.21	☆	☆	☆☆	0.0	None	609-282-2800	4.00	None	None	Vincent Giordano	94
MERRILL MUNI SRS INT; A ⊠	Intermediate Muni	25.5	9.82	1.47	5.31	5.80	7.02	5.4	None	609-282-2800	1.00	0.76	None	Vincent Giordano	88
MERRILL MUNI SRS INT; B	Intermediate Muni	126.2	9.82	1.40	4.98	5.48	6.69	5.1	None	609-282-2800	None	1.07	4.00	Vincent Giordano	88
MERRILL MUNI SRS INT; C	Intermediate Muni	0.1	9.82	1.41	☆	☆	☆	0.0	None	609-282-2800	None	1.00	1.00	Vincent Giordano	94
MERRILL MUNI SRS INT; D	Intermediate Muni	2.8	9.82	1.45	☆	☆	☆	0.0	None	609-282-2800	1.00	None	None	Ken Jacob	94
MERRILL MUNI INS; A ⊠	Insured Muni	1,762.1	7.92	2.05	8.55	6.49	8.06	5.7	None	609-282-2800	4.00	0.42	None	Ken Jacob	84
MERRILL MUNI INS; B	Insured Muni	806.3	7.92	1.86	7.87	5.69	7.24	4.9	None	609-282-2800	None	1.17	4.00	Ken Jacob	88
MERRILL MUNI INS; C	Insured Muni	6.1	7.92	1.85	☆	☆	☆	0.0	None	609-282-2800	None	None	1.00	Ken Jacob	94
MERRILL MUNI INS; D	Insured Muni	27.3	7.92	1.86	☆	☆	☆	0.0	None	609-282-2800	4.00	0.40	None	Ken Jacob	94
MERRILL MUNI LTD MAT; A	Short-Term Muni	551.2	9.92	1.68	4.48	4.00	5.07	3.9	None	609-282-2800	1.00	0.76	None	Peter Hayes	89
MERRILL MUNI LTD MAT; B	Short-Term Muni	128.9	9.92	1.58	4.10	☆	☆	3.5	None	609-282-2800	None	None	4.00	Peter Hayes	92
MERRILL MUNI LTD MAT; C	Short-Term Muni	3.1	9.92	1.71	☆	☆	☆	0.0	None	609-282-2800	None	0.55	1.00	Peter Hayes	94
MERRILL MUNI LTD MAT; D	Short-Term Muni	9.7	9.93	1.75	☆	☆	☆	0.0	None	609-282-2800	1.00	1.30	None	Peter Hayes	94
MERRILL MUNI NATL; A ⊠	General Muni	1,085.1	10.02	2.61	7.96	6.40	8.02	5.9	None	609-282-2800	4.00	None	None	Ken Jacob	84
MERRILL MUNI NATL; B	General Muni	427.9	10.02	2.41	7.25	5.64	7.23	5.2	None	609-282-2800	None	None	4.00	Ken Jacob	88
MERRILL MUNI NATL; C	General Muni	4.6	10.03	2.50	☆	☆	☆	0.0	None	609-282-2800	None	1.15	1.00	Ken Jacob	94
MERRILL MUNI NATL; D	General Muni	21.1	10.03	2.64	☆	☆	8.05	0.0	None	609-282-2800	4.00	1.97	None	Ken Jacob	94
MFS AL MUNI BOND; A	Alabama Muni	85.5	10.43	2.20	7.38	6.34	☆	5.3	637-2929	617-954-5000	4.75	0.75	None	David King	94
MFS AL MUNI BOND; B	Alabama Muni	4.6	10.43	1.99	6.50	☆	☆	4.5	637-2929	617-954-5000	None	1.84	4.00	David King	94
MFS AR MUNI BOND; A	Single State Muni	189.4	9.64	1.11	5.11	5.88	☆	5.5	637-2929	617-954-5000	4.75	0.69	None	David King	94
MFS AR MUNI BOND; A	Single State Muni	7.4	9.64	1.06	4.22	☆	☆	4.5	637-2929	617-954-5000	None	1.76	4.00	David King	93
MFS CA MUNI BOND; A	California Muni	275.8	5.44	2.00	6.99	5.87	8.00	5.7	637-2929	617-954-5000	4.75	1.69	None	David Smith	93
MFS CA MUNI BOND; B	California Muni	31.2	5.44	1.81	5.75	5.75	☆	4.8	637-2929	617-954-5000	None	0.60	4.00	David Smith	93
MFS CA MUNI BOND; C	California Muni	4.0	5.45	1.74	5.91	☆	☆	4.7	637-2929	617-954-5000	None	1.68	1.00	Geoff Schechter	93
MFS FL MUNI BOND; A	Florida Muni	92.8	9.66	1.99	7.12	6.32	☆	5.5	637-2929	617-954-5000	4.75	1.14	None	Geoff Schechter	93
MFS FL MUNI BOND; B	Florida Muni	13.4	9.66	1.80	6.19	☆	☆	4.5	637-2929	617-954-5000	None	1.96	4.00	Geoff Schechter	93
MFS GA MUNI BOND; A	Georgia Muni	75.3	10.40	1.81	6.51	5.75	☆	5.4	637-2929	617-954-5000	4.75	0.02	None	Geoff Schechter	93
MFS GA MUNI BOND; B	Georgia Muni	9.2	10.40	1.50	5.63	☆	☆	4.5	637-2929	617-954-5000	None	1.02	4.00	Geoff Schechter	93
MFS LA MUNI BOND; A ⤴	Louisiana Muni	17.5	9.24	1.53	7.22	☆	8.23	6.1	637-2929	617-954-5000	4.75	1.17	None	Geoff Schechter	93
MFS LA MUNI BOND; B	Louisiana Muni	3.1	9.24	1.35	6.12	☆	☆	5.2	637-2929	617-954-5000	None	1.89	4.00	Geoff Schechter	93
MFS MA MUNI BOND; A	Massachusetts Muni	261.9	10.89	1.93	6.94	5.97	☆	5.9	637-2929	617-954-5000	4.75	1.21	None	David Smith	93
MFS MA MUNI BOND; B	Massachusetts Muni	8.9	10.90	1.84	6.17	☆	7.52	5.2	637-2929	617-954-5000	None	1.93	4.00	David Smith	94
MFS MD MUNI BOND; A	Maryland Muni	145.0	10.84	0.41	5.90	4.82	☆	5.4	637-2929	617-954-5000	4.75	0.22	None	David King	94
MFS MD MUNI BOND; B	Maryland Muni	12.1	10.84	0.32	5.23	☆	☆	4.7	637-2929	617-954-5000	None	1.23	4.00	David King	94
MFS MS MUNI BOND; A ⤴	Single State Muni	82.0	9.19	1.89	6.64	☆	☆	5.9	637-2929	617-954-5000	4.75	0.59	None	Geoff Schechter	93
MFS MS MUNI BOND; B	Single State Muni	10.1	9.20	1.72	5.67	☆	8.11	5.0	637-2929	617-954-5000	None	1.72	4.00	Geoff Schechter	93
MFS MUNI BOND; A	General Muni	1,962.2	10.74	1.40	7.44	6.41	6.38	5.6	637-2929	617-954-5000	4.75	1.04	None	Robert Dennis	84
MFS MUNI BOND; B	General Muni	53.3	10.73	1.20	6.36	☆	☆	4.6	637-2929	617-954-5000	None	2.10	4.00	Robert Dennis	93
MFS MUNI HIGH INC; A ⊠	High-Yield Muni	1,000.1	8.90	3.01	8.59	6.77	8.02	7.4	637-2929	617-954-5000	4.75	1.13	None	Cindy Brown	93
MFS MUNI HIGH INC; B ⊠	High-Yield Muni	67.5	8.90	2.74	7.47	☆	☆	6.4	637-2929	617-954-5000	None	2.16	4.00	Cindy Brown	93
MFS MUNI INCOME; A	General Muni	51.3	8.63	2.34	7.58	☆	☆	6.0	637-2929	617-954-5000	4.75	2.09	None	David Smith	93
MFS MUNI INCOME; B	General Muni	417.9	8.64	2.08	6.45	6.33	7.24	5.0	637-2929	617-954-5000	None	0.89	4.00	David Smith	93
MFS MUNI INCOME; C	General Muni	10.7	8.64	2.10	6.53	☆	☆	5.1	637-2929	617-954-5000	None	1.74	4.00	David Smith	94
MFS MUNI LTD MAT; A	Short-Term Muni	62.4	7.51	1.64	4.68	4.83	☆	3.7	637-2929	617-954-5000	2.50	None	None	Robert Dennis	92
MFS MUNI LTD MAT; B	Short-Term Muni	7.9	7.50	1.47	3.71	☆	☆	3.0	637-2929	617-954-5000	None	1.16	4.00	Robert Dennis	93
MFS MUNI LTD MAT; C	Short-Term Muni	1.8	7.51	1.43	3.87	☆	☆	3.0	637-2929	617-954-5000	None	None	4.00	Robert Dennis	94
MFS NC MUNI BOND; A	North Carolina Muni	430.9	11.47	1.75	6.58	5.48	6.78	5.2	637-2929	617-954-5000	4.75	1.16	None	Geoff Schechter	93

473

FUND NAME	OBJECTIVE	ASSETS ($MIL) 5/31/95	NAV ($/SHR) 6/30/95	QTR	1YR	3YRS	5YRS	10YRS	DIV YLD %	PHONE 800	PHONE In-State	Load	Exp Ratio	Redemption	MANAGER	SINCE
						(Annualized → 3YRS 5YRS 10YRS)							(FEES)	(FEES)		
MFS NC MUNI BOND; B	North Carolina Muni	28.3	11.47	1.56	5.82	☆	☆	☆	4.5	637-2929	617-954-5000	None	1.88	4.00	Geoff Schechter	'93
MFS NC MUNI BOND; C	North Carolina Muni	8.5	11.46	1.58	5.90	☆	☆	☆	4.6	637-2929	617-954-5000	None	1.81	None	Geoff Schechter	'93
MFS NY MUNI BOND; A	New York Muni	150.3	10.55	1.92	7.02	6.60	8.27	☆	5.4	637-2929	617-954-5000	4.75	1.07	None	Geoff Schechter	'93
MFS NY MUNI BOND; B	New York Muni	27.4	10.54	1.61	6.05	☆	☆	☆	4.5	637-2929	617-954-5000	None	1.89	4.00	Geoff Schechter	'93
MFS PA MUNI BOND; A ▥	Pennsylvania Muni	16.5	9.26	1.15	7.04	☆	☆	☆	5.9	637-2929	617-954-5000	4.75	1.89	None	David King	'94
MFS PA MUNI BOND; B	Pennsylvania Muni	23.2	9.28	1.16	6.26	☆	☆	☆	4.9	637-2929	617-954-5000	None	1.01	4.00	David King	'94
MFS SC MUNI BOND; A	South Carolina Muni	172.4	11.86	1.31	6.99	5.71	7.22	8.54	5.3	637-2929	617-954-5000	4.75	1.19	None	David King	'94
MFS SC MUNI BOND; B	South Carolina Muni	13.8	11.86	1.12	6.22	☆	☆	☆	4.5	637-2929	617-954-5000	None	1.90	4.00	David King	'94
MFS TN MUNI BOND; A	Tennessee Muni	118.1	10.28	1.45	6.26	5.71	7.02	☆	5.4	637-2929	617-954-5000	4.75	1.22	None	David King	'94
MFS TN MUNI BOND; B	Tennessee Muni	10.7	10.28	1.37	5.50	☆	☆	☆	4.7	637-2929	617-954-5000	None	1.94	4.00	David King	'94
➤ MFS TX MUNI BOND; A	Texas Muni	17.9	9.90	1.29	7.58	6.75	☆	☆	6.0	637-2929	617-954-5000	4.75	0.02	None	Geoff Schechter	'92
MFS TX MUNI BOND; B	Texas Muni	2.4	9.91	1.10	6.68	☆	☆	☆	5.1	637-2929	617-954-5000	None	1.02	4.00	Geoff Schechter	'93
MFS VA MUNI BOND; A	Virginia Muni	435.4	11.17	2.10	6.89	5.44	6.88	8.02	5.5	637-2929	617-954-5000	4.75	1.16	None	David Smith	'93
MFS VA MUNI BOND; B	Virginia Muni	23.6	11.16	1.92	6.03	☆	☆	☆	4.8	637-2929	617-954-5000	4.75	1.88	4.00	David Smith	'93
MFS VA MUNI BOND; C	Virginia Muni	2.4	11.15	1.93	5.98	☆	☆	☆	4.8	637-2929	617-954-5000	None	1.80	None	David Smith	'94
➤ MFS WA MUNI BOND; A	Washington Muni	15.5	9.68	2.41	9.74	☆	☆	☆	5.9	637-2929	617-954-5000	4.75	0.02	None	David Smith	'92
MFS WA MUNI BOND; B	Washington Muni	2.8	9.68	2.23	8.74	☆	☆	☆	5.5	637-2929	617-954-5000	None	1.02	4.00	David Smith	'93
MFS WV MUNI BOND; A	Single State Muni	130.8	11.29	2.08	6.94	6.06	7.40	8.30	5.5	637-2929	617-954-5000	4.75	1.19	None	David Smith	'93
MFS WV MUNI BOND; B	Single State Muni	10.9	11.29	1.90	6.26	☆	☆	☆	4.7	637-2929	617-954-5000	None	1.91	4.00	David Smith	'93
MGD MUNI; FLAG INV	General Muni	48.0	10.38	2.10	8.14	5.95	5.95	☆	5.2	645-3923	410-637-6819	4.50	0.90	None	R. Alan Medaugh	'90
MGD MUNI; ISI	General Muni	87.1	10.38	2.10	8.14	5.95	7.19	☆	5.2	645-3923	410-637-6819	4.45	0.90	None	R. Alan Medaugh	'90
MIDWEST TX FR INTMDT; A	Intermediate Muni	78.6	10.86	2.29	6.38	6.21	6.95	☆	4.5	443-4249	513-629-2000	2.00	0.99	None	John Goetz	'86
MIDWEST TX FR INTMDT; C	Intermediate Muni	4.8	10.86	2.16	5.85	☆	☆	☆	4.0	443-4249	513-629-2000	None	None	1.00	John Goetz	'94
MIDWEST TX FR OH INS; A	Ohio Muni	75.6	11.99	1.69	7.78	6.37	7.71	8.22	5.3	443-4249	513-629-2000	4.00	0.75	None	John Goetz	'86
MIDWEST TX FR OH INS; C	Ohio Muni	4.2	12.00	1.65	7.33	☆	☆	☆	4.8	443-4249	513-629-2000	None	1.22	1.00	John Goetz	'93
MONITOR OH TAX-FR; INV	Ohio Muni	2.4	21.38	2.43	6.18	4.86	☆	☆	4.5	253-0412	614-463-5580	2.00	1.02	None	William Doughty	'91
MONITOR OH TAX-FR; TR	Ohio Muni	59.5	21.38	2.50	6.44	5.14	6.15	☆	4.7	253-0412	614-463-5580	None	0.77	None	William Doughty	'88
MONTANA TAX-FREE FUND	Single State Muni	16.0	9.66	-1.10	3.40	☆	☆	☆	5.7	562-6637	701-852-5292	None	0.46	4.00	W. Dan Korgel	'92
☞ MONTGOMERY CA TF SH/INT	California Muni	6.0	12.04	1.90	6.03	☆	☆	☆	3.7	572-3863	415-627-2400	None	0.23	None	William Stevens	'93
MORG STAN INSTL MUNI BD	Intermediate Muni	44.3	10.26	1.98	☆	☆	☆	☆	0.0	548-7786	617-557-8000	None	None	None	Lori Cohane	'95
MORGAN GRENFELL MUNI	Intermediate Muni	194.2	10.71	1.99	7.92	7.98	☆	☆	5.7	932-7781	215-989-6611	None	0.54	None	David Baldt	'93
MUIR CA TAX FREE BOND	California Muni	15.4	15.53	1.54	5.11	4.92	☆	☆	4.3	223-7010	415-989-3200	2.00	0.75	None	Mary Schiavone	'94
MUNDER MI TRIPLE TF; Y	Michigan Muni	0.8	9.34	1.89	7.45	☆	☆	☆	5.5	892-4366	None	None	0.31	None	Wendy Harries	'94
MUNDER MI TRIPLE TF; K	Michigan Muni	26.6	9.34	1.82	7.17	☆	☆	☆	5.2	892-4366	None	None	0.56	None	Wendy Harries	'94
MUNDER MI TRIPLE TF; A	Michigan Muni	0.4	9.34	1.82	7.17	☆	☆	☆	5.2	892-4366	None	3.75	0.56	None	Wendy Harries	'94
MUNDER TAX-FREE BOND; K	General Muni	242.4	10.30	1.99	☆	☆	☆	☆	4.5	892-4366	None	None	0.93	None	Wendy Harries	'94
MUNDER TX-FR INTMDT; Y	Intermediate Muni	11.1	10.37	2.54	7.23	☆	☆	☆	4.2	892-4366	None	None	0.70	None	Wendy Harries	'92
MUNDER TX-FR INTMDT; K	Intermediate Muni	337.1	10.37	2.48	6.97	5.00	6.42	☆	4.0	892-4366	None	None	0.95	None	Wendy Harries	'92
MUNDER TX-FR INTMDT; A	Intermediate Muni	4.2	10.36	2.48	6.87	☆	☆	☆	4.0	892-4366	None	3.75	0.95	None	Wendy Harries	'92
MUNI FD CAL INTMDT; INTER	California Muni	15.1	10.36	2.34	6.96	5.63	7.11	☆	5.0	221-8120	None	None	0.20	None	Don Simmons	'93
MUNI FD TEMP INTMDT; SHS	Intermediate Muni	7.5	10.93	2.67	7.25	5.44	7.04	6.51	4.8	221-8120	None	None	0.40	None	Don Simmons	'92
MUNI SECS INC CA; FORT	California Muni	14.8	10.09	2.70	9.07	☆	☆	☆	5.9	245-4770	412-288-1900	1.00	0.25	1.00	Jonathan C. Conley	'92
MUNI SECS INC MI INTMDT	Michigan Muni	60.3	10.68	2.62	7.40	6.43	☆	☆	5.0	245-4770	412-288-1900	3.00	0.50	1.00	Jonathan C. Conley	'91
MUNI SECS INC NY; FORT	New York Muni	22.0	10.08	2.98	7.81	☆	☆	☆	5.8	245-4770	412-288-1900	1.00	0.39	1.00	Jonathan C. Conley	'92
MUNI SECS INC OH; FORT	Ohio Muni	72.6	11.14	2.36	8.31	6.53	☆	☆	5.3	245-4770	412-288-1900	1.00	0.90	1.00	Jonathan C. Conley	'90

Fund	Objective	%	NAV						Yld	Phone	Phone	Load	Exp	Def	Manager	Since
MUNI SECS INC PA; A	Pennsylvania Muni	85.0	11.15	2.84	9.40	6.67	☆	☆	5.5	245-4770	412-288-1900	3.00	0.75	None	Jonathan C. Conley	'90
N&B MUNI SECURITIES TR	Intermediate Muni	43.7	10.61	1.77	5.86	5.39	☆ 6.42	☆	5.4	877-9700	212-476-8800	None	0.65	None	Theresa Havell	'87
N&B NY INS INTMDT FUND	New York Muni	10.8	9.80	2.72	7.67	☆	☆	☆	4.2	877-9700	212-476-8800	None	None	None	Clara DelVillar	'94
NARRAGANSETT INS TX-FREE	Single State Muni	34.3	9.80	2.70	9.82	☆	☆	☆	5.4	453-6864	212-697-6666	4.00	0.02	None	Salvtore DiSanto	'92
NATIONS FL INT; INV A	Florida Muni	2.2	10.35	2.40	7.50	☆	☆	☆	4.4	321-7854	None	3.25	0.73	None	Michele M. Poirier	'92
NATIONS FL INT; INV C	Florida Muni	0.3	10.35	2.33	7.18	☆	☆	☆	4.1	321-7854	None	None	1.13	1.00	Michele M. Poirier	'92
NATIONS FL INT; INV A	Florida Muni	4.7	10.35	2.33	7.18	☆	☆	☆	4.1	321-7854	None	None	1.05	4.00	Michele M. Poirier	'93
NATIONS FL INT; TR A	Florida Muni	43.4	10.35	2.45	7.72	☆	☆	☆	4.6	321-7854	None	None	0.55	None	Michele M. Poirier	'93
NATIONS FL MUNI; INV A	Florida Muni	1.6	9.35	2.62	9.86	☆	☆	☆	5.3	321-7854	None	4.25	0.39	None	Michele M. Poirier	'93
NATIONS FL MUNI; INV N	Florida Muni	0.1	9.35	2.48	☆	☆	☆	☆	0.0	321-7854	None	None	None	5.00	Michele M. Poirier	'94
NATIONS FL MUNI; INV N	Florida Muni	24.2	9.35	2.48	9.27	☆	☆	☆	4.8	321-7854	None	None	0.96	1.00	Michele M. Poirier	'93
NATIONS FL MUNI; TR A	Florida Muni	8.8	9.35	2.50	10.08	6.06	☆	☆	5.5	321-7854	None	3.25	0.21	None	Michele M. Poirier	'93
NATIONS GA INT; INV A	Single State Muni	10.9	10.53	2.42	7.15	5.56	☆	☆	4.5	321-7854	None	None	0.73	None	Michele M. Poirier	'92
NATIONS GA INT; INV C	Single State Muni	2.7	10.53	2.42	6.83	☆	☆	☆	4.2	321-7854	None	None	1.13	1.00	Michele M. Poirier	'92
NATIONS GA INT; INV N	Single State Muni	7.7	10.53	2.42	6.83	☆	☆	☆	4.2	321-7854	None	None	1.05	4.00	Michele M. Poirier	'93
NATIONS GA INT; TR A	Single State Muni	35.9	10.53	2.55	7.37	6.24	☆	☆	4.7	321-7854	None	None	0.55	None	Michele M. Poirier	'92
NATIONS GA MUNI; INV A	Georgia Muni	0.1	9.30	2.52	8.35	☆	☆	☆	5.4	321-7854	None	4.25	0.39	None	Michele M. Poirier	'93
NATIONS GA MUNI; INV C	Georgia Muni	0.1	9.30	2.39	7.75	☆	☆	☆	0.0	321-7854	None	None	None	1.00	Michele M. Poirier	'94
NATIONS GA MUNI; INV N	Georgia Muni	11.7	9.30	2.39	8.55	☆	☆	☆	4.8	321-7854	None	None	0.96	5.00	Michele M. Poirier	'93
NATIONS GA MUNI; TR A	Georgia Muni	0.6	9.30	2.57	7.18	☆	☆	☆	5.5	321-7854	None	None	0.21	None	Michele M. Poirier	'94
NATIONS INT MUNI; INV N	Intermediate Muni	1.0	9.90	2.42	6.85	☆	☆	☆	4.6	321-7854	None	3.25	0.53	4.00	John Kohl	'94
NATIONS INT MUNI; INV C	Intermediate Muni	0.1	9.90	2.34	7.40	☆	☆	☆	0.0	321-7854	None	None	None	1.00	John Kohl	'94
NATIONS INT MUNI; INV A	Intermediate Muni	1.2	9.90	2.35	7.36	5.62	☆	☆	4.3	321-7854	None	None	0.85	None	John Kohl	'94
NATIONS INT MUNI; TR A	Intermediate Muni	67.6	9.90	2.47	7.04	☆	☆	☆	4.8	321-7854	None	None	0.35	None	John Kohl	'94
NATIONS MD INT; INV N	Single State Muni	21.7	10.71	2.67	7.04	☆	☆	☆	4.5	321-7854	None	3.25	0.71	None	John Kohl	'94
NATIONS MD INT; INV N	Single State Muni	2.6	10.71	2.59	7.57	☆	☆	☆	4.2	321-7854	None	None	1.11	1.00	John Kohl	'94
NATIONS MD INT; INV A	Single State Muni	4.5	10.71	2.59	8.41	5.79	☆	☆	4.2	321-7854	None	None	1.03	None	John Kohl	'92
NARRAGANSETT INS; TR A	Maryland Muni	60.4	10.71	2.72	☆	☆	☆	☆	4.7	321-7854	None	None	0.53	None	John Kohl	'92
NATIONS MD MUNI; INV A	Maryland Muni	0.6	9.23	2.24	7.82	☆	☆	☆	5.2	321-7854	None	None	0.39	None	John Kohl	'92
NATIONS MD MUNI; INV C	Maryland Muni	0.1	9.23	2.10	☆	☆	☆	☆	0.0	321-7854	None	None	None	1.00	John Kohl	'93
NATIONS MD MUNI; INV N	General Muni	7.0	9.23	2.10	8.61	☆	☆	☆	4.6	321-7854	None	None	0.96	5.00	John Kohl	'94
NATIONS MD MUNI; TR A	Maryland Muni	1.8	9.23	2.29	8.02	☆	☆	☆	0.0	321-7854	None	4.25	0.21	None	John Kohl	'94
NATIONS MUNI INC; INV A	General Muni	25.1	10.63	2.38	8.02	6.53	☆	☆	5.3	321-7854	None	None	0.79	None	Michele M. Poirier	'92
NATIONS MUNI INC; INV C	General Muni	2.7	10.63	2.38	8.83	5.92	☆	☆	4.8	321-7854	None	None	1.37	1.00	Michele M. Poirier	'92
NATIONS MUNI INC; INV N	General Muni	19.0	10.63	2.38	7.47	☆	☆	☆	4.8	321-7854	None	None	1.37	5.00	Michele M. Poirier	'93
NATIONS MUNI INC; TR A	General Muni	61.8	10.25	2.57	7.16	6.71	☆	☆	5.5	321-7854	None	3.25	0.62	None	Michele M. Poirier	'92
NATIONS NC INT; INV A	Single State Muni	9.6	10.25	2.36	7.15	☆	☆	☆	4.2	321-7854	None	None	0.73	1.00	Michele M. Poirier	'92
NATIONS NC INT; INV C	Single State Muni	1.6	10.25	2.29	7.69	☆	☆	☆	3.9	321-7854	None	None	1.13	4.00	Michele M. Poirier	'92
NATIONS NC INT; INV N	Single State Muni	6.9	10.25	2.29	9.02	☆	☆	☆	3.9	321-7854	None	None	1.05	None	Michele M. Poirier	'93
NATIONS NC INT; TR A	Single State Muni	17.6	10.25	2.41	☆	☆	☆	☆	4.4	321-7854	None	None	0.55	None	Michele M. Poirier	'92
NATIONS NC MUNI; INV A	North Carolina Muni	1.2	9.32	2.30	8.43	☆	☆	☆	5.3	321-7854	None	4.25	0.39	None	Michele M. Poirier	'93
NATIONS NC MUNI; INV C	North Carolina Muni	0.1	9.32	2.16	9.24	☆	☆	☆	0.0	321-7854	None	None	None	1.00	Michele M. Poirier	'94
NATIONS NC MUNI; INV N	North Carolina Muni	28.9	9.32	2.16	7.57	☆	☆	☆	4.8	321-7854	None	None	0.96	5.00	Michele M. Poirier	'93
NATIONS NC MUNI; TR A	North Carolina Muni	1.0	9.32	2.35	7.25	☆	☆	☆	5.5	321-7854	None	None	0.21	None	Michele M. Poirier	'93
NATIONS SC INT; INV A	Single State Muni	16.1	10.43	2.45	7.25	5.96	☆	☆	4.7	321-7854	None	3.25	0.72	None	Michele M. Poirier	'92
NATIONS SC INT; INV C	Single State Muni	5.9	10.43	2.38	7.78	☆	☆	☆	4.4	321-7854	None	None	1.12	1.00	Michele M. Poirier	'92
NATIONS SC INT; INV C	Single State Muni	6.2	10.43	2.38	9.39	☆	☆	☆	4.4	321-7854	None	None	1.04	4.00	Michele M. Poirier	'93
NATIONS SC-INT; TR A	Single State Muni	48.0	10.43	2.50	☆	☆	☆	☆	4.9	321-7854	None	None	0.54	None	Michele M. Poirier	'93
NATIONS SC MUNI; INV A	South Carolina Muni	0.2	9.59	2.50	☆	5.46	☆	☆	5.3	321-7854	None	4.25	0.39	None	Michele M. Poirier	'93
NATIONS SC MUNI; INV C	South Carolina Muni	0.1	9.59	2.34	☆	6.14	☆	☆	0.0	321-7854	None	None	None	1.00	Michele M. Poirier	'94

PERFORMANCE OF MUTUAL FUNDS (continued)

FUND NAME	OBJECTIVE	ASSETS ($MIL) 5/31/95	NAV ($/SHR) 6/30/95	QTR	1YR	3YRS	5YRS	10YRS	DIV YLD %	PHONE 800	In-State	Load	Exp. Ratio	Redemption	MANAGER	SINCE
NATIONS SC MUNI; INV N	South Carolina Muni	10.9	9.59	2.36	8.79	★			4.8	321-7854	None	None	0.96	5.00	Michele M. Poirier	'93
NATIONS SC MUNI; TR A	South Carolina Muni	1.6	9.59	2.55	9.61	★			5.5	321-7854	None	None	0.21	None	Michele M. Poirier	'93
NATIONS SHTM MUNI; INV A	Short-Term Muni	2.8	9.96	2.09	5.68	★			4.1	321-7854	None	1.50	0.52	None	Matt Kiselak	'94
NATIONS SHTM MUNI; INV N	Short-Term Muni	10.4	9.96	2.05	5.52	★			3.9	321-7854	None	None	0.69	None	Matt Kiselak	'94
NATIONS SHTM MUNI; TR A	Short-Term Muni	47.5	9.96	2.14	5.89	★			4.3	321-7854	None	None	0.34	None	Matt Kiselak	'94
NATIONS TN INT; INV A	Single State Muni	8.2	9.97	2.34	7.04	★			4.5	321-7854	None	3.25	0.71	None	Matt Kiselak	'94
NATIONS TN INT; INV C	Single State Muni	0.1	9.97	2.25	☆				0.0	321-7854	None	None	None	1.00	Matt Kiselak	'94
NATIONS TN INT; INV N	Single State Muni	3.4	9.97	2.26	6.72	★			4.2	321-7854	None	None	1.03	4.00	Matt Kiselak	'94
NATIONS TN INT; TR A	Single State Muni	5.8	9.97	2.39	7.25	★			4.7	321-7854	None	None	0.53	None	Matt Kiselak	'94
NATIONS TENNESSEE Muni	Tennessee Muni	0.1	9.46	2.19	9.23	★			5.3	321-7854	None	4.25	0.39	None	Matt Kiselak	'94
NATIONS TN MUNI; INV C	Tennessee Muni	0.1	9.46	2.05	☆				0.0	321-7854	None	None	None	1.00	Matt Kiselak	'94
NATIONS TN MUNI; INV N	Tennessee Muni	6.4	9.46	2.05	8.63	★			4.8	321-7854	None	None	0.96	5.00	Matt Kiselak	'94
NATIONS TX INT; INV A	Single State Muni	0.8	10.09	2.02	6.45	★			4.4	321-7854	None	3.25	0.73	None	Matt Kiselak	'94
NATIONS TX INT; INV C	Single State Muni	0.5	10.09	1.94	☆				0.0	321-7854	None	None	None	1.00	Matt Kiselak	'94
NATIONS TX INT; INV N	Single State Muni	3.2	10.09	1.94	6.13	★			4.1	321-7854	None	None	1.05	4.00	Matt Kiselak	'94
NATIONS TX INT; TR A	Single State Muni	23.2	10.09	2.07	6.66	★			4.6	321-7854	None	4.25	0.55	None	Matt Kiselak	'94
NATIONS TX MUNI; INV A	Texas Muni	0.1	9.28	2.54	8.69	★			5.3	321-7854	None	4.25	0.40	None	Matt Kiselak	'94
NATIONS TX MUNI; INV C	Texas Muni	0.1	9.28	2.39	☆				0.0	321-7854	None	None	None	1.00	Matt Kiselak	'94
NATIONS TX MUNI; INV N	Texas Muni	12.4	9.28	2.39	8.09	★			4.8	321-7854	None	None	0.97	5.00	Matt Kiselak	'94
NATIONS TX MUNI; TR A	Texas Muni	3.3	9.28	2.59	8.90	★			5.5	321-7854	None	None	0.22	None	Matt Kiselak	'94
NATIONS VA INT; INV A	Single State Muni	77.0	10.61	2.62	6.82	6.78	5.54		4.6	321-7854	None	3.25	0.79	None	John Kohl	'94
NATIONS VA INT; INV C	Single State Muni	7.7	10.61	2.55	6.51	★	5.04		4.3	321-7854	None	None	1.19	1.00	John Kohl	'94
NATIONS VA INT; INV N	Single State Muni	111.1	10.61	2.55	6.51	6.89	5.72		4.3	321-7854	None	None	1.11	4.00	John Kohl	'94
NATIONS VA INT; TR A	Single State Muni	162.3	10.61	2.67	7.04	★			4.8	321-7854	None	None	0.61	None	John Kohl	'94
NATIONS VA MUNI; INV A	Virginia Muni	0.4	9.20	2.33	9.09	★			5.3	321-7854	None	4.25	0.39	None	John Kohl	'94
NATIONS VA MUNI; INV C	Virginia Muni	0.1	9.20	2.18	☆				4.8	321-7854	None	None	None	1.00	John Kohl	'94
NATIONS VA MUNI; INV N	Virginia Muni	15.5	9.20	2.19	8.50	★			4.8	321-7854	None	None	0.96	5.00	John Kohl	'94
NATIONS VA MUNI; TR A	Virginia Muni	2.4	9.20	2.38	9.31	★			5.5	321-7854	None	None	0.21	None	John Kohl	'94
NATIONWIDE II TX-FR	General Muni	259.0	10.03	2.03	8.47	7.38	5.88		5.2	848-0920	614-249-7855	None	0.99	5.00	Alpha Benson	'86
ND TAX-FREE FUND ➡	Single State Muni	97.0	8.88	-2.07	1.89	5.34	2.98		5.7	562-6637	701-852-5292	4.25	1.06	4.00	W. Dan Korgel	'89
NEW ENGLAND INT CA; A	California Muni	37.8	7.34	1.33	5.07	★			5.2	888-4823	None	2.50	0.70	None	James Welch	'93
NEW ENGLAND INT CA; B	California Muni	5.8	7.32	0.87	4.01	★			4.5	888-4823	None	None	1.45	4.00	James Welch	'93
NEW ENGLAND INT NY; A	New York Muni	16.4	7.37	2.05	6.25	★			5.3	888-4823	None	2.50	0.70	None	James Welch	'93
NEW ENGLAND INT NY; B	New York Muni	1.4	7.35	1.72	5.32	★			4.6	888-4823	None	None	1.45	4.00	James Welch	'93
NEW ENGLAND MA TX FR; A	Massachusetts Muni	116.3	16.07	1.72	7.64	★	5.85	7.89	5.6	888-4823	None	4.25	0.85	None	James Welch	'88
NEW ENGLAND MA TX FR; B	Massachusetts Muni	5.5	16.05	1.61	7.02	★	5.92	7.58	4.9	888-4823	None	None	1.50	4.00	James Welch	'86
NEW ENGLAND TXEX INC; A	General Muni	197.4	7.35	1.67	7.80	★	5.92	8.59	5.5	888-4823	None	4.50	0.92	None	Nathan Wentworth	'93
NEW ENGLAND TXEX INC; B	General Muni	10.8	7.34	1.46	6.84	★			4.7	888-4823	None	None	1.67	4.00	Nathan Wentworth	'93
NORTH CAROLINA TX FR BD	North Carolina Muni	3.3	10.23	2.01	7.63	★			4.3	525-3863	919-972-9922	None	None	None	Boys,Arnold & Co.,Inc.	'93
NORTHERN FDS INTMDT TXEX	Intermediate Muni	228.4	10.20	2.74	6.73	★			4.0	595-9111	414-271-5885	None	0.85	None	Eric Boeckmann	'94
NORTHERN FDS TAX EXEMPT	General Muni	118.7	10.15	1.90	7.63	★	6.35		4.9	595-9111	414-271-5885	None	0.85	None	Peter Flood	'94
NORTHWEST IDAHO TAX-EX	Single State Muni	5.9	5.15	1.67	9.33	★	5.99		5.0	728-8762	206-734-9900	None	0.75	None	Phelps McIlvaine	'95
NORTHWEST WA TAX-EX	Washington Muni	0.9	4.85	2.84	8.16	★			5.0	728-8762	206-734-9900	None	0.41	None	Phelps McIlvaine	'94
NORWEST AZ TAX-FREE; A ★	Arizona Muni	2.8	9.75	2.75	9.13	★			4.9	338-1348	612-667-8833	3.75	None	None	Margie Grace	'93
NORWEST AZ TAX-FREE; B	Arizona Muni	0.3	9.76	2.66	8.42	★			4.2	338-1348	612-667-8833	None	None	3.00	Margie Grace	'93
NORWEST AZ TAX-FREE; TR	Arizona Muni	0.7	9.75	2.86	9.24	★			4.9	338-1348	612-667-8833	None	None	None	Margie Grace	'93
NORWEST CO TAX-FREE; A ★	Colorado Muni	26.0	9.78	2.76	7.44	★			5.0	338-1348	612-667-8833	3.75	0.07	None	Margie Grace	'93
NORWEST CO TAX-FREE; B	Colorado Muni	5.2	9.79	2.46	6.63	★			4.3	338-1348	612-667-8833	None	0.85	3.00	Margie Grace	'93

Fund	Objective	Net Assets ($Mil)	NAV		☆	☆	☆	☆		Phone	Phone	Max. Load	12b-1	Portfolio Manager	Since
NORWEST CO TAX-FREE; TR	Colorado Muni	24.5	9.78	2.65	7.44	☆	☆	☆	5.0	612-667-8833	338-1348	None	0.11	Margie Grace	'93
NORWEST MN TAX-FREE; A ★	Single State Muni	15.6	10.30	2.31	8.26	5.85	6.72	☆	5.3	612-667-8833	338-1348	3.75	0.61	Pat Hovanetz	'88
NORWEST MN TAX-FREE; B	Single State Muni	5.1	10.30	2.21	7.44	☆	☆	☆	4.5	612-667-8833	338-1348	None	1.31	Pat Hovanetz	'93
NORWEST MN TAX-FREE; C	Single State Muni	1.8	10.30	2.31	8.16	5.23	6.53	☆	5.3	612-667-8833	338-1348	None	0.61	Pat Hovanetz	'93
NORWEST TAX-FR INC; A ★	General Muni	30.8	9.68	2.48	7.79	☆	☆	☆	5.7	612-667-8833	338-1348	3.75	0.60	Bill Jackson	'93
NORWEST TAX-FR INC; A	General Muni	3.7	9.68	2.29	6.98	☆	☆	☆	5.0	612-667-8833	338-1348	None	1.31	Bill Jackson	'93
NORWEST TAX-FR INC; TR	General Muni	94.5	9.68	2.38	7.79	☆	☆	☆	5.7	612-667-8833	338-1348	None	0.60	Bill Jackson	'93
NTH AM FDS NATL MUNI; A	General Muni	8.2	9.37	2.35	6.96	☆	☆	☆	5.4	203-698-0068	334-0575	4.75	0.57	Mary Beth White	'94
NTH AM FDS NATL MUNI; B	General Muni	5.1	9.37	2.14	6.19	☆	☆	☆	4.7	203-698-0068	334-0575	None	1.24	Mary Beth White	'94
NTH AM FDS NATL MUNI; C	General Muni	3.3	9.37	2.14	6.19	☆	☆	☆	4.7	203-698-0068	334-0575	None	1.24	Mary Beth White	'94
NUVEEN AZ VALUE; A	Arizona Muni	1.5	10.31	2.18	☆	☆	☆	☆	0.0	312-917-7810	621-7227	4.50	None	Steve Krupa	'94
NUVEEN AZ VALUE; C	Arizona Muni	0.1	10.23	2.09	☆	☆	☆	☆	0.0	312-917-7810	621-7227	None	None	Steve Krupa	'94
NUVEEN AZ VALUE; R	Arizona Muni	17.9	10.24	2.34	9.19	7.09	☆	☆	5.3	312-917-7810	621-7227	None	0.75	Steve Krupa	'92
NUVEEN CA INS VALUE; A	California Muni	7.1	10.33	1.75	☆	☆	☆	☆	0.0	312-917-7810	621-7227	4.50	1.05	Steve Krupa	'94
NUVEEN CA INS VALUE; C	California Muni	0.3	10.23	1.67	☆	☆	☆	☆	0.0	312-917-7810	621-7227	None	1.80	Steve Krupa	'94
NUVEEN CA INS VALUE; R	California Muni	203.3	10.31	1.83	8.59	6.27	7.96	☆	5.4	312-917-7810	621-7227	None	0.70	Tom Futrell	'90
NUVEEN CA VALUE; A	California Muni	5.6	10.19	1.95	☆	☆	☆	☆	0.0	312-917-7810	621-7227	4.50	1.00	Tom Futrell	'94
NUVEEN CA VALUE; C	California Muni	0.3	10.19	1.76	☆	☆	☆	☆	0.0	312-917-7810	621-7227	None	1.75	Steve Krupa	'94
NUVEEN CA VALUE; R	California Muni	212.9	10.21	1.92	8.09	5.85	7.37	☆	5.7	312-917-7810	621-7227	None	0.71	Steve Krupa	'90
NUVEEN FL VALUE; A	Florida Muni	2.3	10.11	1.92	☆	☆	☆	☆	0.0	312-917-7810	621-7227	4.50	None	Tom Futrell	'94
NUVEEN FL VALUE; C	Florida Muni	0.1	10.10	1.84	☆	☆	☆	☆	0.0	312-917-7810	621-7227	None	None	Tom Futrell	'94
NUVEEN FL VALUE; R	Florida Muni	55.3	10.12	1.98	9.09	6.64	☆	☆	5.1	312-917-7810	621-7227	None	0.75	Steve Krupa	'92
NUVEEN INS MUNI BOND; C	Insured Muni	23.9	10.54	2.15	☆	☆	☆	☆	0.0	312-917-7810	621-7227	4.50	1.00	Steve Krupa	'94
NUVEEN INS MUNI BOND; R	Insured Muni	4.7	10.43	2.10	☆	☆	☆	☆	0.0	312-917-7810	621-7227	None	1.75	Steve Krupa	'94
NUVEEN INS MUNI BOND; R	Insured Muni	761.2	10.50	2.35	9.18	6.99	8.59	☆	5.5	312-917-7810	621-7227	None	0.64	Steve Peterson	'94
NUVEEN MA INS VALUE; A	Massachusetts Muni	2.8	10.20	2.28	☆	☆	☆	☆	0.0	312-917-7810	621-7227	4.50	1.15	Steve Peterson	'93
NUVEEN MA INS VALUE; C	Massachusetts Muni	0.4	10.18	2.09	☆	☆	☆	☆	0.0	312-917-7810	621-7227	None	1.90	Steve Peterson	'94
NUVEEN MA INS VALUE; R	Massachusetts Muni	59.2	10.20	2.35	8.61	6.72	8.16	☆	5.4	312-917-7810	621-7227	None	0.79	Steve Peterson	'93
NUVEEN MA VALUE; A	Massachusetts Muni	1.8	9.69	2.30	☆	☆	☆	☆	0.0	312-917-7810	621-7227	4.50	1.00	Steve Peterson	'94
NUVEEN MA VALUE; C	Massachusetts Muni	0.1	9.65	2.12	☆	☆	☆	☆	0.0	312-917-7810	621-7227	None	1.75	Steve Peterson	'94
NUVEEN MA VALUE; R	Massachusetts Muni	74.0	9.67	2.37	8.31	6.86	8.12	☆	5.6	312-917-7810	621-7227	None	0.75	Ted Neild	'93
NUVEEN MD VALUE; A	Maryland Muni	3.6	10.07	2.69	☆	☆	☆	☆	0.0	312-917-7810	621-7227	4.50	None	Ted Neild	'94
NUVEEN MD VALUE; C	Maryland Muni	1.0	10.06	2.50	☆	☆	☆	☆	0.0	312-917-7810	621-7227	None	None	Ted Neild	'94
NUVEEN MD VALUE; R	Maryland Muni	45.4	10.08	2.85	9.13	6.68	☆	☆	5.2	312-917-7810	621-7227	None	0.75	Ted Neild	'92
NUVEEN MI VALUE; A	Michigan Muni	1.9	10.32	2.45	☆	☆	☆	☆	0.0	312-917-7810	621-7227	4.50	None	Ted Neild	'94
NUVEEN MI VALUE; C	Michigan Muni	0.1	10.30	2.26	☆	☆	☆	☆	0.0	312-917-7810	621-7227	None	None	Ted Neild	'94
NUVEEN MI VALUE; R	Michigan Muni	28.3	10.32	2.41	9.08	7.26	☆	☆	5.2	312-917-7810	621-7227	None	0.75	Ted Neild	'92
NUVEEN MUNI BOND; B	General Muni	2,825.0	9.08	2.21	8.32	6.15	7.60	8.93	5.7	312-917-7810	621-7227	4.50	0.59	Thomas Spalding	'78
NUVEEN NJ VALUE; A	New Jersey Muni	5.2	10.05	2.34	☆	☆	☆	☆	0.0	312-917-7810	621-7227	4.50	None	Steve Peterson	'94
NUVEEN NJ VALUE; C	New Jersey Muni	0.5	10.03	2.15	☆	☆	☆	☆	0.0	312-917-7810	621-7227	None	None	Steve Peterson	'94
NUVEEN NJ VALUE; R	New Jersey Muni	41.5	10.06	2.50	7.82	6.87	☆	☆	5.3	312-917-7810	621-7227	None	0.75	Steve Peterson	'92
NUVEEN NY INS VALUE; A	New York Muni	13.0	10.28	2.37	☆	☆	☆	☆	0.0	312-917-7810	621-7227	4.50	1.05	Dan Solender	'94
NUVEEN NY INS VALUE; C	New York Muni	0.6	10.29	2.47	☆	☆	☆	☆	0.0	312-917-7810	621-7227	None	1.80	Dan Solender	'94
NUVEEN NY INS VALUE; R	New York Muni	347.7	10.29	2.56	8.72	6.84	8.42	☆	5.4	312-917-7810	621-7227	None	0.65	Dan Solender	'94
NUVEEN NY VALUE; A	New York Muni	8.7	10.27	2.45	☆	☆	☆	☆	0.0	312-917-7810	621-7227	4.50	1.00	Dan Solender	'94
NUVEEN NY VALUE; C	New York Muni	0.3	10.29	2.57	☆	☆	☆	☆	0.0	312-917-7810	621-7227	None	1.75	Dan Solender	'94
NUVEEN NY VALUE; R	New York Muni	150.0	10.30	2.49	8.22	6.93	8.37	☆	5.6	312-917-7810	621-7227	None	0.74	Dan Solender	'94

★ NORWEST AZ TAX-FREE; A—The maximum load is currently reduced to 3.25%.
★ NORWEST CO TAX-FREE; A—The maximum load is currently reduced to 3.25%.
★ NORWEST MN TAX-FREE; A—The maximum load is currently reduced to 3.25%.
★ NORWEST TAX-FR INC; A—The maximum load is currently reduced to 3.25%.

PERFORMANCE OF MUTUAL FUNDS (continued)

FUND NAME	OBJECTIVE	ASSETS ($ MIL) 5/31/95	NAV ($/SHR) 6/30/95	QTR	1YR	3YRS	5YRS	10YRS	DIV YLD %	PHONE 800	PHONE In-State	Load	Exp. Ratio	Redemption	MANAGER	SINCE
NUVEEN OH VALUE; A	Ohio Muni	6.6	10.30	2.13	☆	☆	☆	☆	0.0	621-7227	312-917-7810	4.50	1.00	None	Jim Lumberg	'94
NUVEEN OH VALUE; C	Ohio Muni	1.1	10.26	2.04	☆	☆	☆	☆	0.0	621-7227	312-917-7810	None	1.75	None	Jim Lumberg	'94
NUVEEN OH VALUE; R	Ohio Muni	167.2	10.19	2.28	8.74	6.89	☆	8.21	5.5	621-7227	312-917-7810	None	0.73	None	Jim Lumberg	'94
NUVEEN PA VALUE; A	Pennsylvania Muni	2.9	10.08	2.48	☆	☆	☆	☆	0.0	621-7227	312-917-7810	4.50	None	None	Tom O'Shaughnessy	'94
NUVEEN PA VALUE; C	Pennsylvania Muni	0.6	10.08	2.21	☆	☆	☆	☆	0.0	621-7227	312-917-7810	None	None	None	Tom O'Shaughnessy	'94
NUVEEN PA VALUE; R	Pennsylvania Muni	54.5	10.16	2.44	9.54	6.70	☆	☆	5.3	621-7227	312-917-7810	None	0.75	None	Tom O'Shaughnessy	'92
NUVEEN VA VALUE; A	Virginia Muni	3.4	10.17	1.96	☆	☆	☆	☆	0.0	621-7227	312-917-7810	4.50	None	None	Bill Fitzgerald	'94
NUVEEN VA VALUE; C	Virginia Muni	0.5	10.14	1.77	☆	☆	☆	☆	0.0	621-7227	312-917-7810	None	None	None	Bill Fitzgerald	'94
NUVEEN VA VALUE; R	Virginia Muni	57.9	10.17	2.12	9.08	6.88	☆	☆	5.3	621-7227	312-917-7810	4.50	0.75	None	Bill Fitzgerald	'92
111 CORCORAN NC MUNI	North Carolina Muni	39.6	10.33	2.45	8.15	5.67	☆	☆	4.7	422-2080	919-683-7277	4.50	0.69	None	Jim Agnew	'92
ONE FUND TAX-FREE INCOME	General Muni	N/A	10.66	1.78	☆	☆	☆	☆	0.0	578-8078	None	3.00	None	None	Michael Boedeker	'94
ONE GROUP INT TX-FR; A	Intermediate Muni	4.7	10.63	1.53	6.50	5.13	☆	☆	4.8	338-4345	None	4.50	0.73	None	Patrick Morrissey	'94
ONE GROUP INT TX-FR; FID	Intermediate Muni	209.9	10.64	1.68	6.79	5.41	☆	☆	5.1	338-4345	None	None	0.48	None	Patrick Morrissey	'94
ONE GROUP KY MUNI BD; FID	Single State Muni	32.8	9.92	2.30	6.69	☆	☆	☆	4.5	338-4345	None	None	0.70	None	Dave Sivinski	'94
ONE GROUP OH MUNI BD; FID	Ohio Muni	11.9	10.68	1.84	5.82	5.62	☆	☆	4.9	338-4345	None	None	0.78	None	Dave Sivinski	'94
ONE GROUP OH MUNI BD; A	Ohio Muni	81.7	10.65	1.90	6.11	5.77	☆	☆	5.2	338-4345	None	4.50	0.53	None	Dave Sivinski	'94
ONE GROUP TX-FR BD; A	General Muni	10.3	9.72	1.78	6.24	☆	☆	☆	5.7	338-4345	None	4.50	0.79	None	Patrick Morrissey	'94
ONE GROUP TX-FR BD; FID	General Muni	181.4	9.69	1.83	6.49	☆	☆	☆	5.9	338-4345	None	None	0.54	None	Patrick Morrissey	'93
OPPENHEIMER CA TX-EX; A	California Muni	251.3	10.23	2.68	8.66	6.47	7.63	☆	6.0	525-7048	303-671-3200	4.75	0.96	None	Robert Patterson	'94
OPPENHEIMER CA TX-EX; B	California Muni	28.8	10.24	2.48	7.78	☆	☆	☆	5.5	525-7048	303-671-3200	None	1.73	5.00	Robert Patterson	'94
OPPENHEIMER FL TX-EX; A	Florida Muni	13.9	10.96	2.19	9.08	☆	☆	☆	5.8	525-7048	303-671-3200	4.75	0.53	None	Robert Patterson	'93
OPPENHEIMER FL TX-EX; B	Florida Muni	10.8	10.97	2.00	8.14	☆	☆	☆	5.1	525-7048	303-671-3200	None	0.79	5.00	Robert Patterson	'93
OPPENHEIMER MAIN CA; A	California Muni	79.2	12.11	2.78	9.11	6.81	7.90	☆	6.1	525-7048	303-671-3200	4.75	0.54	None	Robert Patterson	'88
OPPENHEIMER MAIN CA; B	California Muni	2.6	12.11	2.61	8.17	☆	☆	☆	5.1	525-7048	303-671-3200	None	1.62	5.00	Robert Patterson	'93
OPPENHEIMER NJ TX-EX; A	New Jersey Muni	6.1	11.03	2.03	8.30	☆	☆	☆	5.9	525-7048	303-671-3200	4.75	None	None	Robert Patterson	'94
OPPENHEIMER NJ TX-EX; B	New Jersey Muni	3.9	11.03	1.94	7.59	☆	☆	☆	5.1	525-7048	303-671-3200	None	0.86	5.00	Robert Patterson	'93
OPPENHEIMER NY TX-EX; A	New York Muni	684.6	12.27	2.12	7.16	5.99	7.75	8.43	5.9	525-7048	303-671-3200	4.75	1.65	None	Robert Patterson	'85
OPPENHEIMER NY TX-EX; B	New York Muni	88.8	12.28	2.01	6.43	☆	☆	☆	5.1	525-7048	303-671-3200	None	0.98	5.00	Robert Patterson	'85
OPPENHEIMER PA TX-EX; A	Pennsylvania Muni	65.8	11.93	2.38	8.57	6.29	7.45	☆	5.8	525-7048	303-671-3200	4.75	1.75	None	Robert Patterson	'93
OPPENHEIMER PA TX-EX; B	Pennsylvania Muni	12.2	11.93	2.18	7.74	☆	☆	☆	5.0	525-7048	303-671-3200	None	0.88	5.00	Robert Patterson	'89
OPPENHEIMER TX-FR BD; A	General Muni	574.1	9.59	1.88	8.14	6.19	7.75	8.76	5.9	525-7048	303-671-3200	4.75	1.69	None	Robert Patterson	'85
OPPENHEIMER TX-FR BD; B	General Muni	63.7	9.58	1.69	7.18	☆	☆	☆	5.4	525-7048	303-671-3200	None	1.05	5.00	Robert Patterson	'93
OPPENHEIMER TXEX INS; A	Insured Muni	73.8	16.68	2.25	7.96	6.23	7.62	☆	5.3	525-7048	303-671-3200	4.75	1.82	None	Robert Patterson	'92
OPPENHEIMER TXEX INS; B	Insured Muni	12.8	16.69	2.06	7.11	☆	☆	☆	4.8	525-7048	303-671-3200	None	1.00	5.00	Robert Patterson	'93
OPPENHEIMER TXEX INT; A	Intermediate Muni	80.2	14.45	2.21	6.41	5.67	7.49	☆	5.2	525-7048	303-671-3200	4.75	2.24	None	Robert Patterson	'93
OPPENHEIMER TXEX INT; C	Intermediate Muni	6.8	14.47	2.00	5.68	☆	☆	☆	4.7	525-7048	303-671-3200	None	0.98	5.00	Robert Patterson	'92
OREGON MUNICIPAL BOND	Single State Muni	26.9	12.37	1.76	6.72	5.32	6.67	☆	4.4	541-9732	503-295-0919	None	0.50	1.00	Huson/Nesbit	'93
OVERLAND CA TX-FR BD; A	California Muni	286.2	10.69	1.65	6.96	6.67	8.01	7.50	5.9	552-9612	415-396-0376	4.75	0.43	None	Wines/Klug	'84/'95
OVERLAND MUNI INCOME; A	General Muni	70.4	10.46	1.46	8.08	6.17	7.43	☆	5.6	552-9612	415-396-0376	4.75	0.95	None	Wines/Sabrell	'88/'88
P HZN CA TX-EX BOND	California Muni	197.5	7.17	1.60	6.89	☆	☆	☆	5.3	332-3863	619-456-9197	3.50	None	None	Kim Michalski	'91/'91
P HZN NATL MUNI BOND	General Muni	2.9	9.79	2.39	9.02	5.98	☆	7.95	5.5	332-3863	619-456-9197	4.50	None	None	Kim Michalski	'84
PAC CAP TXFR SECS; INST	Hawaii Muni	281.4	10.50	2.07	☆	☆	☆	☆	0.0	258-9232	617-722-7868	None	None	None	Yvonne Lim	'94
PAC CAP TXFR SECS; RET	Hawaii Muni	0.6	10.47	2.01	☆	☆	☆	☆	0.0	258-9232	617-722-7868	None	None	None	Yvonne Lim	'94
PAC CAP TXFR SH INT; INST	Short-Term Muni	38.7	10.08	1.66	☆	☆	☆	☆	0.0	258-9232	617-722-7868	4.00	None	None	Yvonne Lim	'94
PAC CAP TXFR SH INT; RET	Short-Term Muni	0.3	10.05	1.61	☆	☆	☆	☆	0.0	258-9232	617-722-7868	2.25	None	None	Yvonne Lim	'94

Fund	Objective	Net Assets	Yield	NAV	1-Yr	3-Yr	5-Yr	10-Yr	Cur Yld	Phone	Phone (Direct)	Load	Exp	CDSC	Manager	Since
PACIFICA CA TAX-FREE	California Muni	167.8	1.83	10.60	7.69	5.99	7.54	☆	5.0	662-8417	212-808-3900	4.50	0.94	None	Richard Carhidi	'95
PACIFICA SH TM CA TAX-FR	California Muni	22.4	1.51	10.06	5.00	☆	☆	☆	4.1	662-8417	212-808-3900	None	0.56	None	Richard Carhidi	'95
PAINEWBR CALIF TX-FR; A	California Muni	177.3	1.52	10.71	7.07	5.21	6.80	☆	5.5	647-1568	None	4.00	0.90	None	Gregory Serbe	'85
PAINEWBR CALIF TX-FR; B	California Muni	32.8	1.24	10.71	6.16	4.38	☆	☆	4.7	647-1568	None	None	1.65	5.00	Gregory Serbe	'91
PAINEWBR CALIF TX-FR; D	California Muni	27.2	1.30	10.70	6.52	☆	☆	☆	5.0	647-1568	None	None	1.39	None	Gregory Serbe	'92
PAINEWBR MUNI HI INC; A	High-Yield Muni	63.8	2.33	10.07	6.60	5.55	7.73	☆	6.0	647-1568	None	4.00	1.03	None	Gregory Serbe	'87
PAINEWBR MUNI HI INC; B	High-Yield Muni	25.9	2.15	10.06	5.81	4.76	☆	☆	5.3	647-1568	None	None	1.79	5.00	Gregory Serbe	'91
PAINEWBR MUNI HI INC; D	High-Yield Muni	23.6	2.21	10.06	6.09	☆	☆	8.42	5.6	647-1568	None	None	1.54	None	Gregory Serbe	'92
PAINEWBR NATL TX-FR; A	General Muni	343.8	1.95	11.37	7.11	5.62	7.24	☆	5.5	647-1568	None	4.00	0.89	None	Serbe/Murphy	'94/'94
PAINEWBR NATL TX-FR; B	General Muni	58.8	1.85	11.37	6.30	4.83	☆	☆	4.8	647-1568	None	None	1.63	5.00	Serbe/Murphy	'94/'94
PAINEWBR NATL TX-FR; D	General Muni	93.4	1.82	11.37	6.57	5.83	7.72	☆	5.0	647-1568	None	None	1.37	None	Serbe/Murphy	'94/'94
PAINEWBR NY TX-FR; B	New York Muni	32.2	1.88	10.36	7.10	5.04	☆	☆	5.3	647-1568	None	4.00	0.75	None	Gregory Serbe	'88
PAINEWBR NY TX-FR; A	New York Muni	14.3	1.70	10.35	6.20	☆	☆	☆	4.6	647-1568	None	None	1.51	5.00	Gregory Serbe	'91
PAINEWBR NY TX-FR; D	New York Muni	20.4	1.76	10.36	6.57	5.87	7.13	☆	4.8	647-1568	None	None	1.27	None	Gregory Serbe	'92
PARAGON LA TAX-FREE	Louisiana Muni	192.3	1.86	10.52	6.55	☆	☆	☆	5.0	None	504-332-5968	4.50	0.65	None	Keith Mooney	'89
PARKSTONE MI MUNI; A	Michigan Muni	38.9	1.97	10.75	6.99	5.79	☆	☆	4.6	451-8377	None	4.00	0.85	4.00	First of Amer Invt Corp	'93
PARKSTONE MI MUNI; B	Michigan Muni	2.2	1.65	10.75	6.29	☆	☆	☆	3.8	451-8377	None	None	None	1.00	First of Amer Invt Corp	'94
PARKSTONE MI MUNI; C	Michigan Muni	0.1	1.01	10.54	☆	☆	☆	☆	0.0	451-8377	None	None	1.00	None	First of Amer Invt Corp	'94
PARKSTONE MI MUNI; INSTL	Michigan Muni	177.4	2.13	10.76	7.33	5.86	☆	☆	4.8	451-8377	None	4.00	None	4.00	First of Amer Invt Corp	'90
PARKSTONE MUNI; A	Intermediate Muni	12.0	1.97	10.39	7.03	5.79	☆	☆	4.0	451-8377	None	None	0.87	1.00	First of Amer Invt Corp	'93
PARKSTONE MUNI; B	Intermediate Muni	0.4	1.84	10.36	6.18	☆	☆	☆	3.2	451-8377	None	None	None	4.00	First of Amer Invt Corp	'94
PARKSTONE MUNI; C	Intermediate Muni	0.1	0.78	10.20	☆	☆	☆	☆	0.0	451-8377	None	None	None	1.00	First of Amer Invt Corp	'94
PARKSTONE MUNI; INSTL	Intermediate Muni	135.3	2.03	10.39	7.26	6.88	6.80	☆	4.2	451-8377	None	None	0.77	None	David Pogran	'88
PARNASSUS CA TX-EX	California Muni	4.4	1.91	15.28	8.66	6.34	☆	☆	5.7	999-3505	415-362-3505	4.50	0.39	None	Team Managed	'92
PAYDEN&RYGEL SH DUR TX; A	Short-Term Muni	16.4	1.56	10.02	☆	☆	☆	☆	0.0	572-9336	213-625-1900	None	0.65	None	Team Managed	N/A
PAYDEN&RYGEL TX EX; A	Intermediate Muni	32.3	1.46	9.32	6.38	5.90	7.30	☆	4.9	572-9336	213-625-1900	None	0.50	None	Team Managed	'94
PHOENIX CA TX EXEMPT; A	California Muni	120.5	1.71	12.73	8.07	5.64	☆	8.30	5.8	243-4361	203-253-1000	4.75	0.85	4.00	James Wehr	'93
PHOENIX CA TX EXEMPT; B	California Muni	0.5	1.58	12.73	☆	☆	☆	☆	0.0	243-4361	203-253-1000	None	None	None	James Wehr	'94
PHOENIX TX-EX BOND; A	General Muni	150.8	2.48	11.00	8.57	6.01	8.39	☆	5.5	243-4361	203-253-1000	4.75	0.96	5.00	James Wehr	'88
PHOENIX TX-EX BOND; B	General Muni	2.3	2.27	11.04	7.81	5.20	☆	☆	4.8	243-4361	203-253-1000	None	1.54	5.00	James Wehr	'94
PIERPONT NY TOT RTN BD	New York Muni	40.9	2.66	10.26	7.08	5.62	☆	☆	4.4	521-5412	212-826-1303	None	None	None	Ebby Gerry	'94
PIERPONT TAX EXEMPT BOND	Intermediate Muni	348.0	2.53	11.61	7.42	☆	7.45	7.49	4.7	521-5412	212-826-1303	None	0.71	None	Ebby Gerry	'92
PILLAR NJ MUNI; A ▦	New Jersey Muni	24.0	2.30	10.48	7.31	☆	☆	☆	4.5	932-7782	None	1.00	0.27	None	Charlene Palmer	'92
PILLAR NJ MUNI; B	New Jersey Muni	21.9	2.33	10.48	7.04	☆	☆	☆	4.3	932-7782	None	4.00	0.52	None	Charlene Palmer	'94
PILOT INTMDT MUNI; A	Intermediate Muni	0.2	2.26	10.37	☆	☆	☆	☆	0.0	817-4568	314-466-3368	None	None	None	Jennifer Wacker	'94
PILOT INTMDT MUNI; PILOT	Intermediate Muni	191.6	2.39	10.38	☆	☆	☆	☆	0.0	817-4568	314-466-3368	None	None	None	Jennifer Wacker	'94
PILOT MUNI BOND; PILOT	General Muni	145.6	2.13	10.66	☆	☆	☆	☆	5.0	817-4568	314-466-3368	4.75	None	None	Jennifer Wacker	N/A
PIMCO ADV TAX-EX; A	California Muni	2.7	2.08	11.70	8.90	☆	☆	☆	4.3	227-7337	203-352-4946	None	1.10	4.75	Team Managed	N/A
PIMCO ADV TAX-EX; C	California Muni	58.6	1.81	11.69	8.00	☆	☆	☆	5.3	227-7337	203-352-4946	1.00	1.80	1.00	Team Managed	'93
PIONEER CA DOUBLE TX-FR	California Muni	7.6	1.75	10.68	8.71	☆	7.24	☆	5.3	225-6292	617-742-7825	3.50	0.36	None	Kathy McClaskey	'93
PIONEER INTMDT TX-FR; A	Intermediate Muni	80.8	2.29	10.19	6.97	☆	☆	☆	4.9	225-6292	617-742-7825	3.50	1.00	None	Kathy McClaskey	'86
PIONEER INTMDT TX-FR; B	Intermediate Muni	2.3	2.07	10.21	5.99	☆	☆	☆	4.0	225-6292	617-742-7825	None	1.84	3.00	Kathy McClaskey	'94
PIONEER MA DOUBLE TX-FR	Massachusetts Muni	4.4	2.00	10.83	9.06	☆	☆	☆	5.1	225-6292	617-742-7825	3.50	0.35	None	Kathy McClaskey	'93
PIONEER NY TRIPLE TX-FR	New York Muni	4.9	2.19	10.83	8.37	☆	☆	☆	5.1	225-6292	617-742-7825	3.50	0.36	None	Kathy McClaskey	'93
PIONEER TAX-FREE INC; A	General Muni	471.8	2.18	11.96	8.03	6.51	8.17	9.45	5.5	225-6292	617-742-7825	4.50	0.91	None	Mark Winter	'86
PIPER FDS MN TAX-EX	Minnesota Muni	140.4	2.53	10.75	9.44	6.78	7.93	☆	5.6	866-7778	612-342-6402	4.00	0.89	None	Reuss/White	'88/'88
PIPER FDS NATL TAX-EX	General Muni	58.5	1.77	10.61	8.53	6.23	7.93	☆	5.3	866-7778	612-342-6402	4.00	0.93	None	Reuss/White	'88/'88
PLANTERS TN TAX-FREE BD	Tennessee Muni	36.9	2.29	10.42	8.48	☆	☆	☆	4.9	242-0242	None	4.00	0.10	None	Robert Eason	'93
PNC OH TX-FR INC; INSTL	Ohio Muni	0.2	2.03	9.90	8.21	☆	☆	☆	5.5	422-6538	None	None	0.10	None	Kimberly A. Burford	'93
PNC OH TX-FR INC; INV A	Ohio Muni	3.4	1.95	9.90	8.03	☆	☆	☆	5.4	422-6538	None	4.50		None	Kimberly A. Burford	'93

PERFORMANCE OF MUTUAL FUNDS (continued)

FUND NAME	OBJECTIVE	ASSETS ($ MIL) 5/31/95	NAV ($/SHR) 6/30/95	QTR	1YR	3YRS	5YRS	10YRS	DIV YLD %	PHONE 800	In-State	Load	Exp. Ratio	Redemption	MANAGER	SINCE
						(Annualized)										
PNC OH TX-FR INC; INV B	Ohio Muni	0.1	9.90	1.76	☆	☆	☆	☆	0.0	422-6538	None	None	None	5.00	Kimberly A. Burford	'94
PNC OH TX-FR INC; SERV	Ohio Muni	5.1	9.90	1.96	7.94	☆	☆	☆	5.3	422-6538	None	None	0.35	None	Kimberly A. Burford	'94
PNC PA TX-FR INC; INSTL	Pennsylvania Muni	1.5	10.14	2.31	8.08	☆	☆	☆	5.2	422-6538	None	None	0.39	None	Douglas Gaylor	'93
PNC PA TX-FR INC; INV A	Pennsylvania Muni	44.9	10.14	2.19	7.59	☆	☆	☆	4.8	422-6538	None	4.50	0.41	None	Douglas Gaylor	'93
PNC PA TX-FR INC; INV B	Pennsylvania Muni	3.2	10.14	2.03	☆	☆	☆	☆	0.0	422-6538	None	None	None	5.00	Douglas Gaylor	'94
PNC PA TX-FR INC; SERV	Pennsylvania Muni	14.5	10.14	2.23	7.80	☆	☆	☆	5.0	422-6538	None	None	0.55	None	Douglas Gaylor	'93
PNC TX-FR INCOME; INSTL	General Muni	0.1	10.44	1.74	8.52	☆	☆	☆	5.1	422-6538	None	None	0.50	None	W. Donald Simmons	'93
PNC TX-FR INCOME; INV A	General Muni	6.9	10.44	1.61	8.02	6.23	7.68	☆	4.7	422-6538	None	4.50	0.95	None	W. Donald Simmons	'90
PNC TX-FR INCOME; SERV	General Muni	3.3	10.44	1.67	8.24	☆	☆	☆	4.9	422-6538	None	None	0.75	None	W. Donald Simmons	'93
PORTICO TX-EX INT; INSTL	Intermediate Muni	23.9	10.14	2.51	6.83	☆	☆	☆	4.2	982-8909	414-287-3710	None	0.60	None	Warren Pierson	'93
PRAIRIE INT MUNI; A	Intermediate Muni	17.2	12.06	2.69	7.27	6.33	7.83	☆	4.6	224-4800	None	3.00	0.06	None	John Erickson	'88
PRAIRIE INT MUNI; B	Intermediate Muni		12.07	2.68	☆	☆	☆	☆	0.0	224-4800	None	None	None	3.00	John Erickson	'95
PRAIRIE INT MUNI; I	Intermediate Muni	349.2	12.07	2.84	☆	☆	☆	☆	0.0	224-4800	None	None	None	None	John Erickson	'95
PRAIRIE MUNI BD; A	General Muni	6.7	12.39	3.10	10.74	7.86	9.03	☆	4.9	224-4800	None	4.50	None	None	John Erickson	'88
PRAIRIE MUNI BD; B	General Muni	0.1	12.40	☆	☆	☆	☆	☆	0.0	224-4800	None	None	None	5.00	John Erickson	'95
PRAIRIE MUNI BD; I	General Muni	242.7	12.38	3.16	☆	☆	☆	☆	0.0	224-4800	None	None	None	None	John Erickson	'95
T ROWE PRICE CA TX-FR BD	California Muni	138.1	10.03	1.58	7.74	6.26	7.73	☆	5.6	638-5660	410-547-2308	None	0.60	None	Mary J. Miller	'90
T ROWE PRICE SUM MUN INC	General Muni	10.1	9.64	2.59	9.21	☆	☆	☆	5.5	638-5660	410-547-2308	None	0.50	None	William T. Reynolds	'93
T ROWE PRICE SUM MUN INT	Intermediate Muni	19.9	9.98	2.79	7.62	☆	☆	☆	4.8	638-5660	410-547-2308	None	0.50	None	Miller/Hill	'93/'94
T ROWE PRICE TX FR SH-IN	Short-Term Muni	455.9	5.31	2.08	5.85	4.85	5.76	5.77	4.3	638-5660	410-547-2308	None	0.59	None	Miller/Hill	'89/'94
T ROWE PRICE TX-FR INC	General Muni	1,361.7	9.33	2.06	8.66	6.89	8.18	8.17	5.7	638-5660	410-547-2308	None	0.59	None	William T. Reynolds	'90
T ROWE PRICE TX-FR INS	Intermediate Muni	87.4	10.56	2.62	7.72	☆	☆	☆	4.6	638-5660	410-547-2308	None	0.65	None	William T. Reynolds	'92
T ROWE PRICE TX-FR FL IN	Florida Muni	53.0	10.31	2.46	7.81	☆	☆	☆	4.5	638-5660	410-547-2308	None	0.60	None	William T. Reynolds	'93
T ROWE PRICE TX-FR GA BD	Georgia Muni	25.6	10.01	1.83	8.54	☆	☆	☆	5.2	638-5660	410-547-2308	None	0.65	None	Mary J. Miller	'93
T ROWE PRICE TX-FR HI YD	High-Yield Muni	918.6	11.78	2.62	8.04	7.15	8.39	9.50	6.2	638-5660	410-547-2308	None	0.79	None	C. Stephen Wolfe	'93
T ROWE PRICE TX-FR MD BD	Maryland Muni	756.1	10.11	2.22	8.30	6.69	7.87	☆	5.7	638-5660	410-547-2308	None	0.57	None	Mary J. Miller	'90
T ROWE PRICE TX-FR NJ BD	New Jersey Muni	61.9	10.77	2.22	8.08	6.83	☆	☆	5.4	638-5660	410-547-2308	None	0.65	None	William T. Reynolds	'91
T ROWE PRICE TX-FR NY BD	New York Muni	124.3	10.48	2.17	7.87	6.79	8.26	☆	5.6	638-5660	410-547-2308	None	0.60	None	William T. Reynolds	'86
T ROWE PRICE TX-FR SH MD	Single State Muni	80.5	5.10	2.06	5.47	☆	☆	☆	3.9	638-5660	410-547-2308	None	0.65	None	Miller/Hill	'93/'94
T ROWE PRICE TX-FR SH VA	Single State Muni	8.6	5.13	2.25	☆	☆	☆	☆	0.0	638-5660	410-547-2308	None	None	None	Charles B. Hill	'94
T ROWE PRICE TX-FR VA BD	Virginia Muni	167.0	10.66	2.02	8.15	6.72	☆	☆	5.4	638-5660	410-547-2308	None	0.65	None	Mary J. Miller	'91
PRINCIPAL PRES INS TX-EX	Insured Muni	18.6	9.91	1.75	8.20	6.27	7.33	☆	4.9	826-4600	414-334-5521	3.50	1.20	None	Vern Van Vooren	'86
PRINCIPAL PRES TAX-EX	General Muni	58.7	8.98	2.15	8.73	6.98	7.98	6.07	5.1	826-4600	414-334-5521	3.50	1.00	None	Vern Van Vooren	'84
PRINCIPAL PRES WI TX-EX	Single State Muni	13.5	9.72	2.17	5.72	☆	☆	☆	5.0	826-4600	414-334-5521	2.50	None	None	Thomas Sancomb	'94
PRINCOR TAX-EX BOND; A	General Muni	180.2	11.67	2.73	8.80	6.28	7.79	☆	5.5	247-4123	515-247-5711	4.75	0.91	None	Garrett/Windsor	'91/'92
PRINCOR TAX-EX BOND; B	General Muni	1.7	11.65	2.47	☆	☆	☆	☆	0.0	247-4123	515-247-5711	None	None	4.00	Garrett/Windsor	'94/'94
PRUDENTIAL BD HI YLD; A	High-Yield Muni	128.6	10.81	2.07	8.27	6.84	7.81	☆	6.7	225-1852	None	3.00	0.69	None	Peter Allegrini	'94
PRUDENTIAL BD HI YLD; B	High-Yield Muni	944.5	10.81	1.97	7.84	6.37	7.35	☆	6.3	225-1852	None	None	1.09	5.00	Peter Allegrini	'94
PRUDENTIAL BD HI YLD; C	High-Yield Muni	3.9	10.81	1.91	☆	☆	☆	☆	0.0	225-1852	None	None	None	1.00	Peter Allegrini	'94
PRUDENTIAL BD INS; A	Insured Muni	87.9	10.92	1.80	8.16	6.17	7.68	☆	5.3	225-1852	None	3.00	0.71	None	Patricia Dolan	'92
PRUDENTIAL BD INS; B	Insured Muni	569.1	10.93	1.70	7.83	5.75	7.27	☆	4.9	225-1852	None	None	1.11	5.00	Patricia Dolan	'92
PRUDENTIAL BD INS; C	Insured Muni	0.5	10.93	1.63	☆	☆	☆	☆	0.0	225-1852	None	None	None	1.00	Patricia Dolan	'94
PRUDENTIAL BD MODIFD; A	Intermediate Muni	11.4	10.58	2.12	6.08	5.96	7.33	☆	4.7	225-1852	None	3.00	1.00	None	Marie Conti	'94
PRUDENTIAL BD MODIFD; B	Intermediate Muni	50.2	10.58	1.92	5.56	5.46	6.87	☆	4.3	225-1852	None	None	1.40	5.00	Marie Conti	'90
PRUDENTIAL BD MODIFD; C	Intermediate Muni	0.2	10.58	1.86	☆	☆	☆	☆	0.0	225-1852	None	None	None	1.00	Marie Conti	'94

Fund	Objective	Assets ($M)	NAV						Phone					Manager	Yr
PRUDENTIAL CA CA INC; A	California Muni	163.1	10.21	2.40	8.45	7.91	☆	6.4	225-1852	None	3.00	None	0.35	None	Christian Smith	'91
PRUDENTIAL CA CA INC; B	California Muni	27.6	10.21	2.30	8.01	☆	☆	6.1	225-1852	None	None	None	1.11	5.00	Christian Smith	'93
PRUDENTIAL CA CA INC; C	California Muni	2.5	10.21	2.24	☆	☆	☆	6.0	225-1852	None	None	None	None	1.00	Christian Smith	'94
PRUDENTIAL CA CA SRS; A	California Muni	68.2	11.41	2.15	8.06	6.26	7.59	5.8	225-1852	None	3.00	None	0.73	None	Christian Smith	'91
PRUDENTIAL CA CA SRS; B	California Muni	110.5	11.41	2.05	7.73	5.86	7.15	5.4	225-1852	None	None	None	1.13	5.00	Christian Smith	'91
PRUDENTIAL CA CA SRS; C	California Muni	0.1	11.41	1.99	☆	☆	☆	0.0	225-1852	None	None	None	None	1.00	Christian Smith	'94
PRUDENTIAL MUNI AZ; A	Arizona Muni	28.9	11.63	1.65	7.79	6.13	7.62	5.4	225-1852	None	3.00	None	0.89	None	Christian Smith	'91
PRUDENTIAL MUNI AZ; B	Arizona Muni	29.6	11.63	1.63	7.36	5.70	7.19	5.0	225-1852	None	None	None	1.29	5.00	Christian Smith	'91
PRUDENTIAL MUNI AZ; C	Arizona Muni	0.1	11.63	1.57	☆	☆	☆	5.0	225-1852	None	None	None	None	1.00	Christian Smith	'91
PRUDENTIAL MUNI FL; A	Florida Muni	125.2	10.00	2.08	8.24	6.48	7.65	6.0	225-1852	None	3.00	None	0.20	None	Marie Conti	'91
PRUDENTIAL MUNI FL; B	Florida Muni	7.0	10.00	1.98	☆	☆	☆	0.0	225-1852	None	None	None	None	5.00	Marie Conti	'94
PRUDENTIAL MUNI FL; C	Florida Muni	10.6	10.00	1.92	7.09	6.19	7.28	5.2	225-1852	None	None	None	0.95	1.00	Marie Conti	'94
PRUDENTIAL MUNI GA; A	Georgia Muni	10.5	11.28	1.23	6.66	5.76	6.84	5.0	225-1852	None	3.00	None	1.30	None	Marie Conti	'94
PRUDENTIAL MUNI GA; B	Georgia Muni	8.4	11.28	1.22	☆	☆	☆	4.6	225-1852	None	None	None	1.70	5.00	Marie Conti	'94
PRUDENTIAL MUNI GA; C	Georgia Muni	0.1	11.28	1.20	☆	☆	☆	0.0	225-1852	None	None	None	None	1.00	Marie Conti	'94
PRUDENTIAL MUNI HI; A	Hawaii Muni	3.1	12.03	2.48	☆	☆	☆	0.0	225-1852	None	3.00	None	None	None	Christian Smith	'94
PRUDENTIAL MUNI HI; B	Hawaii Muni	7.9	12.03	2.37	☆	☆	☆	0.0	225-1852	None	None	None	None	5.00	Christian Smith	'94
PRUDENTIAL MUNI HI; C	Hawaii Muni	0.4	12.03	2.31	☆	☆	☆	0.0	225-1852	None	None	None	None	1.00	Christian Smith	'94
PRUDENTIAL MUNI MA; A	Massachusetts Muni	26.9	11.50	1.90	8.42	6.41	7.93	5.7	225-1852	None	3.00	None	0.87	None	Carla Wrocklage	'91
PRUDENTIAL MUNI MA; B	Massachusetts Muni	29.7	11.50	1.89	7.99	5.99	7.50	5.3	225-1852	None	None	None	1.27	5.00	Carla Wrocklage	'91
PRUDENTIAL MUNI MA; C	Massachusetts Muni	0.1	11.50	1.83	☆	☆	☆	0.0	225-1852	None	None	None	None	1.00	Carla Wrocklage	'94
PRUDENTIAL MUNI MD; A	Maryland Muni	18.1	10.54	1.83	6.23	5.26	6.81	5.2	225-1852	None	3.00	None	0.95	None	Marie Conti	'91
PRUDENTIAL MUNI MD; B	Maryland Muni	23.1	10.55	1.63	5.81	4.84	6.39	4.8	225-1852	None	None	None	1.35	5.00	Marie Conti	'91
PRUDENTIAL MUNI MD; C	Maryland Muni	0.1	10.55	1.57	☆	☆	☆	0.0	225-1852	None	None	None	None	1.00	Marie Conti	'94
PRUDENTIAL MUNI MI; A	Michigan Muni	27.2	11.77	1.30	7.02	6.26	7.64	5.4	225-1852	None	3.00	None	0.91	None	Marie Conti	'95
PRUDENTIAL MUNI MI; B	Michigan Muni	43.0	11.76	1.11	6.50	5.79	7.19	5.0	225-1852	None	None	None	1.31	5.00	Marie Conti	'95
PRUDENTIAL MUNI MI; C	Michigan Muni	0.1	11.76	1.05	6.17	5.18	6.47	0.0	225-1852	None	None	None	None	1.00	Marie Conti	'95
PRUDENTIAL MUNI MN; A	Minnesota Muni	10.4	11.56	1.45	5.75	4.80	6.08	4.9	225-1852	None	3.00	None	1.25	None	Christian Smith	'91
PRUDENTIAL MUNI MN; B	Minnesota Muni	12.5	11.56	1.35	☆	☆	☆	4.5	225-1852	None	None	None	1.65	5.00	Christian Smith	'91
PRUDENTIAL MUNI MN; C	Minnesota Muni	0.1	11.56	1.28	☆	☆	☆	0.0	225-1852	None	None	None	1.00	1.00	Christian Smith	'94
PRUDENTIAL MUNI NC; A	North Carolina Muni	25.9	11.06	1.01	7.06	5.68	7.19	5.5	225-1852	None	3.00	None	0.88	None	Marie Conti	'91
PRUDENTIAL MUNI NC; B	North Carolina Muni	42.8	11.06	0.82	6.54	5.22	6.78	5.1	225-1852	None	None	None	1.28	5.00	Marie Conti	'91
PRUDENTIAL MUNI NC; C	North Carolina Muni	0.1	11.06	0.76	☆	☆	☆	0.0	225-1852	None	None	None	None	1.00	Marie Conti	'94
PRUDENTIAL MUNI NJ; A	New Jersey Muni	46.2	10.86	1.77	7.48	6.10	7.96	5.6	225-1852	None	3.00	None	0.58	None	Carla Wrocklage	'91
PRUDENTIAL MUNI NJ; B	New Jersey Muni	259.2	10.86	1.67	7.05	5.67	7.53	5.2	225-1852	None	None	None	0.98	5.00	Carla Wrocklage	'91
PRUDENTIAL MUNI NJ; C	New Jersey Muni	1.3	10.86	1.61	☆	☆	☆	0.0	225-1852	None	None	None	None	1.00	Carla Wrocklage	'91
PRUDENTIAL MUNI NY; A	New York Muni	163.4	11.82	2.08	7.80	6.46	8.13	5.6	225-1852	None	3.00	None	0.74	None	Carla Wrocklage	'91
PRUDENTIAL MUNI NY; B	New York Muni	171.0	11.82	1.98	7.28	6.02	7.69	5.2	225-1852	None	None	None	1.14	5.00	Carla Wrocklage	'94
PRUDENTIAL MUNI NY; C	New York Muni	0.4	11.82	1.92	☆	☆	☆	0.0	225-1852	None	None	None	None	1.00	Carla Wrocklage	'94
PRUDENTIAL MUNI OH; A	Ohio Muni	51.1	11.78	1.87	7.39	6.36	7.79	5.6	225-1852	None	3.00	None	0.84	None	Christian Smith	'91
PRUDENTIAL MUNI OH; B	Ohio Muni	65.6	11.79	1.77	7.05	5.96	7.37	5.2	225-1852	None	3.00	None	1.24	1.00	Christian Smith	'91
PRUDENTIAL MUNI OH; C	Ohio Muni	0.1	11.79	1.71	☆	☆	☆	0.0	225-1852	None	None	None	None	1.00	Christian Smith	'94
PRUDENTIAL MUNI PA; A	Pennsylvania Muni	47.2	10.45	2.19	7.37	6.41	7.74	5.8	225-1852	None	3.00	None	0.75	None	Carla Wrocklage	'91
PRUDENTIAL MUNI PA; B	Pennsylvania Muni	209.9	10.45	2.09	7.05	5.98	7.30	5.4	225-1852	None	None	None	1.15	5.00	Carla Wrocklage	'91
PRUDENTIAL MUNI PA; C	Pennsylvania Muni	0.3	10.45	2.03	☆	☆	☆	0.0	225-1852	None	None	None	None	1.00	Carla Wrocklage	'91
PRUDENTIAL NATL MUNI; A	General Muni	499.8	15.23	2.10	7.84	6.14	7.99	5.4	225-1852	None	3.00	None	0.77	None	Patricia Dolan	'91
PRUDENTIAL NATL MUNI; B	General Muni	203.8	15.26	1.93	7.40	5.71	7.58	5.0	225-1852	None	None	None	1.17	5.00	Patricia Dolan	'94
PRUDENTIAL NATL MUNI; C	General Muni	0.2	15.26	1.86	☆	☆	☆	5.7	225-1852	None	None	None	None	1.00	Patricia Dolan	'91
PUTNAM AZ TXEX INC; A	Arizona Muni	136.6	8.86	1.49	7.04	5.84	☆	5.7	225-1581	617-292-1000	4.75	None	0.97	None	Howard Manning	'93
PUTNAM AZ TXEX INC; B	Arizona Muni	21.5	8.85	1.34	6.30	☆	☆	5.1	225-1581	617-292-1000	None	None	1.60	5.00	Howard Manning	'93

© Copyright Lipper Analytical Services, Inc.

481

PERFORMANCE OF MUTUAL FUNDS (continued)

FUND NAME	OBJECTIVE	ASSETS ($MIL) 5/31/95	NAV ($/SHR) 6/30/95	QTR	1YR	3YRS	5YRS	10YRS	DIV YLD %	800	In-State	Load	Exp. Ratio	Redemption	MANAGER	SINCE
PUTNAM CA INT TXEX; A	California Muni	6.0	8.29	2.43	4.54	☆	☆	☆	5.4	225-1581	617-292-1000	3.25	None	None	Tom Goggins	'94
PUTNAM CA INT TXEX; B	California Muni	3.7	8.28	2.17	3.73	☆	☆	☆	4.8	225-1581	617-292-1000	None	None	3.00	Tom Goggins	'94
PUTNAM CA TXEX INC; A	California Muni	3,248.5	8.29	1.79	8.58	6.41	7.89	9.02	5.8	225-1581	617-292-1000	4.75	0.68	None	William H. Reeves	'86
PUTNAM CA TXEX INC; B	California Muni	398.6	8.28	1.62	7.86	☆	☆	☆	5.2	225-1581	617-292-1000	None	1.32	5.00	William H. Reeves	'93
PUTNAM CA TXEX INC; M	California Muni	2.8	8.28	1.73	☆	☆	☆	☆	0.0	225-1581	617-292-1000	3.25	None	None	William H. Reeves	'95
PUTNAM FL TXEX INC; A	Florida Muni	271.4	8.95	1.94	8.05	6.06	☆	☆	5.6	225-1581	617-292-1000	4.75	0.91	None	Richard P. Wyke	'90
PUTNAM FL TXEX INC; B	Florida Muni	44.7	8.95	1.77	7.35	☆	☆	☆	4.9	225-1581	617-292-1000	None	1.51	5.00	Richard P. Wyke	'93
PUTNAM INTMDT TXEX; A	Intermediate Muni	7.9	8.11	1.87	4.35	☆	☆	☆	5.7	225-1581	617-292-1000	3.25	None	None	Tom Goggins	'94
PUTNAM INTMDT TXEX; B	Intermediate Muni	5.0	8.18	1.73	3.85	☆	☆	☆	5.1	225-1581	617-292-1000	None	None	3.00	Tom Goggins	'94
PUTNAM MA TXEX II; A	Massachusetts Muni	250.9	9.07	2.04	7.77	6.59	8.53	☆	6.1	225-1581	617-292-1000	4.75	0.96	None	Triet N. Nguyen	'89
PUTNAM MA TXEX II; B	Massachusetts Muni	47.5	9.06	1.88	6.96	☆	☆	☆	5.4	225-1581	617-292-1000	None	1.60	5.00	Triet N. Nguyen	'93
PUTNAM MI TXEX II; A	Michigan Muni	136.1	8.86	1.86	6.62	6.17	7.55	☆	5.9	225-1581	617-292-1000	4.75	0.99	None	Howard Manning	'93
PUTNAM MI TXEX II; B	Michigan Muni	21.1	8.84	1.60	5.90	☆	☆	☆	5.3	225-1581	617-292-1000	None	1.61	5.00	Howard Manning	'93
PUTNAM MN TXEX II; A	Minnesota Muni	98.4	8.80	1.72	6.93	5.97	7.23	☆	5.7	225-1581	617-292-1000	4.75	1.03	None	Howard Manning	'93
PUTNAM MN TXEX II; B	Minnesota Muni	19.7	8.78	1.70	6.19	☆	☆	☆	5.1	225-1581	617-292-1000	None	1.68	5.00	Howard Manning	'93
PUTNAM MUNI INCOME; A	General Muni	848.8	8.80	2.06	7.89	6.72	8.30	☆	6.1	225-1581	617-292-1000	4.75	0.97	None	Richard P. Wyke	'94
PUTNAM MUNI INCOME; B	General Muni	446.4	8.79	1.92	7.27	☆	☆	☆	5.5	225-1581	617-292-1000	None	1.54	5.00	Richard P. Wyke	'94
PUTNAM MUNI INCOME; M	General Muni	2.8	8.79	1.65	☆	☆	☆	☆	0.0	225-1581	617-292-1000	3.25	0.95	None	Tom Goggins	'94
PUTNAM NJ TXEX INC; A	New Jersey Muni	242.9	8.83	2.06	6.95	6.13	7.83	☆	5.7	225-1581	617-292-1000	4.75	0.95	None	Tom Goggins	'93
PUTNAM NJ TXEX INC; B	New Jersey Muni	58.6	8.82	1.90	6.15	☆	☆	☆	5.1	225-1581	617-292-1000	None	1.59	5.00	Tom Goggins	'93
PUTNAM NY INT TXEX; A	New York Muni	2.1	8.12	1.85	3.94	☆	☆	☆	5.6	225-1581	617-292-1000	3.25	0.17	None	Tom Goggins	'94
PUTNAM NY INT TXEX; B	New York Muni	1.4	8.11	1.57	3.31	☆	☆	☆	5.0	225-1581	617-292-1000	None	0.46	3.00	Tom Goggins	'94
PUTNAM NY TXEX INC; A	New York Muni	2,042.5	8.68	0.96	5.97	5.88	7.86	☆	5.9	225-1581	617-292-1000	4.75	0.75	None	David J. Eurkus	'83
PUTNAM NY TXEX INC; B	New York Muni	203.3	8.66	0.77	5.27	☆	☆	☆	5.2	225-1581	617-292-1000	None	1.39	5.00	David J. Eurkus	'93
PUTNAM NY TXEX INC; M	New York Muni	0.2	8.68	0.74	☆	☆	☆	☆	0.0	225-1581	617-292-1000	3.25	None	None	David J. Eurkus	'95
PUTNAM NY TXEX OPPT; A	New York Muni	173.8	8.71	2.56	8.01	6.23	☆	☆	6.1	225-1581	617-292-1000	4.75	0.98	None	Michael F. Bouscaren	'94
PUTNAM NY TXEX OPPT; B	New York Muni	18.4	8.70	2.41	7.21	☆	☆	☆	5.5	225-1581	617-292-1000	None	1.58	5.00	Michael F. Bouscaren	'94
PUTNAM NY TXEX OPPT; M	New York Muni	0.1	8.70	2.36	☆	☆	☆	☆	0.0	225-1581	617-292-1000	3.25	0.99	5.00	Michael F. Bouscaren	'95
PUTNAM OH TXEX II; A	Ohio Muni	193.5	8.81	1.95	7.45	6.22	7.70	☆	5.8	225-1581	617-292-1000	4.75	0.99	None	Tom Goggins	'93
PUTNAM OH TXEX II; B	Ohio Muni	32.8	8.80	1.80	6.80	☆	☆	☆	5.2	225-1581	617-292-1000	None	1.61	5.00	Tom Goggins	'93
PUTNAM PA TXEX INC; A	Pennsylvania Muni	179.0	9.10	2.21	8.15	6.92	8.49	☆	5.8	225-1581	617-292-1000	4.75	0.91	None	Richard P. Wyke	'89
PUTNAM PA TXEX INC; B	Pennsylvania Muni	44.3	9.09	2.04	7.45	☆	☆	☆	5.2	225-1581	617-292-1000	None	1.60	5.00	Richard P. Wyke	'93
PUTNAM TX-FR INC HY; A	High-Yield Muni	465.9	14.14	2.52	7.33	6.53	7.66	☆	6.7	225-1581	617-292-1000	4.75	0.71	None	Triet N. Nguyen	'93
PUTNAM TX-FR INC HY; B	High-Yield Muni	1,464.4	14.14	2.28	6.62	☆	☆	☆	6.0	225-1581	617-292-1000	None	1.45	5.00	Triet N. Nguyen	'88
PUTNAM TX-FR INC HY; M	High-Yield Muni	1.8	14.13	2.46	☆	☆	☆	☆	0.0	225-1581	617-292-1000	3.25	None	None	Triet N. Nguyen	'94
PUTNAM TX-FR INC INS; A	Insured Muni	187.7	14.82	1.76	8.30	☆	☆	☆	5.6	225-1581	617-292-1000	4.75	0.80	None	Richard P. Wyke	'93
PUTNAM TX-FR INC INS; B	Insured Muni	385.6	14.84	1.66	7.68	5.45	6.89	☆	4.9	225-1581	617-292-1000	None	1.53	5.00	Richard P. Wyke	'88
PUTNAM TXEX INC; A	General Muni	2,346.3	8.68	1.11	6.76	5.98	7.87	9.20	6.1	225-1581	617-292-1000	4.75	0.77	None	David J. Eurkus	'83
PUTNAM TXEX INC; B	General Muni	244.3	8.68	0.95	6.18	☆	☆	☆	5.5	225-1581	617-292-1000	None	1.41	5.00	David J. Eurkus	'93
QUEST VALUE CA	California Muni	25.6	10.54	1.55	7.31	6.26	☆	☆	5.1	232-3863	None	4.75	0.61	None	Robert J. Bluestone	'90
QUEST VALUE NATL	General Muni	84.9	10.74	2.19	7.96	6.75	☆	☆	5.4	232-3863	None	4.75	0.43	None	Robert J. Bluestone	'90
QUEST VALUE NY	New York Muni	31.0	10.70	2.42	7.60	6.78	☆	☆	5.2	232-3863	None	4.75	0.65	None	Robert J. Bluestone	'90
RANSON MGD KANSAS	Kansas Muni	131.3	12.07	1.83	6.50	6.50	☆	☆	5.4	345-2363	316-262-4955	4.25	0.70	None	Ranson/Meltzner	'90/'90
RANSON MGD KANSAS INS	Kansas Muni	30.7	12.00	2.49	5.37	☆	☆	☆	4.5	345-2363	316-262-4955	2.75	0.51	None	Ranson/Meltzner	'92/'92
RANSON MGD NEBRASKA	Single State Muni	13.7	10.97	1.91	8.28	☆	☆	☆	5.6	345-2363	316-262-4955	4.25	0.19	None	Ranson/Meltzner	'93/'93

Fund	Objective	Net Assets ($Mil)	NAV	4-Wk %	1-Yr %	3-Yr %	5-Yr %	10-Yr %	Yield %	Phone (800)	Phone (Direct)	Max Chg %	Exp %	Manager	Since
RBB MUNI BD; BEA		52.0	15.34	2.34	8.09	☆	☆		4.2	888-9723	212-878-0600	None	None	Robert Moore	'95
REMBRANDT TX-EX FXD; INV	General Muni	1.2	9.73	1.80	7.16	☆	☆		4.5	443-4725	None	4.50	0.97	Gidley/Pratt	'93/'93
REMBRANDT TX-EX FXD; TR	General Muni	52.4	9.75	1.85	7.39	☆	☆		4.7	443-4725	None	None	0.71	Gidley/Pratt	'93/'93
RIVERSIDE CAP SUNBELT	General Muni	1.7	9.69	-0.91	☆	☆	☆			874-8376	None	3.00	None	Alfred Jordan	'92
RIVERSIDE CAP TN MUNI	Tennessee Muni	21.1	9.84	2.27	5.62	☆	☆		5.1	874-8376	None	3.00	1.19	Alfred Jordan	
ROCHESTER FD MUNICIPALS	New York Muni	2,031.3	17.60	3.46	8.46	7.17	8.67	10.18	6.4	None	716-383-1708	4.00	0.84	Ronald H. Fielding	'83
ROCHESTER LTD TM NY	Single State Muni	512.6	3.23	2.06	5.96	6.51	☆		5.4	None	716-383-1708	2.00	0.89	Ronald H. Fielding	'91
S BERNSTEIN CA MUNI	California Muni	183.8	13.39	2.14	7.09	5.58	5.74		4.8	None	212-756-4097	None	0.70	Investment Policy Group	'90
S BERNSTEIN DIV MUNI	Intermediate Muni	597.9	13.35	2.28	7.40	5.74	6.86		4.8	None	212-756-4097	None	0.67	Investment Policy Group	'89
S BERNSTEIN NY MUNI	New York Muni	434.4	13.34	2.51	7.25	5.74	7.01		4.9	None	212-756-4097	None	0.67	Investment Policy Group	'89
S BERNSTEIN SH DUR CA	California Muni	61.9	12.61	1.70	☆	☆			0.0	None	212-756-4097	None	None	Investment Policy Group	'94
S BERNSTEIN SH DUR DVSFD	Short-Term Muni	102.6	12.62	1.77	☆	☆			0.0	None	212-756-4097	None	None	Investment Policy Group	'94
S BERNSTEIN SH DUR NY	Single State Muni	59.2	12.57	1.57	☆	☆			0.0	None	212-756-4097	None	None	Investment Policy Group	'94
SAFECO ADV INT MUNI; A	Intermediate Muni	1.7	10.40	2.34	☆	☆			0.0	528-6501	206-545-6283	4.75	None	Stephen C. Bauer	'94
SAFECO ADV INT MUNI; B	Intermediate Muni	1.7	10.85	2.15	☆	☆			0.0	528-6501	206-545-6283	None	None	Stephen C. Bauer	'94
SAFECO ADV INT MUNI; C	Intermediate Muni	1.7	10.85	2.24	☆	☆			0.0	528-6501	206-545-6283	None	None	Stephen C. Bauer	'94
SAFECO ADV MUNI BD; A	General Muni	1.9	10.40	2.01	☆	☆			0.0	528-6501	206-545-6283	4.75	None	Stephen C. Bauer	'94
SAFECO ADV MUNI BD; B	General Muni	1.9	10.85	1.81	☆	☆			0.0	528-6501	206-545-6283	None	None	Stephen C. Bauer	'94
SAFECO ADV MUNI BD; C	General Muni	1.9	10.59	1.81	☆	☆			0.0	528-6501	206-545-6283	None	None	Stephen C. Bauer	'94
SAFECO ADV WA MUNI; A	Washington Muni	1.9	10.59	1.88	☆	☆			0.0	528-6501	206-545-6283	4.75	None	Stephen C. Bauer	'94
SAFECO ADV WA MUNI; B	Washington Muni	1.9	10.59	1.69	☆	☆			0.0	528-6501	206-545-6283	None	None	Stephen C. Bauer	'94
SAFECO ADV WA MUNI; C	Washington Muni	1.9	11.61	1.69	☆	☆			0.0	528-6501	206-545-6283	None	None	Stephen C. Bauer	'94
SAFECO CA TX-FR INCOME	California Muni	68.4	10.14	1.95	9.54	6.40	8.04		5.4	426-6730	206-545-5530	None	0.70	Stephen C. Bauer	'83
SAFECO INSURED MUNI BOND	Insured Muni	8.6	10.14	2.13	10.87	☆	8.77		4.9	426-6730	206-545-5530	None	1.08	Stephen C. Bauer	'93
SAFECO INTMDT MUNI BOND	Intermediate Muni	14.6	10.35	2.89	7.10	☆			4.4	426-6730	206-545-5530	None	0.85	Stephen C. Bauer	'93
SAFECO MUNICIPAL BOND	General Muni	498.0	13.47	2.26	9.32	6.30	8.19	9.36	5.7	426-6730	206-545-5530	None	0.56	Stephen C. Bauer	'81
SAFECO WA MUNI BOND	Washington Muni	6.0	10.16	1.85	8.96	☆			4.9	426-6730	206-545-5530	None	1.09	Stephen C. Bauer	'93
SALOMON BROS INT MUN; A	Intermediate Muni	0.3	10.14	2.25	☆	☆			0.0	725-6666	212-783-1301	4.75	None	MaryBeth Whyte	'95
SALOMON BROS INT MUN; B	Intermediate Muni	0.3	10.14	2.05	☆	☆			0.0	725-6666	212-783-1301	5.00	None	MaryBeth Whyte	'95
SALOMON BROS INT MUN; C	Intermediate Muni	0.3	10.14	2.06	☆	☆			0.0	725-6666	212-783-1301	1.00	None	MaryBeth Whyte	'95
SALOMON BROS INT MUN; O	Intermediate Muni	9.5	10.14	2.32	☆	☆			0.0	725-6666	212-783-1301	None	None	MaryBeth Whyte	'95
SALOMON BROS NY MUNI; A	New York Muni	0.3	9.61	2.19	☆	☆			0.0	725-6666	212-783-1301	4.75	None	MaryBeth Whyte	'95
SALOMON BROS NY MUNI; B	New York Muni	0.3	9.61	2.00	☆	☆			0.0	725-6666	212-783-1301	5.00	None	MaryBeth Whyte	'95
SALOMON BROS NY MUNI; C	New York Muni	0.3	9.61	2.00	☆	☆			0.0	725-6666	212-783-1301	1.00	None	MaryBeth Whyte	'95
SALOMON BROS NY MUNI; O	New York Muni	3.2	9.62	2.34	7.27	☆			5.6	725-6666	212-783-1301	None	None	MaryBeth Whyte	'94
SCHWAB INV CA LT TXFR BD	California Muni	91.2	10.42	1.61	7.37	5.83			5.4	838-0650	None	None	0.60	Keighley/Ward	'92/'92
SCHWAB INV CA SH/INTMDT	California Muni	40.5	9.93	2.00	5.35	☆			4.2	838-0650	None	None	0.48	Keighley/Ward	'93/'93
SCHWAB INV LT TXFR BD	General Muni	43.3	10.05	1.92	7.95	☆			5.2	838-0650	None	None	0.51	Keighley/Ward	'92/'92
SCHWAB INV SH/INT TX-FR	Short-Term Muni	53.2	10.01	2.15	5.55	☆			3.9	838-0650	None	None	0.48	Keighley/Ward	'93/'93
SCUDDER CAL TXFREE	California Muni	302.2	10.16	2.16	8.16	6.69	8.33	8.55	5.0	225-2470	617-439-4640	None	0.78	Ragus/Carleton	'90/'83
SCUDDER HI YLD TXFR	High-Yield Muni	288.1	11.71	2.68	8.08	6.80	8.77		6.0	225-2470	617-439-4640	None	0.80	Condon/Manning	'87/'87
SCUDDER LTD TERM TX FR	Short-Term Muni	116.6	11.91	2.15	5.64	☆			4.9	225-2470	617-439-4640	None	None	Patton/Carleton	'94/'94
SCUDDER MASS LTD TX FREE	Single State Muni	48.6	11.92	2.20	6.29	☆			4.5	225-2470	617-439-4640	None	None	Condon/Meary	'94/'94
SCUDDER MASS TX FREE	Massachusetts Muni	302.8	13.43	2.09	8.55	7.54	8.78		5.4	225-2470	617-439-4640	None	0.07	Condon/Meary	'89/'89
SCUDDER MED TRM TXFR	Intermediate Muni	721.7	10.95	2.87	7.52	6.63	7.90		5.0	225-2470	617-439-4640	None	0.63	Carleton/Patton	'86/'90
SCUDDER MGD MUNI BOND	General Muni	759.1	8.52	1.95	8.10	6.63	8.27	8.80	5.7	225-2470	617-439-4640	None	0.63	Carleton/Condon	'86/'88
SCUDDER NY TXFREE	New York Muni	198.0	10.49	2.34	7.71	6.41	8.39	8.30	5.0	225-2470	617-439-4640	None	0.82	Ragus/Carleton	'90/'83
SCUDDER OHIO TXFREE	Ohio Muni	79.7	12.84	2.12	8.18	6.56	8.18		5.4	225-2470	617-439-4640	None	0.50	Carleton/Condon	'95/'88
SCUDDER PENN TXFREE	Pennsylvania Muni	75.2	13.18	2.01	8.30	6.81	8.18		5.5	225-2470	617-439-4640	None	0.50	Carleton/Condon	'95/'88
SECURITY TAX-EXEMPT; A	General Muni	25.2	9.51	1.00	5.78	4.83	6.68	7.10	5.1	888-2461	913-295-3127	4.75	0.82	Jane Tedder	'84

PERFORMANCE OF MUTUAL FUNDS (continued)

FUND NAME	OBJECTIVE	ASSETS ($MIL) 5/31/95	NAV ($/SHR) 6/30/95	QTR	1YR	3YRS	5YRS	10YRS	DIV YLD %	800	In-State	Load	Exp. Ratio	Redemption	MANAGER	SINCE
							(Annualized)						FEES			
SEI TX EX INT-TM MUNI	Intermediate Muni	98.5	10.46	2.07	7.16	5.33	6.41	☆	5.0	342-5734	610-254-1000	None	0.53	None	Blake Miller	'93
SEI TX EX KS; A	Kansas Muni	64.0	10.54	2.05	7.16	6.27	☆	☆	5.4	342-5734	610-254-1000	None	0.21	None	Richard Winton	'95
SEI TX EX MA INTMDT	Massachusetts Muni	6.2	10.20	1.79	6.36	5.41	6.69	☆	4.3	342-5734	610-254-1000	None	0.60	None	Joe Solitto	'95
SEI TX EX PA MUNI; A	Pennsylvania Muni	105.2	10.55	2.09	6.21	5.41	6.69	☆	5.2	342-5734	610-254-1000	None	0.47	None	Peter Pellett	'94
SELIGMAN NJ TXEX; A	New Jersey Muni	74.8	7.52	1.97	7.69	6.25	7.73	☆	5.3	221-7844	212-850-1864	4.75	0.90	None	Thomas G. Moles	'88
SELIGMAN NJ TXEX; D	New Jersey Muni	1.3	7.60	1.73	6.88	☆	☆	☆	4.4	221-7844	212-850-1864	None	1.75	1.00	Thomas G. Moles	'94
SELIGMAN PA TXEX PA; A	Pennsylvania Muni	34.4	7.73	2.15	8.64	6.55	7.73	☆	5.0	221-7844	212-850-1864	4.75	1.16	None	Thomas G. Moles	'86
SELIGMAN PA TXEX PA; D	Pennsylvania Muni	0.3	7.73	1.87	7.63	☆	☆	☆	4.0	221-7844	212-850-1864	None	2.00	1.00	Thomas G. Moles	'94
SELIGMAN PA TXEX CA HY; A	California Muni	48.6	6.42	1.91	7.42	6.53	7.62	9.10	5.8	221-7844	212-850-1864	4.75	0.85	None	Thomas G. Moles	'84
SELIGMAN TXEX CA HY; D	California Muni	0.9	6.42	1.49	6.14	☆	☆	☆	5.0	221-7844	212-850-1864	None	1.74	1.00	Thomas G. Moles	'94
SELIGMAN TXEX CA QLT; A	California Muni	99.5	6.56	1.30	8.29	5.85	7.43	8.36	5.3	221-7844	212-850-1864	4.75	0.81	None	Thomas G. Moles	'84
SELIGMAN TXEX CA QLT; D	California Muni	1.0	6.55	1.04	7.18	☆	☆	☆	4.5	221-7844	212-850-1864	None	1.77	1.00	Thomas G. Moles	'94
SELIGMAN TXEX CO; A	Colorado Muni	56.0	7.27	1.71	6.98	5.99	6.76	☆	5.3	221-7844	212-850-1864	4.75	0.86	Non.	Thomas G. Moles	'86
SELIGMAN TXEX CO; D	Colorado Muni	0.1	7.27	1.53	5.85	☆	☆	☆	5.3	221-7844	212-850-1864	None	1.78	1.00	Thomas G. Moles	'94
SELIGMAN TXEX FL; A	Florida Muni	50.1	7.62	1.58	8.42	6.85	7.89	☆	5.4	221-7844	212-850-1864	4.75	0.42	None	Thomas G. Moles	'86
SELIGMAN TXEX FL; D	Florida Muni	0.8	7.64	1.61	7.75	☆	☆	☆	4.5	221-7844	212-850-1864	None	1.29	1.00	Thomas G. Moles	'94
SELIGMAN TXEX GA; A	Georgia Muni	60.8	7.73	3.00	9.33	6.40	7.80	☆	5.2	221-7844	212-850-1864	4.75	0.73	None	Thomas G. Moles	'87
SELIGMAN TXEX GA; D	Georgia Muni	1.9	7.73	2.60	8.27	☆	☆	☆	4.2	221-7844	212-850-1864	None	1.76	1.00	Thomas G. Moles	'94
SELIGMAN TXEX LA; A	Louisiana Muni	63.7	8.04	1.96	7.67	5.72	7.38	☆	5.4	221-7844	212-850-1864	4.75	0.87	None	Thomas G. Moles	'85
SELIGMAN TXEX LA; D	Louisiana Muni	0.6	8.04	1.80	6.71	☆	☆	☆	4.4	221-7844	212-850-1864	None	1.78	1.00	Thomas G. Moles	'94
SELIGMAN TXEX MA; A	Massachusetts Muni	117.9	7.84	1.86	7.60	6.40	7.96	8.30	5.5	221-7844	212-850-1864	4.75	0.85	None	Thomas G. Moles	'84
SELIGMAN TXEX MA; D	Massachusetts Muni	1.1	7.83	1.39	6.47	☆	☆	☆	4.5	221-7844	212-850-1864	None	1.78	1.00	Thomas G. Moles	'94
SELIGMAN TXEX MD; A	Maryland Muni	57.7	7.87	2.21	8.35	6.39	7.58	☆	5.3	221-7844	212-850-1864	4.75	0.92	None	Thomas G. Moles	'85
SELIGMAN TXEX MD; D	Maryland Muni	0.6	7.88	1.91	7.36	☆	☆	☆	4.2	221-7844	212-850-1864	None	1.80	1.00	Thomas G. Moles	'94
SELIGMAN TXEX MI; A	Michigan Muni	153.8	8.46	1.72	7.60	6.44	7.82	8.95	5.5	221-7844	212-850-1864	4.75	0.84	None	Thomas G. Moles	'84
SELIGMAN TXEX MI; D	Michigan Muni	1.0	8.45	1.38	6.33	☆	☆	☆	4.4	221-7844	212-850-1864	None	1.75	1.00	Thomas G. Moles	'94
SELIGMAN TXEX MN; A	Minnesota Muni	134.3	7.80	1.85	7.01	6.93	7.36	8.18	5.9	221-7844	212-850-1864	4.75	0.85	None	Thomas G. Moles	'84
SELIGMAN TXEX MN; D	Minnesota Muni	2.1	7.80	1.60	5.98	☆	☆	☆	4.9	221-7844	212-850-1864	None	1.74	1.00	Thomas G. Moles	'94
SELIGMAN TXEX MO; A	Missouri Muni	52.8	7.62	1.82	8.44	5.63	7.26	☆	5.2	221-7844	212-850-1864	4.75	0.74	None	Thomas G. Moles	'86
SELIGMAN TXEX MO; D	Missouri Muni	0.4	7.62	1.51	7.28	☆	☆	☆	4.2	221-7844	212-850-1864	None	1.70	1.00	Thomas G. Moles	'94
SELIGMAN TXEX NATL; A	General Muni	109.4	7.51	2.55	8.29	5.85	7.44	9.00	5.4	221-7844	212-850-1864	4.75	0.85	None	Thomas G. Moles	'84
SELIGMAN TXEX NATL; D	General Muni	0.8	7.52	2.37	7.45	☆	☆	☆	4.3	221-7844	212-850-1864	None	1.76	1.00	Thomas G. Moles	'94
SELIGMAN TXEX NC; A	North Carolina Muni	39.1	7.67	1.80	9.65	6.54	7.70	☆	5.3	221-7844	212-850-1864	4.75	0.44	None	Thomas G. Moles	'90
SELIGMAN TXEX NC; D	North Carolina Muni	1.3	7.67	1.72	8.76	☆	☆	☆	4.5	221-7844	212-850-1864	None	1.27	1.00	Thomas G. Moles	'94
SELIGMAN TXEX NY; A	New York Muni	88.4	7.77	2.13	8.18	6.30	7.90	8.52	5.4	221-7844	212-850-1864	4.75	0.87	None	Thomas G. Moles	'84
SELIGMAN TXEX NY; D	New York Muni	0.6	7.78	1.96	7.16	☆	☆	☆	4.4	221-7844	212-850-1864	None	1.81	1.00	Thomas G. Moles	'94
SELIGMAN TXEX OH; A	Ohio Muni	173.6	8.05	1.99	7.50	6.24	7.70	8.75	5.5	221-7844	212-850-1864	4.75	0.84	None	Thomas G. Moles	'84
SELIGMAN TXEX OH; D	Ohio Muni	0.5	8.07	1.68	6.34	☆	☆	☆	4.4	221-7844	212-850-1864	None	1.78	1.00	Thomas G. Moles	'94
SELIGMAN TXEX OR; A	Oregon Muni	60.0	7.60	1.98	7.27	6.09	7.34	☆	5.3	221-7844	212-850-1864	4.75	0.78	None	Thomas G. Moles	'90
SELIGMAN TXEX OR; D	Oregon Muni	1.4	7.60	1.73	6.37	☆	☆	☆	4.4	221-7844	212-850-1864	None	1.72	1.00	Thomas G. Moles	'94
SELIGMAN TXEX SC; A	South Carolina Muni	113.7	7.89	2.08	8.24	5.84	7.45	☆	5.3	221-7844	212-850-1864	4.75	0.83	None	Thomas G. Moles	'87
SELIGMAN TXEX SC; D	South Carolina Muni	1.7	7.88	1.69	7.20	☆	☆	☆	4.3	221-7844	212-850-1864	None	1.74	1.00	Thomas G. Moles	'94
SENTINEL PA TAX-FREE	Pennsylvania Muni	33.4	12.92	1.61	5.72	5.34	6.84	☆	5.0	233-4332	802-229-3761	5.00	1.30	None	Kenneth J. Hart	'93
SENTINEL TAX-FREE INCOME	General Muni	108.6	13.12	1.32	6.61	6.25	☆	☆	5.2	233-4332	802-229-3761	5.00	0.75	None	Kenneth J. Hart	'90
1784 CT TX-EX INC	Connecticut Muni	61.4	10.16	1.76	☆	☆	☆	☆	0.0	252-1784	None	None	None	None	James L. Bosland	'94

Fund	Objective	Net Assets ($Mil)	NAV	(4wk%)	(1yr)	(3yr)	(5yr)	(10yr)	Yield	Phone	Phone (2)	Load	Exp	Load (2)	Manager	Mgr Since
1784 MA TX-EX INC ✱	Massachusetts Muni	82.1	9.79	1.71	6.00	☆	☆	☆	4.8	252-1784	None	None	0.33	None	Susan Sanderson	'93
1784 RI TX-EX INC ✱	Single State Muni	32.5	10.02	1.81	☆	☆	☆	☆	0.0	252-1784	None	None	0.32	None	James L. Bosland	'94
1784 TX-EX MED TM ✱	Intermediate Muni	176.3	10.04	2.15	7.39	☆	☆	☆	0.0	252-1784	None	None	0.48	None	David H. Thompson	'93
SHAWMUT CT INT MUNI; INV	Single State Muni	8.8	9.92	3.04	7.88	☆	☆	☆	4.3	742-9688	508-626-7877	2.00	0.51	None	Robert Gleason	'93
SHAWMUT MA INT MUNI; INV	Massachusetts Muni	8.0	9.89	2.63	7.71	☆	☆	☆	4.4	742-9688	508-626-7877	2.00		None	Robert Gleason	'93
SHORT-TM MUNI; INST SVC	Short-Term Muni	4.8	10.28	2.16	5.26	☆	☆	☆	3.8	245-4770	412-288-1900	None	0.72	None	Jonathan C. Conley	'93
SHORT-TM MUNI; INSTL	Short-Term Muni	222.7	10.28	2.21	5.51	4.11	5.03	5.33	4.0	245-4770	412-288-1900	None	0.47	None	Jonathan C. Conley	'84
SIERRA CA INS INTMDT; A	California Muni	55.5	10.45	1.89	8.71	☆	☆	☆	4.8	222-5852	818-725-0405	4.50	None	4.50	Joseph Piraro	'94
SIERRA CA INS INTMDT; B	California Muni	12.4	10.45	1.68	☆	☆	☆	☆	4.1	222-5852	818-725-0405	5.00	None	5.00	Joseph Piraro	'94
SIERRA CA INS INTMDT; S	California Muni	0.1	10.45	1.70	☆	☆	☆	☆	4.1	222-5852	818-725-0405	5.00	None	5.00	Joseph Piraro	'94
SIERRA CA MUNICIPAL; A	California Muni	414.6	10.53	2.12	7.58	6.21	7.19	☆	5.8	222-5852	818-725-0405	4.50	0.79	4.50	Joseph Piraro	'91
SIERRA CA MUNICIPAL; B	California Muni	6.4	10.53	1.90	☆	☆	☆	☆	5.0	222-5852	818-725-0405	5.00	None	5.00	Joseph Piraro	'94
SIERRA CA MUNICIPAL; S	California Muni	0.1	10.53	1.93	☆	☆	☆	☆	5.0	222-5852	818-725-0405	5.00	None	5.00	Joseph Piraro	'94
SIERRA FL INS MUNI; A	Florida Muni	34.9	9.43	0.30	6.01	☆	☆	☆	5.5	222-5852	818-725-0405	4.50	None	5.00	William Grady	'93
SIERRA FL INS MUNI; B	Florida Muni	3.4	9.43	0.08	☆	☆	☆	☆	4.8	222-5852	818-725-0405	5.00	None	5.00	William Grady	'94
SIERRA FL INS MUNI; S	Florida Muni	0.1	9.43	0.11	☆	☆	☆	☆	4.7	222-5852	818-725-0405	5.00	None	5.00	William Grady	'94
SIERRA NATL MUNI; S	General Muni	276.7	10.76	-0.07	6.32	6.12	☆	☆	5.9	222-5852	818-725-0405	4.50	0.87	4.50	David Johnson	'90
SIERRA NATL MUNI; B	General Muni	4.5	10.76	-0.28	☆	☆	☆	☆	5.2	222-5852	818-725-0405	None	None	5.00	David Johnson	'92
SIERRA NATL MUNI; S	General Muni	0.1	10.76	-0.25	☆	☆	☆	☆	5.2	222-5852	818-725-0405	4.50	None	5.00	David Johnson	'94
SIT MN TAX-FREE INCOME	Minnesota Muni	47.9	10.02	2.02	7.56	☆	☆	☆	5.6	332-5580	612-334-5888	None	None	5.00	Briley/Sit	'93/'93
SIT TX-FR INCOME	General Muni	251.2	9.79	2.35	7.61	6.77	7.43	☆	5.7	332-5580	612-334-5888	None	0.77	None	Briley/Sit	'88/'91
SM BARNEY AZ; A	Arizona Muni	43.3	9.94	1.77	8.32	6.83	7.89	☆	5.3	327-6748	212-723-9218	4.00	0.83	4.00	Lawrence McDermott	'87
SM BARNEY AZ; B	Arizona Muni	22.8	9.94	1.63	7.73	☆	☆	☆	4.8	327-6748	212-723-9218	None	1.35	4.50	Lawrence McDermott	'92
SM BARNEY CA; A	California Muni	420.1	15.59	2.08	9.09	7.15	8.25	8.81	5.6	327-6748	212-723-9218	4.00	0.80	4.00	Joseph Deane	'84
SM BARNEY CA; B	California Muni	137.7	15.59	1.94	8.50	☆	☆	☆	5.1	327-6748	212-723-9218	None	1.32	4.50	Joseph Deane	'92
SM BARNEY FL; A	Florida Muni	16.8	9.89	2.24	8.43	☆	☆	☆	4.9	327-6748	212-723-9218	4.00	0.99	4.00	Lawrence McDermott	'92
SM BARNEY FL; B	Florida Muni	38.8	9.89	2.14	7.91	☆	☆	☆	4.4	327-6748	212-723-9218	None	1.49	4.50	Lawrence McDermott	'92
SM BARNEY INTMDT CA; A	California Muni	23.5	8.21	1.72	6.27	6.05	☆	☆	4.9	327-6748	212-723-9218	2.00	0.75	2.00	Lawrence McDermott	'91
SM BARNEY INTMDT NY; A	New York Muni	57.4	8.25	2.12	6.30	6.01	☆	☆	4.8	327-6748	212-723-9218	2.00	0.65	2.00	Lawrence McDermott	'91
SM BARNEY LTD MUNI; A	Short-Term Muni	63.6	8.11	1.51	5.00	5.08	☆	☆	4.2	327-6748	212-723-9218	2.00	0.80	2.00	Lawrence McDermott	'91
SM BARNEY MA; A	Massachusetts Muni	28.6	12.45	1.97	8.33	5.98	7.57	☆	5.5	327-6748	212-723-9218	4.00	0.81	4.00	Lawrence McDermott	'87
SM BARNEY MA; B	Massachusetts Muni	26.9	12.45	1.83	7.78	☆	☆	☆	5.0	327-6748	212-723-9218	None	1.32	4.00	Lawrence McDermott	'92
SM BARNEY MGD MUNIS; A	General Muni	1,837.7	15.73	2.69	10.97	9.28	9.98	10.06	5.9	327-6748	212-723-9218	4.00	0.71	4.00	Joseph Deane	'88
SM BARNEY MGD MUNIS; B	General Muni	575.5	15.73	2.55	10.38	☆	☆	☆	5.4	327-6748	212-723-9218	None	1.23	2.00	Joseph Deane	'92
SM BARNEY MUNI CA L; A	California Muni	5.4	6.48	1.88	6.72	☆	☆	☆	5.0	None	212-698-5349	2.00	0.19	None	Peter Coffey	'93
SM BARNEY MUNI CA L; C	California Muni	1.7	6.48	1.84	6.43	☆	☆	☆	4.8	None	212-698-5349	None	0.53	None	Peter Coffey	'93
SM BARNEY MUNI CA L; Y	California Muni	0.5	6.48	1.92	6.58	☆	☆	☆	5.0	None	212-698-5349	None	0.35	None	Peter Coffey	'93
SM BARNEY MUNI CA; A	California Muni	163.6	12.36	2.12	8.24	6.47	8.20	☆	6.0	None	212-698-5349	4.00	0.51	4.00	Peter Coffey	'87
SM BARNEY MUNI CA; B	California Muni	0.7	12.36	1.92	☆	☆	☆	☆	0.0	None	212-698-5349	None	None	None	Peter Coffey	'93
SM BARNEY MUNI CA; C	California Muni	6.8	12.35	1.91	7.55	☆	☆	☆	5.4	None	212-698-5349	1.00	1.22	1.00	Peter Coffey	'93
SM BARNEY MUNI FL; A	Florida Muni	13.9	6.63	2.31	8.46	☆	☆	☆	4.9	None	212-698-5349	None	0.20	2.00	Peter Coffey	'93
SM BARNEY MUNI FL; C	Florida Muni	3.0	6.62	2.27	8.01	☆	☆	☆	4.7	None	212-698-5349	1.00	0.52	4.00	Peter Coffey	'93
SM BARNEY MUNI FL; A	Florida Muni	109.7	13.02	2.46	8.73	7.13	☆	☆	5.8	None	212-698-5349	4.00	0.54	1.00	Peter Coffey	'91
SM BARNEY MUNI FL; B	Florida Muni	2.6	13.01	2.26	☆	☆	☆	☆	0.0	None	212-698-5349	None	None	4.50	Peter Coffey	'94
SM BARNEY MUNI FL; C	Florida Muni	3.0	13.01	2.25	8.05	☆	☆	☆	5.2	None	212-698-5349	1.00	1.24	1.00	Peter Coffey	'93
SM BARNEY MUNI GA; A	Georgia Muni	7.5	12.30	3.15	9.76	☆	☆	☆	5.9	None	212-698-5349	4.00	None	None	Peter Coffey	'94
SM BARNEY MUNI GA; B	Georgia Muni	2.9	12.30	2.94	9.12	☆	☆	☆	5.3	None	212-698-5349	None	None	4.50	Peter Coffey	'94
SM BARNEY MUNI GA; C	Georgia Muni	1.6	12.29	3.02	9.18	☆	☆	☆	5.3	None	212-698-5349	1.00	1.00	1.00	Peter Coffey	'94
SM BARNEY MUNI LTD; A	Intermediate Muni	242.5	6.58	1.99	6.94	6.04	7.07	☆	5.6	None	212-698-5349	2.00	0.53	2.00	Peter Coffey	'88
SM BARNEY MUNI LTD; C	Intermediate Muni	28.2	6.58	1.95	6.81	☆	☆	☆	5.3	None	212-698-5349	None	0.88	1.00	Peter Coffey	'93

PERFORMANCE OF MUTUAL FUNDS (continued)

FUND NAME	OBJECTIVE	ASSETS ($ MIL) 5/31/95	NAV ($/SHR) 6/30/95	QTR	1YR	3YRS	5YRS	10YRS (Annualized)	DIV YLD %	PHONE NUMBER 800	PHONE NUMBER In-State	Load	FEES Exp. Ratio	Redemption	MANAGER	SINCE
SM BARNEY MUNI NATL; A	General Muni	402.7	13.46	2.57	8.64	7.21	8.75	☆	6.2	None	212-698-5349	4.00	0.52	None	Peter Coffey	'86
SM BARNEY MUNI NATL; B	General Muni	7.6	13.47	2.46	☆	☆	☆	☆	0.0	None	212-698-5349	None	None	4.50	Peter Coffey	'94
SM BARNEY MUNI NATL; C	General Muni	18.7	13.45	2.37	7.95	☆	☆	☆	5.5	None	212-698-5349	None	1.22	1.00	Peter Coffey	'93
SM BARNEY MUNI NJ; A	New Jersey Muni	59.3	13.40	2.27	8.47	6.72	☆	☆	5.8	None	212-698-5349	4.00	0.44	None	Peter Coffey	'90
SM BARNEY MUNI NJ; B	New Jersey Muni	1.5	13.40	2.24	☆	☆	☆	☆	0.0	None	212-698-5349	None	None	4.50	Peter Coffey	'94
SM BARNEY MUNI NJ; C	New Jersey Muni	3.7	13.39	2.15	7.79	☆	☆	☆	5.2	None	212-698-5349	None	1.17	1.00	Peter Coffey	'93
SM BARNEY MUNI NY; A	New York Muni	84.7	12.98	2.62	8.40	7.06	8.73	☆	5.9	None	212-698-5349	None	0.55	None	Peter Coffey	'87
SM BARNEY MUNI NY; B	New York Muni	4.6	12.98	2.42	☆	☆	☆	☆	0.0	None	212-698-5349	None	None	4.50	Peter Coffey	'94
SM BARNEY MUNI NY; C	New York Muni	6.3	12.97	2.41	7.72	☆	☆	☆	5.3	None	212-698-5349	4.00	None	1.00	Peter Coffey	'93
SM BARNEY MUNI OH; A	Ohio Muni	2.6	12.01	1.70	8.15	☆	☆	☆	5.4	None	212-698-5349	4.00	1.23	None	Peter Coffey	'94
SM BARNEY MUNI OH; B	Ohio Muni	2.3	12.00	1.62	7.58	☆	☆	☆	4.9	None	212-698-5349	None	None	4.50	Peter Coffey	'94
SM BARNEY MUNI OH; C	Ohio Muni	0.7	12.00	1.61	7.45	☆	☆	☆	4.8	None	212-698-5349	None	None	1.00	Peter Coffey	'94
SM BARNEY MUNI PA; A	Pennsylvania Muni	9.1	12.50	2.26	9.19	☆	☆	☆	5.8	None	212-698-5349	4.00	None	None	Peter Coffey	'94
SM BARNEY MUNI PA; B	Pennsylvania Muni	5.9	12.49	2.14	8.58	☆	☆	☆	5.2	None	212-698-5349	None	None	4.50	Peter Coffey	'94
SM BARNEY MUNI PA; C	Pennsylvania Muni	3.6	12.49	2.13	8.54	☆	☆	☆	5.2	None	212-698-5349	None	None	1.00	Peter Coffey	'94
SM BARNEY NJ; A	New Jersey Muni	108.8	12.76	2.52	8.06	6.51	8.23	☆	5.5	327-6748	212-723-9218	4.00	0.89	None	Lawrence McDermott	'88
SM BARNEY NJ; B	New Jersey Muni	57.0	12.76	2.38	7.44	☆	☆	☆	4.9	327-6748	212-723-9218	None	1.40	4.50	Lawrence McDermott	'92
SM BARNEY NY; A	New York Muni	502.6	16.45	2.50	7.93	6.00	7.69	8.54	5.9	327-6748	212-723-9218	4.00	0.77	None	Lawrence McDermott	'84
SM BARNEY NY; B	New York Muni	168.7	16.45	2.36	7.34	☆	☆	☆	5.3	327-6748	212-723-9218	None	1.30	4.50	Lawrence McDermott	'92
SM BARNEY TX-EX INC; A	General Muni	244.9	17.25	2.28	7.66	☆	☆	☆	5.9	327-6748	212-723-9218	4.00	0.84	None	Lawrence McDermott	'92
SM BARNEY TX-EX INC; B	General Muni	759.4	17.25	2.15	7.10	5.78	7.22	☆	5.4	327-6748	212-723-9218	None	1.33	4.50	Lawrence McDermott	'85
SM&R AMER NATL TAX FREE	General Muni	8.2	9.81	2.74	9.02	☆	☆	☆	4.8	231-4639	409-763-2767	4.50	1.11	None	Terry E. Frank	'93
SOUTH DAKOTA TAX-FREE	Single State Muni	4.3	10.04	-0.37	5.20	☆	☆	☆	5.9	562-6637	701-852-5292	4.50	0.46	4.00	W. Dan Korgel	'94
SS RESEARCH CAL TAX; A	California Muni	7.8	7.82	1.37	7.12	☆	☆	☆	5.3	882-3302	617-348-2000	4.50	1.10	None	Paul Clifford	'94
SS RESEARCH CAL TAX; B	California Muni	3.5	7.83	1.30	6.45	☆	☆	☆	4.5	882-3302	617-348-2000	None	1.85	5.00	Paul Clifford	'93
SS RESEARCH CAL TAX; C	California Muni	16.8	7.83	1.55	7.37	6.04	7.49	☆	5.5	882-3302	617-348-2000	None	0.85	None	Paul Clifford	'93
SS RESEARCH CAL TAX; D	California Muni	0.7	7.83	1.17	6.31	☆	☆	☆	4.5	882-3302	617-348-2000	None	1.85	1.00	Paul Clifford	'93
SS RESEARCH FL TAX; A	Florida Muni	3.4	9.40	2.59	7.21	☆	☆	☆	4.8	882-3302	617-348-2000	4.50	None	None	Paul Clifford	'93
SS RESEARCH FL TAX; B	Florida Muni	3.0	9.39	2.41	6.30	☆	☆	☆	4.1	882-3302	617-348-2000	None	None	5.00	Paul Clifford	'93
SS RESEARCH FL TAX; C	Florida Muni	3.5	9.40	2.66	7.47	☆	☆	☆	5.1	882-3302	617-348-2000	None	None	None	Paul Clifford	'93
SS RESEARCH FL TAX; D	Florida Muni	1.3	9.40	2.52	6.41	☆	☆	☆	4.1	882-3302	617-348-2000	None	1.10	1.00	Paul Clifford	'93
SS RESEARCH NY TAX; A	New York Muni	19.9	7.89	1.83	6.10	☆	☆	☆	5.1	882-3302	617-348-2000	4.50	1.10	None	Paul Clifford	'93
SS RESEARCH NY TAX; B	New York Muni	13.1	7.89	1.77	5.31	☆	☆	☆	4.4	882-3302	617-348-2000	None	1.85	5.00	Paul Clifford	'93
SS RESEARCH NY TAX; C	New York Muni	41.1	7.90	2.02	6.35	6.28	7.92	☆	5.3	882-3302	617-348-2000	None	0.85	None	Paul Clifford	'93
SS RESEARCH NY TAX; D	New York Muni	0.8	7.90	1.76	5.30	☆	☆	☆	4.4	882-3302	617-348-2000	None	1.85	1.00	Paul Clifford	'93
SS RESEARCH PA TAX; A	Pennsylvania Muni	7.2	9.38	2.30	7.12	☆	☆	☆	5.0	882-3302	617-348-2000	4.50	None	None	Paul Clifford	'93
SS RESEARCH PA TAX; B	Pennsylvania Muni	4.9	9.38	2.11	6.33	☆	☆	☆	4.2	882-3302	617-348-2000	None	None	5.00	Paul Clifford	'93
SS RESEARCH PA TAX; C	Pennsylvania Muni	3.5	9.39	2.47	7.38	☆	☆	☆	5.2	882-3302	617-348-2000	None	None	None	Paul Clifford	'93
SS RESEARCH PA TAX; D	Pennsylvania Muni	1.1	9.38	2.11	6.33	☆	☆	☆	4.2	882-3302	617-348-2000	None	None	1.00	Paul Clifford	'93
SS RESEARCH TX-EX; A	General Muni	240.4	7.82	1.43	6.24	5.53	7.20	☆	5.1	882-3302	617-348-2000	4.50	1.20	None	Susan Drake	'90
SS RESEARCH TX-EX; B	General Muni	38.2	7.81	1.12	5.32	☆	☆	☆	4.3	882-3302	617-348-2000	None	1.95	5.00	Susan Drake	'93
SS RESEARCH TX-EX; C	General Muni	0.4	7.80	1.37	6.39	☆	☆	☆	5.3	882-3302	617-348-2000	None	0.95	None	Susan Drake	'93
SS RESEARCH TX-EX; D	General Muni	1.2	7.81	1.12	5.32	☆	☆	☆	4.3	882-3302	617-348-2000	None	1.95	1.00	Susan Drake	'93
STAGECOACH CA BOND; A	California Muni	303.3	10.50	1.60	7.94	6.58	☆	☆	5.3	222-8222	None	4.50	0.65	None	Wines/Klug	'92/'92
STAGECOACH CA BOND; B	California Muni	N/A	10.70	1.43	☆	☆	☆	☆	0.0	222-8222	None	None	None	3.00	Wines/Klug	'95/'95

Fund	Objective	Net Assets ($Mil)	NAV	4-Wk %	52-Wk %	3-Yr %	5-Yr %	10-Yr %	Yield %	Tel (in-state)	Tel	Max Load %	12b-1 %	Redemp %	Manager	Mgr Since
STAGECOACH CA INCOME	California Muni	49.5	10.15	1.64	5.35	☆	☆	☆	3.9	222-8222	None	3.00	0.16	None	Milner/Wines	'92/'92
STAND AYER WOOD INT TAX	Intermediate Muni	29.0	20.74	1.96	6.33	☆	☆	☆	4.7	221-4795	617-350-6100	None	0.65	None	Furman/Kubiak	'92/'92
STAND AYER WOOD MA TX-EX	Massachusetts Muni	30.7	20.43	2.01	6.31	☆	☆	☆	4.7	221-4795	617-350-6100	2.50	0.65	None	Furman/Kubiak	'92/'92
STARBURST MUNI INCOME	Intermediate Muni	21.9	10.49	2.19	6.81	6.00	7.35	☆	4.1	239-6669	205-558-6702	4.50	0.75	None	Dan Davidson	'91
STATE BOND TAX EXEMPT FD	General Muni	82.2	10.77	2.28	7.50	6.05	8.36	☆	5.3	437-6663	437-6663	4.50	0.94	None	Keith Martens	'84
STATE BOND TAX-FR INC MN	Minnesota Muni	18.2	10.61	1.94	7.04	5.88	6.83	☆	5.2	437-6663	612-835-0097	4.50	1.00	None	Keith Martens	'88
STATE FARM MUNICIPAL ☑	General Muni	293.3	8.34	2.55	7.72	6.36	7.65	9.01	5.8	None	309-766-2029	None	0.16	None	Kurt Moser	'91
STEINROE HI-YLD MUNI	High-Yield Muni	285.7	11.31	2.33	8.55	5.74	6.99	8.99	5.8	338-2550	None	None	0.76	None	M. Jane McCart	'95
STEINROE INTMDT MUNI	Intermediate Muni	213.0	11.16	2.06	6.59	6.15	7.39	☆	4.9	338-2550	338-2550	None	0.71	None	Joanne Costopoulos	'91
STEINROE MGD MUNI	General Muni	643.4	8.79	1.66	7.12	5.78	7.61	9.21	5.8	338-2550	338-2550	None	0.65	None	M. Jane McCart	'91
STEPSTONE CA TX FR; INSTL	California Muni	10.3	9.39	1.89	8.19	☆	☆	☆	5.1	634-1100	213-236-5698	None	None	None	Robert Bigelow	'94
STEPSTONE CA TX FR; INVST	California Muni	4.8	9.38	1.89	8.20	☆	☆	☆	5.1	634-1100	213-236-5698	3.00	None	None	Robert Bigelow	'94
STI CLASSIC FL; INV	Florida Muni	3.3	10.05	2.01	8.44	☆	☆	☆	4.2	428-6970	None	3.75	None	None	Ron Schwartz	'94
STI CLASSIC FL; TR	Florida Muni	10.0	10.05	2.09	8.67	☆	☆	☆	4.5	428-6970	None	None	None	None	Ron Schwartz	'94
STI CLASSIC GA; INV	Georgia Muni	3.3	9.58	2.15	6.96	☆	☆	☆	4.2	428-6970	None	3.75	None	None	Gay Cash	'94
STI CLASSIC GA; TR	Georgia Muni	12.6	9.56	2.10	7.20	☆	☆	☆	4.4	428-6970	None	None	None	None	Gay Cash	'94
STI CLASSIC INV TX; INV	Intermediate Muni	41.7	11.22	2.27	9.35	8.75	☆	☆	3.8	428-6970	None	3.75	1.14	None	Ron Schwartz	'92
STI CLASSIC INV TX; TR	Intermediate Muni	77.5	11.21	2.37	9.75	☆	☆	☆	4.1	428-6970	None	None	0.75	None	Ron Schwartz	'93
STI CLASSIC TN; INV	Tennessee Muni	1.2	9.40	2.06	8.06	☆	☆	☆	4.6	428-6970	None	3.75	None	None	Ainsley Moses	'94
STI CLASSIC TN; TR	Tennessee Muni	1.7	9.37	1.95	8.10	☆	☆	☆	4.7	428-6970	None	None	None	None	Ainsley Moses	'94
STRONG HIGH YIELD MUNI	High-Yield Muni	169.3	9.66	3.20	7.97	5.66	☆	8.28	7.6	368-1030	414-359-1400	None	None	None	Conlin/Bourbulas	'93/'93
STRONG INS MUNI BD	Insured Muni	42.7	10.55		5.76	5.70	☆	☆	4.9	368-1030	414-359-1400	None	1.00	None	Conlin/Bourbulas	'91/'91
STRONG MUNICIPAL BOND	General Muni	300.5	9.46	-0.35	5.15	4.86	☆	☆	5.7	368-1030	414-359-1400	None	0.80	None	Conlin/Bourbulas	'91/'91
STRONG SH-TM MUNI BD	Short-Term Muni	147.0	9.65	-0.67	0.94	3.37	☆	☆	4.9	368-1030	212-551-5125	None	0.70	None	Conlin/Winston	'94/'94
SUNAMER TAX EX INS; A	Insured Muni	137.6	12.21	1.93	8.53	5.98	☆	☆	5.2	858-8850	212-551-5125	4.75	1.28	None	John Mooney	'94
SUNAMER TAX EX INS; B	Insured Muni	27.4	12.21	1.68	7.69	5.25	☆	☆	4.5	858-8850	212-551-5125	None	2.12	4.00	John Mooney	'94
TAX FREE FUND OF VERMONT	Single State Muni	6.7	9.71	0.99	7.79	6.88	8.71	☆	5.5	675-3333	802-773-0674	4.00	1.66	None	John Pearson	'91
TAX-EXEMPT BD FD AMERICA	General Muni	1,415.8	11.83	2.59	8.75	8.03	☆	☆	5.8	421-4120	714-671-7000	4.75	0.69	None	Multiple Managers	N/A
TAX-FREE FUND FOR UT ●	Single State Muni	27.8	9.60	2.15	9.20	☆	☆	☆	5.7	882-4937	882-4937	4.00	0.03	None	Sterling Jensen	'92
TAX-FREE FUND OF CO	Colorado Muni	217.1	10.28	1.89	7.07	6.43	7.59	☆	5.3	872-2652	212-697-6666	4.00	0.57	None	Christopher Johns	'87
TAX-FREE TRUST OF AZ	Arizona Muni	384.4	10.37	2.04	7.89	6.20	7.69	☆	5.4	437-1020	212-697-6666	4.00	0.70	None	Todd Curtis	'86
THORNBURG INT FL; A	Florida Muni	11.5	11.76	2.13	7.03	☆	☆	☆	5.3	847-0200	505-984-0200	3.50	None	None	Brian McMahon	'94
THORNBURG INT FL; B	Florida Muni	0.3	11.78	1.95	☆	☆	☆	☆	0.0	847-0200	505-984-0200	None	None	3.50	Brian McMahon	'94
THORNBURG INT FL; C	Florida Muni	0.1	11.79	1.95	☆	☆	☆	☆	0.0	847-0200	505-984-0200	None	0.95	None	Brian McMahon	'94
THORNBURG INT NATL; A	Intermediate Muni	214.8	13.05	2.54	7.44	7.05	7.26	7.18	5.3	847-0200	505-984-0200	3.50	None	None	Brian McMahon	'91
THORNBURG INT NATL; B	Intermediate Muni	0.3	13.09	2.77	☆	☆	☆	☆	0.0	847-0200	505-984-0200	None	None	3.50	Brian McMahon	'94
THORNBURG INT NATL; C	Intermediate Muni	1.4	13.07	2.37	☆	☆	☆	☆	4.6	847-0200	505-984-0200	None	0.90	None	Brian McMahon	'91
THORNBURG INT NM; A	Single State Muni	136.6	13.03	2.11	7.05	☆	☆	☆	0.0	847-0200	505-984-0200	3.50	None	None	Brian McMahon	'91
THORNBURG INT NM; B	Single State Muni	0.3	13.03	1.95	☆	☆	☆	☆	0.0	847-0200	505-984-0200	None	None	3.50	Brian McMahon	'94
THORNBURG INT NM; C	Single State Muni	0.1	13.02	1.96	☆	☆	☆	☆	0.0	847-0200	505-984-0200	None	0.95	None	Brian McMahon	'94
THORNBURG LTD CA; A	California Muni	98.2	12.61	2.45	5.12	5.26	6.26	☆	4.6	847-0200	505-984-0200	2.50	None	None	Brian McMahon	'94
THORNBURG LTD CA; B	California Muni	0.3	12.62	2.30	☆	☆	☆	☆	0.0	847-0200	505-984-0200	None	1.00	2.50	Brian McMahon	'94
THORNBURG LTD CA; C	California Muni	0.5	12.62	2.32	☆	☆	☆	☆	0.0	847-0200	505-984-0200	None	None	None	Brian McMahon	'94
THORNBURG LTD NATL; A	Short-Term Muni	908.7	13.37	2.36	5.76	5.72	6.63	☆	4.8	847-0200	505-984-0200	2.50	None	None	Brian McMahon	'84
THORNBURG LTD NATL; B	Short-Term Muni	1.3	13.38	2.21	☆	☆	☆	☆	0.0	847-0200	505-984-0200	None	0.95	2.50	Brian McMahon	'94
THORNBURG LTD NATL; C	Short-Term Muni	1.7	13.40	2.28	☆	☆	☆	☆	0.0	847-0200	505-984-0200	None	None	None	Brian McMahon	'94
TORCHMARK INS TAX-FREE ☑	Insured Muni	2.4	N/A	N/A	N/A	N/A	N/A	N/A	0.0	733-3863	913-236-2050	None	1.00	None	John Holiday	'93
TOWER LA MUNI INCOME	Louisiana Muni	70.2	10.88	2.18	8.31	6.55	8.80	☆	5.3	999-0124	504-533-5100	3.00	0.71	None	Jeff Tanguis	'88
TWEN CENTURY TX-EX INT	Intermediate Muni	80.1	10.28	2.29	6.95	5.68	6.94	☆	4.7	345-2021	816-531-5575	None	0.60	None	Team Managed	N/A
TWEN CENTURY TX-EX LNG	General Muni	55.4	10.23	2.10	8.05	6.11	7.71	☆	5.2	345-2021	816-531-5575	None	0.60	None	Team Managed	N/A

PERFORMANCE OF MUTUAL FUNDS (continued)

FUND NAME	OBJECTIVE	ASSETS ($ MIL) 5/31/95	NAV ($/SHR) 6/30/95	QTR	1YR	3YRS	5YRS	10YRS	DIV YLD %	PHONE 800	PHONE In-State	Load	Redemption	Exp. Ratio	MANAGER	SINCE
						(Annualized)										
TWEN CENTURY TX-EX SHT	Short-Term Muni	58.8	10.06	1.61	5.17	☆	☆	☆	4.1	345-2021	816-531-5575	None	None	None	Laurie S. Kirby	'93
UNITED MUNICIPAL BOND	General Muni	987.3	7.16	1.77	9.51	7.03	8.79	9.92	5.4	913-236-2000	None	4.25	None	0.64	John Holliday	'80
UNITED MUNICIPAL HI INC	High-Yield Muni	378.9	5.23	2.63	8.90	7.98	8.98	☆	6.5	None	913-236-2000	4.25	None	0.76	John Holliday	'86
US NEAR TERM TAX FREE	Short-Term Muni	7.0	10.47	1.74	5.02	5.34	☆	☆	4.1	873-8637	210-308-1234	None	None	None	Creston King	'95
US TAX FREE FUND	General Muni	19.2	11.55	2.37	7.51	6.00	7.23	8.03	5.8	873-8637	210-308-1234	None	None	None	Creston King	'95
USAA CA BOND	California Muni	389.8	10.20	2.49	8.96	6.13	7.65	☆	5.8	382-8722	None	None	None	0.44	Robert Pariseau	'95
USAA FL INCOME	Florida Muni	46.1	9.14	1.98	7.82	☆	☆	☆	5.5	382-8722	None	None	None	0.50	Robert Pariseau	'95
USAA NY BOND	New York Muni	51.6	10.86	2.32	7.36	5.76	7.71	☆	5.8	382-8722	None	None	None	0.50	Kenneth Willman	'90
USAA TAX EX INTMDT-TERM	Intermediate Muni	1,566.7	12.63	2.47	7.61	6.77	7.71	7.83	5.6	382-8722	None	None	None	0.40	Clifford A. Gladson	'93
USAA TAX EX LONG-TERM	General Muni	1,837.5	13.03	2.11	7.28	5.88	7.66	8.60	6.1	382-8722	None	None	None	0.38	Kenneth Willman	'82
USAA TAX EX SHORT-TERM	Short-Term Muni	787.5	10.51	1.58	5.23	4.44	5.53	5.76	4.6	382-8722	None	None	None	0.42	Clifford A. Gladson	'94
USAA TX INCOME	Texas Muni	6.8	10.32	2.51	☆	☆	☆	☆	0.0	382-8722	None	None	None	0.50	Robert Pariseau	'95
USAA VA BOND	Virginia Muni	244.9	10.82	2.04	8.79	6.54	☆	☆	5.9	382-8722	None	None	None	0.50	Robert Pariseau	'95
UST MSTR TX-EX INTMDT	Intermediate Muni	247.8	9.00	3.49	8.86	6.81	7.74	☆	4.4	233-1136	None	4.50	None	0.64	Kenneth M. McAlley	'94
UST MSTR TX-EX LONG	General Muni	84.2	9.42	2.88	13.50	8.94	9.71	☆	4.8	233-1136	None	4.50	None	0.85	Kenneth M. McAlley	'86
UST MSTR TX-EX NY INT	New York Muni	92.3	8.38	2.85	9.01	5.88	6.78	☆	4.1	233-1136	None	4.50	None	0.87	Kenneth M. McAlley	'94
UST MSTR TX-EX SH-TM SEC	Short-Term Muni	45.0	7.01	1.81	4.60	☆	☆	☆	3.9	233-1136	None	4.50	None	0.59	Kenneth M. McAlley	'94
VALUE LINE NY TX EX TR	New York Muni	40.0	9.89	1.76	6.79	5.99	7.95	☆	5.2	223-0818	212-907-1500	None	None	0.87	Team Managed	N/A
VALUE LINE TX EX HI YLD	General Muni	233.1	10.51	2.01	8.16	5.47	7.31	7.95	5.4	223-0818	212-907-1500	None	None	0.61	Team Managed	N/A
VALUESTAR TN TX EX; INV	Tennessee Muni	94.9	9.85	1.26	6.17	☆	☆	☆	4.6	824-3741	None	3.00	None	0.82	Sharon Braune	'95
VANGUARD CA TX-FR INS IN	California Muni	170.8	10.15	2.07	6.84	☆	☆	☆	5.0	662-7447	610-669-1000	None	None	0.19	Ian A. MacKinnon	'94
VANGUARD CA TX-FR INS LG	California Muni	935.8	10.78	1.48	8.31	6.86	8.04	☆	5.6	662-7447	610-669-1000	None	None	0.19	Ian A. MacKinnon	'86
VANGUARD FL INS TX-FR	Florida Muni	361.9	10.50	1.14	8.09	☆	☆	☆	5.4	662-7447	610-669-1000	None	None	0.22	Ian A. MacKinnon	'92
VANGUARD MUNI HIGH YIELD	High-Yield Muni	1,829.3	10.31	1.98	8.72	7.24	8.99	9.69	6.0	662-7447	610-669-1000	None	None	0.20	Ian A. MacKinnon	'81
VANGUARD MUNI INS LG-TM	Insured Muni	1,950.6	11.98	1.65	8.85	6.96	8.46	9.34	5.7	662-7447	610-669-1000	None	None	0.20	Ian A. MacKinnon	'84
VANGUARD MUNI INTMDT-TM	Intermediate Muni	5,293.1	12.98	2.18	7.34	7.11	8.36	8.81	5.3	662-7447	610-669-1000	None	None	0.20	Ian A. MacKinnon	'81
VANGUARD MUNI LIMITED-TM	Short-Term Muni	1,650.3	10.68	2.29	5.82	5.05	6.31	☆	4.4	662-7447	610-669-1000	None	None	0.20	Ian A. MacKinnon	'87
VANGUARD MUNI LONG-TM	General Muni	1,053.2	10.55	2.08	8.88	7.04	8.82	9.43	5.7	662-7447	610-669-1000	None	None	0.20	Ian A. MacKinnon	'81
VANGUARD MUNI SHORT-TM	Short-Term Muni	1,438.5	15.57	1.65	4.61	3.82	4.87	5.38	3.8	662-7447	610-669-1000	None	None	0.20	Ian A. MacKinnon	'81
VANGUARD NJ TX-FR INS LG	New Jersey Muni	741.9	11.35	1.72	8.50	☆	8.46	☆	5.5	662-7447	610-669-1000	None	None	0.21	Ian A. MacKinnon	'88
VANGUARD NY INS TAX-FR	New York Muni	799.4	10.59	1.75	8.19	6.87	8.56	☆	5.5	662-7447	610-669-1000	None	None	0.22	Ian A. MacKinnon	'86
VANGUARD OH TX-FR INSURE	Ohio Muni	175.5	11.22	1.63	8.04	6.89	8.53	☆	5.5	662-7447	610-669-1000	None	None	0.23	Ian A. MacKinnon	'90
VANGUARD PA TX-FR INS LG	Pennsylvania Muni	1,482.1	10.88	1.39	7.78	7.08	8.49	☆	5.7	662-7447	610-669-1000	None	None	0.20	Ian A. MacKinnon	'86
VANKAMP CA INSURED; A	California Muni	143.0	16.85	1.74	7.72	6.43	7.86	☆	5.3	225-2222	708-684-6503	3.25	None	0.78	Joe Piraro	'92
VANKAMP CA INSURED; B	California Muni	19.6	16.85	1.55	6.83	☆	☆	☆	4.5	225-2222	708-684-6503	None	3.00	1.52	Joe Piraro	'93
VANKAMP CA INSURED; C	California Muni	2.8	16.85	1.61	6.96	☆	☆	☆	4.5	225-2222	708-684-6503	None	1.00	1.51	Joe Piraro	'93
VANKAMP FL INSURED; A	Florida Muni	10.1	14.51	1.24	☆	☆	☆	☆	0.0	225-2222	708-684-6503	4.75	None	None	Dave Johnson	'95
VANKAMP FL INSURED; B	Florida Muni	13.5	14.51	1.12	☆	☆	☆	☆	0.0	225-2222	708-684-6503	None	4.00	None	Dave Johnson	'95
VANKAMP FL INSURED; C	Florida Muni	0.1	14.50	1.12	☆	☆	☆	☆	0.0	225-2222	708-684-6503	None	1.00	None	Dave Johnson	'95
VANKAMP INS TAX FREE; A	Insured Muni	1,214.3	18.70	1.92	7.94	6.43	7.99	9.00	5.6	225-2222	708-684-6503	4.75	None	0.88	Joe Piraro	'92
VANKAMP INS TAX FREE; B	Insured Muni	34.3	18.69	1.73	7.13	☆	☆	☆	4.7	225-2222	708-684-6503	None	4.00	1.71	Joe Piraro	'93
VANKAMP INS TAX FREE; C	Insured Muni	3.3	18.70	1.78	7.13	☆	☆	☆	4.7	225-2222	708-684-6503	None	1.00	1.70	Dave Johnson	'95
VANKAMP INS TAX FREE; D	Insured Muni	0.1	18.70	1.87	7.83	☆	☆	☆	5.4	225-2222	708-684-6503	None	0.75	0.97	Joe Piraro	'93
VANKAMP LTD TM MUNI; A	General Muni	16.3	9.94	2.54	7.95	☆	☆	☆	4.8	225-2222	708-684-6503	3.25	None	0.67	Joe Piraro	'94
VANKAMP LTD TM MUNI; B	General Muni	17.3	9.93	2.36	7.16	☆	☆	☆	4.1	225-2222	708-684-6503	None	3.00	1.43	Dave Johnson	'95

Fund	Objective	Net Assets ($mil)	NAV	Dist %	1-Yr	5-Yr	10-Yr	Yld %	Phone	Toll-Free	Load	Exp	CDSC	Manager	Since
VANKAMP LTD TM MUNI; C	General Muni	4.5	9.92	2.25	7.17	☆	☆	4.1	225-2222	708-684-6503	None	1.43	1.00	Dave Johnson	'95
VANKAMP MUNI INC; A	General Muni	519.1	14.95	0.87	7.17	5.59	☆	5.9	225-2222	708-684-6503	4.75	0.99	None	David Johnson	'90
VANKAMP MUNI INC; B	General Muni	169.4	14.95	0.68	6.49	☆	☆	5.1	225-2222	708-684-6503	None	1.70	4.00	David Johnson	'92
VANKAMP MUNI INC; C	General Muni	4.4	14.95	0.68	6.34	☆	☆	5.1	225-2222	708-684-6503	None	1.74	1.00	Dave Johnson	'93
VANKAMP NJ INCOME; A	New Jersey Muni	4.3	14.33	0.84	☆	☆	☆	0.0	225-2222	708-684-6503	4.75	None	None	Dave Johnson	'95
VANKAMP NJ INCOME; B	New Jersey Muni	7.0	14.31	0.65	☆	☆	☆	0.0	225-2222	708-684-6503	None	None	4.00	Dave Johnson	'95
VANKAMP NJ INCOME; C	New Jersey Muni	0.3	14.33	0.72	☆	☆	☆	0.0	225-2222	708-684-6503	None	None	1.00	Dave Johnson	'95
VANKAMP NY INCOME; A	New York Muni	4.1	14.33	0.89	☆	☆	☆	0.0	225-2222	708-684-6503	4.75	None	None	Dave Johnson	'95
VANKAMP NY INCOME; B	New York Muni	9.3	14.33	0.70	☆	☆	☆	0.0	225-2222	708-684-6503	None	None	4.00	Dave Johnson	'95
VANKAMP NY INCOME; C	New York Muni	0.2	14.33	0.70	☆	☆	☆	0.0	225-2222	708-684-6503	None	None	1.00	Dave Johnson	'95
VANKAMP PA TAX FREE; A	Pennsylvania Muni	217.2	16.89	1.05	7.27	6.45	8.27	5.6	225-2222	708-684-6503	4.75	0.90	None	Dave Johnson	'95
VANKAMP PA TAX FREE; B	Pennsylvania Muni	42.5	16.89	0.86	6.54	☆	☆	4.9	225-2222	708-684-6503	None	1.64	4.00	Dave Johnson	'95
VANKAMP PA TAX FREE; C	Pennsylvania Muni	2.8	16.89	0.86	6.54	5.45	8.16	4.9	225-2222	708-684-6503	None	1.63	1.00	Dave Johnson	'89
VANKAMP TX FR HIGH; A	High-Yield Muni	636.5	14.44	1.60	7.77	☆	5.57	6.9	225-2222	708-684-6503	4.75	0.87	None	David Johnson	'93
VANKAMP TX FR HIGH; B	High-Yield Muni	120.5	14.44	1.33	6.87	☆	☆	6.0	225-2222	708-684-6503	None	1.64	4.00	Dave Johnson	'93
VENTURE MUNI PLUS; A	High-Yield Muni	7.2	14.44	1.40	6.95	☆	☆	6.0	279-0279	505-983-4335	None	1.64	1.00	B. Clark Stamper	'94
VENTURE MUNI PLUS; B	High-Yield Muni	45.9	9.21	1.81	☆	☆	7.78	0.0	279-0279	505-983-4335	None	2.07	4.00	B. Clark Stamper	'90
VICTORY NATL MUNI BD	Intermediate Muni	132.9	9.19	1.54	6.29	6.36	7.28	5.8	362-5365	None	4.75	None	None	Paul Toft	'94
VICTORY NY TAX-FREE	New York Muni	6.4	9.78	2.55	6.43	6.32	☆	4.3	362-5365	None	4.75	None	None	Paul Toft	'94
VICTORY OH MUNI BOND	Ohio Muni	16.3	12.68	2.05	6.17	☆	☆	4.8	362-5365	None	4.75	0.91	None	Paul Toft	'95
VIRTUS MD MUNI; INV	Single State Muni	60.0	11.01	2.47	8.78	7.09	7.86	4.7	444-7123	None	None	0.51	None	E. Christian Goetz	'94
VIRTUS MD MUNI; TR	Single State Muni	32.2	10.53	2.00	6.98	5.67	☆	4.2	444-7123	None	None	1.17	2.00	E. Christian Goetz	'94
VIRTUS VA MUNI; INV	Single State Muni	10.4	10.53	2.06	7.24	5.84	☆	4.4	444-7123	None	None	0.92	None	E. Christian Goetz	'94
VIRTUS VA MUNI; TR	Single State Muni	68.6	10.66	2.30	7.28	5.95	☆	4.2	444-7123	None	None	1.15	2.00	E. Christian Goetz	'94
VISION NY TX-FR	New York Muni	34.7	10.66	2.36	7.55	6.14	☆	4.5	836-2211	716-842-4488	4.50	0.90	None	Tom Pierce	'95
VISTA CA INTMDT TAX FREE	California Muni	28.3	9.84	2.84	7.86	☆	☆	4.5	348-4782	None	4.50	0.52	None	Pamela Hunter	'87
VISTA NY INCOME; A	New York Muni	33.9	9.76	1.72	7.02	☆	8.60	5.2	348-4782	None	4.50	0.76	None	Pamela Hunter	'93
VISTA NY INCOME; B	New York Muni	105.0	11.34	2.14	7.10	6.68	☆	5.1	348-4782	None	None	1.51	5.00	Pamela Hunter	'87
VISTA TX FR INCOME; A	General Muni	94.1	11.72	1.31	6.74	7.22	9.29	4.6	348-4782	None	4.50	0.58	None	Pamela Hunter	'93
VLC TR OCEAN STATE TX-EX	Single State Muni	13.8	11.66	1.25	6.02	☆	7.04	5.0	300-1116	401-421-1411	None	1.47	5.00	Samuel Hallowell	'92
VOYAGEUR AZ INS; A	Arizona Muni	42.5	10.37	1.40	6.23	6.45	☆	4.5	553-2143	612-376-7000	4.00	0.88	None	McCullagh/Dougall	'91/'93
VOYAGEUR AZ INS; C	Arizona Muni	0.4	10.68	2.36	9.09	6.89	☆	5.6	553-2143	612-376-7000	4.75	0.72	4.75	McCullagh/Dougall	'94/'94
VOYAGEUR AZ TAX FREE; A	Arizona Muni	2.0	10.20	2.80	8.23	☆	☆	5.3	553-2143	612-376-7000	None	1.50	None	Andrew M. McCullagh, Jr.	'92/'93
VOYAGEUR CA INS; A	California Muni	33.6	10.11	1.45	8.29	☆	☆	5.6	553-2143	612-376-7000	4.75	0.20	4.75	McCullagh/Dougall	'94/'94
VOYAGEUR CA INS; B	California Muni	4.4	10.11	1.33	7.75	☆	☆	5.2	553-2143	612-376-7000	None	0.73	None	McCullagh/Dougall	'87/'93
VOYAGEUR CA TAX FREE; A	California Muni	1.1	10.10	1.54	☆	☆	☆	0.0	553-2143	612-376-7000	4.75	0.66	4.75	Andrew M. McCullagh, Jr.	'94/'94
VOYAGEUR CO TAX FREE; A	Colorado Muni	398.1	10.41	3.09	8.65	7.15	8.08	5.4	553-2143	612-376-7000	3.75	1.80	None	McCullagh/Dougall	'92/'93
VOYAGEUR CO TAX FREE; C	Colorado Muni	0.8	10.41	2.86	7.79	☆	☆	4.5	553-2143	612-376-7000	None	0.44	4.00	McCullagh/Dougall	'94/'94
VOYAGEUR FL INS; A	Florida Muni	251.1	10.39	2.32	9.27	6.87	☆	5.4	553-2143	612-376-7000	4.75	1.00	None	McCullagh/Dougall	'95
VOYAGEUR FL INS; B	Florida Muni	2.2	10.39	2.22	8.80	☆	☆	5.1	553-2143	612-376-7000	2.75	None	None	McCullagh/Dougall	'95
VOYAGEUR FL LTD; A	Florida Muni	0.6	10.32	3.50	7.83	☆	☆	4.3	553-2143	612-376-7000	None	None	4.75	Andrew M. McCullagh, Jr.	'95
VOYAGEUR FL LTD; C	Florida Muni	0.1	10.32	3.31	☆	☆	☆	0.0	553-2143	612-376-7000	4.75	None	None	Andrew M. McCullagh, Jr.	'95
VOYAGEUR FL TAX FREE; A	Florida Muni	2.0	10.21	2.38	☆	☆	☆	0.0	553-2143	612-376-7000	None	None	None	Andrew M. McCullagh, Jr.	'95
VOYAGEUR FL TAX FREE; C	Florida Muni	0.1	10.22	2.26	☆	☆	☆	0.0	553-2143	612-376-7000	None	None	None	Andrew M. McCullagh, Jr.	'95
VOYAGEUR IA TAX FREE; A	Single State Muni	38.8	9.28	2.27	6.21	☆	☆	5.1	553-2143	612-376-7000	3.75	None	None	Howell/Greenshields	'93/'93
VOYAGEUR ID TAX FREE; A	Single State Muni	5.7	10.63	2.12	☆	☆	☆	0.0	553-2143	612-376-7000	3.75	None	None	Elizabeth Howell	'95
VOYAGEUR ID TAX FREE; B	Single State Muni	0.2	10.63	2.09	☆	☆	☆	0.0	553-2143	612-376-7000	None	None	4.00	Elizabeth Howell	'95
VOYAGEUR ID TAX FREE; C	Single State Muni	0.3	10.63	1.93	☆	☆	☆	0.0	553-2143	612-376-7000	None	None	None	Elizabeth Howell	'95

PERFORMANCE OF MUTUAL FUNDS (concluded)

FUND NAME	OBJECTIVE	ASSETS ($ MIL) 5/31/95	NAV ($/SHR) 6/30/95	QTR	1YR	3YRS	5YRS (Annualized)	10YRS	DIV YLD %	PHONE 800	PHONE In-State	Load	Exp. Ratio	Redemption	MANAGER	SINCE
VOYAGEUR KS TAX FREE; A	Kansas Muni	8.8	10.22	2.24	8.01	☆	☆	☆	5.4	553-2143	612-376-7000	4.75	0.06	None	Howell/Greenshields	'92/'92
VOYAGEUR MN INS; A	Minnesota Muni	309.2	10.34	2.17	7.54	6.68	7.82	☆	5.3	553-2143	612-376-7000	4.75	0.61	None	Howell/Greenshields	'90/'93
VOYAGEUR MN INS; C	Minnesota Muni	2.5	10.34	1.98	6.70	☆	☆	☆	4.6	553-2143	612-376-7000	None	1.36	None	Howell/Greenshields	'94/'94
VOYAGEUR MN LTD; A	Single State Muni	72.5	10.96	2.95	6.85	5.54	6.44	☆	4.3	553-2143	612-376-7000	2.75	0.92	None	Howell/Greenshields	'90/'93
VOYAGEUR MN LTD; C	Single State Muni	0.4	10.96	2.76	6.14	☆	☆	☆	3.6	553-2143	612-376-7000	None	1.71	None	Howell/Greenshields	'94/'94
VOYAGEUR MN TAX FREE; A	Minnesota Muni	452.8	12.09	2.16	7.30	6.38	7.60	8.33	5.4	553-2143	612-376-7000	4.75	0.90	None	Howell/Greenshields	'90/'93
VOYAGEUR MN TAX FREE; C	Minnesota Muni	1.8	12.09	1.97	6.40	☆	☆	☆	4.7	553-2143	612-376-7000	None	1.72	None	Howell/Greenshields	'94/'94
VOYAGEUR MO INS; A	Missouri Muni	45.6	10.05	2.46	8.86	☆	☆	☆	5.5	553-2143	612-376-7000	4.75	0.15	None	Howell/Greenshields	'92/'92
VOYAGEUR MO INS; B	Missouri Muni	4.3	10.05	2.33	8.42	☆	☆	☆	5.1	553-2143	612-376-7000	None	0.49	4.00	Howell/Greenshields	'94/'94
VOYAGEUR NATL INS; A	Insured Muni	36.0	10.08	1.88	9.16	6.58	☆	☆	5.6	553-2143	612-376-7000	4.75	0.10	None	McCullagh/Howell	'92/'93
VOYAGEUR NATL INS; B	Insured Muni	0.8	10.08	1.77	8.67	☆	☆	☆	5.2	553-2143	612-376-7000	None	0.48	4.00	McCullagh/Howell	'94/'94
VOYAGEUR ND TAX FREE; A	Single State Muni	36.4	10.49	2.12	8.40	6.69	☆	☆	5.4	553-2143	612-376-7000	4.75	0.46	None	McCullagh/Howell	'91/'91
VOYAGEUR ND TAX FREE; B	Single State Muni	0.2	10.49	2.00	7.85	☆	☆	☆	5.0	553-2143	612-376-7000	None	0.99	4.00	McCullagh/Howell	'94/'94
VOYAGEUR NM TAX FREE; A	Single State Muni	22.2	10.41	2.59	8.18	☆	☆	☆	5.3	553-2143	612-376-7000	3.75	0.29	None	McCullagh/Dougall	'92/'93
VOYAGEUR NM TAX FREE; B	Single State Muni	0.5	10.41	2.31	7.41	☆	☆	☆	4.7	553-2143	612-376-7000	None	0.98	4.00	McCullagh/Dougall	'94/'94
VOYAGEUR OR INS; A	Oregon Muni	19.1	9.56	1.95	8.06	☆	☆	☆	5.3	553-2143	612-376-7000	4.75	None	None	Howell/Greenshields	'93/'93
VOYAGEUR OR INS; B	Oregon Muni	2.0	9.56	1.82	7.42	☆	☆	☆	4.8	553-2143	612-376-7000	None	None	4.00	Howell/Greenshields	'94/'94
VOYAGEUR UT TAX FREE; A	Single State Muni	4.1	10.50	2.27	7.78	☆	☆	☆	5.6	553-2143	612-376-7000	3.75	0.10	None	McCullagh/Dougall	'92/'93
VOYAGEUR WA INS; A	Washington Muni	2.3	9.96	2.65	8.54	☆	☆	☆	5.7	553-2143	612-376-7000	4.75	None	None	Howell/Greenshields	'93/'93
VOYAGEUR WI TAX FREE; A	Single State Muni	24.7	9.37	1.81	7.18	☆	☆	☆	5.1	553-2143	612-376-7000	3.75	None	4.00	McCullagh/Howell	'94/'94
WADDELL & REED MUNI BD	General Muni	28.6	10.33	1.30	7.30	☆	☆	☆	4.3	None	913-236-2000	None	1.94	None	Boston Intl Advisors	'95
WARBG PINCUS NY MUNI BD	New York Muni	81.2	10.35	2.19	6.29	6.12	7.14	☆	4.4	257-5614	212-878-0600	None	0.60	3.00	Christensen/Parente	'92/'92
WARBG PINCUS S-T BD; GAM	Short-Term Muni	1.6	10.01	1.17	☆	☆	☆	☆	0.0	257-5614	212-878-0600	None	None	None	Parante/Van Daalen	'94/'94
WARBG PINCUS S-T BD; INST	Short-Term Muni	17.5	10.00	1.12	☆	☆	☆	☆	0.0	257-5614	212-878-0600	None	0.10	None	Parante/Van Daalen	'94/'94
WARBG PINCUS TAX FREE	General Muni	4.2	10.31	2.35	9.49	7.69	8.72	☆	5.6	888-9723	212-878-0600	None	0.15	None	Robert Moore	'95
WESTCORE AZ INT TX-FR	Single State Muni	24.6	10.62	2.34	7.53	6.42	☆	☆	4.9	392-2673	303-623-2577	3.75	0.31	None	Jack Berryman	'92
WESTCORE CA INTMDT; INSTL	California Muni	1.0	10.06	2.77	8.00	☆	☆	☆	5.0	392-2673	303-623-2577	None	0.09	None	Gerry Wagner	'93
WESTCORE CA INTMDT; RET	California Muni	1.1	10.06	2.77	8.00	☆	☆	☆	5.0	392-2673	303-623-2577	3.50	0.21	None	Gerry Wagner	'93
WESTCORE CO TX-EX	Single State Muni	10.8	10.64	2.66	7.50	6.23	☆	☆	5.0	392-2673	303-623-2577	3.50	0.27	None	Bob Lindig	'91
WESTCORE OREGON TX-EX FD	Oregon Muni	52.3	16.24	1.93	7.95	5.92	7.26	☆	5.2	392-2673	303-623-2577	4.50	0.62	None	Mary Gail Walton	'93
WESTCORE QUALITY TX EX	Intermediate Muni	14.5	15.19	2.51	7.08	☆	☆	☆	4.6	392-2673	303-623-2577	3.50	0.27	None	Mary Gail Walton	'93
WILLIAM PENN PA TAX-FREE	Pennsylvania Muni	110.4	11.00	2.80	8.36	6.83	7.92	☆	5.9	523-8440	610-670-1031	4.75	0.79	None	Miller Anderson & Sherr.	'87
WINTHROP FOCUS MUNI TR	Intermediate Muni	35.6	9.86	2.15	6.12	☆	☆	☆	3.8	225-8011	212-504-4000	None	0.83	4.00	Marybeth Leithead	'93
WM BLAIR LTD TAX-FREE	Short-Term Muni	16.1	9.81	2.64	6.81	☆	☆	☆	4.7	742-7272	312-364-8000	None	None	None	Bentley M. Myer	'94
WOODWARD MI BD; INSTL	Michigan Muni	28.8	10.18	2.38	8.65	☆	☆	☆	4.7	688-3350	None	None	0.53	None	Robert Grabowski	'93
WOODWARD MI BD; RTL	Michigan Muni	21.2	10.16	2.17	8.44	☆	☆	☆	4.8	688-3350	None	4.75	0.53	None	Robert Grabowski	'93
WOODWARD MUNI BD; INSTL	General Muni	52.7	10.27	2.24	8.36	☆	☆	☆	4.7	688-3350	None	None	0.53	None	Robert Grabowski	'93
WOODWARD MUNI BD; RTL	General Muni	13.4	10.27	2.24	8.36	☆	☆	☆	4.7	688-3350	None	4.75	0.53	None	Robert Grabowski	'93
WPG FUNDS TR INTMDT MUNI	Intermediate Muni	13.8	9.91	1.80	6.78	☆	☆	☆	4.2	223-3332	212-908-9500	None	0.85	None	Schwarz/Miller	'93/'93
WRIGHT INC INS TAX FREE	Insured Muni	11.1	11.49	2.20	6.46	5.58	6.84	6.93	4.8	232-0013	203-333-6666	None	0.90	None	Team Managed	N/A

Source: Lipper Analytical Services, Inc. Reprinted by permission of *Barron's National Business and Financial Weekly*, © 1995 Dow Jones & Company, Inc. ALL RIGHTS RESERVED WORLDWIDE.

Tracing Obsolete Securities*

The following is a list of some of the available sources of information on tracing obsolete securities. This list should be useful to those who wonder whether their old securities have any value, to researchers, and to collectors. All of the books listed below should be available in large public libraries or in larger business libraries.

To trace a security, you need to know the name of the company, the date of issue and the state in which the company was incorporated; all three pieces of information should appear on the security. Start with volumes appropriate to the issue date of the security and continue through to the present, if necessary. If the security cannot be found, contact the department that registers corporations in the state in which the company was incorporated. In most states this will be the office of the Secretary of State. They maintain records of name changes and bankruptcies and can usually answer your inquiry quickly; some charge a nominal fee for the service. Call the department to see what their procedures and costs are. You may need to send a copy of the certificate. Do not send the original certificate.

For an introduction to searching obsolete securities, the best guide, now out of print, is:

Cargiulo, Albert F. and Rocco Carlucci.
The Questioned Stock Manual: A Guide to Determining the True Worth of Old and Collectible Securities. New York: McGraw-Hill, 1979, xiv, 193 p.: ill. tables.
Chapters 3 and 4 deal with locating sources of information on securities. Chapter 6 covers the detection and recognition of fraudulent securities and a description of how securities are printed. The appendix contains a table of the top 100 firms, 1917–1977.

For historical data, beginning with colonial times, the Fisher, Scudder, and Smythe manuals are classics. The manuals are still published and the Smythe firm continues to do research into obsolete securities, charging a fee of $50 for each company. They also serve as dealers and appraisers of obsolete securities for collectors. You can contact them at:

R. M. Smythe & Co.
26 Broadway
New York, NY 10004
(212) 943-1880

*Frederick N. Nesta, formerly Director, Marymount Manhattan College Library.

Robert D. Fisher
Manual of Valuable & Worthless Securities: Showing Companies That Have Been Reorganized, Merged, Liquidated or Dissolved, Little Known Companies and Oil Leases. New York: R. M. Smythe, 1926–. 15 v.
First published in 1926 as the *Marvyn Scudder Manual...*, the series was taken over by Robert D. Fisher with vol. 5 in 1937. It has been published by the R. M. Smythe firm since 1971 under the editorship of Robert D. Fisher, Jr. With vol. 6 the series limited itself to securities and the date on which they became worthless. The earlier volumes present brief corporate obituaries. Volume 15, 1984, includes a price guide for collectors of obsolete certificates.

Smythe, Ronald M.
Valuable Extinct Securities: the Secret of the Obsolete Security Business. Unclaimed Money and How to Collect It, With a List of... Extinct Securities of Good Value From the Records of the Four Principal Dealers.... New York: R. M. Smythe, 1929. v, 398 p.
By the author and publisher of *Obsolete American Securities and Corporations*, later the *Robert D. Fisher Manual of Valuable and Worthless Securities*. This list of over 1,500 securities gives due and foreclosure dates and the dates of sale or merger.

Smythe, Roland M.
Obsolete American Securities and Corporations. New York: R. M. Smythe, 1911. liv, 1166 p.: ill.
(*Obsolete American Securities and Corporations*: vol. 2). Pages 1–28 discuss Continental and other early U.S. state and foreign notes and bonds. Twenty plates illustrate some of the bonds discussed. Volume 1 was published in 1904.
Valuable Extinct Securities Guide. 1939 ed. New York: R. M. Smythe, Inc., 1938. 127 p. The first edition was published in 1929 and was the sequel to *Obsolete American Securities and Corporations*.

The books below can be consulted to trace more recent corporate reorganizations:

Capital Changes Reporter for Federal Income Tax Purposes. Clark, NJ: Commerce Clearing House (NJ), 1949–. 6 v., loose-leaf. Securities distributions, taxability of disbursements, splits, offers, rights, etc.

The National Monthly Stock Summary. Jersey City, NJ: National Quotation Bureau, 1926–.
Summary data from the daily service, supplied either from the service or from dealers' lists. Name, par value, exchange, closing price, bids and offerings. May also include shares outstanding, control, reorganization, dividend or other information. Monthly, with bound cumulative volumes issued twice yearly.

Capital Adjustments, Reorganizations and Exchanges, Stock Dividends. Rights and Splits. Englewood Cliffs, NJ: Prentice-Hall, 1980–. 2 v. in 3, looseleaf.
Current changes, disbursements, etc. Includes notes on taxability. Supplements the bound volumes below.

Capital Adjustments: Stock Dividends, Stock Rights, Reorganizations. Englewood Cliffs, NJ: Prentice-Hall, 1962–.
The earlier volumes cover corporate and government securities from early in the century. Updated by looseleaf supplements. Includes name changes, incorporation dates, mergers.

Bank & Quotation Record. Arlington, MA: National News Services, 1928–.
"A publication of the Commercial and Financial Chronicle." Monthly opening and closing prices, highs, lows, etc. Includes equipment trusts, public utility bonds, Chicago Board Options Exchange, foreign exchange rates for the month, CDs, Federal funds, prime banker acceptance rates, commercial paper statistics. Published continuously for over sixty years, it is a fascinating document of American financial history.

FOREIGN CORPORATIONS

Canada

Canadian Mines Register of Dormant and Defunct Companies: Third Supplement.
Toronto: Northern Miner Press Limited, 1976. 108 p. Originally published in 1960.

Survey of Predecessor and Defunct Companies. 3rd ed. Toronto: The Financial Post Corporation Service Group, 1985. 208 p.
Covers over 12,000 companies and spans over 50 years. Lists name changes, removals, the exchange basis for new shares, along with the addresses and telephone numbers of Canadian Federal and Provincial corporate registry offices.

United Kingdom

The Stock Exchange Official Year-Book. London: Macmillan, 1934–.
Contains substantial information on the London Stock Exchange, foreign securities, municipal securities, regulations and statistics and a directory of International exchanges. The main body lists each company with parent/subsidiary note, background, financial data, stock history, voting, dividends. Includes the *Register of Defunct and Other Companies Removed from the Stock Exchange Official Year-Book*, a listing of over 23,000 companies removed from the Official Year-Book since 1875, along with a list of Commonwealth Government and Provincial stocks redeemed or converted since 1940. The Register was published separately until 1980.

Australia

Register of Companies Removed from the Stock Exchanges Official Lists. Sydney: Stock Exchange Research Pty., 1984? 104 p. Lists companies that were traded on one or more Australian exchanges. Historical data, with delistings going back to the early 1930s.

Discount Brokers

The 1995 Discount Broker Survey: A Guide to Commissions and Services

by Marie Swick, Jean Henrich, and Maria Crawford Scott*

Discount brokers continue to compete for customers through an expansion of services offered. The number of no-load mutual funds available at little or no charge through discount firms keeps growing. In addition, more and more discounters are offering low-cost dividend reinvestment, as well as research reports at minimal or no charge.

Information on the commissions charged for a range of trades, as well as services offered, is included in the AAII *Journal*'s annual survey of discount brokerage firms. This year's survey covers 82 firms that refer to themselves as discount firms.

The survey is designed to help individual investors spot the discount brokers that best meet their needs in terms of cost and services. To help make comparisons easier, the listing includes not only the dollar commission for a range of trades, but also the percentage of the transaction that the commission represents.

What does the listing cover?

Commissions

The stock commissions charged by discount brokerage firms vary widely not just by amount, but also by the way in which they are determined. For instance, some discounter's rates are based on the dollar value of the transaction, others' are based on the number of shares in the transaction, some use a combination, and some simply provide a table that lists the prices for various transactions without providing any formulas.

This makes generalized comparisons impossible, since certain firms will be cheaper for some kinds of trades, yet more expensive for others. To help overcome that problem, our listing presents three trades that cover a range of possibilities for the typical individual investor: a modest trade of a higher-priced stock (100 shares at $50 per share, a $5,000 transaction); a large trade (500 shares at $50 per share, a $25,000 transaction); and a modest trade of a low-priced stock (1,000 shares at $5 per share, a $5,000 transaction). Commissions charged by each broker for these trades are presented in total dollars and as a percentage of the total transaction.

The trades reflect commissions for exchange-listed stocks, although most of the firms charge the same rate for stocks traded over the counter; a few, however, do not. The minimum commission amount represents the minimum dollar amount charged for any stock trade by the firm.

At the bottom of the listing, we have indicated the average, the highest, and the lowest charges and percentages for each trade as a point of comparison.

The three transactions should give you some basis for comparing the various firms. However, certain discounts as well as additional charges by some firms may not be reflected in these particular examples. Examples of further discounts offered by a few firms include:

- Trades of a large number of shares, for instance over 1,000 shares per transaction.
- Trades of a large dollar volume. Several firms, in fact, offer special accounts for customers who consistently trade in large volume; these are noted in the listings by a double asterisk.
- Trades made using a computer or touch-tone phone to place the order.

Examples of additional charges that may not be reflected in these examples include:

- Shares that are particularly low-priced, such as those selling for under $5 a share.
- A small number of firms levy extra charges for odd lots (any number of shares less than 100—for instance, a sale of 553 shares consists of five round lots of 100, and an odd lot of 53 shares).
- A small number of firms (indicated by an asterisk in the listing) levy extra charges for non-market orders such as limit and stop orders (a market order is an order to

*Marie Swick is AAII's research analyst. Jean Henrich is associate editor and Maria Crawford Scott is editor of the *AAII Journal*.

Source: Reprinted with permission from the *AAII Journal*, January 1995. The *AAII Journal* is published by the American Association of Individual Investors, 625 N. Michigan Avenue, Chicago, IL 60611. Telephone: 312-280-0170.

buy or sell at the best price available at the time the order is received).

- Some brokers charge extra for special handling, such as transferring an account to or from another broker or registering certificates in the owner's name and mailing it to the owner. These charges are shown in the table under Handling Fees, a "t" after the fee designates an account transfer fee and a "c" designates a fee for registering a stock certificate in the owner's name.

Research and Other Services

Price isn't the sole consideration for most individual investors when selecting a discount broker. Other services provided by the firm are also important considerations.

Two popular services are offered by all of the discount brokers in the survey. All of the firms in the survey have SIPC coverage, which insures (through the Securities Investor Protection Corp.) the securities and cash in customer accounts up to a maximum of $500,000 per customer. In addition, all but six of the firms in the survey have purchased additional protection for their customer accounts. The six firms without additional protection are designated by the symbol ➥ after their names.

All of the firms in the survey also offer self-directed Individual Retirement Accounts.

Other services provided by discount brokerage firms vary, and in the listing we have included information on the most popular ones:

- **Research.** Some discounters offer research information and investment recommendations on various topics, such as the economy, business conditions, and specific companies. In the listing, we have divided research reports into two types: "Standard" denotes reports that are supplied to the firm by an outside source, such as Standard & Poor's or Value Line; "Custom" refers to reports that are researched inhouse by the firm's own analysts. Some brokers subscribe to Wall Street by Fax, a program that provides standard reports to a firm's clients by fax machine. Brokers may charge for standard or custom research information; those that do are noted under Research.

- **Interest on cash balances.** Most investors want assurance that any cash balances are earning interest. Most discount firms pay interest on these funds, although some will only pay interest on amounts above a certain minimum. A sweep account automatically invests cash balances (for instance, funds from the sale of shares) in an interest-bearing money market fund until those funds are reinvested. Money market funds usually pay a higher rate of interest than cash balance accounts that simply earn interest. In the listings, we indicate if a brokerage firm offers a sweep account by the word "Sweep," followed by any minimum amounts required for such an arrangement (note that after this minimum is met, any additional cash, regardless of how small, is swept into the money market fund). If the firm does not offer a sweep account but pays interest on uninvested funds, we use the word "Interest," followed by the minimum amount upon which it pays interest, if a minimum applies.

- **No-load mutual funds.** Many discount firms offer no-load mutual funds for their customers; while many charge a fee for the transaction, some discounters offer a certain number of no-load funds at no charge to the customer. Investors interested in this service should request a list of the funds offered from the discounter, as well as the charges. We have indicated if the firm offers no-load mutual funds by the symbol "NLMF," and we note if a fee is charged on any mutual funds traded.

- **Dividend reinvestment.** Some discount brokers will allow an investor to automatically reinvest dividends through the firm; while many charge for this service, it is not at the standard rates (in which the minimum may apply). The average charge is $2 for each dividend payment that is reinvested. If a firm offers this arrangement, we use the symbol "DRP," and we note if a fee is charged.

- **On-line trading.** Twelve discount brokerage firms offer on-line trading to customers with a computer and modem. A few firms even give discounts on their commissions to trades placed on-line. If a discounter offers an on-line service, we have indicated this by the word "On-Line." In addition, the accompanying box provides more information on the on-line services offered.

Additional Services

While we have listed the most popular services, there are many others offered by discount brokers. Some firms, for instance, have offices in many locations, a consideration for investors who want the reassurance of a local contact. Check with the firm for a list of branch-office locations if this is important to you. Most of the discount brokers listed here have 800 phone numbers, so that calls are toll-free regardless of where they are located.

Most discounters offer current market quotes, but several also have 24-hour touch-tone telephone service that allows quick access to account information, market quotes and trades.

Some firms offer asset management accounts with checkwriting privileges, debit cards, direct deposit of payroll checks and other checks, and ATM access cards.

Most discounters offer the standard broker fare of margin accounts, trading of other instruments (options, bonds, and certificates of deposit, for instance), wire transfers, confirmations of trades and monthly statements.

How to Use the Listing

The listing here is intended to give you a starting point if you are seeking a discount brokerage firm or if you want to see how your current broker stacks up.

Compare the commission charges for the kinds of trades that you are most likely to make, and make note of fees that may be charged for services you are likely to use. Then select several discounters to call for more information. When calling a firm, ask for a commission schedule and a description of the services they offer. Double-check the charges in the listings here—prices change, and although we have made every attempt to provide recent and accurate information, it is best to confirm the charges yourself. You should also check for other charges that may apply to your particular situation; for instance, some firms charge a flat fee to open an account and some charge accounts that remain inactive for a period of time.

In addition, make sure you are comfortable with any firm you choose; our listing does not attempt to rate the financial condition or the service quality of the firms (Tables pp 496–500).

AAII Guide to Discount Brokerage Firms

Telephone	Brokerage Firm	Commission 100 Shares at $50/Share Total: $5,000 ($)	as % of Trade	500 Shares at $50/Share Total: $25,000 ($)	as % of Trade	1,000 Shares at $5/Share Total: $5,000 ($)	as % of Trade	Minimum Comm. ($)	Handling Fees	Research (see keys)	Other Services
800/228-3011	AccuTrade*	31.00	0.62	110.00	0.44	67.00	1.34	31.00	$25.00t	Standard (fee)	Sweep ($1,000); NLMF (fee)
800/228-3011	AccuTrade Direct Access	48.00	0.96	48.00	0.19	48.00	0.96	48.00	$25.00t	Standard (fee)	Sweep ($1,000); NLMF (fee); On-Line
800/221-5873	Andrew Peck	50.00	1.00	72.50	0.29	90.00	1.80	50.00	$35.00c		Sweep; NLMF (fee)
800/328-4076	Arnold Securities	35.75	0.72	130.16	0.52	69.85	1.40	35.00			Interest ($250); NLMF (fee); DRP (fee)
800/368-3668	Aufhauser (K.) & Co.*	28.99	0.58	28.99	0.12	28.99	0.58	28.99	$15.00c	Custom	Sweep ($100); NLMF (fee); On-Line
800/321-1640	Baker & Co.	40.00	0.80	80.00	0.32	55.00	1.10	40.00			Sweep ($500)
800/221-2111	Barry Murphy & Co.	32.50	0.65	62.50	0.25	60.00	1.20	25.00	$50.00t	Standard (fee)	Sweep ($1,000); NLMF (fee); DRP
800/547-6337	Bidwell & Co.	28.00	0.56	60.00	0.24	60.00	1.20	20.00	$10.00c	Standard (fee)	Sweep; NLMF (fee); DRP
800/922-0960	Broker's Exchange	52.50	1.05	160.00	0.64	75.00	1.50	35.00		Standard	Sweep ($100); NLMF (fee)
800/822-2021	Brown & Co.	29.00	0.58	29.00	0.12	29.00	0.58	29.00	$20.00c		Interest ($1,001); On-Line
800/899-6878	Bruno, Stolze & Co.	45.00	0.90	130.00	0.52	75.00	1.50	35.00		Standard	Sweep ($1,000); NLMF (fee)
800/262-5800	Bull & Bear Securities	44.00	0.88	124.00	0.50	70.40	1.41	31.00		Standard	Sweep ($10); NLMF (fee); DRP (fee)
800/621-0392	Burke Christensen & Lewis	34.00	0.68	120.00	0.48	70.00	1.40	34.00			Interest ($1,501)
800/821-4800	Bush Burns Securities	35.00	0.70	35.00	0.14	35.00	0.70	35.00			Interest ($1,000); NLMF (fee)
800/999-3699	Calvert Securities Corp.	50.00	1.00	149.50	0.60	80.00	1.60	45.00		Standard	Sweep; NLMF (fee)
800/435-4000	Charles Schwab	55.00	1.10	155.00	0.62	90.00	1.80	39.00	$15.00c	Custom (fee)	Sweep ($1,000); NLMF (fee); DRP; On-Line
800/292-6637	Consolidated Financial	35.00	0.70	45.00	0.18	59.50	1.19	35.00		Standard	Sweep ($500)
800/222-0124	CoreStates Securities	82.50	1.65	167.50	0.67	82.50	1.65	50.00	$2.50c	Standard	Sweep ($25); NLMF (fee)
813/586-3541	Downstate Discount	48.00	0.96	90.00	0.36	65.00	1.30	39.00			Sweep; NLMF (fee)
800/786-2575	E*Trade Securities	25.00	0.50	25.00	0.10	25.00	0.50	25.00	$20.00t		Sweep ($100); On-Line
800/544-8666	Fidelity Brokerage Services	54.00	1.08	154.50	0.62	88.50	1.77	38.00		Standard (fee)	Sweep; NLMF (fee); On-Line
800/326-4434 ↑	First Union Brokerage	45.00	0.90	140.00	0.56	90.00	1.80	40.00	$15.00c		Interest
800/221-8210	Fleet Brokerage Securities	46.20	0.92	135.55	0.54	67.77	1.36	37.00			Sweep ($500); NLMF (fee)
800/729-7585 ↑	Freeman Welwood & Co.	45.00	0.90	145.00	0.58	70.00	1.40	34.00		Standard	Sweep ($500); NLMF (fee); DRP (fee)

800/634-8518	Icahn & Co.	50.00	1.00	75.00	0.30	60.00	1.20	40.00		Standard	Sweep
800/247-3396	J.D. Seibert & Company	49.00	0.98	140.00	0.56	75.00	1.50	49.00		Standard	Sweep; DRP (fee)
800/233-3411	Jack White & Company	36.00	0.72	48.00	0.19	63.00	1.26	33.00			Sweep ($500); NLMF (fee)
404/522-5766	Jackson Securities, Inc.	40.00	0.80	40.00	0.16	80.00	1.60	40.00		Both	Sweep ($1,000); NLMF (fee)
800/678-2626	Kashner Davidson	50.00	1.00	160.00	0.64	75.00	1.50	45.00	$50.00t	Standard	Sweep ($100)
800/252-0090	Kennedy, Cabot & Co.	33.00	0.66	33.00	0.13	53.00	1.06	33.00			Sweep ($100)
800/688-3462	Lombard Institutional	34.00	0.68	34.00	0.14	34.00	0.68	34.00		Standard (fee)	Sweep; NLMF (fee); DRP (fee)
800/221-3305	Marquette de Bary Co.	42.90	0.86	146.43	0.59	69.85	1.40	20.00	$50.00t	Standard	Sweep ($1,000)
800/366-1500	Marsh Block & Co.	33.86	0.68	50.00	0.20	50.00	1.00	25.00		Both	Sweep ($1,000); NLMF (fee)
800/223-6642	Max Ule	57.00	1.14	195.00	0.78	70.00	1.40	35.00		Standard	Interest ($1,001); DRP; On-Line
800/643-9663	Midwood Discount*	36.50	0.73	36.50	0.15	36.50	0.73	36.50			Sweep; NLMF (fee); DRP
800/621-2627	Mongerson & Co.	35.00	0.70	95.00	0.38	66.00	1.32	30.00		Both	Sweep ($500)
800/621-2627	Mongerson & Co. Premier**	35.00	0.70	65.00	0.26	66.00	1.32	30.00		Both	Sweep ($500)
800/872-0711	Muriel Siebert Share Rates**	75.00	1.50	75.00	0.30	75.00	1.50	75.00		Standard (fee)	Sweep; NLMF
800/872-0711	Muriel Siebert Value Rates	45.00	0.90	113.00	0.45	57.00	1.14	37.50		Standard (fee)	Sweep; NLMF
800/888-3999	National Discount Brokers	30.00	0.60	30.00	0.12	30.00	0.60	30.00	$25.00c	Standard (fee)	Sweep
800/872-6533	Olde Discount	40.00	0.80	100.00	0.40	52.50	1.05	20.00		Custom	Sweep ($1,000)
800/825-5723	PC Financial Net Frequent	40.00	0.80	105.00	0.42	45.00	0.90	40.00			Sweep ($500); NLMF (fee); On-Line
800/825-5723	PC Financial Network	40.00	0.80	140.00	0.56	60.00	1.20	40.00			Sweep ($500); NLMF (fee); On-Line
800/221-1660	Pace Securities	40.00	0.80	75.00	0.30	70.00	1.40	40.00			Sweep ($1,000)
800/421-8395	Pacific Brokerage Services	25.00	0.50	25.00	0.10	25.00	0.50	25.00		Standard	Interest ($400); On-Line
800/772-4400	People's Securities	40.00	0.80	131.00	0.52	69.00	1.38	38.00		Standard	Sweep ($5,000)
800/444-5880	Perelman-Carley & Assoc.	23.00	0.46	25.00	0.10	50.00	1.00	23.00			Interest
800/666-1440	Peremel & Co.	40.00	0.80	70.00	0.28	100.00	2.00	40.00		Standard (fee)	Sweep; NLMF (fee)
800/959-4554	Premier Discount	37.00	0.74	45.00	0.18	55.00	1.10	35.02			Interest ($1,001)
800/782-8871	Prestige Status, Inc.†	28.95	0.58	28.95	0.12	28.95	0.58	28.95			Sweep ($500); DRP
800/247-2752	➜ ProValue	60.00	1.20	173.00	0.69	94.00	1.88	49.00	$50.00t		Sweep ($1,000)
800/221-5220	Quick & Reilly	49.00	0.98	119.50	0.48	60.50	1.21	37.50		Standard	Sweep; NLMF (fee); DRP (fee); On-Line

(continued)

AAII Guide to Discount Brokerage Firms (concluded)

Telephone	Brokerage Firm	Commission 100 Shares at $50/Share Total: $5,000 ($)	as % of Trade	500 Shares at $50/Share Total: $25,000 ($)	as % of Trade	1,000 Shares at $5/Share Total: $5,000 ($)	as % of Trade	Minimum Comm. ($)	Handling Fees	Research	Other Services (see keys)
800/488-0090	R.J. Forbes Group, Inc.	35.00	0.70	35.00	0.14	35.00	0.70	35.00			Sweep; DRP (fee)
800/328-8600	Recom Securities	39.00	0.78	163.00	0.65	75.00	1.50	35.00		Standard	Sweep ($1,000); DRP (fee)
800/676-1848	Rodecker & Co.	72.50	1.45	247.50	0.99	132.50	2.65	50.00		Both	Sweep; DRP
800/488-5195	Royal Grimm & Davis	40.00	0.80	75.00	0.30	70.00	1.40	37.50		Standard	Sweep; DRP (fee); On-Line
718/448-2900	Russo Securities	50.00	1.00	75.00	0.30	100.00	2.00	50.00		Standard	Sweep; DRP
800/283-1950 ↕	Scottsdale Sec Safekeeping	31.50	0.63	49.50	0.20	63.00	1.26	31.50			Interest
800/283-1950 ↕	Scottsdale Sec Supersaver	50.00	1.00	50.00	0.20	50.00	1.00	50.00	$10.00c		Interest
800/283-1950 ↕	Scottsdale Sec Trans & Ship	35.00	0.70	55.00	0.22	70.00	1.40	35.00	$10.00c		Interest
800/732-7678	Seaport Securities Corp.*	34.00	0.68	50.00	0.20	80.00	1.60	34.00		Standard	Sweep; NLMF (fee); DRP (fee)
800/327-3156	Securities Research	45.00	0.90	115.00	0.46	95.00	1.90	35.00		Standard	Sweep ($100); NLMF; DRP (fee)
800/221-4242	Shearman, Ralston	40.00	0.80	110.00	0.44	106.00	2.12	40.00		Standard	Sweep ($100); NLMF (fee); DRP (fee)
800/327-1536	Shochet Securities	65.00	1.30	152.00	0.61	97.00	1.94	40.00		Custom	Sweep
800/455-2211	Spear Securities	48.00	0.96	145.00	0.58	85.00	1.70	38.00		Standard	Sweep; NLMF; DRP
800/726-7401	St. Louis Discount*	37.00	0.74	64.00	0.26	62.40	1.25	37.00		Standard	Sweep
800/222-5520	State Discount	35.00	0.70	45.00	0.18	70.00	1.40	35.00		Standard	Sweep; NLMF (fee); DRP (fee)
800/782-1522	Sterling Investment	45.00	0.90	124.50	0.50	69.50	1.39	40.00		Standard	Sweep; NLMF (fee)
800/421-6563	Stock Mart (The)	35.75	0.72	162.70	0.65	62.87	1.26	30.00			Sweep; DRP
415/853-0817	StockBridge Partners, Inc.	45.00	0.90	85.00	0.34	135.00	2.70	35.10		Standard	Sweep
800/225-6196 ↕	StockCross*	33.50	0.67	67.50	0.27	110.00	2.20	25.09			Interest ($3,001)
614/228-5391	Sweney Carwright & Co.	67.50	1.35	112.50	0.45	67.50	1.35	37.00		Standard	Sweep
800/638-5660 ↕	T. Rowe Price Discount	46.00	0.92	134.00	0.54	80.00	1.60	35.00	$25.00t		Sweep; NLMF (fee)
800/669-4483	Thomas F. White	65.00	1.30	130.00	0.52	65.00	1.30	35.00		Standard (fee)	Sweep; NLMF (fee); DRP (fee)
800/522-3000	Tradex Brokerage	35.00	0.70	95.00	0.38	75.00	1.50	25.00			Sweep ($1,001); DRP (fee)
800/962-5489	Tuttle Securities	55.00	1.10	140.00	0.56	90.00	1.80	40.00		Standard	Sweep; NLMF (fee)

Phone	Firm								Handling Fees	Research	Other Services
800/631-1635	U.J.B. Investor Services	43.00	0.86	98.00	0.39	60.00	1.20	25.00		Standard (fee)	Sweep; NLMF (fee)
800/862-7283	Unified Management Corp.††	54.00	1.08	154.00	0.62	90.00	1.80	38.00	$10.00c, $25.00t	Standard (fee)	Sweep ($101); NLMF (fee); On-Line
800/992-8327	Vanguard Discount	48.00	0.96	135.00	0.54	77.00	1.54	36.25			Sweep; DRP
800/426-8106	Voss & Co.	53.63	1.07	162.70	0.65	104.78	2.10	49.00		Standard	Sweep; DRP (fee)
800/221-7990	Wall Street Discount	35.00	0.70	40.00	0.16	80.00	1.60	35.00		Standard	Interest ($1,001); NLMF (fee)
800/843-9601	Washington Disc Frequent**	25.00	0.50	25.00	0.10	25.00	0.50	25.00	$20.00t		Interest; NLMF (fee)
800/934-4410	Waterhouse Securities	35.00	0.70	111.74	0.45	54.72	1.09	35.00	$25.00c		Sweep ($1,000); NLMF (fee)
800/700-6363	White Discount Securities***	42.00	0.84	42.00	0.17	42.00	0.84	42.00	$25.00t	Standard (fee)	Sweep ($2,000); NLMF (fee); DRP (fee)
800/223-5023	Whitehall Securities Inc.	50.00	1.00	62.50	0.25	125.00	2.50	50.00		Standard	Interest ($2,001)
800/221-3154	York Securities	35.00	0.70	43.00	0.17	53.00	1.06	35.00		Standard	Sweep; NLMF; DRP (fee)
800/433-5132	Young, Stovall	50.00	1.00	136.00	0.54	78.00	1.56	35.00		Standard	Sweep
800/800-3215	Your Discount Broker	35.00	0.70	55.00	0.22	70.00	1.40	35.00		Standard	Sweep; NLMF (fee)
	Average	42.67	0.85	94.52	0.38	68.49	1.37	36.29			
	Highest	82.50	1.65	247.50	0.99	135.00	2.70	75.00			
	Lowest	23.00	0.46	25.00	0.10	25.00	0.50	20.00			

Key to Research and Other Services

Research: Provides research information. **Standard** research is supplied to the firm by outside sources. **Custom** research is supplied by the firm's own analysts.

Other Services

Interest: Pays interest on customers' cash balances. Amounts in parentheses, if any, indicate minimum amount at which interest is paid. If a discount firm offers a sweep account, we do not include information on cash balance interest.

Sweep: Automatically invests cash balances in an interest-bearing money market fund until those funds are reinvested. Money market funds usually pay a higher rate of interest than cash balance accounts that simply earn interest.

NLMF: No-load mutual funds can be purchased through the firm. Note that some firms charge for this, others do not. In addition, the number of funds available varies from firm to firm; check with the firm for a listing of available funds.

DRP: Dividends can be automatically reinvested through the brokerage firm.

On-Line: Trades can be made through computer. For more information on on-line trading, see box on following page.

Key to Handling Fees

c = charge for registering stock certificate in owner's name
t = charge for transferring account to or from another broker

Notes

* Non-market orders are higher
** High volume rates
*** Commissions reflect Calif. branch only; other branches vary

All firms offer self-directed IRAs and SIPC coverage.
† Formerly Aurex Financial Corp.
†† Formerly Unified Brokerage System
➤ Does not insure accounts above the SIPC minimum of $500,000

On-Line Discount Brokers

The table below provides more information concerning the on-line trading services offered by a number of discount brokers. On-line services enable computer users with modems to register trades with a broker through their computers. Commissions are usually the same as the normal brokerage charges, although some firms may offer a discount for on-line trading. Use the telephone numbers provided to request information on any start-up, maintenance, and access fees and additional requirements and services.

Telephone	Brokerage Firm	Name of On-Line Service
800/228-3011	AccuTrade	AccuTrade Direct Access
800/866-6757	Aufhauser	WealthWEB
800/822-2021	Brown & Co.	PCLine
800/334-4455	Charles Schwab	Equalizer, StreetSmart
800/786-2575	E*Trade Securities	E*Trade Securities
800/544-0246	Fidelity	Fidelity On-Line Xpress*
800/223-6642	Max Ule	Max Ule On-Line**
800/262-2294	Pacific Brokerage	Remote Access
800/825-5723	PC Financial Network	PCFN*
800/634-6214	Quick & Reilly	QuickWay
800/487-2339	Royal Grimm & Davis	Traders Express*
800/862-7283	Unified Mgmt. Corp.	Money Manager

*IBM-compatible systems only
**Through CompuServe off brokerage hours only

Bonds and Money Market Instruments

RELATION OF GROSS DOMESTIC PRODUCT, GROSS NATIONAL PRODUCT, NET NATIONAL PRODUCT, NATIONAL INCOME, AND PERSONAL INCOME

[Billions of dollars]

	1993	1994	Seasonally adjusted at annual rates					
			1993	1994				1995
			IV	I	II	III	IV	I
Gross domestic product	**6,343.3**	**6,738.4**	**6,478.1**	**6,574.7**	**6,689.9**	**6,791.7**	**6,897.2**	**6,977.4**
Plus: Receipts of factor income from the rest of the world [1]	136.6	167.1	141.3	145.4	162.1	176.7	184.2	201.9
Less: Payments of factor income to the rest of the world [2]	132.1	178.6	143.3	146.1	169.5	188.8	210.1	219.8
Equals: Gross national product	**6,347.8**	**6,726.9**	**6,476.2**	**6,574.0**	**6,682.5**	**6,779.6**	**6,871.3**	**6,959.5**
Less: Consumption of fixed capital	669.1	715.3	674.0	734.1	698.1	709.9	719.3	730.1
Capital consumption allowances	635.1	680.3	650.3	683.2	669.8	679.4	688.9	697.9
Less: Capital consumption adjustment	−33.9	−35.0	−23.8	−50.9	−28.3	−30.5	−30.5	−32.2
Equals: Net national product	**5,678.7**	**6,011.5**	**5,802.2**	**5,840.0**	**5,984.5**	**6,069.8**	**6,152.0**	**6,229.4**
Less: Indirect business tax and nontax liability	525.3	554.0	539.7	544.7	550.3	557.2	564.0	565.6
Business transfer payments	28.7	30.7	28.6	30.1	30.3	30.8	31.4	31.6
Statistical discrepancy	2.3	−30.9	−16.5	−36.1	−24.0	−21.1	−42.4	−58.6
Plus: Subsidies less current surplus of government enterprises	9.0	.7	11.7	7.4	3.0	−8.0	.4	−2.5
Equals: National income	**5,131.4**	**5,458.4**	**5,262.0**	**5,308.7**	**5,430.7**	**5,494.9**	**5,599.4**	**5,688.4**
Less: Corporate profits with inventory valuation and capital consumption adjustments	485.8	542.7	533.9	508.2	546.4	556.0	560.3	569.7
Net interest	399.5	409.7	389.1	394.2	399.7	415.7	429.2	442.4
Contributions for social insurance	585.6	626.0	597.2	614.7	623.5	628.9	636.7	648.1
Wage accruals less disbursements	20.0	0	0	0	0	0	0	0
Plus: Personal interest income	637.9	664.0	627.7	631.1	649.4	674.2	701.1	723.6
Personal dividend income	181.3	194.3	184.1	185.7	191.7	196.9	202.7	205.5
Government transfer payments to persons	892.6	939.9	908.3	924.2	934.3	945.4	955.8	980.8
Business transfer payments to persons	22.8	23.5	22.7	23.2	23.4	23.6	23.8	24.0
Equals: Personal income	**5,375.1**	**5,701.7**	**5,484.6**	**5,555.8**	**5,659.9**	**5,734.5**	**5,856.6**	**5,962.0**
Addenda:								
Net domestic product	5,674.2	6,023.0	5,804.1	5,840.7	5,991.8	6,081.8	6,177.8	6,247.4
Domestic income	5,126.9	5,469.9	5,264.0	5,309.4	5,438.1	5,506.9	5,625.3	5,706.4
Gross national income	6,345.5	6,757.8	6,492.7	6,610.1	6,706.5	6,800.8	6,913.7	7,018.1

1. Consists largely of receipts by U.S. residents of interest and dividends and reinvested earnings of foreign affiliates of U.S. corporations.

2. Consists largely of payments to foreign residents of interest and dividends and reinvested earnings of U.S. affiliates of foreign corporations.

Source: *Survey of Current Business,* Economic and Statistics Administration, Bureau of Economic Analysis

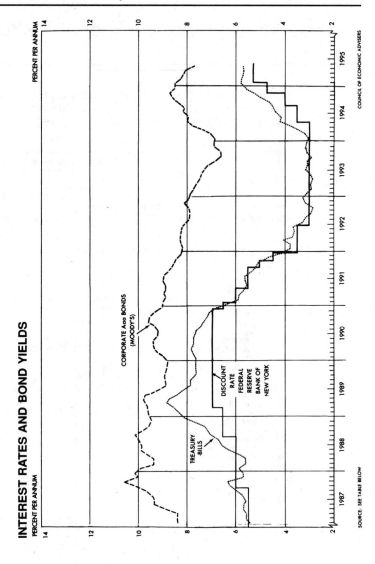

INTEREST RATES AND BOND YIELDS

PERCENT PER ANNUM

PERCENT PER ANNUM

CORPORATE Aaa BONDS (MOODY'S)

TREASURY BILLS

DISCOUNT RATE FEDERAL RESERVE BANK OF NEW YORK

SOURCE: SEE TABLE BELOW

COUNCIL OF ECONOMIC ADVISERS

[Percent per annum]

Period	U.S. Treasury security yields			High-grade municipal bonds (Standard & Poor's)[3]	Corporate Aaa bonds (Moody's)	Prime commercial paper, 6 months[1]	Discount rate (N.Y. F.R. Bank)[4]	Prime rate charged by banks[4]	New-home mortgage yields (FHFB)[5]
	3-month bills (new issues)[1]	Constant maturities[2]							
		3-year	10-year						
1985	7.48	9.64	10.62	9.18	11.37	8.01	7.69	9.93	11.55
1986	5.98	7.06	7.68	7.38	9.02	6.39	6.33	8.33	10.17
1987	5.82	7.68	8.39	7.73	9.38	6.85	5.66	8.21	9.31
1988	6.69	8.26	8.85	7.76	9.71	7.68	6.20	9.32	9.19
1989	8.12	8.55	8.49	7.24	9.26	8.80	6.93	10.87	10.13
1990	7.51	8.26	8.55	7.25	9.32	7.95	6.98	10.01	10.05
1991	5.42	6.82	7.86	6.89	8.77	5.85	5.45	8.46	9.32
1992	3.45	5.30	7.01	6.41	8.14	3.80	3.25	6.25	8.24
1993	3.02	4.44	5.87	5.63	7.22	3.30	3.00	6.00	7.20
1994	4.29	6.27	7.09	6.19	7.97	4.93	3.60	7.15	7.49
1994: May	4.19	6.34	7.18	6.26	7.99	4.92	3.00–3.50	6.75–7.25	7.43
June	4.18	6.27	7.10	6.14	7.97	4.86	3.50–3.50	7.25–7.25	7.62
July	4.39	6.48	7.30	6.19	8.11	5.13	3.50–3.50	7.25–7.25	7.71
Aug	4.50	6.50	7.24	6.19	8.07	5.19	3.50–4.00	7.25–7.75	7.67
Sept	4.64	6.69	7.46	6.33	8.34	5.32	4.00–4.00	7.75–7.75	7.70
Oct	4.96	7.04	7.74	6.50	8.57	5.70	4.00–4.00	7.75–7.75	7.76
Nov	5.25	7.44	7.96	6.96	8.68	6.01	4.00–4.75	7.75–8.50	7.81
Dec	5.64	7.71	7.81	6.76	8.46	6.62	4.75–4.75	8.50–8.50	7.83
1995: Jan	5.81	7.66	7.78	6.53	8.46	6.63	4.75–4.75	8.50–8.50	8.18
Feb	5.80	7.25	7.47	6.24	8.26	6.38	4.75–5.25	8.50–9.00	8.28
Mar	5.73	6.89	7.20	6.10	8.12	6.30	5.25–5.25	9.00–9.00	8.21
Apr	5.67	6.68	7.06	6.01	8.03	6.19	5.25–5.25	9.00–9.00	8.15
May	5.70	6.27	6.63	5.90	7.65	6.07	5.25–5.25	9.00–9.00	....
Week ended: 1995: May 6	5.74	6.54	6.93	6.14	7.89	6.16	5.25–5.25	9.00–9.00	....
13	5.63	6.27	6.66	5.93	7.69	6.06	5.25–5.25	9.00–9.00	....
20	5.71	6.25	6.59	5.85	7.60	6.06	5.25–5.25	9.00–9.00	....
27	5.72	6.14	6.49	5.80	7.51	6.02	5.25–5.25	9.00–9.00	....
June 3	5.64	5.83	6.23	5.79	7.33	5.92	5.25–5.25	9.00–9.00	....

[1] Bank-discount basis.
[2] Yields on the more actively traded issues adjusted to constant maturities by the Treasury Department.
[3] Weekly data are Wednesday figures.
[4] Average effective rate for year; opening and closing rate for month and week.
[5] Effective rate (in the primary market) on conventional mortgages, reflecting fees and charges as well as contract rate and assumed, on the average, repayment at end of 10 years.

Sources: Department of the Treasury, Board of Governors of the Federal Reserve System, Federal Housing Finance Board, Moody's Investors Service, and Standard & Poor's Corporation.

Source: Economic Indicators, Council of Economic Advisers.

INTEREST RATES Money and Capital Markets

Percent per year; figures are averages of business day data unless otherwise noted

Item	1992	1993	1994	1994 Dec.	1995 Jan.	1995 Feb.	1995 Mar.	1995, week ending Mar. 3	Mar. 10	Mar. 17	Mar. 24	Mar. 31
MONEY MARKET INSTRUMENTS												
1 Federal funds[1,2,3]	3.52	3.02	4.21	5.45	5.53	5.92	5.98	5.88	5.93	5.94	5.97	6.06
2 Discount window borrowing[2,4]	3.25	3.00	3.60	4.75	4.75	5.25	5.25	5.25	5.25	5.25	5.25	5.25
Commercial paper[3,5,6]												
3 1-month	3.71	3.17	4.43	6.08	5.86	6.05	6.07	6.05	6.08	6.07	6.05	6.08
4 3-month	3.75	3.22	4.66	6.26	6.22	6.15	6.15	6.13	6.19	6.15	6.14	6.15
5 6-month	3.80	3.30	4.93	6.62	6.63	6.38	6.30	6.28	6.39	6.31	6.27	6.25
Finance paper, directly placed[3,5,7]												
6 1-month	3.62	3.12	4.33	5.93	5.76	5.95	5.95	5.93	5.95	5.95	5.96	5.96
7 3-month	3.65	3.16	4.53	6.12	6.10	6.04	6.03	6.02	6.06	6.04	6.03	6.02
8 6-month	3.63	3.15	4.56	6.17	6.25	6.10	6.04	6.02	6.07	6.03	6.03	6.03
Bankers acceptances[3,5,8]												
9 3-month	3.62	3.13	4.56	6.18	6.12	6.05	6.04	6.03	6.08	6.03	6.02	6.05
10 6-month	3.67	3.21	4.83	6.53	6.45	6.22	6.14	6.12	6.20	6.12	6.11	6.13
Certificates of deposit, secondary market[3,9]												
11 1-month	3.64	3.11	4.38	6.01	5.84	6.01	6.02	6.00	6.02	6.01	6.01	6.04
12 3-month	3.68	3.17	4.63	6.29	6.24	6.16	6.15	6.13	6.20	6.14	6.12	6.15
13 6-month	3.76	3.28	4.96	6.78	6.71	6.44	6.34	6.33	6.41	6.33	6.31	6.34
14 Eurodollar deposits, 3-month[3,10]	3.70	3.18	4.63	6.27	6.23	6.14	6.15	6.13	6.20	6.13	6.13	6.16
U.S. Treasury bills												
Secondary market[3,5]												
15 3-month	3.43	3.00	4.25	5.60	5.71	5.77	5.73	5.74	5.76	5.75	5.72	5.69
16 6-month	3.54	3.12	4.64	6.21	6.21	6.03	5.89	5.91	5.96	5.90	5.87	5.81
17 1-year	3.71	3.29	5.02	6.67	6.59	6.28	6.03	6.07	6.14	6.00	5.97	5.98
Auction average[3,5,11]												
18 3-month	3.45	3.02	4.29	5.64	5.81	5.80	5.73	5.73	5.77	5.76	5.76	5.64
19 6-month	3.57	3.14	4.66	6.21	6.31	6.10	5.91	5.90	6.00	5.92	5.91	5.80
20 1-year	3.75	3.33	4.98	6.75	6.86	6.59	6.16	n.a.	6.16	n.a.	n.a.	n.a.
U.S. TREASURY NOTES AND BONDS												
Constant maturities[12]												
21 1-year	3.89	3.43	5.32	7.14	7.05	6.70	6.43	6.47	6.54	6.39	6.37	6.38
22 2-year	4.77	4.05	5.94	7.59	7.51	7.11	6.78	6.83	6.91	6.71	6.71	6.73
23 3-year	5.30	4.44	6.27	7.71	7.66	7.25	6.89	6.95	7.04	6.81	6.83	6.84
24 5-year	6.19	5.14	6.69	7.78	7.76	7.37	7.05	7.10	7.18	6.95	7.01	7.01
25 7-year	6.63	5.54	6.91	7.80	7.79	7.44	7.14	7.21	7.28	7.03	7.10	7.11
26 10-year	7.01	5.87	7.09	7.81	7.78	7.47	7.20	7.27	7.35	7.11	7.16	7.15
27 20-year	n.a.	6.29	7.49	7.99	7.97	7.73	7.57	7.61	7.68	7.48	7.55	7.51
28 30-year	7.67	6.59	7.37	7.87	7.85	7.61	7.45	7.49	7.56	7.37	7.43	7.40

Composite												
29 More than 10 years (long-term)	7.52	6.45	7.41	7.97	7.93	7.69	7.52	7.56	7.64	7.44	7.50	7.48
STATE AND LOCAL NOTES AND BONDS												
Moody's series[13]												
30 Aaa	6.09	5.38	5.77	6.62	6.55	6.05	5.92	5.98	5.95	5.93	5.82	5.90
31 Baa	6.48	5.83	6.17	7.17	7.05	6.61	6.06	6.10	6.10	6.10	6.02	6.00
32 Bond Buyer series[14]	6.44	5.60	6.18	6.80	6.53	6.22	6.10	6.08	6.18	6.06	6.09	6.07
CORPORATE BONDS												
33 Seasoned issues, all industries[15]	8.55	7.54	8.26	8.73	8.71	8.50	8.35	8.41	8.46	8.27	8.33	8.30
Rating group												
34 Aaa	8.14	7.22	7.97	8.46	8.46	8.26	8.12	8.17	8.22	8.04	8.10	8.08
35 Aa	8.46	7.40	8.15	8.62	8.60	8.39	8.24	8.29	8.35	8.17	8.22	8.19
36 A	8.62	7.58	8.28	8.73	8.70	8.48	8.33	8.39	8.44	8.25	8.32	8.28
37 Baa	8.98	7.93	8.63	9.10	9.08	8.85	8.70	8.76	8.81	8.62	8.69	8.65
38 A-rated, recently offered utility bonds[16]	8.52	7.46	8.29	8.78	8.75	8.55	8.40	8.52	8.43	8.32	8.35	8.40
MEMO												
Dividend–price ratio[17]												
39 Common stocks	2.99	2.78	2.82	2.91	2.87	2.81	2.76	2.79	2.81	2.76	2.73	2.69

1. The daily effective federal funds rate is a weighted average of rates on trades through New York brokers.

2. Weekly figures are averages of seven calendar days ending on Wednesday of the current week; monthly figures include each calendar day in the month.

3. Annualized using a 360-day year for bank interest.

4. Rate for the Federal Reserve Bank of New York.

5. Quoted on a discount basis.

6. An average of offering rates on commercial paper placed by several leading dealers for firms whose bond rating is AA or the equivalent.

7. An average of offering rates on paper directly placed by finance companies.

8. Representative closing yields for acceptances of the highest-rated money center banks.

9. An average of dealer offering rates on nationally traded certificates of deposit.

10. Bid rates for Eurodollar deposits at 11:00 a.m. London time. Data are for indication purposes only.

11. Auction date for daily data; weekly and monthly averages computed on an issue-date basis.

12. Yields on actively traded issues adjusted to constant maturities. Source: U.S. Department of the Treasury.

13. General obligation bonds based on Thursday figures; Moody's Investors Service.

14. State and local government general obligation bonds maturing in twenty years are used in compiling this index. The twenty-bond index has a rating roughly equivalent to Moody's A1 rating. Based on Thursday figures.

15. Daily figures from Moody's Investors Service. Based on yields to maturity on selected long-term bonds.

16. Compilation of the Federal Reserve. This series is an estimate of the yield on recently offered, A-rated utility bonds with a thirty-year maturity and five years of call protection. Weekly data are based on Friday quotations.

17. Standard & Poor's corporate series. Common stock ratio is based on the 500 stocks in the price index.

NOTE. Some of the data in this table also appear in the Board's H.15 (519) weekly and G.13 (415) monthly statistical releases. For ordering address, see inside front cover.

Source: *Federal Reserve Bulletin*, Board of Governors of the Federal Reserve System.

PRIME RATE CHARGED BY BANKS Short-Term Business Loans (percent per year)[1]

Date of change	Rate	Period	Average rate	Period	Average rate	Period	Average rate
1992—July 2	6.00	1992	6.25	1993—Jan.	6.00	1994—Jan.	6.00
1994—Mar. 24	6.25	1993	6.00	Feb.	6.00	Feb.	6.00
Apr. 19	6.75	1994	7.15	Mar.	6.00	Mar.	6.06
May 17	7.25	1992—Jan.	6.50	Apr.	6.00	Apr.	6.45
Aug. 16	7.75	Feb.	6.50	May	6.00	May	6.99
Nov. 15	8.50	Mar.	6.50	June	6.00	June	7.25
1995—Feb. 1	9.00	Apr.	6.50	July	6.00	July	7.25
		May	6.50	Aug.	6.00	Aug.	7.51
		June	6.50	Sept.	6.00	Sept.	7.75
		July	6.02	Oct.	6.00	Oct.	7.75
		Aug.	6.00	Nov.	6.00	Nov.	8.15
		Sept.	6.00	Dec.	6.00	Dec.	8.50
		Oct.	6.00				
		Nov.	6.00			1995—Jan.	8.50
		Dec.	6.00			Feb.	9.00
						Mar.	9.00
						Apr.	9.00

1. The prime rate is one of several base rates that banks use to price short-term business loans. The table shows the date on which a new rate came to be the predominant one quoted by a majority of the twenty-five largest banks by asset size, based on the most recent Call Report. Data in this table also appear in the Board's H.15 (519) weekly and G.13 (415) monthly statistical releases. For ordering address, see inside front cover.

Source: *Federal Reserve Bulletin*, Board of Governors of the Federal Reserve System.

Reported bond volume and trades on NYSE, 1994 (par value in thousands)

	Par value		No. of	Avg. daily	Avg. trade size
	Total	Avg. daily	trades	trades	(thousands)
January	$724,837	$34,516	31,942	1,521	$22.7
February	607,556	31,977	27,283	1,436	22.3
March	780,392	33,930	39,263	1,707	19.9
April	670,002	35,263	35,365	1,861	18.9
May	656,082	31,242	35,834	1,706	18.3
June	555,011	25,228	31,627	1,438	17.5
July	508,652	25,433	27,470	1,374	18.5
August	563,604	24,505	32,785	1,425	17.2
September	549,208	26,153	30,343	1,445	18.1
October	520,591	24,790	29,372	1,399	17.7
November	532,902	25,376	30,517	1,453	17.5
December	528,337	25,159	31,741	1,511	16.6
Year	$7,197,174	$28,560	383,542	1,522	$18.8
		Par value			
High Day		$50,410	May 6		
Low Day		$7,875	November 25		
High Month		$724,837	January		
Low Month		$508,652	July		

Source: New York Stock Exchange *Fact Book.*

Most active bonds on NYSE, 1994

Issue		Par value of reported volume (thousands)
RJR Nabisco Inc.	9¼ s '13	$177,008
General Motors Acceptance	zero coupon '15	175,290
USAir Inc.	12⅞ s '00	157,630
duPont ei de Nemours	6 s '01	144,378
Stone Container Corporation	10¾ s '02	137,662
General Motors Acceptance	zero coupon '12	135,300
Eckerd Corporation	9¼ s '04	118,537
CompUSA Inc.	9½ s '00	115,240
Stone Container Corporation	11½ s '99	112,931
Revlon Consumer Products	9½ s '99	99,439
RJR Nabisco Inc.	8¾ s '05	88,200
RJR Nabisco Inc.	8¾ s '04	83,255
AT&T Corporation	8⅛ s '22	82,138
RJR Nabisco Inc.	8.30 s '99	80,280
Time Warner Inc.	reset notes '02	78,811
General Motors Acceptance	8¼ s '16	77,835
Time Warner Inc.*	8¾ s '15	75,891
RJR Nabisco Inc.	7⅝ s '03	75,007
F&M Distributors	11½ s '03	74,826
Best Buy Company Inc.	8⅝ s '00	74,725
Rally's Hamburgers Inc.	9⅞ s '00	72,794
Stone Container Corporation	10¾ s '97	69,937
Service Merchandise Co.	9 s '04	69,328
Time Warner Inc.	9⅛ s '13	67,006
RJR Nabisco Inc.	8⅝ s '02	65,577
RJR Nabisco Inc.	8 s '00	65,122
Time Warner Inc.	9.15 s '23	64,920
International Business Machines Corp.	6⅜ s '97	64,023
AT&T Corporation	7⅛ s '02	63,679
Tyco Toys Inc.	10⅛ s '02	62,621
Stone Container Corporation	11 s '99	59,825
GPA Delaware Inc.	8¾ s '98	57,762
Chrysler Corporation	13 s '97	53,047
International Business Machines Corp.	6⅜ s '00	51,499
Wheeling-Pittsburgh Corp.	9⅜ s '03	49,744
International Business Machines Corp.	7½ s '13	46,791
International Business Machines Corp.	7¼ s '02	45,641
Long Island Lighting Co.	8.90 s '19	41,869
Stone Container Corporation	11⅞ s '98	40,029
Kaufman & Broad Home	9⅜ s '03	38,651
International Business Machines Corp.	8⅜ s '19	38,077
AT&T Corporation	8⅝ s '31	37,479
Time Warner Inc.	7.45 s '98	36,897
Reliance Group Holdings Inc.	9 s '00	36,563
Safeway Inc.	9.65 s '04	36,484
International Business Machines Corp.	9 s '98	36,463
RJR Nabisco Inc.	disc debs due '01	35,948
General Host Corporation	11½ s '02	35,199
Showboat Inc.	9¼ s '08	34,935
Owens-Illinois Inc.	10 s '02	34,182

* Convertible

Source: New York Stock Exchange *Fact Book*.

Credit Ratings of Fixed Income and Money Market Securities

KEY TO STANDARD & POOR'S CORPORATE AND MUNICIPAL BOND RATING DEFINITIONS

A Standard & Poor's corporate or municipal debt rating is a current assessment of the creditworthiness of an obligor with respect to a specific debt obligation. This assessment may take into consideration obligors such as guarantors, insurers, or lessees.

The debt rating is not a recommendation to purchase, sell or hold a security, inasmuch as it does not comment as to market price or suitability for a particular investor.

The ratings are based on current information furnished by the issuer or obtained by Standard & Poor's from other sources it considers reliable. Standard & Poor's does not perform an audit in connection with any rating and may, on occasion, rely on unaudited financial information. The ratings may be changed, suspended or withdrawn as a result of changes in, or unavailability of, such information, or for other circumstances.

The ratings are based, in varying degrees, on the following considerations:

I. Likelihood of default—capacity and willingness of the obligor as to the timely payment of interest and repayment of principal in accordance with the terms of the obligation;
II. Nature of and provisions of the obligation;
III. Protection afforded by, and relative position of, the obligation in the event of bankruptcy, reorganization or other arrangement under the laws of bankruptcy and other laws affecting creditor's rights.

AAA

Debt rated **AAA** have the highest rating assigned by Standard & Poor's to a debt obligation. Capacity to pay interest and repay principal is extremely strong.

AA

Debt rated **AA** have a very strong capacity to pay interest and repay principal and differ from the highest rated issues only in a small degree.

A

Debt rated **A** have a strong capacity to pay interest and repay principal although

Source: From Standard & Poor's Debt Rating Division.

they are somewhat more susceptible to the adverse effects of changes in circumstances and economic conditions than debts in higher rated categories.

BBB

Debt rated **BBB** are regarded as having an adequate capacity to pay interest and repay principal. Whereas they normally exhibit adequate protection parameters, adverse economic conditions or changing circumstances are more likely to lead to a weakened capacity to pay interest and repay principal for debts in this category than for debts in higher rated categories.

BB, B, CCC, CC

Debt rated **BB, B, CCC,** and **CC** are regarded, on balance, as predominantly speculative with respect to capacity to pay interest and repay principal in accordance with the terms of the obligation. **BB** indicates the lowest degree of speculation and **CC** the highest degree of speculation. While such debts will likely have some quality and protective characteristics, these are outweighed by large uncertainties or major risk exposures to adverse conditions.

C

The rating **C** is reserved for income bonds on which no interest is being paid.

D

Debt rated **D** are in default, and payment of interest and/or repayment of principal is in arrears.

Plus (+) or minus (−)

The ratings from **AA** to **B** may be modified by the addition of a plus or minus sign to show relative standing within the major rating categories.

Provisional Ratings

The letter p indicates that the rating is provisional. A provisional rating assumes the successful completion of the project being financed by the debts being rated and indicates that payment of debt service requirements is largely or entirely dependent upon the successful and timely completion of the project. This rating, however, while addressing credit quality subsequent to completion of the project, makes no comment on the likelihood of, or the risk of default upon failure of, such completion. The investor should exercise his own judgment with respect to such likelihood and risk.

L°

The letter "L" indicates that the rating pertains to the principal amount of those bonds where the underlying deposit collateral is fully insured by the Federal Savings & Loan Insurance Corp. or the Federal Deposit Insurance Corp.

NR

Indicates that no rating has been requested, that there is insufficient information on which to base a rating or that S&P does not rate a particular type of obligation as a matter of policy.

Debt Obligations

Debt Obligations of issuers outside the United States and its territories are rated on the same basis as domestic corporate and municipal issues. The ratings measure the creditworthiness of the obligor but do not take into account currency exchange and other uncertainties.

Bond Investment Quality Standards

Under present commercial bank regulations issued by the Comptroller of the Currency, bonds rated in the top four categories (**AAA, AA, A, BBB,** commonly known as "Investment Grade" ratings) are generally regarded as eligible for bank investment. In addition, the Legal Investment Laws of various states impose certain rating or other standards for obligations eligible for investment by savings banks, trust companies, insurance companies and fiduciaries generally.

KEY TO STANDARD & POOR'S PREFERRED STOCK RATING DEFINITIONS

A Standard & Poor's preferred stock rating is an assessment of the capacity and willingness of an issuer to pay preferred stock dividends and any applicable sinking fund obligations. A preferred stock rating differs from a bond rating inasmuch as it is assigned to an equity issue, which issue is intrinsically different from, and subordinated to, a debt issue. Therefore, to reflect this difference, the preferred stock rating symbol will normally not be higher than the bond rating symbol assigned to, or that would be assigned to, the senior debt of the same issuer.

The preferred stock ratings are based on the following considerations.

I. Likelihood of payment—capacity and willingness of the issuer to meet the timely payment of preferred stock dividends and any applicable sinking fund requirements in accordance with the terms of the obligation.
II. Nature of, and provisions of, the issue.
III. Relative position of the issue in the event of bankruptcy, reorganization, or other arrangements affecting creditors' rights.

AAA

This is the highest rating that may be assigned by Standard & Poor's to a preferred stock issue and indicates an extremely strong capacity to pay the preferred stock obligations.

AA

A preferred stock issue rated **AA** also qualifies as a high-quality fixed income security. The capacity to pay preferred stock obligations is very strong, although not as overwhelming as for issues rated **AAA.**

A

An issue rated **A** is backed by a sound capacity to pay the preferred stock obligations, although it is somewhat more susceptible to the adverse effects of changes in circumstances and economic conditions.

BBB

An issue rated **BBB** is regarded as backed by an adequate capacity to pay the preferred stock obligations. Whereas it normally exhibits adequate protection parameters, adverse economic conditions or changing circumstances are more likely to lead to a weakened capacity to make payments for a preferred stock in this category than for issues in the **A** category.

BB, B, CCC

Preferred stock rated **BB, B,** and **CCC** are regarded, on balance, as predominately speculative with respect to the issuer's capacity to pay preferred stock obligations. **BB** indicates the lowest degree of speculation and **CCC** the highest degree of speculation. While such issues will likely have some quality and protective characteristics, these are outweighed by large uncertainties or major risk exposures to adverse conditions.

CC

The rating **CC** is reserved for a preferred stock issue in arrears on dividends or sinking fund payments but that is currently paying.

C

A preferred stock rated **C** is a non-paying issue.

°Continuance of the rating is contingent upon S&P's receipt of an executed copy of the escrow agreement or closing documentation confirming investments and the cash flows.

D

A preferred stock rated **D** is a non-paying issue with the issuer in default on debt instruments.

NR

NR indicates that no rating has been requested, that there is insufficient information on which to base a rating, or that S&P does not rate a particular type of obligation as a matter of policy.

Plus (+) or Minus (−) To provide more detailed indications of preferred stock quality, the ratings from **AA** to **B** may be modified by the addition of a plus or minus sign to show relative standing within the major rating categories.

The preferred stock rating is not a recommendation to purchase or sell a security, inasmuch as market price is not considered in arriving at the rating. Preferred stock *ratings* are wholly unrelated to Standard & Poor's earnings and dividend *rankings* for common stocks.

MUNICIPAL NOTES

A Standard & Poor's role rating reflects the liquidity concerns and market access risks unique to notes. Notes due in 3 years or less will likely receive a long-term debt rating. The following criteria will be used in making that assessment.

— Amortization schedule (the larger the final maturity relative to other maturities the more likely it will be treated as a note).
— Source of Payment (the more dependent the issue is on the market for its refinancing, the more likely it will be treated as a note).

Note rating symbols are as follows:

SP-1 Very strong or strong capacity to pay principal and interest. Those issues determined to possess overwhelming safety characteristics will be given a plus (+) designation.
SP-2 Satisfactory capacity to pay principal and interest.
SP-3 Speculative capacity to pay principal and interest.

TAX-EXEMPT DEMAND BONDS

Standard & Poor's assigns "dual" ratings to all long-term debt issues that have as part of their provisions a demand or double feature.

The first rating addresses the likelihood of repayment of principal and interest as due, and the second rating addresses only the demand feature. The long-term debt rating symbols are used for bonds to denote the long-term maturity and the commercial paper rating symbols are used to denote the put option (for example, "AAA/A-1 + "). For the newer "demand notes," S&P's note rating symbols, combined with the commercial paper symbols, are used (for example, "SP-1 + /A-1 + ").

KEY TO STANDARD & POOR'S COMMERCIAL PAPER RATING DEFINITIONS

A Standard & Poor's Commercial Paper Rating is a current assessment of the likelihood of timely payment of debt having an original maturity of no more than 365 days.

Ratings are graded into four categories, ranging from **A** for the highest quality obligations to **D** for the lowest. The four categories are as follows:

A

Issues assigned this highest rating are regarded as having the greatest capacity for timely payment. Issues in this category are further refined with the designations 1, 2, and 3 to indicate the relative degree of safety.

A-1 This designation indicates that the degree of safety regarding timely payment is very strong.
A-2 Capacity for timely payment on issues with this designation is strong. However, the relative degree of safety is not as overwhelming as for issues designated **A-1**.
A-3 Issues carrying this designation have a satisfactory capacity for timely payment. They are, however, somewhat more vulnerable to the adverse effects of changes in circumstances than obligations carrying the higher designations.

B

Issues rated **B** are regarded as having only an adequate capacity for timely payment. However, such capacity may be damaged by changing conditions for short-term adversities.

C

This rating is assigned to short-term obligations with a doubtful capacity for payment.

D

This rating indicates that the issue is either a default or is expected to be in default upon maturity.

The Commercial Paper Rating is not a recommendation to purchase or sell a security. The ratings are based on current information furnished to Standard & Poor's by the issuer or obtained from other sources it considers reliable. The ratings may be changed, suspended, or withdrawn as a result of changes in, or unavailability of, such information.

KEY TO MOODY'S MUNICIPAL RATINGS*

Aaa

Bonds which are rated **Aaa** are judged to be of the best quality. They carry the smallest degree of investment risk and are generally referred to as "gilt edge." Interest payments are protected by a large or by an exceptionally stable margin and principal is secure. While the various protective elements are likely to change, such changes as can be visualized are most unlikely to impair the fundamentally strong position of such issues.

Aa

Bonds which are rated **Aa** are judged to be of high quality by all standards. Together with the **Aaa** group they comprise what are generally known as high grade bonds. They are rated lower than the best bonds because margins of protection may not be as large as in **Aaa** securities or fluctuation of protective elements may be of greater amplitude or there may be other elements present which make the long term risks appear somewhat larger than in **Aaa** securities.

A

Bonds which are rated **A** possess many favorable instrument attributes and are to be considered as upper medium grade obligations. Factors giving security to principal and interest are considered adequate, but elements may be present which suggest a susceptibility to impairment sometime in the future.

Baa

Bonds which are rated **Baa** are considered as medium grade obligations; i.e., they are neither highly protected nor poorly secured. Interest payments and principal security appear adequate for the present but certain protective elements may be lacking or may be characteristically unreliable over any great length of time. Such bonds lack outstanding investment characteristics and in fact have speculative characteristics as well.

Ba

Bonds which are rated **Ba** are judged to have speculative elements; their future cannot be considered as well assured. Often the protection of interest and principal payments may be very moderate, and thereby not well safeguarded during both good and bad times over the future. Uncertainty of position characterizes bonds in this case.

B

Bonds which are rated **B** generally lack characteristics of the desirable investment. Assurance of interest and principal payments or of maintenance of other terms of the contract over any long period of time may be small.

Caa

Bonds which are rated **Caa** are of poor standing. Such issues may be in default or there may be present elements of danger with respect to principal or interest.

Ca

Bonds which are rated **Ca** represent obligations which are speculative in a high degree. Such issues are often in default or have other marked shortcomings.

C

Bonds which are rated **C** are the lowest rated class of bonds, and issues so rated can be regarded as having extremely poor prospects of ever attaining any real investment standing.

Con.(—)

Bonds for which the security depends upon the completion of some act or the fulfillment of some condition are rated conditionally. These are bonds secured by (a) earnings of projects under construction, (b) earnings of projects unseasoned in operation experience, (c) rentals which begin when facilities are completed, or (d) payments to which some other limiting condition attaches. Parenthetical rating denotes probable credit stature upon completion of construction or elimination of basis of condition.

KEY TO MOODY'S CORPORATE RATINGS*

Aaa

Bonds which are rated **Aaa** are judged to be of the best quality. They carry the smallest

---

*Note: Those bonds in the **Aa, A, Baa, Ba** and **B** groups which Moody's believes possess the strongest investment attributes are designated by the symbols **Aa 1, A 1, Baa 1, Ba 1** and **B 1.**

Source: Moody's Investors Service, Inc.

*Note: Moody's applies numerical modifiers, **1, 2** and **3** in each generic rating classification from **Aa** through **B** in its corporate bond rating system. The modifier **1** indicates that the security ranks in the higher end of its generic rating category; the modifier **2** indicates a mid-range ranking; and the modifier **3** indicates that the issue ranks in the lower end of its generic rating category.

degree of investment risk and are generally referred to as "gilt edge." Interest payments are protected by a large or by an exceptionally stable margin and principal is secure. While the various protective elements are likely to change, such changes as can be visualized are most unlikely to impair the fundamentally strong position of such issues.

Aa

Bonds which are rated **Aa** are judged to be of high quality by all standards. Together with the **Aaa** group they comprise what are generally known as high grade bonds. They are rated lower than the best bonds because margins of protection may not be as large as in **Aaa** securities or fluctuation of protective elements may be of greater amplitude or there may be other elements present which make the long term risks appear somewhat larger than in **Aaa** securities.

A

Bonds which are rated **A** possess many favorable investment attributes and are to be considered as upper medium grade obligations. Factors giving security to principal and interest are considered adequate but elements may be present which suggest a susceptibility to impairment sometime in the future.

Baa

Bonds which are rated **Baa** are considered as medium grade obligations, i.e., they are neither highly protected nor poorly secured. Interest payments and principal security appear adequate for the present but certain protective elements may be lacking or may be characteristically unreliable over any great length of time. Such bonds lack outstanding investment characteristics and in fact have speculative characteristics as well.

Ba

Bonds which are rated **Ba** are judged to have speculative elements; their future cannot be considered as well assured. Often the protection of interest and principal payments may be very moderate and thereby not well safeguarded during both good and bad times over the future. Uncertainty of position characterizes bonds in this class.

B

Bonds which are rated **B** generally lack characteristics of the desirable investment. Assurance of interest and principal payments or of maintenance of other terms of the contract over any long period of time may be small.

Caa

Bonds which are rated **Caa** are of poor standing. Such issues may be in default or there may be present elements of danger with respect to principal or interest.

Ca

Bonds which are rated **Ca** represent obligations which are speculative in a high degree. Such issues are often in default or have other marked shortcomings.

C

Bonds which are rated **C** are the lowest rated class of bonds and issues so rated can be regarded as having extremely poor prospects of ever attaining any real investment standing.

KEY TO MOODY'S COMMERCIAL PAPER RATINGS

The term "Commercial Paper" as used by Moody's means promissory obligations not having an original maturity in excess of nine months. Moody's makes no representation as to whether such Commercial Paper is by any other definition "Commercial Paper" or is exempt from registration under the Securities Act of 1933, as amended.

Moody's Commercial Paper ratings are opinions of the ability of issuers to repay punctually promissory obligations not having an original maturity in excess of nine months. Moody's makes no representation that such obligations are exempt from registration under the Securities Act of 1933, nor does it represent that any specific note is a valid obligation of a rated issuer or issued in conformity with any applicable law. Moody's employs the following three designations, all judged to be investment grade, to indicate the relative repayment capacity of rated issuers:

Issuers rated **Prime-1** (or related supporting institutions) have a superior capacity for repayment of short-term promissory obligations. Prime-1 repayment capacity will normally be evidenced by the following characteristics:

-Leading market positions in well established industries.

-High rates of return on funds employed.

-Conservative capitalization structures with moderate reliance on debt and ample asset protection.

-Broad margins in earnings coverage of fixed financial charges and high internal cash generation.

-Well established access to a range of financial markets and assured sources of alternate liquidity.

Issuers rated **Prime-2** (or related supporting institutions) have a strong ca-

Source: Moody's Investors Service, Inc.

pacity for short-term promissory obligations. This will normally be evidenced by many of the characteristics cited above but to a lesser degree. Earnings trends and coverage ratios, while sound, will be more subject to variation. Capitalization characteristics, while still appropriate, may be more affected by external conditions. Ample alternate liquidity is maintained.

Issuers rated **Prime-3** (or related supporting institutions) have an acceptable capacity for repayment of short-term promissory obligations. The effect of industry characteristics and market composition may be more pronounced. Variability in earnings and profitability may result in changes in the level of debt protection measurements and the requirement for relatively high financial leverage. Adequate liquidity is maintained.

Issuers rated **Not Prime** do not fall within any of the Prime rating categories.

If an issuer represents to Moody's that its Commercial Paper obligations are supported by the credit of another entity or entities, the name or names of such supporting entity or entities are listed within parentheses beneath the name of the issuer. In assigning ratings to such issuers, Moody's evaluates the financial strength of the indicated affiliated corporations, commercial banks, insurance companies, foreign governments or other entities, but only as one factor in the total rating assessment. Moody's makes no representation and gives no opinion on the legal validity or enforceability of any support arrangement. You are cautioned to review with your counsel any questions regarding particular support arrangements.

KEY TO MOODY'S PREFERRED STOCK RATINGS*

Moody's Rating Policy Review Board extended its rating services to include quality designations on preferred stocks on October 1, 1973. The decision to rate preferred stocks, which Moody's had done prior to 1935, was prompted by evidence of investor interest. Moody's believes that its rating of preferred stocks is especially appropriate in view of the ever-increasing amount of these securities outstanding,

---

*Note: Moody's applies numerical modifiers **1, 2** and **3** in each rating classification from **1** indicates that the security ranks in the higher end of its generic rating category; the modifier **2** indicates a mid-range ranking; and the modifier **3** indicates that the issue ranks in the lower end of its generic rating category.

Source: Moody's Investors Service, Inc.

and the fact that continuing inflation and its ramifications have resulted generally in the dilution of some of the protection afforded them as well as other fixed-income securities.

Because of the fundamental differences between preferred stocks and bonds, a variation of our familiar bond rating symbols is being used in the quality ranking of preferred stocks. The symbols, presented below, are designed to avoid comparison with bond quality in absolute terms. It should always be borne in mind that preferred stocks occupy a junior position to bonds within a particular capital structure.

Preferred stock rating symbols and their definitions are as follows:

aaa

An issue which is rated **aaa** is considered to be a top-quality preferred stock. This rating indicates good asset protection and the least risk of dividend impairment within the universe of preferred stocks.

aa

An issue which is rated **aa** is considered a high-grade preferred stock. This rating indicates that there is reasonable assurance that earnings and asset protection will remain relatively well maintained in the foreseeable future.

a

An issue which is rated **a** is considered to be an upper-medium grade preferred stock. While risks are judged to be somewhat greater than in the **"aaa"** and **"aa"** classifications, earnings and asset protection are, nevertheless, expected to be maintained at adequate levels.

baa

An issue which is rated **baa** is considered to be medium grade, neither highly protected nor poorly secured. Earnings and asset protection appear adequate at present but may be questionable over any great length of time.

ba

An issue which is rated **ba** is considered to have speculative elements and its future cannot be considered well assured. Earnings and asset protection may be very moderate and not well safeguarded during adverse periods. Uncertainty of position characterized preferred stocks in this class.

b

An issue which is rated **b** generally lacks the characteristics of a desirable investment.

Assurance of dividend payments and maintenance of other terms of the issue over any long period of time may be small.

caa

An issue which is rated **caa** is likely to be in arrears on dividend payments. This rating designation does not purport to indicate the future status of payments.

"ca"

An issue which is rated **"ca"** is speculative in a high degree and is likely to be in arrears on dividends with little likelihood of eventual payment.

"c"

This is the lowest rated class of preferred or preference stock. Issues so rated can be regarded as having extremely poor prospects of ever attaining any real investment standing.

KEY TO SHORT-TERM LOAN RATINGS

MIG 1/VMIG 1

This designation denotes best quality. There is present strong protection by established cash flows, superior liquidity support or demonstrated broadbased access to the market for refinancing.

MIG 2/VMIG 2

This designation denotes high quality. Margins of protection are ample although not so large as in the preceding group.

MIG 3/VMIG 3

This designation denotes favorable quality. All security elements are accounted for but there is lacking the undeniable strength of the preceding grades. Liquidity and cash flow protection may be narrow and market access for refinancing is likely to be less well established.

MIG 4/VMIG 4

This designation denotes adequate quality. Protection commonly regarded as required of an investment security is present and although not distinctly or predominantly speculative, there is specific risk.

Issues or the features associated with **MIG** or **VMIG** ratings are identified by date of issue, date of maturity or maturities or rating expiration date and description to distinguish each rating from other ratings. Each rating designation is unique with no implication as to any other similar issue of the same obligor. **MIG** ratings terminate at the retirement of the obligation while **VMIG** rating expiration will be a function of each issue's specific structural or credit features.

Collateralized Mortgage Obligation (CMO) Volatility Ratings

Fitch announces ratings of collateralized mortgage obligation (CMO) volatility. V-Ratings offer a balanced view of the relative volatility of total return, price, and maturity for each CMO tranche.

CMOs are fixed income investments supported by U.S. government agency or whole loan collateral and structured into specific classes of securities known as tranches. All CMOs have high credit quality reflecting their support by federal agency certificates of Fannie Mae, Freddie Mac, or Ginnie Mae, or backing from whole loan collateral rated 'AAA.'

Individual tranches, however, have varying degrees of market risk. CMOs differ from pass-through certificates because cash flows from the collateral are structured to prioritize payment among tranches. Pass-through certificates are sold and priced with an expected yield and maturity based on an assumed mortgage prepayment rate. All pass-through certificate holders share symmetrically in this prepayment risk. CMO tranches are individually priced for expected return, maturity, and assumed prepayment rates based on their unique characteristics. Because cash flows are specifically allocated as part of structuring a new issue CMO, there is an asymmetrical distribution of prepayment risk among the tranches.

V-Rating Definitions

Fitch Indicated Volatility: Low to Moderate

Securities rated V1, V2, or V3 perform predictably over a range of various interest rate scenarios. On balance, total return, price, and cash flow indicators are less volatile than current coupon agency certificates.

V1 The security exhibits relatively small changes in total return, price, and cash flow in all modeled interest rate scenarios.

V2 The security exhibits relatively small changes in total return, price, and cash flow in most modeled interest rate scenarios. Under certain adverse interest rate scenarios, one or more of the indicators are more volatile than securities rated V1.

V3 The security exhibits relatively larger changes in total return, price, and cash flow in all modeled interest rate scenarios. However, on balance, total return, price, and cash flow indicators are less volatile than current coupon agency certificates.

Fitch Indicated Volatility: High

Securities rated V4 or V5 perform less predictably over a range of various interest rate scenarios. On balance, total return, price, and cash flow indicators are more volatile than current coupon agency certificates.

V4 The security exhibits greater changes in total return, price, and cash flow than current coupon agency certificates in all modeled interest rate scenarios. However, most indicators show less volatility than securities rated V5.

V5 The security exhibits substantial changes in total return, price, and cash flow in all modeled interest rate scenarios compared to current coupon agency certificates. Under the most stressful interest rate scenario tests, negative total returns may result.

Source: Fitch Investors Service, Inc., One State Street Plaza, New York, NY 10004.

MAJOR MONEY MARKET AND FIXED INCOME SECURITIES

Type	Interest: When Paid	Marketability	Denominations	Maturity
A. *Interest Fully Taxable* Corporate Bonds and Notes	S[1]	Very good to poor depending on quality	$1,000	1 to 50 years
Corporate Preferred Stock (Pays dividends as a fixed percentage of face value. Dividends not obligatory, but if declared must be paid before that of the common stock. Dividends fully taxable for individuals, but 85% exempt from federal tax for corporations)	Generally quarterly	Good to poor depending on quality	$100 or less	No maturity
Federal Home Loan Mortgage Corporate Bonds	S	Fair	$25,000	Up to 25 years
Federal Home Loan Mortgage Certificates	S	Fair	$100,000	Up to 3 years
Farmers' Home Administration Notes and Certificates	Annual	Fair	$25,000	1 to 25 years
Federal Housing Administration Debentures (Guaranteed by the U.S. Government)	S	Very good	$50	1 to 40 years
Federal National Mortgage Association Bonds	S	Fair	$25,000	2 to 25 years
Government National Mortgage Modified Pass through Certificates (interest plus some repayment of principal, guaranteed by U.S. Government)	Monthly	Good	$25,000	30 years; average life 12 years
Federal Home Loan Bank Bonds and Notes	S	Good	$10,000	1 to 20 years
Export-Import Bank Debentures and Certificates	S	Good	$5,000	3 to 7 years
International Bank for Reconstruction Development (World Bank), Inter-American Development Bank, Asia Development Bank	S	Fair to poor	$1,000	3 to 25 years
Foreign and Eurodollar Bonds and Notes	May be Annual or S	Poor	$1,000 (amounts vary in foreign currencies)	1 to 30 years
Bankers Acceptances (short-term debt obligations (resulting from international trade and guaranteed by a major bank)	Discounted[2] on a 360-day year basis	Fair	$5,000	1 to 270 days
Commercial Paper (short-term debt issued by a major corporation)	Discounted on a 360-day year basis	No secondary market	$100,000 (occasionally smaller)	1 to 270 days
Negotiable Certificates of Deposit (short-term debt issued by banks and which can be sold on the open market)	Interest paid on maturity; 360-day year basis	Fair	$100,000 (occasionally smaller)	30 days to 1 year
Non-negotiable Certificate of Deposit (savings certificates)	Interest paid on maturity; 360-day year basis	Non-negotiable	$500 $10,000	30 months 6 months
Collateralized Mortgage Obligations (CMO)	S or monthly	Good	$1,000	typically 2 to 20 years
Repurchase Agreements (generally short term loans by large investors, secured by U.S. Government or other high quality issues)[3]	Interest paid on maturity; 360-day year basis	No secondary market	$100,000	1 to 30 days (sometimes more)

(continued)

MAJOR MONEY MARKET AND FIXED INCOME SECURITIES *(concluded)*

Type	Interest: When Paid	Marketability	Denominations	Maturity
Zero Coupon Bonds (Bonds stripped of coupons)	Bonds issued at deep discount. Full yield realized at maturity	Good	$1,000 on maturity	1 to 30 years
B. *Interest Exempt from State and Local Income Taxes*				
U.S. Treasury Bonds and Notes	S	Very good	$1,000	1 to 20 years
U.S. Treasury Bills	Discounted on a 360-day basis	Very good	$10,000	90 days to 1 year
U.S. Series EE Savings Bonds[4]	Issued at discount, full interest, paid on maturity	No secondary market: available for resale	$50 minimum $10,000 maximum	10 years (can be redeemed before maturity at reduced yields
U.S. Series HH Savings[5] Bonds	S	No secondary market	$10,000 $15,000 maximum	10 years
Federal Land Bank Bonds	S	Good	$1,000	1 to 10 years
Federal Financing Bank Notes and Bonds	S	Good	$1,000	1 to 20 years
Tennessee Valley Authority Notes and Bonds	S	Fair	$1,000	5 to 25 years
Banks for Cooperatives Bonds	Interest: 360-day year basis	Good	$5,000	180 days
Federal Intermediate Credit Bank Bonds	Interest: 360-day year basis	Good	$5,000	270 days
Federal Home Loan Bank Notes and Bonds	Discounted: 360-day year basis	Good	$10,000	30 to 360-day year basis (some more)
Farm Credit Bank Notes and Bonds	Interest: 360-day year basis	Good	$50,000	270 days (some more)
C. *Interest Exempt from Federal Income Tax*				
State and Local Notes and Bonds (in-State issues, usually exempt from State and local income taxes)	S	Good to fair depending on rating	$5,000	1 to 50 years
Housing Authority Bonds (in-State issues usually exempt from State and local income taxes)	S	Good to fair	$5,000	1 to 40 years

[1] S means semiannually.

[2] A discount means interest paid in advance, thus a 10% discounted security maturing at $10,000 would cost $9,000 to purchase.

[3] Recently some banks have issued repurchase agreements for smaller amounts of money, i.e., several thousands of dollars.

[4] Since November 1982, U.S. Savings Bonds pay variable interest equal to 85% of the 5 year Treasury securities' rate adjusted semi-annually and have a minimum guaranteed rate which is adjustable. The rate applies to bonds held 5 years or more.

[5] Issued in exchange for EE bonds.

U.S. Treasury Bonds, Notes, and Bills: Terms Defined*

U.S. Treasury bonds, notes and bills are interest paying securities representing a debt on the part of the U.S. Government. Treasury bonds have a maturity of over 5 years, while notes mature within 5 to 7 years. Bills are discussed below. Both Treasury bonds and notes are generally issued in minimum denominations of $1,000 and pay interest semiannually. The amount of semiannual interest paid is determined by the coupon rate specified on the bond and is calculated on a 365-day year basis. For a $1,000 face value† bond the interest is given by:

$$\text{semiannual interest} = 1/2 \ (\$1,000 \times \text{coupon rate})$$

Bonds may be priced higher (at a premium) or lower (at a discount) than the face value (par) depending on current interest rates. The *current yield* is the rate the investor receives based on the prices actually paid for a bond. The price is given by:

$$\text{current yield} = \frac{\$1,000 \times \text{coupon rate}}{\text{purchase price}}$$

Thus, a $1,000 face value bond with an 8% coupon rate purchased at $850 has a current yield by:

$$\text{current yield} = \frac{\$1,000 \times 8\%}{\$850} = 9.41\%$$

The *yield to maturity* (YTM) is the yield obtained on taking into account the years remaining to maturity, annual interest payments, and the capital gain (or loss) realized at maturity. It is obtained from special tables.

However, the yield to maturity (YTM) may be found approximately from the formula

$$\text{YTM} = \frac{I + A}{B}$$

I = annual interest rate

$$A = \frac{\$1,000 - M}{N}$$

$$B = \frac{\$1,000 + M}{2}$$

where M = current market price of the bond

N = years remaining to maturity

As an example, a bond ($1,000 face value) has a 10% coupon and is currently priced at $1,100 with 10 years remaining to maturity. What is the approximate YTM?

$$I = \$1,000 \times .1 = \$100 \text{ interest per year}$$

$$A = \frac{\$1,000 - \$1,100}{10} = \$ -10$$

$$B = \frac{\$1,000 + \$1,100}{2} = \$1,050$$

$$\text{YTM} = \frac{\$100 - \$10}{\$1,050} = .0857 = 8.57\%$$

U.S. Treasury bills (T-bills) are U.S. Government debt obligations which mature within one year. They are offered by the Federal Reserve Bank with maturities of 90 days (3-month bills) and 182 days (six-month bills). Nine-month bills and one-year bills are also available. Treasury bills are sold in a minimum denomination of $10,000. Interest is paid by the discount method based on a 360-day year. With the discount method, interest is, in effect, paid at the time the bill is purchased. Thus a 91-day $10,000 bill (face value) with an 8% discount interest rate would provide the buyer with $202.22 ($10,000 × .08 × 91⁄360) interest at the time of purchase. This amount is deducted from the face value of the bill at the time of purchase so the buyer actually pays a net amount of $9,797.78 ($10,000 − $202.22). When the bill matures, the buyer receives $10,000 on redemption.

Since T-bills pay interest at the time of purchase (discount basis) on a 360-day year basis, while bonds (and notes) pay interest semiannually on a 365-day year basis, the two rates cannot be compared directly. To compare the two rates, the discount rate must be converted to the so-called *bond equivalent yield*, given by

$$\text{bond equivalent yield} = \frac{365 \times \text{discount rate}}{360 - (\text{discount rate} \times \text{days to maturity})}$$

As an example, a newly issued 91-day note with a discount rate of 12% has a

$$\text{bond equivalent yield} = \frac{365 \times (.12)}{360 - (.12 \times 91)} = 12.55\%$$

Interest from U.S. Treasury bonds, notes, and bills are subject to federal income tax,

---

*The terms *current yield*, *yield to maturity*, etc. defined in this section are generally applicable to all fixed incomes.

†Face value is the amount of the bond or note payable upon maturity.

but are exempt from state and local income taxes.

bond maturing in June of 1985 and bearing a 10⅜% coupon is indicated by *May '85 10⅜*.

How to Read U.S. Government Bond and Note Quotations

How to Read U.S. Treasury Bill Quotations

TREASURY BONDS AND NOTES

(1) Rate	Maturity (2) Mo/yr	(3) Bid	(4) Asked	(5) Chg	(6) Ask Yld
8½	Feb 92n	100:00	100:02−	1	0.00
7⅞	Mar 92n	100:11	100:13	...	3.25
8½	Mar 92n	100:13	100:15	...	3.18
11¾	Apr 92n	101:00	101:02−	1	3.46
8⅞	Apr 92n	100:27	100:29	...	3.51
6⅝	May 92n	100:18	100:20+	1	3.62

(1) Rate	(2) Days to Mat.	(3) Bid	(4) Asked	(5) Chg	(6) Ask Yld
Feb 27 '92	0	3.59	3.49+	0.09	0.00
Mar 05 '92	7	3.92	3.82+	0.09	3.89
Mar 12 '92	14	3.93	3.83+	0.04	3.90
Mar 19 '92	21	3.93	3.83+	0.06	3.90
Mar 26 '92	28	3.84	3.80+	0.04	3.87
Apr 02 '92	35	3.92	3.88+	0.06	3.96

The above exhibit is an example of U.S. Government bond and note quotations as it appears in *The Wall Street Journal*.

(1) Indicates the coupon rate of interest. Rates are quoted to ⅛ of a percent. Thus 8⅜ means 8.375%. The semiannual interest payments are calculated, as described elsewhere, using this rate.

(2) Indicates the year of maturity and the month in which the bond or note matures. The letter *n* means the security is a note. Otherwise a bond is implied.

(3) The *bid price* per bond or note (the price at which the bond can be sold to the dealer), expressed as a percentage of the face value ($1,000) of the bond. Prices are quoted in terms of 1/32 of a percent. Thus 98.5 means 98 5/32. To find the dollar value of the price, convert 98 5/32 to a decimal (98 5/32 = .98156) and multiply by the face value of the bond to give $981.56 (.98156 × $1,000).

(4) The *ask price* per bond or note (the price at which the dealer will sell the bond). The dollar value is found as indicated above.

(5) The change in the bid price from the closing price of the previous day.

(6) The yield if the bond is held to maturity, based on the ask price.

Some U.S. Treasury bonds can be called back for redemption prior to maturity. These are shown with two dates (under item 2 for example)—*1993–98* indicating that the bonds mature in 1998, but may be called back and redeemed any time after 1993.

Some newspapers (such as *The New York Times*) use a slight modification of the above arrangement, though the various terms have the same meaning as defined above. Thus, a

The above exhibit is an example of Treasury bill quotations as it appears in *The Wall Street Journal*.

(1) The date of maturity.

(2) Days to maturity.

(3) The bid price at market close quoted as a *discount* rate in percent. This bid price is the price at which the dealer will buy the bill. To convert the discount rate to a dollar price use the formula

$$\text{dollar price} = \$10,000 - (\text{discount rate} \times \text{days to maturity} \times .2778)$$

In the above, the discount must be expressed in percent. For example, if the dealer bids 3.82% discount for a bill which matures in 50 days, the dollar price is given by

$$\text{dollar price} = \$10,000 - [3.82 \times 50 \times .2778] = \$9,946.94$$

(4) The asked price at market close expressed as a discount rate in percent. The asked price is the price at which the dealer will sell a bill to a buyer. To convert to a dollar price use the above formula.

(5) The bond equivalent yield expressed in percent. This is calculated (as explained elsewhere) from the asked price expressed as a discount rate. This rate is used to compare T-bill yields to that of bonds, notes and certificates of deposit.

Some newspapers (e.g., *The New York Times*) use a somewhat different arrangement, though the meaning of the terms is the same as defined above. Thus, a bill maturing on June 4, 1981, is indicated as such. Also included in some newspapers is the change in bid price expressed as a discount rate.

How to Read Corporate Bond Quotations*

Corporate bonds are debt securities issued by private corporations. They generally have a face value (the amount due on maturity) of $1,000 and a specified interest rate (coupon rate) paid semiannually. Many corporate bonds have a *call* provision which permits the company to recall and redeem the bond after a specified date. Call privileges are usually exercised when interest rates fall sufficiently. Investors, therefore, cannot count on *locking in* high interest rates with corporate bonds. Bond quality designations used by Moody's and Standard & Poor's are given elsewhere in the Almanac (pp. 509–515).

The following is an example of price quotations for bonds traded on The New York Stock Exchange as they appear in *The Wall Street Journal*.

CORPORATION BONDS

VOLUME, $18,990,000

(1) Bonds		(2) Cur Yld	(3) Vol	(4) High	(5) Low	(6) Close	(7) Net Chg
AlaP	9s2000	14.	6	63	62	63	2
AlaP	8½s01	15.	10	57½	57½	57¼	...
AlaP	8⅞s03	15.	25	60	59½	60	+ ½
AlaP	10⅞05	15.	3	72	72	72	− 2¼

*Yield terms are the same as those defined in the section on U.S. Treasury Bonds, Notes and Bills, p. 519.

(1) Bonds		(2) Cur Yld	(3) Vol	(4) High	(5) Low	(6) Close	(7) Net Chg
AlaP	10½05	15.	12	70½	70½	70½	− 1
AlaP	12⅝10	16.	7	81¼	81⅛	81⅛	− 1⅝

(1) The name of the issue in abbreviated form, followed by the coupon rate of interest in percent (designated by the letter *s*), and the year in which the bond matures. The coupon rate is stated in terms of ⅛ of a percent; 9⅜ means 9.375%.

(2) This is the current yield which is calculated as stated elsewhere. (See U.S. Treasury Bonds, Notes, and Bills, p. 519.)

(3) This item is the number of bonds sold that day.

(4) This is the highest price quoted for the bond sold on that day, expressed as a percentage of face value ($1,000). To convert to dollars, express the price as a decimal and multiply by the face value of the bond. As an example:

$$58½ = (.5850 \times \$1,000.) = \$585$$

(5) This is the lowest price quoted that day. It is converted into dollars as described above.

(6) This is the price at the close of the market that day.

(7) This is the change in the closing price from that of the previous day. To convert to dollars, express as a decimal and multiply by $1,000. Thus, − 1⅞ means a decrease per bond of $18.75 (.01875 × $1,000) from that of the previous day.

TAX EXEMPT VERSUS TAXABLE YIELDS

tax bracket	To equal a tax-free yield of:											
	5½%	6%	6½%	7%	7½%	8%	8½%	9%	9½%	10%	10½%	11%
	a taxable investment has to earn:											
28%	7.64%	8.33%	9.03%	9.72%	10.42%	11.11%	11.81%	12.50%	13.19%	13.89%	14.58%	15.28%
30	7.86	8.57	9.29	10.00	10.71	11.43	12.14	12.86	13.57	14.29	15.00	15.71
31	7.97	8.70	9.42	10.14	10.87	11.59	12.32	13.04	13.77	14.49	15.22	15.94
32	8.09	8.82	9.56	10.29	11.03	11.76	12.50	13.24	13.97	14.71	15.44	16.18
34	8.33	9.09	9.85	10.61	11.36	12.12	12.88	13.64	14.39	15.15	15.91	16.67
36	8.59	9.38	10.16	10.94	11.72	12.50	13.28	14.06	14.84	15.63	16.41	17.19
37	8.73	9.52	10.32	11.11	11.90	12.70	13.49	14.29	15.08	15.87	16.67	17.47
39	9.02	9.84	10.66	11.48	12.30	13.11	13.93	14.75	15.57	16.39	17.21	18.03

Tax Exempt Bonds

Tax exempt (municipal) bonds are issued by state and local governments and are free from federal income tax on interest payments. The bonds are often issued in $5,000 denominations and pay interest semiannually. Capital gains are taxable. In addition, holders of out-of-state bonds may be subject to state and local income taxes of the state in which they reside. For example, a New York City resident holding Los Angeles municipal bonds would be subject to New York State and City income taxes on the interest.

The aproximate taxable equivalent yield of a tax exempt bond is obtained by means of the expression

$$\text{taxable equivalent yield} = \frac{\text{tax exempt yield}}{1 - (F + S + L)}$$

where

F is the federal tax bracket of the investor
S is the state tax bracket of the investor
L is the local tax bracket of the investor

Thus, an investor in the 50% federal bracket, 10% state bracket and 3% local bracket who holds a bond with a current yield of 6% which is exempt from all income taxes would enjoy a taxable equivalent yield (TEY) given by

$$\text{TEY} = \frac{6\%}{1 - (.5 + .1 + .03)} = 16.21\%$$

A taxable yield of 16.21% would be necessary to provide the same yield as the 6% current yield on the tax exempt security.

However, since state and local taxes are deductible in calculating the Federal tax, the exact expression is:

$$\text{taxable equivalent yield} = \frac{\text{tax exempt yield}}{[1 - (S + L)][1 - F]}$$

TYPES OF TAX EXEMPT BONDS AND NOTES

General Obligation bonds, also known as GO's, are backed by a pledge of a city's or state's full faith and credit for the prompt repayment of both principal and interest. Most city, county and school district bonds are secured by a pledge of unlimited property taxes. Since general obligation bonds depend on tax resources, they are normally analyzed in terms of the size of the resources being taxed.

Revenue bonds are payable from the earnings of a revenue-producing enterprise such as a sewer, water, gas or electric system,

airport, toll bridge, college dormitory, lease payments from property rented to industrial companies, and other income-producing facilities. Revenue bonds are analyzed in terms of their earnings.

Limited and Special Tax bonds are payable from the pledge of the proceeds derived by the issuer from a specific tax such as a property tax levied at a fixed rate, a special assessment, or a tax on gasoline.

Municipal notes are short term obligations maturing from 30 days to a year and are issued in anticipation of revenues coming from the sales of bonds (BANS), taxes (TANS), or other revenues (RANS).

Project notes, issued by local housing and urban renewal agencies, are backed by a U.S. Government guarantee and are also tax exempt.

How to Understand Tax Exempt Bond Quotations

Generally the prices of municipal bonds are quoted in terms of the yield to maturity (defined elsewhere) rather than in percentage of face value, as with other bonds. The yield to maturity can be converted to a dollar price if the years remaining to maturity and the rate of interest due are known. Certain tables used for this purpose are given in the *Basis Book* (published by the Financial Publishing Company, 82 Brookline Avenue, Boston, Massachusetts). The books list the dollar price (per $1,000 face value of the bond) corresponding to a given coupon rate, yield, and years to maturity.

Some municipal bonds, however, are quoted directly in terms of percentage of face value. Thus, a bid price (the price at which the dealer will buy the bonds from the investor) of 98⅝ for a $5,000 face value bond can be converted to a dollar price by first converting the bid to a decimal expression (.98625) and then multiplying by the face value of the bond. The result in this case is $4,931.25 (.98625 × $5,000). The same calculation applies to the ask price (the price at which the dealer will sell the bond to the investor).

Prices of tax exempt bonds are not quoted in the daily press. They can be obtained by calling municipal bond dealers. Extensive quotations are given in some relatively expensive publications:

The Blue List
Standard & Poor's
25 Broadway
New York, New York 10004
(212) 770-4600

The Daily Bond Buyer
and
The Weekly Bond Buyer
The Bond Buyer
1 State Street Plaza
New York, New York 10004
(212) 943-8200

Bond Week (Formerly Money Manager)
Institutional Investor
488 Madison Avenue
New York, New York 10022
(212) 303-3300

Government National Mortgage Association (GNMA) Modified Pass Through Certificates

A GNMA Mortgage-Backed Security is a government-guaranteed security which is collateralized by a pool of federally-underwritten residential mortgages. The investor receives a monthly check for a proportionate share of the principal and interest on a pool of mortgages whether or not the payments have actually been collected from the borrowers.

The GNMA Mortgage-Backed Security offers the highest yield of any federally-guaranteed security. In addition, the GNMA security offers a very competitive return in comparison to private corporation debt issues. Moreover, the investor receives a

monthly return on the GNMA guaranteed investment, rather than semi-annual payments as on most bonds. This monthly payment represents a cash flow available for reinvestment and has the effect of increasing the yield on GNMAs by 10 to 18 basis points (a basis point is 0.1%) when compared to the yield equivalent received on a bond investment with the same "coupon" rate but paying interest semi-annually.

On single-family securities (a popular form) the maturity is typically 30 years. However, statistical studies have determined that the average life of a single-family security is approximately 12 years, due to prepayments of principal. Nevertheless, some of the mortgages in any pool are likely to remain outstanding for the full 30-year period.

The minimum size of original individual certificates is $25,000 with increments of $5,000 above that amount.

Due to the uncertainties in the maturity of the above mentioned pass-through certificates, collateralized mortgage obligations (CMOs) have been introduced. CMOs are bonds backed by Ginnie Maes, Freddie Macs, and other mortgage instruments providing investors with a wide choice of maturities ranging from 2 to 20 years. Essentially, the monthly payments from the underlying mortgage instruments are initially allocated to the nearest maturity CMO and subsequently to CMO maturities of successively longer duration. CMO interest payments are made semiannually or monthly.

Components—Dow Jones 20 Bond Average

The Dow Jones Bond Averages are a simple arithmetic average compiled daily by using the New York Exchange closing bond prices. A list of the bonds on which these averages are based follows:

10 Public Utilities

Name	Coupon	Maturity
BellSouth Telcm	6⅜%	2004
Comwlth Ed	7⅝%	2003
Consol Nat Gas	7¼%	2015
Michigan Bell	7%	2012
New York Tel	7⅜%	2011
Pacific Bell	7⅛%	2026
Phil Electric	7⅜%	2001
Potmc Elec Pwr	7%	2018
So. Bell Tel	7⅜%	2010
Tucson Elec	7⅝%	2003

10 Industrials

Name	Coupon	Maturity
AT&T	7⅛%	2002
Beth Steel	6⅞%	1999
Champion Intl	6½%	2011
Chrysler Finl	6½%	1998
DuPont	6%	2001
General Signal	5¾%	2002
IBM	6⅜%	2000
Mead Corp.	6¾%	2012
Occid Petrol	10⅛%	2009
Sears Roebuck	9½%	1999

Source: Reprinted by permission of Barron's *Business and Financial Weekly*, © 1995 Dow Jones & Company, Inc. All Rights Reserved Worldwide.

Components—Barron's Confidence Index

Barron's Confidence Index is the ratio of the average yield to maturity on best grade corporate bonds to the intermediate grade corporate bonds average yield to maturity. A list of the bonds on which the confidence index is based follows:

Best Grade Bonds

Name	Coupon	Maturity
AMBAC Inc	9⅜%	2011
Amoco Co	8⅝%	2016
Campbell Soup	8¾%	2021
Ches & Potom T	7⅞%	2022
Genl RE Cp	9%	2009
IBM	8⅜%	2019
McDonalds	8⅞%	2011
Proc & Gamb	8½%	2009
United Parcel	8⅜%	2020
Wisc El Svc	8⅜%	2026

Intermediate Grade Bonds

Name	Coupon	Maturity
Arco Chem	9.80%	2020
Ariz Pub Svc	8¾%	2024
CSX Corp	8⅝%	2022
Dayton Hud	8⅞%	2022
Delta Airl	9¼%	2022
Eastman K	9.20%	2021
GTE Corp	8¾%	2021
NCNB	9⅜%	2009
Philips Pet	9⅜%	2011
Ralston Purina	9¼%	2009

Source: Reprinted by permission of Barron's *Business and Financial Weekly*, © 1995 Dow Jones & Company, Inc. All Rights Reserved Worldwide.

Monetary Aggregates Defined

Money supply data has been revised and expanded to reflect the Federal Reserve's redefinition of the monetary aggregates. The redefinition was prompted by the emergence in recent years of new monetary assets—for example, negotiable order of withdrawal (NOW) accounts and money-market mutual fund shares—and alterations in the basic character of established monetary assets—for example, the growing similarity of and substitution between the deposits of thrift institutions and those of commercial banks.

M1-A has been discontinued with M1-B now designated as "M-1." M-1 is currency in circulation plus all checking accounts including those which pay interest, such as NOW accounts. M-1 excludes deposits due to foreign commercial banks and official institutions.

M-2 as redefined adds to M1-B overnight repurchase agreements (RPs) issued by commercial banks and certain overnight Eurodollars (those issued by Caribbean branches of member banks) held by U.S. nonbank residents, money-market mutual fund shares, and savings and small-denomination time deposits (those issued in denominations of less than $100,000) at all depository institutions. Depository institutions are commercial banks (including U.S. agencies and branches of foreign banks, Edge Act Corporations, and foreign investment companies), mutual savings banks, savings and loan associations, and credit unions.

M-3 as redefined is equal to new M-2 plus large-denomination time deposits (those issued as in denominations of $100,000 or more) at all depository institutions (including negotiable CDs) plus term

RPs issued by commercial banks and savings and loan associations.

L, the very broad measure of liquid assets, equals new M-3 plus other liquid assets consisting of other Eurodollar holdings of U.S. nonbank residents, bankers acceptances, commercial paper, savings bonds, and marketable liquid Treasury obligations.

Federal Reserve Banks

Board of Governors of the Federal Reserve System, Washington, D.C. 20551

Federal Reserve Bank	Telephone Number	District	Address
BOSTON*	617-973-3000	1	600 Atlantic Avenue, Boston, Massachusetts 02106
NEW YORK*	212-720-5000	2	33 Liberty Street (Federal Reserve P.O. Station), New York, New York 10045
Buffalo Branch	716-849-5000		160 Delaware Avenue, Buffalo, New York 14202 (P.O. Box 961, Buffalo, New York 14240-0961)
PHILADELPHIA	215-574-6000	3	Ten Independence Mall, Philadelphia, Pennsylvania 19106 (P.O. Box 66, Philadelphia, Pennsylvania 19105)
CLEVELAND*	216-579-2000	4	1455 East Sixth Street, Cleveland, Ohio 44114 (P.O. Box 6387, Cleveland, Ohio 44101)
Cincinnati Branch	513-721-4787		150 East Fourth Street, Cincinnati, Ohio 45202-0999 (P.O. Box 999, Cincinnati, Ohio 45201-0999)
Pittsburgh Branch	412-261-7800		717 Grant Street, Pittsburgh, Pennsylvania 15219 (P.O. Box 867, Pittsburgh, Pennsylvania 15230)
RICHMOND*	804-697-8000	5	701 East Byrd Street, Richmond, Virginia 23219 (P.O. Box 27622, Richmond, Virginia 23261)
Baltimore Branch	301-576-3300		502 South Sharp Street, Baltimore, Maryland 21201 (P.O. Box 1378, Baltimore, Maryland 21203)
Charlotte Branch	704-358-2100		530 Trade Street, Charlotte, North Carolina 28202 (P.O. Box 30248, Charlotte, North Carolina 28230)
Culpeper Communications and Records Center	703-829-1600		Mount Pony Rd., State Rte. 658 (P.O. Drawer 20, Culpeper, Virginia 22701)
ATLANTA	404-521-8500	6	104 Marietta Street, N.W., Atlanta, Georgia 30303-2713
Birmingham Branch	205-731-8500		1801 Fifth Avenue, North, Birmingham, Alabama 35283 (P.O. Box 830447, Birmingham, Alabama 35283-0447)
Jacksonville Branch	904-632-1000		800 Water Street, Jacksonville, Florida 32204 (P.O. Box 929, Jacksonville, Florida 32231-0044)
Miami Branch	305-591-2065		9100 Northwest 36th Street, Miami, Florida 33178 (P.O. Box 520847, Miami, Florida 33152-0847)
Nashville Branch	615-251-7100		301 Eighth Avenue, North, Nashville, Tennessee 37203 (P.O. Box 4407, Nashville, Tennessee 37203-4407)
New Orleans Branch	504-593-3200		525 St. Charles Avenue, New Orleans, Louisiana 70130 (P.O. Box 61630, New Orleans, Louisiana 70161-1630)
CHICAGO*	312-322-5322	7	230 South LaSalle Street, Chicago, Illinois 60604 (P.O. Box 834, Chicago, Illinois 60690-0834)
Detroit Branch	313-961-6880		160 W. Fort Street, Detroit, Michigan 48226 (P.O. Box 1059, Detroit, Michigan 48231)
ST. LOUIS	314-444-8444	8	411 Locust Street, St. Louis, Missouri 63102 (P.O. Box 442, St. Louis, Missouri 63166)
Little Rock Branch	501-324-8300		325 West Capitol Avenue, Little Rock, Arkansas 72201 (P.O. Box 1261, Little Rock, Arkansas 72203)
Louisville Branch	502-568-9200		410 South Fifth Street, Louisville, Kentucky 40202 (P.O. Box 32710, Louisville, Kentucky 40232)
Memphis Branch	901-523-7171		200 North Main Street, Memphis, Tennessee 38103 (P.O. Box 407, Memphis, Tennessee 38101)
MINNEAPOLIS	612-340-2345	9	250 Marquette Avenue, Minneapolis, Minnesota 55480
Helena Branch	406-447-3800		100 Neill Avenue, Helena, Montana 59601

Federal Reserve Bank	Telephone Number	District	Address
KANSAS CITY	816-881-2000	10	925 Grand Avenue, Kansas City, Missouri 64198
Denver Branch	303-572-2300		1020 16th Street, Denver, Colorado 80202 (Terminal Annex-P.O. Box 5228, Denver, Colorado 80217)
Oklahoma City Branch	405-270-8400		226 Dean A. McGee Avenue (P.O. Box 25129) Oklahoma City, Oklahoma 73125
Omaha Branch	402-221-5500		2201 Farnam Street, Omaha, Nebraska 68102 (P.O. Box 3958, Omaha, Nebraska 68103)
DALLAS	214-651-6111	11	400 South Akard Street (Station K), Dallas, Texas 75222
El Paso Branch	915-544-4730		301 East Main Street, El Paso, Texas 79901 (P.O. Box 100, El Paso, Texas 79999)
Houston Branch	713-659-4433		1701 San Jacinto Street, Houston, Texas 77002 (P.O. Box 2578, Houston, Texas 77252)
San Antonio Branch	512-224-2141		126 East Nueva Street, San Antonio, Texas 78204 (P.O. Box 1471, San Antonio, Texas 78295)
SAN FRANCISCO	415-974-2000	12	101 Market Street, San Francisco, California 94105 (P.O. Box 7702, San Francisco, California 94120)
Los Angeles Branch	213-683-2300		950 South Grand Avenue, Los Angeles, California 90015 (Terminal Annex-P.O. Box 2077, Los Angeles, California 90051)
Portland Branch	503-221-5900		915 S.W. Stark Street, Portland, Oregon 97025 (P.O. Box 3436, Portland, Oregon 97208)
Salt Lake City Branch	801-322-7900		120 South State Street, Salt Lake City, Utah 84111 (P.O. Box 30780, Salt Lake City, Utah 84125)
Seattle Branch	206-343-3600		1015 Second Avenue, Seattle, Washington 98104 (P.O. Box 3567, Seattle, Washington 98124)

*Additional offices of these Banks are located at Lewiston, Maine 04240; Windsor Locks, Connecticut 06096; Cranford, New Jersey 07016; Jericho, New York 11753; Utica Oriskany, New York 13424; Columbus, Ohio 43216; Columbia, South Carolina 29210; Charleston, West Virginia 25328; Des Moines, Iowa 50306; Indianapolis, Indiana 46206; and Milwaukee, Wisconsin 53201.

Source: Board of Governors of the Federal Reserve System, Washington, D.C. 20551.

Options and Futures

What Are Stock Options?

There are two types of stock options—call and put. A call option is the right to buy a specified number of shares of a stock at a given price before a specific date. A put option is the right to sell a specific number of shares of a stock at a given price before a specific date. Options, unlike a futures contract, are a right *not an obligation* to buy or sell stock. The price at which the stock may be bought or sold is referred to as the exercise (or striking) price. The date at which the option expires is the *expiration* date. The term "in-the-money" option refers to either a call option with an exercise price less than that of the market price of the stock, or a put option with an exercise price above the market price of the stock.

Expiration months are set at intervals of three months for the cycles: the January–April–July–October cycle, February–May–August–November cycle, and the March–June–September–December cycle. Options expire at 11:59 P.M. Eastern Standard Time on the Saturday immediately following the third Friday of the expiration month.

The exercise prices are set at 5 point (dollar) intervals for stocks trading below $50, 10 point intervals for stocks trading between $50 to $200, and 20 point intervals for securities trading above $200. Initial exercise prices are set above and below the price of the security. Thus, if a security is priced at 32½ on the New York Stock Exchange at the time new options are opened, the opening exercise prices would be set at 30 and 40. If the price of the security is close to a standard exercise price, three prices are set: at the standard price, as well as above and below the latter.

Standard option contracts are written for 100 shares of stock of the underlying security. The price at which the seller (writer) agrees to sell an option to the buyer is called the *premium*. The premium is quoted *per share* of the underlying stock so that the price per contract is 100 times the quote.

After the option is issued, the premium will fluctuate with the price of the stocks. With call options the premium will increase with an increase in the price of stock. With put options the premium will increase when the stock price declines. The reason should be clear from the following examples. Assume

that in January a July call option is written at the exercise price of 50 ($50 per share) on the XYZ Corporation stock. We assume that the stock is selling at $51. The call option writer (seller) asks and receives a premium of $2 ($200 per option contract). After brokerage commission on the sale (say $25 per contract) the option writer nets a profit of $175 per contract. The call option buyer pays $200 for the contract plus the commission or $225. Assume that the stock increases to 60 per share. The option holder (buyer) can, in principle, purchase the stock at 50 (the Exercise price) and sell it at 60 netting a profit on transaction of $10 per share (neglecting commissions). Clearly the call option has acquired increased value which will be reflected in the premium (option price). Let us assume that the premium increases from 2 to 10 ($200 to $1,000 per contract). If the option holder now sells the option, he will make a profit (after commissions) of $750 on a $250 investment ($200 premium and $50 commissions).

Alternatively, the option holder may elect to exercise the option and acquire the shares at 50 (the exercise price). The option writer must then deliver 100 shares of XYZ Corporation at $50 per share.

If the stock price drops below the exercise price and remains so until expiration of the option, the call option buyer can lose his entire investment. Sometimes the loss may be reduced if the option is sold before it matures. The holder then is said to have *closed out* his position.

Similar arguments apply to put options. In this case the option holder benefits if the price of the stock decreases below the exercise price. Assume that the above stock drops to 40. The put holder could, in principle, buy the stock at 40 and sell it at 50 (the exercise price) to the put writer. The put holder would make a profit of $10 per share (neglecting commissions). The put premium would reflect this situation and, as a result, increase.

Instead of selling the option and taking a profit, the put holder may elect to exercise the option and sell 100 shares to the put writer who must purchase these shares at the 50 exercise price.

If the market price of the stock is greater than the exercise price when the put option expires, the holder will lose his investment.

Options are traded on the Chicago Board of Options Exchange, the American Stock Exchange, the Pacific Stock Exchange and the Philadelphia Stock Exchange.

How to Read Option Quotations

The following explains option quotations as they appear in *The Wall Street Journal*.

(1)	(2)	(3)	(4)	(5)	(6)	(7)
			—Call—		—Put—	
Option/Strike		Exp.	Vol.	Last	Vol.	Last
Micron	50	Mar	20	12⅝	106	⁵⁄₁₆
62⅝	50	Apr	109	13⅛	110	¾
62⅝	55	Feb	140	7⅞	. . .	. . .
62⅝	55	Mar	137	8⅞	37	⅞
62⅝	55	Apr	148	9¾	1001	1¹⁄₁₆
62⅝	60	Feb	337	2¾	162	¼

Source: Reprinted by permission of *The Wall Street Journal* © Dow Jones and Company, Inc., 1994. ALL RIGHTS RESERVED.

(1) Lists the stock to which the option contract corresponds. The price listed underneath is the closing price of the stock.
(2) Lists the strike price i.e. the price at which the owner of the option can buy or sell the corresponding stock.
(3) Gives the month at which the option expires. All options expire on the third Friday of the expiration month.
(4) Gives the number of option contracts (in this case a call) traded.
(5) Gives the price (premium) per call option at the close of the trading day. Since an option contract is for 100 shares of stock, a contract will trade at 100 times the premium.
(6) Same as 4 above but applies to puts.
(7) Same as 5 above but applies to puts.

Stock Market Futures*

Standard & Poor's 500 Stock Index futures[†] combine the unique aspects of the futures market with the opportunities of stock ownership and stock options by helping many investors manage their inherent stock market risks, and at the same time allowing others to participate in broad market moves. S&P 500 Index futures can play

---

*Although every attempt has been made to insure the accuracy of the information in this section, the Chicago Mercantile Exchange assumes no responsibility for any errors or omissions. All matters pertaining to rules and specifications herein are made subject to and are superseded by official Exchange rules.

[†] Editor's Note: Futures based on the Value Line (Kansas City Exchange) and the New York Stock Exchange (New York Futures Exchange) indices are also traded. The principles are the same as with the S&P 500 futures.

Source: *Opportunities in Stock Futures*, Index and Option Market, Chicago Mercantile Exchange, 444 West Jackson Street, Chicago, IL 60606.

an important role in an individual's or institution's overall market strategy.

Stock ownership is subject to several risks. Lower earnings reports or changes in industry fundamentals can cause severe declines in individual issues. Or, a promising industry or company might drop because the entire market is heading down. A myriad of decisions go into individual stock selection—but the first question is usually what is the state and direction of the entire market.

The introduction of the Standard & Poor's 500 Stock Index contract allows investors to hedge, and therefore, virtually eliminate their portfolio exposure in a declining market without disturbing their holdings. At the same time, others can purchase or sell the contract according to their expectations of future market activity. This simultaneous ability to hedge the risks of stock ownership and to take advantage of broad market moves creates opportunities for everyone with positions in or opinions about the stock market.

A NEW MARKET FOR TODAY'S INVESTOR

S&P 500 Index futures are traded on the Index and Option Market division of the Chicago Mercantile Exchange. One of the largest commodity exchanges in the world, the CME introduced financial futures trading in 1972 when it formed the International Monetary Market to trade contracts in foreign currencies. Later, the IMM added futures contracts in Gold, 90-Day Treasury Bills, Three-Month Domestic Certificates of Deposit, and Three-Month Eurodollar Time Deposits.

THE S&P 500 INDEX

The Standard & Poor's Stock Price Index has been the standard by which professional portfolio managers and individuals have measured their performance for 65 years. Begun in 1917 as an index based on 200 stocks, the list was expanded to 500 issues in 1957.

Currently, the Index is one of the U.S. Commerce Department's 12 leading economic indicators.

The S&P 500 Index is made up of 400 industrial, 40 public utilities, 20 transportation, and 40 financial companies and represents approximately 80% of the value of all issues traded on the New York Stock Exchange.

The S&P 500 Index is calculated by giving more "weight" to companies with more stock issued and outstanding in the market. Basically, each stock's price is multiplied by its number of shares outstanding. This assures that each stock influences the Index with the same importance that it carries in the actual stock market.

The Index is calculated by multiplying the shares outstanding of each of the 500 stocks by its market price. These amounts are then totaled and compared to a 1941–43 base period.

Calculations are performed continually while the market is open for each of the 500 stocks in the Index. The resulting Index is available minute-by-minute via quote machines throughout the world.

WHAT IS FUTURES TRADING?

The practice of buying or selling goods at prices agreed upon today, but with actual delivery made in the future, dates back to the 12th century. In the United States, organized futures exchanges were active as early as the 1840s. Today, the markets offer futures in grains, meats, lumber, metals, poultry products, currencies and interest-bearing securities.

The ability to contract today at a fixed price for future delivery performs two vital economic functions: risk transfer and price discovery.

For example, suppose a producer of cattle sees that someone is willing to buy his animals for delivery six months hence at a price that insures him an adequate profit. He decides to sell his production, with delivery after the animal matures, at the contracted price. In the process, he has locked in a price that is satisfactory to him and has insulated himself against the risk that the price may fall. In other words, he has transferred the risk of lower prices to someone else. Conversely, the purchaser of his animals has locked in his price and is assured that he will not have to pay a higher price in the future. This transaction could take place directly between the two men, or could be accomplished through futures trading at the CME—without the need for buyer and seller to actually meet. The open public trading system at the CME makes it easy to discover what the market currently considers to be a fair price for future delivery.

If the sale takes place on the Chicago Mercantile Exchange, the Exchange guarantees that both parties adhere to their agreement by placing itself and its resources between them. The Exchange thus becomes the buyer and the seller of the contract. This assures both parties that the contract will be carried out because the Exchange stands behind both parts of the agreement.

When delivery day arrives, the product is delivered to designated delivery points and inspected to make sure it is of the quality stipulated by the contract. The seller receives payment at the agreed price and buyer receives the produce.

Since full payment does not occur until the delivery day, the performance of both parties to the contract requires a good faith deposit or performance bond—known as the margin—when the contract is entered. Margins usually amount to a small percentage of the contract's total face value.

This payment differs from margin for stock purchases in that it is not a partial payment. It serves as a guarantee for both buyer and seller that there are sufficient funds on either side to cover adverse price movements that might otherwise bring the ability to meet contract terms into question.

At the close of business each day, each futures position is revalued at the contract's current closing price. This price is compared to the previous day's close (or if an initial position, the purchase or sale price) and the net gain or loss is calculated. Gains and losses are taken or made from the margin account each day in cash. There are no paper gains or losses in futures trading. If a margin account falls below a specified level, futures traders are required to deposit more money to maintain their positions.

All futures market participants should understand the operation of futures markets and consult with a Registered Commodity Representative before opening a futures trading account.

The S&P 500 Index futures contract is quoted in terms of the actual Index, but carries a face value of 500 times the Index. The contract does not move point-for-point with the actual Index, but it stays close enough to act as an effective proxy for the Index, and by extension, for the stock market as a whole.

If, for example, the futures price is quoted at 108.75, then the face value of the contract would be $54,375 (500 × 108.75). Minimum futures price increments, or movements, are .05 of the Index or $25. So if the futures quote is at 108.75, trades can continue to take place at that level, or move to 108.80 or to 108.70, with each .05 move equal to $25.

Trading opens at 9:00 A.M. and closes at 3:15 P.M. (Chicago time) with contracts trading for settlement in March, June, September and December. The final settlement day is the third Thursday of the contract month. At the close of business on that day all open positions have one final mark-to-market calculation—only on this day the expiration of the contract is marked to the actual closing level of the S&P 500 Index itself. Unlike traditional commodities, there is no physical delivery of the underlying commodity or resulting payment for the commodity in S&P 500 futures.

It is this unique cash settlement feature of the S&P 500 futures contract that eliminates the prohibitively expensive costs of delivering 500 individual issues in varying amounts. Since there are little or no delivery costs, investors are assured that there will be no institutional factors to influence the futures contract's price. Thus, the price of the futures contract will reflect the current expectations about the direction of future stock prices. The International Monetary Market division of the CME pioneered this innovative concept in 1981, when its Eurodollar Time Deposit contract became the first cash settlement futures contract ever traded.

The S&P 500 futures contract should be viewed as a complement to equity ownership, not a substitute for it. Among the many benefits of S&P futures is the hedging ability that holders of stock can employ to provide an effective, cost efficient means of protecting security holdings against temporary market declines rather than selling and disturbing stock holdings. In addition, investors find the futures market equally as liquid for both buyers and sellers. Unlike the

stock exchanges, short sellers do not require an up-tic before a trade can take place and there are no additional margin requirements.

SITUATIONS & STRATEGIES

Outright positions, either long or short, spreading and hedging are all uses for S&P futures. The contract also offers an unusually large number of hedging strategies when combined with equity portfolios and options. The following examples will show some of these uses in more detail.

LONG POSITION

Situation: An individual sees that interest rates are declining, the economy is firming and believes the entire market is undervalued. He notes that the S&P 500 futures contract for September delivery is at 108.85 and the actual S&P 500 Index is at 108.70.

It is apparent that most futures market participants also believe a move up is imminent. As supply and demand factors are bal-

Day	Position	Cost	S&P Future Closing Price	Gain or (Loss) Points × $5 (.01 equals 1 point)		Account Balance	Cumulative Gain or (Loss)
1	Long one contract	108.85	108.90	.05	$ 25	$5,025	$ 25
2	same	108.85	108.60	(.30)	(150)	4,875	(125)
3	same	108.85	108.40	(.20)	(100)	4,775	(225)
4	same	108.85	107.00	(1.40)	(700)	4,075	(925)
5	same	108.85	108.00	1.00	500	4,575	(425)
6	same	108.85	108.70	.70	350	4,925	(75)
7	same	108.85	109.50	.80	400	5,325	325
Sub Total Period one		108.85	109.50	65	$325	$5,325	$325

Period one: Our investor was a little off on his timing and his margin account was debited each day that losses occurred. If his margin balance had fallen to the maintenance minimum ($2,000 per contract) in this example he would have been required to make an additional payment to bring his balance back to the initial margin level ($5,000). As it is, he ended the period with a credit of $325 in cash.

Period two: With minor backing and filling, the trend is up and the S&P futures price closes period two at a level of 115.65.

	Position	Cost	S&P Future Closing Price	Gain or (Loss) Points × $5 (.01 equals 1 point)		Account Balance	Cumulative Gain or (Loss)
Sub Total Period Two	Long one contract	108.85	115.65	6.80	$3,400	$8,400	$3,400

Observations: During the first two weeks our investor's judgment of the market was correct and the S&P futures price advanced 680 index points or 6.25%. This translated into a gain of $3,400 on his initial investment of $5,000 or a gain of 68%.

At this point our investor believes that the market is due for a correction and decides to lock in his profit. He calls his RCR and instructs him to "cover" his September long position. His broker will then enter a sell order. After the close of business, the Exchange Clearing House will match the investor's previous long position and his new short position for a net zero position. All margins will be returned with cash credited to the investor's account with his broker the next day. Brokerage commissions have not been included in this example, but they are usually extremely reasonable and generally are quoted to include *both* the purchase and sale of the contract.

anced in an open marketplace, the intrinsic value of the September contract is established. The market is willing to pay a slight premium (.15) for the futures contract over the actual Index.

He calls his Registered Commodity Representative, enters an order to buy one September S&P 500 futures contract at the market and makes a good faith deposit to his account to guarantee his ability to meet his contractual commitment. For purposes of the following example, a margin account balance of $5,000 will be used. Margin requirements for actual positions vary. Individuals should contact their Registered Commodity Representatives for current information.

SHORT POSITION

If, instead of a rising market our investor believed that tight money would increase interest rates and the economy was weakening, he might have concluded that the S&P 500 Index futures price of 108.85 was an overvaluation and that the price was vulnerable to a decline.

one September S&P Index contract to cover his short at the opening.

The opening is down on news that industrial production was weak and his position is covered at 106.55. His gain on his short then amounts to 2.30 at $25 per .05 or $1,150. The money is credited to his account the following day.

REDUCING THE VOLATILITY OF A STOCK PORTFOLIO

One reason for equity ownership is to take advantage of the long-term growth prospects of the company in which stock is purchased. Over time, higher earnings per share might be translated into a higher dividend payout. In the case of a company with a high return on investment and profits that are reinvested in the company's own growth, the expectation is that the growth will be reflected in higher share prices. However carefully constructed and diversified a portfolio may be, it is still subject in varying degrees to the risk that the market will decline. In order to protect principal values in a de-

Day	Position	Cost	S&P Future Closing Price	Gain or (Loss) Points × $5 (.01 equals 1 point)	Account Balance	Cumulative Gain or (Loss)
1	Short one contract	108.85	110.05	(1.20)	$ 600	$4,400	($ 600)
2	same	108.85	112.50	(2.45)	(1,225)	3,175	(1,825)
3	same	108.85	112.00	(.50)	(250)	3,425	(1,575)
4	same	108.85	109.50	(2.50)	(1,250)	4,675	(325)
5	same	108.85	108.75	.75	375	5,050	50
6	same	108.85	107.40	1.35	675	5,725	725
7	same	108.85	107.05	.35	175	5,900	900
Sub Total		108.85	107.05	1.80	$ 900	$5,900	$ 900

In our hypothetical example, the short position eventually worked. If the price had gone to a closing level of 114.85, the investor's account balance would have dropped to the maintenance margin level of $2,000 and he would have been required to add additional funds to bring his balance back to $5,000.

He decides to call his Registered Commodity Representative and enter a sell order for one September S&P 500 Stock Index future. Selling is just as easy as buying in an open outcry market. All bids to buy and offers to sell must be made publicly in the trading arena and are subject to immediate acceptance by any member. This differs greatly from stock exchanges where specialists or market makers require an up-tic from the previous sale to transact a short sale.

Let's again assume the initial margin required is $5,000. The above table shows the status of the short position over the course of seven trading days.

Our investor decides at this point that he wants to cover his short position and lock in his profit. The next morning before the opening of trading, he enters an order to buy

clining market, investors have traditionally sold stock to raise cash or shifted to more defensive issues with less volatility. These tactics very often are short-run solutions that disturb carefully tailored long-run objectives. S&P 500 Index futures can be used to add protection against a market downturn and allow an investor to maintain his equity holdings based on the prospects of the companies rather than the direction of the market.

SHORT HEDGE AGAINST A DIVERSIFIED PORTFOLIO

Situation: An investor owns a well-diversified portfolio with a current market value of $110,000. The S&P 500 futures contract is at 108.85. The market appears weak and the investor believes that there is substantial downside risk during the next three months. He decides to short S&P 500 futures to protect his portfolio.

Action: The S&P 500 futures contract at 108.85 represents a contract value of $54,425 ($500 × 108.85$). In order to protect his portfolio, he sells two contracts ($110,000 divided by $54,425 equals 2.02).

This hypothetical example assumed that the volatility of the portfolio very closely matched that of the market as measured by the S&P 500 futures contract prices. In reality, portfolios may be more or less sensitive to market moves. Statistical regression analysis for individual issues and entire portfolios can be calculated to measure past price volatility relative to the market. Expressed as "beta," it is a statistical measure of past movements which may change in the future. However, it is useful when hedging market risk in portfolios that are more volatile than the market.

tracts to offset the portfolio's greater volatility to the market.

The concept of volatility and hedge ratios also may be applied to industry groupings and individual stocks. However, as the number of individual stock holdings that are being hedged decreases, then the greater is the chance that factors affecting that smaller group will make their prices react differently relative to the market than they have in the past.

ADDITIONAL USES OF THE S&P 500 FUTURES CONTRACT

Spreads: The simultaneous purchase and sale of different contract months to take advantage of perceived price discrepancies is called "spreading." The technique is considered by many to be less volatile than an outright long or short position, and as

Day	Position Short 2 Contracts	Closing Price S&P Contract	Gain or (Loss) Contract Points × $5 × 2 Contracts (.01 equals 1 point)		Value of Stock Portfolio	Portfolio Gain or (Loss)
1	108.85	110.05	(1.20)	($1,200)	$111,213	$1,213
18	108.85	109.50	(.65)	(650)	110,657	657
36	108.85	107.40	1.45	1,450	108,535	(1,465)
54	108.85	106.05	2.80	2,800	107,171	(2,829)
72	108.85	103.10	5.75	5,750	104,190	(5,810)
90	108.85	100.65	8.20	8,200	101,714	(8,286)
Position Closed	108.85	100.65	8.20	$8,200	$101,714	($8,286)

Observations: The market dropped and our investor hedged the cash decline in his portfolio with an offsetting gain in his futures position. Of course, if he were wrong about the direction of the market and it went up, he would have had losses in his futures positions but his stocks may have participated in the advance. The investor throughout this period did not have to disturb his holdings and continued to receive his dividend payments.

Let us assume that the S&P 500 has a beta of 1.00 (that is, a given percentage move in the market gives rise to the same percentage move in the S&P 500) and our hypothetical portfolio has a beta of 1.50. Our portfolio's past market action relative to moves in the market was 50% greater than a given move in the general market. To compensate for this greater volatility, our hedger would require more S&P contracts to offset a greater decline in the value of his portfolio. Known as a hedge ratio, the dollar value of the portfolio is divided by the dollar value of the S&P 500 futures contract, the resulting figure is multiplied by the beta of the portfolio. Using our investor's portfolio and having calculated a beta of 1.5, we arrive at three contracts instead of two when the beta was 1.00:

$$\frac{\$110,000}{54,425} \times 1.5 = 3.03 \text{ contracts}$$

Thus, our investor would have sold three con-

such, spreads generally carry lower margin requirements.

A characteristic of the futures market is that the closest contract date behaves more like the cash market. (In the S&P 500 futures contract, the cash market is the actual S&P 500 Index.) More distant months or back months have a greater component of their price determined by the expectations of what the price will be in the future.

These changing expectations of price levels of the S&P 500 contract into the future creates spreading opportunities. Options strategists will use the S&P 500 futures contract to reduce market risk when writing uncovered puts and calls. Block traders, investment bankers, stock specialists, options principals and anyone with the risk of stock market volatility, now have a vehicle and a well-capitalized liquid market to buy and sell market risk—the Standard & Poor's 500 Stock Index futures contract.

CONTRACT TERMS SUMMARY

Size	500 times the value of the S&P 500 Index
Delivery	Mark-to-market at closing value of the actual S&P 500 Index on Settlement Date
Hours	9:00 AM to 3:15 PM Central Time
Months Traded	March, June, September, December
Clearing House Symbol	SP
Ticker Symbol	SP
Prices	Contract quoted in terms of S&P 500 Index
Minimum Fluctuation in Price	05 ($25)
Limit Move	3.00 ($1,500)
Last Day of Trading	3rd Thursday of Contract Month
Settlement Date	Last Day of Trading

Understanding the Commodities Market

COMMODITY EXCHANGES

A Commodity Exchange is an organized market of buyers and sellers of various types of commodities. It is public to the extent that anyone can trade through member firms. It provides a trading place for commodities, regulates the trading practices of the members, gathers and transmits price information, inspects and governs commodities traded on the Exchange, supervises warehouses that store the commodity, and provides means for settling disputes between members. All transactions must be conducted in a pit on the Exchange floor within certain hours.

FUTURES CONTRACT

A futures contract is a contract between two parties where the buyer agrees to accept delivery at a specified price from the seller of a particular commodity, in a designated month in the future, if it is not liquidated before the contract reaches maturity. A futures contract is not an option; nothing in it is conditional. Each contract calls for a specified amount, and grade of product. For example: *A person buying a February Pork Belly contract at 52.40 in effect is making a*

Source: Commodity Educational Services, Division of Commodity Cassettes, Inc., 778 Frontage Road, Northfield, IL 60093.

legal obligation, now, to accept delivery of 38,000 pounds of frozen Pork Bellies, to be delivered during the month of February, for which the buyer will pay 52.40 per pound.

The average trader does not take delivery of a futures contract, since he normally will close out his position before the futures contract matures. As a matter of fact, a survey conducted by a leading exchange has estimated that less than 3% of the contracts traded are settled by actual delivery.

Editor's Note: The scope of the commodities market has been broadened in recent years to include contracts on financial (debt) instruments (T-bills, bonds, etc.) and composite stock market indices such as Value Line, S&P 500, and the New York Stock Exchange. With the stock market index futures, settlement is made in cash in amount based on the underlying index. Cash, not the securities, is used to offset the long and short positions. The cash value of the contract is defined as the index quotation × 500.

THE HEDGER AND SPECULATOR

A hedger buys or sells a futures contract in order to reduce the risk of loss through price variation. A short hedger sells a futures contract to protect the possible decline in the actual commodity owned by him. A long hedger purchases a futures contract to protect the possible advance in the value of an actual commodity needed to be purchased in the future.

The speculator is an important factor in the volume of future trading today. He, in effect, voluntarily assumes the risk, which the hedger tries to avoid, with the expectations of making a profit. He is somewhat of an insurance underwriter. The largest number of traders on any commodity exchange is the speculator. In order for the hedger to participate, he must have continuous trading interests and activity in the market. This trading activity stems from the role of the speculator, because he involves himself in buying or selling of futures contracts with the idea of making a profit on the advance or decline of prices. The speculator tries to forecast prices in advance of delivery and is willing to buy or sell on this basis. A speculator involves himself in an inescapable risk.

CAN YOU BE A SPECULATOR?

Now, can you be a speculator? Before considering entering into the futures market as a speculator, there are several facts which you should understand about the market and also about yourself. In order to enter into the futures market, you must understand that you are dealing with a margin account.

Margins are as low as 5 to 10% of the total value of the futures contract, so you are obtaining a greater leverage on your capital.

Fluctuations in price are rapid, volatile, and wide. It is possible to make a very large profit in a short period of time, but also, it is possible to take a substantial loss. In fact, surveys taken by the Agricultural Department have shown that up to 75% of the individuals speculating in commodity markets have lost money. This does not mean that some of their trades were not profitable, but after a period of time with a given sum of money they ended up being a loser.

Now taking you as an individual, let us see whether you have the characteristics to become a commodity trader. Number one and the most important is that you do not take money that you have set aside for your future, or money you need daily to support your family or yourself. Number two, and almost equally important, is that you must be willing to assume losses and be willing to assume these losses with such a temperament that it is not going to affect your everyday life. Money used in the futures market should be money that has been set aside for strictly risk purposes, and if this money is not risk capital, your methods of trading could be seriously affected, because you cannot afford to be a loser.

Another very important factor is that you must not feel that you are going to take a thousand, two thousand, five or ten thousand dollars and place this with a brokerage firm and not follow the daily happenings of the market. Price fluctuations are fast, and as stated before, wide, so you must not only be in contact with your Account Executive daily, but know and study the technical facts that may be affecting the particular market in which you are speculating.

The individual who makes his first trade by buying a contract on Monday and selling this contract on the following Wednesday, making six hundred dollars on a $1,000 investment, in a period of two days, suddenly says to himself, *"Where has this market been all my life? Why am I working? Why not just concentrate on this market, if every two days or so I can make six hundred dollars?"* This is a fallacy, since this is an individual that is going to destroy himself and most likely his family. The next trade he will feel confident that because of his first profitable trade the market will always go his way even though he is now showing a loss in his position. He still feels that the market will turn around in his direction. If you become married to a particular commodity futures contract and constantly feel that the losses you are taking at the present time will reverse into profits, you are really fighting the market and in most cases fighting a losing battle. This could lead to disaster. There is a saying that you let your profits ride, but liquidate your losses fast.

In any way that you are uneasy with a position that you are holding, it is better to liquidate it. If, prior to the time of buying or selling a contract, you are not sure that this is the right step to take, do not take it. To protect yourself against this hazard you should pre-decide on every trade and exactly how much you intend to lose.

Another important point is not to involve yourself in too many markets. It is difficult to know all the technical facts and be able to follow numerous markets. In addition, if you are in a winning position, be conservative as to how you add additional contracts or pyramid your position. Being conservative will sometimes cause you to miss certain moves in certain markets and you may feel this to be wrong, but over a long period of time, this conservatism will be profitable to you.

If at this point you feel that you are ready, both financially and mentally to trade commodities, the next step is to begin the actual mechanics of trading a futures contract.

OPENING AN ACCOUNT

The first important factor is to decide which brokerage firm will afford you the best service. To accomplish this, you should do a little research by checking with the various exchanges about different brokerage firms. You should study their advertising, market letters, and other information. These should all be presented in a business-like manner and have no unwarranted claims, such as a guarantee of profit without indicating the possibility of loss.

The brokerage firm must be able to handle orders on all commodity exchanges. Do not pick just any Account Executive in a firm, but one you feel confident to help you make market decisions. Become acquainted with the Account Executive through phone or personal conversations. His knowledge of the factors entering into the market and the understanding of current market trends are important in your final choice.

After making a decision on the brokerage firm and the Account Executive that would be best for you, contact him and have him send you the literature concerning different contracts, and also, any additional information as to his organization. He will then send you the necessary signature cards required by the firm to open an account, and ask you for a deposit of margin money.

You will be trading in regulated commodities, and margin money will be deposited in a segregated fund at the brokerage firm's bank. A segregated account means that the money will only be used for margin and not for expenses of the brokerage firm.

Now you decide to enter into your first trade. Your Account Executive and you decide to enter into a December Live Cattle contract on the Chicago Mercantile Exchange. Your order will be executed as follows: Your Account Executive will place this order with his order desk who will then transmit the order to the floor of the Chicago Mercantile Exchange. There your order will be executed on the trading floor, in the pit. All technical details connected with the transaction will be handled by the brokerage firm.

Upon filling of your order, the filled order will be transmitted back to your Account Executive, who will then contact you, advising you that you have purchased one December Live Cattle contract at a given price. You will also receive a written confirmation on this transaction. You will now show an open position in December Live Cattle on the books of the brokerage firm.

MECHANICS OF A TRADE

Let us go back one step to explain in detail just how your order to buy one December Cattle was handled on the floor of the exchange. All buying and selling in the pit is done by open out-cry, and every price change is reported on the exchange ticker system. Each firm has brokers in the different pits, a pit meaning a trading area for the purpose of buying and selling contracts.

When your order was received on the exchange floor, it was time stamped and then given to a runner. This is a person who takes the order from the desk on the exchange floor and gives it to one of the brokers in the December Cattle trading pit. He is then responsible to the brokerage firm to fill that order, if possible, at the stated price. After filling the order, he then has the runner return it to the desk, where it is time stamped and transmitted back to the order desk at the brokerage house, and the filled order is reported to you.

MARGIN

Futures trading requires the trader to place margin with his brokerage firm. Initial margin is required and this amount varies with each commodity. The minimum margin is established by each commodity exchange. Additional funds are needed when the equity of your account falls below this level. This is known as a maintenance margin call.

All margin calls must be met immediately. Normally you will be given a reasonable amount of time to comply with this request. If you do not comply, the firm has the right to liquidate your trades or a sufficient number of trades to restore your account to margin requirements.

The brokerage firm has the right to raise margin requirements to the customer at any time. This is normally done if the price of the commodity is changing sharply or if it is the brokerage firm's opinion that due to the volatility of the market the margin requirement is not sufficient at that particular time.

Most commodity contracts have a minimum fluctuation and also a maximum fluctuation for any one particular day. For example, if you are trading frozen Pork Bellies on the Chicago Mercantile Exchange the fluctuation is considered in points. A point equals three dollars and eighty cents. This means that if you buy a contract at 52.40 and the next price tick is 52.45, you have made a paper profit of five points or nineteen dollars. The maximum fluctuation on a belly contract is 200 points, so your profit or loss cannot exceed in one day more than 200 points from the previous day's settlement. There are exceptions in some commodity contracts, where the spot month has no limit.

Let us assume that you had originally placed in the hands of your brokerage firm two thousand dollars margin money, and that you and your Account Executive decide to purchase a December Live Cattle contract whose initial margin is $1200 with maintenance of $900.00. After the purchase of the contract your account would show initial margin required $1200 dollars with excess funds of eight hundred dollars. At the end of each day the settlement price of December Cattle would be applied to your purchase price and your account would be adjusted to either an increase due to profit or decrease due to loss in your contract.

Further, assume that in a period of two or three days there is a decline in the price of the December Cattle contract and your account now shows a loss of three hundred dollars. Since maintenance margin is only nine hundred dollars on this contract, you will still show an excess of eight hundred dollars over and above maintenance margin. But, in the next four days suppose there is an additional loss of nine hundred dollars. Your account will now need one hundred dollars to maintain the maintenance margin and four hundred dollars additional in order to bring your account up to initial margin. Your Account Executive, or a man from the margin department of the brokerage firm will then contact you, stating that you must place additional money with the firm in order to maintain the December Cattle contract.

At this point, you must decide whether you should continue with the contract, feeling that it may be profitable in the next few days, and thus sending the brokerage firm the required four hundred dollars to maintain your position, or whether to assume your loss and sell the contract.

Let us assume that you decide to sell your December contract at this point and that the selling price causes a loss of four hundred dollars. Added to this loss would be the commission of forty dollars, so your total loss on the transaction would be four hundred forty dollars. A confirmation and purchase and sales statement will be sent to you, showing the original price paid for the contract, the price for which it was sold, the gross loss of four hundred dollars plus the commision of forty dollars making the total loss four hundred forty dollars, and your new ledger balance on deposit with the firm as fifteen hundred sixty dollars.

As shown in our example, commission was charged only when the contract was closed out. A single commission is charged for each round-turn transaction consisting of the creation and liquidation of a single contract.

CONTROLLED, DISCRETIONARY, AND MANAGED ACCOUNTS

There are two methods of trading your account. The first is the professional approach where you and your Account Executive decide on each trade with no discretion being given directly to your Account Executive. This method was illustrated in the discussion about margins. The second method is called a controlled discretionary or managed account. Under this method, you are giving your Account Executive authorization to trade your account at his discretion at any time and as many times that he considers that a trade should be made. The Chicago Mercantile Exchange, and the Board of Trade have rules governing this type of relationship. The following is an excerpt from the C.M.E. rule regarding controlled, discretionary and managed accounts.

REQUIREMENTS

No clearing member shall accept or carry an account over which any individual or organization, other than the person in whose name the account is carried, exercises trading authority or control, hereinafter referred to as controlled accounts, unless:

The account is initiated with a minimum of $5000°, and maintained at a minimum equity of $3,750°, regardless of

lesser applicable margin requirements. In determining equity the accounts or ledger balances and positions in all commodities traded at the clearing member shall be included. Whenever at the close of any business day the equity, calculated with all open positions figured to the settling price, in any such account is below the required minimum, the clearing member shall immediately notify the customer in person, by telephone or telegraph and by written confirmation of such notice mailed directly to the customer, not later than the close of the following business day. Such notice shall advise the customer that unless additional funds are promptly received to restore the customer's controlled account to no less than $5,000°, the clearing member shall liquidate all of the customer's open futures positions at the Exchange.

In the event the call for additional equity is not met within a reasonable time, the customer's entire open position shall be liquidated. No period of time in excess of five business days shall be considered reasonable unless such longer period is approved in writing by an officer or partner of the clearing member upon good cause shown.

REVIEWING YOUR CONFIRMATIONS AND STATEMENTS

An important factor in trading is that you must be sure that no errors occur in your account. For every trade made you should receive a confirmation, and for every closeout a profit and loss statement known as a Purchase-and-Sale, showing the financial results of each transaction closed out in your account. In addition, a monthly statement showing your ledger balance, your open position, the net profit or loss in all contracts liquidated since the date of your last previous statement, and the net unrealized profit and loss on all open contracts figured to the market should be sent to you.

You should carefully review these statements. Upon receiving a confirmation of a trade you should immediately check its accuracy as far as type of commodity, month, trading price and quantity of contracts. If this does not agree with your original order, it should be immediately reported to the main office of your brokerage firm, and any differences should be explained and adjustments should be made.

If you do not receive a confirmation on a trade after it was orally reported to you by your Account Executive, be sure to contact him and the main office so that if an error was made it can be corrected immediately.

°Minimums can be changed by each exchange, so consult your Account Executive for current regulations.

You should receive written confirmation when you deposit money with your brokerage firm. If within a few days, you have not received this confirmation, report it immediately to the main office of your brokerage firm.

Never assume that an order has been filled until you receive an oral confirmation from your broker. A ticker or a board that you may be observing can be running several minutes behind and is not the determining factor as to whether your trade was executed or not. Until you receive this oral confirmation, never re-enter an order to buy or sell, against that position.

If you receive a confirmation in the mail showing a trade not belonging to you, immediately notify the main office of your brokerage firm and have them explain why this is on a confirmation with your account number. If it is an error, be sure that it is adjusted immediately and a written confirmation sent to you showing the adjustment of the error. If an error is made and it is profitable to you do not consider this any differently than if it was not profitable. Regardless of whether there is a profit or loss, all errors should be immediately reported to the brokerage firm.

Be sure that when you request funds to be mailed from your account that they are received within a few days from the time of your request. If not, contact the accounting department of the brokerage firm to see what is the cause of the delay.

Never make a check out to an individual. Always make your check out to the brokerage firm.

DAY TRADING

Day trading is where there is a buy and sell made during the trading hours on one particular day. Day trading is not considered to be a sound practice for the new speculator and inexperienced trader. Day trading is something that should be executed only by a sophisticated trader who is in frequent communication with the floor, and even then, on a limited basis.

ORDERS

In order to trade effectively in the commodity market there are several basic types of orders. The most common order is a market order. A market order is one which you authorize your Account Executive to buy or sell at the existing price. This is definitely not a predetermined price, but is executed at a bid or offer at that particular moment.

Example: Buy 5 Feb Pork Bellies at the market.

LIMITED OR PRICE ORDERS AND "OB" DESIGNATION

This type of order to buy or sell commodities at a fixed or "limited" price and the ordinary "market" order are the most common types of orders.

Example: Buy Three Jan Silver 463.10. This limit order instructs the floor broker to buy three contracts of January Silver futures at 463.10. Even with this simple order, however, one presumption is necessary—that the market price prevailing when the order enters the pit is 463.10 or higher. If the price is below 463.10, the broker could challenge on the basis that the client may have meant *"Buy Three Jan Silver 463.10 stop."* Therefore, while it is always assumed that a "limit: order means 'or better,'" if possible, it saves confusion and challenges if the "OB" designation is added to the limit price. This is particularly true on orders near the market, or on pre-opening orders with the limit price based on the previous close, because no one knows whether the opening will be higher or lower than the close, i.e., *Buy Three Jan Silver 463.10 OB.*

STOP ORDERS *(Orders having the effect of market orders)*

Buy Stop   Buy stop orders must be written at a price higher than the price prevailing at the time of entry. If the prevailing price for December Wheat is 456 per bushel, a buy stop order must designate a price above 456.

Example: "Buy 20 Dec Wht 456½ Day Stop." The effect of this order is that if December Wheat touches 456½ the order to buy 20 December Wheat becomes a market order. From that point, 456½ on, all the above discussion regarding market orders applies.

Sell Stop   Sell stop orders must be written at a price lower than the price prevailing at the time of entry in the trading pit. If the prevailing price of December Wheat is 456 per bushel, a sell stop order must designate a price below 456.

Example: "Sell 20 Dec Wht 455 Day Stop." If this order enters the trading pit with the above price of 456 prevailing, the order to sell 20 December Wheat becomes a market order. From that point 455 on, all the above discussion regarding market orders applies.

Buy stop orders have several specific uses. If you are short a December Wheat at 456, and wish to limit your loss to ½ cent per bushel, the above buy stop order at 456½ would serve this purpose. However, it is important to realize that such *"stop loss"* orders do not actually limit the loss to exactly ½ cent when *"elected"* or *"touched off"* because they become market orders and must be executed at whatever price the market conditions dictate.

Another use is when you are without a position and believe that, because of chart analysis or for other reasons, a buy of December Wheat at 456½ would signal the beginning of an important uptrend in Wheat prices. Thus, the same order to *"Buy 20 Dec Wheat 456½ Day Stop"* would serve this purpose.

Sell stop orders have the same uses in reverse. That is, if you are long 20 December Wheat at 456 and wish to limit this loss to 1 cent per bushel, the above sell stop order at 455 would serve this purpose, within the limitations of the market order possibilities. Similarly, if you are without a position and believe that a sale of December Wheat at 455 would signal a downtrend in wheat prices, and you wish to be short the market, you could use the order to *"Sell 20 December Wheat 455 Day Stop"* for this purpose.

STOP LIMIT ORDERS *(Variations of stop orders)*

Stop limit orders should be used by you when you wish to give the floor broker a limit beyond which he cannot go in executing the order which results when a stop price is *"elected."*

Example: "Buy 20 Dec Wheat 456½ Day Stop Limit." This instructs the broker that when the price of 456½ is reached and *"elects"* this stop order, instead of making it a market order, it becomes a limited order to be executed at 456½ *(or lower)*, but no higher than 456½. Another possibility:

Example: "Buy One February Pork Belly 58.10 Day Stop Limit 58.25 (or any other price above 58.10)." This instructs the broker that when the price of 58.10 *"elects"* the stop order instead of making it a market order, it becomes a limited order to buy at 58.25 *(or lower)*, but not higher as with any limit order.

Stop limit orders are particularly useful to you when you have no position and wish to enter a market via the stop order, but want to put some reasonable limit as to what you will pay. On the other hand, stop limit orders are not useful to you when you have an open position and wish to prevent a loss beyond a certain point. The reason is that by limiting the broker to a certain price after a *"stop loss"* order is elected, **you also run the risk**

that the market may exceed the limit too fast for the broker to execute. This would leave you with your original position because the broker would have to wait for the return to the limit before executing. With a straight stop *(no limit)* order, the broker must execute *"at the market."*

Example: "Buy One February Pork Belly 58.10 Day Stop Limit 58.25." Suppose the market moves to 58.10 but then only 20 February Pork Bellies are offered at that price. Your broker bids for one at 58.10 but another broker in the pit catches the seller's eye first and buys 20 and your broker misses the sale. Your broker then bids 58.20 but the best offer is 58.30. He bids 58.25, but the offer at 58.30 remains unchanged. Then another broker bids for and buys February Pork Bellies at 58.30 and the market moves on up. Your broker is left with no execution to your order unless the market later declines to your limit making a fill possible.

If you did not have a position you might be disappointed, but you would be unhurt financially. However, if you had a position and were trying to limit your loss you would have defeated your purpose with the stop limit order, if you truly wanted *"out"* after the stop was elected.

Stop limit orders on the sell side have exactly the same uses, advantages and disadvantages as discussed above, but in reverse:

Example: "Sell 20 December Wheat 455 Day Stop Limit." This means that when the market declines to 455 per bushel, the broker may sell at 455 *(or higher)*, but no lower.

Another Example: "Sell One February Pork Belly 58.25 Stop Limit 58.10." This instructs the broker to sell a belly after the stop price of 58.25 is reached and *"elects"* the stop order, but no lower than 58.10.

M.I.T. ORDERS *(Market-if-touched)*

By adding MIT *(Market-if-Touched)* to a limit order, the limit order will have the effect of a market order when the limit price is reached or touched. This type of order is useful to you, when you have an open position and if a certain limit price is reached.

Example: "Sell One September Sugar 950 MIT." The floor broker is told that if and when the price of September Sugar rises to 9½¢ per pound, he is to sell one contract at the market. At this price of 9½¢ all prior discussion on market orders applies.

Under certain market conditions, not

enough contracts are bid at 9½¢ to fill all offers to sell. Thus, you may see your straight limit price appear on the ticker, but your broker fails to make the sale.

But by adding **MIT** to the limit price, you will receive an execution, because the order becomes a market order, if the price is touched. However, the price will not necessarily be a good one in your eyes, since it became a market order when touched.

The same reasoning is true on the buy side of MIT orders but in reverse. Assume you are short one contract of September Sugar, with the prevailing price at 9½¢ per pound and you want to cover or liquidate your short at 9¢.

Example: "Buy One September Sugar 9¢ MIT." If and when the price of September sugar declines to 9¢ per pound, the floor broker must buy one contract at the market. Aside from the disadvantages of any market order, the MIT designation on the buy order prevents the disappointment which might arise if a straight limit buy at 9¢ were entered without the MIT added.

SPREAD ORDERS

As explained in the Glossary, a spread is a simultaneous long or short position in the same or related commodity. Thus a spread order would be to buy one month of a certain commodity and sell another month of the same commodity, or buy one month of one commodity and sell the same or another month of a related commodity.

Example: "Buy 5 July Beans Market and Sell 5 May Beans Market" or "Buy 10 Kansas City Dec Wheat Market and Sell 10 Chicago May Wheat Market."

Another Example: "Buy 5 May Corn Market and Sell 5 May Wheat Market."

In the example of the related commodity spread, normally the reason you would use such a spread, is that you expect to make a profit out of an expected tightness in the Corn Market, in the hope the corn contract will gain in value faster than wheat.

There may be a situation where you have a position either long or short in a commodity and want to change to a nearer or more distant option of the same commodity. For example you are long 5,000 bushels of May Soybeans on May 20 and want to avoid a delivery notice by moving your position forward into the July option. The basic spread order would be:

"Buy 5 July Beans Market and Sell 5 May Beans Market."

Sometimes you may prefer not to use market orders, in which case you use the difference spread.

Example: "Buy 5 July Beans and Sell 5 May Beans July 2¢ Over." Even though the prices of the two options are not specified, the broker is allowed to execute at any time he can do so with July selling at 2¢ or less above May. Over or under designations are a necessity for clarity to the floor broker. Omitting either is like omitting the price.

All orders, except market orders, can be cancelled, prior to execution. Naturally, a market order is executed immediately upon reaching the pit, so its cancellation is almost impossible.

There are other variations of orders, but for you the new speculator, the types mentioned are sufficient for your trading.

Options on Stock Market Indices, Bond Futures, and Gold Futures

STOCK MARKET INDEX OPTIONS

Stock market index related options are options whose prices are determined by the value of a stock market average such as the Standard and Poor (S&P) 500 Index or the New York Stock Exchange Composite Index, among others. Two types of such options are currently traded; index options and index futures options. The former are settled in cash while the latter are settled by delivery of the appropriate index futures contract.

Both types of options move in the same way in response to the underlying market index, thereby providing investors the opportunity to speculate on the market averages. The buyer of a call index option is betting that the underlying market index value will increase significantly above the strike price (before the option expires) so as to provide a profit when the option is sold. On the other hand, the buyer of a put option is speculating that the market index value will fall sufficiently below the strike price before the option expires so as to provide a profit when the put option is sold. Option writers (sellers), on the other hand, assume an opposite position.

While index futures (page 542) also permit speculation on the market averages, index option tend to be less risky since option *buyers* are not subject to margin calls and losses are limited to the price (premium) paid for the option. However, index option writers (sellers), in return for the premium received, are subject to margin calls and are exposed to losses of indeterminate magnitude. However, writers of call options on index *futures* can protect themselves by holding the underlying futures contract.

Index Options

A number of index options based on the broad market averages are now traded:

S&P 100 Index [Chicago Board of Options Exchange (CBOE)]
S&P 500 Index (Chicago Board of Options Exchange)
Major Market Index [American Exchange (Amex)]
Institutional Index (American Exchange)
NYSE Options Index (New York Stock Exchange)
Value Line Index (Philadelphia Exchange)
National OTC Index (Philadelphia Exchange)

A brief description of some of the more important indices follows.

The S&P 100 Index is a so-called weighted index obtained by multiplying the current price of each of the 100 stocks by the number of shares outstanding and then adding all of the products to obtain the weighted sum. The weighted sum is then multiplied by a scaling factor to provide an index of a convenient magnitude. The S&P 500 Index is calculated similarly except that all of the S&P 500 stocks are included.

The NYSE Index is based on the weighted sum of all of the stocks traded on the New York Exchange while the AMEX Index is based on the weighted sum of all of the issues traded on the American Exchange. The Institutional Index consists of 75 stocks most widely held by institutional investors.

The Major Market Index differs from the above in that it is just the simple (unweighted) sum of 20 blue chip stocks multiplied by a factor of one tenth. This index behaves very similarly to the Dow Jones Index.

Generally index options expire on the Saturday following the third Friday of the expiration month. Hence the last trading day is on the third Friday of the expiration month. The price of an index option contract is $100 times the premium as quoted in the financial press.

Example: The July 120 (an option with a strike price of 120 expiring in July) Major Market Index call option is quoted (Exhibit 1) at 3.00. The cost of an option contract is $300 ($100 × 3).

Option premiums consist of the sum of two components; the intrinsic value and the time value. The intrinsic value of a *call* option

EXHIBIT 1 INDEX OPTIONS QUOTATIONS

CHICAGO BOARD

CBOE 100 INDEX

Strike Price	Calls—Last			Puts—Last		
	June	Sept	Dec	June	Sept	Dec
145	15¼	....	....	¹⁄₁₆	1	....
150	13¾	....	....	⅛	1¾	....
155	9⅛	10	....	⁷⁄₁₆	3⅛	....
160	5⅛	9¼	....	1⁷⁄₁₆	4⅝	8¼
165	2⅛	6½	8⅝	3⅞	7¼	10½
170	1¹⁄₁₆	3¾	6	7⅝	12	13½

Total call volume 20846. Total call open int. 62006.
Total put volume 25167. Total put open int. 103733.
The index closed at 163.55, + 1.91.

AMERICAN EXCHANGE

MAJOR MARKET INDEX

Strike Price	Calls—Last			Puts—Last		
	Jul	Oct	Jan	Jul	Oct	Jan
115	5¾	8⅝	10	1⅞	3¾	5½
120	3	5¾	7	4	5⅞	7½
125	1⅛	3¼	....	7⅜	....	....
130	⁷⁄₁₆	2¼	3⅝	....	....	

Total call volume 2351. Total call open int. 14572.
Total put volume 5276. Total put open int. 9593.
The index closed at 118.69, + 1.00.

is $100 times the difference obtained by subtracting the strike price from the current value of the index. The intrinsic value of a *put* option is $100 times the difference obtained by subtracting the current value of the index from the strike price. The time value is the money which an option buyer is willing to pay in the expectation that the option will become more valuable (*increase its intrinsic value*) before it expires. Obviously the time value decreases as the time to expiration decreases.

It should be noted that there is a distinction between exercising an index option and selling an index option to close out a position. Exercising an option gives the holder the right to a cash amount equal to the *intrinsic* value of the option. Hence, the time value of the option is lost. When an option is sold to close out a position, the option holder receives a cash amount equal to the *premium* which contains both the intrinsic value and the time value of the option. Thus, in most cases it is more profitable to sell the option. The profit realized (before commissions and taxes) on the *sale* of an option contract is equal to $100 times the difference obtained by subtracting the premium paid when the option was purchased from the premium received when the option was sold.

Example: On May 24 the CBOE 100 Index was 163.55. In anticipation of a market decline, an investor buys a September 165-put option quoted at 7¼ for a total premium of $725 (7.25 × 100) per option. Assume that on August 10 the puts were selling at a total premium of $850 due to a decline in the CBOE 100 Index to 160.10. If the investor sells the put option he will realize a profit, before commissions and taxes, of $125 (850−725). If the market moves in a contrary direction he could lose his entire investment.

Index Futures Options

Index futures options (also called futures options) are the right to buy (call) or sell (put) the underlying index futures contracts (see page 540). Futures options are currently traded on the New York Futures Exchange and the Chicago Mercantile Exchange. The dollar value of the underlying contract for the New York Futures Exchange option is equal to the New York Stock Exchange Composite Index multiplied by 500 while that for the Chicago Mercantile Exchange option is equal to the S&P 500 Index multiplied by 500. Quotations for futures options as they appear in *The Wall Street Journal* are shown in Exhibit 2. The total futures option premium per option is equal to the quoted value multiplied by 500. Gains and losses are calculated in the same way as index options.

The expiration day of the S&P 500 futures option is on the third Thursday of the expiration month while that for the NYSE futures option is the business day prior to the last business day of the expiration month.

Example: On May 24, 1983, the New York Composite Index is 94.39. An investor expects the Index to increase during the next six months and buys a September 96 futures call option at a total premium of $1750 (3.50 × 500), as indicated in Exhibit 2. Assume that by August 10 the Index is at 100 and that the September call premium is quoted at 8.00 corresponding to a total premium per option of $4000 (8.00 × 500). By selling the option at the current value the investor can realize a profit of $2250 (4000 − 1750) before commissions and taxes.

Example: Assume that on May 24, 1983 when the S&P 500 Index is at 163.43, an investor expects a market decline within six months. He purchases a September 155 S&P put option at a total premium per option of $1150 (2.30 × 500), as indicated in the quotations shown in Exhibit 2. Assume that the Index declines to 150 on August 10 and that the quoted put premium is 6.50 corresponding to a total premium per option of $3250 (6.50 × 500). By selling the option at the current value the investor can realize a profit of $2100 (3250 − 1150), before commissions and taxes.

EXHIBIT 2   FUTURES OPTIONS

CHICAGO MERCANTILE EXCHANGE

S&P 500 STOCK INDEX – Price = $500 times premium.

Strike Price	Calls—Settle			Puts—Settle		
	Jun	Sep	Dec	Jun	Sep	Dec
135	....	....	....	.05	....	....
140	23.90	24.25	....	.05	.45	....
145	18.90	20.20	....	.05	.90	....
150	13.95	15.25	....	.10	1.25	....
155	9.20	11.50	....	.30	2.30	4.50
160	4.95	8.60	....	1.05	3.60	....
165	1.90	5.50	8.75	3.00	5.75	7.80
170	.45	3.50	....	6.50	9.50	....
175	.10	1.80	....	11.15	14.00	....

Estimated total vol. 1,440
Calls: Fri. vol. 766; open int. 6,216
Puts: Fri. vol. 532; open int. 6,552

N.Y. FUTURES EXCHANGE

NYSE COMPOSITE INDEX – Price = $500 times premium.

Strike Price	Calls—Settle			Puts—Settle		
	Jun	Sep	Dec	Jun	Sep	Dec
84	10.90	11.70	....	.05	.40	.75
86	8.90	10.00	11.00	.05	.70	1.50
88	5.95	8.50	9.70	.05	1.00	1.75
90	5.15	7.00	8.30	.25	1.50	2.30
92	3.35	5.50	7.00	.50	2.00	2.95
94	1.95	4.50	6.00	1.15	3.00	3.75
96	.95	3.50	5.00	2.10	3.90	4.95
98	.40	2.75	3.95	3.50	5.25	6.05
100	.15	1.75	3.25	....	6.25	7.00

Estimated total vol. 1,405
Calls: Fri. vol. 844; open int. 4,836
Puts: Fri. vol. 549; open int. 4,801
S&P 500 Index 163.43
New York Composite Index = 94.39

While a number of the same basic concepts apply to both index options and future options, there are differences between the two because the futures options have underlying index futures contracts which are traded on the open market. This makes possible a number of trading strategies with futures options which are not available with index options; for example, simultaneously buying an index futures contract and writing a corresponding call option. Also, for the reason given above, there is a distinction between selling a futures option, the usual procedure, and exercising the option. When a futures option is exercised, the option is exchanged for a position in the index futures market which may result in a loss in the time value of the option.

Investors planning to trade options should read two free booklets available from any of the options exchanges:

Understanding the Risks and Uses of Options
Listed Options On Stock Indices

Subindex Options

Subindex options are based on an index made up of leading publicly traded companies within a specific industry. These options permit speculation on an industry without the necessity of selecting specific stocks within the industry. As with all stock index options they are settled in cash.

U.S. TREASURY BOND FUTURES OPTIONS

Options on U.S. Treasury Bonds (T-Bonds), traded on the Chicago Board of Trade, are the right to buy (call) or sell (put) a T-Bond futures contract. The T-Bond futures contract underlying the option is for $100,000 of Treasury Bonds, bearing an 8% or equivalent coupon, which do not mature (and are non-callable) for at least 15 years. When long term interest rates decline, the value of the futures contract and the call option increases while the value of a put option decreases. The reverse is true when long term rates increase.

Premiums for T-bond futures *options* are quoted in ¹⁄₆₄ of 1% (point): Hence each ¹⁄₆₄ of a point is equal to $15.63 ($100,000 × .01 × ¹⁄₆₄) per option. Thus a premium quote of 2–16 means 2¹⁶⁄₆₄ or (2 × 64 + 16) × $15.63 or $2250.72 per option. It should be noted that prices of T-bond *futures* are quoted in ¹⁄₃₂ (of a point) worth $31.25 per futures contract.

As with options trades in general, the profit (before taxes and commissions) is the premium received (per option) when the option is sold minus the premium paid when the option was purchased.

The last trading day for the options is the first Friday, preceded by at least five business days, in the month *prior* to the month in which the underlying futures contract expires. For example, in 1983 a December option stops trading on November 18, 1983.

GOLD FUTURES OPTIONS

The most widely traded gold futures option is on the New York Comex Exchange. The option is the right to buy (call) or sell (put) a gold futures contract for 100 Troy ounces of pure gold. Both the futures contract and the corresponding call option increase or decrease with the price of gold. Put option premiums move in the opposite direction to the price of gold.

Option premiums are in dollars per ounce of gold. Thus a quoted premium of 2.50 corresponds to total premium of $2500 (2.50 × 100) per option.

The profit (before commissions and taxes) to an option buyer is simply the premium received when the option is sold less the premium paid when the option was purchased.

The last trading day for gold futures options is the second Friday in the month *prior* to the expiration date of the underlying gold futures contract. Thus in 1983 a December option expires on Friday November 11, 1983. Example: In August an investor buys a December 400 (an option with a strike price of 400 on a December gold futures contract) Comex call option quoted at 25.00. The total price per option is $2500 (25.00 × 100).

On November 5, the price of gold has increased and the investor sells the option at a quoted premium of 50.00 or $5000.00 (50 × 100) per option. His profit is $2500 (5000 − 2500).

The Commodities Glossary

Acreage allotment   The portion of a farmer's total acreage that he can harvest and still qualify for government price supports, low interest crop loans and other programs. It currently applies to specialty crops—tobacco, peanuts and extra long staple cotton—for which complex federal marketing orders have been written to control production closely. Before the 1977 farm bill was passed, the same term also applied more loosely to the portion of a farmer's wheat or feed grain acreage for which government payments would be made. A farmer could harvest 100 acres of wheat, for instance, but he'd receive price support payments only for 70 acres if that was his allotment. The allotment in this sense is called "program acreage" in the new farm bill.

Arbitrage   The simultaneous buying and selling of futures contracts to profit from what the trader perceives as a discrepancy in prices. Usually this is done in futures in the same commodity traded on different exchanges, such as cocoa in New York and cocoa in London or silver in New York and silver in Chicago. Some arbitrage occurs between cash markets and futures markets.

Asking price   The price offered by one wishing to sell a physical commodity or a futures contract. Sometimes a futures market will close with an asking price when no buyers are around.

Backwardation   An expression peculiar to New York markets. It means "nearby" contracts are trading at a higher price, or "premium," to the deferreds. See also *Inverted market*.

Basis   A couple of meanings: (1) The difference between the price of the physical commodity (the cash price) and the futures price of that commodity. (2) A geographic reference point for a cash price; for example, the price of a beef carcass is quoted "basic Midwest packing plants."

Bear   A trader who thinks prices will decline. "Bearish" is often used to describe news or developments that have, or are expected to have, a downward influence on prices. A bear market is one in which the predominant price trend is down. Some think this term originated with an old axiom about "selling the skin before you've caught the bear."

Bid   The price offered by one who wishes to purchase a physical commodity or a futures contract. Sometimes a futures market will close with a bid price when no sellers are around.

Broker   An agent who buys and sells futures on behalf of a client for a fee. They work for brokerage firms, some of which have extensive research and analysis departments that occasionally issue trading advice. A few firms have so many customers who follow such advisories that recommendations to buy or sell can influence market prices materially.

Bull   A trader who thinks prices will go up. "Bullish" describes developments that have, or are expected to have, an upward influence on prices. A bull market is one in which the predominant price trend is up. Some theorize this term originally related to a bull's habit of tossing its head upward.

Butterfly   An unusual sort of spread involving three contract months rather than two. Often used to move profits or losses from one year to the next for tax purposes.

Cash   The price at which dealings in the physical commodity take place. Used more sweepingly, it can mean simply the physical commodity itself (as in "cash corn" or "cash lumber"), or refer to a market. For example, the cash hog market is a terminal (or, collectively, all terminals) where live hogs are sold by farmers and bought by meat packers.

Chart   A graph of futures prices (and sometimes other statistical trading information) plotted in such a way that the charter believes gives insight into future price movements. Several futures markets regularly are influenced by buying or selling based on traders' price-chart indications.

Clearing house   The part of all futures exchanges (usually a separate corporation with its own members, fees, etc.) which clears all trades made on the exchange during the day. It matches the buy transactions with the equal number of sell transactions to provide orderly control over who owns what and who owes what to whom. Although futures traders theoretically trade contracts among themselves, the clearing house technically is in the middle of each transaction—being the buyer to every seller and the seller to every buyer. That's how it keeps track of what is going on.

Close   The end of the trading session. On some exchanges, the "close" lasts for several minutes to accommodate customers who have entered buy or sell orders to be consummated "at the close." On those exchanges, the closing price may be a range encompassing the highest and lowest prices of trading consummated at the close. Other exchanges officially use settlement prices as the closing prices.

Source: The *Dow Jones Commodities Handbook*, edited by Dan Ruck, Dow Jones Books, Dow Jones Company, Inc. 1979.

Cold storage Refrigerated warehouses where perishable commodities are stored. In effect, the warehouses are secondary sources of commodities that aren't immediately available from the producers. The Agriculture Department periodically reports the quantities of various commodities stored in warehouses. Futures traders watch these reports to see if the supplies are building or dwindling abnormally fast, which indicates how closely supply and demand are balanced.

Commission The fee charged by a broker for making a trade on behalf of customers.

Contract In the case of futures, an agreement between two parties to make and in turn accept delivery of a specified quantity and quality of a commodity (or whatever is being traded) at a certain place (the delivery point) by a specified time (indicated by the month and year of the contract).

Country Refers to a place relatively close to a farmer where he can sell or deliver his crop or animals. For instance, a country elevator typically is located in a small town and accepts grain from farmers in the immediate vicinity. A country shipping point is a place where farmers in an area combine their marketings for shipment. A country price is the one these elevators, shipping points or whatever pay for the farmers' goods; it's based on the terminal-market prices, less transportation and handling costs.

Covering Buying futures contracts to offset those previously sold. "Short covering" often causes prices to rise even though the overall market trend may be down.

Crop report Estimates issued periodically by the Department of Agriculture on estimated size and condition of major U.S. crops. Similar reports are made on livestock.

Crush The process of reducing the raw, unusable soybean into its two major components, oil and meal. A "crush spread" is a futures spreading position in which a trader attempts to profit from what he believes to be discrepancies in the price relationships between soybeans and the two products. The "crush margin" is the gross profit that a processor makes from selling oil and meal minus the cost of buying the soybeans.

Deferred contracts In futures, those delivery months that are due to expire sometime beyond the next two or three months.

Delivery The tendering of the physical commodity to fulfill a short position in futures. This takes place only during the delivery month and normally takes the form of a warehouse receipt (from an exchange-accredited warehouse, elevator or whatever) that shows where the cash commodity is.

Delivery point The place(s) at which the cash commodity may be delivered to fulfill an expiring futures contract.

Discretionary accounts A futures trading account in which the customer puts up the money but the trading decisions are made at the discretion of the broker or some other person, or maybe a computer. Also known as "managed accounts."

Evening up Liquidating a futures position in advance of a significant crop report or some other scheduled development so as not to be caught on the wrong side of a surprise. In concentrated doses, evening up can cause a bull market to retreat somewhat and a bear market to rebound somewhat.

First notice day The first day of a delivery period when holders of short futures positions can give notice of their intention to deliver the cash commodity to holders of long positions. The number of contracts circulated on first notice day and how they are accepted or not accepted by the longs is often interpreted as an indication of future supply-demand expectations and thus often influence prices of all futures being traded, not just the delivery-month price. This effect also sometimes occurs on subsequent notice days. Rules concerning notices to deliver vary from contract to contract.

F.O.B. Free on Board, meaning that the commodity will be placed aboard the shipping vehicle at no cost to the purchaser, but thereafter the purchaser must bear all shipping costs.

Forward Contract A commercial agreement for the merchandising of commodities in which actual delivery is contemplated but is deferred for purposes of commercial convenience or necessity. Such agreements normally specify the quality and quantity of goods to be delivered at the particular future date. The forward contract may specify the price at which the commodity will be exchanged, or the agreement may stipulate that the price will be determined at some time prior to delivery.

Fundamentalist A trader who bases his buy-sell decisions on supply and demand trends or developments rather than on technical or chart considerations.

Futures Contracts traded on an exchange that call for a cash commodity to be delivered and received at a specified future time, at a specified place and at a specified price. Similar arrangements made directly between buyer and seller are called "forward contracts." They aren't traded on an exchange.

Hedge Using the futures market to reduce the risks of unforeseen price changes that are inherent in buying and selling cash commodities. For example, as an elevator operator buys cash grain from farmer, he can "hedge" his purchases by selling futures contracts; when he sells the cash commodity, he purchases an offsetting number of futures contracts to liquidate his position. If prices rise while he owns the cash grain, he sells the cash grain at a profit and closes out his futures at a loss, which almost aways is no greater than his profit in the cash transaction. If prices fall while he owns the cash grain, he sells the cash grain at a loss but recoups all or almost all of the loss by buying back futures contracts at a price correspondingly lower than at which he first sold them. Some users of commodities assure themselves of supplies of their raw materials at a set price by buying futures, which is another form of hedging. When the time comes to acquire inventories, they can either take delivery on their futures contracts or, more likely, simply buy their supplies in the cash market. Futures-contract prices tend to match cash prices at the time the futures expire, so if cash prices have risen the users' higher costs are offset by profits on their futures contracts.

Hedger   The Commodity Futures Trading Commission says a hedger in a general sense is someone who uses futures trading as a temporary, risk-reducing substitute for a cash transaction planned later in his main line of business. All other futures traders are classified as speculators. There are more legally specific definitions of hedging and hedgers in such markets as grains, soybeans, potatoes and cotton, where limits are placed on the number of contracts speculators may trade or own. The Commission has broadened these limits to allow hedging in closely related, rather than exactly matching, commodities. A sorghum producer, for instance, can use corn futures as a hedging tool where he couldn't before this rule-broadening. The more general distinction between hedgers and speculators may be important to potential traders. Some may want to use a market like interest rate futures to offset some expected heavy borrowing. The government hasn't set any speculative trading limits in those markets, but lenders or company directors are more apt to back a plan to trade futures for hedging purposes rather than speculation.

Inverted market   A futures market where prices for deferred contracts are lower than those for nearby-delivery contracts because of great near-term demand for the cash commodity. Normally, prices of deferred contracts are higher, in part reflecting storage costs.

Last trading day   The day when trading in an expiring contract ceases, and traders must

either liquidate their positions or prepare to make or accept delivery of the cash commodity. After that, there is no more futures trading for that particular contract month and year.

Life of contract   The period of time during which futures trading in a particular contract month and year may take place. This is usually less than a year, but sometimes up to 18 months.

Limit move   The maximum that a futures price can rise or fall from the previous session's settlement price. This limit, set by each exchange, varies from commodity to commodity. Some exchanges have variable limits, whereby the limit is expanded automatically if the market moves by the limit for a certain number of consecutive trading sessions. When prices fail to move the expanded limit, or after a specified period of time, the limits revert to normal.

Liquidation   Closing out a previous position by taking an opposite position in the same contract. Thus, a previous buyer liquidates by selling, and a previous seller liquidates by buying.

Long   A trader who has bought futures, speculating the prices will rise. He is "long" until he liquidates by selling or fulfills his contracts by making delivery.

Margin   The amount of "good faith" money that commodity traders must put in order to trade futures. The margins, set by each exchange, usually amount to 5% to 10% of the total value of the commodity contract. The "initial margin" is the amount of money that must be put up to establish a position in a futures market. Exchanges establish this margin, too, but brokerage firms often require even larger amounts to protect their own financial interests. "Maintenance margin" is the money that traders must put up to retain their position in the futures markets.

Margin call   A request by a brokerage firm that a customer put up more money. That means the market price has gone against the customer's position and the brokerage firm wants the customer to cover his paper loss, which would become a real loss if the position were liquidated.

Nearby contracts   The futures that expire the soonest. Those that expire later are called deferred contracts.

New crop   The supply of a commodity that will be available after harvest. The term also is sometimes used in connection with pigs and hogs because the major farrowing periods in the spring and fall are referred to as "crops." There sometimes are substantial price differences between futures contracts related to new-crop supplies and those related to old-crop supplies.

Nominal price An artificial price—usually the midpoint between a bid and an asked price—that gives an indication of the market price level even though no actual transactions may have taken place at that price.

Old crop The supply from previous harvests.

Open The period each session when futures trading commences. Sometimes the open lasts several minutes to accommodate customers who have placed orders to buy or sell contracts "on the open." On these exchanges, opening prices are reported by the exchange as a range, although these seldom are widely disseminated because of space restrictions in newspapers and periodicals; they are carried on tickers and display panels during that trading day, however.

Open interest Outstanding futures contracts that haven't been liquidated by purchase or sale of offsetting contracts, or by delivery or acceptance of the physical commodity.

Option The right to buy or sell a futures contract over a specified period of time at a set price.

Overbought A term used to express the opinion that prices have risen too high too fast and so will decline as traders liquidate their positions.

Oversold Like "overbought" except the opinion is that prices have fallen too far too fast and so probably will rebound.

Pit The areas on exchange floors where futures trading takes place. Pits usually have three or more levels and can accommodate a large number of traders. On several New York exchanges the trading areas are called rings and consist of open-center, circular tables around which traders sit or stand.

Position A trader's holdings, either long or short. A position limit is the maximum number of contracts a speculator can hold under law; it doesn't apply to bona-fide hedgers, although there really isn't any objective way of telling whether a person in position to hedge actually is hedging or is speculating instead.

Profit taking A trader holding a long position turns paper profits into real ones by selling his contracts. A trader holding a short position takes profits by buying back contracts.

Reaction A decline in prices following a substantial advance.

Recovery An increase in prices following a substantial decline.

Settlement price The single closing price, determined by each exchange's price committee of directors. It is used primarily by the exchange clearing house to determine the need for margin capital to be put up by brokerage-firm members to protect the net position of that firm's total accounts. It's also issued by some exchanges as the official closing price, and it is used to determine the price limits and net price changes on the following trading day. (See also: *Close*.)

Set-aside Acreage withdrawn from crop production for a season and used for soil conservation under a production-control program. Wheat farmers this year must set aside two acres of land for each 10 acres they plant to wheat in order to get any federal price support or disaster aid. The Agriculture Department has also said corn, sorghum and barley producers similarly may be required to set aside some of their acreage if it appears that surpluses will grow too much otherwise.

Short A trader who has sold futures, speculating that prices will decline. He is "short" until he liquidates by buying back contracts or fulfills his contracts by taking delivery.

Short squeeze A situation in which "short" futures traders are unable to buy the cash commodity to deliver against their positions and so are forced to buy offsetting futures at prices much higher than they'd ordinarily be willing to pay.

Speculation Buying or selling in hopes of making a profit. The word connotes a high degree of risk.

Spot The same as cash commodities. Literally, delivery "on the spot" rather than in the future.

Spreads and straddles Terms for the simultaneous buying of futures in one delivery month and selling of futures in another delivery month (or even the simultaneous buying of futures in one commodity and selling of futures in a different but related commodity). One purpose is to profit from perceived discrepancies in price relationships. Another purpose is to transfer current trading profits to some future time to avoid immediate tax liability.

Stop-loss order An open order given to a brokerage firm to liquidate a position when the market reaches a certain price so as to prevent losses from mounting or profits from eroding. Sometimes market price trends are accelerated when concentrations of stop-loss orders are touched off.

Support price A level below which the government tries to keep the agricultural-commodity prices that farmers receive from falling. They're set basically by Congress when farm legislation is passed and adjusted from time to time by the President or Agriculture Secretary. Subsidy payments, commodity purchases, production controls or commodity-secured loans are among the devices used to make up the difference when market prices dip below the support level. Futures and cash prices often tend to remain near the support level when there are large crop surpluses because lower prices keep commodities off the market and higher ones quickly draw willing sellers.

Switch   A trading maneuver in which a trader liquidates his position in one futures delivery and takes the position in another delivery month in expectation that prices will change more rapidly in the second contract than in the first. Thus, a trader might switch out of a position in an October silver futures contract into a position in a December silver futures contract. Warning: Some people use the word "switch" when they mean "spread" or "straddle." Feel free to correct them.

Technical factors   Futures prices often are affected by influences related to the market itself, rather than to supply-demand fundamentals of the commodity with which the market is concerned. For example, if a

market moves up or down the limit several days in succession there frequently is a subsequent "technical reaction" caused in part by the liquidation of contracts held by traders on the wrong side of the price move.

Terminal   Refers to an elevator or livestock market at key distribution points to which commodities are sent from a wide area.

Trading range   The amount that futures prices can fluctuate during one trading session—essentially, the price "distance" between limit up and limit down. If, for instance, the soybean futures price can advance or fall by a maximum of 20 cents per bushel in one day, the trading range is double that, or 40 cents per bushel. In one market, cocoa, price movements are restricted to a daily range of six cents a pound.

Visible supply   The amount of a commodity that can be accounted for and computed accurately, usually because it is being kept in major known storage places.

Warehouse or elevator receipt   The negotiable slip of paper that a short can hand over to fulfill an expiring futures contract's delivery requirement. The receipt shows how much of the commodity is in storage.

Dow Jones Futures and Spot Commodity Indexes

The method for arriving at the Dow Jones Futures and Spot Commodity Indexes differs from some others in the order in which the computations are made. Instead of first weighting each price, then adding them up and finally calculating the percentage or index, this method first turns each price into an index or percentage of its base-year price, then weights each individual index, and finally adds them up. Stated mathematically, the more usual method calculates the percentage relation of one average to another, while the Dow Jones Commodity Index method calculates the average of a set of percentage changes. These two methods do not result in exactly the same figures. However, they are equally valid when used consistently, and the indexes they produce are of the same general magnitude.

The Dow Jones Commodity Index method has two advantages. One is that it saves computation, because the factors or multipliers perform two computations at once. They calculate the individual percentages and weight

them at one stroke. The other advantage is that if you have yesterday's index, you can apply the multipliers to today's individual price changes. Then all you do is add the resulting figures to yesterday's index, or subtract them from it, depending on whether they're up or down. That gives today's index. No need to recalculate the whole thing each day.

As for the weights, they were obtained by the usual mathematical methods. Basically, the weight of each commodity is the percentage of its commercial production value to the total commercial production value of all commodities in the index, in this case for the years 1927–31. In calculating the weights, consideration also was given to the relation between volume of trading in each commodity and its commercial production.

A further refinement was necessary because price changes of the various commodities are quoted in different units. Grain prices change in eighths of a cent, wool prices change in tenths of a cent, and all the other staples in the Dow Jones index move in hundredths of a cent. This adjustment merely required appropriate treatment in each case of the multiplier, so that it would

Source: The *Dow Jones Commodities Handbook*, edited by Dan Ruck, Dow Jones Books, Dow Jones & Company, Inc.

give the right figure for any price change. In the case of grains it meant an adjustment of 20%, since one-tenth is that much smaller than one-eighth. In other cases a mere adjustment of decimal points was sufficient.

The twelve commodities, with the weight of each and the multiplier applied to the price changes of each, are:

	Weight	Multiplier
Wheat	19.5	16
Corn	8	11
Oats	5	13
Rye	4	5
Wool Tops	5.5	4
Cotton	23	10
Cottonseed Oil	4.5	4
Coffee	7	3
Sugar	8.5	27
Cocoa	5	5
Rubber	6	3
Hides	4	3

These are the essentials for calculating the spot index. However, the futures index requires one more set of unusual steps. That's because several times a year an actual quoted "future" disappears. For instance, while early in the year it is possible to buy wheat to be delivered in December, when the month of December actually arrives that "delivery" expires and is no longer quoted.

The result is that futures prices are affected not only by market conditions but also by how close the delivery date looms. Interest charges and other such factors influence them. On July 1, the December delivery is just five months off, but a month later it is only four months away, and a five-month delivery should not, in a precise index, be compared with a four-month delivery.

This problem is overcome by the use of two futures quotations for each commodity. They are combined to produce on each market day the calculated price that would apply to a delivery exactly five months off.

On the first day of July, only the December delivery is used, since it is just five months away and thus no adjustment need be made. On the second day, the two quotations used are those for the same December delivery and the one for May of the following year. The quoted price for December is adjusted by one day's proportion of the difference between it and May's quoted price. Since there are 151 days between December and May (except in leap years) the figure for one day's proportion is 1/151 of the price difference between the two. The resulting fraction is added to December's price, or subtracted from it, depending on whether May is quoted above or below December.

The following day 2/151 of the difference are added or subtracted, the third day 3/151 and so on until December 1, on which day only the May contract's price is used. On December 2, the combination used is May and July, and so on around the year.

To facilitate the work of calculating the futures index every hour of each business day and the spot index once a day, tables have been prepared—resembling somewhat tables of logarithms or bond yields—which give the figures arrived at by multiplying the various quotational units of each commodity by its factor or multiplier. For instance, the tables show the proper multiples for one-eighth, one-quarter, three-eighths, etc., when each is multiplied by each grain's factor or multiplier.

The commodity futures index is published once an hour and as of the close of commodity markets each day on the Dow Jones News Service, where also the spot index is published once daily. Both are published likewise in *The Wall Street Journal*.

Commodity Futures Trading Commission (CFTC)

Federal laws regulating commodity futures trading are enforced by the Commodity Futures Trading Commission. For information on commodity brokers call (202) 254-8630.

National Office

Commodity Futures Trading Commission
2033 K Street, NW
Washington, DC 20581
  Telephone: (202) 254-6387
  Fax: (202) 254-6265
  Public Information: (202) 254-8630

Regional Offices

Eastern Region
1 World Trade Center
New York, NY 10048
  Telephone: (212) 466-2071

Central Region
300 S. Riverside Plaza
Chicago, IL 60606
  Telephone: (312) 353-5990

Southwestern Region
4900 Main Street
Kansas City, MO 64112
  Telephone: (816) 370-3255

Minneapolis Office
510 Grain Exchange Building
Minneapolis, MN 55415
  Telephone: (612) 370-2025

Western Region
10900 Wilshire Boulevard
Los Angeles, CA 90024
  Telephone: (213) 209-6783

The Commodity Futures Trading Commission (CFTC), the Federal regulatory agency for futures trading, was established by the Commodity Futures Trading Commission Act of 1974 (88 Stat. 1389; 7 U.S.C. 4a), approved October 23, 1974. The Commission began operation in April 1975, and its authority to regulate futures trading was renewed by Congress in 1978, 1982, and 1986.

The CFTC consists of five Commissioners who are appointed by the President with the advice and consent of the Senate. One Commissioner is designated by the President to serve as Chairman. The Commissioners serve staggered 5-year terms, and by law no more than three Commissioners can belong to the same political party.

ACTIVITIES

The Commission regulates trading on the 13 U.S. futures exchanges, which offer active futures and options contracts. It also regulates the activities of numerous commodity exchange members, public brokerage houses (futures Commission merchants), Commission-registered futures industry salespeople and associated persons, trading advisers, and commodity pool operators. Some off-exchange transactions involving instruments similar in nature to futures contracts also fall under CFTC jurisdiction.

The Commission's regulatory and enforcement efforts are designed to ensure that the futures trading process is fair and that it protects both the rights of customers and the financial integrity of the marketplace. The CFTC approves the rules under which an exchange proposes to operate and monitors exchange enforcement of those rules. It reviews the terms of proposed futures contracts, and registers companies and individuals who handle customer funds or give trading advice. The Commission also protects the public by enforcing rules that require that customer funds be kept in bank accounts separate from accounts maintained by firms for their own use, and that such customer accounts be marked to present market value at the close of trading each day.

Futures contracts for agricultural commodities were traded in the United States for more than 100 years before futures trading was diversified to include trading in contracts for precious metals, raw materials, foreign currencies, financial instruments, commercial interest rates, and U.S. Government and mortgage securities. Contract diversification has grown in exchange trading in both traditional and newer commodities.

Futures and Securities Organizations

UNITED STATES

Chicago Futures/Options Society
200 E. Randolph
Chicago, IL 60675
  (312) 444-7810

Futures Industry Association, Inc.
2001 Pennsylvania Avenue, NW
Washington, DC 20006
  (202) 466-5460

Source: U.S. Government Manual and the Commodity Futures Trading Commission.

Futures Industry Institute
2001 Pennsylvania Avenue, NW
Washington, DC 20006
(202) 223-1528

Managed Futures Association
182 University Avenue
P.O. Box 761
Palo Alto, CA 94302
(415) 325-4533

Market Technicians Association Inc.
1 World Trade Center
New York, NY 10048
(212) 912-0995

**National Association of Securities
Dealers (NASD)**
1735 K Street, NW
Washington, DC 20006
(202) 728-8000

National Futures Association (NFA)
200 West Madison Street
Chicago, IL 60606
(312) 781-1300
(800) 621-3570

**National Option & Futures Society
Inc.**
170 Old Country Road
Mineola, NY 11501
(516) 739-3414

**North American Securities
Administrators Association,
Inc. (NASAA)**
1 Massachusetts Avenue, NW
Washington, DC 20004
(204) 737-0900

FOREIGN

Canada
**Investment Dealers Association
of Canada**
121 King Street West
Toronto, Ontario M5H 3T8
(416) 364-6133

France
**Association Professionnelle des
Intervenants sur les Marche a Terme**
Bourse du Commerce
2 rue de Viarmes
75001 Paris

Germany
German Futures Trading Association
Bockenheimer Landstrasse 92
D-60323 Frankfurt/M

Japan
**Federation of Bankers Associations
of Japan**
3-1 Marunouchi, 1-chome
Chiyoda-ku, Tokyo 100

Japan Securities Dealers Association
5-8 Kayabacho, 1-chome
Nihonbashi, Chuo-ku
Tokyo 103

Switzerland
**Swiss Commodities, Futures and
Options Association**
11 Route de Drize
P.O. Box 1181
CH-1227 Carouge/Geneva

United Kingdom
European Managed Futures Association
St. Katharine's Way
London E1 9UN

Futures and Options Association
Roman Wall House
1-2 Crutched Friars
London EC3N 2AN

INTERNATIONAL

**International Association of Financial
Engineers**
c/o St. John's University
Department of Finance
Jamaica, NY 11439
(718) 990-6161

**International Federation of Technical
Analysts**
P.O. Box 1347
New York, NY 10009
(212) 912-0995

**International Organization of Securities
Commissions**
800 Square Victoria
P.O. Box 171
Montreal, Quebec H4Z 1C8
(514) 875-8278

**International Swaps and Derivatives
Association, Inc.**
1270 Avenue of the Americas
New York, NY 10020
(212) 332-1200

**International Women's Futures
Association**
141 W. Jackson Boulevard
Chicago, IL 60604
(800) 686-5497

Futures and Options Exchanges

The following pages provide exchange and contract information for most of the world's futures and options exchanges, listed by country in alphabetical order. We have attempted to include every active futures contract in our listing. However, we may have overlooked a few new contracts, or some may be inactive or may not be listed for trading yet. (Because of space limitations, we did not include equity and index option contracts traded on the six U.S. options exchanges. Contact exchanges for specifications.) Details of all contracts are current, to the best of our knowledge, but any area is subject to change. If contract specifications are important to you, **verify our listing with your broker or the exchange.**

Here are further notes about each column:

Contract—The name of the contract is in bold-face type. Type in parentheses indicates whether it is a futures (F), options on futures (OF) or options (O) contract. Many contracts also include a ticker symbol in parentheses.

Contract months—In many cases, active months are the spot month and the next two or three months. Often, we abbreviate that to just "Next 3 months." Some contracts also have serial options, so there is trading in all months even though that may not be indicated.

Trading hourse—All trading periods listed are in local time. In most cases, the first number is a morning time and the last number an afternoon time, but in a day of 24-hour trading, that may not always hold.

Contract size—This is generally self-evident. On indexes, the size is typically the index value multiplied by the number indicated.

Minimum fluctuation—This is the minimum price change or tick value and the amount of money it represents.

Daily limit—Many exchanges do not have daily price limits so this column is not included for all exchanges. For those contracts that do have daily limits, the figure shown is the normal limit that prices can move up or down from the previous day's close. Many exchanges now have variable limit policies which can alter these limits in volatile periods. Also, spot or other nearby contracts often have no limits or have different limits than more distant months.

Date launched—First day or month or year contract was traded, according to the exchange—5-25-43 is May 25, 1943, for example.

Daily volume—The average daily volume for 1994, usually through the end of September. This figure, while not precise for the whole year, gives you an idea about the activity and liquidity of the contract relative to other contracts.

Source: Reprinted with permission of *Futures Magazine*, 219 Parkade, Cedar Falls, Iowa 50613. 319-277-6341.

FUTURES AND OPTIONS EXCHANGES

Australia

Australian Stock Exchange, Derivatives

A division of the Australian Stock Exchange Ltd.
20 Bond St., Sydney, NSW 2000, Australia. 61-2-227-0000; fax 61-2-251-5525
Michael Shepherd, chairman; David White, director, derivatives and marketing development

Contract	Contract months	Trading hours	Contract size	Minimum fluctuation	Date contract launched	Daily Volume
Equities (48 stocks) (O)	Various cycles out 9 months; some out to 3 years	10-12:15, 2-5 Overseas: 5-7	1,000 shares	$0.001	1976	34,000 (total)
Indexes (3 indexes) (O)	Quarterly	10-12:15, 2-5	$10 x index	$0.001	1992	200

Sydney Futures Exchange (SFE)

30-32 Grosvenor St., Sydney, NSW 2000, Australia. 61-2-256-0555; fax 61-2-256-0666
Leslie V. Hosking, chief executive; Bruce C. Hudson, chairman

Contract	Contract months	Trading hours	Contract size	Minimum fluctuation	Date contract launched	Daily volume
Wool (F) (Cash-settled) (WS)	Feb,Apr,Jun,Aug,Oct, Dec out 18 months	10:30-12:30, 2-4	2,500 kg	1¢/kg = A$25	5-11-60	19
90-Day Bank Bills* (F, OF) (IR)	Mar,Jun,Sep, Dec out 3 years	8:30-12:30, 2-4:30	A$500,000 face value	0.01% = A$12	F: 10-17-79 OF: 5-10-85	36,747 3,671
All-Ordinaries Share Price Index* (F, OF) (AO)	Mar,Jun,Sep, Dec out 18 months	9:50-4:10	A$25 x index	1.0 pt. = A$25	F: 2-16-83 OF: 6-18-85	10,855 3,489
3-Year Treasury Bonds* (F, OF) (YB)	Mar,Jun,Sep, Dec out 2 quarters	8:30-12:30, 2-4:30	A$100,000 (12% coupon)	0.01 pt. = A$28	F: 5-17-88 OF: 6-16-85	39,452 2,064
10-Year Treasury Bonds* (F, OF) (XB)	Mar,Jun,Sep, Dec out 2 quarters	8:30-12:30, 2-4:30	A$100,000 (12% coupon)	0.005% = A$44	F: 12-5-84 OF: 11-6-85	27,771 3,523
BHP Share Futures (F) (BP)	Mar,Jun,Sep, Dec out 6 months	9:50-4:10	1,000 shares	1¢ = A$10	5-16-94	104
NCP Share Futures (F) (ME)	Feb,May,Aug, Nov out 6 months	9:50-4:10	1,000 shares	1¢ = A$10	5-16-94	76
NAB Share Futures (F) (NB)	Jan,Apr,Jul, Oct out 6 months	9:50-4:10	1,000 shares	1¢ = A$10	5-16-94	53
WMC Share Futures (F) (MQ)	Mar,Jun,Sep, Dec out 6 months	9:50-4:10	1,022 shares	1¢ = A$10.22**	9-26-94	—
WBC Share Futures (F) (BC)	Jan,Apr,Jul, Oct out 6 months	9:50-4:10	1,000 shares	1¢ = A$10	9-26-94	—
MIM Share Futures (F) (IM)	Jan,Apr,Jul, Oct out 6 months	9:50-4:10	1,000 shares	1¢ = A$10	9-26-94	—
BTR Share Futures (F) (TR)	Mar,Jun,Sep, Dec out 6 months	9:50-4:10	1,000 shares	1¢ = A$10	9-26-94	—

*These contracts are also traded on SFE's overnight screen dealing system, SYCOM, which operates between 4:40 p.m. and 6 a.m. Approximately 10% of SFE turnover is traded on SYCOM.
** Tick size differs from other share futures contracts to be consistent with equity option market.

Austria

Austrian Futures & Options Exchange (OTOB)

Strauchgasse 1-3, P.O. Box 192, A-1014 Vienna, Austria. 43-1-531-65-0; fax 43-1-532-97-40
Christian Imo, CEO

Contract	Contract months	Trading hours	Contract size	Minimum fluctuation	Date contract launched	Daily volume
Equities (6 stocks) (O)	Next 3 months plus last month of next quarter	9-2	50 shares	Varies with price	10-4-91	5,156
Austrian Traded Index (ATX) (F, O)	Next 3 months plus last month of next quarter	9-2	ATS 100 x index	ATS 0.10 = ATS 10	8-7-92	F: 1,406 O: 4,650
Long-term Equity Options (LEOs)	June 1995, June 1996	9-2	ATS 100 x index	ATS 0.10 = ATS 10	6-20-94	57
Austrian Government Bonds (F)	Mar,Jun,Sep,Dec	9-4	ATS 1,000,000	0.01% of contract size = ATS 100	7-9-93	520

(continued)

FUTURES AND OPTIONS EXCHANGES (continued)

Belgium

Belgian Futures and Options Exchange (BELFOX)

Palais de la Bourse, Rue Henry Maus, 2, 1000 Brussels, Belgium. 32-2-512-80-40; fax 32-2-513-83-42
Remi Vermeiren, chairman

Contract	Contract months	Trading hours	Contract size	Minimum fluctuation	Daily Volume
Belgian Government Bonds (F, OF) (BGB, BGO)	Mar,Jun,Sep,Dec	8:30-5	BEF2,500,000 (9% coupon)	0.01 pt. = BEF250	3,074 434
Equities (8 stocks)	Mar,Jun,Sep,Dec	10-4:30	20-100 shares	BEF1	1,211
3-Month BIBOR (F) (BIB)	Mar,Jun,Sep,Dec	8:30-4:30	BEF25,000,000	0.01 pt. = BEF2,500	680
BEL 20 Index (F: BXF, O: BXO)	All months	F: 9:30-4:30 O: 10-4:30	F: 1,000 x Index in BEF O: 100 x Index in BEF	F: 0.10 pt. = BEF100 O: 0.01 pt. = BEF1	412 1,915

Brazil

Bolsa de Mercadorias & Futuros (BM&F)

The Commodities & Futures Exchange, Praca Antonio Prado, 48, Sao Paulo, SP, Brazil 01010-901. 55-11-232-5454; 55-11-239-3531
Manoel Pires da Costa, chairman; Dorival Rodrigues Alves, CEO

Contract	Contract months	Trading hours	Contract size	Minimum fluctuation	Date contract launched	Daily volume
Gold (F, O)	F: All months O: Jan,Mar,May,Jul,Sep,Nov	9:45-4	250 grams	R$0.001/gram = R$0.25	F: 3-14-86 O: 1-31-86	NA 30,485
Gold (F)	All months	9:45-4	1 kg	0.001 pt./gram = US$1	8-27-93	211
IBOVESPA Stock Index (F, OF)	Feb,Apr,Jun Aug,Oct,Dec	9:30-1, 3-4:30	R$0.20 x index	F: 5 pt. = R$1 OF: 1 pt. = R$0.20	F: 2-14-86 OF: 10-21-94	38,174 NA
1-Day Interbank Deposits* (F, OF)	All months	10-1, 3-4:45	R$50,000	F: 0.1 pt. = R$0.05 OF: 0.01 pt. = R$0.005	F: 6-5-91 OF: 10-21-94	110,708 NA
30-Day Interbank Deposits* (F)	All months	10-1, 3-4:45	R$50,000	0.1 pt. = R$0.05	6-5-91	NA
U.S. Dollar (Commercial) (F, O)	All months	10-4:45	US$10,000	R$0.001/US $1,000 = R$0.01	F: 4-23-87 O: 8-16-91	126,591 1,941
U.S. Dollar (Floating) (F, O)	All months	10-4:45	US$10,000	R$0.001/US $1,000 = R$0.01	F: 8-16-91 O: 8-16-91	393 NA
Coffee (Arabica) (F, OF)	F: Mar,May,Jul,Sep,Dec OF: Feb,Apr,Jun,Aug,Nov	10-3:30	100 60-kg bags	0.01 pt/bag = US$1	F: 8-3-89 OF: 9-20-91	344 13,797
Coffee (Robusta) (F)	Jan,Mar,May, Jul,Sep,Nov	10-3:30	100 60-kg. bags	0.05 pt/bag = US$5	3-20-92	NA
Live Cattle (F, OF)	F: Mar,May,Aug,Oct,Dec OF: Feb,Apr,Jul,Sep,Nov	3-4	330 net arrobas**	0.01 pt/15 kg = US$3.30	F: 6-7-91 OF: 7-22-94	17 217
Feeder Cattle (F)	All months	3-4	33 140-kg feeder steers	0.10 pt/steer = US$3.30	6-12-92	NA
Cotton (F)	Mar,Apr,May, Jul,Oct,Dec	11-11:45	28,108.65 lb. (12,750 kg)	0.01 pt./lb = US$281.0865	9-27-91	NA
Soybeans (F)	Jan,Mar,Apr,May, Jul,Aug,Sep,Nov	10:30-3:15	30 metric tons	0.01pt./bag = US$5	7-16-93	NA
Interest Rate Swaps	Minimum of 2, maximum of 730 days	12-6	R$40,000 (minimum final value)	—	3-22-93	26,949
Exchange Rate Swaps	Minimum of 2, maximum of 730 days	12-6	R$40,000 (minimum final value)	—	12-3-93	683
Interest Rate x Exchange Rate Swaps	Minimum of 2, maximum of 730 days	12-6	R$40,000 (minimum final value)	—	12-3-93	17,844
Interest Rate x Gold Swaps	Minimum of 2, maximum of 730 days	12-6	R$40,000 (minimum final value)	—	6-17-94	3
Interest Rate x Reference Rate Swaps	Minimum of 2, maximum of 730 days	12-6	R$40,000 (minimum final value)	—	6-17-94	465

BM&F also trades spot and forward contracts on10-gram gold and spot contracts on 0.225-gram gold.
* Average interest rate calculated by Cetip (Central of Custody and Cash Settlement of Certificates and Bonds).
**R$= Brazilian Real; 1 arroba = 15 kg.

Canada

Montreal Exchange (ME)

The Stock Exchange Tower, 800, Square Victoria, C.P. 61, Montreal, Quebec H4Z 1A9 Canada. (514) 871-2424; fax (514) 871-3531
Claude Bedard, chairman; Gerald A. Lacoste, president and CEO

Contract	Contract months	Trading hours	Contract size	Minimum fluctuation	Daily limit	Date contract launched	Daily volume
1-Month Canadian Bankers' Acceptance (F) (BAR)	First 6 months	8:20-3	C$3,000,000 face value	0.01% = C$25	—	4-16-92	34
3-Month Canadian Bankers' Acceptance (F, OF) (BAX, OBX)	Mar,Jun,Sep,Dec over 2 years	8:20-3	C$1,000,000 face value	0.01% = C$25	—	F: 4-22-88 OF: 4-7-94	7,087 140
10-Year Government of Canada Bond (F: CGB; OF: OGB)	F: Mar,Jun,Sep, Dec over 2 years OF: Monthly	8:20-3	C$100,000	0.01% = C$10	F: 3 pt. = C$3,000	F: 9-15-89 OF: 3-20-91	6,168 41
Government of Canada Bond (O: OBA, OBK, OBV)	3 months plus two in Mar,Jun,Sep, Dec cycle	8:20-4	C$25,000	0.01% of C$100 value		1982	236
Equities (O) (24 stocks)	At least 3 months	9:30-4	100 shares	*	—	1975	2,140
LEAPs (O) (6 stocks)	Expire in Jan. for up to 2 years, 8 mos.	9:30-4	100 shares	*	—	9-21-92	175
PEACs & SPECs (11 stocks)	Original term: 5 years One expiration per stock	9:30-4	1 share	*	—	12-3-92	41,487

*For prices under C$0.10, 0.01; from C$0.10 to C$5, 0.05; over C$5, 0.125.

Toronto Futures Exchange (TFE)

2 First Canadian Place, The Exchange Tower, Toronto, Ontario M5X 1J2 Canada. (416) 947-4487; fax (416) 947-4272
Henry Kneis, chairman; Jim Gallagher, president

Contract	Contract months	Trading hours	Contract size	Minimum fluctuation	Daily limit	Date contract launched	Daily volume
Toronto 35 Stock Index (F) (TXF)	Mar,Jun,Sep,Dec and next 2 months	9:15-4:15	100 x index	0.02 pt. = C$10	13.5 pt. = C$6,750	5-27-87	425
Toronto 100 Stock Index (F) (TOP)	Mar,Jun,Sep,Dec and next 2 months	9:15-4:15	100 x index	0.02 pt. = C$10	16.5 pt. = C$8,250	5-94	42
Silver (O) (SVR)	Next 3 months	9:05-4	100 oz.	Under $5: 25¢ $5-$15: 50¢	—	1-1-83	38

Toronto Stock Exchange (TSE)

2 First Canadian Place, The Exchange Tower, Toronto, Ontario M5X 1J2 Canada. (416) 947-4700; (416) 947-4662
Fred Ketchen, chairman; J. Pearce Bunting, president

Contract	Contract months	Trading hours	Contract size	Minimum fluctuation	Date contract launched	Daily volume
Toronto 35 Index (O) (TXO)	Mar,Jun,Sep,Dec and next 2 months	9:30-4:15	100 x index	Under C10¢, C1¢; C10¢-C$5, C5¢; C$5 and above, C12.5¢	5-27-87	1,021
Toronto 100 Index (O) (TOP)	Mar,Jun,Sep,Dec and next 2 months	9:30-4:15	100 x index	Under C10¢, C1¢ C10¢-C$5, C5¢; C$5 and above, C12.5¢	5-94	42
Toronto 35 Index Participation Units (Units and O) (TIP)	Units: do not expire O: Mar,Jun,Sep, Dec and next 2 months	9:30-4	100 units	Units: C$0.05 O: Under C10¢, C1¢; above C10¢, C5¢	Units: 3-9-90 O: 9-30-91	245,000
LEAPs (O) (10 stocks)	Up to 2 years, Jan. expiration	9:30-4	100 shares	—	9-92	265
Equities (O) (35 stocks)	At least next 6 months	9:30-4	100 shares	—	1975	4,512

Vancouver Stock Exchange (VSE)

609 Granville St., Stock Exchange Tower, Vancouver, B.C., V7Y 1H1 Canada. (604) 689-3334; fax (604) 688-6051
S.R. Sherwood, chairman; D.J. Hudson, president

Contract	Contract months	Trading hours	Contract size	Minimum fluctuation
TCO Equities (O) (24 classes)	One of seven expiry cycles	6:30-1	100 shares	Under C10¢, C1¢; C10¢-C$5, C5¢; C$5-C$35, C12.5¢; C$35 and above, C25¢
TCO Gold (O)	Feb,May,Aug,Nov	6:30-1	10 troy oz.	C$0.10/oz. = C$1

(continued)

FUTURES AND OPTIONS EXCHANGES *(continued)*

The Winnipeg Commodity Exchange (WCE)

500 Commodity Exchange Tower, 360 Main St., Winnipeg, Manitoba R3C 3Z4 Canada. (204) 925-5000; fax (204) 943-5448
B. Hayward, chairman; F. V. Siemens, president

Contract	Contract months	Trading hours	Contract size	Minimum fluctuation	Daily limit	Date contract launched	Daily volume*
Western Domestic Feed Barley (F, OF) (AB)	Feb,May,Aug,Nov	9:30-1:15	20 metric tons	C10¢/ton = C$2	C$5/ton = C$100	F: 1989 OF: 1993	317 5
Canola (F, OF) (RS)	Jan,Mar,Jun, Aug,Sep,Nov	F: 9:30-1:15 OF: 9:30-1:20	20/100 metric tons*	C10¢/ton = C$2/C$10	C$10/ton = C$200/$1,000	F: 1963 OF: 1991	4,652 283
Flaxseed (F, OF) (F)	Mar,May,Jul, Oct,Dec	9:30-1:15	20/100 metric tons*	C10¢/ton = C$2/C$10	C$10/ton = C$200/C$1,000	F: 1904 OF: 1993	387 7
Oats (F) (O)	Mar,May,Jul, Oct,Dec	9:30-1:15	20/100 metric tons*	C10¢/ton = C$2/C$10	C$5/ton = C$100/C$500	1904	215
Rye (F) (R)	Mar,May,Jul, Sep,Dec	9:30-1:15	20/100 metric tons*	C10¢/ton = C$2/C$10	C$5/ton = C$100/C$500	1917	12
Domestic Feed Wheat (F, OF) (W)	Mar,May,Jul, Oct,Dec	9:30-1:15	20/100 metric tons*	C10¢/ton = C$2/C$10	C$5/ton = C$100/C$500	F: 1974 OF: 1992	852 13
Canadian Domestic Feed Barley (F, OF) (BY)	Mar, May, Jul, Sep, Dec	8:30-1:15	20/100 metric tons	C10¢/ton = C$2/C$10	C$5/ton	F: 1993 OF: 1993	91 0

*Trading is in 20-ton job lots and 100-ton board lots; volume figure is based on 20-ton units of trading.

Chile

Santiago Stock Exchange

La Bolsa 64, Casilla 123-D, Santiago, Chile. 56-2-698-2001, 56-2-695-8077; fax 56-2-672-8046
Pablo Irarrázaval Valdés, president

Contract	Contract months	Trading hours	Contract size	Minimum fluctuation	Date contract launched	Daily volume
IPSA Index (F)	All months	9:30-1:20	2,000 x index	0.01 pt.	4-91	NA
U.S. Dollar (F)	Jan,Mar,May, Jul,Sep,Nov	9:30-1:20	US$10,000	US0.10	12-90	NA
Equities (O)	Next 2 months plus 2 from quarterly cycle	9:30-4:30	1 share	—	8-94	NA

China

Beijing Commodity Exchange (BCE)

311 Chonyun Building, No. 8 Beichen East Road, Chaoyang District, Beijing 100101 China. 86-1-492-4956, 86-1-492-6688,
fax 86-1-499-3365, 86-1-493-3183.
Qiao Gang, board chairman; Wu Xiaoqiang, president

Contract	Contract months	Trading hours	Contract size	Minimum fluctuation	Daily limit	Daily volume
Soybeans (F)	Jan,Mar,May, Jul,Sep,Nov	9-11:50, 1-2	10 tons	1 yuan/ton = 10 yuan	1,000 yuan	70
Soybean meal (F)	All months	9-11:50, 1-2	10 tons	1 yuan/ton = 10 yuan	800 yuan	878
Corn (F)	Jan,Mar,May, Jul,Sep,Nov	9-11:50, 1:30-2	10 tons	1 yuan/ton = 10 yuan	400 yuan	NA
Aluminum (F)	All months	10-11:50, 2:20-3	25 tons	10 yuan/ton	5% of settlement price	NA
Plywood (F)	All months	9-11:50, 1:30-3	400 pieces	2 yuan/100 pieces = 8 yuan	800 yuan	NA
T-bonds (F)	Mar,Jun,Sep,Dec	9-11:50, 1:30-3	10,000 yuan	0.02 yuan/100 yuan	200 yuan	46,496
Copper (F)	All months	9-11:50, 1:30-2	25 tons	10 yuan/ton	5% of settlement price	NA
Wheat (F)	Jan,Mar,May, Jul,Sep,Nov	*	10 tons	1 yuan/ton = 10 yuan	500 yuan	NA
Peanuts (F)	Jan,Mar,May, Jul,Sep,Nov	*	10 tons	2 yuan/ton = 20 yuan	1,500 yuan	NA
Green beans, Red beans (F)	Jan,Mar,May, Jul,Sep,Nov	9-11:50, 1:30-3	10 tons	2 yuan/ton = 20 yuan	1,200 yuan	26,745
Polypropylene (F)	All months	1:30-2	10 tons	8 yuan/ton = 80 yuan	2,500 yuan	NA
Sodium Carbonate (F)	All months	9-11:50	10 tons	2 yuan/ton = 20 yuan	600 yuan	NA

*Check with exchange.

Denmark

FUTOP Market — Copenhagen Stock Exchange and the FUTOP Clearing Centre

Copenhagen Stock Exchange, Nikolaj Plads 6, Box 1040, DK-1007 Copenhagen, Denmark. 45-33-93-3366; fax 45-33-12-8613
Sven Caspersen, chairman; Bent Mebus, president

Contract	Contract months	Trading hours	Contract size	Minimum fluctuation	Date contract launched	Daily volume
Danish Government Bonds:						
7% 2004 (F,OF)	Mar,Jun,Sep,Dec	9-3:30	DKK1 million	0.02 pt. = DKK200	9-94	NA
8% 2003 (F,OF)	Mar,Jun,Sep,Dec	9-3:30	DKK1 million	0.02 pt. = DKK200	10-92	F: 2,269 OF: 423
9% 1998 (F)	Mar,Jun,Sep,Dec	9-3:30	DKK1 million	0.05 pt. = DKK500	10-92	621
Mortgage Credit Bonds 6% 2026 (F)	Mar,Jun,Sep,Dec	9-3:30	DKK1 million	0.05 pt. = DKK500	10-93	921
KFX Stock Index (F, OF)	Mar,Jun,Sep,Dec	9-3:30	DKK1 million	0.05 pt. = DKK50	12-89	F: 2,070 OF: 419
Equities (O) (6 stocks)	Mar,Jun,Sep,Dec	9-3:30	100 shares	0.10 pt. = DKK10	12-90	573
3-month CIBOR (F)	Mar,Jun,Sep,Dec	9-3:30	DKK5 million	0.01 pt. = DKK125	9-93	215

Finland

Finnish Options Exchange Ltd.

Erottajankatu 11, SF-00130, Helsinki, Finland. 358-0-601-499; fax 358-0-604-442
Anders Lindeberg, president; Jaakko Soini, vice president, trading

Contract	Contract months	Trading hours	Contract size	Minimum fluctuation	Date contract launched	Daily volume
USD/FIM (O, F)	Every month	10-4	$40,000	FIM0.0001	1989	NA
DEM/FIM (O, F)	Every month	10-4	DM100,000	FIM0.0001	1991	NA
SEK/FIM (O, F)	Every month	10-4	SEK100,000	FIM0.0001	1992	NA
GBP/FIM (O, F)	Every month	10-4	£25,000	FIM0.0001	1993	NA
EEK/FIM (O, F)	Every month	10-4	EEK100,000	FIM0.0001	1993	NA
USDFIM (RS: O, F)	Every month	10-4	$100,000	FIM0.0001	1994	NA
DEMFIM (RS: O, F)	Every month	10-4	DM100,000	FIM0.0001	1994	NA
USDDEM (RS: O, F)	Every month	10-4	$100,000	DM0.0001	1994	NA
DEMEEK (RS: O, F)	Every month	10-4	DM100,000	EEK0.01	1994	NA
3-month Helibor (Forwards)	Mar,Jun,Sep,Dec	10-4	FIM1 million	0.01%	1992	NA
Finnish Government Bond futures:						
11% 1997 (forwards)	Sep,Dec	10-4	FIM1 million	0.01%	1994	NA
9.5% 2004 (forwards)	Sep,Dec	10-4	FIM1 million	0.01%	1994	NA

SOM Finnish Securities and Derivatives Exchange Clearing House

Keskuskatu 7, P.O. Box 926, FIN-00101 Helsinki, Finland. 358-0-13-12-11; fax 358-0-13-12-12-11
Asko Schrey, president; Matti Byman, PR/information

Contract	Contract months	Trading hours	Contract size	Minimum fluctuation	Date contract launched	Daily volume
Finnish Options Index (FOX) (F, O)	Feb,Apr,Jun, Aug,Oct,Dec	10-4	FIM100 x index	F: 0.25 pt. = FIM25; O: Varies*	5-2-88	F: 259 O: 1,640
GBP/FIM (GBP) (F, O)	Mar,Jun,Sep,Dec	10-4	£10,000	0.05 = FIM5	10-26-92	@
SEK/FIM (SEK) (F, O)	Mar,Jun,Sep,Dec	10-4	SEK10,000	0.05 = FIM5	10-26-92	@
DEM/FIM (DEM) (F, O)	Mar, Jun,Sep,Dec	10-4	DM10,000	0.05 = FIM5	10-26-92	@
USD/FIM (USD) (F, O)	Mar,Jun,Sep,Dec	10-4	$10,000	0.05 = FIM5	10-26-92	@
STOX Stock Options (F: 21 stocks, O: 11 stocks)	Mar,Jun,Sep,Dec	10-4	100 shares	Varies**	F: 10-15-90 O: 10-1-93	F: 880 O: 786
Finnish Government Bonds (F)	Mar,Jun,Sep,Dec	10-4	FIM1 million	0.01	1-21-94	277
HBR03 Interest Rates (F)	Mar,Jun,Sep,Dec	10-4	FIM1 million (nominal value)	0.01	1993	NA

* If quote >10.00, 0.10 pt = FIM10. If quote is 10.00-30.00, 0.25 pt. = FIM25. If quote is 30.00 or more, 0.50 pt. = FIM50.
** Futures: If quote < 100, 0.10 pt = FIM10; If quote is 100 or greater, 0.25 pt. = FIM25. Options: If quote < 3.00, 0.10 pt. = FIM10; if 3.00 or greater, 0.25 = FIM25.
@ Combined average daily volume of four currencies is 79.

(continued)

FUTURES AND OPTIONS EXCHANGES *(continued)*

France

Marche a Terme International de France (MATIF)

176 rue Montmartre, 75002 Paris, France. 33-1-40-28-82-82; fax 33-1-40-28-80-01, Telex: 218-362
Gerard Pfauwadel, president; Gilbert Durieux, chief executive

Contract	Contract months	Trading hours	Contract size	Minimum fluctuation	Date contract launched	Daily volume
Long-Term Notional Bond (F, OF) (NNN)**	Mar,Jun,Sep,Dec	9-4:30	FF500,000	F: 0.02% = FF100 OF: 0.01% = FF50	2-86 1-88	225,313 84,111
3-Month PIBOR (F, OF) (PIB)**	Mar,Jun,Sep,Dec	8:30-4	FF5,000,000	F: 0.01% = FF125 OF: 0.005% = FF62.5	9-88 3-90	56,462 15,556
ECU Bond (F) (ECU)**	Mar,Jun,Sep,Dec	9-4:30	100,000 XEU	0.02% = 20 XEU	10-90	2,574
CAC 40 Stock Index (F) (CAC)**	Mar,Jun,Sep,Dec and next two months	10-5	FF200 x index	0.5 pt. = FF100	11-88	30,910
White Sugar (F) (SUC)	Mar,May,Aug, Oct,Dec	10:45-1, 3-7	50 metric tons in bags	US10¢/ton = US$5	5-64*	1,161
Potatoes (F) (PDT)	Nov,Feb,Apr,May	10:30-12:45, 2-4	20 metric tons in bags on pallets	FF0.25/100 kg. = FF50	11-87	100
French Treasury Bond (F) (FLT)	Mar,Jun,Sep,Dec	9-4:30	FF500,000	0.02% = FF100	1-93	0
French Medium-Term Bond (F) (FMT)	Mar,Jun,Sep,Dec	9-4:30	FF500,000	0.01% = FF50	6-93	0

* The sugar contract existed prior to the establishment of MATIF. As a MATIF contract since 1988, it is cleared by the Banque Centrale de Compensation, a MATIF subsidiary.
** Also trades on GLOBEX.

Marche des Options Negociables de Paris (MONEP)

S.C.M.C., 39, rue Cambon, 75001 Paris, France. 33-1-49-27-18-00; fax 33-1-49-27-18-23, Telex: 214 538 F
Alain Morice, chairman

Contract	Contract months	Trading hours	Contract size	Minimum fluctuation	Date contract launched	Daily volume
CAC 40 Stock Index (O) (PX1)	Mar,Jun,Sep,Dec and next 2 months	10-5	FF200 x index	FF0.01/pt. = FF2	11-3-88	11,344
Long-Term CAC 40 Stock Index (O) (PXL)	Mar,Sep up to 2 years	10-5	FF50 x index	FF0.01/pt. = FF0.50	10-17-91	12,496
Equities (O) (44 stocks*)	Mar,Jun,Sep,Dec	10-5	20-500 shares (mostly 100)	FF0.01	9-10-87	11,881

* Includes 12 equity options traded on the "Fixing Group," i.e. through a fixing procedure on the STAMP electronic system.

Germany

DTB Deutsche Terminboerse (Deutsche Boerse AG)

Postal address: 60284 Frankfurt, Street address: Boersenplatz 7-11, 60313 Frankfurt, Germany. 49-69-2101-0; fax 49-69-29977-455,
Telex: 4175 953 dtb d   Gerhard Eberstadt, chairman; Joerg Franke, general manager

Contract	Contract months	Trading hours	Contract size	Minimum fluctuation	Date contract launched	Daily volume
Long-Term Bund (Bund: 8.5-10 years) (F, OF)	F: Mar,Jun,Sep,Dec OF: Feb,May,Aug,Nov	8-5:30	DM250,000 (6% coupon)	0.01 pt. = DM25	F: 11-23-90 OF: 8-16-91	63,440 1,235
Medium-Term Bund (Bobl: 3.5-5 years) (F, OF)	F: Mar,Jun,Sep,Dec OF: Feb,May,Aug,Nov	8-5:30	DM250,000 (6% coupon)	0.01 pt. = DM25	F: 10-4-91 OF: 1-15-93	26,633 225
Extra Long-Term Bund (F) (Buxl: 15-30 years)	Mar,Jun,Sep,Dec	8-5:30	DM250,000 (6% coupon)	0.01 pt. = DM25	3-11-94	787
German Stock Index (DAX) (F, O, OF)	F: Mar,Jun,Sep,Dec O, OF: Next 3 mos. and next 2 mos. of March cycle	9:30-4	F, OF: DM100 x index O: DM10 x index	F: 0.5 pt. = DM50 O: 0.1 pt. = DM1 OF: 0.1 pt. = DM10	F: 11-23-90 O: 8-16-91 OF: 1-24-92	22,306 97,809 203
Equities (O) (16 stocks)	Mar,Jun,Sep,Dec and next 3 months	9:30-4	50 shares	DM0.1 = DM5	1-26-90	42,170
FIBOR (F)	Mar,Jun,Sep,Dec and next 3 months	8:45-5:15	DM1 million	0.01% = DM25	3-18-94	3,324

Hong Kong

Hong Kong Futures Exchange Ltd. (HKFE)

5/F, Asia Pacific Finance Tower, Citibank Plaza, 3 Garden Road, Hong Kong. 852-842-9333; fax 852-810-5089
Ka Chai Leong, chairman; Ivers W. Riley, CEO

Contract	Contract months	Trading hours	Contract size	Minimum fluctuation	Date contract launched	Daily volume*
Gold (F) (HGF)	Feb,Apr,Jun,Aug,Oct,Dec, spot and next 2 months	9-12, 2:30-5:30	100 troy oz.	US10¢/oz. = US$10	8-19-80	4
Hang Seng Stock Index (F, O) (HSI)	Mar,Jun,Sep,Dec, spot and next month	10-2:30, 2:30-4	HK$50 x index	1 index pt. = HK$50	F: 5-6-86 O: 3-5-93	14,500 2,191
3-Month Hong Kong Interbank Offered Rate (HIBOR) (F) (HBR)	Mar,Jun,Sep,Dec up to two years out	9-3:30	HK$1 million	1 pt. = HK$25	2-7-90	0

* Average trading volume from September 1993 to Aug. 31, 1994.

Hungary

Budapest Commodity Exchange

H-1373, P.O. Box 495, 1134 Budapest. 36-1-269-8571, fax 36-1-269-8575
Szergej Keresztesi, president, CEO

Contract	Contract months	Trading hours	Contract size	Minimum fluctuation	Date contract launched	Volume@
Corn (F)	Mar,May,Jul, Sep,Oct,Nov,Dec	10-11:30*	20 metric tons	HUF400/ton = HUF8,000	1989	9,262
Milling Wheat (F)	Jan,Mar,May,Jul, Aug,Sep,Oct,Dec	10-11:30*	20 metric tons	HUF400/ton = HUF8,000	1989	16,242
Feed Wheat (F)	Jan,Mar,May,Jul, Aug,Sep,Oct,Dec	10-11:30*	20 metric tons	HUF400/ton = HUF8,000	1989	1,508
Feed Barley (F)	Mar,May,Jun,Jul, Aug,Sep,Oct,Dec	10-11:30*	20 metric tons	HUF400/ton = HUF8,000	1989	1,508
Black Seed (F)	Mar,May,Sep, Oct,Dec	10-11:30*	20 metric tons	HUF400/ton = HUF8,000	1989	1,779
BL-55 Wheat Flour (F)	Monthly	10-11:30 *	5 metric tons	HUF1,000/ton = HUF5,000	1989	0
Live Hog No. 1 (F)	Monthly	10:30-11:30 **	5,000 kg.	HUF5/kg. = HUF25,000	1991	249
Live Hog No. 2 (F)	Monthly	10:30-11:30 **	5,000 kg.	HUF5/kg. = HUF25,000	1991	42
Deutsche Mark (F) (DEM)	Mar,Jun,Sep,Dec plus 3 mos.	Weekdays, 10:30-11:30	DM1,000	HUF0.01/DM = HUF10	1993	102,758
U.S. Dollar (F) (USD)	Mar,Jun,Sep,Dec plus 3 mos.	Weekdays, 10:30-11:30	US$1,000	HUF0.01/US$ = HUF10	1993	103,576
Yen (F)	Mar,Jun,Sep,Dec plus 3 mos.	Weekdays, 10:30-11:30	¥5 million	HUF0.01/¥100 = HUF500	1994	54
Interest Rates (F)	Mar,Jun,Sep,Dec plus 3 mos.	Weekdays, 10-10:30	3-mo. HUF1 million deposit	1/16%	10-24-94	110

* Trading takes place on Tuesdays, Wednesdays and Thursdays.
** Trading takes place on Tuesdays and Thursdays.
@ Total volume in lots through September 1994.

Budapest Stock Exchange

H-1052 Budapest, Deák F. u. 5. Hungary. 36-1-266-1258; 36-1-117-5226, fax 36-1-118-1737
Jozsef Rotyis, chief executive; Lajos Bokros, president

Contract	Contract months	Trading hours	Contract size	Minimum fluctuation	Date contract launched	Daily Volume
U.S. Dollar/ HUF (F) (USD)	Mar,Jun,Sep,Dec plus next 2 months	11-2	10,000 $/HUF	HUF0.01/$	*	—
Deutsche mark/ HUF (F) (DEM)	Mar,Jun,Sep,Dec plus next 2 months	11-2	20,000 DM/HUF	HUF0.01/DM	*	—
Budapest Stock Exchange Index (F) (BUX)	Mar,Jun,Sep,Dec	11-2	HUF100 x index	60 pt. = HUF6,000	*	—
Short-term Treasury Bills (F) (DWIX)	Mar,Jun,Sep,Dec	11-2	HUF250,000	None*	*	—

* Pending at press time. Check with exchange.

(continued)

FUTURES AND OPTIONS EXCHANGES *(continued)*

Ireland

Irish Futures & Options Exchange (IFOX)

Segrave House, Earlsfort Tce., Dublin 2, Ireland. 353-1-676-7413; fax 353-1-661-4645
Fergus Sheridan, chairman; Michael Whelan, managing director

Contract	Contract months	Trading hours	Contract size	Minimum fluctuation	Date contract launched	Daily volume
Long Gilt (F) (ILG)	Mar,Jun,Sep,Dec	8:30-4:15*	IR£50,000	IR£5	5-89	40
Short Gilt (F) (SGT)	Mar,Jun,Sep,Dec	8:30-4:15*	IR£100,000	IR£10	9-91	1
3-Month Interest Rate (F) (DIB)	Mar,Jun,Sep,Dec	8:30-4:15*	IR£500,000	IR£12.50	5-89	16
ISEQ Index (F) (ISQ)	Mar,Jun,Sep,Dec	8:30-4:15*	IR£10 x index	IR£1	1-90	0

*All contracts have a late trading session from 4:17 to 5:15.

Israel

The Tel Aviv Stock Exchange Ltd. (TASE)

54 Ahad Haam St., Tel Aviv, 65202, Israel. 972-3-567-7411; fax 972-3-510-5379, 972-3-566-1822
Haim Stoessel, chairman; Saul Bronfeld, managing director

Contract	Contract months	Trading hours*	Contract size	Minimum fluctuation	Date contract launched	Daily volume
MAOF-25 Index (O)	2 and 4 months out (odd months)	11-4	100 x index	0.01 = 1 shekel	8-1-93	28,000
U.S. Dollar Exchange Rates (O)	2 and 4 months out (even months)	10:30-11, 4-4:30	10,000 x exchange rate	0.01 = 1 shekel	1-4-94	500

* Trading days are Sunday through Thursday.

Italy

Italian Stock Exchange

Piazza degli Affari, 6, 20123, Milan, Italy. 39-2-724-261, fax 39-2-864-64-323
Benito Boschetto, CEO; Attilio Ventura, president

Contract	Contract months	Trading hours	Contract size	Minimum fluctuation	Date contract launched	Daily volume
MIB 30 Index (F) (MIB30)	Mar,Jun,Sep,Dec	9:30-5:30	ItL100 million	1 index pt.	12-2-94	—

Japan

Kansai Agricultural Commodities Exchange (KANEX)

1-10-14 Awaza, Nishi-ku, Osaka 550, Japan. 81-6-531-7931; fax 81-6-541-9343
Kazuo Shimazaki, president; Eiji Kugano, executive director

Contract	Contract months	Trading hours	Contract size	Minimum fluctuation	Date contract launched	Daily volume
Red Beans (F)	All months	9, 10, 11, 1, 2, 3	2,400 kg.	¥10/30 kg.	10-6-52	14,370
Imported Soybeans (F)	Feb,Apr,Jun, Aug,Oct,Dec	10, 11, 1, 2, 3	30 metric tons	¥10/ton	12-6-76	4,518
Raw Sugar (F, OF)	Jan, Mar, May, Jul, Sep, Nov	F: 9:10, 10:20, 12:50, 1:50, 2:50 OF: 9:30-11:30, 1:30-3:10	50 metric tons	F: ¥0.10/kg. OF: ¥0.05/ kg.*	F: 4-52 OF: 10-91	1,222 323
Refined Sugar (F)	Next 6 months	9:10, 10:20,1:10, 1:50, 2:50	9 metric tons	¥0.10	4-52	12

* Changes to ¥10 per metric ton from the March 1996 contract, therefore: F: ¥10 (1,000 kg), OF: ¥5 (1,000 kg)

Kobe Raw Silk Exchange (KSE)

126 Higashimachi, Chuo-ku, Kobe 650, Japan. 81-78-331-7141; fax 81-78-331-7145
Kan Nanba, president; Haruo Miyairi, managing director

Contract	Contract months	Trading hours	Contract size	Minimum fluctuation	Daily limit	Date contract launched	Daily volume
Raw Silk (F)	Next 6 months	9:15, 11:20, 1:15, 2:50	150 kg.	¥1/kg.	¥200	5-14-51	2,802

Kobe Rubber Exchange (KRE)

49 Harima-cho, Chuo-ku, Kobe 650, Japan. 81-78-331-4211; fax 81-78-332-1622
Takeshi Ohira, chairman; Keiichiro Hayashi, managing director

Contract	Contract months	Trading hours	Contract size	Minimum fluctuation	Date contract launched	Daily volume*
Natural Rubber (F)	Current month, and succeeding 5 months	9:30, 10:30, 1:30, 2:30, 3:30, 5	5,000 kg.	¥0.1	1-16-52	5,183

* 1993 figure.

Nagoya Stock Exchange (NSE)

3-17 Sakae, 3-chome, Naka-ku, Nagoya 460, Japan. 81-52-262-3172; fax 81-52-241-1527.
Yukihiko Satomi, general affairs division

Contract	Contract months	Trading hours	Contract size	Minimum fluctuation	Date contract launched	Daily volume
Option 25 Index (O)	Next 4 months	9-11, 12:30-3:10	¥10,000 x index	Below 100: 0.5 pt. = ¥5,000 Above 100: 1 pt. = ¥10,000	10-17-89	651

Nagoya Textile Exchange

2-15, Nishiki 3 Chome, Nakaku, Nagoya 460, Japan. 81-52-951-2171; fax 81-52-961-6407
Hanshichi Toyoshima, president

Contract	Contract months	Trading hours	Contract size	Minimum fluctuation	Date contract launched	Daily volume
Cotton Yarn (F)	Next 6 months	9:20-10:30, 1:10-2:20	4,000 lb.	¥0.1/lb.	9-51	5,023
Wool Yarn (F)	Next 6 months	9:40-10:50, 1:30-2:40	500 kg.	¥1/kg.	10-51	483
Staple Fiber Yarn (F)	Next 6 months	9:55-11:05, 1:55-3	5,000 lb.	¥0.1/lb.	2-51	59

Osaka Securities Exchange (OSE)

8-16, Kitahama, 1-chome, Chuo-ku, Osaka 541, Japan. 81-6-229-8643; fax 81-6-231-2639
Kyoji Kitamura, president

Contract	Contract months	Trading hours	Contract size	Minimum fluctuation	Date contract launched	Daily volume
Nikkei 225 Stock Average (F, O)	F: Mar,Jun,Sep,Dec O: Next 4 months	9-11 12:30-3	¥1,000 x average	F: ¥10 O: Below ¥1,000, ¥5; above ¥1,000, ¥10	F: 9-3-88 O: 6-12-89	F: 24,338 O: 17,390
Nikkei 300 Stock Average (F, O)	F: Mar,Jun,Sep,Dec O: Mar,Jun,Sep,Dec plus 2 near-term mos.	9-11 12:30-3:15	¥10,000 x index	0.10 pt. = ¥1,000	2-14-94	F: 22,390 O: 1,493

Osaka Textile Exchange

2-5-28 Kyutaro-machi, Chuo-ku, Osaka 541, Japan. 81-6-253-0031; fax 81-6-253-0034
Hiroshi Sugiura, chairman; Khoji Murata, vice chairman

Contract	Contract months	Trading hours	Contract size	Minimum fluctuation	Date contracct launched	Daily volume
Cotton Yarn (20s, 30s, 40s) (F)	Next 6 months	9:45, 10:45, 1:45, 2:45	20s, 30s: 2,000 lb. 40s: 4,000 lb.	¥0.1/lb.	6-11-51	20s: 2,635 30s: NA 40s: 2,336
Staple Fiber Yarn (F)	Next 6 months	9:45, 10:45, 1:45, 2:45	5,000 lb.	¥0.1/lb.	11-1-50	24
Woolen Yarn (F)	Next 6 months	9:20, 11:20, 2:20, 3:20	500 kg.	¥1/kg.	7-1-53	2,133

(continued)

FUTURES AND OPTIONS EXCHANGES *(continued)*

Tokyo Commodity Exchange (TOCOM)

10-8 Nihonbashi Horidomecho, 1-chome, Chuo-ku, Tokyo 103, Japan. 81-3-3661-9191; fax 81-3-3661-7568
Naozo Mabuchi, chairman; Masahiro Omura, senior managing director

Contract	Contract months	Trading hours	Contract size	Minimum fluctuation	Date contract launched	Daily volume
Gold (F)	Current or next odd month; all even months	9-11, 1-3:30	1 kg.	¥1/gram	3-23-82	56,586
Silver (F)	"	9-11, 1-3:30	30 kg.	¥0.1/10 grams	1-26-84	4,620
Platinum (F)	"	9-11, 1-3:30	500 grams	¥1/gram	1-26-84	20,469
Palladium (F)	"	9-11, 1-3:30	1.5 kg.	¥1/gram	8-3-92	3,302
Rubber (F)	Next 6 months	9:45, 10:45, 1:45, 2:45, 3:30	5,000 kg.	¥0.10/kg.	12-12-52	31,405
Cotton Yarn (F)	Next 6 months	8:50, 10:15, 12:50, 3:10	1,814.36 kg.	¥0.10/lb.	9-1-51	10,472
Wool (F)	Next 6 months	8:50, 10:15, 12:50, 3:10	500 kg.	¥1/kg.	10-1-53	188

Tokyo Grain Exchange (TGE)

12-5 Nihonbashi Kakigara-cho, 1-Chome, Chuo-ku, Tokyo 103, Japan. 81-3-3668-9321; fax 81-3-3661-4564
Seiji Mori, chairman; Katsumi Kawamura, president

Contract	Contract months	Trading hours	Contract size	Minimum fluctuation	Date contract launched	Daily volume
U.S. Soybeans (F, OF)	Feb,Apr,Jun, Aug,Oct,Dec	F: 10, 11, 1:10, 2:10 OF: 10-11:45, 1-2:45	30,000 kg.	F: ¥10/1,000 kg OF: ¥5/1,000 kg. or ¥10/1,000 kg.*	F: 3-1-84 OF: 6-3-91	12,388 275
Red Beans (F) (Hokkaido)	Next 6 months	9, 10, 11, 1:10, 2:10, 3:10	80 30-kg. bags (2,400 kg.)	¥10/30 kg.	10-10-52	19,742
Corn (F)	Jan,Mar,May Jul,Sep,Nov	9, 11, 1:10, 3:10	100,000 kg.	¥10/1,000 kg.	4-20-92	13,184
Refined Sugar (F)	Next 6 months	9:05, 10:15, 12:55, 1:55, 2:55	9,000 kg.	¥0.10/kg.	5-7-52	12
Raw Sugar (F, OF) (Before March 1996 contract month)**	Jan,Mar,May Jul,Sep,Nov	F: 9:10, 10:20, 1,2,3 OF: 9:10-11:30, 1-3:15	20,000 kg.	F: ¥0.10/kg. OF: ¥0.05/kg.	F: 5-7-52 OF: 5-6-92	F: 4,542 OF: 149
Raw Sugar (F, OF) (Effective from March 1996 contract month)**	Jan,Mar,May Jul,Sep,Nov	F: 9:10, 10:20, 1,2,3 OF: 9:10-11:30, 1-3:15	50,000 kg.	F: ¥10/1,000 kg. OF: ¥10/1,000kg.	F: 5-7-52 OF: 5-6-92	@ @

* Effective from June 1995 contract and onward month. June 1995 contract for options on U.S. soybean futures was started June 29, 1994.
** March 1996 contract for raw sugar futures was started Aug. 1, 1994. March 1996 contract for options on raw sugar futures will begin Jan. 4, 1995.
@ Volume totals reflect combined raw sugar contracts average daily volume.

Tokyo International Financial Futures Exchange (TIFFE)

1-3-1 Marunouchi, Chiyoda-ku, Tokyo 100, Japan. 81-3-5223-2400; fax 81-3-5223-2450
Taroichi Yoshida, chairman & president; Mamoru Minakuchi, senior managing director

Contract	Contract months	Trading hours	Contract size	Minimum fluctuation	Date contract launched	Daily volume
3-Month Euroyen (F: EY; OF: EYO)	Mar,Jun,Sep,Dec	9-12, 1:30-3:30, 4-6	¥100,000,000	0.01 pt. = ¥10,000	F: 6-30-89 OF: 7-8-91	160,597 2,401
3-Month Eurodollar (F) (EU)	Mar,Jun,Sep,Dec	9-12, 1:30-3:30	US$1,000,000	0.01 pt. = US$25	6-30-89	0
U.S. Dollar/ Japanese Yen (F)(UD)	Mar,Jun,Sep,Dec	9-12, 1:30-3:30	US$50,000	0.05 pt. = ¥2,500	2-15-90	74
1-Year Euroyen (F) (EY1Y)	Mar,Jun,Sep,Dec	9-12, 1:30-3:30, 4-6	¥100,000,000	0.01 pt. = ¥10,000	7-14-92	101

Tokyo Stock Exchange (TSE)

2-1 Nihombashi-Kabuto-Cho, Chuo-ku, Tokyo 103, Japan. 81-3-3666-0141; fax 81-3-3663-0625; Telex: 02522759
Mitsuhide Yamaguchi, president and CEO; Kenichi Isaka, deputy president

Contract	Contract months	Trading hours	Contract size	Minimum fluctuation	Date contract launched	Daily volume*
10-Year Japanese Government Bond (F, OF)	F: Mar,Jun,Sep,Dec OF: Mar,Jun,Sep,Dec plus next 2 mos.	9-11, 12:30-3	¥100,000,000	0.01 pt = ¥10,000	F: 10-19-85 OF: 5-11-90	61,635 6,125
20-Year Japanese Government Bond (F)	Mar,Jun,Sep,Dec	9-11, 12:30-3	¥100,000,000	0.01 pt = ¥10,000	7-8-88	13
Tokyo Stock Price Index (TOPIX) (F, O)	F: Mar,Jun,Sep,Dec O: Monthly	9-11, 12:30-3:10	¥10,000 x Index	F: 1 pt. O: 0.50 pt. = ¥5,000	F: 9-3-88 O: 10-20-89	8,768 154
U.S. T-Bonds (F)	Mar,Jun,Sep,Dec	9-11, 12:30-3	US$100,000	1/32 pt. = US$31.25	12-1-89	458

* 1993 figure.

Malaysia

Kuala Lumpur Commodity Exchange (KLCE)

Fourth Floor, Citypoint, Komplek Dayabumi, Jalan Sultan Hishamuddin, P.O. Box 11260, 50740 Kuala Lumpur, Malaysia.
60-3-293-6822; fax 60-3-274-2215; Telex: MA 31472
Dato' Dr. Syed M.A. Alhady, chairman; Dato' Syed Abdul Jabbar Shahabudin, chief executive officer

Contract	Contract months	Trading hours	Contract size	Minimum fluctuation	Date contract launched	Daily volume
Cocoa (F)	Jan,Mar,May,Jul, Sep,Nov,Dec	11:15-12, 3-7	10 metric tons	US$1/ton = US$10	8-8-88	0
Crude Palm Oil (F)	Next 6 months plus alternate months up to 1 year	11-12:30, 3:30-6	25 metric tons	M$1/ton = M$25	10-23-80	2,301
SMR 20 Rubber (F)	Nearby months plus two distant quarters	10-1, 4-6	10 metric tons	M1/4sen/kg.	3-3-86	0
Tin (F)	Next 4 months plus alternate months up to 1 year	12:15-1, 4-7	5 metric tons	US$5/ton	10-27-87	0
Crude Palm Kernel Oil (F)	Next 6 months plus alternate months up to 1 year	11:15-12:15, 3:15-5:45	25 metric tons	M$1/ton = M$25	10-29-92	2

Netherlands

European Options Exchange (EOE-Optiebeurs)

Rokin 65, 1012 KK Amsterdam, The Netherlands. 31-20-550-4550; fax 31-20-623-0012; Telex: 10955/14596
J.Ch.L. Kuiper, president; U.L. Doornbos, managing director

Contract	Contract months	Trading hours	Contract size	Minimum fluctuation	Date contract launched	Daily volume
Dutch Government Bonds (O, FLEX) (NL, FO)	O: Feb,May,Aug,Nov FLEX: flexible	9-5	DFL10,000 (nominal value)	DFL0.01	6 different bonds FLEX: 3-25-94	3,056 (total)
Notional Bonds (F, OF) (FTO, OOF)	Feb,May,Aug,Nov	9-5	DFL250,000 (nominal value)	DFL0.01	11-11-90	58
EOE Index (F, O) (FTI, EOE)	*	9:30-4:30	F: DFL200 x index O: DFL100 x index	DFL0.10	5-18-87	15,958 (total)
Dutch Top 5 Index (F, O) (FT5, TOP5)	*	9:30-4:30	F: DFL200 x index O: DFL100 x index	DFL0.10	3-21-90	1,844
Eurotop 100 Index (F, O) (FET, E100)	Next 3 months	11-4:30	ECU50 x index	ECU0.10	6-6-91	6
U.S. Dollar (F, O) (FUS, DGX, DXJ)	Next 3 months plus Mar,Jun,Sep Dec	FUS: 9:15-5 DGX: 9:30-5 DXJ: 9:15-5	US$25,000 US$10,000 US$100,000	DFL0.0005 DFL0.05 DFL0.01	FUS: 9-27-91 DGX: 11-18-82 DXJ: 3-20-89	2,011 (total)
Gold (O) (GD)	Next 3 months plus Feb,May,Aug,Nov	9:30-4:30	10 troy oz.	US10¢/oz.	4-2-81	587
Silver (O) (SI)	Next 3 months plus Feb,May,Aug,Nov	9:30-4:30	1,000 troy oz.	US10¢/oz.	3-10-94	26
Dutch Stock (O) (42 stocks)	Different cycles	9:30-4:30	100 shares	DFL0.10	4-4-78	32,227

* Next 3 months plus Jan, Apr, Jul, Oct and 3 years out in October cycle for EOE Index; next 3 months plus 6 months in Jan, Apr, Jul, Oct cycle for Dutch Top 5 Index.

(continued)

FUTURES AND OPTIONS EXCHANGES *(continued)*

Financiele Termijnmarkt Amsterdam N.V. (FTA)

Nes 49, 1012 KD Amsterdam, The Netherlands. 31-20-550-4555; fax 31-20-624-5416
R.F. Sandelowsky, general manager

Contract	Contract months	Trading hours	Contract size	Minimum fluctuation	Date contract launched	Daily volume
Dutch Top 5 Index (F) (FT5)	Next 3 months plus Jan,Apr,Jul,Oct	9:30-4:30	DFL200 x index	0.10 pt. = DFL20	3-21-90	251
EOE Dutch Stock Index	Next 3 months plus Jan,Apr,Jul,Oct	9:30-4:30	DFL200 index	0.05 pt. = DFL10	6-19-87	4,252
Guilder Bonds (F) (FTO)	Mar,Jun,Sep,Dec	9-5	DFL250,000 (7% coupon)	0.01 pt. = DFL25	NA	60
U.S. Dollar/ Guilder (F) (FUS)	Next 3 months plus Mar,Jun,Sep,Dec	9:30-4:30	US$25,000	US5¢ = DFL12.50	NA	60
Eurotop 100 Index (F) (FET)	Next 3 months	9:30-4:30	ECU50 x index	0.10 pt. = ECU5	1991	2

New Zealand

New Zealand Futures & Options Exchange Ltd. (NZFOE)

P.O. Box 6734, Wellesley St., 10th Level, Stock Exchange Centre, Auckland, New Zealand. 64-9-309-8308; fax 64-9-309-8817
Peter Mansell, chief executive

Contract	Contract months	Trading hours	Contract size	Minimum fluctuation	Date contract launched	Daily volume*
90-Day Bank Accepted Bills (F, OF) (BBC)	Mar,Jun,Sep,Dec	8-12 1-5	NZ$500,000	0.01% annum yield	12-2-86	3,273
3-year Government Stock (F, OF) (TYS)	Mar,Jun,Sep,Dec	8-12 1-5	NZ$100,000	0.01	relisted 5-14-93	887
10-Year Government Stock (F,OF) (TEN)	Mar,Jun,Sep,Dec	8-12 1-5	NZ$100,000	0.01	6-7-91	103
NZSE-40 Capital Share Price Index (F, O) (FIF)	Mar,Jun,Sep,Dec	9-12 1:05-4:50	NZ$20 x index	1 pt.	9-23-91	10
Share Options (O) (5 stocks)	Quarterly cycles	9:05-4:45	1,000 shares	—	10-5-90	170
U.S. Dollar (F) (USD)	All months	8:15-12 1:05-4:45	US$50,000	NZ$0.0001/US$1	1-25-85	NA
New Zealand Wool (F) (WFC)	Feb,Apr,Jun, Aug,Oct,Dec	10-12 1:05-3	2,500 kg. x index	1 pt.	5-3-91	NA

* As of December 1993.

Norway

Oslo Stock Exchange (OSLO)

P.O. Box 460, Sentrum, N-0105 Oslo, Norway. 47-22-34-17-00; fax 47-22-41-65-90; Telex: 77242
Erik Jarve, president

Contract	Contract months	Trading hours	Contract size	Minimum fluctuation	Date contract launched	Daily volume
Stock Options (O)	Mar,Jun,Sep,Dec	10-4	100 shares	NOK0.05	5-22-90	2,902
OBX Index (F, O)	All months	10-4	NOK100 x index	F: NOK0.25 O: NOK0.05	F: 9-4-92 O: 6-28-90	21 1,549
10-year Government Bonds S463 (F)	Mar,Jun,Sep,Dec	9-3	NOK1,000,000 nominal	0.01 = NOK100	6-18-93	767
7-year Government Bonds S462 (F)	Mar,Jun,Sep,Dec	9-3	NOK1,000,000 nominal	0.01 = NOK100	2-11-94	168

Philippines

Manila International Futures Exchange Inc. (MIFE)

7/F Producer's Bank Centre, Paseo de Roxas, Makati 1200, The Philippines. 63-2-818-5496, 63-2-818-5533; Fax 63-2-818-5529, 63-2-810-5763
Francisco S. Sumulong Sr., chairman and president

Contract	Contract months	Trading hours	Contract size	Minimum fluctuation	Date contract launched	Daily volume
Sugar (F)	Next 6 months	9:15, 10:15, 1:15, 2:15	112,000 lb.	US2¢	10-20-86	2,207
Soybeans (F)	Next 6 months	9:45, 10:45, 1:45, 2:45	500 60-kg. bags	US50¢	10-20-86	2,941
Copra (F)	Next 6 months	9, 10, 1, 2	20,000 kg.	US1¢	2-1-88	2,538
Coffee (F)	Next 6 months	9:30, 10:30, 1:30, 2:30	5,000 kg.	US5¢	2-1-88	2,372
Interest Rates (F)	Next 4 alternate months	9:30-11:30, 1:30-3:30	10,000 pesos x interest rate	0.01%	10-22-90	45
U.S. Dollar/ Japanese Yen (F)	Spot plus next 3 months	8:30-3*	¥12,500,000	¥0.01	3-1-91	697
U.S. Dollar/ Deutsche Mark (F)	Spot plus next 3 months	8:30-3*	DM125,000	DM0.0001	3-1-91	175
U.S. Dollar/ Swiss Franc (F)	Spot plus next 3 months	8:30-3*	SF125,000	SF0.0001	11-11-91	311
U.S. Dollar/ Peso (F)	Next 4 months	10-3	US$100,000	0.001 pesos	11-3-92	13
British Pound/ U.S. Dollar (F)	Spot plus next 3 months	8:30-3*	£62,500	US$0.0001	3-1-91	409
Dry Cocoon (F)	Next 6 months	11-3	300 kg.	US50¢	7-8-92	2,384

*Hours are 8:30 a.m. to 11 p.m. if a U.S. holiday.

Singapore

Singapore Commodity Exchange Ltd.

111 North Bridge Road #23-04/05, Peninsula Plaza, Singapore 0617. 65-338-5600, fax 65-338-9116, 65-338-9640, 65-338-9676
Patrick Hays, chairman

Contract	Contract months	Trading hours*	Contract size*	Minimum fluctuation*	Date contract launched	Daily volume**
Rubber RSS1 (F)	Single months Quarters out 18 months	10-1, 3:30-5:30	5 metric tons 15 metric tons	S0.25¢/kg.=S$12.50 S0.25¢/kg.=S$37.50	5-27-92	2,500
Rubber RSS3 (F)	(Same as above, but prices in U.S. dollars)					2,800
Rubber TSR 20	Single months Quarters out 18 months	10-1, 3:30-5:30	20 metric tons 60 metric tons	S0.25¢/kg.=S$50 S0.25¢/kg.=S$150	5-27-92	2,200
RCS Index	Spot months plus 8 consecutive months	10-1, 3:30-5:30	5 metric tons	US0.10¢/kg. = US$5	8-30-93	100

*Top line for single months, bottom line for quarters. **Volume in metric tons; 1994 figure.

(continued)

FUTURES AND OPTIONS EXCHANGES *(continued)*

Singapore International Monetary Exchange Ltd. (SIMEX)

1 Raffles Place, No. 07-00, OUB Centre, Singapore 0104. 65-535-7382; fax 65-535-7282; Telex: RS 38000 SINMEX
Elizabeth Sam, chairman; Ang Swee Tian, president

Contract	Contract months	Trading hours	Contract size	Minimum fluctuation	Date contract launched	Daily volume
Japanese Government Bonds (F, OF) (JB)	Mar,Jun,Sep,Dec for 5 quarters	7:45-10:30, 11:30-7:10	¥50,000,000 (10-yr, 6% coupon)	¥0.01= ¥5,000	10-1-93	1,146
Euroyen (F, OF) (EY)	Mar,Jun,Sep,Dec (3-year cycle)	8-11:15, 12:15-7:05	¥100,000,000	0.01 pt. = ¥2,500	10-27-89	27,072
Eurodollar (F, OF) (ED)	Mar,Jun,Sep,Dec (10-year cycle)	7:45-7	US$1,000,000	0.01 pt. = US$25	9-7-84	33,380
Euromark (F) (EM)	Mar,Jun,Sep,Dec (2-year cycle)	10-7:10	DM1,000,000	0.01 pt. = DM25	9-20-90	1,155
Nikkei Stock Average (F, OF) (NK)	Mar,Jun,Sep,Dec for 5 quarters	8-10:15, 11:15-2:15	¥500 x average	5 pt. = ¥2,500	9-3-86	22,491
SIMEX MSCI Hong Kong (F) (HI)	*	10-12:30, 2:30-4	HK$100 x HK Index	1 pt. = HK$100	3-31-93	2
Deferred Spot Dollar/yen (F) (DY)	Mar,Jun,Sep,Dec	8-7	US$100,000	¥0.01/US$	11-1-93	325
Deferred Spot Dollar/mark (F) (UM)	Mar,Jun,Sep,Dec	8:05-7:05	US$100,000	DM0.0001/US$	11-1-93	477
British Pound (F) (BP)	Mar,Jun,Sep,Dec and spot month	8:25-5:15	£62,500	US$0.0002/£ = US$12.50	7-1-86	9
Deutsche Mark (F) (DM)	Mar,Jun,Sep,Dec and spot month	8:20-5:10	DM125,000	US$0.0001/DM = US$12.50	9-7-84	38
Japanese Yen (F) (JY)	Mar,Jun,Sep,Dec and spot month	8:15-5:05	¥12,500,000	US$0.000001/¥ = US$12.50	11-7-84	89
Gold (F) (GD)	Feb,Apr,June, Aug,Oct,Dec	9-5:15	100 troy oz.	US5¢/oz. = US$5	5-2-90	0
Fuel Oil (F) (SF)	Next 9 months	9:30-12:30, 2:30-7	100 metric tons	US10¢/ton = US$10	2-22-89	799

* 2 serial months and Mar, Jun, Sep, Dec on a 5-quarterly month cycle.

South Africa

South African Futures Exchange (SAFEX)

105 Central Street, Houghton Estate 2198, P.O. Box 4406, Johannesburg, 2000, Republic of South Africa. 27-11-728-5960;
fax 27-11-728-5970
Stuart A. Rees, CEO; Russell M. Loubser, chairman

Contract	Contract months	Trading hours	Contract size	Minimum fluctuation	Date contract launched	Daily volume
All Share Index (ALSI) (F, O)	Mar,Jun,Sep,Dec	24 hours	R10 x index	1 pt.	1987	F: 9,487 O: 11,325
All Gold Index (GLDI) (F, O)	Mar,Jun,Sep,Dec	24 hours	R10 x index	1 pt.	1987	F: 3,428 O: 353
JSE Industrial Index (INDI) (F, O)	Mar,Jun,Sep,Dec	24 hours	R10 x index	1 pt.	1987	F: 3,859 O: 1,837
Dollar/Gold Index (DGLD) (F, O)	Mar,Jun,Sep,Dec	24 hours	US$ x R100	US$0.01	1990	F: 12 O: 0
Short-Term Interest (BBF3) (F, O)	Feb,May,Aug,Nov	24 hours	R1,000,000	0.01%= 1 pt.	1988	F: 7 O: 0
Long Bond (E168) (F, O)	Feb,May,Aug,Nov	24 hours	R100,000	0.005% = 1/2 pt.	1987	F: 36 O: 1

Spain

MEFF RENTA FIJA (MEFF-F)

Via Laietana, 58, 08003, Barcelona, Spain. 34-3-412-1128; fax 34-3-268-4769
Josep M. Basañez, chairman; José-Luis Oller, CEO

Contract	Contract months	Trading hours	Contract size	Minimum fluctuation	Date contract launched	Daily volume
90-day MIBOR (F, OF)	F: 8 months in Mar,Jun,Sep,Dec cycle OF: Nearest 4 mos.	9-5:15	10,000,000 pesetas	1 pt. = 250 pesetas	F: 10-22-90 OF: 4-3-92	15,000 1,000
360-day MIBOR (F)	8 months in Mar,Jun,Sep,Dec cycle	9-5:15	10,000,000 pesetas	1 pt. = 1,000 pesetas	10-1-93	2,000
3-Year Government Bonds (F, OF)	F: Mar,Jun,Sep,Dec OF: Nearest 2 mos.	9-5:15	10,000,000 pesetas	1 pt. = 1,000 pesetas	F: 3-16-90 OF: 4-3-92	11,526 0
10-Year Government Bonds (F, OF)	F: Mar,Jun,Sep,Dec OF: Next 2 mos. plus 1 spot mo.	9-5:15	10,000,000 pesetas	1 pt. = 1,000 pesetas	F; 4-10-92 OF: 4-10-92	70,000 8,000

MEFF RENTA VARIABLE (MEFF-V)

Torre Picasso, Planta 26, 28020 Madrid, Spain. 34-1-585-0800; fax 34-1-571-9542
Josep-Manuel Basañez, chairman; Jose Massa, CEO

Contract	Contract months	Trading hours	Contract size	Minimum fluctuation	Date contract launched	Daily volume
IBEX-35 Stock Index (F, O)	All months	10:45-5:15	100 pesetas x index	1 pt. = 100 pesetas	1-14-92	F: 125,000 O: 40,000
Equities (O) (4 stocks)	Mar,Jun,Sep,Dec	10:45-5:15	100 shares	1 ESP/share	2-25-93	2,000

Sweden

OM Stockholm AB (OMS)

Brunkebergstorg 2, Box 16305, S-103 26 Stockholm, Sweden. 46-8-700-0600; fax 46-8-723-1092
Olof Stenhammar, chairman; Per E. Larsson, president

Contract	Contract months	Trading hours	Contract size	Minimum fluctuation	Date contract launched	Daily volume
Swedish OMX Stock Index (F, O)	All months	10-4	SEK100 x index	SEK0.01	F: 4-3-87 O: 12-18-86	6,386 22,544
Stocks (F, O) (24 stocks)	All months	10-4	100 shares	SEK0.01	F: 10-7-88 O: 6-12-85	937 37,364
Notional T-bills (OMvx 180) (F)	Mar,Jun,Sep,Dec	8:30-4	SEK1,000,000	0.01 pt.	9-3-92	15,822
OMr2 Notional Bonds (F)	Mar,Jun,Sep,Dec	8:30-4	SEK1,000,000	0.01 pt.	9-28-92	7,573
OMr5 Notional Bonds (F, O)	Mar,Jun,Sep,Dec	F: 8:30-4 O: 10-4	SEK1,000,000	0.01 pt.	F: 10-28-90 O: 3-4-94	7,922 502
OMr10 Notional Bonds (F)	Mar,Jun,Sep,Dec	8:30-4	SEK1,000,000	0.01 pt.	10-28-90	5,175
MBB5 Mortgage Bonds (F)	Mar,Jun,Sep,Dec	8:30-4	SEK1,000,000	0.01 pt.	5-20-92	1,174
MBB2 Mortgage Bonds (F)	Mar,Jun,Sep,Dec	8:30-4	SEK1,000,000	0.01 pt.	4-14-93	865
CT2 Mortgage Bonds (F)	Mar,Jun,Sep,Dec	8:30-4	SEK1,000,000	0.01 pt.	8-16-91	1,069
CT5 Mortgage Bonds (F)	Mar,Jun,Sep,Dec	8:30-4	SEK1,000,000	0.01 pt.	5-24-91	1,367
IMM-FRA (F)	Mar,Jun,Sep,Dec	8:30-4	SEK1,000,000	0.01 pt.	4-2-93	22,223
OMr-Swap (F)	Mar,Jun,Sep,Dec	8:30-4	SEK1,000,000	0.01 pt.	3-27-92	NA
SB5 Mortgage Bonds (F)	Mar,Jun,Sep,Dec	8:30-4	SEK1,000,000	0.01 pt.	9-1-92	409

(continued)

FUTURES AND OPTIONS EXCHANGES *(continued)*

Switzerland

Swiss Options and Financial Futures Exchange (SOFFEX)

Selnaustrasse 32, CH-8021 Zurich, Switzerland. 41-1-229-2111; fax 41-1-229-2233
Otto E. Nageli, CEO

Contract	Contract months	Trading hours	Contract size	Minimum fluctuation	Date contract launched	Daily volume
Swiss Market Index (F, O)	Next 3 months plus Jan,Apr,Jul,Oct	F: 9:30-1, 1:55-4:15 O: 10-1	F: SF50 x index O: SF5 x index	F: 0.1 pt. = SF5 O: Varies	F: 11-9-90 O: 12-7-88	6,809 26,762
Stocks (O) (12 stocks)	Next 3 months plus Jan,Apr,Jul,Oct	10-1, 1:55-4:15	5 shares	Varies	5-19-88	75,048
Low Exercise Price Options (LEPOs)	Next 2 months of Jan,Apr,Jul,Oct (A cycle)	10-1, 1:55-4:15	5 shares	Varies	—	*
Swiss Government Bonds (F, O)	F: Next 4 mos. of Mar, Jun,Sep,Dec (C cycle) O: Next 2 mos. of March cycle	8:30-5	SF100,000	0.01% = SF10	F: 5-29-92 O: 1-28-94	4,077 300

*Included in stock options total.

United Kingdom

International Petroleum Exchange of London Ltd. (IPE)

International House, 1 St. Katharine's Way, London E1 9UN. 44-171-481-0643; fax 44-171-481-8485; Telex: 927479; "Oiline": 0891 311 311
Philip Lynch, chairman; Peter Wildblood, chief executive

Contract	Contract months	Trading hours	Contract size	Minimum fluctuation	Date contract launched	Daily volume
Brent Crude Oil (F: FB; OF: OB, CB, PB)	F: Next 12 months OF: First 6 mos. of futures	9:31-8:15	1,000 barrels	US1¢/barrel = US$10	F: 6-23-88 OF: 5-11-89	39,486 2,234
Gasoil (F: FP; OF: OP, CP, PP)	F: Up to 18 months OF: First 6 mos. of futures	9:15-5:27	100 metric tons	F: US25¢/ton = US$25 OF: US5¢/ton = $5	F: 4-6-81 OF: 7-20-87	14,705 448
Unleaded Gasoline (F) (FU)	Next 6 months	9:25-5:18	100 metric tons	US25¢/ton = $25	1-27-92	19

London Commodity Exchange (LCE)

1 Commodity Quay, St. Katharine Docks, London E1 9AX. 44-171-481-2080; fax 44-171-702-9923
Michael Jenkins, chairman; Robin Woodhead, chief executive

Contract	Contract months	Trading hours	Contract size	Minimum fluctuation	Date contract launched	Daily volume
Cocoa No. 7 (F, OF)	Mar,May,Jul, Sep,Dec	9:30-12:30, 2-5	10 metric tons	£1/ton	1928	F: 6,289 OF: 390
Coffee (Robusta)(F, OF)	Jan,Mar,May, Jul,Sep,Nov	9:45-12:32, 2:30-5	5 metric tons	$1/ton	1958	F: 5,229 OF: 932
Sugar No. 5 (White) (F, OF)	Mar,May,Aug, Oct,Dec	9:45-7	50 metric tons	F: US10¢/ton OF: 5¢/ton	1983	F: 1,829 OF: NA
Sugar No. 7 (Premium raw) (F)*	Jan,Mar,May, Jul,Oct	10-7:01	50 long tons	F: US0.01¢/lb.	1993	145
Baltic Freight Index (F, OF) (BIFFEX)	Spot month and 2 mos. + Jan,Apr,Jul,Oct	10:15-12:30, 2:30-4:30	$10 x index	1 pt.= $10	1985	F: 167 OF: NA
EEC Wheat (F, OF)	Jan,Mar,May, Jun,Sep,Nov	10:30-12:30, 2:30-4	100 metric tons	5 pence/ton = £5	1929	F: 337 OF: NA
EEC Barley (F, OF)	Jan,Mar,May, Sep,Nov	10:30-12:30, 2:30-4	100 metric tons	5 pence/ton = £5	1929	F: 32 OF: NA
Potatoes (F, OF)	F: Mar,Apr,May, Jun,Nov	11-12:30, 2:30-4	20 metric tons	10 pence/ton = £2	1980	F: 151 OF: NA

*Traded on LCE's proprietary electronic trading system FAST.

London International Financial Futures and Options Exchange (LIFFE)

Cannon Bridge, London EC4R 3XX. 44-171-623-0444; fax 44-171-588-3624; Telex: 893893
Nick Durlacher, chairman; Daniel H. Hodson, chief executive

Contract	Contract months	Trading hours	Contract size	Minimum fluctuation	Date contract launched	Daily volume
Long Gilt (F, OF)	Mar,Jun,Sep,Dec	F: 8-4:15 APT: 4:30-6 OF: 8:02-4:15	£50,000 (nominal value, 9% coupon)	F:£1/32 = £15.625 OF:£1/64 = £7.8125	F: 11-18-82 OF: 3-13-86	86,626 10,410
3-Month Euromark Interest Rate (F, OF)	Mar,Jun,Sep,Dec	F: 8-4:10 APT: 4:25-5:59 OF: 8:02-4:10	DM1,000,000	1 pt. (0.01%) = DM25	F: 4-20-89 OF: 3-1-90	127,054 11,057
3-Month Eurodollar Interest Rate (F, OF)	Mar,Jun,Sep,Dec	F: 8:30-4 OF: 8:32-4	US$1,000,000	1 pt. (0.01%) = US$25	F: 9-30-82 OF: 6-27-85	511 74
3-Month Euroswiss Interest Rate (F, OF)	Mar,Jun,Sep,Dec APT: 4:24-5:55	F: 8:10-4:05 OF: 8:12-4:05	SF1,000,000	0.01 pt. = SF25 OF: 10-15-92	F: 2-7-91 83	6,902
3-Month Sterling Interest Rate (F, OF)	Mar,Jun,Sep,Dec	F: 8:05-4:05 APT: 4:22-5:57 OF: 8:07-4:05	£500,000	1 pt. (0.01%) = £12.50	F: 11-4-82 OF: 11-5-87	65,611 13,883
3-Month ECU Interest Rate (F)	Mar,Jun,Sep,Dec	8:05-4:05	ECU1,000,000	0.01 pt. = ECU 25	10-26-89	2,474
German Government Bonds (F, OF)	Mar,Jun,Sep,Dec	F: 7:30-4:15 APT: 4:20-5:55 OF: 7:32-4:15	DM250,000 (nominal value, 6% coupon)	DM0.01 = DM25	F: 9-29-88 OF: 4-20-89	160,735 36,882
Japanese Government Bonds (F)	Mar,Jun,Sep,Dec	APT: 7-4	¥100,000,000 (6% coupon)	¥0.01 = ¥10,000	4-3-91	2,597
Italian Government Bonds (F, OF)	Mar,Jun,Sep,Dec	F: 8-4:10 APT: 4:21-5:58 OF: 8:02-4:10	ItL200,000,000 (nominal value, 12% coupon)	ItL0.01 = ItL20,000	F: 9-19-91 OF: 10-24-91	53,287 4,797
3-Month Eurolira Interest Rates (F)	Mar,Jun,Sep,Dec	7:55-4:10 APT: 4:23-5:58	ItL1,000,000,000	ItL0.01 = ItL25,000	5-12-92	14,409
FT-SE 100 Index (F)	Mar,Jun,Sep,Dec APT: 4:32-5:30	8:35-4:10	£25 x index = £12.50	0.5 pt.	5-3-84	16,981
FT-SE 100 Index (O) (American Style)	Next 4 months plus Jun,Dec	8:35-4:10	£10 x index	0.5 pt. = £5	5-3-84	18,663
FT-SE 100 Index (O) (European Style)	Next 3 months plus Mar,Jun,Sep,Dec	8:35-4:10	£10 x index	0.5 pt. = £5	2-1-90	*
FT-SE Mid 250 Index (F)	Mar,Jun,Sep,Dec	8:30-4:05	£10 x index	0.5 pt. = £5	2-25-94	135
Equities (O)	Three cycles	8:35-4:10	1,000 shares	0.5 pence/share = £5	4-78	18,669

* Included in FT-SE 100 Index American style options total.

London Metal Exchange (LME)

56 Leadenhall Street, London EC3A 2BJ. 44-171-264-5555; fax 44-171-680-0505; Telex: 8951367
Raj K. Bagri, chairman; David E. King, chief executive

Contract	Contract months	Trading hours*	Contract size	Minimum fluctuation	Date contract launched***	Daily volume
Aluminum (F, OF)	**	11:55, 12:55, 3:35, 4:15	25 metric tons	US50¢/ton = $12.50	6-87	F: 56,463 OF: 4,476
Aluminum Alloy (F)	**	11:45, 1:05, 3:50, 4:30	20 metric tons	US50¢/ton =$12.50	6-10-92	630
Copper (F, OF)	**	Noon, 12:30, 3:30, 4:10	25 metric tons	US50¢/ton = $12.50	4-86	F: 64,491 OF: 7,265
Lead (F, OF)	**	12:05, 12:45, 3:20, 4	25 metric tons	US50¢/ton = $12.50	10-52	F: 7,479 OF: 223
Nickel (F, OF)	**	12:15, 1, 3:45, 4:25	6 metric tons	US$1/ton = $6	4-79	F: 12,987 OF: 446
Tin (F, OF)	**	11:50, 12:40, 3:40, 4:20	5 metric tons	US$1/ton = $5	6-91	F: 4,629 OF: 105
Zinc (F, OF)	**	12:10, 12:50, 3:25, 4:05	25 metric tons	US50¢/ton = $12.50	9-88	F: 20,657 OF: 899

* Each floor trading session lasts 5 minutes, beginning at the time listed. Contracts also are traded electronically via a terminal network order matching system and in open-outcry kerb trading sessions.
** All contracts are traded for any market day between the current day spot and 3 months forward or the next 12 months for lead, nickel aluminum alloy and tin and the next 24 months for aluminum, copper and zinc.
*** Date the contract in its present form was introduced. Trading in some metals goes back to 1883; some contracts were reintroduced after World War II and later replaced by the current contracts.

FUTURES AND OPTIONS EXCHANGES *(continued)*

OMLX, The London Securities & Derivatives Exchange

107 Cannon St., London EC4N 5AD. 44-171-283-0678; fax 44-171-815-8508
Lynton Jones, chief executive

Contract	Contract months	Trading hours	Contract size	Minimum fluctuation	Date contract launched	Daily volume
OMX Index (F, O)	All months	9-3	SEK100 x index	SEK0.01	12-89*	F: 8,464 O: 24,225**
Long OMX Index (O)	Yearly	9-3	SEK100 x index	SEK0.01	4-24-92	
Swedish Stocks (F, O) (24 stocks)	All months	9-3	100 shares	SEK0.01	3-90*	F: 365 O: 50,175**
Long Stocks (O)	Yearly	9-3	100 shares	SEK0.01	3-18-92	

*Traded at OM Stockholm prior to launch at OM London.
** Volume for OMX Index options includes Long OMX Index options; volume for Swedish stock options includes Long Stocks options.

United States

American Stock Exchange (AMEX)

Derivative Securities, 86 Trinity Place, New York, NY 10006. (212) 306-1000; fax (212) 306-1802
Richard F. Syron, chairman and CEO; Jules L. Winters, president and COO
AMEX trades a number of broad-based and sector index options, as well as other derivatives. For contract information, contact exchange.

Chicago Board Options Exchange (CBOE)

400 S. LaSalle St., Chicago, IL 60605. (312) 786-5600; (800) 678-4667; Fax (312) 786-7409; (312) 786-7413
Alger B. Chapman, chairman, CEO; Charles J. Henry, president, COO
The CBOE trades options on stocks and indexes, as well as more exotic options such as LEAPs and Flex options. Check with the exchange for contract specifications.

Chicago Board of Trade (CBOT)

141 W. Jackson Blvd., Chicago, IL 60604-2994. (312) 435-3500; fax (312) 341-3306
Patrick H. Arbor, chairman; Thomas R. Donovan, president & CEO

Contract**	Contract months	Trading hours*	Contract size	Minimum fluctuation	Daily limit	Date contract launched	Daily volume
Corn (F, OF) (C)	Mar,May,Jul, Sep,Dec	9:30-1:15	5,000 bu.	1/4¢/bu. = $12.50	10¢/bu. = $500	F: 1-2-1877 OF: 2-85	47,053 9,197
Wheat (F, OF) (W) (Soft winter)	Mar,May,Jul, Sep,Dec	9:30-1:15	5,000 bu.	1/4¢/bu. = $12.50	20¢/bu. = $1,000	F: 1-2-1877 OF: 11-86	13,418 2,909
Oats (F, OF) (O)	Mar,May,Jul, Sep,Dec	9:30-1:15	5,000 bu.	F: 1/4¢/bu. = $12.50 OF: 1/8¢/bu. = $6.25	10¢/bu. = $500	F: 1-2-1877 OF: 5-90	2,058 96
Soybeans (F, OF) (S)	Jan,Mar,May,Jul, Aug,Sep,Nov	9:30-1:15	5,000 bu.	1/4¢/bu. = $12.50	30¢/bu. = $1,500	F: 10-5-36 OF: 10-84	44,385 12,089
Soybean Meal (F, OF) (SM)	Jan,Mar,May,Jul, Aug,Sep,Oct,Dec	9:30-1:15	100 tons	10¢/ton = $10	$10/ton = $1,000	F: 8-19-51 OF: 2-87	18,345 1,143
Soybean Oil (F, OF) (BO)	Jan,Mar,May,Jul, Aug,Sep,Oct,Dec	9:30-1:15	60,000 lb.	1/100¢/lb. = $6	1¢/lb. = $600	F: 7-17-50 OF: 2-87	18,906 1,119
Diammonium Phosphate (DAP) (F) (FZ)	Mar,Jun,Sep,Dec	8:30-1:15	100 tons	10¢/ton = $10	$10/ton = $1,000	10-18-91	68
Anhydrous Ammonia (F) (NZ)	Mar,Jun,Sep,Dec	8:15-12:45	100 tons	10¢/ton = $10	$10/ton = $1,000	9-11-92	11
U.S. Treasury Bonds (F, OF) (US)	Mar,Jun,Sep,Dec	7:20-2, 5-8:30	$100,000 (8% coupon)	1/32 pt. = $31.25	3 pt. = $3,000	F: 8-22-77 OF: 10-1-82	414,338 117,357
10-Year U.S. Treasury Notes (F, OF) (TY)	Mar,Jun,Sep,Dec	7:20-2, 5-8:30	$100,000 (8% coupon)	1/32 pt. = $31.25	3 pt. = $3,000	F: 5-3-82 OF: 5-85	97,046 27,502
5-Year U.S. Treasury Notes (F, OF) (FV)	Mar,Jun,Sep,Dec	8-2, 5-8:30	$100,000	1/64 pt. = $15.625	3 pt. = $3,000	F: 5-20-88 OF: 5-90	49,408 10,945
2-Year U.S. Treasury Notes (F) (TU)	Mar,Jun,Sep,Dec	7:20-2, 5:20-8:05	$200,000	1/4 of 1/32 pt. = $15.625	1 pt. = $2,000	F: 6-22-90 OF: 4-24-92	3,726 533
30-Day Fed Funds (F) (FF)	All months	7:20-2	$5,000,000	0.01% = $41.67	150 basis pt.	10-3-88	1,401
Municipal Bond Index (F, OF) (MB)	Mar,Jun,Sep,Dec	7:20-2	$1,000 x Bond Buyer Index	1/32 pt. = $31.25	3 pt. = $3,000	F: 6-11-85 OF: 6-87	6,041 105
Flexible U.S. T-bonds (OF) (CG, PG)***	Flexible	7:20-2	$100,000 face value	1/64 pt. = $15.625	3 pt. = $3,000 expands to 4.5	1-8-94	861
Flexible 10-Year U.S. Treasury Notes (OF) (TC, TP)***	Flexible	7:20-2	$100,000 face value	1/64 pt. = $15.625	3 pt. = $3,000 expands to 4.5	1-7-94	214

Contract**	Contract months	Trading hours*	Contract size	Minimum fluctuation	Daily limit	Date contract launched	Daily volume
Flexible 5-Year U.S. Treasury Notes (OF) (FL, FP)***	Flexible	7:20-2	$100,000 face value	1/64 pt. = $15.625	3 pt. = $3,000, expands to 4.5	1-7-94	853
Flexible 2-Year U.S. Treasury Notes (OF) (TUC, TUP)***	Flexible	7:20-2	$100,000 face value	1/2 of 1/64 pt. ($15.625)	3 pt. = $3,000, expands to 4.5	1-7-94	1
Canadian Government Bonds (F, OF) (CN)	Mar,Jun,Sep,Dec	7:20-2	C$100,000 (9% coupon)	1/100 pt. = C$10	3 pt. = C$3,000 expands to 4.5	4-8-94	F: 138 OF: 7
Gold (F) (KI)	Feb,Apr,Jun, Aug,Oct,Dec	7:20-1:40	1 kg. = 32.15 oz.	10¢/oz. = $3.22	$50/oz. = $1,607.50	4-12-83	100
Gold (F) (GH)	Feb,Apr,Jun, Aug,Oct,Dec	7:20-1:40	100 fine troy oz.	10¢/troy oz. = $10	$50/oz. = $5,000	9-13-87	4
Silver (F) (SV)	Next 3 months plus Feb,Apr,June	7:25-1:25, 5-8:30	5,000 troy oz.	1/10¢/oz. = $5	$1/oz. = $5,000	9-14-87	22
Silver (F, OF) (AG)	Feb,Apr,June, Aug,Oct,Dec	7:25-1:25	1,000 troy oz.	1/10¢/oz. = $1	$1/oz. = $1,000	F: 3-16-81 OF: 3-85	335 27
FOSFA International Edible Oils Index (F) (VO)	Feb,May,Aug,Nov	9:30-1:15	100 metric tons x index	25¢/metric ton = $25	$25/metric ton = $2,500@	9-23-94	8
Structural Panel Index (F) (PI)	Jan,Mar,May, July,Sep,Nov	10-1	100,000 sq. ft. (100 MSF)	$0.10/MSF = $10	$15/MSF = $1,500	1-25-94	27
National Catastrophe Insurance (F, OF) (UN)	Mar,Jun,Sep,Dec	8:30-2:30	$25,000 x ratio of losses/premiums	1/10 pt. = $25	10 pt. = $2,500	12-11-92	F: 0 OF: 8
Eastern Catastrophe Insurance (F, OF) (UE)	Mar,Jun,Sep,Dec	8:30-2:30	$25,000 x ratio of losses/premiums	1/10 pt. = $25	10 pt. = $2,500	12-11-92	F: 0 OF: 37
Midwestern Catastrophe Insurance (F, OF) (UM)	Mar,Jun,Sep,Dec	8:30-2:30	$25,000 x ratio of losses/premiums	1/10 pt. = $25	10 pt. = $2,500	3-93	0
Western Catastrophe Insurance (F, OF) (WA)	Mar,Jun,Sep,Dec	8:30-2:30	$25,000 x ratio of losses/premiums	1/10 pt. = $25	10 pt. = $2,500	12-10-93	0
Western Annual Catastrophe Insurance (F, OF) (UM)	Monthly	8:30-2:30	$25,000 x ratio of losses/premiums	1/10 pt. = $25	10 pt. = $2,500	12-10-93	0

* The first times listed for the interest rate and metals contracts are for the regular day session Monday through Friday, Central Standard Time. The second time period is for the evening session Sunday through Thursday evenings. During the summer months when Central Daylight Time is in effect, the trading time for the evening session is one hour later — T-bond futures, for example, trade from 6 p.m. to 9:30 p.m. Sunday-Thursday, Chicago time, when daylight savings time is in effect.
**All CBOT financial products trade on Project A: Hours are 2:30-4:30 p.m.
*** Also European-style exercise.
@ Price limit expandable to $37.50 per metric ton ($3,750 per contract).

Chicago Stock Exchange (CHX)

One Financial Place, 440 S. LaSalle St., Chicago, Ill. 60605-1070. (312) 663-2222; fax (312) 663-2396
Homer J. Livingston Jr., president, CEO; Erwin E. Schulze, chairman
The Chicago Stock Exchange has 3,024 issues available for trading, and members can trade NYSE, AMEX and CHX exclusives and over-the-counter stocks. Average daily share volume for 1994 is 13.15 million shares.

Chicago Mercantile Exchange (CME)

30 S. Wacker Drive, Chicago, IL 60606. (312) 930-1000; fax (312) 930-3439
John F. Sandner, chairman, board of directors; William J. Brodsky, president, CEO

Contract	Contract months	Trading hours	Contract size	Minimum fluctuation	Daily limit	Date contract launched	Daily volume
Cattle, Feeder (F, OF) (FC)	Jan,Mar,Apr,May, Aug,Sep,Oct,Nov	8:45-1	50,000 lb.	2.5¢/cwt. = $12.50	1.5¢/lb. = $750	F: 11-30-71 OF: 1-9-87	1,898 510
Cattle, Live (F, OF) (LC)	Feb,Apr,Jun, Aug,Oct,Dec	8:45-1	40,000 lb.	2.5¢/cwt. = $10	1.5¢/lb. = $600	F: 11-30-64 OF: 10-30-84	14,549 2,566
Hogs, Live (F, OF) (LH)	Feb,Apr,Jun,Jul, Aug,Oct,Dec	8:45-1	40,000 lb.	2.5¢/cwt. = $10	1.5¢/lb. = $600	F: 2-28-66 OF: 2-1-85	5,827 406
Pork Bellies (F, OF) (PB)	Feb,Mar,May, July,Aug	8:45-1	40,000 lb.	2.5¢/cwt. = $10	2¢/lb. = $800	F: 9-18-61 OF: 10-3-86	2,603 133
Broiler Chickens (F) (BR)	Feb,Apr,May,Jun, July,Aug,Oct,Dec	9:10-1	40,000 lb.	2.5¢/cwt. = $10	2¢/lb. = $800	F: 2-7-91 OF: 2-7-91	NA NA
Lumber (F, OF) (Random-length) (LB)	Jan,Mar,May, July,Sep,Nov	9-1:05	160,000 bd. ft.	10¢/1,000 bd. ft. = $16	$5/1,000 bd. ft. = $800	F: 10-1-69 OF: 5-29-87	720 105

(continued)

FUTURES AND OPTIONS EXCHANGES *(continued)*

International Monetary Market Division of the CME (IMM)**

Contract	Contract months	Trading hours	Contract size	Minimum fluctuation	Daily limit***	Date contract launched	Daily volume
Deutsche Mark (F, OF) (DM)	Jan,Mar,Apr,Jun, July,Sep,Oct,Dec*	7:20-2	DM125,000	$0.0001/DM = $12.50	200 pt. 300 pt.	F: 5-16-72 OF: 1-24-84	49,216 26,231
Canadian Dollar (F, OF)	Jan,Mar,Apr,Jun, July,Sep,Oct,Dec*	7:20-2	C$100,000	$0.0001/C$ = $10	200 pt. 300 pt.	F: 5-16-72 OF: 6-16-86	7,186 1,003
Swiss Franc (F, OF) (SF)	Jan,Mar,Apr,Jun, July,Sep,Oct,Dec*	7:20-2	SF125,000	$0.0001/SF = $12.50	200 pt. 300 pt.	F: 5-16-72 OF: 2-25-85	21,859 3,445
British Pound (F, OF) (BP)	Jan,Mar,Apr,Jun, July,Sep,Oct,Dec*	7:20-2	£62,500	$0.0002/£ = $12.50	400 pt. 800 pt.	F: 5-16-72 OF: 2-25-85	14,630 3,707
Japanese Yen (F, OF) (JY)	Jan,Mar,Apr,Jun, July,Sep,Oct,Dec*	7:20-2	¥12,500,000	$0.000001/¥ = $12.50	200 pt. 300 pt.	F: 5-16-72 OF: 3-5-86	28,402 15,655
Australian Dollar (F, OF) (AD)	Jan,Mar,Apr,Jun, July,Sep,Oct,Dec*	7:20-2	A$100,000	$0.0001/A$ = $10	200 pt. 300 pt.	F: 1-13-87 OF: 1-11-88	1,356 40
French Franc (F, OF) (FF)	Mar,Jun,Sep,Dec	7:20-2	FF250,000	$0.0002/FF = $10.00	500 pt.	F: 9-20-93 OF: 9-20-93	244 7
DM/JY Cross Rate (F, OF) (DJ)	Mar,Jun,Sep,Dec	7:20-2	DM125,000	0.01 = ¥1,250	150 pt. None	F: 2-26-92 OF: 2-26-92	0 0
London Interbank Offered Rate (LIBOR) (F, OF) (EM)	F: All months OF: Spot plus next six months	7:20-2	$3,000,000	F: 1 pt. = $25 OF: 1 pt. = $12.50	—	F: 4-5-90 OF: 6-12-91	7,975 435
Treasury Bills (90-day) (F, OF) (TB)	Mar,Jun,Sep,Dec	7:20-2	$1,000,000	1 pt. = $25	—	F: 1-6-76 OF: 4-10-86	4,266 38
1-year T-bills (F, O) (YR)	F: Mar,Jun,Sep,Dec O: Mar,Jun,Sep,Dec plus serial months	7:20-2	$500,000	0.005 = $25	None	3-28-94	F: 6
Eurodollar Time Deposit (F, OF) (ED)	Mar,Jun,Sep,Dec* F: 5 years out OF: 1 1/2 years out	7:20-2	$1,000,000	1 pt. = $25	—	F: 12-9-81 OF: 5-20-85	450,630 117,667
British Pound Rolling Spot (F, OF) (RP)	F: Mar,Jun,Sep,Dec O: All 12 months with weekly expirations	7:20-2	£250,000	1 pt. = $25	—	6-15-93	0
Deutsche Mark Rolling Spot (F, OF) (RD)	F: Mar,Jun,Sep,Dec O: All 12 months with weekly expirations	7:20-2	$250,000	1 pt. = DM25	—	9-14-93	F: 410
Deutsche Mark Currency Forwards (FM)	12 mos. plus 4 in the March cycle	7-2	$250,000	0.001 = DM25	NA	9-12-94	761
3-Month Euromark (F, OF) (EK)	F: Mar,Jun,Sep,Dec O: Mar,Jun,Sep,Dec plus serial month	7:20-2	DM1,000,000	1 pt. = DM25	—	4-26-93	F: 4 OF: 0

* In addition to the months listed, a spot month contract is also traded.
** All IMM contracts are also traded on GLOBEX.
*** For currencies, the top number listed is the opening limit between 7:20 a.m. and 7:35 a.m.; the bottom number is the expanded limit in effect between 7:35 a.m. and 1:45 p.m. There are no daily limits during the last 15 minutes of trading. Contact exchange for details on limits.

Index and Option Market Division of the CME (IOM)

Contract	Contract months	Trading hours	Contract size	Minimum fluctuation	Daily limit	Date contract launched	Daily volume
Nikkei 225 Stock Average (F, OF) (NK)	F: Mar,Jun,Sep,Dec OF: All months	8-3:15	$5 x Average	5 pt. = $25	Varies*	F: 9-25-90 OF: 9-90	2,469 57
S&P 500 Stock Index (F, OF) (SP)	F: Mar,Jun,Sep,Dec OF: All months	8:30-3:15	$500 x index	5 pt. = $25	Varies**	F: 4-21-82 OF: 1-28-83	72,527 18,248
S&P MidCap 400 Index (F, OF) (MD)	Mar,Jun,Sep,Dec	8:30-3:15	$500 x index	0.05 pt. = $25	Varies***	F: 2-13-92 OF: 2-13-92	1,186 23
FT-SE 100 Stock Index (F, OF) (FI)	Mar,Jun,Sep,Dec	8:30-3:15	$50 x index	0.5 pt. = $25	None	F: 10-15-92 OF: 10-15-92	0 0
Goldman Sachs Commodity Index (F, OF) (GI)	Feb,Apr,Jun, Aug,Oct,Dec	8:15-2:15	$250 x index	0.10 pt. = $25	None	F: 7-28-92 OF: 7-28-92	594 228
Russell 2000 Stock Price Index (F, OF) (RL)	F: Mar,Jun,Sep,Dec OF: Feb,Mar,Apr,Jun, Sep,Dec & serial month	8:30-3:15	$500 x index	0.05 pt. = $25	Varies	F: 2-4-93 OF: 2-4-93	170 19
Major Market Index (F, OF) (BC)	Nearest 3 mos. plus next 3 mos. in March cycle	8:15-3:15	$500 x index	0.05 pt. = $25	Varies	F: 9-7-93 OF: 9-7-93	720 5

* 1,000 when Nikkei Average is below 20000, 1,500 when it is between 20005 and 30000, 2,000 when it is above 30005.
** 5 points for first 10 minutes; if price is at limit at end of that period, there is a 2-minute trading halt; then the limit expands to 12 points for 30 minutes; if prices are at that limit after 30 minutes, there is another 2-minute trading halt; then the limit is increased to 20 points.
*** Similar to S&P 500 pattern except that the opening limit is 2 points, then it expands to 4 points and 7 points.

Coffee, Sugar & Cocoa Exchange Inc. (CSCE)

4 World Trade Center, New York, NY 10048. (212) 938-2800; (800) 433-4348; fax (212) 524-9863
Charles H. Falk, chairman; Bennett J. Corn, president

Contract	Contract months	Trading hours	Contract size	Minimum fluctuation	Daily limit	Date contract launched	Daily volume
Brazil Differential Coffee (F) (KB)	Mar,May,Jul, Sep,Dec	9:15-2:05	37,500/lb.	5/100¢/lb. = $18.75	None	6-12-92	0
Cocoa (F, OF) (CC)	Mar,May,Jul, Sep,Dec@	F: 9-2	10 metric tons	$1/ton = $10	$88/ton = $88	F: 1925 OF: 1986	5,874 1,445
Coffee "C" (F, OF) (KC)	Mar,May,Jul, Sep,Dec@	9:15-2:05	37,500 lb.	F: 5/100¢/lb. = $18.75 OF: 1/100¢/lb. = $3.75	F: 6¢/lb.* OF: None	F: 1964 OF: 1986	11,549 1,445
Sugar No. 11 (World) (F, OF) (SB)	Mar,May, Jul,Oct**	10-1:50	112,000 lb.	1/100¢/lb. = $11.20	F: 1/2¢/lb. = $560* OF: None	F: 1914 OF: 1986	18,618 4,058
Sugar No. 14 (F) (SE)	Jan,Mar,May, Jul,Sep,Nov	9:40-1:45	112,000 lb.	1/100¢/lb. = $11.20	1/2¢/lb. = $560*	7-8-85	545
Sugar (F) (White) (WS)	Jan,Mar,May, Jul,Oct	10-1:50	50 metric tons	20¢/ton = $10	$10/ton	10-5-87	0
Cheddar Cheese (F, OF) (EZ)	Feb,May,Jul, Sep,Nov	2:15-3:15	10,500 lbs.	F:10/100¢/lb. = $10.50 OF: 1/100¢/lb. = $4	6¢/lb.*	F: 6-15-93 OF: 6-22-93	4 0
Nonfat Dry Milk (F, OF) (MU)	Feb,May,Jul, Sep,Nov	2:15-3:15	11,000 lbs.	F: 10/100¢/lb. = $11 OF:1/100¢/lb. = $4.40	6¢/lb.*	F: 6-15-93 OF: 6-22-93	4 0

* No limits two nearby months.
** Plus serial options that began trading Feb. 3, 1992.
@ Plus serial options that began trading February 1994.

GLOBEX

30 S. Wacker Drive, Chicago, IL 60606. (312) 930-2397; fax (312) 930-8219
John F. Sandner, chairman; Cynthia A. Pender, executive director
CME and MATIF financial contracts are listed on GLOBEX. Check with exchanges for trading hours. DTB may begin listing contracts on GLOBEX in 1995.

Kansas City Board of Trade (KCBT)

4800 Main St., Suite 303, Kansas City, MO 64112. (816) 753-7500; (800) 821-5228; fax (816) 753-3944; Hotline (800) 821-4444
Don Hills, chairman; Michael Braude, president

Contract	Contract months	Trading hours	Contract size	Minimum fluctuation	Daily limit	Date contract launched	Daily volume
Wheat (F: KW; OF: HC, HP)	Mar,May,Jul, Sep,Dec	F: 9:30-1:15 OF: 9:30-1:20	5,000 bu.	F: 1/4¢/bu.=$12.50 OF: 1/8¢/bu.=$6.25	25¢/bu.= $1,250	F: 6-18-76 OF: 10-30-84	5,986 412
Value Line (F: KV)	Mar,Jun,Sep,Dec	8:30-3:15	500 x index	0.05=$25	20 pt.=$10,000	2-24-82	210
Mini Value Line (F: MV; OF: MVC, MVP)	F: Mar,Jun,Sep,Dec OF: Plus first 2 serial months	8:30-3:15	100 x index	0.05=$5	20 pt.=$2,000	F: 7-29-83 OF: 7-1-92	205 12

MidAmerica Commodity Exchange (MidAm) An affiliate of the Chicago Board of Trade

141 W. Jackson Blvd., Chicago, IL 60604. (312) 341-3000; fax (312) 341-3027
(For key personnel, see Chicago Board of Trade)

Contract	Contract months	Trading hours*	Contract size	Minimum fluctuation	Daily limit	Date contract launched	Daily volume
Cattle, Live (F) (XL)	Feb,Apr,Jun, Aug,Oct,Dec	8:45-1:15	20,000 lbs.	2.5/100¢/lb. = $5	1.5¢/lb. = $300	9-21-78	63
Hogs, Live (F) (XH)	Feb,Apr,Jun, Jul,Aug,Oct,Dec	8:45-1:15	20,000 lbs.	2.5/100¢/lb. = $5	1.5¢/lb. = $300	6-3-74	69
Corn (F, OF) (XC)	Mar,May,Jul, Sep,Dec	9:30-1:45	1,000 bu.	1/8¢/bu. = $1.25	10¢/bu. = $100	F: 10-24-22 OF: 3-21-91	995 17
Oats (F) (XO)	Mar,May,Jul, Sep,Dec	9:30-1:45	1,000 bu.	1/8¢/bu. = $1.25	12¢/bu. = $100	10-24-22	23
Rough Rice (F, OF) (NR)	Jan,Mar,May, Jul,Sep,Nov	9-1:30	2,000 cwt. (200,000 lbs.)	1/2¢/cwt. = $10 OF: 1/4¢/cwt.=$5	30¢/cwt. = $600	F: 9-16-83 OF: 4-10-92	360 29
Soybeans (F, OF) (XS)	Jan,Mar,May, Jul,Aug,Sep,Nov	9:30-1:45	1,000 bu.	1/8¢/bu. = $1.25	30¢/bu. = $300	F: 12-8-40 OF: 2-85	3,210 52
Soybean Meal (F) (XE)	Jan,Mar,May,Jul, Aug,Sep,Oct,Dec	9:30-1:45	20 tons	10¢/ton = $2	$10/ton = $200	1-31-86	17
Wheat (F, OF) (XW) (Soft winter)	Mar,May,Jul, Sep,Dec	9:30-1:45	1,000 bu.	1/8¢/bu. = $1.25	20¢/bu. = $200	F: 10-24-22 OF: 10-84	355 10

(continued)

FUTURES AND OPTIONS EXCHANGES *(continued)*

Contract	Contract months	Trading hours	Contract size	Minimum fluctuation	Daily limit***	Date contract launched	Daily volume
New York Gold (F, OF) (XK)	All months	7:20-1:40	33.2 fine troy oz.	10¢/oz. = $3.32	None	F: 6-8-84 OF: 7-84	110 2
New York Silver (F) (XY)	All months	7:25-1:40	1,000 troy oz.	10/100¢/oz. = $1	None	11-1-82	54
Platinum (F) (XU)	Next 3 months plus Jan,Apr,Jul,Oct	7:10-1:40	25 troy oz.	10¢/oz. = $2.50	$25/oz. = $625	8-17-84	10
U.S. Treasury Bonds (F, OF) (XB)	Mar,Jun,Sep,Dec	7:20-3:15	$50,000 face value	F: 1/32 pt. = $15.62 OF: 1/64 pt. = $7.81	96/32 pt. = $1,500	F: 9-81 OF: 3-22-91	5,565 12
U.S. Treasury Bills (90-day) (F) (XT)	Mar,Jun,Sep,Dec	7:20-2:15	$500,000 face value	1 pt. = $12.50	None	4-2-82	4
U.S. Treasury Notes (F) (XN)	Mar,Jun,Sep,Dec	7:20-3:15	$50,000 face value	1/32 pt. = $15.62	96/32 pt. = $1,500	4-30-93 (relisted)	126
Eurodollar (F) (UD)	Mar,Jun,Sep,Dec	7:20-2:15	$500,000	1 pt. = $12.50	None	8-21-92	33
British Pound (F) (XP)	Mar,Jun,Sep,Dec	7:20-2:15	£12,500	$0.0002/£ = $2.50	None	9-15-83	299
Canadian Dollar (F) (XD)	Mar,Jun,Sep,Dec	7:20-2:15	C$50,000	$0.0001/C$ = $5	None	9-15-83	39
Deutsche Mark (F) (XM)*	Mar,Jun,Sep,Dec	7:20-2:15, 5:20-8:05**	DM62,500	$0.0001/DM = $6.25	None	9-15-83	483
Japanese Yen (F) (XJ)*	Mar,Jun,Sep,Dec	7:20-2:15, 5:20-8:05**	¥6,250,000	$0.000001/¥ = $6.25	None	9-15-83	291
Swiss Franc (F) (XF)	Mar,Jun,Sep,Dec	7:20-2:15	SF62,500	$0.0001/SF = $6.25	None	9-15-83	262

*See trading hours footnote for Chicago Board of Trade. ** Sunday through Thursday.

Minneapolis Grain Exchange (MGE)

400 S. Fourth St., Minneapolis, MN 55415. (612) 338-6212; fax (612) 339-1155
L. Scott Hackett, chairman; James H. Lindau, president

Contract	Contract months	Trading hours	Contract size	Minimum fluctuation	Daily limit	Date contract launched	Daily volume
Wheat (hard red spring) (F: MW; OF: CW, PW)	Mar,May,Jul, Sep,Dec	F: 9:30-1:15 OF: 9:35-1:25	5,000 bu.	F: 1/4¢/bu.=$12.50 OF: 1/8¢/bu.=$6.25	20¢/bu. =$1,000	F: 1-3-1893 OF: 10-30-84	3,046 136
Wheat (white) (F: NW; OF: NC, NP)	Mar,May,Jul, Sep,Dec	F: 9:35-1:20 OF: 9:40-1:30	5,000 bu.	F: 1/4¢/bu.=$12.50 OF: 1/8¢/bu.=$6.25	20¢/bu. =$1,000	F: 9-10-84 OF: 6-24-91	92 43
Frozen Shrimp (white) (F, OF: SH)	Mar,Jun,Sep,Dec	F: 9:40-1:30 OF: 9:45-1:40	5,000 lbs.	F: 1/4¢/lb.=$12.50 OF: 1/8¢/lb.=$6.25	20¢/lb. = $1,000	F: 7-12-93 OF: 7-12-93	10 2
Black Tiger Shrimp F: BT; OF: BT(C), BT(P)	Mar,Jun,Sep,Dec	F: 9:40-1:30 OF: 9:45-1:40	5,000 lbs.	F: 1/4¢/lb.=$12.50 OF: 1/8¢/lb.=$6.25	20¢/lb. =$1,000	F: 11-18-94 OF: 11-18-94	NA NA

New York Cotton Exchange (NYCE)

4 World Trade Center, New York, NY 10048. (212) 938-2702; fax (212) 488-8135
Paul T. Jones II, chairman; Joseph J. O'Neill, president
FINEX: (212) 938-2634; fax (212) 432-0294. Hunt Taylor, chairman
Citrus Associates of the NYCE Inc.: Elliott Seabrook, president
NYFE: (212) 938-4940, (800) THE NYFE; fax (212) 432-0294. Norman Eisler, chairman

Contract	Contract months	Trading hours	Contract size	Minimum fluctuation	Daily limit	Date contract launched	Daily volume
Cotton (F: CT; OF: CO)	Mar,May,Jul, Oct,Dec	10:30-2:40	50,000 lb. (100 bales)	1/100¢/lb. = $5	2¢/lb. = $1,000	F: 9-10-1870 OF: 10-30-84	10,000 3,000

Citrus Associates of the New York Cotton Exchange Inc.

Contract	Contract months	Trading hours	Contract size	Minimum fluctuation	Daily limit	Date contract launched	Daily volume
Frozen Concentrated Orange Juice (F: JO; OF: OJ)	Jan,Mar,May, Jul,Sep,Nov	10:15-2:15	15,000 lb.	5/100¢/lb. = $7.50	5¢/lb. = $750*	F: 10-26-66 OF: 12-19-85	2,500 500

* 10¢/lb. moving price limits allowed on current and next current futures contracts.

FINEX

Contract	Contract months	Trading hours	Contract size	Minimum fluctuation	Daily limit	Date contract launched	Daily volume
U.S. Dollar Index (USDX) (F: DX; OF: DO)	Mar,Jun,Sep,Dec	*	$1,000 x index	0.01 (1 basis pt.) = $10	***	F: 11-20-85 OF: 9-3-86	2,196 197
2-Year Treasury Auction Notes (F) (TW)	All months	8:20-3	$100 x basis pt. of yield	0.005 pt. = $50	None	2-22-89	3
5-Year Treasury Auction Notes (F) (FY)	All months	8:20-3	$100 x basis pt. of yield	0.005 pt. = $50	None	5-6-87	274

Contract	Contract months	Trading hours	Contract size	Minimum fluctuation	Daily limit	Date contract launched	Daily volume
NYFE							
Sterling/D-mark Cross-rate (F) (MP)	Mar,Jun,Sep,Dec	**	£125,000	DM0.001 pt. = DM12.50	None	6-17-94	94
D-mark/yen Cross-rate (F) (MY)	Mar,Jun,Sep,Dec	**	DM125,000	¥0.01 pt. = ¥1,250	None	F: 7-13-94	496
D-mark/krona Cross-rate (F) (MK)	Mar,Jun,Sep,Dec	**	DM125,000	KR0.0005 pt. = KR62.50	None	@	NA
D-mark/Paris Cross-rate (F) (MF)	Mar,Jun,Sep,Dec	**	DM500,000	FF0.0001 pt. = FF50	None	6-17-94	54
D-mark/lira Cross-rate (F) (ML)	Mar,Jun,Sep,Dec	**	DM250,000	ITL0.05 pt. = ITL12,500	None	8-8-94	15
U.S. dollar/pound Cross-rate (F) (YP)	Mar,Jun,Sep,Dec	*	£62,500	$0.0001 pt. = $6.25	None	@	NA
U.S. dollar/D-mark Cross-rate (F) (YM)	Mar,Jun,Sep,Dec	*	DM125,000	$0.0001 pt. = $12.50	None	6-17-94	242
U.S. dollar/yen Cross-rate (F) (YY)	Mar,Jun,Sep,Dec	*	¥12,500,000	$0.000001 pt. = $12.50	None	@	NA
U.S. dollar/Canadian dollar Cross-rate (F) (YD)	Mar,Jun,Sep,Dec	*	C$100,000	$0.0001 pt. = $10	None	@	NA
U.S. dollar/Swiss franc Cross-rate (F) (YF)	Mar,Jun,Sep,Dec	*	SF125,000	$0.0001pt. = $12.50	None	@	NA
NYSE Composite Index (F, OF) (YX)	Mar,Jun,Sep,Dec	9:30-4:15	$500 x index	0.05 pt. = $25	18 pt.	F: 5-6-82 OF: 1-28-83	3,500 150
CRB Futures Price Index (F, OF) (CR)	Mar,May,Jul, Sep,Dec	9:10-2:45	$500 x index	0.05 pt. = $25	None	F: 6-12-86 OF: 10-28-88	500 40

* Hours are 7 p.m. to 10 p.m.; 3 a.m. to 8 a.m.; and 8:05 a.m. to 3 p.m.; The 3 a.m. to 8 a.m. session takes place on the Dublin exchange floor. During Daylight Savings Time, the 7 p.m. session ends at 11 p.m.
** Hours are 7 p.m. to 10 p.m.; 3 a.m. to 9 a.m.; and 9:05 a.m. to 3 p.m.; The 3 a.m. to 9 a.m. session takes place on the Dublin exchange floor. During Daylight Savings Time, the 7 p.m. session ends at 11 p.m.
*** Expanded price limits apply to 15-minute time periods under certain conditions and at certain times. Consult exchange rules.
@ Contracts have been approved, but at press time hadn't started trading.

New York Mercantile Exchange (NYMEX)

4 World Trade Center, New York, NY 10048. (212) 938-2222; fax (212) 938-2985
Daniel Rappaport, chairman; R. Patrick Thompson, president

NYMEX division:

Contract	Contract months	Trading hours	Contract size	Minimum fluctuation	Daily limit	Date contract launched	Daily volume
Palladium (F) (PA)	Mar,Jun,Sep,Dec	8:10-2:20	100 troy oz.	5¢/oz. = $5	$6/oz. = $600	1-22-68	550
Platinum (F: PL; OF: PO)	F: Jan,Apr,Jul,Oct OF: Plus next 3 months	8:20-2:30	50 troy oz.	10¢/oz. = $5	$25/oz. = $1,250	F: 12-3-56 OF: 10-16-90	3,591 383
Heating Oil (F: HO; OF: OH)	F: Next 18 months OF: Next 6 months plus months 9, 12	9:50-3:10	42,000 gal.	0.01¢/gal. = $4.20	F: 4¢/gal. = $1,680 OF: None	F: 11-14-78 OF: 6-26-87	35,255 2,758
New York Harbor Unleaded Gasoline (F: HU; OF: GO)	F: Next 18 months OF: Next 6 months plus months 9, 12	9:50-3:10	42,000 gal.	0.01¢/gal. = $4.20	4¢/gal. = $1,680 OF: None	F: 12-3-84 OF: 3-13-89	29,942 2,755
Gulf Coast Unleaded Gasoline (F) (GU)	Next 18 months	9:40-3:10	42,000 gal.	0.01¢/gal. = $4.20	4¢/gal. = $1,680	9-18-92	0
Crude Oil (F: CL; OF: LO)	F: Next 18 mos. plus months 21, 24, 30, 36 OF: Next 12 & 18, 24, 36	9:45-3:10	1,000 barrels (42,000 gal.)	1¢/barrel = $10	F: $1.50/barrel = $1,500 OF: None	F: 3-30-83 OF: 11-14-86	106.762 23,827
Sour Crude Oil (F) (SC)	Next 18 months	9:35-3:20	1,000 barrels	1¢/barrel = $10	$1.50/barrel = $1,500	2-28-92	0
Natural Gas (F: NG; OF: ON)	F: Next 18 months OF: Next 12 months	10-3:10*	10,000 MMBtu	0.1¢/MMBtu = $10	F: 10¢/MMBtu = $1,000 OF: None	F: 4-2-90 OF: 10-2-92	23,419 1,756
Propane Gas (F) (PN)	Next 15 months	9:55-3:05	42,000 gal.	0.01¢/gal. = $4.20	4¢/gal. = $1,680	8-21-87	298
Heating oil/crude spread (OF) (CH)	Next 6, 9, 12 mos.	9:50-3:10	1,000 barrels each	$0.01/bbl =$10	None	10-7-94	NA
Gasoline/crude spread (OF) (CF)	Next 6, 9, 12 mos.	9:50-3:10	1,000 barrels each	$0.01/bbl =$10	None	10-7-94	NA

*NYMEX also has a 2-minute trading session after the close of its natural gas futures markets with trading in the first four listed months only at prices established during the closing range.

(continued)

FUTURES AND OPTIONS EXCHANGES *(concluded)*

COMEX division:

Contract	Contract months	Trading hours	Contract size	Minimum fluctuation	Daily limit	Date contract launched	Daily volume
Copper (F: HG; OF: HX)	F: All months* OF: Feb,Mar,May,Jul, Sep,Nov,Dec	9:25-2**	25,000 lb.	5/100¢/lb. = $12.50	20¢/lb. = $5,000	F: 7-5-33 OF: 4-7-86	10,816 725
Silver (F: SI; OF: SO)	F: Current + next 2 mo. plus Jan,Mar,May, Jul,Sep,Dec* OF: All months	8:25-2:25**	5,000 troy oz.	F: 1/2¢/oz. = $25 OF: 1/10¢/oz. = $5	$1.50/oz. = $7,500	F: 7-5-33 OF: 10-4-84	23,861 5,238
Gold (F: GC; OF: OG)	F: Current + next 2 mo. plus Feb,Apr,Aug,Oct* OF: All months	8:20-2:30**	100 troy oz.	10¢/oz. = $10	$75/oz. = $7,500	F: 12-31-74 OF: 10-1-82	34,599 6,597
5-Day Gold (O)	Each day based on nearest of Feb,Apr,Jun,Aug,Dec	8:20-2:30**	100 troy oz.	10¢/oz. = $10	None	9-3-91	4
5-Day Silver (O)	Each day based on nearest of Mar,May,Jul,Sep,Dec	8:25-2:25**	5,000 troy oz.	1/10¢/oz. = $5	None	12-10-91	2
5-Day Copper (O)	Each day based on nearest of Mar,May,Jul,Sep,Dec	9:25-2**	25,000 lb.	5/100¢/lb. = $12.50	None	8-10-93	1
Eurotop 100 Stock Index (F: ER; OF: EQ)	Mar,May,Jul,Dec	5:30-11:30*	$100 x index	F: 0.1 pt. = $10 OF: 0.05 pt. = $5	None	F: 10-26-92 OF: 1-8-93	255 0

* Spot, next two months and months listed out to 23 months; 60 months for June, Dec gold futures and July, Dec silver futures.
** Plus 3-minute post-settlement trading session; matched order procedure for closing prices only applies to copper futures.

New York Stock Exchange (NYSE)

11 Wall St., New York, NY 10005. (212) 656-8533; (800) 692-6973; fax (212) 656-8534
Donald J. Solodar, executive VP, fixed income/options; David Krell, VP, options and index products
The NYSE trades index products and equity options. Contact exchange for individual contract specifications.

Pacific Stock Exchange (PSE)

301 Pine St., San Francisco, CA 94104. (415) 393-4000; fax (415) 393-4202
Leopold Korins, chairman, CEO; Robert M. Greber, president, COO
The PSE trades equity options and two index options. Contact exchange for individual contract specifications.

Philadelphia Stock Exchange (PHLX)/Philadelphia Board of Trade (PBOT)

1900 Market St., Philadelphia, PA 19103. (215) 496-5000; (800) 843-7459; fax (215) 496-5653
John J. Wallace, chairman; Nicholas A. Giordano, president, CEO

*Options traded on the PHLX (top line under contract size, fluctuation, date launched), futures on the PBOT (bottom line)
Several index options also are traded on PHLX. Contact the exchange for specifications.*

Contract	Contract months	Trading hours *	Contract size	Minimum fluctuation	Date contract launched
British Pound (O; F: ZB)	O: ** F: Mar,Jun,Sep,Dec plus 2 near-term months	2:30 a.m.-2:30 p.m.	O: £31,250 F: £62,500	$0.0001/£=$3.125 $0.0001/£=$6.25	8-28-87 5-22-87
Canadian Dollar (O; F: ZC)	**	7 a.m.-2:30 p.m.	O: C$50,000 F: C$100,000	US$0.0001/C$=US$5 US$0.0001/C$=US$10	2-11-83 8-8-86
Deutsche Mark (O; F: ZD)	**	2:30 a.m.-2:30 p.m.	O: DM 62,500 F: DM125,000	$0.0001/DM=$6.25 $0.0001/DM=$12.50	2-4-83 8-8-86
Swiss Franc (O; F: ZS)	**	2:30 a.m.-2:30 p.m.	O: SF62,500 F: SF125,000	$0.0001/SF=$6.25 $0.0001/SF=$12.50	1-26-83 8-8-86
French Franc (O; F: ZF)	**	2:30 a.m.-2:30 p.m.	O: FF250,000 F: FF500,000	$0.00002/FF=$5 $0.000002/FF=$10	9-17-84 8-8-86
Japanese Yen (O; DF: ZJ)	**	2:30 a.m.-2:30 p.m.	O: ¥6,250,000 F: ¥12,500,000	$0.000001/¥=$6.25 $0.000001/¥=$12.50	1-14-83 8-8-86
Australian Dollar (O; F: ZA)	**	2:30 a.m.-2:30 p.m.	O: A$50,000 F: A$100,000	US$0.0001/A$=US$5 US$0.0001/A$=US$10	1-19-87 5-22-87
European Currency Unit (O; F: ZE)	**	2:30 a.m.-2:30 p.m.	O: ECU62,500 F: ECU125,000	$0.0001/ECU=$6.25 $0.0001/ECU=$12.50	2-12-86 8-8-86
D-Mark/J-Yen Cross Rates (O) (MYX)	**	2:30 a.m.-2:30 p.m.	DM62,500	¥0.01/DM = ¥625	11-22-91
B-Pound/D-Mark Cross Rates (O) (PMX)	**	2:30 a.m.-2:30 p.m.	£31,250	DM0.0002/£ = DM6.25	9-21-92
B-Pound/J-Yen Cross Rates (O) (PYX)	**	2:30 a.m.-2:30 p.m.	£31,250	¥0.02 = ¥625	***

* Times listed are Eastern Standard Time from 6 p.m. Sunday through 2:30 p.m. Friday. During Eastern Daylight Time, trading is from 7-11 p.m. and 11:30 p.m. through 2:30 p.m. the following day.
** Regular options: Mar, June, Sep, Dec, and two near-term months; month-end options: three nearest months; long-term options: 18, 24, 30 and 36 months (June and December).
*** Not yet trading.

Source: Reprinted with permission of *Futures Magazine*, 219 Parkade, Cedar Falls, Iowa 50613. 319-277-6341.

COMMODITY PRICE CHARTS[1]

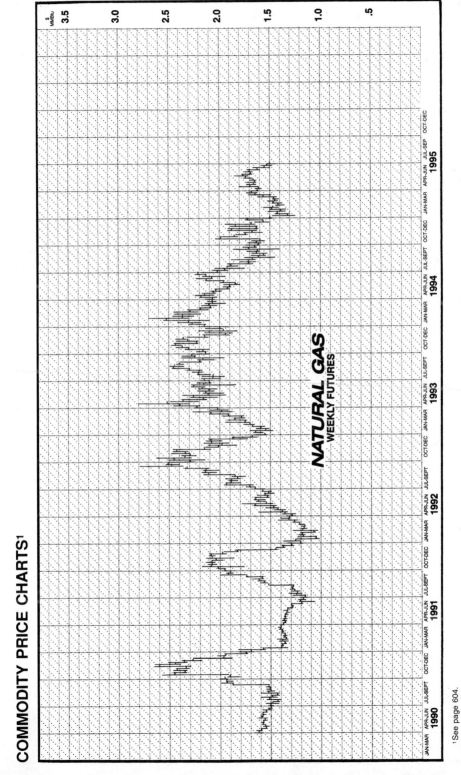

NATURAL GAS
WEEKLY FUTURES

[1] See page 604.

Source: Charts reprinted from: **Commodity Price Charts**, 219 Parkade, Cedar Falls, Iowa 50613.

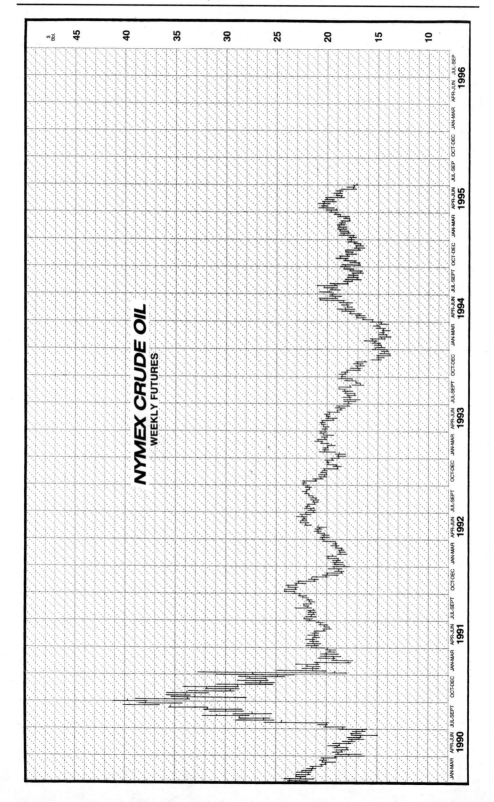

NYMEX CRUDE OIL
WEEKLY FUTURES

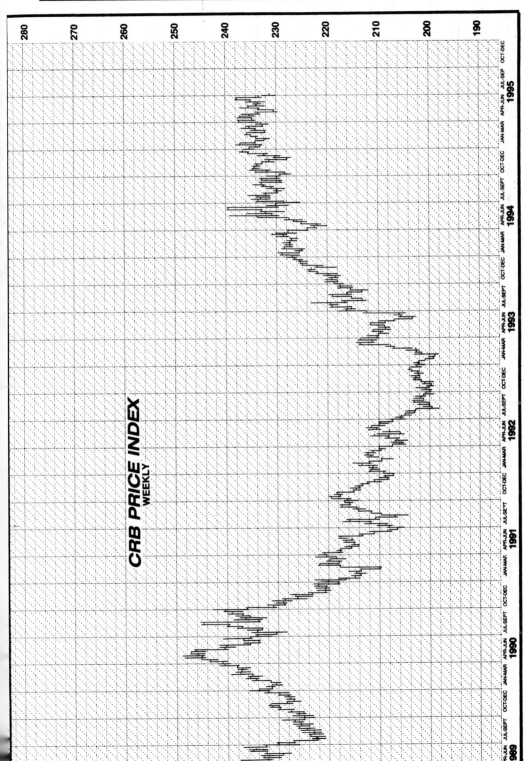

CRB PRICE INDEX
WEEKLY

280 270 260 250 240 230 220 210 200 190

APR-JUN JUL-SEPT OCT-DEC **1989** JAN-MAR APR-JUN JUL-SEPT OCT-DEC **1990** JAN-MAR APR-JUN JUL-SEPT OCT-DEC **1991** JAN-MAR APR-JUN JUL-SEPT OCT-DEC **1992** JAN-MAR APR-JUN JUL-SEPT OCT-DEC **1993** JAN-MAR APR-JUN JUL-SEPT OCT-DEC **1994** JAN-MAR APR-JUN JUL-SEPT OCT-DEC **1995**

Source: Charts reprinted from: **Commodity Price Charts**, 219 Parkade, Cedar Falls, Iowa 50613.

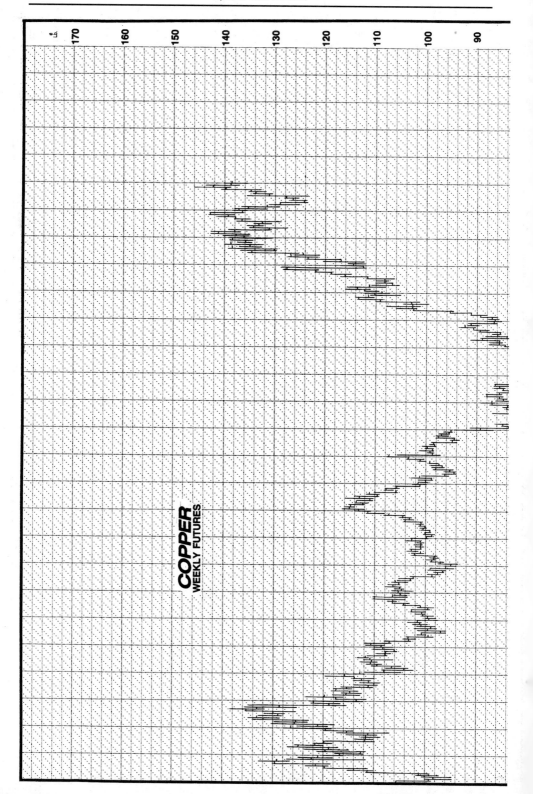

COPPER
WEEKLY FUTURES

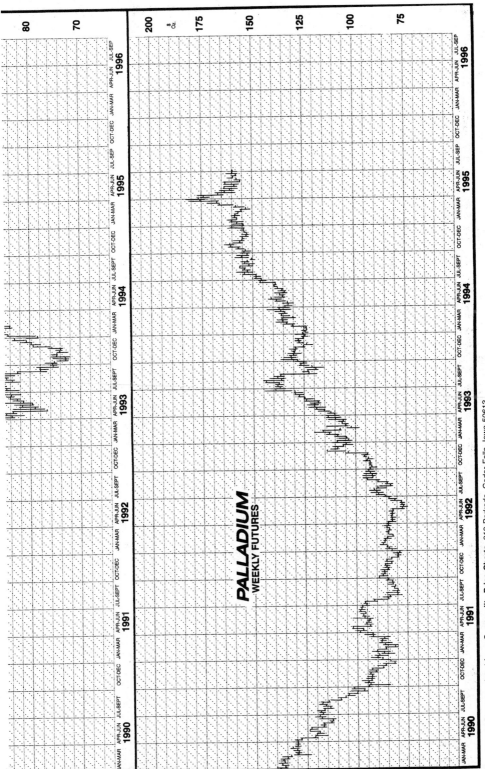

PALLADIUM
WEEKLY FUTURES

Source: Charts reprinted from: Commodity Price Charts, 219 Parkade, Cedar Falls, Iowa 50613.

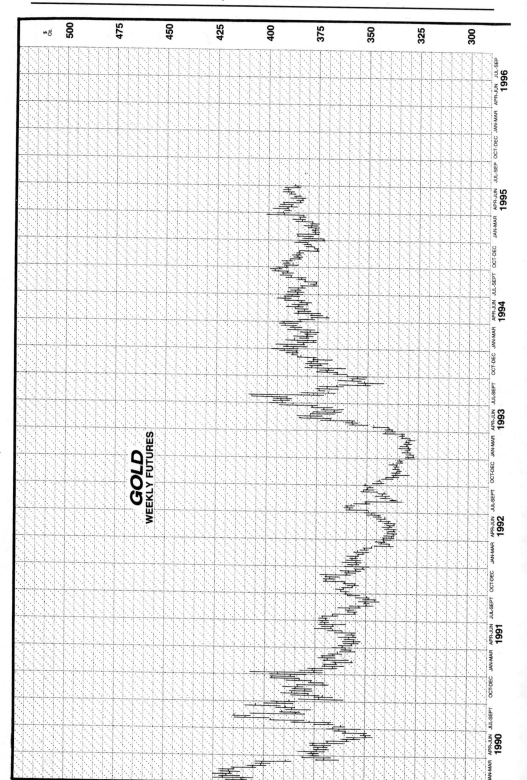

GOLD
WEEKLY FUTURES

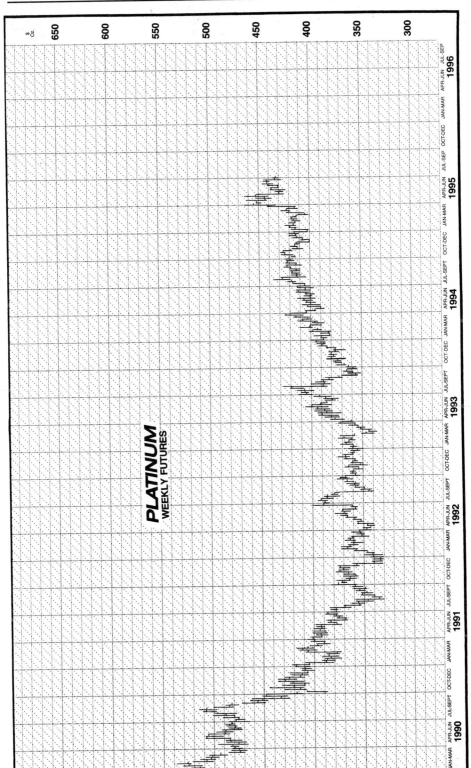

PLATINUM
WEEKLY FUTURES

Source: Charts reprinted from: **Commodity Price Charts**, 219 Parkade, Cedar Falls, Iowa 50613.

COMEX SILVER
WEEKLY FUTURES

$/Oz.

11.0
10.5
10.0
9.5
9.0
8.5
8.0
7.5
7.0

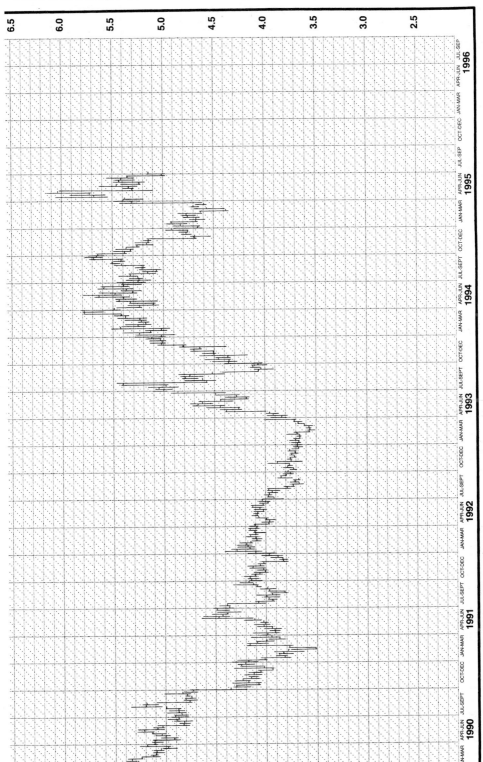

Source: Charts reprinted from: **Commodity Price Charts**, 219 Parkade, Cedar Falls, Iowa 50613.

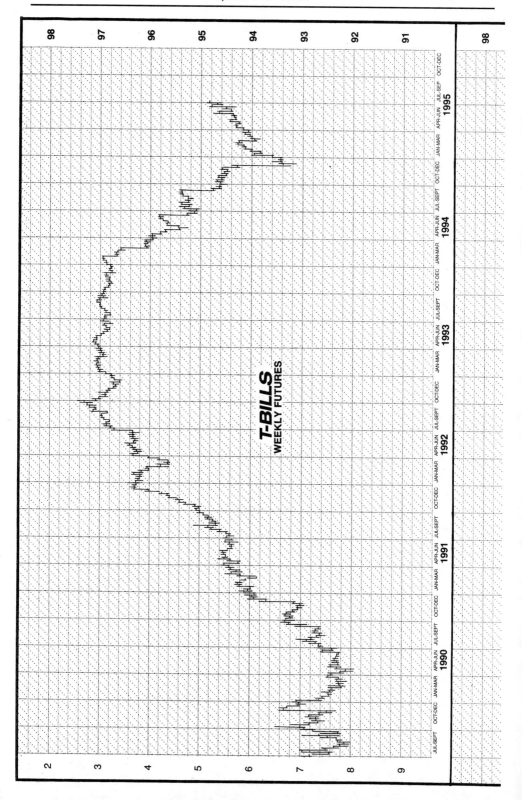

T-BILLS
WEEKLY FUTURES

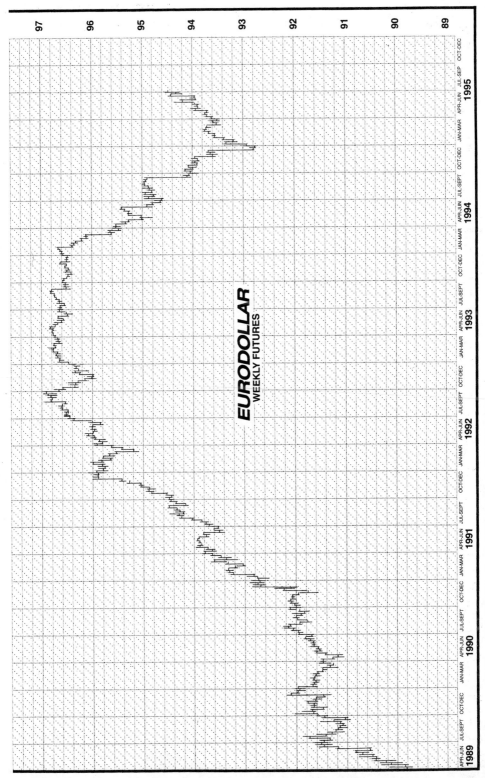

EURODOLLAR
WEEKLY FUTURES

Source: Charts reprinted from: **Commodity Price Charts**, 219 Parkade, Cedar Falls, Iowa 50613.

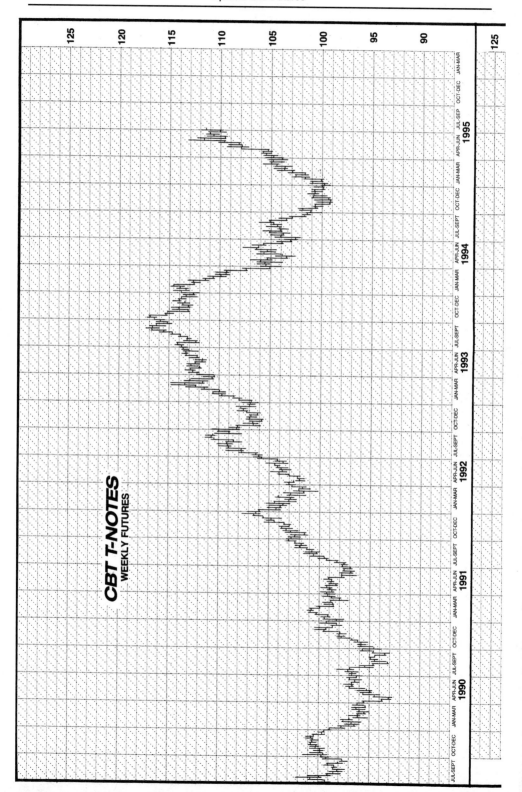

CBT T-NOTES
WEEKLY FUTURES

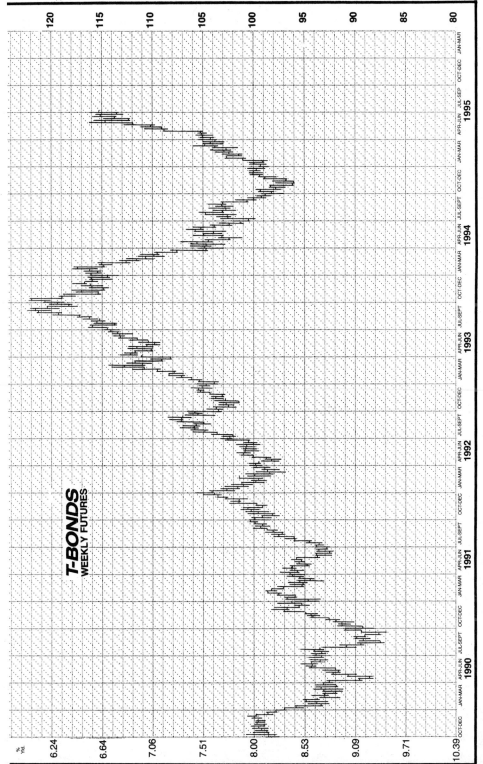

T-BONDS
WEEKLY FUTURES

Source: Charts reprinted from: **Commodity Price Charts**, 219 Parkade, Cedar Falls, Iowa 50613.

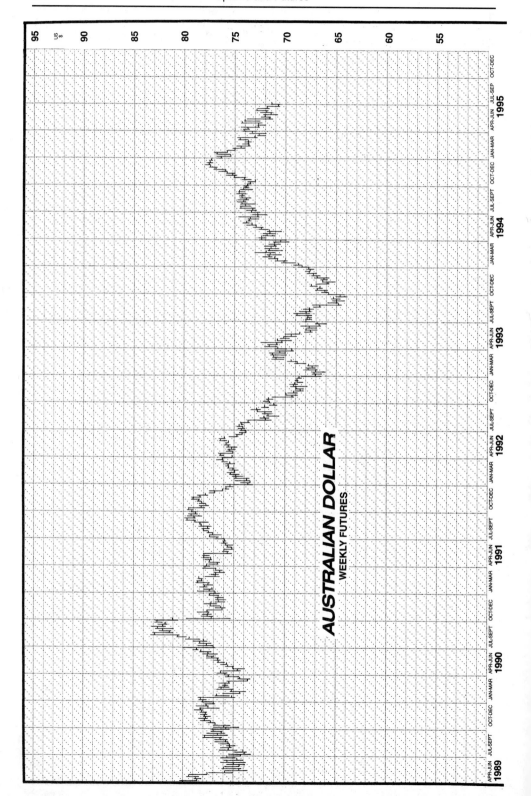

AUSTRALIAN DOLLAR
WEEKLY FUTURES

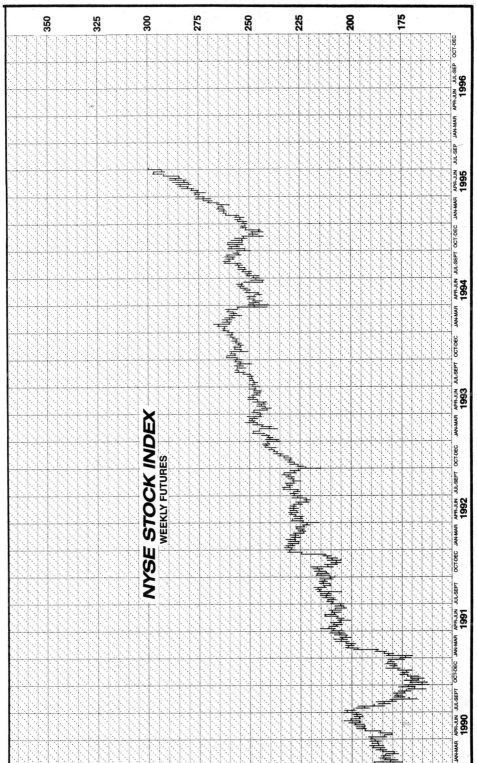

NYSE STOCK INDEX
WEEKLY FUTURES

Source: Charts reprinted from: **Commodity Price Charts**, 219 Parkade, Cedar Falls, Iowa 50613.

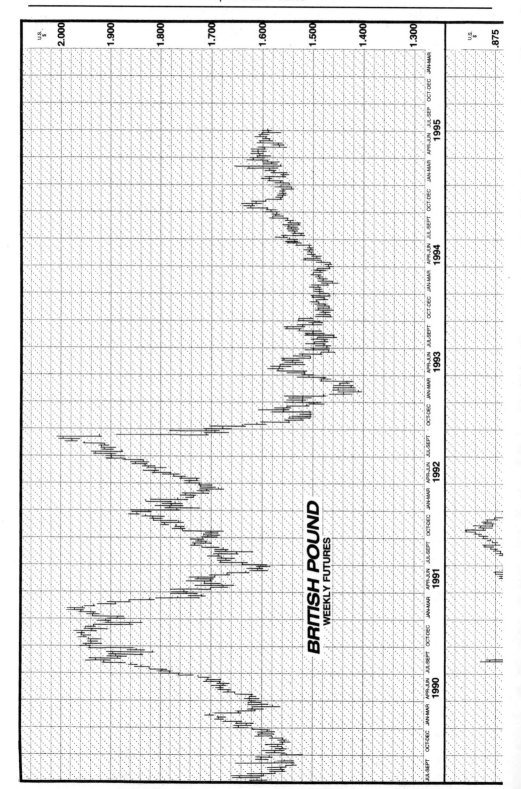

BRITISH POUND
WEEKLY FUTURES

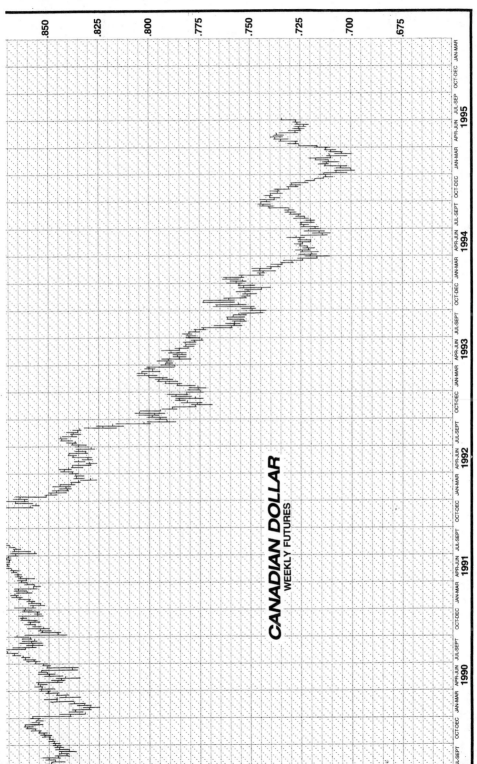

CANADIAN DOLLAR
WEEKLY FUTURES

Source: Charts reprinted from: **Commodity Price Charts**, 219 Parkade, Cedar Falls, Iowa 50613.

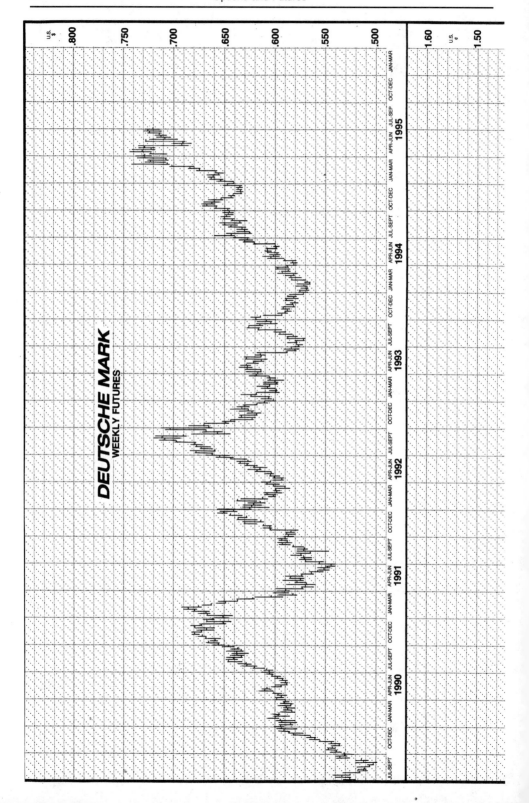

DEUTSCHE MARK
WEEKLY FUTURES

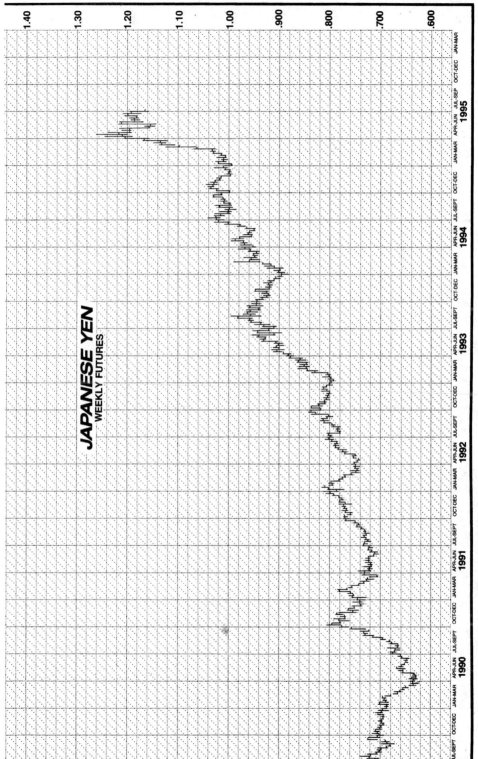

JAPANESE YEN
WEEKLY FUTURES

Source: Charts reprinted from: **Commodity Price Charts**, 219 Parkade, Cedar Falls, Iowa 50613.

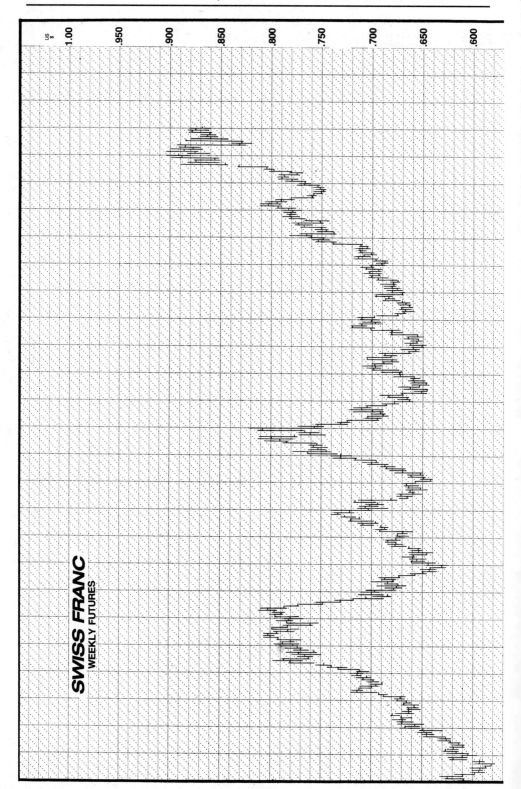

SWISS FRANC
WEEKLY FUTURES

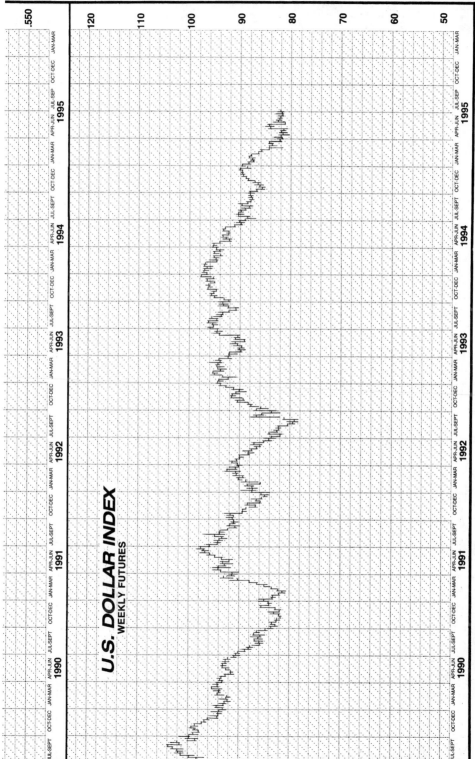

U.S. DOLLAR INDEX
WEEKLY FUTURES

Source: Charts reprinted from: **Commodity Price Charts**, 219 Parkade, Cedar Falls, Iowa 50613.

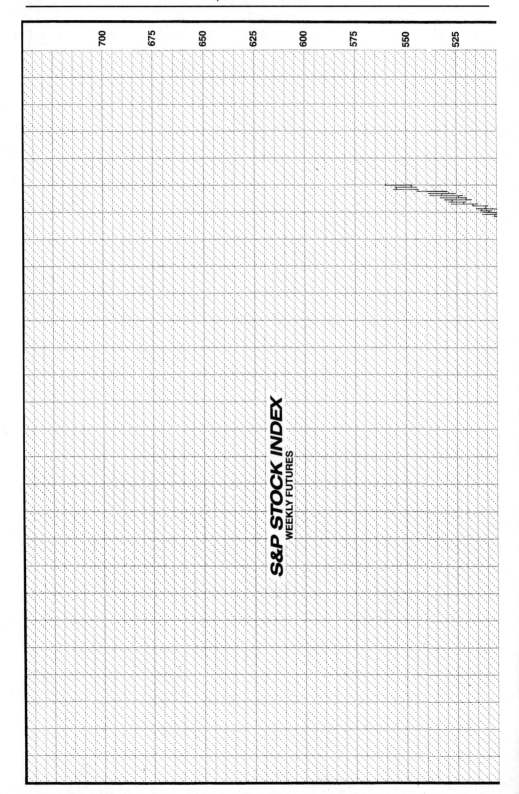

S&P STOCK INDEX
WEEKLY FUTURES

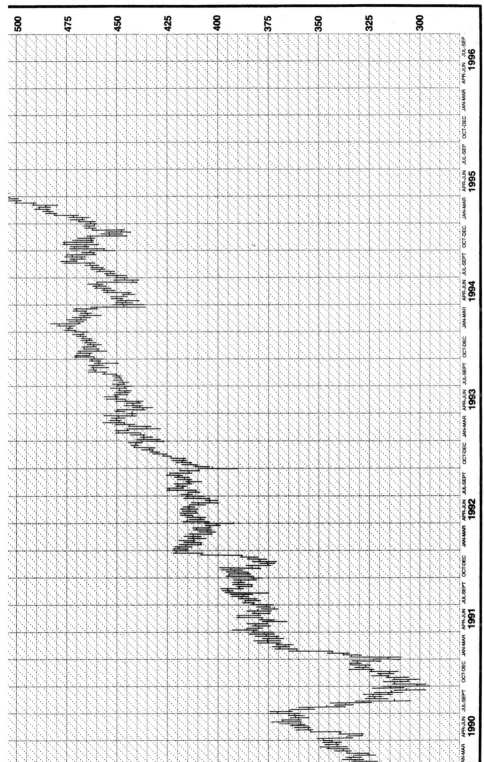

Source: Charts reprinted from: **Commodity Price Charts**, 219 Parkade, Cedar Falls, Iowa 50613.

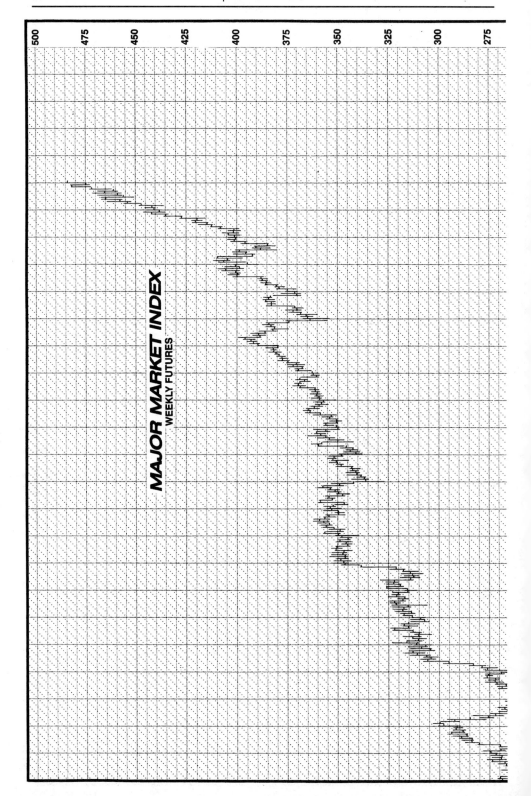

MAJOR MARKET INDEX
WEEKLY FUTURES

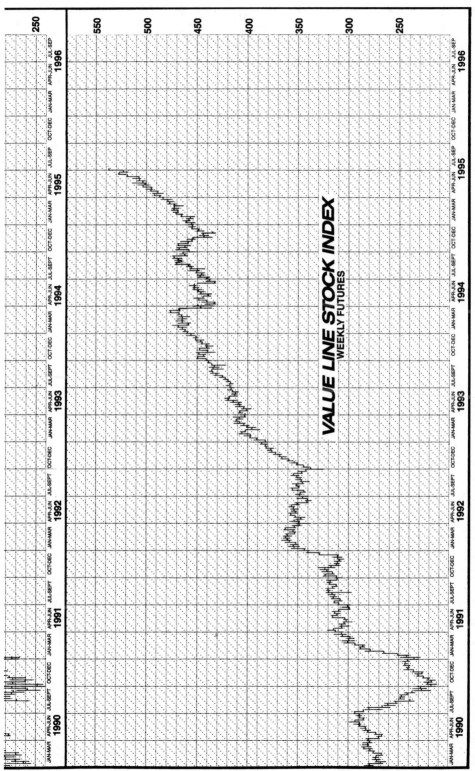

VALUE LINE STOCK INDEX
WEEKLY FUTURES

Source: Charts reprinted from: **Commodity Price Charts**, 219 Parkade, Cedar Falls, Iowa 50613.

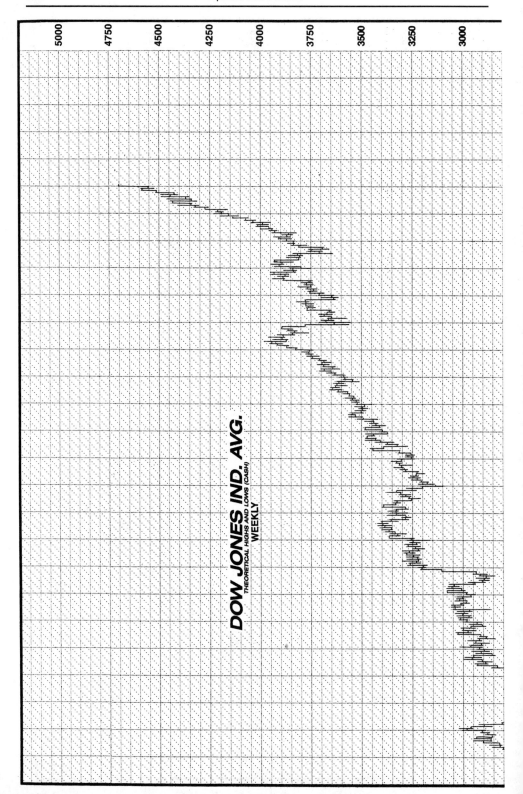

DOW JONES IND. AVG.
THEORETICAL HIGHS AND LOWS (CASH)
WEEKLY

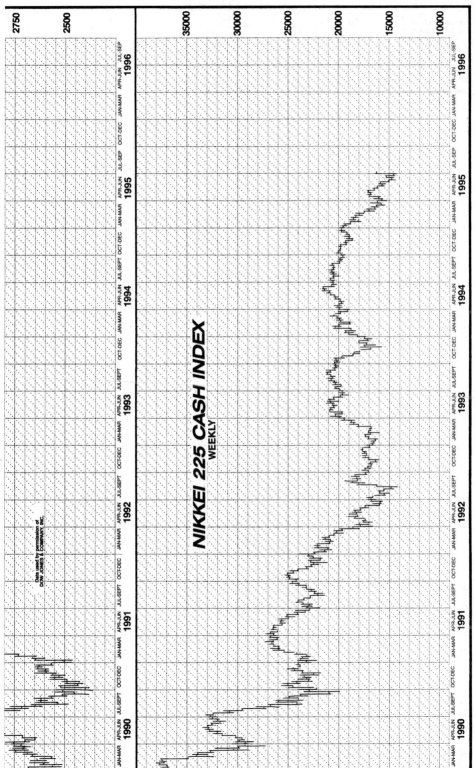

NIKKEI 225 CASH INDEX
WEEKLY

Data used by permission of
DOW JONES & COMPANY INC.

These weekly Charts are plotted through July 7, 1995. Weekly charts are published on a quarterly schedule, and the next mailing is on October 6, 1995. Monthly charts are published semi-annually. The next mailing will be August 11, 1995.

Weekly High, Low & Close Charts of the Nearest Futures Contract: Long-term charts are plotted for the nearest futures contract on a weekly basis. During the week of change-over, the price action of both the expiring contract and the next one are included in the week's range.

Contract months used for plotting CPC weekly and monthly supplements.

Cattle	Feb., April, June, Aug., Oct., Dec.
Hogs	Feb., April, June, July, Aug., Oct., Dec.
Feeder Cattle	Jan., March, April, May, Aug., Sept., Oct., Nov.
Pork Bellies	Feb., March, May, July, Aug.
Corn	March, May, July, Sept., Dec.
Oats	March, May, July, Sept., Dec.
Rice	Jan., March, May, July, Sept., Nov.
Soybeans	Jan., March, May, July, Aug., Sept., Nov.
Soybean Meal	Jan., March, May, July, Aug., Sept., Oct., Dec.
Soybean Oil	Jan., March, May, July, Aug., Sept., Oct., Dec.
Chicago Wheat	March, May, July, Sept., Dec.
K.C. Wheat	March, May, July, Sept., Dec.
Mpls. Wheat	March, May, July, Sept., Dec.

Cotton	March, May, July, Oct., Dec.
Lumber	Jan., March, May, July, Sept., Nov.
Crude Oil	Every month
Gas (Unleaded)	Every month
Heating Oil	Every month
Currencies	March, June, Sept., Dec.
Eurodollar	March, June, Sept., Dec.
Interest Rates	March, June, Sept., Dec.
Stock Indices	March, June, Sept., Dec. (except MMI)
Major Market Index	Every month
Cocoa	March, May, July, Sept., Dec.
Coffee	March, May, July, Sept., Dec.
Orange Juice	Jan., March, May, July, Sept., Nov.
Sugar	March, May, July, Oct.
Copper	March, May, July, Sept., Dec.
Silver	March, May, July, Sept., Dec.
Gold	Feb., April, June, Aug., Oct., Dec.
Palladium	March, June, Sept., Dec.
Platinum	Jan., April, July, Oct.

Source: Charts reprinted from: **Commodity Price Charts,** 219 Parkade, Cedar Falls, Iowa 50613.

Computer Services and Educational Material for Business and Finance

Selected On-Line Business/ Financial Data Bases

On-line data bases are collections of computer stored data which are retrievable by remote terminals. The data bases are collected and organized by a so-called *producer*. The latter provides the data base to a *vendor* who distributes the data by means of a telecommunication network to the user. Often a vendor will offer a large number of different data bases. In some instances the producer and vendor are the same.

Using an on-line data base requires: (1) a *terminal* (a typewriter-like device usually equipped with a video display) to receive data and send commands to the vendor's computers, and (2) a *modem* for coupling the terminal to a telephone line. Printouts (hard copy) of the desired information can be obtained with the aid of electronic printers located at the user's terminal or, alternatively, ordered from the vendor.

The user accesses the data base by dialing a telephone number and then typing (on the terminal keyboard) a password provided by the vendor. Searching the data base is done with special commands and procedures peculiar to each base.

The contents of data bases vary. Some provide statistical data only—usually in the form of time series. Other bases provide bibliographic references and, in some instances, abstracts or the full text of articles.

Specifics concerning data base contents, instructions, and prices are available from vendors. Listed below are some major business data bases and vendors. More complete information concerning data bases is available from the sources given below.

ABI Inform
Provides references on all areas of business management with emphasis on "how-to" information.

Producer: Data Courier Inc. (Louisville, KY)

Vendors: BRS, DIALOG, SDC

Accountants Index
Contains reference information on accounting, auditing taxation, management and securities.

Producer: American Institute of Certified Public Accountants (New York, NY)

Vendor: SDC

American Profile
Provides statistical information on U.S. households including population, income, dependents, and also data on types of businesses in that area.

Producer: Donnelley Marketing (Stamford, CT)

Vendor: Business Information Service

Business Credit Service
Provides business credit and financial information.

Producer: TRW, Inc. (Orange, CA)

Vendor: TRW

Canadian Business and Current Affairs
English language business and popular periodicals

Producer: Micromedia Limited (Toronto, Ontario)

Vendors: DIALOG, CISTI

CIS Index
Contains references and abstracts from nearly every publication resulting from Senate and House Committee meetings since 1970.

Producer: Congressional Information Services, Inc. (Washington, DC)

Vendors: DIALOG, SDC

Commodities
Contains over 41,000 times series of current commodity prices for the U.S., Canada, U.K., and France.

Producer: Wolff Research (London, U.K.)

Vendor: I. P. Sharp

Compendex (Computerized Engineering Index)
Contains over 1 million citations and abstracts to the world wide engineering literature.

Producer: Engineering Information Inc. (New York)

Vendors: BRS, D-STAR, DIALOG

CompuServe, Inc.
Provides references, statistical and full text retrieval of information of personal

interest including health, recipes, gardening, financial and investment data including the Compustat and Value Line data bases.

Producer: CompuServe, Inc. (Columbus, OH)
Vendor: CompuServe

Compustat

Provides very extensive financial data on companies.

Producer: Standard and Poor's Compustat Service, Inc. (Englewood, CO)
Vendors: ADP, Business Information Services, CompuServe, Data Resources, Chase Econometrics/Interactive Data Corp.

Disclosure II

Provides extracts of 10K and other reports filed with the Securities and Exchange Commission.

Producer: Disclosure Inc. (Bethesda, MD)
Vendors: Business Information Services (Control Data), DIALOG, Dow Jones, New York Times Information Services, Mead Data Central.

Dow Jones News/Retrieval Service and Stock Quote Reporters

Contains text of articles appearing in major financial publications including *The Wall Street Journal* and *Barrons*. Quote Service provides quotes on stocks, bonds, mutual funds.

Producer: Dow Jones & Company (New York, NY)
Vendors: BRS, Dow Jones & Company

DRI Capsule/EEI Capsule

Provides over 3700 U.S. social and economic statistical time series such as population, income, money supply data, etc.

Producers: Data Resources, Inc. (Lexington, MA) and Evans Economics Inc. (Washington, DC)
Vendors: Business Information Services, United Telecom Group, I. P. Sharp

Federal Register Abstracts

Provides coverage of federal regulatory agencies as published in the Federal Register.

Producer: Capitol Services (Washington, DC)
Vendors: DIALOG, SDC

GTE Financial System One Quotation Service

Provides current U.S. and Canadian quotations and statistical data on stocks,

bonds, options, commodities and other market data.

Producer: GTE Information Systems (Reston, VA)
Vendor: GTE Information Systems, Inc.

The Information Bank

Provides an extensive current affairs data source consisting of abstracts from numerous English language publications.

Producer: The New York Times Information Service
Vendor: The New York Times Information Service

LEXIS

Contains full text references to a wide range of legal information including court decisions, regulations, government statutes.

Producer: Mead Data Central (New York, NY)
Vendor: Mead Data Central

Media General Financial Services

Provides extensive historical fundamental and technical data and calculations on U.S. publicly owned companies. Also provides data on industries, the financial markets, mutual funds and corporate bonds.

Producer: Media General Financial Services (Richmond, VA)
Vendors: Dow Jones News Retrieval, DIALOG, Thomson Financial Networks, Randall—Helms Fiduciary Consultants, Telescan, Lotus One Source (CD-ROM)

NEXIS

Provides full text business and general news including management, technology, finance, science, politics, religion.

Producer: Mead Data Central (New York, NY)
Vendor: Mead Data Central

PTS Marketing and Advertising Reference Service

Provides citations with abstracts & articles on the marketing and advertising of consumer goods and services.

Producer: Predicast, Inc. (Cleveland, OH)
Vendors: DIALOG, BRS, DATA-STAR

PTS Prompt

Covers world wide business news on new products, market data, etc.

Producer: Predicast, Inc. (Cleveland, OH)
Vendors: ADP, BRS, DIALOG

Quick Quote

Provides current quotations, volume, high-low data for securities of U.S. public corporations.

Producer: CompuServe Inc.

Vendor: CompuServe

Quotron 800

Provides up to the minute quotation and statistics on a broad range of securities such as stocks, bonds, options, commodities.

Producer: Quotron Systems Inc. (Los Angeles, CA)

Vendor: Quotron Systems Inc.

The Source (has been acquired by CompuServe)

Producer: Source Telecomputing (McLean, VA)

Vendor: Source Telecomputing Corp.

Trinet Company Data Base

Provides data on about 250,000 companies in the U.S.

Producer: Trinet, Inc. (Parsippany, NJ)

Vendors: DRI, DIALOG, Mead Data Central

For further information on data bases:

Computer Readable Data Bases, Gale Research (835 Penobscot Building, Detroit, MI 48226) A comprehensive data base and CD-ROM directory, revised annually.

Data Base Vendors

ADP Data Services, Inc.
175 Jackson Plaza
Ann Arbor, MI 48106
313-769-6800

BRS, Inc.
1200 Route 7
Latham, NY 12110
518-783-1161
800-235-1209

Chase Econometrics/Interactive Data Corporation
95 Hayden Avenue
Lexington, MA 02173
617-890-8100

CompuServe, Inc.
5000 Arlington Centre Boulevard
Columbus, OH 43220
614-457-8600
800-848-8990

Data Resources, Inc. (DRI)
1750 K Street NW
Washington, DC 20006
202-663-7720

DIALOG Information Services, Inc.
3460 Hillview Avenue
Palo Alto, CA 94304
415-858-3810
800-334-2564

Dow Jones & Company, Inc.
P.O. Box 300
Princeton, NJ 08540
609-452-2000
800-257-5114

General Electric Information Services Company
401 North Washington Street
Rockville, MD 20850
301-294-5405

GTE Education Services
8505 Freeport Parking
Irving, TX 75063
214-929-3000

Mead Data Central
P.O. Box 933
Dayton, OH 45401
800-227-4908

The New York Times Information Services, Inc.
229 West 43rd Street
New York, NY 10036
800-543-6862

Quotron Systems, Inc.
12731 West Jefferson Boulevard
P.O. Box 66914
Los Angeles, CA 90066
213-827-4600

SDC Search Service/Orbit
8000 Westpark Drive
McLean, VA 22102
703-442-0900
800-456-7248

I. P. Sharp Associates
Exchange Tower
Toronto, Ontario, Canada M5X IE3
416-364-5361
800-387-1588

TRW Information Services Division
505 City Parkway West
Orange, CA 92668
714-385-7000

Noteworthy Software of Interest to Investors

The following provides a brief description of moderately priced software products of special interest to investors.

The EQUALIZER (Charles Schwab & Co., 101 Montgomery Street, San Francisco, CA 94104)

To use this software it is necessary to open an account with the discount brokerage firm of Charles Schwab & Co. The EQUAL-IZER includes the following features:

- access to financial information and data via Dow Jones News Retrieval and Standard and Poor's Marketscope
- price quotes on securities and mutual funds provided by Schwab, Dow Jones, or Warner Communications
- portfolio maintenance and record keeping
- trading capabilities (via Charles Schwab, of course)

This is excellent software for the active investor. The instruction manual which accompanies the software is first class.

QUICKEN (Intuit, 66 Willow Place, Menlo Park, CA 04025)

This is a leading program for maintaining records and managing personal finances. QUICKEN permits users to record deposits, monitor investments, keep track of saving, and print out checks as they become due. The software can also be used for small business and bookkeeping.

A 'help' program is provided which facilitates start up. The instruction manual accompanying QUICKEN is excellent. Also available at bookstores are other manuals.

WEALTHBUILDER (developed for *Money Magazine* by Reality Technologies, Inc., 3624 Market Street, Philadelphia, PA 19104) is a program intended to guide users on the development of investment strategies to meet their goals (home purchase, college education, retirement, etc.). Given the investor's financial goals, risk tolerance, net worth, and the like, the program provides an allocation of investments among equities, mutual funds, bonds, precious metals, and money market funds.

Information for allocating funds among each type of investment is available (for a price) on quarterly updated disks which contain data provided by Standard & Poor. CompuServe, the online data base, now provides a service for users of WEALTHBUILDERS.

The program is recommended for serious financial planning.

MANAGING YOUR MONEY (MECA Ventures, Inc., 355 Riverside Avenue, Westport, CT 06801) is a popular personal financial program providing the following features:

- budget and checkbook program
- a tax estimator
- an estate and insurance planner
- a financial calculator
- a portfolio manager

In addition to the above the program has a built in name filing capability and a word processor.

QUANT IX (Quant Software, 5900 North Port Washington Road, Milwaukee, WI 53217) is an excellent and relatively inexpensive portfolio stock analyzer with record keeping capability. The software also provides for downloading data from CompuServe and Warner Communications. A unique feature is the availability of six different methods for evaluating stocks.

OPTIONS TOOLS DELUX (Richard Kedrow, 25 Illinois Avenue, Schaumburg, IL 60913). This helpful software provides option investors with the capability of calculating theoretical option values using the Black-Scholes and binomial models, hedge ratios, volatility, breakeven values, and covered call analysis.

BUSINESS PLAN GENERATOR (Essex Financial Group, 714 Market Street, Philadelphia, PA 19106) is a very useful computer program intended to help in the development of business plans. The underlying philosophy is that of Dynamic Planning which views planning as an ongoing procedure responding to changes in the business environment, and provides for feedback into the planning process. The program generates all of the expected planning projections; profit and loss statements, balance sheets, cash flows, and numerous financial ratios. The program also permits taking into account the effects of acquisitions. The *Business Plan Generator* requires the use of Lotus 1-2-3 since it functions as an overlay of the latter.

DEALMAKER II (ValueSource, 1939 Grand Avenue, San Diego, CA 92109) is a sophisticated business evaluation program intended for buyers, sellers, and brokers. Other applications include evaluations of businesses for such purposes as marital dissolution, estate and gift taxes, employee stock options, and going public.

Twelve evaluation methods are provided, including book value, liquidation value, discounted earnings, the use of industry P/E ratios, and others.

The program also allows for consideration of projected post acquisition financial statements and for the effects on buyer and seller of different ways of financing the acquisition.

Screening Software

With thousands of companies listed on the exchanges, identifying promising investment opportunities is a daunting task. Fortunately this arduous chore can be greatly facilitated with the screening programs described below.

Investor's Alliance

Investor's Alliance provides a data base service to members comprising nearly 5000 companies traded over the counter and on the exchanges. The data are provided on diskettes which are updated quarterly. However, users can also update more frequently by going online. A screening capability is also included. Though the cost of this service is very modest the available data are surprisingly extensive.

Investor's Alliance, Inc.
219 Commercial Boulevard
Fort Lauderdale, FL 33308-4440
Telephone: 305-491-5100

MarketBase

MarketBase is an impressive software package providing key financial and market data on *all* companies traded in the NYSE, AMEX, and NASDAQ exchanges—over 5200 companies in all. The data spans a five year period. Updates are provided (depending on the subscription terms) on a weekly, monthly, or quarterly basis. Bi-monthly and bi-weekly updates are also available.

Over fifty financial and market criteria are included for screening. Companies may be screened by selecting a combination of criteria; for example, the PE ratio, revenues, earnings growth, market capitalization, SIC Code, and others. *MarketBase* also permits users to define their own selection criteria. Once screened, companies may be further explored by obtaining annual reports, 10-Q, press releases, and other materials by phoning the company. Although *MarketBase* software does not provide phone numbers, these may be obtained by calling the vendor. The software also lacks online communication capability.

MarketBase is an important resource for the serious investor. For further information contact:

MarketBase, Inc.
368 Hillside Avenue
P.O. Box 37
Needham Heights, MA 02194
Telephone: 800-735-0700

Value/Screen

Value/Screen provides access to about 1600 stocks composing the Value Line data base. Reportedly, these account for 90% of all trading on U.S. exchanges. Screening is carried out utilizing a wide variety of financial, market, and rating variables. Provisions are also available for user defined screening criteria. A rather elegant screening option displays particular screening criteria by means of a histogram.

Value/Screen is equipped with an online communications capability providing access to the Dow Jones News Retrieval Services.

Updates are available weekly, monthly, or quarterly. Data can also be down loaded online.

For complete details, contact:

Value Line Publishing, Inc.
711 Third Avenue
New York, NY 10017
Telephone: 800-654-0508

Home Study Course for Investors

Several very good self study courses of interest to investors are worthy of mention here.

CEI FUTURES AND OPTIONS HOME STUDY COURSE (Commodities Educational Institute, 219 Parkade, Cedar Falls, IA 50613) is intended to train professionals and consists of some 21 audio tapes and two binders of notes and supplemental materials. The emphasis of this course is on commodity futures though some attention is given to financial futures and options on futures. Topics covered include the economic function of the futures market, how the futures market works, technical analysis, hedging, rules and regulations, financial futures, stock indexes, options on futures.

Purchasers of this course can attend 5 day work shops held in various cities at reduced rates.

FUTURES TRADING COURSE (Futures Industry Association, 2001 Pennsylvania Avenue, N.W., Washington, D.C. 20006) is comprised of three volumes which cover much of the same ground as the CEI course described above. The Institute also runs seminars and workshops for those wishing to acquire professional qualifications.

HOME STUDY COURSE OF THE AMERICAN ASSOCIATION OF INDIVIDUAL INVESTORS (AAII) (AAII, 625 North Michigan Avenue, Chicago, IL 60611) is an excellent course which provides coverage of the entire field of investments: stocks, bonds, mutual funds, futures, options, real estate, and more. Purchasers of this course receive updated material from time to time. The association also holds comprehensive national investment seminars on topics of current interest which are also available on audio tape. A recent seminar occupied some 25 tapes and is accompanied by a substantial set of notes.

FORBES STOCK MARKET COURSE (Forbes, Inc., 60 Fifth Avenue, New York, NY 10011) is somewhat more elementary than the AAII described above and focuses almost exclusively on the stock market. A small section of the course is devoted to options and warrants. The course should appeal to investors who want a readable basic survey of the equities market.

Employment

Future Employment Opportunities

Every 2 years, the Bureau of Labor Statistics develops projections of the labor force, economic growth, industry output and employment, and occupational employment under three sets of alternative assumptions—low, moderate, and high. These projections cover a 10- to 15-year period and provide a framework for the discussion of job outlook in each occupational statement in the *Handbook*. All of the approximately 250 statements in this edition of the *Handbook* identify the principal factors affecting job prospects, then discuss how these factors are expected to affect the occupation. This chapter uses the moderate alternative of each projection to provide a framework for the individual job outlook discussions.

Population Trends

Employment opportunities are affected by population trends in several ways. Changes in the size and composition of the population between 1992 and 2005 will influence the demand for goods and services. For example, the population aged 85 and over will grow about four times as fast as the total population, increasing the demand for health services. Population changes also produce corresponding changes in the size and characteristics of the labor force.

The U.S. civilian noninstitutional population, aged 16 and over, is expected to increase from about 192 to 219 million over the 1992-2005 period—growing more slowly than it did during the previous 13-year period, 1979-92. However, even slower population growth will increase the demand for goods and services, as well as the demand for workers in many occupations and industries.

The age distribution will shift toward relatively fewer children and teenagers and a growing proportion of middle-aged and older people into the 21st century. The decline in the proportion of teenagers reflects the lower birth rates that prevailed during the 1980's; the impending large increase in the middle-aged population reflects the aging of the "baby boom" generation born between 1946 and 1964; and the very rapid growth in the

number of old people is attributable to high birth rates prior to the 1930's, together with improvements in medical technology that have allowed most Americans to live longer.

Minorities and immigrants will constitute a larger share of the U.S. population in 2005 than they do today. Substantial increases in the number of Hispanics, Asians, and Blacks are anticipated, reflecting immigration, and higher birth rates among Blacks and Hispanics. Substantial inflows of immigrants will continue to have significant implications for the labor force. Immigrants tend to be of working age but of different educational and occupational backgrounds than the U.S. population as a whole.

Population growth varies greatly among geographic regions, affecting the demand for goods and services and, in turn, workers in various occupations and industries. Between 1979 and 1992, the population of the Midwest and the Northeast grew by only 3 percent and 4 percent, respectively, compared with 19 percent in the South and 30 percent in the West. These differences reflect the movement of people seeking new jobs or retiring, as well as higher birth rates in some areas than in others.

Projections by the Bureau of the Census indicate that the West and South will continue to be the fastest growing regions, increasing 24 percent and 16 percent, respectively, between 1992 and 2005. The Midwest population is expected to grow by 7 percent, while the number of people in the Northeast is projected to increase by only 3 percent.

Geographic shifts in the population alter the demand for and the supply of workers in local job markets. Moreover, in areas dominated by one or two industries, local job markets may be extremely sensitive to the economic conditions of those industries. For these and other reasons, local employment opportunities may differ substantially from the projections for the Nation as a whole presented in the *Handbook*. Sources of information on State and local employment prospects are identified on page 620.

Labor Force Trends

Source: *Occupational Outlook Handbook* 1994–1995, U.S. Department of Labor, Bureau of Labor Statistics.

Population is the single most important factor governing the size and composition of

Chart 1

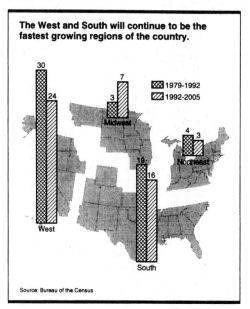

The West and South will continue to be the fastest growing regions of the country.

□ 1979-1992
▨ 1992-2005

Source: Bureau of the Census

America's workers will be an increasingly diverse group as we move toward 2005. White non-Hispanic men will make up a slightly smaller proportion of the labor force, and women and minority group members will comprise a larger share than in 1992. White non-Hispanics have historically been the largest component of the labor force, but their share has been dropping, and is expected to fall from 78 percent in 1992 to 73 percent by 2005. Whites are projected to grow more slowly than Blacks, Asians, and others, but because of their size, whites will experience the largest numerical increase. Hispanics will add about 6.5 million workers to the labor force from 1992 to 2005, increasing by 64 percent. Despite this dramatic growth, Hispanics' share of the labor force will only increase from 8 percent to 11 percent, as shown in chart 3. Blacks, Hispanics, and Asians and other racial groups will account for roughly 35 percent of all labor force entrants between 1992 and 2005.

Women will continue to join the labor force in growing numbers. The percentage increase of women in the labor force between 1992 and 2005 will be larger than the percentage increase in the total labor force, but smaller than the percentage increase for women in the previous 13-year period. In the late 1980's, the labor force participation of women under age 40 began to increase more slowly than in the past. Women were only 42 percent of the labor force in 1979;

the labor force, which includes people who are working, or looking for work. The civilian labor force, 127 million in 1992, is expected to reach 151 million by 2005. This projected 19-percent increase represents a slight slowdown in the rate of labor force growth, largely due to slower population growth (chart 2).

Chart 2

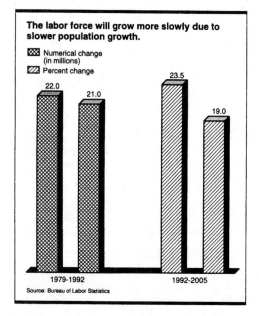

The labor force will grow more slowly due to slower population growth.

▨ Numerical change (in millions)
▨ Percent change

Source: Bureau of Labor Statistics

Chart 3

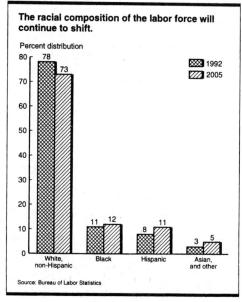

The racial composition of the labor force will continue to shift.

Percent distribution

▨ 1992
▨ 2005

Source: Bureau of Labor Statistics

by 2005, they are expected to constitute 48 percent.

The changing age structure of the population will directly affect tomorrow's labor force. Compared to young workers, the pool of experienced workers will increase. In 1992, the median age of the labor force was 37.2 years; by 2005, it will be 40.5 years.

Between 1979 and 1992, the youth labor force (16 to 24 years of age) dropped by 5 million, a 20-percent decline. In contrast, the number of youths in the labor force will increase by 3.7 million over the 1992–2005 period, reflecting an increase of 18 percent, compared to 19 percent growth for the total labor force. As a result, young people are expected to comprise roughly the same percentage of the labor force in 2005 as in 1992. Among youths, the teenage labor force (16 to 19 years of age) will increase by 31 percent over the 1992–2005 period, a numerical increase of 2.1 million. The labor force 20 to 24 years of age is projected to increase by 12 percent, a numerical increase of 1.6 million. The total youth labor force accounted for 24 percent of the entire labor force in 1979, fell to 16 percent in 1992, and should stay about the same through 2005.

The scenario should be somewhat different for prime-age workers (25 to 54 years of age). The baby boom generation will continue to add members to the labor force, but their share of the labor force peaked in 1985. These workers accounted for 62 percent of the labor force in 1979, and rose significantly to 72 per-

cent in 1992, but should decline slightly to 70 percent by 2005. The proportion of workers in the 25–34 age range will decline dramatically, from 28 percent to 21 percent in 2005. On the other hand, the growing proportion of workers between the ages of 45 and 54 is equally striking. These workers should account for 24 percent of the labor force by the year 2005, up from 18 percent in 1992. Because workers in their mid-forties to mid-fifties usually have substantial work experience and tend to be more stable than younger workers, this could result in improved productivity and a larger pool of experienced applicants from which employers may choose.

The number of older workers, aged 55 and above, is projected to grow about twice as fast as the total labor force between 1992 and 2005, and about 15 times as fast as the number of workers aged 55 and above grew between 1979 and 1992. As the baby boomers grow older, the number of workers aged 55 to 64 will increase; they exhibit higher labor force participation than their older counterparts. By 2005, workers aged 55 and over will comprise 14 percent of the labor force, up from 12 percent in 1992.

In recent years, the level of educational attainment of the labor force has risen dramatically. In 1992, 27 percent of all workers aged 25 and over had a bachelor's degree or higher, while only 12 percent did not possess a high school diploma. The trend toward higher educational attainment is expected to continue. Projected rates of employment growth are faster for occupations requiring higher levels of education or training than for those requiring less.

Three out of the 4 fastest growing occupational groups will be executive, administrative, and managerial; professional specialty; and technicians and related support occupations. These occupations generally require the highest levels of education and skill, and will make up an increasing proportion of new jobs. Office and factory automation, changes in consumer demand, and movement of production facilities to offshore locations are expected to cause employment to stagnate or decline in many occupations that require little formal education—apparel workers and textile machinery operators, for example. Opportunities for those who do not finish high school will be increasingly limited, and workers who are not literate may not even be considered for most jobs.

Those who do not complete high school and are employed are more likely to have low paying jobs with little advancement potential, while workers in occupations requiring higher levels of education have higher incomes. In addition, many of the occupations projected to grow most rapidly between

Chart 4

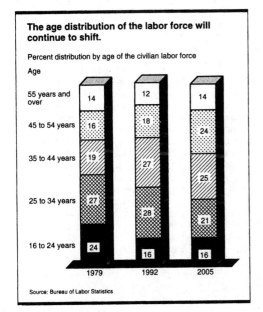

The age distribution of the labor force will continue to shift.

Percent distribution by age of the civilian labor force

Age

Age	1979	1992	2005
55 years and over	14	12	14
45 to 54 years	16	18	24
35 to 44 years	19	27	25
25 to 34 years	27	28	21
16 to 24 years	24	16	16

Source: Bureau of Labor Statistics

1992 and 2005 are among those with higher earnings.

Nevertheless, even slower growing occupations that have a large number of workers will provide many job openings, because the need to replace workers who leave the labor force or transfer to other occupations account for most job openings. Consequently, workers with all levels of education and training will continue to be in demand, although advancement opportunities generally will be best for those with the most education and training.

Employment Change

Total employment is expected to increase from 121.1 million in 1992 to 147.5 million in 2005, or by 22 percent. The 26.4 million jobs that will be added to the U.S. economy by 2005 will not be evenly distributed across major industrial and occupational groups, causing some restructuring of employment. Continued faster than average employment growth among occupations that require relatively high levels of education or training is expected. The following two sections examine projected employment change from both industrial and occupational perspectives. The industrial profile is discussed in terms of wage and salary employment, except for agriculture, forestry, and fishing, which includes self-employed and unpaid family workers. The occupational profile is viewed in terms of total employment (wage and salary, self-employed, and unpaid family workers).

Industrial Profile

The long-term shift from goods-producing to service-producing employment is expected to continue (chart 5). For example, service-producing industries, including transportation, communications, and utilities; retail and wholesale trade; services; government; and finance, insurance, and real estate are expected to account for approximately 24.5 million of the 26.4 million job growth over the 1992–2005 period. In addition, the services division within this sector—which includes health, business, and educational services—contains 15 of the 20 fastest growing industries. Expansion of service sector employment is linked to a number of factors, including changes in consumer tastes and preferences, legal and regulatory changes, advances in science and technology, and changes in the way businesses are organized and managed. Specific factors responsible

Chart 5

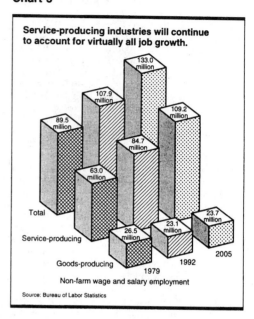

Service-producing industries will continue to account for virtually all job growth.

Non-farm wage and salary employment

Source: Bureau of Labor Statistics

for varying growth prospects in major industry divisions are discussed below.

Service-Producing Industries

Services. Services is both the largest and the fastest growing division within the service-producing sector (chart 6). This division provided 38.6 million jobs in 1992; employment is expected to rise 40 percent to 54.2 million by 2005, accounting for almost two-thirds of all new jobs. Jobs will be found in small firms and in large corporations, and in industries as diverse as hospitals, data processing, and management consulting. Health services and business services are projected to continue to grow very fast. In addition, social, legal, and engineering and management services industries further illustrate this division's strong growth.

Health services will continue to be one of the fastest growing industries in the economy with employment increasing from 9.6 to 13.8 million. Improvements in medical technology, and a growing and aging population will increase the demand for health services. Employment in home health care services— the second fastest growing industry in the economy—nursing homes, and offices and clinics of physicians and other health practitioners is projected to increase rapidly. However, not all health industries will grow at the

Chart 6

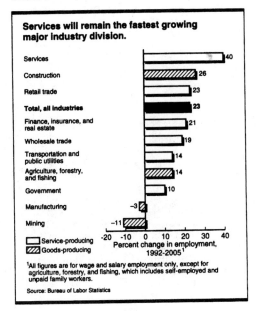

Services will remain the fastest growing major industry division.

	Percent change in employment, 1992-2005[1]
Services	40
Construction	26
Retail trade	23
Total, all industries	23
Finance, insurance, and real estate	21
Wholesale trade	19
Transportation and public utilities	14
Agriculture, forestry, and fishing	14
Government	10
Manufacturing	-3
Mining	-11

☐ Service-producing
▨ Goods-producing

[1]All figures are for wage and salary employment only, except for agriculture, forestry, and fishing, which includes self-employed and unpaid family workers.

Source: Bureau of Labor Statistics

same rate. Despite being the largest health care industry, hospitals will grow more slowly than most other health services industries.

Business services industries also will generate many jobs. Employment is expected to grow from 5.3 million in 1992 to 8.3 million in 2005. Personnel supply services, made up primarily of temporary help agencies, is the largest sector in this group and will increase by 57 percent, from 1.6 to 2.6 million jobs. However, due to the slow-down in labor force participation by young women, and the proliferation of personnel supply firms in recent years, this industry will grow more slowly than during the 1979–92 period. Business services also includes one of the fastest growing industries in the economy, computer and data processing services. This industry's rapid growth stems from advances in technology, world wide trends toward office and factory automation, and increases in demand from business firms, government agencies, and individuals.

Education is expected to add 2.8 million jobs to the 9.7 million in 1992. This increase reflects population growth and, in turn, rising enrollments projected for elementary, secondary, and postsecondary schools. The elementary school age population (ages 5–13) will rise by 2.8 million between 1992 and 2005, the secondary school age (14–17) by 3.4 million, and the traditional postsecondary school age (18–24) by 2.2 million. In addition, continued rising enrollments of older, for-

eign, and part-time students are expected to enhance employment in postsecondary education. Not all of the increase in employment in education, however, will be for teachers; teacher aides, counselors, and administrative staff also are projected to increase.

Employment in social services is expected to increase by 1.7 million, bringing the total to 3.7 million by 2005, reflecting the growing elderly population. For example, residential care institutions, which provide around-the-clock assistance to older persons and others who have limited ability for self-care, is projected to be the fastest growing industry in the U.S. economy. Other social services industries that are projected to grow rapidly include child daycare services and individual and miscellaneous social services, which includes elderly daycare and family social services.

Wholesale and retail trade. Employment in wholesale and retail trade is expected to rise by 19 and 23 percent, respectively; from 6 to 7.2 million in wholesale trade and from 19.3 to 23.8 million in retail trade. Spurred by higher levels of personal income, the fastest projected job growth in retail trade is in apparel and accessory stores, and appliance, radio, television, and music stores. Substantial numerical increases in retail employment are anticipated in large industries, including eating and drinking places, food stores, automotive dealers and service stations, and general merchandise stores.

Finance, insurance, and real estate. Employment is expected to increase by 21 percent—adding 1.4 million jobs to the 1992 level of 6.6 million. The strong demand for financial services is expected to continue. Bank mergers, consolidations, and closings—resulting from overexpansion and competition from nonbank corporations that offer bank-like services—are expected to limit job growth among commercial banks and savings and loan associations. The fastest growing industries within this sector are expected to be holding and investment offices and mortgage bankers and brokers. Insurance agents, brokers, and services are expected to register the largest numerical increase in jobs.

Transportation, communications, and public utilities. Overall employment will increase by 14 percent. Employment in the transportation sector is expected to increase by 24 percent, from 3.5 to 4.3 million jobs. Truck transportation will account for 50 percent of all new jobs; air transportation will account for 29 percent. The projected gains in transportation jobs reflect the continued shift from rail to road freight transportation, rising personal incomes, and growth in foreign trade. In addition, deregulation in the transportation industry has increased personal and business travel options, spurring strong job growth in the passenger transportation arrangement industry, which includes travel agencies. Reflecting laborsaving technology and industry competition, employment in communications is projected to decline by 12 percent. Employment in utilities, however, is expected to grow, adding 117,000 new jobs, highlighted by strong growth in water supply and sanitary services.

Government. Between 1992 and 2005, government employment, excluding public education and public hospitals, is expected to increase 10 percent, from 9.5 million to 10.5 million jobs. Growth will be driven by State and local government. Employment in the Federal Government and U.S. Postal Service is expected to decline by 113,000 and 41,000 jobs, respectively.

Goods-Producing Industries

Employment in this sector has not recovered from the recessionary period of the early 1980's and the trade imbalances that began in the mid-1980's. Although overall employment in goods-producing industries is expected to show little change, growth prospects within the sector vary considerably.

Construction. Construction is expected to increase by 26 percent from 4.5 to 5.6 million. The need to improve the Nation's infrastructure, resulting in increases in road, bridge, and tunnel construction, will offset the slowdown in demand for new housing, reflecting the slowdown in population growth and the overexpansion of office building construction in recent years.

Agriculture, forestry, and fishing. After declining for many decades, overall employment in agriculture, forestry, and fishing is projected to grow by 14 percent, from 1.7 million to 2 million jobs. Strong growth in agricultural services will more than offset an expected continued decline in crops, livestock and livestock products.

Manufacturing. Manufacturing employment is expected to decline by 3 percent from the 1992 level of 18 million. The projected loss of manufacturing jobs reflects productivity gains achieved from increased investment in manufacturing technologies.

The composition of manufacturing employment is expected to shift since most of the jobs that will disappear are production jobs. On the other hand, the number of professional positions in manufacturing firms will increase.

Mining. Mining employment is expected to decline 11 percent from 631,000 to

562,000. Underlying this projection is the assumption that domestic oil production will drop and oil imports will rise, reducing employment in the crude petroleum industry. In addition, employment in coal mining should continue to decline sharply due to the expanded use of laborsaving machinery.

Occupational Profile

Continued expansion of the service-producing sector conjures up an image of a work force dominated by cashiers, retail sales workers, and waiters. Although service sector growth will generate millions of these jobs, it also will create jobs for financial managers, engineers, nurses, electrical and electronics technicians, and many other managerial, professional, and technical workers. As indicated earlier, the fastest growing occupations will be those that require the most formal education and training.

This section furnishes an overview of projected employment in 12 categories or "clusters" of occupations based on the Standard Occupational Classification (SOC). The SOC is used by all Federal agencies that collect occupational employment data, and is the organizational framework for grouping statements in the *Handbook.*

In the discussion that follows, projected employment change is described as growing faster, slower, or the same as the average for

Chart 7

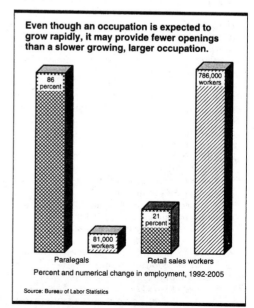

Even though an occupation is expected to grow rapidly, it may provide fewer openings than a slower growing, larger occupation.

86 percent — Paralegals — 81,000 workers

786,000 workers — Retail sales workers — 21 percent

Percent and numerical change in employment, 1992-2005

Source: Bureau of Labor Statistics

all occupations. (These phrases are explained on page 619.) While occupations that are growing fast generally offer good opportunities, the numerical change in employment also is important because large occupations, such as retail sales workers, may offer many more new jobs than a small, fast-growing occupation, such as paralegals (chart 7). For a more detailed discussion of occupational growth, see the discussion of job outlook in the chapter, Keys to Understanding What's in the *Handbook*.

Professional specialty occupations. Workers in these occupations perform a wide variety of duties, and are employed in almost every industry. Employment in this cluster is expected to grow by 37 percent, from 16.6 to 22.8 million jobs, making it the fastest growing occupational cluster in the economy (chart 8). Human services workers, computer scientists and systems analysts, physical therapists, special education teachers, and operations research analysts are among the fastest growing professional specialty occupations.

Service occupations. This group includes a wide range of workers in protective services, food and beverage preparation, health services, and cleaning and personal services. Employment in these occupations is expected to grow by 33 percent, faster than average, from 19.4 to 25.8 million. Service occupations that are expected to experience both fast growth and large job growth include homemaker-home health aides, nursing aides, child care workers, guards, and correction officers.

Technicians and related support occupations. Workers in this group provide technical assistance to engineers, scientists, physicians, and other professional workers, as well as operate and program technical equipment. Employment in this cluster is expected to increase 32 percent, faster than average, from 4.3 to 5.7 million. Employment of paralegals is expected to increase much faster than average as use of these workers in the rapidly expanding legal services industry increases. Health technicians and technologists, such as licensed practical nurses and radiological technologists, will add large numbers of jobs. Growth in other occupations, such as broadcast technicians, will be limited by laborsaving technological advances.

Executive, administrative, and managerial occupations. Workers in this cluster establish policies, make plans, determine staffing requirements, and direct the activities of businesses, government agencies, and other organizations. Employment in this cluster is expected to increase by 26 percent, from 12.1 to 15.2 million, reflecting average growth. Growth will be spurred by the increasing number and complexity of business operations and result in large employment gains, especially in the services industry division. However, many businesses will streamline operations by employing fewer managers, thus offsetting increases in employment.

Like other occupations, changes in managerial and administrative employment reflect industry growth, and utilization of managers and administrators. For example, employment of health services managers will grow much faster than average, while wholesale and retail buyers are expected to grow more slowly than average.

Hiring requirements in many managerial and administrative jobs are becoming more stringent. Work experience, specialized training, or graduate study will be increasingly necessary. Familiarity with computers will continue to be important as a growing number of firms rely on computerized management information systems.

Transportation and material moving occupations. Workers in this cluster operate the equipment used to move people and equipment. Employment in this group is expected to increase by 22 percent, from 4.7 to 5.7 million jobs. Average growth is expected for bus drivers, reflecting rising school enrollments. Similar growth is expected for truck drivers and railroad transportation workers due to growing demand for transportation services. Technological improvements and automation should result in material moving equipment operators increasing more slowly

Chart 8

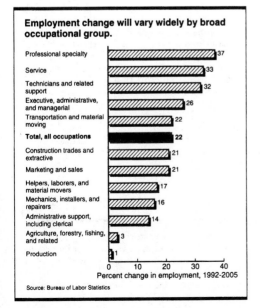

Employment change will vary widely by broad occupational group.

Professional specialty	37
Service	33
Technicians and related support	32
Executive, administrative, and managerial	26
Transportation and material moving	22
Total, all occupations	22
Construction trades and extractive	21
Marketing and sales	21
Helpers, laborers, and material movers	17
Mechanics, installers, and repairers	16
Administrative support, including clerical	14
Agriculture, forestry, fishing, and related	3
Production	1

0   10   20   30   40
Percent change in employment, 1992-2005

Source: Bureau of Labor Statistics

Employment

than the average. Water transportation workers are projected to show little change in employment as technological advances increase productivity.

Construction trades and extractive occupations. Workers in this group construct, alter, and maintain buildings and other structures, and operate drilling and mining equipment. Overall employment in this group is expected to increase 21 percent, about as fast as average, from 3.7 to 4.5 million. Virtually all of the new jobs will be in construction. Spurred by new projects and alterations to existing structures, average employment growth is expected in construction. On the other hand, increased automation, continued stagnation in the oil and gas industries, and slow growth in demand for coal, metal, and other materials will result in a decline in employment of extractive workers.

Marketing and sales occupations. Workers in this cluster sell goods and services, purchase commodities and property for resale, and stimulate consumer interest. Employment in this cluster is projected to increase by 21 percent, from 13 to 15.7 million jobs, about as fast as average. Demand for travel agents is expected to grow much faster than average. Due to strong growth in the industries that employ them, services sales representatives, securities and financial services sales workers, and real estate appraisers will experience faster than average growth. Many part- and full-time job openings are expected for retail sales workers and cashiers due to the large size and high turnover associated with these occupations. Opportunities for higher paying sales jobs, however, will tend to be more competitive.

Helpers, laborers, and material movers. Workers in this group assist skilled workers and perform routine, unskilled tasks. Overall employment is expected to increase by 17 percent, about as fast as average, from 4.5 to 5.2 million jobs. Some routine tasks will become increasingly automated, limiting employment growth among machine feeders and offbearers. Employment of service station attendants will decline, reflecting the trend toward self-service gas stations. Employment of construction laborers, however, is expected to increase about as fast as average, reflecting growth in the construction industry.

Mechanics, installers, and repairers. These workers adjust, maintain, and repair automobiles, industrial equipment, computers, and many other types of equipment. Overall employment in these occupations is expected to grow by 16 percent, from 4.8 to 5.6 million, due to increased use of mechanical and electronic equipment. The fastest growing occupation in this group is expected to be data processing equipment repairers,

reflecting the increased use of these types of machines. Communications equipment mechanics, installers, and repairers, and telephone and cable television line installers and repairers, in sharp contrast, are expected to record a decline in employment due to labor-saving advances.

Administrative support occupations, including clerical. Workers in this largest major occupational group perform a wide variety of administrative tasks necessary to keep organizations functioning smoothly. The group as a whole is expected to grow by 14 percent, from 22.3 to 25.4 million jobs, about as fast as the average. Technological advances are projected to slow employment growth for stenographers and typists and word processors. Receptionists and information clerks will grow faster than average, spurred by rapidly expanding industries such as business services. Because of their large size and substantial turnover, clerical occupations will offer abundant opportunities for qualified jobseekers in the years ahead.

Agriculture, forestry, fishing, and related occupations. Workers in these occupations cultivate plants, breed and raise livestock, and catch animals. Although demand for food, fiber, and wood is expected to increase as the world's population grows, the use of more productive farming and forestry methods and the consolidation of smaller farms are expected to result in only a 3-percent increase in employment, from 3.5 to 3.6 million jobs. Employment of farm operators and farm workers is expected to rapidly decline, reflecting greater productivity; the need for skilled farm managers, on the other hand, should result in average employment growth in that occupation.

Production occupations. Workers in these occupations set up, install, adjust, operate, and tend machinery and equipment and use hand tools to fabricate and assemble products. Little change in the 1992 employment level of 12.2 million is expected due to increases in imports, overseas production, and automation. Relative to other occupations, employment in many production occupations is more sensitive to the business cycle and competition from imports.

Replacement Needs

Most jobs through the year 2005 will become available as a result of replacement needs. Thus, even occupations with little or no employment growth or slower than average employment growth still may offer many job openings.

Replacement openings occur as people leave occupations. Some transfer to other occupations as a step up the career ladder or change careers. Others stop working in order to return to school, assume household responsibilities, or retire.

The number of replacement openings and the proportion of job openings made up by replacement needs varies by occupation. Occupations with the most replacement openings generally are large, with low pay and status, low training requirements, and a high proportion of young and part-time workers. Occupations with relatively few replacement openings tend to be associated with high pay and status, lengthy training requirements, and a high proportion of prime working age, full-time workers. Workers in these occupations generally acquire education or training that often is not applicable to other occupations. For example, among professional specialty occupations, only 38 percent of total job opportunities result from replacement needs, as opposed to 78 percent among production occupations (chart 9).

Interested in More Detail?

Readers interested in more information about projections and detail on the labor force, economic growth, industry and occupational employment, or methods and assumptions should consult the November 1993 *Monthly Labor Review* or *The American Work Force: 1992–2005*, BLS Bulletin 2452. Information on the limitations inherent in economic projections also can be found in either of these two publications. For additional occupational data, as well as statistics on educational and training completions, see the 1994 edition of *Occupational Projections and Training Data*, BLS Bulletin 2451.

Key Phrases in the *Handbook*
Changing employment between 1992 and 2005

If the statement reads . . .	Employment is projected to . . .
Grow much faster than the average	Increase 41 percent or more
Grow faster than the average	Increase 27 to 40 percent
Grow about as fast as the average	Increase 14 to 26 percent
Little change or grow more slowly than the average	Increase 0 to 13 percent
Decline	Decrease 1 percent or more

Opportunities and competition for jobs

If the statement reads . . .	Job openings compared to job-seekers may be . . .
Excellent opportunities	Much more numerous
Very good opportunities	More numerous
Good or favorable opportunities	About the same
May face competition	Fewer
May face keen competition	Much fewer

Chart 9

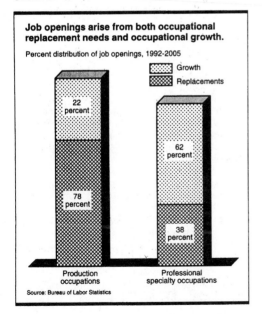

Job openings arise from both occupational replacement needs and occupational growth.

Percent distribution of job openings, 1992-2005

Growth

Replacements

22 percent

78 percent

62 percent

38 percent

Production occupations

Professional specialty occupations

Source: Bureau of Labor Statistics

Where to Find State and Local Job Information

State and local job market and career information is available from State employment security agencies and State Occupational Information Coordinating Committees (SOICC's). State employment security agencies develop occupational employment projections and other job market information. SOICC's provide or help locate labor market and career information. The following list provides the title, address, and telephone number of State employment security agency directors of research and SOICC directors.

Alabama
Chief, Labor Market Information, Alabama Department of Industrial Relations, 649 Monroe St., Room 422, Montgomery, AL 36131. Phone: 205-242-8855.

Director, Alabama Occupational Information Coordinating Committee, Alabama Center for Commerce, Room 364, 401 Adams Ave., P.O. Box 5690, Montgomery, AL 36103-5690. Phone: 205-242-2990.

Alaska
Chief, Research and Analysis Section, Alaska Department of Labor, P.O. Box 25501, Juneau, AK 99802-5501. Phone: 907-465-4500.

Executive Director, Alaska Department of Labor, Research and Analysis Section, P.O. Box 25501, Juneau, AK 99802-5501. Phone: 907-465-4518.

American Samoa
Statistical Analyst, Research and Statistics, Office of Manpower Resources, American Samoa Government, Pago Pago, AS 96799. Phone: 684-633-5172.

Director, American Samoa State Occupational Information Coordinating Committee, Office of Manpower Resources, American Samoa Government, Pago Pago, AS 96799. Phone: 684-633-4485.

Arizona
Research Administrator, Arizona Department of Economic Security, P.O. Box 6123, Site Code 733A, Phoenix, AZ 85005-6123. Phone: 602-542-3871.

Executive Director, Arizona State Occupational Information Coordinating Committee, P.O. Box 6123, Site Code 897J, 1789 West Jefferson St., First Floor North, Phoenix, AZ 85005-6123. Phone: 602-542-6466.

Arkansas
Manager, Labor Market Information, Arkansas Employment Security Division, P.O. Box 2981, Little Rock, AR 72203-2981. Phone: 501-682-3198.

Executive Director, Arkansas Occupational Information Coordinating Committee, Arkansas Employment Security Division, Employment and Training Services, P.O. Box 2981, Little Rock, AR 72203. Phone: 501-682-3159.

California
Chief, Labor Market Information Division, Employment Development Department, P.O. Box 942880, MIC 57, Sacramento, CA 94280-0001. Phone: 916-427-4675.

Executive Director, California Occupational Information Coordinating Committee, 1116 9th St., Lower Level, P.O. Box 94244-2220, Sacramento, CA 95814. Phone: 916-323-6544.

Colorado
Director, Labor Market Information, Colorado Department of Labor and Employment, 393 S. Harlan St., 2nd Floor, Lakewood, CO 80226-3509. Phone: 303-937-4947.

Director, Colorado Occupational Information Coordinating Committee, State Board Community College, 1391 Speer Blvd., Suite 600, Denver, CO 80204-2554. Phone: 303-866-4488.

Connecticut
Director, Research and Information, Employment Security Division, 200 Folly Brook Blvd., Wethersfield, CT 06109. Phone: 203-566-2120.

Executive Director, Connecticut Occupational Information Coordinating Committee, Connecticut Department of Education, 25 Industrial Park Rd., Middletown, CT 06457. Phone: 203-638-4042.

Delaware
Chief, Office of Occupational and Labor Market Information, Delaware Department of Labor, P.O. Box 9029, Newark, DE 19702-9029. Phone: 302-368-6962.

Executive Director, Office of Occupational and Labor Market Information, Delaware Department of Labor, University Office Plaza, P.O. Box 9029, Newark, DE 19714-9029. Phone: 302-368-6963.

District of Columbia
Chief, Division of Labor Market Information, District of Columbia Department of Employment Services, 500 C St. NW., Room 201, Washington, DC 20001. Phone: 202-724-7213.

Executive Director, District of Columbia Occupational Information Coordinating Committee, Department of Employment Security Services, 500 C St. NW., Room 215, Washington, DC 20001. Phone: 202-639-1090.

Florida

Chief, Bureau of Labor Market Information, Florida Department of Labor and Employment Security, 2012 Capitol Circle SE., Room 200, Tallahassee, FL 32399-2151. Phone: 904-488-1048.

Manager, Florida Department of Labor and Employment Security, Bureau of Labor Market Information, 2012 Capitol Circle SE., Hartman Bldg., Suite 200, Tallahassee, FL 32399-0673. Phone: 904-488-1048.

Georgia

Director, Labor Information Systems, Georgia Department of Labor, 148 International Blvd. NE., Atlanta, GA 30303. Phone: 404-656-3177.

Executive Director, Georgia Occupational Information Coordinating Committee, Department of Labor, 148 International Blvd., Sussex Place, Atlanta, GA 30303. Phone: 404-656-9639.

Guam

Administrator, Department of Labor, Bureau of Labor Statistics, Government of Guam, P.O. Box 9970, Tamuning, GU 96911-9970.

Executive Director, Guam State Occupational Information Coordinating Committee, Human Resource Development Agency, Jay Ease Bldg., Third Floor, P.O. Box 2817, Agana, GU 96910. Phone: 671-646-9341.

Hawaii

Chief, Research and Statistics Office, Department of Labor and Industrial Relations, P.O. Box 3680, Honolulu, HI 96813. Phone: 808-548-7639.

Executive Director, Hawaii State Occupational Information Coordinating Committee, 830 Punchbowl St., Room 315, Honolulu, HI 96813. Phone: 808-586-8750.

Idaho

Chief, Research and Analysis, Idaho Department of Employment, 317 Main St., Boise, ID 83735-0670. Phone: 208-334-6169.

Director, Idaho Occupational Information Coordinating Committee, Len B. Jordan Bldg., Room 301, 650 West State St., Boise, ID 83720. Phone: 208-334-3705.

Illinois

Director, Economic Information and Analysis, Illinois Department of Employment Security, 401 South State St., Room 215, Chicago, IL 60605. Phone: 312-793-2316.

Executive Director, Illinois Occupational Information Coordinating Committee, 217 East Monroe, Suite 203, Springfield, IL 62706. Phone: 217-785-0789.

Indiana

Program Manager, Labor Market Information, Indiana Workforce Development, 10 North Senate Ave., Indianapolis, IN 46204. Phone: 317-232-7460.

Executive Director, Indiana Occupational Information Coordinating Committee, 309 West Washington St., Room 309, Indianapolis, IN 46204. Phone: 317-232-8528.

Iowa

Supervisor, Audit and Analysis Department, Iowa Department of Employment Services, 1000 East Grand Ave., Des Moines, IA 50319-0209. Phone: 515-281-8181.

Acting Executive Director, Iowa Occupational Information Coordinating Committee, Iowa Department of Economic Development, 200 East Grand Ave., Des Moines, IA 50309. Phone: 515-242-4890.

Kansas

Chief, Labor Market Information Services, Kansas Department of Human Resources, 401 SW. Topeka Blvd., Topeka, KS 66603-3182. Phone: 913-296-5058.

Director, Kansas Occupational Information Coordinating Committee, 401 Topeka Ave., Topeka, KS 66603. Phone: 913-296-2387.

Kentucky

Branch Manager, Research and Statistics, Department for Employment Services, 275 East Main St., Frankfort, KY 40621. Phone: 502-564-7976.

Information Liaison/Manager, Kentucky Occupational Information Coordinating Committee, Workforce Development Cabinet, 500 Mero St., Capital Plaza Tower, Room 305, Frankfort, KY 40601. Phone: 502-564-4258.

Louisiana

Director, Research and Statistics Section, Louisiana State Department of Labor, P.O. Box 94094, Baton Rouge, LA 70804-4094. Phone: 504-342-3141.

Acting Director, Louisiana Occupational Information Coordinating Committee, P.O. Box 94094, Baton Rouge, LA 70804-9094. Phone: 504-342-5149.

Maine

Director, Division of Economic Analysis and Research, Maine Department of Labor, Bureau of Employment Security, 20 Union St., Augusta, ME 04330. Phone: 207-289-2271.

Acting Executive Director, Maine Occupational Information Coordinating Committee, State House Station 71, Augusta, ME 04333. Phone: 207-624-6200.

Maryland

Director, Office of Labor Market Analysis and Information, Economic and Employment Development, 1100 North Eutaw St., Room 601, Baltimore, MD 21201. Phone: 410-333-5000.

Director, Maryland State Occupational Information Coordinating Committee, State Department of Employment and Training, 1100 North Eutaw St., Room 205, Baltimore, MD 21201. Phone: 410-333-5478.

Massachusetts

Director of Research, Massachusetts Department of Employment and Training, 19 Staniford St., 2nd Floor, Boston, MA 02114. Phone: 617-727-6868.

Director, Massachusetts Occupational Information Coordinating Committee, Massachusetts Division of Employment Security, Charles F. Hurley Bldg., 2nd Floor, Government Center, Boston, MA 02114. Phone: 617-727-6718.

Michigan

Deputy Director, Financial and Management Services, Michigan Employment Security Commission, 7310 Woodward Ave., Detroit, MI 48202. Phone: 313-876-5904.

Executive Coordinator, Michigan Occupational Information Coordinating Committee, Victor Office Center, Third Floor, 201 North Washington Square, Box 30015, Lansing, MI 48909. Phone: 517-373-0363.

Minnesota

Director, Research and Statistics Office, Minnesota Department of Jobs and Training, 390 North Robert St., St. Paul, MN 55101. Phone: 612-296-6546.

Director, Minnesota Occupational Information Coordinating Committee, Department of Jobs and Training, 390 North Robert Street, St. Paul, MN 55101. Phone: 612-296-2072.

Mississippi

Chief, Labor Market Information Division, Mississippi Employment Security Commission, P.O. Box 1699, Jackson, MS 39215-1699. Phone: 601-961-7424.

Director, Mississippi Occupational Information Coordinating Committee Office, 301 West Pearl St., Jackson, MS 39203-3089. Phone: 601-949-2240.

Missouri

Chief, Research and Analysis, Missouri Division of Employment Security, P.O. Box 59,

Jefferson City, MO 65104-0059. Phone: 314-751-3591.

Director, Missouri Occupational Information Coordinating Committee, 400 Dix Rd., Jefferson City, MO 65109. Phone: 314-751-3800.

Montana

Chief, Research and Analysis, Department of Labor and Industry, P.O. Box 1728, Helena, MT 59624-1728. Phone: 406-444-2430.

Program Manager, Montana Occupational Information Coordinating Committee, P.O. Box 1728, 1327 Lockey St., Second Floor, Helena, MT 59624. Phone: 406-444-2741.

Nebraska

Director, Labor Market Information, Nebraska Department of Labor, P.O. Box 94600, Lincoln, NE 68509-4600. Phone: 402-471-9964.

Administrator, Nebraska Occupational Information Coordinating Committee, P.O. Box 94600, State House Station, Lincoln, NE 68509-4600. Phone: 402-471-4845.

Nevada

Chief, Employment Security Research, Nevada Employment Security Department, 500 East Third St., Carson City, NV 89713. Phone: 702-687-4550.

Director, Nevada Occupational Information Coordinating Committee, 1923 North Carson St., Suite 211, Carson City, NV 89710. Phone: 702-687-4577.

New Hampshire

Director, Economic Analysis and Reports, New Hampshire Department of Employment Security, 32 South Main St., Concord, NH 03301-4587. Phone: 603-228-4123.

Director, New Hampshire State Occupational Information Coordinating Committee, 64B Old Suncook Rd., Concord, NH 03301. Phone: 603-228-3349.

New Jersey

Assistant Commissioner, Policy and Planning, New Jersey Department of Labor, Labor and Industry Bldg., P.O. Box CN056, Trenton, NJ 08625-0056. Phone: 609-292-2643.

Staff Director, New Jersey Occupational Information Coordinating Committee, 609 Labor and Industry Bldg., CN056, Trenton, NJ 08625-0056. Phone: 609-292-2682.

New Mexico

Chief, Economic Research and Analysis Bureau, Employment Security Department, P.O. Box 1928, Albuquerque, NM 87103. Phone: 505-841-8645.

Director, New Mexico Occupational Information Coordinating Committee, 401 Broadway NE., Tiwa Bldg., P.O. Box 1928, Albuquerque, NM 87103. Phone: 505-841-8455.

New York
Director, Division of Research and Statistics, New York State Department of Labor, State Campus, Bldg. 12, Room 400, Albany, NY 12240-0020. Phone: 518-457-6181.

Executive Director, New York Occupational Information Coordinating Committee, Department of Labor, Research and Statistics Division, State Campus, Bldg. 12, Room 400, Albany, NY 12240. Phone: 518-457-6182.

North Carolina
Director, Labor Market Information Division, Employment Security Commission of North Carolina, P.O. Box 25903, Raleigh, NC 27611-5903. Phone: 919-733-2936.

Executive Director, North Carolina Occupational Information Coordinating Committee, 1311 Saint Mary's St., Suite 250, P.O. Box 27625, Raleigh, NC 27611. Phone: 919-733-6700.

North Dakota
Director, Research and Statistics, Job Service of North Dakota, P.O. Box 1537, Bismarck, ND 58502-1537. Phone: 701-224-2868.

Coordinator, North Dakota State Occupational Information Coordinating Committee, 1720 Burnt Boat Dr., P.O. Box 1537, Bismarck, ND 58502-1537. Phone: 701-224-2733.

Northern Mariana Islands
Executive Director, Northern Mariana Islands Occupational Information Coordinating Committee, P.O. Box 149, Room N-1, Building N, Northern Mariana College, Saipan, CM 96950. Phone: 670-234-1457.

Ohio
Director, Labor Market Information Division, Ohio Bureau of Employment Services, P.O. Box 1618, Columbus, OH 43215. Phone: 614-752-9494.

Director, Ohio Occupational Information Coordinating Committee, Division of Labor Market Information, Ohio Bureau of Employment Services, 1160 Dublin Rd., Bldg. A, Columbus, OH 43215. Phone: 614-752-6863.

Oklahoma
Director, Research and Planning Division, Oklahoma Employment Security Commission, 2401 North Lincoln, Room 310, Oklahoma City, OK 73105. Phone: 405-557-7116.

Executive Director, Oklahoma Occupational Information Coordinating Committee, Department of Voc/Tech Education, 1500 W. 7th Ave., Stillwater, OK 74074. Phone: 405-743-5198.

Oregon
Assistant Administrator, Research and Statistics, Employment Division, Oregon Department of Human Resources, 875 Union St. NE., Room 207, Salem, OR 97311-9986. Phone: 503-378-3220.

Acting Director, Oregon Occupational Information Coordinating Committee, 875 Union St. NE., Salem, OR 97311. Phone: 503-378-5490.

Pennsylvania
Director, Research and Statistics Division, Department of Labor and Industry, 1213 Labor and Industry Building, Harrisburg, PA 17121. Phone: 717-787-6466.

Director, Pennsylvania Occupational Information Coordinating Committee, Pennsylvania Department of Labor and Industry, 1224 Labor and Industry Bldg., Harrisburg, PA 17120. Phone: 717-787-8646.

Puerto Rico
Director of Bureau of Labor Statistics, Department of Labor and Human Resources, Research and Analysis Division, 505 Munoz Rivera Ave., 17th Floor, Hato Rey, PR 00918. Phone: 809-754-5332.

Director, Puerto Rico Occupational Information Coordinating Committee, 202 Del Cristo St., P.O. Box 366212, San Juan, PR 00936-6212. Phone: 809-723-7110.

Rhode Island
Supervisor, Labor Market Information and Management Services, Rhode Island Department of Employment, 107 Friendship St., Providence, RI 02903. Phone: 401-277-3704.

Director, Rhode Island Occupational Information Coordinating Committee, 22 Hayes St., Room 133, Providence, RI 02908. Phone: 401-272-0830.

South Carolina
Director, Labor Market Information Division, South Carolina Employment Security Commission, P.O. Box 995, Columbia, SC 29202-0995. Phone: 803-737-2660.

Director, South Carolina Occupational Information Coordinating Committee, 1550 Gadsden St., P.O. Box 995, Columbia, SC 29202. Phone: 803-737-2733.

South Dakota
Director, Labor Market Information Division, South Dakota Department of Labor, P.O. Box 4730, Aberdeen, SD 57402-4730. Phone: 605-622-2314.

Director, South Dakota Occupational Information Coordinating Committee, South Dakota Department of Labor, 420 South Roosevelt St., P.O. Box 4730, Aberdeen, SD 57402-4730. Phone: 605-622-2314.

Tennessee

Director, Research and Statistics Division, Tennessee Department of Employment Security, 500 James Robertson Pkwy., 11th Floor, Nashville, TN 37245-1000. Phone: 615-741-2284.

Executive Director, Tennessee Occupational Information Coordinating Committee, 500 James Robertson Pkwy., 11th Floor Volunteer Plaza, Nashville, TN 37219. Phone: 615-741-6451.

Texas

Chief, Economic Research and Analysis, Texas Employment Commission, 1117 Trinity St., Room 208-T, Austin, TX 78778. Phone: 512-463-2616.

Director, Texas Occupational Information Coordinating Committee, Texas Employment Commission Building, 3520 Executive Center Dr., Suite 205, Austin, TX 78731. Phone: 512-502-3750.

Utah

Director, Labor Market Information, Utah Department of Employment Security, P.O. Box 11249, Salt Lake City, UT 84147-1249. Phone: 801-536-7425.

Executive Director, Utah Occupational Information Coordinating Committee-c/o Utah Department of Employment Security, P.O. Box 11249, 140 East 300 South, Salt Lake City, UT 84147. Phone: 801-536-7806.

Vermont

Chief, Policy and Public Information, Vermont Department of Employment and Training, P.O. Box 488, Montpelier, VT 05602. Phone: 802-229-0311.

Director, Vermont Occupational Information Coordinating Committee, 5 Green Mountain Dr., P.O. Box 488, Montpelier, VT 05601-0488. Phone: 802-229-0311.

Virginia

Director, Economic Information Service, Virginia Employment Commission, P.O. Box 1358, Richmond, VA 23211. Phone: 804-786-7496.

Executive Director, Virginia Occupational Information Coordinating Committee, Virginia Employment Commission, 703 East Main St., P.O. Box 1358, Richmond, VA 23211. Phone: 804-786-7496.

Virgin Islands

Director, Virgin Islands Department of Labor, Bureau of Labor Statistics, Labor/Research and Analysis Division, P.O. Box 3359, St. Thomas, U.S. Virgin Islands 00801-3359. Phone: 809-776-3700.

Coordinator, Virgin Islands Occupational Information Coordinating Committee, P.O. Box 3359, St. Thomas, U.S. Virgin Islands 00801. Phone: 809-776-3700.

Washington

Director, Labor Market and Economic Analysis, Washington Employment Security Department, 605 Woodview Dr., SE, Lacey, WA 98503. Phone: 206-438-4800.

Acting Executive Director, Washington Occupational Information Coordinating Committee, c/o Employment Security Department, P.O. Box 9046, Olympia, WA 98507-9046. Phone: 206-438-4803.

West Virginia

Director, Labor and Economic Research Section, West Virginia Bureau of Employment Security, 112 California Ave., Charleston, WV 25305-0112. Phone: 304-348-2660.

Executive Director, West Virginia Occupational Information Coordinating Committee, One Dunbar Plaza, Suite E, Dunbar, WV 25064. Phone: 304-293-5314.

Wisconsin

Director, Bureau of Workforce Policy and Information, Department of Industry, Labor, and Human Relations, P.O. Box 7944, Madison, WI 53707-7944. Phone: 608-266-5843.

Administrative Director, Wisconsin Occupational Information Coordinating Council, Division of Employment and Training Policy, 201 East Washington Ave., P.O. Box 7972, Madison, WI 53707. Phone: 608-266-8012.

Wyoming

Manager, Research and Planning, Employment Security Commission, P.O. Box 2760, Casper, WY 82602-2760. Phone: 307-265-6715.

Executive Director, Wyoming Occupational Information Coordinating Council, Post Office Box 2760, 100 West Midwest, Casper, WY 82602. Phone: 307-265-7017.

U.S. Demographics

Source: Excerpted from *Population Projections of the United States, by Age, Sex, and Race, and Hispanic Origin, 1993 to 2050* by Jennifer Cheeseman Day, U.S. Bureau of the Census, Current Population Reports, Series P25–1104. The tables in this section are from the same source.

Highlights from the Bureau of the Census Middle Series

Population Size and Growth

- In the middle series, the population is projected to reach 276 million by 2000—a growth of 26.9 million or 10.8 percent since 1990. Only during the 1950's were more people added to the Nation's population than are projected to be added during the 1990's.

- The population may top 300 million by 2010. By the middle of the next century, the population may increase to 392 million—more than a 50 percent increase from the 1990 population.

- Despite these large increases in the number of persons in the population, the rate of population growth is projected to decrease during the next six decades by about 50 percent. From 2030 to 2050, the U.S. would grow more slowly than ever before in its history.

Age Distribution

- The age group under 18 may increase about 6 million by the turn of the century, then grow another 20 million by 2050. Even so, this age group's proportion of the total population may never again be as large as it is today.

- During the next decade, the largest growing age group is the 45 to 54 year olds, increasing 44 percent from 1990 to 2000.

- During the next two decades, the rate of population growth of the elderly population (aged 65 and over) is projected to be slower than at any time during this century.

- The most rapidly growing age group would be the 85 and over age group, doubling in size from 1990 to the year 2020, and increasing sixfold by the year 2050.

Race and Hispanic-Origin Distribution

- The race and Hispanic-origin distribution of the U.S. population is projected to change. A combination of three factors contributes to this shift: differential fertility, net immigration, and age distribution among the race and Hispanic-origin groups.

- Although three-quarters of the population was non-Hispanic White in 1990, this group would contribute only 35 percent of the total population growth during this decade. After 2030, the non-Hispanic White population would contribute nothing to the nation's population growth because it would be declining in size.

- The non-Hispanic White share of the U.S. population would steadily fall from 76 percent in 1990 to 72 percent in 2000, 60 percent in 2030, and 53 percent in 2050.

- By the middle of the next century, the Black population would double its 1990 size to 62 million. After 2012, more Blacks than non-Hispanic Whites would be added to the population each year.

- The fastest-growing race/ethnic group (with the highest rate of increase) would be the Asian and Pacific Islander population with annual growth rates that may exceed 4 percent during the 1990's.

- The race/ethnic group adding the largest number of people to the population would be the Hispanic-origin population. In fact, after 1996 the Hispanic population is projected to add more people to the United States every year than would any other race or origin group. By 2010, the Hispanic-origin population may become the second-largest race/ethnic group.

- By the year 2030, the non-Hispanic White population would be less than half of the U.S. population under age 18. In that year, this group would still comprise three-quarters of the 65 and over population.

Components of Change

- Between 1993 and 2050, the aging of the population would cause the annual total number of deaths to increase by about 85 percent, from 2.2 million in 1993 to 4.1 million in 2050. Most of the deaths would occur to the non-Hispanic White population.

- The number of births in the United States is projected to decrease slightly as the century ends, and then increase progressively throughout the projection period. After 2011 the number of births each year would exceed the highest annual number of births ever achieved in the United States during the 20th century.

- In 1995, about 63 percent of all births would be non-Hispanic White, about 1 in 6 would be Black, and 1 in 6 would be of Hispanic origin. By the middle of the 21st century, less than one-half of all births would be non-Hispanic White, 1 in 3 would be Hispanic, 1 in 5 would be Black, and 1 in 10 would be Asian and Pacific Islander.

- The middle series assumes that every year 2 of every 3 people added to the population through net immigration would be Hispanic or Asian, 1 in 5 would be non-Hispanic White, and 1 in 10 would be Black.

- In 1993, almost one-third of the population growth would be caused by net immigration. By 2000, the nation's population is projected to be 7.8 million (2.9 percent) larger than it would have been if there had been no net immigration after July 1, 1992.

Population, by Race and Hispanic Origin: 1990 to 2050

(As of July 1. Resident population)

Year	Total	Race					Not of Hispanic origin, by race			
		White	Black	American Indian[1]	Asian[2]	Hispanic Origin[3]	White	Black	American Indian[1]	Asian[2]
ESTIMATE										
1990	249,415	209,150	30,620	2,075	7,570	22,554	188,559	29,400	1,806	7,096
PROJECTIONS										
Lowest Series										
2050	285,502	214,054	42,026	3,323	26,099	57,643	161,382	38,933	2,807	24,738
Middle Series										
1995	263,434	218,334	33,117	2,226	9,756	26,798	193,900	31,648	1,927	9,161
2000	276,241	226,267	35,469	2,380	12,125	31,166	197,872	33,741	2,055	11,407
2005	288,286	233,343	37,793	2,543	14,608	35,702	200,842	35,793	2,190	13,759
2010	300,431	240,297	40,224	2,719	17,191	40,525	203,441	37,930	2,336	16,199
2020	325,942	254,791	45,409	3,090	22,653	51,217	208,280	42,459	2,641	21,345
2030	349,993	267,457	50,596	3,473	28,467	62,810	210,480	46,934	2,960	26,810
2040	371,505	277,232	55,917	3,894	34,461	75,130	209,148	51,489	3,314	32,424
2050	392,031	285,591	61,586	4,346	40,508	88,071	205,849	56,346	3,701	38,064
Highest Series										
2050	522,098	378,408	79,722	5,039	58,930	128,255	262,855	71,675	4,221	55,093

[1] American Indian represents American Indian, Eskimo, and Aleut.
[2] Asian represents Asian and Pacific Islander.
[3] Persons of Hispanic origin may be of any race.

Percent Distribution of the Population, by Race and Hispanic Origin

(As of July 1. Resident population)

Series and year	Race					Hispanic origin[3]	Not of Hispanic origin, by race			
	Total	White	Black	American Indian[1]	Asian[2]		White	Black	American Indian	Asian
ESTIMATE										
1990.........	100.0	83.9	12.3	0.8	3.0	9.0	75.7	11.8	0.7	2.8
PROJECTIONS										
Lowest Series										
2050.........	100.0	75.0	14.7	1.2	9.1	20.2	56.5	13.6	1.0	8.7
Middle Series										
1995.........	100.0	82.9	12.6	0.8	3.7	10.2	73.6	12.0	0.7	3.5
2000.........	100.0	81.9	12.8	0.9	4.4	11.3	71.6	12.2	0.7	4.1
2005.........	100.0	80.9	13.1	0.9	5.1	12.4	69.7	12.4	0.8	4.8
2010.........	100.0	80.0	13.4	0.9	5.7	13.5	67.7	12.6	0.8	5.4
2020.........	100.0	78.2	13.9	0.9	7.0	15.7	63.9	13.0	0.8	6.5
2030.........	100.0	76.4	14.5	1.0	8.1	17.9	60.1	13.4	0.8	7.7
2040.........	100.0	74.6	15.1	1.0	9.3	20.2	56.3	13.9	0.9	8.7
2050.........	100.0	72.8	15.7	1.1	10.3	22.5	52.5	14.4	0.9	9.7
Highest Series										
2050.........	100.0	72.4	15.3	1.0	11.3	24.6	50.3	13.7	0.8	10.6

[1] American Indian represents American Indian, Eskimo, and Aleut.
[2] Asian represents Asian and Pacific Islander.
[3] Persons of Hispanic origin may be of any race.

State Population Projections: 1995 to 2010

[In thousands. As of July 1. Series A, B, C, and D reflect different interstate migration assumptions. Series A is the preferred series model. For explanation of methodology, see text, section 1]

REGION, DIVISION, AND STATE	1995 Series A	1995 Series B	1995 Series C	1995 Series D	2000 Series A	2000 Series B	2000 Series C	2000 Series D	2010 Series A	2010 Series B	2010 Series C	2010 Series D
U.S.	263,437	263,437	263,435	263,435	276,242	276,242	276,239	276,239	300,430	300,431	300,431	300,430
Northeast	51,441	52,123	51,465	52,507	51,884	53,210	52,329	54,582	53,301	55,102	54,225	58,183
N.E.	13,198	13,601	13,213	13,523	13,216	14,025	13,507	13,996	13,755	14,785	14,212	14,751
ME	1,236	1,276	1,242	1,250	1,240	1,323	1,288	1,270	1,309	1,413	1,375	1,300
NH	1,132	1,183	1,128	1,133	1,165	1,274	1,204	1,163	1,280	1,429	1,350	1,207
VT.	579	593	580	581	592	623	605	596	623	675	644	620
MA	5,976	6,133	5,974	6,159	5,950	6,254	6,032	6,401	6,097	6,495	6,249	6,785
RI	1,001	1,031	1,004	1,029	998	1,060	1,022	1,065	1,034	1,115	1,072	1,126
CT.	3,274	3,385	3,285	3,371	3,271	3,491	3,356	3,501	3,412	3,658	3,522	3,713
M.A	38,243	38,522	38,252	38,984	38,668	39,185	38,822	40,586	39,546	40,317	40,013	43,432
NY.	18,178	18,319	18,184	18,795	18,237	18,504	18,321	19,838	18,546	18,856	18,799	21,761
NJ.	7,931	8,005	7,926	8,040	8,135	8,267	8,165	8,413	8,562	8,681	8,677	9,075
PA.	12,134	12,198	12,142	12,149	12,296	12,414	12,336	12,335	12,438	12,780	12,537	12,596
Midwest. . : . .	61,993	61,469	61,989	62,068	63,836	62,610	63,664	64,075	66,333	64,953	65,982	67,716
E.N.C	43,610	43,258	43,620	43,753	44,806	44,013	44,769	45,220	46,259	45,506	46,242	47,805
OH	11,203	11,103	11,203	11,209	11,453	11,238	11,430	11,479	11,659	11,500	11,661	11,913
IN	5,820	5,766	5,821	5,771	6,045	5,922	6,032	5,929	6,286	6,212	6,274	6,187
IL	11,853	11,770	11,855	11,991	12,168	11,974	12,153	12,533	12,652	12,424	12,621	13,541
MI	9,575	9,512	9,584	9,682	9,759	9,614	9,826	10,040	10,033	9,803	10,160	10,666
WI	5,159	5,107	5,157	5,100	5,381	5,265	5,328	5,239	5,629	5,567	5,526	5,498
W.N.C.	18,383	18,211	18,369	18,315	19,030	18,597	18,895	18,855	20,074	19,447	19,740	19,911
MN	4,619	4,581	4,618	4,591	4,824	4,733	4,814	4,756	5,127	5,020	5,096	5,068
IA	2,861	2,834	2,859	2,851	2,930	2,867	2,867	2,912	2,981	2,946	2,868	3,032
MO	5,286	5,241	5,289	5,279	5,437	5,313	5,459	5,406	5,760	5,489	5,788	5,638
ND	637	634	634	647	643	633	622	663	676	642	626	698
SD.	735	720	732	725	770	737	750	749	815	781	786	805
NE.	1,644	1,626	1,644	1,635	1,704	1,660	1,681	1,680	1,793	1,742	1,734	1,773
KS.	2,601	2,575	2,593	2,587	2,722	2,654	2,684	2,689	2,922	2,827	2,842	2,897
South	91,728	91,387	91,705	90,684	97,244	96,576	96,931	94,503	107,385	106,120	106,852	101,445
S.A.	47,019	46,988	47,070	46,257	50,005	50,015	50,517	48,004	55,321	55,422	56,737	50,976
DE.	718	715	719	705	759	757	770	727	815	834	850	758
MD	5,078	5,081	5,089	5,081	5,322	5,334	5,420	5,334	5,782	5,762	6,008	5,763
DC.	559	564	559	608	537	545	549	640	577	545	584	697
VA.	6,646	6,645	6,644	6,570	7,048	7,060	7,106	6,854	7,728	7,760	7,902	7,318
WV	1,824	1,812	1,819	1,820	1,840	1,811	1,783	1,830	1,842	1,827	1,720	1,835
NC	7,150	7,130	7,143	6,980	7,617	7,588	7,616	7,169	8,341	8,416	8,455	7,438
SC.	3,732	3,727	3,743	3,688	3,932	3,924	3,976	3,808	4,311	4,287	4,378	3,998
GA	7,102	7,120	7,097	6,954	7,637	7,678	7,664	7,249	8,553	8,679	8,732	7,758
FL.	14,210	14,194	14,257	13,851	15,313	15,318	15,633	14,393	17,372	17,312	18,108	15,411
E.S.C	16,019	15,844	15,997	15,823	16,762	16,357	16,633	16,252	17,941	17,412	17,697	16,962
KY.	3,851	3,803	3,842	3,819	3,989	3,883	3,927	3,913	4,160	4,050	4,046	4,064
TN.	5,228	5,166	5,221	5,108	5,538	5,399	5,513	5,222	6,007	5,857	5,980	5,392
AL.	4,274	4,228	4,272	4,225	4,485	4,375	4,471	4,357	4,856	4,677	4,818	4,580
MS	2,666	2,647	2,662	2,671	2,750	2,700	2,722	2,760	2,918	2,828	2,853	2,926
W.S.C	28,690	28,555	28,638	28,604	30,477	30,204	29,781	30,247	34,123	33,286	32,418	33,507
AR.	2,468	2,456	2,462	2,434	2,578	2,557	2,546	2,489	2,782	2,751	2,716	2,592
LA.	4,359	4,334	4,346	4,407	4,478	4,424	4,343	4,592	4,808	4,604	4,471	4,947
OK	3,271	3,265	3,262	3,267	3,382	3,366	3,259	3,353	3,683	3,578	3,352	3,524
TX.	18,592	18,500	18,568	18,496	20,039	19,857	19,633	19,813	22,850	22,353	21,879	22,444
West	58,275	58,458	58,276	58,176	63,278	63,846	63,315	63,079	73,411	74,256	73,372	73,086
Mountain . . .	15,384	15,142	15,323	14,902	16,890	16,339	16,391	15,718	19,093	18,625	18,331	17,359
MT	862	851	855	837	920	894	867	859	996	993	899	906
ID	1,156	1,117	1,152	1,101	1,290	1,200	1,229	1,158	1,454	1,373	1,335	1,282
WY	487	484	484	477	522	512	483	495	596	571	491	534
CO	3,710	3,663	3,683	3,575	4,059	3,957	3,851	3,729	4,494	4,477	4,183	4,000
NM	1,676	1,658	1,670	1,641	1,823	1,780	1,776	1,737	2,082	2,005	2,009	1,939
AZ.	4,072	4,024	4,051	3,978	4,437	4,320	4,404	4,201	5,074	4,891	5,136	4,645
UT.	1,944	1,914	1,936	1,910	2,148	2,079	2,063	2,076	2,462	2,413	2,294	2,442
NV.	1,477	1,431	1,492	1,383	1,691	1,597	1,718	1,463	1,935	1,902	1,984	1,611
Pacific	42,891	43,316	42,953	43,274	46,388	47,507	46,924	47,361	54,318	55,631	55,041	55,727
WA	5,497	5,453	5,504	5,295	6,070	6,025	6,054	5,539	7,025	7,087	6,898	6,005
OR	3,141	3,105	3,147	3,045	3,404	3,340	3,396	3,360	3,876	3,812	3,753	3,360
CA.	32,398	32,892	32,450	33,097	34,888	36,062	35,490	36,689	41,085	42,255	42,075	44,076
AK.	634	642	631	618	699	732	658	666	781	880	754	769
HI	1,221	1,224	1,221	1,219	1,327	1,348	1,326	1,316	1,551	1,597	1,561	1,517

Source: U.S. Bureau of the Census, *Current Population Reports*, series P25-1111.

Source: *Statistical Abstract of the United States*, U.S. Department of Commerce.

Population Projections, by Age—States: 1995 to 2010

[In thousands. As of July 1. Data shown are for series A, the preferred series model; for explanation of methodology, see text, section 1]

REGION, DIVISION, AND STATE	UNDER 18 YEARS			18 TO 44 YEARS			45 TO 64 YEARS			65 YEARS AND OVER		
	1995	2000	2010	1995	2000	2010	1995	2000	2010	1995	2000	2010
U.S.	69,036	71,789	73,619	109,288	109,274	108,058	51,468	59,860	78,651	33,655	35,324	40,099
Northeast	12,593	12,801	12,326	21,056	20,069	18,912	10,523	11,711	14,465	7,272	7,304	7,597
N.E.	3,187	3,191	3,045	5,503	5,154	4,902	2,667	3,018	3,830	1,842	1,853	1,977
ME	303	294	286	504	477	458	257	294	375	172	175	191
NH	288	288	285	482	464	457	228	273	372	135	141	165
VT	148	149	146	245	235	228	116	135	167	70	72	82
MA	1,418	1,420	1,317	2,530	2,358	2,226	1,184	1,329	1,672	844	842	881
RI	238	237	227	414	387	368	195	223	286	154	151	153
CT	792	803	784	1,328	1,233	1,165	687	764	958	467	472	505
M.A	9,406	9,610	9,281	15,553	14,915	14,010	7,856	8,693	10,635	5,430	5,451	5,620
NY.	4,539	4,611	4,439	7,505	7,143	6,735	3,717	4,058	4,846	2,417	2,426	2,525
NJ.	1,951	2,047	2,051	3,232	3,121	2,972	1,658	1,854	2,348	1,091	1,112	1,192
PA.	2,916	2,952	2,791	4,816	4,651	4,303	2,481	2,781	3,441	1,922	1,913	1,903
Midwest.	16,356	16,593	16,340	25,355	25,095	23,799	12,103	13,784	17,282	8,179	8,369	8,912
E.N.C	11,458	11,665	11,467	17,951	17,676	16,660	8,574	9,711	12,035	5,628	5,755	6,097
OH	2,873	2,891	2,778	4,567	4,483	4,159	2,253	2,532	3,103	1,509	1,547	1,618
IN	1,509	1,550	1,534	2,412	2,409	2,278	1,154	1,314	1,636	745	772	836
IL	3,126	3,206	3,198	4,930	4,857	4,642	2,303	2,592	3,225	1,496	1,513	1,589
MI	2,583	2,635	2,621	3,932	3,802	3,569	1,871	2,112	2,567	1,189	1,211	1,278
WI	1,367	1,383	1,336	2,110	2,125	2,014	993	1,161	1,504	689	712	776
W.N.C.	4,898	4,928	4,873	7,404	7,419	7,139	3,529	4,073	5,247	2,551	2,614	2,815
MN	1,243	1,254	1,225	1,921	1,930	1,849	875	1,038	1,370	578	602	683
IA	743	736	705	1,125	1,128	1,061	556	627	767	438	439	449
MO	1,376	1,381	1,371	2,107	2,090	2,006	1,055	1,197	1,546	749	769	837
ND	170	164	163	259	254	250	115	133	170	93	94	93
SD.	211	216	218	285	292	284	132	155	203	105	107	111
NE.	449	452	448	656	663	649	309	354	447	231	236	248
KS.	706	725	743	1,051	1,062	1,040	487	569	744	357	367	394
South	23,875	24,901	25,688	37,959	38,346	37,992	18,090	21,274	28,647	11,809	12,724	15,055
S.A.	11,618	12,217	12,505	19,316	19,402	19,107	9,547	11,255	15,148	6,539	7,130	8,559
DE.	182	191	193	302	305	295	142	164	214	92	99	113
MD	1,317	1,405	1,453	2,159	2,124	2,077	1,033	1,192	1,551	568	602	701
DC.	109	99	102	263	248	261	112	117	142	76	73	72
VA.	1,654	1,745	1,780	2,907	2,923	2,879	1,343	1,576	2,101	742	803	967
WV	432	425	406	724	703	642	389	434	514	280	277	280
NC	1,758	1,862	1,879	3,023	3,045	2,978	1,462	1,713	2,284	908	997	1,199
SC.	980	1,013	1,036	1,569	1,570	1,548	740	867	1,152	443	481	575
GA	1,909	2,030	2,125	3,080	3,153	3,161	1,387	1,656	2,269	726	798	998
FL.	3,277	3,447	3,531	5,289	5,331	5,266	2,939	3,536	4,921	2,704	3,000	3,654
E.S.C	4,157	4,275	4,305	6,574	6,606	6,352	3,232	3,714	4,824	2,058	2,167	2,459
KY.	983	996	982	1,598	1,594	1,490	779	890	1,125	491	509	563
TN.	1,295	1,343	1,343	2,173	2,209	2,151	1,090	1,269	1,674	671	717	839
AL.	1,125	1,183	1,233	1,732	1,736	1,691	858	975	1,264	560	591	667
MS	754	753	747	1,071	1,067	1,020	505	580	761	336	350	390
W.S.C.	8,100	8,409	8,878	12,069	12,338	12,533	5,311	6,305	8,675	3,212	3,427	4,037
AR.	643	657	661	953	960	927	504	578	758	368	383	436
LA.	1,251	1,247	1,282	1,803	1,792	1,766	808	925	1,195	498	515	565
OK	870	875	900	1,313	1,314	1,312	648	739	969	441	454	502
TX.	5,336	5,630	6,035	8,000	8,272	8,528	3,351	4,063	5,753	1,905	2,075	2,534
West.	16,212	17,494	19,265	24,918	25,764	27,355	10,752	13,091	18,257	6,395	6,927	8,535
Mountain	4,376	4,690	4,967	6,410	6,770	6,919	2,848	3,503	4,847	1,750	1,924	2,362
MT	233	242	250	343	356	357	172	203	260	114	117	130
ID	344	373	396	466	512	526	211	262	360	133	143	172
WY	141	145	162	207	218	235	89	108	144	51	51	54
CO	972	1,037	1,054	1,645	1,722	1,728	717	885	1,198	376	415	514
NM	500	540	588	679	705	734	311	374	515	185	204	247
AZ.	1,127	1,213	1,281	1,629	1,673	1,705	759	927	1,305	558	623	783
UT.	684	723	800	803	882	928	286	356	504	172	188	230
NV.	375	417	436	638	702	706	303	388	561	161	183	232
Pacific	11,836	12,804	14,298	18,508	18,994	20,436	7,904	9,588	13,410	4,645	5,003	6,173
WA	1,461	1,589	1,712	2,336	2,464	2,589	1,070	1,342	1,888	631	675	836
OR	811	869	945	1,279	1,328	1,400	631	773	1,026	421	434	504
CA.	9,048	9,779	11,008	14,061	14,327	15,494	5,867	7,077	9,978	3,422	3,704	4,605
AK.	201	221	239	300	319	342	105	129	163	28	31	38
HI	315	346	394	532	556	611	231	267	355	143	159	190

Source: U.S. Bureau of the Census, *Current Population Reports*, series P25-1111.

Source: *Statistical Abstract of the United States,* U.S. Department of Commerce.

Population Projections, by Race—States: 1995 to 2010

[In thousands. As of July 1. Data shown are for series A, the preferred series model; for explanation of methodology, see text, section 1]

REGION, DIVISION, AND STATE	WHITE			BLACK			AMERICAN INDIAN, ESKIMO, ALEUT			ASIAN, PACIFIC ISLANDER		
	1995	2000	2010	1995	2000	2010	1995	2000	2010	1995	2000	2010
U.S.	218,333	226,268	240,293	33,118	35,475	40,227	2,229	2,382	2,718	9,756	12,121	17,188
Northeast	43,381	43,218	43,268	6,263	6,570	7,267	118	108	98	1,678	1,989	2,669
N.E.	12,183	12,120	12,408	691	718	810	32	31	31	291	348	506
ME	1,217	1,220	1,283	5	5	5	6	6	6	8	9	14
NH	1,109	1,137	1,236	7	8	10	2	3	3	14	18	31
VT.	570	582	609	2	3	4	2	2	2	4	5	9
MA	5,445	5,373	5,387	340	352	393	11	10	10	180	215	307
RI.	927	917	933	44	46	51	4	4	4	25	31	46
CT.	2,915	2,891	2,960	293	304	347	7	6	6	60	70	99
M.A	31,198	31,098	30,860	5,572	5,852	6,457	86	77	67	1,387	1,641	2,163
NY.	14,025	13,819	13,542	3,249	3,391	3,705	57	50	43	846	977	1,257
NJ.	6,405	6,445	6,526	1,156	1,242	1,434	14	13	11	356	435	591
PA.	10,768	10,834	10,792	1,167	1,219	1,318	15	14	13	185	229	315
Midwest.	54,306	55,391	56,441	6,249	6,689	7,526	382	411	460	1,055	1,345	1,900
E.N.C.	37,392	38,006	38,350	5,277	5,653	6,379	165	170	174	776	976	1,354
OH	9,806	9,943	9,948	1,253	1,335	1,483	22	22	22	122	152	206
IN	5,275	5,444	5,587	476	514	582	14	15	15	55	72	102
IL	9,603	9,713	9,801	1,843	1,957	2,181	23	22	21	383	476	648
MI	7,958	8,000	7,979	1,417	1,520	1,737	61	63	64	140	176	253
WI	4,750	4,906	5,035	288	327	396	45	48	52	76	100	145
W.N.C.	16,914	17,385	18,091	972	1,036	1,147	217	241	286	279	369	546
MN	4,344	4,498	4,699	104	111	122	58	64	74	113	151	232
IA	2,763	2,816	2,841	57	65	78	8	8	8	33	41	53
MO	4,629	4,737	4,970	581	609	664	20	20	21	56	72	105
ND	600	601	622	4	4	5	28	31	37	5	7	11
SD.	663	685	702	3	4	4	62	74	97	5	7	11
NE.	1,550	1,598	1,669	64	69	76	14	15	16	17	22	31
KS.	2,365	2,450	2,588	159	174	198	27	29	33	50	69	103
South	72,121	75,813	82,386	17,378	18,708	21,297	606	630	677	1,624	2,094	3,024
S.A..	35,962	37,772	40,805	9,960	10,868	12,615	185	194	208	911	1,173	1,691
DE.	570	589	603	132	149	181	3	3	3	14	18	28
MD	3,500	3,546	3,631	1,368	1,514	1,776	13	13	14	196	249	361
DC.	178	176	195	369	349	365	1	1	1	11	12	16
VA.	5,127	5,367	5,743	1,284	1,391	1,592	15	15	15	220	275	378
WV	1,756	1,770	1,768	54	53	50	3	3	3	11	14	20
NC	5,378	5,682	6,125	1,594	1,715	1,916	90	98	109	88	123	190
SC.	2,561	2,677	2,902	1,131	1,207	1,344	9	9	9	31	39	56
GA	5,025	5,346	5,857	1,955	2,139	2,485	13	12	12	109	140	199
FL.	11,867	12,619	13,981	2,073	2,351	2,906	38	40	42	231	303	443
E.S.C	12,690	13,231	14,042	3,166	3,331	3,634	44	45	46	120	155	219
KY.	3,535	3,646	3,769	286	307	345	6	6	6	24	30	40
TN.	4,327	4,563	4,899	845	905	1,014	11	11	11	46	59	83
AL.	3,140	3,284	3,529	1,083	1,139	1,243	18	18	19	33	44	65
MS	1,688	1,738	1,845	952	980	1,032	9	10	10	17	22	31
W.S.C	23,469	24,810	27,539	4,252	4,509	5,048	377	391	423	593	766	1,114
AR.	2,047	2,139	2,311	386	395	412	15	17	18	20	27	41
LA.	2,909	2,953	3,119	1,371	1,427	1,550	19	19	20	60	78	119
OK	2,699	2,770	2,979	244	251	269	276	290	320	52	71	115
TX.	15,814	16,948	19,130	2,251	2,436	2,817	67	65	65	461	590	839
West.	48,525	51,846	58,198	3,228	3,508	4,137	1,123	1,233	1,483	5,399	6,693	9,595
Mountain . . .	14,004	15,248	16,974	436	485	556	589	669	818	354	490	748
MT	798	847	908	2	2	3	55	62	74	6	8	12
ID	1,118	1,242	1,392	5	6	8	18	21	24	15	21	31
WY	467	498	564	4	5	5	12	14	17	4	6	9
CO	3,431	3,733	4,090	156	174	200	34	36	38	89	117	166
NM	1,460	1,574	1,760	32	33	35	159	181	231	25	35	56
AZ.	3,606	3,894	4,379	123	131	143	251	285	348	91	127	204
UT.	1,843	2,017	2,272	14	16	18	33	39	50	54	77	122
NV.	1,281	1,443	1,609	100	118	144	27	31	36	70	99	148
Pacific	34,521	36,598	41,224	2,792	3,023	3,581	534	564	665	5,045	6,203	8,847
WA	4,915	5,360	6,071	164	174	187	101	112	131	318	424	635
OR	2,929	3,139	3,508	54	60	70	47	52	60	111	153	238
CA.	25,701	26,987	30,357	2,512	2,719	3,245	277	276	314	3,908	4,906	7,169
AK.	477	516	543	26	28	29	102	116	150	29	39	59
HI	499	596	745	36	42	50	7	8	10	679	681	746

Source: U.S. Bureau of the Census, *Current Population Reports*, series P25-1111.

Source: *Statistical Abstract of the United States*, U.S. Department of Commerce.

Women in Business: Information Sources

Not only are women starting businesses at twice the rate of men but women owned businesses are also growing in diversity. If the present trend continues, almost 40% of small businesses will be owned by women by the year 2000. As the number of women entrepreneurs continues to increase so does the amount of business related information targeted to them. The following is a selected list of information sources that should prove helpful.

OFFICE OF WOMEN'S BUSINESS
  OWNERSHIP (OWBO)
SMALL BUSINESS ADMINISTRATION
  (SBA)
409 Third Street SE
Washington, DC 20416
SBA Answer Desk: 800-827-5722
  OWBO Tel: 202-205-6673
  TDD: 202-205-7333
  FAX: 202-205-7064

The Office of Women's Business Ownership (OWBO) offers both current and potential women business owners access to a variety of services and resources. These include prebusiness workshops, technical, financial and management information and training conferences on exporting, access to capital, and selling to the Federal Government (see below).

Each SBA office has a women's representative who can explain the resources that are available and provide guidance on how to access them. The regional coordinator for your area will direct you to your local representative. The coordinator's telephone numbers are given below:

ME, VT, MA, NH, CT, RI . . . 617-565-8695
NY, NJ, PR, VI. 716-263-6700
PA, DE, MD, VA, DC, WV . . 215-897-5406
NC, SC, KY, TN, GA, AL,
  MS, FL 404-347-2386
MN, WI, MI, OH, IN, IL. . . . 312-353-5000
                                    Ext. 764
NM, TX, OK, AR, LA 214-767-7858
KS, MO, IA, NE 816-426-5311
MT, ND, SD, WY, UT, CO. . . 303-294-7067
CA, NV, AZ, HI 415-744-8491
WA, OR, ID, AK 206-553-8547

The following are a number of OWBO sponsored programs.

Access to Capital

OWBO sponsors "Access to Capital" conferences throughout the country and markets the SBA guaranteed loan programs including the Small Loan Incentive, which targets small businesses searching for $50,000 or less; and has developed a directory.

Alternative Financing Sources is available to women business owners seeking new sources of capital. To obtain a copy call 202-205-6673.

For businesses needing smaller amounts of capital, the SBA has the Microloan Program that emphasizes small loans up to a maximum of $25,000. This program is not yet available in every state.

Women's Network for Entrepreneurial Training

A national mentoring program, the Women's Network for Entrepreneurial Training (WNET), is available in all 50 states. This program links established women business owners with entrepreneurs whose businesses are ready to grow. Through the year-long, one-on-one mentor relationship, successful women entrepreneurs pass on knowledge, skills, information, inspiration and support.

Demonstration Project Program for Women Business Owners

Currently there are 39 Demonstration Centers in 20 states. Administered by the SBA's Office of Women's Business Ownership, the Demonstration Program provides long-term training and counseling for women interested in either starting or expanding a small business. These Centers provide one to one, woman-to-woman counseling on all aspects of business and include for example, financial management, marketing, accounting, and budgeting information. Each center tailors its style and offerings to the particular needs of its community. These non-profit Centers charge only a nominal charge for their services. Call: 202-205-6673.

Selling to the Federal Government

OWBO sponsors conferences to train women on how to do business with the federal government and encourages women business owners to register on the Procurement

Automated Source System (PASS), Telephone: 202-205-6469, which lists potential small business suppliers for federal agencies and prime contractors. OWBO also refers women business owners to SBA procurement personnel who can assist them in the procedures of selling to the federal government.

OWBO negotiates women-owned procurement goals with each federal department and agency, encouraging procurement officials to seek out women-owned firms to provide the goods and services they need.

Opportunities in the Global Marketplace

Together with SBA's Office of International Trade, OWBO offers training and resources for women entrepreneurs considering expanding their businesses beyond domestic borders.

To prepare women entrepreneurs for the global marketplace, OWBO hosts training conferences, "Women Going International," around the country. Topics include export financing, legal considerations, strategic marketing and a focus on service related businesses.

Small Business Development Centers (SBDCs)

SBDCs are sponsored by SBA in partnership with state and local governments, the educational community and the private sector. They provide high-quality, low-cost assistance, counseling and training to prospective and existing small business owners. To locate the lead SBDC nearest you see page 214.

Offices of Small and Disadvantaged Business Utilization (OSDBU) with Their Women-Owned Business Representatives (WOBREP)

WOMEN-OWNED BUSINESS PROGRAM—Commerce has had a thriving women's business program for many years. The Department of Commerce has increased contract awards to women business owners from $2.8 million in 1980 to more than $30 million in 1993; initiated several procurement conferences for women; published a variety of directories, handbooks and bibliographies; and increased women's representation on Commerce advisory committees and technical programs.

The OSDBU also provides personal consulting for women interested in: selling to the Federal Government, participating in the Small Business Innovation Research and the Technology Transfer Programs, exploring exporting opportunities, researching issues of concern to women business owners, obtaining business related statistics, or joining trade associations. Call: 703-875-1551.

SERVICE CORPS OF RETIRED
    EXECUTIVES (SCORE)
409 Third Street SW
Washington, DC 20024

This organization of volunteers provides counseling to small business people. Volunteers include former or active accountants, business owners, corporation executives and lawyers. To obtain the name of the National SCORE Women's Business Ownership Coordinators nearest you call the National Volunteer Director at 410-266-8746.

STATE SPONSORED WOMEN ASSISTANCE PROGRAMS

Many states have specific programs geared for women-owned businesses. To locate the nearest office call your state's Department of Economic Development, listed in the State Information Guide on page 708.

SELECTED ASSOCIATIONS FOR BUSINESS WOMEN

NATIONAL ASSOCIATION FOR
    FEMALE EXECUTIVES, INC. (NAFE)
30 Irving Place
New York, NY 10003
Tel: 212-477-2200

The National Association for Female Executives, Inc. (NAFE) is the largest businesswomen's organization in the United States. It is a professional association dedicated to the advancement of women in the workplace through education, networking and public advocacy. NAFE functions to support women in business and to help them succeed in achieving their career goals and financial independence.

Among the benefits of membership are a venture capital fund to assist entrepreneurial members; satellite conferences, seminar programs and special events to encourage education and networking; *Executive Female* magazine; low-interest unsecured loan programs, credit card, group health and auto insurance, resume service and "How-To" career guides; flat-fee debt collection service; restaurant discounts plus many other discount services for your business. Membership is $29 per year.

AMERICAN WOMEN'S ECONOMIC DE-
    VELOPMENT CORPORATION (AWED)
71 Vanderbilt Avenue
New York, NY 10169
Tel: 212-688-1900
FAX: 212-692-9296

The American Women's Economic Development Corporation (AWED) is a nonprofit organization providing entrepreneurial women with management training and business counseling. Some of the courses offered by AWED are: Starting Your Own Business, Managing Your Own Business, Finance, as well as Chief Executive Roundtables and a Business Development Roundtable. Admission to AWED training programs is based on an application and a personal interview. Modest fees are charged for the above.

ASSOCIATIONS WITH SIGNIFICANT WOMEN BUSINESS OWNER MEMBERSHIP

AMERICAN ASSOCIATION OF
  UNIVERSITY WOMEN
1111 16th Street, NW
Washington, DC 20036
Tel: 202-785-7700

AMERICAN BUSINESS WOMEN'S
  ASSOCIATION
9100 Ward Parkway
P.O. Box 8728
Kansas City, MO 64114
Tel: 816-361-6621

AMERICAN WOMEN'S SOCIETY OF
  CERTIFIED PUBLIC ACCOUNTANTS
401 N. Michigan Avenue
Chicago, IL 60611
Tel: 312-644-6610

BUSINESS AND PROFESSIONAL
  WOMEN/USA
2012 Massachusetts Avenue, NW
Washington, DC 20036
Tel: 202-293-1100

ASSOCIATION OF BLACK WOMEN
  ENTREPRENEURS, INC.
1301 N. Kenter Avenue
Los Angeles, CA 90049
Tel: 310-472-4927

FEDERALLY EMPLOYED WOMEN
1400 Eye Street, NW
Washington, DC 20005
Tel: 202-898-0994

FEDERATION OF ORGANIZATIONS
  FOR PROFESSIONAL WOMEN
2001 S Street, NW
Washington, DC 20009
Tel: 202-328-1415

FINANCIAL WOMEN INTERNATIONAL
Bethesda, MD 20814-3015
Tel: 301-657-8288
FAX: 301-913-0001

HISPANIC WOMEN'S COUNCIL
5803 East Beverly Boulevard
Los Angeles, CA 90022
Tel: 213-725-1657

INTERNATIONAL WOMEN'S
  FUTURES ASSOCIATION
141 W. Jackson Boulevard
Chicago, IL 60604
Tel: 800-686-5497

LATIN BUSINESS & PROFESSIONAL
  WOMEN
P.O. Box 45-0913
Miami, FL 33245-0913
Tel: 305-446-9222

NATIONAL ASSOCIATION FOR THE
  COTTAGE INDUSTRY
P.O. Box 14850
Chicago, IL 60616
Tel: 312-871-4900

NATIONAL ASSOCIATION OF
  DEMONSTRATING COMPANIES
P.O. Box 1476
Buzzards Bay, MA 02532
Tel: 508-564-5918

NATIONAL ASSOCIATION OF
  INVESTMENT COMPANIES
1111 14th Street, NW
Washington, DC 20005
Tel: 202-289-4336

NATIONAL ASSOCIATION OF
  MINORITY WOMEN IN BUSINESS
906 Grand Avenue
Kansas City, MO 64106
Tel: 816-421-3335
FAX: 816-421-3336

NATIONAL ASSOCIATION OF SMALL
  BUSINESS INVESTMENT COMPANIES
1199 N. Fairfax Street
Alexandria, VA 22314
Tel: 703-683-1601

NATIONAL ASSOCIATION OF WOMEN
  BUSINESS ADVOCATES
Women's Business Resource Program
Ohio Department of Development
77 South High Street
Columbus, OH 43215
Tel: 614-466-4945

NATIONAL ASSOCIATION OF WOMEN
  BUSINESS OWNERS
710 44th Street
Chevy Chase, MD 20815
Tel: 301-951-9411

NATIONAL FEDERATION OF BUSINESS
  & PROFESSIONAL WOMEN CLUBS
2012 Massachusetts Avenue, NW
Washington, DC 20036
Tel: 202-293-1100

NATIONAL FOUNDATION FOR
  WOMEN BUSINESS OWNERS
1100 Wayne Ave.
Silver Springs, MD 20910
Tel: 301-495-4975

NATIONAL WOMEN'S ECONOMIC
  ALLIANCE FOUNDATION
1440 New York Avenue
Washington, DC 20005
Tel: 202-393-5257

NATIONAL WOMEN'S POLITICAL
  CAUCUS
1275 K Street, NW
Washington, DC 20005
Tel: 202-898-1100

9 TO 5: NATIONAL ASSOCIATION
  OF WORKING WOMEN
614 Superior, NW
Cleveland, OH 44113
Tel: 216-566-9308

ORGANIZATION OF CHINESE
  AMERICAN WOMEN
1439 Rhode Island Avenue
Washington, DC 20005
Tel: 202-638-0330

WOMEN'S BUSINESS DEVELOPMENT
  CORPORATION
P.O. Box 658
Bangor, ME 04402-0658
Tel: 207-623-0065

WOMEN'S WORLD BANKING
8 West 40th Street
New York, NY 10018
Tel: 212-768-8513

WOMEN EXECUTIVES IN STATE
  GOVERNMENT
122 C Street, NW
Washington, DC 20001
Tel: 202-628-9374

WOMEN IN FRANCHISING
53 West Jackson Boulevard
Chicago, IL 60604
Tel: 312-431-1467

SOCIETY OF WOMEN ENGINEERS
345 East 47th Street
New York, NY 10017
Tel: 212-705-7855

PUBLICATIONS:

A list of SBA publications and video tapes for starting and managing a small business is available from your local SBA office or by writing: Small Business Directory, P.O. Box 1000, Ft. Worth, TX 76119.

An SBA publication *Women Business Owners: Selling to the Federal Government* is designed to help women business owners by providing them with information about marketing their goods and services to the federal government. Available from your local U.S. Government Bookstore or by mail or telephone from the Superintendent of Documents in Washington, D.C. Telephone: 202-783-3238.

For Women: Managing Your Own Business includes material on business planning, marketing, personnel management, insurance and much more. Available from the Office of Women's Business Ownership by calling 202-205-6673 or the Superintendent of Documents at 202-512-1800.

The Women's Bureau of the U.S. Department of Labor publishes a variety of material for women business owners, including:

A Working Woman's Guide To Her Job Rights
Directory of Non Traditional Training and
  Employment Programs Serving Women
Alternative Work Patterns
State Maternity/Parental Leave Laws
Women Business Owners
Women in Labor Unions

Single copies of publications are available free of charge from the Department of Labor, 200 Constitution Avenue, NW, Washington, D.C. 20210, Telephone: 202-219-6611.

The *Encyclopedia of Women's Associations Worldwide*, edited by L. R. Greenfield, contains thousands of organizations throughout the world concerning women and women's issues. Among the information included are the purpose of the organization, languages of correspondence, publications, conventions, and meetings. Entries are arranged by subject and organized alphabetically. Published by Gale Research Co., 835 Penobscot Building, Detroit, MI 48226.

Women and Credit Histories is available from the Federal Trade Commission (FTC). Telephone: 202-326-2222. This free pamphlet tells you how to establish credit and what to do if you feel you have been unfairly denied credit. Also includes an explanation of your legal credit rights as well as information on how to establish credit.

Entrepreneurial Woman, published by *Entrepreneur Magazine*, contains information appropriate to its title. Address: 2392 Morse Avenue, Irvine, CA 92714-6234. Telephone: 714-261-2325.

Executive Female is the official bimonthly publication of the National Association for Female Executives (NAFE). Issues contain articles on a variety of subjects such as career strategies, the best solutions to management problems, tips from successful entrepreneurs on starting and growing a business, better ways to manage money, your staff, and your company. Membership in NAFE includes a subscription to *Executive Female*. Contact NAFE at 212-477-2200.

50/50 By 2000: The Woman's Guide to Political Power is available from NAFE. Covers such topics as women in politics, and women's issues. Contact NAFE at 212-477-2200.

SELECTED PUBLICATIONS ON FINANCING

In addition to the generally known publications, the following are some lesser known publications which should be of interest to the business woman.

Alternative Financing, prepared by the Office of Women's Business Ownership, contains a listing and description of Federal small business funding sources, organizations active in development finance, as well as a list of loans that are only available in specific states. To obtain a free copy call 202-205-6673.

The State and Small Business, produced by the Office of Advocacy of the Small Business Administration, includes information on sources of financing, state legislation that affects business, and much more. Available through the Superintendent of Documents at 202-512-1800.

Steps to Small Business Financing is an informative booklet developed through a joint project with the American Banker's Association and the National Federation of Independent Business. Available from the American Banker's Association at 202-663-5221.

Investing in Gold and Diamonds

Investing in Gold

Gold has been one of the more widely promoted investment vehicles over the last several years. Prices moved from about $140 per ounce in early 1977 to over $800 in early 1980. However, by August 1985 prices declined to $291 an ounce but climbed to over $380.00 by May 1993. Because of such large fluctuations, the metal has stimulated a great deal of speculative interest among many investors.

Investment in gold can be made in a variety of ways:

Gold bullion (bars and wafers) This can be purchased through many stock brokers, bullion currency dealers, and some investment (mutual fund) companies. The purity of gold is indicated by the fineness. Pure gold has a fineness of 1.000 and corresponds to 24 karats.° Each bar is stamped with the fineness as determined by an assay, the refiner's number, a bar identification number and the weight. A bar fineness of .995 or better is acceptable.

Individuals who accept delivery of gold bars and who subsequently wish to resell must have the bar reassayed prior to sale because of the possibility of adulteration with cheaper metals. Because of the latter possibility, individuals should always buy from reputable dealers, and the bar should bear the stamp of well recognized refiners or assayers. Individuals taking physical possession of the metal also have sales taxes, storage, and insurance costs.

The purchaser may arrange to have the dealer (or agent) retain physical possession of the bullion. In this case, evidence of ownership is provided by a *gold deposit certificate* (receipt) issued by the dealer. Since gold certificates are generally non-negotiable or assignable, there is no loss if it is stolen. The gold deposit certificate method of buying bullion eliminates sales taxes, storage risks (though the dealer will charge a modest storage fee) and the need for assay on resale. It is probably the most convenient way of purchasing gold.

Gold bullion coins Bullion coins are issued in large number by several governments which guarantee their gold content. They have no numismatic value. The best known gold bullion coins are the U.S. Gold One Ounce, South African Krugerrand, Canadian Maple Leaf, Austrian 100 Corona and the Gold Mexican 50 peso. The first three coins have a pure gold content of one ounce. The Austrian Corona has a gold content of .9802 ounce and the Mexican peso 1.2057 ounces. The premium (cost above the gold value) varies from dealer to dealer. For those who do not want to take physical possession, deposit certificates are available for the coins.

One of the largest bullion dealers is Gold Line International (800-289-3325) headquartered in Santa Monica, California. Gold coins can also be purchased at banks where there is generally a very low premium over the gold content value.

Gold stocks The stocks of a number of Canadian and U.S. gold mining companies are traded on the New York (N), American (A) and Over-The-Counter (O) exchanges. Of course, with stocks, the investor is not just buying into gold, but also into the many special problems associated with running a company—production costs, quality of the ore, lifetime of the deposit, etc. However, many gold stocks pay dividends, whereas other gold investments do not pay any return during the holding period.

South African gold mines are traded on the Over-The-Counter Market by means of ADR (American Depository Receipt). ADR is a claim on foreign stocks (South African gold shares, in this case) held by the foreign branches of large U.S. banks. Holders of ADRs are entitled to dividends which, in the case of South African gold shares, may be substantial. The ADRs of these companies are listed in *The Wall Street Journal.*

Mutual funds specializing in gold and precious metals A number of mutual funds specializing in gold and precious metals stocks provide diversification among a number of issues thereby reducing risk associated with any particular stock.

Options on gold stocks Put and call options are available on Homestake

---

° This "karats" is not to be confused with the "carats" that apply to diamonds.

Mining (Chicago Options Exchange) and on ASA Limited (American Options Exchange). These options may be used for leveraged speculation or for hedging existing gold holdings. Holders of call options gain if the gold shares increase, while holders of put options benefit if prices decline.

The Philadelphia Stock Exchange trades a gold/silver option based on an index of seven different stocks in the industry.

Options on gold bullion Put and call options on gold bullion are traded on the International Options Market (IOM) of the Montreal Stock Exchange. IOM options are on 10 ounces of gold. Contract months are Feb/May/Aug/Nov.

Monex (Newport Beach, CA) provides put and call options on 32.15 ounces of gold. The Monex options are not tradeable but can be exercised during the option period. Expiration periods are 30, 60, 90, and 185 days.

Since options are paid in full, they are not subject to margin calls or forced liquidation as is the case with futures contracts. At this time, quotations on bullion options are not available in the daily press.

Gold futures contract Gold futures contracts are obligations to buy or sell 100 ounces of gold on or before a specified date at a specified price. Futures contracts must be exercised if held to maturity, while options contracts need not be exercised if held to maturity. Futures contracts are purchased on margin, and hence, are subject to margin call and possible forced liquidation. They are widely quoted in the financial press, and the market is highly organized.

As with options, futures contracts may be used for leveraged speculation or for hedging. Speculators will buy contracts if they anticipate a price increase or sell contracts in anticipation of a price decrease.

Gold futures are traded on the N.Y. Commodity Exchange, the International Monetary Market of the Chicago Mercantile Exchange, and other markets.

Options on Gold Futures Contracts Options on Gold Futures contracts (the right to buy and sell a gold futures contract rather than the metal) are actively traded on the New York Comex. The futures contract underlying the options is for 100 ounces of gold. Contract months are April/Aug./Dec. Gold futures options premiums are reported daily in *The Wall Street Journal*.

Investing in Diamonds

Diamond prices are very volatile. For example, they have appreciated on the average of about 12.6% over the ten-year period 1969–1979 (compared to a consumer price index of 6.1% during the same period of time). There have been periods (the recession of 1973–1974 and in 1981) when the price of investment quality diamonds slipped as much as 40%. A major factor stabilizing the market is DeBeers, a South African diamond company which handles as much as 80% of the world's diamonds. While the appreciation of diamonds has been impressive, potential buyers should be aware that prices are not quoted in the daily newspapers; therefore, selling the stones at a profit may be difficult. Quotes are available in the *Rappaport Diamond Report*, 15 West 47th Street, New York, NY 10036, (212) 354-0575. Another good source of information on the diamond industry is the Diamond Registry, 580 Fifth Avenue, New York, NY 10036, (212) 575-0444. The registry publishes a monthly newsletter which includes price ranges, trends, and forecasts as well as other pertinent material.

To locate reputable gem dealers check with the Diamond Registry (address above) or the

American Gem Society
1050 East Flamingo Road
Las Vegas, NV 89109
(702) 255-6500

American Diamond Industry
   Association
71 West 47th Street
New York, NY 10036
(212) 575-0525

Buyers should only deal with reputable firms, and the stones should be certified by an independent laboratory such as the Gemological Institute of America, tel: (212) 221-5858 and International Gemological Institute, tel: (212) 398-1700.

Diamonds are ranked in terms of the 4 C's—carat (one carat equals 1/142 ounces in weight), color, clarity, and cut.

Carat For investment purposes the diamond should be more than .5 carat. However, diamonds of more than 2 carats may be difficult to sell.

Color There are six main categories, each with subdivisions:

D,E,F—Colorless
G,H,I,J—Near colorless
K,L,M—Faint yellow

N,O,P,Q,R—Very light yellow
S,T,U,V,W,X,Y,Z—Light yellow
Fancy yellow stone

Color should be in the range from D to H. However, Fancy Yellow Stones often command very high prices because of their scarcity.

Clarity Although bubbles, lines, and specks (inclusions) are natural to diamonds, they may interfere with the passage of light through the diamond. With a 10X magnification, a professional appraiser can grade the diamond according to the ten clarity grades:

> **FL**—Flawless
> **IF**—Internally flawless
> **VVS-1, VVS-2**—Very, very slight inclusions

VS-1, VS-2—Very slight inclusions
SI-1, SI-2—Slight inclusions
I-1, I-2, I-3—Imperfect

Investment grade stones should be in the range FL to VS-2.

Cut There are several types of cuts—oval, marquise, pear shaped, round brilliant and emerald. Round brilliant stones are preferred for investment purposes. Proportions are important, and the preferred values are:

> Depth % (total depth divided by girdle diameter): 57% to 63%.
> Table (table diameter divided by girdle diameter): 57% to 66%.
> Girdle thickness should be neither very thick nor very thin.

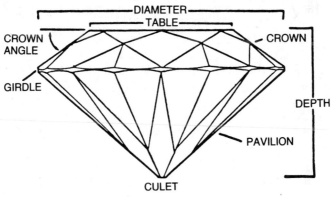

THE ROUND BRILLIANT DIAMOND

MEDIAN SALES PRICE OF SINGLE-FAMILY HOMES (in thousands of dollars)

Metropolitan Area*	1992	1993	1994	1994 (Not Seasonally Adjusted)				1995
				I	II	III	IV	Ir
Akron, OH	$79.3	$83.2	$84.9	$81.6	$86.6	$86.5	$83.3	$83.9
Albany/Schenectady/Troy, NY	111.4	112.3	112.0	112.5	110.3	113.0	112.3	106.6
Albuquerque, NM	92.0	100.4	110.0	103.1	108.5	112.5	114.5	110.8
Amarillo, TX	58.1	63.2	64.5	63.6	65.9	63.9	63.8	67.8
Orange Cnty. (Anaheim/Santa Ana MSA), CA**	230.9	217.2	211.0	206.2	211.0	213.9	212.2	205.1
Appleton/Oshkosh/Neenah, WI	71.0	75.4	80.6	78.6	80.0	83.3	80.2	82.4
Atlanta, GA	89.5	91.8	93.6	93.1	93.8	94.0	93.4	94.4
Atlantic City, NJ	109.1	106.7	107.6	104.9	111.8	105.7	107.3	106.2
Aurora/Elgin, IL	118.8	121.7	124.4	124.2	124.0	124.7	124.9	123.3
Austin/San Marcos, TX	83.8	91.3	96.2	95.5	95.0	97.0	97.3	98.5
Baltimore, MD	113.4	115.7	115.4	115.7	118.8	115.9	108.8	109.5
Baton Rouge, LA	73.6	75.9	77.4	78.4	76.2	77.9	77.1	79.8
Beaumont/Port Arthur, TX	61.5	63.2	65.0	65.6	66.7	65.4	61.8	61.7
Biloxi/Gulfport, MS	62.4	67.2	70.9	72.4	68.0	70.3	72.9	71.1
Birmingham, AL	90.9	96.5	100.2	99.5	100.1	100.8	100.1	99.7
Boise City, ID	83.1	91.4	99.0	97.3	97.0	102.0	101.0	98.0
Boston, MA	171.1	173.2	179.3	170.6	181.3	187.3	176.6	175.1
Bradenton, FL	82.1	86.5	88.3	86.4	88.6	86.9	90.3	87.6
Buffalo/Niagara Falls, NY	81.7	83.5	82.3	82.4	81.9	82.0	83.7	82.2
Canton, OH	71.1	75.4	77.5	76.3	79.4	74.4	80.1	77.8
Cedar Rapids, IA	71.9	78.0	82.8	80.6	80.5	84.0	84.9	79.7
Champaign/Urbana/Rantoul, IL	66.6	69.7	74.1	68.0	74.8	76.4	74.3	78.1
Charleston, SC	82.3	89.9	91.6	91.3	92.3	90.5	92.0	92.6
Charleston, WV	70.3	74.8	78.6	72.4	80.2	80.6	78.1	82.6
Charlotte/Gastonia/Rock Hill, NC/SC	102.2	106.1	106.5	104.0	106.8	110.4	104.6	100.0
Chattanooga, TN/GA	73.0	73.6	77.5	76.1	77.4	79.0	77.7	76.3
Chicago, IL	136.8	142.0	144.1	135.9	144.5	151.9	141.6	143.3
Cincinnati, OH/KY/IN	88.6	91.4	96.5	93.6	96.6	98.7	96.4	94.6
Cleveland, OH	90.7	95.0	98.5	94.2	99.3	100.7	98.1	93.2
Colorado Springs, CO	86.9	93.7	104.2	97.9	103.4	109.1	105.5	104.6
Columbia, SC	84.7	85.1	86.6	82.9	87.7	90.0	84.9	86.9
Columbus, OH	91.0	91.8	94.8	92.8	97.4	94.4	93.6	92.8
Corpus Christi, TX	67.5	70.5	74.1	71.7	74.1	74.9	75.1	69.4
Dallas, TX	91.3	94.5	95.0	95.1	96.3	95.4	92.3	90.6

Davenport/Moline/Rock Island, IA/IL	54.8	58.3	61.8	60.8	60.6	63.5	61.9	60.6
Dayton/Springfield, OH	81.2	82.1	84.2	82.5	85.7	85.5	81.9	84.6
Daytona Beach, FL	66.2	67.8	69.0	66.2	70.5	70.7	68.3	68.2
Denver, CO	96.2	104.7	116.8	111.2	114.8	121.6	119.0	120.8
Des Moines, IA	73.0	78.8	81.7	77.4	81.5	85.0	82.0	84.1
Detroit, MI	81.3	86.0	87.0	85.7	87.2	87.7	87.0	90.5
El Paso, TX	67.5	71.8	75.3	73.6	74.4	77.6	75.4	74.6
Eugene/Springfield, OR	79.7	84.4	96.2	90.1	95.9	101.3	96.7	99.8
Fargo/Moorhead, ND/MN	70.7	75.5	77.6	78.2	74.7	78.8	78.3	82.1
Ft. Lauderdale/Hollywood/Pompano Beach, FL	99.1	103.1	103.1	100.1	104.8	104.8	101.8	101.9
Ft. Myers/Cape Coral, FL	71.1	77.1	77.8	78.9	77.2	77.8	77.7	73.1
Ft. Worth/Arlington, TX	80.2	82.9	82.5	83.5	82.3	82.7	81.5	80.0
Gainesville, FL	79.1	82.9	84.6	82.1	84.5	82.7	89.3	82.3
Gary/Hammond, IN	76.1	82.8	87.2	84.1	87.6	87.4	88.3	85.1
Grand Rapids, MI	73.1	76.5	76.9	76.6	76.4	77.3	77.8	76.9
Green Bay, WI	72.9	81.5	86.6	84.4	85.7	89.2	86.3	87.5
Greensboro/Winston-Salem/High Point, NC	88.4	94.7	96.6	95.9	95.3	96.7	98.9	98.3
Greenville/Spartanburg, SC	82.9	84.9	87.4	83.0	87.9	89.1	88.5	86.8
Hartford, CT	141.1	135.3	133.4	132.9	134.0	135.1	130.8	126.0
Honolulu, HI	349.0	358.5	360.0	355.0	365.0	368.0	357.0	349.0
Houston, TX	80.3	80.9	80.5	79.5	82.6	81.2	78.1	77.2
Indianapolis, IN	83.7	86.6	90.7	90.5	92.4	90.0	89.2	88.6
Jacksonville, FL	76.8	77.1	81.9	79.7	81.5	83.6	82.3	80.7
Kalamazoo, MI	69.6	71.1	74.8	74.7	76.2	73.9	73.9	80.0
Kansas City, MO/KS	79.5	83.6	87.1	84.9	86.8	88.6	87.7	88.5
Knoxville, TN	80.1	85.3	89.2	88.6	88.1	89.9	90.1	88.8
Lake County, IL	119.6	130.1	130.8	128.8	132.5	135.6	124.5	135.3
Lansing/East Lansing, MI	69.9	73.2	75.5	73.0	74.6	76.6	77.1	73.9
Las Vegas, NV	104.3	108.2	110.5	110.4	109.9	110.8	111.0	111.6
Lexington/Fayette, KY	78.7	82.5	87.5	83.0	86.9	90.0	88.6	87.0
Lincoln, NE	67.7	72.5	76.6	74.1	73.9	80.6	77.6	78.1
Little Rock-N. Little Rock, AR	N/A	N/A	75.0	74.5	75.7	72.7	76.8	78.8
Los Angeles Area, CA**	210.8	195.4	189.1	191.6	190.9	191.1	182.7	177.1
Louisville, KY/IN	69.5	74.5	80.5	77.8	81.3	81.6	80.9	82.3
Madison, WI	94.9	104.6	116.0	111.5	115.1	120.0	116.2	114.5

(continued)

MEDIAN SALES PRICE OF SINGLE-FAMILY HOMES (in thousands of dollars) (concluded)

Metropolitan Area*	1992	1993	1994	1994 (Not Seasonally Adjusted)				1995
				I	II	III	IV	Ir
Melbourne/Titusville/Palm Bay, FL	$74.8	$75.3	$76.7	$74.9	$76.9	$78.2	$76.9	$73.7
Memphis, TN/AR/MS	85.3	87.0	86.3	85.6	87.0	86.7	85.1	81.6
Miami/Hialeah, FL	97.1	98.8	103.2	105.0	102.0	103.0	103.3	102.6
Milwaukee, WI	97.0	104.1	109.0	106.5	110.4	111.1	106.6	108.8
Minneapolis/St. Paul, MN/WI	94.2	98.2	101.5	100.0	101.0	103.2	101.5	103.7
Mobile, AL	64.8	68.2	69.9	69.5	71.7	68.3	69.6	68.8
Montgomery, AL	79.7	83.2	82.2	81.7	81.4	83.4	82.1	80.6
Nashville, TN	88.8	90.4	96.5	95.2	95.5	96.1	99.5	99.5
New Haven/Meriden, CT	145.8	142.5	139.6	137.6	141.5	144.1	135.0	131.9
New Orleans, LA	73.6	76.8	76.9	75.4	76.9	77.4	77.8	74.4
New York/N. New Jersey/Long Island, NY/NJ/CT	172.7	173.2	173.2	170.3	174.6	177.4	168.7	167.0
Bergen/Passaic, NJ	187.6	188.4	192.7	188.3	193.5	199.4	187.2	191.8
Middlesex/Somerset/Hunterdon, NJ	168.9	168.8	170.7	161.1	174.8	175.6	166.6	164.8
Monmouth/Ocean, NJ	139.2	137.1	137.0	135.2	137.5	140.2	133.8	132.8
Nassau/Suffolk, NY	158.6	159.2	159.3	158.8	161.2	161.7	154.6	153.3
Newark, NJ	184.4	185.1	187.3	181.4	191.0	192.4	181.8	183.1
Norfolk/Virginia Bch/Newport News, VA	94.8	98.2	103.8	104.7	104.9	103.7	101.6	99.4
Ocala, FL	56.2	57.8	59.5	58.1	57.9	62.8	59.6	57.5
Oklahoma City, OK	61.6	64.9	66.7	67.6	66.6	66.5	65.7	65.6
Omaha, NE/IA	69.4	72.7	75.6	72.8	75.1	78.0	75.8	76.6
Orlando, FL	87.6	90.1	90.7	89.9	91.8	91.9	89.2	89.1
Pensacola, FL	67.2	71.9	76.4	74.8	78.0	78.1	74.6	79.1
Peoria, IL	59.1	63.2	67.9	65.9	69.4	68.7	66.6	61.2
Philadelphia, PA/NJ	117.0	118.0	119.5	116.8	119.5	124.7	115.4	113.4
Phoenix, AZ	86.8	89.1	91.4	89.2	91.1	93.2	92.0	91.6
Pittsburgh, PA	78.6	82.2	80.7	80.0	84.3	80.8	76.8	77.2
Portland, OR	97.7	106.0	116.9	111.2	117.6	118.7	120.0	120.6
Providence, RI	118.5	116.3	116.4	115.6	116.6	117.7	115.2	112.8
Raleigh/Durham, NC	105.9	109.2	115.2	110.1	112.3	116.0	124.5	118.6
Reno, NV	117.9	126.3	133.6	130.7	132.2	137.6	133.5	132.2
Richland/Kennewick/Pasco, WA	84.2	101.9	111.3	105.3	113.1	118.9	108.1	113.5
Richmond/Petersburg, VA	93.9	94.1	95.4	94.0	93.4	95.0	99.2	99.9
Riverside/San Bernardino, CA**	136.2	134.4	129.1	131.0	129.4	128.9	127.2	122.6
Rochester, NY	84.7	84.8	85.6	85.3	86.5	85.7	84.8	82.1

Rockford, IL	75.7	81.3	84.9	82.5	83.9	87.1	85.8	84.9
Sacramento, CA**	134.0	129.2	124.5	127.4	126.2	122.0	121.4	120.2
Saginaw/Bay City/Midland, MI	N/A	58.3	58.9	59.2	58.7	60.4	57.0	54.8
Saint Louis, MO/IL	83.2	84.8	85.0	83.2	86.6	85.9	82.9	83.3
Salt Lake City/Ogden, UT	76.5	84.9	98.0	92.8	95.6	103.2	102.2	103.0
San Antonio, TX	70.4	77.0	78.2	76.8	78.7	79.3	77.4	76.0
San Diego, CA**	183.1	176.9	176.0	176.9	178.6	175.9	170.7	172.1
San Francisco Bay Area, CA**	259.3	254.4	255.6	251.4	260.9	258.3	248.9	244.5
Sarasota, FL	93.2	94.1	97.0	97.1	95.1	98.9	97.9	100.8
Seattle, WA	145.7	150.2	155.9	152.9	155.7	158.4	156.4	155.1
Shreveport, LA	66.3	69.0	70.2	68.8	70.5	70.7	70.9	66.2
Sioux Falls, SD	69.0	74.8	80.1	77.8	80.3	81.2	80.1	83.7
South Bend/Mishawaka, IN	62.9	63.6	64.7	65.6	69.1	60.9	61.6	62.2
Spokane, WA	76.3	85.5	94.6	90.7	94.1	95.0	97.3	92.6
Springfield, IL	67.7	72.6	75.8	71.5	77.9	76.5	74.4	74.1
Springfield, MA	115.1	112.4	107.7	108.4	110.1	108.9	100.8	N/A
Springfield, MO	62.8	68.1	73.0	69.3	73.2	73.4	75.5	75.4
Syracuse, NY	80.4	84.7	83.1	82.1	83.5	84.8	81.4	83.2
Tacoma, WA	107.8	113.5	118.9	115.0	119.1	121.4	119.4	118.6
Tallahassee, FL	87.3	92.5	97.8	95.7	98.7	98.0	98.7	98.9
Tampa/St. Petersburg/Clearwater, FL	72.6	75.0	76.2	74.3	75.3	77.0	78.2	72.2
Toledo, OH	71.5	72.3	73.8	72.8	75.7	75.6	69.4	72.5
Topeka, KS	64.7	67.5	63.3	66.4	64.0	62.3	61.4	59.3
Trenton, NJ	138.1	133.4	131.3	128.9	129.8	139.5	126.3	122.6
Tucson, AZ	N/A	88.2	95.4	92.8	94.8	96.1	98.5	97.9
Tulsa, OK	68.3	71.3	74.1	73.5	73.1	76.3	73.3	72.9
Washington, DC/MD/VA	157.8	158.3	157.9	154.9	159.1	160.3	155.8	150.1
Waterloo/Cedar Falls, IA	47.2	50.5	53.1	48.1	51.7	55.5	55.0	55.3
W. Palm Beach/Boca Raton/Delray Beach, FL	114.1	114.6	117.6	114.0	114.7	121.7	120.0	113.8
Wichita, KS	68.6	71.4	73.7	73.4	74.5	73.8	72.5	72.6
Wilmington, DE/NJ/MD	117.2	N/A	N/A	N/A	N/A	N/A	N/A	N/A
Worcester, MA	128	129	130.6	129.2	130.2	132.8	130	128.9
Youngstown/Warren, OH	57.6	61.2	63.1	66.3	63.4	61.9	61.9	60.9

* All areas are metropolitan statistical areas (MSA) as defined by the U.S. Office of Management and Budget as of 1992. They include the named central city and surrounding areas.
** Provided by the California Association of REALTORS®. N/A Not Available   r   Revised

© 1995 NATIONAL ASSOCIATION OF REALTORS®

Source: Reprinted with permission from the REAL ESTATE OUTLOOK: Market Trends and Insights, NATIONAL ASSOCIATION OF REALTORS®, Washington, DC.

APARTMENT CONDOS AND CO-OPS

Year		United States	Northeast	Midwest	South	West	United States	Northeast	Midwest	South	West
		Unit Volume Seasonally Adjusted Annual Rate					Median Sales Price Not Seasonally Adjusted				
1992		366,000	78,000	67,000	115,000	106,000	$84,900	$103,200	$75,800	$69,600	$107,100
1993		401,000	86,000	73,000	131,000	111,000	83,500	99,200	76,400	69,000	103,500
1994		437,000	96,000	75,000	145,000	120,000	87,100	100,100	86,200	69,200	106,600
1994	I	438,000	95,000	78,000	141,000	124,000	$87,000	$103,000	$85,000	$68,900	$106,900
	II	443,000	96,000	75,000	149,000	123,000	88,300	101,700	85,500	70,700	111,500
	III	445,000	102,000	75,000	146,000	122,000	86,800	99,700	87,000	68,500	102,800
	IV	422,000	93,000	71,000	146,000	111,000	86,200	96,700	87,100	68,600	105,300
1995	I r	403,000	94,000	69,000	134,000	106,000	85,800	95,300	87,700	68,000	106,600

r *Revised*

Source: Reprinted with permission from the *REAL ESTATE OUTLOOK: Market Trends and Insights*, NATIONAL ASSOCIATION OF REALTORS®, Washington, DC.

© 1995 NATIONAL ASSOCIATION OF REALTORS®

HOUSING AFFORDABILITY

Year		Median Priced Existing Single-Family Home	Mortgage Rate*	Monthly P & I Payment	Payment as % Income	Median Family Income	Qualifying Income**	Affordability Indices		
								Composite	Fixed	ARM
1992		$103,700	8.11%	$615	20.0%	$36,812	$29,523	124.7	120.1	145.0
1993		106,800	7.16	578	18.8	36,959	27,727	133.3	128.4	154.9
1994		109,800	7.47	612	19.3	38,105	29,392	129.6	120.1	147.0
1994	Apr	$109,100	7.21%	$593	19.1%	$37,341	$28,466	131.2	123.8	150.3
	May	109,900	7.52	616	19.7	37,437	29,566	126.6	117.4	146.4
	Jun	113,300	7.54	636	20.3	37,532	30,540	122.9	112.7	138.8
	Jul	112,400	7.68	640	20.4	37,628	30,713	122.5	112.8	138.4
	Aug	113,000	7.76	648	20.6	37,723	31,117	121.2	111.8	136.7
	Sep	108,900	7.74	624	19.8	37,819	29,930	126.4	116.0	141.0
	Oct	107,500	7.76	617	19.5	37,914	29,602	128.1	116.4	142.9
	Nov	108,700	7.72	621	19.6	38,010	29,817	127.5	113.6	141.3
	Dec	109,100	7.97	639	20.1	38,105	30,653	124.3	112.4	136.7
1995	Jan	108,100	7.94	631	19.8	38,246	30,285	126.3	112.0	138.2
	Feb	107,000	8.19	639	20.0	38,387	30,695	125.1	113.9	137.0
	Mar r	107,900	8.24	648	20.2	38,528	31,099	123.9	115.7	136.9
	Apr p	108,400	8.14	645	20.0	38,669	30,951	124.9 This Month	118.0 Month Ago	136.7 Year Ago
Apr p	Northeast	$134,100	7.70%	$765	21.6%	$42,516	$36,698	115.9	112.2	110.4
	Midwest	88,500	7.91	515	15.4	40,044	24,720	162.0	161.2	161.4
	South	93,800	7.79	540	18.8	34,516	25,903	133.3	133.6	130.3
	West	145,400	7.89	845	25.3	40,129	40,557	98.9	100.1	99.0

*Effective rate on loans closed on existing homes – Federal Housing Finance Board. Regional interest rate from HSH Associates, Butler, NJ

**Based on current lending requirements of the Federal National Mortgage Association using a 20% down payment.

r Revised   p Preliminary

Source: Reprinted with permission from the *REAL ESTATE OUTLOOK: Market Trends and Insights*, NATIONAL ASSOCIATION OF REALTORS®, Washington, DC.

FIRST-TIME HOMEBUYER AFFORDABILITY

Year		Starter Home Price	10% Down Payment	Loan Amount	Effective Interest Rate*	Effective I Rate Plus PMI	Monthly Payment	Prime First-Time Median Income	Qualifying Income	Affordability Indices	
										First-Time Buyer	Composite
1992		$88,100	$8,810	$79,290	8.11%	8.36%	$602	$23,133	$28,887	80.1	124.7
1993		90,800	9,080	81,720	7.16	7.41	566	23,475	27,186	86.4	133.3
1994		93,300	9,330	83,970	7.47	7.72	600	24,203	28,792	84.1	129.6
1994	I	$91,500	$9,150	$82,350	6.91%	7.16%	$557	$23,657	$26,724	88.5	136.7
	II	94,200	9,420	84,780	7.42	7.67	603	23,839	28,929	82.4	127.2
	III	94,700	9,470	85,230	7.74	7.99	625	24,021	29,990	80.1	123.5
	IV	92,100	9,210	82,890	7.82	8.07	612	24,203	29,389	82.4	126.9
1995	Ir	91,500	9,150	82,350	8.12	8.37	626	24,469	30,030	81.5	125.5

Effective rate on loans closed on existing homes – Federal Housing Finance Board
r Revised

Source: Reprinted with permission from the *REAL ESTATE OUTLOOK: Market Trends and Insights*, NATIONAL ASSOCIATION OF REALTORS®, Washington, DC.

OFFICE REAL ESTATE MARKET: Selected Cities*

ATLANTA, GEORGIA: Office

Atlanta, Georgia

MARKET DATA

Inventory (sf)	Class A CBD	Class A Outside CBD	Class B CBD	Class B Outside CBD
Total	32,557,821	65,587,671	-	-
Vacant	4,604,947	6,966,543	-	-
Vacancy Rate	14.1%	10.6%	-	-
Vacant Sublease	n/a	n/a	-	-
Under Construction	n/a	360,000	-	-
Substantial Rehab	n/a	n/a	-	-
Net Absorption	588,827	1,951,377	-	-

Rental Rates ($/sf)

	CBD	Outside CBD	CBD	Outside CBD
Lowest	19.56	19.83	12.57	12.60
Highest	21.12	20.38	13.78	13.08
Weighted Average	20.77	19.05	n/a	12.54

Sales Prices ($/sf)

	CBD	Outside CBD	CBD	Outside CBD
Lowest	80.00	50.00	16.00	20.00
Highest	175.00	118.00	60.00	45.00
Weighted Average	n/a	n/a	n/a	n/a

Operating Expenses ($/sf)

	CBD	Outside CBD	CBD	Outside CBD
Lowest	6.89	6.36	5.00	4.50
Highest	9.30	8.73	8.00	7.00
Weighted Average	n/a	n/a	n/a	n/a

Tax Expenses ($/sf)

	CBD	Outside CBD	CBD	Outside CBD
Lowest	n/a	n/a	n/a	n/a
Highest	n/a	n/a	n/a	n/a
Weighted Average	n/a	n/a	n/a	n/a

Utility Rates:	CBD $1.85 per sf	**Parking Ratio:**	CBD - 1 per 500 sf
	Outside CBD $1.85 per sf		Outside CBD - 1 per 250 sf
	Not Separately Metered		

Standard Work Letter: n/a, typically based on dollars per square foot

Operating Cost Escalation: Base Year

Rate of Return:	Cap Rate: n/a	**Mortgage Money Supply:** Moderate
	IRR: n/a	**Prime Source of Financing:** Insurance Companies, REITs

Cumulative Discount Rate: 20%
Landlord Concessions
Parking, Rental Abatement, Moving Allowance, Interior Improvements

Leasing Activity Profile
Major Activity - Fortune 500 Firms, Business Services, Sales, Finance/Banking, Energy
Minor Activity - Legal/Accounting, Insurance, Government

OUTLOOK

Absorption	Up 6-10%
Construction	Up 1-5%
Vacancies	Down 1-5%
Rental Rates	Up 1-5%
Landlord Concessions	Same
Sales Class A CBD	n/a
Prices Outside CBD	n/a
Class B CBD	n/a
Outside CBD	n/a

1994 REVIEW

The approaching 1996 Olympic Games are providing some short-term relief to the troubled Atlanta CBD office market. The downtown's net absorption of 589,000 sq. ft. in 1994 reflected a number of users needing offices convenient to the Olympic venues, but only for a 24 to 30 month period. With Downtown vacancy above 14 percent for Class "A", such accommodations are plentiful. The north suburban markets, though, are booming, especially along the newly opened Georgia 400 corridor. Suburban net absorption approached two million sq. ft. and brought rents onto a par with the downtown towers. Investment interest in Atlanta was brisk, with foreign investors and REITs especially active.

1995 FORECAST

Build-to-suit activity, already gathering momentum, should be accelerating in 1995. The intense construction activity associated with the Olympic preparation is driving up development costs, and these in turn will be putting pressure on rents, especially in the hot markets on the north side of town. Absorption is forecast to be up between six and 10 percent this year. The long-term prospects for the downtown market are cloudy, though. Once Olympic users have departed, the serious imbalance in the CBD will once again pinch more severely.

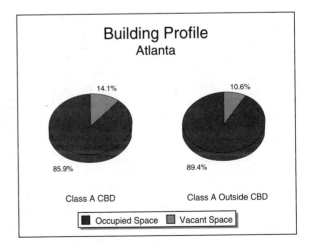

Building Profile
Atlanta

14.1% / 85.9% — Class A CBD
10.6% / 89.4% — Class A Outside CBD

Occupied Space ■ Vacant Space

Source: Reprinted from the 1995 edition of *Comparative Statistics of Industrial and Office Real Estate Markets* with permission of the Society of Industrial and Office REALTORS®.

*See Glossary of Terms on page 666.

Chicago, Illinois: Office

Chicago, Illinois

Market Data

Inventory (sf)	Class A		Class B	
	CBD	Outside CBD	CBD	Outside CBD
Total	43,921,738	24,639,208	47,218,100	31,858,380
Vacant	6,593,124	3,544,001	9,781,171	5,510,874
Vacancy Rate	15.0%	14.4%	20.7%	17.3%
Vacant Sublease	568,793	795,781	1,031,623	375,586
Under Construction	0	0	0	0
Substantial Rehab	0	0	0	0
Net Absorption	3,059,403	276,535	483,030	-376,033
Rental Rates ($/sf)				
Lowest	8.00	13.50	4.50	10.00
Highest	48.03	33.32	34.00	17.50
Weighted Average	26.83	24.50	18.19	18.73
Sales Prices ($/sf)				
Lowest	70.00	n/a	18.00	30.00
Highest	140.00	n/a	60.00	75.00
Weighted Average	n/a	n/a	n/a	n/a
Operating Expenses ($/sf)				
Lowest	4.50	3.75	3.00	2.00
Highest	7.50	7.96	7.40	6.54
Weighted Average	n/a	n/a	n/a	n/a
Tax Expenses ($/sf)				
Lowest	3.78	1.12	2.25	.66
Highest	10.71	7.50	8.20	5.92
Weighted Average	n/a	n/a	n/a	n/a

Utility Rates:	CBD $1.40 per sf	Parking Ratio:	CBD - n/a
	Outside CBD $1.00 per sf		Outside CBD - 1 per 250 sf
	Separately Metered		

Standard Work Letter: $20.00 per sf, typically based on dollars per square foot	Operating Cost Escalation: Base Year and Stop - Net lease with passthru

Rate of Return:	Cap Rate: n/a	Mortgage Money Supply: Moderate
	IRR: n/a	Prime Source of Financing: Insurance Companies, Commercial Banks, Pension Funds

Cumulative Discount Rate: 10-30%
Landlord Concessions
Lease Assumptions, Moving Allowance, Interior Improvements

Leasing Activity Profile
Major Activity - Fortune 500 Firms, Insurance, Business Services, Sales, Finance/Banking, Government, Healthcare
Minor Activity - Legal/Accounting, Engineering/Architecture, Energy

Outlook

Absorption		Down 1-5%
Construction		Up 1-5%
Vacancies		Down 1-5%
Rental Rates		Up 1-5%
Landlord Concessions		Same
Sales	Class A	CBD	Up 6-10%
Prices		Outside CBD	Up 6-10%
	Class B	CBD	Up 1-5%
		Outside CBD	Up 1-5%

1994 Review

Pent-up demand made its effects felt, especially in Chicago's downtown Class "A" offices, during 1994. A broad-based uptick in business activity in the region, plus a perceived tightening in the most desirable locations, prompted large tenants to scramble for space. Top quality CBD offices saw their vacancies plummet from 21.7 percent to 15.0 percent in just a year. Suburban Class "A" vacancy dropped one percentage point over the year. Rents did not adjust upward much, though, and tenants can still find attractive leasing packages in the market including moving allowances and assumption of existing lease obligations.

1995 Forecast

Suburban markets west and north of the city will likely be seeing speculative construction returning during 1995. Large blocks of space, 100,000 sq. ft. and up, are in short supply. Though layoffs continue at major employers like Amoco and Ameritech, office jobs growth in the MSA is projected for the balance of the decade. SIOR's local reporters see effective rents rising in the coming year, and Class "A" office values making an upward move of six to 10 percent. Forecasts of single-digit vacancies in the near future may prove overly optimistic, but the ongoing recovery of the Chicago market is well established.

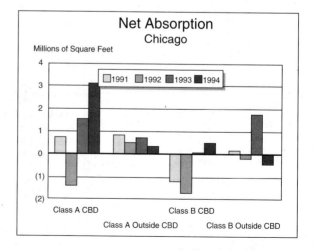

Net Absorption
Chicago
Millions of Square Feet

Legend: 1991 | 1992 | 1993 | 1994

Class A CBD   Class B CBD
Class A Outside CBD   Class B Outside CBD

Houston, Texas: Office

Houston, Texas

Market Data

Inventory (sf)	Class A CBD	Class A Outside CBD	Class B CBD	Class B Outside CBD
Total	25,653,000	36,547,000	6,318,000	43,284,000
Vacant	3,926,000	4,352,000	2,023,000	9,184,000
Vacancy Rate	15.3%	11.9%	32.0%	21.2%
Vacant Sublease	3,000,000	3,000,000	3,000,000	3,000,000
Under Construction	0	0	0	0
Substantial Rehab	0	0	0	0
Net Absorption	244,000	510,000	-200,000	-1,576,000

Rental Rates ($/sf)				
Lowest	12.50	12.00	10.50	9.25
Highest	24.00	23.00	14.00	13.00
Weighted Average	15.97	13.81	11.93	11.65

Sales Prices ($/sf)				
Lowest	60.00	45.00	38.00	27.00
Highest	90.00	65.00	65.00	55.00
Weighted Average	75.00	55.00	51.00	41.00

Operating Expenses ($/sf)				
Lowest	6.50	6.00	6.50	6.25
Highest	8.00	8.00	7.50	7.00
Weighted Average	7.25	7.00	7.00	6.50

Tax Expenses ($/sf)				
Lowest	1.75	1.50	1.75	1.25
Highest	2.50	3.00	2.50	2.00
Weighted Average	2.25	2.35	2.25	1.65

Utility Rates:	CBD $2.00 per sf Outside CBD $1.25 per sf Not Separately Metered	**Parking Ratio:**	CBD - 1 per 1,500 sf Outside CBD - 1 per 300 sf

Standard Work Letter: $15.00 per sf, typically based on dollars per square foot

Operating Cost Escalation: Base Year

Rate of Return: Cap Rate: 10.5% IRR: 15.0%

Mortgage Money Supply: Tight
Prime Source of Financing: Owner Financing

Cumulative Discount Rate: 5-15%
Landlord Concessions
Parking, Moving Allowance, Interior Improvements

Leasing Activity Profile
Major Activity - n/a
Minor Activity - Fortune 500 Firms, Legal/Accounting, Insurance, Business Services, Sales, Finance/Banking, Engineering/Architecture, Government, Energy

Outlook

Absorption	Up 1-5%
Construction	Down 1-5%
Vacancies	Down 1-5%
Rental Rates	Same
Landlord Concessions	Same
Sales	Class A CBD	Up 1-5%
Prices	Outside CBD	Up 1-5%
	Class B CBD	Up 1-5%
	Outside CBD	Up 1-5%

1994 Review

A decade after the collapse of the energy price bubble, Houston's office vacancy remains close to 20 million sq. ft. Twelve million sq. ft. of available sublease space compounds the woes. Approximately 750,000 sq. ft. of net absorption brought Class "A" occupancies up to 86.7 percent in 1994. But the situation for Class "B" properties deteriorated even further. Corporate downsizing remained a factor as oil and gas companies continued their consolidation. Occasionally, though, this means jobs being brought to Houston from elsewhere. Houston did add 35,000 non-agricultural jobs in the past year, but needs more than 100,000 additional office jobs just to set the stage for market equilibrium.

1995 Forecast

An acceleration of office job growth, to an annual rate of 2.5 percent from 1995 through 1998, is forecast to make gradual inroads on Houston's oversupply. SIOR's local respondent sees a modest increase in absorption for 1995, and expects renewed interest in office investments to advance sales prices slightly. A great deal depends upon Houston's potential as a business services center in the NAFTA era. The city is already aggressively pursuing efforts in that respect. Economic diversification is a necessary long-range strategy, but that is easier to articulate than to accomplish.

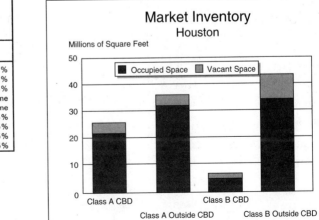

Market Inventory
Houston
Millions of Square Feet

Legend: ■ Occupied Space ■ Vacant Space

Class A CBD
Class A Outside CBD
Class B CBD
Class B Outside CBD

Los Angeles - Central, California: Office

Los Angeles-Central, California

Market Data

| Inventory (sf) | Class A | | Class B | |
	CBD	Outside CBD	CBD	Outside CBD
Total	25,000,000	-	9,000,000	-
Vacant	6,200,000	-	1,900,000	-
Vacancy Rate	24.8%	-	21.1%	-
Vacant Sublease	1,870,000	-	55,000	-
Under Construction	0	-	0	-
Substantial Rehab	-1,743,000	-	-532,000	-
Net Absorption	0	-	0	-
Rental Rates ($/sf)				
Lowest	10.00	15.00	9.00	12.00
Highest	26.00	27.00	14.00	18.00
Weighted Average	18.00	16.00	13.00	15.00
Sales Prices ($/sf)				
Lowest	40.00	35.00	35.00	30.00
Highest	120.00	90.00	70.00	75.00
Weighted Average	105.00	80.00	65.00	60.00
Operating Expenses ($/sf)				
Lowest	10.00	n/a	6.50	6.00
Highest	12.00	n/a	9.00	8.00
Weighted Average	11.00	n/a	8.00	7.50
Tax Expenses ($/sf)				
Lowest	n/a	n/a	n/a	n/a
Highest	n/a	n/a	n/a	n/a
Weighted Average	n/a	n/a	n/a	n/a

Utility Rates: CBD $1.50-2.00 per sf Outside CBD $1.50-2.00 per sf Not Separately Metered	**Parking Ratio:** CBD - 1 per 1,000 sf Outside CBD - 1 per 333 sf
Standard Work Letter: $25.00 per sf, typically based on dollars per square foot	**Operating Cost Escalation:** Base Year
Rate of Return: Cap Rate: 10.0%-11.0% IRR: 12.0%-15.0%	**Mortgage Money Supply:** Tight **Prime Source of Financing:** Owner Financing

Cumulative Discount Rate: 15-25%
Landlord Concessions
Parking, Rental Abatement, Lease Assumptions, Moving Allowance, Interior Improvements

Leasing Activity Profile
Major Activity - Government
Minor Activity - Fortune 500 Firms, Legal/Accounting, Insurance, Business Services, Sales, Finance/Banking

Outlook

Absorption	Up 1-5%
Construction	Up 1-5%
Vacancies	Down 1-5%
Rental Rates	Up 1-5%
Landlord Concessions	Up 11-15%
Sales Class A CBD	Same
Prices Outside CBD	Same
Class B CBD	Same
Outside CBD	Same

1994 Review

The Los Angeles CBD office market was dead in the water in 1994. Vacancy rose to 23.8 percent because of substantial occupancy losses in both Class "A" and Class "B" space. The aggregate losses amounted to an estimated 2.2 million sq. ft. for the year, reflecting L.A.'s still substantial job erosion in the FIRE sector, trade, and major Fortune 500 employers. Rents stagnated below $20 per sq. ft. on average, and discounts of 25 percent from quoted rent levels were available to tenants as inducements to make deals in these troubled times. Both downtown and the mid-Wilshire corridor have been battered in the market contraction.

1995 Forecast

Most observers look for the Southern California economy to turn around in 1995, posting the first gains in net employment since the onset of the area's worst crunch in the post-World War II era. For the office market, the outlook is more sanguinary than sanguine. Lease rates should continue down as the sublet space drives prices, and Class "B" tenants take advantage of upgrade opportunities. Only government-oriented users are expected to show an appetite for expansion. Though buyers are active in the market, price levels are characteristic of bottom-fishers who have moved in from healthier cities.

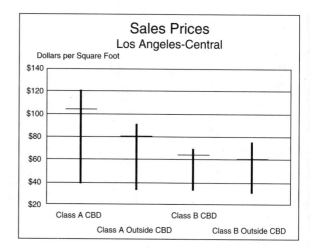

Sales Prices
Los Angeles-Central
Dollars per Square Foot

New Jersey - Central/Northern, New Jersey: Office

Northern 11 Counties - New Jersey

Market Data

	Class A		Class B	
Inventory (sf)	**CBD**	**Outside CBD**	**CBD**	**Outside CBD**
Total	-	85,467,000	-	65,627,000
Vacant	-	10,954,000	-	14,649,000
Vacancy Rate	-	12.8%	-	22.3%
Vacant Sublease	-	794,000	-	940,000
Under Construction	-	500,000	-	0
Substantial Rehab	-	300,000	-	0
Net Absorption	-	783,000	-	683,000

Rental Rates ($/sf)				
Lowest	-	16.50	-	10.00
Highest	-	28.00	-	20.00
Weighted Average	-	20.73	-	16.96

Sales Prices ($/sf)				
Lowest	-	65.00	-	30.00
Highest	-	80.00	-	60.00
Weighted Average	-	70.00	-	45.00

Operating Expenses ($/sf)				
Lowest	-	3.75	-	3.50
Highest	-	6.50	-	5.50
Weighted Average	-	5.00	-	4.70

Tax Expenses ($/sf)				
Lowest	-	1.75	-	1.25
Highest	-	3.50	-	2.50
Weighted Average	-	2.50	-	1.80

Utility Rates:	CBD n/a	**Parking Ratio:**	CBD - n/a
	Outside CBD $1.25 per sf		Outside CBD - 1 per 250 sf
	Not Separately Metered		

Standard Work Letter: $15.00 per sf, typically based on dollars per square foot

Operating Cost Escalation: Base Year

Rate of Return:	Cap Rate: n/a
	IRR: 13.0%

Mortgage Money Supply: Tight
Prime Source of Financing: Insurance Companies, REITs

Cumulative Discount Rate: n/a%
Landlord Concessions
Parking, Rental Abatement, Lease Assumptions, Moving Allowance, Interior Improvements

Leasing Activity Profile
Major Activity - Fortune 500 Firms, Insurance, Finance/Banking
Minor Activity - Legal/Accounting, Business Services, Sales, Engineering/Architecture, Energy

Outlook

Absorption	Up 1-5%
Construction	Up 1-5%
Vacancies	Down 1-5%
Rental Rates	Same
Landlord Concessions	Same
Sales Class A CBD	n/a
Prices Outside CBD	Same
Class B CBD	n/a
Outside CBD	Same

1994 Review

Northern New Jersey, consisting of eleven counties within 75 miles of Times Square, has led the New York metropolitan region's economic rebound in 1994. Leasing activity, however, is still reported sluggish. Net occupancy rose 1.5 million sq. ft., but this is only one percent of the market's vast inventory of space. Corporate downsizing is very much in evidence still. Key indicators like the 17 percent vacancy rate and quoted lease rates of $20 per sq. ft. or less are unmistakeable signs of lingering trouble in commercial offices here.

1995 Forecast

An influx of "tirekickers" appeared in the market late in 1994, possibly a harbinger of an upsurge in leasing for 1995. The highway corridors of I-287 in Middlesex County and I-80 in Bergen County, and the Hudson River waterfront in Jersey City stand to benefit most from the regional employment recovery. Corporate downsizing in telecommunications and pharmaceuticals poses continuing risk that, as markets begin to stabilize, large blocks of owner-users space could be returned to the market. Required IRRs of 13 percent suggest that investors' have factored that risk into their purchase offers.

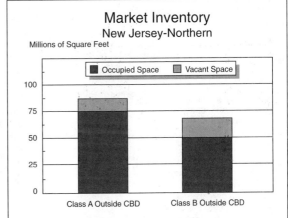

Market Inventory
New Jersey-Northern
Millions of Square Feet

Legend: ■ Occupied Space   ■ Vacant Space

(Bar chart: Class A Outside CBD, Class B Outside CBD)

New York - Brooklyn/Queens, New York: Office

Brooklyn and Queens, New York

Market Data

Inventory (sf)	Class A		Class B	
	CBD	Outside CBD	CBD	Outside CBD
Total	64,821,542	-	-	-
Vacant	8,186,205	-	-	-
Vacancy Rate	12.6%	-	-	-
Vacant Sublease	n/a	-	-	-
Under Construction	n/a	-	-	-
Substantial Rehab	n/a	-	-	-
Net Absorption	-898,385	-	-	-
Rental Rates ($/sf)				
Lowest	n/a	18.00	13.00	11.00
Highest	n/a	25.00	16.00	14.00
Weighted Average	n/a	n/a	n/a	n/a
Sales Prices ($/sf)				
Lowest	n/a	n/a	n/a	n/a
Highest	n/a	n/a	n/a	n/a
Weighted Average	n/a	n/a	n/a	n/a
Operating Expenses ($/sf)				
Lowest	11.00	11.00	10.00	10.00
Highest	13.00	13.00	12.00	12.00
Weighted Average	n/a	n/a	n/a	n/a
Tax Expenses ($/sf)				
Lowest	4.00	4.00	3.50	3.50
Highest	5.00	5.00	4.50	4.50
Weighted Average	n/a	n/a	n/a	n/a

Utility Rates:	CBD $150.00 per sf	Parking Ratio:	CBD - n/a
	Outside CBD $150.00 per sf		Outside CBD - n/a

Standard Work Letter: $27.50 per sf, typically based on dollars per square foot	Operating Cost Escalation: Base Year
Rate of Return: Cap Rate: 9.0%-11.0% IRR: n/a	Mortgage Money Supply: Moderate Prime Source of Financing: Commercial Banks

Cumulative Discount Rate: 20%
Landlord Concessions
Parking, Rental Abatement, Interior Improvements

Leasing Activity Profile
Major Activity - n/a
Minor Activity - Fortune 500 Firms, Legal/Accounting, Insurance, Business Services, Sales, Government

Outlook

Absorption	Down 1-5%
Construction	Same
Vacancies	Up 1-5%
Rental Rates	n/a
Landlord Concessions	Same
Sales Class A CBD	Down 1-5%
Prices Outside CBD	Up 1-5%
Class B CBD	Down 6-10%
Outside CBD	Down 1-5%

1994 Review

At the trough of the New York City business cycle, the "outer boroughs" of Brooklyn and Queens, across the East River from Manhattan, saw any possible space demand sponged up by the attractive rents available in Midtown and Downtown. At this point, tenants are merely playing a checker game. Some backfilling of space is occurring, but the vacancy rate is high and likely to stay that way. The occupancy decline for 1994 amounted to almost 900,000 sq. ft. in these boroughs, the after-effects of the sharp employment losses of the early Nineties.

1995 Forecast

The coming year should see the second consecutive rise in employment for New York City, as a gradual recovery in the economy takes hold. Service sector employment will benefit Manhattan first, though, and the Brooklyn/Queens market will see little if any new demand. These locations depend upon back-office operations of financial firms, law offices oriented primarily to litigation, and government agencies. None are expected to show sharp increases in 1995. Much of the economic development in the boroughs has been supported by good city/state governmental cooperation in the past. The incoming gubernatorial administration has already locked horns with the mayor's office, however, and that does not bode well for office recovery in the boroughs.

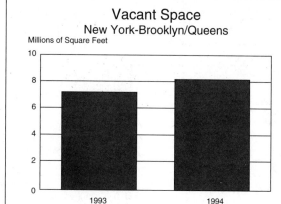

Vacant Space
New York-Brooklyn/Queens
Millions of Square Feet

MANHATTAN, NEW YORK: Office

York

(sf)	Class A		Class B	
	Midtown	Downtown	Midtown	Downtown
	175,800,000	79,600,000	75,600,000	28,700,000
	25,300,000	14,300,000	13,000,000	7,600,000
y Rate	14.4%	18.0%	17.2%	26.5%
Sublease	4,713,000	1,255,000	477,000	464,000
Construction	110,000	1,741,000	0	0
tantial Rehab	0	0	0	0
Absorption	-1,420,000	-283,000	364,000	-440,000

ntal Rates ($/sf)

Lowest	11.50	11.00	8.00	7.50
Highest	68.00	45.00	40.00	30.00
Weighted Average	33.60	30.10	19.60	19.10

Sales Prices ($/sf)

Lowest	16.80	18.10	36.00	5.80
Highest	264.90	18.10	216.70	77.30
Weighted Average	68.15	18.10	62.40	42.50

Operating Expenses ($/sf)

Lowest	7.00	7.00	5.00	5.00
Highest	12.00	12.00	10.00	10.00
Weighted Average	8.50	8.50	8.50	8.50

Tax Expenses ($/sf)

Lowest	8.50	7.00	5.00	3.50
Highest	12.00	10.00	9.00	5.00
Weighted Average	9.00	8.50	7.50	4.00

Utility Rates:	CBD $2.00 per sf Outside CBD $n/a per sf Separately Metered	**Parking Ratio:**	CBD - n/a Outside CBD - n/a
Standard Work Letter: $45.00 per sf, typically based on dollars per square foot		**Operating Cost Escalation:** Base Year	
Rate of Return:	Cap Rate: n/a IRR: n/a	**Mortgage Money Supply:** Tight **Prime Source of Financing:** Commercial Banks, Pension Funds	

Cumulative Discount Rate: 20-25%
Landlord Concessions
Rental Abatement, Moving Allowance, Interior Improvements

Leasing Activity Profile
Major Activity - Fortune 500 Firms, Legal/Accounting, Insurance, Business Services, Sales, Finance/Banking, Engineering/Architecture
Minor Activity - Government

Outlook

Absorption		Up 1-5%
Construction		Up 1-5%
Vacancies		Up 1-5%
Rental Rates		Up 1-5%
Landlord Concessions		Down 1-5%
Sales	Class A CBD	Up 6-10%
Prices	Outside CBD	Up 6-10%
	Class B CBD	Up 6-10%
	Outside CBD	Up 6-10%

1994 REVIEW

The nation's largest office market was stirring in 1994, but divergent trends were seen in its two principal districts. Midtown saw net absorption of 4.5 million sq. ft., and a modest rise in Class "A" asking rents. Sales prices in Midtown also revealed returning confidence, with the first transactions at $200 per sq. ft. or higher since the market crash of the late Eighties. Wall Street, however, suffered another year of contraction in its employment base and reduced profitability at the investment houses. Virtually no change in occupancy was registered, with rents weak and concession packages ample.

1995 FORECAST

Slow improvement in supply/demand fundamentals is forecast for 1995 and succeeding years. An office employment growth rate for Manhattan of about one percent per year is most probable for the late Nineties. Rental rates are likely to improve once again in Midtown and, given the proximity of these markets, Downtown will begin to stir in another 18 to 24 months. Investors are already positioning themselves for a market recovery, and SIOR's reporter not unreasonably expects prices to rise by as much as 10 percent this year. Some pain lingers in this market, but New York's stature as a world city should serve it well in the years ahead.

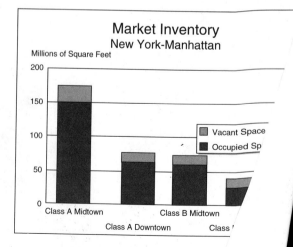

Market Inventory
New York-Manhattan
Millions of Square Feet

SAN FRANCISCO, CALIFORNIA: Office

San Francisco, California

MARKET DATA

Inventory (sf)	Class A		Class B	
	CBD	Outside CBD	CBD	Outside CBD
Total	32,635,000	5,587,000	15,887,000	12,678,000
Vacant	2,775,000	389,000	2,174,000	1,312,000
Vacancy Rate	8.5%	7.0%	13.7%	10.3%
Vacant Sublease	721,000	79,000	132,000	57,000
Under Construction	0	0	0	0
Substantial Rehab	0	0	0	0
Net Absorption	595,000	175,000	180,000	-412,000
Rental Rates ($/sf)				
Lowest	16.00	12.00	11.00	12.00
Highest	46.00	26.00	25.00	24.00
Weighted Average	22.00	17.00	16.00	15.00
Sales Prices ($/sf)				
Lowest	78.00	136.00	55.00	143.00
Highest	78.00	148.00	94.00	143.00
Weighted Average	78.00	142.00	76.00	143.00
Operating Expenses ($/sf)				
Lowest	8.50	8.00	8.00	6.50
Highest	13.00	11.00	10.00	8.00
Weighted Average	10.00	9.00	9.25	8.25
Tax Expenses ($/sf)				
Lowest	1.20	1.10	.75	.50
Highest	3.00	2.00	2.20	1.40
Weighted Average	1.80	1.50	1.60	1.10

Utility Rates:	CBD $1.65 per sf	**Parking Ratio:**	CBD - 1 per 3,500 sf
	Outside CBD $1.65 per sf		Outside CBD - 1 per 1,000 sf
	Not Separately Metered		
Standard Work Letter: $35.00 per sf, typically based on dollars per square foot		**Operating Cost Escalation:** Base Year	
Rate of Return: Cap Rate: 9.5%-10.0%		**Mortgage Money Supply:** Tight	
IRR: n/a		**Prime Source of Financing:** Syndication	

Cumulative Discount Rate: n/a%
Landlord Concessions
Rental Abatement, Moving Allowance, Interior Improvements

Leasing Activity Profile
Major Activity - Business Services, Finance/Banking, Government, Non-profit Groups
Minor Activity - Fortune 500 Firms, Legal/Accounting, Sales, Engineering/Architecture

Outlook

Absorption	Up 1-5%
Construction	Same
Vacancies	Down 6-10%
Rental Rates	Up 1-5%
Landlord Concessions	Down 6-10%
Sales Class A CBD	Up 6-10%
Prices Outside CBD	Up 6-10%
Class B CBD	Up 1-5%
Outside CBD	Up 1-5%

(m...
only ...
lateral m...
Francisco o...
below the 10 ...
"A" space tighte...
available. Require...
programs encouraged ...
Rental rates varied little ...
the prime user sectors (FIR...
and government) showed virt...
employment change. Asian inves...
from Hong Kong, Taiwan, Singapo...
and South Korea, were the heaviest investors in office buildings locally during
1994.

1995 FORECAST

Bay Area employment recovery is projected to follow only a shallow upward slope in 1995 and 1996, indicating only a slim reduction in San Francisco's vacancy rate. Suburban markets to the north of the Golden Gate and on the east side of the Bay compete for tenants, and the city suffers from business migratory trends presently favoring the Pacific Northwest and Intermountain states. Nevertheless, San Francisco is one of America's true business gateway cities and will benefit as Asian business activity grows again. Major urban development projects are revitalizing the city, and the market shows promise for the later Nineties.

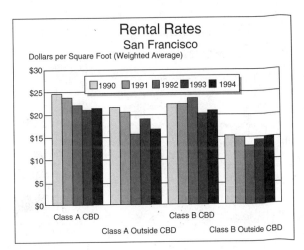

Rental Rates
San Francisco
Dollars per Square Foot (Weighted Average)

Legend: 1990, 1991, 1992, 1993, 1994

Categories: Class A CBD, Class A Outside CBD, Class B CBD, Class B Outside CBD

Tucson, Arizona: Office

Tucson, Arizona

Market Data

Inventory (sf)	Class A		Class B	
	CBD	Outside CBD	CBD	Outside CBD
Total	490,423	2,312,548	941,800	2,477,833
Vacant	85,781	284,068	225,949	316,272
Vacancy Rate	17.5%	12.3%	24.0%	12.8%
Vacant Sublease	5,000	25,000	2,500	20,000
Under Construction	0	0	0	0
Substantial Rehab	0	0	0	40,000
Net Absorption	19,332	4,315	-10,761	125,430

Rental Rates ($/sf)				
Lowest	17.85	14.00	12.50	12.00
Highest	20.50	20.50	15.00	15.00
Weighted Average	18.75	16.25	13.75	14.00

Sales Prices ($/sf)				
Lowest	n/a	41.00	n/a	40.00
Highest	n/a	68.00	n/a	60.00
Weighted Average	n/a	57.00	n/a	49.00

Operating Expenses ($/sf)				
Lowest	6.85	6.30	5.75	5.40
Highest	7.30	7.10	6.30	6.45
Weighted Average	7.00	6.55	5.95	5.75

Tax Expenses ($/sf)				
Lowest	2.25	1.20	1.25	.95
Highest	2.85	2.30	1.80	1.75
Weighted Average	2.35	1.70	1.55	1.45

Utility Rates: CBD $1.50-1.75 per sf
Outside CBD $1.50-1.75 per sf
Not Separately Metered

Parking Ratio: CBD - 1 per 250 sf
Outside CBD - 1 per 200 sf

Standard Work Letter: $18.00 per sf, typically based on dollars per square foot

Operating Cost Escalation: Base Year

Rate of Return: Cap Rate: 10.0%-10.5%
IRR: 12.0%-15.0%

Mortgage Money Supply: Ample
Prime Source of Financing: Insurance Companies, Owner Financing, Commercial Banks, SBA Funding

Cumulative Discount Rate: 5%
Landlord Concessions
Parking, Interior Improvements

Leasing Activity Profile
Major Activity - Legal/Accounting, Insurance, Business Services, Sales, Engineering/Architecture
Minor Activity - Fortune 500 Firms, Finance/Banking, Government, Energy

Outlook

Absorption	Up 6-10%
Construction	Up 1-5%
Vacancies	Down 11-15%
Rental Rates	Up 11-15%
Landlord Concessions	Same
Sales Class A CBD	Same
Prices Outside CBD	Up 11-15%
Class B CBD	Same
Outside CBD	Up 11-15%

1994 Review

Tucson enjoyed another year of substantial improvement in its office market. Its vacancy rate dropped from 17 percent in 1993 to 14.7 percent at the time of this survey. The tightening market means that tenants needing 10,000 sq. ft. units have only 14 options in the MSA, eight of which are downtown. Rental rates have begun to move upward, but at less than $1.00 per sq. ft. in the past year. Tucson gained 13,300 jobs in 1994 (5.0 percent), and the economy is clearly in high gear. Businesses are migrating to the area. Most office acquisitions have been by owner-users who can readily justify the prices of suburban properties, which are still under $70 per sq. ft.

1995 Forecast

Build-to-suit opportunities will be commonplace in 1995, owing to the lack of large space blocks. Sales prices and lease rates are expected to continue to rise through 1996, accelerating as the market tightens. User-driven construction will include 20 to 35 percent expansion space, which will be available short-term to the general market. Confidence in the market's ability to grow in the near future is expressed in cap rates of approximately 10 percent, but an appreciation of Tucson's volatility can be seen in the 12 to 15 percent discount rates applied to forecasted income streams in IRR analysis.

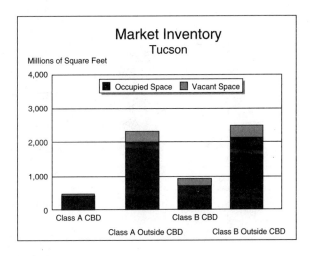

Market Inventory
Tucson

Millions of Square Feet

Legend: Occupied Space / Vacant Space

X-axis categories: Class A CBD, Class B CBD, Class A Outside CBD, Class B Outside CBD

INDUSTRIAL REAL ESTATE MARKET: Selected Cities*

Atlanta, Georgia: Industrial

Atlanta, Georgia

Market Data

Inventory (sf)	Central City	Suburban
Total	27,140,000	266,770,000
Vacant	4,650,000	32,310,000
Vacancy Rates	17.1%	12.1%
Under Construction	0	7,500,000
Net Absorption	1,110,000	12,830,000

Site Prices ($/sf)	Central City	Suburban
Improved Sites		
Less than 2 acres	n/a	2.00-3.50
2 to 5 acres	1.50 2.50	2.00-3.50
5 to 10 acres	n/a	1.75-3.00
Over 10 acres	n/a	1.75-3.00
Unimproved Sites		
Less than 10 acres	n/a	1.00-3.00
10 to 100 acres	.50-1.25	1.00-2.50
Over 100 acres	n/a	.50-1.50

Prime Source of Financing: REITs, Pension Funds

Mortgage Money Supply: Ample

Current Trends

Composition of Absorption
Warehouse/Distr.	85.0%
Manufacturing	10.0%
High Tech/R&D	5.0%

Composition of Inventory
Warehouse/Distr.	85.0%
Manufacturing	10.0%
High Tech/R&D	5.0%

Rate of Construction
Warehouse/Distr.	Up 11-15%
Manufacturing	Up 6-10%
High Tech/R&D	Up 6-10%

Dollar Volume - Sales
Warehouse/Distr.	Up 11-15%
Manufacturing	Up 6-10%
High Tech/R&D	Up 6-10%

Dollar Volume - Leases
Warehouse/Distr.	Up 11-15%
Manufacturing	Up 6-10%
High Tech/R&D	Up 6-10%

Outlook

Sales Prices
Warehouse/Distr.	Up 11-15%
Manufacturing	Up 6-10%
High Tech/R&D	Up 6-10%

Lease Prices
Warehouse/Distr.	Up 11-15%
Manufacturing	Up 6-10%
High Tech/R&D	Up 6-10%

Site Prices Up 6-10%

Absorption
Warehouse/Distr.	Up 20%
Manufacturing	Up 6-10%
High Tech/R&D	Up 6-10%

Construction
Warehouse/Distr.	Up 6-10%
Manufacturing	Up 6-10%
High Tech/R&D	Up 6-10%

Dollar Volume - Sales Up 11-15%

Dollar Volume - Leases Up 6-10%

	Sales Prices ($/sf)		Gross Lease Prices ($/sf)		Construction	Vacancy
	Central City	Suburban	Central City	Suburban	($/sf)	Indicators
Less than 5,000 sf	27.00-32.00	40.00-50.00	3.25-4.25	3.75-5.50	45.00-55.00	Substantial Shortage
5,000 to 19,999 sf	22.00-27.00	35.00-40.00	2.75-4.00	3.25-5.00	30.00-40.00	Substantial Shortage
20,000 to 39,999 sf	18.00-22.00	23.00-30.00	2.50-3.50	2.00-4.25	25.00-30.00	Moderate Shortage
40,000 to 59,999 sf	17.00-20.00	20.00-22.00	2.25-2.75	2.75-4.00	20.00-25.00	Moderate Shortage
60,000 to 99,999 sf	15.00-18.00	18.00-20.00	2.00-2.50	2.50-3.50	18.00-20.00	Substantial Shortage
More than 99,999 sf	14.00-18.00	16.00-19.00	2.00-2.25	2.00-3.25	17.00-18.00	Substantial Shortage
High Tech/R&D	45.00-65.00	50.00-75.00	6.50-7.50	6.00-9.00	35.00-60.00	Balanced Market

	Warehouse & Factories		Research & Developent	
	Central City	Suburban	Central City	Suburban
Real Estate Taxes	.45	.28	.70	.40
Insurance (Fire & Liability)	.07	.07	.10	.10
Structural & Roof Maintenance	n/a	n/a	n/a	n/a
Common Area Maintenance	.05	.25	.50	.50

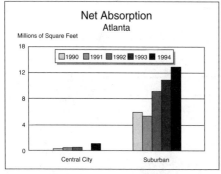

Net Absorption
Atlanta
Millions of Square Feet
□ 1990 ▨ 1991 ▨ 1992 ▨ 1993 ■ 1994
Central City   Suburban

1994 Review

Demand for industrial space in Atlanta surged again in 1994, reaching an estimated 14 million sq. ft. Atlanta's economy created more than 200,000 new jobs since 1991, generating demand for a variety of commercial properties. Vacancy, at an average of 12.6 percent, is still relatively high by national standards, but the market's ability to soak up excess space has been clearly demonstrated. REITs were active purchasers of Atlanta industrial property in 1994, and with the added competition for quality properties, cap rates declined.

1995 Forecast

Speculative development in the Atlanta industrial market is among the strongest in the nation. SIOR's correspondent reported that at the end of 1994, there were 16 new properties under construction and 17 more set to break ground. Most of these buildings were significantly preleased: usually 40 percent of the square footage was committed. New development will continue to be concentrated in the quadrants north and west of downtown.

Source: Reprinted from the 1995 edition of *Comparative Statistics of Industrial and Office Real Estate Markets* with permission of the Society of Industrial and Office REALTORS®.

*See Glossary of Terms on page 666.

Chicago, Illinois: Industrial

Chicago, Illinois

Market Data

Inventory (sf)

	Central City	Suburban
Total	180,000,000	555,000,000
Vacant	18,500,000	51,000,000
Vacancy Rates	10.3%	9.2%
Under Construction	200,000	5,500,000
Net Absorption	-2,815,000	7,415,000

Site Prices ($/sf)

	Central City	Suburban
Improved Sites		
Less than 2 acres	1.50-6.00	3.00-5.00
2 to 5 acres	2.00-6.00	3.00-4.50
5 to 10 acres	2.00-4.00	2.25-4.00
Over 10 acres	1.50-4.00	2.00-3.25
Unimproved Sites		
Less than 10 acres	n/a	n/a
10 to 100 acres	n/a	1.00-1.50
Over 100 acres	n/a	.50-1.00

Prime Source of Financing: Insurance Companies, Commercial Banks, Pension Funds

Mortgage Money Supply: Ample

Current Trends

Composition of Absorption
Warehouse/Distr.	75.0%
Manufacturing	23.0%
High Tech/R&D	2.0%

Composition of Inventory
Warehouse/Distr.	62.0%
Manufacturing	31.0%
High Tech/R&D	7.0%

Rate of Construction
Warehouse/Distr.	Same
Manufacturing	Up 1-5%
High Tech/R&D	Same

Dollar Volume - Sales
Warehouse/Distr.	Up 6-10%
Manufacturing	Up 6-10%
High Tech/R&D	Same

Dollar Volume - Leases
Warehouse/Distr.	Up 1-5%
Manufacturing	Up 1-5%
High Tech/R&D	Same

Outlook

Sales Prices
Warehouse/Distr.	Up 6-10%
Manufacturing	Up 1-5%
High Tech/R&D	Same

Lease Prices
Warehouse/Distr.	Up 6-10%
Manufacturing	Up 6-10%
High Tech/R&D	Same

Site Prices Up 11-15%

Absorption
Warehouse/Distr.	Up 6-10%
Manufacturing	Up 1-5%
High Tech/R&D	Up 6-10%

Construction
Warehouse/Distr.	Up 6-10%
Manufacturing	Up 6-10%
High Tech/R&D	Up 6-10%

Dollar Volume - Sales Up 1-5%

Dollar Volume - Leases Up 6-10%

	Sales Prices ($/sf)		Net Lease Prices ($/sf)		Construction	Vacancy
	Central City	Suburban	Central City	Suburban	($/sf)	Indicators
Less than 5,000 sf	34.00	55.00	4.00	5.00	n/a	Balanced Market
5,000 to 19,999 sf	27.00	42.00	3.50	4.00	42.00-46.00	Balanced Market
20,000 to 39,999 sf	25.00	36.00	3.00	3.60	34.00-38.00	Balanced Market
40,000 to 59,999 sf	20.00	32.50	3.00	3.50	29.00-32.00	Moderate Shortage
60,000 to 99,999 sf	15.00	30.00	2.60	3.25	25.00-27.50	Moderate Shortage
More than 99,999 sf	13.00	28.00	2.25	3.30	21.00-24.50	Substantial Shortage
High Tech/R&D	n/a	35.00-45.00	5.00-8.00	4.50-8.00	65.00-70.00	Moderate Oversupply

	Warehouse & Factories		Research & Development	
	Central City	Suburban	Central City	Suburban
Real Estate Taxes	1.35	.80-1.75	2.50	2.00-4.00
Insurance (Fire & Liability)	.08	.08	.10	.10
Structural & Roof Maintenance	.15	.15	.15	.15
Common Area Maintenance	.35	.35	.50	.50

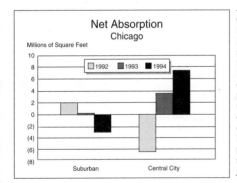

Net Absorption
Chicago
Millions of Square Feet

Legend: 1992, 1993, 1994

Categories: Suburban, Central City

1994 Review

Chicago is one of the nation's leading industrial centers with more than 500,000 jobs in the manufacturing sector and a massive 735 million sq. ft. inventory. Major manufacturing industries include electrical and non-electrical machinery, printing and publishing, chemicals and food products. Just over 60 percent of Chicago's industrial market is comprised of warehouse/distribution space. Manufacturing makes up about 30 percent of the inventory while the small high-tech sector accounts for just seven percent. Net absorption in 1994 totaled 4.6 million sq. ft., up about 10 percent from 1993. During 1994, 2.5 million sq. ft. of speculative construction was completed, mostly in northeast DuPage County, northeast Will County, Lake County and southern Wisconsin.

1995 Forecast

Chicago should experience another year of improving demand in 1995. Net absorption in most property types is expected to rise steadily, allowing for equally strong sale and lease increases. Over the long-term, Chicago's industrial market will continue to shift from manufacturing to warehouse/distribution and high-tech facilities, and from the close-in locations to the further suburbs. The entrance of more capital as result of REIT activity is a big bright spot for the market. As financing from traditional sources returns, new development will gain momentum.

Houston, Texas: Industrial

Houston, Texas

Market Data

Inventory (sf)	Central City	Suburban
Total	70,000,000	200,000,000
Vacant	15,000,000	16,000,000
Vacancy Rates	21.4%	8.0%
Under Construction	0	2,000,000
Net Absorption	1,000,000	2,000,000

Site Prices ($/sf)	Central City	Suburban
Improved Sites		
Less than 2 acres	1.50-6.00	.70-5.00
2 to 5 acres	1.50-6.00	.70-5.00
5 to 10 acres	1.25-5.00	.70-4.00
Over 10 acres	1.00-5.00	.50-4.00
Unimproved Sites		
Less than 10 acres	1.50-5.00	.25-2.50
10 to 100 acres	.75-3.00	.20-2.00
Over 100 acres	n/a	.10-1.00

Prime Source of Financing: Insurance Companies, Commercial Banks, Owner Financing

Mortgage Money Supply: Tight

Current Trends

Composition of Absorption
Warehouse/Distr.	50.0%
Manufacturing	48.0%
High Tech/R&D	2.0%

Composition of Inventory
Warehouse/Distr.	50.0%
Manufacturing	37.0%
High Tech/R&D	13.0%

Rate of Construction
Warehouse/Distr.	Up 1-5%
Manufacturing	Same
High Tech/R&D	Same

Dollar Volume - Sales
Warehouse/Distr.	Up 6-10%
Manufacturing	Up 6-10%
High Tech/R&D	Same

Dollar Volume - Leases
Warehouse/Distr.	Up 1-5%
Manufacturing	Up 1-5%
High Tech/R&D	Same

Outlook

Sales Prices
Warehouse/Distr.	Up 1-5%
Manufacturing	Same
High Tech/R&D	Up 1-5%

Lease Prices
Warehouse/Distr.	Up 1-5%
Manufacturing	Up 1-5%
High Tech/R&D	Up 1-5%

Site Prices n/a

Absorption
Warehouse/Distr.	Up 11-15%
Manufacturing	Up 11-15%
High Tech/R&D	Up 1-5%

Construction
Warehouse/Distr.	Up 11-15%
Manufacturing	Same
High Tech/R&D	Same

Dollar Volume - Sales Up 11-15%

Dollar Volume - Leases Up 11-15%

	Sales Prices ($/sf)		Lease Prices ($/sf)		Construction	Vacancy
	Central City	Suburban	Central City	Suburban	($/sf)	Indicators
Less than 5,000 sf	20.00-40.00	15.00-45.00	2.50-4.00	2.50-4.00	25.00-45.00	Balanced Market
5,000 to 19,999 sf	20.00-35.00	15.00-35.00	2.00-4.00	2.20-4.00	20.00-40.00	Balanced Market
20,000 to 39,999 sf	18.00-30.00	15.00-35.00	2.00-3.55	2.00-3.50	20.00-35.00	Balanced Market
40,000 to 59,999 sf	15.00-30.00	15.00-30.00	2.00-3.85	2.00-3.25	18.00-30.00	Moderate Shortage
60,000 to 99,999 sf	12.00-25.00	12.00-25.00	1.80-3.00	1.80-3.00	17.00-28.00	Substantial Shortage
More than 99,999 sf	12.00-20.00	12.00-25.00	1.80-2.80	1.80-2.80	15.00-25.00	Substantial Shortage
High Tech/R&D	15.00-50.00	15.00-50.00	3.50-8.00	3.50-8.00	25.00-50.00	Balanced Market

	Warehouse & Factories		Research & Development	
	Central City	Suburban	Central City	Suburban
Real Estate Taxes	.45-.60	.45-.65	.45-.60	.45-.65
Insurance (Fire & Liability)	.09-.15	.09-.15	.10-.18	.10-.18
Structural & Roof Maintenance	.06-.12	.06-.12	.06-.12	.06-.12
Common Area Maintenance	.12-.35	.12-.35	.15-.40	.25-.40

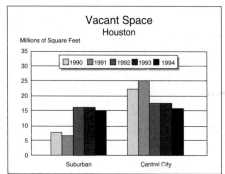

Vacant Space
Houston
Millions of Square Feet
□1990 ■1991 ■1992 ■1993 ■1994
Suburban   Central City

1994 Review

Occupancy increased in Houston's massive 270 million sq. ft. market during 1994. Job growth was brisk last year, though not equally distributed throughout all industries. The energy-dominated manufacturing and mining sectors reported declines, but trade, transportation, and especially services enjoyed robust increases. These gains stimulated demand for industrial space, allowing net absorption to reach three million sq. ft. Sales activity was particularly brisk in 1994: the dollar volume was reportedly up by a range of six to 10 percent.

1995 Forecast

NAFTA's positive effects should materialize in Houston in 1995. Transportation, manufacturing, and services are all expected to benefit from the loosening of trade restrictions with Mexico. As job growth advances, net absorption of warehouse/distribution and manufacturing space is projected to rise. SIOR's reporters expect a 10-to-15 percent increase in demand for industrial space in the coming year. Speculative development will be limited to a few projects north and northwest of downtown.

Los Angeles - Central, California: Industrial

Los Angeles Central and Suburban, California

Market Data

Inventory (sf)	Central City	Suburban
Total	322,000,000	-
Vacant	34,770,000	-
Vacancy Rates	10.8%	-
Under Construction	3,000,000	-
Net Absorption	-638,000	-

Site Prices ($/sf)	Central City	Suburban
Improved Sites		
Less than 2 acres	9.00-30.00	-
2 to 5 acres	9.00-20.00	-
5 to 10 acres	7.00-15.00	-
Over 10 acres	6.00-13.00	-
Unimproved Sites		
Less than 10 acres	n/a	-
10 to 100 acres	n/a	-
Over 100 acres	n/a	-

Prime Source of Financing: Commercial Banks

Mortgage Money Supply: Ample

Current Trends

Composition of Absorption	
Warehouse/Distr.	75.0%
Manufacturing	20.0%
High Tech/R&D	5.0%
Composition of Inventory	
Warehouse/Distr.	75.0%
Manufacturing	20.0%
High Tech/R&D	5.0%
Rate of Construction	
Warehouse/Distr.	Same
Manufacturing	Same
High Tech/R&D	Same
Dollar Volume - Sales	
Warehouse/Distr.	Up 25%
Manufacturing	Up 25%
High Tech/R&D	Up 25%
Dollar Volume - Leases	
Warehouse/Distr.	Up 12%
Manufacturing	Up 12%
High Tech/R&D	Up 12%

Outlook

Sales Prices	
Warehouse/Distr.	Down 6-10%
Manufacturing	Down 6-10%
High Tech/R&D	Down 6-10%
Lease Prices	
Warehouse/Distr.	Up 6-10%
Manufacturing	Up 6-10%
High Tech/R&D	Up 6-10%
Site Prices	Down 6-10%
Absorption	
Warehouse/Distr.	Up 6-10%
Manufacturing	Up 6-10%
High Tech/R&D	Up 6-10%
Construction	
Warehouse/Distr.	Up 1-5%
Manufacturing	Up 1-5%
High Tech/R&D	Up 1-5%
Dollar Volume - Sales	Up 11-15%
Dollar Volume - Leases	Up 1-5%

	Sales Prices ($/sf)		Net Lease Prices ($/sf)		Construction	Vacancy
	Central City	Suburban	Central City	Suburban	($/sf)	Indicators
Less than 5,000 sf	n/a	-	5.00-7.00	-	40.00	Substantial Oversupply
5,000 to 19,999 sf	50.00-70.00	-	4.50-6.00	-	27.00	Substantial Oversupply
20,000 to 39,999 sf	40.00-60.00	-	3.50-5.00	-	25.00	Substantial Oversupply
40,000 to 59,999 sf	35.00-50.00	-	3.00-4.50	-	19.00	Moderate Oversupply
60,000 to 99,999 sf	30.00-45.00	-	3.00-4.00	-	18.00	Balanced Market
More than 99,999 sf	25.00-35.00	-	2.50-4.00	-	14.00	Moderate Shortage
High Tech/R&D	60.00-80.00	-	-	-	45.00	n/a

	Warehouse & Factories		Research & Developent	
	Central City	Suburban	Central City	Suburban
Real Estate Taxes	.45	-	n/a	-
Insurance (Fire & Liability)	.06	-	n/a	-
Structural & Roof Maintenance	.06	-	n/a	-
Common Area Maintenance	.03	-	n/a	-

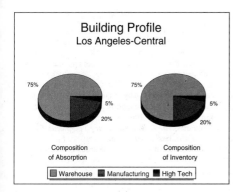

Building Profile
Los Angeles-Central

Composition of Absorption: 75% / 20% / 5%
Composition of Inventory: 75% / 20% / 5%

Legend: ■ Warehouse ■ Manufacturing ■ High Tech

1994 Review

Toward the end of 1994 Los Angeles' battered economy showed some signs of life. After losing 35,000 jobs during the first seven months of the year, the county's employment base finally stabilized. The residual effects of national GDP growth and the return of some foreign investment, particularly from China, helped to stem the tide of employment losses. In addition, the number of companies announcing relocation also diminished. Job growth was too weak in 1994 to generate demand for industrial space: net absorption for the year was negative.

1995 Forecast

Rising employment in trade, business services, and the entertainment industries will just barely outstrip the declines in manufacturing in 1995. Since 75 percent of Central Los Angeles' industrial inventory is comprised of warehouse/distribution properties, the production job losses will not be fatal to the market. Improving net absorption in 1995 should firm lease rates but sales prices will continue to fall. About three million sq. ft. of space was under construction at the end of 1994, although none of it was speculative.

New Jersey - Central, New Jersey: Industrial

Central New Jersey (Mercer, Middlesex, Monmouth and Somerset Counties)

Market Data

Inventory (sf)	Central City	Suburban
Total	-	n/a
Vacant	-	21,350,000
Vacancy Rates	-	n/a
Under Construction	-	2,000,000
Net Absorption	-	5,450,000

Site Prices ($/sf)	Central City	Suburban
Improved Sites		
Less than 2 acres	-	6.50
2 to 5 acres	-	6.00
5 to 10 acres	-	5.50
Over 10 acres	-	5.00
Unimproved Sites		
Less than 10 acres	-	n/a
10 to 100 acres	-	n/a
Over 100 acres	-	n/a

Prime Source of Financing: Insurance Companies, Commercial Banks

Mortgage Money Supply: Moderate

Current Trends

Composition of Absorption	
Warehouse/Distr.	n/a
Manufacturing	n/a
High Tech/R&D	n/a

Composition of Inventory	
Warehouse/Distr.	n/a
Manufacturing	n/a
High Tech/R&D	n/a

Rate of Construction	
Warehouse/Distr.	Up 11-15%
Manufacturing	Same
High Tech/R&D	Down 6-10%

Dollar Volume - Sales	
Warehouse/Distr.	Up 11-15%
Manufacturing	Same
High Tech/R&D	Down 6-10%

Dollar Volume - Leases	
Warehouse/Distr.	Up 11-15%
Manufacturing	Same
High Tech/R&D	Down 6-10%

Outlook

Sales Prices	
Warehouse/Distr.	Up 11-15%
Manufacturing	Same
High Tech/R&D	Same

Lease Prices	
Warehouse/Distr.	Up 11-15%
Manufacturing	Same
High Tech/R&D	Same

Site Prices	Same

Absorption	
Warehouse/Distr.	Up 11-15%
Manufacturing	Up 6-10%
High Tech/R&D	Down 6-10%

Construction	
Warehouse/Distr.	Up 11-15%
Manufacturing	Same
High Tech/R&D	Same

Dollar Volume - Sales	Up 11-15%
Dollar Volume - Leases	Up 11-15%

	Sales Prices ($/sf)		Lease Prices ($/sf)		Construction	Vacancy
	Central City	Suburban	Central City	Suburban	($/sf)	Indicators
Less than 5,000 sf	-	45.00	3.50	6.00	55.00	n/a
5,000 to 19,999 sf	-	40.00	3.00	5.25	50.00	n/a
20,000 to 39,999 sf	-	40.00	3.00	5.00	40.00	n/a
40,000 to 59,999 sf	-	40.00	2.50	4.25	36.00	n/a
60,000 to 99,999 sf	-	32.00	2.50	4.25	33.00	n/a
More than 99,999 sf	-	35.00	2.50	4.00	33.00	n/a
High Tech/R&D	-	60.00	7.50	7.00	75.00	Balanced Market

	Warehouse & Factories		Research & Development	
	Central City	Suburban	Central City	Suburban
Real Estate Taxes	1.00	.45-.75	1.50	1.00
Insurance (Fire & Liability)	.08-.12	.08-.12	.10-.15	.10-.15
Structural & Roof Maintenance	.10-.20	.10-.20	.10-.20	.10-.20
Common Area Maintenance	.25	.25	.25	.25

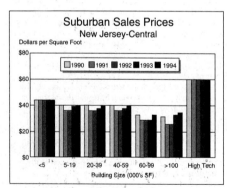

Suburban Sales Prices
New Jersey-Central

Dollars per Square Foot

Legend: 1990 1991 1992 1993 1994

Building Size (000's SF): <5, 5-19, 20-39, 40-59, 60-99, >100, High Tech

1994 Review

Large distribution centers were in strong demand in the Central New Jersey office market in 1994. The dollar volume of both sales and lease transactions for this property type advanced by a range of 11 to 15 percent and kicked off a round of build-to-suit activity. This was the first year in many to see significant new construction. Net absorption totaled 5.5 million sq. ft. for the year, less than 1993's seven million sq. ft. but enough to lower the supply of vacant space.

1995 Forecast

Wariness among Central New Jersey's largest manufacturers in the pharmaceutical industry will limit net absorption of light industrial space in 1995. In contrast, demand for distribution facilities should be up by as much 15 percent. New development is underway in South Brunswick and the Exit 8A area of the New Jersey Turnpike: SIOR's correspondent reports two million sq. ft. under construction at the end of 1994 and more planned for 1995.

New Jersey - Northern, New Jersey: Industrial

Northern New Jersey (Bergen, Essex, Hudson, Passaic, Sussex, Union, and Warren Counties)

Market Data

Inventory (sf)	Central City	Suburban
Total	n/a	n/a
Vacant	n/a	43,000,000
Vacancy Rates	n/a	n/a
Under Construction	n/a	250,000
Net Absorption	n/a	16,900,000

Site Prices ($/sf)	Central City	Suburban
Improved Sites		
Less than 2 acres	7.00	7.00
2 to 5 acres	6.00	6.50
5 to 10 acres	5.00	6.50
Over 10 acres	n/a	6.00
Unimproved Sites		
Less than 10 acres	n/a	n/a
10 to 100 acres	n/a	n/a
Over 100 acres	n/a	n/a

Prime Source of Financing: Insurance Companies, Commercial Banks

Mortgage Money Supply: Moderate

Current Trends

Composition of Absorption
Warehouse/Distr.	80.0%
Manufacturing	10.0%
High Tech/R&D	10.0%

Composition of Inventory
Warehouse/Distr.	n/a
Manufacturing	n/a
High Tech/R&D	n/a

Rate of Construction
Warehouse/Distr.	Up 6-10%
Manufacturing	Same
High Tech/R&D	Down 6-10%

Dollar Volume - Sales
Warehouse/Distr.	Up 6-10%
Manufacturing	Same
High Tech/R&D	Down 6-10%

Dollar Volume - Leases
Warehouse/Distr.	Up 6-10%
Manufacturing	Same
High Tech/R&D	Down 6-10%

Outlook

Sales Prices
Warehouse/Distr.	Up 6-10%
Manufacturing	Same
High Tech/R&D	Same

Lease Prices
Warehouse/Distr.	Up 6-10%
Manufacturing	Same
High Tech/R&D	Same

Site Prices — Same

Absorption
Warehouse/Distr.	Up 11-15%
Manufacturing	Up 6-10%
High Tech/R&D	Same

Construction
Warehouse/Distr.	Up 1-5%
Manufacturing	Same
High Tech/R&D	Same

Dollar Volume - Sales Up 6-10%

Dollar Volume - Leases Up 6-10%

	Sales Prices ($/sf)		Lease Prices ($/sf)		Construction	Vacancy
	Central City	Suburban	Central City	Suburban	($/sf)	Indicators
Less than 5,000 sf	45.00	63.00	5.00	6.50	55.00	Balanced Market
5,000 to 19,999 sf	35.00	56.00	4.50	6.00	50.00	Balanced Market
20,000 to 39,999 sf	35.00	52.00	4.00	5.50	40.00	Balanced Market
40,000 to 59,999 sf	30.00	42.00	3.75	5.00	36.00	Balanced Market
60,000 to 99,999 sf	25.00	42.00	3.50	5.00	33.00	Balanced Market
More than 99,999 sf	25.00	38.00	3.50	5.00	33.00	Moderate Shortage
High Tech/R&D	n/a	65.00	n/a	7.00	75.00	Balanced Market

	Warehouse & Factories		Research & Development	
	Central City	Suburban	Central City	Suburban
Real Estate Taxes	1.00	.75-.90	1.50	1.00
Insurance (Fire & Liability)	.08-.12	.08-.12	.10-.15	.10-.15
Structural & Roof Maintenance	.10-.20	.10-.20	.10-.20	.10-.20
Common Area Maintenance	.25	.25	.25	.25

Warehouse Outlook
New Jersey-Northern

1994 Review

After four years of weak demand and declining values, Northern New Jersey's industrial market turned in an impressive performance in 1994. SIOR's correspondent reports 16 million sq. ft. of net absorption for the year, a dramatic rise from 1993's 6.3 million sq. ft. A rebounding economy fueled demand for distribution space in the seven-county market: some manufacturing companies were expanding as well. The dollar volume of warehouse/ distribution transactions was up about 10 percent in 1994.

1995 Forecast

Net absorption should continue to rise in 1995. Demand for warehouse/distribution space is projected to rise by 11 to 15 percent, while manufacturing absorption increases by six to 10 percent. Such robust activity should put some upward pressure on rents and sales prices. Although more than 40 million sq. ft. was available at the end of 1994, a shortage of large (100,000 sq. ft. or greater) quality space could emerge over the next 12 months.

NEW JERSEY - SOUTHERN, NEW JERSEY: INdustrIAL

Southern New Jersey (Burlington, Camden, Gloucester Counties)

MARKET DATA

Inventory (sf)	Central City	Suburban
Total	-	30,301,892
Vacant	-	1,662,153
Vacancy Rates	-	5.5%
Under Construction	-	329,000
Net Absorption	-	n/a

Site Prices ($/sf)	Central City	Suburban
Improved Sites		
Less than 2 acres	-	1.70
2 to 5 acres	-	1.70
5 to 10 acres	-	1.40
Over 10 acres	-	1.38
Unimproved Sites		
Less than 10 acres	-	1.00
10 to 100 acres	-	.90
Over 100 acres	-	.85

Prime Source of Financing: Insurance Companies, Commercial Banks, Owner Financing

Mortgage Money Supply: Moderate

CURRENT TRENDS

Composition of Absorption
Warehouse/Distr.	85.0%
Manufacturing	5.0%
High Tech/R&D	10.0%

Composition of Inventory
Warehouse/Distr.	80.0%
Manufacturing	10.0%
High Tech/R&D	10.0%

Rate of Construction
Warehouse/Distr.	Up 1-5%
Manufacturing	Same
High Tech/R&D	Same

Dollar Volume - Sales
Warehouse/Distr.	Same
Manufacturing	Same
High Tech/R&D	Same

Dollar Volume - Leases
Warehouse/Distr.	Up 1-5%
Manufacturing	Up 1-5%
High Tech/R&D	Up 1-5%

Outlook

Sales Prices
Warehouse/Distr.	Same
Manufacturing	Same
High Tech/R&D	Same

Lease Prices
Warehouse/Distr.	Up 6-10%
Manufacturing	Up 6-10%
High Tech/R&D	Up 6-10%

Site Prices Same
Absorption
Warehouse/Distr.	Same
Manufacturing	Same
High Tech/R&D	Same

Construction
Warehouse/Distr.	Same
Manufacturing	Same
High Tech/R&D	Same

Dollar Volume - Sales Up 1-5%

Dollar Volume - Leases Up 1-5%

	Sales Prices ($/sf)		Lease Prices ($/sf)		Construction	Vacancy
	Central City	Suburban	Central City	Suburban	($/sf)	Indicators
Less than 5,000 sf	-	n/a	-	3.50-5.00	40.00-60.00	Moderate Shortage
5,000 to 19,999 sf	-	n/a	-	3.50-5.00	40.00-45.00	Moderate Shortage
20,000 to 39,999 sf	-	n/a	-	3.25-4.25	35.00-40.00	Balanced Market
40,000 to 59,999 sf	-	n/a	-	3.25-4.25	30.00-35.00	Moderate Oversupply
60,000 to 99,999 sf	-	n/a	-	3.50-4.00	25.00-32.00	Moderate Shortage
More than 99,999 sf	-	n/a	-	3.00-4.00	24.00-27.00	Substantial Shortage
High Tech/R&D	-	n/a	-	5.50	n/a	Balanced Market

	Warehouse & Factories		Research & Development	
	Central City	Suburban	Central City	Suburban
Real Estate Taxes	-	.25-.90	-	n/a
Insurance (Fire & Liability)	-	.05-.13	-	n/a
Structural & Roof Maintenance	-	n/a	-	n/a
Common Area Maintenance	-	.25-.40	-	n/a

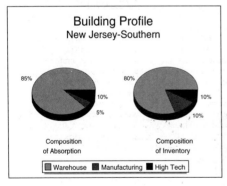

Building Profile
New Jersey-Southern

85% / 10% / 5% — Composition of Absorption

80% / 10% / 10% — Composition of Inventory

Legend: ■ Warehouse ■ Manufacturing ■ High Tech

1994 REVIEW

Vacancy in the Southern New Jersey industrial market fell considerably in 1994. As of year-end, the 30.3 million sq. ft. inventory was just 5.5 percent vacant, down from 13 percent in 1993. The market is dominated by warehouse/distribution space, demand for which received a boost from the improving national economy. Several REIT purchases took place in 1994 but the dollar volume of sales transactions was essentially unchanged from the year before. Lease prices were up, however, suggesting an imminent increase in values and activity.

1995 FORECAST

Another solid year of net absorption is projected for the southern New Jersey market in 1995. While demand is not likely to exceed 1994's total, it should keep pace. Speculative development is already underway in Gloucester County, as ground has been broken on a 229,000 sq. ft. warehouse/ distribution facility. During the second quarter of 1995 construction is set to begin on a 100,000 sq. ft. light industrial/warehouse building.

New York - Brooklyn/Queens, New York: Industrial

Brooklyn/Queens, New York

Market Data

Inventory (sf)	Central City	Suburban
Total	330,000,000	-
Vacant	39,000,000	-
Vacancy Rates	11.8%	-
Under Construction	0	-
Net Absorption	17,000,000	-

Site Prices ($/sf)	Central City	Suburban
Improved Sites		
Less than 2 acres	10.00-20.00	-
2 to 5 acres	8.00-15.00	-
5 to 10 acres	7.00-15.00	-
Over 10 acres	6.00-15.00	-
Unimproved Sites		
Less than 10 acres	n/a	-
10 to 100 acres	n/a	-
Over 100 acres	n/a	-

Prime Source of Financing: Commercial Banks

Mortgage Money Supply: Moderate

Current Trends

Composition of Absorption	
Warehouse/Distr.	80.0%
Manufacturing	15.0%
High Tech/R&D	5.0%
Composition of Inventory	
Warehouse/Distr.	60.0%
Manufacturing	30.0%
High Tech/R&D	10.0%
Rate of Construction	
Warehouse/Distr.	n/a
Manufacturing	n/a
High Tech/R&D	n/a
Dollar Volume - Sales	
Warehouse/Distr.	Up 1-5%
Manufacturing	Down 6-10%
High Tech/R&D	Same
Dollar Volume - Leases	
Warehouse/Distr.	Down 1-5%
Manufacturing	Down 6-10%
High Tech/R&D	Down

Outlook

Sales Prices	
Warehouse/Distr.	Up 1-5%
Manufacturing	Same
High Tech/R&D	Up 1-5%
Lease Prices	
Warehouse/Distr.	Down 1-5%
Manufacturing	Down 6-10%
High Tech/R&D	Same
Site Prices	Up 1-5%
Absorption	
Warehouse/Distr.	Up 1-5%
Manufacturing	Down 6-10%
High Tech/R&D	Same
Construction	
Warehouse/Distr.	Same
Manufacturing	Same
High Tech/R&D	Same
Dollar Volume - Sales	Same
Dollar Volume - Leases	Same

	Sales Prices ($/sf)		Gross Lease Prices ($/sf)		Construction	Vacancy
	Central City	Suburban	Central City	Suburban	($/sf)	Indicators
Less than 5,000 sf	30.00-35.00	-	4.50-7.00	-	45.00	Substantial Shortage
5,000 to 19,999 sf	18.00-23.00	-	4.00-5.50	-	40.00	Moderate Shortage
20,000 to 39,999 sf	20.00-30.00	-	4.00-5.00	-	37.00	Balanced Market
40,000 to 59,999 sf	20.00-30.00	-	3.25-4.50	-	35.00	Balanced Market
60,000 to 99,999 sf	18.00-25.00	-	3.00-4.25	-	32.00	Moderate Oversupply
More than 99,999 sf	18.00-25.00	-	3.00-4.25	-	30.00	Moderate Oversupply
High Tech/R&D	35.00-45.00	-	4.50-5.50	-	100.00	Balanced Market

	Warehouse & Factories		Research & Development	
	Central City	Suburban	Central City	Suburban
Real Estate Taxes	1.50-3.00	-	2.25-2.75	-
Insurance (Fire & Liability)	.20-.30	-	.20-.30	-
Structural & Roof Maintenance	.20	-	.20	-
Common Area Maintenance	n/a	-	n/a	-

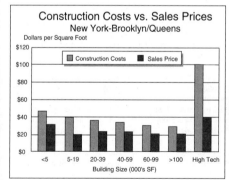

Construction Costs vs. Sales Prices
New York-Brooklyn/Queens

Dollars per Square Foot

Legend: Construction Costs, Sales Price

Building Size (000's SF): <5, 5-19, 20-39, 40-59, 60-99, >100, High Tech

1994 Review

The accelerated pace of job growth in the greater New York region buoyed demand for industrial space in Brooklyn and Queens. About 17 million sq. ft. was absorbed in 1994, lowering the vacancy in this massive 330 million sq. ft. inventory to 11.8 percent, the lowest average in more than five years. Smaller buildings — those ranging between 25,000 and 75,000 sq. ft. — were in the strongest demand. Net absorption of larger facilities remained slow. Sales and lease prices firmed for warehouse/distribution space but rates for manufacturing properties declined again.

1995 Forecast

New York's regional economic recovery is largely driven by the formation of small companies. This trend is reflected in the Brooklyn-Queens industrial market where small space-users continue to generate the lion's share of net absorption. During 1995, SIOR's reporter expects demand for warehouse/distribution space, especially properties under 10,000 sq. ft. to increase by about five percent. Production jobs will continue to leave the city in 1995, depressing demand for manufacturing facilities.

New York - Manhattan, New York: Industrial

New York - Manhattan, New York

Market Data

Inventory (sf)	Central City	Suburban
Total	n/a	-
Vacant	n/a	-
Vacancy Rates	n/a	-
Under Construction	n/a	-
Net Absorption	n/a	-

Site Prices ($/sf)	Central City	Suburban
Improved Sites		
Less than 2 acres	n/a	-
2 to 5 acres	n/a	-
5 to 10 acres	n/a	-
Over 10 acres	n/a	-
Unimproved Sites		
Less than 10 acres	n/a	-
10 to 100 acres	n/a	-
Over 100 acres	n/a	-

Prime Source of Financing: Commercial Banks, Owner Financing

Mortgage Money Supply: Moderate

Current Trends

Composition of Absorption	
Warehouse/Distr.	n/a
Manufacturing	n/a
High Tech/R&D	n/a
Composition of Inventory	
Warehouse/Distr.	n/a
Manufacturing	n/a
High Tech/R&D	n/a
Rate of Construction	
Warehouse/Distr.	Same
Manufacturing	Same
High Tech/R&D	Same
Dollar Volume - Sales	
Warehouse/Distr.	Up 6-10%
Manufacturing	Up 6-10%
High Tech/R&D	Same
Dollar Volume - Leases	
Warehouse/Distr.	Down 1-5%
Manufacturing	Up 1-5%
High Tech/R&D	Same

Outlook

Sales Prices	
Warehouse/Distr.	Up 6-10%
Manufacturing	Up 6-10%
High Tech/R&D	Up 1-5%
Lease Prices	
Warehouse/Distr.	Up 6-10%
Manufacturing	Up 6-10%
High Tech/R&D	n/a
Site Prices	n/a
Absorption	
Warehouse/Distr.	n/a
Manufacturing	n/a
High Tech/R&D	n/a
Construction	
Warehouse/Distr.	n/a
Manufacturing	n/a
High Tech/R&D	n/a
Dollar Volume - Sales	n/a
Dollar Volume - Leases	n/a

	Sales Prices ($/sf)		Gross Lease Prices ($/sf)		Construction	Vacancy
	Central City	Suburban	Central City	Suburban	($/sf)	Indicators
Less than 5,000 sf	30.00-120.00	-	5.00-20.00	-	n/a	Moderate Oversupply
5,000 to 19,999 sf	20.00-120.00	-	5.00-20.00	-	n/a	Moderate Oversupply
20,000 to 39,999 sf	20.00-100.00	-	4.50-15.00	-	n/a	Balanced Market
40,000 to 59,999 sf	20.00-100.00	-	4.50-15.00	-	n/a	Balanced Market
60,000 to 99,999 sf	15.00-100.00	-	4.00-15.00	-	n/a	Moderate Shortage
More than 99,999 sf	10.00-100.00	-	3.50-15.00	-	n/a	Moderate Shortage
High Tech/R&D	n/a	-	n/a	-	n/a	Balanced Market

	Warehouse & Factories		Research & Development	
	Central City	Suburban	Central City	Suburban
Real Estate Taxes	n/a	-	n/a	-
Insurance (Fire & Liability)	n/a	-	n/a	-
Structural & Roof Maintenance	n/a	-	n/a	-
Common Area Maintenance	n/a	-	n/a	-

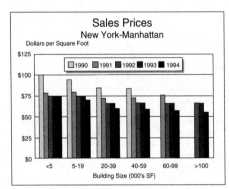

Sales Prices
New York-Manhattan
Dollars per Square Foot

Legend: 1990, 1991, 1992, 1993, 1994

Building Size (000's SF): <5, 5-19, 20-39, 40-59, 60-99, >100

1994 Review

New York City's industrial market stabilized in 1994 but remains relatively soft. Manufacturing jobs contracted at a much slower pace last year than they had during the recession, stemming the tide of vacated properties returning to the market. Advances in the printing and publishing and textiles industries helped to prop up the production economy. The dollar volume of sales transactions was up by a range of six to 10 percent for the year but leasing activity reported a slight decline.

1995 Forecast

Much of the land zoned industrial lies dormant in New York City. With taxes and labor rates too high for most goods-producing industries, the manufacturing sector is witnessing a long-term and permanent decline. City officials now plan to convert much of the under-utilized property to other uses. During 1995, an improved economic picture should allow for modest improvement in demand. Sales prices should increase again and for the first time in several years, lease rates will be up as well.

Industrial Real Estate Market

Tucson, Arizona: Industrial

Tucson, Arizona

Market Data

Inventory (sf)	Central City	Suburban
Total	7,805,136	-
Vacant	1,069,881	-
Vacancy Rates	13.7%	-
Under Construction	35,000	-
Net Absorption	358,407	-

Site Prices ($/sf)	Central City	Suburban
Improved Sites		
Less than 2 acres	1.75	-
2 to 5 acres	1.50	-
5 to 10 acres	1.40	-
Over 10 acres	1.20	-
Unimproved Sites		
Less than 10 acres	.50	-
10 to 100 acres	.20	-
Over 100 acres	.10	-

Prime Source of Financing: Insurance Companies

Mortgage Money Supply: Moderate

Current Trends

Composition of Absorption	
Warehouse/Distr.	40.0%
Manufacturing	25.0%
High Tech/R&D	35.0%
Composition of Inventory	
Warehouse/Distr.	30.0%
Manufacturing	30.0%
High Tech/R&D	40.0%
Rate of Construction	
Warehouse/Distr.	Up 25%
Manufacturing	Same
High Tech/R&D	Same
Dollar Volume - Sales	
Warehouse/Distr.	Down 1-5%
Manufacturing	Down 1-5%
High Tech/R&D	Down 6-10%
Dollar Volume - Leases	
Warehouse/Distr.	Up 11-15%
Manufacturing	Up 1-5%
High Tech/R&D	Same

Outlook

Sales Prices	
Warehouse/Distr.	Up 1-5%
Manufacturing	Up 1-5%
High Tech/R&D	Up 1-5%
Lease Prices	
Warehouse/Distr.	Up 6-10%
Manufacturing	Up 11-15%
High Tech/R&D	Up 11-15%
Site Prices	Up 6-10%
Absorption	
Warehouse/Distr.	Up 11-15%
Manufacturing	Up 6-10%
High Tech/R&D	Up 6-10%
Construction	
Warehouse/Distr.	Up 30%
Manufacturing	Up 1-5%
High Tech/R&D	Up 6-10%
Dollar Volume - Sales	Up 25%
Dollar Volume - Leases	Same

	Sales Prices ($/sf)		Net Lease Prices ($/sf)		Construction	Vacancy
	Central City	Suburban	Central City	Suburban	($/sf)	Indicators
Less than 5,000 sf	35.00	-	4.44	-	35.00	Substantial Shortage
5,000 to 19,999 sf	30.00	-	4.20	-	30.00	Substantial Shortage
20,000 to 39,999 sf	28.00	-	3.96	-	30.00	Substantial Shortage
40,000 to 59,999 sf	25.00	-	3.36	-	28.00	Moderate Shortage
60,000 to 99,999 sf	25.00	-	3.00	-	26.00	Balanced Market
More than 99,999 sf	23.00	-	2.76	-	22.00	Balanced Market
High Tech/R&D	35.00	-	4.80	-	45.00	Moderate Shortage

	Warehouse & Factories		Research & Development	
	Central City	Suburban	Central City	Suburban
Real Estate Taxes	.07	-	.09	-
Insurance (Fire & Liability)	.02	-	.03	-
Structural & Roof Maintenance	.01	-	.01	-
Common Area Maintenance	.02	-	.12	-

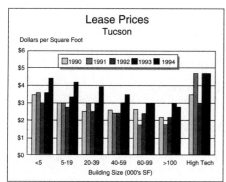

Lease Prices
Tucson
Dollars per Square Foot

1990 1991 1992 1993 1994

Building Size (000's SF)
<5 5-19 20-39 40-59 60-99 >100 High Tech

1994 Review

Tucson's economy is booming. The decision by Hughes to consolidate nearly all its missile production to Tucson and the recent award to Hughes of a $1.0 billion Tomahawk missile contract bode extremely well for the manufacturing sector. Software and teleservice companies have also moved to Tucson, taking advantage of low operating costs vis-a-vis California. A little more than one million sq. ft. was available for sale or lease at the end of 1994, not enough to handle increasing demand, according to SIOR's reporter.

1995 Forecast

With fewer properties to choose from, many users have opted to build their own facilities. About 50,000 sq. ft. of speculative construction has been proposed for the Park and Ajo area, 210,000 sq. ft. is planned in the Airport submarket and 50,000 sq. ft. is under consideration in the Palo Verde/I-10 corridor. Only 35,000 sq. ft. was under construction at the end of 1994 and it is difficult to predict how much of the proposed development will proceed in 1995. Although demand appears strong, financing terms are still relatively unattractive.

Glossary of Terms

DEMOGRAPHICS

Population. The 1994 population projection for the MSA. Figures are based on data from Urban Decision Systems.

Population Growth Rate. The annual percentage change in populations between 1994 and 1999 for the MSA. Figures are based on data from Urban Decision Systems.

Unemployment Rate. The percent of labor force unemployed in August 1994 as published by the Bureau of Labor Statistics in Employment and Earnings.

Median Household Income. The estimated median household income for 1994 as published by Urban Decision Systems.

Cost of Living Index. Measures relative price levels for consumer goods and services in participating areas, as published by American Chamber of Commerce Researchers Association (ACCRA).

Demographic Rankings. This ranks local statistics against other U.S. Metropolitan markets.

INDUSTRIAL MARKETS

Prime Industrial Building. A prime industrial building is in the top 25 percent of the most desired industrial properties in a given market area. Such buildings are considered to be for general purpose uses such as industrial, research, warehouse and/or manufacturing.

Central City/Suburban. Since the definition of urban and suburban varies widely, it is the responsibility of the individual survey respondent to reflect his or her area's particular characteristics.

Total Inventory. Total square footage (sq. ft.) of rentable industrial space, vacant and occupied, ready for tenant finish. Includes owner occupied space.

Vacant Inventory. Total square footage of vacant rentable industrial space, including sublease.

Net Absorption. Net change in occupied space.

Under Construction. Industrial space in construction stages; ground has been broken. Does not include planned projects.

Construction Costs. Construction costs reflect only hard construction costs such as general contractor, overhead, and profit, but exclude architectural and engineering fees, financing fees, and mortgage/brokerage fees for both construction and permanent financing.

Lease Prices. A gross lease is one in which the tenant's rent includes real estate taxes, fire and extended coverage insurance, as well as maintenance of the roof structure and outside walls. A net lease is one in which the tenant assumes the operating expenses of the leased premises.

Improved Sites. Improved sites are in the top 25 percent of overall desirability of the existing inventory. Such sites are in a "ready-to-build" condition and are essentially level and graded and serviced with all necessary utilities. Rail service may or may not be available.

Unimproved Sites. These sites are also in the top 25 percent of overall desirability of the existing inventory and zoned for industrial use. Streets and utilities may not yet be installed, but are reasonably close and available. Rail service may or may not be available.

Prime High-Technology Building. Generally, high-technology (high-tech) buildings are 50 percent or more office, fully air-conditioned, 12-18' clear height, have extensive landscaping and parking, and are architecturally impressive. In some areas of the country where high-tech industries are not prevalent, this building could be used as a showroom or as pure office. These properties are sometimes called "flex buildings."

Operating Expenses. Outlays pertaining to real estate operations, exclusive of tenant's on-going businesses costs. Includes building payroll, maintenance, utilities, insurance, general and administrative costs, etc. Expessed in dollars per sq. ft., annually. [Note: survey questionnaire did not define this item for reporters, and local practices vary. Please refer inquiries about specifics to local reporters.]

Real Estate Taxes. Local property taxes on land and building, expressed in dollars per sq. ft., annually.

OFFICE MARKETS

CBD. Central Business District space located near the historical urban core, commonly associated with traditional government and financial districts in most cities.

Outside CBD. Outside the CBD includes both suburban area and "urban clusters" with areas of high office space concentrations that often rival nearby CBDs.

Class "A." Excellent locations, high-quality tenants, high-quality finish, well-maintained, professionally managed, and usually new, or old buildings that are competitive with new buildings.

Class "B." Good location, professionally managed,

fairly high-quality construction and tenancy. Class "B" buildings generally show very little functional obsolescence and deterioration.

Total Inventory. Total square footage (sq. ft.) of rentable space, vacant and occupied, ready for tenant finish. Includes owner occupied space.

Vacant Inventory. Total square footage of vacant rentable space, including sublease.

Current Construction. Total square footage presently under construction includes any space that will be available for occupancy before the end of 1993.

Substantial Rehabilitation. Repair/replacement of building interior finish and/or systems requiring temporary displacement of tenants.

Net Absorption. Net change in occupied stock.

Rental Rate. Minimum, maximum, and weighted average quoted gross rental rate for competitive office space in each class, in U.S. dollars per square foot($/sq. ft.).

Gross Rental. Services included in the rental rate vary from market to market.

Sales Prices. Minimum, maximum, and weighted average sales prices for competitive office space in each class, in U.S. dollars per square foot ($/sq. ft.).

Weighted Average Rental Rate. Average quoted rental rate weighted by the vacant space available at the rental rate, in each class.

Average Utility Rates. Figures presented are dollars per square foot per year.

Standard Work Letter. Sometimes called a construction rider, this refers to the work that the landlord will do for the tenant, typically to finish out the interior of the space.

Typical Parking Ratio. The ratio refers to the availability of parking spaces per number of square feet leased by a tenant.

Operating Cost Escalation. Operating cost escalation refers to the procedure used to adjust rents over the term of a lease.

Cumulative Discount Rate. The rental rate discount factor is the cumulative effect of landlord lease concessions on gross rental rates. It is expressed as a percentage of base rent.

Operating Expenses. Outlays pertaining to real estate operations, exclusive of tenant's on-going businesses costs. Includes building payroll, maintenance, utilities, insurance, general and administrative costs, etc. Expressed in dollars per sq. ft., annually. [Note: survey questionaire did not define this item for reporters, and local practices vary. Please refer inquiries about specifics to local reporters.]

Real Estate Taxes. Local property taxes on land and building, expressed in dollars per sq. ft., annually.

Cap Rate. Rate of return to real estate investment, expressed as a ratio of net operating income to sales price. Excludes the impact of mortgage.

Internal Rate of Return. The annualized rate of return on investment capable of being generated over a period of ownership, including the periodic cash flows and the ultimate termination of the investment. Discounts all returns to equal the original investment. In practice, often used synonymously with **discount rate** to indicate the return on capital used to convert all future receipts into net present value.

MISCELLANEOUS TERMS

Maquiladora. The twin plant operation that has grown up along the U.S./Mexico border, in which goods are shipped into Mexico for assembly and finishing work using lower cost labor, and then are distributed through the U.S. market. Import duties are payable only on the imputed value added in the assembly process. The Maquiladora program served as a spring board for U.S./ Mexico trade cooperation, which has culminated in the North American Free Trade Agreement. The treaty agreements under NAFTA will eventually supercede the Maquiladora arrangements.

FIRE Sector. An acronym standing for Finance, Insurance and Real Estate, one of the major industry groupings in the Standard Industrial Classification system established by the U.S. Department of Commerce.

Backfilling. A colloquialism referring to the re-leasing of space once occupied by a tenant that has relocated elsewhere.

Source: Reprinted from the 1995 edition of *Comparative Statistics of Industrial and Office Real Estate Markets* with permission of the Society of Industrial and Office Realtors®.

Real Estate Investment Trusts (REITs)

The real estate investment trust, or REIT (pronounced "reet"), is the best way for many investors to invest in commercial real estate. As an investment vehicle, the REIT combines the best features of real estate and stocks. It gives an investor a practical and efficient means to include professionally managed real estate in an investment portfolio.

The REIT industry began its fourth decade in 1990. Because of the industry's overall maturity and performance over the last three decades, REITs can be viewed as "all-weather" investments. REITs will become the vehicle of choice for many investors throughout the 1990s.

This brochure answers fundamental questions about REITs and is designed for investors, financial planners, stock brokers, the media and the general public.

WHAT IS A REIT?

A REIT is essentially a corporation or trust that combines the capital of many investors to acquire or provide financing for all forms of real estate. A REIT serves much like a mutual fund for real estate in that retail investors obtain the benefit of a diversified portfolio under professional management. Its shares are freely traded, often on a major stock exchange.

A corporation or trust that qualifies as a REIT generally does not pay corporate income tax to the Internal Revenue Service (IRS). This is a unique feature and one of the most attractive aspects of a REIT. Most states honor this federal treatment and do not require REITs to pay state income tax. This means that nearly all of a REIT's income can be distributed to shareholders, and there is no double taxation of the income to the shareholder. Unlike a partnership, a REIT cannot pass its tax losses onto its investors.

WHAT QUALIFIES A REIT?

In order for a corporation or trust to qualify as a REIT, it must comply with certain provisions within the Internal Revenue Code. As required by the Tax Code, a REIT must:

• be a corporation, business trust or similar association;

Source: *Real Estate Investment Trusts: Frequently Asked Questions About REITS,* National Association of Real Estate Investment Trusts, Inc., 1129 Twentieth Street, N.W., Washington, D.C. 20036.

• be managed by a board of directors or trustees;
• have shares that are fully transferable;
• have a minimum of 100 shareholders;
• have no more than 50 percent of the shares held by five or fewer individuals during the last half of each taxable year;
• invest at least 75 percent of the total assets in real estate assets;
• derive at least 75 percent of gross income from rents from real property, or interest on mortgages on real property;
• derive no more than 30 percent of gross income from the sale of real property held for less than four years, securities held for less than one year or certain prohibited transactions;
• pay dividends of at least 95 percent of REIT taxable income.

WHY WERE REITS CREATED?

REITs were created to provide investors with the opportunity to participate in the benefits of ownership of larger-scale commercial real estate or mortgage lending, and receive an enhanced return, because the income is not taxed at the REIT entity level. This means that a diverse range of investors can realize investment opportunities otherwise available only to those with larger resources. This opportunity first became available when President Eisenhower signed the real estate investment trust tax provisions into law in 1960. The basic provisions of this law remain unchanged, although there have been a number of improvements to the law over the past 30 years.

The REIT industry has benefitted from tax reform initiatives enacted in the 1980s. These initiatives eliminated the incentive of tax-sheltered real estate vehicles and promoted a return to the fundamentals of capital formation and investment in real estate for income and appreciation. A tax change in 1986 allowed REITs to manage their properties directly, and a 1993 change removes a significant barrier to pension plan investment in REITs.

WHO INVESTS IN REITS?

Thousands of investors, both U.S. and non-U.S., own shares of REITs. So do pension funds, endowment funds, insurance companies, bank trust departments and mutual funds.

An individual who chooses to invest in a REIT seeks to achieve current income distributions and long-term stock appreciation potential. An investor also has the benefit of liquidity, if needed.

IMPORTANT DIFFERENCES: REITS VS. PARTNERSHIPS

	REITs	Partnerships
Liquidity	Yes, most REITs are listed on stock exchanges	No, when liquidity exists, generally much less than REITs
Minimum Investment Amount	None	Typically $2,000–$5,000
Reinvestment Plans	Yes, including some at discounts	No
Ability to Leverage Investments without Incurring UBIT for Tax-Exempt Accounts	Yes, this makes REITs suitable for individual IRAs, KEOGH and other pension plans	No
Investor Control	Yes, investors re-elect directors and, in some cases, approve advisors annually	No, controlled by general partner who cannot be easily removed by limited partners
Independent Directors	Yes, stock exchange rules or state law typically requires majority to be independent of management	No
Beneficial Ownership	At least 100 shareholders required–most REITs have thousands	Shared between any number of limited and general partners
Ability to Grow by Additional Public Offerings of Stock or Debt	Yes	No
Ability to Pass Losses on to Investors	No	Yes
Information to Investors	Form 1099	Form K-1
Subjects investors to state taxes	No	Yes

REIT shares typically may be purchased from $2 to $40 each, with no minimum purchase required.

ARE REITS LIMITED PARTNERSHIPS?

No. REITs are not partnerships. There are important organizational and operational differences between REITs and limited partnerships.

One of the major differences between REITs and limited partnerships is how annual tax information is reported to investors. An investor in a REIT receives IRS Form 1099 from the REIT, indicating the amount and type of income received during the year. An investor in a partnership receives a very complicated IRS Schedule K-1.

The oversight/corporate governance features of a REIT are believed to be far superior to those of a partnership.

Other important differences between REITs and limited partnerships are shown in the accompanying chart.

HOW MANY REITS ARE THERE?

There are over 250 REITs operating in the United States today. Their assets total over 61 billion. Over 80 percent of these trade on the national stock exchanges:

- New York Stock Exchange—136 REITs
- American Stock Exchange—65 REITs
- NASDAQ National Market System—24 REITs

In addition, there are dozens of REITs that are not traded on a stock exchange. The balance of this booklet discusses publicly-traded REITs.

HOW ARE REIT STOCKS VALUED?

Like all companies whose stocks are publicly traded, REIT share prices are quoted daily. To determine a value for these shares, typical analysis involves one or more of the following criteria:

- Anticipated total return from the stock, calculated from the anticipated price change and the prevailing yield;
- Current prevailing dividend yield relative to other yield-oriented investments (e.g., bonds, utility stocks);
- Dividend coverage from funds from operations;
- Management quality structure;
- Anticipated growth (or lack thereof) in funds from operations per share; and
- Underlying asset value of the real estate and/or mortgages, and other assets.

WHAT TYPES OF REITS ARE THERE?

The REIT industry has a diverse profile, which offers many attractive opportunities to investors. REIT industry analysts often classify REITs in one of three investment approaches:

Equity REITs own real estate. Their revenue comes principally from rent. REIT industry investments in property ownership have increased steadily for 30 years.

Mortgage REITs loan money to real estate owners. Their revenue comes principally from interest earned on their mortgage loans. Some mortgage REITs also invest in residuals of mortgage-based securities.

Hybrid REITs combine the investment strategies of both equity REITs and mortgage REITs.

REITs can also be distinguished by...

Type of Property...

Some REITs invest in a variety of property types—shopping centers, apartments, warehouses, office buildings, hotels, etc. Other REITs specialize in one property type only, such as shopping centers or factory outlet stores. Health care REITs specialize in health care facilities: hospitals, including acute care, rehabilitation and psychiatric, medical office buildings, nursing homes, and congregate and assisted living centers.

Geographic Focus...

Some REITs invest throughout the country. Others specialize in one region only, or even a single metropolitan area.

WHO DETERMINES A REIT'S INVESTMENTS?

A REIT's investments are determined by its board of directors or trustees. Directors are elected by, and responsible to, the shareholders. In turn, the directors appoint the management personnel. REIT directors are typically well-known and respected members of the real estate, business and professional communities.

HOW ARE REITS MANAGED?

REITs employ professional management, individuals who are hired and periodically reviewed by the REIT's board of directors. REIT managers are selected based upon their extensive real estate background and expertise. REITs can be either internally managed or externally advised.

WHAT MAKES A REIT ATTRACTIVE TO INVESTORS?

In addition to avoiding double taxation and requiring no minimum investment, REITs also offer investors:

- Current income: usually stable and often provides an attractive return;
- Liquidity: shares of publicly traded REITs are readily converted into cash because they are traded on the major stock exchanges;
- Professional management: REIT managers are skilled, experienced real estate professionals;
- Portfolio diversification: minimizes risk;
- Performance Monitoring: A REIT's performance is monitored on a regular basis by independent directors of the REIT, independent analysts, independent auditors, and the business and financial media. This scrutiny provides the investor a measure of protection and more than one barometer of the REIT's financial condition.

HOW DO I INVEST IN A REIT?

An individual may invest in a publicly traded REIT, which in most cases is listed

INDUSTRY PROFILE
REIT Type by Market Capitalization
August 31, 1994

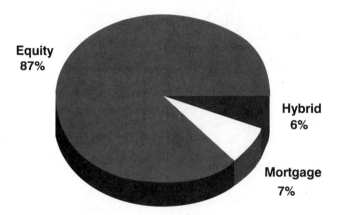

Equity
87%

Hybrid
6%

Mortgage
7%

$43.5 BILLION REIT INDUSTRY PROFILE
by Property Investment Strategy
August 31, 1994

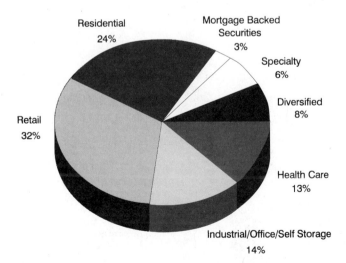

Residential
24%

Mortgage Backed
Securities
3%

Specialty
6%

Diversified
8%

Retail
32%

Health Care
13%

Industrial/Office/Self Storage
14%

on a major stock exchange, by purchasing shares through a stock broker. An investor can enlist the services of a broker, investment advisor or financial planner to help analyze his or her financial objectives. These individuals also may be able to recommend an appropriate REIT for the investor. An investor can also contact a REIT directly for a copy of the company's annual report, prospectus and other financial information. In addition, investors can diversify their investment further by buying shares in a mutual fund that specializes in investing in real estate securities.

Potential investors may contact the National Association of Real Estate Investment Trusts® (NAREIT) for a free listing of all publicly traded REITs, with exchange symbols, and a list of educational publications available, as well as a list of the mutual funds that primarily invest in REITs.

For more information, contact NAREIT, 1129 Twentieth Street, N.W., Suite 705, Washington, D.C., 20036, (202) 785-8717.

PUBLICLY TRADED REITS

Symbols

NEW YORK STOCK EXCHANGE

	Symbols
Agree Realty	ADC
American Health Properties, Inc.	AHE
American Industrial Property Investors	IND
Americana Hotels and Realty Corporation	AHR
Amli Residential Properties, Inc.	AML
Apartment Investment & Management Company	AIV
Arbor Property Trust	ABR
Asset Investors Corporation	AIC
Associated Estates Realty Corporation	AEC
Avalon Properties, Inc.	AVN
BRE Properties, Inc.	BRE
BRT Realty Trust	BRT
Bay Apartment Communities, Inc.	BYA
Beacon Properties Corp.	BCN
Bedford Property Investors, Inc.	BED
Berkshire Realty Company, Inc.	BRI
Bradley Real Estate, Inc.	BTR
Burnham Pacific Properties, Inc.	BPP
CBL & Associates Properties, Inc.	CBL
CRIIMI MAE, Inc.	CMM
CRI Liquidating REIT, Inc.	CFR
CV REIT	CVI
CWM Mortgage Holdings, Inc.	CWM
Cali Realty Corporation	CLI
California Real Estate Investment Trust	CT
Camden Property Trust, Inc.	CPT
Capstead Mortgage Corporation	CMO
Capstone Capital Corporation	CCT
Carr Realty Corporation	CRE
Charles E. Smith Residential Realty	SRW
Chateau Properties, Inc.	CPJ
Chelsea GCA Realty Inc.	CCG
Commercial Net Lease Realty, Inc.	NNN
Colonial Property Trust	CLP
Columbus Realty Trust	CLB
Cousins Properties Incorporated	CUZ
Crescent Real Estate Equity	CEI
Crown American Realty Trust	CWN
DeBartolo Realty	EJD
Developers Diversified Realty Corporation	DDR
Duke Realty Investments, Inc.	DRE
EQK Realty Investors I	EKR
EastGroup Properties	EGP
Equity Residential Properties Trust	EQR
Essex Property Trust	ESS
Evans Withycombe Residential, Inc.	EWR
Excel Realty Trust	XEL
Factory Stores of America, Inc.	FAC
Federal Realty Investment Trust	FRT
First Industrial Realty Trust, Inc.	FR
First Union Real Estate Equity and Mortgage Investments	FUR
Franchise Finance Corp. of America	FFA
G & L Realty Corp.	GLR
Gables Residential Trust	GBP
General Growth Properties, Inc.	GGP
Glimcher Realty Trust	GRT
HRE Properties	HRE
Health Care Property Investors, Inc.	HCP
Health Care REIT	HCN
Health & Retirement Properties Trust	HRP
Healthcare Realty Trust, Inc.	HR
Highwoods Properties, Inc.	HIW
Home Properties of New York	HME
Homeplex Mortgage Corporation	HPX

Symbols

	Symbols
Horizon Outlet Centers	HGI
IRT Property Company	IRT
Irvine Apartment Communities	IAC
JDN Realty Corporation	JDN
JP Realty, Inc.	JPR
Kimco Realty Corporation	KIM
Kranzco Realty Trust, Inc.	KRT
LNH REIT, Inc.	LHC
LTC Properties, Inc.	LTC
Lexington Corporate Properties	LXP
Liberty Property Trust	LRY
MGI Properties	MGI
Macerich Company, The	MAC
Malan Realty Investors	MAL
Manufactured Home Communities, Inc.	MHC
Mark Centers Trust	MCT
McArthur/Glen Realty Corporation	MCG
Meditrust	MT
Merry Land & Investment Company, Inc.	MRY
Mid-America Apartment Communities, Inc.	MAA
Mid-America Realty Investments	MDI
Mills Corporation, The	MLS
Mortgage and Realty Trust	MRT
National Golf Properties, Inc.	TEE
National Health Investors, Inc.	NHI
Nationwide Health Properties, Inc.	NHP
New Plan Realty Trust	NPR
Oasis Residential, Inc.	OAS
Omega Healthcare Investors, Inc.	OHI
PIMCO Commercial Mortgage Securities Trust	PCM
Paragon Group, Inc.	PAO
Post Properties, Inc.	PPS
Price REIT, The Class B	RET
Prudential Realty Trust	PRT
Prudential Realty Trust (Capital Shares)	PRT P
ROC Communities, Inc.	RCI
RPS Realty Trust	RPS
Real Estate Investment Trust of California	RCT
Realty Income Corporation	O
Realty ReFund Trust	RRF
Regency Realty Corporation	REG
Resource Mortgage Capital, Inc.	RMR
Rockefeller Center Properties, Inc.	RCP
Santa Anita Realty Enterprises, Inc.	SAR
Saul Centers, Inc.	BFS
Security Capital Industrial Trust	SCN
Security Capital Pacific Trust	PTR
Simon Property Group	SPG
Sizeler Property Investors, Inc.	SIZ
South West Property Trust	SWP
Spieker Properties, Inc.	SPK
Starwood Lodging	HOT
Storage Equities, Inc.	SEQ
Storage Trust Realty	SEA
Storage USA	SUS
Summit Properties Trust	SMT
Sun Communities, Inc.	SUI
TIS Mortgage Investment Company	TIS
Tanger Factory Outlet Centers, Inc.	SKT
Taubman Centers, Inc.	TCO
Thornburg Mortgage Asset Corporation	TMA
Town and Country Trust, The	TCT
Transcontinental Realty Investors, Inc.	TCI
TriNet Corporate Realty Trust, Inc.	TRI
Tucker Properties Corporation	TUC
United Dominion Realty Trust	UDR
Universal Health Realty Income Trust	UHT

Symbols

Urban Shopping Centers, Inc.	URB
Vornado Realty Trust	VNO
Walden Residential Properties, Inc.	WDN
Weeks Corporation	WKS
Weingarten Realty Investors	WRI
Wellsford Residential Property Trust, Inc.	WRP

AMERICAN STOCK EXCHANGE

ASR Investments Corporation	ASR
Alexander Haagen Properties, Inc.	ACH
America First REIT, Inc.	AFR
American Real Estate Investment Corporation	REA
Angeles Mortgage Investment Trust	ANM
Angeles Participating Mortgage Trust	APT
Arizona Land Income Corporation	AZL
Banyan Hotel Investment Fund	VHT
Banyan Short Term Income Trust	VST
Boddie-Noell Restaurant Properties, Inc.	BNP
Brandywine Realty Trust	BDN
California Jockey Club	CJ
CenterPoint Properties Corporation	CNT
Commercial Assets Inc.	CAX
Copley Properties, Inc.	COP
Franklin Advantage Real Estate Income Fund	FAD
Franklin Real Estate Income Fund	FIN
Franklin Select Real Estate Income Fund	FSN
Grove Real Estate Asset Trust*	GRE
HMG/Courtland Properties	HMG
Income Opportunity Realty Trust	IOT
Koger Equities, Inc.	KE
Landsing Pacific Fund	LPF
MIP Properties	MIP
Meridian Point Realty Trust IV	MPD
Meridian Point Realty Trust VI	MPF
Meridian Point Realty Trust VII	MPG
Meridian Point Realty Trust VIII	MPH
Metropolitan Realty Corporation	MET
Mid-Atlantic Realty Trust	MRR
North American Trust, Inc.	NAM
One Liberty Properties, Inc.	OLP
PMC Commercial Trust	PMCTS
PS Business Parks	PSB
Pacific Gulf Properties, Inc.	PAG
Partners Preferred Yield	PYA
Partners Preferred Yield II	PYB
Partners Preferred Yield III	PYC
Pennsylvania Real Estate Investment Trust	PEI
Pittsburgh & West Virginia Rail Road	PW
Presidential Realty Corporation	PDL A
Presidential Realty Corporation (Class B)	PDL B
Property Capital Trust	PCT
Public Storage Properties VII, Inc.	PSH
Public Storage Properties IX, Inc.	PSK
Public Storage Properties X, Inc.	PSL
Public Storage Properties XI, Inc.	PSM
Public Storage Properties XII, Inc.	PSN
Public Storage Properties XIV, Inc.	PSP

Symbols

Public Storage Properties XV, Inc.	PSQ
Public Storage Properties XVI, Inc.	PSU
Public Storage Properties XVII, Inc.	PSV
Public Storage Properties XVIII, Inc.	PSW
Public Storage Properties XIX, Inc.	PSY
Public Storage Properties XX, Inc.	PSZ
RYMAC Mortgage Investment Corporation	RM
Resort Income Investors, Inc.	RII
Storage Properties, Inc.	PSA
United Mobile Homes, Inc.	UMH
Vanguard Real Estate Fund I	VRO
Vanguard Real Estate Fund II	VRT
Washington Real Estate Investment Trust	WRE
Western Investment Real Estate Trust	WIR

NASDAQ NATIONAL MARKET SYSTEM

Allied Capital Commercial Corporation	ALCC
Banyan Strategic Land Fund II	VSLF
Banyan Strategic Realty Trust	VLANS
Chicago Dock and Canal Trust, The	DOCKS
Continental Mortgage & Equity Trust	CMETS
Crocker Realty Investors, Inc.	CRKR
Equity Inns, Inc.	ENNS
Felcor Suite Hotels	FLCO
INVG Mortgage Securities Corporation	INVG
Innkeepers USA Trust	NKPR
Jameson Inns, Inc.	JAMS
Mellon Participating Mortgage Trust	MPMTS
Meridian Point Equity Trust '83	MPTBS
Monmouth Real Estate Investment Trust	MNRTA
National Income Realty Trust	NIRTS
Nooney Realty Trust, Inc.	NRTI
Price REIT, The	PRET
Prime Residential Inc.	PRES
Prime Retail, Inc.	PRME
RFS Hotel Investors, Inc.	RFSI
Shurgard Storage Centers	SHUR
USP Real Estate Investment Trust	USPTS
Vinland Property Trust	VIPTS
Winston Hotels	WINN

NASDAQ SUPPLEMENTAL LIST

Cedar Income Fund, Ltd.	CEDR
Crocker Realty Investors	CRKR
Royale Investments, Inc.	RLIN

OTHER OVER-THE-COUNTER

Arlington Realty Investors	RYNMS
Central Realty Investors	CMRT
Century Realty Trust	CRLTS
Fifty Associates	FFTY
First REIT of New Jersey	FRET
First Washington Realty Trust	FWSH
Harbor American Health Care Trust, Inc.	HAHC
Ivey Properties	IVPP
Investors Real Estate Trust	IRET
Medical Properties	MPP
Peregrine Real Estate Trust	CWLES
Real Estate Fund Investment Trust	REFI

*traded on American emerging companies market

Source: National Association of Real Estate Trusts, Inc., 1129 20th Street, N.W., Washington, D.C. 20036.

Glossary of Real Estate and REIT Terms

This glossary of terminology used in conjunction with discussions of real estate investment trusts has been prepared by the Research Department of the National Association of Real Estate Investment Trusts. Credit should be given to Realty Income Trust, a NAREIT member, which produced a glossary of terms upon which NAREIT drew heavily.

Acceleration clause A condition in a loan contract or mortgage note which permits the lender to demand immediate repayment of the entire balance if the contract is breached or conditions for repayment occur, such as sale or demolition.

Accrued interest or rent An amount of interest or rent which has been earned but which may not have been received in the same period as earned. On many short-term first mortgages, accrued interest is not received in cash until permanent financing is obtained.

Acquisition loan See C&D loan.

Advisor A REIT's investment advisor (usually pursuant to a renewable one-year contract) provides analysis of proposed investments, servicing of the portfolio, and other advisory services. Fee limits for advisory services are prescribed by many state securities regulators. Also spelled "adviser."

Amortization The process of retiring debt or recovering a capital investment through scheduled, systematic repayments of principal; that portion of fixed mortgage payment applied to reduction of the principal amount owed.

Anchor tenant An important tenant, usually with an excellent credit rating (also known as a triple-A tenant), which takes a large amount of space in a shopping center or office building and is usually one of the first tenants to commit to lease. The anchor tenant usually is given lower rent because of the desirability of having that tenant at the property, both because of its credit rating and its ability to generate traffic.

Appraisal An opinion by an expert of the value of a property as of a specified date, supported by the presentation and analysis of relevant data. The appraisal may be arrived at by any or all of three methods: the cost approach (cost to reproduce), the market approach (comparison with other similar properties), or the income approach (capitalization of actual or projected income figures).

Assessed value The value of a property which is assigned to it by a taxing authority for purposes of assessing property taxes; often assessed value bears a fixed relationship by local statute to market value.

Asset swaps See swap program.

Assets Anything of value owned by the company. Assets are either financial, as cash or bonds; or physical, as real or personal property. For REIT tax purposes, more than 75% of the trust's assets must be property owned or securities backed by real estate.

Assumption of mortgage When the responsibility for repaying existing indebtedness secured by property is "assumed" by the second purchaser. In most jurisdictions, this relieves the first owner of the original obligations, at least to the extent that can be satisfied by sale of this asset after foreclosure.

Attribution More than 50% of a REIT's shares cannot be held by fewer than six people (otherwise it becomes a personal holding company for tax purposes). When someone has indirect control over someone else's shares (such as a trustee over shares held for the benefit of another) then "control" for personal holding company purposes may be "attributed." This complicated legal topic of "attribution" arises, however, only when the REIT's shares are held by a few.

Audit An examination of the financial status and operations of an enterprise, based mostly on the books of account, and undertaken to assure conformity to generally accepted accounting principles and to secure information for, or to check the accuracy of, the enterprise's balance sheet, income statement, and/or cash flow statement.

Balloon mortgage A mortgage loan which provides for periodic payments, which may include both interest and principal, but which leaves the loan less than fully amortized at maturity, requiring a final large payment which is the "balloon." Usually the term does not apply to an "interest only" loan whose full principal is due upon maturity or upon call during its life.

Bankrupt When liabilities exceed assets, Federal laws enable the entity to dissolve in an orderly fashion (Chapter VII), or permit a court officer to restructure the company into a survivor "going business" (Chapter X), or permit existing management to do the same under court supervision (Chapter XI), or to do so despite the preferred position of secured creditors if real property is the only asset of the business (Chapter XII).

Source: National Association of Real Estate Investment Trusts, 1129 Seventeenth Street, N.W., Washington, D.C. 20036.

Beneficial owner   The person who ultimately benefits from ownership of shares or other securities—in contrast to "nominees" (often pseudonyms for control of investment professionals so as to facilitate security transactions without having to track down beneficial owners to participate in each step of the procedures).

Blue sky laws   State laws regulating conditions of sale of securities of companies (particularly those just starting out of the "clear blue sky") for the protection of the investing public. National stock exchange rules usually supersede state laws pursuant to a "blue chip" exemption contained in such state laws. The federal securities laws dovetail with state laws and pertain to publicly held companies, primarily as to accounting and disclosure practices.

Bond   A debt certificate which (a) represents a loan to a trust, (b) bears interest, and (c) matures on a stated future date. Short term bonds (generally with a maturity of five years or less from the date of issuance) are often called notes. See debentures.

Book value per share   Shareholder equity as adjusted to tangible net worth (assets minus liabilities plus paid-in capital) per share outstanding.

Borrower   A person or entity who received something of value, ordinarily money, and is obligated to pay it back, as the debtor to the creditor, usually pursuant to a note or "IOU" containing terms and conditions.

Broker   A person who is paid to act as an intermediary in connection with a transaction, in contrast to a dealer or principal who buys or sells for his own account. In the REIT world, the term "broker" usually refers to a real estate salesman, although the term is also used for "stockbrokers" too.

Building lien   An encumbrance upon the property by the contractor or subcontractors. Also known as a "mechanic's" or "materialman's" lien.

Building permit   Written permission by the local municipality (usually through the building inspector or other agent) allowing construction work on a piece of property in accordance with plans which were submitted and conforming to local building codes and regulations.

Business trust   An unincorporated business in which assets are given to trustees for management to hold or to sell, as investments. The business trust form was first fully developed in Massachusetts, under common law, and the term "Massachusetts business trust" is sometimes used to describe entities formed in other states. It is a form of business through a trustee or trustees who hold legal title to the property of the business. Capital contributions are made to the trustees by the beneficiaries whose equitable title and interest in the property of the trust are evidenced by trust certificates, usually called shares of beneficial interest. The earnings of the trust are paid to them, as dividends are paid to stockholders. The beneficiaries generally enjoy limited liability, as the control and management of the trust rests solely with the trustees, but the trust form or organization can be distinguished from a corporation. Early REIT tax laws relied on this distinction to define eligible real estate operations.

Capital gain   The amount by which the net proceeds from resale of a capital item exceed the adjusted cost (or "book value") of the asset. If a capital asset is held for more than twelve months before disposition it is taxed on a more favorable basis than a gain after a shorter period of time.

Capitalization rate   The rate of return utilized to value a given cash flow, the sum of a Discount Rate and a Capital Recapture Rate. It is applied to any income stream with a finite term over which the invested principal is to be returned to the investor or lender.

Cash flow   The revenue remaining after all cash expenses are paid, i.e., non-cash charges such as depreciation are not included in the calculation.
   Cash flow per share. Cash flow divided by the common shares outstanding. Shareholders must make this computation themselves since the SEC has prohibited companies from stating this calculation.
   Net cash flow. Generally determined by net income plus depreciation less principal payments on long-term mortgages.

Cash on cash return   The "cash flow" from a property expressed as a percentage of the cash "equity" invested in a property.

Chapter X   See bankrupt.

Collateral   An item of value, such as real estate or securities, which a borrower pledges as security. A mortgage gives the creditor the right to seize the real estate collateral after non-performance of the debtor.

Commitment   A promise to make an investment at some time in the future if certain specified conditions are met. A REIT may charge a fee to the borrower at the time of making the commitment. A REIT's level of commitments minus expected repayments can be regarded as an indication of future funding requirements.
   "Take-out" commitment is one provided by the anticipated long-term lender, usually

with complicated terms and conditions that must be met before the "take-out" becomes effective.

"Gap" commitment is an anticipated short-term loan to cover part of the final "take-out" that the long-term lender refuses to advance until certain conditions are met (like 90% rent-up of an apartment after construction is completed). The amount above the "floor" or basic part of the loan is the "gap," and the gap commitment is issued to enable the construction lender to make a construction loan commitment for the full amount of the take-out loan instead of only for the "floor" amount.

"Standby" commitment is one that the lender and borrower doubt will be used. It exists as reassurance to a short-term construction lender that if, after completion of a building, the borrower cannot find adequate long-term "take-out" financing, the construction lender will be repaid.

Compensating balances   Money which is sometimes required by banks to be held in checking accounts by borrowers, as part of their loan agreement.

Condominium   A form of fee ownership of whole units or separate portions of multi-unit buildings which facilitates the formal filing, recording and financing of a divided interest in real property. The condominium concept may be used for apartments, offices and other professional uses. See cooperatives.

Conduit tax treatment   So long as most (if not all) earnings are passed along by an entity, then federal taxation is avoided at the entity's level. REITs, mutual funds, and certain kinds of holding companies are eligible for "conduit tax treatment" under certain conditions.

Constant   The agreed-upon periodic (usually monthly) payment to pay the face interest rate, with any residual amount going to amortize the loan.

Construction and development loan (C&D)   A short-term loan for the purpose of constructing a building, shopping center, or other improvement upon real estate, or developing a site in preparation for construction. A C&D loan is normally disbursed in increments (called *draws* or *draw-downs*) as building proceeds, rather than in a single disbursement, and is conditioned upon compliance with a variety of factors. It is usually repaid with the proceeds of the permanent loan. A land loan or purchase and development loan is sometimes made for the purpose of acquiring unimproved vacant land, usually as a future building site and for financing improvements to such land (street, sewers, etc.) as a prerequisite to construction of a building upon the site.

Contingent interest   Interest on a loan that is payable only if certain conditions occur, in contrast to interest that becomes an accrued liability (whether or not paid) at a specific time.

Cooperative   A form of ownership whereby a structure is owned by a corporation or trust with each individual owner holding stock in the corporation representative of the value of his apartment. Title to the apartment is evidenced by a proprietary lease which often does not qualify as adequate collateral for some lenders.

Cost-to-carry   The concept specified by the accounting profession to be used by REITs in computing anticipated interest cost on debt needed to "carry" non-earning or partially-earning assets until they're restored to earning status or sold.

Current liabilities   Money owed and due to be paid within one year.

Dealer   Someone who buys property with the purpose of selling it at a profit rather than holding it as an investment. A dealer's profits are taxed at the ordinary income rate rather than the capital gains rate regardless of how long the property is held for resale (in contrast to the investor who sells a property after a year and pays at the capital gains rate). A REIT is not permitted to be a dealer unless it is willing to pay a 100% tax on gains from such sales in the year in which it is deemed to be a dealer; sales of foreclosed property do not fall within this definition. See principal.

Debenture   An obligation which is secured only by the general credit of the issuing trust, as opposed to being secured by a direct lien on its assets, real estate or otherwise. A debenture is a form of a bond.

Declaration of trust   Similar to articles of incorporation for a corporation, this document contains rules for operation of the trust, selection of its governing trustees, etc., and is the keystone of a REIT.

Deed   A legal instrument which conveys title from one to another. It must be (a) made between competent parties (b) have legally sound subject matter (c) correctly state what is being conveyed (d) contain good and valuable consideration (e) be properly executed by the parties involved and (f) be delivered to be valid.

Deed in lieu of foreclosure   The device by which title to property is conveyed from the mortgagor (borrower) to the mortgagee (lender) as an alternative to foreclosure. While this procedure can transfer effective control more quickly, many lenders eschew it because undiscovered prior liens (from a workman who was never paid but hadn't gotten around to filing his valid, but late, claim for example) remain enforceable in contrast to the more formal foreclosure procedures which wipe out prior claims after due notice.

Deferred maintenance   The amount of repairs that should have been made to keep a property in good running condition, but which have been put off. The term contemplates the desirability of immediate expenditures, although it does not necessarily denote inadequate maintenance in the past.

Deficiency dividend   The process of paying an "extra" dividend after the close of the fiscal year so as to comply with REIT tax requirements to pay out more than 90% of income. See dividend.

Depreciation   The loss in value of a capital asset, due to wear and tear which cannot be compensated for by ordinary repairs, or an allowance made to allow for the fact that the asset may become obsolete before it wears out. The purpose of a depreciation charge is to write off the original cost of an asset by equitably distributing charges against its operation over its useful life, matching "cost" to the period in which it was used to generate earnings. Depreciation is an optional noncash expense recognizable for tax purposes. If the REIT pays out more than its taxable earnings, then it is distributing a "return of capital" or-as is commonly stated in the industry—"paying out depreciation."

Development loans   See construction and development loan.

Dilution   The situation which results when an increase occurs in a company's outstanding securities without a corresponding increase in the company's assets and/or income.

Discount rate   An interest rate used to convert a future system of payments into a single present value. See capitalization rate.

Dividend or distribution   The distribution of cash or stock to shareholders of a company which is made periodically as a means of distributing all or a portion of net income or cash flow. Technically, a dividend can be paid only from net taxable income, so many REITs distribute cash and later characterize their distributions as capital gains or a tax-free return of capital if net taxable income is less than the cash paid out.

Dividend or distribution yield   The annual dividend or distribution rate for a security expressed as a percent of its market price. For most REITs, the "annualized" rate is the previous quarter's distribution times four, regardless of how the distribution is characterized.

Draw   A request from a borrower to obtain partial payment from the lender pursuant to a loan commitment. The lender reassures himself that the borrower has completed the required steps (such as putting in the concrete properly) before advancing money. Often, the borrower submits bills from subcontractors, which are then "paid" by the lender after inspecting the subcontractor's work. In such cases, the check is usually made out to the subcontractor but must be signed by the borrower, too, so that the lender ends up only with one borrower. See construction and development loan.

Effective borrowing costs   The cost of borrowing after adjustment for compensating balances or fees in lieu of compensating balances, and selling expenses in the case of publicly sold debt.

Encumbrance   A legal right or interest in real estate which diminishes its value. Encumbrances can take a number of forms, such as easements, zoning restrictions, mortgages, etc.

Entrepreneur   An individual who is responsible for a commercial or real estate activity who takes a certain risk of loss in a transaction for the right to enjoy any profit which may result.

Equity   The interest of the shareholders in a company as measured by their paid-in capital and undistributed income. The term is also used to describe (i) the difference between the current market value of a property and the liens or mortgages which encumber it or (ii) the cash which makes up the difference between the mortgage(s) and the construction or sale price.

Equity leveraging   The process by which shares are sold at a premium above book value (in anticipation of greater earnings).

Equity participation   Usually, the right of an investor to participate to some extent in the increased value of a project by receiving a percentage of the increased income from the project. If a REIT were to participate in a percentage of the net income of a venture (such as the shopping center's owner/lessor), then it could be deemed to be a partner in an active business. Thus, most REIT leases spell out the "equity participation" as a percentage of gross receipts or sales (which is a more stable measure of sales activity, anyway, and one readily identifiable from the lessor's federal income tax statement).

Escrow   A deposit of "good faith" money which is entrusted to a third party (often a bank) until fulfillment of certain conditions and agreements, when the escrow may be released or applied as payment for the purchase of property or for services rendered.

Estoppel certificate An instrument used when a mortgage or lease is assigned to another. The certificate sets forth the exact remaining balance of the lease or mortgage as of a certain date and verifies any promises to tenants that may have been made by the first owner for which the second owner may be held accountable.

Exculpatory clause A clause which relieves one of liability for injuries or damages to another. Exculpatory clauses are placed in REIT documents with the intention of eliminating personal liability of its trustees, shareholders and officers.

Expenses The costs which are charges against current operations on earnings of a building, company or other reporting entity. They may have been "paid out" in cash, or accrued to be paid later, or charged as a bookkeeping procedure to reflect the "using up" of assets (as in depreciation) utilized in the production of income during the period of current operations.

Face value The value which is shown on the face of an instrument such as a bond, debenture or stock certificate. The "face rate" of a debt instrument is often known as its "coupon rate."

Fair market value See market value.

Fee or fee simple Title to a property which is absolute, good and marketable; ownership without condition.

Fiduciary A relationship of trust and confidence between a person charged with the duty of acting for the benefit of another and the person to whom such duty is owed, as in the case of guardian and ward, trustee and beneficiary, executor and heir.

First mortgage That mortgage which has a prior claim over all other liens against real estate. In some jurisdictions, real estate taxes, mechanics liens, court costs, and other involuntary liens may take priority over such a contractual lien: title companies "clear" properties so as to reassure first mortgage lenders (and owners) of their uncontested position and to guarantee them of that position under certain conditions.

Fiscal year The 12-month period selected as a basis for computing and accounting for a business. A fiscal year need not coincide with the calendar year, except for all REITs initially qualifying for special tax treatment after 1976.

Fixed assets Assets, such as land, buildings and machinery, which cannot be quickly converted into cash. For REITs, most "fixed assets" are real property although some (like furniture in an apartment lobby) may be personal property.

Fixed charges Those interest charges, insurance costs, taxes and other expenses which remain relatively constant regardless of revenue. See net lease.

Floating rate A variable interest rate charged for the use of borrowed money. It is determined by charging a specific percentage above a fluctuating base rate, usually the prime rate as announced by a major commercial bank.

Floor loan A portion or portions of a mortgage loan commitment which is less than the full amount of the commitment and which may be funded upon conditions less stringent than those required for funding the full amount, or the "ceiling" of the loan. For example, the floor loan, equal to perhaps 80% of the full amount of the loan, may be funded upon completion of construction without any occupancy requirements, but substantial occupancy of the building may be required for funding the full amount of the loan, which is referred to as the "ceiling." See commitment, gap.

Foreclosure The legal process of enforcing payment of a debt by taking the properties which secure the debt, once the terms of the obligation are not followed. Upon foreclosure, the entire debt might not be fully discharged by transfer and disposition of the property (as determined by the courts). If so, a "deficiency judgment" may be obtained, at which point the lender is like any other creditor in attempting to get the debtor to pay the deficiency. Collection of the deficiency judgment in major real estate transactions is rare, but it becomes a major factor in negotiations if the borrower decides to return to the real estate business in the future.

Fully diluted earnings The hypothetical earnings per share of a company, computed after giving effect to the number of shares which would be outstanding if all convertible debt and warrants were exercised, and also to any reduction in interest payments resulting from such exercise.

Gap commitment See commitment, gap. Also see floor loan.

General lien A lien against the property of an individual or other entity generally, rather than against specific items of realty or personal property.

Ground lease See sale-leaseback.

Holding company A corporation that owns or controls the operations of various other companies. Many REITs were sponsored by bank or insurance holding companies whose subsidiary companies advise and manage REITs, pursuant to contracts with the REIT's trustees.

Independent contractor A firm hired to actively manage property investments. A tax-qualified REIT must hire an independent contractor to manage and operate its property, so as to distinguish itself as an investor rather than an active manager.

Income property Developed real estate, such as office buildings, shopping centers, apartments, hotels and motels, warehouses and some kinds of agricultural or industrial property, which produce a flow of income—in contrast to non-income generating real estate like raw land which would be bought and held for a speculative profit upon resale or development.

Indenture The legal document prepared in connection with, for example, a bond issue, setting forth the terms of the issue, its specific security, remedies in case of default, etc. It may also be called the "deed of trust."

Indentured trustee A trustee, generally the trust department of a major bank, which represents the interest of bondholders under a publicly offered issue.

Insider A person close to a trust who has intimate knowledge of financial developments before they become public knowledge.

Interest rate The percentage rate which an individual pays for the use of borrowed money for a given period of time.

Intermediate-term loan A loan for a term of three to ten years which is usually not fully amortized at maturity. Often, developers will seek interim loans by which to pay off construction financing, in anticipation of obtaining long-term financing at a later date on more favorable terms, either because long-term rates decline generally or because the project can show an established, stable earnings history.

Interim loan A type of loan which is to be repaid out of the proceeds of another loan. Ordinarily, not self-liquidating (amortized), the lender evaluates the risk of obtaining refinancing as much as the period risk. See C&D loans.

Investment advisor See advisor.

Joint venture The entity which is created when two or more persons or corporate entities join together to carry out a specific business transaction of real estate development. A joint venture is usually of limited duration and usually for a specific property; it can be treated as a partnership for tax purposes. The parties have reciprocal and paralleling rights and obligations.

Junior mortgage loan Any mortgage loan in which the lien and the right of repayment are subordinate to that of another mortgage

loan or loans. A "second mortgage" is a junior mortgage. "Third, fourth," etc. mortgages are always deemed to be secondary.

Land loan See construction and development loan.

Land-purchase leaseback See sale-leaseback.

Late charge The charge which is levied against a borrower for a payment which was not made in a timely manner.

Lease A contract between the owner of property (lessor) and a tenant (lessee) setting forth the terms, conditions and consideration for the use of the property for a specified period of time at a specified rental. See sale-leaseback and net lease.

Leasehold improvements The cost of improvements or betterments to property leased for a period of years, often paid for by the tenant. Such improvements ordinarily become the property of the lessor (owner) on expiration of the lease; consequently their cost is normally amortized over the life of the lease if the lessor pays for them.

Leverage The process of borrowing upon one's capital base with the expectation of generating a profit above the cost of borrowing.

Liability management The aspect of the management of a company concerned with the planning and procurement of funds for investment through the sale of equity, public debt and bank borrowings. In the REIT industry, the phrase contrasts to "asset management" or the real estate side of the business.

Line of credit Usually, an agreement between a commercial bank and a borrower under which the bank agrees to provide unsecured credit to the borrower upon certain terms and conditions. Normally, the borrower may draw on all or any part of the credit from time to time.

Limited partnership A partnership which limits certain of the partners' (the limited partners) liability to the amount of their investment. At least one partner (the "general partner") is fully liable for the obligations of the partnership and its operations, usually with the limited partners participating as investors only.

Loan loss reserve A reserve set up to offset asset values in anticipation of losses that are reasonably expected. Initially, REITs had insufficient operating experience to anticipate losses in any one class of investments or for a portfolio as a whole, so tax authorities would not permit substantial contributions toward a reserve as an allowable period expense. When difficulties arose, the conversion of short-term loans to longer-term property holdings required some form of recognition of likely losses in the financial statements. A novel procedure for REITs was devised by requiring, for book purposes, computation of additions to the reserve based in part on the probable cost of sustaining the troubled assets over the longer period of time necessary to "cure" the problem. Also known as "allowance for losses."

Loan run-off The rate at which an existing mortgage portfolio will reduce (or "run-off") to zero if no new loans are added to the portfolio.

Loan swaps See asset swaps.

Long-term mortgage Any financing, whether in the form of a first or junior mortgage, the term of which is ten years or more. It is generally fully amortized.

Loss carry forwards The net operating loss (NOL) incurred in prior years, which may be applied for tax purposes against future earnings, thereby reducing taxable income. For REITs (which must pay out most of their taxable income), NOLs can be carried forward eight years; for non-REIT-taxed companies, NOL can be carried forward for only seven years.

Market value The highest price in terms of money which a property will bring in a competitive and open market under all conditions requisite to a fair sale—the buyer and the seller each acting prudently, knowledgeably, and at arm's length. See appraisal.

Moratorium A period in which payments of debts or other performance of a legal obligation is suspended temporarily, usually because of unforeseen circumstances which make timely payment or performance difficult or impossible. This forebearance can be whole or partial.

Mortgage A publicly recorded lien by which the property is pledged as security for the payment of a debt valid even beyond death ("mort" is death in French). In some states a mortgage is an actual conveyance of the property to the creditor until the terms of the mortgage are satisfied. While there is always a "note" secured by a mortgage document, both the note and mortgage instrument are commonly called "the mortgage." For types, see: first, junior, short-term, long-term, wrap-around and construction and development mortgage definitions.

Mortgage banker A non-depository lender who makes loans secured by real estate and then usually packages and sells those loans in large groups to institutional investors, pursuant to a "long-term commitment" he has negotiated with the life insurance company or other institutional investor. Mortgage bankers frequently arrange to service these mortgages for the out-of-town institutions, collecting regular payments, keeping the lender up to date on the progress of the loan, escrowing payments for taxes and insurance premiums, and, if necessary, administering foreclosure proceedings. Many REITs were sponsored by mortgage bankers.

Mortgage constant The total annual payments of principal and interest (annual debt service) on a mortgage with level-payment amortization schedule, expressed as a percentage of the initial principal amount of the loan.

Mortgagee in possession A lender or one who holds a mortgage who has taken possession of a property in order to protect an interest in the property. Usually, this is done with commercial properties as to which rents, management fees and other disbursements continue even if the mortgage is in default. The possession must be taken with the consent of the mortgagor (or a court, in cases of foreclosure) and the mortgagee must be careful to do only those things to the property that the mortgagor (or court) will agree to accept, should it resume its role as a creditworthy owner.

Net income The dollar amount that remains after all expenses, including taxes, are deducted from gross income. For regular companies, it is also called after-tax profit, the "bottom line" figure of how a company has performed with its investors' money. For REITs, it is net taxable income which, if fully distributed, is not taxed.

Net lease A lease, sometimes called a net-net (insurance and taxes) or even a net-net-net lease (insurance, taxes, and maintenance) in which the tenant pays all costs, including insurance, taxes, repairs, upkeep and other expenses, and the rental payments are "net" of all these expenses. See lease and fixed charges.

Net worth The remaining asset value of a property company or other entity after deduction of all liabilities against it.

Non-accrual loans See non-earning investments.

Non-earning investments The category of loans or investments which are not earning the originally anticipated rate of return. Some may be characterized as "partially earning." When interest is recorded as earned rather than as received (accrued interest), "non-accrual investments" are those which management expects not to receive interest as originally contemplated. In the vernacular, non-earning investments are "problem loans" or "troubled properties."

Non-qualified REIT   A REIT that was formerly qualified, or conducts its affairs as if it is qualified, but that has elected for the tax year in question to be treated like a normal business corporation for tax purposes. Thus, some restraints (primarily against active management and holding property for sale) are lifted, while REIT conduit tax treatment is lost.

Occupancy rate   The amount of space or number of apartments or offices or hotel rooms which are rented as compared with the total amount or number available. The rate is usually expressed as a percentage.

Operating expenses   Expenses arising out of or relating to business activity such as interest expense, professional fees, salaries, etc.

Operating income   Income received directly from business activity in the normal course, as contrasted with capital gains income, or other extraordinary income.

Option   A right to buy or lease property at a certain specified price for specified terms. Consideration is typically given for the option, which is exercisable over a limited time span. If the option is not exercised, the consideration is forfeited. A loan to a developer secured by his option to obtain real estate is considered a "qualified" REIT asset.

Origination   The process by which a loan is created, including the search for (or receipt of) the initial plans, the analysis and structuring of the proposed financing, and the review and acceptance procedures by which the commitment to make the investment is finally issued.

Overage income   Rental income above a guaranteed minimum depending on a particular level of profit or retail sales volume by the tenant, payable under the terms of a lease.

Participations   A lender often "participates out" or sells a portion of his loan to another lender while retaining a portion and managing the investment. REITs buy real estate secured participations as well as originating them.

Par value   The face value assigned to a security when it is issued. The stated par value of a security generally has nothing to do with its market or book value.

Passivity   The state of owning investments but not actively managing them (as a property management firm does for the investor) or engaging in trading the securities (like a broker or dealer). This "passivity" test is implicit behind several of the REIT tax requirements.

Pension funds   Money which is accumulated in trust to fund pensions for companies or unions and which is frequently invested in part in real estate. A co-mingled real estate pension fund account is managed, usually under contract to a financial institution, much like a REIT except that its shares are not publicly traded but instead sold to other pension funds.

Permanent financing   See long-term loan.

Point   An amount which represents 1% of the maximum principal amount of an investment. Used in connection with a discount from, or a share of, a principal amount deducted at the time funds are advanced, it represents additional compensation to the lender.

Portfolio   The investments of a company, including investments in mortgages and/or ownership of real property. REIT portfolios usually consist of equity in property, short-term mortgages, long-term mortgages and/or subordinated land sale-leasebacks.

Portfolio turnover   The average length of time from the funding of investments until they are paid off or sold.

Preferred shares   Stocks which have prior claim on distributions (and/or assets in the event of dissolution) up to a certain definite amount before the shares of beneficial interest are entitled to anything. As a form of ownership, preferred shares stand behind senior subordinated and secured debtholders in dissolution, as well as other creditors.

Prepayment penalty   The penalty which is imposed on the borrower for payment of the mortgage before it is due. Often a mortgage contains a clause specifying that there is to be no prepayment penalty, or limits the prepayment penalty to only the first few years of the mortgage term.

Price earnings ratio   A ratio which consists of the market price divided by current annualized earnings per share. Such a computation is now found in most daily stock listings. For REITs, annualization of quarterly earnings is computed by multiplying the most recent distribution by four, regardless of the distribution's later characterization as a dividend, return-of-capital, or capital gains.

Prime lending rate   The rate at which commercial banks will lend money from time to time to their most creditworthy customers, used as a base for most loans to financial intermediaries such as REITs.

Principal   The buyer or seller in a real estate transaction as distinguished from an agent.

Principal   The sum of money loaned. The amount of money to be repaid on a loan excluding interest charges.

Prior lien   A lien or mortgage ranking ahead of some other lien. A prior lien need not itself be a first mortgage.

Pro forma   Projected or hypothetical as opposed to actual as related, for example, to a balance sheet or income statement.

Problem investments   See non-earning investments.

Prospectus   A document describing an investment opportunity; the detailed description of new securities which must be supplied to prospective interstate purchasers under the Securities Act of 1933.

Provision for loan losses   Periodic allocation of funds to loan loss reserves in recognition of a decline in the value of a loan or loans in a trust's portfolio due to a default on the part of the borrowers.

Proxy   An authorization given by a registered security holder to vote stock at the annual meeting or at a special meeting of security holders.

Purchase and leaseback   See sale-leaseback.

Pyramiding   In stock market transactions, this term refers to the practice of borrowing against unrealized "paper" profits in securities to make additional purchases. In corporate finance, it refers to the practice of creating a speculative capital structure by a series of holding companies, whereby a relatively small amount of voting stock in the parent company controls a large corporate system. In real estate, it refers to the practice of financing 100% or more of the value of the property.

Qualified assets   Assets which meet tax requirements for special REIT tax treatment, i.e. real property. In any tax year, 75% of a REIT's assets must be invested in real property, either through ownership or by securities secured by real estate. A "partially qualified" asset is one that qualifies under the 90% test of being a passive investment in a security, but not under the 75% real estate test.

Qualified income   That portion of income which is classified as interest, rents, or other gain from real property, as spelled out in the REIT tax laws.

Raw land   Land which has not been developed or improved.

RCA   See revolving credit agreement.

Real estate investment trust (REIT, pronounced "reet")   A trust established for the benefit of a group of investors which is managed by one or more trustees who hold title to the assets for the trust and control its acquisitions and investments, at least 75% of which are real estate related. A major advantage of a REIT is that no federal income tax need be paid by the trust if certain qualifications are met. Congress enacted these special tax provisions to encourage an assembly method, which is essentially designed to provide for investment in real estate what the mutual provided for investment in securities. The REIT provides the small investor with a means of combining his funds with those of others, and protects him from the double taxation that would be levied against an ordinary corporation or trust.

Revolving credit agreement (or "revolver")   A formal credit agreement between a group of banks and a REIT, the terms of which are reviewed periodically when it is "rolled over" or "revolved" or refinanced by a similar agreement. For many trusts, "revolvers" have replaced informal lines of credit extended by individual banks to REITs, thereby providing a uniform (and usually restrictive) approach by all creditors, reassuring each bank that others in the RCA would not be paid off preferentially.

Registration statement   The forms filed by a company with the Securities and Exchange Commission in connection with an offering of new securities or the listing of outstanding securities on a national exchange.

Reserves for loss   See loan loss reserve.

Return of capital   A distribution to shareholders in excess of the trust's earnings and profits, usually consisting of either depreciation or repayment of principal from properties or mortgages held by the trust. Each shareholder receiving such a distribution is required to reduce the tax basis of his shares by the amount of such distribution. For financial accounting purposes, what constitutes a return of capital may differ from that determined under Federal income tax requirements.

Return on equity   A figure which consists of net income for the period divided by equity and which is normally expressed as a percentage.

Right of first refusal   The right or option granted by a seller to a buyer, to have the first opportunity of acquiring a property.

Rights offering   The privilege extended to a shareholder of subscribing to additional stock of the same or another class or to bonds, usually at a price below the market and in an amount proportional to the number of shares already held. Rights must be exercised within a time limit and often may be sold if the holder does not wish to purchase additional shares.

Sale-leaseback   A common real estate transaction whereby the investor buys property from, and simultaneously leases it back to, the seller. This enables the previous owner (often a developer) to "cash out" on an older property while retaining control.

Land sale-leaseback-this procedure, made common by several REITs that specialize in the transaction, affects only the land under income-producing improvements (such as shopping centers, etc.)-leaving the depreciable improvements in the hands of those who might benefit from the tax consequences. Since the improvements were probably financed with the proceeds of a first mortgage which remains in effect, the rights of the new investor are made second, or junior, to those of the first mortgage holder. Hence the common phrase "subordinated land sale-leaseback." In return for accepting a less secure position, the new investor usually obtains an "overage" clause whereby additional rent is paid anytime gross income of the shopping center (or whatever) exceeds a pre-determined floor.

Seasoned issues   Securities of large, established companies which have been known to the investment public for a period of years, covering good times and bad.

Second mortgages   See junior mortgage loan.

Secured mortgages   See junior mortgage loan.

Secured debt   For REITs, senior mortgage debt secured by specific properties. In case of default on "nonrecourse" debt, the lender may assume property ownership but may not pursue other assets of the lender.

Senior mortgage   A mortgage which has first priority.

Senior unsecured debt   Funds borrowed under open lines without security. Most bank lines to REITs were unsecured.

Shares of beneficial interest   Tradable shares in a REIT. Analogous to common stock in a corporation.

Shareholders' equity   Primarily money invested by shareholders through purchase of shares, plus the accumulation of that portion of net income that has been reinvested in the business since the commencement of operations.

Short-term mortgage   A loan upon real estate for a term of three years or less, bearing interest payable periodically, with principal usually payable in full at maturity.

Sinking fund   An arrangement under which a portion of a bond or preferred stock issue is retired periodically, in advance of its fixed maturity. The company may either purchase a stipulated quantity of the issue itself, or supply funds to a trustee or agent for that purpose. Retirement may be made by call at a fixed price, or by inviting tenders, or by purchase in the open market.

Sponsor   The entity which initiated the formation of a REIT and usually acts (often via a subsidiary) as investment advisor to the trust thereafter. The sponsor puts the reputation of its institution on the line for the REIT and usually arranges lines of credit, provides support services and, occasionally, compensating balances.

Spread   Difference between percentage return on an investment and cost of funds to support the investment.

Standby commitment   See commitment, standby.

Standing loan   Usually not amortized, the loan is secured by completed property that has not yet been refinanced with a "permanent" long-term mortgage.

Subordinated debt   Debt which is junior to secured and unsecured senior debt, it may be convertible into shares of beneficial interest for REITs. Senior subordinated debt is senior to other subordinated debt.

Subordinated ground lease   See sale-leaseback.

Swap program   A procedure for reducing debt (by a troubled REIT) by trading an asset to the creditor in return for cancellation of part of a loan to the REIT. Often a cash premium payment is made in addition to reduction of the debt. The premium may then be distributed to the other creditors pro rata. The amount of the cash premium, or the ratio of cash-to-debt reduction to be applied against the value of the asset, is sometimes determined by a sealed-bid "auction" process as set forth in the "revolving credit agreement" between the creditors and the REIT. See RCA.

Syndicate   A group of investors who transact business for a limited period of time and sometimes with a single purpose. It is a short-term partnership.

Take-out commitment   See commitment.

Tax shelter   The various aspects of an investment which offer relief from income taxes or opportunities to claim deductions from taxable income. Although tax shelters are an important facet of real estate investment, they do not have a direct influence on REIT investment choices because qualified trusts are exempt from income taxes.

Usury   The charging of interest rates for the use of money higher than what's allowed by local law.

Warrants   Stock purchase warrants or options give the holder rights to purchase shares of stock, generally running for a longer period of time than ordinary subscription rights given shareholders. Warrants are often attached to other securities, but they may be issued separately or detached after issuance.

Working capital   Determined by subtracting current liabilities from current assets. It represents the amount available to carry on the day-to-day operation of the business.

Work-out   When a borrower has problems, the process undertaken by the lender to help the borrower "work out" of the problems becomes known itself as a "work out." The presumption during a "work out" is that the borrower will eventually resume a more normal debtor's position once problems are solved within (presumably) a reasonably short time.

Wrap-around mortgage   A type of junior mortgage used to refinance properties on which there is an existing first mortgage loan. The face amount of the wrap-around loan is equivalent to the unpaid balance on the existing mortgage plus cash advanced to the property owner upon funding. Such loans carry a higher interest rate than the existing mortgage. The wrap-around lender assumes the obligation to maintain payments of principal and interest on the existing mortgage so as to enhance his right to make claim from his secondary position.

Yield   In the stock market, the rate of annual distribution or dividend expressed as a percentage of price. Current yield is found by dividing the market price into the distribution rate in dollars. In real estate, the term refers to the effective annual amount of income which is being accrued on an investment expressed as a percentage of its value.

100 LEADING NATIONAL ADVERTISERS

Rank 1993	Rank 1992	Company	Headquarters	Total U.S. ad spending 1993	1992	% chg	Unmeasured spending 1993	1992	% chg	Total measured media 1993	1992	Measured magazine & newspaper 1993	1992	% chg	Measured TV, cable & radio 1993	1992	% chg
1	1	Procter & Gamble Co.	Cincinnati	$2,397.5	$2,164.3	10.8	$1,096.1	$989.5	10.8	$1,301.4	$1,174.8	$205.6	$179.7	14.4	$1,095.7	$995.0	10.1
2	2	Philip Morris Cos.	New York	1,844.3	1,977.5	-6.7	843.2	904.1	-6.6	1,001.1	1,073.4	224.0	239.7	-6.6	729.8	773.8	-5.7
3	3	General Motors Corp.	Detroit	1,539.2	1,345.2	14.4	411.6	359.7	14.4	1,127.6	985.5	398.5	312.5	27.5	727.9	669.4	8.7
4	4	Sears, Roebuck & Co.	Chicago	1,310.1	1,166.3	12.4	714.2	635.5	14.7	596.5	530.8	222.1	193.6	14.7	374.3	337.0	11.1
5	5	PepsiCo	Purchase, N.Y.	1,038.9	929.6	11.8	405.2	371.9	11.8	633.7	557.7	14.3	8.0	78.6	611.5	545.9	12.0
6	6	Ford Motor Co.	Dearborn, Mich.	958.3	794.8	20.6	214.7	178.1	20.6	743.6	616.7	279.7	215.9	29.5	463.6	400.2	15.8
7	18	AT&T Corp.	New York	812.1	623.7	30.2	296.8	227.9	30.2	515.3	395.8	107.3	95.7	12.1	406.9	299.7	35.8
8	10	Nestle SA	Vevey, Switzerland	793.7	731.1	8.6	387.1	356.6	8.6	406.6	374.5	132.3	127.8	3.5	274.2	246.4	11.3
9	11	Johnson & Johnson	New Brunswick, N.J.	762.5	717.4	6.3	376.5	354.2	6.3	386.0	363.2	57.8	68.9	-16.2	328.2	294.2	11.6
10	7	Chrysler Corp.	Highland Park, Mich.	761.6	756.3	0.7	166.8	165.6	0.7	594.8	590.7	177.9	174.6	1.9	416.3	415.9	0.1
11	8	Warner-Lambert Co.	Morris Plains, N.J.	751.0	751.0	-0.0	494.1	491.9	-0.0	256.9	259.1	28.2	30.6	-7.7	228.6	228.4	0.1
12	12	Unilever NV	London/Rotterdam	738.2	690.4	6.9	276.4	258.5	6.9	461.8	431.9	113.9	93.0	22.5	347.7	338.8	2.6
13	9	McDonald's Corp.	Oak Brook, Ill.	736.6	743.6	-0.9	325.9	329.0	-0.9	410.7	414.6	8.6	8.9	-3.3	387.9	393.2	-1.4
14	16	Time Warner	New York	695.1	637.9	9.0	326.8	299.9	9.0	368.3	338.0	141.9	113.1	25.5	225.9	224.0	0.9
15	14	Toyota Motor Corp.	Toyota City, Japan	690.4	648.9	6.4	207.1	194.7	6.4	483.3	454.2	161.0	137.0	17.5	322.1	316.8	1.7
16	21	Walt Disney Co.	Burbank, Calif.	675.7	553.0	22.2	270.3	262.1	22.2	405.4	290.9	90.3	61.9	45.9	314.3	226.6	38.7
17	15	Grand Metropolitan	London	652.9	646.3	1.0	365.6	361.9	1.0	287.3	284.4	69.8	64.5	8.1	211.8	213.8	-0.9
18	17	Kellogg Co.	Battle Creek, Mich.	627.1	630.3	-0.5	213.2	214.3	-0.5	413.9	416.0	9.3	8.3	12.4	404.6	407.7	-0.8
19	13	Eastman Kodak Co.	Rochester, N.Y.	624.7	686.0	-8.9	419.7	460.9	-8.9	205.0	225.1	27.9	45.9	-39.3	176.4	178.2	-1.0
20	25	Sony Corp.	Tokyo	589.0	517.0	13.9	212.2	186.3	13.9	376.8	330.7	190.1	169.3	12.3	185.4	160.8	15.3
21	23	J.C. Penney Co.	Dallas	585.2	537.4	8.9	319.4	293.3	8.9	265.8	244.1	101.7	100.8	0.9	164.1	143.2	14.5
22	19	General Mills	Minneapolis	569.2	572.3	-0.5	139.8	140.6	-0.5	429.4	431.7	33.9	20.9	62.0	394.6	410.3	-3.8
23	22	Kmart Corp.	Troy, Mich.	558.2	537.7	3.8	264.2	254.5	3.8	294.0	283.2	153.4	155.7	-1.5	140.1	127.1	10.2
24	20	Anheuser-Busch Cos.	St. Louis	520.5	556.6	-6.5	208.2	197.6	5.4	312.3	359.0	12.8	27.1	-52.7	288.3	321.0	-10.2
25	24	American Home Products Corp.	New York	501.6	529.0	-5.2	220.7	185.1	19.2	280.9	343.9	35.6	26.6	34.0	245.2	317.3	-22.7
26	26	RJR Nabisco	Winston-Salem, N.C.	499.4	496.2	0.6	199.8	248.1	-19.5	299.6	248.1	82.9	63.5	30.5	197.1	155.0	27.2
27	31	Nissan Motor Co.	Tokyo	413.1	370.7	11.4	87.4	78.5	11.4	325.7	292.2	115.2	85.2	35.2	210.4	206.2	2.0
28	30	May Department Stores Co.	St. Louis	403.6	382.7	5.5	40.4	38.3	5.5	363.2	344.4	317.5	309.8	2.5	45.7	34.5	32.5
29	37	Matsushita Electric Industrial Co.	Osaka, Japan	385.1	312.0	23.4	192.7	156.1	23.4	192.4	155.9	68.2	49.8	37.0	121.6	103.3	17.8
30	27	Ralston Purina Co.	St. Louis	372.8	411.5	-9.4	238.6	263.4	-9.4	134.2	148.1	37.2	51.1	-27.3	96.9	96.9	-0.0
31	29	Hershey Foods Corp.	Hershey, Pa.	366.3	383.0	-4.3	271.1	288.2	-5.9	95.2	94.8	10.6	10.1	5.0	84.6	84.6	-0.0
32	33	Honda Motor Co.	Tokyo	354.4	349.1	1.5	96.4	95.0	1.5	258.0	254.1	79.6	70.9	12.3	178.2	182.8	-2.6
33	28	Coca-Cola Co.	Atlanta	341.3	392.0	-12.9	153.6	158.6	-3.2	187.7	233.4	9.1	20.5	-55.7	176.8	211.1	-16.3
34	35	Mars Inc.	McLean, Va.	337.6	320.4	5.4	167.1	158.6	5.4	170.5	161.8	8.9	11.7	-24.4	161.4	149.9	7.7
35	39	American Express Co.	New York	324.8	294.6	10.3	94.2	109.0	-13.6	230.6	185.6	95.9	86.4	11.0	134.6	99.0	35.9
36	38	H.J. Heinz Co.	Pittsburgh	318.9	299.2	6.6	239.2	242.0	-1.2	79.7	57.2	8.0	8.6	-7.4	71.7	48.5	47.8
37	43	Circuit City Stores	Richmond, Va.	308.5	261.1	18.1	46.3	26.1	77.4	262.2	235.0	210.8	187.9	12.2	51.5	47.1	9.2
38	34	U.S. Government	Washington	304.4	342.4	-11.1	123.0	138.4	-11.1	181.4	204.0	72.7	73.6	-1.2	108.1	129.8	-16.7
39	32	Sara Lee Corp.	Chicago	299.7	359.2	-16.6	157.5	188.8	-16.6	142.2	170.4	30.3	35.2	-13.9	111.8	134.9	-17.2
40	77	MCI Communications Corp.	Washington	297.4	162.2	83.3	89.2	56.8	57.0	208.2	105.4	12.7	4.1	213.8	194.8	100.8	93.3
41	36	Colgate-Palmolive Co.	New York	287.4	315.5	-8.9	198.5	217.9	-8.9	88.9	97.6	22.4	13.1	70.5	66.5	83.4	-21.1
42	49	Nike Inc.	Beaverton, Ore.	281.4	230.9	21.9	143.3	117.6	21.9	138.1	113.3	46.0	40.0	15.1	90.6	73.1	24.0
43	42	R.H. Macy & Co.	New York	280.5	270.4	3.7	68.1	65.7	3.7	212.4	204.7	192.7	177.4	8.7	19.3	27.2	-29.1
44	46	Hasbro Inc.	Pawtucket, R.I.	277.3	244.7	13.3	55.5	49.0	13.3	221.8	195.7	12.4	10.9	13.4	209.4	184.8	13.3
45	40	SmithKline Beecham	London	269.7	291.8	-7.6	156.4	175.1	-7.6	113.3	116.7	7.5	9.9	-24.5	105.8	106.8	-0.9

Rank	'92 Rank	Company	Headquarters													
46	48	Dayton Hudson Corp.	Minneapolis	266.7	230.9	15.5	55.9	48.4	210.8	182.5	145.0	121.8	19.1	64.9	60.1	8.0
47	56	Sprint Corp.	Shawnee Mission, Kan.	264.8	207.6	27.6	113.9	98.9	150.9	108.7	26.2	14.1	86.3	124.5	94.4	31.9
48	51	Wal-Mart Stores	Bentonville, Ark.	251.9	222.4	13.3	145.4	128.4	106.5	94.0	19.1	20.1	-4.8	87.3	73.8	18.3
49	41	Bristol-Myers Squibb Co.	New York	250.2	280.1	-10.7	119.6	133.9	130.6	146.2	26.4	32.6	-19.1	104.2	113.5	-8.2
50	54	Levi Strauss & Co.	San Francisco	248.9	213.0	16.8	145.3	124.4	103.6	88.6	13.5	19.4	-30.3	39.5	68.3	31.1
51	44	Quaker Oats Co.	Chicago	246.5	257.0	-4.1	130.7	136.2	115.8	120.8	27.9	31.9	-12.5	87.7	88.6	-1.0
52	47	News Corp.	Sydney	243.5	233.5	4.3	60.9	58.4	182.6	175.1	59.2	47.5	24.7	122.9	126.8	-3.1
53	53	Schering-Plough Corp.	Madison, N.J.	233.1	214.0	8.9	114.2	110.6	118.9	103.4	36.8	20.5	79.4	82.1	82.9	-1.0
54	52	Mazda Motor Corp.	Hiroshima, Japan	228.0	215.4	5.8	61.3	57.9	166.7	157.5	45.2	66.0	-31.5	121.5	91.4	32.9
55	65	Tandy Corp.	Fort Worth, Texas	223.1	183.3	21.7	107.0	87.9	116.1	95.4	68.2	72.1	-5.5	47.9	23.1	107.4
56	50	Federated Department Stores	Cincinnati	223.0	226.3	-1.4	44.6	27.1	178.4	199.2	159.0	179.8	-11.6	19.4	19.4	0.2
57	60	U.S. dairy farmers	Arlington, Va.	215.1	192.1	12.0	98.9	88.3	116.2	103.8	8.4	16.6	-49.4	106.1	85.7	23.8
58	59	S.C. Johnson & Son	Racine, Wis.	209.9	194.6	7.9	97.6	90.5	112.3	104.1	7.2	17.9	-59.8	105.0	86.0	22.1
59	45	General Electric Co.	New York	204.8	251.6	-18.6	108.0	132.6	96.8	119.0	43.9	60.2	-27.2	51.7	57.1	-9.5
60	70	Mattel	Hawthorne, Calif.	201.1	173.0	16.3	60.7	52.2	140.4	120.8	13.0	16.3	-20.6	127.4	104.4	22.0
61	69	Joh. A. Benckiser GmbH	Ludwigshafen, Germany	199.2	173.4	14.9	99.6	86.7	99.6	86.7	56.2	35.1	60.0	43.4	51.6	-15.9
62	76	Clorox Co.	Oakland, Calif.	198.3	162.9	21.7	59.5	48.9	138.8	114.0	21.2	14.8	44.0	117.5	99.3	18.4
63	58	Adolph Coors Co.	Golden, Colo.	197.8	195.0	1.5	81.1	72.2	116.7	122.8	4.1	6.5	-36.6	107.5	113.5	-5.3
64	57	ITT Corp.	New York	196.2	206.8	-5.1	144.2	152.0	52.0	54.8	29.7	26.3	13.0	21.8	28.0	-21.9
65	62	Helene Curtis Industries	Chicago	192.6	189.5	1.6	80.9	79.6	111.7	109.9	28.9	27.9	3.6	82.8	82.0	0.9
66	75	Paramount Communications	New York	185.3	166.3	11.4	73.2	65.7	112.1	100.6	37.3	24.7	50.6	73.3	74.7	-1.9
67	63	ConAgra	Omaha	183.2	188.4	-2.8	101.1	104.0	82.1	84.4	21.0	12.6	66.4	61.0	70.9	-13.9
68	61	Ciba-Geigy	Basel, Switzerland	182.7	191.2	-4.4	105.5	110.4	77.2	80.8	31.1	41.4	-24.9	46.1	39.4	17.1
69	64	IBM Corp.	Armonk, N.Y.	171.8	186.2	-7.7	78.7	85.3	93.1	100.9	60.6	78.8	-23.1	31.8	21.5	48.0
70	105	Citicorp	New York	169.8	107.9	57.4	40.0	29.1	129.8	78.8	57.7	40.9	41.1	72.1	37.7	91.3
71	74	Broadway Stores	Los Angeles	169.5	166.4	1.9	48.1	47.2	121.4	119.2	109.2	110.2	-0.9	12.1	9.0	35.4
72	82	Wendy's International	Dublin, Ohio	168.3	142.6	18.0	37.0	34.1	131.3	108.5	1.1	0.8	26.8	127.9	105.4	21.4
73	71	Gillette Co.	Boston	167.2	171.6	-2.6	71.9	84.1	95.3	87.5	23.0	21.7	6.1	72.2	65.8	9.8
74	67	Goodyear Tire & Rubber Co.	Akron, Ohio	163.1	178.1	-8.5	79.9	103.3	83.2	74.8	26.0	16.9	54.5	57.0	57.8	-1.5
75	90	Roll International	Los Angeles	160.1	133.1	20.3	32.1	26.7	128.0	106.4	127.9	106.3	20.4	0.1	0.2	-43.7
76	78	Philips NV	Eindhoven, The Netherlands	158.3	161.6	-2.1	78.9	80.6	79.4	81.0	20.5	22.4	-8.5	58.8	58.6	0.3
77	55	Campbell Soup Co.	Camden, N.J.	150.1	209.7	-28.4	50.0	69.9	100.1	139.8	25.5	51.8	-50.8	74.6	88.1	-15.3
78	85	Upjohn Co.	Kalamazoo, Mich.	146.5	138.0	6.2	61.6	58.0	84.9	80.0	31.2	12.3	152.8	53.7	67.6	-20.5
79	94	Bayer AG	Leverkusen, Germany	145.3	125.9	15.4	59.8	51.8	85.5	74.1	7.7	4.9	55.6	77.8	69.1	12.7
80	88	Wm. Wrigley Jr. Co.	Chicago	144.9	134.0	8.2	26.1	14.7	118.8	119.3	4.8	8.8	-46.0	113.3	109.9	3.1
81	68	American Stores Co.	Salt Lake City, Utah	143.0	177.0	-19.2	44.8	55.4	98.2	121.6	40.5	60.7	-33.3	56.6	60.4	-6.2
82	66	American Brands	New York	142.7	178.2	-19.9	79.3	85.5	63.4	92.7	44.6	69.0	-35.3	12.5	11.9	4.8
83	83	Marriott International	Washington	132.6	138.8	-4.4	86.2	90.2	46.4	48.6	37.4	37.2	0.5	8.8	11.0	-19.9
84	84	AMR Corp.	Dallas	131.3	138.6	-5.3	39.4	39.4	91.9	101.4	50.3	68.2	-26.3	41.6	33.1	25.7
85	80	CPC International	Englewood Cliffs, N.J.	129.4	145.4	-11.0	84.1	101.8	45.3	43.6	5.0	5.3	-4.5	40.2	38.3	5.0
86	111	Apple Computer	Cupertino, Calif.	129.1	99.0	30.4	62.0	54.5	67.1	44.5	36.0	35.9	0.4	31.1	8.2	279.3
87	86	Seagram Co.	Montreal	126.8	136.9	-7.4	40.6	35.0	86.2	101.9	48.4	51.6	-6.2	34.3	44.9	-23.6
88	98	Dr Pepper/Seven-Up Cos.	Dallas	125.5	115.3	8.9	44.4	40.8	81.1	74.5	1.2	0.6	119.0	79.8	73.6	8.3
89	73	Dow Chemical Co.	Midland, Mich.	125.1	168.0	-25.5	32.0	43.0	93.1	125.0	35.2	49.4	-28.8	57.9	75.6	-23.4
90	93	Loews Corp.	New York	124.5	128.8	-3.3	55.0	56.9	69.5	71.9	34.6	37.8	-8.6	7.3	7.7	-5.8
91	119	Visa International	San Francisco	122.5	95.2	28.6	30.6	27.1	91.9	68.1	8.8	3.7	138.7	83.1	64.5	28.9
92	112	Kimberly-Clark Corp.	Irving, Texas	119.8	99.0	21.1	24.8	20.5	95.0	78.5	29.2	24.3	20.3	65.8	54.2	21.5
93	97	U.S. Shoe Corp.	Cincinnati	118.8	117.7	1.0	52.3	64.7	66.5	53.0	19.2	11.2	71.8	47.2	41.6	13.4
94	114	Imasco	Montreal	117.6	98.8	19.1	47.0	39.5	70.6	59.3	0.2	0.4	-38.6	68.2	56.7	20.3
95	151	B.A.T Industries	London	116.9	73.7	58.6	52.5	33.1	64.4	40.6	35.6	21.1	69.2	8.0	9.1	-12.2
96	107	Daimler-Benz AG	Stuttgart, Germany	116.6	100.8	15.7	30.2	26.1	86.4	74.7	47.4	45.9	3.2	38.9	28.6	36.2
97	129	Bally Manufacturing Corp.	Chicago	115.1	85.3	34.9	62.9	46.6	52.2	38.7	10.1	7.4	35.3	42.0	31.1	35.0
98	110	Pfizer Inc.	New York	114.9	99.2	15.8	56.3	54.6	58.6	44.6	13.4	7.7	75.1	45.1	37.0	22.2
99	102	Mitsubishi Motors Corp.	Tokyo	113.4	109.2	3.9	23.7	22.8	89.7	86.4	20.6	21.7	-4.9	69.1	64.7	6.8
100	79	Delta Air Lines	Atlanta	113.1	147.2	-23.2	28.3	36.8	84.8	110.4	49.9	55.1	-9.5	32.0	52.7	-39.3

Notes: Dollars are in millions. 1992 rankings are adjusted to reflect the figures shown. Sources: Measured media from Competitive Media Reporting. Unmeasured spending figures are AA estimates.

This ranking reprinted from Ad Age's 100 Leading National Advertisers special issue, Sept. 28, 1994.

Source: Reprinted with permission from the January 2, 1995 issue of *Advertising Age.* Copyright 1995 by Crain Communications Inc.

100 LEADING MEDIA COMPANIES

Rank 1993	Rank 1992	Company	Headquarters	Total media revenue 1993	Total media revenue 1992	% chg	Newspaper revenue 1993	Newspaper revenue 1992	Magazine revenue 1993	Magazine revenue 1992	TV & radio revenue 1993	TV & radio revenue 1992	Cable TV revenue 1993	Cable TV revenue 1992	Other media revenue 1993	Other media revenue 1992
1	1	Time Warner	New York	$5,719.4	$5,559.4	2.9			$2,070.4	$2,024.4			$3,649.0	3,535.0		
2	2	Capital Cities/ABC	New York	5,512.3	5,011.2	10.0	$568.7	$546.2	328.3	318.1	$3,882.3	$3,593.6	733.0	553.3		
3	3	Tele-Communications Inc.	Denver	4,153.0	3,574.0	16.2							4,153.0	3,574.0		
4	4	CBS Inc.	New York	3,510.1	3,503.0	0.2					3,510.1	3,503.0				
5	6	Gannett Co.	Arlington, Va.	3,472.0	3,301.1	5.2	2,844.0	2,689.2			397.2	370.6			$230.8	$241.3
6	7	Advance Publications	Newark, N.J.	3,266.0	3,190.2	2.4	1,800.0	1,748.0	970.0	975.0			496.0	467.2		
7	5	General Electric Co.	Fairfield, Conn.	3,102.0	3,363.0	-7.8					3,008.0	3,283.0	94.0	80.0		
8	8	Times Mirror Co.	Los Angeles	2,681.9	2,723.4	-1.5	1,980.7	1,943.2	230.8	233.7		107.9	470.4	438.6		
9	9	News Corp.	Sydney	2,651.8	2,467.8	7.5	138.8	139.8	600.0	600.0	1,426.0	1,149.0			487.0	579.0
10	10	Knight-Ridder	Miami	2,068.6	1,996.3	3.6	2,068.6	1,996.3								
11	12	New York Times Co.	New York	2,019.7	1,773.3	13.9	1,537.9	1,307.0	394.5	386.1	75.5	70.5			11.8	9.7
12	11	Cox Enterprises	Atlanta	1,940.8	1,836.4	5.7	804.0	765.7	1.8	1.8	427.0	425.2	708.0	643.7		
13	13	Tribune Co.	Chicago	1,825.4	1,703.2	7.2	1,229.4	1,176.2			596.0	527.0				
14	14	Viacom International	New York	1,819.0	1,638.8	11.0					181.8	168.9	1,637.2	1,469.9		
15	16	Turner Broadcasting System	Atlanta	1,761.6	1,609.6	9.4							1,761.6	1,609.6		
16	15	Hearst Corp.	New York	1,738.7	1,631.4	6.6	720.0	701.0	800.0	720.0	218.7	210.4				
17	17	Thomson Corp.	Toronto	1,604.0	1,529.6	4.9	718.0	701.0	886.0	828.6						
18	18	Washington Post Co.	Washington	1,384.2	1,361.0	1.7	692.3	677.6	332.5	347.1	177.4	162.2	182.0	174.1		
19	19	Continental Cablevision	Boston	1,177.2	1,113.5	5.7							1,177.2	1,113.5		
20	25	Comcast Corp.	Bala Cynwyd, Pa.	1,095.4	728.2	50.4							1,095.4	728.2		
21	21	Reed Elsevier	London	1,070.0	1,040.4	2.8			1,070.0	1,040.4						
22	22	Dow Jones & Co.	New York	1,069.8	1,008.5	6.1	1,069.8	1,008.5								
23	20	E.W. Scripps	Cincinnati	1,062.6	1,079.5	-1.6	517.7	556.2			284.3	277.3	260.6	246.0		
24	23	Advo Inc.	Windsor, Conn.	856.6	787.6	8.8									856.6	787.6
25	24	Reader's Digest Association	Pleasantville, N.Y.	804.1	760.5	5.7			804.1	760.5						
26	27	Ziff Communications	New York	718.0	620.0	15.8			645.0	556.0					73.0	64.0
27	28	International Data Group	Framingham, Mass	715.4	616.0	16.1			715.4	616.0						
28	30	Cablevision Systems Corp.	Woodbury, N.Y.	666.7	572.5	16.5							666.7	572.5		
29	26	Valassis Communications	Livonia, Mich.	661.4	684.0	-3.3									661.4	684.0
30	29	Meredith Corp.	Des Moines, Iowa	628.9	572.7	9.8			480.1	463.2	105.2	106.0	43.6	3.5		
31	33	Providence Journal Co.	Providence, R.I.	560.0	535.0	4.7	130.0	120.0			150.0	140.0	280.0	275.0		
32	31	McGraw-Hill	New York	545.3	542.7	0.5			445.6	439.0	99.7	103.7				
33	34	A.H. Belo Corp.	Dallas	544.8	515.9	5.6	335.6	314.7			209.2	201.2				
34	32	Westinghouse Electric Corp.	Pittsburgh	538.4	540.1	-0.3					538.4	540.1				
35	35	Media News Group	Houston	515.0	515.0	0.0	515.0	515.0								
36	36	Chronicle Publishing Co.	San Francisco	491.0	486.0	1.0	261.0	264.0			111.0	109.0	119.0	113.4		
37	38	Media General	Richmond, Va.	488.2	470.6	3.7	307.1	299.0	1.6	1.7	54.1	52.5	125.4	117.4		
38	40	Cablevision Industries Corp.	Liberty, N.Y.	481.8	442.0	9.0							481.8	442.0		
39	37	Freedom Newspapers	Irvine, Calif.	479.0	473.6	1.1	393.0	389.6			86.0	84.0				
40	41	Central Newspapers	Indianapolis	466.6	433.6	7.6	466.6	433.6								
41	45	Harte-Hanks Communications	San Antonio, Texas	463.5	423.3	9.5	306.1	290.2			27.8	25.7			129.6	107.4
42	42	Multimedia Inc.	Greenville, S.C.	456.2	432.6	5.5	135.9	132.5			155.7	155.7	164.6	144.4		
43	39	Zuckerman media properties**	New York	452.1	443.0	2.1	246.7	238.0	205.4	205.0						
44	43	K-III Holdings	New York	445.7	432.0	3.2	121.0	119.8	324.7	312.2						
45	50	Gaylord Entertainment Co.	Nashville	442.1	392.3	12.7					152.1	137.5	290.0	254.8		
46	47	Landmark Communications	Norfolk, Va.	436.6	412.0	6.0	283.0	277.0	15.0	14.0	46.0	42.1	92.6	78.9		
47	44	McClatchy Newspapers	Sacramento, Calif.	433.7	425.9	1.8	433.7	425.9								
48	49	Pulitzer Publishing Co.	St. Louis	426.9	398.4	7.2	290.1	285.0			136.8	113.4				
49	48	Matra Hachette	Paris	422.0	403.0	4.7			422.0	403.0						
50	58	Chris-Craft Industries	New York	412.0	307.9	33.8					412.0	307.9				

Rank	Company	Headquarters	1994	1993	% chg
51	USA Network	New York	380.0	364.0	4.4
52	Copley Newspapers	La Jolla, Calif.	365.0	377.0	-3.2
53	Cowles Media Co.	Minneapolis	358.2	334.6	7.1
54	Crown Media	Dallas	353.4	306.9	15.2
55	Paragon Communications	Dallas	338.2	316.0	7.0
56	Sammons Communications	Stamford, Conn.	332.1	304.2	9.2
57	Journal Register Co.	Trenton, N.J.	330.0	326.0	1.2
58	Donrey Media Group	Fort Smith, Ark.	329.8	322.4	2.3
59	Adelphia Communications Corp.	Coudersport, Pa.	319.0	305.2	4.5
60	Falcon Holding Group	Los Angeles	315.0	306.1	2.9
61	Paramount Communications*	New York	314.0	247.4	26.9
62	Journal Communications	Milwaukee	305.1	291.3	4.7
63	Lee Enterprises	Davenport, Iowa	304.7	292.8	4.1
64	Century Communications Corp.	New Canaan, Conn.	302.2	281.0	7.5
65	Blade Communications	Toledo, Ohio	295.0	204.9	44.0
66	Heritage Media Corp.	Dallas	291.2	250.9	16.1
67	Enquirer/Star Group	Lantana, Fla.	289.2	265.7	8.8
68	TeleCable Corp.	Norfolk, Va.	286.7	268.0	7.0
69	National Geographic Society	Washington	285.9	293.6	-2.6
70	Morris Communications	Augusta, Ga.	284.5	282.0	0.9
71	3M	St. Paul, Minn.	280.0	260.0	7.7
72	New World Communications Group	Atlanta	262.0	260.0	0.8
73	CMP Publications	Manhasset, N.Y.	259.0	215.4	20.2
74	Seattle Times Co.	Seattle	249.0	245.0	1.6
75	Forbes Inc.	New York	245.1	229.8	6.7
76	Houston Industries	Houston	244.1	235.8	3.5
77	Petersen Publishing Co.	Los Angeles	230.7	221.5	4.2
78	Discovery Communications	Bethesda, Md.	226.0	172.0	31.4
79	Lenfest Group	Pottstown, Pa.	225.0	200.0	12.5
80	Dispatch Printing Co.	Columbus, Ohio	221.5	213.0	4.0
81	Univision Holdings	New York	214.0	195.2	9.6
82	Times Publishing Co.	St. Petersburg, Fla.	214.0	207.0	3.4
83	Great American Communications	Cincinnati	205.2	205.2	0.0
84	Infinity Broadcasting Corp.	New York	204.5	150.2	36.2
85	InterMedia	San Francisco	201.2	180.0	11.8
86	Lifetime Television	New York	197.4	176.7	11.7
87	Patrick Media Group	Chicago	190.0	175.0	8.6
88	General Media International	New York	178.1	178.1	0.0
89	Telemundo Group	New York	178.0	154.0	15.6
90	Marvel Entertainment Group	New York	175.3	138.8	26.3
91	Arts & Entertainment Network	New York	174.2	135.8	28.3
92	LIN Broadcasting Corp.	Kirkland, Wash.	168.4	164.8	2.2
93	Hollinger Inc.	Toronto	166.8	155.1	7.5
94	Pittway Corp.	Northbrook, Ill.	166.0	163.0	1.2
95	Macromedia	Hackensack, N.J.	165.0	154.3	5.7
96	Park Communications	Ithaca, N.Y.	163.1	148.5	9.2
97	Wenner Media	New York	162.2	149.6	8.2
98	Howard Publications	Oceanside, Calif.	161.9	158.0	1.9
99	Crain Communications	Chicago	161.0	151.6	3.6
100	International Family Entertainment	Virginia Beach, Va.	156.3	129.8	20.4

Notes: Dollars are in millions. All figures are net revenues and Ad Age estimates. 1992 rankings are adjusted to reflect the figures shown. Some figures for 1992 were adjusted either by Ad Age or the company to reflect continuing operations. **1993 returns are restated by AA to reflect 12 months. *Includes U.S. News & World Report, Atlantic Monthly and New York Daily News.

This ranking reprinted from 100 Leading Media Companies special report, AA, August 8, 1994.

Source: Reprinted with permission from the January 2, 1995 issue of Advertising Age. Copyright 1995 by Crain Communications Inc.

TOP 100 MAGAZINES BY GROSS REVENUE

Rank 1993	1992	Magazine	Headquarters	Total revenue	'93-92 % chg	Ad revenue	Ad pages	Subscriber revenue	Newsstand revenue	Paid circulation	Parent company
1	1	TV Guide	Radnor, Pa.	$966,606	3.0	$322,163	2,761.88	$398,692	$245,751	14,122,915	News Corp.
2	2	People	New York	722,241	4.0	367,421	3,074.55	156,602	198,218	3,446,569	Time Warner
3	3	Time	New York	614,110	-1.3	344,237	2,031.89	242,807	27,066	4,100,280	Time Warner
4	4	Sports Illustrated	New York	545,535	-3.0	301,961	2,033.96	228,110	15,464	3,356,729	Time Warner
5	5	Reader's Digest	New York	500,418	5.8	131,338	955.38	346,265	22,815	16,261,968	Reader's Digest Association
6	6	Parade	New York	410,669	-8.6	410,669	715.32	0	0	36,956,730	Advance Publications
7	7	Newsweek	New York	408,109	-1.0	260,673	2,102.03	122,826	24,610	3,156,192	Washington Post Co.
8	8	Better Homes & Gardens	Des Moines	321,219	-2.1	188,720	1,399.85	121,104	11,395	7,600,960	Meredith Corp.
9	10	Good Housekeeping	New York	302,889	4.6	206,943	1,589.71	65,608	30,338	5,162,597	Hearst Corp.
10	11	PC Magazine	New York	299,918	5.4	249,770	6,736.29	39,103	11,045	1,039,720	Ziff Communications
11	9	U.S. News & World Report	Washington	298,231	1.1	202,114	2,186.13	88,151	7,966	2,281,369	Mortimer Zuckerman
12	13	Business Week	New York	262,946	3.1	217,535	3,499.72	39,517	5,894	883,718	McGraw-Hill
13	12	Family Circle	New York	247,472	-4.1	163,228	1,570.25	34,324	49,920	5,114,030	New York Times Co.
14	19	National Enquirer	Lantana, Fla.	235,292	20.5	27,894	860.16	18,771	188,627	3,403,330	Enquirer/Star Group
15	14	Ladies' Home Journal	Des Moines	233,730	6.0	127,828	1,402.04	87,667	18,235	5,153,565	Meredith Corp.
16	18	Woman's Day	New York	226,667	7.6	146,335	1,630.84	26,714	53,618	4,858,625	Hachette Filipacchi
17	16	Forbes	New York	218,070	1.3	173,785	3,814.71	29,063	5,222	770,008	Forbes Inc.
18	17	Cosmopolitan	New York	216,573	1.4	140,844	1,833.90	15,478	60,251	2,627,491	Hearst Corp.
19	15	National Geographic	Washington	215,124	-1.1	46,779	314.89	168,286	59	8,015,495	National Geographic Society
20	25	Star Magazine	Tarrytown, N.Y.	197,128	22.2	15,572	603.91	14,547	167,009	2,957,915	Enquirer/Star Group
21	22	Fortune	New York	193,654	13.3	149,223	2,793.88	39,263	5,168	786,619	Time Warner
22	21	USA Weekend	New York	182,697	6.7	182,697	711.96	0	0	17,830,242	Gannett Co.
23	20	Money	New York	178,123	3.0	98,456	1,282.99	64,005	15,662	2,100,039	Time Warner
24	23	McCall's	New York	177,084	4.2	102,487	1,137.86	64,236	10,361	4,605,441	New York Times Co.
25	24	Playboy	Chicago	168,176	1.4	45,953	676.14	81,359	40,664	3,402,617	Playboy Enterprises
26	30	PC Week	Medford, Mass.	161,966	27.1	161,966	6,037.61	0	0	6,309	Ziff Communications
27	27	Glamour	New York	154,572	4.6	101,979	1,718.40	16,550	36,043	2,304,769	Advance Publications
28	26	Vogue	New York	153,048	2.9	112,129	2,566.38	14,284	26,635	1,250,008	Advance Publications
29	28	Southern Living	Birmingham, Ala.	151,699	8.3	87,657	1,469.23	53,604	10,438	2,368,678	Time Warner
30	29	Redbook	New York	151,364	12.2	94,510	1,310.33	38,056	18,798	3,345,451	Hearst Corp.
31	31	Rolling Stone	New York	114,076	-0.0	71,520	1,641.37	26,405	16,151	1,236,525	Wenner Media
32	36	New York Times Magazine	New York	110,654	8.9	110,654	2,852.64	0	0	1,767,836	New York Times Co.
33	38	Golf Digest	Trumbull, Conn.	109,535	12.2	66,832	1,343.63	37,127	5,576	1,461,566	New York Times Co.
34	41	Country Living	New York	108,865	17.9	64,937	1,194.97	22,986	20,942	1,977,214	Hearst Corp.
35	33	Consumer Reports	Yonkers, N.Y.	108,368	-3.8	0	0.00	104,543	3,825	4,859,995	Consumers Union of U.S.
36	47	Entertainment Weekly	New York	107,539	28.7	48,795	1,109.34	52,355	6,389	1,066,141	Time Warner
37	45	Computerworld	Framingham, Mass.	107,531	25.5	100,828	4,046.25	6,703	0	139,652	International Data Group
38	37	Modern Maturity	Lakewood, Calif.	105,568	4.4	52,225	223.05	53,343	3,975	22,226,063	AARP
39	35	Parents	New York	104,526	-2.2	68,129	1,398.82	32,422	12,125	1,776,470	Gruner & Jahr Publications
40	32	Cable Guide & Total TV	Horsham, Pa.	104,458	-8.0	26,864	286.76	77,594	0	5,494,987	TVSM
41	52	The New Yorker	New York	99,259	25.2	70,572	2,254.09	24,499	4,188	808,545	Advance Publications
42	49	CRN/Computer Reseller News	Manhasset, N.Y.	98,202	39.8	98,202	7,343.03	0	0		CMP Publications
43	49	PC World	San Francisco	96,902	18.0	67,183	2,475.87	23,352	6,367	915,326	International Data Group
44	46	Soap Opera Digest	New York	95,837	12.0	13,697	577.84	26,655	55,485	1,437,758	K-III Holdings
45	42	Prevention	Emmaus, Pa.	95,031	4.9	28,935	669.38	53,971	12,125	3,220,763	Rodale Press
46	40	PC Computing	Foster City, Calif.	94,271	-0.8	70,835	2,971.09	18,113	5,323	875,768	Ziff Communications
47	39	Penthouse	New York	90,787	-6.2	27,479	675.62	12,418	50,890	1,201,692	General Media
48	48	Computer Shopper	New York	89,915	7.7	73,071	7,858.73	5,547	11,297	504,212	Ziff Communications
49	34	Life	New York	85,330	-23.1	30,402	481.31	41,081	13,847	1,625,096	Time Warner
50	51	Car and Driver	Troy, Mich.	83,958	4.8	60,237	1,133.58	17,593	6,128	1,055,403	Hachette Filipacchi

Rank	'93	Magazine	City	% chg	Gross ($000)					Circulation	Publisher
51	44	Travel & Leisure	New York	-5.8	83,587	1,154.97	51,172	582	31,833	1,010,939	American Express Co.
52	43	Vanity Fair	New York	-6.5	83,063	1,247.84	57,327	14,348	11,388	1,157,725	Advance Publications
53	53	Sunset	Menlo Park, Calif.	2.8	81,330	1,204.77	53,715	3,394	24,221	1,441,506	Time Warner
54	50	Elle	New York	0.5	81,049	1,356.45	54,006	10,830	16,213	924,429	Hachette Filipacchi
55	54	Smithsonian	Washington	1.4	79,035	832.54	39,922	342	38,771	2,212,418	Smithsonian Institution
56	60	Seventeen	New York	11.1	78,681	1,014.35	40,069	13,146	25,466	1,940,601	K-III Holdings
57	57	Architectural Digest	Los Angeles	27.3	78,423	1,104.27	35,749	8,082	34,592	1,000,592	Advance Publications
58	67	InfoWorld	San Mateo, Calif.	16.6	77,225	3,337.00	75,750	0	1,475	11,510	International Data Group
59	59	Golf Magazine	New York	5.1	75,158	1,076.58	48,261	4,834	22,063	1,221,554	Times Mirror Co.
60	94	Harper's Bazaar	New York	55.6	74,603	1,573.47	57,296	8,092	9,215	738,403	Hearst Corp.
61	57	Woman's World	Englewood Cliffs, N.J.	1.8	73,522	240.00	3,914	69,608	0	1,216,925	Bauer Publishing Co.
62	58	Ebony	Chicago	2.3	73,181	941.75	39,724	7,274	26,183	1,939,500	Johnson Publishing Co.
63	80	MacUser	Foster City, Calif.	25.7	71,469	2,415.19	58,432	3,458	9,579	452,443	Ziff Communications
64	56	Mademoiselle	New York	-6.1	71,276	1,274.96	48,692	11,463	11,121	1,218,985	Advance Publications
65	55	Byte	Peterborough, N.H.	-8.0	71,018	2,814.00	54,099	5,581	11,338	511,325	McGraw-Hill
66	63	Self	New York	3.0	69,433	1,084.47	45,013	13,107	11,313	1,314,315	Advance Publications
67	67	Macworld	San Francisco	8.0	69,353	2,230.00	54,790	4,766	9,797	427,097	International Data Group
68	64	Bride's & Your New Home	New York	0.8	67,705	2,973.57	59,699	6,900	1,106	296,776	Advance Publications
69	62	Inc.	Boston	-0.2	67,541	1,136.07	54,527	1,519	11,495	647,211	Goldhirsh Group
70	66	GQ	New York	0.4	66,647	1,489.95	47,246	11,637	7,764	711,476	Advance Publications
71	70	Endless Vacation	Indianapolis	6.5	66,345	264.75	5,937	0	60,408	929,356	Resort Condominiums International
73	78	Travel Weekly	Secaucus, N.J.	14.6	65,881	4,839.48	64,572	0	1,309	50,335	Reed Elsevier
74	65	Field & Stream	New York	-2.0	65,522	662.40	32,623	1,905	30,994	2,007,901	Times Mirror Co.
74	72	New York	New York	5.4	64,436	2,293.36	43,404	5,048	15,984	434,029	K-III Holdings
75	85	House Beautiful	New York	16.8	63,335	829.28	42,777	6,030	14,528	1,009,446	Hearst Corp.
76	76	The Economist	New York	8.5	61,983	2,706.00	33,569	3,675	24,739	245,093	Economist Newspapers North America
77	83	Highlights for Children	Columbus, Ohio	7.7	60,716	0.00	0	0	60,716	2,568,359	Highlights for Children
78	76	Popular Science	New York	4.4	60,550	791.00	31,941	6,158	22,451	1,815,819	Times Mirror Co.
79	81	Modern Bride	New York	6.2	60,359	2,632.99	50,525	6,576	3,258	351,712	Reed Elsevier
80	86	Barron's	New York	10.7	59,686	1,656.00	27,115	15,468	17,103	262,702	Dow Jones & Co.
81	73	Jet	Chicago	0.2	58,969	1,023.00	20,227	8,182	30,560	974,764	Johnson Publishing Co.
82	77	Road & Track	Detroit	0.1	57,908	1,040.78	40,049	6,646	11,213	750,093	Hachette Filipacchi
83	82	Globe	Boca Raton, Fla.	0.7	56,849	70.00	1,059	54,826	964	1,011,117	Globe Communications Corp.
84	74	Bon Appetit	Los Angeles	-3.9	56,405	909.02	31,072	4,117	21,216	1,294,945	Advance Publications
85	75	Popular Mechanics	New York	-4.4	55,604	698.84	31,668	5,736	18,200	1,386,951	Hearst Corp.
86	69	Sporting News	St. Louis	-12.0	55,503	471.99	9,119	3,984	42,400	526,208	Times Mirror Co.
87	84	Muscle & Fitness	Woodland Hills, Calif.	0.5	54,981	1,469.72	31,413	18,620	4,948	534,307	Weider Publications
88	87	Gourmet	New York	4.0	54,511	1,097.56	36,320	3,819	14,372	906,299	Advance Publications
89	132	MacWeek	San Francisco	55.5	53,656	4,129.09	52,853	0	803	8,114	Ziff Communications
90	89	New Woman	Manhasset, N.Y.	6.9	53,533	836.95	24,308	15,936	13,289	1,314,294	K-III Holdings
91	122	Windows	Manhasset, N.Y.	45.2	52,062	2,778.02	39,223	4,563	8,276	386,918	CMP Publications
92	113	CommunicationsWeek	Manhasset, N.Y.	37.1	51,578	2,691.24	51,426	152	0	1,062	CMP Publications
93	106	Home	New York	24.1	50,956	802.96	29,624	2,542	18,790	1,043,964	Hachette Filipacchi
94	90	Conde Nast Traveler	New York	1.8	50,569	1,004.38	36,730	1,229	12,610	866,557	Advance Publications
95	88	Motor Trend	Los Angeles	-1.6	50,460	790.50	29,216	6,050	15,194	932,881	Petersen Publishing Co.
96	93	HFD-The Weekly Home Furnishings	New York	4.5	50,349	4,200.00	49,376	0	973	25,607	Capital Cities/ABC
97	117	YM	New York	36.2	49,891	454.70	15,875	12,096	21,920	1,701,615	Gruner & Jahr Publications
98	96	Parenting	San Francisco	7.7	49,749	1,055.61	34,819	1,248	13,682	805,512	Time Warner
99	100	Electronic Engineering Times	Manhasset, N.Y.	12.7	49,154	3,796.09	49,000	9	145	941	CMP Publications
100	99	Us	New York	7.4	48,925	544.58	19,563	13,770	15,592	1,110,056	Wenner Media

Notes: Dollars are in thousands. Figures are gross rate card rates and undiscounted subscription and newsstand prices and are AA estimates.

This ranking reprinted from the Ad Age 300 special report, AA, June 20, 1994.

Source: Reprinted with permission from the January 2, 1995 issue of *Advertising Age*. Copyright 1995 by Crain Communications Inc.

TOTAL MEASURED U.S. AD SPENDING BY CATEGORY & MEDIA

Rank	Category	Year	Total ad spending	Consumer magazine	Sunday magazine	Local newspaper	National newspaper	Outdoor	Network TV	Spot TV	Syndicated TV	Cable TV networks	Network radio	National spot radio
1	Retail	1993	$8,082.3	$213.5	$126.0	$4,930.5	$10.5	$155.2	$491.7	$1,589.9	$48.4	$114.2	$119.0	$283.5
		1992	7,669.7	177.8	127.1	4,893.8	11.6	80.4	441.5	1,548.4	25.3	63.3	71.3	229.2
2	Automotive	1993	7,754.5	1,056.4	31.3	2,413.8	120.1	55.0	1,533.6	2,103.9	64.4	235.5	37.8	102.7
		1992	5,922.7	1,037.9	30.0	913.0	110.8	47.6	1,578.8	1,855.2	50.0	147.0	50.9	101.5
3	Business & consumer services	1993	5,259.4	616.2	45.3	1,579.5	364.9	86.7	971.4	1,040.8	64.5	247.8	70.8	171.4
		1992	4,689.4	499.7	34.2	1,364.1	292.4	83.2	853.2	1,105.4	55.8	145.8	79.5	176.1
4	Entertainment & amusements	1993	3,749.9	82.6	3.9	634.6	9.6	69.0	1,152.9	1,411.2	108.6	168.5	13.9	95.1
		1992	3,122.0	63.7	36.3	389.3	9.0	62.8	1,035.5	1,236.0	84.6	105.8	15.1	84.0
5	Foods	1993	3,442.8	467.7	46.3	21.9	0.7	8.8	1,341.8	890.6	293.4	246.0	52.6	72.9
		1992	3,495.9	457.3	51.3	29.1	1.3	10.4	1,471.3	881.1	305.4	181.3	34.4	72.9
6	Toiletries & cosmetics	1993	2,608.4	812.2	34.3	10.3	2.7	1.7	1,139.9	275.1	152.3	160.3	7.3	12.2
		1992	2,430.7	721.8	27.7	8.5	3.5	1.8	1,110.3	273.8	119.3	143.2	7.0	13.8
7	Drugs & remedies	1993	2,294.7	365.9	38.6	120.7	20.7	13.0	942.4	341.6	195.7	164.4	71.2	20.4
		1992	2,135.6	293.9	30.3	87.1	10.7	12.5	935.5	379.1	158.1	110.7	95.3	22.4
8	Travel, hotels & resorts	1993	2,030.5	369.0	44.3	852.3	117.2	41.0	205.3	211.6	12.8	87.0	22.3	67.6
		1992	2,241.1	332.5	51.0	1,097.6	110.4	38.8	199.1	247.6	7.7	51.6	35.9	68.9
9	Direct response companies	1993	1,404.8	711.3	369.9	59.7	47.5	1.3	38.7	59.9	55.4	26.7	27.5	7.1
		1992	1,364.3	600.5	373.2	95.5	41.3	0.9	70.7	85.8	24.2	31.3	36.7	4.2
10	Candy, snacks & soft drinks	1993	1,286.7	63.6	1.8	12.5	1.3	9.0	549.0	294.8	148.4	121.1	44.9	40.3
		1992	1,249.7	68.1	4.0	13.5	3.0	7.2	578.6	297.4	113.2	90.4	30.5	43.9
11	Insurance & real estate	1993	1,242.3	120.2	16.7	623.1	41.3	28.0	170.5	142.4	13.3	37.8	17.9	31.1
		1992	966.2	135.5	11.2	395.7	49.8	22.4	164.5	118.9	7.1	22.4	14.5	24.1
12	Apparel	1993	1,090.5	509.9	41.1	14.9	4.3	5.2	302.4	84.0	38.1	75.4	2.1	13.1
		1992	1,068.0	492.9	27.8	13.9	5.7	5.7	339.7	78.8	27.2	55.3	8.9	12.0
13	Sporting goods, toys & games	1993	990.9	170.1	1.5	4.1	2.0	0.2	270.2	273.7	122.1	145.0	0.0	1.9
		1992	884.7	168.5	3.4	6.5	2.2	0.2	241.9	259.2	107.6	92.2	0.7	2.3
14	Publishing & media	1993	806.6	213.6	9.2	165.6	10.2	33.3	48.7	183.2	30.0	40.4	28.1	44.3
		1992	806.9	202.0	14.7	237.1	14.5	33.6	41.8	162.8	8.3	25.1	22.2	44.8
15	Computers, office equipment	1993	799.8	365.7	6.6	45.8	120.3	2.1	156.8	21.4	12.7	34.3	8.5	25.4
		1992	737.1	347.8	3.9	55.0	134.5	2.6	125.2	22.0	6.7	21.6	1.5	16.4
16	Beer & wine	1993	779.0	38.4	2.8	7.3	1.9	37.2	352.8	204.5	24.0	62.4	6.4	41.3
		1992	850.8	63.5	5.1	12.3	1.9	36.0	365.6	203.5	27.5	53.9	7.2	74.3
17	Household equipment & supplies	1993	696.7	139.9	9.8	8.3	0.6	0.2	291.5	117.8	54.2	59.6	10.5	4.4
		1992	678.0	162.0	14.8	18.3	2.2	0.4	290.7	93.7	41.2	46.7	3.3	4.8
18	Soaps, cleansers & polishes	1993	668.4	72.8	1.2	0.8	0.7	0.0	348.6	91.1	73.0	70.6	7.1	2.4
		1992	596.4	71.4	5.1	3.0	0.3	0.3	295.2	107.8	54.1	48.2	6.4	4.8
19	Electronic entertainment	1993	432.4	105.4	6.6	10.5	3.6	0.6	111.2	71.5	56.2	46.7	12.8	7.5
		1992	412.3	113.0	5.0	35.1	4.9	0.8	116.7	67.3	22.5	33.6	8.3	5.1

#	Category	Year												
20	Jewelry & cameras	1993	353.4	167.0	6.3	6.0	7.7	1.5	106.0	22.8	9.3	25.1	0.0	1.9
		1992	341.2	156.3	9.0	6.8	7.8	2.1	109.6	18.6	7.0	20.6	1.3	2.1
21	Cigarettes	1993	340.2	210.1	22.5	5.7	0.8	101.1	0.0	0.0	0.0	0.0	0.1	0.0
		1992	382.1	224.0	26.9	6.6	0.8	123.5	0.0	0.1	0.0	0.0	0.2	0.1
22	Building materials	1993	336.9	86.2	6.2	44.2	1.4	0.5	65.1	68.5	4.3	52.9	0.9	6.7
		1992	338.5	83.2	7.7	49.0	1.7	0.9	86.6	65.5	6.4	27.3	2.8	7.5
23	Gasoline, lubricants & fuels	1993	309.9	22.2	3.5	5.5	5.1	10.5	56.9	137.7	5.4	23.0	1.8	38.4
		1992	307.5	17.9	0.9	9.9	3.6	6.9	70.7	135.0	4.5	16.7	0.6	41.0
24	Household furnishings	1993	301.8	144.0	13.9	37.7	0.9	0.1	48.5	30.2	14.4	8.2	1.4	2.7
		1992	255.2	122.6	11.2	41.3	1.2	0.1	37.6	26.1	6.5	4.5	0.0	4.1
25	Horticulture & farming	1993	229.4	22.8	17.2	52.8	1.5	0.1	35.2	47.1	3.8	24.2	3.3	21.5
		1992	215.5	19.4	14.0	48.4	1.3	0.4	27.0	53.2	2.7	18.5	8.0	22.8
26	Liquor	1993	218.4	165.8	12.4	2.5	5.5	24.8	0.0	0.0	0.0	0.0	1.1	6.2
		1992	236.3	185.4	8.8	8.4	5.8	21.2	0.0	2.1	0.0	0.0	1.4	3.2
27	Pets & pet foods	1993	195.0	42.1	3.0	11.6	0.2	0.0	74.3	19.8	11.3	27.1	2.4	3.1
		1992	171.2	34.0	1.8	7.0	0.2	0.0	68.8	27.5	12.2	16.8	1.8	1.1
28	Freight	1993	148.7	44.9	0.3	5.6	12.6	0.1	43.9	25.9	0.1	9.4	0.2	5.7
		1992	151.6	34.7	0.0	5.9	14.2	0.5	54.4	32.5	0.0	4.8	0.2	4.3
29	Industrial materials	1993	124.0	36.1	0.2	3.1	6.6	0.4	43.2	9.1	0.5	12.7	11.7	0.4
		1992	122.8	45.8	0.1	7.6	8.7	1.2	41.1	10.6	1.0	4.6	1.8	0.2
30	Business propositions	1993	46.6	26.8	0.7	6.3	9.8	0.2	0.0	1.8	0.4	0.4	0.2	0.3
		1992	39.6	27.0	0.6	1.9	7.2	0.7	0.0	1.6	0.0	0.1	0.2	0.3
31	Airplanes (not travel)	1993	18.1	8.0	0.0	1.4	6.8	0.0	0.0	0.5	0.0	1.2	0.0	0.2
		1992	21.9	12.3	0.0	2.7	5.2	0.1	0.0	0.5	0.0	1.0	0.0	0.1
32	Other	1993	308.3	120.1	1.6	76.5	95.5	9.2	0.0	1.2	3.0	1.2	0.0	0.0
		1992	351.6	132.8	5.0	56.4	96.2	49.7	0.5	2.9	0.5	6.6	1.0	0.1
	Total	1993	48,351.2	7,590.5	925.1	11,774.8	1,034.4	696.0	10,892.7	9,773.5	1,620.1	2,329.0	583.6	1,131.6
		1992	44,256.7	7,105.1	941.9	9,920.1	963.7	655.0	10,752.5	9,399.7	1,286.6	1,590.5	549.1	1,092.4

Notes: Dollars are in millions. Local newspaper growth was affected by expanded measurement of classified advertising in 1993. Source: Competitive Media Reporting. Categories are Industry classes as defined by CMR.

This ranking reprinted from Ad Age's 100 Leading National Advertisers special issue, Sept. 28, 1994.

Source: Reprinted with permission from the January 2, 1995 issue of *Advertising Age*. Copyright 1995 by Crain Communications Inc.

Business Information Directory

General Reference Sources

Business Information Sources by Lorna M. Daniells. A classic source of information covering such topics as finance, industry, statistics, management, marketing and much more. Published by the University of California Press, Berkeley and Los Angeles, California.

Business Organizations, Agencies and Publications Directory, lists organizations, agencies and information services that promote, coordinate, and regulate commercial activity in the U.S. Gale Research Co., 835 Penobscot Building, Detroit, MI 48226.

Directory of Marketing Research Houses and Services is an annual available from the American Marketing Association, 250 South Wacker Drive, Chicago, IL 60606.

Encyclopedia of Banking and Finance, is a comprehensive source on subjects indicated in the title. Bankers Publishing Co., 210 South Street, Boston, MA.

Encyclopedia of Business Information Sources edited by James Woy. A wide range of information sources are listed under 1,100 alphabetically arranged business subjects. Easy identification of key live, print, and electronic sources of information. Also covers subjects of current interest, new technologies, and new industries in addition to basic business subjects. Available from Gale Research Co., 835 Penobscot Building, Detroit, MI 48226.

Encyclopedia of Business Information Sources: Europe, edited by M. Balachandran covers business information sources from more than 50 Eastern and Western European countries. Sources are listed under alphabetically arranged business subjects and then by type of resources. There is also a section in which these entries are arranged by title or organization name. Available from Gale Research Co., 835 Penobscot Building, Detroit, MI 48226.

Encyclopedia of Information Systems and Services. Provides comprehensive international coverage of computer-based information systems and services. Includes details on information providers, access services, sources of information, and support services. Listings are arranged in a single volume covering about 5,000 information organizations, systems, and services located in the United States and some 70 other countries. More than 30,000 organizations, services and products are identified. Published by Gale Research Co., 835 Penobscot Building, Detroit, MI 48226.

Guide to American Directories, published by B. Klein Publications, Inc., P.O. Box 8503, Coral Springs, FL 33065.

Lesko's Info Power contains thousands of sources of free and low cost information covering a wide variety of subjects such as investments, businesses, job opportunities and much more. Published by Information USA, P.O. Box E, Kingston, MD 20895.

National Directory of Addresses and Telephone Numbers. A national business directory that lists all SEC registered companies, major accounting and law firms, banks, and financial institutions, associations, unions, etc. Included are 50,000 fax numbers. Published by Omnigraphics, Penobscot Building, Detroit, MI 48226.

Standard Rate and Data Service provides information on periodical circulation and advertising rates. Published by Standard Rates and Data Service, Inc., 5201 Old Orchard Road, Skokie, IL 60077-1021.

Statistical Abstract of the United States, published annually by the Bureau of the Census, is the standard summary on the social, political, and economic statistics of the United States. It includes data from both government and private sources. Appendix I gives a comprehensive list of sources. Available from the Superintendent of Documents, Government Printing Office, Washington, DC 20402.

The *United States Government Manual* is an annual publication. It describes the organization, purposes, and programs of most government agencies and lists top personnel. Available from the Superintendent of Documents, Government Printing Office, Washington, DC 20402.

Washington Information Directory is an annual publication listing, by topic, organizations and publications which provide information on a wide range of subjects. It also lists congressional committee assignments, regional federal offices, embassies, and state and local officials. Published by the Congressional Quarterly, Inc., 1414 22nd Street NW, Washington, DC 20037.

Who Knows: A Guide to Washington Experts, Washington Researchers, 2612 P Street NW, Washington, DC 20007.

Professional and trade organizations and publications are a major source of contacts and information. Key directories to these sources are listed below.

Directories in Print, contains more than 16,000 detailed entries on directories published in the United States and Canada. Directories outside the U.S. and Canada are listed in *International Directories in Print* and city and state directories are listed in *City and State Directories in Print.* Available from Gale Research Co., 835 Penobscot Building, Detroit, MI 48226.

Encyclopedia of Associations contains detailed entries on over 22,000 active organizations, clubs, and other non-profit organizations. Available from Gale Research Co., 835 Penobscot Building, Detroit, MI 48226.

The Gale Directory of Publications and Broadcast Media, a guide to newspapers, magazines and other periodicals, as well as radio, television and cable companies. Available from Gale Research Co., 835 Penobscot Building, Detroit, MI 48226.

National Trade and Professional Associations of the United States. A comprehensive listing of professional trade and labor associations, including addresses, membership size, publications by the associations, and convention schedules. An annual published by Columbia Books, 1212 New York Avenue NW, Washington, DC.

Standard Periodical Directory covers U.S. and Canadian periodicals. Published by Oxbridge Communications, Inc., 150 Fifth Avenue, New York, NY 10011.

The World Guide to Trade Associations gives a comprehensive national and international listing of associations. Published by R. R. Bowker Co., 245 West 17th Street, New York, NY 10011.

Ulrich's International Periodical Directory covers both domestic and foreign periodicals. Published by R. R. Bowker Co., 245 West 17th Street, New York, NY 10011.

World Business Directory edited by Linda Irvin contains information on more than 130,000 companies interested in international trade opportunities. Lists contact, financial, and business information and includes an Alphabetic Index, SIC Index and Product Index. Available from Gale Research Co., 835 Penobscot Building, Detroit, MI 48226.

Population information on all aspects of national and world population is provided by the Population Reference Bureau, Inc., 1875 Connecticut Avenue NW, Washington, DC 20009.

BUSINESS AND ECONOMICS INFORMATION

Government publications referred to below may be obtained from the Government Printing Office (GPO), Washington, DC 20402, unless otherwise indicated.

Census Catalog and Guide is an annual one-step guide to Census Bureau resources. Includes explanations of the censuses and surveys of business, manufacturing, and population, names and phone numbers of over 1,600 sources of assistance—Census Bureau specialists, State and local agencies, and private companies.

Business and economic information is provided by the following key references.

Annual Survey of Manufacturers. General statistics of manufacturing activity for industry groups, individual industries, states, and geographical regions are provided. (GPO)

County Business Patterns is an annual publication on employment and payrolls, which includes a separate paperbound report for each state. (GPO)

Current Industrial Reports are a series of over 100 monthly, quarterly, semiannual, and annual reports on major products manufactured in the United States. For subscription, contact the Bureau of the Census, U.S. Department of Commerce, Washington, DC 20233. (GPO)

The Economic Bulletin Board of the Department of Commerce includes same day postings of data provided by both the Bureau of Labor Statistics and the Bureau of Economic Analysis. There are updates from the Bureau of the Census on the principal indicators, monetary statistics and foreign trade. For information call (202) 482-1986.

Economic Indicators is a monthly summary-type publication prepared by the Council of Economic Advisers. It contains charts and tables on national output, income, spending, employment, unemployment, wages, industrial production, construction, prices, money, credit, federal finance, and international statistics. (GPO)

Federal Reserve Bulletin is a monthly issued by the Federal Reserve System, containing articles and very extensive tabulated data on all aspects of the monetary situation, credit, mortgage markets, interest rates, and stock and bond yields. Available from the Board of Governors, Federal Reserve System, Washington, DC 20551.

Foreign Trade is a Bureau of the Census publication giving monthly reports on U.S. foreign trade. (GPO)

Monthly Labor Review. This monthly publication provides articles and statistics on employment, productivity, wages, earnings, prices, wage settlements, and work stoppages. (GPO)

Population: Current Report is a series of monthly and annual reports covering population changes and socioeconomic characteristics of the population. (GPO)

Quarterly Financial Report for Manufacturing, Mining, and Trade Corporations is issued by the Bureau of the Census of the U.S. Department of Commerce. It covers corporate financial statistics including sales, profits, assets, and financial ratios, classified by industry group and size. (GPO)

Retail Sales: Current Business Report is a weekly report which provides retail statistics. (GPO)

State and Metropolitan Area Data Book contains information on personal income, population characteristics, business, health, and crime among other topics. Prepared by the Bureau of the Census. (GPO)

Survey of Current Business is a major publication which is supplemented on a weekly basis with *Current Statistics*. The publication contains articles as well as comprehensive statistics on all aspects of the economy, including data on the GNP, employment, wages, prices, finance, foreign trade, and production by industrial sector. (GPO)

Wholesale Trade, Sales and Inventories: Current Business Report provides a monthly report on wholesale trade. (GPO)

U.S. Global Outlook is a new (1995) publication intended as an annual review of major markets for U.S. exports. The first edition reviews seven major industrial sectors: medical equipment, computer hardware and software, motor vehicles and parts, paper products, and information services.

U.S. Occupational Outlook is a biannual providing information on employment opportunities, and projections. (GPO)

U.S. CORPORATE INFORMATION

The major sources of information on publicly held corporations (as well as government and municipal issues) are:

Moody's Investor Services, Inc., owned by Dun & Bradstreet, 99 Church Street, New York, NY 10007, and

Standard & Poor's Corp., owned by McGraw-Hill, 25 Broadway, New York, NY 10004.

Standard & Poor's *Corporate Records* and Moody's *Manuals* are large multivolume works published annually and kept up to date with current reports. The services provide extensive coverage of industrials, public utilities, transportation, banks, and financial companies. Also included are municipal and government issues.

In addition, the above corporations provide computerized data services and magnetic tapes. Compustat tapes, containing major corporate financial data, are available from Investor's Management Services, Inc., Denver, CO, a subsidiary of Standard & Poor's. Time-sharing access to Compustat and other financial data bases is available through Interactive Data Corporation, Waltham, MA.

Media General Financial Services, 301 East Grace Street, Richmond, VA, 23219, maintains a data base of corporate and industry information on 5500 companies. It can be accessed via Dow Jones News Retrieval, Dialog, Thomson Financial Networks, Randall-Helms Fiduciary Consultants, Lotus One Source (CD-ROM). Media General Financial Services also provides data on the financial markets, mutual funds and corporate bonds.

The Media General Financial Services proprietary product line also includes direct sales of its data through magnetic tapes, diskettes, custom research applications, specialized screening and report services.

DISCLOSURE II, available from Disclosure, Inc. (5161 River Road, Bethesda, MD 20816), provides an on line data base of corporate information for some 10,000 companies. Disclosure II can be used via the Dow Jones Retrieval Service, New York Times Information Service, Lockheed's DIALOG Information Services, Inc., ADP, CompuServe, among others.

Also available from Disclosure is MICRO/SCAN: Disclosure II, a monthly diskette service which provides information on dividends per share, 4-year growth rate in earnings per share, price/book value, etc. For information call 800-638-8076.

The 10-K and other corporate reports are filed with the Securities and Exchange Commission and are available at local SEC offices, investor relations departments of publicly traded companies, as well as various private services, such as Disclosure Inc. which provides a complete microfiche service. *The SEC News Digest,* formerly published by the government, is now available from Disclosure, Inc. (address above). Included in the *Digest* is a daily listing of 8K reports, a daily Acquisitions of Securities Report, as well as information about what's happening inside the SEC.

Disclosure Inc. has two additional services helpful for researching a corporation. Through the *SEC Watch Service* any report filed by a company with the SEC can be retrieved while corporate information such as prospective supplements and tender offers can be retrieved through the *SEC Research Service*.

Betchel Information Service located at 1801 Research Boulevard, Rockville, MD 20850 is another SEC document retrieval service. The Index of financial documents is updated several times a day.

Major trade directories include the annual *Thomas Register of American Manufac-*

turers (published by Thomas Publishing Company, 1 Pennsylvania Plaza, New York, NY 10005) and Dun & Bradstreet's *Reference Book of Manufacturers*.

Thomas Register includes in two volumes an alphabetical listing of manufacturers, giving address, phone number, product, subsidiaries, plant location, and an indication of assets. Dun & Bradstreet's *Reference Book* covers similar information, including sales and credit. Dun & Bradstreet's *Million Dollar Directory* series provides data on U.S. companies whose net worth is $1,000,000 and up, including information on privately held corporations; also published is a companion volume the *Billion Dollar Directory* which tracks America's corporate families.

How to Find Information About Private Companies includes strategies for private company investigation, sources for private company intelligence, and how to find information about private companies. Published by Washington Researchers, 2612 P Street NW, Washington, DC 20007.

The *Corporate Directory*, published by Cambridge Information Group, 7200 Wisconsin Avenue, Bethesda, MD 20814 is a two volume compendium of over 9500 public companies. Included is such information as corporate officers, majority stockholders, SIC members, major subsidiaries, P/E ratio, etc.

Monitor Publishing, 104 Fifth Avenue, New York, NY 10011 publishes four directories that list, among other items, names, titles, and addresses of the managers of the listed companies in the U.S. and abroad. The volumes are: *The Corporate 1000* (a quarterly), *The Financial 1000*, *The Over-the-Counter 1000*, and *The International 1000*. Monitor also publishes the *Blue Book of Canadian Business*.

Directory of Investment Research, an annual published by Nelson Publishing, 1 Gateway Plaza, Port Chester, NY lists security analysts with a subject specialty, top corporate officers, and brokerage firms researching a given company.

Register of Corporations is published by Standard & Poor's Corp., 345 Hudson Street, New York, NY 10014.

Directory of Corporate Affiliations and International Directory of Corporate Affiliations are references to the structure of major domestic and international corporations. Published by National Register Publishing Company, 3004 Glen View Road, Wilmette, IL 60091.

How to Find Company Intelligence in State Documents provides information filed by companies with the state governments and also business related data collected by the states. Washington Researchers Publishing, 2612 P Street NW, Washington, DC 20007.

How to Find Information About Companies: The Corporate Intelligence Source Book provides information on sources helpful in researching either private or public companies. Available from Washington Researchers Publishing. (See above for the address.)

Ward's Business Directory of U.S. Private and Public Companies. Company profiles on over 142,000 private and public U.S. businesses—over 90% of which are privately held. Available from Gale Research, Inc., 835 Penobscot Building, Detroit, MI 48226.

Future earnings projections of listed companies based on surveys by securities analysts are provided by Lynch, Jones, and Ryan, 345 Hudson Street, New York, NY 10013.

Zacks Investment Research, Inc., 155 North Wacker Drive, Chicago, IL 60606 also provides future earnings projections.

The Corporate Finance Sourcebook, published by the National Register Publishing Company, Macmillan Directory Division, P.O. Box 609, Wilmette, IL 60091, provides information on sources of capital, financial intermediaries and specialized financial sources.

Information on foreign corporations is provided in *World Trade Data Reports*, distributed by the District Offices of the U.S. Department of Commerce.

TRACKING FEDERAL GOVERNMENT DEVELOPMENTS

Commerce Business Daily (CB). This daily provides information on contract awards and subcontract opportunities, Defense Department awards, and surplus sales. *CB* is available on-line from: United Communications Group, 8701 Georgia Avenue, Silver Springs, MD 20910; DIALOG Information Services, 3460 Hillview Avenue, Palo Alto, CA 94304; or Data Resources, Inc., 2400 Hartwell Avenue, Lexington, ME 02173. Available from the Superintendent of Documents, Government Printing Office, Washington, DC 20402.

Federal Register. This daily provides information on federal agency regulations and other legal documents. Available from the Superintendent of Documents, Government Printing Office, Washington, DC 20402.

CQ Weekly Report. This major service follows every important piece of legislation through both houses of Congress and reports on the political and lobbying pressures being applied. Available from the Congressional Quarterly Service, 1414 22nd Street, Washington, DC 20037.

Daily Report for Executives. A daily series of reports giving Washington developments that affect all aspects of business operations. Available from the Bureau of National

Affairs, Inc., 1231 25th Street NW, Washington, DC 20037.

The Bureau of National Affairs, Inc. (address above) and the *Commerce Clearing House, Inc.* (4025 West Peterson Avenue, Chicago, IL 60646), publish a large number of valuable weekly loose-leaf reports covering developments in all aspects of law, government regulations, and taxation.

INDEX PUBLICATIONS

Indexes of a wide variety of articles appearing in periodicals, trade presses, and financial services dealing with corporations, industry, and finance are given in the following:

Business Periodicals Index published by H. W. Wilson Co., 950 University Avenue, Bronx, NY.

Funk and Scott Index of Corporations and Industries, published by Predicast, Inc., 11001 Cedar Street, Cleveland, OH 44141.

Major newspaper indexes are:

Wall Street Journal Index published by Dow Jones & Co., Inc., 22 Cortlandt Street, New York, NY 10007 (monthly).

New York Times Index published by the New York Times Company, 229 W. 43rd Street, New York, NY 10036 (semimonthly, cumulates annually).

TRACKING ECONOMIC INDICATORS

Composite Index of Leading Economic Indicators: Each month the Bureau of Economic Analysis compiles this data from the 12 leading economic indicators. This material appears each month in the *Bureau's Survey of Current Business* available by subscription from:

Superintendent of Documents
Government Printing Office
Washington, DC 20402
202-512-1800

Consumer Price Index (CPI) (changes in cost of goods to customers): For these monthly reports prepared by the Bureau of Labor Statistics write:

Bureau of Labor Statistics
Department of Labor
Postal Square Building
2 Massachusetts Avenue NE
Washington, DC 20212

CPI 24 hour hotline: 202-606-7828.

Producer Price Index (PPI) (measures changes in prices received in primary markets by producers). For monthly reports write:

Bureau of Labor Statistics
Department of Labor
Postal Square Building
2 Massachusetts Avenue NE
Washington, DC 20212

PPI 24 hour hotline: 202-606-7828.

Available from the Bureau of Labor Statistics (BLS) are press releases on *State and Metropolitan Area Unemployment* (issued monthly), the *Employment Cost Index* (issued quarterly), and the *Employment Situation Study* (released monthly). To subscribe write:

Bureau of Labor Statistics
Department of Labor
Postal Square Building
2 Massachusetts Avenue NE
Washington, DC 20212

Unemployment Insurance Claims Weekly may be obtained by calling or by writing:

Employment and Training Administration
Department of Labor
Postal Square Building
2 Massachusetts Avenue NE
Washington, DC 20212

Releases on the *Money Supply* (Report H-6, issued weekly) and on *Consumer Credit* (Report G-19, issued monthly) may be obtained from the

Publications Services
Federal Reserve Board
Washington, DC 20551
202-452-3244

Personal Consumption Expenditure Deflator is prepared monthly by the Bureau of Economic Analysis of the Department of Commerce. This information appears in a press release *Personal Income and Outlays* and can be obtained in writing from the

Public Information Office Order Desk
Bureau of Economic Analysis
Department of Commerce
Washington, DC 20230

For information call 202-523-0777.

Monthly Trade Report (index of retail sales and accounts receivable) is compiled by the Bureau of the Census and published in *Current Business Reports* as part of what is known as the BR series. Also available are *Current Business Reports Wholesale Trade* and *Current Business Reports Selected Services.* To subscribe contact the Superintendent of Documents (address given below). For a sample copy call: 301-763-4100.

Value of New Construction Put in Place is a Census Bureau monthly report (part of the

C-30 Series) which charts the dollar amount of new construction. It is available on an annual subscription basis from the Superintendent of Documents, Government Printing Office, Washington, DC 20402. For a sample copy call: 301-457-1605.

Joint Economic Committee of Congress Reports

Reports on the economic issues studied by the Joint Economic Committee are available free of charge from:

Joint Economic Committee of Congress
Dirksen Senate Office Building
Washington, DC 20510
202-224-5171

TRACKING CONGRESSIONAL ACTION

Congressional action information can be obtained from several sources. The Legis Office will provide information on whether legislation has been introduced, who sponsored it, and its current status. For House or Senate action, call 202-225-1772.

Cloakrooms of both houses will provide details on what is happening on the floor of the chamber.

House cloakrooms:
Democrat 202-225-7330
Republican 202-225-7350

Senate cloakrooms:
Democrat 202-224-4691
Republican 202-224-6391

ASSISTANCE FROM U.S. GOVERNMENT AGENCIES

The **Office of Business Liaison (OBL)** serves as the focal point for contact between the Department of Commerce and the business community. Through the *Business Assistance Program* individuals and firms are guided through the entire government complex. Other services include dissemination of information and reports such as *Outlook*.

Write Office of Business Liaison, U.S. Department of Commerce, Washington, DC 20230. This office is also a focal point for handling inquiries for domestic business information.

OBL telephone numbers:
Office of the Director . . (202) 482-3942
Office of Private Sector
Initiatives 3717
Business Assistance
Program 3176
TDD . . . . 5691[4]

Industry experts in the International Trade Administration can provide specifics about an industry.

Country experts in the Department of State provide up to date economic and political information on countries throughout the world, as well as background reports on specific countries. For information contact:

Country Desk Officers
U.S. Department of State
2201 C Street NW
Washington, DC 20520
Telephone: 202-647-4000

Major Bureau of Labor Statistics Indicators are available daily from a recorded message at 202-606-7828.

Economic news and highlights of the day are provided by phone from the Department of Commerce. For economic news call 202-393-4100. For news highlights call 202-393-1847.

The Energy Information Center will provide free information on energy and related matters. Write National Energy Information Center, Forrestal Building, 1000 Independence Avenue SW, Washington, DC 20585. Call 202-586-8800.

Technical and scientific information are provided by the **National Technical Information Service** of the Department of Commerce, 5285 Port Royal, Springfield, VA 22161, which handles requests about government-sponsored research of all kinds. There is a basic charge to research a subject. For information call 703-487-4600.

The **Census Bureau** produces detailed statistical information for the U.S. Information is available on population, housing, agriculture, manufacturing, retail trade, service industries, wholesale trade, foreign trade, mining, transportation, construction, and the revenues and expenditures of state and local governments. The Bureau also produces statistical studies of many foreign countries.

Bureau of the Census: Information Sources

As the Federal Government's principal fact-finding agency, the Census Bureau collects, processes, analyzes, and disseminates statistics on important aspects of the Nation's social and economic life.

TELEPHONE CONTACTS FOR DATA USERS

Frequently called numbers[1]

Census Customer Services	
(Data product & ordering information for	
computer tapes, CD-ROMs, microfiche,	
& some publications).	457-4100
FAX (General Information)	457-4714
(Orders only)	457-3842
TDD.	457-4611
Agriculture Information	1-800-523-3215
Business Information	1-800-541-8345
Census-BEA Bulletin Board	457-2310
Census Job Information (Recording)	457-4499
Census Personnel Locator.	457-4608
Congressional Affairs	457-2171
Data Centers (DUSD)	457-1305
FastFax (DUSD).	1-900-555-2FAX
Foreign Trade Information	457-3041/2311
Internet (General Information)—(DUSD) . . .	457-1242
Library.	457-2511
Population Information	457-2422 / 2435 (TTY)
Public Information Office (Press)	457-2794
Technical Support (CD-ROM Products)	457-1324

Census regional offices

(Information services, data product information)

Atlanta, GA	404-730-3833/3964 (TDD)
Boston, MA	617-424-0510/0565 (TDD)
Charlotte, NC	704-344-6144/6548 (TDD)
Chicago, IL	708-562-1740/1791 (TDD)
Dallas, TX	214-767-7105/7181 (TDD)
Denver, CO	303-969-7750/6769 (TDD)
Detroit, MI	313-259-1875/5169 (TDD)
Kansas City, KS	913-551-6711/5839 (TDD)
Los Angeles, CA.	818-904-6339/6249 (TDD)
New York, NY.	212-264-4730/3863 (TDD)
Philadelphia, PA	215-597-8313/8864 (TDD)
Seattle, WA	206-728-5314/5321 (TDD)
Regional Office Liaison—FLD	457-2032

Other key contacts

1990 Census Tabulations & Publications—	
U.S.: Gloria Porter (DMD).	457-4019
Puerto Rico & Outlying Areas:	
Lourdes Flaim (DMD)	457-4023
1992 Economic Census—Paul Zeisset/	
Robert Marske (EPCD)	457-4151

2000 Census Plans—	
Catherine Keeley (DIR)	457-4036
Bulletin Board (Technical assistance)—	
DUSD	457-1242
CENDATA (Online service)—DUSD.	457-1214
Census & You (Newsletter)—	
Neil Tillman (DUSD).	457-1221
Census Catalog—John McCall (DUSD). . . .	457-1221
Census History—Les Solomon (DUSD)	457-1167
Census Records (Age search)—	
DPD	812-285-5314
Conferences/Exhibits—	
Joanne Dickinson (DUSD)	457-1191
Confidentiality & Privacy—	
Jerry Gates (PPDO).	457-2516
County & City, State & Metropolitan Area	
Data Books—Wanda Cevis (DUSD).	457-1166
Economic Studies—Arnold Reznek (CES) . .	457-1856
Education Support—	
Dorothy Jackson (DUSD)	457-1210
FastFax (General Information)—DUSD	457-1242
Freedom of Information Act—	
Gary Austin (PPDO).	457-2532
Historical Statistics—DUSD	457-1166
Legislation—Thomas Jones (PPDO)	457-2512
Litigation—Nick Birnbaum (PPDO)	457-2490
Microdata Files—	
Carmen Campbell (DUSD)	457-1139
Monthly Product Announcement	
(Newsletter)—Mary Kilbride (DUSD)	457-1221
Statistical Abstract—Glenn King (DUSD) . . .	457-1171
Statistical Briefs—	
Robert Bernstein (DUSD)	457-1221
Statistical Research—	
C. Easley Hoy (SRD).	457-4978
User Training—DUSD	457-1210

Internet:	
Census-BEA Bulletin Board	
(Telnet)	cenbbs.census.gov
Gopher	gopher gopher.census.gov
FTP	ftp ftp.census.gov
World Wide Web	http://www.census.gov

Business Economics

Agriculture

Crops & Livestock Statistics—	
Linda Hutton (AGFS)	763-8569
Farm Economics—James Liefer (AGFS) . . .	763-8514
General Information—	
Sharon Powers (AGFS).	1-800-523-3215
Irrigation Statistics—	
John Blackledge (AGFS)	763-8560
Laboratory—Dave Peterson (AGFS)	763-8260

Outreach—Quentin Coleman (AGFS)	763-8561
Puerto Rico, Virgin Islands, Guam,	
Northern Marianas, & American Samoa—	
Kent Hoover (AGFS)	763-8564

Communications & utilities

Census—Dennis Shoemaker (SVSD)	457-2786
Current Programs—	
Tom Zabelsky (SVSD)	457-2766

Business Economics *(concluded)*

Construction

Building Permits—Linda Hoyle (MCD) 457-1321
Census—Pat Horning (MCD) 457-4680
Construction in Metro Areas—
  Joseph Gilvary (MCD) 457-4666
Housing Starts & Completions—
  David Fondelier (MCD). 457-4703
Residential Characteristics, Price Index,
  Sales—Steve Berman (MCD) 457-4666
Residential Improvements & Repairs—
  Joe Huesman (MCD). 457-1605
Value of New Construction—
  George Roff (MCD) 457-1605

Finance, insurance, & real estate

Census—SVSD 457-2777

Foreign trade

Data Services—Reba Higbee (FTD). . . 457-3041/2227
Shipper's Declaration—
  Hal Blyweiss (FTD) 457-1086

Manufacturing

Concentration—Andy Hait (MCD) 457-4769
Exports From Manufacturing
  Establishments—Philippe Morris (MCD) . . 457-4761
Financial Statistics (Quarterly Financial
  Report)—Ronald Lee (AGFS) 763-5435
Fuels & Electric Energy Consumed, &
  Production Index—Pat Horning (MCD) . . . 457-4680

To contact any of the specialists by mail, use their
name, the division, and the address—Bureau of
the Census, Washington, DC 20233. To receive
copies of *U.S. Bureau of the Census Telephone
Contacts for Data Users,* contact Customer Services (301-457-4100).

Key to Office Abbreviations

AGFS	Agriculture & Financial Statistics Division
CAO	Congressional Affairs Office
DMD	Decennial Management Division
DPD	Data Preparation Division
DSD	Demographic Surveys Division
DSMD	Demographic Statistical Methods Division
DSSD	Decennial Statistical Studies Division
DUSD	Data User Services Division
EPCD	Economic Planning & Coordination Division
ESMPD	Economic Statistical Methods & Programming Division
FLD	Field Division
FTD	Foreign Trade Division
GEO	Geography Division
GOVS	Governments Division
HHES	Housing & Household Economic Statistics Division
MCD	Manufacturing and Construction Division
PIO	Public Information Office
POP	Population Division
PPDO	Program & Policy Development Office
SRD	Statistical Research Division
SVSD	Services Division
TCO	Telecommunications Office
TMO	CASIC Technologies Management Office
2KS	Year 2000 Research & Development Staff

Industries:
  Electrical & Transportation Equipment,
  Instruments, & Miscellaneous—
  Bruce Goldhirsch (MCD) 457-4817
  Food, Textiles, & Apparel—
  Judy Dodds (MCD) 457-4651
  Metals & Industrial Machinery—
  Kenneth Hansen (MCD) 457-4755
  Wood, Furniture, Paper, Printing,
  Chemicals, Petroleum Products, Rubber,
  & Plastics—Michael Zampogna (MCD). . 457-4810
Monthly Shipments, Inventories, & Orders—
  Kathy Menth (MCD) 457-4832
Technology, Innovation, Research &
  Development, Capacity, & Pollution
  Abatement—Elinor Champion (MCD) 457-4701

Retail trade

Advance Monthly—
  Ronald Piencykoski (SVSD) 457-2713
Census—SVSD 457-2687
Monthly Report—Irving True (SVSD). 457-2706
Monthly Sales (24-hour recording) 457-1089
Quarterly Financial Report—
  Ronald Lee (AGFS) 763-5435

Services

Census—Jack Moody (SVSD) 457-2689
Current Reports—
  Thomas Zabelsky (SVSD) 457-2766

Transportation

Census—Dennis Shoemaker (SVSD) 457-2786
Commodity Flow Survey—
  John Fowler (SVSD) 457-2108
Truck Inventory & Use—
  Bill Bostic (SVSD) 457-2797
Warehousing & Trucking—
  Tom Zabelsky (SVSD) 457-2766

Wholesale trade

Census—John Trimble (SVSD). 457-2694
Current Sales & Inventories—
  Nancy Piesto (SVSD). 457-2779
Quarterly Financial Report—
  Ronald Lee (AGFS) 763-5435

Special topics

Assets/Expenditures—
  Sheldon Ziman (AGFS) 1-800-541-8345
Business Investment—
  Charles Funk (AGFS) 763-2542
Census Products—Robert Marske /
  Paul Zeisset (EPCD) 457-4151
Characteristics of Business Owners—
  Valerie Strang (AGFS) 763-5726
County Business Patterns—
  Paul Hanczaryk (EPCD) 457-2580
Enterprise Statistics—
  Eddie Salyers (AGFS) 763-7234
Industry & Commodity Classification—
  James Kristoff (EPCD) 457-2813
Mineral Industries—
  Patricia Horning (MCD) 457-4680
Minority- & Women-Owned Businesses—
  Valerie Strang (AGFS) 763-5726
Puerto Rico & Outlying Areas—
  Kent Hoover (AGFS) 763-8564
Quarterly Financial Report—
  Ronald Lee (AGFS) 763-5435

Demographics & Population

(1990 Census, 2000 Census—also see "Other Key Contacts")

Aging Population, U.S.—POP 457-2378
Ancestry—POP 457-2403
Apportionment—POP 457-2381
Child Care—Martin O'Connell /
  Lynne Casper (POP) 457-2416
Children—Donald Hernandez (POP) 457-2465
Citizensip—POP. 457-2403
Commuting, Means of Transportation,
  & Place of Work—Phil Salopek /
  Celia Boertlein (POP). 457-2454
Crime—Gail Hoff (DSD). 457-3925
Current Population Survey:
  General Information—DUSD 457-4100
  Questionnaire Content—
  Ron Tucker (DSD) 457-3806
  Sampling Methods—
  Preston Waite (DSMD) 457-4287
Demographic Surveys
  (General information)—DSD 457-3811
Disability—Jack McNeil /
  Bob Bennefield (HHES) 763-8300/8578
Education—POP. 457-2464
Education Surveys—
  Richard Schwartz (DSD) 457-3800
Equal Employment Opportunity Data—
  Tom Scopp (HHES) 763-8199
Fertility & Births—Martin O'Connell /
  Amara Bachu (POP) 457-2416
Foreign Born—POP 457-2403
Group Quarters Population—
  Denise Smith (POP) 457-2378
Health Surveys—Robert Mangold (DSD) . . . 457-3879
Hispanic & Ethnic Statistics—POP 457-2403
Homeless—Annetta Clark (POP) 457-2378
Household Estimates—POP. 457-2465
Households & Families—
  Steve Rawlings (POP) 457-2465

Immigration (Legal / Undocumented) &
  Emigration—Edward Fernandez (POP) . . 457-2103
Journey to Work—Phil Salopek /
  Gloria Swieczkowski (POP) 457-2454
Language—POP. 457-2464
Longitudinal Surveys—
  Sarah Higgins (DSD) 457-3801
Marital Status & Living Arrangements—
  Arlene Saluter (POP) 457-2465
Metropolitan Areas (MA's):
  Population—POP. 457-2422
  Standards—James Fitzsimmons (POP) . . 457-2419
Migration—Kristin Hansen (POP) 457-2454
National Estimates & Projections—POP . . . 457-2422
Outlying Areas—Michael Levin (POP) 457-2327
Place of Birth—Kristin Hansen (POP) 457-2454
Population Information—POP. . . 457-2422/2435 (TTY)
Prisoner Surveys—Gail Hoff (DSD). 457-3925
Puerto Rico—Lourdes Flaim (DMD) 457-4023
Race Statistics—POP 457-2453/2402
Reapportionment & Redistricting—
  Marshall Turner, Jr. (DIR) 457-4039
Sampling Methods, Decennial Census—
  Henry Woltman (DSSD) 457-4199
School District Data—Jane Ingold (POP). . . 457-2408
Special Demographic Surveys—
  Sarah Higgins (DSD) 457-3801
Special Population Censuses—
  Elaine Csellar (FLD) 457-1429
Special Tabulations—Rose Cowan (POP) . . 457-2408
State & County Estimates—POP 457-2422
State Projections—POP. 457-2422
Undercount, Demographic Analysis—
  Gregg Robinson (POP) 457-2103
Veterans' Status—
  Thomas Palumbo (HHES) 763-8574
Women—Denise Smith (POP) 457-2378

Geographic Concepts

1980 Census Map Orders—
  Ann Devore (DPD) 812-288-3192
1990 Census Maps—DUSD. 457-4100
Annexations & Boundary Changes—
  Joseph Marinucci (GEO) 457-1099
Area Measurement—GEO 457-1099
Census County Divisions—
  Cathy McCully (GEO) 457-1099
Census Designated Places—
  Nancy Torrieri (GEO) 457-1099
Census Geographic Concepts—GEO 457-1099
Census Tracts—Cathy Miller (GEO) 457-1099
Centers of Population—
  Lourdes Ramirez (GEO). 457-1073
Congressional Districts:
  Address Allocations—GEO 457-1050
  Boundaries—Cathy McCully (GEO) 457-1099
Federal Geographic Data Committee—
  Fred Broome (GEO) 457-1056
Fee-Paid Block Splits—Joel Miller (GEO) . . . 457-1099
FIPS Codes—Virgeline Davis (GEO). 457-1099
Internal Points—Tony Costanzo (GEO) 457-1073
Master Address File—Dan Sweeney (GEO). . 457-1106

Metropolitan Areas—
  James Fitzsimmons (POP) 457-2419
Outlying Areas—Virgeline Davis (GEO) 457-1099
Population Circles (Radii)—
  Rick Hartgen (GEO). 457-1128
Postal Geography—Rose Quarato (GEO) . . 457-1128
School Districts—Dave Aultman (GEO) 457-1099
State Boundary Certification—
  Louise Stewart (GEO) 457-1099
TIGER System:
  Future Plans & Products—GEO. 457-1100
  Products—Larry Carbaugh (DUSD) 457-1242
  Thematic Mapping—Tim Trainor (GEO). . . 457-1101
Urban/Rural Residence—POP 457-2381
Urbanized Areas & Urban / Rural Concepts—
  Nancy Torrieri (GEO) 457-1099
Voting Districts—Cathy McCully (GEO) 457-1099
ZIP Codes:
  Demographic Data—DUSD. 457-4100
  Economic Data—Anne Russell (SVSD). . . 457-2687
  Geographic Relationships—
  Rose Quarato (GEO) 457-1128

Governments

Criminal Justice—Alan Stevens (GOVS) . . . 457-1550
Education
  Elementary-Secondary—
    Larry MacDonald (GOVS) 457-1563
  Post-Secondary—
    John Monaco (GOVS). 457-1106
Federal Expenditure Data—
  Robert McArthur (GOVS) 457-1565

Finance & Employment:
  General—Henry Wulf (GOVS). 457-1486
  Eastern States—
    George Beaven (GOVS) 457-1529
    Western States—Russell Price (GOVS) . . 457-1488
Governmental Organization—
  David Kellerman (GOVS) 457-1586
Taxation—Henry Wulf (GOVS) 457-1486

Housing

American Housing Survey—
  Edward Montfort (HHES) 763-8551
  John Cannon (DSD) 457-3877
  Census—Robert Bonnette (HHES) 763-8553
Components of Inventory Change Survey—
  Barbara Williams (HHES) 763-8551
Housing Affordability—Peter Fronczek /
  Howard Savage (HHES). 763-8165

Market Absorption/Residential Finance—
  Anne Smoler / Ellen Wilson (HHES) 763-8165
New York City Housing & Vacancy Survey—
  Peter Fronczek (HHES) 763-8165
Vacancy Data—Alan Friedman /
  Robert Callis (HHES). 763-8165

Income, Poverty, & Wealth

Consumer Expenditures—
  Ron Dopkowski (DSD) 457-3914
Household Wealth—T. J. Eller /
  Wallace Fraser (HHES) 763-8578
Income Statistics—HHES 763-8576
Poverty Statistics—HHES 763-8578
Survey of Income & Program Participation
  (SIPP)—Judy Eargle (HHES) 763-8375

General Information—
  Enrique Lamas (DSD) 457-3819
Microdata Files—
  Carmen Campbell (DUSD) 457-1139
Statistical Methods—
  Vicki Huggins (DSMD) 457-4192

International Statistics

Africa, Asia, Latin America, North America, &
  Oceania—Patricia Rowe (POP). 457-1358
Aging Population—Kevin Kinsella (POP) . . . 457-1371
China, People's Republic—Loraine West /
  Christina Harbaugh (POP) 457-1360
Europe, Former Soviet Union—Marc Rubin (POP)457-1362

Health—Karen Stanecki (POP). 457-1406
International Data Base—
  Peter Johnson (POP). 457-1403
International Visitors—
  Gene Vandrovec (PIO). 457-2816
Women in Development—
  Patricia Rowe (POP) 457-1358

Labor Force

Commuting, Means of Transportation, &
  Place of Work—Phil Salopek /
  Celia Boertlein (POP). 457-2454
Employment & Unemployment—
  Thomas Palumbo (HHES) 763-8574

Journey to Work—Phil Salopek /
  Gloria Swieczkowski (POP) 457-2454
Occupation & Industry Statistics—HHES . . . 763-8574

National, State, & Local Data Centers

Business/Industry Data Centers—DUSD . . . 457-1305
Clearinghouse for Census Data Services—
  Larry Carbaugh (DUSD). 457-1242

National Census Information Centers—
  Barbara Harris (DUSD) 457-1305
State Data Center Program—
  Tim Jones (DUSD) 457-1305

[1]Use area code 301 unless otherwise noted. Names of individuals given above are subject to change.
Source: U.S. Bureau of the Census, *Telephone Contacts for Data Users.*

Information Sources in the U.S. Department of Commerce:
Quick Reference List[1]

**GENERAL INFORMATION, PROCUREMENT, AND
PUBLIC AFFAIRS OFFICES**

Aeronautical and Nautical
  Chart Sales . . . . (301) 436-6980
Bidder's List . . . . (202) 482-3387
Business Assistance . . . . (202) 482-3176
Commerce Speakers . . . . (202) 482-1360
Consumer Affairs . . . . (202) 482-5001
Copyright Information* . . . . (202) 707-3000
Economics and Statistics
  Administration . . . . (202) 482-2235
Economic Bulletin Board . . . . (202) 482-1986
Economic Development
  Administration . . . . (202) 482-5113
Energy Related Inventions
  Evaluation . . . . (301) 975-5500
Federal Procurement Conferences . . . (703) 274-6471
Fishery Management Plans . . . . (301) 713-2334
International Trade Administration. . . . (202) 482-3808
Malcolm Baldrige Quality Award . . . . . (301) 975-2036
MBDA ABELS System for
  Procurement . . . . (202) 482-2025
Metric Information . . . . (301) 975-3690
Minority Business Development
  Agency (MBDA) . . . . (202) 482-4547
National Institute of Standards and
  Technology (NIST) . . . . (301) 975-2000
National Technical Information Service
  Sales Desk . . . . (703) 487-4650
National Telecommunications and   ,
  Information Administration . . . . (202) 482-1551
National Ocean Service . . . . (202) 482-6090
National Weather Service . . . . (301) 713-0622
NIST Research Information . . . . (301) 975-2790
Patent Information . . . . (703) 308-HELP
Patent Regional Information . . . . (703) 308-3924
Procurement Forecast . . . . (202) 482-1472
Sea Grant Research . . . . (301) 713-2438
Small Business Administration
  Answer Desk . . . . (800) 827-5722
Small Business Innovation Research
  (SBIR) . . . . (301) 763-4240
Small Business Set Asides . . . . (202) 482-3387
Small Business Technology
  Assistance . . . . (301) 975-6343
Standards Code and Information
  Program . . . . (301) 975-4029
Technology Administration . . . . (202) 482-1397
U.S. Travel and Tourism
  Administration . . . . (202) 482-0137
Women-Owned Business . . . . (202) 482-5614

PUBLICATIONS

"Business America" Magazine . . . . . . (202) 482-3251
"Commerce Business Daily" . . . . (202) 482-0632
"Survey of Current Business" . . . . . . (202) 606-9900

STATISTICS

Business Cycles . . . . (202) 606-5365
Capital Investment . . . . (202) 606-5308
Export Statistics . . . . (202) 482-2185
Foreign Travelers to U.S. . . . . (202) 482-4028
Gross Domestic Product . . . . (202) 606-9700
Housing Starts . . . . (301) 763-5731
Income Data . . . . (301) 763-8579
International Investment . . . . (202) 606-9800
International Trade Balance . . . . (202) 606-9545
Leading Economic Indicators . . . . (202) 606-5365
National Economic, Social &
  Environmental Data Bank
  (Domestic) . . . . (202) 482-1986
Personal Income, Outlays and
  Savings . . . . (202) 606-5301
Personal Income by County . . . . (202) 606-5360
Population . . . . (301) 763-5002
Price Indexes . . . . (202) 606-9700
Regional Projections . . . . (202) 606-5344
Retail Trade Data . . . . (301) 763-5294

TRADE AND EXPORTS

Advocacy Center . . . . (202) 482-3896
Business Information Service for the
  Newly Independent States . . . . (202) 482-4655
District Export Councils . . . . (202) 482-2975
Eastern Europe Business Information
  Center . . . . (202) 482-2645
Export Contact List Service . . . . (202) 482-2505
Export Licensing Voice Information
  System (ELVIS) . . . . (202) 482-4811
Export License Application and
  Information Network (ELAIN) . . . . . (202) 482-4811
Export Promotion Coordination . . . . . (202) 482-4501
Export Trading Companies . . . . (202) 482-5131
Fish Exports . . . . (301) 713-2328
Foreign Availability . . . . (202) 482-0074
Foreign Trade Zones . . . . (202) 482-2862
Industry/Products Information . . . . (202) 482-1461
International Trade Administration . . . . (202) 482-3808
Latin America/Caribbean Business
  Development Center . . . . (202) 482-0841
National Trade Data Bank . . . . (202) 482-1986
System for Tracking Export License
  Application (STELA) . . . . (202) 482-2752
Trade Information Center, for any
  information on Federal programs
  and activities that support U.S.
  exports . . . . (202) 482-0543
                           (800) USA-TRAD
               or (800) 482-8723

WEATHER

Climate for Farming . . . . (301) 713-1677
Historic Weather Conditions
  w/certified copies . . . . (704) 271-4800
Selected Cities Forecast . . . . (703) 260-0806
Tide Predictions . . . . (301) 713-2815

---

[1] All (301) 763 . . . telephone numbers have been changed to (301) 457.
*Administered by the Library of Congress.

COMMODITIES: SOURCES OF GOVERNMENT INFORMATION

Information on various commodities may be obtained by calling the following:

Office of Industries
International Trade Commission
Telephone: 202-205-3296

Bureau of Mines
Ferrous and Nonferrous Metals
Telephone: 202-501-9465
Industrial Minerals
Telephone: 202-501-9401

Crops Bulletin Board
Department of Agriculture
Telephone: 1-800-523-3215

Crops Statistics
Bureau of the Census
Telephone: 301-523-8567

Metals and Minerals
Trade Development
Telephone: 202-482-5157

Minerals Industries
Bureau of the Census
Telephone: 301-523-5938

Industry and Commodity Classification
Bureau of the Census
Telephone: 301-457-1314

Federal Agricultural Service: Commodity and Marketing Divisions
Dairy, Livestock and
Poultry 800-523-3215
Grain and Feed
Division 800-523-3215
Horticulture and Tropical
Products 800-523-3215
Oilseed and Oilseed
Products 301-457-4634
Tobacco, Cotton and
Seeds 800-523-3215
Forest Products 202-205-0957

Available through the Government Printing Office (202-512-1800) are the Bureau of the Census Publications, *U.S. Imports, U.S.A. Commodities by Country* and *U.S. Exports Schedule 13, Commodities by Country.*

DOING BUSINESS WITH THE FEDERAL GOVERNMENT

Publications

The publications listed below may be purchased from the Government Printing Office (GPO) at 202-512-1800.

Catalogue of Federal Domestic Assistance provides grant information on more than 50 agencies.

Doing Business with the Federal Government contains helpful material for marketing products or services to the Government, i.e., how to make products known, how and where to obtain the necessary forms and papers to get started, and how to bid on Government contracts. It also provides a geographical listing of Business Service Centers that have information about contract opportunities, as well as whom to contact and where to go for the information needed to sell to individual Government agencies. A list of Business Service Centers is given below.

The *Commerce Business Daily* tells, for example, what products and services the Government is buying, which agencies are buying, due dates for bids, how to get complete specifications. Each weekday, the *Commerce Business Daily* gives a complete listing of products and services wanted by the U.S. Government. Each listing includes product or service, along with a short description, name and address of agency, deadline for proposals or bids, phone number to request specifications, and solicitation numbers of product or service needed. Issued Monday through Friday.

The *Federal Acquisition Regulation* (FAR) is the primary source of procurement regulations used by all Federal agencies in their acquisition of supplies and services. It sets forth all the provisions and clauses that are used in Government contracting. Because the clauses in a specific solicitation for bids refer to a numbered provision of FAR rather than providing the full text, the FAR is necessary to understand the solicitation. Subscription service consists of a basic manual and supplementary material for an indeterminate period.

The *United States Government Purchasing and Sales Directory* contains an alphabetical listing of the products and services bought by all military departments and a separate listing for civilian agencies. It also includes an explanation of the ways in which the Small Business Administration can help a business obtain Government prime contracts and subcontracts, data on Government sales of surplus property, and comprehensive descriptions of the scope of the Government market for research and development.

The *General Services Subcontracting Directory* is designed to aid small business professionals interested in subcontracting opportunities within the Department of Defense (DOD). The guide is arranged alphabetically by state and includes the name and address of each current DOD prime contractor as well as the product or services being provided to DOD. It also includes the name and telephone number for each DOD Small Business Liaison Officer who knows what the subcontracted products and services are, what the prime contracting firm has purchased in the past, what it is presently purchasing, and what it may be planning to purchase in the future.

The *Federal Register* provides the official version of public regulations issued by the Federal agencies. It also includes announcements of grants and other funding information, as well as data on the availability of Government contracts.

U.S. GENERAL SERVICES ADMINISTRATION (GSA): BUSINESS SERVICE CENTERS

The Business Service Centers are a one stop, one point of contact for information on General Services Administration and other Government contract programs. The primary function is to provide advice on doing business with the Federal Government. The Centers provide information, assistance, and counseling and sponsor business clinics, procurement conferences, and business opportunity meetings.

Many Government purchases must be made from a GSA "Federal Supply Schedule"—a list of vendors from which agencies can place their orders directly with contractors at pre-established prices. Business representatives interested in selling products and services to the Government should contact the nearest Business Service Center given above.

BUSINESS ASSISTANCE PROGRAM: COMMERCE DEPARTMENT

The Business Assistance program is designed to shorten the time it takes a businessperson to track down information within the labyrinth of government bureaus and agencies. Business Assistance Program staffers can provide information or direct inquiries to the proper authority on such subjects as regulatory changes, government programs, services, policies, and even relevant government publications for the business community. For information call 202-482-3176 or write: Business Assistance Program Business Liaison Office, Department of Commerce, Washington, DC 20230.

FEDERAL INFORMATION CENTER (FIC)

The FIC is a focal point for obtaining information about the federal government and often about state and local governments. A member of the center's staff can either provide information or direct inquiries to an expert who can.

BUSINESS SERVICE CENTER

Region	Area of Service	Telephone
National Capitol	District of Columbia, nearby Maryland, Virginia	202-708-5804
1	Connecticut, Maine, Massachusetts, New Hampshire, Rhode Island, and Vermont	617-565-8100
2	New Jersey, New York, Puerto Rico, and Virgin Islands	212-264-1234
3	Delaware, Pennsylvania, West Virginia, Virginia, Maryland (except for D.C. metropolitan area)	215-597-9613
4	Alabama, Florida, Georgia, Kentucky, Mississippi, North Carolina, South Carolina, and Tennessee	404-331-5103
5	Illinois, Indiana, Ohio, Michigan, Minnesota, and Wisconsin	312-353-5383
6	Iowa, Kansas, Missouri, and Nebraska	816-926-7203
7	Arkansas, Louisiana, New Mexico, Oklahoma, and Texas	817-334-3284
8	Colorado, Montana, North Dakota, South Dakota, Utah, and Wyoming	303-236-7408
9	California (northern), Hawaii, and Nevada (except Clark County)	415-744-5050
	Arizona, Los Angeles, California (southern), and Nevada (Clark County only)	213-894-3210
10	Alaska, Idaho, Oregon, and Washington	206-931-7956

To call the Center, dial the telephone number given below for your metropolitan area. The Center is open from 9 A.M. to 5 P.M., local time, unless otherwise noted. If you are not in one of the areas listed, call (301) 722-9000.

Alabama
Birmingham, Mobile . . . . (800) 366-2998
Alaska (8 A.M.–4 P.M.)
Anchorage. . . . . (800) 729-8003
Arizona
Phoenix . . . . (800) 359-3997
Arkansas
Little Rock. . . . . (800) 366-2998

California
Los Angeles, San Diego,
San Francisco, Santa Ana,
Sacramento . . . . (800) 726-4995

Colorado
Colorado Springs, Denver, Pueblo . . . (800) 359-3997

Connecticut
Hartford, New Haven . . . . (800) 347-1997

Florida
Fort Lauderdale, Jacksonville, Miami,
Orlando, St. Petersburg, Tampa,
West Palm Beach . . . . (800) 347-1997

Georgia
Atlanta . . . . (800) 347-1997

Hawaii (7 A.M.–3 P.M.)
Honolulu . . . . (800) 733-5996

Illinois
Chicago . . . . (800) 366-2998

Indiana
Gary . . . . (800) 366-2998
Indianapolis . . . . (800) 347-1997

Iowa
All locations . . . . (800) 735-8004

Kansas
All locations . . . . (800) 735-8004

Kentucky
Louisville . . . . (800) 347-1997

Louisiana
New Orleans . . . . (800) 366-2998

Maryland
Baltimore . . . . (800) 347-1997

Massachusetts
Boston . . . . (800) 347-1997

Michigan
Detroit, Grand Rapids . . . . (800) 347-1997

Minnesota
Minneapolis . . . . (800) 366-2998

Missouri
St. Louis . . . . (800) 366-2998
All other locations . . . . (800) 735-8004

Nebraska
Omaha . . . . (800) 366-2998
All other locations . . . . (800) 735-8004

New Jersey
Newark, Trenton . . . . (800) 347-1997

New Mexico
Albuquerque . . . . (800) 359-3997

New York
Albany, Buffalo, New York,
Rochester, Syracuse . . . . (800) 347-1997

North Carolina
Charlotte . . . . (800) 347-1997

Ohio
Akron, Cincinnati, Cleveland,
Columbus, Dayton, Toledo . . . . (800) 347-1997

Oklahoma
Oklahoma City, Tulsa . . . . (800) 366-2998

Oregon
Portland . . . . (800) 726-4995

Pennsylvania
Philadelphia, Pittsburgh . . . . (800) 347-1997

Rhode Island
Providence . . . . (800) 347-1997

Tennessee
Chattanooga . . . . (800) 347-1997
Memphis, Nashville . . . . (800) 366-2998

Texas
Austin, Dallas, Fort Worth,
Houston, San Antonio . . . . (800) 366-2998

Utah
Salt Lake City . . . . (800) 359-3997

Virginia
Norfolk, Richmond, Roanoke . . . . . . (800) 347-1997

Washington
Seattle, Tacoma . . . . (800) 726-4995

Wisconsin
Milwaukee . . . . (800) 366-2998

Users of Telecommunications Devices for the Deaf (TDD/TTY) may call toll-free from any point in the United States by dialing (800) 326-2996.

State Information Guide

Regional Manufacturers Directories

Connecticut/Rhode Island Manufacturers Directory
Commerce Register, Inc.
190 Godwin Avenue
Midland Park, NJ 07432

Main/New Hampshire/Vermont Directory of Manufacturers
Commerce Register, Inc.
190 Godwin Avenue
Midland Park, NJ 07432

Harris Publishing Co.
2057 Aurora Road
Twinsburg, OH 44087

Maryland/DC/Delaware Manufacturers Directory
Harris Publishing Co.
2057 Aurora Road
Twinsburg, OH 44087

Midwest Manufacturers Directory
Harris Publishing Co.
2057 Aurora Road
Twinsburg, OH 44087

New York Metro Directory of Manufacturers
Commerce Register, Inc.
190 Godwin Avenue
Midland Park, NJ 07432

New England Manufacturers Directory
Harris Publishing Co.
2057 Aurora Road
Twinsburg, OH 44087

New York Upstate Directory of Manufacturers
Commerce Register, Inc.
190 Godwin Avenue
Midland Park, NJ 07432

Northwest Manufacturers Directory
Harris Publishing, Co.
2057 Aurora Road
Twinsburg, OH 44087

Northern California
Database Publishing Company
P.O. Box 70024
Anaheim, CA 92825-0024

Manufacturers' News, Inc.
1633 West Central Street
Evanston, IL 60201

State Sales Guides
Dun & Bradstreet, Inc.
299 Park Avenue
New York, NY 10171

Southeast Manufacturers Directory
Harris Publishing Co.
2057 Aurora Road
Twinsburg, OH 44087

Southern California Business Directory and Buyer's Guide
Database Publishing Company
P.O. Box 70024
Anaheim, CA 92825-0024

Manufacturers' News, Inc.
1633 West Central Street
Evanston, IL 60201

Upstate New York Directory of Manufacturers
Commerce Register Inc.
190 Godwin Avenue
Midland Park, NJ 07432

West and Southwest Manufacturers Directory
Harris Publishing Co.
2057 Aurora Road
Twinsburg, OH 44087

Small Business Assistance Publications

Directory of Federal and State Business Assistance—A Guide for New and Growing Companies, presents full descriptions to financial, management, innovation, and information programs and services established to help both large and small firms in their day-to-day operations. To order write the National Technical Information Service, 5285 Port Royal Road, Springfield, VA 22161 or call 703-487-4650.

Directory of Incentives for Business Investment and Development in the U.S., The Urban Institute Press, available from United Press of America, 4720 Boston Way, Lanham, MD 20706. State by state guide to economic business incentives. Included are descriptions of state assistance and financial assistance programs.

How to Do Business with the States: A Guide for Vendors. A list of primary state entities with independent purchasing authority and information. Includes a listing of states that publish vendor guides and vendor commodity definition guidelines. Available from the Council of State Governments. Call: 800-800-1910.

Monthly Checklist of State Publications, Superintendent of Documents. Washington, DC 20402. A monthly list of documents and publications received from the States.

State Administrative Officials Classified by Function, Council of State Governments, Iron Works Pike, P.O. Box 1190, Lexington, KY 40578. Names, titles, telephone numbers and addresses of state officials and administrators.

State and Local Government Purchasing is available from the Council of State Governments. A resource to a better understanding of laws, regulations and procedures associated with the acquisition of goods and services. Call: 800-800-1910.

State and Metropolitan Area Data Book is prepared by the Bureau of the Census of the U.S. Department of Commerce. Presents a wide variety of information on States and metropolitan areas in the United States. Available from the Government Printing Office by calling 202-512-1800.

State Executive Directory is available from Carroll Publishing at 1058 Thomas Jefferson Street, NW., Washington, D.C. 20007. Telephone: 202-333-8620. Contains names, titles, addresses and phone numbers.

The States and Small Business: A Directory of Programs and Activities. A guide to state programs designed to assist small business. Includes sources of financing, new state legislation affecting business and more. Prepared by the Office of Advocacy, U.S. Small Business Administration and available from the Superintendent of Documents at 202-512-1800.

Business/Industry Data Centers (BIDC's) and State Data Centers (SDC's)[1]

Business/Industry Data Centers (BIDC's) offer assistance in business related matters. Such assistance includes information gathering, location of expert help, and guidance on new technologies. Most of these centers also are able to offer other types of assistance, such as market feasibility, or at least link businesses with appropriate contacts.

Access to the many statistical products available from the Bureau of the Census is provided through the services of the joint federal-state cooperative State Data Center Program. Through the Program, the Bureau furnishes statistical products, training in the data access and use, technical assistance, and consultation to states which, in turn, disseminate the products and provide assistance in their use.

Below we list the SDC and BIDC lead agency contacts. All States except Alaska

[1] Names of contacts are subject to change.

have SDC's. Asterisks (°) identify States that also have BIDC's. In some States, one agency serves as the lead for both the SDC and the BIDC; we list the BIDC separately where there is a separate agency serving as the lead.

Alabama—Annette Watters,
University of Alabama 205-348-6191
*Arizona—Betty Jeffries,
Department of Security 602-542-5984
Arkansas—Sarah Breshears, University of Arkansas at Little Rock 501-569-8530
California—Linda Gage,
Department of Finance 916-322-4651
Colorado—Rebecca Picaso,
Department of Local Affairs 303-866-2156
Connecticut—Bill Kraynak,
Office of Policy & Management. 203-566-8285
*Delaware—Staff, Development Office. . 302-739-4271
District of Columbia—Gan Ahuja,
Mayor's Office of Planning 202-727-6533
*Florida—Valerie Jugger,
State Data Center 904-487-2814
BIDC—Nick Leslie,
Department of Commerce 904-487-2971
Georgia—Marty Sik,
Office of Planning & Budget 404 050-0911
Guam—Art De Oro,
Department of Commerce 671-646-5841
Hawaii—Jan Nakamoto,
Department of Business, Economic
Development, & Tourism 808-586-2493
Idaho—Alan Porter,
Department of Commerce 208-334-2470
Illinois—Suzanne Ebetsch,
Bureau of the Budget 217-782-1381
*Indiana—Laurence Hathaway,
State Library. 317-232-3733
BIDC—Carol Rogers,
Business Research Center. 317-274-2205
Iowa—Beth Henning, State Library . . . 515-281-4350
Kansas—Marc Galbraith,
State Library. 913-296-3296
*Kentucky—Ron Crouch, Center for
Urban & Economic Research 502-852-7990
Louisiana—Karen Paterson,
Office of Planning & Budget 504-342-7410
*Maine—Jean Martin,
Department of Labor 207-287-2271
*Maryland—Robert Dadd/
Jane Traynham, Department of
State Planning 410-225-4450
*Massachusetts—Valerie Conti,
University of Massachusetts 413-545-3460
Michigan—Eric Swanson, Department
of Management & Budget 517-373-7910
*Minnesota—David Birkholz,
State Demographer's Office 612-296-2557
BIDC—David Rademacher,
State Demographer's Office 612-297-3255
*Mississippi—Rachael McNeely,
University of Mississippi. 601-232-7288
BIDC—Bill Rigby, Division of
Research & Information Systems . . . 601-359-2674
*Missouri—Kate Graf, State Library . . . 314-751-1823
BIDC—Terry Maynard, Small
Business Development Centers 314-882-0344
*Montana—Patricia Roberts,
Department of Commerce 406-444-2896

Nebraska—Jerome Deichert,
University of Nebraska-Omaha 402-595-2311
Nevada—Laura Witschi, State Library. . 702-687-8327
New Hampshire—Thomas J. Duffy,
Office of State Planning 603-271-2155
*New Jersey—Connie O. Hughes,
Department of Labor 609-984-2593
*New Mexico—Kevin Kargacin,
University of New Mexico. 505-277-6626
BIDC—Bobby Leitch,
University of New Mexico. 505-277-2216
*New York—Staff, Department of
Economic Development 518-474-1141
*North Carolina—Staff, State Library . . 919-733-3270
North Dakota—Richard Rathge,
North Dakota State University. 701-231-8621
Northern Mariana Islands—Juan Borja,
Department of Commerce & Labor. . . 670-322-0874
*Ohio—Barry Bennett,
Department of Development 614-466-2115
*Oklahoma—Jeff Wallace,
Department of Commerce 405-841-5184
Oregon—George Hough,
Portland State University 503-725-5159
*Pennsylvania—Diane Shoop,
Pennsylvania State University
at Harrisburg 717-948-6336
Puerto Rico—Irmgard Gonzalez
Segarra, Planning Board 809-728-4430
Rhode Island—Paul Egan,
Department of Administration 401-277-6493
South Carolina—Mike MacFarlane,
Budget & Control Board. 803-734-3780
South Dakota—DeVee Dykstra,
University of South Dakota. 605-677-5287
Tennessee—Charles Brown,
State Planning Office. 615-741-1676
Texas—Steve Murdock,
Texas A&M University 409-845-5115
*Utah—Brenda Weaver,
Office of Planning & Budget 801-538-1036
Vermont—Sybil McShane,
Department of Libraries 802-828-3261
*Virginia—Dan Jones,
Virginia Employment Commission . . . 804-786-8308
Virgin Islands—Frank Mills,
University of the Virgin Islands 809-776-9200
*Washington—David Lamphere, Office
of Financial Management. 206-586-2504
*West Virginia—Mary C. Harless,
Office of Community & Industrial
Development 304-558-4010
BIDC—Randy Childs, Center for
Economic Research 304-293-7832
*Wisconsin—Robert Naylor,
Department of Administration 608-266-1927
BIDC—Michael Knight,
University of Wisconsin-Madison. . . . 608-265-3044
Wyoming—Wenlin Liu, Department
of Administration & Fiscal Control . . . 307-777-7504

State Information Offices*

Alabama
STATE CAPITOL, MONTGOMERY, AL 36130
(205) 242-8000

INFORMATION OFFICES

Commerce/Economic Development
Alabama Development Office
401 Adams Avenue
Montgomery, AL 36130

Department of Economic & Community
Affairs
401 Adams Avenue
Montgomery, AL 36130

Corporate
Secretary of State
P.O. Box 5616
Montgomery, AL 36103

Taxation
Department of Revenue
Gordon Persons Building
50 Ripley Street
Montgomery, AL 36132

State Chamber of Commerce
Business Council of Alabama
2 N. Jackson Street
P.O. Box 76
Montgomery, AL 36101

International Commerce
Department of International Trade
Alabama Development Office
401 Adams Avenue
Montgomery, AL 36130

Banking
State Banking Department
101 S. Union Street
Montgomery, AL 36130

Securities
Alabama Securities Exchange Commission
770 Washington Street
Montgomery, AL 36130

Labor and Industrial Relations
Department of Industrial Relations
649 Monroe Street
Montgomery, AL 36130

Alabama Department of Labor
Administrative Building
1789 Congressman W. L. Dickinson Drive
National Guard Credit Union
Montgomery, AL 36130

Insurance
Department of Insurance
135 S. Union Street
Montgomery, AL 36130

Uniform Industrial Code
Alabama Development Office
401 Adams Street
Montgomery, AL 36130

INDUSTRIAL AND BUSINESS DIRECTORIES

Alabama Directory of Mining and Manufacturing, Alabama Development Office, State Capitol, Montgomery, AL 36130

---

*See page 208 for Small Business Administration Regional Office telephone numbers.

Alabama Industrial Directory, Alabama Development Office, State Capitol, Montgomery, AL 36130
Alabama Manufacturers Register, Manufacturers' News, Inc., 1633 W. Central Street, Evanston, IL 60201
Alabama International Trade Directory, Alabama Development Office, State Capitol, Montgomery, AL 36130
Top Businesses in Alabama, State Capitol, Montgomery, AL 36130
Birmingham Industrial Directory, Birmingham Chamber of Commerce, 1914 6th Avenue, Birmingham, AL 35203

Alaska

STATE CAPITOL, JUNEAU, AK 99811
(907) 465-2111

INFORMATION OFFICES

Commerce/Economic Development
Department of Commerce & Economic Development
P.O. Box 110800
Juneau, AK 99811-0800
Corporate
Department of Commerce & Economic Development
Corporation Section
P.O. Box 110808
Juneau, AK 99811-0808
Taxation
Department of Revenue
P.O. Box 110420
Juneau, AK 99811-0420
State Chamber of Commerce
Alaska State Chamber of Commerce
310 2nd Street
Juneau, AK 99801
International Commerce
Office of International Trade
3601 C Street
Anchorage, AK 99503-5934
Banking
Division of Banking, Securities and Corporations
Department of Commerce & Economic Development
P.O. Box 110808
Juneau, AK 99811-0808
Securities
Division of Banking, Securities and Corporations
Department of Commerce and Economic Development
P.O. Box 11808
Juneau, AK 99811-0808
Labor and Industrial Relations
Department of Labor
P.O. Box 21149
Juneau, AK 99802-1149

Insurance
Division of Insurance
Department of Commerce and Economic Development
P.O. Box 110805
Juneau, AK 99811-0805
Uniform Industrial Code
Uniform Commercial Code Office
Division of Management
Department of Natural Resources
P.O. Box 107005
Anchorage, AK 99510-7005

INDUSTRIAL AND BUSINESS DIRECTORIES

Alaska/Hawaii Manufacturers Directory, Manufacturers' News, Inc., 1633 W. Central Street, Evanston, IL 60201
Alaska Petroleum and Industrial Directory, 409 W. Northern Lights Boulevard, Anchorage, AK 99603

Arizona

STATE CAPITOL, PHOENIX, AZ 85007
(602) 542-4331

INFORMATION OFFICES

Commerce/Economic Development
Department of Commerce
3800 N. Central Avenue
Phoenix, AZ 85012
Corporate
Arizona Corporation Commission
1200 W. Washington Avenue
Phoenix, AZ 85007
Taxation
Department of Revenue
1600 W. Monroe
Phoenix, AZ 85007
State Chamber of Commerce
Arizona State Chamber of Commerce
1221 E. Osborn Road
Phoenix, AZ 85014
Banking
Banking Department
2910 N. 44th Street
Phoenix, AZ 85018
Insurance
Insurance Department
2910 N. 44th Street
Phoenix, AZ 85018
Securities
Arizona Corporation Commission
1300 W. Washington Avenue
Phoenix, AZ 85007
International Commerce
International Trade
Department of Commerce
3800 N. Central Avenue
Phoenix, AZ 85012

Labor and Industrial Relations
Industrial Commission
800 W. Washington Street
Phoenix, AZ 85007

INDUSTRIAL AND BUSINESS DIRECTORIES

Arizona Industrial Directory, Phoenix Chamber of Commerce, 201 N. Central Avenue, Phoenix, AZ 85073; Database Publishing, P.O. Box 70024, Anaheim, CA 92825-0024. Manufacturers' News, 1633 Central Street, Evanston, IL 60201

Arizona USA International Trade Directory, Arizona State Department of Commerce, 3800 N. Central Avenue, Phoenix, AZ 85012

Directory of Arizona Manufacturers, Phoenix Chamber of Commerce, 201 N. Central Avenue, Phoenix, AZ 85073

Arkansas

STATE CAPITOL, LITTLE ROCK, AR 72201
(501) 682-3000

INFORMATION OFFICES

Commerce/Economic Development
Arkansas Industrial Development
Commission
Big Mac Building
One State Capitol Mall
Little Rock, AR 72201

Corporate
Secretary of State
Corporations Department
State Capitol
Little Rock, AR 72201

Taxation
State Revenue Office
Department of Finance and
Administration
Joel Y. Ledbetter Building
7th and Wolfe Streets
Little Rock, AR 72201

State Chamber of Commerce
Arkansas State Chamber of Commerce
410 South Cross
Little Rock, AR 72201

International Commerce
Arkansas Industrial Development
Commission
Big Mac Building
One State Capitol Mall
Little Rock, AR 72201

Banking
State Bank Department
323 Center Street
Tower Building
Little Rock, AR 72201

Securities
Arkansas Securities Department
Heritage West Building
201 East Markham
Little Rock, AR 72201

Labor and Industrial Relations
Arkansas Department of Labor
10421 West Markham
Little Rock, AR 72205

Insurance
Arkansas Insurance Department
400 University Tower Building
Little Rock, AR 72204

Ombudsman
State Claims Commission
State Capitol
Little Rock, AR 72201

INDUSTRIAL AND BUSINESS DIRECTORIES

Arkansas Directory of Manufacturers, Arkansas Industrial Development Commission, One State Capitol Mall, Little Rock, AR 72201; Manufacturers' News, Inc., 1633 W. Central Street, Evanston, IL 60201

Arkansas State and County Economic Data (annual), Research and Public Service, Division of Regional Economic Analysis, 2801 South University, Little Rock, AR 72204

California

STATE CAPITOL, SACRAMENTO, CA 95814
(916) 332-9900

INFORMATION OFFICES

Commerce/Economic Development
Trade and Commerce Agency
801 K Street
Sacramento, CA 95814

Corporate
Secretary of State
1500 11th Street
Sacramento, CA 95814

Taxation
Board of Equalization
450 N Street
Sacramento, CA 95814

P.O. Box 942877
Sacramento, CA 94279-0001

State Chamber of Commerce
California Chamber of Commerce
P.O. Box 1736
Sacramento, CA 95812-1736

International Commerce
California State World Trade
Commission
801 K Street
Sacramento, CA 95814

Banking
State Banking Department
111 Pine Street
San Francisco, CA 94111-5613
Securities
Department of Corporations
980 8th Street
Sacramento, CA 95814
Labor and Industrial Relations
Department of Industrial Relations
455 Golden Gate Avenue
San Francisco, CA 94102

P.O. Box 420603
San Francisco, CA 94142
or
1121 L Street
Sacramento, CA 95814
Insurance
Department of Insurance
300 South Spring Street–South Tower
Los Angeles, CA 90013
or
770 L Street
Sacramento, CA 95814

INDUSTRIAL AND BUSINESS DIRECTORIES

California Handbook, California Institute of Public Affairs, P.O. Box 189040, Sacramento, CA 95818

California International Trade Register, Database Publishing Company, P.O. Box 70024, Anaheim, CA 92825-0024; Manufacturers' News, Inc., 1633 W. Central Street, Evanston, IL 60201

California Manufacturers Register, Database Publishing Company, P.O. Box 70024, Anaheim, CA 92825-0024; Manufacturers' News, Inc., 1633 W. Central Street, Evanston, IL 60201

California Services Register, Database Publishing Company, P.O. Box 70024, Anaheim, CA 92825-0024; Manufacturers' News, Inc., 1633 W. Central Street, Evanston, IL 60201

San Francisco County Commerce and Industry Directory, Database Publishing Company, P.O. Box 70024, Anaheim, CA 92825-0024; Manufacturers' News, Inc., 1633 W. Central Street, Evanston, IL 60201

Southern California Business Directory and Buyers Guide, Database Publishing Company, P.O. Box 70024, Anaheim, CA 92825-0024; Manufacturers' News, Inc., 1633 W. Central Street, Evanston, IL 60201

INFORMATION OFFICES

Commerce/Economic Development
Office of Business Development
World Trade Center
1625 Broadway
Denver, CO 80202
Corporate
Secretary of State
Civic Center Plaza
1560 Broadway
Denver, CO 80202
Taxation
Colorado Department of Revenue
Department of Revenue
1375 Sherman Street
Denver, CO 80203
State Chamber of Commerce
Colorado Association of Commerce and Industry
1776 Lincoln Street
Denver, CO 80203
International Commerce
Office of Business Development
International Trade Office
1625 Broadway
Denver, CO 80202
Banking
Division of Banking
1560 Broadway
Denver, CO 80202
Securities
Division of Securities
Department of Regulatory Agencies
1580 Lincoln Street
Denver, CO 80203
Labor and Industrial Relations
Division of Labor
1515 Arahoe
Denver, CO 80202-2117
Insurance
Division of Insurance
1560 Broadway
Denver, CO 80202
Uniform Commercial Code
Commercial Recordings Division
1560 Broadway
Denver, CO 80202

INDUSTRIAL AND BUSINESS DIRECTORIES

Directory of Colorado Manufacturers, Business Research Division, Graduate School of Business Administration, Campus Box 420, University of Colorado, Boulder, CO 80309; Manufacturers' News, Inc., 1633 W. Central Street, Evanston, IL 60201

Colorado

STATE CAPITOL, DENVER, CO 80203
(303) 866-5000

Connecticut

STATE CAPITOL, HARTFORD, CT 06106
(203) 566-4840

INFORMATION OFFICES

Commerce/Economic Development
Department of Economic
  Development
865 Brook Street
Rocky Hill, CT 06067

Corporate
Secretary of State
Corporations Division
30 Trinity Street
Hartford, CT 06106

Taxation
Department of Revenue Services
92 Farmington Avenue
Hartford, CT 06105

State Chamber of Commerce
Connecticut Business and Industry
  Association
370 Asylum Street
Hartford, CT 06103

International Commerce
Department of Economic
  Development
865 Brook Street
Rocky Hill, CT 06067

Banking
Department of Banking
44 Capitol Avenue
Hartford, CT 06106

Securities
Divisions of Securities & Business
  Investments
Department of Banking
44 Capitol Avenue
Hartford, CT 06106

Labor and Industrial Relations
Department of Labor
200 Folly Brook Boulevard
Wethersfield, CT 06109

Insurance
Department of Insurance
P.O. Box 816
Hartford, CT 06142

Uniform Industrial Code
Department of Economic
  Development
865 Brook Street
Rocky Hill, CT 06107

Business Ombudsman
Department of Economic Development
865 Brook Street
Rocky Hill, CT 06067

INDUSTRIAL AND BUSINESS DIRECTORIES

Classified Business Directory—State of Connecticut, Connecticut Directory Co., Inc., 322 Main Street, Stamford, CT 06901

Connecticut Classified Business Directory, Connecticut Directory Co., Inc., 322 Main Street, Stamford, CT 06901

Connecticut Service Directory, George D. Hall Co., 50 Congress Street, Boston, MA 02109

Directory of Connecticut Manufacturers, Harris Publishing Co., 2057 Aurora Road, Twinsburg, OH 44087

Directory of Connecticut Manufacturing Establishments, Connecticut Department of Labor, 200 Folly Brook Boulevard, Wethersfield, CT 06109

Delaware

LEGISLATIVE HALL, DOVER, DE 19901
(302) 739-4101

INFORMATION OFFICES

Commerce/Economic Development
Delaware Economic Development Office
99 Kings Highway
P.O. Box 1401
Dover, DE 19903

Corporate
Secretary of State
Corporations Department
Townsend Building
P.O. Box 898
Dover, DE 19903

Taxation
Department of Finance
Division of Revenue
Carvel State Office Building
820 N. French Street
Wilmington, DE 19801

International Commerce
Delaware Economic Development
  Office
99 Kings Highway
P.O. Box 1401
Dover, DE 19903

State Chamber of Commerce
Delaware State Chamber of
  Commerce, Inc.
One Commerce Center
Wilmington, DE 19801

Banking
State Bank Commission
Department of State
Thomas Collins Building
P.O. Box 1401
Dover, DE 19903

Labor and Industrial Relations
Division of Industrial Affairs
Department of Labor
Carvel State Office Building
820 N. French Street
Wilmington, DE 19801

Insurance
State Insurance Commission
841 Silver Lake Boulevard
Rodney Building
Dover, DE 19901

INDUSTRIAL AND BUSINESS DIRECTORIES

Delaware Directory of Commerce and Industry, Delaware State Chamber of Commerce, One Commerce Center, Wilmington, DE 19801; Manufacturers' News, Inc., 1633 W. Central Street, Evanston, IL 60201

Florida

STATE CAPITOL, TALLAHASSEE, FL 32399
(904) 488-1234

INFORMATION OFFICES

Commerce/Economic Development
Department of Commerce
Collins Building
107 W. Gaines Street
Tallahassee, FL 32399-2000
Division of Economic
Development
Department of Commerce
Collins Building
Tallahassee, FL 32399-2000
Corporate
Secretary of State
Division of Corporations
409 E. Gaines Street
Tallahassee, FL 32301
Taxation
Department of Revenue
Carlton Building
Tallahassee, FL 32399-0100
State Chamber of Commerce
Florida Chamber of Commerce
P.O. Box 11309
Tallahassee, FL 32302-3309
International Commerce
Florida Department of Commerce
Division of International Trade and
Development
Collins Building
107 W. Gaines Street
Tallahassee, FL 32399-2000
Banking
Florida Department of Banking
& Finance
The Capitol
Tallahassee, FL 32399-0350
Securities
Florida Department of Banking &
Finance
Division of Securities
The Capitol
Tallahassee, FL 32399-0350
Labor and Industrial Relations
Florida Department of Labor and
Employment Security
303 Hartman Building

2012 Capital Circle, SE
Tallahassee, FL 32399-2152
Insurance
Florida Department of Insurance
The Capitol
Tallahassee, FL 32399-0300
Commercial Information Services
Florida Department of State
Bureau of Information Services
409 E. Gaines Street
Tallahassee, FL 32301
Business Ombudsman
Florida Department of Commerce
Bureau of Business Assistance
Collins Building
107 W. Gaines Street
Tallahassee, FL 32399

INDUSTRIAL AND BUSINESS DIRECTORIES

Florida Manufacturers Register, Manufacturers' News, Inc., 1633 W. Central Street, Evanston, IL 60201
South Florida International Trade and Services Directory 1990, World Trade Center Miami, One World Trade Plaza, 80 SW 8th St., Suite 1800, Miami, FL 33130
Directory of International Manufacturing and Commercial Operations in Florida, Florida Department of Commerce, Division of International Trade and Development, Collins Building, Tallahassee, FL 32399-2000
Directory of Florida Industries, Harris Publishing Co., 2057 Aurora Road, Twinsburg, OH 44087

Georgia

STATE CAPITOL, ATLANTA, GA 30334
(404) 656-2000

INFORMATION OFFICES

Commerce/Economic Development
Department of Industry, Trade, and
Tourism
P.O. Box 1776
285 Peachtree Center Avenue, N.E.
Atlanta, GA 30301-1776
Corporate
Business Services and Regulations
Division
Secretary of State
2 Martin Luther King Jr. Drive, S.E.
Atlanta, GA 30334
Taxation
Department of Revenue
270 Washington Street, S.W.
Atlanta, GA 30334

State Chamber of Commerce
Business Council of Georgia
233 Peachtree Street
Atlanta, GA 30303-2705

International Commerce
Department of Industry and
Trade
P.O. Box 1776
285 Peachtree Center Avenue
Atlanta, GA 30303-1776

Banking
Department of Banking and
Finance
2990 Brandywine Road
Atlanta, GA 30341

Securities
Business Services and Regulations
Division
Secretary of State
2 Martin Luther King Jr. Drive, S.E.
Atlanta, GA 30334

Labor and Industrial Relations
Department of Labor
148 International Boulevard
Atlanta, GA 30303

Insurance
Office of Commissioner of
Insurance
2 Martin Luther King Jr. Drive, S.E.
Atlanta, GA 30334

INDUSTRIAL AND BUSINESS DIRECTORIES

Georgia Manufacturers Register, Manufacturers' News, Inc., 1633 W. Central Street, Evanston, IL 60201

Georgia Manufacturing Directory, Department of Industry, Trade, and Tourism, P.O. Box 1776, 285 Peachtree Center Avenue, Atlanta, GA 30301-1776

Georgia World Trade Directory, Business Council of Georgia, 233 Peachtree Street, Atlanta, GA 30303

Georgia Manufacturers Directory, Harris Publishing Co., 2057 Aurora Road, Twinsburg, OH 44087

Industrial Sites in Georgia, Georgia Power Company, Box 4545, Atlanta, GA 30303

Georgia International Trade Directory, Department of Industry, Trade, and Tourism, P.O. Box 1776, 285 Peachtree Center Avenue, Atlanta, GA 30301-1776

Georgia Directory of International Services, World Congress Institute, 1 Park Place S, Fulton Federal Building, Atlanta, GA 30303

International Companies with Facilities in Georgia, Department of Industry, Trade, and Tourism, P.O. Box 1776, 285 Peachtree Center Avenue, Atlanta, GA 30301-1776

Hawaii

STATE CAPITOL, HONOLULU, HI 96813
Information Office (808) 586-0221

INFORMATION OFFICES

Commerce/Economic Development
Business, Development & Marketing
Division
737 Bishop Street
Honolulu, HI 96813

Department of Commerce and
Consumer Affairs
1010 Richards Street
Honolulu, HI 96813

Corporate
Department of Commerce and
Consumer Affairs
Business Registration Division
P.O. Box 40
Honolulu, HI 96810

Taxation
Department of Taxation
830 Punchbowl Street
Honolulu, HI 96813

State Chamber of Commerce
Chamber of Commerce of Hawaii
1132 Bishop Street
Honolulu, HI 96813

International Commerce
International Business Center of Hawaii
201 Merchant Street
Honolulu, HI 96813

Hawaii Foreign-Trade Zone No. 9
Pier 2
Honolulu, HI 96813

Banking
Financial Institutions Division
Department of Commerce and
Consumer Affairs
1010 Richards Street
Honolulu, HI 96813

Securities
Financial Institutions Division
Department of Commerce and
Consumer Affairs
1010 Richards Street
Honolulu, HI 96813

Labor and Industrial Relations
Department of Labor and Industrial
Relations
830 Punchbowl Street
Honolulu, HI 96813

Insurance
Insurance Division
Department of Commerce and
Consumer Affairs
1010 Richards Street
Honolulu, HI 96813

Business Ombudsman
Office of the Ombudsman
465 S. King Street
Honolulu, HI 96813

INDUSTRIAL AND BUSINESS DIRECTORIES

Directory of Manufacturers, State of Hawaii, Chamber of Commerce of Hawaii, Dillingham Building, 1132 Bishop Street, Honolulu, HI 96813

Hawaii Business Directory, Hawaii Business Directory, Inc., 1164 Bishop Street, Honolulu, HI 96813

Idaho

STATE CAPITOL, BOISE, ID 83720
(208) 334-2411

INFORMATION OFFICES

Mailing address for all state offices is:
Statehouse
Boise, ID 83720

Commerce/Economic Development
Department of Commerce
700 W. State Street
Boise, ID 83720

Corporate
Secretary of State
State Capitol
Boise, ID 83720

Taxation
Department of Revenue and Taxation
800 Park Boulevard
Boise, ID 83722

State Chamber of Commerce
Idaho Association of Commerce
and Industry
805 West Idaho
Boise, ID 83702

International Commerce
Department of Commerce
700 W. State Street
Boise, ID 83720

Banking
Department of Finance
700 W. State Street
Boise, ID 83720

Securities
Department of Finance
700 W. State Street
Boise, ID 83720

Labor and Industrial Relations
Department of Labor and Industrial
Services
277 N. 6th Street
Boise, ID 83720

Insurance
Department of Insurance
700 W. State Street
Boise, ID 83720

Uniform Industrial Code
Department of Labor and Industrial
Services
277 N. 6th Street
Boise, ID 83720

Business Ombudsman
Department of Commerce
700 W. State Street
Boise, ID 83720

INDUSTRIAL AND BUSINESS DIRECTORIES

Idaho Manufacturing Directory, Center for Business and Research, University of Idaho, Moscow, ID 83843; Manufacturers' News, Inc., 1633 W. Central Street, Evanston, IL 60201

Idaho Opportunities, Department of Commerce, 700 W. State Street, Boise, ID 83720

Illinois

STATE HOUSE, SPRINGFIELD, IL 62706
(217) 782-2000

INFORMATION OFFICES

Commerce/Economic Development
Department of Commerce and
Community Affairs
620 E. Adams Street
Springfield, IL 62701

Corporate
Secretary of State
Business Services
Michael Howlett Building
Springfield, IL 62756

Taxation
Department of Revenue
101 W. Jefferson Street
Springfield, IL 62794

State Chamber of Commerce
Illinois State Chamber of Commerce
311 S. Wacker Drive
Chicago, IL 60606

International Commerce
Department of Commerce and
Community Affairs
100 W. Randolph Street
Chicago, IL 60601

Banking
Department of Financial Institutions
100 W. Randolph Street
Chicago, IL 60601

Securities
Secretary of State
900 S. Spring Street
Springfield, IL 62704

Labor and Industrial Relations
Department of Labor
One W. Old State Capitol Plaza
Springfield, IL 62701

Department of Commerce and
Community Affairs
620 E. Adams Street
Springfield, IL 62701

Insurance
Department of Insurance
320 W. Washington Street
Springfield, IL 62767
Uniform Industrial Code
Secretary of State
Uniform Commercial Code
Michael Howlett Building
Springfield, IL 62756
Business Ombudsman
Attorney General
500 South Second Street
Springfield, IL 62706

INDUSTRIAL AND BUSINESS DIRECTORIES

Chicago Cook County and Illinois Industrial Directory, Manufacturers' News, Inc., 1633 W. Central Street, Evanston, IL 60201
Illinois Industrial Directory, Harris Publishing Co., 2057 Aurora Road, Twinsburg, OH 44087
Illinois Manufacturers Directory, Manufacturers' News, Inc., 1633 W. Central Street, Evanston, IL 60201
Illinois Services Directory, Manufacturers' News, Inc., 1633 W. Central Street, Evanston, IL 60201
Development Finance Programs, Department of Commerce and Community Affairs, 620 E. Adams, Springfield, IL 62701

Indiana

STATE HOUSE, INDIANAPOLIS, IN 46204
(317) 232-3140

INFORMATION OFFICES

Commerce/Economic Development
Department of Commerce
1 N. Capitol Avenue
Indianapolis, IN 46204
Corporate
Secretary of State
Corporation Section
Indiana Government Center South
Indianapolis, IN 46204
Taxation
Department of Revenue
100 N. Senate Avenue
Indianapolis, IN 46204
State Board of Tax Commissioners
150 W. Market Street
Indianapolis, IN 46204
State Chamber of Commerce
Indiana Chamber of Commerce
1 N. Capitol Avenue
Indianapolis, IN 46204

International Commerce
International Trade Division
Indiana Department of Commerce
1 N. Capitol Avenue
Indianapolis, IN 46204
Banking
Department of Financial Institutions
Indiana Government Center South
Indianapolis, IN 46204
Securities
Secretary of State
Securities Commission
1 N. Capitol Avenue
Indianapolis, IN 46204
Labor and Industrial Relations
Indiana Department of Labor
Indiana Government Center South
Indianapolis, IN 46204
Insurance
Indiana Department of Insurance
311 W. Washington Street
Indianapolis, IN 46204
Uniform Industrial Code
Secretary of State
Uniform Commercial Code Division
Indiana Government Center South
Indianapolis, IN 46204
Business Ombudsman
Business Ombudsman Office
Department of Commerce
1 N. Capitol Avenue
Indianapolis, IN 46204

INDUSTRIAL AND BUSINESS DIRECTORIES

Harris Indiana Industrial Directory, Harris Publishing Co., 2057 Aurora Road, Twinsburg, OH 44087
Indiana Industrial Directory, Harris Publishing Co., 2057 Aurora Road, Twinsburg, OH 44087
Indiana Manufacturers Directory, Manufacturers' News, Inc., 1633 W. Central Street, Evanston, IL 60201

Iowa

STATE CAPITOL, DES MOINES, IA 50319
(515) 281-5011

INFORMATION OFFICES

Commerce/Economic Development
Department of Economic Development
200 E. Grand Avenue
Des Moines, IA 50309
Corporate
Secretary of State
Corporation Division
Hoover Building
Des Moines, IA 50319

Taxation
Department of Revenue and Finance
Hoover Building
Des Moines, IA 50319
International Commerce
Department of Economic Development
200 E. Grand Avenue
Des Moines, IA 50309
Banking
Department of Commerce
Banking Division
200 E. Grand Avenue
Des Moines, IA 50309
Iowa Housing Finance Authority
200 E. Grand Avenue
Des Moines, IA 50309
Securities
Department of Commerce
Insurance Division
Securities Bureau
Lucas Building
Des Moines, IA 50319
Labor
Department of Employment Service
Division of Industrial Services
1000 E. Grand Avenue
Des Moines, IA 50319
Bureau of Labor
1000 E. Grand Avenue
Des Moines, IA 50319
Insurance
Department of Commerce
Insurance Division
Lucas Building
Des Moines, IA 50319

INDUSTRIAL AND BUSINESS DIRECTORIES

Iowa Manufacturers Directory, Harris Publishing Co., 2057 Aurora Road, Twinsburg, OH 44087

Iowa Manufacturers Register, Iowa Department of Economic Development, 200 E. Grand Avenue, Des Moines, IA 50309; Manufacturers' News, Inc., 1633 W. Central Street, Evanston, IL 60201

Doing Business in Iowa, Iowa Department of Economic Development, 200 E. Grand Avenue, Des Moines, IA 50309

Kansas

STATE CAPITOL BUILDING, TOPEKA, KS 66612
(913) 296-0111

INFORMATION OFFICES

Commerce/Economic Development
Department of Commerce
700 S.W. Harrison Street
Topeka, KS 66603-3712

Corporate
Secretary of State
State House
Corporation Department
Topeka, KS 66612
Taxation
Department of Revenue
Docking State Office Building
915 Harrison Street
Topeka, KS 66612-1588
State Chamber of Commerce
Kansas Chamber of Commerce
and Industry
835 S.W. Topeka Boulevard
Topeka, KS 66603
International Commerce
Department of Commerce
700 S.W. Harrison Street
Topeka, KS 66603-3712
Banking
Banking Department
700 Jackson Street, S
Topeka, KS 66603-3796
Securities
Securities Commissioner of Kansas
618 S. Kansas
Topeka, KS 66603-3804
Labor and Industrial Relations
Department of Human Resources
401 Topeka
Topeka, KS 66603-3182
Insurance
Insurance Department
420 S.W. 9th Street
Topeka, KS 66612-1678
Business Ombudsman
Department of Commerce
700 S.W. Harrison Street
Topeka, KS 66603-3712

INDUSTRIAL AND BUSINESS DIRECTORIES

Directory of Kansas Manufacturers and Products, Kansas Department of Commerce, 700 S.W. Harrison Street Topeka, KS 66603-3712; Manufacturers' News, Inc., 1633 W. Central Street, Evanston, IL 60201

Kansas Association Directory, Kansas Department of Commerce, 700 S.W. Harrison Street, Topeka, KS 66603-3712

Kansas Aerospace Directory, Kansas Department of Commerce, 700 S.W. Harrison Street, Topeka, KS 66603-3712

Kansas Agribusiness Directory, Kansas Department of Commerce, 700 S.W. Harrison Street, Topeka, KS 66603-3712

Kansas Directory of Commerce, Wichita Eagle Beacon, 825 E. Douglas, Wichita, KS 67202-3512

Kansas International Trade Resource Directory, Kansas Department of Commerce,

700 S.W. Harrison Street, Topeka, KS
66603-3712
Kansas Job Shop Directory, Kansas Department of Commerce, 700 S.W. Harrison
Street, Topeka, KS 66603-3712

Kentucky

STATE CAPITOL, FRANKFORT, KY 40601
(502) 564-3130

INFORMATION OFFICES

Commerce/Economic Development
Kentucky Economic Development
  Cabinet
Capital Plaza Office Tower
Frankfort, KY 40601
Corporate
Office of Secretary of State
Corporation Division
Capitol Building
Frankfort, KY 40601
Taxation
Kentucky Revenue Cabinet
Fair Oaks Lane
Frankfort, KY 40601
State Chamber of Commerce
Kentucky Chamber of Commerce
Versailles Road
P.O. Box 817
Frankfort, KY 40602
International Commerce
Kentucky Economic Development
  Cabinet
Office of International Marketing
Capitol Plaza Tower
Frankfort, KY 40601
Banking
Kentucky Department of Financial
  Institutions
Division of Banking and Thrift Institutions
477 Versailles Road
Frankfort, KY 40601
Securities
Kentucky Department of Financial
  Institutions
Division of Securities
477 Versailles Road
Frankfort, KY 40601
Labor and Industrial Relations
Kentucky Labor Cabinet
The 127 Building
Frankfort, KY 40601
Insurance
Kentucky Department of Insurance
229 West Main Street
P.O. Box 517
Frankfort, KY 40602
Uniform Industrial Code
Kentucky Department of Housing,
  Buildings, and Construction
The 127 Building
Frankfort, KY 40601

Business Ombudsman
Kentucky Department of Existing
  Business and Industry
Capitol Plaza Tower
Frankfort, KY 40601

INDUSTRIAL AND BUSINESS DIRECTORIES

Kentucky Industrial Directory, Harris Pub-
lishing Co., 2057 Aurora Road, Twinsburg,
OH 44087
Kentucky International Trade Directory,
Kentucky Economic Development Cabinet,
Capitol Plaza Tower, Frankfort, KY 40601
Kentucky Directory of Manufacturers, Ken-
tucky Economic Development Cabinet,
Capitol Plaza Tower, Frankfort, KY 40601
Kentucky Manufacturers Register, Manufac-
turers' News, Inc., 1633 W. Central Street,
Evanston, IL 60201; Harris Publishing,
Co., 2057 Aurora Road, Twinsburg, OH
44087

Louisiana

STATE CAPITOL, BATON ROUGE, LA 70804
(504) 342-7015

INFORMATION OFFICES

Commerce/Economic Development
Department of Economic Development
P.O. Box 94185
Baton Rouge, LA 70804-9185
Corporate
Secretary of State
Division of Corporation
P.O. Box 94125
Baton Rouge, LA 70804-9125
Taxation
Department of Revenue and Taxation
P.O. Box 3440
Baton Rouge, LA 70823
State Chamber of Commerce
Louisiana Association of Business
  and Industry
P.O. Box 80258
Baton Rouge, LA 70898
International Commerce
Department of Economic Development
Office of International Trade, Finance
  and Development
100 France Street
P.O. Box 94185
Baton Rouge, LA 70804
Banking
Department of Economic Development
Office of Financial Institutions
8401 United Plaza Boulevard
P.O. Box 94095
Baton Rouge, LA 70804

Securities
Louisiana Securities Commission
1100 Poydras Street
325 Loyola Avenue
New Orleans, LA 70163

Labor and Industrial Relations
Department of Labor
P.O. Box 94094
Baton Rouge, LA 70804-9094

Insurance
Office of Insurance Rating Commission
P.O. Box 94157
Baton Rouge, LA 70804

Uniform Industrial Code
Department of Economic Development
P.O. Box 94185
Baton Rouge, LA 70804-9185

Department of Labor
Department of Labor
P.O. Box 94094
Baton Rouge, LA 70804-9094

Business Ombudsman
Department of Economic Development
P.O. Box 94185
Baton Rouge, LA 70804-9185

INDUSTRIAL AND BUSINESS DIRECTORIES

Louisiana Manufacturers Register, Manufacturers' News, Inc., 1633 W. Central Street, Evanston, IL 60201

Louisiana Directory of Manufacturers, Department of Economic Development, 101 France Street, Baton Rouge, LA 70802; Harris Publishing Co., 2057 Aurora Road, Twinsburg, OH 44087

Louisiana International Trade Directory, World Trade Center, 2 Canal Street, New Orleans, LA 70130

Maine

State House, Augusta, ME 04333
(207) 289-1110

INFORMATION OFFICES

Commerce/Economic Development
Department of Economic and
Community Development
193 State Street
State House Station #59
Augusta, ME 04333

Corporate
Department of State
Division of Corporations
State House Station #101
Augusta, ME 04333

Private Development Associations
Maine Development Foundation
45 Memorial Circle
Augusta, ME 04330

Taxation
Bureau of Taxation
Department of Administrative &
Financial Services
State House Station #24
Augusta, ME 04333

State Chamber of Commerce
Maine State Chamber of Commerce and
Industry
126 Sewall Street
Augusta, ME 04330

International Commerce
Department of Economic and
Community Development
193 State Street
State House Station #59
Augusta, ME 04333

Banking
Bureau of Banking
Hallowell Annex
Correspondence to:
State House Station #36
Augusta, ME 04333-0036

Securities
Bureau of Banking
Securities Division
State House Station #121
Augusta, ME 04333

Labor and Industrial Relations
Department of Labor
Bureau of Labor Standards
State House Station #45
Augusta, ME 04333

Insurance
Bureau of Insurance
Hallowell Annex
Hallowell, ME 04347
Correspondence to:
State House #34
Augusta, ME 04333

INDUSTRIAL AND BUSINESS DIRECTORIES

Maine Marketing Directory, Department of Economic and Community Development, State House Station #59, Augusta, ME 04333

Maine/New Hampshire/Vermont Directory of Manufacturers, Inc., Commerce Register, 190 Godwin Avenue, Midland Park, NJ 07432; Harris Publishing Co., 2057 Aurora Road, Twinsburg, OH 44087

Maine Manufacturing Directory, Tower Publishing Company, 34 Diamond Street, Portland, ME 04101; Manufacturers' News, Inc., 1633 W. Central Street, Evanston, IL 60201

Maryland

State House, Annapolis, MD 21401
(410) 974-3901

INFORMATION OFFICES

Commerce/Economic Development
Department of Economic and
Employment Development
217 E. Redwood Street
Baltimore, MD 21202

Corporate
State Department of Assessments
and Taxation
301 W. Preston Street
Baltimore, MD 21201

Taxation
Comptroller of the Treasury
Louis L. Goldstein Treasury Building
P.O. Box 466
Annapolis, MD 21404-0466

State Chamber of Commerce
Maryland Chamber of Commerce
60 West Street
Annapolis, MD 21401

International Commerce
Department of Economic and
Employment Development
Maryland International Division
World Trade Center
401 East Pratt Street
Baltimore, MD 21202

Maryland Port Administration
World Trade Center
401 East Pratt Street
Baltimore, MD 21202

Banking
State Banking Commissioner
Department of Licensing and Regulation
501 St. Paul Place
Baltimore, MD 21202

Securities
Division of Securities
Office of the Attorney General
200 St. Paul Place
Baltimore, MD 21202

Labor and Industrial Relations
Department of Licensing and Regulation
Division of Labor and Industry
501 St. Paul Place
Baltimore, MD 21202

Insurance
Maryland Insurance Administration
Department of Licensing and Regulation
501 St. Paul Place
Baltimore, MD 21202

Business Ombudsman
Department of Economic and
Employment Development
Manufacturing and Business Assistance
217 East Redwood Street
Baltimore, MD 21202

INDUSTRIAL AND BUSINESS DIRECTORIES

Maryland Manufacturers Directory, Harris
Publishing Co., 2057 Aurora Road, Twinsburg, OH 44087

Maryland/D.C. Manufacturers Directory,
Manufacturers' News, Inc., 1633 W. Central Street, Evanston, IL 60201

Technology Resource Guide...Maryland,
Corporate Technology Information Ser-
vices, Inc., Suite 200, 12 Alfred Street,
Woburn, MA 01801

Massachusetts

STATE HOUSE, BOSTON, MA 02133
General Information: (617) 727-2121

INFORMATION OFFICES

Commerce/Economic Development
Executive Office of Economic Affairs
2101 McCormack Building
1 Ashburton Place
Boston, MA 02108

Office of Business Development
Executive Office of Economic Affairs
1 Ashburton Place
Boston, MA 02108

Corporate
Secretary of State
Corporations Division
1 Ashburton Place
Boston, MA 02108

Taxation
Accounting Bureau/Department
of Revenue
Leverett Saltonstall Building
100 Cambridge Street
Boston, MA 02204

International Commerce
Office of International Trade and
Investment
100 Cambridge Street
Boston, MA 02202

Banking
Division of Banks and Loan Agencies
100 Cambridge Street
Boston, MA 02202

Securities
Secretary of State
Securities Division
1 Ashburton Place
Boston, MA 02108

Labor and Industrial Relations
Executive Office of Labor
1 Ashburton Place
Boston, MA 02108

Department of Labor and Industries
Executive Office of Labor
100 Cambridge Street
Boston, MA 02202

Insurance
Division of Insurance
470 Atlantic Avenue
Boston, MA 02110-2208

INDUSTRIAL AND BUSINESS DIRECTORIES

Directory of Directors in the City of Boston and Vicinity, Bankers Service Co., 14 Beacon Street, Boston, MA 02108

Directory of Massachusetts Manufacturers, George D. Hall Co., 50 Congress Street, Boston, MA 02109

Massachusetts Directory of Manufacturers, Commerce Register Inc., 190 Godwin Avenue, Midland Park, NJ 07432

Massachusetts Industrial Directory, Harris Publishing Co., 2057 Aurora Road, Twinsburg, OH 44087

Massachusetts Service Directory, George D. Hall Co., 50 Congress Street, Boston, MA 02109

Massachusetts State Industrial Directory, State Industrial Directories Corp., 2 Penn Plaza, New York, NY 10001

Michigan

STATE CAPITOL, LANSING, MI 48913
(517) 373-1837

INFORMATION OFFICES

Commerce/Economic Development
Michigan Jobs Commission
Customer Assistance and Research
201 N. Washington Square
Victor Office Center
Lansing, MI 48913

Corporate
Corporation and Securities Bureau
6546 Mercantile Way
Lansing, MI 48909

Taxation
Bureau of Collection
Department of Treasury
Treasury Building
P.O. Box 30199
Lansing, MI 48909

State Chamber of Commerce
Michigan State Chamber of Commerce
600 S. Walnut
Lansing, MI 48933

International Commerce
Michigan International Office
Department of Commerce
525 W. Ottawa Street
P.O. Box 30225
Lansing, MI 48909

Banking
Financial Institutions Bureau
Department of Commerce
Grand Plaza
206 E. Michigan

P.O. Box 30224
Lansing, MI 48909

Securities
Corporation and Securities Bureau
Department of Commerce
6546 Mercantile Way
P.O. Box 30199
Lansing, MI 48909

Labor and Industrial Relations
Bureau of Employment Relations
Department of Labor
State of Michigan Plaza Building
1200 Sixth Street
Detroit, MI 48226

Department of Labor
Victor Office Center
201 North Washington
P.O. Box 30015
Lansing, MI 48909

Insurance
Ottawa Building
P.O. Box 30220
Lansing, MI 48913

Business Ombudsman
Michigan Jobs Commission
Customer Assistance and Research
Victor Office Center
Lansing, MI 48913

INDUSTRIAL AND BUSINESS DIRECTORIES

Michigan Industrial Directory, Harris Publishing Co., 2057 Aurora Road, Twinsburg, OH 44087

Michigan Manufacturers Directory, Manufacturers' News, Inc., 1633 W. Central Street, Evanston, IL 60201

Minnesota

STATE CAPITOL, ST. PAUL, MN 55155
(612) 296-6013

INFORMATION OFFICES

Commerce/Economic Development
Department of Trade and Economic Development
500 Metro Square
121-7th Place East
St. Paul, MN 55101-2146

Minnesota Department of Commerce
Commerce Building
133 E. 7th Street
St. Paul, MN 55101

Corporate
Secretary of State
Domestic or Foreign Corporations
180 State Office Building
St. Paul, MN 55155

Taxation
Department of Revenue
10 River Park Plaza
St. Paul, MN 55146
State Chamber of Commerce
Minnesota Chamber of
Commerce
480 Cedar Street
St. Paul, MN 55101
International Commerce
Minnesota Trade Office
1000 World Trade Center
St. Paul, MN 55101
Banking
Minnesota Department of
Commerce
Banking Division
Commerce Building
133 E. 7th Street
St. Paul, MN 55101
Securities
Minnesota Department of
Commerce
Registration Unit
Commerce Building
133 E. 7th Street
St. Paul, MN 55101
Labor and Industrial Relations
Minnesota Department of Labor
and Industry
443 Lafayette Road
St. Paul, MN 55155
Insurance
Minnesota Department of
Commerce
Policy Analysis Division
Commerce Building
133 E. 7th Street
St. Paul, MN 55101
Business Ombudsman
Department of Trade and Economic
Development
Small Business Assistance Office
500 Metro Square
121-7th Place East
St. Paul, MN 55101-2146

INDUSTRIAL AND BUSINESS DIRECTORIES

Minnesota Directory of Manufacturers, Manufacturers' News, Inc., 1633 W. Central Street, Evanston, IL 60201; State Industrial Directories Corp., 2 Penn Plaza, New York, NY 10001

Minnesota Manufacturers' Register, Manufacturers' News, Inc., 1633 W. Central Street, Evanston, IL 60201

Mississippi

OFFICE OF THE GOVERNOR, JACKSON, MS
39205-0139
(601) 359-3150

INFORMATION OFFICES

Commerce/Economic Development
Mississippi Department of Economic
and Community Development
P.O. Box 849
Jackson, MS 39205
Corporate
Secretary of State
P.O. Box 136
Jackson, MS 39205
Taxation
Tax Commission
102 Woolfolk Building
P.O. Box 22828
Jackson, MS 39225
State Chamber of Commerce
P.O. Box 1849
Jackson, MS 39205-1849
Banking
Department of Banking and
Consumer Finance
1206 Woolfolk State Office
Building
P.O. Drawer 23729
Jackson, MS 39225-3729
International Commerce
Department of Economic and
Community Development
P.O. Box 849
Jackson, MS 39205
Securities
Secretary of State's Office
Securities Division
P.O. Box 136
Jackson, MS 39205
Labor and Industrial Relations
Employment Security Commission
1520 W. Capitol Street
P.O. Box 1699
Jackson, MS 39215-8711
Insurance
Department of Insurance
1804 Sillers Building
P.O. Box 79
Jackson, MS 39205

INDUSTRIAL AND BUSINESS DIRECTORIES

Mississippi Manufacturers' Directory, Research Division, Department of Economic and Community Development, P.O. Box 849, Jackson, MS 39205; Manufacturers' News, Inc., 1633 W. Central Street, Evanston, IL 60201

Missouri

STATE INFORMATION CENTER, JEFFERSON
CITY, MO 65102
(314) 751-2000

INFORMATION OFFICES

Commerce/Economic Development
Department of Economic Development
Community and Economic Development
P.O. Box 118
Jefferson City, MO 65102

Corporate
Secretary of State
Corporations Division
600 West Main Street
P.O. Box 778
Jefferson City, MO 65102

Taxation
Department of Revenue
Division of Taxation and Collections
Truman State Office Building
P.O. Box 629
Jefferson City, MO 65105

State Chamber of Commerce
Missouri Chamber of Commerce
428 East Capitol Avenue
P.O. Box 149
Jefferson City, MO 65102

International Commerce
International Business Development
Community and Economic Development
Truman State Office Building
P.O. Box 118
Jefferson City, MO 65102

Banking
Missouri Division of Finance
Truman State Office Building
P.O. Box 716
Jefferson City, MO 65102

Securities
Office of the Secretary of State
Securities Division
600 West Main Street
P.O. Box 778
Jefferson City, MO 65102

Labor and Industrial Relations
Missouri Dept. of Labor & Industrial
  Relations
3315 West Truman Boulevard
Jefferson City, MO 65109

Insurance
Missouri Division of Insurance
Truman State Office Building
P.O. Box 690
Jefferson City, MO 65102

Uniform Industrial Code
Missouri Division of Labor Standards
P.O. Box 449
Jefferson City, MO 65102

INDUSTRIAL AND BUSINESS DIRECTORIES

Contacts Influential: Commerce and Industrial Directory (for Kansas City Area), Contacts Influential, Inc., 2405 Grand Avenue, Kansas City, MO 64108

Missouri Manufacturers' Register, Manufacturers' News, Inc., 1633 W. Central Street, Evanston, IL 60201

Missouri Directory of Manufacturers, Harris Publishing Co., 2057 Aurora Road, Twinsburg, OH 44087

Montana

STATE CAPITOL, HELENA, MT 59620
(406) 444-3111

INFORMATION OFFICES

Commerce/Economic Development
Department of Commerce
1424 9th Avenue
Helena, MT 59620-0501

Census and Economic Information Center
Department of Commerce
1429 9th Avenue
Helena, MT 59620-0501

Corporate
Secretary of State
Business Services Bureau
State Capitol Building
Helena, MT 59620-2801

State Chamber of Commerce
Montana Chamber of Commerce
P.O. Box 1730
Helena, MT 59624

International Commerce
International Trade Office
Montana Department of Commerce
1424 9th Avenue
Helena, MT 59620-0501

Banking
Commissioner of Financial Institutions
Montana Department of Commerce
1520 East 6th Avenue
Helena, MT 59620-0543

Securities
Securities Division
State Auditor's Office
Sam Mitchell Building
Helena, MT 59620-0301

Labor and Industrial Relations
Commissioner's Office
Montana Department of Labor
  & Industry
Lockey and Roberts
Helena, MT 59620-1501

Insurance
Insurance Department
State Auditor's Office
Sam Mitchell Building
Helena, MT 59620-0301

Uniform Commercial Code
Secretary of State
Uniform Commercial Code Bureau
State Capitol Building
Helena, MT 59620-2801

Business Ombudsman
Small Business Advocate
Montana Department of Commerce
1424 9th Avenue
Helena, MT 59620-0501

INDUSTRIAL AND BUSINESS DIRECTORIES

Montana Manufacturers Directory, Department of Commerce, 1424 9th Avenue, Helena, MT 59620; Manufacturers' News, Inc., 1633 W. Central Street, Evanston, IL 60201

Montana Business & Industrial Location Guide, Department of Commerce, 1424 9th Avenue, Helena, MT 59620

Nebraska

STATE CAPITOL, LINCOLN, NE 68509
(402) 471-2311

INFORMATION OFFICES

Commerce/Economic Development
Department of Economic Development
301 Centennial Mall South
P.O. Box 94666
Lincoln, NE 68509-4666
Corporate
Secretary of State
Corporation Division
P.O. Box 94608
Lincoln, NE 68509-4608
Taxation
Department of Revenue
301 Centennial Mall South
P.O. Box 94818
Lincoln, NE 68509-4818
State Chamber of Commerce
Nebraska Chamber of Commerce
and Industry
1320 Lincoln Mall
P.O. Box 95128
Lincoln, NE 68509
International Commerce
Nebraska Department of Economic
Development
Business Recruitment Division
P.O. Box 94666
Lincoln, NE 68509-4666
Banking
Department of Banking and Finance
The Atrium
1200 N Street
Lincoln, NE 68509-5006
Securities
Department of Banking and Finance
The Atrium
1200 N Street
P.O. Box 95006
Lincoln, NE 68509-5006

Labor and Industrial Relations
Nebraska Department of Labor
550 South 16th Street
P.O. Box 94600
Lincoln, NE 68509-4600
Insurance
Department of Insurance
The Terminal Building
941 O Street
Lincoln, NE 68508
Uniform Industrial Code
Uniform Commercial Code Division
301 Centennial Mall South
P.O. Box 95104
Lincoln, NE 68509-5104
Business Ombudsman
One-Stop Center
Department of Economic
Development
P.O. Box 94666
Lincoln, NE 68509-4666

INDUSTRIAL AND BUSINESS DIRECTORIES

A Directory of Lincoln, Nebraska Manufacturers, Lincoln Chamber of Commerce, 1221 N Street, Lincoln, NE 68508

Nebraska Manufacturers Register, Manufacturers' News, Inc., 1633 W. Central Street, Evanston, IL 60201

Directory of Nebraska Manufacturers and Their Products, Nebraska State Department of Economic Development, P.O. Box 94666, Lincoln, NE 68509-4666

Directory of Manufacturers for the Omaha Metropolitan Area, Omaha Economic Development Council, 1301 Harney, Omaha, NE 68102

Directory of Major Employers for the Omaha Area, Omaha Economic Development Council, 1301 Harney, Omaha, NE 68102

Nevada

STATE CAPITOL, CARSON CITY, NV 89710
(702) 687-5670

INFORMATION OFFICES

Commerce/Economic Development
Department of Business & Industry
1665 Hot Springs Road
Carson City, NV 89710

Commission on Economic Development
5151 S. Carson Street
Carson City, NV 89710
Corporate
Secretary of State
Capitol Complex
Carson City, NV 89710

Taxation
Department of Taxation
1340 S. Curry Street
Carson City, NV 89710
State Chamber of Commerce
Nevada Chamber of Commerce
Association
P.O. Box 3499
Reno, NV 89505
International Commerce
Commission on Economic
Development
International Office
3770 Howard Hughes Parkway #295
Las Vegas, NV 89158
Banking
Financial Institutions Division
406 E. Second Street
Carson City, NV 89710
Securities
Secretary of State
Capitol Complex
Carson City, NV 89710
Labor and Industrial Relations
Labor Commission
1445 Hot Springs Road
Carson City, NV 89710

Department of Industrial Relations
1390 S. Curry Street
Carson City, NV 89710
Insurance
Insurance Department
1665 Hot Springs Road
Carson City, NV 89710

INDUSTRIAL AND BUSINESS DIRECTORIES

Directory of Nevada Mine Operations, Division of Mine Inspection, Department of Industrial Relations, 1380 S. Curry Street, Carson City, NV 89710
Nevada Industrial Directory, Gold Hill Publishing Co., Inc., P.O. Drawer F, Virginia City, NV 89440; Manufacturers' News, Inc., 1633 W. Central Street, Evanston, IL 60201

New Hampshire

STATE HOUSE, CONCORD, NH 03301
(603) 271-1110

INFORMATION OFFICES

Commerce/Economic Development
Department of Resources and Economic Development
Division of Economic Development
172 Pembroke Road
Concord, NH 03302

Corporate
Secretary of State
Corporations Division
State House Annex
Concord, NH 03301
Taxation
Board of Taxation
61 S. Spring Street
Concord, NH 03301

Department of Revenue Administration
61 S. Spring Street
Concord, NH 03301
State Chamber of Commerce
Business and Industry Association of
New Hampshire
122 N. Main Street
Concord, NH 03301
International Commerce
Department of Resources & Economic
Development
Division of Economic Development
172 Pembroke Road
Prescott Park—Concord, NH 03302
Banking
Banking Department
State of New Hampshire
169 Manchester Street
Concord, NH 03301

New Hampshire Banking Association
125 N. Main Street
Concord, NH 03301
Securities
Insurance Department, Securities
Division
State of New Hampshire
State House
Concord, NH 03301
Labor and Industrial Relations
Department of Employment Security
State of New Hampshire
32 S. Main Street
Concord, NH 03301

Department of Labor
95 Pleasant Street
Concord, NH 03301
Insurance
Insurance Department
State of New Hampshire
169 Manchester Street
Concord, NH 03301
Standard Industrial Code
Department of Employment Security
State of New Hampshire
32 S. Main Street
Concord, NH 03301

INDUSTRIAL AND BUSINESS DIRECTORIES

Made in New Hampshire, New Hampshire Office of Industrial Development, Department of Resources, Concord, NH 03301

Maine/New Hampshire/Vermont Industrial Directory, Harris Publishing Co., 2057 Aurora Road, Twinsburg, OH 44087

New Hampshire Manufacturing Directory, Tower Publishing Company, 34 Diamond Street, Portland, ME 04111

New Jersey

STATE HOUSE, TRENTON, NJ 08625
(609) 777-2500

INFORMATION OFFICES

Commerce/Economic Development
Department of Commerce and
Economic Development
20 W. State Street, CN 820
Trenton, NJ 08625

Division of Travel and Tourism
20 W. State Street, CN 826
Trenton, NJ 08625

Economic Development Authority
Capitol Place One, CN 990
200 S. Warren Street
Trenton, NJ 08625
Corporate
Secretary of State
Division of Commercial Recording
820 Bear Tavern Road, CN 308
W. Trenton, NJ 08625
Taxation
Department of Treasury
Division of Taxation
50 Barrack Street, CN 240
Trenton, NJ 08625
State Chamber of Commerce
New Jersey State Chamber of
Commerce
1 State Street Square
50 W. State Street
Trenton, NJ 08608
International Commerce
Division of International Trade
28 W. State Street, CN 836
Trenton, NJ 08625-0836
Banking
Department of Banking
20 W. State Street, CN 040
Trenton, NJ 08625
Securities
Bureau of Securities
2 Gateway Center
Newark, NJ 07102
Labor and Industrial Relations
Department of Labor and Industry
John Fitch Plaza, CN 110
Trenton, NJ 08625
Insurance
Department of Insurance
20 W. State Street, CN 325
Trenton, NJ 08625

Business Ombudsman
Department of State
State House, CN 300
Trenton, NJ 08625

INDUSTRIAL AND BUSINESS DIRECTORIES

New Jersey Manufacturers Directory, Manufacturers' News, Inc., 1633 W. Central Street, Evanston, IL 60201; Harris Publishing Co., 2057 Aurora Road, Twinsburg, OH 44087

The New Jersey Directory of Manufacturers, Commerce Register, Inc., 190 Godwin Avenue, Midland Park, NJ 07432

New Mexico

STATE CAPITOL, SANTA FE, NM 87503
(505) 827-3000

INFORMATION OFFICES

Commerce/Economic Development
Economic Development Department
Joseph M. Montoya Building
1100 S. St. Francis Drive
Santa Fe, NM 87503
Corporate
State Corporation Commission
P.E.R.A. Building
P.O. Drawer 1269
Santa Fe, NM 87504-1269
Taxation
Taxation and Revenue Department
P.O. Box 630
Joseph M. Montoya Building
1100 S. St. Francis Drive
Santa Fe, NM 87504-0630
State Chamber of Commerce
Association of Commerce and Industry
of New Mexico
4001 Indian School NE
Albuquerque, NM 87110
International Commerce
Trade Division
Economic Development Department
Joseph M. Montoya Building
1100 S. St. Francis Drive
Santa Fe, NM 87503
Banking
Financial Institutions Division
Regulation and Licensing Department
725 St. Michael's Drive
Santa Fe, NM 87503
Securities
Securities Division
Financial Institutions Division
Regulation and Licensing Department
725 St. Michael's Drive
Santa Fe, NM 87503

Labor and Industrial Relations
Department of Labor
1596 Pacheco Street
Aspen Plaza Building
Santa Fe, NM 87504
Insurance
State Corporation Commission
P.E.R.A. Building
P.O. Drawer 1269
Santa Fe, NM 87504

INDUSTRIAL AND BUSINESS DIRECTORIES

New Mexico Manufacturing Directory, Manufacturers' News, Inc., 1633 W. Central Street, Evanston, IL 60201
New Mexico Directory of Manufacturers, Economic Development Division, New Mexico Economic Development, Joseph M. Montoya Building, 1100 S. St. Francis Drive, Santa Fe, NM 87503

New York

STATE CAPITOL, ALBANY, NY 12224
(518) 474-2121

INFORMATION OFFICES

Commerce/Economic Development
Department of Economic Development
One Commerce Plaza
Albany, NY 12245

Division of Regional Economic
Development
One Commerce Plaza
Albany, NY 12245
Corporate
Secretary of State
162 Washington Avenue
Albany, NY 12231
Taxation
Department of Taxation and Finance
State Campus Building #9
Albany, NY 12227
State Chamber of Commerce
Business Council of New York State
152 Washington Avenue
Albany, NY 12210
Small Business Advisory Board
Division for Small Business
1515 Broadway
New York, NY 10036
International Commerce
Department of Economic Development
1515 Broadway
New York, NY 10036
Banking
Department of Banking
194 Washington Avenue
Albany, NY 12210

Labor and Industrial Relations
Department of Labor
State Campus
Albany, NY 12240
Insurance
Department of Insurance
Empire State Plaza
Agency Building #1
Albany, NY 12257
Uniform Commercial Code
Department of State
107 Washington Avenue
Albany, NY 12231
Business Ombudsman
Department of Economic Development
Division for Small Business
1515 Broadway
New York, NY 10036

INDUSTRIAL AND BUSINESS DIRECTORIES

New York Manufacturers' Directory, Harris Publishing Co., 2057 Aurora Road, Twinsburg, OH 44087; Manufacturers' News, Inc., 1633 W. Central Street, Evanston, IL 60201
The New York State Directory, Cambridge Information Group, 7200 Wisconsin Avenue, Bethesda, MD 20814-9777

North Carolina

GENERAL ASSEMBLY
STATE LEGISLATIVE BUILDING
RALEIGH, NC 27601-1096
(919) 733-1110 (government information)
733-7928 (legislators)

INFORMATION OFFICES

Commerce/Economic Development
Department of Commerce
430 N. Salisbury Street
Raleigh, NC 27603-5900
Corporate
Secretary of State
Corporation Division
300 N. Salisbury Street
Raleigh, NC 27603-5909
Taxation
Department of Revenue
501 N. Wilmington Street
Raleigh, NC 27604-8001
State Chamber of Commerce
North Carolina Citizens for Business
and Industry
P.O. Box 2508
Raleigh, NC 27602
International Commerce
International Development
Department of Commerce
430 N. Salisbury Street
Raleigh, NC 27603

Banking
Banking Commission
Department of Commerce
430 N. Salisbury Street
Raleigh, NC 27603
Securities
Secretary of State
Securities Division
300 N. Salisbury Street
Raleigh, NC 27603-5909
Labor and Industrial Relations
Department of Labor
4 W. Edenton Street
Raleigh, NC 27601-1092
Insurance
Department of Insurance
430 N. Salisbury Street
Raleigh, NC 27603-5908

INDUSTRIAL AND BUSINESS DIRECTORIES

North Carolina Manufacturers Register, Manufacturers' News, Inc., 1633 W. Central Street, Evanston, IL 60201

North Carolina Manufacturers Directory, George D. Hall Co., 50 Congress Street, Boston, MA 02109; Harris Publishing Co., 2057 Aurora Road, Twinsburg, OH 44087

North Dakota

STATE CAPITOL, BISMARCK, ND 58505
(701) 224-2000

INFORMATION OFFICES

Commerce/Economic Development
Economic Development & Finance
1833 East Bismarck Expressway
Bismarck, ND 58504
Corporate
Office of the Secretary of State
Corporation Department
600 East Boulevard Avenue
Bismarck, ND 58505-0500
Taxation
Tax Department
600 East Boulevard Avenue
Bismarck, ND 58505-0599
State Chamber of Commerce
Greater North Dakota Association
State Chamber of Commerce
Box 2639
2000 Shafer Street
Bismarck, ND 58502
International Commerce
International Trade
Economic Development & Finance
1833 East Bismarck Expressway
Bismarck, ND 58504

Banking
State Banking Commission
600 East Boulevard Avenue
Bismarck, ND 58505-0510
Securities
Securities Commissioner
600 East Boulevard Avenue
Bismarck, ND 58505
Labor and Industrial Relations
State Commissioner of Labor
600 East Boulevard Avenue
Bismarck, ND 58505
Insurance
Insurance Commissioner
600 East Boulevard Avenue
Bismarck, ND 58505-0320
Uniform Industrial Code
Secretary of State
600 East Boulevard Avenue
Bismarck, ND 58505-0500

INDUSTRIAL AND BUSINESS DIRECTORIES

North Dakota Directory of Manufacturers and Food Processors, Economic Development & Finance, 1833 East Bismarck Expressway, Bismarck, ND 58504

Ohio

STATE HOUSE, COLUMBUS, OH 43215
(614) 466-3455
State Operator: (614) 466-2000

INFORMATION OFFICES

Commerce/Economic Development
Ohio Department of Development
77 S. High Street
P.O. Box 1001
Columbus, OH 43266-0101
Corporate
Secretary of State
Corporation Section
30 E. Broad Street
Columbus, OH 43266-0418
Taxation
Department of Taxation
30 E. Broad Street
Columbus, OH 43266-0420
State Chamber of Commerce
Ohio Chamber of Commerce
35 E. Gay Street
Columbus, OH 43215-1192
International Commerce
Ohio Department of Development
International Trade Division
77 S. High Street
P.O. Box 1001
Columbus, OH 43266-0101

Banking
Ohio Department of Commerce
Division of Banks
77 S. High Street
Columbus, OH 43266-0544

Securities
Ohio Department of Commerce
Division of Securities
77 S. High Street
Columbus, OH 43266-0544

Labor and Industrial Relations
Ohio Department of Industrial Relations
2323 W. Fifth Avenue
P.O. Box 825
Columbus, OH 43266-0567

Insurance
Ohio Department of Insurance
2100 Stella Court
Columbus, OH 43266-0566

Uniform Industrial Code
Industrial Commission of Ohio
Division of Safety and Hygiene
246 N. High Street
Columbus, OH 43266-0589

Business Ombudsman
Ohio Department of Development
Small and Developing Business Division
Minority Business Development Division
77 S. High Street
P.O. Box 1001
Columbus, OH 43266-0101

INDUSTRIAL AND BUSINESS DIRECTORIES

Akron, Ohio Membership Directory and Buyers Guide, Akron Regional Development Board, 1 Cascade Plaza, Akron, OH 44308-1192

The Chamber Directory, Toledo Area Chamber of Commerce, 218 Huron Street, Toledo, OH 43604

Manufacturers Directory, Columbus Regional Information Service, 37 North High Street, Columbus, OH 43215-3181

Ohio Industrial Directory, Harris Publishing Co., 2057 Aurora Road, Twinsburg, OH 44087

Ohio Manufacturers Directory, Manufacturers' News, Inc., 1633 W. Central Street, Evanston, IL 60201

Oklahoma

STATE CAPITOL, OKLAHOMA CITY, OK 73105
(405) 521-2011

INFORMATION OFFICES

Commerce/Economic Development
Department of Commerce
P.O. Box 26980
Oklahoma City, OK 73126-0980

Corporate
Secretary of State
State Capitol
Oklahoma City, OK 73105

Taxation
Tax Commission
M. C. Connors Building
2501 N. Lincoln Boulevard
Oklahoma City, OK 73105

State Chamber of Commerce
Oklahoma State Chamber of Commerce
330 N.E. 10th Street
Oklahoma City, OK 73104-3200

International Commerce
International Trade Division
Department of Commerce
6601 Broadway Extension
P.O. Box 26980
Oklahoma City, OK 73126

Banking
Oklahoma Banking Department
4100 N. Lincoln Boulevard
Oklahoma City, OK 73105

Securities
Oklahoma Securities Commission
Will Rogers Building
2401 N. Lincoln Boulevard
Oklahoma City, OK 73105

Labor and Industrial Relations
Oklahoma Labor Department
4001 N. Lincoln Boulevard
Oklahoma City, OK 73105

Insurance
Insurance Commission
1901 N. Walnut Street
P.O. Box 53408
Oklahoma City, OK 73152-3408

Uniform Industrial Code
Universal Commercial Code Division
County Clerk's Office
County Court House
Oklahoma City, OK 73102

INDUSTRIAL AND BUSINESS DIRECTORIES

Oklahoma Directory of Manufacturers and Processors, Department of Commerce, P.O. Box 26980, Oklahoma City, OK 73126-0980.

Oklahoma Manufacturers Register, Manufacturers' News, Inc., 1633 W. Central Street, Evanston, IL 60201

Oregon

STATE CAPITOL, SALEM, OR 97310
(503) 986-1388

INFORMATION OFFICES

Commerce/Economic Development
Economic Development Department
775 Summer Street N.E.
Salem, OR 97310

Corporate
Corporation Division
Office of Secretary of State
Commerce Building
158 12th Street N.E.
Salem, OR 97310
Taxation
Department of Revenue
Revenue Building
955 Center Street
Salem, OR 97310-0210
International Commerce
International Trade Division
Economic Development Department
One World Trade Center
121 S.W. Salmon
Portland, OR 97204
Banking
Division of Finance and Corporate
  Securities
Department of Consumer and
  Business Services
21 Labor and Industries Building
Salem, OR 97310
Securities
Division of Finance and Corporate
  Securities
Department of Consumer and
  Business Services
21 Labor and Industries Building
Salem, OR 97310
Labor and Industry
Bureau of Labor and Industries
800 N.E. Oregon Street
Portland, OR 97232
Insurance
Insurance Division
Department of Consumer and
  Business Services
Labor and Industries Building
Salem, OR 97310
Uniform Industrial Code
Building Codes Division
Department of Consumer and
  Business Services
1535 Edgewater N.W.
Salem, OR 97310

INDUSTRIAL AND BUSINESS DIRECTORIES

Directory of Oregon Manufacturers, International Trade Directory, and *Directory of Oregon Wood Products Manufacturers*, Economic Development Department, 775 Summer Street, N.E., Salem, OR 97310; Manufacturers' News, Inc., 1633 W. Central Street, Evanston, IL 60201
Oregon Business Directory, American Directory Publishing Co., Inc., 5711 S. 86th Circle, P.O. Box 27347, Omaha, NE 68127
Oregon Manufacturers Register, Database Publishing Company, P.O. Box 70024, Anaheim, CA 92825-0024

Pennsylvania

MAIN CAPITOL BUILDING, HARRISBURG, PA
17120
(717) 787-2121

INFORMATION OFFICES

Department of Commerce
Department of Commerce
Office of the Secretary
Forum Building
Harrisburg, PA 17120

Office of International Development
Department of Commerce
Forum Building
Harrisburg, PA 17120

Office of Program Management
Department of Commerce
Forum Building
Harrisburg, PA 17120

Business Resource Network
Department of Commerce
Forum Building
Harrisburg, PA 17120

Office of Technology Development
Department of Commerce
Forum Building
Harrisburg, PA 17120
International Commerce
Department of Commerce
Office of International Development
Forum Building
Harrisburg, PA 17120
Corporate
Department of State
Bureau of Corporations
308 North Office Building
Harrisburg, PA 17120
Taxation
Department of Revenue
P.O. Box 8903
Harrisburg, PA 17105
State Chamber of Commerce
Pennsylvania Chamber of Business
  and Industry
417 Walnut Street
Harrisburg, PA 17101-1596
Banking
Department of Banking
333 Market Street
Harristown II
Harrisburg, PA 17101-2290
Securities
Securities Commission
East Gate Office Building
1010 N. 7th Street
Harrisburg, PA 17102
Labor and Industrial Relations
Department of Labor & Industry
Labor & Industry Building
7th & Forester Streets
Harrisburg, PA 17120

Insurance
Department of Insurance
1321 Strawberry Square
Harrisburg, PA 17120

INDUSTRIAL AND BUSINESS DIRECTORIES

Pennsylvania Directory of Manufacturers, Commerce Register, 190 Godwin Avenue, Midland Park, NJ 07432

Pennsylvania Industrial Directory, Harris Publishing Co., 2057 Aurora Road, Twinsburg, OH 44087

Pennsylvania Manufacturers Register, Manufacturers' News, Inc., 1633 W. Central Street, Evanston, IL 60201

Rhode Island

STATE HOUSE, PROVIDENCE, RI 02903
(401) 277-2000

INFORMATION OFFICES

Commerce/Economic Development
Department of Economic Development
7 Jackson Walkway
Providence, RI 02903
Taxation
Division of Taxation
Department of Administration
One Capitol Hill
Providence, RI 02908
Corporate
Secretary of State
Corporation Department
100 N. Main Street
Providence, RI 02903
State Chamber of Commerce
Rhode Island Chamber of Commerce
30 Exchange Terrace
Providence, RI 02903
International Commerce
Rhode Island Department of Economic Development
7 Jackson Walkway
Providence, RI 02903
Banking
Department of Business Regulation
Banking Division
233 Richmond Street
Providence, RI 02903
Securities
Department of Business Regulation
Banking Division
233 Richmond Street
Providence, RI 02903
Labor and Industrial Relations
Department of Labor
220 Elmwood Avenue
Providence, RI 02907

Insurance
Department of Business Regulation
Insurance Division
233 Richmond Street
Providence, RI 02903
Business Ombudsman
Business Development Division
Department of Economic Development
7 Jackson Walkway
Providence, RI 02903

INDUSTRIAL AND BUSINESS DIRECTORIES

Rhode Island Directory of Manufacturers, Department of Economic Development, 7 Jackson Walkway, Providence, RI 02903; Manufacturers' News, Inc., 1633 W. Central Street, Evanston, IL 60201

South Carolina

GOVERNOR'S OFFICE
STATE HOUSE, COLUMBIA, SC 29211
(803) 734-9818
State Operator (803) 734-1000

INFORMATION OFFICES

Commerce/Economic Development
South Carolina State Department of Commerce
P.O. Box 927
1201 Main Street
Columbia, SC 29202
Taxation
Department of Revenue
P.O. Box 125
Columbia Mill Building
Columbia, SC 29214
Corporate
Secretary of State
P.O. Box 11350
Columbia, SC 29211
State Chamber of Commerce
South Carolina Chamber of Commerce
1201 Main Street
Columbia, SC 29202
International Commerce
South Carolina Department of Commerce
1201 Main Street
P.O. Box 927
Columbia, SC 29202
Labor and Industrial Relations
South Carolina Department of Labor, Licensing, and Regulation
Landmark Center, 3600 Forest Drive
P.O. Box 11329
Columbia, SC 29211-1329
Insurance
South Carolina Department of Insurance
1612 Marion Street
P.O. Box 100105
Columbia, SC 29202-3105

Banking
  State Treasurer's Office
  Wade Hampton Building
  Banking Operations
  P.O. Drawer 11778
  Columbia, SC 29211
Securities
  Secretary of State
  Securities Division
  P.O. Box 11350
  1205 Pendleton Street
  Columbia, SC 29201
Business Ombudsman
  SC Department of Consumer Affairs
  P.O. Box 5757
  2801 Devine Street
  Columbia, SC 29250-5757

INDUSTRIAL AND BUSINESS DIRECTORIES

Industrial Directory of South Carolina, South
  Carolina Department of Commerce, P.O.
  Box 927, 1201 Main Street, Columbia, SC
  29202; Manufacturers' News, Inc., 1633 W.
  Central Street, Evanston, IL 60201

South Dakota

STATE CAPITOL, PIERRE, SD 57501-5070
(605) 773-3011

INFORMATION OFFICES

Commerce/Economic Development
  Governor's Office of Economic
    Development
  711 Wells Avenue
  Pierre, SD 57501

  Department of Commerce and
    Regulation
  910 E. Sioux
  Pierre, SD 57501
Corporate
  Secretary of State
  Corporation Division
  Capitol Building
  Pierre, SD 57501
Taxation
  Department of Revenue
  Kneip Building
  Pierre, SD 57501
State Chamber of Commerce
  Industry & Commerce Association
    of South Dakota
  P.O. Box 190
  Pierre, SD 57501
International Commerce
  Governor's Office of Economic
    Development
  711 Wells Avenue
  Pierre, SD 57501

Banking
  Department of Commerce and Regulation
  Division of Banking
  105 S. Euclid
  Pierre, SD 57501
Securities
  Department of Commerce and Regulation
  Division of Securities
  910 E. Sioux
  Pierre, SD 57501
Labor and Industrial Relations
  Department of Labor
  Division of Labor and Management
  Kneip Building
  Pierre, SD 57501
Insurance
  Department of Commerce and Regulation
  Division of Insurance
  910 E. Sioux
  Pierre, SD 57501

INDUSTRIAL AND BUSINESS DIRECTORIES

*South Dakota Manufacturers and Processors
  Directory,* Governor's Office of Economic
  Development, 711 Wells Avenue, Pierre,
  SD 57501; Manufacturers' News, Inc., 1633
  W. Central Street, Evanston, IL 60201
South Dakota Export Directory, Governor's
  Office of Economic Development, 711
  Wells Avenue, Pierre, SD 57501

Tennessee

STATE CAPITOL, NASHVILLE, TN 37243-0001
(615) 741-2001

INFORMATION OFFICES

Commerce/Economic Development
  Department of Economic and
    Community Development
  Rachel Jackson Building
  320 6th Avenue North
  Nashville, TN 37243-0405
Corporate
  Secretary of State
  Records Division
  James K. Polk Building
  Nashville, TN 37243-0306
Taxation
  Department of Revenue
  1200 Andrew Jackson Building
  500 Deaderick Street
  Nashville, TN 37242-1099
International Commerce
  Department of Economic & Community
    Development
  International Sales & Marketing
  Rachel Jackson Building
  320 6th Avenue North
  Nashville, TN 37243-0405

Banking
Department of Financial Institutions
John Sevier Building
500 Charlotte Avenue
Nashville, TN 37243-0705
Securities
Department of Commerce &
Insurance
Securities Division
500 James Robertson Parkway
Nashville, TN 37243
Labor and Industrial Relations
Department of Labor
710 James Robertson Parkway
Nashville, TN 37243-0661
Insurance
Department of Commerce &
Insurance
Insurance Division
500 James Robertson Parkway
Nashville, TN 37243
Business Ombudsman
Department of Economic &
Community Development
Business & Industry Services Division
Rachel Jackson Building
320 6th Avenue North
Nashville, TN 37243-0405

INDUSTRIAL AND BUSINESS DIRECTORIES

Directory of Tennessee Manufacturers, M.
Lee Smith Publishers, 162 Fourth Avenue,
P.O. Box 198867, Nashville, TN 37219;
Manufacturers' News, Inc., 1633 W. Central Street, Evanston, IL 60201

Texas

STATE CAPITOL, AUSTIN, TX 78701
State Information: (512) 463-4630

INFORMATION OFFICES

Commerce/Economic Development
Texas Department of Commerce
P.O. Box 12728, Capitol Station
Austin, TX 78711
Corporate
Secretary of State
P.O. Box 12697
Austin, TX 78711
Taxation
Comptroller of Public Accounts
P.O. Box 13528
Austin, TX 78711-3528
State Chamber of Commerce
Texas State Chamber of Commerce
900 Congress Avenue
Austin, TX 78711-3528

Rio Grande Chamber of Commerce
P.O. Box 1499
Weslaco, TX 78599-1499
International Commerce
Texas Department of Commerce
P.O. Box 12728, Capitol Station
Austin, TX 78711
Banking
Texas Department of Banking
2601 N. Lamar
Austin, TX 78705-4294
Securities
State Securities Board
P.O. Box 13167
Austin, TX 78711-3167
Licensing and Regulation
P.O. Box 12157
Austin, TX 78711
Insurance
Texas Department of Insurance
P.O. Box 149104
Austin, TX 78711-9104
Uniform Industrial Code
Secretary of State
Uniform Commercial Code Section
P.O. Box 12697
Austin, TX 78711

INDUSTRIAL AND BUSINESS DIRECTORIES

Dallas Business Guide, Greater Dallas Chamber of Commerce, 1201 Elm Street, Dallas, TX 75270-2014
Directory of Texas Manufacturers, Bureau of Business Research, University of Texas at Austin, TX 78712
Fort Worth Directory of Manufacturers, Fort Worth Area Chamber of Commerce, 777 Taylor Street, Fort Worth, TX 76102-4997
Texas Manufacturers Register, Manufacturers' News, Inc., 1633 W. Central Street, Evanston, IL 60201

Utah

STATE CAPITOL, SALT LAKE CITY, UT 84114
(801) 538-3000

INFORMATION OFFICES

Commerce/Economic Development
Department of Commerce
160 East 300 South
Salt Lake City, UT 84111

Division of Business and Economic
Development
160 East 300 South
Salt Lake City, UT 84111

Office of Planning & Budget
Data Resources Section
116 Capitol Building
Salt Lake City, UT 84114

Corporate
Division of Corporations
Heber M. Wells Building
160 E. 300 South
Salt Lake City, UT 84111

Taxation
Utah State Tax Commission
Heber M. Wells Building
160 E. 300 South
Salt Lake City, UT 84134

International Commerce
International Business
　Development
Division of Business &
　Economic Development
160 East 300 South
Salt Lake City, UT 84111

Banking
Financial Institutions
324 S. State
P.O. Box 89
Salt Lake City, UT 84110-0089

Securities
Division of Securities
Heber M. Wells Building
P.O. Box 45811
Salt Lake City, UT 84111

Labor and Industrial Relations
Industrial Commission of Utah
Heber M. Wells Building
160 E. 300 South
Salt Lake City, UT 84111

Insurance
Department of Insurance
3110 State Office Building
Salt Lake City, UT 84114

Licensing
Division of Occupational and
　Professional Licensing
160 East 300 South
P.O. Box 45802
Salt Lake City, UT 84145-0802

Uniform Industrial Code
Employment Security/
　Job Service
140 East 300 South
Salt Lake City, UT 84111

INDUSTRIAL AND BUSINESS DIRECTORIES

Utah Directory of Business and Industry,
Utah Division of Business and Economic
Development, 140 East 300 South, Salt
Lake City, UT 84111; Manufacturers'
News, Inc., 1633 W. Central Street, Evans-
ton, IL 60201

Vermont

STATE HOUSE, MONTPELIER, VT 05602
(802) 828-3333

INFORMATION OFFICES

Commerce/Economic Development
Agency of Development and
　Community Affairs
Department of Economic
　Development
109 State Street
Montpelier, VT 05602

Corporate
Secretary of State
Corporation Department
26 Terrace Street
Montpelier, VT 05602

Taxation
Department of Taxes
Agency of Administration
109 State Street
Montpelier, VT 05602

International Commerce
Agency of Development and
　Community Affairs
Pavillion Office Bldg.
109 State Street
Montpelier, VT 05609

State Chamber of Commerce
Vermont State Chamber of
　Commerce
P.O. Box 37
Montpelier, VT 05602

Insurance
Department of Banking and Insurance
89 Main Street
Montpelier, VT 05602

Banking
Department of Banking and Insurance
89 Main Street
Montpelier, VT 05602

Securities
Department of Banking and Insurance
89 Main Street
Montpelier, VT 05602

Labor and Industrial Relations
Department of Labor and Industry
National Life Building
Montpelier, VT 05602

Uniform Commercial Code
Department of Banking and Insurance
89 Main Street
Montpelier, VT 05602

Business Ombudsman
Agency Development and
　Community Affairs
Department of Economic
　Development
109 State Street
Montpelier, VT 05602

INDUSTRIAL AND BUSINESS DIRECTORIES

Maine/New Hampshire/Vermont Directory of Manufacturers, Commerce Register Inc., 190 Godwin Avenue, Midland Park, NJ 07432

Vermont Manufacturing Directory, Tower Publishing, 34 Diamond Street, Portland, ME 04112; Manufacturers' News, Inc., 1633 W. Central Street, Evanston, IL 60201

Vermont Directory of Manufacturers, Vermont Agency of Development and Community Affairs, Montpelier, VT 05602

Vermont Yearbook, The National Survey, Chester, VT 05143

Virginia

STATE CAPITOL, RICHMOND, VA 23219
(800) 422-2319

INFORMATION OFFICES

Commerce/Economic Development
Department of Economic Development
P.O. Box 798
1021 East Cary Street
Richmond, VA 23206-0798
Corporate
State Corporation Commission
Tyler Building
1300 East Main Street
Richmond, VA 23219
Taxation
Department of Taxation
2200 W. Broad Street
P.O. Box 1880
Richmond, VA 23282-1880
State Chamber of Commerce
Virginia Chamber of Commerce
9 South Fifth Street
Richmond, VA 23219
International Commerce
Department of Economic Development
P.O. Box 798
1021 East Cary Street
Richmond, VA 23206-0798
Banking
State Corporation Commission
Bureau of Financial Institutions
Tyler Building
1300 East Main Street
Richmond, VA 23219
Securities
State Corporation Commission
Division of Securities and
Retail Franchising
Tyler Building
1300 East Main Street
Richmond, VA 23219

Labor and Industrial Relations
Department of Labor and Industry
Powers-Taylor Building
13 S. 13th Street
Richmond, VA 23219
Insurance
State Corporation Commission
Bureau of Insurance
Tyler Building
1300 East Main Street
Richmond, VA 23219
Employment and Unemployment Information
Virginia Employment Commission
Economic Information Services Division
703 E. Main Street
Richmond, VA 23219
Consumer Ombudsman
Department of Agriculture and Consumer
Services
Division of Consumer Affairs
P.O. Box 1163
Richmond, VA 23209

INDUSTRIAL AND BUSINESS DIRECTORIES

Virginia Industrial Directory, Chamber of Commerce, 9 South Fifth Street, Richmond, VA 23219

Virginia Manufacturers Directory, Manufacturers' News, Inc., 1633 W. Central Street, Evanston, IL 60201

MacRAE's State Industrial Directory North Carolina/South Carolina/Virginia, MacRAE's Industrial Directories, 817 Broadway, New York, NY 10003

Washington

101 GENERAL ADMINISTRATION BUILDING,
OLYMPIA, WA 98504
(206) 753-5630

INFORMATION OFFICES

Commerce/Economic Development
Department of Trade and Economic
Development
906 Columbia St. S.W.
P.O. Box 4830
Olympia, WA 98504
Corporate
Secretary of State
Corporate Division
505 E. Union
Olympia, WA 98504
Taxation
Department of Revenue
412 General Administration Building
P.O. Box 47450
Olympia, WA 98504-7450

State Chamber of Commerce
Association of Washington Business
1414 S. Cherry Street
Olympia, WA 98501

International Commerce
Department of Trade & Economic
  Development
Domestic & International Trade Division
2600 Westin Building
2001 Sixth Avenue
Seattle, WA 98121

Banking
General Administration Building
Banking and Consumer Finance
1400 S. Evergreen Park Drive
P.O. Box 41200
Olympia, WA 98504-1200

Securities
Department of Licensing Building
Att: Securities Division
405 Black Lake Boulevard
Olympia, WA 98504

Labor and Industrial Relations
Department of Labor & Industries
Employment Standards—Apprenticeship
Crime Victims Division
P.O. Box 44520
Olympia, WA 98504-4520

Insurance
Insurance Commissioner's Office
Insurance Building
P.O. Box 40255
Olympia, WA 98504-0255

Uniform Commercial Code
Department of Licensing
Business License Services
405 Black Lake Boulevard
Olympia, WA 98504

Business Ombudsman
Department of Trade & Economic
  Development
Business Assistance Center
919 Lakeridge Way, S.W.
Olympia, WA 98504

INDUSTRIAL AND BUSINESS DIRECTORIES

Business Assistance in Washington State, Washington State International Trade Directory, Department of Trade and Economic Development, 906 Columbia Street, SW, P.O. Box 48300, Olympia, WA 98504-8300

Directory of Advanced Technology Industries in Washington State, Economic Development Partnership for Washington State, 18000 Pacific Highway South, Seattle, WA 98188

Minority Women Business Enterprises, Office of Minority Women Business Enterprises, 406 S. Water Street, Olympia, WA 98504

Washington Manufacturers Register, Times Mirror Press, P.O. Box 7440, Newport Beach, CA 92658

Washington Forest Industry Mill Directory (1984), Department of Natural Resources, 1065 S. Capitol Way, Olympia, WA 98504

Directory of Washington Mining Operations, Department of Natural Resources, P.O. Box 47007, Division of Geology, Olympia, WA 98504-7007

Washington Manufacturers Register, Database Publishing Company, P.O. Box 70024, Anaheim, CA 92825-0024; Manufacturers' News, Inc., 1633 W. Central Street, Evanston, IL 60201

West Virginia

STATE CAPITOL, CHARLESTON, WV 25305
(304) 558-3456

INFORMATION OFFICES

Commerce/Economic Development
West Virginia Development Office
Building 6, Capitol Complex
Charleston, WV 25305

Corporate
Secretary of State
Corporate Division
Building 1, Capitol Complex
1900 Washington Street East
Charleston, WV 25305

Taxation
Department of Tax and Revenue
Building 6, Capitol Complex
Charleston, WV 25305

State Chamber of Commerce
P.O. Box 2789
1101 Kanawha Valley Building
Charleston, WV 25330-2789

International Commerce
West Virginia Development Office
Building 6, Capitol Complex
Charleston, WV 25305

Banking
Division of Banking
1900 Washington Street East,
  Capitol Complex
Charleston, WV 25305

Securities
Auditor's Office
Building 1, Capitol Complex
Charleston, WV 25305

Labor and Industrial Relations
Division of Labor
1900 Washington Street East
Building 1, Capitol Complex
Charleston, WV 25305

Insurance
Insurance Commission
2019 Washington Street East,
  Capitol Complex
Charleston, WV 25305

Uniform Industrial Code
Secretary of State
1900 Washington Street East
Building 1, Capitol Complex
Charleston, WV 25305

Business Ombudsman
West Virginia Development Office
Building 6, Capitol Complex
Charleston, WV 25305

INDUSTRIAL AND BUSINESS DIRECTORIES

West Virginia Manufacturers Directory, Harris Publishing Co., 2057 Aurora Road, Twinsburg, OH 44087; Manufacturers' News, Inc., 1633 W. Central Street, Evanston, IL 60201

Wisconsin

STATE CAPITOL, MADISON, WI 53702
(608) 266-2211

INFORMATION OFFICES

Commerce/Economic Development
Department of Development
123 W. Washington Avenue
Box 7970
Madison, WI 53707-7970

Corporate
Secretary of State
Corporate Division
30 W. Miffin Street
Box 7848
Madison, WI 53707-7848

Taxation
Department of Revenue
125 S. Webster Avenue
P.O. Box 8933
Madison, WI 53708-8933

State Chamber of Commerce
Wisconsin Association of Manufacturers and Commerce
501 E. Washington Avenue
Box 352
Madison, WI 53701

International Commerce
International Business Services
Department of Development
Box 7970
123 W. Washington Avenue
Madison, WI 53707-7970

Banking
Banking, Office of the Commissioner
101 E. Wilson Avenue
P.O. Box 7876
Madison, WI 53707-7876

Securities
Securities—Office of the Commissioner
101 E. Wilson Avenue
Box 1768
Madison, WI 53701-1768

Labor and Industrial Relations
Department of Industry, Labor, and Human Relations
201 E. Washington Avenue
P.O. Box 7946
Madison, WI 53707-7946

Insurance
Office of the Commissioner of Insurance
121 E. Wilson Street
Box 7873
Madison, WI 53707-7873

Uniform Industrial Code
Department of Industry, Labor and Human Relations
201 E. Washington Avenue
Box 7969
Madison, WI 53707

Business Ombudsman
Small Business Ombudsman
Department of Development
123 W. Washington Avenue
Box 7970
Madison, WI 53707

INDUSTRIAL AND BUSINESS DIRECTORIES

Classified Directory of Wisconsin Manufacturers, Wisconsin Association of Manufacturers and Commerce, 501 E. Washington Avenue, Box 352, Madison, WI 53701; State Industrial Directories Corp., 2 Penn Plaza, New York, NY 10001

Wisconsin Exporters Directory, Wisconsin Department of Development, 123 W. Washington Avenue, Box 7920, Madison, WI 53707

Wisconsin Manufacturers Register, Manufacturers' News, Inc., 1633 W. Central Street, Evanston, IL 60201

Wisconsin Local Development Organizations (annual), Wisconsin Department of Development, 123 W. Washington Avenue, Box 7970, Madison, WI 53707

Wisconsin Services Directory, Wisconsin Association of Manufacturers and Commerce, 501 E. Washington Avenue, Box 352, Madison, WI 53701

Wyoming

STATE CAPITOL, CHEYENNE, WY 82002
(307) 777-7220

INFORMATION OFFICES

Commerce/Economic Development
Department of Commerce
Division of Economic and Community Development
Barrett Building
Cheyenne, WY 82002

Corporate
Secretary of State
Corporate Division
State Capitol
Cheyenne, WY 82002
Taxation
Department of Revenue and Taxation
Herschler Building
Cheyenne, WY 82002
International Commerce
International Trade Office
Herschler Building
Cheyenne, WY 82002
Banking
State Examiner
Herschler Building
Cheyenne, WY 82002
Securities
Secretary of State
Securities Division
State Capitol
Cheyenne, WY 82002
Labor and Industrial Relations
Department of Employment
Herschler Building
Cheyenne, WY 82002
Insurance
Insurance Commission
Herschler Building
Cheyenne, WY 82002
Business Ombudsman
Division of Economic and Community
  Development
Barrett Building
Cheyenne, WY 82002

INDUSTRIAL AND BUSINESS DIRECTORIES

Wyoming Directory of Manufacturing and Mining, Manufacturers' News, Inc., 1633 W. Central Street, Evanston, IL 60201

Puerto Rico

CAPITOL, SAN JUAN, PR 00901
(809) 724-6040 (House of Representatives)
(809) 724-2030 (Senate)

INFORMATION OFFICES

Commerce/Economic Development
Puerto Rico Department of Economic
  Development and Commerce
P.O. Box 4435
San Juan, PR 00902

Puerto Rico Planning Board
P.O. Box 41119
San Juan, PR 00940

Government Development Bank
P.O. Box 42001
Minillas Station
San Juan, PR 00940

Economic Development Bank
P.O. Box 5009
San Juan, PR 00919-5009

Puerto Rico Tourism Company
P.O. Box 4435
San Juan, PR 00902
Taxation
Puerto Rico Department of Treasury
P.O. Box S-4515
San Juan, PR 00902

Office of Industrial Tax Exemption
P.O. Box 2519
San Juan, PR 00919
International Commerce
Foreign Export
P.O. Box 362350
San Juan, PR 00936
Chamber of Commerce
Chamber of Commerce Puerto Rico
P.O. Box 3789
San Juan, PR 00902
Puerto Rico Manufacturers Association
P.O. Box 192410
San Juan, PR 00919
Securities
Office of the Commissioner of Financial
  Institutions
Centre Europa Building
1492 Ponce de León Avenue
San Juan, PR 00907
Labor and Industrial Relations
Puerto Rico Labor Relations Board
P.O. Box 4048
San Juan, PR 00905

National Labor Relations Board
Federal Building
Carlos E. Chardon Street
San Juan, PR 00918
Insurance
Office of the Insurance Commissioner
P.O. Box 8330
San Juan, PR 00910

Puerto Rico Insurance Companies
  Association, Inc.
P.O. Box 3395
San Juan, PR 00936
Uniform Industrial Code
Department of Labor and Human
  Resources
505 Muñoz Rivera Avenue
Prudencio Rivera Martínez Building
San Juan, PR 00918
Business Ombudsman
Ombudsman Office
1205 Ponce de León Avenue
Banco de San Juan
San Juan, PR 00907-3995
International Commerce
Puerto Rico Department of Commerce
External Trade Promotion Program
P.O. Box S 4275
San Juan, PR 00902

US Department of Commerce
International Trade Administration
Carlos E. Chardon Street
Federal Building
San Juan, PR 00918

Puerto Rico Chamber of Commerce
International Trade Division
P.O. Box 3789
San Juan, PR 00902

Banking

Puerto Rico Bankers Association
820 Banco Popular Center
San Juan, PR 00918

INDUSTRIAL AND BUSINESS DIRECTORIES

Puerto Rico Official Industrial and Trade Directory, Witcom Group, Inc., P.O. Box 2310, San Juan, PR 00902

The Businessman's Guide to Puerto Rico, Puerto Rico Almanacs, Inc., P.O. Box 9582, Santurce, PR 00908

Index

J

K

L

M

Other books of interest to you from Irwin *Professional Publishing*...

SOROS
The Life, Times, and Trading Secrets of the World's Greatest Investor
Robert Slater

On George Soros:

"No other investor has produced better results for such a long period—not Peter Lynch, not Warren E. Buffett."

—Business Week

He has been called **"The World's Most Successful Investor."** Enter the world of George Soros and discover his 31 most closely guarded trading secrets. This fascinating story of the remarkable life, stunning accomplishments, and unique personal vision of George Soros, the world's premier investor, probes the unique investment philosophy, strategies, methods, and tactics that have given Soros enormous influence over world financial markets. (300 pages)
ISBN: 0-7863-0361-1

THE IRWIN GUIDE TO USING THE WALL STREET JOURNAL, FIFTH EDITION
Michael B. Lehmann

A one-of-a-kind tool for understanding *The Wall Street Journal*. It presents a thorough and practical education for making informed business and investment decisions, and includes highlights of the best investor tips and expanded discussion of derivatives. (400 pages)
ISBN: 0-7863-0483-9

STOCK FOR THE LONG RUN
A Guide to Selecting Markets for Long-Term Growth
Jeremy J. Siegel

"One of the Best Business Books of 1994. The book belongs on every investor's shelf."

—Business Week

Financial expert, Jeremy Siegel, of the Wharton School of the University of Pennsylvania offers solid strategies for long-term investment success, showing investors how to understand and interpret the movements of the market over time. *Stocks for the Long Run* includes a detailed description of market performances since 1802—including nearly 100 original charts and graphs—providing a unique perspective on returns and market fluctuations and examines the economic, political, and fiscal changes that affect the stock market, such as deficits, taxes, and inflation. (250 pages)
ISBN: 1-55623-804-5

THE IRWIN INVESTOR'S HANDOOK 1995 EDITION
Edited by Phyllis S. Pierce

Investors and financial planners rely on each new edition of this *Handbook* to help them make accurate calculations for capital gains, dividends, yields, and returns on investments. It's the only complete hardcopy source of market statistics available. (200 pages)
ISBN: 0-7863-0430-8

Available in fine bookstores and libraries everywhere!